49TH EDITION

KOVELS' Antiques & Collectibles PRICE GUIDE 2017

Black Dog
& Leventhal
Publishers
New York

Cover design by Chrisopher Lin

Front cover photographs, from left to right:
Furniture, pie safe, walnut, punched tin
Rosenthal, coffeepot, warmer, flash design, Dorothy Hafner, 1900s
Political, button, jugate, Hoover, Curtis

Back cover photographs, top to bottom:
Toy, pram, Felix the Cat, tin lithograph, Spain
Bottle, target ball, Gevelot, Paris, c.1895
Tiffany, lamp, Daffodil

Spine:
Orphan Annie, toy, Orphan Annie & Sandy, tin, windup

Black Dog & Leventhal Publishers
Hachette Book Group
1290 Avenue of the Americas
New York, NY 10104

www.hachettebookgroup.com
www.blackdogandleventhal.com

First Edition: September 2016

Black Dog & Leventhal Publishers is an imprint of Hachette Books, a division of Hachette Book Group.
The Black Dog & Leventhal Publishers name and logo are trademarks of Hachette Book Group, Inc.

The publisher is not responsible for websites (or their content) that are not owned by the publisher.
The Hachette Speakers Bureau provides a wide range of authors for speaking events.
To find out more, go to www.HachetteSpeakersBureau.com or call (866) 376-6591.

Print book interior design by Sheila Hart Design, Inc.

ISBN: 978-0-316-31532-6

Printed in the United States of America

WW
10 9 8 7 6 5 4 3 2 1

BOOKS BY RALPH AND TERRY KOVEL

American Country Furniture, 1780–1875

A Directory of American Silver, Pewter, and Silver Plate

Kovels' Advertising Collectibles Price List

Kovels' American Antiques 1750–1900

Kovels' American Art Pottery

Kovels' American Collectibles 1900–2000

Kovels' American Silver Marks, 1650 to the Present

Kovels' Antiques & Collectibles Fix-It Source Book

Kovels' Antiques & Collectibles Price Guide

Kovels' Bid, Buy, and Sell Online

Kovels' Book of Antique Labels

Kovels' Bottles Price List

Kovels' Collector's Guide to American Art Pottery

Kovels' Collector's Guide to Limited Editions

Kovels' Collectors' Source Book

Kovels' Depression Glass & Dinnerware Price List

Kovels' Dictionary of Marks— Pottery and Porcelain, 1650 to 1850

Kovels' Guide to Selling, Buying, and Fixing Your Antiques and Collectibles

Kovels' Guide to Selling Your Antiques & Collectibles

Kovels' Illustrated Price Guide to Royal Doulton

Kovels' Know Your Antiques

Kovels' Know Your Collectibles

Kovels' New Dictionary of Marks— Pottery and Porcelain, 1850 to the Present

Kovels' Organizer for Collectors

Kovels' Price Guide for Collector Plates, Figurines, Paperweights, and Other Limited Edition Items

Kovels' Quick Tips: 799 Helpful Hints on How to Care for Your Collectibles

Kovels' Yellow Pages: A Resource Guide for Collectors

The Label Made Me Buy It: From Aunt Jemima to Zonkers— The Best-Dressed Boxes, Bottles, and Cans from the Past

BOOKS BY TERRY KOVEL AND KIM KOVEL

Kovels' Antiques & Collectibles Price Guide

INTRODUCTION

This has been another year of the weak "collecting economy" that started in 2008. However, once again, prices are a little better than last year, and record prices were set as bidders fought for the best of the best, especially the best of collectibles and art made after 1950. (See page ix for a list of this year's record prices.) The changes in the way antiques are collected, thanks to the Internet, cell phones, tablets, computers, and other electronic ways to buy and sell have taken over a large part of the action. And lifestyle and modern design has changed some of the demands. In the past, older collectors (now over 60) wanted collections of as many different toys or plates as possible or a house furnished with only country furniture—a quantity of good to excellent examples was the goal. Now the goal is a perfect piece. There is new interest in "design" and there are museum exhibits and collectors who display and explain modern teapots, unfamiliar furniture, even kitchen hot water pots and corkscrews as good or bad "design." It is a hard term to define since everything is designed by someone. But it seems to include what today is considered to be great design in any category including painting, sculpture, jewelry, kitchen tools, cars, packaging, advertising, clothing, and more. That has shifted some buyers' attention in the antique and vintage collector's world to great graphics, unique jewelry, unusual chairs and tables, glass, silver, pottery, and even medical devices. The most apparent change of interest in the 2016 era is condition. This has altered the pricing for many antiques especially for furniture (refinishing), mechanical banks and other metal collectibles (amount of original paint and no damage), and bottles, glass, and ceramics (no chips, no cracks, no flaws, and no repairs—no matter how old.) And there is a surprising opposite interest in repaired pieces from years ago like stapled export porcelain. "Go-withs" are now a collecting category. Buyers want broken goblet stems made into candleholders or damaged 18th century porcelain teapots with silver spouts added as replacements. It may be just part of the way being "green" and recycling has influenced the concerns of collectors. We can brag that antique collectors were the first serious recyclers.

Since 1953, the year we published our first book, the antiques world has been going from one or two antiques shows in a city per year to almost one every week. But with so many new online ways to buy and sell antiques—and the weak economy—many shows have been discontinued. Auctions of expensive antiques used to be held in New York, Chicago, and a few other large cities. Small towns had "farm auctions" held outside a farmhouse, or a local auctioneer who sold antiques, tractors, and tools in the barn. There were no malls, no Internet shops, sales, or auctions. Today many major cities have auction houses that run sales at their galleries with online access that reaches buyers in every country. And major auctions are also online from London, Paris, Hong Kong, and sometimes from the home of a special collection. Every day there are dozens of auctions you can watch and place bids on from your computer or phone. And there are several online auction sites that advertise and list the coming auctions, then handle the competing bids in real time. There are also timed auctions usually for one type of collectible like bottles that are online for a specified length of time, usually about two weeks.

Our first book, *Kovels' Dictionary of Marks: Pottery & Porcelain*, was one of just 60 titles about antiques announced that year. In 1969, there were about 200 new books. Now few books about collectibles and antiques are published, but much of the old and new information previously found in old books, company catalogs, and advertisements is now online. Our years of newspaper columns and questions, newsletters, special reports, books of marks, and other writings are now on our website, Kovels.com. Some can be found with an online search.

The economic problems that started in 2008 with the stock market crash and housing bust spread to other investments, including antiques and collectibles. There is still a saying that if you buy antiques, they go up in value every year and are a good investment. That is only half true. If you buy the right antiques and sell at the right time, they sell for higher prices than you paid, even when you factor in inflation. Consider this: Our first price book lists a Diamond Dyes cabinet for $50. In the early months of 2008, the same cabinet sold for $1,112 to $2,633. In 2012, two Diamond Dyes cabinets were listed, one at $540, the other $550—very low prices. In 2013, common Diamond Dyes cabinets were $407, $1,320, and $1,540. In 2014, the cabinet featuring Children with Balloons was $896, the Governess was $1,560, and Washer Woman was $720. In 2015, Evolution of Woman was $360; Maypole, $1,596; Children with Balloons, $2,400; and Blond Fairy, $1,112. Last year Children Skipping Rope was $617, Children with Balloons was $472, Governess $531, Maypole $531, Prism $660, and Washer Woman with a blue background $1680. And in this year's book there are two cabinets: Evolution of Woman sold for $423 and Washer Woman with a blue background sold for $495. There are twelve original designs used on the tin fronts of these cabinets. The cabinets have been so popular that there are now fake cabinets in a slightly smaller size and copies of the tin panel from the cabinet door being sold as vintage signs.

The past year has seen little change in the influence of the worldwide recession. It is still affecting the values of antiques and collectibles. There seem to be more shows closing or joining other shows and there are many more auction bidders because of the added activities online. Almost every auction is online as well as on the phone and most also have a live group of bidders at the sale. But many auctions end up with unsold pieces.

It has become more difficult to sell vintage collections of figurines, small advertising items like tape measures or glass shoes. Pressed glass is priced so low it is selling a bit better. Carnival glass rarities are hitting all-time highs while common pieces are difficult to sell. Prices for items offered on eBay are still low, and many items don't sell. In 2012, prices leveled for things with international appeal, like Chinese porcelain and ivory. The best pieces are high priced.

The endangered species laws for the sale of antique and new ivory have caused great confusion. New rules from the U.S. Fish and Wildlife Service went into effect July 6, 2016. They prohibit the importation of most African elephant ivory except for items made with ivory parts, such as musical instruments used in orchestras, items that are part of a traveling exhibition, a household move or inheritance (with special criteria), and ivory for law enforcement or scientific purposes. Also exempt are furniture, firearms, and other antiques that have less than seven ounces of ivory. "Bona fide" antiques (age proven by a professional appraisal or verifiable document) are exempt as well. But most African elephant ivory, including antique ivory, still can't be imported. We tried to list the parts of the law that affect collectors, but we suggest you read the long and complicated regulations at https://10172-presscdn-0-75-pagely.netdna-ssl.com/wp-content/uploads/2016/06/final-rule-african-elephant-4d.pdf. Some ivory items including antiques have been seized and crushed because some feel allowing anything ivory to be sold suggests that ivory is valuable and living elephants are being killed for profit. Many EPA laws forbid the sale of parts of endangered species including elephants (ivory), rhinoceros (horns), eagles (feathers), tigers and other cats (skins), and even some types of turtles (shells). There is also pressure to do what is politically correct and this may cause an unexpected legal problem even if it is an historic item. Sales of vintage Ku Klux Klan items, caricatures of black, Irish, Chinese and Jewish people on postcards or joke figurines are criticized and result in bad publicity or removal of the item(s) from a sale. A group of drawings from the

Japanese-American camps during World War II were pulled from an auction because protesters thought it would be too emotional. They wanted to have the drawings put into a special museum exhibit. Beware of anything that mentions Muslims or their religion in a derogatory manner. Legal auctions of historic antique guns caused controversy and unpleasant publicity and the laws covering guns, ammunition, and even antique firearms are being argued by many government groups.

From 2013 to 2015, Chinese bidding slowed down for all but top-quality pieces. From 2008 to 2016, Hummel, Royal Doulton figurines and character jugs, "country furniture" with peeling paint, and "brown furniture" like period Chippendale desks have gone way down in value. And by 2016 auction houses led the way to accepting only higher-priced items. Sotheby's and Christies won't sell antiques or art worth less than thousands of dollars in their important sales. Some advertising auctions want items over $500 or $1,000. Large advertising signs, enameled metal signs, die-cut cardboard advertising, auto-related pieces, even small oil cans and other small tins with great graphics, as well as rock 'n' roll and travel posters are up but only if in very good to excellent condition. Unfortunately many items are repaired and restored before being sold and the only way to know is to contact a person before the sale and ask. It is often not part of the catalog description. Malls and shops have been closing but shows and shops seem to have better prices than they could get seven years ago. Collectors and dealers agree that "good stuff sells" and well-run shows, shops, and sales are doing "OK." Usable furniture in good condition and decorative "smalls" are selling for expected prices. And 1890s oak dining tables that were hard to sell are starting to attract more buyers because of the low prices. The "best" of every type of antique or collectible is in demand. Some auctions get prices that are close to retail. But easy-to-find antiques are at about one-third of retail because the Internet has revealed the large, worldwide supply.

There is still a problem with bids from China. Some bidders refused to honor their bids and instead asked for a price reduction—or just didn't pay for or pick up a purchase. Often the sale price is reported online at the time of the auction bid, but there is rarely a public announcement that the bid was not honored. The auction houses selling expensive art and antiques now require a cash deposit before the sale that will be forfeited if a buyer does not honor a bid.

Kovels' Antiques and Collectibles Price Guide 2017 has current, reliable information, plus edited content. The book has 2,500 new color photographs and 25,000 prices. You will also find more than 200 facts of interest and tips about care and repair. Each photograph is shown with a caption that includes the description, price, and source. The book has color tabs and color-coded paragraphs that make it easy to find listings, and it uses a modern, readable typestyle. More than 750 paragraphs introduce separate price categories. They give history and descriptions that help identify an unknown piece. We make some changes in the paragraphs every year to indicate new owners, new distributors, company closures, or new information about production dates. We added two new categories, Gameboard and Pyrex. All of the antiques and collectibles priced here were offered for sale during the past year, most of them in the United States. Other prices came from sales that accepted bids from all over the world. Almost all auction prices given include the buyer's premium, because that is part of what the buyer paid. Very few include local sales tax and the extra charges involving phone bids, online bids, credit cards, or shipping.

READ THIS FIRST

This is a book for the buyer and the seller. We check prices, visit shops, shows, and flea markets, read hundreds of publications and catalogs, check Internet sales, auctions, and other online services, and decide which antiques and collectibles are of most interest to most collectors in the United States. We concentrate on the average pieces in any category. Sometimes high-priced items are included so you can see that special rarities are very valuable. Prices of some items were very high because a major collection by a well-known collector of top-quality pieces were auctioned. Auction houses like to have huge sales of things that belonged to one well-known collector or expert. Many catalogs now feature the name and biography of the collector and advertise the auction with the collector's name in all the ads. This year there were major sales of collections of toys, banks, guns, Martin Brothers pottery, and exceptional artists' personal collections. A few famous bottle collections were auctioned at online-only bottle auctions. Single collector auctions of dolls, Victorian glass, lamps with leaded glass shades, and Tiffany of all types were well advertised and prices were high. There was even an important collection of 1,000 glass toothpick holders.

Most listed pieces cost less than $10,000. The highest price in this book is $1,066,000 for a Tiffany lamp with Oriental Poppy shade, c.1910. The lowest price is $2 for two bottle caps: Wash & Return Bottles Daily and Pure Fresh Milk. The largest antique is a 195-inch art nouveau backbar and front bar, with mirrors and stained glass, that sold for $7,260. There are several pieces that were just ½ inch: A political charm with portraits of Grant & Colfax sold for $347. A Mickey Mouse stick pin brought $115.

Many unusual, unique, and weird things are included. This year, we list an embalming machine sold for $153, a Chicago police paddy wagon went for $840, a prison door with iron box lock that was used for solitary confinement at Berks County Prison sold for $266, a Tilden & Hendricks candy wrapper from 1876 auctioned for $448, a suit of armor sold for $78,400, and a wooden telephone booth with glass folding doors sold for $400.

Of major interest today, and getting the highest prices, are antique guns and ammunition, the best of modern furniture, and modernist jewelry by artists like Calder or Bertoia. Early comic books in excellent condition are selling at high prices, and the comics that include the first appearance of Batman, Superman, and other superheroes or first issues like Action No. 1 are selling for thousands of dollars. The original pieces of art from the covers of important comic books or magazines are selling as art, not collectibles, and artists like Norman Rockwell sell for very, very high prices.

There are still bargains to be had, some that have been emerging as "collectibles" over the last seven years. Big is still "big." Groups of small figurines or sets of plates are very hard to sell. But large-scale accent pieces with colors and lines that blend in with modern furnishings—pieces like huge crocks, floor vases, centerpieces, bronze sculptures, large posters and garden statuary—attract decorators as well as the owners of large homes. Blue and white, the colors favored in the 17th and 18th centuries, are back, turquoise and black and white are this year's decorator favorites. Anything from clothes and glass to ceramics and furniture in the "newest style" between the 1950s and 2000 is hot. They are all going up in price and attracting new, younger buyers. Iron objects like bookends, doorstops, pots and pans, even snow eagles and carnival shooting targets are getting harder to find and sell quickly. But costume jewelry is the most popular item we see selling at shows and online. Prices for pieces marked with important makers' names can sell for as much as $1,500 to $2,500. A few very popular collectibles of the past, like Roseville and Rookwood pottery, Mexican silver jewelry, and almost any clear glass have come down in price for all but the largest and most important pieces.

The meltdown price of sterling silver the last few years made it profitable to melt many pieces. Hundreds of coin silver items, especially spoons and no-name sterling serving dishes and flatware, disappeared in the meltdown craze. Sterling by well-known companies or designers like Tiffany, Gorham, and Liberty now get top dollar. And very modern unfamiliar shapes make tea services saleable at high prices. Ordinary traditional services are low priced. Almost all coin silver spoons and serving pieces that were not destroyed are hard to sell for more than melt-down price even if in perfect, useable condition.

Art as investment is the latest trend for millionaires and billionaires. The prices of very important art has been rising faster than most traditional investments like real estate or stocks and bonds. And the buyer has the added prestige of great taste, sophistication, and bragging rights for owning a one-of-a-kind masterpiece. The highest price for a famous painting this year was Paul Gaugin's *Nafea Faa Ipoipo (When Will You Marry?)* which sold for nearly $300 million. Quality and works of recognized artists sell high because collectors consider it an "investment" that will increase in value. Works by contemporary studio potters that are made in non-traditional shapes are now popular. Teapots and vases are not made to be used, but are one-of-a-kind, large, and often colorful sculptures. Tiffany lamps have become so expensive there are now rising prices for all other leaded glass lamps like Handel, Pairpoint, Moe Bridges, and Pittsburgh. Norman Rockwell's oil paintings are selling for thousands of dollars and his prints are selling for hundreds of dollars to those who like the art but have less money. Mixed metal furniture from the 1950s and later by Paul Evans is setting records. A polychrome steel cabinet with painted wood and gold leaf trim sold for $287,500. A decorated pine Spitler blanket chest, made in about 1800, sold for $356,500. Wooden furniture by George Nakashima is popular and expensive. Authentic Western and American Indian items are steadily rising in price. Even some souvenirs made for tourists are wanted. There is more interest and rising prices for TV, radio and computer collectibles. Unique celebrity-related photographs, autographs, clothing, or belongings like baseballs or guitars can start bidding wars. Vintage watches by Rolex and Patek Philippe are in demand and prices are getting higher, especially for those made after 1926, when the first waterproof models were made. Many are bought to wear, not just to display. Additions to the auction sales that started less than 10 years ago are designer purses by makers like Hermès or Chanel and special edition sneakers made by Nike and other name brands. These are selling for hundreds to thousands of dollars and are not really collected but are bought to use or to resell to make a profit.

Kovels' Antiques and Collectibles Price Guide prices have gotten younger over the past 49 years. Most items in our original book were made before 1860, so they were more than a century old. Today we list pieces made as recently as 2000, and there is great interest in furniture, glass, ceramics, and good design made since 1950.

The book is more than 590 pages long and crammed full of prices and photographs. We try to have a balanced format—not too many items that sell for over $5,000. We list a few very expensive pieces so you can realize that a great paperweight may cost $10,000 but an average one is only $25. Nearly all prices are from the American market for the American market. Only a few European sales are reported. We don't include prices we think result from "auction fever." We do list verified bargains. There are more items under $10 than in any of our price books written in the past fifteen years.

The index is computer-generated. Use it often. It includes categories and much more. For example, there is a category for Celluloid. Most celluloid will be there, but a toy made of celluloid may be listed under Toy and also indexed under Celluloid. There are also cross-references in the listings and in the paragraphs. But some searching must be done. For example, Barbie dolls are in the Doll category; there is no Barbie category. And when you look at "doll, Barbie," you find a note that "Barbie" is under "doll, Mattel, Barbie" because Mattel makes Barbie dolls and most dolls are listed by maker.

All photographs and prices are new. Antiques and collectibles pictured are items that were offered for sale or sold for the amount listed in 2015–2016. Auction prices include the buyer's premium. Wherever we had extra space on a page, we filled it with tips about the care of collections and other useful information. Don't discard this book. Old Kovels' price guides can be used in the coming years as a reference source for price changes and for tax, estate, and appraisal information.

The prices in this book are reports of the general antiques market. As we said, every price in the book is new. We do not estimate or "update" prices. Prices are either realized prices from auctions, completed sales, or they're asking prices. We know that a buyer may have negotiated an asking price to a lower selling price, but we report asking prices. We do not pay dealers, collectors, or experts to estimate prices. If the price is from an auction, it includes the buyer's premium if one is charged; but prices do not include sales tax. If a price range is given, at least two identical items were offered for sale at different prices. Price ranges are found only in categories like Pressed Glass, where identical items can be identified. Some prices in *Kovels' Antiques & Collectibles Price Guide* may seem high and some low because of regional variations, but each price is one you could have paid for the object somewhere in the United States. Internet prices from sellers' ads or listings are avoided. Because so many non-collectors sell online but know little about the objects they are describing, there can be inaccuracies in descriptions. Sales from well-known Internet sites, shops, and sales, carefully edited, are included.

If you are selling your collection, do not expect to get retail value unless you are a dealer. Wholesale prices for antiques are 30 to 40 percent of retail prices. The antiques dealer must make a profit or go out of business. Internet auction prices are less predictable—because of an international audience and "auction fever," prices can be higher or lower than retail.

RECORD PRICES

Record prices for antiques and collectibles make news every year. We report those that relate to the entries in this book. We do not include record prices for works of art that are often seen in museums, like oil paintings, antique sculptures, or very recent work by modern artists unless the artist also worked in decorative arts. Our list is a snapshot of the collectors' market.

ADVERTISING

Gasoline sign: $164,700 for a gas station sign, "Musgo Gasoline - Michigan's Mile Maker," with a portrait of an Indian in full headdress in the center, c.1940, 48-in. diameter. Morphy Auctions, Denver, Pennsylvania.

CLOCK & WATCHES

E. Howard No. 43 clock: $254,100 for an E. Howard & Company No. 43 floor regulator clock, with reverse painted glass astronomical dial, sweep minute hand, 5-hour numbers, in a carved walnut case, 105 inches high. Fontaine's Auction Gallery, Pittsfield, Massachusetts.

FURNITURE

Spitler decorated blanket chest: $356,500 for a Shenandoah Valley of Virginia blanket chest, yellow pine, paint decorated by Johannes Spitler, with inverted hearts & crescents, and lovebirds perched on tulip design, dovetailed case, wrought-iron strap hinges, interior lidded till, c.1800, 23 x 47 1/2 x 21 1/4 in., Jeffrey S. Evans, Mt. Crawford, Virginia.

Paul Evans furniture: $287,500 for a Paul Evans cabinet with wavy front made of welded polychrome steel, painted wood and slate, 2 doors, 23K gold leaf and welded signature. Rago Auctions, Lambertville, New Jersey.

GLASS

Flask GI-119: $133,000 for a cobalt blue GI-119 flask, Columbia with Liberty Cap on the front and American Eagle on back, pontil, Kensington Glass Works, Pennsylvania, 1830-1840, pint. Glass Works Auctions, Lambertville, New Jersey.

Paul Evans cabinet: $287,500

Tagliapietra sculptural glass vessel: $46,875 for the sculptural vessel "Medusa," by Lino Tagliapietra, Murano, Italy, 2007, blown, battuto and inciso glass, signed, 20 x13 in., Rago Auctions, Lambertville, New Jersey.

Christian Dior perfume bottle: $67,650 for a limited edition 1957 perfume bottle, "J'appartiens a Miss Dior" (I Belong to Miss Dior), figural dog-shaped bottle with 16-in. silk box shaped like a doghouse. Created to celebrate the 10th anniversary of the House of Dior, signed "Tien Dior." Perfume Bottles Auctions, New York.

JEWELRY

Most expensive diamond: $57,500,000 for the largest blue diamond in the world, 14.62 ct., "The Oppenheimer Blue," (named after its former owner, Sir Philip Oppenheimer) mounted in a platinum ring, with trapeze-shaped diamond on either side. Christie's, Geneva, Switzerland.

Most expensive green diamond sold at auction: $16,818,983 for the "Aurora Green" mounted in a gold ring surrounded by circular-cut pink diamonds. Christie's, Hong Kong.

Bracelet: $7.2 million for an Art Deco sapphire and diamond bracelet by Cartier. Christie's, Hong Kong.

Pair of ruby earrings: $11.6 million for a pair of Burmese oval-shaped ruby earrings of 10.02 and 9.09 ct. by Etcetera. Christie's, Hong Kong.

LAMPS

Chihuly chandelier: $200,000 for a Dale Chihuly chandelier made of white, clear, and amber blown glass, and steel armature, made in Seattle, Washington, in 2004, 120 x 60 x 58 in., Rago Auctions, Lambertville, New Jersey.

MISCELLANEOUS

Most expensive biscuit: $22,968 for a wheat biscuit that survived the sinking of the R.M.S. Titanic in 1912, found in the survivor's kit of the Titanic's lifeboat, the square biscuit made by Spillers & Bakers stamped with the brand name and "Pilot," 3 ½ x 3 ½ in., Henry Aldridge & Son's, Wiltshire, England.

Titanic dinner menu: $118,750 for a first class dinner menu from the April 14, 1912, voyage of the R.M.S. Titanic. Heritage Auctions, Dallas, Texas.

John Lennon guitar: $2,410,000 for a John Lennon original 1962 J-160E Gibson Acoustic guitar. Julien's Auctions, Beverly Hills, California.

Superman lunchbox and thermos: $20,400

Superman lunchbox: $20,400 for a Superman lunchbox with original Universal thermos, 1954. Morphy Auctions, Denver, Pennsylvania.

PAINTINGS & PRINTS

Cassius Coolidge painting: $658,000 for the Cassius Coolidge painting "Poker Game," signed C.M. Coolidge, dated copyright 1894, oil on canvas painting of 4 dogs playing poker, smoking pipes & cigars and drinking. Sotheby's, New York.

Carl Kahler painting: $826,000 for the Carl Kahler painting "My Wife's Lovers," an oil on canvas painting of cats, considered the "world's greatest cat painting," commissioned in 1891 by Kate Birdsall Johnson to create the very large painting picturing 42 of her 350 cats. Sotheby's, New York.

PAPER

Any piece of Judaica: $9,322,000 for the complete Babylonian Talmud or "Oral Law," printed by Daniel Bomberg in Venice, a collection of hundreds of years of rabbinical discussion and debate explaining laws of the Bible. One of 14 complete 16th century sets to survive. Sotheby's, New York.

Amazing Fantasy No. 15 comic book: $454,100 for the 1962 Amazing Fantasy No. 15 comic book with the first appearance of Spider-Man, near mint condition. Heritage Auctions, Dallas, Texas.

Single Inverted Jenny stamp: $1,351,250 for a single "Inverted Jenny" stamp issued on May 10, 1918, with the image of the Curtiss JN-4 airplane in the center upside down. Sold May 31, 2016, by Siegel Auction Galleries, New York.

Stoneware water cooler: $483,000

POTTERY & PORCELAIN

American stoneware: $483,000 for a stoneware water cooler with stepped bunghole and open handles, incised cobalt blue federal eagle with spread wings and shield across its chest, attributed to Henry Remmey, Sr. or Jr., Baltimore, Maryland, c.1812–29, 19 ½ in. 17, 2015, Crocker Farm, Sparks, Maryland.

Van Briggle: $275,000 for a Van Briggle Lorelei vase with 2-color glaze, 1902, marked AA Van Briggle 17/1902/III, 10 ¼ x 4 ½ in., Rago Auctions, Lambertville, New Jersey.

SPORTS

Babe Ruth New York Yankees contract: $549,000 for the 1922 Babe Ruth New York Yankees contract. Goldin Auctions, at NYY Steakhouse, New York.

Michael Jordan collectible: $173,240 for Michael Jordan's final Bulls regular season jersey, worn on April 18, 1998. Goldin Auctions, Runnermede, New Jersey.

Mickey Mantle rookie card: $585,800 for a 1952 Topps Mickey Mantle rookie card. Heritage Auctions, Dallas, Texas.

Ted Williams jersey: $183,000 for the 1955 Ted Williams game-used Red Sox road jersey with matching pants MEARS A-9. Goldin Auctions, at NYY Steakhouse, New York.

TEXTILES

Political memorabilia: $185,000 for an 1844 double-sided jugate banner with color portraits for presidential candidate James K. Polk with his running mate George M. Dallas, 76 x 75 in., Heritage Auctions, Dallas, Texas.

Hermès Birkin handbag: $300,168 for a Hermès signature Birken handbag made with white matte Himalayan crocodile leather, 18K white gold and diamond hardware. Christie's, Hong Kong.

Judy Garland's Wizard of Oz dress: $1,565,000 for the dress worn by Judy Garland as Dorothy in *The Wizard of Oz*, blue & white gingham pinafore dress, fitted bodice and full skirt, with cotton blouse. Bonhams, New York.

Political jugate banner, 1844: $185,000

TOYS, DOLLS, & BANKS

Bing Jupiter passenger train set: $48,000 for a Bing "Jupiter" passenger train set, with engine & tender, sleeping car, & dining car, gauge III set, 4-4-0 live steam locomotive, 22 in. (engine & tender). Bertoia Auctions, Vineland, New Jersey.

Märklin toy train tunnel: $84,000 for a Märklin train tunnel with mountain scape, railed slopes, mountain side houses and top tower, hand painted, railed base has lamps at entrance, Germany, 29 x 13 in., Bertoia Auctions, Vineland, New Jersey.

Märklin object: $493,292 for a miniature toy workshop representing the Märklin company from 1905 in Göppengen, the biggest toy Märklin ever made, 49 x 34 x 27 in. Auktionshaus Hohenstaufen, Germany.

KOVELS OFFER EVEN MORE PRICE INFORMATION SOURCES

Website: Kovels.com

Join the community of collectors at Kovels.com to keep up on more in the buy-sell world of antiques. You should register, but there is no charge for most of the information on the site, years of answers to questions from collectors who read our newspaper column, and over 1,000,000 searchable prices from past years. Other information, including a database of pottery and porcelain marks and makers and another of silver marks and makers, is available for a fee.

Newsletter: *Kovels on Antiques and Collectibles*

You already know this book is a great overall price guide for antiques and collectibles. Each entry is current, every photograph is new, and all prices are accurate. There is also another Kovel publication designed to keep you up-to-the-minute in the world of collecting. Things change quickly. Important sales produce new record prices. Fakes appear. Rarities are discovered. To keep up with developments, you can read *Kovels on Antiques and Collectibles,* our monthly newsletter. It is now available by subscription in two forms, a print edition that is mailed and an electronic format that is available via an online subscription at Kovels.com. Both provide the identical newsletter, with current information and photos useful to collectors. The electronic edition gives you access to over ten years of newsletter archives, too. Each newsletter is filled with color photographs, about forty per issue. The newsletter reports prices, trends, auction results, Internet sales, and other news for collectors (see the back page of this book to order).

HOW TO USE THIS BOOK

There are a few rules for using this book. Each listing is arranged in the following manner: CATEGORY (such as silver), OBJECT (such as vase), DESCRIPTION (as much information as possible about size, age, color, and pattern). Some types of glass, pottery, and silver are exceptions to this rule. These are listed CATEGORY, PATTERN, OBJECT, DESCRIPTION. All items are presumed to be in good condition and undamaged, unless otherwise noted. In most sections, if a maker's name is easily recognized like Gustav Stickley we include it near the beginning of the entry. If the maker is obscure, the name may be near the end.

- You will find silver flatware in either Silver Flatware Plated or Silver Flatware Sterling. There is also a section for Silver Plate, which includes coffeepots, trays, and other plated holloware. Most solid or sterling silver is listed by country, so look for Silver-American, Silver-Danish, Silver-English, etc.

Silver jewelry is listed under Jewelry. Most pottery and porcelain is listed by factory name, such as Weller or Wedgwood; by item, such as Calendar Plate; in sections like Dinnerware or Kitchen; or in a special section, such as Pottery-Art, Pottery-Contemporary, Pottery-Midcentury, etc.

- Sometimes we make arbitrary decisions. Fishing has its own category, but hunting is part of the larger category called Sports. We have omitted most guns except toy guns. These are listed in the Toy category. It is not legal to sell weapons without a special license, so guns are not part of the general antiques market. Air guns, BB guns, rocket guns, and others are listed in the Toy section. Everything is listed according to the computer alphabetizing system.
- We made several editorial decisions. A butter dish is a "butter." A salt dish is called a "salt" to differentiate it from a saltshaker. It is always "sugar and creamer," never "creamer and sugar." Where one dimension is given, it is the height; or if the object is round, it's the diameter. The height of a picture is listed before width. Glass is clear unless a color is indicated.
- Some antiques terms, such as "Sheffield" or "Pratt," have two meanings. Read the paragraph headings to know the definition being used. All category headings are based on the vocabulary of the average person, and we use terms like "mud figures" even if not technically correct. Some categories are known by several names. Pressed glass is also called pattern glass or EAPG (Early American pattern glass). We use the name pressed glass because much of the information found in old books and articles use that name.
- This book does not include price listings for fine art paintings, antiquities, stamps, coins, or most types of books. Comic books are listed only in special categories like Superman, but original comic art and cels are listed in their own categories.
- Prices for items pictured can be found in the appropriate category. Look for the matching entry with the abbreviation "Illus." The color photograph will be nearby.
- Thanks to computers, the book is produced quickly. The last entries are added in June; the book is available in September. But human help finds prices and checks accuracy. We read everything at least five times, sometimes more. We edit more than 40,000 entries down to the 25,000 entries found here. We correct spelling, remove incorrect data, write category paragraphs, and decide on new categories. We proofread copy and prices many times, but there may be some misspelled words and other errors. Information in the paragraphs is updated each year and this year more than 38 updates and additions were made.
- Prices are reported from all parts of the United States, Canada, Europe, and Asia, converted to U.S. dollars at the time of the sale. The average rate of exchange on June 1, 2016, was $1 U.S. to about $1.31 Canadian, €0.90 (euro), and £0.69 (British pound). Prices are from auctions, shops, Internet sales, shows, and even some flea markets. Every price is checked for accuracy, but we are not responsible for errors. We cannot answer your letters asking for price information, but please write if you have any requests for categories to be included or any corrections to the paragraphs or prices. You may find the answers to your other questions at Kovels.com.
- When you see us at shows, auctions, house sales, and flea markets, please stop and say hello. Don't be surprised if we ask for your suggestions. You can write to us at P.O. Box 22192-K, Beachwood, OH 44122, or visit us on our website, www.Kovels.com.

TERRY KOVEL AND KIM KOVEL
July 2016

ACKNOWLEDGMENTS

For the past nine years our publisher, Black Dog & Leventhal, and its president, J.P. Leventhal, have helped us continue to rethink, redesign, and improve *Kovels Antiques & Collectibles Price Guide.* There are many changes in technology that speeded production, improved the quality of pictures and made it easier to read and use. We changed to color photos, automatic index, easy to read type styles, and added features like marks, tips, sidebars of added information, and even a special section with information to help explain the how and why of buying and selling antiques and collectibles using new technologies. Thanks to J.P. Leventhal; Lisa Tenaglia, our editor; Ankur Ghosh, our production editor; and Kara Thornton for publicity. Mary Flower, Robin Perlow, and Cynthia Schuster Eakin did copyediting and proofreading for the entire book and found the tiniest of errors.

Thanks to Sheila Hart, who put all the prices, photographs, and paragraphs together and created the look and layout of *Kovels' Antiques & Collectibles Price Guide 2017*, and Janet Dodrill who outlined the images for print.

The details and hard work required to record prices, assemble photos and information, check accuracy and spelling, and solve many other problems are all done by our Kovels' staff. We thank Darlene Craven, Katie Karrick, Liz Lillis, Beverly Malone, Tina McBean, Renee McRitchie, and Erika Risley, who recorded prices, a difficult task because they had to put each price in the proper one of the over 700 categories. Special thanks to three other staff members. Cherrie Smrekar recorded the record prices all year long and created that list as well as tackling tips and sidebars. Lauren Rafferty, our photo editor, made sure each of the 2,500 pictures was captioned and credited properly, as well as approving the quality of pictures. Gay Hunter has been the in-house editor for dozens of years and each year she finds better ways to control the problems. Her year-round job includes spellchecking the prices as they are recorded and making sure we have pictures for each section. She also updates the paragraphs. And most of all she keeps us all on schedule so the final book comes out on time. And very, very special thanks to our daughter, Kim Kovel, who is in charge of technology, finance, advertising, and the business side of Kovels. She is also our expert on the Fifties and newer collectibles and other "younger" pieces now included in the book. This, our 49th edition of *Kovels' Antiques and Collectibles Price Guide*, is possible only because so many of us created it.

CONTRIBUTORS

The world of antiques and collectibles is filled with people who have answered our every request for help. Dealers, auction houses, and shops have given advice and opinions, supplied photographs and prices, and made suggestions for changes. Many thanks to all of them:

Photographs and information were furnished by: Accurate Auctions, Ahlers & Ogletree Auction Gallery, Alex Cooper Auctioneers, Allard Auctions, Bamfords Auctioneers and Valuers Ltd., Bertoia Auctions, Bill & Jill Insulators, Brunk Auctions, California Auctioneeers & Appraisers, Case Antiques Inc., Clars Auction Gallery, Copake Auction Inc., Cordier Auctions & Auctioneers, Cottone Auctions, Cowan's Auctions, Crocker Farm, Crown Auctions, Dirk Soulis Auctions, DuMouchelles Art Gallery,

Eagle Cap Collectibles Auction, Early American History Auctions, Early Auction Co., Ewbank's, Fairfield Auction, Fox Auctions, Fryer & Brown Auctioneers, Garth's Auctioneers & Appraisers, Glass Works Auctions, Great Estates Auctioneers & Appraisers, Guyette & Deeter, Hake's Americana & Collectibles, Heritage Auctions, Hess Auction Group, Humler & Nolan, James D. Julia, Inc., Jaremos Estate Liquidators, Jeffrey S. Evans & Associates, Los Angeles Modern Auctions (LAMA), Manifest Auctions, Martin Auction Co., McMasters Harris Auction Co., Milestone Auctions, Morphy Auctions, Mossgreen Pty. Ltd., Neal Auction Co., Nest Egg Auctions, New Orleans Auction Galleries, NH Button Auctions, Norman C. Heckler & Co., North American Auction Co., Old Barn Auction, Open-Wire Insulator Services, Palm Beach Modern Auctions, Perfume Bottles Auction, , Phillips, Potter & Potter Auctions Rago Arts and Auction Center, Replacements, Ltd., Rich Penn Auctions, Robert Edward Auctions, RSL Auction, Ruby Lane, Sam Scott Pottery, Selkirk Auctioneers & Appraisers, Showtime Auction Services, Skinner, Inc., Stephenson's Auction, Strawser Auction Group, The Cobbs Auctioneers, The Stein Auction Co., Theriault's, Thomaston Place Auction Galleries, Tradewinds Antiques & Auctions, Treadway Toomey Auctions, Vintage Costume Jewels, Wickliff Auctioneers, Wm Morford Antiques, Woody Auction, and Wright.

The contact information for these people is at the back of this book on page 562.

To the others who knowingly or unknowingly contributed to this book, we say thank you: Alderfer, Aspire Auctions, Auction Gallery of the Palm Beaches, Augusta Auctions, Belhorn Auctions, Billings Auction, Bonhams, Bremo Auctions, Bruhns Auction Gallery, Chandler's International Auction & Estate Sales, Christie's, Christiana Auction Gallery, Clifford A. Wallach, Concept Art Gallery, Cresent City Auction Gallery, CRN Auctions, Dallas Auction Gallery, Ripley Auctions, Don Presley Auction, Doyle, East Coast Auctions, Elite Decorative Arts, Faganarms, Inc., Freeman's, Fusco Auctions, Golden Memories Auction Co., Grogan & Co., *Heisey News,* Heisey Collectors of America, , Horst Auctioneers, Hyde Park Country Auctions, Hollywood Poster Auction, J. Levine Auction & Appraisal, Jackson's International Auctioneers, Just Art Pottery, John McInnis Auctioneers, Kejaba Treasures, Kaminski Auctions, Keystone Auctions, Leighton Galleries, Leland Little Auctions, Leonard Auction, Leslie Hindman Inc., Lewis & Maese Antiques & Auctions, Link Auction Galleries, Manor Auctions, Michaan's Auctions, Morton Auctioneers, Mosby & Co. Auctions, O'Gallerie, Old World Auction, *Pole Top Discoveries,* Pook & Pook, Quinn's Auction Galleries, Rachel Davis Fine Arts, Rush Antiques, Simpson Galleries, Sotheby's, Stair Galleries, Stuart Kingston Inc., Susanin's Auctions, Time and Again Galleries, Tom Harris Auction, Trader Fred's, Treadway Gallery, Trocadero, Uniques & Antiques Auction Sales, Weschler & Son, Westport Auction, and other sites.

A. WALTER made pate-de-verre glass under contract at the Daum glassworks from 1908 to 1914. He decorated pottery during his early years in his studio in Sevres, where he also developed his formula for pale, translucent pate-de-verre. He started his own firm in Nancy, France, in 1919. Pieces made before 1914 are signed *Daum, Nancy* with a cross. After 1919 the signature is *A. Walter Nancy*.

Bowl, Nude Woman, Curled Up, Signed, 1940s, 9 In. 7234
Dish, Crab, Green To Blue, Brown To Yellow, 8 In. 5000
Dish, Moth, 3-Sided, Signed, 2 ¼ x 6 ¾ In. 950
Dish, Scarab, Black & Red, Yellow Base, c.1920, 5 In. 1480
Paperweight, Bird, Signed, 1920s, 4 x 4 x 3 In. .... *illus* 1875
Paperweight, Henri Berge, 2 Lizards Entwined, Leaf Base, 3 ⅝ In. 6132
Tray, Crab, Sea Plants, Mottled, 6-Sided, Art Nouveau, 10 In. .... *illus* 2588
Tray, Figural Bumblebee On Edge, Cream, Oval, Signed, 4 In. 2074

ABC plates, or children's alphabet plates, were most popular from 1780 to 1860, but are still being made. The letters on the plate were meant as teaching aids for children learning to read. The plates were made of pottery, porcelain, metal, or glass. Mugs and other items were also made with alphabet decorations.

Bowl, Jack & Jill, Transferware, Germany, 1900s, 7 ⅝ In. 60
Mug, Fish, Gun, Kittens, Multicolor, Handleless, Ceramic, 3 In. 150
Mug, Madrid, Spain, Brown, Brownhills Pottery, c.1880, 2 ¾ In. 300
Mug, Robinson Crusoe, Making A Boat, Brownhills Pottery, c.1880, 2 ⅞ In. 300
Plate, Blue, Clock, Numbers, Calendar, Staffordshire, 1887, 6 ⅞ In. 275
Plate, Children Playing, For My Nephew, Pearlware, c.1850, 5 ¾ In. 250
Plate, Children, Dog, Parrot, Germany, 5 ⅞ In. 29
Plate, Elephant, Jumbo, Tin, Embossed, c.1880, 5 ½ In. 95
Plate, God Gives All Things To Industry, Woman Seated, Garden, 6 ¼ In. 135
Plate, Little Strokes Fell Great Oaks, Raised Foot, Man With Ax, c.1850, 6 In. 130
Plate, Men On Horses, Shooting, J. & G. Meakin, c.1850, 5 ½ In. 75
Plate, Oriental Hotel, Building, On River, Transferware, c.1880, 7 ⅜ In. 105
Plate, Robinson Crusoe, Finding The Footprints, Goat, Chocolate Brown, c.1880, 7 ¼ In. 225
Plate, Sheep Dog, Seated In Front Of Fence, Staffordshire, England, c.1870, 7 ½ In. 375
Plate, What Fruit Does Our Sketch Represent, Black Figures, 1840s, 6 In. 170

ABINGDON POTTERY was established in 1908 by Raymond E. Bidwell as the Abingdon Sanitary Manufacturing Company. The company started making art pottery in 1934. The factory ceased production of art pottery in 1950.

Candlestick, Double Scroll, Gilt, c.1940, 4 ½ In., Pair 35
Console, Bird Of Paradise, Flowered Branch, Panels, Cream, 14 x 5 In. 40
Urn, Curved Handles, Flared Rim, White, 9 x 7 In. 40
Vase, 2-Tone, Black, Yellow, Jonquil, Foil Label, 8 In. 121
Vase, Fan Shape, Integral Flower Frog, Mauve, Paper Label, 1940s, 7 x 5 x 4 In. 49
Vase, Handles, Tassel, Footed, Pink, 8 ⅝ x 6 In. .... *illus* 42
Vase, Pink, Anchor, 10 In. 28
Vase, Urn Shape, Handles, Blue Glaze, c.1945, 15 In. 115
Wall Shelf, Scalloped Shell, Acanthus Lower Finial, White, c.1942, 9 x 7 x 3 In. 79

ADAMS china was made by William Adams and Sons of Staffordshire, England. The firm was founded in 1769 and became part of the Wedgwood Group in 1966. The name *Adams* appeared on various items through 1998. All types of tablewares and useful wares were made. Other pieces of Adams may be found listed under Flow Blue and Tea Leaf Ironstone.

TRADE MARK
ADAMS
ENGLAND

Bowl, Vegetable, Octagonal, Lid, Flower Finial, Crane, Blue Flowers, 8 ½ x 6 ¼ In. 50
Cup & Saucer, Farmers Prayer, Flower & Leaf Trim 125
Cup & Saucer, Flower & Leaf Border, In God Is Our Trust 125
Eggcup, Pink Rose Sprays, Blue Ground, Double, c.1935 15
Eggcup, Red Bud, Blue Leaves, 3 ¾ In. 8
Eggcup, Red Flower, Blue Leaves, Gilt Trim, Double, 3 ¾ In. 15
Pitcher, Milk, Adams' Rose, Flowers, Leaves, 7 ½ In. .... *illus* 118
Plate, Landing Of Columbus, Transferware, Blue & White, 10 In. .... 125 to 135
Plate, Pearlware, Early Adams Rose, c.1830, 9 ¼ x 9 ½ In., 5 Piece 95
Plate, White House, Flow Blue, c.1900, 10 ¼ In. 125
Teapot, Adams' Rose, Scrolled Spout, 8 ¾ In. 385
Tobacco Jar, Kids Around Table, Dickensware, c.1910, 5 x 6 In. 99

A. Walter, Paperweight, Bird, Signed, 1920s, 4 x 4 x 3 In.
$1,875

Rago Arts and Auction Center

A. Walter, Tray, Crab, Sea Plants, Mottled, 6-Sided, Art Nouveau, 10 In.
$2,588

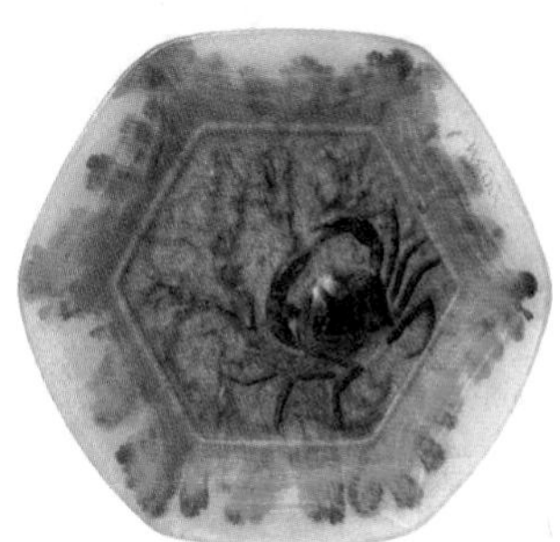

Early Auction Company

Abingdon, Vase, Handles, Tassel, Footed, Pink, 8 ⅝ x 6 In.
$42

Ruby Lane

This is an edited listing of current prices. Visit **Kovels.com** to check thousands of prices from previous years and sign up for free information on trends, tips, reproductions, marks, and more.

Adams, Pitcher, Milk, Adams' Rose, Flowers, Leaves, 7 ½ In.
$118

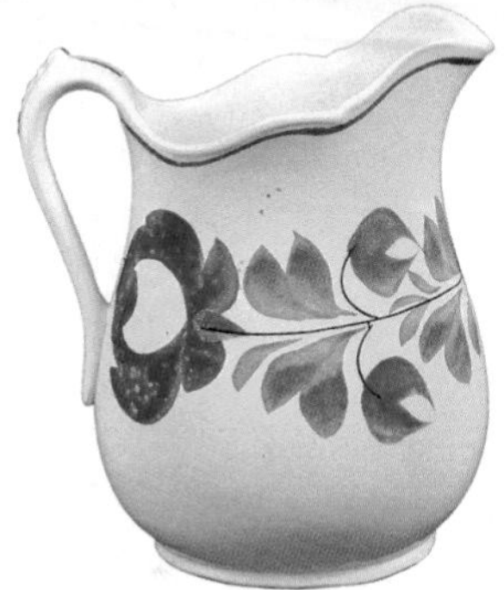

Hess Auction Group

Advertising, Banner, Yardley's Old English Lavender, Woman, Basket, Lavender, 1920s, 30 x 35 In.
$173

Hake's Americana & Collectibles

Advertising, Bench, Star Brand Shoes, Oak, Punched Logo In Backing, Brass Studs, 69 x 39 In.
$580

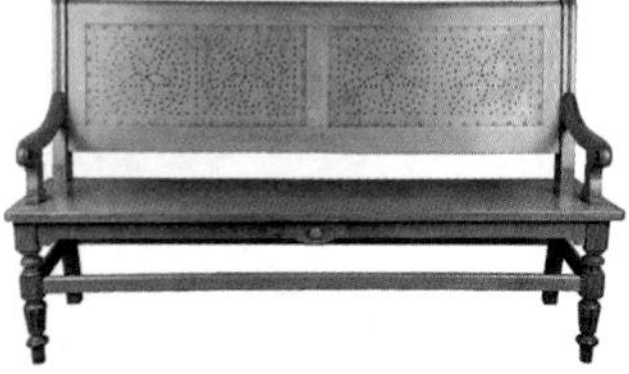

Morphy Auctions

Advertising, Bin, Big Johnson's Log Cabin Coffee, Tin Lithograph, Painted, 18 x 28 x 24 In.
$3,660

Morphy Auctions

ADVERTISING containers and products sold in the old country store are now all collectibles. These stores, with crackers in a barrel and a potbellied stove, are a symbol of an earlier, less hectic time. Listed here are many advertising items. Other similar pieces may be found under the product name, such as Planters Peanuts. We have tried to list items in logical places, so enameled tin dishes will be found under Graniteware, auto-related items in the Auto category, paper items in the Paper category, etc. Store fixtures, cases, signs, and other items that have no advertising as part of the decoration are listed in the Store category. The early Dr Pepper logo included a period after "Dr," but it was dropped in 1950. We list all Dr Pepper items without a period so they alphabetize together. For more prices, go to kovels.com.

Ashtray & Matchbook Holder, Statler Hotel, Glossy Green Glaze, 1950s, 5 In. Diam. 22
Ashtray, Clay-Adams Co., Skull Shape, 3 x 3 x 4 In. 180
Ashtray, Shell Oil, Compliments Of Petersburg Shell Service Station, Uhl, 2 ½ In. 58
Ashtray, U.S. Cold Storage, Snowman, Round, Green, White, Black, 5 x 5 In. 60
Banner, Alfa Romeo, Flag, Badge, 1970s, 30 x 42 In. 625
Banner, Firestone Tires, 9.95, Nylon, Cloth, Red, White, Blue, 1950s, 36 x 70 In. 90
Banner, Remington, America's Oldest Gun Makers, Rifle, Silk, Tassels, 1955, 35 x 21 In. 240
Banner, Sideshow, Cow With 5 Legs, Alive, Painted, Brackets, 96 x 68 In. 3000
Banner, Sideshow, Peggy The Cow With 5 Legs, Born Alive, Cow In Pasture, 96 x 118 In. 720
Banner, Sideshow, See Otis Jordan, Frog Boy, Alive, Cloth, F. Johnson, 94 x 114 In. 4920
Banner, Sideshow, World Champion Sword Swallower, Alive, Canvas, 138 x 114 In. 1200
Banner, Yardley's Old English Lavender, Woman, Basket, Lavender, 1920s, 30 x 35 In. ....*illus* 173
Barrel, Tobacco, Wigwam Fine Cut, Label, Stencil, Tax Stamp, Lid, 13 x 12 In. 510
Baseball Scorer, Murray Hill Club Whiskey, Figural Catcher's Mitt, Celluloid, 3 In. 164
Bench, Star Brand Shoes, Oak, Punched Logo In Backing, Brass Studs, 69 x 39 In. ....*illus* 580
Bin, Big Johnson's Log Cabin Coffee, Tin Lithograph, Painted, 18 x 28 x 24 In. ....*illus* 3660
Bin, Luxury Coffee, Pine, Hinged, Slant Lid, Yellow Paint, Stenciled Label, 1800s, 32 x 22 In. 540
Bin, Scull's Sterling Coffee, Tin Lithograph, 22 x 19 In. 413
Bobbin's Head, Col. Sanders, KFC, Figural, Glasses, Cane, White Suit 127
Books may be included in the Paper category.
Bottles are listed in their own category.
Bottle Openers are listed in their own category.
Box, see also Box category.
Box, Beech-Nut Brand, Chewing Gum, Wood, 12 ½ x 24 In. 120
Box, Black Maria Chewing Tobacco, 10 Cents, Native Woman, Wood, 1930, 11 x 7 In. 207
Box, Cereal, Sugar Pops, Display, Cowboy, Guy Madison, Cardboard, 20 x 15 In. 282
Box, Cigar, Champions, World Champion Portraits, 1897, Allen & Ginter, 9 ¾ x 5 In. ....*illus* 648
Box, Display, King Collar Button Co., Gold Leaf Decal, Wood, 6 x 6 In. 114
Box, Fairway Oats, Cardboard, Multicolor Graphic, 3 Lb., 9 ½ x 5 ¼ In. ....*illus* 207
Box, Fairy Soap, Wood, Winged Fairies, Cream, Red, 3 x 10 x 1 ¼ In. 115
Box, Home Plate Oats, Cardboard, Baseball Scene, Multicolor, 1 Lb., 7 x 4 In. ....*illus* 863
Box, Martha Washington Oats, Cardboard, Multicolor Graphic, 9 ½ x 5 ½ In. ....*illus* 184
Box, Portage Rolled Oats, Cardboard, Indians Carrying Canoe, Cylindrical, 10 x 6 In. ....*illus* 242
Box, Seed, Rice's, Wood Display, Multicolor Label, 4 x 11 x 6 ½ In. 316
Box, Shipping, Evinrude Motors, Outboard Marine & Mfg. Co., 1940s, 43 x 20 In. 240
Box, Silver Gem Chewing Gum, Flying Woman, Children, Candy, Wood, Lid, 8 In. 180
Box, Uncle Sam's Oat Flakes, Cardboard, Red, White, Blue, Cylindrical, 10 x 5 In. ....*illus* 316
Box, Wigwam Oats, Cardboard, Indian Village, Multicolor, 9 ½ x 5 ½ In. ....*illus* 776
Broom Holder, Chas. Brown Grocery Co., Cincinnati, Ohio, 40 x 21 In. 428
Broom Holder, Woods Norway, Pine Syrup, 2-Sided, Blackboard, c.1890 428
Bucket, Heinz Mince Meat, Wood, Lid, Bail Handle, Label, 20 Lb., 10 x 10 In. .... 485 to 1265
Cabinet, Dental, Peroxigen Toilet Articles, Tin Litho, Girl, Brushing Teeth, 20 x 14 In. ....*illus* 1553
Cabinet, Diamond Dyes, Evolution Of Woman, 30 ½ x 28 ½ In. 423
Cabinet, Diamond Dyes, Washer Woman, Tin, c.1910, 30 x 23 In. 495
Cabinet, Humphrey's Specifics, Pine, Tin Panels, Interior Drawers, 21 x 28 x 10 In. ....*illus* 298
Cabinet, Rit Dye, Slant Front, 3 Drawers, Color Samples, Metal, 11 ¼ x 14 ¼ In. 180
Cabinet, Spool, Belding Brothers & Co., 7 Drawers, Maple, c.1900, 21 x 20 In. 850
Cabinet, Spool, Clark's O.N.T., 7 Drawers, Ruby Glass, Hardware, 29 x 23 In. 1140
Cabinet, Spool, Coats & Clark, Metal, Blue, c.1800, 10 x 24 x 14 In. 345
Cabinet, Spool, J. & P. Coats', 4 Drawers, Lift Top, Oak, 30 x 20 x 12 In. 295
Cabinet, Spool, J. & P. Coats', Mahogany, 6 Drawers, 22 ¼ x 22 ¼ In. 375
Cabinet, Spool, Star Mercerized, Fast Colors-Will Boil, 4 Drawers, Metal, c.1900, 15 x 14 In. 395
Calendars are listed in their own category.
Can, Co-Op Household Oil, Squeezable, Lead Top, Gray, White, 2 x 4 In. 20
Can, Finol Household Oil, Standard, Red, White, Blue, Squeezable, 1970s, 4 In. 18
Can, Republic Motor Oil, Eagle, Shield, Red, White, Blue, 6 x 4 In. 242
Can, Singer Sewing Machine Oil, Green, Red, c.1920 65

Advertising, Box, Cigar, Champions, World Champion Portraits, 1897, Allen & Ginter, 9 ¾ x 5 In.
$648

Robert Edwards Auctions

Advertising, Box, Fairway Oats, Cardboard, Multicolor Graphic, 3 Lb., 9 ½ x 5 ¼ In.
$207

Wm Morford

Advertising, Box, Home Plate Oats, Cardboard, Baseball Scene, Multicolor, 1 Lb., 7 x 4 In.
$863

Wm Morford

Punchboards
Handmade punchboards were used in the eighteenth century. It was not until the twentieth century that printed boards were made. The first patent dates from 1905. Punchboards, advertising enticements that gave you the prize indicated by the piece you punched out of the board, were all the rage into the 1930s. Their popularity and sales declined during World War II, and many states said they were illegal because the process was a form of gambling. Some are still made today.

Advertising, Box, Martha Washington Oats, Cardboard, Multicolor Graphic, 9 ½ x 5 ½ In.
$184

Wm Morford

Advertising, Box, Portage Rolled Oats, Cardboard, Indians Carrying Canoe, Cylindrical, 10 x 6 In.
$242

Wm Morford

Advertising, Box, Uncle Sam's Oat Flakes, Cardboard, Red, White, Blue, Cylindrical, 10 x 5 In.
$316

Wm Morford

Advertising, Box, Wigwam Oats, Cardboard, Indian Village, Multicolor, 9 ½ x 5 ½ In.
$776

Wm Morford

Advertising, Cabinet, Dental, Peroxigen Toilet Articles, Tin Litho, Girl, Brushing Teeth, 20 x 14 In.
$1,553

Wm Morford

Peanut Butter Invented
The Kellogg Brothers were the first to invent peanut butter, but they failed to patent it.

Advertising, Cabinet, Humphrey's Specifics, Pine, Tin Panels, Interior Drawers, 21 x 28 x 10 In.
$298

Showtime Auction Services

Advertising, Crock, Heinz's Currant Jelly, Stoneware, Lid, Bail Handle, 10 Lb., 7 ½ In.
$684

Showtime Auction Services

Advertising, Dispenser, Blue-Jay Corn Plasters, Man In Rocker, Tin, Die Cut, 6 x 14 x 6 In.
$655

Showtime Auction Services

Advertising, Dispenser, Kel-Ola Syrup, Flowers, Ceramic Ball Pump
$2,166

Showtime Auction Services

Advertising, Dispenser, Ward's Lemon Crush, Figural, Lemon, Raised Letters, Pump, 14 In.
$1,544

James D. Julia Auctioneers

Canisters, see introductory paragraph to Tins in this category.
Cards are listed in the Card category.
Case, Display, Cigarette, Wood, Glass, Ogden's Guinea Gold, 33 In. 519
Change Receiver, see also Tip Tray in this category.
Change Receiver, Andy Gump Cigars, Wood Base, Glass Top, Multicolor, 7 ¼ x 7 ¼ In. 805
Charger, Lord Calvert, Superb American Whiskey, Scroll, Cream, Gold, Metal, 23 In. 60
Cheese Scale, Standard Computing, Red, Round Wood Base, 13 x 16 In. 210
Christmas Tree, Feather, Light-Up, Black Top Hat Base, LaSalle Hat Co., 26 In. 325
Cigar Box, Kit Carson, Imperials, Wood, Cowboy On Horse, Gun, 6 ½ x 4 In. 288
Cigar Cutter, Bauer's Kidney Gin, Figural Pig, Cast Iron, Pull-Down Tail, 7 x 4 In. 399
Cigar Cutter, Country Gentleman 5 Cents, American Thoroughbred, Counter, 5 x 3 In. 240
Cigar Cutter, Glenwood 10 Cents, Lighter, Top Globe, 17 x 9 In. 1952
Cigar Cutter, Que Placer, Mild Blend Habanas, 8 In. 180
Cigar Cutter, Robert Burns Cigars, Conway Cigar Co., Counter, c.1910, 6 x 5 In. 120
Cigar Cutter, Rocky Ford, Mechanical, Cast Iron, Dispenses Wood Match, 8 x 11 In. 1495
Cigarette Holder, Racing Mechelen, Soccer Ball, Tin, Mechanical, 1938 251
Clocks are listed in their own category.
Cloth, Rub-No-More Frolic, Mother Elephant, Bathing Baby, Litho On Oilcloth, 32 x 30 In. 837
Clothes Wringer, American Wringer Co., Good Will Soap, Wood, Box, 4 x 8 In. 242
Cooler, Dr Pepper, Drink Dr Pepper, Good For Life, Trunk, Handles, Green, Metal, 14 In. 510
Crock, Heinz Plum Butter, Stoneware, Lid, Bail Handle, Vegetables On Label, 36 Oz. 1026
Crock, Heinz Raspberry Jelly, Standard Quality, Lid, Bail Handle, Stoneware, Label, 9 In. 418
Crock, Heinz's Currant Jelly, Stoneware, Lid, Bail Handle, 10 Lb., 7 ½ In. *illus* 684
Cuspidor, Havana, All Famous Havana 5 Cent Cigars, Trumpet Rim, Brass, 9 x 10 In. 30
Dispenser, Blue-Jay Corn Plasters, Man In Rocker, Tin, Die Cut, 6 x 14 x 6 In. *illus* 655
Dispenser, Buckeye Root Beer, Ceramic, Urn Shape, Pump, White, Green, 14 In. 1342
Dispenser, Daggett's Orangeade, Soda Syrup, Textured Glass, Green, 14 In. 519
Dispenser, Formacone Formaldehyde, Pinecone Shape, Prevents Disease, 11 In. 300
Dispenser, Fowler's Cherry Smash, Cherry Shape, Pump, Ceramic, 15 In. 2745
Dispenser, Hershey's Honey Bar, 1 Cent, Iron, Northwestern Corp., c.1925, 13 In. 561
Dispenser, Kel-Ola Syrup, Flowers, Ceramic Ball Pump *illus* 2166
Dispenser, Malted Grape-Nuts, Chocolate Drink, Yellow, Glass Lid, c.1926, 7 x 15 In. 180
Dispenser, McCormick Tea, Teapot Form, Black, White Letters, Spigot, Hall, 13 In. 120
Dispenser, Straw, Hires Root Beer, Cast Iron, Footed, c.1911, 5 x 10 In. 494
Dispenser, Sundae, Curtiss Baby Ruth, Automatic Hot Fudgester, Lid, 10 In. 270
Dispenser, Syrup, Ward's Orange Crush, Ceramic, Figural, Pump, 8 x 14 In. 1140
Dispenser, Ward's Lemon Crush, Figural, Lemon, Raised Letters, Pump, 14 In. *illus* 1544
Display, A Point To Remember, Kleanbore, Dog, Pointer, Cardboard, 1933, 34 x 43 In. 1938
Display, Alka-Seltzer, Tin Lithograph, Tape Dispenser, Counter, 12 x 7 x 11 In. 122
Display, Blue-Jay Corn Plasters, Tin, Drawers, Woman Tending To Her Feet, 9 x 13 In. 270
Display, Cabinet, Putnam Dyes, Tin, 5 x 12 x 8 In. *illus* 149
Display, Dentyne Gum, Majorette, Feathered Hat, Red, White, Tin, 7 ½ x 3 In. 450
Display, Diadem Hair Pins, Wood, Slanted, Counter, 17 In. 120
Display, Edison Mazda Lamps, Woman, Lightbulb, Cardboard, 1920s, 68 x 23 In. *illus* 575
Display, Figural, Cowboy Boot, Leather, Western Store, 29 x 17 In. 36
Display, Grape-Nuts, Dizzy Dean, Pitching Baseball, Die Cut, 1930s 2629
Display, Great Atlantic & Pacific Tea Co., Couple On Tricycle, Die Cut, 1883, 7 x 10 In. 21
Display, Hamm's Beer, Figural, Black & White Bear, Styrofoam, c.1960, 27 x 18 x 62 In. 90
Display, Hanes Merrichild Sleeper, Young Boy, Puppy, Composition, Base, 22 In. 228
Display, Hoover Vacuum, Green Dust Figure, Rubber, 1960s, 6 In. 180
Display, Join The Big Bear Drinking Brotherhood Of Hamm's, Bear, Rotating, 76 x 54 In. 6710
Display, Kellogg's Corn Flakes, Seated Woman, Sweetheart Of The Corn, Die Cut, 42 In. 330
Display, King Collar Button Co., Figural Collar Button, 1890s, 9 ½ In. 600
Display, Life Savers, 5 Cents, Candy Mints, Candy Drops, Blue, Tin, 11 ½ x 10 In. 330
Display, Life Savers, Tin Lithograph, Black & White, After Eating After Smoking, 13 x 6 In. 244
Display, Lime Cola, It's Definitely Good, Bottle, Wood, Counter, 16 x 6 In. 153
Display, M&M's Candy, Figural, Red Character, Air Salute, Wheel Base, 20 x 42 In. 210
Display, Manischewitz Kosher Wine, Figural Hand On Grape Cluster, 7 x 11 In. 420
Display, McGregor Happy Foot, Molded, Sock, Composition, Gold Color, 1930s, 8 In. *illus* 569
Display, Munyon's Homeopathic Home Remedies, Tin, Drawers, c.1910, 12 x 14 In. *illus* 549
Display, Old Crow Kentucky Bourbon, Figural Crow, Tux & Hat, 10 In. 120
Display, Owl Casting, Iron, Oak Shield, Mills Novelty Co., 1900s, 22 x 16 In. 153
Display, Poll-Parrot Shoes, Papier-Mache Parrot, Perched, Multicolor, 36 In. 900
Display, Thomas Inks, Ask For Me, Figural Black Cat, Plaster, 20 ½ In. 840
Display, Watta Pop, Figural, Polar Bear, Chalkware, Lollipop Holder, 8 x 7 In. 275
Display, Watta Pop, Polar Bear, Chalkware, 5 x 8 In. *illus* 660

Advertising, Display, Cabinet, Putnam Dyes, Tin, 5 x 12 x 8 In.
$149

Showtime Auction Services

Advertising, Display, Edison Mazda Lamps, Woman, Lightbulb, Cardboard, 1920s, 68 x 23 In.
$575

Wm Morford

Advertising, Display, McGregor Happy Foot, Molded, Sock, Composition, Gold Color, 1930s, 8 In.
$569

Hake's Americana & Collectibles

Advertising, Display, Munyon's Homeopathic Home Remedies, Tin, Drawers, c.1910, 12 x 14 In.
$549

Morphy Auctions

Advertising, Display, Watta Pop, Polar Bear, Chalkware, 5 x 8 In.
$660

Showtime Auction Services

Advertising, Display, Whistle Soda, Hand, Full Unopened Bottle, Figural, Iron, Wall Mount, 10 In.
$1,121

Wm Morford

Display, Whistle Soda, Hand, Full Unopened Bottle, Figural, Iron, Wall Mount, 10 In. ....*illus* 1121
Dolls are listed in their own category.
Door Pull, Double Cola, Red, Orange, Gold Swirl Accents, 1930s, 12 In. 240
Door Push, Canada Dry Ginger Ale, The Best Of Them All, Hand, Bottle, 4 x 12 In. 200
Door Push, Hamm's Beer, Theo. Hamm Brewing Co., Porcelain, 15 x 4 In. 1591
Door Push, Pop Kola, America's Finest Cola, Bottle, Tin Lithograph, 3 x 8 In. 125
Door Push, Rainbo Is Good Bread, Blue, White, Red, 26 ½ x 3 In. 60
Door Push, Sunbeam Bread, Batter Whipped, Tin Lithograph, 1950s, 20 x 9 In. 300
Door Push, Yankee Doodle, Root Beer, Bottle, Red, White, Blue, Tin, 4 x 12 In. 175
Fans are listed in their own category.
Figure, Bob's Big Boy, Restaurant, Standing, Holding Burger, 43 In. 1200
Figure, Dog, RCA, Nipper, Molded Rubber, Plastic, Black & White, 36 In. 671
Figure, Doughboy Flour, Mechanical, Rabbit In World War I Uniform, Salutes, 26 In. 1680
Figure, J.I. Case, Old Abe, War Eagle, Perched On Globe, Cast Iron, c.1865, 57 In. 4750
Figure, Penfold Golf, Figural Golfer, Plaster, Argyle Sweater Vest, Hat, 1930s, 19 In. 1195
Figure, Punch, Cigar Store, Standing Smoking, Jester Outfit, Cast Zinc, 1885, 19 In. 80663
Firecrackers, Kent, Cherry Flash, Salutes, Marshmallow Shape, Box, 1946, 3 x 4 In. 330
Firecrackers, Salutes, Silver Flash, Box, 1920s, 3 x 3 In. 600
Firecrackers, Star Brand, Glittercrackers, Salutes, Box, 3 x ⅝ In. 330
Firecrackers, Warrior Brand, Macau, Logo Salutes, Box, 5 x 2 In. 60
Gun Rack, Savage Stevens Fox, World Famous Rifles & Shotguns, Wood, 20 x 29 In. 538
Ice Cream Cup, Tarzan, Animals, Panels, Waxed, Lily-Tulip Cup Corp., 1930s, 3 In. ....*illus* 173
Illustration, Alka-Seltzer, Oil On Canvas, 2 Woman Chatting, 1900s, 43 x 33 In. 2151
Illustration, Cream Of Wheat, Oil On Canvas, Children, Chalkboard, 1900s, 29 x 18 In. 2271
Illustration, Jergens Face Powder, Sweet Siren You, Mixed Media, Paper, c.1942, 11 x 8 In. 1793
Illustration, Laros Lingerie, Oil On Masonite, Woman, Nightgown, c.1940, 33 x 22 In. 1783
Jar, Almonds, Nutritious Delicious, 5 Cents, Lid, Clear Glass, Round, Pedestal, 14 In. 214
Jar, Bowers Three Thistle Snuff, Stoneware, Cobalt Letters, Rolled Rim, 14 x 11 In. 185
Jar, Display, Chicos Spanish Peanut, Tin Lithograph Lid, Embossed, 10 In. ....*illus* 671
Jar, Heinz Vinegar, Cylindrical, Label, Stopper, Glass, Pontil, 35 In. 1265
Jar, Lutted S.P. Cough Drops, Clear Glass, Log Cabin Shape, Lid, 8 x 7 In. 171
Jug, Citro, The Thirst Quencher, 5 Cents, Glass, Paint, Cylindrical, Funnel Top, 13 In. 90
Jug, Heinz Dill Vinegar, Blue Ceramic, Red, Label, 5 In. 270
Jug, Heinz Pickling Distilled Vinegar, Keystone, Handle, Stopper, 3 In. 60
Label, Cigar Box, Old Abe, Lincoln's Portrait, c.1930, 6 ½ x 2 ¼ In. 10
Label, Cigar, Mark Twain, Liked By All, Portrait, Stone Chromolithograph, 1800s, 9 x 7 In. 50
Label, Proof, Gum, Adams Chewing Gum, Tutti Frutti, Woman, Gown, Updo, Paper 108
Laird's Apple Brandy, Pourer, 4 x 2 ½ In. 45
Lamps are listed in the Lamp category.
Match Dispenser, Economy Stove Co., Cast Iron, Copper Flash, 4 ½ x 4 ½ In. ....*illus* 390
Match Holder, Fly, Wendel Meyer, Cast Iron, Simpson Iron Co........*illus* 513
Megaphone, Ted's Creamy Root Beer, Ted Williams, Holding Bat, Yellow, 1950s........ 598
Menu Board, Angler's Inn, Hotel, It's Always Time For A Guinness, Chalkboard, 34 x 59 In. 3088
Menu Sign, Drink Cherry Smash, A True Fruit Blend, Round Top, 18 In. 427
Menu, Soda Fountain, We Sell Wamsutta Ginger Ale, Indian, Bow, Tin, 11 x 29 In. 1938

Advertising mirrors of all sizes are listed here. Pocket mirrors range in size from 1 ½ to 5 inches in diameter. Most of these mirrors were given away as advertising promotions and include the name of the company in the design.

Mirror, Ammon & Person, Baby Brand Butterine, Oval, Celluloid, 3 x 2 In. 316
Mirror, Classic Cream Dove Peanut Butter, Boy In Overalls, Holding Jar, Oval, 3 In. 278
Mirror, Ginger Ale, Red Rock, Woman, Roses, Drinking, Oval, Celluloid, 3 x 2 In. 575
Mirror, Good For 10 Cents In Trade, Elk Cafe, Cortland, N.Y., Celluloid........ 300
Mirror, J.I. Case Threshing Machine Co., Celluloid, 1 ¾ x 2 ¾ In. ....*illus* 120
Mirror, Little Rock Railway, Woman Exiting Trolley Car, Celluloid, 3 x 2 In. ....*illus* 2415
Mirror, Meet Me At The Eagle Hotel, Nude Woman, By Ocean, 2 x 3 In. 150
Mirror, Mellon's Cafe, Baseball Club, Oval, Celluloid, 1912, 3 x 2 In. 371
Mirror, Neave's Foods For Infants & Invalids, Running Boy, Holding Container, 1910, 2 In. 115
Mirror, Put Roses In Your Cheeks, Drink Hires Root Beer, Woman, Celluloid, 3 In. 230
Mirror, Roller Rink, Excelsior, Woman On Skates, Round, 2 In. 431
Mug, Jac. Ruppert's Lager Beer, Display, Label Under Glass, 9 ¾ In. 2400
Mug, Metz Bro's Lager Beer, Etched, 6 In. 405
Page Folder, Trethaway Bros., Tin Lithograph, Our Specialty, 12 x 3 In. 456
Pail, Buffalo Brand Peanut Butter, Bail Handle, Wood Lid, 10 ½ x 12 In. 173
Pail, Bully Boy Tobacco, P. Lorillard Co., Label, Wood, Metal Lid, 11 x 13 In. 480
Pail, Hoody's Famous Peanut Butter, Children, Teeter-Totter, Tin Lithograph, 3 ⅜ x 4 In. 345

Advertising, Ice Cream Cup, Tarzan, Animals, Panels, Waxed, Lily-Tulip Cup Corp., 1930s, 3 In.
$173

Hake's Americana & Collectibles

Advertising, Jar, Display, Chicos Spanish Peanut, Tin Lithograph Lid, Embossed, 10 In.
$671

Morphy Auctions

Advertising, Match Dispenser, Economy Stove Co., Cast Iron, Copper Flash, 4 ½ x 4 ½ In.
$390

Showtime Auction Services

Advertising, Match Holder, Fly, Wendel Meyer, Cast Iron, Simpson Iron Co.
$513

Showtime Auction Services

Advertising, Mirror, J.I. Case Threshing Machine Co., Celluloid, 1 ¾ x 2 ¾ In.
$120

Showtime Auction Services

TIP

Any lithographed can with a picture is of more value than a lithographed can with just names. Any paper-labeled can that can be dated before 1875 is rare. Any ad that pictures an American flag or a black person has added value.

Store Signs

Some old store signs were lithographed directly on tin and made to look like a picture with a wooden frame. The Grape-Nuts sign picturing a girl and her St. Bernard is one of the best known examples.

Advertising, Mirror, Little Rock Railway, Woman Exiting Trolley Car, Celluloid, 3 x 2 In.
$2,415

Wm Morford

Advertising, Print, Budweiser, Lithograph, Woman, Eagle, Frame, 26 ½ x 36 ½ In.
$1,708

Morphy Auctions

Advertising, Print, Centlivre's Nickel Plate Beer, Chromolitho, Couple, Railroad Car, 29 x 25 In.
$244

Morphy Auctions

Advertising, Print, Eberhardt & Ober Brewing Co., Lithograph, Factory, Frame, 45 x 34 In.
$854

Morphy Auctions

Advertising, Roly Poly, Mayo's Cut Plug Tobacco, Dutchman, Tin Litho, Multicolor, 7 x 6 In.
$219

Wm Morford

TIP
Don't keep identification on your key ring. If it is lost, it's an invitation for burglars to visit.

Pail, Jackie Coogan Peanut Butter, Tin Lithograph, c.1919, 3 ½ x 3 ¾ In. 230
Pail, Skippy Peanut Butter, Lithograph, Multicolor, Tin, 12 Oz., 3 x 3 ½ In. 127
Pail, Swift's Peanut Butter, Premium Quality, Peanuts, Yellow, Blue, Lid, Tin, 25 Lb., 10 In. 30
Paperweight, Zepp Photo Service, Figural, Camera, Cast Iron, Black, 3 x 3 In. 316
Pin Holder, Thompson Meters, Cloisonne Porcelain, Enamel Lid, Round, 1 ½ x 2 In. 127
Pin, Flintkote Roofing, Black Cat, Night Time Roof, Yellow Stripe, c.1899, 1 ½ In. 115
Pin, N.Y. State Horticultural Society, Apple Shape, Red, Pinback, 1942, 1 ¼ In. 12
Pin, Teddy Bear Bread, Figural, Die Cut, Tin Lithograph, Eyeglasses, c.1912, 2 In. 170
Plate, El Gallo, Ruy Lopez, Rooster, Key West Cigar, Vienna Art, 10 In. 244
Print, Budweiser, Lithograph, Woman, Eagle, Frame, 26 ½ x 36 ½ In. .... *illus* 1708
Print, Centlivre's Nickel Plate Beer, Chromolitho, Couple, Railroad Car, 29 x 25 In. .... *illus* 244
Print, Eberhardt & Ober Brewing Co., Lithograph, Factory, Frame, 45 x 34 In. .... *illus* 854
Print, Fairy Soap, Little Sweethearts, Boy Giving Flower To Girl, Frame, 1901, 23 x 31 In. 30
Printer's Proof, Class, Cigar 5 Cents, Peacock, Full Plumage, Frame, 17 x 25 In. 570
Printer's Proof, Owl Cigars, Now 5 Cents, 2 Owls, Perched, Cigar, 12 x 8 In. 150
Puzzle, Tip Top Bread, Town Scene, 1950s.......... 20
Rack, Curtiss Penny Candies, Use Your Cents, Tin, 10 ½ In. 180
Rack, Kotex, Nurse Holding Box, Tin Lithograph, 1920s, 25 x 20 In. 518
Rack, Tootsie Roll, 5 Cents, Black, Yellow, 13 ½ x 10 ½ In. 420
Ring, Honeycomb Kid, Post, 24K Gold, Montana Map, 1966, Adjustable 115
Ring, Kellogg's, Baseball Game, Silvered Metal, 2 Baseballs, Plastic Cover, 1949.......... 115
Roly Poly, Mayo's Cut Plug Tobacco, Dutchman, Tin Litho, Multicolor, 7 x 6 In. .... *illus* 219
Salt & Pepper Shakers are listed in their own category.
Scales are listed in their own category.
Shelf, Sunshine Biscuits, Always Ask For Sunshine Biscuits, Metal, 15 x 20 In. 510
Sign, 7Up, Get Real Action, 7Up Your Thirst Away, Light-Up, Round, 15 x 3 In. 630
Sign, 7Up, We Proudly Serve 7Up, It Likes You, Green, Red, Tin, c.1945, 13 x 32 In. 360
Sign, 7Up, You Like 7Up, It Likes You, Tin, Frame, Oval, 40 x 29 In. 330
Sign, AC Spark Plugs, Blue, Red, White, Tin, 18 x 9 In. 300
Sign, Adams Fruit Gum, Woman Holding Cherries, Masonite, 15 x 10 In. 60
Sign, Ajax Beer, Glass, Metal Frame, Neon, 20 x 12 x 6 In. 1375
Sign, Alexander, The Man Who Knows, Alexander The Great Face, c.1910, 27 x 41 In. 170
Sign, Alka-Seltzer, Woman, Holding Stack Of Boxes, Oil On Canvas, c.1950, 33 x 29 In. 1076
Sign, Ask For Jersey Ice Cream, Girl, Red Bow In Hair, Tin Lithograph, 6 x 14 In. 265
Sign, Baby Label Bread, Baby In High Chair, Blue, White, Red, Porcelain, 36 x 15 In. 285
Sign, Barker's Powder, Horse & Cattle, Farm With Healthy Animals, Litho, Frame, 25 x 21 In. 518
Sign, Bartlett's Blacking, Leather, Man, Black Boy Valet, Chromolithograph, c.1863, 12 x 15 In. 1554
Sign, Bears' Honeydew Cigarettes, Elephant, Yellow, Orange, Porcelain, 13 x 18 In. 86
Sign, Beeman's Pepsin Gum, Aids Digestion, Yellow & Red, Tin, 17 x 2 ½ In. 390
Sign, Benjamin Moore & Co., Figural Paint Bucket & Brush, Plastic, 25 In. 150
Sign, Blasco Husky Batter, Tin, Embossed, Dog On Battery, Handmade, 21 x 15 In. 1500
Sign, Blue Diamond Brand, Hood River Apples, Glass Front, Frame, 12 x 22 In. 30
Sign, Bond Bread, The Home-Like Loaf, Black & Yellow, Porcelain, 18 x 14 In. 200
Sign, Bowey's Root Beer, Sweating Mug, Barrel Dispenser, Painted Metal, 1930s, 8 x 10 In. 230
Sign, Buffalo Brewing Bohemian Beer, Tin, Gesso Frame, 32 ½ In. .... *illus* 11400
Sign, Bull Durham, 1 Oz. Bag 5 Cents, Bull, Yellow, Blue, Tin, Embossed, 9 x 12 In. 660
Sign, Bullet Board, Winchester Double W, Frame, 58 x 40 In. .... *illus* 23800
Sign, Burma-Shave, 2-Sided, 40 x 17 ½ In. .... *illus* 200
Sign, Bus Depot, Santa Fe Trail System, Blue, Keyhole Shape, 2-Sided, Blue, 26 x 23 In. 7800
Sign, Buster Brown Shoes, Plastic, Rubberized, 3-D, Buster Dog, c.1950, 27 x 22 In. .... *illus* 580
Sign, Cafe Salada, Can Shape, White, Blue, Yellow, Porcelain, 12 x 12 In. 510
Sign, Call For A Botl'O Orange, & Other Flavors, Bottle, Tin, 12 x 24 In. 275
Sign, Camel Lights, Joe Camel, Smoking Cigarette, Tin, Marked, 17 x 28 In. 30
Sign, Campbell's Soup, Kids, Batter, Outfielder, Die Cut, c.1969, 42 In., Pair.......... 92
Sign, Canada Dry, Beverages, Green, Red, White, Porcelain, 1950s, 30 x 10 In. 200
Sign, Carter's Union Suits For Boys, Cardboard, Easel, Boy On Scooter, 15 x 14 In. .... *illus* 207
Sign, Cascarets Bowel Candy Cathartic, Canvas, Sleeping Woman, c.1900, 29 x 42 In. .... *illus* 1708
Sign, Chalkboard, Golden Cola, Refreshing As A Cup Of Coffee, Cup, 20 x 28 In. 366
Sign, Chateau De Fonfel, Vin Sans Pareil, Woman, Grapevines, Frame, 42 x 28 In. 1235
Sign, Chesterfield Cigarettes, Cooler, Cigarette Pack Shape, Cardboard, 22 In. 150
Sign, Cincinnati Stove Works, Woman On Horseback, Cast Iron, 1903, 27 x 42 In. 5520
Sign, Columbia Dry Batteries, They Last Longer, Tin, 9 x 3 ½ In. 420
Sign, Columbia Records, Vinyl Record Shape, Grooves, Porcelain, 1920s, 28 In. 3000
Sign, Continental Insurance Co. Of New York, Self-Framed, Tin Litho, 20 x 30 In. .... *illus* 793
Sign, Corner, Schulze's Butter-Nut Bread, Sweet As A Nut, Porcelain, 17 x 22 In. 175
Sign, Cream Of Wheat, Health Authorities Urge Hot Cereal, Paper, Frame, 1920s, 27 x 37 In. 366

Advertising, Sign, Buffalo Brewing Bohemian Beer, Tin, Gesso Frame, 32 ½ In.
$11,400

Showtime Auction Services

Advertising, Sign, Bullet Board, Winchester Double W, Frame, 58 x 40 In.
$23,800

Showtime Auction Services

Advertising, Sign, Burma-Shave, 2-Sided, 40 x 17 ½ In.
$200

Showtime Auction Services

Advertising, Sign, Buster Brown Shoes, Plastic, Rubberized, 3-D, Buster Dog, c.1950, 27 x 22 In.
$580

Morphy Auctions

Advertising, Sign, Carter's Union Suits For Boys, Cardboard, Easel, Boy On Scooter, 15 x 14 In.
$207

Wm Morford

Advertising, Sign, Cascarets Bowel Candy Cathartic, Canvas, Sleeping Woman, c.1900, 29 x 42 In.
$1,708

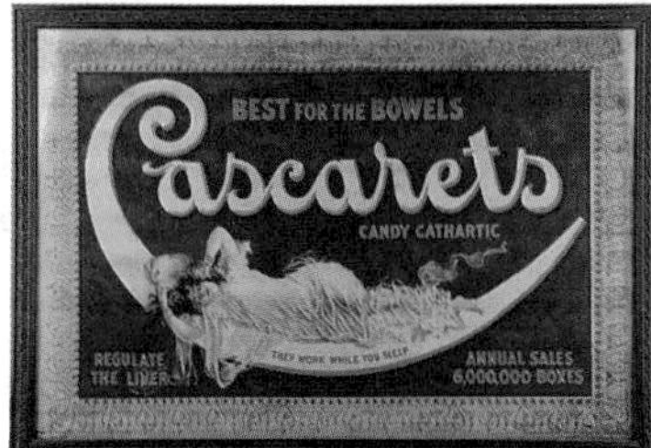

Morphy Auctions

Advertising, Sign, Continental Insurance Co. Of New York, Self-Framed, Tin Litho, 20 x 30 In.
$793

Morphy Auctions

Advertising, Sign, Dr. D. Jayne's Tonic Vermifuge, Reverse Glass, Frame, c.1880, 12 x 14 In.
$4,370

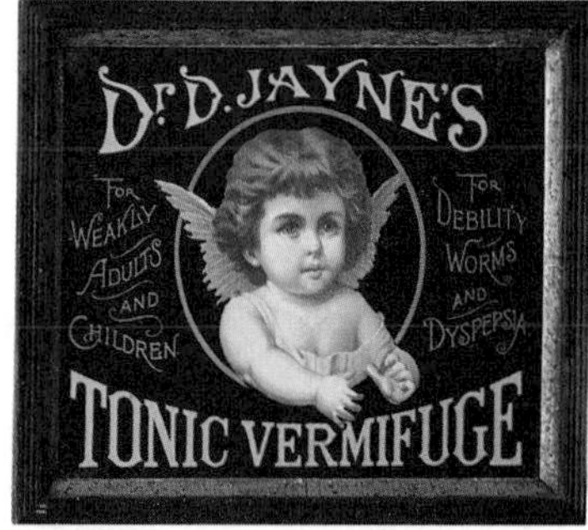

Wm Morford

Advertising, Sign, Drink Grape Ola, Tin Lithograph, Embossed, W.F. Robertson, 1920s, 13 x 19 In.
$392

Hake's Americana & Collectibles

Advertising, Sign, Eagle, Figural, Old Abe Civil War Mascot, Case, Carved, c.1885, 27 x 9 In.
$6,518

James D. Julia Auctioneers

Advertising, Sign, Euthymol Toothpaste, Parke Davis & Co., Easel, Cardboard, 9 ¾ x 5 In.
$265

Wm Morford

Advertising, Sign, Ghiradelli's Chocolate & Cocoa, Girl, Doll, Tea Party, Tin, Self-Framed, 23 x 28 In.
$2,678

Showtime Auction Services

Advertising, Sign, Grand Rapids Brush, Cardboard, Lady Liberty, Horse Brushes, 15 x 20 In.
$1,140

Showtime Auction Services

Sign, Curtiss Candies, Butterfinger, Rich In Dextrose, Yellow, Black, Tin, 10 x 28 In. 390
Sign, Daggett & Ramsdell's Cold Cream, Woman, Cardboard, Frame, 12 x 22 In. 150
Sign, Don't Whittle Corns, Use Blue-Jay Corn Plasters, Old Man, Tin, c.1925, 14 x 4 In. 330
Sign, Dr Pepper, 3-D, Cardboard, Girl With Bottle, 1940s, 18 x 15 In. 1778
Sign, Dr Pepper, Drink A Bite To Eat At 10 2 4, Bottle, Frame, 58 x 22 In. 1560
Sign, Dr Pepper, Tic Tic Toc, Get A Cold Doc, Woman, Bottle, Cardboard, 32 x 19 In. 120
Sign, Dr. D. Jayne's Tonic Vermifuge, Reverse Glass, Frame, c.1880, 12 x 14 In. .... *illus* 4370
Sign, Drink A Punch & Judy Cocktail, It Recuperates, Red, Celluloid, c.1910, 12 x 7 In. 1020
Sign, Drink Cherry Blush, Cherries Only Rival, Tin, Cherry Branch, Red, Green, 9 x 6 In. 456
Sign, Drink Double Cola, Scroll, Black, Yellow, Red, Oval, Tin, Flange, 18 ½ x 15 In. 390
Sign, Drink Dr Pepper, Good For Life!, Tin Lithograph, Brick Design, c.1939, 12 x 29 In. 780
Sign, Drink Ginseng Liqueur, Long Life Tonic, Flower Border, Bottle, Tin, 12 x 9 In. 230
Sign, Drink Grape Ola, Tin Lithograph, Embossed, W.F. Robertson, 1920s, 13 x 19 In. .... *illus* 392
Sign, Drink Nesbitt's Orange, 5 Cents, Bottle Shape, 1940s, 44 x 12 In. 1200
Sign, Drink Speed-Ball, The Delicious Drink, Woman, Tin, Curled Corners, 1907, 10 x 10 In. 1254
Sign, Drugstore, W.H. Wentland Manor, Drugs, Yellow, Red, Tin, 12 x 23 In. 180
Sign, Eagle, Figural, Old Abe Civil War Mascot, Case, Carved, c.1885, 27 x 9 In. .... *illus* 6518
Sign, Early Times Whiskey, Tin Lithograph, Backwoods Distillery, Ky., 24 In. 1725
Sign, Eastside Beer, Woman Holding Glass, Yellow Roses, Lithograph, Frame, 21 x 17 In. 270
Sign, Enjoy Hires Root Beer, Healthful Delicious, Bottle, Blue, Yellow, Tin, 10 x 28 In. 458
Sign, Esslinger Premium Beer, Logo, Bottle Cap Shape, Plastic, Light-Up, Box, 15 In. 700
Sign, Euthymol Toothpaste, Parke Davis & Co., Easel, Cardboard, 9 ¾ x 5 In. .... *illus* 265
Sign, Eyeglasses, Figural, Blue Eyes, Metal, Plaster, 41 x 19 In. 1200
Sign, F.W. Woolworth & Co., Entrance, Red, Gold Lettering, Frame, Glass, 12 x 25 In. 150
Sign, Farm Stand, Watermelon Shape, Ice Cold, Paint, 2-Sided, Pine, 1800s, 14 x 31 In. 1778
Sign, Father John's Medicine, A Body Builder, Bottle, Portrait, Paper, Frame, 12 x 40 In. 114
Sign, Fig Newton, National Biscuit Company, Lithograph, Frame, 12 x 23 In. 60
Sign, Firestone, Paper Lithograph, Trio Girls, Multicolor Graphic, c.1910, 24 x 16 In. 2645
Sign, Flying A Gasoline, Round, Winged Letter A, Red, White, Black, 11 ¼ In. 150
Sign, Foster Freeze, Little Foster, Ice Cream Cone Mascot, 1950s, 9 x 11 In. 600
Sign, Free If You Guess Your Weight, Green, Black & Orange, Frame, 18 x 12 In. 183
Sign, Fresh Milk, RS Titwill, Metal, Painted, c.1900, 13 x 20 ½ In. 360
Sign, Fudgicle, Toast To Good Health, 5 Cents, Girl & Boy, Cardboard, Easel, 20 x 17 In. 330
Sign, Ganong's Chocolate Bars, 5 Cents, Children, Candy, Lithograph, Frame, 15 ½ x 25 In. 210
Sign, General Electric, Appliances Television, Round, Reverse On Glass, Light-Up, 15 In. 240
Sign, Get HEP For Yourself, Bottle, Oval, 2-Sided, Flange, 18 x 13 In. 210
Sign, Ghiradelli's Chocolate & Cocoa, Girl, Doll, Tea Party, Tin, Self-Framed, 23 x 28 In. .... *illus* 2678
Sign, Glenwood-Inglewood Spring Water, Woman, Long Red Hair, Paper, Frame, 25 x 22 In. 180
Sign, Golden West Coffee, Drink More Coffee, Cardboard, 26 x 38 In. 142
Sign, Grand Rapids Brush, Cardboard, Lady Liberty, Horse Brushes, 15 x 20 In. .... *illus* 1140
Sign, Grand Republic Flour, Woman Baker, Paper, 25 ½ x 18 In. 840
Sign, Grape-Nuts, Tin Lithograph, To School Well Fed On Grape-Nuts, 20 x 30 In. .... *illus* 915
Sign, Grapette Soda, Enjoy Grapette Soda, Black, Red, White, Tin, Oval, 16 x 27 In. 510
Sign, Green Giant, Niblets, Corn, Playing Tuba, c.1951, 22 x 17 In. 28
Sign, Greenfield's Chocolates, Woman With Hat Boxes, Paper, 1911, 23 x 13 In. 120
Sign, H.P. Hood & Sons, Milk, Cow, Green, White, Porcelain, Round, 1900, 30 In. 1800
Sign, Hamm's Beer, Enjoy Baseball With Hamm's, Scoreboard, Frame, 36 x 31 In. 519
Sign, Hankey's Farm Boy Bakery Products, Cream, Blue, Celluloid, Tin, 13 x 6 In. 46
Sign, Heinz 57 Ketchup, Girl, Straw Hat, Holding Tomatoes, Cardboard, Frame, 20 x 10 In. 633
Sign, Heinz Olive Oil, Heinz Malt Vinegar, For Perfect Salads, Paper, Frame, 12 x 15 In. 257
Sign, Heinz, Pure Food Products, 57 Varieties, Pickle, Round, 11 ¼ In. 30
Sign, Helmar Turkish Cigarettes, Egyptian Woman Profile, Cardboard, 17 x 28 In. 300
Sign, Hershey's Ice Cream, The Purest Kind, Yellow, Red, Porcelain, 10 x 15 In. 1389
Sign, Hickman-Ebbert Co., Horse, Wagon, Boy & Girl, Tin, Self-Framed, 38 x 26 In. .... *illus* 1547
Sign, Hi-Plane Tobacco, 10 Cents, Black, Green, Tin, 35 In. 180
Sign, Hires Root Beer, Black, Yellow, Cardboard, c.1910, 15 x 10 In. 545
Sign, Hires Root Beer, For Thirst & Pleasure, Round, Light Blue, Black, Tin, 23 In. 480
Sign, Holbrook Polar Brand, Ice Cream Sodas, 2-Sided, Flange, 15 x 9 In. 90
Sign, Honeymoon Special, White Ground, Blue Letters, Moon Face, Round, 18 In. 410
Sign, Hoover Co., Starry Night, 2 Kids & Dog, Watercolor On Board, 1937, 21 x 16 In. 896
Sign, Hopkins & Allen, Prairie Girl, Cowgirl, Revolver, Lithograph, 1910, 29 In. 2000
Sign, Horse Stable, Horse Head, Patrick Henry Quinn, Paint, Cast Iron, 1880, 22 x 38 In. 1938
Sign, Husky, Figural Dog, Motor Oil, Blue, White, Porcelain, 72 x 16 In., 2 Piece 7200
Sign, In Bottles Only, Cherry Blossoms, A Blooming Good Drink, Tin, 20 x 10 In. 510
Sign, Jackson Brewing, Dorothy Dandridge, Microphone, Bottle, 1950s, 21 x 28 In. 777
Sign, Jell-O, Now Tastes Twice As Good!, Cardboard, Easel, 31 x 21 In. 480

Advertising, Sign, Grape-Nuts, Tin Lithograph, To School Well Fed On Grape-Nuts, 20 x 30 In.
$915

Morphy Auctions

Advertising, Sign, Hickman-Ebbert Co., Horse, Wagon, Boy & Girl, Tin, Self-Framed, 38 x 26 In.
$1,547

Showtime Auction Services

Advertising, Sign, John M. Meehan, Groceries, Meats & Provisions, Cardstock, Embossed, 18 x 13 In.
$316

Wm Morford

Advertising, Sign, Mother's Oats, Raises Boy Like That, Wrapped In Tiger Pelt, Paper, Frame, 1901, 17 x 25 In.
$149

Showtime Auction Services

Advertising, Sign, Owensboro Wagon, Tin Litho, Hickman-Ebbert, Apple Tree, c.1906, 38 x 26 In.
$2,565

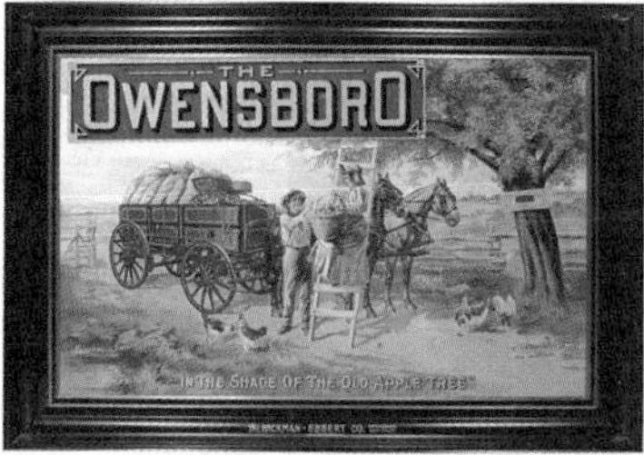

Showtime Auction Services

Advertising, Sign, Rough On Rats, Household Troubles, Paper, Under Glass, Frame, 24 x 18 In.
$298

Showtime Auction Services

Advertising, Sign, Runkel's Cocoa, Blue & White, Enameled Porcelain, 6 x 18 In.
$546

Wm Morford

Advertising, Sign, Sandow Cigars, 5 Cents, Body Builder, Embossed, String Hanger, 3 x 4 ½ In.
$518

Wm Morford

Advertising, Sign, Reddy Kilowatt, I Work For Pennies A Day, Cardboard, 28 x 22 In.
$89

Showtime Auction Services

A

Advertising, Sign, Satin Skin Powder, 4 Tints, Flesh, White, Pink, Brunet, Frame, 35 x 45 In.
$427

Morphy Auctions

Advertising, Sign, Spina Soap, Devil, Jointed, Smoking, Cardboard, Die Cut, Frame, 34 x 20 In.
$2,128

Wm Morford

Advertising, Sign, Squeeze Soda, Boys Playing Ball, Die Cut, Cardboard Litho, Frame, 18 x 22 In.
$336

Morphy Auctions

Advertising, Sign, Thirsty?, Just Whistle, 5 Cents, Boy, Actual Bottle Cutout, Easel, 27 x 14 In.
$374

Wm Morford

Advertising, Sign, Whistle Soda, Soda Bottle, 12 Ounces, 5 Cent, Litho, Cardboard, 1939, 9 x 31 In.
$244

Morphy Auctions

Advertising, Sign, Winchester, Tin Litho, Dead Ducks, Antlers, Alexander Pope, 30 x 36 In.
$4,600

James D. Julia Auctioneers

Advertising, Sign, Your Uncle Says Buy Ambrosia Chocolate Bark, Uncle Sam, Frame, 15 x 7 In.
$345

Wm Morford

Advertising, Stringholder, Swifts Pride Soap, Tin Lithograph, 2-Sided, 15 ½ x 30 In.
$18,975

Wm Morford

Sign, Jell-O, Tastes Twice As Good, Woman Holding Plate Of Jello, 32 x 22 In. 180
Sign, Jewelers, Watches, Jewelry, Clocks, Pocket Watch Shape, Zinc, 15 x 20 In. 1080
Sign, John M. Meehan, Groceries, Meats & Provisions, Cardstock, Embossed, 18 x 13 In. ....*illus* 316
Sign, Johnson Sea-Horse Outboard Motors, Noble Hardware Co., Tin, 20 x 14 In. 750
Sign, Johnson Sea-Horse, Outboard Motors, Spinner, Neon, c.1930, 18 x 18 In. 300
Sign, Kellogg's Corn Flakes, Girl Eating Cereal, Tree Stump, 1920s, 28 x 23 In. 30
Sign, Kleanbore, .22 Cartridges, Scout Holding Rifle, Cardboard, 1932, 24 x 32 In. 510
Sign, Kraft, Pex Chicken Feed, I Get The Milk-Bank Boost, Chicken, Tin, 19 x 14 In. 120
Sign, La Deva Havana Cigar, Excellent Quality, Woman Profile, Hat, Tin, 12 x 18 In. 300
Sign, Leaf Spearmint Chewing Gum, The Flavor Lingers Longer, Tin Lithograph, 9 x 25 In. 150
Sign, Leo Ouellet, Watch, Painted Roman Numerals, Cast Iron, Gilt, 20 In. 584
Sign, Lily Rye, Rubel-Lilienfeld Co., Red, Black, Reverse On Glass, 26 x 34 In. 480
Sign, Lincoln Weldealer, Arc Welding Equipment, Yellow, Red, Black, Tin, 17 x 30 In. 210
Sign, Lucky Strike, Jim Bottomley, Swinging Bat, Die Cut, Frame, 1929, 23 x 42 In. 777
Sign, Made In Detroit, Posselius Bros. Furniture Mfg. Co., Wood, 1895, 49 x 11 In. 330
Sign, Marguerite Havana Cigars, Tin Litho, Marguerite Taking Flower, 1911, 11 x 14 In. 108
Sign, Mecca Cigarettes, Stylish Girl, Multicolor, Paper Lithograph, c.1912, 20 x 11 In. 575
Sign, Medo-Land, Ice Cream Cone Shape, Steel, Die Cut, 2-Sided, Bracket, 19 x 40 In. 855
Sign, Molar, Figural, Teeth Extracted 25 Cts, Artificial Teeth, Wood, Gilt Top, 16 x 11 In. 10665
Sign, Mona Motor Oil, Barnsdall, Blue, White, Red, Wood Frame, 18 x 72 x 1 In. 1320
Sign, Mother's Oats, Raises Boy Like That, Wrapped In Tiger Pelt, Paper, Frame, 1901, 17 x 25 In. ..*illus* 149
Sign, Moxie Nerve Food, Elegant Woman, Cardstock, Embossed, Die Cut, 6 x 4¾ In. 604
Sign, Mutz's Mortgage, Black, Scrollwork, Cast Iron, Mounted, 14 x 16 In. 90
Sign, National Ale, Monk, Drinking Stein Of Beer, Tin Lithograph, 23 x 17 In. 360
Sign, Nectar Tea, Cup & Saucer Shape, White, Green, Porcelain, 21 x 13 In. 480
Sign, Nehi, Drink Nehi Beverages, Ice Cold, Bottle, Red, Yellow, Tin, 12 x 30 In. 390
Sign, New Home, Buy The Light Running Sewing Machine, Dog, Cardboard, 6 x 38 In. 288
Sign, Newly Renovated Large Rooms, 48 x 24 In. 672
Sign, No Smoking, Policeman Holding Sign, Figural, Resin, 17 x 20 In. 275
Sign, Oh Boy Gum, It's Pure, 1 Cent, Yellow, Blue, Red, Tin, 14 x 10 In. 420
Sign, Old Gold Cigarettes, Carol Lombard, In Chair Smoking, Easel, 1934, 31 x 42 In. 657
Sign, Old Gold Cigarettes, Taste Great Straight, Display Topper, Red, Yellow, 25 x 8 In. 90
Sign, Old Kentucky Tavern, Tavern Time, Pocket Watch Shape, Glass Cover, 17 x 14 In. 120
Sign, Oliver St. John, Temple Bar, Dublin, Irish Guinness Stout, Wood, Chalkboard, 45 x 49 In. . 1779
Sign, Orange Miami, Buvez, Un Breuvage De Qualite, Bottle, Tin, France, 1963, 29 x 14 In. 60
Sign, Our American Lady, Hamilton-Brown Shoe Co., Paper, Frame, 1925, 20 x 26 In. 150
Sign, Owensboro Wagon, Tin Litho, Hickman-Ebbert, Apple Tree, c.1906, 38 x 26 In. ....*illus* 2565
Sign, Owl Cigar Now 5 Cents, Cardboard, Back Mounted Eyes, 12 x 10 In. 748
Sign, Pearl Cream Ale, Beer, Gold Filigree, Green, Tin Lithograph, 1¼ x 13¼ In. 30
Sign, Pennsylvania Dutch, Birch Beer, It's Wonderful Good, Amish Man, Tin, 10 x 15 In. 120
Sign, Penny Scale, Weight, Silhouettes, Fat, Skinny, Just Right, Porcelain, 10 x 9 In. 604
Sign, Peppers Hygrade Ginger Ale, Let Us Serve You, Celluloid, Oval, 7 x 5 In. 90
Sign, Philip Morris, Pack, Box, Johnny The Bellboy, Cigarettes, Cardboard, 44 In. 60
Sign, Pocket Watch, Repairing, Clocks On Rim, Paint, Iron, Sheet Metal, 2-Sided, 26 In. 780
Sign, Popsicles, 5 Cents Sold Here, A Frozen Drink On A Stick, Orange, Tin, 3 x 10 In. 354
Sign, Post Office, Millers Mills, Wood, Silver On Black, Curved, N.Y., 11 x 45 In. 246
Sign, Post Toasties, Don't Forget Your Post Toasties, Cloth, Frame, 62 x 14 In. 660
Sign, Powell's Breakfast Cocoa, Victorian Woman, Reverse Glass, Chain, 11 x 8 In. 330
Sign, Powerlube Motor Oil, Tiger, Blue & Yellow, Porcelain, 60 x 36 In. 2400
Sign, Red Crown Gas, Paddle Shape, Center Crown, Porcelain, 2-Sided, 14 x 17 In. 1140
Sign, Red Goose Shoes, Red Goose, Red, Yellow, Tin Lithograph, 16 x 9½ In. 180
Sign, Reddy Kilowatt, I Work For Pennies A Day, Cardboard, 28 x 22 In. ....*illus* 89
Sign, Remington Autoloading Rifle, .25 Cal., Coyote On Rifle, Cardboard, 1910, 12 In. 660
Sign, Remington UMC, Woman Aiming Rifle, String Hanging, 1913, 19 x 15 In. 390
Sign, Reynolds Pianos, Sonora, Clear As A Bell, Yellow, Paint, Metal, 48 x 29 In. 60
Sign, Rising Sun Stove Polish, Girl, Bows, Lace Dress, Paper, 30 x 22 In. 780
Sign, Rochelle Club Beverages, Decidedly Better, Bottle, Tin, Embossed, 12 x 24 In. 336
Sign, Rolling Rock, On Tap, Horse & Horseshoe, Reverse On Glass, Round, 15 In. 180
Sign, Rough On Rats, Household Troubles, Paper, Under Glass, Frame, 24 x 18 In. ....*illus* 298
Sign, Royal Crown Cola, Bottle, Tin, Frame, 36½ x 16 In. 330
Sign, Royal Crown Cola, Figural Bottle, Tin, 1962, 59 x 16 In. 90
Sign, Runkel's Cocoa, Blue & White, Enameled Porcelain, 6 x 18 In. ....*illus* 546
Sign, Ryan Aeronautical Co., Sales, Service, Airplane, Porcelain Over Steel, c.1940, 9 x 12 In. 295
Sign, Saloon, The Colorado Bakery, Victorian Woman Portrait, c.1890, 18 x 14 In. 777
Sign, Sandow Cigars, 5 Cents, Body Builder, Embossed, String Hanger, 3 x 4½ In. ....*illus* 518
Sign, Satin Skin Powder, 4 Tints, Flesh, White, Pink, Brunet, Frame, 35 x 45 In. ....*illus* 427

Advertising, Teakettle, Griswold, Size 2, Marked, Use Erie Ware The Best, 3 ½ In.
$247

Cordier Auctions

Advertising, Telephone, Stromberg-Carlson, Candlestick, Metal, Carbon Composition, 3 x 2 In.
$518

Wm Morford

Advertising, Tin, All American Cookies, Lakeside Biscuit Company, Football Players, Litho, 6 In.
$345

Wm Morford

Advertising, Tin, Allen's Sanitary Tooth-Ease, Paper Label, Le Roy, N.Y., 4 x 7 ¾ In.
$242

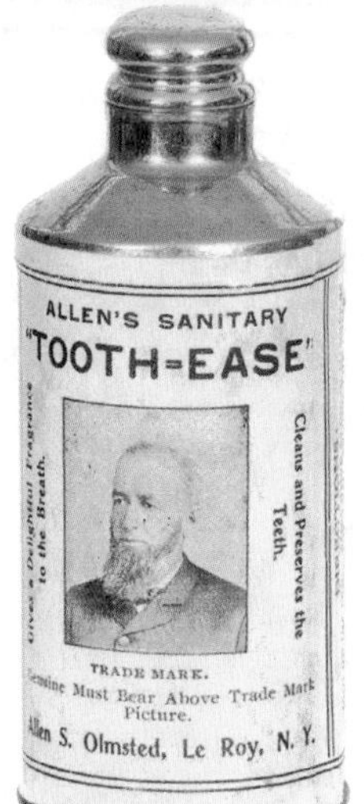

Wm Morford

Advertising, Tin, Green Turtle Cigars, Lithograph, Smoking Turtle Trademark, 5 ¼ x 7 ½ In.
$184

Wm Morford

Advertising, Tin, Honey Moon Tobacco, Couple Seated On Moon, Tin Litho, Pocket, 5 x 3 In.
$748

Wm Morford

Sign, Sheldon Gas Co., Red, Cream, Blue, Porcelain, Round, 16 In. Diam. 270
Sign, Sheppard Campbell Wholesale Oysters, Oyster Shape, 29 x 45 In. 2074
Sign, Sidewalk, Poll-Parrot Shoes, For Boys & Girls, Parrot In Boots, 22 x 46 In. 798
Sign, Sidewalk, Turnbull's Green Mountain Ice Cream, 2-Sided, Iron Frame, 20 x 34 In. 900
Sign, Smoke Royal Token, 10 Cent Cigar, 2 Nude Women, Paper, Frame, 21 x 26 In. 270
Sign, Smoke The White Label, 5 Cent Cigars, Box Of Cigars, Tin, Hanging, 14 x 10 In. 150
Sign, Smoke The Wizard Cigar, Blue, Silverleaf, Wood Frame, 1920s, 25 x 14 In. 580
Sign, Sober-Up It's A Life Saver, Woman On Deck, Bottle, Easel Back, 10 x 15 In. 125
Sign, Southern White Lead, Dutch Boy Paint, Seated Dutch Boy, Can, Tin, 14 x 27 In. 3135
Sign, Spalding, Hockey Equipment, Play To Win, Player, Cardboard, 1940s, 15 x 22 In. 837
Sign, Spiffy Soda, Make Mine Spiffy, A Swell Cola Drink, Boy, Tin Lithograph, 10 x 6 In. 345
Sign, Spina Soap, Devil, Jointed, Smoking, Cardboard, Die Cut, Frame, 34 x 20 In. *illus* 2128
Sign, Squeeze Soda, Boys Playing Ball, Die Cut, Cardboard Litho, Frame, 18 x 22 In. *illus* 336
Sign, Squeeze, Hits The Spot, Archer Girl, Hold Your Squeeze Today?, Cardboard, 21 x 15 In. 183
Sign, Squirrel Brand, Salted Peanuts, Squirrel Eating, Cardboard, 13 x 12 In. 300
Sign, Standard Ethyl Gasoline, Chevron, White, Blue, Enamel, Hanging, 21 x 28 In. 420
Sign, Standard Varnish Works, The Man Who Knows, Tin, 16 ½ x 10 ¼ In. 720
Sign, Star Plug Tobacco, Sold Here, Enameled 5-Color, 12 x 24 In. 776
Sign, Studebaker Authorized Service Parts, Enamel On Metal, 2-Sided, c.1932, 48 x 25 In. 1950
Sign, Sweet Caporal Cigarettes, Soldier, Red & Gold Metallic, c.1915, 17 x 30 In. 717
Sign, Swift's Hams, Cardboard, Multicolor Graphics, Frame, 33 x 24 In. 2875
Sign, Texaco, Sky Chief, Red, Green, Tin, 2-Sided, 30 In. Diam. 2242
Sign, The Apple Tree Restaurant, Alligatored Paint, Tin, Wood Frame, 72 x 15 In. 840
Sign, The Rexall Store, Black, White, Porcelain, Rounded Edges, 39 x 8 In. 480
Sign, The Rexall Store, Drugs, Burlingame & Stahl, Leaded Glass, 63 x 26 In. 912
Sign, Thirsty?, Just Whistle, 5 Cents, Boy, Actual Bottle Cutout, Easel, 27 x 14 In. *illus* 374
Sign, Thirsty?, Just Whistle, Demand The Genuine, Hand, Holding Bottle, 13 x 19 In. 180
Sign, This Way To Your Weight, Guess Your Weight, Wall, Wood, Light-Up, Wood, 35 x 19 In. 610
Sign, Thompson's Liqueur, Sloe Gin, An Excellent Astringent, Glass Mirror, 7 x 19 In. 30
Sign, Tootsie Rolls, Appetizingly Delicious, Yellow, Blue, Tin Lithograph, 9 x 19 In. 108
Sign, Trivoli Beer, On Tap, Carved Burl, Marching Golfers, 15 x 13 In. 300
Sign, Trufruit Flavored Soda, 5 Cents Large Glass, Metal, Wood, Light-Up, 8 x 12 In. 115
Sign, Turkish Trophies Cigarettes, Woman, Istanbul Skyline, Frame, 1930s, 37 x 27 In. 1159
Sign, Twang Root Beer, Save Caps For Premiums, Bottle Cap, Tin, Round, 14 In. 275
Sign, UMC Cartridges, Shooting Gallery, Bull's Eye, Bull Head Shape, Tin Litho, 27 x 19 In. 1793
Sign, Valvoline Lubricants, Custom Built, Black, Orange, Green, Tin, 18 x 36 In. 1080
Sign, Vender Bie's Ice Cream, Hand Holding Cone, 2-Sided, Porcelain, 18 x 28 In. 2400
Sign, Wallpapers & Decorations, John Gilkes & Sons, Color Litho, c.1900, 55 x 39 In. 184
Sign, Waterman's Ideal Fountain Pen, 2 Boys, Tin Over Cardboard, 13 x 9 In. 600
Sign, Weber Lifelike Fly Rod Lures, For All Fresh Water Game Fish, 1920s, 30 x 37 In. 397
Sign, Wheaties, Whole Wheat Flakes, Boy, Cereal Box, Easel, 1930s, 20 x 16 ½ In. 420
Sign, Whistle Orange Soda, Thirsty? Just Whistle, Bottle, 5 Cents, Cardboard, 31 x 9 In. 125
Sign, Whistle Soda, Soda Bottle, 12 Ounces, 5 Cent, Litho, Cardboard, 1939, 9 x 31 In. *illus* 244
Sign, White Horse, Pennsylvania Motor Oil, 100 Percent, Pure, White, Green, 19 x 25 In. 600
Sign, Whizzer, Wing Logo, Red, Yellow, Blue, Metal, Light-Up, Box, 25 x 5 In. 300
Sign, Winchester Fishing Lures, Sold Here, Fish Shape, Cardboard, 20 x 14 In. 1680
Sign, Winchester, Tin Litho, Dead Ducks, Antlers, Alexander Pope, 30 x 36 In. *illus* 4600
Sign, Wright, Hoists, Trolleys, Cranes, Cast Iron, Black, Gold Letters, 36 x 8 In. 338
Sign, Wrigley's Juicy Fruit Chewing Gum, A Daisy Gum, Girl, Daisies, Paper, 12 x 20 In. 228
Sign, Wurlitzer Music, Listen To Your Favorite Band, Paper, Frame, 1940s, 23 x 30 In. 270
Sign, Yes I Said 10 Cents, Model Smoking Tobacco, Man, Porcelain, 34 x 11 In. 900
Sign, Your Uncle Says Buy Ambrosia Chocolate Bark, Uncle Sam, Frame, 15 x 7 In. *illus* 345
Spoon, Sherwin-Williams, Cover The Earth, Figural Frog Handle, Paint Can, c.1900, 5 In. 132
Standee, Elvis Presley, Comeback Special, TV Performance, 1968, 22 x 28 In. 1793
Standee, Speedy Alka-Seltzer, Multicolor, Cardboard, Die Cut, 1960s, 63 In. 460
Standee, The Seven Year Itch, Marilyn Monroe, Subway Grate, 1955, 40 x 78 In. 8050
Stool, Cane Seat, Schenley's Red Label Whiskey, Right Because It's Light, 35 In. 60
Stringholder, Red Goose Shoes, Tin Goose, Red & White, Die Cut 1254
Stringholder, Shinola Shoe Polish, Stenciled, Hanging, Wood, Metal, 17 x 8 In. 230
Stringholder, Spool, Heinz, 57 Varieties, Pickle, Hanging, Tin, Green, 18 x 17 In. 1140
Stringholder, Swifts Pride Soap, Tin Lithograph, 2-Sided, 15 ½ x 30 In. *illus* 18975
Syrup, Drink Green River, Yellow & Green, Ball Shape, Lid, Ball Finial, 8 x 16 In. 390
Syrup, Drink Hires, It's Pure, Hourglass Shape Dispenser, Pump 684
Tap Handle, Chocolate Meltdown, Pennsylvania Brewing Co., Porcelain, 13 In. 108
Tap Handle, Dogfish Head Brewery, Bottle In Sharks Mouth, Porcelain, 14 In. 87
Teakettle, Griswold, Size 2, Marked, Use Erie Ware The Best, 3 ½ In. *illus* 247

Advertising, Tin, Roly Poly, Mayo's Tobacco, Mammy, Litho, Smoking, Corncob Pipe, 7 x 6 In.
$460

Wm Morford

Advertising, Tin, Walter Baker Original Cocoa, Display, Embossed Cover, Paper Label, ½ Lb.
$150

Showtime Auction Services

Advertising, Toy, Washing Machine, Wonder Washer, Victor Mfg., Agitator, Salesman's Sample, 16 In.
$1,112

James D. Julia Auctioneers

Advertising, Trade Stimulator, Uncle Sam, Eyes Move, Composition Head, Hands, Cloth, 29½ In.
$3,540

Bertoia Auctions

Tin Trays
The tin advertising tray was first used in the 1880s and is still popular.

Advertising, Tray, Lebanon Brewing Co., Beer, Ale & Porter, C.M. Coolidge, 1910, 11 x 13 In.
$1,416

Hess Auction Group

TIP
Get a big mailbox so when you are away your mail will not be seen from the street.

Advertising, Trash Can, Bennet Receptacles, Pressed Steel, Insert, Salesman's Sample, 1950s, 7 In.
$293

Hake's Americana & Collectibles

A

Akro Agate, Tea Set, Teapot, Cup & Saucer, Sugar, Creamer, 3 Plates, Slag Glass, Green, Child's
$145

Ruby Lane

Alabaster, Lamp, 3 Draped Females, Dome Light, Marble Base, Continental, c.1900, 54 In., Pair
$11,685

Skinner, Inc.

Amber Glass, Pitcher, Pilgrim, 1960s, 4 ½ x 2 ¾ In.
$18

Ruby Lane

Telephone, Stromberg-Carlson, Candlestick, Metal, Carbon Composition, 3 x 2 In. .... *illus* 518
Thermometers are listed in their own category.

Advertising tin cans or canisters were first used commercially in the United States in 1819 and were called tins. Today the word *tin* is used by most collectors to describe many types of containers, including food tins, biscuit boxes, roly poly tobacco containers, gunpowder cans, talcum powder sprinkle-top cans, cigarette flat-fifty tins, and more. Beer Cans are listed in their own category. Things made of undecorated tin are listed under Tinware.

Tin, All American Cookies, Lakeside Biscuit Company, Football Players, Litho, 6 In. .... *illus* 345
Tin, Allen's Sanitary Tooth-Ease, Paper Label, Le Roy, N.Y., 4 x 7¾ In. .... *illus* 242
Tin, Aspirin, Plee-Zing, Blue, White, Red, Tin Lithograph, 1¼ x 2 In. 184
Tin, Beacon Java Coffee, Boyd Leeds & Co., Lighthouse, Yellow, Red, 13 x 22 In. 480
Tin, Biscuit, Big Sioux, Chief, Red, Black, White, Lid, 7 x 9 In. 150
Tin, Biscuit, Crumpsall's, Mail Cart Shape, Simulated Spoke Wheels, England, 7 In. 590
Tin, Biscuit, Huntley & Palmers, Artist Pallet Shape, Artist Painting, 7 x 2 x 9 In. 89
Tin, Biscuit, Huntley & Palmers, Cairo, 6-Sided Table, Multicolor, c.1902, 6½ x 7¼ In. 115
Tin, Biscuit, Huntley & Palmers, Lantern Shape, England, 9½ In. 30
Tin, Cadette Baby Talc, Toy Soldier Shape, 7¼ x 2¼ x 1¼ In. 196
Tin, Camel Cigarettes, R.J. Reynolds Tobacco Co., 5¾ x 4¼ In. 18
Tin, Coburn & Co., Allspice, Red, Eggshell Blue, Square, c.1890, 6½ x 9½ In. 240
Tin, Colburn's Mustard, Phila, Lid, White, Green, Red, Leaf Borders, Round 270
Tin, Dan Patch, Roasted Coffee, Horse, Cylindrical, Bail Handle, 11 In. 330
Tin, Derby's Peter Pan, Peanut Butter, Free Sample, Round, 2¼ x 1⅝ In. 35
Tin, Eve, Cut Cube Tobacco, Eve & Leaf, Considering Fruit Tree, 3¾ In. 119
Tin, Fire, Nordlinger-Charleton Fireworks Co., Lid, c.1880, 3 In. 120
Tin, Fountain Tobacco, Penn Tobacco Co., Multicolor, Tin Lithograph, 6¼ x 5¼ In. 604
Tin, Golden Pheasant Condom, Cardboard Box, 4 Individual Tins, 3½ x 2¼ In. 104
Tin, Green Turtle Cigars, Lithograph, Smoking Turtle Trademark, 5¼ x 7½ In. .... *illus* 184
Tin, Griffon, Blade Box, The Improved Safety Razor, 2⅛ x 1⅛ In. 295
Tin, Hindoo Plug Tobacco, Multicolor Lithograph, Pocket, 3½ x 3½ In. 633
Tin, Hi-Plane, Tobacco, 4 Engine, Red Ground, White, Lettering, Pocket, 4¼ x 3 In. 403
Tin, Honey Moon Tobacco, Couple Seated On Moon, Tin Litho, Pocket, 5 x 3 In. .... *illus* 748
Tin, Ivanhoe, Ground Cinnamon, Castle, Blue, White, Yellow, 3 x 2¼ In. 58
Tin, L.A.W. Sliced Plug, Tobacco, Rounded Corners, Yellow, 4½ In. 1140
Tin, Mason's Black Crows, Candy Drops, Green, Orange, Crow, House, 3¼ x 4 In. 253
Tin, Milk Maid Java & Mocha Coffee, Pail, Lid, Bail Handle, Green, Gold, 12 x 7 In. 390
Tin, Mohican Coffee, Profile Indian Chief, Headdress, Blue, Red, White, Lid 240
Tin, Murad Turkish Cigarettes, Woman Holding Up Tray, Oval, 13 x 19 In. 2850
Tin, Old Black Joe, Axle Grease, Black & White, Cylindrical, Lid, Lb. 240
Tin, Our Own Brand, Roasted Coffee, Blue & White, Bail Handle, 10½ In. 210
Tin, Possum Cigars, 3 For 10 Cents, Good & Sweet, Red, Possum, Lid, 5 x 5 In. 200
Tin, Powow Brand Salted Peanuts, Indian Chief, Round, Green, Orange, Tin, 1909, 9 x 8 In. 300
Tin, Roly Poly, Mayo's Tobacco, Mammy, Litho, Smoking, Corncob Pipe, 7 x 6 In. .... *illus* 460
Tin, Royal Sugar Cone, Red & Black, Lid, Bail Handle, 15¼ In. 125
Tin, Sunny South, Sweet Milk Chocolate Peanuts, Black Woman, Red Hat, 3 x 8 In. 230
Tin, Sunset Trail, Cigar, Multicolor Graphic, Western Scenes, Cowboys, 5½ x 6 In. 1553
Tin, Sunshine Coffee, Enterprise Coffee Co., Girl, Umbrella, Blue & White, 5¾ x 4¼ In. 300
Tin, The Gem Safety Razor, Man With Razor, Green, Black, Cylindrical, Lid, 2⅜ In. 148
Tin, Three Knights, Condom, Black, Cream, Knights, On Horseback, Tin, Square, Rounded 138
Tin, Twin Ports Coffee, Multicolor Graphic, Eimon Mercantile Co., 6 x 4 In. 1265
Tin, United Stores, Nursery Candies, Nursery Rhyme Characters, Animals, 3 x 6 In. 316
Tin, Walter Baker Original Cocoa, Display, Embossed Cover, Paper Label, ½ Lb. .... *illus* 150
Tin, Zingo Sweets, Race Car Logo, Candy, Blue, Orange, Red, Round, 10 x 12 In. 345

Advertising tip trays are decorated metal trays less than 5 inches in diameter. They were placed on the table or counter to hold either the bill or the coins that were left as a tip. Change receivers could be made of glass, plastic, or metal. They were kept on the counter near the cash register and held the money passed back and forth by the cashier. Related items may be listed in the Advertising category under Change Receiver.

Tip Tray, Benjamin Franklin Insurance Co., Profile, Tin Lithograph, Round, 1930s, 4 In. 60
Tip Tray, Cottolene, Workers, Picking Cotton, Black Border, c.1910, 4¼ In. 75
Tip Tray, D.R. Ginn M.D., Dog, Flower & Bird Border, Tin, c.1900, 3 x 4 In. 65
Tip Tray, Drink Lemon Kola, 5 Cents In Bottles At Fountains, Yellow, Red, 4⅜ In. Diam. 120
Tip Tray, Fairy Soap, Girl Sitting On Soap Bar, Tin, Round, c.1910, 4¼ In. 98

Tip Tray, Lemon Kola, 5 Cents, Bottles, Fountain, Red, Yellow, Tin, Round, 4 ⅜ In. 225
Tip Tray, Miller High Life, Flying Ducks, Red Border, 1950s, 4 x 6 In. 40
Tip Tray, Old Reliable Coffee, Woman, Flowers, c.1910 150
Tip Tray, Soul Kiss Perfume, Maiden, Picking Flower Petals, Tin, Round, c.1900, 4 In. 175
Tip Tray, Zipp's Cherri-O Soda, Multicolor Graphics, Tin Lithograph, Round, 12 In. 719
Tobacco Cutter, 5 Brothers Tobacco Works, Cast Iron, 18 x 7 In. 480
Toy, Washing Machine, Wonder Washer, Victor Mfg., Agitator, Salesman's Sample, 16 In. .... *illus* 1112
Trade Stimulator, Uncle Sam, Eyes Move, Composition Head, Hands, Cloth, 29 ½ In. .... *illus* 3540
Trash Can, Bennet Receptacles, Pressed Steel, Insert, Salesman's Sample, 1950s, 7 In. ...... *illus* 293
Tray, Congress Beer, Haberle Brewing Co., Enameled Porcelain, Over Steel, Round, 15 In. 6670
Tray, Daeufer Lieberman Beer, Yellow, Red, Tin Lithograph, Oval, 12 ½ x 15 In. 219
Tray, Great Western Champagne, Woman Seated, Bottle Cork, 13 x 13 In. 50
Tray, Lebanon Brewing Co., Beer, Ale & Porter, C.M. Coolidge, 1910, 11 x 13 In. .... *illus* 1416
Tray, Lebanon Brewing Co., Woman With Horse, Tin Lithograph, Oval, 1905, 17 x 14 In. 1298
Tray, Lion Beer, Quality In Every Drop, Woman With Roses, Holding Glass, 13 In. 225
Tray, NuGrape, A Flavor You Can't Forget, Hand Holding Bottle, 1920s, 13 ½ In. 125
Tray, Orange Crush, Round, Bottles Pointing Inward, Red, Blue, c.1945, 12 In. 180
Tray, Ortlieb's Lager Beer Ale, Round, Woman Holding Glass, Round, Blue, 12 In. 180
Tray, Red Raven, Ask The Man, Red Bird, Naked Child Reaching For Bottle, Round, 12 In. 175
Tray, Russ Bros Velvet Ice Cream, Cake, Cones, Fruit, Round, 14 ¼ In. 60
Tray, Thompson's Ice Cream, Children At Table, Tin Lithograph, 1919, 13 In. 400
Tray, Tip, see Tip Trays in this category.
Tray, Wrigley's Spearmint Gum, Happy To Serve You, Arrow Head, 13 x 11 In. 420
Vending Case, Johnson's Flavor Toasted Nuts, Metal, Decals, Turntable, 1950s, 32 x 54 In. 244
Vending Machine, 7Up, 10 Cents, 35 Slider, Green & White, 1950s, 30 x 42 In. 976
Vendor Box, Cracker Jack, With Prize, The More You Eat, The More You Want, 12 x 19 In. 210
Whiskbroom Holder, American Steel Farm Fences, Tin Lithograph, 4 ¼ x 1 ¾ In. 265
Window, Rolls-Royce, Stained Glass, Metal Frame, Jeweled Accents, 23 x 42 x ¾ In. 300

AGATA glass was made by Joseph Locke of the New England Glass Company of Cambridge, Massachusetts, after 1885. A metallic stain was applied to New England Peachblow, which the company called Wild Rose, and the mottled design characteristic of agata appeared. There are a few known items made of opaque green with the mottled finish.

Tumbler, Deep Pink To Salmon Pink, New England, c.1888, 3 ¾ x 2 In. 225
Vase, Dimpled Body, Pinched Rim, Pink To White, New England, 6 ¼ In. 895
Vase, Oval, Stick Neck, Pink To Rose, Blossoms, New England, 9 ½ In. 350
Vase, Pink To Ivory, Flowers, Shape, Stem, c.1887, 7 ½ In. 1400

AKRO AGATE glass was founded in Akron, Ohio, in 1911 and moved to Clarksburg, West Virginia, in 1914. The company made marbles and toys. In the 1930s it began making other products, including vases, lamps, flowerpots, candlesticks, and children's dishes. Most of the glass is marked with a crow flying through the letter *A*. The company was sold to Clarksburg Glass Co. in 1951. Akro Agate marbles are listed in this book in the Marble category.

Ashtray, Blue, Marbleized, Leaf Shape, c.1930, 4 In. 21
Cup & Saucer, Octagonal, Chalane Blue, Child's 20
Cup, Green, Horizontal Panels, Vertical Rings, Tapered, 2 ½ In. 12
Flowerpot, Jadite, Marbleized, Ribbed Rim, c.1940, 2 ¾ In. 35
Lamp, Custard, Caramel Swirls, Cut Stars, Square Foot, 1940s, 21 In., Pair 165
Planter, Jonquil, Blue Swirled Milk Glass, 5 ¼ x 3 x 2 In. 17
Pot, Ribbed Rim, Yellow, 21 x 2 In. 18
Tea Set, Teapot, Cup & Saucer, Sugar, Creamer, 3 Plates, Slag Glass, Green, Child's .... *illus* 145
Tea Set, Teapot, Sugar & Creamer, Cobalt Blue & White, Child's, 3 Piece 95
Vase, Cornucopia, Blue & White, Ribbed, c.1935, 3 ¼ In. 18

ALABASTER is a very soft form of gypsum, a stone that resembles marble. It was often carved into vases or statues in Victorian times. There are alabaster carvings being made even today.

Bust, Child, Wearing Bonnet, Carved, 13 x 6 In. 270
Bust, Girl, Wearing, Bonnet, Drying Eyes, Holding Basket, Broken Handle, 11 In. 93
Bust, Maiden, Gazing Sideward, Draped Flower Garland, Rocky Base, c.1900, 21 In. 1750
Bust, Peasant Woman, Cap, Italy, 10 x 9 ½ In. 204
Bust, Woman, Flower Strewn Hair, Bare Shoulders, Italy, c.1900, 26 In. 1416
Bust, Woman, Gilded Laurel Crown, Italy, c.1900, 16 ½ In. 268
Bust, Woman, Head Turned, 18 In. 184
Bust, Woman, Renaissance Costume, Micro Mosaic, Platform, c.1890, 15 x 14 In. 984

Amberina, Vase, Stork, New England Glassworks, c.1884, 4 ½ In.
$345

Early Auction Company

American Encaustic, Tile, Portrait, Woman, Bonnet, Green, c. 1925, 6 ¼ In.
$125

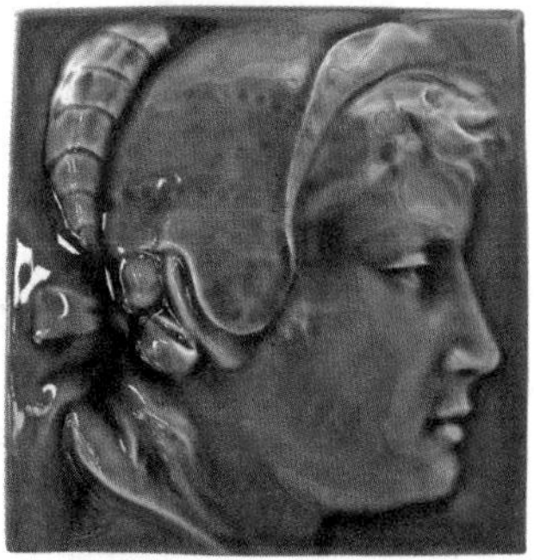

Ruby Lane

Tax Donations

If you plan to give your collection to a museum and get a tax deduction, you must find the proper museum. Your gift must fit into the museum's collection and be displayed most of the time. Museums want pieces that fill gaps in their collections and are given without too many restrictions. But you might want to set rules for any future sale of the items. Perhaps ask that the money from a sale be used to purchase another item for the same collection.

Animal Trophy, Bearskin, Black Bear, Head, Claws, c.1980, 64 In.
$570

Garth's Auctioneers & Appraisers

Animal Trophy, Bison Head, Brown Hair, Horns, Glass Eyes, Mounted, 41 x 21 In.
$1,185

James D. Julia Auctioneers

Animal Trophy, Elk, Head, 12-Point Rack, Mounted, c.1950, 33 In.
$570

Selkirk Auctioneers & Appraisers

Bust, Woman, Veiled, Smiling, Hair Flowing Over Shoulder, Socle Base, 1800s, 23 In. 196
Bust, Young Girl, Looking Down, Headdress, Necklace, 12 x 12 In. 281
Chandelier, 1-Light, Bowl Shape Shade, Gold Hanging Cords, 23 x 12 In. 984
Chandelier, 1-Light, Louis XVI, Bronze, Center Globe, c.1905, 20 x 14 In. 787
Chandelier, 6-Light, Art Deco, Bronze, Red, Extending Up, c.1910, 26 x 24 In. 968
Chandelier, 6-Light, Art Deco, Bronze, Shades, Flower Center, c.1920, 34 x 30 In. 363
Chandelier, 6-Light, Stone Bowl, Gilt Bronze Braided Ropes, Leaf Arms, 35 x 29 In. 625
Chandelier, 7-Light, Baronial Style, Metal, Bowl, Pierced, Scrolled Frame, 53 x 31 In. 937
Chandelier, 7-Light, Louis XVI, Corona, Torches, Ribbon, Laurels, 30 x 25 In. 2299
Chandelier, 12-Light, Bronze, Gilt, Fluted Stem, Flower Chain, Bowl, c.1900, 51 In. 1500
Ewer, Neoclassical, Carved, Grape, Leaf, Beast Handles, 37 x 14 In., Pair........ 264
Figurine, 2 Wrestlers, Classical, 15 x 8 In. 292
Figurine, Classical Woman, Sandals, Knee-Length Dress, Flower Garlands, 33 x 12 In. 3720
Figurine, Napoleon, Standing, Uniform, Continental, 25 In. 1195
Figurine, Native American Man, Parrot, Wood Base, Alvin Marshal, 27 ½ In. 150
Figurine, Penitent Magdalene, Seminude, Kneeling, Cross In Hands, Skull, 1800s, 16 In. 1681
Figurine, Queen Louise Of Prussia, Marble Base, Adolfo Cipriani, 28 In. 861
Figurine, Renaissance Woman, Beatrice, Holding Rose, Carrying Book, Italy, 30 In. 800
Figurine, Woman, Classical, Looking Down, 32 In. 1210
Figurine, Woman, Robes, Left Hand On Book, 27 x 7 ½ In. 242
Figurine, Woman, Seated, Neoclassical, Gilt Bronze, Mounted As Lamp, c.1900, 18 x 11 In. 1500
Figurine, Woman, Standing, Holding Basket Of Flowers, 30 In. 185
Figurine, Woman, Windswept, K. Hofman, 17 ¼ x 11 ¾ In. 484
Figurine, Young Boy, Reading, 17 In. 3105
Group, Madonna & Child, Lamb, 22 ½ x 8 In. 1800
Group, Psyche Revived By Cupid's Kiss, After Antonio Canova, 16 ⅜ In. 547
Group, Snow Owls, Abraham Anghik, 24 x 24 In. 744
Group, The Wrestler, 2 Wrestlers Grappling, 17 x 16 In. 236
Group, Woman, Kneeling, Holding Up Skirts, Art Nouveau, 14 x 11 In. 402
Jardiniere, 3 Cherubs, Rocky Base, Urn, Carved Vines, Flowers, 17 x 11 In. 885
Lamp Base, Campana Urn Form, Leaf Carved Rim, Ribbed Socle, Stepped Base, 15 In. 308
Lamp, 3 Draped Females, Dome Light, Marble Base, Continental, c.1900, 54 In., Pair........ *illus* 11685
Lamp, Electric, Figural, Rebecca At The Well, Woman Seated On Wall, 24 x 10 In. 426
Lamp, Figural, Woman Dipping Toe In Pool, 20 In. 625
Lemon, c.1900, 3 In. 40
Pedestal, Carved, Fluted Column, Round Revolving Top, 44 x 10 In. 300

ALUMINUM was more expensive than gold or silver until the 1850s. Chemists learned how to refine bauxite to get aluminum. Jewelry and other small objects were made of the valuable metal until 1914, when an inexpensive smelting process was invented. The aluminum collected today dates from the 1930s through the 1950s. Hand-hammered pieces are the most popular.

Candy Dish, Rose Pattern, Handle, Crimped Rim, Barricini, 1950s, 7 x 7 In. 14
Charger, Art Deco, Ring Of Zodiac Signs, Hammered Finish, Arthur Armour, 18 In. 198
Ice Bucket, Diving Helmet Shape, Marked Livorno 1894, 12 x 9 In. 400
Ice Bucket, Raised Bamboos Shoots, Handles, Everlast, 1950s, 6 x 11 In. 49
Mailbox, Stand, Victorian, Cast, Crown Surmount, Lobed Column Support, 1900s, 46 x 15 In. .. 308
Tray, 2 Swivel Trays, Embossed Flowers & Scrolls, Crimped Edge, c.1950, 14 In. 27
Tray, Hammered, Wood Insert Handles, Marked, Buenilum, 1950s, 11 In. 14

AMBER, *see Jewelry category.*

AMBER GLASS is the name of any glassware with the proper yellow-brown shading. It was a popular color just after the Civil War and many pressed glass pieces were made of amber glass. Depression glass of the 1930s–50s was also made in shades of amber glass. Other pieces may be found in the Depression Glass, Pressed Glass, and other glass categories. All types are being reproduced.

Ashtray, Triangular, Footed, c.1950, 3 x 4 x 4 In. 55
Basket, Split Handle, 4 ½ x 4 ½ x 5 In. 14
Bowl, Boat Shape, Square Footed, Bohemian, c.1920, 5 x 6 x 3 ¼ In. 150
Cake Plate, Pedestal, 1970s, 11 x 2 ¾ In. 20
Candy Dish, Lid, Paneled, Scalloped Foot, 7 x 5 In. 49
Compote, Lid, Diamond Point Pattern, 12 In. 27
Cruet, Thumbprint, Ruffled Rim, Applied Handle, Stopper, 1800s, 6 ¼ In. 119
Dish, Pumpkin Shape, Ribbed, Stem Handle, 3 x 5 In. 5
Dresser Jar, Stopper, Twisted, Square Base, 10 ½ In. 83

Mantel, Adam Style, Fluted Pilasters, Carved Urns, Scrollwork, 57 x 84 In. 1045
Mantel, Cherubs, Swags, Woman's Head, Torso, 76 x 63 ½ In. 3510
Mantel, Federal, Carved, Painted Green, Serpentine Cornice, c.1812, 66 x 93 In. .... *illus* 8610
Mantel, Figural, Atlas, Italian Renaissance Style, Carved Walnut, 1800s, 48 x 20 In. 688
Mantel, George III, Painted, Parcel Gilt, Egg & Dart Beading, Swags, 57 ½ x 71 In. 1920
Mantel, George III, Pine, C-Scrolls, Leaves, Egg & Dart, 54 x 63 In. 1459
Mantel, George III, Pine, Silvered Gesso, 57 x 61 In. 383
Mantel, Tile Inserts, Green, 62 x 50 ¾ In. 322
Medicine Cabinet, Glass Latching Door, Shelves, Product Containers, 1800s, 25 x 17 In. 334
Model, Georgian Revival House, William Whitney Lewis, c.1915, 33 x 59 In. 3120
Model, Ipswich House, Composition Over Wood, Pigment, Plastic Windows, 23 x 27 In. 437
Model, Spiral Staircase, Stained Wood, Turned Balusters, 22 ½ x 13 ¾ In. 281
Model, Staircase, Black Marble Plinth, 20th Century, 28 x 32 In. 1845
Ornament, Cast Metal, Geometric, Louis Sullivan, Frame, c.1890, 12 x 12 In. 2125
Ornament, Lion's Head, Copper, Molded, 19th Century, 22 x 37 In. 1534
Ornament, Mask, Aztec, Headdress, Copper, Patina, Commodore Hotel, 1900s, 35 x 33 In. .*illus* 4062
Ornament, Medallion, George Washington Profile, Cast Iron, c.1858, 36 x 30 In. 4375
Ornament, Swan, Cast Iron, Standing, Wings Back, Scrollwork, 1800s, 21 x 30 In. .... *illus* 1464
Ornament, Wood, Carved, Ecclesiastical, Leaves, Berries, 17 x 11 ¾ In. 130
Overmantel Mirror, Aesthetic, Multicolor, Parcel Gilt, Gesso, Mask Crest, 67 x 55 In. 563
Overmantel Mirror, Black Paint, Gilt, 2 Sections, Beveled Edge, c.1870, 83 x 59 In. 460
Overmantel Mirror, Classical, Gilt Wood, Triptych, Turned, Leaves, c.1890, 87 x 35 In. 649
Overmantel Mirror, Federal, Giltwood, Sections, Pilasters, Eglomise Panels, c.1800, 36 x 57 In. 2460
Overmantel Mirror, French Empire Style, 1980s, 76 x 45 In. 267
Overmantel Mirror, Neoclassical, Painted, Parcel Gilt, Lilies, Maidens, 61 x 30 In. 615
Panel, Bone Inlay, Mother-Of-Pearl, Birds, Branches, Boxwood, 30 x 17 In., Pair 1071
Panel, Directoire, Pine, Carved, Painted, Parcel Gilt, Swags, Leaves, c.1800, 43 x 14 In. 984
Panel, Half Round, Zinc Over Steel, Conical Rays, Fan Shape, 1800s, 13 x 22 In., Pair 830
Panel, Painted, Reserves Of Ruins, Flower Bouquets, Italy, 79 x 25 In., Pair 1230
Panel, Teakwood, Carved, Tigers, Leaves, India, c.1900, 15 x 24 In., Pair 888
Pediment, Cast Iron, Yellow, 15 ½ x 10 ½ In., Pair 510
Pediment, Chippendale, Parcel Gilt, Mahogany, Carved, Dragons, Gesso, c.1800, 12 x 26 In. 590
Post, Cast Iron, Fluted Tapered Columns, Squared Base, c.1860, 54 x 8 In., Pair 295
Roof Finial, Rooster, Redware, Molded, Inset Glass Shards, Barrel Tile, 18 x 15 In. 826
Roof Finial, Terra-Cotta, Pineapple Shape, Italy, 1900, 17 x 11 ¾ In., 3 Piece 625
Roof Tile, Bearded Sage, Child In Arms, 19 x 7 In. 153
Roof Tile, Bucking Horse, Yellow, Green, 11 ⅓ In. 63
Roof Tile, Camel, 5 Figures Riding, Multicolor, 16 x 12 In. 120
Roof Tile, Deity Riding Monkey With Peach, 13 x 13 ½ In. 360
Roof Tile, Foo Dog, Multicolor, 15 ½ x 15 In. 295
Roof Tile, Foo Dog, Staff Pole, Slate, Chinese, 1800s, 18 x 17 In. 250
Roof Tile, Glazed Pottery, Man, Standing On Curved Base, Chinese, c.1600, 11 ½ In. 538
Roof Tile, Immortal Riding Foo Dog, 1800s, 10 x 10 In. 402
Roof Tile, Koi Fish, Yellow, Green Glaze, Wood Stand, 11 x 6 ½ In., Pair 687
Roof Tile, Ming Warrior, Terra-Cotta, Multicolor Enamel, Chinese, 1800s, 14 x 4 ½ In. 180
Roof Tile, Owl, Terra-Cotta, Multicolor, Glass Eyes, 17 x 14 In. 770
Roof Tile, Rooster, Green, Yellow, 13 ½ x 10 ⅕ In., Pair 270
Roof Tile, Woman & Child, Multicolor, 25 x 23 In. 94
Roundel, 2 Female Musicians, Classical, Stone, England, 1950-90, 31 ½ In. 3307
Screens are also listed in the Fireplace and Furniture categories.
Shutter Lock, Iron, Spiral, 18th Century, 7 ½ In., Pair 150
Sign, 9th Ave., W. 39 St., Enamel, Cobalt Blue, White, Humpback, 23 x 12 In. 117
Spigot, Brass, Mounted On Oak Carved Panel, 39 x 13 In., Pair 313
Street Light, Cast Iron, Square Base, Globe, Leaves, c.1900, 114 x 24 In. 720
Telephone Booth, Wood, Glass Folding Doors, 83 x 30 In. 400
Transom, Softwood, Carved, Ebonized, Carp, Terrapin, Swirls, c.1890, 13 x 76 In., Pair 133
Valance, Gilt, Stenciled, Landscape, House, Harbor, Boat, 15 ¼ x 42 In., Pair 2340
Wall Bracket, Eagle, Spread Wings, Shelf, Carved Gilt Gesso & Wood, 1800s, 23 x 30 In., Pair ... 4920
Wall Bracket, Walnut, Carved, Bust, Man's Face, Beard, Demilune Top, c.1850, 11 x 10 In. *illus* 896
Wall Bracket, Wood, Baroque Style, Gilt, Carved, Pierced Leaves, Flowers, 19 In., Pair 937
Window Cornice, Walnut, Parcel Gilt, Cartouche, Leaves, Shells, c.1865, 15 x 88 In. 2091
Window Grate, Central Medallion, Cast Iron, 28 ½ x 18 In., Pair 246
Window Grate, Half Circle, Sunburst, 46 x 24 In. 205
Window Grille, Demilune, Peacock, Iron, 56 x 26 ½ In. 409

Architectural, Gate, Cast Iron, Lambs Under Willow Tree, Nesting Doves, 1800s, 30 x 28 In.
$1,098

Neal Auctions

Architectural, Mantel, Federal, Carved, Painted Green, Serpentine Cornice, c.1812, 66 x 93 In.
$8,610

Skinner, Inc.

Architectural, Ornament, Mask, Aztec, Headdress, Copper, Patina, Commodore Hotel, 1900s, 35 x 33 In.
$4,062

Neal Auctions

TIP

Having a garage (tag) or house sale? Use a fanny pack worn in front to keep your money. Be sure to have lots of change, bills and coins, for the sale.

Architectural, Ornament, Swan, Cast Iron, Standing, Wings Back, Scrollwork, 1800s, 21 x 30 In.
$1,464

Neal Auctions

Architectural, Wall Bracket, Walnut, Carved, Bust, Man's Face, Beard, Demilune Top, c.1850, 11 x 10 In.
$896

Neal Auctions

Arita, Vase, Double Gourd, Blue & White, Figures, Landscape, Flared Rim, c.1700, 15 In.
$237

James D. Julia Auctioneers

AREQUIPA POTTERY was produced from 1911 to 1918 by the patients of the Arequipa Sanatorium in Marin County, north of San Francisco. The patients were trained by Frederick Hurten Rhead, who had worked at the Roseville Pottery.

Figurine, Bulldog, Black, White & Brown Matte Glazes, Impressed Logo, 4 ¼ In. 885
Figurine, Bulldog, Blue, White, Brown, 4 ¼ In. 750
Tile, Bear, 6 x 6 In. 425
Tile, Castle, 6 x 6 In., 3 Piece 850
Tile, Circular Pattern, Quarter Circle At Corners, 6 x 6 In., Pair 450
Tile, Fruit, 6 x 6 In. 600
Tile, Yin Yang, 6 x 6 In., 3 Piece 650
Vase, Blue, Cylinder, 1912, 6 In. 650
Vase, Blue, Mermaid, Shark, 4 ¼ x 5 ½ In. 2900
Vase, Green, Brown, White Froth, 1913, 3 ¼ x 3 In. 450
Vase, Green, Mottled, 3 ½ x 3 ½ In. 650
Vase, Mottled Glaze, Stamped, Vase Under Tree, c.1913, 3 ¼ x 3 In. 563
Vase, Yellow-White, 4 ¼ In. 300

ARGY-ROUSSEAU, *see G. Argy-Rousseau category.*

ARITA is a port in Japan. Porcelain was made there from about 1616. Many types of decorations were used, including the popular Imari designs, which are listed under Imari in this book.

Bowl, Lid, Handles, Poppies, Red Ground, Underplate, c.1930, 7 x 6 In. 135
Bowl, Namban, Blue & White, Panels, Figures, Patterns, Rolled Rim, Octagonal, c.1800, 8 In. ... 735
Bowl, Round, Open Work, Blue Border, Lid, c.1950, 5 ½ In. 75
Canister, Stylized Flowerpots, Multicolor, Lid, 8 In. 298
Charger, Blue & White, Birds, Lotus Pond, Flowers, 21 In. 6234
Charger, Blue & White, Fish Scales, Bamboo Shoots, Brown Trim, c.1900, 12 In. 91
Cup & Saucer, Stylized Bat Design, Blue, Red 88
Cup, Sake, Pheasant, Lake, Leaves, Flowers, Footed, Pair 89
Dog, Shi, Blue & White, Mirror Image, 8 ¼ x 10 ½ In., Pair 60
Incense Holder, Prunus Branch, Blue, Gold, Moon Shape, c.1950, 3 x 2 In. 29
Plate, Blue & White, Paneled, Lobed, Brown Rim, 8 In. 280
Plate, Blue & White, Trees, Crosshatch Pattern, 10 In. 50
Plate, Mountains, Sea, Boats, Blue, White, 19th Century, 9 In. 150
Vase, Double Gourd, Blue & White, Figures, Landscape, Flared Rim, c.1700, 15 In. .... *illus* 237
Vase, Reticulated, Porcelain, Royal Blue, White, 1926-89, 11 ½ In. .... *illus* 89

ART DECO, or Art Moderne, a style started at the Paris Exposition of 1925, is characterized by linear, geometric designs. All types of furniture and decorative arts, jewelry, book bindings, and even games were designed in this style. Additional items may be found in the Furniture category or in various glass and pottery categories, etc.

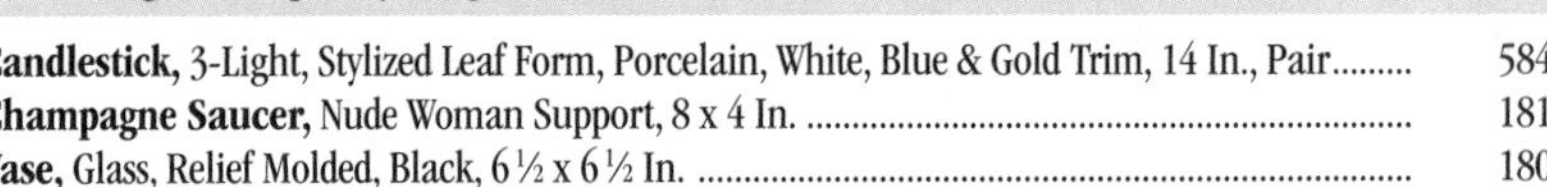

Candlestick, 3-Light, Stylized Leaf Form, Porcelain, White, Blue & Gold Trim, 14 In., Pair 584
Champagne Saucer, Nude Woman Support, 8 x 4 In. 181
Vase, Glass, Relief Molded, Black, 6 ½ x 6 ½ In. 180

ART GLASS, *see Glass-Art category.*

ART NOUVEAU is a style of design that was at its most popular from 1895 to 1905. Famous designers, including Rene Lalique and Emile Galle, produced furniture, glass, silver, metalwork, and buildings in the new style. Ladies with long flowing hair and elongated bodies were among the more easily recognized design elements. Copies of this style are being made today. Many modern pieces of jewelry can be found. Additional Art Nouveau pieces may be found in Furniture or in various glass categories.

Centerpiece, Fish Amid Waves, Mermaid, Water Child, After H. St. Larche, 9 x 19 In. 840
Chamberstick, Figural, Woman Languishing, Gilt Metal, 6 In. 72
Compote, Pressed Glass, Gilt Metal Mount, Marked Orvit, 5 ¾ x 10 In. 420
Ewer, Gilt Bronze Mount, Red Marble, After P. Aube, 5 x 5 ⅜ In. 540

ART POTTERY, *see Pottery-Art category.*

AURENE PIECES *are listed in the Steuben category.*

AUSTRIA *is a collecting term that covers pieces made by a wide variety of factories. They are listed in this book in categories such as Royal Dux or Porcelain.*

AUTO parts and accessories are collectors' items today. Gas pump globes and license plates are part of this specialty. Prices are determined by age, rarity, and condition. Collectors say "porcelain sign" for enameled iron or steel. Signs and packaging related to automobiles may also be found in the Advertising category. Lalique hood ornaments may be listed in the Lalique category.

Bottle, Oil, Sunoco, Glass, Spout, Blue & Yellow Label, Qt., 14 In. 120
Cabinet, Mobiloil, Milk Glass Globe, Embossed Gargoyle, Shelves, 86 x 24 In. 5100
Can, Amalie Oil, Wood Handle, Red, Yellow, Pennsylvania, c.1960, 5 Gal. 150
Can, Esso Motor Oil, Red, White, Black, 5 Qt., 6¾ x 9 In. 53
Can, Golden Flash Motor Oil, Plane, Orange, Black, Metal 960
Can, Joco Oils Motor Oil, White, Blue, Red Letters & Border, Gal., 8 x 6¾ In. 330
Can, National Benzole Mixture, Embossed, Pressure Cap, 2 Gal., 13 x 9½ In. 120
Can, Pennzoil, Logo, United Airlines Mainliner Airplane, Gal. 99
Can, Phil Rite Double Safe, Red, Hose, 10 x 18 In. 90
Can, Polarine, Summer/Winter Scene, Car, Yellow, 5 Gal., 13 x 9 In. 720
Can, Quaker State Oil, Medium, Phinny Bros. Co., c.1910, 5 Gal. 200
Can, Record Motor Oil, Yellow, Red Text, ½ Gal., 7¾ In. 660
Can, Shafer Oil & Refining Company, Deep Rock, Gal., 11 In. 162
Can, Veltex Motor Oil, Yellow, Fletcher Oil Co., c.1940, ½ Gal., 8 x 6 x 3 In. 195
Cart, Lubester, 2 15-In. Porcelain Signs, Red, 51 x 34 In. 2160
Collage, U.S.A Map, License Plate For Each State, Frame, 51 x 31 In. 976
Decelerometer, Ammco Tools, Inc., Model 7350, Measures Rate Of Deceleration, 8 In. 60
Display Board, Ford Model T Timer, 41 Timers, Easel Frame, 38 x 26 In. 397
Display, Firestone Tires, Tin Lithograph & Rubber, Tire & Base, 2 Parts, 30 x 33 In. 397
Display, Rack, Mobiloil, World's Best Known, 29 x 26 In. 600
Display, Trico Wiper Blades, Woman, Driving, 6 Slots, 11 x 19 In. 660
Door, Paddy Wagon, Chicago Police, Wood, Metal, Window, Bars, 24 x 49 In. 840
Gas Pump, Bowser, Red Sentry, Crank & Dial, 72 In. 330
Gas Pump, Clear Vision, Cylindrical, 10 Gal. 960
Gas Pump, Dixie, Ethyl, Confederate Flag, Light-Up Globe, Yellow, Brass Nozzle, 78 In. 2745
Gas Pump, G&B Model 66, Blind, Cast Iron Door, Red, 82 In. 244
Gas Pump, Pennsylvania Curb, White Hose, G&B Brass Nozzle 540
Gas Pump, Super Shell, Yellow, Red, Light-Up Plastic Globe, 1989, 71 In. 840
Globe, Standard Oil Flame, Glass, Metal Base, 21 x 13 In. 780
Globe, Standard Oil Gold Crown, Embossed Milk Glass, 16 x 16 In. 570
Grill, Mercedes, Advertising Display, 1980s, 19½ x 26 In. ....*illus* 265
Hat, Gas Attendant, Black, Brim, 7½ In. 180
Hood Ornament, Flying Lady, Chrome, 1950s, 13½ x 7 In. 240
Hood Ornament, Propeller, Chrome, 7½ x 5½ In. 74
Hood Ornament, Winged, Model A, 4 x 9½ In. 215
Horn, Brass, Le Testophone, Musical, 4 Trumpets, France, 24 In. 480
License Plate Attachment, Mobilgas, Pegasus, Red, Embossed, c.1930, 4¾ x 6½ In. 150
License Plate Attachment, Westinghouse, Orange Porcelain, Steel, 5⅓ x 10¼ In. 84
License Plate Attachment, Yellowstone Park Wyoming, 3 Bears, Mountain, 4¾ x 10¼ In. 540
License Plate, Blue, Pennsylvania, 1906, 6½ x 8 In. 531
License Plate, Illinois, Black, Cream, 1910 150
License Plate, Massachusetts, Blue & White, 1909 125
License Plate, Pennsylvania, Black & Yellow, 1911 175
License Plate, Rhode Island, State Police, 100, Ocean State, Metal, 1973-82, 6 x 12 In. 127
License Plate, White, Pennsylvania, 1909, 6½ x 10½ In. 201
Lubester Top, Texaco Motor Oil, Red, Glass Tubes, 17 x 5 In. 420
Meter, Air & Water, Eco Islander, Red Porcelain, Key, 56½ In. 3300
Mobil Oil, Glass Quart Bottles, Floor Stand, Spouts & Stopper Lids, 1930s, 16 x 29 In., 6 Pack 570
Oil Strainer, Tinned Copper, Brass Lever, 1900s, 9 In. ....*illus* 39
Parking Meter, Gold Color, Round Top, Half Circle, Two Hour Time Limit, 57½ x 14 In. 49
Parking Meter, Nickels & Dimes, Gold Color, Round Pedestal Base, 1960s, 17 In. 270
Poster, Woco Pep, Pep Makes A Winner!, Ball Player, King Of Motor Fuel, 1940, 12 x 26 In. 214
Pump, Gilbarco, Red, 58 x 20 In. 600
Pump, Oil Change, Wayne Pump Co., Yellow, Red, Shell Pen Motor Oil, Model 90 300
Rack, Cans, Conoco Oil, 43 In. 720
Radio, Atlas, Heavy Duty Extra Capacity Battery, c.1960, 10 x 13 In. 660
Sign, Atlantic, Gasoline Pump, Enamel, Brass Grommets, 1950s, 9 x 13 In. 127
Sign, Auto Club, So. Cal., Sweetwater 6, Yerington 57, Arrow, Diamond Shape, Enamel, 26 x 26 In. 427
Sign, Braender Tires, The Tire To Tie To, Bulldog, Porcelain Flange, Orange, 19 In. 458
Sign, Bridge, 10 Dollar Fine, Warning, Driving Faster Than A Walk, Ohio, 1800s, 15 x 31 In. 240
Sign, Bus Stop, Salmon Color, Oval, Cast Iron, 2-Sided, 9½ x 12½ In. 330
Sign, California Route 66, Green & White, Reflective Border, 38 x 38 In. 458

TIP
Windows in outside doors should be covered with grillwork or made of unbreakable glass.

Arita, Vase, Reticulated, Porcelain, Royal Blue, White, 1926-89, 11½ In.
$89

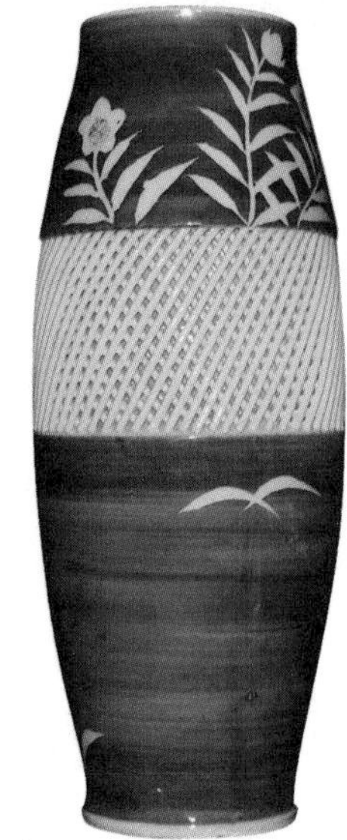

Ruby Lane

Auto, Grill, Mercedes, Advertising Display, 1980s, 19½ x 26 In.
$265

Ruby Lane

The Red Kettle
In 1891 a Salvation Army captain set up a crab pot on the wharf in San Francisco to collect money for the poor. It was so successful, the Salvation Army started using the now famous red kettle across the country.

A

Auto, Oil Strainer, Tinned Copper, Brass Lever, 1900s, 9 In.
$39

Ruby Lane

TIP
If it seems too good to be true, it usually is! Trust your instincts when buying antiques. Experienced collectors notice many little signs of repair or reproduction, often without realizing it.

Auto, Traffic Light, Electric, Metal, 3 Lenses, Green, Yellow, Red, 36 x 10 In.
$178

James D. Julia Auctioneers

Autumn Leaf, Grease Jar, Lid, Gold Trim, 4 x 5 In.
$25

Ruby Lane

Autumn Leaf, Salt & Pepper, Shaped Handle, 1936-76, 4½ In.
$39

Ruby Lane

Autumn Leaf, Teapot, Nautilus, Anniversary Pot, 1996, 6¾ In.
$99

Ruby Lane

Azalea, Teapot, Lid, Gold Finish, Noritake, 5 x 8 ½ In.
$203

Ruby Lane

Baccarat, Perfume Bottle, Cut Crystal, Applied Green Agate Jewels, Stopper, c.1844, 6 ¾ In.
$590

Brunk Auctions

Baccarat, Tumbler, Paperweight Panel, Enameled Rose & Pansy, Diamond Point Design, 3 ⅞ In.
$1,185

James D. Julia Auctioneers

Sign, Chevrolet, Blinking Owl, It's Wise To Choose Six, 35 x 22 In. 12720
Sign, Conoco Gasoline, Colonial Minuteman, Round, Enamel, Yellow, 2-Sided, 25 In. Diam....... 2074
Sign, Curb, En-Ar-Co Motor Oil, White Rose, Boy, Blackboard, c.1917, 46 x 28 In 5100
Sign, Gilmore Lion Head Motor Oil, Roaring Lion, Tin Lithograph, Frame, 30 x 12 In. 1037
Sign, Goodrich Tires, Slow Down, Safety First, Round, Red & White, Enamel, 26 In. Diam. 336
Sign, Hudson Parts-Service, DSL, Blue, White Text, Red, 30 x 42 ½ In. 2160
Sign, Kerrville Bus Co. Depot, Shield Shape, Blue & White, Enamel, 2-Sided, 22 x 18 In. 458
Sign, Nash, Authorized Service, Enamel, Shield Shape, Blue, 17 x 27 In. 732
Sign, One-Way, Police Department, Arrow, White, Black Letters, 2-Sided, c.1930, 8 x 30 In. 115
Sign, Route 32 Hawaii, Black & White, Embossed, Rounded Triangle, Enamel, 16 x 16 In. 366
Sign, Standard Oil, Grease Gun Display, Service Garage, Enamel, 35 x 32 In. 3050
Stand, Air Pump, Air Whip, Free Air, Re Metal, Bell Base, 92 In. 122
Thermometer, Skelly, Go Modern & Save, Round, Convex, c.1950, 18 In. Diam........ 390
Thermometer, Wanda Motor Oil, Beige, Red, 38 x 7 ½ In 1680
Thermometer, William Tell Motor Oil, Hits The Spot, 38 ¾ x 8 ¼ In. 840
Tool Box, Bomb Shape, Bantam Proto Power, Blackhawk, Red Metal, Wheels, 1948, 32 x 11 In. 1037
Traffic Light, Electric, Metal, 3 Lenses, Green, Yellow, Red, 36 x 10 In. ....*illus* 178
Traffic Light, Marbelite Co., Inc., 36 In. 146
Traffic Signal, 3-Sided, Pole Stand, Light-Up, Flashes, 64 ½ In. 1140
Uniform, Jumpsuit, STP, White, Logo, Paxton Turbo Indy 500, 1967, Size M........ 210

AUTUMN LEAF pattern china was made for the Jewel Tea Company beginning in 1933. Hall China Company of East Liverpool, Ohio, Crooksville China Company of Crooksville, Ohio, Harker Potteries of Chester, West Virginia, and Paden City Pottery, Paden City, West Virginia, made dishes with this design. Autumn Leaf has remained popular and was made by Hall China Company until 1978. Some other pieces in the Autumn Leaf pattern are still being made. For more prices, go to kovels.com.

Bowl, Nesting, 3 Piece 58
Bowl, Vegetable, 9 In. 30
Bowl, Vegetable, Oval, 10 In. 22
Cake Plate, Gold Rim, 9 In. 16
Cake Safe, Wire Clamps, c.1935........ 75
Casserole, Lid, Handles, 3 ½ Qt., 12 x 9 x 6 In. 125
Cookie Jar, Handles, Ribbed, Lid, c.1936........ 160
Cup & Saucer **10**
Custard Cup, 3 ½ In., 6 Piece........ 29
Grease Jar, Lid, Gold Trim, 4 x 5 In. ....*illus* 25
Jug, Ball, 80 Oz........ 38
Jug, Ball, Ice Lip, 7 ½ In. 35
Pie Plate, 9 ¾ In. 14
Plate, Bread & Butter, 6 In. 6
Platter, 11 ⅜ In. 25
Platter, 13 ⅝ In. 28
Punch Set, Bowl, 12 Cups 320
Salt & Pepper, Handles, 4 ½ In. 39
Salt & Pepper, Shaped Handle, 1936-76, 4 ½ In. ....*illus* 39
Teapot, Airflow, 22K Gold, Trim, Footed........ 180
Teapot, Aladdin, Infuser........ 89
Teapot, Aladdin, Lid, 11 x 6 In. 48
Teapot, Mini, French, 4 ½ In. 72
Teapot, Nautilus, Anniversary Pot, 1996, 6 ¾ In. ....*illus* 99
Teapot, Newport, Lid, Handle, 6 ¼ In. 85
Teapot, T-Ball Square, Lid, 5 ½ In. 72
Tureen, Nautilus, Rolled Handles 120
Watering Can, c.1990, 6 In. 75

AVON *bottles are listed in the Bottle category under Avon.*

AZALEA dinnerware was made for Larkin Company customers about 1915 to 1941. Larkin, the soap company, was in Buffalo, New York. The dishes were made by Noritake China Company of Japan. Each piece of the white china was decorated with pink azaleas.

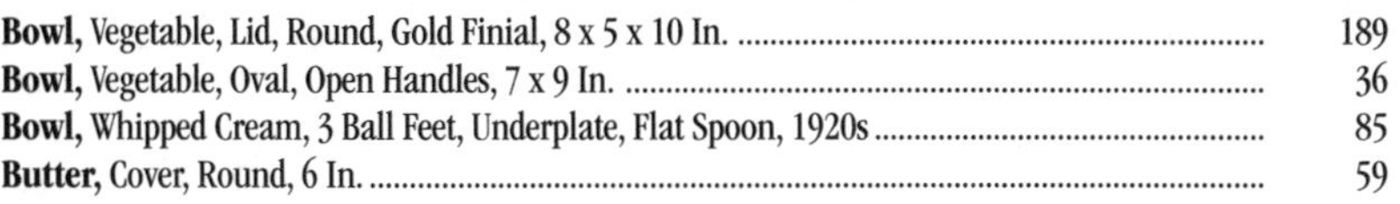

Bowl, Vegetable, Lid, Round, Gold Finial, 8 x 5 x 10 In. 189
Bowl, Vegetable, Oval, Open Handles, 7 x 9 In. 36
Bowl, Whipped Cream, 3 Ball Feet, Underplate, Flat Spoon, 1920s........ 85
Butter, Cover, Round, 6 In. 59

Badge, California Game Patrol, Shield, Bear, Bronze, Copper, Irvine & Jachens S. F., 2 In.
$161

Ruby Lane

Badge, Fireman, NYFD, Maltese Cutout Shape, Pin, Catch, New York City, 1930s, 2⅛ In.
$231

Ruby Lane

Bank, Cash Register, Uncle Sam's Savings, Key, Novelty Co., 4 ¾ In.
$18

Hess Auction Group

Bank, Mechanical, Boy On Trapeze, Cast Iron, Japanned Base, Barton Smith Co., c.1888
$9,600

Bertoia Auctions

TIP
Never repaint an old bank. It lowers the resale value.

Bank, Mechanical, Jonah & The Whale, Painted, Iron, Shepard Hardware, Pat. 1890, 10 In.
$1,298

Hess Auction Group

Bank, Mechanical, Postman, Tin Lithograph, Burnette, England, c.1927
$295

Bertoia Auctions

Celery Dish, 10 In. 179
Cup & Saucer 14
Plate, Dinner, 10 In. 20
Platter, Oval, 8 x 11 In. 55
Shaker, Berry Shape, 6 ½ In. 30
Sugar & Creamer 135
Teapot, Finial, 5 In. 203
Teapot, Lid, Gold Finish, Noritake, 5 x 8 ½ In. .... *illus* 203

BACCARAT glass was made in France by La Compagnie des Cristalleries de Baccarat, located 150 miles from Paris. The factory was started in 1765. The firm went bankrupt and began operating again about 1822. Cane and millefiori paperweights were made during the 1845 to 1880 period. The firm is still working near Paris making paperweights and glasswares.

Bottle, Vanity, Etched Flowers, 4 ¾ In. 156
Candlestick, Crystal, Waisted, Fluted Sides, 6 In., Pair 240
Candlestick, Oxygene, Emerald Green Cup, Acid Etched Mark, Sawtooth Pedestal, 10 In., Pair .. 437
Champagne Cooler, Crystal, 9 x 8 In. 360
Champagne Cooler, Maxim, Crystal, 9 x 8 In. 420
Chandelier, 6-Light, Gilt Bronze, Reeded, Hanging Prisms, Sprays, c.1950, 28 x 19 In. 2460
Chandelier, 12-Light, Gilt Bronze, Crystal, 2 Tiers, Prism Sprays, 1900s, 40 x 29 In. 4182
Cocktail Set, Shaker, Martini Glasses, Thomas Bastide, 9 ½ In., 5 Piece 600
Decanter, Ring Foot, Paneled Sides, Square Neck, Round Stepped Stopper, 12 In. 488
Decanter, Tapered, Paneled, Stopper, Marked, c.1950, 8 ¾ In. 461
Decanter, Teardrop Stopper, Squat, Ruby To Clear, Arched Pattern, Drip Like, 8 x 5 In. 460
Figurine, Cat, Lying Down, Black Crystal, 3 x 4 ½ In. 90
Figurine, Falcon, On Outcrop, 10 In. 414
Figurine, Polar Bear, Crystal, 6 ½ In. 120
Figurine, Shark, Fins, Pointy Nose, Clear, Swimming, Rocky Base, 1900s, 19 In. 500
Flute, Champagne, Mille Nuits, Knopped, Matte Stem, Base, Mathias, 11 ½ In., Pair 153
Goblet, Crystal, Montaigne, 7 In., 6 Piece 150
Goblet, Water, Lyra, Crystal, 7 ½ In., 24 Piece 1920
Ice Bucket, Rotary Pattern, Tapered, Molded, c.1981, 9 x 8 In. 676
Paperweight, Dahlia Rose, White Ground, Marked, Box, c.1980, 2 ½ In. 750
Paperweight, Millefiori, Red, White, Blue, Flowers, Stars, 2 ¼ In. 675
Paperweight, Millefiori, Stamped, 1 ¾ x 2 ½ In. 270
Paperweight, Sulphide, Woodrow Wilson Portrait, Yellow, c.1972, 3 In. 200
Perfume Bottle, Cut Crystal, Applied Green Agate Jewels, Stopper, c.1844, 6 ¾ In. .... *illus* 590
Perfume Bottle, Cyclamen, For Elizabeth Arden, Crystal, Pyramidal Stopper, Pin, 1938, 5 In. .. 590
Rose Bowl, Pontils, Small Mouth, Wide Rim, 1900s, 6 ½ In. 189
Star, Etched Stamp, 5 ½ In. 155
Tumbler, Double Old-Fashioned, Harmonie, Crystal, 4 In., 6 Piece 480
Tumbler, Paperweight Panel, Enameled Rose & Pansy, Diamond Point Design, 3 ⅞ In. .... *illus* 1185
Vase, Deep To Light Purple, Hexagonal Opening, Thomas Bastide, 8 ¼ x 6 ¼ In. 545
Vase, Harmonie, Cylindrical, Furrowed Side, Acid Etched Mark, 8 x 3 In. 184
Vase, Oceanie, Ruby Glass, Millefleur, Abstract Base, Horseshoe Cutout Rim, 8 In. 438
Vase, Square, Clear, Red Acid Etched Overlay, Sunflower Design, c.1900, 8 In. 717
Vase, Stepped, Twisted Shape, Clear, Flared Foot, 1900s, 9 In. 875
Vase, Tornado, Tapered, Molded Swirl Opening, Box, 1900s, 15 x 9 In. 1722
Vase, Translucent Amber, Cameo Wisteria Vines, Opalescent, Round Shoulder, 13 In. 474
Wine Cooler, Moulin Rouge, Molded Crystal, Gilt, Paneled, Tapered, c.1990, 9 In. 861
Wine, Massena, Crystal, Furrowed Texture, Etched, 7 x 3 ¼ In., 8 Piece 472

BADGES have been used since before the Civil War. Collectors search for examples of all types, including law enforcement and company identification badges. Well-known prison or law enforcement badges are most desirable. Most are made of nickel or brass. Many recent reproductions have been made.

California Game Patrol, Shield, Bear, Bronze, Copper, Irvine & Jachens S. F., 2 In. .... *illus* 161
Deputy Sheriff, Pewter, California, Bear, 1 ⅝ x 2 ⅛ In. 150
Deputy Sheriff, Sterling Silver, Star Shape, 2 ⅛ x 2 ½ In. 143
Fireman, NYFD, Maltese Cutout Shape, Pin, Catch, New York City, 1930s, 2 ⅛ In. .... *illus* 231
Indian Police, Sterling Silver, Shield Shape, Bow & Arrows, 1 ⅞ x 2 ⅜ In. 300
Patrolman, Mobile & Ohio R.R., Silvered Brass, C.H. Hanson Co., c.1920, 2 ¼ In. 153
Police, Railroad, Santa Fe, Shield Shape, Gold Color, Blue Enamel, 2 x 3 In. 175
Race Car Driving, Indianapolis 500 Pit, 1st Post War Race, 1946, 1 x 2 In. 3825
Ribbon, Major General William T. Sherman, G.A.R., Metal, Cannon, Star, 1891, 5 In. 115

BANKS of metal have been made since 1868. There are still banks, mechanical banks, and registering banks (those that show the total money deposited on the face of the bank). Many old iron or tin banks have been reproduced since the 1950s in iron or plastic. Some old reproductions marked *Book of Knowledge, John Wright*, or *Capron* may be listed. Pottery, glass, and plastic banks are also listed here. Mickey Mouse and other Disneyana banks are listed in Disneyana. We have added the M numbers based on *The Penny Bank Book: Collecting Still Banks* by Andy and Susan Moore and the R numbers based on *Coin Banks by Banthrico* by James L. Redwine. Several early mechanical banks from a renowned private collection were sold at auction for very high prices in 2015. We have listed some of the exceptional banks as well as prices for average banks.

Alarm Clock, Alarm Safety Deposit Vault, Tin, Red, c.1930, 3 ¼ In. 60
Animal Face, Top Hat, Circus Club Mallows, Tin Lithograph, Cylindrical, Canada, 7 In. 944
Asian Shrine, Silvered Lead, Japan, c.1930, 3 ¾ In. 450
Auto, 4 Passengers, Spoke Wheels, Cast Iron, Red Paint, A.C. Williams, c.1920, 7 In. 300
Bank Building, 6-Sided, Japanned Finish, 2 ¼ In. 266
Bank Building, English Counting House, Child, Bulldog, Tellers, Windows, Footed, Cast Iron, 6 x 6 In. 660
Bank Building, Home Savings, Dog Finial, Cast Iron, J. & E. Stevens, M 1237, c.1891, 5 x 4 In. . 148
Bank Building, Home Savings, Iron, Ornate Roof, Orange, Brown, 6 In. 420
Basilica Of Our Lady Of Scherpenheuvel, Coppered Lead, Germany, M 1487, 1930s, 4 In. 270
Battleship Maine, White, Cast Iron, M 1439, 10 In. 472
Bear With Top Hat, Collar, Spelter, c.1925, 5 ¼ In. 192
Black Boy, 2 Faces, Smiling, Draped Head, Cast Iron, A.C. Williams, M 84, 3 In. 90
Book, Thy Kingdom Come, Cast Iron, Embossed, Lid Opens, Slot, 3 ½ In. 210
Building, Bungalow, Front Porch, Cast Iron, Green & Gray Paint, 1918, 4 x 6 x 8 In. 330
Building, Cast Iron Roof, Grey Iron Mfg. Co., 1903, 3 ½ x 3 In. 59
Building, Gingerbread, House, Children, Woman, Cast Iron, Paint, M 1029, 4 ½ x 4 In. 1500
Building, Villa, Cylindrical Towers, Finial, Japanned, Kyser & Rex, M 1179, c.1894, 5 In. 590
Calvin Coolidge, Do As Coolidge Does, Save, Ceramic, Bronze Finish, c.1924, 5 In. 834
Captain Kidd, Cast Iron, Holding Shovel, Next To Tree, M 38, 6 In. .... 150 to 428
Cash Register, Uncle Sam's Savings, Key, Novelty Co., 4 ¾ In. .... *illus* 18
Cat With Ball, Cast Iron, A.C. Williams, M 352, c.1910, 6 In. 189
Chocolat Menier, Kiosk, Dome Top, Blue, Tin Litho, Tray, France, c.1930, 10 In. 207
Church, Tin Lithograph, Yellow, Tall Steeple, Red Roof With Cross, 6 In. 118
Coin Purse, Boy Looking Out, Parian Bisque, Flowers, Germany, c.1910, 3 ½ In. 240
Cucumber, Pottery, 7 ½ In. 177
Donation, Abraham Lincoln Brigade, Cardboard, Metal Lids, Liberty Bell, c.1938, 5 In. 173
Duck, Stretched Wings, Orange Beak, Hubley, M 624, 5 In. 413
Eggman, Caricature Of Wm. Howard Taft, Top Hat, Cast Iron, Arcade, M 108, c.1910, 4 In. 1200
Elephant, Gray Paint, Red & Gold Highlights, Hubley, 4 ¾ In. 89
Gas Pump, Cast Iron, Red Paint, Square Base, Globe Top, M 1485, 6 In. 200
Geisha, Kimono, Seated, Playing Instrument, Pillow Base, Cast Iron, Hubley, 7 In. 180
General Butler, Cast Iron, J. & E. Stevens, M 54, c.1880, 7 In. .... 300 to 472
Give Me A Penny, Black Man, Standing, Cast Iron, Paint, Screw, Hubley, M 166, 1902, 5 ½ In. .. 180
Globe On Claw Feet, Hinged Door, Copper Flash, Cast Iron, Kenton, M 812, c.1910, 5 In. 240
Globe On Wood Base, Metal, Paper, Miller Bank Service, M 791, c.1930, 4 ¼ In. 192
Goodyear Zeppelin Hangar, Logo, Duralumin, 7 ¼ In. 266
Goose, Sewer Tile, W. Smith, Superior Clay Products, Uhrichsville, Ohio, 16 In. 540
Gourd, Pottery, Tan Glaze, Blue Flowers, Leaves, Incised, c.1900, 4 ½ In. 94
Graf Zeppelin, Cast Iron, Ribbed, Silver Paint, A.C. Williams, M 1428, c.1930, 6 ½ In. 249
Hansel & Gretel House, Tin Lithograph, Key Lock Roof, Stollwerck, M 1016, 2 ½ In. 118
Hen On Nest, Spelter, Germany, c.1925, 4 ½ In. 216
Humpty Dumpty, Alice In Philcoland, Ceramic, American Bisque, 6 In. 36
Independence Hall, Centennial, Enterprise, M 1242, 1875, 9 ¼ x 10 ¼ In. 409
Indian Chief Bust, 4-Post, Cast Iron, c.1890, 4 ¾ In. 450
Lion, Tail Right, Standing, Cast Iron, A.C. Williams, 1920s, 3 ¾ In. 53
Mascot, Young Baseball Player, Standing On Baseball, Cast Iron, Hubley, 1915, 6 In. 7200

Mechanical banks were first made about 1870. Any bank with moving parts is considered mechanical. The metal banks made before World War I are the most desirable. Copies and new designs of mechanical banks have been made in metal or plastic since the 1920s. The condition of the paint on the old banks is important. Worn paint can lower a price by 90 percent.

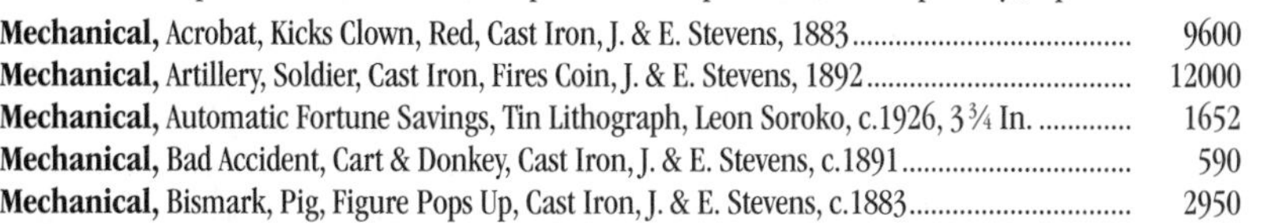

Mechanical, Acrobat, Kicks Clown, Red, Cast Iron, J. & E. Stevens, 1883 9600
Mechanical, Artillery, Soldier, Cast Iron, Fires Coin, J. & E. Stevens, 1892 12000
Mechanical, Automatic Fortune Savings, Tin Lithograph, Leon Soroko, c.1926, 3 ¾ In. 1652
Mechanical, Bad Accident, Cart & Donkey, Cast Iron, J. & E. Stevens, c.1891 590
Mechanical, Bismark, Pig, Figure Pops Up, Cast Iron, J. & E. Stevens, c.1883 2950

Bank, Mechanical, Roller Skating, Cast Iron, Kyser & Rex, c.1880
$120,000

Bertoia Auctions

Bank, Pig, Pottery, Brown & Red Mottle Glaze, 2 x 3 ½ In.
$295

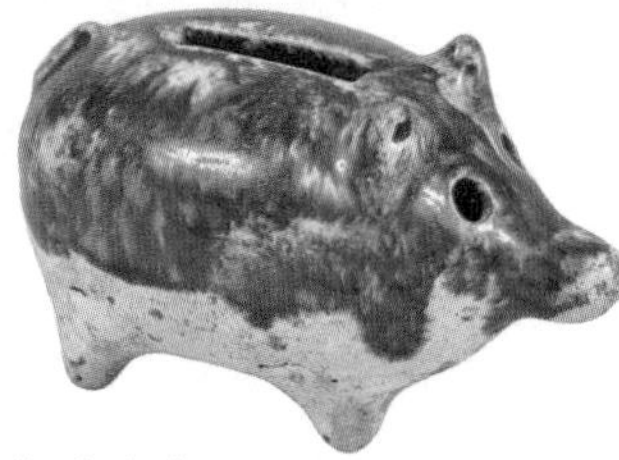

Hess Auction Group

Bank, Pig, Seated, Cast Iron, A.C. Williams, M 582, 1910-34, 3 x 4 ½ In.
$30

Hess Auction Group

TIP
Collector preference has changed in mechanical bank collecting. The rarest banks were most expensive from the 1950s to the 1980s. Now collectors want condition more than rarity and almost perfect paint.

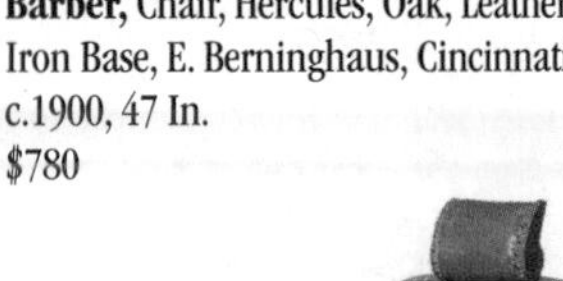

Barber, Chair, Hercules, Oak, Leather, Iron Base, E. Berninghaus, Cincinnati, c.1900, 47 In.
$780

Garth's Auctioneers & Appraisers

Barber, Chair, Paidar, Green Porcelain Base, Armrests, Leather, Accessories, 48 x 46 In.
$1,037

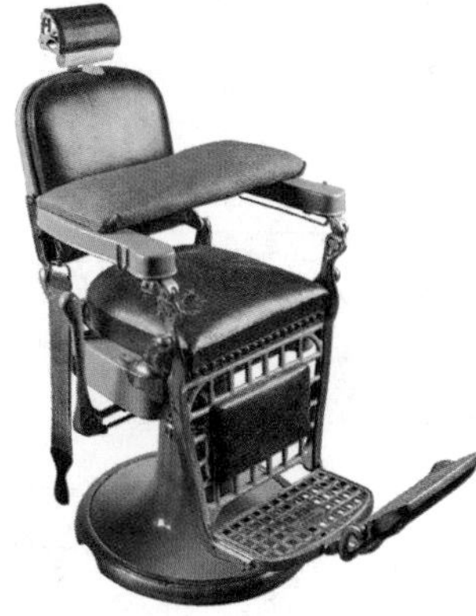

Morphy Auctions

Barber, Steamer, Hot Towel, Vulcan, Nickel Plated, 20 x 57 In.
$488

Morphy Auctions

Mechanical, Boy On Trapeze, Cast Iron, Japanned Base, Barton Smith Co., c.1888 .... *illus* 9600
Mechanical, Boy Robbing Bird's Nest, Green Brown, Cast Iron, J. & E. Stevens, 1906 42000
Mechanical, Boy Robbing Bird's Nest, Stealing Eggs, On Tree Limb, J. & E. Stevens, 7 In. 11353
Mechanical, Boys Stealing Watermelons, Key, Kyser & Rex, c.1885, 6 ½ x 5 In. 2106
Mechanical, Bread Winner, 3 Figures, Honest Labor Bread, Cast Iron, J. & E. Stevens, 1886 72000
Mechanical, Bulldog, Coin On Nose, Swallows, Cast Iron, J. & E. Stevens, 1880 6000
Mechanical, Bulldog, Red Blanket, Cast Iron, J. & E. Stevens 472
Mechanical, Bunker Hill, Monument, Zigzag Path, Cast Iron, Wood, 16 In. 10620
Mechanical, Cabin, Black Man In Doorway, Coin On Roof, Man Flips, 1885, 5 x 3 In. 420
Mechanical, Cabin, Black Man, Roof Coin Slot, Broom Turns, Cast Iron, 4 x 4 In. 863
Mechanical, Circus Ticket Collector, Barrel, H.L. Judd Co., c.1879 944
Mechanical, Clown On Globe, Round Footed Base, Cast Iron, J. & E. Stevens, c.1890, 9 In. 1793
Mechanical, Creedmoor, Soldier Shooting, Spiked Helmet, Brass, J. & E. Stevens 1298
Mechanical, Dapper Dan, Minstrel Dances, Tin Lithograph, Windup, Marx, 1925 708
Mechanical, Darktown Battery, Black Boys Playing Baseball, Cast Iron, Paint, 10 In. 1938
Mechanical, Dentist, Pulls Tooth & Falls Back, Gas Bag, J. & E. Stevens, c.1880, 6 In. 10755
Mechanical, Eagle & Eaglets, Perched, Open Wings, Cast Iron, Stopper, 6 x 9 In. .... 172 to 300
Mechanical, Elephant, Howdah, White, Hubley, c.1930 384
Mechanical, Frog, Little Frog Kicks Coin To Big Frog, Cast Iron, J. & E. Stevens, 1872 6000
Mechanical, Girl Skipping Rope, Squirrel, J. & E. Stevens, c.1890 5900
Mechanical, Hall's Liliput, Cast Iron, J. & E. Stevens 325
Mechanical, Hold The Fort, Artillery Action, Cast Iron 36000
Mechanical, Home Bank, Dormers, Red & Yellow Paint, Cast Iron, J. & E. Stevens, c.1872 413
Mechanical, Humpty Dumpty, Cast Iron, Painted, Shepard Hardware, c.1884, 7 ¾ x 6 In. 519
Mechanical, Indian Shooting Bear, Cast Iron, J. & E. Stevens, 10 In. .... 2700 to 4720
Mechanical, John Bull's Money Box, Dog Jumps, Iron, Sydenham & McOustra, 1909 22800
Mechanical, Jolly Negro, Open Mouth, Cast Iron, Red, Black, Yellow Paint, 6 In. 325
Mechanical, Jolly Nigger, Cast Iron, Painted, Figural Black Man Bust, 1890s, 6 x 7 In. 383
Mechanical, Jonah & The Whale, Painted, Iron, Shepard Hardware, Pat. 1890, 10 In. .... *illus* 1298
Mechanical, Jumbo On Wheels, Cast Iron, Embossed Saddle, Head Nods, J. & E. Stevens 295
Mechanical, Lion & 2 Monkeys, Single Peanut, Cast Iron, Kyser & Rex 649
Mechanical, Magician, Makes Coin Disappear, Cast Iron, J. & E. Stevens 944
Mechanical, Mammy & Child, Kyser & Rex, Pat. 1884 3540
Mechanical, Man Holding Fortune Dial, Cast Iron, Wood Base, 15 In. 1440
Mechanical, Mason, Cast Iron, Shepard Hardware, 7 ½ In. 1422
Mechanical, Mason, Tradesman, Brick Wall, Cast Iron, Shepard Hardware Co., 1887 26400
Mechanical, Milking Cow, Red, Bailey Pedestal Series, Cast Iron, J. & E. Stevens, 1888 39000
Mechanical, Octagonal Fort, Cannon, c.1880 1652
Mechanical, Organ, Cat & Dog, Monkey In Yellow & Red Suit, Hat Tips, Kyser & Rex 148
Mechanical, Owl, Turns Head, Brown, Cast Iron, Glass Eyes, J. & E. Stevens 325
Mechanical, Owl, Turns Head, Perched On Log, J. & E. Stevens, 7 ¼ In. 600
Mechanical, Paddy & The Pig, Sitting, J. & E. Stevens, c.1885 2950
Mechanical, Penny Pineapple, Hawaii, Open Mouth, Hand Out, 8 ¾ In. 270
Mechanical, Piano, Cast Iron, Nickel Finish, Embossed, E.M. Roche, 5 ¾ In. 384
Mechanical, Pig In Highchair, J. & E. Stevens, Pat. 1897 561
Mechanical, Postman, Tin Lithograph, Burnette, England, c.1927 .... *illus* 295
Mechanical, Punch & Judy, On Stage, Curtain, Pull Lever, Painted, c.1884 885
Mechanical, Queen Victoria, Porcelain Over Cast Iron, c.1897 4425
Mechanical, Race Course Bank, Coin Starts Race, Cast Iron, J. & E. Stevens, 1871 20400
Mechanical, Roller Skating, Cast Iron, Kyser & Rex, c.1880 .... *illus* 120000
Mechanical, Rooster, Cast Iron, Crowing Motion, Kyser & Rex, 1880s 885
Mechanical, Santa Claus, Chimney, Tosses Coin In, Cast Iron, Shepard Hardware, 1889 590
Mechanical, Speaking Dog, Girl In Red Dress, Cast Iron, J. & E. Stevens, 1885, 7 ½ x 7 In. 1140
Mechanical, Springing Cats, Mouse, Lead, Wood, Wooden Base, 1882 33000
Mechanical, Strong Box, Brass, Bail Handle, Ball Feet, 7 x 9 ½ In. 295
Mechanical, Tabby, Cat On Egg, Chick, Cast Iron, c.1886 384
Mechanical, Tammany, Man In Chair, Blue Jacket, Brown Pants, J. & E. Stevens, 6 x 4 In. 275
Mechanical, Teddy & The Bear, Man With Rifle, Bear In Tree Stump, 10 In. 1080
Mechanical, Trick Dog, Cast Iron, Green Clown, 6-Part Base, Shepard Hardware 266
Mechanical, Trick Dog, Cast Iron, Multicolor, Hubley, c.1930, 7 ¼ x 8 ½ In. 266
Mechanical, Trick Pony, Cast Iron, Shepard Hardware 531
Mechanical, William Tell, Cast Iron, J. & E. Stevens, Pat. 1896 502
Mechanical, World's Fair, Columbus & Indian Chief, Cast Iron, J. & E. Stevens 384
Officer, Cadet, Blue Uniform, Cast Iron, Hubley, 5 ¾ In. 324

Palace, Columns, Double Staircase, Steeple, Cast Iron, Paint, Gilt, Ives US., 1885, 8 x 8 In. 1320
Parrot Head, Penny, Green, Yellow, Orange, Blue, Germany, Spelter 660
Pig, Brown Mottled Glaze, Pottery, 6 ½ In. 142
Pig, Ceramic, Faux Leather, Brown, Slot, Curled Tail, c.1950, 11 x 19 In. 212
Pig, Chalkware, Standing, Painted Trim, c.1900, 12 x 17 In. 885
Pig, Glazed Pottery, Brown & Yellow Mottled, 3 ½ x 5 In. 118
Pig, Iron, White, France, 9 ½ x 19 In. 2520
Pig, Pottery, Brown & Red Mottle Glaze, 2 x 3 ½ In. .... *illus* 295
Pig, Seated, Cast Iron, A.C. Williams, M 582, 1910-34, 3 x 4 ½ In. .... *illus* 30
Polish Rooster, Looking Sideways, Full Body, Cast Iron, Paint, Gilt, M 541, 6 In. 1440
Punch & Judy, Theater, Children, Organ Grinder, Dancing Bear, Tin Lithograph, 3 In. 118
Register, Donald Duck Dime, Yellow Border, Tin Lithograph, 1939, 3 In. 185
Sack, 2 Pigs, Silvered Lead, Germany, c.1925, 3 ¼ In. 72
Safe, Cast Iron, Interior Drawers, c.1890, 7 x 9 In. 205
Safe, Dewey, Cast Iron, Arcade, c.1902, 5 ¼ In. 540
Safe, National, Combination, Cast Iron, 4 x 5 In. 175
Safe, Stork, Carrying Bundle, Cast Iron, J.M. Harper, c.1907, 5 ¾ In. 900
Santa, Holding Staff, On Snowball, Parian Bisque, Germany, c.1900, 3 ½ In. 900
Santa, With Tree, Red Suit & Hat, Cast Iron, Paint, Hubley, M 61, c.1920, 6 In. 600
Savings Chest, Van Elyen-Henstep, Cast Iron, M 948, c.1890, 6 ½ x 4 ½ In. 205
Sewing Machine, Singer, Stand, Dome Top, Shelves, Tin Litho, Germany, M 1368, c.1910, 5 In. 428
Stoneware, White Flint Glaze, Cobalt Blue Band, 4 ¼ In. 59
Street Clock, Columnar, Round Face, Marquee, Cast Iron, Paint, M 1548, c.1920, 6 In. 270
Swiss Cottage, Stollwerck's Chocolate, Tin Lithograph, Key Lock Roof, 3 ¼ In. 89
Teddy Roosevelt Bust, Pedestal, Coin Slot, In Uniform, Cast Iron, Paint, 1919, 5 In. 168
Teepee, Sitting Indian, Spelter, Germany, c.1920, 5 In. 300
Transvaal Money Box, Cast Iron, Gentleman, Beard, Pipe, Top Hat, 6 In. 212
Trolley, Bank Marquee, Cutout Windows, Cast Iron, Paint, M 1472, c.1889, 4 ½ In. 330
U.S. Mail Bank, Mailbox, Cast Iron, Red Paint, O.B. Fish, M 834, 1903, 7 In. 360
Uncle Sam, Red, White, Blue, Painted, Wood, c.1940, 4 In. 330
Whiskey Bottle, Seagram's 5 Crown, Glass, Wood Slot Cap, 28 x 9 In. 60
World's Fair Administration Building, Red Trim, Combination, Cast Iron, M 1072, 6 x 6 In. . 384
You Can Bank On Osborn Molding Machines, Nickel Finish, 2 In. 236

BARBER collectibles range from the popular red and white striped pole that used to be found in front of every shop to the small scissors and tools of the trade. Barber chairs are wanted, especially the older models with elaborate iron trim.

Chair, Eugene Berninghaus, Climax, Oak, Swivel Base, 1880, 44 ½ x 28 In. 363
Chair, Hercules, Oak, Leather, Iron Base, E. Berninghaus, Cincinnati, c.1900, 47 In. .... *illus* 780
Chair, Koken, Child's, 46 x 19 In. 789
Chair, Koken, Child's, Porcelain Base, Leather Seat, Carved Wood Horse Head 1710
Chair, Koken, Cream Tufted Leather, Head & Footrest, U.S.A., 36 x 49 ½ In. 1560
Chair, Koken, President, Leather, Metal, Black & White, Mad Men Era, 1950s, 41 In. 854
Chair, Paidar, Green Porcelain Base, Armrests, Leather, Accessories, 48 x 46 In. .... *illus* 1037
Chalkboard, Figural, Red Headed Barber, Holding Scissors & Comb, Earrings, Sign, 71 In. 1037
Pole, 3 Spiraling Stripes, Red, White, Blue, Ball Top, c.1900, 74 In. 840
Pole, Blue & Red, Round Finial, Turned, 70 x 15 In. 1521
Pole, Electric, Glass, Red, White, Blue, 27 In. 120
Pole, Electric, Spinning, Light-Up, Wall Mount, Porcelain Top, Glass, Windup, 34 In. 330
Pole, Elite Barber Shop, Porcelain, Leaded Glass, Globe, Red, White, Gilt, 85 In. 4275
Pole, Glass Cylinder, Red & White, Electrified, John Oster Manufacturing, 20 ½ x 10 ½ In. 192
Pole, Multicolor, Wood, 65 In. 760
Pole, Pine, Turned & Painted, Red, White, Blue, c.1890, 30 In. 3555
Pole, Porcelain, Globe, Illuminated, Rotating, Wall Mount, Koken, 36 In. 780
Pole, Red, White & Blue, 94 In. 1111
Pole, Sign, Porcelain, Cream & Green, Lamp Pole, Spinner, Top Globe, 15 x 82 In. 2160
Pole, Wood, Turned, Painted, Black & Silver Spiral, Acorn Finials, Iron Brackets, 36 In. 1722
Shaving Mirror, Mahogany, Satinwood, Sailor's, Compact, Slides Open, 5 ¼ x 3 ¼ In. 123
Shaving Mirror, Mahogany, Shape, Drawer, 20 x 15 In. 183
Shaving Stand, Metal, Lift Top Mirror, Drawer, 2 Doors, Casters, 37 x 18 ¾ In. 500
Sign, Barber Shop, Porcelain, Curved, Striped, Red, White, Blue, 24 x 18 In. 360
Sign, J.A. Kleiser Shaving & Hair Cutting Parlor, Wood Flange, Red, White, Blue, 15 x 42 In. 3900
Sign, Vegederma For The Hair, Woman, Gentlemen, Paper, 1903, 20 x 29 In. 7410
Steamer, Hot Towel, Vulcan, Nickel Plated, 20 x 57 In. .... *illus* 488
Towel Sterilizer, Nickel Plated Copper, Gas Burner, Enameled Base, c.1920 1500

TIP
Splint baskets should have an occasional light shower. Shake off the excess water. Dry the basket in a shady spot.

Basket, Gathering, Oak, Brown, Blue, Red, 1800s, 11 x 14 ¾ In.
$266

Cripple Creek Auctions

Basket, Nantucket, Swing Handle, Wood Bottom, Copper Nails, Robinson, 1800s, 7 x 11 In.
$3,851

James D. Julia Auctioneers

Basket, Shigeru Shinomiya, Bamboo, Bulbous, Sensuji Style, Lacquer Flower Holder, 8 ½ In.
$246

Skinner, Inc.

Basket, Splint, Oak, Oval, Bentwood Handle & Wrapped Rim, 8 ½ In.
$94

Hess Auction Group

Basket, Splint, Oak, Red, Lid, Urn Shape, Handles, 21 x 8 ½ In.
$201

Cripple Creek Auctions

Batman, Mug, Milk Glass, Batman Pictured On Both Sides, Westfield, 1966
$12

Ruby Lane

BAROMETERS are used to forecast the weather. Antique barometers with elaborate wooden cases and brass trim are the most desirable. Mercury column barometers are also popular with collectors. It is difficult to find someone to repair a broken one, so be sure your barometer is in working condition.

Aneroid, Carved Oak, Leafy Scrolls, Thermometer, Germany, c.1900, 25 In. 188
Aneroid, Giltwood, Carved Fruit, Leaf Scrolls, Italy, 1900s, 30 x 17 In. 738
Banjo, Chiesa Keizer & Co., Rosewood, Mother-Of-Pearl Inlay, c.1890, 40 x 12 In. 300
Banjo, Regency Style, Mahogany, Urn Finial, Round Dials, 46 x 12 In. 250
Banjo, Rosewood, Inlay, Engraved Steel Dial, c.1900, 27 In. 177
Ebonized Frame, Boule Inlay, France, 1800s, 23 x 23 In. 307
Holosteric, Round, Signed PHBN, France, c.1920, 5 In. 61
Stick, 2 Engraved Panels, Carved Rosewood, Brass, Leaf Carved Base, c.1805, 36 In. 1476
Stick, Ebonized, Brass Box, Canted Silver Scales, Barley Twist, c.1700, 35 In. 1197
Stick, G. Broggi Warranted, George III Rectangular Steel Dial, 35 ½ x 4 ½ In. 420
Stick, Mahogany, Bowfront, Inscribed, Carpenter & Westley, England, c.1835, 38 In. 750
Stick, Spencer Browning Co., Brass Gimbaled, Wall Mount, Arch Top, 1800s, 37 In. 1920
Stick, Thermometer, Georgian, Burl, Silver Dial, Narrow Throat, Scotland, 1800s, 36 In. 590
Thermometer, Eiffel Tower, Metal, Fretwork, France, 21 In. 940
Thermometer, Giltwood, Flaming Torch, Fluted, Wreath, Pierced Scroll, c.1790, 40 In. 1125
Thermometer, Giltwood, Leaves, Pinecone Finial, Fluted Urn Crest, c.1750, 41 In. 1187
Thermometer, Hygrometer, Mahogany Case, Wheel, Mirror, c.1850, 49 In. 406
Thermometer, Walnut, Brass Plates, Latin Inscriptions, Branches, France, 37 In. 196
Wheel, Banjo, Satinwood, Round Dial, c.1810, 46 In. 674
Wheel, J. Giobbie, Hepplewhite, Inlaid Mahogany, Marked, c.1800, 39 x 10 In. 338
Wheel, Langley Tunbridge Wells, Victorian, Rosewood, Signed, 39 ½ x 12 ½ In. 60
Wheel, Mahogany, Banjo Shape, Inlaid Trim, Hygrometer, Thermometer, Mirror, 44 x 12 In. 210
Wheel, Marine Themed, Brass Dial, Carved Mahogany, Fowled Anchor, 14 ½ In. 1966

BASEBALL *collectibles are in the Sports category, except for baseball cards, which are listed under Baseball in the Card category.*

BASKETS of all types are popular with collectors. American Indian, Japanese, African, Nantucket, Shaker, and many other kinds of baskets may be found in other sections. Of course, baskets are still being made, so a collector must learn to judge the age and style of a basket to determine its value. Also see Purse.

Appalachian, White Oak Splint, Handle, 1800s, 17 x 15 In. 450
Apple, Pine, Painted Flowers, White Ground, Bentwood Handle, c.1910, 8 x 10 In. 90
Armadillo, Scale-Like Pattern, Tan, 8 ¾ x 12 ¾ In. 150
Bee Skep, Coil, Rye Straw, Pennsylvania, 1800s, 12 ½ x 17 In. 561
Carved Oak Handles, Oak Splint Weave, c.1870, 30 x 17 In. 150
Cheese, Bamboo, Woven Splint, Bentwood Handle, Wrapped Rim, 12 x 13 In. 12
Cheese, Red Paint, 19th Century, 11 ¼ In. 584
Cheese, Splint, Woven Oak, Round, Bentwood Wrap Rim, Hexagonal Base, 7 x 21 In. 165
Coil, Grass Weave, 17 In. 47
Coil, Lid, Rye Straw, Down Blanket Storage, Pa., 19th Century, 31 x 22 In. 201
Coil, Rye Straw, Schnitz Basket For Dried Apples, 1800s, 26 In. 47
Drying, Apple Schnitz, Splint, Woven Oak, Rectangular Wood Frame, Pegged, 3 ½ x 47 In. 154
Egg, Splint, Woven Oak, Green Paint, Oval Shape, Bentwood Handle, 8 x 10 ½ In. 413
Egg, Wire, Bulbous, Loop Feet, Fixed Wire Wrapped Handle, 1800s, 12 x 8 ½ In. 325
Egg, Wire, Fixed Bail Handle, Bulbous, Round Footed Base, 1800s, 11 x 9 In. 130
Field, Splint, Woven Oak, Bentwood Wrapped Rim, Conical, 2 Carved Handles, c.1900, 16 In. 189
Field, Wire, Fixed Handle, Bulbous, Loop Footed Base, 1800s, 23 x 20 In. 266
Field, Woven, Oak Splint, Double Oval Bentwood Wrapped Rim, Cutout Handles, 30 x 21 In. 266
Fruit, Rye Straw, Coil Footed, Pa., 19th Century, 4 ¾ x 10 ¾ In. 354
Gathering, Oak, Brown, Blue, Red, 1800s, 11 x 14 ¾ In. .... *illus* 266
Gathering, Splint, Oak, Carved Handles, Round Wrapped Rim, 14 ½ x 22 In. 384
Harvest, Splint, Hickory, Square Base, Round Rim, Arched Handles, New England, 10 x 32 In. 215
Ikebana, Bamboo, Woven, Round, Long Neck, Flared Rim, Japan, 23 In. 189
Ikebana, Bulbous, Braided Arching Handle, Japan, 16 ½ In. 105
Indian Snake Charmer, Tapered, Lid, Painted Black Lizards, Rattan Handles, 31 x 16 In. 271
Market, Oak, Woven, Splint, Bentwood Handle, Wrapped Rim, Blue Dyed Bands, 12 x 11 In. 224
Nantucket, Round, 2 Heart Cutout Handles, Turned Mahogany Bottom, c.1897, 4 x 8 In. 1107
Nantucket, Splint, Turned Wood Base, Bentwood Handles, Francis H. Brown, 10 x 18 In. 615

Nantucket, Swing Handle, Wood Bottom, Copper Nails, Robinson, 1800s, 7 x 11 In. .... *illus* 3851
Picnic, Handle, Flowers, Dark Brown, Chinese, 15 ½ x 15 In. 12
Purse, Tin, New England Style, Carved Fish Clasp, Hinged, Wood Handle, 10 x 7 In. 46
Round, 2 Handles, Yellow, 1800s, 19 ½ x 14 In. 468
Rye Straw, Pediment Base, 9 x 14 ½ In. 45
Rye Straw, Round, Coiled, Lid, Carved Handles, Bentwood Rim Base, 11 x 17 In. 561
Rye, Norwegian Folk Art, Fretwork, Scalloped, Flowers, Fruit, c.1900, 9 x 9 x 3 In. 295
Sewing, Nantucket, Mahogany Pedestal, Wrapped Top Rim, Turned Ash Foot, 10 In. Diam. 2074
Shigeru Shinomiya, Bamboo, Bulbous, Sensuji Style, Lacquer Flower Holder, 8 ½ In. ....*illus* 246
Splint, Ash, Double Swing Handle, New England, 1800s, 22 ½ x 16 ½ In. 103
Splint, Double Lidded, Fixed Handle, c.1960, 8 ¼ x 11 x 8 In. 369
Splint, Oak, 3 Handles, 21 ½ x 9 ½ In. 80
Splint, Oak, Oval, Bentwood Handle & Wrapped Rim, 8 ½ In. .... *illus* 94
Splint, Oak, Red, Lid, Urn Shape, Handles, 21 x 8 ½ In. .... *illus* 201
Splint, Woven Oak, Egg Or Berry, Bentwood Handle, c.1900, 5 x 6 In. 561
Splint, Woven Oak, Oval, Triple Wrap Handle, Bentwood Trim, 1800s, 11 x 11 In. 118
Splint, Woven, Swing Handle, New England, c.1900, 7 In. 240
Storage, Rye Straw, Coil, Bulbous, Tilted, Pa., 19th Century, 19 x 18 In. 177
Woven, Dyed, Lid, Round Top, Square Base, 8 ¼ x 10 In. 71

BATCHELDER
LOS ANGELES

BATCHELDER products are made from California clay. Ernest Batchelder established a tile studio in Pasadena, California, in 1909. He went into partnership with Frederick Brown in 1912 and the company became Batchelder and Brown. In 1920 he built a larger factory with a new partner. The Batchelder-Wilson Company made all types of architectural tiles, garden pots, and bookends. The plant closed in 1932. In 1936 Batchelder opened Batchelder Ceramics, also in Pasadena, and made bowls, vases, and earthenware pots. He retired in 1951 and died in 1957. Pieces are marked *Batchelder Pasadena* or *Batchelder Los Angeles*.

Corbel, Reader, High Relief, Red Clay, 5 ¾ x 5 ¾ In., Pair 300
Tile, Dutch Boy & Girl, Dog Pulling Cart, Trees, Windmills, Impressed, 5 ½ x 17 ½ In. 295
Tile, Grapevine, White, 3 x 3 In. 100
Tile, Griffin, Brown, Circle, 5 ¾ x 5 ¾ In. 100
Tile, Lion, Purple, 3 x 3 In. 70
Tile, Peacock, Grooming, Brown, In Circle, 5 ¾ x 5 ¾ In. 100
Tile, Squirrel, Branch, Berries, Brown, Blue Ground, 3 x 3 In. 200
Tile, Turkey, Purple, Multicolor, Grooming, 4 x 4 In. 375

BATMAN and Robin are characters from a comic strip by Bob Kane that started in 1939. In 1966, the characters became part of a popular television series. There have been radio and movie serials that featured the pair. The first full-length movie was made in 1989.

Action Figure, Fused Plastic Chest Emblem, Vinyl, Canada, Mego, 1976, 12 ½ In. 288
Belt, Utility, Bat Belt, Plastic, Chromed Plastic Buckle, Gun, Cuffs, Box, 1976, 8 x 14 In. 374
Blanket, Quilted, Batman & Robin Running, Cotton, c.1966, 62 x 84 In. 348
Cake Pan, Batman, Hands On Hips, Wilton, 1989 25
Comic Book, Batman & Robin, Riding Tricycles, June-July, 1945 506
Comic Book, No. 9, February-March, Joker, Bill Finger, Jack Burnley Cover, 1942 633
Comic Book, No. 40, April-May, Joker Cover, Bill Finger, Jack Burnley Cover, 1947 462
Comic Book, No. 55, October-November, Joker Cover & Story, Bill Finger Story, 1949 406
Display, Burry's Cookies, Batmobile, Batman & Robin, Molded Plastic, 1966, 32 x 48 In. 1518
Figurine, Penguin, Open Umbrella, Glass, 1976, 6 In. 28
Game, Batman Game, Board, Milton Bradley, 1966, 10 x 19 In. 36
Game, Shooting Arcade, Plastic Gun, Villain Portrait Target, Box, 1977, 6 x 8 In. 348
Lunch Box, Thermos, Batman & Robin, Embossed Metal, Villains, Aladdin, 1966, 7 In. 2465
Mask, Specs, Glasses, Figural Bat Design, Batman & Robin Card, 1966, 3 x 6 In. 115
Model Kit, Batman Holding Bat-A-Rang, Plastic Pieces, Assembly, Box, 1964 115
Model Kit, Robin The Boy Wonder, National Periodical Publications, Aurora, 1966 115
Mug, Caped Crusader, 2-Sided, Milk Glass, Westfield, c.1966 15
Mug, Milk Glass, Batman Pictured On Both Sides, Westfield, 1966 .... *illus* 12
Pillowcase, Batman & Robin, Comic Book Graphics, Plastic Bag, 1966, 7 x 11 In. 173
Puppet, Joker, Printed Fabric, Vinyl Head, Ideal, 10 In. 380
Shaker, Figural, Arms Crossed, 4 ½ In. 12
Slippers, Batman & Robin, Running, Pow, Thud, Wham, Faux Leather, Blue, 1966, 6 ½ In. 105
Toy, Car, Batman Driving, Movable Arms, Tin Lithograph, Friction, Yanoman, Box, 6 In. 10030
Toy, Play Set, Figures, Bat Plane, Bat Car, Ideal, Box, 1960s, 13 ½ x 20 ½ In. 10247

Battersea, Box, Enamel, Flowers, Blue, Small
$476

Ruby Lane

Bauer, Pitcher, Undertray, Turquoise, 2 Piece
$177

California Auctioneers & Appraisers

Beatles, Pendant, Figure, Googly Eyes, Guitar, Goldtone, 1964, 2 ¼ x 2 ⅛ In.
$59

Ruby Lane

TIP

Dentists recommend brushing with a soft toothbrush, but hard toothbrushes are better for some jobs. Cemetery preservationists use hard toothbrushes to clean old tombstones. They are good for other cleaning jobs, too.

Beehive, Plate, Portrait, Marie De Medici, Flower Border, Gilt, Royal Vienna, 9 In.
$1,610

Early Auction Company

Beehive, Plate, Portrait, Woman, Silver Overlay, Royal Vienna, Marked, 9½ In.
$1,450

Ruby Lane

Beehive, Stein, Painted, Monk Holding Keg, Inlaid Lid, Brass, Royal Vienna, ⅛ Liter
$2,040

Fox Auctions

BATTERSEA enamels, which are enamels painted on copper, were made in the Battersea district of London from about 1750 to 1756. Many similar enamels are mistakenly called Battersea.

Box, Enamel, Flowers, Blue, Small............*illus* 476
Candlestick, Enamel, Painted Sprigs, Multicolor Flowers, Scalloped Bobeches, 10 x 5 In., Pair.. 553
Tieback, Women's Portraits, Urns, Courting Couples, Brass Frame, 2 In., 6 Piece............ 510

BAUER pottery is a California-made ware. J.A. Bauer bought Paducah Pottery in Paducah, Kentucky, in 1885. He moved the pottery to Los Angeles, California, in 1909. The company made art pottery after 1912 and introduced dinnerware marked *Bauer* in 1930. The factory went out of business in 1962 and the molds were destroyed. Since 1998, a new company, Bauer Pottery Company of Los Angeles, has been making Bauer pottery using molds made from original Bauer pieces. The pottery is now made in Highland, California. Most pieces are marked "2000." Original pieces of Bauer pottery are listed here. See also the Russel Wright category.

Cal-Art, Vase, Ruffled, Fan, Teal, 8 In. 136
Flowerpot, Stepped, Yellow, Flared, 3½ In. 30
Kitchenware, Cookie Jar, Green............ 200
Kitchenware, Teapot, Aladdin, White, 4 Cup, 10½ In. 150
La Linda, Bowl, Fruit, Pink, 5¼ In., 4 Piece............ 60
Monterey, Creamer, Cobalt Blue, Ball Shape, 2¾ In. 79
Monterey, Pitcher, Water, Red, 7 In. 125
Pitcher, Undertray, Turquoise, 2 Piece............*illus* 177
Plain, Salt & Pepper, Pink Speckled, Egg Shape, 2⅝ In. 14
Ring, Bowl, Cereal, Yellow, 5 In. 38
Ring, Carafe, Lid, Wood Handle, Turquoise............ 85
Ring, Creamer, Gray, 3¾ In. 42
Ring, Mixing Bowl, Chocolate Brown, 9⅞ In. 199
Ring, Mixing Bowl, Jade Green, 9½ In. 78
Ring, Mixing Bowl, Mustard Yellow, 11 In. 110
Ring, Mixing Bowl, Orange, 6 In. 44
Ring, Mixing Bowl, Pumpkin Glaze, 8½ x 4½ In. 35
Ring, Mixing Bowl, Yellow, 8 In. 29
Ring, Pitcher, Light Blue, 2 Qt., 5½ In. 125
Ring, Pitcher, Orange, Qt., 5¾ In. 75
Ring, Sugar & Creamer, Maroon............ 75
Swirl, Jardiniere, Green, 7 In. 125
Swirl, Planter, Pink Speckle, 7 In. 45
Swirl, Vase, Globular, Green, 7 In. 150

BAVARIA is a region in Europe where many types of porcelain were made. In the nineteenth century, the mark often included the word *Bavaria*. After 1871, the words *Bavaria, Germany*, were used. Listed here are pieces that include the name *Bavaria* in some form, but major porcelain makers, such as Rosenthal, are listed in their own categories.

Bowl, Dresden Flowers, Reticulated Sides, Oval, c.1945, 10 x 7 In. 94
Compote, Spray, Roses, Tulips, Gilt Trim, Schumann Arzberg, 7½ x 3½ In. 48
Cup & Saucer, Demitasse, Gold Bouquets, Violets, Winterling China............ 18
Jug, Ball Shape, Corn, Brown, Yellow, c.1900, 6¼ In. 207
Muffineer, Blossoms, Spray, Gilded Top, 5 In. 116
Plate, Empress Pattern, Lattice Border, Gilt, Schumann, 9 In. 65
Plate, Salad, Roses, Gilt Trim, 7½ In. 12
Plate, Soldier, Rearing Horse, Gold Trim, Bareuther Waldsassen, 4 x 4 In. 10
Plate, Violets, Yellow Border, Signed Hauk, 8½ In. 30
Plate, White, Gold Rim, Gold Filigree Border, Heimrich & Co., 11¼ In. 708
Vase, Grapes, Leaves, Footed, Yellow, Green, A. Koch, 8½ In. 68
Vase, Green, Silver Thistles, Shouldered, Heinrich & Co., c.1900, 8 In. 360

BEADED BAGS *are included in the Purse category.*

BEATLES collectors search for any items picturing the four members of the famous music group or any of their recordings. Because these items are so new, the condition is very important and top prices are paid only for items in mint condition. The Beatles first appeared on American network television in 1964. The group disbanded in 1971. Ringo Starr and Paul McCartney are still performing. John Lennon died in 1980. George Harrison died in 2001.

Album, Beatles '65, Capitol Records, Group, Holding Open Umbrellas............ 30

Album, Beatles At The Hollywood Bowl, Ticket Stubs, 1977 65
Album, Sgt. Pepper's Lonely Hearts Club Band, Capitol Records 45
Binder, 3-Ring, Transfer Image Of Band, NEMS Enterprises, c.1964 100
Bracelet, Celluloid Portraits, Metal, c.1965, 6 In. 139
Charm, John Lennon, Bust, Sterling Silver, c.1960, 1 ¼ In. 129
Doll, Ringo Starr, Hard Plastic, Rubber Head, Drum, 1964, 4 ½ In. 77
Glass, Ringo, John, Paul, George, Portrait, Apple Corp., Ltd., 4 Piece 61
Harmonica, Storage Box, The Beatles, Get The Beat, Blister Card, 1964, 8 x 11 In. 506
Lunch Box, Embossed Metal, Member Portraits, Guitars, 1965 626
Magazine, Beatlemania, Vol. 1, No. 1, 10 ¼ x 14 In. 19
Necktie, Black, White, Man Sleeping, I Call Your Name, Silk, 4 x 57 In. 27
Necktie, Man, Hard Hat, Silver Moon & Stars, House, Hard Day's Night, Silk, 4 x 57 In. 80
Notebook, Beatles In Front Of Blue Brick Wall, Autographs, 8 ½ x 11, 1964 45
Paint Set, Paint Your Own Beatle, P. McCartney, By Number, Box, 1964, 14 x 19 In. 1670
Pendant, Figure, Googly Eyes, Guitar, Goldtone, 1964, 2 ¼ x 2 ⅛ In. ....*illus* 59
Pin, Portraits, Brass, 1964, 2 In. Diam. 65
Plate, Beatles Live In Concert, Band Playing, Blue, Black, White, Delphi, 8 In. 24
Purse, Clutch, Vinyl, Black, Portraits, Facsimile Signatures, Zipper Top, Strap, Dame, 10 In. 221
Puzzle, Yellow Submarine, 100 Piece, Jaymar, 1968, 13 x 18 In., Pair 211
Tin, Talc, Lithograph, Photo Of Band, With The Beatles, Stuffed Donkey, 1964, 8 In. 316
Watch, Portraits, The Beatles, Leather Band, Fossil, 9 In. 50
Water Color Set, Yellow Submarine, 6 Pictures, King Features, 1968, 9 x 11 In. 278
Wig, Bag, Header Card, Lowell Toy Mfg., c.1964, 9 ¾ x 12 In. 209

BEEHIVE, Austria, or Beehive, Vienna, are terms used in English-speaking countries to refer to the many types of decorated porcelain bearing a mark that looks like a beehive. The mark is actually a shield, viewed upside down. It was first used in 1744 by the Royal Porcelain Manufactory of Vienna. The firm made what collectors call Royal Vienna porcelains until it closed in 1864. Many other German, Austrian, and Japanese factories have reproduced Royal Vienna wares, complete with the original shield or beehive mark. This listing includes the expensive, original Royal Vienna porcelains and many other types of beehive porcelain. The Royal Vienna pieces include that name in the description.

Box, Portrait, Green, Gilt, 2 ¼ x 4 ¾ In. 575
Charger, Square Reserve, Floating Nudes, Fuchsia Border, Gilt Filigree, 14 ½ In. 813
Dish, Art Nouveau, Blue, Gilt, Romantic Scene, Ackermann & Fritze, Royal Vienna, 15 In. 94
Figurine, Napoleon, Horse, 13 x 12 In. 276
Jug, Portrait, Woman, Clematis Vines, Gold Flowers, Leaves, Red, Oval, Handle, 9 In. 805
Plaque, Der Fischer, Fisherman, Royal Vienna, Signed A. Heinrich, 1800s, 9 ½ x 6 In. 661
Plaque, Meditation, Woman Portrait, Gilt Border, Cobalt Blue, Royal Vienna, 14 x 14 In. 863
Plate, Dancing Maidens, Flowers, Gilt Accents, Transfer, 10 ⅛ In. 23
Plate, Mother & Children, Garden, Gilt Geometric Border, 9 ⅜ In. 720
Plate, Portrait, Marie De Medici, Flower Border, Gilt, Royal Vienna, 9 In. ....*illus* 1610
Plate, Portrait, Woman, Silver Overlay, Royal Vienna, Marked, 9 ½ In. ....*illus* 1450
Plate, Seated Maiden, Sea, Lyre, Green Border, Raised Dots, 6 In. 345
Plate, Woman, Butterfly, Garden, Gilt Geometric Border, 9 ½ In. 990
Plate, Woman, Classical Interior, Cobalt Blue Border, 9 ½ In., 2 Piece 944
Plate, Woman, Garden, Cherubs, Gilt Geometric Border, 9 ½ In. .... 660 to 720
Stein, Painted, Monk Holding Keg, Inlaid Lid, Brass, Royal Vienna, ⅛ Liter ....*illus* 2040
Tea Caddy, Cherub, Woman, Woodland, Lid, Gold Finial, 4 ¾ In. 281
Tea Set, Teapot, Sugar & Creamer, Cup & Saucer, Tray, 6 Piece 276
Tea Set, Teapot, Sugar & Creamer, Gilt, Bacchanalian, Blue Ground, Gilt, 3 Piece 3540
Tea Set, Teapot, Sugar, Creamer, 2 Cups, Saucers, Tray, Landscapes, 8 Piece 1875
Teapot, Children Playing, Cobalt Blue Ground, Gilt Metal, 7 ¾ In. 688
Teapot, Cobalt Blue, Winged Dolphin Figural Handle, Signed Kramer, 8 x 6 ½ In. 480
Urn, Blue, Cartouche, Handles, Nymph, Landscape, Royal Vienna, 8 ⅝ In. 134
Vase, Lid, Egg Shape, Gilt Handles, Blue Beehive Mark, Royal Vienna, Austria, c.1900, 19 In. 236
Vase, Lid, Portrait, Burgundy, Signed Geyer, 16 ½ In. 738
Vase, Medallion, Gilt Border, Portrait, Woman, Scarf, Acanthus, Flowers, 19th Century, 5 In. 544
Vase, Mythological Scene, Nessus Abducting Deianeira, Bulbous, Royal Vienna, 12 In. 109
Vase, Oval, Gold, Pink, Red, Group Of Men, Footed, Marked, 6 ½ In. 1300
Vase, Putti With Compote, Nude, Landscape, Gilt, Signed Donath, 13 ¾ In. 1187
Vase, Solitude, Seminude Woman, Auburn Hair, Gold Band, Royal Vienna, Wagner, 12 In. 1770
Water Pot, Peach Bloom, Rounded Sides, Pinched Neck, Flared Rim, c.1900, 3 x 5 In. 124

BEER BOTTLES *are listed in the Bottle category under Beer.*

Bell, Brass, Hotel, Elephant's Head, Push Bone Tusks, Key Wind Bell Rings, 3 x 6 In.
$604

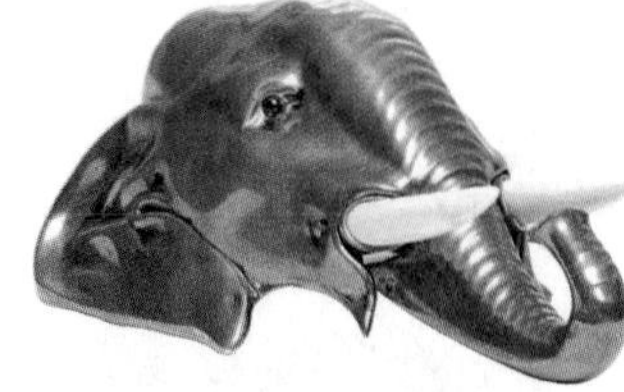

Wm Morford

TIP
Install locks on all garage doors and windows.

Bell, Bronze, Carved, Engraved, 8 Emblems, Double Dragon Finials, 19th Century, Chinese, 9 ½ in.
$474

James D. Julia Auctioneers

Bell, Cast Bronze, Plantation, Clapper, Iron Yoke Supports, c.1850, 17 In. Diam.
$3,660

Neal Auctions

Bennington, Flask, Brown & Blue Mottle Glazed, Book Shape, 5 ¾ In.
$708

Hess Auction Group

Bennington, Flask, Coachman, Toby, Yellowware, Mottled Rockingham Glaze, 1849, 10 ¾ In.
$531

Hess Auction Group

Barber Bottles

Barber bottles are available in all kinds of glass: pressed, carnival, milk, cut, opalescent, overlay, and other art glass. Many have enameled designs or acid-etched decorations. They are sometimes labeled with the customer's name, or with the contents, such as "Bay Rum" or "Witch Hazel." They often come in pairs and occasionally have a matching vase for shaving paper. The vases are rare today.

BEER CANS are a twentieth-century idea. Beer was sold in kegs or returnable bottles until 1934. The first patent for a can was issued to the American Can Company in September of that year, and Gotfried Kruger Brewing Company, Newark, New Jersey, was the first to use the can. The cone-top can was first made in 1935, the aluminum pop-top in 1962. Collectors should look for cans in good condition, with no dents or rust. Serious collectors prefer cans that have been opened from the bottom.

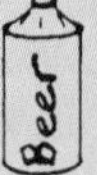

Altes Beer, Gold, Black, Cone Top, c.1948 100
Bub's Beer, It's The Grain, Red, White, 1950s, Cone Top 400
Copper Club Beer, Cone Top, Green, Copper, c.1950 115
Griesedieck Bros. Light Lager, Flat Top, Red, Gold 25

BELL collectors collect all types of bells. Favorites include glass bells, figural bells, school bells, and cowbells. Bells have been made of porcelain, china, or metal through the centuries.

Brass, Diva Oil Lamp, Etched, Bells Of Sarna, Tag, 3 In. 24
Brass, Embossed Flowers, Scalloped, Wood Stand, Stepped Base, 18 In. 139
Brass, Hand, Turned Maple Handle, 1800s, 9 In. 59
Brass, Hotel, Elephant's Head, Push Bone Tusks, Key Wind Bell Rings, 3 x 6 In. .... *illus* 604
Brass, Hotel, Figural Owl, Perched, 6 ¼ In. 510
Brass, Neoclassical, Service, 19 In. 50
Brass, Water Carrier, Etched, Enameled, Bells Of Sarna, India, 1940s, 2 ½ In. 10
Bronze, Altar, Engraved, Precious Emblems, Deep Black, Tibet, 1800s, 7 In. 62
Bronze, Armature Stand, Applied Dragon Motif, 18 x 9 In. 96
Bronze, Carved, Engraved, 8 Emblems, Double Dragon Finials, 19th Century, Chinese, 9 ½ In. .... *illus* 474
Bronze, Cast, Dolphin Frame, 40 In. 1653
Bronze, Chinese, 1800s, 10 In. 281
Bronze, Hand, Striker, Arch, Asiatic, 18 ¼ x 15 In. 238
Bronze, Mission, Round Handle, 1818, 9 ¼ x 5 ¾ In. 115
Bronze, Temple Elephant Bell, Thailand, 1800s, 12 x 7 ⅗ In. 230
Cast Bronze, Plantation, Clapper, Iron Yoke Supports, c.1850, 17 In. Diam. .... *illus* 3660
Cast Iron, Hotel, Copper Flashed, Sphere, Rotating, Footed Shaped Base, 5 x 5 In. 480
Cast Iron, Strap Hoop Handle, c.1850, 6 x 4 In. 45
Glass, Pear Shape, Bohemian, 6 In. 35
Hammer, Silencer, Carved Wood Stand, Lacquer, Japan, 15 In. 615
Metal, Service, Mechanical, Mounted On Wood, 10 In. 30
Silver, Metal, Tortoise, Figural, Upward Gazing, Windup, Grey & Co., 1922, 5 ½ In. 1243
Silver, Windmill Shape, Spinning Motion, Dutch, 7 ½ In. 184
Sleigh, 21 Brass Bells, Fender Washers, Leather Strap, c.1910, 80 In. 170
Sleigh, 23 Double Graduated Cast Brass, 1 ¼ In. Leather Strap, 76 In. 170
Temple, Chime, Painted, Birds, Branches, Flowers, Key Fret, 5 Graduated Sizes, 8 x 4 In. 362
Wood, Laminated Metal, Paul Evans, Phil Powell, 11 ¼ x 2 ½ In. 1875
Wrought Iron, Sheep, Switzerland, 15 x 11 In. 298

BELLEEK china was made in Ireland, other European countries, and the United States. The glaze is creamy yellow and appears wet. The first Belleek was made in 1857. All pieces listed here are Irish Belleek. The mark changed through the years. The first mark, black, dates from 1863 to 1890. The second mark, black, dates from 1891 to 1926 and includes the words *Co. Fermanagh, Ireland.* The third mark, black, dates from 1926 to 1946 and has the words *Deanta in Eirinn*. The fourth mark, same as the third mark but green, dates from 1946 to 1955. The fifth mark (second green mark) dates from 1955 to 1965 and has an *R* in a circle added in the upper right. The sixth mark (third green mark) dates from 1965 to 1981 and the words *Co. Fermanagh* have been omitted. The seventh mark, gold, was used from 1981 to 1992 and omits the words *Deanta in Eirinn*. The eighth mark, used from 1993 to 1996, is similar to the second mark but is printed in blue. The ninth mark, blue, includes the words *Est. 1857* and the words *Co. Fermanagh Ireland* are omitted. The tenth mark, black, is similar to the ninth mark but includes the words *Millennium 2000* and *Ireland*. It was used only in 2000. The eleventh mark, similar to the millennium mark but green, was introduced in 2001. The twelfth mark, black, is similar to the eleventh mark but has a banner above the mark with the words *Celebrating 150 Years*. It was used in 2007. The thirteenth trademark, used from 2008 to 2010, is similar to the twelfth but is brown and has no banner. The fourteenth mark, the Classic Belleek trademark, is similar to the twelfth but includes Belleek's website address. The Belleek Living trademark was introduced in 2010 and is used on items from that giftware line. The word *Belleek* is now used only on the pieces made in Ireland even though earlier pieces from other countries were sometimes marked *Belleek*. These early pieces are listed by manufacturer, such as Ceramic Art Co., Haviland, Lenox, Ott & Brewer, and Willets.

Basket, Oval, 4 Strand, Applied Flowers, Flowering Vines, 10 x 6 x 2 In. 149
Chalice, White, Purple Flowers & Leaves, Gilt, High Glaze, Round Foot, c.1898 191
Coffeepot, Shamrock, Cob Luster, 5th Mark, Green, 6 ¾ In. 52

Bennington, Jug, Stylized Leaf, Stoneware, Salt Glaze, Lug Handle, E. & L.P. Norton, 2 Gal., 14 In.
$150

Cowan Auctions

Bennington, Pitcher, Dark Luster Rockingham Glaze, Molded Flower Sprigs, 6-Sided, 9 ¾ In.
$180

Cowan Auctions

Bennington, Pitcher, Flint Enamel, Yellow, Brown, Green, Alternate Rib, Marked, 1850s, 10 In.
$180

Cowan Auctions

Bicycle, H.B. Smith Machine, Pony Star, High Wheel Safety, c.1888, 24-In. Wheels
$16,380

Copake Auction

Bicycle, Harley-Davidson, Pedal, Pressed Steel Fenders, Fake Tank, Spring Seat, 43 In.
$275

Morphy Auctions

Bicycle, Monark, Boy's, Balloon, B.F. Goodrich Tires, Stewart Warner Cadet Speedometer, 1947
$848

Copake Auction

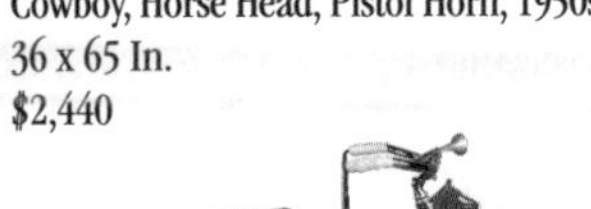

Bicycle, Monark, Gene Autry, Girl's, Cowboy, Horse Head, Pistol Horn, 1950s, 36 x 65 In.
$2,440

Morphy Auctions

Bicycle, Singer Cycle Co., Tandem, Removable Front, Humbers Pat., Eng., 1886, 40 x 80 In.
$10,237

Copake Auction

Bicycle, Tandem, Rear Steering, Male-Female, c.1920
$234

Copake Auction

Bicycle, Western Flyer, Green, Leather Seat, Men's, Marked Ca 1950, 40 In.
$156

Garth's Auctioneers & Appraisers

Ford Charcoal

Henry Ford invented charcoal briquettes. They were made from leftover scraps of wood from Model T car manufacturing.

Cornucopia, Shamrock, White, Gold Trim, 9th Mark, Blue, 11½ x 7 In. 18
Dish, Shell Shape, Pink Rim With Gold Trim, 2nd Mark, Black, 1891-1926, 9⅝ In. 40
Figurine, Irish Wolfhound, White, Marked Belleek Collector's Society, 7⅜ In. 52
Flower Holder, White, Marked Belleek, 5½ In. 287
Honey Pot, Shamrock, Cob Luster, 6th Mark, Green, 5¾ In. 24
Jug, Aberdeen, Mother-Of-Pearl Luster, 3rd Mark, Black, 1926-46, 7 In. 86
Jug, Nautilus Shell Shape, White, 1st Mark, Black, 1863-90, 5¼ In. 63
Pitcher, Bulbous, Tapered Neck, Wavy Spout, Curved Handle, Fluted, Flowers, c.1891, 9 In. 777
Pitcher, Shamrock, 2nd Mark, Black, 3½ In. 86
Plate, Hexagonal, Lace Pattern, Basket Weave, Stylized Twig Handle, c.1890, 11 In. Diam. 203
Platter, Floral, White & Brown, Brown Mark, 15⅝ In. 57
Shell Plateau, White, Pink Tint, Gold Highlights, 2nd Mark, Black, 1891-1926, 4⅝ In. 80
Sugar, Ivy, Cob Luster, 3rd Mark, Black, 1926-46, 3¾ In. 6
Sugar, Shell Shape, White, 1st Mark, Black, 1863-90, 6½ In. 207
Teapot, Tridacna, 1st Mark, Black, 1863-1890, 7¾ In. 172
Tray, Tridacna, White, 2nd Mark, Black, 1891-1926, 15 x 14 In. 373
Trinket Box, Acorn, Cob Luster, 3rd Mark, Black, 1926-46, 3½ In. 74
Vase, Leaves & Berries, Painted, 1903, 5 x 4½ In. 178
Vase, Oval, Parrots, Perched On Branches, Blossoms, Purple, Green, Gold, 18 In. 460
Vase, Spill, Flying Fish, White, 1st Mark, Black, 1863-90, 4¼ In. 230
Vase, Spill, Lily Of The Valley, White, 2nd Mark, Black, 1891-1926, 6⅝ In. 34

BENNINGTON ware was the product of two factories working in Bennington, Vermont. Both the Norton Company and Lyman Fenton & Company were out of business by 1896. The wares include brown and yellow mottled pottery, Parian, scroddled ware, stoneware, graniteware, yellowware, and Staffordshire-type vases. The name is also a generic term for mottled brownware of the type made in Bennington.

Candlestick, Flint Enamel Glaze, Organic Shape Bobeches, Tripod Foot, 8 In. 330
Candlestick, Flint Enamel Mottled Glaze, Column Shape, c.1860, 9½ In. 150
Crock, E. & L.P. Norton, Bennington, Vermont, 4, 1800s, 11 x 12 In. 263
Crock, Salt Glaze Stoneware, Cobalt Blue Leaf, Impressed Mark, 1800s, 4 Gal., 11 x 12 In. 180
Flask, Brown & Blue Mottle Glazed, Book Shape, 5¾ In. .... *illus* 708
Flask, Coachman, Toby, Yellowware, Mottled Rockingham Glaze, 1849, 10¾ In. .... *illus* 531
Flask, Flint Enamel, Molded Tavern Scene, c.1850, 6 In. 92
Jar, Storage, Lid, Gothic Style, Flint Enamel Mottled Glaze, 1800s, 13 x 11 In. 330
Jug, Stylized Leaf, Stoneware, Salt Glaze, Lug Handle, E. & L.P. Norton, 2 Gal., 14 In. .... *illus* 150
Pitcher, Dark Luster Rockingham Glaze, Molded Flower Sprigs, 6-Sided, 9¾ In. .... *illus* 180
Pitcher, Flint Enamel, Yellow, Brown, Green, Alternate Rib, Marked, 1850s, 10 In. .... *illus* 180
Tieback, Flint Enamel Glaze, 10-Point Stars, Flowers, 4½ In., 2 Pair 270

BERLIN, a German porcelain factory, was started in 1751 by Wilhelm Kaspar Wegely. In 1763, the factory was taken over by Frederick the Great and became the Royal Berlin Porcelain Manufactory. It is still in operation today. Pieces have been marked in a variety of ways.

Plate, Das Palais Des Prinzen Carl, Gilt Border & Scrollwork, Stars, c.1820, 8 In. Diam. 1625
Plate, Pierced Border, Flowers, Leaves, Multicolor, c.1890, 9 In. Diam., Pair 1063
Platter, Relief Modeled, Head Of Woman, Sea Green, Blue, 17 x 13¾ In. 420
Tureen, Lid, Animals, Insects, Woven Texture Band, Gilt, Bacchus Finial, c.1870, 14 x 12 In. 777

BESWICK started making pottery in Staffordshire, England, in 1894. The pottery became John Beswick Ltd. in 1936. The company became part of Royal Doulton Tableware, Ltd. in 1969. Production ceased in 2002 and the John Beswick brand was bought by Dartington Crystal in 2004. Figurines, vases, and other items are being made and use the name Beswick. Beatrix Potter figures were made from 1948 until 2002. They shouldn't be confused with Bunnykins, which were made by Royal Doulton.

Beatrix Potter, Character Jug, Old Mr. Brown, Squirrel Handle, BP 3C, 3 In. 155
Beatrix Potter, Figurine, Amiable Guinea Pig, BP 2A, 4 In. 225
Beatrix Potter, Figurine, Diggory Delvet, Mole, 1982, 3 In. 70
Beatrix Potter, Figurine, Duchess, Holding Flowers, Gold Back Stamp, BP2, c.1955 428
Beatrix Potter, Figurine, Miss Moppet, BP 2A, 1960s, 3 In. 99
Beatrix Potter, Figurine, Mr. Benjamin Bunny, Holding Pipe, Riding Crop, 1970s, 4 In. 75
Beatrix Potter, Figurine, Old Mr. Brown, 3¼ In. 55
Beatrix Potter, Figurine, Ribby, BP 2A, 3½ In. 81
Beatrix Potter, Figurine, Timmy Tiptoes, BP 2A, c.1960, 3½ In. 54
Beatrix Potter, Figurine, Tom Kitten, 1948, 3½ In. 75
Beatrix Potter, Group, Flopsy, Mopsy & Cottontail, 2¾ x 3 In. 158

Bowl, No. 300, Asymmetrical, Squared, Double Strap, Ivory Matte Glaze, 1934, 10 In. 45
Figurine, 2 Birds, No. 926, Orange, 1950s, 5 ½ x 5 In. 115
Figurine, Cat, Seated, Ginger, No. 1031, 4 ½ In. 115
Figurine, Champion Newton Tinkle Jersey Cow, No. 1345, 4 x 6 In. 100
Figurine, Dog, Afghan Hound, Hajubah Of Davlen, Golden Brown, 7 x 5 In. 135
Figurine, Dog, Collie, A. Gredington, c.1968, 3 x 4 In. 78
Figurine, Dog, Collie, No. 1814, c.1960, 3 ¼ x 4 ½ In. 78
Figurine, Dog, Dachshund, Black, 3 ½ In. 45
Figurine, Dog, Doberman Pinscher, Annastock Lance, 6 x 6 ½ In. 92
Figurine, Dog, English Spaniel, White, Sitting, 5 ¾ In. 55
Figurine, Dog, Golden Retriever, No. 41, 1970s, 5 x 8 In. 125
Figurine, Dog, Irish Setter, Sugar Of Wendover, 5 ¾ x 8 ¼ In. 96
Figurine, Dog, Old English Sheep Dog, No. 2232, Sitting, 11 In. 250
Figurine, Dog, Scottish Terrier, Black, 2 x 3 In. 48
Figurine, Horse & Rider, Huntsman, 9 x 8 ½ In. 195
Figurine, Horse, Brown, Glossy, 8 x 10 In. 75
Figurine, Horse, Head Down, Black & Gray, 6 x 8 In. 160
Figurine, Lion Cub, 1967, 4 x 6 In. 95
Figurine, Mallard Duck, No. 756-1 & 2, Pair 110
Jug, No. 137, Ball Shape, 4 ½ In. 39
Relish, 3 Sections, Cabbage Leaf Shape, Tomato, 10 In. 50
Salt & Pepper, Sairey Gamp & Mr. Micawber, 3 In. 35
Teapot, Sairey Gamp, Umbrella Handle, Polka Dot Tie, No. 691, 1954, 5 x 7 In. 157
Vase, Ballerina, No. 1287, 4-Sided, Trumpet, Peach, Mint Glaze, 11 In. 89
Vase, Rabbits, Jumping, No. 677, Palm Trees, Rusty Brown Matte Finish, 1938, 7 In. 63
Vase, Ribbed, Scalloped Top, Wavy Design, Footed, 1920s, 9 In. 135
Vase, Tulip, Oval, Footed, 6 ¼ In. 67

BETTY BOOP, the cartoon figure, first appeared on the screen in 1931. Her face was modeled after the famous singer Helen Kane and her body after Mae West. In 1935, a comic strip was started. Her dog was named Bimbo. Although the Betty Boop cartoons ended by 1938, there was a revival of interest in the Betty Boop image in the 1980s and new pieces are being made.

Ashtray, Betty & Bimbo, Sitting On Edge, Iridescent, Fleischer Studios, Japan, 1930s, 3 x 4 In. 175
Cards, Playing, Betty In Front Of Curtain, Diamond Ground, 1932, 3 ½ x 2 In. 75
Doll, Ballerina, Tutu, Box, Marty Toys, 1986, 12 In. 55
Doll, Cloth, Red Dress & Shoes, Holding Roses, 11 In. 15
Doll, Composition, Green Leaf Type Dress, Fleischer Studios, 1931, 14 In. 3500
Doll, Wood, String-Jointed, Red Dress, U.S.A., 4 In. 90
Figurine, Composition, Red & Orange, Fleischer Studios, c.1931, 14 In. 230
Nodder, Bisque, Molded Hair, Japan, 7 In. 50
Wall Pocket, Betty & Bimbo, Red Dress, Barn, 1930s 95

BICYCLES were invented in 1839. The first manufactured bicycle was made in 1861. Special ladies' bicycles were made after 1874. The modern safety bicycle was not produced until 1885. Collectors search for all types of bicycles and tricycles. Bicycle-related items are also listed here.

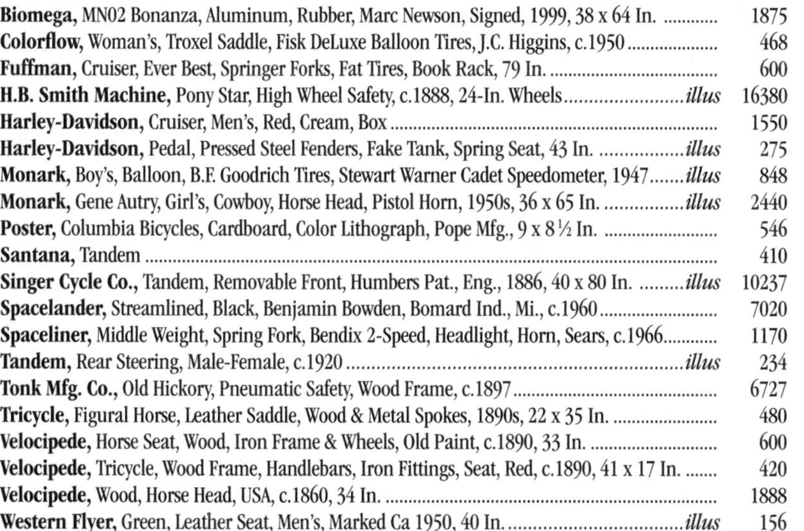

Biomega, MN02 Bonanza, Aluminum, Rubber, Marc Newson, Signed, 1999, 38 x 64 In. 1875
Colorflow, Woman's, Troxel Saddle, Fisk DeLuxe Balloon Tires, J.C. Higgins, c.1950 468
Fuffman, Cruiser, Ever Best, Springer Forks, Fat Tires, Book Rack, 79 In. 600
H.B. Smith Machine, Pony Star, High Wheel Safety, c.1888, 24-In. Wheels .... *illus* 16380
Harley-Davidson, Cruiser, Men's, Red, Cream, Box 1550
Harley-Davidson, Pedal, Pressed Steel Fenders, Fake Tank, Spring Seat, 43 In. .... *illus* 275
Monark, Boy's, Balloon, B.F. Goodrich Tires, Stewart Warner Cadet Speedometer, 1947 .... *illus* 848
Monark, Gene Autry, Girl's, Cowboy, Horse Head, Pistol Horn, 1950s, 36 x 65 In. .... *illus* 2440
Poster, Columbia Bicycles, Cardboard, Color Lithograph, Pope Mfg., 9 x 8 ½ In. 546
Santana, Tandem 410
Singer Cycle Co., Tandem, Removable Front, Humbers Pat., Eng., 1886, 40 x 80 In. .... *illus* 10237
Spacelander, Streamlined, Black, Benjamin Bowden, Bomard Ind., Mi., c.1960 7020
Spaceliner, Middle Weight, Spring Fork, Bendix 2-Speed, Headlight, Horn, Sears, c.1966 1170
Tandem, Rear Steering, Male-Female, c.1920 .... *illus* 234
Tonk Mfg. Co., Old Hickory, Pneumatic Safety, Wood Frame, c.1897 6727
Tricycle, Figural Horse, Leather Saddle, Wood & Metal Spokes, 1890s, 22 x 35 In. 480
Velocipede, Horse Seat, Wood, Iron Frame & Wheels, Old Paint, c.1890, 33 In. 600
Velocipede, Tricycle, Wood Frame, Handlebars, Iron Fittings, Seat, Red, c.1890, 41 x 17 In. 420
Velocipede, Wood, Horse Head, USA, c.1860, 34 In. 1888
Western Flyer, Green, Leather Seat, Men's, Marked Ca 1950, 40 In. .... *illus* 156

Bing & Grondahl, Cake Plate, Violets & Berries, Gold Trim, Open Dolphin Handles, 10 ¼ In.
$75

Ruby Lane

Bing & Grondahl, Figurine, Boy With Dog, 5 x 3 ½ In.
$125

Ruby Lane

Birdcage, Metal, Pagoda Shape, 3 Tiers, Red, Gilt, Porcelain Feeders, Base, 1900s, 85 x 20 In.
$2,337

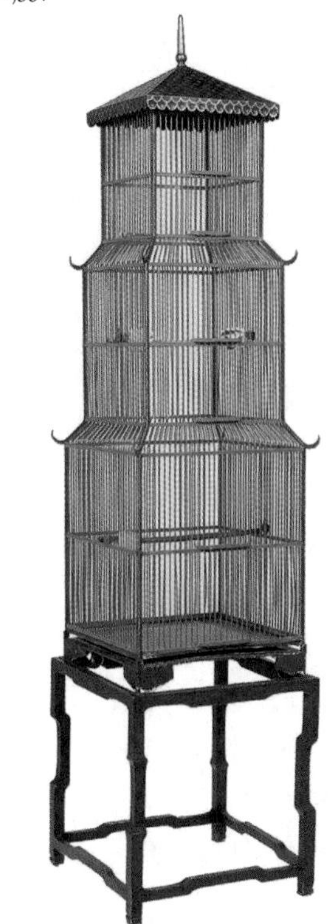

New Orleans (Cakebread)

Birdcage, Pine, Wirework, Gothic House, Columns, Peaked Roof, Italy, c.1900, 44 x 40 x 23 In.
$649

Brunk Auctions

Bisque, Figurine, Woman, Man, Bohemian, Painted, Gilt, J. Moehling, c.1860, 22 x 8 In., Pair
$437

New Orleans (Cakebread)

Black, Figurine, Uncle Tom, Little Eva On Knee, Staffordshire, 11 In.
$118

Hess Auction Group

BING & GRONDAHL is a famous Danish factory making fine porcelains from 1853 to the present. Underglaze blue decoration was started in 1886. The annual Christmas plate series was introduced in 1895. Dinnerware, stoneware, and figurines are still being made today. The firm has used the initials *B & G* and a stylized castle as part of the mark since 1898. The company became part of Royal Copenhagen in 1987.

B&G KJØBENHAVN MADE IN DENMARK

Bowl, 2 Mice, Red Eyes, 5 In. 63
Cake Plate, Violets & Berries, Gold Trim, Open Dolphin Handles, 10 ¼ In. .... *illus* 75
Coffee Set, Coffeepot, Cream & Sugar, Sea Gulls, Blue, White, 3 Piece 152
Figurine, Boy With Dog, 5 x 3 ½ In. .... *illus* 125
Figurine, Cat, Reclining, Tan, 4 ½ x 3 ½ In. 45
Figurine, Child, Who Is Calling, 1960s, 6 In. 72
Figurine, Girl With Doll, 7 ⅜ In. 30
Figurine, Sealyham Terrier, White, 6 ¼ In. 72
Figurine, Shepherdess, 3 Sheep, c.1950, 10 ¼ In. 185
Figurine, The Cobbler, 9 In. 62
Group, Dancing Couple, 8 x 5 In. 36
Group, Woman Milking Cow, Cat, Blue Dress, 1950s, 7 ¾ In. 172
Teapot, Sea Gulls, Blue, White, 6 ½ x 10 In. 102

BINOCULARS of all types are wanted by collectors. Those made in the eighteenth and nineteenth centuries are favored by serious collectors. The small, attractive binoculars called opera glasses are listed in their own category.

Binolux, 7x35, Compass, Leather Case 46
Bushnell, 7x21, Insta Focus, Leather Case 54
Eduardo Augusto Pereira Oculista No. 90, Leather Barrels & Case, c.1900, 4 x 3 In. 83
Goerz, 9x, Trieder Binocle, Germany 195
Kmart, 7x35, Plastic, Case, Hong Kong 30
Lemaire, Adjustable, Leather Case, c.1900, 5 x 4 In. 75
Merchant Marines, Black Finish, Paris, 6 ¼ x 5 In. 50
Ofuna, 7x50, Black Leather Case, Occupied Japan, c.1945 50
Sans Streiffe No. 810, 7x35, 4 Lens Caps, Case, Japan 39
Trojan, Leather Case, c.1945, 5 ½ x 3 ½ In. 25

BIRDCAGES are collected for use as homes for pet birds and as decorative objects of folk art. Elaborate wooden cages of the past centuries can still be found. The brass or wicker cages of the 1930s are popular with bird owners.

3 Domed Sections, Green, Wrought Iron Stand, France, 63 x 27 In. 468
Gothic Style, Wirework Domes, Crenellated Cornice, Arched, Carved, Gilt, 1800s, 36 x 34 In. 861
Iron, White, Shepard's Hook, 62 In. 24
Lacquered Bamboo, Perch, Cloisonne Bowls, Metal Hook, 26 In. 246
Mahogany, Carved, Iron, Center Dome, Lateral Domes, Neoclassical Style, 1900s, 32 x 30 In. 369
Mahogany, Regency Style, Barrel Vault Top, 41 x 30 In. 188
Metal, 2 Parts, Rectangular, Stand, Casters, 32 x 22 In. 70
Metal, Octagonal, Hinged, Green, Gilt, Victorian, 86 x 49 In. 9749
Metal, Pagoda Shape, 3 Tiers, Red, Gilt, Porcelain Feeders, Base, 1900s, 85 x 20 In. .... *illus* 2337
Metal, Rectangular, Peaked Roof, Victorian, 79 ¾ x 36 In. 500
Paint, 3 Domed Sections, 29 x 26 In. 250
Pine, Iron, Pointed Arch, 2 Feeding Drawers, Victorian, Gothic, 28 x 27 In. 307
Pine, Wirework, Gothic House, Columns, Peaked Roof, Italy, c.1900, 44 x 40 x 23 In. .... *illus* 649
Round, Twig Top, 43 ½ x 22 In. 360
Tin, Crown Top, Hanging Loop, Round Bars, Sliding Door, Perch, Containers, 1800s, 21 In. 649
Tin, Gable Roof, Deer Head Ornament, Chimney Handle, Stevens & Brown, 14 x 17 In. 531
Tin, Removable Base, Glass Feeder, Painted, Stevens & Brown, 21 In. 502
Tin, Round, Hanging, Bar Perches, Feeder Cup, 1800s, 15 ½ In. 295
Wood, 3 Sections, Dome Top, 27 x 13 In. 117
Wood, Wire, Double Dome, Pinecone Finials, Victorian, 36 ½ x 33 In. 390
Wood, Wire, House, Federal Façade, 2 Turrets, Victorian, 23 x 31 x 16 In. 420
Wrought Iron, Square, Hanging, 15 x 17 In. 120

BISQUE is an unglazed baked porcelain. Finished bisque has a slightly sandy texture with a dull finish. Some of it may be decorated with various colors. Bisque gained favor during the late Victorian era when thousands of bisque figurines were made. It is still being made. Additional bisque items may be listed under the factory name.

Bowl, Figural Support, Cherubs, Gilt, Continental, 12 ¼ In. 63
Bust, Woman, Wearing Flower Adorned Hat, Square Base, 1800s, France, 31 In. 984
Figurine, Athlete, Holding Baton, Continental, c.1910, 22 x 5 ½ In. 687
Figurine, Child Holding Cross, Globe, Octagonal Base, France, 29 x 11 In. 900
Figurine, Man & Woman, 18th Century Dress, Multicolor, Continental, 1800s, 20 x 8 In., Pair... 390
Figurine, Man, Woman, 17th Century Dress, Vion & Baury, 16 ¾ In., Pair 300
Figurine, Nude, Kneeling, Adjusting Hair, A.K. Tutter For Hutschenreuther, 13 x 7 In. 156
Figurine, People Of Russia Series, Man, Kalmyk, 1930, 11 ½ In. 5750
Figurine, People Of Russia Series, Woman, Ostyak From Obdorsk, 10 In. 3750
Figurine, Woman, Man, Bohemian, Painted, Gilt, J. Moehling, c.1860, 22 x 8 In., Pair........ *illus* 437
Group, 2 Men, Long Coats, Beards, Germany, 12 In. 188
Group, After Louis Cyffle, 4 Men, Tub Aloft, Girl, Tambourine, 27 x 8 ¾ In. 1200
Group, Centaur, Nude Maiden, Ginori, 15 ¼ In. 400
Group, Farewell Kiss, Wife Climbs Ladder To Kiss Soldier, Attributed To Gardener, 1800s, 9 In. .. 3750
Group, Man Leaning In For Kiss, Woman Rejecting, Basket Of Flowers, 1800s, 8 In. 554
Group, Nude Warriors Carrying Nude Maiden, Ginori, Italy, 17 ½ In. 276
Group, Shoemaker & Boy, 8 ½ x 9 In. 180
Holy Water Font, Mary In Flower Encrusted Gothic Arch, High Glaze, 14 x 8 In. 178
Mustard Pot, Shell & Coral Base, Turtle Lid, Turtle Head Ladle Handle, c.1900, 4 In. 106
Plaque, Ariadne On Panther, Nude Woman, Upswept Hair, 1814, 14 ¼ In. 726
Sculpture, Eagle Head, White, Germany, 7 ½ In. 6

BLACK memorabilia has become an important area of collecting since the 1970s. The best material dates from past centuries, but many recent items are also of interest. F & F is the mark used on plastic made by Fiedler & Fiedler Mold & Die Works, Inc. in the 1930s and 1940s. Objects that picture a black person may also be listed in this book under Advertising, Sign; Bank; Bottle Opener; Cookie Jar; Doll; Salt & Pepper; Sheet Music; Toy; etc.

Automaton, Musician, Plays Tune, 2 Dancers, Cabin Box, Crank, D.A.A. Buck Co., 9 In. 2091
Brush Doll, Red Cap, Red Bodice, Woonsocket Brush Co., 1925, 5 x 2 In. 41
Brush Doll, White Cap, Black Jacket, White Buttons, 7 ¾ x 1 ½ In. 58
Cookie Jars are listed in the Cookie Jar category.
Figurine, Black Man Carrying Water Buckets On Back, Metal, Paint, 11 x 14 In. 257
Figurine, Uncle Tom, Little Eva On Knee, Staffordshire, 11 In. .... *illus* 118
Figurine, Wax, Woman Vegetable Seller, Head Wrap, 7 ¾ x 3 In. 153
Garden Hose Connector, Black Man Standing, Overalls & Hat, Painted Steel, 30 In. 200
Nodder, Man, Bowler Hat, Bowtie, Suspenders, Papier-Mache, 40 x 16 In. 1560
Poster, Uncle Tom's Cabin, Stone Litho, Jess Yo Come Along N Laff, c.1910, 89 x 40 In. 830
Slave Badge, No. 585, Charleston, South Carolina, Mechanic, 1804, 2 ½ In. 840
Smoking Stand, Black Man, Butler, Red Jacket, Long Legs, Holding Tray, 35 In. 399
Table, Side, Flower Shape, Crouching Black Boy Support, Gilt Base, c.1900, 22 In., Pair.......... 1875
Toys are listed in the Toy category

BLENKO GLASS COMPANY is the 1930s successor to several glassworks founded by William John Blenko in Milton, West Virginia. In 1933, his son, William H. Blenko Sr., took charge. The company made tablewares and vases in classical shapes. In the late 1940s it hired talented designers and made innovative pieces. The company made a line of reproductions for Colonial Williamsburg. It is still in business and is best known today for its decorative wares and stained glass. All products are made to order.

Ashtray, Rooster, On Weather Vane, Blue, 1950s, 3 ½ In. 28
Bowl, Amberina, Ruffled Rim, 12 Multicolor Glass Balls, 6 ¾ x 15 In. 107
Pitcher, Asymmetrical, Bulbous, Flared Rim, Loop Handle, Yellow, Blue, 1960s, 7 In. 50
Pitcher, Crackle Glass, Blue, 5 ⅝ x 6 ¾ In. .... *illus* 15
Vase, Blue, Genie, Stopper, Blown, 23 x 6 In. 178
Vase, Opalescent, Milky To Clear, Red Rim, c.1970, 13 x 3 ½ In. 357

BLOWN GLASS, *see Glass-Blown category.*

BLUE GLASS, *see Cobalt Blue category.*

BLUE ONION, *see Onion category.*

BLUE WILLOW, *see Willow category.*

Blenko, Pitcher, Crackle Glass, Blue, 5 ⅝ x 6 ¾ In.
$15

Ruby Lane

Boch Freres, Vase, Flowers, Leaves, Art Deco, 12 x 7 In.
$110

Ruby Lane

Boehm, Everglades Kite, Birds On Tree Stump, Eating Snails, Shaped Base, Signed, c.1980, 21 In.
$2,596

Brunk Auctions

This is an edited listing of current prices. Visit **Kovels.com** to check thousands of prices from previous years and sign up for free information on trends, tips, reproductions, marks, and more.

Boehm, Giant Panda Cub, 6 ½ x 8 In.
$96

Stephenson's Auction

Bone, Corkscrew, Carved Lion's Head Handle, Silver Plate Leafy Caps, Metal Screw
$154

DuMouchelles Art Gallery Art Gallery

Bookends, Magnolia Blossoms, Yellow, Syroco Wood, 1940s, 7 x 5 ½ x 2 ¼ In.
$41

Ruby Lane

TIP

When shelving books, leave room for air flow. The books should be about a half-inch from the wall or back of the shelf unit. They should not be packed together tightly.

BOCH FRERES factory was founded in 1841 in La Louviere in eastern Belgium. The wares resemble the work of Villeroy & Boch. The factory closed in 1985. M.R.L. Boch took over the production of tableware, but went bankrupt in 1988. Le Hodey took over Boch Freres in 1989, using the name Royal Boch Manufacture S.A. It went bankrupt in 2009. A new managing director is now running the company.

BOCH FRERES KERAMIS MADE IN BELGIUM

Plate, Working Peasants, Oxen, Blue & White, Marked, 11 In. .... 220 to 225
Vase, Flowers, Leaves, Art Deco, 12 x 7 In. .... *illus* 110
Vase, Gres Keramis, Bottle Shape, Multicolor Enamel, 1920s, 11 ½ In. 523
Vase, Gres Keramis, Flower Garland, Charles Catteau, Belgium, 1920s, 10 x 10 In. 500
Vase, Yellow, Stylized Leaves, 14 ¾ x 10 In. 281

BOEHM is the collector's name for the porcelains of Edward Marshall Boehm. In 1953 the Osso China Company was reorganized as Edward Marshall Boehm, Inc. The company is still working in England and New Jersey. In the early days of the factory, dishes were made, but the elaborate and lifelike bird figurines are the best-known ware. Edward Marshall Boehm, the founder, died in 1969, but the firm has continued to design and produce porcelain. Today, the firm makes both limited and unlimited editions of figurines and plates.

Boehm MADE IN U.S.A.

Bengal Tiger, Mid-Leap, Open Jaw, 15 x 19 In. 625
Black Capped Chickadee, Holly, Berries, 6 ¾ x 11 In. 707
Blue Grosbeak, Perched On Oak Branch, Acorns, 11 ¼ In. 230
Bobwhite Quail, 2 Birds, 2 Chicks, Green Plant Shape Support, 11 x 15 In. 125
Centerpiece, Porcelain, Icaria Peony, White, Green, 8 x 20 In. 738
Common Tern, Bisque, Broad Wings, Tree Trunk, Hatchling, 3 Eggs, Pebbles, 14 x 13 In. 484
Doves, Fan-Tailed, White, Branch, 6 ½ x 6 ½ In., 3 Piece 215
Downy Woodpecker, 2 Birds, Feeding Young, Stump, Trumpet Lily Vine, Wood Base, 14 In. 334
Everglades Kite, Birds On Tree Stump, Eating Snails, Shaped Base, Signed, c.1980, 21 In. .*illus* 2596
Flamingos, Signed Helen Boehm, 1987, 13 x 15 In. 375
Flower Bouquet, Pink Blooms, Green Grass, Bowl, 13 In. 461
Giant Panda Cub, 6 ½ x 8 In. .... *illus* 96
Giraffe, 14 In. 400
Her First Pony, Red Shirt, Brown & White Pony, c.1986, 10 ¾ x 10 In. 276
Horse, Rearing, Brown, 13 x 11 In. 124
Marie Antoinette, Peach Underskirt, Blue Overdress, Fan, 13 In. 492
Meadow Lark, 8 ½ In. 212
Mourning Doves, 2 Birds, Perched On Stump, Leaves, Round Foot, 14 In. .... 74 to 173
Ornithological, Long Legs, Pointed Beak, 21 In., Pair 188
Paphiopedilum, Hummingbird, Perched, Wings Up, Orchid, 5 x 7 In. 219
Parula Warblers, Bisque, Branch, Pink Vine, Ladybugs, 15 ¾ x 8 ½ In. 363
Pheasant, Golden Oriental, Oval Base, 8 x 15 In. 2990
Plate, Various Woodland & Bird Designs, Gilt Rim, 10 Piece 120
Red Shouldered Hawk, Wings Open, Landing, 26 ¼ x 20 ½ In. 2700
Rhododendron, Yellow, Butterfly, Branch, 9 ¾ In. 553
Robin, Perched On Rock, Daffodils, 11 In. 633
Rubrum Lilies, Stones, Moss, 10 ¾ In. 523
Shafter Flicker, Bisque, Yellow, Chipmunk, Mushrooms, 12 x 10 ½ In. 363
Snowy Owl, Branches, Pinecones, 19 ¼ x 13 ½ In. 861
Towhee, Perched On Stump, Among Mushrooms, 7 ⅝ In. 265
Tufted Titmouse, 2 Birds, Flowering Branch, Wintertime, 13 In. 299
Western Bluebirds, Bisque, Male, Female, Yellow Flowers, Marked, 17 x 18 In. 1089
White-Throated Sparrow, 9 ¼ In. 106

BONE includes those articles made of bone not listed elsewhere in this book.

Corkscrew, Carved Lion's Head Handle, Silver Plate Leafy Caps, Metal Screw .... *illus* 154
Effigy Figure, Woman, Sailor Carved, 6 x 1 ½ In. 118

BOOKENDS have probably been used since books became inexpensive. Early libraries kept books in cupboards, not on open shelves. By the 1870s bookends appeared, especially homemade fret-carved wooden examples. Most bookends listed in this book date from the twentieth century. Bookends are also listed in other categories by manufacturer or material. All bookends listed here are pairs.

Apple, Pear, Murano Glass, Blue, Green, Clear, c.1950, 6 In. 149
Art Deco, Discus Thrower, Bronze, Pompeiian Bronze Co., c.1925, 8 ½ x 5 In. 330
Bird, Side Glancing, Green Over Tan Matte Glaze, Square Base, 1931, 6 In. 374

B

Birds, Perched, Cast Iron, Painted, 5 In.	104
Boy & Girl, Bronze, Carrying Books, Signed, c.1920, 7 In.	188
Boy On Rocking Horse, Toys On Floor, Cast Iron, Judd Co., 6 In.	30
Brass, Dog, Stack Of Books, 5 In., Pair	25
Broadside Ship, Waves, Blue Matte Crystalline Glaze, 1935, 5 In.	259
Bronze, Egyptian Style, Stone Wall, Throne, 9 ¼ In., Pair	177
Bronze, Man, Slumped Over Donkey, After James Earl Fraser, 8 In., Pair	100
Buddha, Bronze, Seated, Meditation Pose, Japan, 7 ½ x 6 ½ In.	240
Cactus, Mottled Green Over Tan Matte Glaze, Round Base, 1941, 4 In.	345
Cornucopia Basket, Tan Over Brown Glaze, Square Base, 1920, 5 In.	138
Court Women, Hennin Hat, Seated, Reading Book, Bronze, Max Le Verrier, 6 x 18 In.	1179
Crow, Perched, Leaves, Pottery, Blue Matte Glaze, Shaped Base, 1922, 5 In.	288
Devil Horse, Pottery, Spanish Red Glaze, Kenton Hills Pottery, 7 In.	173
Dog, Spaniel, Pointer, Brass, Oblong Base, 1940s, 5 x 7 In., Pair	150
Double Owl, Standing On Book, Green Matte Glaze, Pottery, 1927, 7 In.	1610
Double Penguin, Standing Side By Side, Brown Glaze, Pottery, 1928, 6 In.	288
Elephant, Bronze, Drinking, Compartment, Jennings Brothers, 6 ½ x 5 In.	240
Fish, Glass, Heisey	50
Fisherman, Iron, Gloucester, 8 ½ In.	60
Flat, Relief, After Rodin's The Thinker, 5 In.	38
Flowers, Cast Iron, Orange, Green, Blue, Black Ground, Arched, Art Deco, 4 In.	384
Fruit, Figural, Pottery, Grapes, Lemons, Wiener Werkstatte, 3 ¾ x 6 In.	83
Gerdago Girl, Art Deco, Red, Gold, Metal, c.1927, 7 In.	495
Hammered Metal, Lucite, Aluminum, Jump Gates, 6 ½ x 6 In.	220
Horse Head, Glass, Heisey	190
Horse Head, Pottery, Nubian Black Glaze, Open Mouth, 1928, 6 In.	288
Horse Head, Pottery, Wine Madder Glaze, Open Mouth, Squared Mane, 1954, 6 In.	196
Hound Dog, Pottery, Nubian Black Glaze, Looking Down, Floppy Ears, 1938, 5 In.	460
House, Cast Iron, In Woods, Garden, Bradley & Hubbard, 6 In.	118
Hugh Acton, Chrome, Cylindrical, 6 x 3 In., Pair	60
Impalas, Wood Carved, Antlers, 6 ¼ x 3 ¾ In.	60
Indian Chief, Bronze, B. Altman & Co., 7 ¼ x 4 ½ In.	276
Koala Bear, Tree, Glazed Earthenware, Square Base, Inscribed, Australia, c.1900, 5 ½ In.	947
Lion Of Lucerne, Bronze, Cast Iron, 4 ¾ x 7 In.	176
Magnolia Blossoms, Yellow, Syroco Wood, 1940s, 7 x 5 ½ x 2 ¼ In. *illus*	41
Mallard, Redhead Duck, Carved & Painted, Molded Round Base, 5 x 4 In.	523
Man & Horse, Armor, Silver Plate, 9 ½ x 7 In.	148
Man, Bronze, Seminude, Thinker, Green Patina, Square Base, 1914, 9 In.	3000
Medieval Maidens, Spelter, Cone Shape Hat, Reading, c.1930, 6 x 7 In.	1945
Monks Reading Books, Bronze, Red Robes, 7 x 4 ½ In.	153
Native Americans, Metal, Headdress, 8 x 7 In.	149
Nude, Kneeling, Spelter, Bronzed, Notched Base, Art Deco, 1920-30, 5 In. *illus*	225
Nude Bronze, Sitting, Hand On Knee, Art Nouveau, Armor Bronze, c.1925	125
Nude Warrior Leaning On Warrior, Composite, Arm Raised, Green, 10 In.	50
Owl, Sitting On Book, Black Forest, Carved, Germany, c.1940, 5 ½ x 4 ½ In.	189
Panther, Pottery, Reclining On Book, Green Over Tan Glaze, 1937, 6 In.	288
Pelicans, Brass, Scalloped Base, Art Deco, Hagenauer, c.1928, 5 x 5 x 3 In.	368
Seal, Looking Up, Rock Shape Base, Aventurine Glaze, 1922, 7 In.	1725
Seashell, 1950-60, 5 ½ x 7 In. *illus*	77
Seated Couple, Porcelain, Victorian, Tree Stumps, 7 In., Pair	35
Seated Woman, Reading, Bronze, Marble Base, Max Le Verrier, 8 ½ x 3 In.	165
Skyscraper Shape, Onyx, Green, Black, Leaf, Art Deco, 6 x 5 In.	182
Small Child, Hugs Goose, Metal, Reticulated Octagonal Screen, 8 x 7 In., Pair	423
St. Francis Of Assisi, Pottery, Kneeling, Bird, Brown & Gray Glaze, 1945, 7 In.	230
Tanager Bird, Cast Iron, On Branch, Bradley & Hubbard, 6 In.	89
Tribal Figure, Onyx, Carved, Brown & Tan, 6 ½ x 2 x 3 In.	24
Warrior, Bronze, Robe, Sword, Palm Tree, Desert, 8 x 4 ½ In.	115
Wisdom, Bronze, Man, Book Open On Lap, 9 x 5 In.	172
Woman Reclining, Reading, Pottery, Mottled Gray Glaze, 1916, 6 In.	518
Wrestlers, Bronze, Stepping To Side, Head Down, Japan, 7 x 6 In.	400

BOOKMARKS were originally made of parchment, cloth, or leather. Soon woven silk ribbon, thin cardboard, celluloid, wood, silver, tortoiseshell, and metals were used. Examples made before 1850 are scarce, but there are many to be found dating before 1920.

Blue Ribbon, Sterling Silver Angels At Each End, 8 In.	95
Brass, Figural, Bird On Branch, Italy, 7 x 3 In.	35

TIP

To remove the musty odor from old books, try this. Leather-covered books should be wiped with a mixture of equal parts alcohol and water. The pages of the books should be warmed. Stand the books on edge, open them, and blow-dry them with a portable hair dryer on high heat.

Bookends, Nude, Kneeling, Spelter, Bronzed, Notched Base, Art Deco, 1920-30, 5 In. $225

Ruby Lane

Bookends, Seashell, 1950-60, 5 ½ x 7 In. $77

Ruby Lane

Bookmark, Hewlett Packard Computer, Sterling Silver, Tiffany, 1997, 2 ½ x 2 In. $225

Ruby Lane

Bossons, Wall Plaque, Old Timer, 1960s, 6 x 6 In.
$125

Ruby Lane

Bottle, Barber, Mary Gregory, Girl, Flowers, Aqua Blue Glass, 8 In.
$57

Showtime Auction Services

Bottle, Beer, F. Gleason, 1852, Stoneware, Gray, Incised, Cobalt Blue, 9 ¾ In.
$161

Glass Works Auctions

Celluloid, Silver Owl, Victorian, England, c.1880, 3 ⅛ In. 250
Chromolithograph, Embossed, Victorian Couple, Ernest Nester, London, 6 x 2 In. 6
Chromolithograph, Mary, Joseph, Jesus, 5 ¾ x ⅜ In. 5
Cross-Stitch, Cling To Hold, Cross, Flowers, 11 ½ x 2 In. 5
Die Cut, Embossed, Lilacs, Girl, Verse, 6 x 2 ⅜ In. 18
Enameled, Unicorn, Multicolor, Shepherd's Hook, 1980s, 5 In. 12
Gold Plated, Monkey, Holding Banana, c.1970, 3 In. 10
Hewlett Packard Computer, Sterling Silver, Tiffany, 1997, 2 ½ x 2 In. .... *illus* 225
Mauchlineware, Old Church, c.1933, 5 x 1 In. 138
Mother-Of-Pearl, Anchor, 1800s, 2 ¾ x 1 In. 573
Sterling Silver, Cornucopia, Reed & Barton, 2 ¾ x 1 ⅝ In. 45
Sterling Silver, Flower, Scrolls, Monogram, S. Kirk & Sons, 2 ½ x 1 In. 36
Sterling Silver, Heart, Openwork, Napier, 4 ½ x 1 In. 85
Sterling Silver, Scrolled, Leaves, Pierced, George K. Webster, c.1915, 3 ¼ In. 175
Sterling Silver, Teddy Bear, Figural, Tiffany & Co., 1984, 1 ¾ x 1 In. 90

BOSSONS character wall masks (heads), plaques, figurines, and other decorative pieces were made by W.H. Bossons, Limited, of Congleton, England. The company was founded in 1946 and closed in 1996. Dates shown are the date the item was introduced.

BOSSONS

Wall Mask, Dog, Boxer, Black, Tan, Studded Collar, 1960s, 4 In. 85
Wall Mask, Dog, Scottie, Black, 5 x 3 ¼ In. 75
Wall Mask, Guardsman, 1986, 7 x 4 In. 65
Wall Mask, Mr. Bumble, c.1969, 5 In. 40
Wall Mask, Mr. Micawber, c.1964, 5 ¾ In. 88
Wall Mask, Old Salt, c.1971, 5 ¼ In. 45
Wall Mask, Sarah Gamp, 5 In. 55
Wall Mask, Smuggler, Cap, Eye Patch, 5 ½ In. 45
Wall Mask, Tibetan, 5 ¼ In. 30
Wall Mask, Tyrolean, Hat, Beard, Pipe, 1960s, 6 In. 75
Wall Plaque, Koala, Baby, Climbing Tree Trunk, 10 In. 115
Wall Plaque, Old Timer, 1960s, 6 x 6 In. .... *illus* 125
Wall Pocket, Japanese Woman, Red Headpiece, Closed Eyes, c.1958, 6 ½ x 4 In. 225
Wall Pocket, Woodpecker, Tree Trunk, Babies, c.1968, 11 x 5 In. 39

BOSTON & SANDWICH CO. *pieces may be found in the Sandwich Glass category.*

BOTTLE collecting has become a major American hobby. There are several general categories of bottles, such as historic flasks, bitters, household, and figural. ABM means the bottle was made by an automatic bottle machine after 1903. Pyro is the shortened form of the word *pyroglaze*, an enameled lettering used on bottles after the mid-1930s. This form of decoration is also called ACL or applied color label. Several major collections of bottles sold at auction in 2015. Prices for some of the exceptional bottles are listed here as well as prices for average bottles. For more prices, go to kovels.com.

Avon started in 1886 as the California Perfume Company. It was not until 1929 that the name Avon was used. In 1939, it became Avon Products, Inc. Avon has made many figural bottles filled with cosmetic products. Ceramic, plastic, and glass bottles were made in limited editions.

Avon, Christmas Stocking, Christmas Surprise, Green, Red Ball Lid, 1970s, 3 x 2 In. 7
Avon, Pumpkin Coach, Hearts & Vines, Paper Label, c.1976, 1 ¾ x 2 ½ x 3 In. 10
Barber, Amethyst, Holly, Bulbous, Swollen Stick Neck, Stopper, 8 In. 120
Barber, Aqua Opalescent, Drape, Shaped Body, Stick Neck, Rolled Rim, 8 In. 210
Barber, Bristol Glass, Blue, Yellow, Flowers, Smokestack Bottom, Ring Foot, 8 In. 114
Barber, Cranberry Opalescent, Coin Spot, Swollen Stick Neck, 8 In. 114
Barber, Cranberry Opalescent, Spatter, Fountain Shape, 8 In. 57
Barber, Cranberry Opalescent, Swirl, Melon Shape, Stick Neck, Rolled Rim, 7 ¼ In. 57
Barber, Mary Gregory, Girl, Flowers, Aqua Blue Glass, 8 In. .... *illus* 57
Barber, Milk Glass, Green Neck, White Body, Flowers, Stopper, 7 In. 89
Barber, Opalescent, Pale Blue Veining, Shaped Stick Neck, Stopper, 8 In. 630
Barber, Vegederma, Purple, Enamel Woman, Long Hair, Swollen Stick Neck, Stopper, 8 In. 627
Barber, Yellow Opalescent, Swirl, Bulbous, Stick Neck, Rolled Rim, 7 ¼ In. 371

Beam bottles were made to hold Kentucky Straight Bourbon, made by the James B. Beam Distilling Company. The Beam series of ceramic bottles began in 1953.

Beam, Opalescent Milk Glass, Round, Embossed, Paper Label, c.1957, 11 In. 22

Bottle, Bitters, David Andrews Vegetable Jaundice, Aqua, Tombstone Form, 8 ¼ In.
$2,070

Glass Works Auctions

Bottle, Bitters, Herb's Wild Cherry Bark, Amber, Label Under Glass, Double Collar, 8 In.
$1,840

Glass Works Auctions

Bottle, Bitters, I & LM Hellman, St. Louis, Mo., Amber, Embossed Panel Frames, 8 ⅞ In.
$748

Glass Works Auctions

Bottle, Bitters, John Moffat, Phoenix, Price 1 Dollar, Olive Amber, Outward Rolled Lip, 5 ¼ In.
$978

Glass Works Auctions

Bottle, Bitters, John W. Steele's Niagara Star, Fletcher, Hoag & Steele, Semi-Cabin, Amber, 10 In.
$1,840

Glass Works Auctions

Bottle, Bitters, Original Pocahontas, Y. Ferguson, Barrel, Blue Aqua, c.1870, 9 ¼ In.
$3,163

Glass Works Auctions

Bottle, Bitters, Pig, Suffolk, Philbrook & Tucker, Boston, Amber, Double Collar, 10 In.
$1,170

Norman Heckler & Company

Bottle, Cosmetic, Genuine Bear's Oil, Growth & Beauty Of Hair, Walking Bear, Aqua, 3 In.
$403

Glass Works Auctions

Bottle, Decanter, Cobalt Blue Ribs, Flared Base, Applied Neck Ring, Pillar Mold, Pontil, 8 In.
$805

Glass Works Auctions

Bottle, Demijohn, Olive, Bulbous, Applied Rim, Pontil, 1800s, 20 In.
$150

Cowan Auctions

Bottle, Flask, Double Eagle, Deep Sapphire Blue, Pontil, Sheared & Tooled Lip, Pt.
$16,415

Glass Works Auctions

Bottle, Flask, Double Eagle, Green Aqua, Sheared Mouth, Pontil, Pt.
$1,989

Norman Heckler & Company

Bottle, Flask, Eagle, Zanesville, Ohio, J. Shepard & Co., Masonic Arch, Blue Aqua, c.1840, Pt.
$863

Glass Works Auctions

Bottle, Flask, Scroll, Blue Aqua, Corset Waist, Pontil, c.1835, Pt.
$518

Glass Works Auctions

Beer, Ale, Olive Amber, Lady's Leg Neck, Double Collar, England, 7 In. 81
Beer, Anheuser-Busch Lager, Pre-Prohibition, O. Meyer & Co., 9 ½ In. 120
Beer, Carling's Red Cap Ale, Label, Green, Canada, 12 Oz., 9 ¼ In. 15
Beer, Edelweiss, Schoenfofen Brewing, Embossed, c.1908, 12 Oz., 9 ½ In. 18
Beer, F. Gleason Lemon Beer, Stoneware, Gray Brown, Salt Glaze, Blue Letters, 8 ¼ In. 150
Beer, F. Gleason, 1852, Stoneware, Gray, Incised, Cobalt Blue, 9 ¾ In. ....*illus* 161
Beer, Grolsch, Amber Glass, Swing Top, 3 Piece.......... 6
Beer, Hyde Park, St. Louis, Paper Label, Embossed, Amber Glass, 9 ½ In. 50
Beer, I.P.A. India Pale Ale, Green, Portrait, John Labatt, Label, c.1945, 9 ¼ In. 20
Beer, Long's Champagne Beer, Cincinnati, Ohio, Yellow Amber, 10-Sided, Double Collar, 9 In. ... 863
Beer, Minck Brewing Co., Richmond, Brown, 9 ¼ In. 12
Beer, Original Budweiser, C. Conrad, 9 ½ In. 60
Beer, Peru Beer, Dark Amber, 9 ½ In. 35
Beer, R & H Pilsner Beer, Amber, Label, Double Ringed Neck, c.1930, 12 Oz.......... 55
Beer, R. Portner, Embossed, Tivoli Trade Mark, Blob Top, 7 ¾ In. 1050
Beer, Rocky Mountain, Anaconda Brewing Company, Label, c.1933, 12 x 3 In. 30
Beer, West End BRG & Co., Utica, N.Y., Embossed, Aqua, 12 Oz., 9 ¾ In. 25
Bininger, A.M. & Co., No. 19 Broad St., New York, Shaded Olive, Handle, 8 In. 1495
Bininger, A.M. & Co., No. 19 Broad St., New York, Yellow Amber, Jug, Handle, 8 In. 633
Bitters, American Life, P.E. Iler, Tiffin, Ohio, Cabin, Amber, Rounded Shoulders, 8 ¾ In. 4600
Bitters, Baker's Orange Grove, Semi-Cabin, Strawberry Puce, Sloping Collar, 9 ⅜ In. 2300
Bitters, Baker's Orange Grove, Semi-Cabin, Yellow Amber, Spiral Corners, 9 ½ In. 546
Bitters, Barrel, Cobalt Blue, Flattened Lip, 10 In. 2185
Bitters, Berkshire, Amann & Co., Cincinnati, O., Pig Shape, Tobacco Amber, 10 ¼ In. 5463
Bitters, Berkshire, Amann & Co., Cincinnati, O., Pig Shape, Yellow Amber, 9 ½ In. 3738
Bitters, Bourbon Whiskey, Barrel, Salmon, Apricot Tone, Squared Collar, 9 ¼ In. 878
Bitters, Brown's Celebrated Indian Herb, Patented 1868, Indian Princess, Dark Amber, 12 In. ... 1495
Bitters, Bryant's Stomach, Olive Green, 8-Sided, Lady's Leg Neck, 12 ¼ In. 2415
Bitters, Caldwell's Herb, Great Tonic, Golden Yellow Amber, 3 Indented Sides, 12 ¼ In. 489
Bitters, Clarke's Vegetable Sherry Wine, Aqua, Sloping Collar, ½ Gal., 11 ⅜ In. 1035
Bitters, Constitution, Seward & Bentley, Buffalo, N.Y., A.M.S.2, Amber, Paneled, 9 ⅜ In. 2645
Bitters, David Andrews Vegetable Jaundice, Aqua, Tombstone Form, 8 ¼ In. ....*illus* 2070
Bitters, Doyle's Hop, 1872, Cluster Of Hops, Semi-Cabin, Deep Amber, Double Collar, 9 ⅞ In. 575
Bitters, Dr. Hill's, Restorative, Strengthening, Farmer, N.Y., Amber, Arched Panels, 9 ½ In. 5175
Bitters, Dr. J. Hostetter's Stomach, Lemon Yellow, Olive Tone, Arched Sides, 9 In. 1265
Bitters, Dr. J. Samson's Strengthening, Amber, Arched Sides, Sloping Collar, 9 In. 633
Bitters, Dr. Stephen Jewett's Celebrated Health Restoring, Yellow Amber, 8-Sided, 7 ⅜ In. 3163
Bitters, Dr. Wheeler's Sherry Wine, Shaded Grass Green, Rounded Shoulder, 7 ⅞ In. 920
Bitters, Drake's Plantation, X, Patented 1862, Cabin, 6 Log, Ginger Ale, 9 ⅞ In. 1495
Bitters, Drake's Plantation, X, Patented 1862, Cabin, 6 Log, Strawberry Puce, 10 In. 345
Bitters, Great American Herb Tonic, Dr. Morgan, Philadelphia, Semi-Cabin, Amber, 10 ⅜ In. 4600
Bitters, Greeley's Bourbon Whiskey, Barrel, Apricot Puce, Flattened Rim, 9 ⅜ In. 863
Bitters, Greeley's Bourbon, Barrel, Olive Green, Flattened Lip, 9 ⅜ In. 3738
Bitters, Greeley's Bourbon, Barrel, Olive Green, Ginger Ale Tone, Squared Collar, 9 ¼ In. 1755
Bitters, Greeley's Bourbon, Barrel, Olive Shaded To Topaz, Flattened Rim, 9 ¼ In. 3450
Bitters, Greeley's Bourbon, Barrel, Smoky Copper Topaz, 9 In. 431
Bitters, Greeley's Bourbon, Barrel, Smoky Topaz, Flattened Lip, 9 ⅜ In. 920
Bitters, H.P. Herb Wild Cherry, Reading, Pa., Semi-Cabin, Yellow, Olive Tone, 10 In. 6325
Bitters, Herb's Wild Cherry Bark, Amber, Label Under Glass, Double Collar, 8 In. ....*illus* 1840
Bitters, Holtzermann's Patent Stomach, Cabin, Orange Amber, Shaded, 9 ½ In. 1610
Bitters, I & LM Hellman, St. Louis, Mo., Amber, Embossed Panel Frames, 8 ⅞ In. ....*illus* 748
Bitters, Jackson's Aromatic Life, Grass Green, Arched Panels, Sloping Collar, 9 In. 2875
Bitters, Jno. Moffat, Phoenix, Price 1 Dollar, New York, Yellow Amber, Rolled Lip, 5 ⅝ In. 6900
Bitters, John Moffat, Phoenix, Price 1 Dollar, Clear, Rolled Lip, Pontil, 5 ⅝ In. 1150
Bitters, John Moffat, Phoenix, Price 1 Dollar, Olive Amber, Outward Rolled Lip, 5 ¼ In. ......*illus* 978
Bitters, John Moffat, Phoenix, Price 2 Dollars, New York, Olive Amber, Rolled Lip, 6 ¾ In. 2415
Bitters, John Root's, 1834, Buffalo, N.Y., Semi-Cabin, Amber, Sloping Collar, 10 ¼ In. 5175
Bitters, John Root's, 1834, Buffalo, N.Y., Semi-Cabin, Blue Green, 10 ¼ In. 1380
Bitters, John W. Steele's Niagara Star, Fletcher, Hoag & Steele, Semi-Cabin, Amber, 10 In. ..*illus* 1840
Bitters, Kagy's Superior Stomach, Yellow Olive Amber, Case, Sloping Collar, 9 ½ In. 1265
Bitters, Kelly's Old Cabin, Patented 1863, Cabin, Yellow Amber, Sloping Collar, 9 ¼ In. 2106
Bitters, Kimball's Jaundice, Troy, N.H., Olive Amber, Sloping Shoulders & Collar, 7 In. 1638
Bitters, McKeever's Army, Civil War Drum, Cannonballs On Shoulder, Amber, 10 ½ In. 4025
Bitters, Napoleon Cocktail, Dingens Brothers, Buffalo, Drum, Lady's Leg Neck, 10 In. 8050
Bitters, Napoleon, 1866, Dingens Brothers, Buffalo, N.Y., Semi-Cabin, Amber, 10 In. 2875

Bottle, Flask, Scroll, Yellow Amber, Sheared Mouth, Pontil, Louisville, Ky., Pt.
$322

Norman Heckler & Company

Bottle, Fruit Jar, F. & J. Bodine, Philadelphia Pa., Aqua, Sheared Mouth, Wire Clamp, Qt.
$431

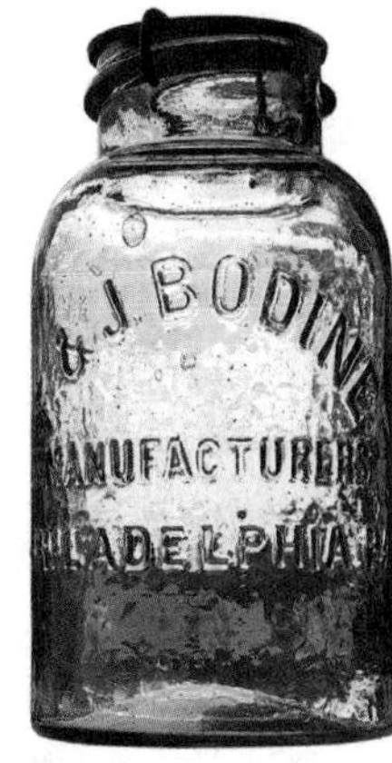

Glass Works Auctions

Bottle, Fruit Jar, J.D. Willoughby, Pat., Jan. 4, 1859, Cornflower Blue, Metal Stopper, ½ Gal.
$690

Glass Works Auctions

Bottle, Fruit Jar, Mason's Patent Nov 30th, 1858, Cross, Orange Amber, Zinc Lid, ½ Gal.
$431

Glass Works Auctions

Bottle, Fruit Jar, Nonpareil, Patented July 17, 1866, Green Aqua, Tin Closure, Qt.
$556

Norman Heckler & Company

Bottle, Ink, Umbrella, 8-Sided, Sapphire Blue, Inward Rolled Lip, c.1850, 32 ⅜ In.
$2,300

Glass Works Auctions

Bitters, National, Ear Of Corn, Patent 1867, Amber, 12 ¾ x 2 ¾ In. 172
Bitters, National, Ear Of Corn, Patent 1867, Blue Aqua, Double Collar, 12 ½ In. 7480
Bitters, National, Ear Of Corn, Patent 1867, Yellow Amber, Topaz Tone, 12 ¼ In. 690
Bitters, OK Plantation, Patented 1863, Amber, 3-Sided, Tapered, Sloping Collar, 11 In. 1840
Bitters, Old Sachem & Wigwam, Barrel, Blue Aqua, Horizontal Ribs, 9 ⅞ In. 4313
Bitters, Old Sachem & Wigwam, Barrel, Shaded Pink Puce, Ribbed, 9 ⅜ In. 10925
Bitters, Original Pocahontas, Y. Ferguson, Barrel, Blue Aqua, c.1870, 9 ¼ In. .... *illus* 3163
Bitters, Pig, Suffolk, Philbrook & Tucker, Boston, Amber, Double Collar, 10 In. .... *illus* 1170
Bitters, Pineapple, W & Co., N.Y., Deep Amber, Double Collar, 8 ½ In. 575
Bitters, Romaine's Crimean, 1863, Semi-Cabin, Indented, Amber, Sloping Collar, 10 In. 1725
Bitters, Royal Italian, Shield, Crown, F. Gianelli, Genova, Amethyst, Tapered, 13 ½ In. 805
Bitters, Simon's Centennial, Bust, George Washington, Amber, Rolled Rim, 10 ⅛ In. 3163
Bitters, Solomon's Strengthening & Invigorating, Savannah, Blue, Arched Panels, 9 ⅝ In. 1265
Bitters, Suffolk, Philbrook & Tucker, Boston, Pig, Yellow Amber, 10 In. 805
Bitters, That's The Stuff, Barrel, Golden Amber, Horizontal Ribs, 10 In. 1840
Bitters, Wampoo, Blum, Siegel & Bro., New York, Yellow Amber, Indented Panels, 9 ⅝ In. 431
Bitters, Warner's Safe, Safe, Orange Amber, Rounded Shoulder, Double Collar, 9 ½ In. 805
Bitters, William Allen's Congress, Semi-Cabin, Blue Green, Sloping Collar, 10 ¼ In. 4025
Bitters, William Allen's Congress, Semi-Cabin, Yellow Amber, Sloping Collar, 10 ¼ In. 3163
Black Glass, Champagne, Olive Amber, Cylindrical, Tapered Neck, Sloping Collar, 12 ⅜ In. 497
Black Glass, Dutch, Onion, 1700s, 7 ½ In. 234
Blown, Carboy, Amber, Oval, Tapered Spout, Concave Base, 1800s, 18 In. 443
Blown, Globular, Olive Green, Applied Collar, Pontil, 10 ½ x 7 ¾ In. 527
Blown, Globular, Orange Amber, Applied Yellow Green Blob Top, 7 ¾ In. 1287
Blown, Wine, Horse's Hoof, Deep Olive Green, Painted Portrait, Netherlands, 6 In. 644
Coca-Cola bottles are listed in the Coca-Cola category.
Cologne, Alabaster Over Rosaline, Footed, Collar, Swirling Ribs, Murano, 10 In. 354
Cologne, Cobalt Blue, Ribbed, Blown, Stopper, 6 ½ In. 71
Cologne, Cranberry Flashed, Cylindrical, Enamel, Gilt, Stopper, Myers-Neffe, c.1890, 7 In. 649
Cologne, Cut Glass, Blue To Clear, Flowers & Leaves, Cylindrical, Faceted Stopper, 7 In. 59
Cologne, Painted, Flowers, Leaves, Jesus, Blown, Pewter Collar & Cap, 8 In. 502
Cordial, Wishart's Pine Tree Tar, Phila., Pine Tree, Yellow, Olive, 7 ⅝ In. 575
Cosmetic, Dr. Leon's Electric Hair Renewer, Amethyst, Panels, Cylindrical Neck, 7 ¼ In. 1093
Cosmetic, Dr. Tebbetts' Physiological Hair Regenerator, Pink Puce, Paneled, 7 ½ In. 690
Cosmetic, Genuine Bear's Oil, Growth & Beauty Of Hair, Walking Bear, Aqua, 3 In. .... *illus* 403
Cure, Dr. Craig's Kidney, Embossed Kidney, Orange Amber, Double Collar, 9 ¾ In. 2070
Decanter, Cobalt Blue Ribs, Flared Base, Applied Neck Ring, Pillar Mold, Pontil, 8 In. .... *illus* 805
Decanter, Green, Hobnail, Fluted, Square, Melon Ribbed Shoulder, Stopper, 3-Piece Mold, Pt. ... 3510
Demijohn, Amber, Globular, Squat, 18 In. 240
Demijohn, Green, 18 In. 263
Demijohn, Green, New Hampshire, 15 In. 292
Demijohn, Olive, Bulbous, Applied Rim, Pontil, 1800s, 20 In. .... *illus* 150
Figural, Penguin, Blown Glass, Red Feet & Beak, Paper Label, Bols, 3 ¾ In. 65
Figural, Violin, Amber Shaded To Yellow, Wood Handle, Metal Pegs, c.1893, 14 In. 374
Figural, Whiskbroom, 6 x 3 In. 110
Flask, 16 Vertical Ribs, Sapphire Blue, Sheared Mouth, Pontil, ½ Pt. 3218
Flask, Amethyst, Expanded Diamond, Blown, Stiegel Type, Pocket, 4 ¾ In. 649
Flask, Anchor & Sheaf Of Grain, Calabash, Blue, Double Collar, Qt. 4888
Flask, Cannon, A Little More Grape, Teal, Pt. 978
Flask, Carved Figure, Leaves, Lotus Petals, Round, Pinched Mouth, Handles, 6 x 11 x 10 In. 2000
Flask, Concentric Ring Eagle, Canteen Form, Yellow Green, Sheared, Pt. 1872
Flask, Concentric Ring Eagle, Green, Sheared, Pontil, Qt. 6325
Flask, Cornucopia & Urn, Olive Amber, Basket Of Fruit, Blown, 5 ½ In. 106
Flask, Double Eagle, Aqua, Sheared Mouth, Pontil, Pt. 1053
Flask, Double Eagle, Blue Aqua, Pontil, Qt. 345
Flask, Double Eagle, Blue Aqua, Sheared Tooled, Pontil, Pt. 431
Flask, Double Eagle, Deep Olive, Applied Ring Mouth, Qt. 690
Flask, Double Eagle, Deep Sapphire Blue, Pontil, Sheared & Tooled Lip, Pt. .... *illus* 16415
Flask, Double Eagle, Grass Green, Applied Ring Mouth, Qt. 1150
Flask, Double Eagle, Green Aqua, Sheared Mouth, Pontil, Pt. .... *illus* 1989
Flask, Double Eagle, Light Cobalt Blue, Ring Mouth, Pt. 1287
Flask, Eagle & Anchor, Blue Green, Shaded, Sheared, Pontil, Pt. 805
Flask, Eagle & Anchor, Yellow, Olive Tone, Double Collar, Pt. 5850
Flask, Eagle & Banner, Blue Aqua, Oval, Ring Mouth, Pt. 702
Flask, Eagle & W.C. & Cornucopia, Blue Aqua, Pontil, ½ Pt. 1638
Flask, Eagle & Willington, Blue Green, Sloping Collar, Pt. 2530

Bottle, Ink, Umbrella, 8-Sided, Smoky Olive Green, Inward Rolled Lip, Pontil, 2 ½ In.
$518

Glass Works Auctions

Bottle, Milk, Polar Bear Ice Cream, Garden Farm Dairy, Enamel Label, 10 x 4 In.
$115

Wm Morford

Snuff Bottles
At the same time the Chinese were developing small bottles to hold snuff, Europeans were creating snuff boxes, which have also become collectibles. The Chinese needed bottles rather than boxes, according to historians, because Chinese apparel had no pockets. The bottles, with their sealed stoppers, could be hidden up a sleeve.

Bottle, Poison, Diamond Pattern, Cobalt Blue, Tooled Lip, Stopper, Label, c.1895, 9 In.
$403

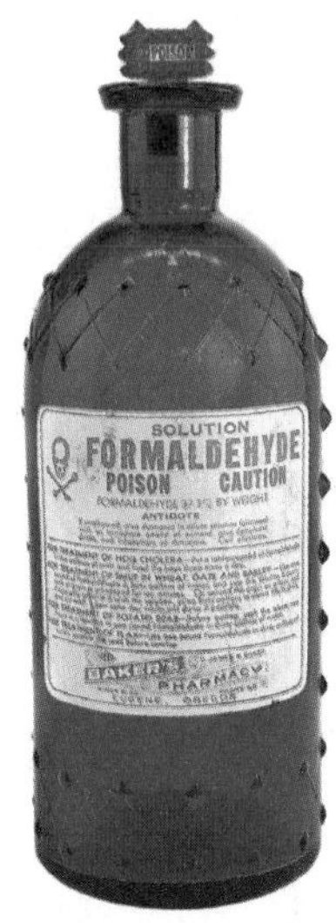

Glass Works Auctions

Bottle, Poison, Raised Diamonds, Smoky Teal, Flattened Lip, 4 ½ In.
$633

Glass Works Auctions

Bottle, Poison, Skull & Crossed Bones, DP Co., Coffin Shape, Hobnails, Cobalt Blue, 1870-90, 7 ⅛ In.
$4,388

Norman Heckler & Company

Bottle, Poison, Skull, Embossed Poison, Pat June 26th, 1894, Cobalt Blue, 4 In.
$3,450

Glass Works Auctions

Bottle, Scent, Sunburst, Cobalt Blue, Sheared & Tooled Lip, Pontil, c.1830, 2 ¾ In.
$288

Glass Works Auctions

Bottle, Snuff, Agate, Carved Monkeys, Butterfly, Round, Red Stone Stopper, c.1900, 3 In.
$1,007

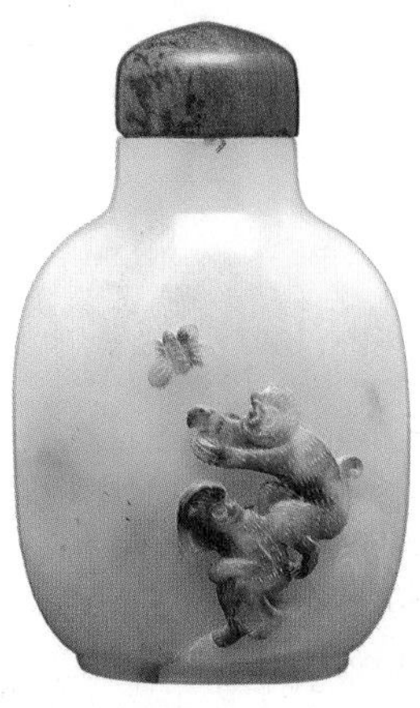

James D. Julia Auctioneers

Bottle, Snuff, Amethyst, Relief Carved, Birds, Flowers, Chinese, 1800s, 2 In.
$124

James D. Julia Auctioneers

Bottle, Snuff, Peking Glass, Reverse Painted, Kingfisher, Branch, Inscribed, Gui Xianggu, 3 In.
$813

Neal Auctions

Bottle, Soda, A. Raab, Tamaqua, Pa., Shaded Green, Slug Plate, Double Collar, 7 In.
$242

Glass Works Auctions

Flask, Eagle & Willington, Olive Green, Sheared & Tooled Lip, Pt. 316
Flask, Eagle & Willington, Yellow Olive, Double Collar, Pt. 633
Flask, Eagle, Zanesville, Ohio, J. Shepard & Co., Masonic Arch, Blue Aqua, c.1840, Pt. *illus* 863
Flask, Figural, Clam Shell, Cobalt Blue, Threaded Mouth, Tin Cap, 5 ½ In. 556
Flask, Flora Temple & Horse, Red Puce, Double Collar, Handle, Qt. 633
Flask, For Pike's Peak, Prospector & Hunter, Aqua Tint, Pt. 2106
Flask, For Pike's Peak, Prospector & Hunter, Ice Blue, Double Collar, ½ Pt. 253
Flask, For Pike's Peak, Prospector, Eagle, Lime Green, ½ Pt. 2223
Flask, Franklin & Dyott, Tobacco Amber, Puce Tone, Sheared, Pontil, Pt. 18720
Flask, Franklin & Franklin, Blue Green, Sheared, Qt. 19550
Flask, Girl On Bicycle & Eagle, Lemon Yellow, Olive Tone, Pt. 9775
Flask, Horse Pulling Cart & Eagle, Yellow Olive, Sheared, Pontil, Pt. 748
Flask, Horseman & Hound, Yellow Amber, Ring Mouth, Pt. 936
Flask, Hunter & Fisherman, Calabash, Golden Amber, Sloping Collar 265
Flask, Hunter & Fisherman, Calabash, Shaded Teal, Sloping Collar, Qt. 748
Flask, Jackson & Eagle, Blue Aqua, Sheared & Tooled, Pontil, Pt. 3163
Flask, Jackson & Eagle, Green Aqua, Sheared & Tooled, Pontil, Pt. 1035
Flask, Jackson & Flowers, Blue Aqua, Sheared & Tooled, Pontil, Pt. 5750
Flask, Jenny Lind & Glass House, Calabash, Cornflower Blue, Blob Top 805
Flask, Jenny Lind & Glass House, Calabash, Yellow Olive Green, Qt. 9945
Flask, Jenny Lind, Calabash, Teal Green, Double Collar, Qt. 1380
Flask, Jenny Lind, Calabash, Yellow Olive, Double Collar, Qt. 2760
Flask, Kossuth & Frigate, Bust, Yellow Amber, Blob Top, Qt. 2925
Flask, Lafayette & Clinton, Shaded Yellow Olive, Side Ribs, Sheared, Pt. 2185
Flask, Lafayette & Liberty Cap, Yellow Olive Amber, ½ Pt. 1521
Flask, Lafayette & Liberty, Yellow Amber, Sheared & Tooled, ½ Pt. 1093
Flask, Log Cabin & Flag, Hard Cider, Aqua, Sheared, Pontil, Pt. 11700
Flask, Masonic & Eagle, Clear, Amethyst Striation, Sheared, Pt. 2300
Flask, Masonic & Eagle, Golden Amber, Shaded, Tooled Lip, Zanesville, Pt. 805
Flask, Masonic & Eagle, Orange Amber, Sheared Mouth, Pt. 995
Flask, Masonic & Eagle, Pale Blue Green, Zanesville, Pt. 644
Flask, Masonic & Eagle, Red Amber, Sheared, Pontil, Pt. 863
Flask, Masonic, Clasped Hands & Eagle, Citron, Calabash, Sloping Collar, Qt. 690
Flask, Pitkin Type, 20 Vertical Ribs, Twisted, Olive Green, Sheared Mouth, 5 ⅝ In. 748
Flask, Pitkin Type, 30 Ribs, Swirled To Left, Olive Green, Inward Rolled Mouth, 6 ⅜ In. 1287
Flask, Scroll, Blue Aqua, Corset Waist, Pontil, c.1835, Pt. *illus* 518
Flask, Scroll, Blue Aqua, Corset Waist, Sheared, Qt. 748
Flask, Scroll, Citron, Applied Ring Mouth, Qt. 1840
Flask, Scroll, Cobalt Blue, Applied Ring Mouth, Pontil, Qt. 9200
Flask, Scroll, Cobalt Blue, Double Collar, Iron Pontil, Pt. 8775
Flask, Scroll, Deep Chocolate Amber, Applied Ring Mouth, Pontil, Qt. 920
Flask, Scroll, Golden Amber, Sheared, Pontil, Qt. 1610
Flask, Scroll, Green Aqua, Corset Waist, Tooled Lip, Pt. 863
Flask, Scroll, Light To Medium Cobalt Blue, Sheared, Pontil, Qt. 2070
Flask, Scroll, Yellow Amber, Sheared Lip, Pontil, Pt. 863
Flask, Scroll, Yellow Amber, Sheared Mouth, Pontil, Louisville, Ky., Pt. *illus* 322
Flask, Soldier & Dancer, Yellow Olive, Ring Mouth, Pt. 585
Flask, Success To The Railroad, Horse & Cart, Aqua, Sheared, Pt. 1287
Flask, Success To The Railroad, Horse & Cart, Forest Green, Pt. 4680
Flask, Success To The Railroad, Locomotive, Apricot, Sheared, Pt. 702
Flask, Sunburst, Emerald Green, Tapered, Ribbed Sides, Pt. 585
Flask, Sunburst, Golden Amber, Sheared, Pontil, Pt. 2645
Flask, Sunburst, Olive Amber, Tapered, Horizontal Ribs On Sides, Pt. 8775
Flask, Sunburst, Puce, Sheared, Pontil, ½ Pt. 3218
Flask, Sunburst, Shaded Emerald Green, Shaped Ribbed Sides, Pt. 1093
Flask, Union, Clasped Hands & Cannon, Olive Yellow, Ring Mouth, Pt. 2457
Flask, Union, Clasped Hands & Cannon, Orange Amber, Ring Mouth, Pt. 690
Flask, Union, Clasped Hands & Eagle, Deep Amber, Double Collar, Pt. 219
Flask, Union, Clasped Hands & Eagle, Yellow Olive, Sloping Collar, Qt. 2415
Flask, Union, Clasped Hands, Sapphire Blue, Shaded, Qt. 5625
Flask, Washington & Eagle, Green Aqua, Sheared & Tooled, Pt. 575
Flask, Washington & Jackson, Yellow Olive, Sheared, Pontil, Pt. 633
Flask, Washington & Monument, Copper, Apricot Tone, Pt. 3510
Flask, Washington & Monument, Pale Orange Puce, Ribbed Sides, Qt. 1495
Flask, Washington & Monument, Pink Amethyst, Ribbed Sides, Qt. 2530
Flask, Washington & Sailing Ship, Yellow Amber, Pontil, Pt. 4888

Flask, Washington & Taylor, Cobalt Blue, Sheared, Pontil, Qt. 3450
Flask, Washington & Taylor, Emerald Green, Sloping Collar, Qt. 575
Flask, Washington & Taylor, Never Surrenders, Medium To Deep Claret, Sloping Collar, Qt. 6435
Flask, Washington, Father Of His Country, Teal, Qt. 863
Flask, Wheat Price, Bushy Haired Bust, Fairview Works, Blue Green, Ribbed, Pt. 8050
Food, Blueberry Preserves, Amber, Cylindrical, Fluted Shoulder, Double Collar, 11 3/8 In. 497
Fruit Jar, F. & J. Bodine, Philadelphia Pa., Aqua, Sheared Mouth, Wire Clamp, Qt. .... *illus* 431
Fruit Jar, J.D. Willoughby, Pat., Jan. 4, 1859, Cornflower Blue, Metal Stopper, 1/2 Gal. .... *illus* 690
Fruit Jar, Mason's Patent Nov 30th, 1858, Cross, Orange Amber, Zinc Lid, 1/2 Gal. .... *illus* 431
Fruit Jar, Nonpareil, Patented July 17, 1866, Green Aqua, Tin Closure, Qt. .... *illus* 556
Fruit Jar, Petal, Grass Green, 10-Panel Shoulder, Wide Rolled Rim, Iron Pontil, Qt. 1610
Fruit Jar, Star, 5-Point Star, Wreath Of Fruit, Blue Aqua, Metal Lid, Zinc Screw Band, Qt. 230
Fruit Jar, Trademark Lightning, Shaded Yellow Olive, Wire Closure, Qt. 345
Gin, Case, Yellow Olive, Dip Mold, Outward Rolled Lip, Magnum, 17 5/8 In. 1610
Gin, Charles' London Cordial, Green, Sloping Collar, Case, 9 1/2 In. 374
Gin, London Jockey Club House, Horse & Rider, Dark Grass Green, Sloping Collar, 9 5/8 In. 575
Gin, London Jockey Club House, Horse & Rider, Square, Beveled, Pontil, 9 3/8 In. 1989
Household, Kinne's Improved Washing Preparation, Ashford, Conn., Aqua, Cylindrical, 11 In. . 1170
Ink, 12-Sided, Dark Olive Amber, Sheared, Pontil, 1 3/4 In. 1170
Ink, 12-Sided, Emerald, Yellow Tone, Fluted Shoulders, Stretched Spout, Master, 9 1/2 In. 7605
Ink, Blake & Herring, N-Y, Umbrella, 8-Sided, Blue Green, Inward Rolled Lip, 3 In. 2691
Ink, Cone, Draped, Cobalt Blue, Label Panel, Double Ring Collar, 4 In. 2340
Ink, Cylindrical, Fluted Sides, Teal Green, Sheared Mouth, 1 1/2 x 1 7/8 In. 761
Ink, David's & Black, New York, Teal, Cylindrical, Sloping Collar, Crimped Spout, Qt. 1150
Ink, Fahnestock's Neutral, Blue Aqua, 6 Concave Panels, Flattened Rim, 6 In. 633
Ink, Farley's, 8-Sided, Yellow Amber, Flared Mouth, Master, 3 5/8 In. 585
Ink, G & R's Carmine, Aqua, Cylindrical, Inward Rolled Lip, 2 7/8 In. 978
Ink, Harrison's Columbian, 8-Sided, Sapphire Blue, Inward Rolled Lip, 1 1/2 In. 1521
Ink, Harrison's Columbian, Light Green, Cylindrical, Flared Double Collar, Master, 7 In. 748
Ink, Jones' Empire, N.Y., 12-Sided, Emerald Green, Squared Collar, Master, 5 3/4 In. 9360
Ink, Teakettle, 8-Sided, Sapphire Blue, Ground Mouth, Metal Collar & Cap, 2 In. 1872
Ink, Umbrella, 8-Sided, Deep Cherry Red, Inward Rolled Lip, Pontil, 2 1/2 In. 1265
Ink, Umbrella, 8-Sided, Emerald Green, Sheared Mouth, Pontil, 2 1/2 In. 920
Ink, Umbrella, 8-Sided, Golden Amber, Inward Rolled Lip, Pontil, 2 3/8 In. 196
Ink, Umbrella, 8-Sided, Grape Amethyst, Tooled Mouth, 2 1/2 In. 702
Ink, Umbrella, 8-Sided, Old Amber, Sheared & Tooled, Pontil, 2 3/8 In. 242
Ink, Umbrella, 8-Sided, Sapphire Blue, Inward Rolled Lip, c.1850, 32 3/8 In. .... *illus* 2300
Ink, Umbrella, 8-Sided, Smoky Olive Green, Inward Rolled Lip, Pontil, 2 1/2 In. .... *illus* 518
Ink, Umbrella, 8-Sided, Yellow, Topaz Tone, Inward Rolled Mouth, Iron Pontil, 2 1/4 In. 1053
Ink, Warren's Congress, 8-Sided, Forest Green, Sloping Collar With Ring, Spout, 7 1/4 In. 7020
Ink, Waters, Troy, N.Y., 6-Sided, Aqua Tapered, Inward Rolled Lip, Pontil, 2 3/4 In. 690
Medicine, Apothecary, Blue & White Crystalline Glaze, Lid, Blossom Handles, 8 In., Pair 115
Medicine, Apothecary, Cobalt Blue, Blown, Elongated Neck, Mushroom Stopper, 11 In., Pair...... 201
Medicine, Apothecary, Lid, Clear, 1800s, 15 In., Pair 175
Medicine, Apothecary, Porcelain, Opium, Quinine, Colchique, A. Saluiae, 5 In., 4 Piece........ 168
Medicine, Apothecary, Tin, Blue, White, Beaker Shape, Birds, Leaves, Cross, 10 1/2 In., Pair........ 240
Medicine, Curtis & Perkins' Cramp & Pain Killer, Bangor, Me., Aqua, Cylindrical, 4 5/8 In. 115
Medicine, Doctor Geo. W. Blocksom, Druggist, Zanesville, Blue Aqua, 12-Sided, 8 In. 978
Medicine, Doctor P. Hall's Cough Remedy, Cornflower Blue, Rolled Lip, 4 3/4 In. 230
Medicine, Dr. Birmingham's Anti Bilious Blood Purifier, Blue Green, Cylindrical, 8 1/2 In. 2925
Medicine, Dr. G.W. Phillip's Diarrhea Syrup, Cincinnati, O, Blue Aqua, 6 In. 1035
Medicine, Dr. J.S. Wood's Elixir, Albany, NY, Blue Green, Tombstone Form, 8 3/4 In. 2185
Medicine, Dr. Perkins' Syrup, Albany, Blue Green, Square, Arched Shoulder, 9 1/4 In. 13800
Medicine, Dr. Robertson's Family Medicine, Prepared Only By T.W. Dyott, Aqua, 5 In. 4388
Medicine, Dr. S.S. Fitch & Co., 714 Broadway, N.Y., Aqua, Wide Rolled Lip, 2 3/4 In. 127
Medicine, Dr. Wistar's Balsam Of Wild Cherry, Deep Blue Aqua, 8-Sided, 6 1/4 In. 104
Medicine, G.W. Stone's Mesmeric Nerve Restorative, Boston, Aqua, Double Collar, 6 In. 1989
Medicine, Hanbury Smith, Druggist, Aqua, Oval, Blob Top, 7 5/8 In. 431
Medicine, Indian Medical Spring Water, Indian's Head, Cobalt Blue, Cylindrical, 10 1/2 In. 1955
Medicine, J. Starkweather's Hepatic Elixir, Upton, Mass., Aqua, 6-Sided, Sloping Collar, 6 3/8 In. . 1265
Medicine, Jones Cholagogue, J.D. Park, Cincinnati, Blue Aqua, Double Collar, 6 3/4 In. 518
Medicine, Lindsey's Blood Searcher, Hollidaysburg, Olive, Arched Panels, 9 3/8 In. 3450
Medicine, Longley's Panacea, Yellow Olive, Rectangular, Beveled, Double Collar, 6 In. 1170
Medicine, Loomis's Cream, Liniment, Emerald Green, Corset Waist, Rolled Lip, 4 5/8 In. 2430
Medicine, Milk Of Magnesia, Chas. H. Phillips Chemical Co., Cobalt Blue, 7 x 3 In. 12
Medicine, Morse's Celebrated Syrup, Prov. R.I., Emerald Green, 9 1/2 In. 3163

Bottle, Soda, H. Nash & Co., Root Beer, Cincinnati, Blue, 12-Sided, Blob Top, 8 1/2 In.
$1,093

Glass Works Auctions

Bottle, Soda, Seeters Vichy & Carbonated Beverages, Lion, Yellow Green, Hutchinson, 7 In.
$345

Glass Works Auctions

Bottle, Target Ball, Gevelot, Paris, Cobalt Blue, Diamond, Center Band, c.1895, 3 In.
$460

Glass Works Auctions

Bottle, Whiskey, Casper's, Made By Honest North Carolina People, Cobalt Blue, 12 In.
$690

Glass Works Auctions

Bottle, Whiskey, Old Rye, Christytown Pottery, Stoneware, Albany Slip, Teat Spouts, 7 In.
$9,000

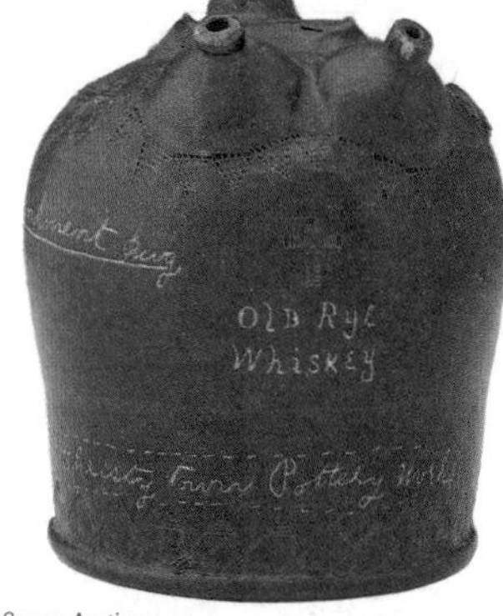

Cowan Auctions

Bottle Opener, Donkey, Cast Iron, Original Paint, c.1950, 3 In.
$85

Ruby Lane

Medicine, P.T. Wright & Co., Ague Mixture, Philada., Aqua, Indented, Double Collar, 7 In. 230
Medicine, Parvin's Tonic Mixture, Aqua, Streaky, Arched Shoulder, Pontil, 6⅛ In. 805
Medicine, Pike & Osgood, Alternative Syrup, Boston, Olive Amber, Stoddard, 8½ In. 10530
Medicine, Prof. H.K. Flagg's Balm Of Excellence, Aqua, 6-Point Star, Double Collar, 5 In. 184
Medicine, R.E. Woodward's Vegetable Tincture, South Reading, Mass., Aqua, 8-Sided, 6 In. 1380
Medicine, Rev. W. Clark's European Cough Remedy, Aqua, Sloping Collar, 7½ In. 374
Medicine, Rohrer's Expectoral Wild Cherry Tonic, Yellow Amber, Tapered, 10½ In. 489
Medicine, Seaver's Joint & Nerve Liniment, Straw Yellow, Olive Tone, Flared Lip, 4 In. 1725
Medicine, Skerritt's Oil, B. Wheeler, W. Henrietta, N.Y., Green, Cylindrical, 7¼ In. 2645
Medicine, Smith's Green Mountain Renovator, East Georgia, Vt., Olive Amber, 7 In. 1872
Medicine, Swaim's Panacea, Philada, Grass Green, Fluted, Double Collar, 8 In. 546
Medicine, W.W. Clark's Infallible Worm Syrup, Phila., Aqua, Cylindrical, Rolled Lip, 4 In. 104
Medicine, White's Hair Restorative, Pale Aqua, Oval, Sloping Collar, Pontil, 6⅜ In. 138
Medicine, Wm. S. Merrell & Co., Druggists, Cincinnati, Aqua, Oval, Applied Lip, 7⅞ In. 316
Milk, Borden, Amber, Portrait, Square, Qt., 9 In. 18
Milk, Community Dairy, Red Plastic Neck Holder, Half Gal., 10½ In. 20
Milk, Glockhoff Dairy, Direct From Farm To You, Pyro Glaze, 1940s, Qt. 68
Milk, Polar Bear Ice Cream, Garden Farm Dairy, Enamel Label, 10 x 4 In. .... *illus* 115
Milk, Quality Chekd, Check Mark In Q, Brown, Wavy Vertical Lines, ½ Gal. 19
Milk, R.L. Schmid, Fredericks, Pa., Embossed, Half Pint 105
Milk, Sunshine Dairy, Sun, Orange Pyro, c.1927, Qt. 35
Mineral Water, Avon Spring Water, Red Amber, Double Collar, Qt. 4313
Mineral Water, B. Bick & Co., Cincinnati, B, Cornflower, 10-Sided, Pontil, 7⅜ In. 316
Mineral Water, Buffums, Cobalt Blue, 10-Sided, Sloping Collar, Iron Pontil, 7⅝ In. 633
Mineral Water, Byronic Acid Spring Water, Teal, Iron Pontil, Double Collar, Qt. 4025
Mineral Water, Capt. H. Niehaus, Cincinnati, B, Blue Aqua, 10-Sided, Blob Top, 7¼ In. 207
Mineral Water, Coon & Spencer's Nectarian, Cobalt Blue, 8-Sided, Blob Top, 8¼ In. 1380
Mineral Water, F. Gleason, Rochester, Cobalt Blue, Ten Pin, Sloping Collar, 8⅜ In. 489
Mineral Water, F. Gleason, Rochester, N.Y., Sapphire Blue, Blob Top, 7¾ In. 489
Mineral Water, Gardner & Landon, Sharon, Sulphur Water, Olive Green, Qt. 978
Mineral Water, Geo. H. Tobey, Cincinnati, T, Blue Aqua, Sloping Collar, 7⅜ In. 173
Mineral Water, Highrock Congress Spring, 1767, Rock, C & W, Saratoga, N.Y., Amber, Pt. 403
Mineral Water, Iodine Spring Water, L, South Hero, Vt., Yellow Amber, Double Collar, Qt. 1610
Mineral Water, J & A Dearborn, New York, Sapphire Blue, 8-Sided, Blob Top, 6⅞ In. 242
Mineral Water, J. Whitney, Richfield Springs, Sulphur Water, Yellow Olive, Blob Top, Pt. 1150
Mineral Water, John & G.J. Postel, Cincinnati, Green Aqua, Sloping Collar, Pontil, 7¼ In. 161
Mineral Water, Knickerbocker, Boughton & Chase, Rochester, N.Y., Blue, Blob Top, 7¼ In. 316
Mineral Water, Magnetic Spring, Henniker, NH, Yellow Amber, Double Collar, Qt. 1265
Mineral Water, Oak Orchard, Acid Springs, Alabama, Genesee Co., N.Y., Blue Green, Qt. 546
Mineral Water, Old Saratoga, Quaker Springs, Emerald Green, Sloping Collar, Pt. 1093
Mineral Water, Round Lake, Saratoga Co., N.Y., Red Amber, Sloping Collar, Qt. 8050
Mineral Water, Rutherford's Premium, Cincinnati, Sapphire Blue, 10-Sided, 7½ In. 2185
Mineral Water, Rutherford's, Cin., Aqua, Sloping Collar, Pontil, 6⅝ In. 3738
Mineral Water, Seal Rock Spring, Silas Gurney, Boston, Teal, Cylindrical, Sloping Collar, Qt. 644
Mineral Water, Star Spring Co., Saratoga, N.Y., 5-Point Star, Green, Pt. 690
Mineral Water, Syracuse Springs, D, Excelsior, New York, Amber, Double Collar, ½ Pt. 460
Mineral Water, The Excelsior, J. Doudall, Avondale, Green, 8-Sided, Blob Top, 7½ In. 2875
Mineral Water, W. Wilke & Co., Cin., O., This Bottle Is Never Sold, Aqua, 10-Sided, 7⅝ In. 127
Mineral Water, Washington Spring Co., Bust Of George Washington, Green, Pt. 431
Perfume bottles are listed in their own category.
Pickle, Bunker Hill, Skilton Foote & Cos., Lighthouse Form, Yellow Olive, 11⅜ In. 1610
Pickle, Cathedral, 6-Sided, Arched Lattice Windows, Teal, 11½ In. 690
Poison, Diamond Pattern, Cobalt Blue, Tooled Lip, Stopper, Label, c.1895, 9 In. .... *illus* 403
Poison, Embossed Poison, Cobalt Blue, Cylindrical, Raised Diamonds, Flattened Lip, 11 In. 633
Poison, Raised Diamonds, Smoky Teal, Flattened Lip, 4½ In. .... *illus* 633
Poison, Skull & Crossed Bones, DP Co., Coffin Shape, Hobnails, Cobalt Blue, 1870-90, 7⅛ In. *illus* 4388
Poison, Skull, Embossed Poison, Pat June 26th, 1894, Cobalt Blue, 4 In. .... *illus* 3450
Sarsaparilla, Dr. Guysott's Compound Extract Of Yellow Dock, Blue, 9½ In. 5175
Sarsaparilla, John Bull Extract, Louisville, Ky., Aqua, Sloping Collar, Iron Pontil, 9 In. 431
Sarsaparilla, Old Dr. Townsend's, New York, Blue Green, Sloping Collar, 9¾ In. 345
Sarsaparilla, Turner's, Buffalo, N.Y., Blue Aqua, Bubbles, Sloping Collar, 12½ In. 920
Scent, Bohemian, Green Cut To Clear, Gilt Decoration, 4 In. 584
Scent, Cameo Glass, Teardrop, Opal Over Clear Over Red, Flowers, Gorham, c.1890, 4 In. 708
Scent, Sunburst, Cobalt Blue, Sheared & Tooled Lip, Pontil, c.1830, 2¾ In. .... *illus* 288
Seal, Deep Olive Amber, T. Perkins, Wine, Sloping Collar, String Rim, 12⅞ In. 878
Seal, Deep Yellow Olive, I Mascarene 1748, Wine, Long Neck, Sheared, String Lip, 9⅝ In. 1638

Seal, Olive Green, D Wells 1764, Wine, Oval, Sheared, Applied Ring, 11 ¼ In. 14040
Seal, Yellow Olive Amber, R+H 1765, Wine, Ring Mouth, Pewter Band, Dip Mold, 8 In. 2875
Snuff, Agate, Amber, White, Relief Carved Grasshopper, Beet, Chinese, c.1910, 3 In. 240
Snuff, Agate, Carved Monkeys, Butterfly, Round, Red Stone Stopper, c.1900, 3 In. ....*illus* 1007
Snuff, Agate, Milky Tan, Incised, Ducks, Lotus Pool, Pink Glass Stopper, 1800s, 2 In. 390
Snuff, Agate, Milky Tan, Mask & Mock Ring Handles, Coral Stopper, Chinese, 2 ⅜ In. 120
Snuff, Agate, Translucent, Carved, Birds In Flight, Flowers, Red Mark, 3 x 2 In. 104
Snuff, Amber, Carved Shoulders, Beast Head Handles, Flared Foot Ring, 2 ⅝ In. 500
Snuff, Amethyst, Relief Carved, Birds, Flowers, Chinese, 1800s, 2 In. ....*illus* 124
Snuff, Bamboo Root, Flattened Circle, Foo Dog Masks, Stopper, c.1800, 1 ⅓ In. 533
Snuff, Banded Agate, Tan, Yellow, White, Flat, Round, Jadeite Stopper, c.1800, 2 ¾ In. 480
Snuff, Cloisonne, 4 Swimming Ducks, Flowers, Attached Spoon In Lid, Footed, 2 ½ In. 247
Snuff, Glass, Enamel, White, Butterfly, Mantis, Flowers, c.1915, 2 ½ In. 720
Snuff, Glass, Red Carved Overlay, Fruit, Tapering Oval, Flat Rim, c.1800, 2 In. 125
Snuff, Glass, Snowflake Ground, Red Overlay, Oval Foot, Blue Stopper, Black Collar, 2 ¼ In. 600
Snuff, Glass, White Cut To Red, Overlapping Petals, Oval, Green Stopper, 3 ¼ x 2 In. 506
Snuff, Ivory, Carved, Scholar Under Tree, 2 Women, Round, Shouldered, c.1890, 3 In. 75
Snuff, Lapis, Bird Among Palm Plants, Rock Formation, Agate Stopper, 3 x 1 ¾ In. 115
Snuff, Lapis, Foo Dog, Carved, 1900s, 2 ½ In. 173
Snuff, Malachite, Buddha, Rock Formation, Flowers, 2 ⅜ In. 62
Snuff, Malachite, Fish Shape, Ball Stopper, 2 ⅜ In. 150
Snuff, Malachite, Gourd Shape, Leaves, Tendrils, 2 ¾ In. 325
Snuff, Mother-Of-Pearl, Dragon, Peacock, Mosaic Style, Faceted, Stopper, 3 ½ x ¾ In. 109
Snuff, Peking Glass, Aquamarine, Etched Songbirds, 3 In. 326
Snuff, Peking Glass, Dragons, Carved, Blue To Clear, Flattened Oval, Stopper, 3 In. 178
Snuff, Peking Glass, Red Overlay, Dragon, Lotus, Scholar, Oval Foot, 19th Century, 2 ⅜ In. 276
Snuff, Peking Glass, Reverse Painted, Kingfisher, Branch, Inscribed, Gui Xianggu, 3 In. .....*illus* 813
Snuff, Porcelain, Red, White, Catching Demon, Jadeite Stopper, Chinese, 2 ⅞ In. 180
Snuff, Rock Crystal, Carved, Rectangular, Green Stopper, Chinese, 2 ⅛ In. 600
Snuff, Seed Pod, Silver Mount, Chalcedony Stopper, Wood Stand, 1800s, 2 In. 415
Snuff, White, Blue, Man, Smallpox, Fan, Hugging, Green Stone Stopper, Chinese, 2 ⅞ In. 1080
Soda, A. Raab, Tamaqua, Pa., Shaded Green, Slug Plate, Double Collar, 7 In. ....*illus* 242
Soda, Boyd, Balt., Torpedo, Light Smoky Topaz, Sloping Collar, 9 In. 8625
Soda, C.B. Owens Root Beer, Sapphire Blue, 12-Sided, Blob Top, 8 ⅜ In. 1380
Soda, C.W. Rider, Watertown, N.Y., Teal, Blob Top, Hutchinson, 6 ¾ In. 1380
Soda, Carpenter & Cobb, Knickerbocker, Saratoga Springs, Light Green, 10-Sided, 7 ⅜ In. 633
Soda, D. McCoy's Root Beer, Cincinnati, Shield, Cobalt Blue, Blob Top, Pontil, 8 In. 9200
Soda, E. Bigelow & Co., Soda Water, Springfield, Mass., Sapphire Blue, Blob Top, 7 In. 805
Soda, Fr. Goosmann & Co. Root Beer, Blue Aqua, 12-Sided, Blob Top, 8 ⅞ In. 2530
Soda, H. & C. Overdick, Cincinnati, Cobalt Blue, 12-Sided, Blob Top, 8 ¾ In. 3450
Soda, H. Nash & Co., Root Beer, Cincinnati, Blue, 12-Sided, Blob Top, 8 ½ In. ....*illus* 1093
Soda, J. Rother, Baltimore Glass Works, Torpedo, Black Amethyst, 9 In. 5175
Soda, Seeters Vichy & Carbonated Beverages, Lion, Yellow Green, Hutchinson, 7 In. ....*illus* 345
Soda, Stromeyer's Grape Punch, Clear, Label, Metal Cap, 12 ½ In. 330
Soda, Sun Rise, Ribbed, Tazewell Mfg. Co., c.1970, 10 Oz. 10
Soda, Vin Fizz, Clear Glass, Label, Metal Cap, 11 ½ In. 300
Storage, Deep Yellow Amber, Wide Mouth, Flared Rim, Pontil, Stoddard, N.H., 7 ¾ In. 2185
Target Ball, Gevelot, Paris, Cobalt Blue, Diamond, Center Band, c.1895, 3 In. ....*illus* 460
Target Ball, Glasshutten Charlottenburg, Clear, Lattice, Center Band, Sheared, 2 ¾ In. 546
Whiskey, Amber, Silver Overlay, Bows & Shield Design, Monogram, 11 ½ In. 600
Whiskey, Backbar, Lotus Club, Etched, Bulbous, Stick Neck, Loop Handle, Stopper, 10 In. 120
Whiskey, Casper's, Made By Honest North Carolina People, Cobalt Blue, 12 In. ....*illus* 690
Whiskey, Glendisco, B, Rum, Label Under Glass, Fluted Neck, Backbar, 10 ½ In. 920
Whiskey, H.A. Graef's Son, N.Y., Canteen, Chartreuse Green, Double Collar, 6 ⅝ In. 316
Whiskey, Indian Princess, Mohawk, Pure Rye, Pat. Feb 11 1868, Amber, 12 ¼ In. 3163
Whiskey, J T Gayen, Altona, Cannon, Amber, Tapered, Blob Top, 13 ⅝ In. 1380
Whiskey, Jug, Puce, Applied Mouth, Handle, 9 ⅜ In. 150
Whiskey, King Edward Reserve, Barrel, Amber, Sloping Collar, Internal Threading, 8 ½ In. 345
Whiskey, Old Rye, Christytown Pottery, Stoneware, Albany Slip, Teat Spouts, 7 In. ....*illus* 9000
Whiskey, Old Wheat, S.M. & Co., Yellow Amber, Teardrop, Double Collar, Pontil, 9 ⅜ In. 161
Whiskey, Perrine's Ginger, Embossed Apple, Semi-Cabin, Amber, 9 ¾ In. 316
Whiskey, Pig, Figural, Good Old Bourbon In A Hogs, Yellow Amber, 6 ½ In. 288
Whiskey, SSW & Co., Amber, Chestnut Form, Ring Mouth, Handle, Pontil, 8 ⅝ In. 4600
Wine, Green Bubbly, Bulbous, Stick Neck, Cap, 20 In. 1000
Wine, Los Angeles Wine Co., Red Amber, Megaphone Shape, Tooled Mouth, 13 ½ In. 242
Wine, Onion, Deep Yellow Olive Amber, Squat, String Lip, Pontil, Magnum, 6 ⅞ In. 6900

Bottle Opener, Dragon Head, Munich Beer, Germany, 1960s, 4 In.
$45

Ruby Lane

Bottle Opener, Fish, Mother-Of-Pearl, Flexible, c.1940, 5 ½ In.
$149

Ruby Lane

Bottle Stopper, Wood, Kissing, Couple, Mechanical, 6 ¼ x ½ In.
$50

Ruby Lane

BOTTLE CAPS for milk bottles are the printed cardboard caps used since the 1920s. Crown caps, used after 1892 on soda bottles, are also popular collectibles. Unusual mottoes, graphics, and caps from bottlers that are out of business bring the highest prices.

Baker & Son Dairy, Windmill, Blue, Red, 1 ½ In., 50 Piece	6
Bunten's Pure Milk, Maplewood Farm, Blue, Red, Paper, 1961, 2 In., 25 Piece	7
Clifford Coldy, Pure Milk, Green Fields, Red Cows, 1930s, 1 ½ In., 2 Piece	7
Green Acres Farm, Red, Black, 1950s, 2 ¼ In., 10 Piece	6
Hulburt Farm Dairy, Red, White, Paper, 1940-60, 1 ¾ In., 6 Piece	6
Maple Leaf Dairy, Red, Green, 1950s, 2 In., 8 Piece	12
Mellin's Food, For Infants & Invalids, Paper, 1897, 1 ¼ In.	10
Null's Dairy, Chocolate Eye's Drinks, Black Girl, Red Shirt, 5 Piece	49
Pure Raw Milk, Green, Red Dot, Cardboard, 1 ¾ In., 12 Piece	6
Saco Dairy, Raw Milk, Blue, White, c.1910, 1 ⅝ In.	15
Wash & Return Bottles Daily, Pure Fresh Milk, 1 ½ In., 2 Piece	2
White Cross Heavy Cream, Waxed Cardstock, 2 ¼ In., 10 Piece.	6

BOTTLE OPENERS are needed to open many bottles. As soon as the commercial bottle was invented, the opener to be used with the new types of closures became a necessity. Many types of bottle openers can be found, most dating from the twentieth century. Collectors prize advertising and comic openers.

Antler, Silver, John Hasselbring, 11 In.	135
Bakelite, Marbled Brown, Can't Slip, 4 In.	26
Bakelite, Red, 5 ¾ In.	25
Bottle Shape, Sterling Silver, Corkscrew, Pat. 1897, 2 ¾ In.	145
Bust Of Farmer, Wood, Double Handle, France, 1930s	42
Cornish Pisky, Brass, 5 In.	45
Crown, Finger Pull Corkscrew, Brass, 5 In.	95
Dog, Poodle, Sitting, Brass, Italy, c.1955, 4 ⅝ In.	39
Donkey, Cast Iron, Original Paint, c.1950, 3 In. *illus*	85
Dragon Head, Munich Beer, Germany, 1960s, 4 In. *illus*	45
Fish, Articulated, Abalone Inlay, c.1950, 6 In.	65
Fish, Mother-Of-Pearl, Flexible, c.1940, 5 ½ In. *illus*	149
Goose, Metal, Scott Products, 5 ½ In.	45
Jockey Hat, Yellow, Scott Products, 1960s, 3 ½ x 2 ¼ In.	55
Lizard, Silver Plated, International Silver, c.1980, 7 x 3 In.	26
Mallard Duck, Cast Iron, c.1950, 2 ¾ In.	24
Man In Top Hat, Wood, Carved, Anri, 1960s, 4 In.	45
Man's Portrait, Embossed Metal, Wing Armed Corkscrew, Italy, 7 ½ In.	20
Nude, Bronze, Long Hair, 4 In.	65
Nude, Cast Iron, 8 In.	29
Owl, Sterling Silver, Gorham, 3 ⅞ In.	295
Pretzel, Cast Iron, Brown, Salt Specks, 1951, 3 x 2 In.	48
Progressus, Metal, Wall Mount, c.1965, 3 x 1 ½ In.	15
Prussian Helmet, Brass, 2 ¼ x 2 In.	65
Rooster, Cast Iron, Red Paint, 3 ¾ x 2 ½ In.	12
Sterling Silver, Amnesty Pattern, Weidlich Co., 1940, 5 ¾ In.	25
Sterling Silver, Flowers, Web, 6 ⅞ In.	97
Sterling Silver, Grand Duchess Pattern, Towle, 6 ¼ In.	145
Sterling Silver, Pyramid Pattern, Georg Jensen, 4 ¼ In.	193
Sterling Silver, Rococo, Raised Beads, 4 In.	75
Sterling Silver, Web Silver Co., 6 In.	35

BOTTLE STOPPERS are made of glass, metal, plastic, and wood. Decorative and figural stoppers are used to replace the original cork stoppers and are collected today.

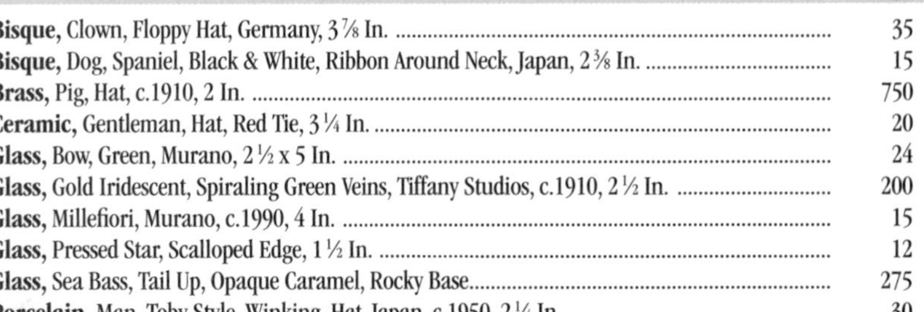

Bisque, Clown, Floppy Hat, Germany, 3 ⅞ In.	35
Bisque, Dog, Spaniel, Black & White, Ribbon Around Neck, Japan, 2 ⅜ In.	15
Brass, Pig, Hat, c.1910, 2 In.	750
Ceramic, Gentleman, Hat, Red Tie, 3 ¼ In.	20
Glass, Bow, Green, Murano, 2 ½ x 5 In.	24
Glass, Gold Iridescent, Spiraling Green Veins, Tiffany Studios, c.1910, 2 ½ In.	200
Glass, Millefiori, Murano, c.1990, 4 In.	15
Glass, Pressed Star, Scalloped Edge, 1 ½ In.	12
Glass, Sea Bass, Tail Up, Opaque Caramel, Rocky Base	275
Porcelain, Man, Toby Style, Winking, Hat, Japan, c.1950, 2 ¼ In.	30

Bottle Stopper, Wood, Man, Raises Head, Mouth Opens, Mechanical, Anri, c.1950, 5 In.
$35

Ruby Lane

Box, Bride's, Bentwood, Oval, Orange, Painted, Flowers, Leaves, c.1830, 6 ½ x 12 x 7 In.
$502

Hess Auction Group

Box, Game, Bronze, Enameled Plaques, Mahogany Tray, Bun Feet, Chips, 8 x 6 x 2 In.
$1,599

Skinner, Inc.

TIP

Don't buy a collector something for the collection. Buy a book about the collectible or something related to the collection, like a T-shirt picturing a bank for a bank collector.

B

Porcelain, Sea Captain, Pipe, Beard, Cap, 4 x 3 In. 48
Silver Plate, Cartouche, Scalloped Edge, c.1940, 2 In. 40
Silver Plate, King Francis Pattern, Reed & Barton, Fruit Basket, 3 ½ In. 65
Sterling Silver, Parrot, 2 ½ In. 195
Sterling Silver, Woman, Domed Cap, Germany, c.1907, 2 In. 100
Wood, Couple, Kissing, Anri 24
Wood, Dancing Bear, Black Forest, Germany, 3 ½ In. 110
Wood, Dog, Pug, Glass Eyes, Black Forest, c.1900, 2 In. 132
Wood, Eagle, Open Wings, Shoebutton Eyes, c.1920, 4 In. 95
Wood, Kissing, Couple, Mechanical, 6 ¼ x ½ In. .... *illus* 50
Wood, Man, Playing Drums, Mechanical, Italy 12
Wood, Man, Raises Head, Mouth Opens, Mechanical, Anri, c.1950, 5 In. .... *illus* 35
Wood, Woman, Laughing, Babushka, Black Forest, 1960s, 5 In. 42

BOXES of all kinds are collected. They were made of thin strips of inlaid wood, metal, tortoiseshell, embroidery, or other material. Additional boxes may be listed in other sections, such as Advertising, Battersea, Ivory, Shaker, Tinware, and various Porcelain categories. Tea Caddies are listed in their own category.

Altar, Wood, Leaves, Carved, Continental, 10 x 12 ¾ In. 199
Ammunition, Wood, Military, Shotgun Shells, Handles, 7 x 27 In. 92
Apple, Softwood, Feather Grain Painted, Pa., 1800s, 4 x 12 In. 885
Apple, Softwood, Red Paint, Square, Plank Sides, Molded Base, 1800s, 3 x 11 x 11 In. 224
Apple, Wood, Inset Panels, Scalloped Border, Flared Rim & Foot, Black & Red, c.1875, 9 x 9 In. . 1599
Art, Hardwood, Hinged, Oval, Stuck Out Tongue Handle, Stewart Paul, 1951, 6 x 10 ½ In. 1599
Artist Paint, Mahogany, Inlaid Conch Shell, Spandrels, Stringing, 2 ½ x 13 ½ In. 628
Bible, Wood, Carved, Initialed In Front AK, Continental, 1800s, 10 x 12 In. 351
Birch, Dovetailed, Red & Black Vinegar Sponged Decoration, Lock, 2 Handles, 13 x 30 In. 360
Bride's, Ash & White Wood, Stenciled Flowers, Leaves, Green, Oval, Lid, 1853, 10 x 18 In. 1304
Bride's, Bentwood, Oval, Orange, Painted, Flowers, Leaves, c.1830, 6 ½ x 12 x 7 In. .... *illus* 502
Bride's, Bentwood, Painted, Hound Chasing Fox, Forest, Roses, Lid, 1800s, 7 x 16 In. 246
Bronze, Art Nouveau, Gilt, Coffin Shape, Lid, 5 x 6 ½ In. 88
Bronze, Enameled, Gilt, Portrait, Blue, Signed Heriche, 2 ⅜ x 6 ½ In. 341
Bronze, Hinged Lid, Putto Gazing At Bird, Wheat Bundle, 2 ¼ x 5 In. 210
Burled Maple, Rosewood, Dovetail Construction, Signed Christopher Maier, 10 x 4 ¼ In. 150
Candle, Mahogany, Sliding Panel, George III, c.1785, 18 x 5 x 4 In. 375
Candle, Oak, Hinged Lid, Tapered Shape, Wall Mount, George III, c.1810, 16 x 6 ½ In. 142
Candle, Softwood, Paint, Flowers, Leaves, Slide Lid, 1800s, 8 x 12 In. 443
Candle, Wall, Walnut, Dark Stained, 12 x 12 ¼ In. 300
Candy, Marines, America's Defenders, Die Cut, Marine Holding Rifle, 1942, 2 x 3 x 6 In. 511
Candy, Our Gang, Spanky Photo, Group, 1935, 2 x 4 x 1 In. 173
Casket, Wood, Hinged Fall, Interior Drawers, Painted, Scroll, Armorial, 1700s, 12 x 15 In. 2750
Casket, Wood, Tortoiseshell, Toupee Feet, Silk Tufted Lining, Oval, France, 1800s, 11 x 8 In. 554
Cherry Inlay, Heart, Star, Horse, Knife, Fork, Spoon, Slide Lid, Initials H.B.H., 19 x 8 In. 354
Cigar, Inlaid Dragons, Pearl, Paw Feet, Initials JMN, Hinged Lid, 1932, 3 x 8 In. 935
Cigar, Tortoiseshell, Silver Mount, Keyhole Escutcheon, Wood Lining, 1800s, 7 x 6 In. 1020
Cigar, Wood, Black Forest, Seated Elk, Thatched House, 7 ½ x 9 In. 344
Cigar, Wood, Chip Art, Slide Lid, 1888, 5 x 1 x 1 In. 225
Cigarette, Sculpted Glass, Brass, Green, Bird Shape Handle, Art Deco, 5 ½ x 6 ¼ In. 345
Clothesline, Wood, House Shape, Folk Art, c.1910, 22 x 14 In. 384
Coffer, Bog Oak, Zinc Liner, Carved Leaf Design, 1500s, 21 ½ x 48 In. 800
Coffer, Rosewood, Brass Mounted, Engraved Isabel, Lined, Gothic Revival, 1800s, 7 In. 531
Decanter, Mahogany, Elongated Hexagon, Velvet Lined, 1800s, 10 ½ x 10 In. 235
Decanter, Mahogany, Line Inlaid, Panels, Checked Border, Lined, Lift Lid, c.1810, 9 x 11 In. 750
Display Case, Gilt Brass, Beveled Glass Insert, Leaf Design, Velvet Liner, Hinged Lid, 8 x 6 In. 92
Document, Black, Gold, Brass Handle, Lock, Key, Hinged Lid, 1800s, 9 x 6 x 4 In. 145
Document, Carved Oak, Carved Frieze, Iron Hardware, Projected Lid, c.1665, 8 x 18 In. 369
Document, Cherry, Dovetailed, Key, Hinged Lid, c.1860, 5 x 12 x 6 In. 425
Document, Lacquer, Bird On Plum Tree, Branches, Gold Flecks, Lift Lid, c.1900, 6 x 11 In. 210
Document, Lacquer, Flowers, Red & Black, Iron Bail Handles & Hinge, c.1826, 9 x 10 In. 118
Document, Mother-Of-Pearl Inlay, Canted Corners, Bronze Handles, 15 ¾ x 19 In. 153
Document, Oak, Carved Arabesques, Lift Sloped Lid, England, 17th Century, 11 x 26 In. 677
Document, Papered, Sewn Edges, Painted Peonies, Brass Hinge, Handles, Chinese, 22 x 14 In. . 47
Document, Pine, Lollipop Handle, Faux Mahogany Grain, Green Trim, Slide Lid, c.1810, 19 In. 360
Document, Wood, Block Print Wallpaper, Wire Latch, Dome Lid, c.1860, 5 x 14 In. 120
Document, Wood, Paint, Strawberries & Flowers, Black Ground, 1800s, 5 x 18 In. 118
Document, Wood, Red & Black Sponge Paint, Brass Bail Handle, Dome Lid, c.1830, 7 x 18 In. .. 250

Box, Hat, Wallpaper, Blue, Village Scene, Chickens, Label, Mrs. Crary, 1800s, 12 x 18 In.
$224

Hess Auction Group

Box, Knife, Mahogany, Inlay, Fitted Interior, Hinged Lid, Federal, 15 x 11 In., Pair
$2,607

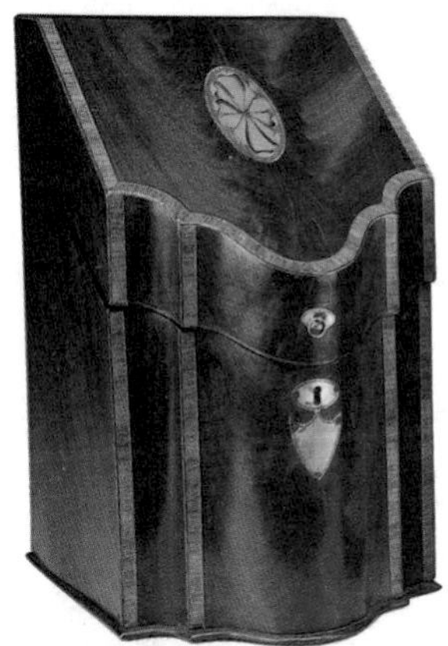

James D. Julia Auctioneers

Box, Knife, Mahogany, Urn Shape, Stepped Dome Top, Finial, George III, 1800s, 27 In., Pair
$3,198

Skinner, Inc.

TIP

Check wall-hung and glass shelves regularly to be sure they have not loosened or bent.

Box, Pipe, Tiger Maple, Carved, Pierced Heart, Scrolls, Drawer, Pinwheel, 1700s, 20 x 5 In.
$1,235

James D. Julia Auctioneers

TIP

If you discover a cache of very dirty antiques and you are not dressed in work clothes, make yourself a temporary cover-up from a plastic garbage bag.

Box, Trinket, Glass, Bronze Ormolu Mounts, Hinged Lid, Lion's Mask, Handle, France, 3 x 5 In.
$305

DuMouchelles Art Gallery

Boy Scout, Canteen, Aluminum, Green, Canvas, Strap
$65

Ruby Lane

Bradley & Hubbard, Letter Holder, Bronze, Patina, Marked, B & H, c.1890, 5 x 6 x 4 In.
$300

Ruby Lane

Bradley & Hubbard, Plaque, Portrait, Painted, Woman With Flowing Hair, 8 ½ In.
$325

Ruby Lane

Bradley & Hubbard, Lamp, Metal Overlay Shade, 8 Panels, Flowers, Brass Base, 22 In.
$625

Ruby Lane

Dresser, Bronze, Gilt, Leather, Coffin Shape, Scrolled Straps, 9 x 5 ½ In.	500
Dresser, Onyx, Sterling Silver, Jasper Group, England, 1922, 1 ⅞ x 6 In.	60
Dresser, Renaissance Revival, Bronze, Gilt, Coffin Shape, Relief Scrolling, 7 ½ x 4 ½ In.	938
Dresser, Sterling Silver, George V, Hinged Lid, Neoclassical Style, Monogram, 1912, 1 x 4 x 2 In.	98
Game, Bronze, Enameled Plaques, Mahogany Tray, Bun Feet, Chips, 8 x 6 x 2 In. *illus*	1599
Glass, Octagonal, Brass Mount, Engraved, Hinged Lid, 4 x 5 In.	390
Glove, Mahogany, Marquetry, Flowers, Line Inlay, 11 ¾ x 5 In.	178
Glove, Rosewood, Ivory Mount, Brass Rivets, Dome Lid, 3 ½ x 10 ⅝ In.	175
Hat, Stetson, Red, Winter Scene, Art Deco, 1920s, 13 x 12 x 7 In.	95
Hat, Vinyl Covered, Snap Latches, Pinup Girl Design, Carrying Handle, 1950s, 8 x 16 In.	115
Hat, Wallpaper, Bentwood, Merchant's Exchange, New York, c.1850, 11 x 18 In.	266
Hat, Wallpaper, Blue Ground, Castle Ruins Scene, People, Camels, 13 x 17 In.	59
Hat, Wallpaper, Blue Ground, Squirrel, Landscape, 11 ½ x 20 In.	71
Hat, Wallpaper, Blue, Village Scene, Chickens, Label, Mrs. Crary, 1800s, 12 x 18 In. *illus*	224
Hat, Wallpaper, White & Green Flower Design, Oval, 1831, 11 x 16 In.	106
Hat, Wood, Painted, Red, Flowers, Round, Lid, 1800s, 11 x 16 In.	106
Incense, Lacquer, Gold, Silver Prunus, Flowers, Drawer, Japan, 1912, 7 x 8 ¾ In.	1045
Jewelry, Casket Shape, Tortoiseshell, Gilt, Cabriole Feet, Hinged Lid, c.1875, 5 x 8 In.	1250
Jewelry, Chinoiserie, Painted, France, c.1890, 12 x 14 In.	450
Jewelry, Gilt Bronze, Porcelain, Figures, Scroll Corners, Top Shape Feet, c.1900, 5 x 8 In.	2175
Jewelry, Gilt Metal, Relief Decoration, Cherubs, Fruit, Scrolled Feet, Lift-Off Tray, 8 x 7 In.	504
Jewelry, Porcelain, Enamel, Gilt Bronze, Cherub Handle, Rosettes, Hinged Lid, c.1890, 15 x 14 In.	9560
Jewelry, Porcelain, Gilt, Ormolu, Enamel, Blue, Flowers, Swag, France, 3 ½ x 10 In.	120
Jewelry, Porcelain, Gilt, Pink, Claw Feet, France, 3 ¼ x 5 ½ In.	144
Jewelry, Wood, Carved, Footed, 9 x 12 In.	60
Jewelry, Wood, Log Cabin Shape, Diamond Shingled, Front Door, Window, 1800s, 12 x 14 In.	677
Kindling, Softwood, Grain Painted, 3 Interior Compartments, Footed, Pa., 1800s, 24 x 70 In.	708
Knife, Federal, Mahogany, Fruitwood Inlay, 13 ¾ x 8 ½ In., Pair	1045
Knife, Lacquer, Gold, Phoenix, Flowers, Velvet, 2 Handles, George III, c.1800, 14 x 9 In.	240
Knife, Mahogany Veneer, Shell Inlay, Shell Medallion, Georgian, c.1800, 15 x 9 In.	324
Knife, Mahogany Veneer, Shell Inlay, Shield Shape Escutcheon, Georgian, 15 x 9 In.	240
Knife, Mahogany, Banded Inlay, Sloped, Hinged, Lid, 14 x 9 In.	246
Knife, Mahogany, Inlay, c.1875, 14 ½ x 9 In.	123
Knife, Mahogany, Inlay, Fitted Interior, Hinged Lid, Federal, 15 x 11 In., Pair *illus*	2607
Knife, Mahogany, Inlay, George III, c.1775, 14 ¾ x 9 In., Pair	1500
Knife, Mahogany, Inlay, Rosewood, Crossbanded, Fitted, George III, c.1800, 14 x 10 In., Pair	2250
Knife, Mahogany, Medallion, Inlay, George III, 15 x 9 In.	216
Knife, Mahogany, Satinwood Inlay, Panels, Shaped, Georgian, 14 x 11 In.	214
Knife, Mahogany, Urn Shape, Stepped Dome Top, Finial, George III, 1800s, 27 In., Pair *illus*	3198
Knife, Scrolled & Pierced, Square Sides, Painted, c.1825, 6 x 12 x 9 In.	338
Leather, Brass Tacks, Trunk Form, Printed Paper Inside, Blue Dots, Dome Lid, 8 x 18 x 9 In.	215
Leather, Camphorwood, Paint, Red, Flower Borders, Brassbound, Chinese, c.1850, 15 x 33 In.	431
Leather, Embossed, Serpentine Edge, Tooled Leaves, Arabesque, Iron, 6 ½ x 22 In.	1968
Letter, Mahogany, Fruitwood, Marquetry, Leaves, 12 ⅜ x 8 ¾ In.	220
Letter, Oak, Hinged, Doors, Dividers, England, c.1900, 11 x 12 In.	121
Letter, Oak, Slant Front, Bronze Inkwells, 1800s, 14 x 17 In.	302
Milk, Gray Green Paint, Marked Floral Green Spring, 13 x 11 In.	150
Picnic, Lacquer, Gilt, Fruiting Grapevines, Sparrows, Bamboo, Loop Handle, 8 x 5 In.	312
Pill, 18K Gold, Relief Cat Decoration, Ruby Inset Collar, Spring-Loaded Lid, 2 x 1 In.	1968
Pill, Art Deco, 14K Yellow Gold, Platinum Wreath, Black & Cream Enameling, Oval, 2 ¾ In.	885
Pipe, Tiger Maple, Carved, Pierced Heart, Scrolls, Drawer, Pinwheel, 1700s, 20 x 5 In. *illus*	1235
Pipe, Wall, Mahogany, Shaped Crest, Dovetailed Drawer, 22 x 6 In.	360
Powder, Art Nouveau, Carved, Pink, Flowers, St. Louis, 4 In.	360
Powder, Filigree, Stone, Inset Cut Glass, Blue, White, 4 In.	125
Powder, Lid, Woman, Figural, Pedestal, Parrot, Squat, Pink, White, Porcelain, 1800s, 5 In.	69
Powder, Silver, Flowers, Leaves, Spring-Loaded Lipstick Compartment, Bright Cut, 2 In.	83
Rosewood, Scrolls, Sliding Panel, Buddhist Emblems, Silk Lined, 31 x 4 In.	237
Sailor's, Mahogany, Geometric Inlay, Chamfered Lid, 1800s, 12 x 8 In.	369
Sailor's, Wood, Writing Surface, Compartments, Carved Stars & Pinwheel Lid, 1800s, 7 x 17 In.	308
Scholar's, Stacking, 4 Tiers, Handle, Brass Corners, Chinese, 13 ½ x 7 In.	2750
Shoeshine, Iron, Camel Base Foot Rest, Black Paint, Strap Hinge Lid, 13 x 13 In.	120
Shoeshine, Stand, Cabinet, Art Nouveau Pyrography, Grain Painted, Hinged Door, 26 In.	330
Softwood, Painted, Pennsylvania Dutch Designs, Dome Lid, D. Ellinger, 1941, 6 x 13 In.	2950
Stationary, Silver Overlay, ½ Barrel Shape, Rococo Style, Coated Cotton Lid, 12 x 9 In.	259
Stationery, George III, Mahogany, 14 In.	125

Brass, Bust, Boy Smoking Cigarette, Hat, Art Nouveau, Signed, Zelezny, c.1900, 3 ½ x 3 In.
$480

Ruby Lane

Brass, Letter Holder, Fish, Embossed, Wood Base, England, c.1900, 5 ¾ x 5 In.
$45

Ruby Lane

Bristol, Vase, Pansies, Yellow, 7½ In.
$32

Ruby Lane

Bronze, Censer, Qilin, Head Extended, Hinged Tail Reservoir, Chinese, 1800s, 5 In.
$360

Selkirk Auctioneers & Appraisers

TIP
Dust your bronze, then try the Chinese method of polishing. Rub the bronze with the palm of your hand. This puts a little oil on the metal.

Bronze, Mirror, Gilt, 8 Lobed, Mythical Beasts, Grapevines, Flower Shape, Knob, Chinese, 7 In.
$1,416

Brunk Auctions

Bronze, Plaque, Honey Bee, Honeycomb Rondel, Raised Border, Patina, Round, c.1910, 32 In.
$10,455

Skinner, Inc.

Sterling Silver, Etched, Venice Canal, Hinged Lid, Buccellati, 1900s, 5 ½ x 7 In. 2295
Storage, Basswood & White Pine, Putty Design, Wire Handles, Dome Lid, c.1830, 11 x 24 In. 930
Storage, Book Shape, Grain Painted, Diamond Shape Escutcheon, Hinged Lid, 11 x 9 In. 652
Storage, Camphorwood, Mother-Of-Pearl Inlay, Scallop Skirt, Lid, c.1890, 6 x 12 In. 86
Storage, Coca, Carved, Scallop Shell Shape, Flowers, Hinged Lid, Spain, 1700s, 6 x 9 In. 2040
Storage, Flame Mahogany, Shaped Base, Mirror Veneers, Striped Inlay, Stencil, 7 x 12 ½ In. 242
Storage, Lacquer, Black, Brass Mounts, Boating Scene, Trays, Hinged Lid, 5 x 23 In. 613
Storage, Oak, Carved, Brass, Sunbursts & Leaves, Hinged Fold-Back Lid, 1800s, 6 x 15 In. 431
Storage, Padouk, Slide Drawer, Side Handles, Brass Mounts, Hinged Lid, 1800s, 21 x 10 In. 1185
Storage, Softwood, Heart Design, Slide Lid, 1800s, 4 x 12 ½ In. 266
Storage, Vinegar Grain Painted, Caramel & Brown, Hinged Dome Lid, Lock, 1800s, 9 x 18 In. 420
Storage, Wood, Painted Folk Art Scenes, Hudson River, Flowers, 1800s, 14 x 19 In. 502
Storage, Wood, Rectangular, Painted Flowers & Fruits, Basket Weave Ground, 11 In. 593
Strong, Iron Clad, Lid, Handles, Painted Black, 1700s, 19 x 30 In. 1770
Strong, Wells Fargo, Wood, Green Paint, Stenciled, Iron Hardware, Leather, 1870s, 10 x 21 In. 6100
Tantalus, Ebony, Brass Bound, 4 Decanters, Cordials, 10 x 12 In. 275
Tantalus, Mahogany, 5 Gilt Decanters, England, 8 x 10 In. 300
Tantalus, Mother-Of-Pearl Inlay, 4 Decanters, 15 Glasses, Etched Leaves, 10 ¾ x 12 ½ In. 375
Tantalus, Victorian, Oak, 6 Shot Glasses, Secret Compartment, 3 Bottles, 10 Piece 188
Tobacco, Brass, Engraved, Hinged, Leaf Scrolls, Shield, Lions, Crown, Dutch, c.1777, 7 x 2 In. 195
Tobacco, Canted Corners, Stepped Base, Octagonal Lid, Round Knob, Iron, 7 x 5 In. 185
Trinket, Bentwood, Painted, Stylized Flower On Lid, Red Ground, Oval, 1800s, 2 x 4 ½ In. 325
Trinket, Black Lacquer, Gilt, Hinged Lid, Paw Feet, Garden, Figures, c.1840, 6 In. 295
Trinket, Capo-Di-Monte Style, Molded Cherubs, Reticulated Lid, Scroll Feet, c.1800s, 4 x 7 In. 448
Trinket, Chest Shape, Softwood, Paint, Black, Red, Trim Panels, Dome Lid, c.1800, 3 x 5 In. 649
Trinket, Gilt Brass, Cased Glass, Orange Enameled Leaves, Handles, Footed, c.1900, 5 In. 800
Trinket, Gilt Metal, Silvered, Peasants Harvesting Hay, Grapes, Bracket Feet, c.1910, 3 x 8 In. 593
Trinket, Glass, Bronze Ormolu Mounts, Hinged Lid, Lion's Mask, Handle, France, 3 x 5 In. *illus* 305
Trinket, Mixed Wood, Hinged Lid, Canted, Pinwheels, Fans, Lovebird, c.1890, 8 x 10 In. 431
Trinket, Porcelain, Square, White, Green Jungle Leaves, Toucan Handle, Lid, Hermes, 6 x 3 In. 475
Trinket, Round, Black Opal, Flower Design, Leaves, Red, Green, Brown, 1926, 8 In. Diam. 4140
Trinket, Sevres Style, Seated Couple, Turquoise, Gilt Scroll, Hinged Lid, c.1890, 7 In. Diam. 538
Trinket, Softwood, Paint, Blue, White Trim, Flowers, Leaves, Wire Hinges, c.1800, 4 x 8 In. 177
Trinket, Vine Handle, Round, Rose Shape, Shaped Petals, Budding Vine Foot, Lid, 1800s, 3 x 3 In. 531
Trinket, Wood, Lid With Canted Edges, Star & Fan Inlay, 1800s, 8 x 12 In. 246
Trinket, Wood, Paint, Center Tree, Flowers, A.P., Tin Hasp, Wire Hinges, Lid, 1800s, 11 x 9 In. 4130
Wall, Mixed Wood, Red Paint, Arched Backboard, 1800s, 8 x 12 In. 472
Wall, Wood, Smoke Grained Paint, Lollipop Hanger, Open Well, c.1900, 15 x 5 In. 1185
Wallpaper Over Wood, Board, Stripe, Green, Red, Tan, White, Oval, Lid, 8 x 15 x 12 In. 576
Wood, Blue & White Porcelain Panels, Keyhole, 7 x 12 In. 403
Wood, Feather Grain Design, Stenciled, Lid, Lock, 1800s, 4 x 13 x 9 In. 130
Wood, Oak, Inlaid Bands, 3 Colors, English Style Lock, Dovetailed, 13 x 9 In. 47
Wood, Panels, 5 Drawers, Each Painted, Country Scenes, Flip Top, Mirror, 12 x 6 ¼ In. 123
Wood, Pine, Painted, Feathered Design, Blue, Brass Pulls, c.1825, 4 x 8 x 4 In. 2214
Wood, Pine, Painted, Red Over Orange, Dovetailed, c.1850, 11 x 29 x 14 In. 219
Wood, Pine, Red Over Yellow Grain Painting, Stenciled, House, c.1830, 12 x 25 In. 813
Wood, Pine, Sponge Paint, Block Printed Wallpaper, Varnish, Dome Lid, 12 x 19 In. 125
Wood, Seed, Red Paint, Hinged Slant Lid, Interior Compartments, 10 Drawers, 1800s, 8 x 28 In. 2478
Wood, Tax Stamps, Painted, Flowers, Franklin County Juvenile Center Detention Home, 8 x 5 In. 561
Wood, Walnut, Velvet Lined, Crowned Double Armorial, Birds, Vines, 3 ½ x 12 In. 2400
Wood, Yew, Boulle Style, Engraved Brass, Mother-Of-Pearl, Tortoiseshell, c.1900, 11 x 8 In. 570
Work, Calamander, Brassbound, Shield, Drawers, Velvet Lined, Lift Lid, c.1900, 8 x 14 In. 738
Writing, Desk, Walnut, Burl, Shaped, Curved Side, Lift Dome Lid, 1800s, 6 x 9 x 6 In. 397
Writing, George I, Walnut, Drop Front, Sliding Supports, Drawer, c.1720, 13 x 17 In. 767
Writing, Mahogany, Brass Shield, Engraved, Lifting Tray, 11 x 8 In. 276
Writing, Oak, Jacobean, Hinged Slant Lid, Carved Swirls, Molded Edge, c.1700, 25 x 15 In. 201

BOY SCOUT collectibles include any material related to scouting, including patches, manuals, and uniforms. The Boy Scout movement in the United States started in 1910. The first Jamboree was held in 1937. Girl Scout items are listed under their own heading.

Ax, Marked, Be Prepared, Sheath, Collins, 14 ½ In. 65
Belt, Khaki Fabric, Metal Buckle, Insignia, Pat Aug. 13, 1912 & Feb. 25, 1913, 37 In. 20
Book, Den Mother's Den Book, 160 Pages, 1962, 7 x 5 In. 8
Book, Music & Bugling, Merit Badge Series, 36 Pages, 1947, 5 ½ x 8 In. 10
Bowl, World Jamboree, Idaho, USA, Logo, Mountains, 1967, 6 ¾ In. 20

Canteen, Aluminum, 2 Flap Case, Shoulder Strap, 1950s, 7 ½ In. 36
Canteen, Aluminum, Green, Canvas, Strap *illus* 65
Fire Starter Kit, Hot Spark, Red Vinyl Case 20
Handbook For Boys, 1st Edition, 30th Printing, 1938 80
Handbook, 11th Edition, 1998 9
Hat, Garrison Type, Olive Green, Insignia, 1960s, 11 x 4 ¾ In. 14
Knife, 4 Blades, Folding, Logo, Imperial 35
Knife, Hunting, Insignia, Leather Sheath, 8 ½ In. 70
Mug, W.D. Boyce Council Scout Show, Porcelain, 1991 10
Patch, Valley Forge Pilgrimage, BSA, Pennsylvania, Red, White, Blue, 1971 13
Pin, 2 Scouts, 1st Annual Boy Scout Celebration, 1918, 1 ¾ In. 374
Pin, Celluloid, We're Backing Boy Scouts, Red, White, Blue, Logo, 1960s, ⅞ In. 18
Pin, Fleur-De-Lis, BS Of A, c.1911, 1 ½ In. 29
Pin, Heart Shape, Red Enameled Fleur-De-Lis, 14K Gold, C Clasp, 1 In. 40
Plaque, Wolf's Head, Over Crescent Shape Banner, Boy Scouts, Cast Iron, 19 x 12 In. 246
Utensils, Spoon, Fork, Knife, Stainless Steel, Imperial, Logo, Case, 1950s 19
Whistle, Bronze, Cylindrical, c.1909, 2 ⅝ In. 165
Whistle, Nickel Plate, Insignia, USA, 2 In. 15

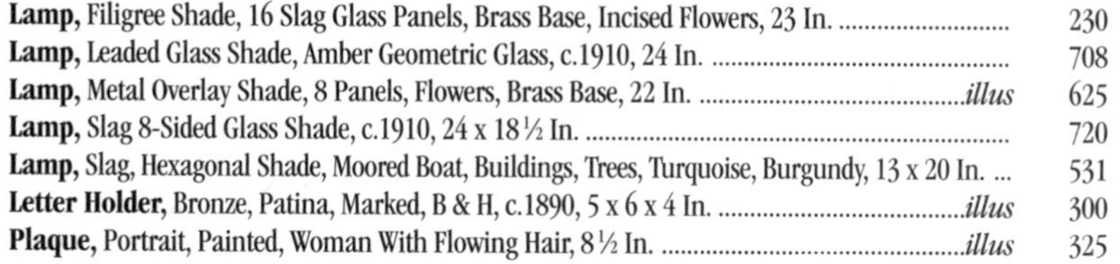

BRADLEY & HUBBARD is a name found on many metal objects. Walter Hubbard and his brother-in-law, Nathaniel Lyman Bradley, started making cast iron clocks, tables, frames, andirons, bookends, doorstops, lamps, chandeliers, sconces, and sewing birds in 1854 in Meriden, Connecticut. The company became Bradley & Hubbard Manufacturing Company in 1875. Charles Parker Company bought the firm in 1940. Bradley & Hubbard items may be found in other sections that include metal.

Lamp, Filigree Shade, 16 Slag Glass Panels, Brass Base, Incised Flowers, 23 In. 230
Lamp, Leaded Glass Shade, Amber Geometric Glass, c.1910, 24 In. 708
Lamp, Metal Overlay Shade, 8 Panels, Flowers, Brass Base, 22 In. *illus* 625
Lamp, Slag 8-Sided Glass Shade, c.1910, 24 x 18 ½ In. 720
Lamp, Slag, Hexagonal Shade, Moored Boat, Buildings, Trees, Turquoise, Burgundy, 13 x 20 In. ... 531
Letter Holder, Bronze, Patina, Marked, B & H, c.1890, 5 x 6 x 4 In. *illus* 300
Plaque, Portrait, Painted, Woman With Flowing Hair, 8 ½ In. *illus* 325

BRASS has been used for decorative pieces and useful tablewares since ancient times. It is an alloy of copper, zinc, and other metals. Additional brass items may be found under Bell, Candlestick, Tool, or Trivet.

Alms Dish, Adam & Eve, Gothic Script, Hammered Sides, 13 ¼ In. 1556
Alms Dish, Nuremberg, Annunciation, Punched Border, 17 ½ In. 2334
Basket, Wirework, Woven, Rollover Rim, 3 ½ x 10 ¾ In. 120
Bed Warmer, Metal Handle, Round, Heart Cutout Design, 1800s, 34 In. 62
Bowl, Footed, Applied Decoration, Asia, 5 x 12 In. 24
Bowl, Scroll Handle, 11 ½ In. 63
Bucket, Coal, Victorian, High Relief, 33 ½ In. 125
Bust, Boy Smoking Cigarette, Hat, Art Nouveau, Signed, Zelezny, c.1900, 3 ½ x 3 In. *illus* 480
Card Case, Writhing Dragon, Mount Fuji, Phoenix, Etched, c.1900, 3 ½ In. 1071
Chalice, Gilt Wash, Lid, 11 x 4 In. 236
Chestnut Roaster, Incised Star, Geometric Hinged Lid Pan, Wood Shaft, 43 ½ x 12 In. 94
Coal Bin, Hinged Lid, Relief Picture Of Tavern Scenes, 17 x 24 In. 69
Coffee Set, Coffeepot, Sugar & Creamer, Lacquer, Banded, Tommy Parzinger, 16 x 4 ¾ In. 240
Dish, Alms, St. George, Slaying Dragon, Wide Rim, Flowers, Round, 14 Diam. 544
Dish, Dwarfs Standing, Holding Each End, Round, 7 x 3 In. 120
Diver Helmet, Miniature, 7 In. 48
Doorknocker, Inscribed, Met Peynen Dve De Weerelt 1567, Man, Sack, 6 ½ x 5 In. 145
Figurine, Krishna, Dancing On Serpent Kaliya, Patina, 7 x 2 ¾ In. 94
Gong, Asian, 19 ¼ In. 47
Jam Pan, Folding Handle, Impressed, Hiram Hayden, Ct., c.1834, 16 ½ x 14 In. 123
Jardiniere, Bamboo, 4-Footed, 8 ½ In. 63
Jardiniere, Baroque, Oval, Lobed Body, Lion Mask, Paw Feet, 6 x 13 In. 480
Jardiniere, Oval, Winged Cherub Heads, Snake Handles, Footed, Italy, c.1800, 10 x 21 In. 780
Jug, Applied C-Scroll Handle, Lid, 19 x 15 In. 396
Kettle Stand, Cabriole Front Legs, Pierced Heart Design, Wrought Iron Frame, 1800s, 18 In. 63
Kettle, Apple, Iron Hanger, Copper Rivets, c.1870, 25 x 17 In. 180
Lectern, Eagle, Perched On HalfHemisphere, Spread Wings, Cast, 21 ½ x 19 ½ In. 353
Letter Holder, Fish, Embossed, Wood Base, England, c.1900, 5 ¾ x 5 In. *illus* 45
Letter Stand, Inkwell, Porcelain, Scrolling, Footed, 9 x 9 In. 240

Bronze, Sculpture, Abstract, Curtis Jere, 1969, 14 x 10 In.
$915

Palm Beach Modern Auctions

Bronze, Sculpture, Barye, Antoine-Louis, Tigre Qui Marche, Walking Tiger, Marble, 1891, 10 x 17 In.
$2,750

Rago Arts and Auction Center

Bronze, Sculpture, Berge, Edward, Wildflower, Signed, American Art Foundry, 7 In.
$1,000

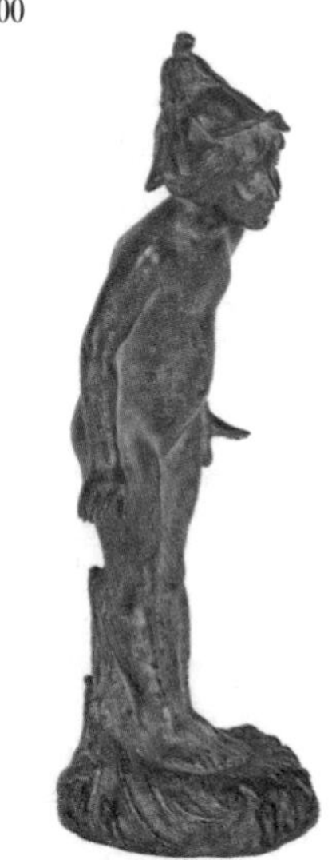

Rago Arts and Auction Center

This is an edited listing of current prices. Visit **Kovels.com** to check thousands of prices from previous years and sign up for free information on trends, tips, reproductions, marks, and more.

Bronze, Sculpture, Bergman, Franz, Stag, Cold Paint, Vienna, c.1915, 11 x 7 ½ In.
$2,375

New Orleans (Cakebread)

Bronze, Sculpture, Bergman, Man, Female Slave, Carpet, Namgreb, c.1900, 7 x 9 In.
$2,460

Skinner, Inc.

Bronze, Sculpture, Buddha, Amida, Seated, Double Lotus, Lacquer, Gilt, 1800s, 14 In.
$3,396

James D. Julia Auctioneers

Liqueur Set, 6 Glasses, Tray, Nickel Plated, Female Nude Stems, Karl Hagenauer, 7 Piece 1230
Mortar & Pestle, Flared Rim, Ring Foot, Banded, Dumbbell Shape Pestle, 1800s, 4 ½ In. 63
Planter, Art Deco, Pierced Ovals, Leaves, Scrolls, Draped Urn, c.1930, 18 x 48 In. 1062
Plaque, Relief, Lohengrin & Elsa, Bright Finish, 11 x 8 In. 150
Prayer Wheel, White Metal, Bone, Wood Handle, 1800s, 10 In. 92
Safety Pin, Style Of Carl Aubock, Opens, 36 In. 750
Samovar, Ebonized Handles, Claw Feet, 21 In. 156
Sculpture, Bird, Sergio Bustamante, 28 ¾ x 25 In. 1320
Sculpture, Figural, Toero, Miguel Berrocal, Stamped, 1970s, 11 ½ x 8 In. 3000
Sculpture, Prancing Colt, Cube Base, 66 x 24 In., Pair 1430
Sculpture, Sailing Ship, 3 Masts, C. Jere, 34 x 34 In. 247
Sculpture, Wall, 11 Flying Birds, 34 x 48 In. 338
Shade, Punched, Cone Shape, Repousse Ships, Beaded Fringe, Newcomb, 3 ½ x 5 ¾ In. 153
Spoon Mold, Pewter, Impressed 2, 2 Sections, 1800s, 10 In. 130
Taper Jack, Tooled Base, Continental, Early 1700s, 8 ½ In. 660
Tie Rack, 5 Plated Hooks, Indian Profile Cast, Painted, 6 ½ x 12 In. 219
Tipstaff, Crown Shape Top, Shaped Handle, Gilt Lacquer, c.1875, 10 x 2 In. 937
Tobacco Box, Copper Secondary, Engraved, Hunt Scenes, 4 Seasons, Oval, Dutch, 6 In. 281
Towel Rack, Edwardian, 3 Dowels, 34 ¾ x 26 ½ In. 420
Urn, Gilt, Copper Repousse, J.G. & Sons, England, c.1890, 10 ½ In. 210
Vase, Nickel Plate, Flavio Gill, 13 x 12 In. 240
Vase, Pedestal Base, Handles, Chinese, c.1880, 10 In. 60
Wine Cooler, Oval, Paw & Ball Feet, Lion's Head Ring Handles, c.1810, 15 x 24 In. 1625

BRASTOFF, *see Sascha Brastoff category.*

BREAD PLATE, *see various silver categories, porcelain factories, and pressed glass patterns.*

BRIDE'S BOWLS OR BASKETS were usually one-of-a-kind novelties made in American and European glass factories. They were especially popular about 1880 when the decorated basket was often given as a wedding gift. Cut glass baskets were popular after 1890. All bride's bowls lost favor about 1905. Bride's bowls and baskets may also be found in other glass sections. Check the index at the back of the book.

Cranberry Glass, Cased, Silver Plate Frame, 12 x 9 ½ In. 184
Cranberry Glass, Clear Rigaree, Rockford Silver Plate Stand, 2 Handles, 9 ¾ In. 173
Cranberry Ruffled Bowl, Silver Plate Frame, E.G. Webster, c.1890, 13 x 11 In. 210
Filigree Openwork Basket, Cartouches, Silver Frame, Reed & Barton, 17 x 13 In. 500
Flowers, Bead Trim, Handle, Silver Plate Frame, 10 x 10 In. 31
Pink Glass, Gilt Garland, Tassels, Footed, England, c.1890, 9 x 8 ¼ In. 180
Repousse Decoration, Leaves, 3 x 4 ¼ In., Pair 338
Repousse Flowers, Putti, Continental, 4 x 12 ½ In. 554
Ruffled, Cranberry Glass, Leaves, Silver Plate Flame, James W. Tufts. Co., 13 In. 172
Satin Glass, Enameled, Ruffled Rim, Silvered Handle, c.1890, 12 x 11 ¾ In. 180

BRISTOL glass was made in Bristol, England, after the 1700s. The Bristol glass most often seen today is a Victorian, lightweight opaque glass that is often blue. Some of the glass was decorated with enamels.

Bottle, White, Rectangular Bottles, Gilded Corners, Square Stopper, 4 ½ x 2 ½ In. 61
Bottle, White, Teardrop Stoppers, Flower Swags, 11 ½ x 4 In., Pair 92
Box, Victorian, Small Portrait, Frosted, Translucent Dog Finial, 8 ½ x 9 ½ In. 123
Vase, Greek, Chariots, Horses, Decoration, 17 ¾ In., Pair 281
Vase, Pansies, Yellow, 7 ½ In. .... *illus* 32
Vase, White Birds, Flowers, Landscape, 10 ¾ In., Pair 36

BRITANNIA, *see Pewter category*

BRONZE is an alloy of copper, tin, and other metals. It is used to make figurines, lamps, and other decorative objects. Bronze lamps are listed in the Lamp category. Pieces listed here date from the eighteenth, nineteenth, and twentieth centuries.

Ashtray, Fish Swimming, Swirling Water, Blue Eye, Round, 3 ¾ In. 1035
Book Holder, Renaissance Revival, Slide, Reticulated, Columns, Lion's Head, Dragons, 23 x 5 In. 121
Bowl, Applied Putti & Cherubs, Playing, Rolling, Climbing, 10 x 16 ½ In. 189
Bowl, Carved Landscape Scene, Gilt, Wide Rim, Ring Foot, 3 ½ In. 3705
Bowl, Center, 2 Nude Women, Hoisting Themselves Over Edge, 8 x 15 In. 3910
Bowl, Gilt, Pedestal Foot, Eagle Handles, Stippled, Leaf Border, c.1900, 8 x 10 In. 1000

Bronze, Sculpture, Buddha, Head, Gilt, Curled Hair Knots, Long Earlobes, Thai, c.1900, 12 In.
$570

Selkirk Auctioneers & Appraisers

Bronze, Sculpture, Cannon, Relief, Maiden, Suit Of Armor, Wood Base, Gorham, 1800s, 14 In., Pair
$2,583

Skinner, Inc.

Bronze, Sculpture, Caravanniez, A., Medieval Figure In Armor, Barbedienne Foundry, 17 In.
$1,920

Cowan Auctions

TIP
Don't keep a house key in an obvious spot in the garage.

Bronze, Sculpture, De Tirtoff, Romain, Emerald Vase, Maiden, Vase Over Head, 1988, 24 In.
$2,460

Skinner, Inc.

Bronze, Sculpture, Ibex, Standing, Amethyst Crystals, Cold Paint, Austria, c.1890, 7 In.
$300

Cowan Auctions

TIP
Be careful when cleaning bronze figurines, lamp bases, bowls, etc. Never use steel wool, stiff brushes, or chemicals.

Bronze, Sculpture, Kalish, Max, US Army Officer, Walter Reed, c.1910, 17 In.
$2,562

DuMouchelles Art Gallery

Bronze, Sculpture, Mene, P.J., Elk, Tree Stump, Marble Base, c.1850, 14 ½ In.
$472

Brunk Auctions

Bronze, Sculpture, Psyche, Seminude, Seated, Bent Knee, Wings, Drape, France, c.1850, 9 In.
$660

Cowan Auctions

Bronze, Sculpture, Reverie, Bust, Porcelain, Gilt, Marble Base, J.M. Mengue, c.1913, 14 In.
$2,625

Rago Arts and Auction Center

TIP
Never wash a bronze. Never use metal polish on a bronze. Dust frequently.

Brushpot, Wavy Shaped, 16 Luohans, Cast, 3 ⅜ In. 356
Bust, After Morer, Salammbo, Turquoise, Glass, 17 ½ x 9 ¾ In. 4800
Bust, Athena Promachos, Greek Style, 7 ¼ x 9 ¾ In. 450
Bust, Bissell, Geo. E., Abraham Lincoln, Marble Plinth, c.1900, 20 In. 980
Bust, Catlett, Elizabeth, Singing Head, Woman, Bun, 1968, 5 ½ x 9 In. 16000
Bust, Froget, The Cardinal, 1800s, 8 x 5 In. 123
Bust, Head Of An African, 12 x 12 In. 840
Bust, Jacobs, Henri, Art Nouveau, 22 In. 250
Bust, Maiden, Carved White Marble, Bonnet, Bodice, Leaves, Marble Base, c.1900, 27 In. 1968
Bust, Man, Pointy Nose, Downcast Gaze, 19 ¾ In. 250
Bust, Russell, Charles M., Indian, Feathers In Hair, Square Marble Base, 9 ½ x 8 In. 342
Bust, Schiele, E., Selbstibildnis, Self-Portrait, Stamped, 1980, 11 x 7 In. 2838
Bust, Villanis, Emmanuel, Head Wrap, France, 9 ½ In. 1188
Bust, Wilhelm I, Signed, C. Steffens, c.1875, 10 In. 510
Bust, Woman, Gazing To Side, Hair Up, Bare Shoulders, Austria, c.1900, 20 In. 1062
Bust, Zeus Head, Curly Hair, Full Beard, Stand, 9 In. 549
Casket, Renaissance Revival, Dore, Leaves, Scroll, Putti, Stepped Edge, 1800s, 6 x 5 In. 106
Censer, Elephant Head Feet, Strap Handles, Tripod, Brown, 1700s, 6 ½ In. 618
Censer, Gilt, Flaring Rim, L-Shape Handles, Footed, Oval, c.1700, 7 In. 4740
Censer, Globe Shape, Tapered Neck, Scroll Handles, Mask Feet, Dragons, 18 x 19 In. 19600
Censer, Gold Inlay, Brown, Square, Bulging Sides, 2 Handles, Footed, 4 x 8 ½ In. 237
Censer, Gold Splashes, Monster Head Handles, Squat, Tripod, 10 In. 830
Censer, Goose, Lid, Standing, 10 x 12 In. 278
Censer, Lid, Turtle Knop, Japan, c.1910, 3 ¼ x 4 ¾ In. 150
Censer, Pierced Dome Lid, Dragon Finial, Stylized Leaves, Panels, Handles, 17 In. 870
Censer, Pierced Lid, Foo Dogs, Brocade Spheres, Squat, Footed, 1800s, 14 x 12 In. 988
Censer, Qilin, Head Extended, Hinged Tail Reservoir, Chinese, 1800s, 5 In. ....*illus* 360
Censer, Quatrelobed, Upright S-Shape Handles, Tripod, Bulbous Feet, 14 In. 711
Centerpiece, Art Nouveau, Gilt, Cobalt Blue Insert, France, 10 ½ x 26 In. 1380
Centerpiece, Bowl, Masks, Flower Swags, Serpent Handles, Round Foot, c.1890, 12 In. 3750
Centerpiece, Gilt, Gadrooned Bowl, Cartouches, Putti Supports, c.1900, 7 x 18 In. 2500
Centerpiece, Gilt, Tazza Supported By Nude Woman, 2 Tritons, Turtles, 21 ½ x 22 In. 3760
Chair, Anthropomorphic, Alejandro Colunga, Cold Painted, c.1980, 9 x 5 In. 1107
Charger, Sorenson, Carl, Arts & Crafts, Concentric Circles, 15 In. 91
Cup, Wine, Ritual, Tripod, Wide Rim, Greek Key Banding, Symbols, 6 x 7 In. 296
Decanter, Pinecone Stopper, 18 ½ In. 83
Dish, Vide-Poches, Art Nouveau, Albert Marionnet, France, 4 ¾ x 8 ½ In. 780
Epergne, Empire, Gilt, Reticulated Gallery, Fruit-Filled Bowls, 7 x 34 In. 8437
Epergne, Gilt, 3 Sections, Baluster Galleries, Reeded Edge, c.1890, 43 x 18 In. 3500
Epergne, Silvered, 3 Sections, Pierced Gallery, Ribbon, Scroll Feet, c.1900, 2 x 36 In. 1875
Ewer, Putti, Snake Entwined Handles, Gilt, Octagonal Base, 24 In. 813
Ewer, Silvered Putti, Carts, Cherubs On Handles, Continental, 21 x 10 In., Pair 400
Ewer, Triton, Bacchus, Neoclassical, Water & Wine, After John Flaxman, 18 In. 1024
Garniture, Gilt, Ebonized Wood, Eagles, Spheres, Column, Base, c.1890, 28 In., Pair 875
Garniture, Red Griotte Marble, Dragon Handles, Masks, Shaped Base, c.1865, 22 In., Pair 2337
Hand Mirror, Classical Figures, Leafy Scrolls, Putti, Reticulated Handle, c.1880, 13 In. 523
Hand Mirror, Handle, Symbols, Pine Tree, Cranes, Turtle, Bamboo Design, 11 x 7 In. 23
Incense Burner, Gilt, Qulin, Snarling, Hinged Head, Clouds, Snake, Claw Feet, 1600s, 9 In. 8766
Incense Burner, Group Of Devils, Japan, 20 x 15 In. 5865
Incense Burner, Hanging, Patinated, Eagle On Pine Branch, c.1900, 16 x 26 In. 2460
Jardiniere, Cranes, Rounded Rim, Paneled, Drop Handles, 9 ¼ x 10 ½ In. 302
Jardiniere, Gilt, Scrolling Handles, Bacchic Heads & Vine Leaves, Fluted Foot, c.1885, 9 In. 433
Jardiniere, Roaring Dragons, Tapered Sides, Frothy Waves, 14 ¼ x 20 In. 3341
Letter Rack, 4 Sections, Stepped, Acanthus, 9 ½ x 12 ¾ In. 157
Mirror, Gilt, 8 Lobed, Mythical Beasts, Grapevines, Flower Shape, Knob, Chinese, 7 In. ....*illus* 1416
Mirror, Scalloped Edge, Relief Flying Birds, Leaves, Silk Tassel, Chinese, 2 ¾ In. 100
Model, Cradle, Curule Base, Gilt Wreath, Gold Satin Lined, Dore Trim, c.1900, 6 x 6 In. 1250
Mortar, Mask, Swags, Human Head Handles, Italy, 8 In. 1556
Pail, Asperges, Medieval Style, Religious Figures, Inscription, 1800s, 11 x 5 In. 593
Pitcher, Ritual, Animal Handle, Wavy Rim, Inlaid Silver, Banding, c.1800, 3 x 6 In. 154
Placard Stand, Gilt, Top Loading, On Pole, Triangular Pedestal, 65 x 23 In. 142
Plaque, Eagle, Spread Wings, Head Turned, Perched On Arrows, Verdigris, 10 x 36 In. 1185
Plaque, Female Nude, Long Hair, Musician, 18 ¾ x 14 ½ In. 780
Plaque, Honey Bee, Honeycomb Rondel, Raised Border, Patina, Round, c.1910, 32 In. ....*illus* 10455
Plaque, Mack, B., Mother, Nude Infant, Relief, 33 x 26 ½ In. 1342
Plaque, Woman, Tray Of Fruit, Gadrooned Border, Patina, 19 In. 123

Sculpture, 2 Dogs, Hounds, Prowling, Hunting, Naturalistic Base, c.1850, 5 ½ x 15 In. 461
Sculpture, 2 Dogs, Tavern, Wood Bench & Table, Sausage, Geschutzt, 1 ½ x 2 ¾ In. 242
Sculpture, 2 Girls, Nude, Playing Leapfrog, Oval Base, Germany, c.1900, 17 In. 1978
Sculpture, 2 Women, 1 Holding Letter, Rocky Base, 1900s, 19 ½ In. 863
Sculpture, A La Fontain, Woman & Child, Water Pitcher, Girl Drinking, c.1900, 30 In. 2375
Sculpture, Abstract, Curtis Jere, 1969, 14 x 10 In. ....*illus* 915
Sculpture, Abstract, Torso, Jean Arp, 1956, 16 ½ x 6 In. 960
Sculpture, Allegorical Figures, French Empire, Column, Gilt Plaques, Dore, 12 In., Pair 4062
Sculpture, Aloysius Gonzaga As Young Boy, Seated, Round Base, c.1890, 37 In. 922
Sculpture, Amadio, Metello, Narcissus, Verdigris Patina, 25 x 9 In. 922
Sculpture, Amendola, G.B., Notary, Umbrella, 21 ¼ x 8 In. 1830
Sculpture, Angel, Nude Woman, Spread Wings, Round Stepped Base, 24 In. 1830
Sculpture, Arabian Rug Dealer, Man Spreading Out Rug, 6 ½ x 7 In. 1265
Sculpture, Arson, Alphonse, 2 Birds, 8 x 7 In. 115
Sculpture, Artemis, Nude, Goddess Of Hunting, Stag, Denmark, 20 ½ x 17 In. 5250
Sculpture, Audubon, Eagle, Stretching Wings, 17 x 14 In. 726
Sculpture, Autumn Harvest, Woman With Rake, Patina, France, c.1900, 16 In. 563
Sculpture, Baboon Mother & Baby, On Her Back, Patina, 9 x 9 In. 1062
Sculpture, Baigneuse, Patina, After Etienne Maurice Falconet, c.1890, 15 ¾ In. 354
Sculpture, Baker, Bryant, Pioneer Woman, Brown Patina, Marble Base, 1927, 17 ½ In. 1003
Sculpture, Barthelemy, Bone, Lute Players, 1920s, 9 x 3 ½ In. 484
Sculpture, Barye, Antoine-Louis, Cat, Seated, Signed, 2 ½ In. 1298
Sculpture, Barye, Antoine-Louis, Pheasant, Standing, Stone Base, 13 x 21 In. 750
Sculpture, Barye, Antoine-Louis, Tigre Qui Marche, Walking Tiger, Marble, 1891, 10 x 17 In. *illus* 2750
Sculpture, Barye, Elephant, Trotting, 5 x 5 ½ In. 1076
Sculpture, Barye, Lion & Wild Boar, 10 x 18 In. 4305
Sculpture, Barye, Lion, Climbing Mound, 5 In. 984
Sculpture, Bear, Eating Grapes, Russia, 12 ¾ x 6 ½ In. 726
Sculpture, Bearden, J., Harry Box, Koosh Ball Shape, Painted Steel, Fused, 14 x 20 In. 2176
Sculpture, Benkei, Seated, Leg Outstretched, Holds Bell, Gilt Flowers, 13 ½ In. 11688
Sculpture, Berge, Edward, Nude Boy, Looking Down, Green, 8 In. 984
Sculpture, Berge, Edward, Nude Girl Holding Hat, 7 ½ In. 1353
Sculpture, Berge, Edward, Wildflower, Signed, American Art Foundry, 7 In. ....*illus* 1000
Sculpture, Bergman, Franz, Stag, Cold Paint, Vienna, c.1915, 11 x 7 ½ In. ....*illus* 2375
Sculpture, Bergman, Man, Female Slave, Carpet, Namgreb, c.1900, 7 x 9 In. ....*illus* 2460
Sculpture, Bergman, Owl Standing On Books, Cold Paint, 3 ¾ x 1 ¾ In. 172
Sculpture, Boar, Running, Tail Up, Brown, 1900s, 8 x 13 In. 830
Sculpture, Bonduel, L., L'Alerte, Nude Man On Ground, 1889, 21 ¼ x 30 ½ In. 1875
Sculpture, Bone, Mephistopheles, 10 ½ In. 2214
Sculpture, Bonheur, I., 2 Rams, Peyrol Foundry, c.1870, 8 x 14 x 5 In. 5580
Sculpture, Boomer, Bob, Native American Woman, 3 Baskets, 1997, 19 ½ x 8 ½ In. 690
Sculpture, Boomer, Bob, Native American Woman, Robe, 1984, 11 ½ x 7 ½ In. 258
Sculpture, Bouval, Maurice, Blacksmith, Patina, Signed, 25 ½ In. 767
Sculpture, Boy Pushing Wheelbarrow, 8 ½ x 12 ½ In. 100
Sculpture, Boyce, R., Proteus, Nude, Bubbles In Hair & Beard, Zebrawood Base, 1964, 8 In. 492
Sculpture, Brilliant, Fredda, 3 Graces, Signed, 1900s, 13 In., 3 Piece 826
Sculpture, Bronco Buster, Cowboy On Bucking Bronco, Marble Base, 21 In. 519
Sculpture, Brown, D., 2 Flying Ducks, Marble Base, 15 ½ x 22 ½ In. 124
Sculpture, Buddha, Amida, Seated, Double Lotus, Lacquer, Gilt, 1800s, 14 In. ....*illus* 3396
Sculpture, Buddha, Disciples, Hands In Prayer, Lotus Bases, 16 ½ In., Pair 720
Sculpture, Buddha, Head, Gilt, Curled Hair Knots, Long Earlobes, Thai, c.1900, 12 In. ......*illus* 570
Sculpture, Buddha, Seated, Lotus Position, Hands In Meditation Gesture, 15 In. 593
Sculpture, Buddha, Seated, Shaped Outswept Feet, Flower, Square Base, 3 x 3 In. 488
Sculpture, Buddha, Standing, Right Hand In Abhaya, Wood Base, Thailand, c.1800, 15 x 3 In. 469
Sculpture, Cannon, Relief, Maiden, Suit Of Armor, Wood Base, Gorham, 1800s, 14 In., Pair ...*illus* 2583
Sculpture, Caravanniez, A., Medieval Figure In Armor, Barbedienne Foundry, 17 In. ....*illus* 1920
Sculpture, Carone, Nicolas, Standing Woman's Torso, Legs, Feet, No Head, 12 x 4 In. 2520
Sculpture, Cat, Egyptian, 5 In. 100
Sculpture, Cat, Egyptian, 18 ¼ In. 461
Sculpture, Cavalry Man, Cowboy Standing On Rock, Aiming Rifle, 1984, 7 x 11 In. 314
Sculpture, Cellini, Benvenuto, Mercury, Patina, Italy, 26 x 7 In. 406
Sculpture, Chargant, Taureau, Bull, Tail Up, Head Down, Striding, Base, c.1910, 9 x 15 In. 2125
Sculpture, Chaudet, Antoine-Denis, Shepherd Phorbus Rescuing Oedipus, c.1910, 17 x 6 In. 676
Sculpture, Chaudet, Cupid, Playing, Butterfly, 1800s, 9 x 7 ¾ In. 549
Sculpture, Cheyenne Warrior On Horseback, Holding Spear, 1900s, 20 In. 735
Sculpture, Chinese Scholar, Robed, Seated, Gilt, Lucite Stand, 8 x 5 ½ In. 11800

Bronze, Sculpture, Sappho, Moreau, Mathurin, Relief Plaque, Signed, 24 x 26 In.
$1,230

Skinner, Inc.

Bronze, Sculpture, Six, Michael, Pheasants, Cold Paint, Austria, c.1900, 9 x 19 In.
$840

Cowan Auctions

Bronze, Sculpture, The Dancer, Woman Holding Drape, Signed, Slate Base, c.1900, 17 In.
$1,481

James D. Julia Auctioneers

Ever "Read" a Statue?
Sculptors follow a historic set of rules for making a statue of a rider on horseback. If the horse is standing on all four legs, and the rider mounted, the rider is a national hero. If the horse has three legs on the ground and a mounted rider, the rider died as a result of battle injuries. If the horse has only two legs on the ground, and a mounted rider, the rider died in battle. And if the rider is standing beside the horse, the horse and rider were killed.

Bronze, Sculpture, Tiger, Roaring, Inlaid Stone Eyes, Marked, Japan, c.1890, 8 ½ x 19 In.
$861

New Orleans (Cakebread)

Bronze, Sculpture, Weems, K. L., Kangaroo, Signed, 20th Century, 13 x 20 In.
$6,325

Cottone Auctions

Bronze, Sculpture, Wright, Russel, Seal, Whoozoo, U.S.A., 1930, 3 x 3 In.
$625

Rago Arts and Auction Center

Sculpture, Chinese Woman, Holding Urn, 19th Century, 5 In. 400
Sculpture, Chiparus, C.H., Dancer, Marble Base, 16 ½ x 15 In. 10200
Sculpture, Chiparus, D., Dancer, Art Deco Woman, Verdigris Patina, Green Marble, 8 x 15 In. .. 570
Sculpture, Chope, Ed, Eagles In Battle, Multicolor, 52 x 26 In. 3900
Sculpture, Chope, Who's Catch, Eagle, Spread Wings, Bass, c.1993, 36 ¾ In. 5400
Sculpture, Claudion, Courting Couple, Stepped Marble Base, Marked, c.1900, 14 x 16 x 7 In. ... 738
Sculpture, Cleopatra, Seated, Holding Fan, Base, France, c.1890, 29 In. 5000
Sculpture, Clodion, Claude Michel, Bacchanalian Group, Patina, 21 In. 1416
Sculpture, Colinet, J.R., Andalusian Dancer, Poppies In Hair, Lion Skin, Marble Base, 29 In. 5366
Sculpture, Consagra, Pietro, Bozzetto I, 1966, 8 ¼ x 6 In. 4200
Sculpture, Continental, Bird, Nest, 2 ¾ x 3 In. 480
Sculpture, Cotterill, Tim, Owl, Big Foot, 1998, 3 ½ x 10 ¼ In. 1089
Sculpture, Courting Peasant Couple, Marble Base, 14 x 13 In. 156
Sculpture, Cowboy On Bronco, Whip, Rearing, Bronco Buster, Marble Base, 21 x 17 In. 489
Sculpture, Cronqvist, Lena, Girl, Bowl, Signed, 8 x 5 ½ In. 3444
Sculpture, Dana, Girl, Bench, Reading, Book, Signed, 35 x 31 In. 1200
Sculpture, Dancer, Bending To Lift Hem Of Skirt, c.1910, 20 x 10 In. 687
Sculpture, Dancer, Midriff Gown, Leg Extended Back, Arm Draped, Marble Base, 13 x 15 In. 316
Sculpture, Dancer, Wearing Boots, Feathered Hat, Midriff Dress, Globe Base, 21 In. 173
Sculpture, David, Jose Maria, Walrus, Long Tusks, 13 ¼ In. 11670
Sculpture, Davidson, Jim, Little Golfer, Cold Paint, Marked, 48 In. 1599
Sculpture, De Tirtoff, Romain, Emerald Vase, Maiden, Vase Over Head, 1988, 24 In. ....*illus* 2460
Sculpture, Deity, Ushnishavijaya, 8 Arms, Wood Stand, 9 In. 1680
Sculpture, Dog, Greyhound, Reclining, Crossed Paws, c.1825, 6 x 3 ¾ In. 270
Sculpture, Dog, Scottie, Standing, Ears Up, Tail Straight Up, Cast, Art Deco, c.1940, 8 In. 92
Sculpture, Dog, Terrier, Playing With Snail, Rocky Base, c.1880, 4 ½ x 7 In. 277
Sculpture, Dolphins, Leaping From Water, Round Marble Base, 23 In., Pair 105
Sculpture, Dragon, Coiled, Flaming Pearl Of Wisdom, Cast, Chinese, 2 x 2 ½ In. 293
Sculpture, Dragon, Gothic Revival, Spread Wings, Scrolling Rail, 21 ¾ In. 406
Sculpture, Dragon, Incense Burner, Koro, Inset Cover, Engraved Scales, Flower Tile, 9 In. 354
Sculpture, Draped Woman, 2 Children, Oval Wood Base, France, 1910, 13 In. 720
Sculpture, Drouot, E., Slave Fighting Tiger, 26 In. 1875
Sculpture, Drouot, Edouard, Samson, Verdigris Patina, Signed, 23 In. 738
Sculpture, Ducks, In Water, In Tree, Ducklings, France, 13 ½ x 13 In. 265
Sculpture, Dying Gaul, 1700s, 13 x 29 In. 1180
Sculpture, Egyptian Cat, Seated On Haunches, Curled Tail, Wood Base, 6 In. 4886
Sculpture, Elephant, Trunk Up, Ivory Tusks, Black Marble Base, c.1900, 15 x 23 In. 1464
Sculpture, Erte, Astra, Art Deco, Woman, Necklace, Teal Skirt, c.1987, 19 x 10 ½ In. 2299
Sculpture, Erte, Fireleaves, Multicolor, 1988, 19 In. 2400
Sculpture, Erte, Wedding, Multicolor, France, 1986, 16 x 17 In. 3000
Sculpture, Erte, Woman, Swinging Arms, Blue Dress, 1980, 15 ½ In. 2125
Sculpture, Farnese Bull, 20 x 16 ¾ In. 4275
Sculpture, Fells, Augusta, For Youngest, Child Face, Medallion, Cast, 1982, 7 x 2 In. 544
Sculpture, Female Torso, Nude, 20th Century School, 12 x 5 In. 720
Sculpture, Ferrand, Ernest Justin, Pair Of Lovers, Signed, c.1900, 17 ¼ In. 600
Sculpture, Ferville-Suan, Charles, La Fraicheur, Draped Man, Standing Over Snake, 37 In. 2706
Sculpture, Filgner, V., Conductor, Arm Raised, 14 In. 60
Sculpture, Fix-Masseau, Pierre Felix, Le Secret, Foundry Mark, c.1900, 11 x 2 ½ In. 2952
Sculpture, Flowers In Vase, Gilt, 22 x 9 ½ In. 522
Sculpture, Foley, J.H., Oliver Goldsmith, 20 In. 5250
Sculpture, Fontana Delle Tartarughe, 4 Warriors In Training, Turtles, c.1890, 25 x 12 In. 1250
Sculpture, Fortuna, Raised Arm, Foot On Wheel, Marble Column Base, 1900s, 34 In. 461
Sculpture, Fremiet, Cat, Sitting, 5 In. 338
Sculpture, Frontier Justice, Native American On Horseback, Base, 1900s, 23 x 14 In. 615
Sculpture, Gagne, Boy, Playing Marbles, Kneeling, c.1875, 8 x 5 x 7 In. 675
Sculpture, Gambler, Bust Of Wild West Sheriff, Rope, 4 Aces, Marble Base, 14 In. 1220
Sculpture, Gilt, Kubera, God Of Wealth, Sino-Tibetan, Double Lotus Throne, 11 In. 4130
Sculpture, Grant, Speed, Bucking Horse, Rider, 1970, 16 ½ x 10 In. 900
Sculpture, Grausman, Philip, Bean, Spouting, 1965, 5 x 4 In. 1320
Sculpture, Grediaga Kieff, Abstract, 3-Part Loops, Marble Base, 17 ½ In. 4556
Sculpture, Gregoire, Emile, Woman, Seated, Embroidering, Alabaster, Bone, France, 1800s 1800
Sculpture, Greyhound, Seated, Verdigris Patina, Square Base, 1900s, 33 x 11 In. 1125
Sculpture, Gross, Chaim, Tumbler, Veined Marble Base, 10 x 8 In. 720
Sculpture, Hagenauer, African Boy, Seated, 1940s, 3 ½ In. 281
Sculpture, Hare, Running, Cold Paint, 1 ½ x 4 ⅝ In. 124
Sculpture, Harvest Time, Indians, Harvest, Dog, Lazy Susan, 16 ½ x 16 ½ In. 273

Sculpture, Hear, See, Speak No Evil, Monkeys, Bench, 30 x 34 In. 1652
Sculpture, Herrmann, James, Turtle, American Box, 2 x 8 In. 748
Sculpture, Hollow Figure, Bent Knee, Arm Overhead, c.1980, 20 x 8½ In. 726
Sculpture, Hopkins, Mark, Boys, Baseball, Flying Hat, Signed, 5 x 8¾ In. 152
Sculpture, Horse, Rearing, Marble Base, 10 x 14 In. 407
Sculpture, Horse, Reclining, Head Up, Leg Stretched Out, Patina, 5 x 8 In. 812
Sculpture, Houston, Horse, Walking, Signed, 73½ x 80 In. 1045
Sculpture, Hunolt, Jim, Emerging, Gold, Smooth, 10¾ x 8¾ In. 230
Sculpture, Hunolt, Jim, Reclining Lovers, Red, Glossy, 1900s, 7½ x 18¼ In. 373
Sculpture, Huntsman On Horseback, 2 Dogs, Wolf, Russia, c.1890, 9 x 22 In. 50000
Sculpture, Ibex, Standing, Amethyst Crystals, Cold Paint, Austria, c.1890, 7 In. *illus* 300
Sculpture, Ihlenfeld, K., Modernist Tree Meets Octopus, Patina, 14½ x 12 In. 82
Sculpture, Immaculata, After Paul Maximilien Landowski, 18½ In. 3000
Sculpture, Kalish, Max, US Army Officer, Walter Reed, c.1910, 17 In. *illus* 2562
Sculpture, Kauba, C., Frontier Justice, Horse & Rider, 1900s, 23 x 14 In. 358
Sculpture, Kauba, C., How-Kola, Brave On Horseback, Rearing Horse, 1900s, 20 x 13 In. 605
Sculpture, Kauba, C., Indian Chief, Headdress, Holding Shotgun, 26 x 14 In. 570
Sculpture, Kessanlis, Male Genitalia, 3 x 3¾ In. 1020
Sculpture, King, William, Adult Dressing Child, 1974, 11½ x 8½ In. 1200
Sculpture, Kley, L., Boy, Floppy Hat, Hands On Waist, 1903, 10¾ In. 438
Sculpture, Kowalczewski, Paul Ludwig, Diana With Hound, Forest, Agate Base, 12 x 7 In. 295
Sculpture, Kramer, H., Horse, 1980, 9 x 9¾ In. 305
Sculpture, Lady Godiva, Horse, Sitting Side Saddle, Flowing Hair, Marble, c.1870, 20 In. 2769
Sculpture, Lanceray, Eugene, Cowboy On Horse, Signed, 8¼ x 8¼ In. 2091
Sculpture, Lanceray, Eugene, Trick Rider, Horse, Rider, 11 In. 6765
Sculpture, Lane, Artis, Couple, Arms Out, Hands On Waist, 1982, 26½ x 24 In. 6250
Sculpture, Last Cavalryman, Erik Christiansen, 1987, 6½ x 6 In. 60
Sculpture, Laurent, E., Fisherman, A Day's Catch, Parcel Gilt, Signed, c.1870, 24 In. 594
Sculpture, Lebourg, C., Piper, Dancing, 40 x 17 In. 5795
Sculpture, Lemarquier, Young Faun, Patinated, Marble Base, c.1900, 20 x 12 In. 799
Sculpture, Lequesne, Eugene L., Dancing Faun, Cast, Brown Patina, Paris, 11 In. 748
Sculpture, Lion, Seated, Cast, 1900, 3 x 1½ In. 60
Sculpture, Lost Girls, Auguste Moreau, 15 x 5¾ In. 720
Sculpture, Mack, B., Golfer, Waist Up, Swinging Club, Frame, 36 x 45 In. 1440
Sculpture, Mack, B., Nude Woman, Seated, Shoulder-Length Hair, 30½ x 35½ In. 1822
Sculpture, Maiden, Winged, Seminude, Reaching Out, Pedestal, Germany, c.1875, 15 In. 615
Sculpture, Makahala, 6-Armed Deity, With Consort, Lotus Base, Gilt, c.1900, 11 x 8 In. 1320
Sculpture, Manuel, M., Mule, Head Looking Down, Ears Back, Signed 1841, 4 x 8 In. 400
Sculpture, McVey, William Mozart, Ram, Brown Patina, Monogram, Marble Base, 13 x 5 In. 978
Sculpture, Meadmore, C., Rune Brown Patina, Marble Base, 1995, 9 x 10 In. 9375
Sculpture, Mene, P.J., Elk, Tree Stump, Marble Base, c.1850, 14½ In. *illus* 472
Sculpture, Mercie, Antonin, David & Goliath, Brown Patina, 18½ In. 1892
Sculpture, Mercury, Nude, Seated, Rocky Base, Italy, c.1885, 13 In. 1384
Sculpture, Michelangelo, Bust, Sideward Glancing, Marble Base, c.1890, 23 x 14 In. 3444
Sculpture, Monk, Seated, Gilt, Paper Blessing Inside, 6 x 4 In. 661
Sculpture, Moreau, A., 2 Girls Gathering Flowers, Signed, 18 x 9 In. 750
Sculpture, Moreau, A., Woman, Sheer Dress, Calla Lilies, 36 x 11 In. 1599
Sculpture, Morelli, Eugene, Birds On Branch, White Breast, Black, Yellow, 9 x 4¾ In. 316
Sculpture, Morelli, Eugene, Ridgeline Kestrel, Marble Base, 18¾ x 6¾ In. 1725
Sculpture, Morris, John, Man In Thought, Cubist Style, 12 x 8¾ In. 430
Sculpture, Moses, Seated, Draped Clothes, Long Beard, Marble Pedestal, c.1910, 27 x 9 In. 1125
Sculpture, Mozart, Standing, Holding Violin & Bow, c.1880, 23 In. 1483
Sculpture, Nataraja Shiva, Standing Within Ring Of Fire, India, 21½ x 19 In. 360
Sculpture, Nude Woman, Bent Backwards, On Knees, Shadowbox, Frame, 22 x 17 In. 210
Sculpture, Nude Woman, Seated On Lily Pad, Looking Over Shoulder, c.1900, 11 x 16 In. 9831
Sculpture, Nude, Bent Figure, 65½ x 12 In. 615
Sculpture, Ophelia, Art Nouveau, Gilt, Foundry Mark, c.1900, 6¾ x 4½ In. 676
Sculpture, Osborne, Leo, Whale Tail, Dips Back Into Water, 4 x 6¾ In. 181
Sculpture, Pan Playing Flute, Grape Leaf Wreath, c.1900, 31 x 17 In. 2074
Sculpture, Pan, Art Nouveau, Nude, Playing Flute, 16 x 13 In. 204
Sculpture, Pandora, Standing, Draped Robe, Holding Box, Square Base, c.1895, 24 In. 1000
Sculpture, Panther, Striding, Dark Patina, Sloped Marble Base, c.1925, 25 In. 12868
Sculpture, Parks, B., Whoops, Man Riding Horse, Following Horse, Jumping Cacti, 27 In. 540
Sculpture, Pavlos, A., Boy Holding Puppies, 13⅓ In. 1125
Sculpture, Pavlos, A., Couple Skiing, 25½ In. 2000
Sculpture, Peacock, Cold Paint, Green, 3¼ x 3⅝ In. 124

Bronze, Urn, Campana, Handles, Satyr Heads, Medusa, Grapes, Marble Base, c.1835, 15 In.
$812

New Orleans (Cakebread)

Bronze, Vase, Usubata, Swirling Dragons, Chasing Sacred Pearl, Japan, c.1900, 12 x 9 In.
$437

New Orleans (Cakebread)

TIP

Don't use bleaching cleansing powders or disinfectant floor-washing products that contain chlorine in a room that has bronze figures on display. Chlorine harms bronzes.

TIP
Taking part in the arts by going to shows, galleries, auctions, museums, craft, carpentry, or painting classes and lectures, and maybe even garage sales, to search for collectibles has a positive impact on your health and well-being according to a recent British study.

Brownies, Puzzle, Skating, Snowballing, Cardboard, Characters, 24 Pieces, 11 x 13 In., 2 Box Set
$138

Wm Morford

Brush, Bowl, Pink, Speckled, c.1950, 8 In.
$22

Ruby Lane

Buck Rogers, Toy, Gun, U-235 Atomic Pistol, Metal, Silver Finish, Daisy, Box, 1945, 10 In.
$219

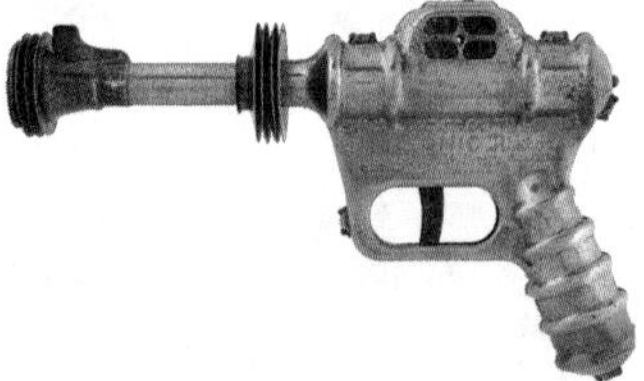

Hake's Americana & Collectibles

Sculpture, Pernot, Henri, Surprise, Satyr Terme, Putti, Patina, c.1900, 32 x 12 In. 1845
Sculpture, Poertnel, Otto, Woman, 2 Dogs, Art Deco, Patina, Marble Base, 18 x 20 In. 1800
Sculpture, Pool, Princess & The Frog, Nude Seated Princess, 1925, 5 In. 554
Sculpture, Presset, Henri, Torsotuya, Torso, 1964, 13 x 3 ½ In. 720
Sculpture, Prince, Roger, 5 Men In Hats, 1964, 18 x 10 In. 5457
Sculpture, Psyche, Seminude, Seated, Bent Knee, Wings, Drape, France, c.1850, 9 In. ....*illus* 660
Sculpture, Qilin, Striding, Head & Tail Up, 1900s, 20 x 23 In. 5819
Sculpture, Rancoulet, Parents, Toddler, Basket, Walking, 15 ¼ In. 279
Sculpture, Renaissance Woman, Dress, Waistcoat, Holding Spindle, c.1890, 22 In. 1625
Sculpture, Reverie, Bust, Porcelain, Gilt, Marble Base, J.M. Mengue, c.1913, 14 In. ....*illus* 2625
Sculpture, Ring Tail Lemur, Reticulated Figure, Curled Tail, 32 In. 1150
Sculpture, Robert Graham, Moca Torso, Woman, Nude, c.1992, 11 x 4 ½ In. 5000
Sculpture, Robert Graham, Woman, Nude, Seated, Chair, Elisa, 3 ½ x 2 ¼ In. 2375
Sculpture, Rocchi, Gualberto, Adam & Eve, Nude, 1981, 26 x 13 ¾ In. 302
Sculpture, Roman Scholar, Holding Scroll, Gilt, Marble Step Base, 21 x 8 In. 489
Sculpture, Salmones V, Holding Up Baby With Arms Out, 43 In. 1337
Sculpture, Samurai, Full Armor, Surcoat, Birds, Holding Katana, Wood Base, 20 In. 7792
Sculpture, Sappho, Moreau, Mathurin, Relief Plaque, Signed, 24 x 26 In. ....*illus* 1230
Sculpture, Sea Creature, Holding Shell, Marble Base, 7 x 5 In. 594
Sculpture, Sea Turtle, Hatchling, Emerging From Egg, 3 In. 345
Sculpture, Seated Buddha, Double Lotus Base, Holding Bowl, 16th Century, 12 x 9 In. 3500
Sculpture, Secret, 4 Nude Women, Leaning In, Heads Together, 24 x 20 In. 8258
Sculpture, Seifert, V., Boy Blacksmith, Signed, Marble Socle Base, 6 In. 310
Sculpture, Shepherdess, Flock Of Spring Lambs, Stepped Marble Base, c.1910, 17 x 17 In. 2214
Sculpture, Shinabarger, T., Full Curl, Ram's Bust, Green Marble Support, 16 ½ x 10 ½ In. 1941
Sculpture, Shinabarger, T., Gentleman Of Sage, Buck, Marble Support, Wood Base, 19 x 10 In. 1493
Sculpture, Six, Michael, Pheasants, Cold Paint, Austria, c.1900, 9 x 19 In. ....*illus* 840
Sculpture, Snake Charmer, Gilt, Woman, Curled Hair, Nude Torso, c.1900, 19 x 4 ½ In. 726
Sculpture, Snake Dancer, Woman, Snake Skin Dress, Arms Up, Ivory Comb, c.1920, 23 In. 43555
Sculpture, Sphinx, Cold Paint, Alabaster Base, 4 ½ x 7 In. 253
Sculpture, Sphinx, Seated, Winged, Gilt, 1800s, 8 x 3 ¼ In. 276
Sculpture, Stallion, Standing, Rectangular Base, Patina, France, 1900s, 25 x 30 In. 1250
Sculpture, Sweeten, R., Ram Skull, 5 x 9 In. 118
Sculpture, Tarrac A., Battle Of Chapultepec, Eagle, Sunburst, Men, 19 ¾ x 8 In. 544
Sculpture, Telephone, Marble Top, Scroll, Leaves, Rach, Oscar, 40 ½ x 28 In. 750
Sculpture, Teppanom, Gilt, Kneeling, Hands In Prayer, Steeple Crown, Taiwan, 13 In. 488
Sculpture, The Dancer, Woman Holding Drape, Signed, Slate Base, c.1900, 17 In. ....*illus* 1481
Sculpture, Tiger, Roaring, Inlaid Stone Eyes, Marked, Japan, c.1890, 8 ½ x 19 In. ....*illus* 861
Sculpture, Tiot, Dog, Seated, Head Up, Cast, France, c.1900, 40 In., Pair 1298
Sculpture, Tucker, W., Bridge Shape, Promise, 8 ½ x 2 ½ In. 1440
Sculpture, Two Young Lovers, Eutrope Bouret, 17 x 6 ½ In 1200
Sculpture, Unterberger, F., Armor, Weapon, Standing, 18 In. 1694
Sculpture, Vainqueur Du Derby, Winner Of Derby, Jockey, Riding Horse, c.1879, 16 In. 288
Sculpture, Van Tongeren, Herek, Theatro XXVI, Arches, 3 Structures, 1986, 11 x 10 In. 2040
Sculpture, Weems, K. L., Kangaroo, Signed, 20th Century, 13 x 20 In. ....*illus* 6325
Sculpture, Winder, Rudolf, Dog, Reclining, Paint, Square Base, Austria, 1800s, 4 x 10 In. 345
Sculpture, Winged Cherub, Crouched, Bow, Looking Down, 15 ½ x 23 In. 363
Sculpture, Winged Mercury, Red Marble Base, 20 x 14 In. 1464
Sculpture, Winged Putto, Holding Bow, Crouching, 1800s, 15 x 25 In. 2360
Sculpture, Winged Victory, Soldier, Holding Sword & Shield, Marble Base, c.1890, 31 In. 2000
Sculpture, Woman, Draped, Column, Lion Heads At Base, 1875, 19 ½ In. 923
Sculpture, Woman, Holding Gilt Floral Wreath Above Head, 1800s, 40 In. 4687
Sculpture, Wright, Russel, Seal, Whoozoo, U.S.A., 1930, 3 x 3 In. ....*illus* 625
Sculpture, Yros, Saint, 4 Chicks, Chasing Frog, Gilt, Signed, 1900s, 6 x 5 ½ In. 625
Sculpture, Zygmunt, Joan, Mountain Bluebird On Aspen, 13 ½ x 5 In. 747
Stirrup Cup, Thyton, Patina, Stag's Head, Silvered Eyes, Antlers, 7 x 5 In. 142
Tazza, Empire, Shallow Tray, Incised Classical Figure, Figural Masks, 1800s, 15 In. 400
Tazza, Sphinx, Egyptian Revival, 16 x 15 ½ In. 584
Temple Lion, Seated, Patina, c.1900, 40 x 16 In. 2706
Tray, Archaic, Cast, Shang Dynasty, Scrollwork, Chinese, 1700s, 24 x 15 In. 240
Trophy, Patina, Loop Handles, Cup Shape, Centaurs, Italian Grand Tour, c.1880, 15 In. 1000
Urn, Campana, Handles, Satyr Heads, Medusa, Grapes, Marble Base, c.1835, 15 In. ....*illus* 812
Urn, Dragons, Masks, Pear Shape, Handles, 1800s, 16 In. 840
Urn, Garniture, Egyptian Revival, Polished, Vase Shape, Sphinx Handles, 15 x 8 In., Pair 984
Urn, Gilt, Classical Figures, Faux Marble Base, 14 x 7 ½ In., Pair 1000
Urn, Louis XVI Style, Fluted, Females Handles, Cartouches, Masks, 1900s, 15 x 9 In. 61

Urn, Porcelain, Cobalt Blue, Swirl Fluting, Handles, Lid, Shaped Base, c.1900, 24 In. 687
Urn, Ribbed, Mask Shape Handles, Relief Band, Classical Figures, 11 ¼ x 6 ½ In. 184
Urn, Silvered, Classical Figures, Handles With Female Bust, 47 x 20 In. 434
Vase, Applied Crabs, Compressed, Ring Foot, Flared Rim, Green, 9 In. 4740
Vase, Art Deco, Woman's Face & Hair Around Base, 1900s, 14 ¼ x 6 ½ In. 184
Vase, Art Nouveau, Woman's Profile, Gilt, Curved Body, c.1915, 14 ½ In. 800
Vase, Balciar, Gerald, Bit Of Honey, Signed, Mid 1900s, 11 ¼ In. 960
Vase, Cobalt Porcelain, Trumpet Shape, Dore Festoon, Scroll Banding, Round Foot, 22 In. 793
Vase, Coustaury, L., Art Nouveau, Children, Signed, c.1910, 12 ½ In. 1045
Vase, Enamel, Two Figural Handles, Chinese, 24 x 15 In. 400
Vase, Figural, Maiden, Flowing Skirt, Intertwined Blossoming Branches, c.1900, 29 In. 4355
Vase, Flowers, Grasses, Japan, 8 In. 150
Vase, Frieze Relief, Satyr Busts, Twisted Vine Handles, Pedestal Foot, 7 x 12 In. 613
Vase, Gurschner, Arts & Crafts, Celtic Design, Marked, c.1908, 7 ½ In. 600
Vase, Ikebana Usubata, Broad Rim, Diapered Panel, Japan, 1800s, 10 x 11 In. 184
Vase, Inlaid Mixed Metals, Lantern, Flowers, Oval, Pedestal, Rolled Rim, 13 In. 2922
Vase, Landscape, Silver, Copper, Inlay, c.1920, 10 In. 308
Vase, Lobed, Long Neck, Relief Dragon, c.1900, 18 In., Pair 300
Vase, Monster Handles, Champleve Enamel Bands, Ring Foot, c.1900, 14 In. 267
Vase, Nimal Head Handles At Neck, Animals, Archaic Script, 14 In. 275
Vase, Peacock, Horn Shape, 13 ½ In. 70
Vase, Red, Bird, Sun, Japan, 8 x 8 In. 125
Vase, Relief Design, Birds, Rounded Bottom, Saucer Foot, Rolled Rim, c.1890, 10 In. 69
Vase, Saucer Foot, Scrollwork, Cicada, Projecting Flanges, c.1800, 12 In. 124
Vase, Trumpet Shape, Taotie Mask Banding, Splayed Foot, Flanges, 18 In. 525
Vase, Usubata, Swirling Dragons, Chasing Sacred Pearl, Japan, c.1900, 12 x 9 In. .... *illus* 437
Wine Jug, Pear Shape, Mask Handles, Rings, Loop Handle, 8 ¼ In. 295

BROWNIES were first drawn in 1883 by Palmer Cox. They are characterized by large round eyes, downturned mouths, and skinny legs. Toys, books, dinnerware, and other objects were made with the Brownies as part of the design.

Candy Container, On A Pear, Papier-Mache, 3 ½ x 3 ¼ In. 125
Candy Dish, Gymnasts, Porcelain, 6 In. 93
Doll, Policeman, Cloth, 6 ½ In. 38
Plate, Bouncing, Trampoline Held By Two Men, 4 ⅞ In. 40
Puzzle, Skating, Snowballing, Cardboard, Characters, 24 Pieces, 11 x 13 In., 2 Box Set .... *illus* 138
Rattle, Brownie Heads, Sterling Silver, Mother-Of-Pearl Handle, 2 ½ x ¾ In. 595
Toilette Set, Soap Dish, Toothbrush Holder, Wash Bowl, Chamber Pot, 5 Piece 385

BRUSH-MCCOY, *see Brush category and related pieces in McCoy category.*

BRUSH POTTERY was started in 1925. George Brush first worked in 1901 in Zanesville, Ohio. He started his own pottery in 1907, but it burned to the ground soon after. In 1909 he became manager of the J.W. McCoy Pottery. In 1911, Brush and J.W. McCoy formed the Brush-McCoy Pottery Co. After a series of name changes, the company became The Brush Pottery in 1925. It closed in 1982. Old Brush was marked with impressed letters or a palette-shaped mark. Reproduction pieces are being made. They are marked in raised letters or with a raised mark. Collectors favor the figural cookie jars made by this company. Because there was a company named Brush-McCoy, there is great confusion between Brush and Nelson McCoy pieces. Most collectors today refer to Brush pottery as Brush-McCoy. See McCoy category for more information.

BRUSH WARE
MARK

Bowl, Pink, Speckled, c.1950, 8 In. .... *illus* 22
Frog, Green, White Throat, 15 In. 173
Vase, Geometric Jewel Design, Fat Bottom, 8 ½ In. 266

BUCK ROGERS was the first American science fiction comic strip. It started in 1929 and continued until 1967. Buck has also appeared in comic books, movies, and, in the 1980s, a television series. Any memorabilia connected with the character Buck Rogers is collectible.

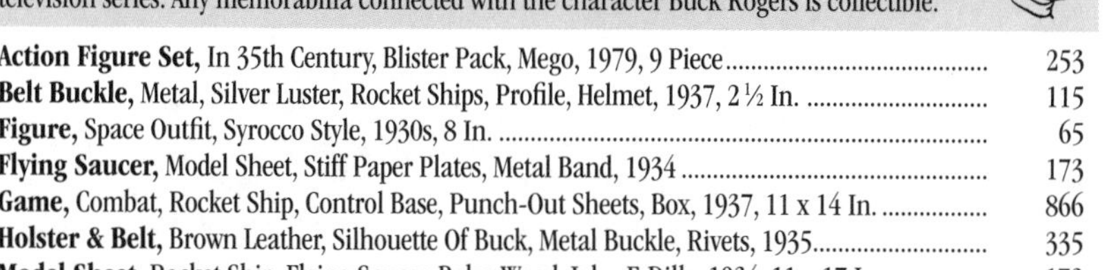

Action Figure Set, In 35th Century, Blister Pack, Mego, 1979, 9 Piece 253
Belt Buckle, Metal, Silver Luster, Rocket Ships, Profile, Helmet, 1937, 2 ½ In. 115
Figure, Space Outfit, Syrocco Style, 1930s, 8 In. 65
Flying Saucer, Model Sheet, Stiff Paper Plates, Metal Band, 1934 173
Game, Combat, Rocket Ship, Control Base, Punch-Out Sheets, Box, 1937, 11 x 14 In. 866
Holster & Belt, Brown Leather, Silhouette Of Buck, Metal Buckle, Rivets, 1935 335
Model Sheet, Rocket Ship, Flying Saucer, Balsa Wood, John F. Dille, 1934, 11 x 17 In. 173
Pocketknife, Celluloid Grip, Buck In Rocket Ship, Camillus Cutlery Co., c.1935, 3 In. 383

Buffalo Pottery Deldare, Charger, An Evening At Ye Lion Inn, 1908, 13 ½ In.
$435

Ruby Lane

Burmese, Pitcher, Tankard, Thomas Hood Verse, Enamel Flowers, Applied Handle, 9 In.
$3,738

Early Auction Company

Burmese, Vase, Jack-In-The-Pulpit, Acid Finish, Crimped Rim, Mt. Washington, 14 In.
$230

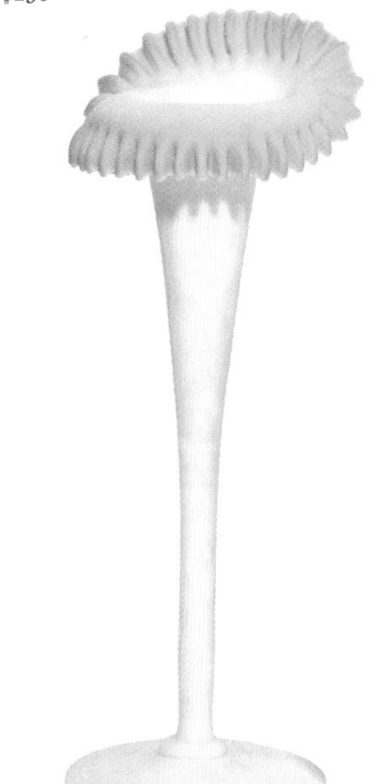

Early Auction Company

Burmese, Vase, Optic Ribbed, Applied Flower, Drip Rim, 4 Reeded Feet, Mt. Washington, 8 In.
$6,785

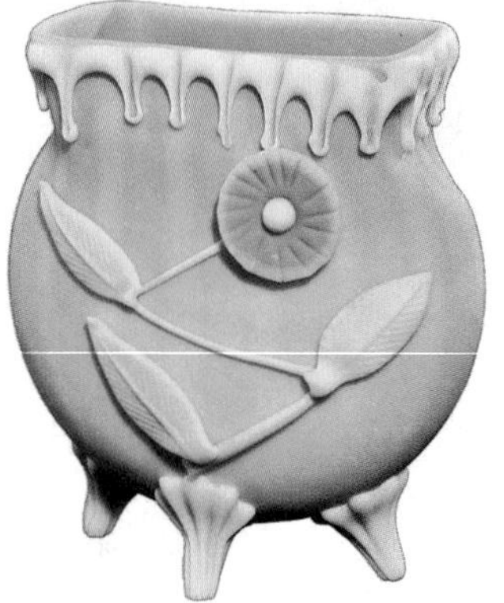

Early Auction Company

Burmese, Vase, Pink Shaded To Yellow, Trefoil Top, Flowers, Leaves, Gilt, Mt. Washington, 10½ In.
$863

Early Auction Company

Burmese, Vase, Satin, Oval, Trifold Rim, Raspberry Prunt, 3 Reeded Feet, Mt. Washington, 7 In.
$144

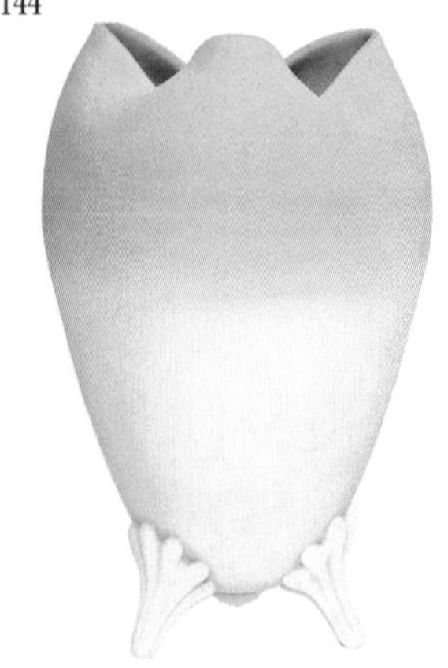

Early Auction Company

Ring, Birthstone, Brass, Sapphire Blue Faceted Stone, Initial C, 1934, Adjustable 191
Ring, Brass, Initial P, Ruby Stone, Premium, 1934, Adjustable 575
Ring, Glow, Sylvania, Plastic Light Bulb, Brass Base, Lightning Bolts, c.1953 173
Ring, Repeller Ray, Solar Scouts, Premium, Brass Finish, 1936 569
Rocket Ship, Multicolor, Tin Lithograph, Windup, Box, 1934, 12 In. 1139
Tablet, Cardboard, Illustrated, Among The Depth Men Of Neptune, 1930s, 7 x 8 In. 173
Toy, Flash Blast Attack Ship, Cast Metal, Painted, Blast Attack, Tootsietoy, Box, 1937, 4½ In. 304
Toy, Gun, U-235 Atomic Pistol, Metal, Silver Finish, Daisy, Box, 1945, 10 In. .... *illus* 219
Toy, Storybook, Kellogg's, Envelope, Color Art, Robot, Paper, 1933, 6 x 8 In. 165
Toy, Water Pistol, Liquid Helium, Orange & Yellow, 7½ In. 660
Toy, Water Pistol, Liquid Helium, Steel, Bulbous Body, Copper Finish, Daisy, 7¼ In. 253
Toy, Water Pistol, Liquid Helium, Steel, Lithograph, Bulbous Body, XZ-44, 1936, 7 In. 455
Uniform, In 25th Century, Dr. Elias Huer, Jacket, Pants, c.1981 633
Watch, Pocket, Buck Holding Gun, Embossed Back, Silver Case 720

BUFFALO POTTERY was made in Buffalo, New York, after 1902. The company was established by the Larkin Company, famous manufacturers of soap. The wares are marked with a picture of a buffalo and the date of manufacture. Deldare ware is the most famous pottery made at the factory. It has either a khaki-colored or green background with hand-painted transfer designs.

BUFFALO POTTERY

Cup & Saucer, Lune, Blue, Demitasse 8
Pitcher, Blue Man, White Ground, Marked John Paul Jones, 10 In. 94
Pitcher, Cinderella, Horse-Drawn Carriage, Laurel Leaves, c.1910 245
Pitcher, Rip Van Winkle, c.1907, 5⅞ In. 475
Plate, Dinner, Lune, 9 In. 19
Platter, LaFrance Rose, 15 x 11 In. 49
Platter, Lune, Oval, 10½ In. 37
Platter, Willow Transfer, c.1909, 14 x 11 In. 165

BUFFALO POTTERY DELDARE

Bowl, Fallowfield Hunt, The Death, Hunters, Dogs, c.1908, 9 In. 850
Bowl, Ye Village Tavern, Men Around Table, Drinking, c.1908, 9 In. 450
Cake Plate, Ye Village Gossips, Cutout Leafy Handles, c.1908, 11 In. 450
Charger, An Evening At Ye Lion Inn, 1908, 13½ In. .... *illus* 435
Cup & Saucer, Gentleman, Cane, Houses, 1909 125
Plate, Ye Village Street, c.1908, 7 In. 125
Tea Tile, Breaking, c.1908, 6½ In. Diam. 150
Teapot, Lid, Village Life In Ye Olden Days, Hexagonal, c.1909, 7 In. 185

BUNNYKINS, *see Royal Doulton category.*

BURMESE GLASS was developed by Frederick Shirley at the Mt. Washington Glass Works in New Bedford, Massachusetts, in 1885. It is a two-toned glass, shading from peach to yellow. Some pieces have a pattern mold design. A few Burmese pieces were decorated with pictures or applied glass flowers of colored Burmese glass. Other factories made similar glass also called Burmese. Related items may be listed in the Fenton category, the Gundersen category, and under Webb Burmese.

Pitcher, Tankard, Thomas Hood Verse, Enamel Flowers, Applied Handle, 9 In. .... *illus* 3738
Vase, Jack-In-The-Pulpit, Acid Finish, Crimped Rim, Mt. Washington, 14 In. .... *illus* 230
Vase, Leaf & Vine Decoration, Bulbous, Mt. Washington, 4 In. 144
Vase, Optic Ribbed, Applied Flower, Drip Rim, 4 Reeded Feet, Mt. Washington, 8 In. .... *illus* 6785
Vase, Pink Shaded To Yellow, Trefoil Top, Flowers, Leaves, Gilt, Mt. Washington, 10½ In. .... *illus* 863
Vase, Satin, Egyptian Urn Form, 2 Angular Handles, Mt. Washington, 6½ In. 230
Vase, Satin, Oval, Trifold Rim, Raspberry Prunt, 3 Reeded Feet, Mt. Washington, 7 In. .... *illus* 144
Vase, Shouldered, Thistles, Pink, Gold, 7 In. 1638
Vase, Stick Neck, Shaded, Bamboo Design, Gold Trim, 10¼ In., Pair 1150
Vase, Stick, Wild Rose Spray, Thomas Hood Verse, Mt. Washington, 8 In. 1725
Water Set, Tankard Form, Acid Finish, 9-In. Pitcher, 7 Piece 345

BUSTER BROWN, the comic strip, first appeared in color in 1902. Buster and his dog, Tige, remained a popular comic and soon became even more famous as the emblem for a shoe company, a textile firm, and other companies. The strip was discontinued in 1920. Buster Brown sponsored a radio show from 1943 to 1955 and a TV show from 1950 to 1956. The Buster Brown characters are still used by Brown Shoe Company, Buster Brown Apparel, Inc., and Gateway Hosiery.

Bank, Good Luck Horseshoe, Buster Brown & Tiger, Cast Iron, c.1920, 4¼ In. 83
Comic Strip, Color, Chicago Sunday Tribune, Frame, May 3, 1903, 19 x 25 In. 25

Buster Brown, Sign, Buster & Tige, Tin Litho, Begging Tige, Biscuit, c.1910, 39 In.
$2,465

Hake's Americana & Collectibles

Buster Brown, Toy, Rolly-Dolly, Buster Brown, Composition, Jointed Head, 1904 Pat., 7 ½ In.
$131

Hake's Americana & Collectibles

Buster Brown, Toy, Spinner, Buster Spinning Plate, Tin, Windup, Germany, c.1915, 7 In.
$2,360

Bertoia Auctions

Butter Chip, Brown Transfer, Dogwood, Scrolls, Gildea & Walker, England, c.1883, 2 ½ In.
$63

Ruby Lane

Butter Chip, Pink Luster, Abstract Flowers, Green & Orange Accents, 1850s, 4 In.
$39

Ruby Lane

Button, Gouache On Paper, Under Glass, Female Bather, Painted, France, c.1790, 1 ½ In.
$203

New Hampshire Button Auctions

TIP

Put a wide-angle viewer in a solid outside door so you can see who is there before opening the door.

Button, Inaugural, George Washington, Copper, Long Live The President, Raised Letters, c.1790
$2,825

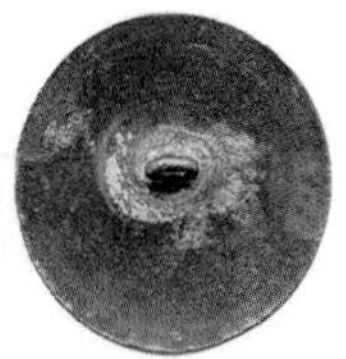

New Hampshire Button Auctions

Buttonhook, Sterling Silver, Edwardian, Glove, Claydon Robbin & Co., c. 1910, 3 ¼ In.
$21

Ruby Lane

Calendar Paper, 1916, Pabst Extract, Yard Long, Woman Standing, Frame, 7 x 37 In.
$314

Showtime Auction Services

"Unique" Collectible

Looking for a different kind of collection? Save cat and dog feeding bowls that speak for themselves with animal pictures or words. Because they are all low round bowls they look best on the floor, on a low shelf, or even on the stairs.

Calendar Plate, 1978, Homes, Carriage, Brown, Alfred Meakin, 9 In.
$15

Ruby Lane

Cambridge, Rose Point, Candlestick, Clear, 6 x 7 In., Pair
$110

Ruby Lane

Cambridge Pottery, Tile, King Lear, Lady, Brown, 6 In., Pair
$145

Ruby Lane

Figure, Buster, Arm Around Tige, Cast Iron, A.C. Williams Co., c.1920, 7 In. 192
Helium Balloon Inflator, Buster's Head, Fiberglass Head, 64 In. 143
Mirror, Buster, Holding Shoe, Tige On Hind Legs, c.1912, 2¾ In. 230
Mirror, Buster, Holding Shoe, Tige, Celluloid, 2¼ In. 275
Nodder, Buster Brown, Papier-Mache, 1900s, 6 In. 395
Sign, Buster & Tige, Tin Litho, Begging Tige, Biscuit, c.1910, 39 In. .... *illus* 2465
Sign, Buster Brown Shoes, For Boys-For Girls, Buster & Tige, Tin, 14 x 40 In. 600
Toy, Rolly-Dolly, Buster Brown, Composition, Jointed Head, 1904 Pat., 7½ In. .... *illus* 131
Toy, Spinner, Buster Spinning Plate, Tin, Windup, Germany, c.1915, 7 In. .... *illus* 2360
Toy, Spinner, Buster Spins Arms, Balls At Ends, Tin, Windup, Germany, c.1915, 7 In. 1298

BUTTER CHIPS, or butter pats, were small individual dishes for butter. They were the height of fashion from 1880 to 1910. Earlier as well as later examples are known.

Brown Transfer, Dogwood, Scrolls, Gildea & Walker, England, c.1883, 2½ In. .... *illus* 63
California Poppy, Santa Fe Railroad, 3⅜ In. 75
Flowers, Majolica, Pale Turquoise, Wedgwood, Marked 95
Green Leaf Pattern, Basket Weave Ground, Majolica 40
Pink Flower, Bud, Stem, Raised Rim, Gold Trim, Royal Copenhagen, 3¾ x 2½ In. 28
Pink Luster, Abstract Flowers, Green & Orange Accents, 1850s, 4 In. .... *illus* 39
Tea Leaf, Alfred Meakin, 2 x 2 In. 12
Tea Leaf, Coupe, Wedgwood, 2½ x 2½ In. 14
Tea Leaf, Mellor Taylor, 2½ x 2½ In. 9
Tea Leaf, Red Cliff, 2 x 2 In. 9

BUTTER MOLDS *are listed in the Kitchen category under Mold, Butter.*

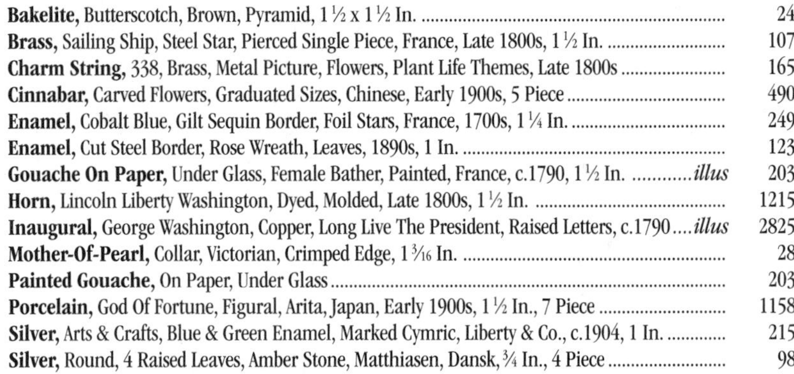

BUTTON collecting has been popular since the nineteenth century. Buttons have been used on clothing throughout the centuries, and there are millions of styles. Gold, silver, or precious stones were used for the best buttons, but most were made of natural materials, like bone or shell, or from inexpensive metals. Only a few types favored by collectors are listed for comparison.

Bakelite, Butterscotch, Brown, Pyramid, 1½ x 1½ In. 24
Brass, Sailing Ship, Steel Star, Pierced Single Piece, France, Late 1800s, 1½ In. 107
Charm String, 338, Brass, Metal Picture, Flowers, Plant Life Themes, Late 1800s 165
Cinnabar, Carved Flowers, Graduated Sizes, Chinese, Early 1900s, 5 Piece 490
Enamel, Cobalt Blue, Gilt Sequin Border, Foil Stars, France, 1700s, 1¼ In. 249
Enamel, Cut Steel Border, Rose Wreath, Leaves, 1890s, 1 In. 123
Gouache On Paper, Under Glass, Female Bather, Painted, France, c.1790, 1½ In. .... *illus* 203
Horn, Lincoln Liberty Washington, Dyed, Molded, Late 1800s, 1½ In. 1215
Inaugural, George Washington, Copper, Long Live The President, Raised Letters, c.1790 .... *illus* 2825
Mother-Of-Pearl, Collar, Victorian, Crimped Edge, 1 3/16 In. 28
Painted Gouache, On Paper, Under Glass 203
Porcelain, God Of Fortune, Figural, Arita, Japan, Early 1900s, 1½ In., 7 Piece 1158
Silver, Arts & Crafts, Blue & Green Enamel, Marked Cymric, Liberty & Co., c.1904, 1 In. 215
Silver, Round, 4 Raised Leaves, Amber Stone, Matthiasen, Dansk, ¾ In., 4 Piece 98

BUTTONHOOKS have been a popular collectible in England for many years and are now gaining the attention of American collectors. The buttonhooks were made to help fasten the many buttons of the old-fashioned high-button shoes and other items of apparel.

Silvertone, Art Nouveau, 5¼ In. 19
Sterling Silver, Asymmetrical Baroque Scroll Handle, c.1890, 7⅞ In. 95
Sterling Silver, Edwardian, Glove, Claydon Robbin & Co., c. 1910, 3¼ In. .... *illus* 21
Sterling Silver, Flowers, Scrolling, Monogram, c.1910, 8¾ In. 95
Sterling Silver, Poppies, Bows, Art Nouveau, Adie & Lovekin Ltd., 1905, 6½ In. 118
Sterling Silver, Raised Flowers, Scrolls, 3⅜ In. 22
Sterling Silver, Scrolls, Monogram, Tiffany & Co., c.1905, 7 In. 175

BYBEE POTTERY of Bybee, Kentucky, was started by Webster Cornelison. The company claims it started in 1809, although sales records were not kept until 1845. The pottery is still operated by members of the sixth generation of the Cornelison family. The handmade stoneware pottery is sold at the factory. Various marks were used, including the name *Bybee*, the name *Cornelison*, or the initials *BB*. Not all pieces are marked. A mark shaped like the state of Kentucky with the words *Genuine Bybee* and similar marks were also used by a different company, Bybee Pottery Company of Lexington, Kentucky. It was a distributor of various pottery lines from 1922 to 1929.

Bank, Pig, Gray, 5⅝ In. 16

Centerpiece, Blue, White, Spongeware, 3¾ x 10 In. 38
Rooster, Red, White, Spongeware, 1960s, 3¾ In. 22
Vase, Blue, Redware, 1920s, 9¾ In. 125
Vase, High Shoulders, Green, Teal, 5 x 3 In. 26
Vase, Ruffled Rim, Blue, 3¾ In. 64

CALENDARS made to hang on the wall or to be displayed on a desk top have been popular since the last quarter of the nineteenth century. Many were printed with advertising as part of the artwork and were given away as premiums. Calendars with guns, gunpowder, or Coca-Cola advertising are most prized.

1906, Nature's Remedy Cures Constipation, Dyspepsia, Cardboard, Lithograph, 10 x 7 In. 575
1909, Poppies & Lily Of The Valley, Die Cut, Embossed, Gold Trim, 15 x 10 In. 22
1916, Pabst Extract, Yard Long, Woman Standing, Frame, 7 x 37 In. .... *illus* 314
1936, Trailmobile, Owl, Truck, Cardboard, 11 x 17 In. 115
1948, Pinup, Harold's Club Elvgren, Aiming To Please, Cardstock, 12 x 15 In. 204
1950, Sturtevant Motor Parts, Pinup Girl, Metal Strips, 33½ x 16 In. 50
1957, Pinup, Glamour Gal Proverb, Jayne Mansfield, Spiral Bound, 16 x 34 In. 115
January, Bible Stories, Wood Panel, c.1900, 17⅜ x 13¼ In. 800

CALENDAR PLATES were popular in the United States as advertising giveaways from 1906 to 1929. Since then, a few plates have been made every year. A calendar and the name of a store, a picture of flowers, a girl, or a scene were featured on the plate.

1909, Pink Roses, J.H. Otterness Co., Pope Gosser China, 8¼ In. 35
1909, Water Lilies, Nebraska, Person & Dewitt, 22K Gold Trim, 9 In. 72
1910, 4 Seasons, Homer Laughlin, 9 In. 30
1910, Gibson Girl, Bows, 9 In. 109
1911, Building, 22K Gold Flowers, Flatbush Trust Co., 8½ In. 40
1911, Girl, Apple Basket, Rose Border, Carnation McNicol, 8¼ In. 95
1912, Grape Bunch Border, Liberty Bell, American Flags, Sundial, 8¼ In. 85
1912, Owl On Book, A & M French Drugs, 8½ In. 95
1916, Indian Girl, I.M. Adler, 7⅜ In. 48
1920, Girl Driving Car, Bluebirds, 8¼ In. 90
1956, Windmill, Ship, Flowers, Scrolls, Taylor, Smith & Taylor, 10 In. 18
1962, Geometric Lines, Flowers, Gilt, 10 In. 20
1963, Medallion, Laurel Leaf Garland, Gilt, 10 In. 25
1965, Zodiac, Church, Brown, Royal Staffordshire, 9 In. 25
1976, Astrology, Rural Scene, Red, White, Alfred Meakin, 9 In. 12
1976, Bicentennial, Red, White, Blue, Eagle, Flags, 9⅛ In. 22
1978, Homes, Carriage, Brown, Alfred Meakin, 9 In. .... *illus* 15
1978, Samurai Warriors, Wedgwood, 10 In. 24
1980, Scrolls, Currier & Ives, 10 In. 14
1981, Horses, Wedgwood, 10 In. 25

CAMARK POTTERY started out as Camden Art Tile and Pottery Company in Camden, Arkansas. Jack Carnes founded the firm in 1926 in association with John Lessell, Stephen Sebaugh, and the Camden Chamber of Commerce. Many types of glazes and wares were made. The company was bought by Mary Daniel in the early 1960s. Production ended in 1983.

Bowl, Lilac Lavender Matte Glaze, Melon Ribbed, Rose Shape, 1930-40 31
Plaque, Horse Head, 1930s, 7½ In. 165
Sugar & Creamer, Art Deco, Gilt, Pale Yellow, 2 Piece 45
Vase, Blossom Shape, Olive Green Matte, Handles, 5¾ x 7 In. 28
Vase, Combination Color Matte Glaze, Yellow, Green, Blue, 9½ In. 120
Vase, Yellow To Blue To Green, Flared Lip, 9½ In. 120

CAMBRIDGE GLASS COMPANY was founded in 1901 in Cambridge, Ohio. The company closed in 1954, reopened briefly, and closed again in 1958. The firm made all types of glass. Its early wares included heavy pressed glass with the mark *Near Cut*. Later wares included Crown Tuscan, etched stemware, and clear and colored glass. The firm used a *C* in a triangle mark after 1920.

Amethyst Pinch, Tumbler, 2 Oz. 10
Apple Blossom, Dish, Handles, 7 x 5 In. 24
Caprice, Bowl, Oval, Midnight Blue, Footed, 11¼ In. 85
Caprice, Bowl, Ruffled, 4-Footed, Clear, 10 In. 18
Caprice, Bowl, Square, Handles, 7 In. 25
Caprice, Candleholder, 3-Light, 10¾ In. 55

Cameo Glass, Box, Windmill, Mountains, Amethyst Cut To Clear, Kralik, Czechoslovakia, 1920s, 3 In.
$225

Ruby Lane

Cameo Glass, Perfume Bottle, Elongated Teardrop, Cloisonne Screw Cap, c.1890, 6¾ In.
$1,416

Brunk Auctions

Cameo Glass, Pitcher, Grape Clusters, Leaves, Amethyst Over Cream, Shaped Handle, DeLatte, 15 In.
$2,300

Early Auction Company

C

Cameo Glass, Tumbler, Amethyst, Trees In Landscape, Signed, c.1915, 3 ¾ In.
$219

Ruby Lane

Cameo Glass, Vase, Bird, Attacking Hare, Red Over Clear, Acid Cut, c.1900, 9 ¼ x 5 In.
$899

Ruby Lane

Cameo Glass, Vase, Cascading Blossoms, Mauve, Frosted, Signed, Pertusot, France, 3 ¾ In.
$56

Early Auction Company

Caprice, Goblet, Water, Stem, Moonlight Blue, 7 In. 34
Caprice, Torte Plate, Moonlight Blue, Footed, Scalloped, 11 In. 35
Caprice, Tumbler, Footed 15
Chantilly, Cruet, Stopper, 7 In. 150
Chantilly, Relish, 3 Sections, 7 x 2 In. 30
Cleo, Cup, Green 10
Cleo, Plate, Salad, Moonlight Blue, 7 In. 21
Crown Tuscan, Relish, 3 Sections, 3 Handles, Clear, Pink, 7 ¾ In. 32
Decagon, Cup & Saucer, Green 23
Decagon, Plate, Dessert, Green, 6 In. 11
Decagon, Tray, Moonlight Blue, Center Handle, 10 ½ In. 35
Diane, Tray, Center Handle, 11 In. 87
Elaine, Sugar, Footed, Handles, 3 In. 25
Flower Frog, Draped Woman, Light Emerald Green, 13 In. 80
Harvest, Bowl, Centerpiece, Oval, Marigold, 12 In. 45
Harvest, Creamer, Blue, 4 In. 22
Harvest, Pitcher, Water, Blue 45
Harvest, Spooner, Blue 35
Martha, Plate, Scalloped, 11 ¼ In. 26
Plainware, Pitcher, Moonlight Blue, Footed, 5 In. 90
Portia, Relish, 5 Sections 40
Portia, Sugar & Creamer 45
Rose Point, Butter, Cover, Open Handles, 5 In. 125
Rose Point, Candleholder, 2-Light, 6 x 8 In. 65
Rose Point, Candleholder, Ram's Head, 4 ½ In. 185
Rose Point, Candlestick, Clear, 6 x 7 In., Pair .... *illus* 110
Rose Point, Cocktail Shaker, 46 Oz., 13 ½ In. 395
Rose Point, Creamer 20
Rose Point, Dish, Pickle, 9 ½ In. 52
Rose Point, Ice Bucket, Swing Handle, 5 ¾ In. 99
Rose Point, Nappy, Handle, 5 In. 55
Rose Point, Relish, 3 Sections, Handles, 12 x 7 ½ In. 70
Rose Point, Relish, 3 Sections, Loop Handle, Scalloped Edge, 6 ½ In. 50
Rose Point, Relish, Handles, 7 In. 35
Rose Point, Salt & Pepper 60
Rose Point, Sugar & Creamer 50
Rose Point, Tumbler, Water, Footed, 7 In., 10 Oz. 38
Wildflower, Candy Dish, Lid, Finial, 5 ¼ x 5 ¼ In. 120
Wildflower, Sugar & Creamer 22
Wildflower, Vase, Flared, Footed, 11 In. 95

CAMBRIDGE POTTERY was made in Cambridge, Ohio, from about 1895 until World War I. The factory made brown glazed decorated artwares with a variety of marks, including an acorn, the name *Cambridge*, the name *Oakwood*, and the name *Terrhea*.

Pitcher, Blended Glaze, Footed, 12 In. 300
Pitcher, Dark Green Matte Glaze, Leaf & Berry, Cylindrical, 6 x 4 In. 165
Pitcher, Green Matte Glaze, Molded Leaves & Berries, Squat, 7 x 10 In. 150
Pitcher, Trumpet Flowers, Vines, c.1910, 5 ½ In. 125
Planter, Brown Glaze, Palm Frond, c.1900, 5 In. 145
Tile, King Lear, Lady, Brown, 6 In., Pair .... *illus* 145
Vase, Brown, Handle, Leaves On Branch, 3 x 5 ½ In. 55

CAMEO GLASS was made in much the same manner as a cameo in jewelry. Parts of the top layer of glass were cut away to reveal a different colored glass beneath. The most famous cameo glass was made during the nineteenth century. Signed cameo glass pieces by famous makers are listed under the glasswork's name, such as Daum, Galle, Legras, Mt. Joye, Webb, and more. Others, signed or unsigned, are listed here.

Bowl, Orange Flowers, Leaves, Yellow Textured Ground, Gilt, Undulating Rim, 8 In. 711
Bowl, Tulips, Peach, Green, Orange, Rolled Rim, Boda, Signed, 5 x 7 In. 58
Box, Flowers, Green Leaves, Goldtone Lid, V.S. Lorraine, Marked, 4 x 6 ½ In. 188
Box, Windmill, Mountains, Amethyst Cut To Clear, Kralik, Czechoslovakia, 1920s, 3 In. .... *illus* 225
Jug, Silver Plate Mounted, Green Leaves, Fuchsia Buds, 13 ⅞ x 5 In., Pair 911
Perfume Bottle, Citron, Opal Flowers & Butterfly, Teardrop, Flip Cap, 3 ¼ In. 575
Perfume Bottle, Elongated Teardrop, Cloisonne Screw Cap, c.1890, 6 ¾ In. .... *illus* 1416
Perfume Bottle, Falcon's Head, Opal Cut To Citron, Silver Cap, Laydown, T. Starr, 7 In. 7763

Pitcher, Grape Clusters, Leaves, Amethyst Over Cream, Shaped Handle, DeLatte, 15 In. ......*illus* 2300
Tumbler, Amethyst, Trees In Landscape, Signed, c.1915, 3¾ In. ......*illus* 219
Vase, Bird, Attacking Hare, Red Over Clear, Acid Cut, c.1900, 9¼ x 5 In. ......*illus* 899
Vase, Birds, Purple, Landscape, Signed, France, c.1930, 8 In. 2065
Vase, Bleeding Heart, Green, Pink, Gilt Sunbursts, Icicle Band, Swollen, 3¼ In. 5333
Vase, Cascading Blossoms, Mauve, Frosted, Signed, Pertusot, France, 3¾ In. ......*illus* 56
Vase, Cut Glass, Green Ground, Oval, Red Petals, Grape Leaves, 7¾ x 6¾ In. 300
Vase, Flat Sided, Blue Cut Scene, Pine At Shore, Signed, Lamartine, 7¾ In. 374
Vase, Flowers, Pink & White, Leaves, Gilt, Pinwheels, Green Ground, Tapered, 12 In. 10665
Vase, Green, Orange, Brown, Round Foot, 9¼ x 3 In. 2520
Vase, Landscape, House, Violet, Iridescent, Barry Sautner, 1981, 9½ In. 677
Vase, Mauve, Rolling Hills, Cottages, Valley, Arsall, c.1940, 27 x 9 In. 922
Vase, Mountainous Landscape, Orange, Pink, Green, 10 In. 605
Vase, Red, White, Carved Flowers, Butterfly, Stourbridge, England, c.1880, 5 In. ......*illus* 1245
Vase, Ruffled Rim, Acid Cut, Butterflies, Pine Needles, Signed Carl Goldberg, 6½ In. 302
Vase, Seahorses, Seaweed, Fish, Shells, Green, Gourd Shaped, Barry Sautner, 1981, 10 In. 800
Vase, Shouldered, Citron, Opal Cut Wild Rose, Butterfly, Band At Foot, 5 In. 374
Vase, Squat, Dazzled Orange Ground, Paddle Shape Rays, 7¾ x 7½ In. 480
Vase, Stemmed Flowers, Purple Frosted, Icicle Border, Bell Shape, Ring Foot, 3 In. 775
Vase, Summer Scene, Landscape, Bronze Band, Legras, 11 In. 375
Vase, Swollen, Pear Shape, Fuchsia Flowers, Pink, Orange, Amber, 1900s, 10 In. 92
Vase, White Flowers & Leaves, Blue Ground, Genie Bottle, 9 In. 2311
Vase, White Flowers, Vines, Green Leaves, Fuchsia Ground, Burgun & Schverer, 6 In. ......*illus* 5333

CAMPAIGN *memorabilia are listed in the Political category.*

CAMPBELL KIDS were first used as part of an advertisement for the Campbell Soup Company in 1904. The kids were created by Grace Drayton, a popular illustrator of the day. The kids were used in magazine and newspaper ads until about 1951. They were presented again in 1966; and in 1983, they were redesigned with a slimmer, more contemporary appearance.

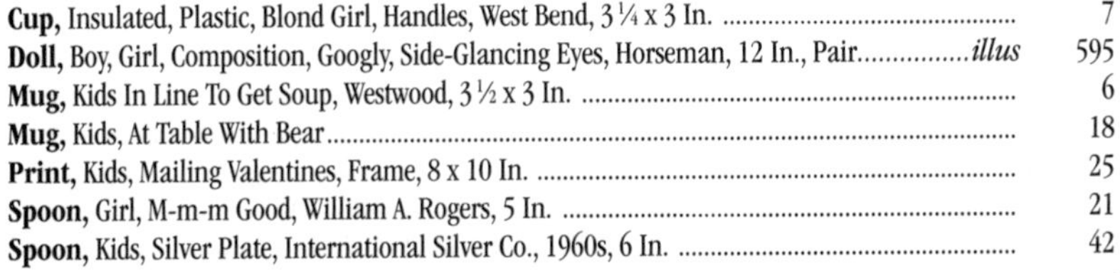

Cup, Insulated, Plastic, Blond Girl, Handles, West Bend, 3¼ x 3 In. 7
Doll, Boy, Girl, Composition, Googly, Side-Glancing Eyes, Horseman, 12 In., Pair......*illus* 595
Mug, Kids In Line To Get Soup, Westwood, 3½ x 3 In. 6
Mug, Kids, At Table With Bear...... 18
Print, Kids, Mailing Valentines, Frame, 8 x 10 In. 25
Spoon, Girl, M-m-m Good, William A. Rogers, 5 In. 21
Spoon, Kids, Silver Plate, International Silver Co., 1960s, 6 In. 42

CANDELABRUM refers to a candleholder with more than one arm to hold many candles; a candlestick is designed to hold one candle. The eccentricity of the English language makes the plural of candelabrum into candelabra.

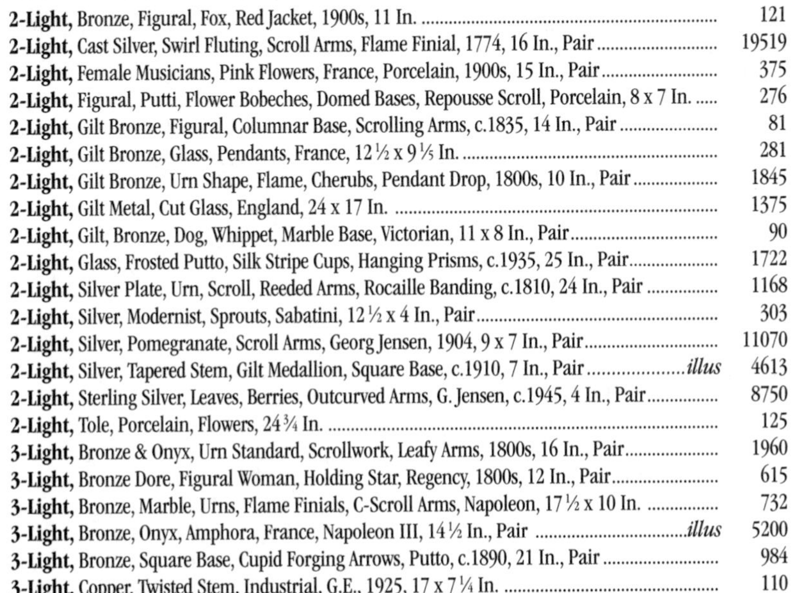

2-Light, Bronze, Figural, Fox, Red Jacket, 1900s, 11 In. 121
2-Light, Cast Silver, Swirl Fluting, Scroll Arms, Flame Finial, 1774, 16 In., Pair...... 19519
2-Light, Female Musicians, Pink Flowers, France, Porcelain, 1900s, 15 In., Pair...... 375
2-Light, Figural, Putti, Flower Bobeches, Domed Bases, Repousse Scroll, Porcelain, 8 x 7 In. 276
2-Light, Gilt Bronze, Figural, Columnar Base, Scrolling Arms, c.1835, 14 In., Pair...... 81
2-Light, Gilt Bronze, Glass, Pendants, France, 12½ x 9⅕ In. 281
2-Light, Gilt Bronze, Urn Shape, Flame, Cherubs, Pendant Drop, 1800s, 10 In., Pair...... 1845
2-Light, Gilt Metal, Cut Glass, England, 24 x 17 In. 1375
2-Light, Gilt, Bronze, Dog, Whippet, Marble Base, Victorian, 11 x 8 In., Pair...... 90
2-Light, Glass, Frosted Putto, Silk Stripe Cups, Hanging Prisms, c.1935, 25 In., Pair...... 1722
2-Light, Silver Plate, Urn, Scroll, Reeded Arms, Rocaille Banding, c.1810, 24 In., Pair...... 1168
2-Light, Silver, Modernist, Sprouts, Sabatini, 12½ x 4 In., Pair...... 303
2-Light, Silver, Pomegranate, Scroll Arms, Georg Jensen, 1904, 9 x 7 In., Pair...... 11070
2-Light, Silver, Tapered Stem, Gilt Medallion, Square Base, c.1910, 7 In., Pair......*illus* 4613
2-Light, Sterling Silver, Leaves, Berries, Outcurved Arms, G. Jensen, c.1945, 4 In., Pair...... 8750
2-Light, Tole, Porcelain, Flowers, 24¾ In. 125
3-Light, Bronze & Onyx, Urn Standard, Scrollwork, Leafy Arms, 1800s, 16 In., Pair...... 1960
3-Light, Bronze Dore, Figural Woman, Holding Star, Regency, 1800s, 12 In., Pair...... 615
3-Light, Bronze, Marble, Urns, Flame Finials, C-Scroll Arms, Napoleon, 17½ x 10 In. 732
3-Light, Bronze, Onyx, Amphora, France, Napoleon III, 14½ In., Pair ......*illus* 5200
3-Light, Bronze, Square Base, Cupid Forging Arrows, Putto, c.1890, 21 In., Pair...... 984
3-Light, Copper, Twisted Stem, Industrial, G.E., 1925, 17 x 7¼ In. 110
3-Light, Empire Style, Brass, Patinated Metal, Winged Victory Shape, Scroll, 27 x 9 In. 437

Cameo Glass, Vase, Red, White, Carved Flowers, Butterfly, Stourbridge, England, c.1880, 5 In.
$1,245

Ruby Lane

Cameo Glass, Vase, White Flowers, Vines, Green Leaves, Fuchsia Ground, Burgun & Schverer, 6 In.
$5,333

James D. Julia Auctioneers

Campbell Kids, Doll, Boy, Girl, Composition, Googly, Side-Glancing Eyes, Horseman, 12 In., Pair
$595

Ruby Lane

Candelabrum, 2-Light, Silver, Tapered Stem, Gilt Medallion, Square Base, c.1910, 7 In., Pair
$4,613

Skinner, Inc.

Candelabrum, 3-Light, Bronze, Onyx, Amphora, France, Napoleon III, 14 ½ In., Pair
$5,200

Ruby Lane

Candelabrum, 3-Light, Girandole, Bronze, Tree Of Life, Hanging Prisms, c.1845, 22 In.
$366

Neal Auctions

3-Light, Gilt Bronze, Cut Glass, Tiers, Swags, Prisms, Drops, c.1935, 24 In., Pair 1045
3-Light, Gilt Bronze, Figural, Nudes, Vines, Branches, 16 In., Pair 1000
3-Light, Gilt Bronze, Flame Finial, Scroll Arms, Urn, Twist Column, 19 In., Pair 1230
3-Light, Gilt Bronze, Marble, Column, Flowers, Motteau, Louis XVI Style, 17 x 8 In., Pair 2952
3-Light, Gilt Bronze, Marble, Twisted Rope Scrolls, Urn, Tripartite Base, 23 In., Pair 2214
3-Light, Gilt Bronze, Signed E.T. Hurley, 1918, 15 In., Pair 492
3-Light, Girandole, Bronze, Tree Of Life, Hanging Prisms, c.1845, 22 In. .... *illus* 366
3-Light, Girandole, Gilt Bronze, Brass, Crystal, Tree Of Life, c.1840, 14 ½ In. 366
3-light, Ormolu, Figural, Louis XV Style, c.1890, Pair 2640
3-Light, Ormolu, Putti, Leafy Arms, Marble Base, Louis XVI Style, 18 ½ In., Pair 923
3-Light, Porcelain, Prancing Horse, Leaves, 7 x 8 In., Pair 369
3-Light, Silver Plate, Faceted Baluster Stem, Spiral Leaf Branches, 17 In., Pair 2250
3-Light, Silver Plate, Removable Lights, Stephenson & Sons, 19 ½ x 15 In. 468
3-Light, Silver Plate, Tapered, Urn Shape Socket, Scroll Arms, Boulton, England, 21 x 19 In., Pair 1000
3-Light, Silver Plate, Twisted Reeded Arms, Shell Bobeches, Sheffield, 1800s, 23 In., Pair 1076
3-Light, Silver, Buttercup Pattern, Turned Stem, Scroll Arms, Gorham, c.1899, 13 In., Pair 922
3-Light, Silver, Edwardian, Baluster Stem, Square Foot, c.1900, 16 In., Pair 2500
3-Light, Silver, George III, Knopped Stem, Flowers, Scrolls, c.1767, 19 In., Pair 5000
3-Light, Silver, Interchangeable, Gadrooned Arms, Gorham, 13 x 11 In. 212
4-Light, Aesthetic, Cast, Chain Swags, Red Marble Base, c.1890, 19 ½ In., Pair 270
4-Light, Brass, Lion Head, Claw Foot, Stepped Base, 21 ¼ In., Pair 937
4-Light, Bronze Dore, Tripartite, Winged Griffin, Cornucopia Arms, 1900s, 27 In., Pair 2000
4-Light, Bronze, Gilt, Putti, Marble Base, 20 ½ x 12 In. 308
4-Light, Bronze, Marble, Pink, Louis XIV, c.1800, 21 In. 363
4-Light, Cut & Molded Glass, Glass Coin Swags, 22 ½ In., Pair 875
4-Light, Gilt Bronze, Baluster Stem, Tripartite, Scroll Arms, c.1835, 21 In., Pair 1625
4-Light, Gilt Bronze, Marble, Hoof Foot, Twisted Arms, Goats Head, c.1835, 28 In., Pair 1000
4-Light, Gilt Metal, Sevres Style, 16 In., Pair 281
4-Light, Porcelain, Flower Encrusted, White Ground, Cherubs, 19 ½ x 9 ¾ In. 500
4-Light, Porcelain, Gilt Bronze, Oval Urns, Rose Bush Arms, c.1900, 23 In., Pair 2750
4-Light, Silver Plate, 3 Camels, Griffins, Elkington & Co., Victorian, 21 ⅞ In., Pair 3890
4-light, Silver, Center Bowl, Rococo Style, c.1905, Pair 1440
4-Light, Silver, George I Style, Scroll Arms, Spool Nozzles, 1929, 15 In., Pair 7417
4-Light, Silver, Raised Scrolling, Stamped, Germany, 8 ¼ x 14 In. 184
4-Light, Wood, Tole, Flowering Urn, Scrolling Branches, Multicolor, 16 ¾ x 14 In., Pair 544
5-Light, Art Nouveau, Silver Plate, 15 ¼ In., Pair 150
5-Light, Bronze, Heron Finial, Leopard Feet, Marble Base, French Empire, 28 In. .... *illus* 649
5-Light, Bronze, Red Marble, Nymph, Tree Trunk, Leaves, 25 ¾ x 14 In., Pair 1337
5-Light, Bronze, Regency, Birds, Crane, Turtle, 26 ¼ x 8 ¾ In. 600
5-Light, Gilt Bronze, Cut Glass, Louis XVI, 27 ½ In. 1375
5-Light, Gilt Bronze, Pierced Scroll Feet, Columnar, Putto, Globe, c.1890, 22 In., Pair 922
5-Light, Gilt Bronze, Reeded Stem, Leaves, Scroll, Piercing, Paw Feet, 27 In., Pair 1722
5-Light, Gilt Bronze, Scroll Branches, Acorn, Oak Leaves, Figure, 1900s, 40 In. 2500
5-Light, Gilt Bronze, Winged Figure, Angels, Empire Style, 1800s, 30 In., Pair 3125
5-Light, Malachite, Gilt Bronze, Scrollwork Arms, c.1900, 16 x 8 In., Pair 468
5-Light, Marble, Carved, Gilt Metal, France, 1800s, 24 x 15 In., Pair 480
5-Light, Neoclassical, Gilt Metal, Onyx, Stepped Base, 24 ½ In., Pair 406
5-Light, Patinated Bronze, Composite Stone Base, Neoclassical Style, 23 In., Pair 338
5-Light, Porcelain, Central Stem, 4 Scrolling Arms, Flower Candle Cups, 23 x 13 In. 2987
5-Light, Putti, Circular Marble Center Column, 26 x 13 ¼ In. 2500
5-Light, Red Marble, Gilt Bronze, Urns, Acanthus, Flower Garland, Ribbons, 28 x 12 In. 3125
5-Light, Silver Plate, Rococo Style, Leafy Arms, Reeded, Flower Foot, 1900s, 28 In., Pair 1875
5-Light, Silver Plate, Square Base, 18 ¼ x 16 ¼ In. 123
5-Light, Sterling Silver, Acanthus Covered Scroll Arms, Fisher Silversmiths, 17 In. 375
5-Light, Wrought Iron, Arts & Crafts, Goberg, Germany, 1910, 13 x 13 In. .... *illus* 165
6-Light, Brass, Glass, Pendants, 30 ½ In. 138
6-Light, Brass, Nickel, Figural Reindeer, Antlers Hold Candles, 1900s, 39 x 27 In., Pair 1875
6-Light, Gilt Bronze, Boy Holding Spyglass, Ormolu, Flowers, 29 In., Pair 2299
6-Light, Gilt Bronze, Female Masks, Paw Feet, Napoleon III, c.1870, 30 ½ In. 3890
6-Light, Gilt Bronze, Figural, Leaves, Flowers, Putto, Black, 27 x 12 ½ In. 273
6-Light, Gilt Bronze, Fluted Columns, Paw Feet, Triangle Base, 1800s, 27 In., Pair 819
6-Light, Gilt Bronze, Scroll Branches, Putto, Flower Head Base, c.1890, 27 In., Pair 1500
6-Light, Gilt Bronze, Scroll Branches, Seated Putto, c.1890, 32 In., Pair 6000
6-Light, Gilt Bronze, Standing Putto, Scroll Branches, Fluted Column, 27 In., Pair 2000
6-Light, Ormolu, Swan Shape Arms, Turned Stem, Socle, c.1810, 29 In., Pair 6150
7-Light, Brass, Lilies, Urn, Knopped Shafts, 27 x 17 In. 153

Candelabrum, 5-Light, Bronze, Heron Finial, Leopard Feet, Marble Base, French Empire, 28 In.
$649

Ruby Lane

Candelabrum, 5-Light, Wrought Iron, Arts & Crafts, Goberg, Germany, 1910, 13 x 13 In.
$165

Ruby Lane

Candlestick, Bronze, Water Nymphs, Holding Lily Pad, Art Nouveau, France, c.1900, 12 In., Pair
$379

Ruby Lane

Candlestick, Gilt, Cherub, Stalk, Flower Shape Cup, Leaves, France, 1890s, 8 In.
$150

Ruby Lane

Candlestick, Pricket, Yellow, Lotus, Lei Wen Border, Porcelain, Chinese, c.1890, 11 x 5 In., Pair
$3,555

James D. Julia Auctioneers

Candlestick, Silver Plate, Jugendstil, Openwork Whiplash, Germany, c.1910, 11 x 4 In., Pair
$312

New Orleans (Cakebread)

Candlestick, Silver, Openwork Base, Dominick & Haff, 11 In.
$259

Early Auction Company

Candlestick, Steel, Forged, Fabricated, Blackened, Albert Paley, Stamped, 2001, 13 ½ x 6 In., Pair
$5,313

Rago Arts and Auction Center

TIP
If your home is water-damaged, ask friends to help. Time is critical. Hire a company that specializes in water-damage restoration. Experts have the necessary equipment to circulate air to keep out mold, mildew, and fungi.

Candy Container, Belsnickle, Holding Tree, Felt Coat, Rabbit Fur Beard, Germany, 1930s, 7 In.
$325

Ruby Lane

Candy Container, Desk, School Daze, Wood, Metal, Judi's Sweet Shoppe, 1970s, 5 x 4¾ In.
$55

Ruby Lane

7-Light, Gilt Bronze, Scroll Branches, Urn, Handles, Swept Feet, c.1900, 38 In., Pair 3750
8-Light, Bronze, Gilt, Satyr, Garland, Leaves, Vines, Marble Base, c.1890, 42 In. 3125
8-Light, Gilt Bronze, Figural, Lion, Scrolled Crest, Reticulated Foot, 35 In., Pair 594
9-Light, Gilt Bronze, Figure Holding Cornucopia, Belle Epoque Style, 27 In., Pair 919
9-Light, Parcel Gilt, Crystal, 38½ x 19 In., Pair 4375
9-Light, Porcelain, Figural, Ariadne & Bacchus, Cornucopia, 24¾ In. 2375
16-Light, Cut Glass, Thistle Sconce, Scroll Branches, Column, c.1950, 54 In., Pair 2750

CANDLESTICKS were made of brass, pewter, glass, sterling silver, plated silver, and all types of pottery and porcelain. The earliest candlesticks, dating from the sixteenth century, held the candle on a pricket (sharp pointed spike). These lost favor because in times of strife the large church candlesticks with prickets became formidable weapons, so the socket was mandated. Candlesticks changed in style through the centuries, and designs range from Classical to Rococo to Art Nouveau to Art Deco.

Altar, Baroque Style, Gilt Brass, Baluster, Flared Fluted Border, 24½ In., Pair 195
Bisque, Porcelain, Gilt Bronze, Figural, Man, Woman, Basket, Flowers, 6 In. 100
Brass, Baroque, Tiered Urn, Segmented Stem, Octagonal Base, 16 x 5 In., Pair 30
Brass, Baroque, Winged Cherub Heads, Domed Hexagonal Base, 11½ x 7 In., Pair 360
Brass, Cobra, Figural, Lotus Candleholder, 8¼ In., Pair 125
Brass, Disc Foot, Stick Neck, Conical Cup, Conjoined Letters JMP, 1910, 13 In., Pair 3450
Brass, Gothic Revival, Gilt, c.1875, 34¼ In., Pair 2918
Brass, Pricket, Repousse, c.1880, 39 In., Pair 960
Brass, Queen Anne, Petal Base, 18th Century, 7¾ In., Pair 465
Brass, Queen Anne, Petal Shape Bobeche, Stepped Base, c.1700s, 8 In., Pair 998
Brass, Reversed Beehive In Stem, Push-Up, 1800s, 11 In., Pair 81
Brass, Shaped Drip Catcher, Knob & Ball Stem, Petal Base, England, 7¾ In., Pair 277
Brass, Stepped Base, Incised Vines, Scroll, 1800, 8 In., Pair 615
Brass, Tiered Urn & Vase Stems, Dome Base, 18½ In., Pair 120
Brass, Turned Stem, Bell Foot, Square Footed Base, Spain, c.1800, 9 In., Pair 154
Bronze, Figural Seahorse Stem, Round Base, Cylinder Cup, Hurley, 1905, 7 In., Pair 1380
Bronze, Marble, Acanthus Leaves, Lion's Head Supports, Baroque Style, 26 x 6 In., Pair 861
Bronze, Marble, Gilt, Square Base, 4¾ In., Pair 88
Bronze, Reeded Stem, Molded Leaves, Dolphin Feet, Tripartite Foot, c.1835, 14 In., Pair 687
Bronze, Seahorse Base, Stick Stem, Cylindrical Cup, E.T. Hurley, 1914, 13 In., Pair 1495
Bronze, Water Nymphs, Holding Lily Pad, Art Nouveau, France, c.1900, 12 In., Pair .... *illus* 379
Burnished Copper & Glass, Sunburst, M. Brazier-Jones, 1990, 27 In. 1437
Cast Iron, Pricket, Black Enameled, Fluted, Tapered, 1800s, 40 x 38 In., Pair 974
Cast Silver, Shells, Roses, Leaves, Twisted Stem, Hexagonal Base, 1766, 12 In., Pair 7807
Cloisonne, White Elephant, Gilt Saddle, Lotus Flower, Bells, 17½ In. 553
Cloisonne, White Ground, Painted Dragons, Flowers, Chinese, 12 In., Pair 120
Cloisonne, Wisteria, Blue, Green, Yellow, Votive, 3½ In. 83
Copper, Pricket, Repousse, Claw Feet, 23½ x 6 In., Pair 94
Copper, Silver Plate, Shells, Dolphins, Shell Shape Base, c.1870, 18 In. 125
Coromandel, Triangle Shape Base, Cartouches, Applied Scroll Feet, 29 In., Pair 5835
Cut Glass, Gilt Metal, Square Base, Beading, 9 In., Pair 175
Decoupage, Gilt White Metal Capital, Base, Urn Shape, Cherubs, Garlands, 9 In., Pair 224
Frog, Pottery, Holding Shell Above Head, 5½ In., Pair 59
Gilt, Cherub, Stalk, Flower Shape Cup, Leaves, France, 1890s, 8 In. .... *illus* 150
Gilt Bronze, Flambeaux Finial, Pierced Handles, Fluted Stem, Square Base, 7 In., Pair 5505
Gilt Bronze, Ogee Shape Base, Paw Footed Ribbed Vases, Napoleon III, 13 x 6 In., Pair 1375
Gilt Bronze, Rock Crystal, Reeded Stem, Fluted Cups, Leaves & Berries, 7 In., Pair 1353
Gilt Bronze, Triangular Platform, Egyptian Masks, Paw Feet, Empire, 9 In., Pair 177
Gilt Bronze, Tulip, Jewels, 3 Legs, c.1910, 15⅜ In. 15000
Gilt Metal, Ebonized, Pricket, Circular Candle Cup, 18¼ In., Pair 183
Gilt Metal, Palm Tree Standard, Leaf Base, Hounds, 12½ In., Pair 693
Glass, Frosted, Iridescent, Blown, White, Stick Shape, Flared Foot, c.1950, 15 In., Pair 431
Glass, Green, Twist, 15 x 6 In., Pair 90
Ivy, Pottery, White Ground, 3½ x 6½ In., Pair 59
Lucite, Taper To Square Base, 10 x 2 In., Pair 48
Majolica, Blackmoors, Feathered Headdress, Pink, Yellow, Italy, 26 x 7 In., Pair 83
Malachite, Silver, Rolled Rim, Cylindrical Stem, Gilt, Round Foot, 7 In. 197
Mercury Glass, Etched Stripes, Flowers, 10½ x 4¾ In. 150
Narwhal Tusk, Pricket, Naturally Spiraled, Bronze Base, 51 In., Pair 8437
Oak, Barley Twist, Ebonized, Round Base, England, 12½ In., Pair 61
Ormolu, Bronze, Satyr Mask, Flame Finial, Hoof Feet, Directoire Style, 16 x 8½ In. 5700
Patina, Bronze, Gilt, Leaf Cast Sconce, Hexagonal Stem, Lotus, Leaves, 14 In., Pair 2752

Pewter, Baluster Stem, Wide Rim, Stepped Round Pedestal Base, 1800s, 10 In., Pair 236
Pine, Figural, George & Martha Washington, Paint, Conical Hat Sockets, 9 In., Pair.......... 720
Porcelain, Cherub & Cart, Blue, White, Votive, Moore Bros., 7 x 8 ½ In., Pair.......... 180
Porcelain, Foo Dog, Flowers, Bell Shape Cup, Gilt Rim, Chinese, 1800s, 6 In., Pair.......... 2500
Porcelain, Gilt Bronze, Figure, Carrying Box, Branches, Flowers, c.1890, 9 In., Pair 1125
Porcelain, Morning Glory Flower, Figural, Leaves, Blue Gloss Glaze, 1922, 7 In., Pair.......... 115
Porcelain, Mother & Child, 12 ½ In., Pair.......... 47
Porcelain, Old Imari, Gilt, Royal Crown Derby, 10 ½ x 5 ¼ In., Pair.......... 1045
Porcelain, Portraits, Jeweled, Bronze Mount, Blue Celeste, Sevres, 15 In., Pair.......... 3444
Porcelain, Seahorses Around Stem, Triangular Base, Brown Glaze, 1916, 4 In., Pair.......... 173
Porcelain, Women Riding Horses, Blue, White, Denmark, 11 x 10 In. 369
Porcelain, Yellow, Asian Medallion, Peaches, Chinese, 15 In., Pair.......... 236
Pricket, Yellow, Lotus, Lei Wen Border, Porcelain, Chinese, c.1890, 11 x 5 In., Pair ....*illus* 3555
Red Amber, Cone Shape, Knop Socket, Round Flattened Base, 3 ¼ In. 3218
Silver Plate, Contemporary, Columnar, Square Base, 19 ¾ In., Pair.......... 48
Silver Plate, Corinthian Column, Square Base, England, 12 ⅜ In., Pair 438
Silver Plate, Corinthian Column, Stepped Base, Godinger, 11 In., Pair.......... 150
Silver Plate, Jugendstil, Openwork Whiplash, Germany, c.1910, 11 x 4 In., Pair..........*illus* 312
Silver Plate, Spiral Form, 12 Taper Receptacles, 5 ¼ x 5 In. Diam.......... 25
Silver Plate, Square Pedestal Foot, Beaded Design, Shaped Cup, 1800s, 12 In., Pair.......... 49
Silver, Art Nouveau, Poppy, Flower Shape Sconce, Drip Cup, Germany, 9 ½ In., Pair 2091
Silver, Art Nouveau, Woman, Flowing Dress, Cornucopia Sconce, 13 In., Pair 800
Silver, Baluster Shape, Weighted, Footed, 7 In., Pair.......... 150
Silver, Baluster Stem, Square Base, Raised Gadrooned Rim, Armorial, 1742, 6 In., Pair 8783
Silver, Disc Shape, Repousse, Spike Center, Spain, c.1900, 9 In. Diam.......... 469
Silver, Eigle Jensen, S-Shape Base, Trumpet Shape, Denmark, 1950s, 6 x 5 In., Pair.......... 154
Silver, Embossed, Fruit & Leaves, Hammered Spots, Flared Foot, 1902, 8 In., Pair.......... 9831
Silver, Enamel, Columnar, Puiforcat, France, 1857, 6 ½ x 3 ¾ In., Pair.......... 363
Silver, Figural Stem Representing The Seasons, Germany, 10 In., 4 Piece 1750
Silver, Figural, Woman Seminude, Vase On Head, Austria, c.1880, 15 In., Pair 2400
Silver, George III, Jenkins & Timm, 1892, 11 ⅜ In., Pair 1945
Silver, George III, Square Sconce, Bat Wing Fluting, Gadrooned, 1764, 10 In., Pair 6246
Silver, George III, Tapered, Fluted, Round Foot, M. Bolton, c.1808, 11 In., Pair 2125
Silver, Georgian, William Fountain & Daniel Pontiflex, London, 1793, 12 In., 4 Piece.......... 3355
Silver, Gilt, Tapered, Gadroon, Acanthus, Matthew Boulton, Old Sheffield, 14 x 6 In., Pair.......... 593
Silver, Openwork Base, Dominick & Haff, 11 In. ....*illus* 259
Silver, Ship's, Baluster Stem, Gadrooned, Square Base, Shield, 1766, 6 In., Pair.......... 7417
Silver, Urn Shape Sconce, Tapered Stem, Flared Foot, Federal Style, 10 In., Pair.......... 800
Steel, Forged, Fabricated, Blackened, Albert Paley, Stamped, 2001, 13 ½ x 6 In., Pair..........*illus* 5313
Sterling Silver, 2 Dragons Support, Scalloped Pedestal, Leaves, c.1870, 2 ½ In., Pair.......... 1067
Sterling Silver, Adam Style, Chased, Reticulated, Dominick & Haff, N.Y., c.1925, 10 In. 497
Sterling Silver, Columnar, Tapering, Fluted, Cavetto Base, Saucer Nozzle, c.1965, 13 In., Pair... 799
Sterling Silver, Corinthian Column, Fluted Shaft, Cylindrical Pedestal, c.1810, 1 x 5 In., Pair .. 1375
Sterling Silver, Squared, Footed, Stepped Rim, Bobeche, Chased Flowers, 14 x 4 ¾ In. 507
Sterling Silver, Victorian, Columnar, Stepped Base, Beaded, Flare Rim, 1894, 11 In., Pair 375
Turned Wood, Round Base, Dark Stain, 12 ¼ In., Pair.......... 50
Wood, Baluster Post, Round Ejection Holes, Flared Capstan Base, 1600s, 5 In. 799
Wood, Distressed, Turned, Blue, 31 ½ x 8 In., Pair 544
Wood, Taper, Braided Stem, Blue Details, 8 x 4 ¾ In., Pair.......... 168

CANDLEWICK *items may be listed in the Imperial Glass and Pressed Glass categories.*

CANDY CONTAINERS have been popular since the late Victorian era. Collectors have long favored the glass containers, but now all types, including tin and papier-mache, are collected. Probably the earliest glass container sold commercially was the Liberty Bell made in 1876 for sale at the Centennial Exposition. Thousands of designs were made until the cost became too high in the 1960s. By the late 1970s, reproductions were being made and sold without the candy. Containers listed here are glass unless otherwise described. A Belsnickle is a nineteenth-century figure of Father Christmas. Some candy containers may be listed in Toy or in other categories.

Barney Google, Embossed Glass, Painted, 3 ¾ x 2 In. 288
Baseball Player, Uniform, Glove, Holding Ball, 11 In. 2151
Bearded Man, Elderly, Gesso, Bail Handle, Sequins, Snow, 4 x 5 In. Diam.......... 90
Belsnickle, Holding Tree, Felt Coat, Rabbit Fur Beard, Germany, 1930s, 7 In. ....*illus* 325
Boy On Skis, Porcelain, Glass Eyes, Red Snowsuit, Hat.......... 863
Cat, Papier-Mache, Black, Red, Yellow, Mischievous Smile, Collar, 6 In. 270
Child On Sled, Bisque Head, Pink Coat, Leggings, Red Scarf, Germany, 7 In. 2360
Christmas, Pelz Nichol, St. Nicholas, Composition, Cotton, Metal Staff, 12 In. 1003

Candy Container, Fad-A-Way Ball Gum, Baseball Pitcher Graphic, c.1915, 7 ¾ x 4 ¾ In.
$648

Robert Edwards Auctions

Candy Container, Golfer, Papier-Mache, Cardboard, Wood, Metal Club, Germany, c.1940, 7 In.
$195

Ruby Lane

Candy Container, Santa Claus, Holding Feather Tree, Papier-Mache, Yellow, 8 ½ In.
$384

Hess Auction Group

Cane, Green Nephrite, Gold Threading, Ruby, Diamonds, Hardwood, Faberge, Marked, 36 In.
$11,800

Tradewinds Antiques + Auctions

Cane, Rose Quartz, Bulldog Head, Macassar Ebony Shaft, Faberge, c.1900, 35 ¼ In.
$9,440

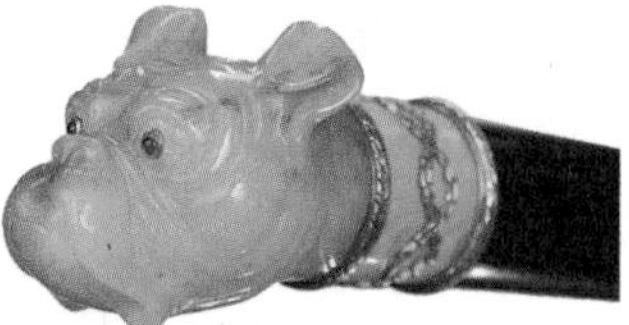

Tradewinds Antiques + Auctions

Cane, Shark Vertebrae, Serpent, Swallowing Sailor, Glass Eyes, Brass Tip, c.1850, 35 In.
$1,111

James D. Julia Auctioneers

TIP

If you find a damaged glass candy container don't discard it. Keep the cap. A collector with a bottle without a cap will want to buy yours.

Christmas, Santa Claus On Reindeer, Leather Harness, Felt Saddle, Dresden Stars, 12 In. 3540
Christmas, Santa Claus, Composition, Curly Fur Beard, Red Robe, Holds Fur Sprig, 15 In. 708
Christmas, Santa Claus, Papier-Mache Face, Red Coat, Sack, Germany, 27 In. 5036
Christmas, St. Nicholas, Sitting On Log, Blue Robe, White Trim, Tree Sprig, 9 In. 1888
Colonial Couple, Composition, Sitting On Bench, 7 x 7 In. 384
Desk, School Daze, Wood, Metal, Judi's Sweet Shoppe, 1970s, 5 x 4¾ In. ....*illus* 55
Dog, Figural, Papier-Mache, Fur, Amber Glass Eyes, Removable Head, c.1890, 9 In. 456
Doll In Crib, Bisque Head, Oval Bed, Gold Silk Bedding, Gebruder Heubach, 13 In. 295
Fad-A-Way Ball Gum, Baseball Pitcher Graphic, c.1915, 7¾ x 4¾ In. ....*illus* 648
Flower Basket, 2 Putti, Cluster Applied Rosettes, Upright Handle, c.1890, 8 In. 64
Golfer, Papier-Mache, Cardboard, Wood, Metal Club, Germany, c.1940, 7 In. ....*illus* 195
Halloween, Witch, Black Dress & Bonnet, Holding Sack, Cardboard, 8 In. 90
Horse, Sparkplug, Barney Google's Horse, Figural, Embossed Glass, Painted, 3 x 4 In. 230
Jack-O'-Lantern, Articulated Arms, Papier-Mache, Germany, 7½ In. 475
Jitney Bus, Glass, Tin Roof, Spoke Wheels, 4 In. 295
Lamb, Standing, Paint, Fabric On Body, Bow Around Neck, 6 In. 546
Santa Claus, Celluloid Face, Net Body, Red, 9½ In. 75
Santa Claus, Holding Feather Tree, Papier-Mache, Yellow, 8½ In. ....*illus* 384
Turkey, Papier-Mache, Atco Co., 7 In. 125
Veggie Boy, Kewpie Type Head, Hands On Hips, Papier-Mache, c.1910, 4 In. 375

CANES and walking sticks were used by every well-dressed man in the nineteenth century, but by World War I the style had changed. Today canes are used by few but the infirm. Collectors prize old canes made with special features, like hidden swords, whiskey flasks, or risqué pictures seen through peepholes. Examples with solid gold heads or made from exotic materials are among the higher-priced canes. See also Scrimshaw.

Agate, Triangular, Eagle Crest, White Enamel Collar, Cranes, Patridgewood, 35 In. 1416
Bakelite, Camera, Midget, Coronet, Hardwood Shaft, Tin Plate, c.1920, 35½ In. 7670
Brass, Telescope, 4-Draw, Boat Logo, Black Painted Hardwood Shaft, 35¾ In. 708
Carved Steer Head, Glass Eyes, 1900s, 35 In. 51
Ebony, Ivory Collar, African American Man Smoking Cigar, 26¼ In. 182
Gold, Gold Quartz, 8 Panels, Gen. Samuel Breck, Presentation, c.1872, 35¾ In. 10030
Gold, Gold Quartz, A.G. Beebe 1869, 8 Panels, Rosewood Shaft, 35¾ In. 6490
Gold, Gold Quartz, Koa Wood, General Samuel Breck, 1872, 35¾ In. 10030
Green Nephrite, Gold Threading, Ruby, Diamonds, Hardwood, Faberge, Marked, 36 In. ....*illus* 11800
Horn, Wood, Carved, Indian Beads, Boot With Metal Toe, c.1900, 36 In. 124
Ivory, Ball, Curved, Stepped, Malacca, Silver Collar, 36 In. 325
Ivory, Elephant Head Handle, Trunk Turned Up, Silver Collar, Malacca Wood Shaft, 37 In. 3735
Ivory, Faces Of The World, Silver Collar, Natural Briarwood Shaft, c.1880, 35⅓ In. 1298
Ivory, Greyhound, L Handle, Silver Collar, c.1885, 35½ In. 708
Ivory, Young Woman, Feathered Hat, Silver Collar, Faux Bamboo, c.1916, 34 In. 220
Jade, Snakewood Shaft, 14K Gold Collar, Maker's Mark, Russia, c.1900, 36½ In. 9440
Mahogany Handle, Violin, Horsehair Bow, Ebony Seats, Maple Board, Austria, c.1860, 34 In. ... 8850
Porcelain, St. Cloud, White, Cobalt Blue, Scrolls, Leaves, Silver Collar, c.1700, 33½ In. 1298
Rock Crystal, Gold, Blue Enamel, Ribbon, c.1900, 36 In. 3540
Rose Quartz, Bulldog Head, Macassar Ebony Shaft, Faberge, c.1900, 35¼ In. ....*illus* 9440
Shark Vertebrae, Serpent, Swallowing Sailor, Glass Eyes, Brass Tip, c.1850, 35 In. ....*illus* 1111
Silver Collar, Snakewood Shaft, Camel, Automaton, Tongue Sticks Out, c.1890, 35 In. 1888
Silver Handle, 2 Birds, Flowers, Wing Shape, 2½ In. 52
Silver Handle, Malacca Shaft, Inscribed Initials, 1884, Marked Tiffany & Co., 35 In. 590
Silver On Bronze, Horse Head & Jockey Handle, Exotic Wood, Rubber Ferrule, c.1875, 37 In. ... 485
Silver, Overlaid Copper Birds, 2 Copper Swallows, c.1895, 35 In. 325
Swagger Stick, Ebony, Flowers, Ivory, Silver Collar, 1900s, 34¾ In. 402
Walking Stick, Carved Ivory Portrait Handle, Civil War Soldier, Silver Collar, 1896, 34 In. 4780
Walking Stick, Carved Wood, Basket Weave Handle, Flowers, Scotland, c.1900, 35½ In. 255
Walking Stick, Concealed Sword, Ebonized Wood, Carved, Inlaid Bone, 36 In. 360
Walking Stick, Cylindrical, Brass Collar, Inscribed William S. Greene, 1800s, 41 In. 605
Walking Stick, Entwined Snake, Snake Head Hand Grip, Carved Eyes, 1800s, 35 In. 356
Walking Stick, Goat Horn Handle, Alpine, Iron Point, Inscribed Interlacken, 66¾ In. 300
Walking Stick, Gold Eagle's Head Handle, Engraved, Wood Shaft, c.1880, 36½ In. 5378
Walking Stick, Gold Handle, Gold Quartz, Vignettes, Rosewood Shaft, c.1850, 34 In. 8750
Walking Stick, Hand Holding Hatching Bird, Tapered Stick, 1800s, 32 In. 474
Walking Stick, Hardwood, Carved Serpents, Geometric Collar, c.1920, 33 In. 184
Walking Stick, Man, Carved, Beaded Eyes, c.1900, 36 In. 295
Walking Stick, Mother-Of-Pearl Handle, Stones River Battlefield, Snake Head, Wood, 35 In. 1080
Walking Stick, Silver Handle, Chrysanthemum Design, Gilt Dragons, Chinese, 34 In. 116

Walking Stick, Walnut, Entwined Snakes, Carved Handle, c.1900, 36 In. 184
Walking Stick, Whalebone, Ebony, Clasped Fist Handle, Scallop Cuff, 1800s, 37 In. 1020
Walking Stick, Wood, Black, Elephant Head, Curled Trunk, 36 In. 275
Walking Stick, Wood, Egyptian Style, Carved Lotus, Silver Inlay 180 to 330
Walrus Ivory, Cannon Handle, Hardwood Shaft, c.1875, 37 In. 560
Walrus Ivory, Housefly Handle, Malacca Shaft, Silver Collar, c.1885, 35 ½ In. 236
Whale Tooth, Silver Collar, Hardwood Shaft, Inscribed K.H. Butts, 1886, 34 In. 295
Wood, Carved, Bird Finial, Stars, Heart & Hand, 1800s, 34 In. 708
Wood, Man In Shell Hat, Mother-Of-Pearl Inlay, Solomon Islands, c.1910, 35 In. 300
Wood, Nautical Turk's Head Knot, Rope Twist, 35 In. 2006

CANTON CHINA is blue-and-white ware made near the city of Canton, in China, from about 1795 to the early 1900s. It is hand decorated with a landscape, building, bridge, and trees. There is never a person on the bridge. The "rain and cloud" border was used. It is similar to Nanking ware, which is listed in this book in its own category.

Basket, Fruit, Underplate, Pierced, Scene, c.1800, 10 x 11 In., 2 Piece *illus* 293
Basket, Willow, Chestnut, Landscape, Pierced Latticework, 4 x In. 420
Bowl, Vegetable, Dome Lid, Oval, Flared Footed Base, Handles, 8 x 13 In. 325
Bowl, Vegetable, Lid, 1800s, 3 ½ x 9 In. 142
Garden Seat, Famille Rose, Figures, Peonies, Butterflies, Hexagonal, c.1825, 19 In., Pair 14540
Ginger Jar, 1800s, 7 ½ In. 118
Jug, Cider, Lid, Foo Dog Finial, Loop Handle, c.1835, 9 In. *illus* 1180
Pitcher, 19th Century, 1800s, 8 ½ In. *illus* 165
Pitcher, Flared Base, c.1860, 12 In. 1298
Platter, 4 Sections, 1800s, 13 x 15 ½ In. 553
Platter, Chamfered, Houses, Trees, Lakes, 14 ¾ x 16 In., Pair 360
Platter, Covered Well & Tree, 1800s, 5 ½ x 14 x 11 In. 461
Platter, Hills, Pagodas, Landscape, Octagonal, 1800s, 15 x 18 In. 502
Platter, Houses, Boats, Octagonal, c.1800, 16 In. 192
Platter, Oval, Pagodas, Trees, Bridge, c.1905, 14 ½ x 12 In. 299
Platter, Pagoda, Landscape, Octagonal, 1800s, 16 x 20 In. 708
Teapot, Lid, Twisted Asparagus Handle, Pagodas, 1800s, 7 In. 127
Tureen, Dome Lid, Flower Finial, Oval, Twisted Handles, Pagoda, 10 x 12 In. 460
Tureen, Lid, Flower Finial, Twist Handles, Pagoda, Trees, Oval, 1900s, 11 x 12 In. 431
Tureen, Lid, Oriental, Gourd Stem Handle, Boar's Head Handles On Base, 8 x 13 In. 443

CAPO-DI-MONTE porcelain was first made in Naples, Italy, from 1743 to 1759. The factory moved near Madrid, Spain, and operated there from 1771 until 1821.The Ginori factory of Doccia, Italy, acquired the molds and began using the crown and *N* mark. It eventually became the modern-day firm known as Richard Ginori, often referred to as Ginori or Capo-di-Monte. This company also used the crown and *N* mark. Richard Ginori was purchased by Gucci in 2013. The Capo-Di-Monte mark is still being used.

N

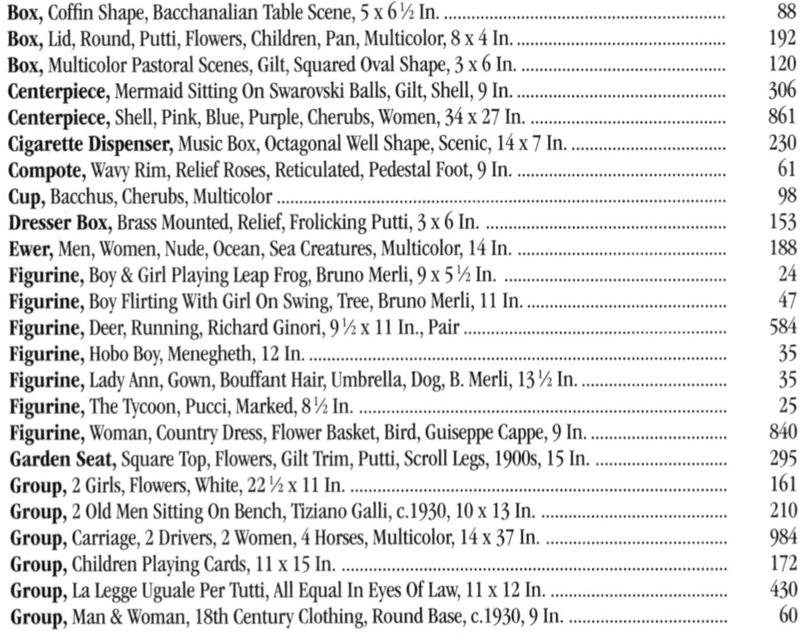

Box, Coffin Shape, Bacchanalian Table Scene, 5 x 6 ½ In. 88
Box, Lid, Round, Putti, Flowers, Children, Pan, Multicolor, 8 x 4 In. 192
Box, Multicolor Pastoral Scenes, Gilt, Squared Oval Shape, 3 x 6 In. 120
Centerpiece, Mermaid Sitting On Swarovski Balls, Gilt, Shell, 9 In. 306
Centerpiece, Shell, Pink, Blue, Purple, Cherubs, Women, 34 x 27 In. 861
Cigarette Dispenser, Music Box, Octagonal Well Shape, Scenic, 14 x 7 In. 230
Compote, Wavy Rim, Relief Roses, Reticulated, Pedestal Foot, 9 In. 61
Cup, Bacchus, Cherubs, Multicolor 98
Dresser Box, Brass Mounted, Relief, Frolicking Putti, 3 x 6 In. 153
Ewer, Men, Women, Nude, Ocean, Sea Creatures, Multicolor, 14 In. 188
Figurine, Boy & Girl Playing Leap Frog, Bruno Merli, 9 x 5 ½ In. 24
Figurine, Boy Flirting With Girl On Swing, Tree, Bruno Merli, 11 In. 47
Figurine, Deer, Running, Richard Ginori, 9 ½ x 11 In., Pair 584
Figurine, Hobo Boy, Menegheth, 12 In. 35
Figurine, Lady Ann, Gown, Bouffant Hair, Umbrella, Dog, B. Merli, 13 ½ In. 35
Figurine, The Tycoon, Pucci, Marked, 8 ½ In. 25
Figurine, Woman, Country Dress, Flower Basket, Bird, Guiseppe Cappe, 9 In. 840
Garden Seat, Square Top, Flowers, Gilt Trim, Putti, Scroll Legs, 1900s, 15 In. 295
Group, 2 Girls, Flowers, White, 22 ½ x 11 In. 161
Group, 2 Old Men Sitting On Bench, Tiziano Galli, c.1930, 10 x 13 In. 210
Group, Carriage, 2 Drivers, 2 Women, 4 Horses, Multicolor, 14 x 37 In. 984
Group, Children Playing Cards, 11 x 15 In. 172
Group, La Legge Uguale Per Tutti, All Equal In Eyes Of Law, 11 x 12 In. 430
Group, Man & Woman, 18th Century Clothing, Round Base, c.1930, 9 In. 60

TIP
Don't stack cups. If you must do it, separate the two cups with a piece of paper or felt.

C

Canton, Basket, Fruit, Underplate, Pierced, Scene, c.1800, 10 x 11 In., 2 Piece
$293

Thomaston Place Auction

Canton, Jug, Cider, Lid, Foo Dog Finial, Loop Handle, c.1835, 9 In.
$1,180

Brunk Auctions

Canton, Pitcher, 19th Century, 1800s, 8 ½ In.
$165

Hess Auction Group

This is an edited listing of current prices. Visit **Kovels.com** to check thousands of prices from previous years and sign up for free information on trends, tips, reproductions, marks, and more.

Capo-Di-Monte, Jardiniere, Pedestal, Painted, Figures, Landscape, Italy, 15 x 39 In.
$610

DuMouchelles Art Gallery

Capo-Di-Monte, Plaque, Mythological Scene, Frame, 1800s, 15 x 19 In.
$270

Cowan Auctions

Group, Man, Woman, Naval Hat, Horse Drawn Carriage, 1800s, 12 x 14 In. 118
Group, Men & Woman Drinking, Table, 20 x 12 In. 861
Group, Piano Recital, Italy, 31 ½ In. 1968
Group, Piano, Lute, 3 Figures, Green Piano, Carpet, 11 x 18 In. 1003
Group, Pool Players, 4 People, Green Table, Tag, 12 x 22 In. 461
Jardiniere, Pedestal, Painted, Figures, Landscape, Italy, 15 x 39 In. .... *illus* 610
Plaque, Battle Scene, Fortress, Horse, Wounded Figure, Relief, 1700s, 22 In. 1353
Plaque, Mythological Scene, Frame, 1800s, 15 x 19 In. .... *illus* 270
Plaque, Octagonal, Adam & Eve, Angel, 8 ½ x 7 In. 492
Platter, Crest In Center, Classical Scene On Border, 21 x 14 ½ In. 250
Stand, Jardiniere, Putti, Musical Instruments, Bruno Merli, 27 ½ x 13 In. 726
Tankard, Lid, Satyrs, Figures, Relief, Twisted Handle, Putti Finial, 1800s, 10 In. 296
Tankard, Porcelain Relief, Battle Scene, Winged Helmet Lid, Loop Handle, 1 Liter........ 420
Tureen, Man & Standing Up Dog Finial, Gilt, 4-Footed, 14 ½ x 13 ½ In. 2706
Urn, Figural Handles, Relief Putti, Blue, White, 1900s, 9 ½ x 7 In. 122
Vase, Frolicking Figures, Cherubs, Ram's Heads, Italy, c. 1900, 9 In. 118
Vase, Putti Handles, Lovers In Garden, Dolphin Fish, Flowers, 37 x 18 In. 430

CAPTAIN MARVEL was introduced in February 1940 in Whiz comic books. An orphan named Billy Batson met the wizard, Shazam, and whenever he said the magic word he was transformed into a superhero. A movie serial was released in 1940. The comic was discontinued in 1954. A second Captain Marvel appeared in 1966, a third in 1967. Only the original was transformed by shouting "Shazam."

Comic Book, Marvel Comics Group, No. 25, March 1973 158
Figure, Captain America, Super-Flex Bendee, Rubber, Card, 1966, 6 x 9 In. 974
Figure, Captain Marvel Jr., Standing In Uniform, Kerr, Box, 6 In. 398
Figure, Mary Marble, Kerr, Fawcett Publications, Box, 6 In. 383
Figure, R.W. Kerr, 1946, 6 ½ In. 886
Ring, Brass Finish, Adjustable, Lightning Bolts, Compass, c.1946........ 345
Toy, Car, Captain America Driver, Friction, Tin Lithograph, Marx........ 288
Toy, Racers Set, Windup, Tin Lithograph, Automatic Toy Co., Box, 4 Piece........ 307
Tricycle, Thor Driver, Tin Lithograph, Star Shield, Vinyl, Windup, 1968, 3 x 4 In. 214
Wristwatch, Captain Marvel, Stainless Steel, Windup, Leather Band, 1948, 9 In. .... *illus* 195

CAPTAIN MIDNIGHT began as a network radio show in September 1940. The first comic book appeared in July 1941. Captain Midnight was really the aviator Captain Albright, who was to defeat the Nazis. A movie serial was made in 1942 and a comic strip was published for a short time. The comic book version of Captain Midnight ended his career in 1948. Radio premiums are the prized collector memorabilia today.

Badge, Decoder, Secret Squadron, Pinback, c.1940, 2 x 1 In. 52
Badge, Flight Patrol, Skelly, Propeller Shape, Brass, 1940s, 2 x 1 In. 45

CARAMEL SLAG, *see Imperial Glass category.*

CARDS listed here include advertising cards (often called trade cards), baseball cards, playing cards, and others. Color photographs were rare in the nineteenth century, so companies gave away colorful cards with pictures of children, flowers, products, or related scenes that promoted the company name. These were often collected and stored in albums. Baseball cards also date from the nineteenth century, when they were used by tobacco companies as giveaways. Gum cards were started in 1933, but it was not until after World War II that the bubble gum cards favored today were produced. Today over 1,000 cards are issued each year by the gum companies. Related items may be found in the Christmas, Halloween, Movie, Paper, and Postcard categories.

Advertising, Accident Bank, H. Partridge & Co., Boston, Mass., 3 ¼ x 5 ¼ In. 1534
Advertising, Andrew's Pearl Baking Powder & Pure Spices, Boy Escaping Crowd........ 12
Advertising, Astrich Brothers, Basket Of Flowers, Chromolithograph, c.1881, 7 x 5 In. 45
Advertising, Clark's O.N.T. Spool Cotton, Victorian Girls, Hugging, c.1890, 7 x 5 In. 18
Advertising, Dark Town Battery Bank, Baseball, c.1888........ *illus* 5760
Advertising, Estey Organ Co., Man Singing To Woman, c.1880, 3 x 5 In. 5
Advertising, Farmers' Friend, Owl, Nest In Tree, 1891, 3 x 4 ¾ In. 5
Advertising, Fisk's Japanese Soap, Man With Umbrella, Temple, 1875 10
Advertising, Folks You Meet, Punster, 4 x 6 In. 8
Advertising, Grandmother's A&P Condensed Milk, Weaned Calf, c.1899 3
Advertising, Humpty Dumpty Toy Savings Bank, Broadhead & Hamlin, Syracuse, 5 x 3 In. 649
Advertising, J.C. Davis' Old Soap, Chromolithograph, Girl, Doll, Boy, Kite, 1880s, 4 x 3 In. 11
Advertising, Lion Coffee, Boy Sitting On Russian Wolf........ 40

Advertising, Magic Yeast Cakes, E.W. Gillett Mfg., Couple In Rowboat, 7 x 5 In.	12
Advertising, Mason Toy Savings Bank, Jacobs, Whitcomb & Co., 3 ¼ x 5 In.	502
Advertising, Ricksecker's Perfumes, Powder, Soap, New Orleans Expo, 7 x 5 In.	27
Advertising, Springfield Institution For Savings, Girl At Desk	5
Advertising, Trick Pony Bank, H. Partridge & Co., Boston, 3 ¼ x 5 ½ In.	207
Advertising, Washburn-Crosby Flour, Cow & Calf, Food Bags, 6 x 4 In.	10
Advertising, Well's Rough On Rats, Family Chasing Rat, 5 x 8 In.	45
Advertising, Wheeler & Wilson, No. 8 Sewing Machine, Wagon, Family, 1800s, 5 x 3 In.	20
Advertising, White Sewing Machine, Easter Bunny, Boy, Egg Hunt	64
Advertising, Wide-Awake Cigars, Uncle Sam, American Eagle, Embossed, 10 x 6 In.	12
Advertising, Yuco Breakfast Food, Kids Eating, Girl In Window	12
Baseball, Bob Gibson, No. 514, Topps, 1959	125
Baseball, Brooks Robinson, Topps, No. 439, 1959	40
Baseball, Carl Yastrzemski, Topps, No. 461, 1970	24
Baseball, Christy Mathewson, New York Giants, Topps, No. 408, 1961	49
Baseball, Duke Snider, Topps, No. 150, 1956	65
Baseball, Ernie Banks, Chicago Cubs, Topps, No. 510, 1965	34
Baseball, Frank Howard, Outfield, Topps, No. 40	25
Baseball, Frank Robinson, Cincinnati Reds, Topps, No. 120, 1965	20
Baseball, Hank Aaron, Milwaukee Braves, Topps, No. 390, 1963	1320
Baseball, Jackie Robinson, Leaf, No. 79, 1948	10800
Baseball, Juan Marichal, Pitcher, San Francisco Giants, Topps, No. 370, 1969	12
Baseball, Ken Griffey Jr., Rookie, Fleer, No. 548, 1989	20
Baseball, Mickey Mantle, No. 50, Topps, 1966	960
Baseball, Mickey Mantle, Yankees, Topps, No. 311, 1952	120000
Baseball, Mike Schmidt, Rookie, No. 615, Topps, 1973	230
Baseball, Roberto Clemente, Rookie, No. 164, Topps, 1955	1287
Baseball, Ron Santo, 3rd Base, Chicago Cubs, Topps, No. 110, c.1965	15
Baseball, Steve Carlton, Rookie, No. 477, Topps, 1965	230
Baseball, Willie Mays, Giants, Topps, No. 200, 1967	179
Baseball, Willie Mays, No. 1, Topps, 1966	4200
Baseball, Willie McCovey, 1st Base, San Francisco Giants, Topps, No. 50, 1971	40
Basketball, Bill Bradley, New York Knicks, Topps, No. 37, 1975	10
Basketball, Bob Cousy, Boston Celtics, Fleer, No. 49, 1961	125
Basketball, Chris Mullin, Golden State Warriors, Rookie, Fleer, No. 77, 1986	40
Basketball, Earl Monroe, New York Knicks, Topps, No. 73, 1972	15
Basketball, George Gervin, San Antonio Spurs, Topps, No. 73, 1977	20
Basketball, John Havlicek, Boston Celtics, Topps, No. 100, 1974	15
Basketball, Julius Erving, New York Nets, All Star, Topps, No. 200, 1974	40
Basketball, Kareem Abdul-Jabbar, Milwaukee Bucks, Topps, No. 1, 1974	25
Basketball, Lew Alcindor, No. 25, Topps, 1969	3900
Basketball, Phil Jordan, New York Knickerbockers, Fleer, No. 24, 1961	23
Basketball, Robert Parish, Golden State Warriors, Rookie, Topps No. 111, 1977	25
Basketball, Wilt Chamberlain, Los Angeles Lakers, Topps, No. 250, 1974	35
Football, Bob Griese, Miami Dolphins, Autographed, Topps, No. 161, 1969	80
Football, Don Meredith, Dallas Cowboys, Topps, No. 74, 1963	59
Football, Don Webb, Boston Patriots, Topps, No. 21, 1965, 2 ½ x 4 In.	50
Football, Frank Gifford, New York Giants, Topps, No. 74, 1960	40
Football, Fred Biletnikoff, Oakland Raiders, Topps, No. 106, 1967	30
Football, Jim Brown, No. 62, Topps, 1958	600
Football, Jim Taylor, Green Bay Packers, Topps, No. 160, 1968	15
Football, Joe Montana, Rookie, San Francisco 49ers, Topps, No. 216, 1981	99
Football, Joe Montana, San Francisco 49ers, Topps, No. 488, 1982	25
Football, Johnny Unitas, Baltimore Colts, Topps, No. 150, 1974	20
Football, Len Dawson, Kansas City Chiefs, Topps, No. 96, 1964	30
Football, Steve Van Buren, Philadelphia Eagles, Bowman Small, No. 45, 1952	80
Greeting, Birthday, 5 Years Old, Bear, Cart Of Flowers, Standup, 1940s, 8 x 6 In.	59
Greeting, Birthday, Goldilocks, Blue Flowered Dress, 1949, 4 ¾ x 5 ¾ In.	8
Greeting, Easter, Couple, Leaning Against Tree, Holding Hands, Tulips, c.1930, 4 x 5 In.	12
Greeting, Good Wishes, Edwardian, Faux Ribbon, Flowers, c.1900, 3 x 5 In.	15
Greeting, New Baby, Baby, Yellow Sleeper, Clown Doll, Die Cut, Embossed, 5 x 7 In.	14
Greeting, St. Patrick's Day, Boy, Dressed In Green, Hat, Walking Stick, Shamrocks, 7 x 5 In.	15
Greeting, Valentine, Boy, Red Pane, Rose Garland, 7 x 5 In.	18
Greeting, Valentine, Mother, Hearts, Violets, Paramount, 1945, 4 x 5 ½ In.	5
Greeting, Valentine, To My Love, Rose Bouquet, Doves, Germany, c.1900, 4 x 2 In.	18
Greeting, Valentine, Women, Auto, Embossed Litho, 3-D Heart, Popup, Victorian, 6 x 6 In.	50

Captain Marvel, Wristwatch, Captain Marvel, Stainless Steel, Windup, Leather Band, 1948, 9 In.
$195

Ruby Lane

Card, Advertising, Dark Town Battery Bank, Baseball, c.1888
$5,760

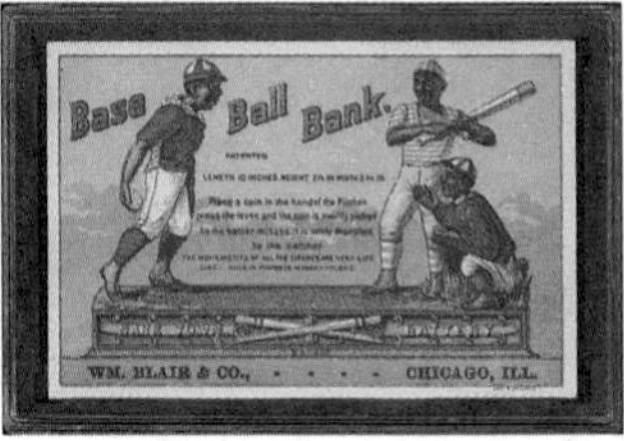

Robert Edwards Auctions

Carnival Glass, Bushel Basket, Aqua, Opalescent, Handles, Footed, Northwood, c.1910, 5 In.
$138

Jeffrey S. Evans

TIP

Do not hide a key outside the house, not even in a key-holding stone. Burglars are smart.

Carnival Glass, Grapevine, Dish, Iridescent Amber Body, Ruffled Rim, Fenton, 8 ¾ In.
$29

Early Auction Company

Carnival Glass, Iris, Pitcher, Water, Marigold, Colorless Handle, Dugan, 11 In.
$80

Jeffrey S. Evans

Carnival Glass, Trout & Fly, Bowl, Crimped Rim, Green, Millersburg, 1909-11, 2 ½ x 9 In.
$345

Jeffrey S. Evans

Carnival Glass, Two Flowers, Dish, Blue, 3 Applied Feet, Ruffled Rim, Fenton, 4 x 11 In.
$75

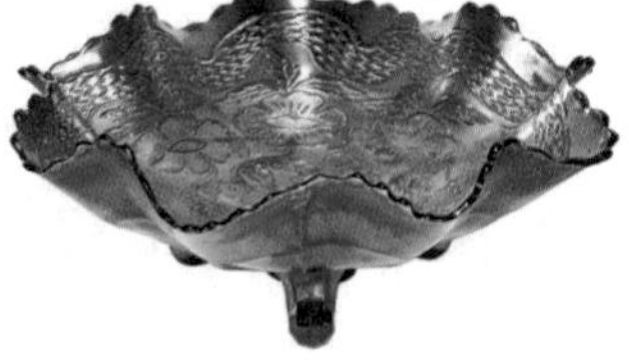

Early Auction Company

CARDER, *see Aurene and Steuben categories.*

CARNIVAL GLASS was an inexpensive, iridescent pressed glass made from about 1907 to about 1925. More than 1,000 different patterns are known. In September 2014 an important collection was sold and resulted in very high prices. Some of them are included here. Carnival glass is currently being reproduced.

Acanthus, Bowl, Ruffled, Pumpkin Marigold, 8 ¾ In. 85
Acorn Burrs & Bark pattern is listed here as Acorn Burrs.
Acorn Burrs, Berry Bowl, Green, 6 Piece 69
Acorn Burrs, Berry Set, Purple, 7 Piece 495
Acorn Burrs, Punch Cup, Green, 6 Piece 67
Acorn Burrs, Spooner, Marigold 185
Acorn Burrs, Spooner, Purple 235
Acorn Burrs, Sugar, Lid, Purple 285
Acorn Burrs, Tumbler, Marigold 85
Apple Blossom Twigs, Bowl, Ruffled Edge, White, 9 In. 265
Apple Blossom Twigs, Bowl, Ruffled, Peach Opal, 8 ½ In. 235
Apple Blossom Twigs, Plate, Purple 345
Apple Panels, Creamer, Marigold 47
Apple Tree, Tumbler, Marigold, 6 Piece 66
April Showers, Vase, Blue, Flared & Ruffled Rim, 6 ¾ In. 185
April Showers, Vase, Blue, Ruffled, 11 ⅜ In. 95
April Showers, Vase, Green, Footed, 11 In. 135
Aramis, Whimsy, Hat Shape, Marigold 67
Asters, Chop Plate, Marigold, 12 In. 80
Autumn Acorns, Bowl, Ruffled, Blue, 9 ¼ In. 115
Autumn Acorns, Bowl, Ruffled, Marigold 68
Banded Medallion & Teardrop pattern is listed here as Beaded Bull's-Eye.
Basket Of Roses, Bonbon, Purple Stippled, Handles 565
Battenburg Lace No. 1 pattern is listed here as Hearts & Flowers.
Battenburg Lace No. 2 pattern is listed here as Captive Rose.
Battenburg Lace No. 3 pattern is listed here as Fanciful.
Beaded Acanthus, Pitcher, Marigold 145
Beaded Bull's-Eye, Vase, Marigold, 7 ¼ In. 87
Beaded Bull's-Eye, Vase, Purple, Flared, 8 ½ In. 165
Beaded Cable, Rose Bowl, Blue, 3-Footed 185
Beaded Cable, Rose Bowl, Custard, Ball Feet 115
Beaded Medallion & Teardrop pattern is listed here as Beaded Bull's-Eye.
Beaded Shell, Mug, Blue 135
Beauty Bud, Vase, Cylindrical, Marigold, 9 ¼ In. 39
Bell & Beads, Bowl, Ruffled, Purple, 6 ¾ In. 115
Big Basketweave, Basket, Marigold, Handle 57
Big Basketweave, Vase, Blue, 10 ¼ In. 265
Big Basketweave, Vase, White, Flared, 11 ¼ In. 165
Birds & Cherries, Bonbon, Handles, Purple 145
Birds & Cherries, Compote, Green, Ruffled 95
Birds & Cherries, Compote, Pumpkin Marigold 85
Birds on Bough pattern is listed here as Birds & Cherries.
Blackberry A pattern is listed here as Blackberry.
Blackberry Bramble, Compote, Amethyst 77
Blackberry Wreath, Bowl, 3-In-1 Edge, Amethyst, 7 ¼ In. 145
Blackberry Wreath, Bowl, Ice Cream, Amethyst, Millersburg, 9 ¾ In. 85
Blackberry Wreath, Bowl, Ruffled, Green, 6 In. 134
Blackberry Wreath, Bowl, Ruffled, Green, Millersburg, 8 ¾ In. 45
Blackberry, Basket, Ruffled Open Edge, Marigold 65
Blackberry, Basket, Sides Up, Open Edge, Blue 87
Broken Arches, Punch Set, Marigold, 10 Piece 795
Bushel Basket, Aqua, Opalescent, Handles, Footed, Northwood, c.1910, 5 In. .... *illus* 138
Butterflies, Bonbon, 2 Handles, Marigold 72
Butterfly & Berry, Berry Bowl, Amethyst, 3-Footed 77
Butterfly & Berry, Butter, Cover, Marigold 165
Butterfly & Berry, Spooner, Marigold 65
Butterfly & Berry, Vase, Amber, 9 ¾ In. 135
Butterfly & Fern, Tumbler, Amethyst 38
Butterfly & Plume pattern is listed here as Butterfly & Fern.

Cactus Leaf Rays pattern is listed here as Leaf Rays.
Captive Rose, Bowl, Amethyst, Ruffled Edge 135
Captive Rose, Plate, Green, 9 ⅛ In. 1150
Checkerboard, Goblet, Amethyst 295
Cherries & Little Flowers, Tumbler, Collar Base, Blue 37
Cherries, Bow, Ruffled Edge, Peach Opal, 6 In. 57
Cherry Chain, Bowl, Ruffled Edge, Marigold, 6 In. 42
Cherry Chain, Ice Cream Bowl, White 245
Cherry Chain, Plate, Pumpkin Marigold, 6 ⅜ In. 115
Cherry, Bowl, Footed, Marigold 115
Cherry, Creamer, Ruby, Fenton 58
Chrysanthemum, Compote, Red, Ribbon Rim, Footed, Fenton, 6 ½ In. 12
Coin Dot, Bowl, Orange, Amethyst, Candy Ribbon Border, 8 ½ In. 24
Coin Dot, Rose Bowl, Amethyst 105
Columbine, Water Set, Amethyst, 7 Piece 725
Concord, Bowl, 3-In-1 Edge, Marigold 265
Cosmos & Cane, Tumbler, White 150
Crab Claw, Tumbler, Marigold 37
Crab Claw, Water Set, Marigold, 5 Piece 315
Dahlia, Berry Bowl, Purple 57
Dahlia, Butter, Cover, Footed, Marigold 325
Dahlia, Creamer, Marigold 155
Daisy & Drape, Vase, Splayed Feet, Marigold 395
Daisy & Lattice Band pattern is listed here as Lattice & Daisy.
Daisy & Plume, Rose Bowl, Stemmed, Marigold 57
Daisy & Plume, Rose Bowl, White, Raspberry Interior 595
Daisy Band & Drape pattern is listed here as Daisy & Drape.
Dandelion, Mug, Handle, Aqua Opalescent 1150
Diamond & Daisy, Tumbler, Marigold 65
Diamond & Rib, Vase, Amethyst, 11 ½ In. 63
Diamond Point & Daisy pattern is listed here as Cosmos & Cane.
Diamond Point, Pitcher, Water, Amber 23
Diamond Point, Tumbler, Amber 15
Diamond Point, Vase, Green, 10 ⅝ In. 95
Diamond Point, Vase, Pumpkin Marigold, 10 ¼ In. 110
Diamond Point, Vase, Squat, Amethyst, 6 ½ In. 85
Dogwood & Marsh Lily pattern is listed here as Two Flowers.
Dogwood Sprays, Bowl, Dome Footed, Marigold, 9 In. 145
Double Stem Rose, Bowl, Dome Footed, Amethyst 165
Dragon & Lotus, Bowl, Ice Cream Shape, Blue, 8 ¾ In. 185
Dragon & Lotus, Bowl, Spatula Foot, Amethyst 195
Drapery Variant, Vase, Pumpkin Marigold, 8 ½ In. 145
Drapery, Bowl, Tricornered, Marigold 145
Drapery, Rose Bowl, Aqua Opalescent 125
Fanciful, Plate, Blue, 9 In. 595
Fanciful, Plate, White, 9 In. 285
Feather & Hobstar pattern is listed here as Inverted Feather.
Field Flower, Candy Dish, Fenton, 7 ½ In. 6
Fish & Flowers pattern is listed here as Trout & Fly.
Frosted Block, Plate, White, 9 In. 85
Fruits & Flowers, Bonbon, Footed, 2 Handles, Blue 165
Fruits & Flowers, Bowl, Ruffled Edge, Amethyst, 6 In. 57
Fruits & Flowers, Bowl, Ruffled Edge, Blue, 7 ¼ In. 145
Garland, Compote, Scalloped Edge, Blue, Indiana Glass, 7 ½ In. 10
Garland, Rose Bowl, Footed, Marigold 67
Golden Harvest, Wine, Purple 40
Good Luck, Bowl, Ruffled Edge, Blue 385
Good Luck, Bowl, Ruffled Edge, Pastel Marigold, 9 In. 345
Good Luck, Plate, Green, 9 In. 775
Grape & Cable, Berry Set, Green, 5 Piece 495
Grape & Cable, Bonbon, Green, Stippled 225
Grape & Cable, Bowl, Ball Feet, Green, 7 ¾ In. 115
Grape & Cable, Bowl, Crimped, Green, Northwood, 10 ¾ In. 92
Grape & Cable, Bowl, Crimped, Round, Green, 8 In. 40
Grape & Cable, Bowl, Dessert, Green, Northwood, 4 ⅞ In. 23

Carnival Glass, Wide Panel, Epergne, 4 Trumpets, Green, Northwood, c.1909, 16 x 11 ½ In.
$287

Jeffrey S. Evans

Carousel, Horse, Jumper, Wood, Daniel C. Muller, Early 20th Century, 42 x 45 In.
$8,900

Ruby Lane

Carousel, Pig, Prancer, Carved, Saddle, Bow On Tail, Repaint, c.1890, 27 x 39 x 33 In.
$1,440

Garth's Auctioneers & Appraisers

Carriage, Stroller, Wicker, Movable Hood, Upholstered Interior, 1890s, 50 x 40 In.
$244

Morphy Auctions

Cash Register, National, Model, Saloon, Brass, Embossed, Dolphin, Marble Shelf, c.1905, 27 x 18 In.
$519

Morphy Auctions

Castor Jar, Silver Plate, Double, Pressed Inserts, Scenes, Glass Containers, Victorian, Derby Silver, 1800s
$127

Early Auction Company

TIP
Do not wash or rinse gold-decorated glass with very hot water or strong soap. It will remove some of the gold.

Grape & Cable, Bowl, Dessert, Marigold, Northwood, 4 In. 39
Grape & Cable, Bowl, Ruffled Edge, Marigold, 7 ½ In. 56
Grape & Cable, Butter, Cover, Green 245
Grape & Cable, Candlestick, Dome Base, Pair 575
Grape & Cable, Compote, Lid, Purple 375
Grape & Cable, Hatpin Holder, Marigold 265
Grape & Cable, Hatpin Holder, Purple 255
Grape & Cable, Plate, Amethyst, Northwood, 2 x 8 ¾ In. 115
Grape & Cable, Plate, Spatula Feet, Marigold, 9 In. 165
Grape & Cable, Powder Jar, Green 365
Grape & Cable, Sherbet, Pastel Marigold 45
Grape & Cable, Spooner, Purple 115
Grape & Cable, Sweetmeat, Amethyst 275
Grape & Cable, Tumbler, Amethyst, Northwood 32
Grape & Cable, Tumbler, Marigold, Northwood 33
Grape & Cable, Water Set, Electric Purple, 7 Piece 535
Grape & Cable, Whimsy, Hat Shape, Marigold 75
Grape & Leaf, Dish, Green, 4 Pedestal Legs, Scalloped Rim, 1970s, 12 x 8 In. 25
Grape Delight pattern is listed here as Vintage.
Grape Leaves, Bowl, Ruffled Edge, Purple, 7 In. 135
Grape Wreath, Bowl, Ruffled Edge, Marigold, 7 In. 95
Grapevine, Dish, Iridescent Amber Body, Ruffled Rim, Fenton, 8 ¾ In. .... *illus* 29
Grapevine, Tumbler, Purple 74
Greek Key, Bowl, Dome Footed, Green 135
Greek Key, Plate, Flared, Green 450
Harvest Time pattern is listed here as Golden Harvest.
Hearts & Flowers, Bowl, Ruffled Edge, White, 9 In. 265
Hearts & Flowers, Compote, Ruffles, Marigold 35
Hearts & Flowers, Compote, White 165
Hearts & Flowers, Plate, Flared, Ribbed, Purple, 9 In. 475
Heavy Grape, Bowl, Scalloped Edge, 6 ¼ In. 135
Heavy Grape, Chop Plate 95
Heavy Iris, Water Set, Electric Purple, 7 Piece 2300
Heirloom Sunset, Butter, Cover, Round, Red Sunset 82
Heirloom Sunset, Pitcher, Red Sunset, Indiana Glass, 40 Oz. 112
Hobnail pattern is listed in this book as its own category.
Hobstar & Feather, Chop Plate, Frosted, Millersburg, 12 In. 105
Hobstar Band, Tumbler, Marigold 37
Hobstar, Creamer, Purple 165
Hobstar, Punch Cup, Amethyst, Smith Glass 13
Holly & Berry, Bowl, Blue, Green, Northwood, 9 In. 6
Holly, Compote, Goblet Shape, Marigold 40
Holly, Plate, Blue, 9 ¾ In. 675
Honeycomb & Beads, Bowl, Crimped Edge, Peach Opal, 7 ¼ In. 57
Illusion, Bonbon, 2 Handles, Marigold 67
Imperial Grape, Compote, Olive Green 150
Imperial Grape, Cup & Saucer, Marigold 67
Imperial Grape, Decanter, Electric Purple 465
Imperial Grape, Plate, Aqua, 9 ¼ In. 295
Imperial Grape, Wine, Pumpkin Marigold, 6 Piece 235
Intaglio pattern is listed here as Hobstar & Feather.
Inverted Double Diamond, Double Salt, Marigold 205
Inverted Feather, Spooner, Amethyst, Cambridge 235
Iris, Pitcher, Water, Marigold, Colorless Handle, Dugan, 11 In. .... *illus* 80
Iris, Wine, Jeannette, 4 In. 15
Lattice & Daisy, Water Set, Marigold, 7 Piece 395
Lattice & Grape, Tumbler, Blue 65
Lattice & Grape, Water Set, Blue, 7 Piece 565
Lattice & Grapevine pattern is listed here as Lattice & Grape.
Leaf & Beads, Nut Dish, Footed, Sunflower Interior, Green 135
Leaf & Beads, Rose Bowl, Rayed Interior, Green 165
Leaf Rays, Nappy, Handle, Purple 95
Leaf Rays, Nappy, Ruffled Edge, Electric Purple, Handle 135
Lily Pons, Nappy, Amber, Indiana Glass, 7 In. 10
Lily Pons, Relish, Amber, Indiana Glass, 9 ½ In. 8

Little Flowers, Berry Bowl, Green 65
Loganberry, Bonbon, Amber, Indiana Glass, 7 In. 12
Long Thumbprint, Vase, Pumpkin Marigold, 11 ½ In. 80
Long Thumbprint, Vase, Squat, Amethyst, 7 In. 67
Maple Leaf, Berry Bowl, Marigold 35
Melon & Fan pattern is listed here as Diamond & Rib.
Memphis, Punch Cup, Purple, Pair 57
Morning Glory, Funeral Vase, Pumpkin Marigold, 15 In. 595
Nesting Swan, Bowl, Purple 475
Nippon, Bowl, Ruffled Edge, Basketweave Back, Marigold 245
Old Fashion Flag pattern is listed here as Iris.
Open Rose, Bowl, Marigold Footed, 4 x 7 ¾ In. 12
Pansy & Leaf, Bowl, Amethyst, Dugan, 8 ½ In. 59
Peacock & Urn, Bowl, Ice Cream, Marigold, Scalloped 125
Peacock At The Fountain, Sugar, Lid, Purple 165
Princess, Punch Bowl, Sawtooth Rim, Blue, Indiana Glass, 12 In. 113
Princess, Punch Cup, Amber, Footed, 2 ⅜ In. 8
Princess, Punch Cup, Blue, Indiana Glass 7
Raspberry, Tumbler, Green 45
Rays & Ribbons, Bowl, Crimped Edge, Amethyst, Millersburg, 9 ½ In. 135
Rose & Ruffles pattern is listed here as Open Rose.
Roses & Loops pattern is listed here as Double Stem Rose.
Split Diamond, Butter, Cover, Marigold 15
Stippled Diamond & Flower pattern is listed here as Little Flowers.
Stippled Leaf & Beads pattern is listed here as Leaf & Beads.
Stippled Rays, Bowl, Northwood, 8 ½ In. 6
Stippled Ribbons & Rays pattern is listed here as Rays & Ribbons.
Sunflower & Wheat pattern is listed here as Field Flower.
Sunflower pattern is listed here as Dandelion.
Swirl Hobnail, Rose Bowl, Purple, Millersburg 150
Three Fruits, Plate, Ribbed, Dark Marigold 125
Three Fruits, Plate, Ribbed, Purple 145
Trout & Fly, Bowl, Crimped Rim, Green, Millersburg, 1909-11, 2 ½ x 9 In. .... *illus* 345
Two Flowers, Dish, Blue, 3 Applied Feet, Ruffled Rim, Fenton, 4 x 11 In. .... *illus* 75
Vintage, Goblet, Water, Marigold 14
Vintage, Nappy, Crimped, Marigold, 9 In. 16
Vintage, Punch Bowl, Marigold, 11 ⅞ In. 232
Vintage, Rose Bowl, White 85
Wide Panel, Epergne, 4 Trumpets, Green, Northwood, c.1909, 16 x 11 ½ In. .... *illus* 287
Wild Grapes pattern is listed here as Grape Leaves.
Windsor, Juice, Blue, Federal Glass, 4 ⅜ In. 8

CAROUSEL or merry-go-round figures were first carved in the United States in 1867 by Gustav Dentzel. Collectors discovered the charm of the hand-carved figures in the 1970s, and they were soon classed as folk art. Most desirable are the figures other than horses, such as pigs, camels, lions, or dogs. A stander has all four feet on the carousel platform; a prancer has both front feet in the air and both back feet on the platform; a jumper has all four feet in the air and usually moves up and down.

Carriage, Stylized Swans, 2 Bench Seats, Multicolor, 1900s, 56 x 31 In. 819
Cat, Jumper, White, Yellow Eyes, Saddle, Gustave Bayol, France, c.1875, 30 x 37 In. 2299
Goat, Prancer, Carved, White, Saddle, Dentzel, 67 x 63 In. 12650
Goat, Prancer, Pine, Painted, Charles Looff, c.1900, 56 x 45 In. 7800
Horse, Jumper, Brown, White Saddle, Red Bridle, 48 x 8 ¼ In. 605
Horse, Jumper, Red & Blue Saddle, 56 x 64 In. 240
Horse, Jumper, Wood, Daniel C. Muller, Early 20th Century, 42 x 45 In. .... *illus* 8900
Horse, Prancer, Wood, Painted, Horsehair Tail, Lily, England, c.1900, 73 x 53 In. 840
Horse, Wood, Hair Tail, Glass Eyes, Ebonized Base, c.1900, 44 x 43 x 12 In. 922
Pig, Prancer, Carved, Saddle, Bow On Tail, Repaint, c.1890, 27 x 39 x 33 In. .... *illus* 1440
Rabbit, Jumper, Saddle, Ribbon, Glass Eyes, c.1960, 68 x 51 In. 615

CARRIAGE means several things, so this category lists baby carriages, buggies for adults, horse-drawn sleighs, and even strollers. Doll-sized carriages are listed in the Toy category.

Buggy Seat, Black Paint, Shaped Splats, Woven Seat, Stretchers, 1800s, 33 x 34 In. 338

Castor Set, 2 Cobalt Blue Sauce Dishes, Silver Frame, Victorian
$575

Early Auction Company

Castor Set, 7 Bottles, Amberina Glass, Etched Flowers, Silver Plated Frame, 16 ½ In.
$1,955

Early Auction Company

Cauldon, Plate, Chinese Scene, 1902, 10 ¼ In.
$32

Ruby Lane

Celadon, Bowl, Shrimp & Sauce, Rolled Scalloped Rim, Pedestal Base
$120

Celadon, Brush Washer, Jade, Lotus Shape, Tied Branches, Smiling Frog, c.1890, 6 ½ In.
$2,470

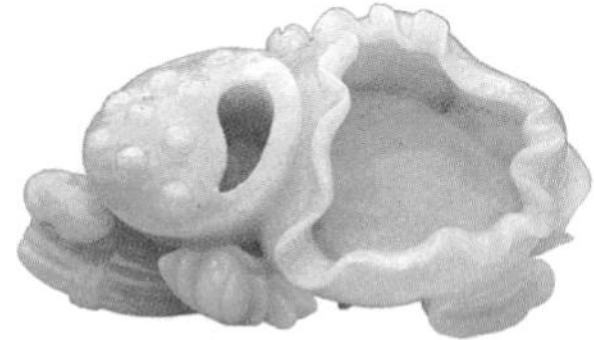

James D. Julia Auctioneers

Celadon, Plate, Flowers, Butterflies, Fish, 19th Century, 10 In. Diam.
$595

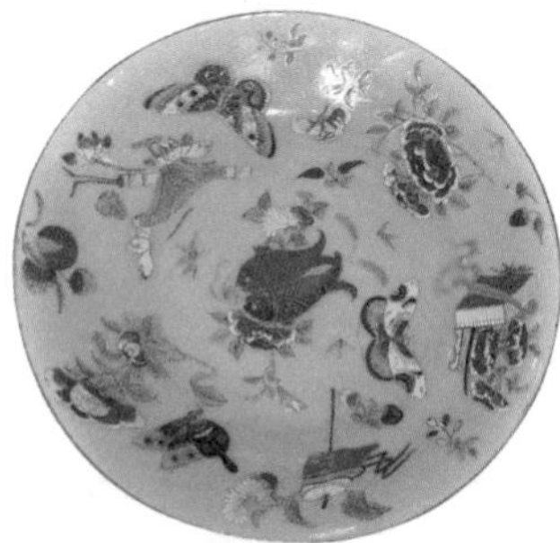

Ruby Lane

TIP

To find a small crack in porcelain or glass, try this. Put the piece on a table. Tap it with your fingernail. A cracked piece gives off a dull thud, a perfect piece will "ring." Learn to recognize the sound by practicing on some pieces you know are broken.

Sleigh, Red & Black Paint, Curved Runners, Push Handle, 1800s, Child's, 37 x 18 In. 266
Stroller, Wicker, Movable Hood, Upholstered Interior, 1890s, 50 x 40 In. .... *illus* 244

CASH REGISTERS were invented in 1884 because an eye on the cash was a necessity in stores of the nineteenth century, too. John and James Ritty invented a large model that resembled a clock and kept a record of the dollars and cents exchanged in the store. John Patterson improved the cash register with a paper roll to record the money. By the early 1900s, elaborate brass registers were made. More modern types were made after 1920.

American, Model 522, Brass, Marble Base, Receipt Side, Festoon Marquee, 1911 485
National, Brass, Signed Marquee, W.B. Goodyear, 902011W Over 356, 22 x 21 In. 177
National, Model 52 ¼, Brass, Marble Base, Scroll Marquee, Side Receipt 1680
National, Model 95, Brass, 3 Drawers, Wood Base, Hand Crank, 1903, 26 x 27 In. 510
National, Model 130, Nickel, Scroll Design, Marquee, 1905, 19 In. 1037
National, Model 211, Copper Flashed, Candy Store, Scrolling Leaves, 1908 995
National, Model 216, Bronze, Copper Finish, Fleur-De-Lis, 1909, 21 x 16 In. 1220
National, Model 311, Bronze, Mount Purchased, Dolphins, 1908, 10 x 21 In. 570
National, Model 313, Bronze, Dolphins, Marble Till Shelf, 15-Key, c.1914, 18 x 17 In. 480
National, Model 425, Bronze, Empire Design, Oak Base, Embossed, 1915, 25 x 28 In. 427
National, Model 452, Bronze, Empire Design, Crank, Wood Base, c.1909, 24 x 27 In. 960
National, Model 592, Floor, Nickel Plate, Wood, Empire Design, 1910, 69 x 29 In. 4880
National, Model 1054, Embossed, Metalwork On Case, 23 In. 360
National, Model, Saloon, Brass, Embossed, Dolphin, Marble Shelf, c.1905, 27 x 18 In. .... *illus* 519
Ticket Receipt Box, National Cash Register, Cast Iron, Brass Finish, 6 x 6 In. 182

CASTOR JARS for pickles are glass jars about six inches in height, held in special metal holders. They became a popular dinner table accessory about 1890. Each jar had a top that was usually silver or silver plate. The frame, also of a silver metal, had a handle that arched above the jar and a hook that held a pair of tongs. By 1900, the pickle castor was out of fashion. Many examples found today have reproduced glass jars in old holders. Additional pickle castors may be found in the various Glass categories.

Pickle, Clear Jar, Bird, Flowers, Silver Plate, Tongs, 6 ¼ x 12 In. 48
Pickle, Hobnail, Vaseline, c.1890, 4 ½ In. 95
Silver Plate, Double, Pressed Inserts, Scenes, Glass Containers, Victorian, Derby Silver, 1800s .... *illus* 127

CASTOR SETS holding just salt and pepper castors were used in the seventeenth century. The sugar castor, mustard pot, spice dredger (shaker), bottles for vinegar and oil, and other spice holders became popular by the eighteenth century. These sets were usually made of sterling silver. The American Victorian castor set, the type most collected today, was made of silver plated Britannia metal. Colored glass bottles were introduced after the Civil War. The sets were out of fashion by World War I. Be careful when buying sets with colored bottles; many are reproductions. Other castor sets may be listed in various porcelain and glass categories in this book.

2 Bottles, Victorian Frame, Cobalt Blue Pickle Castor, 2 Sauce Dishes 173
4 Bottles, Cut Glass, Spoon, S. Wolfenden Bolton, 7 ¾ x 6 In. 92
5 Bottles, Cranberry Glass, Coin Dot, Silver, Bird, Floral Handle, 19 In. 120
5 Bottles, Cut Glass Cruets, Heraldic Design, Center Post, Charles T. Fox, 1840, 10 In. 472
5 Bottles, Etched Glass, Silver, Oval Handle, 17 x 7 In. 41
5 Bottles, Ruby Glass, Silver, 16 In. 118
6 Bottles, Square, Cut Glass, Silver Plate, Keyhole Handle, 8 x 7 In. 82
6 Bottles, Vase Shape, Cut Glass, Silver Plate, Crest, England, 10 x 6 In. 180
7 Bottles, Amberina Glass, Etched Flowers, Silver Plated Frame, 16 ½ In. .... *illus* 1955
7 Bottles, Cut Glass, Diamond, Silver Plate, Etched Flowers, 16 ¾ x 6 ½ In. 120
7 Bottles, Cut Glass, Flowers, Pomegranates, Acorns, Leaves, Silver, 9 x 7 In. 186
2 Cobalt Blue Sauce Dishes, Silver Frame, Victorian .... *illus* 575

CATALOGS *are listed in the Paper category.*

CAUGHLEY porcelain was made in England from 1772 to 1814. Caughley porcelains are very similar in appearance to those made at the Worcester factory. See the Salopian category for related items.

Dish, Blue & White Transfer, River Scene, Diaper Border, Gilt, c.1790, 9 x 9 In. 81
Sauceboat, Blue & White, Landscape, 3 ⅜ x 5 ½ In., Pair 531

CAULDON Limited worked in Staffordshire, Great Britain, and went through many name changes. John Ridgway made porcelain at Cauldon Place, Hanley, until 1855. The firm of John Ridgway, Bates and Co. of Cauldon Place worked from 1856 to 1859. It became Bates, Brown-Westhead, Moore and Co. from 1859 to 1862. Brown-Westhead, Moore and Co. worked from 1862 to 1904. About 1890, this firm started using the words *Cauldon* or *Cauldon Ware* as part of the mark. Cauldon Ltd. worked from 1905 to 1920, Cauldon Potteries from 1920 to 1962. Related items may be found in the Indian Tree category.

Bowl, Flow Blue, Flowers, Curlicues, 14 x 6 In. 240
Cup & Saucer, Flower Bouquets, Pink Border, Gilt Rim, White Ground, 12 Piece 676
Plate, Chinese Scene, 1902, 10 ¼ In. .... *illus* 32
Plate, Trout, Cobalt Blue Border, Gilt, Shaped Rim, Filigreed, 9 In. 67
Plate, Woman, Geese, Country Farm, Blossoming Trees, Gilt Flower Rim, 10 In. 61

CELADON is the name of a velvet-textured green-gray glaze used by Chinese, Japanese, Korean, and other factories. This section includes pieces covered with celadon glaze with or without added decoration.

Bowl, Flared Rim, Incised Flower Petal, Round Foot, 5 In. 181
Bowl, Impressed Flowers, 3 x 17 In. 780
Bowl, Impressed Flowers, Ribbed Sides, 3 x 13 ¼ In. 420
Bowl, Shrimp & Sauce, Rolled Scalloped Rim, Pedestal Base .... *illus* 120
Bowl, Sloping Sides, Copper Rim, Flower Relief Rondel, Fan Shape Panels, 7 In. 420
Bowl, Wood Box, Japan, 3 ½ x 8 In. 185
Brush Washer, Jade, Lotus Shape, Tied Branches, Smiling Frog, c.1890, 6 ½ In. .... *illus* 2470
Censer, Ming Style, Carved Flowers, 3 Glazed Feet, Chinese, 4 x 11 In. 708
Charger, Carved Flowers & Scrolling, Sea Green, Shaped Edge, 1800s, 17 In. Diam. 296
Charger, Flared Rim, Incised Lotus Scroll Design, Shaped Edge, 17 In. Diam. 1062
Charger, Longquan, Fluted, Scalloped Rim, Lotus, Chinese, 12 ¾ In. 750
Dish, Painted, White Flowers, Glazed, Punch'ong, Footed, Korea, 1 ¼ x 4 In. 472
Figurine, Foo Dog, White Glaze, Opposing, On Plinth, Pup, Ball, 12 x 8 In., Pair 719
Figurine, Guanyin, Flowing Robes, Holding Rosary, Mottled, 7 In. 1853
Incense Burner, Brown Glaze Top, Double Loop Handles, Animal Head Feet, 8 In. 413
Jar, Compressed Globular, Carved Peony Banding, Leaves, Scroll, 6 In. 1558
Jar, Guan, Ming Style, Carved Peonies, Tendrils, Recessed Base, Footed, 6 x 9 In. 885
Planter, Bonsai, Applied Blue Decoration, 4 Splayed Legs, Japan, 1800s, 5 x 15 In. 148
Plate, Flowers, Butterflies, Fish, 19th Century, 10 In. Diam. .... *illus* 595
Plate, Flowers, Peaches, Green, 1800s, 8 ¼ In., 8 Piece 185
Plate, Symbol Medallion, 5 Bats, 9 ¼ In. 120
Scepter, White To Green, Hardstone, Shaped Handle, c.1900, 16 x 4 In. 12980
Vase, Blue & White Decoration, Flat Lip, 17 ¼ In. 373
Vase, Bottle Shape, Bulbous, Cylindrical Neck, Molded Dragon, Marked, 12 ½ In. .... *illus* 1230
Vase, Carved, Flowers, Central Band, Wavy Ground, 7 ¼ In. .... *illus* 590
Vase, Compressed Globular, Flared Neck, Brown Crackles, 7 In. 4740
Vase, Globular, Flared Rim, Ring Of Petals, Round Foot, 1900s, 10 x 7 In. 1235
Vase, Hu Shape, Incised, Lotus Flowers, Leaves, Ruyi, Dragon Handles, c.1900, 18 In. 4800
Vase, Lotus Shape, Fluted, Leaves, Blue-Green Glaze, 1800s, 8 ¼ x 5 In. 1121
Vase, Ming Style, Molded, Pear Shape, Handles, Rings, Chrysanthemum Border, 12 In. 2124
Vase, Olive Green, China, 12 In. 281
Vase, Pear Shape, Incised Banding, Leaves, Ruyi Border, Dragons, 11 In. 740
Vase, Reeded, 1800s, 5 ¾ x 5 ½ In. 123
Vase, Rolled Rim, Saucer Foot, Dragons, Clouds, Pearls, c.1900, 15 In. 4693
Vase, Squat, Glazed, Cranes, Key Fret Border, Lotus Petals, 5 ½ x 6 In. 109
Vase, Squat, Ring Foot, Green, Orange Band On Foot & Rim, 1800s, 5 x 6 In. 397
Vase, White Leaves, Flowers, Fruit, Bulbous, Bell Foot, Trumpet Neck, 1800s, 15 In., Pair 937
Vase, White Leaves, Flowers, Herons, 14 x 9 In., Pair 1464
Water Dropper, Duck, Rope, Korea, 1970s, 5 ½ In. .... *illus* 121

CELLULOID is a trademark for a plastic developed in 1868 by John W. Hyatt. Celluloid Manufacturing Company, the Celluloid Novelty Company, Celluloid Fancy Goods Company, and American Xylonite Company all used celluloid to make jewelry, games, sewing equipment, false teeth, and piano keys. The name *celluloid* was often used to identify any similar plastic. Celluloid toys are listed under Toy.

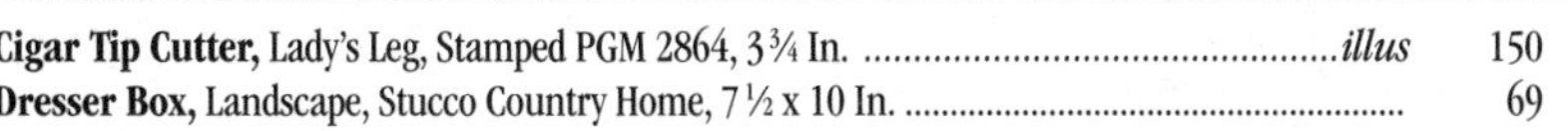

Cigar Tip Cutter, Lady's Leg, Stamped PGM 2864, 3 ¾ In. .... *illus* 150
Dresser Box, Landscape, Stucco Country Home, 7 ½ x 10 In. 69

Celadon, Vase, Bottle Shape, Bulbous, Cylindrical Neck, Molded Dragon, Marked, 12 ½ In.
$1,230

Skinner, Inc.

Celadon, Vase, Carved, Flowers, Central Band, Wavy Ground, 7 ¼ In.
$590

Brunk Auctions

Celadon, Water Dropper, Duck, Rope, Korea, 1970s, 5 ½ In.
$121

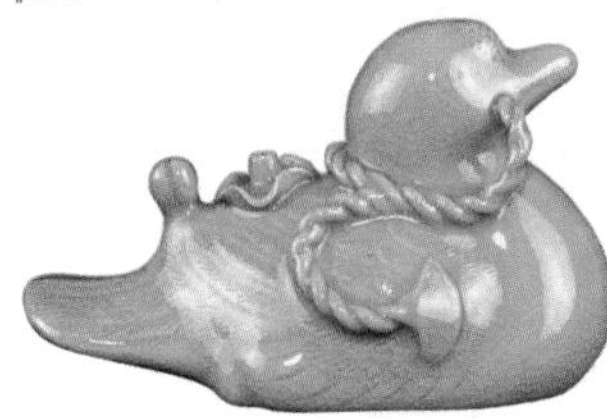

Ruby Lane

C

Celluloid, Cigar Tip Cutter, Lady's Leg, Stamped PGM 2864, 3 ¾ In.
$150

Showtime Auction Services

Chalkware, Figurine, Cat, Seated, Yellow Cream Stripes, Black Ground, c.1885, 15 ½ In.
$677

Skinner, Inc.

Charlie Chaplin, Toy, Raises Hat & Foot, Swings Cane, Tin, Windup, Germany, c.1918, 8 In.
$708

Bertoia Auctions

Dresser Set, Child's, Mirror, Combs, Brushes, Powder Box, Satin-Lined Box, 10 Piece 89
Figurine, Wooden Bird, Celluloid Leaves, 3 ¾ In. 30
Mirror, Magician Thurston Portrait, Imps Whispering, Oval, Pocket, 1920, 2 ¾ In. 676
Pin, Sweetheart Soldier, Articulated, World War II, 4 x 4 In. 69

CELS *are listed in this book in the Animation Art category.*

CERAMIC ART COMPANY of Trenton, New Jersey, was established in 1889 by Jonathan Coxon and Walter Scott and was an early producer of American belleek porcelain. It became Lenox, Inc. in 1906. Do not confuse this ware with the pottery made by the Ceramic Arts Studio of Madison, Wisconsin.

Mug, Tyg, Cherubs, Scrolled Handles, 1889, 6 In. 695
Vase, Carnation, Dark, Gilt Shoulders, White Body, 10 x 4 ¾ In. 495
Vase, Gold, Maroon, Cyclamen, 11 ½ x 7 In. 525

CERAMIC ARTS STUDIO was founded about 1940 in Madison, Wisconsin, by Lawrence Rabbett and Ruben Sand. Their most popular products were molded figurines. The pottery closed in 1955. Do not confuse these products with those of the Ceramic Art Co. of Trenton, New Jersey.

Ewer, Beaker Shape, Loop Handle, Grapes, Flowers, c.1900, 14 x 7 In. 122
Figurine, Comedy & Tragedy, Betty Harrington, 10 In., Pair 300
Head Vase, Becky, Green Stripes, 1950, 5 ½ In. 75
Sauceboat, Jasperware, Green, Horse, Oval Foot, 2 x 4 ½ In. 60
Vase, Bud, Triple, Bamboo, Multicolor, Man, Woman, c.1945, 7 In. 45

CHALKWARE is really plaster of Paris decorated with watercolors. One type was molded from Staffordshire and other porcelain models and painted and sold as inexpensive decorations in the nineteenth century. This type is very valuable today. Figures of plaster, made from about 1910 to 1940 for use as prizes at carnivals, are also known as chalkware. Kewpie dolls made of chalkware will be found in their own category.

Ashtray, Boxer, Green Grass Base, 1940s, 9 x 7 In. 29
Bank, Apple, Bull's-Eyes, White, 3 ¼ In. 935
Buck's Head, Paint, Sideways Glancing, Round Wall Mount, c.1950, 11 ½ In. 118
Bust, Native American, Tribal Chief, Bearclaw Necklace, 29 In., Pair 427
Centerpiece, Fruit-Filled Urn, Multicolor, c.1960, 18 In. 40
Figurine, Cat, Seated, Curled Tail, Red Ears, 19th Century, 7 ¼ In. 738
Figurine, Cat, Seated, Painted Collar With Hanging Bells, c.1885, 7 In. 360
Figurine, Cat, Seated, Yellow Cream Stripes, Black Ground, c.1885, 15 ½ In. .... *illus* 677
Figurine, Dog, German Shepherd, Seated, c.1940, 10 In. 22
Figurine, Dog, King Charles Spaniel, Brown Spots, Red Collar, c.1885, 7 In., Pair 277
Figurine, Dog, Poodle, Standing, White, Painted Highlights, Base, c.1880, 7 ½ x 5 In. 90
Figurine, Dog, Puppy, Reclining, Bug On Back, c.1935, 2 x 2 ¾ In. 32
Figurine, Dove, Painted, Cherry Branch Base, c.1885, 11 ¼ In., Pair 570
Figurine, Dove, Perched On Stump, Cherry Branch, 11 ½ In. 177
Figurine, Indian Chief, Headdress, Hand On Brow, Countertop, 21 In. 330
Figurine, Indian, Lone Wolf, Feather, Bust, Chalkware, Painted, c.1907, 13 x 8 In. 228
Figurine, Lamb & Ewe, Reclining, White, c.1860, 8 x 7 x 4 In. 385
Figurine, Our Lady Of Fatima, 12 ½ In. 225
Figurine, Pig, Standing, Ears Up, Cream, Painted Brown Features, 6 x 10 In. 194
Figurine, Rabbit, Spotted, Black, Red, Gold, 19th Century, 5 ¾ In. 861
Figurine, Reclining Lamb & Ewe, White, c.1860, 8 x 7 x 4 In. 385
Figurine, Squirrel, Painted, Yellow, Red & Black Splashes, 1800s, 6 ½ x 3 In. 1046
Figurine, Stag, Reclining, Paint, Smoke Design, Oval Base, c.1885, 6 ¼ In., Pair 649
Figurine, Victorian Woman, Red Dress, Pacini Novelty Co., c.1950, 11 ½ In. 39
Pincushion, Bulldog, Sitting, Japan, 2 ¾ In. 48
Plaque, Galloping Horses, Black, Gilt Manes, 1950s, 20 x 15 In. 89
Plaque, Kissing Angel Fish, White, Red Lips, 1954, 5 x 5 In. 34
Salt & Pepper, Black & White, Base, Raised Tail, 2 ¼ In. 14

CHARLIE CHAPLIN, the famous comedian, actor, and filmmaker, lived from 1889 to 1977. He made his first movie in 1913. He did the movie *The Tramp* in 1915. The character of the Tramp has remained famous, and in the 1980s appeared in a series of television commercials for computers. Dolls, candy containers, and all sorts of memorabilia with the image of Charlie's Tramp are collected. Pieces are being made even today.

Candy Container, Charlie Next To Glass Barrel, 3 x 2 In. 115
Doll, Composition Head, Molded Hair & Mustache, Cloth Body, Cane, Amberg, 12 In. 425
Marionette, Plaster, Paint, Suit, Hat, Tie, Certificate 60
Toy, Balancing Bicycle, Painted, Multicolor, Tin Lithograph, 8 x 7 In. 100
Toy, Raises Hat & Foot, Swings Cane, Tin, Windup, Germany, c.1918, 8 In. .... *illus* 708
Toy, Walker, Charlie Holding Cane, Brim Hat, Box, Germany, 7 x 3 In. 1200
Toy, Walker, Tin, Felt Suit, Cane, Clockwork, Box, Germany, 6 ½ In. 826

CHARLIE McCARTHY was the ventriloquist's dummy used by Edgar Bergen from the 1930s. He was famous for his work in radio, movies, and television. The act was retired in the 1970s. Mortimer Snerd, another Bergen dummy, is also listed here.

Book, Story Of, Eleanor Packer Story, Henry E. Vallely Art, Whitman, 1938 163
Doll, Composition Shoulder Head, Painted, Muslin Body, Effanbee, c.1935, 18 In. .... *illus* 336
Doll, Ventriloquist, Composition Head, Molded Hair, Cloth Body, 15 In. 180
Radio, Majestic, Bakelite, Ivory, Charlie, Seated, c.1938, 6 x 7 x 6 In. 682
Ring, Figural, 18K Gold Plate, Die Cut Image, Name, 1938 173
Toy, Benzene Buggy, Charlie Driving Car, Tin, Windup, Marx, 1938, 7 In. .... 240 to 538
Toy, Charlie, Wobbly Walker, Mouth Opens, Tin Litho, Windup, Marx, Box, 8 In. .... 108 to 384
Toy, Coupe, Charlie & Mortimer Snerd, Tin Litho, Windup, Box, 1939, 16 In. 2277
Toy, Private Car, Mortimer Snerd, Car, Striped, Tin, Clockwork, Marx, 16 In. 1121

CHELSEA porcelain was made in the Chelsea area of London from about 1745 to 1769. Some pieces made from 1770 to 1784 are called Chelsea Derby and may include the letter *D* for *Derby* in the mark. Ceramic designs were borrowed from the Meissen models of the day. Pieces were made of soft paste. The gold anchor was used as the mark, but it has been copied by many other factories. Recent copies of Chelsea have been made from the original molds. Do not confuse Chelsea porcelain with Chelsea Grape, a white pottery with luster grape decoration. Chelsea Keramic is listed in the Dedham category.

Bonbonniere, Hinged Lid, Children, Dog, Kaleidoscope, Multicolor, Gold, c.1760, 2 In. 6831
Dish, Cabbage, Leaf Shape, Ruffled Edge, Curved Stem Handle, Green, White, c.1755, 9 In. 179
Plate, Sunflower, 2 Overlapping Leaves, Stalk Handle, c.1755, 8 ⅝ In., 2 Piece 7780
Vase, Green, Oval, Lion's Heads In Relief At Ends, W.P.S. Griffin, 1881, 7 x 12 In. 1476
Vase, Oxblood Glaze, Swollen Shoulder, Cylindrical Neck, Marked, H. Robertson, 8 In. 3321
Vase, Shouldered, Oval, Cylinder Neck, Red Oxblood Glaze, 1880s, 7 ½ x 4 In. 2250

CHELSEA GRAPE pattern was made before 1840. A small bunch of grapes in a raised design, colored with purple or blue luster, is on the border of the white plate. Most of the pieces are unmarked. The pattern is sometimes called Aynsley or Grandmother. Chelsea Sprig is similar but has a sprig of flowers instead of the bunch of grapes. Chelsea Thistle has a raised thistle pattern. Do not confuse these Chelsea patterns with Chelsea Keramic Art Works, which can be found in the Dedham category, or with Chelsea porcelain, the preceding category.

Plate, Tab Handles, Blue Luster, c.1800, 10 In. 70
Sugar & Creamer, Copper Luster, Scalloped 115

CHINESE EXPORT porcelain comprises the many kinds of porcelain made in China for export to America and Europe in the eighteenth, nineteenth, and twentieth centuries. Other pieces may be listed in this book under Canton, Celadon, Nanking, Rose Canton, Rose Mandarin, and Rose Medallion.

Basin, Landscape, Figures, Cartouches, Flowers, Overhang Rim, Bats, 1800s, 15 In. 598
Bowl, Blue & White, Pagodas, Blue Rim, 10 In. 495
Bowl, Centerpiece, Famille Verte, Tapered, Round Foot, Gilt, Peacocks, Flowers, 14 In. 153
Bowl, Crest Of Luttrell, Flowers, Gilt, Ring Foot, c.1765, 6 x 6 In., Pair 281
Bowl, Famille Rose, Hunt Scenes, Flowers, Wide Rim, Ring Foot, 1800s, 11 In. 1500
Bowl, Famille Rose, Mandarin, Figures, Scrolling Flowers, c.1790, 5 x 11 ½ In. 2074
Bowl, Famille Rose, Peach Branches, Bats, Clouds, Scallop Border, c.1760, 16 In. 220
Bowl, Famille Rose, Squat, Ring Foot, Millefleur Gilt Ground, 6 x 2 In., Pair 948
Bowl, Fish, Famille Verte, Oval, Western Wing Story, 1800s, 14 x 16 In. .... *illus* 4130
Bowl, Fruit, Scalloped Rim, Chrysanthemum Branches, 4 ⅜ x 7 ⅝ In. 960
Bowl, Imperial Yellow & Green, Lobed, Green Dragons, Foot Ring, 5 In. 4920
Bowl, Punch, Declaration Of Independence, Shield, Eagle, c.1817, 5 x 12 In. .... *illus* 5228
Bowl, Purple & Orange Landscape, 3 Men, Butterflies, Footed, 8 ⅞ In. 138
Bowl, Square Cartouches, Flower Clusters, Fleur-De-Lis Band, 10 ½ x 4 In. 302

Charlie McCarthy, Doll, Composition Shoulder Head, Painted, Muslin Body, Effanbee, c.1935, 18 In.
$336

Theriault's

Chinese Export, Bowl, Fish, Famille Verte, Oval, Western Wing Story, 1800s, 14 x 16 In.
$4,130

Brunk Auctions

Chinese Export, Bowl, Punch, Declaration Of Independence, Shield, Eagle, c.1817, 5 x 12 In.
$5,228

Skinner, Inc.

Chinese Export, Charger, Figures In Garden, Green, Chenghua Mark, c.1600, 13⅝ In.
$7,688

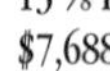

Neal Auctions

Chinese Export, Cup & Saucer, Armorial, Welsh Family Arms, Gilt Spearheads, 1800s, 2 x 5 In.
$720

Cowan Auctions

TIP

People sometimes hide "treasures" in their homes and when they die the family has no idea where to look for them. Check the "clothes chutes" where laundry items could be dropped to the basement, then check for nails inside the chute that have string on them. We heard of a man who found a plastic bottle at the end of a string with $500 cash in it.

Box, Lid, Famille Jaune, Green, Purple, Phoenix, Dragon, Waves, c.1800, 4 x 3 In. 356
Box, Lid, Famille Rose, Round, Blossoms, Leaves, Branches, Bats, 1900s, 2 x 4 In. 494
Charger, Dragon & Phoenix, c.1900 1200
Charger, Famille Verte, Center Reserve, Emperor, Courtiers, Palace Scene, 24 In. 738
Charger, Figures In Garden, Green, Chenghua Mark, c.1600, 13⅝ In. .... *illus* 7688
Charger, Lobed, Yellow Panels, Gilt Dragons, Flaming Pearls, c.1890, 2 x 19 In. 1000
Charger, Octagonal, Flowers, Leaves, White Ground, Gold Trim, 14½ In. Diam. 570
Chocolate Pot, Lid, Cylindrical, Pistol Grip Handle, Fish Spout, Crest, 1700s, 7 In. 308
Creamer, Lid, Gilt, White Flowers, 4½ In. 50
Cup & Saucer, Armorial, Welsh Family Arms, Gilt Spearheads, 1800s, 2 x 5 In. .... *illus* 720
Cup, Famille Rose, Lotus, Libation, Pink Petals, Yellow, Green, c.1908, 5 x 7 In. 500
Cup, Famille Rose, Millefleur, Gilt Rim, Marked, 2½ In., Pair 17700
Cup, Wine, Famille Rose, Bell Shape, Flowers, Ring Foot, 1900s, 3 x 3 In., Pair 153
Dish, Blue & White, Figures, Waterscape, Lozenge Shape, c.1900, 11 x 9 In. 126
Dish, Famille Rose, 8 Treasures, Flower Roundel, Emblems, 7 In. Diam. 1250
Dish, Famille Rose, Chrysanthemum & Butterfly Scroll, Waves, 1700s, 9 In. 276
Dish, Famille Rose, Peonies Branches, Chrysanthemums, 5 In. Diam., Pair 309
Dish, Famille Rose, Shell Shape, Peonies, Butterfly Wings, c.1805, 10 x 10 In. 196
Dish, Hundred Antiques, Famille Verte, Dragons, 8¼ In., Pair 472
Dish, Lid, Famille Rose, Peach Of Immortality Finial, Flowers, Gilt, 3 x 5 In. 150
Ewer, Famille Rose, Monk's Cap Shape, Loop Handle, Lotus, Bats, Dragons, 7 In. 1235
Figurine, Cat, Green, 1800s, 9 In. 4270
Figurine, Elephant, Standing, Head Turned, Seat On Back, Blanket, Trunk Up, 7 In. 475
Figurine, Foo Star, Famille Rose, Standing, Holding Child, Marked, 20 In. 545
Figurine, Guanyin, Seated, Famille Rose, Coral Cloak, Gilt, Lotus, Vines, c.1900, 9 In. 237
Figurine, Parrot, Rockwork Base, Green, Yellow Glaze, c.1700, 7½ In., Pair .... *illus* 215
Figurine, Peacock, Perched, Rockwork Base, Multicolor, 1800s, 16 x 6 In., Pair 875
Figurine, Phoenix, Famille Rose, Sweeping Tail, Perched On Branch, 14 In. 830
Figurine, Phoenix, Pink Breast, 14 In. 246
Figurine, Rooster, Standing, Pierced Tree Trunk, c.1900, 12 In., Pair 5625
Flask, Famille Rose, Moon Shape, Straight Neck, Chilong Handles, 1800s, 10 In., Pair 194
Ginger Jar, Cover, Famille Rose, Auspicious Procession, 1900s, 14 x 8¼ In., Pair 500
Ginger Jar, Famille Verte, Oval, Figures, Gardens, Kite, Dome Lid, 10 In. 1375
Ginger Jar, Lid, Children & Adults, Round, Bulbous, Finial, 1800s, 8½ In. 173
Hat Stand, Famille Rose, Cylindrical, Openwork, Courtyard, Figures, c.1900, 12 In. 356
Hat Stand, Famille Rose, The Hundred Antiques, Cylindrical, Pierced, 1800s, 11 In. 119
Jar, Burnt Orange, White Koi Fish, 1900s, 13½ In. 86
Jar, Famille Rose, Women, Children, Activities, Yongzheng Mark, c.1925, 8 In. .... *illus* 2832
Jar, Famille Verte, Mythical Beasts, Paneled Landscape, 16½ In., Pair 3304
Jar, Lid, Blue, Landscape Reserves, People, Finial, 10 In. 188
Jar, Lid, Famille Rose, Hexagonal Barrel Shape, Relief, Fruits, 1800s, 12 In. 370
Jardiniere, Famille Verte, Square, Round Aperture, Squat Feet, 1800s, 8 x 5 In. 545
Jardiniere, Montieth, Multicolor, Landscape, 8 x 19 In. 125
Lantern, 6-Sided, Blue, White, Flowers, People, Landscapes, 15½ In., Pair 1169
Mug, Cylindrical, Saucer Foot, Pink Flowers, Blue & White, Loop Handle, 5 In. 336
Mug, Glorious Victory At Culloden, Medallion, Duke Of Cumberland, c.1750, 6 In. .... *illus* 3567
Pitcher, Fluted, Flower Border, Water Landscapes, Exotic Birds, c.1750, 9 In. 277
Planter, Stand, Famille Jaune, Warriors, Landscape, Yellow Ground, 8 x 8 In., Pair 2242
Plate, Armorial, Octagonal, Arms Of Watson, Flowers, Fan, Crown, c.1750, 9 In. Diam. .... *illus* 937
Plate, Central Medallion, Orange Fitzhugh, Animals, 1800, 8 In., 4 Piece 625
Plate, Famille Rose, 3 Reserves, Butterflies, Birds, Flowers, Triangular, 11 In. 295
Plate, Famille Rose, Bats, Roundels, Swastikas, Yellow Ground, 9 In. Diam. 371
Plate, Famille Verte, Bird & Flower, Double Circle, 8⅜ In. 492
Plate, Japanese Market, Orange Rim, Blue, White Ground, Umbrella, 9 In. 1500
Plate, Martin Luther, Portrait, Grisaille, Cartouche, Putti Heads, c.1750, 9 In. 1750
Plate, Tobacco Leaf Pattern, Scalloped Edges, c.1750-60, 9 In., Pair 1888
Plate, Yellow Fitzhugh, Plants, Animals, 8½ In. 5937
Plate, Yellow Fitzhugh, Red Outline, 4 Sections, Center Medallion, c.1800, 8 In. 5937
Platter, Armorial, Blue, White, Butterflies, Leaves, c.1890, 11¾ In., Pair 937
Platter, Blue & White, Serpentine Edge, Panels, Peonies, Pomegranates, c.1765, 17 In. 615
Platter, Famille Rose, Flowering Vine Border, Flowers, Vases, c.1790, 15 x 12 In. 687
Platter, Famille Rose, Oblong, Ogee Edge, Flowers, c.1800, 16 x 12 In. 593
Platter, Famille Rose, Octagonal, Outdoor Scene, Upturned Rim, 1700s, 16 x 13 In. .... *illus* 896
Platter, Flowers, Blue & White, Oval, Shaped Rim, 14 x 11 In., Pair 431
Platter, Garden Scene, Blue & White, 8-Sided, c.1950, 11 x 14½ In. .... *illus* 480

Chinese Export, Figurine, Parrot, Rockwork Base, Green, Yellow Glaze, c.1700, 7 ½ In., Pair
$215

Skinner, Inc.

Chinese Export, Jar, Famille Rose, Women, Children, Activities, Yongzheng Mark, c.1925, 8 In.
$2,832

Brunk Auctions

Chinese Export, Mug, Glorious Victory At Culloden, Medallion, Duke Of Cumberland, c.1750, 6 In.
$3,567

Skinner, Inc.

Whistler Was Broke

James Whistler, the famous painter, sold his house and his collection of Chinese porcelains to pay legal bills. He sued an art critic for libel and won, but he wasn't awarded enough to cover his legal fees.

Chinese Export, Plate, Armorial, Octagonal, Arms Of Watson, Flowers, Fan, Crown, c.1750, 9 In. Diam.
$937

New Orleans (Cakebread)

Chinese Export, Platter, Famille Rose, Octagonal, Outdoor Scene, Upturned Rim, 1700s, 16 x 13 In.
$896

Neal Auctions

Chinese Export, Platter, Garden Scene, Blue & White, 8-Sided, c.1950, 11 x 14 ½ In.
$480

Selkirk Auctioneers & Appraisers

Chinese Export, Platter, Scalloped, Tobacco Leaf Pattern, Multicolor, c.1800, 17 x 14 In.
$1,968

Cowan Auctions

Chinese Export, Platter, Shield Crest, Monogram, Grapevine Rim, Blue & Gilt, c.1810, 17 In.
$677

Cowan Auctions

Compulsive Collecting

A famous child prodigy who could spell at age 1, read at 1½, and speak Greek and Latin by 3 enrolled at Harvard when he was 11 and then worked as a college professor. But he left teaching and worked only menial jobs while spending most of his time on his collecting passion, streetcar transfers. He died at 46. His story is told in psychology textbooks. Other geniuses who collected trivial objects are also used as examples in studies of compulsive behavior. So is it a compulsive obsession to have a large collection of firecracker labels or doorknobs—but not if the collection is million-dollar paintings or rare coins?

Chinese Export, Vase, Famille Verte, 3 Dragons, Yellow Ground, Clouds, 1800s, 17 ¾ In.
$2,596

Brunk Auctions

Chinese Export, Vase, Figural, Goldfish, Lotus Blossoms, Painted, 16 In.
$861

Cowan Auctions

Chinese Export, Vase, Kuci Kung, Interlocking Panels, Pierced, Flowers, 1800s, 8 In.
$593

James D. Julia Auctioneers

Platter, Orange Fitzhugh, Oval, Central Medallion, Animals, 14 x 18 In. 1120
Platter, Oval, Rose Border, Moth Medallion, Orange Peel Glaze, c.1850, 14 x 16 In. 180
Platter, Scalloped, Tobacco Leaf Pattern, Multicolor, c.1800, 17 x 14 In. *illus* 1968
Platter, Shield Crest, Monogram, Grapevine Rim, Blue & Gilt, c.1810, 17 In. *illus* 677
Platter, Tobacco Leaf, Flowers, Scrolling Ferns, 1700s, 13 In. 2813
Punch Bowl, 4 Reserves, Quilted Border, 4 x 10 In. 480
Punch Bowl, Famille Rose, Armorial, Spearhead Band, c.1755, 11 In. 3750
Punch Bowl, Famille Rose, Figures, Key Design Border, c.1850, 16 In. Diam. 623
Punch Bowl, Famille Rose, Flowers, Garlands, White Ground, 1900s, 5 ½ x 12 In. 148
Punch Bowl, Figures, Water's Edge, Birds, Diapered Rim, c.1790, 6 ½ x 15 In. 1778
Punch Bowl, Hunt Scene, Porcelain, 15 ¾ In. 2420
Punch Bowl, Silver, Gilt, Repousse Chrysanthemums, Scalloped, c.1880, 15 In. Diam. 14340
Saucer, Famille Rose, 2 Coiling Dragons, 5 Claws, Flaming Pearl, 9 In. Diam. 975
Teapot, Band Of Scholar's Objects, Buddhist Elements, Gilt, 4 ¾ In. 246
Teapot, Famille Rose, Butterflies, Flat Shoulder, Curved Spout, c.1900, 5 x 6 In. 62
Teapot, Landscapes, Blue & White, Gold Trim, Molded Spout & Handle, 8 In. 144
Teapot, Multicolor Enamel, Flower Swags, Urns, c.1790, 5 x 8 In. 142
Teapot, Multicolor Enamel, Red Spearhead Border, Flowers, 6 ½ x 8 In. 212
Trinket Box, Flowers, Underglaze Blue, Multicolor, c.1900, 2 ½ x 4 In. 90
Tureen, Famille Rose, Lid, Open Crown Knop, Plumed Handles, 1700s, 11 In. 938
Tureen, Lid, Armorial, Finial, Handles, 1700s, 8 x 12 In. 450
Tureen, Lid, Birds, Flowers, Baskets, Blue Ground, Panels, 1800s, 10 x 9 In. 240
Tureen, Oblong, Round Medallions, Animal Finial, 7 ½ x 4 ¾ In. 302
Tureen, Platter, Man, Goats, Lake, Estate, Lid, Blue, White, 16 In. 375
Tureen, Sauce, Leaves, Mask Handles, c.1790, 4 ½ x 7 In. 1875
Tureen, Stand, Lid, Parrots, Pomegranates, 1700s, 5 In., Pair 12500
Tureen, Tray, Blue & Gold, Leaves, 11 x 14 In. 244
Vase, Basket Weave, 6 Serpentine Reserves, 10 x 4 ½ In. 2074
Vase, Beaker Shape, Flared Rim, Children, Village, Blue & White, 18 In. 551
Vase, Blue & White, Flaring Mouth, Foo Dog, 17 ½ x 7 ¼ In., Pair 305
Vase, Blue & White, Key Fret Border, Figures, Landscape, 1800s, 21 x 11 In. 799
Vase, Bottle, Medallions, Beaded Texture, Blue, White, Pagoda, 1800s, 12 In., Pair 1845
Vase, Crackle Glaze, Blue & White, Trumpet Neck, 16 In. 259
Vase, Cylindrical, Trumpet Rim, Landscape, Grapevines, c.1900, 10 In. 375
Vase, Famille Jaune, Yenyen, Yellow Mottled Ground, Pheasant, c.1800, 15 x 8 In. 7080
Vase, Famille Rose, Beauties In Garden, 13 In. 750
Vase, Famille Rose, Bottle Shape, Stick Neck, Peony Sprays, c.1800, 7 In., Pair 779
Vase, Famille Rose, Dragon Handles, c.1900, 24 x 10 In. 1107
Vase, Famille Rose, Gilt Handles, Figures, Pavilion, c.1945, 23 In. 200
Vase, Famille Rose, Hexagonal, Panels, Peaches, Pomegranates, Pink, 18 In. 119
Vase, Famille Rose, Magpies, Prunus Flowers, Branches, 10 In., Pair 865
Vase, Famille Rose, Pear Shape, Elephant Head Handles, Landscape, 15 In. 207
Vase, Famille Rose, Stoneware, Crackle Ivory, Foo Dogs, Dragons, c.1900, 24 In. 119
Vase, Famille Rose, Turquoise Ground, Flowers, Bats, Trumpet Neck, c.1900, 13 In. 3555
Vase, Famille Verte, 3 Dragons, Yellow Ground, Clouds, 1800s, 17 ¾ In. *illus* 2596
Vase, Famille Verte, Birds, Butterflies, Paneled, 17 ½ In., Pair 2242
Vase, Famille Verte, Bottle, Squat, Inverted Neck, Immortals, Leaves, c.1890, 7 In. 593
Vase, Famille Verte, Flowering Prunus Branches, Bamboo, 18 In. 590
Vase, Famille Verte, Lotus, Hand Holding Cornucopia, 1800s, 14 ½ In. 885
Vase, Figural, Goldfish, Lotus Blossoms, Painted, 16 In. *illus* 861
Vase, Flat Shoulder, Rolled Rim, Scalloped Edge, Birds, Trees, 1800s, 10 In. 741
Vase, Hundred Butterfly Design, Trumpet Shape, 1800s, 18 In. 711
Vase, Kuci Kung, Interlocking Panels, Pierced, Flowers, 1800s, 8 In. *illus* 593
Vase, Lid, Famille Rose, Foo Dog Finial, Dragon Handles, c.1810, 10 In. 2125
Vase, Lid, Hunting Scene, Flatt Shape, Ruyi Head Finial, Handles, 17 x 9 In. 838
Vase, Red Splash Flambe, Bottle Shape, Incised, Marked, c.1870 2280
Vase, Triple Gourd, Famille Verte, Flowers, Bats, Pierced Stand, 1900s, 21 In., Pair 1230
Warming Dish, Lid, Famille Rose, 6 ¼ x 14 In 345
Wine Cup, Famille Rose, Dragons, Phoenix, Tiger Feet, c.1800, 5 x 6 In. 356

CHINTZ is the name of a group of china patterns featuring an overall design of flowers and leaves. The design became popular with English makers about 1928. A few pieces are still being made. The best known are designs by Royal Winton, James Kent Ltd., Crown Ducal, and Shelley. Crown Ducal and Shelley are listed in their own sections.

Anemone Blue, Teapot, Lid, Countess, Royal Winton, 4 Cup, 4 ¾ In. 427

Apple Blossom Pink, Dish, Shell Shape, James Kent, 5 In. 38
Apple Blossom Pink, Plate, Dinner, Scalloped, James Kent, 10 In. 119
Apple Blossom Pink, Relish, 2 Sections, James Kent, 6 ¼ In. 132
Balmoral, Cup & Saucer, Royal Winton 74
Balmoral, Plate, Dinner, Royal Winton, 10 In. 174
Briar Rose, Cup & Saucer, Royal Albert 28
Clevedon, Platter, Oval, Royal Winton, 10 In. 134
Florida Plate, Exotic Bird, Mauve Ground, 8-Sided, c.1930, 8 ¼ In. 59
Florita, Nut Dish, James Kent, 3 ⅝ In. 46
Hazel, Jam, Lid, Underplate, Royal Winton 362
Julia, Tea Set, Tray, Teapot, Creamer, Sugar, Toast Rack, Flowers, Gilt, Royal Winton, c.1950, 8 x 11 In. *illus* 220
Kew, Nut Dish, Round, Pierced Handles, Royal Winton, 5 ⅝ In. 62
Marigold, Bowl, Nut, Lord Nelson Ware, 1930s, 6 ½ x 4 ½ In. .... *illus* 10
Richmond, Teapot, Countess, Royal Winton, 1930s, 6 x 8 ½ In. .... *illus* 245
Rosalynde, Bonbon, Oval, James Kent, 9 In. 78
Rosalynde, Cup & Saucer, Footed, James Kent 50
Rosalynde, Nut Dish, James Kent, 5 x 5 In. 69
Rosalynde, Plate, Salad, James Kent, 7 ⅞ In. 32
Summertime, Sugar Shaker, Flared Base, Royal Winton, 1932-60s, 3 ½ In. .... *illus* 75
Sunshine, Plate, Dinner, Royal Winton, 9 ⅞ In. 87

CHOCOLATE GLASS, sometimes mistakenly called caramel slag, was made by the Indiana Tumbler and Goblet Company of Greentown, Indiana, from 1900 to 1903. It was also made at other National Glass Company factories. Fenton Art Glass Co. made chocolate glass from about 1907 to 1915. More recent pieces have been made by Imperial and others.

Cactus, Butter, Cover, Greentown, 5 ¼ x 7 ¼ In. 145
Cactus, Sauce, Greentown, 4 In. 25
Eggcup, Chicken, Imperial 53
Figurine, Hoot Less Owl, Imperial, 4 In. 40
Figurine, Woodchuck, Imperial, 3 In. 38
Leaf Bracket, Dish, 3-Sided, 3-Toed, Handle, Greentown, 3 ⅝ In. 45
Leaf Bracket, Dish, 3-Sided, Footed, Loop Handle, Greentown, 4 In. 52
Pitcher, Water, Serenade, Greentown, 7 ½ In. .... *illus* 290
Scalloped Flange, Vase, Chocolate, Trumpet, Footed, Greentown, 6 In. 65
Wild Rose & Bowknot, Toothpick Holder, Scalloped Rim, c.1901, 1 ¾ In. .... *illus* 156

CHRISTMAS collectibles include not only Christmas trees and ornaments listed below, but also Santa Claus figures, special dishes, and even games and wrapping paper. A Belsnickle is a nineteenth-century figure of Father Christmas. A kugel is an early, heavy ornament made of thick blown glass, lined with zinc or lead, and often covered with colored wax. Christmas collectibles may also be listed in the Candy Container category. Christmas trees are listed in the section that follows.

Belsnickle, Blue Hooded Coat, Holding Sprig, Papier-Mache, Germany, c.1900, 9 In. 213
Belsnickle, Pulling Sleigh, Toys, Green Coat, Papier-Mache, Composition, Wood, 16 In. 1180
Belsnickle, Santa Claus, Chalkware, Snow Flecks, Tiny Tim On Back, Penn. Dutch, 9 In. 2124
Belsnickle, Santa Claus, Hunchback, Composition, Fur, Flecked Coat, Basket, Twig, 9 In. 2950
Button, Hamburgers, Santa Claus, Chimney, Moon, St. Louis Button Co., c.1919, 1 ¼ In. 405
Button, Home Again, Wanamaker's, Santa Claus, Piloting Biplane, c.1911, 1 ½ In. 569
Button, Santa, Meet Me At Abele's, Holly Leaves, Red Berries, No Hat, 1 ¼ In. .... *illus* 153
Candle Chime, Nativity Base, Tin Lithograph, 12 In. 59
Candy Containers are listed in the Candy Container category.
Doll, Santa Claus, Composition Body, Red Boots, Rosy Cheeks, 18 In. 125
Doll, Santa Claus, Fabric Face, Painted, Cloth Body, Red Jacket, Hat, 1920, 29 In. 150
Figure, Creche, St. Joseph, Wax, Glass Eyes, Walking Stick, Neapolitan, 23 In. 354
Figure, Display, Santa Claus, Composition, 33 x 10 In. 672
Figure, Drummer Boy, Standing On Drum Pedestal, Drum, 72 In. 180
Figure, Santa Claus, Art Deco, Nickel Plated, 1940s, 16 ½ x 10 In. 276
Figure, Santa Claus, Hitchhiking, On Vacation, Plastic Fiberglass, 73 In. 180
Lamp, Oil, Santa Claus, Opaque White Glass, Red, Gold, Black, 1877, 10 In. .... *illus* 3835
Lantern, Santa Claus Face, Paper Inserts, Mica Flecks, Germany, 8 ½ In. .... *illus* 561
Lantern, Santa Claus Head, Candle, Papier-Mache, Wire Handle, Germany, 5 In. .... *illus* 767
Mold, Santa Claus Holding Toy Sack, Mahogany, King Cole, Canton, Oh., 13 In. 885
Nodder, Father Christmas, Composition, Fur, Felt, Tree, Candles, Clockwork, 22 In. 4720
Nodder, Santa Claus, Composition, 1950s, 5 ¼ In. 65
Nodder, Santa Claus, Composition, Glass Eyes, Mohair Beard, Fur Coat, Tree, Windup, 26 In. 1770

Chintz, Julia, Tea Set, Tray, Teapot, Creamer, Sugar, Toast Rack, Flowers, Gilt, Royal Winton, c.1950, 8 x 11 In.
$220

Jeffrey S. Evans

Chintz, Marigold, Bowl, Nut, Lord Nelson Ware, 1930s, 6 ½ x 4 ½ In.
$10

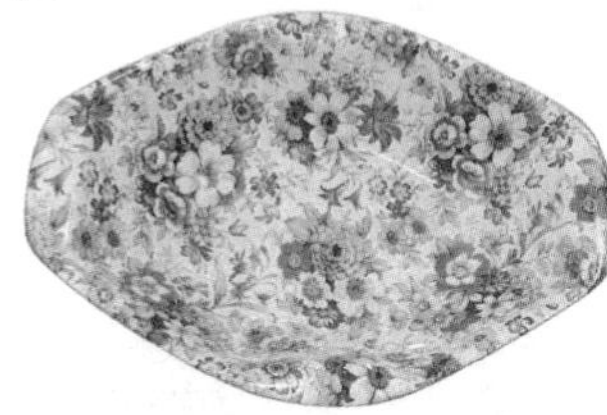

Ruby Lane

Chintz, Richmond, Teapot, Countess, Royal Winton, 1930s, 6 x 8 ½ In.
$245

Ruby Lane

Chintz, Summertime, Sugar Shaker, Flared Base, Royal Winton, 1932-60s, 3 ½ In.
$75

Ruby Lane

C

Chocolate Glass, Pitcher, Water, Serenade, Greentown, 7 ½ In.
$290

Strawser Auction Group

Chocolate Glass, Wild Rose & Bowknot, Toothpick Holder, Scalloped Rim, c.1901, 1 ¾ In.
$156

Jeffrey S. Evans

Christmas, Button, Santa, Meet Me At Abele's, Holly Leaves, Red Berries, No Hat, 1 ¼ In.
$153

Hake's Americana & Collectibles

TIP
Store fragile Christmas tree ornaments in plastic resealable bags. Be sure there is some air in the bag when you zip it. This air bubble protects like bubble wrap.

Nodder, Santa Claus, Felt, Holding Tree, 8 In. 18
Nodder, Santa Claus, Sitting, Watch In Hand, Composition, Fur, Red Felt, Germany, 16 In. 649
Pin, Merry Christmas, East Rockaway National Bank, Santa Claus, Holly, c.1910, 1 ½ In. 34
Postcard, Santa Claus, May Your Christmas Be Bright, S. Schmucher, 1912 49
Poster, Uncle Sam, Buy Christmas Seals, Fight Tuberculosis, 1926, 31 In. 266
Print, Santa Claus, Thomas Nast's Night Before Christmas, Lithograph On Cloth, 29 In. 472
Textile, Printed, Cotton, Stocking, Cut & Sew Instructions, S.H. Howe, 1889, 29 In. .... *illus* 590
Toy, Father Christmas Pulling, Candy Basket On Sled, Tin Lithograph, Germany, 4 In. 5015
Toy, Roly Poly, Santa Claus, Painted, Schoenhut, 9 In. .... *illus* 1062
Toy, Santa Claus, Celluloid, Lead, Walker, TN, Occupied Japan, c.1948, 6 In. .... *illus* 450
Toy, Santa Claus, Driving Wicker Car, Composition, Rabbit Fur Beard, Germany, 10 In. .... *illus* 590
Toy, Santa Claus, Sleigh, 2 Reindeer, White, Red Trim, Cast Iron, Hubley, 16 In. 8260
Toy, Santa Claus, Sleigh, Goats, Althof Bergmann, 18 In. 2655
Toy, Santa Claus, Toys, Head Rocks, Paper & Cloth Over Wood, Clockwork, 18 In. 3245
Toy, Sleigh, Santa Claus & 2 Reindeer, Paper On Wood, 1890s, Bliss, 18 In. 1003

CHRISTMAS TREES made of feathers and Christmas tree decorations of all types are popular with collectors. The first decorated Christmas tree in America is claimed by many states, including Pennsylvania (1747), Massachusetts (1832), Illinois (1833), Ohio (1838), and Iowa (1845). The first glass ornaments were imported from Germany about 1860. Paper and tinsel ornaments were made in Dresden, Germany, from about 1880 to 1940. Manufacturers in the United States were making ornaments in the early 1870s. Electric lights were first used on a Christmas tree in 1882. Character light bulbs became popular in the 1920s, bubble lights in the 1940s, twinkle bulbs in the 1950s, plastic bulbs by 1955. In this book a Christmas light is a holder for a candle used on the tree. Other forms of lighting include light bulbs. Other Christmas collectibles are listed in the preceding section.

Feather, Berries, Candle Clips, Round Wood Base, Germany, 35 In. 649
Feather, Forest Green, Red Berries, Wood Base, Swags, Germany, 72 In. 2360
Feather, Wood Base, Germany, 44 In. .... *illus* 595
Feather, Wood Stencil Base, Bulbs, Garlands, Germany, Vintage, 52 In. .... *illus* 354
Feather, Wood Stenciled Base, Germany, 37 In. 295
Ornament, Alligator, Multicolor, Hook In Mouth, Dresden, 4 In. 384
Ornament, Angel, Wood, Holds Banner, Glory Be, Gold Wings, Erzgebirge, 19 In. 885
Ornament, Baby Jesus, Manger, Wax, Gold Halo, Dresden Bed, Woven Wire, 3 In. 118
Ornament, Bell, May Your Christmas Be Delightful, Precious Moments, 1985, 3 In. 10
Ornament, Carousel Horse, Rabbit, Sterling, Cazenovia Abroad, Box, 4 x 3 In., 2 Piece 242
Ornament, Dog, Hound, Picking Up Scent, Tail In Air, Brown, Dresden, Germany, 3 In. 384
Ornament, Dog, Pug, Yellow Bandanna, Dresden, 2 ¾ In. 266
Ornament, Dog, Wolfhound, Dresden, 4 In. 89
Ornament, Eddie Cantor, Glass, Red Chenille Arms & Legs, 6 In. 266
Ornament, Jockey, On Horseback, Brown House, Saddle Stirrups, Dresden, 3 In. 443
Ornament, Keystone Cop, Elongated Legs, Glass, 5 In. 177
Ornament, Kugel, Amber, Grape Cluster, Blown Glass, Germany, 3 ½ In. 118
Ornament, Kugel, Amber, Pear Shape, Blown Glass, Germany, 3 In. 4425
Ornament, Kugel, Blue, Ribbed Egg Shape, 4 In. 21240
Ornament, Kugel, Cobalt Blue, Ball Shape, Blown Glass, 3 In. 65
Ornament, Kugel, Cobalt Blue, Ball Shape, Blown Glass, 5 ¼ In. 130
Ornament, Kugel, Cobalt Blue, Grape Cluster, 4 In. 443
Ornament, Kugel, Dark Green, Blown Glass, Cap, 10 In. 561
Ornament, Kugel, Gold, Ball Shape, Blown Glass, 3 ¾ In. 35
Ornament, Kugel, Gold, Ball Shape, Crackle Glass, Germany, 6 ¼ In. 12
Ornament, Kugel, Gold, Blown Glass, Cap, 10 In. 443
Ornament, Kugel, Gold, Egg Shape, Blown Glass, Germany, 6 ¼ In. 767
Ornament, Kugel, Gold, Turnip Shape, Ribbed, Loop, Germany, 4 ½ In. 130
Ornament, Kugel, Golden Orange, Blown Glass, Ribbed, Germany, 2 ¾ In. .... *illus* 649
Ornament, Kugel, Grape Cluster, Green, Blown Mold, 4 In. .... *illus* 266
Ornament, Kugel, Grape Cluster, Red, Blown Glass, Germany, 4 ¾ In. .... *illus* 4425
Ornament, Kugel, Green, Ball Shape, Blown Glass, 4 ½ In. .... 47 to 65
Ornament, Kugel, Red, Diamond Shape, Panels, Loop, Germany, 4 ½ In. 384
Ornament, Kugel, Silver, Ribbed Egg Shape, 3 ½ In. 649
Ornament, Lady Steeplechase Rider, Black Hat, Velvet Dress, Germany, 3 In. 295
Ornament, Long-Ear Hog, Pointy Ears, Curly Tail, Dresden, 4 In. 354
Ornament, Mickey & Minnie Mouse, Glass, Black Details, 3 ½ In., Pair 472
Ornament, North Atlantic Flounder, Metal, Silver Shaded To Gold, 3 ½ In. 295
Ornament, Peacock, Spread Fan, Blue, Green, Gold, Dresden, 4 In. 708

Christmas, Lamp, Oil, Santa Claus, Opaque White Glass, Red, Gold, Black, 1877, 10 In.
$3,835

Bertoia Auctions

Christmas, Lantern, Santa Claus Face, Paper Inserts, Mica Flecks, Germany, 8 ½ In.
$561

Bertoia Auctions

Christmas, Lantern, Santa Claus Head, Candle, Papier-Mache, Wire Handle, Germany, 5 In.
$767

Hess Auction Group

TIP

Never burn Christmas greens in the fireplace. The wood will send sparks up the chimney, and some evergreens burn so hot they could cause a fire in the flue or a buildup of creosote in the chimney.

Christmas, Textile, Printed, Cotton, Stocking, Cut & Sew Instructions, S.H. Howe, 1889, 29 In.
$590

Hess Auction Group

Christmas, Toy, Roly Poly, Santa Claus, Painted, Schoenhut, 9 In.
$1,062

Bertoia Auctions

Christmas, Toy, Santa Claus, Celluloid, Lead, Walker, TN, Occupied Japan, c.1948, 6 In.
$450

RSL Auction

Christmas, Toy, Santa Claus, Driving Wicker Car, Composition, Rabbit Fur Beard, Germany, 10 In.
$590

Bertoia Auctions

Christmas Tree, Feather, Wood Base, Germany, 44 In.
$595

Ruby Lane

Christmas Tree, Feather, Wood Stencil Base, Bulbs, Garlands, Germany, Vintage, 52 In.
$354

Hess Auction Group

Christmas Tree, Ornament, Kugel, Golden Orange, Blown Glass, Ribbed, Germany, 2 ¾ In.
$649

Hess Auction Group

Christmas Tree, Ornament, Kugel, Grape Cluster, Green, Blown Mold, 4 In.
$266

Hess Auction Group

Christmas Tree, Ornament, Kugel, Grape Cluster, Red, Blown Glass, Germany, 4 ¾ In.
$4,425

Hess Auction Group

TIP
Dust glass Christmas ornaments with a feather duster.

Christmas Tree, Stand, Cast Iron, American Water Motor Co., Ohio, c.1920, 10 x 15 In.
$75

Ruby Lane

Christmas Tree, Stand, Santa Claus, Poured Concrete, 11 In.
$118

Bertoia Auctions

Ornament, Peanut Face Man, Glass, Chenille Arms & Legs, Germany, 6 In. 1180
Ornament, Santa Claus, In Airplane, Glass, Tinsel Rope, Composition, 7 In. 154
Ornament, Silver Bell, Blown Glass, Reeded Bottom, Germany, 10 x 9 In. 59
Ornament, Snow Baby, Cotton, Crepe Paper, Composition, Googly Eyes, 6 In. 94
Ornament, Snowflake Shape, Sterling Silver, Gorham, 3 ½ In., 12 Piece 529
Ornament, Stork, Silver, Long Legs, Dresden, 3 In. 266
Ornament, Swordfish, Golden Brown, Dresden, 6 In. 354
Ornament, Wax Baby, Silver Sebnitz Coach, Dresden Wheels, 3 In. 148
Stand, Cast Iron, American Water Motor Co., Ohio, c.1920, 10 x 15 In. *illus* 75
Stand, Cast Iron, Light-Up, Bulbs, Painted Trees, North Mfg. Co., 1933, 14 In. 75
Stand, Santa Claus, Poured Concrete, 11 In. *illus* 118
Sticker, Wall, Vinyl, Merry Merry, Die Cut, Ornaments, M. Minter, 8 x 48 In. 60

CHROME items in the Art Deco style became popular in the 1930s. Collectors are most interested in high-style pieces made by the Connecticut firms of Chase Brass & Copper Co., Manning-Bowman & Co., and others.

Basket, Pierced, Handle, Farberware, Krome Kraft, 11 x 5 In. 15
Box, Tissue, Embossed, Wall Mount, 10 x 5 x 2 In. 45
Canister Set, Engraved, Flour, Sugar, Tea, Coffee, Beauty Ware, 1950s 22
Canister Set, Manhattan Pattern, Ribbed, Black Lids, Red Knobs, 1940s, Largest 7 In., 3 Piece *illus* 50
Carafe, Insulated, Hinged, Hook Handle, Aladdin, c.1950, 11 In. 95
Carafe, Mid Century Modern, Hinged, Insulated, Handle, Aladdin, c.1950, 11 ½ In. 95
Cocktail Ball, Tray, Art Deco, Pierced, Chase, 1930s, Ball 3 ⅜ In., Tray 6 ⅜ In. *illus* 68
Cocktail Shaker, Arched Handle, Spout, Krome Kraft Farber Bros., 11 In. 110
Cocktail Shaker, Bell Shape, Wood Handle, c.1937, 11 In. 95
Condiment Server, Ferris Wheel, Extended Handles, 8 Glass Dishes, c.1950, 24 In. 1230
Figure, Penguin, Holding Tray, Art Deco, Plated Brass, c.1930, 6 ¼ x 3 In. 210
Lamp, Electric, Art Deco, Stepped Base, Adjustable Domed Shade, 1930s, 14 In. 395
Tray, Teak Base, Milbern Creations, 14 x 5 In. 24
Wine Taster, Tab Handle, France, 4 In. 30

CIGAR STORE FIGURES of carved wood or cast iron were used as advertisements in front of the Victorian cigar store. The carved figures are now collected as folk art. They range in size from counter type, about three feet, to over eight feet high.

Black Man, Carved, Painted, Hat, Holding Cigars, 1800s, 16 x 9 In. 4148
Black Man, Derby Hat, Red Coat, Holding Cigars, Wood, 1800s, 27 In. 1652
Blackamoor, Carved, Black Cap, Waistcoat, Striped Pants, 49 x 15 In. 2440
Indian Maiden, Red, White & Blue Skirt, 1800s, 82 x 16 In. *illus* 22800
Indian Maiden, Robe, Headdress, Holding Cigars, c.1880, 72 x 20 In. 25000
Indian Princess, Holding Tobacco Leaves, Pine, Painted, 61 In. 12000
Indian, Carved, Painted, Holding Cigars, Tomahawk, 1800s, 62 In. 8400
Indian, Chief, Carved Wood, F. Gallagher, 16 x 72 In. 330
Indian, Holding Revolver & Rifle, Wood, Painted, c.1910, 70 In. 600
Indian, Tomahawk In Belt, Cut Steel, Painted, c.1900, 54 In. 15000

CINNABAR is a vermilion or red lacquer. Pieces are made with tens to hundreds of thicknesses of the lacquer that is later carved. Most cinnabar was made in the Orient.

Box, 9 Dragons, 3 Claws Each, Waves, Incised 6 Character Mark, 6 ¼ In. 5842
Box, Blossom Shape, Figure, Flowers, Yellow Ground, c.1900, 12 In. 1599
Box, Figures, Landscape, 1 ½ x 5 ½ In. 48
Box, Flat Lid, Round, Squat, Engraved Trees & Leaf Design, c.1950, 5 x 12 In. 85
Box, Flowers, Landscape In Reserve, Latch, 6 x 12 In. 35
Box, Landscape, Pagoda, Ocean, Mountains, Scrolling Vines, 6 ¾ In. 847
Box, Lid, Carved Lotus & Plants, Rosewood Stand, 1700s, 4 x 3 In. 2963
Box, Lid, Carved, Figures In Courtyard, Blue Enamel Interior, c.1905, 6 x 4 In. 109
Box, Lid, Peach Shape, Carved Flowers & Leaves, 1700s, 6 x 6 In. 1235
Box, Lid, Peach Shape, Carved, Scholars, Diamond Diaper Pattern, 5 ½ In. 437
Box, Lift Lid, Carved, Immortals, Landscape, Square, 4 Scroll Legs, 5 ¾ x 4 In. 360
Box, Peach Shape, Carved, Brocade Pattern, Flowers, Leaves, 1700s, 6 x 6 In. *illus* 1185
Box, Rectangular, Dragon, 1 ¾ x 4 ½ In. 40
Box, Round, Lid, Lobed, Carved, Figures, Pavilions, Fruit, Green Paint, 7 In. 2205
Box, Shaped, Carved, Lotus, Aquatic Plants, Rosewood Stand, 1700s, 4 ¼ x 3 ¼ In. *illus* 2963
Box, Water Dragon, Fish, Foo Dogs, 7 ¼ In. 938

Chrome, Canister Set, Manhattan Pattern, Ribbed, Black Lids, Red Knobs, 1940s, Largest 7 In., 3 Piece
$50

Ruby Lane

Chrome, Cocktail Ball, Tray, Art Deco, Pierced, Chase, 1930s, Ball 3 ⅜-In., Tray 6 ⅜ In.
$68

Ruby Lane

Cigar Store Figure, Indian Maiden, Red, White & Blue Skirt, 1800s, 82 x 16 In.
$22,800

Showtime Auction Services

Cinnabar, Box, Peach Shape, Carved, Brocade Pattern, Flowers, Leaves, 1700s, 6 x 6 In.
$1,185

James D. Julia Auctioneers

Cinnabar, Box, Shaped, Carved, Lotus, Aquatic Plants, Rosewood Stand, 1700s, 4 ¼ x 3 ¼ In.
$2,963

James D. Julia Auctioneers

Cinnabar, Tray, Carved, Scene Of Scholars, Mountains, Relief Border, 1800s, 14 x 11 In.
$431

Cowan Auctions

Civil War, Battle Rattle, From CSS Kate, Wood, 8 x 7 ½ In.
$1,020

Cowan Auctions

Civil War, Belt Plate, Pennsylvania Reserve Brigade, Stamped, Coat Of Arms, 1850s, 3 x 2 In.
$738

Skinner, Inc.

Civil War, Cap, Forage, Model 1858, Leather Visor, Chin Strap, Brass Buttons, Bugle, c.1865
$1,845

Skinner, Inc.

Civil War, Drum, Snare, Eagle, American Shield, Motto, Randolph Light Infantry, 17 In.
$2,370

James D. Julia Auctioneers

TIP

Clarice Cliff pieces marked in black are worth two to three times as much as pieces marked in any other color.

Civil War, Jacket, Artillery Shell, Blue Broadcloth, Worsted Tape, Brass Buttons, c.1865, Size 4
$1,722

Skinner, Inc.

Clarice Cliff, Cafe Au Lait, Vase, Balloon Trees, Multicolor, Spread Foot, 13 x 7 In.
$976

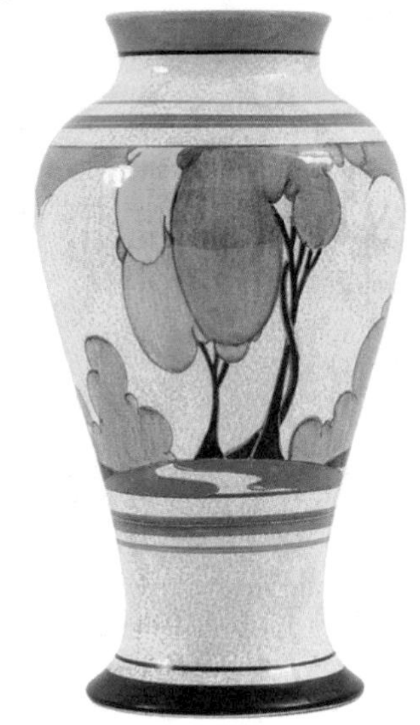

Palm Beach Modern Auctions

Clarice Cliff, Celtic Harvest Wheatsheaf, Platter, Newport Makers Mark, c.1937, 12 ¾ In.
$400

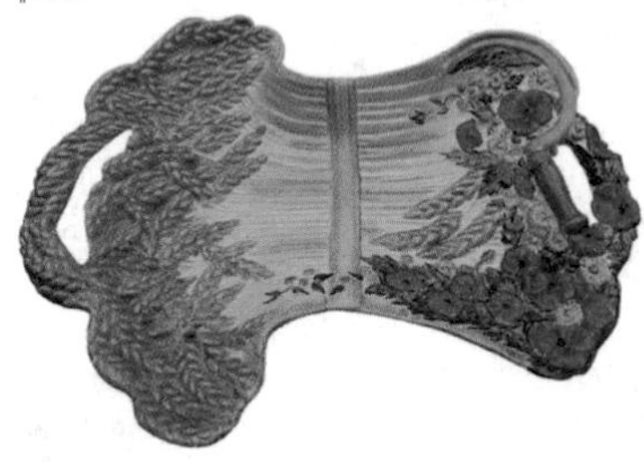

Ruby Lane

Censer, Foo Dog Finial, Handles, Wood Stand, 14¾ x 13 In. 172
Dish, High Relief, Figures, Garden, Barbed Rim, Flowering Branches, 8 In. 236
Figure, Armored Horse, Saddle, Key Fret Border, Chinese, 10 x 11 In. 529
Jar, Flower Carving, High Relief, 4½ In., Pair 98
Plate, Carved, Immortal Riding Dragon, Scrolling Leaves, Shaped Rim, 1800s, 9 In. 556
Plate, Carved, Leaves, Peonies, Rockery, Lotus, Scrolling Vine Border, 12 In. 124
Teapot, Symbols Of Good Fortune, Leaves, 4 x 7½ In. 3900
Tray, Carved, Scene Of Scholars, Mountains, Relief Border, 1800s, 14 x 11 In. .... *illus* 431
Vase, Bird, Flowers, Gold Rim, 1900s, 13 x 6 In. 126
Vase, Black, Carved, Flowers, Birds, 7½ x 4 In. 118
Vase, Carved In Relief, Flowers, Landscape, 12½ In. 215
Vase, Dragon, 6¾ x 3½ In., Pair 258
Vase, Incised, Woman, Garden, Pond, Carved Handles, 18 In. 338
Vase, Mountain Scene, Carved, 1900s, 9¾ x 5¼ In., Pair 805

CIVIL WAR mementos are important collector's items. Most of the pieces are military items used from 1861 to 1865. Be sure to avoid any explosive munitions.

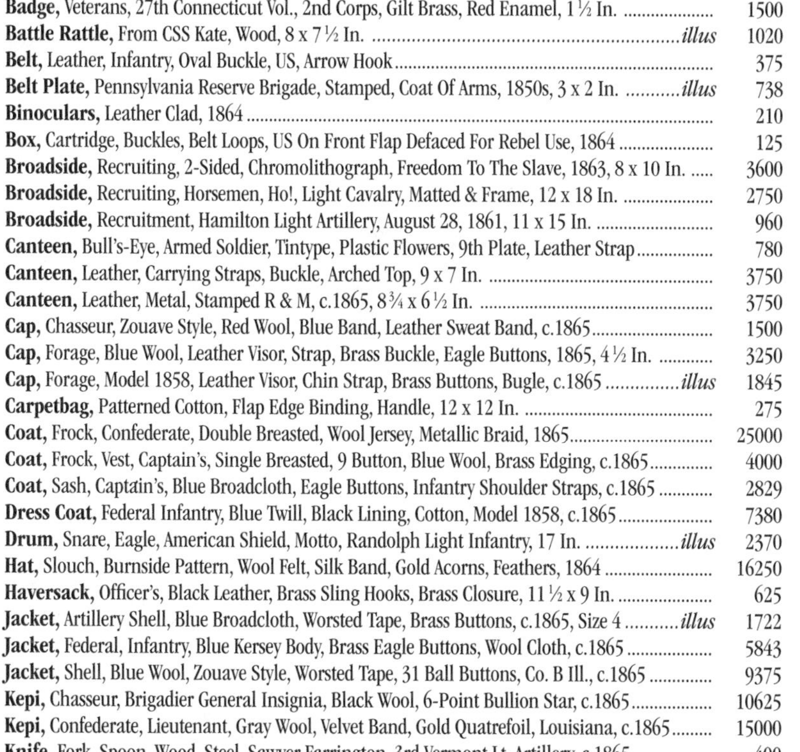

Badge, Veterans, 27th Connecticut Vol., 2nd Corps, Gilt Brass, Red Enamel, 1½ In. 1500
Battle Rattle, From CSS Kate, Wood, 8 x 7½ In. .... *illus* 1020
Belt, Leather, Infantry, Oval Buckle, US, Arrow Hook 375
Belt Plate, Pennsylvania Reserve Brigade, Stamped, Coat Of Arms, 1850s, 3 x 2 In. .... *illus* 738
Binoculars, Leather Clad, 1864 210
Box, Cartridge, Buckles, Belt Loops, US On Front Flap Defaced For Rebel Use, 1864 125
Broadside, Recruiting, 2-Sided, Chromolithograph, Freedom To The Slave, 1863, 8 x 10 In. 3600
Broadside, Recruiting, Horsemen, Ho!, Light Cavalry, Matted & Frame, 12 x 18 In. 2750
Broadside, Recruitment, Hamilton Light Artillery, August 28, 1861, 11 x 15 In. 960
Canteen, Bull's-Eye, Armed Soldier, Tintype, Plastic Flowers, 9th Plate, Leather Strap 780
Canteen, Leather, Carrying Straps, Buckle, Arched Top, 9 x 7 In. 3750
Canteen, Leather, Metal, Stamped R & M, c.1865, 8¾ x 6½ In. 3750
Cap, Chasseur, Zouave Style, Red Wool, Blue Band, Leather Sweat Band, c.1865 1500
Cap, Forage, Blue Wool, Leather Visor, Strap, Brass Buckle, Eagle Buttons, 1865, 4½ In. 3250
Cap, Forage, Model 1858, Leather Visor, Chin Strap, Brass Buttons, Bugle, c.1865 .... *illus* 1845
Carpetbag, Patterned Cotton, Flap Edge Binding, Handle, 12 x 12 In. 275
Coat, Frock, Confederate, Double Breasted, Wool Jersey, Metallic Braid, 1865 25000
Coat, Frock, Vest, Captain's, Single Breasted, 9 Button, Blue Wool, Brass Edging, c.1865 4000
Coat, Sash, Captain's, Blue Broadcloth, Eagle Buttons, Infantry Shoulder Straps, c.1865 2829
Dress Coat, Federal Infantry, Blue Twill, Black Lining, Cotton, Model 1858, c.1865 7380
Drum, Snare, Eagle, American Shield, Motto, Randolph Light Infantry, 17 In. .... *illus* 2370
Hat, Slouch, Burnside Pattern, Wool Felt, Silk Band, Gold Acorns, Feathers, 1864 16250
Haversack, Officer's, Black Leather, Brass Sling Hooks, Brass Closure, 11½ x 9 In. 625
Jacket, Artillery Shell, Blue Broadcloth, Worsted Tape, Brass Buttons, c.1865, Size 4 .... *illus* 1722
Jacket, Federal, Infantry, Blue Kersey Body, Brass Eagle Buttons, Wool Cloth, c.1865 5843
Jacket, Shell, Blue Wool, Zouave Style, Worsted Tape, 31 Ball Buttons, Co. B Ill., c.1865 9375
Kepi, Chasseur, Brigadier General Insignia, Black Wool, 6-Point Bullion Star, c.1865 10625
Kepi, Confederate, Lieutenant, Gray Wool, Velvet Band, Gold Quatrefoil, Louisiana, c.1865 15000
Knife, Fork, Spoon, Wood, Steel, Sawyer Farrington, 3rd Vermont Lt. Artillery, c.1865 400
Medical, Bag, Leather, Union Army Physician, c.1865, 12 x 18 In. 270
Pillow, Remembrance, With Love 1864, Velvet, Beading, Gimp Edging, 6 x 8 In. 89
Requisition Book, Gettysburg, Lemuel Norton, Dec. 1862-June 1863, 5 x 10 In. 600
Spurs, Cavalry Officer's, Gilded Brass, Cast Flower Design, 1861, 5 In. 1125
Stove, Sibley, Sheet Iron, Tapered, Union Army 6th Corps, Antietam, 29 x 18 In. 400
Tin Cup, Handle, Painted, Charles Briggs, Company K, 36th Mass. Vol., 4 In. 923

CKAW, *see Dedham category.*

CLARICE CLIFF was a designer who worked in several English factories, including A.J. Wilkinson Ltd., Wilkinson's Royal Staffordshire Pottery, Newport Pottery, and Foley Pottery after the 1920s. She is best known for her brightly colored Art Deco designs, including the Bizarre line. She died in 1972. Reproductions have been made by Wedgwood.

Autumn, Plate, Marked, 1933, 9 In. 435
Bizarre, Bowl, Triangles, Black, Red, Yellow, Signed, 5 In. 285
Bizarre, Cup & Saucer, Triangles, Signed 235
Bizarre, Pitcher, Black Matte Ground, Berried Handle, Leaves, 7½ x 7¼ In. 190
Bizarre, Vase, Marigold, Blue, 8 x 4¼ In. 4500
Cafe Au Lait, Plate, Octagonal, Red Rim, Marked, 9 In. 550

Clarice Cliff, Harvest, Basket, Oval, Arched Handle, Flowers, Stamped, 1940s, 9 x 6 In.
$575

Ruby Lane

Clarice Cliff, Ophelia, Sugar, Lid, Flowers, Newport Pottery Company, England, c.1945, 4 x 6 In.
$41

Ruby Lane

Clarice Cliff, Tonquin, Toast Holder, 4 Slice, Brown Transfer, Staffordshire, England, 1935, 7 In.
$45

Ruby Lane

TIP

Electric toasters, coffeepots, and some furniture are made with chrome, a plated metal. The plating is soft and thin. Abrasives shouldn't be used in cleaning. Clean chrome with a mild soap or detergent and soft cloth, then use an all-metal cleaner for the shine.

Clock Vocabulary
Originally a clock was used to tell time and had a bell or other sound-making parts, while a timepiece kept time but was silent. Today people tend to call all sorts of timekeepers "clocks," including wall clocks, shelf clocks, and church tower clocks.

Clock, Advertising, American Safety Razor, Ever-Ready, Tin, Embossed, 8-Day, 13 x 18 In.
$2,280

Showtime Auction Services

Clock, Advertising, Dr Pepper, Thanks, Reverse Paint, Good For Life, 1930s, 22 x 17 In.
$2,745

Morphy Auctions

TIP
A grandfather clock should be cleaned, oiled, and adjusted every five years. It is important to keep the clock level if it is to keep accurate time.

Cafe Au Lait, Vase, Balloon Trees, Multicolor, Spread Foot, 13 x 7 In. ... *illus* 976
Celtic Harvest Wheatsheaf, Platter, Newport Makers Mark, c.1937, 12¾ In. ... *illus* 400
Crocus, Bizarre, Candlestick, Signed, 4½ In., Pair ... 230
Crocus, Cup & Saucer, Wilkenson's ... 201
Crocus, Pin Tray, Tan Rim, Stretched Flowers, Signed, 3 In. ... 110
Crocus, Pitcher, Athens Shape, Brown Base, 6½ In. ... 220
Crocus, Plate, Octagonal, c.1932, 5½ In. ... 115
Diamonds, Bizarre, Pin Tray, Black, Orange, Signed, 3 In. ... 165
Fantasque, Bizarre, Jug, Flowers, Landscape, Bright, 9½ x 8 In. ... 960
Fantasque, Pitcher, Flowers, Landscape, 9⅛ In. ... 480
Figurine, Gnome, Sitting Under Mushroom, 4½ In. ... 205
Gayday, Bizarre, Cup & Saucer, Flowers, Marked ... 225
Geometric Flowers, Bizarre, Bowl, Blue, Yellow, Orange, 4⅛ x 8¼ In. ... 120
Geometric Flowers, Bizarre, Vase, Blue, Yellow, Orange, 8¾ In. ... 300
Gibraltar, Bizarre, Pin Tray, Blue Band, Signed, 3½ In. ... 295
Glendale, Honey Pot, Lynton Shape, Lid, c.1936, 3½ In. ... 245
Harvest, Basket, Oval, Arched Handle, Flowers, Stamped, 1940s, 9 x 6 In. ... *illus* 575
Ophelia, Sugar, Lid, Flowers, Newport Pottery Company, England, c.1945, 4 x 6 In. ... *illus* 41
Ravel, Gravy Boat, Squared Spout, 2¾ In. ... 105
Red Roofs, Plate, Marked, 9 In. ... 139
Rose, Plate, Scalloped Corner, Green, Red, 9 In. ... 325
Secrets, Ashtray, Stamped 1936, 4½ In. ... 205
Tonquin, Bone Dish, Crescent Shape, Green, c.1930, 3 x 6 In. ... 28
Tonquin, Toast Holder, 4 Slice, Brown Transfer, Staffordshire, England, 1935, 7 In. ... *illus* 45

CLEWELL was made in limited quantities by Charles Walter Clewell of Canton, Ohio, from 1902 to 1955. Pottery was covered with a thin coating of bronze, then treated to make the bronze turn different colors. Pieces covered with copper, brass, or silver were also made. Mr. Clewell's secret formula for blue patinated bronze was burned when he died in 1965.

Vase, Copper Clad Ceramic, Brown Patina Shaded To Green, Incised, 9 In. ... 384
Vase, Copper Clad Ceramic, Brown Shaded To Green Patina, Incised, 4½ In. ... 325
Vase, Copper Clad, Brown, Green, Incised Mark, 17½ In. ... 1625
Vase, Copper Clad, Maple Leaves, Stamped, 7 x 5 In. ... 875

CLIFTON POTTERY was founded by William Long in Newark, New Jersey, in 1905. He worked there until 1909 making lines that included Crystal Patina and Clifton Indian Ware. Clifton Pottery made art pottery until 1911 and then concentrated on wall and floor tile. By 1914, the name had been changed to Clifton Porcelain and Tile Company. Another firm, Chesapeake Pottery, sold majolica marked *Clifton Ware*.

Vase, Bulbous, Stick Neck, Geometric Designs, 11½ In. ... 150
Vase, Green Glaze, Bulbous, c.1906, 4½ In. ... 420
Vase, Mottled Green Crystalline Glaze, Shouldered, 10 In. ... 250

CLOCKS of all types have always been popular with collectors. The eighteenth-century tall case, or grandfather's, clock was designed to house a works with a long pendulum. The name on the clock is usually the maker but sometimes it is a merchant or other craftsman. In 1816, Eli Terry patented a new, smaller works for a clock, and the case became smaller. The clock could be kept on a shelf instead of on the floor. By 1840, coiled springs were used and even smaller clocks were made. Battery-powered electric clocks were made in the 1870s. A garniture set can include a clock and other objects displayed on a mantel.

Advertising, AC Fire Ring, Spark Plugs, Round Face, Fire Border, Orange, 20 x 20 In. ... 330
Advertising, Alarm, Chew Friendship Cut Plug, Screaming Face, Footed, c.1886, 4 x 5 In. ... 1080
Advertising, American Safety Razor, Ever-Ready, Tin, Embossed, 8-Day, 13 x 18 In. ... *illus* 2280
Advertising, Arm & Hammer, Church & Co.'s, Box Shape, Muscle Arm, c.1910, 3 x 4 In. ... 153
Advertising, Burnett's Extract, Baird, Wood, Red, Cabinet, Round Face, c.1893, 19 In. ... 4183
Advertising, Coon Chicken, Good Eat'n Anytime, Black Man, Porcelain, Neon, 28 x 18 In. ... 2745
Advertising, Dr Pepper, Bottle Cap Shape, Red, White, Black, 11 In. Diam. ... 150
Advertising, Dr Pepper, Thanks, Reverse Paint, Good For Life, 1930s, 22 x 17 In. ... *illus* 2745
Advertising, Drink Dr Pepper, 5 Cents, Good For Life, Square, 1930s, 22 x 17 In. ... 2318
Advertising, Drink Orange Crush, Electric, Orange, White, Light-Up, Square, 15½ In. ... 210
Advertising, Enjoy Squirt, Never An After Thirst, Bottle, Lemon, Glass, Light-Up, 15 In. ... 270
Advertising, Eyewater, Cures Without Pain, Baird, Cabinet, Round, c.1890s ... 3346
Advertising, Gem Damaskeene, Razor, 1 Dollar, Pendulum, Wall, Wood, 28 x 23 In. ... 1342
Advertising, General Electric, Refrigerator, Monitor Top, c.1929, 5 x 8½ In. ... 427

Clock, Animated Picture, Music, 14 Movements, Cutouts, Keys, France, c.1870, 13 x 16 In.
$7,980

Theriault's

Clock, Annular, Urn Shape, Enamel, Classical Figures, Gilt, Rings, Alabaster Base, c.1915, 7 In.
$1,353

New Orleans (Cakebread)

Clock, Behrens, P., Wall, Railroad Station, Copper, Glass, Enameled Metal, c.1910, 10 In.
$1,125

Rago Arts and Auction Center

Clock, Blinking Eye, Lion, Cast Iron, Painted, Bradley & Hubbard, c.1880, 10 In.
$5,605

Bertoia Auctions

Clock, Bracket, Boardroom, Sheraton, Mahogany, Marquetry, 8 Bells, c.1890, 36 In.
$2,460

Skinner, Inc.

Clock, Carriage, Brass, Glass, Bamboo Style Case, Hour Repeater, Double Dial, France, 6 In.
$3,555

James D. Julia Auctioneers

Clock, Cartier, Sterling Silver, Blue Enamel, Art Deco, Gold Color Face, Marked, 1927, 5 In.
$11,210

Brunk Auctions

Clock, Cuckoo, Carved Wood, Hanging Rabbit, Pheasant, Stag Head, Leaves, Round Dial, 14 x 24 In.
$180

Fox Auctions

Clock, Figural, Dog, Mechanical, Pendulum, Tongue Moves, Painted, 7 ½ In.
$180

Showtime Auction Services

Clock, Figural, Earth Goddess, Putti, Winter, Summer, Gilt, Porcelain, Paris, 1815, 20 x 14 In.
$984

New Orleans (Cakebread)

Clock, I. Noguchi, Hawkeye Measured Time, Timer Knob, Model L, Bakelite, c.1932, 6 In.
$5,000

Los Angeles Modern Auctions

Clock, Jacob Petit Style, Paris, Scrolled Feet, Gilt, Turk, Lounging, c.1850, 18 x 10 In.
$468

New Orleans (Cakebread)

Clock, Marsh, Williams & Co., Mahogany, Half Columns, Reverse Painted, 1800s, 33 x 18 In.
$1,920

Cowan Auctions

Clock, Munger, Asa, Shelf, Mahogany, Stovepipe Pillars, Portraits, Iron Dial, 1832, 39 In.
$39,100

Cottone Auctions

Clock, Pedro Friedeberg, 3-Legged Table Clock, Blue, Gilt Mahogany, c.1968, 11 x 8 In.
$6,875

Los Angeles Modern Auctions

Clock, Regulator, Carved Case, Center Crest, Turned Finials, Brass Case, Vienna, 50 In.
$3,444

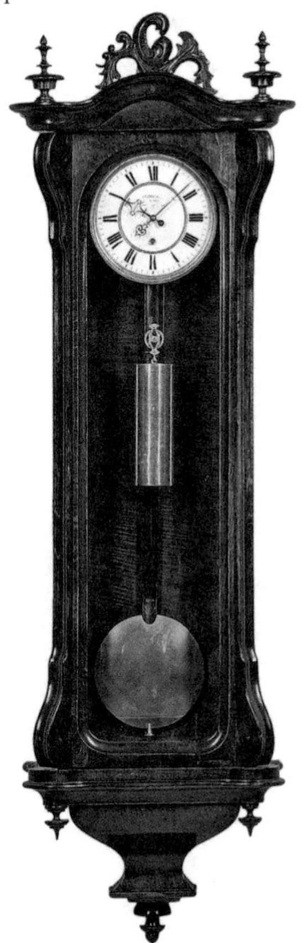

Skinner, Inc.

Advertising, Goulding's Manures, Best For All Crops, Case, Haven Clock Co., 1800s, 32 x 18 In. 330
Advertising, Iroquois Beer, Profile Of Indian Chief, Square, Metal Case, 14 ½ In. 159
Advertising, Kendall Motor Oils, Spinner, Red, Black, Green, Glass, Light-Up, 20 In. Diam. 684
Advertising, Mercury Kiekhaefer Outboards, Black, Orange, Light-Up, c.1960, 12 x 24 In. 300
Advertising, Parry Buggies, Etched Buggy, Wood, Glass Case, Octagonal, 17 x 26 In. 1482
Advertising, Perfection Leather Oil, Baird, Pendulum, Black Paint, Round Face, 18 x 32 In. 2032
Advertising, Squirt Fountain Service, Squirt Quenches Quicker, Boy, Bottle, Neon, 26 x 14 In. 1342
Advertising, Sun Crest, Sun Shape, Wavy Rim, Signed Mickey Mantle, 1950s, 11 In. 568
Advertising, Sunbeam, Girl Eating Toast, Bread, White, Blue, Light-Up, 15 In. Diam. 570
Advertising, Time For Dairy Queen, Cone, Blue, White, Metal Frame, Light-Up, 16 In. Diam. 460
Advertising, Time Her Rite Barn Clock, Cow, Square, Milking Machine Timers, 14 x 14 In. 360
Advertising, We Sell Eerie Hollow Ware, Up To Time, Skillet Shape, Nickel Plate, 11 x 15 In. 3705
Alarm, Cartier, Beveled Glass, Round Stepped Base, 8-Day, Swiss, 4 x 3 In. 384
Alarm, Louis XVI Style, Silver Plate, Pendula D'Officier, Travel Case, c.1910, 4 x 3 In. 94
Animated Picture, Music, 14 Movements, Cutouts, Keys, France, c.1870, 13 x 16 In. *illus* 7980
Annular, Urn Shape, Enamel, Classical Figures, Gilt, Rings, Alabaster Base, c.1915, 7 In. *illus* 1353
Ansonia, Shelf, Figural, Woman Holding Flowers, Spelter, c.1890, 23 x 18 In. 272
Ansonia, Viscount, Shelf, Regulator, Crystal, 8-Day, Time & Strike, c.1905, 15 x 8 In. 390
Ansonia, Walnut Inlaid Cherry Floral Case, 8-Day, Octangular, Stick & Ball, 34 x 18 In. 106
Banjo, Waltham, Wood, Glass Dial, Reverse Paint, On Glass, Eagle Finial, 21 In. 240
Baroque Style, Silver Plate, Brass, Pilasters, Arabesques, Putto, 24 x 6 In. 861
Behrens, P., Wall, Railroad Station, Copper, Glass, Enameled Metal, c.1910, 10 In. *illus* 1125
Black Forest, Cuckoo, Carved Wood, Leaves, Deer, Antlers, Germany, 23 x 14 In. 427
Black Forest, Mountain Goats, Leaves, Branches, Door, 8-Day, 32 x 27 In. 3630
Blinking Eye, Lion, Cast Iron, Painted, Bradley & Hubbard, c.1880, 10 In. *illus* 5605
Bracket, Boardroom, Sheraton, Mahogany, Marquetry, 8 Bells, c.1890, 36 In. *illus* 2460
Bracket, George III, Mahogany, Ogee Caddy Top, Brass Handle, Arched Door, 20 In. 5522
Bracket, Mahogany, Brass, Molded Arch, Carrying Handle, Fish Scale Panels, c.1800, 18 In. 1479
Canfield Bro. & Co., Gilt Bronze, Champleve, Enamel, Portico, Double Face, 28 In. 1298
Carriage, Brass, Champleve, Round Dial, Multicolor, Shaped Feet, c.1900, 3 ½ x 2 In. 1187
Carriage, Brass, Glass, Bamboo Style Case, Hour Repeater, Double Dial, France, 6 In. *illus* 3555
Carriage, Brass, Lacquered, Gorge Cased, Reeded Columns, Top Handle, c.1885, 7 In. 1483
Carriage, Geneva Clock Co., Sterling, Green Guilloche Enamel, White Face, Swiss 1020
Carriage, Gilt Brass, Grape & Vine Leaf Design, Footed, c.1900, 7 x 4 In. 1375
Carriage, Gilt Brass, Porcelain, Bamboo Pattern Case, Handle, Red Enamel, c.1885, 4 In. 946
Carriage, Travel, Mayer, Bronze Dore, Guilloche, Rococo Style, Velvet Sash, 3 x 3 In. 106
Carrien, Louis XIV, Marble, Bronze, Woman, Children, Shelf, c.1880, 22 x 20 In. 2420
Cartel, Gilt Bronze, Cartouche Shape, Leaves, Flower Head, Lattice, c.1900, 20 In. 3750
Cartel, Louis XVI Style, Bronze, Fluted Base, Leaf Finial, Grillwork, c.1880, 24 x 12 In. 799
Cartier, Desk, Oval, White Face, Roman Numerals, Paris, 2 ½ x 5 ½ In. 330
Cartier, Sterling Silver, Blue Enamel, Art Deco, Gold Color Face, Marked, 1927, 5 In. *illus* 11210
Causard, Shelf, Gilt Bronze, Scrolled Leafy Support, Lovebird Finial, Signed, 1800s, 14 In. 1353
Chelsea, Shelf, Babro, No. 31, Mahogany Case, Massachusetts, c.1905, 9 ¾ In. 177
Chelsea, Shelf, Ship's Bell, Yacht Wheel, Ebonized Wood Base, Backplate, 17 ½ In. 1062
Chime, Pagoda Top, Fluted, Corinthian Columns, Scroll Feet & Apron, c.1900, 109 In. 5535
Cuckoo, Carved Wood, Hanging Rabbit, Pheasant, Stag Head, Leaves, Round Dial, 14 x 24 In. *illus* 180
Currier, Edmund, Looking Glass, Dovetail, Reverse Paint, Twist Columns, c.1825, 38 In. 9840
Didisheim Goldschmidt Fils & Co., Transfers, Paint, Celluloid, Frame, Tripod, 4 x 4 In. 230
DRGM, Bracket, Time & Strike, Oak Case, Bronze Paw Feet, Shelf, c.1870, 19 x 12 In. 207
Eastlake Style, Walnut, Strike & Chime, Carving, Gallery Top, Barometer, 36 x 17 In. 115
Eibel, H., Walnut, Carved, Curved Pediment, Wall, 60 In. 1320
Figural, Black Man's Face, Smiling, Green Hat, Tie Pendulum, Eyes Move, 9 In. 450
Figural, Dog, Mechanical, Pendulum, Tongue Moves, Painted, 7 ½ In. *illus* 180
Figural, Earth Goddess, Putti, Winter, Summer, Gilt, Porcelain, Paris, 1815, 20 x 14 In. *illus* 984
Figural, Mercury Standing On Rocks, Winged Helmet, Bronze Dore, c.1835, 19 x 12 In. 1230
Figural, Race Car, Desk Piece, Steel, Patina, Germany, Prewar, 6 ¾ In. 425
Gilbert Co., Oak, Mission Style, Square Face, Slatted Design, Shelf, 15 x 5 In. 489
Guelin, A., Louis XVI Style, Painted, Flowers, Leaves, Lucerne, Shelf, c.1900, 21 x 11 In. 1320
Hermes, LeCoultre, Travel Alarm, Brass, Back Crocodile Case, Swiss, 4 ⅜ In. 1180
Hills, Goodrich & Co., Shelf, Ogee, Mahogany Veneer, President's House, c.1850, 31 In. 800
Howard Miller, Brass & Wood, Sun Shape, Round Face, Wall, 1960s, 13 In. Diam. 219
Howard Miller, Teakwood, Painted Metal, 19 In. 998
Howard, E., Regulator, Keyhole, Rosewood, Reverse Painted, 31 ½ In. 3998
Howard, E., Regulator, Rosewood, Half Round Molding, 8-Day, c.1870, 28 ½ In. 1107
I. Noguchi, Hawkeye Measured Time, Timer Knob, Model L, Bakelite, c.1932, 6 In. *illus* 5000
J.E. Caldwell & Co., Faience, Galle Style, Enamel, Gilt, Flowers, Leaves, Wall, 1800s, 27 In. 1046

Clock, Shelf, Duval, Boulle, Faux Tortoiseshell, Brass Case, Flame & Urn Finial, c.1870, 24 In.
$2,583

Skinner, Inc.

Clock, Shelf, Gilt Metal, Cut Glass, Porcelain Dial, Bun Feet, Glass Dome, France, 18 In.
$1,080

Cowan Auctions

Clock, Shelf, Pendulum Chime, Westminster, Herschede Canterbury, 10 ½ x 20 ½ In.
$165

Hess Auction Group

Clock, Shelf, Skeleton, Brass, Pierced, Silvered Ring, Mahogany Base, c.1890, 13 ½ In.
$738

Skinner, Inc.

Clock, Shelf, Willard, A., Mahogany, Fretwork, Glazed Door, Eglomise Mat, c.1820, 35 In.
$3,321

Skinner, Inc.

Clock, Sinclair, Chelsea, Gothic Arch, Intaglio Thistle, Hardy & Hayes, 12 x 8 In.
$1,581

Early Auction Company

Clock, Stickley, G., Shelf, Elm, Brass, Copper, Leaded Glass, Red Decal, c.1902, 21 x 14 In.
$21,250

Rago Arts and Auction Center

Clock, Tall Case, Classical, Mahogany, Poplar, Broken Arch, Fluted Columns, c.1820, 100 In.
$1,920

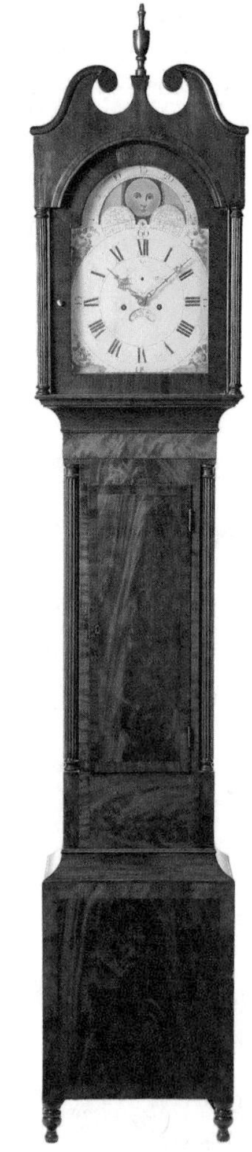

Garth's Auctioneers & Appraisers

Clock, Tall Case, Parzinger, Lacquered Wood, Lime Green, Square, Pyramid Finial, 1960s, 84 x 11 In.
$10,000

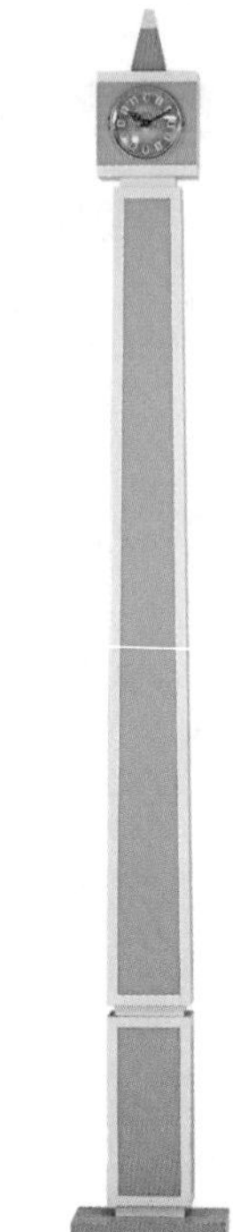

Rago Arts and Auction Center

Clock, Tall Case, Regulator, Engraved Brass Dial, Plated Pendulum, Oak Case, c.1875, 100 In.
$4,920

Skinner, Inc.

Jacob Petit Style, Paris, Scrolled Feet, Gilt, Turk, Lounging, c.1850, 18 x 10 In. ....*illus* 468
Jaeger-LeCoultre, Atmos Marina, Brass, Square, Seascape, 9 x 7 In. 1920
Jaeger-LeCoultre, Shelf, Atmos, Rhodium Plated, Model 540, Box, 8 x 9 In. 2473
Japy Freres, Louis XVI Style, Fruitwood, Gilt Metal Leaf Accents, Shelf, 14 In. 431
Jerome & Co., Wall, Inlaid Wood, Reverse Painted, Pendulum, 8-Day, 28 x 17 In. 180
Juvet & Co., Terrestrial Globe, Brass Tripod Stand, Dolphin Feet, Shelf, c.1880, 31 In. 11685
Juvet & Co., Terrestrial Globe, Stylized Flower Column, Claw Feet, c.1880, 46 In. 6150
Kroeber, Gallery, Maltese, Turned Buttons, Wood Bezel, c.1890, 28 In. 246
Lantern, Brass, Leaf Frets, Turned Columns, Spire Finial, c.1900, 9 In. 217
Luman Watson, Mahogany, Arched Pediment, Half Columns, Painted Dial, Shelf, 36 x 18 In. .. 240
Lyre, Mahogany, Carved Finial, Pillow Molding, 8-Day, Time Only Movement, c.1825, 38 In. 1722
Marine, Octagonal, Mahogany, Brass Bezel, 30-Hour Time & Strike, c.1847, 13 In. 584
Marsh, Williams & Co., Mahogany, Half Columns, Reverse Painted, 1800s, 33 x 18 In. .....*illus* 1920
Munger, Asa, Shelf, Mahogany, Stovepipe Pillars, Portraits, Iron Dial, 1832, 39 In. ....*illus* 39100
New Haven, Wall, Southern Gum Case, 30-Day, Chimes, Seconds Dial, c.1900, 35 In. 375
Pedro Friedeberg, 3-Legged Table Clock, Blue, Gilt Mahogany, c.1968, 11 x 8 In. ....*illus* 6875
Pilgrim, Tole, Standing With Cane, Clock On Chest, Square Base, 16 In. 214
Pillar & Scroll, Wood, Drawer, Pierced, Engraved, Japan, c.1850, 15 In. 1107
Pitkin, Levi, Regulator, Cherry, Dovetail, 8-Day, Passing Strike Movement, c.1800, 53 In. 22140
Portico, Empire Style, Bronze Dore, Patina, Leaves, Columns, France, c.1876, 20 x 9 In. 2214
Punch, Factory, International Time Recording, Wood Case, c.1910, 15 x 46 In. 270
Regulator, Carved Case, Center Crest, Turned Finials, Brass Case, Vienna, 50 In. ....*illus* 3444
Sessions, Ebonized Wood, Faux Marble Columns, Shelf, c.1910, 11 x 16 In. 72
Seth Thomas, Brass Movement, 8-Day, Wood Veneers, Gold Leaf Columns, Shelf, 33 x 19 In. 212
Seth Thomas, Course, Bakelite, Metal Frame, Window, c.1942, 8½ x 12 In. 615
Seth Thomas, Mahogany Veneered, Time & Strike, Shelf, 16 x 11 In. 159
Seth Thomas, Porcelain, Glass Door, Orchids, Pink, Blue, Shelf, Dresden, 16 x 12 In. 118
Seth Thomas, Shelf, Brass, 8-Inch Dial, Time & Bell Strike, c.1900, 10½ x 10 In. 182
Seth Thomas, Shelf, Mahogany, Cornucopias, Flowers, Stenciled, Shelf, c.1835, 31 In. 861
Shelf, Art Nouveau, Patinated Metal, Curved Feet, c.1900, 15 x 8½ In. 360
Shelf, Black Marble, Bronze, Portico, Columns, Mask Medallions, Cherubs, c.1834, 18 In. 553
Shelf, Boulle Style, Gilt, Brass, Tortoiseshell, Waisted Case, Enamel Dial, 1800s, 30 In. 1479
Shelf, Brass, Skeleton, Gothic Revival, Sir Walter Scott, Dog, 1800s, 18 x 11¼ In. 1210
Shelf, Bronze Dore, Figural Apollo, Lyre, Holding Scroll, Wreath, c.1835, 30 x 19 In. 2214
Shelf, Bronze, Louis XV Style, Mask, Pierced Scroll Border, Flowers, c.1890, 24 In. 799
Shelf, Bronze, Silvered, Dome Top, Soldier, Urn, Columns, Plinth, c.1890, 27 x 12 In. 6375
Shelf, Cathedral Shape, Pierced Rose Window, Arched, c.1850, 21 In. 1582
Shelf, Charles X, Marble, Gilt, Diana, Bow, Hound, Stepped Base, Scroll Feet, c.1835, 19 In. 937
Shelf, Duval, Boulle, Faux Tortoiseshell, Brass Case, Flame & Urn Finial, c.1870, 24 In. .....*illus* 2583
Shelf, Eastlake Style, Oak, c.1890, 23 In. 102
Shelf, Eastlake, Black Slate, Red Marble Trim, Gold, Brass Movement, 10 x 13 In. 150
Shelf, Figures, Hunched Over, Clock On Back, Parcel Gilt, Beaded, c.1800, 21 In. 1045
Shelf, Gilt Bronze, Champleve, Glass, Arched Case, Urn Finial, Spool Feet, c.1900, 20 In. 2000
Shelf, Gilt Bronze, Flowers, Ribbons, Columns, Finials, Gladiator, c.1889, 29 x 13 In. 1898
Shelf, Gilt Bronze, Malachite Base, Flowers, Arched, Leaves, Vines, Butterfly, c.1800, 11 In. 1230
Shelf, Gilt Bronze, Porcelain, Figural, Urn, Flowers, Figures, Enamel Dial, c.1885, 25 In. 3362
Shelf, Gilt Metal, Cut Glass, Porcelain Dial, Bun Feet, Glass Dome, France, 18 In. ....*illus* 1080
Shelf, Gilt Metal, Porcelain, Rounded Base, Cherubs, Crest, Garland, Blue, c.1890, 18 In. 1722
Shelf, Louis XV, Spelter, Marble, Chariot, Horse, c.1890, 21 x 23 In. 1150
Shelf, Louis XV, Spelter, Standing Woman, Pink Marble Base, Paris, c.1895, 22 x 11 In. 363
Shelf, Mahogany, Library, Glass Case, Molded Cornice, Ogee Base, Bun Feet, 9 In. 3956
Shelf, Marble, Bronze Dore, Square, Beading, Fluted, Columns, Lunette Crest, c.1800, 18 In. 1476
Shelf, Medieval Style, Cast Bronze, Bell Shape, Inscription, Enamel, c.1900, 12 In. 210
Shelf, Napoleon III, Gilt Bronze, Molded Feet, Porcelain Plaque, Flowers, 15 x 16 In. 500
Shelf, Napoleon III, Marble Base, Diane De Gabies Figure, F. Barbedienne, 22 x 13 In. 984
Shelf, Neoclassical, Fruitwood, Parcel Gilt, Glazed Panels, Scroll Feet, Austria, c.1790, 23 In. 750
Shelf, Pendulum Chime, Westminster, Herschede Canterbury, 10½ x 20½ In. ....*illus* 165
Shelf, Pillar & Scroll, Memorial Scene, Turned Feet, Pennsylvania, c.1830, 31 In. 11685
Shelf, Quarter Striking, Starbursts, Porcelain Dial, Spring Powered, Bun Foot, c.1850, 22 In. 4305
Shelf, Regency, Carved Rosewood, Brass Inlay, Bowed Reeded Top, c.1835, 12 x 7 In. 1000
Shelf, Silver Gilt, Red Guilloche, Enamel, Arched, Pearl Border, Faux Shagreen Case, 3 In. 1143
Shelf, Silvered Bronze, Winged Victory, Blowing Horn, Owl, Round Dial, c.1900, 32 In. 2750
Shelf, Skeleton, Brass, Pierced, Silvered Ring, Mahogany Base, c.1890, 13½ In. ....*illus* 738
Shelf, Willard, A., Mahogany, Fretwork, Glazed Door, Eglomise Mat, c.1820, 35 In. ....*illus* 3321
Sinclair, Chelsea, Gothic Arch, Intaglio Thistle, Hardy & Hayes, 12 x 8 In. ....*illus* 1581
Skeleton, Glass Dome, Wood Base, Blue & White Enamel, Scrolled, c.1860, 17 In. 584

Clock, Tall Case, Robert Danton, Japanned, Brass Dial, 8-Day, c.1700, 91 In.
$3,422

Brunk Auctions

Cloisonne, Cup Holder, Gilt Silver, Sawtooth Rim, Handle, Russia, c.1915, 3 x 4 In.
$3,300

Alex Cooper

Cloisonne, Kovsh, Silver Gilt, Flowers & Scrolls, N. Strulev, Russia, c.1900, 3½ In.
$1,169

Skinner, Inc.

Cloisonne, Planter, Gilt Bronze, Scrolling Vine & Lotus, Paneled, Blue Ground, 9 ½ In., Pair
$3,851

James D. Julia Auctioneers

Cloisonne, Sugar Basket, Gilt Silver, Handle, Marked, 11th Artel, Russia, c.1908, 4 In.
$4,500

Alex Cooper

Cloisonne, Tea Caddy, Lid, 14-Sided Cube, Crimson Clouds, Dragon, Phoenix, c.1900, 5 x 4 In.
$360

Selkirk Auctioneers & Appraisers

TIP

Never run an ad that says "Call after 6 p.m." It is an announcement that you are away from the house during the day.

Slave, Blond Wood, Inlay, Marquetry, Roman Numerals, Glass Door, Dutch, 12 x 38 In. 1003
Standard Novelty Co., Night-Light, Octagonal, Nickel Plate, Handle, Oil, c.1886, 6 In. 338
Stickley, G., Shelf, Elm, Brass, Copper, Leaded Glass, Red Decal, c.1902, 21 x 14 In. .... *illus* 21250
Tall Case, Bailey, Banks & Biddle, Silvered & Gilt Dial, Mahogany, c.1900, 97 x 28 In. 885
Tall Case, Burr Walnut, Musical, Bombe Base, Time & Strike, Holland, 119 x 25 In. 10762
Tall Case, Classical, Mahogany, Poplar, Broken Arch, Fluted Columns, c.1820, 100 In. .... *illus* 1920
Tall Case, G. Brown, Walnut, Flat Cornice, Tombstone Door, Brass Dial, Boston, 83 In. 5228
Tall Case, George III Style, Mahogany, Carved, Broken Arch Bonnet, Brass, c.1800, 97 x 21 In. .. 854
Tall Case, George III Style, Mahogany, Sphere Finials, Scroll Cornice, 90 In. 625
Tall Case, George III, Chinoiserie, Figures, Pagoda Top, Panel Door, c.1790, 103 In. 3750
Tall Case, Georgian Style, Chinoiserie, Battery Operated, Faux Face, 1900s, 90 x 17 In. 478
Tall Case, Herschede, F., Neoclassical, Mahogany, Columns, Brass Movement, 92 In. 1232
Tall Case, Herschede, Mahogany, Broken Pediment Crest, 79 x 21 In. 540
Tall Case, J. Albert, Walnut, Inlay, Swan Neck, Flame Finials, Spandrels, c.1795, 97 In. 4920
Tall Case, Louis XV Style, Pine, Painted, Ogee Crown, Repousse Face, 1800s, 96 x 20 In. 308
Tall Case, Mahogany, Arched Pediment, Paneled, Beveled Glass Door, c.1925, 101 In. 875
Tall Case, Oak, Carved, Scroll Pediment, Figural Mask, Brass Dial, c.1900, 103 x 20 In. 7380
Tall Case, Oak, Rounded Top & Brass Face, Germany, c.1920, 77 x 20 In. 330
Tall Case, Parzinger, Lacquered Wood, Enameled Metal, Square Face, 1960s, 86 In. 4063
Tall Case, Parzinger, Lacquered Wood, Lime Green, Square, Pyramid Finial, 1960s, 84 x 11 In. ..... *illus* 10000
Tall Case, Pine, Paint, Broken Arch Pediment, Canted Corners, Turned Feet, c.1810, 95 In. 625
Tall Case, Regency, Mahogany, Shell Carved, Lyre, Gothic Arch, Paint, c.1830, 86 x 20 In. 2006
Tall Case, Regulator, Engraved Brass Dial, Plated Pendulum, Oak Case, c.1875, 100 In. ..... *illus* 4920
Tall Case, Robert Danton, Japanned, Brass Dial, 8-Day, c.1700, 91 In. .... *illus* 3422
Tall Case, Ward, A., Maple, Arched Door, Brass & Silvered Dial, N.Y., c.1740, 83 In. 9840
Tall Case, Wingate, Birch, Maple, Fretwork, Crossbanding, French Feet, c.1820, 89 In. 6150
Terry, Eli & Sons, Pillar & Scroll, Mahogany, Pine, Landscape Tablet, c.1825, 33 In. 938
Terry, Eli, Shelf, Pillar & Scroll, Mahogany, Scrolling Crest, Finials, c.1825, 37 In. 600
Terry, S.B., Regulator, Mahogany, Wood Bezel, Skeletonized, 3 Pillars, c.1840, 35 In. 3690
Terry, S.B., Torsion, Octagonal, Rosewood, 8-Day, Pat. Oct. 5th 1852, 12 In. 677
Tiffany Clocks that are part of desk sets made by Louis Comfort Tiffany are listed in the Tiffany category. Clocks sold by the store Tiffany & Co. are listed here.
Travel, Bailey, Banks & Biddle, Art Deco, 14K Yellow Gold, Delphia 15 Jewel 502
Travel, Cartier, Gold, Round, Hinged Stand, Quartz Movement, Alarm, Box, 4 x 3 In. 427
Travel, Miller & Buckley, 14K Yellow Gold, Steel Movement, Lemnia 15 Jewel 1151
Wag-On-Wall, Brass, Tin Dial, Repousse Birds, Flowers, Pendulum, c.1890, 60 In. 406
Wag-On-Wall, Weight & Pendulum, Arched Crest, Flowers, Cream & Red, 1800s, 7 In. 384
Wall, Eastlake, Oak, Carved Pediment, Pendulum, 42 x 15 In. 720
Wall, Gilt Bronze, Leaves, Cartouche, Oval Plaque, Door, France, c.1880, 25 x 12 In. 1331
Wall, Howard Miller, Spike, Model 2202-D, 1952, 18 ½ In. 1823
Wall, Renaissance Revival, Walnut, Cartouche Shape, Fruit Basket, c.1890, 58 x 40 In. 4750
Waltham, Regulator, Arch Top, Egg & Dart, Ben Franklin Bust, c.1900, 73 In. 3444
Waumsley, Mahogany, Round, Painted Face, Wall, 1900, 18 In. 240
Willard, Aaron, Shelf, Mahogany, Fret Top, Splayed Feet, 8-Day, c.1800, 39 In. 7380
Wooden, Hourglass, Tartanware, Victorian, 5 ⅜ x 3 In. 120
Wooding, Edmund, Shelf, Column & Splat, 3 Women, 30-Hour, East West, c.1830, 30 In. 1046

CLOISONNE enamel was developed during the tenth century. A glass enamel was applied between small ribbons of metal on a metal base. Most cloisonne is Chinese or Japanese. Pieces marked *China* were made after 1900.

Basket, Fruit, Jadeite & Hardstone Fruit, 22 x 10 In. 1416
Beaker, Flowers, Geometric Patterns, Marked Nikolai Alekseev, c.1910, 5 ½ In. 5000
Beaker, Winged Griffins, Stippled Gilt, Marked Alder, Russia, 1877, 6 In. 2750
Bowl, Brass Rim, Blue, Pink Flowers, 4 ¾ x 15 ¼ In. 92
Bowl, Inverted Bell Shape, Flared Rim, Lotus Flowers, Turquoise, 11 In. Diam. 875
Bowl, Phoenix, Dragons, Blue, Fishbowl Shape, Red Border, Medallions, 8 x 9 In. 181
Bowl, Squat, Flared Neck, Geometric Bands, Panels, Russia, 1908-17, 2 x 3 In. 1875
Box, Band Inserts, Flowers, Leaves, Blue, Star Shape Medallions, 1800s, 11 x 5 In. 180
Box, Dome Lid, Pink Rose, Silver Gilt, Bracket Feet, Russia, c.1896-1908, 2 ¾ In. 4250
Box, Dome Lid, Round, Saucer Foot, Stylized Flowers, Scroll, Gilt, 1800s, 4 In. Diam. 216
Box, Figural, Mandarin Ducks, Lid, Feather, Scrolling, 4 ¾ x 6 In., Pair 615
Box, Lid, Flower Shape, Shou Symbol, Bats, Lotus, Gilt, 4 In. Diam. 556
Box, Round, Magpie, Plum Blossoms, Blue, Flowers, 14 In. 2500
Box, Silver, White Flowers, Blue, Green, Footed, Russia, 2 x 3 In. 738
Censer, Lid, Foo Dog Finial, Globular, Handles, Beast Head, Feet, Turquoise, 11 In. 375
Censer, Square Shape, Tapered, Rounded Corners, Bird, Flowering Tree, 4 x 4 In. 1920

Censer, Stand, Globular, Shaped Foot, Handles, Lotus Blossoms, Vines, 6 In. 1481
Censer, Tripod, Squat, Pierced Wood Lid, Upright Handles, Lotus Pods, 5 In. 3555
Centerpiece, Bowl, Dragon Handles, Flowers, Pierced Rim, Mask Feet, c.1900, 11 x 19 In. 1625
Charger, Crane, Sky, Clouds, Landscape, China, Wood Stand, 1900s, 25 In. 747
Charger, Dragon, Flower Shape Edges, Central Medallion, 5-Clawed Dragon, 1900s, 14 In. 302
Charger, Teal Ground, Trumpet-Shape Orange Flowers, Japan, 13 ½ In. 240
Cup Holder, Gilt Silver, Sawtooth Rim, Handle, Russia, c.1915, 3 x 4 In. .... *illus* 3300
Cups, Tumbler, Gray Ducks, Scrolls, Scrolls, Gilt Interior, 2 In., Pair 7282
Dish, Flared Flower Shape, Gilt Rim, Lotus Roundel, Prunus, Multicolor, 8 In. Diam. 1000
Dish, Partridge, Storks, Enameled Center, Blue Ground, Japan, c.1910, 11 ¾ In. 236
Egg, Flowers, Birds, Chinese, Late 20th Century, 19 In. 125
Figurine, Camel, Open Mouth, Saddle Comes Off, Blue, Red, Gilt, 23 x 19 In. 687
Figurine, Horse, Copper, Back Legs Bent, Dragons, Leaves, 1900s, 16 x 16 In. 1210
Figurine, Horse, Prancing, Blue, Green, Gilt Hooves, 15 ¾ x 19 In., Pair 747
Figurine, Horse, Standing, Removable Saddle, Wood Stand, c.1950, 15 In., Pair 988
Figurine, Koi Fish, Black Eyes, Open Mouth, Hollow, Wave Shape Stand, 10 x 3 In. 118
Figurine, Pig, Standing, Blue, Red, Gilt, Phoenixes & Dragons, c.1920, 11 x 23 In. 711
Figurine, Qilin, Reclining, Tendrils, Dragons, Red Ground, Pierced Stand, c.1900, 5 x 8 In. 750
Figurine, Rhinoceros, Lapis Blue, Archaic Style, Gilt Copper Hollow Shape, 12 x 21 In. 448
Goblet, Flower Scroll, Textured Ground, Gilt, Spread Foot, Russia, c.1910, 7 In. 7768
Group, 2 Parrots, Gourd, 16 ¼ In. 5000
Incense Burner, Duck, Wing Shape Lid, Multicolor Enamel, Gilt, 10 x 9 In., Pair 614
Jar, Black, Flowers, Green, 1900s, 11 ½ x 6 In. 150
Jar, Lid, Flowers, Blue, White, Footed, 5 In. 75
Jar, Peonies, Chrysanthemums, Long Foot, Yellow Ground, Turquoise, 13 x 8 In. 738
Kovsh, Hook Shape Handle, Scroll, Leaves, Multicolor, Russia, 1908-17, 6 In. 4250
Kovsh, Silver Gilt, Flowers & Scrolls, N. Strulev, Russia, c.1900, 3 ½ In. .... *illus* 1169
Kovsh, Silver, 2-Headed Eagle, Russia, 2 ⅝ x 4 In. 492
Letter Opener, Gilt, Silver, Blue Handle, Fitted Case, 10 ½ In. 1968
Planter, Gilt Bronze, Scrolling Vine & Lotus, Paneled, Blue Ground, 9 ½ In., Pair .... *illus* 3851
Planter, Oval, Lobed, Flared Rim, Lotus Scrolls, Shaped Feet, 1800s, 11 x 6 In. 216
Salt Chair, Turquoise, Beaded Borders, Stippled Gilt, V. Agafonov, 1890, 2 ½ In. 1250
Salt, Master, Shaded Enamel, 8 Lobed Panels, Russia, c.1900, 2 ½ In. 3750
Screen, Black, White Flowers, Snowy Slope, Birds, 7 ¼ x 13 In. 633
Spoon, Silver Gilt, Pan Slavic Style, Twist Handle, Russia, 1908-17, 4 ½ In. 1250
Stationery Holder, Medieval Building, Gabled Ends, Kneeling Figures, 9 x 11 In. 3120
Sugar Basket, Gilt Silver, Handle, Marked, 11th Artel, Russia, c.1908, 4 In. .... *illus* 4500
Tazza, Bronze Trim, Elephant Head, Lotus Plants, 2 Ducks, Blue, c.1910, 7 x 12 In. 1000
Tea & Coffee Spoons, Silver Gilt, Leaves, Red, White, Blue, Box, Russia, 5 In., 24 Piece 4982
Tea Caddy, Lid, 14-Sided Cube, Crimson Clouds, Dragon, Phoenix, c.1900, 5 x 4 In. .... *illus* 360
Teapot, Blue, Dragon Handle, Tibet, 13 x 16 In. 472
Teapot, Figural, Buddha, Purple, Gilt, White, 3 x 6 In. 108
Teapot, Goose, Figural, 8 x 8 ½ In. 180
Tray, Enamel, White Celadon Jade, Buckle-Shape Dragon Handles, 12 x 8 ¾ In. 1180
Vase, 2 Conjoined Pilgrim Flasks, Flying Dragons, Narrow Neck, Square Foot, 16 x 15 In. 1476
Vase, 6 Panels, Blue Ground, Multicolor, Chinese, 39 x 16 In., Pair 1098
Vase, 6 Panels, Cranes, Mountains, Landscapes, 12 ½ In. 375
Vase, Black Ground, Pink Chrysanthemum, Chinese, 1800s, 12 In. 84
Vase, Black, Cranes, Flowers, Japan, 6 x 4 In., Pair 82
Vase, Black, Swirling Dragon, Bottle Shape, Japan, 5 ⅞ In. 308
Vase, Blue, Flowers, Birds, Leaves, Banding, Ayashi Kodenji, Japan, 3 ½ In., Pair 2300
Vase, Bottle Shape, Scrolling Vines & Flowers, Splay Foot, 1900s, 5 x 3 In. 2074
Vase, Brass, Yellow, Cherry Blossoms, 9 ¾ x 4 In. 488
Vase, Bronze, Purple, Green, Black, Flowers, Lid, Handles, 20 In. 805
Vase, Camel Shape, Blue, 7 ½ In., Pair 100
Vase, Double Fish Shape, Oval, Enamel, Gilt Bronze Banding, Chinese, 12 x 10 In. .... *illus* 4720
Vase, Double Gourd, Flowers, Butterflies, 9 ¼ x 5 In. 180
Vase, Double, Conjoined, Lotus Blooms, Archaistic Designs, Buddhist Symbols, 13 In. .... *illus* 1778
Vase, Elongated, Multicolor Irises, Blue Ground, Japan, c.1860, 18 In. 531
Vase, Flared Rim, 5 Dragons, Flaming Pearl, Waves, c.1900, 13 In. 1838
Vase, Flattened Shoulder, Wisteria Blooms, Branches, Leaves, 1800s, 3 In. .... *illus* 1353
Vase, Flowers & Butterflies, Elongated Oval, Flared Foot, Pinched Neck, 10 In. 207
Vase, Gilt Rim, Foot, Hunting Scenes, Landscape, Chinese, 12 In. 260
Vase, Globular, Prunus Branches, Bamboo, Chrysanthemums, Red, c.1900, 9 In. 738
Vase, Hexagonal, Birds, Prunus, Flowers, Butterflies, Lotus, Multicolor, 15 x 7 In. 92

Cloisonne, Vase, Double Fish Shape, Oval, Enamel, Gilt Bronze Banding, Chinese, 12 x 10 In.
$4,720

Brunk Auctions

Cloisonne, Vase, Double, Conjoined, Lotus Blooms, Archaistic Designs, Buddhist Symbols, 13 In.
$1,778

James D. Julia Auctioneers

Cloisonne, Vase, Flattened Shoulder, Wisteria Blooms, Branches, Leaves, 1800s, 3 In.
$1,353

Skinner, Inc.

Cloisonne, Vase, Tree, White Flowers, Hammered Copper, Moriage, Ando, Japan, 1930s, 7 x 9 In.
$1,050

Ruby Lane

TIP
Don't hang valuable old clothing on wire hangers. This puts a strain on the shoulders. Store clothing flat or folded on a shelf.

Clothing, Hat, Bowler, Lining, Franklin Simon Co., 21 ½ In.
$86

Showtime Auction Services

Clothing, Hat, Military, Shako, Felt, Leather, Wool Pompom, 79th Infantry, France, 1812, 8 In.
$4,600

Cowan Auctions

Vase, Multicolor, Dragon Handles, Chinese, 17 ½ In., Pair 450
Vase, Multicolor, Teal Ground, Chinese, 20 In. 360
Vase, Peacock, Flowers, Dark Blue, 1900s, Japan, 8 In. 861
Vase, Pink & White Iris, Green Leaves, Yellow, Japan, 10 In., Pair 374
Vase, Red Iridescent, Japan, 7 ½ In. 90
Vase, Ribbed, Flower Heads, Figures, Emblems, Flared Rim, c.1900, 15 In. 980
Vase, Shouldered, Tapered, Rolled Rim, Green, Peony, Leafy Branch, 11 In., Pair 153
Vase, Square, Panels, Shouldered, Block Foot, Dragons, Lotus, Ring Handles, 11 In., Pair 7110
Vase, Tapered, Rounded Shoulders, Flared Lip, Bird, Grass, Flowers, c.1900, 6 In. 185
Vase, Tree, White Flowers, Hammered Copper, Moriage, Ando, Japan, 1930s, 7 x 9 In. .... *illus* 1050
Vodka Cup, Silver Gilt, Panels, Birds, Flowers, Mint Green, White Swan, Russia, 2 In. 8048

CLOTHING of all types is listed in this category. Dresses, hats, shoes, underwear, and more are found here. Other textiles are to be found in the Coverlet, Movie, Quilt, Textile, and World War I and II categories.

Blouse, Rayon, Crepe, Beaded, Sequined, Blue, Whimsical Scrolls, Size XL, c.1930 60
Boots, Untanned Leather, Brown, Wood Trees, 1900s, Men's, Size 10-10 ½ 283
Cap, Yellow Cab Driver, Black & Yellow, Size 7 ⅜ 270
Cape, Wool, Cashmere, Faux Fur Trim, Italy, 36 In. 270
Chasuble, Needlepoint Panels, Gothic Revival Design, Silk, Linen, Black, Silver, 1800s 369
Coat, Fur, Dark Brown, Taffeta Lined, Notched Lapels, Pockets, ¾ Sleeves, Size 8, 22 In. 562
Coat, Leopard Print Fabric, Mink Trim, 40 In. 210
Coat, Mink, Blond, Satin Collar, Pockets, c.1960, Size Medium 75
Coat, Mink, Chocolate Brown, Notched Collar, Pockets, Back Slit, Full Length, Size 6, 47 In. 5500
Coat, Mink, Silk Lined, Belt, Embroidered Design, Ellisberg 184
Coat, Mink, Stroller, Brown, Stand-Up Collar, Bishop's Sleeve, Size 4-6, 27 In. 663
Coat, Mouton, Chocolate Brown, Annis Furs, 1940s, Size 16 60
Coat, Wool, Double Breasted, Red Orange, Round Collar & Lapel, Belt, c.1970, Size 3 390
Dress Bag, Louis Vuitton, Canvas, Round Shoulders, Gold LV Monogram, Zipper, 60 x 24 In. 272
Dress, Beads, Sequined Rose Appliques, Car Wash Hemline, Silk, Lime Green, 1930s, 59 In. 495
Dress, Delphos, Silk, Pleated, Murano Glass Beadwork, Belt, Mariano Fortuny, c.1910, 55 In. 3690
Hat, Bowler, Lining, Franklin Simon Co., 21 ½ In. .... *illus* 86
Hat, Military, Shako, Felt, Leather, Wool Pompom, 79th Infantry, France, 1812, 8 In. .... *illus* 4600
Hat, Straw, Faux Pearls, Metallic Thread Flowers, Label, Christine, c.1945, 7 x 5 In. 85
Hat, Western, Dakota, Silver Belly Color, Resistol, Original Box, c.1960, Man's, Size 7 .... *illus* 115
Jacket, Black Persian Lamb, Fox Collar, Ciner, 26 ½ In. 540
Jacket, Blue Silk Ground, Floral Blooms, Butterflies, Chinese, c.1910, 3 In. .... *illus* 371
Jacket, Evening, Black Wool, Silk, Escada, Size 44 148
Jacket, Leather, Beaded Multicolor Flowers, Fringe, Antler Buttons, c.1915, Man's, 28 In. 240
Jacket, Mink, Snakeskin Trim, Notched Collar, Hook Closure, Lined, 1980s, Size 6 .... *illus* 1375
Jacket, Purple Silk, Damask Design, Peony Roundels, Flowers, Chinese, c.1920, 54 In. 2074
Jacket, Sheared, 2-Tone, Ruffles, Akhesa, France, 21 In. 450
Jacket, Silk, Embroidered, Peaches, Bats, Wan Pattern, Chinese, c.1900, 26 In. .... *illus* 5535
Robe, Black, Embroidered Roundels, Flowers, c.1930, 40 In. 237
Robe, Blue Silk, Brocade Woven, Embroidery, Gold Dragons, Flaming Pearl, c.1900, 55 In. 5500
Robe, Fragment, Silk, Brocade, Gold, Blue, 1700s, 24 ¼ x 38 ¾ In. 2070
Robe, Quilted, Knotted Fabric Buttons, Pink, Made For Marshall Field, Size 14 65
Scarf, Blue, Red, Butterfly, Peter Max, 20 x 20 In. 73
Scarf, Chanel, Woman Wearing Necklaces, 34 x 34 In. 74
Scarf, Hermes, Kenya, Silk, 35 x 35 In. 270
Scarf, L'Automne, Cream Profile, Dark Green Ground, YSL, 35 x 35 In. 240
Scarf, L'Hiver, Black Profile, White & Blue Ground, Red Accent, YSL, 35 x 35 In. 330
Scarf, Silk, Brides De Gala, Horse Bridles, Yellow, Cream, Gray, Hermes, 35 x 35 In. 176
Scarf, Silk, Circus, Multicolor, Blue Ground, Hermes, 35 ½ x 35 ½ In. 154
Scarf, Silk, Flowers, Light Blue Ground, Emilio Pucci, Italy, 35 x 5 In. 143
Scarf, Silk, Grand Manege, Ribbons, Bridles, Henri D'Origny, 35 x 35 In. 165
Scarf, Silk, Sauvagine De Vol, Blue Ground, Red Border, Hermes, Box, c.1950, 35 x 35 In. 132
Scarf, Tibet, Silk Twill, Black, Yellow, Auburn, Green, Blue, C. Latham, Hermes, 35 x 35 In. 190
Scarf, White Ground, Red Border, Cartier, 35 x 32 In. 50
Scarf, Yellow, Lines, Vase, Bernard Buffet, 30 x 30 In. 98
Shop Smock, Kiekhaefer Mercury, Logo Patch Front & Back, Size 44 T 240
Swimsuit, Woman's, Geometric Pattern, Magenta, Green, Gottex, 1960s, Size 6 325
Top Hat, Beaver, House Of Bernstein, Knox Hat Mfg., Est.1876, 21 ½ In. .... *illus* 120
Top Hat, Collapsible, Silk, Black, c.1900, Size 6 ¼ 225
Wig, Barrister's, Horsehair, Gray Hair, Mesh Foundation, Label, England, c.1900 720

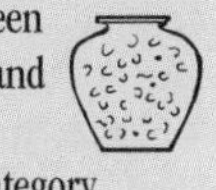

CLUTHRA glass is a two-layered glass with small bubbles and powdered glass trapped between the layers. The Steuben Glass Works of Corning, New York, first made it in 1920. Victor Durand of Kimball Glass Company in Vineland, New Jersey, made a similar glass from about 1925. Durand's pieces are listed in the Durand category. Related items are listed in the Steuben category.

Vase, Kimble, Round Body, Burnt Orange, Opalescent, Signed, 8 In. 259
Vase, Shouldered, White Opalescent, Rolled Rim, 8 In. 520
Vase, Yellow, Orange, Kimball Glass, c.1931, 4 x 4 In. .... *illus* 250

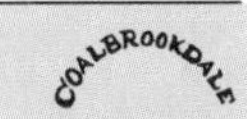

COALBROOKDALE was made by the Coalport porcelain factory of England during the Victorian period. Pieces are decorated with floral encrustations.

Basket, Potpourri, Pierced Lid, Flowered Handle, c.1825, 6 x 7 x 5 In. 475
Basket, Woven, Multicolor Flowers, Gilt, Handle, 10 x 5 In. 972
Dresser Jar, Flowers, Rocaille Gold, Handles, 1850s, 6 In. 402
Potpourri, Pierced Lid, Rose Finial, Handles, Handles, c.1850, 6 ½ In. 295
Sucrier, Flowers, Butterflies, Lady Bugs, 2 Double Handles, c.1850, 7 x 6 In. 945
Sucrier, Scalloped Shell, Lid, Blue Leaves, Bird Finial, Footed, c.1825, 3 x 5 In. 250
Teapot, Scalloped Shell, Green Leaves, Bail Handle, c.1820, 1 ¼ Cup, 6 In. 325
Vase, Rococo Revival Style, Flowers, Multicolor, Footed, c.1849, 5 ½ In. 1700

COALPORT ware was made by the Coalport Porcelain Works of England beginning about 1795. Early pieces were unmarked. About 1810–25 the pieces were marked with the name *Coalport* in various forms. Later pieces also had the name John Rose in the mark. The crown mark was used with variations beginning in 1881. The date 1750 is printed in some marks, but it is not the date the factory started. Coalport was bought by Wedgwood in 1967. Coalport porcelain is no longer being produced. Some pieces are listed in Indian Tree.

Bowl, Lid, Jeweled, Leaf Handles, Pink Ground, Band Of Stars, c.1890, 5 In. 1046
Box, Heart Shape, Woman's Portrait, Gilt Leaves, Green Ground, Jewels, c.1893, 5 In. 2706
Box, Hexagonal, Round Central Portrait, Girl, Medallions, Jewels, c.1890, 6 In. 2583
Box, Lid, Cushion, Ivory Ground, Opals, Rubies, Turquoise Jewels, Cartouche, c.1890, 4 In. 554
Box, Lid, Globe Shape, Semiprecious Stones, Gold Ground, 4 ¾ In. 1845
Box, Lid, Globular, Turquoise Jewels, Gold Ground, Center Enamel Jewel, c.1890, 4 In. 2706
Box, Lid, Jeweled, Flat, Round, Turquoise Enamel, Gold Ground, 2 ½ In. 461
Box, Lid, Jeweled, Oval Ivory Ground, Semiprecious, 1800s, 4 ¼ In. 1046
Box, Lid, Jeweled, Round, Pink Ground, Scrolled Leaves, 5 In. 800
Box, Lid, Jeweled, Round, Turquoise Enamel, Gold Ground, c.1890, 2 ½ In. .... *illus* 461
Box, Lid, Jeweled, Shell Shape, Gold Ground, Turquoise, c.1890, 3 ¾ In. 1107
Cup & Saucer, Batwing Pattern, c.1900 86
Dessert Set, Tray, 6 Plates, Gilt, Shaped Edges, Parcel Gilt, Imari, 10 x 9 In., 7 Piece 181
Dish, Sweetmeat, Scalloped, Molded, Footed, Gilt, Scrolling, Leaves, Green Rim, 12 x 8 In. 81
Figurine, Harriet, Pink Gown & Shawl, Fan, 3 ¼ In. 39
Inkwell, Stand, Insert Pot, Gold, Turquoise Enamel, Crown Mark, c.1890, 5 In. .... *illus* 2214
Perfume Bottle, Heart Shape, Blue Ground, Silver Plate, Blue Cap, 4 ¾ In. 413
Plate, Gilded, Shreve Crump & Low, 10 ¼ Diam., 12 Piece 219
Plate, Gilt, Exotic Birds, Insects, Red Ground, 10 ½ In., Pair 60
Plate, Gilt, Green, 9 In., 12 Piece 615
Plate, Soup, Central Sprig, Gilt Roundel, Blue Ribbon Border, c.1785, 8 ½ In. 155
Scent Bottle, Hinged Lid, Multicolor, Jeweled, Oval, c.1890, 4 ½ In. 861
Slipper, Porcelain, Jeweled, Gold Ground, Turquoise Enamel, c.1890, 5 In. 554
Slipper, Porcelain, Jeweled, Ivory Ground, Semiprecious Stones, Gold Field, c.1790, 4 In. 1353
Tea Canister, Gold, Turquoise Jewels, Square, Leaf Scroll Handles, c.1890, 7 In. 1107
Tea Canister, Jeweled, Cover, Pink Ground Border, Ivory Body, Gilt, c.1890 523
Tureen, Lid, Stand, Oval, Beaded, Flowers, Gilt, Handles, Scroll Feet, c.1825, 7 x 10 In. 188
Vase, Bottle Shape, Jeweled, Mask Handles, Pink Ground, Turquoise Enamel, 6 ½ In. 1230
Vase, Bottle Shape, Landscape, Gold & Pink, Turquoise Jewels, Handles, c.1890, 8 In. .... *illus* 4305
Vase, Flat, Enamel, Medallion, Gold Orb, Salopian Ware Mark, c.1875, 6 x 6 In., Pair .... *illus* 214
Vase, Jeweled, Scrolled Handles, Yellow Ground, Mottled Multicolor, 6 In. 338
Vase, Lid, Jeweled, Bottle Shape, Glazed, Landscape Cartouche, c.1890, 6 ¾ In. .... 215 to 554
Vase, Lid, Jeweled, Scenic, Pierced Leaves, Handles, Landscape, c.1890, 7 In. 615
Vase, Lid, Jeweled, Yellow Ground, Gold Field, Turquoise Enamel, 1800s, 7 ¾ In. 615
Vase, Lid, Potpourri, Jeweled, Squat, Handles, Landscape, 5 In., Pair 1107
Vase, Lid, Ruby Ground, Coastal Scene Cartouche, Bulbous, Square Handles, c.1890, 6 In. 1230

Clothing, Hat, Western, Dakota, Silver Belly Color, Resistol, Original Box, c.1960, Man's, Size 7
$115

Allard Auctions

Clothing, Jacket, Blue Silk Ground, Floral Blooms, Butterflies, Chinese, c.1910, 3 In.
$371

James D. Julia Auctioneers

Clothing, Jacket, Mink, Snakeskin Trim, Notched Collar, Hook Closure, Lined, 1980s, Size 6
$1,375

New Orleans (Cakebread)

Clothing, Jacket, Silk, Embroidered, Peaches, Bats, Wan Pattern, Chinese, c.1900, 26 In.
$5,535

Skinner, Inc.

TIP
Changing temperatures bother a grandfather clock. An inside corner is the best place for the clock.

C

Clothing, Top Hat, Beaver, House Of Bernstein, Knox Hat Mfg., Est.1876, 21 ½ In.
$120

Showtime Auction Services

Cluthra, Vase, Yellow, Orange, Kimball Glass, c. 1931, 4 x 4 In.
$250

Ruby Lane

Coalport, Box, Lid, Jeweled, Round, Turquoise Enamel, Gold Ground, c.1890, 2 ½ In.
$461

Skinner, Inc.

COBALT BLUE glass was made using oxide of cobalt. The characteristic bright dark blue identifies it for the collector. Most cobalt glass found today was made after the Civil War. There was renewed interest in the dark blue glass in the late 1930s and dinnerware was made.

Vase, Flowers, Leaf Sprays, 12 In. 106
Vase, Trumpet, Silver Mount, Grapes, Grape Leaves, Florence, Round Foot, 11 In. 704

COCA-COLA was first served in 1886 in Atlanta, Georgia. It was advertised through signs, newspaper ads, coupons, bottles, trays, calendars, and even lamps and clocks. Collectors want anything with the word *Coca-Cola*, including a few rare products, like gum wrappers and cigar bands. The famous trademark was patented in 1893, the *Coke* mark in 1945. Many modern items and reproductions are being made.

Bank, Drink Coca-Cola, Work Refreshed, Ice Cold, Vending Machine, Box, 1950s, 6 In. 150
Bar Stool, Cast Iron, Red Leather Cushion, Chrome Seat, 30 In. 270
Bookmark, Heart Shape, Victorian Woman, Drinking, Celluloid, 1898 622
Bottle Carrier, Stadium, Drink Coca-Cola, Steel, Upright Handle, Red & White, 12 x 12 In. 153
Bottle Holder, Shopping Cart, Enjoy Coca-Cola While You Shop, Place Bottle Here, 5 x 5 In. 150
Bottle Opener, Have A Coke, It's The Real Thing, Stainless Steel, Ekco, c.1970, 3 In. ....*illus* 12
Bottle Machine, Model 39B, 15 Cent, Red Paint, Vendo Co., Kansas City, 58 x 27 In. 1062
Calendar, 1916, Seated Girl, Holding Bottle, Hat, Roses, Frame, 15 x 34 In. 700
Calendar, 1918, Miss June Caprice, Holding Glass, Hat, Fur Collar, 14 x 10 In. 50
Calendar, 1941, Girl Sitting On Log, Holding Coke Bottle, 20 ½ In. 90
Can Opener, Drink Coca-Cola, Have A Coke, Steel, Ekco, 1960, 3 ¾ In. ....*illus* 10
Cash Register, National, Drink Coca-Cola, 5 Cents, Brass Top Sign, Wood Base, 10 x 21 In. 780
Cash Register, National, Model 717, Drink Coca-Cola, 5 Cents, 1924, 16 x 21 In. 1220
Clock, Ice Cold Coca-Cola, Spinner, Light-Up, Yellow, Red, Convex Glass, 20 In. 300
Clock, Neon, Metal, Glass, Ice Cold, Script Logo, Octagonal, Art Deco Style, 18 In. 1800
Clock, Regulator, Calendar Date, 5 Cents, Sold Here, Sessions, 1925, 36 x 18 In. ....*illus* 850
Cooler, AM Radio, Drink Coca-Cola, Ice Cold, Red & White, 9 ½ In. 300
Cooler, Drink Coca-Cola, In Bottles, Red, Spout, Latching Top, Cavalier, 19 x 18 In. 120
Cooler, Drink Coca-Cola, Refreshing & Reliable, Metal Handle, 18 x 13 In. 120
Cooler, Red, Metal, Drink Coca-Cola In Bottles, Textured, 18 x 18 In. 151
Crate, Bottle Carrier, Wooden, Red Paint, 24 Slots, 1971, 19 x 12 x 4 In. ....*illus* 25
Decal, Window, Drink Coca-Cola, Please Pay When Served, Round, 1930s, 15 In. 780
Dispenser, Outboard Motor, Drink Coca-Cola, Ice Cold, Red, White, 1950s, 12 x 22 In. 488
Dispenser, Soda, There's Nothing Like A Coke, Barrel Shape, 3 Spigots, Claw Foot, 32 In. 840
Display, Drink Coca-Cola, Extra Bright Refreshment, Birds, Cardboard, 1956, 40 x 20 In. 549
Doll, Uniform, Cap, Side-Glancing Eyes, Buddy Lee, c.1930, 13 In. 210
Door Push, Come In! Have A Coca-Cola, Red, Yellow, Porcelain, Oval, 4 x 11 In. 300
Doorstop, Bellhop, Holding Coca-Cola Tray, Full Body, 2 Piece, Round Base, c.1898, 9 In. 2370
Fan, Hand, Drink Coca-Cola, Geisha, Bamboo, Paper, Handle, 15 x 10 In. ....*illus* 385
Ice Pick, Bottle Opener, Wood Handle, Red Coca-Cola Logo, 10 In. ....*illus* 45
Lamp Shade, Hanging, Milk Glass, Metal Tassel, White, Red, Green, 1930s, 14 x 10 In. 660
Lamp, Delicious With Food, Coke Brightens Every Bite, Glasses, c.1968, 14 In. 1440
Lamp, Stained Glass, Hanging, 16 x 17 In. 2700
Match Striker, Drink Coca-Cola, Strike Match Here, Round, Red, Yellow, 1939, 4 x 4 In. 652
Matchbook Holder, Tin, Logo, Be Really Refreshed, Matchbooks, 6 ¾ In. .... 192 to 270
Menu Board, Delicious & Refreshing, Chalkboard, Tin, 27 In. 120
Menu Board, Drink Coca-Cola, Wood, 24 ½ x 14 In. 660
Menu Holder, Table Side, Stainless Steel, Coke Bottles, 17 x 6 In. 397
Mirror, Bottles, Metal Holder, 7 ½ x 3 In. 98
Mirror, Girl, Big Hat, Flowers, Celluloid, Pocket, 1911, 2 ½ x 1 ½ In. 202
Mirror, Pocket, 1907, 2 ¾ x 1 ¾ In. 671
Mirror, Pocket, Drink Coca-Cola, Woman, Holding Up Glass, Oval, 1907, 2 In. 286
Mirror, Pocket, Woman, Sitting At Table, Holding Glass, 1909, 2 In. 262
Perfume Bottle, Glass, Clear, Bottle Shape, Flattened Glass & Cork Stopper, 4 In. 96
Pin, Service, 10K Yellow Gold, Pink & Clear Chip Stones, Coke Bottle, Frame 79
Poster, All Set At Our Home, Boy Holding 6-Pack, Gold Frame, 27 x 56 In. 450
Poster, Pause A Minute, Refresh Yourself, Woman Holding Bottle, 1920s, 22 x 14 In. 780
Poster, Talk About Refreshing, 2 Women, Lounge Chairs, Frame, 1943, 63 x 34 In. 540
Poster, Time Out For Coke, Drink Coca-Cola, Woman, Bottle, Dog, 1950, 38 ½ x 22 In. 240
Refrigerator, Drink Coca-Cola, Please Pay Clerk, Serve Yourself, Red, 23 x 53 In. 1920
Sign, Bottle Shape, Coca-Cola Trade Mark Register, Enameled Porcelain, 16 x 5 In. 265
Sign, Bottle, Round Button, Metal, Red, White, 12 In. 60
Sign, Coca-Cola Bottling Company, Plant In Oklahoma, Metal, Dumore, 27 x 12 In. 90
Sign, Coupon, Coca-Cola, 5 Cent, Woman In Gown, Holding Fan, Frame, 1904, 16 x 13 In. 210

Coalport, Inkwell, Stand, Insert Pot, Gold, Turquoise Enamel, Crown Mark, c.1890, 5 In.
$2,214

Skinner, Inc.

Coalport, Vase, Bottle Shape, Landscape, Gold & Pink, Turquoise Jewels, Handles, c.1890, 8 In.
$4,305

Skinner, Inc.

Coalport, Vase, Flat, Enamel, Medallion, Gold Orb, Salopian Ware Mark, c.1875, 6 x 6 In., Pair
$214

DuMouchelles Art Gallery

Coca-Cola, Bottle Opener, Have A Coke, It's The Real Thing, Stainless Steel, Ekco, c.1970, 3 In.
$12

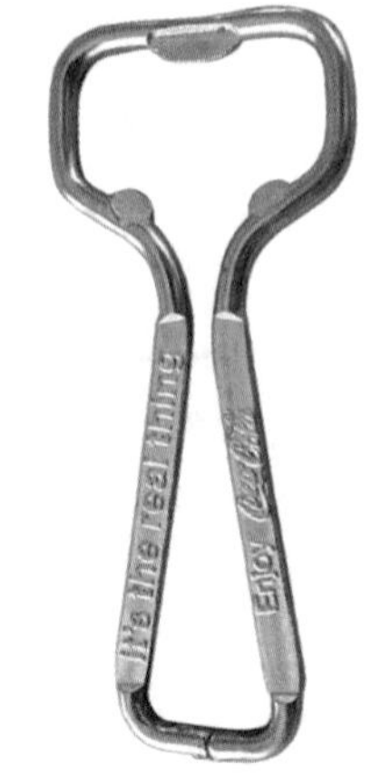

Ruby Lane

Coca-Cola, Can Opener, Drink Coca-Cola, Have A Coke, Steel, Ekco, 1960, 3 ¾ In.
$10

Ruby Lane

Coca-Cola, Clock, Regulator, Calendar Date, 5 Cents, Sold Here, Sessions, 1925, 36 x 18 In.
$850

Ruby Lane

Coca-Cola, Crate, Bottle Carrier, Wooden, Red Paint, 24 Slots, 1971, 19 x 12 x 4 In.
$25

Ruby Lane

Coca-Cola, Fan, Hand, Drink Coca-Cola, Geisha, Bamboo, Paper, Handle, 15 x 10 In.
$385

Ruby Lane

Coca-Cola, Ice Pick, Bottle Opener, Wood Handle, Red Coca-Cola Logo, 10 In.
$45

Ruby Lane

Coca-Cola, Tray, 1930, Bather Girl, Tin, 10 ½ x 13 ¼ In.
$366

Morphy Auctions

Coffee Mill, Cherrywood & Pewter, Iron Crank Handle, Dovetailed Case, 1800s, 10 In.
$71

Hess Auction Group

TIP
Baking soda and vinegar or lemon juice can be used to remove rust.

Coffee Mill, Enterprise, 2 Wheel, No. 2, Cast Iron, Red Paint, Pat. Oct. 21, 73, 12 x 10 In.
$410

Thomaston Place Auction

Coffee Mill, Enterprise, 2 Wheel, Red, Pat. 1898, 1904, 18 x 17 x 24 In.
$2,745

Morphy Auctions

Sign, Delicious & Refreshing, Bottles, Tin, 6-Pack, Red, White, 1954, 11 x 12 In. 1185
Sign, Drink Coca-Cola, 2 Glasses, Wood, Metal, Gold, Red, White, 1930s, 11 In. 570
Sign, Drink Coca-Cola, Bottle In Circle, Porcelain, Hanging, 1939, 60 x 45 In. 1342
Sign, Drink Coca-Cola, Bottle, Wood, Metal Trim, Triangular, c.1938, 20 x 19 In. 540
Sign, Drink Coca-Cola, Fountain Service, Porcelain, Curved Bottom, 14 In. 540
Sign, Drink Coca-Cola, Here's Refreshment, Wood, Horseshoes, Metal Bottle, 16 x 11 In. 450
Sign, Drink Coca-Cola, Sam's Soft Drinks, Tin, Red Paint, Frame, c.1923, 30 x 72 In. 319
Sign, Drink Coca-Cola, Sidewalk, 2-Sided, Porcelain, Fountain Machine, 1941, 25 x 26 In. 1920
Sign, Drink Coca-Cola, Sign Of Good Taste, Button, Red, White, Yellow, 24 In. 480
Sign, Drink Coca-Cola, Wherever Thirst Goes, Girl In Rowboat, Cardboard, c.1942, 57 x 28 In. 854
Sign, Drugs, Soda, Drink Coca-Cola, Porcelain, Red, White, Mint Green, 1950s, 30 x 18 In. 600
Sign, Enjoy Ice Cold, Coke Bottle, Red, White, Tin Lithograph, 1950s, 7 ½ x 54 In. 720
Sign, Gentlemen At Soda Fountain, Top Hat, Magazine, Frame, 22 x 18 In. 30
Sign, Santa Claus, Holding Bottles & Sign, Stand-Up, Cardboard, 1950s, 11 ½ In. 150
Sign, Take Home A Carton, Red, Yellow, 1940s, 54 x 18 In. 600
Sign, Things Go Better With Coke, Tin Lithograph, Red & White, 1960s, 12 x 30 In. 184
Sign, Tired?, Coca-Cola Relieves Fatigue, 5 Cent, Druggist, Soda Jerk, Frame, 22 x 12 In. 1320
Soda Chest, Refrigerator, Swivel Wheels, 34 ½ In. 450
Thermometer, Coca-Cola, Bottle Shape, Trade Mark Registered, Tin, Embossed, 17 In. 52
Thermometer, Drink Coca-Cola In Bottles, Button Top, Red, White, Tin, 1950s, 9 x 3 In. 175
Thermometer, Drink Coca-Cola In Bottles, Round, Red & White, Glass Cover, 12 In. 150
Thermometer, Drink Coca-Cola, Delicious & Refreshing, Wood, Arched, 1915, 21 In. 228
Thermometer, Drink Coca-Cola, Sign Of Good Taste, Red, White, Round, 12 In. 120 to 150
Tip Tray, 1906, Delicious, Refreshing, Woman Holding Glass, Round, Tin, 4 ¼ In. 312 to 360
Tip Tray, 1914, Betty, Woman In Bonnet, Tin Lithograph, Oval, 4 ¼ x 6 In. 180
Tip Tray, 1920, Woman In Yellow Dress, Hat, Tin Lithograph, Oval, 4 ½ x 6 In. 270
Toy, Bottle Truck, Every Bottle Sterilized, Pressed Steel, 1930s, 11 In. 510
Toy, Truck, Corvair, Flat Bed, Tin, Yellow, White, Red Logo, Friction, Japan, 6 x 8 In. 480
Toy, Truck, Delivery, Pressed Steel, Yellow, Lithographed Bottles, Marx, 17 In. 300
Toy, Truck, Drink Coca-Cola, Buddy L, Yellow, Box, 1950s, 15 ¼ In. 450
Toy, Truck, Metal, Red, 4 Full Cases Of Bottles, 4 Empty Cases, Smith-Miller, 13 ½ In. 630
Tray, 1903, Woman In Gown, Seated, Holding Bottle, Flower Border, 6 In. 720
Tray, 1914, Woman, Tying Bonnet, Drink, Delicious & Refreshing, 13 x 10 In. 252
Tray, 1916, Elaine, Seated, Holding Glass, Hat, Roses, Metal, 8 ½ x 19 In. 180 to 310
Tray, 1922, Girl Holding Glass, Hat, 13 ¼ In. 570
Tray, 1929, Woman, In Yellow Bathing Suit, Floral Wrap, Tin, 13 x 10 In. 156
Tray, 1930, Bather Girl, Tin, 10 ½ x 13 ¼ In. *illus* 366
Tray, 1936, Woman In Gown, Seated Holding Glass, Tin, Square, 10 x 13 In. 397
Tray, 1942, Woman Leaning Against Car, Holding Bottle, Woman Driver, 13 In. 210
Tray, Pretzel, Countertop, Aluminum, 3 Figural Coke Bottle Feet, 4 x 9 ½ In. 108
Vending Machine, 5 Cents, Drink Coca-Cola, Red & White, Glasco, 37 x 41 In. 336
Vending Machine, 6 Cents, Jacobs Mailbox, Red & White, 1950s, 29 x 54 In. 3355
Vending Machine, 10 Cents, Bottles, Red & White, 36 In. 570
Vending Machine, 10 Cents, Drink Coca-Cola In Bottles, Bottle, Boy, 1940s, 24 x 39 In. 1220
Vending Machine, 10 Cents, Drink Coca-Cola In Bottles, Red, White, Vendo, 59 In. 1952 to 4800
Vending Machine, Cavalier 51, 1950s, 65 ½ x 24 ¾ In. 726
Vending Machine, Gumball, Always Coca-Cola, 1 Cent, 5 Cent, Countertop, 8 x 17 In. 60
Vending Machine, Red & Green, Arched Top, Bottles, c.1941, 65 In. 6000
Wall Pocket, Pressed Paper, Cardboard, Red, Green, Gold, c.1932, 9 x 12 x 3 In. 177
Watch Fob, Sterling Silver, Embossed Bottle, Leaves, Shaped, 2 In. 114

COFFEE MILLS are also called coffee grinders, although there is a difference in the way each grinds the coffee. Large floor-standing or counter-model coffee mills were used in the nineteenth-century country store. Small home mills were first made about 1894. They lost favor by the 1930s. The renewed interest in fresh-ground coffee has produced many modern electric mills and hand mills and grinders. Reproductions of the old styles are being made.

Charles Parker Co., 2 Wheels, Cast Iron, Blue, Red, Gilt, Flowers, c.1897, 13 In. 2160
Cherrywood & Pewter, Iron Crank Handle, Dovetailed Case, 1800s, 10 In. *illus* 71
Colonial, Wrightsville Hardware Co., Cast Iron, Wood, Dovetailed, 1905, 11 x 6 x 6 In. 155
Elgin National, 2 Wheel, Eagle Finial, Cast Iron, Red Paint, 22 x 11 In. 345
Enterprise, 2 Wheel, No. 2, Cast Iron, Red Paint, Pat. Oct. 21, 73, 12 x 10 In. *illus* 410
Enterprise, 2 Wheel, Red, Pat. 1898, 1904, 18 x 17 x 24 In. *illus* 2745
Enterprise, Cast Iron, Handle, 12 x 7 In. 90
Grand Union, Wood, Cast Iron, Tin, Red, Factory Scene, Wall Mount, 12 x 4 In. 374
Landers, Frary & Clark, Cast Iron, Red Paint, Decals, Drawer, Crank, Wood Base, 12 In. 360

Red, Drawer, Marked 1873, 18 x 12 In. 247
Ubero, Cast Iron, Wall Mount, Wood Base, Tin, Ubero Selected Coffee, 12 x 4 In. 316

COIN SPOT is a glass pattern that was named by collectors for the spots resembling coins, which are part of the glass. Colored, clear, and opalescent glass was made with the spots. Many companies used the design in the 1870–90 period. It is so popular that reproductions are still being made.

Cruet, Cranberry Opalescent, Applied Colorless Handle, Cut Facet Stopper, 6 In. .... 275 to 450
Pitcher, Water, White Opalescent, 9 ¼ x 9 In. 30
Syrup, White Opalescent, Swirl, Metal Spout, Northwood, c.1875, 6 In. 79

COIN-OPERATED MACHINES of all types are collected. The vending machine is an ancient invention dating back to 200 B.C., when holy water was dispensed from a coin-operated vase. Smokers in seventeenth-century England could buy tobacco from a coin-operated box. It was not until after the Civil War that the technology made modern coin-operated games and vending machines plentiful. Slot machines, arcade games, and dispensers are all collected.

Arcade, 1 Cent, Hitler, Poison The Rat, Countertop, World War II, 23 ½ In. 10200
Arcade, 4-Square, Wood, Red & Black Crackle Paint, 2 Games, 1950s, 68 x 30 In. 1464
Arcade, Charlie & Mabel, In The Park, Wood, Pink & White, 72 In. 4575
Arcade, Claw Machine, Crane, Empire State Building, 1 Cent, Wood, Wheels, 69 In. 2440
Arcade, Electric Shock, How Much Can You Take, 1 Cent, Metal, Red, 17 x 9 In. 610
Arcade, Electricity Is Life, Horseshoe Shocker, 1 Cent, Cast Iron, c.1900, 18 x 14 In. 3965
Arcade, Esco, Cupid's Arrow Machine, Painted Wood, 1 Cent, c.1929, 60 In. .... *illus* 1586
Arcade, Golf For Two, 1 Cent, Wood & Metal, Drawer, Chester Pollard, 24 x 20 In. 8540
Arcade, Horse Kiddy Ride, Ride Sandy, Tooled Leather Saddle, 55 x 21 In. 510
Arcade, Love Pilot, Cupid, 5 Cents, Personality Tester, Wood, Glass, 1938, 84 In. 3050
Arcade, Lunar Rescue, 25 Cents, Joystick, Sega, 1970s, 36 ½ x 29 ½ In. 6600
Arcade, Marquee, Iron, Light-Up, Moving Pictures, Naked Woman, Scroll, 29 In. 1342
Arcade, Player Piano, 25 Cent Coinola, Drums, Cymbals, Xylophone, Stool, 60 x 59 In. 2745
Arcade, Poison This Rat, 3 Pills, Hitler, 1 Cent, Flipball, Wood, c.1941, 17 x 24 In. 1952
Arcade, Submarine Kiddy Ride, 25 Cent, Electric, Metal, Silver, Blue, 72 x 48 In. 1342
Automatic Banjo Machine, Encore, Oak Cabinet, 12 Music Rolls, Key, 78 x 24 In. 25200
Coin Sorter, Wood, 4 Drawers, Crank Handle, 15 x 23 x 10 ½ In. 1200
Fortune Teller, Grandmother Predictions, 10 Cent, 88 In. 18000
Fortune Teller, Mlle. Zita, 1 Cent, Wood, Metal Legs, c.1900, 74 In. 10980
Fortune Teller, Oak, Metal, Head Figure, Learn Your Future, 1 Cent, 23 x 25 In. 732
Fortune Teller, Oracle Of Life, 1 Cent, Oak, Nickel Plated Casting, Light-Up, Key, 92 x 28 In. 1585
Fortune Teller, Sheik, 1 Cent, Hexagonal Booth, Red & Green, 79 In. 2745
Fortune Teller, Wake The Wizard, Crystal Ball Style, 25 Cents, 9 x 14 In. 150
Music Box, Polyphon, Disc, Crest, Wood Case, 50 ½ x 27 In. 2091
Music Box, Regina, Wood Case, Crank, Double Comb, 15 ½-In. Discs, 23 In. .... *illus* 1560
Mutoscope, Boxing Movie, Real Moving Pictures, 1 Cent, 74 In. 6000
Mutoscope, Movie Reel, 5 Cents, Coin Drawer, Marquee Top, Red, 50 In. 570
Mutoscope, Pictures Of Interesting Girls, 1 Cent, Wood, Metal, 1904, 55 x 21 In. 10370
Mutoscope, Real Movies, 1 Cent, Warner Bros. Stretchbra, c.1930, 16 x 73 In. 1342
Pinball, Air Aces, Stand, Multicolor, Bally Mfg., Chicago, c.1960, 70 x 29 In. 418
Pinball, Little Pro Golf, 10 Cent, Southland Engineering Inc., 1965, 66 x 51 In. 2074
Pinball, Sportsman, Hunting Skill, 5 Cent, Wood, Jennings, 1933, 40 x 39 In. 854
Pinball, Super Par Golf, Chicago Coin, Lights Up, Key, 70 x 25 x 57 In. .... *illus* 1464
Pinball, World Series Baseball, 5 Cent, Rock-Ola RMC, c.1936, 36 x 40 In. 1586
Skill, Baker, Kicker & Catcher, 1 Cent, Try Your Skill, 5 Balls, Wood, c.1920, 19 In. 458
Skill, Barn Yard, 1 Cent, Countertop, Penny Gumball, Keys, 17 ½ In. 1320
Skill, Basketball, 1 Cent, Vest Pocket, Flip Ball, c.1929, 17 x 9 In. 671
Skill, Bat-A-Ball, 5 Balls, Pin Drop Field, 1 Cent, Wood, c.1946, 60 In. 1220
Skill, Challenger Rocket Patrol, 5 Cents, 29 x 15 x 9 In. 270
Skill, Football Kicker & Catcher, Wood Case, 1930s, 17 ½ In. 510
Skill, Goalee, Chicago Coin, 2 Players, 5 Cent, Cabinet, 37 x 44 In. 3300
Skill, Goalee, Chicago Coin, Two Can Play, 1 Cent, 1954, 81 x 45 In. 2074
Skill, Kicker, Catcher, 1 Cent, Field, Paint, Key, 16 x 17 ½ In. 1200
Skill, Lung Tester, 1 Cent, Strong Man, Glass Tube, Column Base, 72 In. 2074
Skill, Mills Novelty, Target Practice, 1 Cent, Pin Field, Key, 20 In. 330
Skill, Mutoscope, Al Jolson, Drop Card, Cast Iron, Red, Gilt, c.1900, 76 In. .... *illus* 6710
Skill, National Baseball, 1 Cent, Wood, Brass, Glass, Paper Field, c.1928, 21 x 20 In. 488
Skill, Olympic Puncher, 1 Cent Strength Tester, The Manly Art!, Cast Iron, 1905, 81 In. 9760
Skill, Shoot The Bear, Rifle, Shooting Gallery, 5 & 25 Cent, Stand, 80 x 43 In. 2745

Coin-Operated, Arcade, Esco, Cupid's Arrow Machine, Painted Wood, 1 Cent, c.1929, 60 In.
$1,586

Morphy Auctions

Coin-Operated, Music Box, Regina, Wood Case, Crank, Double Comb, 15 ½-In. Discs, 23 In.
$1,560

Cowan Auctions

TIP
Keep basement windows locked at all times.

C

Coin-Operated, Pinball, Super Par Golf, Chicago Coin, Lights Up, Key, 70 x 25 x 57 In.
$1,464

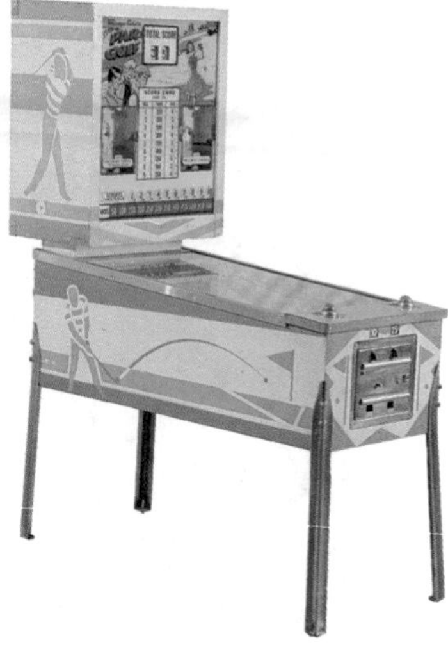

Morphy Auctions

Coin-Operated, Skill, Mutoscope, Al Jolson, Drop Card, Cast Iron, Red, Gilt, c.1900, 76 In.
$6,710

Morphy Auctions

Coin-Operated, Slot, Jackpot Belle, Buckley, Chrome, Halftop, Crisscross, c.1948, 16 x 26 In.
$793

Morphy Auctions

Coin-Operated, Slot, Mills, Baseball, 5 Cent, Wood Case, c.1929, 16 x 26 In.
$3,050

Morphy Auctions

Coin-Operated, Trade Stimulator, Field Mfg., 4 Jacks, 1 Cent, Countertop, c.1929, 14 ½ x 19 In.
$671

Morphy Auctions

Coin-Operated, Trade Stimulator, Hit Me, Poker, 5 Cent, 5 Reel, Gum Vendor, 1930s, 12 x 11 ½ In.
$893

Showtime Auction Services

Coin-Operated, Trade Stimulator, Mills, Bell Boy, Cast Aluminum, Reel Strips, 1931
$2,040

Showtime Auction Services

Coin-Operated, Vending, Gum, Baker Boy, Metal, Name Plate, Manikin Vendor Co., 1920s, 16 In.
$4,740

James D. Julia Auctioneers

Skill, Shuffleboard, Marvel Play, 8 Pucks, 25 Cent, Wood, c.1967, 148 x 50 In. 1220
Skill, Steeplechase, 5 Cents, Tiers, Red, Yellow, Countertop, 20 In. 540
Skill, Strength Tester, Pull Tiger's Tail, Make Him Roar, 1 Cent, Iron, 1928, 62 In. 11590
Skill, Target Practice, Clown Shooter, Pistol, 1 Cent, Metal, Yellow, 68 In. 2318
Skill, Target Practice, Revolver, Hitler's Mouth, 1 Cent, Wood, Metal, 18 x 23 In. 3355
Skill, Target Shooting, Rifle Range, Genco's Gun Club, 10 Cents, 1950s, 30 x 72 In. 420
Slot, Black Beauty, 25 Cent, Escalator Bell, Wood, Blue, 27 In. 1098
Slot, Bursting Cherry, 5 Cent, Blue, Yellow, Red, Wood Base, 1938, 16 x 25 In. 1220
Slot, Cocktail Waitress, 5 Cent, 3 Reel Bell Machine, Star Bell, 1948, 71 In. 26840
Slot, Comet Roll-A-Top, 5 Cent, Rotary Escalator, Jackpot Window, 25 x 16 In. 690
Slot, Golden Nugget, Golden Doll, 10 Cent, 3-Reel Escalator Bell, 25 In. 840
Slot, Golden Nugget, Golden Doll, 25 Cent, Escalator Bell, 1955, 27 x 17 In. 1098
Slot, Jackpot Belle, Buckley, Chrome, Halftop, Crisscross, c.1948, 16 x 26 In. ....*illus* 793
Slot, Jackpot, Dice, Yellow, Horse Heads, 25 Cent, Wood Base, 1935, 16 x 17 In. 7320
Slot, Jennings Club, 50 Cent, Chief, Club Bell, Wood Console, 1946, 60 In. 3050
Slot, Jennings, 5 Cent, Blue, Red, Silver, Brown, 28 x 15 ¼ In. 690
Slot, Jennings, Electrovender, Fortune Reels, 5 Cent, Wood Cabinet, 48 In. 1464
Slot, Mills, Baseball, 5 Cent, Wood Case, c.1929, 16 x 26 In. ....*illus* 3050
Slot, Mills, Red Cherry, Black Cherry, 5 Cent, Aluminum, 1930s, 16 x 23 In. 612
Slot, Mills, Silent Skyscraper, 10 Cent, Gooseneck Bell, c.1933, 16 x 25 In. 900
Slot, Mills, World's Fair Century, 25 Cent, Escalator Bell, Blue, c.1933, 15 x 29 In. 1320
Slot, QT, Dutch Woman, Standing, 5 Cents, Blue & Gold, Bell, c.1947, 19 x 56 In. 2160
Slot, Rol-A-Top, 5 Cent, Cherry Front, Escalator Bell, Multicolor, c.1938, 15 x 27 In. 3900
Slot, Tic-Tac-Toe, Jennings Chief, 5 Cents, Escalator Bell, c.1946, 15 ½ x 28 In. 840
Strength Tester, Hercules Figure, Ball Grip, Wood Case, 1 Cent, Footed, 1929, 71 x 21 In. 2440
Strength Tester, I.D. Test Of Strength, Wood & Metal Case, Red & White, 16 x 22 In. 275
Strength Tester, Turn His Head, Ladies Do You Have Strength & Beauty, Pull Rope 9600
Telescope Viewer, Scenic, 10 Cent, Cast Iron Base, Black Pedestal, 66 In. 2440
Trade Stimulator, 7 Grand, 5, 10, 25 Cent, Wood, Glass, Dice Game, 1948, 17 x 14 In. 458
Trade Stimulator, American Eagle, 1 Cent, 3 Reel, Blue & White, Keys, 9 ½ In. 360
Trade Stimulator, Card Machine, 1 Cent, Wood Case, Pedestal, 1902 21000
Trade Stimulator, Fey The Ace, Dice Game, Silver, Red, c.1929, 10 x 10 In. 5100
Trade Stimulator, Field Mfg., 4 Jacks, 1 Cent, Countertop, c.1929, 14 ½ x 19 In. ....*illus* 671
Trade Stimulator, Groetchen Tool, Imp, 3 Reel, 1 Cent, Gumball, 6 ½ In. 180
Trade Stimulator, Hit Me, Poker, 5 Cent, 5 Reel, Gum Vendor, 1930s, 12 x 11 ½ In. ....*illus* 893
Trade Stimulator, Horse Racing, Les Petits Chevaux, Token, Cast Iron, 1932, 19 In. 2745
Trade Stimulator, Jennings, Puritan Girl, 25 Cent, Cast Aluminum, 1928 1140
Trade Stimulator, Jennings, Puritan Girl, 5 Cent, Cast Metal, Woman, c.1928, 10 In. 915
Trade Stimulator, Mills, Bell Boy, Cast Aluminum, Reel Strips, 1931 ....*illus* 2040
Trade Stimulator, Puritan Gum, 1 Cent, Countertop, Jackpot, 9 x 10 ¾ In. 570
Trade Stimulator, Rock-Ola, Horse Race Game, 1 Cent, c.1933, 14 ½ x 12 In. 1680
Trade Stimulator, Rock-Ola, Radio Wizard, 5 Cent, Brown Metal, 11 x 10 In. 1159
Trade Stimulator, Table Pinball Poker, 5 Cent, Wood Case, Metal, c.1936, 13 x 22 In. 488
Trade Stimulator, Tower, Countertop, 1 Cent, 5 Cents, 10 Cents, Wood Case, 22 In. 4500
Vending, Be Healthier Electric Nerve & Muscle Massage, 1 Cent, 20 x 62 In. 6100
Vending, Button, Black & Red Marquee, Drop 10 Cents In Slot, 1905, 14 x 6 In. 915
Vending, Candy Bars, Heath Sales Co., 3 Columns, Key, 29 ½ x 16 In. 270
Vending, Candy, Southern Automatic Candy Co., Wood, Deco Design, 74 x 34 In. 6000
Vending, Chewing Gum, Pulver, 1 Cent, Traffic Cop, Red Porcelain, 21 In. 1098
Vending, Cigarette, 5 & 10 Cents, Dark Red, Chrome, Oval Mirror, 74 x 28 In. 1586
Vending, Condom, Blue, White & Red, Paint, Metal, 1960s, 30 In. 150
Vending, Cupid's Post, Get Your Letters Here, 1 Cent, Postman, c.1925, 72 In. 1830
Vending, Fantail, Fresh-Tasty, 1 Cent, 5 Cents, Norris Master, 1933, 16 In. 1830
Vending, Foot Vibrator, 5 Cents, A Treat For Golfers Tired Feet, 44 x 19 In. 1680
Vending, Gum, Baker Boy, Metal, Name Plate, Manikin Vendor Co., 1920s, 16 In. ....*illus* 4740
Vending, Gum, Zeno, 1 Cent, Yellow Porcelain, Black Lettering, 17 In. ....*illus* 580
Vending, Gumball, 10 Cent, Northwestern Sunoco, Blue, Yellow, 8 x 17 In. 120
Vending, Gumball, Manikin Baker Boy, 1 Cent, Red, Green, 1928, 16 x 11 In. 3355
Vending, Gumball, Premier, Baseball Card, 1 Cent, Oak, Red, c.1969, 13 x 13 In. 305
Vending, Jackson Gumball, 1 Cent, Flared Glass Globe, Burgundy, Gold, 19 In. 1464
Vending, Kodak Film, 620 Film, 1 Shilling, Red, Yellow, Keys, England, 43 In. 570
Vending, Kotex Sanitary Pad, 5 Cent, Wall Mount, Black, 15 x 5 ½ In. 580
Vending, Li'l Abner Vendar-Bar, Steel, Candy, Glass Window, 1949, 12 x 23 In. 380
Vending, Matchbook, 1 Cent, Edward's Mfg., 1920s, 13 In. 420
Vending, Matchbox, 1 Cent, Cast Iron, Glass Dome, Footed, 1916, 17 In. 1830
Vending, Matchbox, 2 Boxes 5 Cents, Countertop, Cigar Cutter, c.1911, 13 x 6 In. 976

Coin-Operated, Vending, Gum, Zeno, 1 Cent, Yellow Porcelain, Black Lettering, 17 In.
$580

Morphy Auctions

Comic Art, Silhouettes, Jiggs & Maggie, Wood Cutouts, 2-Sided, 1920s Comic Characters, 25 In.
$94

Hess Auction Group

Compact, Copper, Painted, Woman Undressing, Interior Erotic Scene, Snakeskin Puff, 3 ½ In.
$156

Treadway Toomey Galleries

Consolidated, Shade, Opal Glass, Grapes, Round, c.1900, 9 x 4 In.
$156

Jeffrey S. Evans

TIP
Never leave a note outside explaining that you are not at home.

Cookbook, Julia Child & Company, 1st Edition, Softcover, Illustrated, 1978, 244 Pages
$25

Ruby Lane

Cookbook, Someone's In The Kitchen With Dinah, Hardcover, 1971, 10 x 6 In., 180 Pages
$25

Ruby Lane

Vending, Napkin, 1 Cent, Swami Napkin Dispenser, Fortune, 8 ½ In. 660
Vending, Peanut, 1 Cent, Columbus Model 46, Glass Globe, 1946, 8 x 14 In. 300
Vending, Peanut, 1 Cent, Exhibit Supply Co., Countertop, Red, Black, 10 In. 150
Vending, Peanut, 1 Cent, Octagonal, Bell Bottom Base, c.1930, 13 ½ In. 780
Vending, Peanut, Smilin' Sam From Alabam, Red, Gold, Bust, Bald Head, Key 540
Vending, Perfume, 1 Cent, Wood, Wall Mount, Mirror, 7 x 12 In. 330
Vending, Perfume, 10 Cent, 3 Scents, Restroom, Pink, Square, 1950s, 12 x 12 In. 153
Vending, Phonograph, Edison, 1 Cent, Crank, Wax Cylinders, Keys, 56 In. 7800
Vending, Popcorn, Figural, Robot, 25 Cent, Plain & Butter, c.1980, 29 x 57 In. 660
Vending, Postage Stamp, 10 Cent, 25 Cent, Crank Handles, 14 In. 120
Vending, Razor Blade, 10 Cent, 4 Column, Key, 19 In. 270
Vending, Relax-A-Lator, Floor Foot Massager, Step Up For Pick Up, 10 Cent, 51 In. 1037
Vending, Stamp, 5 Cent, 10 Cent, Porcelain, Red, White Blue, Uncle Sam, 20 x 8 In. 90
Vending, Tom's Toasted Peanuts, 5 Cent, Delicious Sandwiches, 1950s, 19 x 61 In. 793
Vending, Toothbrush, 25 Cent, DuPont, Porcelain, Brush Your Cares Away, 31 In. 90
Vending, Viking Cigarettes, Sheet Metal, Gold & Tan Enamel, 55 x 30 In. 72

COLLECTOR PLATES are modern plates produced in limited editions. Some may be found listed under the factory name, such as Bing & Grondahl, Royal Copenhagen, Royal Doulton, and Wedgwood.

Al Hirschfield, Lena Horne, 12 In. 125
Confederate States Of America, Dedication To Robert E. Lee 32
Konigszelt & Bayern, The 12 Dancing Princesses, 1986, 8 In. 14
Norman Rockwell, Old Man Winter, Gold Trim, 9 ¼ In. 15
Reco, Little Miss Muffet, 1981, 8 ½ In. 18
Thames & Hudson, Zoe's Cat, 11 ¼ In. 18

COMIC ART, or cartoon art, includes original art for comic strips, magazine covers, book pages, and even printed strips. The first daily comic strip was printed in 1907. The paintings on celluloid used for movie cartoons are listed in this book under Animation Art.

Book Art, Monkees, No. 5, Pen & Ink, Jose Delbo, Oct. 1967, 11 ¼ x 14 ¼ In. 139
Cover, Original Art, Action Comics No. 1, Superman, 1942, 12 ½ x 17 In. 51750
Panel, Snoopy, Black Marker, On Paper, Signed Charles Schulz, Frame, 12 ¾ x 12 ¾ In. 720
Silhouettes, Jiggs & Maggie, Wood Cutouts, 2-Sided, 1920s Comic Characters, 25 In. ....*illus* 94
Strip, Blondie, Fiancee's Father Mr. Bumstead, 1930, 18 x 4 In. 20913
Strip, Calvin & Hobbes, Eat Vegetables?, Yecchh!, Mat, 1987, 16 x 8 In. 47800
Strip, Felix The Cat, Ink Drawing, Patrick Sullivan, 5 x 24 In. 1920
Strip, Peanuts, Snoopy, Lucy, Mat, 1963, 27 x 5 ½ In. 31070
Strip, Superman, No. 8070, Wayne Boring, Pen & Ink, Oct. 29, 1964, 7 x 19 ½ In. 139
Sunday, Felix The Cat, Safe If I Don't Get A Blowout, 12 Panels, March 24, 1935, 17 x 22 In. 5693
Sunday, Henry, Doctor With Tools, 11 Panels, Sept. 28, 1958 115
Sunday, Nancy, April Fool's Handbag, Ernie Bushmiller, 14 Panels, April 2, 1944, 20 x 27 In. 449
Sunday, Popeye Thimble Theater, Boxing, Matted, Frame, 1935, 26 x 28 In. 31070
Sunday, Star Wars, Princess Leia, Imperial Servant, Russ Manning, 1979, 17 x 24 In. 2530

COMMEMORATIVE items have been made to honor members of royalty and those of great national fame. World's Fairs and important historical events are also remembered with commemorative pieces. Related collectibles are listed in the Coronation and World's Fair categories.

Box, U.S. Bicentennial, Round Enamel Seals, Delaware, Hawaii, Bulgari, Italy, 7 ½ x 4 ¼ In. 1936
Button, Great Baltimore Fire Of 1904, Buildings In Flames, Celluloid, 1 ¾ In. 115
Medal, 1936 Olympics, Ribbon, Germany, 3 ¾ In. 96
Medallion, Queen Victoria, 60 Years Of Reign, Bronze, 2 In. 78
Memorial Plaque, Sinking Of USS Maine, Bronze, C. Keck, c.1898, 13 x 17 ½ In. 561
Print, Silk, Historic Souvenir Of The Louisiana Purchase, St. Louis, 1904, 17 x 11 In. 153
Watch, Zep, Graf Zeppelin, Around The World Flight, Silvering, 1929, 2 In. 253

COMPACTS hold face powder. A woman did not powder her face in public until after World War I. By 1920, the beauty parlor, permanent waves, and cosmetics had become acceptable. A few companies sold cake face powder in a box with a mirror and a pad or puff. Soon the compact was designed by jewelers and made of gold, silver, and precious materials. Cosmetic companies began to sell powder in attractive compacts of less valuable metal or plastic. Collectors today search for Art Deco designs, famous brands, compacts from World's Fairs or political events, and unusual examples. Many were made with companion lipsticks and other fittings.

Cartier, Baguette Diamonds, Rubies, 14K Gold, Art Deco, Sunburst, Pouch, 4 x 3 In. 2645

C

Cartier, Gold, Burmese, Baguette Ruby Design, Engraved Hallmarks, 1920s, 3 x 2 ¼ In. 3278
Classical Scene, Beveled Mirror, Italy, 3 x 2 ½ In. 180
Copper, Painted, Woman Undressing, Interior Erotic Scene, Snakeskin Puff, 3 ½ In. .... *illus* 156
Elsa Peretti, 18K Gold, Heart Shape, Mirror, Halston, 1970s, 3 ¼ In. 3198
Enamel Mount, The Gleaners, After Millet, 3 x 4 In. 300
Metal Flower, Blue Sequin Rim, Green Inner Border, Mirror, Round, 3 ¾ In. 12
Portrait, Woman, Hat, Round, Mirror, France, 1 x 1 ½ In. 60
Silver, Enamel Romantic Scene, Leaves, Mirror, Powder Compartment, Italy, 3 x 3 In. 196
Silver, Enamel, Courting Couple, Landscape, Shell Shape, 3 ½ x 3 ½ In. 156
Silver, Enamel, Gold Wash, Helios, Chariot, Dawn, Flowers, 3 ¾ x 3 In. 270
Silver, Enamel, Sunset, Seascape, Sea Gull, 2 ½ In. 120
Silver, Enamel, Waterfall, Picnic, Woman, Children, Lake, c.1890, 4 x 3 ½ In. 1029
Silver, Hammered, Flowers, Japan, 3 In. 31
Van Cleef & Arpels, 14K Gold, Platinum, Diamond Ballerina, Sapphire, 3 x 2 In. 9225

CONSOLIDATED LAMP AND GLASS COMPANY of Coraopolis, Pennsylvania, was founded in 1894. The company made lamps, tablewares, and art glass. Collectors are particularly interested in the wares made after 1925, including black satin glass, Cosmos (listed in its own category in this book), Martele (which resembled Lalique), Ruba Rombic (1928–32 Art Deco line), and colored glasswares. Some Consolidated pieces are very similar to those made by the Phoenix Glass Company. The colors are sometimes different. Consolidated made Martele glass in blue, crystal, green, pink, white, or custard glass with added fired-on color or a satin finish. The company closed for the final time in 1967.

Shade, Opal Glass, Grapes, Round, c.1900, 9 x 4 In. .... *illus* 156
Vase, Cream Ground, Pastel Dancing Bacchantes, Gold Base, 12 In. 150
Vase, Katydid Insect, Purple Stain, 7 x 8 In. 72
Vase, Lovebirds, Berry Branches, Aqua, Pink, Oval, c.1926, 10 ½ In. 229
Vase, Pink, Goldfish, Relief, 9 ¼ In. 344

CONTEMPORARY GLASS, *see Glass-Contemporary.*

COOKBOOKS are collected for various reasons. Some are wanted for the recipes, some for investment, and some as examples of advertising. Cookbooks and recipe pamphlets are included in this category.

Better Homes & Gardens Junior Cook Book, 1955 55
Better Homes & Gardens, New Cook Book, Binder Style, Red & White Checkered, 1968 50
Betty Crocker, Pie Cover, 5-Ring Binder, Golden Press, 480 Pages, 1972 65
Betty Crocker's Good & Easy Cook Book, Spiral Bound, 1954 25
Betty Crocker's New Picture Cook Book, 5-Ring Binder Style, 1961 32
Cook's Tour Of Mississippi, Jackson Daily News, Spiral Bound, 1981, 6 ½ x 7 In., 206 Pages 18
Crisco, Recipes For Good Eating, Proctor & Gamble, Paperback, 1945, 8 x 5 In., 64 Pages 12
Fannie Farmer, Food & Cookery For The Sick & Convalescent, 1913, 7 x 5 In., 305 Pages 35
First United Methodist Church, Something For Everyone, 1989, 5 x 7 In. 10
General Foods, All About Home Baking, Hardcover, Plaid, 1936 22
Good Housekeeping, Hardcover, 1973, 811 Pages 35
Good Provider's Cook Book, Paperback, 7 ¾ x 5 In., 64 Pages 10
Graham Kerr, Galloping Gourmet, Doubleday & Co., Hardcover, 1969, 284 Pages 15
Julia Child & Company, 1st Edition, Softcover, Illustrated, 1978, 244 Pages .... *illus* 25
London Family Cook & Town & Country Housekeeper's Guide, 1811, 8 x 5 In., 634 Pages.. 400
Melting Pot Of Mennonite Cookery, Hardcover, 1975 45
Modern Family, Meta Given, J.G. Ferguson & Assoc., Hardcover, 1943, 938 Pages 65
Someone's In The Kitchen With Dinah, Hardcover, 1971, 10 x 6 In., 180 Pages .... *illus* 25

COOKIE JARS with brightly painted designs or amusing figural shapes became popular in the mid-1930s. Many companies made them and collectors search for cookie jars either by design or by maker's name. Listed here are examples by the less common makers. Major factories are listed under their own names in other categories of the book, such as Abingdon, Brush, Hull, McCoy, Metlox, Red Wing, and Shawnee. See also the Disneyana category.

Alice In Wonderland, Porcelain, Arms Up, Blue & White Dress, 1950s, 13 In. .... *illus* 690
Apple, Red, Green Stem, Maurice Of California, c.1963, 11 In. 24
Bear Beau, Marked, Metlox, c.1980, 11 In. 35
Buick Convertible, Red, White Seats & Tires, Glenn Appleman, Signed, 15 In. 540
Casper Friendly Ghost, Figural, Glazed Ceramic, 1960s, 14 In. 278
Dinosaur, T-Rex, Sinclair Oil, Green Paint, Glazed Ceramic, 1942, 13 In. 1200
Flintstones, Figural, Dino Carrying Golf Bag, Glazed Ceramic, 1960s, 6 x 12 In. 173

Cookie Jar, Alice In Wonderland, Porcelain, Arms Up, Blue & White Dress, 1950s, 13 In.
$690

James D. Julia Auctioneers

Cookie Jar, Little Red Riding Hood, Holding Basket, Cape, Metlox Potteries, c.1960, 13 In.
$374

James D. Julia Auctioneers

Cookie Jar, Peter Pan, Sitting, Green, White, Gold Paint, Hat, c.1960, 11 In.
$92

James D. Julia Auctioneers

Cookie Jar, Raggedy Andy, Figural Head, Hat Shape Lid, Bowtie, Bobbs-Merrill Co., c.1965, 11 In.
$69

James D. Julia Auctioneers

Cookie Jar, Yogi Bear, Ceramic, Standing, Hat & Tie, Sign, Marked, Hanna-Barbera, c.1961, 13 In.
$218

James D. Julia Auctioneers

Coors, Salt & Pepper, Wheat, 4 ⅝ x 2 ¼ In.
$30

Ruby Lane

Little Red Riding Hood, Holding Basket, Cape, Metlox Potteries, c.1960, 13 In. .... *illus* 374
Penguin, Yellow Scarf, Metlox, 11 ¾ In. 95
Peter Pan, Sitting, Green, White, Gold Paint, Hat, c.1960, 11 In. .... *illus* 92
Pixie Head, Red Pointed Hat, Gilner & Gonder, c.1955 20
Raggedy Andy, Figural Head, Hat-Shape Lid, Bowtie, Bobbs-Merrill Co., c.1965, 11 In. .... *illus* 69
Superman, In Phone Booth, Porcelain, Removable Top, 1978, 13 x 7 In. 313
Yogi Bear, Ceramic, Standing, Hat & Tie, Sign, Marked, Hanna-Barbera, c.1961, 13 In. .... *illus* 218
Yogi Bear, Felt Tongue Sticking Out, Green Tie, 14 In. 131

COORS ware was made by the Coors Porcelain Company of Golden, Colorado, a company founded with the help of the Coors Brewing Company. Its founder, John Herold, started the Herold China and Pottery Company in 1910. The company name was changed in 1920, when Herold left. Dishes were made from the turn of the century. Coors stopped making nonessential wares at the start of World War II. After the war, the pottery made ovenware, teapots, vases, and a general line of pottery, but no dinnerware—except for special orders. The company is still in business making industrial porcelain. For more prices, go to kovels.com.

COORS
U.S.A.

Bowl, Pour Spout, Putty, 16 In. 80
Salt & Pepper, Wheat, 4 ⅝ x 2 ¼ In. .... *illus* 30
Urn, Mint Green, Creamy Interior, Trophy Shape, 5 ½ x 7 ½ In. 25
Vase, Art Deco, Blue, Circle Handles From Mouth To Foot, 8 x 9 In. 22
Vase, Pink, 9 ½ x 5 In. 22

COPELAND pieces listed here are those that have a mark including the word *Copeland* used between 1847 and 1976. Marks include *Copeland Spode* and *Copeland & Garrett.* See also Copeland Spode, Royal Worcester, and Spode.

Bust, Lover, Parian, Socle, Inscribed R. Monti, 1871, 13 In. 554
Cup & Saucer, Bridge, Houses, Flower Border, Red & White, Transferware 28
Figurine, Bisque, Miss Ellie Vide Water Babies, Joseph Durham, 3 ¼ In. 354
Figurine, Miss Ellie, Nude, Flowing Hair, Leaves, Rocky Base, White, Parian, c.1875, 20 In. *illus* 861
Pitcher, 3 Eagles, Flags, Crossed Arrows, Gilt, 1876 Centennial Memorial, 9 In. .... *illus* 1320
Plate, The Roller, Interlaced Lattice, White, Gilt, Blue, Copeland & Garrett, 9 ¼ In. 272
Vase, Centennial, Arrow, Shield, 9 ¼ x 8 ¾ In. 1785

COPELAND SPODE appears on some pieces of nineteenth-century English porcelain. Josiah Spode established a pottery at Stoke-on-Trent, England, in 1770. In 1833, the firm was purchased by William Copeland and Thomas Garrett and the mark was changed. In 1847, Copeland became the sole owner and the mark changed again. W.T. Copeland & Sons continued until a 1976 merger when it became Royal Worcester Spode. The company was bought by the Portmeirion Group in 2009. Pieces are listed in this book under the name that appears in the mark. Copeland, Royal Worcester, and Spode have separate listings.

COPELAND
SPODE
ENGLAND

Cup, Figural Tulip, Loop Stem Handle, Square Base, Green, Red, Yellow, 1800s, 3 In. 120
Pitcher, Blue & White, Jasperware, Chicago Commemorative Design, 1893, 9 In. 371
Plate, Leaf Gilt Rim, White Ground, c.1910, 9 In., 7 Piece 127

COPPER has been used to make utilitarian items, such as teakettles and cooking pans, since the days of the early American colonists. Copper became a popular metal with the Arts & Crafts makers of the early 1900s, and decorative pieces, like desk sets, were made. Other pieces of copper may be found in Arts & Crafts, Bradley & Hubbard, Kitchen, Roycroft, and other categories.

Ashtray, Cigarette Dispenser, Figural Elephant, Flashed, 9 x 6 In. 257
Ball, Geodesic, 16 ½ x 16 ½ In. 206
Basin, Narrow Neck, Flared Rim, Flowers, Palms, Arabic Prayer, India, 1800s, 8 In. 492
Bed Warmer, Brass Plug, Rein Kupfer, 1900s, 11 x 8 x 4 In. 65
Bowl, Gilt, Scalloped, Winged Cherubs, Urn Shape, Scroll Leaf Feet, 17 ½ x 19 In. 1500
Bowl, Patterned, India, 7 ½ In. 738
Box, Wrought, Hammered, R.B. Reitz, 7 x 4 In. 319
Bucket, Hammered, 19 x 24 In. 400
Bucket, Padded Swing Handle, Side Handles, Wraparound Lip, 5 Gal., 1800s, 14 x 13 In. 450
Cauldron, Apple Butter, Stand, 20 ¾ In. 184
Cauldron, Wrought Iron Handle, 1800s, 21 ½ x 28 ½ In. 610
Chafing Dish, Stand, Hammered, Scrolled Legs, Hares, Oak, Heinrich, c.1890, 11 x 21 In. .*illus* 2460
Coal Scuttle, Lift Lid, Ring Handle, Dovetailed, 1800s, 13 x 16 In. 120
Cooking Bath, Handles, Perforated Insert, Oval, 6 ½ x 23 In. 97
Figure, Dachshund, Formica Base, Hungary, c.1950, 2 ½ x 4 In. 360

Copeland, Figurine, Miss Ellie, Nude, Flowing Hair, Leaves, Rocky Base, White, Parian, c.1875, 20 In.
$861

Skinner, Inc.

Copeland, Pitcher, 3 Eagles, Flags, Crossed Arrows, Gilt, 1876 Centennial Memorial, 9 In.
$1,320

Cowan Auctions

TIP

Polish brass, copper, or pewter only once or twice a year.

Copper, Chafing Dish, Stand, Hammered, Scrolled Legs, Hares, Oak, Heinrich, c.1890, 11 x 21 In.
$2,460

Skinner, Inc.

Copper, Kettle, Apple Butter, Crimped Seams, Rolled Rim, Iron Bail Handle, 1800s, 13 x 20 In.
$502

Hess Auction Group

Copper, Teakettle, Dovetail Joints, Brass Arms Support Handle & Spout, c.1825, 10 x 13 ½ In.
$150

Ruby Lane

Copper, Teakettle, Swing Handle, Crimped Seams, Dome Lid, Schaum, c.1814, 12 ½ In.
$2,124

Hess Auction Group

Copper, Tray, Hammered, Cutouts, Raised Design, G. Stickley, Als Ik Kan Stamp, 1905, 19 In.
$2,625

Rago Arts and Auction Center

Coralene, Vase, Blue Mother-Of-Pearl Body, Split, Folded Rim, Seaweed, Amber Feet, 6 ¼ In.
$115

Early Auction Company

Cordey, Figurine, Woman's Bust, Dresden Lace, 1940s, 7 ½ In.
$24

Ruby Lane

Corkscrew, Wood, Carved Portrait, Iron Hobs, Double Handle, France, 1930s
$42

Ruby Lane

Figure, Horse, Running, 17 x 13 In. 117
Figurine, Shepherdess, Urn On Shoulder, Painted, 1900s, 21 ½ x 7 In. 125
Frame, Arts & Crafts, Hammered, Honeycomb Texture, Reticulated Leaves, 22 x 17 ½ In. 106
Fudge Warmer, Stoneware Pits, Side Handles, Spout, Cutouts, Richardson, c.1915, 12 In. 660
Hand Warmer, Openwork, Dome Lid, Phoenix, Peonies, Handle, Chinese, 6 ¾ In. 1464
Hand Warmer, Reticulated Lid, Octagonal, 2 Handles, Panels, Lotus, Bats, 7 In. 1778
Humidor, Hammered, Round, Tapered Lid, Finial, Old Mission, Kopperkraft, 6 In. 460
Kettle, Apple Butter, Crimped Seams, Rolled Rim, Iron Bail Handle, 1800s, 13 x 20 In. *illus* 502
Kettle, Apple Butter, Rolled Rim, Wrought Iron Handles, c.1890, 9 x 14 ½ In. 177
Kettle, Apple Butter, Wrought Iron Bail Handle, 1800s, 17 x 25 In. 189
Kettle, Lid, Wrought Iron Bail Handle, 1800s, 15 x 16 ½ In. 94
Kettle, Water, Dome Lid, Cylindrical, Bail Handle, Shaped Spout, 1800s, 16 In. 71
Kettle, Wrought Iron Bail Handle, Riveted Iron Tabs, 1800s, 14 ¾ x 20 In. 295
Mirror, Hammered Frame, Raised Ovals, Strapwork Corners, Arts & Crafts, 15 x 13 In. 3198
Molds are listed in the Kitchen category.
Pail, Iron Bail Handle, Wood Turned Grip, Rolled Rim, Concaved, 1800s, 10 x 12 In. 384
Pail, Rolled Rim, Iron Swivel Bail Handle, Tapered Seam Tabs, 1800s, 7 x 13 In. 413
Pitcher, Hammered, Wrought Iron, Stickley Brothers, c.1910, 14 ¼ x 7 In. 625
Pitcher, Thumb Grip, c.1880, 6 In. 96
Plaque, Seminude Male Warrior, Sword, Oak Frame, 6 ¼ x 14 In. 390
Plate, Etched, Magi On Camels, Star Of Bethlehem, 1922, 6 x 4 In. 633
Pot, Cooking, Dovetailed Sides, Brass Handles & Spigot, c.1850, 19 x 18 In. 922
Sconce, Hammered, Curled Corners, c.1910, 9 x 3 In. 128
Sculpture, 4 Molds Of Heads, Cast Iron Frame, 12 ½ x 30 In. 720
Sculpture, Abstract, Welded, c.1970, 37 x 8 ½ In. 106
Stock Pot, 2-Tone, Handles, Spigot, Lid, Hammered, Interior Mesh Basket, 1900s, 16 x 15 In. 799
Tea Set, Coffeepot, Tray, Sugar, Jug, Green & White Mosaic, 4 Piece 366
Tea Set, Teapot, Creamer, Sugar, Lid, Tray, c.1930, 8 ½ In. 240
Teakettle, Dovetail Joints, Brass Arms Support Handle & Spout, c.1825, 10 x 13 ½ In. *illus* 150
Teakettle, Oval, Dome Lid, Gooseneck Spout, Swing Handle, c.1800, 12 In. 106
Teakettle, Swing Handle, Crimped Seams, Dome Lid, Schaum, c.1814, 12 ½ In. *illus* 2124
Teakettle, Swing Handle, Mushroom Finial, Dome Lid, Gooseneck Spout, 1800s, 13 In. 502
Tobacco Box, Oval, Engraved Clipper Ship, Mermaid, Hinged Lid, c.1800, 5 In. 130
Tray, Hammered, Cutouts, Raised Design, G. Stickley, Als Ik Kan Stamp, 1905, 19 In. *illus* 2625
Tray, Hammered, Oval, Shaped Handles, Brown Patina, Gustav Stickley, 11 x 23 In. 633
Tray, Hammered, Rounded Corners, Twisted Handles, Gustav Stickley, 12 x 15 In. 690
Urn, Arts & Crafts, Repousse, Ball Support, Round Foot, 13 ⅞ x 8 ¾ In. 90
Vase, Hammered, Cylindrical, Signed, Japan, c.1910, 7 In. 180
Vase, Hand Hammered, Black, Drips, 8 In., 4 Piece 613
Vase, Relief, Tapered, Leaves, Berries, Ribbons, 1900s, 16 ¾ x 10 In. 246
Vase, Swollen Bottom, Stick, Rolled Rim, Hammered, Monogram, Jarvie, 1900s, 12 In. 1875
Wall Decoration, Blacksmith Shop, Carriage, Curtis Jere, 1970s, 50 x 20 In. 375
Wall Decoration, Ship, Clipper, 4 Masts, Sails, Rowboats, C. Jere, 30 x 42 In. 424
Watch Holder, Restauration Period, Chased, Ebonized Base, Inscription, 1894, 9 x 9 In. 177
Wine Cooler, Brass Overlay, Oak Leaves, Acorns, 8 ½ x 8 In., Pair 250
Wine Vat, Brass, Wood, Pout, Handles, Aude Region, France, 50 Liter, 24 x 19 In. 660

COPPER LUSTER *items are listed in the Luster category.*

CORALENE glass was made by firing many small colored beads on the outside of glassware. It was made in many patterns in the United States and Europe in the 1880s. Reproductions are made today. Coralene-decorated Japanese pottery is listed in the Japanese Coralene category.

Biscuit Jar, Lid, Blue, Coralene Apple Branch Decoration, Silver Plate, 6 In. 148
Jam Jar, Cranberry, Coralene Flower & Leaf Decoration, Bail Handle, 6 In. 75
Pitcher, Pink Cased Glass, Coralene Overlay, Dark Pink To Pink, 7 ¾ In. 83
Tumbler, Aquamarine Opalescent, White Flower, Butterfly, 7 In. 144
Vase, Blue Mother-Of-Pearl Body, Split, Folded Rim, Seaweed, Amber Feet, 6 ¼ In. *illus* 115
Vase, Glass, Tapering Neck, Bulbous, Opalescent Dense Coralene, 11 ½ In., Pair 217
Vase, Iris, Purple, Pink, Green Leaves, 7 In. 928
Vase, Lime Flowers, Dark Green Ground, 3-Footed, 8 ½ In. 3248

CORDEY China Company was founded by Boleslaw Cybis in 1942 in Trenton, New Jersey. The firm produced gift shop items. In 1969 it was acquired by the Lightron Corp. and operated as the Schiller Cordey Co., manufacturers of lamps. About 1950 Boleslaw Cybis began making Cybis porcelains, which are listed in their own category in this book.

Figurine, Woman's Bust, Dresden Lace, 1940s, 7 ½ In. *illus* 24

CORKSCREWS have been needed since the first bottle was sealed with a cork, probably in the seventeenth century. Today collectors search for the early, unusual patented examples or the figural corkscrews of recent years.

2 Lion Heads, Pewter, Makoulpa, 3 In. 34
Anchor, Brass, Sailboat Holder, Germany, c.1970, 5 ¼ x 2 ⅞ In. 45
Anchor, Grapes, Rope, Embossed, Brass, Germany, 5 x 4 In. 101
Boar Tusk, Sterling Mounts, Rococo Motif, 6 x 5 In. 295
Boot, Sterling Silver, R. Blackington, c.1930, 4 In. 295
Bottle, Champagne, Bottle Opener, Brass.......... 245
Brass, Iron, Rotary, Eclipse, Marble Base, 17 ¾ x 13 ½ In. 258
Dove Handle, Marked, MH, Denmark, 3 x 4 In. 60
Farmer Portrait, Carved Wood, Double Handle, Cylindrical, France, 1930s.......... 42
German Shepherd Head, Syroco, 1940s, 8 x 2 ½ In. 145
Lady's Leg, Boots, Blue Stripes, Celluloid, Legally Registered.......... 650
Loop, Folding, Steel, Victorian, c.1850, 2 x 5 In. 85
Napoleonic Design, Steel, Brass, France, c.1875, 5 ½ In. 175
Sterling Silver, Repousse, 3 x 5 In. 143
Vine Branch, Worm Holes, Laurent Siret, c.1950, 5 ½ x 3 In. 19
Wine Waiter, Silver Plate, Double Lever Sommelier, Aldo Colombo, Italy, 8 In. 78
Wood, Carved Portrait, Iron Hobs, Double Handle, France, 1930s.......... *illus* 42

CORONATION souvenirs have been made since the 1800s. Pottery, glass, tin, silver, and paper objects with a picture of the monarchs and date have been sold at many coronations. The pieces that mention King Edward VIII, the king who was never crowned, are not rare; collectors should be sure to check values before buying. Related pieces are found in the Commemorative category.

Ashtray, Edward VIII, Portrait, Shield Shape, Gilt, England, 1937, 6 x 5 In. 65
Beaker, Czar Nicholai II & Czaritza Alexandra Feodorovna, 2-Headed Eagle, 1896, 4 x 4 In. 380
Beaker, Edward VII & Alexandra Portraits, Salt Glazed, Doulton, c.1902, 5 x 3 In. 53
Cup, Enamel, Cup Of Sorrows, Dragon Crest, Strapwork, Gilt Band, Russia, 1896, 4 In. .... *illus* 403
Goblet, Queen Elizabeth II, Cut Glass, England, 8 ½ In., Pair.......... 125
Loving Cup, George VI, Coat Of Arms, Gilt Lion Handles, Minton, 1937, 4 ½ In. 269
Mug, George V, Queen Mary, Portraits, Crown, Long May They Live, 1911, 3 In. 70
Mug, King George VI, Queen Elizabeth, Portrait, Laurel Wreath, Meakin, 1937.......... 59
Mug, Queen Elizabeth II, Coat Of Arms, Flags, Collingwoods China, 1953, 3 ¼ In. 15
Mug, Queen Elizabeth II, Yellow Gold, 1953.......... 45
Pitcher, George VI & Queen Elizabeth, Princess Elizabeth, Orange, Blue, 1937, 5 ½ In. 150
Pitcher, King Edward VII, Queen Alexandra, Cherubs, Angels, Paneled, 1902, 5 In. 125
Plate, Edward VII, Queen Alexandra, Portraits, Coat Of Arms, Scalloped Rim, 1902, 9 In. 150
Plate, King Edward VIII, Flags, Portrait, Braided Gilt Border, 1937, 10 In. 95
Plate, Queen Elizabeth II, Portrait, Flags, Paneled Rim, Flowers, 1953, 8 ¾ In. 25
Thimble, George V, Queen Mary, Silver, Buckingham Palace, Westminster Abbey, 1911.......... 310

COSMOS is a pressed milk glass pattern with colored flowers made from 1894 to 1915 by the Consolidated Lamp and Glass Company. Tablewares and lamps were made in this pattern. A few pieces were also made of clear glass with painted decorations. Other glass patterns are listed under Consolidated Lamp and also in various glass categories. In later years, Cosmos was also made by the Westmoreland Glass Company.

Butter, Cover, Flower Border Base, Flower Finial, Round, 6 x 8 In. 165
Condiment, Flowers, Footed, Silver Plated Handles, Eagle Finial, 6 x 6 ½ In. 189
Lamp, Electric, Pastel Flowers, Pink Rim Shade, 17 In. 595
Lamp, Kerosene, Pink, Blue, Yellow Flowers, Yellow Top, c.1900, 9 ½ In. 180
Lamp, Oil, Globular, Pink, Blue, Yellow Flowers, Footed, c.1890, 5 x 2 ½ In. 45
Pitcher, Water, Pink, Yellow, Blue Flowers, Applied Handle, Pink Neck, 9 ½ In. 205
Tumbler, Pastel Flowers, Fishnet Ground, 3 ¾ In., 4 Piece.......... 60
Water Set, Pitcher, 6 Tumblers, Opaque White, Enamel Flowerheads, c.1900, 9 In. & 4 In. .... *illus* 180

COVERLETS were made of linen or wool during the nineteenth century. Most of the coverlets date from 1800 to the 1880s. There was a revival of hand weaving in the 1920s and new coverlets, especially geometric patterns, were made. The earliest coverlets were made on narrow looms, so two woven strips were joined together and a seam can be found. The weave structures of coverlets include summer and winter, double weave, overshot, and others. Jacquard coverlets have elaborate pictorial patterns that are made on a special loom or with the use of a special attachment. Quilts are listed in this book in their own category.

Blue, Red, Yellow, Star & Block, Fringe, c.1850, 74 x 89 In. 118
Blue, White, Checks, Fringe, 1800s, 80 x 84 In. 205

Coronation, Cup, Enamel, Cup Of Sorrows, Dragon Crest, Strapwork, Gilt Band, Russia, 1896, 4 In.
$403

Early Auction Company

Cosmos, Water Set, Pitcher, 6 Tumblers, Opaque White, Enamel Flowerheads, c.1900, 9 In. & 4 In.
$180

Jeffrey S. Evans

Coverlet, Jacquard, 4 Color, A. Kump Hanover 1842, S.B. Sproul, York County, 82 x 90 In.
$198

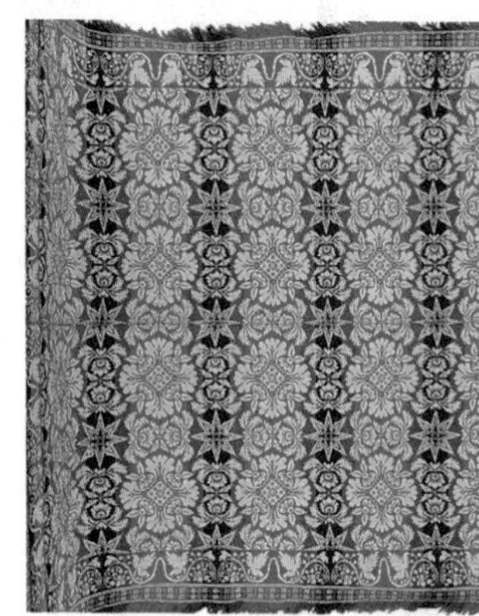

Hess Auction Group

This is an edited listing of current prices. Visit **Kovels.com** to check thousands of prices from previous years and sign up for free information on trends, tips, reproductions, marks, and more.

Early Coverlet Colors

The wool of black sheep was used for black. For other colors, wool was dyed. Indigo was used for blue, cochineal (a Mexican insect) for scarlet. Red came from madder root, and goldenrod and sumac made yellow. Alder bark made tan; hickory or walnut hulls were used to make dark brown.

Coverlet, Jacquard, 4 Color, Floral, Geometric Border, 2 Piece, Lancaster, 1848, 80 x 96 In.
$295

Hess Auction Group

Coverlet, Jacquard, 4 Color, J. Gordon Keagy's Factory, Bedford, Penn., c.1850, 86 x 79 In.
$311

Hess Auction Group

Coverlet, Jacquard, Eagle Corner, Peacocks, Wool, Cotton, Matthew Rattray, 1845, 74 x 89 In.
$300

Garth's Auctioneers & Appraisers

Coverlet, Jacquard, Flowers, Leaves, Bird Corners, Henry Oberly, c.1850, 82 x 95 In.
$295

Hess Auction Group

Coverlet, Jacquard, Red & Natural, Flowers, Leaves, Border, c.1950, 82 x 96 In.
$266

Hess Auction Group

Coverlet, Jacquard, Rose & Leaf Wreath, Womelsdorf, Signed Oberly, 1839, 83 x 92 In.
$767

Hess Auction Group

Coverlet, Jacquard, Star & Flower, Bird & Tree Border, Henry Philbey, 1834, 72 x 87 In.
$885

Hess Auction Group

Cowan, Bowl, Ivory, Blue Interior, Scalloped, Seahorse Ends, Footed, c.1926, 4 ½ x 16 x 6 In.
$200

Ruby Lane

Cowan, Flower Frog, Laurel, Figural, Draped Woman, Swags, Ivory, 1925, 10 ¼ In.
$290

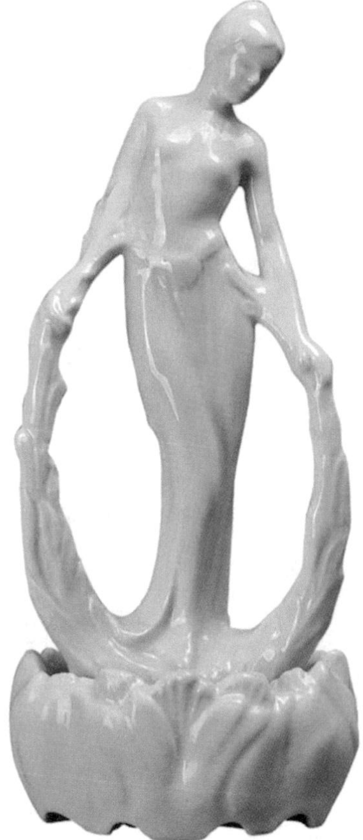

Ruby Lane

Cotton, Wool, Corner Block, C. Wiand, Allentown, 1856, 110 x 98 In. 2980
Double Weave, Block & Harness Pattern, Indigo & Natural, J. Alexander, 88 x 74 In. 615
Jacquard, 4 Color, A. Kump Hanover 1842, S.B. Sproul, York County, 82 x 90 In. *illus* 198
Jacquard, 4 Color, Floral, Geometric Border, 2 Piece, Lancaster, 1848, 80 x 96 In. *illus* 295
Jacquard, 4 Color, J. Gordon Keagy's Factory, Bedford, Penn., c.1850, 86 x 79 In. *illus* 311
Jacquard, 4 Color, Signed, J. Gordon Keagy's Factory, Bedford County, c.1850, 86 x 79 In. 311
Jacquard, Blue & White, Block & Floral Medallion, Fringe, 2 Piece, 1800s, 78 x 68 In. 123
Jacquard, Blue Wool, Star & Flower, White Cotton, Henry Keener, c.1843, 94 x 80 In. 290
Jacquard, Circles, Red, Blue, Wool, Cotton, c.1843, 84 x 105 In. 375
Jacquard, Cream, Red, Blossoms, Wool, Linen, c.1850, 88 x 79 In. 366
Jacquard, Eagle Corner, Peacocks, Wool, Cotton, Matthew Rattray, 1845, 74 x 89 In. *illus* 300
Jacquard, Flowers, Leaves, Bird Corners, Henry Oberly, c.1850, 82 x 95 In. *illus* 295
Jacquard, Peacocks, Fountain, Flower Border, Red, Green, Brown, 1800s, 84 x 98 In. 165
Jacquard, Red & Natural, Flowers, Leaves, Border, c.1950, 82 x 96 In. *illus* 266
Jacquard, Red, Blue, Cream, J. Witmer Manor Township, Anna Mellinger, 1843, 96 x 77 In. 424
Jacquard, Red, Blue, Green, Fringe, William Ney, c.1870, 86 x 86 In. 260
Jacquard, Red, Blue, Signed H. Dissinger Manheim, Lancaster County, 1836, 84 x 94 In. 904
Jacquard, Red, Cream, Signed, Made By P.H. For S.R. & L.M. T. Bethel, 1840, 76 x 82 In. 254
Jacquard, Red, Green, Blue, Flower Border, Wool, Cotton, John Kachel, c.1843, 90 x 86 In. 300
Jacquard, Red, Green, Blue, Rose & Star, Wool, Cotton, Joseph Klar, 100 x 88 In. 300
Jacquard, Red, J. Hausman, Berks County, Lobachsville, 1853, 73 x 87 In. 192
Jacquard, Red, White, Stars, Flowers, Double Cloth, 1846, 95 x 87 In. 785
Jacquard, Rose & Leaf Wreath, Womelsdorf, Signed Oberly, 1839, 83 x 92 In. *illus* 767
Jacquard, Star & Flower, Bird & Tree Border, Henry Philbey, 1834, 72 x 87 In. *illus* 885
Jacquard, U.S. Capitol, Wreaths, Flags, Stars, Wool, Cotton, 1846, 77 x 83 In. 420
Jacquard, Woven, Flowers, Fringed, Red, Tan, Blue, Signed, c.1850, 84 x 94 In. 1003
Red, Blue, Plaid, Fringe, 88 x 73 In. 205
True Boston Town & Christians & Heathens, Multicolor, 1800s, 88 x 78 In. 293
Wool, Cotton, Double Weave, Hempfield Railroad, Trains, Cars, c.1850, 83 In. 1188

COWAN POTTERY made art pottery and wares for florists. Guy Cowan made pottery in Rocky River, Ohio, a suburb of Cleveland, from 1913 to 1931. A stylized mark with the word *Cowan* was used on most pieces. A commercial, mass-produced line was marked *Lakeware*. Collectors today search for the Art Deco pieces by Guy Cowan, Viktor Schreckengost, Waylande Gregory, or Thelma Frazier Winter.

Ashtray, Ram, Blue Glaze, E. Eckhardt, 5 ½ In. 404
Bowl, Ivory, Blue Interior, Scalloped, Seahorse Ends, Footed, c.1926, 4 ½ x 16 x 6 In. *illus* 200
Candleholder, Flying Fish, Antique Green Crystalline Glaze, 8 ¼ In., Pair 236
Charger, Blue, Birds, 15 ½ In. 92
Charger, Thunderbird, Egyptian Blue, 15 ½ In. 132
Figurine, Horse, Brown, c.1931, 9 In. 47
Flower Frog, Blue, Signed, c.1925, 8 x 3 ½ In. 115
Flower Frog, Laurel, Figural, Draped Woman, Swags, Ivory, 1925, 10 ¼ In. *illus* 290
Flower Holder, Repose, White, Impressed Logo, 6 ⅜ In. 189
Group, Indian Man, Woman With Baby On Back, F. Luis Mora, 17 In., Pair 1250
Paperweight, Elephant, Turquoise Glaze, Impressed, Logo, Margaret Postgate, 4 ½ In. 295
Plaque, The Hunt, Horse & Rider, Jumping Fence, V. Schreckengost, c.1931, 11 In. 980
Vase, Bulbous, Scroll Handles, Swirl Banding, Turquoise Blue, 6 In. 3680
Vase, Iridescent Blue & Green, Glossy At Shoulders, 8 In. 48
Vase, Raised Squirrel, Heron, Pheasant, Brown, Turquoise, Round, W. Gregory, 8 In. 1875

CRACKER JACK, the molasses-flavored popcorn mixture, was first made in 1896 in Chicago, Illinois. A prize was added to each box in 1912. Collectors search for the old boxes, toys, and advertising materials. Many of the toys are unmarked.

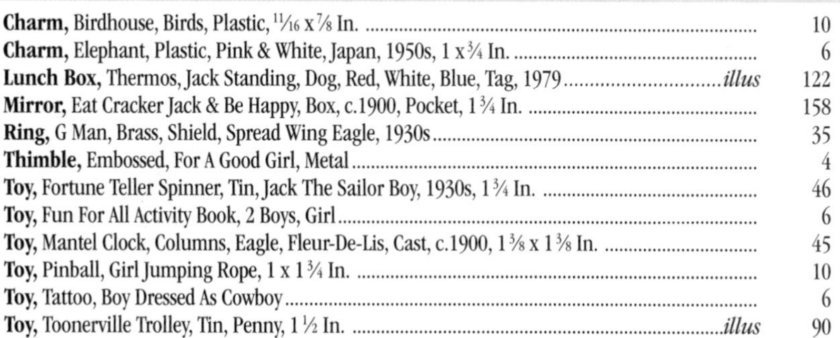

Charm, Birdhouse, Birds, Plastic, $^{11}/_{16}$ x ⅞ In. 10
Charm, Elephant, Plastic, Pink & White, Japan, 1950s, 1 x ¾ In. 6
Lunch Box, Thermos, Jack Standing, Dog, Red, White, Blue, Tag, 1979 *illus* 122
Mirror, Eat Cracker Jack & Be Happy, Box, c.1900, Pocket, 1 ¾ In. 158
Ring, G Man, Brass, Shield, Spread Wing Eagle, 1930s 35
Thimble, Embossed, For A Good Girl, Metal 4
Toy, Fortune Teller Spinner, Tin, Jack The Sailor Boy, 1930s, 1 ¾ In. 46
Toy, Fun For All Activity Book, 2 Boys, Girl 6
Toy, Mantel Clock, Columns, Eagle, Fleur-De-Lis, Cast, c.1900, 1 ⅜ x 1 ⅜ In. 45
Toy, Pinball, Girl Jumping Rope, 1 x 1 ¾ In. 10
Toy, Tattoo, Boy Dressed As Cowboy 6
Toy, Toonerville Trolley, Tin, Penny, 1 ½ In. *illus* 90

Cracker Jack, Lunch Box, Thermos, Jack Standing, Dog, Red, White, Blue, Tag, 1979
$122

Morphy Auctions

Cracker Jack, Toy, Toonerville Trolley, Tin, Penny, 1 ½ In.
$90

Milestone Auctions

Crackle Glass, Vase, Neon Yellow, Rectangular, 10 x 2 ½ In.
$35

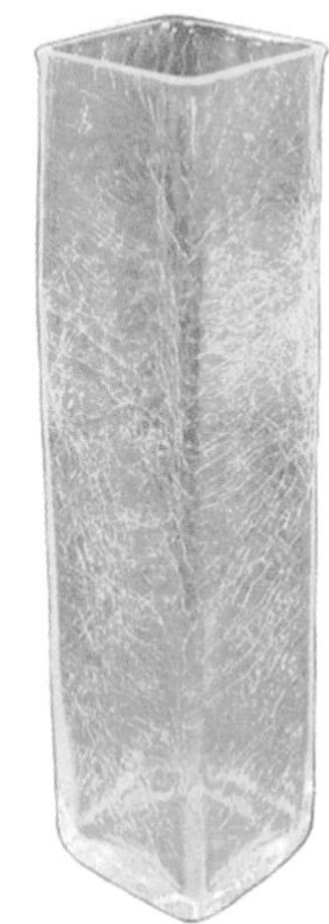

Ruby Lane

Cranberry Glass, Barber Bottle, Daisy & Fern, Opalescent, Pouring Stopper, L.G. Wright, 6 ½ In.
$128

Ruby Lane

Cranberry Glass, Pocket Watch Holder, Egg Shape, Enamel, Gilt Metal Frame, Bird Finial, 11 In.
$708

Hess Auction Group

Cranberry Glass, Vase, White Opalescent Hobnail, Shaded, Ruffled Edge, Footed, 8 x 6 In.
$125

Ruby Lane

Toy, Top, Metal & Wood, Yellow, Red 15
Whistle, Metal 32

CRACKLE GLASS was originally made by the Venetians, but most of the wares found today were made since the 1800s. The glass was heated, cooled, and refired so that many small lines appeared inside the glass. Most was made from about 1930 to 1980, although some is made today. The glass is found in many colors, but collectors today pay the highest prices for amberina, cranberry, or ruby red. Cobalt blue is also popular. More crackle glass may be listed in those categories in this book.

Vase, Arhat Figures, Raised Beaded Halos, Tapered, Japan, 1800s, 12 ½ In. 240
Vase, Neon Yellow, Rectangular, 10 x 2 ½ In. .... *illus* 35

CRANBERRY GLASS is an almost transparent yellow-red glass. It resembles the color of cranberry juice. The glass has been made in Europe and America since the Civil War. It is still being made, and reproductions can fool the unwary. Related glass items may be listed in other categories, such as Rubina Verde.

Barber Bottle, Daisy & Fern, Opalescent, Pouring Stopper, L.G. Wright, 6 ½ In. .... *illus* 128
Bowl, Brides, Vaseline, Opalescent Center, 3 ¼ x 11 In. 181
Bowl, Courting Scenes, Man, Woman, Dog, Gazebo, 2 ½ x 5 In., 12 Piece 1089
Bowl, Ruby To Clear, Scalloped Rim, Fan & Flowers, Star, c.1980, 4 x 10 In. 98
Bowl, White Flowers, Cameo, Attributed To Thomas Webb & Sons, c.1890, 2 x 4 In. 363
Bowl, Wide Scalloped Rim, Kidney-Shaped Cuts, Etched & Gilt Flowers, 6 x 8 In. 302
Creamer, Silver Plate, Bear Head Shape Lid, Clear Handle, 9 ¼ In. 375
Creamer, Silver Plate, Eagle Head Shape Lid, Clear Handle, 9 ½ In. 375
Decanter, Art Nouveau, Silver Overlay, Gothic G Monogram, 10 ¾ In. 726
Decanter, Art Nouveau, Silver Overlay, Grape Leaves, 6 ¼ In. 847
Decanter, Duck, Figural, Brass & Glass Stand, Karel Palda, c.1935, 9 x 10 ¼ In. 423
Epergne, Flower Blooms, Vaseline Stems, 5 Branches, 22 x 13 In. 307
Epergne, Opalescent, Ruffled Trumpet, 20 x 12 ⅕ In. 484
Epergne, Silver Base, White & Gilt Overlay, 10 Prisms, 12 ¾ x 8 ½ In. 540
Garniture, Etched, Prisms, 10 ¾ In. 263
Goblet, Gilt Scrolls, Vines, Hexagonal Shaft, Starburst, Bohemia, 4 ½ In., 7 Piece 302
Luster, 5 Panels, Flowers, Portraits, Cut Glass Prisms, Gilt, 12 ½ x 5 ¼ In. 3025
Pitcher, Ruby To Clear, Hobstar & Diamond, Stick, Bell Foot, Handle, c.1905, 16 In. 98
Plate, Etched, 4 Cartouches, 14 In. 59
Pocket Watch Holder, Egg Shape, Enamel, Gilt Metal Frame, Bird Finial, 11 In. .... *illus* 708
Vase, Air Bubbles, Boat Shape, Cut Edges, 4 x 6 x 3 In. 374
Vase, Bud, Edwardian Sterling, Crosshatched Diamonds, 5 In. 181
Vase, Cameo Portraits, Gilt, 10 x 2 ¾ In., Pair 1089
Vase, Candy Cane White Stripe, Ruffled Rim, 11 ½ x 6 In. 86
Vase, Cornucopia, Gilt Bronze Dolphin, 9 ¼ In. 149
Vase, Cut To Clear, Trumpet Shape, Geometric Patterns, c.1900, 9 In. 400
Vase, Cylindrical, Porcelain Plaque, Gilt Enamel, Raised Foot, c.1890, 15 In., Pair 837
Vase, Figural Procession, 11 ¾ x 5 ½ In. 484
Vase, Gilt, Playful Putti, Trumpet Shape Neck, 19 ¾ x 4 ½ In., Pair 3932
Vase, Mary Gregory Style, 11 ¾ x 5 ¼ In., Pair 605
Vase, Portrait, Round Foot, 13 In., Pair 313
Vase, Red To Clear, Swirls, Dots, Bulbous, Trumpet Neck, Round Foot, 1900s, 11 In. 156
Vase, Trumpet, Gilt Bronze Mount, France, 20 In., Pair 750
Vase, White Opalescent Hobnail, Shaded, Ruffled Edge, Footed, 8 x 6 In. .... *illus* 125

CREAMWARE, or queensware, was developed by Josiah Wedgwood about 1765. It is a cream-colored earthenware that has been copied by many factories. Similar wares may be listed under Pearlware and Wedgwood.

Basket, Underplate, Reticulated, Handles, England, 8 x 10 ½ In. .... *illus* 1119
Basket, Underplate, Reticulated, Scrolled Leafy Handles, 4 ½ x 10 In., 2 Piece 1089
Bowl, Liverpool Transfer, Cream & Brown, Flared Rim, Round Foot, c.1800, 5 x 9 In. 236
Bowl, Washington, Franklin, Nautical, Ship Inside, Transfer, Liverpool, 3 x 7 In. 1845
Candlestick, Bees, Daisies, Folded Over Cup & Corners, England, c.1900, 7 In., Pair .... *illus* 165
Coffeepot, Lid, Pear Shape, Loop Handle, Painted Flower Clusters, Center Rose, c.1780, 10 In. *illus* 431
Creamer, Courting Couple, Pine Trees, Red Decoration, White Ground, 5 In. 50
Pitcher & Bowl, Ship, Peace, Plenty & Independence, Eagle, Transfer, 9 ½ In. 4613
Pitcher, George Washington With Map Of America, Ship, Compass, Liverpool, 9 ½ In. 2829
Pitcher, Ship, 3-Masted, Commerce Unshackled By War, Transfer, Liverpool Pottery, 9 In. 1845
Pitcher, Ship, 3-Masted, Ship Packet, James Barrett In Wreath, Transfer, Liverpool, 9 In. 1968

Plaque, Admiral Nelson, Relief, Molded, c.1805 ... 875
Plate, Angel, Looking Back At Baby, Leafy Rim, Bohemia, 9 In., Pair ... 75
Plate, Scalloped Plate, Multicolor Enamel, Inscriptions About Freedom, Dutch, c.1790, 9 In. ... 60
Platter, Sepia Eagle, Monogram, Herculaneum, 10 ¼ In. ... 420
Sauceboat, Lid, Oval Base, Rope Twist Handle, Ivy Borders, England, c.1800, 6 x 7 In., Pair ... 148
Stirrup Cup, Figural, Fox Head Shape, Red, Orange, Black, 1800s, 4 In., Pair ... 2000
Tea Caddy, Dome Lid, Marbleized Mocha, Cylindrical Collar, Ogee Shoulder, 5 In. ... 201
Tea Canister, Lid, Lead Glazed, Multicolor, Staffordshire, c.1765, 4 In. ... 677
Teapot, Dome Lid, Rose Pattern, Loop Handle, Gooseneck Spout, Footed, 1700s, 9 In. ... 154

CROWN DERBY is the name given to porcelain made in Derby, England, from the 1770s to 1935. Andrew Planche and William Duesbury established Crown Derby as the first china-making factory in Derby. Pieces are marked with a crown and the letter *D* or the word *Derby*. The earliest pieces were made by the original Derby factory, while later pieces were made by the King Street Partnerships (1848–1935) or the Derby Crown Porcelain Co. (1876–90). Derby Crown Porcelain Co. became Royal Crown Derby Co. Ltd. in 1890. It is now part of Royal Doulton Tableware Ltd.

Bowl, Avesbury, 5 ¼ In., 12 Piece ... 80
Dish, Orange Flowers, Green Leaves, Dark Wavy Border, 11 ½ In. ... 475
Figurine, Bird, Blue, Gilt, 6 In. ... 40
Figurine, Fox, Blue, White, 4 ¼ x 2 ¼ In. ... 50
Figurine, Frog, Gilt, Red, Blue, 3 ½ x 3 In. ... 60
Urn, Multicolor, Pink Flowers, 11 ½ In. ... 50
Vase, Blown Out, Orange & Blue Flowers, 7 In. ... 350
Vase, Gilt, Multicolor, Cream Ground, c.1880, 11 In. ... 100

CROWN DUCAL is the name used on some pieces of porcelain made by A.G. Richardson and Co., Ltd., of Tunstall and Cobridge, England. The name has been used since 1916. Crown Ducal is a well-known maker of chintz pattern dishes. The company was bought by Wedgwood in 1974.

Platter, Cobalt Blue Band, Gold Flowers & Leaves, 14 In. ... 45
Saucer, Blue Flowers, Birds, Scalloped Edge ... 9

CROWN MILANO glass was made by the Mt. Washington Glass Works about 1890. It was a plain biscuit color with a satin finish decorated with flowers and often had large gold scrolls. Not all pieces are marked.

Biscuit Jar, Metal Lid, Squat, Melon Ribbed, Stippled Flowers, Gold Enamel Vines, 6 In. ... *illus* 173
Marmalade, Silver Lid, Holly Leaves, Red Berries, Diamond Design, Marked ... 575
Pitcher, Pressed Body, Raised Lines & Beading, Flowers, Twisted Handle, 8 In. ... 593
Vase, Flowers, Scrolls, Cream Shaded To Tan, Melon Ribbed, Fold-Down Rim, 14 In. ... 1725
Vase, Flowers, White Ground, Tapered, Curled Handles At Rim, 10 In. ... 2963
Vase, Gourd Shape, Stick Neck, Enameled Flowers, Gilded Scroll, Cartouche, 13 In. ... 474
Vase, Opal Body, Floral Gilt, Cut Fingers, 3 Ball Feet, Logo, 5 ¾ In. ... *illus* 690
Vase, Opal Paneled Body, Thistle, Applied Handles, 8 In. ... 805
Vase, Opal, Enameled Flowers, Gold Scrollwork, Tapered, Stretched Rim, 14 In. ... 3163
Vase, Red & Yellow Flowers, Gold Trim, Bulbous Foot, Lattice, Tri-Cut Rim, 11 In. ... 4600
Vase, Squat, Bulbous Mouth, Ruffle Rim, Gilt Fern Design, Blossoms, c.1890, 7 In. ... 3585

CROWN TUSCAN *pattern is included in the Cambridge glass category.*

CRUETS of glass or porcelain were made to hold vinegar, oil, and other condiments. They were especially popular during Victorian times and have been made in a variety of styles since the eighteenth century. Additional cruets may be found in the Castor Set category and also in various glass categories.

Cranberry Glass, Thumbprint, 7 x 4 In. ... 20
Cut Glass, Cut Daisies, Thumbprint Handle, Faceted Stopper, c.1910, 5 ½ In. ... *illus* 50
Double, Oil & Vinegar, Transfer, Butterflies, Ferns, Pottery, Staffordshire, c.1880, 7 In. ... *illus* 385
Glass, Gray Tint, Hand-Pulled Lip With Spout, Hollow Handle, 7 ½ In. ... 345
Glass, Opaque Blue, Chrysanthemum Sprig, Pressed Glass Stopper, c.1899, 7 In. ... 150
Glass, Raspberry, Diamond Quilted, 7 ¼ x 3 ½ In. ... 60
Glass, Shamrocks, 4-Leaf Clover, Gold, Green, Pontil, Faceted Stopper, 1890s, 4 In. ... *illus* 325
Glass, Silver Overlay, Grid, Pointed Stopper, 8 ½ x 3 In. ... 150
Opalescent Glass, Lattice Pattern, Yellow, Frosted Ribbed Handle, 7 In. ... 125
Ruby Glass, Clear Handle, Clear Stopper, 6 x 3 ½ In. ... 20
Ruby Stained, Clear, Loop Handle, Beach Souvenir, Stopper, U.S. Glass Co., 1903, 8 In. ... *illus* 204
Satin Glass, Cranberry To Opaque, Daisy, Opaque Stopper, 7 In. ... 40
Silver, Horn, Nordic Motifs, Norway, 2 ½ In. ... 40

Creamware, Basket, Underplate, Reticulated, Handles, England, 8 x 10 ½ In.
$1,119

Ahlers & Ogletree

Creamware, Candlestick, Bees, Daisies, Folded Over Cup & Corners, England, c.1900, 7 In., Pair
$165

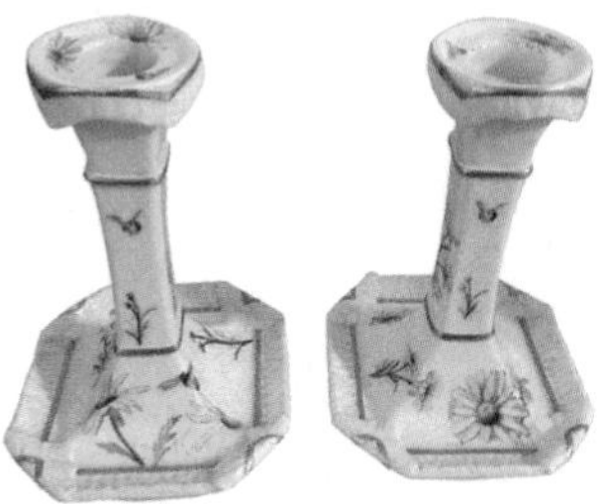

Ruby Lane

Creamware, Coffeepot, Lid, Pear Shape, Loop Handle, Painted Flower Clusters, Center Rose, c.1780, 10 In.
$431

Skinner, Inc.

Crown Milano, Biscuit Jar, Metal Lid, Squat, Melon Ribbed, Stippled Flowers, Gold Enamel Vines, 6 In.
$173

Early Auction Company

Crown Milano, Vase, Opal Body, Floral Gilt, Cut Fingers, 3 Ball Feet, Logo, 5 ¾ In.
$690

Early Auction Company

Cruet, Cut Glass, Cut Daisies, Thumbprint Handle, Faceted Stopper, c.1910, 5 ½ In.
$50

Ruby Lane

Cruet, Double, Oil & Vinegar, Transfer, Butterflies, Ferns, Pottery, Staffordshire, c.1880, 7 In.
$385

Ruby Lane

CT GERMANY was first part of a mark used by a company in Altwasser, Germany (now part of Walbrzych, Poland), in 1845. The initials stand for C. Tielsch, a partner in the firm. The Hutschenreuther firm took over the company in 1918 and continued to use the *CT*.

C.T.

Dish, Curved Handle, Pink Flowers, Gilt Border, 1900-20, 8 x 10 In. 55
Fish Service, Oval Platter, 12 Plates, Fish, Sea Life, Blue Swags, 13 Piece 302
Tray, 2 Sections, Ruffled Rim, Center Handle, Yellow Flowers, Ferns, 1890, 10 In. 95

CUP PLATES are small glass or china plates that held the cup while a diner of the mid-nineteenth century drank coffee or tea from the saucer. The most famous cup plates were made of glass at the Boston and Sandwich factory located in Sandwich, Massachusetts. There have been many new glass cup plates made in recent years for sale to gift shops or collectors of limited editions. These are similar to the old plates but can be recognized as new.

Glass, Amethyst, Roman Rosette, c.1840, 5 ⅜ In. 300
Glass, Bird In Flight, Scalloped Border, Azure Blue, 4 In. 27
Glass, Central Scrolls, Stippled, Heart Border, 3 ½ In. 57
Glass, Fleur-De-Lis, Trefoils, Scalloped Edge, 3 ¼ In. 86
Glass, Ship, Shield & Star Border, Scalloped & Pointed Border, 3 ½ In. 46
Glass, Sulfide, Profile, Man In Uniform, Diamond Ground, Scalloped, c.1840, 3 ½ In. 120
Pearlware, Butterfly, Scalloped Rim, c.1830, 3 ⅜ In. 57
Pearlware, Calico Sprig, Transfer, Blue & White, 3 ¼ In. 85
Porcelain, Boat, Landscape, Stairs To Statue, Transfer, Staffordshire, c.1875, 4 In. 100
Porcelain, Errand Boy, Double Transfer, Wilkie's, Staffordshire, c.1825, 3 ½ In. 195
Porcelain, Flower Sprigs, Red, Blue, Green, Embossed, Staffordshire, 1800s, 4 In. 55
Porcelain, Flowers, Leaves, Netting Ground, Blue, White, 3 ⅞ In. 100
Porcelain, Pagodas, Temple, Sailboat, Lavender, Flower Border, 4 ¼ In. 26
Porcelain, Pasture Scene, Cows, Blue Transfer, Staffordshire, c.1850, 4 In. 95
Porcelain, Shirley House, Stringing Border, Enoch Wood & Sons, c.1830, 4 In. 250
Winter View Of Pittsfield, Massachusetts, Blue Transfer, Impressed Clews, 4 ¾ In. .... *illus* 177

CURRIER & IVES made the famous American lithographs marked with their name from 1857 to 1907. The mark used on the print included the street address in New York City, and it is possible to date the year of the original issue from this information. Earlier prints were made by N. Currier and use that name from 1835 to 1847. Many reprints of the Currier or Currier & Ives prints have been made. Some collectors buy the insurance calendars that were based on the old prints. The words *large, small,* or *medium folio* refer to size. The original print sizes were very small (up to about 7 x 9 in.), small (8.8 x 12.8 in.), medium (9 x 14 in. to 14 x 20 in.), large (larger than 14 x 20 in.). Other sizes are probably later copies. Other prints by Currier & Ives may be listed in the Card category under Advertising and in the Sheet Music category. Currier & Ives dinnerware patterns may be found in the Adams or Dinnerware categories.

American Winter Scenes, Horse Drawn Sleigh, F.F. Palmer, 1854, 16 x 24 In. .... *illus* 923
Autumn Fruits, Walnut Frame, 13 x 18 In. .... *illus* 118
Four Seasons Of Life, Middle Age, Parsons & Atwater, Frame, 1868, 16 x 18 In. 145
Fox Hunting, The Meet, Lithograph, Frame, 1870, 15 x 20 In. 650
Horses At The Ford, 1867, Frame, 24 x 20 In. 1100
Josephine, Mahogany Frame, 1865, 22 x 17 In. 135
Minnehaha Falls, Mat, Frame, 19 x 22 ¼ In. .... *illus* 188
Straw-Yard, Winter, Medium Folio, Lithograph, Frame, 20 x 22 In. 750
The Fireman Always Ready, Signed, 1858, 20 ¼ x 15 ½ In. 375
Three Little Sisters, Frame, 1862, 19 x 15 In. 2800
Village Blacksmith, N. Currier, Frame, 9 ¾ x 14 In. 795
Woodcock Shooting, N. Currier, Frame, 1852, 20 x 25 In. 575

CUSTARD GLASS is a slightly yellow opaque glass. It was made in England in the 1880s and was first made in the United States in the 1890s. It has been reproduced. Additional pieces may be found in the Cambridge, Fenton, and Heisey categories. Custard glass is called *Ivorina Verde* by Heisey and other companies.

Argonaut, Centerpiece, Footed, 10 ½ x 5 x 6 In. 50
Chrysanthemum Sprig, Bowl, Ruffled Rim, 4 Scroll Feet, 10 x 7 x 5 In. 18
Chrysanthemum Sprig, Toothpick Holder, Scalloped Foot & Rim, Marked, 3 In. .... *illus* 99
Finecut & Roses, Rose Bowl, Nutmeg Details, Crimped Rim, 4 x 3 In. 55
Glass, Louis XV, Spooner, 4 Curved Feet 23
Harvard, Toothpick Holder, Beaded Panels, Ruffled Band, 2 ¾ In. 40

Cruet, Glass, Shamrocks, 4-Leaf Clover, Gold, Green, Pontil, Faceted Stopper, 1890s, 4 In.
$325

Ruby Lane

Cruet, Ruby Stained, Clear, Loop Handle, Beach Souvenir, Stopper, U.S. Glass Co., 1903, 8 In.
$204

Jeffrey S. Evans

TIP
Cruet tops for American glass pieces are almost always cut or pressed, not blown.

Cup Plate, Winter View Of Pittsfield, Massachusetts, Blue Transfer, Impressed Clews, 4 ¾ In.
$177

Hess Auction Group

Currier & Ives, American Winter Scenes, Horse Drawn Sleigh, F.F. Palmer, 1854, 16 x 24 In.
$923

Cowan Auctions

Currier & Ives, Autumn Fruits, Walnut Frame, 13 x 18 In.
$118

Hess Auction Group

Currier & Ives, Minnehaha Falls, Mat, Frame, 19 x 22 ¼ In.
$188

Garth's Auctioneers & Appraisers

Custard Glass, Chrysanthemum Sprig, Toothpick Holder, Scalloped Foot & Rim, Marked, 3 In.
$99

Woody Auction

Cut Glass, Bowl, Hobnail, 3 Roundels, Flowers, Fluted Foot, England, 1800-10, 3 ½ x 5 In.
$175

Ruby Lane

Cut Glass, Decanter, Cobalt Blue Cut To Clear, Brilliant, 14 In.
$153

Hess Auction Group

Cut Glass, Decanter, Green Cut To Clear, Circular & Banded, Diamond Shape Stopper, 12 In.
$488

Neal Auctions

Lampshade, Cone Shape, Embossed Flowers, Rosette, 1930s, 15 ¼ In. 675
Louis XV, Cruet, 5 ½ In. 30
Maize is its own category in this book.
Petit-Point, Vase, Flowers, Harrach, c.1900, 12 In. 423
Poinsettia Lattice, Bowl, Ruffled Sawtooth Edge, 3-Footed, c.1900, 9 In. 165

CUT GLASS has been made since ancient times, but the large majority of the pieces now for sale date from the American Brilliant period of glass design, 1875 to 1915. These pieces have elaborate geometric designs with a deep miter cut. Modern cut glass with a similar appearance is being made in England, Ireland, Poland, and the Czech and Slovak republics. Chips and scratches are often difficult to notice but lower the value dramatically. A signature on the glass adds significantly to the value. Other cut glass pieces are listed under factory names, like Hawkes, Libbey, and Sinclaire.

Basket, Hobstar, Double Notched Handle, 11 x 11 In. 298
Biscuit Jar, Hobstar, Globular, Silver Reticulated Flower Handle, Everted Rim, c.1906, 5 In. 400
Biscuit Jar, Starburst, 9 ½ In. 76
Bowl, Alhambra, Clear, Tooth Cut Rim, Clear, 8 In. Diam., c.1900 677
Bowl, Figural, Swan, Silver Tail, Head & Neck, 9 x 13 In. 2530
Bowl, Flint, Strawberry Diamond, Fan, 8 ½ In. 427
Bowl, Flower Head Banding, Clear, c.1900, 8 In. Diam. 61
Bowl, Hobnail, 3 Roundels, Flowers, Fluted Foot, England, 1800-10, 3 ½ x 5 In. .... *illus* 175
Bowl, Hobstars, Fans, Diamonds, Buttons, Notched Rim, c.1900, 8 In. Diam. 179
Bowl, Hobstars, Sunbursts, Engraved Diamonds, Scalloped Rim, c.1900, 9 In. Diam. 246
Bowl, Molded Vine & Berry, Hobstar, Sterling Silver Rim, Flared, c.1898, 9 In. 125
Bowl, Ormolu Mount, Female Masks, Scroll Handles, c.1875, 16 x 16 ¾ In. 5312
Bowl, Stars & Hobnails, Zigzag Edge, Scalloped Rim, 1900s, 9 In. Diam. 276
Castor, Sugar, Barrel Shape, Starburst, Scallops, Pierced Lid, Silver Rim, c.1900, 5 In. 72
Cologne Bottle, Strawberry Diamond & Fan, Lapidary Stopper, Cape Cod Glass Co., 8 In. 177
Cologne Bottle, Uranium Glass, Cane Pattern, Bulbous, Lapidary Stopper, 9 In. 1416
Compote, Hobstars & Crosshatch, Scalloped Rim, Faceted Stem, Notch Base, c.1900, 11 In. 287
Compote, Serpentine Rim, Diamond Cut Star Burst, 10 x 9 In. 118
Decanter, Amethyst Cut To Clear, Cathedral Shape, Tapered, Stopper 118
Decanter, Cobalt Blue Cut To Clear, Brilliant, 14 In. .... *illus* 153
Decanter, Green Cut To Clear, Circular & Banded, Diamond Shape Stopper, 12 In. .... *illus* 488
Decanter, Regency Cut, Diamond Point, Stopper, Bulbous, Neck Rings, 1800s, 12 In., Pair 1168
Decanter, Strawberry, Mushroom Stopper, Pittsburgh, Pa., 1820s, 10 In. 502
Decanter, Wine & Spirit, Club Shape, Faceted Stopper, Flared Rim, c.1810, 10 In. 194
Dresser Jar, Sterling Silver Repousse Enamel, Violets, Ray Star In Bottom, 2 x 2 In. 118
Goblet, Water, Square Base, c.1900, 4 ¾ In., 14 Piece 300
Humidor, Lid, Hobstar, Rolled Rim, Round, 7 x 5 In. 92
Ice Bucket, Colonna, Upright Handles, Scalloped Rim, c.1900, 6 x 7 In. 188
Jar, Hobstar, Diamond & Fan, Sterling Silver Repousse Lid, 6 ¾ In. 329
Jar, Lid, Cylindrical, Molded Line Design, Silver Lid, Etched Leaves, c.1920, 7 In. 313
Pitcher, Alhambra, Greek Key Border, Tooth Cut Rim, Honeycomb Handle, c.1900, 12 In. 11070
Pitcher, Beaker, Silver Spout & Cuff, Repousse Flowers, C-Scroll Handle, c.1900, 12 In. 500
Pitcher, Clear, Flared Bottom, Loop Handle, Sterling Silver Collar, Wavy Spout, 10 In. 118
Pitcher, Russian Cut, Swollen, Tapering, Notched Rim, c.1910, 7 In. 191
Punch Bowl, Sawtooth Rim, Flared Pedestal Foot, c.1900, 9 x 10 In. 1188
Punch Bowl, Stand, Ladle, Buffalo Pattern, Sawtooth, Scalloped Rim, Pinwheels, 15 x 14 In. 826
Punch Bowl, Star & Hobstar, 2 Parts, Scalloped Rim, Scalloped Bell Foot, c.1900, 12 In. 150
Punch Bowl, Yellow, Harvard, Panels, Flowers, Scalloped Rim, Trumpet Base, c.1900, 10 In. 431
Scent Bottle, Globular, Hearts, Sterling Silver Hinged Lid, Fern Leaves, c.1900, 6 In. 777
Tray, Ice Cream, Brilliant, Stars & Hobstars, Handles, Zigzag Scallop Rim, c.1900, 14 In. 753
Tray, Lattice Design, Rosettes, Scalloped Rim, Clear, c.1900, 11 In. Diam. 861
Vanity Jar, Round, Bulbous, Sterling Silver Indian Head Lid, c.1905, 3 In. 657
Vase, Brunswick Pattern, Clear, Round Foot, Tapered, Zigzag Ruffle Rim, 12 ½ In. 83
Vase, Globular, Hobstar, Triangles, Sterling Flower Vine Rim, c.1900, 6 ¼ In. 369
Vase, Globular, Trumpet Neck, 2 Handles, Russian Cut Design, c.1910, 7 In. 359
Vase, Green Cut To Clear, Fans, Cross-Hatching, Star Cuts, Flared, 7 ½ In. .... *illus* 85
Vase, Hobstars, Diapered Triangles, Goblet Shape, Zigzag Rim, Footed, c.1900, 13 In. 306
Vase, Stars & Hobnails, Trumpet Shape, Square Pedestal, Zigzag Rim, c.1900, 16 In. 521
Vase, Stick, Bulbous Bottom, Wavy Paneled, Enamel, Gilt, Flowers, c.1890, 16 In. 35
Vase, Wheel Cut, Flower Heads, Fluted Windows, Thumbprint Rim, Gorham, 12 x 6 In. 118
Wine, Square Base, c.1900, 4 In., 14 Piece 180

CYBIS porcelain is a twentieth-century product. Boleslaw Cybis came to the United States from Poland in 1939. He started making porcelains in Long Island, New York, in 1940. He moved to Trenton, New Jersey, in 1942 as one of the founders of Cordey China Co. and started his own company, Cybis Porcelains, about 1950. The firm is still working. See also Cordey.

CYBIS

Figurine, Flamenco Dancer, White Dress, Red Ruffles, Red Shoes, 15 In. 246
Figurine, Owl, Yellow Eyes, Yellow Talons, Stump, 17 ¼ In. 250
Figurine, Seated Woman, Floral Headdress, Striped Skirt, 18 x 11 In. 1476

CZECHOSLOVAKIA is a popular term with collectors. The name, first used as a mark after the country was formed in 1918, appears on glass and porcelain and other decorative items. Although Czechoslovakia split into Slovakia and the Czech Republic on January 1, 1993, the name continues to be used in some trademarks.

PEASANT ART INDUSTRY MADE IN CZECHOSLOVAKIA

CZECHOSLOVAKIA GLASS

Atomizer, Cranberry Cut To Clear, Gilt, c.1920, 8 ¾ In. 2460
Lamp Globe, Ewer Shape, Green, Painted Flowers, Pair 24
Perfume Bottle, Amethyst, Square, Rounded Corners, Disc Stopper, 7 In. 420
Perfume Bottle, Art Deco, Black, Openwork Malachite Stopper, Nude, Leaves, 7 x 4 In. 354
Perfume Bottle, Atomizer, Art Deco, Black Cut To Clear, 1930s, 8 In. 2460
Perfume Bottle, Atomizer, Art Deco, Black, 1920s, 5 In. 5228
Perfume Bottle, Black, Green Monkeys, c.1930, 7 ¼ In. 8610
Perfume Bottle, Gazelle, Matte Finish, Flower Stopper, c.1930, 6 ½ In. .... *illus* 472
Perfume Bottle, Hoffman, Amber, Gilt Metal, Portrait, 1920s, 8 ½ In. 2091
Perfume Bottle, Hoffman, Black, Cylindrical, Classical Women, 7 In. 2706
Perfume Bottle, Hoffman, Brown, Frosted, Bird, Nude, 1920s, 5 In. 5843
Perfume Bottle, Hoffman, Coral Red, Frosted, Nude, 1920s, 4 ⅜ In. 5843
Perfume Bottle, Ruby, Bakelite Roses, Gilt Metal, 1920s, 7 ½ In. 8610
Perfume Bottle, Trio, Blue To Clear, Jeweled Holder, c.1920, 4 In. 738
Vase, Art Deco, Red, Figures, Hoffman Style, 7 ¾ x 6 In. 210
Vase, Black, Relief, Flowers, 5 ½ In., Pair 50
Vase, Gold Iridescent, Fold Over Rim, 7 x 8 ½ In. 216
Vase, Quatrefoil, Gilt Trim, Scrolls, Multicolor, Bun Feet, 8 x 3 ½ In., Pair 847

CZECHOSLOVAKIA POTTERY

Figurine, Horse, Rider, Porcelain, 15 ½ In. 281
Pitcher, Figural, Toucan, Ditmar Urbach, 9 x 7 ½ In. 240
Vase, Gold, Cobalt Blue, Flowers, Karlsbad Porcelain Factory, 1916, 8 ⅝ In. .... *illus* 325

DANIEL BOONE, a pre–Revolutionary War folk hero, was a surveyor, trapper, and frontiersman. A television series, which ran from 1964 to 1970, was based on his life and starred Fess Parker. All types of Daniel Boone memorabilia are collected.

Belt Buckle, Brass, Daniel Boone, Relief, Oval, 1960s 21
Souvenir Spoon, Old Kentucky Home, Sterling Silver, 5 ⅝ In. .... *illus* 45
Toy, Canoe, Figures, Plastic, Yellow, Red, Blue, 1964, 10 In. 35
Toy, Figure, Daniel Boone, Hat, Rifle, Horse, Hartland, 10 In. 20

D'ARGENTAL is a mark used in France by the Compagnie des Cristalleries de St. Louis. The firm made multilayered, acid-cut cameo glass in the late nineteenth and twentieth centuries. D'Argental is the French name for the city of Munzthal, home of the glassworks. Later the company made enameled etched glass.

D'argental

Perfume Bottle, Leaves, Blue, Cameo, 6 ½ x 3 In. 875
Vase, Boats, Water, Multicolor, Crimped Rim, Flattened Oval, 6 In. 958
Vase, Brown, Violet, Branches, Berries, 7 ⅞ In. 223
Vase, Clematis Blossoms, Vine, Dark Amethyst, Blue, Elongated Oval, 6 In. 403
Vase, Cobalt Blue Neck, Blue Flowers, Yellow, Blue Foot, Cameo, 4 In. 350
Vase, Landscape, River & Trees, Blue, Purple Overlay, Swollen, Ring Foot, c.1920, 10 In. 1000
Vase, Purple Flowers, Cameo, 5 ½ In. 350
Vase, Purple Rose Leaves, Thorns, Yellow Ground, 11 ¾ In. 840
Vase, Raspberry Blush, Berries, Leaves, Yellow, High Shoulders, c.1920, 7 In. 320
Vase, Red Flowers, Leaves, Yellow Ground, 5 ½ In. 70
Vase, Scenic, Island, Palm Trees, Water, Mottled Indigo, Tapered, 9 ¾ In. 805
Vase, Shooting Star Wildflowers, Cobalt Blue, Yellow Matte, Trumpet Neck, 4 In. 403
Vase, Tapered, Sycamore, Amber, Brown Leaves, Branches, Overlay, c.1910, 8 In. 938
Vase, Yellow, Central Band, Flowers, Cameo, 12 In. 1700

Cut Glass, Vase, Green Cut To Clear, Fans, Cross-Hatching, Star Cuts, Flared, 7 ½ In.
$85

Ruby Lane

Czechoslovakia Glass, Perfume Bottle, Gazelle, Matte Finish, Flower Stopper, c.1930, 6 ½ In.
$472

Brunk Auctions

Czechoslovakia Pottery, Vase, Gold, Cobalt Blue, Flowers, Karlsbad Porcelain Factory, 1916, 8 ⅝ In.
$325

Ruby Lane

Daniel Boone, Souvenir Spoon, Old Kentucky Home, Sterling Silver, 5 ⅝ In.
$45

Ruby Lane

Daum, Vase, Red Poppies, Wheel Carved, Cameo, Martele, Incised, c.1900, 8 In.
$7,500

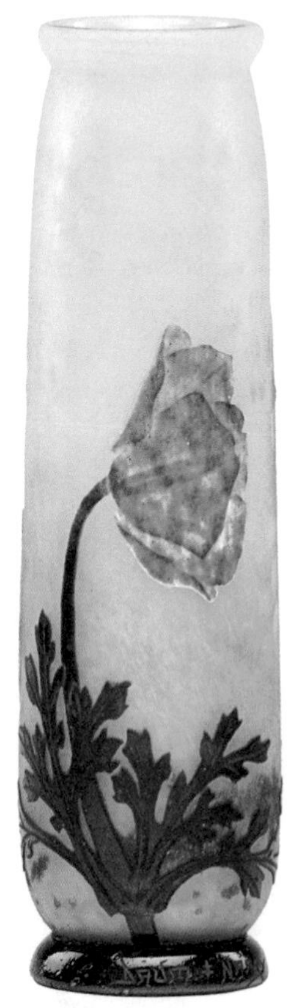

Rago Arts and Auction Center

DAUM, a glassworks in Nancy, France, was started by Jean Daum in 1875. The company, now called *Cristalleries de Nancy*, is still working. The *Daum Nancy* mark has been used in many variations. The name of the city and the artist are usually both included. The term *martele* is used to describe applied decorations that are carved or etched in the cameo process.

Bowl, Boats, Venetian Scene, 3 ¼ In. 1170
Bowl, Harbor, Sailboats, Windmills, Cottages, 8 x 3 In. 1404
Bowl, Les Figues, Pate-De-Verre, 8 x 12 In. 2160
Bowl, Morning Glories, Leaves, White, Gray, Green, Frosted Ground, Enamel, Cameo, 6 In. 2015
Bowl, Pate-De-Verre, Amber, Blue Mottled, Butterfly, 5 ¾ x 7 ¾ In. 584
Bowl, Red Flowers, Stems & Leaves, Butterfly, Gold Trim, Etched, Ground, Squat, 8 In. 5333
Bowl, Tinted Green, Wide Zigzag Rim, Tapered, 1930s, 4 x 8 In. 144
Box, Lid, Enamel, Leaves, Amble Mottled Ground, Cameo, Squared, Squat, 3 In. 556
Creamer, Flowers, Gold Trim, Cameo, Textured Ground, Silver Foot, Handle & Hinged Lid, 4 In. 948
Figurine, Rabbit, Pate-De-Verre, Orange, 5 x 4 ¾ In. 210
Flacon, Smelling, Emerald Over Clear, Etched, Enamel, Gold Trim, Stopper, c.1892, 3 In. 767
Lamp, Hanging, 4-Light, Flowers, Leaves, Purple, Cameo, 16 In. 1380
Lamp, Hanging, Cameo Glass Globe, Leaf & Berry Design, Brass Acanthus Leaf Fixture, 16 In. 2250
Lamp, Winter Scene, Trees, Snow, Baluster Stem, Spread Foot, Mushroom Shade, 18 In. 16590
Perfume Bottle, Enameled, Red Flowers, Green, c.1900, 5 In. 5535
Perfume Bottle, Green Shaded To Rose To Amethyst, Flowers, Cameo, c.1895, 4 In. 2360
Pitcher, Ships On Water, Windmill, Blue & White, Frosted, Textured, Tapered, 8 In. 1150
Plaque, Venus Drape, Reclining Woman, Amber, Relief Carved, Olivier Brice, 1900s, 12 In. 1315
Powder Jar, Flowers, Yellow, Green, Frosted Ground, Acid Cut, Silver Lid, Squat, 5 In. 185
Salt, Road By Water, Sailboats, Blue & White, Frosted, Bucket Form, Raised Handles, 2 In. 748
Sculpture, Crystal Flame, Clear, Bell Shape Base, Signed, c.1980, 19 In. 115
Sculpture, Torso, Clear & Frosted Glass, 3 ½ In. 120
Tray, Le Figues, Pate-De-Verre, 17 In. 1320
Tray, Pate-De-Verre, Frog, 1 ½ x 6 ½ In. 300
Tumbler, Bleeding Heart Flowers, Shaded & Mottled Ground, Barrel Form, 3 ½ In. 1150
Vase, Berries, Leaves, Footed, Brown, Yellow, Orange, Cross Of Lorraine, 6 In. 1755
Vase, Blossoms, Leaves, Butterfly, Dragon, Mottled Indigo, 3-Sided, Gold Trim, Cameo, 7 In. 920
Vase, Bronze Mounted, Medallions, Swags, 4-Footed, 28 ½ In. 375
Vase, Bulbous, Flared Rim, Ring Foot, Iron, Cage Glass, Circles, Yellow, Blue Mottled, 9 x 9 In. 750
Vase, Chipped Ice, France, 1900s, 11 ½ In. 615
Vase, Crocus Flowers, Stems, Frosted Ground, Red Cameo, Tapered, Round Shoulder, 6 In. 2370
Vase, Diamond Shape, Pinched Sides, Cameo Bellflowers, Mottled, Red, Amber, Green, 5 In. 1955
Vase, Fall Landscape, Shouldered, Signed, 9 ½ In. 12677
Vase, Flowers, Etched, Enamel Decoration, Cameo, Gold Trim, France, 1890s, 11 x 4 In. 750
Vase, Flowers, Frosted, Clear Shaded To Yellow To Pink, Blue & Gold Trim, Square, 5 In. 1265
Vase, Flowers, Green Leaves, Mottled Tan Ground, Cameo, Bulbous, Tapered, 4 ½ In. 1725
Vase, Frosted Green Glass, Pink Enameled Berries, Branches, Cameo, 13 In. 767
Vase, Fuchsias, Acid Etched, Footed, 3-Sided Rim, Signed, 12 In. 5557
Vase, Gold Enamel Flowers, Paix Et Peu, Frosted Indigo Ground, Signed, 3 ¼ In. 489
Vase, Green Tinted Glass, Twisted Quatrefoil Shape, Rolled Rim, 1930s, 11 x 11 In. 345
Vase, Green, Pink Cameo Flowers, Leaves, Smokestack, Stick Neck, Flared Rim, 16 In. 10369
Vase, Iris, Purple, Green Leaves, Stick Neck, Flared Rim, Signed, 4 ¾ In. 2925
Vase, Lake, Trees, Sailboats, Mountains, Mottled Orange Sunset Sky, 12 In. 2074
Vase, Landscape, Trees, Yellow, Green, Orange, Flared Rim, Signed, 13 ¾ In. 9360
Vase, Majorelle, Mottled Purple & Pink, Iron Banded Frame, Stylized Leaves, 9 ¾ In. 2161
Vase, Majorelle, Wrought Iron Mount, Amber, 10 x 6 ½ In. 630
Vase, Mushrooms, Pine Tree Limbs, Mottled Yellow, Cream Ground, Tapered, Signed, 16 In. 11850
Vase, Oval, Green, Mauve, Grapevine, Cluster, Geometric, Martele Panels, Cameo, 5 In. 374
Vase, Pillow Shape, Birches At Dawn, Purple Landscape, 4 ¾ In. 2340
Vase, Pillow Shape, Citrus Mottled Colors, Cut Berries, Branch, Enamel, Cameo, 4 x 4 ¾ In. 2300
Vase, Pink Flowers, Green Leaves, Purple Shaded To Green, Bulbous, Long Neck, 10 In. 7110
Vase, Poppies, Stems & Leaves, Butterflies, Cameo, Orange, Yellow, Round, Stick Neck, 8 In. 5925
Vase, Red Flowers, Clear, Cased Yellow Inside, Fire Polished, Oval, Red Foot, 5 ¾ In. 1422
Vase, Red Orchids, Mottled Brown Shaded To Yellow Shaded To Cream, Cinched Base, 3 In. 2548
Vase, Red Poppies, Wheel Carved, Cameo, Martele, Incised, c.1900, 8 In. .... *illus* 7500
Vase, Sailboats, Harbor, Sunset, Rolled Rim, 8 ¼ In. 2340
Vase, Silver Dollar Plants, Acid Texture Frosted Ground, Cream, Green Mottled, Bulbous, 4 In. 3259
Vase, Snow On Trees, Village, Church, Blue, Marked, 7 ¾ In. 4972
Vase, Square, Violet Flowers, Leaves, Gilt Highlights, Inscribed, Pontil, 1890-96, 4 In. .... *illus* 2460
Vase, Thistle, Gilded & Enamel, Purple Ground, Bulbous, Round Foot, Saucer Neck, 3 ½ In. 830

Daum, Vase, Square, Violet Flowers, Leaves, Gilt Highlights, Inscribed, Pontil, 1890-96, 4 In.
$2,460

Skinner, Inc.

Davenport, Jug, Imari, Hydra Head, Octagonal, Handle, 1825, 4 In.
$110

Ruby Lane

Davy Crockett, Mug, Fire-King, White, Red, 3 ¼ In.
$10

Ruby Lane

TIP

Never leave your house keys on your key chain when an attendant parks your car.

Daum History

Cut and enameled glass, often with heraldic crests, was made by Daum at first. In 1885 Daum's sons Auguste (1853–1909) and Antonin (1864–1930) introduced Art Nouveau–style pâte-de-verre and cameo glass. Pieces were decorated with flowers, landscapes, and other natural forms. In 1900 Daum joined Emile Gallé and Louis Majorelle to found the École de Nancy. Daum started making free-form clear glass in the 1950s. It reintroduced pâte-de-verre glass in 1966, using contemporary designs. Daum glass is still being made.

De Vez, Vase, Cameo, Brown & Red, Grape Clusters, Leaves & Vines, Cream To Red, Stippled, 7 In.
$652

James D. Julia Auctioneers

Decoy, Black Duck, Original Paint, Ward Brothers, Maryland, 1936
$17,250

Guyette, Schmitd & Deeter

Decoy, Canada Goose, Preening, Original Paint, Ward Brothers, 1968
$13,800

Guyette, Schmitd & Deeter

Dedham, Dolphin, Plate, Blue, White, Blue Mark, c.1900, 8 ½ In.
$738

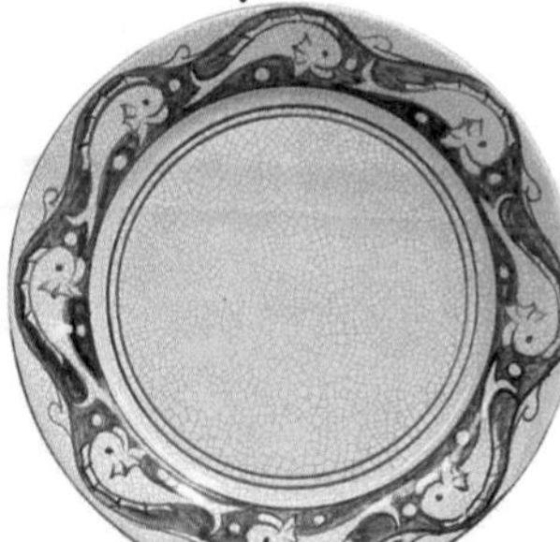

Skinner, Inc.

Dedham, Lobster, Plate, Seaweed, Blue, White, Blue Mark, c.1900, 8 ½ In.
$431

Skinner, Inc.

Dedham, Oak Leaves, Pitcher, Blue, White, Loop Handle, Blue Mark, 1929, 5 ½ In.
$338

Skinner, Inc.

TIP

When packing a piece of pottery for shipping, look at the shape. If it has a hollow space larger than one inch across, fill the space with sponge foam or bubble wrap.

Vase, Trees, Mottled Green & Brown, Blown-Out, Mottled Fiery Orange & Yellow Sky, 17 In. 9480
Vase, Trees, Mottled, Textured Brown Shaded To Orange To Blue, Cylindrical, Cameo, 9 In. 4631
Vase, Urn Shape, Cushion Foot, Opaque, Cerulean Blue, Stylized Flowers, c.1900, 7 In. 896
Vase, Venice, Gondolas, River, Cylindrical, 8 ½ In. 1755
Vase, White Flowers, Footed, Padded & Wheel Carved, Cylindrical, 17 In. 4680
Vase, Wild Roses, Cranberry, Green, Frosted, Textured, Green Foot & Rim, Martele, 7 In. 2074
Vase, Winter Landscape, Pillow Form, Scalloped Rim, Cross Of Lorraine, 9 In. 4972

DAVENPORT pottery and porcelain were made at the Davenport factory in Longport, Staffordshire, England, from 1793 to 1887. Earthenwares, creamwares, porcelains, ironstone, and other ceramics were made. Most of the pieces are marked with a form of the word *Davenport*.

Cup & Saucer, Flowers, Leaves, Vines, Diamond Diapering Pattern, Pink, c.1875 229
Jug, Imari, Hydra Head, Octagonal, Handle, 1825, 4 In. .... *illus* 110
Plate, Children Playing, Garden, Scalloped Edge, Red Transferware, c.1840, 9 In. 250
Plate, Dessert, Scalloped, Molded Rim, Gilt, Cobalt Blue & White Border, Grape Leaves, 9 In., Pair 184
Plate, Man, Carrying Urn, Church, Lake, Scalloped, Marked, 8 ½ In. 48
Platter, River Church, Flower Border, Blue & White Transfer, c.1825, 15 x 12 In. 415
Teapot, Woman, Milking Cow, Cobalt Blue & White, Child's, 5 ¾ In. 85

DAVY CROCKETT, the American frontiersman, was born in 1786 and died in 1836. The historical character gained new fame in 1954 when the Walt Disney television show ran a series of episodes featuring Fess Parker as Davy Crockett. Coonskin caps and buckskins became popular and hundreds of different Davy Crockett items were made.

Bowl, Slanted Sides, Davy, Cow, Red, Fire-King, 4 ¾ In. 45
Clock, Pendulum, Davy, Kneeling, Holding Rifle, Pressed Wood, c.1955, 7 In. Diam. 172
Cookie Jar, Figural, Brush Pottery, c.1956, 10 ½ In. 395
Dime Bank, Frontier, Tin Lithograph, 1950s, 2 ½ x 2 ½ In. 115
Hat, Faux Fur, Child's, 1950s 30
Mug, Fire-King, White, Red, 3 ¼ In. .... *illus* 10
Mug, Milk, Blue Graphics, Famous Frontiersman, Hazel Atlas, 1950s 15
Ring, Plastic, Blue Cameo, c.1955, Size 3 35
Talking Book, Davy & The Indians, 78 RPM, John Winston Co., 1955 40
Tumbler, Davy On Horse, Raised Arm With Rifle, 4 ¾ In. 20
Wallet, Davy Wearing Coonskin Cap, Western Scenes, Plastic, 3 x 3 In. 40

DE MORGAN art pottery was made in England by William De Morgan from the 1860s to 1907. He is best known for his luster-glazed Moorish-inspired pieces. The pottery used a variety of marks.

Bowl, Carnations, Panels, Turquoise & Blue, 7 ¾ In. 919
Dish, Wide Flower Border, Central Tulips, Blue, Green, 11 ¼ In. 8500
Tile, Flowers, Multicolor, 6 ½ x 6 ½ In. 400
Tile, Stylized Carnations, Leaves, Blue, Green, Lavender, Frame, 26 In. 984

DE VEZ was a signature used on cameo glass after 1910. E. S. Monot founded the glass company near Paris in 1851. The company changed names many times. Mt. Joye, another glass by this factory, is listed in its own category.

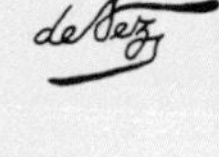

Vase, Cameo, Brown & Red, Grape Clusters, Leaves & Vines, Cream To Red, Stippled, 7 In. ..*illus* 652

DECORATED TUMBLERS *may be by maker or design or in Advertising, Coca-Cola, Pepsi-Cola, Sports, and other categories.*

DECOYS are carved or turned wooden copies of birds, fish, or animals. The decoy was placed in the water or propped on the shore to lure flying birds to the pond for hunters. Some decoys are handmade; some are commercial products. Today there is a group of artists making modern decoys for display, not for use in a pond. Many sell for high prices.

Black Duck, Original Paint, Ward Brothers, Maryland, 1936 .... *illus* 17250
Bluebill Duck, Glass Eyes, Keel Weight, Evans, 1920s, 7 ½ x 15 In. 218
Bluebill Duck, Tack Eyes, Mason Decoy Factory, 1920s, 6 ¾ x 13 ½ In. 58
Blue-Winged Teal, Painted, White Head Crescent, Button Eyes, Ojibway, Minn., 5 x 11 In. 188
Canada Goose, Brown, Tan, Painted, Carved, 11 x 20 In. 156
Canada Goose, Carved, Wings, Painted, 1950s, 23 In. 987

Canada Goose, George Harvey, 11 x 26 In. 604
Canada Goose, Hollow, Painted, Feathered Sides, New Jersey, 1900s, 9 x 21 In. 360
Canada Goose, Preening, Original Paint, Ward Brothers, 1968 .... *illus* 13800
Canada Goose, Snuggled Head, Painted Feathering, Glass Eyes, Michigan, 1940s, 7 x 21 In. 240
Canvasback Drake, Painted, Scalloped Feathers, Turned Head, Ira Hudson, c.1910, 17 x 9 In. 738
Canvasback Duck, Carved, Glass Eyes, Pratt, 1950s, 7 ½ x 14 ½ In. 161
Canvasback Duck, Carved, Glass Eyes, Schmidt, 1960s, 9 ¾ x 23 ¼ In. 58
Duck, Gray Paint, Brown, Black, White, 18 In. 546
Goose, 19 x 32 In. 468
Lake Erie Canvasback Drake, Bobtail, Wood, Painted Eyes, Ohio, c.1910, 6 x 15 In. 250
Mallard Drake, Glass Eyes, Paul Berry, c.1980, 15 x 6 In. 85
Mallard Drake, Tin, Paint, Square Base, 7 In. 118
Merganser, Walter Cross, Nova Scotia, 20 In. 47
Merganser, White, Gray, Green Head, Horsehair Tuft, Red Breast, Black Spots, 17 In. 338
Pigeon, Wood, Paint, Raised Feather, Glass Eyes, c.1900, 15 x 11 In. 313
Pintail Drake, Tilted Head, Ward Brothers, Painted, 1930s 4398
Redhead Duck, Tack Eyes, Mason Decoy Factory, 1930s, 6 ¾ x 13 ½ In. 69
Swan, Carved, Painted, 39 x 19 In. 234
Widgeon Drake, Wood, Painted, Raised Wing Tips, Glass Eyes, M. Pirnie, Mich., 1940s, 13 In. 313
Wood Duck, Ben Schmidt, Painted, 14 In. 122

DEDHAM POTTERY was started in 1895. Chelsea Keramic Art Works was established in 1872 in Chelsea, Massachusetts, by members of the Robertson family. The factory closed in 1889 and was reorganized as the Chelsea Pottery U.S. in 1891. The firm used the marks *CKAW* and *CPUS*. It became the Dedham Pottery of Dedham, Massachusetts. The factory closed in 1943. It was famous for its crackleware dishes, which picture blue outlines of animals, flowers, and other natural motifs. Pottery by Chelsea Keramic Art Works and Dedham Pottery is listed here.

DEDHAM POTTERY

Azalea, Plate, 10 In. 96
Butterfly & Flower, Plate, Blue & White Glaze, 8 ¼ In. 369
Dolphin, Plate, Blue, White, Blue Mark, c.1900, 8 ½ In. .... *illus* 738
Grape, Plate, 8 ½ In., 7 Piece 302
Lobster, Plate, Seaweed, Blue, White, Blue Mark, c.1900, 8 ½ In. .... *illus* 431
Mushroom, Dish, Toast, Lid, Blue & White, 8 ½ In. 431
Oak Leaves, Pitcher, Blue, White, Loop Handle, Blue Mark, 1929, 5 ½ In. .... *illus* 338
Rabbit, Bowl, 6 In. 60
Rabbit, Bowl, Blue & White, 8 In. 154
Rabbit, Celery Dish, Blue & White, Oval, 10 In. 185
Rabbit, Plate, 7 ¾ In. 25
Rabbit, Plate, 8 ½ In. 50
Rabbit, Plate, Blue & White, 10 In. 123
Rabbit, Plate, Bread & Butter, 6 In. .... 138 to 148
Rabbit, Platter, Oval, 17 ½ In. .... 2689 to 3256
Rabbit, Tray, Oval, 12 ½ x 7 ¼ In. 300
Swan, Plate, Blue & White, Stamped, c.1935, 10 In. 185
Toadstool, Plate, 8 ¾ In. 70
Turkey, Plate, Blue & White, 8 ¼ In. 246
Turtle, Teapot, Blue, White, Blue Mark, c.1935, 5 In. .... *illus* 861
Vase, Brown Volcanic Glaze, Green Flambe On Mouth, Swollen, Incised HCR, 6 ⅞ In. .... *illus* 4920
Vase, Crackled Beige Glaze, Mossy Green Glaze Dripped On Shoulder, c.1900, 9 In. 615
Vase, Frothy Cream & Tan Over Slate, Experimental, Hugh Robertson, 10 In. 1230
Vase, Nude Woman Standing, Blue & White Crackled Glaze, H. Robertson, 9 In. .... *illus* 10455
Vase, Oxblood & Green Flambe Glazes, Volcanic Ground, Bulbous, 8 ½ In. 5535
Vase, Oxblood, Hugh Robertson, 8 x 3 In. 700
Vase, Yellow Brown, Hugh Robertson, 7 ½ In. 400

DEGUE is a signature acid etched on pieces of French glass made by the Cristalleries de Compiegne in the early 1900s. Cameo, mold blown, and smooth glass with contrasting colored rims are the types most often found.

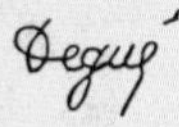

Vase, Clear, Frosted Green, Intertwined Circle Design, Globular, Flat Flared Rim, 1920, 5 In. 335
Vase, Dark Pink To Purple, Drip Design, Oval, Round Foot, Rolled Rim, c.1925, 17 In. 438
Vase, Elongated Oval, Pedestal Foot, Beige, Red & Purple Flower Overlay, c.1920, 23 In. 2500
Vase, Green, Etched, Frosted Design, Round Foot, Flared Rim, c.1930, 7 In. 65
Vase, Pear Shape, Ring Foot, Flared Rim, Peach Enamel, Green, Black Grapevines, c.1900, 22 In. 1375
Vase, Trees, Etching, Blue, 1925, 18 x 10 In. .... *illus* 5800

Dedham, Turtle, Teapot, Blue, White, Blue Mark, c.1935, 5 In.
$861

Skinner, Inc.

Dedham, Vase, Brown Volcanic Glaze, Green Flambe On Mouth, Swollen, Incised HCR, 6 ⅞ In.
$4,920

Skinner, Inc.

Dedham, Vase, Nude Woman Standing, Blue & White Crackled Glaze, H. Robertson, 9 In.
$10,455

Skinner, Inc.

D

Degue, Vase, Trees, Etching, Blue, 1925, 18 x 10 In.
$5,800

Ruby Lane

Delft, Candlesticks, Salt Holder, 2-Sided Girl, Wood Base, 18th Century, 9-In. Candlestick
$1,476

Ruby Lane

Delft, Condiment Set, Salt, Pepper, Mustard, Hand Painted, Blue, Elesva, 6-In. Tray, 5 Piece
$70

Ruby Lane

Delft, Dish, Lobed, Figures, Landscape, Chinoiserie, Manganese, Blue, c.1710, 13 In.
$984

Skinner, Inc.

Delft, Snuff Jar, Flowers, Scrolls, Medallion, Inscribed Havanna, Brass Lid, 1700s, 12 In.
$1,599

Skinner, Inc.

Dental, Cabinet, Mahogany, Drawers, Glass Doors, American Cabinet, c.1910, 58 x 41 In.
$1,062

New Orleans (Cakebread)

Old Delft, New Delft

You can learn to tell old delft from new. Delft crumbles and chips easily, so old delft dishes and tiles should show some signs of wear. The blue decorations on old delft are slightly darker. Old wares are much thicker and heavier than new ones. New pieces have much whiter bodies and much clearer designs. But the easiest way to judge whether your delft is old or new is to compare it with a new, fresh-from-the-gift-shop piece of delft.

Dental, Chair, Patient's, Walnut, Leather, Swivel, Style Of W.D. Allison Co., c.1910, 50 x 23 In.
$168

Wickliffe Auctioneers

DELATTE glass is a French cameo glass made by Andre Delatte. It was first made in Nancy, France, in 1921. Lighting fixtures and opaque glassware in imitation of Bohemian opaline were made. There were many French cameo glassmakers, so be sure to look in other appropriate categories.

Bowl, Flowers, Stylized Leaves, Rose, Violet, Crimped Rim, c.1910, 7¾ In. 350
Vase, Bottle Shape, Yellow, Blue, Signed, 11 In. 325
Vase, Bulbous, Stick Neck, Brown Flowers & Vines, Yellow Ground, 18 In. 600
Vase, Flower, Purple, Pink Ground, Oval, Cameo, 6 x 3¼ In. 175
Vase, Orange, Red, Parrot, Footed, c.1925, 10 In. 220
Vase, Sailing Ship, High Waves, Black, Signed Jarvil Nancy, 7 x 5½ In. 250

DELDARE, *see Buffalo Pottery Deldare.*

DELFT is a special type of tin-glazed pottery. Early delft was made in Holland and England during the seventeenth century. It was usually decorated with blue on a white surface, but some was polychrome, decorated with green, yellow, and other colors. Most delftware pieces were dishes needed for everyday living. Figures were made from about 1750 to 1800, and are rare. Although the soft tin-glazed pottery was well-known, it was not named delft until after 1840, when it was named for the city in Holland where much of it was made. Porcelain became more popular because it was more durable and Holland gradually stopped making the old delft. In 1876 De Porceleyne Fles factory in Delft introduced a porcelain ware that was decorated with blue and white scenes of Holland that reminded many of old delft. It became popular with the Dutch and tourists. By 1990 all of the blue and white porcelain with Dutch scenes was made in Asia, although it was marked *Delft*. Only one Dutch company remains that makes the traditional old-style delft with blue on white or with colored decorations. Most of the pieces sold today were made after 1891, and the name *Holland* usually appears with the Delft factory marks. The word *Delft* appears alone on some inexpensive twentieth- and twenty-first century pottery from Asia and Germany that is also listed here.

Bottle, Water, Sheep, Standing, Tree, A.A.E., Blue & White, Stone Buildings, c.1750, 9 In. 8783
Bowl, Baptism Of Jesus By John The Baptist, Blue & White, Shaped Rim, 4 x 13 x 11 In. 400
Bowl, Blue & White, Stylized Flowers & Leaves, Shrub, Insect, Banding, 1700s, 11 In. 840
Bowl, Fruit, Pierced Star, Blue, White, Scalloped Edges, 3-Footed, Floral Reserves, 1764, 8 In. 420
Bowl, Multicolor, Blue Underglaze Painting, Footed, c.1730, 3¾ x 7¾ In. 177
Bowl, Punch, Footed, Blue Flowers, Purple Detail, c.1800, 4 x 9 In. 472
Candlesticks, Salt Holder, 2-Sided Girl, Wood Base, 18th Century, 9-In. Candlestick ....*illus* 1476
Charger, Blue & White, Dot & Lattice Border, Landscape, Bird, c.1750, 14 In. 554
Charger, Blue & White, Flower Head Center, Leaves, Scrolled Vines, c.1720, 13 In. Diam. 554
Charger, Blue & White, Flowers, Ocher Enamel Rim, Ribbed Border, Scroll, 1700s, 13 In. 923
Charger, Blue & White, Peacock, Ocher Enamel Rim, Leaf Border, Floral Urn, c.1750, 12 In. 554
Charger, Blue & White, Urn, Bouquet, Peacock-Shape Feather Fan Behind Urn, Holland, 1700s, 12 In. 338
Charger, Chinoiserie, Lattice & Dash Border, Garden Landscape, Figure Fence, c.1750, 13½ In. 523
Charger, Fruit & Leaf Border, Center Floral Garden, Fence, Bird, Multicolor, 1700s, 13¾ In. 400
Charger, Green, Red Enamel Accents, Flower Basket Center, 1800s, 13 In. 224
Charger, House, Flowers, Yellow, Blue, Burgundy, 12¼ In. 585
Charger, Multicolor, Alternating Flowers, Lattice Border, Landscape, Bird, c.1750, 14 In. 369
Charger, Multicolor, Double Ogee Shape, Stylized Flower, Blue Lines, 1700s, 14 In. 472
Charger, Peacock, Leaf Border, Urn, Flowers, Ocher Enamel Rim, 1700s, 14 In., Pair........ 492
Charger, Zigzag, Alternating Flower & Leaf Border, Flowers In Urn, Multicolor, 14 In. 431
Condiment Set, Salt, Pepper, Mustard, Hand Painted, Blue, Elesva, 6-In. Tray, 5 Piece ....*illus* 70
Dish, Blue & White, Lobed, Paneled Figure & Leaf Border, Landscape, c.1690, 14 In. 1968
Dish, Blue & White, Peacock Pattern, Scrolls, Gilt Rim, c.1900, 10 In. Diam. 31
Dish, Figures, Landscape, Flowers, Trellis Diaperwork, Multicolor, 1¾ x 12 In., Pair 1121
Dish, Lobed, Figures, Landscape, Chinoiserie, Manganese, Blue, c.1710, 13 In. ....*illus* 984
Dish, Trefoil, Cherubs In Landscape, Blue, 2 Stretched Sides, Reticulated Dividers, 6 x 8 In. 150
Dish, Underplate, Pumpkin Shape, 11¼ x 9½ In. 234
Figurine, Hound, Baying, Seated, Blue, White, Gold Speckles, Teeth Bared, c.1715, 8 In. 15615
Flower Brick, Holes In Top For Stems, 1700s, 3¼ x 6¼ In. 4484
Jar, Blue & White, Lid, Birds & Leaves, Ribbed, Octagonal, Acorn Finials, 20 x 10 In., Pair........ 1104
Jar, Blue & White, Lid, Peacocks, Flowers, Ribbed, Octagonal, 25 x 11½ In. 523
Jar, Drug, Apollo Head, Diascord T.A., Blue & White, Ring Foot, Rolled Rim, 1717, 12 In. 8198
Lamp, Banquet, Burner, Finial, Painted Flowers, Dutch, c.1890, 36 In. 354
Melon Tureen, Lid, Stand, Leafy Vine Finial, Hendrik Van Hoorn, c.1800, 7 In., Pair........ 11875
Plaque, Blue & White, Earthenware, Shield Shape, Figures In Cart, 1800s, 22 x 16 In. 800
Plaque, Pictorial, After Wouwerman, Blue & White, Shaped Edge, 16 x 22 In. 978
Plate, Flower, Leaves, Cream Ground, Orange, Blue, Green, 1700s, 9 In. Diam. 165
Plate, Llama Figure, Reclining In Pasture, Zigzag Border, Painted, c.1710, 6½ In. Diam. 119

Depression Glass, Cherry Blossom, Pitcher, Pink, Pedestal Base, 1930s, 7 In.
$55

Ruby Lane

Depression Glass, Miss America, Relish, Pink, 4 Section, Sawtooth Edge, c.1936, 9 In.
$25

Ruby Lane

Depression Glass, Ocean Wave, Sugar & Creamer, Green, Rippled, 3 In. Diam.
$35

Ruby Lane

Cherry Blossom

Cherry Blossom is one of the popular Depression glass patterns. The pattern was made by Jeannette Glass Company, Jeannette, Pennsylvania, from 1930 to 1939. Full dinner sets, serving pieces, and a child's set were made in a range of colors. Pieces were made in Crystal, Delphite (opaque blue), Green Jadite, Pink, and Red. Reproductions have been made.

Depression Glass, Old Colony, Relish, Pink, 5 Section, Scalloped Rim, c.1936, 10 x 5 In.
$30

Ruby Lane

Depression Glass, Oyster & Pearl, Candlestick, Vitrock, Green & White, Anchor Hocking, 1930s, 3 In.
$40

Ruby Lane

Depression Glass, Stippled Grape, Candy Jar, Raised Grapes, Dark Green, Brown, Clear, 8 In.
$19

Ruby Lane

Plate, Soup, Earthenware, Glazed, Landscape, Multicolor, 12 In. 83
Platter, Blue & White, Group Looking Out To Sea, Boat, 12¾ x 11 In. 74
Platter, Blue & White, Mythical Creature, 13¾ In. 246
Posset Pot, Blue Underglaze, Flowers, Fruit, Bird, Handles, Spout, 1700s, 5 x 7½ In. 142
Shaving Bowl, Multicolor Flowers, Leaves, Serpentine Edge, 3¼ x 12¼ In. 71
Snuff Jar, Flowers, Scrolls, Medallion, Inscribed Havanna, Brass Lid, 1700s, 12 In. ....*illus* 1599
Stein, Pewter Lid, Multicolor Flowers, Purple Sponged Accents, Monogram, c.1800, 7 In. 420
Tankard, Turned Bands, Spread Foot, Strap Handle, Blue & White, Banner, 1663, 5 In. 78077
Vase, Blue & White, Oval, Lobed, Chinese Decorations, Dutch, 6¾ x 4½ In. 480
Vase, Gilt, Swirl, Squat Neck, 6¼ In. 423
Vase, Multicolor, Octagonal Beaker Shape, Cottage, Yellow Scroll Border, Dutch, 9 x 5 In. 480
Vase, Octagonal, Fluted, Birds, Butterflies, Rabbit Among Flower Gardens, c.1850, 21 In. 369
Vase, Rounded, Tapered, Flowers, Rockwork, Wave Banded Rim, 8¼ x 5¾ In. 600
Water Bottle, Blue & White, Elongated Neck, Spout, Bulbous Body, Flowers Heads, c.1760, 9 In. . 1168

DENTAL cabinets, chairs, equipment, and other related items are listed here. Other objects may be found in the Medical category.

Cabinet, Golden Oak, Mirrored Back, Porcelain Pulls, Rotary Base, Pat. 1895, 55 x 26 In. 2128
Cabinet, Mahogany, Drawers, Glass Doors, American Cabinet, c.1910, 58 x 41 In. ....*illus* 1062
Cabinet, Oak, 3 Doors, 10 Drawers, 67 x 29 In. 2360
Cabinet, Oak, Fitted Interior, Accessory Dental Instruments, 12 x 14 In. 129
Chair, Patient's, Walnut, Leather, Swivel, Style Of W.D. Allison Co., c.1910, 50 x 23 In. ....*illus* 168
Tool Set, 6 Tools, Bone Handles, Box, 1800s, 6 x 3 In. 132

DENVER is part of the mark on an American art pottery. William Long of Steubenville, Ohio, founded the Lonhuda Pottery Company in 1892. In 1900 he moved to Denver, Colorado, and organized the Denver China and Pottery Company. This pottery, which used the mark *Denver*, worked until 1905, when Long moved to New Jersey and founded the Clifton Pottery. Long also worked for Weller Pottery, Roseville Pottery, and American Encaustic Tiling Company. Do not confuse this pottery with the Denver White Pottery, which worked from 1894 to 1955 in Denver.

Bowl, Water Lilies, Brown, Green Glaze, c.1900, 3½ x 11 In. 895
Pitcher, Brown & Green Glaze, Neighbors Around Fence, c.1902, 7 x 5 In. 125

DEPRESSION GLASS is an inexpensive glass that was manufactured in large quantities during the 1920s and early 1930s. It was made in many colors and patterns by dozens of factories in the United States. Most patterns were also made in clear glass, which the factories called *crystal*. If no color is listed here, it is clear. The name *Depression glass* is a modern one and also refers to machine-made glass of the 1940s through 1970s. Sets missing a few pieces can be completed through the help of a matching service.

Ballerina pattern is listed here as Cameo.
Basket pattern is listed here as No. 615.
Block pattern is listed here as Block Optic.
Block Optic, Cup & Saucer, Green, Hocking Glass 13
Block Optic, Mug, Green, Hocking Glass, 2¾ In. 31
Block Optic, Sandwich Plate, Pink, Hocking Glass, 10¼ In. 22
Bouquet & Lattice pattern is listed here as Normandie.
Cameo, Butter, Cover, Hocking Glass 198
Cameo, Grill Plate, Green, Hocking Glass, 10½ In. 11
Cameo, Plate, Square, Green, Hocking Glass, 8⅜ In. 49
Cameo, Sherbet, Green, Hocking Glass, 3⅛ In. 11
Candlewick pattern is listed in the Imperial Glass category.
Caprice pattern is included in the Cambridge Glass category.
Cherry Blossom, Butter, Green, Jeannette Glass, 6 In. 13
Cherry Blossom, Pitcher, Pink, Pedestal Base, 1930s, 7 In. ....*illus* 55
Colonial Fluted, Saucer, Green, Federal Glass 3
Columbia, Bowl, Ruffled Edge, Federal Glass, 10½ In. 17
Columbia, Bread Plate, Federal Glass, 6 In. 4
Columbia, Cup & Saucer, Federal Glass 23
Cube pattern is listed here as Cubist.
Cubist, Sherbet, Pink, Jeannette Glass, 2 x 3 In. 8
Daisy pattern is listed here as No. 620.
Dancing Girl pattern is listed here as Cameo.
Diamond pattern is listed here as Miss America.
Diana, Bowl, Cereal, Pink, Federal Glass, 5 In. 8

Diana, Creamer, Amber, Federal Glass ... 8
Diana, Cup, Amber, Federal Glass ... 6
Diana, Plate, Bread & Butter, Pink, Federal Glass, 6 In. ... 3
Diana, Platter, Amber, Oval, Federal Glass ... 12
Doric, Creamer, Pink, Jeannette Glass, 4 In. ... 15
Doric, Salt & Pepper, Pink ... 38
Dutch Rose pattern is listed here as Rosemary.
Fan Fold, Napkin Holder, 4 x 4 In. ... 62
Fire-King, Bowl, Vegetable, Turquoise, 8 In. ... 17
Flat Diamond pattern is listed in the Imperial Glass category.
Fortune, Bowl, Pink, Hocking Glass, c.1937, 4 ½ In. ... 6
Georgian, Berry Bowl, Green, Federal Glass, 4 ½ In. ... 8
Iris & Herringbone pattern is listed here as Iris.
Iris, Butter, Jeannette, 5 ¾ In. ... 12
Line 300 pattern is listed in the Paden City category as Peacock & Wild Rose.
Lorain pattern is listed here as No. 615.
Lovebirds pattern is listed here as Georgian.
Luanna, Vase, Bud, Pink, Morgantown Glass Co., 9 ¾ In. ... 60
Madrid, Plate, Amber, Luncheon, Federal Glass, 8 In. ... 6
Madrid, Sherbet, Amber, Cone Shape, Federal Glass ... 5
Mayfair, Plate, Salad, Amber, Federal Glass, 6 ¾ In. ... 6
Miss America, Pitcher, Pink, Hocking Glass, 7 ½ In. ... 138
Miss America, Relish, Pink, 4 Section, Sawtooth Edge, c.1936, 9 In. ... *illus* 25
Miss America, Water Goblet, Pink, Square Footed, Hocking Glass, 5 In., 6 Piece ... 98
Moondrops pattern is listed in the New Martinsville category.
Moonstone, Cup & Saucer, Anchor Hocking ... 9
Moonstone, Sugar & Creamer, Anchor Hocking ... 13
No. 615, Plate, Luncheon, Yellow, Indiana Glass, 8 ½ In. ... 19
No. 620, Cup & Saucer, Green, Indiana Glass ... 4 to 5
No. 620, Plate, Dinner, Green, Indiana Glass, 9 ⅜ In. ... 5
No. 620, Plate, Salad, Green, Indiana Glass, 7 ⅜ In. ... 3
Normandie, Cup & Saucer, Yellow, Federal Glass ... 9
Normandie, Grill Plate, Yellow, Federal Glass, 11 In. ... 13
Normandie, Plate, Dinner, Plate, Yellow, 11 In. ... 50
Normandie, Sherbet, Yellow, Federal Glass, 2 ¾ In. ... 9
Ocean Wave, Sugar & Creamer, Green, Rippled, 3 In. Diam. ... *illus* 35
Old Cafe, Candy Dish, Ruby, Tab Handles, Hocking Glass, c.1938, 8 ¾ In. ... 22
Old Colony, Relish, Pink, 5 Section, Scalloped Rim, c.1936, 10 x 5 In. ... *illus* 30
Oyster & Pearl, Candlestick, Vitrock, Green & White, Anchor Hocking, 1930s, 3 In. ... *illus* 40
Patrician, Plate, Salad, Federal Glass, 7 ½ In. ... 12
Peacock & Wild Rose pattern is listed in the Paden City category.
Pebbled Rim, Cup & Saucer, Pink ... 8
Pioneer, Bowl, Crimped, Federal Glass, 11 ¼ In. ... 6
Pioneer, Sandwich Plate, Smoke, Federal Glass, 11 In. ... 12
Princess, Butter, Pink, Tab Handles, Hocking Glass, 7 ½ In. ... 36
Radiance pattern is listed in the New Martinsville category.
Rope pattern is listed here as Colonial Fluted.
Rosemary, Bowl, Federal Glass, 5 In. ... 5
Royal Lace, Creamer, Hazel Atlas, 4 In. ... 53
Shell, Bowl, Cereal, Jadite, 6 In. ... 38
Shell, Cup & Saucer, Jadite ... 32
Spoke pattern is listed here as Patrician.
Stippled Grape, Candy Jar, Raised Grapes, Dark Green, Brown, Clear, 8 In. ... *illus* 19
Sunflower, Ashtray, Green, Jeannette Glass ... 9
Waffle pattern is listed here as Waterford.
Waterford, Butter, Cover, Hocking Glass, 6 ½ x 4 In. ... 19

DERBY has been marked on porcelain made in the city of Derby, England, since about 1748. The original Derby factory closed in 1848, but others opened there and continued to produce quality porcelain. The Crown Derby mark began appearing on Derby wares in the 1770s.

Candlestick, Marble, Columns, Tuscan Shape, Slate & Marble Plinth, 1790, 22 In., Pair ... 10312
Cup & Saucer, Flowers, Trailing Leaves, Blue, Gilt, c.1815 ... 465
Figurine, Basket Shepherds, Pierced Rocaille, c.1765, 10 In., Pair ... 2500
Figurine, Cat, Sitting Up, Scroll Base, Tortoise Shell, Purple, Tan, White, c.1758, 4 In. ... 5855
Plate, Birds, Branches, Red, Blue, Green, Gilt Edge, c.1785, 7 In. ... 60

TIP
Dishes don't match in many modern sets. The dinner plate may have a plain colored rim, salad plate a rim with a geometric design in blending colors. When you stack the plates in a pile, largest at the bottom, the plate rims are next to each other making a new design. Do the same thing; assemble a set in many patterns and similar colors.

Dick Tracy, Badge, Secret Service Patrol, Sergeant, Brass, Quaker Oats, 1938, 2 ¾ In.
$50

Ruby Lane

Dinnerware, Currier & Ives, Casserole, Cover, Handles, Royal China, 1 ¼ Qt., 11 x 3 In.
$78

Ruby Lane

This is an edited listing of current prices. Visit **Kovels.com** to check thousands of prices from previous years and sign up for free information on trends, tips, reproductions, marks, and more.

Dinnerware, Currier & Ives, Gravy Boat, Underplate, Blue, Royal China, 5 ¾ & 8 In.
$34

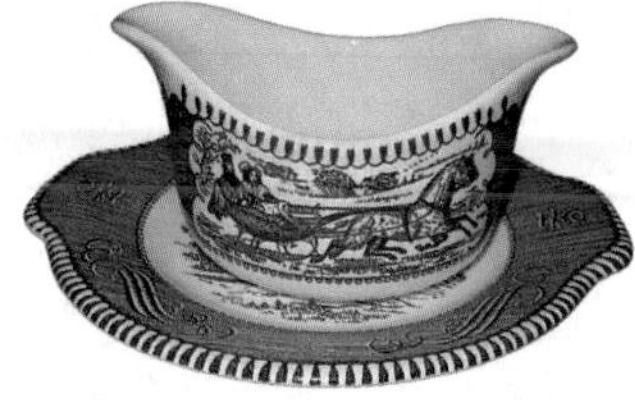

Ruby Lane

Dinnerware, Currier & Ives, Plate, Cake, Blue, Royal China, 10 x 11 ⅝ In.
$14

Ruby Lane

Dinnerware, Fair Winds, Plate, Dinner, Alfred Meakin, 10 ⅝ In.
$6

Ruby Lane

Dinnerware, Moss Rose, Egg Cup, Eggshell, Homer Laughlin, 1940s, 3 ¾ In.
$30

Ruby Lane

Urn, Campana, Imari Decoration, Serpentine Handles, Gold Leaf, c.1820, 7 x 5 ½ In. 196
Vase, Bulbous Body, Narrow Neck, Handles, Flowers, c.1810, 4 In. 199
Vase, Eel Trap, Bulrushes, Ducks, Purple, Gray, Chelsea, 10 In., Pair 6875
Vase, Trumpet, Beaded Borders, Purple, Orange, Gilt, Leaves, Round Foot, c.1825, 5 In. 88
Vase, Warwick, Forest Green, Gold, Armorial, Fruit Still-Life, c.1830, 13 ½ In. 2375
Wine Jug, Lid, Bulbous, Shaped Handle, Flower Sprays, Gilt Borders, c.1815, 11 In. 700

DICK TRACY, the comic strip, started in 1931. Tracy was also the hero of movies from 1937 to 1947 and again in 1990, and starred in a radio series in the 1940s and a television series in the 1950s. Memorabilia from all these activities are collected.

Badge, Secret Service Patrol, Brass, Inspector General, Portrait, Star, 1938, 2 ½ In. .... 221 to 278
Badge, Secret Service Patrol, Sergeant, Brass, Quaker Oats, 1938, 2 ¾ In. .... *illus* 50
Button, Tracy, Junior, Celluloid, c.1933, 1 In. 144
Comic Book, Chains Of Crime, Chester Gould, 1936 253
Figure, Resin, 13 In. 95
Poster, Movie Serial, Dick Tracy Returns, 15 Chapter, 1938, 27 x 41 In. 505
Wristwatch, Hand In Pocket, Holding Gun, Leather Band, Box, 1935 .... 383 to 460

DICKENS WARE *pieces are listed in the Royal Doulton and Weller categories.*

DINNERWARE used in the United States from the 1930s through the 1950s is listed here. Most was made in potteries in southern Ohio, West Virginia, and California. A few patterns were made in Japan, England, and other countries. Dishes were sold in gift shops and department stores, or were given away as premiums. Many of these patterns are listed in this book in their own categories, such as Autumn Leaf, Azalea, Coors, Fiesta, Franciscan, Hall, Harker, Harlequin, Red Wing, Riviera, Russel Wright, Vernon Kilns, Watt, and Willow. For more prices, go to kovels.com. Sets missing a few pieces can be completed through the help of a matching service.

Autumn Monarch, Bowl, Vegetable, Johnson Brothers, 8 ¼ In. 19
Azalea, Plate, Dinner, Crooksville, 10 In. 20
Blue Bonnet, Chop Plate, Harmony House, 12 ½ In. 28
Blue Bonnet, Creamer, Harmony House, 3 In. 37
Bristol, Plate, Bread & Butter, Castleton, 6 In. 20
Buttercup, Plate, Bread & Butter, Edwin Knowles, 6 In. 10
Charisma, Sugar & Creamer, Mikasa 32
Currier & Ives, Casserole, Cover, Handles, Royal China, 1 ¼ Qt., 11 x 3 In. .... *illus* 78
Currier & Ives, Gravy Boat, Underplate, Blue, Royal China, 5 ¾ In. & 8 In. .... *illus* 34
Currier & Ives, Plate, Cake, Blue, Royal China, 10 x 11 ⅝ In. .... *illus* 14
Delrose, Sugar & Creamer, Flintridge Of California 48
Dorchester, Sugar, Lid, Johnson Brothers 52
Fair Winds, Plate, Dinner, Alfred Meakin, 10 ⅝ In. .... *illus* 6
Fantasy Apple, Plate, Dinner, Blue Ridge, 9 In. 17
Friendly Village, Cup & Saucer, Johnson Brothers, 16 Piece 35
Fruit Sampler, Cup & Saucer, Johnson Brothers 14
Golden Wheat, Soup, Dish, Homer Laughlin, 7 In. 11
Grapevine, Berry Bowl, Edwin Knowles, 5 In. 14
Grapevine, Plate, Dinner, Edwin Knowles, 10 In. 21
Heumann, Bowl, Vegetable, Lid, Handles, Maddock & Sons, 11 x 7 In. 64
Heumann, Platter, John Maddock & Sons, 15 x 10 In. 50
Honey Gold, Chop Plate, Taylor Smith & Taylor, 1970s, 12 In. 15
Leona, Platter, Oval, Noritake, 16 x 12 In. 50
Madras, Gravy Boat, Underplate, Alfred Meakin 28
Malvern, Soup, Dish, Johnson Brothers, 8 In. 34
Margaret Rose, Soup, Dish, Johnson Brothers, 8 In. 37
Melody, Bowl, Cereal, Square, Johnson Brothers, 6 In. 12
Moderntone, Plate, Dinner, Shell Pink, Hazel Atlas, 8 ⅞ In. 7
Moderntone, Soup, Dish, Pastel Blue, Handles, Hazel Atlas, 6 x 2 In. 9
Moderntone, Soup, Dish, Shell Pink, Handles, Hazel Atlas, 6 x 2 In. 11
Moss Rose, Egg Cup, Eggshell, Homer Laughlin, 1940s, 3 ¾ In. .... *illus* 30
Poppy & Rose, Cup & Saucer, Decal, Homer Laughlin, 2 ⅝ In. .... *illus* 16
Priscilla, Bowl, Dessert, Household Institute, 1930s, 5 ¼ In. 12
Southern Plantation, Gravy Boat, Underplate, Johnson Brothers 50
Spring Rose, Bowl, Vegetable, Round, Homer Laughlin, 8 In. 32
Spring Rose, Cup & Saucer, Homer Laughlin 14
Spring Song, Creamer, Homer Laughlin 36
Spring Song, Cup & Saucer, Homer Laughlin 30

Small Butter Dish

Butter pats are round dishes 3 ½ inches in diameter that held a square pat of butter at a dinner table. It can be confused with an ashtray, salt dish, doll dish, and even a saucer. There is an indentation in a saucer to hold a cup. A butter pat often has a rim.

Dinnerware, Poppy & Rose, Cup & Saucer, Decal, Homer Laughlin, 2 ⅝ In.
$16

Ruby Lane

Dinnerware, Verna, Dish, Leaf Shape, Handle, Blue Ridge, 10 x 9 ¾ In.
$75

Ruby Lane

Dinnerware, Wild Strawberry, Plate, Dinner, Blue Ridge, 9 ¼ In.
$23

Ruby Lane

Dionne Quintuplets, Doll Set, Composition, Original Outfits, Rompers, Bonnets, Box, 1930s, 7 In.
$895

Ruby Lane

Dionne Quintuplets, Doll Set, Composition, Wig, Name Pin, Basket, Madame Alexander, 8 In., 6 Piece
$390

Morphy Auctions

Dirk Van Erp, Vase, Gourd Shape, Hammered Copper, Patina, c.1911, 7 x 6 In.
$3,000

Rago Arts and Auction Center

Dirk Van Erp, Vase, Red Warty, Hammered Copper, Windmill Stamp, 1915-29, 8 x 7 ½ In.
$6,250

Rago Arts and Auction Center

Dionne Quintuplets, Doll Set, Madame Alexander, Original Clothes, Seesaw, 7 In.
$2,520

Ruby Lane

TIP

Go to antiques shows early; there may be plenty of antiques left at the end of the show, but the dealers are tired and not as eager to talk to customers.

Disneyana, Cookie Jar, Ludwig Von Drake, Mortarboard Lid, American Bisque, 1961, 9 In.
$173

Hake's Americana & Collectibles

Disneyana, Display, Mickey Mouse, Composition, Relief, Frame, Old King Cole, c.1935, 50 In.
$1,150

Hake's Americana & Collectibles

Disneyana, Doll, Minnie Mouse, Rag, Velveteen Covered, Wire Inserts, Metal Eyes, Felt, 6 In.
$744

Norman Heckler & Company

Sunnyvale, Plate, Dinner, Castleton, 1950s, 10 5/8 In. 33
Trousseau, Cup & Saucer, Castleton 51
Trousseau, Cup, Castleton 28
Verna, Dish, Leaf Shape, Handle, Blue Ridge, 10 x 9 3/4 In. .... *illus* 75
Wild Strawberry, Plate, Dinner, Blue Ridge, 9 1/4 In. .... *illus* 23
Yellow Nocturne, Plate, Dinner, Blue Ridge, 10 In. 31
Yellow Nocturne, Platter, Blue Ridge, 13 In. 73

DIONNE QUINTUPLETS were born in Canada on May 28, 1934. The publicity about their birth and their special status as wards of the Canadian government made them famous throughout the world. Visitors could watch the girls play; reporters interviewed the girls and the staff. Thousands of special dolls and souvenirs were made picturing the quints at different ages. Emilie died in 1954, Marie in 1970, Yvonne in 2001. Annette and Cecile still live in Canada.

Calendar, 1944, Girls, Nest In Tree, Frame, 13 x 16 In. 60
Doll, 5 Babies, Composition, Human Hair, Madame Alexander, 14 In. 1950
Doll Set, Composition, Original Outfits, Rompers, Bonnets, Box, 1930s, 7 In. .... *illus* 895
Doll Set, Composition, Wig, Name Pin, Basket, Madame Alexander, 8 In., 6 Piece .... *illus* 390
Doll Set, Madame Alexander, Original Clothes, Seesaw, 7 In. .... *illus* 2520
Doll's Crib, 1934, 6 x 19 1/4 In. 338
Fan, Girls In Highchairs, Wood Handle, 1934, 8 x 8 In. 49
Handkerchief, Bonnets & Bows, Blue, Pink, Signed, Tom Lamb, 8 x 8 In. 45
Handkerchief, Girls, Bears, Dolls, Blue, Red, 8 1/4 x 8 1/4 In. 55
Picture, Girls, On Stomachs, Frame, 10 x 13 In. 35
Pillow Cover, Burlap, Portraits, Maple Leaves, Pine Trees, Rising Sun, 1930s, 15 x 11 In. 55
Postcard, Girls, Sitting On Curb, Dr. Dafoe, World Copyright N.E.A., 1936, 5 x 3 In. 24
Soap, Figural, Castile, 1930s, 3 1/2 In., 5 Piece 49
Spoon, Girl, Name, On Handle, Silver Plate, Carlton, 1930s, 6 In., 5 Piece 50

DIRK VAN ERP was born in 1860 and died in 1933. He opened his own studio in 1908 in Oakland, California. He moved his studio to San Francisco in 1909 and the studio remained under the direction of his son until 1977. Van Erp made hammered copper accessories, including vases, desk sets, bookends, candlesticks, jardinieres, and trays, but he is best known for his lamps. The hammered copper lamps often had shades with mica panels.

Bookends, Copper, Monogrammed, MGR, 5 3/4 x 6 In. 307
Bowl, Squat, Inward Rounded Rim, 2 3/4 x 9 1/2 In. 615
Lamp, Copper, Hammered, 4-Panel Mica Shade, Ball Shape, c.1908, 15 x 14 In. 6500
Lamp, Copper, Hammered, 4-Panel Mica Shade, c.1920, 12 1/2 x 12 In. 3500
Vase, Gourd Shape, Hammered Copper, Patina, c.1911, 7 x 6 In. .... *illus* 3000
Vase, Hammered Copper, Red, Shouldered, Flat Rim, c.1900, 7 x 8 In. 3750
Vase, Red Warty, Hammered Copper, Windmill Stamp, 1915-29, 8 x 7 1/2 In. .... *illus* 6250

DISNEYANA is a collectors' term. Walt Disney and his company introduced many comic characters to the world. Collectors search for examples of the work of the Disney Studios and the many commercial products modeled after his characters, including Mickey Mouse and Donald Duck, and recent films, like *Beauty and the Beast* and *The Little Mermaid*.

Badge, Store, Mickey Mouse, Sincerely Yours, Mickey Mouse, Celluloid, 3 1/2 In. 219
Bank, Mickey & Minnie Mouse, In Wagon, Canister, Tin Lithograph, 1930s, 4 In. 316
Bank, Mickey & Minnie Mouse, Treasure Chest, Tin Litho, Minnie, Digging, 1930s, 2 x 3 In. 230
Bank, Mickey Mouse, Dime Register, Tin Litho, Gold Border, 1939, 3 x 3 In. 201
Book, Mickey Mouse, Magic Carpet, Softcover, Whitman, 1935, 3 1/2 x 4 In. 209
Boots, Davy Crockett Indian Fighter, Tan Leather, Fringe, Fur Trim, Box, c.1955, Size 13 230
Bowl, Mickey & Minnie Mouse, Green Rim, Glazed, 1930s, 7 In. Diam. 115
Button, Mickey Mouse Movie Club, Cheer Leader, Officer, 1930s, 2 1/4 In. 3795
Button, Mickey Mouse, As Santa, Meet Me At Hank's Toyland, 1932, 1 1/4 In. 306
Canister Set, Mickey & Minnie Mouse, China, Box, Japan, 1930s, 9 Piece 3897
Carousel Figure, Mickey Mouse, Wood, Walking, Carved, Painted, France, 1930s, 23 x 49 In. 7475
Cel, see Animation Art category.
Clock, Donald Duck Holding Clock, Ceramic, Painted, 1950s, 7 1/2 x 9 In. 115
Clock, Mickey Mouse, Wristwatch Shape, 9 1/2 x 36 In. 120
Comic Book, Uncle Scrooge, No. 386, March, 4-Color, Del Publishing, Carl Barks Story, 1952 280
Cookie Jar, Ludwig Von Drake, Mortarboard Lid, American Bisque, 1961, 9 In. .... *illus* 173
Display, Donald Duck, Bust, Sailor Cap, Lollipops, Composition, 1940s, 6 x 8 In. 1341
Display, Mickey Mouse, Composition, Relief, Frame, Old King Cole, c.1935, 50 In. .... *illus* 1150
Doll, Davy & Polly Crockett, Plastic, Sleep Eyes, Box, Fortune Toy, 1955, 7 In., Pair 168

Disneyana, Figurine, Centaurette, Fantasia, Ceramic, Painted, Glazed, Vernon Kilns, 8 In.
$506

Hake's Americana & Collectibles

Disneyana, Toy, Mickey Mouse, Rocker, Wood, Painted, Walt Disney Enterprises, c.1935, 35 x 23 In.
$417

Hake's Americana & Collectibles

Disneyana, Toy, Mickey Mouse, Telephone, Candlestick, Pressed Steel, N.N. Hill, c.1934, 7 In.
$380

Hake's Americana & Collectibles

Disneyana, Toy, Mickey Mouse, Whirligig, Balls Spin, Celluloid, Tin, Windup, Borgfeldt, 7 In.
$944

Bertoia Auctions

Disneyana, Wallpaper, Mickey & Minnie Mouse, Frame, 1930s, 25 x 38 In.
$230

Hake's Americana & Collectibles

Disneyana, Wastebasket, Mickey Mouse, Minnie & Friends, Boat, Tin Lithograph, 1936, 10 x 11 In.
$629

Norman Heckler & Company

Doll, Automaton, Mother & Child, Head Nods, Arms Lift, Phalibois, c.1880, 24 In.
$17,360

Theriault's

Doll, Buddy L, Phillips 66 Service Station Man, Lil Phil, 12 In.
$240

Showtime Auction Services

D

Doll, Carved Bone, Boy, Ink Drawn Features, Pin & Dowel Joints, Cap, Necktie, 1800s, 7 In.
$342

Theriault's

Doll, Door Of Hope, Wood Head, Cloth Body, Jointed Hips & Shoulders, c.1910, 12 In.
$2,128

Theriault's

Doll, Dressel, Uncle Sam, Bisque Socket Head, Glass Eyes, Composition, 10 In.
$502

Bertoia Auctions

Doll, Mickey Mouse, Fun-E-Flex, Wood Body, Flexible Metal Arms, Legs, 1930s, 7 In. 362
Doll, Mickey Mouse, Pie Eyes, Whiskers, Felt Ears, Steiff, 18 In. 1080
Doll, Minnie Mouse, Rag, Velveteen Covered, Wire Inserts, Metal Eyes, Felt, 6 In. .... *illus* 744
Doll, Pinocchio, Felt Face, Cloth Body, Painted Hair & Eyes, 16 In. 660
Doll, Snow White, Composition, Socket Head, Flirty Eyes, Black Mohair, Ideal, 1938, 22 In. 570
Drum, Mickey Mouse & Disney Friends, Tin Lithograph, Strap, Drumsticks, 1930s, 6 x 4 In. 127
Feeding Dish, Mickey, Banging Drum, Alphabet Border, Bavaria, c.1932, 7 ¾ In. 172
Figurine, Bambi, Standing, Sideward Glancing, Glazed Ceramic, 1947, 6 x 8 In. 230
Figurine, Centaurette, Fantasia, Ceramic, Painted, Glazed, Vernon Kilns, 8 In. .... *illus* 506
Figurine, Cinderella, Lovely Dress For Cinderelly, Glass Dome, 8 x 5 In. 431
Figurine, Donald Duck, Golfing, Checkered Hat, Club, Ceramic, Zaccagnini, c.1947, 8 In. 949
Figurine, Geppetto, Ceramic, Painted, Glazed, Brayton Laguna, c.1939, 8 In. 417
Figurine, Hippopotamus, Fantasia, Painted, Glazed Ceramic, Vernon Kilns, 1940, 5 ¼ In. 285
Figurine, Horace Horsecollar, Clarabelle Cow, Wood, Keith Kaonis, 1981, 10 In., 2 Piece............ 886
Figurine, Jiminy Cricket, Ceramic, Painted, Glazed, Brayton Laguna, c.1939, 5 ½ In. 380
Figurine, Mickey Mouse, Celluloid, Raised Hand, c.1949, 7 In. 172
Figurine, Mickey Mouse, Playing Banjo, Porcelain, Black & White, Rosenthal, 1932, 3 In. 575
Figurine, Minnie Mouse, Looking Down Shyly, Rosenthal, Germany, c.1932, 3 ¼ In. 3061
Figurine, Pinocchio, Looking Over Shoulder, School Books, Glazed, 1947, 6 In. 115
Figurine, Snow White, 7 Dwarfs Only, Chalkware, 7 Piece 195
Figurine, Snow White, 7 Dwarfs, Ceramic, 1947, 9 In., 5 ½ To 6 In. 374
Figurine, Tinkerbell, Standing, Slightly Bent Forward, Head Tilted, Wings, 1992, 10 In. 1076
Flashlight, Mickey Mouse, Mickey & Minnie In Woods, Tin Litho, Metal Cap, 6 In. 75
Footstool, Donald Duck, Angry Donald, Long Bill, Painted, Wood, 1930s, 7 x 15 In. 127
Game, Mickey Mouse, Bagatelle, Wood, Label, Marks Bros., c.1930, 12 x 23 x 5 In. 190
Game, Snow White & The Seven Dwarfs, Bagatelle, Chad Valley, England, 1949, 15 In. 361
Juicer & Cup, Mickey, Hands On Hips, Black, Blue Pants, Green Border, Germany, 1932 115
Lobby Card Set, Snow White & Seven Dwarfs, Glossy, 1958, 11 x 14 In., 8 Piece 115
Lunch Box, Disneyland, Castle, Rides, Metal, Aladdin, c.1957 230
Map, Disneyland, Linen Mounted, Theme Park, Characters, c.1958, 30 x 45 ¼ In. 127
Marionette, Donald Duck, Carved Wood, Sailor's Uniform, 22 In. 120
Match Holder, 3 Little Pigs, Singing, Dancing, Enameled, Red, Black, 1930s, 1 ½ x 1 ¼ In. 95
Movie Theater Display, Mickey Mouse, Steamboat Willie, Light-Up, Wood, 32 x 24 In. 854
Mug, Mickey Mouse, Dancing, Paragon, 1930s, 3 In. 173
Pail, Mickey Mouse, Tin Lithograph, Boat, Airplane, Happynak, 1950s, 5 In. 173
Panel, Mickey Mouse, Leaping Mickey, Harp Shape, Painted Wood, 1930s, 17 x 33 In. 285
Pencil Case, Mickey Mouse, Musical Mouse, Tin Litho, Piano, Saxophone, 1930s, 4 x 8 In. 2234
Pencil Sharpener, Pluto, Sitting, Bakelite, Round, 1930s, 1 In. 26
Perfume Bottle, Mickey Mouse, Porcelain, Gold, Face In Circle, Japan, 4 ¾ In. 369
Pin, Mickey Mouse, Enamel On Brass, Early 1930s, 1 ¼ In. 221
Pitcher, King Of Hearts, From Alice In Wonderland, Ceramic, Regal China, c.1951, 7 In. 281
Poster, Movie, Donald Duck, Chips Ahoy, Linen Mounted, 1956, 27 x 41 In. 765
Purse, Mickey Mouse, Whiting & Davis, Child's, c.1935 199
Purse, Minnie Mouse, Mesh, Painted Frame, Cohn & Rosenberger, c.1934, 2 ½ x 3 ¼ In. 173
Purse, Minnie, Mickey, Enameled, Chain, Snap Case, Cohn & Rosenberger, c.1934, 3 x 3 In. 207
Push Puppet, Donald Duck, Plastic, Kohner Brothers, 1960, 2 ½ In. 22
Radio, Snow White & Seven Dwarfs, Composition, 7 ½ x 7 ½ In. 540
Radio, Snow White & Dwarfs, Wood Frame, Acorn Knobs, Emerson, 1939, 11 x 8 In. 2280
Roadster, Mickey Mouse, Disney Parade, Tin Litho, Driver Mickey, Windup, 1950s, 11 In. 192
Rocking Chair, Mickey & Minnie Mouse, Painted, Kroehler, 1930s, Child's, 16 ½ x 27 In. 727
Rug, Mickey & Minnie, Airplane, Donald With Parachute, Frame, 48 x 30 In. 270
Shovel, 3 Little Pigs, Dancing, Tin Lithograph, Green, Ohio Art Co., c.1930, 11 In. 136
Shovel, Mickey & Minnie On Beach, Tin Litho, Wood Handle, Ohio Art, 1930s, 6 x 7 x 21 In. 595
Shovel, Mickey & Minnie, Pluto, Tin Litho, Beach Scene, 1930s, 7 x 12 In. 345
Sprinkling Can, 3 Little Pigs, Playing Instruments, Tin Lithograph, Blue, Ohio Art, 6 In. 379
Sprinkling Can, Mickey & Minnie, Tin Litho, 1930s, 3 x 6 In. 173
Sprinkling Can, Snow White & Seven Dwarfs, Tin Lithograph, Ohio Art, 6 ½ In. 173
Stickpin, Mickey Mouse, Embossed Mickey, Silvered Brass, Oval, 1932, ½ In. 115
Sugar, White Rabbit Lid, Red Heart, From Alice In Wonderland, Regal China, 5 ½ In. 281
Tea Set, Mickey & Minnie Mouse, Lusterware, Japan, Box, 1950s, 11 Piece 306
Tea Set, Snow White & The Seven Dwarfs, Tin Litho, Box, Ohio Art, Child's, 8 Piece.................. 186
Teapot, Donald Duck, Figural, Lid, Ceramic, Long Bill, Arm Handle, 8 In. 360
Teapot, Mad Hatter, Alice In Wonderland, Figural, c.1951, 9 ½ x 7 ½ In. 702
Tin, Mickey & Minnie, Just Married, Lid, Round, Wilson Bros., 6 ¼ In. 100
Tin, Mickey Mouse, Nephew, Sports, Hinged Lid, Hexagonal, Belgium, 1930s, 6 x 6 In. 90
Tin, Mickey Mouse, Superfine Mickey Mouse Cocoa, 1930s, 3 x 6 In. 209

Tin, Snow White, Dwarfs, Biscuit, Disneyland, Tin Lithograph, Hinged Lid, 1940, 8 x 13 In. 443
Toy, 3 Little Pigs, Drum, 2 Violins, Felt, Clockwork, Schuco, Germany, 4½ In., 3 Piece 413
Toy, Donald Duck, Crazy Car, Tin, Plastic, Windup, Marx, 1950s, 6 In. 216
Toy, Donald Duck, Drummer, Tin, Multicolor, Windup, Linemar, 5¾ In. 200
Toy, Donald Duck, Marching, With 3 Nephews, Rubber Rifles, Tin, Linemar, Box, 10 In. 561
Toy, Donald Duck, Skier, Tin & Plastic, Paint, Windup, 10¼ In. 60
Toy, Donald Duck, Whirligig, Celluloid, Multicolor, Windup, Japan, 7¼ In. 225
Toy, Dopey, Walker, Tin Lithograph, Clockwork, Yellow, Marx, Box, 8 In. 207
Toy, Mickey & Minnie Mouse, Acrobats, Celluloid Figures, Box, 14 In. 330
Toy, Mickey & Minnie Mouse, Handcar, Windup, 8 In. 240
Toy, Mickey Mouse, 2 Cardboard Mickey Figures, Metal Wheels, Bells, c.1934, 9 x 7 In. 569
Toy, Mickey Mouse, Airplane, Mickey Mouse Express, Tin Litho, Marx, 9½ In. 325
Toy, Mickey Mouse, Magician, The Great Mickey, Battery Operated, Linemar, 10 In. 413
Toy, Mickey Mouse, Pail, Beach Scene, Tin Lithograph, Bail Handle, 5¾ In. 425
Toy, Mickey Mouse, Race Car, Tin Lithograph, Blue, Mickey Driving, Windup, c.1936, 4 In. 120 to 270
Toy, Mickey Mouse, Rocker, Wood, Painted, Walt Disney Enterprises, c.1935, 35 x 23 In. .....*illus* 417
Toy, Mickey Mouse, Roller Skater, Tin Lithograph, Windup, Linemar, 6½ In. 500
Toy, Mickey Mouse, Telephone, Candlestick, Pressed Steel, N.N. Hill, c.1934, 7 In. ....*illus* 380
Toy, Mickey Mouse, Train, Mickey Mouse Express, Tin Litho, Windup, Box, 1950s, 10 x 10 In. 459
Toy, Mickey Mouse, Truck, Mousekemovers, Tin Lithograph, Friction, 8½ In. 480
Toy, Mickey Mouse, Washing Machine, Hand Crank, Footed, Tin, Ohio Art Co., 8 In. 175
Toy, Mickey Mouse, Washing Machine, Tin Litho, Crank, Plunger, Box, 1930s, 4 x 8 In. 1139
Toy, Mickey Mouse, Watering Can, Tin Litho, Loop Handle, Saxophone, Ohio Art Co., 9 In. 100
Toy, Mickey Mouse, Whirligig, Balls Spin, Celluloid, Tin, Windup, Borgfeldt, 7 In. ....*illus* 944
Toy, Mickey Mouse, Xylophone, Tin Lithograph, Windup, 5¾ In. 200
Toy, Mickey, Train Car, Stoker, Holding Shovel, Composition, Lionel, c.1935 253
Toy, Minnie Mouse, Doll, Fun-E-Flex, Wood, U.S.A., 6¾ In. 100
Toy, Minnie Mouse, Seamstress, Seated In Rocker, Multicolor, Tin, Windup, 7 In. 175
Toy, Pinocchio, Acrobat, Rocking Base, Tin Litho, Windup, Marx, 17 x 11 In. 236
Toy, Pinocchio, Doll, Composition Head, Wood Body, Ideal, Box, 7½ In. 75
Toy, Pinocchio, Figure, Wood, Paint, Jointed, Hat, Tie, Ideal, 19 In. 600
Toy, Pinocchio, Walker, Pronounced Nose, Tin Litho, Multicolor, Windup, Marx, 8½ In. 148
Toy, Pinocchio, Walking, Eyes Move, Tin Lithograph, Windup, Marx, Box, 8½ In. 649
Toy, Pluto, Drum Major, Holding Cane, Playing Kazoo, Tin, Windup, Linemar, Box, 6½ In. 360
Toy, Roller Coaster, Shooting Gallery, Fun House, Tin, Windup, Chein, 1950s, 20 x 10 In. 230
Wallpaper, Mickey & Minnie Mouse, Frame, 1930s, 25 x 38 In. ....*illus* 230
Wastebasket, Mickey Mouse, Minnie & Friends, Boat, Tin Lithograph, 1936, 10 x 11 In. .....*illus* 629
Watch, Pocket, Full Body, Chrome Metal Case, Ingersoll, 1939, 2 In. 253
Wristwatch, Donald Duck, Gold Luster, 3 Vinyl Bands, Box, Bradley, 1970s 218
Wristwatch, Snow White, 7 Dwarfs, Braided Strap, c.1939 121

DOCTOR, *see Dental and Medical categories.*

DOLL entries are listed by marks printed or incised on the doll, if possible. If there are no marks, the doll is listed by the name of the subject or country or maker. Notice that Barbie is listed under Mattel. G.I. Joe figures are listed in the Toy section. Eskimo dolls are listed in the Eskimo section and Indian dolls are listed in the Indian section. Doll clothes and accessories are listed at the end of this section. The twentieth-century clothes listed here are in mint condition.

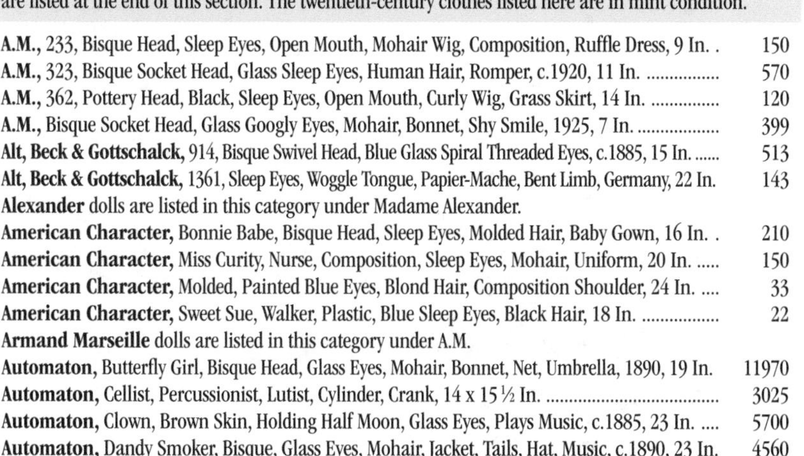

A.M., 233, Bisque Head, Sleep Eyes, Open Mouth, Mohair Wig, Composition, Ruffle Dress, 9 In. . 150
A.M., 323, Bisque Socket Head, Glass Sleep Eyes, Human Hair, Romper, c.1920, 11 In. 570
A.M., 362, Pottery Head, Black, Sleep Eyes, Open Mouth, Curly Wig, Grass Skirt, 14 In. 120
A.M., Bisque Socket Head, Glass Googly Eyes, Mohair, Bonnet, Shy Smile, 1925, 7 In. 399
Alt, Beck & Gottschalck, 914, Bisque Swivel Head, Blue Glass Spiral Threaded Eyes, c.1885, 15 In. 513
Alt, Beck & Gottschalck, 1361, Sleep Eyes, Woggle Tongue, Papier-Mache, Bent Limb, Germany, 22 In. 143
Alexander dolls are listed in this category under Madame Alexander.
American Character, Bonnie Babe, Bisque Head, Sleep Eyes, Molded Hair, Baby Gown, 16 In. . 210
American Character, Miss Curity, Nurse, Composition, Sleep Eyes, Mohair, Uniform, 20 In. 150
American Character, Molded, Painted Blue Eyes, Blond Hair, Composition Shoulder, 24 In. 33
American Character, Sweet Sue, Walker, Plastic, Blue Sleep Eyes, Black Hair, 18 In. 22
Armand Marseille dolls are listed in this category under A.M.
Automaton, Butterfly Girl, Bisque Head, Glass Eyes, Mohair, Bonnet, Net, Umbrella, 1890, 19 In. 11970
Automaton, Cellist, Percussionist, Lutist, Cylinder, Crank, 14 x 15½ In. 3025
Automaton, Clown, Brown Skin, Holding Half Moon, Glass Eyes, Plays Music, c.1885, 23 In. 5700
Automaton, Dandy Smoker, Bisque, Glass Eyes, Mohair, Jacket, Tails, Hat, Music, c.1890, 23 In. 4560
Automaton, English Bulldog, Mechanical, Papier-Mache, Movable Jaw, Wheels, c.1890, 12 x 22 In. 738

Doll, French, Bisque Swivel Head, Sculpted Sideburns, Glass Eyes, Kid Body, c.1875, 15 In.
$1,120

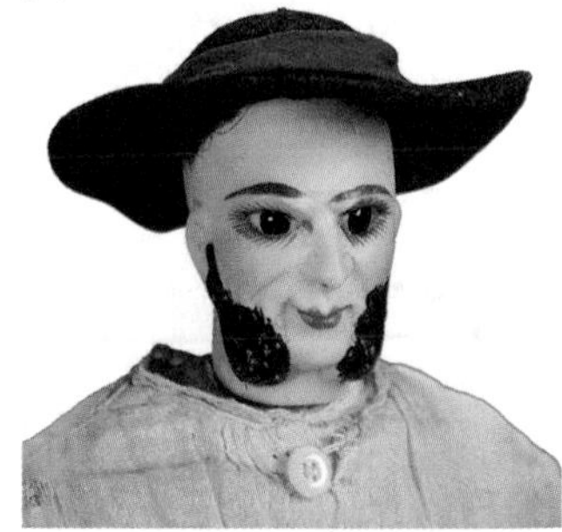

Theriault's

Doll, Gebruder Heubach, Bisque, Wrinkles, Muslin Body, Native American, c.1910, 13 In.
$1,792

Theriault's

Doll, German, Gentleman, Wood, Carved, 1 Piece Head & Torso, Glued Hair, Jointed, 34 In.
$5,415

Theriault's

Doll, German, Wax, Woman, Spinning Wheel, Silk Flowers, Glass Dome, c.1850, 8 In.
$168

Theriault's

Doll, Grodner-Tal, Wood, 1 Piece Head & Body, Dowel, Jointed, German, c.1840, 11 In.
$6,720

Theriault's

Doll, Izannah Walker, Cloth, Oil-Painted Face, Hair, Stitch-Jointed, Costume, c.1865, 18 In.
$32,480

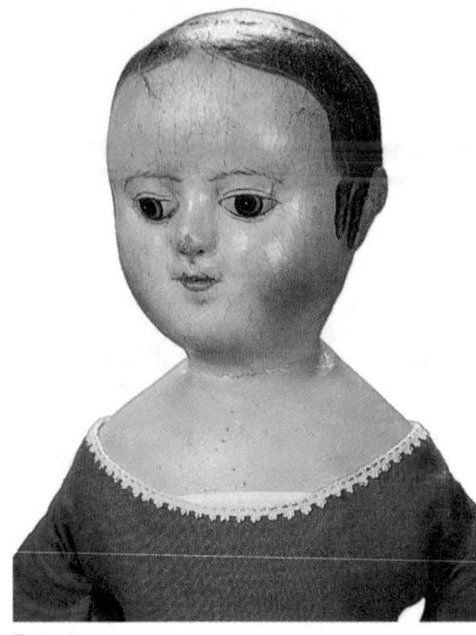

Theriault's

Doll, Japanese, Gosho, Martial Arts Student, Wood, Gofun, Sword, Maruhei, c.1930, 10 In.
$952

Theriault's

Doll, Japanese, Gosho, Wood, Carved, Gofun, Painted, Human Hair, Silk Robe, 14 In.
$21,280

Theriault's

Doll, K * R, 102, Boy, Bisque Socket Head, Composition, Wood, Ball-Jointed, c.1910, 12 In.
$26,880

Theriault's

Doll, Kathe Kruse, Cloth, Pressed & Oil-Painted Features, Jointed, Germany, c.1920, 16 In.
$5,040

Theriault's

Automaton, Girl Skipping Rope, China Doll, Cloth Dress, Tin Podium, 1890s, 5 ¾ In. 6490
Automaton, Mother & Child, Head Nods, Arms Lift, Phalibois, c.1880, 24 In. .... *illus* 17360
Automaton, Musician, Rocking Boat, Patrolling Guard, Windmill, Glass Dome, 19 ½ x 19 In. .. 1140
Automaton, Musicians, Lute, Cloth Base, 9 ¾ x 10 ½ In. 438
Automaton, Singing Bird, 2 Birds, Brass Cage, Domed, Germany, 11 In. 720
Automaton, Singing Bird, Cherubs, Instruments, Scrolling Leaves, Flowers, 2 ½ x 4 In. 1466
Automaton, Troubadour, Violin, Bisque Head, Glass Eyes, Mohair, Silk Costume, 1865, 15 In. ... 4560
Automaton, Vive La France, Bisque Head, Mohair, Balancing On Globe, Flag, 1889, 24 In. 9690
Automaton, Whistler, 2 Men, Instruments, He's A Jolly Good Fellow, K. Griesbaum, 14 x 12 In. . 620
Automaton, Whistler, Shabby Man, Hands In Pockets, Nods Head, K. Griesbaum, 15 x 3 In. 295
Automaton, Woman, Fan, Bisque Head, Glass Eyes, Mohair, Lorgnette, Lifts Fan, c.1890, 24 In. 6720
Barbie dolls are listed in this category under Mattel.
Benedictine Nun, Walker, Plastic, Turning Head, 1950s, 15 In. 95
Bergmann dolls are also in this category under S & H and Simon & Halbig.
Black dolls are also included in the Black category.
Bru Jne, Bebe, Bisque Swivel Head, Glass Eyes, Kid Body, Auburn Mohair, c.1885, 36 In. 22230
Bru Jne, Bisque Socket Head, Brevete Face, Kid Body, Paperweight Eyes, Silk Dress, 15 In. 5000
Bru Jne, Bisque Swivel Head, Amber Eyes, Lamb's Wool Wig, Plump Kid Body, 1882, 15 In. 9690
Bru Jne, Bisque Swivel Head, Blue Glass Eyes, Dimple, Kid Body, Human Hair, c.1885, 29 In. 14820
Buddy L, Phillips 66 Service Station Man, Lil Phil, 12 In. .... *illus* 240
Bullwinkle, Talking, Cloth, Stuffed, Vinyl Head & Antlers, Pull Ring, Mattel, Box, 11 In. 256
Bye-Lo, Bisque Head, Sleep Eyes, Cloth Body, Bonnet, Baby, 16 In. 240
Carved Bone, Boy, Ink Drawn Features, Pin & Dowel Joints, Cap, Necktie, 1800s, 7 In. .... *illus* 342
Cloth, Adams Sisters, Columbia Rag, Oil Cloth, Painted Features, Original Dress, N.Y., 30 In. 2360
Cloth, Charming Chase, Molded Face, Painted Hair, Stockinet, Jointed, 13 In. 480
Cloth, Embroidered Face, Wool Suit, Jointed, c.1900, 18 In. 125
Cloth, Maggie Bessie, Painted Face, Rosy Cheeks, c.1895, 17 In. 7800
Cloth, Soldier, Felt, Shoebutton Eyes, Jointed, Blue Uniform, Wood Sword, Boots, 18 In. 561
Composition, Sleep Eyes, Mohair Wig, Ideal, Box, 1930s, 17 In. 732
Denamur, Bisque Socket Head, Golden Brown Skin, Amber Eyes, Mohair, c.1888, 20 In. 3990
Door Of Hope, Wood Head, Cloth Body, Jointed Hips & Shoulders, c.1910, 12 In. .... *illus* 2128
Dressel, Uncle Sam, Bisque Socket Head, Glass Eyes, Composition, 10 In. .... *illus* 502
E.H. Germany, Braided Wig, Cloth Pin-Jointed Body, Bisque Lower Arms, 12 In. 49
Eden Bebe, Bisque Socket Head, Glass Eyes, Mohair, Folklore Costume, c.1900, 14 In. 1482
Effanbee, Barbara Ann, Composition, Sleep Eyes, Open Mouth, Teeth, Human Hair, 17 In. 400
Effanbee, Patsy Joan, Composition, Curly Mohair Wig, Sleep Eyes, Hat, 16 In. 180
Effanbee, Patsy Ann, Composition, Green Sleep Eyes, Brass Heart Bracelet, 19 In. 121
Effanbee, Patsy Lou, Composition, Brown Sleep Eyes, Blush, 22 In. 132
Effanbee, Skippy, Composition Socket Head, Painted Hair, Pug Nose, Uniform, 1935, 14 In. 171
Effanbee, Skippy, Composition, Molded, Painted Features, Brown Shorts, Tie, 13 ½ In. 118
Folk Art, Cloth Body, Wood Face, Painted, Leather Hands & Feet, 1800s, 23 In. 118
Football Player, Composition Head, Molded Hair, Smiling, Cloth Body, Jersey, Felt Helmet......... 375
French, Bisque Head, Paperweight Eyes, Long Human Hair, Composition, Festival Dress, 9 In. .. 510
French, Bisque Shoulder Head, Blue Glass Eyes, Lamb's Wool Wig, Music Box, 1890, 13 In. 513
French, Bisque Socket Head, Glass Sleep Eyes, Human Hair, Bourgogne Costume, c.1930, 21 In. 855
French, Bisque Swivel Head, Blue Glass Eyes, Mohair Wig, Kid Poupee Body, 1860, 16 In. 5244
French, Bisque Swivel Head, Blue Glass Eyes, Mohair Wig, Purple Silk Gown, c.1865, 13 In. 4332
French, Bisque Swivel Head, Sculpted Sideburns, Glass Eyes, Kid Body, c.1875, 15 In. .... *illus* 1120
French, Cloth Swivel Head, Side-Glancing Eyes, Mohair, Muslin, Alsatian Costume, 1930, 16 In. 399
Fura, Celluloid, Black Forest Region, Sleep Eyes, Bollenhut Hat, 13 In. 25
G.I. Joe figures are listed in the Toy category.
Gaultier, Bebe, Bisque Socket Head, Paperweight Eyes, Wood Body, Closed Mouth, 7 In. 711
Gaultier, Bebe, Bisque, Brown Eyes, Wood, Composition, Jointed, Lamb's Wool Muff, 14 In. 3540
Gaultier, Bisque Head, Glass Eyes, Dimple, Human Hair, Composition, Jointed, 1888, 24 In. 4560
Gaultier, Bisque Socket Head, Kid Body, Mohair Wig, Paperweight Eyes, Closed Mouth, 16 In. ... 950
Gaultier, Bisque Swivel Head, Glass Eyes, Poupee Body, Kid, Wedding Gown, c.1875, 20 In. 2850
Gebruder Heubach dolls may also be listed in this category under Heubach.
Gebruder Heubach, Bisque Socket Head, Glass Sleep Eyes, Mohair, Composition, 1915, 12 In. . 570
Gebruder Heubach, Bisque, Wrinkles, Muslin Body, Native American, c.1910, 13 In. .... *illus* 1792
German, Bisque Head, Brown Glass Sleep Eyes, Mohair, Silk Ribbon Bonnet, 1927, 20 In. 1995
German, Bisque Head, Chubby Face, Blue Side-Glancing Googly Eyes, Mohair, c.1920, 7 In. 570
German, Bisque Head, Paperweight Eyes, Blond Mohair Wig, Composition Body, 17 In. 1320
German, Bisque Head, Sleep Eyes, Curly Mohair, Composition Body, Festival Dress, 14 In. 90
German, Bisque Socket Head, Ebony Color Skin, Brown Sleep Eyes, Fleece Wig, 1912, 20 In. 5130
German, Gentleman, Wood, Carved, 1-Piece Head & Torso, Glued Hair, Jointed, 34 In. .... *illus* 5415
German, Soldier, Bisque Shoulder Head, Painted Hair, Mustache, Muslin Body, c.1890, 7 In. 855
German, Wax, Woman, Spinning Wheel, Silk Flowers, Glass Dome, c.1850, 8 In. .... *illus* 168

Doll, Kestner, 221, Toddler, Bisque, Googly Eyes, Mohair, Wood, Composition, Jointed, 12 In.
$3,920

Theriault's

Doll, Lenci, Dutch Girl, Felt, Pressed, Mohair Curls, Felt Costume, Wood Clogs, 17 In.
$826

Bertoia Auctions

D

Doll, Miss Curity, Nurse, Socket Head, Composition, Blue Sleep Eyes, Blonde Mohair Wig, 1940s, 21 In.
$912

Theriault's

Doll, Ravca, Aged Man, Stockinet, Stitched Face, Mohair Wig, Straw Filled, c.1930, 18 In.
$1,254

Theriault's

Doll, Simon & Halbig, 1358, Black, Bisque Socket Head, Wig, Composition, c.1900, 13 In.
$3,360

Theriault's

Doll, Simon & Halbig, Bisque Head, Hair Wig, Composition, Ball-Jointed, c.1900, 23 In.
$47,600

Theriault's

Doll, Steiner, Bebe, Bisque Socket Head, Glass Eyes, Mohair Wig, Composition, c.1884, 8 In.
$17,920

Theriault's

Doll, Troll, Hard Plastic, Fuzzy Hair, Felt Outfit, Thomas Dam, Box, 1960s
$30

Doll, Ventriloquist, Happy Hazzard, 12 Functions, McElroy Brothers, 1930s, 42 In.
$49,450

Crown

Gibson Girl, Emma Clear, Teal Dress, Tilted Hat, Blond, Cloth, Porcelain 375
Grodner-Tal, Wood, 1-Piece Head & Body, Dowel, Jointed, German, c.1840, 11 In. ....*illus* 6720
Half Dolls are listed in the Pincushion Doll category.
Handwerck, 109, Bisque Socket Head, Sleep Eyes, Open Mouth, Composition Body, 22 In. 240
Herman Munster, Hard Plastic Body, Vinyl Head, Rooted Hair, Box, 1964, 5 x 8 In. 561
Hertel & Schwab, 163, Googly, Bisque Head, Glass Side-Glancing Sleep Eyes, 12 In. 2779
Heubach, see also Gebruder Heubach.
Heubach, 300, Bisque Head, Toddler Body, Blond Wig, Composition, 16 In. 210
Heubach, 7975, Bisque Head, Jointed Composition Body, Bonnet, Jumper, 12 In. 1200
Heubach, Baby Stuart, Bisque Socket Head, Intaglio Eyes, Composition, Bonnet, 6 In. 150
Heubach, Boy, Bisque, Intaglio Eyes, Human Hair, Wood, Composition, High Knee Joints, 17 In. . . 590
Heubach, Whistling Jim, Bisque Head, Sculpted Hair, Puckered Rim, Sailor Outfit, 1915, 13 In. 684
Ideal, Deanna Durbin, Composition, Sleep Eyes, Open Mouth, Human Hair, Jointed, 24 In. 200
Ideal, Samantha, Bewitched, Posable, Sparkle Dress, Hat, Broom, Box, 1965, 10 x 14 In. 1898
Ideal, Saucy Walker, Plastic, Saran Wig, Sleep Eyes, Open Mouth, 2 Teeth, c.1955, 22 In. 345
Indian Dolls are listed in the Indian category.
Izannah Walker, Cloth, Oil-Painted Face, Hair, Stitch-Jointed, Costume, c.1865, 18 In. .....*illus* 32480
J.D.K. Dolls are also listed in this category under Kestner.
Japanese, Beautiful Lady, Wood, Gofun, Glass Eyes, Kimono, c.1900, 20 In. 3920
Japanese, Gosho, Martial Arts Student, Wood, Gofun, Sword, Maruhei, c.1930, 10 In. ....*illus* 952
Japanese, Gosho, Monkey Trainer & Monkey, Wood, Gofun, Silk, Papier-Mache Monkey, 12 In. . 3472
Japanese, Gosho, Wood, Carved, Gofun, Painted, Human Hair, Silk Robe, 14 In. ....*illus* 21280
Japanese, Ningyo Of Tenjin, Wood, Sculpted, Gofun, Silk, Brocade, c.1915, 13 In. 896
Japanese, Puppet, Osome, Bunraku Character, Wood, Gofun, Tie-Dyed Silk, Velvet, 45 In. 6160
Jester, Bisque Clown Face, Painted Wood Legs, Holds Cymbals, Claps When Squeezed, 12 In. 826
Jumeau, Bebe Triste, Jester, Pressed Bisque Socket Head, Blue Glass Eyes, Boy, c.1885, 33 In. 22230
Jumeau, Bebe, Bisque Head, Paperweight Eyes, Open Mouth, Human Hair, Jointed Body, 33 In. 660
Jumeau, Bebe, Bisque Socket Head, Composition Body, Mohair Wig, Open Mouth, Teeth, 18 In. 650
Jumeau, Bebe, Bisque Socket Head, Glass Eyes, Mohair Wig, Composition, c.1890, 11 In. 7900
Jumeau, Bisque Head, Brown Paperweight Eyes, Pierced Ears, Mohair, Jointed, Bebe, 23 In. 1416
Jumeau, Bisque Head, Full Cheeks, Glass Enamel Eyes, Mohair, Ball-Jointed, 1878, 12 In. 9120
Jumeau, Bisque Socket Head, Glass Eyes, Human Hair, Jointed Composition Body, 1888, 24 In. . 3420
Jumeau, Fashion, Bisque Swivel Head, Glass Eyes, Mohair Wig, Kid Body, 1878, 17 In. 2736
K * R, 101, Marie, Bisque Head, Blue Eyes, Blond Braided Wig, Composition Body, 10 In. 830
K * R, 101, Marie, Bisque Socket Head, Painted Eyes, Mohair, Ball-Jointed, c.1910 1938
K * R, 101, Peter, Bisque Socket Head, Painted Eyes, Pouty Mouth, Curly Skin Wig, 8 In. 420
K * R, 102, Boy, Bisque Socket Head, Composition, Wood, Ball-Jointed, c.1910, 12 In. ....*illus* 26880
K * R, 114, Gretchen, Bisque Socket Head, Pout, Composition, Ball-Jointed, 1910, 10 In. 2052
K * R, 114, Hans, Bisque Head, Painted, Blond Wig, Wood, Composition, Jointed, 23 In. 885
K * R, 116, Baby, Domed Bisque Socket Head, Sculpted Hair, Glass Sleep Eyes, c.1912, 15 In. 855
K * R, Bisque Socket Head, Sleep Eyes, Dimples, Open Mouth, Mohair, Jointed, 14 In. 200
Kathe Kruse, Cloth, Boy, Molded Head & Separate Thumb, Blue Pinafore, Straw Hat, 15 In. 1180
Kathe Kruse, Cloth, Girl, Swivel Head, Jointed Shoulders & Hips, Blond Mohair, 14 In. 531
Kathe Kruse, Cloth, Molded Hair & Face, Painted, Red Hat, 17 In. 49
Kathe Kruse, Cloth, Molded Painted Hair, Red Dress, c.1910, 17 In. 510
Kathe Kruse, Cloth, Pressed & Oil-Painted Features, Jointed, Germany, c.1920, 16 In. ....*illus* 5040
Kathe Kruse, Du Mein, Sand Baby, Stockinet, Molded, Painted, Weighted, 20 In. 1180
Kathe Kruse, Synthetic Head, Human Hair Wig, Cloth Body, Painted Features, Signed, 14 In. ... 125
Kestner Dolls are also in this category under J.D.K.
Kestner, 18, Bisque Head, Glass Eyes, Ball-Jointed, Composition Body, Closed Mouth, 29 In. 3088
Kestner, 221, Toddler, Bisque, Googly Eyes, Mohair, Wood, Composition, Jointed, 12 In. .....*illus* 3920
Kestner, 307, Bisque, Glass Eyes, Blond Mohair, Jointed Shoulders & Hips, 8 In. 450
Kestner, Asian Boy, Bisque, Brown Sleep Eyes, Black Human Hair, Silk Costume, 16 In. 2242
Kestner, Baby Jean, Bisque Socket Head, Glass Sleep Eyes, Lamb's Wool Wig, 1915, 19 In. 456
Kestner, Bisque Head, Open Mouth, Blond Mohair Wig, Kid Body, Brown Eyes, c.1900, 23 In. 270
Kestner, Bisque, Baby, Blue Eyes, Rosy Cheeks, White Dress, Germany, Marked 200
Kestner, Shoulder Head, Sleep Eyes, Open Mouth, Blond Wig, Kid Body, Gusseted, 21 In. 210
Kestner, Toddler, Bisque Socket Head, Glass Sleep Eyes, Teeth, Blond Mohair, c.1918, 10 In. 684
Kewpie Dolls are listed in the Kewpie category.
Kley & Hahn, Toddler, Bisque Head, Smile, Brown Intaglio Eyes, Painted Hair, Jointed, 20 In. ... 590
Lenci, Dutch Girl, Felt, Pressed, Mohair Curls, Felt Costume, Wood Clogs, 17 In. ....*illus* 826
Lenci, Girl, Felt, Pouty, Side-Glancing Eyes, Mohair Wig, Pink Dress, Hat, Purse, 17 In. 480
Lerch, Papier-Mache, Shoulder Head, Molded Features, Cloth & Leather Body, c.1860, 31 In. 1652
Limbach, Bisque, Articulated, Painted Blond Hair, Pouty Mouth, Germany, 4¾ In. 62
Little Lulu, Cloth, Stuffed, Linen, Felt Hat, Ribbon, Braided Hair, Knickerbocker, 1940s, 18 In. .. 177
Madame Alexander, Amy, Hard Plastic, Floss Hair, Loop Curls, Little Women Series, 14 In. 240
Madame Alexander, Baby Genius, Composition, Plastic, Cloth, Christening Gown, 17 In. 102

Doll, Ventriloquist, Walking, Carved Wood, Slot Jaw, Winks, Spitter, c.1955, 50 In.
$2,415

Crown

Doll Clothes, Dress & Bonnet, Linen, Drop Waist, Embroidered, Lace, Sash, c.1885, For 12-In. Doll
$896

Theriault's

Doorstop, Boy, Holding Fruit Basket, Hollow Half Round, Paint, c.1920, 9 ¼ In.
$474

James D. Julia Auctioneers

Doorstop, Cat, Modernistic, Figural, Cast Iron, Black Paint, Hubley, 5 x 10 In.
$655

Showtime Auction Services

Doorstop, Cat, Seated, Paint, Cast Iron, Hubley, 9 In.
$177

Hess Auction Group

Madame Alexander, Ballerina, Plastic, Blond Wig, Pink Satin & Tulle Dress, 22 In. 424
Madame Alexander, Jeannie Walker, Brown Sleep Eyes, 1940s, 18 In. 55
Madame Alexander, Lissy, Bride, Jointed, White Dress & Veil, 1950s, 11 ½ In. 124
Madame Alexander, Little Genius, Composition, Brown Sleep Eyes, Mohair, 1940s, 18 In. 99
Madame Alexander, Scarlett, Composition, Green Velvet Coat, Human Hair, 1939, 15 In. 800
Madame Alexander, Sonja Henie, Skater, Composition, Socket Head, Hair, Box, 1945, 21 In. 741
Marionette, Albert Einstein, Plaster, Paint, White Lab Coat, Vest, Certificate, 26 In. 60
Martha Chase, Mammy, Stockinet Body, White Apron, Red Head Scarf, c.1900, 26 In. 4920
Mattel, Barbie, Ash Blond, Pink Lips, Pink & Green Bathing Suit, Box, 1970 300
Mattel, Barbie, Blond Bubble Cut, Red Swimsuit, Heels, Stand, Booklet, Box, 1963 325
Mattel, Barbie, Blond Ponytail, Swimsuit, Black Stripes, 35th Anniversary, Box........ 20
Mattel, Barbie, Blond, Malibu, Box, 1970 226
Mattel, Barbie, Blond, Polka Dot Dress, White Boots, 1966 45
Mattel, Barbie, Brunette Bubble Cut, Green & Black Long Dress 55
Mattel, Barbie, No. 3, Brunette Ponytail, Babydoll Nightgown, 1960........ 350
Mattel, Barbie, No. 4, Brunette Ponytail, Striped Swimsuit 400
Mattel, Barbie, Pale Blond, Orange Lips, Striped Swimsuit, Box, 1965........ 795
Mattel, Barbie, Short Red Hair, Side-Glancing Eyes, Red Dress, 1965........ 195
Mattel, Barbie, Strawberry Blond Bubble Cut, Pink Lips, Red Swimsuit, c.1964........ 38
Mattel, Ken, Blond, Open Hands, Print Shirt, Brown Pants, 1968, 12 In. 40
Mego Corp., Sonny & Cher, White Shirt, Jeans, Long Red Dress, 1976, 12 In. 58
Miss Curity, Nurse, Socket Head, Composition, Blue Sleep Eyes, Blonde Mohair Wig, 1940s, 21 In. *illus* 912
Mr. Magoo, Plastic, Green Felt Jacket, Hat, 1962, 15 ½ In. 120
Nun, Composition, Sleep Eyes, Lashes, Closed Mouth, Habit, 21 In. 150
Paper dolls are listed in their own category.
Papier-Mache, Black Man, Minstrel, Playing Banjo, Velvet Base, Gilt Ball Feet, France, 31 In. ... 9120
Papier-Mache, Clown, Socket Head, Glass Sleep Eyes, White Mohair, Butterflies, c.1890, 13 In. . 684
Papier-Mache, Eden Clown, Socket Head, Blue Glass Eyes, Hat, Mohair Wig, c.1890, 15 In. 798
Papier-Mache, Girl, Flowers, Swivel Head, Enamel Eyes, Mohair, Mechanical, c.1850, 11 In. 4902
Papier-Mache, Girl, Sculpted Hair, Painted Eyes, Muslin, Germany, c.1820, 6 In. 2052
Papier-Mache, Monkey, Playing Harp, Brown Glass Eyes, Fangs, Mohair, c.1880, 18 In. 22800
Parian, Dancing Woman, Red Dress, Lace, Revolves On Lead Base, Pull String, Germany, 9 In. . 236
Pincushion dolls are listed in their own category.
Porcelain, Shoulder Head, Cloth Body, Bisque Arms & Legs, Silk Gown, Painted Boots, 12 In. ... 89
Puppet, Policeman, Fabric Body, Hat, Bowtie, Smiling, c.1905, 23 ½ In. 542
Ravca, Aged Man, Stockinet, Stitched Face, Mohair Wig, Straw Filled, c.1930, 18 In. ....*illus* 1254
S & H dolls are also listed here as Bergmann and Simon & Halbig.
S.F.B.J., 238, Bisque Head, Jewel Eyes, Open Mouth, Teeth, Human Hair, Wood Body, 19 In. 1560
S.F.B.J., Bisque Socket Head, Sleep Eyes, Composition & Wood Body, Open Mouth, 14 In. 300
Schoenhut, Clown, Wood, Green, Purple, Hat, 10 In. 75
Schoenhut, Miss Dolly, Wood, Sleepy Eyes, Mohair Wig, Mouth Opens, Spring-Jointed, 16 In. ... 125
Schoenhut, Wood, Carved Socket Head, Blue Eyes, Blond Mohair, Spring-Jointed, 15 In. 969
Schoenhut, Wood, Intaglio Eyes, Mohair Wig, Jointed, Cotton Dress, Pinafore, 18 In. 850
Schoenhut, Wood, Socket Head, Brown Sleep Eyes, Mohair Wig, Spring-Jointed, 1911, 22 In. 399
Shirley Temple dolls are included in the Shirley Temple category.
Simon & Halbig dolls are also listed here under Bergmann and S & H.
Simon & Halbig, 719, Bisque Socket Head, Sleep Eyes, Pouty, Dimple, Mohair, Kid Body, 18 In. 750
Simon & Halbig, 887, Bisque, Swivel Head, Glass Sleep Eyes, Mohair, Layette, c.1890, 6 In. 1083
Simon & Halbig, 1078, Child, Brown, Bisque Head, Open Mouth, Black Mohair, Hat, 13 In. 570
Simon & Halbig, 1159, Flapper, Bisque Socket Head, Glass Sleep Eyes, Mohair, 13 In. 912
Simon & Halbig, 1294, Bisque Head, Sleep Eyes, Curly Mohair, Composition, Walks, 19 In. 330
Simon & Halbig, 1358, Black, Bisque Socket Head, Wig, Composition, c.1900, 13 In. ....*illus* 3360
Simon & Halbig, Asian, Bisque Head, Composition, Wig, Sleep Eyes, Open Mouth, 17 In. 1950
Simon & Halbig, Asian, Bisque Socket Head, Sleep Eyes, Black Mohair, Jointed, 19 In. 850
Simon & Halbig, Asian, Bisque, Glass Eyes, Swivel Neck, Black Mohair, Kimono, 5 In. 420
Simon & Halbig, Bisque Head & Body, Blond Wig, Blue Eyes, Bonnet, 6 In. 830
Simon & Halbig, Bisque Head, Glass Eyes, Lashes, Blond Wig, Composition Body, 42 In. 3555
Simon & Halbig, Bisque Head, Glass Sleep Eyes, Dimple, Mohair, Jointed, c.1900, 12 In. 627
Simon & Halbig, Bisque Head, Hair Wig, Composition, Ball-Jointed, c.1900, 23 In. ....*illus* 47600
Simon & Halbig, Bisque Socket Head, Glass Sleep Eyes, Mohair, Composition, 1910, 18 In. 8550
Simon & Halbig, Bisque, Socket Head, Sleep Eyes, Blond Human Hair, Marked, c.1912, 13 In. .. 1008
Simon & Halbig, Girl, Bisque Head, Blue Sleep Eyes, Open Mouth, Wood, Composition Body, 22 In. ... 236
Sonneberg, Bisque Socket Head, Glass Eyes, Mohair Wig, Composition Body, c.1884, 17 In. 1036
Sonneberg, Mary, Bisque Socket Head, Glass Eyes, Mohair, Lamb, Box, c.1890, 7 In. 2736
Steiner, Bebe, Bisque Socket Head, Glass Eyes, Mohair Wig, Composition, c.1884, 8 In. ......*illus* 17920
Steiner, Bisque Socket Head, Glass Eyes, Mohair, Jointed, Bonnet, 1889, 24 In. 4560
Sweet Dolly, Plastic, Saran Hair, Sleep Eyes, 16 In. 55

Talking, Dr. Seuss, Cat In The Hat, Vinyl Head, Cloth Body, Mattel, Box, 1970, 11 In. 173
Terri Lee, Hard Plastic, Blond Wig, Straw Hat, Red Striped Outfit, Box, 16 In. 195
Theroude, Papier-Mache, Glides, Enamel Eyes, White Mohair Wig, 1850, 17 In. 5700
Troll, Hard Plastic, Fuzzy Hair, Felt Outfit, Thomas Dam, Box, 1960s.......... *illus* 30
Ventriloquist Dummy, Black Girl, Wood, Carved, Painted, Braided Hair, Cloth Arms, Legs, 25 In. 708
Ventriloquist, Happy Hazzard, 12 Functions, McElroy Brothers, 1930s, 42 In. .... *illus* 49450
Ventriloquist, Walking, Carved Wood, Slot Jaw, Winks, Spitter, c.1955, 50 In. .... *illus* 2415
Wax, Blue Inset Eyes, Linen, Horsehair Stuffing, Silk Gown & Bonnet, c.1890, 12 In. 295
Wax, Woman, Shoulder Head, Cloth Body, Blue Glass Eyes, Blue Wool Suit, 1880s, 16 In. 472
Wood, Queen Anne Style, 1-Piece Head & Torso, Human Hair, Spoon Arms & Legs, 17 In. 1180
Wood, Queen Anne Style, Painted, Gesso, Human Hair, Antique Fabric, c.1800, 19 In. 1416

DOLL CLOTHES

Dress & Bonnet, Linen, Drop Waist, Embroidered, Lace, Sash, c.1885, For 12-In. Doll.......... *illus* 896
Dress, Cream & Aqua Silk & Brocade, Blue Bonnet, 2 Piece, 15 In. 207
Jeans, Red & White Striped Top, c.1960 55
Outfit, Ken, Doctor, Hankie, Bag, Stethoscope, Pants, Jacket, No. 793.......... 45

DONALD DUCK *items are included in the Disneyana category.*

DOORSTOPS have been made in all types of designs. The vast majority of the doorstops sold today are cast iron and were made from about 1890 to 1930. Most of them are shaped like people, animals, flowers, or ships. Reproductions and newly designed examples are sold in gift shops.

2 Quail, On Branch In Tall Grass, Fred Everett, Hubley, 7 In. 826
3 Geese, Walking, Oval Base, Cast Iron, Hubley, 8 ¼ In. 360
3 Gypsy Street Singers, Painted, Cast Iron, Hubley, 7 In. 885
Aunt Jemima, Hands On Hips, Wide Eyes, Red, Yellow, Cast Iron, 10 In. 1652
Babe Ruth, Figural, Swinging Bat, Uniform, Round Green Base, Cast Iron, 1940s, 9 In. 167
Bathing Beauties, 2 Bathers Under Parasol, Fish, Art Deco, Cast Iron, Hubley, 11 In. 413
Bear, Standing, Dunce Hat, Silver Paint, Round Base, Cast Iron, c.1920, 20 In. 593
Bellhop, Black, White Uniform, Luggage, Cast Iron, Creations Co., 7 ½ In. 1416
Bellhop, Uniform, Green, Yellow, Judd & Co., 8 ½ In. 927
Black Child, Reaching Up, Nude, Cast Iron, Base, c.1900, 17 x 7 In. 554
Black Man Sitting On Cotton Bale, Striking Match, Cast Iron & Metal, 9 x 7 In. 1888
Black Man Sitting On Cotton Bale, Top Hat, Cast Iron, c.1900, 8 ¾ In. 750
Boy, Holding Fruit Basket, Hollow Half Round, Paint, c.1920, 9 ¼ In. .... *illus* 474
Buddha, Draped Robe, Legs Crossed, Cast Iron, 9 In. 1180
Butler, Blue Uniform, Black Bowtie, Checkered Floor Base, Bradley & Hubbard, 11 In. 325
Cabin, Edgar Allen Poe, Cast Iron, Bradley & Hubbard, 6 ½ In. 649
Calla Lilies, Leaves, Blue Vase, Base, Hubley, 7 x 5 ¼ In. 413
Cap'n Eri, Standing In Boat, Holding Oar, Yellow Raincoat, Paint, Cast Iron, c.1920, 7 In. 889
Cat, Modernistic, Figural, Cast Iron, Black Paint, Hubley, 5 x 10 In. .... *illus* 655
Cat, Seated, Paint, Cast Iron, Hubley, 9 In. .... *illus* 177
Cat, Sitting, Black, Lean Tall Figure, Ears Pointed Up, Cast Iron, c.1920, 10 In. 356
Claw Foot, Cast Iron, 14 ¾ In. 36
Dahlias, Basket, Cast Iron, 1920s, 9 x 7 In. 135
Daisy Bowl, Rounded Bouquet, Green Bowl, Cast Iron, Hubley, 7 ½ In. 236
Dog, Black & White, Fido Collar, Pillow, Hubley, 5 ½ x 7 ½ In. 369
Dog, Bloodhound, Iron, Skinny, Curved Body, Sitting Up, Tail Curled Up, c.1920, 15 In. 356
Dog, Boston Terrier, Cast Iron, Hubley, 10 ¼ x 10 ⅛ In. 97
Dog, Boston Terrier, Sitting With Paw Up To Door, Full Figure, Cast Iron, 10 In. 270
Dog, Boston Terrier, Standing, Cast Iron, Hubley, 10 In. .... *illus* 236
Dog, Bull Mastiff, Standing, Paint, Cast Iron, 10 ½ In. 570
Dog, Deco, Orange, Paint Geometrics, Art Deco Style, Cast Iron, 7 ¼ In. .... *illus* 295
Dog, English Setter, Cast Iron, Hubley, 15 ½ x 18 ½ In. 97
Dog, French Bulldog, Seated, Full Figure, Black & White, Cast Iron, Hubley, 1939, 7 x 8 In. 150
Dog, French Bulldog, Sitting, Bug Eyes, Large Ears, Cast Iron, Hubley, 8 In. 240
Dog, Gray, Bone In Mouth, 8 In. 75
Dog, Pekingese, Brown, Cast Iron, Hubley, 9 ¾ In. 531
Dog, Pointer, Paw Up, Pointing Tail, Cast Iron, Paint, 14 In. 150
Dog, Scottie, Cast Iron, Hubley, 11 x 8 ⅜ In. 60
Dog, Spaniel, Seated, Multicolor, Square Base, Majolica, c.1890, 9 ½ In. 2640
Dog, Wolfhound Borzoi, Standing, Cream & Black Paint, Cast Iron, Hubley, 9 ⅞ In. 120
Dolly Dimple, Googly Eyes, Yellow Dress & Bonnet, Cast Iron, Hubley, 7 ¾ In. 236
Door Porter, William IV, Flowers, Instruments, Paint, Bronze, Porcelain, 18 x 7 In., Pair.......... 1353
Duck, Top Hat, Walking, Wings Folded Behind Back, Square Base, Cast Iron, 8 In. 660

Check the Screws

Boston Terrier iron doorstops are so popular they have been reproduced. Look at the heads of screws that join the two halves of the body. If they are Phillips-head screws, it's a modern copy.

D

Doorstop, Dog, Boston Terrier, Standing, Cast Iron, Hubley, 10 In.
$236

Bertoia Auctions

Doorstop, Dog, Deco, Orange, Paint Geometrics, Art Deco Style, Cast Iron, 7 ¼ In.
$295

Bertoia Auctions

Doorstop, Flowers, Gladiolas, Cast Iron, Hubley, No. 489, 10 In.
$295

Bertoia Auctions

Doorstop, Parlor Maid, Cocktails On Tray, Cast Iron, Impressed FISH, Hubley, c.1920, 9 In.
$2,666

James D. Julia Auctioneers

Doorstop, Poinsettia, Clay Pot, Square Base, Cast Iron, Paint, Judd Co., 10 x 5 In.
$649

Bertoia Auctions

Doorstop, Red Riding Hood, Wolf, Embossed, Cast Iron, Nuydea Foundry, c.1920, 10 In.
$2,370

James D. Julia Auctioneers

Dutch Girl, 2 Flower Baskets, 2 Braids, 9 x 5¾ In. 73
Elephant, Coconut Tree, Upturned Trunk, Cast Iron, 1922, 10 In. 360
Elephant, Standing, Multicolor Blanket, Shaped Base, Paint, Iron, c.1900, 10 x 12 In. 615
Elephant, Trunk Down, Tusks, Base, Cast Iron, Bradley & Hubbard, 9¾ In. 944
Elk, Stag, Antlers, Leaves, 16 In. 120
Fighting Cock, Duckling, Angry Rooster, Ruffled Feathers, Duck, Cast Iron, 9 In. 900
Fisherman, Jacket, Hat, 6 In. 95
Flamingo, Standing Among Reeds, Shaded Pink, Green, Cast Iron, Hubley, 10 In. 885
Flapper Girl, Brown Dress, Flowers At Waist, Hat, Cast Iron, E.O.M. Co., Toledo, 12 In. 590
Flowers, Gladiolas, Cast Iron, Hubley, No. 489, 10 In. .... *illus* 295
Frog, Sitting In Grass, Profile, Grin, Flattened, Green Paint, Cast Iron, c.1920, 7 x 4½ In. 415
Fruit Bowl, Multicolor, Hubley, 7 x 7 In. 266
Geisha, Playing Instrument, Kneeling, Flowered Base, Cast Iron, Hubley, 7 x 6 In. 266
George Washington, Leaning On Draped Pedestal, Holding Hat, Cast Iron, 13 In. 885
Goldenrod, Yellow, Green Grass Base, Cast Iron, Hubley, 7 In. 325
Golfer, Putting, Red Jacket, Knickers, Cast Iron, Hubley, 8⅜ In. 295
Golfer, Putting, Yellow & Green Paint, Iron, Hubley, c.1920, 8¼ In. 533
Grandpa Rabbit, Side-Glancing Eyes, Red Jacket, Cast Iron, 8½ In. 413
Grape Leaves, Cast Iron, 13 x 6 In. 12
Greyhound, White Paint, Cast Iron, 10 x 15½ In., Pair 180
Hill Clutch, Foundry Man, Holding Pot, Cap, Gloves, Goggles, Full Figure, Iron, 8 x 6 In. 228
Horse, Standing, Hubley, 10½ x 11⅝ In. 194
House, Saltbox, Long Pitched Roof, Blue, Red Chimney, Cast Iron, 5 In. 384
Judy, Seated, Holding Punch, Paint, Cast Iron, 11¾ In. 2950
Koala Bear, Black, Yellow Stripes, Orange Ears & Base, Cast Iron, Taylor Cook, 5¾ In. 295
Lighthouse, Cape Hatteras, Black & White Paint, Striped, Cast Iron, c.1925, 21 In. 1778
Lion, Clay, Impressed Factory Mark, Lee Clay Products, 5½ x 11½ In. 510
Little Red Riding Hood, Round Base, Cast Iron, Hubley, 9½ In. 150
Mammy, Hands On Hip, Apron, Full Figure, Paint, Cast Iron, c.1910, 13 In. .... 239 to 485
Mammy, Red Polka Dot Bandanna, Maid Uniform, Hands On Hips, Cast Iron, 1930s, 12 In. 270 to 413
Marigolds, White Ribbed Vase, Blue Stripes, Cast Iron, Hubley, 7¾ In. 325
Marquis De Lafayette, Cast Iron, 11⅝ x 5 In. 61
Mary Quite Contrary, Full Figure, Holding Flowers & Water Can, Iron, 8 x 15 In. 270
Messenger Boy, Holding Art Deco Flowers, Cast Iron, Red & Black Base, Fish, Hubley 531
Mexican Guitarist, Wide Brimmed Hat, Cast Iron, Littco, 11¾ In. 1121
Monkey, Sitting, Full Figure, Paint, Cast Iron, Wood Base, 9 In. 240
Mrs. Ally Sloper, Holding Children, Dog, 11½ In. 1416
Narcissus, 3-Footed Striped Pot, Garland, Cast Iron, Hubley, 7½ In. 295
Nasturtiums, Black & White Striped Flowerpot, Cast Iron, Hubley, 8 In. 295
Old Salt Man Of Sea, Fisherman, Yellow Rainsuit, Full Figure, Cast Iron, 6 x 15 In. 450
Old Salt, Yellow Jacket, Net, Iron, Littco, 11¼ In. 85
Old Woman, Flower Basket, Parasol, Cast Iron, Bradley & Hubbard, 11 In. 885
Owl, Paint, Green, White, Cast Iron, Bradley & Hubbard, 15¾ In. 1062
Parlor Maid, Cocktails On Tray, Cast Iron, Impressed FISH, Hubley, c.1920, 9 In. .... *illus* 2666
Parrot, Taylor Cat, Deco Style, Taylor Cook, Marked, c.1930, 10 x 4 In. 1770
Peacock, Blue, Yellow, Red, 6 x 6 In. 60
Peacock, Full Open Tail, Blue Shaded To Green To Yellow, Cast Iron, 6½ In. 708
Penguin, Full Figure, Bowtie & Top Hat, Black & White, Cast Iron, Hubley, 4 x 10 In. 540
Penguin, Wearing Bowtie, Standing, Head Up, Base, Cast Iron, 10½ In. 300
Peter Rabbit, Standing, Eating Carrot, Paw In Pocket, 9⅜ In. .... 236 to 270
Petunias & Asters, 2-Tone Pastels, Weave Basket, Hubley, 9½ x 6½ In. 472
Pheasant, Grassy Base, Cast Iron, Fred Everett, Hubley, 8½ In. 502
Pig, Standing, Brown Spots, Paint, Oval Base, Cast Iron, 6 x 9 In. 1180
Pilgrim Boy, Arm Raised, 8¾ x 5⅜ In. 36
Pirate, Pack Over Shoulder, Paint, Knife On Belt, Walking, Cast Iron, 1920, 12 x 10 In. 593
Poinsettia, Clay Pot, Square Base, Cast Iron, Paint, Judd Co., 10 x 5 In. .... *illus* 649
Poinsettia, Red, Cast Iron, Judd, 9 In. 220
Poppies & Cornflowers, Multicolor, Paint, Hubley, 7 x 6½ In. 295
Punch, Seated, Dog Toby, Cast Iron, 12½ x 8½ In. 4130
Rabbit, In Garden, Picket Fence, Paint, Cast Iron, Albany Foundry Co., 6¼ In. 142
Rabbit, Pushing Wheelbarrow, Blue Overalls, Cast Iron, Littco, 11⅝ In. 1121
Rabbit, Sitting, White, Cast Iron, 9 In. 160
Rabbit, Standing On Hind Legs, Cast Iron, Bradley & Hubbard, 15 In. 1534
Red Riding Hood, Standing With Wolf, Paint, Round Base, Cast Iron, c.1920, 8 In. 494
Red Riding Hood, Wolf, Embossed, Cast Iron, Nuydea Foundry, c.1920, 10 In. .... *illus* 2370

Rooster, Crowing, Multicolor, Cast Iron, 13 In. 372
Rumba Dancer, Cast Iron, 10 ¾ In. 242
Sailor, Standing, Legs Apart, Hands On Hips, Cap, Round Base, Paint, Cast Iron, 1800s, 6 In. 492
Senorita With Basket Of Flowers, Yellow Dress, Teal Shawl, Cast Iron, 11 In. 266
Sheep, Black Paint, Cast Iron, 10 ¼ In. 229
Sheep, Paint, White, Turquoise Base, Cast Iron, c.1885, 7 ½ x 10 ½ In. 185
Snooper, Detective, Black Trench Coat, Long Nose, Magnifying Glass, Iron, 13 In. 1062
Snowy Owl, Bradley & Hubbard, W. Meriden Ct., 15 ½ In. 1989
Soldier, Flower In Rifle, Paint, Red Jacket & Hat, Round Base, Iron, 1920, 13 In. 2370
Soldier, Hessian, Marching, Helmet, Rectangular Base, Cast Brass, 8 ½ In. 115
Southern Belle, Hair In Bun, Holding Flowers & Hat, Cast Iron, Albany Foundry, 11 In. 177
Southern Belle, Holding Hat, Paint, Cast Iron, c.1900, 11 In. 165
Squirrel, Seated, Holding Nut, Green Paint, Cast Iron, Hubley, 9 In. 531
Stork, Drinking From Ewer, 10 ½ x 7 ¾ In. 109
Swallows, Perched On Holly Bush, Paint, Hubley, 8 ¾ x 7 In. 1003
Tropical Woman With Fruit Basket On Head, Green, Coral Apron, Cast Iron, 12 In. 384
Tulips, Floppy, Art Deco Vase, Cast Iron, Hubley, 10 In. 59
Turkey, Cast Iron, Bradley & Hubbard, 12 ½ In. 5015
Turkey, Multicolor, Paint, Bradley & Hubbard, 12 ½ In. 2006
Uncle Sam, Full Figure, Half Round Base, Paint, Top Hat, Hands On Waist, c.1940, 16 In. 1481
Uncle Sam, Hands On Hips, Round Base, For The Open Door, Cast Iron, 1920s, 12 In. .... *illus* 21240
Woman, With Muff, Black & White Dress & Coat, Cast Iron, Albany Foundry, 9 ½ In. 443

DOULTON pottery and porcelain were made by Doulton and Co. of Burslem, England, after 1882. The name *Royal Doulton* appeared on the company's wares after 1902. Other pottery by Doulton is listed under Royal Doulton.

Butter Chip, Elaine, Brown Transferware, c.1887, 3 Piece .... *illus* 60
Figurine, Mephistopheles, Multicolor Enamel, c.1890, 12 ½ In. 461
Jardiniere, Blue Flower & Leaf Band, Cobalt, Basket Weave Band, Lambeth, 7 x 9 In. 108
Jardiniere, Spades, High Gloss Blue Green Ground, Lambeth, 1905, 11 x 13 In. 300
Umbrella Stand, Blue Embroidery-Like Design, Brown Ground, Lambeth, 22 In. 240
Urn, Gilt, Portrait, Cartouche, Cobalt, Burslem, 11 ¾ In. 605
Vase, Blue, Green, Blossoms, Beige, High Shoulders, Lambeth, Stoneware, 8 x 5 In., Pair 240
Vase, Cream, Pink Flowers, Green Leaves, Handles, Burslem, 14 ½ In. 127
Vase, Decorated Floral Band, Lambeth, Stoneware, 10 x 4 In. 121
Vase, Decorated Leafy Band, White Flowers, Cobalt, Stoneware, Lambeth, 10 x 4 In. 121
Vase, Stick, Tapestry, Amber, Mustard, Blue, 11 x 5 In. 99
Vase, Tapestry, Butterflies, Flowers, Cobalt, Burslem Chine Ware, 1900, 14 In., Pair 369
Water Cooler, Bas Relief, Children, Blue, Green, Cream, Lambeth, 13 In. 129

DRESDEN and Meissen porcelain are often confused. Porcelains were made in the town of Meissen, Germany, beginning about 1706. The town of Dresden, Germany, has been home to many decorating studios since the early 1700s. Blanks were obtained from Meissen and other porcelain factories. Some say porcelain was also made in Dresden in the early years. Decorations on Dresden are often similar to Meissen, and marks were copied. Some of the earliest books on marks confused Dresden and Meissen, and that has remained a problem ever since. The Meissen "AR" mark and crossed swords mark are among the most forged marks on porcelain. Meissen pieces are listed in this book under Meissen. German porcelain marked "Dresden" is listed here. Irish Dresden and Dresden made in East Liverpool, Ohio, are not included in this section.

DRESDEN S GERMANY

Bone Dish, Leaf Shape, Raised Roses, Gold Rim, c.1945, 4 x 2 In. 35
Bowl, Centerpiece, Shaped Rim, Reticulated, Flowers, Footed, 13 In. 214
Bowl, Scalloped, Flowers, 4-Legged, Von Schierholz, 8 ½ x 8 In. 182
Bowl, White Ground, Scalloped, Gilt Rim, Reticulated, Flowers, Courting Scene, 11 x 8 In. 118
Centerpiece, Figural, 4 Cherubs Holding Vessel, Von Schierholz, 15 In. 150
Centerpiece, Figural, Bowl, Putti Supports, Gilt Work, Flowers, c.1915, 20 In. .... *illus* 1168
Compote, Painted, Pierced Bowl, 4 Seated Putti, Marked, c.1910, 14 ½ x 11 In. 300
Cup & Saucer, Flowers, Gilt Trim, c.1869 .... 85 to 95
Cup & Saucer, Flowers, Multicolor, Scrolled Gilt Border, Demitasse 60
Dresser Box, Round, Reticulated, Dome Lid, Flowers, Openwork, Gilt, 4 x 4 In. 122
Dresser Box, Round, Squat, Shaped, Figural Cherubs On Lid, Flowers, Gilt, 7 In. 244
Figurine, Bird On Branch, Blue & Yellow Bird, 3 In. 944
Figurine, Elk, Bellowing, 3 In. 266
Figurine, Horse, Carriage, Woman Passenger, Flowers, Grass, 9 ½ x 19 ½ In. 944
Figurine, Monkey, Seated, Tree Stump, Carl Thieme, c.1901, 15 ¾ x 11 ½ In. 1331
Figurine, Napoleon Bonaparte, Black Hat & Boots, Marked, 11 In. 123
Figurine, Roman Soldier, Seated, Holding Rolled Document, c.1890, 7 In. 875

Doorstop, Uncle Sam, Hands On Hips, Round Base, For The Open Door, Cast Iron, 1920s, 12 In.
$21,240

Bertoia Auctions

Doulton, Butter Chip, Elaine, Brown Transferware, c.1887, 3 Piece
$60

Ruby Lane

Dresden, Centerpiece, Figural, Bowl, Putti Supports, Gilt Work, Flowers, c.1915, 20 In.
$1,168

New Orleans (Cakebread)

D

Duncan & Miller, Sanibel, Plate, Salad, Blue Opalescent, Curved Shell, 1940s, 9 x 8 In.
$40

Ruby Lane

Duncan & Miller, Swan, Dish, Green & Clear, 9 x 12 In.
$35

Ruby Lane

Duncan & Miller, Swirl, Bowl, 2-Ply, Gold Highlights, c.1902, 4 x 8 In.
$40

Ruby Lane

TIP

If you receive a package of glass antiques during cold weather, let it sit inside for a few hours before you unpack it. The glass must return to room temperature slowly or it may crack.

Group, Cherubs, Flower Crowns, 19th Century, 7 x 5 ½ x 8 In. 250
Group, Figural, Seated Woman, Gown, Children, 7 In. 153
Jar, Encrusted Fruit, Flowers, Doves, Pheasants, Schneeballen, 15 In., Pair........ 2250
Nodder, Chinese Man, Moving Head, Hands & Tongue, 10 In. 553
Plate, Cartouches, Dog, Horse, Flowers, Blue, Purple, Lamm, 11 In. 92
Plate, Dinner, Salad, White Ground, Floral Bouquet, c.1950, 10 & 7 ¾ In., 18 Piece........ 96
Plate, Flower Sprays, Blue Spots, Gilt Border, 10 ½ In., 12 Piece........ 153
Plate, Lattice, Flowers, Reticulated Edge, 8 In. Diam., 9 Piece 215
Tureen, 4 Country Scenes, 2 Handles, Handled Lid, 4-Footed, 14 x 13 ¾ In. 125
Urn, Panel, Group, Landscape, Gilt, Yellow, Purple, 15 x 8 ½ In. 210
Vase, Lid, Gilt, Multicolor Enamel, Putti, Crown, Crest, Flowers, Swags, Carl Thieme, 35 In. 2460
Wall Bracket, Flowers, Gilt, Rococo Style, Figural Scenes, 1800s, 9 In., Pair 531

DUNCAN & MILLER is a term used by collectors when referring to glass made by the George A. Duncan and Sons Company or the Duncan and Miller Glass Company. These companies worked from 1893 to 1955, when the use of the name *Duncan* was discontinued and the firm became part of the United States Glass Company. Early patterns may be listed under Pressed Glass.

Amberette, Bowl, Round, 8 In. 46
Andover, Goblet, Water, 7 In. 10
Astral, Tumbler, Iced Tea, 6 ¼ In. 8
Belfast, Goblet, Water, 5 ⅞ In. 11
Bridal Bow, Wine, 4 ¾ In. 19
Buttercup, Sherbet, 5 ¼ In. 26
Button Panel, Punch Cup, 2 ⅜ In. 18
Canterbury, Celery Dish, 10 ½ In. 34
Canterbury, Nappy, 7 ¼ In. 14
Canterbury, Relish, 3 Sections, Round, 8 In. 18
Caribbean, Bowl, Flared, 12 ½ In. 46
Caribbean, Plate, Dinner, Blue, 9 In. 19
Chantilly, Creamer, 3 ⅝ In. 43
Chantilly, Relish, 3 Sections, Round, 8 In. 57
Charmaine Rose, Relish, 3 Sections, 12 In. 23
Charmaine Rose, Tumbler, Iced Tea, c.1950, 6 ⅝ In. 14
Clematis, Tray, Round, 12 In. 20
Concerto, Plate, Luncheon, 8 ¾ In. 7
Concerto, Sherbet, 4 ⅞ In. 6
Dogwood, Sherbet, 3 ½ In. 8
Essex, Plate, Salad, 7 ½ In. 14
Eternally Yours, Goblet, Water, 1940s, 7 ½ In. 26
First Love, Bowl, Crimped, Round, 10 ½ In. 25
First Love, Cup & Saucer, c.1940........ 26
First Love, Goblet, Water, c.1935, 6 ⅞ In. 26
First Love, Jug, 80 Oz., 9 In. 269
Francis First, Goblet, Water, 8 In. 15
Garland, Goblet, Water, 7 ¼ In. 23
Grape, Pitcher, Milk Glass, c.1950, 60 Oz., 6 In. 37
Indian Tree, Candlestick, 3 ⅜ In. 17
Indian Tree, Cup & Saucer, c.1940........ 40
Indian Tree, Goblet, Water, 7 ⅞ In. .... 23 to 26
King Arthur, Punch Bowl, 11 ⅞ In. 86
Laurel Wreath, Cordial, 3 ⅝ In. 33
Laurel Wreath, Plate, Luncheon, 8 ⅝ In. 7
Magnolia, Compote, 6 ⅜ In. 27
Magnolia, Goblet, 5 ⅝ In. 20
Magnolia, Sherbet, 4 ½ In. 12
Murano, Bowl, Folded Edge, 13 In. 21
Queen's Lace, Plate, Salad, 7 ½ In. 13
Queen's Lace, Tumbler, Iced Tea, 6 ⅝ In. 12
Radiance, Plate, Salad, 7 ½ In. 10
Radiance, Sherbet, 4 ¾ In. 11
Rhythm, Goblet, Water, c.1950, 6 ¾ In. 7
Rhythm, Plate, Salad, 1950s, 7 ½ In. 13
Ridgewood, Cocktail, 4 ⅞ In. 6
Ridgewood, Goblet, Water, 6 ⅝ In. 12
Sandwich, Goblet, Water, Amber, 5 ¾ In. 8
Sandwich, Tumbler, Iced Tea, Amber, 5 ½ In. 15

St. Charles, Goblet, Water, 1950s, 5¾ In. 35
Sanibel, Plate, Salad, Blue Opalescent, Curved Shell, 1940s, 9 x 8 In. *illus* 40
Swan, Dish, Green & Clear, 9 x 12 In. *illus* 35
Swirl, Bowl, 2-Ply, Gold Highlights, c.1902, 4 x 8 In. *illus* 40
Tiara, Cocktail, 5½ In. 12

DURAND art glass was made from 1924 to 1931. The Vineland Flint Glass Works was established by Victor Durand and Victor Durand Jr. in 1897. In 1924 Martin Bach Jr. and other artisans from the Quezal glassworks joined them at the Vineland, New Jersey, plant to make Durand art glass. They called their gold iridescent glass Gold Luster.

Bowl, Beveled, Square, 6 x 11 In. 35
Bowl, Center, Golden Red Finish, Rainbow Aurora, 14½ In. 325
Compote, Peacock Feather, Etched Rose, Vines, Cobalt Blue, White, Yellow Stem, 4 x 12 In. 265
Ginger Jar, Green & White Crackle Design, Gold Iridescent, Shouldered, Lid, 8 In. 1304
Salt, Marigold, Golden Threads, White Combed Petals, Edged Green, Round, 1 x 3 In. 92
Vase, Blue Iridescent, Flared, Rim, Tapered, Signed, Engraved Signature, 8 In. 529
Vase, Blue Iridescent, Gold Accents, Genie Bottle, Stick Neck, Rolled Rim, c.1925, 12 In. 1089
Vase, Blue Iridescent, Green, Threaded, Shouldered, Tapered, Gilt, c.1930, 8 In. 750
Vase, Gold & Pink Iridescent, 15½ x 8½ In. 373
Vase, Gold Iridescent, Platinum & Orange, Bulbous, Trumpet Neck, Signed, 6 In. 356
Vase, Gold Luster, Tapered, Green Hears, Iridescent Vines, Gold Interior, Signed, 8 In. 460
Vase, Iridescent, Calcite, Gold, Magenta, Scalloped Rim, 9½ x 3½ In. 173
Vase, Iridescent, Green, Blue, 14½ In. 250
Vase, King Tut, Blue, 1920s, 12 x 6 In. 813
Vase, King Tut, Gold Iridescent, Opal Coiling, Shouldered, Flared Rim, Marked, 8¾ In. 546
Vase, Olive Green Pulled Feathers, Aurene Gold Over Mustard Yellow, 7 In. 590
Vase, Orange Luster, Green Leafy Vines, Squat, Trumpet Neck, c.1930, 6 In. 625
Vase, Peacock Feather, 5 Opals, Ruby Ground, Shouldered, Flared Rim, 9 In. 518
Vase, Pedestal Foot, Slender, Flaring, Gold Iridescent, Opaque To Translucent, 16 In. 593
Vase, Red, Crackle, Bulbous, 9¾ In. 1345
Vase, Trumpet, Blue Footed, Blue & White Opal Pulled Feather, 12½ In. *illus* 920
Vase, Yellow Pulled Feather, Green & Orange Iridescent, Gold Threading, Flared Rim, 11 In. 1185

ELFINWARE is a mark found on Dresden-like porcelain that was sold in dime stores and gift shops. Many pieces were decorated with raised flowers. The mark was registered by Breslauer-Underberg, Inc., of New York City in 1947. Pieces marked *Elfinware Made in Germany* had been sold since 1945 by this importer.

Elfinware

Ewer, Applied Flowers, Moss, Handle, Germany, 2⅛ x 2 In. 12
Figurine, Grand Piano, Applied Flowers, Moss, 3⅓ x 4½ In. 5
Hatpin Holder, Applied Flowers, Pink, 3 Openings, c.1900, 4 x 3 In. 125
Potpourri, Lid, Reticulated, Applied Flowers, Green Moss, 4½ x 1½ In. 72

ELVIS PRESLEY, the well-known singer, lived from 1935 to 1977. He became famous by 1956. Elvis appeared on television, starred in twenty-seven movies, and performed in Las Vegas. Memorabilia from any of the Presley shows, his records, and even memorials made after his death are collected.

Lobby Card, Spinout, MGM, 1966, 14 x 10 In. 45
Pen, Wood Guitar-Shape Case, 7½ x 2½ In. 25
Photo Corniche, Black & White, 1950s, 27½ x 19½ In. *illus* 550
Photograph, Lithograph, Holding Guitar, Head Tilted, 1950s, 27 x 19 In. 450
Plate, Looking At A Legend, Delphi, 1990, 8½ In. 15
Record, All Shook Up, RCA, 45 RPM, 1957 7
Ukette, Plastic Ukulele, Music Box, Elvis Image, Yellow & Red, c.1957, 15 x 5 In. 938

ENAMELS listed here are made of glass particles and other materials heated and fused to metal. In the eighteenth and nineteenth centuries, workmen from Russia, France, England, and other countries made small boxes and table pieces of enamel on metal. One form of English enamel is called *Battersea* and is listed under that name. There was a revival of interest in enameling in the 1930s and a new style evolved. There is now renewed interest in the artistic enameled plaques, vases, ashtrays, and jewelry. Enamels made since the 1930s are usually on copper or steel, although silver was often used for jewelry. Graniteware is a separate category, and enameled metal kitchen pieces may be included in the Kitchen category. Cloisonne is a special type of enamel and is listed in its own category.

Bowl, Blue, 5 Sets Of Schooling Fish, Nekrasoff, 11¾ In. 120
Bowl, Courting Couples, Gilt Metal Mount, Support, Round Base, Austria, 8 In. 1250

Durand, Vase, Trumpet, Blue Footed, Blue & White Opal Pulled Feather, 12½ In.
$920

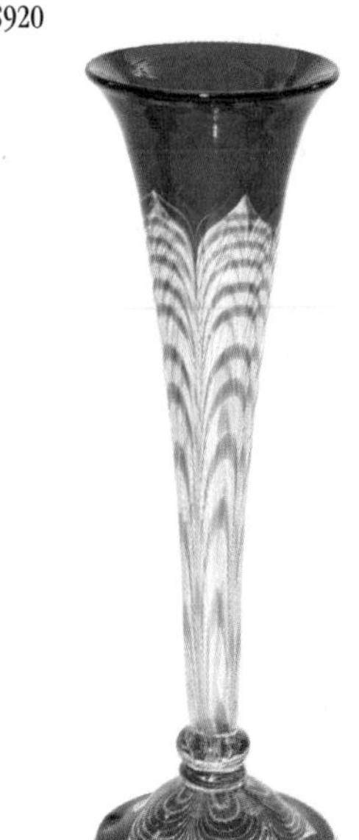

Early Auction Company

Elvis Presley, Photo Corniche, Black & White, 1950s, 27½ x 19½ In.
$550

Ruby Lane

Enamel, Box, Copper, Hinged, Moonlit Scene, Tooled Foil Inset, Frank Marshall, 7 x 5 In.
$3,186

Humler & Nolan

Enamel, Box, Lid, Sterling Silver, Hammered, Flowers, Turquoise, G. Twichell, 5 In.
$6,195

Humler & Nolan

Enamel, Letter Holder, Copper, Hammered, Sailing Ship Medallion, Incised Twichell, 4 x 6 In.
$1,185

James D. Julia Auctioneers

Enamel, Plaque, Woman, Holding Jewelry Box, Flowing Robes, Arm Up, Limoges, Frame, 1800s, 8 x 5 In.
$354

Brunk Auctions

Bowl, Seaside, 12 In. 338
Bowl, Silver, Dragon Shape Handles, Marius Hammer, Norway, 1910, 4 In. 2500
Bowl, The Cavern, Copper, Silver Leaf, Mildred Watkins, Cleveland, Ohio, 1¾ x 7½ In. 1375
Box, Copper, Blue, Pink, Round, Lid, France, 4¾ In. 406
Box, Copper, Hinged, Moonlit Scene, Tooled Foil Inset, Frank Marshall, 7 x 5 In. ....*illus* 3186
Box, Figural, Goose, Silver, Couple, Landscape, Multicolor, 6 In. 1500
Box, Lid, Enamel, Bronze, Black, White, Scrolls, Figures, Footed, Limoges, c.1900, 6 x 4 In. 350
Box, Lid, Sterling Silver, Hammered, Flowers, Turquoise, G. Twichell, 5 In. ....*illus* 6195
Box, Metal, Hinged Lid, Cobalt, Filigree, 4-Footed, France, 6 In. 1500
Card Case, Art Nouveau, Silver Gilt, Red, Sergey Agafonov, c.1900, 3¾ x 2¼ In. 9000
Card Case, Hinged Lid, Cut Corner, Blue, Silver Center Panel Flowers, Art Deco, 4 x 2½ In. 780
Card Case, Silver, Courting Couple, Lake, 3⅝ x 2¼ In. 188
Censer, Rounded Rectangle, Brass Swing Handles, Elephants, Birds, Chinese, 5 x 7 In. 1560
Compote, Gilt, Courting Couple, Jeweled Support, Austria, 6½ In. 875
Condiment Set, Grasshoppers, 7 Wells, Round, Wood Case, Chinese, 1900s, 13 In. 123
Cup & Saucer, Sake, Pink, Flowers, Vines, 2 Piece 47
Ewer, Cherubs, Landscape, Multicolor, Tan, Austria, 9 In. 1750
Figurine, Knight, Horseback, Sword Up, Mixed Metals, Signed Brian Rodden, 18½ x 17½ In. ... 400
Goblet, Green Glass, Medieval Figures, Dancing, Grapevines, Gilded, c.1900, 10 In. 554
Letter Holder, Copper, Hammered, Sailing Ship Medallion, Incised Twichell, 4 x 6 In. ....*illus* 1185
Necessaire, Courting Couple, Pink, Gilt Metal Mount, Continental, 4 In. 531
Necessaire, Woman, Portrait, Green, Gilt Metal Mount, Continental, 4 In. 750
Plaque, Copper, Harlequin, France, c.1900, 11 x 6 In. 132
Plaque, Copper, Midcentury Modern, Abstract, Jane Hammel, 6 x 4 In. 168
Plaque, Copper, Standing Man, France, 5¼ x 3⅜ In 438
Plaque, Pilange, Woman, Arms Up, Doris Hall, 27 x 24½ In. 1560
Plaque, The Concert, Ruth Raemisch, 11¼ x 10½ In. 1560
Plaque, Underwater Scene, Bather, Fish, Red Hair, Doris Hall, 11¾ x 15 In. 840
Plaque, Woman In Hat, White Dress, Blue Wall, Doris Hall, 12 x 12 In. 840
Plaque, Woman, Holding Jewelry Box, Flowing Robes, Arm Up, Limoges, Frame, 1800s, 8 x 5 In. . *illus* 354
Plaque, Young Aristocrat, France, 4⅝ x 3¼ In. 307
Salt Cellar, Kovsh, Pastel, Shaded Flowers, Beaded Trim, Russia, 1½ x 3½ In. 1062
Sculpture, Abstract, Red, Rafael Consuegra, 72½ x 34 In. 2091
Sugar Basket, Silver, Oval Lobbed Panels, Gustav Klingert, Russia, c.1900, 5¼ In. 1875
Sugar Tongs, Floral Decoration, Gilt Washed Interior, Antip Kuzmichev, Russia, 1800s 338
Tray, Scalloped Oval, Young Women, Bathing Parlor, Cherubs, 1900, 16¾ In. 5250
Vase, 2 Decorated Bands, Handles, Multicolor, 12 x 8½ In. 156
Vase, Bronze, Gourd Shape Body, Trumpet Neck, Cone Shape Foot, Dragons, 15¼ In. 246
Vase, Copper, Cobalt, Man & Woman Profiles, White, France, 7 In., Pair 531
Vase, Man In Landscape, Copper, P. Sernet, France, c.1890, 3¾ In. ....*illus* 450
Vase, Opaline Glass, Songbird, Leafy Branch, Gilt Ball Feet, 12½ In., Pair 500
Vase, Portrait, Blue, Woman, France, 3 In. 118
Vase, Red, Dragons, 7½ x 7½ In., Pair 144
Vase, Woman, Brown Landscape Ground, Dark Green Neck & Foot, 6 In., Pair 750
Wall Hanging, Abstract, Rectangles, Starburst, Diamond Shape, Christos, 1974, 30 x 31 In. 125

ERPHILA is a mark found on Czechoslovakian and other pottery and porcelain made after 1920. This mark was used on items imported by Ebeling & Reuss, Philadelphia, a giftware firm that was founded in 1866 and out of business sometime after 2002. The mark is a combination of the letters *E* and *R* (Ebeling & Reuss) and the first letters of the city, Phila(delphia). Many whimsical figural pitchers and creamers, figurines, platters, and other giftwares carry this mark.

Handpainted ERPHILA Czechoslovakia

Biscuit Jar, Man, Pink Outfit, 1880s 25
Figurine, Boy Riding Goat, 5½ x 5 In., Pair 78
Figurine, Dancers, Blue Dress, Yellow Cape, 1886, 6½ In. 25
Figurine, Dog, Terrier, Black & White, Marked, 4 x 5 In. 48
Syrup, Underplate, Dorset, Cheery Chintz, Multicolor, 2 Piece 35
Tray, Woman, Long Dress, Cherub, Multicolor, 10 In. 35
Vase, Woman, Walking, Basket On Head, Child, Brown, 7 In. ....*illus* 130

ES GERMANY porcelain was made at the factory of Erdmann Schlegelmilch from 1861 to 1937 in Suhl, Germany. The porcelain, marked *ES Germany* or *ES Suhl*, was sold decorated or undecorated. Other pieces were made at a factory in Saxony, Prussia, and are marked *ES Prussia*. Reinhold Schlegelmilch made the famous wares marked *RS Germany*.

Bowl, Mother-Of-Pearl Finish, Gold Highlights, 4 x ½ In. 36
Plaque, Woman, Swallows, Beaded Band, Scalloped Edge, c.1900, 9 In. 89

ESKIMO artifacts of all types are collected. Carvings of whale or walrus teeth are listed under Scrimshaw. Baskets are in the Basket category. All other types of Eskimo art are listed here. In Canada and some other areas, the term *Inuit* is used instead of Eskimo.

Arrow, Bird, Chip Carved, 1800s, 30 In. 62
Basket, Attu, Woven Grass, Green, Red & Brown Yarn, Conical Lid, Knob, 1800s, 9 x 7 In. 504
Basket, Passamaquoddy, Swing Handles, Red, Blue, Yellow Paint, Lid, c.1900, 19 x 11 In. 296
Basket, Trinket, Lid, Coiled, Polar Bear Finial, Walrus Ivory, 3 ½ x 4 In. .... *illus* 708
Carving, Hunter, Kayak, Wood, Animal Skin, 5 ¾ x 28 ½ In. 570
Doll, Cloth, Bead Design, Seal Gut Skin Dress, Siberia, c.1900, 9 x 6 In. 247
Figurine, Seal Hunter, Soapstone, Gray, 7 ¾ x 7 In. 149
Figurine, Walrus, Stone, Paquita, 9 ¼ x 12 ¾ In. 1584
Knife, Story, Bone, Caribou Carvings, 7 In. 120
Mask, Cedar, Carved, Painted, c.1910, 11 x 6 ½ In. .... *illus* 237
Pipe, Bone, Etched, Geometric Zoomorphic Design, Curved, Dovetail Bowl, c.1860, 13 In. 1541
Pipe, Walrus Ivory, Carved, Fossilized, c.1900, 12 ¼ In. 1200
Spoon, Sheep Horn, Carved, Ring & Dot, 9 ⅝ In. 984
Tobacco Container, Antler, Carved, Incised, Scenes, Wood Plug, 1800s, 3 x 5 In. .... *illus* 1020
Trinket Box, Wood, Lift Lid, Applied Figures, Shaped Feet, Greenland, c.1905, 7 x 4 In. .... *illus* 1046

FABERGE was a firm of jewelers and goldsmiths founded in St. Petersburg, Russia, in 1842, by Gustav Faberge. Peter Carl Faberge, his son, was jeweler to the Russian Imperial Court from about 1870 to 1917. The rare Imperial Easter eggs, jewelry, and decorative items are very expensive today.

ФАБЕРЖЕ
КФ

Bowl, Silver, Gold Wash, Scalloped Foot, Gadrooned, Multicolor Enamel, c.1926, 2 x 3 ¾ In. 805
Caviar Server, Cobalt Cut To Clear, 18 ½ x 9 In. 546
Cigarette Case, Silver, Guilloche Enamel, Lavender, Double-Headed Eagle, 2 ½ x 3 ½ In. 5747
Cufflinks, Diamond Border, Enamel, 14K, Anchor, Blue, c.1900 3327
Cufflinks, Diamond, Enamel, Oval, Michael Perchin, c.1900 3025
Cufflinks, Jade, Nephrite, 14K, Round, Gold X, August Fredrik Hollming, c.1900 3025
Cup, Agate, X Form, Reeded Silver, Green, c.1915, 1 ¾ x 3 ¾ In. 1452
Kovsh, Dragon's Head, Reticulated Handle As Tail, Silver Gilt, Cloisonne, c.1910, 6 In. 14760
Match Safe, Egg Shape, Royal Blue Enamel, Engine Turned, Gold Band, 2 In. 5500
Pillbox, Blue Guilloche, Hinged Lid, Round, 8-Point Star, 2 ½ In. 2722
Pillbox, Silver, Engine Turned, Sapphire Cabochons, Henrik Wingstrom, 1 ½ In. 2178
Pin, Diamond, 3 Oval Cabochon Sapphires, August Holmstom, c.1900 6050
Vodka Cup, Cloisonne, Lobed Sections, Flowers, Blue, Red, Parrot Shape Handle, 2 ¼ In. 9581

FAIENCE refers to tin-glazed earthenware, especially the wares made in France, Germany, and Scandinavia. It is also correct to say that faience is the same as majolica or Delft, although usually the term refers only to the tin-glazed pottery of the three regions mentioned.

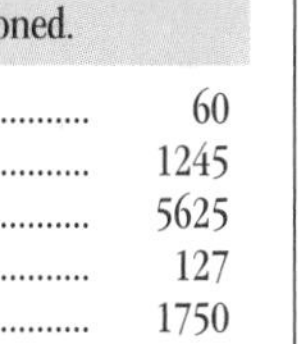

Bulb Forcer, Lavender Harbor Scene, Gold Trim, Demilune Shape, 5 x 10 In. 60
Charger, Battle Scene, Armored Soldiers, Horses, Continental, 12 In. 1245
Charger, Cluster Of 3 Fish, Eel, Aquatic Plants, Shells, Insects, 15 In. 5625
Ewer, Enameled, Glazed, Shells, Footed Base, Marked, 13 ¾ x 7 In. 127
Jardiniere, Gilt Bronze Mount, Group In Landscape, Continental, 25 In. 1750
Plate, Figural Scene, Renaissance Style Border, Multicolor, Signed AD, 14 In. 98
Stand, Walking Stick, Blue, Cylindrical Body, Stylized Leaves, England, c.1910, 24 In. 615
Tureen, Lid, Squash, Smaller Squash Finial, c.1800, 11 In. 5250
Vase, Fleur-De-Lis Shape, Multicolor, 13 x 8 ¼ In., Pair 380
Vase, Lid, Yellow Flowers, Marked, France, 1800s, 15 ¼ In., Pair 450
Vase, Moth, Blue & Red, Rolled Rim, California Faience Co., 1920s, 5 x 5 In. .... *illus* 1500
Vase, Swollen Top, Pinched Waist, Ring Foot, Slip Trail Flowers, c.1902, 9 In. 1440

FAIRINGS are small souvenir boxes and figurines that were sold at country fairs during the nineteenth century. Most were made in Germany. Reproductions of fairings are being made, especially of the famous *Twelve Months after Marriage* series.

Box, Trinket, Mother, Child, Hurdy-Gurdy, 2 Piece, Porcelain, Paint, c.1880, 3 x 3 In. .... *illus* 95
Box, Woven Base, Dog Laying In Grass, Black & White, 19th Century, 3 ½ x 1 ¾ x 2 In. 75
Figurine, Midnight's Holy Hour, Mother & Baby In Bed, Father Standing, 1880s, 3 x 3 In. .. *illus* 99
Figurine, When A Man Marries, Woman In Bed, Man Holding Baby, Conta & Boehme 69
Pin Dish, 2 Pigs, In Front Of Camera, 3 ½ In. 45
Trinket Box, Carved Wood Log, Figural Gnome On Lid, Long Beard, Hinged Lid, 5 x 3 In. 120
Trinket Box, Red Riding Hood, Dog, Fence, Dresser, Conta & Boehme, c.1875, 3 ½ x 3 x 2 In. ... 101

FAIRYLAND LUSTER *pieces are included in the Wedgwood category.*

Enamel, Vase, Man In Landscape, Copper, P. Sernet, France, c.1890, 3 ¾ In.
$450

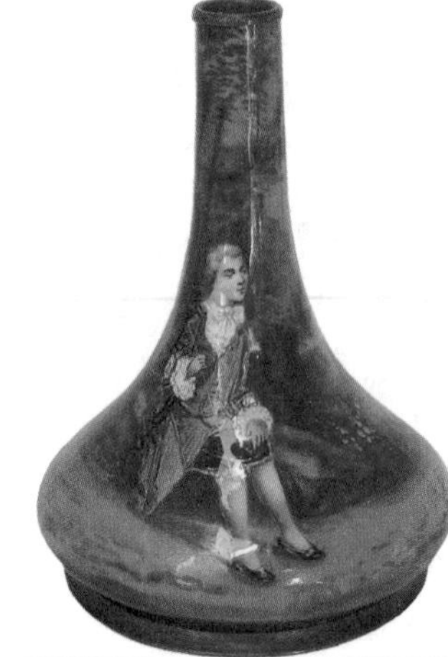

Ruby Lane

Erphila, Vase, Woman, Walking, Basket On Head, Child, Brown, 7 In.
$130

Ruby Lane

Eskimo, Basket, Trinket, Lid, Coiled, Polar Bear Finial, Walrus Ivory, 3 ½ x 4 In.
$708

Hess Auction Group

Eskimo, Mask, Cedar, Carved, Painted, c.1910, 11 x 6 ½ In.
$237

James D. Julia Auctioneers

Eskimo, Tobacco Container, Antler, Carved, Incised, Scenes, Wood Plug, 1800s, 3 x 5 In.
$1,020

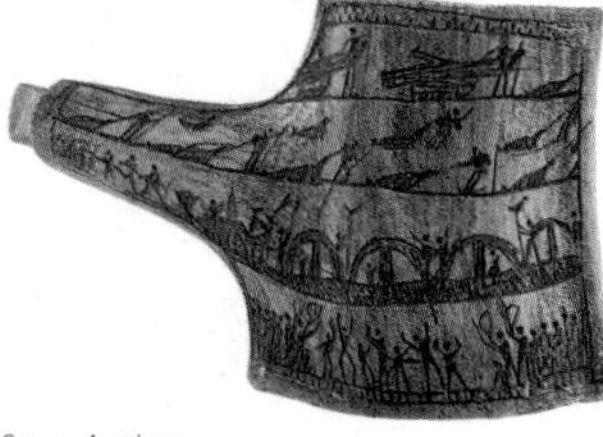

Cowan Auctions

Eskimo, Trinket Box, Wood, Lift Lid, Applied Figures, Shaped Feet, Greenland, c.1905, 7 x 4 In.
$1,046

Cowan Auctions

TIP

Gummed tags can be removed by heating the tag with a hair dryer, then loosening it with a flat knife.

FAMILLE ROSE, *see Chinese Export category.*

FANS have been used for cooling since the days of the ancients. By the eighteenth century, the fan was an accessory for the lady of fashion and very elaborate and expensive fans were made. Sticks were made of ivory or wood, set with jewels or carved. The fans were made of painted silk or paper. Inexpensive paper fans printed with advertising were giveaways in the late nineteenth and early twentieth centuries. Electric fans were introduced in 1882.

Advertising, Apple Gum, Juicy!, 5 Cents, Apple Shape, 15 x 9 In. 60
Black Lacquer, Regency, Rounded, Hydrangea, Turned, 19th Century, 16 x 10¾ In., Pair.......... 303
Carved, Plum Branches, Center Cartouche, Silk Ribbon, Chinese Export, Frame, c.1800, 6 x 8 In. 625
Electric, Air Castle, Tabletop, 2 Blades, Metal, 16½ In. 60
Electric, Dominion, Tabletop, 5 Blades, Teal, Jet Air, 1950s, 11½ In. 60
Electric, Emerson, Brass Blades, 1900s, 13 x 10 In. 218
Electric, Fitzgerald, Black, Brass, 13¼ x 10¼ In. 52
Electric, Gilbert, Desk, Light Blue, Multispeed, Swivels, Art Deco Style, 16 In. 150
Electric, Kenmore, Black, Green, Silver, 10¼ x 9 In. 22
Metalwork Frame, Enameled Flowers, Stand, Box, 10½ x 19 In. 500
Painted, Lacquer Ribs, Reserves, Famille Rose, Silk, Bone, Canton, 1800s, 17 In. ....*illus* 431
Paper, Couples, Musicians, Painted, 2-Sided, 11 x 20 In. 75
Silk, Embroidered, Gold Plated Filigree, Box, 12 In. 105
Tortoiseshell, Brise, Relief Carved, Village Scene, Chinese, Frame, 7 x 12 In. 2952
Tortoiseshell, Pierced Spines, Painted Silk, Wood Nymph, Cobwebs, Fairies, 16 x 26 In. 984

FAST FOOD COLLECTIBLES *may be included in several categories, such as Advertising, Coca-Cola, Toy, etc.*

FEDERZEICHNUNG, *see Loetz category.*

FENTON ART GLASS COMPANY was founded in 1905 in Martins Ferry, Ohio, by Frank L. Fenton and his brother, John W. Fenton. They painted decorations on glass blanks made by other manufacturers. In 1907 they opened a factory in Williamstown, West Virginia, and began making glass. The company stopped making art glass in 2011 and assets were sold. A new division of the company makes handcrafted glass beads and other jewelry. Copies are being made from leased original Fenton molds by an unrelated company, Fenton's Collectibles. The copies are marked with the Fenton mark and Fenton's Collectibles mark. Fenton is noted for early carnival glass produced between 1907 and 1920. Some of these pieces are listed in the Carnival Glass category. Many other types of glass were also made. Spanish Lace in this section refers to the pattern made by Fenton.

Aqua Crest, Vase, Fan Shape, 8 In. 36
Aqua Crest, Vase, Ruffled, Bulbous, 7¾ In. 48
Butterfly & Berry, Basket, Topaz Opalescent, 7 In. 45
Coin Dot, Vase, Blue Opalescent, Crimped Edge, 6½ In. 124
Cranberry Opalescent, Pitcher, Water, Honeycomb, c.1950, 9 x 7 In. 44
Crystal Crest, Vase, Footed, White, Footed, 4 In. 60
Emerald Crest, Compote, Milk Glass, Ruffled, 4 In. 49
Fairy Lamp, Burmese, Dogwood, Matte Glass Lamp, Dome, Glass Center, Folded Rim Base, 6 In. 69
Figurine, Bird, Wing Ding, Painted, Sticker, 3¼ In. 25
Figurine, Hummingbird, Amberina, Base, 5 In. 48
Figurine, Hummingbird, Green, Iridescent, 4 In. 23
Figurine, White Carnival Bird, Flowers, 4 In. 39
Georgian, Creamer, Amber.......... 10
Hobnail, Butter, Cover, Milk Glass, Round, 5 In. 71
Hobnail, Cake Plate, Crimped Edge, Turquoise, 12 In. 852
Hobnail, Cake Plate, Milk Glass, Ruffled Rim, Pedestal, 12 In. 124
Hobnail, Slipper, Amber, 6 In. 14
Hobnail, Sugar, White Opalescent, Footed, Handles.......... 23
Hobnail, Top Hat, Blue, 2 In. 21
Hobnail, Vase, Footed, Topaz Opalescent, Ivy Ball, 4¾ In. 64
Mother's Day, Plate, Iridescent Amethyst, Madonna & Child, 1971, 7¾ In. 9
Paperweight, Bird, Satin, Tail Up, 6 x 5 In. 38
Peacock, Vase, Periwinkle Blue, Flared Cup Top, 12 In. 611
Priscilla, Sugar & Creamer, Green.......... 52
Rib & Holly Sprig, Compote, Marigold, Flared & Crimped Rim, 4 In. 20
Silver Crest, Basket, 11 In. 55
Silver Crest, Bowl, Spanish Lace, 10 x 4 In. 31
Silver Crest, Candy Dish, Lid, Footed, 6 In. 200

Silver Crest, Compote, 9 In. 28
Silver Crest, Compote, Lid, c.1955, 9 ¼ x 6 ¾ In. 36
Spruce Green, Rose Bowl, 3 In. 42
Thumbprint, Basket, Ruby, 8 x 8 In. 28
Thumbprint, Creamer, Amber, 4 In. 18
Thumbprint, Creamer, Colonial Pink, 4 In. 31
Thumbprint, Epergne, 3-Horn, Colonial Blue, 10 x 9 In. 250
Vase, Abstract Design, Leaves, Twigs, 11 In. 180
Vase, Red, Pulled Feather Design, Blue Disc Foot, Stick Neck, Flared Rim, 7 In. *illus* 3680
Waterlily, Pitcher, Custard, 7 In. 64

FIESTA, the colorful dinnerware, was introduced in 1936 by the Homer Laughlin China Co., redesigned in 1969, and withdrawn in 1973. It was reissued again in 1986 in different colors and is still being made. New colors, including some that are similar to old colors, have been introduced. One new color is introduced in March every year. The simple design was characterized by a band of concentric circles beginning at the rim. Cups had full-circle handles until 1969, when partial-circle handles were made. Harlequin and Riviera were related wares. For more prices, go to kovels.com.

Apricot, Cup 16
Apricot, Cup & Saucer 12
Apricot, Gravy Boat 72
Apricot, Platter, 11 In. 32
Chartreuse, Sugar & Creamer 45
Cobalt Blue, Chop Plate, 15 In. 20
Cobalt Blue, Gravy Boat 40
Cobalt Blue, Nappy, 9 ½ In. 10
Gray, Plate, 9 In. 11
Green, Bowl, Footed, 12 In. 70
Green, Mixing Bowl, No. 1 140
Green, Plate, 3 Sections, 10 ½ In. 20
Ivory, Mixing Bowl, No. 7 170
Ivory, Plate, 6 In. 5
Ivory, Plate, 10 In. 18
Ivory, Tumbler, Juice, 3 ½ In. 15
Medium Green, Bowl, Fruit, 4 ¾ In. 170
Medium Green, Gravy Boat 55
Medium Green, Nappy, 8 ½ In. 55
Medium Green, Salt & Pepper, Ball Shape 55
Medium Green, Sugar & Creamer 150
Red, Chop Plate, 13 In. 20
Red, Gravy Boat 45
Red, Mixing Bowl, No. 2, 1936-42, 4 x 5 ⅞ In. *illus* 200
Red, Sugar & Creamer 35
Rose, Chop Plate, 15 In. 25
Rose, Mug, Porky Pig, Looney Tunes *illus* 12
Rose, Sugar & Creamer 20
Turquoise, Cup & Saucer 26
Turquoise, Mixing Bowl, No. 7 150
Turquoise, Plate, 3 Sections, 10 ½ In. 15
Yellow, Bowl, 11 ¾ In. 60
Yellow, Cup & Saucer 19 to 21
Yellow, Mixing Bowl, No. 5 30
Yellow, Plate, 9 In. 12
Yellow, Plate, Dinner, 10 ½ In. 15 to 23
Yellow, Sugar & Creamer 30
Yellow, Sugar, Lid 15 to 18

FINCH, *see Kay Finch category.*

FINDLAY ONYX AND FLORADINE are two similar types of glass made by Dalzell, Gilmore and Leighton Co. of Findlay, Ohio, about 1889. Onyx is a patented yellowish white opaque glass with raised silver daisy decorations. A few rare pieces were made of rose, amber, orange, or purple glass. Floradine is made of cranberry-colored glass with an opalescent white raised floral pattern and a satin finish. The same molds were used for both types of glass.

Bowl, Red Base, Opalescent Flowers, 2 ¾ x 7 ½ In. 633

Faience, Vase, Moth, Blue & Red, Rolled Rim, California Faience Co., 1920s, 5 x 5 In.
$1,500

Rago Arts and Auction Center

New Fiesta

Fiesta pottery has been reissued since 1986. Collectors call it New Fiesta or Post 86 Fiesta.

Fairing, Box, Trinket, Mother, Child, Hurdy-Gurdy, 2 Piece, Porcelain, Paint, c.1880, 3 x 3 In.
$95

Ruby Lane

Fairing, Figurine, Midnight's Holy Hour, Mother & Baby In Bed, Father Standing, 1880s, 3 x 3 In.
$99

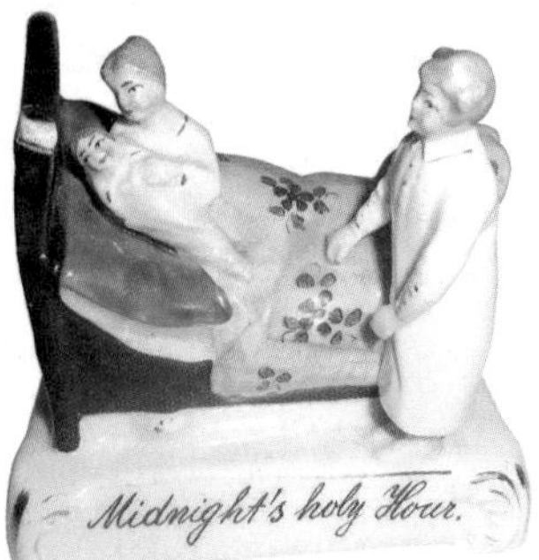

Ruby Lane

Fan, Painted, Lacquer Ribs, Reserves, Famille Rose, Silk, Bone, Canton, 1800s, 17 In.
$431

Cowan Auctions

Fenton, Vase, Red, Pulled Feather Design, Blue Disc Foot, Stick Neck, Flared Rim, 7 In.
$3,680

Early Auction Company

Fiesta, Red, Mixing Bowl, No. 2, 1936-42, 4 x 5 ⅞ In.
$200

Ruby Lane

Fiesta, Rose, Mug, Porky Pig, Looney Tunes
$12

Findlay, Celery, Onyx, Opal Body, Ribbed Cylindrical Neck, Round Bottom, Silver Flowers, 6 In.
$345

Early Auction Company

Findlay, Spooner, Floradine, Translucent Cranberry Glass, White Flowers, 4 ¼ In.
$201

Early Auction Company

Firefighting, Grenade, Hand Grenade, H In Shield, Cobalt Blue, Hobnail, 6 In.
$1,035

Glass Works Auctions

Firefighting, Helmet, High Eagle Tooled Leather, Chief, Cairns & Bro, Velvet Liner, c.1900, 15 x 9 In.
$895

Ruby Lane

Firefighting, Horn, Speaking, Silver Plate, Helmet Braid, c.1910, 24 In.
$1,888

Brunk Auctions

Celery, Onyx, Opal Body, Ribbed Cylindrical Neck, Round Bottom, Silver Flowers, 6 In. ......*illus* 345
Pitcher, Onyx, Fluted Neck, 4 ¾ In. 395
Shaker, Onyx, Opal, Bulbous, Ribbed Neck, 5 ½ x 3 ¼ In. 395
Spooner, Floradine, Translucent Cranberry Glass, White Flowers, 4 ¼ In. ....*illus* 201
Spooner, Onyx, Ball Shape, 4 x 4 ½ In. 295
Sugar, Lid, Onyx, Ivory, Globular, 5 ¾ In. 175

FIREFIGHTING equipment of all types is wanted, from fire marks to uniforms to toy fire trucks. It is said that every little boy wanted to be a fireman or a train engineer 75 years ago and the collectors today reflect this interest.

Ax, Oak Handle, 1950s, 16 In. 118
Bucket, Copper, Riveted, Cylindrical, Swing Bail Handle, Monogrammed, 1800s, 13 x 14 In. 388
Bucket, Leather, Brown, Handle, Marked M.A.R., 20 In. 113
Bucket, Leather, Canvas, Brass Buttons, 1900s, 15 ¾ x 7 ½ In. 287
Bucket, Leather, George Washington, Urn, Protection In Danger, c.1800, 13 In. 2390
Bucket, Leather, Green Paint, Top Handle, Banner, Prescott, 1800s, 19 In. 354
Bucket, Leather, Handle, Metal Rim, Red Paint, c.1810, 10 ½ In. 469
Bucket, Leather, Paint, Shaking Hands, J.B. Kittridge No. 2, F.F.C., c.1800, 13 In. 4740
Bucket, Leather, Strap Handle, c.1850, 12 x 11 In. 295
Bucket, Red, Stenciled Flower Basket, Gilt, Silver, Black, Bail Handle, 9 ½ x 11 In. 130
Extinguisher, Hero Can Fire Extinguisher, Red, White, Canada, 1940s, 5 In. 28
Fire Mark, Cast Iron, Embossed FA, Painted, Philadelphia, 1800s, 11 ½ In. 295
Grenade, Hand Grenade, H In Shield, Cobalt Blue, Hobnail, 6 In. ....*illus* 1035
Helmet, High Eagle Tooled Leather, Chief, Cairns & Bro, Velvet Liner, c.1900, 15 x 9 In. ......*illus* 895
Helmet, Leather, Black, No. 4, Eagle, Cairns & Bro, 8 ¼ x 10 ¾ In. 460
Horn, Speaking, Silver Plate, Helmet Braid, c.1910, 24 In. ....*illus* 1888
Horn, Speaking, Silver Plate, Relief Engine Co., No. 2, New Rochelle, c.1910, 22 In. 1298
Hydrant, Iron, Red, Rope Twist, Shields, 30 In. 60
Lantern, Brass, Wheel Cut, Acid Etched, Pawtucket, Pat. J. Sangster, 1862, 18 In. ....*illus* 2470
Pumper Lantern, Gilt Brass, Glass, Geo W. Frantz, Eagle Finial, Dome, c.1890, 21 In. ....*illus* 9225
Siren, Fire Engine, Red, Bell Shape, Mounting Bracket, 9 ½ x 16 ½ In. 240
Siren, Fire Station, Red Paint, Cast Iron, Pressed Steel, Federal Electric Co., 11 x 13 ½ In. 94
Trumpet, Speaking, Presentation, Silver Plate, 1880, 18 x 6 ½ In. 2875

FIREPLACES were used to cook food and to heat the American home in past centuries. Many types of tools and equipment were used. Andirons held the logs in place, firebacks reflected the heat into the room, and tongs were used to move either fuel or food. Many types of spits and roasting jacks were made and may be listed in the Kitchen category.

Andirons, Art Deco Style, Stylized Leaves, S-Curve Stem, Fluted Base, Gilt Metal, 21 In. 2214
Andirons, Art Deco, Dolphin, Steel, Iron, Tapered, Pierced Standard, Scrolled Feet, 34 x 30 In. .. 1845
Andirons, Black Men, Hands On Knees, 17 ½ x 17 In. 322
Andirons, Brass & Iron, Steeple Top, Sphere, Arched Feet, c.1790, 19 x 18 In. 711
Andirons, Brass, Claw Foot, 27 ¼ In. 48
Andirons, Brass, Double Lemon Top, Seamed, 19th Century, 19 In. 281
Andirons, Brass, Federal, Faceted Spire, Ball, Spurred Legs, Ball Feet, c.1800, 26 In. 360
Andirons, Brass, Figural, Zeus, Hera, Atop 3 Sirens, Grotesque Mask, 37 x 19 In. 518
Andirons, Brass, Iron, Block Shape, Square Top, Arched Feet, c.1925, 17 x 25 In. 546
Andirons, Brass, Lion Head At Center, Twist Bulb Finial, 23 ½ x 10 In. 246
Andirons, Brass, Scalloped, Turned Finials, Ball & Claw Feet, 21 x 10 ½ In. 91
Andirons, Brass, Steeple Top, Cabriole Legs, Ball Feet, Fretwork, c.1800, 27 x 12 In. 3198
Andirons, Bronze, Cupids, Holding Kindling, Pierced Base, Paw Feet, c.1875, 36 x 20 In. 2214
Andirons, Bronze, Egyptian Style, Continental, 34 x 13 In. 780
Andirons, Bronze, Patina, Scroll & Urn, France, 26 x 16 In. 177
Andirons, Bronze, Renaissance Revival, Reticulated Sphere, Flowers, 25 x 12 ½ In. 364
Andirons, Cast Iron, Brownie, Hands On Hips, Marked, Freihofer, 8 x 16 In. 180
Andirons, Cast Iron, Classical, Serpentine Dolphins, Bradley & Hubbard, 14 x 8 In. 837
Andirons, Cast Iron, Duck Decoy, Black Paint, Arched Feet, c.1920, 11 x 15 In. 593
Andirons, Cast Iron, Duck, 11 x 19 ½ In. 351
Andirons, Cast Iron, Grant & Ben Franklin Busts, 7 x 15 In. 345
Andirons, Cast Iron, Hessian Soldier, Red Coat, Black Pants, Yellow Boots, 12 x 24 In. 165
Andirons, Cast Iron, Indian, Headdress, Tunic, Crossed Arms, Scroll Feet, 13 In. 246
Andirons, Cast Iron, Pierced Brass Rondels, Thistle Design, 25 x 19 In. 207
Andirons, Cast Iron, Seated Ducks, Glass Eyes, 11 x 15 In. 840
Andirons, Cast Iron, Tito Lucifer, Cone Shape, Philippe Starck, 11 x 15 In. 1187
Andirons, Cast Iron, Whippet, 27 ¾ In. 2856

Firefighting, Lantern, Brass, Wheel Cut, Acid Etched, Pawtucket, Pat. J. Sangster, 1862, 18 In.
$2,470

James D. Julia Auctioneers

Firefighting, Pumper Lantern, Gilt Brass, Glass, Geo W. Frantz, Eagle Finial, Dome, c.1890, 21 In.
$9,225

Skinner, Inc.

Fireplace, Fireback, George Washington Bust Medallion, Cast Iron, c.1790, 21 x 21 In.
$5,535

Skinner, Inc.

Fireplace, Screen, Leaded Stained Glass, Victorian Woman, Flowers, c.1900, 44 x 36 In.
$593

James D. Julia Auctioneers

Fireplace, Screen, Satinwood, Cane, Portrait Medallion, Oval Frame, c.1910, 34 x 19 In.
$1,353

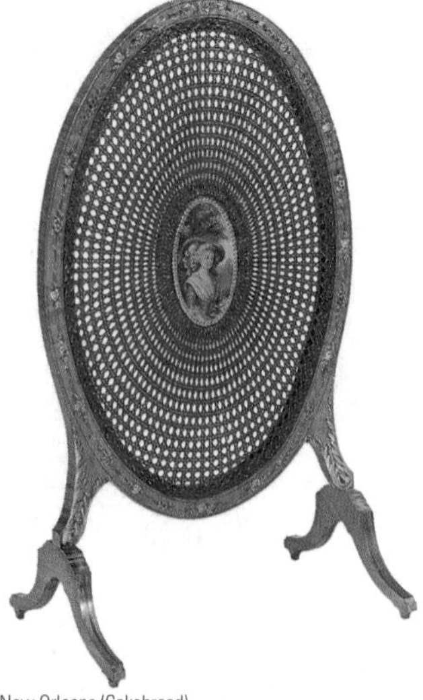

New Orleans (Cakebread)

Andirons, Chrome, Enameled Steel, Glass, Style Of Jacques Adnet, 15 ½ x 22 ½ In. 1000
Andirons, Coiled Dolphins, Urn-Shape Finials, 28 ¼ In. 1000
Andirons, Copper, Iron, Prairie School, Stylized Trees, c.1925, 19 ½ x 11 In. 1875
Andirons, George II Style, Squat Bulbous Tops, Urn Finials, Paw Feet, c.1910, 20 In. 355
Andirons, Gilt Bronze, Man & Woman, Swags, Cherubs, Leaves, 1800s, 35 In. 1750
Andirons, Horseshoe Shape Finial, Shaped Standard, c.1900, 15 In. 60
Andirons, Iron, Projecting Platform, Vinework, Supports, c.1800, 18 In. 338
Andirons, Iron, Sitting Cat, Silhouette Design, Pierced Eyes & Mouth, 13 x 14 In. 593
Andirons, Lion, Double Scroll, Mirrored, 20 ½ x 13 In. 847
Andirons, Metal & Iron, Lemon Top Finials, Columnar Shaft, Claw & Ball Feet, c.1790, 20 In. .. 615
Andirons, Steel, Brass, Tulip Shape, Arch, Scroll, 1900s, 19 x 8 ½ In. 215
Andirons, Wrought Iron, Knife Blade, Brass Urn Finials, c.1790, 17 x 9 ½ In. 59
Andirons, Wrought Iron, Ring Handles, Scrolled Top & Base, c.1900, 31 ½ x 25 In. 553
Andirons, Wrought Iron, Rustic Style, Twisted, 29 ½ In. 76
Bellows, Blue & White Delft Mounted, Wood, Brass, Family, Cottage, 17 ½ x 7 In. 840
Bellows, Brass, Carved, Man's Face, Leaves 142
Bellows, Painted, Baskets Of Flowers, Ferns, Red Border, Brass Nozzle, 1800s, 19 In. 277
Bellows, Turned Brass Spout, Yellow, Stenciled, Gold, Flowers, Leaves, c.1850, 18 In. 93
Bellows, Walnut, Carved, Harpy Handle, Marriage Of Cupid & Psyche, 26 x 12 ¾ In. 1088
Box, Log, Brass, Drinking, Card Players, Ramshackle Background, 18 x 17 In. 94
Chenets, Andirons, Belle Epoque, Argente, Urns, Flame Finial, Neoclassical, 15 x 14 In. 553
Chenets, Andirons, Bronze Dore, Scrolled & Pierced, Rocaille, Peasant Child, c.1900, 18 x 16 In. 1875
Chenets, Andirons, Bronze, Cupid, Vase, Ribbons, Grape Leaves, Ram's Head, 1800s, 27 In. 3690
Chenets, Andirons, Bronze, Fruit Basket, Flame Finial, Columnar Frieze, 1800s, 15 In. 2214
Chenets, Andirons, Bronze, Gilt, Louis XV Style, Flowers, Scroll, c.1890, 18 x 50 In. 813
Chenets, Andirons, Bronze, Urn Shape, Flame Finial, Lion's Paw Feet, c.1900, 13 x 13 In. 492
Chenets, Andirons, Cast Iron, Egyptian Revival, Pharaoh Head, 19th Century, 17 x 3 x 4 In. 375
Chenets, Andirons, Gilt Bronze, Louis XVI Style, Acorn Finials, c.1880, 11 x 12 In. 584
Chenets, Andirons, Gilt Bronze, Louis XVI Style, Fluted Column, Leaves, Swags, 19 x 16 In. 1599
Chenets, Andirons, Gilt Bronze, Napoleon III, Fluted Column, Laurel Swags, 15 x 8 In. 799
Chenets, Andirons, Gilt Bronze, Napoleon III, Pierced Rocaille, Billet Bar, c.1870, 17 x 25 In. ... 1000
Chenets, Andirons, Gilt Bronze, Urn Shape Finial, 11 ¼ x 12 ¾ In. 250
Chenets, Andirons, Silvered Bronze, Louis XV Style, 15 ½ In. 845
Coal Bucket, Brass, 16 x 10 In. 24
Coal Bucket, Staved, Brass Trim, Paw Feet, 14 ½ In. 59
Coal Scuttle, Scoop, Brass, Round Foot, Wood Turned Handle, 21 x 13 In. 130
Coal Scuttle, Tole, Black, Poppies, Daisies, Leaves, Knob, 4-Footed, 17 x 18 In. 49
Coal Scuttle, Tole, Gray, Cylindrical, Handles, Lid, 15 x 14 In. 24
Coal Scuttle, Tole, Lift Top, Calla Lilies, Black Ground, Gilt, Handles, Claw Feet, 25 x 15 In. 94
Coal Scuttle, Victorian, Tole, 2 Handles, Masks On Knees, Painted, Cast Iron Feet, 23 x 11 In. ... 236
Fender, Brass, Pierced, Claw Feet, 3 Bands, 11 ½ x 50 In. 60
Fender, Brass, Wirework Front Panel, Paw Feet, Tongs, Shovel, c.1890, 48 x 12 In. 448
Fender, Brass, Wirework, Serpentine, Urn Finials, Paw Feet, c.1950, 16 x 48 In. 391
Fender, Bronze Dore, Arched Ends, Lyres, Lunettes, Pierced, Medallions, c.1835, 7 x 39 In. 584
Fender, Copper, Red Leather Padded Corners, England, 18 x 63 In. 330
Fender, Gilt Bronze, Baluster Fluted Columns, Flowers, Leaf, 1800s, 82 x 13 In. 230
Fender, Iron & Leather, Openwork Spirals, Brass Tacks, Pleated Seat, c.1910, 24 x 83 In. 1673
Fender, Iron Wirework, Serpentine, Brass Top Rail, Swag & Grillwork, c.1810, 40 x 13 In. 590
Fender, Oak, Barley Twist, 14 x 43 In. 109
Fender, Restauration, Chenets, Adjustable, Rod Shape, Scrolling, Dog Finials, 41 x 8 In. 375
Fender, Sheet Iron, Wire, Bow Front, c.1810, 7 x 44 In. 148
Fender, Tole, Grapevine, Grapes, Mesh, 16 x 38 In. 96
Fireback, Basket Of Flowers On Draped Stand, Cast Iron, Shaped Top, 20 x 16 In. 308
Fireback, Cast Iron, Tombstone, Phoenix Rising, Great Fire In Boston, 1760, 31 In. 4305
Fireback, George Washington Bust Medallion, Cast Iron, c.1790, 21 x 21 In. .... *illus* 5535
Fireback, Tudor Style, Cast Iron, Lion Passant Quadrant, Thistle, c.1900, 26 x 30 In. 1968
Fireboard, Beadboard Panels, Carved Green Applied Leaves, c.1890, 34 x 36 In. 861
Guard, Brass, Fan Shape, Pierced, Leaf Frame, Folding, 29 x 41 ½ In. 196
Guard, French Empire, Gilt Bronze, Egyptian Style, Sphinx Busts, 11 x 42 In. 1353
Hearth Stand, False Drawers, Cast Handles, Scroll & Dart Skirt, Legs, 1800s, 19 x 18 In. 35
Mantel is listed in the Architectural category.
Peat Bucket, George III, Mahogany, Reeded, Banded Body, Brass Loop Handle, c.1800, 16 In. ... 944
Roaster, Iron, Dome Lid, Rod & Hooks, 1800s, 11 x 7 In. 325
Screen, Arts & Crafts, Iron, Copper, Embossed Portrait Panel, Schiller Goethe, 46 x 31 In. 295
Screen, Bronze, Pierced & Scrolled, Cornucopia, Flowers, Scroll Feet, c.1910, 30 x 29 In. 593
Screen, Bronze, Wire, Rocaille Serpentine Frame, Handle, Putto On Swing, c.1910, 31 x 23 In. . 984
Screen, Bronze, Wire, Serpentine Crest, Handle, Flowers, Leaves, Tendrils, c.1910, 28 x 10 In. ... 3444

Screen, Classical Revival, Walnut, Carved, Arched Crest, Needlepoint, 43 x 35 In. 183
Screen, Copper, Embossed, Wrought Iron, Warrior Bust, 42 x 57 In. 984
Screen, Diamond Pattern, Iron Base, Wire, Brass Cap, Hand Forged, c.1890, 12 x 30 In. 413
Screen, Edwardian, Mahogany, Needlepoint, Flower Spray, 38 ¼ x 25 In. 60
Screen, Flowers, Cast Iron, Painted, 43 x 32 ½ In. 409
Screen, French Style, Brass, Fan Shape, Scalloped Edge, 26 x 38 In. 210
Screen, George III, Satinwood, Mahogany Stringing, Walnut Inlay, c.1790, 43 x 19 In. 59
Screen, Gilt Bronze, Pierced Legs, Rocaille & Scroll, Handle, Flame Pot, c.1910, 31 x 28 In. 2091
Screen, Gilt Bronze, Torches, Cut Corner Top, Pierced Crest, Hoof Feet, c.1900, 30 x 29 In. 875
Screen, Gothic, Oak, Carved, Lions, 50 x 34 In. 5175
Screen, Leaded Stained Glass, Victorian Woman, Flowers, c.1900, 44 x 36 In. *illus* 593
Screen, Leather, Hunt Scene, Horses, Riders, Black Painted Frame, c.1960, 35 x 39 In. 120
Screen, Louis XVI Style, Gilt Metal, Figural Mounts, Crossed Torch, 31 x 30 In. 1353
Screen, Louis XVI Style, Giltwood, Crest, Acorn Finials, Needlework Scene, 37 x 19 In. 738
Screen, Pole, Needlepoint, Cherry, Adjustable, Shield Shape, Agnus Dei, Tripod Base, 53 In. 420
Screen, Pole, Needlepoint, George III Style, Mahogany, Carved, Frame, Birds, 50 In. 180
Screen, Pole, Needlepoint, King Arthur, Dragon, Tripod Base, Claw Feet, 66 x 18 In. 127
Screen, Pole, Needlework Panel, Flowers, Silk, Turned Mahogany, Tripod Base, 56 In. 738
Screen, Rococo Style, Bronze, Wire, Scroll Surround, Rocaille Handle, c.1900, 32 x 29 In. 2952
Screen, Satinwood, Cane, Portrait Medallion, Oval Frame, c.1910, 34 x 19 In. *illus* 1353
Screen, Wire, Bronze, Louis XV Style, Angels Warming Hands, 27 x 29 x 7 In. 522
Screens are also listed in the Architectural and Furniture categories.
Surround, Neoclassical, Oak, Carved, Molded Crown, Shelf, 1800s, 82 x 60 In. 1007
Tongs, Brass Turned Handle, Iron, 1820, 29 In. 74
Tongs, Cast Iron, Owl Handle, 1800s, 27 In. 71
Tool Set, Brass, Stand, Tongs, Shovel, Poker, England, 1800s, 28 In., 4 Piece 71
Tool Set, Bronze, Umbrella Shape Holder, Poker, Shovel, Tongs, Brush, c.1890, 35 In. 750
Tool Set, Chrome, Brush, Dust Pan, Poker, Tongs, Art Deco, 12 In. 45
Tool Set, Chromed Steel, Caliber, Virginia Metalcrafters, 33 x 9 ¼ In. 770
Tool Set, Hanging Rack, Esherick, Wood, Iron, Copper, 1960, 60 x 16 In., 4 Piece *illus* 27500
Tool Set, Iron, Cast, Brush, Tongs, Scoop, Poker, Cylindrical Handles, 27 x 12 In. 303
Tool Set, Steel & Brass, Tongs, Poker, Shovel, Leaf Pierced Handles & Pan, 30 In. 786
Trammel, Sawtooth, Adjustable, Wrought Iron, 1800s, 28 ½ To 44 In. *illus* 130
Trammel, Wrought Iron, Saw Tooth, Adjustable, 1800s, 21 To 28 In. 94

FISCHER porcelain was made in Herend, Hungary. The wares are sometimes referred to as Herend porcelain. The pottery was originally founded in Herend in 1826 and was bought by Moritz Fischer in 1839. Fischer made replacement pieces for German and Far Eastern dinnerware and later began making its own dinnerware patterns. Figurines were made beginning in the 1870s. The company was nationalized in 1948. Martin's Herend Imports, Inc., began importing Herend china into the United States in 1957. The company was privatized in 1993 and is now in business as Herend.

MF

Bonbonniere, Queen Victoria Pattern, Round, Flowers, Gilt, 1900s, 2 ½ x 3 In. 46
Box, Blue Garland, Globe Shape, Fish Shape Finial, Lid, 9 ½ x 6 ⅓ In. 219
Cachepot, Bouquet, Fuchsia Flowers, Ruffled Rim, Gilt Band, Squat, Openwork, 4 x 5 In. 61
Chop Plate, Flowers & Butterflies, Basket Texture, Gilt Edge, Wavy Rim, 1900s, 15 x 14 In. 938
Dish, Rothschild Bird Pattern, Shell Shape, White, Multicolor, c.1910, 4 x 9 In., Pair 708
Ewer, Cream Ground, Brown Mottled, Gilt, Round Body, Pinch Center, c.1910, 7 ½ x 12 In. 69
Figurine, 2 Ducks, Entwined Heads, Fishnet Design, Multicolor, Gilt, c.1980, 8 In. 2000
Figurine, Butterfly & Daisy, Multicolor, 4 In. 72
Figurine, Giraffes, Entwined Necks, Blue & White Pattern, 8 x 5 ½ In. 676
Figurine, Moose, Standing, Black & White, Fishnet Pattern, Gilt Hooves & Antlers, 5 In. *illus* 732
Figurine, Nude Woman, Draped, Looking Into Hand Mirror, White High Glaze, c.1920, 16 In. 359
Figurine, Owl, Perched On Stylized Branch, Orange Fishnet, Marked, 5 In. 92
Figurine, Rabbit, Fishnet, Blue, Gold Leaf Nose, 12 x 7 ½ In. 605
Figurine, Stag, Head Up, Mouth Open, Fishnet Design, Gilt Antlers, 1900s, 11 In. 875
Figurine, Swans, Cuddling, Red & White, Purple, Pink, Blue Wings, 7 ¾ x 4 ½ In. 277
Figurine, Toldi & The Bull, Man Holding Down Bull, Stamped, 9 x 17 In. 219
Figurine, Victorian Woman, Pink Frilly Dress, Playing Guitar, c.1900, 15 In. 329
Figurine, Woman, Playing Guitar, Purple Ruffled Dress, 14 In. 375
Fish Platter, Blue Garland, 24 x 9 ½ In. 407
Group, Mare, Calf, Green, Blue, White, Gold Hooves, 12 ½ x 13 In. 1125
Jar, Imari, Rooster Finial, Signed Jossef Gluck, 10 x 6 In. 800
Jug, Flowers, Butterflies, Fan Leaves, Blue, 13 In. *illus* 1500
Perfume Bottle, Queen Victoria, Butterfly Finial, 5 In. 331
Planter, Printemps, Scalloped Border, Blue, Flowers, Marked, 6 x 10 In. 363
Tea Set, Teapot, 2 Cup & Saucer, Sugar & Creamer, Tray, Gallery, Pink, 8 Piece 1353

Fireplace, Tool Set, Hanging Rack, Esherick, Wood, Iron, Copper, 1960, 60 x 16 In., 4 Piece
$27,500

Rago Arts and Auction Center

TIP
Wear cotton gloves when cleaning any type of metal. Oils in the skin will leave a mark.

Fireplace, Trammel, Sawtooth, Adjustable, Wrought Iron, 1800s, 28 ½ To 44 In.
$130

Hess Auction Group

F

Fischer, Figurine, Moose, Standing, Black & White, Fishnet Pattern, Gilt Hooves & Antlers, 5 In.
$732

DuMouchelles Art Gallery

Fischer, Jug, Flowers, Butterflies, Fan Leaves, Blue, 13 In.
$1,500

Ruby Lane

Fishing, Lure, Bass-A-Lure, Shakespeare, 3 Hooks, Glass Eyes, Perch, Kalamazoo, Box
$305

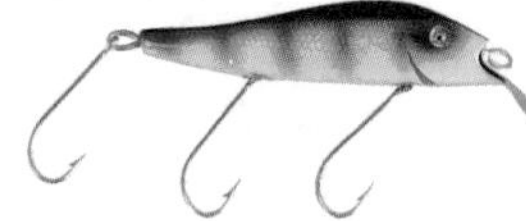

Morphy Auctions

Appraising Lures
There are sites online that will appraise antique fishing lures from a posted picture.

Tray, Serving, Chinese Bouquet, Green, Gilt, White Ground, Twig Handles, 14 In. 201
Tray, Serving, Divided, Birds, Green Handles, 13 x 9 In. 279
Tureen, Applied Roses, Lemon Finial, Green Flowers, 9 ¼ x 11 ½ In. 258
Tureen, Tray, Red Head Bird Finish, Green Handles, Blue Trim, Birds, 9 ½ x 13 In. 1168
Tureen, Underplate, Birds, Lemon Finial, 15 In. 875
Tureen, Underplate, Birds, Purple Rose Finial, 12 x 15 In. 688
Vase, Bud, Beige, Brown, Handles, 10 ½ x 5 ¾ In. 126
Vase, Regency Style, White, Footed, Square Base, Gilt Accents, 7 x 6 In. 178

FISHING reels of brass or nickel were made in the United States by 1810. Bamboo fly rods were sold by 1860, often marked with the maker's name. Lures made of metal, or metal and wood, were made in the nineteenth century. Plastic lures were made by the 1930s. All fishing material is collected today and even equipment of the past thirty years is of interest if in good condition with original box.

Bait Bucket, Tole, Black Paint, Flowers, Liner, 2 Handles, 7 x 13 In. 225
Creel, Wicker, Leather Strap, 15 x 8 In. 126
Creel, Wicker, Leather, Shoulder Strap, c.1945, 14 x 5 ½ In. 125
Eel Tongs, Oak, Chamfered Corners, Nail Teeth, c.1800, 21 In. 100
Fish Gig, 5 Barbs, Socket Handle, Wood Pole, Handwrought, c.1850, 73 x 4 In. 55
Lure, Bass-A-Lure, Shakespeare, 3 Hooks, Glass Eyes, Perch, Kalamazoo, Box........ *illus* 305
Lure, Creek Chub, Wood, Glass Eyes, 3 Hooks, Box, 1950s, 5 In. 45
Lure, Dreadnought, Moonlight Bait Co., Brass, Nickel, Spinners, Box, c.1912, 4 In. .... *illus* 29280
Lure, Kautzky Mfg., Lazy Ike, Articulated, Wood, Diver, c.1950, 2 ¾ In. 50
Lure, Pfueger, Pal-O-Mine, Wood, Jointed, 4 ½ In. 24
Lure, Shakespeare, Marty's Mighty Mouse, Double Treble Hook, Box, 2 ⅝ In. 50
Lure, Shakespeare, Musky Pad-Ler, Wood, 3 Hooks, Pressed Eyes, 1936, 3 ¾ In. 90
Lure, Suick Co., Thriller, 3 Treble Hooks, 1956, 7 In. 17
Lure, Wiggle Tail Minnow Co., Wood, Glass Eyes, Front Spinner, Detroit, c.1912, 3 In. .... *illus* 23180
Lure, Wood, Green, 3 In. 16
Lure, Wood, South Bend, ¾ In. 18
Manual, Fishing With Hook & Line, For Anglers, Pictorial Cover, Frank Forrester, 7 x 4 In. 1298
Minnow Trap, Willow, 48 In. 58
Outboard Motor, Johnson, Sea-Horse, TN 5 HP, Metal Stand, c.1950, 11 x 39 In. .... *illus* 580
Reel, Brass Star Back, Walnut, Rosewood Handles, c.1910, 4 x 3 x 3 In. 350
Reel, Fin-Nor, Fly No. 3........ 320
Reel, Fly, Raised Pillar, Brass, 1800s, 2 In. 40
Reel, Klondike, Salmon, Mahogany, Brass, Marked, c.1900, 6 ¼ In. 200
Reel, Martin, Automatic Retrieving, 1950s, 3 x 2 In. 43
Reel, Penn Peer, c.1970, 3 x 5 ½ In. 35
Reel, Salmon, Rubber, Silver, Orange, Black, Click, Philbrook & Paine, c.1880, 4 In. .... *illus* 12200
Reel, Shakespeare, Closed Cast, Pushbutton Spin, 1960s........ 24
Tackle Box, Bob-Bet, Metal, Green, Round, Walter S. Cole, 1940s, 4 ½ In. 25
Tackle Box, Cricket Cage, Marine Mesh, Cylindrical, Metal, Gray Paint, Hinged, c.1915, 6 In. 95
Tackle Box, D Shape, Copper, Coil Spring, Marked, BM, c.1875, 3 ¾ x 4 ¾ x 3 In. 400
Tackle Box, Pressed Cork, Green & Metal Frame, Oberlain, 1950s, 14 x 7 x 6 In. 35

FLAGS *are included in the Textile category.*

FLASH GORDON appeared in the Sunday comics in 1934. The daily strip started in 1940. The hero was also in comic books from 1930 to 1970, in books from 1936, in movies from 1938, on the radio in the 1930s and 1940s, and on television from 1953 to 1954. All sorts of memorabilia are collected, but the ray guns and rocket ships are the most popular.

Casting Set, Electric Ladle, Paint, Home Foundry Mfg., Box, 1934, 9 x 16 In. 404
Comic Book, On The Planet Mongo, Whitman, No. 1110, Don Moore, 1934........ 183

FLORENCE CERAMICS were made in Pasadena, California, from World War II to 1977. Florence Ward created many colorful figurines, boxes, candleholders, and other items for the gift shop trade. Each piece was marked with an ink stamp that included the name *Florence Ceramics Co*. The company was sold in 1964 and although the name remained the same, the products were very different. Mugs, cups, and trays were made.

Bust, Shen, Gold, White Jacket, 1940s, 8 x 5 ¾ In. 260
Figurine, Camille, Aqua Blue, Net Lace Shawl, 1953, 9 x 6 In. 35
Figurine, Matilda, Aqua, 8 ½ In. 95
Figurine, Scarlet O'Hara, Gray Dress, Green Hat, Bow, Muff, 8 ¾ In. 200
Figurine, Vivian, Pink Dress........ 200

Fishing, Lure, Dreadnought, Moonlight Bait Co., Brass, Nickel, Spinners, Box, c.1912, 4 In.
$29,280

Morphy Auctions

Fishing, Lure, Wiggle Tail Minnow Co., Wood, Glass Eyes, Front Spinner, Detroit, c.1912, 3 In.
$23,180

Morphy Auctions

Fishing, Outboard Motor, Johnson, Sea-Horse, TN 5 HP, Metal Stand, c.1950, 11 x 39 In.
$580

Morphy Auctions

Fishing, Reel, Salmon, Rubber, Silver, Orange, Black, Click, Philbrook & Paine, c.1880, 4 In.
$12,200

Morphy Auctions

Folk Art, Jigger, Man With Top Hat, Sheet Metal, Painted, Iron Rod, Wood Ball, c.1850, 20 In.
$3,000

Cowan Auctions

Folk Art, Squirrel On Tree Stump, Mixed Materials, Gold Painted, c.1950, 27 In.
$210

Garth's Auctioneers & Appraisers

Folk Art, Toy, 2 Women, Churning Butter, Jointed, Wood, Pull String Movement, c.1850, 4 In.
$560

Theriault's

Folk Art, Whirligig, Civil War Union Soldier, Pine, Tin, Paint, Sword Shape Paddles, 24 In.
$16,800

Garth's Auctioneers & Appraisers

Fostoria, Coin, Vase, Red, Footed, 1958-82, 8 In.
$55

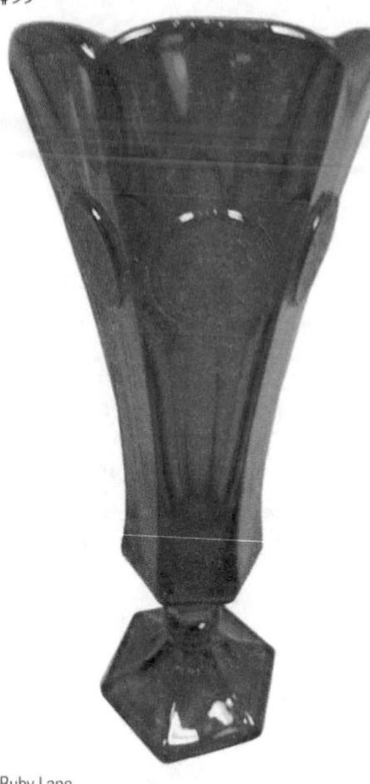

Ruby Lane

Franciscan, Apple, Cup & Saucer, 1940s
$14

Ruby Lane

Franciscan, El Patio, Toast & Jam Set, Green, Yellow, 7 ¼ x 5 ½ In.
$32

Ruby Lane

Vase, Figural, Asian Girl, Holding Fan, 8 x 4 ¾ In. 22
Vase, Girl, White Dress, 7 In. 75

FLOW BLUE was made in England and other countries about 1830 to 1900. The dishes were printed with designs using a cobalt blue coloring. The color flowed from the design to the white body so that the finished piece has a smeared blue design. The dishes were usually made of ironstone china. More Flow Blue may be found under the name of the manufacturer.

Bowl, Ironstone, Fluted, Gold Trim, 13 x 6 In. 118
Bowl, Lid, Oval, Shaped, White, Blue Flowers, Leaves, Gilt Scroll Handles, c.1890, 6 In. 72
Cup & Saucer, Chapoo, Ironstone, J. Wedgwood, 6 In. 71
Jardiniere, Bulbous, Cushion Foot, Scallop Rim, Flowers, Gilt, c.1920 72
Pitcher & Bowl, Gilt, Briar, Middleport Pottery, 12 ½ In. 126
Plate, Cashmere, Ironstone, Signed F. Morley & Co., 7 In., 5 Piece 177
Plate, Flowers, Riley, 1800s, 8 ¾ In. 35
Platter Set, Flower Festoon Band, Scalloped Rim, 9 x 14 In., 4 Piece 153
Platter, Oval, Flowers, Scalloped, Ford & Sons, c.1900, 16 ½ x 12 In. 229

FLYING PHOENIX, *see Phoenix Bird category.*

FOLK ART is also listed in many categories of this book under the actual name of the object. See categories such as Box, Cigar Store Figure, Paper, Weather Vane, Wooden, etc.

Abraham Lincoln, Paint, Standing, Carved, Elongated, Stepped Base, 33 In. 593
Barn, Green, White, Doors, Peaked Roof, 20 x 15 In. 94
Barrel, Pig, Metal Straps, Metal Face & Legs, 26 ½ x 12 In. 375
Bellows, Painted, Hilly Landscape, Mustard, Green, Red Ground, Flowers, 1800s, 19 In. 3900
Bird Tree, Branches, Carved, Shadowbox Frame, c.1900, 25 x 29 In. 1298
Bird Tree, Mushroom, Birds On Branches, Carved, Platform, c.1900, 12 x 13 In. 885
Bird Tree, Wood, Painted, Birds, Butterfly, Squirrels, Birdhouses, C. Snyder, 16 In. 83
Bird, 6 Birds On Branches, Painted Accents, c.1950, 7 ½ x 10 In. 500
Bird, Carved, Red & Black Paint, Dome, Wood Base, 4 In. 384
Bird, Swallowtail, Wood, Painted, Bernier, Maine, c.1900, 6 ½ In. 1875
Birdhouse, House Shape, White, Green Roof, 10 x 18 In. 146
Birdhouse, Steep Pitched Roof, 2 Windows, Door, 21 x 21 In. 59
Black Man, Standing, Holding Splitting Wedge, Hat, Carved, Shaped Base, 12 ½ In. 177
Black Man, Watermelon, Wood Base, Pedestal, J. Murphy, 62 x 20 In. 175
Bust, Abe Lincoln, Water Soaked Currency, 6 ¼ In. 400
Bust, Admiral Dewey, Water Soaked Currency, 5 In. 500
Bust, Female, Yellow Dress, Red Ruffle, Long Hair, 27 x 22 In. 1500
Chicken, Iron, Figural, Repurposed Farm Equipment Parts, 1900s, 23 x 28 In., Pair 480
Civil War Soldier, At Attention, Flag, Musket, Bayonet, Carved, Wire Fence, 1800s, 10 In. 531
Cup, Gourd Shape, Carved, Clipper Ship, Geometric & Flower Design, 1861, 2 x 5 In. 165
Dog, Chihuahua, Wood, Stamped, My Dog Tiger, Silvio Zoratti, c.1960, 10 x 15 In. 480
Dolphin, Wood, Arched, Nose & Tail Pointed Down, 23 x 30 In. 738
Dove, On Perch, Detailed Eyes, Pine, c.1885, 21 x 17 In. 2250
Draft Horses On Wheels, Pulling Wagon, Carved Wood, 9 x 23 In. 502
Eagle, Perched On Book, Spread Wings, Head Down, Wood, Paint, Glass Eyes, 16 x 25 In. 2760
Eagle, Wood, Painted, On Rock Base, c.1900, 20 In. 63
Fish, Painted, Hanging On Chain, Glass & Painted Eyes, c.1970, 9 In. 240
Indian, Wearing Cowboy Hat, Skates, Rocket, Wood, Painted, 15 In. 30
Jardiniere, Wood, Pinecone Decorated, Tapered Outward, c.1910, 14 ½ x 22 In. 625
Jigger, Man With Top Hat, Sheet Metal, Painted, Iron Rod, Wood Ball, c.1850, 20 In. .... *illus* 3000
Monkey, Carved, Leather Britches, Leg & Arm Up, 37 In. 119
Owl, Tin, Head Turned, 17 In. 82
Parrot, Standing, Carved Wood, Painted, Multicolor, Base, 8 In. 384
Patriot, Standing Man, Top Hat, Holding Sword & Flag, Carved, Block Base, 1894, 11 In. 4148
Plaque, Eagle, Spread Wing, Carved Wood, Glass Eyes, Gold Paint, c.1950, 24 In. 210
Retablo, Religious, Exorcism, Paint On Tin Panel, Frame, c.1880, South America, 17 x 13 In. .. 780
Rooster, Red, Yellow, Wood, 19th Century, 9 ½ x 6 ¼ In. 660
Sand Bottle, Eagle, 36-Star Flag, Garland, Mrs. S.J. Stott, Andrew Clemens, c.1890, 7 In. 19200
Sand Bottle, Eagle, 36-Star Flag, Garland, Multicolor, Andrew Clemens, 1883, 7 ¼ In. 18000
Snake, Articulated Joints, Wood, On Canvas Strip, c.1885, 42 ½ In. 875
Squirrel On Tree Stump, Mixed Materials, Gold Painted, c.1950, 27 In. .... *illus* 210
Tiger, Wood, Schimmel Style, Painted, Jonathan Bastian, 6 ¼ x 12 ½ In. 354
Toy, 2 Women, Churning Butter, Jointed, Wood, Pull String Movement, c.1850, 4 In. .... *illus* 560
Turkey, Standing, Open Beak, Head Up, Carved, Paint, Wood Base, 36 In. 2006
Whirligig, Airplane, Tin, Josh Hinkley, 1920s, 30 x 22 In. 1638

Whirligig, Black Soldier, Artillery Uniform, Wood Stand, Base, c.1870, 15 In. 861
Whirligig, Civil War Union Soldier, Pine, Tin, Paint, Sword Shape Paddles, 24 In. .... *illus* 16800
Whirligig, Man Sawing Wood, 1920, 23 x 22 In. 93
Whirligig, Sailor, Silhouette, 2 Paddles, Wood, Painted, Nantucket, 1898, 18 In. 1140
Whirligig, Tommy-Totem, Wood, Cardboard, Howard See, 10 x 4 ½ In. 120
Whirligig, Windmill, Wood, Painted, 23 In. 266
Woodpecker, Red Headed, Black Feathers, Wood, 10 x 6 ½ In. 907

FOOTBALL *collectibles may be found in the Card and the Sports categories.*

FOSTORIA glass was made in Fostoria, Ohio, from 1887 to 1891. The factory was moved to Moundsville, West Virginia, and most of the glass seen in shops today is a twentieth-century product. The company was sold in 1983; new items will be easily identifiable, according to the new owner, Lancaster Colony Corporation. Additional Fostoria items may be listed in the Milk Glass category.

American, Bowl, Inverted Rim, 7 In. 36
American, Cup & Saucer 10
American, Ice Bucket, 6 ½ In. 35
American, Plate, Salad, 7 In. 6
American, Sherbet, Flared, Footed 5
American, Vase, Milk Glass, Flared, Footed, 8 ½ In. 30
Arlington, Banana Stand, Milk Glass, 7 ¾ In. 53
Baroque, Saucer 3
Brocaded Palms, Vase, Green 115
Camellia, Plate, Luncheon, 8 ½ In. 11
Celestial, Bowl, 5 In. 7
Century, Compote, Lid, 6 In. 22
Chintz, Torte Plate, 13 ¼ In. 48
Coin, Ashtray, Ruby, 7 ½ In. 15
Coin, Nappy, Amber, Handle 12
Coin, Vase, Red, Footed, 1958-82, 8 In. .... *illus* 55
Colony, Bowl, Console, Rolled Edge, 9 In. 28
Colony, Bowl, Footed, 6 x 10 In. 38
Colony, Cake Salver, Footed, 12 In. 65
Colony, Iced Tea, 12 Oz. 12
Colony, Plate, Salad, 7 In. 7
Colony, Relish, 3 Sections, Oval, Handles, 10 In. 18
Colony, Sugar & Creamer 12
Diamond Sunburst, Compote, Lid, Square Footed, Milk Glass, 8 In. 119
Fairfax, Cup, Blue, Footed 10
Fairfax, Cup, Topaz, Footed 4
Fairfax, Plate, Salad, Green, 7 ½ In. 3
Fairfax, Plate, Salad, Rose, 7 ½ In. 7
Heather, Cup & Saucer 13
Jenny Lind, Tray, Dresser, Milk Glass, 11 ¼ In. 50
Lafayette, Relish, 2 Sections 9
Lido, Plate, 7 In. 6
Lido, Plate, 8 ½ In. 9
Needlepoint, Tumbler, Green, Opalescent Rim, 3 x 3 ½ In., 8 Piece 106
Priscilla, Plate, Amber, 7 ½ In. 5
Romance, Plate, 7 ½ In. 4
Sprite, Cup & Saucer 22

FOVAL, *see Fry category.*

FRAMES *are included in the Furniture category under Frame.*

FRANCISCAN is a trademark that appears on pottery. Gladding, McBean and Company started in 1875. The company grew and acquired other potteries. It made sewer pipes, floor tiles, dinnerware, and art pottery with a variety of trademarks. It began using the trade name *Franciscan* in 1934. In 1936, dinnerware and art pottery were sold under the name *Franciscan Ware.* The company made china and cream-colored, decorated earthenware. Desert Rose, Apple, El Patio, and Coronado were best sellers. The company became Interpace Corporation and in 1979 was purchased by Josiah Wedgwood & Sons. The plant was closed in 1984, but a few of the patterns are still being made. For more prices, go to kovels.com.

Apple, Bowl, Vegetable, Lid, 9 ¾ x 4 ¼ In. 36

Franciscan, Starburst, Bowl, Vegetable, Divided, Atomic Decoration, 8 ¼ In.
$39

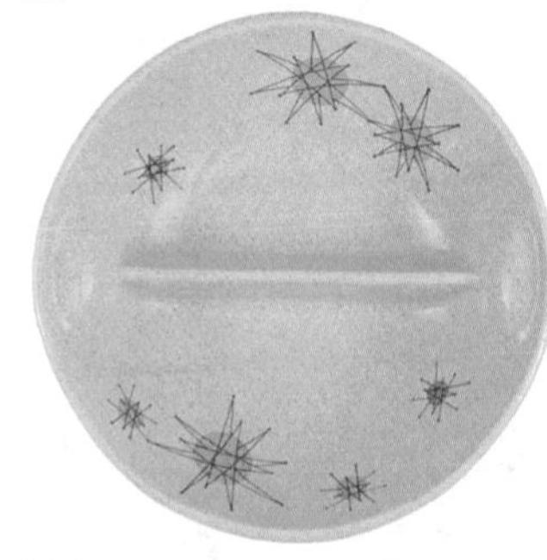

Ruby Lane

Frankart, Figurine, Woman, Standing, Bronzed, 8 ½ In.
$121

Great Estates Auctioneers

TIP
Remove stains from old ceramic vases by scrubbing with salt.

Frankoma, Figurine, Bull, Green, Ada Clay, 2 x 3 ¼ In.
$290

Dirk Soulis Auctions

Fraternal, Elks, Sign, BPOE, Elk's Head, Roman Numeral Clock, Porcelain, Round, 30 In.
$350

Manifest Auctions

Fraternal, Lions Club, Pin, Bow, Sterling, Lion Pendant Charm, Marked, 1950s, 1 9/16 In.
$45

Ruby Lane

Fraternal, Masonic, Cuff Links, Gold, Blue Enamel, Embossed, Bar, England, 3/4 x 1/2 In.
$379

Ruby Lane

TIP

Don't use your mother's maiden name, the town you or your parents were born in, or other personal information when asked for a security question with an online account. The answers can be easily found in a geneology search.

Apple, Cup & Saucer, 1940s ... *illus* 14
Apple, Relish, Oval, Divided, 10 3/8 In. ... 12
Autumn Leaves, Casserole, Lid, 2 Qt. ... 24
Desert Rose, Bowl, Vegetable, 8 In. ... 22
Desert Rose, Cake Plate, Pedestal, 8 x 3 3/4 In. ... 38
Desert Rose, Coffeepot, Lid, 9 In. ... 35
Desert Rose, Gravy Boat, Underplate, 2 Spouts, 9 x 6 x 4 In. ... 35
Desert Rose, Teapot, Lid, 4 1/4 x 6 In. ... 25
El Patio, Toast & Jam Set, Green, Yellow, 7 1/4 x 5 1/2 In. ... *illus* 32
Mandarin, Teapot, Lid, Footed, 7 1/2 x 9 In. ... 68
Starburst, Bowl, Vegetable, Divided, Atomic Decoration, 8 1/4 In. ... *illus* 39
Starburst, Butter, Lb. ... 58
Starburst, Cup & Saucer ... 9
Starburst, Gravy Boat, Underplate ... 18
Starburst, Platter, Oval, 12 In. ... 55
Starburst, Soup, Dish ... 20

FRANKART INC., New York, New York, mass-produced nude "dancing lady" lamps, ashtrays, and other decorative Art Deco items in the 1920s and 1930s. They were made of white lead composition and spray-painted. *Frankart Inc.* and the patent number and year were stamped on the base.

Ashstand, Nude, Holding Glass Bowl, c.1925, 8 1/2 x 10 In. ... 700
Bookends, Boy, Dog, 1930s ... 94
Bookends, Dutch Children, c.1934, 5 x 5 x 3 In. ... 119
Bookends, Scottie Dog, Cast Metal, Marked, 1920s, 5 x 6 1/2 In. ... 155
Bust, Woman, Long Hair, Flowered Headband, Base, 5 x 6 1/2 In. ... 95
Figurine, Woman, Standing, Bronzed, 8 1/2 In. ... *illus* 121
Lamp, Art Deco, Nude Woman, Arms Outstretched, Enameled Metal, 10 1/2 x 6 In. ... 390
Lamp, Cranberry Glass, Enameled Metal, Glass, Bakelite, 2 Standing Women, 13 1/2 x 8 In. ... 3375
Lamp, Nude, Fan Base, Spelter, 1920s, 13 x 4 x 3 In., Pair ... 250
Lamp, Nude, Silhouette, Outstretched Arms, c.1930, 10 1/2 In. ... 750
Lamp, Nudes, Back To Back, Pink Square Crackle Glass Shade, 13 In. ... 1500
Nude, Holding Glass Tray, Spelter, c.1925, 8 1/2 In. ... 145
Sculpture, Jazz Player, 1930s, 9 In. ... 150

FRANKOMA POTTERY was originally known as The Frank Potteries when John F. Frank opened shop in 1933. The factory is now working in Sapulpa, Oklahoma. Early wares were made from a light cream-colored clay from Ada, Oklahoma, but in 1956 the company switched to a red clay from Sapulpa. The firm made dinnerware, utilitarian and decorative kitchenwares, figurines, flowerpots, and limited edition and commemorative pieces. John Frank died in 1973 and his daughter, Joniece, inherited the business. Frankoma went bankrupt in 1990. The pottery operated under various owners for a few years and was bought by Joe Ragosta in 2008. It closed in 2010. The buildings, assets, name, and molds were sold at an auction in 2011.

Candleholder, Art Deco, Standing Nude, Flowing Drapery, Gerald Smith, c.1930, 11 x 8 In. ... 150
Figurine, Bull, Green, Ada Clay, 2 x 3 1/4 In. ... *illus* 290
Figurine, Dog, English Setter, Prairie Green, c.1940, 8 x 5 1/2 In. ... 190
Trivet, Flag, Flag Of Freedom, c.1977, 6 3/8 In. ... 22

FRATERNAL objects that are related to the many different fraternal organizations in the United States are listed in this category. The Elks, Masons, Odd Fellows, and others are included. Also included are service organizations, like the American Legion, Kiwanis, and Lions Club. Furniture is listed in the Furniture category. Shaving mugs decorated with fraternal crests are included in the Shaving Mug category.

Elks, Sign, BPOE, Elk's Head, Roman Numeral Clock, Porcelain, Round, 30 In. ... *illus* 350
Lions Club, Pin, Bow, Sterling, Lion Pendant Charm, Marked, 1950s, 1 9/16 In. ... *illus* 45
Masonic, Cane, Figures, Symbols, Clasped Hands, Diamonds, Animals, Flowers, 34 In. ... 540
Masonic, Charm, Daisy, Rose Gold, Silver Pyramids, Engraved Symbols, 19th Century ... 188
Masonic, Charm, Gold, Silver & Niello Pyramids, Symbols, England, 1800s, 3/4 In. ... 219
Masonic, Cuff Links, Gold, Blue Enamel, Embossed, Bar, England, 3/4 x 1/2 In. ... *illus* 379
Masonic, Fob, 10K Yellow Gold, Enameled Accents, 1 3/4 x 1 In. ... 189
Masonic, Fob, Claw Charm, Egyptian Revival, Citrine Sphinx, Frame, 1800s, 1 1/2 In. ... 240
Masonic, Paperweight, Metal, Symbols, 6 1/2 x 5 In. ... *illus* 29
Masonic, Ring, 14K Rose Gold, European Cut Diamond, W.E. Monogram, Size 8 1/4 ... 124
Masonic, Staff, Master's, Wood, Organic & Twist Carving, 44 In. ... 480
Masonic, Sword, Knights Templar, Gilt, Etched Blade, Helmet Pommel, Scabbard, 37 In. ... 118

Masonic, Sword, Momento, Mori, Bone, Brass, Skull & Crossbones, Sheath, c.1910, 35 In. 148
Odd Fellows, Apron, Silk, Painted Symbols, c.1810, 17 ½ x 15 In. 120
Odd Fellows, Badge, Pin, Ribbon, Memorial, 2-Sided, Tassel Trim, 9 ½ x 2 In. ....*illus* 38
Odd Fellows, Podium, Lodge, Pine, Crackled Red & Yellow Paint, Gavels, Chain, 33 In. 480
Order Of The Garter, Match Safe, Aluminum, Acanthus, Woven, Cartouche, Hinged 71
Ring, Tau Epsilon Phi, 4 Emeralds, 18 Pearls, Solitaire, Penn State, 2 In. 161
Society Of The Cincinnati Insignia, Virginia Eagle, Cast 18K Gold, Enamel, 1906, 20 In. 2360

FRY GLASS was made by the H.C. Fry Glass Company of Rochester, Pennsylvania. The company, founded in 1901, first made cut glass and other types of fine glasswares. In 1922 it patented a heat-resistant glass called Pearl Ovenglass. For two years, 1926–1927, the company made Fry Foval, an opal ware decorated with colored trim. Reproductions of this glass have been made. Depression glass patterns made by Fry may be listed in the Depression Glass category. Some pieces of cut glass may also be included in the Cut Glass category.

Pitcher, Lemonade, Goblets, Green Handle, Stems, 10 x 5 ¾ In. 472
Tea Set, Teapot, 6 Cups & Saucers, Opalescent, 13 Piece 208
Vase, Jade Green, Trumpet Shape, Frilly Ruffled Rim, Round Foot, 18 In. 115
Vase, Swing, Black, c.1920, 16 In. 195

FULPER POTTERY COMPANY was incorporated in 1899 in Flemington, New Jersey. It made art pottery from 1909 to 1929. The firm had been making bottles, jugs, and housewares from 1805. Doll heads were made about 1928. The firm became Stangl Pottery in 1929. Stangl Pottery is listed in its own category in this book.

Basket, Multicolor, Flower Lid, Handles, 9 ½ In. 142
Bowl, Green, Oval, 8 In. 43
Doorstop, Sleeping Cat, Flambe Mirrored Black, Ivory Glaze, c.1916, 5 x 9 ½ In. 413
Jar, Lid, Blue Flambe Glaze, Open Glaze Bubbles, Foot Ring, 3 ¾ x 5 ½ In. 118
Lamp, Boudoir, Glazed, Ballerina, Scalloped Tutu, Mask, Swan, 1920s, 15 x 8 In. ....*illus* 250
Lamp, Vasekraft, Mirror Black & Cat's-Eye Flambe Glaze, c.1915, 19 x 17 In. ....*illus* 10000
Urn, Mirror Black, Copper Dust Flambe, Round Foot, 15 x 7 ½ In. 313
Urn, Pink, Blue, Flambe, Round, Pedestal Foot, Shouldered, Handles At Neck, c.1915, 10 In. 625
Vase, Artichoke Leaf, Flambe Glaze, Green, Brown, Ring Foot, c.1915, 6 x 9 In. ....*illus* 469
Vase, Blue & Purple Mottled Glaze, Jug Handles, 6 ½ In. 125
Vase, Bronze Green Matte Glaze, Glossy Cream, Molded, Ribbed, Shouldered, c.1910, 7 In. 431
Vase, Brown Speckled Over Green, Oval, 12 x 7 In. 361
Vase, Chinese Blue Flambe, Matte Glaze, Ink Stamp, c.1910, 15 x 10 In. ....*illus* 5625
Vase, Cobalt Blue Flambe Glaze, Round, Shouldered, Flat Rim, c.1915, 10 x 10 In. 1750
Vase, Cucumber Crystalline Glaze, 2 Angular Handles, Horizontal Shoulder Line, 5 In. 94
Vase, Cucumber Over Ivory Matte Glazes, Stamped, c.1910, 7 ¾ In. 424
Vase, Famille Rose Glaze, Tapered Neck, Footed, Incised Mark, 11 ½ In. 59
Vase, Frothy Copper Duct Crystalline, Flared Foot & Rim, c.1910, 14 x 6 In. 3750
Vase, Frothy Crystalline Glaze, Cylindrical, High Rounded Shoulder, 15 x 5 ½ In. 1500
Vase, Green Flambe Glaze Over Oatmeal, Bulbous, Buttressed Neck, 5 In. 230
Vase, Green, Yellow, Speckled Red, Pear Shape, Ring Foot, c.1810, 11 ½ x 7 ½ In. 1625
Vase, Leopard Skin Crystalline Glaze, Green, Cylindrical, Marked, 11 In. 173
Vase, Leopard Skin Crystalline Glaze, Reticulated, Green, Handles, Cylindrical, c.1910, 14 In. ... 3750
Vase, Mirror Black Glaze, Tulip, Lobed, Shaped Saucer Foot, Bulbous, 12 In. 1953
Vase, Mirror Black Over Mahogany & Ivory Flambe, Pear Shape, 7-Sided, Lobes, 10 In. 173
Vase, Mustard Matte Glaze, Bulbous, Squat, Ring Foot, Frothy Crystalline, 1910, 8 x 10 In. 4688
Vase, Rose Glaze, Red, Circle Design, Reeded Neck, Trumpet Rim, c.1915, 14 In. ....*illus* 2500
Vase, Wisteria Glaze, Purple, Blue, Smokestack Shape, Buttress, Gold, 8 In. 219

FURNITURE of all types is listed in this category. Examples dating from the seventeenth century to the 2000s are included. Prices for furniture vary in different parts of the country. Oak furniture is most expensive in the West; large pieces over eight feet high are sold for the most money in the South, where high ceilings are found in the old homes. Condition is very important when determining prices. These are NOT average prices but rather reports of unique sales. If the description includes the word *style*, the piece resembles the old furniture style but was made at a later time. It is not a period piece. Small chests that sat on a table or dresser are also included here. Garden furniture is listed in the Garden Furnishings category. Related items may be found in the Architectural, Brass, and Store categories.

Armchairs are listed under Chair in this category.
Armoire, Adam Style, Walnut, Carved, 5 Drawers, Paneled Back, Sides, c.1890, 79 x 53 In. 1180
Armoire, Applied Carving, 3 Mirrored Doors, 2 Drawers, 1900-20s, 88 x 55 In. 100
Armoire, Art Deco, Ebony, Mahogany, Dessin Fournier, 78 x 59 In. 240

Fraternal, Masonic, Paperweight, Metal, Symbols, 6 ½ x 5 In.
$29

Ruby Lane

Fraternal, Odd Fellows, Badge, Pin, Ribbon, Memorial, 2-Sided, Tassel Trim, 9 ½ x 2 In.
$38

Ruby Lane

Fulper, Lamp, Boudoir, Glazed, Ballerina, Scalloped Tutu, Mask, Swan, 1920s, 15 x 8 In.
$250

Rago Arts and Auction Center

Fulper, Lamp, Vasekraft, Mirror Black & Cat's-Eye Flambe Glaze, c.1915, 19 x 17 In.
$10,000

Rago Arts and Auction Center

Fulper, Vase, Artichoke Leaf, Flambe Glaze, Green, Brown, Ring Foot, c.1915, 6 x 9 In.
$469

Rago Arts and Auction Center

Fulper, Vase, Chinese Blue Flambe, Matte Glaze, Ink Stamp, c.1910, 15 x 10 In.
$5,625

Rago Arts and Auction Center

Fulper, Vase, Rose Glaze, Red, Circle Design, Reeded Neck, Trumpet Rim, c.1915, 14 In.
$2,500

Rago Arts and Auction Center

Furniture, Armoire, French Provincial, Carved, Panel Doors, Open Spokes, c.1910, 80 x 53 In.
$738

Skinner, Inc.

Furniture Made Here
The center of furniture manufacturing in the United States in the late nineteenth century was Grand Rapids, Michigan.

TIP
Brown shoe polish is good to cover scuffs and slight damage on furniture.

Furniture, Armoire, French Provincial, Cherry, Arched Pediment, Doors, 1800s, 91 x 59 In.
$923

Skinner, Inc.

Furniture, Armoire, Louis XV Style, Provincial, Pine, Carved, Continental, 1800s, 87 x 55 In.
$600

Cowan Auctions

Armoire, Art Nouveau, Mirror, Pierced, Flowers, 3 Doors, 80 x 42 In. 840
Armoire, Belle Epoque, Ormolu, Parquetry, Inlay, Mirrored Doors, c.1900, 87 x 80 In. 549
Armoire, Edwardian, Mahogany Inlay, Bowfront, Crown, Doors, 1900s, 82 x 76 In. 431
Armoire, Elm, 2 Doors, 2 Drawers, Chinese Painted, 75 x 37 In. 125
Armoire, Empire, Carved Walnut, Long Drawer, Ormolu Columns, 66 x 22 In. 1353
Armoire, Flower Carving, 2 Doors, 82 x 40 In. 188
Armoire, French Provincial, Carved, 4 Interior Shelves, Serpentine Apron, 81 x 60 In. 949
Armoire, French Provincial, Carved, Panel Doors, Open Spokes, c.1910, 80 x 53 In. .... *illus* 738
Armoire, French Provincial, Cherry, Arched Pediment, Doors, 1800s, 91 x 59 In. .... *illus* 923
Armoire, French Provincial, Cherry, Molding, Inlay, Paneled Doors, 1800s, 90 x 60 In. 677
Armoire, French Provincial, Fruitwood, Cornice, Carved Door, Scroll Feet, 1800s, 79 x 44 In. 1968
Armoire, French Provincial, Fruitwood, Cornice, Paneled Doors, Shelves, c.1850, 90 x 54 In. 1230
Armoire, French Provincial, Fruitwood, Domed Cornice, Arched Doors, 88 x 54 In. 812
Armoire, Louis Philippe, Carved Walnut, c.1925, 91 x 60 In. 184
Armoire, Louis Philippe, Walnut, Carved, Rounded Crown, Bracket Feet, 1800s, 84 x 55 In. 593
Armoire, Louis XV Style, Provincial, Pine, Carved, Continental, 1800s, 87 x 55 In. .... *illus* 600
Armoire, Louis XV, Acanthus Leaf Crest, 2 Mirrored Doors, 104 x 59 In. 750
Armoire, Louis XV, Flowers, Birds, Panel Doors, Cabriole Legs, 90 x 58 ½ In. 1107
Armoire, Louis XV, Inlay, Rosewood, Double Flower Marquetry, Bombe Sides, 73 ½ x 50 In. 184
Armoire, Louis XV, Oak, Carved, Fielded Panel Doors, Brass Escutcheons, Cabriole, 85 x 67 In. . 522
Armoire, Louis XVI Style, Bird's-Eye Maple, Cherry, Carved, Mirror Door, c.1890, 88 x 45 In. 492
Armoire, Mahogany, 2 Paneled Doors, Interior Drawers, Carved Cornice, 90 x 57 In. 885
Armoire, Michael Graves, Kyoto Collection, Painted Wood, Arkitektura, 1990s, 50 x 54 In. 1250
Armoire, Neoclassical, Walnut, Stepped Cornice, 2 Doors, Drawers, c.1840, 101 x 85 In. 2689
Armoire, Oak, 2 Doors, 2 Drawers, 82 ½ x 60 In. 484
Armoire, Ormolu Mounts, 4 Shelves, 72 In. 338
Armoire, Provincial, Oak, 2 Doors, Arched, Cabriole Legs, 19th Century, 93 ½ x 62 In. 726
Armoire, Provincial, Painted, Paneled Doors, Applied Accents, Block Feet, 1900s, 92 x 65 In. 799
Armoire, Renaissance Revival, Arch Pediment, Shell Crest, Urn Finials, Mirror, 101 x 58 In. 671
Bar Cart, 2 Round Teak Trays, Wheels, 27 ¼ In. 247
Bar Cart, Aldo Tura, Goatskin, Brass, Drop Leaf, Brass Wheels, c.1960, 31 x 30 In. 544
Bar Cart, Aldo Tura, Lacquered, Goatskin, Drop Down Sides, 39 x 19 In. 605
Bar Cart, Cesare, Lacca, Walnut, Cross Supports, Wheels, 33 x 36 ½ In. 545
Bar Cart, J. Adnet, 2 Tiers, Nickeled Brass, Glass Rod, Mirrored Glass, 24 x 23 In. 1000
Bar Cart, J. Adnet, Nickel Plated Brass, Mahogany, Mirror, Doors, 1950s, 32 x 34 In. .... *illus* 5625
Bar Cart, J. Quinet, 3 Tiers, Brass, Smoked Glass, Casters, France, 1960s, 23 x 28 In. 2500
Barrel, Rum, Victorian, Staved Oak, Brass Branded, Hinged Lid, 37 x 26 In. 3250
Barstool, Claudio Salocchi, Fiberglass, Adjustable, Orange, 54 ¾ In. 726
Barstool, H. Bertoia, 428, Midcentury Modern, Wire, 4 Piece 2600
Barstool, Lucite, Curved Backrest, Pierced, Tubular Footrest, c.1970, 34 x 17 ½ In., Pair 484
Barstool, Rectangular Back, Trapezoid Seat, Turned Legs, 50 ½ x 14 In., 4 Piece 369
Basket, Chestnut, Adam Style, Lid, Brass Covered, Oval, Ring Pulls, Rosettes, 23 x 12 In. 1375
Bed Steps, Mahogany, Carved, Lift Top, Leather Treads, c.1850, 27 x 30 In. .... *illus* 980
Bed Steps, Mahogany, Contemporary, Brass Handles, Cutout Feet, 20 x 18 In. 184
Bed Steps, Satinwood, Tooled Leather, Cylindrical, Pullout Step, 1800s, 17 In. 242
Bed Steps, Victorian, Mahogany, Ogee Front, Green Tooled Leather, 27 x 18 In. 923
Bed Steps, William IV, Mahogany, Leather Treads, Chamber Pot Compartment, 25 In. .... *illus* 854
Bed Steps, Wood, Gray Paint, 32 x 19 ½ In. 54
Bed, Brass, Frosted Flower & Scroll Panels, 70 x 58 In. 225
Bed, Canopy, Federal, Mahogany, Posts, Carved Ribbon, Marlboro Feet, c.1810, 86 x 72 In. 1800
Bed, Canopy, George III Style, Mahogany, Urn Finials, Block Feet, 1900s, 86 x 89 In. 605
Bed, Canopy, Neoclassical, Cherry, Mahogany, Acanthus Carved, Brass Feet, 106 x 93 In. 3690
Bed, Canopy, Walnut, Carved, Tapered Posts, Casters, 102 ½ x 80 In. 544
Bed, Chelsea, Brass Rivets, Upholstered Headboard, Oak Rails, 55 x 85 In. 531
Bed, Cone Shape, G. Nakashima, Walnut, Birch Plywood, 1965, 75 x 78 In. 9375
Bed, Contemporary, Mahogany, Sleigh, Restauration Style, 45 x 86 In. 1062
Bed, Directoire, Multicolor, Pyramidal Crest, Paneled Back, c.1910, 44 x 82 In., Pair 1187
Bed, Four-Poster, Cherry, Acorn Finial, c.1875, 82 ½ x 36 In., Pair 584
Bed, Four-Poster, Mahogany, Swan Neck Pediment, Baluster, Sheaths, 1900s, 80 x 65 In. 369
Bed, Four-Poster, Rococo Style, Hardwood, Cartouche & Leaf Headboard, Twist Post, 92 x 86 In. 799
Bed, Four-Poster, Walnut, Barley Twist Posts, Carved Shield, c.1810, 92 x 77 In. .... *illus* 3050
Bed, G. Nakashima, Walnut, Platform, c.1950, 54 x 75 ½ In. 2500
Bed, Gothic Revival, Mahogany, Low-Post, Pierced Headboard, c.1830, 65 x 79 In. 1230
Bed, Half-Tester, Belle Epoque, Silvered Brass, France, c.1900, 108, 83 In. 1500
Bed, Half-Tester, Rococo Revival, Segmented Turned Post, Crest, Roundel, c.1875, 63 x 83 In. 1599
Bed, Henry II Style, Walnut, Carved, Broken-Arch, Paneled Headboard, Double, 56 x 75 In. 148

Furniture, Bar Cart, J. Adnet, Nickel Plated Brass, Mahogany, Mirror, Doors, 1950s, 32 x 34 In.
$5,625

Rago Arts and Auction Center

Furniture, Bed Steps, Mahogany, Carved, Lift Top, Leather Treads, c.1850, 27 x 30 In.
$980

Neal Auctions

Furniture, Bed Steps, William IV, Mahogany, Leather Treads, Chamber Pot Compartment, 25 In.
$854

Neal Auctions

TIP

Don't lock furniture with antique locks. If they stick, it is almost impossible to open the door or drawer without damaging the wood.

Furniture, Bed, Four-Poster, Walnut, Barley Twist Posts, Carved Shield, c.1810, 92 x 77 In.
$3,050

Neal Auctions

Furniture, Bed, Headboard, Carved, Curtains, Footboard, Painted, Continental, 1800s, 71 x 51 In.
$300

Cowan Auctions

Vernis Martin Finish

Vernis Martin is a type of lacquer developed in France about 1720 that was used by the Martin brothers. A color, usually green, was added to varnish and applied to the surface of a piece of wooden furniture. Gold dust was added to some of the undercoats and elaborate decorations were added to the top coat. The technique has been copied but often with gold-colored, not real, gold dust.

Bed, Headboard, Carved, Curtains, Footboard, Painted, Continental, 1800s, 71 x 51 In. ...... *illus* 300
Bed, Herter Bros., Victorian, Mahogany, Burl Walnut, Marquetry, c.1880, 76 x 66 In. 3776
Bed, Iron Head & Footboard, Painted Faux Wood Veneer, Flowers, 60 x 60 In. 177
Bed, Louis Philippe, Fruitwood, Slatted Back, Outscrolled Arms, Ogee, c.1850, 34 x 78 In. 1168
Bed, Louis XV Style, Enameled Iron, Brass, Serpentine Arch, King, 59 x 76 x 83 In. 275
Bed, Louis XV, Beech, Arched, Carved, White, Upholstered, Cabriole Legs, 47 x 73 In. 123
Bed, Louis XVI Style, Brass, Arched Headboard & Footboard, Urn, c.1900, 54 x 74 In. 178
Bed, Louis XVI Style, Giltwood, Carved, Scrolled Cane Ends, c.1900, 54 x 90 In. 1084
Bed, Neoclassical, Curly Maple, Cannonball Posts, Turned Legs, Child's, c.1830, 33 x 49 In. 420
Bed, Neoclassical, Faux Wood, Parcel Gilt, Shield Crest, Flowering Urns, 1800s, 71 x 74 In. 437
Bed, Renaissance Revival Style, Canopy, Ribbed Frame, Barley Twists, 98 x 88 In. 3000
Bed, Sleigh, Louis XVI Style, Fruitwood, Padded Back, Scroll Headboard, c.1910, 65 x 85 In. 1722
Bed, Sleigh, Mahogany, Carved, Front Rail, Tuned Bun Feet, c.1850, 42 x 38 In. 325
Bed, Sleigh, Neoclassical, Mahogany, Pine, Veneers, Rope Rails, c.1870, 45 x 82 In. 219
Bed, Victorian, Iron Frame, Black Paint, Brass Finials, c.1890, Twin, 54 x 75 In., Pair 1121
Bed, Walnut, Arched Headboard, Burl Paneled, Continental, 2 Joined To Make King Size 2562
Bed, Wrought Iron, Headboard, Footboard, 2 Rails, Curlicues, 77x 55 In. 250
Bedroom Set, Chest, Dresser, Stand, Yellow Front, White Frame, Broyhill, 3 Piece 1375
Bench, Arts & Crafts, Oak, Through Tenon Stretcher, c.1910, 18 x 42 In., Pair 531
Bench, Astral, Cherry, Slatted Back, Continuous Seat, c.1979, 12 Ft. 2400
Bench, Bootjack, Gray Paint, c.1962, 45 ½ In. 160
Bench, Bucket, Mortised Shelves, Lebanon County, Pa., 37 x 12 x 42 In. 295
Bench, Bucket, Poplar, Old Gray Paint, Nailed Construction, Cutout Ends, 31 x 50 In. 840
Bench, Bucket, Softwood, Tan Paint, Molded Sink Top, Shelf, Arched Feet, 1800s, 31 x 45 In. 1534
Bench, Bucket, Walnut, Shaped Back, 2 Shelves, Arched Feet, American, 38 x 37 x 17 In. 1560
Bench, Bugatti, Walnut, Copper, Brass, Medallion, Arms, c.1900, 31 x 48 In. .... *illus* 13750
Bench, Chest, Caasapanca, Hinged Lid, Walnut, Carved, Figures, Spain, 1600s, 37 x 72 In. 1845
Bench, Elk Horn, Leather Covered, Intertwined Elk Antler Base, 1900s, 16 x 52 In. 1476
Bench, Elm, Mortised Construction, Chinese, c.1900, 21 x 68 In. 180
Bench, Finn Juhl, Tak, Enameled Steel, Brass, Branded Bovirke, 1950s, 16 x 89 In. 8750
Bench, Flemish Style, Oak, Padded, 8 Turned, Tapered Legs, Stretchers, c.1910, 20 x 103 In. 1968
Bench, French Provincial Style, Carved Apron, Cabriole Legs, Scroll Feet, 17 x 47 x 15 In. 984
Bench, G. Nakashima, Spindle Back, Hickory, Rosewood, 1989, 33 x 66 In. 10625
Bench, George III Style, Mahogany, Chinese Chippendale, Padded Seat, 20 x 37 In. 343
Bench, Greta Magnusson Grossman, Basket Weave, 1952, 65 x 16 In. 1500
Bench, Hall, French Provincial, Medieval Style, Oak, Carved, Lift Seat, 1700s, 45 x 51 In. 366
Bench, Hall, Restoration Style, Cherry, Rounded Carved Arms, Tapered Legs, 25 x 33 In. 178
Bench, Hall, Walnut, Scrolled Pediment, Mirror Back, 2 Drawers, 100 x 62 In. 1920
Bench, Louis XV Style, Walnut, Needlepoint Covering, X-Stretcher, 1800s, 30 x 36 In. 800
Bench, Louis XVI Style, Cane Seat, Carved Apron, Fluted Legs, Top Shape Feet, 21 x 35 In. 338
Bench, Max Gottschalk, Leather, Yellow, Circles, Rolled, Branded, c.1965, 27 x 59 In. 2500
Bench, Modern Surfboard Design, Red Leather, Tube Supports, 70 x 18 In. 240
Bench, Modern, Pace Collection, Glass 1220
Bench, Mortise Legs, Skirt, Shaped Cutout Legs, Mustard Grain Painted, 1800s, 19 x 54 In. 1062
Bench, Neoclassical Style, Mahogany, Upholstered, Scroll Arms, Flared Legs, 32 x 86 In. 531
Bench, Oak, Carved, Scrolled, Acanthus Handholds, England, 1800s, 37 x 84 In., Pair 2214
Bench, Peinte, Louis XVI Style, Padded, Beaded Apron, Top-Shape Feet, c.1900, 19 x 35 In. 338
Bench, Piano, Duet, Victorian, Padded Seats, Tapered Ledge, Chas. Wadman, 1800s, 24 x 34 In. 150
Bench, Piano, Needlepoint, 21 x 38 In. 180
Bench, Red Lacquer, Carved, Blossom Border, Cane, Landscape, Chinese, Republic Period 300
Bench, Serge Castello, Chrome Metal, Wool Mohair, c.2000, 18 x 48 In. 240
Bench, Softwood, Red Ocher Paint, Beaded Crest, Open Backrest, 1800s, 33 x 72 In. .... *illus* 3776
Bench, Wegner, Johannes Hansen, Oak, Cane, Metal Label, Denmark, 1960s, 18 x 26 In. 2500
Bench, Wegner, Johannes Hansen, Teak, Branded, 1960s, 12 x 63 In. 6875
Bench, Window, George III, Mahogany, c.1750-90, 24 x 44 In. 1750
Bench, Windsor, Mixed Wood, Plank Seat, Spindle Back, Carved Grips, c.1800, 30 x 81 In. 7670
Bench, Windsor, Pine Plank Seat, Painted, Spindle Back, 1800s, 33 x 108 In. 1770
Bookcase, 4 Glass Doors, 4 Carved Inset Panel Doors, Egg & Dart Crown, 99 x 90 In. 1375
Bookcase, Aesthetic Revival, Walnut, Burl, Ebonized, Glass Doors, 1870s, 48 x 16 In. 531
Bookcase, Amboyna, 2 Doors, Domed Cornice, Brass Band, Bun Feet, c.1890, 91 x 50 In. 3000
Bookcase, Arts & Crafts, Oak, 4 Shelves, 2 Doors, 66 x 54 In. 424
Bookcase, Arts & Crafts, Oak, Mortised Shelves, Cutout Clovers, c.1915, 29 x 31 In., Pair 480
Bookcase, Arts & Crafts, Walnut, 2 Doors, Panes, Shelves, Block Feet, c.1950, 54 x 55 In. 360
Bookcase, Barrister, Globe-Wernicke, 2 Stacks, Glazed Doors, 40 x 34 ½ In. 333
Bookcase, Barrister, Oak, 53 x 34 In. 313
Bookcase, Cabinet, French Provincial, Louis XII Style, Beech, Carved, 70 x 21 In. 519

Furniture, Bench, Bugatti, Walnut, Copper, Brass, Medallion, Arms, c.1900, 31 x 48 In.
$13,750

Rago Arts and Auction Center

Furniture, Bench, Softwood, Red Ocher Paint, Beaded Crest, Open Backrest, 1800s, 33 x 72 In.
$3,776

Hess Auction Group

Furniture, Bookcase, Federal, Mahogany, Drop Front, Desk, 2 Doors, Inlay, 1807, 98 x 53 In.
$5,490

Neal Auctions

Names for Mission-Style Furniture

Craftsman was the name used by Gustav Stickley. Furniture by other makers was called Arts & Crafts, Crafts-Style, Hand-Craft, Mission, Quaint, or Roycroft. To add to the confusion, the family name was used by Gustav's relatives.

Furniture, Bookcase, Lifetime, Oak, Single Door, 6-Pane, c.1910, 45 x 30 In.
$1,750

Rago Arts and Auction Center

Furniture, Bookcase, Revolving, Mahogany, Inlay, Fretwork, Shelves, Edwardian, 33 x 22 In.
$366

Neal Auctions

Furniture, Bookrack, Arts & Crafts, Oak, Cutout Sides, c.1910, 46 x 22 In.
$390

Garth's Auctioneers & Appraisers

Furniture, Buffet, Deux-Corps, Pearwood, Doors, Shelves, Door-Length Hinges, c.1900, 89 In.
$840

Selkirk Auctioneers & Appraisers

Furniture, Cabinet, Display, Hardwood, Glass, Brass & Mother-Of-Pearl Inlay, Japan, 54 In.
$1,610

Cottone Auctions

Furniture, Cabinet, Display, Mahogany, Robert Mitchell Furniture Co., c.1906, 64 x 44 In.
$660

Cowan Auctions

Furniture, Cabinet, Display, Vitrine, Oak, Glass, Wheeled Feet, 4 Shelves, 41 x 63 In.
$305

Morphy Auctions

Furniture, Cabinet, Edwardian, Mahogany, Doors, Shelves, Multiple Drawers, 1800s, 83 x 42 In.
$1,750

Neal Auctions

Furniture, Cabinet, G. Nelson, Rosewood, Aluminum, Drawers, Herman Miller, 1952, 40 x 19 In.
$5,625

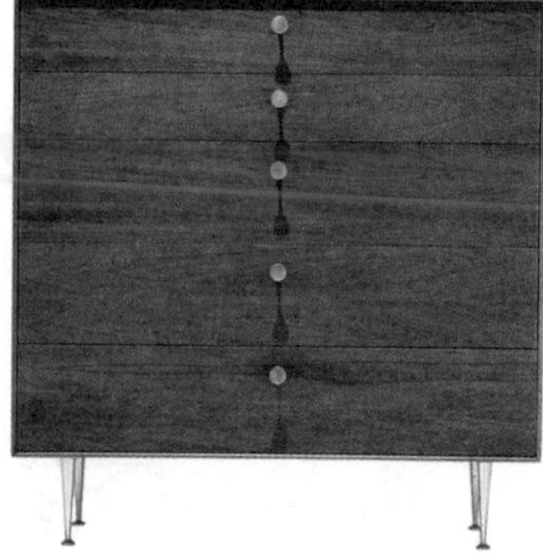

Wright (Chicago)

Furniture, Cabinet, G. Stickley, Oak, 2 Doors, Glass Panels, Branded, Label, c.1912, 64 x 41 In.
$5,312

Rago Arts and Auction Center

TIP

Go green. Refinish and restore old furniture. It saves up to 95 percent of the energy needed to make a new piece, and it is probably less expensive.

Bookcase, Cabinet, William IV, Mahogany, Grille Cupboard Doors, Shelves, c.1850, 78 x 43 In. . 1230
Bookcase, Esherick, Walnut, Graduated Shelves, Paoli, Pa., 1930s, 99 x 35 In. 10625
Bookcase, Federal, Mahogany, Drop Front, Desk, 2 Doors, Inlay, 1807, 98 x 53 In. *illus* 5490
Bookcase, G. Stickley, 2 Paneled Doors, Mullions, Gothic Arches, c.1901, 53 x 75 In. 15340
Bookcase, G. Stickley, Oak, 2 Doors, Paned, Gallery, Copper Handles, c.1904, 56 x 49 In. 3705
Bookcase, George III, White, 90 x 102 In. 1800
Bookcase, J. Stickley, Arts & Crafts, Oak, 3-Shelf Interior, Dual Mullioned, 54 x 45 In. 1464
Bookcase, Lifetime, Oak, Single Door, 6-Pane, c.1910, 45 x 30 In. *illus* 1750
Bookcase, Mahogany, 2 Parts, Gadroon Cornice, Doors, Paw Feet, c.1835, 86 x 41 In. 1000
Bookcase, Mahogany, 2 Shelf, Drawer, 42 x 20 In. 219
Bookcase, Mahogany, Carved, Glass Door, 3 Sections, 94 x 88 In. 960
Bookcase, Mahogany, Marble Top, Ebonized, Inlay, Open Shelves, 52 x 69 In. 1479
Bookcase, Mahogany, Pierced Broken Swan Neck Crest, Glazed Doors, c.1810, 92 In. 2125
Bookcase, Revolving, Danner, 2 Shelves, 58 ½ x 24 In. 833
Bookcase, Revolving, Mahogany, Inlay, Fretwork, Shelves, Edwardian, 33 x 22 In. *illus* 366
Bookcase, Revolving, Oak, Spindled Gallery Top, Divided Sections, Slats, c.1900, 52 x 20 In. 554
Bookcase, Revolving, Walnut, 2 Tiers, Tripod Base, Gallery, c.1950, 53 x 23 In., Pair 3501
Bookcase, Walnut Veneer, Curved Sides, Open Shelf Compartments, c.1910, 34 x 41 In. 5000
Bookcase, Walnut, Arched Cornice, Glazed Door, Hinged Fall, c.1715, 82 x 30 In. 2500
Bookcase, Walnut, Domed, Molded Cornice, Glazed Doors, Drawers, Cupboard, 87 x 57 In. 1187
Bookcase, Walnut, Hinged Door, Carved Panel, Shelves, 1960s, 36 x 55 In. 104
Bookcase, Walnut, Open, From Louis Philippe Armoire, Bracket Feet, c.1850, 84 x 58 In. 948
Bookrack, Arts & Crafts, Oak, Cutout Sides, c.1910, 46 x 22 In. *illus* 390
Bookrack, Tier, Inlaid Paterae On Sides, V-Shape Shelves, 31 x 22 In. 293
Bookstand, Bronze, Shaped Foot, Fluted Baluster Stem, Angled Panel, Patina, 14 x 11 In. 362
Bracket, Hardwood, Mother-Of-Pearl, Carved, Middle-Eastern, 37 ½ x 13 In. 780
Bracket, Victorian, Carved, Flowers, Shells, 11 x 13 In., Pair 210
Bracket, Victorian, Gilt, Carved Deer, 14 x 11 In., Pair 960
Bracket, Victorian, Gilt, Velvet, Lion Masks, 16 x 8 ½ In. 450
Breakfront, Federal Style, Mahogany, Swan Neck Crest, Drawer, Glass Doors, 83 x 55 In. 600
Breakfront, Oak, Dome Cornice, Carved Shell, Glass Doors, c.1900, 105 x 81 In. 5000
Buffet, Cherry, 2 Drawers, 2 Cupboard Doors, Fan Carved, c.1850, 47 x 51 In. 1187
Buffet, Deux-Corps, Pearwood, Doors, Shelves, Door-Length Hinges, c.1900, 89 In. *illus* 840
Buffet, French Provincial Style, Fruitwood, Drawers, Cupboards, 41 x 63 In. 937
Buffet, French Provincial, Fruitwood, Drawers, Cupboard Doors, c.1850, 50 x 53 In. 812
Buffet, Fruitwood, Cupboard Doors, Shaped Panel, Carved Urn, c.1805, 37 x 54 In. 2091
Buffet, Henri III, Upper Doors, Frieze Drawers, Double Cupboard, Fluted Columns, 91 x 59 In. . 369
Buffet, Midcentury Modern, 2 Shelves, 4 Doors, Denmark, 65 x 95 In. 2214
Buffet, Pierre Debs, Inlaid Diamond Pattern, 4 Doors, 29 ½ x 72 In. 476
Buffet, Provincial Louis XV Style, Fruitwood, Walnut, Burl Drawers, Doors, 37 x 50 In. 1230
Buffet, Provincial Louis XV Style, Oak, Carved, Paneled Glazed Doors, c.1900, 102 x 71 In. 2460
Buffet, Provincial Louis XV Style, Painted, Drawers, Paneled Doors, 45 x 58 In. 1353
Bureau, Bombe, Paint, Slant Front, Shaped Top, Cabriole Legs, c.1890, 42 x 38 In. 750
Bureau, Dressing, Neoclassical, Parcel Gilt, Mahogany, Mirror, Columns, c.1840, 88 x 45 In. 738
Bureau, Dutch Walnut, Bombe, Fall-Front, Fitted Interior, 3 Drawers, 39 ½ x 48 In. 2745
Bureau, Federal, Maple, Inlay, Crossbanded Borders, 4 Drawers, French Feet, 39 x 21 In. 861
Bureau, French Style, 8 Drawers, 2-Toned, Metal Fitting Mounts, Pulls, 42 x 16 In. 265
Bureau, Mahogany, Marquetry, Slant Front, Kettle Shape Base, Paw Feet, c.1790, 43 x 43 In. 1875
Bureau, Mahogany, Slant Front, Cubby Holes, Stretcher Shelf, Bun Feet, c.1810, 48 x 49 In. 5658
Bureau, Napoleon III, Rosewood, 2 Doors, Slant Front, Fluted Legs, c.1875, 70 x 36 In. 3750
Bureau, Neoclassical, Figured Mahogany, Marble, Paneled Doors, Shelves, c.1840, 84 x 42 In. 767
Bureau, Walnut, Bombe, Inlaid Flowers, Urns, Leaves, c.1800, 55 x 43 In. 4338
Cabinet, Adam Style, Multicolor, Ebonized, Painted, Asian Figure, Fluted, 30 x 31 In. 1845
Cabinet, Art Deco, Pedestal, Rounded Front, Glass Doors, 64 x 34 In. 625
Cabinet, Bamboo, 2 Doors, 2 Drawers, 55 x 37 In. 187
Cabinet, Baroque, Carved, Walnut, Italy, 36 ½ x 29 ¼ In. 5210
Cabinet, Biedermeier, Elm, Triangular Uprights, Drop Front, Door, 1800s, 81 x 44 In. 1476
Cabinet, Black, Porcelain, Gilt Bronze, Courting Couples, 2 Doors, 89 x 36 ¾ In. 4556
Cabinet, Bookcase, Federal, Cherry, Poplar, 2 Sections, Glass Pane Doors, 1800s, 87 x 45 In. 2124
Cabinet, Bookcase, Gothic Revival, Mahogany, Carved, Glazed Doors, Molding, 94 x 99 In. 2360
Cabinet, Chestnut, Linenfold, Carved, Wrought Iron, 2 Sections, c.1900, 62 x 38 In. 254
Cabinet, Chinoiserie, French Style, Red Paint, Glass Front, Rounded Front, Gilt, 65 x 25 In. 115
Cabinet, Cordial, Victorian, Ebonized Walnut, Gilt, Mother-Of-Pearl, c.1890, 11 x 13 In. 1046
Cabinet, Corner, Doors, 2 Shelves, Tiered, Flowers, Green, 21 x 17 In., Pair 366
Cabinet, Demijohn, Federal, Mahogany, Shaped Top, Brass Bail Handles, 21 x 25 In. 266
Cabinet, Display, Aesthetic Revival, Openwork Shelves, Beveled Glass, Carved, 83 x 57 In. 1380

Furniture, Cabinet, Hundred Boys, Red Lacquer, Scenic Panels, Cloisonne, c.1800, 62 In.
$3,555

James D. Julia Auctioneers

Furniture, Cabinet, James Mont, Wood, Carved & Silvered, Caryatids, Mirror, 1960s, 31 x 76 In.
$3,625

Rago Arts and Auction Center

Furniture, Cabinet, L. & J.G. Stickley, Oak, Doors, Glass, Shelves, Decal, c.1912, 62 x 44 In.
$5,000

Rago Arts and Auction Center

F

Furniture, Cabinet, Louis Philippe, Mahogany, Removable Boxes, Leather Drop Fronts, c.1850, 66 In.
$1,476

New Orleans (Cakebread)

Furniture, Cabinet, Mahogany, Domed Cornice, Glazed Doors, Flower Inlay, c.1790, 89 x 68 In.
$1,500

New Orleans (Cakebread)

TIP

A drawer that is stuck can be helped by heat. Remove any nearby drawers, then aim a blow dryer set on medium at the wood. Once the drawer is opened, rub the runners with paraffin or a candle.

Cabinet, Display, Art Deco, Red Glass, Brass Mounted, Lighted, Siegel Paris, 35 23 In. 3050
Cabinet, Display, British Telephone Booth, Red, Glass Windows, 4 Shelves, 73 x 30 In. 725
Cabinet, Display, Federal, Mahogany, Drawers, Doors, Mullions, 1800s, 41 x 36 In. 630
Cabinet, Display, French Style, Gilt Bronze, c.1900, 34 x 22 In. 960
Cabinet, Display, Gothic Revival, Cast Brass, Crystal Steeple, c.1870, 30 x 11 In. 1140
Cabinet, Display, Hardwood, Glass, Brass & Mother-Of-Pearl Inlay, Japan, 54 In. ....*illus* 1610
Cabinet, Display, Louis XVI Style, Walnut, Gilt Bronze, Floral Roping, 1800s, 40 x 32 In. 492
Cabinet, Display, Mahogany, Robert Mitchell Furniture Co., c.1906, 64 x 44 In. ....*illus* 660
Cabinet, Display, Oak, Carved, Bowfront, Curved Glass, c.1900s, 61 x 49 In. 305
Cabinet, Display, Parcel Gilt, Wrought Iron Open Scroll, Electrified, 79 x 39 In. 153
Cabinet, Display, Victorian, Oak, Carved, Curved Glass, Paw Feet, c.1900, 69 x 56 In. 296
Cabinet, Display, Victorian Style, Mahogany, 2 Lower Shelves, 3 Upper, Pierced Sides, 60 x 20 In. 60
Cabinet, Display, Vitrine, Oak, Glass, Wheeled Feet, 4 Shelves, 41 x 63 In. ....*illus* 305
Cabinet, Ebonized, Slate Top, Ormolu, Brass, Leaf Swags, Doors, c.1870, 41 x 17 In., Pair 7500
Cabinet, Edwardian, Mahogany, Doors, Shelves, Multiple Drawers, 1800s, 83 x 42 In. ....*illus* 1750
Cabinet, Edwardian, Satinwood, Mahogany, Inlay, 2 Glazed Doors, Glass Shelves, 72 x 47 In. 826
Cabinet, Filing, Card Catalog, Oak, 18 Drawers, Yawman & Erbe Mfg., 52 ½ x 33 In. 550
Cabinet, Filing, Oak, 3 Sections, 15 Drawers, Pittsburgh Desk & Chair Co., 51 x 22 In. 247
Cabinet, Filing, Oak, 8 Drawers, Sole Makers, 42 x 27 In. 220
Cabinet, G. Nelson, Rosewood, Aluminum, Drawers, Herman Miller, 1952, 40 x 19 In. ....*illus* 5625
Cabinet, G. Stickley, Oak, 2 Doors, Glass Panels, Branded, Label, c.1912, 64 x 41 In. ....*illus* 5312
Cabinet, Georgian Style, Walnut, Broken-Arch Pediment, Doors, J & B Blower, 84 x 36 In. 240
Cabinet, Gio Ponti, Figured Walnut, 2 Slide Doors, Singer & Sons, c.1959, 27 x 79 In. 10000
Cabinet, Gun, Oak, Wrought Iron Hardware, Carved Figures, Flowers, 1900s, 81 x 51 In. 540
Cabinet, H. Probber, Glass, Laminate, Shelf, 22 ½ x 42 In. 270
Cabinet, Hundred Boys, Red Lacquer, Scenic Panels, Cloisonne, c.1800, 62 In. ....*illus* 3555
Cabinet, Hunt, Stag's Head, Hunting Dogs, Scrolls, Leaves, Shelves, 4 Drawers, 106 x 106 In. 7500
Cabinet, Italian Renaissance, Baroque, Walnut, Lift Top, Iron Hinges, c.1700, 41 x 51 In. 4484
Cabinet, James Mont, Wood, Carved & Silvered, Caryatids, Mirror, 1960s, 31 x 76 In. ....*illus* 3625
Cabinet, L. & J.G. Stickley, Oak, Doors, Glass, Shelves, Decal, c.1912, 62 x 44 In. ....*illus* 5000
Cabinet, Library, Louis XVI Style, Inlay, Kingwood, Tulipwood, Bronze Gallery, 67 x 60 In. 1230
Cabinet, Linen, Provincial, Directoire, Fruitwood, Cupboard Doors, Paneled, 39 x 56 In. 1250
Cabinet, Louis Philippe, Mahogany, Removable Boxes, Leather Drop Fronts, c.1850, 66 In. *illus* 1476
Cabinet, Louis XVI Style, Mahogany, Marble Top, Drawer, Cupboard Doors, c.1910, 40 x 50 In. . 2214
Cabinet, Louis XVI Style, Oak, Mahogany, Marble Top, Pierced Gallery, 50 x 56 In., Pair 4920
Cabinet, Mahogany, 2 Doors, Square Knobs, 1950s, 22 ½ x 24 In. 1154
Cabinet, Mahogany, Carved, Marble Top, Henredon, 30 x 43 In. 1250
Cabinet, Mahogany, Domed Cornice, Glazed Doors, Flower Inlay, c.1790, 89 x 68 In. ....*illus* 1500
Cabinet, Mahogany, Drawers, Yawman Mfg. Co., 70 x 33 In. 960
Cabinet, Mahogany, Marble Top, Demilune, Cupboard Doors, Ormolu, c.1900, 38 x 77 In. 8125
Cabinet, Mahogany, Paneled Doors, Carved, Gilt Paint, 1960s, 64 x 87 In. 1998
Cabinet, Michael Graves, Stained, Painted, Branded, Ink Stamped, Drexel, 1989, 50 x 65 In. 1250
Cabinet, Multicolor, Frieze Drawers, Paneled Door, Block Feet, 36 x 40 In. 1187
Cabinet, Neoclassical, Mahogany, Broken-Scroll Pediment, Rosettes, Urn Finial, 66 x 37 In. 120
Cabinet, Oak, 2 Sections, 3 Doors, Carved Panels, Columns, Drawers, 52 x 50 In. 413
Cabinet, Oxbow, Flowers, Bracket Feet, 1900s, 34 ½ x 41 x 13 In. 430
Cabinet, Paolo Buffa, Marquetry, 6 Drawers, Tapered Legs, Midcentury Modern 3965
Cabinet, Papier-Mache, Chinoiserie, Figures, Wood Panel Doors, c.1890, 20 x 18 In. 625
Cabinet, Pier, Directoire Style, Painted, Faux Marble Top, Bronze, 32 x 94 In. 413
Cabinet, Pine, Double Paneled Doors, Pilasters, Ball Feet, Ornaments, c.1865, 25 x 36 In. 110
Cabinet, Pine, Molded Cornice, 4 Paneled Cupboard Doors, c.1910, 88 x 87 In. 1168
Cabinet, Provincial, Multicolor, Cupboards, Painted, Faux Paneling, Square Legs, 37 x 47 In. ... 468
Cabinet, Provincial, Tuscan Style, Doors, Columnar Pilasters, Drawer, Paneled Doors, 80 x 37 In. 461
Cabinet, Queen Anne Style, Walnut, 3 Shelves, Shaped Top, Doors, 60 x 24 In. 330
Cabinet, Regency, Satinwood, Amber Patina, Ebonized Trim, Doors, c.1810, 17 x 20 In. 1250
Cabinet, Renaissance Revival, Ebonized, Marble Top, Drawer, Door, Brass, c.1890, 43 x 48 In. .. 1200
Cabinet, Renaissance Revival, Oak, Carved, Columns, B. Favard, c.1900, 66 x 34 In. ....*illus* 1140
Cabinet, Roadkill, Graham, Metal, Wood, Doors, Holographic Image, 91 x 36 In. ....*illus* 3375
Cabinet, Robsjohn-Gibbings, Walnut, Stained, Bleached, Widdicomb, 33 x 36 In. 1125
Cabinet, Rustic, Beveled Cornice, Hinged Doors, Round Pulls, Shelf, 32 x 52 In. 380
Cabinet, Sewing, Mahogany, Drawers, Fold-Out Top, Door, Stretcher, 1800s, 35 x 15 In. 150
Cabinet, Shanxi, Elm, Red Lacquered, Figural Scene, 2 Doors, c.1860, 43 x 37 In. 593
Cabinet, Side, Regency, Mahogany, 15 Doors, Plinth, 19th Century, 77 x 49 ½ In. 1845
Cabinet, Side, Regency, Rosewood, Bowfront, Open Center Bay, Shelves, 39 x 74 In. 3550
Cabinet, Spice, Walnut, Molded Cornice, Hinged Panel, Drawers, c.1775, 19 x 17 x 8 In. 799
Cabinet, Tambour, Povl Dinesen, Teak, Drawers, Foil Label, Denmark, 1960s, 31 x 75 In. 2625

Furniture, Cabinet, Renaissance Revival, Oak, Carved, Columns, B. Favard, c.1900, 66 x 34 In. $1,140

Selkirk Auctioneers & Appraisers

Furniture, Cabinet, Roadkill, Graham, Metal, Wood, Doors, Holographic Image, 91 x 36 In. $3,375

Rago Arts and Auction Center

TIP

Don't put plastic covers on wooden furniture. The plastic may melt onto the wood and harm the finish. Don't even leave a plastic tablecloth on a table for more than a month.

Furniture, Cabinet, Walnut, Tabletop, Carved Openwork, Curved Legs, 1973, 32 x 23 In. $1,063

Rago Arts and Auction Center

Furniture, Candlestand, Cherry, Shaped Top, Turned Post, Tripod Base, c.1810, 26 x 16 In. $1,046

Skinner, Inc.

Furniture, Candlestand, Queen Anne, Cherry, Tray Top, Drawer, Pad Feet, c.1770, 26 x 16 In. $2,133

James D. Julia Auctioneers

Furniture, Cellarette, Georgian Style, Mahogany, Brass, Tole Liner, 8-Sided, 27 x 19 In. $1,220

Neal Auctions

Furniture, Cellarette, Stand, Federal, Walnut, Dovetailed, Drink Slide, c.1800, 37 x 19 In. $30,680

Brunk Auctions

Furniture, Chair Set, Butterfly, Ferrari-Hardoy, Bonet, Kurchan, 38 x 31 In., 5 Piece
$500

Los Angeles Modern Auctions

Furniture, Chair Set, Plank Seat, Geo. Hay, Chair Cabinet Coffin Maker, York, Pa., 31 In., 6
$480

Garth's Auctioneers & Appraisers

Furniture, Chair, Anglo-Portuguese, Chippendale Style, Ball & Claw Feet, c.1790, 41 In., Pair
$1,722

Skinner, Inc.

Furniture, Chair, Anglo-Portuguese, Mahogany, Carved, 1800s, Pair
$2,091

Neal Auctions

Furniture, Chair, Arne Jacobsen, Egg, Aluminum, Swivel, Fritz Hansen, 1960s, 39 In.
$2,760

Cottone Auctions

Furniture, Chair, Belter, Lady's, Rococo, Rosewood, Fountain Elms Pattern,c.1855, 40 In.
$5,120

Neal Auctions

Furniture, Chair, Bergere, Empire Style, Mahogany, Bronze Mounted, Busts, Closed Arms
$3,438

Neal Auctions

Furniture, Chair, Bergere, Federal, Mahogany, Rosettes, Tufted Velvet Upholstery, c.1820, 39 In.
$2,074

Neal Auctions

Furniture, Chair, Black Forest Type, Dwarf, Grapevines, 47 x 20 In.
$1,560

Fox Auctions

Cabinet, Tortoise, Ebonized, Hinged Top, Cupboard, Pierced Heart, 1600s, 55 x 33 In. 12500
Cabinet, Vitrine, Georgian Style, Mahogany, Glazed Doors, Glass Shelves, 1900s, 92 x 47 In. 1180
Cabinet, Vitrine, Mahogany, 6 Shelves, Baker Furniture, 92 x 46 In. 250
Cabinet, Walnut, Faux Marble, Demilune, Flower Banding, Figures, c.1890, 36 x 52 In. 3198
Cabinet, Walnut, Gilt, Inlaid Leaves, Rosettes, Panel Door, Fluted Columns, 41 x 80 In. 3747
Cabinet, Walnut, Tabletop, Carved Openwork, Curved Legs, 1973, 32 x 23 In. .... *illus* 1063
Cabinet, Wegner, Oak, Rosewood, Matte Chrome Steel, Mobler, 1960s, 31 x 79 In. 3750
Cabinet, White Pine, Tabletop, Molded Crest, Glazed Door, Block Feet, 1700s, 29 x 24 In. 799
Cabinet, Wood, Red Lacquer, Carved, Reticulated Panel Doors, Pierced, c.1800, 33 x 43 In. 738
Cabinet, Writing, 2 Doors, Writing Panel, Gilt Garden Scenes, Chinese, 51 x 24 In. 1200
Caddy, Wine, Queen Anne, Mahogany, Shaped Top, Cutout Handle, 23 x 23 In. 207
Candlestand, Cherry, Shaped Top, Turned Post, Tripod Base, c.1810, 26 x 16 In. .... *illus* 1046
Candlestand, Cherry, Shaped Top, Vase & Ring-Turned Stem, Tripod Legs, c.1780, 26 x 17 In. .. 492
Candlestand, Chippendale Style, Tilt Top, Mahogany, Ball & Claw Feet, Round, 23 x 13 In. 301
Candlestand, Chippendale, Cherry, Beaded, Cabriole Legs, c.1785, 26 x 14 In. 162
Candlestand, Chippendale, Cherry, Tilt Top, Dish Rim, Pedestal, Ball & Claw Feet, 28 In. 1416
Candlestand, Chippendale, Maple, Shaped Curly Top, Tripod Base, Mass., 1725, 23 x 14 In. 300
Candlestand, Federal, Cherry, Tilt Top, Birdcage Support, Spider Legs, 28 x 19 In. 472
Candlestand, Federal, Tiger Maple, Plank Top, Pedestal, Tripod Base, 28 x 21 In. 587
Candlestand, George III, Mahogany, Hexagonal Top, Scroll Support, 39 x 14 In. 2359
Candlestand, Georgian, Mahogany, Rosehead Nail, Leather Top, Pedestal, c.1800, 28 x 20 In. .. 177
Candlestand, Mahogany, Round Top, Baluster Stem, Cabriole Feet, c.1790, 27 x 22 In. 234
Candlestand, Mahogany, Square Top, Pierced Gallery, Pierced Legs, c.1790, 28 x 12 In. 750
Candlestand, Mixed Wood, Red Finish, Adjustable, Shoe Feet, Square Top, 27 In. 142
Candlestand, Queen Anne, Cabinet, Shells, Square Top, 3-Part Base, 1765, 25 x 16 In. 3259
Candlestand, Queen Anne, Cherry, Tray Top, Drawer, Pad Feet, c.1770, 26 x 16 In. .... *illus* 2133
Candlestand, Queen Anne, Round Top, Turned Standard, Cabriole Legs, 1800s, 26 x 17 In. 219
Candlestand, Standard, Carved, Gilt Paint, c.1700, 42 In. 620
Candlestand, Tilt Top, Cherry, Vase & Ring Turned, Tripod Cabriole Legs, c.1775, 26 In. 922
Candlestand, Victorian, Walnut, Bowed Sided, Tapered Support, c.1870, 36 x 10½ In., Pair 468
Candlestand, Walnut, Dished Tilt Top, Birdcage Support, Cabriole Legs, c.1775, 29 In. 3321
Candlestand, Wood, Red Paint, Butter Churn Base, Cutting Board Top, 1800s, 29 x 20 In. 73
Cane Holder, Pine, 39 In. 201
Canterbury, American Rosewood, c.1840, 22¼ x 15 In. 236
Canterbury, Edwardian, Mahogany, Inlay, Harp Shape, Curved Legs, Slats, 23 x 22 In. 625
Canterbury, Regency Style, Lacquer, Drawer, Block Feet, Curved Top, Spindles, 24 In. 344
Canterbury, Regency, Rosewood, Dovetailed Drawer, Casters, 1800s, 20 x 18 In. 1121
Canterbury, Rosewood, Carved, Lyre Shape Dividers, Turned Legs, England, 21 x 15 In. 366
Canterbury, Rosewood, Pierced Lyre Shape Dividers, Turned Feet, c.1860, 17 x 22 In. 735
Canterbury, Rosewood, Pierced, Frieze Drawer, Baluster Legs, c.1850, 21 x 20 In. 629
Canterbury, Victorian, Mahogany, 3 Compartments, X Shape Supports, c.1900, 22 In. 492
Canterbury, Victorian, Rosewood, Drawer, Spindle Frame, Casters, 1800s, 18 x 20 In. 215
Captain's Bar, Teak, Fold-Out Bar, 3 Drawers, Ice Trays, Midcentury Modern, 35 x 71 In. 412
Cart, Magazine, Teak, Rolling, Canvas Sling, Denmark, 19 x 20 In. 36
Cart, Tile Top, Smoky Maple, Round, Black, Green, Red, 17¾ x 32 In. 2074
Case, Liqueur, Napoleon III, Walnut, Inlay, Serpentine, Banding, Cartouche, c.1860, 11 x 13 In. 1353
Cassone, Baroque, Cedar, Pokerwork, Figures, Beasts, Hinged Lid, c.1690, 25 x 72 In. 5000
Cassone, Baroque, Walnut, Carved, Wrought Iron Hinges, Hasp, Till, 1600s, 25 x 60 In. 1770
Cassone, Walnut, Hinged Lid, Gadrooned, Griffins, Urn, Iron Handles, c.1690, 23 x 68 In. 1476
Cellarette, George III, Mahogany, Oval, Bail Handles, Casters, c.1800, 28 x 24 In. 2205
Cellarette, George III, Mahogany, Oval, Hinged Top, Fan Shape Fluting, Reeded, 21 x 27 In. 9438
Cellarette, Georgian Style, Mahogany, Brass, Tole Liner, 8-Sided, 27 x 19 In. .... *illus* 1220
Cellarette, Mahogany, Brass Bound, 8-Sided, Lined Interior, 1800s, 29 x 18 In. 861
Cellarette, Mahogany, Sarcophagus, Chamfered Corners, Melon Feet, 1800s, 22 x 30 In. 1348
Cellarette, Oak, Brass Bands, Oval, Lion's Head Handles, Copper Liner, 11 x 22 In. 660
Cellarette, Regency, Mahogany, Breadboard Ends, Zinc Lined Interior, c.1810, 24 x 17 In. 562
Cellarette, Regency, Mahogany, Sarcophagus Shape, Hinged, Metal Lined, c.1810, 21 x 28 In. .. 1476
Cellarette, Regency, Rosewood, Ormolu, Sarcophagus Shape, Flower Head, 31 x 19 In. 5899
Cellarette, Stand, Federal, Walnut, Dovetailed, Drink Slide, c.1800, 37 x 19 In. .... *illus* 30680
Chair Set, Art Deco, Birch, Carved, Upholstered High Back, Splayed Legs, 39 In., 6 671
Chair Set, Art Deco, Rosewood, Upholstered Back, Seat, Brass Tacking, France, 37 In., 6 4484
Chair Set, Balloon Back, Plank Seat, Green, Flowers, Gold & Black Trim, 1800s, 32 In., 6 708
Chair Set, Balloon Back, Plank Seat, Multicolor Flowers, Leaves, Red, Blue, White, 17 In., 6 236
Chair Set, Brno, Mies Van Der Rohe, Upholstered Seat, Back, Chrome Arms, Legs, Knoll, 4 1000
Chair Set, Butterfly, Ferrari-Hardoy, Bonet, Kurchan, 38 x 31 In., 5 Piece .... *illus* 500
Chair Set, Cane Back, Cushion, Continuous Arm, Ward Bennett, 4 1100

Furniture, Chair, Black Lacquer, Parcel Gilt, Mother-Of-Pearl Inlay, 34 In., Pair
$512

Neal Auctions

Furniture, Chair, Butterfly, Ferrari-Hardoy, Leather, c.1957, 3 x 35 In.
$1,045

Skinner, Inc.

Furniture, Chair, Campeche, Ottoman, Mahogany, Carved, Leather Upholstery, Arms, 1900s
$6,710

Neal Auctions

This is an edited listing of current prices. Visit **Kovels.com** to check thousands of prices from previous years and sign up for free information on trends, tips, reproductions, marks, and more.

F

Furniture, Chair, Carved, Lacquered, Continuous Arm, Chinese, c.1900, 34 x 20 In.
$230

Cottone Auctions

Furniture, Chair, Cockfighting, Oak, Curved Back, Black Paint, Leather Slip Seat, c.1830, 33 In.
$527

Thomaston Place Auction

Furniture, Chair, Coconut, Curved, Steel, Fiberglass, Leather, Herman Miller, 1950s, 34 In.
$2,625

Rago Arts and Auction Center

Chair Set, Chippendale Style, Scrolled Crest, Gothic Pierced Splat, 2 Armchairs, 40 In., 8 700
Chair Set, Contemporary, Ebonized Beech, Leather, Poltrona Frau, 37 In., 8 944
Chair Set, Eames, Bikini, Eiffel Tower Base, Midcentury Modern, 6 2684
Chair Set, Eastward, Cherry, Ash, Signed Thos. Moser, 39 x 21 In., 4 1800
Chair Set, Ettore Sottsass, Modern, Mandarin, Metal Arms, Legs, Padded Seat, Back, 5 650
Chair Set, Fornasetti, Starburst, 1989, 37 ½ x 16 In., 8 6710
Chair Set, George III, Mahogany, Pierced Splat, Shaped Crest Rail, 1700s, 38 In., 10 5750
Chair Set, Hitchcock, Ebonized Wood, Blank Paint, Stenciled Flowers, Rush Seat, 33 In., 4 248
Chair Set, Irish Chippendale, Mahogany, Shell Carved Crest, Pierced Splat, 38 In., 6 2006
Chair Set, Louis XV Style, Mahogany, Cane, Leather, Carved Crest, 38 In., 6 1500
Chair Set, Midcentury Modern, Rosewood, Hiels O. Moller, 2 Armchairs, 10 3750
Chair Set, Milo Baughman, Modern, Seat Cushion, Padded Arms, Chrome, 2 Armchairs, 6 1100
Chair Set, Modern, Richard Schultz, Arms, Woven Back, Seat, 3 1037
Chair Set, Neoclassical, Mahogany, Gondola, Curved Crest Rail, Francois Signouret, 31 In., 6 ... 1185
Chair Set, Paulin, Ribbon, Mushroom Ottoman, Stretch Upholstery, Painted Wood, 1970s, 4 7500
Chair Set, Plank Seat, Geo. Hay, Chair Cabinet Coffin Maker, York, Pa., 31 In., 6 .... *illus* 480
Chair Set, Regency, Multicolor, Gold Leaf, Carved Back, Hoof Feet, 2 Armchairs, 35 In., 10 2500
Chair Set, Saarinen, Midcentury Modern, Tulip, Pedestal Side Chair, 4 1830
Chair Set, Teak, Horizontal Back Rail, Faux Leather Cushion, 30 In., 8 842
Chair Set, Tiger Maple, Concave Crest, Acanthus Scroll Splat, Cane Seat, 33 In., 6 1968
Chair Set, Tiger Maple, Painted, Crest Tablet, Pierced Splat, Cane Balloon Seat, 34 In., 4 2214
Chair Set, Whitewashed, 39 ½ x 21 In., 6 312
Chair Set, Windsor, Fanback, 25 In., 4 1102
Chair Set, Windsor, Sack Back, Continuous Arm, Green Paint, David Smith, 40 In., 4 720
Chair, Adrian Pearsall, Lounge, Upholstered, Arms 2318
Chair, Adrian Pearsall, Midcentury Modern, Craft Associates, 40 x 33 In., Pair 357
Chair, Aesthetic Revival, Walnut, Owl Carved Arm Supports, Upholstered, c.1875, 35 In. 3444
Chair, Anglo-Portuguese, Chippendale Style, Ball & Claw Feet, c.1790, 41 In., Pair .... *illus* 1722
Chair, Anglo-Portuguese, Mahogany, Carved, 1800s, Pair .... *illus* 2091
Chair, Arne Jacobsen, Egg, Aluminum, Swivel, Fritz Hansen, 1960s, 39 In. .... *illus* 2760
Chair, Art Deco, Barrel Back, Wood, Upholstered, Curved Back Legs, France, 27 In. 677
Chair, Art Deco, Mahogany, Carved, Upholstered, France, c.1930, 35 In., Pair 767
Chair, Art Deco, Troy, Sunshade, Chrome, Tubular Frame, Wood Arms, 1930s, 31 In., Pair 242
Chair, Banister Back, Rush Seat, Shaped Crest, Turned Supports, Brown Paint, 1700s, 44 In. 502
Chair, Barcelona, Mies Van Der Rohe, Leather, Chrome, Knoll, Pair 6100
Chair, Beech, Floral Upholstery, Arms, 34 In. 118
Chair, Belter, Lady's, Rococo, Rosewood, Fountain Elms Pattern, c.1855, 40 In. .... *illus* 5120
Chair, Benhardt, Leather, 38 x 33 In. 500
Chair, Bergere, Directoire, Paint, Outswept Back, Upholstered, Closed Arms, c.1790, 36 In. 2583
Chair, Bergere, Ebonized, Curved Crest, Downswept, Closed Arms, 1900s, 35 In., Pair 1750
Chair, Bergere, Empire Style, Beech, Gilt, Molded Crest, Upholstered, Closed Arms, 41 In. 1200
Chair, Bergere, Empire Style, Mahogany, Bronze Mounted, Busts, Closed Arms .... *illus* 3438
Chair, Bergere, Federal, Mahogany, Rosettes, Tufted Velvet Upholstery, c.1820, 39 In. .... *illus* 2074
Chair, Bergere, Louis Philippe, Mahogany, Closed Arms, 36 x 25 In. 500
Chair, Bergere, Louis XV Style, Fruitwood, Cane, Serpentine Seat, Closed Arms, 21 In. 615
Chair, Bergere, Louis XV Style, Ivory Paint, Upholstered, Carved, Closed Arms, 35 In., Pair 687
Chair, Bergere, Louis XV Style, Mahogany, Gilt, Upholstered, Closed Arms, 1900s, 41 In. 275
Chair, Bergere, Louis XV Transitional, Mahogany, Domed, Padded Back, Closed Arms, 44 In. 437
Chair, Bergere, Ottoman, Louis XV Style, Multicolor, Bolster, Closed Arms, 1900s, 32 In. 1168
Chair, Bergere, Ottoman, Louis XVI Style, Multicolor, Cushion, Closed Arms, 45 In. 18450
Chair, Bergere, Rectangular Back, Scroll Crest, Swan Neck Uprights, Closed Arms, c.1850 492
Chair, Bergere, Regency, Paneled Frame, Buttoned Leather, Closed Arms, Casters, c.1825 8160
Chair, Bergere, Shaped Crest, Cabriole Legs, Upholstered, Closed Arms, 1900s, 37 In., Pair 1080
Chair, Bergere, Victorian, Mahogany, Carved, Pierced Crest, Upholstered, Closed Arms, 27 In. 178
Chair, Bergere, Victorian, Rosewood, Parcel Gilt, Closed Arms, c.1850 4279
Chair, Biedermeier, Fruitwood, Reclining, Upholstered, Arms, c.1830, 41 x 28 In. 3068
Chair, Black Forest Type, Dwarf, Grapevines, 47 x 20 In. .... *illus* 1560
Chair, Black Lacquer, Parcel Gilt, Mother-Of-Pearl Inlay, 34 In., Pair .... *illus* 512
Chair, Black Leather, Chrome, Italy, 1970s, 26 ½ x 23 In., Pair 184
Chair, Black Paint, Banister Back, Turned Finials & Stretchers, Arms, 1700s, 46 In. 384
Chair, Black Paint, Shaped Crest Rail, Vase Shape Splat, Scroll Arms, Dunlap, N.H., 41 In. 1353
Chair, Bucket, Overman, Swivel, Black Vinyl, Pedestal Base, 4-Footed, 27 x 28 In., Pair 150
Chair, Butterfly, Ferrari-Hardoy, Leather, c.1957, 33 x 35 In. .... *illus* 1045
Chair, Campaign, Lucite, Chrome, Yellow Slings, Brass, Adjustable, 1970s, 28 ½ x 23 In. 402
Chair, Campaign, Tooled Leather, Mahogany, Brass, 44 ½ x 27 In. 3750
Chair, Campeche, Federal Style, Mahogany, Carved, Scrolled Crest, Leather Sling Seat, 1900s..... 1315

Furniture, Chair, Corner, Chippendale, Elm, Upholstered, Pierced Gothic Slats, 32 In.
$295

Brunk Auctions

Furniture, Chair, Corner, Queen Anne, Mahogany, Vase Shape Splat, Front Slipper Foot, 31 In.
$240

Garth's Auctioneers & Appraisers

Furniture, Chair, D. Knorr, Enameled Steel, Upholstered, Knoll Associates, 1940s, 28 x 22 In.
$2,125

Rago Arts and Auction Center

Furniture, Chair, Dan Johnson, Gazelle, Bronze, Caning, c.1958, 27 x 24 In.
$13,750

Los Angeles Modern Auctions

Furniture, Chair, Eames, Lounge, Aluminum, Vinyl, Arms, Herman Miller, 1958, 28 x 34 ½ In.
$953

Jim Wroda

Furniture, Chair, Esherick, Ash, Cherry, Saddle Leather Seat, Tapered Legs, 1957, 31 In.
$6,875

Rago Arts and Auction Center

Furniture, Chair, F. & H. Campana, Harumaki, Aluminum, Carpet, Rubber, c.2004, 34 x 24 In.
$9,375

Los Angeles Modern Auctions

Furniture, Chair, Frank Lloyd Wright, Johnson Wax, Upholstered, Arms, Cassina, 1992, 35 In.
$1,169

Skinner, Inc.

Furniture, Chair, Friedeberg, Mahogany, Carved, Gilt, Paint, Butterfly Back, Footed, 1983, 38 In.
$4,063

Rago Arts and Auction Center

Furniture, Chair, G. Nelson, Kangaroo, Steel, Upholstered, Herman Miller, 1955, 37 x 40 In.
$7,500

Wright (Chicago)

Furniture, Chair, G. Stickley, Square, Shaped Back, Plank Armrest, Block Legs, c.1901, 42 In.
$500

Rago Arts and Auction Center

Furniture, Chair, Georgian Style, Burl, Pierced Splat, Outscrolling Arms, 40 In.
$562

New Orleans (Cakebread)

Chair, Campeche, Mahogany, Cane Back, Seat, Scroll Arms, Curule Base, 37 x 23 In. 1314
Chair, Campeche, Ottoman, Mahogany, Carved, Leather Upholstery, Arms, 1900s .... *illus* 6710
Chair, Campeche, Pine, Carved, Tilt Back, Sling Seat, Morocco, 1900s, 34 x 22 In., Pair 474
Chair, Carolean Style, Fruitwood, Tall Padded Back, Seat, Stretcher, 1800s, 44 In., 6.......... 1125
Chair, Carved, High Back, Two Tall Faces, Hot Pink Vinyl Seat, Witco, 59 x 23 ½ In. 137
Chair, Carved, Lacquered, Continuous Arm, Chinese, c.1900, 34 x 20 In. .... *illus* 230
Chair, Chesterfield, Leather, Button Tufted, Brass Nails, Ball Feet, Arms, 31 x 46 In., Pair 1586
Chair, Chinoiserie, Pierced Back, Arms, Cane Seat, Turned Legs, 1900s, 38 In., Pair.......... 1000
Chair, Chippendale Style, Mahogany, Cabriole Legs, Carved Splat, Arms, Child's 360
Chair, Chrome, Sleigh Base Frame, Upholstered, Wood Armrests, Thayer Coggin, 40 x 31 In. 259
Chair, Club, Art Deco Style, Leather, Upholstered Back, Seat, Lacquer Arms, 1900s, 26 x 30 In. .. 780
Chair, Club, Art Deco, Leather, France, c.1930, 34 x 32 In. 322
Chair, Club, Leather, Brown, Casters, 29 ½ In. 376
Chair, Club, Leather, Rolled Arms, France, 1890s, 36 x 30 In., Pair 1167
Chair, Club, Mohair, Arms, c.1930s, 32 x 28 In., Pair.......... 660
Chair, Club, Paulin, Groovy Chair, Crescent Shape Split, c.1973, 26 x 30 In., Pair 2057
Chair, Club, Wassily, Brown Leather Bands, Chrome, Stendig, 29 x 31 In. 106
Chair, Coat Of Arms, Needlepoint Seat, 1800s, 48 x 19 In. .... 1210 to 1815
Chair, Cockfighting, Oak, Curved Back, Black Paint, Leather Slip Seat, c.1830, 33 In. .... *illus* 527
Chair, Coconut, Curved, Steel, Fiberglass, Leather, Herman Miller, 1950s, 34 In. .... *illus* 2625
Chair, Conversation, Renaissance Style, Carved Back, Splayed Seat, Cushion, 48 x 26 In. 173
Chair, Corner, Chippendale, Elm, Upholstered, Pierced Gothic Slats, 32 In. .... *illus* 295
Chair, Corner, Conversation, Victorian, Walnut, Tufted, Baluster Legs, c.1890, 37 x 52 In. 2988
Chair, Corner, Huanghuali, Pierced Splats, Cabriole Legs, Chinese, c.1750, 35 x 29 In. 5899
Chair, Corner, Queen Anne Style, Beech, Cane Back & Seat, Slats, Arms, c.1900, 29 In. 89
Chair, Corner, Queen Anne Style, Mahogany, Shaped Splats, Upholstered Seat, Drexel.......... 150
Chair, Corner, Queen Anne, Mahogany, Vase Shape Splat, Front Slipper Foot, 31 In. .... *illus* 240
Chair, Corner, Rococo, Walnut, 31 ½ x 22 In. 375
Chair, D. Knorr, Enameled Steel, Upholstered, Knoll Associates, 1940s, 28 x 22 In. .... *illus* 2125
Chair, Dan Johnson, Gazelle, Bronze, Caning, c.1958, 27 x 24 In. .... *illus* 13750
Chair, Danish Modern Style, Beech, Carved, Curved Arms, c.1950, 33 x 25 In., Pair 504
Chair, Desk, Fanny, Saporiti, Flip Top, File Separators, Postmodern, 1993, 2 Piece 1037
Chair, Desk, Metamorphic, Mahogany, Foldover, Pivoting, Spindles, c.1854, 29 x 36 In. 1045
Chair, Director's, Alessandro Albrizzi, Fabric Seat, Back, Arms, Pair.......... 1300
Chair, Eames, Bikini, Eiffel Tower Base, Midcentury Modern, Pair.......... 125
Chair, Eames, DKR, Enameled Steel, Vinyl, Eiffel Tower Base, 1966, 22 x 32 In. 437
Chair, Eames, La Fonda, Fiberglass, Aluminum, Vinyl, c.1962, 21 x 29 In. 698
Chair, Eames, LCM, Dyed Ash Plywood, Chrome Plated, c.1948, 27 x 27 In. 476
Chair, Eames, Lounge, Aluminum, Vinyl, Arms, Herman Miller, 1958, 28 x 34 ½ In. .... *illus* 953
Chair, Eames, Lounge, Cast Aluminum, Leather, Plastic, 1969, 26 x 39 In. 539
Chair, Eames, Lounge, Ottoman, Rosewood, Leather, Aluminum, 1956, 34 x 32 In. 4375
Chair, Eames, Lounge, Ottoman, Rosewood, Midcentury Modern 2100
Chair, Eames, RAR, Fiberglass, Rope Edge, Birch, Steel, 1950, 25 x 27 In. 1397
Chair, Eames, Vinyl, Aluminum, Black, Horizontal Stripes, 33 x 20 In., Pair.......... 1200
Chair, Eero Aarnio, Lounge, Midcentury Modern, Metal Base, Woven Back, Seat 475
Chair, Esherick, Ash, Cherry, Saddle Leather Seat, Tapered Legs, 1957, 31 In. .... *illus* 6875
Chair, F. & H. Campana, Harumaki, Aluminum, Carpet, Rubber, c.2004, 34 x 24 In. .... *illus* 9375
Chair, Fauteuil, Henri II Style, Oak, Carved, Pierced Crest Rail, Spindle Splat, 1800s, 28 In. 178
Chair, Fauteuil, Louis XIII Style, Mahogany, Upholstered, Arms, c.1850, 46 In., Pair.......... 750
Chair, Fauteuil, Louis XIII Style, Oak, Carved, Upholstered Arms, 1800s, 49 x 27 In. 237
Chair, Fauteuil, Louis XV Giltwood, Padded Back, Molded Frame, Arms, 1700s, 37 In., Pair 5166
Chair, Fauteuil, Louis XV Style, Fruitwood, Shaped, Upholstered, c.1810, 39 x 26 In. 687
Chair, Fauteuil, Louis XV Style, Giltwood, Flower Carved Crest, Upholstered, 41 In., Pair 593
Chair, Fauteuil, Louis XVI Style, Giltwood, Rope-Twist Frame, Arms, c.1910, 39 In., Pair.......... 1476
Chair, Fauteuil, Louis XVI Style, Gray Paint, Padded Arms, Upholstered, c.1900, 35 In., Pair....... 660
Chair, Fauteuil, Louis XVI Style, Multicolor, Padded Back, Arms, Seat, c.1810, 34 In., Pair 3444
Chair, Fauteuil, Mahogany, Padded Back, Arms, Gilt Maiden's Head, c.1790, 35 In., Pair.......... 1250
Chair, Fauteuil, Neoclassical, Painted, Parcel Gilt, Upholstered Arms, 1800s, 35 x 24 In., Pair 1353
Chair, Fauteuil, Regency, Fruitwood, Carved, Crest, Upholstered, Flat Back, Arms, c.1790.......... 1793
Chair, Fauteuil, Restauration, Fruitwood, Crest Rail, Reeded Arms, c.1810, 36 In., Pair.......... 1187
Chair, Fauteuil, Rope Carved, Garland Crest, Arms, Upholstered, c.1890, 39 In., Pair.......... 1168
Chair, Fauteuil, Walnut, Backswept Crest, Arms, Saber Legs, Upholstered, c.1835, 36 In., Pair 984
Chair, Finn Juhl, Lounge, Teak, Brass, Upholstered, France & Sons, 1950s, 29 x 27 In., Pair 5938
Chair, Folding, Scottish, Oak, Carved, 29 ½ x 14 In. 180
Chair, Folke Ohlsson Style, Danish Modern Style, Wood Frame, Cushions, 29 x 33 In. 311
Chair, Frank Lloyd Wright, Johnson Wax, Upholstered, Arms, Cassina, 1992, 35 In. .... *illus* 1169

Furniture, Chair, Hand, Laminated Spruce, Carved, Style Of Pedro Friedeberg, c.1985, 36 In.
$5,000

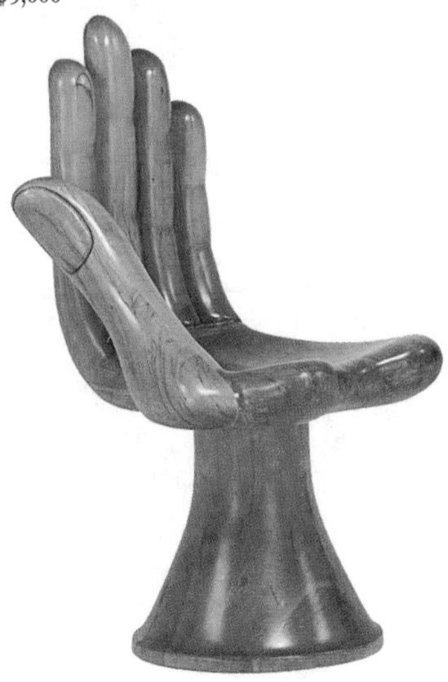

Rago Arts and Auction Center

Furniture, Chair, Hans Olsen, Lounge, Teak, Upholstery, Fried Egg, Asymmetrical, 1956, 41 In.
$6,875

Wright (Chicago)

Furniture, Chair, Horn, Inlaid Diamond & Star Shapes, Attributed To Wenzel Friedrich, 34 In.
$1,904

Showtime Auction Services

Furniture, Chair, Jeanneret, Lounge, Teak, Upholstered Seat, Cane, Block Arms, 1950s, 29 In.
$6,250

Rago Arts and Auction Center

Furniture, Chair, Ladder Back, 5-Slat Back, Rush Seat, Arms, Delaware Valley, 1700s, 43 In.
$708

Brunk Auctions

Furniture, Chair, Louis XVI Style, Carved, Gilt, Upholstered, Open Arms, Gilt, c.1900, 42 In.
$354

Brunk Auctions

Furniture, Chair, Mahogany, Carved Shield Back, Serpentine Front, c.1800, 39 x 22 In.
$130

Hess Auction Group

Furniture, Chair, Midcentury Modern, Rattan, Bentwood, Suede Upholstery, 34 In.
$165

Hess Auction Group

Furniture, Chair, Ming Style, Rosewood, Horseshoe Back, Pierced Splat, Arms, 39 x 20 In., Pair
$1,778

James D. Julia Auctioneers

Furniture, Chair, Neoclassical, Mahogany, Carved, Upholstered Seat, Arms, c.1845
$1,107

Neal Auctions

Furniture, Chair, Nutting, Brewster, Maple, Carved, Arms, Branded, 46 ½ In.
$3,600

Fairfield Auction

Furniture, Chair, Oak, Turned Stiles, Spindles, Box Stretcher, Carver, c.1670, 40 In.
$2,074

James D. Julia Auctioneers

Furniture, Chair, Office, Wegner, Teak, Leather, Steel, Castors, Swivel, 1955, 30 In.
$27,500

Wright (Chicago)

Furniture, Chair, Piano, Biedermeier, Mahogany, Fanback, Adjustable Seat, c.1825, 32 In.
$305

Neal Auctions

Furniture, Chair, Queen Anne, Walnut, Vase Shape Splat, Hoop Arms, Phila., c.1760, 42 In.
$2,963

James D. Julia Auctioneers

Furniture, Chair, R. Riemerschmid, Pine, Wicker, Arch Front, Curved Arms, c.1905, 33 In.
$3,125

Rago Arts and Auction Center

Furniture, Chair, Regency, Cane Seat, Back, Open Arms, Downswept Handholds, c.1810, 34 In.
$450

Cowan Auctions

Furniture, Chair, Robert Venturi, Grandmother's Tablecloth, Plywood, Fabric, c.1981, 38 In.
$6,150

Skinner, Inc.

Chair, French Provincial, Wood, Cane, Shaped Arms, Cabriole Legs, 38 x 25 In., Pair 184
Chair, French Style, Mahogany, Upholstered Back, Seat, Shaped Crest, Pair 300
Chair, French Style, Upholstered, Round Back, Padded Scrolled Armrests, 35 x 26 In., Pair 83
Chair, Friedeberg, Mahogany, Carved, Gilt, Paint, Butterfly Back, Footed, 1983, 38 In. *illus* 4063
Chair, Fruitwood, Leather, Tub Shape, 1900s, 28 ¾ x 28 In., Pair 3500
Chair, G. Nelson, Kangaroo, Steel, Upholstered, Herman Miller, 1955, 37 x 40 In. *illus* 7500
Chair, G. Stickley, Arts & Crafts, Oak, Open Arms, Back Rail, c.1910, 41 x 25 In. 472
Chair, G. Stickley, Square, Shaped Back, Plank Armrest, Block Legs, c.1901, 42 In. *illus* 500
Chair, George III Style, Carved Wood, Baroque Scrolling, Rosettes, Arms, 40 x 30 In. 253
Chair, George III, Mahogany, Serpentine Crest Rail, Upholstered, Arms, c.1760, 40 In., Pair 6490
Chair, George III, Mahogany, Shaped Crest, Pierced Splat, Hook Arms, 1700s, 38 In. 812
Chair, Georgian Style, Burl, Pierced Splat, Outscrolling Arms, 40 In. *illus* 562
Chair, Gilt, Scroll Carved Wings, Keyhole Design, Demilune Seat, c.1980, 38 x 27 In. 423
Chair, Giovanni Offredi, Lounge, Midcentury Modern, Leather, Chrome, Pair 3172
Chair, H. Bertoia, Diamond Mesh, Chrome Finish, 33 x 27 In. 137
Chair, H. Probber, Lounge, Architectural Series, No. 248, Pair 3050
Chair, Haimi, Midcentury Modern, Finland, 28 x 23 In. 154
Chair, Half Spindle, Green, Pennsylvania, 1800s, 33 ½ In. 24
Chair, Hall, George III, Mahogany, Oval Paneled Back, Prince Of Wales, Square Legs 1577
Chair, Hall, Gothic Revival, Oak, Pierced & Carved Stiles, Splat & Legs, c.1850, 68 In., Pair 12500
Chair, Hand, Laminated Spruce, Carved, Style Of Pedro Friedeberg, c.1985, 36 In. *illus* 5000
Chair, Hans Olsen, Lounge, Bikini, Modern, Molded Wood, Black Vinyl, Pair 2900
Chair, Hans Olsen, Lounge, Teak, Upholstery, Fried Egg, Asymmetrical, 1956, 41 In. *illus* 6875
Chair, Harry Balmer, Postmodern, Sculptural, Narrow Vertical Slat, Metal Legs 2400
Chair, Hat, Wood, Red & Black Lacquer, Square Arms, Box Stretcher, c.1800, 46 In., Pair 1476
Chair, Heywood-Wakefield, Lounge, Deck, Folding, Wood, c.1910, 38 x 55 In., Pair 2816
Chair, High Back, Damask Upholstery, Arched Crest, Carved, Outswept Arms, 42 x 40 In. 242
Chair, High Back, Folke Paalson, Red Dyed Wood, Arms, Turned Birch, 1960s, 41 In. 127
Chair, Hill Manufacturing, Lucite, Round Back, Waterfall Base, Side, 31 x 18 In. 212
Chair, Hill Manufacturing, Lucite, Scrolled Back, Tubular Arms, 40 x 24 In., Pair 484
Chair, Horn Arms & Legs, Leather Seat, 19th Century, 27 x 36 In. 1400
Chair, Horn, Inlaid Diamond & Star Shapes, Attributed To Wenzel Friedrich, 34 In. *illus* 1904
Chair, Huanghuali, Square, Railed Back, Marble Roundel, c.1900, 30 x 21 In. 1071
Chair, Ib Kofod-Larsen, Lounge, Upholstered, Seat, Arms, Stretchers, Ottoman, c.1960 900
Chair, Ib Kofod-Larsen, Lounge, Walnut Frame, Stretchers, Upholstered, Tufted, 39 x 30 In. 920
Chair, Irish Chippendale Style, Mahogany, Carved, Needlepoint, Upholstered, c.1900, 43 In. 885
Chair, Italian Mod, Anigre Wood, Removable Cover Cushions, 39 x 17 In., Pair 153
Chair, Jacaranda Wood, Red Leather, Ottoman, 1970s, 39 x 26 ½ In. 1035
Chair, Jacobean Style, Spindles, Carved, Pierced Crest, Splat, c.1920, 54 x 29 In. 120
Chair, Jacobean Style, Wood, Needlepoint Tapestry, Flowers, c.1920, 41 x 20 In. 426
Chair, Jeanneret, Lounge, Teak, Upholstered Seat, Cane, Block Arms, 1950s, 29 In. *illus* 6250
Chair, Jeanneret, Lounge, Teak, Upholstered, Cane, India, 29 x 21 In., Pair 15000
Chair, Jeanneret, Scissor, Birch, Aluminum, Webbing, Upholstered, Knoll, 1950s, 31 In., Pair 3750
Chair, John Stuart, Lounge, Ottoman, Button Tufted, Chrome Feet, 37 x 31 In. 383
Chair, Kezu, By Dakota Jackson, Leather, Open Arm, Tapered Legs, 37 x 25 In., Pair 425
Chair, Klismos, Bronze, c.1980, 27 x 18 In., Pair 4750
Chair, Lacquered, Mohair, 1950s, 35 x 23 In., Pair 575
Chair, Ladder Back, 5-Slat Back, Rush Seat, Arms, Delaware Valley, 1700s, 43 In. *illus* 708
Chair, Ladder Back, Acorn Finials, Arms, Child, c.1800, 22 In. 75
Chair, Le Corbusier, Tubular Chrome, Leather, Arms, Black, c.2000, 27 x 30 In., Pair 1440
Chair, Leather, Rolled Arms, Arched, c.1960, 30 x 36 In. 187
Chair, Louis Ghost, Black & White, Elliptical Back, Arms, Kartell, 2002, 37 In., Pair 360
Chair, Louis Philippe, Walnut, Rounded Crest, Padded Back, Flat Arms, c.1850, 36 In. 937
Chair, Louis XV Style, Giltwood, Carved, Open Arms, Upholstered, 39 In. 472
Chair, Louis XV, Softwood, Carved, Painted, Needlepoint Upholstery, Arms, 41 In., Pair 600
Chair, Louis XVI Style, Carved, Gilt, Upholstered, Open Arms, Gilt, c.1900, 42 In. *illus* 354
Chair, Louis XVI Style, Cream Paint, Gilt, Upholstered, Open Arms, c.1900, 43 In., Pair 531
Chair, Louis XVI Style, Desk, Mahogany, Padded Back, Seat Cushion, 1900s, 43 In. 1599
Chair, Louis XVI Style, Multicolor, Padded Back, Molded Frame, 36 In., Pair 1125
Chair, Louis XVI Style, Multicolor, Padded Tapered Back, Seat, 1900s, 38 In. 468
Chair, Louis XVI, Giltwood, Curved Crest, Round Seat, Square Back, 35 ½ x 23 In. 1342
Chair, Lounge, Black Vinyl, Cocoon Shape, Black Laminate Base, 37 x 32 In. 110
Chair, Lounge, Danish Modern, High Back, Upholstered, Wood Frame, 40 x 26 In. 165
Chair, Lounge, Modern, Saporiti, Upholstered Seat, Back, Arms, Neck Pillow, Pair 1100
Chair, Lounge, Tubular Chrome, Faux Fur, No Arms, c.1970, 29 x 25 In. 900
Chair, Lounge, Tufted Seat & Back, Chrome Frame, Midcentury Modern, 28 x 24 In., Pair 247

Furniture, Chair, Robert Venturi, Queen Anne, Grandmother's Tablecloth, Plywood, 1986, 39 In.
$3,750

Rago Arts and Auction Center

Furniture, Chair, Robert Venturi, Queen Anne, Plywood, Yellow Laminate, Knoll, 38 x 27 In.
$1,230

Skinner, Inc.

Furniture, Chair, Rococo Revival, Rosewood, Cornucopia, Attributed To Belter, c.1855, 46 In.
$33,688

Neal Auctions

F

Furniture, Chair, Rococo Revival, Rosewood, Rosalie Without Grapes, c.1865, 38 In., Pair
$1,353

New Orleans (Cakebread)

Furniture, Chair, Rococo, Rosewood, Elaborate Carved Back, Upholstered Seat, c.1860
$420

DuMouchelles Art Gallery

Furniture, Chair, Rohlfs, Hall, Oak, Cutouts, Beaded Seat, Openwork Legs, c.1900, 47 In.
$18,750

Rago Arts and Auction Center

Chair, Machine Age Style, Curved Tubular Steel, Faux Leather Seat & Back, 29 In., Pair 677
Chair, Mahogany, Blond, Interwoven, Reeded, Shaped Legs, Square Arms, 40 In., Pair 1875
Chair, Mahogany, Carved Shield Back, Serpentine Front, c.1800, 39 x 22 In. .... *illus* 130
Chair, Mahogany, Georgian Style, Pierced Skirt, Fret-Carved Legs, c.1900, 39 In. 492
Chair, Mahogany, Pierced Splat, Shaped Crest, Ball & Claw Feet, c.1900, 39 In., Pair 225
Chair, Mahogany, Pierced Wheel Back, Molded Arms, Square Legs, Spade Feet, 38 In., Pair 1750
Chair, Mahogany, Scrolled Seat & Back, Curule Supports, Padded Arms, c.1850, 38 In. 398
Chair, Mahogany, Writing Arm, Drawer, Neoclassical, 1850s, 38 In. 446
Chair, Maple, Ash, 4 Spindles, Ring-Turned Posts, Woven Seat, 38 x 15 In. 5843
Chair, Marcel Breuer, B33, Chrome Frame, Laced Black Leather Back, Seat, Knoll, 32 In. 344
Chair, McCobb, Lounge, Splayed Back Legs, Curved Top, Upholstered, 33 x 34 In. 587
Chair, Midcentury Modern, Rattan, Bentwood, Suede Upholstery, 34 In. .... *illus* 165
Chair, Mies Van Der Rohe, Barcelona, X Frame, Leather, c.1929, 30 x 29 In. .... 2250 to 8505
Chair, Mies Van Der Rohe, MR20, Stainless Steel, Wicker Seat, Knoll, 1927, 33 x 22 In. 265
Chair, Milo Baughman, Lounge, Chrome, Upholstered, Thayer Coggin, 27 In., Pair 1200
Chair, Milo Baughman, Lounge, Modern, Upholstered, Chrome Curved Base, Pair 1830
Chair, Milo Baughman, Ottoman, Scoop, c.1953, 27 x 27 ½ In. 544
Chair, Ming Style, Rosewood, Horseshoe Back, Pierced Splat, Arms, 39 x 20 In., Pair .... *illus* 1778
Chair, Modern, Padded Seat, Upper Back, Arms, Brazil 900
Chair, Neoclassical Style, Walnut, Lovebird & Trophy Crest, Ram's Head Arms, 37 In. 437
Chair, Neoclassical, Mahogany, Carved Crest Rail, Fan Shape Splat, Padded Seat, 35 In., Pair 676
Chair, Neoclassical, Mahogany, Carved, Upholstered Seat, Arms, c.1845 .... *illus* 1107
Chair, Nico Zographos, Lounge, Wool Upholstery, Stainless Steel, 32 x 24 In., Pair 240
Chair, Norman Cherner, Bentwood, Yellow Vinyl Seat, Back, 31 x 20 In. 127
Chair, Norman Cherner, Walnut, Enameled Plywood, Arm, Plycraft, 1950s, 31 In., Pair 2250
Chair, Nutting, Brewster, Maple, Carved, Arms, Branded, 46 ½ In. .... *illus* 3600
Chair, Oak, Cane, Arms, England, 36 x 28 In. 212
Chair, Oak, Carved, Leafy Back, Serpentine Seat, Hairy Paw Feet, 41 x 18 In. 165
Chair, Oak, Turned Stiles, Spindles, Box Stretcher, Carver, c.1670, 40 In. .... *illus* 2074
Chair, Office, Dunbar, Swivel, Brass Pedestal Base, 25 x 27 In., Pair 495
Chair, Office, Wegner, Teak, Leather, Steel, Castors, Swivel, 1955, 30 In. .... *illus* 27500
Chair, Paulin, Lounge, Ribbon, Midcentury Modern 3750
Chair, Paulin, Sling, Blue, 1963, 38 x 32 In. 3438
Chair, Philippe Starck, Lounge, Modern, Doctor Sonderbar, Pair 2440
Chair, Piano, Biedermeier, Mahogany, Fanback, Adjustable Seat, c.1825, 32 In. .... *illus* 305
Chair, Pineapple Shape Splats, Yellow, Green, 41 ½ In. 146
Chair, Poltrona Frau, Aqua Leather, Oval Cushion, Polished Steel Swivel Base, 33 In. 1722
Chair, Porter, Carved Walnut, Upholstered, 64 x 27 In. 840
Chair, Provincial, Louis XV Style Fruitwood, Padded Back, Floral Crest, c.1810, 38 In., Pair 343
Chair, Provincial, Louis XV Style, Needlework Upholstery, Open Arms, 35 In., Pair 413
Chair, Queen Anne, Walnut, Vase Shape Splat, Hoop Arms, Phila., c.1760, 42 In. .... *illus* 2963
Chair, R. Lowey, Barcalounger, c.1966, 43 x 37 ½ In. 5312
Chair, R. Riemerschmid, Pine, Wicker, Arch Front, Curved Arms, c.1905, 33 In. .... *illus* 3125
Chair, Red Paint, Concave Crest Rail, Vase Shape Splat, Urn Finials, Arms, Conn., 46 In. 4305
Chair, Regency Style, Mahogany, Carved, Multicolor, Reproduction, 40 In. 236
Chair, Regency, Cane Seat, Back, Open Arms, Downswept Handholds, c.1810, 34 In. .... *illus* 450
Chair, Regency, Ebonized, Turned Crest Rail, Painted Panel, Downswept Arms, 31 In., Pair 1750
Chair, Renaissance Revival Style, Leather, Carved, Scrolling Arms, 48 x 25 In. 1116
Chair, Renaissance Revival, Carved, Claw Feet, 6 Faces, Arms, 67 x 30 In. 968
Chair, Renaissance Revival, Mahogany, Dolphins, Arms, 38 ½ x 19 ½ In. 120
Chair, Renaissance Revival, Savonarola Style, Shaped, Carved Crest Rail, 34 x 27 In. 492
Chair, Renaissance Style, Parcel Gilt, Carved Ears, Embroidery, Arms, 52 In., Pair 861
Chair, Risom, Sculpted Wood, Linen & Cotton Upholstery, 31 x 22 In. 92
Chair, Robert Venturi, Grandmother's Tablecloth, Plywood, Fabric, c.1981, 38 In. .... *illus* 6150
Chair, Robert Venturi, Queen Anne, Grandmother's Tablecloth, Plywood, 1986, 39 In. .... *illus* 3750
Chair, Robert Venturi, Queen Anne, Plywood, Yellow Laminate, Knoll, 38 x 27 In. .... *illus* 1230
Chair, Rocker, is listed under Rocker in this category.
Chair, Rococo Revival, Rosewood, Cornucopia, Attributed To Belter, c.1855, 46 In. .... *illus* 33688
Chair, Rococo Revival, Rosewood, Rosalie Without Grapes, c.1865, 38 In., Pair .... *illus* 1353
Chair, Rococo, Rosewood, Elaborate Carved Back, Upholstered Seat, c.1860 .... *illus* 420
Chair, Rohlfs, Hall, Oak, Cutouts, Beaded Seat, Openwork Legs, c.1900, 47 In. .... *illus* 18750
Chair, Ron Arad, Wool Upholstery, Soft Big Easy, 1988, 36 x 47 In. 1800
Chair, Rosewood, Henry Clay Pattern, Crest, Concave, Open Arms, c.1850, 43 In., Pair 7380
Chair, Rosewood, Rounded Reticulated Back, Folding, Brass Mounts, 44 In., Pair 861
Chair, Safari, Arne Norell, Rosewood, 28 x 26 ¼ In. 1353
Chair, Salon, Bugatti, Orientalism, Ebonized Wood, Metals, Bone, c.1915, 36 In. 8700

Furniture, Chair, Sam Maloof, Executive, Swivel, Walnut, Leather, 1984, Signed, 53 x 29 In. $8,750

Los Angeles Modern Auctions

Furniture, Chair, Shaker, Maple, Ladder Back, Tape, Acorn Finials, Arms, Mt. Lebanon, c.1880, 41 In. $960

Wright (Chicago)

Furniture, Chair, Strap, Robsjohn-Gibbings, Walnut, Linen, Widdicomb, c.1960, 30 x 25 In. $2,760

Selkirk Auctioneers & Appraisers

Furniture, Chair, Theater, Maple, Iron, Gold, Bronze B, Heywood-Wakefield, c.1924, 33 In., Pair $531

Brunk Auctions

Furniture, Chair, Valet, Wegner, Maple, Teak, Brass, Lyre Shape Back, 1953, 21 In. $9,600

Wright (Chicago)

Furniture, Chair, Wainscot, Oak, Carved Crest Rail, Box Stretcher, England, c.1685, 40 In. $738

Skinner, Inc.

Furniture, Chair, Walnut, Carved, Grapes, Scrolling, Face Carved Crest, Italy, c.1880, 47 In. $427

DuMouchelles Art Gallery

Furniture, Chair, Walnut, Carved, Scrolled Pierced Splat, Slip Seat, c.1790, 38 In., Pair $6,765

Skinner, Inc.

Furniture, Chair, Wegner, Lounge, Oak, Cane, Brass, Leather, Arms, Denmark, 1956, 27 x 38 In. $2,750

Wright (Chicago)

F

Furniture, Chair, Windsor, Birdcage, Bamboo Turnings, Painted, Phila., c.1810, 35 In. $1,625

Garth's Auctioneers & Appraisers

Furniture, Chair, Windsor, Brace Back, Shield Seat, Black, Green, New Eng., 1800s, 35 x 19 In. $59

Hess Auction Group

Furniture, Chair, Windsor, Comb Back, Carved Crest, Plank Seat, Turnings, Arms, c.1775, 40 In. $3,444

Skinner, Inc.

Furniture, Chair, Windsor, Comb Back, Nutting, Paper Label, 44 ½ In. $390

Fairfield Auction

Furniture, Chair, Windsor, Fanback, 7 Spindles, Carved, H-Stretcher, Pa., 1800s, 38 In. $3,690

Skinner, Inc.

Furniture, Chair, Windsor, Fanback, Spindles, Carved Ears, Pa., c.1790, 16 x 34 In. $708

Hess Auction Group

Furniture, Chair, Windsor, Low Back, Saddle Seat, Continuous Arm, Old Paint, 1700s, 29 In. $4,425

Hess Auction Group

Furniture, Chair, Windsor, Sack Back, 7 Spindles, Painted, Black Over Green, Arms, 37 In. $360

Cowan Auctions

Furniture, Chair, Windsor, Sack Back, Maple, Butternut, Spindles, Writing Arm, c.1775, 35 In. $2,370

James D. Julia Auctioneers

Chair, Sam Maloof, Executive, Swivel, Walnut, Leather, 1984, Signed, 53 x 29 In. .... *illus* 8750
Chair, Sam Maloof, Walnut, 7 Curved Flat Spindles, Arms, Tufted Leather Pad, 43 In. 13530
Chair, Savonarola, Walnut, Carved, Sunburst, Folding Back, Front, Arms, Italy, 37 x 26 In. 584
Chair, Schou Andersen, Midcentury Modern, 28 ½ x 21 ½ In. 184
Chair, Sedan, Louis XV, Mahogany, Kingwood Banded, Inlay, Vines, Urns, 65 ¾ x 28 In. 854
Chair, Shaker, Maple, Ladder Back, Tape, Acorn Finials, Arms, Mt. Lebanon, c.1880, 41 In. . *illus* 960
Chair, Sheraton Style, Multicolor, Crest, Pierce Splat, Padded Arms, Seat, 39 In., Pair................ 468
Chair, Shoe Shape, Red, Animal Print, 40 x 40 ½ In. 176
Chair, Slipper, Aesthetic Revival, Gilt, Painted, Reticulated Back, Upholstered Seat, 1800s.......... 299
Chair, Slipper, Michael Taylor, Mahogany, Tufted Seat Cushions, Baker Furniture, 33 x 24 In. ... 357
Chair, Slipper, Wormley, Lacquered Mahogany, Upholstered, Dunbar, 1960s, 33 x 24 In., Pair 2125
Chair, Slipper, Wormley, Mahogany, Upholstered, Cushion, Dunbar, 1960s, 33 x 24 In., Pair...... 1875
Chair, Spanish Colonial Style, Red, Arms, 48 ¼ x 28 ½ In. 500
Chair, Splint Back, Seat, Base Stretcher, Pair 198
Chair, Square Crest, Bats & Dragons Splat, Low Back, Arms, c.1910, Chinese, 36 In., Pair 300
Chair, Strap, Robsjohn-Gibbings, Walnut, Linen, Widdicomb, c.1960, 30 x 25 In. .... *illus* 2760
Chair, Swivel, Barrel Back, Leatherette Upholstery, Midcentury Modern, c.1960, Pair 540
Chair, Table, Pine, Ash, Tilt, Scrolled Supports, Trestle, Compartment, c.1775, 43 In. Diam. 2214
Chair, Thayer Coggin, Lounge, Chrome Metal, Sleigh Base, Upholstered, Wood Arms, 40 In. 403
Chair, Theater, Maple, Iron, Gold, Bronze B, Heywood-Wakefield, c.1924, 33 In., Pair .... *illus* 531
Chair, Tiger Maple, Arched Back Slats, Woven Splint Seat, Turned Legs, 1800s, 33 In. 72
Chair, Transit, Eileen Gray, Lacquer, Nickeled Brass, Leather, Ecart International, 32 x 42 In. 3750
Chair, Tub, Louis XV Style, Double Cane Back, Arm Supports, Cushion, France, 35 In. 944
Chair, Upholstered Hand, Red, Yellow, Lime, Blue, 1960s 156
Chair, V. Kagen, Lounge, Mohair, Blue, Plexiglas, Omnibus, 35 x 32 In. 60
Chair, Valet, Wegner, Maple, Teak, Brass, Lyre Shape Back, 1953, 21 In. .... *illus* 9600
Chair, Victorian, John Jilliff, Walnut Frame, Cushion Back, Seat, Arms, c.1880, Pair 1020
Chair, Victorian, Mahogany, Cockfighting, Leather Upholstery, Padded Top Rail, 34 In. 1845
Chair, W. Platner For Knoll, Lounge, Wire Support, Winged Seat, Velvet, 38 x 41 In., Pair........... 7475
Chair, W. Platner, Wire Base, Back, Cushion Seat, Crest, Midcentury Modern, Pair 1600
Chair, Wainscot, Oak, Carved Crest Rail, Box Stretcher, England, c.1685, 40 In. .... *illus* 738
Chair, Walnut Frame, Cushioned Seat, Back, Arms, Pair 210
Chair, Walnut, Cane Seat, Splat, Block & Turned Side Rails, Legs, Stretchers, 48 x 18 In. 148
Chair, Walnut, Carved, Grapes, Scrolling, Face Carved Crest, Italy, c.1880, 47 In. .... *illus* 427
Chair, Walnut, Carved, Scrolled Pierced Splat, Slip Seat, c.1790, 38 In., Pair...................... *illus* 6765
Chair, Walnut, Crest, Shell, Scroll Terminals, Pierced Splat, Beaded Legs, c.1775, 40 In. 1045
Chair, Wassily, Black Leather, Chrome Frames, 30 x 26 In., Pair 563
Chair, Wegner, Lounge, A.P. Stolen, Tall Back, Oak, Teak, Upholstered, 1960s, 42 x 35 In. 7500
Chair, Wegner, Lounge, Oak, Cane, Brass, Leather, Arms, Denmark, 1956, 27 x 38 In. .... *illus* 2750
Chair, Wendell Castle, Fiberglass, Molar, Red Orange, Gel Coated, c.1970, 24 x 30 In. 1452
Chair, Wendell Castle, Lounge, Molar, White Molded Plastic, Pair 1600
Chair, William & Mary Style, Scrolled Handholds, Upholstered, c.1910, 45 x 30 In., Pair............ 492
Chair, William & Mary, Banister Back, Turned Stiles, Woven Seat, Arms, 45 In. 531
Chair, William & Mary, Carved, Black Paint, Cane, Arms, Pierced Crest, 53 x 25 In. 369
Chair, Windsor, 7 Spindles, Bamboo Turnings, New England, 1800s, 37 In. 83
Chair, Windsor, Birdcage, 1820s, Pair 225
Chair, Windsor, Birdcage, Bamboo Turnings, Painted, Phila., c.1810, 35 In. .... *illus* 1625
Chair, Windsor, Black Paint, New England, Arms, c.1900 920
Chair, Windsor, Brace Back, Shield Seat, Black, Green, New Eng., 1800s, 35 x 19 In. .... *illus* 59
Chair, Windsor, Comb Back, Carved Crest, Plank Seat, Turnings, Arms, c.1775, 40 In. .... *illus* 3444
Chair, Windsor, Comb Back, Nutting, Paper Label, 44 ½ In. .... *illus* 390
Chair, Windsor, Fanback, 7 Spindles, Carved, H-Stretcher, Pa., 1800s, 38 In. .... *illus* 3690
Chair, Windsor, Fanback, Spindles, Carved Ears, Pa., c.1790, 16 x 34 In. .... *illus* 708
Chair, Windsor, Fanback, Wood, Carved, Rustic Finish, Leather Seat, 35 x 19 In., Pair................ 130
Chair, Windsor, Hoop Back, 1800s, 39 In. 117
Chair, Windsor, Hoop Back, Green, 35 In., Pair 263
Chair, Windsor, Hoop Back, Spindles, Bamboo Turned, Red Paint, Scroll Arms, 35 In. 649
Chair, Windsor, Hoop Back, Wood, Paint, Yellow Flowers, Shaped Splat, 1800s, 17 In. 708
Chair, Windsor, Low Back, Saddle Seat, Continuous Arm, Old Paint, 1700s, 29 In. .... *illus* 4425
Chair, Windsor, Sack Back, 7 Spindles, Painted, Black Over Green, Arms, 37 In. .... *illus* 360
Chair, Windsor, Sack Back, Maple, Butternut, Spindles, Writing Arm, c.1775, 35 In. .... *illus* 2370
Chair, Windsor, Sack Back, Red Stain, Shaped Saddle Seat, c.1790, 33 In. 861
Chair, Wing, Empire, Mahogany, Carved, Shell Crest, Arms, Upholstered, 35 x 29 In. 246
Chair, Wing, George III, Mahogany, Padded Back, Seat, Outscrolled Arms, c.1790, 47 In. 468
Chair, Womb, Eero Saarinen, Upholstered, 2 Cushions, Knoll, 1960s, 36 x 40 In., Pair 2832
Chair, Wood, Carved, Men Drinking From Steins Back, Shaped Seat, Turned Legs, 36 In. ....*illus* 540

Furniture, Chair, Wood, Carved, Men Drinking From Steins Back, Shaped Seat, Turned Legs, 36 In.
$540

Fox Auctions

Furniture, Chair, Wood, Paint, Gilt, Bone & Mother-Of-Pearl Inlay, Egyptian Revival, 43 In.
$2,440

Neal Auctions

Furniture, Chair, Woven Splint Seat, Splat Back, Black Paint, 1700s, 41 In., Pair
$83

Cripple Creek Auctions

FURNITURE

Furniture, Chaise Longue, G. Nelson, Steel, Upholstered, Herman Miller, 1954, 69 x 30 In. $10,000

Wright (Chicago)

Furniture, Chest, Baroque, Walnut, Figural Carving, Drawers, Lion Paw Feet, 1800s, 40 x 58 In. $7,380

F

Skinner, Inc.

Furniture, Chest, Blanket, Pine, Molded Lid, Painted, Ball Feet, Continental, 1800s, 16 x 33 In. $308

Cowan Auctions

Furniture, Chest, Dower, Lid, Compass, Tulips, Name Plate, Berks County, c.1810, 28 x 50 In. $3,776

Hess Auction Group

Furniture, Chest, Dower, Painted, Decorated Arched Panels, Geometric, Pa., 1809, 24 x 53 In. $5,900

Hess Auction Group

Furniture, Chest, George I Style, Oyster Veneer, Concentric Circles, 4 Drawers, 23 x 22 In. $944

Brunk Auctions

Furniture, Chest, Hepplewhite, Cherry, Pine, Reeded Drawers, Cutout Feet, c.1810, 34 x 43 In. $250

Garth's Auctioneers & Appraisers

Furniture, Chest, Mahogany, Scrolls & Flower Inlay, Drawers, Dutch, c.1785, 31 x 36 In. $1,353

New Orleans (Cakebread)

Furniture, Chest, Mahogany, Veneer, Mirror, Drawers, Ebonized, Stencil, c.1823, 65 x 36 In. $4,305

Skinner, Inc.

Furniture, Chest, Neoclassical, Grain Painted, 4 Drawers, Mushroom Knobs, 47 x 42 In. $240

Cowan Auctions

Furniture, Chest, Neoclassical, Mahogany, Drawers, Columns, Boston, c.1825, 50 x 46 In. $676

New Orleans (Cakebread)

Chair, Wood, Paint, Gilt, Bone & Mother-Of-Pearl Inlay, Egyptian Revival, 43 In. .... *illus* 2440
Chair, Wood, Rex, Niko Kralj, Folding, Horizontal Slat Back, Midcentury Modern 300
Chair, Wormley, Midcentury Modern, Bentwood, 15 ½ x 15 ¾ In. 484
Chair, Woven Splint Seat, Splat Back, Black Paint, 1700s, 41 In., Pair .... *illus* 83
Chair, Wrought Iron, Brass, Strapwork Lattice Seat, Downswept Arms, c.1900, 35 In., Pair 1187
Chaise Longue, G. Nelson, Steel, Upholstered, Herman Miller, 1954, 69 x 30 In. .... *illus* 10000
Chaise Longue, Gray & White, Scrolled Back, Stretchers, c.1925, 35 ½ x 48 In., Pair 1452
Chaise Longue, Le Corbusier Style, Cow Pattern, Chrome, 63 x 21 In. 625
Chaise Longue, Louis XV Style, Fruitwood, Double Domed, Padded Back, 38 x 70 In. 984
Chaise Longue, Louis XV, Cabriole Legs, France, 19th Century, 39 x 67 In. 900
Chaise Longue, MDF Italia, Stainless Steel, Leather Upholstery, Italy, 2000s, 25 x 53 In. 3125
Chaise Longue, Modern, Brazilian Rosewood Frame, X Shape Metal, Cowhide, 31 x 53 In. 968
Chaise Longue, Poul Kjaerholm, Cane, Chrome Steel, Fritz Hansen, 1965, 34 x 60 In. 5000
Chaise Longue, Queen Anne, Walnut, Veneer, Oak, Cushion Seat, c.1800, 38 x 62 In. 236
Chaise Longue, Teak, Copper, Upholstered, 1960s, 37 x 27 x 60 In. 1250
Chest, 6-Board, Mustard Yellow Putty Paint, Lift Top, Cutout Base, c.1825, 25 x 40 In. 2583
Chest, Art Deco Style, Tiger Maple, Checkered, 3 Drawers, Brass Pulls, 36 x 45 In. 299
Chest, Baroque, Pine, Carved, Lift Top, 1700s, 31 x 44 In. 413
Chest, Baroque, Walnut, Figural Carving, Drawers, Lion Paw Feet, 1800s, 40 x 58 In. .... *illus* 7380
Chest, Birch, Flata Cove, 6 Graduated Drawers, Bracket Feet, c.1800, 55 x 33 x 17 In. 2829
Chest, Black Lacquer, Chinese, c.1950, 24 x 20 In. 150
Chest, Blanket, Blue Sponge Paint, Pine, Poplar, Paneled, Drawers, Hinged Lid, 33 x 45 In. 19200
Chest, Blanket, Carved, Continental, Shoe Feet, 1600s, 17 x 35 In. 1053
Chest, Blanket, Chippendale, Oak, Drawer, Pierced Brasses, Iron Side Handles, 22 x 30 In. 390
Chest, Blanket, Chippendale, Pine, Old Blue Paint, Strap Hinges, Bracket Feet, 44 In. 1080
Chest, Blanket, Chippendale, Pine, Paint, Tombstone Panels, Tulips, c.1790, 29 x 52 In. 2625
Chest, Blanket, Chippendale, Poplar, Pine, Batten Ends, Square Feet, c.1800, 23 x 47 In. 590
Chest, Blanket, Hardwood, Dovetail, Turned Feet, 2 Drawers, 19th Century, 34 x 47 In. 156
Chest, Blanket, Mustard Paint, 6-Board, Dovetailed, Chamfered Base, c.1850, 27 x 43 In. 922
Chest, Blanket, Painted, Multicolor, Flowers, Village, Germany, c.1838, 22 ½ x 25 In. 484
Chest, Blanket, Pine, Anna Habekern, Red & Black Paint, Pennsylvania, 28 x 50 In. 1440
Chest, Blanket, Pine, Molded Lid, Painted, Ball Feet, Continental, 1800s, 16 x 33 In. .... *illus* 308
Chest, Blanket, Pine, Molded Lift Top, Interior Till, Bracket Feet, 1800s, 21 x 38 In. 858
Chest, Blanket, Pine, Old Salmon Paint, Breadboard Ends, Turned Legs, Till, 26 x 42 In. 270
Chest, Blanket, Poplar, Sponge Decorated, Molded, Turned Feet, 26 x 42 In. 420
Chest, Blanket, Round Mirrored Pieces, Latticework, 49 x 27 In. 156
Chest, Blanket, Sheraton, Blue Paint, Molded Top, Turned Legs, c.1820, 26 x 20 In. 237
Chest, Blanket, Sheraton, Pine, Poplar, Grain Painted, Paneled, Turned Legs, 24 x 41 In. 330
Chest, Blanket, Sheraton, Tiger Maple, Hinged Lid, Pie Board Ends, Turnip Feet, 20 x 28 In. 1416
Chest, Blanket, Smoke Decorated, Hinged Lid, Base Molding, Interior Till, 17 x 33 In. 360
Chest, Blanket, Softwood, Feather Grain Paint, Gold Stencil, c.1849, 17 x 26 In. 885
Chest, Blanket, Softwood, Marbleized Paint Design, Quote, 1800s, 12 x 19 In. 767
Chest, Blanket, Softwood, Painted, Red Ground, Multicolor Tulips, L.E.B., 1844, 18 x 25 In. 5605
Chest, Blanket, Softwood, Red, Molded Lid, Stepped Till, Turned Feet, 1800s, 16 x 27 In. 443
Chest, Blanket, Walnut, Chippendale Style, Hinged Lid, Bracket Feet, c.1810, 7 x 12 In. 1185
Chest, Blanket, Walnut, Shaped Apron, Turned Feet, 12 x 14 In. 540
Chest, Blanket, Walnut, Sulphur Inlay, Molded Lid, Iron Strap Hinges, 1700s, 9 x 18 In. 27140
Chest, Blanket, Wood, Paint, Pinwheel, Red, Molded Hinged Lid, Plank Feet, 1800s, 17 x 24 In. . 1888
Chest, Blanket, Wood, Painted, Molded Lid, Urn, Flowers, Vine Border, c.1820, 22 x 45 In. 9840
Chest, Butler's, Georgian Style, Mahogany, Pullout Surface, Drawers, 1800s, 29 x 28 In. 338
Chest, Butler's, Regency Style, Mahogany, Drawers, Foot Shape Feet, Slippers, 61 x 21 In. 5192
Chest, Campaign, Teak, 2 Parts, Recessed Pulls, Brass Banding, Handles, c.1890, 35 x 35 In. 2214
Chest, Carved, Painted, Multicolor, Panel Doors, Drawers, 37 ½ x 48 ½ In. 677
Chest, Cedar, Walnut, Paneled Sides, Bun Feet, c.1930, 23 x 45 In. 150
Chest, Cedar, Walnut, Paneled, Flat Front Base, Lane, 1960s, 19 x 42 In. 184
Chest, Charles II Style, Oak, Carved, Lid, Panels, Flowers, Drawer, Stile Feet, 29 x 46 In. 431
Chest, Cherry, Reeded Crest, Bowfront, Drawer, 1820s, 43 x 41 In. 1210
Chest, Chippendale Style, Figured Mahogany, 4 Drawers, Brass Handles, 1900s, 36 x 55 In. 180
Chest, Chippendale, Cherry, 3 Under Locking Drawers, 3 Graduated Drawers, 42 x 44 In. 220
Chest, Chippendale, Dovetail, 6 Drawers, Bracket Feet, 42 x 43 ½ In. 440
Chest, Chippendale, Walnut, Yellow Pine, 5 Drawers, Fluted Columns, c.1800, 38 x 43 In. 4956
Chest, Dower, Baroque, Walnut, Carved, Flowers, Paw Feet, c.1700, 22 x 43 In. 1887
Chest, Dower, Chippendale, Pine, Fish, Leopard, Strap Hinges, c.1775, 27 x 51 In. 1283
Chest, Dower, Lid, Compass, Tulips, Name Plate, Berks County, c.1810, 28 x 50 In. .... *illus* 3776
Chest, Dower, Oak, Bail Handles, Scrolled Feet, Scalloped Apron, 24 ½ x 44 ½ In. 303
Chest, Dower, Oak, Gilt, Carved, Sunburst, Arches, Leaves, Lion, 18 x 50 In. 1815

Furniture, Chest, Neoclassical, Pine, Poplar, Painted, 5 Drawers, Ohio, c.1830, 46 x 42 In.
$5,400

Garth's Auctioneers & Appraisers

Furniture, Chest, Neoclassical, Tiger Maple, Cherry, Outset Drawer, 1800s, 47 x 41 In.
$431

Cowan Auctions

Furniture, Chest, Parzinger, Wood, Lacquer, Brass Studs, Glass, Drawers, 1960s, 21 x 24 In.
$3,625

Rago Arts and Auction Center

TIP

Touching up gilding does not change value if it is done by an expert.

Furniture, Chest, Seed, Mixed Wood, Grain Painted, 37 Drawers, John Boyer, 1800s, 22 x 19 In.
$17,700

Hess Auction Group

Furniture, Chest, Sheraton, Tiger Maple, Half Columns, 4 Graduated Drawers, 45 x 42 In.
$1,464

Neal Auctions

Furniture, Chest, Sugar, Federal, Cherry, Hinged, Divider, Drawer, 1800s, 29 x 30 In.
$3,304

Brunk Auctions

Furniture, Chest, Sugar, Walnut, Hinged Top, Drawer, Turned Legs, Tenn., c.1825, 36 x 29 In.
$5,192

Case Auctions

Furniture, Chest, Tiger Maple, Cherry, Gallery, 4 Drawers, Columns, 1800s, 52 x 43 In.
$420

Cowan Auctions

Furniture, Chest-On-Chest, Mahogany, Carved, Drawers, Bracket Feet, c.1770, 84 x 42 In.
$11,070

Skinner, Inc.

Furniture, Commode, Corner, Chippendale, Mahogany, Splats, Arms, Upholstered, c.1790, 33 In.
$185

Cowan Auctions

Furniture, Commode, Neoclassical Style, Mahogany, Bronze, Russia, c.1910, 34 x 38 In., Pair
$8,438

Neal Auctions

Furniture, Credenza, Walnut, Carved, Drawers, Doors, Figural Mounts, Italy, 1800s, 35 x 40 In.
$1,845

Skinner, Inc.

Chest, Dower, Painted, Decorated Arched Panels, Geometric, Pa., 1809, 24 x 53 In. ....*illus* 5900
Chest, Dower, Softwood, Lid, Pie Board Ends, Flowers, Iron Hinges, c.1800, 51 x 22 In. 2478
Chest, Dower, Softwood, Painted, Arched Panels, Molded Lid, Bracket Feet, 1806, 23 x 53 In. 3540
Chest, Elizabethan Revival, Oak, Paneled Drawers, Pilasters, Bun Feet, 1800s, 38 x 40 In. 923
Chest, Empire, 4 Drawers, Keyholes, 40 x 35 In. 605
Chest, English Oak, Lift Top, Dovetailed Case, Brass Bail Handles, 10 x 21 In. 165
Chest, Federal, Cherry Case, 4 Tiger Maple Drawers, Bowfront, c.1820, 41 x 42 In. 1888
Chest, Federal, Inlaid Cherry, Pine, 5 Drawers, c.1810, 43 x 40 In. 1652
Chest, Federal, Mahogany, Scroll Backsplash, Spiral Twist Columns, c.1820, 45 x 44 In. 562
Chest, Federal, Mahogany, Sheraton Style, Oval Corners, Beaded Drawers, c.1810, 36 x 40 In. ... 615
Chest, Federal, Maple, 4 Drawers, Mushroom Handles, Bowfront, c.1925, 42 x 42 In. 357
Chest, Flowers, Multicolor, White Ground, Drawers, 29 x 25 In., Pair 1145
Chest, French Provincial, Louis Philippe, Oak, Carved, Doors, Drawers, 1800s, 59 x 31 In. 326
Chest, George I Style, Oyster Veneer, Concentric Circles, 4 Drawers, 23 x 22 In. ....*illus* 944
Chest, George III, Mahogany, Ogee Molded Top, 4 Graduated Drawers, 35 x 32 In. 2366
Chest, George III, Oak, Mahogany, Drawers, Slide, Starburst Inlay, c.1790, 35 x 41 In. 2000
Chest, George III, Walnut, Banding, 5 Drawers, Bracket Feet, c.1790, 33 x 35 In. 1476
Chest, George III, Yew, Oyster Burl, Inlaid Flowers, Scroll, 5 Drawers, 36 ½ x 27 In. 1331
Chest, Georgian Style, Mahogany, 5 Drawers, Shaped Apron, Block Feet, 45 x 30 In. 219
Chest, Georgian, Burl Walnut, Oak, 2 Over 3 Graduated Drawers, c.1790, 36 x 38 In. 3480
Chest, Georgian, Veneer, Incised Brasses, Bracket Base, Graduated Drawers, 38 x 39 In. 369
Chest, Grain Painted, Mixed Wood, Shaped Gallery, Drawers, Bracket Feet, 49 x 42 In. 330
Chest, Hepplewhite, Cherry, Pine, 4 Drawers, Beaded Edges, French Feet, 39 x 36 In. 540
Chest, Hepplewhite, Cherry, Pine, Reeded Drawers, Cutout Feet, c.1810, 34 x 43 In. ....*illus* 250
Chest, Louis XVI Style, Kingwood, Marble Top, Bowed Top, Drawers, 50 x 25 In. 1168
Chest, Mahogany, Bowfront, 6 Drawers, Splayed Feet, Sabots, Ormolu, 49 x 40 In. 1250
Chest, Mahogany, Bracket Feet, Graduated Drawers, Beaded, c.1775, 30 x 18 In. 529
Chest, Mahogany, Projecting Drawers, Pineapple Carved Pillars, Paw Feet, c.1835, 53 x 51 In. .. 615
Chest, Mahogany, Scrolls & Flower Inlay, Drawers, Dutch, c.1785, 31 x 36 In. ....*illus* 1353
Chest, Mahogany, Veneer, Mirror, Drawers, Ebonized, Stencil, c.1823, 65 x 36 In. ....*illus* 4305
Chest, Metal, White, Inlaid Indian Agate Stones, Velvet Lined, Footed, 1900s, 19 x 24 In. 687
Chest, Midcentury, Bowfront, Straight Case, 4 Drawers, 1970s, 39 x 34 In. 726
Chest, Midcentury, Walnut Veneer, Mayan Line, Tribal Design, Bassett, 1960s, 45 x 40 In. 181
Chest, Mixed Wood, Paneled Sides, Geometric Inlay, 5 Dovetailed Drawers, 10 x 10 In. 390
Chest, Mule, Pine, 2 Drawers, Cutout Feet, 40 x 40 ½ In. 220
Chest, Mule, Pine, Molded Hinged Lid, 2 Drawers, Shaped Cutout Feet, 42 x 42 In. 300
Chest, Mule, William & Mary, Pine, Red Stain, Molded Lid, Till, 1700s, 34 x 38 In. 3120
Chest, Neoclassical, Figured Mahogany, Ebonized, 3 Drawers, 19th Century, 32 x 32 In. 236
Chest, Neoclassical, Grain Painted, 4 Drawers, Mushroom Knobs, 47 x 42 In. ....*illus* 240
Chest, Neoclassical, Mahogany, Drawers, Columns, Boston, c.1825, 50 x 46 In. ....*illus* 676
Chest, Neoclassical, Mahogany, Recessed Drawers, Scroll Back, Carved, c.1820, 54 x 45 In. 3198
Chest, Neoclassical, Pine, Poplar, Painted, 5 Drawers, Ohio, c.1830, 46 x 42 In. ....*illus* 5400
Chest, Neoclassical, Tiger Maple, Cherry, Outset Drawer, 1800s, 47 x 41 In. ....*illus* 431
Chest, Oak Paneled, Hinged, Iron Strapwork, Germany, c.1850, 25 x 49 In. 177
Chest, Oak, 6 Drawers, c.1915, 30 x 48 In. 178
Chest, Oak, 6-Board, Lunette Frieze, Bootjack Ends, c.1700, 25 x 53 In. 1046
Chest, Oak, Banded Top, 8 Drawers, Paneled, Shaped Bracket Feet, 1700s, 38 x 23 In. 687
Chest, Oak, Domed Carved Panels, Strap Hinges, England, c.1763, 23 ½ x 48 In. 397
Chest, Oak, Molded Edge, 2 Over 3 Drawers, Paneled Front, 1700s, 35 x 36 In. 876
Chest, Paint Decorated, Dome Top, Thomas Matteson, Vermont, c.1835, 13 x 26 In. 7080
Chest, Parzinger, Wood, Lacquer, Brass Studs, Glass, Drawers, 1960s, 21 x 24 In. ....*illus* 3625
Chest, Pine, 3 Drawers, c.1840, 12 ¾ x 9 ¼ In. 377
Chest, Pine, Grain Painted, Nut Brown, Pine, Drawer, Lift Top, Bracket Feet, 33 x 36 In. 1046
Chest, Pine, Grain Painted, Red Orange & Black, 4 Drawers, Cutout Feet, 39 x 39 In. 3998
Chest, Pine, Red Paint, Hinged Top Over 3 Drawers, Cutout Feet, Brass Pulls, 54 x 36 In. 2460
Chest, Queen Anne, Bandy Legs, 5 Drawers, 58 x 40 In. 994
Chest, Queen Anne, Maple, 2 Parts, Shell Carved, Cabriole Legs, Pad Feet, 1700s, 75 x 39 In. 861
Chest, Queen Anne, Walnut, Banded Top, 5 Drawers, Bun Feet, 1700s, 35 x 38 In. 4428
Chest, Regency, Mahogany, Bowfront, String Banding, Bracket Feet, c.1810, 38 x 45 In. 799
Chest, Rustic, Pine, Dovetailed, Hinged, Candle Box Interior, James Vickery, 1885, 18 x 36 In. ... 330
Chest, Seed, Mixed Wood, Grain Painted, 37 Drawers, John Boyer, 1800s, 22 x 19 In. ....*illus* 17700
Chest, Sewing, Regency Style, Anglo-Indian, Bone, Wood, Sarcophagus Shape, 1800s, 12 x 8 In. . 593
Chest, Sheraton, Cherry, Bowfront, 4 Cock-Beaded Drawers, Scallop Skirt, c.1825, 42 x 40 In. ... 1298
Chest, Sheraton, Curly Maple, 4 Graduated Drawers, Brass Bail Handles, 40 x 41 In. 3000
Chest, Sheraton, Tiger Maple, Half Columns, 4 Graduated Drawers, 45 x 42 In. ....*illus* 1464
Chest, Sheraton, Tiger Maple, Pine, Chestnut, Cock-Beaded, Inlay, Drawers, 1800s, 39 x 42 In. .. 720

Furniture, Credenza, Wormley, Walnut, Brass, Drawers, Doors, Dunbar, c.1958, 30 x 72 In.
$8,610

Skinner, Inc.

Furniture, Cupboard, Corner, Cherry, Doors, Drawers, 5 Shelves, Brass Latches, c.1820, 94 x 48 In.
$4,248

Case Auctions

Furniture, Cupboard, Corner, Hanging, Blind Door, Painted, Shelves, Pa., 1800s, 37 x 31 In.
$1,062

Hess Auction Group

Furniture, Cupboard, Corner, Hanging, Walnut, Molding, Door, Carved, Shelves, c.1780, 50 In.
$4,956

Brunk Auctions

Furniture, Cupboard, Corner, Painted, 12-Pane Paneled Door, Pa., c.1810, 86 x 46 In.
$3,835

Hess Auction Group

Furniture, Cupboard, Corner, Pine, 2 Sections, Open Top, Shelves, Door, 1800s, 87 x 52 In.
$390

Garth's Auctioneers & Appraisers

Chest, Snakeskin Veneer, 3 Drawers, Paw Feet, 25 x 30½ In. 3120
Chest, Sugar, Cherry, Lift Top, Drawer, Turned Feet, Compartments, c.1835, 30 x 36 In. 1168
Chest, Sugar, Federal, Cherry, Hinged, Divider, Drawer, 1800s, 29 x 30 In. .... *illus* 3304
Chest, Sugar, Walnut, Hinged Top, Drawer, Turned Legs, Tenn., c.1825, 36 x 29 In. .... *illus* 5192
Chest, Tansu, Red Lacquer, 3 Drawers, Wrought Iron Hardware, Japan, c.1900, 24 x 36 In. 240
Chest, Teak, Ebonized, Brass Mounted, Lift Top, Bun Feet, c.1800, 28 x 53 In. 236
Chest, Tiger Maple, Cherry, Gallery, 4 Drawers, Columns, 1800s, 52 x 43 In. .... *illus* 420
Chest, Victorian, Chestnut, Elm, Brass Pulls, Sidelock, 6 Drawers, c.1880, 50 x 33 x 18 In. 850
Chest, Vine & Flower Bone Inlay, 4 Drawers, Bone Knobs, 30 x 39 x 16 In. 1230
Chest, Walnut, 3 Drawers, Ring Handles, Reeded Columns, Continental, 35 x 49 In. 1375
Chest, Walnut, 3 Over 2 Over 5 Graduated Drawers, Brass Pulls, Pa., 1784, 64 In. 6150
Chest, Walnut, Gadrooned & Fluted Moldings, Hinged Top, Coat Of Arms, 27 x 65 In. 1750
Chest, Walnut, Glass Top, 6 Drawers, Casters, Widdicomb, c.1950, 47½ x 34 In. 726
Chest, Walnut, Sandwich Top, String Inlay, 4 Drawers, c.1790, 38½ x 19 In. 389
Chest, Walnut, Veneer, 5 Drawer, Cavalier, c.1950, 44 x 38 In., Pair.......... 1089
Chest, William & Mary, Walnut, Figured, Pierced Brasses, Patinated, c.1700, 60 x 41 In. 1770
Chest, Wood, Chinoiserie, Serpentine, Slate Top, 4 Drawers, Scenes, c.1865, 37 x 43 In. 1045
Chest, Wood, Painted, Putti, 3 Drawers, Urn & Scroll Design, 1800s, 37 x 50 In. 1375
Chest, Yellow Pine, Blue Paint, Cut Nails, 40 x 49 In. 1652
Chest-On-Chest, Burl, Dentil Cornice, 3 Short Over 4 Long Drawers, 73 x 46 In. 2013
Chest-On-Chest, Chippendale, Mahogany, Cherry, Bonnet Top, Serpentine, Fan, 93 x 44 In. 8360
Chest-On-Chest, George III, Mahogany, Molded Cornice, String Inlay, c.1800, 77 x 45 In. 1750
Chest-On-Chest, Kittinger, Georgian, Mahogany, 7 Drawers, 68 x 39 In. 625
Chest-On-Chest, Mahogany, Carved, Drawers, Bracket Feet, c.1770, 84 x 42 In. .... *illus* 11070
Chest-On-Frame, Needlepoint, Red Flowers, Green Leaves, Lift Top, Fruitwood, 44 x 30 In. 2829
Chest-On-Frame, Queen Anne Style, Maple, North Shore Shape, 1800s, 66 x 42 In. 1920
Chiffonier, Regency, Rosewood, Brass Grill Doors, Roses, Gilt Columns, 61 x 40 In. 1483
Choir Stall, Italian Style, Carved, Griffins, H Shape, Support Wall, 1800s, 42 x 50 In. 308
Coat Rack, Hanging, Oak, Carved Lion's Head Brackets, Armorial Shield, c.1950, 14 x 41 In. 150
Coat Rack, Iron, Curlicues, 84 In. 59
Coat Rack, Mahogany, Ring-Turned Post, Acorn Finial, Turned Pegs, 3-Footed, 69 In. 976
Coat Rack, Metal, Leather Wrapped Pole, 4 Hooks, Fleur-De-Lis Finial, Foot, 81 x 15 In. 201
Coat Rack, Neoclassical, Mahogany, Carved, Mirror, Serpentine Supports, 78 x 38 In. 519
Coffer, Altar, Huanghuali, Carved, Drawers, Dragon, Brass Handles, 1800s, 35 x 44 In. 6457
Coffer, Elm, Red Lacquer, Mortised, Scroll Ends, Scalloped, Chinese, c.1900, 30 x 26 In. 300
Coffer, Fruitwood, Banded, Hinged, Storage Space, Escutcheon, Shaped Feet, 31 x 52 In. 3198
Coffer, Jacobean, Oak, Carved, Hinged Lid, England, 26 x 50 In. 776
Coffer, Oak, Carved Lunettes, Hinged Lid, Strap Hinges, Bootjack Ends, Lock, 15 x 25 In. 356
Coffer, Oak, Carved, Diamonds, Medallions, Lock Plate, 33½ x 58½ In. 307
Coffer, Oak, Inlay, Paneled Top, Front, Diamond Shapes, Lunette Frieze, 1800s, 26 x 51 In. 308
Coffer, Oak, Joined, Paneled Cover, Carved, 1800s, 20 x 38 In. 246
Coffer, Renaissance Revival, Walnut, Arched Lid, Griffins, Leaf Scrolls, 33 x 40 In. 248
Coffer, Walnut, Carved, Painted, Red, Gilt, Iron Strap Hinges, Continental, 20 x 11 In. 1722
Commode, Biedermeier Style, Bronze Mounted, Lined Drawers, c.1950, 10¾ x 14 In. 178
Commode, Biedermeier, Burl, Satinwood, Marble Round Top, Ogee Drawer, 40 x 41 In. 2706
Commode, Biedermeier, Elm, Figured Panels, Banded Edge, c.1840, 36 x 48 In. 1353
Commode, Bombe, Louis XV Style, Rosewood, Marble, Marquetry, Ormolu, 34 x 46 In. 1169
Commode, Bombe, Mahogany, Marble Top, 4 Drawers, Ormolu, Dutch, 35 x 39 In. 885
Commode, Chippendale, Mahogany, Pullout, Brass Carrying Handles, 30 x 22 In. 236
Commode, Corner, Chippendale, Mahogany, Splats, Arms, Upholstered, c.1790, 33 In. .... *illus* 185
Commode, Dutch, Marquetry, Flowers, 3 Drawers, Scalloped Edges, 32 x 34 In. 3068
Commode, Empire Style, Mahogany, Figured, Fossilized Marble Top, Drawers, 37 x 48 In. 1673
Commode, Empire, Mahogany, Drawers, Pilasters, Head Capitals, c.1810, 37 x 51 In. 1500
Commode, Fruitwood, Mahogany, Banded, Inlay, Scroll, 3 Drawers, c.1900, 36 x 51 In. 1250
Commode, Fruitwood, Marble Top, Painted, France, 28 x 21 In. 180
Commode, Georgian Style, Mahogany, Fruitwood Inlay, 33 x 39 In. 540
Commode, Georgian Style, Mahogany, Square Legs, 32 x 22 In., Pair 1375
Commode, Georgian Style, Mahogany, Tray Type Gallery, c.1850, 30 x 10 In. 210
Commode, Gray Marble Top, Asian Landscape, Bombe Front, 2 Drawers, 49 x 34 In. 813
Commode, Kingwood & Marble, Banded, Cabriole Legs, Sabots, 34 x 51 In. 1968
Commode, Lift Top, Pine, Drawer, Door, 29 x 18 In. 117
Commode, Louis Philippe, Mahogany, Chamfered Corners, 4 Drawers, Block Feet, 31 x 22 In. 1434
Commode, Louis XV Style, Cherry, Stepped Edge, Serpentine Top, Drawers, 1900s, 32 x 38 In. 385
Commode, Louis XV Style, Chinoiserie, Marble Top, Drawers, Cabriole Legs, 35 x 34 In. 1000
Commode, Louis XV Style, Fruitwood, Drawers, Composite Marble Top, 33 x 37 x 16 In. 430
Commode, Louis XV Style, Gilt Bronze, 2 Drawer, Verde Antico Marble, 33 x 45 x 20 In. 676

Furniture, Cupboard, Corner, Pine, Painted, Shaped Interior Shelves, 78 x 53 x 25 In.
$3,360

Garth's Auctioneers & Appraisers

Furniture, Cupboard, Corner, Sheraton, Grain Painted, Cornice, Glass Pane Doors, 89 x 56 In.
$2,832

Hess Auction Group

TIP
A rolltop on a rolltop desk can be repaired with window-shade material. Glue the slats to the material with white glue. Be careful; this is not an easy repair and slats must be spaced properly.

Furniture, Cupboard, Court, Oak, Carved, Inlay, Columns, Shelf, England, c.1700s, 57 x 51 In.
$11,685

Skinner, Inc.

Furniture, Cupboard, Door, Blue Paint, Nailed Case, 1800s, 64 x 31 In.
$413

Hess Auction Group

Furniture, Cupboard, Hanging, Chippendale Style, Walnut Inlay, Vine, Pa., c.1980, 31 x 21 In.
$236

Brunk Auctions

Furniture, Cupboard, Nutting, Sunflower, Oak, Carved, Drawers, Doors, Branded, 50 x 57 In.
$4,080

Fairfield Auction

Furniture, Cupboard, Double, Shaker, Pine, Blue Paint, Doors, 10 Drawers, Meeting House, 77 In.
$67,200

Wright (Chicago)

Furniture, Cupboard, Pine, Pewter, Painted, 3 Shelves, Drawers, 1800s, 81 x 61 In.
$480

Cowan Auctions

Furniture, Cupboard, Step Back, Pine, Worn Paint, 8 Panes, Paneled Doors, c.1825, 81 x 50 In.
$3,840

Garth's Auctioneers & Appraisers

Furniture, Desk, Cabinet, Carved, Compartments, J. Moore, Renaissance Revival, c.1875, 66 In.
$4,305

Skinner, Inc.

Commode, Louis XV Style, Kingwood, Marble Top, 4 Drawers, Cabriole Legs, 33 x 45 In. 813
Commode, Louis XV Style, Kingwood, Veneers, Parquetry, Marble Top, Drawers, 33 x 43 In. 3960
Commode, Louis XV Style, Painted, Green Ground, Floral Sprays, Cabriole Legs, 30 x 22 In. 270
Commode, Louis XV Style, Pine, 3 Drawers, Brass Handles, 1800s, 36½ x 34½ In. 1694
Commode, Louis XV Style, Walnut, Figured, Bronze Mounts, Italy, 31 x 32 In. 649
Commode, Mahogany, Marble Top, Molded Edge, Brass Banding, c.1810, 50 x 36 In. 2214
Commode, Multicolor, Scenic, Cherubs, Scroll Border, Fitted Case, Italy, 1800s, 36 x 49 In. 1845
Commode, Neoclassical Style, Mahogany, 3 Drawers, Gold Urn & Scrolls, 31 x 32 In. 250
Commode, Neoclassical Style, Mahogany, Bronze, Russia, c.1910, 34 x 38 In., Pair *illus* 8438
Commode, Neoclassical Style, Mahogany, Marble Top, Brass Gallery, c.1910, 33 x 31 In. 1100
Commode, Neoclassical Style, Marquetry, Mahogany, Drawers, 30 x 39 In. 1187
Commode, Neoclassical, Fruitwood, Inlaid Animal, 3 Drawers, c.1790, 34 x 27 In. 2000
Commode, Neoclassical, Mahogany, 4 Drawers, Fluted Supports, Leaves, c.1810, 34 x 48 In. 937
Commode, Painted, Multicolor, Flowers, Drawers, Shaped Top, c.1910, 30 x 23 In., Pair 750
Commode, Provincial, Cherry, Marble Top, Drawers, c.1810, 30 x 44 In. 1625
Commode, Regency Style, Fruitwood, 3 Long Drawers, Scrolled Toes, 31 x 32 In. 1000
Commode, Regency Style, Kingwood, Marble Top, Bombe Case, Drawers, 1800s, 34 x 54 In. 1375
Commode, Regency, Chestnut, Bowfront, Bombe Case, Bracket Feet, 41 x 55 In. 8302
Commode, Regency, Mahogany, Brass, Marble Top, Bombe Case, c.1790, 35 x 51 In. 7500
Commode, Rococo, Mahogany Veneer, Pine, Serpentine Front, Drawers, 32 x 40 In. 2400
Commode, Rosewood, Marble Top, Breakfront, Inlaid Waterscape, Stars, c.1790, 35 x 45 In. 5166
Commode, Sauteuse, French Provincial, Walnut, Serpentine Top, Paneled, 1800s, 35 x 43 In. 1560
Commode, Scroll & Urn Design, Serpentine Front, 3 Drawers, Italy, 1800s, 38 x 52 In. 1968
Commode, Walnut, Mahogany, Banded Top, Medallion, Drawers, c.1790, 36 x 50 In. 3000
Cradle, Chippendale, Oak, Hooded, Raised Panels, Finial Post, c.1790, 31 x 38 In. 230
Cradle, Gothic Revival, Walnut, Cane Panels, Arched Bonnet, Turned Frame, 48 x 45 In. 60
Cradle, Mahogany, Oval, Turned Spindles, Serpentine Trestle Legs, Victorian, 39 x 50 In. 185
Cradle, Pine, Oak, Panels, Carved, Hinged Canopy, Leaves, Thistle, 1600s, 30 x 38 In. 255
Cradle, Walnut, Paneled, Canted Sides, Knob Finials, Rockers, Inscribed 1673, 27 x 40 In. 800
Cradle, Wicker, Multicolor, Canopy, Pierced, Rocking, c.1900, 63 x 41 In. 153
Credenza, Baroque, Walnut, Cupboard, Panel Doors, Bracket Feet, c.1690, 44 x 62 In. 7500
Credenza, Kittinger, Mahogany, 4 Drawers, 2 Doors, 59½ x 20 In. 500
Credenza, Midcentury, 3 Sections, 6 Doors, Chinese, 30 x 99½ In. 55
Credenza, Midcentury, 4 Doors, Brown Lacquer, 2 Drawers, Pierre Cardin, 30 x 74 In. 847
Credenza, Painted, Faux Marble, Paneled, Doors, Interior Shelves, 1800s, 44 x 53 In. 1680
Credenza, Walnut, 2 Doors, Drawers, Open Shelf, Zinc Pulls, Risom, 72 x 26 In. 380
Credenza, Walnut, Carved, Drawers, Doors, Figural Mounts, Italy, 1800s, 35 x 40 In. *illus* 1845
Credenza, Wormley, Walnut, Brass, Drawers, Doors, Dunbar, c.1958, 30 x 72 In. *illus* 8610
Cupboard Bootjack, Base, Bucket, Green, 1800s, 44 x 17 In. 351
Cupboard Over Chest, Softwood, Chantelle Painted Surface, Cornice, 1800s, 89 x 33 In. 1180
Cupboard, Bonnetiere, Louis XIV Style, Multicolor, Mirrored Door, c.1910, 79 x 18 In. 275
Cupboard, Bonnetiere, Provincial, Cherry, Domed Cornice, c.1850, 96 x 53 In. 812
Cupboard, Chimney, Pine, Green & Yellow Paint, Paneled Door, 77 x 20 In. 510
Cupboard, Chippendale, Walnut, 2 Sections, Rosehead Nails, c.1810, 88 x 49 In. 1534
Cupboard, Corner, Blue Paint, Molded Cornice, Double Paneled Door, 1800s, 82 x 36 In. 738
Cupboard, Corner, Cherry, Brass Hardware, 5 Shelves, 94 x 48 x 24 In. 4248
Cupboard, Corner, Cherry, Dentil Molding, 2 Paneled Doors, Brass H Hinges, 79 x 42 In. 1230
Cupboard, Corner, Cherry, Doors, Drawers, 5 Shelves, Brass Latches, c.1820, 94 x 48 In. *illus* 4248
Cupboard, Corner, Green Painted Interior, 2 Doors, 4 Shelves, 77 x 36 In. 180
Cupboard, Corner, Hanging, Blind Door, Painted, Shelves, Pa., 1800s, 37 x 31 In. *illus* 1062
Cupboard, Corner, Hanging, Stepped Cornice, Arched Wood Hook Back, c.1910, 40 x 25 In. 725
Cupboard, Corner, Hanging, Walnut, Molding, Door, Carved, Shelves, c.1780, 50 In. *illus* 4956
Cupboard, Corner, Maple, Pine, Molded Cornice, 2 Doors, Inset Panels, Shelves, 79 x 45 In. 270
Cupboard, Corner, Paint Decorated, Paneled Doors, Shelves Inside, 89 x 51 In. 660
Cupboard, Corner, Painted, 12-Pane Paneled Door, Pa., c.1810, 86 x 46 In. *illus* 3835
Cupboard, Corner, Pine, 2 Sections, Open Top, Shelves, Door, 1800s, 87 x 52 In. *illus* 390
Cupboard, Corner, Pine, 3 Shelves, Dentil Molding, Chamfered Doors, 62 x 41 In. 168
Cupboard, Corner, Pine, Green Painted, Windmill On Door, Shaped Legs, 1800s, 60 x 29 In. 120
Cupboard, Corner, Pine, Painted, Shaped Interior Shelves, 78 x 53 x 25 In. *illus* 3360
Cupboard, Corner, Sheraton, Grain Painted, Cornice, Glass Pane Doors, 89 x 56 In. *illus* 2832
Cupboard, Corner, Softwood, Grain Painted, York County, 1800, 75x 61 In. 1062
Cupboard, Corner, Tiger Maple, Hinged Paneled Doors, Cutout Base, c.1810, 80 x 41 In. 3444
Cupboard, Corner, Walnut, Paneled Doors, Painted Shelf Interior, 1800s, 79 x 48 In. 240
Cupboard, Corner, Yellow, Glass Door, Paneled Door, 42 x 29 In. 994
Cupboard, Court, Oak, Carved, Inlay, Columns, Shelf, England, c.1700s, 57 x 51 In. *illus* 11685
Cupboard, Door, Blue Paint, Nailed Case, 1800s, 64 x 31 In. *illus* 413

Cupboard, Double, Shaker, Pine, Blue Paint, Doors, 10 Drawers, Meeting House, 77 In. ..... *illus* 67200
Cupboard, Federal, Cherry, Inlay, Arched Glazed Doors, Paneled Doors, 93 x 43 In. 37760
Cupboard, Hanging, Chippendale Style, Walnut Inlay, Vine, Pa., c.1980, 31 x 21 In. .... *illus* 236
Cupboard, Hanging, Grain Painted, Burnt Sienna, Paneled Door, 3 Shelves, 24 x 19 In. 369
Cupboard, Jelly, Louis XII Style, Oak, Carved, Raised Panel Door, 1800s, 30 x 25 In. 336
Cupboard, Jelly, Pine, Carved, Serpentine Gallery, 1800s, 57 x 26 In. 474
Cupboard, Jelly, Walnut, Scroll Cut Gallery, 2 Drawers, Ripple Edges, c.1840, 57 x 44 In. 216
Cupboard, Louis XVI Style, Fruitwood, Brass Gallery, Shelf, 1800s, c.1810, 35 x 14 In. 178
Cupboard, Nutting, Sunflower, Oak, Carved, Drawers, Doors, Branded, 50 x 57 In. .... *illus* 4080
Cupboard, Oak, 2 Glass Doors Applied Mountains, 2 Doors, Slide Out Tray, 78 x 48 In. 275
Cupboard, Oak, Corner, Paneled Door, 2 Shelves, 1800s, 38 x 29 In. 246
Cupboard, Oak, Joined, Marquetry Door, Turned Supports, 49 x 48 In. 3444
Cupboard, Oak, Wrought Iron, Linenfold, 1900s, 61 In. 472
Cupboard, Paneled Sides 2 Doors, Shaped Apron, Straight Legs, 50 x 45 In. 330
Cupboard, Pine, Paint Decorated, Orange Sponge, 2 Plank Doors, American, 1800s, 33 In. 720
Cupboard, Pine, Pewter, Painted, 3 Shelves, Drawers, 1800s, 81 x 61 In. .... *illus* 480
Cupboard, Playhouse Style, White House, Glass Windows, Berg, 1984, 34 x 40 In. 153
Cupboard, Renaissance Style, Carved, Figural Court Scene, Shelf, Drawers, 68 x 78 In. 2645
Cupboard, Softwood, Painted, Paneled Doors, Interior Shelves, Stiles, Drawer, 75 x 56 In. 1534
Cupboard, Softwood, Step Back, Chantelle Paint, Doors, Spice Drawers, 1800s, 84 x 50 In. 1416
Cupboard, Spanish Colonial Style, Walnut, Carved, Fielded Square Panels, 1900s, 36 x 35 In. .. 153
Cupboard, Step Back, Butternut, Walnut, 2 Sections, Raised Panel Doors, Pa., 85 x 59 In. 625
Cupboard, Step Back, Pine, Distressed Paint, 2 Single-Board Doors, 70 x 27 In. 210
Cupboard, Step Back, Pine, Worn Paint, 8 Panes, Paneled Doors, c.1825, 81 x 50 In. .... *illus* 3840
Cupboard, Walnut, Molded Cornice, Arched Flat Panel Door, Shelf, 1700s, 32 x 20 In. 1180
Cupboard, Welsh, Cornice, 3 Shelves, 3 Drawer Case, Open Base, 1900s, 78 x 72 In. 584
Daybed, Barcelona, Mies Van Der Rohe, Leather, Walnut, Stainless Steel, 1990s, 25 x 77 In. 2750
Daybed, G. Jalk, P. Jeppesen, Convertible, Teak, Upholstered, 1960s, 29 x 80 In. 4062
Daybed, G. Nakashima, Walnut, Birch Plywood, No Arms, 1964, 10 x 72 In. 6250
Daybed, Gianni Songia, Rosewood, Leather, 1963, 78 In. 825
Daybed, Leather, Cream, Handle Shape Ends, 82 x 32 In. 1188
Daybed, Louis XVI, Square Headboard & Footboard, 45 x 82 In. 2125
Daybed, Louis XVI, Walnut, Carved, Brass Tack, Reeded Frame, c.1890, 35½ x 75 In. 307
Daybed, Spanish Style, Pine, Carved, End Panels, Turned Legs, Front Rail, 24 x 67 In. 154
Daybed, William & Mary Style, Oak, Carved, Tufted Cushion, 68 x 21 In. 406
Desk, Architect's, George III, Mahogany, Carved, Ratchet Support, Drawer, c.1810, 29 x 36 In. ... 677
Desk, Arne Hovmand-Olsen, Hanging, 3 Drawers, Flip Top, Midcentury Modern, 12 x 59 In. 1500
Desk, Butler's, Mahogany, 2 4-Glass Panel Doors, Pullout Desk, 3 Drawers, 96 x 42 In. 600
Desk, Butler's, Mahogany, Brass, False Drawers, Fold Down Desk, c.1900, 38 x 32 In. 1125
Desk, Butler's, Mahogany, Reeded Tambour Doors, Columns, Hinged Doors, c.1810, 47 x 41 In. 1476
Desk, Butler's, Walnut, Burl, 3 Drawers, Pillar Columns, Scroll Feet, Casters, 49 x 43 In. 358
Desk, Cabinet, Carved, Compartments, J. Moore, Renaissance Revival, c.1875, 66 In. .... *illus* 4305
Desk, Carlton House, Mahogany, Tulipwood, Leather, Gillows, c.1890, 42 x 52 In. .... *illus* 6150
Desk, Carlton House, Satinwood, Scenes, Dovetailed, Leather, 1800s, 39 x 53 In. .... *illus* 3068
Desk, Carved Wood, Bone Flowers Decoration, Letter Rack, Drawer, 42 x 26 In., 2 Piece 375
Desk, Chippendale, Slant Front, Mahogany, Pine, Drawers, Center Prospect, c.1800, 43 x 38 In. 688
Desk, Danish Modern, Wood, Tapered Legs, 7 Drawers, 29 x 53 In. 366
Desk, Davenport, Eastlake, Walnut, Carved, Arched Back, Open Shelf, Leather, 48 x 27 In. 385
Desk, Davenport, Walnut Burl, Fretwork, Drawer, Leather Surface, Victorian, 36 x 23 In. 1968
Desk, Drop Front, Cherry, Concave Drawers, Shells, Cabriole Legs, c.1750, 42 x 35 In. 4305
Desk, Empire, Mahogany, Ormolu Mount, Leather Top, 1800s, 30 x 56 In. 430
Desk, Federal Style, Mahogany, Tambour Doors, Columns, c.1900, 46 x 34 In. 354
Desk, Filing Cabinet, Waterfall Desk Top, Rust Lacquer, 3 Drawers, Italy, 29 x 78 In. 2299
Desk, Fruitwood, Plank Top, Rounded, Kneehole, Cabriole Legs, c.1890, 30 x 70 In. 615
Desk, G. Stickley, Drop Front, Oak, Fitted Interior, Wormholes, c.1907, 45 x 36 In. .... *illus* 738
Desk, George II Style, Chinoiserie, Red & Gold Paint, 5 Drawers, Pad Feet, 30 x 56 In. 1063
Desk, Gregg Fleishman, Laminated Birch, Red Enamel, Interlocking Design, 29 x 60 In. 242
Desk, Hepplewhite Style, Beacon Hill, Inlay, Faux Leather, c.1960, 48 x 28 In. .... *illus* 360
Desk, Hepplewhite, Slant Front, Walnut, Dovetailed, Cock-Beaded, 47 x 42 In. 765
Desk, Jean Prouve, Patina, 2 Seats, c.1920.. 11875
Desk, Kneehole, Walnut, 7 Drawers, 1700s, 30 x 35 In. 300
Desk, Larkin, Oak, Carved, Oval Mirror, Cupboard Door, Drawer, c.1900, 72 x 58 In. 237
Desk, Limbert, Arts & Crafts, Drawer, Copper Pulls, Cane Side Panels, 30 x 45 In. 1416
Desk, Limbert, Drop Front, Wood, Shelves, Cutouts, Doors, c.1905, 54 x 38 In. .... *illus* 8125
Desk, Louis Philippe, Walnut, Carved, Cubbyholes, Shelves, Drawer, 1800s, 46 x 50 In. 533
Desk, Louis XV, Fruitwood, Leather Top, Drawers, Cabriole Legs, 1700s, 31 x 57 In. 1875

Furniture, Desk, Carlton House, Mahogany, Tulipwood, Leather, Gillows, c.1890, 42 x 52 In.
$6,150

Skinner, Inc.

Furniture, Desk, Carlton House, Satinwood, Scenes, Dovetailed, Leather, 1800s, 39 x 53 In.
$3,068

Brunk Auctions

Furniture, Desk, G. Stickley, Drop Front, Oak, Fitted Interior, Wormholes, c.1907, 45 x 36 In.
$738

Skinner, Inc.

Furniture, Desk, Hepplewhite Style, Beacon Hill, Inlay, Faux Leather, c.1960, 48 x 28 In.
$360

Garth's Auctioneers & Appraisers

Furniture, Desk, Limbert, Drop Front, Wood, Shelves, Cutouts, Doors, c.1905, 54 x 38 In.
$8,125

Rago Arts and Auction Center

Furniture, Desk, Musical, Cherry, String Instrument, J.C. Burgner, Wm. Paton, 1819, 50 x 43 In.
$62,720

Case Auctions

Furniture, Desk, Vargueno, Drop Front, Baroque, Carved, Walnut Inlay, c.1700, 56 x 42 In.
$9,188

Neal Auctions

Desk, Louis XV, Leather Top, Gold Tooled, 1940s, 68 x 35 In. 2000
Desk, Louis XV, Slant Front, Gallery Top, Courting Couple, 3 Drawers, 47 x 30 In. 4270
Desk, Mahogany, Inlay, Leather Surface, Stand, c.1955, 24 x 20 In. 390
Desk, Mahogany, Inset Leather, Banding, Tapered Square Legs, c.1890, 30 x 44 In. 2091
Desk, Mahogany, Inset Leather, Drawers, Splayed Legs, Brass Casters, 29 x 64 In. 750
Desk, Mahogany, Kneehole, 3 Drawers, Brass Pulls, Pedestals, c.1875, 30 x 53 In. 738
Desk, Mahogany, Leather Top, Drawers, Hobbs & Co., 1800s, 30 x 47 In. 1476
Desk, Majorelle, Mahogany, Fruitwood, Inlay, c.1900, 50 x 41 ¼ In. 1625
Desk, Maria Pergay, Stainless Steel, Drawers, France, 1970s, 30 x 79 x 32 In. 28750
Desk, Midcentury, Chrome, Teak, 2 Drawers, Alternating Panels, Rods, 31 x 54 In. 3025
Desk, Milo Baughman, Chrome Steel, Painted Wood, John Stuart Label, 1970s, 29 x 54 In. 875
Desk, Mother-Of-Pearl Inlay, Lacquered, England, c.1850, 37 x 24 In. 1315
Desk, Musical, Cherry, String Instrument, J.C. Burgner, Wm. Paton, 1819, 50 x 43 In. *illus* 62720
Desk, Oak, Marquetry, Flowers, Bows, Kidney Shape, Casters, c.1890, 35 x 29 In. 299
Desk, P. Evans, Directional, Double Pedestal, Chrome Steel, Walnut Burl, 1970s, 29 x 84 In. 4687
Desk, Partners, 2 Pedestals, Mahogany, Inset Leather, Drawers, c.1890, 30 x 59 In. 738
Desk, Partners, Oak, Leather Inset, Drawers, Turned Legs, c.1900, 36 x 60 In. 1125
Desk, Partners, Oak, Pegged, Drawers, Turned Legs, c.1850, 34 x 59 x 58 In. 676
Desk, Pedestal, Georgian, Mahogany, Marquetry, Drawers, Paneled Cupboard, 35 x 56 In. 812
Desk, Pedestal, Louis XVI Style, Bronze, Inlay, Leather Blotter, Drawers, 1900s, 83 x 44 In. 1250
Desk, Plantation, Walnut, Carved, Hinged Cornice, Drawer, Arched Niche, 58 x 42 In. 657
Desk, Plantation, Walnut, Cove Molded Cornice, 2 Doors, 3 Drawers, 48 x 43 In. 1152
Desk, Planter's, Cherry, 2 Part, Panel Door, Drawer, Turned Legs, c.1850, 57 x 25 In. 119
Desk, Queen Anne, Walnut, Fitted Interior, Conforming Frame, 38 x 31 In. 767
Desk, Regency Style, Leather Lined, Tambour Door, Pullout Slide, Woman's, 35 x 32 In. 354
Desk, Regency, Drop Front, Maple, Arched Trestle Stretcher, 45 x 22 In. 320
Desk, Roll Top, 4 Drawers, 36 x 26 In. 172
Desk, Schoolmaster's, Slant Front, Pine, Gallery Back, Tapered Legs, Fitted, 48 x 30 In. 125
Desk, Schoolmaster's, Slant Front, Softwood, Shaped Gallery, Quill Holders, 44 x 31 In. 83
Desk, Slant Front, Cherry, 4 Drawers, Fitted Interior, Fan Carved, Ogee Bracket Feet, 42 In. 1230
Desk, Slant Front, Pine, Red Paint, Gallery, Hinged, Drawers, 1800s, 39 x 32 In. 480
Desk, Vargueno, Drop Front, Baroque, Carved, Walnut Inlay, c.1700, 56 x 42 In. *illus* 9188
Desk, Vargueno, Drop Front, Oscar Bach, Walnut, Wrought Iron, 1920s, 38 x 21 In. *illus* 10000
Desk, Vargueno, Drop Front, Spanish Colonial, Walnut, Carved, Inlay, 15 x 22 In. 2706
Desk, Victorian, Ebonized Wood, Bamboo, Pomegranates, Reticulated, Japan, 54 x 48 In. 2070
Desk, Victorian, Mahogany, Crossbanded, Pierced Brass Gallery, Casters, 41 x 53 In. 1577
Desk, Warehouseman's, Slant Front, Mahogany, Carved, 3 Drawers, Trestle Base, 47 x 84 In. 296
Desk, Wood, Kidney Shape Top, Pierced Brass Gallery, Stars, Sabots, c.1890, 30 x 39 In. 812
Desk-Bookcase, Federal, Document Drawer, Paneled Doors, Columns, 1811, 93 x 39 In. 3540
Desk-Bookcase, Sheraton, Cherry, Pine, Slant Front, Lid, Drawer, c.1835, 68 x 33 In. *illus* 281
Desk-Bookcase, William & Mary Style, Burl, Veneer, Doors, Drawers, 89 x 43 In. *illus* 767
Dinette Set, Table, 2 Chairs, Black Iron, Parcel Gilt, Acorn Finials, Italy, 41 x 16 In. 3025
Dining Set, Midcentury Modern, Maple, Table, 6 Chairs, Padded, Baker Furniture 2160
Dining Set, Table, 4 Chairs, Cast, Welded Aluminum, 1970s, 29 x 36 In. 2875
Dresser, Art Nouveau, Walnut, Mahogany, Myrtle, Doors, Glass Portico, Inlay, 78 x 33 In. 748
Dresser, Charles II, Oak, Molded, Doors, Drawers, Block Feet, 1600s, 36 x 71 In. 6250
Dresser, Eastlake, Walnut, Carved, Marble Top, Dropwell, Arched Crest, Mirror, 82 x 53 In. 896
Dresser, Ebonized, X Shape Handles, 3 Drawers, James Mont Style, 30 x 20 In. 303
Dresser, Faux Bamboo Style, Carved Pediment, Mirror, Marble, 86 x 61 In. 316
Dresser, Federal Style, Mahogany, Painted Mahogany, Swivel Mirror, Paul Weise, 72 x 35 In. 420
Dresser, Florence Knoll, Birch, Light Green Stain, 3 Drawer, Louvered, c.1950, 28 x 36 In. 364
Dresser, Frankl, Stained Wood, Plated Metal, 7 Drawers, 1940s, 45 x 40 In., Pair 4375
Dresser, French Provincial, Fruitwood, Plate Shelves, Drawers, Doors, c.1850, 89 In. *illus* 799
Dresser, G. Nakashima, Tall Origins, Walnut, Brass, Elm Burl, Widdicomb, 50 x 47 In. 3625
Dresser, G. Nakashima, Walnut, 4 Drawers, 1958, 30 x 36 In. 4062
Dresser, G. Nakashima, Walnut, 6 Drawers, Plank Overhang Top, 1965, 32 x 83 In. 25000
Dresser, Henri II Style, Walnut, Carved, Mirrored Marble Top, Drawers, 81 x 51 In. 385
Dresser, John Stuart, Midcentury Modern, Rosewood, 6 Drawers, Chrome Frame, 28 x 77 In. 590
Dresser, McCobb, 8 Drawers, Planner Group, c.1950, 41 ¾ x 60 In. 1000
Dresser, Midcentury Modern, Cherry, 2-Sided, Brass Cap Feet, 32 x 60 In. 176
Dresser, Midcentury Modern, White, Green Case, Drawers, Kittinger, Buffalo, 33 x 45 In. 615
Dresser, Oak, 2 Sections, Scalloped Cornice, Plate Rails, Drawers, Shelves, 1800s, 80 x 60 In. 660
Dresser, Rougier, Chrome, White, 6 Drawers, Canada, c.1960s, 30 x 72 In. 1210
Dresser, Victorian, Walnut, Bowfront, Bracket Feet, 33 x 45 In. 150
Dresser, Walnut, Bowfront, Glass Top, 6 Drawers, Widdicomb, c.1950, 29 ½ x 67 In. 1089
Dresser, Walnut, Louvered Doors, 6 Drawers, Turned Legs, Brass, 1960s, 30 x 54 In. 299

Item	Price
Dresser, Welsh, George III, Oak, Pine, Molded Cornice, Iron Hooks, Shelves, c.1800, 84 x 72 In.	1320
Dresser, Welsh, Oak, Paneled Drawers, Rosehead Nails, Turned Legs, Stretchers, 32 x 50 In.	2006
Dresser, Wig, Rococo Revival, Rosewood, Marble Top, Pierced Crest, c.1870, 93 x 49 In.	1722
Dry Bar, Carved Panels, Hinged Top, Fitted Interior, Bun Feet, 44 x 54 In.	220
Dry Sink, 2-Tone Green & Yellow, 33 ½ x 35 In.	702
Dry Sink, Pink & Poplar, Grain Painted, Backsplash Shelf, 2 Doors, 38 x 43 In.	900
Dry Sink, Red, 2 Doors, 52 x 21 In.	117
Dry Sink, Walnut, High Back, Shelf, Doors, Interior Shelves, Cutout Feet, 1800s, 40 x 49 In.	660
Dry Sink, Work Slide, Painted, Mustard, Tapered Legs, 34 x 41 In.	805
Dumbwaiter, George III, Mahogany, 3 Graduated Shelves, Tripod Base, 45 In.	366
Dumbwaiter, George III Style, Mahogany, 3 Dished Tiers, Arch Legs, Slipper Feet, 40 In.	184
Dumbwaiter, Georgian Style, Mahogany, 3 Graduated Turned Shelves, Tripod, 40 x 23 In.	105
Easel, Artist's, Beech, Carved, Serpentine Through Tenons, Adjustable, 1900s, 64 x 25 In.	178
Easel, Baroque, Leaf Carved Frame, Rosettes, Gilt, Painted, Folding, c.1900, 64 In.	354
Easel, Gilt, Peacock, Twist Turn Poles, Owl, Leaves, Ball & Claw, 70 x 24 In.	2520
Easel, Sheraton Style, Wood, Rotating, Adjustable, Spindle Column, 81 x 30 In.	885
Easel, Victorian Style, Mahogany, Carved, Folding, Adjustable Painting Support, 68 In.	531
Etagere, Biedermeier, Mahogany, Ebonized Wood, Round Shelves, 1800s, 55 In.	554
Etagere, Bronze, Gilt & Marble, 3 Tiers, Pierced Galleries, Ball Feet, c.1900, 30 x 14 In.	875
Etagere, Mahogany, Corner, 3 Tiers, Barley Twist Legs, Button Feet, 1800s, 51 x 31 In.	735
Etagere, Mahogany, Marble, Arched Crest, Mirror, Drawers, c.1890, 98 x 48 In.	830
Etagere, Regency, Mahogany, 3 Tiers, Drawers, Supports, Casters, c.1810, 43 In.	984
Etagere, Regency, Mahogany, Frieze Drawer, Edwards & Roberts, 1820, 54 ½ x 21 In.	4375
Etagere, Rococo Revival, Rosewood, Shelves, Mirrors, Brooks, c.1865, 85 x 56 In. *illus*	4674
Etagere, Rococo Revival, Walnut, Lyre Shape Pierced Crest, Galleries, c.1850, 68 x 42 In.	177
Etagere, Rococo, Rosewood, Marble Top, Cabinet, Carved Fruit, c.1875, 100 x 55 In.	5000
Footrest, Cast Iron, Camel, Walking, Wood Round Base, 9 In.	50
Footstool, Classical, Mahogany, Needlepoint Seat, Braid Trim, Reeded Base, 17 In. *illus*	563
Footstool, Embroidered, Green Ground, Red Dragon, Gold Velvet, 25 x 17 In.	156
Footstool, French Style, Walnut, Upholstered Top, Cabriole Legs, 13 x 16 x 20 In.	270
Footstool, Louis XV Style, Walnut, Serpentine Top, Rocaille Shells, c.1910, 15 x 12 In.	123
Footstool, Mahogany, Rectangular Top, Beaded Edge, Splayed Legs, 1800s, 4 x 10 In.	142
Footstool, Needlepoint, Yellow, Bun Feet, 14 ½ x 12 ½ In., Pair	125
Footstool, Rococo, Mahogany, Carved, Flowers, Cabriole Legs, c.1850, 11 x 14 In.	185
Footstool, Victorian, Rococo Revival, Rosewood Frame, Carved, Upholstered, 12 x 17 In.	118
Frame, Fruitwood, Mahogany, Flat, 25 x 21 ¾ In.	210
Frame, Giltwood, Beaded, Pierced, Leafy, Scroll, 18 ⅛ x 15 ½ In.	1020
Frame, Giltwood, Gesso, Deep Reeded Molding, 23 ½ x 20 ¼ In.	1020
Frame, Regency, Giltwood, Beaded, Scroll, Leaves, 22 x 18 ¾ In.	240
Gong, Stand, Ebonized Wood, Carved, Reticulated, Gilt, Victorian, Japan, 50 x 26 In.	920
Hall Stand, Arts & Crafts, Oak, Cutouts, Cupboard, Mirror, 77 x 40 In.	747
Hall Stand, Bamboo, Mirror, Shelves, 18th Century, 70 x 35 ½ In.	288
Hall Stand, Black Forest Style, Tree, Bears, Mirror, Umbrella Holder, 1900s, 72 In. *illus*	510
Hall Stand, Oak, Carved, Arched Fan Crest, Center Mirror, Wood Hooks, Tray, 89 x 36 In.	415
Hall Stand, Twig Frame, Birch Branches, Plank Seat, Framed Mirror Back, 76 x 19 In.	180
Hall Stand, Victorian, Golden Oak, Mirror, Iron Hooks, 1800s, 78 x 43 In.	385
Hall Stand, Victorian, Mirror, Carved Crest, Walnut, c.1850, 90 x 46 In.	368
Hall Tree, Art Nouveau, Burl, Oak, Carved Ogee Planks, Panels, Marquetry, 87 x 32 In.	748
Hall Tree, Oak, Cast Iron, Hat, Coat, Umbrella Stand, C.R. Mackintosh, c.1900, 73 In. *illus*	32500
Hall Tree, Wood, Iron, Nickel Plate, 8 Hooks, Round Shelf, Enamel Base, c.1910, 84 In.	840
Highboy, Cherry, Valanced Skirt, Cabriole Legs, Drawers, Pad Feet, c.1750, 88 x 38 In.	2583
Highboy, Chippendale, Mahogany, Bonnet Top, Split Swan Neck, 7 Drawers, 85 x 41 In.	907
Highboy, Queen Anne, Mahogany, Drawers, Bonnet Top, Carved, c.1750, 80 x 39 In. *illus*	2880
Highboy, Queen Anne, Walnut, Molded Cornice, Herringbone Banding, c.1710, 68 x 41 In.	5412
Highboy, William & Mary, Mahogany, Fruitwood, Drawers, Twist Legs, 1700s, 55 In. *illus*	1045
Highchair, Ladder Back, Mixed Wood, Turned Finials & Legs, Stretcher, 1700s, 38 In.	384
Highchair, Maple, Red Paint, Slats, Splint Seat, Arms, New Eng., c.1790, 38 x 22 In. *illus*	492
Huntboard, Federal, Walnut, Poplar, Pine, Cut Nail, c.1810, 36 x 59 In.	2242
Kneeler, Prie-Dieu, Ebonized, Upholstered, Barley Twist Supports, 1800s, 34 x 19 In.	178
Kneeler, Prie-Dieu, French Empire Style, Ebonized, Pierced Cross, Upholstered, 35 In.	207
Kneeler, Prie-Dieu, Rosewood, Reticulated Crest, Rope Twist, Upholstered, 1860, 40 x 22 In.	1960
Kneeler, Prie-Dieu, Walnut, Carved, Upholstered, Curved Arms, Cross Splat, 35 x 20 In.	431
Ladder, Rolling, Pine, 8-Tread, Mortised Side Rails, Iron Wheels, c.1890, 98 In.	738
Lap Desk, Black Walnut, Brass Mounted, Green Leather, 7 x 20 In.	363
Lap Desk, Brass Inlay, Faux Leather Surface, Pen Tray, Inkwell, 1800s, 14 x 9 In.	444
Lap Desk, Campaign, Camphorwood, Brass Bound, Pen Slot, Bottle, 1800s, 21 x 25 In.	185

Furniture, Desk, Vargueno, Drop Front, Oscar Bach, Walnut, Wrought Iron, 1920s, 38 x 21 In.
$10,000

Rago Arts and Auction Center

Furniture, Desk-Bookcase, Sheraton, Cherry, Pine, Slant Front, Lid, Drawer, c.1835, 68 x 33 In.
$281

Garth's Auctioneers & Appraisers

Furniture, Desk-Bookcase, William & Mary Style, Burl, Veneer, Doors, Drawers, 89 x 43 In.
$767

Brunk Auctions

F

Furniture, Dresser, French Provincial, Fruitwood, Plate Shelves, Drawers, Doors, c.1850, 89 In.
$799

New Orleans (Cakebread)

Furniture, Etagere, Rococo Revival, Rosewood, Shelves, Mirrors, Brooks, c.1865, 85 x 56 In.
$4,674

New Orleans (Cakebread)

Furniture, Footstool, Classical, Mahogany, Needlepoint Seat, Braid Trim, Reeded Base, 17 In.
$563

Neal Auctions

Furniture, Hall Stand, Black Forest Style, Tree, Bears, Mirror, Umbrella Holder, 1900s, 72 In.
$510

Garth's Auctioneers & Appraisers

Furniture, Hall Tree, Oak, Cast Iron, Hat, Coat, Umbrella Stand, C.R. Mackintosh, c.1900, 73 In.
$32,500

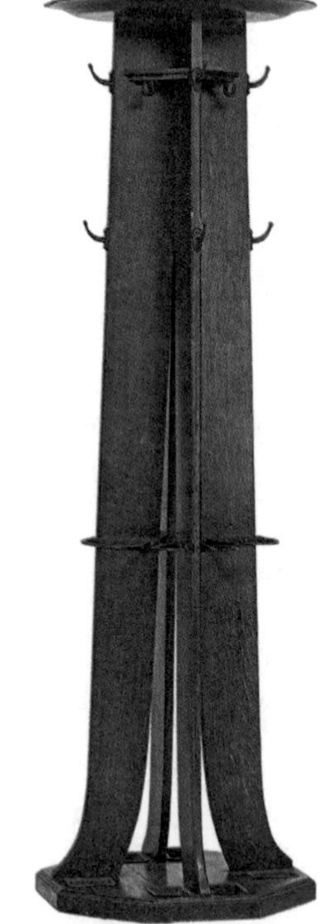

Rago Arts and Auction Center

Furniture, Highboy, Queen Anne, Mahogany, Drawers, Bonnet Top, Carved, c.1750, 80 x 39 In.
$2,880

Garth's Auctioneers & Appraisers

Furniture, Highboy, William & Mary, Mahogany, Fruitwood, Drawers, Twist Legs, 1700s, 55 In.
$1,045

New Orleans (Cakebread)

Furniture, Highchair, Maple, Red Paint, Slats, Splint Seat, Arms, New Eng., c.1790, 38 x 22 In.
$492

Skinner, Inc.

Lap Desk, Leather, Fold-Out Stationary Rack, 3 x 10 ½ In. 184
Lap Desk, Mahogany, Fitted Roll Top Tambour, Foldover Lid, c.1800, ... 854
Lap Desk, Papier-Mache, Mother-Of-Pearl Inlay, 13 x 10 In. 212
Lap Desk, Tulipwood, Ebonized Wood, Bronze Accents, Sloping Lid, c.1900, 11 In. 185
Lap Desk, William IV, Campaign Style, Mahogany, Brass, Bramah Lock, c.1840, 20 x 11 In. 430
Lectern, Renaissance Revival, Oak, Slanted, Drawer, 2 Graduated Shelves, 47 x 39 In. 553
Library Ladder, Edwardian Style, Maple, Leather, Folding, 6 Steps, 1900s, 81 x 12 In. 2214
Library Ladder, Stained, Modern, 84 x 20 ½ In. 875
Library Ladder, Wood, Serpentine Stringer, 4 Rounded Steps, 40 x 18 ½ In. 307
Library Shelves, Victorian, Mahogany, 5 Shelves, Carved, Cherub Head, 83 x 55 In. 1495
Library Steps, George III Style, Pine, 5 Steps, Turned Balustrades, 1900s, 85 x 39 In. 984
Library Steps, George III, Faux Wood, Acorn Finials, Base, Casters, 97 x 90 In. 4880
Library Steps, Mahogany, 4 Steps, England, 45 x 15 In. 600
Library Steps, Wood & Metal, Quarter Spiral, 41 In. 250
Linen Press, American Classical, Mahogany, 2 Doors, 4 Drawers, c.1820, 94 x 48 In. 3355
Linen Press, Cherry, 2 Shaped Doors, 4 Drawers, 81 x 39 In. 1404
Linen Press, Federal, Cherry, Outset Molded Cornice, 5 Drawers, Splayed Legs, 84 x 49 In. 960
Linen Press, Federal, Mahogany, 3 Inlaid Panels Over Hinged Doors, 4 Drawers, 87 In. 1107
Linen Press, George III Style, Mahogany, Paneled Doors, Drawers, c.1850, 68 x 43 In. 625
Linen Press, George III, Figured Mahogany, 2 Case, c.1800, 76 x 50 In. 1534
Linen Press, Georgian, Mahogany, Paneled Doors, Drawers, Rod, c.1810, 74 x 55 In. 984
Linen Press, Georgian, Oak, Dentil Cornice, Arched & Paneled Doors, Drawers, 79 x 75 In. 544
Linen Press, Mahogany, 2 Doors, Stepped Cornice, Drawers, c.1885, 85 x 53 In. 750
Linen Press, Mahogany, Cove Molded Cornice, Paneled Doors, Drawers, c.1850, 83 x 54 In. 937
Linen Press, Mahogany, Dentil Molded Cornice, 2 Doors, 3 Drawers, 80 x 38 In. 324
Linen Press, Mahogany, Molded Cornice, Doors, Arched Panel, Bun Feet, c.1865, 92 x 55 In. 1353
Love Seat, Donald Deskey, Upholstered, Arms, Chrome, Royal Chrome, c.1935, 26 In. .... *illus* 720
Love Seat, Louis XVI Style, Upholstered, Gilt Frame, c.1880, 32 x 48 In. 425
Love Seat, Milo Baughman Style, Chrome Frame, Tufted Upholstery, 1970s, 62 x 34 In. 230
Love Seat, Robsjohn-Gibbings, Walnut, Upholstered, Widdicomb, 1950s, 33 x 53 In. 2375
Love Seat, Victorian Style, Mahogany, Shaped Crest, Tufted Upholstery, 44 x 53 In. 480
Lowboy, Queen Anne, Oak, Molded Edge, 3 Drawers, Cabriole Legs, c.1790, 28 x 32 In. 468
Lowboy, William & Mary Style, Wood, Paint, Molded Lid, Cutout Skirt, Finials, 24 In. 590
Mirror, Antler Mounted, Round, 25 x 25 In. 1080
Mirror, Art Deco, Wood, Gilt, Paint, Square Pediment, Fruit Basket, 1930s, 53 x 30 In. 127
Mirror, Art Nouveau, Parcel Gilt, Leaves, Woman Feeding Peacock, 22 ½ x 36 In. 120
Mirror, Baldachin Crest, Old Mirror Plate, Italy, 7 ½ x 40 In. 2196
Mirror, Baroque, Giltwood, Scrolling Pierced Frame, Shell Cresting, 105 x 68 In. 6875
Mirror, Baroque, Giltwood, Square, Open Scrollwork, Carved Leaves, 21 x 21 In. 812
Mirror, Baroque, Stamped Brass, Beveled, c.1875, 22 ¾ x 12 ¾ In. 369
Mirror, Belle Epoque, Giltwood, Ribbons, Reeded, Pierced Bowknot, c.1900, 72 x 45 In. 615
Mirror, Biedermeier, Giltwood, Pediment Top, Neoclassical Ornament, c.1800, 34 x 14 In. 399
Mirror, Bronze, Sunburst, Glass Cabochons, Zodiac Emblems, M. Brazier-Jones, 38 In. 11498
Mirror, Carved Deal, Egg & Dart Frame, Rocaille, Broken-Arch Crest, c.1900, 47 x 51 In. 738
Mirror, Carved, Black Paint, Frame, Neoclassical Urns, Reverse Painted, 40 x 30 In. 183
Mirror, Cherry, Scroll Crest, Etched Grapes, Vines, Bird, Red Wash, 1700s, 15 x 10 In. 1722
Mirror, Cheval, G. Thonet, Beech, Brass, Austria, c.1904, 68 x 34 In. 3000
Mirror, Cheval, Stand, Mahogany, Columns, Ringed, 1880s, 61 x 31 In. 1650
Mirror, Cheval, Victorian, Walnut, Arched Crest, Inlaid Flowers, 70 x 31 In. 1107
Mirror, Chinese Chippendale Style, Giltwood, Pierced Surround, Rocaille, 1900s, 43 x 24 In. 468
Mirror, Chinoiserie, Black Paint, Octagonal, Flowers, 47 x 34 In. 344
Mirror, Chippendale Style, Gilt Scrolling, Leaved, Bird Crest, c.1980, 62 x 32 In. 660
Mirror, Chippendale, Mahogany, Phoenix Crest, Giltwood, Scroll Cutout Frame, 38 x 21 In. 236
Mirror, Chippendale, Maple, Giltwood, 38 x 20 In. 307
Mirror, Column, Parcel Gilt, Corinthian Capitals, Italy, 1800s, 40 x 36 In. 1572
Mirror, Courting, Cherry, Reverse Painted, Fruit Bowl, Lollipop Top, 15 x 8 In. .... *illus* 2489
Mirror, Courting, Mahogany, Half Round, Reverse Painted, Flowers, c.1830, 19 In. 185
Mirror, Cut Glass, Bellflowers, Octagonal Frame, Leaf Base, 48 x 29 In. 547
Mirror, Door, Phil Powell, Twig Fretwork, 69 x 31 In. 1625
Mirror, Dressing, Oak, Turned Swivel Supports, Shaped Base, 18 x 22 In. 48
Mirror, Dressing, Oscar Onken, Folding, Oak, 3-Part, Label, c.1910, 75 x 75 In. .... *illus* 780
Mirror, Dressing, Queen Anne, Pine, Japanned, Chinoiserie, Drawer, Slant Front, 1800s, 42 In. . 240
Mirror, Edwardian, Giltwood, Shield Shape, Urn Crest, Swags, c.1910, 42 x 18 In., Pair 2952
Mirror, Egyptian Revival, Reverse Painted, Giltwood, Beveled, c.1810, 40 x 24 In. 2706
Mirror, Empire Style, Painted, Ormolu, Arched Pediment, Columns, 1900s, 42 x 27 In. 148
Mirror, Empire, Parcel Gilt, Lacquer, Applied Gesso, Rectangular, 43 ½ x 21 ½ In. 184

Furniture, Love Seat, Donald Deskey, Upholstered, Arms, Chrome, Royal Chrome, c.1935, 26 In.
$720

Garth's Auctioneers & Appraisers

Furniture, Mirror, Courting, Cherry, Reverse Painted, Fruit Bowl, Lollipop Top, 15 x 8 In.
$2,489

James D. Julia Auctioneers

Furniture, Mirror, Dressing, Oscar Onken, Folding, Oak, 3-Part, Label, c.1910, 75 x 75 In.
$780

Garth's Auctioneers & Appraisers

This is an edited listing of current prices. Visit **Kovels.com** to check thousands of prices from previous years and sign up for free information on trends, tips, reproductions, marks, and more.

Furniture, Mirror, Fun House, Carnival, Wood Frame, Blue, Lighted Marquee, 1930s, 81 x 33 In.
$1,159

Morphy Auctions

Furniture, Mirror, George II, Walnut, Giltwood, Broken-Arch, Scroll, Swags, c.1800, 52 x 26 In.
$1,250

New Orleans (Cakebread)

Furniture, Mirror, Lyre Shape, Giltwood, Gesso, Eagle Heads, Carved, c.1810, 42 In.
$923

Neal Auctions

Mirror, Federal Style, Giltwood, 3-Way, Reverse Painted, Eagles, c.1910, 32 x 62 In., Pair........... 799
Mirror, Federal, Mahogany, Reverse Painted, House, Column Frame, 35 x 20 In. 201
Mirror, Federal, Pine, Fisheye, Spread Wing Eagle Crest, 1800s, 46 In. 500
Mirror, Federal, Reverse Painted, Dancing Girl, Applied Turnings, c.1880, 34 x 20 In., Pair........ 210
Mirror, Folk Art, Teal, White, Leaves, Scrolls, 71 x 45 ¼ In. 303
Mirror, French Empire, Parcel Gilt, Multicolor Gesso, Pointed Pediment, Columns, 28 x 21 In. . 296
Mirror, French Provincial Style, Fruitwood, Arched, Candleholders, 1700s, 50 x 51 In. 812
Mirror, French Window Shape, Gothic Style Arch, Mullions, 66 x 33 In. 368
Mirror, Fun House, Carnival, Wood Frame, Blue, Lighted Marquee, 1930s, 81 x 33 In. ....*illus* 1159
Mirror, George II, Giltwood, Pitch Pediment, Crossed Eagle's Head Crest, 1700s, 52 x 29 In. 861
Mirror, George II, Walnut, Giltwood, Broken-Arch, Scroll, Swags, c.1800, 52 x 26 In. ....*illus* 1250
Mirror, George III, Mahogany, Oval, Pierced, Carved, 28 x 16 In. 266
Mirror, George III, Rosewood, Adjustable, Pivot, Oval, S-Scroll Supports, Trestle Base, 22 In. 531
Mirror, George III, Walnut, Parcel Gilt, Broken Swan Neck Pediment, 1790, 52 x 25 In. 1500
Mirror, Georgian Style, Giltwood, Metal, Oval, Urn Finial, Scroll, Beading, 60 x 31 In. 250
Mirror, Georgian Style, Mahogany Veneer, Parcel Gilt Scrollwork Trim, Crest, 49 x 29 In. 738
Mirror, Giltwood, Arched Crest, Flowers, Serpentine Marble Top, c.1865, 138 x 43 In., Pair......... 4500
Mirror, Giltwood, Beaded Liner, Pierced Arrow Crest, Wheat, c.1790, 33 x 17 In. 1045
Mirror, Giltwood, Beaded, Cherub's Crest, Cabochon, Flower Swags, c.1890, 67 x 42 In. 1845
Mirror, Giltwood, Belle Epoch, Oval, Lovebirds Crest, Pierced Leaves, c.1890, 43 x 25 In. 1722
Mirror, Giltwood, Carved & Pierced, Rocaille, Roses, Scroll, Shells, c.1870, 40 x 22 In. 1187
Mirror, Giltwood, Carved Leaves, Fluted, Overhanging Crest, c.1890, 75 x 38 In. 2214
Mirror, Giltwood, Carved, Acorns, Grapes, Reeded Columns, c.1810, 46 x 29 In. 1169
Mirror, Giltwood, Cherubs, Gold Paint, Finesse Originals, c.1972, 60 x 31 In. 570
Mirror, Giltwood, Cornice, Tablet, Apollo & Chariot, Mummy Heads, c.1810, 60 x 39 In. 738
Mirror, Giltwood, Cushion, Beveled, Acanthine, Pierced Flower Crest, c.1900, 55 x 36 In. 3198
Mirror, Giltwood, Cushion, Egg & Dart Molding, Acanthus, Crests, c.1900, 52 x 40 In. 1500
Mirror, Giltwood, Flower & Leaf Carved Crest, Finials, Beaded Frame, c.1890, 73 x 50 In. 2375
Mirror, Giltwood, Flowers, 8-Sided, Pierced Rocaille Crest, Shell, c.1890, 49 x 30 In. 2460
Mirror, Giltwood, Flowers, Baluster Columns, Leopard Masks, Victorian, 65 x 48 In. 2373
Mirror, Giltwood, Fluted, Carved Leaves, Scroll, Draped Leaf Crest, c.1890, 75 x 38 In. 2214
Mirror, Giltwood, Gesso, Urn, Flowers, Italy, 41 x 26 In., Pair.. 1125
Mirror, Giltwood, Grape Leaf, Scroll, Urn, Beaded Border, 85 x 42 In. 1125
Mirror, Giltwood, Molded Frame, Flowers, Serpentine Crest, Shells, c.1890, 55 x 32 In. 1187
Mirror, Giltwood, Oval, 31 x 38 In. 180
Mirror, Giltwood, Pierced Scrollwork, Cabochon Corners, Leaves, c.1900, 57 x 36 In. 2152
Mirror, Giltwood, Pierced Scrollwork, Shell Shape Crests, Flower Basket, 58 x 28 In. 593
Mirror, Giltwood, Pierced, Carved, Angels, Shells, Scroll, Leaves, 1700s, 45 x 51 In. 6250
Mirror, Giltwood, Pierced, Oval, Rocaille, Hoho Birds, Pagoda Crest, Bells, 1900s, 55 x 32 In. 2125
Mirror, Giltwood, Ribbon Surround, Painted Landscape, c.1940, 88 x 33 In. 1375
Mirror, Giltwood, Scroll, Egg & Dart Molding, Arched, Putti Crest, c.1890, 66 x 36 In. 1750
Mirror, Giltwood, Scroll, Fluted Frame, Vines, Fruit Basket Crest, 1900s, 61 x 27 In., Pair........... 937
Mirror, Giltwood, Scrolled Frame, Serpentine Crest, Pierced Rocaille, c.1890, 69 x 45 In. 1722
Mirror, Girandole, Icicles, Trailing Vines, 38 x 17 In. 960
Mirror, Gray Stain, 3 Swags, Cherub Faces, Rounded Corners, France, 96 x 48 In. 1250
Mirror, Italian Style, Giltwood, Gesso, Multicolor, Pierced Pagoda, Painted Scene, 37 x 17 In. ... 185
Mirror, Lined Pine, Lyre Shape, Leaves, Blossoms, Classical Mask, c.1810, 86 x 52 In. 1599
Mirror, Louis XIV, Giltwood, Gesso, Pierced, Openwork Pediment, Birds, 30 x 18 In. 531
Mirror, Louis XV Style, Giltwood, Pierced Scrollwork, Putto, Garlands, c.1890, 49 x 25 In. 1750
Mirror, Louis XV, Giltwood, Gesso, Pierced Crest, Beaded Liner, Flowers, 43 x 28 ½ In. 153
Mirror, Louis XVI Style, Composite, Giltwood, Putti, Urn, Flowers, Ribbons, 74 x 43 In. 1169
Mirror, Louis XVI Style, Giltwood, Beveled, Ribbon Crest, Birds, Garlands, 74 x 44 In. 1722
Mirror, Louis XVI Style, Parcel Gilt, Pinecone Gilt Rests, Beaded Liner, 48 x 27 In. 875
Mirror, Louis XVI, Giltwood, Urn, Leaves, Reeded, 46 ½ x 29 In. 363
Mirror, Louis XVI, Parcel Gilt, Paint, Swags, Lyres, Flower Crest, c.1790, 71 x 42 In. 3444
Mirror, Lyre Shape, Giltwood, Gesso, Eagle Heads, Carved, c.1810, 42 In. ....*illus* 923
Mirror, Mahogany, Gesso, Scrolling Crest, Concave Shell, c.1880, 16 x 10 In. 277
Mirror, Mahogany, Ormolu Trim, Brass Finials, 19th Century, 72 x 33 In. 461
Mirror, Metal, Reverse Painted, Flowers, Scroll, Pierced, Portraits, Dancers, 27 x 19 In. 1875
Mirror, Mixed Wood, Painted, Half Round Crest, Reeded Frame, c.1810, 32 x 22 In. 248
Mirror, Napoleon III Style, Giltwood, Shell Shape Cartouche, Molded Frame, 63 x 42 In. 1250
Mirror, Napoleon III, Giltwood, Arched Crest, Shells, Molded Frame, c.1865, 59 x 39 In. 1875
Mirror, Napoleon III, Giltwood, Gesso, Arched Crest, Winged Women, c.1890, 73 In. 9375
Mirror, Neoclassical Style, Beaded, Acanthine, Crest, Feathered Arrow, Urn, 79 x 40 In. 399
Mirror, Neoclassical Style, Carved, Giltwood, Reverse Painted, Columns, c.1910, 45 x 27 In. 180
Mirror, Neoclassical Style, Flower Crest, Scroll Pediment, Garlands, 1800s, 55 x 29 In. 2091

Mirror, Neoclassical Style, Giltwood, Carved, Arched Crest, Garlands, c.1910, 78 x 56 In. 1195
Mirror, Neoclassical Style, Giltwood, Cushion, Pierced, Torch, Belle Epoque, 59 x 37 In. 2337
Mirror, Oak, Grapevines, Squared, Card Bird Crest, c.1895, 50 x 33 In. 420
Mirror, Oak, Medicine Cabinet, Towel Rack, Shelves, Bar, Wall Mount, 18 x 67 In. 30
Mirror, Octagonal, Beveled, Blue Mirrored Border, 45 x 27 In. 281
Mirror, Paolo Buffa, Maple, Clear & Green Glass, Italy, 1950s, 51 x 31 In. 3750
Mirror, Parcel Gilt, Scroll Carved Panels, Black, Square, Italy, c.1690, 37 x 31 In. 3690
Mirror, Pier, Carved, Giltwood, Rosette Corners, c.1810, 49 x 29 In. .... *illus* 610
Mirror, Pier, Giltwood, 18th Century Style Painted Seascape, Castle, 63 In. 185
Mirror, Pier, Giltwood, Marble Console, Pierced Crest, Relief Fruit, Garland, 102 x 28 In. 1067
Mirror, Pier, Giltwood, Molded Shadowbox, Shell & Scroll, Leaves, c.1800, 70 x 46 In. 875
Mirror, Pier, Giltwood, Ribbons, Flower Basket, Pierced Crest, c.1950, 59 x 32 In. 1625
Mirror, Pier, Louis Philippe, Giltwood, Egg & Dart Molded Frame, c.1850, 60 x 24 In. 799
Mirror, Pier, Louis XV, Parcel Gilt, Love Awakening, c.1880, 78 ½ x 52 ½ In. 1220
Mirror, Pier, Louis XVI Style, Giltwood, Ogee Frame, River Scene, 64 x 29 In. 1067
Mirror, Pier, Louis XVI Style, Parcel Gilt, Inset Oval, Oil On Panel, c.1910, 60 x 48 In. 3000
Mirror, Pier, Louis XVI, Parcel Gilt, Berried Laurel Leaves, Sage, 59 x 50 ½ In. 605
Mirror, Pier, Marble Top Table, Rococo Style, Carved Stretcher, 147 x 58 In. 3000
Mirror, Pier, Planter, Venetian Rococo Style, Parcel Gilt, Painted, Shelves, 200 x 46 In. 1845
Mirror, Pier, Rococo Revival, Giltwood, Scroll & Shell Carved Crest, c.1875, 118 x 42 In. 922
Mirror, Planter, Henri II Style, Walnut, Stoneware, Spindled Cornice, 110 x 60 In. 488
Mirror, Queen Anne, Mahogany, Scrolled Crest, Rectangular Frame, c.1750, 16 x 9 In. 277
Mirror, Queen Anne, Mahogany, Scrolling Crest, Molded Frame, c.1775, 15 x 9 In. 615
Mirror, Ravanaya, Indian Figures, Gods, Leaves, 46 x 30 ½ In. 406
Mirror, Red Lacquer Border, Giltwood, Leaves, 35 x 16 In. 212
Mirror, Regency, Giltwood, Convex, Molded, Giltwood Frame, England, 1800s, 16 ½ In. 354
Mirror, Renaissance Revival, Blackamoor Figures, 90 x 77 In. 1963
Mirror, Restauration, Painted, Molded, Carved Leaf Shield, Garland, c.1810, 27 x 23 In. 343
Mirror, Rococo Style Frame, Slip Finish, Carved, Openwork, 50 x 18 In. 219
Mirror, Rococo Style, Gilded, Pierced, Carved Frame, c.1910, 51 x 35 In. 360
Mirror, Rococo Style, Giltwood, Curved Frame, Scrolls, Leaves, Openwork, 66 x 42 In. 500
Mirror, Rococo, Giltwood, Pierced Leaf & Scroll Crest, Grapes, c.1875, 62 x 56 In. 625
Mirror, Rococo, Giltwood, Round Top, Molded Frame, Shells, Scroll, c.1765, 28 x 23 In. 1187
Mirror, Shaker, Maple, Shelf, Peg Holes, Brass, 25 x 14 In. 2215
Mirror, Shaving, Chrome, Adjustable, Beveled, Brush Holder, Rubberset Co., 1920s, 17 In. 185
Mirror, Shaving, Regency, Satinwood, Cross Banded, String Inlay, Swivel, Drawers, 24 x 23 In. . 118
Mirror, Shield Shape, Engraved Scrolling & Diapering, c.1950, 24 x 16 In., Pair 1875
Mirror, Silver Gilt, Beveled, Leaf Designed, 38 x 29 In. 72
Mirror, Silvered Metal, Harp Shape, Cherub Gazing Down, Birds, Bust, c.1900, 21 In. 1500
Mirror, Stand, 2 Parts, Arched Crest, Fluted Columns, Cartouche, Leaves, c.1870, 112 x 44 In. .. 593
Mirror, Sunburst, Giltwood, Argente, Round, Molded Rabbit, 31 x 31 In. 800
Mirror, Tiger Maple, Rectangular, Molded Frame, 1800s, 24 x 29 In. 210
Mirror, Tin, Pediment, Scrolled, Thimble Drops, Drawer, Portraits, c.1900, 18 x 13 In. 240
Mirror, Tortoiseshell, Ebonized Wave Edge Molding, c.1900, 29 x 21 In. 1625
Mirror, Venetian Style, Etched, Beveled, Leaf Molded Crest, 47 x 25 In. 500
Mirror, Venetian Style, Shield Shape, Sprays, Beveled Edge, 31 x 18 In., Pair 1168
Mirror, Venetian Style, Tapered Shield, Cut Scalloping, Leaf Sprays, 47 x 22 In. 492
Mirror, Venetian, Cut, Engraved Flowers, Basket, Beveled, c.1940, 60 x 35 In. 1845
Mirror, Venetian, Etched Glass, Beveled, Beaded, Leaf Crest, 48 x 28 In. .... *illus* 549
Mirror, Venetian, Etched, Oval, Beveled, Heart Crest, Leaf Cut Plate Border, 61 x 35 In. 861
Mirror, Walnut, Etched Daisy Accents, Metallic Gold Inlay, Gallery Top, 51 x 66 In. 300
Mirror, Wood Frame, Reverse Painted Glass, Church, Smoke Design, 1800s, 20 x 12 In. 514
Mirror, Wood, Arched Crest, Attached Antlers & Horns Frame, c.1975, 68 x 34 In. 660
Mirror, Wood, Ebonized, Gilt, Carved, Leaves, Shelf, Beaded Rim, Victorian, 30 x 12 In. 71
Mirror, Wood, Silver Paint, Carved Swag, Ribbons, c.1900, 45 x 27 In. 325
Ottoman, Barcelona, Mies Van Der Rohe, Leather, Stainless Steel, 1990s, 25 x 23 In. 2000
Ottoman, Dakota Jackson, Pincushion, c.1990, 20 x 32 In. 180
Ottoman, Empire, Rolled Feet, 1800s, 22 x 31 In. 105
Ottoman, J.L. Moller, 18 x 19 In. 99
Ottoman, Kilim Upholstery, Padded, Hinged, Interior Storage, Bun Feet, c.1890, 21 x 36 In. 799
Ottoman, Octagonal, Skirted, Tufted, 15 ½ x 37 In. 270
Ottoman, Woven, Rolled Feet, Mackenzie Childs, 25 x 23 In. 83
Overmantel Mirror, see Architectural category.
Parlor Set, Louis XV Style, Giltwood, Flower Carved Crests, Upholstered, Sofa, 4 Chairs 1250
Pedestal, Art Nouveau, Rosewood, Fruitwood, Flower Branch Inlay, Shelves, 47 x 14 In. 984
Pedestal, Blackamoor, Carved, Multicolor, Giltwood, Scalloped Top, 31 x 16 In. 1750

Furniture, Mirror, Pier, Carved, Giltwood, Rosette Corners, c.1810, 49 x 29 In.
$610

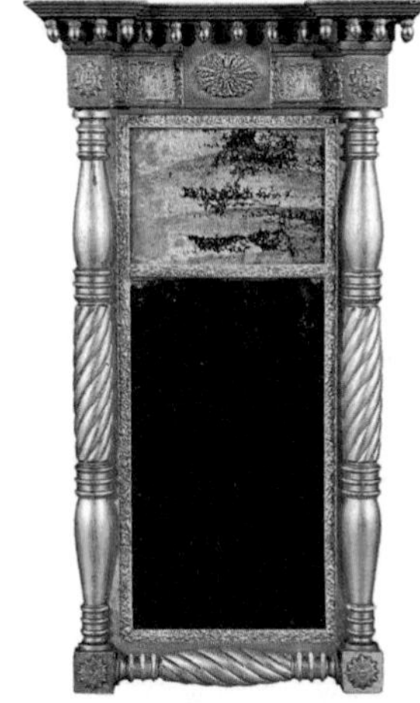

Neal Auctions

Furniture, Mirror, Venetian, Etched Glass, Beveled, Beaded, Leaf Crest, 48 x 28 In.
$549

DuMouchelles Art Gallery

Furniture, Pedestal, Marble, Gilt Bronze Mounts, 19th Century, 41 x 12 In.
$978

Cottone Auctions

F

Furniture, Pedestal, Neogrecque, Walnut, Ebonized, Incised, Gilt, Kilian Brothers, c.1890, 41 In.
$3,798

Neal Auctions

Furniture, Pie Safe, Cherry, Punched Tin, 16 Pinwheels, Gallery Back, 1800s, 64 x 42 In.
$3,186

Hess Auction Group

Furniture, Pie Safe, Mixed Wood, Punched Tin Panels, Drawers, Shelves, 1800s, 57 x 38 In.
$413

Hess Auction Group

Pedestal, Chrome, Cylindrical, P. Mayen, c.1970, 44¾ x 12 In. 333
Pedestal, French Provincial, Walnut, Wine Press Screw, Carved, 1800s, 48 x 10½ In. 185
Pedestal, French Provincial, Walnut, Wine Press Screw, Octagonal Base, 52 x 14 In. 400
Pedestal, Gilt Bronze, Porcelain, Onyx, Square Revolving Top, Bird, c.1900, 44 In. 2375
Pedestal, Giltwood, Carved Fruit & Scroll, Tapered Standard, Fluted, Putto, 1600s, 59 In. 1500
Pedestal, Greek Revival, Cypress, Carved, Tapered Doric Form, Louisiana, 34 x 12 In. 308
Pedestal, Ivory Veneered, Ebonized, Glass Top, Shields, Helmets, c.1890, 19 x 46 In. 3750
Pedestal, Louis XV Style, Gilt Bronze, Figured Marble, Hercules Mask, c.1890, 47 In. 1121
Pedestal, Marble, Carved, Doric Column, Ring Turned, 1900s, 39½ x 10 In. 593
Pedestal, Marble, Fluted Column, Egg & Dart Base, Gilt, 37 x 11 In. 246
Pedestal, Marble, Gilt Bronze Mounts, 19th Century, 41 x 12 In. ....*illus* 978
Pedestal, Modern, Lucite Case, 3 Wood Tiers, 25 x 12 In. 71
Pedestal, Neoclassical Style, Alabaster, Carved, Ring Turned, France, c.1910, 43 x 11 In. 98
Pedestal, Neoclassical, Ebonized, Parcel Gilt, Marble Top, 43 x 13 In. 3000
Pedestal, Neogrecque, Walnut, Ebonized, Incised, Gilt, Kilian Brothers, c.1890, 41 In. ....*illus* 3798
Pedestal, Onyx, Gilt Bronze, Tapered Standard, Cove Molded, Shells, c.1910, 49 x 18 In. 2375
Pedestal, Triangular Glass Top, Iron, 3-Footed, 54½ In., Pair.......... 437
Pedestal, Victorian, Mahogany, Shell Frieze, Twisted Column, Garland, 37 x 15 In. 861
Pedestal, Wood Base, Papier-Mache Kneeling Blackamoor, Skirt, Gilt, c.1935, 20 In. 1353
Pedestal, Wood, Figural, Female Legs In Miniskirt, 38 x 15 In. 312
Pedestal, Wood, Paint, Carved, Shaped Top, Kettle Shape Base, Shelf, Gilt, c.1890, 48 In. 1168
Pew, Church, Oak, Embossed, Cutout Accents, Cross, Fleur-De-Lis, 25 x 40 In. 150
Pew, Pine, Spanish Colonial Style, Multicolor, c.1900, 26 x 122 In., Pair 1375
Pew, Pine, Spanish Colonial Style, Multicolor, c.1900, 28 x 124 In., Pair 2500
Pew, Pine, Spanish Colonial Style, Turned Slats, Multicolor, c.1900, 36 x 110 In. 250
Pie Safe, 2 Paneled Doors, Square Legs, 1800s, 70 x 41 In. 1408
Pie Safe, Cherry, 12 Punched Tin Panels, Circles, Cutout Feet, c.1880, 47 x 42 x 21 In. 720
Pie Safe, Cherry, Punched Tin, 16 Pinwheels, Gallery Back, 1800s, 64 x 42 In. ....*illus* 3186
Pie Safe, Door, 4 Diamond Shape Openings, c.1900, 27 x 15 In. 117
Pie Safe, Mixed Wood, 2 Doors, 6 Punched Tin Panels, Stars, Cutout Feet, 54 x 44 In. 660
Pie Safe, Mixed Wood, Punched Tin Panels, Drawers, Shelves, 1800s, 57 x 38 In. ....*illus* 413
Pie Safe, Poplar, Brown & Cream Paint, Punched Tin Panels, Glazed Doors, 76 In. ....*illus* 2040
Pie Safe, Walnut, 12 Punched Tin Panels, Stars, Drawer, Square Nails, 60 x 41 In. 930
Pie Safe, Walnut, Pine, Punched Tin Panels, Brown Paint, Backsplash, 1800s, 59 x 44 In. 1020
Pie Safe, Walnut, Punched Tin, Shelves, Drawer, 2 Doors, Tenn., c.1850, 46 x 42 In. ....*illus* 3540
Planter, Adirondack Twig, 28 x 14 In. 994
Planter, Louis XV Style, Cherry, Carved, Copper Lined, Stretcher Shelf, 30 x 37 In. 549
Rack, Baking, Iron, Brass Mounts, Scrolled Ironwork, Brass Wheat Shafts, 1900s, 84 x 85 In. 1375
Rack, Bread, French Provincial, Walnut, Carved, Turned Spindles, 1800s, 38 x 31 In. 956
Rack, Drying, Herb, Oak, Center Column, 3 Folding Arms, Spider Legs, 1800s, 60 In. 308
Rack, Drying, Softwood, 2 Sections, Hinged, Mortis, Pegged, 1800s, 50 x 32 In. 71
Rack, Drying, Softwood, Mortised, Pegged, Natural Finish, c.1810, 44 x 43 In. 201
Rack, Magazine, Art Deco, Chrome, Fred Farr, Red Bakelite Handle, Revere, 18 x 12 In. 225
Rack, Magazine, Iron, Openwork Leaves, Twist Handle, 20 x 13 In. 60
Rack, Quilt, Walnut, Arched Trestle Sides, Turned Rails, c.1890, 31 x 26 In. 122
Recamier, Regency, Square Scroll Back, 1 Scrolled Arm, Tapered Lobed Legs, 38 x 24 In. 461
Recamier, Rosewood, Carved Crest, Serpentine Seat, Closed Arms, c.1865, 37 x 37 In. 4674
Recamier, Scrolled Back, Flat Cabriole Legs, 38½ x 70 In. 307
Rocker, Adirondack Twig, Lacquer, Branches, Owl's-Eye Crest, Splat, 27 x 25 In. 108
Rocker, Arts & Crafts, Oak, Spindle Sides, 37 x 26 In. 99
Rocker, Bentwood, Ebonized, Oval Cane Back, Seat, Scroll Arms, Thonet, c.1890.......... 732
Rocker, Eames, Bikini, Mesh & Tweed, Rosewood, 1950s, 27½ x 18½ In. 605
Rocker, Hans Olsen, 1963, 38½ x 35 In. 375
Rocker, L. & J.G. Stickley, Oak, 5 Vertical Slats, Upholstered Seat, 1900s, 32 x 18 In. 60
Rocker, Maison Jansen, Chrome Tubing, Black, c.1960s, 42½ x 23 In. 968
Rocker, Quartersawn Oak, Carved, Shieldback, Carved Putti, Oak Leaf, Arms, 39 x 31 In. 132
Rocker, Rustic, Twig, Woven, Brown, 32¼ x 40½ In. 270
Rocker, Shaker, Tiger Maple, Ladder Back, Arms, Mushroom Caps, c.1820, 45 In. ....*illus* 2640
Rocker, Square Crest, Carved Splat, Landscape, Upholstered Seat, c.1890.......... 344
Rocker, V. Kagan, Sculpted Walnut, Upholstered, 1970s, 39 x 32 In. 6250
Rocker, Windsor, Comb & Sack Back, Black Paint, New England, 42 In. ....*illus* 708
Rocker, Yellow Paint, Stenciled Fruit, Mahogany Arms, Grain Painted Seat, c.1830, 45 In. 277
Room Divider, Blackened Steel, Mahogany, Signed, Albert Paley, 1991, 84 x 138 In. 22500
Room Divider, Le Corbusier, Plastic Drawers, France, c.1956, 59½ x 70 In. 10000
Screen, 2-Panel, Lacquered, Mother-Of-Pearl, Peacocks, Landscape, Japan, c.1890, 70 x 67 In. . 780
Screen, 3-Panel, Art Deco, Fountain & Flowers, Carved, Painted, 84 x 72 In. 2272

Furniture, Pie Safe, Poplar, Brown & Cream Paint, Punched Tin Panels, Glazed Doors, 76 In. $2,040

Cowan Auctions

Furniture, Pie Safe, Walnut, Punched Tin, Shelves, Drawer, 2 Doors, Tenn., c.1850, 46 x 42 In. $3,540

Case Auctions

Furniture, Rocker, Shaker, Tiger Maple, Ladder Back, Arms, Mushroom Caps, c.1820, 45 In. $2,640

Wright (Chicago)

Furniture, Rocker, Windsor, Comb & Sack Back, Black Paint, New England, 42 In. $708

Hess Auction Group

Furniture, Screen, 3-Panel, G. Stickley, Leather Inserts Over Slats, c.1905, 69 x 65 In. $1,875

Rago Arts and Auction Center

Furniture, Screen, 3-Panel, Leather, Scene, Man, 2 Maidens, Castle, 1800s, 54 x 68 In. $711

James D. Julia Auctioneers

Furniture, Screen, Table, Hardwood, Porcelain, Frame, River, Openwork Scrolls, c.1900, 18 x 29 In. $5,843

Skinner, Inc.

Furniture, Secretary, Maple, Walnut, Inlay, Carved, Fruit Pulls, Shelves, Ohio, c.1890, 88 In. $1,046

Cowan Auctions

F

Furniture, Secretary, Roll Top, 2 Sections, Arched Crest, Glass Doors, c.1890, 108 x 45 In.
$1,778

James D. Julia Auctioneers

Furniture, Server, Federal, Mahogany, Carved, Divided Drawer, Brass Pulls, c.1818, 36 x 33 In.
$1,968

Skinner, Inc.

Furniture, Server, Sheraton, Mahogany, Bird's-Eye Maple, Inlay, New Eng., c.1815, 50 In.
$1,020

Garth's Auctioneers & Appraisers

Screen, 3-Panel, Canvas, Chinoiserie Style, Cockerel, Flowers, Carved, c.1910, 83 x 72 In. 937
Screen, 3-Panel, G. Stickley, Leather Inserts Over Slats, c.1905, 69 x 65 In. .... *illus* 1875
Screen, 3-Panel, Leather, Scene, Man, 2 Maidens, Castle, 1800s, 54 x 68 In. .... *illus* 711
Screen, 3-Panel, Louis XV Style, Fruitwood, Carved, Tapestry Panels, Rocaille, 78 x 75 In. 1353
Screen, 3-Panel, Marvin Arenson, Aluminum, Impressed, Fish, Plants, c.1950, 72 x 62 In. 3025
Screen, 3-Panel, Marvin Arenson, Folding, Painted 600
Screen, 3-Panel, Victorian, Leather, Bouquet, Urn, Brass Studded, c.1900, 69 x 67 In. 500
Screen, 4-Panel, French Toile, Red, White, 58 x 56 In. 120
Screen, 4-Panel, Fringe, Damask, Burlap, Salmon, c.1985, 71 x 96 In. 660
Screen, 4-Panel, Leather, Landscape, Arched Top, Women, Farming, Ducks, 69 x 70 In. 968
Screen, 4-Panel, Marionettes, Yellow, Fornasetti, Italy, c.1950, 51 x 56 In. 1560
Screen, 4-Panel, Neoclassical Style, Shaped Crest, Painted, 1900s, 84 x 28 In. 1845
Screen, 4-Panel, Red Lacquer, Painted Birds, Trees, Palace, Chinese, c.1950, 72 In. 600
Screen, 6-Panel, Chinese Court Scene, Figures, Black Lacquer, 84 x 94 ½ In. 420
Screen, 6-Panel, Eames, Walnut, c.1957, 34 ¼ x 57 ¾ In. 1458
Screen, 6-Panel, Prunus Branches, Gold Leaf Paper, Ink, 1900s, 37 x 80 ¾ In. 461
Screen, 8-Panel, Ebonized Wood Panels, Dragon, Floral, Bird, 96 In. 500
Screen, Baroque, Leatherette, Brass Bosses, Serpentine Top, Scrollwork, 67 x 67 In. 922
Screen, French Aubusson, Tapestry, Gilt, 44 ¼ x 25 ¼ In. 976
Screen, Gilt, Silk Brocade, Wreath Crest, Fluted Uprights, c.1850, 41 x 26 In. 750
Screen, Jade, Pierced, Immortal Figure, Gilt Calligraphy, 26 x 19 In. 1100
Screen, Pole, Shield Shape, Mahogany, Fabric, Tripod Base, c.1840, 59 In. 120
Screen, Regency, Mahogany Frame, Caster Feet, Jacquard Panel, c.1810, 39 x 22 In. 94
Screen, Table, Hardwood, Porcelain, Frame, River, Openwork Scrolls, c.1900, 18 x 29 In. ... *illus* 5843
Screens are also listed in the Architectural and Fireplace categories.
Secretary, Biedermeier, Drop Front, Figured Walnut, Austria, c.1830, 56 x 41 ½ In. 472
Secretary, Biedermeier, Roll Top, Birch, 2 Part, 84 x 47 ½ In. 1140
Secretary, Chippendale, Drop Front, Mahogany, Doors, Drawers, 89 x 40 In. 384
Secretary, Corner, Blue, 4 Doors, 6 Drawers, Norway, 76 x 37 In. 594
Secretary, Cornice, 2 Glass Doors, 2 Wood Doors, 43 x 23 In. 585
Secretary, Drop Front, Chinoiserie, Glass Doors, Maddox Of Jamestown, 78 x 32 In. 1200
Secretary, Eastlake, Walnut, Pine, 2 Glass Doors, 2 2-Paneled Doors, 86 In. 450
Secretary, Empire Style, Drop Front, Mahogany, Ebonized, Drawer, c.1850, 61 x 41 In. 1845
Secretary, Empire Style, Drop Front, Mahogany, Marble Top, 56 x 38 In. 676
Secretary, Empire, Drop Front, Poplar, 2 Paneled Doors, 2 Drawers, 75 x 40 In. 648
Secretary, George III, Drop Front, Mahogany, Glazed Doors, 1700s, 87 x 42 In. 1722
Secretary, Louis Philippe, Drop Front, Rosewood, Carved, Gallery, 1800s, 48 x 35 In. 458
Secretary, Mahogany, Paneled Doors, Interior Shelves, c.1800, 86 x 42 In. 660
Secretary, Maple, Walnut, Inlay, Carved, Fruit Pulls, Shelves, Ohio, c.1890, 88 In. .... *illus* 1046
Secretary, Neoclassical, Roll Top, Mahogany, Jacob Style, Glazed Doors, 93 x 48 In. 5658
Secretary, Painted, Shaped Cornice, Cabinet, Fitted Interior, Drawers, 1700s, 88 x 46 In. 1560
Secretary, Pine, 2 Glazed Doors, 5 Drawers, England, 80 ½ x 38 In. 351
Secretary, Regency Style, Drop Front, Mahogany, Glass Doors, 1800s, 92 x 47 In. 923
Secretary, Renaissance Revival, Rosewood, Cylinder, Paneled Doors, c.1875, 64 x 35 In. 1000
Secretary, Rococo, Cream Paint, Flowers, Shell Carved Crest, 3 Drawers, 64 ½ x 45 In. 1586
Secretary, Roll Top, 2 Sections, Arched Crest, Glass Doors, c.1890, 108 x 45 In. .... *illus* 1778
Secretary, Roll Top, Rosewood, Broken-Arch Pediment, Doors, c.1865, 103 x 48 In. 1845
Secretary, Rosewood, Bonnet Top, Finials, Doors, Scalloped Mirrors, c.1865, 75 x 34 In. 2952
Secretary, Slant Front, Mahogany, 2 Parts, Projecting Cornice, Pillars, c.1825, 97 x 54 In. 1107
Secretary, Slant Front, Mahogany, Gallery, Urn, Cupboard, Warrior, c.1790, 69 x 46 In. 1230
Secretary, Widdicomb, Birch, 6 Drawers, 7 Letter Slots, 1989, 60 x 41 In. 726
Semainier, Giltwood, Mirrored, 7 Drawers, 49 x 20 In. 330
Server, Anglo-Colonial, Hardwood, Gallery, Drawers, Doors, 1800s, 52 x 68 In. 1722
Server, Baroque, 2 Paneled Drawers, Turned Trestle Shape Base, 36 x 66 In. 2242
Server, Cherry, Scrolled Backsplash, Frieze Drawer, Turned Ball Feet, 1800s, 33 x 39 In. 429
Server, Edwardian, Adam Style, Mahogany, Urn, Swag Carved Frieze, c.1900, 37 x 67 In. 1180
Server, Empire Style, Fruitwood, Marble Top, Frieze Drawers, c.1890, 37 x 89 In. 2000
Server, Federal, Mahogany, Bird, Pullout, Bottle Drawers, c.1800, 41 x 44 In. 15990
Server, Federal, Mahogany, Carved, Divided Drawer, Brass Pulls, c.1818, 36 x 33 In. .... *illus* 1968
Server, Federal, Mahogany, Veneer, Lion Mask Pulls, c.1810, 36 x 37 In. 2360
Server, G. Stickley, Oak, 3 Drawers, Rivets, Hammered Iron, Brand Mark, 40 x 48 In. 1800
Server, Mahogany, Carved, Molded Top, Drawers, Ball Feet, c.1810, 34 x 37 In. 956
Server, Mahogany, Fruitwood, Drawers, Cupboard Doors, Star Inlay, Bracket Feet, 42 x 82 In. ... 2250
Server, Mahogany, Reeded Edge, 4 Drawers, Turned Reeded Legs, c.1810, 36 x 36 In. 4920
Server, Mahogany, Scrolled Backsplash, Drawer, Ring-Turned Legs, West Indies, 55 x 57 In. 2745
Server, Neoclassical, Mahogany, Figured Backboard, Scroll Sides, Drawers, 57 x 47 In. 799

Furniture, Settee, Chippendale, Mahogany, Ball & Claw Feet, Upholstered, 1800s, 53 x 56 In.
$1,200

Garth's Auctioneers & Appraisers

Furniture, Settee, Regency, Mahogany, Sleigh Shape Frame, Scroll Arms, c.1850, 32 x 55 In.
$922

New Orleans (Cakebread)

Furniture, Settee, Rolled Arms, Mahogany, Inlay, Paw Feet, Dutch, c.1850, 71 In.
$800

Skinner, Inc.

Furniture, Settee, Satinwood, Cane, Painted, Flowers, Reserves, England, 1800s, 33 x 53 In.
$1,673

Neal Auctions

Furniture, Sofa, Empire, Mahogany, Molded Back, Scroll Arms, Upholstery, 37 x 93 In.
$100

Hess Auction Group

Furniture, Sofa, G. Nelson, Marshmallow, Steel, Naugahyde, Herman Miller, 1956, 52 x 31 In.
$17,500

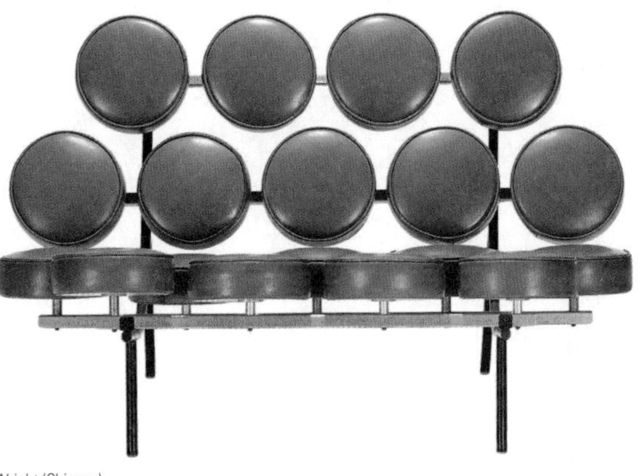

Wright (Chicago)

F

Furniture, Sofa, Mahogany, Carved, Scroll Arms, Upholstered, c.1830, 78 x 36 In.
$1,912

Neal Auctions

Furniture, Speaker, Charles & Ray Eames, Stephens Tru-Sonic, 1956, 29 x 23 x 16 In.
$3,750

Los Angeles Modern Auctions

Furniture, Stand, Corner, Pine, Marble Top, Carved, Gilt, Continental, c.1800, 32 x 20 In.
$570

Garth's Auctioneers & Appraisers

Furniture, Stand, Fruitwood, Gallery, Drawer, Cupboard, Hoof Feet, c.1890, 33 x 18 In.
$1,500

New Orleans (Cakebread)

Furniture, Stand, Magazine, Bamboo, Lacquer, Japan, c.1915, 33 x 16 In.
$461

New Orleans (Cakebread)

Furniture, Stand, Music, Wharton Esherick, Cherry, Sculpture, Carved, 1962, 44 x 20 In.
$26,250

Rago Arts and Auction Center

Furniture, Stand, Pedestal, Blue, 6 Graduated Wood Shelves, Tin Galleries, 62 x 24 In.
$189

Hess Auction Group

Furniture, Stand, Plant, 2 Tiers, Green Paint, 1800s, 28 x 46 In.
$767

Hess Auction Group

Server, Regency Style, Mahogany, D-Shape Top, Drawers, Grapevines, c.1900, 37 x 88 In. 3000
Server, Sheraton, Mahogany, Bird's-Eye Maple, Inlay, New Eng., c.1815, 50 In. .... *illus* 1020
Server, Wrought Iron, Linenfold, Doors, Long Drawer, 1900s, 41 In. 1298
Settee, Bergere, Louis XV Style, Domed, Padded Back, Seat, Closed Arms, 32 In. 218
Settee, Biedermeier, Fruitwood, Cane Seat, Fanback, Scroll Arms, Tapered Legs, 35 x 50 In. 2596
Settee, Chinoiserie Style, Ebonized Wood, Gilt Accents, c.1800, 32 x 57 In. 861
Settee, Chippendale Style, Mahogany, Outscrolled Arms, Stretchers, 34 x 57 In., Pair 1080
Settee, Chippendale, Mahogany, Ball & Claw Feet, Upholstered, 1800s, 53 x 56 In. .... *illus* 1200
Settee, Empire Revival, Mahogany, Tablet Crest, Sleigh Arms, Upholstered, 34 x 89 In. 1185
Settee, Empire Style, Beech, Carved, Paw Feet, Triple Fiddleback, c.1910, 34 x 46 In. 492
Settee, Empire Style, Mahogany, Carved, Serpentine High Back, Scroll Arms, 48 x 55 In. 652
Settee, Empire, Mahogany, Horsehair Upholstery, Reeded Back Rail, c.1840, 34 x 63 In. 1680
Settee, Faux Bamboo, Turned Beech, Padded Seat, 2 Bolsters, c.1770, 79 In. 8750
Settee, Federal Style, Mahogany, Reeded Spindles, Downswept Arms, c.1900, 35 x 68 In. 1599
Settee, French Provincial, Louis Philippe, Cherry, Triple Back, Rush Seat, c.1850, 40 x 67 In. 305
Settee, French Provincial, Louis XVI Style, Oak, Carved, Instruments, Garlands, 63 x 48 In. 356
Settee, Fruitwood, Box Shape, Double Cane Back, Top Shape Feet, c.1890, 41 x 71 In. 1230
Settee, Fruitwood, Padded Back, Molded Frame, Scroll Arms, Fluted Legs, c.1805, 35 x 67 In. 812
Settee, Fruitwood, Padded, Outswept Sides, Panel Frame, Saber Legs, c.1850, 38 x 92 In. 4000
Settee, George III Style, Mahogany, Double Chairback, Chippendale, Crest, 39 In., Pair 2460
Settee, Hepplewhite, Mahogany, Curved Padded Back, Undulating Arms, c.1900, 35 x 63 In. 1107
Settee, Louis Philippe, Cherry, Triple Back, Tablet Crest, Arched Splats, Rush Seat, 67 In. 305
Settee, Louis XV Style, Cream Paint, Domed Back, Carved Crest, Arms, Upholstered, 38 x 76 In. 799
Settee, Louis XV Style, Giltwood, Carved Shells & Flowers, Upholstered, 43 x 58 x 23 In. 1045
Settee, Louis XVI Style, Beech, Cane Back & Sides, Upholstered, 41 x 71 x 30 In. 472
Settee, Louis XVI Style, Multicolor, Padded Back, Arms, Tapered Legs, c.1810, 36 x 50 In. 2952
Settee, Mahogany, Marquetry, Backswept Crest, Arms, Saber Legs, c.1900, 37 x 37 In. 687
Settee, Mahogany, Outscrolled Arms, H-Shape Stretchers, 1800s, 40 x 71 In. 1168
Settee, Neoclassical, Fruitwood, Parcel Gilt, Paint, Cane Back, Seat, Italy, 39 x 69 In., Pair 3690
Settee, Painted, Flowers, Mixed Wood, Half Spindles, Scroll Arms, c.1830, 33 x 76 In. 1750
Settee, Panel Frame, Flower Crest, Padded Back, Scroll Arms, Peg Feet, 1800s, 44 x 64 In. 1187
Settee, Ralph Lauren, Os De Mouton, Wing Back, Upholstered, c.1900, 50 x 56 In. 2151
Settee, Regency, Mahogany, Sleigh Shape Frame, Scroll Arms, c.1850, 32 x 55 In. .... *illus* 922
Settee, Renaissance Revival, Oak, Carved, Spindle Gallery, Paneled Back, c.1890, 58 x 73 In. 615
Settee, Restauration, Fruitwood, Paneled Back, Crest Rail, Closed Arms, c.1810, 34 x 61 In. 937
Settee, Rolled Arms, Mahogany, Inlay, Paw Feet, Dutch, c.1850, 71 In. .... *illus* 800
Settee, Satinwood, Cane, Painted, Flowers, Reserves, England, 1800s, 33 x 53 In. .... *illus* 1673
Settee, Victorian Style, Rosewood, Carved, Serpentine Back, Upholstered, 1900s, 36 x 59 In. 732
Settee, Walnut, Carved, Triple Serpentine Back, Bowed Seat, c.1890, 36 x 57 In. 492
Settee, Wendell Castle, Molar Group, White, Gel-Coated, c.1969, 26 x 49 In. 3932
Settee, Windsor, Raised Crest, Arms, Carved, Turned Stretchers, 31 x 82 In. 4425
Settle, Arrow Back, Half Spindle, Turned Legs, Black Paint, Stencil, 1800s, 34 x 72 In. 308
Settle, French Provincial, Pine, Carved Panels, Arms, 49 x 88 In. 431
Settle, George III, Oak, Arched Shape Panels, Cabriole Legs, 74 In. 394
Settle, George III, Oak, Mahogany, Crossbanded, Lozenge Detail, 34 x 66 In. 2334
Settle, William & Mary, Oak, Plank Top, 28 x 36½ In. 1556
Shelf, Bracket, Jigsaw Work, Dog, Ladder, Birds In Trees, Gold Paint, c.1910, 23 In., Pair 60
Shelf, Bracket, Regency, Giltwood, 10¾ x 10 In., Pair 275
Shelf, Corner, Mahogany, 2 Tiers, Curved Cabinet, Inlaid Doors, 1800s, 31½ In. 215
Shelf, Display, Mirror Back, Gilt, Exotic Tree, Scrolling Vine, Shelves, 67 x 24 In., Pair 6250
Shelf, Elm, Mortised Construction, 3 Shelves, Slab Sides, Scroll Carving, 69 x 77 In. 375
Shelf, George III, Figured Mahogany, Shaped Top, Bottom, Hanging, c.1800, 44 x 43 In. 531
Shelf, Hanging, Pine, Grain Painted, Shaped Sides, 4 Shelves, 2 Drawers, 44 x 28 In. 1230
Shelf, Hanging, Whale End, Pine, Bittersweet Paint, 4 Shelves, New England, 36 x 29 In. 420
Shelf, P. Evans, City Scape, Wall Mount, Chrome Steel, 1970s, 14 x 48 In. 1375
Shelf, Pine, Overhanging Top, Shelves, Blue Paint, Hanging, c.1910, 31 x 31 In. 410
Shelf, Sheraton Style, Mahogany, 3 Tiers, Molded, Turned Supports, Casters, 48 x 72 In. 266
Sideboard, Arts & Crafts, Beveled Mirror, Scrolled Supports, c.1900, 56 x 60 In. 305
Sideboard, Burl Walnut, Drawers, Side Doors, Scrolling, Bun Feet, 39 x 72 In. 354
Sideboard, Cherry, 3 Drawers, Brass Ring Pulls, Doors, Square Feet, 1970s, 34 x 58 In. 150
Sideboard, Curly Maple, Cherry, Pine, 5 Drawers, 4 Doors, c.1840, 54 x 78 In. 688
Sideboard, Directoire Style, Shelf, Gilt, Pierced Gallery, Fluted Spindles, 50 x 42 In. 403
Sideboard, Elm, Walnut, Rectangular Canted, Bracket Feet, 42 x 55 In. 738
Sideboard, Federal Style, Mahogany, Inlay, Serpentine, Veneer, 1900s, 39 x 65 In. 1298
Sideboard, Finn Juhl, Sliding Doors, Basket Weave, 5 Legs, 1956, 78 x 18 In. 3750
Sideboard, Flame Mahogany Veneer, Silver & Linen Drawers, 39 x 73 In. 620

Furniture, Stand, Portfolio, Rosewood, Reticulated, Brass, Ratchet, c.1850, 39 In.
$2,390

Neal Auctions

TIP
Put a little furniture polish on a damp cloth when you dust wooden furniture. You won't have to polish as often.

Furniture, Stand, Rootwood, 3 Display Areas, 1800s, 18 x 12 In.
$711

James D. Julia Auctioneers

Furniture, Stand, Shaker, Cherry, Cast Steel Plate, Tripod, Round Top, Tapered Stem, 24 x 15 In.
$12,000

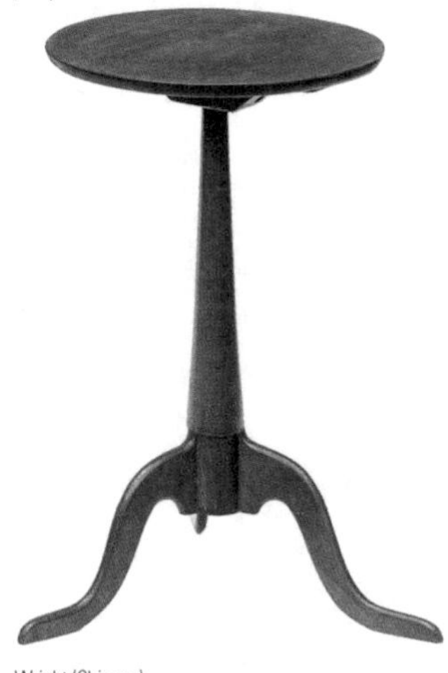

Wright (Chicago)

TIP

A paste made of instant coffee crystals and water can be used to "paint" a scratch on dark furniture.

Furniture, Stand, Sheraton, Tiger Maple, Single-Board Top, Drawer, c.1830, 27 x 19 In.
$978

Cottone Auctions

Furniture, Stool, Flemish Style, Mahogany, Padded Top, Turned Legs, c.1910, 21 x 28 In.
$500

New Orleans (Cakebread)

Furniture, Stool, V. Kagan, Steel, Enamel, Upholstery, Triangular Seat, 1970s, 16 In., Pair
$5,313

Rago Arts and Auction Center

Sideboard, French Empire, Metal Mounted, Granite Top, 36 ½ x 97 ¾ In. 732
Sideboard, French Provincial, Walnut, Carved, Drawers, c.1850, 44 x 60 In. 415
Sideboard, George III, Mahogany, Satinwood Inlay, 3 Drawers, c.1775, 36 x 72 In. 3025
Sideboard, Hepplewhite, Mahogany, Fruitwood Inlay, 35 x 51 In. 840
Sideboard, Louis Philippe, Cherry, Drawers, Cupboard Doors, Plinth Base, 1800x, 41 x 54 In. 1067
Sideboard, Louis Philippe, Cherry, Marble Top, Drawers, Cupboards, c.1850, 42 x 59 In. 592
Sideboard, Louis XIII Style, Walnut, Carved, Drawers, Iron Hinges, c.1830, 46 x 54 In. 474
Sideboard, Louis XV Style, Cherry, Inlay, Carved, Serpentine Top, Paneled Doors, 39 x 82 In. 385
Sideboard, Louis XV, French Provincial, Flowers, Leaves, Doors, 3 Drawers, 42 ¾ x 51 In. 510
Sideboard, Louis XVI, Walnut, 2 Fielded Panel Doors, Turned Legs, 39 x 59 In. 676
Sideboard, Mahogany, 2 Drawers, Turned Legs, Stretcher Shelf, c.1810, 12 x 12 In. 1225
Sideboard, Mahogany, 3 Drawers, 4 Doors, Rope Twist Columns, 1840s, 44 x 71 In. 290
Sideboard, Mahogany, Carved, Backsplash, Scroll Supports, c.1810, 57 x 73 In. 717
Sideboard, Mahogany, Drawers, Doors, Bottle Drawers, c.1825, 46 x 67 In. 1045
Sideboard, Mahogany, Inlay, Shaped Top, Incurved Cabinet Doors, Drawer, 37 x 69 In. 500
Sideboard, Mahogany, Pedestal, Stepped Top, Drawer, Door, c.1840, 60 x 97 In. 7072
Sideboard, Mahogany, Scroll Back, Carved, Figured Columns, c.1825, 56 x 61 In. 3444
Sideboard, McCobb, 4 Drawers, Metal Frame, Cane Shelf, Calvin Group, 30 x 48 In. 518
Sideboard, McCobb, Hanging Cabinet, 4 Black Leather Doors, 31 x 77 In. 1071
Sideboard, Neoclassical Revival, Quartersawn Oak, Mirror, Scroll Supports, c.1900, 53 x 60 In. 246
Sideboard, Oak, Carved, Display Shelf, Lower Cabinet, Scotland, 96 x 67 In. 620
Sideboard, Pine, Barley Twist, 3 Drawers, 2 Doors, 2 Shelves, 36 x 71 In. 363
Sideboard, Renaissance Revival, Fruitwood, Steer Skull, Drawers, Doors, c.1890, 43 x 63 In. 492
Sideboard, Server, Federal Style, Walnut, Doors, Drawers, 36 x 38 In. 1062
Sideboard, Sheraton Style, Bowfront, Mahogany, Drawers, Cabinet, c.1875, 37 x 60 In. 375
Sideboard, Teak, 2 Drawers, Cabinet Doors, Ring Pulls, Shelves, c.1970, 29 x 49 In. 138
Sideboard, Teak, Wegner, Sculpted, A-Frame, 6 Drawers, Shelves, Ry Mobler, 71 x 71 In. 2473
Sideboard, Walnut, 2 Parts, Carved Crest, Cartouche, Marble, Columns, c.1865, 81 x 66 In. 2952
Sideboard, Wegner, Sliding Doors, Basket Weave, 1965, 78 ¾ x 19 In. 5000
Sofa, Adrian Pearsall, Walnut, Slate, 1970s, 29 ½ x 85 ½ In. 431
Sofa, Camelback, Mahogany, Blue Velvet, Stretchers, Scroll Arms, 34 x 77 In. 150
Sofa, Camelback, Mahogany, Scroll Arms, Carved Rosettes, Serpentine Apron, 36 x 83 In. 1250
Sofa, Chesterfield, Leather, Brown, 75 x 34 In. 1188
Sofa, Chesterfield, Leather, Button Tufting, Brass Nailheads, Bun Feet, 27 x 76 In. 1064
Sofa, Chesterfield, Leather, Tufted, Brown, 80 x 32 In., Pair 2700
Sofa, Chesterfield, Sleeper, Aubergine Glaze Leathers, Tufting, 76 x 37 In. 431
Sofa, Chippendale Style, Camelback, Mahogany, Serpentine Front, 1900s, 35 x 84 In. 344
Sofa, Darrell Landrum, Wrought Iron, c.1955, Diamonds, Triangles, 26 x 84 In. 6683
Sofa, Dunbar, Button Tufted Bench, Rectangular, 1 Arm, 4-Footed, 29 x 81 In. 2975
Sofa, Empire, Mahogany, Molded Back, Scroll Arms, Upholstery, 37 x 93 In. ....*illus* 100
Sofa, Federal, Mahogany, Sheraton Style, Stepped Crest Rail, Arms, c.1800, 39 x 82 In. 1016
Sofa, French Style, Carved Wood, Leaf Scrolls, Shaped Crest Rail, 41 x 85 In. 1093
Sofa, G. Nelson, 3 Cushion, Metal Feet, Upholstered, Herman Miller, 82 x 32 In. 1035
Sofa, G. Nelson, Marshmallow, Steel, Naugahyde, Herman Miller, 1956, 52 x 31 In. ....*illus* 17500
Sofa, George III Style, Mahogany, Domed Back, Downswept Sides, Acanthus, 37 x 68 In. 625
Sofa, George III, Gilt, Husk Carved, Rosette, 8 Fluted Tapered Legs, 1780, 70 In. 10000
Sofa, Knoll Shape, Veraseta Rose Silk Damask Upholstery, Domed Back, 44 x 90 In. 922
Sofa, Louis XV Style, Paint, Parcel Gilt, Carved Crest, Guilloche, Scroll Arms, 40 x 59 In. 1722
Sofa, Louis XV, Walnut Frame, Mohair, Acanthus, Flowers, Scroll Arms, 82 In. 605
Sofa, Mahogany, Box Shape, Molded Crest Rail, Scroll Arms, Lyres, c.1835, 25 x 87 In. 1000
Sofa, Mahogany, Bronze, Tubular Crest Rail, Upright Columns, 1800s, 34 x 84 In. 1076
Sofa, Mahogany, Carved Crest, Scroll Arms, Cornucopia Paw Feet, c.1825, 35 x 85 In. 1230
Sofa, Mahogany, Carved, Cylindrical Crest Rail, Acantine Scrolls, Dolphin Arms, 34 x 91 In. 1952
Sofa, Mahogany, Carved, Scroll Arms, Upholstered, c.1830, 78 x 36 In. ....*illus* 1912
Sofa, McCobb, 3 Cushions, Arms, c.1960, 98 In. 2812
Sofa, Midcentury, Quilted Brown Leather, Low Profile Arms, 6 Chrome Legs, 32 x 88 In. 968
Sofa, Midcentury, Scrolled, Padded Back, Low Arms, 4-Cushion Back, Velvet, 26 x 97 In. 726
Sofa, Milo Baughman, Chrome, Flat Bar, Upholstered, Selig, c.1960, 85 x 32 In. 1003
Sofa, Milo Baughman, Tufted, Naugahyde, c.1970s, 90 x 23 In. 544
Sofa, Milo Baughman, Vinyl, Tapered Wood Legs, Thayer Coggin, 1960s, 29 x 76 In. 748
Sofa, Peter Hvidt, Midcentury Modern, Collapsible Arms, Upholstered 1464
Sofa, Risom, Blue Green Scrim Upholstery, Tufted Back, Label, 1960s, 32 x 78 In. 2360
Sofa, Risom, Midcentury Modern, U-251, Upholstered, Walnut, 1955, 33 x 52 In. 649
Sofa, Rococo Revival, Rosewood, Serpentine, Carved Crest, Cabriole Legs, c.1850, 43 x 78 In. 2337
Sofa, V. Kagan, Bilbao, Serpentine Shape Seat, Orange, 38 x 95 In. 2299
Sofa, V. Kagan, Modern, Sectional, Omnibus, 2 Sections, Upholstered 4880

Sofa, V. Kagan, Shorty, Stainless Steel, Microfiber, 2000s, 29 x 98 In. 8125
Sofa, Wegner, Johannes Hansen, Chrome Steel, Upholstered, 1980s, 27 x 85 In. 2500
Sofa, Widdicomb, Oriental Style, 3 Cushion, Low Back, Arms, 80 In. 1320
Sofa, Wormley, La Gondola, c.1957, 84 In. 8125
Sofa, Wormley, Walnut, Upholstered, 1960s, 31 x 86 In. 1188
Speaker, Charles & Ray Eames, Stephens Tru-Sonic, 1956, 29 x 23 x 16 In. .... *illus* 3750
Stand, Boxwood Inlay, 3 Drawers, Ormolu Accents, Drawer Pulls, France, 29 x 14 In. 207
Stand, Cabinet, 3 Drawers, Pedestal Base, Kent Coffey, Pair 600
Stand, Cherry, 3 Graduated Drawers, Turned Legs, Blown Glass Pulls, 1840, 29 x 26 In. 300
Stand, Corner, Pine, Marble Top, Carved, Gilt, Continental, c.1800, 32 x 20 In. .... *illus* 570
Stand, Drawer, Cherry, Blue Paint, Square, Oval Corners, Tapered Legs, c.1800, 27 x 18 x In. 676
Stand, Empire Style, Mahogany, Carved, Marble Top, Drawer, 30 x 17 In. 504
Stand, Federal, Tiger Maple, 2 Drawers, Pa., c.1810, 29 x 22 In. 531
Stand, Federal, Tiger Maple, Shaped Top, Turreted Corners, Drawers, c.1800, 28 x 17 In. 2032
Stand, Figured Hardwood, 2 Tiers, Quin Dynasty, Chinese, 33 In. 2596
Stand, Fishbowl, Green Glass, 2 Lamps, Lozenge Shape, Asian Scenes, 48 x 24 In. 562
Stand, Flower, George III, Satinwood, Inlay, 3 Tiers, Glass Wells, 42 x 25 ¾ In., Pair 8125
Stand, Folio, Renaissance Revival, Walnut, 2 Tiers, Ebonized, Pierced, c.1890, 50 x 23 In. 1067
Stand, Folio, Walnut, Turned Adjustable Supports, c.1890, 47 x 31 In. 1121
Stand, French Empire, Mahogany, Marble Top, Carved, Drawer, 30 x 16 In. 584
Stand, Fruitwood, Gallery, Drawer, Cupboard, Hoof Feet, c.1890, 33 x 18 In. .... *illus* 1500
Stand, H. Probber, Ebony, Brass, 1 Drawer, Doors, 25 ½ x 36 In., Pair 968
Stand, Jardiniere, Hardwood, Round Marble Top, Pierced Apron, Dragons, 1800s, 19 In. 389
Stand, Jardiniere, Louis XVI, Ormolu Mounted, Mahogany, Gallery, 17 x 25 In. 8750
Stand, Kettle, George III, Mahogany, Round Dish Top, Ring-Turned Stem, c.1790, 24 In. 937
Stand, Lamp, Marquetry, Tilt Top, Inlaid Figures, Nighttime Sky, Spiral Base, 29 In. 237
Stand, Lectern, Venice Style, Walnut, Carved, Tripod Base, 53 x 24 In. 360
Stand, Louis Philippe, Cherry, Carved, Drawer, Cupboard Door, Bracket Feet, 33 x 17 In. 148
Stand, Louis Philippe, Walnut, Marble, Carved, Drawers, Plinth Base, 1800s, 35 x 15 In. 119
Stand, Magazine, Bamboo, Lacquer, Japan, c.1915, 33 x 16 In. .... *illus* 461
Stand, Mahogany, Marble Top, Pierced Brass Gallery, Bulbous Legs, c.1810, 28 x 19 In. 937
Stand, McCobb, Drawer, Shelf, Black Metal Legs, c.1950, 22 x 18 In., Pair 625
Stand, Midcentury, Walnut Veneer, Mayan, Tribal Pulls, Bassett, 1960s, 45 x 40 In., Pair 272
Stand, Music, Edwardian, Lyre, Inlay, Cornucopia, Flowers, 32 In. 154
Stand, Music, Victorian, 51 x 27 ¾ In. 277
Stand, Music, Wharton Esherick, Cherry, Sculpture, Carved, 1962, 44 x 20 In. .... *illus* 26250
Stand, Neoclassical Style, Giltwood, Carved, Round Marble Top, Scroll Feet, c.1890, 16 In. 5250
Stand, Parzinger, Mahogany, Green Lacquer, Cabinet, Brass, 1960s, 22 x 21 In., Pair 4500
Stand, Pedestal, Blue, 6 Graduated Wood Shelves, Tin Galleries, 62 x 24 In. .... *illus* 189
Stand, Plant, 2 Tiers, Green Paint, 1800s, 28 x 46 In. .... *illus* 767
Stand, Plant, Art Deco, Forged Iron Bowl, Acanthus, Signed, Paul Kiss, Paris, 29 In. 3304
Stand, Plant, Black & White Marble Top, Painted Cast Iron Base, c.1910, 22 ½ In. 120
Stand, Plant, Eastlake Style, Pedestal, Scrolled Pillars, 3-Part Base, 58 x 16 In. 277
Stand, Plant, Green Onyx, Gilt Metal, Beadwork, Greek Key Band, Leaf Apron, c.1900, 44 In. 615
Stand, Plant, Napoleon III, Burl, Ebonized, Oval Top, Gilt Gargoyles, c.1875, 34 In. 937
Stand, Plant, Oak, Round, Turned Stem, Carved Swirling Leaves, Tripod Base, 38 x 20 In. 780
Stand, Plant, Rosewood, Pierced Frieze & Stretcher, Molded Feet, 1900s, 41 x 17 In., Pair 1125
Stand, Plant, Wrought Iron, Copper Basin, Painted, 47 x 14 In., Pair 552
Stand, Plant, Wrought Iron, Rose, Branch, 45 x 18 In. 180
Stand, Portfolio, Adjustable Slatted Rack, Turned Supports, Casters, 45 ½ x 26 In. 1000
Stand, Portfolio, Mahogany, Slatted Rack, Baluster Stem, Arched Legs, c.1850, 44 x 29 In. 1348
Stand, Portfolio, Rosewood, Reticulated, Brass, Ratchet, c.1850, 39 In. .... *illus* 2390
Stand, Rootwood, 3 Display Areas, 1800s, 18 x 12 In. .... *illus* 711
Stand, Rosewood, Serpentine Marble Top, Cupboard, Flowers, Ormolu, 1900s, 34 x 18 In., Pair. 1187
Stand, Scan Coll, Rosewood, Shaped Top, Pullout Shelf, Drawers, Denmark, 29 x 21 In., Pair 363
Stand, Shaker, Cherry, Cast Steel Plate, Tripod, Round Top, Tapered Stem, 24 x 15 In. .... *illus* 12000
Stand, Shaving, French Empire, Metal, Oval Swivel Mirror, Dolphin, Tray, 50 ½ In. 156
Stand, Shaving, Queen Anne Style, Mahogany, 3 Drawer, Adjustable Mirror, 1800s, 26 x 20 In. .. 236
Stand, Sheraton, Cherry, Maple, Square Top, Drawer, Turned Legs, c.1820, 27 x 21 In. 415
Stand, Sheraton, Drawer, Yellow, New England, 1800s, 38 x 17 In. 321
Stand, Sheraton, Tiger Maple, Single-Board Top, Drawer, c.1830, 27 x 19 In. .... *illus* 978
Stand, Smoking, Art Deco, Penguin Pedestal, Garret Thew, c.1929, 21 ¾ In. 132
Stand, Smoking, Arts & Crafts, Hammered, Ashtray, Candleholder, Snuffer, 25 x 10 In. 65
Stand, Smoking, Carved, High Relief Man In Medallion, Drawer, 34 x 15 In. 272
Stand, Smoking, Hammered Bronze, Cast, Marble Top, 1800s, 28 x 16 In. 240
Stand, Tripod, George II, Mahogany, Piecrust Rim, Reeded Stem, 1800s, 22 x 14 In. 5535

Furniture, Stool, Wharton Esherick, Hickory, Redgum, Cherry, Signed, 1962, 17 x 12 ½ In.
$8,125

Rago Arts and Auction Center

Furniture, Table, Bamboo, Chinese, Wood Top, 1800s, 22 x 10 In.
$59

James D. Julia Auctioneers

Furniture, Table, Center, Mahogany, Marble, Carved, Dog, Cincinnati, c.1875, 42 In.
$420

Cowan Auctions

TIP

Try the new electrostatic dust cloths to remove dust from waxed and polished furniture.

Furniture, Table, Center, Renaissance Revival, Walnut, Marble, Trestle, c.1870, 30 x 42 In.
$3,081

James D. Julia Auctioneers

Furniture, Table, Coffee, Art Deco Style, Chrome, Maple, Plate Glass, 2 Tiers, 18 x 47 x 26 In.
$468

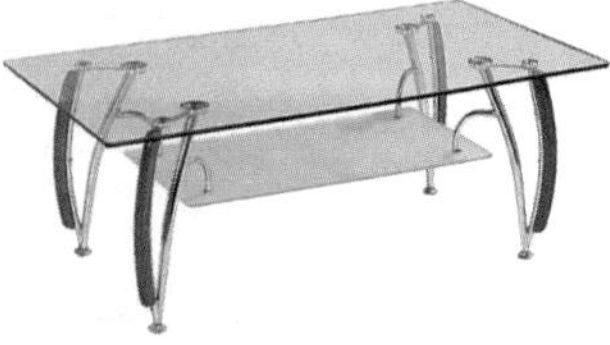

New Orleans (Cakebread)

Furniture, Table, Coffee, G. Nakashima, Walnut, Rosewood, Plank Top, 1988, 15 x 50 In.
$18,750

Rago Arts and Auction Center

Furniture, Table, Coffee, P. Evans, Cityscape, Burl, Brass, Glass, 1970s, 16 x 42 In.
$3,936

New Orleans (Cakebread)

TIP

Rotate your dining room, kitchen, and coffee table on your birthday. If you remember to do this each year the furniture will fade evenly.

Stool, Curly Maple, Alligatored, C-Scroll Legs, c.1840, 10 x 17 In., Pair 344
Stool, Drafting, Wendell Castle, Laminated Walnut, Suede, Carved, 1977, 46 x 17 In. 5938
Stool, Flemish Style, Mahogany, Padded Top, Turned Legs, c.1910, 21 x 28 In. .... *illus* 500
Stool, Francis Mair, Wicker, Iron Frame, Round, 1960s, 17 x 15 In., Pair 276
Stool, Fruitwood, Padded Seat, Leaf Carved Apron, Cabriole Legs, Stretchers, 19 x 47 In. 468
Stool, George II, Mahogany, Drop-In Seat, Cabochon Carved Legs, 17 x 23 In. 1250
Stool, Gout, Wood Spindles, Folding, Black Paint, 21 x 19 In. 60
Stool, Laboratory, Chrome, Adjustable, 1950s, 25 In. 162
Stool, Louis XV Style, Padded, Shaped Apron, Cabriole Legs, Scrolled Toes, 13 x 14 In. 615
Stool, Mahogany, Bowed Seat, Lattice Sides, Inlay, Vase, X-Frame, c.1890, 22 In. 235
Stool, Mahogany, George II, Upholstered, Cabriole Legs, Paw Feet, c.1750, 19 x 22 In. 625
Stool, Oak, Carved, Box Joint, Figural Mask, Compartment, Splayed Legs, 17 x 18 In., Pair 800
Stool, Oak, Dished Seat, Octagonal Baluster Legs, Mouse, Block Feet, c.1928, 15 x 16 In. 2555
Stool, Oak, Plank Seat, Carved Frieze, Splayed Legs, Lift Top, Interior, 1600s, 17 x 19 In. 523
Stool, P. Evans, Patchwork, Torchcut, Welded, Steel, Upholstered, 1960s, 28 ½ x 16 In. 6875
Stool, Regency Style, Giltwood, Curved Legs, Stretcher, Upholstered, 20 x 19 In. 2337
Stool, Regency, Oak, X-Frame, Cane Seat, Overscrolled Ends, Paterae, Bun Feet, 17 x 21 In. 4325
Stool, Rococo Style, Giltwood, Scroll Arms, 4 Carved Putti, Cabriole Legs, 28 In. 1500
Stool, Sori Yanagi, White, 3-Legged, 1954, 15 x 20 In., Pair 1875
Stool, Table, Knoll, Midcentury Modern, Wire, Wood, Stacking, 4 Piece 1100
Stool, Tove & Edvard Kindt-Larsen, Wood, Leather, Round, Open Back, 25 In., 3 Piece 11500
Stool, Tripod, Inlaid Oak & Leaf, Turned Legs, 14 In. 11
Stool, Tudor Style, Jointed, Shaped Apron, Splayed Legs, Stretcher, 19 x 18 In., Pair 677
Stool, V. Kagan, Brass, Triangle Shape, Upholstered, 1900s, 15 ¾ x 21 In., Pair 847
Stool, V. Kagan, Steel, Enamel, Upholstery, Triangular Seat, 1970s, 16 In., Pair .... *illus* 5313
Stool, Walnut, Mortise Legs, Shaped Scalloped Skirt, 1800s, 7 x 14 In. 236
Stool, Wharton Esherick, Hickory, Redgum, Cherry, Signed, 1962, 17 x 12 ½ In. .... *illus* 8125
Stool, Windsor, Black, Oval Seat, Bamboo Turning, Stretchers, Pa., 1800s, 21 x 15 In. 1180
Table Base, Modern, Cast Aluminum, Stylized Woman's Crossed Legs, Bent Knees, 16 x 17 In. .. 581
Table, Aalto, Bentwood, White, Shelf, Finland, 1932, 23 x 23 ½ In., Pair 1375
Table, Aesthetic Revival, G. Viardot, Inlay, Walnut, Rosewood, 2 Tiers, c.1910, 29 x 21 In. 308
Table, Alabaster, Round, Lobed Urn, 21 ¼ x 16 ½ In. 338
Table, Altar, Hardwood, Carved, Stylized Bats, Clouds, Drawers, 15 x 62 In. 295
Table, Altar, Hardwood, Paneled Top, Scrolled Ends, Shaped Skirt, Chinese, 37 x 49 In. 17700
Table, Altar, Huanghuali, Scroll Ends, Pierced Apron, Dragons, Pearl, 1800s, 33 x 49 In. 2727
Table, Altar, Huanghuali, Upturned Ends, Molded Edges, Ruyi Brackets, 32 x 45 In. 5844
Table, Altar, Pine, Shaped Apron, Stretchers, Red Lacquer, Chinese, c.1900, 34 x 78 In. 150
Table, Armani, Ebonized, 2 Leaves, Round, 29 ¾ x 71 In. 1680
Table, Art Nouveau, Galle, Marquetry, Crane, Fruitwood, Serpentine Top, Shelf, 33 x 29 In. 554
Table, Asian, Mahogany, Shaped Stretchers, Drawers, 25 x 34 In. 120
Table, Asian, Pedestal, Hexagonal, Pierced Apron, Shaped Stretchers, 30 x 19 In. 130
Table, Bamboo, Chinese, Wood Top, 1800s, 22 x 10 In. .... *illus* 59
Table, Banded, Rounded Corners, Urn Pedestals, Tripod Legs, 3 Leaves, 29 x 93 In. 366
Table, Baroque, Walnut, Battened Top, Scalloped Front Stretcher, 1600s, 24 x 33 In. 590
Table, Bench, Mixed Wood, Paint, Round Scrub Top, Baton Supports, Pegged, c.1800, 47 In. 885
Table, Biedermeier, Elm, Figured Round Top, Tilting, 3-Part Base, c.1835, 31 x 49 In. 1375
Table, Biedermeier, Walnut, Drum Shape Top, 3-Part Base, Drawer, c.1810, 19 In., Pair 800
Table, Bistro, Black Laminate Top, Chrome Base, Round, Knoll, 1960s, 30 x 28 In. 52
Table, Bistro, Industrial, Cast Iron, Granite Top, Trestle, Stretcher, c.1910, 28 x 40 In. 504
Table, Bistro, Thonet Style, Mixed Wood, Bentwood Base, c.1910, 43 x 26 In. 156
Table, Blackamoor Pedestal, Gondola, Paw Feet, 39 ¼ x 13 ½ In. 2400
Table, Book, Revolving, 3 Tiers, Parquetry, Flowers, Baluster Gallery, c.1880, 31 x 21 In. 378
Table, Bouillotte, Kingwood, Marble Top, Round, Banding, Inlaid Leaves, c.1910, 29 x 36 In. 799
Table, Brutalist, Welded Metal, Beveled Glass Top, Oval, Silas Seadel, 62 x 21 In. 259
Table, Burl, Marquetry, Demilune, Drawers, Bronze, Pierced Apron, 1800s, 31 x 37 In. 1230
Table, Butterfly, William & Mary, Cherry, Pine, Drawer, Turned Legs, 38 In. 813
Table, Card, Chairs, Midcentury Modern, Slide Out Cup Holders, Leather, 30 x 36 In., 5 Piece 1003
Table, Card, Cherry, Serpentine Front, Braided Edge, Reeded Turned Legs, c.1810, 30 x 36 In. 738
Table, Card, D-Shape Flip Top, String Inlay Apron, Square Legs, c.1790, 36 x 18 In. 649
Table, Card, Federal, Cock-Beaded, Drawer, Tapered Legs, Stringing, c.1800, 28 x 28 In. 738
Table, Card, George III, Sheraton Style, Mahogany, Demilune, Gateleg, c.1790, 30 In. 738
Table, Card, Mahogany, Inlay, 36 x 17 ¾ In. 497
Table, Card, Sheraton, Mahogany, Carved Leaves, Spiral Legs, Ball Feet, c.1820, 30 x 34 In. 283
Table, Carved Wood, Marble Top, Reticulated Griffin Legs, Stretcher, 21 x 26 In., Pair 472
Table, Center, Ebony, Bone, Turned Legs, Undertier Baluster Gallery, c.1900, 30 x 39 In. 3125
Table, Center, Empire Style, Walnut, Marble Top, Ormolu Masks, Winged Lions, 36 x 54 In. 9225

Furniture, Table, Coffee, P. Evans, Metal, Glass, Marked, PE, 1972, 16 x 60 x 34 In.
$5,625

Los Angeles Modern Auctions

Furniture, Table, Coffee, P. Evans, Upside Down Loop, Steel, Wood, Slate, c.1971, 16 x 36 In.
$23,750

Rago Arts and Auction Center

Furniture, Table, Coffee, Robsjohn-Gibbings, Mahogany, Bleached, Openwork, 1940s, 16 x 48 In.
$1,000

Rago Arts and Auction Center

Furniture, Table, Coffee, W. Platner, Nickeled Wire Base, Glass Top, Knoll, 16 x 40 In.
$489

Cottone Auctions

Furniture, Table, Coffee, Willy Rizzo, Stainless Steel, Lacquer, Swivel Bar, c.1971, 47 To 53 In.
$5,535

Skinner, Inc.

Furniture, Table, Console, Italian Rococo Style, Faux Marble, Pierced Apron, Putto Legs, 31 x 41 In.
$1,342

Neal Auctions

Furniture, Table, Dining, Amboyna, Marquetry, Burl Top, Leaves, Trestle, c.1875, 30 x 14 In.
$625

New Orleans (Cakebread)

Furniture, Table, Dining, Federal, Cherry, 2 Sections, Walnut, Poplar, 1800s, 29 x 55 In.
$531

Brunk Auctions

F

Furniture, Table, Dining, Lucite, Glass Top, Stepped Pedestal Base, 1960s-70s, 54 In.
$295

Brunk Auctions

Furniture, Table, Dressing, Mahogany, Drawers, Carved, Cabriole Legs, c.1750, 26 x 22 In.
$39,975

Skinner, Inc.

Furniture, Table, Dressing, Pine, Yellow Paint, Dovetail Drawers, New Eng., c.1850, 42 x 36 In.
$1,560

Garth's Auctioneers & Appraisers

Furniture, Table, Drop Leaf, Cherry, Turned Legs, Gateleg, c.1825, 48 x 21 In. Closed
$431

Cowan Auctions

Table, Center, Gilt Bronze, Round Marble Top, Busts, Swirl Stretcher, c.1950, 37 x 23 In. 3500
Table, Center, Giltwood, Inset Glass Over Embroidery, Flowers, Mask, 1800s, 32 x 54 In. 5000
Table, Center, Giltwood, Onyx Top, D Ends, Pierced Laurel Leaf Frieze, c.1890, 32 x 43 In. 3000
Table, Center, Herter Bros., Rosewood, Inlay, Shaped, Turned Legs, Stretcher, 31 x 32 In. 7865
Table, Center, Louis XV, Walnut, Hinged Top, Drawer, Hoof Feet, c.1760, 28 x 32 In. 2500
Table, Center, Mahogany, Marble Top, Ormolu, Cherubs, Festoons, c.1900, 30 x 44 In. 2250
Table, Center, Mahogany, Marble Top, Pierced Brass Gallery, Square Legs, c.1910, 32 x 44 In. 1722
Table, Center, Mahogany, Marble, Carved, Dog, Cincinnati, c.1875, 42 In. ....*illus* 420
Table, Center, Mahogany, Round Marble Top, Ormolu Band, Fluted Legs, 1900s, 32 x 32 In. 687
Table, Center, Porcelain, 2 Parts, Painted, Flowers, White, Round, 38 x 27 In. 117
Table, Center, Renaissance Revival, Walnut, Marble, Trestle, c.1870, 30 x 42 In. ....*illus* 3081
Table, Center, Round, Marquetry, Flower Baskets, Hexagonal Pedestal, c.1915, 30 x 44 In. 1230
Table, Center, Stained Wood, Faux Marble, Round, c.1975, 30¾ In. 500
Table, Center, Swiss Alpine, Oak, Pine, Drawer, Battens, Pins, Splayed Legs, 31 x 49 In. 1107
Table, Charles Limbert, Cross Stretchers, Tapered Legs, c.1910, 26 x 22 In. 518
Table, Chess, Checkerboard Top, Cabriole Legs, Shaped Stretchers, Drawer, 30 x 21 In. 180
Table, Chinese Style, Red Lacquer Screen Top, Incised, Painted Birds, 15 x 38 In. 1180
Table, Chinese, Rosewood, Rouge Marble Top, Medial Shelf, Claw Feet, c.1880, 23 x 21 In. 660
Table, Chippendale Style, Mahogany, Tripod, Tilting Round Top, Piecrust Edge, 30 x 33 In. 2214
Table, Coffee, 12-Sided Top, Beveled Glass, Helix Shape Lucite Base, 16 x 36½ In. 247
Table, Coffee, Adrian Pearsall, Wood Base, Shaped Glass Top, 16 x 51 x 33 In. 230
Table, Coffee, Art Deco Style, Chrome, Maple, Plate Glass, 2 Tiers, 18 x 47 x 26 In. ....*illus* 468
Table, Coffee, Birch Veneer, Smoked Glass, Square Metal Base, c.1970, 18 x 39 In. 363
Table, Coffee, Bronze, Glass, Cupid Shape Supports, Oval Top, Italy, 1900s, 22 x 51 In. 289
Table, Coffee, Bronze, Pewter Clad Wood, Chinoiserie, Square Legs, c.1936, 18 x 47 In. 6562
Table, Coffee, Contemporary, Wood, Inset Glass Top, Semi-Circular Base, 17 x 34 In. 270
Table, Coffee, Faux Travertine, Square, Paneled Top, Bracket Shape Legs, 18 x 48 In. 148
Table, Coffee, Fornasetti, Transfer Decorated, Lacquered Wood, Mahogany, 18 x 47 In. 1250
Table, Coffee, Fornasetti, Transfer, Lacquered Wood, Mahogany, 1950s, 18 x 48 In. 625
Table, Coffee, Frankl, Enameled Cork, Stained, Lacquered Mahogany, 1940s, 14 x 71 In. 2250
Table, Coffee, G. Nakashima, Black Walnut, Slab, Shelf, 1957, 14 x 66½ In. 20000
Table, Coffee, G. Nakashima, Walnut, Rosewood, Plank Top, 1988, 15 x 50 In. ....*illus* 18750
Table, Coffee, H. Probber, Nuclear, 2 Piece, Wood, Black, C Shape, c.1975, 14 x 47 In. 544
Table, Coffee, Harvey Ellis, Cherry, Storage, Drawers, Stickley, 19 x 40 In. 720
Table, Coffee, Hollywood Regency, 6-Point Concave Stretcher, 1960s, 15 x 40 In. 272
Table, Coffee, Huanghuali, Splay Apron, Carved Flowers, Claw Feet, 1700s, 14 x 34 In. 10714
Table, Coffee, I. Noguchi, Biomorphic, Triangular Glass Top, Wood Arms, 15 x 49 In. 240
Table, Coffee, Italian Style, Glass Top, Bending Reeds Base, 18 x 29 In. 270
Table, Coffee, J. Greene, Stained, Geometric Shape, Walnut, Rosewood, 16 x 67 In. 750
Table, Coffee, Jane Kennedy, Glass Top, c.1974, 16 x 72 x 48 In. 4062
Table, Coffee, Karl Springer, Round Legs, Metal, Lucite, 17½ x 48 In. 4575
Table, Coffee, Lily, Metal Flower Shapes, Round Base, Arthur Court, 17 x 48 In. 1342
Table, Coffee, Louis XV, Cherry, Cane, Wide Skirt, Cabriole Legs, 17 x 46 In. 184
Table, Coffee, Louis XV, Gilt Bronze, Glass Top, Leaf Carved Cabriole Legs, 16 x 48 In. 9687
Table, Coffee, Low Honed Travertine, Square, 1970s, 16 x 39½ x 39½ In. 770
Table, Coffee, Mahogany, Bowed Drop Leaves, Scrolled Legs, Casters, 1940s, 20 x 43 In. 83
Table, Coffee, McCobb, Maple, Square Top, Tapered Turned Legs, 1960s, 18 x 36 In. 276
Table, Coffee, Midcentury Modern, Kittinger, Lotus Style, Muller & Barringer, 14 x 48 In. 270
Table, Coffee, Midcentury Modern, Mirrored, 20th Century, 17½ x 40 In. 236
Table, Coffee, Mies Van Der Rohe, Barcelona, Chrome, Glass Top, Knoll, 17 x 36 In. 330
Table, Coffee, Milo Baughman, Rosewood, Oval, Metal Legs, Coggin, 13 x 60 x 30 In. 374
Table, Coffee, Milo Baughman, Walnut Veneer, Checkerboard, Metal Base, 16 x 65 In. 288
Table, Coffee, Minguren, G. Nakashima, Figured Walnut, 1975, 17 x 28 x 26 In. 12500
Table, Coffee, Octagonal Base, Multicolor, Round, 17 x 48 In. 2375
Table, Coffee, P. Evans, Cityscape, Burl, Brass, Glass, 1970s, 16 x 42 In. ....*illus* 3936
Table, Coffee, P. Evans, Metal, Glass, Marked, PE, 1972, 16 x 60 x 34 In. ....*illus* 5625
Table, Coffee, P. Evans, Round Marble Top, Steel Spread Base, 1960s, 16 x 30 In. 10000
Table, Coffee, P. Evans, Upside Down Loop, Steel, Wood, Slate, c.1971, 16 x 36 In. ....*illus* 23750
Table, Coffee, Philip & Kelvin LaVerne, Chin Ying, Bronze, Pewter, 1960s, 17 x 70 In. 13750
Table, Coffee, Philip & Kelvin LaVerne, Onyx, Rectangular Sides, Notches, c.1975, 52¼ x 27½ In. 212
Table, Coffee, Robsjohn-Gibbings, Glass Top, Leaf, Stretcher, c.1950, 16 x 53 x 26½ In. 8750
Table, Coffee, Robsjohn-Gibbings, Mahogany, Bleached, Openwork, 1940s, 16 x 48 In. ....*illus* 1000
Table, Coffee, Rosewood, Steel Inlay, Biomorphic, 14½ x 54 In. 316
Table, Coffee, Slate, Gilt Metal, Village, River, Branch Shape Legs, 22 x 41 x 35 In. 2750
Table, Coffee, Stone, Lacquered Top, Brass Base, Scroll Feet, Round, c.1970, 17 x 40 In. 92
Table, Coffee, Tiger Maple, Contemporary, Natural Finish, Splayed Legs, 18 x 33 In. 127

Table, Coffee, V. Kagan, Glass Tile Top, Walnut, Swirl Base, 1950s, 55 x 34 In. 20000
Table, Coffee, W. Platner, Nickeled Wire Base, Glass Top, Knoll, 16 x 40 In. .... *illus* 489
Table, Coffee, Walnut, Raised Molded Edge, Lower Shelf, Turned Legs, 1960s, 19 x 58 In. 230
Table, Coffee, Willy Rizzo, Stainless Steel, Black Glass, 13 ½ x 38 In. 420
Table, Coffee, Willy Rizzo, Stainless Steel, Lacquer, Swivel Bar, c.1971, 47 To 53 In. .... *illus* 5535
Table, Conrad Schultz, Mahogany, Marble Top, Serpentine, Shell Carved, Beaded, 29 x 45 In. 330
Table, Console, Art Deco Style, Wrought Iron, Marble, Rope Molding, 1900s, 38 x 24 In. 717
Table, Console, Art Deco, Walnut, Veneer, D-Shape, Incurved Legs, Base, c.1965, 29 x 53 In. 2250
Table, Console, Baroque, Giltwood, Marble Top, Molded Edge, Scrolled, 40 x 53 In. 2337
Table, Console, Chippendale, Mahogany, Chestnut, Fretwork, Rhode Island, 20 x 34 In. 3120
Table, Console, Empire Style, Mahogany, Mirror, Ebonized, Turret Feet, 1900s, 62 x 44 In. 1107
Table, Console, Federal, Mahogany, 49 x 24 In. 219
Table, Console, Florentine, Faux Marble Top, Black, Leaves, 72 x 16 In. 423
Table, Console, Georgian Style, Mahogany, Carved Apron, Cabriole Legs, Ireland, 31 x 48 In. 688
Table, Console, Gilt, Black Painted, Wrought Iron, Marble, Scrolled Stretcher, 35 x 56 In. 590
Table, Console, Gio Ponti, Flip Top, Stained, Lacquered Walnut, Brass, 1960s, 30 x 65 In. 11875
Table, Console, Historic Natchez, Mahogany, Marble Top, Henredon, 41 x 55 In. 600
Table, Console, Italian Rococo Style, Faux Marble, Pierced Apron, Putto Legs, 31 x 41 In. .. *illus* 1342
Table, Console, K. Bitting, Faux Parchment, Fiberboard, Painted, c.2000, 29 x 60 In. 1800
Table, Console, Louis XV Style, Giltwood, Marble Top, Fruit Spray, c.1850, 32 x 24 In. 1168
Table, Console, Louis XVI Style, Marble Top, Pierced Carved Frieze, Medallion, 31 x 28 In. 1722
Table, Console, Marble Top, Gilt Base, Cabriole Legs, Molded Apron, 1960s, 38 x 60 In. 1006
Table, Console, Marble Top, Inlay, Scalloped, Mirrored Drawers, c.1870, 34 x 49 In. 270
Table, Console, Mirror, Venetian, 92 x 23 In. 540
Table, Console, Neoclassical, Demilune, Pine, Birds, Wings Up, 34 x 41 In. 750
Table, Console, P. Evans, Directional, Cityscape, Mirror, Chrome, Steel, 1970s, 70 x 48 In. 8750
Table, Console, Parcel Gilt, Louis XVI, Demilune Marble Top, Mirror, 85 x 50 In. 671
Table, Console, Parzinger, Cabinet, Drawer, Splayed Legs.......... 3500
Table, Console, Parzinger, Walnut, Laminate, Square Gallery, X Legs, 1960s, 33 x 37 In. 2875
Table, Console, Pine, Plank Top, Shaped Apron, 3 Drawers, Lower Shelf, 31 x 61 In. 438
Table, Console, Regency, Mahogany, 2 Drawers, 68 ½ x 13 ¾ In. 2250
Table, Console, Rosewood, Rope-Twist Edge, Bulbous Spiral Legs, 1800s, 35 x 55 In. 3125
Table, Console, Rosewood, Serpentine Marble Top, Flowers, Mirror, c.1865, 39 x 63 In. 2337
Table, Console, Venetian, Faux Marble, Painted, Serpentine, 1800s, 37 x 48 In., Pair 2988
Table, Console, Walnut, String Inlay, 3 J-Shape Legs, Curved Base, c.1910, 32 x 48 In. 3000
Table, Console, Wood, Neogothic Style, Carved, Drawers, Shaped Legs, Guatemala, 26 x 64 In. .. 625
Table, Contemporary, Wrought Iron, Cast Stone, Paneled, X-Shape Base, 37 x 42 In. 984
Table, Corner, Brass, Lucite, Round, 21 x 20 In., Pair 738
Table, Corner, Grain Painted, Fan Shape Top, Curved Apron, Lower Shelf, 1800s, 35 x 30 In. 390
Table, Corner, Renaissance Revival, Columns, Ebonized, Brass, Gilt, c.1890, 32 x 37 In. 406
Table, Danish Modern, Teak, Round Top, Black Laminate, Tripod Base, 18 x 14 In., Pair 253
Table, Demilune, Elm, Red Lacquer, Scrolled Legs, Stretcher Base, c.1900, 33 x 51 In. 129
Table, Dining, Amboyna, Marquetry, Burl Top, Leaves, Trestle, c.1875, 30 x 14 In. .... *illus* 625
Table, Dining, Andre Arbus, Wood Top, 9 Terra-Cotta Spaced Squares, Brass Sabots.......... 6000
Table, Dining, Arne Jacobsen, Rosewood, Aluminum, Label, F. Hansen, 1960s, 28 x 57 In. 2625
Table, Dining, Art Nouveau, Walnut, Carved, Molded Legs, France, c.1900, 29 x 51 In. 236
Table, Dining, Chippendale Style, Round Top, Gadrooned Edge, 1900s, 29 x 56 In. 600
Table, Dining, Drop Leaf, Extension, Round, Cabriole Legs, Hand Crank, 29 x 59 In. 316
Table, Dining, Drop Leaf, George III, Mahogany, Ball & Claw Feet, c.1770, 28 x 42 In. 423
Table, Dining, Eero Saarinen, Tulip, White, Round, Enamel, c.1995, 29 x 42 In. 1154
Table, Dining, Farm, French Elm, Frieze Drawer, Square Legs, 1800s, 28 x 65 In. 786
Table, Dining, Federal, Cherry, 2 Sections, Walnut, Poplar, 1800s, 29 x 55 In. .... *illus* 531
Table, Dining, French Provincial, Farm, Fruitwood, Plank Top, 1800s, 30 x 78 In. 2125
Table, Dining, French Provincial, Farm, Oak, 3 Frieze Drawers, Square Legs, 78 In. 584
Table, Dining, G. Nakashima, Walnut, Plank Top, Round Legs, 1960, 42 x 72 In. 10625
Table, Dining, George III, Mahogany, Dished Tilt Top, Flower Shape, c.1790, 27 x 35 In. 1260
Table, Dining, Georgian Style, Mahogany, Inlay, Pedestal, Saber Legs, 29 x 59 In. 492
Table, Dining, Glass Top, Rectangle, Industrial, 32 x 63 In. 175
Table, Dining, Glass, Irving Rosen For Pace, 28 x 96 In. 1045
Table, Dining, Jacobean Style, Walnut, Oak, Crossbanded, Gadrooned, Carved, 97 x 61 In. 780
Table, Dining, John Mortensen, Modern, Rosewood, Pedestal Bases, 2 20-In. Leaves 800
Table, Dining, Louis XIII Style, Oak, Carved, Barley Twist Legs, Stretcher, 1800s, 29 x 55 In. 338
Table, Dining, Lucite, Glass Top, Stepped Pedestal Base, 1960s-70s, 54 In. .... *illus* 295
Table, Dining, Mahogany, 2 Pedestals, Turned Columns, Reeded Legs, 1800s, 28 x 43 In. 2373
Table, Dining, Mahogany, 3 Pedestals, Columnar Stem, Splayed Legs, 1900s, 30 x 117 In. 600
Table, Dining, Mahogany, Bulbous Columnar Stem, Splayed Legs, c.1890, 30 x 103 In. 3500

TIP

Treat your tables to custom-fit glass tops. They will save the finish and make you a more relaxed hostess, knowing that wet glass will not damage the tabletops.

Furniture, Table, Drop Leaf, Chippendale, Cherry, Square Fluted Legs, c.1750, 27 x 38 In.
$830

James D. Julia Auctioneers

Furniture, Table, Drop Leaf, Provincial, Pine, Painted, Tapered Legs, 29 x 70 In.
$687

New Orleans (Cakebread)

Furniture, Table, Drop Leaf, Sheraton, Tiger Maple, c.1835, 36 x 18 In., 11-In. Leaves
$240

Garth's Auctioneers & Appraisers

Furniture, Table, Drop Leaf, Stickley Bros., Gateleg, Decal, c.1910, 30 x 46 In., Open
$1,500

Rago Arts and Auction Center

Furniture, Table, Drum, Regency, Oak, Working & False Drawers, Leather, c.1840, 40 In.
$1,107

Skinner, Inc.

Furniture, Table, Galle, Walnut, Inlaid Grass, Leaves, 3 Tiers, Shaped Legs, 33 x 27 In.
$2,214

Skinner, Inc.

House of Cards

Charles and Ray Eames, famous for furniture and other designs in the 1950s and after, invented the game House of Cards. It was a deck of large cards that could be used to build "houses."

Table, Dining, McCobb, Walnut, Extension, 4 Leaves, 30 x 72 In. 476
Table, Dining, Modern, Saporiti, Glass, Metal, Cast Round Base 750
Table, Dining, Oak, Farm Style, Overhang Top, Plank Apron, Block Legs, 59 x 32 In. 214
Table, Dining, Oak, Plank Top, Frieze Drawer, Box Stretcher, 1600s, 31 x 108 In. 1750
Table, Dining, Provincial, Louis XV Style, Mahogany, Drawer Leaves, 32 x 39 x 60 In. 461
Table, Dining, Regency Style, Mahogany, Round, Banded, 4 Turned Supports, 31 x 79 In. 3690
Table, Dining, Renaissance Revival, Oak, Fluted Apron, Griffins, Claw Feet, c.1890, 30 In. 7500
Table, Dining, Round, Black Forest, Oak, Leaves, Wolf Head, 27 x 52 In. 625
Table, Dining, Tiger Oak, Carved, Ball & Claw Feet, c.1900, 44 x 44 In. 153
Table, Dining, Walnut, Inlaid Star, Banding, Draw End, Square Legs, c.1890, 32 x 36 In. 8302
Table, Dining, Walnut, Tempered Glass, Giovanni Michelucci, 1980s, 30 x 59 In. 9375
Table, Directoire, Mahogany, Telescopic, Gilt Bronze, Channel Splay Leg Base, 30 x 18 In. 246
Table, Drafting, Adjustable, Iron, Pedestal Base, Scallop Stretcher, 31 ¾ x 48 In. 968
Table, Drafting, Oak, Iron, Drafting Lamp, Hamilton, 48 x 34 In. 585
Table, Drafting, Wood, Hinged Cast Iron Tripod Base, c.1900, 47 In. 156
Table, Dressing, Bird's-Eye Maple, Pine, Cherry, Mirror, Drawers, Casters, 1800s, 69 x 35 In. 330
Table, Dressing, Georgian, Oak, 3 Dovetailed Drawers, c.1800, 29 x 34 In. 590
Table, Dressing, Lifting Center, Mirror, 2 Compartments, c.1910, 30 x 34 In. 196
Table, Dressing, Louis XV Style, Walnut, Inlay, Serpentine Crotcheted Top, 1800s, 29 x 28 In. 267
Table, Dressing, Mahogany, Drawers, Carved, Cabriole Legs, c.1750, 26 x 22 In. .... *illus* 39975
Table, Dressing, Mahogany, Mirror, Scrolled Supports, 4 Drawers, Scroll Feet, 61 In. 375
Table, Dressing, Neoclassical, Mahogany, Carved, Dolphin Crest, Trestle Base, 71 x 48 In. 770
Table, Dressing, Neoclassical, Mahogany, Pine, Drawers, Glass Pulls, c.1830, 43 x 39 In. 188
Table, Dressing, Pine, Yellow Paint, Dovetail Drawers, New Eng., c.1850, 42 x 36 In. .... *illus* 1560
Table, Drop Leaf, Cherry, Turned Legs, Gateleg, c.1825, 48 x 21 In. Closed .... *illus* 431
Table, Drop Leaf, Chippendale, Cherry, Square Fluted Legs, c.1750, 27 x 38 In. .... *illus* 830
Table, Drop Leaf, George III Style, Mahogany, Gateleg Support, 30 x 67 In. 2952
Table, Drop Leaf, George III, Mahogany, Bowed Ends, Pad Feet, c.1790, 28 x 22 In. 625
Table, Drop Leaf, Hepplewhite, 19th Century, 29 x 42 In. 180
Table, Drop Leaf, Hepplewhite, Maple, Tapered Legs, c.1800, Drop Leaves, 28 x 55 In. 610
Table, Drop Leaf, Hepplewhite, Style, Floral Inlay, Banded, Drawer, 27 x 42 In. 644
Table, Drop Leaf, Provincial, Pine, Painted, Tapered Legs, 29 x 70 In. .... *illus* 687
Table, Drop Leaf, Queen Anne Style, Mahogany, Oval Leaves, Tapered Legs, 28 x 41 In. 500
Table, Drop Leaf, Sheraton, Tiger Maple, c.1835, 36 x 18 In., 11-In. Leaves .... *illus* 240
Table, Drop Leaf, Stickley Bros., Gateleg, Decal, c.1910, 30 x 46 In., Open .... *illus* 1500
Table, Drop Leaf, Walnut, Drawer, Box Stretcher, Bun Feet, 31 x 28 ½ In. 555
Table, Drum, African, Cowhide, Animal Hoof, 20 ¼ x 29 ½ In. Diam. 363
Table, Drum, George III, Boxwood, String, Inlay, Mahogany, 1800, 28 ½ In. 1093
Table, Drum, Glass Top, Mounted Animal Hide, 22 x 28 In. 125
Table, Drum, Regency, Oak, Working & False Drawers, Leather, c.1840, 40 In. .... *illus* 1107
Table, Eames, Surfboard, Elliptical, Herman Miller, 1950s, 89 x 29 In. 590
Table, Eastlake, Walnut, Carved, Granite Top, Figural Support, Cabriole Legs, 30 x 27 In. 336
Table, Ebonized Mahogany, Gallery Top, Drawer, Ormolu, France, c.1900, 16 x 32 In. 207
Table, Egyptian Revival, Gray Lacquer, Goat's Head, Gold, Red, Stretcher, 1970, 72 x 24 In. 1500
Table, Empire Style, Burl, Marble Top, Ormolu Applied, Round Top, 29 x 21 In. 500
Table, Empire Style, Mahogany, Onyx Round Top, Maiden's Heads, c.1910, 26 x 33 In. 1353
Table, Extension, Walnut, Banded Top, Round, Dolphin Supports, c.1950, 78 ½ In. 687
Table, Farm, Blue Gray Paint, Removable Top, Shaped Skirt, 1800s, 29 x 88 In. 420
Table, Farm, Cherry, Carved, Drawer, Cabriole Legs, 1800s, 30 x 78 In. 1185
Table, Farm, Chippendale, Walnut, Pine Board Top, Drawers, Beaded Skirt, c.1785, 31 x 61 In. .. 1534
Table, Faux Marble, Octagonal & Square Stones Inset, Panels, c.1900, 30 x 33 In. 1968
Table, Figured Mahogany, Brass, Oval, 3 Tiers, c.1890, 34 x 30 In. 1003
Table, Folding, Metal, Green, 30 x 31 In. 146
Table, Formica, Pink, 37 x 31 In. 24
Table, Frankl, Cork, Walnut, Brass, 2 Leaves, 29 x 72 In. 960
Table, French Provincial, Cherry, Draw End, Shaped Apron, Cabriole Legs, 1800s, 61 x 122 In. .. 676
Table, French Provincial, Farm, Cherry, Drawers, Cabriole Legs, 30 x 78 In. 1353
Table, French Provincial, Fruitwood, Dough Trough, Banded Ends, 1800s, 63 x 32 In. 799
Table, French Provincial, Fruitwood, Molded Edge, Scallop Frieze, 1800s, 20 x 31 In. 1000
Table, Fruitwood, Inlay, Continental, Urn, Vines, Ribbons, 30 ½ x 36 In. 960
Table, Fruitwood, Mahogany, Frieze Drawers, Ring-Turned Legs, c.1890, 30 x 126 In. 2091
Table, G. Nakashima, Wepman, Flame Walnut, 12 ½ x 21 In. 2040
Table, Galle, Walnut, Inlaid Grass, Leaves, 3 Tiers, Shaped Legs, 33 x 27 In. .... *illus* 2214
Table, Game, Federal, Bird's-Eye Maple, Mahogany, Foldover, c.1800, 36 x 36 In. 2953
Table, Game, Federal, Mahogany, Flame Veneer, Inlaid Wavy Birch, Elliptical, 29 In. 2337
Table, Game, Foldover, Inlay, Compartment, Ireland, c.1850, 30 x 33 In., Open .... *illus* 4920

Table, Game, Fruitwood, Demilune Top, Hinged, Square Legs, Tapered, c.1850, 29 x 43 In. 861
Table, Game, Fruitwood, D-Shape, Frieze, Scrolled Legs, 28½ x 44 In. 1020
Table, Game, George III, Drop Leaf, Mahogany, Leather, Drawer, c.1790, 36 x 20 In. .... *illus* 1315
Table, Game, George III, Mahogany, Foldover, Leather Lined, Surface, 1700s, 28 x 34 In. 354
Table, Game, George III, Mahogany, Hinged, Serpentine, Rope Twist Edge, c.1775, 28 x 36 In. 430
Table, Game, George III, Mahogany, Serpentine Top, Leaf Edge, c.1700, 29 x 36 In. 1875
Table, Game, Half Circle, Green Felt, Extendable Leg Support, 37 In. 500
Table, Game, Hepplewhite, Flame Birch, Maple, Inlay, Tapered Legs, c.1810, 29 x 36 In. ..... *illus* 593
Table, Game, Hepplewhite, Mahogany, Pine, Oval Corners, Oval Inlay, 28 x 35 In. 1560
Table, Game, Louis XV Style, Fruitwood, Removable Panel, Chessboard, 30 x 41 In. 468
Table, Game, Louis XV Style, Mahogany, Fruitwood, Bronze Ormolu, c.1980, 32 x 41 In. 330
Table, Game, Louis XV Style, Multicolor, Inset Leather, Cabriole Legs, c.1850, 28 x 30 In. 1107
Table, Game, Louis XVI, Mahogany, Demilune, Brass Band, Fluted Legs, c.1790, 31 x 43 In. 750
Table, Game, Mahogany Veneer, Carved, Gilt Leaf, Paw Feet, c.1818, 29 x 37 In. .... *illus* 3075
Table, Game, Mahogany, Dished Edge, Inlaid Chessboard, Tapered Legs, c.1890, 38 x 25 In. 2214
Table, Game, Mahogany, Stencil, Foldover Top, Carved Pedestal, Paw Feet, c.1825, 30 x 36 In. ... 1107
Table, Game, Mahogany, Stenciled, Vase Shape Pedestal, Paw Feet, c.1825, 29 x 36 In. 553
Table, Game, Marquetry, Walnut, Figured, Foldover, Drawer, 1800s, 37 x 24 In. 649
Table, Game, Pine, Shaped Top, Checkerboard, Black & Red Paint, Turned Legs, 25 x 26 In. 780
Table, Game, Rosewood, Richard Shultz, Chrome Legs, Bands, Knoll, 26 x 34 In. 236
Table, Game, Thonet, Flip Top, Felt, Bentwood, France, c.1915, 28 x 38 In. .... *illus* 1920
Table, Game, Turned Legs, Flip Top, Round, Green Felt, 30 x 33 In. 242
Table, Game, Victorian, Walnut, c.1875, 21 x 24 In. 182
Table, Game, Walnut, Oak Inlay, Checkerboard, Card Suits, c.1900, 28 x 31 In. .... *illus* 3444
Table, Game, William IV, Marble Top, Malachite Chessboard, Fluted Legs, c.1850, 31 x 30 In. 2952
Table, Garrison Rousseau, Shagreen Veneer, c.1980, 17 x 60 In. 1200
Table, George II, Mahogany, Single Drawer, 20 x 25¾ In. 1440
Table, George III, Mahogany, Eared Hinge Top, Gadrooned, Cabriole Legs, 29 In. 2967
Table, George III, Mahogany, Hinged Dish Top, Fluted Column, Tripod, 26 x 29 In. 27528
Table, George III, Mahogany, Pierced Gallery, Paterae, X-Stretcher, 28 x 34 In. 17697
Table, Gilt, Mahogany, Columnar, Drexel, 30 x 18 In. 522
Table, Gio Ponti, Figured Italian Walnut, Rosewood, Italy, c.1931, 23 x 35 In. 15000
Table, Glass Top, Round, Carved Figural Support, 4 Swans, 28½ x 48 In. 1000
Table, Glass Top, Sunburst, Z Shape Stiles, 18 x 41½ In. 1936
Table, Gothic Revival, Rosewood, Marble, Drop Finials, c.1845, 36 In. .... *illus* 30750
Table, Green Shagreen Veneer, Square Top, Legs, 20th Century, 94 x 99 In., Pair........ 1534
Table, H. Probber, Mahogany, 2 Leaves, 29 x 66 In. 840
Table, Hardwood, Carved, Pierced Skirt, Burl Inset Top, Chinese, 33 x 27 In. .... *illus* 649
Table, Hardwood, Rosewood, Cloisonne Inset Round Panels, Chines, c.1900, 18 x 47 In. 2242
Table, Harvest, Hepplewhite, Red Paint, 3-Board Top, Beaded, Tapered Legs, 28 x 62 In. 590
Table, Harvest, Pine, Trestle Base, 2-Board Top, 138 x 35 In. 1180
Table, Harvest, Walnut, Plank Top, X-Shape Leg Supports, Stretcher, 31 x 180 In. 2478
Table, Hippopotamus, Dan Dailey, Oval Glass Top, Blue Glass Hippo, 56 x 17 In. 6000
Table, Jacobean Style, Oak, Carved, Paw Feet, Hastings Table Co., 30 x 144 In. 3318
Table, Jean Marie Massaud, Heaven, Woven Metal Base, Glass Round Top, 30 x 48 In. 875
Table, Karl Springer, Tapered Cube, 15 x 41 In. 246
Table, Kitchen, Lucite, Pedestal, Glass Top, 28¾ In. 273
Table, Lacquer, Rectangular, c.1900, 31 x 91 In. 4000
Table, Library, Arts & Crafts, Limbert, Oak, Drawer, Shelves, Medial Shelf, 30 x 45 In. 360
Table, Library, Baroque, Chestnut, Drawer, Leaf Frieze, Turned Legs, c.1690, 29 x 65 In. 5000
Table, Library, Baroque, Walnut, Chestnut, Frieze Drawers, Scroll Legs, 31 x 80 In. 3750
Table, Library, Baroque, Walnut, Oak, Carved, Leaves, Drawers, Skirt, c.1700, 33 x 87 In. 5900
Table, Library, Baroque, Walnut, Oak, Saint Peter, Joseph, Stretcher, 46 x 25¾ In. 4252
Table, Library, Chestnut, Walnut, Carved, Leaf Frieze, Turned Legs, c.1690, 29 x 66 In. 5000
Table, Library, Italian Renaissance Style, Walnut, Griffin Supports, Shield, 32 x 90 In. 649
Table, Library, Mahogany, 2 Tiers, Revolving, Leather Top, Saber Legs, c.1900, 30 x 36 In. 148
Table, Library, Mahogany, Serpentine, Shaped Apron, Cabriole Legs, c.1890, 29 x 51 In. 2000
Table, Library, Oak, Round Corners, Frieze Drawer, Scroll, Spiral Legs, c.1900, 31 x 48 In. 711
Table, Library, Regency, Mahogany Veneer, 2 Friezes, Drawers, 1800s, 54 x 28 In. 295
Table, Library, Regency, Rosewood Veneer, Inlay, Drawers, c.1800, 29 x 54 In. 369
Table, Library, Regency, Rosewood, Inset Leather Surface, Paneled Frieze, 1800s, 29 x 55 In. 984
Table, Library, Renaissance Revival, Carved Walnut, c.1875, H-Stretcher, 29¾ x 71 In. 1353
Table, Library, Renaissance Revival, Oak, Urn Shape End Supports, c.1920, 32 x 96 In. 720
Table, Library, Renaissance Revival, Walnut, Scroll Stem, Paw Feet, c.1900, 32 x 85 In. 4375
Table, Library, Renaissance Style, Birch, Carved, Drawer, Trestle, c.1940, 30 x 54 In. 267
Table, Library, Walnut, Burl, Tapered Legs, Curved Stretcher Base, c.1890, 31 x 144 In. 1200

Furniture, Table, Game, Foldover, Inlay, Compartment, Ireland, c.1850, 30 x 33 In., Open
$4,920

Skinner, Inc.

Furniture, Table, Game, George III, Drop Leaf, Mahogany, Leather, Drawer, c.1790, 36 x 20 In.
$1,315

Neal Auctions

Furniture, Table, Game, Hepplewhite, Flame Birch, Maple, Inlay, Tapered Legs, c.1810, 29 x 36 In.
$593

James D. Julia Auctioneers

Furniture, Table, Game, Mahogany Veneer, Carved, Gilt Leaf, Paw Feet, c.1818, 29 x 37 In.
$3,075

Skinner, Inc.

Furniture, Table, Game, Thonet, Flip Top, Felt, Bentwood, France, c.1915, 28 x 38 In.
$1,920

Selkirk Auctioneers & Appraisers

TIP
To remove white rings on wooden tabletops, use paste wax and 0000-grade steel wool. Rub with the grain. Buff with a wad of cheesecloth.

Furniture, Table, Game, Walnut, Oak Inlay, Checkerboard, Card Suits, c.1900, 28 x 31 In.
$3,444

New Orleans (Cakebread)

Furniture, Table, Gothic Revival, Rosewood, Marble, Drop Finials, c.1845, 36 In.
$30,750

New Orleans (Cakebread)

Table, Library, William IV, Mahogany, Leather Inset, Frieze Drawers, c.1850, 30 x 54 x 45 In. 738
Table, Library, William IV, Mahogany, Oak, Leather, Turned Legs, c.1835, 31 x 72 In. 3250
Table, Louis XV Style, Argente, Marble Top, Lattice, Pendant Shell, Stretcher, 32 x 56 In. 625
Table, Louis XV Style, Carved, Multicolor, Marble Top, Cabriole Legs, c.1890, 29 x 32 In. 3750
Table, Louis XV Style, Fruitwood, Scalloped Frieze, Hoof Feet, c.1810, 30 x 53 In. 1125
Table, Louis XV Style, Giltwood, Turtle Shape Top, Shell Carving, c.1910, 30 x 40 In. 562
Table, Louis XVI Style, Giltwood, Marble Top, Leaf Pierced Frieze, Stretcher, 32 x 40 In. 984
Table, Louis XVI Style, Kingwood, Drawers, Inlay, Gilt Bronze, Plaque, 30 x 45 In. 369
Table, Louis XVI Style, Multicolor, Marble Top, Pierced Guilloche Frieze, 33 x 44 In. 1187
Table, Lucite, Staple Shape, 38 x 21 In., Pair 313
Table, Magazine, X-Shape, Widdicomb, c.1950, 22 ½ x 29 In. 424
Table, Mahogany, Aluminum Legs, Round Top, Claw Foot, Mozer, 1998, 30 x 28 In. .... *illus* 2625
Table, Mahogany, Satinwood, Oval Panel, Drawer, c.1890, 28 x 24 In. .... *illus* 1125
Table, Mahogany, Scalloped End, C-Scroll Supports, c.1840, 28 x 22 In. 553
Table, Maitland Smith, Tessellated Fossil, Inlaid Brass, 20 x 26 In. 173
Table, Malachite, Inlay, Parcel Gilt, Continental, 30 x 26 In. .... *illus* 1783
Table, Maple, Cone Shape Legs, Angelo Mangiarotti, c.1970, 28 x 48 ½ In. 3000
Table, Marble Top, Cloverleaf Shape, Pedestal Base, Aluminum, 37 x 36 ½ In. 220
Table, Marble Top, Silver Beige Ripples, Toffee Border, 40 ½ x 24 In. 2040
Table, Mark Hampton, Modern, Bamboo Mounted Black Walnut, Lacquer, 28 x 63 In. 3600
Table, McCobb, Cane Lower Shelf, Calvin Group, 19 x 28 In. 150
Table, Mirror, Kidney Shape, Karl Springer, c.1970, 16 x 28 ½ In., Pair 12500
Table, Mirror, Louis XVI Style, Carved, Gilt Scroll Crest, Demilune, c.1950, 30 x 40 In. 720
Table, Modern, Black Metal, Half Round Top, Trestle Shape Base, 1900s, 24 x 16 In. 177
Table, Modern, Saporiti, Wood, Glass, Metal, Pair 549
Table, Napoleon III, Ebonized, Mahogany, Pierced Brass Gallery, Butterfly, 27 x 18 In. 1107
Table, Napoleon III, Kingwood, Marble Top, Gallery, Drawer, 29 x 19 In. 1107
Table, Napoleon III, Marble Top, Guilloche Banding, Shelf, c.1890, 28 x 32 In. .... *illus* 1230
Table, Neoclassical Revival, Mahogany, Round Marble Top, Fluted Stem, 1800s, 22 x 36 In. 770
Table, Neoclassical Style, Fruitwood, Ebonized Edge, Drawer, c.1850, 28 x 33 In. .... *illus* 1845
Table, Neogothic, Cast Iron, Arches, Black Painted Base, Stone Top, c.1880, 32 x 27 In. 330
Table, Nesting, French Provincial Style, Fruitwood, Scalloped, 25 x 21 In., 3 Piece .... *illus* 687
Table, Nesting, Galle, Walnut, Inlaid Flowers, Arched Feet, c.1900, 28 & 27 In., 2 Piece 1599
Table, Nesting, Gianfrano Frattini, Interchangeable Black Or White Laminate Top, 4 Piece 2196
Table, Nesting, Mahogany, Banded Round Top, Lattice, Guilloche Inlaid Flowers, 28 In., Pair 593
Table, Nesting, Sheraton Style, Mahogany, Multicolor, Painted, Flowers, 14 x 20 In., 3 Piece 104
Table, Occasional, Bronze, Glass, Round, Walter Lamb, 15 x 24 In. 1586
Table, Octagonal Top, Knickers & Boots Shape Legs, Landform Base, 26 x 25 In. 1875
Table, Onyx, Champleve, Bronze Mountings, Paw Feet, 25 x 16 In. 1875
Table, P. Evans Style, Mixed Metal Patchwork, Brown, Yellow, 16 x 16 In. 480
Table, Partners, Writing, Neoclassical, Fruitwood, Walnut, Heraldic Emblem, 32 x 45 In. 1750
Table, Pembroke, Adam Style, Satinwood, Inlay, Painted, Drawer, 26 x 32 In. 944
Table, Pembroke, Cherry, Serpentine, Cross Stretchers, c.1780, 29 x 37 In. 614
Table, Pembroke, George III, Mahogany, Oak, Drawer, Stretcher, 1700s, 27 x 27 In. 720
Table, Pembroke, Mahogany, Crossbanded, Reeded Legs, c.1810, 30 x 36 In. 984
Table, Phil Powell, Walnut, Sculpted, New Hope, Pa., 1960s, 18 x 31 In. .... *illus* 9375
Table, Phil Powell, Walnut, Turned, Slate, New Hope, Pa., 1960s, 23 x 15 In. 2625
Table, Philip & Kelvin LaVerne, Chan, Chinese Scene, c.1965, 17 x 35 In. .... *illus* 7380
Table, Pier, Burl Veneer, Frieze Drawer, Ogee Supports, 1830s, 34 In. 649
Table, Pier, Empire Style, Mahogany, Marble, Gilt Bronze, Caryatids, 36 x 53 In. 2460
Table, Pier, Empire Style, Multicolor, Fluted Frieze, Mirrored Back, Scrolling, 37 x 50 In. 1187
Table, Pier, George III, Giltwood, Marble Top, Demilune, Fluted Frieze, 34 x 54 In. 5899
Table, Pier, George IV, Mahogany, Marble Top, C-Scroll Cabriole Legs, Plinth, 37 x 50 In. 633
Table, Pier, George IV, Oak, Pierced Quatrefoil Open Frieze, Footed, 31 x 39 In. 2949
Table, Pier, Mahogany, Gilt, Stenciled Frieze, Columns, Paw Feet, 1825, 37 x 42 In. 3750
Table, Pier, Parcel Gilt, Mahogany, Stencil, Marble Top, Columns, c.1825, 36 x 45 In. 4674
Table, Pier, Rosewood, Bronze, Marble, Mirror, c.1810, 36 x 36 In. .... *illus* 7170
Table, Pine, Marble Top, Carved Drawers, Acanthus, Paw Feet, Italy, 33 x 48 In. 1722
Table, Porcelain, Putti, Winged Soldiers, Inset Plaques, Style Of Carl Thieme, 33 x 23 In. 625
Table, Postmodern, Center Hall, Pucci De Rossi, 28 ½ x 45 x 32 In. 2196
Table, Provincial, Mario Villa, Painted Patera, Swag, Masque Banding, 1800s, 30 x 43 In. 2214
Table, Reading, George IV, Mahogany, Hinged Ratcheted Top, Book Rest, 31 In. 1285
Table, Refectory, Baroque, Walnut, 2-Board Top, Wrought Iron, Spain, 70 x 29 In. 4720
Table, Refectory, Baroque, Walnut, Removable Top, Battened Ends, Italy, 33 x 83 In. 3776
Table, Refectory, French Provincial, Oak, Scalloped Frieze, Drawer, 1800s, 30 x 70 In. 1625
Table, Refectory, Provincial, Tapered Legs, Stretchers, England, 31 x 108 In. 1220
Table, Regency, Grain Painted, Parcel Gilt Bronze Mounts, Top Rotates, c.1810, 23 In. 944

Furniture, Table, Hardwood, Carved, Pierced Skirt, Burl Inset Top, Chinese, 33 x 27 In.
$649

Brunk Auctions

Furniture, Table, Mahogany, Aluminum Legs, Round Top, Claw Foot, Mozer, 1998, 30 x 28 In.
$2,625

Rago Arts and Auction Center

Furniture, Table, Mahogany, Satinwood, Oval Panel, Drawer, c.1890, 28 x 24 In.
$1,125

New Orleans (Cakebread)

Furniture, Table, Malachite, Inlay, Parcel Gilt, Continental, 30 x 26 In.
$1,783

New Orleans (Cakebread)

Furniture, Table, Napoleon III, Marble Top, Guilloche Banding, Shelf, c.1890, 28 x 32 In.
$1,230

Skinner, Inc.

Furniture, Table, Neoclassical Style, Fruitwood, Ebonized Edge, Drawer, c.1850, 28 x 33 In.
$1,845

New Orleans (Cakebread)

Furniture, Table, Nesting, French Provincial Style, Fruitwood, Scalloped, 25 x 21 In., 3 Piece
$687

New Orleans (Cakebread)

Furniture, Table, Phil Powell, Walnut, Sculpted, New Hope, Pa., 1960s, 18 x 31 In.
$9,375

Rago Arts and Auction Center

Furniture, Table, Philip & Kelvin LaVerne, Chan, Chinese Scene, c.1965, 17 x 35 In.
$7,380

Skinner, Inc.

Furniture, Table, Pier, Rosewood, Bronze, Marble, Mirror, c.1810, 36 x 36 In.
$7,170

Neal Auctions

Furniture, Table, Sewing, Black Lacquer, Gilt, 8-Sided Top, Drawer, Foldover, c.1910, 29 In.
$1,896

James D. Julia Auctioneers

Furniture, Table, Sewing, Mahogany, Satinwood, Pineapple Carved Legs, c.1805, 31 x 23 In.
$1,000

Neal Auctions

Furniture, Table, Sewing, Papier-Mache, Mother-Of-Pearl, Inlay, Casters, c.1850, 30 x 21 In.
$1,102

Neal Auctions

Table, Regency, Mahogany, Reeded Edge & Legs, Stationery Flap, 29 x 30 In. 7865
Table, Regency, Satinwood, Banded Rosewood, Lyre Shape Trestle, Saber Legs, 29 x 39 In. 4182
Table, Renaissance Revival, Mahogany, Carved, Gadrooned Edge, c.1890, 33 x 38 In. 1353
Table, Roche Bobois, Travertine, Round Glass Top, 28 ½ x 47 ½ In. 276
Table, Rococo Style, Multicolor, Verde Antico Marble Top, 33 x 45 In. 687
Table, Rosewood, Gilt Bronze, Serpentine Marble Top, Busts, c.1905, 31 x 20 In. 2500
Table, Round, Regency Style, Mahogany, Gilt Band Top, Shelf, Saber Legs, 29 x 29 In. 750
Table, Rustic, Twig & Chip Carved, 2 Tiers, Ben Davis, 28 In. 4250
Table, Sawbuck, Pine, Breadboard Top, X-Crossed Legs, Stretchers, 29 x 44 x 72 In. 938
Table, Sewing, Black Lacquer, Gilt, 8-Sided Top, Drawer, Foldover, c.1910, 29 In. .... *illus* 1896
Table, Sewing, Federal, Mahogany, Walnut, Inlay, Drawers, Reeded Legs, Mass., 30 x 20 In. 360
Table, Sewing, Japanned, Empire, Lift Top, Black, Gold, Trestle Base, Claw Feet, 30 x 25 In. 715
Table, Sewing, Lacquer, Hinged Lid, Black, Gold, Flowers, Lyre-Shape Trestle, c.1850, 28 x 25 In. 600
Table, Sewing, Lacquer, Scalloped Edge, Turned Pedestal, Cabriole Tripod Base, 19 x 16 In. 990
Table, Sewing, Mahogany, Hinged Top, Fitted Interior, Drawer, 1800s, 19 x 19 In. 510
Table, Sewing, Mahogany, Satinwood, Pineapple Carved Legs, c.1805, 31 x 23 In. .... *illus* 1000
Table, Sewing, Papier-Mache, Mother-Of-Pearl, Inlay, Casters, c.1850, 30 x 21 In. .... *illus* 1102
Table, Sewing, Regency, Rosewood, Carved, Twist-Turned Pedestal, c.1820, 29 x 14 In. 236
Table, Sewing, Sheraton, Mahogany, 2 Drawers, Wood Knobs, Brass Inlay, c.1815, 30 x 18 In. ... 1067
Table, Sewing, Sheraton, Mahogany, Inlay, Bag, c.1810, 29 x 22 In. .... *illus* 2074
Table, Sewing, Victorian, Trumpet Shape, Mahogany, Sandalwood Inset, Pedestal, 27 x 17 In. ... 242
Table, Sewing, William IV, Drawers, Cubbies, Urn Shape Pedestal, Carved Feet, 30 ½ x 20 ½ In. . 120
Table, Shaker, Butternut, Drawers, Overhanging Top, Tapered Legs, 1800s, 29 x 41 In. 277
Table, Side, Art Deco, Sunburst Veneer, Round Top, Flared Legs, Scroll Feet, c.1945, 33 In. 4000
Table, Side, Bamboo, Shelf, Lacquered, 19th Century, 31 x 13 x 13 In. 600
Table, Side, Bronze, 8-Sided White Marble Top, Tripod Base, Paw Feet, c.1865, 30 x 21 In. 861
Table, Side, Bronze, Malachite Top, Flower Scrollwork Frieze, 1900s, 31 x 16 In. 5750
Table, Side, C. Aubock, Walnut, Sliced Log, Brass, Austria, 1950s, 18 ¾ x 39 In. 2875
Table, Side, Copper Tiles, Storage Cube, Metal Tacks, 21 ½ x 17 In. 248
Table, Side, Directoire Style, Marble, Pierced Gallery, Concave, Drawers, 31 x 22 In. 676
Table, Side, Dutch Baroque, Cream, 34 x 47 In. 2375
Table, Side, Edwardian, Mahogany, Panel, Leafy Scroll Inlay, Pad Feet, c.1910, 27 x 16 In. 584
Table, Side, Federal, Maple, Painted, Drawer, Plank Top, Square Legs, 1800s, 27 In. 295
Table, Side, French Provincial, Fruitwood, Drawer, Shaped Skirt, c.1790, 28 x 32 In. 2375
Table, Side, French Provincial, Fruitwood, Ring-Turned Bulbous Legs, c.1790, 27 x 21 In. 1000
Table, Side, Fruitwood, Banded Top, Scallop Frieze, Drawer, 1900s, 29 x 34 In. 615
Table, Side, Fruitwood, Canted Corners, Inlaid Banding, Square Legs, c.1780, 32 x 43 In. 687
Table, Side, Fruitwood, Marble Top, Bowed Front, Cabriole Legs, c.1915, 29 x 51 In. 676
Table, Side, Fruitwood, Shaped Gallery, Cupboard Door, Flemish Toes, c.1890, 32 x 22 In. 2500
Table, Side, George III, Padouk, Crossbanded, Kidney Shape, Block Legs, 31 x 48 In. 3146
Table, Side, Gilt Bronze, Onyx Top, Winged Women, Paw Feet, c.1890, 30 x 19 In. 1476
Table, Side, Giltwood, Porcelain Plaque, Portrait, Austrian Duchesse Du Maine, 29 In. .... *illus* 3355
Table, Side, Japanned, Black & Gilt, Pierced Fretwork Gallery, Door, 35 x 13 In. 10814
Table, Side, Kidney Shape, Courting Scene, Painted, 29 x 21 x 13 In. 430
Table, Side, Louis XV Style, Kingwood, Parquetry, Gilt, Serpentine, c.1900, 32 x 31 In. 3750
Table, Side, Louis XV Style, Mahogany, Gilt Bronze, Tambour Doors, Shelf, c.1900, 32 In. 687
Table, Side, Mahogany, Marble, Brass Gallery, Drawer, Reeded Supports, c.1905, 30 x 29 In. 1168
Table, Side, Mahogany, Octagonal, Pierced Gallery, c.1790, 30 x 29 In. 3750
Table, Side, Mahogany, Round Marble Top, Column Legs, Bun Feet, 26 x 20 In., Pair 1750
Table, Side, Marble Top, Shaped, Drawer, Carved Flower Spray, Shelf, c.1850, 40 x 55 In. 1168
Table, Side, McCobb, Maple, Drawer, Lower Shelf, Turned Tapered Legs, 1960s, 19 x 27 In. 138
Table, Side, Napoleon III, Fruitwood, Flower Shape Inlaid Lift Top, Sabots, c.1870, 27 In. 812
Table, Side, Neoclassical, Mahogany, Demilune, Top Shape Feet, c.1800, 30 x 36 In., Pair 1500
Table, Side, P. Evans, Aluminum, Slate, Scored, Welded, Dyed, 1970s, 17 x 17 In., Pair .... *illus* 21250
Table, Side, Philip & Kelvin LaVerne, 6-Sided, Chinese Scene, 1960s, 16 x 18 In. .... *illus* 6765
Table, Side, Regency, Mahogany, Marble Top, Ormolu Frieze, Mirror, c.1810, 38 x 40 In. 2125
Table, Side, Rococo, Fruitwood, Marble Top, Pierced, Cabriole Legs, c.1760, 35 x 59 In. 4750
Table, Side, Rosewood, Kidney Shape, Spindle Stretcher, Splayed Legs, c.1890, 29 x 34 In. 553
Table, Side, Sheraton Style, Drawer, c.1800, 15 x 22 In. 182
Table, Side, Silvertone, Oval, Glass Top, Shelf Below, 35 x 24 In. 188
Table, Side, Umbo, Plastic, Modular, Bright Orange, 17 ½ x 11 ½ In. 303
Table, Side, Walnut, Plank Top, Turned Legs, Carved Frieze, Spain, 1700s, 32 x 42 In. 1582
Table, Side, Walnut, Shaped, Cabriole Legs, Slipper Feet, 1800s, 28 In. 338
Table, Side, Walnut, Travertine, Singer & Sons, 16 x 24 In. 184
Table, Side, Wood, Cloisonne Panel Top, Flowers, Square Legs, c.1900, 23 x 26 In. 1476
Table, Side, Wormley, Rosewood, Brass, Murano Glass Tiles, Slatted Base, 1950s, 21 x 26 In. *illus* 2375
Table, Silas Seandel, Composite, Bronze, Glass, 2000s, 22 x 30 In. 3125

Table, Spanish Baroque, Walnut, Wrought Iron Mounted, Trestle, Stretchers, 28 x 28 In. 1534
Table, Spanish Provincial, Pine, Oval, Turned Legs, Box Stretcher, 1800s, 32 x 42 x 81 In. 2952
Table, Spanish, Oak, Lyre Shape Supports, Scrolling Iron Stretcher, 1800s, 30 x 32 In. 2750
Table, Stickley Bros., Arts & Crafts, Oak, Round Top, Lower Shelf, c.1910, 30 x 30 In. 720
Table, Tavern, 2-Board Top, Pie Board Ends, Drawer, Turned Legs, 1700s, 29 x 35 In. 1003
Table, Tavern, English Oak, Plank Top, Turned Bulbous Legs, Stretcher, 1700s, 28 x 42 In. 738
Table, Tavern, Maple, Pine, Breadboard Ends, Drawer, Stretcher, c.1750, 27 x 47 x 30 In. 4305
Table, Tavern, Maple, Single-Board Top, Turned Legs, Button Feet, 1700s, 27 x 27 In. 413
Table, Tavern, Mixed Wood, Stretcher, Round Top, Splayed Legs, 1700s, 25 x 28 In. 1180
Table, Tavern, Nutting, Queen Anne, Branded, 24 x 21 In. ....*illus* 540
Table, Tavern, Oak, Plank Top, Carved, Baluster Legs, Box Stretcher, 1600s, 87 x 35 In. 1599
Table, Tavern, Pine, 3-Board Top, Painted Stretcher Base, Beaded Skirt, 1700s, 41 x 28 In. 3068
Table, Tavern, Tiger Maple, Oval, Turned Legs, Pegged, Cherry Skirt, c.1790, 26 x 31 In. 590
Table, Tavern, Tiger Maple, Overhanging Scrub Top, Turned Legs, c.1775, 26 x 26 x 23 In. 1722
Table, Tavern, Victorian Style, Cast Iron, Mahogany, Round, Pierced Decoration, 28 x 23 In. 237
Table, Tavern, William & Mary, Maple, Oval Top, Turned Legs, 1735, 37 x 29 In. 889
Table, Tea, George III, Satinwood, Crossbanded, Marquetry, Demilune Medallion, 30 In. 433
Table, Tea, George III, Single-Board Top, Fretwork Stretcher, c.1790, 22 x 26 In. 1415
Table, Tea, Lacquer, Carved, Reserves, Sages In Garden, Chinese, c.1900, 34 x 22 In. ....*illus* 468
Table, Tea, Regency, Mahogany, Banded, Hinged Top, Brass Lines, 30 x 36 In. 786
Table, Tea, Round, Lions, Birds, Fruit, Knobbed Stem, Palm Leaves, 23 In. Diam. 972
Table, Tea, Tilt Top, Chippendale Style, Mahogany, Shaped Edge, Reeded Post, 28 x 32 In. 460
Table, Tea, Tilt Top, Chippendale Style, Piecrust Edge, Birdcage, 29 x 32 In. 299
Table, Tea, Tilt Top, Queen Anne, Mahogany, Serpentine Edges, c.1790, 28 x 32 In. ....*illus* 237
Table, Tea, Tilt Top, Queen Anne, Walnut, Birdcage Support, Pedestal, c.1760, 30 x 36 In. 3540
Table, Tea, Walnut, 8-Sided, Pierced Gallery, Spiral Post, Snake Feet, 1700s, 31 x 31 In. 720
Table, Tessellated Fossil Box, On Stand, Brass Handles, Maitland Smith, 20 x 16 In. 454
Table, Tile Top, Oak, Santa Barbara Mission Scene, Turned Legs, 16¾ x 24 In. 732
Table, Tilt Top, Biedermeier, Fruitwood, Ebonized Border, c.1825, 31 x 40 In. ....*illus* 590
Table, Tilt Top, Chippendale, Tripod Base, Shell Carved Knees, Claw Feet, 1700s, 28 x 29 In. 472
Table, Tilt Top, George III, Mahogany, Yew, Inlaid Tablet, Column, 28 x 46 In. 593
Table, Tilt Top, Hardwood, Oval, Carved Flowers, Leaves, Grapes, Scroll Feet, 1800s, 31 In. 1681
Table, Tilt Top, Mahogany, Piecrust Edge, Turned, Ball Feet, 1800s, 29 x 32 In. ....*illus* 295
Table, Tilt Top, Metal, Painted Hunt Scene, 8-Sided, Cast Tripod Base, Verdigris, 43 x 24 In. 1534
Table, Tilt Top, Piecrust, Reticulated, Shell Carving, Tripod Base, 28 x 32 In. 472
Table, Tilt Top, Rosewood, Octagonal, Molded Frieze, Notched Border, Paw Feet, 29 x 55 In. 750
Table, Tilt Top, Victorian, Molded, Rosewood, Carved, Tripod, Lobed Shaft, 29 x 47 In. 2967
Table, Tole, Glass Top, Scrolled Wrought Iron, 17¾ x 40 In. 302
Table, Traccia, Meret Oppenheim, Ultramobile Collection, Metal Bird Talon Feet......................... 5185
Table, Tray, Cherry, Drawer, Inlaid Mariners Compass, Square Legs, c.1800, 28 x 27 In. 677
Table, Tray, Hunt, Mahogany, Campaign Style, Brass Handles, 27 x 28 In. 968
Table, Tray, Oval Cutout Handles, Rectangular, c.1960, 31 x 26 In. 274
Table, Tray, Tole, Parcel Gilt, Scene, Abbey Ruins, c.1840, 18 x 31 x 24 In. ....*illus* 984
Table, Tray, Turned Feet, Gallery Back & Sides, Cutout Handles, 26 x 15 In. 213
Table, Trestle, Walnut, Vase Shape Supports, Carved Stretcher, 1800s, 26 x 39 In. 184
Table, Tulipwood, Gilt Bronze, Porcelain, Cabriole Legs, 28¾ x 28 In. 486
Table, Turned Legs, Drawer, Wales, 20th Century, 31 x 60 In. 800
Table, Victorian, Mahogany, Marble Top, Oval, Carved Legs, 23 x 22 In. 360
Table, Victorian, Spool, Upholstered, 20½ x 16¼ In. 60
Table, W. Platner, Chromed Metal, Glass, Knoll, 18 x 16 In. ....*illus* 793
Table, Walnut, 2 Drawers, Turned Legs, c.1880, 33 x 21 In. 2673
Table, Walnut, 2 Pedestals, Columnar, Ribbed & Fluted, Paw Feet, 1700s, 28 x 116 In. 4750
Table, Walnut, Marquetry, Parquetry, St. George Slaying Dragon, c.1900, 28 x 27 In. 400
Table, Walnut, Pierced Lyre Shape Trestle Base, Scrolling Iron Stretcher, 20 x 63 In. 430
Table, Whist Counting, Cast Iron, Painted, Counting Pegs, John Gill, c.1863................................ 732
Table, William & Mary Style, Gateleg, Planked Top, Stretcher, c.1890, 43 x 54 In. 369
Table, William & Mary Style, Walnut, Marquetry, Drawer, Twist Legs, 1800s, 28 x 28 In. 492
Table, Wood, Carved, Godogan, Niels Van Eijk, Miriam Vander Lubbe... 3750
Table, Work, Bird's-Eye Maple, Cherry, Poplar, Drawer, Turned Shaft, c.1840, 27 In. 219
Table, Work, Cabriole Legs, Drawer, Tooled & Gilt Green Leather, 1700s, 27 x 31 In. 708
Table, Work, Drop Leaf, Mahogany, Drawers, Turned Stem, Reeded Legs, c.1815, 30 x 20 In. 1169
Table, Work, Federal, Mahogany, Reeded Swelled Legs, Drawer, c.1810, 29 x 20 In. 1968
Table, Work, Fruitwood, Frieze Drawers, Stretcher Base, 1800s, 33 x 60 In. 800
Table, Work, Hepplewhite, Drop Leaf, Red Paint, Overhang, Drawer, 27 x 41 In. 308
Table, Work, Mahogany, Drawers, Lyre Shape Support, 29 x 22 In. 336
Table, Work, Mahogany, Drawers, Turned Tapered Legs, 30 x 19 In. 510
Table, Work, Mahogany, Wood Gallery, Drawers, Turned Legs, Victorian, 38 x 48 In. 431

Furniture, Table, Sewing, Sheraton, Mahogany, Inlay, Bag, c.1810, 29 x 22 In.
$2,074

James D. Julia Auctioneers

Furniture, Table, Side, Giltwood, Porcelain Plaque, Portrait, Austrian Duchesse Du Maine, 29 In.
$3,355

DuMouchelles Art Gallery

Furniture, Table, Side, P. Evans, Aluminum, Slate, Scored, Welded, Dyed, 1970s, 17 x 17 In., Pair
$21,250

Rago Arts and Auction Center

F

Furniture, Table, Side, Philip & Kelvin LaVerne, 6-Sided, Chinese Scene, 1960s, 16 x 18 In.
$6,765

Skinner, Inc.

Furniture, Table, Side, Wormley, Rosewood, Brass, Murano Glass Tiles, Slatted Base, 1950s, 21 x 26 In.
$2,375

Rago Arts and Auction Center

Furniture, Table, Tavern, Nutting, Queen Anne, Branded, 24 x 21 In.
$540

Fairfield Auction

Furniture, Table, Tea, Lacquer, Carved, Reserves, Sages In Garden, Chinese, c.1900, 34 x 22 In.
$468

New Orleans (Cakebread)

Furniture, Table, Tea, Tilt Top, Queen Anne, Mahogany, Serpentine Edges, c.1790, 28 x 32 In.
$237

James D. Julia Auctioneers

Furniture, Table, Tilt Top, Biedermeier, Fruitwood, Ebonized Border, c.1825, 31 x 40 In.
$590

Brunk Auctions

Furniture, Table, Tilt Top, Mahogany, Piecrust Edge, Turned, Ball Feet, 1800s, 29 x 32 In.
$295

Hess Auction Group

Furniture, Table, Tray, Tole, Parcel Gilt, Scene, Abbey Ruins, c.1840, 18 x 31 x 24 In.
$984

New Orleans (Cakebread)

Table, Work, Pine, Red Paint, Marble Top, Biscuit Slab, Lid, Tapered Legs, 1800s, 37 x 30 In. 2006
Table, Work, Victorian, Drop Leaf, Cabinet, Lift Top, Compartments, 1800s, 31 x 41 In. 861
Table, Work, Walnut, Drawers, Turned Legs, Stretcher Base, Spain, 1800s, 28 x 48 In. 308
Table, Wormley, Cube, Walnut, Dunbar, 18 x 18 In., Pair 615
Table, Wormley, Sheaf Of Wheat................ 1220
Table, Writing, Baroque, Walnut, Carved Drawer, Scroll Cut Trestle, 1600s, 30 x 45 In. 492
Table, Writing, Burl, Kidney Shape Top, Columnar Standards, Scroll Feet, 1800s, 26 x 42 In. 540
Table, Writing, Figured Mahogany, Cantilever, Adjustable, 1830s, 31 x 44 In. 295
Table, Writing, George III, Mahogany, Figured, c.1810, 32 x 41 x 23½ In. 649
Table, Writing, Gothic, Walnut, c.1870, 51 x 30½ In. 10698
Table, Writing, Louis Philippe Style, Oak, Carved, Drawer, Stretcher, 1800s, 30 x 48 In. 237
Table, Writing, Louis XIII Style, Oak, Carved, Drawer, Bobbin Legs, 29 x 36 In. 237
Table, Writing, Louis XV Style, Mahogany, Kingwood, Banded, Drawer, 24 x 40 x 24 In. 492
Table, Writing, Louis XV Style, Walnut, Inset Leather, Drawers, Pullout, 1900s, 30 x 69 In. 488
Table, Writing, Louis XVI, Mahogany, Satinwood, Leather, Brass Banding, 30 x 51 In. 1722
Table, Writing, Louis-Philippe, Elm, Glazed Cabinet Doors, Drawers, c.1860, 59 x 34 In. 1107
Table, Writing, Renaissance Revival, Homer Style, Carved, Scrolling, Drawer, 30 x 55 In. 3998
Table, Writing, Tulipwood, Birch, Inlay, Stretcher, Russia, 28½ x 36 In. 1070
Table, Wrought Iron, San Jose Pottery Tile, Plant Cipher, 1930s, 17 x 37 In. .... *illus* 5000
Tabouret, Empire Style, Mahogany, Gilt Bronze, X-Stretcher, Paw Feet, c.1900, 20 In., Pair........ 9375
Tabouret, Oak, Hexagonal Top, Gadrooned, Lion Mask Legs, Paw Feet, c.1900, 20 x 21 In. 490
Tea Cart, Bamboo, Wheels, Circles, Round Trays, 33 x 25 In. 205
Tea Cart, Beech, Oak, Carved, 3 Shelves, Casters, France, c.1910, 36 x 30 In. 123
Tea Cart, Brass, Lattice Rims, 2 Smoky Glass Shelves, 3 Wheels, Folds, France, 29 In. 122
Tea Cart, Louis XVI Style, Oak, Silver Plate, Ice Bowl, Bottle Holders, 35 x 38 In. .... *illus* 500
Tea Cart, Wegner, Teak, Round Legs, Medial Shelf, Casters, Denmark, c.1950, 24 x 28 In. 180
Tea Cart, William IV, Mahogany, 3 Tiers, Turned Legs, Bulbous Feet, c.1810, 45 x 48 In. 1960
Teapoy, Neoclassical, Mahogany, 8-Sided Case, Acanthus, Casters, 1800s, 28 x 17 In. 2928
Teapoy, Regency, Rosewood, Carved, Sarcophagus Shape, Lotus Standard, c.1810, 28 x 17 In. ... 738
Teapoy, Victorian, Gothic, Oak, Leaves, Spiral Fluting, c.1860, 28 x 19 In. 1751
Teapoy, William IV, Rosewood, Box Shape, Lid, Pedestal, Glass Cups, c.1810, 29 In. .... *illus* 861
Tete-A-Tete, Edwardian, Oak, Carved, Opposing Seats, Spindle Backs, c.1910, 28 x 53 In. 185
Tete-A-Tete, Egyptian Revival, Parcel Gilt, Upholstered Central Armrest, 31 x 47 In. 400
Tete-A-Tete, Rococo Revival, Rosewood, Carved, Swivels, c.1850, 44 x 77 In. .... *illus* 3068
Tie Press, Mahogany, Inlay, Hinged, Acme, c.1900, 5 x 9 In. 48
Tray, Stand, Blackamoor, Standing On Hands, Walnut, 1800s, 32 In., Pair................ 4305
Tray, Stand, Papier-Mache, Scalloped, Leaves, Birds, Gilt On Black, Iron Base, c.1841................ 460
Tray, Stand, Regency, Tole, Red, Painted Castle, Landscape, Gilt Grape Edge, 30 x 30 In. 1045
Umbrella Stand, Black, Square, Cutout Top, Cast Iron, Cabriole Legs, Paw Feet, 26 x 13 In. 600
Umbrella Stand, Fornasetti, Metal, Serigraphed, Musical Instruments, Italy, c.1955, 26 In. 1353
Umbrella Stand, Fornasetti, Transfer Decorated, Enameled Metal, Brass, 1960s, 23 x 10 In. 1125
Umbrella Stand, Hall, Oak, Brass, 40 x 22 In. 750
Umbrella Stand, Jack Tar, Iron, Multicolor, 1800s, 21 x 17½ In. 1638
Umbrella Stand, Old Leather Boot, Fiberglass, Brown Paint, 23 In. 106
Umbrella Stand, Stoneware, Snow Boot Shape, Brown, 24 x 12 In. 180
Umbrella Stand, Victorian, Leaves, 8 Round Slots, Handle, Iron, Cast, 25 x 17 In. 360
Urn, Knife, Mahogany, Inlaid, Reeding, Bowknots, Swags, Cone Finial, c.1890, 31 In., Pair......... 2091
Urn, Mantel, Onyx, Pedestal, Leaf Scroll Handles, Plinth, France, 1800s, 9½ In., Pair 300
Vanity, Art Deco, Marble, Zinc, Lower Shelf, Beveled Mirror, Vinyl Stool, 2 Piece 303
Vanity, Stool, Herman Miller, 29½ x 56½ In. 300
Vitrine, French Style, Stepped Cornice, Demilune Glass Panel, Stretcher, c.1960, 70 x 22 In. 210
Vitrine, Galle, Ombelle, Walnut, Flowers, Butterfly, Inlay, c.1900, 48 x 26 In. .... *illus* 10000
Vitrine, Louis XV Style, Gilt, Festoons, Curved Glass Panels, 55 In. .... *illus* 300
Vitrine, Louis XV Style, Mahogany, Glass Panel, Hinged Lid, 1900s, 30 x 43 In. 1353
Vitrine, Mahogany, Gilt Bronze, Oval, Marble Top, Glass Door, c.1915, 59 x 28 In. 4375
Vitrine, Mahogany, Glazed Panel Top, Ormolu Edge, Hinged, Lotus, c.1900, 33 x 38 In. 1500
Vitrine, Mahogany, Hinged Top, Scrolling Leaf Ormolu, Reeded Legs, c.1890, 30 x 38 In. 2214
Vitrine, Mahogany, Ormolu, Demilune, Baby Satyrs, 2 Shelves, 16 x 5 In., 57 x 37 In. 4537
Vitrine, Painted, Bronze Ormolu, Brass Trim, Door, Courting Scenes, 1800s, 71 x 38 In. 600
Vitrine, Rococo, Multicolor, Parcel Gilt Mirror, Scrolling Crest, Door, 145 x 62 In. 2375
Vitrine, Walnut, Gilt Bronze, Marble Top, Panel Door, Turned Feet, c.1900, 71 x 29 In. 3125
Wall Unit, P. Evans, Cityscape, Gold, Silver, Tiles, Smoked Glass, c.1950, 80 x 48 In. .... *illus* 1200
Wardrobe, 2 Flat Panel Doors, Bracket Base, 3 Shelves, 60 x 41 In. 118
Wardrobe, Art Nouveau, Oak, 3 Doors, Shelves, c.1900, 88 x 60 In. 150
Wardrobe, Painted, Pastel, Gilt, Broken-Arch Pediment, Paneled Doors, 1800s, 75 x 43 In. 300
Wardrobe, Perriand, Pine, White Paint, Black Metal, Sliding Doors, 68 x 58 In. 2520

TIP

To make a new marble tabletop look old, wipe it with vinegar a few times. The dull finish of old tops came from repeated washings.

F

Furniture, Table, W. Platner, Chromed Metal, Glass, Knoll, 18 x 16 In.
$793

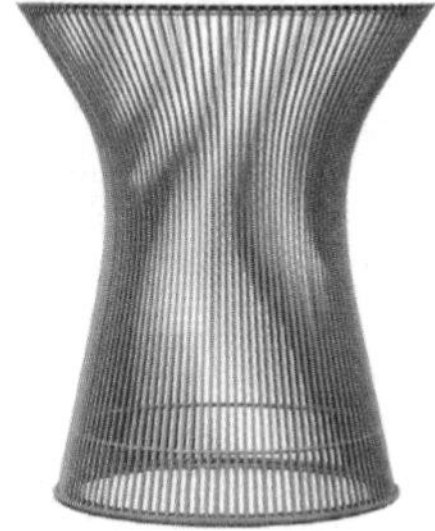

Palm Beach Modern Auctions

Furniture, Table, Wrought Iron, San Jose Pottery Tile, Plant Cipher, 1930s, 17 x 37 In.
$5,000

Rago Arts and Auction Center

Furniture, Tea Cart, Louis XVI Style, Oak, Silver Plate, Ice Bowl, Bottle Holders, 35 x 38 In.
$500

New Orleans (Cakebread)

This is an edited listing of current prices. Visit **Kovels.com** to check thousands of prices from previous years and sign up for free information on trends, tips, reproductions, marks, and more.

FURNITURE

Furniture, Teapoy, William IV, Rosewood, Box Shape, Lid, Pedestal, Glass Cups, c.1810, 29 In.
$861

Skinner, Inc.

Furniture, Tete-A-Tete, Rococo Revival, Rosewood, Carved, Swivels, c.1850, 44 x 77 In.
$3,068

Brunk Auctions

Furniture, Vitrine, Galle, Ombelle, Walnut, Flowers, Butterfly, Inlay, c.1900, 48 x 26 In.
$10,000

Rago Arts and Auction Center

Furniture, Vitrine, Louis XV Style, Gilt, Festoons, Curved Glass Panels, 55 In.
$300

Cowan Auctions

Furniture, Wall Unit, P. Evans, Cityscape, Gold, Silver, Tiles, Smoked Glass, c.1950, 80 x 48 In.
$1,200

Selkirk Auctioneers & Appraisers

Furniture
George Nakashima learned traditional joinery skills from a Japanese carpenter in a U.S. internment camp in Idaho during World War II.

Furniture, Wardrobe, Schrank, Painted, Paneled Doors, Columns, Lancaster, c.1780, 88 x 89 In.
$31,860

Hess Auction Group

Furniture, Washstand, Blanket Box, Shaker, Pine, Cabinet, Lift Lid, Peg Feet, c.1845, 52 In.
$3,600

Wright (Chicago)

Is It a Marriage?
If you have a two-part piece of furniture like a highboy or secretary-desk, the two parts should match in every way: wood grain, dovetailing, and other construction details. If they do not, it is possible that the piece is a "marriage." The parts originally came from two different pieces later joined together by a dealer. Recently we saw a "divorce"—a Victorian dresser split into a mirror and two small chests of drawers.

Wardrobe, Schrank, Painted, Paneled Doors, Columns, Lancaster, c.1780, 88 x 89 In. ....*illus* 31860
Wardrobe, Schrank, Red Milk Paint, Stepped Cornice, Doors, Drawers, c.1780, 90 x 87 In. 8850
Wardrobe, Veneer, Inlay Banding, Panel Doors, Shelves, 1900s, 77 x 72 In. 413
Washstand, Arts & Crafts, Oak, Marble Top, Green Tile, 2 Candle Shelves, c.1910, 45 x 36 In. 215
Washstand, Blanket Box, Shaker, Pine, Cabinet, Lift Lid, Peg Feet, c.1845, 52 In. ....*illus* 3600
Washstand, Federal, Mahogany, Drawer, 1800s, 20 x 16 In. 234
Washstand, Federal, Mahogany, Sheraton Style, Backsplash, Drawers, c.1810, 40 x 35 In. 799
Washstand, Mahogany, Bronze, Gallery Backsplash, Ladder Top, Cone Feet, 1800s, 39 In. 242
Washstand, Marble Top, Frieze Drawer, Door, Casters, c.1875, 30 x 36 In. 246
Washstand, Neoclassical, Mahogany, Pine, Poplar, Gallery, Columns, Drawer, Doors, 40 x 28 In. 313
Washstand, Sheraton, Wood, Paint, Bowfront, Backsplash, Shelf, Drawer, c.1840, 35 In. ....*illus* 356
Washstand, Turned Legs, Drawer, Towel Bars, Bottom Shelf, 33 x 24 In. 104
Washstand, Victorian Renaissance, Walnut, Marble Top, Reeded Columns, Casters, 32 x 36 In. 77
Washstand, Wrought Iron, Tin Leaves, Candlestand, Copper Bowl, 85 In. 3112
Wastebasket, Arts & Crafts, Stickley Style, Quartersawn Oak Slats, Handles, 17 x 15 In. 380
Wastebasket, G. Stickley, Oak, Staves, Metal Bands, Rivets, Red Decal, c.1907, 14 In. ....*illus* 2375
Wastebasket, Mirror Panels, Rosettes, Velvet Lined, 20¾ x 13¾ In. 165
Wet Bar, Molded Surround, Brass Foot Rail, Sink Set Up, 71 x 18 In. 995
Whatnot Shelf, Regency, Rosewood, 3 Tiers, Ring & Baluster Turnings, 1800s, 31 In. 531
Whatnot Shelf, Regency, Rosewood, 4 Tiers, Turned Supports, Drawer, c.1800, 52 x 19 In. 2000
Window Seat, George III Style, Giltwood, Scroll Arms, Fluted Legs, c.1890, 26 x 46 In. 750
Window Seat, George III, Giltwood, 28½ x 54 In. 1375
Window Seat, Louis XVI Style, Fruitwood, Scroll Arms, Upholstered, c.1900, 27 x 49 In. 800
Window Seat, Regency Style, Mahogany, Padded Seat, Sides, 1900s, 32 x 56 In. 799
Wine Cooler, George IV, Mahogany, Parcel Gilt, Gothic Tracery, c.1830, 18½ x 25 In. 7500
Wine Cooler, Table, Marble Top, Inset Copper Bottle Holders, c.1790, 28 x 18 In. 1168

G. ARGY-ROUSSEAU is the impressed mark used on a variety of glass objects in the Art Deco style. Gabriel Argy-Rousseau, born in 1885, was a French glass artist. In 1921, he formed a partnership that made pate-de-verre and other glass. The partnership ended in 1931 and he opened his own studio. He worked until 1952 and died in 1953.

G-ARGY-ROUSSEAU

Ashtray, Cranberry, Scalloped Border, Pate-De-Verre, c.1925, 6 In. 1112
Bowl, Red Berry Clusters, Leaves, Pate-De-Verre, 3 x 3 In. 2185
Ceiling Light, Large Flower Head, Chains For Suspension, 12 In. 7665
Night-Light, Orange Anemone, Mottled Ground, Pate-De-Verre, Iron Base, 8 In. 5333
Vase, Apple Picker, Apple Trees, Yellow Apples, Rolled Rim, 1920s, 10 x 6 In. ....*illus* 15000
Vase, Bramble Leaves, Spider Web, Spider, Bulbous, Pink, Green, 4½ In. 8888
Vase, Ogives, Stylized Leaf Panels, Blue Green, Flared, Signed, 7 In. 5036
Vase, Overlapping Leaves, Flower Rim, Tapered, Gray, Mottled Purple, 10 In. 8295
Vase, Poppies, Long Stems, Orange, Red, 7 In. 8230
Vase, Tall Pheasant Tail Feathers, Mottled Cream, Orange Brown, 6 In. 6221
Vase, Yellow, Brown & White Flowers, Mottled Cream Ground, Tapered, 6 In. 4740

GALLE was a designer who made glass, pottery, furniture, and other Art Nouveau items. Emile Galle founded his factory in France in 1874. After Galle's death in 1904, the firm continued to make glass and furniture until 1931. The *Galle* signature was used as a mark, but it was often hidden in the design of the object. Galle cameo and other types of glass are listed here. Pottery is in the next section. His furniture is listed in the Furniture category.

Gallé

Bowl, Green, Frosted, Encircling Ferns, Cameo, Rough Wave Rim, Saucer Foot, 5 In. Diam. 593
Bowl, Hydrangeas, Pink, White Ground, Elongated Oval, Pinched Rim, 11 In. 1034
Bowl, Shell Shape, Clear Brown, 6½ In. 840
Decanter, Amber, Enamel Man & Woman Carrying Basket, Faceted Stopper, 13 In. 1185
Dessert Stand, Round, Gilt Bronze, Yellow, Blue Flowers, 3 Tiers, Cameo, 28¾ In. 4840
Figurine, Cat, Seated, Yellow, Blue Circles, Hearts, Signed, c.1890, 13 x 11 In. ....*illus* 1750
Inkwell, Lid, Earth Tone Flowers, Frosted Ground, 1½ x 4 In. ....*illus* 690
Lamp, Domed Shade, Violet, Amber, Metal Floral Overlay, Bronze Base, Stork, 19 In. ....*illus* 1968
Lamp, Mountains, Pines, Eagles On Shade, Sky, Frosted Yellow Ground, 22 In. ....*illus* 9200
Perfume Bottle, Drum Shape, Cased Red Brown, Cameo, Etched, Rose Ground, c.1900, 4¼ In. ... 767
Perfume Burner, Etched, Engraved, Cameo, Footed, Brass Burner, c.1910, 6½ In. ....*illus* 1121
Plate, Chardons De Lorraine, Smoky, Pink Enameled, Upturned End, Thistles, Gilt, 3 x 12 In. ... 184
Sconce, Red, Flowering Cactus, Frosted Yellow Ground, Cameo, Bronze Frame, 11 x 8 In. 2844
Sugar, Purple & Red Flame Bands, Amber Ground, Flowers, Clear Handles, Cameo, 3 x 7 In. 21330
Vase, Acid Carved, Pink Cameo Flowers, Maroon Leaves, Yellow To Cream, 11½ In. ....*illus* 1896
Vase, Amber Flowers & Stems, Blown-Out, Frosted Yellow Ground, Oval, 9½ In. 11850
Vase, Banjo Shape, Fern Design, Green, Brown, Signed, 7½ In. 474

Furniture, Washstand, Sheraton, Wood, Paint, Bowfront, Backsplash, Shelf, Drawer, c.1840, 35 In.
$356

James D. Julia Auctioneers

Furniture, Wastebasket, G. Stickley, Oak, Staves, Metal Bands, Rivets, Red Decal, c.1907, 14 In.
$2,375

Rago Arts and Auction Center

G.Argy-Rousseau, Vase, Apple Picker, Apple Trees, Yellow Apples, Rolled Rim, 1920s, 10 x 6 In.
$15,000

Rago Arts and Auction Center

Galle, Figurine, Cat, Seated, Yellow, Blue Circles, Hearts, Signed, c.1890, 13 x 11 In.
$1,750

Rago Arts and Auction Center

Galle, Inkwell, Lid, Earth Tone Flowers, Frosted Ground, 1½ x 4 In.
$690

Early Auction Company

Galle, Lamp, Domed Shade, Violet, Amber, Metal Floral Overlay, Bronze Base, Stork, 19 In.
$1,968

Cowan Auctions

Vase, Berry Vine, Leaves, Lavender, Frosted Cream Ground, Saucer Foot, 12 In. 6518
Vase, Birch Tree Catkins, Brown, Green, Cameo, Bulbous, Cylinder Neck, 1900s, 6 In. 1000
Vase, Blue, Purple Acid Cut Flowers, Frosted Yellow Ground, Flared Rim, Cameo, 6 In. 2075
Vase, Brown & Green Trees, Cream Shaded To Salmon Ground, Oval, Flared, 15¾ In. 4148
Vase, Brown, Purple, Amber, Leaves, Acid Cut, Fire Polished, Scalloped Rim, Cameo, 11 In. 11850
Vase, Bud, Gold, Pink, Cameo, Squat Base, Tapered Neck, c.1910, 4½ In. 480
Vase, Bud, Ocher, Leaves & Berries, Cameo, 5¼ In. 484
Vase, Bud, Poppy Design, Orange, White Swirl, Cameo, Round, Stick Neck, c.1900, 7 In. 403
Vase, Budding & Flowering Branches, Red, Pink, Cream, Cameo, 18¾ x 5½ In. 3600
Vase, Catkin Stalks, Brown & Green, Frost Pink, Bulbous, Cameo, Cylindrical Neck, 4 In. 316
Vase, Clear, Green Flowers & Leaves, Cameo, 10 In. 63
Vase, Cream, Purple Flower Branch Overlay, Beaker, Smokestack, Cameo, c.1900, 10 In. 1000
Vase, Cylindrical, Ring Foot, Brown, Green, Red, Flowers, Branches, Cameo, c.1900, 18 In. 3540
Vase, Deep Purple Trees, Pond, Fence, Frosted White To Peach, Oval, Ring Foot, Cameo, 11 In. .. 4148
Vase, Dome Shape, Flared Rim, Squat, Cranberry To Red, Yellow, Cameo, Frosted, c.1900, 8 In. . 2006
Vase, Enamel, Brown Glass, Flowers, Dragonfly, Spiral Ribbed, Ring Foot, 9¾ In. .... *illus* 5036
Vase, Frosted Yellow Ground, Brown Leaves, Red Flowers, Round, Roll Rim, 7 In. 8591
Vase, Gold Trees, Cream & Purple Ground, 18½ In. 2250
Vase, Iris, Purple, Yellow Ground, Elongated Oval, Cameo, Marked, 9 In. 2578
Vase, Lavender & Green Flowers, Peach Ground, Swollen Shoulder, Green Foot, 9⅜ In. 2074
Vase, Lavender, Smoky Cream Ground, Carved, Cameo, Pedestal Base, c.1900, 13¼ In. 1298
Vase, Leaves, Brown, Cameo, 9⅝ x 4⅜ In. 840
Vase, Lilies, Spread Foot, Cameo, Signed, 18 In. .... *illus* 5463
Vase, Mottled Amber, Butterflies, Bubbles, Purple Top, Signed, Smokestack Shape, 14 In. 32588
Vase, Mountain Vista, Conifer Trees, Green, Blue, Amethyst, Cameo, 10 In. 2714
Vase, Narrow Neck, Ornamental Ferns, Olive Green, Gold, Cameo, 23½ x 7½ In. 2498
Vase, Oleander Flowers, Stem & Leaves, Amber, Pink, Frosted Yellow, Cameo, 14 In. 3555
Vase, Orange Seed Pods, Leafy Branches, White, Orange, Cameo, Pear Shape, 4 In. 345
Vase, Pear Shape, Square Wavy Rim, Fire Polished, Orange Flowers, Green Cameo, 9 In. 2074
Vase, Pedestal, Oak Leaves, Brown, Green, Peach Matte Ground, 6 x 5½ In. 443
Vase, Pendant Branches, Opaque To Rose, Cameo, 13⅜ x 5 In. 960
Vase, Purple Flowers, White Ground, 9½ In. 813
Vase, Purple Fuchsia, Blown-Out, Frosted Yellow Ground, Flared Rim, 11½ In. 8295
Vase, Purple Leaves & Berries, Thorny Branches, Frosted Yellow Ground, Pear Shape, 9 In. 2963
Vase, Purple Pine Trees, Blue Mountains, Cream Frosted Ground, Shouldered, 8 In. 3259
Vase, Purple, White, Cameo, 3½ x 4 In. 480
Vase, Purple, Yellow Ground, Reeds, Flowers, Cameo, Octagonal Foot, Signed, 4½ In. 363
Vase, Red & Pink Fuchsia, Blown-Out, Frosted Cream Shaded To Yellow Ground, 12 In. 11850
Vase, Red & Pink, Cyclamen Flowers, Yellow Ground, Cameo, Swollen, Tapered, 9 In. 2666
Vase, Red, Leaves, Pink Bleeding Heart, Frosted Ground, Cylindrical, Bell Foot, Cameo, 10 In. ... 2252
Vase, Red, Wheel Carved Honeysuckle, Yellow Ground, Shaded, Tapered, Wide Rim, 5 In. 1778
Vase, Red, Yellow, Silver Rim, Leaves, Cameo, 2¾ In. 295
Vase, Round Foot, Flowers, Praying Mantis, Blue Glass Beads, Rolled Rim, Cameo, c.1900, 6 In. 1673
Vase, Scenic, Cameo, Scenic, Footed, 6¼ In. 780
Vase, Square, Multicolor Enameled Flowers, Cameo, 12 In. 3000
Vase, Stick, Prunelles, Blue & Violet Flowers, Pale Yellow Ground, c.1920, 14 x 4 In. 847
Vase, Sunset Scene, Grasses, 9 x 6¼ In. 1440
Vase, Twilight Landscape, Mountains, Trees, Yellow Sky, Cameo, Signed, c.1910, 10¼ In. 2583
Vase, Yellow Water Lilies, Vaseline To Brown, Cameo, 10 x 6 In. 2520

GALLE POTTERY was made by Emile Galle, the famous French designer, after 1874. The pieces were marked with the initials *E. G.* impressed, *Em. Galle Faiencerie de Nancy*, or a version of his signature. Galle is best known for his glass, listed above.

Dog, Pug, Seated, Yellow, Blue & White Hearts, Circles & Flowers, Glass Eyes, 14 In. 1230
Powder Box, Purple Flowers, Marked, 5 In. Diam. 760

GAME collectors like all types of games. Of special interest are any board games or card games. Transogram and other company names are included in the description when known. Other games may be found listed under Card, Toy, or the name of the character or celebrity featured in the game. Gameboards without the game pieces are listed in the Gameboard category.

Addams Family, Plastic Player Pieces, Board, Box, Lid, 1964, 10 x 20 In. 984
Bag Toss, Black Man, Open Mouth, Red Lips, Striped Shirt, 1900s, 21½ x 11 In. 1521
Bagatelle, Green Hornet, Double Action, Cardboard, Plastic, Box, 1966, 12 x 17 In. 2214
Board, Cribbage, Whalebone, Whale Shape, Shell Panels, 1800s, 13 In. 584
Board, Dealer's Choice, Used Car Dealership, Parker Brothers, 1972 .... *illus* 50

Board, Game Of Merry Christmas, Markers, Money, Dice, Parker Bros., 1890, 24 In. 5605
Board, Parcheesi, Wooden, Inlaid, Center Medallion, Wired Back, Hanging, c.1880, 22 x 22 In. *illus* 875
Board, Spinning Wheel, Yale, Harvard, Red, Blue, Yellow, 1900s, 25 ½ x 26 ½ In. 1170
Box, Burl Walnut, Inlay, Ebonized, Compartments, Gilt Metal Lid, Chips, c.1910, 2 x 12 In. 215
Chess Set, Blue, White, Pewter, Franklin Mint, Civil War, 1983, 32 Piece, 13 x 13 In. 149
Chess Set, Box, Enamel, Silver, Gilt, Cabochons, Blue, Wood, Hinged Lid, 5 x 12 In. 7813
Chess Set, Box, Staunton Pattern, Ivory, Red, Fort Shape 2918
Chess Set, Chinoiserie, Black, Beige, Figures, Buildings, 9 x 22 In. 563
Chess Set, Ivory Pieces, Wood Board, 18 ½ x 18 ½ In. 402
Chess Set, Ivory, Onyx, 14 x 14 In. 177
Chess Set, Jadeite, 12 x 15 ½ In. 118
Chess Set, Maple, Walnut, 33 Piece, Elliot Franz Sandow, 19 ⅜ x 19 ⅜ In. 850
Chess Set, Sterling Silver, Silver Gilt, Inlay, Winged Paw Feet, Cartouche, Spain, 4 x 18 In. 1830
Chinese Checkers, 36 Various Stone Marbles, Wood Board, 20 In. 168
Chinese Checkers, Malachite, Bone, Chess, 8 ¼ In. 450
Creature From The Black Lagoon, Mystery, Spinner, Box, Hasbro, Board, 1963, 10 x 19 In. ... 1708
Croquet Set, Stand, Mahogany, Victorian, 10 Mallets, Turned Legs, Brass Markers, 1870, 37 In. 4668
Cue Holders, Wall Mount, Inlay, Continental, 60 x 13 ¼ In., Pair 500
Dartboard, Bull's-Eye, Layered Pressed Paper, Iron, Red White & Blue Paint, c.1900, 7 In. 618
Darts, Board, Black, White, Red, Blue, Green Ground, 21 x 21 In. 497
Disneyland Monorail Game, Walt Disney, Board, Box, 1960 40
Dominoes, Rosewood, Silver Pips, Pins, Lines, Inset Silver Eagle, Box, W. Spratling, 8 In. 1722
Dominoes, Rosewood, Walnut Case, Hinged Lid, Scoring Holes, Cartier, 14 x 4 ½ In. 840
Game Of Cycling, Pawns & Spinner, Parker Brothers, Box, c.1900, 15 x 9 In. 180
Gee-Wiz, Horse Racing, Wolverine, Box, 1923, 16 x 6 x 3 In. 75
Hockey, Canadian Bobby Hull, Cardboard, Players, Goals, Flippers, c.1963, 22 x 39 In. 195
Innocence Abroad, Lithograph, Spinner, 7 Wood Pieces, Box, Parker Brothers, Board, 10 In. ... 148
Mahjong, 144 Ebony & Bone Tiles, Carved, Lacquered Case, 12 x 9 ¼ In. ....*illus* 580
Mahjong, Mahogany, Cased, Handle, Doors, Drawers, Bamboo, Bone Tiles, 1800s, 7 x 9 In. 974
Ouija, Board, Mystifying Oracle, Pancetta Box, William Fuld, 1919, 12 x 18 In. ....*illus* 212
Puzzle, Dexterity, Monkey Pool Players, Embossed Tin, Germany, c.1900s, 1 ½ In. ....*illus* 145
Race Horse, 5 Pony Race, Mechanical, Handle, Die Cast Metal, Tetrarcho, 30 x 10 In. 183
Rifleman, Holding Rifle, Box, 1959, 9 ½ x 19 In. 115
Rock'em Sock'em Robots, Plastic, Marx, Box, 1973 195
Roulette Wheel, O'Neill, Wood, Numbered Slots, Round, Spins, Metal, Chicago, 31 In. ......*illus* 1830
Sea Hunt, Diving Masks, Guns, Fishing Rods, Vinyl Fish, Board, Box, c.1960, 15 x 24 In. 633
Sea Hunt, Ideal Water Sport For Pools, Lakes, Oceans, Fish, Masks, Box, c.1960, 28 In. 633
Skittles, Clown, Composition, Paper Label, Germany, 23 In., 5 Piece 7080
Table Top Croquet Set, Mallets, Hoops, Balls, 1940s, Case 18 x 8 In. 425
Target Figure, Clown, Arcade, Canvas, Baseball Toss, 14 In. ....*illus* 90
Target, Eagle, Cast Iron, Painted Feathers, Red, White & Blue Bull's-Eye, Stand, 15 In. 1722
Target, Straight Arrow, Magnetic Arrows, Box, National Biscuit Co., 11 x 14 In. 253
Tiddlywinks, Cardboard, Multicolor Graphic Cats, Milton Bradley, 12 x 9 In. 230
Time Tunnel, Board, Spinner, Ideal, Box, 1966, 10 x 20 In. 984
Wheel, Gambling, Carnival, Star Shape, Metal Spokes, Wood, Black, Red, c.1910, 25 In. ......*illus* 767
Wheel, Gambling, Cream, Stand, 75 x 24 In. 175
Wheel, Gambling, Wood & Iron, Blue & White Paint, Mounted, Stand, c.1910, 48 x 29 In. 300
Wheel, Red, Yellow, Stand, 37 x 24 In. 146
Yacht Race, Die Cut Pieces, Spinner, Board, McLoughlin Bros., Pat. 1887, 17 In. 826

GAME PLATES are plates of any make decorated with pictures of birds, animals, or fish. The game plates usually came in sets consisting of twelve dishes and a serving platter. These sets were most popular during the 1880s.

Birds, Gold Encrusted, Turquoise Trim, Bavaria, 10 ¼ In., 12 Piece 700
Drake & Hen Duck, Barnyard, Flow Blue, Crimped, Copeland, c.1910, 10 ½ In. 89
Duck In Flight, Scalloped Rim, Solis, Limoges, 9 ½ In. 95
Ducks In Pond, Rocks, Ruffled Rim, Gilt, Limoges, 8 ¾ In. 43
Ducks, Swimming, Fox, Rose Border, Transfer, Wedgwood, c.1903, 10 ⅜ In. 107
Elks, In Meadow, Scalloped Green Border, Dornheim, c.1890, 12 In. 75
Fish, Gilded Grillwork Border, Spode, c.1890, 8 ¾ In., 8 Piece 1500
Game Birds, Sleeping Dog, Under Bushes, Pink Luster, c.1800, 8 In. 85
Partridge, On Branch, Oval, Johnson Brothers, 11 x 10 In. 55
Ring-Necked Pheasant, Meadow, Scalloped & Beaded Rim, Germany, c.1900, 8 In. 70
Ruffed Grouse, Dark Blue Ground, Gilt Border, Germany, 12 In. 70
Trout, Scalloped Edge, Tressemann & Vogt, Limoges, c.1898, 9 In. 125
Woodcock, Brown To Green To Blue Rim, Scalloped, Bavaria, 12 ½ In. 125

Galle, Lamp, Mountains, Pines, Eagles On Shade, Sky, Frosted Yellow Ground, 22 In.
$9,200

Early Auction Company

Galle, Perfume Burner, Etched, Engraved, Cameo, Footed, Brass Burner, c.1910, 6 ½ In.
$1,121

Brunk Auctions

Galle, Vase, Acid Carved, Pink Cameo Flowers, Maroon Leaves, Yellow To Cream, 11 ½ In.
$1,896

James D. Julia Auctioneers

Galle, Vase, Enamel, Brown Glass, Flowers, Dragonfly, Spiral Ribbed, Ring Foot, 9 ¾ In.
$5,036

James D. Julia Auctioneers

Galle, Vase, Lilies, Spread Foot, Cameo, Signed, 18 In.
$5,463

Cottone Auctions

Game, Board, Dealer's Choice, Used Car Dealership, Parker Brothers, 1972
$50

Ruby Lane

GAMEBOARD collectors look for just the board without the game pieces. The boards are collected as folk art or decorations. Gameboards that are part of a complete game are listed in the previous category.

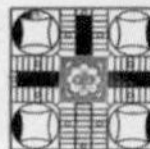

Backgammon, Inlay, Hinge, 5 ¾ x 12 In. 24
Backgammon, Red, White, Person In Field, 18 x 18 In. 614
Checkers & Parcheesi, Painted, Applied Walnut Edge, c.1890, 18 ½ In. *illus* 2337
Checkers & Parcheesi, Red, Yellow, Wood, 17 ¾ x 7 ¾ In. 1287
Checkers & Parcheesi, Wood, Decoupage Flowers, c.1880, 17 x 17 In. 240
Checkers, Black, Red, 19 ¼ x 25 ¼ In. 117
Checkers, Black, White, Black Border, 16 x 19 ½ In. 321
Checkers, Black, White, Horse, Pony, 12 ¼ x 26 In. 1404
Checkers, Blue, Wood, Green & Yellow Paint, Molded Ends, 18 x 13 In. 150
Checkers, Chess, Red, Cream, Butterfly, Folk Art, 1800s, 14 ¾ x 26 In. 1521
Checkers, Cream, Black, 15 x 14 ¾ In. 906
Checkers, Diamond Border, Marble, Round, Italy, 1800s, 20 In. Diam. 780
Checkers, Eglomise, Multicolor, Carved Oak Frame, c.1895, 17 x 17 In. 184
Checkers, Green, White, Beavers, Maple Leaves, c.1890, 31 x 19 In. *illus* 2214
Checkers, Pine, Black & Yellow Paint, Scrolling Vine Border, 1800s, 17 x 17 In. 1778
Checkers, Red, Black, 1800s, 20 ¼ x 33 ½ In. 176
Checkers, Slate, Engraved, Paint, 15 ¼ x 15 ½ In. 526
Checkers, Softwood, Paint, Green, Black & Yellow, Slide Lid, 1800s, 15 x 15 In. 767
Checkers, Standard Oil, Board & Chips, Black & Red, Standard Size 90
Parcheesi, Folding, Red, Blue, Yellow, White, 22 x 21 In. 1404
Parcheesi, Home, Red, Brown, Yellow, 18 x 17 ¾ In. 1440
Parcheesi, Horseshoe, Lion's Head, 20 ½ x 20 ½ In. 2106
Parcheesi, Multicolor, 1800s, 17 ½ In. 1170
Parcheesi, Painted, Black Edge, Red, Yellow, Green, Orange, Blue, c.1890, 20 x 20 In. *illus* 6765
Parcheesi, Pine, Painted, Gordon Eldred, May 12, 1935, Climax, Michigan, 28 x 24 In. 3250

GARDEN FURNISHINGS have been popular for centuries. The stone or metal statues, urns and fountains, sundials, small figurines, and wire, iron, or rustic furniture are included in this category. Many of the metal pieces have been made continuously for years.

Arbor, 2 Pedestals, Arch, Metal, Painted, 3 Sections, 103 x 82 In. 156
Arbor, Lattice Panels, Peaked Roof, Metal, Painted, 3 Sections, 103 x 60 In. 281
Bench, Acanthus Leaf, Marble, Carved, c.1910, 17 x 55 In. 1088
Bench, Adirondack Style, 61 x 27 In. 585
Bench, American Fern Pattern, Pierced, Branchwork Legs, Cast Iron, 1800s, 24 x 55 In. 1225
Bench, Curtain Pattern, 3-Part Back, Rosette Crest, Arms, Iron, Fortune Label, 1800s *illus* 1107
Bench, Curved Flower Back, Green Paint, Cast Iron, c.1890, 30 x 45 In. 1320
Bench, Empire Style, Birch, Carved, Pierced Double Swan, Arms, 1900s, 39 x 52 In., Pair 861
Bench, Fern & Blackberry, Black Painted, Cast Iron, c.1875, 73 In. 4750
Bench, Fern Pattern, White, Cast Iron, c.1900, 33 x 56 x 23 In. 1107
Bench, Gothic Revival, Quatrefoil, Scroll Arms, Cast Iron, c.1850, 35 x 55 In. 3696
Bench, Gothic, Pierced Scrolling Leafy Back, 67 ¾ In. 4750
Bench, Leaf & Berry, Hoof Feet, Cast Iron, Wexford Foundry, 38 ½ x 48 In. 2722
Bench, Leaves, Branches, White Arms, Cast Iron, 52 x 73 In. 847
Bench, Leaves, White, Cast Iron, 73 x 52 In. 847
Bench, Lily Of The Valley, White, Cast Iron, Coalbrookdale, 62 x 23 ½ In. 3159
Bench, Medallions, Wood Slats, Painted Black, 36 x 36 In. 500
Bench, Neo-Gothic, Diamond, Quatrefoil, Honeycomb Seat, 35 x 39 In., Pair 4500
Bench, Oak, Curved Seat, English, 108 In. 4680
Bench, Openwork Leaves, Scallop Back, Griffon Legs, Cast Iron, c.1850, 28 x 42 In. 1103
Bench, Oval, Medallions, Irises, Leaves, Victorian, 37 ¾ x 38 In. 2187
Bench, Regency, Wire, Continuous Back, Rolled Arms, Wrought Iron Frame, 1800s, 31 x 69 In. 6144
Bench, Serpentine Back, Leaves & Flowers, Cast Iron, 32 x 43 In. 640
Bench, Slatted Oak Seat, Scrolling Leaves, Lattice Frame, Cast Iron, 34 x 26 In. 550
Bench, Tree Limb, Rustic, Paint, Hoof Feet, 34 ½ x 72 In., Pair 968
Bench, Twisting Vines, Brown Paint, Cast Iron, 30 x 50 x 17 In. 480
Bench, Victorian Style, White Paint, Festoon, Pierced, Cast Metal, c.1950, 36 x 45 In. 633
Bench, Welded Horseshoes, Iron, 20th Century, 36 ¼ x 47 ½ In. 272
Bench, Wood Slats, Hairpin Iron Frame, Arthur Umanoff, 44 x 26 ½ In. 660
Bird Feeder, Cold Paint Nest, Eggs, Flowers, Grass, Birds On Rim, Bronze, Austria, 10 In. 2963
Birdbath, Baluster Column, Ogee Bowl, Square Base, Carved Marble, 36 x 26 In. 562
Birdbath, Cupid Holding Shell Over Head, Lead, 28 In. 450
Birdbath, Putti Holding Bowl, Round Base, Neoclassical Style, 29 In. 281

Game, Board, Parcheesi, Wooden, Inlaid, Center Medallion, Wired Back, Hanging, c.1880, 22 x 22 In.
$875

Ruby Lane

Game, Mahjong, 144 Ebony & Bone Tiles, Carved, Lacquered Case, 12 x 9 ¼ In.
$580

Ruby Lane

Game, Ouija, Board, Mystifying Oracle, Pancetta Box, William Fuld, 1919, 12 x 18 In.
$212

Hess Auction Group

Game, Puzzle, Dexterity, Monkey Pool Players, Embossed Tin, Germany, c.1900s, 1 ½ In.
$145

Ruby Lane

Game, Roulette Wheel, O'Neill, Wood, Numbered Slots, Round, Spins, Metal, Chicago, 31 In.
$1,830

Morphy Auctions

Game, Target Figure, Clown, Arcade, Canvas, Baseball Toss, 14 In.
$90

Showtime Auction Services

Game, Wheel, Gambling, Carnival, Star Shape, Metal Spokes, Wood, Black, Red, c.1910, 25 In.
$767

Hess Auction Group

Gameboard, Checkers & Parcheesi, Painted, Applied Walnut Edge, c.1890, 18 ½ In.
$2,337

Skinner, Inc.

Gameboard, Checkers, Green, White, Beavers, Maple Leaves, c.1890, 31 x 19 In.
$2,214

Skinner, Inc.

Gameboard, Parcheesi, Painted, Black Edge, Red, Yellow, Green, Orange, Blue, c.1890, 20 x 20 In.
$6,765

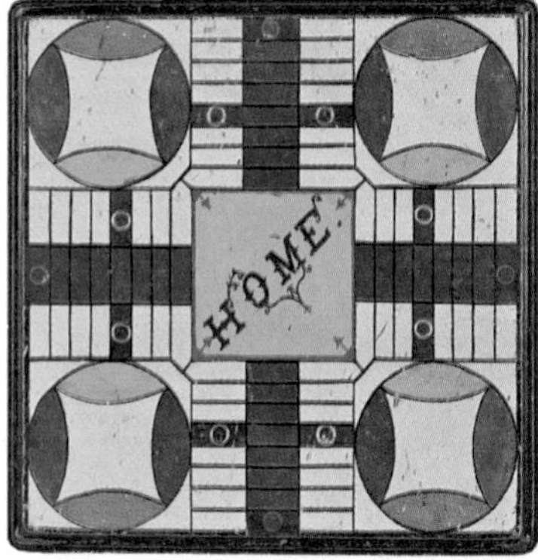

Skinner, Inc.

G

GARDEN

Garden, Bench, Curtain Pattern, 3-Part Back, Rosette Crest, Arms, Iron, Fortune Label, 1800s
$1,107

Neal Auctions

Garden, Boot Scraper, Dog, Dachshund, Black Paint, Iron, 8 x 21 ½ In.
$142

Hess Auction Group

Garden, Figure, Lion, Standing, Zinc, A.B. & W.T. Westervelt, N.Y., c.1890, 50 x 75 In.
$2,040

Garth's Auctioneers & Appraisers

TIP

You can keep your antique birdbath clear of algae if you put a few pre-1982 pennies in the water. The copper discourages algae. Friends will probably toss in more money thinking you have a wishing well. They do it in every mall.

Birdbath, Reclining Tiger, Carved Sandstone, c.1890, 8 ¼ x 15 In. 18880
Birdbath, Ruffled Bowl, Fluted Column, Stepped Base, Iron, 28 x 16 ½ In., Pair 397
Birdhouse, Clapboard, Shingles, White, 17 ½ x 12 In. 480
Birdhouse, Georgian Manor, Arched Windows, Wirework, Hinged Doors, c.1890, 24 x 31 In. 492
Birdhouse, House Shape, Lattice Windows, Green, 15 x 17 In. 30
Birdhouse, Wood, House Shape, 2-Story, Tin Roof, Wraparound Porch, 26 ½ x 21 In. 266
Boot Scraper, 2 Men Sawing Log, Paint, Full Body, Iron, Integral Base, c.1900 1185
Boot Scraper, Banjo Player, Oval Bowl, Horseshoe Shape, Cast Iron, c.1900, 13 In. 177
Boot Scraper, Cat, Black, Seated, Tail Curled In, Cast Iron, 7 In. 50
Boot Scraper, Cat, Paint, Iron, 15 ½ x 10 In. 380
Boot Scraper, Dog, Dachshund, Black Paint, Iron, 8 x 21 ½ In. .... *illus* 142
Boot Scraper, Duck Shape, Cast Iron, 13 ½ In. 325
Boot Scraper, Duck Shape, Scraper On Back, Iron, Gold Paint, c.1885, 14 In. 390
Boot Scraper, Duck, Decoy, Cast Iron, 7 ⅜ x 14 ½ In. 276
Boot Scraper, Frog & Fish Footman, Invitation, Alice In Wonderland, Iron, 2-Sided, 9 In. 561
Boot Scraper, Grasshopper, Wedge Base, Iron, Green Paint, c.1900, 7 x 16 In. 1235
Boot Scraper, Hen, Seated, Mounted, Iron, Wood Base, Cast, 9 In. 125
Boot Scraper, Pig, Iron, 6 x 10 In. 351
Boot Scraper, Whimsical Cat, Tail Up, Black Paint, Iron, Wood Base, 10 ¼ In. 443
Chair, Fern Design, Shaped Openwork Back & Arms, Dished Seat, c.1900, 35 In., Pair 1107
Chair, Gothic, Arched Backs, Interlace, Iron, Versha England, 12 Piece 5835
Chair, Lounge, Metal, Wire Mesh, Wheels, Russell Woodard, 33 x 70 In., Pair 1080
Chair, Woven, Hammered, Ball Finials, Disc Feet, Iron, 38 x 23 ¾ In. 151
Chair, Woven, Oval Back, Curved Arms, Iron, 41 ¾ x 30 ¾ In., Pair 544
Chaise Longue, Iron, Shell, Acanthus, 35 ½ x 57 In. 2000
Dining Set, Steel, Round Table, 6 Chairs, 26 ¾ x 58 In. 1000
Figure, Angel, Dark Green, Black, Acanthus, Wall, Curled Hair, Marble, 51 x 12 In., Pair 1573
Figure, Black Boy Fishing, Cement, Painted, c.1920, 17 x 8 In. 60
Figure, Black Man, Wearing Overalls, Cast Iron, Paint, Square Base, 45 In. 610
Figure, Caught In Storm, Girl, Bracing Herself, Marble, 1900s, 45 x 20 In. 2952
Figure, Dionysus, Wreath Of Grapes, Leaning On Stump, Cast Iron, c.1890, 60 In. 4500
Figure, Dog, Seated, Oval Base, Painted Metal, 37 In., Pair 688
Figure, Dog, Whippet, Reclining, Iron, Black Paint, 17 x 37 In., Pair 2750
Figure, Dog, Whippet, Reclining, White Paint, Cast Iron, c.1890, 17 x 38 In., Pair 1250
Figure, Eiffel Tower, Cast Iron, 53 ½ x 52 In. 847
Figure, Elk, Standing, Fur Details, Cast Iron, 15 ¾ In. 826
Figure, Foo Dog, Crouching, Front Paws On Pup, Bronze, 29 x 43 In., Pair 6125
Figure, Hound, Molossian, Seated, Docked Tail, Carved Sandstone, 52 x 32 x 35 In. 6000
Figure, Lion, Standing, Zinc, A.B. & W.T. Westervelt, N.Y., c.1890, 50 x 75 In. .... *illus* 2040
Figure, Pixie, Cement, 20 In., Pair 298
Figure, Rabbit, Resting, Long Ears, Concrete, 20th Century, 7 ¾ x 14 In. 91
Figure, Snail, Shell On Back, Lead, 7 ½ x 11 In. 210
Figure, Turkey, Spread Tail, Lead, 11 In. 210
Figure, Virgin Mary, Kneeling In Prayer, Bronze, c.1900, 40 In. 1188
Figure, Woman, Dolphin, Cast Stone, 50 In. 1328
Figure, Woman, Standing, Holding Basket, Dress, Cast Stone, c.1990, 54 In. 431
Figure, Woman's Head, Laying On Side, Looking Up, Stone, 12 x 6 ½ In. 28
Fountain Head, Cherub, Lips Pursed, Bronze, Marinelli Foundry, c.1950, 15 x 11 ¾ In. 847
Fountain Head, Jumping Fish, Mouth Open, Scroll Base, Lead, 14 In. 413
Fountain, 3 Putti Support, Marble, 1870s, 24 x 23 In. 1669
Fountain, Boy Playing Flute, Bronze, Green Patina, 23 In. 546
Fountain, Boy, Holds Shell Over Head, Birds, 31 In. 212
Fountain, Cherub Holding Basket, Cast Iron, Continental, 81 x 45 In. .... *illus* 5312
Fountain, Crocodile Shape, Metal, Head Up, Tail Curled, Arched Back, 43 In. 2250
Fountain, Fish, Upright, Open Mouth, 2 Small Side Fish, Carved, Stone, 1900s, 43 In. 236
Fountain, Frog Boy, Nude Boy Hold Frogs, Standing On Ball, Edith Barrette Parsons, 24 In. 10620
Fountain, Frog, Lily Pad Design, Egrets, Boy, Fish, Cast Iron, Zinc, c.1880, 72 In. x 96 In. 2666
Fountain, Girl Holding Daisy As Umbrella, Water Sprays From Top, Cast Metal, 21 In. 173
Fountain, Mask, Open Mouth, Marble, Variegated, 1900s, 15 ½ x 14 ½ In. 2125
Fountain, Mermaid & Dolphin, Garlands, Lotus Base, Lead, England, 32 In. 800
Fountain, Putti & Fish, Frog & Turtle Pan, Egret Base, Iron, J.W. Fiske, 1800s, 72 In. .... *illus* 4864
Fountain, Renaissance, Bronze, Porcelain, Landscape, Nude Women, 77 x 33 In. 6534
Fountain, Scalloped Basin, Floral Spray, Johnson Brothers Hanley Ltd., 22 x 17 In. 132
Fountain, Seated Nude Woman, In Seashell, Fish, Janet Scudder Style, 46 x 30 In. 3894
Fountain, Sousaphone, Cooking Pot, Trumpets, Horns, Ed Haugevik, Linda Spirit, 80 In. 767

Fountain, Turtle Shape, Bronze, 10 x 25 In. 5250
Fountain, Wall, Mask Of Medusa, Arched Back, Carved Limestone, 79 x 64 In. 11250
Fountain, Woman, Robes, Bronze, 59 x 26 In. 1107
Fountain, Young Boy, Holding Shell, Rockwork Base, Round Basin, Stone, 48 x 47 In. 359
Gate Weight, Bell Shape, Red Paint, Iron, 1800s, 6 In. 60
Gate, Cedar, Lattice, 37 x 80½ In. 82
Gate, Central Medallion Flower Shape, 6 Bars, 1800s, 35 x 48 In. 205
Gate, Gilt Details, 4 Panels, Wrought Iron, Marked B.F. Paris, France, 1800s, 74 x 111 In. 3328
Gate, Heart Shape Curlicues, White, Iron, 38 x 47 In. 117
Gate, Lyre, Flowers, Scrolls, Penn., Wrought Iron, 1800s, 45 x 33 In. *illus* 544
Gate, Pointed Tips, Arches, Iron, 26 x 25 In., Pair 363
Gatepost Finial, Tiger, Head, Heavy Brow, Iron, 17 In. 7391
Gazebo, Ivy Leaves, 6 Panels, Iron, 96 x 66 In. 212
Group, Dog, Whippets, Collars, Oval Base, Stylized Grass, Cast Stone, 15 x 11 In. 2040
Hitching Post, Black Boy, Cast Iron, Paint, c.1850, 44 In. 900
Hitching Post, Black Man, Vest, Hat, Holding Ring, Paint, Cast Iron, Base, 38½ In. 948
Hitching Post, Boy On Cotton Bale, Overalls, Cast Iron, c.1890, 44 x 16 In. *illus* 625
Hitching Post, Horse Head Shape, Ring In Mouth, Iron, 15 x 11 In. 276
Hitching Post, Horse Head, Black Paint, Cast Iron, 1800s, 64 In. *illus* 531
Hitching Post, Horse Head, Cast Iron, 10 x 8 In. 86
Hitching Post, Horse Head, Iron, 53 In. 351
Hitching Post, Horse Head, Turned Column Stem, Square Base, Cast Metal, c.1950, 48 In. 489
Hitching Post, Lion Head, Black Paint, Cast Iron, 1800s, 10½ x 8½ In. 189
Hitching Post, Man, Standing On Cotton Bale, Green Pants, Suspenders, Iron, 44 x 16 In. 875
Hitching Ring, Lion Head, Ring In Mouth, Cast Iron, Wall Mount, 1800s, 12 x 8 In. 142
Hose Reel, Gothic, Wrought Iron, 10-In. Round Reel, 19½ x 13 In. 60
Jardiniere, Basket Weave, Cream, Giltwood, Metal Insert, 25 x 27½ In. 375
Jardiniere, Figural, Porters Carrying Tasseled Sack, Paw Feet, Bronze, 14½ x 18 In. 305
Jardiniere, Lattice, Acanthus, Cream, Cast Iron, Late 1900s, 10½ x 15½ In. 242
Jardiniere, Neoclassical, Flared Rim, Fluted Body, Round Foot, Iron, 26¾ x 14¾ In. 181
Jardiniere, Shell Shape Dish, C-Scroll Supports, 3-Part Base, 48½ x 47 In. 3600
Jardiniere, Swags, On Stand, Octagonal Base, Black, Cast Iron, 67 x 20 In., Pair 2891
Jardiniere, Urn Shape, Black Painted Bases, Cast Iron, 14 x 15 In., Pair 720
Jardiniere, Whiskey Barrel Style, 8 In. 38
Lawn Jockey, Black Man, Standing, Holding Lantern, Cast Iron, 38 In. 413
Lawn Jockey, Railroad Lantern, Red Pants, White Hat, Cast Stone, c.1905, 44 In. 489
Patio Set, Table, 4 Chairs, Wrought Iron, Woodard, 29 x 61 In. 300
Pergola, White Paint, Arched Canopy, Scrolls, Pierced, Metal, c.1910, 120 In. 1572
Plant Stand, see also Furniture, Stand, Plant
Planter, Angel, Wings, Paw Feet, Marble, Carved, c.1900, 11½ x 27½ In. 1250
Planter, Bathtub Shape, Pink Marble, Bronze Claw Feet, c.1890, 3½ x 8¼ In. 1080
Planter, Blue, White Enamel, Flared Rim, Applied Lion Masks, Cast Iron, 1800s, 26 x 25 In. 10240
Planter, Champleve, Multicolor, Band Of Phoenix, Tiger, Dragon, Bronze, Chinese, 20 x 16 In. 92
Planter, Clamshell Encrusted, Round Bowl, Pedestal, 55 In. 1159
Planter, Concrete, Rounded Lip, Flared Sides, White, 16 x 19 In., Pair 1188
Planter, Demilune Outline, Gadrooned, Stepped Base, Stone, c.1890, 18 x 36 In. 3500
Planter, Demilune, Urns, Swags, Gray, Lead, 10 x 17 In., Pair 726
Planter, Dragon, Birds, Leaves, Bowl On Pedestal, Bronze, c.1900, 34 In. 500
Planter, Egyptian Boy, Basket On Head, Fiberglass, 25 x 77 In. 90
Planter, Iron, Wirework, 2 Tiers, Top Jardiniere, Scroll Feet, c.1950, 34 x 33 In. 299
Planter, Louis XIV, Octagonal, 8 Legs, Bronze, c.1900, 33 x 25 In. 484
Planter, Metal Strapwork, 2 Tiers, Scrolled Base, Baskets, c.1900, 57 x 34 In. 750
Planter, Multitiered, 12 Round Holders, Adjustable Arms, Cast Iron, Victorian, 40 x 26 In. 581
Planter, Napoleon III, Ebonized Wood, Inlay, Ormolu, 6¾ x 17 In. 252
Planter, Openwork, Green, Urn Shape, Handles, Metal, 29 x 27 In. 125
Planter, Oval, Ogee Shape, Plinth Base, Carved, Stone, 1800s, 12½ x 59 In. 3750
Planter, Paw Feet, Lion's Head Ring Handles, Stars, Copper & Brass, 1700s, 15 In., Pair 3000
Planter, Ram's Heads, Cement, 26 x 16 In. 234
Planter, Regency Style, Tole, Red Paint, Gold Accents, Ring Handles, Paw Feet, 11 In. 1020
Planter, Square, Curved Feet, Brass Handles, Flowering Tree, Teak, c.1950, 17 x 16 In. 104
Planter, Urn, Cast Iron, White Paint, c.1860, 26 x 21½ In. *illus* 266
Rain Drum, Cylindrical, Cast Frogs On Rim, Bronze, 16 x 21 In. 1081
Screen, Arbor, Iron, 74 x 74 In. 97
Sculpture, Dog, Seated, Long Ears & Tail, Stone, Shaped Base, 32 x 19 In. *illus* 2583
Seat, Asparagus Bunch, Pink Ribbon, Majolica, Italy, 18 x 13 In. 219
Seat, Barrel Shape, White, Porcelain, Chinese, 19½ x 13 In., Pair 600

Garden, Fountain, Cherub Holding Basket, Cast Iron, Continental, 81 x 45 In.
$5,312

Neal Auctions

Garden, Fountain, Putti & Fish, Frog & Turtle Pan, Egret Base, Iron, J.W. Fiske, 1800s, 72 In.
$4,864

Kamelot

Garden, Gate, Lyre, Flowers, Scrolls, Penn., Wrought Iron, 1800s, 45 x 33 In.
$544

Kamelot

Garden, Hitching Post, Boy On Cotton Bale, Overalls, Cast Iron, c.1890, 44 x 16 In.
$625

Neal Auctions

Garden, Hitching Post, Horse Head, Black Paint, Cast Iron, 1800s, 64 In.
$531

Hess Auction Group

Garden, Planter, Urn, Cast Iron, White Paint, c.1860, 26 x 21 ½ In.
$266

Hess Auction Group

Garden, Sculpture, Dog, Seated, Long Ears & Tail, Stone, Shaped Base, 32 x 19 In.
$2,583

Skinner, Inc.

Garden, Settee, Fern, Arms, Cast Iron, Kramer Bros., Oh., c.1890, 35 x 58 In.
$1,470

Neal Auctions

Garden, Sundial, Woman, Bronze, Lucie Richards, Roman Bronze Works, 1917, 15 In.
$3,998

Skinner, Inc.

Gaudy Dutch, Cup & Saucer, Single Rose, 5 ½ In.
$189

Hess Auction Group

Gaudy Dutch, Cup & Saucer, War Bonnet, 5 ½ In.
$266

Hess Auction Group

Gaudy Dutch, Plate, Carnation, 8⅜ In.
$413

Hess Auction Group

Seat, Drum Shape, Blue & White, Flowers, Porcelain, c.1950, 19 x 13 In. 518
Seat, Famille Rose, Cutout Top, Panels, Butterflies, Flowers, Hexagonal, c.1810, 19 In. 1888
Seat, Famille Rose, Interior Courtyard Scene, Pink & Green, 14 x 14 In. 59
Seat, Famille Rose, Scenes, Porcelain, 18 x 12 ½ In. 625
Seat, Figural, Elephant, White, Multicolor Saddle, Ceramic, 22 x 23 In. 188
Seat, Flowers, Birds, Barrel Shape, Porcelain, Painted, Chinese, 19 In. 270
Seat, Green Glaze, Reticulated Wan Symbols, Pierced, Hexagonal, 1900s, 18 In., Pair 799
Seat, Hexagonal, Barrel Shape, Blue & White, Pierced Tops, Porcelain, c.1900, 19 In., Pair.......... 1873
Seat, Pillow Shape, White, Green Rope Trim, Tassels, Terra-Cotta, 13 ¼ In. 363
Seat, Porcelain, Maroon, Green Flowers, Birds, Chinese, 18 x 14 In. 118
Seat, Rose Medallion, Cutout Top, Sides, Hexagonal, Chinese, 19 In. 1534
Seat, Stool, Terra-Cotta, Tasseled, Pin & White Glaze, Tufted Top, Italy, 1900s, 15 In. 159
Seat, Turtle Shape, Yellow, Cream, Asian, Composition, 27 x 17 In. 70
Settee, Curved, Steel, 33 ¾ x 72 ½ In. 375
Settee, Fern, Arms, Cast Iron, Kramer Bros., Oh., c.1890, 35 x 58 In. ....*illus* 1470
Settee, Gothic Arch & Rose, White, Cast Iron, Washington Iron Works, Buffalo, 36 In. 554
Settee, Gothic Revival, White, Iron, 33 ½ x 56 In. 3120
Sprinkler, Art Deco, Mermaid, 2-Sided, Green, Yellow, 14 ¾ In. 5605
Sprinkler, Mallard, Standing On Shell, Cast Iron, Bradley & Hubbard, 12 ¾ In. 4720
Sprinkler, Sprinkling Bozo, Monkey, 2-Sided, Die Cut Steel, 30 x 8 In. 204
Stand, 3 Tiers, 4 Legs, Iron, Wire, 50 x 33 In. 49
Stand, Scroll, Iron, Metal, Glass, 21 x 15 In. 234
Stand, Topiary, Green, Ball Finial, Oval Medallions, 65 x 22 In. 720
Stand, Topiary, Iron, Reeded, Rosettes, Lion's Head Mounts, 26 ½ In. 91
Stand, Topiary, Twigs, Cone, 38 x 20 ½ In., Pair.......... 120
Stand, Twig Shape, Green, 29 ½ x 18 In., Pair.......... 960
Stool, Frog Shape, Cushion On Back, White, Green Rope Trim, Yellow Tassels, 17 x 24 In. 130
Sundial, Knights In Armor, Plinth Base, Pierced Gnomon, Stone, 1800s, 30 x 37 In. 2250
Sundial, Pewter, Roman Numerals, Directionals, Weathered, J. Cutler, c.1790, 9 In. Square 840
Sundial, Round, Minute & Hours Scales, Countries, Compass, Bronze, c.1745, 8 x 14 In. 2500
Sundial, Square Column, Pierced Gnomon, Base, Stone, Bronze, 55 In. 2250
Sundial, Woman, Bronze, Lucie Richards, Roman Bronze Works, 1917, 15 In. ....*illus* 3998
Sundial, Ye Know Not The Hour, Tapered Plinth, Cast Stone, 42 x 24 In. 660
Table, Art Nouveau, Spiraled Legs, Bronze, Faux Marble Top, c.1930, 28 x 29 In. 960
Table, Neoclassical Style, Round Stone Top, Lyre Support, Cast Iron, c.1910, 30 x 18 In. 406
Table, Pierced Round Top, Serpentine Griffin Legs, Shelf, Cast Iron, 1800s, 29 In. 490
Table, Potting, Wood Plank, Iron Base, 6 Cast Iron Spoke Wheels, France, 31 x 69 In. 2432
Table, Round Top, Barley Twist Pedestal, Claw Footed, Marble, c.1900, 30 x 31 In. 1800
Table, Square Top, Turned Column, Square Base, Zinc, Bronze, 31 x 35 ½ In. 1331
Table, Winged Lion Supports, Bevel Edge, Carrara Marble, Carved, 1800s, 36 x 76 In. 35670
Urn, Campana Shape, Lion's Head Handles, Chrysanthemums, Scrolls, Bronze, 19 x 14 In. 2091
Urn, Campana Shape, Lotus, Reeded, Egg & Dart Trim, Cast Iron, c.1900, 28 In., Pair.......... 625
Urn, Double Swan Handle, Cobalt Blue High Glaze, 16 ½ x 17 In., Pair.......... 175
Urn, Drapes, Iron, 8 ¼ x 7 ½ In., Pair.......... 240
Urn, Fruiting Rims, Fluted & Gadrooned, Square Base, Stone, 24 x 23 In., Pair.......... 2250
Urn, Iron, Petal Ends, Pedestal Base, Red Paint, 1800s, 16 ½ In. 142
Urn, Laurel Swags, Berries, Masks, Pineapple Finial, Cast Iron, c.1900, 30 In. 545
Urn, Lobed Body, Leaves, Square Pedestal, Black Paint, Cast Iron, c.1900, 31 In., Pair 885
Urn, Neoclassical Style, Foldover Rim, Pedestal Foot, Metal, 44 In., Pair 625
Urn, Stands, Iron, 36 x 20 In., Pair 553
Urn, Swag Decoration, Flame Finial, Square Plinth Base, Stone, 31 ½ In. 875
Urn, Swags, Masks, Pineapple Finial, Laurel Leaf, Satyr, Bacchus Mask, Iron, 30 x 17 In. 544
Urn, Tazza Shape, 3 Parts, Woman Masks, Cast Iron, c.1890, 39 In., Pair.......... 1625
Urn, Urn, Pierced Scroll Handles, Molded Rim, Cast Iron, c.1850, 55 x 21 In., Pair.......... 4674
Urn, Victorian, Iron, White, 18 ½ x 36 ½ In. 960
Urn, White, Lobed, Marble, 1900s, 21 x 21 ½ In., Pair.......... 1625
Watering Pail, 2 Handles, Tin, Cast, Iron, 20 ½ x 19 ¼ In. 210
Wheelbarrow, French Provincial, Carved Spoke Wheel, Oak, Iron, 23 x 68 ½ In. 307

GAUDY DUTCH pottery was made in England for the American market from about 1810 to 1820. It is a white earthenware with Imari-style decorations of red, blue, green, yellow, and black. Only sixteen patterns of Gaudy Dutch were made: Butterfly, Carnation, Dahlia, Double Rose, Dove, Grape, Leaf, Oyster, Primrose, Single Rose, Strawflower, Sunflower, Urn, War Bonnet, Zinnia, and No Name. Other similar wares are called Gaudy Ironstone and Gaudy Welsh.

Bowl, Butterfly, Flowers, Leaves, Blue Rim, 8 ½ In 212

TIP
Some types of stone and metal remain free of organic stains if they're left in partial sunlight and heat, but not if in deep shade.

Gaudy Dutch, Plate, Dinner, Single Rose, Soft Paste, Red, Green, Blue Flowers, Leaves, 9 ¾ In.
$118

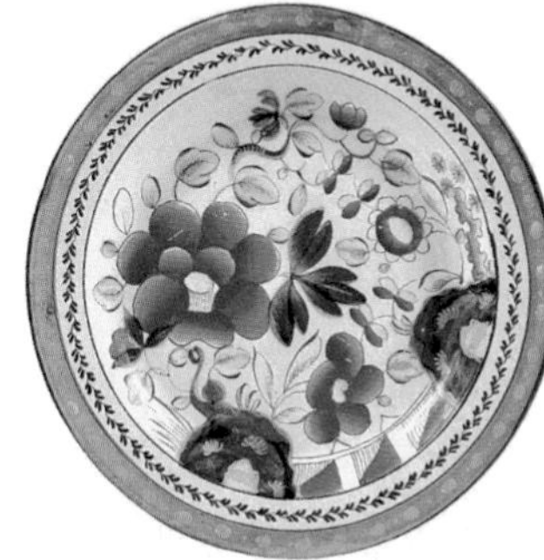

Hess Auction Group

Gaudy Dutch, Plate, Toddy, Grape, 6 ¼ In.
$1,180

Hess Auction Group

Gaudy Dutch, Plate, Urn, 7 ⅜ In.
$212

Hess Auction Group

TIP

If you are searching flea markets and yard sales, don't offer too little for a treasure. Being too cheap will mean that you may not hear about other similar items the dealer has not yet set out for sale. Offer a low but fair price, usually 20 percent off the market price.

Gaudy Dutch, Sugar, Lid, Grape, 5 ¼ x 7 ½ In.
$224

Hess Auction Group

Gaudy Dutch, Sugar, Lid, Sunflower, Clamshell Handles, 5 ½ x 5 ½ In.
$354

Hess Auction Group

Gaudy Dutch, Waste Bowl, Oyster, Soft Paste, 2 ¾ x 5 ½ In.
$325

Hess Auction Group

Creamer, Oyster, Helmet Shape, 5 ½ x 4 ¾ In. 885
Cup & Saucer, Grape, 5 ¾ In. 266
Cup & Saucer, Oyster, 5 ½ In. 472
Cup & Saucer, Single Rose, 5 ½ In. .... *illus* 189
Cup & Saucer, Sunflower, 5 ½ In. 266
Cup & Saucer, War Bonnet, 5 ½ In. .... *illus* 266
Cup Plate, War Bonnet, 4 ¼ In. 708
Plate, Carnation, 8 ⅜ In. .... *illus* 413
Plate, Dinner, Single Rose, Soft Paste, Red, Green, Blue Flowers, Leaves, 9 ¾ In. .... *illus* 118
Plate, Double Rose, 10 In. 443
Plate, Soup, War Bonnet, Black, Orange, Green, 8 ½ In., 4 Piece 1320
Plate, Toddy, Butterfly, 5 ⅝ In. 1003
Plate, Toddy, Grape, 6 ¼ In. .... *illus* 1180
Plate, Urn, 7 ⅜ In. .... *illus* 212
Sugar, Lid, Grape, 5 ¼ x 7 ½ In. .... *illus* 224
Sugar, Lid, Sunflower, Clamshell Handles, 5 ½ x 5 ½ In. .... *illus* 354
Waste Bowl, Oyster, Soft Paste, 2 ¾ x 5 ½ In. .... *illus* 325
Waste Bowl, Sunflower, Leaves, Red, Blue, Green, Ring Foot, 7 In. 295

GAUDY IRONSTONE is the collector's name for the ironstone wares with the bright patterns similar to Gaudy Dutch. It was made in England for the American market after 1850. There may be other examples found in the listing for Ironstone or under the name of the ceramic factory.

Bowl, Vegetable, Open, Strawberry & Floral, 2 ¼ x 9 ½ In. 177
Coffeepot, Pinwheel, Paneled, 9 ¼ In. .... *illus* 590
Coffeepot, Pinwheel, Paneled, Square Handle & Spout, 9 ¼ In. 443
Creamer, Pinwheel, Loop Handle, Flared Spout, Spread Foot, 5 ¾ In. 443
Pitcher, Cream, Pinwheel, 5 ¾ In. 207
Pitcher, Cream, Pinwheel, Paneled, 5 ½ In. 325
Platter, Blackberry, 13 ½ x 10 In. 236
Platter, Pinwheel, Cobalt Blue, Iron Red, White Ground, 10 ¼ x 13 ½ In. 165
Tureen, Lid, Flowers, Leaves, Twig Handles, Grape Finial, 10 x 8 In. 384
Waste Bowl, Seeing Eye, 3 ¾ x 5 ⅜ In. 35

GAUDY WELSH is an Imari-decorated earthenware with red, blue, green, and gold decorations. Most Gaudy Welsh was made in England for the American market. It was made from 1820 to about 1860.

Creamer, Grape & Leaf, Paneled, 6 In. 106
Cup Plate, Floral, 3 ⅝ In., 5 Piece 41
Pitcher, Milk, Floral & Leaves, 5 ¼ In. .... *illus* 83

GEISHA GIRL porcelain was made for export in the late nineteenth century in Japan. It was an inexpensive porcelain often sold in dime stores or used as free premiums. Pieces are sometimes marked with the name of a store. Japanese ladies in kimonos are pictured on the dishes. There are over 125 recorded patterns. Borders of red, blue, green, gold, brown, or several of these colors were used. Modern reproductions are being made.

Bowl, Scalloped Rim, 3 x 10 ½ In. 24
Cup & Saucer, 6 Piece 26
Plate, Geishas, Fans, Blue Scalloped Rim, 8 ½ In. 24
Plate, Geishas, Landscape, 8 Scalloped Sections, Red Rim, 7 ½ In., Pair 50
Saucer, Geishas, Landscape, Pagodas, 5 ½ In., 4 Piece 25
Sugar, Lid, Orange Kimono, 3 ¾ In. 28

GENE AUTRY was born in 1907. He began his career as the "Singing Cowboy" in 1928. His first movie appearance was in 1934, his last in 1958. His likeness and that of the Wonder Horse, Champion, were used on toys, books, lunch boxes, and advertisements.

Book, Better Little Book, Mystery Of Paint Rock Canyon, No. 1425, 1947, 3 x 4 ½ In. 32
Book, Gene Autry & The Redwood Pirates, 248 Pages, Whitman Publishing, 1946, 5 x 8 In. 45
Button, I Saw Gene Autry, Nov. 1-11, Boston Garden Rodeo, Photo, 1940s, 1 In. 86
Photograph, Gene, On Horseback, Truck & Trailer, 6 x 4 In. 85
Toy, Cap Gun, Holster, Horse Head Grip, 1950s, 9 ½ In. 100
Toy, Repeating Cap Pistol, Jr. Model, Cast Iron, Pearlized Grip, Box, 1940s, Kenton 190
View-Master Reel, Gene, Champion, c.1950 6

GIBSON GIRL black-and-blue decorated plates were made in the early 1900s. Twenty-four different 10 ½-inch plates were made by the Royal Doulton pottery at Lambeth, England. These pictured scenes from the book *A Widow and Her Friends* by Charles Dana Gibson. Another set of twelve 9-inch plates featuring pictures of the heads of Gibson Girls had all-blue decoration. Many other items also pictured the famous Gibson Girl.

Plate, A Quiet Dinner With Dr. Bottles, 10 ½ In. 75
Plate, Message From Outside World, 10 ½ In. .... 115 to 125
Plate, Mr. Waddles Arrives Late, Card Filled, 10 ½ In. 125
Plate, She Finds Some Consolation In Her Mirror, c.1901, 10 ½ In. .... *illus* 145
Plate, She Goes To The Fancy Dress Ball As Juliet, 10 ½ In. 140
Plate, She Looks For Relief Among Some Of The Old Ones, 10 ½ In. 130
Plate, Some Think She Has Remained In Retirement Too Long, 10 ½ In. 220
Plate, They Go Fishing, 10 ½ In. 118
Tray, Gibson Girl In Christmas White Fur, Holly Berries, Tin, c.1890, 16 x 13 In. 175

GIRL SCOUT collectors search for anything pertaining to the Girl Scouts, including uniforms, publications, and old cookie boxes. The Girl Scout movement started in 1912, two years after the Boy Scouts. It began under Juliette Gordon Low of Savannah, Georgia. The first Girl Scout cookies were sold in 1928.

Bank, Dime Register, Silvertone, 1930s, 2 ¾ x 2 ½ In. 85
Bracelet, Silver & Goldtone, 2 Trefoils, Spring-Loaded Hinge, 1957 .... *illus* 38
Charm, Senior Roundup, Sterling Silver, 1962, ¾ In. 35
Cup, Collapsing, Aluminum, Insignia, 1950s, 2 ½ In. 22
Doll, Effanbee, Sleep Eyes, Jointed, Rooted Hair, Green Uniform, 1965, 8 ¼ In. 39
Handbook, Green Hard Cover, Illustrations, 464 Pages, 1930, 5 x 7 In. .... *illus* 17
Handbook, Intermediate Program, Hardcover, 1949.......... 28
Uniform, Jumper, Blouse, Green, Size 10.......... 18

GLASS factories that are well known are listed in this book under the factory name. This category lists pieces made by less well-known factories. Additional pieces of glass are listed in this book under the type of glass, in the categories Glass-Art, Glass-Blown, Glass-Bohemian, Glass-Contemporary, Glass-Midcentury, Glass-Venetian, and under the factory name.

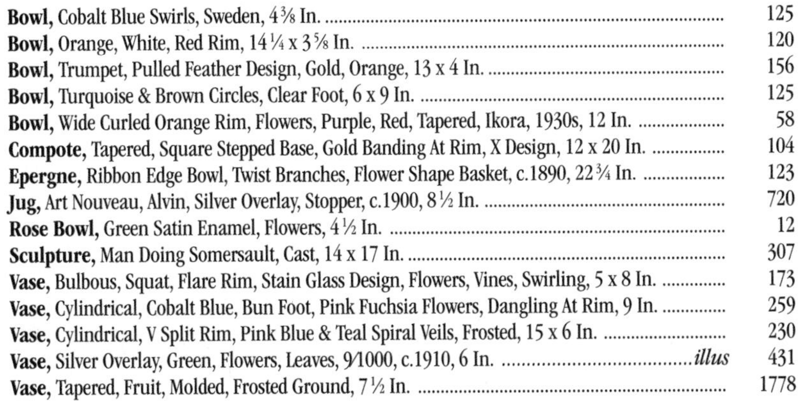

Bowl, Cobalt Blue Swirls, Sweden, 4 ⅜ In. 125
Bowl, Orange, White, Red Rim, 14 ¼ x 3 ⅝ In. 120
Bowl, Trumpet, Pulled Feather Design, Gold, Orange, 13 x 4 In. 156
Bowl, Turquoise & Brown Circles, Clear Foot, 6 x 9 In. 125
Bowl, Wide Curled Orange Rim, Flowers, Purple, Red, Tapered, Ikora, 1930s, 12 In. 58
Compote, Tapered, Square Stepped Base, Gold Banding At Rim, X Design, 12 x 20 In. 104
Epergne, Ribbon Edge Bowl, Twist Branches, Flower Shape Basket, c.1890, 22 ¾ In. 123
Jug, Art Nouveau, Alvin, Silver Overlay, Stopper, c.1900, 8 ½ In. 720
Rose Bowl, Green Satin Enamel, Flowers, 4 ½ In. 12
Sculpture, Man Doing Somersault, Cast, 14 x 17 In. 307
Vase, Bulbous, Squat, Flare Rim, Stain Glass Design, Flowers, Vines, Swirling, 5 x 8 In. 173
Vase, Cylindrical, Cobalt Blue, Bun Foot, Pink Fuchsia Flowers, Dangling At Rim, 9 In. 259
Vase, Cylindrical, V Split Rim, Pink Blue & Teal Spiral Veils, Frosted, 15 x 6 In. 230
Vase, Silver Overlay, Green, Flowers, Leaves, 9/1000, c.1910, 6 In. .... *illus* 431
Vase, Tapered, Fruit, Molded, Frosted Ground, 7 ½ In. 1778

GLASS-ART. Art glass means any of the many forms of glassware made during the late nineteenth or early twentieth century. These wares were expensive when they were first made and production was limited. Art glass is not the typical commercial glass that was made in large quantities, and most of the art glass was produced by hand methods. Later twentieth-century glass is listed under Glass-Contemporary, Glass-Midcentury, or Glass-Venetian. Even more art glass may be found in categories such as Burmese, Cameo Glass, Tiffany, and other factory names.

Bowl, Black, Etched Band Of Overlapping Circles, Art Deco, France, 5 ½ In. 215
Bowl, Flygsfors, Conquille, Paul Kedelv, 1950s, 10 ½ x 5 In. .... *illus* 200
Compote, Cranberry, Mottled, Muller Freres, 8 ¼ In. 150
Ewer, Lavender & Green, Footed, Straight-Up Spout, Handle, Swollen, 1925, 21 In. 3000
Ewer, Yellow, Brown Spots, Blue Drip, Smokestack, Handle, Upturned Spout, c.1923, 13 In. 1875
Platter, Round, Orange Powdered Glass, Yellow, Red, Violet, c.1925, 18 In. Diam. 438
Tumbler, Green, Etched Gold Vines, White Enameled Berries, c.1900, 5 In. 359
Vase, Art Deco, Etched, Gilt, 10 x 6 In. 118
Vase, Art Nouveau, Green Iridescent, Silver Plate Footed Base, Handles, 17 ½ x 9 In. 2040
Vase, Art Nouveau, Pewter Stylized Mounts, Green Iridescent, White, Gray, Orange, 13 x 8 In. 299

Gaudy Ironstone, Coffeepot, Pinwheel, Paneled, 9 ¼ In.
$590

Hess Auction Group

Gaudy Welsh, Pitcher, Milk, Floral & Leaves, 5 ¼ In.
$83

Hess Auction Group

Gibson Girl, Plate, She Finds Some Consolation In Her Mirror, c.1901, 10 ½ In.
$145

Ruby Lane

TIP

Don't sticky-tape a top on a teapot. The decoration may come off with the tape. Secure a top with dental wax or earthquake wax.

Girl Scout, Bracelet, Silver & Goldtone, 2 Trefoils, Spring-Loaded Hinge, 1957
$38

Ruby Lane

Girl Scout, Handbook, Green Hard Cover, Illustrations, 464 Pages, 1930, 5 x 7 In.
$17

Ruby Lane

Glass, Vase, Silver Overlay, Green, Flowers, Leaves, 9/1000, c.1910, 6 In.
$431

Neal Auctions

Vase, Art Nouveau, Silver Overlay, Gold Iridescent, Gingko Leaf, c.1900, 4 In. 590

Vase, Beaker, Rounded Flare Foot, Amber, Tan, Blue, Green, Red, Drip Design, 1900s, 10 In. 750

Vase, Bottle Shape, Cut, Stained, Gilded, Scroll Band, Flowers, Persian Revival, c.1900, 6 In. 123

Vase, Bulbous, Cylinder Neck, Red Iridescent, Black Design Collar, Gold, c.1900, 6 In. 15000

Vase, Custard Swirl, Gilt Rim, Victorian, 7¾ x 5 In. 270

Vase, Dimpled, Folded Rim, Amber, Pink, Blue, Pulled Feather, c.1900, 10 In. 478

Vase, Globular, Cylindrical Neck, Yellow, Carved Plum Blossoms, c.1910, 8 x 4 In. *illus* 444

Vase, Globular, Stick Neck, Faceted, Oval Bands, Red To Clear, Stars, Pad Base, c.1900, 11 In. 1494

Vase, Iridescent, Blue, Pink, Red, Pulled Feather, Bell Shape, Ruffled Rim, c.1920, 6 In. 300

Vase, Jades, Pink & Mauve Powdered, Violet, Orange, Footed, Pear, c.1928, 20 In. 3000

Vase, Jugendstil, Bronze Mounted, Iridescent, Oil Spot, Tapered, 3 Arms, Tripod Base, 11 In. 554

Vase, Paperweight, Clear, Painted Pink & White Flowers, Green Leaves, Orient & Flume, 8 In. 330

Vase, Pewter Mount, Iridescent, Purple & Yellow Swirls, Austria, c.1924, 6½ x 6½ In. 390

Vase, Salmon, Blown-Out, Stepped Iron Rod Panels, 2 Hoops, Lorraine, 15 In. 738

Vase, Shouldered, Green, Etched Design, Overlay, c.1925, 13 In. 2000

Vase, Square, Gilt Stand, Turquois, Enameled Flowering Stems, c.1900, 11 In. 313

Vase, Stylized Flowers, Opal, Pink, Red, Blue Tendrils, Iridescent Red Interior, Lotton, 1976, 8 In. *illus* 604

Vase, Tapers, Reverse Paint, Landscape, Trees, Buildings, Marcel Goupy, 8¾ x 5 In. 1694

Vase, Trumpet, Round Foot, Orange To White, Violet Band, Red Beads, c.1925, 10 In. 3000

Vase, Yellow, Gilt Interior, Lead Luster, Flared Neck, c.1925, 8 In. 299

GLASS-BLOWN. Blown glass was formed by forcing air through a rod into molten glass. Early glass and some forms of art glass were hand blown. Other types of glass were molded or pressed.

Bell, Garden, Flared, Green, 15 x 17 In. 610

Bottle, Deep Yellow Olive, Shaft & Globe Form, Applied String Lip, 5⅛ In. 8775

Bowl, Marine Reliquary Series, David New-Small, Aquatic Creatures, 8 In. 248

Bowl, Tartan Pattern, Pink, Yellow, Ruffle Pleated Rim, Frosted Shells Foot, 3 x 7 In. 1304

Compote, Lid, Ruby Red, Clear Controlled Bubble Finial & Stem, 10 x 6 In. 30

Compote, Ribbed Bowl, Baluster Stem, Pinched Rim, Pillar Mold, 7 x 9 In. 120

Decanter, Canary Yellow, 6-Sided, Concave Panels, Pinched Waist, Doughnut Lip, 10 In. 690

Decanter, Cobalt Blue, 8 Fluted Bottom Panels, Tapered, Doughnut Lip, 10⅜ In. 690

Demijohn, Green, Marked 1787, 20½ In. 854

Pitcher, Swirl Design, Lid, 9½ In. 175

Smoke Bell, Clear, Spherical Finial, 13 x 13 In. 12

Smoke Bell, Green, Applied Cylindrical Finial, Flared Base, 11 x 9¾ In. 18

Sugar, Double Mound Lid, Cobalt Blue Flint, Paneled, Scallop Rim, Finial, 7 In. 189

Sugar, Lid, Cobalt Blue, Gallery Rim, Flattened Finial, Pittsburgh, 6 x 5 In. *illus* 380

Vase, Amethyst, Paneled Base, Flared Out Rim, 6¾ In. 4305

Vase, Flowers, Red, Yellow, Orange Ground, Rolled Rim, M. Peiser, 1975, 14 x 9 In. *illus* 2015

Vase, Gold Iridescent, Pulled Feather, Dome Foot, Trumpet, Moire Fern, 1900s, 9 In. 239

Vase, Red & Blue Loops, White Ground, Bulbous, Trumpet Neck, Ruffled Rim, 8 In. 1422

Vase, Red, Pink, Silver, Chris Hawthorne, Port Orford, Ore., 15 x 19 In. 563

Vase, Tangerine, Yellow, Purple Mottle, Bell Shape, Pedestal Foot, c.1920, 7 In. 717

GLASS-BOHEMIAN. Bohemian glass is an ornate overlay or flashed glass made during the Victorian era. It has been reproduced in Bohemia, which is now a part of the Czech Republic. Glass made from 1875 to 1900 is preferred by collectors.

Beaker, Footed, White To Cranberry, 5 In. 198

Bowl, Blown, Raised Enamel Blue Birds Of Paradise, Gilt, 11¼ In. 132

Bowl, Cut Crenellated Rim, Enameled Birds & Butterflies, c.1875, 8¾ In. 369

Bowl, Double Handle, Gilt, Leaves, Graf Harrach, 4 x 10 In. 544

Bowl, Melon Shape, Yellow Opalescent, Crimped Rim, Textured Body, Kralik, 9 x 12 In. 177

Bowl, Pedestal, Curled, Crimped, Red, Rendskopr Pepita, 10½ x 4½ In. 484

Box, Potpourri, Cut, Lavender To Clear, Metal Mesh Lid, 4¾ x 7 In. 74

Candy Dish, Acorn, Leaf, Cut Diamond, Undertray, 8 x 7 In., Pair 5490

Cologne Bottle, White Cased Over Cranberry Glass, Cut Windows, Stopper, 7½ In. 354

Decanter Set, Blue Glass Barrel Decanters, Ball Stoppers, Jester, 10 Piece 181

Decanter Set, Palda, Enameled Panels, Blue, Green, Amethyst, Intaglio Bands, 11 x 4 In. 345

Decanter, Blue To Clear, Bottle Shape, Leaf Gilding, c.1880, 11 In. 741

Decanter, Cobalt Blue, Jeweled, Stopper, 19 In. 738

Decanter, Green To Clear, Hexagonal Panels, Stick Neck, Stopper, c.1850, 12 In. 148

Decanter, Paint, Winged Creatures, Swags, Faceted Stopper, c.1900, 10 In., Pair 369

Decanter, Ship's, Ruby, Crystal, Squat Shape, Faceted Base, Cut Diamond, 8½ x 6 In. 148

Ewer, Gilt, Cobalt Blue, Stopper, 11 In. 24

Garniture, Table Casket, 2 Candlesticks, Gilt, Enamel, Green, 3 Piece 457
Goblet, Blue, Hunting Scenes, Deer, Engraved, 5 ½ In., Pair 215
Goblet, Blue, Yellow, Clear Stems, 7 ¾ In., 8 Piece 625
Goblet, Ruby Cut To Clear, 9 ¾ In., 6 Piece 100
Lamp, Shade, Cobalt Blue Cut To Clear, Mushroom Shape, Etched, 24 In. 247
Liqueur Serving Set, Gilt, Cobalt Blue, Decanter, 4 Goblets, Tray, 6 Piece 115
Perfume Bottle, Count Von Buquoy, Red Hyalith, Fan Shape, Gilt, Stopper, c.1810, 6 In. 531
Perfume Bottle, Enamel Overlay, Gilt, Stopper, Bohemia, c.1880, 7 ½ In. 540
Perfume Bottle, Nude, Cherubs, Swans, Enamel, Gold, Lobmeyr, c.1880, 5 In. 2091
Perfume Bottle, Pink Cut To Clear, Enamel & Gilt Stopper, Lobmeyr, c.1875, 9 In. ....*illus* 944
Tumbler, Pilsner, Ruby Cut To Clear, Blown, Wheel Etched, Animals, 1800s, 9 ¼ In., Pair 130
Urn, Brass Mount, Cobalt Cut To Clear, 16 x 9 In. Pair 747
Vanity Box, Faceted, Clear Lavender, Lid, Finial, c.1930, 4 In. 200
Vase, 6 Facets, Cobalt Blue, Gold Band, Birds, 12 ¼ In. 313
Vase, Basalt, Parcel Gilt, Birds, Flowers, Blue On Black, Graf Harrach, 1800s, 14 x 6 In., Pair 1331
Vase, Blue Martele, Rounded Collar, Wilhelm Kralik, c.1900, 8 ¾ In. 363
Vase, Blue, Cut Glass, Gilt, 15 In. 984
Vase, Bottle, Green, Silvered, Applied Green Threading, Kralik, c.1900, 11 In. 127
Vase, Bottle, Texture, Metal Figural Cattail, Leaves, Green Iridescent, Blue, Kralik, 8 In. 173
Vase, Bulbous, Ruffled Rim, Flowers, Multicolor, 8 In. 235
Vase, Cased, Rectangular, Canted Corners, Cranberry Glass Over Milk Glass, 9 x 4 In., Pair 605
Vase, Cobalt Blue, Gilt Scroll, Women In Rose Garden, c.1855, 19 In., Pair 1625
Vase, Cobalt Cut To Clear, Fluted, Round Foot, 20 In., Pair 2500
Vase, Cranberry To Clear Twist, Gilt, 13 ½ x 4 In. 726
Vase, Cut, Flashed, Amber, Ruby, Flower Panels, 14 ⅛ In. 244
Vase, Cylindrical, Clear Textured, Violet Overlay Egyptian Scene, c.1930, 10 In. 568
Vase, Cylindrical, Purple Cut To Clear, 11 ¾ In. 63
Vase, Globular, Tube Neck, Red Enamel, Gilt Leaves, Branches, c.1900, 12 In. 250
Vase, Green Glass, Cameo, Trumpet Shape, Sliver Plated Griffin Form, 20 ½ x 8 In. 461
Vase, Green Iridescent, Bronze Mount, Leaves, 12 ¾ x 3 ½ In. 605
Vase, Green, Iridescent, Brown Striations, 6 ¼ x 4 ½ In. 212
Vase, Iridescent, Blue, Pulled Indigo, Purple Pulled Feather, Pallme-Konig, 12 ½ x 5 ¾ In. 242
Vase, Kralik, Art Nouveau, Pulled Rim, Pewter, Amethyst, Silver Gold Design, 10 ½ x 7 In. 443
Vase, Light Green Iridescent, Square, Twist, 8 ¾ x 5 ½ In. 181
Vase, Mint Green, Gilt Enamel, Flowers, Leaves, Butterflies, c.1920, 20 ¼ In. 424
Vase, Pillow, Moser Style, Guppies, Coral, 4-Footed, 6 x 5 ½ In., Pair 363
Vase, Portrait, Oval Porcelain Reserve, Translucent Green, Gilt, c.1875, 12 In., Pair ....*illus* 1064
Vase, Red & Green Mottled, Raised Gold Flower & Leaf Design, c.1900, 8 In. 431
Vase, Reverse Etched Moon, Cameo, Fritz Heckert, 11 ½ In. 540
Vase, Ruby Glass, Applied Green Decoration, Flared Segmented Top, Kralik, 9 ½ x 4 In. 35
Vase, Slender Trumpet Shape, Ruby Color, Scroll, Scallop Foot, c.1900, 22 In., Pair 4750
Vase, Tube, Green, Thorny, Leafy Flower, Wilhelm Kralik, c.1925, 6 ¾ x 4 ¾ In. 363
Vase, White, Karl Anton, Hieroglyphs, Green Dome Vase, 13 In. 181
Water Sprinkler, Gilt, Yellow, Deer, Flowers, 9 ¼ x 10 In. 181

GLASS-CONTEMPORARY includes pieces by glass artists working after 1970. Many of these pieces are free-form, one-of-a-kind sculptures. Paperweights by contemporary artists are listed in the Paperweight category. Earlier studio glass may be found listed under Glass-Midcentury or Glass-Venetian.

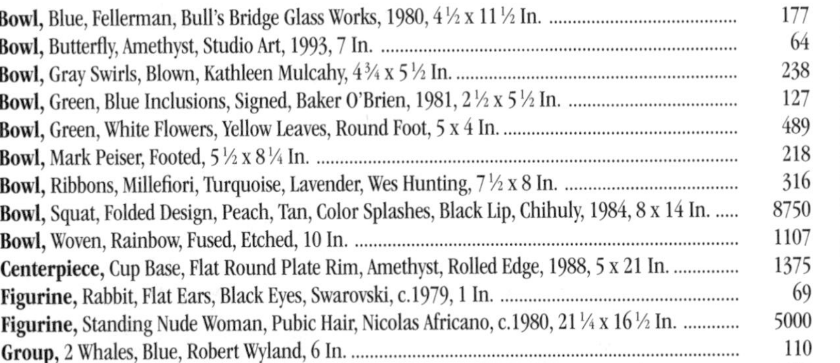

Bowl, Blue, Fellerman, Bull's Bridge Glass Works, 1980, 4 ½ x 11 ½ In. 177
Bowl, Butterfly, Amethyst, Studio Art, 1993, 7 In. 64
Bowl, Gray Swirls, Blown, Kathleen Mulcahy, 4 ¾ x 5 ½ In. 238
Bowl, Green, Blue Inclusions, Signed, Baker O'Brien, 1981, 2 ½ x 5 ½ In. 127
Bowl, Green, White Flowers, Yellow Leaves, Round Foot, 5 x 4 In. 489
Bowl, Mark Peiser, Footed, 5 ½ x 8 ¼ In. 218
Bowl, Ribbons, Millefiori, Turquoise, Lavender, Wes Hunting, 7 ½ x 8 In. 316
Bowl, Squat, Folded Design, Peach, Tan, Color Splashes, Black Lip, Chihuly, 1984, 8 x 14 In. 8750
Bowl, Woven, Rainbow, Fused, Etched, 10 In. 1107
Centerpiece, Cup Base, Flat Round Plate Rim, Amethyst, Rolled Edge, 1988, 5 x 21 In. 1375
Figurine, Rabbit, Flat Ears, Black Eyes, Swarovski, c.1979, 1 In. 69
Figurine, Standing Nude Woman, Pubic Hair, Nicolas Africano, c.1980, 21 ¼ x 16 ½ In. 5000
Group, 2 Whales, Blue, Robert Wyland, 6 In. 110
Lamp, Opal Multi Flora, White Flowers, Leaves, Iridized, Finial, Charles Lotton, 22 ¾ In. 2360
Obelisk, Green Spiral, Cut Glass Rectangles, Bronze Pedestal, 1990, 57 In. 341
Obelisk, Square Base, Striped, 17 ¼ In., Pair 250

Glass-Art, Bowl, Flygsfors, Conquille, Paul Kedelv, 1950s, 10 ½ x 5 In.
$200

Glass-Art, Vase, Globular, Cylindrical Neck, Yellow, Carved Plum Blossoms, c.1910, 8 x 4 In.
$444

James D. Julia Auctioneers

Glass-Art, Vase, Stylized Flowers, Opal, Pink, Red, Blue Tendrils, Iridescent Red Interior, Lotton, 1976, 8 In.
$604

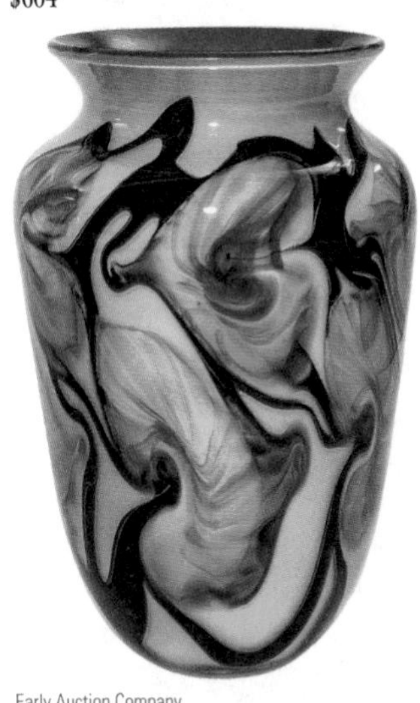

Early Auction Company

G

Glass-Blown, Sugar, Lid, Cobalt Blue, Gallery Rim, Flattened Finial, Pittsburgh, 6 x 5 In.
$380

Norman Heckler & Company

Glass-Blown, Vase, Flowers, Red, Yellow, Orange Ground, Rolled Rim, M. Peiser, 1975, 14 x 9 In.
$2,015

James D. Julia Auctioneers

Glass-Bohemian, Perfume Bottle, Pink Cut To Clear, Enamel & Gilt Stopper, Lobmeyr, c.1875, 9 In.
$944

Brunk Auctions

Paperweight, Paul Stankard, Flower, Ant, Berries, Root People, 2 ½ x 3 In. .... *illus* 2125
Perfume Bottle, Caged Multi Flora, Neodymium, Fuchsia, C. Lotton, 1993, 10 In. 944
Pitcher, Rose Blown, Integral Handle, Labino, Etched, 1978, 4 ½ x 4 ¼ In. 236
Plaque, Vase Of Flowers, Fused, Etched Signature, M. & F. Higgins, 11 x 14 In. .... *illus* 563
Sculpture, Cactus Flower, Glass Needles, Blossoms, Glass Base, J. Perkins, 10 x 11 In. 369
Sculpture, Crystal, Internal Pink & Orange Veil, Signed Labino, 1977, 6 ¼ In. .... *illus* 3220
Sculpture, Disc, Blue, Purple Stylized Moth, Dreutler & Zirnsack, 1994, 20 In. 720
Sculpture, Emergence Series, Dominick Labino, 1983, 7 ¼ x 2 ½ In. .... *illus* 3500
Sculpture, Figural, Standing Man, Green & Clear, Laminated, 1980s, 30 x 9 In. 1875
Sculpture, Lapis Blue, Seaform, Teal, Dale Chihuly, 1985, 25 x 19 In., 4 Piece 13750
Sculpture, Patchwork Wizard Teapot, Murrine, R. Marquis, 1984, 15 x 8 In. .... *illus* 11250
Sculpture, Red Bowl Shape, Dale Chihuly, 26 ½ In. 10000
Sculpture, Red Cone, Purple Ribbons, Martin Blank, 18 x 25 In. 3250
Sculpture, Round, White, Green, Red, Peter VanderLaan, 13 ½ In. 250
Sculpture, Sympathetic Movement, Bent Loops, Calcedonia, Blue Foot, 1968, 8 x 6 In. 2963
Sculpture, Teapot, Lid, Circle Handle, Purple Swirl Stripes, R. Marquis, 1978, 4 x 6 In. 1875
Sculpture, Triangular, Red, Yellow, Ross Neder, 33 x 29 In. 500
Sculpture, Yellow 2-Tier Piccolo, Scroll Arms & Feet, D. Chihuly, 1996, 14 In. .... *illus* 1536
Slipper, High Top, Combed Design, Crystal Rigaree Trim, Curled Toe, 3 x 5 In. 359
Vase, Amber, Red & White Blossoms, Swirling Leaves, C. Lotton, 10 In. 403
Vase, Aurene Blue Daffodils, Lily Of The Valley, Kathy Orme, Orient & Flume, c.1977, 11 In. 472
Vase, Aventurine, Round, Metallic Green, Pink Flowers, C. Lotton, 10 In. 518
Vase, Bark Texture, Red, Green, 14 ½ In. 177
Vase, Battuto Incalmo, Purple, Red, Blue, Etched Sonma Blomdahl 2001, 18 x 12 In. 3250
Vase, Bell Bottom, Orange, Pulled Green & Silvery Black Feathers, D. Lotton, 5 x 8 In. 150
Vase, Blown, Blue Flowers, 1998, 8 ½ In. 246
Vase, Blue Iridescent, Exaggerated Ribs, Signed, Labino, 9 In. .... *illus* 230
Vase, Blue, Red, Swirls, Inclusions, William Morris, 19 In. 10000
Vase, Blue, White Flowers, Orient & Flume, 5 ½ In. 184
Vase, Bulbous, Green Feather Design, Blue Tips, Tribal, Lotton, 1977, 6 In. 345
Vase, Bulbous, Pearl Green, Gold Inclusions, Leafy Wreath, Lotton, 9 In. 690
Vase, Cameo, Under The Sea, Angelfish, Coral, Teal Blue, Enamel, Tapered, 8 In. 207
Vase, Cylindrical, Blanket, Blue Ground, Red & Black Swirl, Chihuly, 1984, 13 In. 16250
Vase, Cylindrical, Shouldered, Rolled Foot, Blue, Landscape, J. Nygren, 1988, 8 In. 500
Vase, Double Gourd, Pink Blossoms, Blue Aurene, Green, C. Lotton, 6 In. 374
Vase, Double, Multicolor, Stylized Flower Shapes, Lotton, 1994, 9 x 5 ½ In. 540
Vase, Drop Fern, Pink, Green Iridescent Leaves, Herringbone Design, 9 In. 431
Vase, Feathers, Iridescent, Blue, Cobalt Blue, Orient & Flume, 5 x 6 ½ In. 354
Vase, Flower Shape, Ebony Leaves, Dangling Vines, Gold Matte, C. Zweifel, 12 In. 207
Vase, Folded, Ruffled Rim, Green Lip Wrap, Speckled Design, Chihuly, 2001, 10 In. .... *illus* 10000
Vase, Globe Shape, Fern Leaves, Ruby Chevrons, C. Lotton, 1986, 7 x 7 In. 230
Vase, Globe Shape, Pink Flowers, Leaves, Fold-Down Collar, 1981, 5 x 6 In. 259
Vase, Globe, Cylinder Neck, King Tut Design, Pink, Green, 7 x 7 In. 431
Vase, Gold Circles, Blue Stripes, 7 In. 125
Vase, Golden Leaves & Vines, Cobalt Blue, Magenta, Gourd, 1990, 10 In. 564
Vase, Gourd, Mandarin Red, Wide Rolled Rim, C. Lotton, 1984, 3 In. 374
Vase, Gourd, Pink Streaked Flowers, Green Leaves, C. Lotton, 10 In. 575
Vase, Gourd, Shiny Aurene Gold, Water Lily Pods, Green, Blue, Vines, 4 x 5 In. 259
Vase, Iridescent, Plum, Tree, Millefiori Flowers, Orient & Flume, 5 In. 300
Vase, Iridescent Mauve Hearts, Vines, Peach Ground Over Red, Charles Lotton, 4 ½ In. 266
Vase, Lino Tagliapietra, Effetre Internationale, Murano, 1982, 9 x 6 In. .... *illus* 1250
Vase, Massimiliano Schiavon, Blown, Murano, c.1971, 13 x 13 In. .... *illus* 1063
Vase, Meadow Landscape, Red Poppies, Richard Satava, 1999, 14 ½ In. 826
Vase, Metallic Copper Leaves, Purple, Fuchsia, Round, Fold-Back Rim, 6 In. 345
Vase, Metamorfosi, Houshu, Murano Canes, Yoichi Ohira, 2001, 7 x 5 In. 21250
Vase, Molded, John Lewis, 1989, 12 x 15 In. 1200
Vase, Multi Flora, Pink Flowers, Green, Blue Ground, Charles Lotton, 1987, 10 ¾ In. 885
Vase, Multicolor, Geometric, Peter Ridabock, c.1991, 14 ¾ x 5 ½ In. 252
Vase, Oval, Green Vines & Leaves, Flowers, Pink, Purple, Fuchsia, 1986, 10 In. 805
Vase, Oval, Pink Streaked Flowers, Green Leaves, Ruby Glass, 10 In. 575
Vase, Paperweight, Lupines, Round, Tapered, Crystal, Multicolor Flowers, 1984, 5 x 6 In. 403
Vase, Planetary, Crackle Blue & Gold Foil Orb, Planets, Urn, 5 x 4 In. 431
Vase, Purple Matte Iridescence, Tapered, Flared Top, c.1981, 8 x 6 In. 130
Vase, Red & Purple Swirls, Metallic, Lundberg Studios, 7 x 5 ½ In. 276
Vase, Red, Yellow, Purple, Toots Zunsky, 24 ½ In. 15000
Vase, Ribbons, Millefiori, Turquoise, Lavender, Wes Hunting, 11 x 8 In. 316

Glass-Bohemian, Vase, Portrait, Oval Porcelain Reserve, Translucent Green, Gilt, c.1875, 12 In., Pair
$1,064

Early Auction Company

Glass-Contemporary, Paperweight, Paul Stankard, Flower, Ant, Berries, Root People, 2 ½ x 3 In.
$2,125

Rago Arts and Auction Center

Glass-Contemporary, Plaque, Vase Of Flowers, Fused, Etched Signature, M. & F. Higgins, 11 x 14 In.
$563

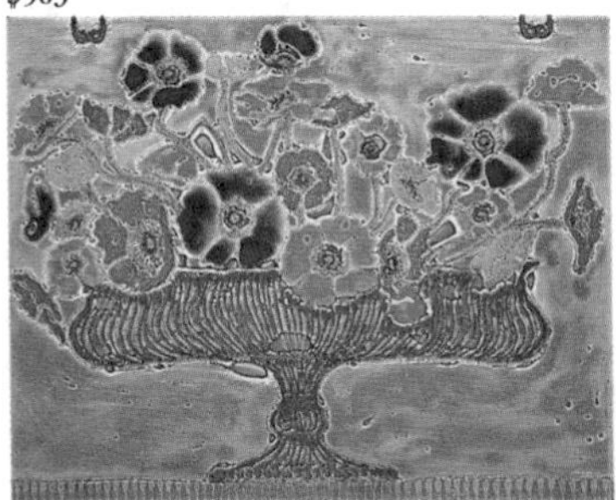

Rago Arts and Auction Center

Glass-Contemporary, Sculpture, Crystal, Internal Pink & Orange Veil, Signed Labino, 1977, 6 ¼ In.
$3,220

Early Auction Company

Glass-Contemporary, Sculpture, Emergence Series, Dominick Labino, 1983, 7 ¼ x 2 ½ In.
$3,500

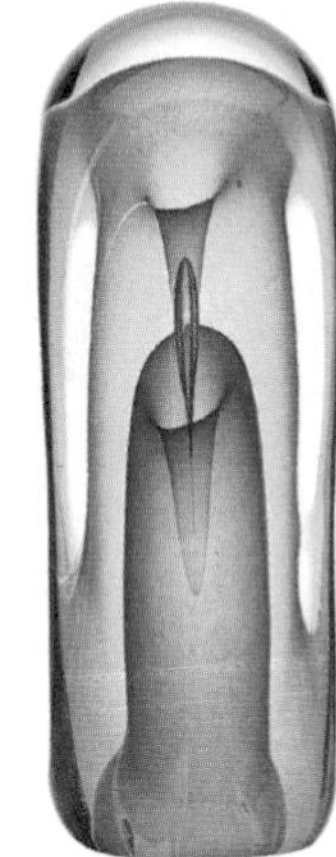

Rago Arts and Auction Center

Glass-Contemporary, Sculpture, Patchwork Wizard Teapot, Murrine, R. Marquis, 1984, 15 x 8 In.
$11,250

Rago Arts and Auction Center

Glass-Contemporary, Sculpture, Yellow 2-Tier Piccolo, Scroll Arms & Feet, D. Chihuly, 1996, 14 In.
$1,536

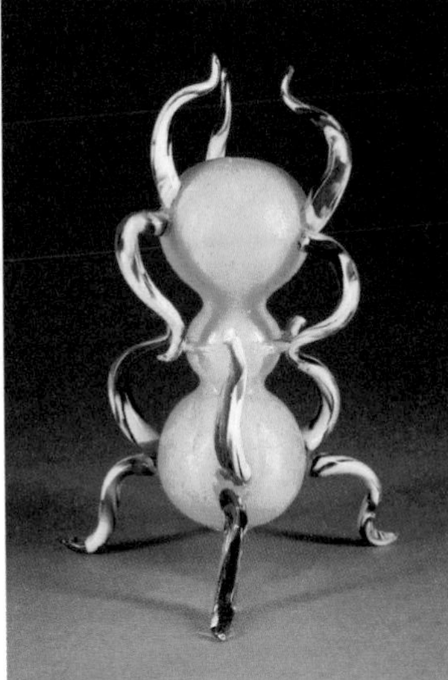

Neal Auctions

Glass-Contemporary, Vase, Blue Iridescent, Exaggerated Ribs, Signed, Labino, 9 In.
$230

Early Auction Company

Glass-Contemporary, Vase, Folded, Ruffled Rim, Green Lip Wrap, Speckled Design, Chihuly, 2001, 10 In.
$10,000

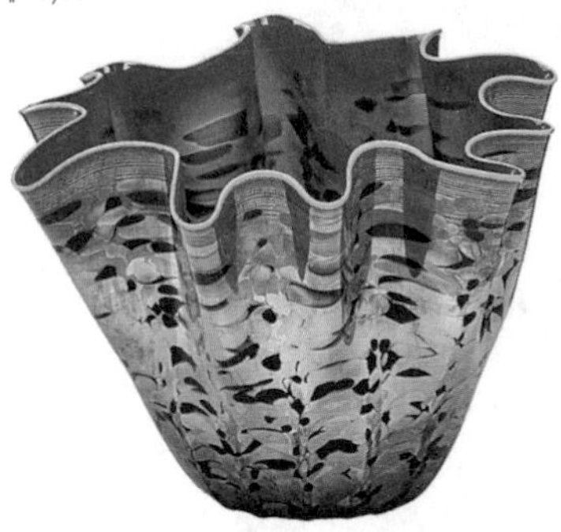

Rago Arts and Auction Center

Glass-Contemporary, Vase, Lino Tagliapietra, Effetre Internationale, Murano, 1982, 9 x 6 In.
$1,250

Rago Arts and Auction Center

Glass-Contemporary, Vase, Massimiliano Schiavon, Blown, Murano, c.1971, 13 x 13 In.
$1,063

Rago Arts and Auction Center

Glass-Midcentury, Vase, Trumpet, Red Body, Silver Vertical Design, Signed Nash Chintz, 12 In.
$805

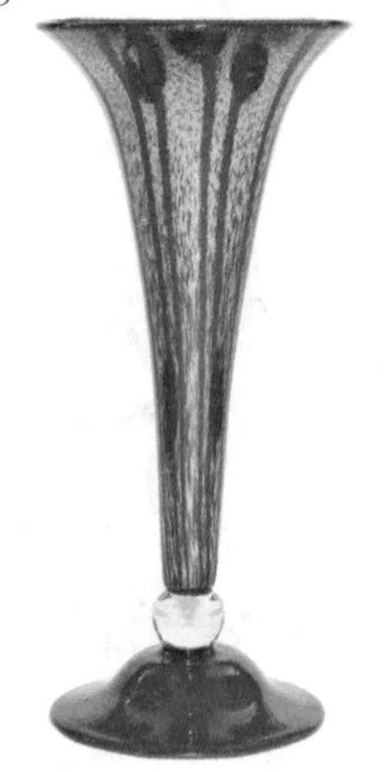

Early Auction Company

Vase, Round, Ruby Red, White Inclusions, Swirl, D. Labino, 4 x 4 In. 345
Vase, Ruby Serpentine, Split Leaves, Stems, Gold, Aurene, C. Lotton, 9 In. 920
Vase, Salmon Pink, Clear, Molded Overlay, Arches & Wings, 1975, 6 In. 748
Vase, Shouldered, Iridescent Pin, Flowers, Leaves, C. Lotton, 10 x 8 In. 575
Vase, Shouldered, Oval, Ruby Red, Leafy Wreath, Ebony Vines, 1983, 10 In. 575
Vase, Trumpet, Applied Leaves, Iridescent Green, Oil Spot, Dennis Mullen, 13 In. 614
Vase, Verre De Soie, Green Mottled Leaves, Insects, Black Vines, 7 In. 316
Vase, Winter, Snow Falling, Forest, Trumpet Shape, Round Foot, Orient & Flume, 8 x 5 In. 288
Vase, Wisteria, Ruby, Blue & Yellow Feathers, Chains, Charles Lotton, 1988, 7 x 7 In. 502
Vase, Wisteria, Swollen Cylinder, Amber, Pink Feather Design, Gold, 11 In. 403

GLASS-CUT, *see Cut Glass category.*

GLASS-DEPRESSION, *see Depression Glass category.*

GLASS-MIDCENTURY refers to art glass made from the 1940s to the early 1970s. Some glass factories, such as Baccarat or Orrefors, are listed under their own categories. Earlier glass may be listed in the Glass-Art and Glass-Contemporary categories. Italian glass may be found in Glass-Venetian.

Bowl, Clear, Blue & Red Inclusions, Air Trap, Round Rim, Tapered, A. Thuret, 5 x 7 In. 863
Bowl, Stylized Fish, Coral, Etched Bubbles, Waylande Gregory, 5 ½ x 2 ¼ In. 130
Decanter, Smoked Glass, Chicken Shape Stopper, Kaj Franck, Finland, c.1960, 12 In. 510
Sculpture, Pulcino Bird, Green, Murrines, Millefiori Eyes, Copper Feet, c.1960, 12 In. 4751
Sculpture, Soap Bubble, Green, Kaj Franck, Finland, c.1954, 7 ⅛ x 5 ¾ In. 851
Vase, 3 Tubes At Rim, Circles Design, Pink, Red, Yellow, Clear, c.1955, 15 In. 750
Vase, Agate Swirl, Purple, Mauve, Brown, Mark Peiser, 8 In. 192
Vase, Blown, Applied Leaf Blades, Dark Gray Air Bubbles, H. Navarre, 11 In. 4000
Vase, Blue Flower, Leaves, Ruby Ground, Swollen, Rolled Rim, Josh Simpson, 1949, 6 In. 523
Vase, Blue Iridescent, King Tut Swirls, Swollen, Squat, Ruffled Rim, Austria, 7 ¾ In. 2161
Vase, Bulbous, Squat, Yellow & Blue Waves, Amethyst Glass, 1971, 4 x 5 In. 359
Vase, Clear, Air Trap Inclusions, Twisted Base, Tapered, Signed, G. Nyman, 1950s, 6 In. 288
Vase, Clear, Etched, 2 Matadors & Charging Bull, Tapered, c.1950, 11 x 8 In. 69
Vase, Clear, Cased Threaded Design, Bottle Shape, Lattimo, 1954, 7 In. 173
Vase, Cordee, Oval, Raised Ropes Design, Clear To Ruby Base, France, c.1965, 11 In. 308
Vase, Elongated Oval, Wide Rim, Burgundy Red, Aurene Blue, Zipper Design, 8 In. 115
Vase, Green Dragged Loop, Gold Iridescent Zipper Design, Cream, Tapered, Swollen, 7 In. 533
Vase, Green, Bulbous, Narrow Neck, Inverted Lip, Marvin Lipofsky, 1960, 11 x 8 In. 2125
Vase, Iridescent Purple, Pulled Feathers, 9 ⅛ x 4 ½ In. 272
Vase, Lime Green, Blue, Purple, Stylized Flowers, Mark Peiser, 1971, 9 ¼ In. 288
Vase, Trumpet, Red Body, Silver Vertical Design, Signed Nash Chintz, 12 In. .... *illus* 805

GLASS-PRESSED, *see Pressed Glass category.*

GLASS-VENETIAN. Venetian glass has been made near Venice, Italy, since the thirteenth century. Thin, colored glass with applied decoration is favored, although many other types have been made. Collectors have recently become interested in the Art Deco and fifties designs. Glass was made on the Venetian island of Murano from 1291. The output dwindled in the late seventeenth century but began to flourish again in the 1850s. Some of the old techniques of glassmaking were revived, and firms today make traditional designs and original modern glass. Since 1981, the name *Murano* may be used only on glass made on Murano Island. Other pieces of Italian glass may be found in the Glass-Contemporary and Glass-Midcentury categories of this book.

Aquarium, Fish, Blue, 11 ¼ x 8 In. 360
Bowl, Black & Clear Ribbon, 6 ½ x 13 ½ In. 165
Bowl, Bubbles, Round Foot, Iridescent Ball Support, 11 x 15 In. 324
Bowl, Clamshell, Iridescent, Ercole Barovier, c.1940, 7 ¾ x 14 ¾ In. 900
Bowl, Conical, Bell Shape Foot, Lavender, Green Trim, Tagliapietra, 1989, 6 x 9 In. 875
Bowl, Light Green, Flattened Rim, Opalescent White Interior, 8 x 8 ½ In. 250
Bowl, Millefiori, Round, Green, Royal Blue, Murano, Rosewood Stand, 5 ½ In. 543
Bowl, Pink Efesco, Air Inclusions, c.1960, 4 x 13 ½ In. 288
Bowl, Ribbon, Pink, Clear, 10 ½ x 12 ½ In. 403
Bowl, Ruby Red, Gold Flecks, Dot Design, Spiral Air Bubble, Murano, 1960s, 3 x 5 In. 127
Bowl, Wheel Cut Glass, Yellow, Alfredo Barbini, 2 ¾ x 8 ¼ In. 120
Centerpiece, Frosted Battuto Base, Laura Diaz De Santillana, 11 ½ x 15 In. 302
Charger, Inverno, Pale Blue, White Tree Center, Venini, 1997, 14 In. 813
Dish, Alternating Pink & White, Latticinio, Murano, Signed Venini, Italy, 6 ¾ In. 125

Figurine, 2 Birds, On Branch, Clear, Amber, Murano, Signed, 1980s, 10¾ In. 275
Figurine, Bird, Blue, Green, Amber, Murano, Angelo Seguso, 18¼ In. 348
Figurine, Bird, On Its Back, Wings Forming Circle In Lap, Head Up, Venini, 7 In. 633
Figurine, Cactus, Vase Base, Seguso, Murano, 11 x 5 In. .... *illus* 938
Figurine, Cockatoo, Clear, Green, White, c.1950, 17 In. 150
Figurine, Dolphin, Blue, Green, Purple, 10 x 15 In. 120
Figurine, Dolphin, Pink, Blue, Purple, Clear, 20 In. 188
Figurine, Duck, Preening, Violet, Pink, Crystal, Striped Effect, Sticker, 8¼ x 11 In. 104
Figurine, Duck, Red Head, Black Handle, 1984, 12 x 13 In. 1140
Figurine, Fish, Ribbon-Like Fins, Blue, 3 Seaweed Stalks, Green, Round Base, 13½ In. 156
Figurine, Gazelle, Clear, Amber Horns, c.1970, 19 In. 250
Figurine, Gentleman, Fancy Coat, Knickers, Buckled Shoes, 12½ In. 100
Figurine, Pantolone, Fulvio Bianconi, Murano, Italy, c.1950, 15 In. .... *illus* 938
Figurine, Pintail Duck, Clear Over Blue, 6 x 8 In. 179
Figurine, Woman Carrying Urn On Head, Black, Green, 12 In. 63
Fishbowl, Multicolor, Clear, Elio Raffaeli, 20th Century, 8 x 8⅜ In. 600
Jug, Cockerel, Applied Colored Glass, Handle, Signed, Ermanno Nason, 1984, 14 In. .... *illus* 1353
Lamp, Millefiori, Ruby Red, White, Dots, Mushroom Shape, Murano, c.1970, 14 In. 322
Lamp, Pendant, Glass, Brass, Anzolo Fuga, 1950s, 19½ x 7½ In., Pair 2750
Mirror, Trapezoidal, Rope Turned, Loop Handle, Brass Connectors, 15 In. 246
Orb, Half-Circle Cut Back, Amethyst, Internal Bubble, 14½ x 10 In. 1080
Orb, Internal Bubble Channels, Oval Black Base, 14 x 10 In. 1020
Perfume Bottle, Blue Overlay, Millefiori, Murano, c.1950, 7½ In. .... *illus* 354
Pitcher, Dog Shape, Blue Accents, c.1900, 9½ In. 2543
Sculpture, Embryo, Shaped, Sommerso Crystal, Livio Seguso, c.1975, 13 x 7 In. 1188
Sculpture, First Trophy, Coffeepot Top, Trumpet Foot, R. Marquis, 1986, 19 In. .... *illus* 11875
Sculpture, Head, Round Black Plinth, Clear, Loredana Rosin, c.1985, 21 In. 984
Sculpture, Horse, Blue, Yellow, Walter Furlan, 13 x 23 In. 540
Sculpture, Saturno, Sculpture Of Saturn, Fuchsia To Purple, Tagliapietra, 1987, 9 x 21 In. 2375
Sculpture, Silver Nitrate & Clear, Standing Figure, Arms Over Head, Dino Rosin, 27 x 11 In 3327
Sculpture, Sommerso Glass Stones Internally, Blue, Bubbles, 24 x 9 In. 2880
Sculpture, Teardrop, Blue, Green, Pink, Clear, 11½ x 4 In. 180
Sculpture, Woman With Dove, 4 Arms, Juan Ripolles, 2002, 27½ x 13 In. 977
Smoking Set, Thick Glass, Lighter, Ashtray, Blue, Magenta 148
Tazza, Etched Ships, Dolphin Supports, c.1930, Pair 1680
Vase, Amber, Clear, Loose Checks, Fulvio Bianconi, Italy, c.1950, 9 x 6½ In. 6765
Vase, Applied Face, Green, Red Eyes, Black Nose, Blue Lips, Vetro Artistico, 12 x 7 In. 382
Vase, Applied Wave Handles, Gold Flecking, Pink, 13 In. 270
Vase, Balloon Shape, Clear & Green, Stripes, L. Tagliapietra, 1999, 17 In. .... *illus* 23750
Vase, Battuto, Blown, Tapered, Rounded, Yellow, Green, Red, Murano, c.1990, 18 In. 2000
Vase, Blown, Lino Tagliapietra, Italy, Signed, 1990s, 23 x 11 In. 18750
Vase, Bottle Shape, Green Smudge, Scavo Murano, 10 x 5¼ In. 96
Vase, Bottle Shape, Green Smudge, Scavo Murano, 12 x 4½ In. 132
Vase, Bottle Shape, Tapio Wirkkala, c.1966, 4 x 4½ In. 780
Vase, Bottle, Clear, Multicolor Dots Design, Rolled Flare Rim, c.1958, 17 In. 1375
Vase, Bottle, Curved Stick Neck, Multicolor, D. Martens, Murano, c.1960, 15 In. 8750
Vase, Bulb Shape, High Triangular Handles, Ribbed, Narrow Neck, 8½ In. 720
Vase, Bulbous Tri-Lobed, Stick Neck, Multicolor Splashes, Powell, 1997, 38 In. 18750
Vase, Cased Amber, Deep Red Layers, Flavio Poli, 11⅜ In. 1080
Vase, Clear, Green, Blue, Fishes, Gino Cenedese, Murano, 1977, 7½ x 8 In. 390
Vase, Dorico Corniola, Barovier & Toso, Murano, c.1960, 13 x 5½ In. .... *illus* 4688
Vase, Fulvio Bianconi, Paper Label, 3-Line Acid Etched, Fasce Orizzontali, 1950s, 8½ x 7 In. 7500
Vase, Green Iridescent, Black Overlay, Exterior Bulges, C. Scarpa, Murano, c.1950, 5 In. .... *illus* 1968
Vase, Handkerchief, Transparent, Amethyst, Fulvio Bianconi, c.1950s, 11 x 13½ In. 1140
Vase, Luigi Onesto, Italy, c.1970, 9½ x 4½ In. 1080
Vase, Narrow Mouth, Concentric Circles, Cobalt Blue, Clear, Murano, 11 In. 246
Vase, Oblong Shape, Ruby Red, Handkerchief Rim, Venini, 6½ x 12 In. 403
Vase, Occhi, Murrine, Fused, Tobia Scarpa, Venini, Murano, 12 In. .... *illus* 4888
Vase, Oval, Bubbly, 2 Decorative Ball Shape Handles, Tan, Clear, 15 In. 875
Vase, Oval, Milky White, Blue Band Top To Bottom, 1980s, 9¼ In. 185
Vase, Patchwork Design, Pink, Blue, Red, Yellow, 13 In. 480
Vase, Riccardo Licata Venini, Blown, Murrine, Doppio Incalmo, Murano, c.1956, 10 x 4 In. 4063
Vase, Scozzese, Fulvio Bianconi, 3-Line Acid Etched, 9¾ x 4 In. 2176
Vase, Sommerso, Tulip Shape, Yellow & Green, Murano, c.1950, 10 In. 246
Vase, Square Prismatic Shape, Blue To Green, Murano, 7 In. 183
Vase, Trumpet Shape, Ruffled Rim, Rainbow Tinted, Fluted, Murano, c.1940, 14 In. 120

Glass-Venetian, Figurine, Cactus, Vase Base, Seguso, Murano, 11 x 5 In.
$938

Rago Arts and Auction Center

Glass-Venetian, Figurine, Pantolone, Fulvio Bianconi, Murano, Italy, c.1950, 15 In.
$938

Rago Arts and Auction Center

Glass-Venetian, Jug, Cockerel, Applied Colored Glass, Handle, Signed, Ermanno Nason, 1984, 14 In.
$1,353

New Orleans (Cakebread)

G

Glass-Venetian, Perfume Bottle, Blue Overlay, Millefiori, Murano, c.1950, 7 ½ In.
$354

Brunk Auctions

Glass-Venetian, Sculpture, First Trophy, Coffeepot Top, Trumpet Foot, R. Marquis, 1986, 19 In.
$11,875

Rago Arts and Auction Center

Glass-Venetian, Vase, Balloon Shape, Clear & Green, Stripes, L. Tagliapietra, 1999, 17 In.
$23,750

Rago Arts and Auction Center

Glass-Venetian, Vase, Dorico Corniola, Barovier & Toso, Murano, c.1960, 13 x 5 ½ In.
$4,688

Rago Arts and Auction Center

Glass-Venetian, Vase, Green Iridescent, Black Overlay, Exterior Bulges, C. Scarpa, Murano, c.1950, 5 In.
$1,968

Skinner, Inc.

Glass-Venetian, Vase, Occhi, Murrine, Fused, Tobia Scarpa, Venini, Murano, 12 In.
$4,888

Cottone Auctions

Goebel, Egg Timer, Friar Tuck, Brown Matte, Marked, W. Germany, 3 In.
$65

Ruby Lane

GLASSES for the eyes, or spectacles, were mentioned in a manuscript in 1289 and have been used ever since. The first eyeglasses with rigid side pieces were made in London in 1727. Bifocals were invented by Benjamin Franklin in 1785. Lorgnettes were popular in late Victorian times. Opera Glasses are listed in the Opera Glass category.

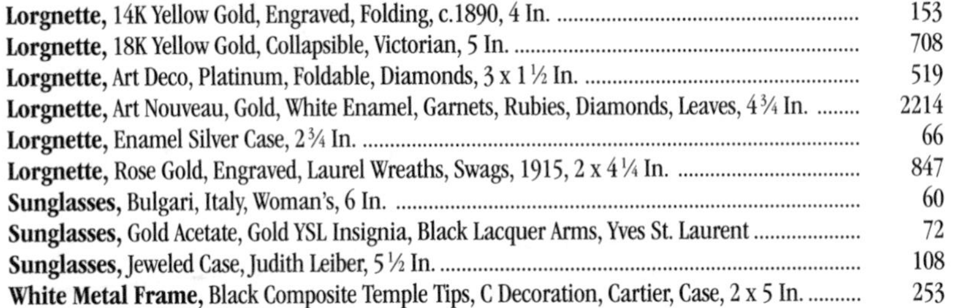

Lorgnette, 14K Yellow Gold, Engraved, Folding, c.1890, 4 In. 153
Lorgnette, 18K Yellow Gold, Collapsible, Victorian, 5 In. 708
Lorgnette, Art Deco, Platinum, Foldable, Diamonds, 3 x 1 ½ In. 519
Lorgnette, Art Nouveau, Gold, White Enamel, Garnets, Rubies, Diamonds, Leaves, 4 ¾ In. 2214
Lorgnette, Enamel Silver Case, 2 ¾ In. 66
Lorgnette, Rose Gold, Engraved, Laurel Wreaths, Swags, 1915, 2 x 4 ¼ In. 847
Sunglasses, Bulgari, Italy, Woman's, 6 In. 60
Sunglasses, Gold Acetate, Gold YSL Insignia, Black Lacquer Arms, Yves St. Laurent 72
Sunglasses, Jeweled Case, Judith Leiber, 5 ½ In. 108
White Metal Frame, Black Composite Temple Tips, C Decoration, Cartier, Case, 2 x 5 In. 253

GLIDDEN POTTERY worked in Alfred, New York, from 1940 to 1957. The pottery made stoneware, dinnerware, and art objects.

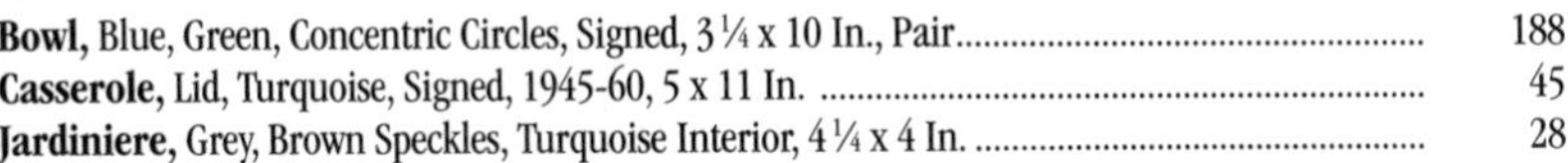

Bowl, Blue, Green, Concentric Circles, Signed, 3 ¼ x 10 In., Pair 188
Casserole, Lid, Turquoise, Signed, 1945-60, 5 x 11 In. 45
Jardiniere, Grey, Brown Speckles, Turquoise Interior, 4 ¼ x 4 In. 28

GOEBEL is the mark used by W. Goebel Porzellanfabrik of Oeslau, Germany, now Rodental, Germany. The company was founded by Franz Detleff Goebel and his son, William Goebel, in 1871. It was known as F&W Goebel. Slates, slate pencils, and marbles were made. Soon the company began making porcelain tableware and figurines. Hummel figurines were first made by Goebel in 1935 and are now being made by another company. Goebel is still in business. Old pieces marked *Goebel Hummel* are listed under Hummel in this book.

Decanter, Red Friar Tuck, No. KL 96, 3 Line Stylized Bee, 10 ¼ In. 125
Egg Timer, Friar Tuck, Brown Matte, Marked, W. Germany, 3 In. .... *illus* 65
Figurine, Angel With Lantern, Blue Hooded Coat, Wings, 1970s, 3 ½ In. 80
Figurine, Bear With Honey Pot, Brown, Red, W. Germany, 1970s .... *illus* 32
Figurine, Bird, Robin, Tree Limb, 3 ⅝ In. 68
Figurine, Half Doll, Yellow Flowered Bonnet, Hands Away, Looped Braid, 4 In. 169
Figurine, Kitten, Ladybug On Paw, Gray, 2 ¼ In. 28
Figurine, Lamb, 3 ¼ In. 43
Plaque, Goldfinch, Oval, F. Kirchner, 1975, 6 x 5 In. 35
Salt & Pepper, Cat, Scarf Around Neck, Purple, Chartreuse, c.1960, 2 ¾ In. 39
Sugar, Creamer, Friar Tuck, Tray 76
Trinket Box, Bird, Black, Gray, Round, 6 In. 105

GOLDSCHEIDER was founded by Friedrich Goldscheider in Vienna in 1885. The family left Vienna in 1938 and the factory was taken over by the Germans. Goldscheider started factories in England and in Trenton, New Jersey. The New Jersey factory started in 1940 as Goldscheider–U.S.A. In 1941 it became Goldscheider–Everlast Corporation. From 1947 to 1953 it was Goldcrest Ceramics Corporation. In 1950 the Vienna plant was returned to Mr. Goldscheider and the company continues in business. The Trenton, New Jersey, business, called Goldscheider of Vienna, imports all of the pieces.

Candelabrum Lamp, Nude Woman In Ring, Faux Candles, Austria, 1930s, 22 x 13 In. .... *illus* 1375
Figurine, Ballet Dancer, Red & Black Costume, Ruffled Tiered Tutu, Black Base, c.1935, 8 In. ... 1375
Figurine, Butterfly Dancer, Marked, Josef Lorenzi, 18 ½ In. .... *illus* 3422
Figurine, Dancer, Woman, Purple, Blue, Green, Skirt, Hat, Round Footed Base, c.1935, 17 In. ... 6563
Figurine, Dancing Spanish Woman, Holding Up Skirt, Fanned, Flower Urns, c.1930, 21 In. 3000
Figurine, Masquerade Ball, Woman, Black & Red Gown, Hat, Holding Mask, 1935, 15 In. 938
Figurine, Woman, Flower Flapper Dress, Hat, Strappy Shoes, Green Pedestal, c.1930, 19 In. 6250
Figurine, Young Man Tipping His Hat, Holding Cane, Suitcase, 1920s, 11 In. 246

GOLF, *see Sports category.*

GONDER CERAMIC ARTS, INC., was opened by Lawton Gonder in 1941 in Zanesville, Ohio. Gonder made high-grade pottery decorated with flambe, drip, gold crackle, and Chinese crackle glazes. The factory closed in 1957. From 1946 to 1954, Gonder also operated the Elgee Pottery, which made ceramic lamp bases.

Bookends, Horse Head, Red Flambe Glaze, 10 In. 195
Figurine, Asian, Man, Jar, Woman, Holding Fan, Forest Green Glaze, Foil Label, 10 In., Pair 89

Goebel, Figurine, Bear With Honey Pot, Brown, Red, W. Germany, 1970s
$32

Ruby Lane

Goldscheider, Candelabrum Lamp, Nude Woman In Ring, Faux Candles, Austria, 1930s, 22 x 13 In.
$1,375

Rago Arts and Auction Center

Goldscheider, Figurine, Butterfly Dancer, Marked, Josef Lorenzi, 18 ½ In.
$3,422

Humler & Nolan

This is an edited listing of current prices. Visit **Kovels.com** to check thousands of prices from previous years and sign up for free information on trends, tips, reproductions, marks, and more.

G

Gouda, Humidor, Damascus, Shell Finial, Green, Cobalt, Yellow, 7 In.
$400

Ruby Lane

Gouda, Vase, Beek, Green, Rust, Cobalt Blue, Black, 1920s, 3 ½ In.
$150

Ruby Lane

Graniteware, Bucket, Blue & White Swirl, Black Trim, Lid, Wire Bail Handle, Wood Grip, 7 In.
$53

Hess Auction Group

Vase, Cornucopia, Swirled Fronds, Scalloped Edge, Brown Drip Glaze, 7 In. 15
Vase, Ming Yellow, 4-Sided, 7 ¾ In. 50
Vase, Pillow, Crane, Blue Luster Glaze, 9 x 4 x 2 In. 55
Vase, Pink & Green Glaze, Trumpets, Swans, 8 In. 20
Vase, Stylized Horn, Base, Speckled Pink, 7 ¼ In. 20
Vase, Stylized Peacock Feather Shape, Scalloped, Wine Brown, 11 x 11 x 2 In. 75

GOOFUS GLASS was made from about 1900 to 1920 by many American factories. It was originally painted gold, red, green, bronze, pink, purple, or other bright colors. Many pieces are found today with flaking paint, and this lowers the value.

Bowl, Carnations, Stems, Red, Gold, Scalloped, Sawtooth Edge, c.1900, 10 ½ In. 45
Bowl, Narcissus Spray, Red & Gold On Clear, 6 ¾ In. 59
Bowl, Red & Gold Intaglio, Cherries, Branches, Ruffled, 10 In. 65
Bowl, Red Roses, Gold, Lattice, c.1900, 9 In. 20
Mug, Tennessee Rose, American Flag, c.1897 18
Pickle Jar, Flowers, Red & Gold, 12 ½ In. 90
Pin, Holly, Berries, Reverse Carved, Embossed Silver Frame, c.1940, 1 x 1 In. 45
Plate, Red & Gold Cherries, Leaf Border, 11 In. 58
Plate, Red Apples, Leaves, Scrolls, Flowers & Lattice Border, c.1900, 8 ½ In. 35
Rose Bowl, Puffy Roses, Pink & Green, 5 ½ In. 38
Vase, Pink Parrot, Shouldered, 1800s, 12 ½ In. 78
Vase, Puffy Poppies, Red & Gold Paint, 7 In. 40

GOUDA, Holland, has been a pottery center since the seventeenth century. Two firms, the Zenith pottery, established in the eighteenth century, and the Zuid-Hollandsche pottery, made the brightly colored art pottery marked *Gouda* from 1898 to about 1964. Other factories followed. Many pieces featured Art Nouveau or Art Deco designs. Pattern names in Dutch, listed here, seem strange to English-speaking collectors.

Bowl, Stylized Flowers, Multicolor, Aqua Exterior, 6 x 2 ½ In. 75
Creamer, Flowers, Multicolor, Zuid, Holland, 3 x 3 In. 65
Flower Frog, Hunze Pattern, Yellow, Blue, Round, 4 ¼ x 3 ¾ In. 90
Humidor, Damascus, Shell Finial, Green, Cobalt, Yellow, 7 In. .... *illus* 400
Humidor, Damascus, Textured, Green, Yellow, Cobalt Blue, Shell Finial, 7 In. 400
Mug, Art Nouveau Design, Barrel Shape, Yellow, Red, Green, 4 ¾ In. 65
Nappy, Bertino Pattern, Multicolor Flowers, c.1931, 7 ½ In. 65
Planter, Tulips, Yellow, Orange, Purple, Flared Edge, 1950s, 6 ¾ x 5 In. 38
Vase, Beek, Green, Rust, Cobalt Blue, Black, 1920s, 3 ½ In. .... *illus* 150
Vase, Desire Royal Pattern, Footed, Tapered, c.1953, 7 In. 270

GRANITEWARE is enameled tin or iron used to make kitchenware since the 1870s. Earlier graniteware was green or turquoise blue, with white spatters. The later ware was gray with white spatters. Reproductions are being made in all colors. There is a second definition of the word *graniteware* meaning a blue speckled pottery. Only the metal graniteware is listed here.

Bucket, Blue & White Swirl, Black Trim, Lid, Wire Bail Handle, Wood Grip, 7 In. .... *illus* 53
Bucket, Brown, Lid, Large Swirl, Wire Ball Handle, Wood Finial, 6 In. 118
Bucket, Emerald Green, Lid, Large Swirl, Blue Trim, Bail Handle, Wood Grip, 6 ½ x 6 In. 142
Bucket, Emerald Green, Lid, Large Swirl, Wire Bail Handle, Wood Grip, 5 x 5 In. 177
Coffeepot, Blue & White Swirl, Hinged Lid, 9 In. 200
Coffeepot, Brown & White Swirl, Black Trim, 8 ½ In. .... *illus* 142
Coffeepot, Brown Relish, Copper & Brass Trim, Signed L&G Mfg., 8 ¾ In. 90
Coffeepot, Emerald Green, Blue Swirl Trim, 9 ¼ In. 200
Coffeepot, Flowers, Butterflies, Bird, Hinged Lid, Curved Spot, 1800s, 10 In. 225
Coffeepot, Gray, Gray Swirls, Hinged Lid, 8 ½ In. 45
Coffeepot, Gray, Tin Dome Hinged Lid, L&G Mfg. Co., 5 ½ In. .... *illus* 24
Colander, Brown Agate, Large Swirl, Brown Trim, Wire Handles, 4 ¼ x 10 ¼ In. 41
Dinner Carrier, Stacked, Mottled, 3 Tiers, Warming Base, Handle, 14 x 7 In. 153
Double Boiler, Cream & Green, Lid, 5 ½ x 8 ¾ In. 25
Double Boiler, Emerald Green, Blue Trim, Lid, Handles, 11 ½ x 6 In. 212
Funnel, Robin's-Egg Blue, White Interior, Rolled Edge, 6 In. 45
Grater, Robin's-Egg Blue, White Speckled, Wire Legs & Handle, 8 In. 65
Jug, Syrup, White, Multicolor Castle Scene, Pewter Trim, Figural Finial, 8 In. 212
Kettle, Green & White Swirl, Lid, Blue Trim, Wire Bail Handle, Wood Grip, 8 In. .... *illus* 177
Ladle, Emerald Green, Large Swirl, Blue Trim, Handle, 15 ¾ x 6 In. 236
Lunch Pail, Blue Enamel, Lid, Tin Swing Handle, Iron Finial, 8 In. .... *illus* 30

Lunch Pail, Brown, White Speckled, Bail Handle, Ridges, 4 x 4 ½ In. 32
Lunch Pail, Gray Mottled, Oval, Tin Swing Handle, Dome Lid, 7 ¾ x 10 In. 18
Measure, Cobalt & White Swirl, 4 x 5 ½ In. 135
Mixing Bowl, Blue & White Swirl, 9 ¾ x 4 ¾ In. 52
Pan, Roasting, Black, White Speckled, Lid, 16 x 12 x 7 In. 70
Salt Box, Hanging, Gray Mottled, Arched Back, Eyelet, El-An-Ge, 11 x 7 In. 142
Slop Bucket, White, Black Trim, Bail Handle, Label, Flintstone, 15 In. 90
Strainer, Black, White Speckled, 10 ¾ In. 39
Strainer, Gray, Handle, 6 ¼ In. Diam., 4-In. Handle 27
Strainer, White, Speckled, 3-Footed, 8 x 3 In. 20
Tea Steeper, Cobalt Blue, Medium Swirl, Tin Lid, Wood Finial, 4 ½ In. 83
Teapot, Gray, Medium Mottled, Pewter Trim, 8 ¼ In. 47
Teapot, Tin Lid, Medium Brown Mottle, Wood Finial, 6 In. 82
Teapot, White, Multicolor Flowers, Leaves, Pewter Trim, 9 ¼ In. 200
Tub, Brown, Gray Interior, Handles, Pedestal Base, 18 x 13 In. 98
Watering Can, Blue & White, Raised Star, Top & Side Handle, 15 In. 95

GREENTOWN glass was made by the Indiana Tumbler and Goblet Company of Greentown, Indiana, from 1894 to 1903. In 1899, the factory became part of National Glass Company. A variety of pressed glass was made. Additional pieces may be found in other categories, such as Chocolate Glass, Holly Amber, Milk Glass, and Pressed Glass.

Cactus, Sauce, Chocolate, Scalloped Rim, 4 In. 28
Cord Drapery, Pitcher, Footed, 5 In. 30
Dewey, Creamer, Canary Yellow, 3-Footed, 5 In. 45
Figurine, Dolphin, Beaded, Chocolate, c.1900, 6 In. 250

GRUEBY FAIENCE COMPANY of Boston, Massachusetts, was founded in 1894 by William H. Grueby. Grueby Pottery Company was incorporated in 1907. In 1909, Grueby Faience went bankrupt. Then William Grueby founded the Grueby Faience and Tile Company. Grueby Pottery closed about 1911. The tile company worked until 1920. Garden statuary, art pottery, and architectural tiles were made until 1920. The company developed a green matte glaze that was so popular it was copied by many other factories making a less expensive type of pottery. This eventually led to the financial problems of the pottery. Cuerda seca and cuenca are techniques explained in the Tile category. The company name was often used as the mark, and slight changes in the form help date a piece.

Humidor, Lid, Blue Matte Glaze, Round Body, Raised Shoulder Design, Veins, 4 In. 1534
Tile, 2 Trees In Landscape, Green & Brown, Blue, Matte, Oak Frame, c.1904, 6 x 6 In. 3075
Tile, 2-Masted Ship, Frame, Square, Boston, c.1905, 8 In. .... *illus* 2000
Tile, Geometric, Green, Ivory, Blue, Yellow, 9 x 9 In. 1170
Tile, Lion, Beneath Trees, Matte Glaze, White Clay Body, 4 x 4 In. 590
Tile, Moorish, Blue, Green, Yellow, 9 x 9 In. 1170
Tile, Rabbit, Glazed Ceramic, Green, Blue, Brown, Signed, 6 In. 7930
Tile, Trees In Landscape, Green, Blue, Glazed, Square, c.1906, 6 In. 1046
Vase, Bulbous, Squat, Cylindrical Neck, Rolled Rim, Green, Yellow Blossoms, 1905, 13 In. 8125
Vase, Crocuses, Curdled Blue Glaze, Wide Mouth, Rolled Rim, c.1905, 8 ½ x 7 In. 1375
Vase, Curdled Mustard Glaze, Carved Leaves, Oval, Erickson, c.1905, 10 x 6 In. .... *illus* 1875
Vase, Green Glaze, Embossed Leaf Design, Squat Shape, Paper Label, 4 ¾ In. 649
Vase, Green Matte Glaze, Leaves & Buds, Shouldered, Rolled Rim, c.1905, 23 x 8 In. .... *illus* 10000
Vase, Green, Raised Blossoms, Squat, Leaves, Long Neck, Erickson, 12 In. 2250
Vase, Leaves, Buds, Bulbous, Tapered Neck, c.1900, Circle Faience Stamp, 7 ½ x 4 ½ In. 1500
Vase, Melon Shape, Ring Foot, Leaves & Flower Buds, Green, c.1905, 12 x 8 In. 6875
Vase, Relief Banded, 7 Upright Leaves, Stems, Fleur-De-Lis, 12 x 12 ¾ In. 3600
Vase, Tapered, Bulbous Shoulder, Flat Rim, Yellow Glaze, Leaf Pattern, c.1900, 6 In. 1875
Vase, Tapered, Lobed, Shaped Rim, Green, Yellow Buds, c.1905, 8 x 5 In. 2875
Vase, Urn Shape, Flared Rim, Ring Foot, Leaves, Curdled Green Glaze, c.1900, 10 In. 2000

GUN, *see Toy.*

GUSTAVSBERG ceramics factory was founded in 1827 near Stockholm, Sweden. It is best known to collectors for its twentieth-century artwares, especially Argenta, a green stoneware with silver inlay. The company broke up and was sold in the 1990s.

Gustafsberg

Dish, Argenta, Flower Inlay, Scalloped Edge, 4 In. 65
Figurine, Girl, Mei, Lisa Larson, Foil Label, 1970s, 3 ¾ In. 98
Tray, Argenta, Bouquet Inlay, 5 In. Diam. 100
Vase, Argenta, Blue Flambe Glaze, 3 Inlay Crowns, 5 x 3 x 3 In. 75

Graniteware, Coffeepot, Brown & White Swirl, Black Trim, 8 ½ In.
$142

Hess Auction Group

Graniteware, Coffeepot, Gray, Tin Dome Hinged Lid, L&G Mfg. Co., 5 ½ In.
$24

Hess Auction Group

Graniteware, Kettle, Green & White Swirl, Lid, Blue Trim, Wire Bail Handle, Wood Grip, 8 In.
$177

Hess Auction Group

G

Graniteware, Lunch Pail, Blue Enamel, Lid, Tin Swing Handle, Iron Finial, 8 In.
$30

Hess Auction Group

Grueby, Tile, 2-Masted Ship, Frame, Square, Boston, c.1905, 8 In.
$2,000

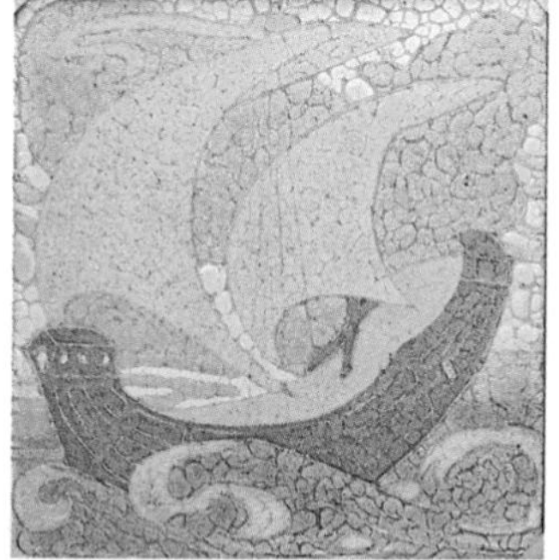

Rago Arts and Auction Center

Grueby, Vase, Curdled Mustard Glaze, Carved Leaves, Oval, Erickson, c.1905, 10 x 6 In.
$1,875

Rago Arts and Auction Center

Vase, Argenta, Flower Inlays, Flared, Footed, 5 In. 250
Vase, Argenta, Hashtag Inlay, Cylindrical, 3 ½ In. 80
Vase, Blood Red, Green Speckled, Shouldered, Marked, 8 x 5 In. 850
Vase, Squat, Flat Rim, Flowers, Butterflies, Blue & White, c.1902, 3 ¾ In. 288
Vase, Stylized Fish, Blue Matte Glaze, Paper Label, Kage, 4 ⅞ In. 293
Vase, Tapered, Bulbous Shoulder, Incised Grapes, Blue & White, c.1900, 17 In. 1150
Vase, Variegated Brown Glaze, Striped, Shouldered, S. Lindberg, 4 In. 167

HAEGER POTTERIES, INC., Dundee, Illinois, started making commercial artwares in 1914. Early pieces were marked with the name *Haeger* written over an *H*. About 1938, the mark *Royal Haeger* was used in honor of Royal Hickman, a designer at the factory. The firm closed in 2016. See also the Royal Hickman category.

Haeger

Ashtray, Shell, Brown, 8 ¼ x 6 In. .... *illus* 28
Candleholder, Marbled Blue Green, Petal Shape, c.1960, 6 x 3 In., Pair 25
Cookie Jar, Yellow, Red Hippopotamus, 1960s, 8 ½ x 6 ½ In. 34
Figurine, Bunch O' Collie Pups, Amber Glaze, c.1945, 5 x 9 In. 265
Jardiniere, Turquoise, Fluted, Double Handle, Round Foot, 14 In., Pair 113
Mixing Bowl, Scalloped Trim, Textured, Mustard, 7 ⅝ In. 25
Pitcher, Pink, Rolled Rim, 6 In. 14
Planter, Footed, Ribbed, Beige, c.1960, 6 ¼ x 5 ¼ In. 18
Planter, Panther, Black, 9 x 4 x 3 In. 35
Planter, Sage Green, Attached Underplate, 10 x 3 ½ In. 16
Vase, Art Deco, Blue, 7 x 8 ¼ In. .... *illus* 115
Vase, Bud, Stick Neck, Orange Peel Glaze, 1970s, 9 ¾ In. 35
Vase, Bulbous, Collared Rim, Orange Peel Glaze, c.1950, 5 ½ In. 39
Vase, Bulbous, Stick Neck, Orange Peel Glaze, 15 In. 76
Vase, Lily Shape, Yellow Green, 14 x 6 ¾ In., Pair 90
Vase, Peacock, Blue, Pink, c.1940, 15 x 15 ½ In. 112
Vase, Peacock, Pink, Blue, Marked, Royal, 1940s, 15 In. .... *illus* 101

HALF-DOLL, *see Pincushion Doll category.*

HALL CHINA COMPANY started in East Liverpool, Ohio, in 1903. The firm made many types of wares. Collectors search for the Hall teapots made from the 1920s to the 1950s. The dinnerware of the same period, especially Autumn Leaf pattern, is also popular. The Hall China Company merged with Homer Laughlin China Company in 2010. Autumn Leaf pattern dishes are listed in their own category in this book.

HALL'S SUPERIOR QUALITY KITCHENWARE

Arizona, Bowl, Vegetable, 8 x 8 In. 27
Arizona, Creamer, 6 Oz., 3 In. 21
Arizona, Plate, Dinner, 11 In. 9
Arizona, Plate, Salad, 8 In. 10
Blue, Teapot, Hook Lid, Gold Trim, 6 x 4 ½ In. .... *illus* 45
Bouquet, Bowl, Vegetable, 8 x 8 In. 41
Bouquet, Butter, Cover, Winged, ¼ Lb. 199
Bouquet, Casserole, Lid, Oval, 2 Qt. 123
Bouquet, Celery Dish, 11 ⅞ In. 32
Bouquet, Coffeepot, Lid, 5 Cup, 8 ¼ In. 209
Bouquet, Cup & Saucer, Footed 9
Bouquet, Eggcup, Double, 4 ¼ In. 32
Bouquet, Gravy Boat 27
Bouquet, Plate, Bread & Butter, 6 ⅜ In. 7
Bouquet, Teapot, Modern Shape, Lid, 4 Cup, 4 ⅝ In. 319
Bowknot Pink, Teapot, Lid, 4 Cup, 4 ¼ In. 65
Buckingham, Cup & Saucer, Footed 10
Cactus, Coffeepot, Lid, Viking, 10 Cup, 7 ¾ In. 42
Caprice, Cup & Saucer 11
Caprice, Plate, Bread & Butter, 6 ⅜ In. 7
Caprice, Plate, Dinner, 11 In. 33
Caprice, Platter, Oval, 15 In. 44
Caprice, Sugar & Creamer 35
Century Fern, Bowl, Dessert, 6 ½ In. 9
Concord, Bowl, Cereal, 6 ¼ In. 8
Concord, Cup & Saucer 7
Concord, Plate, Dinner, 10 ½ In. 8

Grueby, Vase, Green Matte Glaze, Leaves & Buds, Shouldered, Rolled Rim, c.1905, 23 x 8 In.
$10,000

Rago Arts and Auction Center

TIP

You can list only your phone number and not your street address in the local phone book. Ask your phone company. Good idea for a known collector.

Haeger, Ashtray, Shell, Brown, 8 ¼ x 6 In.
$28

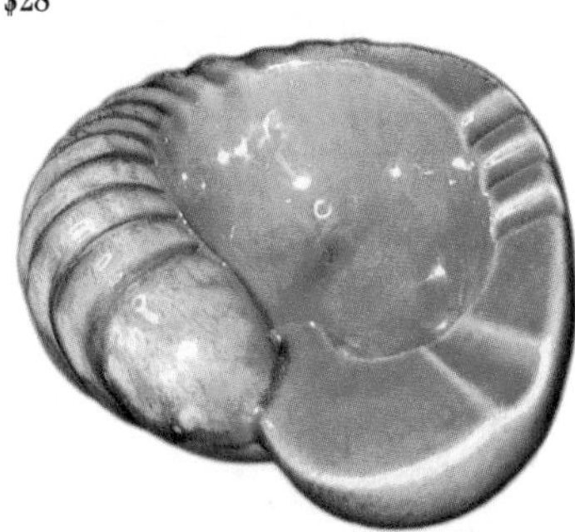

Ruby Lane

Run a Successful Garage Sale

Run a garage sale: clean the house and get extra cash. Most newspapers offer a garage sale kit that explains what to do. Better yet, join friends and have a big, big sale. Try to find someone who had sales before. Learn about security needed, helpers, and city permits. A few tips. Run an ad online and in the local paper. Put up signs large enough to read from a moving car. Set up sorted displays, clothes in one place, toys in another. Mark everything with masking tape or a label that's hard to remove. Have an electric outlet to test any electrical items. Price things low enough. Don't let anyone in your house for any reason. Keep cash in a secure box with one person watching it.

Haeger, Vase, Art Deco, Blue, 7 x 8 ¼ In.
$115

Ruby Lane

Haeger, Vase, Peacock, Pink, Blue, Marked, Royal, 1940s, 15 In.
$101

Ruby Lane

Hall, Blue, Teapot, Hook Lid, Gold Trim, 6 x 4 ½ In.
$45

Ruby Lane

Hall, Radiance, Casserole, Lid, c.1930, 8 ¼ In.
$42

Ruby Lane

Hall, Red Poppy, Platter, Black Leaves, 13 ½ In.
$32

Ruby Lane

Hall, Tulip, Bowl, Salad, Cook Coffee Co., 9 In.
$18

Ruby Lane

Save the Label

Save all labels and written information found on antiques to help determine the history of the object. Do not remove labels. To copy a bottle label, you can try rolling the bottle on a scanner bed at the scan speed. It is easier than it sounds. Put a wide rubber band on the bottle if it has embossed lettering. It helps make a smoother roll.

Halloween, Decoration, Maid, Jack-O'-Lantern Head, Die Cut Cardboard, Germany, 1920s, 8 x 3 In.
$90

Ruby Lane

Halloween, Decoration, Scarecrow, Owl, Moon, 3-D, Folds Out, Beistle Co., c.1950, 8 x 8 In.
$125

Ruby Lane

TIP

Fishing line is strong and almost invisible and can be used to tie fragile items to a base or wall. This will prevent damage from earthquakes, two-year-olds, and dogs with wagging tails.

Crocus, Bean Pot, Handle, 3 Qt., 6 In. ... 329
Crocus, Bowl, Vegetable, 9 In. ... 35
Crocus, Jug, Ball, 64 Oz., 5 ¼ In. ... 210
Crocus, Mug, Flagon Style, 4 ⅝ In. ... 47
Crocus, Plate, Dinner, 10 ¼ In. ... 219
Crocus, Salt & Pepper, Teardrop Shape ... 109
Crocus, Teapot, Lid, Car Shape ... 259
Dutch Couple, Teapot, Lid, Windmill, Target, 8 Cup, 5 ¼ In. ... 35
Flair, Candlestick, 4 ½ In. ... 19
Flair, Cup & Saucer ... 8
Frost Flowers, Bowl, Vegetable, 8 x 8 In. ... 16
Frost Flowers, Cup & Saucer ... 11
Gold Lace, Casserole, 9 In. ... 76
Gold Lace, Cookie Jar, Lid, 7 ½ In. ... 30
Harlequin, Butter, Cover, Winged, ¼ Lb. ... 189
Harlequin, Soup, Dish, Lugged, 9 In. ... 42
Heather Rose, Bowl, Vegetable, 9 In. ... 31
Heather Rose, Cup & Saucer ... 8
Heather Rose, Jug, Utility, 40 Oz., 5 ½ In. ... 44
Heather Rose, Pie Plate, 9 In. ... 40
Mt. Vernon, Platter, 11 ½ In. ... 12
Mulberry, Platter, Oval, 17 In. ... 46
Mulberry, Sugar ... 22
Mums, Cup & Saucer ... 6
Mums, Gravy Boat ... 29
Mums, Plate, Luncheon, 9 ⅛ In. ... 33
Old Rose, Creamer, Empire, 7 Oz., 3 ¼ In. ... 13
Phoenix Green, Bowl, Vegetable, Round, 8 In. ... 26
Poppy, Bowl, Vegetable, Round, 9 In. ... 38
Poppy, Cup & Saucer ... 48
Poppy, Teapot, Lid, Streamline, 4 Cup, 5 In. ... 259
Primrose, Bowl, Vegetable, Oval, 10 In. ... 20
Primrose, Cake Plate, 9 ½ In. ... 33
Primrose, Creamer, 8 Oz., 2 ⅞ In. ... 16
Primrose, Cup & Saucer, Footed ... 8
Primrose, Jug, Rayed, 32 Oz., 5 ½ In. ... 42
Primrose, Plate, Dinner, 10 ⅛ In. ... 10
Primrose, Platter, Oval, 13 In. ... 40
Radiance, Casserole, Lid, c.1930, 8 ¼ In. ... *illus* 42
Red Poppy, Cup & Saucer ... 34
Red Poppy, Jug, Ball, 64 Oz., 5 ½ In. ... 149
Red Poppy, Pepper, Platinum Trim, Handle, c.1940, 5 In. ... 16
Red Poppy, Platter, Black Leaves, 13 ½ In. ... *illus* 32
Red Poppy, Platter, Oval, 11 In. ... 47
Red Poppy, Salt & Pepper, Teardrop ... 40
Red Poppy, Shaker, Platinum Ring, Bulbous, c.1940, 5 In. ... 17
Red Poppy, Soup, Dish, Rim, 8 ½ In. ... 15
Red Poppy, Teapot, Lid, Aladdin, 4 Cup, 4 ⅜ In. ... 239
Refrigerator Ware, Casserole, Lid, Yellow, Round, 2 Qt. ... 54
Refrigerator Ware, Pitcher, Lid, Yellow & White ... 60
Royal Rose, Casserole, Lid, 2 Qt. ... 54
Royal Rose, Salt & Pepper ... 40
Silhouette, Casserole, Medallion, Lid, 1 ¾ Qt., 8 ¼ In. ... 76
Silhouette, Plate, Salad, 7 ⅜ In. ... 41
Silhouette, Salt & Pepper, 5 Band ... 98
Tulip, Bowl, Dessert, 5 ⅝ In. ... 10
Tulip, Bowl, Salad, Cook Coffee Co., 9 In. ... *illus* 18
Tulip, Cup & Saucer ... 12
Tulip, Sugar, Lid, 3 ⅛ In. ... 47

HALLOWEEN is an ancient holiday that has changed in the last 200 years. The jack-o'-lantern, witches on broomsticks, and orange decorations seem to be twentieth-century creations. Collectors started to become serious about collecting Halloween-related items in the late 1970s. The papier-mache decorations, now replaced by plastic, and old costumes are in demand.

Costume, Ben Cooper, James Bond 007, Hat, Domino Mask, Tuxedo, Box, 1966, Size L ... 190
Costume, Spider-Man, Rayon, Vacuform Mask, Marvel Comics, Box, 1970, Size 12-14 ... 115

Decoration, Maid, Jack-O'-Lantern Head, Die Cut Cardboard, Germany, 1920s, 8 x 3 In. ....*illus* 90
Decoration, Scarecrow, Owl, Moon, 3-D, Folds Out, Beistle Co., c.1950, 8 x 8 In. ....*illus* 125
Jack-O'-Lantern, Papier-Mache, Face, Eyes Missing, 1940s, 4 ½ x 4 ½ In. ....*illus* 45
Jack-O'-Lantern, Papier-Mache, Wire Handles, Graduated, 4-7 In., Set Of 4.............................. 1888
Jack-O'-Lantern, Tin, Hinged Lid, Handle, Punched, Folk Art, c.1900, 10 In. 649
Lantern, Devil's Head, Pointy Chin, Composition, Paper Insert, Bail Handle, 5 In. 1770
Lantern, Witch, Sooty Face, Pilgrim Hat, Paper Inserts, Handle, Germany, 5 In. 561
Postcard, Startled Woman, Cow With Jack-O'-Lanterns On Horns, Slogan, J. Bien, 1910 .....*illus* 22
Pumpkin Head Man, Vegetable Man, Orange & Black Velvet Suit, Victorian, 20 In. 2950
Torch, Parade, Jack-O'-Lantern, Tin, Wood Shaft, c.1910, 6 x 27 In. ....*illus* 1888

HAMPSHIRE pottery was made in Keene, New Hampshire, between 1871 and 1923. Hampshire developed a line of colored glazed wares as early as 1883, including a Royal Worcester–type pink, olive green, blue, and mahogany. Pieces are marked with the printed mark or the impressed name *Hampshire Pottery* or *J.S.T. & Co., Keene, N.H.* Many pieces were marked with city names and sold as souvenirs.

Loving Cup, Green Matte Glaze, 3 Handles, 5 In. 125
Vase, Arts & Crafts, Blue Matte Glaze, Flowers, Leaves, 6 ½ x 4 ¾ In. 345
Vase, Arts & Crafts, Blue Matte Glaze, Stripes, Cylinder, Tapered, Pinched Neck, 8 x 4 In. 276
Vase, Green Matte Glaze, Bulbous, 5 ½ In. 145
Vase, Green Matte Glaze, Handles, Pedestal, 6 x 7 ¾ In. 185
Vase, Green Matte Glaze, Ribbed, 3 ¼ x 6 ¾ In. 145
Vase, Leaf Blade Surround, Bugs, Green Matte Glaze, 7 In. 708
Vase, Molded Leaf Design, Dark & Light Brown Matte Glaze, Rounded Shoulder, 7 In. 403
Vase, Mottled Blue Glaze, Arts & Crafts, 4 ¼ x 4 ¾ In. 185

HANDEL glass was made by Philip Handel working in Meriden, Connecticut, from 1885 and in New York City from 1893 to 1933. The firm made art glass and other types of lamps. Handel shades were made not only of leaded glass in a style reminiscent of Tiffany but also of reverse painted glass. Handel also made vases and other glass objects.

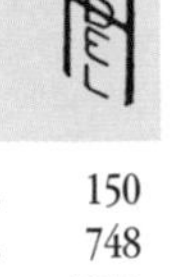

Bowl, Yellow Acid Cut To Clear, Cameo, Signed, 7 x 2 ½ In. 150
Humidor, Native American Portrait, Green, Opal Inside, Cylindrical, Flip Lid, 6 In. 748
Humidor, Teroma, Chipped Ice Ground, Bamboo Trees, Jungle Birds, Round, Lid, 8 In. 3081
Lamp, Arts & Crafts, Frosted Glass Shade, Amber Mottled, Leaves, Bronze Stand, 22 x 14 In. 3480
Lamp, Caramel Slag Shade, Metal Bamboo Overlay, Bronze Base, Art Nouveau Foot, 66 In. 4444
Lamp, Chipped Ice Shade, Daffodils, Bronze Base, 25 x 18 In. ....*illus* 8740
Lamp, Chipped Ice Shade, Exotic Birds, Multicolor, Red Ground, Bronze Base, 24 In. 8295
Lamp, Chipped Ice Shade, Yellow Daffodils, Shaded Black & Green, Bronze Urn Base, 24 In. 10073
Lamp, Cylindrical Glass Shade, Daisies, Etched, Metal Base, c.1910, 16 In. ....*illus* 2500
Lamp, Desk, Chipped Ice Shade, Autumn Woods Scene, Bronze Base, 14 x 11 In. 690
Lamp, Domed Shade, Aquarium, Fish, Green, Yellow, Brown, Mermaid Base, 23 In. 32750
Lamp, Domed Shade, Egyptian Ruins, Urn Base, 25 In. 5850
Lamp, Domed Shade, Tulips, Leaves, Purple, Green, Ribbed Stem, 23 In. ....*illus* 4148
Lamp, Electric, Metal Base, Arts & Crafts Glass Shade, 15 x 7 In. 1080
Lamp, Flowered Shade, Multicolor, Open 3-Part Base, Marked, 22 In. 5265
Lamp, Hanging, Gold Chipped Ice Globe, Trees, Birds, Bronze Cap, Chain & Tassel, 29 In. 4014
Lamp, Lake & Sunset, Red, Black, 24 x 18 In. 3220
Lamp, Trees In Landscape, Patinated Forest Base, 23 In. 12500
Lamp, White Glass Shade, Bronze Base, Pull Chain, c.1910, 14 In. 177
Lamp, Wisteria Shade, Blue, Green, Openwork Top, Bronze Tree Trunk Base, 31 In. 20145
Lamp, Yellow Orange Glass, Metal Hawaiian Sunset Overlay, Bronze Spread Base, 17 In. 1422
Vase, Teroma, Landscape, Pink Sky, Sailboats, Green, Hexagonal Mouth, 11 x 4 In. 272

HARDWARE, *see Architectural category.*

HARKER POTTERY COMPANY was incorporated in 1890 in East Liverpool, Ohio. The Harker family had been making pottery in the area since 1840. The company made many types of pottery but by the Civil War was making quantities of yellowware from native clays. It also made Rockingham-type brown-glazed pottery and whiteware. The plant was moved to Chester, West Virginia, in 1931. Dinnerware was made and sold nationally. In 1971 the company was sold to Jeannette Glass Company, and all operations ceased in 1972. For more prices, go to kovels.com.

Alpine, Bowl, Vegetable, Round, 8 In. 18
Alpine, Cup & Saucer 12
Alpine, Platter, Oval, 13 In. 20

Halloween, Jack-O'-Lantern, Papier-Mache, Face, Eyes Missing, 1940s, 4 ½ x 4 ½ In.
$45

Ruby Lane

Halloween, Postcard, Startled Woman, Cow With Jack-O'-Lanterns On Horns, Slogan, J. Bien, 1910
$22

Ruby Lane

Halloween, Torch, Parade, Jack-O'-Lantern, Tin, Wood Shaft, c.1910, 6 x 27 In.
$1,888

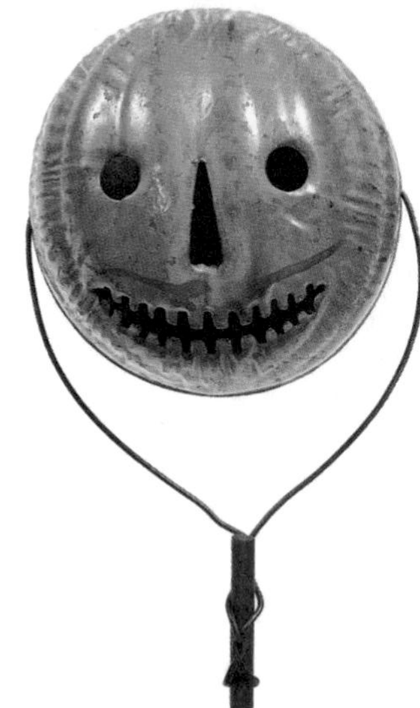

Hess Auction Group

Handel, Lamp, Chipped Ice Shade, Daffodils, Bronze Base, 25 x 18 In. $8,740

Cottone Auctions

Handel, Lamp, Cylindrical Glass Shade, Daisies, Etched, Metal Base, c.1910, 16 In. $2,500

Rago Arts and Auction Center

Handel, Lamp, Domed Shade, Tulips, Leaves, Purple, Green, Ribbed Stem, 23 In. $4,148

James D. Julia Auctioneers

Amy, Cup & Saucer, Footed ... 16
Bermuda, Bowl, Vegetable, Round, 8 In. ... 14
Bermuda, Creamer, 8 Oz., 2 In. ... 9
Bermuda, Plate, Bread & Butter, 6 In. ... 4
Bermuda, Platter, Oval, 12 In. ... 33
Bermuda, Platter, Oval, 16 In. ... 45
Blue Dane, Cup & Saucer ... 8
Blue Mist, Cup & Saucer ... 8
Bouquet, Cup & Saucer ... 13
Bridal Rose, Bowl, Cereal, Lugged, 6 ¾ In. ... 16
Bridal Rose, Cup & Saucer ... 19
Bridal Rose, Gravy Boat, Underplate ... 78
Bridal Rose, Plate, Bread & Butter, 6 In. ... 8
Bridal Rose, Plate, Dinner, 10 In. ... 20
Bridal Rose, Platter, Oval, 11 In. ... 47
Chesterton, Creamer, Celadon, 8 Oz., 2 ¼ In. ... 14
Chesterton, Cup & Saucer, Blue ... 8
Chesterton, Cup & Saucer, Celadon ... 12
Chesterton, Gravy Boat, Celadon ... 53
Chesterton, Plate, Bread & Butter, Blue, 6 ¼ In. ... 6
Chesterton, Plate, Dinner, Celadon, 10 In. ... 24
Chesterton, Platter, Celadon, Oval, 13 In. ... 26
Chesterton, Soup, Dish, Blue, 8 In. ... 6
Cock O'Morn, Butter, Cover, Coral, ¼ Lb. ... 22
Cock O'Morn, Cup & Saucer, Coral ... 6
Cock O'Morn, Cup & Saucer, Yellow ... 9
Corinthian, Dish, Vegetable, Ivory, Teal Lid, Gadroon Rim, Backstamp ... *illus* 100
Dainty Flower, Bowl, Vegetable, Round, Blue, Swirl, 8 In. ... 18
Dainty Flower, Cup & Saucer, Blue, Swirl ... 21
Dainty Flower, Platter, Oval, Blue, Swirl, 13 In. ... 24
Dresden Duchess, Plate, Salad, 7 ¼ In. ... 11
Early American, Plate, Bread & Butter, Square, 6 ⅝ In. ... 14
Early Morn, Plate, Salad, 7 In. ... 6
Early Morn, Platter, Oval, 13 In. ... 13
Everglades, Plate, Salad, 7 ¼ In. ... 7
Everglades, Platter, Oval, 13 In. ... 21
Forget-Me-Knot, Cup & Saucer ... 13
Godey Prints, Cup & Saucer ... 15
Godey Prints, Plate, Dessert, 7 ⅜ In. ... 8
Godey Prints, Sugar & Creamer ... 48
Golden Dawn, Casserole, Round, 1 ½ Qt. ... 45
Golden Dawn, Cup & Saucer ... 6
Homestead, Platter, Oval, 13 In. ... 28
Ivy Wreath, Bowl, Dessert, 5 ¾ In. ... 6
Ivy Wreath, Bowl, Vegetable, Divided, Oval, 10 In. ... 22
Ivy Wreath, Butter, Cover, ¼ Lb. ... 38
Ivy Wreath, Creamer ... 12
Ivy Wreath, Cup & Saucer ... 4
Ivy Wreath, Plate, Salad, 7 ¼ In. ... 6
Ivy Wreath, Platter, Oval, 11 In. ... 14
Ivy, Bowl, Cereal, Lugged, 6 ¾ In. ... 26
Ivy, Bowl, Dessert, 5 ⅝ In. ... 8
Ivy, Bowl, Vegetable, Round, 8 In. ... 32
Ivy, Cake Plate, Handles, 11 In. ... 46
Ivy, Cup & Saucer ... 16
Ivy, Plate, Bread & Butter, 6 ¼ In. ... 6
Ivy, Plate, Dinner, 10 In. ... 22
Ivy, Platter, Oval, 12 In. ... 30
Ivy, Platter, Oval, 16 In. ... 58
Ivy, Salt & Pepper ... 82
Ivy, Teapot, Lid, 4 Cup, 3 ⅜ In. ... 234
Laurelton Aqua, Butter, Cover, ¼ Lb. ... 18
Laurelton Aqua, Coffeepot, Lid, 5 Cup ... 32
Laurelton Aqua, Creamer ... 15
Laurelton Aqua, Cup & Saucer ... 13
Laurelton Aqua, Plate, Dinner, 10 In. ... 9
Laurelton Aqua, Platter, Oval, 14 In. ... 21

Harker, Corinthian, Dish, Vegetable, Ivory, Teal Lid, Gadroon Rim, Backstamp
$100

Ruby Lane

Harker, Mugs, Mother & Dad, Pink, Blue, Cameoware, 3 x 4 ½ In., Pair
$20

Harker, Pitcher, Tulips, 5 ½ In.
$20

Ruby Lane

Harker, Springtime, Plate, Salad, 1950s, 7 ⅜ In.
$6

Ruby Lane

Harlequin, Teapot, Orange, Homer Laughlin, 1940-42, 10 x 6 In.
$149

Ruby Lane

Hatpin, Brass, Mosaic, 9 ¼ x 1 ¼ In.
$120

Ruby Lane

Hatpin, Etruscan Gold Work, 1 In.
$125

Ruby Lane

Hatpin, Rhinestone, Amethyst, Clear, Concentric Circles, 1 ½ In.
$57

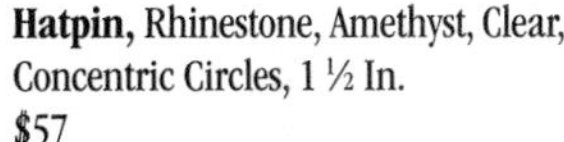

Ruby Lane

Hatpin, Sterling Silver, Man, Hat, Feather, c.1900, 1 x ¾ In.
$52

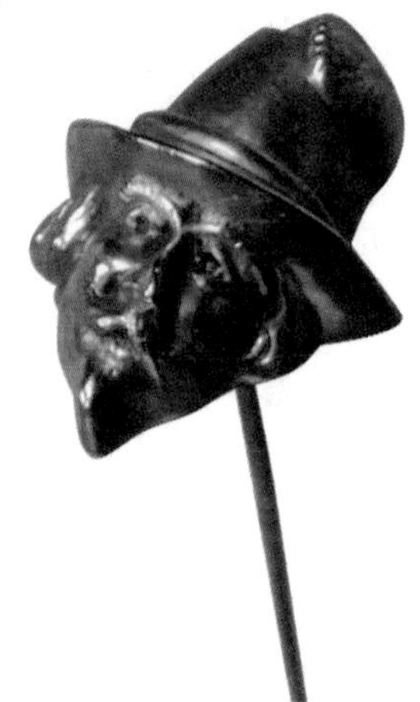

Ruby Lane

TIP

Dust the backs and tops of your framed pictures once a year.

White House Christmas Card
A 1963 White House Christmas card signed by President and Mrs. Kennedy in mint condition sold for $14,640 at a Goldin auction in New York in May 2016. Only 15 are known to exist.

Hatpin Holder, Child, Pierrot, Dog, Germany, 7 ⅛ In.
$295

Ruby Lane

Hatpin Holder, Porcelain, Bavarian, Cylindrical, Forget-Me-Nots, 4 ½ In.
$89

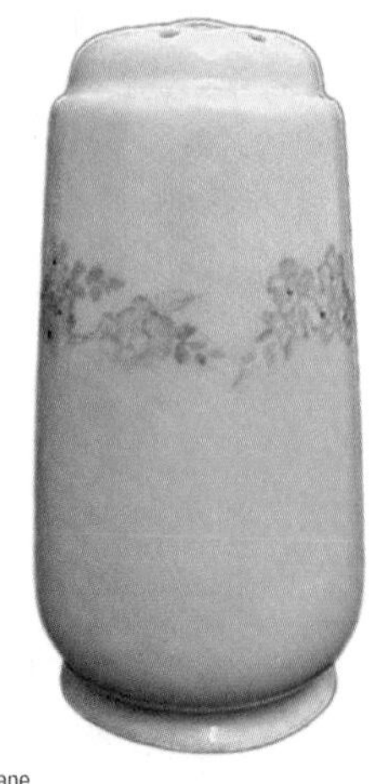

Ruby Lane

Laurelton Beige, Bowl, Cereal, 6 ¾ In. 6
Laurelton Beige, Bowl, Vegetable, Round, 9 In. 23
Laurelton Beige, Sugar, Lid, 2 ¾ In. 16
Leaf Swirl, Bowl, Vegetable, Round, 8 In. 16
Leaf Swirl, Creamer, 8 Oz., 3 ⅜ In. 14
Leaf Swirl, Cup & Saucer 8
Leaf Swirl, Platter, Oval, 13 In. 15
Leaf Swirl, Sugar, Lid 17
Lemon Tree, Bowl, Vegetable, Round, 8 In. 21
Lemon Tree, Platter, Oval, 13 In. 18
Magnolia, Platter, Oval, 13 In. 32
Mugs, Mother & Dad, Pink, Blue, Cameoware, 3 x 4 ½ In., Pair .... *illus* 20
Peacock Alley, Bowl, Vegetable, Divided, Oval, 10 In. 46
Peacock Alley, Cup & Saucer 6
Peacock Alley, Gravy Boat 42
Peacock Alley, Pitcher, Lid, 7 ⅞ In. 46
Peacock Alley, Plate, Bread & Butter, 5 ⅞ In. 5
Peacock Alley, Plate, Dinner, 10 In. 13
Peacock Alley, Salt & Pepper 33
Persian Key, Bowl, Vegetable, Divided, 10 ⅜ In. 24
Persian Key, Cup & Saucer 9
Persian Key, Plate, Dinner, 10 ¼ In. 10
Pitcher, Tulips, 5 ½ In. .... *illus* 20
Springtime, Plate, Salad, 1950s, 7 ⅜ In. .... *illus* 6
White Cap, Cup & Saucer 13

HARLEQUIN dinnerware was produced by the Homer Laughlin Company from 1938 to 1964, and sold without trademark by the F. W. Woolworth Co. It has a concentric ring design like Fiesta, but the rings are separated from the rim by a plain margin. Cup handles are triangular in shape. Seven different novelty animal figurines were introduced in 1939. For more prices, go to kovels.com.

Chartreuse, Cup & Saucer, After Dinner 90
Gray, Plate, 6 ¾ In. 6
Gray, Plate, Dinner, 9 In. 18
Light Green, Plate, 6 ¾ In. 6
Light Green, Soup, Dish, 8 In. 23
Maroon, Figurine, Penguin 229
Maroon, Platter, Oval, 13 In. 30
Mauve Blue, Gravy Boat 21
Mauve Blue, Syrup 250
Medium Green, Bowl, Oatmeal, 6 ⅜ In. 16
Red, Creamer, Ball, 8 Oz., 2 ¾ In. 38
Red, Syrup 110
Rose, Butter, Cover, ½ Lb. 143
Rose, Cup & Saucer 16
Rose, Cup & Saucer, After Dinner 20
Rose, Plate, Bread & Butter, 6 ¼ In. 6
Rose, Platter, Oval, 11 In. 16
Spruce Green, Syrup 160
Teapot, Orange, Homer Laughlin, 1940-42, 10 x 6 In. .... *illus* 149
Turquoise, Butter, Cover, ½ Lb. 126
Turquoise, Cup 5
Turquoise, Gravy Boat 16
Yellow, Cup 9
Yellow, Cup & Saucer 9
Yellow, Pitcher, Tankard, 24 Oz., 4 ⅞ In. 33
Yellow, Syrup 110
Yellow, Teapot, Lid, 3 Cup, 4 ⅞ In. 139

HATPIN collectors search for pins popular from 1860 to 1920. The long pin, often over four inches, was used to hold the hat in place on the hair. The tops of the pins were made of all materials, from solid gold and real gemstones to ceramics and glass. Be careful to buy original hatpins and not recent pieces made by altering old buttons.

Bone, Mouse, Curled Tail, Carved, 1 ½ In. 48
Brass, Mosaic, 9 ¼ x 1 ¼ In. .... *illus* 120

Celluloid, Beige, Brown, Leaves, Rhinestones, c.1930, 6 In. 42
Celluloid, Question Mark Shape, Pale Green, c.1900, 7 ¼ In. 65
Copper, Filigree, Globular, 9 In. 164
Coral, Teardrop Shape, 10K Yellow Gold, c.1880, 2 ¾ In. 150
Dragonflies, Carnival Glass, Purple 85
Enamel, Guilloche, Pink Rose, Painted, 9 In. 22
Etruscan Gold Work, 1 In. .... *illus* 125
Glass Pearl, Sterling Silver, 1940s, 3 ½ In. 65
Glass, Faceted, Black, 6 ½ In. 14
Lapis Lazuli, Brass, c.1910, 3 ¾ In. 55
Mother-Of-Pearl, Snake, Victorian, 9K Gold, 8 ¼ In. 235
Porcelain, Pink Roses, Blue Border, Bavaria, 5 In. 101
Rhinestone, Amethyst, Clear, Concentric Circles, 1 ½ In. .... *illus* 57
Rhinestones, Snowman, Red, Black, Blue, 1950s, 2 ¼ In. 30
Sterling Silver, Man, Hat, Feather, c.1900, 1 x ¾ In. .... *illus* 52
Sterling Silver, Victorian, c.1890, 8 In. 98

HATPIN HOLDERS were needed when hatpins were fashionable from 1860 to 1920. The large, heavy hat required special long-shanked pins to hold it in place. The hatpin holder resembles a large saltshaker, but it often has no opening at the bottom as a shaker does. Hatpin holders were made of all types of ceramics and metal. Look for other pieces under the names of specific manufacturers.

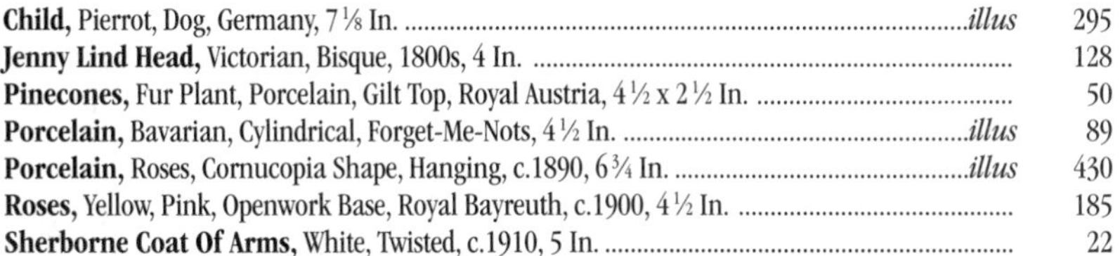

Child, Pierrot, Dog, Germany, 7 ⅛ In. .... *illus* 295
Jenny Lind Head, Victorian, Bisque, 1800s, 4 In. 128
Pinecones, Fur Plant, Porcelain, Gilt Top, Royal Austria, 4 ½ x 2 ½ In. 50
Porcelain, Bavarian, Cylindrical, Forget-Me-Nots, 4 ½ In. .... *illus* 89
Porcelain, Roses, Cornucopia Shape, Hanging, c.1890, 6 ¾ In. .... *illus* 430
Roses, Yellow, Pink, Openwork Base, Royal Bayreuth, c.1900, 4 ½ In. 185
Sherborne Coat Of Arms, White, Twisted, c.1910, 5 In. 22

HAVILAND china has been made in Limoges, France, since 1842. The factory was started by the Haviland Brothers of New York City. Pieces are marked *H & Co., Haviland & Co.*, or *Theodore Haviland*. It is possible to match existing sets of dishes through dealers who specialize in Haviland china. Other factories worked in the town of Limoges making a similar chinaware. These porcelains are listed in this book under Limoges.

HAVILAND& CO.

Basket, Daisies, Hand Painted, Gold Trim, c.1894, 3 ½ x 5 ¼ In. .... *illus* 235
Bowl, Vegetable, Lid, Oval, Pink & Blue Flowers, c.1915, 12 In. 150
Bowl, Vegetable, Monceau, Gold Link Edge, Oval, 9 ½ In. 65
Bread Tray, Open Gilt Handles, Grapes, Leaves, Oval, 13 x 7 In. 85
Cake Plate, Flowers, Blue, Swirled Lip, c.1900, 9 ¾ In. 35
Celery Dish, Pink Flower Border, Central Bouquet, Open Handles, c.1895, 11 x 5 In. 75
Chop Plate, Poppies, Gold Lattice, c.1880, 13 ½ In. 275
Cup & Saucer, Demitasse, Blue Flowers, Gold Edge, c.1890.......... 50
Cup & Saucer, Trees, Insects On Rim, Blue, Gray, Gold Trim, 1893-1931 .... *illus* 89
Dish, Cabbage Leaf, Mint Green, Ruffled Edge, Gold Handle, c.1890, 7 x 6 In. 75
Dish, Strawberries, Green Leaves, Gold Trim, c.1890, 11 x 7 In. 25
Gravy Boat, Underplate, Blue Flowers, Fern, Round, c.1892.......... 125
Plate, Camellia Pattern, 6 ½ In., 4 Piece.......... 43
Plate, Deer & Quail, Stream, Fall, c.1890, 9 ½ In. 60
Plate, Gainsborough, Gold Trim, 8 ¼ In. 19
Plate, Scalloped Gilt Edge, Pink Flowers, 8 ½ In. 35
Platter, Pink Buds, Scalloped Edge, c.1920, 12 In. 60
Punch Bowl, Flowers, Blue & Yellow, Gold Trim, France, 6 ⅜ x 14 ⅞ In. .... *illus* 165
Spooner, Pink & White Flowers, Piecrust Base, Fluted, 4 ⅝ In. 64
Trinket Box, Domed Lid, Oval, Bird, Spread Wings, Gold Border, 2 ¾ x 1 ¼ In. 98
Tureen, Lid, Cobalt Blue, Gilt, Handles, Scrolling Leaves, c.1883, 7 In. 131
Vase, Cylindrical, Gold Rose & Trim, Soft Green, 4 x 2 In. 100
Vase, White, Flowering Branch, Yellow Blossoms, Round Foot, 1900s, 8 In. 59

HAVILAND POTTERY began in 1872, when Charles Haviland decided to make art pottery. He worked with the famous artists of the day and made pottery with slip glazed decorations. Production stopped in 1885. Haviland Pottery is marked with the letters *H & Co.* The Haviland name is better known today for its porcelain.

H&C°

Jardiniere, Applied Flowers, Pale Pink, Green, Brown, Footed, 16 x 8 In. 6800
Jardiniere, Houses, River, Chickens, Emile-Justin Merlot, 1875, 8 ⅞ x 13 In. 1694

TIP

It is easy to glue pieces of broken china. Use a new fast-setting but not instant glue. Position the pieces correctly, then use tape to hold the parts together. If the piece needs special support, lean it in a suitable position in a box filled with sand.

H

Hatpin Holder, Porcelain, Roses, Cornucopia Shape, Hanging, c.1890, 6 ¾ In.
$430

Ruby Lane

Haviland, Basket, Daisies, Hand Painted, Gold Trim, c.1894, 3 ½ x 5 ¼ In.
$235

Ruby Lane

Haviland, Cup & Saucer, Trees, Insects On Rim, Blue, Gray, Gold Trim, 1893-1931
$89

Ruby Lane

Haviland, Punch Bowl, Flowers, Blue & Yellow, Gold Trim, France, 6 3/8 x 14 7/8 In.
$165

Ruby Lane

Haviland Pottery, Vase, Barbotine, Scene, Houses On Riverbank, Signed, Merlot, 9 x 13 In.
$1,652

Humler & Nolan

Haviland Pottery, Vase, Enameled Flowers, Leafy Stems, Shouldered, Chaplet, c.1895, 15 x 8 In.
$8,750

Rago Arts and Auction Center

TIP

When restoring antiques or houses, take color pictures before and after for records of colors used, exact placement of decorative details, and insurance claims.

Jardiniere, Triple Openings, Terra-Cotta, Signed Maurice Bocquet, c.1880, 19 x 13 In. 3850
Vase, Barbotine, Scene, Houses On Riverbank, Signed, Merlot, 9 x 13 In. .... *illus* 1652
Vase, Enameled Flowers, Leafy Stems, Shouldered, Chaplet, c.1895, 15 x 8 In. .... *illus* 8750
Vase, Rabbit, Brown, Blue, Philibert-Leon Couturier, c.1880, 13 1/2 x 7 1/2 In. 3850

HAWKES cut glass was made by T. G. Hawkes & Company of Corning, New York, founded in 1880. The firm cut glass blanks made at other glassworks until 1962. Many pieces are marked with the trademark, a trefoil ring enclosing a fleur-de-lis and two hawks. Cut glass by other manufacturers is listed under either the factory name or in the general Cut Glass category.

Bowl, Festoon, 7 x 4 In. 595
Bowl, Festoon, Cut Glass, 1876-1917, 4 x 8 In. .... *illus* 595
Bowl, Hobstar, Swirl Panel Design, Scalloped Edge, Signed, c.1900, 9 1/2 In. Diam. 1107
Bowl, Sunburst & Thumb, Signed, 6 1/2 In. 75
Centerpiece, Warwick, Footed, Trefoil Mark, 10 x 4 In. 1250
Champagne Flute, Delft Diamond, 6 3/8 In. .... *illus* 50
Cologne, Venetian Pattern, Silver Stopper, Monogram, 1880, 7 In. 708
Compote, Sheraton, Marked, 6 3/4 In. 550
Cordial, Satin Iris, Square Base, Marked, 5 In., 6 Piece 400
Cruet, Cut Glass, Queens Pattern, 5 3/4 In. 150
Decanter, Crystal, Faceted Ball Shape Stopper, Acid Etched Mark, Silver Label, 11 In., Pair 173
Decanter, Palermo, Flared Lip, Bulbous, 8 In. 195
Decanter, Tapered, Lid, Enameled, Duck, Over Water, Cattails, Silver Mounts, c.1920, 12 In. 108
Match Holder, Hobstar & Diamonds, Cloverleaf Logo, 2 1/4 In. 78
Nappy, Canton, 5 7/8 x 1 1/2 In. 45
Pitcher, Glasses, Diamond, 5 x 6 In., Glasses, 3 3/4 In., 7 Piece 450
Pitcher, Hobstar & Fan, Bulbous, Loop Handle, Pinched Neck, Scalloped Rim, c.1890, 8 In. 127
Plate, Dessert, Cut Crystal, 8 In., 12 Piece 180
Powder Jar, Chrysanthemum, Lid, Silver Band, Signed, 5 1/2 x 5 In. 895
Sherbet, Delft Diamond, 5 In., 6 Piece 90
Tankard, Lemonade, Wheel Carved Design, Silver, Hinged Lid, Strainer Spout, 9 1/4 In. 177
Vase, Aberdeen, Sawtooth Rim, 8 x 6 In. 799
Vase, Ferns & Flowers, Trumpet, Footed, 12 1/4 In. 130
Vase, Navarre, Cut, Glass, 1880-1917 .... *illus* 300
Vase, Navarre, Cylindrical, c.1890, 12 In. 300
Wine, Strawberry, 5 1/4 In. 48

HEAD VASES, generally showing a woman from the shoulders up, were used by florists primarily in the 1950s and 1960s. Made in a variety of sizes and often decorated with imitation jewelry and other lifelike accessories, the vases were manufactured in Japan and the U.S.A. Less elaborate examples were made as early as the 1930s. Religious themes, babies, and animals are also common subjects. Other head vases are listed under manufacturers' names and can be located through the index in the back of this book.

Dog's Head, Inarco, Japan, 1960s, 6 x 6 1/2 In. .... *illus* 45
Girl, Blond, Hat, Multicolor, 6 In. 67
Girl, Teenage, Blond, Neck Scarf, Green Shirt, Inarco, Japan, 5 1/2 In. 48
Lady, Glamour Girl, Open Eyes, Blue, 1950s, 6 3/4 In. .... *illus* 24
Lady, Hat With Bow, Napco, 1950-70, 9 1/2 In. .... *illus* 325
Lady, Teal Blue, Curls, Bow, Napco .... *illus* 60
Woman, Blond, Brimmed Purple Hat, Eyelashes, Rose On Neck, Napco, c.1950, 5 3/4 In. 45
Woman, Blond, Red Lips, Pearls, Black Hat, Blue Bow, Rubens, 6 In. 42
Woman, Tilted Hat, Curls, c.1940, 8 1/2 In. 76

HEDI SCHOOP Art Creations, North Hollywood, California, started about 1945 and was working until 1954. Schoop made ceramic figurines, lamps, planters, and tablewares.

Centerpiece, Free-Form, 6 Sections, Multicolor, Marked, c.1950, 11 x 2 In. 139
Figurine, Asian Musician & Dancer, Green, Stepped Base, 10 In. 125
Figurine, Asian Woman, Holding Flowers, 12 1/2 In. 69
Figurine, Peasants, Man, Woman, Blue Outfits, Baskets, 13 In. 220
Figurine, Senorita, Blue Dress, Baskets, 12 3/4 In. 125
Figurine, Temple Dancers, Hats, Fans, c.1940, 12 In. 295
Pitcher, White, Pink & Gold Ridges, Pillow Shape, Loop Handle, 6 x 6 x 3 In. 45
Plaque, Cat Face, Long Hair, 7 x 7 In. 89
Plaque, Cat, Face, Square, 8 1/2 In. .... *illus* 89
Plaque, Cat, Sitting, Stripes, 7 x 7 In. 80
Vase, Asian Man & Woman, Ribbed, 10 In. 65

Hawkes, Bowl, Festoon, Cut Glass, 1876-1917, 4 x 8 In.
$595

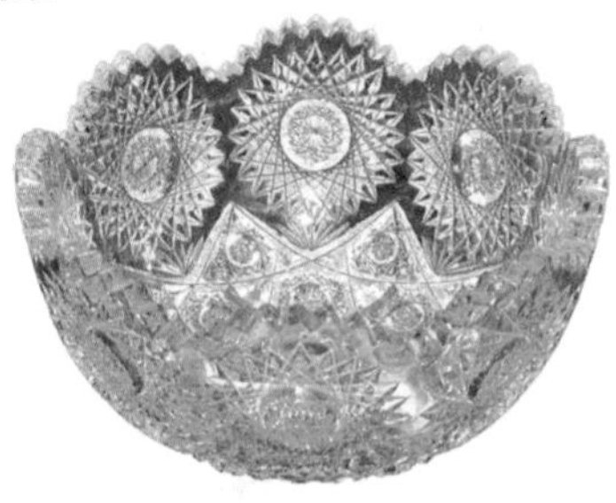

Ruby Lane

Hawkes, Champagne Flute, Delft Diamond, 6 ⅜ In.
$50

Ruby Lane

Hawkes, Vase, Navarre, Cut, Glass, 1880-1917
$300

Ruby Lane

Head Vase, Dog's Head, Inarco, Japan, 1960s, 6 x 6 ½ In.
$45

Ruby Lane

Head Vase, Lady, Glamour Girl, Open Eyes, Blue, 1950s, 6 ¾ In.
$24

Ruby Lane

Head Vase, Lady, Hat With Bow, Napco, 1950-70, 9 ½ In.
$325

Ruby Lane

Head Vase, Lady, Teal Blue, Curls, Bow, Napco
$60

Ruby Lane

Hedi Schoop, Plaque, Cat, Face, Square, 8 ½ In.
$89

Ruby Lane

Heintz Art, Humidor, Lid, Bronze, Patinated, Sterling Overlay, Marked, c.1912, 6 In.
$523

Nest Egg Auctions

H

Heisey, Bead Swag, Bowl, Green, c.1899, 8 ¼ In.
$49

Ruby Lane

Heisey, Fandango, Butter, Cover, Diamond Swag, Scalloped Dish, Ball Finial, c.1900, 5 x 7 In.
$125

Ruby Lane

Heisey, Old Sandwich, Console, Sahara, 4 ¼ x 11 In. Diam.
$85

Ruby Lane

TIP

Do not use lemon-scented detergent or dishwasher "soap" when washing glassware or china with painted decorations, like 1950s cocktail glasses or labeled canister sets. The ingredient that smells like lemons makes the detergent acidic, and it eventually fades the decorations and makes items worthless to collectors. The heat of dishwasher water also damages pieces.

HEINTZ ART METAL SHOP used the letters *HAMS* in a diamond as a mark. In 1902, Otto Heintz designed and manufactured copper items with colored enamel decorations under the name Art Crafts Shop. He took over the Arts & Crafts Company in Buffalo, New York, in 1903. By 1906 it had become the Heintz Art Metal Shop. It remained in business until 1930. The company made ashtrays, bookends, boxes, bowls, desk sets, vases, trophies, and smoking sets. The best-known pieces are made of copper, brass, and bronze with silver overlay. Similar pieces were made by Smith Metal Arts and were marked *Silver Crest*. Some pieces by both companies are unmarked.

Candlestick, Bronze, Petal Cup, Flattened Base, Silver Overlay Border, 14 ⅝ In., Pair 431
Flowers, Vase, Sterling On Bronze, 4 ⅝ In. 50
Humidor, Lid, Bronze, Patinated, Sterling Overlay, Marked, c.1912, 6 In. ..... *illus* 523
Vase, Flowers, Leaves, Sterling On Bronze, 6 x 3 In 307
Vase, Leaves, Flowers, Sterling On Bronze, Marked, 10 ½ x 3 ½ In. 150
Vase, Peacock, Sterling On Bronze, c.1912, 10 In. 369
Vase, Tree, Sterling On Bronze, c.1912, 3 ½ In. 246

HEISEY glass was made from 1896 to 1957 in Newark, Ohio, by A. H. Heisey and Co., Inc. The Imperial Glass Company of Bellaire, Ohio, bought some of the molds and the rights to the trademark. Some Heisey patterns have been made by Imperial since 1960. After 1968, they stopped using the *H* trademark. Heisey used romantic names for colors, such as Sahara. Do not confuse color and pattern names. The Custard Glass and Ruby Glass categories may also include some Heisey pieces.

Animal, Colt, Kicking 55
Animal, Colt, Standing ..... 35 to 55
Animal, Dog, Scottie 30
Animal, Donkey 60
Animal, Giraffe, Head Turned 100
Animal, Goose, Wings Down 100
Animal, Goose, Wings Out 20
Animal, Plug Horse 60
Animal, Rabbit, Head Up 220
Animal, Ringneck Pheasant 30
Aristocrat, Candlestick, 7 In., Pair 35
Banded Flute, Candlestick, Saucer Foot 20
Bead Swag, Bowl, Green, c.1899, 8 ¼ In. ..... *illus* 49
Christos, Decanter, Silver Overlay, Stopper 55
Coarse Rib, Sugar & Creamer, Lid 26
Cobel, Cocktail Shaker, Rooster Head, Stopper 15
Creole, Iced Tea, Footed, Alexandrite 225
Crystolite, Bowl, Flowers, Flared, 12 In. 10
Crystolite, Candleholder, c.1940, 4 x 4 ¾ In. 14
Crystolite, Cocktail Shaker 75
Crystolite, Cordial 80
Crystolite, Pitcher, Water, Lip, ½ Gal. 35
Crystolite, Sugar & Creamer, Tray, Individual 25
Crystolite, Vase, Urn, 7 In. 130
Double Rib & Panel, Basket, Hawks Cutting 75
Double Rib & Panel, Cruet 30
Empress, Ashtray, Cobalt Blue 150
Empress, Plate, Tangerine, 6 In. 75
Empress, Sugar & Creamer, Dolphin, Footed 32
Empress, Sugar & Creamer, Tray, Individual 32
Empress, Sugar, Moongleam 15
Fandango, Butter, Cover, Diamond Swag, Scalloped Dish, Ball Finial, c.1900, 5 x 7 In. ..... *illus* 125
Fandango, Nappy, 9 ½ In. 55
Fish, Match Holder, 3 In. 140
Flamingo, Basket, Columns, Diamond Makers Mark, 8 ¼ In. 30
Flamingo, Basket, Double Rib & Panel 45
Flamingo, Ladle, Mayonnaise 30
Flamingo, Sugar & Creamer, Octagonal 25
Greek Key, Banana Split 20
Greek Key, Goblet, Straight 75
Greek Key, Jelly, Footed, Handles 32
Greek Key, Punch Cup 35
Greek Key, Tankard, Qt. 60
Groove & Slash, Butter, Cover 130

TIP
Never bid at an auction if you have not previewed the items.

Heisey, Ring Band, Pitcher, Custard Glass, Gilt, 5 x 5 ½ In.
$47

Ruby Lane

Heisey, Sunburst, Hair Receiver, Clear, Bulbous, c.1910, 4 ½ In.
$18

Ruby Lane

Heisey, Warwick, Vase, Horn Of Plenty, Cornucopia, Cobalt Blue, 9 In.
$175

Ruby Lane

Hobnail, Tumbler, Amber, Doyle & Co., 1880s, 3 ⅞ x 2 ½ In.
$49

Ruby Lane

Hobnail, Vase, Light Pink Shaded To Black, Frosted, Graduated Hobnails, 1950s, 8 In.
$18

Ruby Lane

Holly Amber, Sugar, Lid, 6 ½ In.
$805

Early Auction Company

Holly Amber, Toothpick Holder, 2 ½ x 2 ½ In.
$115

Early Auction Company

Holt-Howard, Dish, Cottage Cheese, Lid, Kissing Kittens Finial, Bow Rim, 1959
$55

Ruby Lane

Holt-Howard, Lipstick Holder, Daisy 'Dorable, 6-Petaled Flower, Girl With Fan, 1960, 3 x 3 In.
$73

Ruby Lane

TIP
When moving, stuff glasses and cups with crumpled paper, then wrap in bubble wrap.

Hopalong Cassidy, Plate, Black, White Horse, W.S. George, 9 ½ In.
$110

Ruby Lane

Hopalong Cassidy, Skirt, Plastic, Fringe, 16 ½ x 21 ½ In.
$72

Ruby Lane

Horn, Map, Engraved, Paint, New York City, Ships, Hunting, Strap, Plug, 1760s, 20 In.
$4,920

Skinner, Inc.

The First TV Dinner

The TV dinner was introduced in 1953. Almost none of the original boxes and aluminum trays exist.

Item	Price
Ipswich, Tumbler, Footed, 12 Oz.	14
Kohinoor, Ashtray, Zircon, 3 In.	70
Lariat, Bonbon, 7 In.	13
Lariat, Nappy, 7 In.	10
Lariat, Nut Dish, 4 ¼ In.	13
Lariat, Relish, 3 Sections	23
Lariat, Sugar & Creamer	28
Lariat, Sugar & Creamer, Tray, Individual	22
Lodestar, Celery Dish, 10 In.	45
Moongleam, Basket, Double Rib & Panel	45
Moongleam, Basket, Octagonal	90
Moongleam, Ladle, Mayonnaise	50
Nail, Nappy, 4 In.	70
Narrow Flute, Sugar & Creamer	25
New Era, Relish, 3 Sections	25
Old Queen Anne, Cruet, 2 Oz.	105
Old Queen Anne, Nappy, Flared, 8 In.	65
Old Sandwich, Ashtray	12 to 30
Old Sandwich, Console, Sahara, 4 ¼ x 11 In. Diam. *illus*	85
Old Sandwich, Cruet	30
Old Williamsburg, Candlestick, Light Marigold, 8 ¾ In., Pair	25
Old Williamsburg, Champagne	8
Old Williamsburg, Claret	14
Old Williamsburg, Goblet	12
Orchid, Candlestick, 3 In.	31
Orchid, Decanter, Oval, Sterling Silver Stopper, c.1950, 8 In.	115
Panel & Sunburst, Dish, Jelly, Beaded, Footed	25
Pentagon, Relish, 6 In.	15
Petal, Sugar & Creamer	13
Pillows, Salt & Pepper, Gold	110
Pillows, Toothpick Holder	50
Pineapple & Fan, Compote, Square, 7 In.	90
Pineapple & Fan, Tankard, ½ Pint	15
Pineapple & Fan, Vase, Emerald Gold, 6 In.	20
Pinwheel & Fan, Basket, 7 In.	100
Pinwheel & Fan, Nappy, 8 In.	150
Plantation, Bowl, 12 In.	72
Plantation, Champagne	20
Plantation, Cruet, 3 Oz.	30
Plantation, Dish, 4 Sections, Pineapples, 8 In.	65
Plantation, Gardenia Bowl, 12 In.	25
Plantation, Relish, 3 Sections, 11 In.	15
Plantation, Vase, 5 ½ In.	30
Princess, Salt, Marigold, 3-Footed, 3 3/16 In.	55
Priscilla, Mustard, Lid	20
Priscilla, Sugar & Creamer, Flared	24
Punch Bowl, Scalloped Sawtooth Rim, Pedestal Flared Foot, c.1950, 12 x 14 In.	253
Punty & Diamond Point, Compote, 8 ½ In.	105
Punty & Diamond Point, Cruet, Stopper, 6 Oz.	30
Punty Band, Spooner	25
Puritan, Butter, Cover	25
Queen Ann, Relish, Etched Orchid, 3 Sections, 7 In.	5
Queen Ann, Saucer Candle Base, 6 In., Pair	32
Recessed Panel, Candy Jar, 1 Lb.	45
Regency, 2-Light Candle Block, Pair	25
Regency, Puff Box, Lid	55
Ribbed Octagon, Sugar & Creamer	25
Ridgeleigh, Cocktail Shaker, Qt.	105
Ridgeleigh, Dish, Jelly, Tricornered	16
Ridgeleigh, Nappy, 4 ½ In.	14
Ridgeleigh, Nappy, 6-Sided, 4 In.	10
Ridgeleigh, Sugar & Creamer, Tray, Individual	25
Ridgeleigh, Tumbler	140
Ring Band, Pitcher, Custard Glass, Gilt, 5 x 5 ½ In. *illus*	47
Sahara, Ladle, Mayonnaise	35
Stanhope, Sugar & Creamer, Red Knobs	60
Sugar & Creamer, Lid, Silver Banded Interior Pub Scene, Maker's Mark, 5 In.	30

Sunburst, Hair Receiver, Clear, Bulbous, c.1910, 4 ½ In. *illus* 18
Sunflower, Tumbler 65
Sussex, Finger Bowl, Cobalt 65
Sussex, Goblet, 8 Oz. 35
Sweet Ad-O-Line, Goblet 100
Touraine, Sherbet, Amberina 160
Touraine, Toothpick Holder, Ruby Stain 500
Tudor, Cruet, Stopper, c.1930, 6 Oz., 6 In. 38
Twist, Celery Dish, 3 Sections, Moongleam, 13 In. 20
Twist, Compote, Moongleam 25
Twist, Cup & Saucer, Moongleam 25
Twist, Dish, Mayonnaise, Square Base, Moongleam 45
Twist, Plate, Dinner, Moongleam, 10 ½ In. 190
Twist, Plate, Moongleam, 9 In. 35
Urn, Toothpick Holder 110
Waldorf Astoria, Toothpick Holder 25
Warwick, Vase, Horn Of Plenty, Cornucopia, Cobalt Blue, 9 In. *illus* 175
Waverly, Bowl, Etched Orchid, Crimped, 10 In. 8
Waverly, Bowl, Gardenia, Etched Orchid, 12 In. 15
Waverly, Ice Bucket, Handles, Orchid Etch 75
Waverly, Plate, Rose Etch, 8 In. 25
Waverly, Salver, Footed, Orchid Etch, 13 In. 65
Waverly, Vase, Fan, Rose Etch, 7 In. 35
Yeoman, Plate, Victory Etch, 8 In. 165
Yeoman, Sugar & Creamer, Oval 24

HEREND, *see Fischer category.*

HEUBACH is the collector's name for Gebruder Heubach, a firm working in Lichten, Germany, from 1840 to 1925. It is best known for bisque dolls and doll heads, the principal products. The company also manufactured bisque figurines, including piano babies, beginning in the 1880s, and glazed figurines in the 1900s. Piano Babies are listed in their own category. Dolls are included in the Doll category under Gebruder Heubach and Heubach. Another factory, Ernst Heubach, working in Koppelsdorf, Germany, also made porcelain and dolls. These will also be found in the Doll category under Heubach Koppelsdorf.

Figurine, Dancing Girl, Pleated Skirt, Turquoise, Blond Hair, c.1900, 6 ¼ In. 199
Figurine, Dog, Begging, White, 4 ½ In. 157
Figurine, Dog, English Bulldog, Muzzled, Brown, White, Sitting, c.1920, 2 ½ In. 50
Figurine, Dog, Terrier, Black & White, Open Mouth, c.1890, 3 x 6 In. 215
Figurine, Nude, On Bear, 6 ½ x 5 ½ In. 197
Plaque, Reverie, Woman, Red Hair, Draped, Gilt Frame, c.1900, 8 x 5 In. 2500
Tobacco Jar, Boy Clown Head, Hat, Ruffled Collar, c.1895, 5 ½ x 3 ½ In. 550

HISTORIC BLUE, *see factory names, such as Adams, Ridgway, and Staffordshire.*

HOBNAIL glass is a style of glass with bumps all over. Dozens of hobnail patterns and variants have been made. Clear, colored, and opalescent hobnail have been made and are being reproduced. Other pieces of hobnail may also be listed in the Duncan & Miller and Fenton categories.

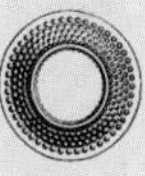

Ashtray, 4 In., 5 Piece 29
Banana Boat, Footed, Milk Glass, 9 x 12 x 3 In. 40
Basket, Handle, 4-Footed, Yellow, Greener & Co., c.1885, 7 x 4 In. 145
Basket, Handle, Westmoreland, 10 x 8 x 8 In. 38
Basket, White Twisted Ribbed Handle, Blue Diamond, Ruffled Edge, 10 ½ In. 85
Bowl, Cranberry To Clear, Crimped, 4 x 2 In. 150
Bowl, Crown Point Rim, Milk Glass, Footed, 8 x 6 In. 26
Cake Stand, Pedestal, Amber, Columbia Glass, 10 x 6 ¾ In. 225
Cologne Bottle, Blue Opalescent, Wrisley, Anchor Hocking, Paper Label, c.1940, 6 ½ In. 48
Cruet, Vaseline, Hobbs, Brockunier, c.1890, 7 ½ In. 90
Goblet, Water, Blue Opalescent, 5 ⅞ In. 29
Goblet, Water, Duncan & Miller, c.1940, 5 ⅞ In. 13
Goblet, Water, Milk Glass, 5 ½ In. 12
Nappy, Moonstone, Opalescent, Heart Shape, Anchor Hocking, 1940s, 6 x 6 ¼ In. 25
Pitcher, Blue, White Applied Handle, Stick Neck, Ruffled Opening, 10 In. 79
Pitcher, Milk Glass, Anchor Hocking, Pt., 1950s, 4 ¾ In. 15
Plate, Opalescent, 8 In. 8

Howdy Doody, Toy, Dancing Howdy, Bob Smith At Piano, Tin Lithograph, Windup, Unique Art, 9 In.
$549

Morphy Auctions

TIP

Be sure to take any labels off your glass and archive them, as the acid in the labels will permanently etch the glass.

Hull, Cornucopia, Tokay, Pink Grapes, Green Leaves, 6 ½ x 11 In.
$55

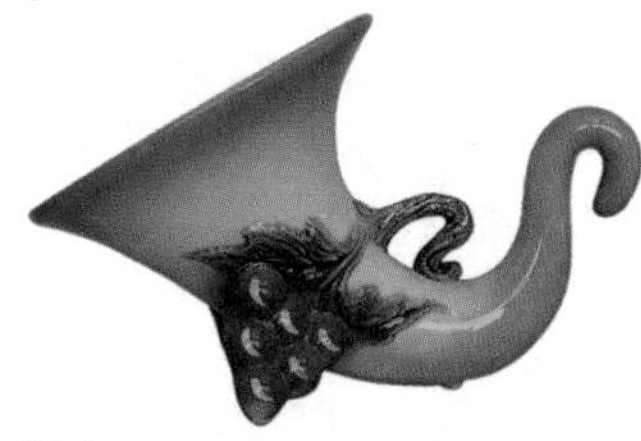

Ruby Lane

Hull, Ewer, Bowknot, Marked, 6 ¼ In.
$70

Ruby Lane

Hull, Pitcher, Butterfly, Flowers, Blue Interior, 8 ¾ x 8 ¼ In.
$55

Ruby Lane

Hull, Vase, Double, Woodland, 1950, 8 ½ In.
$48

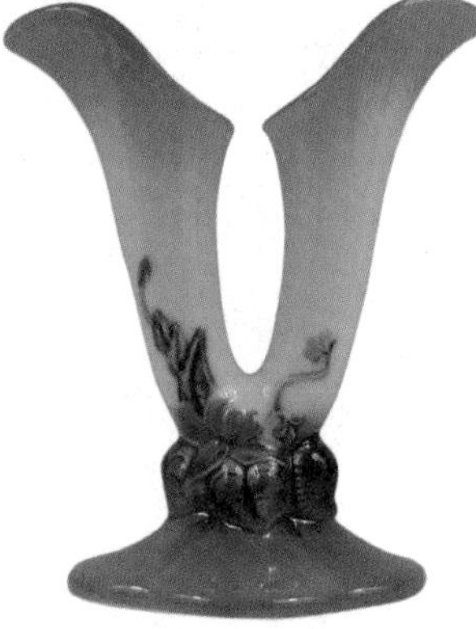

Ruby Lane

Hummel, Figurine, No. 128, Baker, Last Bee, 5 In.
$18

Hess Auction Group

Punch Bowl, Footed, Duncan & Miller, 9 ½ In. 88
Punch Cup, Duncan & Miller, 2 ⅜ In. 8
Relish, 3 Sections, Tab Handles, Duncan & Miller, c.1950, 12 In. 12
Relish, Clover Shape, Opalescent White, Moonstone, Anchor Hocking, c.1943, 6 ½ In. 35
Rose Bowl, Footed, Ruby, Imperial, c.1925, 6 x 3 In. 45
Rose Bowl, Marigold.......... 225
Sherbet, Duncan & Miller, 3 ¼ In. 16
Shoe, Iridescent, 6 In. 25
Sugar & Creamer, Blue Opalescent 46
Top Hat, Blue Opalescent, Duncan & Miller, 2 ⅝ In. 15
Top Hat, Duncan & Miller, 2 ¾ In. 20
Torte Plate, Duncan & Miller, c.1945, 13 ½ In. 45
Tray, White Opalescent, Pedestal, 8 x 2 ¼ In. 32
Tumbler, Amber, Doyle & Co., 1880s, 3 ⅞ x 2 ½ In. ....*illus* 49
Tumbler, Barrel, Green, Anchor Hocking, 12 Oz., 1960s, 4 In. 30
Tumbler, Duncan & Miller, 10 Oz., 5 In. 10
Vase, Black Amethyst, Ruffled Rim, L.E. Smith, 1940s, 8 In. 35
Vase, Crimped & Ruffled, Yellow, Kanawha Cased, 1960s, 5 In. 19
Vase, Crimped, Blue Opalescent, Duncan & Miller, 4 ¼ In. 19
Vase, Fan Shape, Footed, Blue Opalescent, 1940s, 4 In. 25
Vase, Ivy Ball, Duncan & Miller, 1940s, 6 ¼ In. 28
Vase, Ivy Ball, Duncan & Miller, 1940s, 7 ¼ In. 47
Vase, Ivy Ball, Footed, Crimped, Blue Opalescent, Duncan & Miller, 6 ¾ In. 45
Vase, Light Pink Shaded To Black, Frosted, Graduated Hobnails, 1950s, 8 In. ....*illus* 18
Vase, Pink, Frosted, Flared Rim, 1950s, 8 In. 18

HOCHST, or Hoechst, porcelain was made in Germany from 1746 to 1796. It was marked with a six-spoke wheel. Be careful when buying Hochst; many other firms have used a very similar wheel-shaped mark. Copies have been made from the original molds.

Figurine, Nude Woman, Melchior, 1700s, 6 ½ x 3 ½ In. 1750
Figurine, Turkish Orchestra, Horn Player, 7 ½ x 2 ½ In. 190
Figurine, Woman, Yellow Skirt, White Overcoat, 4 ¾ x 2 In. 385
Figurine, Young Boy, No Shoes, Basket, 4 ¾ x 2 In. 385
Group, Woman, Flowered Dress, Sitting, Cherub, c.1900, 8 ½ x 6 In. 195
Group, Woman, Off The Shoulder Dress, Winged Cherub, 8 ½ x 6 ⅝ In. 175

HOLLY AMBER, or golden agate, glass was made by the Indiana Tumbler and Goblet Company of Greentown, Indiana, from January 1, 1903, to June 13, 1903. It is a pressed glass pattern featuring holly leaves in the amber-shaded glass. The glass was made with shadings that range from creamy opalescent to brown-amber.

Butter, Tapered Dome Lid, 6 x 7 ½ In. 403
Cake Plate, Square, Beaded Edge, Pedestal Base, 4 ¼ In. 5963
Compote, Paneled, Beaded Bands, Pedestal Base, Tapered Dome Lid, 8 In. 201
Creamer, Bulbous Opal & Beaded Bands, 4 In. 316
Cruet, Vinegar, Paneled, Ribbed & Beaded Stopper, 6 ½ In. 690
Dish, Pickle, Beaded Bands, Oval, Domed Foot, 4 ½ x 7 ½ In. 1265
Parfait, Bulbous Opal & Beaded Bands, Tapered, Footed, Greentown, 6 In., Pair.......... 460
Relish, Oval, 7 ½ In. 115
Salt & Pepper, Bulbous Opal & Beaded Bands, 3 ¼ In. 978
Sandwich, Tray, Decoration In Concentric Squares, Square, Beaded Edge, 7 ½ In. 345
Sugar, Lid, 6 ½ In..........*illus* 805
Toothpick Holder, 2 ½ x 2 ½ In. ....*illus* 115

HOLT-HOWARD was an importer that started working in New York City in 1949 and moved to Stamford, Connecticut, in 1955. The company sold many types of table accessories, such as condiment jars, decanters, spoon holders, and saltshakers. Its figural pieces have a cartoon-like quality. The company was bought out by General Housewares Corporation in 1968. Holt-Howard pieces are often marked with the name and the year or *HH* and the year stamped in black. The *HH* mark was used until 1974. The company also used a black and silver paper label. Holt-Howard production ceased in 1990, and the remainder of the company was sold to Kay Dee Designs. In 2002, Grant Holt and John Howard started Grant-Howard Associates and made a new piece, a retro pixie cookie jar marked *GHA* that sold from a mail order catalog. Other retro pixie pieces were made until 2006. Similar pieces are being made today by Grant Holt, one of the founders, and are marked *GHA*.

Bowl, Cereal, Red Interior, Marked, 1962, 6 In., 4 Piece 36

Candle Climber, Angel, Gold Accents, 4 In., Pair 24
Candle Climber, Pixie Elves, Iridescent, 3 In., Pair 39
Candleholder, Bride, Groom, c.1959, 4½ In. 79
Candleholder, Winking Santa Claus, Loop Handle, Paper Label, 1950s 15
Coffeepot, Cantaloupe, Lid, 1960s, 10½ In. 45
Dish, Bird, 2 Sections, Blue, Green, Paper Label, 1960, 8 x 6 In. 55
Dish, Cottage Cheese, Lid, Kissing Kittens Finial, Bow Rim, 1959 *illus* 55
Flower Frog, White, Scalloped Edge, Paper Label, 1958, 3½ In., Pair 18
Jar, Cottage Cheese, Kissing Kittens, Bow Rim, c.1959 65
Lipstick Holder, Daisy 'Dorable, 6-Petaled Flower, Girl With Fan, 1960, 3 x 3 In. *illus* 73
Mug, Coq Rouge, 3¾ In., 3 Piece 24
Mug, 3-Dollar Bill, Richard Nixon, 1972, 3½ In. 55
Nut Dish, Lid, 3½ x 3 In. 18
Pencil Holder, Daisy Dorable, Holding Flower, c.1959, 4 x 4 In. 125
Salt & Pepper, Cabbage Green, 2¾ In. 14
Salt & Pepper, Figural, Tomato Shape, Red, 3 x 2½ In. 12
Salt & Pepper, Grape Bunches, Purple, 2½ x 3½ In. 16
Salt & Pepper, Mice, Ribbon On Tail, Brown, 4⅜ In. 41
Salt & Pepper, Pear Shape, 3¼ In. 12
Salt & Pepper, Pigtail Blond Girl, Glancing Boy, 4½ x 3¾ In. 110
Salt & Pepper, Pixie, Boy & Girl, 4½ x 3¾ In. 110
Salt & Pepper, Rabbits, Pink Flowers, Side-Glancing Eyes, Label, 1958, 3 In. 58
Salt & Pepper, Santa Claus, Winking, c.1960, 4¾ In. 22
Stringholder, Kitty, Plaid Bow, Label, 1950s 85
Sugar & Creamer, Cantaloupe, c.1960 30
Sugar & Creamer, Holly Berry, Ribbed, 1959 16
Teabag Holder, Coq Rouge, Paper Label, 1960s, 4½ x 3¾ In., 3 Piece 35

HOPALONG CASSIDY was a character in a series of twenty-eight books written by Clarence E. Milford, first published in 1907. Movies and television shows were made based on the character. The best-known actor playing Hopalong Cassidy was William Lawrence Boyd. His first movie appearance was in 1919, but the first Hopalong Cassidy film was not made until 1934. Sixty-six films were made. In 1948, William Boyd purchased the television rights to the movies, then later made fifty-two new programs. In the 1950s, Hopalong Cassidy and his horse, named Topper, were seen in comics, records, toys, and other products. Boyd died in 1972.

Binoculars, Die Cast, Decal, 1950s 85
Button, Saving Rodeo, Straw Boss, Star, Silver Foil, 1½ In. 139
Button, Vote For Hoppy, Profile Photo, Black & White, c.1950, 1¼ In. 443
Candy Container, Saddlebag Design, Cardboard, Leather, Topps, 1950, 3 x 6 In. 230
Cowboy With Lasso, Rocking Base, Tin Lithograph, Windup, 11¼ In. 236
Picture Gun, Theatre, Model No. 492, Stephens Products Co. 30
Plate, Black, White Horse, W. S. George, 9½ In. *illus* 110
Skirt, Plastic, Fringe, 16½ x 21½ In. *illus* 72
Trading Cards, Wild West Trading Cards, Post Cereals, c.1951 230

HORN was used to make many types of boxes, furniture inlays, jewelry, and whimsies.

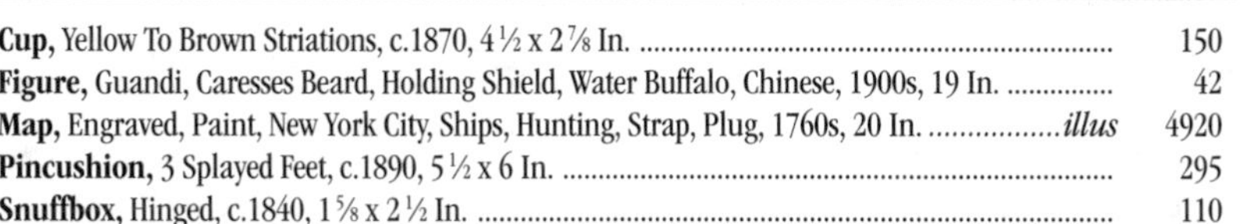

Cup, Yellow To Brown Striations, c.1870, 4½ x 2⅞ In. 150
Figure, Guandi, Caresses Beard, Holding Shield, Water Buffalo, Chinese, 1900s, 19 In. 42
Map, Engraved, Paint, New York City, Ships, Hunting, Strap, Plug, 1760s, 20 In. *illus* 4920
Pincushion, 3 Splayed Feet, c.1890, 5½ x 6 In. 295
Snuffbox, Hinged, c.1840, 1⅝ x 2½ In. 110

HOWARD PIERCE began working in Southern California in 1936. In 1945, he opened a pottery in Claremont. He moved to Joshua Tree in 1968 and continued making pottery until 1991. His contemporary-looking figurines are popular with collectors. Though most pieces are marked with his name, smaller items from his sets often were not marked.

Bust, Woman, Elongated Neck, Speckled Glaze Hair, Brown Glaze, 7 x 3 In. 90
Figurine, Owl, Brown, Black Eyes, Marked, 5 In. 65
Figurine, Quail Family, Brown Glaze, Speckled Chest, 1950s, 5 In., 3 In., 2 In., 3 Piece 68
Figurine, Roadrunner, Gray, White, Black, 12 x 4 In. 125
Flower Frog, Quail On Branch, Gray, White, 6½ In. 50
Vase, Fantail Goldfish, Cameo, Tan & Brown Jasperware, c.1957, 4 In. 129

Hummel, Figurine, No. 174, She Loves Me, She Loves Me Not, Three Line, 4½ In.
$18

Hess Auction Group

TIP
Hummel figurines should be washed in liquid detergent and water, half and half.

Hutschenreuther, Figurine, Musicians Of Bremen, Donkey, Dog, Cat, Rooster, 1948-70, 7¾ In.
$595

Ruby Lane

Hutschenreuther, Group, 3 Ducks, 9½ x 16½ In.
$795

Ruby Lane

Hutschenreuther, Platter, Oval, Barn, Pond, 9 x 24 ½ In.
$795

Ruby Lane

Imari, Dish, Flowers, Iron Red, Orange, Flowerhead Center, Swag Border, c.1800, 5 In. Diam.
$1,353

Skinner, Inc.

Imari, Garniture, 3 Vases, Trumpet & 2 Covered, Porcelain, Chinese Export, 1700s, 10 ½ In.
$1,416

Brunk Auctions

Country Name in Marks

If the name of a country is on the bottom of a plate, it was probably made after 1891. The U.S. government passed a law requiring the name of the "country of origin" be written on pottery or porcelain pieces imported into the United States. Some countries, like England, used the country's name years earlier. If "England" is the mark, the dish may have been made as early as 1850. The words *Made in . . .* were usually used after 1915.

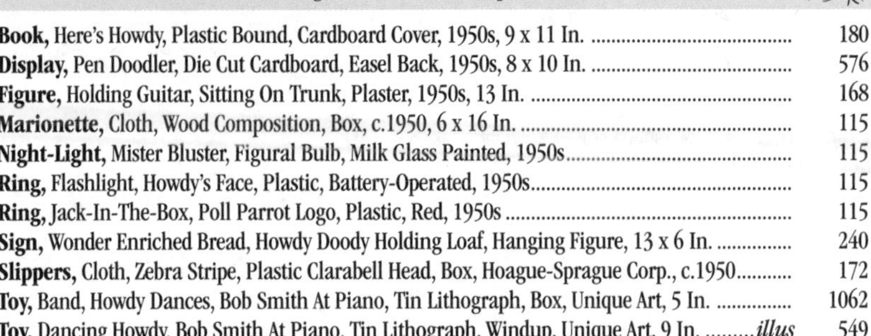

HOWDY DOODY and Buffalo Bob were the main characters in a children's series televised from 1947 to 1960. Howdy was a redheaded puppet. The series became popular with college students in the late 1970s when Buffalo Bob began to lecture on campuses.

Book, Here's Howdy, Plastic Bound, Cardboard Cover, 1950s, 9 x 11 In. 180
Display, Pen Doodler, Die Cut Cardboard, Easel Back, 1950s, 8 x 10 In. 576
Figure, Holding Guitar, Sitting On Trunk, Plaster, 1950s, 13 In. 168
Marionette, Cloth, Wood Composition, Box, c.1950, 6 x 16 In. 115
Night-Light, Mister Bluster, Figural Bulb, Milk Glass Painted, 1950s 115
Ring, Flashlight, Howdy's Face, Plastic, Battery-Operated, 1950s 115
Ring, Jack-In-The-Box, Poll Parrot Logo, Plastic, Red, 1950s 115
Sign, Wonder Enriched Bread, Howdy Doody Holding Loaf, Hanging Figure, 13 x 6 In. 240
Slippers, Cloth, Zebra Stripe, Plastic Clarabell Head, Box, Hoague-Sprague Corp., c.1950 172
Toy, Band, Howdy Dances, Bob Smith At Piano, Tin Lithograph, Box, Unique Art, 5 In. 1062
Toy, Dancing Howdy, Bob Smith At Piano, Tin Lithograph, Windup, Unique Art, 9 In. .... *illus* 549

HULL pottery was made in Crooksville, Ohio, from 1905. Addis E. Hull bought the Acme Pottery Company and started making ceramic wares. In 1917, A. E. Hull Pottery began making art pottery as well as the commercial wares. For a short time, 1921 to 1929, the firm also sold pottery imported from Europe. The dinnerware of the 1940s (including the Little Red Riding Hood line), the matte wares of the 1940s, and the high gloss artwares of the 1950s are all popular with collectors. The firm officially closed in March 1986.

Ashtray, Prancing Deer, Brown Drip Glaze, 1950s, 8 In. Diam. 14
Avocado, Bowl, Vegetable, 2 Sections, Oval, 11 In. 15
Avocado, Plate, Bread & Butter, 6 ¾ In. 6
Bank, Corky Pig, Turquoise, Brown, Marked, c.1978, 9 x 8 In. 69
Blossom Flite, Candlestick, Handle, 3 In. 96
Brown Drip, Casserole, Duck Lid, 2 Qt., 9 In. 65
Brown Drip, Casserole, Lid, Round, Qt., 8 In. 16
Brown Drip, Cup & Saucer 8
Brown Drip, Jug, 52 Oz., 6 ½ In. 16
Brown Drip, Mug, 3 ½ In. 9
Brown Drip, Piggy Bank, Sitting 89
Brown Drip, Piggy Bank, Standing 64
Brown Drip, Plate, Dinner, 10 ⅝ In. 24
Brown Drip, Plate, Fish Shape, 11 In. 117
Brown Drip, Salt & Pepper, Mushroom Shape, 3 ¾ In. 21
Brown Drip, Sugar, Lid, 3 In. 13
Brown Drip, Teapot, Lid, 5 Cup, 5 In. 33
Cornucopia, Tokay, Pink Grapes, Green Leaves, 6 ½ x 11 In. .... *illus* 55
Ewer, Bowknot, Marked, 6 ¼ In. .... *illus* 70
Heartland, Creamer 16
Heartland, Plate, Dinner, 10 ¼ In. 7
Iris, Jardiniere, Pink, Blue, 4 x 4 ½ In. 95
Little Red Riding Hood, Bank, Poppy Spray, 6 ¾ In. 729
Little Red Riding Hood, Creamer, Poppy, 5 In. 145
Little Red Riding Hood, Match Holder, Blue Dress, 5 ⅞ In. 1198
Little Red Riding Hood, Pitcher, Red Poppy Up, 32 Oz., 8 In. 269
Little Red Riding Hood, Salt & Pepper, Red Flower, 3 In. 82
Little Red Riding Hood, Teapot, Lid, Spray, 4 Cup 219
Magnolia, Cornucopia, Yellow, Matte Glaze, 8 In. 92
Magnolia, Ewer, Footed, Yellow, Matte Glaze, 5 In. 31
Open Rose, Vase, Footed, Double Loop Handles, 4 ¾ In. 31
Parchment & Pine, Creamer, Loop Handle, 3 Oz., 2 ½ In. 36
Pitcher, Butterfly, Flowers, Blue Interior, 8 ¾ x 8 ¼ In. .... *illus* 55
Serenade, Ewer, Footed, Yellow Matte Glaze, 13 ¼ In. 278
Serenade, Mug, Yellow Matte Glaze, 5 ¼ In. 114
Sunglow, Casserole, Lid, Pink, Round, 1 ¼ In. 45
Tangerine, Pitcher, Barrel Shape, 32 Oz., 6 ⅝ In. 21
Tawny Ridge, Butter, ¼ Lb. 16
Tawny Ridge, Creamer, 6 Oz., 2 ¼ In. 14
Tokay, Basket, Handle, Footed, Tuscany White, 12 In. 136
Tokay, Dish, Leaf Shape, Pink, Green, Marked, c.1960, 14 x 11 In. 18
Tokay, Dish, Leaf Shape, Tuscany White, 12 ½ In. 42
Tulip, Ewer, Footed, Handle, Blue, 8 In. 72
Vase, Double, Woodland, 1950, 8 ½ In. .... *illus* 48

Wild Flower, Cornucopia, Blue & Pink, 6 3/8 x 7 1/2 In. 27
Woodland, Basket, Footed, Twig Handle, Blue-Green, Glossy, 10 1/2 In. 139
Woodland, Candleholder, Peach-Pink Matte Glaze, 3 3/4 In. 38
Woodland, Creamer, Aladdin Style, Peach-Pink, Glossy, 6 Oz., 2 7/8 In. 53
Woodland, Jardiniere, Leaf Handles, Peach-Pink, Glossy, 5 x 7 In. 84
Woodland, Teapot, Lid, Peach-Pink, Glossy, 5 Cups, 4 3/4 In. 134

HUMMEL figurines, based on the drawings of the nun M.I. Hummel (Berta Hummel), were made by the W. Goebel Porzellanfabrik of Oeslau, Germany, now Rodental, Germany. They were first made in 1935. The *Crown* mark was used from 1935 to 1949. The company added the *bee* marks in 1950. The *full bee*, with variations, was used from 1950 to 1959; *stylized bee*, 1957 to 1972; *three line mark,* 1964 to 1972; *last bee*, sometimes called *vee over gee*, 1972 to 1979. In 1979 the V bee symbol was removed from the mark. *U.S. Zone* was part of the mark from 1946 to 1948; *W. Germany* was part of the mark from 1960 to 1990. The Goebel *W. Germany* mark, called the *missing bee* mark, was used from 1979 to 1990; *Goebel, Germany*, with the crown and *WG*, originally called the *new mark*, was used from 1991 through part of 1999. A new version of the bee mark with the word *Goebel* was used from 1999 to 2008. A special *Year 2000* backstamp was also introduced. Porcelain figures inspired by Berta Hummel's drawings were introduced in 1997. These are marked *BH* followed by a number. They were made in the Far East, not Germany. Goebel discontinued making Hummel figurines in 2008 and Manufaktur Rodental took over the factory in Germany and began making new Hummel figurines. Hummel figurines made by Rodental are marked with a yellow and black bee on the edge of an oval line surrounding the words *Original M.I. Hummel Germany.* The words *Manufaktur Rodental* are printed beneath the oval. Manufaktur Rodental was sold in 2013 and new owners have taken over. Hummel Manufaktur GmbH is the new company. Other decorative items and plates that feature Hummel drawings have been made by Schmid Brothers, Inc., since 1971.

Ashtray, No. 114, Let's Sing, Stylized Bee, 4 3/4 In. 69
Bookends, No. 14A & 14B, Bookworms, Incised Crown Mark, 5 3/4 In. 386
Clock, No. 441, Call To Worship, Missing Bee, 1988, 13 In. 120
Clock, No. 442, Chapel Time, Missing Bee, 11 1/4 In. 150
Figurine, No. 10/1, Flower Madonna, Open Halo, Full Bee, 9 1/2 In. 195
Figurine, No. 20, Prayer Before The Battle, Full Bee, 4 1/2 In. 155
Figurine, No. 47 3/0, Goose Girl, Full Bee, 3 3/4 In. 50
Figurine, No. 51, Village Boy, Stylized Bee, 3 7/8 In. 40
Figurine, No. 58, Playmates, Full Bee, 4 In. 65
Figurine, No. 64, Shepherd Boy, Full Bee, 6 In. 167
Figurine, No. 70, Holy Child, Full Bee, 7 1/2 In. 899
Figurine, No. 127, Doctor, Goebel, Box, 4 3/4 In. 139
Figurine, No. 128, Baker, Last Bee, 5 In. .... *illus* 18
Figurine, No. 131, Street Singer, Small Stylized Bee, 5 In. 178
Figurine, No. 132, Star Gazer, Stylized Bee, 5 In. 145
Figurine, No. 141, Apple Tree Girl, Stylized Bee, 4 In. 38
Figurine, No. 142 3/0, Apple Tree Boy, Stylized Bee, 4 In. 45
Figurine, No. 171, Little Sweeper, Stylized Bee, 4 1/2 In. 90
Figurine, No. 174, She Loves Me, She Loves Me Not, Missing Bee, 4 1/2 In. 32
Figurine, No. 174, She Loves Me, She Loves Me Not, Three Line, 4 1/2 In. .... *illus* 18
Figurine, No. 176/0, Happy Birthday, Full Bee, 5 1/2 In. 245
Figurine, No. 184, Latest News, Full Bee 586
Figurine, No. 197/1, Be Patient, Crown Mark, 6 1/2 In. 65
Figurine, No. 204, Weary Wanderer, Full Bee, 6 In. 176
Figurine, No. 214, Serenade, Last Bee, 3 1/4 In. 27
Figurine, No. 328, Carnival Fastnacht, Missing Bee, 6 In. 39
Figurine, No. 334, Homeward Bound, Missing Bee, 5 3/4 In. 48
Figurine, No. 798, Forever Yours, Full Bee, 4 In. 39
Lamp, No. 111, Wayside Harmony, Full Bee, 10 In. 148
Lamp, No. 223, To Market, Full Bee, 9 In. 186
Plate, Annual Christmas, Boy On Sled, Lantern, 1975, 7 1/2 In. 35

HUTSCHENREUTHER PORCELAIN FACTORY was founded by Carolus Magnus in Hohenburg, Bavaria, in 1814. A second factory was established in Selb, Germany, in 1857. The company made fine quality porcelain dinnerware and figurines. The mark changed through the years, but the name and the lion insignia appear in most versions. Hutschenreuther became part of the Rosenthal division of the Waterford Wedgwood Group in 2000. Rosenthal was bought by Sambonet Paderno Industries, headquartered in Orfento, Novaro, Italy, in 2009.

LORENZ HUTSCHEN REUTER GERMANY

Charger, Roses, Rococo Style, Stems, Leaves, Handles, c.1950, 13 In. 129
Figurine, Bison, Signed, 12 1/2 x 17 1/2 In. 369

Imari, Punch Bowl, Alternating Flowers & Shishi Reserves, Wood Stand, c.1900, 15 In.
$861

Neal Auctions

Imari, Punch Bowl, Orange, Blue Leaves, Landscape Panels, Figures, Arita Mark, 1800s, 6 x 16 In.
$3,500

New Orleans (Cakebread)

TIP
Put pads between stacked plates. Don't stack too many in one pile.

Imari, Vase, Dome Lid, Japan, c.1880, 18 1/2 In., Pair
$492

Cowan Auctions

TIP

Remove handles from casement windows to make them burglarproof. But keep them nearby so you can get out in an emergency.

Indian, Bag, Maliseet, Beaded, Hearts, Flowers, Silk Ribbon Trim, c.1850, 6 x 5 ½ In.
$296

James D. Julia Auctioneers

Indian, Bag, Plateau, Beaded, Red Rose Design, Buckskin Trim, c.1935, 13 x 11 In.
$184

Allard Auctions

Indian, Bag, Sioux, Hide, Beaded, Geometric Designs, c.1890, 14 ½ x 23 ½ In.
$3,600

Cowan Auctions

Figurine, Dancing Woman, Nude, On Tiptoe On Gold Ball, 13 ½ In. 238
Figurine, Dancing Woman, On 1 Knee, Arm Up, 11 In. 163
Figurine, Discus Thrower, Woman, Signed, Tutter, 8 In. 525
Figurine, Dog, Boxer, Brown, 1950s, 5 ½ In. 140
Figurine, Flower Bringer, Green Vest, Striped Pants, c.1890, 5 ¼ In. 375
Figurine, Musicians Of Bremen, Donkey, Dog, Cat, Rooster, 1948-70, 7 ¾ In. .... *illus* 595
Figurine, Nude Boy, Riding Kicking Horse, 7 ¾ x 8 In. 120
Figurine, Nude, Holding Gold Ball, 10 In. 200
Figurine, Nude, Raised Arms, Bent Leg, Ball Base, 8 ½ In. 495
Figurine, Ring Around The Rosie, 8 In., Pair 177
Figurine, Woman With Fan, Red Dress, Blond, Paper Label, 7 ½ In. 170
Gravy Boat, Gold, Black, White, Underplate, 1900s 25
Group, 3 Ducks, 9 ½ x 16 ½ In. .... *illus* 795
Group, Sitting Duck, Inflight Duck, Granget, c.1970, 15 In. 1999
Napkin Ring, Blue & White, Stylized Flower, Scrolling Vine 18
Plaque, Grecian Lovers, Admiring Roses, Signed Wagner, Frame, 5 ¾ x 4 In. 531
Plaque, Man, Smoking Pipe, Gray Beard, Hat, Paper Label, 1800s, 7 x 5 In. 1395
Plate, Berry & Flower Wreath Border, Scalloped Edge, c.1900, 9 ¼ In. 85
Plate, Dinner, Cobalt & Gold Border, White Ground, 10 In., 12 Piece 700
Plate, Pink Flowers, Yellow Centers, Gold Rim, Signed, Cummings, 7 ¾ In. 65
Platter, Mill, Winding Road, Pond, Oval, Margaret Surber, 24 x 9 In. 750
Platter, Oval, Barn, Pond, 9 x 24 ½ In. .... *illus* 795
Platter, Shells, 24K Gold Highlights, Oval, Surber, 22 x 9 In. 795
Vase, Pink, Blue, Yellow Flowers, Gold Rim, Cylindrical, c.1960, 4 ⅝ x 4 In. 65

ICONS, special, revered pictures of Jesus, Mary, or a saint, are usually Russian or Byzantine. The small icons collected today are made of wood and tin or precious metals. Many modern copies have been made in the old style and are being sold to tourists in Russia and Europe and at shops in the United States. Rare, old icons have sold for over $50,000. The riza is the metal cover protecting the icon. It is often made of silver or gold.

Christ The Pantocrator, Halo, Bible, Red, Blue, Russia, 18th Century, 16 x 11 In. 1168
Jesus, Bust, Agony, Blood Dripping, Column & Plinth, Spain, 1800s, 23 In. 295
John The Warrior, Multicolor Tempera, Wood Panel, Russia, 12 ½ x 10 ¼ In. 266
Joseph & Christ, Statue, Multicolor Robes, Seated Christ In Hand, c.1800, 34 In. 1750
Kazan Mother Of God, Multicolor Tempera, Wood Panel, Gilt, Russia, c.1600s, 12 x 10 In. 885
Mary, Silver Plate, Painted Faces, Enameled Halos, 12 x 9 ¾ In. 369
Pokrov Madonna, Saints, Kovcheg Panel, Byzantine Style, Russia, 12 x 9 ¾ In. 9840
Resurrection & Descent To Hades, 12 Holy Feasts, 13 Panels, Paint, Gilt, c.1900, 14 x 12 In. . 1000
St. Alexander Nevsky, Tempura On Wood Panel, Prince Of Kiev, Engraved, c.1995, 9 x 7 In. 687
St. Augustine, Multicolor Tempera, Wood Panel, Russia, 9 ¼ x 4 ½ In. 425
St. Kyriake, Silver Mounted, Ottoman Empire Hallmarks, c.1900, 8 ¾ x 6 ½ In. 615
St. Michael, Russia, 19th Century, 15 ½ x 12 ½ In. 1170
St. Nicholas, Holding Book, Kovcheg Panel, Label, Wood Frame, Russia, 35 x 42 In. 5166
St. Nicholas, Jesus, Mary, Robes, Bible, Hand Up, Russian, Frame, c.1890, 16 x 13 In. 750
St. Nicholas, Multicolor Tempera, Gilt, Wood Panel, Russia, c.1800, 8 x 5 In. 1133
St. Nicholas, Silver Oklad, Cyrillic Mark, A. Stepanov, Moscow, c.1890, 12 x 11 In. 16590
St. Patrick, Holding Building & Staff, Wood, Gesso, Carved, 19th Century, 15 ½ In. 445
Stone, Figure, Madonna & Child, Limestone Carved, French Gothic, c.1300, 30 In. 13200
Travel Altar, Leatherette, Leaded Light, Fleur-De-Lis, Mary, Joseph, Jesus, Lily, 1894, 7 x 4 In. 215
Triptych, Mother Of God In Life, Russia, c.1900, 14 x 17 In. 1476
Virgin & Child, Wall Shrine, Carved, Gilded, Tabernacle Frame, Italy, 1800s, 28 x 11 In. 1440

IMARI porcelain was made in Japan and China beginning in the seventeenth century. In the eighteenth century and later, it was copied by porcelain factories in Germany, France, England, and the United States. It was especially popular in the nineteenth century and is still being made. Imari is characteristically decorated with stylized bamboo, floral, and geometric designs in orange, red, green, and blue. The name comes from the Japanese port of Imari, which exported the ware made nearby in a factory at Arita. Imari is now a general term for any pattern of this type.

Bowl, Blue & White, 2 Encircled Carp Center, Leaves, Scalloped Rim, 12 In. Diam. 85
Bowl, Bronze, Rust Color, Blue Flowers, Handles, Neoclassical Base, 1900s, 9 x 9 ½ In. 60
Bowl, Crane, Spear Shape Leaves, Straight-Sided, Gilt, Blue Ground, 10 ⅞ x 4 ⅜ In. 246
Bowl, Dome Lid, Round, Squat, Flowering Branches, Reeded Ball Finial, 5 x 7 In. 98
Bowl, Figures, Trees, Flowers, Gilt Leaf Handles, Openwork Foot, 1800s, 22 x 15 In. 3250
Bowl, Flowers, Scrolling Leaves, Wide Rim, Cobalt Blue, Red, Green, 11 In. Diam. 98
Bowl, Gilt Bronze Mount, Red Flowers, White Ground, Blue Accents, 9 ½ x 16 In. 177

Bowl, Red, Blossoms, Central Chrysanthemum, Panels, Japan, 15 ½ In. 750
Bowl, Red, Blue, c.1913-26, 4 ½ x 10 In. 265
Bowl, Scalloped Rim, Flowers, White Exterior, Wood Base, c.1910, 3 ½ x 9 ¾ In. 120
Bowl, Scalloped, Flower Shape, Diaper Pattern, Flowers, Medallion, 10 In. 423
Bowl, Swirling Panels Of Flowers, Ring Foot, Wide Rim, c.1900, 4 x 6 In. 150
Box, Porcelain, Round, Seated Person Finial, Red, Green, 4 ½ In. 195
Brushpot, Blue, Branch, Leaf, Medallions, Red Flowers, 6 ¼ x 5 In., Pair.......... 181
Charger, 3 Flowers & Leaves In Center, 17 In. 154
Charger, 3 Red Sections, 3 Blue Sections, 18 In. 246
Charger, Cross Design Center, Flowers, Cobalt Blue, Red, Wavy Rim, 1800s, 13 In. 61
Charger, Figures, Bench, Flower Border, Multicolor, 1800s, 18 In. 153
Charger, Flower Shape Medallions, Red & Gilt Scroll Border, 1800s, 18 In. 183
Charger, Flowerpot Center, Plants, Scalloped Rim, Cobalt Blue, Red, 1800s, 12 In. 244
Charger, Multicolor Enamel, Alternating Sections, Chrysanthemums, Peacocks, 18 In. 173
Charger, Petal Shape Rim, Winged Phoenix, Panels, 18 ¼ In. 425
Charger, Round, Turned Out Rim, Medallion, Potted Flowers, Bird, c.1980, 27 In. 1250
Charger, Shallow Bowl, Central Flowerpot, Panels, Branches, Grass, 1800s, 22 In. 1008
Dish, Chrysanthemum, Ruyi & Flower Lappets, Footed, 1700s, 9 ¼ In. 59
Dish, Flowering Trees, Carp, Stylized Pool, Multicolor, 1700s, 4 x 21 In. 413
Dish, Flowers, Iron Red, Orange, Flowerhead Center, Swag Border, c.1800, 5 In. Diam. .... *illus* 1353
Garden Seat, Barrel Shaped, Pierced Cash Symbols, Multicolor, 18 In., Pair.......... 858
Garniture, 3 Vases, Trumpet & 2 Covered, Porcelain, Chinese Export, 1700s, 10 ½ In. .... *illus* 1416
Jar, Temple, Multicolor Enamel Over Porcelain, Gilt, 1897, 24 In. 502
Jardiniere, Flowers, Tapered, Flat Wide Rim, c.1880, 10 ½ x 14 In. 120
Pitcher, Red, Blue, Dragon Legs, c.1820, 7 In. 84
Plate, Flowers, Urn, Bouquet, 12 In. 59
Plate, Lobed, Serpentine Rim, Seascape, Ruyi Head Reserves, c.1860, 9 x 1 In., 6 Piece 307
Plate, Scalloped, Gilt Accents, Japanese Character Marks, 8 ½ In., 6 Piece.......... 288
Plate, Soup, Blue Glaze, Red Overglaze, Gilt Peonies, Bamboo, Scrolled Border, 9 In., 4 Piece..... 615
Platter, Cobalt Blue, Iron Red, Reserves, Oval, Japan, 1800s, 11 x 9 In. 84
Platter, Hexagonal, 6 Sections, Birds, Cranes, Kites, Ribbon Swags, 18 ¼ In. 605
Platter, Oval, Flowerpot On Table, Scalloped Rim, 1800s, 15 In. 153
Platter, Oval, Shaped Rim, Cobalt Blue, Iron Red, Cream, Flowers, 1800s, 14 In., Pair 750
Punch Bowl, Alternating Flowers & Shishi Reserves, Wood Stand, c.1900, 15 In. .... *illus* 861
Punch Bowl, Orange, Blue Leaves, Landscape Panels, Figures, Arita Mark, 1800s, 6 x 16 In. *illus* 3500
Umbrella Stand, Cylindrical, Flowering Branch, Bird, c.1880, 24 x 9 In. 510
Vase, 2 Phoenix, Bamboo, Peony, Dome Lid, Lion Dog Finial, c.1700, 17 In. 876
Vase, Blue & Red Glaze, Gilt Leaves, Paneled, Brass Fittings, Japan, 17 x 11 In. 121
Vase, Dome Lid, Japan, c.1880, 18 ½ In., Pair.......... *illus* 492
Vase, Double Gourd, Seated Couple, Landscape, Straight Neck, Raised Foot, 12 In. 185
Vase, Flared Rolled Rim, Flowers, Red, White, Blue, Center Circle, c.1900, 10 In. 30
Vase, Flowers, Landscape, Cartouche, Medallions, Leaves, Round Foot, 13 x 4 In. 242
Vase, Stick Neck, 1800, 30 In. 369

IMPERIAL GLASS CORPORATION was founded in Bellaire, Ohio, in 1901. It became a subsidiary of Lenox, Inc., in 1973 and was sold to Arthur R. Lorch in 1981. It was sold again in 1982, and went bankrupt in 1984. In 1985, the molds and some assets were sold. The Imperial glass preferred by the collector is freehand art glass, carnival glass, slag glass, stretch glass, and other top-quality tablewares. Tablewares and animals are listed here. The others may be found in the appropriate sections.

IMPERIAL

Candlewick, Punch Set, Bowl & Underplate, 12 Cups, Ladle, 15 Piece.......... 12
Candlewick, Relish, 4 Sections, Round, 9 ½ In. 15
Candlewick, Sugar & Creamer 21
Cape Cod, Cruet, Stopper, 4 In. 16
Cape Cod, Goblet, Water, 5 ½ In. 4
Cape Cod, Plate, Salad, 8 In. 7
Cape Cod, Relish, 4 Sections, Round, Handle.......... 21
Cosmos, Compote, Ruffled Edge, Marigold, 4 ½ In. 33
Daisy & Button, Toothpick Holder, Marigold.......... 112
Embossed Rose, Vase, Amethyst, Shouldered, 6 In. 35
Fashion, Pitcher, Marigold, 8 ½ In. 56
Fashion, Punch Cup, Marigold 32
Fashion, Tumbler, Marigold.......... 27
Luster Rose, Bowl, Scalloped Edge, 3-Footed, Marigold.......... 35
Luster Rose, Butter, Cover, Green 145
Luster Rose, Spooner, Handles, Green.......... 85

Indian, Basket, Apache, Squat, Shouldered, Coiled, c.1910, 7 x 8 ½ In.
$336

Cowan Auctions

Indian, Basket, Karok, Tobacco, Dome Lid, Handle, Diagonal Diamonds, c.1910, 8 x 6 In.
$316

Allard Auctions

American Indian Jewelry
Early jewelry worn by American Indians was made for their use in ceremonies and as portable wealth. Later jewelry was made to sell to tourists. In 1935 Congress tried to promote development in Indian communities. New silversmiths were trained, and guilds and cooperatives were formed. Indian jewelry became more artistic and more expensive. After World War II, new Indian artists made jewelry pieces with a modern look using traditional materials. Indian trade jewelry is lighter in weight and more highly polished than older jewelry. It is often decorated with arrows, suns, thunderbirds, and other traditional designs.

Indian, Basket, Pomo, Coiled, Triangle Designs, White Seed Beads, c.1900, 2 x 4 In.
$863

Allard Auctions

Indian, Basket, Pomo, Gift, Feathers, 8 x 3 ½ In.
$1,680

Cowan Auctions

Indian, Basket, Yokuts, Woven, Band Of Diamond Shapes, c.1935, 4 x 10 ¾ In.
$984

Cowan Auctions

Indian, Bonnet, Sioux, Hide, Beaded, Lined, Child's, c.1900, 5 ½ In.
$1,440

Cowan Auctions

Pansy, Creamer, Footed, Marigold 19
Provincial, Goblet, Water, Amethyst, 5 ⅝ In. 11
Provincial, Goblet, Water, Olive Green, 5 ⅝ In. 9
Provincial, Sherbet, Olive Green, 4 ½ In. 5
Simplicity, Goblet, Water, 6 In. 25
Tiger Lily, Pitcher, Pink, 7 ⅝ In. 82
Tree Bark, Pitcher, Tankard, Marigold, 8 ½ In. 40
Vintage Grape, Cordial, Amber, 4 In. 25
Vintage Grape, Goblet, Water, Amber, 5 ⅜ In. 28
Vintage, Sherbet, Blue 23

INDIAN art from North and South America has attracted the collector for many years. Each tribe has its own distinctive designs and techniques. Baskets, jewelry, pottery, and leatherwork are of greatest collector interest. Eskimo art is listed under Eskimo in this book.

Bag Panel, Yakama, Beaded, Curved Flowers, Hide Backing, 1900s, 14 ½ x 12 In. 295
Bag, Apache, Hide, Beaded, Zigzag, Brown, Orange, Brown Danglers, 8 In. 1845
Bag, Apache, Hide, Pink & Green Beads, Fringe, Tin Cone Danglers, 10 x 4 In. 984
Bag, Blackfoot, Beaded Hide, Multicolor, Long Strap, c.1890, 9 x 8 In. 1560
Bag, Chippewa, Beaded, Flowers, c.1925, 5 x 4 ¾ In. 156
Bag, Lakota, Hide, Beaded, Red, Turquoise, Birds, Rawhide Slats, Tin Cones, 11 ½ In. 369
Bag, Maliseet, Beaded, Hearts, Flowers, Silk Ribbon Trim, c.1850, 6 x 5 ½ In. .... *illus* 296
Bag, Plateau, Beaded, Red Rose Design, Buckskin Trim, c.1935, 13 x 11 In. .... *illus* 184
Bag, Sioux, Hide, Beaded, Geometric Designs, c.1890, 14 ½ x 23 ½ In. .... *illus* 3600
Bandolier, Chippewa, Cloth, Beads, Orange, Teal, Flowers, Tassels, 38 x 12 In. 1722
Bandolier, Great Lakes, Pink & Purple Flowers, Leaves, White & Pink Ground, 37 In. 1599
Bandolier, Northern Plains, Deer Hoof, Braided Hide, Green Yarn, Beads, c.1920, 23 In. 480
Bandolier, Ojibwe, Cloth, Flowers, White Ground, Red & Gray Wool Tassels, 44 x 12 In. 984
Basket, Apache, Burden, Multicolor, Hide Straps, Fringe, Red Dye, c.1900, 11 x 14 In. 1800
Basket, Apache, Gathering, Bucket Shape, Reinforced Rim, Rawhide Lashing, c.1880, 16 In. 593
Basket, Apache, Squat, Shouldered, Coiled, c.1910, 7 x 8 ½ In. .... *illus* 336
Basket, Chitimacha, Lid, Worm Track, Double Weave, Black, Red, Natural, C. Darden, 7 x 5 In. 777
Basket, Chitimacha, Single Weave, Bowl Shape, Red, Yellow, Black, Ada Thomas, 5 x 10 In. 976
Basket, Hupa, Cylindrical, Stars, Diamonds, Openwork Bands, Tan, Brown, c.1920, 11 In. 1076
Basket, Karok, Tobacco, Dome Lid, Handle, Diagonal Diamonds, c.1910, 8 x 6 In. .... *illus* 316
Basket, Miwok-Paiute, Coiled, Geometric Shapes, Stars, Diamonds, c.1910, 5 x 10 In. 3585
Basket, Monache, Early 1900s, 7 ½ x 13 ½ In. 720
Basket, Mono, Cooking, Flared Rim, Zigzag Pattern, Rectangle Banding, c.1900, 17 In. 2151
Basket, Panamint, Bottleneck, Stacked Triangles, Lizards, c.1910, 3 ½ x 6 ½ In. 1230
Basket, Pima, Coiled, Fret Pattern, Flared, 12 x 3 In. 472
Basket, Pima, Coiled, Pictorial, Woven Bowl, Flared, Spread Wing Eagles, c.1920, 15 In. 2629
Basket, Pima, Woven, Snake Pattern, Braided Rim, 8 x 5 In. 638
Basket, Pomo, Coiled, Triangle Designs, White Seed Beads, c.1900, 2 x 4 In. .... *illus* 863
Basket, Pomo, Gift, Feathers, 8 x 3 ½ In. .... *illus* 1680
Basket, Pomo, Treasure, Coiled, Boat Shape, Clamshell Bead Rim, Feathers, c.1910, 3 x 9 In. ... 2629
Basket, Quinault, Coiled, Red & Green Design, Flared Bottom, c.1950, 11 In. 70
Basket, Skokomish, Storage, Twined, Cylindrical, Rectangles, Animals, c.1910, 14 In. 6274
Basket, Tohono O'Odham, Woman, Oval, Yucca, Devil's Claw, Bear Grass, c.1940, 10 x 13 In. 472
Basket, Yokuts, Woven, Band Of Diamond Shapes, c.1935, 4 x 10 ¾ In. .... *illus* 984
Belt Buckle, Hopi, Silver, Curved, Geometric Patterns, Lawrence Saufkie, 3 x 2 In. 212
Belt, Navajo, Concha, Hammered, Tooled, Turquoise Center, 33 In. 575
Belt, Navajo, Concha, Coin Silver, Hammered, Tooled, Stones, Leather, c.1910, 48 In. 4631
Belt, Navajo, Scalloped, Round & Bar Shape Links, Rectangular Buckle, Woman's, 32 In. 259
Belt, Pictorial, Silver, Buckle, 9 Plates, Turquoise, Coral, Mother-Of-Pearl, Bone Inlay, 43 In. 767
Belt, Plains, Leather Panel, Beads, Blue, Blue & White X, Pink Border, 39 In. 1599
Belt, Plateau, Leather Panel, 5-Point Stars, Arrowheads, Chevrons, 38 In. 431
Belt, Southern Plains, Concha, Leather, Rocker Engraved Brass, 28 In. 4920
Blanket, Navajo, Chief's, 3rd Phase, Tan, Brown, Red, Geometric Pattern, c.1915, 52 x 60 In. 1845
Blanket, Navajo, Chief's Style, Red, Black, White, Diamond Center, c.1910, 59 x 49 In. 865
Blanket, Navajo, Diamond Shapes, Lightening, Homespun Yarn, Multicolor, 77 x 47 In. 403
Blanket, Navajo, Ganado Transitional, Serape, Diamonds, White, Black, Salmon, 53 x 87 In. ... 720
Blanket, Navajo, Symmetrical Design, Homespun Wool, Natural Dye, c.1900, 64 x 44 In. 403
Bolo, Zuni, Silver, Turquoise, Dangles, Stamped, Bear Paw Mark, c.1935, 3 x 3 In. 431
Bonnet, Sioux, Hide, Beaded, Lined, Child's, c.1900, 5 ½ In. .... *illus* 1440
Bottle, Milk, Tlingit, Basketry, Woven Diamonds, Cap, Early 1900s, 5 In. .... *illus* 92
Bow, Modoc, Multicolor, c.1890, 42 In. 1320

Indian, Bottle, Milk, Tlingit, Basketry, Woven Diamonds, Cap, Early 1900s, 5 In.
$92

Allard Auctions

Indian, Bowl, Omaha, Effigy, Burl, Carved, Animal Head, 4 Brass Tacks, 1800s, 12 x 5 In.
$9,225

Skinner, Inc.

Indian, Box, Micmac, Lid, Quilled, Birch, 4 Triangular Boxes In Round Box, c.1900, 5 x 12 In.
$1,680

Cowan Auctions

Indian, Box, Northwest Coast, Bent, Totemic Animals, Pigment Trace, 1800s, 11 x 10 In.
$28,290

Skinner, Inc.

Indian, Chair, Micmac, Quilled, Birch Bark, Maple, Hardwood, Geometrics, c.1850, 34 ½ In.
$1,440

Cowan Auctions

Indian, Doll, Northern Plains, Hide, Beaded, c.1890, 11 ½ In.
$900

Cowan Auctions

TIP

Nineteenth-century Indian blankets are generally not restored by museums. They stabilize them, mount them on backing fabric to avoid further damage, and hang or frame them. There is some thought that even the dirt may be wanted in its original state in the future.

Indian, Dress Yoke, Yakima, Beaded, On Canvas, Cotton & Hide Ties, c.1900, 25 In.
$900

Cowan Auctions

Indian, Dress, Plains, Trade Cloth, Dentalium Shells, Ribbon, Brass Hawk Bells, Girl's, 41 In.
$2,583

Skinner, Inc.

Indian, Dress, Sioux, Velveteen, Cowrie Shell Yoke, Red Ribbon Trim, c.1900, 29 ½ In.
$510

Cowan Auctions

Indian, Hat, Northwest Coast, Basketry, Painted, Nuu-Chah-Nulth, c.1890, 6 x 13 In.
$1,169

Skinner, Inc.

Indian, Katsina, Hopi, Wood, Carved, Multicolor, 7 ¾ In.
$1,230

Skinner, Inc.

Indian, Mittens, Wagon Driver, Buffalo Hide, Cloth Lined, c.1900, 16 x 10 In., Pair
$115

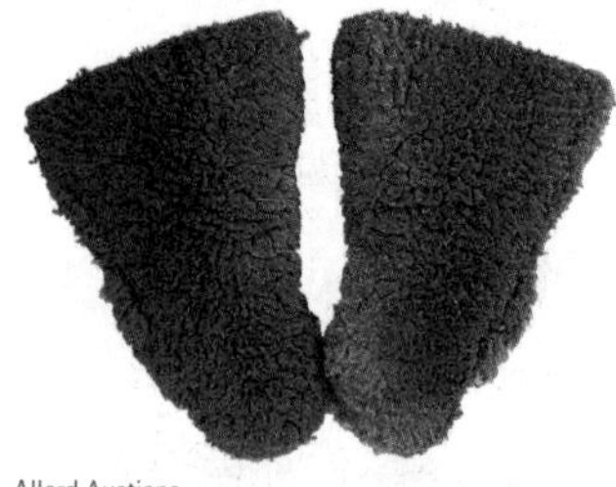

Allard Auctions

Indian, Moccasins, Blackfoot, Beaded, Geometrics, Crosses, Buffalo Hide, c.1890, 10 ½ In.
$3,321

Skinner, Inc.

Bowl, Apache, Basket, Coiled, Figures & Animals, Checkered Rim, c.1910, 16 In. 4780
Bowl, Apache, Basket, Geometric Design, People, Animals, Wide Rim, 1800s, 5 x 15 In. 2655
Bowl, Hopi, Nampeyo Of Hano, Multicolor, c.1890, 3 x 9 In. 5400
Bowl, Hopi, Out-Turned Rim, Pierced Knob, Birds, Cream, Black, c.1920, 10 In. 5378
Bowl, Northeastern, Burl, Oval, Pierced Handles, Amber Color Patina, 1800s, 18 x 15 In. 2280
Bowl, Omaha, Effigy, Burl, Carved, Animal Head, 4 Brass Tacks, 1800s, 12 x 5 In. ....*illus* 9225
Bowl, Yokuts, Basket, Multicolor, c.1915, 8 ½ x 17 ½ In. 1599
Box, Micmac, Lid, Quilled, Birch, 4 Triangular Boxes In Round Box, c.1900, 5 x 12 In. ....*illus* 1680
Box, Naskapi, Bentwood, Lid, Oval, Curved, Spruce Root Laps, c.1850, 21 x 9 In. 415
Box, Northwest Coast, Bent, Totemic Animals, Pigment Trace, 1800s, 11 x 10 In. ....*illus* 28290
Buckle, Navajo, Sterling Silver, Turquoise, Coral, Claw Shape, 4 ½ x 3 In. 531
Button, Zia, Painted, Bird, Convex Earthenware, Arizona, Early 1900s, 1 ½ In. 68
Cane, Southeast, Carved Salamander, Wood Shaft, c.1900, 35 ½ In. 330
Cape, Northern Plains, Dentalium Shell, Beads, Ribbon, Fringe, Woman's, 1890, 16 x 30 In. 7800
Chair, Micmac, Quilled, Birch Bark, Maple, Hardwood, Geometrics, c.1850, 34 ½ In. ....*illus* 1440
Cheyenne, Belt Buckle, Beadwork, Buffalo, Multicolor, Steel Plate, Leather, L. Holley, 4 x 3 In. .. 81
Club, Plains, Double-Headed, Stone, Wrapped With Quilled Slats, c.1880, 36 x 21 In. 1440
Cradle, Sioux, Beaded, Buffalo Hide, Quilled Bands, Wool, Flour Sack, c.1890, 39 In. 2160
Cradleboard, Lakota Sioux, Beaded, Flags, Buffalo, Turtles, Peace Pipes, 21 x 9 In. 625
Cup, Horn, Central Plains, Quill-Wrapped Rawhide Slats, Tin, Feather Danglers, 14 In. 984
Cup, Horn, Northwest Coast, Relief Carved Animal Head, 4 ½ x 3 In. 4305
Cup, Maya, Cylindrical, Ribbing, Red, Blue Gesso, Carved Glyphs, Mica Specks, 10 x 7 In. 2151
Doll, Mohave, Pottery, Red, Black, Beaded Necklace, Wood Cradleboard, c.1885, 7 In. 1912
Doll, Northern Plains, Hide, Beaded, c.1890, 11 ½ In. ....*illus* 900
Dress Yoke, Plateau, Beaded, Hide Fringe, Shoulder Ties, c.1900, 12 ¾ x 16 In. 504
Dress Yoke, Yakima, Beaded, On Canvas, Cotton & Hide Ties, c.1900, 25 In. ....*illus* 900
Dress, Plains, Trade Cloth, Dentalium Shells, Ribbon, Brass Hawk Bells, Girl's, 41 In. ....*illus* 2583
Dress, Sioux, Beaded Hide, Sinew Sewn, Beaded, Multicolor, Fringe, c.1900, 36 In. 3900
Dress, Sioux, Velveteen, Cowrie Shell Yoke, Red Ribbon Trim, c.1900, 29 ½ In. ....*illus* 510
Effigy Jar, Molded Parrot Head, Feathers, Geometric Shapes, Red, Black, c.1400, 18 In. 1793
Effigy Pitcher, Tesuque, Bulbous, 2 Spouts, Upright Handle, Swirl Design, c.1890, 9 In. 1500
Effigy, Mohave, Molded Arms, Pottery, Painted, c.1915, 9 In. 1169
Figure, Cochiti, Man, Singer, Cross Necklace, Canteen, Black, Cream, c.1890, 15 In. 2750
Gauntlets, Deer Hide, Beaded, Fringed, Flower Pattern, c.1935, 12 x 7 In. 165
Gauntlets, Northern Plains, Beaded Hide, c.1890, 13 In. 780
Hair Drop, Northern Plains, Quilled Hide, c.1880, 25 In. 600
Hair Ornament, Plains, Beadwork, c.1920, 7 ½ In. 71
Hat, Northwest Coast, Basketry, Painted, Nuu-Chah-Nulth, c.1890, 6 x 13 In. ....*illus* 1169
Headdress Roach, Porcupine Hair, Fiber Base, c.1900, 18 In. 375
Hide Scraper, Crow, Elk Horn, 4-In. Hook, c.1930, 14 In. 156
Hide Scraper, Plains, Elk Antler, Thunderbird, Geometric Designs, 1800s, 13 ½ In. 2880
Jar, Acoma, Multicolor, Multiple Designs, c.1900, 10 x 11 ½ In. 3480
Jar, Acoma, Pottery, Abstract 2-Headed Bird, Cream, Black, 10 In. 738
Jar, Cochiti, 4 Panels, Diagonal Pattern, 8 ¼ x 10 ½ In. 984
Jar, Hopi, Tulip Design, Multicolor, Hattie Carl, c.1920, 6 x 11 In. 165
Jar, San Ildefonso, Blackware, Gray, Squat, M. Martinez & Popovi Da, c.1957, 6 In. Diam. 720
Jar, San Ildefonso, Bulbous, Black On Red, Plumed Medallions, c.1890, 10 In. 2988
Jar, Santo Domingo, Globe Shape, Lozenges, 6-Point Stars, Black, Beige, c.1890, 17 In. 7768
Jar, Zuni, Applied Frog, c.1900, 8 ½ x 12 ½ In. 3567
Jar, Zuni, Triangles, Band Of Ovals, Feathers, Black, Rust, Bulbous, c.1885, 9 In. 6871
Katsina, Hopi, Hilili, Multicolor, c.1965, 15 ½ In. 540
Katsina, Hopi, Rooster Style, Takawee, Red, Blue, Yellow, Label, 10 In. 550
Katsina, Hopi, Wood, Carved, Multicolor, 7 ¾ In. ....*illus* 1230
Katsina, Malo Hopi, Wood, Carved, Red, Blue, c.1950, 8 ½ In. 450
Katsina, Navajo, Early Morning Singer, Sterling Silver, Jeffery Castillo, 4 ½ In. 180
Katsina, Navajo, Sterling Silver, Turquoise, David R. Freeland Jr., 9 In. 660
Knife Sheaf, Ojibwa, Yellow Ground, Flowers, Beaded, Tin Cone Danglers, c.1830, 11 In. 830
Knife Sheath, Beaded, Leather Strip, Buttons, Dew Claws, Cowrie Shells, c.1890, 16 x 5 In. 2400
Ladle, Feast, Great Lakes, Effigy, Rounded Scoop, Bird Shape Handle, 15 x 8 In. 600
Ladle, Great Lakes, Maple, Wide Bowl, Pierced Handle, Carved, Hook, c.1865, 11 In. 356
Laundry Stick, Penobscot, Birch, Chip Carved, Hearts & Diamonds, 1800s, 28 In. 296
Legging Panels, Plains, Feed Sack Backing, Beaded, Geometric, c.1885, 15 x 11 In. 220
Leggings, Ute, Beaded Hide, Sinew, Tanned, Fringe, Yellow, Green, c.1980, 33 In. 2880
Manta, Hopi, Wedding Embroidered, Spun Cotton, 4-Ply Yarn, c.1890, 59 x 50 In. 9600
Mittens, Wagon Driver, Buffalo Hide, Cloth Lined, c.1900, 16 x 10 In., Pair ....*illus* 115
Moccasins, Apache, Deer Skin, Hard Sole, Blue & Yellow Paint, Beaded, c.1890, 10 In. 830

Indian, Moccasins, Lakota, Hide, Beaded, Buffalo Tracks, Geometrics, Cloth Lining, 10 In.
$800

Skinner, Inc.

Indian, Moccasins, Sioux, Hide, Beaded, Green, Red, White, c.1910, 11 In.
$780

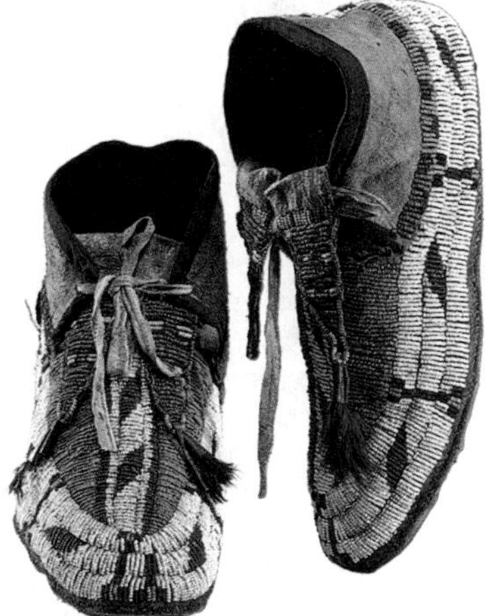

Cowan Auctions

Indian, Necklace, Pueblo, Turquoise, 4 Strands, Graduated, Nuggets, c.1950, 30 In.
$677

Cowan Auctions

Indian, Pendant, Plains, Cloth, Beaded Figures, Thunderbird, Hide Strap, E. Borein, 13 In.
$3,444

Skinner, Inc.

Indian, Pillow, Plateau, Eagle, 32-Star Flag, Buckskin, Glass & Metallic Beads, c.1900, 18 In.
$4,305

Skinner, Inc.

Indian, Pin, Navajo, Silver, Turquoise & Coral Stones, Circular Pattern, 1970s, 4 ⅜ x 4 In.
$316

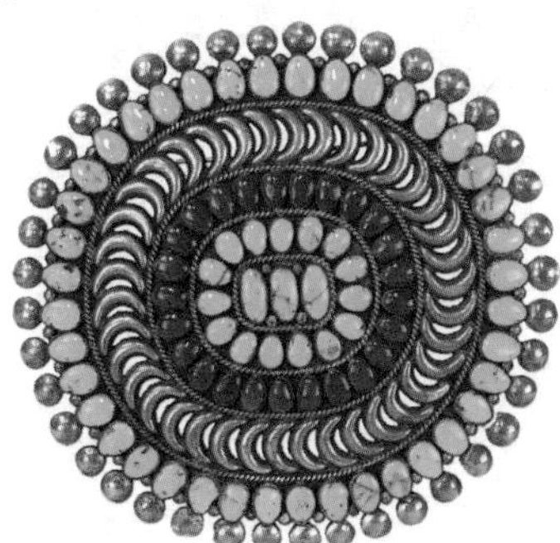

Allard Auctions

Skookum Apple Heads
Skookum Indian dolls were made with apple heads from about 1915 to 1920 and had no feet. The body was a block of wood. In the 1920s, a few had shoes. In the 1930s, leather-over-wood moccasins were used. Composition masks were used as part of the heads from the late teens to the 1940s.

Indian, Pin, Zuni, Silver, Rainbow Dancer, Mosaic Inlay, 1970s, 3 ⅜ x 1 ¾ In.
$288

Allard Auctions

Indian, Pipe, Sioux, Catlinite Bowl, Quilled Stem, c.1900, 26 In.
$2,520

Cowan Auctions

TIP

If garage windows are painted, burglars won't be able to tell if cars are home or not. Use translucent paint to get light in the closed garage, if it has an entrance to your house.

Indian, Pitcher, Anasazi, Chaco, Black On White, Pottery, Prehistoric, 6 x 5 In.
$431

Allard Auctions

Indian, Rattle, Nuu-Chah-Nulth, Wood, Multicolor Paint, c.1910, 9 In.
$1,200

Cowan Auctions

Indian, Rug, Navajo, Feather & Water Bug, Classic Border, c.1970, 79 x 63 In.
$1,150

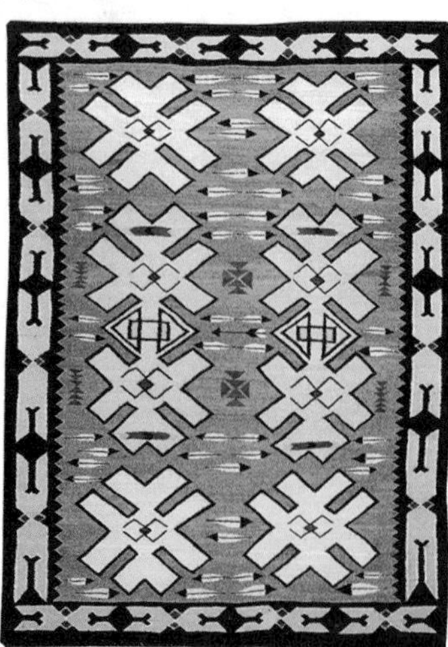

Allard Auctions

Indian, Rug, Navajo, Geometric, Stars, Diamonds, Greek Key Border, c.1935, 121 x 57 In.
$3,000

Cowan Auctions

Indian, Rug, Navajo, Raised Outline, Twill Weave, Oxblood, Gray, White, 24 x 17 ½ In.
$225

Ruby Lane

TIP

Small collectibles can be hung as window-shade pulls.

Indian, Saddlebag, Sioux, Beaded, Hide, Flags, Canvas Back, c.1910, 21 x 13 In., Pair
$5,100

Cowan Auctions

Indian, Tobacco Bag, Sioux, Hide, Beaded, Fringe, c.1885, 30 In.
$1,680

Cowan Auctions

Indian, Tomahawk, Pipe, Plains, Forged & Pierced Head, Label, Owned By Spotted Tail, 17 In.
$5,843

Skinner, Inc.

Moccasins, Blackfoot, Beaded, Geometrics, Crosses, Buffalo Hide, c.1890, 10 ½ In. ....*illus* 3321
Moccasins, Central Plains, Beaded Hide, c.1890, 10 ½ In. 1440
Moccasins, Cheyenne, Red, Yellow, Green Fringe, Beading, 10 In. 1845
Moccasins, Delaware, Beaded Hide, c.1900, Child's, 5 ½ In. 330
Moccasins, Delaware, Hide, Cloth, Silk Applique, Tulip Bead Design, 8 ½ In. 554
Moccasins, Kiowa, Red, Yellow, Green, Fringe, Seed Beads, 1900, 10 In. 1476
Moccasins, Lakota, Hide, Beaded, Buffalo Tracks, Geometrics, Cloth Lining, 10 In. ....*illus* 800
Moccasins, Sioux, Hide, Beaded, Green, Red, White, c.1910, 11 In. ....*illus* 780
Moccasins, Sioux, Hide, Fully Beaded, Blue, Red, Yellow, Geometric Designs, c.1910, 10 In. 800
Necklace, Pueblo, Turquoise, 4 Strands, Graduated, Nuggets, c.1950, 30 In. ....*illus* 677
Olla, Apache, Basket, Vertical Banding, Dog Design, Shouldered, c.1905, 14 In. 2160
Olla, Apache, Figural, Outlined, Stacked Crosses, Wolves, Dogs, c.1910, 15 x 14 In. 9225
Olla, San Ildefonso, Multicolor, Globe Shape, Spiraled Flowers, Geometric, c.1890, 10 x 12 In. .. 2760
Olla, Zuni, Pot, Painted Design, Bulbous, Cream, Brown, Orange, c.1900, 9 x 11 In. 1920
Pants, Sioux, Beaded, Buttons, Suspender Holes, Boy's, c.1890, 16 In. 3120
Pendant, Plains, Cloth, Beaded Figures, Thunderbird, Hide Strap, E. Borein, 13 In. ....*illus* 3444
Pillow, Plateau, Eagle, 32-Star Flag, Buckskin, Glass & Metallic Beads, c.1900, 18 In. ....*illus* 4305
Pin, Navajo, Silver, Turquoise & Coral Stones, Circular Pattern, 1970s, 4 ⅜ x 4 In. ....*illus* 316
Pin, Zuni, Silver, Rainbow Dancer, Mosaic Inlay, 1970s, 3 ⅜ x 1 ¾ In. ....*illus* 288
Pipe Bowl, Anishinaabe Steatite, Catlinite Inlay, Geometrics, T-Shape, c.1890, 8 x 4 In. 720
Pipe Bowl, Sioux, Catlinite, Twisted Stem, Masonic Square, Compass, c.1904, 7 x 26 In. 960
Pipe Tomahawk, Western Plains, Forged Head, Piercing, Multicolor, c.1900, 29 x 17 In. 9600
Pipe, Plains, Pewter Bowl, Ash Stem, File Branding, c.1875, 21 ½ In. 738
Pipe, Sioux, Catlinite Bowl, Quilled Stem, c.1900, 26 In. ....*illus* 2520
Pipe, Western Great Lakes, Steatite Bowl, Lead Inlay, Round Ash Stem, c.1875, 27 ½ In. 492
Pitcher, Anasazi, Chaco, Black On White, Pottery, Prehistoric, 6 x 5 In. ....*illus* 431
Pitcher, San Ildefonso, Bulbous, Loop Handle, Blackware, Avanyu Animal, c.1925, 5 In. 2271
Possible Bag, Sioux, Beaded, Quilled, Late 1800s, 15 ½ x 23 In. 1680
Post, New Mexico, Carved Wood, Scull & Crossbones, Footprints, Horse, Arrows, Paint, c.1940, 50 In. 360
Pot, Fermenting, Tarahumara, Earthenware, 13 x 14 In. 188
Pouch, Apache, Beaded, Hourglass, Fringe, 13 In. 923
Pouch, Ute, Beaded, Rounded, Geometric Patterns, White, Blue, Red, Brass Beads, 4 x 3 In. 738
Pouch, Western Plateau, Envelope Style, Parfleche, Buffalo Hide Tie, c.1890, 25 x 12 In. 1320
Quiver, Mandan, Northern Plains, Beaded Hide, Sinew Sewn, Multicolor, 45 x 26 In. 11400
Rattle, Nuu-Chah-Nulth, Wood, Multicolor Paint, c.1910, 9 In. ....*illus* 1200
Rug, Navajo, Black Border, Gray Field, 54 x 87 In. 492
Rug, Navajo, Brown, Tan, Black, Triangles, Geometric, 59 x 32 In. 187
Rug, Navajo, Feather & Water Bug, Classic Border, c.1970, 79 x 63 In. ....*illus* 1150
Rug, Navajo, Geometric, Stars, Diamonds, Greek Key Border, c.1935, 121 x 57 In. ....*illus* 3000
Rug, Navajo, Gray, Brown, Beige, Serrated Chevrons, Triangular Border, 64 x 25 In. 296
Rug, Navajo, Raised Outline, Twill Weave, Oxblood, Gray, White, 24 x 17 ½ In. ....*illus* 225
Rug, Navajo, Red, White, Brown, Tan, Diamond Step Pattern, 74 x 44 In. 830
Rug, Wheels & Heart Pattern, Red, White, c.1861, 108 x 80 In. 192
Saddlebag, Sioux, Beaded, Hide, Flags, Canvas Back, c.1910, 21 x 13 In., Pair............*illus* 5100
Saddle Blanket, Blackfoot, Beaded, Thread Sewn, Beads, Multicolor, c.1910, 48 x 31 In. 584
Saddle Blanket, Cree, Beaded Wool, Twine, Cane Beads, Tassels, Bells, c.1890, 57 x 36 In. 960
Saddle Blanket, Navajo, Eye Dazzler, Wool, Natural Dye, Multicolor, c.1920, 42 x 23 In. 276
Saddle Blanket, Navajo, Twill Weave, Red Stripes, Interlocking Diamonds, c.1810, 49 x 30 In. . 237
Santa Clara, Vase, Wedding, Matte Dragon Decoration, Glossy Black Glaze, 9 In. 188
Seed Jar, Hopi, Red & Black Paint, Cream Buff Slip, Semicircle Design, c.1890, 13 In. 3250
Seed Jar, San Ildefonso, Ball Shape, Carved, Orange, Stippled Buff Ground, c.1970, 4 In. 2629
Skirt, Anishinaabe, Black Ground, Beaded Flowers, Vining, c.1890, 31 x 33 In. 900
Society Bag, Plains, Beaded, Quilled, Buffalo Hide, Sinew Sewn, c.1890, 6 ½ x 5 In. 5400
Spoon, Bear Head Effigy, Carved Wood, Triangular Bowl, Curved Handle, c.1810, 20 In. 1185
Spoon, Great Lakes, Carved Wood, Incised Heart & Diamonds, c.1880, 8 x 2 In. 356
Spoon, Iroquois, Effigy, Walnut, Chip Carved, Stylized Bird Handle, c.1890, 10 x 4 In. 593
Spoon, Northwest Coast, Horn, Stylized Animal Head Handle, c.1875, 17 In. 984
Tobacco Bag, Blackfoot, Beaded Hide, c.1890, 28 ½ In. 900
Tobacco Bag, Cree, Beaded Hide, c.1890, 23 ½ In. 780
Tobacco Bag, Sioux, Hide, Beaded, Fringe, c.1885, 30 In. ....*illus* 1680
Tomahawk, Lakota, Bronze Head, Ash Staff, Brass Wire Wrapped, 18 ¾ In. 3444
Tomahawk, Pipe, Plains, Forged & Pierced Head, Label, Owned By Spotted Tail, 17 In. ......*illus* 5843
Totem Pole, Tlingit, Carved, Paint, Beaver Mask, Human, Hands Clasped, c.1890, 15 In. 2074
Trunk, Sioux, Parfleche, Multicolor, Geometric Patterns, c.1900, 9 x 15 In., Pair............ 4200
Vase, Acoma, Bulbous, Traditional Design, Stylized, 6 In. 464
Vase, Acoma, Shouldered, Tapered, Stylized Birds, c.1915, 9 x 11 In. 510
Vase, Zia, Birds, Leaves, Triangles, Bulbous, Tapered, Handles, Orange, c.1930, 7 In. 1554

Stolen Art & Antiques
It is said that art and antiques worth a total of $6 billion are stolen each year.

Indian, Vest, Anishinaabe, Beaded, Flowers, Leaves, Pearl Buttons, c.1900, 18 ½ x 38 In.
$1,800

Cowan Auctions

Indian, Vest, Blackfoot, Canvas, Beaded, Checkered Pattern, 2 Crosses, c.1890, 22 In.
$3,567

Skinner, Inc.

Indian, Vest, Quillwork, Indians On Horseback, Flags, Trade Cloth, 1920-30
$1,870

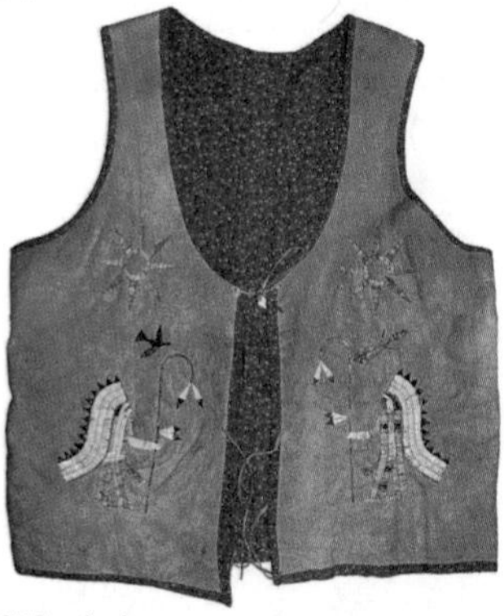

Old Barn Auctions

I

Indian, Wall Pocket, Wyandot, Beaded, Inscribed, Iriquoian, c.1890, 7 x 4 In.
$22

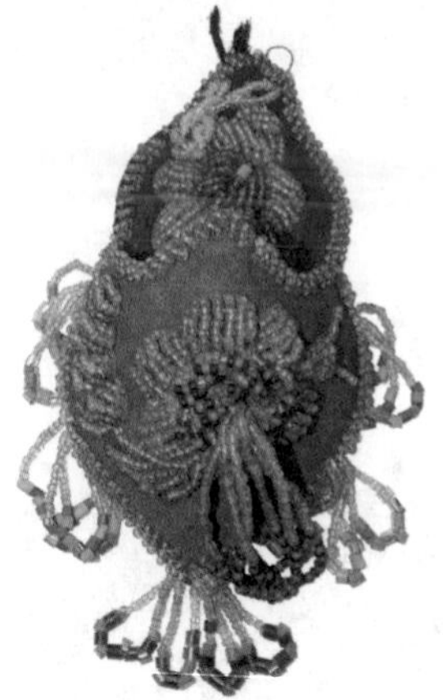

Old Barn Auctions

Indian, Weaving, Navajo, Crystal, c.1910, 73 x 47 In.
$960

Cowan Auctions

TIP

Wool weavings like Indian rugs attract moths. Wool weavings should be turned twice a year. Some say you should also spray them with moth repellent. At least put them outside in the sunlight for a few hours each summer and fall.

Vest, Anishinaabe, Beaded, Flowers, Leaves, Pearl Buttons, c.1900, 18 ½ x 38 In. ... *illus* 1800
Vest, Blackfoot, Canvas, Beaded, Checkered Pattern, 2 Crosses, c.1890, 22 In. ... *illus* 3567
Vest, Quillwork, Indians On Horseback, Flags, Trade Cloth, 1920-30 ... *illus* 1870
Wall Pocket, Wyandot, Beaded, Inscribed, Iriquoian, c.1890, 7 x 4 In. ... *illus* 22
War Bonnet, Beaded, Feathered, Red Felt, Red & Black Feathers, 62 x 15 In. ... 156
Weaving, Navajo, Crystal, c.1910, 73 x 47 In. ... *illus* 960
Weaving, Navajo, Diamonds, Triangles, Red, Yellow Black, c.1900, 89 x 56 In. ... *illus* 2040
Weaving, Navajo, Red Ground, Multicolor Designs, c.1890, 85 x 66 In. ... 1200
Weaving, Navajo, Storm Pattern, Center Figure Holding 2 Birds, c.1930, 57 x 65 In. ... 2520
Weaving, Navajo, Tan Ground, Brown Zigzag Border, Stylized Flower Design, c.1915, 98 x 63 In. ... 1020
Whimsy, Beaded Box, Purse Shape, Hot Pink, Dangles, 5 ¼ x 3 ½ In. ... *illus* 44
Whimsy, Boot Shape, Beaded, Drops, Pink, Blue, c.1865, 6 ½ x 4 ¾ In. ... *illus* 44
Whimsy, Broom Holder, Fabric, Beadwork, Scalloped Top, 1906, 8 x 8 In. ... *illus* 66
Whimsy, Comb Holder, Beaded, Happy Bay, Bird Design, c.1860, 9 x 4 ½ In. ... *illus* 44
Whimsy, Cushion, Trilobe, Beaded, Pink, Moose Head, Mohawk, 9 x 10 In. ... *illus* 44
Whimsy, Double Oval Frames, Green, Beaded, Flowerheads, 12 x 9 ½ In. ... *illus* 55
Whimsy, Horseshoe, Beaded, Brown, Good Luck From Niagara Falls, c.1900, 7 x 6 In. ... *illus* 44
Whimsy, Photo Frame, Drops, Beads, Arched Top, 1800s, 11 x 8 In. ... *illus* 77

INDIAN TREE is a china pattern that was popular during the last half of the nineteenth century. It was copied from earlier Indian textile patterns that were very similar. The pattern includes the crooked branch of a tree and a partial landscape with exotic flowers and leaves. Green, blue, pink, and orange were the favored colors used in the design. Coalport, Spode, Johnson Brothers, and other firms made this pottery.

Berry Bowl, Warwick, 5 ½ In. ... 18
Bowl, Cereal, Meakin, 6 ¼ In. ... 12
Bowl, Vegetable, Lid, Round, Meakin ... 75
Bowl, Vegetable, Oval, Aynsley, 10 In. ... 45
Bowl, Vegetable, Oval, Salem, 9 In. ... 17
Bowl, Vegetable, Round, Pink, Syracuse, 7 In. ... 23
Bowl, Vegetable, Round, Scalloped, Royal Doulton, 9 ½ In. ... 135
Chop Plate, Pink, Syracuse, 12 In. ... 86
Chop Plate, Scalloped, Royal Doulton, 12 In. ... 175
Coffeepot, Lid, Aynsley, 5 Cup, 7 ⅜ In. ... 182
Creamer, Beaded, Coalport, 3 ⅜ In. ... 50
Creamer, Spode, 3 In. ... 77
Cup & Saucer, Coalport ... 10
Cup & Saucer, Demitasse, Minton ... 28
Cup & Saucer, Footed, Noritake ... 23
Cup & Saucer, Footed, Orange, Spode ... 33
Cup & Saucer, Footed, Royal Doulton ... 24
Cup & Saucer, Footed, Royal Grafton ... 41
Cup & Saucer, Green Key, Ridgway ... 11
Cup & Saucer, Johnson Brothers ... 10
Cup & Saucer, Maruta ... 15
Cup & Saucer, Meakin ... 12
Cup & Saucer, Pink, Syracuse ... 13
Cup & Saucer, Salem ... 11
Cup & Saucer, Scalloped, Coral, Coalport ... 29
Gravy Boat, Underplate, Aynsley ... 191
Gravy Boat, Underplate, Meakin ... 42
Plate, Bread & Butter, Aynsley, 6 ½ In. ... 8
Plate, Bread & Butter, Beaded, Coalport, 6 In. ... 8
Plate, Dinner, Gold Trim, Aynsley, 10 ½ In. ... 36
Plate, Dinner, Meakin, 10 In. ... 9
Plate, Dinner, Minton, 9 ¾ In. ... 76
Plate, Dinner, Plate, Johnson Brothers, 10 In. ... 23
Plate, Dinner, Ribbed Rim, Orange, Spode, 10 ¼ In. ... 60
Plate, Dinner, Ridgway, 10 In. ... 8
Plate, Dinner, Scalloped, Coral, Coalport, 10 In. ... 54
Plate, Dinner, Scalloped, Royal Doulton, 10 ¾ In. ... 31
Plate, Luncheon, Coral, Coalport, 9 In. ... 9
Plate, Luncheon, Gold Trim, Aynsley, 8 ¼ In. ... 13
Plate, Luncheon, Johnson Brothers, 9 In. ... 15
Plate, Luncheon, Noritake, 8 ¾ In. ... 13
Plate, Luncheon, Scalloped, Royal Grafton, 8 ¾ In. ... 8

Indian, Weaving, Navajo, Diamonds, Triangles, Red, Yellow Black, c.1900, 89 x 56 In.
$2,040

Cowan Auctions

Indian, Whimsy, Beaded Box, Purse Shape, Hot Pink, Dangles, 5 ¼ x 3 ½ In.
$44

Old Barn Auctions

Indian, Whimsy, Boot Shape, Beaded, Drops, Pink, Blue, c.1865, 6 ½ x 4 ¾ In.
$44

Old Barn Auctions

Indian, Whimsy, Broom Holder, Fabric, Beadwork, Scalloped Top, 1906, 8 x 8 In.
$66

Old Barn Auctions

Indian, Whimsy, Comb Holder, Beaded, Happy Bay, Bird Design, c.1860, 9 x 4 ½ In.
$44

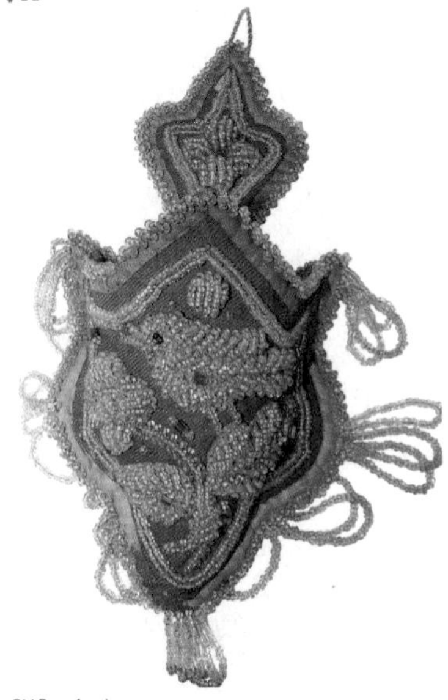

Old Barn Auctions

Indian, Whimsy, Cushion, Trilobe, Beaded, Pink, Moose Head, Mohawk, 9 x 10 In.
$44

Old Barn Auctions

Indian, Whimsy, Double Oval Frames, Green, Beaded, Flowerheads, 12 x 9 ½ In.
$55

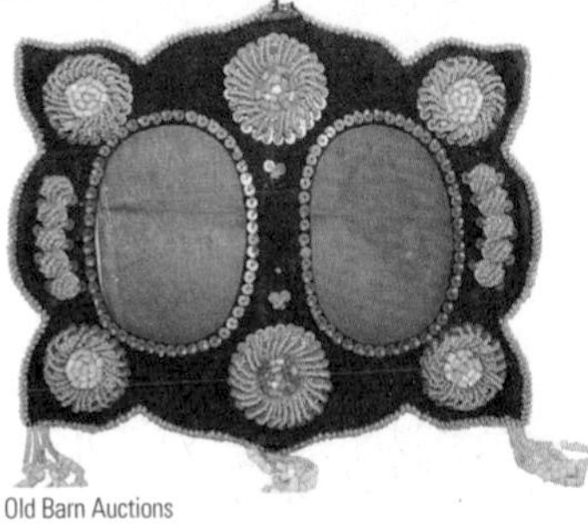

Old Barn Auctions

Indian, Whimsy, Horseshoe, Beaded, Brown, Good Luck From Niagara Falls, c.1900, 7 x 6 In.
$44

Old Barn Auctions

Indian, Whimsy, Photo Frame, Drops, Beads, Arched Top, 1800s, 11 x 8 In.
$77

Old Barn Auctions

I

Indian Tree, Teapot, Lid, Spode, c.1730, 6 ½ In.
$185

Ruby Lane

Inkstand, Mahogany, Brass, Standish, Cut Glass Wells, Bronze Lids, Regency, c.1815, 7 x 14 In.
$359

Neal Auctions

Inkwell, Figural, Dog, Glass Eyes, Hinged Lid, Terra-Cotta, c.1890, 5 ½ In.
$676

Ruby Lane

Insulator, H.G. Co., Petticoat, Beehive, Purple, CS145
$2,200

Open-Wire Insulator Services

Plate, Luncheon, Wedgwood, 9 In. 38
Plate, Salad, Coral, Coalport, 8 In. 31
Platter, Oval, Aynsley, 15 In. 112
Platter, Oval, Meakin, 16 In. 72
Platter, Oval, Minton, 21 In. 332
Platter, Oval, Scalloped, Brown, Maruta, 12 In. 55
Relish, Pink, Syracuse, 8 In. 18
Teapot, Lid, Spode, c.1730, 6 ½ In. .... *illus* 185

INKSTANDS were made to be placed on a desk. They held some type of container for ink, and possibly a sander, a pen tray, a pen, a holder for pounce, and even a candle to melt the sealing wax. Inkstands date to the eighteenth century and have been made of silver, copper, ceramics, and glass. Additional inkstands may be found in these and other related categories.

2 Pheasants, Long Tail Feathers, Elongated Niche, 2 Wells, Austria, 8 x 21 In. 968
Boulle, Double, Standish, Curved Pen Tray, Glass Wells, Footed, 14 x 8 In. 266
Brass, Art Nouveau, 2 Wells, Pen Rest, Hinged Lids, Geschultz, c.1895, 14 x 6 In. 591
Brass, Emu Egg, Figures, Emu, Kangaroo, Chased, c.1920, 11 In. 246
Brass, Inlay, 2 Wells, 1 Drawer, England, 1800s, 14 ½ x 9 In. 118
Brass, Oak, Blue Jasper Blotter, Strapwork Design, Glass Wells, Plaque, 13 In. 989
Brass, Standish, Quill Holder, 2 Covered Wells, Acorn Finials, Peg Feet, 7 In. 185
Bronze, Encrier, Stand, Pounce Pot, Quill Compartments, Dome Lid, 15 x 7 In. 212
Bronze, Figure, Slate Base, 2 Inkwells, 11 ½ x 14 ½ In. 246
Bronze, Gilt Wells, Encrier, Tomb Of Lorenzo De Medici, c.1900, 23 x 30 In. 562
Bronze, Rooster, Fence, 2 Wells, A. Bossu, 11 x 6 In. 195
Gilt Bronze, Marble, Empire, Pen Holder, Eagle Finial, 16 ½ In. 469
Gilt Bronze, Standish, Empire Style, Classical Bust, Marble Plinth, 1800s, 8 In. 246
Gilt Metal, 2 Wells, Footed, France, c.1900, 9 In. 72
Iron, Postal Scale, Judd Mfg. Co., 1880s, 7 x 6 In. 105
Mahogany, Brass, Standish, Cut Glass Wells, Bronze Lids, Regency, c.1815, 7 x 14 In. .... *illus* 359
Mother-Of-Pearl Inlay, Black, Gilt, Papier-Mache, 2 Wells, c.1850, 29 x 15 In. 478
Pewter, Double Hinged Lid, Interior Compartments, Footed, 1800s, 7 x 5 In. 130
Porcelain, Flower Crusted, 2 Wells, Lids, Green, Pink, Yellow, 8 ⅝ In. 215
Silver Plate, 2 Wells, Heraldic Crest, 3 ½ x 6 ½ In. 94
Silver Plate, Standish, Stepped, Bun Feet, Acorn Finial, Crest, 1800s, 7 x 4 In. 75
Silver, 2 Crystal Wells, Sheffield, England, 1870s, 5 ½ x 12 In. 575
Tortoiseshell, Brass Monkey & Bird, Drawer, Leaf Handles, Claw Feet, 7 x 20 In. 600
Wood, Ebonized, Brass Handle, Grape Leaves, Drawers, Bun Feet, 6 ½ x 13 In. 181

INKWELLS, of course, held ink. Ready-made ink was first made about 1836 and was sold in bottles. The desk inkwell had a narrow hole so the pen would not slip inside. Inkwells were made of many materials, such as pottery, glass, pewter, and silver. Look in these categories for more listings of inkwells.

Art Deco, Copper Colored, Footed, Flip Lid, Jennings Brothers, 4 x 4 x 2 In. 60
Black Forest, Doberman Head, Carved, Lourdes, 1800s, 4 x 3 x 4 In. 335
Black Man, Short Hair & Beard, Straw Hat, Austria, 3 ½ x 4 ½ In. 484
Bleu De Hue Style, Blue, White, Asian Men In Garden, c.1900, 3 x 5 In. 125
Brass, Cockatoo Shape, Gilt, Round Leaf Base, Urn, Masks, 7 x 3 ½ In. 275
Brass, Coconut Shell, Indian, Sitting Cross Legged, Club, Bell, 7 x 6 In. 1867
Brass, Crane Shape Supports, Round Base, 7 ½ In. 210
Brass, Stand, Flowers, Scrolls, Glass, Beveled Glass, Waffled, 3 ½ x 2 ¾ In. 100
Bronze, Art Nouveau, Square, Hinged, Peacock, Star, Pinecones, 5 x 5 x 4 In. 165
Bronze, Bust, Yaroslav The Wise, Grand Prince Of Kiev, Hinged, Marble Base, 7 In. 144
Bronze, Cat's Head, Open Mouth, Teeth Showing, Hinged Neck, Bow, c.1910, 4 In. 677
Bronze, Crab, Hinged Shell, 1910, 7 ½ x 7 In. 5490
Bronze, Dionysus, Vases, c.1880, 14 x 7 x 10 In. 210
Bronze, Figural, Armadillo, 3 ½ x 7 In. 720
Bronze, Fish, Carp, 8 ½ In. 369
Bronze, Owl, Bat, Cold Painted, 5 In. 149
Bronze, Pottery, Oval, Scalloped, Sailing Ships, Sea Gulls, 6 x 15 ½ In. 1210
Ceramic, 2 Nude Women, Reclining, Blue High Glaze, c.1926, 3 x 10 In. 161
Clambroth Glass, White, Stopper, 5 x 4 In. 12
Copper Overlay, Lid, Art Nouveau, Curves, c.1900, 5 x 3 x 3 In. 475
Copper, Glass, Cylindrical, Pierced Lid, Spread Foot, Repousse, 7 x 1 ½ In. 589
Enamel, Bell Shape, Flower Finial, Hinged Metal Lid, Cherry Blossoms, 3 ½ In. 232

Figural, Dog, Glass Eyes, Hinged Lid, Terra-Cotta, c.1890, 5 ½ In. ... *illus*	676
Gilt Bronze, Baby & Cabbage, Movable Arms, Milk Glass, Tripod Base, 4 In.	649
Gilt Bronze, Marble, Encrier, Eagle, 2 Wells, 8 x 15 In.	469
Gilt Bronze, Neoclassical, Relief, Long Necked Bird At Corners, 4 x 3 In.	225
Gilt, Art Nouveau, Head Of Woman At Corner, Flowing Hair, 11 x 3 In.	118
Glass, Bohemian, Round Knob Top, Purple Iridescent, Wilhelm Kralik, 4 ½ In.	484
Glass, Dark Olive, 3 Mold, Diamond Pattern, Round, 1 ½ x 2 In.	118
Glass, Iridescent, Ice Pack Shape, Brass Mounted, 4 x 6 In.	60
Hobnail, Wheel Cut, Brass, Brass Hinged Top, 5 In.	275
Iron, Bronze, U.S. Mail, 2 Dogs By Mailbox, Lift Front, 5 ½ In.	100
Iron, Turtle, Black Boy, Riding Back Finial, Red Cap, Red Shell, 5 In.	240
Pewter, Art Nouveau, Signed Pierre-Adrien Dalpayrat, France, 3 In.	708
Porcelain, Oak Leaves & Acorn, Round Dish, Lid, Green Glaze, 1904, 5 In.	219
Porcelain, Putti, Two Baskets, White, Italy, 5 In.	38
Silver Plate, Eagle's Head, Beaded Edge, Drawer, Hinged Lid, England, 4 ½ x 3 In.	72
Silver Plate, Steel, Horse Hoof, Rearing Horse Finial, England, 1899, 5 ½ In.	219
Silver, Deer Antler Finial, 2 Beavers, 4 Ball Feet, Russia, 3 In.	800
Silver, Square Base, Lid, Floral Repousse, Jacobi & Jenkins, 3 x 6 In.	118
Silver, Water Lily, Round Base, Lily Pads, Blossom, Bud, 1839, 7 In.	2342
Spelter, Patina, Mahogany, Alligator Penholders, 1800s, 7 x 5 In.	185
Steel, Medieval Helmet, Pierced Visor, Cut & Chased, Shield Base, 6 x 7 In.	375
Tortoiseshell, Red, Cut Glass, Inlaid Lid, Dished Stand, 4 ½ x 9 In.	1277
Wood, Blackamoor Head, Carved, Painted, Glass Eyes, Porcelain Pot, c.1890, 6 x 5 In.	984
Wood, Turned & Painted, Stenciled Eagles, 6 Quill Holes, c.1850, 3 ½ In.	738

INSULATORS of glass or pottery have been made for use on telegraph or telephone poles since 1844. Thousands of styles of insulators have been made. Most common are those of clear or aqua glass; most desirable are the threadless types made from 1850 to 1870.

Brookfield, No. 9, Dark Olive Amber	67
Brookfield, No. 9, Green & Amber	22
Brookfield, No. 9, New York, Light Amethyst	34
California, Amethyst, Green Streaks	952
Diamond, Amethyst	392
Diamond, Dark Royal Purple	112
Diamond, Light Green	33
E.C. & M. Co. SF, Cobalt Blue	1045
F.M. Locke, Blue Aqua	3245
H.G. Co. Natco, Peacock Blue	1265
H.G. Co., Petticoat, Beehive, Purple, CS145 ... *illus*	2200
Hemingray, D-512, Rainbow Carnival Iridescent	101
Hemingray, Mickey Mouse, Aqua, Milky Swirls ... *illus*	418
Hemingray, No. 19, Cobalt Blue, Embossed USA	179
Hemingray, No. 19, Golden Amber, Embossed USA	100
Hemingray, No. 19, Purple, No Name	146
Hemingray, No. 19, Sapphire Blue, Embossed Made In USA	532
Hemingray, Yellow Olive Green, Pat. 1893	1485
Lowex, 512, Bubbly Amber	45
Mulford & Biddle, U.P.R.R., Threadless, Dark Blue, Embossed, c.1867	1925
Patent, Reversed Letters, Yellow Olive, Cone Shape, Bulbous Neck Ring, 5 In.	761
Pierce, Pluto, Aqua, 1890s	3740
Porcelain, Cooke's Sleeve, England, 1845 ... *illus*	320
Westinghouse, Aqua, Dome Bubble	605

IRISH BELLEEK, *see Belleek category.*

IRON is a metal that has been used by man since prehistoric times. It is a popular metal for tools and decorative items like doorstops that need as much weight as possible. Items are listed here or under other appropriate headings, such as Bookends, Doorstop, Kitchen, Match Holder, or Tool. The tool that is used for ironing clothes, an iron, is listed in the Kitchen category under Iron and Sadiron.

Anvil, Jeweler's, 1800s, Black, Rust, 4 ¾ x 1 ½ In.	35
Ashtray, Isamu Noguchi, Rounded Triangle Shape, c.1957, 7 ¾ x 8 In.	12150
Book Press, Incised Decoration, France, 1800s, 14 x 12 In.	49
Book Press, Plate, Wheel, Wood, c.1895, 14 ¼ x 11 In.	154
Bootjack, Bull Head, 1930, 10 ¼ x 4 ⅔ In.	40

Insulator, Hemingray, Mickey Mouse, Aqua, Milky Swirls
$418

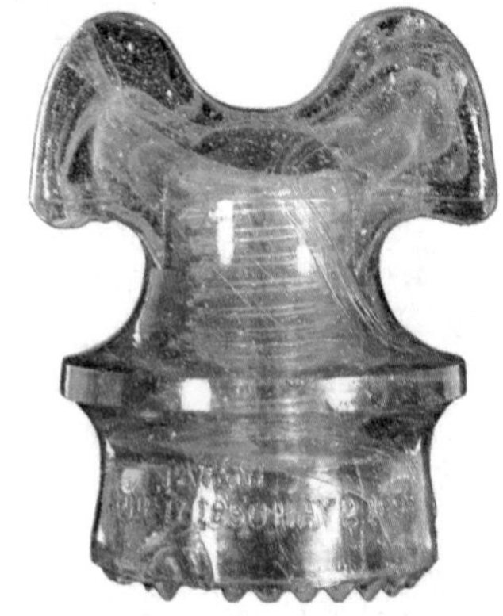

Bill + Jill Insulators

Insulator, Porcelain, Cooke's Sleeve, England, 1845
$320

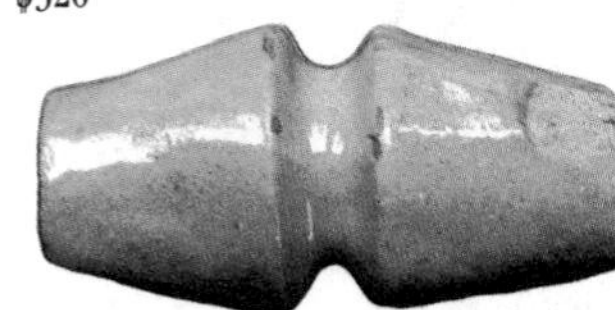

Eagle Cap Collection Auction

Iron, Bootjack, Naughty Nellie, 10 In.
$270

Showtime Auction Services

TIP

Don't brag about the value of your collection to strangers. It might lead to extra interest by the local burglary groups.

Iron, Figure, Cadeau, Man Ray, Brass Nails On Sole, Signed, 1974, 7 In.
$1,750

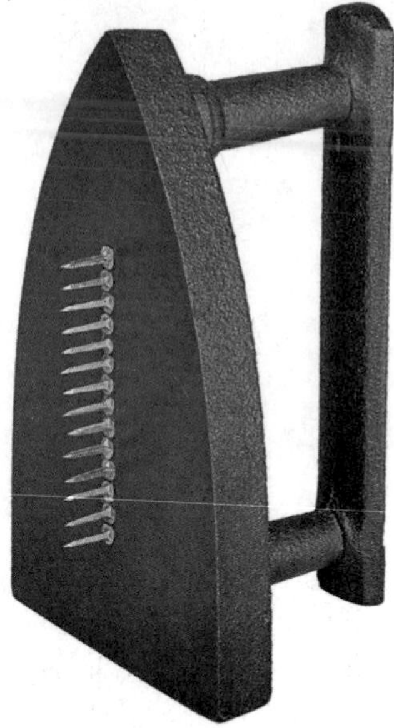

Rago Arts and Auction Center

Iron, Figure, Eagle, Base, Cast, 1700s, 10 x 16 ½ In.
$3,650

Ruby Lane

Iron, Grid, Rotating, Round, Wrought, 1800s, 28 x 11 ½ In.
$142

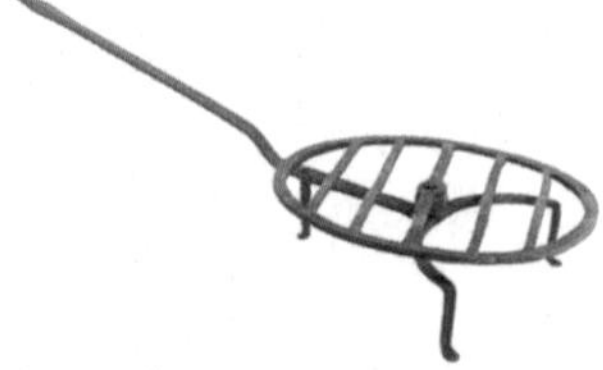

Hess Auction Group

Bootjack, Naughty Nellie, 10 In. .... *illus* 270
Bootjack, Naughty Nellie, Paint, Reclining Woman, Legs Spread, c.1900, 10 ½ In. 224
Bowl, Starburst, 1900s, 11 ½ x 22 ½ In. 1375
Box, Crusades Scene, Soldiers, Praying, Wood Interior, Denmark, 3 ½ x 8¾ In. 112
Brackets, Openwork, 1800s, 53 x 40 ½ In. 643
Bucket, Wrought Handle, Brass Pail, Copper Rivets, Rolled Rim, c.1800, 10 In. 354
Buddha, Standing, Chinese, 25 In. 300
Call Box, Police & Telegram, Blue Paint, Gamewell Co., New York, 19 ½ In. 177
Candleholder, Revolving Top, Rivets, Wrought, 54 In. 1751
Cannon Packer Ball, Chain, Loop Handle, 1800's, 42 In. 395
Cigar Cutter, Woman, Dress, Bustled, 2 In. 330
Cover, Coal Chute, Concentric Circles, Address Marked, Round, 18 In. 300
Cover, Coal Chute, Concentric Rings Of Circles, Round, 16 In. 210
Cover, Coal Chute, Concentric Rings Of Rectangles, 17 ½ In. 270
Cover, Coal Chute, Concentric Rings, Round, Adam Happel Inc., 17 ¼ In. 420
Cover, Coal Chute, Overlapping Rings, Round, 7 Worth St., 17 ½ In. 390
Cross, Mary, Open Work, Angels, Wood Base, 49 x 24 In. 522
Crown Hook, 8 Hooks, Standing Doves, Pierced Tails, Scrollwork, 11 x 14 In. 425
Figure, Cadeau, Man Ray, Brass Nails On Sole, Signed, 1974, 7 In. .... *illus* 1750
Figure, Eagle, Base, Cast, 1700s, 10 x 16 ½ In. .... *illus* 3650
Figure, Horse Head, Bit For Attaching Reins, Wood Wall Plaque, c.1890, 12 In. 420
Figure, Majordomo, Servant, Full Uniform, Judd Co., 8 In. 443
Figure, Rabbit, Seated, Fur Details, White Paint, Gray Eyes, c.1930, 12 x 11 In. 185
Gong, Handwrought, Peel Shape, Inverted Heart Shape, 1700s, 18 ½ In. 295
Grid, Rotating, Round, Wrought, 1800s, 28 x 11 ½ In. .... *illus* 142
Jug, Enamel, Blue, Handle, Spigot, 18 x 19 In 85
Manhole Cover, Map Of Chandigarh, India, Inscribed, Le Corbusier, c.1960, 25 x 4 In. ..... *illus* 4375
Ornament, Cross, Angels, Heart, Display Case, France, 36 x 18 In. .... *illus* 593
Panel, Oak Leaf, Acorns, 28 x 10 ½ In. 720
Room Heater, 8-Sided, Enameled, Chinoiserie, Bamboo, Ruby Glass, c.1890, 33 x 17 In. 369
Safe, Black Alpine, Wheels, Paint, Boat Scene, c.1890, 18 x 19 x 28 In. 420
Safe, Central Safe Co., Gray, Steel Wheels, Rolls Sideways, 20 x 17 x 28 In. 210
Safe, Floor, York Safe & Lock Co., c.1900, 29 x 20 x 19 In. 1350
Safe, Landscape, Combination, Alpine Safe & Lock Co., Ohio, c.1888, 28 x 18 In. 420
Sculpture, 4 Evangelists, Octagonal Base, Square Foot, Paint, c.1875, 28 In., 4 Piece 1770
Sculpture, Abstract, Crown Of Standing Biomorphic Figures, 17 x 8 ½ In. 1476
Sculpture, Abstract, Wood Base, Incised, Warren, 1965, 20 In. 968
Sculpture, Czar, Marble Base, Russia, c.1875, 15 In. 1599
Sculpture, Dancers, Holding Hands, Circle, 17 ½ x 20 In. 400
Sculpture, Eagle, Gilt, Spread Wings, Wood Base, 1800s, 16 x 31 In. 400
Sculpture, Eagle, Pole Top, Spread Wings, Head Turned, Perched, c.1800s, 15 x 15 In. 1067
Sculpture, Eagle, Spread Wings, Head Turned, Gilt, Embossed, c.1800, 35 x 57 In. 7110
Sculpture, Eagle, Standing, Spread Wings, 42 x 80 In. 5625
Sculpture, Eagle, Wings Spread, Crag, 19 In., Pair 234
Sculpture, Face, Wavy Hair, Scarf, White, 11 ½ x 20 In. 409
Sculpture, Hand, Straight Fingers, 1900s, 16 x 6 ½ In. 272
Sculpture, Horse Head, Mahogany Pedestal, c.1900, 58 x 15 ¼ In. 854
Sculpture, Horse Head, Steeplechase, Green & Yellow Paint, 12 x 21 In. 236
Sculpture, Lion, Lying Down, England, 15 x 27 In. 450
Sculpture, North Wind God, 17 x 25 In. 351
Sculpture, North Wind God, Painted White, 21 x 25 In., Pair 82
Sculpture, Snake, Coiled Tail, Wrought, 1800s, 24 In. 3540
Sculpture, Steer Head, White, 19 x 8 In. 351
Sculpture, Top Hat, 1920s, 11 x 15 In. 760
Shooting Gallery Target, Eagle, H.C. Evans & Co., 13 x 10 In. 936
Star, Pierced, 8 In., 16 Piece 47
Stringholder, Ice Skater, Raised Arm & Leg, Fence, Judd Co., 7 In. 1416
Stringholder, Woman At Mirror, Long White Dress, Judd Co., 8 In. 1062
Teapot, Arari Kama, Hobnail, 6 x 7 In. 24
Teapot, Lid, Longevity Crane, Flowers, Bronze, Mixed Metal, Japan, c.1850, 8 In. .... *illus* 533
Teapot, Square, Lid, Hut, Mountain, Monk, Cliff, Handle, Japan, c.1950, 8 In. 533
Teapot, Tetsubin, Handle, Round, Bird, Trees, Brass Lid, Japan, 9 x 8 In. 154
Wall Pocket, Cherub, Leaves, 19 x 15 In. 61
Weight, Duck Shape, Surface Oxidation, c.1900, 8 ½ x 16 In. 554
Windmill Weight, Buffalo, 11 x 15 ½ In. 585
Windmill Weight, Crescent Moon, Eclipse, Stand, Fairbanks, Morse & Co., Chicago, 10 In. 1288

Windmill Weight, Dempster Horse, Black, c.1910, 12 x 16½ In. 292
Windmill Weight, Dempster Horse, White, c.1910, 11 x 15½ In. 292
Windmill Weight, Eagle, 15 x 7 In. 936
Windmill Weight, Horse, Painted, White, Green Base, Dempster Mill Manu. Co., 18 In. 523
Windmill Weight, Horse, Standing, Base, 1800s, 17 x 18 In. 384
Windmill Weight, Horseshoe, 12 x 8 In. 1755
Windmill Weight, Rooster, 21 x 19 In. 205
Windmill Weight, Rooster, Elgin Wind Power & Pump, 17 x 20 In. 1287
Windmill Weight, Rooster, Hummer E 184, Elgin Wind Power & Pump, c.1900, 10 In. ......*illus* 474
Windmill Weight, Rooster, Paint, Rainbow Tail, Elgin Wind Power & Pump Co., Ill., 19 In. 738
Windmill Weight, Rooster, Painted, Black, Red & Yellow Head, Elgin Wind Power, 18 In. 1722
Windmill Weight, Star, U.S. Wind Engine & Pump Co., Batavia, Ill., c.1900, Stand, 14 In. 738
Wreath, Laurel, Painted White, 28 x 23 In., Pair 117

IRONSTONE china was first made in 1813. It gained its greatest popularity during the mid-nineteenth century. The heavy, durable, off-white pottery was made in white or was decorated with any of hundreds of patterns. Much flow blue pottery was made of ironstone. Some of the decorations were raised. Many pieces of ironstone are unmarked, but some English and American factories included the word *Ironstone* in their marks. Additional pieces may be listed in other categories, such as Chelsea Grape, Chelsea Sprig, Flow Blue, Gaudy Ironstone, Mason's Ironstone, Staffordshire, and Tea Leaf Ironstone.

Basin, Side Handles, 1800s, 20½ x 12½ In 321
Bowl, Flow Blue Transfer, Reticulated, Lion Paw Feet, Wide Wavy Rim, 5 x 9 In. 1888
Coffeepot, Blue Wheat Pattern, Ceres Shape, Elsmore & Forster, 10 In. ....*illus* 106
Dispenser, Sherry In Cartouche, Burgundy, Gold Trim, Barrel Form, Oval, Bung, 13 x 12 In. 180
Mug, Peg Tops, 3 Children Spinning Tops, Painted, Child's, 2⅝ In. ....*illus* 59
Pitcher, Red & Blue Flowers, Vines, Trees, Octagonal, 10 In. 85
Plate, Alphabet, Nursery Tales, Old Mother Hubbard, Transfer, England, 7 In. ....*illus* 118
Plate, Butcher Shop Advertising, Tongue, Edwardian, c.1910, 11 In. 120
Plate, Crusoe Viewing The Island, Alphabet Border, Boat, Sailor, Signed, 8 In. Diam. 83
Platter, Black & White, Grisaille, Narrows From Port Hamilton, 1800s, 13 x 17 In. 86
Platter, Flow Blue Transfer, Hong Kong, 12 x 16 In. ....*illus* 236
Platter, Flow Blue, 14 x 12 In. 60
Platter, No. 2, Oval, Impressed Elsmore & Foster, 14¾ x 19 In. 30
Platter, Shaped Rim, Blue & White, Flowers & Leaves Border, c.1910, 16 x 12 In. 44
Potpourri, Cream Glaze, Reticulated, Lovebirds, Bouquet Finial, Handles, 13 x 13 In. 354
Syrup, Pewter Lid, Flow Blue Transfer, Lobed, Saucer Foot, Loop Handle, 7 x 9 In. 106
Tureen, Dome Lid, Flow Blue Transfer, Spread Foot, Oval, Loop Handle, 6 x 11 In. 472
Tureen, Underplate, Double Handles, Imari Style, Gilt Scrolling, 12 x 13 In. 115

ISPANKY figurines were designed by Laszlo Ispanky, who began his American career as a designer for Cybis Porcelains. In 1966, he established his own studio in Pennington, New Jersey; since 1976, he has worked for Goebel of North America. He works in stone, wood, or metal, as well as porcelain. The first limited edition figurines were issued in 1966.

Bust, Serenity, Blond, Cape, c.1970, 4½ In. 45
Figurine, Cinderella, Scrubbing Floor, Bucket, Numbered, 1960s, 12 x 8 In. 650
Figurine, Girl, Sitting, Blond Braids, Hat, Flowers On Lap, 8 In. 250
Figurine, Woman, Seminude, Brown Hair, Flowing Hair Ribbon, Necklace, 8 In. 100
Figurine, Woman, Yellow Dress, Cape, Tree Stump, 9 In. 60
Vase, 2 Seminudes, Panels, Square, 1950s, 11 x 6 In. 125

IVORY from the tusk of an elephant is thought by many to be the only true ivory. To most collectors, the term *ivory* also includes such natural materials as walrus, hippopotamus, or whale teeth or tusks, and some of the vegetable materials that are of similar texture and density. Other ivory items may be found in the Scrimshaw and Netsuke categories. Collectors should be aware of the recent laws limiting the buying and selling of elephant ivory and scrimshaw.

Box, Carved Peonies, Wicker Body, Chrysanthemum Lid, Japan, 1800s, 7 x 4 In. 1599
Box, Prisoner-Of-War, Filigree, Multicolor Ink, Hinged Lid, Handle, c.1810, 3 x 6 In. 480
Card Case, Foo Dogs, Deer, Monkeys, Cranes, Village Scene, Carved, 1800s, 4 In. 1558
Carving, Village Scene, Reticulated, Figures, Boats, Trees, Pagodas, 7 x 15 In. 738
Clamshell, Figures Inside, Japan, 1¼ x 3 In. 156
Fan, Brise, Birds, Flowers, Mother-Of-Pearl & Bronze Pin, Pierced Leaves, 1800s, 10 In. 818
Figurine, Bridge, Dragons, Scroll, Openwork, Carved, 1800s, 9 In. 185
Figurine, Crucifix, Head Back, c.1790, 11 In. 2140

Iron, Manhole Cover, Map Of Chandigarh, India, Inscribed, Le Corbusier, c.1960, 25 x 4 In.
$4,375

Rago Arts and Auction Center

TIP
To clean small pieces of iron, try soaking them in white vinegar for 24 to 48 hours.

Iron, Ornament, Cross, Angels, Heart, Display Case, France, 36 x 18 In.
$593

New Orleans (Cakebread)

TIP
Ivory will darken if kept in the dark. Keep a piano open so the keys will be in natural light. Keep figurines, chess sets, and other ivory in the open.

Iron, Teapot, Lid, Longevity Crane, Flowers, Bronze, Mixed Metal, Japan, c.1850, 8 In.
$533

James D. Julia Auctioneers

TIP
Never use chlorine bleach on ironstone dishes. It will cause the glaze to flake off.

Iron, Windmill Weight, Rooster, Hummer E 184, Elgin Wind Power & Pump, c.1900, 10 In.
$474

James D. Julia Auctioneers

Ironstone, Coffeepot, Blue Wheat Pattern, Ceres Shape, Elsmore & Forster, 10 In.
$106

Hess Auction Group

Figurine, Crucifix, Head Hung Low, 1700s, 9 ½ In. 1556
Figurine, Fisherman, Heavy Net, Japan, 1900s, 6 x 2 ¼ In. 460
Figurine, Geisha, Bondage, Erotica, 1900s, 6 x 2 ½ In. 258
Figurine, Geisha, Wrapped Box, Fruit Basket, Multicolor, Japan, 9 x 3 In. 345
Figurine, Horse, Walking, Head Down, Stand, Chinese, 2 x 3 In. 48
Figurine, Jesus, Corpus Christi, 7 ½ In. 625
Figurine, Man, 2 Boys, Feeding Chickens, Basket, Round Carved Base, 6 In. 1013
Figurine, Man, Asian, 6 x 2 In. 69
Figurine, Man, Skeleton, Seated, Holding Necklace, 1900s, Chinese, 4 ½ In. 184
Figurine, Man, Toy, Robes, Japan, 2 x 1 ½ In. 120
Figurine, Queen Elizabeth, Standing, Holding Orb, Continental, Carved, 1800s, 13 In. 1680
Figurine, Saint George, Dragon, Horse, Spear, 9 x 5 ½ In. 540
Figurine, Seated Buddha, Chinese, 1800s, 5 x 4 In. 488
Figurine, Ship, Wood Base, 5 x 10 In. 488
Figurine, Silver Mount, Virgin, Winged Cherub On Base, Portugal, 8 ½ In. 1000
Figurine, Woman Holding Chrysanthemum Flower, Stand, Chinese, 10 In. 240
Figurine, Woman, Geisha, Parasol, Carved, 7 ½ x 2 ¼ In. 1220
Group, 3 Immortals, Stepped Plaza, Wood, Chinese, 1900s, 16 x 17 ¾ In. 920
Group, Father & Son, Bald, Sandals, 5 ½ x 2 ½ In. 258
Group, Indian Royalty In Howdah, Elephant, 1900s, 6 ¾ x 2 ¼ In. 402
Mystery Ball, Carved, Flowers, Dragons, Reticulated, c.1900, 2 ½ In. Diam. 253
Okimono, Carved Figure, Ono, Gathering Of Demons, Rocks, Octopus, 5 ½ In. 1558
Okimono, Carved Figure, Skeleton, 2 Toads, Monkey, Skull, Lotus Leaf, c.1900, 3 In. 1968
Panel, Joined, Triumph Of Poseidon, Austria, 1700s, 11 x 14 ½ In. 8750
Pipe, Dragon, 1900s, 1 ½ x 6 In. 95
Plaque, Marriage Of Mary & Joseph, France, 1800s, 8 ½ x 12 In. 1000
Scepter, Masks, Teeth, Africa, 55 ¼ x 4 In. 2400
Tree, Flowers, Chinese, 1800s, 9 ½ x 2 ½ In. 276
Triptych, Figural, Mary Queen Of Scotts, Skirts Open, Attendants Pledging, 7 ¾ In. 3750
Triptych, Figural, St. Joan Of Arc, Armor Suit Opens, Scenes Of Life, 8 ½ In. 2750
Triptych, Figural, Virgin & Child, Robes Open, Christ Carrying Cross, 8 In. 3750
Triptych, St. John The Baptist, St. Claire, France, 1800s, 4 ¼ x 5 ¼ In. 813
Tusk, African Elephant, Nude Woman, Palm Trees, Stepped Wood Base, 30 x 3 In. 492
Tusk, Carved, Water Buffalo, Elephant, Rhinoceros, Lion, 3 x 7 ¾ In. 316
Tusk, Elephant, Village Scene No. 1, Cameroon, 26 ½ x 5 In. 126
Tusk, Elephant, Village Scene No. 2, Cameroon, 27 x 4 In. 172
Tusk, Hide, Wood, Man, 42 x 5 ½ In. 540
Vase, Pierced Diaperwork, Spread Rim, Handles, Hexagonal, Scroll Base, 1800s, 8 In. 194

JACK-IN-THE-PULPIT vases, shaped like trumpets, resemble the wildflower named jack-in-the-pulpit. The design originated in the late Victorian years. Vases in the jack-in-the-pulpit shape were made of ceramic or glass.

Vase, Cobalt Blue, Green, Craquelle Border, Rainbow Colors, 12 x 9 In. 115
Vase, Golden Aurene, Drizzled Web Design, Craquelle, 12 x 8 In. 345
Vase, Pulled Feather, Green, Gold Over White, Ruffled, Craquelle, 10 In. 374

JADE is the name for two different minerals, nephrite and jadeite. Nephrite is the mineral used for most early Oriental carvings. Jade is a very tough stone that is found in many colors from dark green to pale lavender. Jade carvings are still being made in the old styles, so collectors must be careful not to be fooled by recent pieces. Jade jewelry is found in this book under Jewelry.

Amulet, Carved, Reticulated, Lotus Flower, Characters, Wood Stand, 2 ¼ In. 224
Animal, White, Qilin, 2 ½ In. 5625
Archer's Ring, Mythical Animal, 4 Characters, White, Russet Marks, Carved, 1 In. 1544
Ax Blade, Ceremonial, Center Disc, Carved Qilong & Lingzi, Symbols, Stand, 7 x 3 In. 242
Basket, Jadeite, Overflowing, Fruit, Flowers, 1900s, 19 In. 3750
Belt Buckle, White, 2 Parts, Pierced, Basket Weave Design, Dragon Head, 1700s, 5 In. 2779
Boat, Junque, White, Sail, Single Mast, Carved Hardwood Stand, 7 In. 11543
Boulder, Relief Carved, 2 Men, Trees, Pagodas, Wood Stand, Chinese, 1900s, 7 x 7 In. .... *illus* 563
Bowl, Carved, Translucent, Celadon To Apple Green, Flared Rim, 2 x 4 In. 181
Bowl, Pale Green, Brown Inclusions, Wide Rim, Ring Foot, 5 In. Diam. 3555
Bowl, Spinach Green, Translucent, Black Mottled Flecks, Wood Stand, 1700s, 4 x 8 In. 483
Box, Lid, Pierced, Squat, Shaped, Carved Flowers, Dragons, Vines, c.1900, 5 x 4 In. 2666
Box, Mottled Green & White, Peach Shape, Leaves, Bird Finial, c.1800, 5 x 5 In. 738
Brush Washer, Mottled White, Gnarled Tree Trunk Shape, Pine Branches, Squirrel, 5 In. 4940

Brush Washer, Spinach Green, Flat Globe Shape, Dragons, Flaming Pearl, Chinese, 7 In. 1869
Brush Washer, White, Carved, Peach, 5 In. 5625
Censer, Mottled Gray, Lavender, Dragon Lug Handles, Lid, Scrollwork, Stand, c.1900, 10 In. 2214
Censer, Squat, Openwork, Bats, Taotie Masks, Feline Finial, Ring Foot, 3 ⅝ In. Diam. 296
Compote, Green, Round, Saucer Foot, Dangling, Dragon Rings, Lid, Phoenix, 22 In. 4014
Cup, 2 Handles, 1 ¾ x 5 In. 1968
Cup, Carved, Kui Dragon Shape Handles, Wood Stand, 3 ½ In. 922
Cup, Celadon, 2 ⅜ In. 750
Cup, Wine, Ox Head Shape Foot, Nephrite, Spinach, Chinese, 10 In. 124
Disc, Carved, Scroll Design, Raised Bumps, 2 In. 254
Disc, White, Reticulated, Moving Wheel Center, Dragons, Scroll, 2 In. 618
Figurine, Buddha's Hand, White Jade, Trailing Vines, 5 Monkeys, 9 In. 5000
Figurine, Cat, Resting, Carved, Tail Curled Around Body, White, 1 ½ In. 466
Figurine, Crane, Standing, Branch In Mouth, White, 3 ¼ In. 625
Figurine, Duck, Carved, 2 In. 215
Figurine, Exotic Bird, Tall Upright Tail, Rocky Base, Wood Stand, 1800s, 10 In., Pair 487
Figurine, Foo Dog, Celadon, Seal, 1 ½ x 2 In. 242
Figurine, Goose, Sitting, Millet, Wood Stand, 1 ¾ In. 1220
Figurine, Guanyin, Standing, Celadon, Chinese, 1900s, 5 ¼ In. 120
Figurine, Horse, Reclining, Looking Backward, Footed Base, 10 x 17 In. 2440
Figurine, Horse, White, Running, Saddle, Stand, 1800s, 5 x 10 In. 246
Figurine, Madonna, Praying, On Globe, Plinth, 1930s, 6 ½ In. 250
Figurine, Ox, Seated, Wood Stand, 8 x 4 In. 812
Figurine, Peking Duck, White, Turned Head, Holding Flower, Wood Base, 1 x 1 In. 1156
Figurine, Reclining Qulin, Flowering Branch, 2 ½ x 4 ½ In. 1320
Figurine, Robed Figure, Koi Fish, 8 ½ x 5 In. 96
Group, 2 Cats & Dragonfly, White, Round Stepped Wood Stand, 1700s, 3 x 2 In. 4750
Group, 2 Horses, Reclining, Facing Each Other, Gray Green, c.1900, 4 x 4 In. 2779
Group, Laughing Twins, White, He He Er Xian, Holding Box, Toad, Lotus, 1700s, 2 x 2 In. 1625
Hairpin, Translucent Greenish White, Pine Tree Finial, c.1600, 7 In. 124
Lock, Inward Facing Dragons, Horses, Willows, Scroll, 2 ⅝ In. 1062
Magnifying Glass, Belt Hook Handle, Pierced, Carved, Dragon, 3 ½ x 7 ½ In. 976
Paperweight, Sheep Crouching, 1 ½ x 2 ¾ In. 123
Pendant, Carved, Melon, Tendrils Around Fruit, Pale Yellow, Russet Veins, c.1860, 2 In. ......*illus* 471
Pillow, Boy Shape, Lotus Draped, Arms Folded, Kneeling, Head Up, c.1800, 7 x 8 In. ....*illus* 1185
Pitcher, 1800s, 1 ¼ x 3 ¼ In. 1230
Plaque, Celadon, Round, Pierced, Birds, Bamboo, 3 ½ In. 625
Plaque, Oval, Incised, Immortals, Clouds, 2 ¾ In. 336
Sachet, Squirrels, Grapevines, Spinach, 2 ¾ In. 560
Seal, Mottled White, Buddhist Lion & Cub Finial, Square, Carved, 5 x 4 In. 5925
Seal, Spinach, Dragon, Incised Scales, Square Base, 4 x 4 ½ In. 6250
Seal, White Dragon, Sanskrit, Chinese, 2 ¼ In. 8125
Table Screen, Spinach, Flowers, Calligraphy, 6 x 5 In. 5535
Teapot, Flower Decoration, 3 ½ x 6 ½ In. 120
Teapot, Lid, Melon Shape, Blooming Branches, Curved Handle, Spout, 3 x 5 ½ In. 184
Urn, Lid, Carved Taotie, Ring Handles, Lotus Finial, Square Flared Foot, 6 ½ In. 127
Urn, Octagonal, Ring Handles, Reticulated Lid, Pierced, Cranes, c.1800, 14 x 12 In. 3690
Vase, Carved, Taotic Masks, Dragon Shape Handles, Ring Foot, 1800s, 6 In. 5558
Vase, Jadeite, Elephant Head Handles, Openwork, Leaves, Green Flecks, 10 ½ In. 3250
Vase, Lavender, Round, Scaled Scroll Legs, Leaf Handles, Lid, Wood Base, 14 In. 3555
Vase, Magnolia Shape, Flowering Buds, Petal Rim, Fungus, Light Green, 4 ½ In. 356
Vase, Serpentine, Green, Purple, Hand Carved, 13 x 7 In. 300
Vase, White, Disc Shape, Elephant Handles, Flowers, Splay Foot, Lid, c.1900, 11 In. 17290
Wedding Box, White, Mottled Green, Flower Shape, Lid, Bats, Lotus, c.1800, 3 x 6 In. 2952

JAPANESE WOODBLOCK PRINTS *are listed in this book in the Print category under Japanese.*

JASPERWARE can be made in different ways. Some pieces are made from a solid-colored clay with applied raised designs of a contrasting colored clay. Other pieces are made entirely of one color clay with raised decorations that are glazed with a contrasting color. Additional pieces of jasperware may also be listed in the Wedgwood category or under various art potteries.

Creamer, Horses, Hunters, Dogs, Deer, Blue, White, Copeland Spode, c.1890, 4 In. 165
Teapot, Blue, Classical Women, Dancing, Copeland Spode, 5 ½ x 8 ¼ In. .... *illus* 195
Vase, Oval, Classically Dressed Figures, Griffins, Triangular Pedestal, 16 In., Pair 1125

Ironstone, Mug, Peg Tops, 3 Children Spinning Tops, Painted, Child's, 2 ⅝ In.
$59

Hess Auction Group

Ironstone, Plate, Alphabet, Nursery Tales, Old Mother Hubbard, Transfer, England, 7 In.
$118

Hess Auction Group

Ironstone, Platter, Flow Blue Transfer, Hong Kong, 12 x 16 In.
$236

Hess Auction Group

Jade, Boulder, Relief Carved, 2 Men, Trees, Pagodas, Wood Stand, Chinese, 1900s, 7 x 7 In.
$563

Selkirk Auctioneers & Appraisers

J

Jade, Pendant, Carved, Melon, Tendrils Around Fruit, Pale Yellow, Russet Veins, c.1860, 2 In.
$471

Ruby Lane

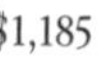

TIP
Don't put a message on your answering machine indicating when you will return.

Jade, Pillow, Boy Shape, Lotus Draped, Arms Folded, Kneeling, Head Up, c.1800, 7 x 8 In.
$1,185

James D. Julia Auctioneers

Jasperware, Teapot, Blue, Classical Women, Dancing, Copeland Spode, 5 ½ x 8 ¼ In.
$195

Ruby Lane

JEWELRY, whether made from gold and precious gems or plastic and colored glass, is popular with collectors. Values are determined by the intrinsic value of the stones and metal and by the skill of the craftsmen and designers. Victorian and older jewelry has been collected since the 1950s. More recent interests are Art Deco and Edwardian styles, Mexican and Danish silver jewelry, and beads of all kinds. Copies of almost all styles are being made. American Indian jewelry is listed in the Indian category. Tiffany jewelry is listed here.

Armlet, Art Nouveau, 14K Gold, Amethyst, Engraved, Carter, Howe & Co., 8 ¾ In. 861
Belt Buckle, Dragon, 14K White Gold, Diamonds, Chinese, c.1930, 2 ½ x 1 ½ In. 1416
Belt Buckle, Heart, Open, 18K Gold, 4 Leather Straps, Elsa Peretti, Tiffany, 2 ½ In. 1353
Belt Buckle, Silver, Engraved Gold-Washed Arabesques, Coins, Boyd, 6 x 2 ½ In. .... *illus* 9200
Bracelet & Earrings, Bakelite, Red, Black, Alternating Lozenges, 1 ½-In. Earrings 154
Bracelet & Earrings, Oval Links, 14K Gold, Paloma Picasso, Tiffany & Co., 7 In. 1534
Bracelet & Earrings, Stylized Lilies, Minoan Style, 18K Gold, Zolotas, 8 x ¾ In. 2583
Bracelet & Pin, Bakelite, Acorns, Oak Leaves, Red, Brown, Hinged Bracelet, c.1935, 4-In. Pin.... 461
Bracelet & Ring, Rope Twist, 18K Gold, Diamonds In Steel Squares, Charriol, 6 ¾ In. 984
Bracelet, 3 Strands, Tassels, 18K Gold, 3 Diamonds, 3 Sapphires, c.1950, 9 ½ In. 1080
Bracelet, 4 Charms, Double Chain Link, Slide Clasp, 14K Gold, Retro, 7 ½ In. 633
Bracelet, 7 Oval Plaques, Landscape, Mosaic, Ropework Rim, Gold, 7 In. .... *illus* 2214
Bracelet, 11 Sapphires, Diamonds, Spray Design, Silver Over Gold, Victorian, 6 ½ In. 1230
Bracelet, 14K Gold, Hinged, Diamonds, Victorian 1593
Bracelet, 18K Yellow Gold, Multi Chain, Open Heart, Toggle Closure, Tiffany, 7 In. 1180
Bracelet, Bakelite, Bangle, Butterscotch, Ribbon Clamp, Black, Red, Green Pleats, 6 In. 1107
Bracelet, Bakelite, Bangle, Gum Drop, Butterscotch, Multicolor Triangles, 1950s, 8 In. 523
Bracelet, Bakelite, Bangle, Hinged, Stylized Flower, Opaque Green, 6 In. 923
Bracelet, Bakelite, Bangle, Philadelphia, Butterscotch, Red, Green, Black, c.1935, 6 In. 3198
Bracelet, Bakelite, Charms, 4 Footballs, 4 Beer Bottles, 3 Hot Dogs On Buns, Chain, 7 In. 369
Bracelet, Bangle, 18K Gold, 5 Knots, Diamonds, Renato Aldo Cipullo, 2 ½ In. 708
Bracelet, Bangle, 18K Gold, Alternating Diamonds, Rubies, Riker Bros., 7 ½ In. 1845
Bracelet, Bangle, Cameo, Coral, Engraved, 14k Gold, Aesthetic, 1890s 1209
Bracelet, Bangle, Citrine, Topaz, Amethyst, Diamonds, Lavin, 2 ⅝ In. 10800
Bracelet, Bangle, Hinged, Gold, Amethysts, Diamonds, Beaded, C. Giuliano, 6 In. .... *illus* 8610
Bracelet, Bangle, Hinged, Stylized Leaves, Butterfly, 15K Gold, Enamel, c.1890, 2 In. 492
Bracelet, Bangle, Jadeite, Polished, Chinese, 3 In. 185
Bracelet, Basket Weave, 18K Gold, Diamonds, Roberto Coin Appassionata Collection, 7 In. 3540
Bracelet, Bombe Center, Flowers, Emeralds, Sapphire, Rubies, 18K, Gubelin, 1950s, 7 In. ..*illus* 15130
Bracelet, Cameo, Coral, Enamel, Silver, Gold, Busts, Vines, France, 1800s, 7 x 1 In. .... *illus* 1125
Bracelet, Cuff, Hinged, Tapered, Knot & Braid, John Broden, Victorian, 7 ¼ In. 4305
Bracelet, Cuff, Sterling, Signed, Peretti, Tiffany & Co., 1978, 2 ¼ In. 322
Bracelet, Fancy Link Chain, 18K White Gold, Diamond, Samuel Getz, 7 In. 1353
Bracelet, I.D., Curb Links, 18K Gold, Slide In Clasp, Safety Catch, Man's, 8 In. 2714
Bracelet, Link, 18K Gold, Enamel, Gemstone, Renaissance Revival, Carlo Giuliano, 7 In. ...*illus* 6765
Bracelet, Link, Bar, Alternating Diamond Set Flowers, 18K Gold, Jabel, 1900s, 7 In. 1250
Bracelet, Link, Belt & Buckle Design, Hermes, c.1980, 7 ½ In. 1120
Bracelet, Link, Double Cable 18K Gold, White Gold Clasp, Marked, Morelli, 7 In. 403
Bracelet, Link, Flowers, 6 Moonstone Cabochons, Oval, 18K Gold, G.J. Hunt, 7 In. 3567
Bracelet, Link, Round, Polished, 14K Gold, Retro, 20th Century, 7 In. 1200
Bracelet, Link, Scrolling Flowers, Leaves, Berlin Ironwork, 6 ½ In., Pair .... *illus* 1476
Bracelet, Link, Silver, Blue, Guilloche Enamel, Starburst, David Andersen, c.1925, 7 In. 189
Bracelet, Link, Silver, Rectangle, Square, Carnelian, Guilloche, David Andersen, 7 ½ In. 183
Bracelet, Lion's Head, 10K Gold, Oval Links, Diamond, Victorian, 7 In. 384
Bracelet, Mesh, 4 Flat Strands, 18K Gold, 5 Emeralds, Box Clasp, 1900s, 7 ½ In. 810
Bracelet, Moonlight Grapes, Silver, Beaded Clusters & Leaves, G. Jensen, 7 ½ In. 1476
Bracelet, Pearl, Silver, Clasp, Engraved, Mikimoto, 7 In. 380
Bracelet, Plaques, 6 Lapis, Round, Leafy Links, Square, Sapphires, E. Oakes, 7 In. 5228
Bracelet, Platinum, Diamonds, Sapphires, Art Deco, 7 ¼ In. 4780
Bracelet, Portrait, Bust, Watercolor On Ivory, Gold Mount, 3 Link Chains, Amethyst 1845
Bracelet, Round & X, Link, 18K Gold, Paloma Picasso, Tiffany & Co., 7 ¼ In. 2337
Bracelet, Scarab, 14K Gold, 7 Semiprecious Stones, Lobster Clasp, Retro, 7 In. 295
Bracelet, Signal Flags, I Love You, Enamel, 18K Gold, 7 In. .... *illus* 2706
Bracelet, Snake, Coiled, 18K Gold, Garnet Eyes, Victorian, 2 ½ x 1 ¼ In. 2478
Bracelet, Strap, Latticework, 18K Blackened Gold, Diamond, Colored Diamond, 6 ¾ In. 5166
Buckle, Dragon, Cloisonne, Silver, 1920s, 2 x 1 ½ In. 75
Buckle, Silver, Oval, Stylized Cutout Figures, Antonio Pineda, c.1950, 5 ½ In. 400
Buckle, US Militia, Oval, Eagle, Motto, Brass, c.1830 1599
Cameo, St. Antonia, Jesus, Silver, c.1935, 1 ½ x 2 In. 295

Charm, 4-Leaf Clover, 14K Gold, Pearls, Ruby, Retro, 1 ½ x 1 ½ In. 288
Charm, Man In The Moon, 2 Faces, Silver, c.1900, ¾ In. 367
Chatelaine Belt Hook, Sterling, Embossed Flower, Leaves, Tiffany, 3 x 4 ½ In. 115
Chatelaine, Watch, Hunter Case, 14K Yellow Gold, Seed Pearls, 1700s, 1 ¼ In. .... *illus* 2091
Cigarette Case, Silver Hinged, Horizontal Bands, Gold Wash, Napier, 4 ¾ x 3 In. 95
Cigarette Case, Silver, Rose Gold, Ribbed, Curved, Sapphire Cabochon, 3 ¾ x 3 In. 581
Cigarette Case, Silvertone, Push Button, Brocade Fabric, Butterflies, 1950s, 3 x 4 In. 25
Clip, Fur, Gold & Rhodium Plated Metal, Rhinestones, Boucher, c.1950, 1 ⅞ In. .... *illus* 68
Clip, Watch, Radiator Grille, Black Lacquer, 18K Gold, Turquoise, Van Cleef & Arpels, 2 In. 7380
Cuff Links & Tie Bar, Brushed, 14K White Gold, Square Sapphires, L. Piccard 414
Cuff Links, 4 Vices, Drinking, Women, Cards, Horses, 18K Gold, Enamel, Edwardian .... *illus* 1968
Cuff Links, 14K White Gold, Yellow Color, Art Deco, Belais Brothers, c.1917, 1 In. 159
Cuff Links, Acorn, Lapis Nuts, 18K Gold, Schlumberger, Tiffany 2829
Cuff Links, Cameo Style, Man, Woman, Embracing, Goldtone, Dante, 1950s, 1 In. 85
Cuff Links, Coins, 1901 10 Dollar Liberty Eagle, 22K Gold, 14K Gold Mount, 1 In. .... *illus* 6250
Cuff Links, Jade Tablet, Buff Top, Bezel Set, Engraved 14K Gold Frame, Toggle, ½ In. 338
Cuff Links, Knot Ends, Polished & Rope Twist, 18K Gold, Schlumberger, Tiffany 1845
Cuff Links, Lion's Head, 14K Gold, Diamonds, 1 x 1 In. 531
Cuff Links, Mallards, Pheasants, Reverse Painted Glass, 18K Gold, ½ In. 923
Cuff Links, Nut & Bolt, Sterling Silver, Tiffany & Co. 492
Cuff Links, Owl, 14K Gold, Diamond Eyes, c.1960 .... *illus* 1500
Cuff Links, Pillow Form, Silver, Georg Jensen, c.1950, 1 ⅝ In. 369
Cuff Links, Playing Cards, Mother-Of-Pearl, 18K Gold .... *illus* 549
Cuff Links, Ribbed, Classical Design, 18K Gold, Tiffany & Co., ¾ x 1 In. 472
Cuff Links, Snake, Gold, Coiled Around Freshwater Pearl, Art Nouveau 984
Earrings, 18K Gold, Paisley, Bombe Shape, Clip-On, Elsa Peretti, Tiffany, 1 ½ x ¾ In. 856
Earrings, Alhambra Hoop, 18K Gold, Clip-On, Van Cleef & Arpels, 1 ½ x 1 ½ In. 2626
Earrings, Blossoms, Silver, Hinged Omega Backs, Clip-On, A. Cummings, 1994, 1 x 1 In. 330
Earrings, Cameo, Coral, 14K Rose Gold, Twist Border, Victorian, 1 In. 130
Earrings, Diamond, 18K Gold, Convertible, Henry Dunay, Pair 3000
Earrings, Diamonds, Peridots, 18K Gold, DiModolo, 1 ½ In. 661
Earrings, Ewer, Micro Mosaic, Gold, Chains, Pearls, 1 ½ In. .... *illus* 5226
Earrings, Flower Head, 14K White Gold, Amethyst, 12 Encircling Diamonds, 1900s 570
Earrings, Hematite Drop, Suspended From Bezel-Set Diamond, R. Boivin, 1 In. 3198
Earrings, Hoop, 18K Gold, Hammered, Ribbed, Cartier, 1970s, 1 ¼ In. 1845
Earrings, Intaglio, Blue Glass, Classical Scene, Hammered Gold, Pearl, E. Locke, 1 In. 4305
Earrings, Love, 18K White Gold, Diamond, Screw Detail, Cartier, ¾ In. 2829
Earrings, Pendant, 18K Gold, Porcelain Beads, Pink & Green Tourmalines, Chandra, 1 ¼ In. 2337
Earrings, Pendant, 18K Gold, Rock Crystal, Ruby, Cultured Pearl, Diamonds, 1 ½ In. 2583
Earrings, Pendant, 18K White Gold, Diamond Melee, Marked, Miseno, 1 In. 800
Earrings, Pendant, 18K White Gold, Rock Crystal Drop, Pearl Flower Chain, Art Deco, 2 ½ In. .. 861
Earrings, Pendant, Diamonds, Foil-Back, Blackened Silver, 14K Gold Mounts, 2 ⅜ In. .... *illus* 984
Earrings, Pendant, Gemstones, Day & Night, Gold, Cannetille Work, 2 ½ In. .... *illus* 1845
Earrings, Pendant, Glass, Plique-A-Jour, Art Nouveau Revival, Trifari, c.1970, 5 In. & 1 In. 120
Earrings, Pendant, Gold Bar, Amber Bead, Hammered Top, Janiye, 2 In. 600
Earrings, Pendant, Ruby, Diamonds, 14K Gold, Silver, Austria-Hungary, c.1910, ½ In. 1150
Earrings, Pendant, Urns, Gold, Applied Beads, Ropework, Etruscan Revival, 2 In. 2337
Earrings, Pendant, Water Pitcher, Bulbous, Long Neck, Wire Handle, Spratling, c.1940, 1 In. 60
Earrings, Quilted, 18K Gold, Brushed, Textured, Clip-On, Henry Dunay, 1 ¼ In. 1353
Earrings, Rock Crystal, Ruby, Flower Cabochon, 18K & 14K Gold, Clip-On, Tambetti, 1 In. 584
Earrings, Roundels, Square Cushion, Beaded Border, 18K Gold, John Hardy, ½ x ½ In. 265
Earrings, Starburst, 11 Rubies, 10 Diamonds, 14K Gold, Tiffany, 1900s, 1 In. 2640
Earrings, Starfish, Pink Tourmaline, Diamonds, 18K Gold, Gunther Weinz, ½ In. 1107
Earrings, Stylized Horses, Semi-Hoop, Enamel, Silvertone Metal, Clip-On, ½ x ¾ In. 207
Earrings, Teardrop, 18K Gold, Clip-On, Elsa Peretti, Tiffany & Co., 1 In. 1230
Earrings, Teardrop, Ribbed, 18K Gold, Lalaounis, Greece, Clip-On, 1 ¾ In. .... *illus* 1353
Earrings, Trefoil Scroll, 18K Gold, Satin Finish, Omega Back, Clip-On, A. Cummings, 1 In. 738
Earrings, Trinity, 3 Entwined Rings, 18K Tricolor Gold, Cartier, ⅞ In. 1545
Earrings, V-Rope, 18K Gold, Schlumberger, Tiffany & Co., 1 ¼ In. .... *illus* 1968
Earrings, X Pattern, 18K White Gold, Blue Enamel Accent, Pomi, Italy, 1 In. 330
Earrings, X Studs, 18K Gold, Tiffany, ½ x ½ In. 340
Earrings, Yellow Sapphire, 18K Gold, Tiffany & Co. 756
Hair Ornament, 14K Gold, 2 Tines, Scroll Finial, Victorian, 4 ½ x 1 In. 218
Hairpin, Silver, 6 Freshwater Pearls, 11 Rose Cut Diamonds, Scotland, 2 ½ In. 413
Hatpins are listed in this book in the Hatpin category.

Jewelry, Belt Buckle, Silver, Engraved Gold-Washed Arabesques, Coins, Boyd, 6 x 2 ½ In.
$9,200

James D. Julia Auctioneers

Jewelry, Bracelet, 7 Oval Plaques, Landscape, Mosaic, Ropework Rim, Gold, 7 In.
$2,214

Skinner, Inc.

Jewelry, Bracelet, Bangle, Hinged, Gold, Amethysts, Diamonds, Beaded, C. Giuliano, 6 In.
$8,610

Skinner, Inc.

Jewelry, Bracelet, Bombe Center, Flowers, Emeralds, Sapphire, Rubies, 18K, Gubelin, 1950s, 7 In.
$15,130

Skinner, Inc.

TIP

If you live in a damp climate, keep a small lightbulb lit in each closet to retard mildew.

Jewelry, Bracelet, Cameo, Coral, Enamel, Silver, Gold, Busts, Vines, France, 1800s, 7 x 1 In.
$1,125

Rago Arts and Auction Center

Jewelry, Bracelet, Link, 18K Gold, Enamel, Gemstone, Renaissance Revival, Carlo Giuliano, 7 In.
$6,765

Skinner, Inc.

Jewelry, Bracelet, Link, Scrolling Flowers, Leaves, Berlin Ironwork, 6 ½ In., Pair
$1,476

Skinner, Inc.

Man-Made Sapphires

The Linde star sapphire patented in 1949 was first made in blue, white, or black. Later, over 14 colors were made. These man-made sapphires and rubies have stars with six rays. Union Carbide of Cleveland developed the stone but stopped production in 1974. Other companies now make the product.

Jewelry, Bracelet, Signal Flags, I Love You, Enamel, 18K Gold, 7 In.
$2,706

Skinner, Inc.

Jewelry, Chatelaine, Watch, Hunter Case, 14K Yellow Gold, Seed Pearls, 1700s, 1 ¼ In.
$2,091

Skinner, Inc.

Jewelry, Clip, Fur, Gold & Rhodium Plated Metal, Rhinestones, Boucher, c.1950, 1 ⅞ In.
$68

Vintage Costume Jewelry

Jewelry, Cuff Links, 4 Vices, Drinking, Women, Cards, Horses, 18K Gold, Enamel, Edwardian
$1,968

Skinner, Inc.

Jewelry, Cuff Links, Coins, 1901 10 Dollar Liberty Eagle, 22K Gold, 14K Gold Mount, 1 In.
$6,250

Selkirk Auctioneers & Appraisers

Jewelry, Cuff Links, Owl, 14K Gold, Diamond Eyes, c.1960
$1,500

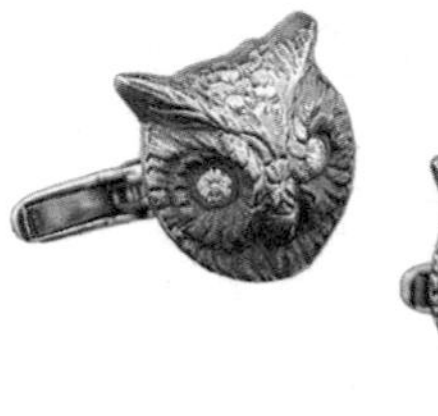

New Orleans (Cakebread)

Jewelry, Cuff Links, Playing Cards, Mother-Of-Pearl, 18K Gold
$549

Neal Auctions

Jabot, 18K Gold, Enamel, Frog Shape Terminals, David Webb, 2 ½ In.	1722
Lavaliere, Pendant, Ribbed, Diamonds, Rope Chain, Floral Caps, 18K Gold, 19 In.	3000
Locket, 4 Picture Frames, Leaves, 14K Gold, Art Nouveau, c.1890, 2 ½ x 3 In.	2530
Locket, 18K Gold, Enamel, Portrait Of Woman, Bessie C. Paterson, 1914, 12 ½ In.	1200
Locket, Memorial, Gold, Hairwork, Seed Pearls, Anna M. DeWint, Box, c.1890, 3 In.	677
Locket, Roman Soldier Profile, Oval, Monogram, 18K Gold, Victorian, 1 ¼ In.	357
Necklace & Bracelet, Cuff, Citrine, Black Molded, Bands, Open End, Inna, 4 x 4 In.	250
Necklace Shortener, Bow, Aquamarine, Emerald Cut, Pearl, 1950s, 2 ¼ x 1 In.	1534
Necklace, 9K Rose Gold, Tusk & Claw, Victorian	450
Necklace, 18K Yellow Gold Chain, Pearls, Toggle Clasp, Elsa Peretti, Tiffany, 15 In.	575
Necklace, Beads, 20 Green Hardstones, 18K Gold, Boule Clasp, Verdura, 17 In.	1968
Necklace, Beads, Murano Glass, 26 In.	120
Necklace, Bean, 18K Gold, Elsa Peretti, Tiffany & Co., 16 In.	1230
Necklace, Bean, Suspended From Chain, 18K Gold, E. Peretti, Tiffany & Co., 30 In.	800
Necklace, Bracelet & Earrings, Blossoms, Silver, Buccellati, Box, 21-In. Necklace	984
Necklace, Chain, Link, Curb, 14K Gold, Gems, Amethyst, Citrine Cabochons, 25 In.	2583
Necklace, Chain, Link, Oval, Scrolled & Navette, 18K Gold, Art Nouveau, France, 65 In.	8610
Necklace, Chain, Platinum, Seed Pearls, Rose Cut Diamond Clasp, Edwardian, 38 In.	3198
Necklace, Choker, Faux Pearl, 2 Strands, Gripoix Bow, Purple Glass, Chanel, 1970s, 19 In.	1794
Necklace, Collar, 14K Gold, Emeralds, Diamonds, 3 ⅜ x 16 ½ In. *illus*	1535
Necklace, Diamonds, Jewels, Chain Link, Iradj Moini	1342
Necklace, Diamonds, Rubies, 18K White Gold, Pave Links, Art Deco, 16 ¼ In.	7475
Necklace, Kinetic, Sculptural, Silver, Smoky Citrine, C. Kriegman, 1969, 5 ½ x 2 ½ In.	750
Necklace, Lariat, Trinity Slide, 18K Tricolor Gold, Knot End, Cartier, 18 In.	1230
Necklace, Lavalier, Sapphire, 2 Freshwater Pearls, 10K Gold, Art Nouveau, 16 In.	161
Necklace, Locket, Monogram, Butterflies, 14K Gold, Enamel, Hinged, 1899, 1 In.	738
Necklace, Locket, Pearl, Goldtone, Repousse, Book Chain, Flower Links, Victorian, 16 In.	210
Necklace, Pearls, 73 Graduated, Ivory Luster, Rose Tint, Mikimoto, 17 In.	510
Necklace, Pendant, Jade, Deer, Gourds, Diamonds, 18K Gold, Ropework, 2 ¼ x 24 In. *illus*	1845
Necklace, Pendant, Mourning, Cameo, Woman, Black Agate, Twisted Wire, 20-In. Chain	216
Necklace, Pendant, Panier De Fruits, Fruit Basket, Glass, Frosted, Blue, Lalique, 1922, 2 In.	123
Necklace, Pendant, Pearls, Moonstone, Silver Leaves, Sandheim, 26 In.	1138
Necklace, Sapphire, 18K Gold, Lorraine Schwartz	1342
Necklace, Silver, Leaf Links, Amethysts, Los Castillo, Taxco, c.1950, 16 In. *illus*	480
Necklace, Snaffle Bit, Diamonds, Link Chain, White Gold, Gucci, 1 ⅜ x 16 In. *illus*	1599
Necklace, Swags, Chain, 14K Gold, Gem Set, Suspended Drops, Pearls, Art Nouveau, 16 In.	1722
Necklace, Watch, Rock Crystal, Platinum, Diamonds, Paperclip Chain, Art Deco, 29 In.	6765
Pendant, Amethyst Cabochons, Pink Tourmaline Drop, Arts & Crafts, F. Hale, 2 ½ In. *illus*	1845
Pendant, Bacchante, Enamel, Diamonds, 18K Gold, Etruscan Revival, 3 In. *illus*	3198
Pendant, Bicolor Gold, Round Diamonds, Edwardian Style, 1 x 1 In.	330
Pendant, Boulder, Opal, Sterling Silver, Australia, 2 x 3 ¼ In.	302
Pendant, Cameo, Coral, Bacchante, Grapes, Carved, Gold Frame, 1 ¾ In.	1722
Pendant, Cameo, Double, Oval, 14K Gold, Chased Scroll, Victorian, 2 ½ x 1 In.	195
Pendant, Cameo, Hardstone, Demeter, Wheat, Gold Ropework Border, Beaded, 2 In.	615
Pendant, Cameo, Hardstone, Renaissance Woman, Gold & Pearl Frame, Oval, 3 In.	1046
Pendant, Cameo, Paste, Silver Gilt, Man's Profile, Prize Medal, Bail, Pin, 1770, 2 In. *illus*	1000
Pendant, Chain, Starfish, 18K Yellow Gold, Elsa Peretti, Tiffany, 2 x 1 ½ In.	552
Pendant, Circle, 18K Gold, 17-In. Gold Chain, Marked, Movado, 1 ¼ In.	277
Pendant, Citrine, Pear Shape, 14K Gold, 1900s, 1 x 2 In.	375
Pendant, Cluster Of Grapes, Lavender Jadeite, 20th Century, 4 In.	240
Pendant, Cross, Reliquary, Engraved, Opens To Compartment, Gold, 3 ½ In. *illus*	2706
Pendant, Danse Rythme Sans Fin, 18K, Cloisonne, S. Delaunay, Artcurial, 1 ⅝ x 3 In. *illus*	6250
Pendant, Diamond, Oval, Pave Set, 18K White Gold, Trace Link Chain, Tiffany, 1 In.	1107
Pendant, Gourds, Jade, Carved, Diamonds, Pearls, Link Chain, Art Deco, 18 In.	1330
Pendant, Hamsa, Hand, Articulated, 18K Gold, Jade, Cipullo, 2 In.	3750
Pendant, Heart, Amethyst, Diamond Frame & Bow, Platinum Over Gold, Edwardian, 2 In.	3690
Pendant, Heart, Diamonds, 18K Gold, Clip-On, Charles Krypell, 1 ½ x 1 In.	1269
Pendant, Jade, 2 Deer, 2 x 2 ½ In.	3750
Pendant, Jade, White, Butterfly, Reticulated Oval Wings, Lotus, 1800s, 2 In.	4870
Pendant, Key, 18K Gold, Carnelian, Cultured Pearl, Silk Cord, A. Cummings, 3 x 33 In.	4613
Pendant, Lavaliere, 14K Gold, Accent Diamond, Seed Pearls, Art Nouveau, 1 ½ In.	213
Pendant, Lavaliere, Platinum Over Gold, Round Diamond, Art Deco, ¾ x ½ In.	242
Pendant, Leaves, Articulated, Diamond, Turquoise Drop, 14K Gold, LeVian, 2 In.	413
Pendant, Lover's Eye Portrait, Reverse Braided Hair, Gilt, Gold Frame, 1 ⅝ In. *illus*	8610
Pendant, Madonna & Child, 2-Sided, Tagua Nut, Oval, Openwork, c.1800, 3 x 2 In.	1020
Pendant, Micro Mosaic, Doves, Cherub, 18K Gold, Compartments, 2 ½ In. *illus*	984

Jewelry, Earrings, Ewer, Micro Mosaic, Gold, Chains, Pearls, 1 ½ In.
$5,226

Skinner, Inc.

Jewelry, Earrings, Pendant, Diamonds, Foil-Back, Blackened Silver, 14K Gold Mounts, 2 ⅜ In.
$984

Skinner, Inc.

Jewelry, Earrings, Pendant, Gemstones, Day & Night, Gold, Cannetille Work, 2 ½ In.
$1,845

Skinner, Inc.

This is an edited listing of current prices. Visit **Kovels.com** to check thousands of prices from previous years and sign up for free information on trends, tips, reproductions, marks, and more.

J

Jewelry, Earrings, Teardrop, Ribbed, 18K Gold, Lalaounis, Greece, Clip-On, 1 ¾ In.
$1,353

Skinner, Inc.

Jewelry, Earrings, V-Rope, 18K Gold, Schlumberger, Tiffany & Co., 1 ¼ In.
$1,968

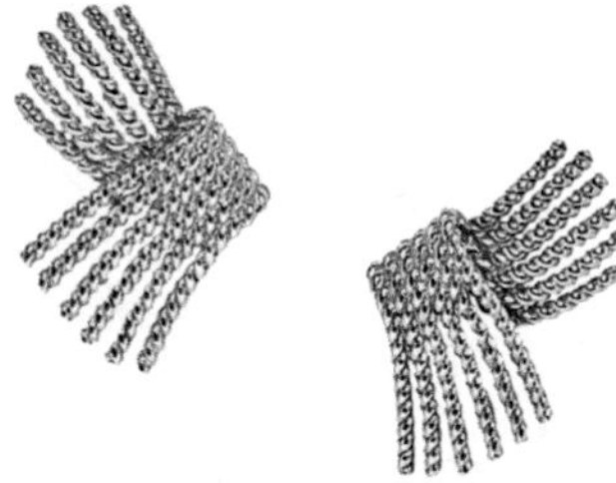

Skinner, Inc.

Jewelry, Necklace, Collar, 14K Gold, Emeralds, Diamonds, 3 ⅜ x 16 ½ In.
$1,535

Skinner, Inc.

TIP

Avoid salt water and chlorine when wearing good jewelry. They can erode the metal and dim the shine on the stones. Hair spray and perfume also make many gemstones dull.

Pendant, Nymph, Swans, Cattails, 14K Gold, Plique-A-Jour Enamel, Diamonds, 2 ¼ In. 1845
Pendant, Open Heart, 18K Yellow Gold, Elsa Peretti, Tiffany, Turquoise Pouch, 1 ½ x 1 In. 575
Pendant, Orange Tree, Silver, Cutout, Enamel, Tassel, Chain, E. David, c.1930, 6 In. 5228
Pendant, Phantom Quartz, Diamond, 18K Gold, Tom Munsteiner, Samuel Getz, 17 In. 2460
Pendant, Pierced Drop Bezel Set, Diamonds, Link Chain, Edwardian, 3 ¼ x 22 ½ In. 2706
Pendant, Pin, Bee, Flower Bouquet, Tricolor Gold, Diamonds, Enamel, 2 x 1 ½ In. ....*illus* 1230
Pendant, Pin, Dragonfly, Pearl, Emeralds, Diamonds, Ruby Accents, 18K Gold, 2 ½ In. ......*illus* 2337
Pendant, Pin, Dragonfly, Platinum, Diamond, Sapphire Eyes, Tiffany & Co., 2 x 2 In. 2829
Pendant, Platinum, Pierced Pear Shape Diamonds, Pearls, Edwardian, 2 x 21 In. 4612
Pendant, St. Christopher, 18K Gold, Cartier, 1 In. 821
Pendant, Star, Chain Fringe, Seed Pearl, 14K Gold, Oval, Victorian, 2 ¾ In. 184
Pendant, Watch, 239 Pave Diamonds, Platinum Over Gold, Winding Crown, Victorian, 1 In. 1920
Pendant, Zodiac Signs, Calendar Page, 14K Yellow Gold, Round, Bail, Tiffany, 1 ½ In. 690
Pin & Earrings, Fan Design, Polished & Florentine 14K Gold, Marked, LFC 780
Pin & Earrings, Flower, Coral & Green Enamel, Topaz Rhinestones, Weiss, 1960s, 2 ½ In. 55
Pin & Earrings, Pearls & Enamel, Dangling Fringe, Shaped Box, Victorian 2040
Pin & Earrings, Snakes, 18K, Enamel, Diamond, Pearl, Ruby Eyes, 1 ½ & 2 In. ....*illus* 1353
Pin, 9 Sapphires, 14K Gold Lattice, Diamond Shape, Pearl Frame, Art Nouveau, 1 ⅜ In. 308
Pin, 14K Gold Frame, Geometric Applique, Seed Pearl, Victorian, 3 ½ x 16 ½ In. 83
Pin, 14K Gold, Amethyst, Oval Cut, Seed Pearls, Victorian, 1 x ¾ In. 207
Pin, 14K Rose Gold, Openwork, Cobalt Blue Enamel Reserves, Victorian, 1 ¼ In. 159
Pin, 14K White Gold, Diamond, 3 Sapphires, Art Deco, ½ x 2 ½ In. 183
Pin, 14K Yellow Gold, Leaf Shape, Matte Finish, Marked, Tiffany, 2 x 1 ½ In. 354
Pin, 18K Yellow Gold, Heart Shape Ribbon, Paloma Picasso, Tiffany, 1 ¼ In. 354
Pin, Amethyst, 14K Bicolor Gold, Open Scrollwork, Victorian, 1 ¼ In. 401
Pin, Bakelite, Bananas & Cherries, Suspended, Leaf Back, c.1935, 4 In. 400
Pin, Bakelite, Red Frog Playing Green Guitar, Articulated Arm, c.1935, 3 In. 861
Pin, Bar Ribbon, Diamonds, Pearls, Rubies, 14K Gold, Austria-Hungary, c.1900, 2 In. 518
Pin, Bar, 14K White Gold, Filigree, Blue Enamel, Diamond, Art Deco, 2 ¼ In. 189
Pin, Bar, Diamonds, 14K Rose Gold, Open Scrolls, Victorian, 1 ¾ x ½ In. 144
Pin, Bar, Platinum Over 18K White Gold, 5 Diamonds, c.1905, 3 x ½ In. 270
Pin, Bar, Platinum, Filigree, 5 Round Cut Diamonds, Art Deco, 2 ½ In. 219
Pin, Beads, Turquoise, Lapis, 18K Gold, Tiffany & Co., 1 ⅝ In. ....*illus* 1230
Pin, Bee, Diamonds, Emerald Eyes, 18K Bicolor Gold, H. Rosenthal, 1 x 1 ¼ In. 1725
Pin, Beetle, Diamonds, Ruby Eyes, Emeralds, Silver Over Gold Mount, 2 ⅛ In. ....*illus* 1722
Pin, Bird Of Paradise, Sapphire, Green Cabochon Head, 18K Gold, Mauboussin, 2 In. 1046
Pin, Bird On Branch, Silver, Turquoise Eye, Taxco, Mexico, 4 ¾ In. 185
Pin, Bird, Flowers, Diamonds, Rubies, Sapphires, Emeralds, Onyx, Art Deco, 1 ⅜ In. ....*illus* 3690
Pin, Blackamoor, Black Enamel, Rhinestone, Faux Pearl, Goldtone, Marked, c.1960, 3 In. 149
Pin, Bow, 14K Gold, Retro, 2 x 1 ¼ In. 247
Pin, Bow, Platinum, Onyx, Diamonds, Art Deco, 2 ¼ In. 1599
Pin, Branch, Lapis, Jade Beads, 14K Gold, Potter & Mellen, 2 ¾ x 1 In. 265
Pin, Buckle, Aquamarine & Diamond, Platinum, Marzo, c.1935, ½ x 1 ¼ In. 1375
Pin, Butterfly, 15K Gold, Diamond, Cabochon Ruby Eyes, c.1890, 1 ½ x 2 ½ In. 10147
Pin, Butterfly, Amethyst, Tsavorite Garnet, Diamonds, 18K Gold, Jean Vitau, 1 ¾ In. 1722
Pin, Butterfly, Rubies, Diamonds, Sapphires, Emeralds, 18K Gold, 1900s, 1 x 2 In. 840
Pin, Calla Lily, 10K Gold, Enameled, Pearl, Diamond, Victorian, 1 ½ In. 183
Pin, Cameo, Hardstone, Maiden, Headdress, Gold Frame, Split Pearls, 2 ⅛ In. ....*illus* 984
Pin, Cameo, Sardonyx, 18K Gold, Diamonds, Woman, Elizabethan Dress, c.1880, 3 In. ......*illus* 1353
Pin, Cameo, Shell, 14K Gold Frame, Engraved Scrolls, Victorian, 2 x 1 ¾ In. 253
Pin, Cameo, Shell, Jupiter, Leaf & Branch Frame, Compartment, Gold, 2 ⅝ x 2 ⅜ In. ....*illus* 1230
Pin, Cameo, Shell, Mercury, Handing Baby To Woman, Silver, S. Dweck, 2 ½ x 2 In. 81
Pin, Cameo, Shell, Silver, Woman, Hair Wreath, Necklace, Diamond, Oval, 1800s, 2 In. ......*illus* 83
Pin, Cameo, Shell, Woman & Cottage Near River & Bridge, Ornate Gold Frame, 2 In. 84
Pin, Cameo, Triple, Moonstone, Ceres, Diana, Minerva, Platinum, Frame, Art Deco, 2 In. 7380
Pin, Cat, 14K Gold Wire, Emerald Eyes, Retro, 1 ¾ x 1 In. 212
Pin, Caterpillar, 18K Gold, Citrine, Diamond Antennae, R. Wander, Pair, 2 x 2 In. ....*illus* 3198
Pin, Chameleon, Sapphires, Diamond, Blackened 18K Gold, S. Getz, 2 ⅜ In. ....*illus* 4305
Pin, Chapeau, Green Beryl, 15K Gold, Globe Finial, Engraved Flowers, c.1900, 3 ½ In. 124
Pin, Circle, 18K Gold, Silver, Pearl, Garnet, Turquoise, Diamonds, Portuguese, 2 ¼ In. ....*illus* 640
Pin, Circle, Maple Leaves, 14K Gold, Silvertone Pearls, Victorian, 1 x 1 In. 138
Pin, Crescent 14K Gold, Diamonds, Victorian, 2 ½ In. 1062
Pin, Cross, 18K Gold, Round Diamonds & Emeralds, 1900s, 2 ¼ x 2 In. 1560
Pin, Dahlia, 18K Gold, Textured Petals, 3 Diamonds, Lunati Gioielli, 2 In. 780
Pin, Diamond, Jade, Art Deco, Lacloche Freres, 1920s, 3 In. 1209
Pin, Diamond, Sapphire, 18K Bicolor Gold, Filigree, Art Deco, 1 ¾ In. 805

Jewelry, Necklace, Pendant, Jade, Deer, Gourds, Diamonds, 18K Gold, Ropework, 2 ¼ x 24 In.
$1,845

Skinner, Inc.

Jewelry, Pendant, Amethyst Cabochons, Pink Tourmaline Drop, Arts & Crafts, F. Hale, 2 ½ In.
$1,845

Skinner, Inc.

Jewelry, Pendant, Cross, Reliquary, Engraved, Opens To Compartment, Gold, 3 ½ In.
$2,706

Skinner, Inc.

Jewelry, Necklace, Silver, Leaf Links, Amethysts, Los Castillo, Taxco, c.1950, 16 In.
$480

Garth's Auctioneers & Appraisers

Jewelry, Pendant, Bacchante, Enamel, Diamonds, 18K Gold, Etruscan Revival, 3 In.
$3,198

Skinner, Inc.

Jewelry, Pendant, Danse Rythme Sans Fin, 18K, Cloisonne, S. Delaunay, Artcurial, 1 ⅝ x 3 In.
$6,250

Neal Auctions

Jewelry, Necklace, Snaffle Bit, Diamonds, Link Chain, White Gold, Gucci, 1 ⅜ x 16 In.
$1,599

Skinner, Inc.

Jewelry, Pendant, Cameo, Paste, Silver Gilt, Man's Profile, Prize Medal, Bail, Pin, 1770, 2 In.
$1,000

Rago Arts and Auction Center

Jewelry, Pendant, Lover's Eye Portrait, Reverse Braided Hair, Gilt, Gold Frame, 1 ⅝ In.
$8,610

Skinner, Inc.

Jewelry, Pendant, Micro Mosaic, Doves, Cherub, 18K Gold, Compartments, 2 ½ In.
$984

Skinner, Inc.

Jewelry, Pendant, Pin, Bee, Flower Bouquet, Tricolor Gold, Diamonds, Enamel, 2 x 1 ½ In.
$1,230

Skinner, Inc.

Jewelry, Pendant, Pin, Dragonfly, Pearl, Emeralds, Diamonds, Ruby Accents, 18K Gold, 2 ½ In.
$2,337

Skinner, Inc.

Jewelry, Pin & Earrings, Snakes, 18K, Enamel, Diamond, Pearl, Ruby Eyes, 1 ½ & 2 In.
$1,353

Skinner, Inc.

Jewelry, Pin, Beads, Turquoise, Lapis, 18K Gold, Tiffany & Co., 1 ⅝ In.
$1,230

Skinner, Inc.

Jewelry, Pin, Beetle, Diamonds, Ruby Eyes, Emeralds, Silver Over Gold Mount, 2 ⅛ In.
$1,722

Skinner, Inc.

Jewelry, Pin, Bird, Flowers, Diamonds, Rubies, Sapphires, Emeralds, Onyx, Art Deco, 1 ⅜ In.
$3,690

Skinner, Inc.

Jewelry, Pin, Cameo, Hardstone, Maiden, Headdress, Gold Frame, Split Pearls, 2 ⅛ In.
$984

Skinner, Inc.

Pin, Dog, Long Hair, Goldtone Metal, Marked, Trifari, 1 ¾ x 2 In. 29
Pin, Dome, 14K Rose Gold, Round Sapphires, Retro, 1 ½ x 1 ½ In. 460
Pin, Donkey, Pulling Man On Flower Cart, Silver, Enamel, M. De Taxco, 1 ½ In. 60
Pin, Dragonfly, Shakudo, Oval, 14K Gold Reed Mount, Potter & Mellen, 1 ⅝ In. 2337
Pin, Draped Chains, Turquoise, Pear Shape Pendant, 15K Gold, Victorian, c.1900, 2 x 2 In. 671
Pin, Duck, Sapphire Cabochons, Diamond Accents, 18K Gold, Aletto Bros., 1 In. 2091
Pin, Emerald, Intaglio, 18K Gold, Cushion Cabochon, Pearl, Elizabeth Gage, 2 In. 2583
Pin, Enamel, Plique-A-Jour, Woman, Upswept Hair, Gold, Art Nouveau, 1 In. 984
Pin, Equestrian, Trotting Horse, Ruby Eye, 14K Gold, 1 ½ x 1 In. 301
Pin, Fan, White Glass, Gold Plated, Trifari, c.1966, 2 ½ x 1 ½ In. 100
Pin, Fibula, Zoomorphic Designs, Wirework, 14K Gold, Scandinavian Revival, c.1870, 4 In. 5842
Pin, Filigree, 14K White Gold, Aquamarine, Lozenge Shape, Art Deco, 1 ½ x 1 In. 173
Pin, Filigree, 14K White Gold, Round Cut Diamonds, Sapphire, Art Deco, 2 x 1 In. 236
Pin, Filigree, Platinum, Gold, Rose Cut Diamonds, Sapphires, Oval, Art Deco, 1 ¼ x 2 In. 345
Pin, Flower, 14K Gold, 4 Round Rubies, Yellow, Curled Petals, Stem, Cartier, Italy, 1 In. *illus* 590
Pin, Flower, Diamonds, Baguette, Colored Diamonds, Platinum, 18K Gold, Tiffany, 3 In. 23370
Pin, Flower, Diamonds, Platinum, Edwardian, Van Cleef & Arpels, 1 In. 5310
Pin, Flower, Enamel Petals, Pink, Diamond Center, 14K Gold, Victorian, 1 x 1 In. 552
Pin, Flower, Enamel, Diamonds, Ruby, 18K, Enamel Petals, Marked, Mauboussin, 2 ½ In. *illus* 1353
Pin, Flower, Peridot, 2 Baroque Freshwater Pearls, 14K Gold, Arts & Crafts, 1 In. 492
Pin, Flower, Silvertone, Openwork Leaves, Aurora Borealis Rhinestones, Coro, 2 ⅞ x 2 In. *illus* 35
Pin, Flowers, Blue Guilloche Enamel, Pearl, Diamond, Pierced Platinum, Edwardian, 1 ½ In. 1968
Pin, Flowers, Platinum, Diamonds, Old Mine Cut, c.1905, 3 x 1 ½ In. 1320
Pin, Frog, 18K Textured Gold, Sapphire Eyes, Emerald Spots, Judith Leiber, 1 ⅜ In. 415
Pin, Grape Leaf, 18K Textured Gold, Sapphire Cluster Center, Tiffany & Co., Italy 523
Pin, Greek Key, Platinum, Diamonds, Filigree, Oval, Edwardian, 1 ½ In. 661
Pin, Horseshoe, 14K Gold, Reticulated, Sapphires, Diamonds, Victorian, 1 ¾ In. 502
Pin, Iris, 18K Gold, Green Enamel Stem, Pearl Petals, Marcus & Co., 2 In. 6139
Pin, Jabot, Rubies, Sapphires, 14K Gold, Filigree, Etruscan Revival, Victorian, 3 ¼ In. 190
Pin, Leaves, Cultured Pearls, Bezel Set Sapphire, 14K Gold, Art Nouveau, 2 In. 138
Pin, Lily, Enamel, Textured Goldtone, Marked Monet, 3 ¼ x 2 ¾ In. 32
Pin, Lion, Holding Drum, Onyx, Diamond, Sapphire Eyes, 18K Gold, 2 ½ In. *illus* 1107
Pin, Locket, Cameo, Woman Facing Left, Black & White, Gold, Pearl Frame, 1 ½ In. 216
Pin, Locket, Silver, Oval, Suspended From 3-Leaf Bar, G. Jensen, 1944, 2 In. 90
Pin, Mask, Mythical Animal, Carved Bone, Silver, Applied Abalone Shell, 2 x 2 In. 311
Pin, Memento Mori, Scene, Blue Glass, Mother-Of-Pearl Urn, Victorian, 1 ½ x 1 In. 59
Pin, Micro Mosaic, St. Peter's Square, Vatican, 14K Gold, Etruscan Style, 1800s, 2 In. 1409
Pin, Moonlight Blossom, Silver, Beaded Swirls, G. Jensen, No. 159, 1 ¾ In. 510
Pin, Mourning, Shovel, Horseshoe On Handle, 14K Gold, Quartz, Amy Flett, 2 ½ In. 540
Pin, Octagonal, Openwork Frame, Platinum, 48 Diamonds, European Cut, 1 ¼ In. 780
Pin, Opal, Oval, 3-Sided 18K Gold Mount, Repousse Scrolls, Art Nouveau, 1 ¾ In. 984
Pin, Pansy, Enamel, Cobalt Blue & Green, 18K Gold, 2 ¼ x 1 ⅛ In. *illus* 960
Pin, Pansy, Platinum, 18K White Gold, Oscar Heyman, Tiffany & Co., 1 ⅜ In. *illus* 12980
Pin, Panther, 18K Gold, Emerald Eyes, Panthere De Cartier, 2 In. 2091
Pin, Peach On Branch, 18K Gold, Buccellati, 1 ¾ In. 2460
Pin, Peacock, Rhinestones, Chain Tails, Crystals, Beads, Avon, 2004, 7 x 2 ½ In. *illus* 45
Pin, Pendant, Ceres, Enamel, Diamonds, Silver Over Gold Mount, Limoges, 2 ¼ In. *illus* 1107
Pin, Pendant, Whiplash Design, Diamonds, White Gold, Art Nouveau, 1 ¼ In. 932
Pin, Pinwheel, Inset Opal, Art Smith, 2 ½ In. 802
Pin, Portrait, 3 Women, Louis XVI Style, Silver Over Gold, Diamond Rim, Tiffany, 1 In. 1968
Pin, Portrait, 18K Gold, Enamel, Rose Cut Diamonds, Rubies, Round, 1800s, 1 ¼ In. 813
Pin, Purple, Red, White Cabochons, Crystals, Silver Metal, Chanel, 2 ½ x 2 ½ In. *illus* 187
Pin, Rooster, 18K Bicolor Gold, Patek Philippe, 3 In. *illus* 4059
Pin, Rose, White Porcelain, 18K Gold Leaves, Diamonds, Chanel, 2 ¼ x 2 ⅛ In. 3585
Pin, Sailfish, Fishing Rod, Gold, Enamel, Seed Pearls, Ruby Eye, Sloan, c.1940, 4 In. 1845
Pin, Sapphire, Pear Shape, Onyx, Diamond, 18K Gold, Clip, Robert Paoli, 13 x 9 In. 3690
Pin, Scroll, 14K Yellow Gold, Round Diamonds, Sapphires, Pearls, Victorian, 1 ½ x 1 In. 212
Pin, Sombrero Hat Shape, Sterling Silver, Eagle Mark, Taxco Mexico, 1960s, 1 ¼ In. *illus* 20
Pin, Sphere, 18K Gold, Applied Wire Twist Accents, Victorian, 1 ½ In. 461
Pin, Spiral, Silver, Elongated, Art Smith, 3 In. 1001
Pin, Spray, Amethyst, Ruby, 14K Gold Retro, 2 ¾ x 2 ¾ In. 690
Pin, Star Of David, Mother-Of-Pearl, c.1955, 2 x 2 In. 39
Pin, Starburst, 14K Gold, Seed Pearls, Victorian, 1 ¼ In. 195
Pin, Stylized Owl's Head, Sapphires, Cabochons, Diamonds, 14K Rose Gold, Retro, 2 In. 1107
Pin, Stylized Pinwheel, Inset Opal, Art Smith, 2 ½ In. 699
Pin, Toucan, Enamel, Diamond Eye, 18K Gold, Marked, Bulgari, 2 In. *illus* 2583

Jewelry, Pin, Cameo, Sardonyx, 18K Gold, Diamonds, Woman, Elizabethan Dress, c.1880, 3 In.
$1,353

Skinner, Inc.

Jewelry, Pin, Cameo, Shell, Jupiter, Leaf & Branch Frame, Compartment, Gold, 2 ⅝ x 2 ⅜ In.
$1,230

Skinner, Inc.

Jewelry, Pin, Cameo, Shell, Silver, Woman, Hair Wreath, Necklace, Diamond, Oval, 1800s, 2 In.
$83

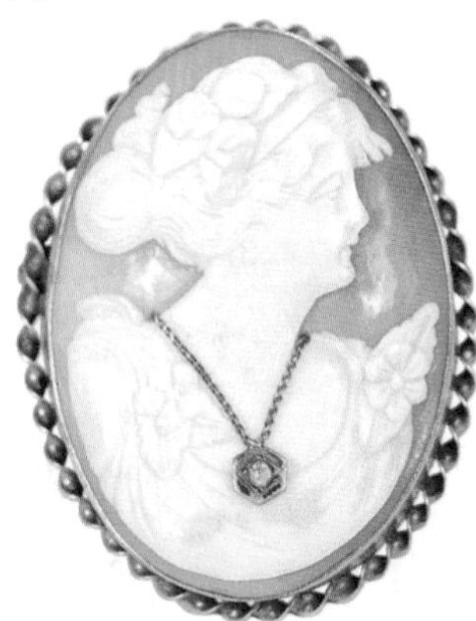

Hess Auction Group

Jewelry, Pin, Caterpillar, 18K Gold, Citrine, Diamond Antennae, R. Wander, Pair, 2 x 2 In.
$3,198

Skinner, Inc.

Jewelry, Pin, Chameleon, Sapphires, Diamond, Blackened 18K Gold, S. Getz, 2 ⅜ In.
$4,305

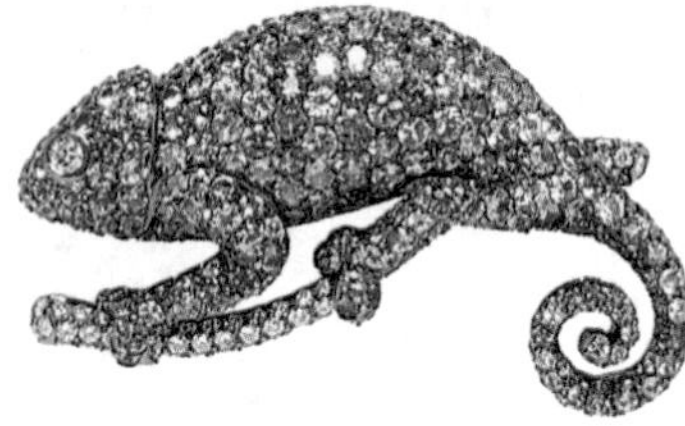

Skinner, Inc.

Jewelry, Pin, Circle, 18K Gold, Silver, Pearl, Garnet, Turquoise, Diamonds, Portuguese, 2 ¼ In.
$640

Neal Auctions

Jewelry, Pin, Flower, 14K Gold, 4 Round Rubies, Yellow, Curled Petals, Stem, Cartier, Italy, 1 In.
$590

Brunk Auctions

Jewelry, Pin, Flower, Enamel, Diamonds, Ruby, 18K, Enamel Petals, Marked, Mauboussin, 2 ½ In.
$1,353

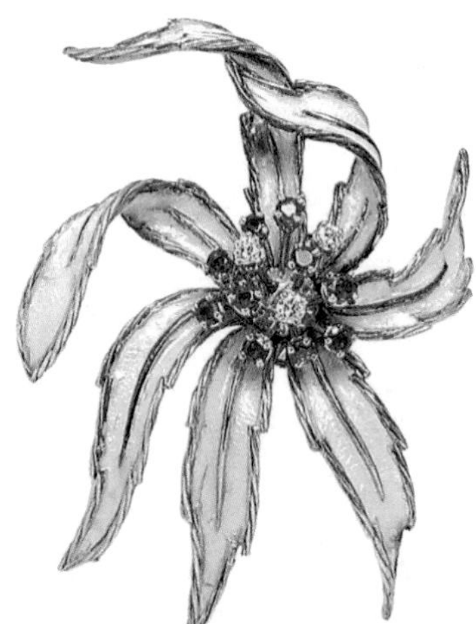

Skinner, Inc.

Jewelry, Pin, Flower, Silvertone, Openwork Leaves, Aurora Borealis Rhinestones, Coro, 2 ⅞ x 2 In.
$35

Vintage Costume Jewelry

Jewelry, Pin, Lion, Holding Drum, Onyx, Diamond, Sapphire Eyes, 18K Gold, 2 ½ In.
$1,107

Skinner, Inc.

Jewelry, Pin, Pansy, Enamel, Cobalt Blue & Green, 18K Gold, 2 ¼ x 1 ⅛ In.
$960

DuMouchelles Art Gallery

Pin, Tulip, 18K Textured Gold, Diamond & Emerald Stamens, Cartier, 2 In. 2829
Pin, Turquoise Cabochon, 14K Gold, Open Scrolling, Victorian, 1 ¼ x 1 ¼ In. 153
Pin, Violet, Purple Enamel, Diamond Edges, 14K Gold, Art Nouveau, 1 ⅜ In. 1722
Pin, Well & Grapevine, 18K Bicolor Gold, Enamel, Diamonds, Rubies, 1900s, 2 x 2 In. 1000
Pin, Wild Rose, Blue Enamel, Diamonds, Platinum, 18K Gold, Boucheron, 1950s, 2 In. ...... *illus* 4920
Pin, Wimbledon's Here, 2 Rackets, 2 Balls, Swallow, Silver, 1900s, 1 ¾ In. 100
Pin, Wreath, 18K Gold Fronds, 13 Diamonds, Tiffany & Co., Italy, 2 In. 1722
Pin, Wreath, Flowers, Ribbons, Diamonds, 14K White Gold, Retro, 1 ½ x 1 ¼ In. 1725
Ring, 3 Synthetic Rubies, Leaf Garland, 14K Gold, Arts & Crafts, Size 5 590
Ring, 4 Twisted Ropes, 18K Gold, Tiffany & Co., Size 6 ½.......... 826
Ring, 10K Gold, Black Onyx Tablet, European Cut Diamond, Art Deco, Man's, Size 6 319
Ring, 14K Gold, 0.25 Carat Round Diamond, Egyptian Revival, Woman's Head, Size 4........ *illus* 649
Ring, Alhambra, Tiger's-Eye, Quartz, Diamond, 18K Gold, Van Cleef & Arpels, 6 ¾ In. 1722
Ring, Amethyst, Round Cut Diamonds, 18K Gold, Bulgari, Size 6.......... 1581
Ring, Angel Skin Coral, Double Arch, 18K Gold, Flattened, Nina, Size 7.......... 372
Ring, Aquamarine, Emerald Cut, 18K Gold, Ball Ornaments, Retro, Size 6 ½.......... 826
Ring, Aquamarine, Faceted, Oval, 18K Gold, c.1950, Size 6 ½ In. 1000
Ring, Band, 11 Square Diamonds, 9 Emeralds, Channel Set, Oscar Heyman, Size 8 ½ 2460
Ring, Band, 18K Tricolor Gold, 6 Interlocking, Cartier, Size 5 ½.......... 519
Ring, Band, 18K White Gold, Bulgari, Size 11 ½.......... 738
Ring, Band, Double, 18K Gold, Stamped Bulgari Logo, Size 6.......... 502
Ring, Band, Flexible, 18K Bicolor Gold, Marina B., Size 6 ½.......... 861
Ring, Cameo, Shell, Skull, Bandanna, Rhodium-Plated, Diamond Melee, Size 7.......... 1230
Ring, Citrine, Platinum, 18K Gold, Edwardian, Size 5 817
Ring, Coral, Woman's Profile, Oval, Carved, 18K Gold, Art Nouveau, Size 5.......... 277
Ring, Crab, 22K Gold, Boris Le Beau, Size 10.......... 1476
Ring, Diamond, Round Cut, 14K Gold, Victorian, Size 5.......... 425
Ring, Diamond, Surrounded By Rubies, 18K White Gold, Art Deco, Size 6 ½ 6490
Ring, Diamonds, Round Brilliant Cut, 18K Gold, Renato Aldo Cipullo, Size 5 590
Ring, Diamonds, Sapphire, Platinum Filigree, Art Deco, Bailey Banks & Biddle, Size 5 ½ 2301
Ring, Diamonds, Sunburst, 14K Gold, c.1950, Size 5 2754
Ring, Dome, 18K Gold, Round Diamonds, Midcentury, Size 6 ¾.......... 826
Ring, Dome, Black Opal Cabochon, 14K Gold, Victorian, Size 6 ¼.......... 543
Ring, Dome, Glass, Black Opaque, Lalique, Size 7.......... 58
Ring, Double Arch, Cross Design, 18K Yellow Gold, Tiffany, Size 5 633
Ring, Engagement, Diamond, 14K Gold, White Gold Filigree, Art Deco, Size 4 ¾ 519
Ring, Fire Opal Cabochons, Diamonds, 18K Gold, Buccellati, Size 7 1770
Ring, Flower, Gold, Round Diamond, Ruby & Diamond Jacket, 1900s, Size 6 ½ In. 600
Ring, Gladiator, 14K Rose Gold, Chocolate, White Diamond, Le Vian, Size 7 1230
Ring, Jade, Sphere, 14K Rose Gold, Squared Prongs, c.1960, Size 6 ¼ In. 299
Ring, Leaves, 14K Gold, Carved Jade Disc, Art Deco, Size 6 ¼ 242
Ring, Leaves, 18K Pink & Green Gold, Turquoise, Oval Cabochon, Retro, Size 7 342
Ring, Lion's Head, 14K Gold, Diamonds, BaumF, Man's, Size 9 ½.......... 543
Ring, Love Band, 18K Gold, 8 Stylized Screw Heads, Marked, Cartier, Box, Size 5.......... 575
Ring, Mizpah, Diamond In Star, 18K Gold, c.1891, Size 5 ½ In. 780
Ring, Moss Agate, 14K Gold, Stepped Mount, Beading, Art Deco, Size 10 ½.......... 276
Ring, Mourning, Amethyst, Rectangular, 18K Gold Mount, Enamel, 1737, Size 5 ¼.......... 1046
Ring, Mourning, Gold, Hairwork Urn, Enamel, Oval, Inscribed, Box, c.1890, 1 In. 800
Ring, Orb, Sterling Silver, Perforated, 1950s, 5 ½ In. 62
Ring, Otter, Holding Diamond, 18K Gold, Marked, G. Appleby, Size 7 366
Ring, Platinum Filigree, Diamonds, Round, Brilliant Cut, Sapphire Trim, Art Deco, Size 6 ½...... 826
Ring, Platinum, Alternating Rows, Diamonds, Baguette, Round Cut, Retro, Size 6 ½.......... 319
Ring, Platinum, Diamonds, 8 Step Cut Synthetic Sapphires, Pierced, Filigree, Size 9.......... *illus* 7670
Ring, Platinum, European Cut Diamond, 9 Diamonds, 4 Sapphires, Art Deco, Size 7 .... *illus* 984
Ring, Platinum, Undulated Open Design, Diamonds, Emeralds, Art Deco, Size 6 ½.......... 8260
Ring, Ruby, Oval, 8-Diamond Surround, 18K Gold Mount, 2 Diamonds, c.1850, Size 8.......... 584
Ring, Sapphire, Oval, Round Cut Diamonds, 18K White Gold, Gregg Ruth, Size 6 ½ 3068
Ring, Sapphires, Cut Diamond, 14K Gold, Art Deco, Size 7 ½ - 8.......... 2124
Ring, Sterling, 22K Yellow Gold, Pear Shape Rubies, Diamonds, Peter Schmid, Size 6 ½.......... 413
Ring, Sterling, Gold, Enamel, Amethyst, Stained Glass Design, E. Pardon, Size 7 ½ In. .... *illus* 1500
Ring, Stylized Flower, Pearl, 12-Diamond Surround, 18K Gold, Victorian, Size 8.......... 800
Ring, Synthetic Ruby, Diamonds, White Gold, Platinum, Edwardian, Size 5.......... 1093
Ring, Topaz, Rectangular, Step Cut, Gold, Brazil, c.1950, Size 6 ½ In. 375
Ring, White Coral Cabochon, 14K Gold, Midcentury, Size 7 679
Sautoir, 2 Chains, 18K Gold, Faceted Sapphire Beads, Pearl Tassels, 53 In. 3075
Stickpin, Bee, 14K Gold, Sapphire, Diamonds, Edwardian Style.......... 288

Jewelry, Pin, Pansy, Platinum, 18K White Gold, Oscar Heyman, Tiffany & Co., 1 ⅜ In.
$12,980

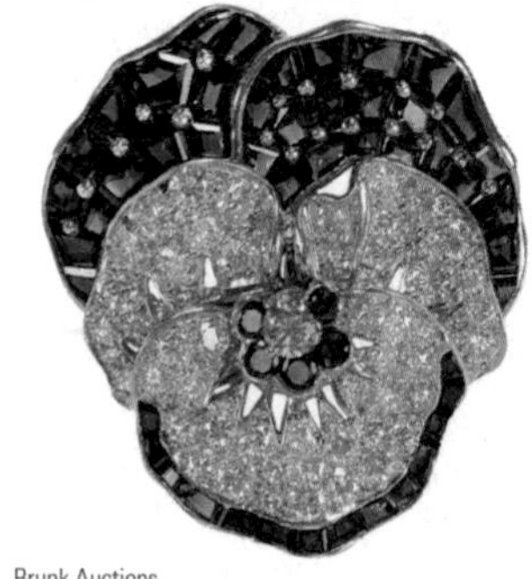

Brunk Auctions

Jewelry, Pin, Peacock, Rhinestones, Chain Tails, Crystals, Beads, Avon, 2004, 7 x 2 12 In.
$45

Vintage Costume Jewelry

Jewelry, Pin, Pendant, Ceres, Enamel, Diamonds, Silver Over Gold Mount, Limoges, 2 ¼ In.
$1,107

Skinner, Inc.

Jewelry, Pin, Purple, Red, White Cabochons, Crystals, Silver Metal, Chanel, 2 ½ x 2 ½ In.
$187

Heritage Auctions Galleries

Jewelry, Pin, Rooster, 18K Bicolor Gold, Patek Philippe, 3 In.
$4,059

Skinner, Inc.

Jewelry, Pin, Sombrero Hat Shape, Sterling Silver, Eagle Mark, Taxco Mexico, 1960s, 1 ¼ In.
$20

Ruby Lane

Jewelry, Pin, Toucan, Enamel, Diamond Eye, 18K Gold, Marked, Bulgari, 2 In.
$2,583

Skinner, Inc.

Jewelry, Pin, Wild Rose, Blue Enamel, Diamonds, Platinum, 18K Gold, Boucheron, 1950s, 2 In.
$4,920

Skinner, Inc.

Jewelry, Ring, 14K Gold, 0.25 Carat Round Diamond, Egyptian Revival, Woman's Head, Size 4
$649

Brunk Auctions

Jewelry, Ring, Platinum, Diamonds, 8 Step Cut Synthetic Sapphires, Pierced, Filigree, Size 9
$7,670

Brunk Auctions

Jewelry, Ring, Platinum, European Cut Diamond, 9 Diamonds, 4 Sapphires, Art Deco, Size 7
$984

New Orleans (Cakebread)

Jewelry, Ring, Sterling, Gold, Enamel, Amethyst, Stained Glass Design, E. Pardon, Size 7 ½ In.
$1,500

Rago Arts and Auction Center

Jewelry, Stickpin, Fly, Lapis Lazuli, 18K Gold, Platinum
$244

Neal Auctions

Stickpin, Cameo, Tiger Eye, Warrior Profile, Gold Plated, 2 ⅝ In. 49
Stickpin, Carnelian, Intaglio, Man Harvesting Grapes, Gold Ropework, Beaded, ½ In. 400
Stickpin, Fan, Enameled Veins, 14K Gold, 3 In. 605
Stickpin, Fly, Lapis Lazuli, 18K Gold, Platinum.......... *illus* 244
Stickpin, Seahorse, Pearls, Peridot, 14K Gold, Victorian, 2 ½ In. 151
Stickpin, Seahorses, Peridot, Faceted, Pearls, 14K Gold, Victorian, 2 In. 177
Stickpin, Snake, Diamond, Opal Bead, 14K Gold, J.E. Caldwell, 3 In. 1107
Tie Clip, Dragon, 22K Gold, 2 x ½ In. 183
Tie Clip, Duck, In Flight, Crimped, Essex Crystal, Painted, Goldtone, 2 ½ In. 24
Tobacco Cutter, Cigar, Ivory Tusk, Metal, 6 ½ x 1 In. 180
Watches are listed in their own category.
Watch Chain, Link, Paperclip & Oval, 14K Rose Gold, Engraved, 14 In. 1353
Wristwatches are listed in their own category.

JOHN ROGERS statues were made from 1859 to 1892. The originals were bronze, but the thousands of copies made by the Rogers factory were of painted plaster. Eighty different figures were created. Similar painted plaster figures were produced by some other factories. Rights to the figures were sold in 1893, and the figures were manufactured until about 1895 by the Rogers Statuette Co. Never repaint a Rogers figure because this lowers the value to collectors.

Group, Council Of War, 1868, 24 x 15 In. .... *illus* 649
Group, One More Shot, Wounded To The Rear, 1865, 24 x 10 In. .... *illus* 118
Group, Sleepy Hollow, Ichabod Crane, Katrina Van Tassel, 1868, 15 x 15 In. .... *illus* 148

JOSEF ORIGINALS ceramics were designed by Muriel Joseph George. The first pieces were made in California from 1945 to 1962. They were then manufactured in Japan. The company was sold to George Good in 1982 and he continued to make Josef Originals until 1985. The company was sold two more times. The last owner went bankrupt in 2011.

Figurine, Ballerina, Chartreuse Tutu, Foil Sticker, 1960s, 7 ¾ In. 35
Figurine, Birthday Angel, Age 7, Green Dress, Doll, c.1980, 4 ¼ In. 18
Figurine, Birthday Angel, Age 10, Holding Book, Sticker, 5 In. 35
Figurine, Birthday Angel, Age 16, Miss Ingenue, Blue Dress, Roses, 6 In. 30
Figurine, Boy, Angel, Graduate, c.1960, 4 In. 25
Figurine, Boy, Pajamas, Holding Snowman, 4 ½ In. 18
Figurine, Cat, Seating, Bell Around Neck, Brown, 4 ½ In. 12
Figurine, Chipmunk, Holding Acorn, 1970s, 3 ¼ In. 35
Figurine, Girl, Brown Outfit, Muff, Green Roses, Gilt Accents, 5 ¾ In. 79
Figurine, Girl, February, Purple Gown & Flower, Amethyst, 4 In. 15
Figurine, Girl, November, Peach Dress, Bouquet, Topaz Rhinestones, 4 In. 24
Figurine, Girl, October, Blue Dress, Pink Flower & Stone, 4 In. 23
Figurine, Girl, Wednesday, Pigtails, Crying, Holding Doll, Pink Dress, 5 In. 85
Figurine, Miss Hawaii, Pineapple, Black Eyes, Foil Label, 4 In. 49
Figurine, Ostrich, Foil Sticker, 5 ¼ In. 30
Figurine, Secret Pal, Holding Fan, Green Dress, 3 ¾ In. 29
Figurine, Secret Pal, Pixie, Crescent Moon, 5 In. 95
Figurine, Skunk, Folded Hands, 1970s, 3 In. 28
Figurine, Woman, Green Dress, Butterflies, Heart Necklace, 9 In. 87
Music Box, Betsy Ross, Holding Flag, God Bless America, 7 In. 139
Music Box, Girl, Blue Flowered Dress, Goose, Oh My Darling Clementine, 6 In. 48
Music Box, Woman, Green Dress, Floppy Hat, Come To The Cabaret, 1950s, 7 In. 44

JUDAICA is any memorabilia that refers to the Jews or the Jewish religion. Interests range from newspaper clippings that mention eighteenth- and nineteenth-century Jewish Americans to religious objects, such as menorahs or spice boxes. Age, condition, and the intrinsic value of the material, as well as the historic and artistic importance, determine the value.

Box, Wood, Folk Art, Carved Star Of David, Brass Handles, c.1850, 10 x 7 x 6 In. 120
Candleholder, Sabbath, Silver Plate, Footed Base, Acanthus Leaves, 1800s, 12 In., Pair 345
Cup, Elijah, Passover, Silver, Lion, Hebrew Text, Ball Feet, Germany, 1850s, 4 In. 615
Cup, Passover, Matzo, Herbs, Lamb, Marked Posen, Germany, c.1880, 8 ½ In. 1722
Etrog Container, Silver, Round, Marked, Germany, 1700s, 5 ¼ In. 1200
Etrog Container, Silver, Snowflake Cabochons, 7 ½ In. 312
Kiddush Cup, Medallion, Flower, Signed, Russia, 1 ½ In. 38
Kiddush Cup, Silver, Flowers, Engraving, Octagonal Base, 5 ½ In. 720
Kiddush Cup, Silver, Grape Cluster, 3 ½ In. 12
Kiddush Cup, Silver, Russia, c.1874, 4 In. 74
Kiddush Cup, Village, Flowers, Engraved, Silver, Russia, 1950s, 2 In. 70

John Rogers, Group, Council Of War, 1868, 24 x 15 In.
$649

Woody Auction

John Rogers, Group, One More Shot, Wounded To The Rear, 1865, 24 x 10 In.
$118

Woody Auction

John Rogers, Group, Sleepy Hollow, Ichabod Crane, Katrina Van Tassel, 1868, 15 x 15 In.
$148

Woody Auction

Item	Price
Kiddush Fountain, Grape Bunches, 6 Goblets, Silver, Footed, 12 In.	1500
Lamp, Sabbath, Brass, Double Eagle, Polish, 1700s, 14 x 8 In.	420
Lamp, Sabbath, Silver, 6-Light, Leaves, Pendants, Simon Woortman, c.1830, 13 In.	4500
Lamp, Sabbath, Silver, High Relief Repousse, Italy, 1700s, 13 x 7 ½ In.	4800
Lamp, Sabbath, Silver, Single Torah Finial, c.1890, Germany, 22 x 12 In.	1200
Menorah, 9-Light, Tree Shape, Silver Plate, 17 ½ x 20 In.	180
Menorah, Heads Of Lions, Stars Of David, Copper, Gold Inlay, 10 x 10 In.	2350
Menorah, Repousse, 4 Scrolling Feet, Italy, c.1960, 14 ½ x 14 ½ In.	605
Menorah, Urn Shape Holders, Repousse Back, Lion, 10 ½ x 14 In.	1320
Mezuzah, Silver, Cloisonne, Flowers, Shin, c.1925, 7 ⅞ x 2 ⅜ In.	840
Mezuzah, Yaccov Heller, Israel's 50th Anniversary, Wall, Houses, 11 x 3 ½ In.	360
Prayer Tallit Bag, Brown Velvet, Embroidery, Star Of David, Flowers, c.1925, 10 In.	120
Prayer Tallit Bag, Red Velvet, Raised Embroidery, Morocco, c.1925, 10 In.	270
Pushke, Alexander III, Bracket Feet, Engraved, Bands, Leaves, Russia, 1893, 3 x 3 In.	1476
Seder Plate, Brass, 3 Tiers, 6 Indentations On Top Plate, 4 Cast Figures, 12 x 14 In.	2040
Spice Box, Silver, Fruit Shape, Bird Finial, Wire Stem, Leaf Shape Base, 1820, 5 In.	1200
Spice Box, Silver, Pear Shape, Hinged Lid, Round Base, Polish, c.1820, 6 ¼ In.	1168
Spice Tower, Cast Filigree Panels, 4 Soldiers, Scroll Feet, V. Schuller, Germany, 9 In.	8400
Spice Tower, Rectangular, Castle Turret Form, Conical Steeple, c.1770, 10 In.	4200
Spice Tower, Silver, Castle Shape, Flag On Steeple, Hinged Top, 7 x 2 In.	495
Tanakh, Written Torah, Silver Cover, Semiprecious Stones, I.M. Fain, Israel, 1953, 6 x 4 In.	219
Textile, Wedding, Embroidery, Flowers, Leaves, Hebrew Text, Tangier, c.1900, 31 x 31 In.	1200
Torah Crown, Silver, Flowers, Urn Finial, Repousse, 6 Ribs, Polish, 1900s, 14 In.	5400
Torah Finial, Silver, Crown, Openwork, Scrolls, Fluting, Bells, Bird, Yiddish, 16 ½ In., Pair	1250
Torah Pointer, Silver, Bone Insert, Amber Cabochons, Russia	338
Torah Pointer, Silver, Filigree Body, Figural Pointing Hand Tip, 9 ¼ In.	414
Torah Pointer, Star Of David, Pointer Finger, Hand, 6 ¼ In.	228

JUGTOWN POTTERY refers to pottery made in North Carolina as far back as the 1750s. In 1915, Juliana and Jacques Busbee set up a training and sales organization for what they named Jugtown Pottery. In 1921, they built a shop at Jugtown, North Carolina, and hired Ben Owen as a potter in 1923. The Busbees moved the village store where the pottery was sold to New York City. Juliana Busbee sold the New York store in 1926 and moved into a log cabin near the Jugtown Pottery. The pottery closed in 1959. It reopened in 1960 and is still working near Seagrove, North Carolina.

Item	Price
Bowl, Blue Interior, Marked, 3 x 5 ¼ In.	30
Bowl, Orange Glaze, Wide Rolled Rim, Strong Taper, Footed, Stamped, 5 x 13 In.	81
Bowl, Salt Glaze, Beige, Wide Flat Rim, Angular, Tapered, Ring Foot, 5 x 10 In.	173
Bowl, Turquoise, Red, Mauve, Wide Rim, Tapered, Ring Foot, 1940s, 4 x 10 In.	311
Urn, Stoneware, Chinese Blue Persian Glaze, Marked, 15 ¾ x 11 In. *illus*	10000
Vase, Blue, Mottled Wine & Turquoise Glaze, 1940s, 5 In.	207
Vase, Dogwood, White Glaze, Beaker, Pinched Neck, Blossoms, 8 In.	109
Vase, Egg Shape, Blue, Red Spats, Flat Rim, 1940s, 6 In.	368
Vase, Egg Shape, High Shoulder, Tapered, Mirror Black, Stamped, 6 ½ In.	104
Vase, Lily, White Glaze, 4 Foldover Handles At Neck, Stamped, c.1962, 10 In.	242
Vase, Sung, Orange, Yellow Slip, Loop Handles At Shoulder, Swollen, c.1930, 7 In.	242
Vase, Trumpet Shape, White, Cobalt Blue Interior, Stamped, 6 ½ x 8 In.	207
Vase, Turquoise Glaze, Dappled Red, Frogskin Interior, Bulbous, Trumpet Neck, 8 In.	311

JUKEBOXES play records. The first coin-operated phonograph was demonstrated in 1889. In 1906 the Automatic Entertainer appeared, the first coin-operated phonograph to offer several different selections of music. The first electrically powered jukebox was introduced in 1927. Collectors search for jukeboxes of all ages, especially those with flashing lights and unusual design and graphics.

Item	Price
AMI, Model DE 40, Music For You, Wood, Metal, Domed Plastic, 20 Records, 60 x 29 In.	210
AMI, Remote, Wall Box, 5 Cents, 10 Cents, 25 Cents, 15 ½ In.	180
Cinematone, Console, 1 Cent, Man & Woman, 12 Records, 1939, 21 x 44 In.	1952
Phonette, Wall Mount, Metal, 6 Minutes, 5 Cents, Red, Silver, 1950s, 7 ½ x 6 In.	125
Seeburg, Model 100 MC, Multi-Coin, Phonograph, Arched Top, 20 Button, 54 In.	1952
Seeburg, Model 1000, Music System, Light Blue, 50's Design, 14 x 22 In.	450
Seeburg, Model M-100C, 100 Songs, Curved Top, Multi Coin, c.1952, 54 x 36 In.	1098
Seeburg, Select-O-Matic, Model M-100B, 100 Selections, Wood, Glass, 1950, 34 x 53 In.	420
Speaker, Seeburg, Model RS2-12, Remote, Teardrop, Blue Mirrors, c.1948, 31 x 17 In. *illus*	915
Wurlitzer, Model 700, Multicolor Design, Metallic Mesh, c.1940, 57 x 34 In.	3050
Wurlitzer, Model 700, Phonograph, Multi-Coin, 24 Selections, 78 RPM, 55 x 32 In. *illus*	4575

Jugtown, Urn, Stoneware, Chinese Blue Persian Glaze, Marked, 15 ¾ x 11 In.
$10,000

Rago Arts and Auction Center

Jukebox, Speaker, Seeburg, Model RS2-12, Remote, Teardrop, Blue Mirrors, c.1948, 31 x 17 In.
$915

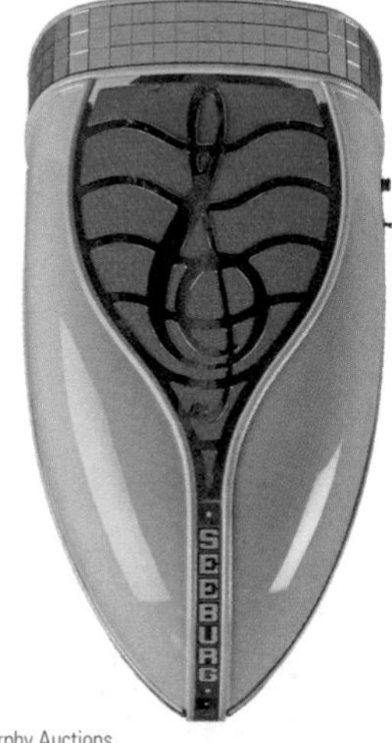

Morphy Auctions

Jukebox, Wurlitzer, Model 700, Phonograph, Multi Coin, 24 Selections, 78 RPM, 55 x 32 In.
$4,575

Morphy Auctions

Wurlitzer, Model 1015, 5 Cents, 24 Selections, 24 In. 1560
Wurlitzer, Model 1015, Bubble Tubes, 24 Selections, Arched, 1940s, 59 x 32 In. 6793
Wurlitzer, Model 1015, Bubbler, Arched Top, 33 x 25 x 60 In. 5100
Wurlitzer, Model 1080, Multi Coin, Horseshoe Shape, Stars, Wood, Blue, 34 x 58 In. 5490
Wurlitzer, Remote Selector, 12 ¾ x 8 ½ In. 115

KATE GREENAWAY, who was a famous illustrator of children's books, drew pictures of children in high-waisted Empire dresses. She lived from 1846 to 1901. Her designs appear on china, glass, napkin rings, and other pieces.

Match Safe, Couple Under Umbrella, Fence, Branches, c.1890, 3 In. 150
Napkin Ring, Boy On Bench, Holding Baton, c.1885 570
Napkin Ring, Girl, Umbrella, Boy, Rolling Hoop, Marked, Tufts 1200
Toothpick Holder, Woman, Barrel, Silver Plated, 4 ¾ x 4 In. 359
Tray, 4 Scenes, Engraved, Pewter, c.1885, 7 ½ In. 132

KAY FINCH CERAMICS were made in Corona del Mar, California, from 1935 to 1963. The hand-decorated pieces often depicted whimsical animals and people. Pastel colors were used.

Kay Finch CALIFORNIA

Cat, Reclining, Closed Eyes, Twisted Tail, 3 x 3 In. 40
Cookie Jar, Pink Cat, Flower Bow, 11 ½ x 8 In. 570
Figurine, Afghan Hound Dog, 13 ½ x 12 In. 330
Figurine, Angel, Hands Folded, Blue Wings & Collar, Blond Hair, 3 ⅞ In. 54
Figurine, Angel, Raised Arms, Blond Hair, Blue Wings & Flowers, 4 ¼ In. 48
Figurine, Baby Bird, Chocolate Brown Glaze, 1940s, 4 ½ In. 35
Figurine, Bird, Pink Matte Glaze, 4 ½ In. 43
Figurine, Cat, Lying Down, Closed Eyes, 3 x 3 In. 40
Figurine, Dog, Cocker Spaniel, Metallic Silver Glaze, 8 x 6 In. 240
Figurine, Dog, Doggie, No. 5301, Blue Bow, Purple Highlights, Marked, 4 ½ In. 349
Figurine, Dog, Freeman McFarland Yorkie, Cream, 10 x 10 ½ In. 36
Figurine, Dog, Poodle, Beggar, White Pearlescent, Purple Flowers, Stamped, 12 x 9 ½ In. 360
Figurine, Dog, Poodle, Gold Bow, White Pearlized, 4 ½ In. 185
Figurine, Dog, Skye Terrier, 11 x 10 ¼ In. 54
Figurine, Doggie, White, Blue Bow, 4 ½ x 5 ½ In. .... *illus* 349
Figurine, Owl, Ma Ma Tootie, Brown, 5 ¾ In. 45
Figurine, Woman, Cape, Muff, Lavender Flowers, 1950s, 7 In. 48
Pin Dish, Bulldog, Glossy Brown, 4 ¾ x 4 ¾ In. 78

KAYSERZINN, *see Pewter category.*

KELVA glassware was made by the C. F. Monroe Company of Meriden, Connecticut, about 1904. It is a pale, pastel-painted glass decorated with flowers, designs, or scenes. Kelva resembles Nakara and Wave Crest, two other glasswares made by the same company.

KELVA

Dresser Box, 6-Pointed Star, Mottled Brown, Blue Flowers, 3 ¼ x 3 ½ In. 236
Dresser Box, Mottled Blue, Pink, Yellow, White Flowers, 2 ½ x 4 ½ In. 206
Dresser Box, Mottled Pink, Coral, White Flowers, 3 x 4 ½ In. 183
Vase, Opalescent, Grey, Apple Blossoms, Long Tapering Neck, Footed, Gilt, 9 In. 181

KENTON HILLS POTTERY in Erlanger, Kentucky, made artwares, including vases and figurines that resembled Rookwood, probably because so many of the original artists and workmen had worked at the Rookwood plant. Kenton Hills opened in 1939 and closed during World War II.

Vase, Flared Rim, Peace Doves, Carrying Ribbon, Cream, Green, Blue, 9 In. 345
Vase, Pear Shape, Trumpet Neck, Leaves, Geometric Design, Cream, Green, Blue, 13 In. 489

KEW BLAS is the name used by the Union Glass Company of Somerville, Massachusetts. The name refers to an iridescent golden glass made from the 1890s to 1924. The iridescent glass was reminiscent of the Tiffany glass of the period.

KEW-BLAS

Candlestick, Amber Iridescent, Feathered, Spread Foot, Bulbous, Flare Rim, c.1920, 9 In. 138
Vase, 4-Pointed Rim, Cylindrical, Green Pulled Feather, Iridescent Gold, c.1910, 11 In. 492
Vase, Gold Iridescent, Peach, Pink, Footed Baluster, Stem, Ruffled Rim, c.1900, 12 In. 250
Vase, Gourd Shape, Iridescent Gold, Optical Ribbing, Magenta & Blue Highlights, 8 In. 173
Vase, Green Iridescent Pulled Design, Gold, Pulled Crown Rim, Flared Foot, 10 In. 356
Vase, Pink & Green, Union Glass Co., 6 In. 446
Vase, Shouldered, Rolled Rim, Tapered, Green & Gold Pulled Feather, c.1910, 8 ½ In. 431

Kay Finch, Figurine, Doggie, White, Blue Bow, 4 ½ x 5 ½ In.
$349

Ruby Lane

Kewpie, Bisque, Bellhop, Painted, Crepe Paper Costume, Germany, c.1915, 4 ½ In.
$504

Theriault's

Kewpie, Bisque, Seated At Tea Table, Folded Arms, Goebel, Germany, c.1915, 4 In.
$1,232

Theriault's

Kewpie, Lighter, Bisque, Brass, Raised Frolicking Figures, Germany, c.1920, 4 In.
$1,232

Theriault's

Kitchen, Butter, Stamp, Wheat Sheath, Ferns, 1800s, 4 ½ In.
$59

Hess Auction Group

Kitchen, Cabbage Cutter, Cherry, Heart Cutouts, Red Wash, c.1890, 19 x 7 In.
$3,690

Skinner, Inc.

KEWPIES, designed by Rose O'Neill, were first pictured in the *Ladies' Home Journal*. The figures, which are similar to pixies, were a success, and Kewpie dolls and figurines started appearing in 1911. Kewpie pictures and other items soon followed. Collectors search for all items that picture the little winged people.

Bisque, Bellhop, Painted, Crepe Paper Costume, Germany, c.1915, 4 ½ In. ....*illus* 504
Bisque, Boy, Bowtie, Pigeon Toed, Japan, 1920s, 4 ½ In. 65
Bisque, Bride & Groom Huggers, c.1920s, 3 ½ In. 175
Bisque, Confederate Soldier, Gun, Red Hat, Label, c.1914, 4 ½ In. 475
Bisque, Crawling, Crying, 4 x 3 In. 32
Bisque, Holding 3 Wrapped Presents, Enesco, 4 ¼ In. 32
Bisque, Huggers, Side-Glancing Eyes, Black Boots, c.1920, 3 ½ In. 95
Bisque, Lawyer, Couple, Holding Green Book, 3 ½ In. 450
Bisque, Lying Down, Head In Hand, Winking, Lefton, 3 x 2 In. 25
Bisque, Lying On Tummy, Crying, 3 x 2 ½ In. 18
Bisque, Mandolin Player, Green Basket, Germany, c.1910, 2 ¼ In. 575
Bisque, Movable Arms, Japan, 1920s, 1 ¾ In. 15
Bisque, Seated At Tea Table, Folded Arms, Goebel, Germany, c.1915, 4 In. ....*illus* 1232
Bisque, Side-Glancing Eyes, Paper Hat, Jointed, Signed, Germany, 4 ½ In. 75
Bisque, Sitting, Crossed Legs, Leaning Back, Lefton, 3 In. 15
Bisque, Sitting, Playing With Toes, 3 ½ In. 24
Bisque, Starfish Hands, Side-Glancing Eyes, Belly Sticker, Signed, 5 In. 133
Bisque, Traveler, Umbrella, Suitcase, Eyelashes, 3 ½ In. 175
Bowl, Kewpies Crawling, Kicking, Playing, Gold Trim, c.1912, 7 ¾ In. 195
Composition, Painted Face, Cotton Dress, 13 In. 100
Lighter, Bisque, Brass, Raised Frolicking Figures, Germany, c.1920, 4 In. ....*illus* 1232
Plate, Kewpie Baby In Pink Petal Flower, Verse, c.1973, 8 In. 26
Powder Dispenser, Composition, Jointed, Heart Shape Label, c.1913, 7 In. 99
Vase, Figural, Big Eyes, Foil Label, Lefton, 1950s, 7 In. 38
Vase, Sucking Thumb, 1950s, Lefton, 4 x 3 In. 35

KING'S ROSE, *see Soft Paste category.*

KITCHEN utensils of all types, from eggbeaters to bowls, are collected today. Handmade wooden and metal items, like ladles and apple peelers, were made in the early nineteenth century. Mass-produced pieces, like iron apple peelers and graniteware, were made in the nineteenth century. Also included in this category are utensils used for other household chores, such as laundry and cleaning. Other kitchen wares are listed under manufacturers' names or under Advertising, Iron, Tool, or Wooden.

Board, Cutting, Pig Shape, Wood, Hanging Hole In Tail, 7 ½ x 13 In. 177
Board, Cutting, Stylized Heart, 1800s, 8 x 18 ½ In. 234
Board, Slaw, Walnut, Heart Handle, 19 x 6 ½ In. 142
Bottle Corker, Nickel Plated, Yankee, Stippled Panels, Vines, Flowers, c.1895, 7 x 13 In. 135
Bowl Holder, Fruitwood, Revolving, Turned, Slipper Feet, England, c.1790, 13 x 10 In. 119
Bowl, Pottery, Cream, Cobalt Flowers, Ear Handles, Round Knob, Lid, 5 x 6 ¼ In. 61
Box, Cutlery, Bird's-Eye Maple, Center Handle, 2 Cutout Hearts, 2 Hinged Lids, 6 x 12 In. 1046
Bread Caddy, Mahogany, Horse Head Handles, Reeded Wheels, c.1810, 8 x 19 In., Pair........................ 3000
Broiler, Footed, Pad Feet, Iron, Grate, Long Handle, End Ring, 1897, 22 x 12 In. 236
Broiler, Rotating, Iron, 30 In. 93
Broiling Rack, Iron, Flat Strips, Sea Hooks, 2 Prong Easel Legs, 1800s, 14 x 13 In. 212
Butcher Block, Maple, c.1905, 32 x 25 In. 182
Butcher Block, Removable Legs, 24 x 25 In. 47
Butter Mold, look under Mold, Butter in this category.
Butter Paddle, Lollipop Handle, 3-In. Print, 1900s, 6 x 11 ⅝ In. 160
Butter Stamp, 2-Horn Cow, Water, Tree, Chip Carved, Crimped Edge, c.1870, 4 ½ x 3 ¾ In. 65
Butter Stamp, 6-Petal Flower, Applied Turned Handle, 5 ¼ x 4 ¼ In. 531
Butter Stamp, Stylized Tulip, Crescent, Maple, Turned, 1800s, 4 ¾ x 4 ¾ In. 2006
Butter Stamp, Tulip, 2 8-Petal Flowers, Turned Ball Handle, Oval, 1842, 4 x 6 ¼ In. 5605
Butter, Stamp, Wheat Sheath, Ferns, 1800s, 4 ½ In. ....*illus* 59
Cabbage Cutter, Cherry, Crescent Moon Cutout, 2 Blades, Molded Stiles, 1800s, 25 x 9 In. 89
Cabbage Cutter, Cherry, Heart Cutouts, Red Wash, c.1890, 19 x 7 In. ....*illus* 3690
Cabbage Cutter, Cherry, Pinwheel Cutout, Pennsylvania, 1800s, 17 x 7 In. ....*illus* 2000
Cabbage Cutter, Walnut, Heart Cutout, Hanging Eyelet, Single, Blade, 1800s, 19 ¾ x 7 In. 266
Cake Pan, Santa Claus Face, Tin, Round, 1920s, 8 In. 40
Canister, Lid, Flour, Tin, Swivel Bail Handles, Red, Gold Stencil, c.1890, 31 x 19 In. 354
Canister, Peaked Lid Smoke Decorated, Tin, Cylindrical, Bail Handles, 24 In. 165

Cauldron, Cast Iron, Bulbous, Flat Rim, Ball Feet, c.1900, 13 x 18 In.	127
Cheese Coaster, Mahogany, Divided, 1800-50, 17 In., Pair	625
Cheese Dish, Lid, Transfer Printed, Blue & White, S. Hancock & Sons, 6 ¾ x 11 In.	30
Cheese Mold, Punched, Diamond Form, Rolled Rim, Triangular Feet, Tin, 1800s, 5 x 8 In.	95
Cheese Press, Buckeye Press, Poplar, Red Paint, Gold Stencil, Stone & Collins, 26 In.	240
Cheese Scale, Wood, Painted, Weights, Emile Chapet Fromagier, c.1900, 30 x 45 In.	420
Churn, Pine, Oak, Lid, c.1905, 30 ½ In.	109
Churn, Pottery, Drippy Alkaline Glaze, 1 Lug & 1 Strap Handle, 1988, 4 Gal., 18 In.	184
Churn, Side Crank, Treen, Barrel Shape, 1850s, 15 x 8 In.	345
Churn, Wood Dasher, Gillsville, Georgia, 5 Gal., 18 In.	75
Coffee Grinders are listed in the Coffee Mill category.	
Coffee Mills are listed in their own category.	
Colander, Redware, John Bell, Impressed Mark, c.1850, 4 ¾ x 10 In.	780
Condiment Jar, Spoon, Figural, Felix The Cat, Tail Handle, Black, White, 1930s, 4 In.	168
Cookie Board, Walnut, Carved Medallion, Flower Basket, 1800s, 11 x 11 In.	469
Cookie Cutter, Elephant Shape, Tin, G. Endriss, 7 ¼ x 10 ½ In. *illus*	1121
Cookie Cutter, Horse & Rider, Coon Hat, Tin, 10 x 9 ½ In.	55
Cookie Cutter, Horse & Rider, Tin, Grasp Handle, 6 x 7 In.	50
Cookie Cutter, Horse, Full Trotting, Tin, Platform, Rolled Edges, Signed, 8 x 12 In.	885
Cookie Cutter, Horse, Tin, On Base Plate, Handle, Pennsylvania, 1800s, 8 x 10 In. *illus*	153
Cookie Cutter, Mermaid, Tin, 5 In.	69
Cookie Cutter, Snowman, Tin, 4 In.	38
Cookie Cutter, Square, Trotting Horse, Tin, Signed, Thomas Mills & Bro., 7 x 12 In.	502
Cookie Mold, Hen On Nest, Tail Feather, 19th Century, 10 ¼ x 9 In.	240
Cookie Mold, Lady Wearing A Dress, Tennis Racket, Iron, c.1875, 4 x 5 In.	210
Cookie Mold, Springerle, 30 Card Form, Birds, Flowers, c.1890-1920, 13 x 9 In.	160
Cookie Mold, Swan, Stag, Woman, 2 Men, Dog, 1800s, 8 ¾ x 15 ¾ In.	240
Cookie Press, Aluminum, Pastry Tips, Plates, Mirro, 5 ⅜ In.	18
Cutlery Tray, Walnut, Serpentine Sides, Divider, Heart Cutout Handle, 1800s, 8 x 15 In.	325
Dough Box, Louis XVI, Oak, Cherry, c.1830, 28 x 49 In.	184
Dough Box, Pine, Blue Green Over Red Paint, Wavy Lines, High Legs, 1800s	2625
Dough Box, Wood, Fitted Lid, 4 Turned Legs, Splayed, 29 x 39 In.	142
Dough Scraper, Cone Shape Brass Handle, Incised Ring, Arched Iron Blade, c.1850, 4 In.	1180
Dough Tray, Softwood, Sloped Sides, Dovetail Construction, Braces, Red, 23 ¾ x 12 ½ In.	110
Dutch Oven, Tapered, Hanger Ears, 3-Footed, Pine Grove Furnace, c.1780-1820, 8 x 13 In.	55
Egg Basket, Wire, Tapered Sides, Drop Handles, 1800s, 10 ¼ x 14 ½ In.	35
Food Steamer, Tin, Copper Brass Plate, Applied Loop Handles, 1800s, 7 ¾ In.	130
Fork, Flesh, 17th Regiment, Iron, Wood Case, Britain, c.1779, 18 ½ In.	1845
Fork, Flesh, Wrought Iron, Flattened Handle, Scrolled Hook, Signed H.R. Fetter, 13 In.	118
Fork, Roasting, 3 Prongs, Wrought Iron, Flattened Handle, Hanging Hole, 1800s, 32 In.	59
Frying Pan, Punched Decoration, Wrought Iron, c.1820-70, 48 x 16 In.	30
Griddle, Hanging, Curved Arm, Wrought Iron, c.1780-1820, 15 x 14 ¾ In.	110
Griddle, Iron, Footed, c.1790-1820, 3 ½ x 15 In.	150
Griddle, Iron, Griswold No. 109, Erie	60
Herb Grinder, Cast Iron, Deep Tray, Legs, 2 Discs With Wood Handles, 20 x 5 x 5 In.	308
Herb Press, Wood, Long Spoon Shape Lever, Raised Dots, Cloud Scrolls, 24 ¾ x 37 ½ In.	181
Icebox, Lucite, Midcentury, Octagonal, Round Interior, Beveled, Alessandro Albrizzi, 11 x 11 In.	248
Icebox, Stand, Rosewood, Metal Bands, Carved, Removable Top, 1800s, 28 x 23 In. *illus*	3555
Iron, Grid, Wrought, Rotating, Flattened Handle, Ring Finial, Tripod Base, 26 x 15 In.	118
Iron, Rosewood Handle, S-Scroll Supports, Finials, Iron & Brass, c.1810, 7 In. *illus*	2370
Kettle Tilter, Handle, Acorn Finial, Wrought Iron, 1700s, 15 x 9 In. *illus*	354
Kettle, Gypsy, 3-Footed, Cast Iron, Marked MML, 8 Quart, 16 x 11 In.	210
Kettle, Lid, Wrought Iron, 3 Legs, Bail Handle, 1700s, 13 ½ In. *illus*	83
Kettle, No. 5, Iron, Tin Lid, Bail Handle, Marietta, Pa., 6 ½ In.	59
Ladle, Curly Maple, Oval, Short Handle, Heart, PPS, Dated 1802, 5 ½ In.	720
Ladle, Wrought Iron, Brass Bowl, Copper Rivets, Rattail Handle, 1800s, 15 In.	94
Ladle, Wrought Iron, Brass Bowl, Flat Punched Handle, 1800s, 18 In.	165
Match Holders can be found in their own category.	
Match Safes can be found in their own category.	
Meat Rack, Iron, Smokehouse, 4-Part Hanger, 5 Hooks, c.1820, 18 x 10 In.	160
Meat Trammel, Iron, 3 Hooks, Adjustable Arm, Diamond Piece Work, 24 x 36 In.	150
Meat Trammel, Iron, Adjustable, 4 Hooks, Rattail Hook, Germany, 1770-1810, 24 x 9 In.	240
Mixer, Milk Shake, Hamilton Beach, Green Porcelain, Enamel, Countertop, 20 In.	300
Mixer, Milk Shake, Light Green, Hamilton Beach, 12 x 10 In.	322
Mixer, Milk Shake, Soda Fountain, Countertop, Red Metal, 14 x 12 x 18 In.	120
Mixing Bowl, Blue Heaven Atomic, Fire-King *illus*	10
Molds may also be found in the Pewter and Tinware categories.	

TIP
Never store an iron pan while it is damp. To be sure it is dry, heat it on a stove burner for a minute.

Kitchen, Cabbage Cutter, Cherry, Pinwheel Cutout, Pennsylvania, 1800s, 17 x 7 In.
$2,000

Hess Auction Group

Kitchen, Cookie Cutter, Elephant Shape, Tin, G. Endriss, 7 ¼ x 10 ½ In.
$1,121

Hess Auction Group

Kitchen, Cookie Cutter, Horse, Tin, On Base Plate, Handle, Pennsylvania, 1800s, 8 x 10 In.
$153

Hess Auction Group

K

Kitchen, Icebox, Stand, Rosewood, Metal Bands, Carved, Removable Top, 1800s, 28 x 23 In.
$3,555

James D. Julia Auctioneers

Kitchen, Iron, Rosewood Handle, S-Scroll Supports, Finials, Iron & Brass, c.1810, 7 In.
$2,370

James D. Julia Auctioneers

Kitchen, Kettle Tilter, Handle, Acorn Finial, Wrought Iron, 1700s, 15 x 9 In.
$354

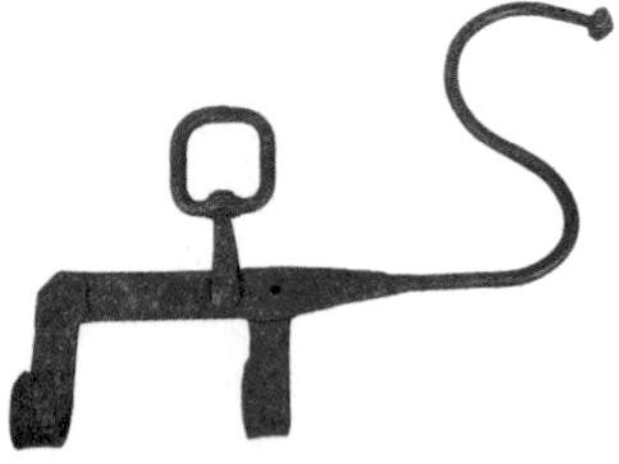

Hess Auction Group

Iron Pans Smooth

Vintage cast-iron pans were hand-cast in sand, while modern pieces are made by a different method that leaves a rough surface. The old ones bring the highest prices.

K

Mold, Butter, Crosshatched Heart, Wood, Domed, Brown Paint, Reeded Edges, 3 x 6 In. 330
Mold, Butter, Wheat Pattern, Double Mold, Dovetailed, 1800s, 6 x 4 x 4 In. 115
Mold, Candy, Chocolate, 28 Disc Shape Molds, Wilbur, 14 x 8 In., 3 Piece.............. 47
Mold, Cheese, Heart Shape, Punched Tin, Pennsylvania, 1800s, 4 In. ....*illus* 153
Mold, Cheese, Round, Punch Tin, Footed, Swivel Hanging Ring Handles, 1800s, 3 x 6 In. 153
Mold, Fish, Lead Glaze, Manganese Sponging, Willoughby Smith, 12 In. 247
Mold, Maple Sugar, Double Heart, Softwood, c.1840-60, 11 ¾ x 4 ½ In. 190
Mold, Turk's, Manganese Mottled Glaze, 1800s, 3 x 8 ½ In. 12
Mold, Candle, see Tinware category.
Mold, Ice Cream, see also Pewter category.
Mortar & Pestle, Brass Foot, 5 ¾ x 8 ¾ In., 2 Piece.............. 60
Mortar & Pestle, Corn Grinding, c.1770-1870, 11 In. 375
Mortar & Pestle, Horizontal Banding, c.1850, 6 x 5 In. 195
Mortar & Pestle, Walnut, 10 In. 90
Mortar & Pestle, Wood, Maple, Black Paint, Oval, Flat Ring Foot, Elliptical Handle, c.1820, 7 In. 237
Oven, Egg Shape, Dome Lid, Finial, Reticulated Scrolling, 4-Footed, Iron, 19 x 21 In. 302
Oyster Shucker, Hand-Forged Iron Blade, Wood Log, 7 ½ In. 96
Pan, Copper, Half Circle, Civil War Motif, 1800s, 12 x 17 In. 70
Pan, Fish Poaching, Copper, Brass, Interior Aluminum Lift Out Tray, 1900s, 5 ½ x 28 In. 183
Pan, Plett, Griswold, No. 34, Cast Iron, 7 Round Indentations..............*illus* 90
Pan, Gem, Griswold, No. 50, Hearts & Star, 7 ¼ In. ....*illus* 825
Pan, Poaching, Lid, Iron, Lift Out Tray, France, Early 20th Century, 6 ½ x 25 ½ x 7 In. 73
Pan, Sauce, Handle, 3-Footed, Wrought Iron, 10 ½ x 22 In. 85
Pantry Box, Ash & Pine, Round, Blue, Lap Joined, Iron Tacks, Pegs, Lid, c.1830, 5 x 11 In. 593
Pantry Box, Bentwood, Paint, Round, Red, Flowers, Hearts, Rosettes, 1800s, 4 x 6 In. 531
Pantry Box, Bentwood, Round, Lapped Seams, Yellow Paint, Lid, c.1860, 4 x 8 ½ In. 270
Pantry Box, Bentwood, Round, Painted Geometric Design & Flowers, Lid, 1800s, 7 x 12 In. 413
Pantry Box, Pine, Blue Paint, Oval, Scrolling Leaves, Flowers, L. Dotter, 1782, 18 x 12 In. 259
Peel, Carved Wood, Fan & Pinwheel Design, Paddle Shape, 1800s, 17 ½ In. 224
Pepper Mill, Painted, Parcel Gilt, 2 Parts, 1970, 50 ½ x 6 In. 180
Pie Board, Softwood, Round, 1800s, 28 x 22 In. 201
Pie Crimper, Brass, Turned Baluster Handle, Ball Finial, 1800s, 5 ½ In. ....*illus* 50
Pie Crimper, Turned Wood Handle, Brass Collar, Wheel, Iron Shaft, 1800s, 9 ½ In. 30
Pie Crimper, Wax-Inlaid Stars, Flowers, Bands, Turned Handle, 1800s, 9 ¼ In. ....*illus* 523
Pie Crimper, Wrought Iron, Turned Maple Handle, Curved Shaft, 1800s, 7 ¼ In. 130
Pie Crimper, Wrought Iron, Wood Handle, Brass Collar, Signed, John Derr, 8 ¼ In. 2006
Pot Warmer, Hearth, Wrought Iron, Brass, Clip-On, Adjustable Slide, 1800s, 17 x 12 In. 18
Pot, Gypsy, Cast Iron, 3 Legs, 15 x 10 ½ In. ....*illus* 30
Pot, Lid, Ceramic, 4-Hen Finial, Blue, Cream, Handles.............. 36
Potato Washer, Wood, Square, Cutout Handles, Ribbed Stats, c.1900, 22 x 21 In. 708
Rack, Roasting, Wrought Iron, 2 Adjustable Bars, 9 Hooks, Arched Legs, Penny Feet, 29 In. 492
Rack, Utensil, Wrought Iron, Roosters, Scrolled Flowers, Dome Top, 5 Hooks, 22 x 27 In. 472
Reamers are listed in their own category.
Recipe Box, Colonial Home, Blue Paint, Signed, H. Musser, 1970s, 6 x 4 In. 24
Roaster, Wrought Iron, Adjustable Hooks & Ring, Tripod Base, Penny Feet, 13 In. 450
Roasting Fork, Iron, Adjustable, Wrapped Hook Handle, 3-Footed, c.1890, 31 In. 130
Rolling Pin, Glass, Cobalt Blue, Painted, For My Mother, 2 Clipper Ships, 13 ¼ In. ....*illus* 53
Rolling Pin, Glass, Cylindrical, Handles, Amethyst, c.1890, 15 In. 60
Rolling Pin, Stoneware, Stenciled Cobalt Blue Flowers, Wood Shaft, 15 In. ....*illus* 94
Saffron Box, Lehn, Turned, Painted, Canister Shape, Strawberry, Salmon Ground, 4 x 3 In. 472
Salt & Pepper Shakers are listed in their own category.
Salt Box, Softwood, Grain Decorated, Arched Back, Hinged Slant Lid, 11 x 13 In. 2360
Salt Box, Walnut, Cutout Backboard, Hanging Eyelet, Drawer, Hinged Lid, c.1901, 14 x 9 In. 212
Salt Box, Wood, Blue Paint, Dovetailed, Arched Back, Canted Hinged Lid, 10 ½ In. 338
Saw Board, Walnut, Blade, Cutout Crest, Scroll Iron Thumb Nut, 1800s, 22 x 7 In. 118
Scoop, Burl Maple, Carved Flared Handle, Shaped End, Pierced Heart, c.1850 5 In. 415
Scoop, Measuring, Red & White Wood Handle, Androck, ¼ Cup, 8 x 2 In. 12
Scoop, Wood, Varnished, c.1850, 14 ¼ x 4 ½ In. 90
Sieve & Pestle, Cone Shape, Aluminum, Wear-Ever, 1950s.............. 24
Sieve, Brass, W.S. Typer Co., c.1900-20, 12 ½ x 4 In. 60
Skillet, Cast Bell Metal, 3 Legs, Handle, Stamped Boston, J. Davis, c.1810, 9 x 24 In. ....*illus* 738
Skillet, Griswold, No. 8, Spider Logo, Erie, 15 ¼ In. ....*illus* 1320
Skillet, Half Spherical Shape Bowl, Flattened Hook Handle, Wrought Iron, c.1810, 20 x 31 In. .. 165
Skillet, Iron, Flat Bevel Handle, Hook Finial, Tapered Sides, Tripod Base, 14 x 23 In. 148
Skillet, Lid, Iron, Griswold, No. 8, Large Letter.............. 144
Skillet, Lid, Iron, Griswold, No. 10, Small Letter.............. 92
Skillet, Lid, Iron, Griswold, No. 12, Large Letter.............. 373

Kitchen, Kettle, Lid, Wrought Iron, 3 Legs, Bail Handle, 1700s, 13 ½ In.
$83

Hess Auction Group

Kitchen, Mixing Bowl, Blue Heaven Atomic, Fire-King
$10

Kitchen, Mold, Cheese, Heart Shape, Punched Tin, Pennsylvania, 1800s, 4 In.
$153

Hess Auction Group

Kitchen, Pan, Plett, Griswold, No. 34, Cast Iron, 7 Round Indentations
$90

Showtime Auction Services

Kitchen, Pan, Gem, Griswold, No. 50, Hearts & Star, 7 ¼ In.
$825

Cordier Auctions

Kitchen, Pie Crimper, Brass, Turned Baluster Handle, Ball Finial, 1800s, 5 ½ In.
$50

Hess Auction Group

Kitchen, Pie Crimper, Wax-Inlaid Stars, Flowers, Bands, Turned Handle, 1800s, 9 ¼ In.
$523

Skinner, Inc.

Kitchen, Pot, Gypsy, Cast Iron, 3 Legs, 15 x 10 ½ In.
$30

Hess Auction Group

Kitchen, Rolling Pin, Glass, Cobalt Blue, Painted, For My Mother, 2 Clipper Ships, 13 ¼ In.
$53

Hess Auction Group

K

Kitchen, Rolling Pin, Stoneware, Stenciled Cobalt Blue Flowers, Wood Shaft, 15 In.
$94

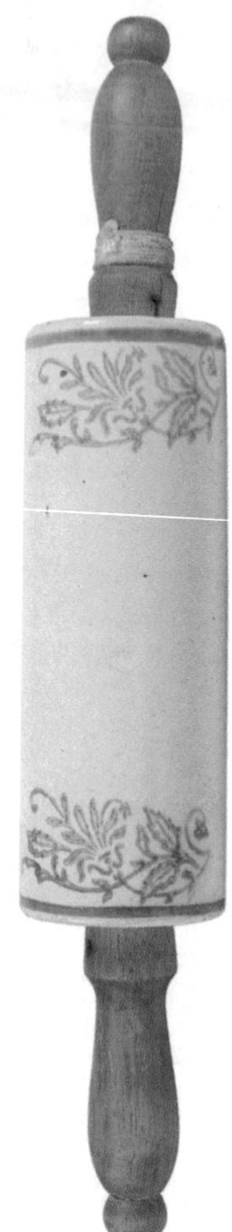

Hess Auction Group

Kitchen, Skillet, Cast Bell Metal, 3 Legs, Handle, Stamped Boston, J. Davis, c.1810, 9 x 24 In.
$738

Skinner, Inc.

Kitchen, Skillet, Griswold, No. 8, Spider Logo, Erie, 15 ¼ In.
$1,320

Cordier Auctions

Skimmer, Wrought Iron, Brass Bowl, Flat Handle, Hanging Hook, c.1800, 16 In. 130
Spatula, Wrought Iron, Flat Punched Handle, Keyhole Shaped Blade, 1800s, 20 In. 94
Spice Box, Cherry, Hanging Eyelet, Double Arch Crest, Slant Lid, Drawer, 1800s 590
Spice Box, Demilune Back, Landscape Scene, 4 ½ x 3 In. 88
Spice Box, Drawer, Red Paint Trace, Lollipop Handle, Berks County, c.1820, 13 In. 708
Spice Box, Red Paint, Slide Lid, Dovetailed, 1800s, 4 x 5 x 11 In. 207
Spice Box, Softwood, Hanging, Arched, Heart Cutout, Hinged Slant Lid, 1800s, 11 x 16 In. 2242
Spice Box, Walnut, 2 Drawers, Spinning Tin Drum, Compartments, Lift Lid, c.1890, 8 x 12 In. . 240
Spice Box, Walnut, Slide Lid, Cherry Baseboard, Compartmented Interior, 1800s, 14 x 8 In. 236
Spice Box, Walnut, Slide Lid, Reeded, Brass Mushroom Finial, Molded Edge, 1800s, 5 x 9 In. 165
Spice Box, Wood, Red Stain, Hinged Lid, Molded Base, 5 Compartments, c.1877, 14 x 5 In. 246
Spoon Rack, Shaped Ends, Scalloped Valances, Mortised Shelf, Red, 1840-90, 7 x 23 In. 150
Spoon, Tasting, Punched, Brass Bowl, Round To Flattened Iron Handle, 10 In. 94
Strainer, Milk Cheese, Cylindrical, Pierced, Handles, Collar Base, 1800s, 7 x 9 In. 59
Stringholder, Bee Skep Shape, Cast Iron, Painted Black, 6 ½ In. 59
Sugar Cutters, Wrought Iron, Scissor Action, Brass Inlay, c.1800, 5 ¼ In. 130
Sugar, Lid, Tin, Red Flowers & Buds, Leaves, Cream Band, Pomegranates, c.1800, 3 ½ In. 1107
Teapot, Spice Of Life, Metal Lid, 6-Cup, Corning Ware, c.1975, 5 ¼ In. ....*illus* 15
Teakettle, Iron, Cone Shape, Bail Handle, Twigs, Kinko Sennin Riding Carp, 10 In. 2727
Toaster, 2 Rails, Arched Pan, Rivets, 3-Footed, Maple Wood Handle, Iron, c.1880, 19 x 8 In. 110
Toaster, Iron, Rectangular, 4 Bars, Berries, 19 ½ In. 205
Toaster, Scrolled Feet, 2 Half Circle Racks, Wrought Iron, c.1800-50, 5 ½ x 9 In. 70
Toaster, Swivel, Wrought Iron, Flattened Handle, Hook Terminal, 1800s, 20 x 14 In. 189
Toaster, Swivel, Wrought Iron, Footed Base, Flat Handle, 2 Bar Racks, 1800s, 14 x 14 In. 236
Trammel, Kettle, Iron, Sawtooth, Wrapped Hook, Ball Handle, 20 x 5 In. 120
Tray, Art Nouveau, Apple Slice Shape, Woman, Flowing Gown, Harp, Cast Iron, c.1890, 9 In. 625
Tray, Tin Lithograph, Town Of Playing Cards, Oval, Piero Fornasetti, 13 ½ x 17 ¾ In. 420
Tray, Tin Lithograph, Yellow, Abstract, Rectangular, Piero Fornasetti, 22 ¾ x 18 In. 840
Tray, Utensil, Walnut, Dovetailed, Scalloped Edges, Center Handle, 1800s, 6 x 16 In. 266
Trivet, see Trivet category.
Tub, Salting, French Provincial, Oak, Beech, Carved, Lift Top, Square Legs, 19 x 18 In. 215
Vegetable Slicer, Mechanical, Wood, Catawissa Specialty Mfg. Co., 1898, 23 x 3 In. 12
Washboard, Wood, Tin, Dubl Handi, Columbus, Ohio, 18 x 8 ½ In. 22
Washing Machine, Gifford's Improved Revolving, Box, Crank, Paint, 42 x 35 In. 399
Washing Machine, Maytag Hand Washer, Wood, Agitator, Wringer, 1920s, 4 Legs, 46 In. 240
Washing Machine, Woman's Friend, Wood, Iron, Wringer, Bluffton, Oh., 1920s, 41 x 44 In. 210

KNIFE collectors usually specialize in a single type. In the 1960s, the United States government passed a law that required knife manufacturers to mark their knives with the country of origin. This seemed to encourage the collectors, and knife collecting became an interest of a large group of people. All types of knives are collected, from top quality twentieth-century examples to old bone- or pearl-handled knives in excellent condition.

Cassowary Bone, Carved Handle, Bird Head, New Guinea, 14 ½ In. 62
Crooked, Cherry, Scrolling Chip Carved Handle, Iron Blade, Wire Wrap, c.1840, 9 In. 830
Dagger, Caugcho, Silver Hilt & Scabbard, Flowers, Solingen Blade, 7 ½ In. 246
Dagger, Hilt, Scabbard, Red Coral, Gold Writing, Turquoise, 9-In. Blade, 14 ½ In. 2460
Dagger, Khanjar, Engraved Sheath, Hilt, Indo-Persian, 8-In. Blade, 13 In. 738
Dagger, Silver & Niello Mounted Kindjal, Russia, c.1900, 14 In. 2550
Dirk, Naval, Flowers, Japan, c.1883, 13 In. 584
Fixed Blade, Tactical, MTech USA Xtreme, 11 In. 106
Flint, Serrated Edge, Bone Handle, Native American, 12 ¼ In. 156
Hibben Machete Blade IV, Sheath, 17 ½ In. 148
Khyber, Eared, Bone Hilt, Brass Scabbard, 11 In. 307
Kindjal, Carved Bone, Double Edge, Leather Scabbard, Sterling, Turquoise Cabochons, 15 x 2 In. 460
Kris, Bone Pommel, Copper Scabbard, Wavy Steel Blade, Philippines, 14 In. 215
Pocket, 14K Gold, Scissors, Nail File, Stainless Steel Blade, Cartier, 2 ¾ In. 260
Pocket, Victorian, Sterling Silver, Arts & Crafts, 2 Blades, 5 In. 175

KNOWLES, *Taylor & Knowles items may be found in the KTK and Lotus Ware categories.*

KOSTA, the oldest Swedish glass factory, was founded in 1742. During the 1920s through the 1950s, many pieces of original design were made at the factory. Kosta and Boda merged with Afors in 1964 and created the Afors Group in 1971. In 1976, the name Kosta Boda was adopted. The company merged with Orrefors in 1990 and is still working.

Sculpture, Etched, Woman With Lute, Vicke Lindstrand, Sweden, c.1920, 8 ⅜ x 6 ⅛ In. 450
Vase, Can Can, Blown, Round Pedestal, Rings, Bowl, Flat Rim, Green, Pink, Red, 11 x 11 In. 397

Vase, Clear, Blue Swirl Lines, Rim, Kjell Engman, Kosta Boda, 7 x 8 In. 102
Vase, Mask & Serpent Design, Swollen Top, Curved Rim, 14 In. 149
Vase, Swollen Stem, Cup Shape Top, Flat Rim, Pink, Green, Red, Mottled Design, 11 x 9 In. 153
Vase, White, Painted Face Outline, Ulrica Hydman-Vallien, Kosta Boda, 5 ½ x 8 In. 96

KPM refers to Berlin porcelain, but the same initials were used alone and in combination with other symbols by several German porcelain makers. They include the Konigliche Porzellan Manufaktur of Berlin, initials used in mark, 1823–47; Meissen, 1723–24 only; Krister Porzellan Manufaktur in Waldenburg, after 1831; Kranichfelder Porzellan Manufaktur in Kranichfeld, after 1903; and the Krister Porzellan Manufaktur in Scheibe, after 1838.

K.P.M

Bowl, Lattice Design, Twist Rope At Foot, Pink Roses, Leaves, Flared Gilt Rim, c.1930, 8 In. 84
Bowl, Lid, Pink, White, Cupid Finial, Holding Gilt Grades, 11 In. 500
Bowl, Stand, Reticulated, c.1850, 9 ½ x 13 ⅝ In. .... *illus* 3200
Cachepot, Classical Reclining Figures, Pink Ground, Brown Transfer Scene, 6 x 6 ¼ In., Pair.... 115
Centerpiece, 2 Parts, Underglaze Blue, 4-Legged, 15 x 26 In. 1440
Centerpiece, Putto & Child Faun, Holding Shell Bowl, Pink, White, 10 x 10 In. 120
Ewer, Cobalt Blue, Gilt, 2 Goats On Rim, Round Foot, 9 x 8 In. 922
Figurine, Cossack Warrior, Blue Scepter Mark, Black Iron Cross, c.1910, 11 ¼ In., Pair.......... 531
Group, 2 Putti, 1 Holding Lyre, 1 Holding Book, Scroll & Quill, Horn, Gilt, c.1910, 5 x 7 In. 717
Lithophane, see also Lithophane category.
Plaque, Boy Whispering To Girl, Carrying Chamberstick, Carved Frame, c.1900, 11 x 8 In. 3690
Plaque, Child With Lamb, Gilded Frame, Cartouche Ornaments At Corners, c.1890, 7 x 12 In. .. 738
Plaque, Children Talking, Painted, Frame, Germany, c.1890, 9 ½ x 7 In. 3120
Plaque, Hagar & Ishmael In The Desert, After Emanuel Krecenc Liska, Frame, 7 x 12 In. 1610
Plaque, Hand Painted, Woman, Profile, Halo, Oval, Frame, 11 x 14 In. 1560
Plaque, Katherine The Great, Gold Dress, Shawl, Gold Frame, 20 x 23 In. .... *illus* 2074
Plaque, Maiden, Long Braid, Holding Flowers, Frame, Mark, 13 x 8 In. 6150
Plaque, Roman Ruins, Women & Children, Pillars, Carved & Gilded Frame, c.1900, 8 x 10 In. . 6150
Plaque, Ruth Harvesting Grain, Incised Scepter Mark, Giltwood Frame, 16 x 11 In. .... *illus* 5175
Plaque, Sorceress, Robed Woman, Horned Headdress, Cauldron, Gilt Frame, c.1900, 12 x 8 In. . 5000
Plaque, To Be Good, Inscribed, Bien Etre, Woman, Long Hair, Kimono, 12 x 7 In. 6765
Plaque, Woman, Seated In Garden, Frame, c.1900, 12 In. 11070
Plaque, Woman, Stringed Instrument, Foreign Girl, Long Dark Hair, Frame, c.1880, 15 In. 6875
Plaque, Women In Parlor, Frame, 1800s, 11 ¾ x 14 In. 805
Teapot, Flowers, Multicolor, Gilt Accents, 5 In. 549
Tureen, Flowers, Putti Finial, Underplate, Lid, 16 In. 1256
Vase, Dome Lid, Woman Bust Handles, Bow, Arrows, Round Foot, c.1900, 20 In. 8125

KTK are the initials of the Knowles, Taylor & Knowles Company of East Liverpool, Ohio, founded by Isaac W. Knowles in 1853. The company made many types of utilitarian wares, hotel china, and dinnerware. It made the fine bone china known as Lotus Ware from 1891 to 1896. The company merged with American Ceramic Corporation in 1928. It closed in 1934. Lotus Ware is listed in its own category in this book.

K.T.&K. CHINA

Jug, Stoneware, Old Maryland Pure Rye Whiskey, 1881, 7 ½ x 6 In. 104
Pitcher, Milk, Lid, Daffodils, Ironstone, 1919-26, 5 ⅞ In. 69
Pitcher, Milk, Moss Rose, Ironstone, 1870s, 6 ½ In. 75
Vase, Tiger, Brown, Green, 10 ½ x 6 ¼ In. 650

KU KLUX KLAN items are now collected because of their historic importance. Literature, robes, and memorabilia are seen at shows and auctions. Laws passed in 1870 and 1871 caused the decline of the Klan. A second group calling itself the Ku Klux Klan emerged in 1915. There are still local groups using the name.

Knife, Fiery Cross, Open Bible, Klansman, Brass, Steel, Taylor Cutlery, 1980, 6 In. 36
Patch, Chain Stiched, Red, White, 1920s, 4 ½ In. Diam. 100
Pocket Knife, KKK, Brass, Klan Member Figure, 1920s, 3 In. 382
Sheet Music, Yes Uncle Sam We're Coming 10 Million Strong, Abe Nace, c.1924, 9 x 11 In. 250
Token, Death Before Dishonor, God Save The South, Skull, Fiery Cross, Aluminum, 1971.......... 85

KUTANI porcelain was made in Japan after the mid-seventeenth century. Most of the pieces found today are nineteenth-century. Collectors often use the term *Kutani* to refer to just the later, colorful pieces decorated with red, gold, and black pictures of warriors, animals, and birds.

九谷

Cat, Reclining, Gilt, Red Color, 12 In. 192
Ginger Jar, Red, Light Pink Reserve, Landscape, Figures, 15 In. 732
Jar, Blue, White Doves, Pink Chrysanthemums, 12 In. 97

Kitchen, Teapot, Spice Of Life, Metal Lid, 6-Cup, Corning Ware, c.1975, 5 ¼ In.
$15

Ruby Lane

KPM, Bowl, Stand, Reticulated, c.1850, 9 ½ x 13 ⅝ In.
$3,200

Ruby Lane

KPM, Plaque, Katherine The Great, Gold Dress, Shawl, Gold Frame, 20 x 23 In.
$2,074

James D. Julia Auctioneers

Invest in Collectibles

If you invest in collectibles, remember the rules. Buy the best you can, buy perfect items, and care for them so they remain perfect. Provenance (written history) adds value, as does a signature. Try to spot the trends influenced by news events, such as the death of a celebrity.

K

KPM, Plaque, Ruth Harvesting Grain, Incised Scepter Mark, Giltwood Frame, 16 x 11 In.
$5,175

Early Auction Company

L.G. Wright, Hobnail, Rose Bowl, Ruby Glass, 3 x 4 ¼ In.
$40

Ruby Lane

L.G. Wright, Moon & Stars, Compote, Flared, Amber, 6 ¼ x 7 ¾ In.
$25

Ruby Lane

TIP

A glass vase or bowl can be cleaned with a damp cloth. Try not to put the glass in a sink filled with water. Hitting the glass on a faucet or the sink is a common cause of breakage.

Jardiniere, Hanging, Peacock, Art Nouveau Metal Mounts, Riessner, Stellmacher & Kessel, 18 In. 1188
Patch Box, Peach Shape, Symbols, Red, Orange, Signed, 2 ½ In. 165
Plate, Blue Green, Scalloped Edge, 9 In., 12 Piece 30
Tray, Quatrefoil, Court Carriage, Gilt, 14 ½ x 11 In. 630
Vase, Gilt, Red, Musicians, Courtyard, Flowers, Birds, 18 In. 123
Vase, Lion-Shape Handles, Samurai, Pine Bough, Flowers, Lappets, c.1890, 16 In. 598
Vase, Rounded, Tapered, 2 Child Scholars, Scroll, Garden, Birds, Flowers, 14 In. 100

L.G. WRIGHT Glass Company of New Martinsville, West Virginia, started selling glassware in 1937. Founder "Si" Wright contracted with Ohio and West Virginia glass factories to reproduce popular pressed glass patterns like Rose & Snow, Baltimore Pear, and Three Face, and opalescent patterns like Daisy & Fern and Swirl. Collectors can tell the difference between the original glasswares and L.G. Wright reproductions because of colors and differences in production techniques. Some L.G. Wright items are marked with an underlined *W* in a circle. Items that were made from old Northwood molds have an altered Northwood mark—an angled line was added to the *N* to make it look like a *W*. Collectors refer to this mark as "the wobbly W." The L.G. Wright factory was closed and the existing molds sold in 1999.

W

Argonaut Shell, Toothpick Holder, Blue Opalescent, Footed, 3 In. 18
Cabbage Leaf, Goblet, 6 In. 16
Cherry, Creamer, Green, 4 ½ In. 14
Daisy & Button, Bowl, Oval, 4-Footed, Amber, 5 In. 10
Daisy & Button, Creamer, Amber, 3 ½ In. 13
Daisy & Button, Goblet, Green, 6 ⅛ In. 13
Daisy & Button, Pitcher, Amber, 48 Oz., 8 ⅜ In. 36
Daisy & Button, Plate, Dinner, Amber, 10 ⅜ In. 14
Daisy & Button, Punch Bowl, Amber, 13 In. 138
Daisy & Button, Punch Cup, Amber, 2 ½ In. 6
Daisy & Button, Salt Dip, 3-Sided, Ruby, 2 ⅜ In. 16
Daisy & Button, Toothpick Holder, Amber, 2 ½ In. 10
Daisy & Button, Tray, Fan Shape, Amber, 10 ½ In. 18
Daisy & Button, Tumbler, Amber, 8 Oz., 3 ⅝ In. 14
Daisy & Button, Wine, Green, 4 ⅞ In. 7
Daisy & Cube, Creamer, Amber, 3 In. 14
Daisy & Cube, Sugar, Handles, Amber, 2 ¾ In. 14
Daisy & Fern, Pitcher, Oval, Cranberry, 64 Oz., 9 ⅝ In. 178
Daisy & Fern, Tumbler, Cranberry, 10 Oz., 4 In. 36
Diamond Quilted, Wine, Green, 4 ¾ In. 13
Double Ring, Wine, Ruby, 5 In. 21
Eyewinker, Creamer, Ruby, 3 ½ In. 18
Eyewinker, Goblet, Water, Amber, 6 ¼ In. 19
Eyewinker, Salt Dip, Ruby, 2 In. 9
Hobnail, Rose Bowl, Ruby Glass, 3 x 4 ¼ In. *illus* 40
Jersey Swirl, Wine, Blue, 4 ¼ In. 15
Lion, Sugar, Lid, 7 In. 92
Milk Glass, Bowl, Oval, Footed, 5 x 2 In. 17
Mirrors & Roses, Goblet, Water, Ruby, 6 ¾ In. 27
Mirrors & Roses, Pickle Jar, Ruby, 4 ⅝ In. 32
Moon & Stars, Ashtray, Green, 8 In. 19
Moon & Stars, Compote, Amber, 7 In. 19
Moon & Stars, Compote, Crimped, Blue, 5 ½ In. 18
Moon & Stars, Compote, Flared, Amber, 6 ¼ x 7 ¾ In. *illus* 25
Moon & Stars, Goblet, Water, Amber, 9 Oz., 5 ⅞ In. 12
Moon & Stars, Goblet, Water, Amethyst, 5 ¾ In. 31
Moon & Stars, Goblet, Water, Ruby, 5 ⅞ In. 37
Moon & Stars, Goblet, Water, Vaseline, Opalescent, 6 In. 62
Moon & Stars, Salt Dip, Ruby, 2 ¼ In. 16
Moon & Stars, Wine, 4 ½ In. 30
Moon & Stars, Wine, Ruby, 4 ½ In. 24
Panel Grape, Creamer, Footed, 10 Oz., 4 ⅜ In. 15
Panel Grape, Goblet, Water, 5 ⅞ In. 16
Panel Grape, Goblet, Water, Ruby, 5 ⅞ In. 37
Panel Grape, Wine, 4 In. 7
Panel Grape, Wine, Ruby, 4 In. 14
Paneled Thistle, Creamer, Footed, 3 ⅜ In. 18
Paneled Thistle, Goblet, Water, 5 ½ In. 12
Paneled Thistle, Relish, 7 ⅛ In. 13

Paneled Thistle, Sugar, Lid. 22
Paneled Thistle, Toothpick Holder, 2 ½ In. 11
Priscilla, Nappy, Crimped, Amber, 6 ½ In. 12
Priscilla, Wine, 4 ⅝ In. 8
Strawberry & Currant, Wine, Amber, 4 ⅞ In. 6
Three Faces, Compote, 4 ¼ In. 45
Three Faces, Goblet, Water, 6 ⅜ In. 24
Three Faces, Shaker, Metal Lid, 5 In. 56
Three Faces, Sugar, Footed, 5 ⅞ In. 23
Three Faces, Toothpick Holder, 2 ½ In. 18
Three Faces, Wine, 5 ½ In. 22
Thumbprint, Tumbler, Amber, 8 Oz., 3 ⅝ In. 13
Westward Ho, Compote, Lid, Oval, 8 ⅞ In. 62
Westward Ho, Spooner, 7 ¾ In. 45
Wild Rose, Wine, Blue, 5 In. 21
Wildflower, Creamer, Amber, 4 ¾ In. 10
Wildflower, Goblet, Water, Amber, 5 ⅞ In. 8
Wildflower, Plate, Luncheon, 9 x 9 In. 13
Wildflower, Sugar, Lid, Footed, Amber, 7 ½ In. 15
Wildflower, Wine, Amber, 5 In. 9

LACQUER is a type of varnish. Collectors are most interested in the Chinese and Japanese lacquer wares made from the Japanese varnish tree. Lacquer wares are made from wood with many coats of lacquer. Sometimes the piece is carved or decorated with ivory or metal inlay.

Bowl, Oblong, Medallion, Gilt, Scroll, Double Handle, 6 ¼ x 5 ¾ In. 484
Bowl, Red Interior, Carved Exterior, 1 ¾ x 3 ½ In., 8 Piece 30
Box, Estate Scene, Multicolor, Russia, 2 ¼ x 5 ¾ In. 69
Box, Fairytale, Boy, Horse, Hinge, Lid, Russia, 1 x 4 In. 156
Box, Hinged Lid, Geometric Decoration, Brass Lock Plate, 4 ⅛ x 14 ¼ In. 960
Box, Horse Drawn Sleigh Ride, Russia, c.1880, 4 ½ x 2 ½ In. 123
Box, Lid, 3 Cranes, Flying Over Trees, Shore, Gold, Silver, Black, 2 x 10 In. 311
Box, Lid, Black, Round, Cranes, Flock, Craggy Mountain, Pavilion, 1 ¼ x 4 In. 2460
Box, Lid, Round, Bats & Lotus Blooms, Ocean, Basket Weave Ground, 10 In. Diam. 988
Box, Lid, Round, Dragon Holding Bowl, Lotus & Scrolling Vine, 10 In. Diam. 741
Box, Lid, Round, Ring Foot, Carved, Burgundy, Figures, Mountains, Flowers, 1800s, 5 In. 1753
Box, Necklace, Lid, Dragons, Flaming Pearls, Swastika Coin, Lotus, Chinese, 10 In. *illus* 1185
Box, Orange, Green, Rounded Sides, Chin Mark, 4 ½ x 10 ¼ In. 278
Box, Outdoor Scenes, People Walking, c.1900, 2 x 7 In. 150
Box, Red, Carved, Vines, Flowers, Chinese, c.1925, 10 In. 615
Box, Scholar's, Mixed Metal, Cranes, Landscape, Japan, 9 ½ x 9 ½ In. 1342
Box, Wealthy Landowner, Peasants, Hinge, Ivan Zubkov, Russia, 1930, 7 ¾ x 5 ½ In. 5250
Box, Work, Octagon, Courtly Figures, Tray, Compartments, Drawer, 1800s, 14 In. 311
Box, Writing, Gold Cranes & Pines, Rectangular, Lid, Japan, c.1900, 6 x 9 In. 1045
Candy Box, Red, Apple Shape, 5 Compartments, Chinese, c.1890, 11 In. 270
Charger, Red & Black, Zodiac Animals In Circle, 15 ½ In. 12
Kimono Box, Inner Tray, Honeycomb Design, Bronze Plates, Lift-Off Lid, 15 x 24 In. 974
Tray, Black, Flowers, Leaves, Japan, 11 ½ x 9 In. 118
Tray, Black, Round, Shallow Walls, Red Edge, Handle, 12 ⅞ In. 308
Trunk, Red, Chinese, 25 x 13 In. 175
Vase, Abalone Inlay, Eagle Chasing Bird, Pine Trees, Copper Collar, 14 x 6 ⅛ In. 360
Vase, Red, Carved, Chinese, 12 In. 276

LADY HEAD VASE, *see Head Vase.*

LALIQUE glass and jewelry were made by Rene Lalique (1860-1945) in Paris, France, between the 1890s and his death in 1945. Beginning in 1921 he had a manufactuing plant in Alsace.The glass was molded, pressed, and engraved in Art Nouveau and Art Deco styles. Most pieces were marked with the signature *R. Lalique*. Lalique glass is still being made. Most pieces made after 1945 bear the mark *Lalique*. After 1980 the registry mark was added and the mark became *Lalique ® France*. In the prices listed here, this is indicated by Lalique (R) France. Some pieces that are advertised as ring dishes or pin dishes were listed as ashtrays in the Lalique factory catalog and are listed as ashtrays here. Names of pieces are given here in French and in English. Jewelry made by Rene Lalique is listed in the Jewelry category.

R.LALIQUE

Ashtray, Square, Serpentine Border, Beveled Edges, Serpentine Design, Engraved, 4 x 4 In. 121
Atomizer, Drapee Dansant, Draped Dancers, Frosted, Nude, Garlands, Metal Top, 6 In. 354

Lacquer, Box, Necklace, Lid, Dragons, Flaming Pearls, Swastika Coin, Lotus, Chinese, 10 In.
$1,185

James D. Julia Auctioneers

Lalique Glassware
Lalique made many types of glassware, including vases, tableware, perfume bottles, jewelry, figurines, hood ornaments, clocks, and lamps. The most famous are decorated with classical figures.

Lalique, Perfume Bottle, Bouchon Cassis, Black Currant, Green, Clear, R. Lalique, 1920, 4 In.
$25,000

Rago Arts and Auction Center

Lalique, Perfume Bottle, Dahlia, Frosted Green, Mushroom Shape Stopper, 8 In.
$1,185

James D. Julia Auctioneers

Lalique, Perfume Bottle, Epines, Swirling Thorns, Blue, R. Lalique France, 1920, 3 ¾ In.
$767

Brunk Auctions

Lalique, Plate, Poissons, Fish, Opalescent, Signed, Lalique, c.1950, 10 ¾ In.
$270

Cowan Auctions

Lalique, Vase, 2 Masks & Handles, Bronze, Smoky Topaz Glass, 1925, 11 x 12 In.
$125,000

Rago Arts and Auction Center

TIP

The best defense against a burglary is a nosy neighbor.

Blotter, Rocker, Cerises, Cherries, Frosted, Blue Patina, 7 In. 988
Blotter, Rocker, Feuilles D'Artichaut, Artichoke Leaves, Frosted, Blue Patina, 7 In. 1067
Bookends, Hirondelk, Swallow, Glass, Frosted, 6 ¼ In. 250
Bowl, Centerpiece, Champs Elysees, Frosted, Clear, Marc Lalique 800
Bowl, Centerpiece, Luxembourg, Cherubs Dancing, Garlands, 10 ½ In. 1599
Bowl, Champs Elysees, Frosted, Clear, Leaf Shape, 7 ¼ x 18 In. 1080
Bowl, Chene, Oak Leaves, Clear, Frosted, 4 x 7 ¾ In. 270
Bowl, Framboises, Raspberries, Purple Frosted & Clear Glass, Box, 8 ½ x 13 In. 3750
Bowl, Gui, Mistletoe, Opalescent Glass, Signed, 12 In. Diam. 148
Bowl, Igor, Tripod Base, Frosted Finish Fish, Marked, 5 ¾ x 7 ¾ In. 136
Bowl, Luxembourg, Cherub, Frosted, High Relief, Garland, 8 ½ x 10 ½ In. 2160
Bowl, Marguerites, Daisies, Overlapping Flowers On Rim, 2 ¾ x 14 ½ In. 360
Bowl, Nemours, Flower Heads, Frosted, Black Centers, 4 x 10 In. .... 480 to 1215
Bowl, Paquerettes, Daisies, Signed, 3 ⅞ x 1 ¼ In. 150
Bowl, Perruches, Parakeets, Opalescent, Gray, Encircling Molded Parrots, 1931, 10 In. 2629
Bowl, Pinsons, Finches, Frosted, Vines, Inscribed Lalique France, 9 ¼ In. 212
Bowl, Plumes, Feathers, Scalloped Rim, 4 x 9 ¾ In. 390
Box, Bureau, Marguerites, Frosted Daisy Pattern Lid, D'Orsay, 4 In. 118
Box, Chat, Cat Face, 2 x 4 In. 300
Candleholder, 3 Anemones, Flower Heads, Signed, 3 In., Pair 115
Candlestick, Mesanges, 2 Birds In Floral Wreath, Frosted & Clear, 1943, 7 In., Pair 461
Caviar Set, Cup, Holder, Bowl, Fish Shape Finial, Lid, 10 x 7 ¾ In., 4 Piece 840
Centerpiece, Miroir Cygnes, Mirror Swans, Etched, Oval, c.1960, 32 In. 4425
Champagne Flute, Ange, Angel, Clear, Frosted, 8 In., 4 Piece 390
Clock, Naiades, Nymphs, Flowing Hair Circles Dial, Blue Patina, Incised R. Lalique, 5 In. 1476
Compote, Frosted Pedestal, Straight-Sided, Clear Bowl, 8 ¾ x 9 ¾ In. 270
Compote, Nogent, Frosted Birds, On Pedestal, Clear Bowl, 3 ½ x 5 ½ In. .... 150 to 212
Compote, Nogent, Pedestal, Clear Bowl On 4 Sparrows' Backs, Round Foot, Signed, 3 x 6 In. 115
Decanter, Argos, 4 Wine Glasses, 11 In. 330
Dresser Box, Enfants, Children, Frosted Glass, 4 In. 210
Dresser Box, Frosted, Clear, Squat, Embossed Lid, Finial, 3 ¼ x 5 ½ In. 150
Figurine, 2 Femmes, 2 Women, Arms, Knees Raised, 5 ½ In. 150
Figurine, 2 Nude Woman, Dancers, Frosted & Clear, Round Base, c.1980, 10 In. 413
Figurine, Cerf, Stag, Lying Down, Frosted & Clear, 10 x 8 ½ In. 246
Figurine, Chien, Dog, Yorky, Frosted, Seated, 2 ¾ x 4 ¼ In. 120
Figurine, Chrysis, Nude Woman, Kneeling, Leaning Backward, Round Base, c.1931, 5 In. 2000
Figurine, Coq Nain, Rooster, Smoky Topaz, Tail Up, c.1928, 8 In. 2625
Figurine, Cygne, Swan, Frosted Glass Cut To Clear, Incised, 1900s, 9 ½ In. 3075
Figurine, Danseuse Bras Baisse, Dancer With Raised Arm, Frosted, 9 In. .... 210 to 360
Figurine, Dinosaurie, Dinosaur, Green Frosted, Marked, France Sticker, 3 x 6 In. 115
Figurine, Madonna & Child, Standing, Clear, Black Glass Base, 15 In. 431
Figurine, Madonna & Enfant, Madonna & Child, Standing, Frosted Glass, Halo, 15 In. 488
Figurine, Panthere, Panther, Zeila, Molded Black Glass, 4 ½ x 14 ½ In. .... 960 to 720
Figurine, Polar Bear, Seated, Clear & Frosted, 6 x 7 In. .... 115 to 300
Figurine, Sea Turtle, Frosted, 4 x 10 ¾ In. 660
Figurine, Siren, Opalescent, Blue, Woman Seated, Seminude, Fins, c.1920, 4 In. 2750
Figurine, Sparrow, Frosted, 3 x 4 ½ In., Pair 180
Goblet, Wine, Bordeaux, Phalsbourg, 6 ½ In., 10 Piece 600
Hood Ornament, Faucon, Falcon, Bird, Radiator Cap Bezel, Wood Base, c.1925, 8 x 5 In. 1875
Hood Ornament, Tete D'Aigle, Eagle Head, Profile, Frosted, 1928, 5 x 6 In. .... 259 to 540
Ice Bucket, Nude Dancers, High Relief, Leaves, Vines, Frosted Glass, Handles, 1900s, 9 In. 1003
Medallion, Saint Christophe, Child On Shoulders, Frosted Intaglio, Radiant Lines, 5 In. 2074
Paperweight, Bison, Frosted Glass, 4 x 5 In. 180
Perfume Bottle, Bouchon Cassis, Black Currant, Green, Clear, R. Lalique, 1920, 4 In. ......*illus* 25000
Perfume Bottle, Clairefontaine, Frosted Lily-Of-The-Valley Stoppers, Signed, 4 ½ In. 83
Perfume Bottle, Clear, Medallions, Classical Nudes, 7 ¾ In. 252
Perfume Bottle, Coty, Amber, Frosted Glass, Sepia Classical Women, Stopper, c.1921 In. 1416
Perfume Bottle, Dahlia, Frosted Green, Mushroom Shape Stopper, 8 In. ....*illus* 1185
Perfume Bottle, Dans La Nuit, In The Night, Stars, Royal Blue, Frosted, Stopper, 3 In. 142
Perfume Bottle, Epines, Swirling Thorns, Blue, R. Lalique France, 1920, 3 ¾ In. ....*illus* 767
Perfume Bottle, For D'Orsay Mystere, Lizards, Black Glass, Block, Stopper, 1912, 3 ¾ In. 708
Perfume Bottle, Globe Shape, Frosted Double Flower Stopper, 6 ½ In. 192
Perfume Bottle, Grande Pomme, Frosted Glass, 5 ½ In. 330
Perfume Bottle, Lepage, Frosted, Clear, Amber, 2 Nudes, Square Stopper, 1920, 5 x 2 In. 7500
Perfume Bottle, Moulin Rouge, Clear & Frosted Glass, 6 ¾ In. 210
Perfume Bottle, Salamandres, Salamanders, Clear & Green, Circles, Stopper, c.1914, 4 In. 1500

Perfume Bottle, Stopper, Etched Serpent, Snake Head Finial, Clear & Orange, c.1920, 3 In. 2750
Plate, Amber, Frosted, Molded Flower Rim, 13 In. 189
Plate, Fleurons, Flowers, Swirling Petals, Opalescent, c.1935, 11 In. 1062
Plate, Poissons, Fish, Opalescent, Signed, Lalique, c.1950, 10 ¾ In. .... *illus* 270
Platter, Martigues, Fish, Amber, Molded Swirling Fish, c.1920, 14 ¼ In. 2813
Scent Bottle, Pivot, Stylized Leaves On Shoulder, Gray Patina, Flower Stopper, 3 In. 5036
Vase, 2 Masks & Handles, Bronze, Smoky Topaz Glass, 1925, 11 x 12 In. .... *illus* 125000
Vase, 3 Jaguars, Frosted, Clear, Molded, 1900s, 11 x 8 In. 1230
Vase, Archers, Etched Nude Male Archers, Raptors, Etched, Round, Tapered, Amber, 11 x 11 In. . 7475
Vase, Aurora, Frosted & Clear, V Shape, Signed, Numbered, Original Box, 13 x 12 In. 6250
Vase, Avallon, Birds On Branches, Berries, Sepia Glass, c.1927, 6 x 6 In. 3000
Vase, Bacchantes, Encircling Female Nudes, Frosted, Signed, 9 ½ x 8 In. 2722
Vase, Bagatelle, Lovebirds, Leaves, Frosted, Etched Base, 6 ¾ In. .... *illus* 384
Vase, Blue Glass, Cylindrical, Angled Rim, Signed, 6 x 2 ½ In. 153
Vase, Ceylan, Lovebirds, Leafy Vines, Frosted Yellow Glass, Flat Rim, 1924, 10 In. .... *illus* 16250
Vase, Ceylon, 2 Parakeets, Intertwined Branches, Tapered, Opalescent, c.1924, 10 In. .... 6335 to 6562
Vase, Claude, Frosted Glass, Bulbous Base, Narrow Neck, Disc Rim, 13 ½ In., Pair 600
Vase, Clear & Frosted, Flared, Molded Lotus Leaves, Leaf Tip Rim, c.1945, 9 In. 750
Vase, Clear & Frosted, Pale Blue, Molded Berry Branches, Flare Rim, c.1930, 8 In. 2988
Vase, Courges, Squash & Vines, Blue, Bulbous, Tapered, Impressed Lalique, 7 ¼ In. 4740
Vase, Crystal & Frosted, 8 Bathing Beauties, Nude, Ribbed Texture, 10 x 8 In. 1035
Vase, Dahlias, Bulbous, Squat, Molded Flower Heads, Blue, Black Enamel, c.1923, 5 In. 2500
Vase, Dampierre, Protruding Birds, Clear & Frosted, 5 In. 270
Vase, Domremy, Thistles, Opalescent, Light Blue Patina, Etched R. Lalique, 8 In. 1482
Vase, Double Dove, Flared, Frosted, Twisted, Fluted Shape, Engraved, 5 In. 230
Vase, Formose, Swirling Carp, Ball Shape, Fish, c.1924, 7 x 6 In. .... 2280 to 3000
Vase, Grignon, Stylized Wheat, Deep Amber, Elongated Oval, Molded Fan Design, 1932, 7 In. 2500
Vase, Gui, Mistletoe, Leaves & Berries, Opalescent, Blue Patina, Round, R. Lalique, 7 In. 1155
Vase, High Relief Opalescent Leaves, Berries, Cylindrical, Clear, 7 In. 474
Vase, Ingrid, Clear & Frosted Glass, 10 ½ x 9 In. .... 728 to 1680
Vase, Insects, Frosted, Green & Blue, Round, Tapered, Rolled Rim, 1913, 11 In. 10888
Vase, Le Mans, Amber, Beige, Swirling Design, Ball Shape, Saucer Foot, c.1931, 4 In. 2868
Vase, Leaves, Flattened Oval, Narrow Mouth, Molded, Opalescent Glass, 1900s, 6 In. 338
Vase, Milan, Ball Shape, Pinched Neck, Molded Leaves, Blue, White Patina, c.1929 43750
Vase, Orleans, Flower Head Repeating Border, Frosted Body, Flared, Footed, c.1910, 7 In. 1888
Vase, Perles, Pearls, 3 Rows Of Draped Strands, Frosted, Oval, Signed R. Lalique, 5 In. 865
Vase, Perruches, Band Of Parakeets, Opalescent Glass, Flat Rim, Blue & Clear, 1924, 9 ½ In. 2280
Vase, Rampillon, Cabochons & Flowers, Ring Foot, Molded Diamond Shapes, 1927, 5 In. 1416
Vase, Ronces, Brambles, Thorny Vines, Frosted, Blue Patina, Oval, Etched R. Lalique, 9 In. 1422
Vase, Ronces, Thorny Vines, Oval, Opalescent, Green Patina, Etched, 1921, 9 x 5 In. .... *illus* 3250
Vase, Satyrs, Frolicking In Vines, Molded Glass, Frosted, High Relief, 1900s, 7 In. 584
Vase, Sauge, Sage Leaves, Frosted Glass, Green Patina, Gourd, Rolled Rim, c.1923, 10 In. 3000
Vase, Soudan, 3 Bands Of Gazelles, Opalescent, Amber Patina, Pear Shape, 1928, 7 x 5 ½ In. 1375
Vase, St. Tropez, Leaves & Berries, Frosted, Polished, Blue, Tapered, Script R. Lalique, 7 In. 1235
Vase, Sylvie, 2 Birds, Clear, Frosted, 8 ½ In. 390
Vase, Tanega, Clear & Green, Molded Leaf At Shoulder, c.1985, 14 ¼ In. 2475
Vase, Tanzania Zebra, Black, Molded Leaves, Banded, 1900s, 8 ½ In. 2124
Vase, Tourbillions, Molded, Enameled, Limited Edition, 8 ¼ x 7 ¾ In. 3000
Vase, Tourbillons, Whirlwind, Frosted Yellow Amber, Geometric Pattern, 1926, 8 x 8 In. .... *illus* 30000
Vase, Tulipes, Tulips, Opalescent, Blue Patina, Molded Flowers, Round, 1927, 8 x 8 In. 2500
Vase, Yasna, Furrows, Molded & Frosted, Square, Tapered, 8 x 6 In. 518
Wall Bracket, Deer, Leaping, Clear & Frosted, c.1945, 10 In., Pair 2000

LAMPS of every type, from the early oil-burning Betty and Phoebe lamps to the recent electric lamps with glass or beaded shades, interest collectors. Fuels used in lamps changed through the years; whale oil (1800–40), camphene (1828), Argand (1830), lard (1833–63), turpentine and alcohol (1840s), gas (1850–79), kerosene (1860), and electricity (1879) are the most common. Other lamps are listed by manufacturer or type of material.

Aladdin, Kerosene, B-63, Clear Glass, Short Lincoln Drape 3797
Art Deco, Funnel Shades, Metal, Painted Green, K.E.M. Weber, c.1930, 45 In., 3 Piece 276
Bouillotte, French Tole Peinte & Brass, 2-Light, c.1900, 20 x 14 x 7 In. 492
Bouilotte, Electric, 3-Light, Louis XVI Style, Gilt Bronze, Gadrooned Drop Cups, 13 In., Pair 1968
Bradley & Hubbard Lamps are included in the Bradley & Hubbard category.
Chandelier, 1-Light, Hans-Agne Jakobsson, Graduated Bentwood, Frame, c.1950, 14 ½ In. 180
Chandelier, 1-Light, Wrought Iron, Banded Basket Shape, Ball Finial Ring, 47 x 29 In. 1000
Chandelier, 3-Light, Art Deco, Frosted Lights, Bronze, Patinated, 24 x 24 In. 1298

TIP

Spray the inside of a glass flower vase with a nonstick product made to keep food from sticking to cooking pots. This will keep the vase from staining if water is left in too long.

Lalique, Vase, Bagatelle, Lovebirds, Leaves, Frosted, Etched Base, 6 ¾ In.
$384

Hess Auction Group

Lalique, Vase, Ceylan, Lovebirds, Leafy Vines, Frosted Yellow Glass, Flat Rim, 1924, 10 In.
$16,250

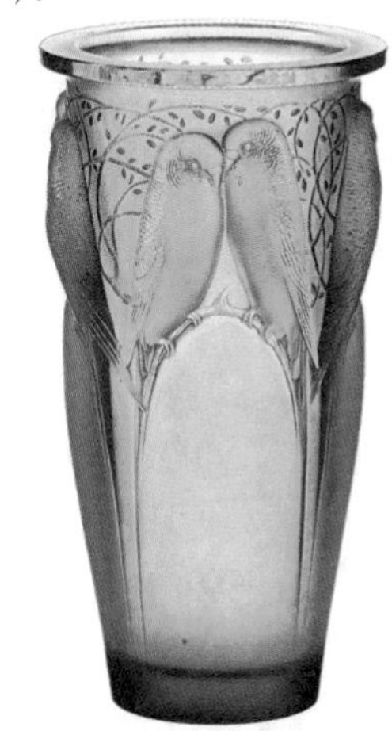

Rago Arts and Auction Center

This is an edited listing of current prices. Visit **Kovels.com** to check thousands of prices from previous years and sign up for free information on trends, tips, reproductions, marks, and more.

L

Lalique, Vase, Ronces, Thorny Vines, Oval, Opalescent, Green Patina, Etched, 1921, 9 x 5 In.
$3,250

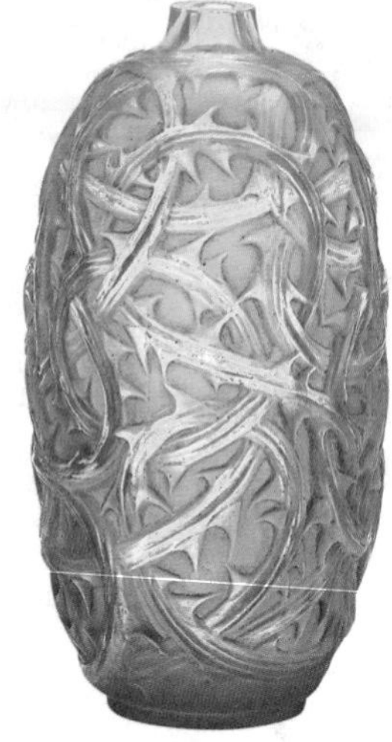

Rago Arts and Auction Center

Lalique, Vase, Tourbillons, Whirlwind, Frosted Yellow Amber, Geometric Pattern, 1926, 8 x 8 In.
$30,000

Rago Arts and Auction Center

Lamp, Chandelier, 3-Light, Bronze, Cut Glass Drops, Molded Chain, Argand, c.1830, 41 In.
$5,412

New Orleans (Cakebread)

Chandelier, 3-Light, Baroque, Wood, Painted, Metal, Turned Standard, 47 x 25 In. 5000
Chandelier, 3-Light, Bronze, Cut Glass Drops, Molded Chain, Argand, c.1830, 41 In. ....*illus* 5412
Chandelier, 3-Light, Ceramic, Stone Grapevine, Brass Chains, Canopy, Electrified, 39 x 19 In. .. 8675
Chandelier, 3-Light, Gilt Bronze, Scroll Arms, Vines, Etched Shades, 1800s, 46 x 25 In. 490
Chandelier, 3-Light, Rococo Style, Bronze Dore, Putti, Wreaths, Leaf Scrolling, 24 x 16 In. 552
Chandelier, 4-Light, 4-Point Stag Antler, Arms, Mermaid Center, Leaves, 13 ½ x 29 In. 1140
Chandelier, 4-Light, Arts & Crafts, Patinated Metal, Slag Glass, c.1910, 34 ½ x 22 In. 3000
Chandelier, 4-Light, Arts & Crafts, Winged Dragons, Gothic Revival, Wrought Iron, 25 x 18 In. 602
Chandelier, 4-Light, Brass, Spherical, Pierced Islamic Medallions, Arms, Chain, 41 x 17 In. 1250
Chandelier, 4-Light, Bronze, Glass Inverted Bell Shade, Chain, Pierced Swags, 30 x 12 In. 676
Chandelier, 4-Light, Dome, Art Deco, Acid Cutback, Molded Metal, Hanging Chain, 18 In. 259
Chandelier, 4-Light, French Provincial, Wrought Iron, Tin, c.1900, 21 x 30 In. 61
Chandelier, 4-Light, Gilt Bronze, Bacchus Masks, Dolphins, Argand, c.1810, 60 x 26 In. ...*illus* 21250
Chandelier, 4-Light, Gilt Metal, Glass, Pierced Fleur-De-Lis, Lyre Shape, c.1900, 40 x 21 In. 123
Chandelier, 4-Light, Iron, Gothic, Chain, 26 x 22 In. 242
Chandelier, 4-Light, Metal, Air Balloon Shape, Openwork, Strips, Paint, 27 x 13 In. 375
Chandelier, 4-Light, Neoclassical, Basket Shape, Swags Of Drops, Metal, 32 x 32 In. 338
Chandelier, 4-Light, Nickeled Brass, Frosted Glass, Parzinger, 1950s, 38 x 21 In. ....*illus* 5000
Chandelier, 4-Light, Tole, Wheat, Grass, Pods, Gilt, Frederick Cooper Style, 21 x 14 In. 272
Chandelier, 4-Light, Woman's Body, Antlers, Wood, Gesso, Lusterweibchen, 19 x 27 In. 1440
Chandelier, 5-Light, Blue Opaline Glass, 25 ½ In. 488
Chandelier, 5-Light, Crystal, Bulbous Diamond Cut Shaft, Hanging Prisms, 1900s, 20 x 19 In. . 1353
Chandelier, 5-Light, Cut Glass, Down Curved Arms, Spiral Twist Shaft, c.1890, 41 x 31 In. 1250
Chandelier, 5-Light, Louis XIV Style, Bronze, Fluted Vase Shape Standard, 22 x 25 In. 1625
Chandelier, 5-Light, Murano Glass, Cream, Purple, Green, c.1960, 24 x 26 In. 303
Chandelier, 5-Light, Murano Glass, Scroll Arms, Venetian, 28 x 22 In. 1560
Chandelier, 6-Light, Adirondack, Antler, 2 Tiers, Drip Sleeves, 30 x 41 In. 1331
Chandelier, 6-Light, Art Deco, Bronze, c.1920, 46 x 24 In. 2178
Chandelier, 6-Light, Art Deco, Frosted Shades, Copper, Flower Base, c.1930, 28 x 29 In. 1476
Chandelier, 6-Light, Baroque Style, Giltwood, Reeded Standard, S-Shape Arms, 36 x 26 In. 1625
Chandelier, 6-Light, Bronze, Gilt, Glass Bowl, Swags, Masks, Teardrop Shades, c.1900, 28 In. 1250
Chandelier, 6-Light, Candle, Tin, Painted Green, 24 x 24 In. 1888
Chandelier, 6-Light, Chrome, Slinky Shape, Lightolier, c.1970, 26 x 23 In. 188
Chandelier, 6-Light, Cut Glass Coin Chain & Pendants, Continental, 39 ½ In. 9375
Chandelier, 6-Light, Cut Glass, Diamond Cut, Spear Prisms, Faceted Drops, c.1890, 36 In. 1750
Chandelier, 6-Light, Cut Molded Glass, Hanging Prisms & Spears, S-Shape Arms, 47 x 30 In. ... 6562
Chandelier, 6-Light, Empire Style, Cut Glass Coins Chain, Glass Bowl, 22 x 22 In. 544
Chandelier, 6-Light, Empire, Bronze, Leaf Molded Arms, Acorn Finial, Electrified, 32 x 30 In. ... 553
Chandelier, 6-Light, French Art Deco, Rosewood, Copper, Frosted Glass Bowls, 28 x 29 In. 1476
Chandelier, 6-Light, Fruit Shape Glass, Wrought Iron, 20 x 23 In. 313
Chandelier, 6-Light, Gilt Brass, Crystal Sprays Of Drops, Prisms, 5 Tiers, c.1950, 29 x 26 In. 984
Chandelier, 6-Light, Gilt Brass, Scroll Arms, Pierced Wreaths, Canopy, Prisms, c.1910, 30 In. 1230
Chandelier, 6-Light, Gilt Bronze, Glass, Hanging Prisms, Beaded Swags, 1900s, 38 x 24 In. 1625
Chandelier, 6-Light, Gilt Bronze, Medallions, Scroll Arms, Drops, Swags, c.1950, 37 x 33 In. 1168
Chandelier, 6-Light, Gilt, Bronze, Bowl, Chains, Shaped Arms, Swan Heads, 24 x 20 In. 750
Chandelier, 6-Light, Gothic, Gilt Bronze, Leaf Pendant Finial, Fret, Chains, c.1875, 40 x 18 In. 1875
Chandelier, 6-Light, Iron, Black, Cage Shape, Candlecups, Upswept Arms, 29 x 34 In. Diam. 242
Chandelier, 6-Light, Lacquer, Gilt, Bronze, Chain Sections, Shaped Bowl, Pineapple, 23 x 18 In. 1125
Chandelier, 6-Light, Louis XIV Style, Bronze, Crystal, Bronze Arms, Drop Strands, 27 x 20 In. ... 750
Chandelier, 6-Light, Louis XVI Style, Basket Shape, Bronze, Crystal, Ribbons, 38 x 25 In. 1353
Chandelier, 6-Light, Lucite, Brass, 42 x 22 In. 375
Chandelier, 6-Light, Modern, Brass, Glass, 20 x 22 In. 330
Chandelier, 6-Light, Murano, Acanthus Leaf Drops, Floral Pedestal, Electrified, 28 ½ In. 708
Chandelier, 6-Light, Parasol Shape, Asian Style, Tole, 30 x 32 In. 660
Chandelier, 6-Light, Porcelain, Putti, Flowers, Pastel Colors, 32 x 19 In. 923
Chandelier, 6-Light, Purple Grape Clusters, 31 x 18 In. 375
Chandelier, 6-Light, Regency Style, Chinoiserie, Red Tole, Silver Gilt, Pagoda Base, 31 x 27 In. 799
Chandelier, 6-Light, Regency, Red Tole, Inverted Pagoda Base, Gilt Chains, c.1830, 23 x 27 In. . 676
Chandelier, 6-Light, Tole, Swan Shape, France, 14 x 22 In. 540
Chandelier, 6-Light, Venetian Glass, Amber To Clear, Bulbous Tapering Post, 26 x 18 In. 472
Chandelier, 6-Light, Venetian Glass, Hand Blown, Gold Flecks, Leaf & Tendrils, 33 x 33 In. 719
Chandelier, 8-Light, 8 4-Point Deer Antlers, 4 4-Point Antler Supports, Canopy, Chain, 34 In. ... 793
Chandelier, 8-Light, Art Nouveau, Brass, Bronze, 38 x 18 In. 615
Chandelier, 8-Light, Brass & Crystal, Glass Sleeves, Spire, Prism Sprays, 1900s, 34 x 24 In. 799
Chandelier, 8-Light, Bronze, Gilt, Masks, 1900s, 28 In. 3500
Chandelier, 8-Light, Bronzed, Prisms, 26 x 29 ½ In. 396

Chandelier, 8-Light, Candle, Iron, S-Shape Arms, Tapered Cone Pendant, c.1800, 14 x 32 In. ... 1067
Chandelier, 8-Light, Gilt Bronze, Chains, 34 ½ x 20 ½ In. 2750
Chandelier, 8-Light, Gilt Bronze, Cut Glass, 2 Tiers, Prisms, Sprays, Drops, c.1950, 43 In. 4920
Chandelier, 8-Light, Gilt Bronze, Foo Dog Heads, Arms, Ribbons, Swags, c.1910, 33 x 29 In. 4674
Chandelier, 8-Light, Giltwood, S-Curve Branches, 3 Tiers, Flowers, Garland, c.1900, 56 In. 5676
Chandelier, 8-Light, Iron & Tole, Baroque Style, Scroll Arms, Leaves, 63 x 40 In. 375
Chandelier, 8-Light, Lacquered Brass, Pierced Spherical Bowl, Glass Shades, c.1890, 43 In. 1500
Chandelier, 9-Light, Cut Glass, Basket Mount, Prisms, Branches, Drops, c.1953, 33 x 24 In. 937
Chandelier, 9-Light, Flared Marble Shades, Relief Medallion, Chained Figure, Bird, 28 x 16 In. 625
Chandelier, 9-Light, Gilt Brass, Clusters Of Multicolor Blown Glass Balls, 28 x 22 In. 375
Chandelier, 9-Light, Pressed Glass Bobeche, Column, Cut Prisms, Swags, Brass, c.1930, 24 In. . 360
Chandelier, 10-Light, Brass, Pierced Baluster Stem, Scrolling Branches, c.1900, 38 x 25 In. 884
Chandelier, 10-Light, Continental, Giltwood, Scaled Dolphins, Shells, 28 x 47 In. 2057
Chandelier, 10-Light, Counter Weight, 57 x 27 In. 375
Chandelier, 10-Light, Frosted Floral Shades, White, Silver, 36 x 24 In. 214
Chandelier, 10-Light, Giltwood, Iron, Prisms, 5 Tiers, Bead Swags, Scroll Arms, 38 x 25 In. 2500
Chandelier, 10-Light, Louis XIV, Silk, Beaded Tin, c.1910, 26 x 26 In. 666
Chandelier, 10-Light, Metal Tubing, Loops, France, c.1950, 42 x 28 In. 600
Chandelier, 12-Light, Aluminum, Amber Glass Cone Shades, Leafy Arms, 1940s, 25 x 36 In. 3750
Chandelier, 12-Light, Belle Epoque, Gilt Bronze, Drip Pans, Electrified, c.1885, 33 In. ......*illus* 1968
Chandelier, 12-Light, Bronze, c.1900, 34 x 29 In. 390
Chandelier, 12-Light, Cut Glass, Metal, Scrolling Prism, 2 Tiers, Swags, 41 In. 1000
Chandelier, 12-Light, Empire, Gilt Bronze, Canopy Crest, Shells, Bell, Flame Finial, 44 x 29 In. 4575
Chandelier, 12-Light, Glass, Gilt Bronze Mounts, Hanging Pendants, Swags, c.1905 3750
Chandelier, 12-Light, Louis XV, Bronze, Gilt, Crystal, Acanthus, Urn, 33 ½ x 23 In. 1573
Chandelier, 12-Light, Louis XV, Gilt, Open Cage, Leaves, Rosettes, 36 x 36 In. Diam. 968
Chandelier, 12-Light, Metal, Faux Candles, Scrolls, Hammered Canopy, Chain, 33 x 42 In. 1845
Chandelier, 12-Light, Tiered, Brass, Scroll Arms, Hexagonal Vase, Chain, c.1900, 40 In. 593
Chandelier, 16 Light, Giltwood, Ring, Glass Coin Chains, 58 x 41 In. 3000
Chandelier, 16-Light, 12 Gas, 4 Electric, Blue Glass Shade, c.1890, 32 x 32 In. 968
Chandelier, 16-Light, Baroque Style, Baluster, Tiered S-Shape Arms, 37 x 31 In. 984
Chandelier, 16-Light, Sevres Style, 5 Cherubs, Vines, Bouquets, Blue, 50 x 52 In. 605
Chandelier, 18-Light, Electric, Sputnik Shape, Chrome, Glass 732
Chandelier, 25-Light, Glass, 2 Tiers, Prisms, Swags Of Drops, Sprays, c.1965, 30 x 31 In. 2337
Chandelier, 36-Light, Gold Metal Expanded Vertical Spiral, Gino Sarfatti, No. 2040 19000
Chandelier, Artichoke Shape, Chrome, Enameled, Copper, Plastic, 1960s, 19 x 24 In. ....*illus* 3625
Chandelier, Brutalist, Tom Greene, Electric, 31 x 24 In. 915
Chandelier, Glass Prisms, Frosted & Clear, Triangular, 3 Tiers, Goldtone, 20 x 29 In. 165
Chandelier, Glass Prisms, Pendant, Fountain Shape, 3 Tiers, 26 x 22 In. 1320
Chandelier, Glass Teardrop Prisms, White & Clear, 2 Tiers, 25 x 20 In. 248
Chandelier, Glass, Hanging In Sheets, Chromed Metal, Murano, c.1980, 15 x 12 In. 390
Chandelier, Glass, Metal Framework, Clear Leaves, Chain, Italy, 1900s, 16 In. Diam. 1107
Chandelier, Globe Shape, Glass, Electric, Emil Stejnar, 19 In. Diam. 2700
Chandelier, Slag Glass, Spelter, Panels, Landscape Scenes, c.1910, 15 x 28 In. 356
Chandelier, Sputnik Style, Glass, Metal, Electric, 1960s, 60 x 40 In. 10000
Chandelier, Venetian Blue & Clear Glass, Beads, 59 x 24 In. 3000
Electric, 2-Light, Amber Elephant Finial, Cold Painted, Metal, Octagonal Base, 33 In. 113
Electric, 2-Light, Opaline Glass, Gilt Bronze, White, Pull String, 33 In., Pair 750
Electric, 3-Light, Mother-Of-Pearl Snail-Shape Shell Shades, Tripod Leaf Base, c.1910, 17 In. ... 840
Electric, 7 Lucite Rods, Vertical, Banded, Stepped Wood Base, 2 Sockets, Drum Shade, 16 In. 185
Electric, Alabaster, 3 Graces, Domed Shade, Cherubs, c.1885, 29 x 17 In. ....*illus* 1952
Electric, Angelo Lelli Arredoluce, Acrylic, Brass, Enameled Steel, 1950s, 17 x 7 In. ....*illus* 2125
Electric, Angelo Lelli, Cobra, Adjustable, Brass, Enamel, Metal, 1960s, 24 x 4 In. ....*illus* 4688
Electric, Arredoluce, 3-Light, Triennale, Nickeled Brass, Enameled Metal, 1960s, 62 In. 6250
Electric, Art Deco, Marble, Carved, Elephant, Holding Milk Glass Shade, 19 x 16 In., Pair.......... 1778
Electric, Art Deco, Mica, Patinated Metal, Glass, France, 1920s, 20 x 9 ½ In. 813
Electric, Art Deco, Seated Nude Holding Frosted Ball, Bronze Tone Pedestal, 20 In., Pair 218
Electric, Art Deco, Star Shape, Frosted, c.1920, 13 x 16 In. 91
Electric, Art Glass, Mushroom Shape, Brown Spots, Metal Base, 1900s, 15 x 11 In. 138
Electric, Art Nouveau, Gilt Metal, Slag Glass Shade, c.1910, 13 x 8 In. 270
Electric, Art Nouveau, Tole, Elephant Ear Plant Base, Morning Glories, Birds, c.1900, 63 x 17 In. 2706
Electric, Arteluce, Aluminum Shade, Rotating Knee Joint, Wall Mounted, c.1970, 4 ½ In. 177
Electric, Arts & Crafts, Copper Shade, Hammered, Oak Base, c.1910, 31 In. 472
Electric, Ballroom Fixture, Mirrored, Motorized, 14 x 24 In. 1440
Electric, Bergboms, Brass, Leather, Linen Shade, 1960s, 46 x 16 In. 1000
Electric, Brass Plated, Alter Stick Shape, Columnar, Tripartite Base, c.1965, 40 x 8 In., Pair....... 861

Lamp, Chandelier, 4-Light, Gilt Bronze, Bacchus Masks, Dolphins, Argand, c.1810, 60 x 26 In.
$21,250

Neal Auctions

Lamp, Chandelier, 4-Light, Nickeled Brass, Frosted Glass, Parzinger, 1950s, 38 x 21 In.
$5,000

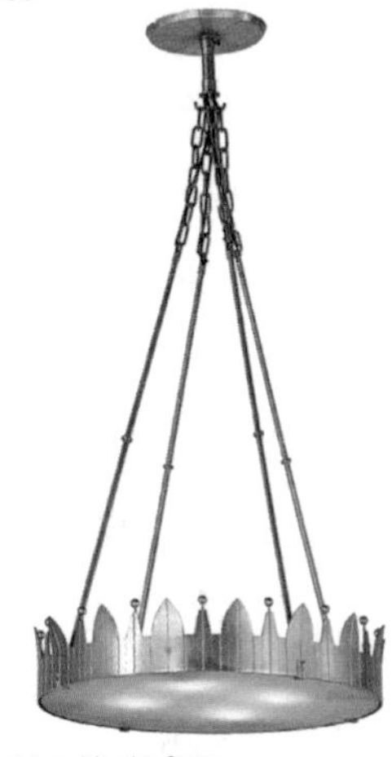

Rago Arts and Auction Center

Lamp, Chandelier, 12-Light, Belle Epoque, Gilt Bronze, Drip Pans, Electrified, c.1885, 33 In.
$1,968

New Orleans (Cakebread)

L

Lamp, Chandelier, Artichoke Shape, Chrome, Enameled, Copper, Plastic, 1960s, 19 x 24 In.
$3,625

Rago Arts and Auction Center

Lamp, Electric, Alabaster, 3 Graces, Domed Shade, Cherubs, c.1885, 29 x 17 In.
$1,952

Neal Auctions

Lamp, Electric, Angelo Lelli Arredoluce, Acrylic, Brass, Enameled Steel, 1950s, 17 x 7 In.
$2,125

Rago Arts and Auction Center

Lamp, Electric, Angelo Lelli, Cobra, Adjustable, Brass, Enamel, Metal, 1960s, 24 x 4 In.
$4,688

Rago Arts and Auction Center

TIP

When cleaning a chandelier, do not spin it around. This could damage the wiring or the chain holding it. Instead of moving the fixture, move your ladder around it.

Lamp, Electric, Bronze, 2 Arabs, Tent, Cold Painted, Marble Base, Signed, Chotka, 16 x 11 In.
$9,263

James D. Julia Auctioneers

Lamp, Electric, Chicago Mosaic, Leaded Shade, Flowers, Leaves, Tree Trunk Base, 23 In.
$830

James D. Julia Auctioneers

Lamp, Electric, Cut Glass, Harvard Pattern, Domed Shade, Prisms, c.1905, 24 In.
$1,470

Neal Auctions

Lamp, Electric, Duffner & Kimberly, Elizabethan, Square Leaded Shade, Metal Base, 19 In.
$17,183

James D. Julia Auctioneers

Electric, Brass, Enameled, 3-Light, Linen Shade, T.H. Robsjohn-Gibbings, 1950s, 56 x 20 In., Pair 10000
Electric, Brass, Pierced Domed Shade, Cattail & Bird Design, Stepped Base, c.1910, 22 x 13 In. . 178
Electric, Bright Orange, Globe, Glossy, Pottery, 27 x 13 In., Pair 330
Electric, Bronze, 2 Arabs, Tent, Cold Painted, Marble Base, Signed, Chotka, 16 x 11 In. ..... *illus* 9263
Electric, Bronze, Art Nouveau Curves, 4 Iridescent Shades, Hearts, Vines, Austria, 28 In. 448
Electric, Bronze, Green Patinated, Figural, Nude Dancers, Schnittmann, 1948, 10 ½ In. 531
Electric, Bronze, Tole Shade, Molded Arms, Round Base Engine Turned Design, c.1910, 26 In. .. 738
Electric, Caramel Slag Glass, 6 Panels, Satin Glass, Patinated Spelter Base, 23 x 17 In. 260
Electric, Cast Iron, Open, Vase Shape, 1900s, 21 ½ x 20 In. 363
Electric, Ceiling, Beaded Crystal, Dome Shape, 10 In., Pair 600
Electric, Ceramic, Crackle Glaze, Blue, Tanner & Kenzie, 24 ½ x 9 ¼ In., Pair 302
Electric, Chalkware, Goddess Pomona, Robes, Holding Fruit, Cornucopia, Flute, c.1950, 60 x 12 In. .. 847
Electric, Charles Lotton, Frosted White, Pink Flowers, Bell Shade, Finial, 1989, 28 In. 230
Electric, Chicago Mosaic, Leaded Shade, Flowers, Leaves, Tree Trunk Base, 23 In. .... *illus* 830
Electric, Chimpanzee, Holds Stem, 3-Light, Bronze, 18 ½ In. 343
Electric, Chinese Official, Court Attire, Porcelain, Argo Light Co., 1940s, 34 In. 92
Electric, Chrome Stacked Ball, 1970s, 25 ½ x 6 In., Pair 275
Electric, Chrome, Extendable Arched Arm, Marble Base, Stendig, Italy, 1960s, 105 In. 885
Electric, Chrystiane Charles, Bambou, 3-Light, Brass, France, 1978, 25 x 14 In. 2250
Electric, Classique, Chipped Ice Shade, Ocean, Moon, Urn Stem, Hexagonal Foot, 1918, 22 In. . 4014
Electric, Contemporary, Faux Tortoiseshell Lucite Shade, Double Socket, Brass, 26 x 19 In. 602
Electric, Couple, Sheep, Porcelain, Violin, Ball Shade, Pierced, Latticework, c.1810, 34 In. 799
Electric, Cut Glass, Drop Prisms, Spears, Saucer Zigzag Foot, Bulb Top, c.1900, 13 In. 127
Electric, Cut Glass, Etched, Domed Shade, Prisms, 1880s, 14 ½ In. 270
Electric, Cut Glass, Harvard Pattern, Domed Shade, Prisms, c.1905, 24 In. .... *illus* 1470
Electric, Dancing Girl, Millefiori Glass Ball, Dancer, Ivorine Face, Gold Finish, Italy, 9 x 5 In. ... 483
Electric, Duffner & Kimberly, Caramel Slag, Green Fish Scale Border, Ribbed Base, 23 In. 4261
Electric, Duffner & Kimberly, Elizabethan, Square Leaded Shade, Metal Base, 19 In. .... *illus* 17183
Electric, Duffner & Kimberly, Iris, Granite Glass, Pink, Purple, Green, Peacock Base, 28 In. 3555
Electric, Duffner & Kimberly, Leaded Slag Glass, Geometric, Metal Base, 1900s, 34 In. ..... *illus* 1250
Electric, Duffner & Kimberly, Thistle Shade, Purple, Green, Amber, Bronze Base, 20 In. 17775
Electric, Empire Style, Ormolu, Brass, Pierced, Scrolling Leaf Base, Roundels, c.1910, 72 x 16 In. 207
Electric, Floor, Brass, Pyramid Shape Shade, Square Base, Chapman Lamp Co., 40 ½ In. 250
Electric, Floor, Curtis Jere, Chrome Vertical Cutout Track Design, 63 In. 950
Electric, Floor, Nickeled Brass, Marble, Mica Shade, Mutual Sunset, 1930s, 57 In. .... *illus* 1875
Electric, Floor, Reggiani, Chrome Post, Glass Domed Shade, Round Base, 80 ½ In. 1300
Electric, Flos Arco, Adjustable Arch, Stainless Frame, Aluminum Globe Shade, 1962, 92 x 86 In. 546
Electric, Fostoria, Gilt Brass, Stylized Heart-Shape Tubular Harp, Swing Light, 14 x 9 ⅞ In. 546
Electric, Gilt Metal, Curlicues, Round Base, 22 In. 38
Electric, Gilt Metal, Marble, Urn Shape, Ram's Head Handles, Swags, c.1900, 23 In., Pair 984
Electric, Gilt Metal, Slag Glass Panels, Vase Shape, Dogwood Flowers, 21 x 16 In. 780
Electric, Gorham, Leaded Glass, Sprays, Geometric, Bronze Tree Trunk Base, 20 In. .... *illus* 5333
Electric, Hanging, 3-Light, Verner Panton, Spiral Triple SP3, Cellidor, Monofilament, 1960s, 87 x 22 In. . 7500
Electric, Hanging, John Morgan, Leaded Slag Glass, Chain, Acorns, 1900s, 35 x 30 In. ...... *illus* 6875
Electric, Hanging, National Mazda Lamps, Lightbulb, Black & Yellow, 21 x 21 In. 240
Electric, Hanging, Opaline Glass, Handkerchief Shape, 11 In. 312
Electric, Hanging, Verner Panton Style, Semi Globe Shape Aluminum, Lightolier, 10 x 16 In. ... 81
Electric, Imari Bottle, Red, White, Dragon, 32 In., Pair 1500
Electric, Industrial Design, Accordion Arm, Metal, 15 ½ In. 198
Electric, Jacques Adnet, Stitched Leather, Brass, Vellum Shade, 1960s, 57 x 18 In. 3000
Electric, Jean Rispal, Walnut, Linen, Floor, c.1950, 68 x 20 x 11 In. .... *illus* 7500
Electric, Jefferson, Chipped Ice Shade, Pond, Trees, Hills, Textured Bulbous Base, 23 In. 2779
Electric, Jefferson, Reverse Painted Glass, Landscape, Multicolor, c.1910, 23 x 18 In. 1020
Electric, Jo Hammerborg, Teak, Brass, Glass, Fog & Morup, Denmark, c.1960, 13 In. .... *illus* 800
Electric, Kurt Verson, Brushed Aluminum, Flip-Flop, Off Center, c.1940, 61 ¾ x 16 ¾ In. 726
Electric, Leaded Glass, Cast Bronze Art Nouveau Base, Verdigris, 22 x 20 In. 3134
Electric, Leaded Slag Glass Shade, Geometric, Metal Tree Base, Suess, c.1900, 24 In. .... *illus* 13750
Electric, Leaded Slag Glass, Blue, Bulb Shape, Hanging, 36 x 14 In. 437
Electric, Lisa Johansson-Pope, Frosted Glass, Mushroom Shape, 1950s, 17 x 10 In., Pair. 1438
Electric, Lucite, Block, Lattice, After Karl Springer, 19 x 7 5/16 In., Pair 847
Electric, Marble, Bronze, Urn Shape, Dionysus Head, Pierced Base, c.1910, 30 In., Pair 1250
Electric, Marble, Horned Goats, 17 ¼ In. 281
Electric, Marble, Variegated, Flared Shade, Molded Base, 1900s, 24 x 7 In., Pair 717
Electric, McKee, Art Deco, Danse De Lumere, Figural, Frosted Amber Glass, Cast, 11 x 10 In. 702
Electric, Metal, Crane, Stretched Fabric, Leaf Shades, 67 x 36 In. 110
Electric, Midcentury Modern, Acrylic, Brass, Cylinder Shape, 30 In., Pair 423

Lamp, Electric, Duffner & Kimberly, Leaded Slag Glass, Geometric, Metal Base, 1900s, 34 In.
$1,250

Rago Arts and Auction Center

Lamp, Electric, Floor, Nickeled Brass, Marble, Mica Shade, Mutual Sunset, 1930s, 57 In.
$1,875

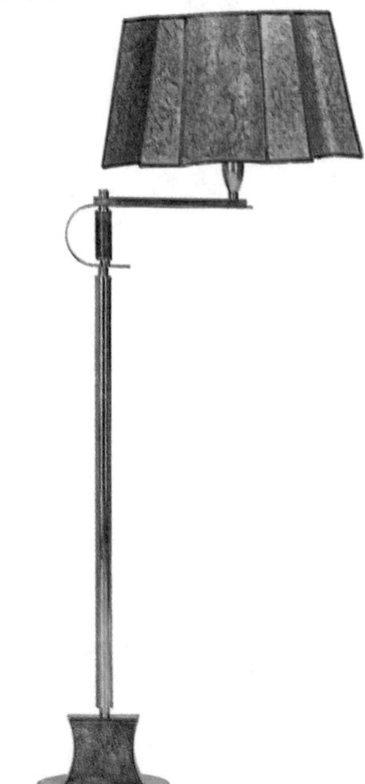

Rago Arts and Auction Center

TIP

When rewiring an old Arts and Crafts lamp, use fabric-covered wire that looks very much like the silk-wrapped cord used at the turn of the twentieth century.

TIP
Use a soft-bristle paint brush to dust lampshades.

Lamp, Electric, Gorham, Leaded Glass, Sprays, Geometric, Bronze Tree Trunk Base, 20 In.
$5,333

James D. Julia Auctioneers

Lamp, Electric, Hanging, John Morgan, Leaded Slag Glass, Chain, Acorns, 1900s, 35 x 30 In.
$6,875

Rago Arts and Auction Center

Big Three Lampmakers
Collectors' most wanted names in early-twentieth-century American electric lamps are Tiffany, Handel, and Pairpoint. The three companies made glass lampshades in Art Nouveau and Art Deco styles. Lamp bases were usually bronze. Table lamps by the "big three" sell for the highest prices, but there are similar, signed lamps by less famous makers.

Electric, Midcentury Modern, Chrome, Acrylic, Lucite, 4 Posts, Italy, 30 In. 500
Electric, Miller & Co., 4-Panel Caramel Slag Glass, Single Socket, Signed, 19 x 12 x 12 ½ In. 311
Electric, Modernist, Ice Cube, 9 Glass Cubes, Brass, Geotano Sciolari, Lightolier, 17 x 17 In. 59
Electric, Moe Bridges, Reverse Painted Shade, Ocean, Moon, Urn Base, Handles, 23 In. .....*illus* 1778
Electric, Moe Bridges, Reverse Painted, Bronze Base, 21 x 15 In. 800
Electric, Murano Glass, Egg Shape, Lucite Base, Chrome, c.1975, 25 ¾ In. 847
Electric, Murano Glass, Ribbed, Metal, 31 ½ In., Pair 1634
Electric, O. Bach, Bronze, 3 Classical Figures, Gold Iridescent Cypriot Ball Shade, 18 In. 2370
Electric, Oscar Bach, Leaded Glass Shade, Sphinxes, Pyramids, Metal Base, 28 In. 8750
Electric, Painted Metal, Urn On Cube, Bright Flowers, Blue Ground, 40 In., Pair 125
Electric, Parker, Caramel Slag Glass Panels, Metal Overlay, Swirls, Ribbons, Urn Base, 22 In. 2161
Electric, Pendant, Artichoke, Poul Henningsen, Copper, Chrome, Louis Poulsen, 24 x 30 In. 3599
Electric, Porcelain, Pink, Green, Flower Swags, Pull Strings, 29 In. 200
Electric, Rattan, Heywood-Wakefield, Crisscross Design, Fabric Lined, c.1900, 18 In. ....*illus* 338
Electric, Reverse Painted, 8 Panels, Mountainous Landscape Scene, Light-Up Base, 26 x 18 In. 189
Electric, Reverse Painted, Domed Frosted Glass Shade, Pittsburgh Lamp Co., c.1920, 23 x 17 In. 915
Electric, Stiffel, Chrome, Genie Bottle Shape, 4 Ball Feet, 25 In., Pair 303
Electric, Tole, Fruit, Square Base, 25 In. 125
Electric, Tole, Green, Black Cityscape Transfer, Parchment Shades, c.1950, 22 x 14 In., Pair 312
Electric, Torchere, Modernist, Max Bill, Painted White, Round Base, 65 In., Pair 1708
Electric, Urn Shape, Cranberry Glass, Metal Mounts, Murano, 1960s, 38 ½ x 8 In., Pair 358
Electric, Urn Shape, Gilt Metal, Marble Mount, Acanthus, 33 ¼ In., Pair 188
Electric, Urn Shape, Porcelain, Famille Jaune, 20 ½ In., Pair 125
Electric, W. Prosper, Copper, Tall Stem, Flared Uplighter Shade, 1982, 79 In., Pair 6335
Electric, Wilkinson, Lily Pond, Leaded Shade, Striated, Leaves, Lily Pad Feet, 30 In. ....*illus* 2666
Electric, Wood, Carved, Sculptural, Gold Leaf Base, Top, James Mont, 33 ½ In., Pair 750
Gasolier, 3-Light, Brass, Coppered, Lacquer, Butterflies, Flowers, Urns, Birds, c.1880, 35 In. 1500
Gasolier, 3-Light, Bronze, Fluted Stem, Flowers, Leaves, Arms, Glass Shades, c.1870, 45 In. 937
Gasolier, 4-Light, Brass, Gilt, Glass, Archer, Warner, Miskey, c.1865, 26 In. ....*illus* 1968
Gasolier, 4-Light, Cut & Frosted Glass, Vase Shape, Ball Shades, Spear Prisms, c.1865, 40 In. 1476
Gasolier, 6-Light, Cut Glass, Fluted Stem, Hanging Spears, Scroll Arms, c.1890, 43 x 35 In. 2250
Gasolier, 6-Light, Pierced Brass Corona, Strands Of Drops, Scroll Arms, c.1890, 35 x 29 In. 738
Gasoliers, Leafy Canopy, Grapevines, Lion, Grotesque Masks, 55 x 37 In., Pair 6405
Grease, Betty, Sheet Iron, Wrought Iron, Twisted Shaft, Wick Pick, Hanging, 1800s, 4 In. 71
Handel Lamps are included in the Handel category.
Hanging, French Provincial, Tin, Rectangular, c.1910, 22 x 12 In. 212
Kerosene, Banquet, Silver Plated, Etched Spherical Shade, c.1890, 36 In. 302
Kerosene, Overlay, Amethyst Cut To Clear, Font, Brass Stem, Marble Base, 9 In., Pair 295
Kerosene, Putti, Green, Urn Shape, 29 x 7 In. 595
Mushroom, Midcentury Modern, Frosted Glass, Polished Chrome, 17 x 5 ¼ In., Pair 726
Oil, Astral, Cut Glass Shade, Spear Prisms, Column Shaft, Marble Base, 1800s, 23 In. 185
Oil, Bronze, Round Well, Spout, Birds, Banded, Reeding, Circular Foot, 8 ½ In. 91
Oil, Bronze, Winged Figure, Boat Shape, Paw Feet, Square Base, c.1885, 4 x 10 In. 1593
Oil, Cranberry Glass, Brass Burner, Plume & Atwood, c.1890, 28 x 11 In. 151
Oil, Cranberry Glass, Hobnail, Pull-Down, Marching Shade, Brass, c.1895, 36 x 16 In. 1089
Oil, Glass Font, Ruby Cut To Clear, Grapes, Leaves, Fluted Brass & Marble Base, 12 In., Pair........ 180
Oil, Gone With The Wind, Delft Decoration, Mythical Beasts, Brass Fittings, Scrolled, 33 In. 920
Oil, Opaline Glass, Blue, Enamel, Pendants, Globe Shape Above Vase Shape, 27 In., Pair 1375
Oil, Student, Brass Harvard Base, Maroon Ribbed Glass Shade, Opal Liner, 20 In. 1035
Oil, Student, Glass, Rubina, Frosted, Hobnail, Square Marble Base, 21 ½ In. 173
Oil, World Globe Shade, Reticulated Brass Base, Marble Shaft, Bradley & Hubbard, 1829, 24 In. 720
Pairpoint Lamps are in the Pairpoint category.
Perfume, Chorus Girl, Top Hat, Standing Near Urn, Art Deco, Germany, 10 In. ....*illus* 1968
Perfume, Diana The Huntress, Crescent Moon Headdress, 2 Gazelles, Porcelain, Metal, 9 In. 584
Piano, Brass, Frosted Cranberry Glass Shade, Flowers, Pierced Font Holder, Spiral Feet, 66 In. .. 984
Piano, Brass, Onyx, Glass Ball Shade, Faux Jewels, Grapevine, Cabriole Legs, c.1890, 66 x 14 In. . 799
Rushholder, Alpine Candle, Scrolled Spring Support, Wrought Iron, Tripod Base, 1800, 27 In. . 826
Sconce, 1-Light, Art Deco, Stained Glass, Green, Red, Purple, Yellow, Pair, 21 ½ x 33 In. 302
Sconce, 1-Light, Brass, Embossed, Candle, Rococo, Wall Plaque, Shells, 15 ¼ x 10 In. 424
Sconce, 1-Light, Bronze, Leaf & Scroll Backplate, Putti, Cornucopia, 1800s, 12 x 9 In., Pair....... 1875
Sconce, 1-Light, Bronze, Silvered, Frosted Shade, Flowers, 2 Birds, c.1925, 12 In., Pair.......... 6929
Sconce, 1-Light, Candle, Sheet Iron, Shield Back, Crimped, c.1800, 12 x 7 In., Pair 1007
Sconce, 1-Light, Gaucho Spur, 12 ½ In., Pair 625
Sconce, 1-Light, Gilt, Metal, Leaf Molded Backplate, Leaf Arms, c.1935, 17 x 7 In., Pair 625
Sconce, 1-Light, Gilt Bronze, Griffin-Shape Arm, Glass Shade, Gas, 1800s, 7 In., Pair ....*illus* 1952
Sconce, 1-Light, Tin, Fan, 12 In. 322

Lamp, Electric, Jean Rispal, Walnut, Linen, Floor, c.1950, 68 x 20 x 11 In.
$7,500

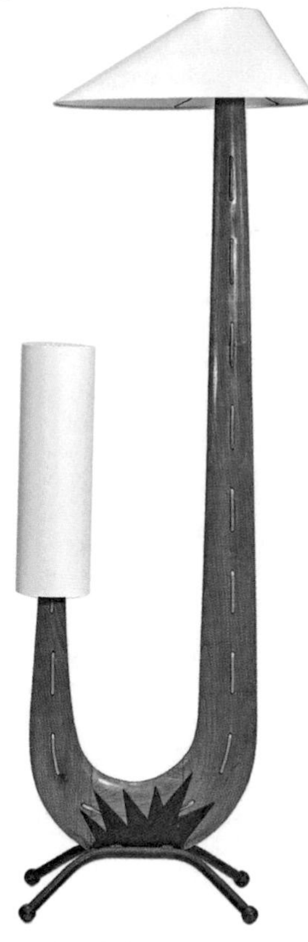

Los Angeles Modern Auctions

TIP
Outdoor lights help prevent crimes, but install them high enough so they are difficult to unscrew.

Lamp, Electric, Jo Hammerborg, Teak, Brass, Glass, Fog & Morup, Denmark, c.1960, 13 In.
$800

Skinner, Inc.

Lamp, Electric, Leaded Slag Glass Shade, Geometric, Metal Tree Base, Suess, c.1900, 24 In.
$13,750

Rago Arts and Auction Center

Lamp, Electric, Moe Bridges, Reverse Painted Shade, Ocean, Moon, Urn Base, Handles, 23 In.
$1,778

James D. Julia Auctioneers

Lamp, Electric, Rattan, Heywood-Wakefield, Crisscross Design, Fabric Lined, c.1900, 18 In.
$338

Skinner, Inc.

Lamp, Electric, Wilkinson, Lily Pond, Leaded Shade, Striated, Leaves, Lily Pad Feet, 30 In.
$2,666

James D. Julia Auctioneers

Lamp, Gasolier, 4-Light, Brass, Gilt, Glass, Archer, Warner, Miskey, c.1865, 26 In.
$1,968

New Orleans (Cakebread)

Lamp, Perfume, Chorus Girl, Top Hat, Standing Near Urn, Art Deco, Germany, 10 In.
$1,968

Skinner, Inc.

Lamp, Sconce, 1-Light, Gilt Bronze, Griffin-Shape Arm, Glass Shade, Gas, 1800s, 7 In., Pair
$1,952

Neal Auctions

Lamp, Solar, Gothic, Brass Mounted, Crystal, Pierced Chimney Holder, Marble, c.1840, 37 In.
$956

Neal Auctions

Lamp, Whale Oil, Pewter Gimble, Saucer Base, Hanging Ring, Swivel Font, 6 In.
$47

Hess Auction Group

Sconce, 2-Light, Bronze, Quiver Backplate, Urns, Flames, Scroll Arms, 1900s, 16 In., Pair 492
Sconce, 2-Light, Ebonized, Brass, Modern, Javelin Shape, 33 ½ x 4 ½ In., Pair 1125
Sconce, 2-Light, Federal, Bronze, Gilt, Eagle, Feathered, Laurel Swag, 12 x 10 In., Pair 968
Sconce, 2-Light, George III, Giltwood, Fluted Back, Leaves, Anthemion, c.1770, 40 In., Pair 4720
Sconce, 2-Light, Gilt Bronze, Leafy Scroll Backplate & Arms, 19 x 11 In., Pair 368
Sconce, 2-Light, Gilt Bronze, Leafy, Fruit, Scroll Arms, S-Scroll Backplate, 35 In., Pair 3165
Sconce, 2-Light, Gilt Bronze, Quiver Shape, Arrows, Leafy Scrolled Arms, 1900s, 19 In., Pair 1476
Sconce, 2-Light, Gilt Metal, Glass, Scroll Branches, Urn, Bird, 1900s, 15 ½ In., Pair 1000
Sconce, 2-Light, Gilt Metal, Leafy Vine, 27 ½ x 16 ¾ In., Pair 250
Sconce, 2-Light, Gilt Metal, Porcelain, Applied Flowers, 18 In. 75
Sconce, 2-Light, Gilt Metal, Rock Crystal, Urn, Scrolling Arms, Flowers, Pendants, 26 x 13 In. ... 125
Sconce, 2-Light, Giltwood, Oval Mirror, Scrolled Arms, Pierced, c.1860, 26 x 16 In., Pair 2706
Sconce, 2-Light, Iron, Flower Shape Backplate, Circle Design, Scroll Arms, 1800s, 17 In., Pair ... 150
Sconce, 2-Light, Iron, Mirror, Frosted, Arched, 15 ¾ x 9 In. 605
Sconce, 2-Light, Louis XV, Ormolu, Acanthus Covered Branches, 17 In., Pair 750
Sconce, 2-Light, Louis XVI Style, Gilt, Bronze, Scroll Branches, Putti, c.1890, 21 In., Pair 1062
Sconce, 2-Light, Metal, Rock Crystal, Flower Sprays, Branches, Drops, 1900s, 26 In., Pair 4428
Sconce, 2-Light, Metal, Silvered, Urn, Scroll Arms, Neoclassical Style, 16 x 7 ½ In., Pair 250
Sconce, 2-Light, Painted Metal, Sheaf Of Wheat Backplates, 1900s, 31 x 13 In., Pair 468
Sconce, 2-Light, Parcel Gilt, Monkey, Vest, Fruit, Italy, 1900s, 21 ¼ x 15 ¾ In. 242
Sconce, 2-Light, Parcel Gilt, Quiver Backplate, Swan, Carved Cups, c.1935, 23 In., Pair 1353
Sconce, 2-Light, Shield Shape, Wall, Mirror Back, 24 x 95 In., Pair 360
Sconce, 2-Light, Silver Plate, Tapered Back, Twisted Arms, c.1910, 11 x 13 In., Set Of 4 1250
Sconce, 2-Light, Wrought Iron, Curlicues, Electric, 1800s, 15 x 11 x 5 In., Pair 338
Sconce, 3-Light, Empire, Silvered Metal, Arrow, Feather, Circle, 29 In. 750
Sconce, 3-Light, Gilt Bronze, Leaf Branches, Roses Crest, Crystal Drops Spray, 22 In., Pair 676
Sconce, 3-Light, Gilt Bronze, Leafy Branches, 26 x 16 ½ In., Pair 3422
Sconce, 3-Light, Gilt Metal, Basket, Leafy Branches, 3 Scrolling Arms, 14 x 14 In., Pair 177
Sconce, 3-Light, Gilt Metal, Glass, 19 In. 406
Sconce, 3-Light, Gilt Wood, Iron, Daisy, 13 ¾ x 22 In., Pair 875
Sconce, 3-Light, Giltwood, Glass, Metal, Vase Shape, Leaves, Drops, c.1935, 15 x 11 In., Pair 625
Sconce, 3-Light, Giltwood, Mirror, Pierced Crest, Shells, Flowers, c.1850, 31 x 17 In., Pair 1062
Sconce, 3-Light, Sheet Iron, Punched, Scrolled Heart, Lunette, Lobed Top, c.1800, 11 x 11 In. ... 1422
Sconce, 3-Light, Shield, 2 Swords, 41 ½ x 22 In. 110
Sconce, 4-Light, Baccarat Cut Crystal Garlands & Drops, 27 x 18 In. 2440
Sconce, 4-Light, Ormolu, Cut Glass, Jasperware, 1900s, 43 x 31 In., Pair 2750
Sconce, 5-Light, Brass, Tassels, Intertwined Bellflowers, Leaf Arms, Prisms, 31 x 18 In., Pair 799
Sconce, 5-Light, Gilt Bronze, Crystal, Lyre Back, Scroll Arms, Prisms, 1900s, 27 In., Pair 1845
Sconce, 5-Light, Gilt Bronze, Fluted Nozzles, Scroll Arms, Urn, Mask, c.1890, 41 In., Pair 4375
Sconce, 5-Light, Gilt Bronze, Pierced Shield, Cabochons, Branches, Mask, 14 x 13 In., Pair 750
Sconce, 7-Light, Wrought Iron, Cluster Of Branches Shape, 1900s, 62 x 33 In., Pair 424
Sconce, Baronial Style, Silvered, Giltwood, Backplates, Acanthus, Italy, 21 x 13 In., Pair 1375
Sconce, Brass, Lily Pan, Tommaso Barbi, 17 In. 127
Sconce, Candle, 5-Light, Gilt, Iron, Oval Laurel, Berry, 15 x 11 In., Pair 544
Sconce, Candle, Tin, Arched, Crimped Top, Tooled Reflectors, Demilune Base, 13 x 4 In., Pair. .. 492
Sconce, Candle, Tin, Mirror Back, Oval Panels, Saucer Base, 1800s, 16 ½ x 7 In., Pair 826
Sconce, Electric, 1-Light, Art Deco, Frosted Glass Inserts, 13 x 7 ½ In. 375
Sconce, Louis XVI, Bronze, 3 Spindles, Finial, Shaped Wall Plate, c.1910, 14 x 11 In., Pair 182
Sconce, Meissen Style, Oval, Cove Molded Frame, Sculpted Flowers, c.1900, 22 x 13 In., Pair 687
Sconce, Murano Glass, Grapevine, Pink, Green, 11 ¾ x 6 ½ In. 424
Sconce, Parcel Gilt, Mirrored, Leaf Bracket, Blackamoor Figure, Basket, 1800s, 36 In., Pair 2337
Sconce, Rock Crystal, 27 In., Pair 3042
Sconce, Victorian, Bronze, Gargoyle, c.1890, 23 x 14 In. 605
Solar, Gothic, Brass Mounted, Crystal, Pierced Chimney Holder, Marble, c.1840, 37 In. ..... *illus* 956
Tiffany Lamps are listed in the Tiffany category.
Tizio, Metal, Adjustable Neck, Raised Arm, Round Foot, Artemide, 20 x 29 In. 94
Torchere, 2-Light, Mahogany, Bronze, Marble Top, Pierced, Fluted Stem, c.1910, 41 In., Pair 676
Torchere, Art Deco, Tapered, Wrought Iron, 79 x 18 In. 4000
Torchere, Blackamoor, Multicolor, Italy, 1800s, 51 x 20 ½ In. 3500
Torchere, Brass, Reticulated Bowl, Masks, Leaves, Columnar, Pedestal, c.1880, 57 In., Pair 750
Torchere, Bronze, Tripod Base, Palmettes, Lion's Heads, Paw Feet, 61 In., Pair 6125
Torchere, Empire Style, Mahogany, Ebonized, Gilt, Busts, Burl Top, Hoof Feet, 40 x 12 In. 598
Torchere, French Empire, Beads, Mesh, Wood, Blue, Ram's Head Masks, 59 ½ In. 1815
Torchere, Georgian, Mahogany, Tripod, 56 In., Pair 375
Torchere, Gilt Bronze, Gothic, Tapered Triangular, Tracery, Quatrefoils, 1800s, 55 In. 1386
Torchere, Gilt Bronze, Marble Top, Openwork Scroll, Masks, Fretwork, c.1910, 40 In., Pair 3824

Torchere, Louis XVII, Bronze, Fluted Columns, Cherubs, Claws, c.1900, 100 x 21 In., Pair 5142
Torchere, Parcel Gilt & Wood, Swans, Columnar Stem, Flowers & Scroll, c.1905, 72 In., Pair 1500
Whale Oil, Back Cut Prisms, Gilt Standard, Marble Base, 23 x 9 In. 2806
Whale Oil, Canary Glass, Etched Flower Panels, Tapered, 8-Sided Foot, 9 In., Pair 144
Whale Oil, Pewter Gimble, Saucer Base, Hanging Ring, Swivel Font, 6 In. .... *illus* 47
Whale Oil, Sinumbra, Bronze, Gilt, Column Standard, Frosted Glass, Electrified, c.1830, 27 In. .. *illus* 777
Whale Oil, Sinumbra, Frosted Glass, Flowers, Glass Pendants, Marble, 30 In. 1150
Whale Oil, Sinumbra, Frosted Glass, Grapes, Pendants, 30 In. 374

LAMPSHADE

Bell Shape, Glass, Etched, 13 In. 147
Glass, Dragonfly, Leaded, Green, Multicolor, c.1980, 13 x 24 In. 500
Glass, Hurricane, Paisley, Berry, Persian, 22 ⅝ x 8 ¼ In. 540
Globe, Glass, Ball Shape, Blue & White Swirl Design 270
Leaded Glass, Overlay, Moorish Style, 6 x 19 ½ In. 12625
Leaded Slag Glass, Grapes, 28 Panels, 24 In. 161
Leaded Slag Glass, Green, Arts & Crafts, 24 In. 460
Leaded Slag Glass, Purple Tulips, Leaves, 14 x 25 In. 115
Leaded Slag Glass, Red Tulips, 12 Panels, Arts & Crafts, 15 ½ x 25 ½ In. 115
Leaded, Fruit & Parrot, Red, Green, Purple, 26 In. 287

LANTERNS are a special type of lighting device. They have a light source, usually a candle, totally hidden inside the walls of the lantern. Light is seen through holes or glass sections.

4-Light, Neoclassical Style, Bronze, Glass, Smoke Bell, Pierced Swags, Laurel, 30 x 11 In. 687
4-Light, Neoclassical Style, Carriage Shape, Metal, Swags, Scrollwork, Leaf Finials, 73 x 24 In. . 1750
12-Light, Baroque, Giltwood, Pierced, Birds, Perching, Flowers, 32 x 24 In. 1089
Barn, Nickel Over Brass, Embossed On Glass Globe, N.C.L. Co., Salesman's Sample, 5 x 4 In. 2530
Brass, Ball Shape, Pierced, Buddhist Deities, Flowers, Cabochons, c.1900, 11 In. Diam. 124
Brass, Birdcage Shape, 1900s, 23 ½ x 11 ¾ In. 3250
Candle, Copper, Tin, Pierced, Hinged Door, Ring Carry Handle, c.1800, 18 x 5 ½ In. 425
Candle, Dome Top, Wire Ring Handle, Tin, Wire Guards, 1800s, 16 In. 354
Candle, Punched Tin, Cylindrical, Conical Top, Ring, Hinged Door, 1800s, 16 In. 325
Candle, Punched Tin, Half Round, Glass Pane Door, Loop Handle, Hanging Ring, 16 x 8 In. 413
Candle, Tin, Punched, Cylindrical, Hinged Door, Cone Top, Hanging Ring, 1800s, 12 In. 354
Globe, Red Glass, Adlake-Dero, Caged, Bail Handle, 1961, 9 ½ In. 236
Hall, 4-Light, Bronze, Glass, Inverted Bell Shade, Pinecone Finial, Leaves, 30 In. 676
Hall, 9-Light, Louis XVI, Gilt Metal, 4 Sections, Leaves, Finials, Rams, Berries, 47 x 21 In. 2420
Hall, Amber Blown Glass, Inverted Bell, Chain, Bird Head Hook, 1800s, 24 In., Pair 799
Hall, Bronzed Iron, Elongated Hexagonal, Shaped Cornice, Opaque Panels, c.1900, 46 In. 2175
Hall, Cranberry Glass, Globe Shape, Painted Flowers, c.1890, 21 x 6 In. 151
Hall, Cranberry Glass, Swirl, Globe Shape, Pull Down, c.1890, 28 x 8 In. 151
Hanging, Arts & Crafts, Green Slag Glass, Verdigris Case, Seahorses, 12 x 7 In. 426
Hanging, Bronze, Patinated, Finials Cupola, Hexagonal, Arched Panes, Pine, 40 x 14 In 492
Hanging, French Deco, Iron, Lucite Panels, Blue, Circles, 22 ½ x 12 ⅛ In. 847
Hanging, Middle Eastern Style, 49 x 21 In., Pair 312
Hanging, Reverse Painted, Bamboo, 2 Tiers, Interior Sconces, Chinese, 18 x 14 In. 188
Iron, G. Stickley, Windowpane, Iron, Amber Glass, Hammered, c.1910, 16 x 11 In. .... *illus* 10625
Kerosene, Adlake Lamp, Non-Sweating, Chicago PRR, Red Globe, Swing Handle, 14 In. 266
Onion, Tin, Whale Oil Burner, Squat, Glass Globe, 14 In. 502
Street, Copper, Iron Mount, Glass Sides, Finial, c.1900, 96-In. Pole, 37 x 17 In. 413
Street, Sheet Metal, Cast Iron, Glass, 3-Socket Candelabra, c.1900, 34 In. 266
Tin, Cylindrical, Conical Top, Dormer Vents, Horn Panes, Stamped, 5 W R, c.1900, 17 In. 431
Tin, Glass, Vaclite, c.1913, 10 In. 175
Tin, Mirrored Back, Glass, Cylindrical, Hurricane Shade, Wire Handle, Kerosene, 1800s, 17 In. .. 177
Tin, Pierced Work, Candle, Hinged Door, Ring Handle, c.1830, 15 x 5 ½ In. 230
Tin, Red, Pointed Dome Top, Leaves, Gilt, 31 In. 123
Victorian, Blue Satin Glass, Pull-Down, Hand Painted, Birds, Flowers, c.1895, 18 x 12 In. 484
Wrought Iron, Rosettes, Swags, Tapered, 35 In., Pair 1750

LE VERRE FRANCAIS is one of the many types of cameo glass made by the Schneider Glassworks in France. The glass was made by the C. Schneider factory in Epinay-sur-Seine from 1918 to 1933. It is a mottled glass, usually decorated with floral designs, and bears the incised signature *Le Verre Francais.*

Le Verre Francais

Bowl, Flowers, Orange, Brown, C. Schneider, c.1930, 4 ¼ x 7 In. 420
Ewer, Draperies Pattern, Swags, Mottled Violet & Yellow, Handle, 18 In. 2074

Lamp, Whale Oil, Sinumbra, Bronze, Gilt, Column Standard, Frosted Glass, Electrified, c.1830, 27 In.
$777

Neal Auctions

Lantern, Iron, G. Stickley, Windowpane, Iron, Amber Glass, Hammered, c.1910, 16 x 11 In.
$10,625

Rago Arts and Auction Center

Leather, Saddle, Parade, Silver Mounts, Blevins Buckle, Pat. Pending, Wyo., c.1825, 28 In.
$830

James D. Julia Auctioneers

L

TIP
Rub salt inside old tea and coffee cups to remove stains.

Leeds, Bowl, American Eagle, Shield, Cranberry Transfer, Feathered Blue Edge, 8 In.
$351

Thomaston Place Auction

Leeds, Cup Plate, Pearlware, Patriotic, Eagle, 13 Stars, Blue Feather Edge, c.1825, 3 In.
$480

Cowan Auctions

Leeds, Pepper Pot, Green Feather Edge, Soft Paste, Dome Lid, Flared Foot, 4 ¼ In.
$201

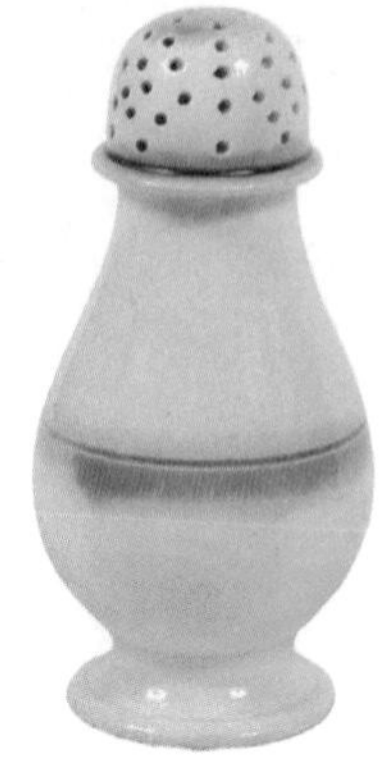

Hess Auction Group

Lamp, Ceiling, Chats, Band Of Cats, Mottled Orange, Brown Bands, 12 In. 8888
Lamp, Electric, Mottled Pink, Yellow Flowers & Bands, 14 In. 1185
Lampshade, Art Deco, Papillons, Turquoise, Orange, Butterflies, c.1925, 6 x 4 In. 826
Tazza, Mottled Yellow & Orange, Red, Violet Overlay, Flowers, 1927, 4 In. 1063
Vase, 3 Leaf Panels, Cobalt Shaded To Pale Blue, Tapered, Footed, 12 In. 1476
Vase, Allover Nested Arcs, Mottled Purple Shaded To Clear, Oval, Footed, 16 In. 1729
Vase, Beige, Brown, Orange, Plant, Rolled Rim, c.1922, 11 In. Diam. 854
Vase, Companulas, Stylized Flowers, Mottled Violet & Orange, 25 In. 3200
Vase, Frosted Yellow Body, Geometric Cut, Band Of Cats, Signed, 12 ½ In. 518
Vase, Halbrans Pattern, Mottled Brown Ducks In Flight, Yellow, Oval, 21 In. 3851
Vase, Hyacinth, Mottled Orange, Rounded Square, Pedestal Foot, 19 In. 8295
Vase, Libellules Pattern, Dragonflies, Mottled Green, Orange, Leaves, Blue, 18 In. 4740
Vase, Mottled Brown Berries, Vines, Orange, Swollen, Tapered, 10 In. 1788
Vase, Orange To Brown Stalks, Dazzled Yellow Ground, 15 ⅛ In. 1320
Vase, Orange, Mottled Brown, White Satin Ground, 6 ½ x 3 ¾ In., Pair 1210
Vase, Papillon Pattern, Mottled Orange, Butterflies, Bulbous Bottom, 20 In. 4444
Vase, Purple Flowers, Footed, c.1930, 11 x 4 In. 1440
Vase, Red Flowers, Cascading Berries, Frosted, Mottled Pink & Blue, Footed, 12 In. 1659
Vase, Squat, Papillons, Blue To White, Red Acid-Etched Butterflies, c.1925, 5 In. 2629
Vase, Stick Neck, Bulbous Body, Clear, Blue Thread Design, c.1920, 24 In. 1195
Vase, Stick, Smokestack, Flare Rim, Flowers, Yellow, Red, 1930, 26 In. 1625
Vase, Sunburst, Sun Rays, Blue Mottle, Ovals, Violet Round Foot, 7 In. 1185
Vase, Swans, Under Branch, c.1930, 12 x 7 ½ In. 2040
Vase, Tobacco Leaf, Mottled White & Orange, Trumpet Mouth, 16 In. 1422
Vase, Tortues, Turtles, Honeycomb Pattern, Mottled Orange, 20 In. 4740
Vase, Yellow To Orange, Violet Overlay, Big Cats, Drip, Oval, c.1923, 19 In. 9375

LEATHER is tanned animal hide and has been used to make decorative and useful objects for centuries. Leather objects must be carefully preserved with proper humidity and oiling or the leather will deteriorate and crack. This damage cannot be repaired.

Attache Case, Must De Cartier, Burgundy, Brass Hardware, Monogram, 11 ½ x 15 ½ In. 649
Box, Tan, Etched, Rawhide Tie, 13 x 27 In. 59
Bucket, Brass Mount, Red, Horse Head, 19 ½ In. 88
Saddle, Parade, Silver Mounts, Blevins Buckle, Pat. Pending, Wyo., c.1825, 28 In. ....*illus* 830
Saddle, Sport, Circle Y Bob Marshall, Tooled, 16 In. 747
Saddle, Western, Black, Hand Chased Silver Decoration, 1930-40 4305
Sculpture, 2 Seated Men Playing Go, Liu Miao Chan, Taiwan, 1986, 11 ¾ x 19 ½ In. 1342
Trinket Box, Pietra Dura, Table On Patio Scene, Lid, 2 x 7 In. 110

LEEDS pottery was made at Leeds, Yorkshire, England, from 1774 to 1878. Most Leeds ware was not marked. Early Leeds pieces had distinctive twisted handles with a greenish glaze on part of the creamy ware. Later ware often had blue borders on the creamy pottery. A Chicago company named Leeds made many Disney-inspired figurines. They are listed in the Disneyana category.

LEEDS POTTERY

Basin, Blue & Tan Acorn, Bud & Leaf Design, Trailing Vine Border, Soft Paste, 4 ⅜ x 14 In. 354
Berry Bowl, Lid, Underplate, Ladle With Drain Holes, Yellow Raspberry Vines, 6 x 8 In. 144
Bowl, American Eagle, Shield, Cranberry Transfer, Feathered Blue Edge, 8 In. ....*illus* 351
Bowl, Vegetable, Green Feather Edge, Flowers & Leaves, Multicolor, Shaped Rim, 8 x 6 In. 590
Bowl, Vegetable, Green Feather Edge, Rectangular, Canted Corners, 12 x 9 In. 118
Charger, Blue Feather Edge, Flowers, Leaves, Tan, Blue, Green, Scalloped Border, 12 ¼ In. 177
Coffeepot, Sunflower Design, Blue & White, Wavy Rim, Saucer Foot, 11 In. 502
Creamer, Double Bulbous, Loop Handle, Flowers & Leaves, Cream, Blue, Green, 4 In. 71
Cup & Saucer, Woods, Flowers, Leaves, Blue Border, Yellow, Tan, Green Band, 5 ¾ In. 118
Cup Plate, Pearlware, Patriotic, Eagle, 13 Stars, Blue Feather Edge, c.1825, 3 In. ....*illus* 480
Mug, Cylindrical, Loop Handle, Molded Base, Mocha Earthworm Design, Soft Paste, 5 In. 944
Pepper Pot, Cylindrical, Dome Lid, Flared Footed Base, Blue Feather Edge, 4 ½ In. 266
Pepper Pot, Green Feather Edge, Soft Paste, Dome Lid, Flared Foot, 4 ¼ In. ....*illus* 201
Pitcher, Barrel Shape, Loop Handle, Mocha Earthworm Design, Banded, Stripes, 8 In. 153
Plate, Green Feather Edge, Peafowl, Yellow, Tan, Brown, 8 ⅞ In. ....*illus* 413
Plate, Toddy, Cottage Pattern, Green Feather Edge, 6 ¼ In. 413
Plate, Toddy, Peafowl, Blue, Yellow, Brown, Green Feather Edge, Leaves, 6 In. 83
Platter, Blue Feather Edge, Embossed Leaves, Shells & Scroll Border, Wavy Rim, 13 In. 71
Platter, Green Feather Edge, Oval, Soft Paste, Impressed Anchor Mark, 13 x 17 ½ In. 94
Platter, Oval, Green Feather Edge, Flat Edge, Shaped Rim, 13 x 17 In. 189
Sauce, Leaf Shape, Blue Feather Edge, Soft Paste, 6 In. 118

Sugar, Lid, Flowers, Leaves, Scrolls, Oval, Scrolled Handles, Yellow, Tan, Green, Blue, 5 In. 325
Tankard, Blue & Green Sponge Decoration, Incised Bands At Rim, 6 In. .... *illus* 384
Teapot, Lid, Creamware, Cylindrical Shape, Beaded Borders, Double Handles, 1700s, 7 In. 308
Teapot, Lid, Creamware, Globe Shape, Leaf Spout, Man Pouring Olive Oil, c.1790, 4 In. 308

LEFTON is a mark found on pottery, porcelain, glass, and other wares imported by the Geo. Zoltan Lefton Company. The company began in 1941. George Lefton died in 1996 and the company was sold in 2001. The company mark has changed through the years, but because marks have been used for long periods of time, they are of little help in dating an object.

Ashtray, Holly, 4 In. 36
Bell, Angel, Figural, Red, White, 4 ½ In. 30
Bell, Christmas Angel, Holding Tree, 4 ½ In. 30
Butter, Cover, Bluebird, Paper Label, 1950s, 4 x 6 ¼ In. 75
Figurine, Woman, Blue Dress & Hat, Fan, Flowers, Leaves, Paper Label, 7 ¾ In. 18
Plate, Deviled Egg, 12 Wells, Roosters Salt & Pepper, Dark Green, Pink, 9 In. .... *illus* 35
Salt & Pepper, Christmas Angel, Boy, Girl, Blond Hair, Gilt Accents, Label, 3 ¾ In. 18
Salt & Pepper, Owl Shape, Yellow Blue, Teardrop Indents, Japan, 3 x 3 In. 18

LEGRAS was founded in 1864 by Auguste Legras at St. Denis, France. It is best known for cameo glass and enamel-decorated glass with Art Nouveau designs. Legras merged with Pantin in 1920 and became the Verreries et Cristalleries de St. Denis et de Pantin Reunies.

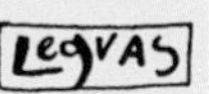

Vase, Amber Glass, Bowed Front, Raspberries, Cream Painted Ground, Cameo, 8 In. 480
Vase, Blossoming Branches, Mottled Green & Blue Shaded To Opal, Tapered, 9 ¼ In. 690
Vase, Blown, Etched, Enamel Birds In Flight, Rounded, Tapered, Signed, 21 In. .... *illus* 1000
Vase, Bulbous, Stick Neck, Swollen Lip, Trees, Pond, Green, Lavender, Pink, 11 In. 1185
Vase, Cameo Glass, Scenic, Square, Signed, France, c.1910, 6 ¾ In. 400
Vase, Cameo, Enamel, Chevron Band, Diamond Spears, Yellow, Brown, Tapered, 11 In. 230
Vase, Cascading Maple Leaves, Translucent Red, Indigo Accents, Shouldered, 11 In. 690
Vase, Chevron Vines, Cone Flowers, Cobalt Blue, White, Pear Shape, Textured Ground, 9 In. 207
Vase, Dark Green, Acid Etched Radiating Lines & Fans, Bulbous, Art Deco, c.1920, 9 ½ In. 738
Vase, Enamel, Trees, Meadow Scene, Pinched Top, Signed, 1878, 9 x 4 In. 242
Vase, Green Acid Cut Cameo, Mottled White, Frosted Citrine, Pond, Trees, Handles, 10 In. 830
Vase, Green Leaves, Cream Ground, Cameo, 19 x 7 In. 1080
Vase, Intaglio, Raised Opalescent Body, Leaves, Branches, Brown, Green, 7 In. 374
Vase, Medallion, Swan, Cattails, Black Scrolls, Mottled Yellow Shaded To Blue, 14 In. 741
Vase, Poppy, Leaves, Mottled Fiery Red & Orange Over Frosted Green, Tapered, 14 In., Pair 460
Vase, Rose Bowl Shape, Folded Rim, Amber, Enameled Winter Landscape, c.1900, 4 In. 717
Vase, Stick, Butterscotch, Amber, Brown & Purple Overlay, Seaweed, Leaves, Cameo, 7 ¾ In. 363
Vase, Tapered Bowl, Relief Cut, Blossoming Branches, Gilt Border, 14 x 4 In. 960
Vase, Yellow Green Rippled Ground, Leafy Wreath, Cherries, Gold, Rounded, 8 In. 288

LENOX porcelain is well-known in the United States. Walter Scott Lenox and Jonathan Coxon founded the Ceramic Art Company in Trenton, New Jersey, in 1889. In 1896 Lenox bought out Coxon's interest, and in 1906 the company was renamed Lenox, Inc. The company makes porcelain that is similar to Irish Belleek. In 2009, after a series of mergers, Lenox became part of Clarion Capital Partners. The marks used by the firm have changed through the years, so collectors can date the ceramics. Related pieces may also be listed in the Ceramic Art Co. category.

Bowl, Vegetable, Lid, Handles, Golden Wreath, 9 In. 165
Candlestick, Holly & Berry, Ribbed Foot, Gilt, 4 ¾ In., Pair 45
Canister, Lid, Cobalt Blue Glaze, Silver Overlay, Trellis Design, Bell Shape, c.1900, 7 In. 625
Cup & Saucer, Bouquet, Multicolor 18
Cup & Saucer, Ribbed, Gold Trim 36
Dish, Shell Shape, Scroll Handle, Green Leaf Mark, 9 x 5 In. 23
Dish, Swan Shape, Gold Beak, 12 x 8 In. 112
Figurine, Governor's Garden Party, Blue Dress, Fan, 8 ½ In. 25
Figurine, Jeweled Fish, c.1990, 7 ½ In. 52
Plate, Dinner, Golden Wreath, 10 ½ In. 24
Plate, Horse, Gold Scrolled Band, W.H. Morley, c.1920, 10 ½ In. 500
Salt & Pepper, Rooster, Rise N' Shine, 24K Gold Accents, 3 ¼ In. 18
Vase, Cylindrical, Ming Pattern, c.1920, 12 ½ In. 85
Vase, Wisteria, Birds, Yellow, Red, Cylindrical, 14 In. 78
Votive Candleholder, Openwork Scrolls, 1 ¾ x 2 ½ In. 16
Votive Candleholder, Roses & Hummingbirds, Embossed, 2 In. 23

Leeds, Plate, Green Feather Edge, Peafowl, Yellow, Tan, Brown, 8 ⅞ In.
$413

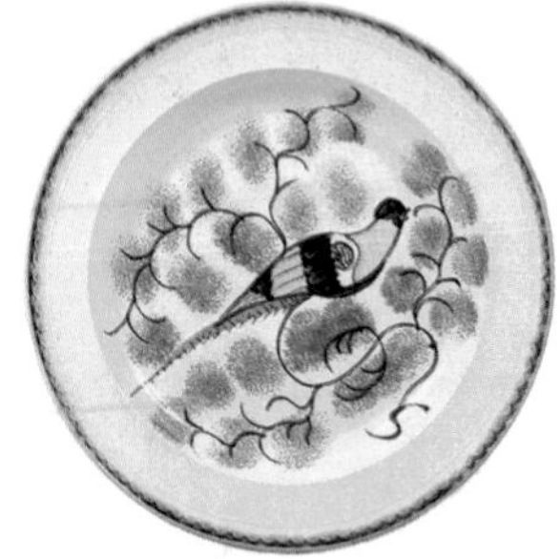

Hess Auction Group

Leeds, Tankard, Blue & Green Sponge Decoration, Incised Bands At Rim, 6 In.
$384

Hess Auction Group

Lefton, Plate, Deviled Egg, 12 Wells, Roosters Salt & Pepper, Dark Green, Pink, 9 In.
$35

L

TIP

Dealers who sell in booths at shows avoid taking sets of china and large paintings. Both are difficult to pack and ship and attract only a limited number of buyers. Large paintings cannot fit in the average house with 8-foot ceilings. Sets of dishes with gold trim can't go in a dishwasher or microwave.

Legras, Vase, Blown, Etched, Enamel Birds In Flight, Rounded, Tapered, Signed, 21 In.
$1,000

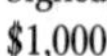

Rago Arts and Auction Center

Libbey, Perfume Bottle, Emerald Cut To Clear, Flowers, Gilded Neck, Stopper, c.1900, 7 In.
$1,534

Brunk Auctions

Libbey, Vase, Lily, Amberina, Ribbed Ball Stem, Ruffled Rim, 10 ¾ In.
$1,495

Early Auction Company

LETTER OPENERS have been used since the eighteenth century. Ivory and silver were favored by the well-to-do. In the late nineteenth century, the letter opener was popular as an advertising giveaway and many were made of metal or celluloid. Brass openers with figural handles were also popular.

Angled Striated Design, Sterling Silver, Bent-Over Handle, Italy, 6 ½ In. 98
Art Deco, Bronze, Steinbock, Austria, c.1925, 6 ¾ In. 175
Bee & Blooming Plum, Repousse, Sterling Silver, Tiffany, 8 In. 599
Calvert Pattern, Sterling Silver, Repousse, S. Kirk & Son, 1927, 5 ¾ In. 55
Coat Of Arms, Flag, Sterling Silver, Enschede, 6 ½ In. 75
Cross, Sterling Silver, Webster, 1965, 7 In. 50
Fish, Sterling Silver, c.1900, 10 ½ In. 100
Flowers, Cloverleaf, Brass, Mosaic, 1800s, 9 In. 360
Flowers, Engraved St. Andrew Lodge, Sterling Silver, 1898, 8 ½ In. 250
Flowers, Repousse, Sterling Silver, S. Kirk & Son, 5 In. 69
Mosaic, Flowers, Brass Openwork, Curved Blade, Italy, 19th Century, 9 In. 340
Nobleman On Rearing Horse, Beggar, Brass, c.1860, 9 In. 350
Painted Bird, Stainless Steel, Wood Handle, Red Case, 6 ½ In. 10
Rose Point, Sterling Silver, Wallace & Sons, c.1934, 7 In. 85
Scottish Terrier, Brass Colored Finish, McClelland Barclay, c.1930, 8 In. 88
Sterling Silver, Mother-Of-Pearl, c.1890, 5 ¾ In. 88
Sterling Silver, Turquoise Inlaid Bear Claws, Marked, KLB, 7 In. 240
Sterling Silver, Turquoise Stone, c.1950, 6 ½ In. 94
Totem Pole, Bone, Multicolor, c.1950, 7 In. 75
Twisted Handle, Metal, Goldtone, Enamel Flowers, Green Stone, 4 ¾ In. 48
U.S. Coins, Embedded In Lucite, 1970s, 9 ½ In. 15
Woman's Head, Nouveau, Flowers, Bronze, 10 ¼ In. 125

LIBBEY Glass Company has made many types of glass since 1888, including the cut glass and tablewares that are collected today. The stemwares of the 1930s and 1940s are once again in style. The Toledo, Ohio, firm was purchased by Owens-Illinois in 1935 and is still working under the name Libbey Inc. Maize is listed in its own category.

Bowl, Amberina, Round, Fold Down Top, Cranberry Shaded To Swirled Amberina, Signed.......... 288
Bowl, Center, Cut Glass, Black Overlay, 4 ½ x 14 In. 540
Box, Lid, Amberina, Round, Tapered, Clear Amber Teardrop Finial, 4 In. 403
Goblet, Black Figural Animal Stems, 5 ¼ x 2 ⅛ In., 3 Piece.......... 120
Perfume Bottle, Cobalt Blue, Engraved To Clear, Peacock, Flowers, Ball Stopper, 1920s, 8 In. ... 767
Perfume Bottle, Emerald Cut To Clear, Flowers, Gilded Neck, Stopper, c.1900, 7 In. ....*illus* 1534
Pitcher, Blue Threaded, Nash, 10 In. 108
Vase, Amberina, Optic Ribbed, Applied Amber Handles, Paper Label, 8 ½ In. 144
Vase, Amberina, Optic Ribbed, Cinched Neck, Flared Ruffled Rim, 6 In. 144
Vase, Amberina, Optic Ribbed, Wide Flared Out & Flattened Rim, 5 In. 431
Vase, Lily, Amberina, Ribbed Ball Stem, Ruffled Rim, 10 ¾ In. ....*illus* 1495

LIGHTERS for cigarettes and cigars are collectible. Cigarettes became popular in the late nineteenth century, and with the cigarette came matches and cigarette lighters. All types of lighters are collected, from solid gold to the first of the recent disposable lighters. Most examples found were made after 1940. Some lighters may be found in the Jewelry category in this book.

Alfred Dunhill, Gold Plated, Pinstripe, Rollagas, Switzerland, 2 ½ x 1 In. 75
Art Nouveau, Sterling, Nude Woman, Waves, Dolphin Handle, c.1900, 4 ½ In. ....*illus* 1046
Cartier, Pink, Yellow Gold Clad, Diamond, Initials RHA, 2 x 1 ½ In. 2850
Cartier, Silver Gilt, Black Enamel, Flip Top, Art Deco, France, c.1930, 1 ⅜ In. 2486
Chrome, Table, Ribbed, Japan, c.1950, 2 ½ In. 22
Cigar, Black Man, Claw Foot, Bust, Cigar In Mouth, Talon Base, 9 ½ In. 1020
Cigar, Owl, Perched, Brass, Round Base, 4 ½ In. 114
Cigar, Seal, Figural, Silver Plate, Posed On Rock, Ball On Nose, 5 In. 120
Cigar, Silver, Caricature Devil Figure, Pointed Horns, Smiling, 1911, 2 ¾ In. 1434
Dunhill, 14K Yellow Gold, Ribbed Body, Signed, 1900s, 2 In. 472
Dunhill, Aquarium, Painted Fish, Water Plants, Rocks, Silver Mounts, 3 x 4 In. 2486
Dunhill, Gold Plated, Rollagas, Hatch Finish, Presentation Box, 2 ½ x 1 In. 190
Eclydo, Snakeskin Design, Silvertone, Watch Embedded In Front, 1950s, 1 ⅝ x 1 ½ In. 125
Ronson, Adonis Model, 14K Yellow Gold, Streamline Design, Monogram, 2 x 1 ¾ In. 604
Zippo, Engraved Plaid Pattern, Chrome, 1964 32
Zippo, There Is No Gravity The World Sucks, Vietnam War 70

LIGHTNING RODS AND LIGHTNING ROD BALLS are collected. The glass balls were at the center of the rod that was attached to the roof of a house or barn to avoid lightning damage. The balls were made in many colors and many patterns.

Arrow, Blue Quilt Raised Ball, Twigs, Copper Roof Base, 71 In. 118
Arrow, Running Horse, Light Blue Ball, Twist, 71 x 21 In. 240
Arrow, White, Ribbed, Grape Ball, 79 In. 100
Amber, Diamond Quilted, 4 ½ In. 30
Ball, Clear, Pressed Glass, 5 ¼ In. *illus* 25
Ball, Milk Glass, Opaque White, 3 ¼ x 3 ¾ In. *illus* 35
Clear, Fitter Ends, 5 ¼ x 4 In. 25
Cobalt Blue, 4 ½ In. 24
Copper, Spiral, Tripod, Amber Glass Ball, 19th Century, 62 In. *illus* 195
Ruby Glass, 4 ½ In. 18

LIMOGES porcelain has been made in Limoges, France, since the mid-nineteenth century. Fine porcelains were made by many factories, including Haviland, Ahrenfeldt, Guerin, Pouyat, Elite, and others. Modern porcelains are being made at Limoges. The word *Limoges* as part of the mark is not an indication of age. Haviland, one of the Limoges factories, is listed as a separate category in this book.

Apothecary, Multicolor, Gilt, 11 x 5 ⅛ In., 10 Piece 615
Basket, Reticulated, Gilt, Green, Pedestal, Cherubs, Leaves, c.1850, 14 In. *illus* 923
Bowl, Grapes, Leaves, Footed, Signed AK France, c.1960, 8 ½ x 3 ½ In. 30
Cachepot, Neoclassical Style, Blue Ground, Red Accents, Shell Shape Handles, 7 In., Pair 431
Centerpiece, Pink, Couple Fishing, Pierced Scroll Rim & Handles, Footed, c.1895, 6 x 17 In. 553
Cup, 2 Handles, Pedestal Foot, Black, Gray, Gold, Masks, Scroll, 1800s, 4 x 7 In. 525
Hand, Mirror, Plaque, Minerva Holding Shield, Spear, Owl, Flower Heads, 4 In. 1775
Pitcher, Blackberries, Leaves, Flowers, Gilt Beaded Square Handle, 5 ¾ x 9 In. 125
Plaque, Pate-Sur-Pate, Blue, Woman, Child, Dancing, Signed, 7 x 5 In. 156
Plaque, Work Horse, Painted Tile, Harness & Reins, Standing In Field, Frame, 17 x 14 In. 618
Plate, Cobalt Blue Border, Raised Gilt, Flowers, Ahrenfeldt, c.1900, 8 ½ In., 11 Piece *illus* 584
Plate, Deviled Egg, 6 Wells, Scalloped Rim, Gold Trim, 5 ½ x 8 In. *illus* 25
Plate, Horse, Green, Black Bridle, Gilt Border, Signed Dubois, c.1900, 11 ½ In. 363
Plate, Repeating Gilt Border Banding, Flowers, William Guerin & Co., 1900s, 9 In., 12 Piece 219
Plate, Uncle Remus, Green, Blue Multicolor Scenes, France, 1900s, 8 ½ In., 11 Piece 738
Tankard, Ewer, Painted, Grapes, Leaves, J.D. Guthrie, T & V, c.1910, 14 x 7 In. 336
Tureen, Flowers, Leaves, Gilt, Leaf Finial, 12 x 12 In. 184
Tureen, Flowers, Multicolor, White Ground, Gilt, 12 x 12 In. 184
Vase, Ferns, Bamboo, Black, Orange, Green Glaze, Round, Flattened Shape, 1882, 11 In. 460
Vase, Loon, Rocky Shore, Horn Upswept Handles, Round Foot, High Gloss, 12 In. 1035
Vase, Portrait, Woman, Oval Medallion, Cherub, Gilt Border, Yellow, Pinched Neck, 14 In. 711
Vase, Tapered, Multicolor Flowers, Gilt, Squared Base, Tressemann & Vogt, c.1900, 14 In. 210
Vase, White Ground, Flared, Rolled Mouth, Metal Gilt, Oval, 1890s, 22 ½ In. 389

LINDBERGH was a national hero. In 1927, Charles Lindbergh, the aviator, became the first man to make a nonstop solo flight across the Atlantic Ocean. In 1932, his son was kidnapped and murdered, and Lindbergh was again the center of public interest. He died in 1974. All types of Lindbergh memorabilia are collected.

Bookends, Bronze, The Aviator, 1929, 6 x 4 ½ In. 75
Calendar, Plane Flying Over City, 1929, Salesman's Sample, 14 ½ x 22 In. 122
Medal, Bronze, Airplane, Captain, Aeronautical Chamber Of Commerce, 2 ½ x 3 In. 118
Poster, He Knew He Could & He Made Good, Plane, Eiffel Tower, Purple, Orange, 30 x 43 In. 3660
Tapestry, Portrait, Planes, New York & Paris Skylines, 62 ½ x 25 ½ In. 183
Toy, Airplane, Spirit Of St. Louis, Red, White, Blue, Celluloid, 6 ½ In. 270

LITHOPHANES are porcelain pictures made by casting clay in layers of various thicknesses. When a piece is held to the light, a picture of light and shadow is seen through it. Most lithophanes date from the 1825–75 period. A few are still being made. Many lithophanes sold today were originally panels for lampshades.

3 Figures In 1700s Costume, Candleholder, Iron Frame, c.1830, 15 x 6 In. *illus* 1125
Courting Couple, Stamped, M. Ruge, SGDG, France, c.1885, 4 ½ In. *illus* 336
Panel, Cast Iron Frame, Grape & Vine, Candleholder, 1880s, 16 In. 1404
Panel, Erotic, Figures, 2 ⅛ x 1 ¾ In., 6 Piece 750
Plaque, Biblical Scene, 11 x 7 In. 49

Lighter, Art Nouveau, Sterling, Nude Woman, Waves, Dolphin Handle, c.1900, 4 ½ In.
$1,046

Skinner, Inc.

Lightning Rod, Ball, Clear, Pressed Glass, 5 ¼ In.
$25

Ruby Lane

Lightning Rod, Ball, Milk Glass, Opaque White, 3 ¼ x 3 ¾ In.
$35

Ruby Lane

TIP

Switch dishwasher detergent brands periodically. This helps to keep the inside of the dishwasher and the dishes free of any chemical buildup.

Lightning Rod, Copper, Spiral, Tripod, Amber Glass Ball, 19th Century, 62 In.
$195

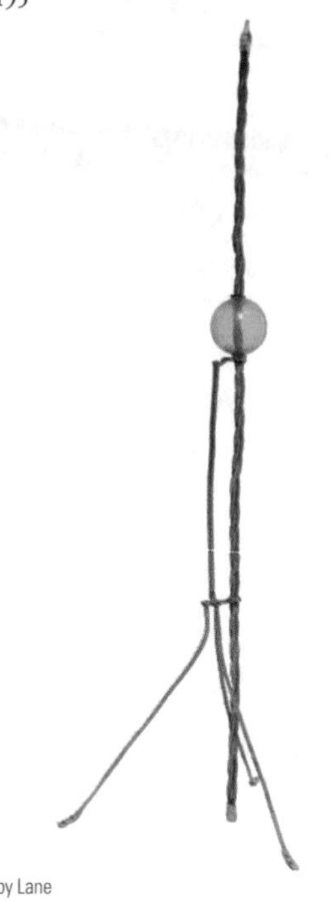

Ruby Lane

Limoges, Basket, Reticulated, Gilt, Green, Pedestal, Cherubs, Leaves, c.1850, 14 In.
$923

Skinner, Inc.

Limoges, Plate, Cobalt Blue Border, Raised Gilt, Flowers, Ahrenfeldt, c.1900, 8 ½ In., 11 Piece
$584

New Orleans (Cakebread)

Plaque, Gothic Cathedral Interior, 6 x 4 ¼ In., 3 Piece 220
Shade, 5 Opal Panels, Relief Scenes, Children, Brass Frame, Signed, PPM, 8 In. .... *illus* 345
Vase, Dragon, Chinese, 7 ½ In. 123
Window, Leaded, Beer Maker, Equipment, Holland, 11 ½ In. 153

LIVERPOOL, England, has been the site of many pottery and porcelain factories since the eighteenth century. Color-decorated porcelains, transfer-printed earthenware, stoneware, basalt, figurines, and other wares were made. Sadler and Green made print-decorated wares starting in 1756. Many of the pieces were made for the American market and feature patriotic emblems, such as eagles and flags. Liverpool pitchers are called Liverpool jugs by collectors.

Jug, Black Transfer, Full Sail, 9 ¾ In. 363
Jug, Black Transfer, Washington Commemorative, 10 ½ In. 826
Jug, Green, Black Transfer, Ship Caroline, James Leech, Eagle, 1800s, 10 ½ In. 302
Jug, Mourning Of George Washington, White, Transfer, 1800s, 10 In. 514
Jug, Naval War 1812, Black Transfer, HMS Reindeer, US Marines, 8 In. .... *illus* 2223
Jug, Washington & Lafayette, 1824, 6 ¼ x 4 In. .... *illus* 1968
Jug, Woman & Children, Black Transfer, Soft Paste, 5 ¾ In. 157

LLADRO is a Spanish porcelain. Brothers Juan, Jose, and Vicente Lladro opened a ceramics workshop in Almacera in 1951. They soon began making figurines in a distinctive, elongated style. In 1958 the factory moved to Tabernes Blanques, Spain. The company makes stoneware and porcelain figurines and vases in limited and unlimited editions. Dates given are first and last years of production. Marks since 1977 have the added word "Daisa," the acronym for the company that holds the intellectual property rights to Lladro figurines.

LLADRÓ®

Bust, Madonna's Head, Gres, No. 2264, 1994-2000, 9 x 6 In. 96
Figurine, Andean Flute Player, Gres, No. 2174, 1987-90, 11 ½ In. 180
Figurine, Bridal Bell, Bride Holding Bouquet, 1995, 3 x 9 In. .... *illus* 122
Figurine, Cinderella, No. 2523, 1972-98, 10 In. .... *illus* 285
Figurine, Deer, No. 1064, 1969-86, 6 ½ In. 150
Figurine, Dog's Birthday, Girl Holding Cake, Puppy, No. 1045, 1987, 7 ½ In. .... *illus* 60
Figurine, El Greco, No. 5359, 1986-90, 12 ½ In. 150
Figurine, Garden Classic, Young Woman, Umbrella, Puppy, No. 7617, 1991, 9 In. .... *illus* 120
Figurine, Geisha, No. 4807, 1972-93, 12 ¼ In. 90
Figurine, Girl With Piglets, Seated, Head Scarf, Basket, No. 4572, 1969-85, 10 ½ In. 161
Figurine, Girl With Wheelbarrow, Bisque, No. 4816, 1972-81, 9 In. 210
Figurine, Girl, Pan & Ducks, No. 5074, 1980-97, 6 ½ In. 330
Figurine, Island Beauty, Gres, No. 2172, 1987-90, 10 ½ In. 210
Figurine, Jester's Serenade, No. 5932, 1993-94, 14 In. 450
Figurine, Lady Empire, No. 4719, 1970-79, 18 ½ x 12 In. 180
Figurine, Meal Time, No. 6190, Box, 1995-98, 7 ½ In. 300
Figurine, Musketeer Athos, No. 6121, Box, 1994-96, 9 ½ In. 72
Figurine, Oriental Forest, No. 6396, 1997-2001, 14 In. 360
Figurine, Pensive Harlequin, No. 6434, 1997-99, 13 ½ x 8 ½ In. 330
Figurine, Physician, Woman, Holding Thermometer, No. 5197, 13 In. .... *illus* 120
Figurine, Professor, No. 5208, 1984-89, 12 ½ In. 180
Figurine, Queen Elizabeth II, Horse, No. 1275, 1974-86, 17 ½ In. .... *illus* 488
Figurine, Rosita, No. 2085, 1974-83, 14 In. 96
Figurine, Startled, No. 5614, 1989-91, 8 ¾ In. 120
Figurine, Stroll In The Sun, No. 6542, 1998-2001, 13 ¼ In. 300
Figurine, Summer Stroll, No. 7611, 1991, 8 In. 84
Figurine, Susan & The Doves, No. 5156, 1982-91, 13 ¼ In. 150
Figurine, Teruko, No. 1451, 1983-2013, 10 ¼ In. 180
Figurine, The Little Kiss, No. 2086, 1978-85, 11 In. 72
Figurine, Valencian Boy, No. 1400, 1982-88, 11 ½ In 210
Figurine, Woman With Hat, Gres, No. 1330, 1976-83, 22 In. 600
Figurine, Woman With Umbrella, No. 4805, 1972-81, 16 ¾ In. 360
Figurine, Young Woman In Trouble, Bisque, No. 4912, 1974-85, 10 ¾ In. 120
Group, A Mother's Way, No. 5946, 1993-96, 11 ¼ In. 390
Group, A Successful Hunt, No. 5098, 1980-93, 18 In. 1920
Group, At The Ball, No. 5398, 1986-91, 13 ¾ In. 210
Group, Car In Trouble, Geese, Couple In Car, No. 1375, 1978-87, 16 In. 3000
Group, Circus Train, Engine, 2 Cars, A. Ramos, No. 1517, 1987-94, 12 ½ x 25 In. 1722
Group, Elk Family, No. 5001, 1978-81, 9 In. 270
Group, Garden Party, No. 1578, 1988-99, 23 x 22 In. 3000

Group, Graceful Duo, Gres, No. 2073, 1977-94, 21 ½ x 9 ½ In. 450
Group, Hansom Carriage, No. 1225, 1972-75, 13 ½ x 24 In. 2640
Group, Horses, No. 1021, 1969-2007, 19 ½ In. 960
Group, Just One More, No. 5899, 1992-97, 8 ½ In. 330
Group, Life's Small Wonders, Gres, No. 2296, 1995-2004, 15 x 7 ¾ In. 240
Group, Love In Bloom, No. 5292, 1985-98, 9 ½ In. 150
Group, Mother, Seated, 2 Children, Boy & Girl, No. 4864, 1974-79, 15 In. 184
Group, Musical 19th Century, No. 1085, 1969-73, 17 x 10 In. 330
Group, Quiet Conversation, No. 1868, 2001-13, 17 ½ x 12 In. 554
Group, Royal Slumber, No. 6385, 1997-2000, 17 ¼ x 12 ¼ In. 660
Group, Sailor's Serenade, No. 5276, 1985-88, 13 x 6 In. 270
Group, Sleep Tight, No. 5900, 1992-97, 7 ¾ In. 210
Group, Southern Charm, No. 5700, 1990-97, 9 ½ In. 840
Group, The Desert People, Camels, Guide, Rider, No. 3555, 1982-86, 21 ½ x 17 In. 1230
Group, The Hunt, No. 1308, 1974-84, 17 ¾ In. 1920
Group, Wedding Cake, No. 5587, 1989-96, 13 ¼ In. 300
Group, Where To Sir?, No. 5952, 1993-98, 12 x 24 In. 900
Group, Will You Marry Me?, No. 5447, 1987-94, 11 ¼ x 10 ¾ In. 330

LOETZ glass was made in many varieties. Johann Loetz bought a glassworks in Klostermuhle, Bohemia (now Klastersky Mlyn, Czech Republic), in 1840. He died in 1848 and his widow ran the company; then in 1879, his grandson took over. Most collectors recognize the iridescent gold glass similar to Tiffany, but many other types were made. The firm closed during World War II.

Loetz Austria

Basket, Clear Bubble Glass, Blue Iridescent Cattail, Leaves, Wavy Foot, c.1918, 12 In. 400
Basket, Gold Iridescent, White Opal, Upright Handle, Polished Pontil, c.1910, 16 In. .... *illus* 370
Bowl, Vaseline, Blue Pulled Feathers, Titania, c.1900, 11 In. 2500
Centerpiece, Bronze Mount, Ruffled, Crimped, Iridescent Amethyst, 9 ½ x 9 ½ In. 423
Centerpiece, Cranberry, Crimped, Architectural Legs, Berried Laurel Swags, 8 ¾ x 14 ¾ In. 544
Lamp, Bronze, Hammered, 2 Owl Supports, Square Base, Cream Oil Spot Shade, 18 In. 3851
Lamp, Hanging, Gold Iridescent, Oil Spot Design, Purple, Red Threading, Bulb Shape, 12 In. 948
Lamp, Oil, Bronze, Curved Stem, Leaf Foot, Blue Phanomen Font, Papillon Ball Shade, 29 In. 3555
Pitcher, Iridescent Green, Formosa, Bronze Mount, 8 ¾ In. 363
Sprinkler, Gold Iridescent Oil Spot, Papillon, Pinched, Stretched Lip, Silver Overlay, 9 In. 4148
Vase, 3 Low Deep Dimples, Magenta, Gold, Candia Silberiris, Textured, 8 x 6 In. 173
Vase, Aurene Blue Ovals, Textured Green Ground, Argus, Pinched, Ruffled Rim, 5 x 5 In. 3105
Vase, Blue Green, Threading, Gold Iridescent Overtones, c.1900, 20 x 10 In. 2242
Vase, Blue Iridescent Waves, Silver Rim & Overlay, Phanomen, Art Deco Geometrics, 5 In. 2963
Vase, Blue Shoulder, Silvery Gold Pulled Designs, Phanomen, 3 ¼ In. 1652
Vase, Blue, Iridescent, 3 Applied Yellow Tendrils, Phanomen, Pinched Oval, 4 In. 2779
Vase, Bulbous, Squat, Pinched Sides, Platinum & Gold Iridescent Wavy Bands, 4 In. 948
Vase, Bulbous, Tapered, Dimpled, Gold Iridescent Crackle, Candia Papillon, 7 x 8 In. 230
Vase, Chalice Shape, Iridescent Cobalt Blue, Papillon Design, c.1925, 5 In. 246
Vase, Cobalt, Phanomen, 2 ⅞ In. 563
Vase, Conch Shell Shape, Gold Iridescent, 4 ⅝ x 7 ½ In. 270
Vase, Conch Shell, Stylized Seaweed Foot, Gold Iridescent, Oil Spot, Papillon, 12 In. .... *illus* 1185
Vase, Cream, Controlled Bubbles, Octopus, Brown Ground, Flowers, Oval, Flared Neck, 9 In. 3088
Vase, Creta Papillon, Ruffled Rim, Blue Gold Pattern, 7 ¾ In. 212
Vase, Gold Iridescent, Oil Spot Design, Sterling Flower Overlay, Oval, Folded Rim, 8 In. 3555
Vase, Gold Iridescent, Silver Overlay Flower, Pinched Folded Rim, Green, Pink, 6 In. 948
Vase, Green & Gold Iridescent, Quatrefoil, Applied Handles, 6 x 4 In. 544
Vase, Green To Silver, Iridescent, Bulb Shape, Inch Worm Shape Ribbon Handles, 12 In. 1250
Vase, Green, Iridescent Oil Spots, Silver Overlay Flowers, Squat, c.1905, 3 In. .... *illus* 550
Vase, Green, Oil Spot, 4 Applied Handles Pulled From Pinched Base, c.1900, 5 x 6 In. 5290
Vase, Iridescent Amber Glass, Pulled Waves, Aelous, Squat, Pinched Sides, 1902, 3 x 4 In. 575
Vase, Iridescent Flowers, Multicolor, Gilt, 8 ¾ x 3 In. 272
Vase, Iridescent Glass, Applied Banding, Polished Rim, Inscribed Austria, 7 ¼ In. 311
Vase, Iridescent, Silver Overlay, Flowers, Folded Rim, Austria, c.1900, 9 x 5 In. .... *illus* 2750
Vase, Light Green, Red Iridescent Flame Pattern, Titania, Oval, 7 In. 4740
Vase, Magenta Halos, Opal Blue, Green Lames, Medici, Pinched Bottom, 5 In. 1150
Vase, Oil Spot, Blue & Bronze Iridescent, Silver Overlay Iris, Medici, Pinched, 11 ¾ In. 7410
Vase, Oil Spot, Flared Rim, 3 ½ x 3 ½ In. 190
Vase, Oil Spot, Iridescent Gold, Crimper Rim, 4 ¾ x 5 ½ In. 211
Vase, Oil Spot, Pulled Feather, Ruffle Top, Multicolor, Purple To Green, 11 x 4 ½ In. 413

Limoges, Plate, Deviled Egg, 6 Wells, Scalloped Rim, Gold Trim, 5 ½ x 8 In.
$25

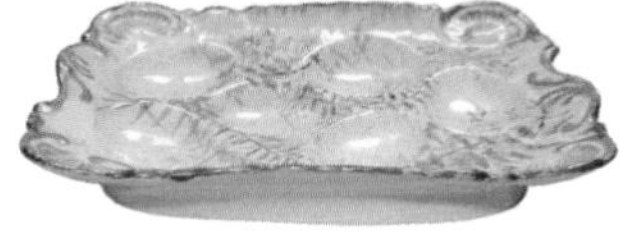

Lithophane, 3 Figures In 1700s Costume, Candleholder, Iron Frame, c.1830, 15 x 6 In.
$1,125

New Orleans (Cakebread)

Lithophane, Courting Couple, Stamped, M. Ruge, SGDG, France, c.1885, 4 ½ In.
$336

Theriault's

L

Lithophane, Shade, 5 Opal Panels, Relief Scenes, Children, Brass Frame, Signed, PPM, 8 In.
$345

Early Auction Company

Liverpool, Jug, Naval War 1812, Black Transfer, HMS Reindeer, US Marines, 8 In.
$2,223

Thomaston Place Auction

Liverpool, Pitcher, Washington & LaFayette, 1824, 6 ¼ x 4 In.
$1,968

Early American History Auctions

TIP

Take off your rings and bracelets before you start to wash figurines or dishes.

Lladro, Figurine, Bridal Bell, Bride Holding Bouquet, 1995, 3 x 9 In.
$122

Ruby Lane

Lladro, Figurine, Cinderella, No. 2523, 1972-98, 10 In.
$285

Ruby Lane

Lladro, Figurine, Dog's Birthday, Girl Holding Cake, Puppy, No. 1045, 1987, 7 ½ In.
$55

Ruby Lane

Lladro, Figurine, Garden Classic, Young Woman, Umbrella, Puppy, No. 7617, 1991, 9 In.
$120

DuMouchelles Art Gallery

Lladro, Figurine, Physician, Woman, Holding Thermometer, No. 5197, 13 In.
$120

Ruby Lane

Vase, Opal Ground, Brown & Pink Marble, Gilt Rim, Oval Shape, Flat Rim, 1889, 10 In. 123
Vase, Papillon, Cobalt Blue, Gold Highlights, 9 x 5 ½ In. 502
Vase, Papillon, Red Shading Into Yellow, Inward Folded Rim, Dimpled, 9 In. 403
Vase, Peach, Blue, Bands, Platinum Iridescent Oil Spots, Cytisus, Pinched Waist, 8 In. 3792
Vase, Peacock, Green Iridescent, Silver Threading, 4 Peacock Eyes, c.1899, 8 In. ....*illus* 5800
Vase, Phanomen, Bronze Ground, Platinum Iridescent Band, Blue, Swirl, Ruffled Neck, 5 In. 2074
Vase, Platinum Iridescent Crackle, Pink, Diaspora, Beaker Shape, Flared Foot & Lip, 9 In. 3555
Vase, Platinum Iridescent Drip Design, Swirls, Bronze Ground, Tapered, Shouldered, 11 In. 7110
Vase, Platinum Iridescent Swirls, Spheres, Gold & Blue, Bronze Ground, Folded Rim, 7 In. 1778
Vase, Platinum Iridescent, Wavy Bands, Amber, Silver Overlay, Shouldered, 10 In. 5629
Vase, Purple Swirls, Light Green To Blue, Lavender Interior, Swollen Neck, 4 In. 2666
Vase, Rainbow, Square, Dimpled, Angular Ribbing, Blue, Yellow, Red, c.1890, 8 In. ....*illus* 461
Vase, Red Features, Combed Waves, Iridescent Blues, Green, Phanomen, Flattened Rim, 8 In. ... 2185
Vase, Red Pulled Feather, Silver Highlights, Orange Ground, Tapered, Shouldered, 7 ¼ In. 3259
Vase, Red To Yellow, Iridescent Flames, Silver Filigree Collar, c.1900, 12 ¼ In. 5750
Vase, Round, Dimpled, Ruffled Rim, Oil Spot, Astraea, Green, Orange, Yellow, 4 x 4 In. 633
Vase, Scenic, Tri-Lobed, Panoramic Mountain Scene, Iridescent, Blue To Amber, 7 ½ x 5 In. 277
Vase, Shouldered, Tapered, Wide Rim, Rose Pink, Golden Blue Flames, Medici, Drip, 3 In. 863
Vase, Silver Overlay, Lilies, Leaves, Logo, Creta Papillon, Alvin Silver Co., 4 ½ In. 413
Vase, Silver Overlay, Tidal Wave Design, Titania, Cobalt Blue, Green, Urn Shape, 4 In. 1380
Vase, Silver Overlay, Yellow Ground, 10 ¼ In. 3500
Vase, Squat, Wide Roll Rim, Green, Threaded Weaving, Ribbed, Iridescent, 5 x 7 In. 115
Vase, Sunset, Pink & Green Iridescent, Reeds, c.1899, 10 ¼ In. 625
Vase, Texas, Prussian Blue Shaded To Chartreuse, Gold Cattails, Leaves, 8 ½ In. 354
Vase, Titania, Sterling Overlay, Carrageen Body, Caramel To Yellow, Pinched Rim, 9 x 5 In. 3894
Vase, Yellow Interior, Blue Exterior, Irregular Shape, 3 ¼ In. 313

LONE RANGER, a fictional character, was introduced on the radio in 1932. Over three thousand shows were produced before the series ended in 1954. In 1938, the first Lone Ranger movie was made. The latest movie was made in 2013. Television shows were started in 1949 and are still seen on some stations. The Lone Ranger appears on many products and was even the name of a restaurant chain for several years.

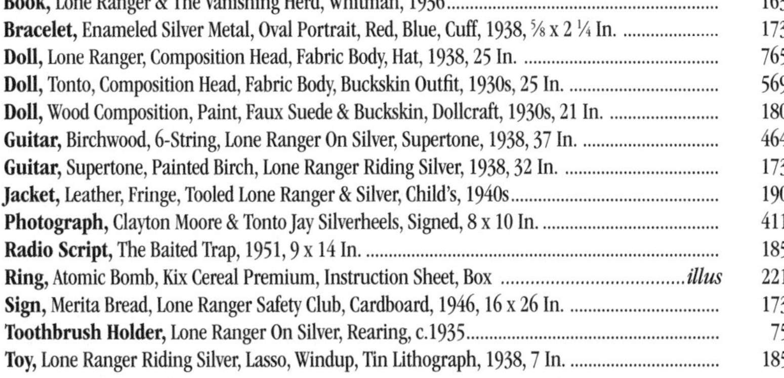

Book, Lone Ranger & The Vanishing Herd, Whitman, 1936........ 163
Bracelet, Enameled Silver Metal, Oval Portrait, Red, Blue, Cuff, 1938, ⅝ x 2 ¼ In. 173
Doll, Lone Ranger, Composition Head, Fabric Body, Hat, 1938, 25 In. 765
Doll, Tonto, Composition Head, Fabric Body, Buckskin Outfit, 1930s, 25 In. 569
Doll, Wood Composition, Paint, Faux Suede & Buckskin, Dollcraft, 1930s, 21 In. 180
Guitar, Birchwood, 6-String, Lone Ranger On Silver, Supertone, 1938, 37 In. 464
Guitar, Supertone, Painted Birch, Lone Ranger Riding Silver, 1938, 32 In. 173
Jacket, Leather, Fringe, Tooled Lone Ranger & Silver, Child's, 1940s........ 190
Photograph, Clayton Moore & Tonto Jay Silverheels, Signed, 8 x 10 In. 411
Radio Script, The Baited Trap, 1951, 9 x 14 In. 185
Ring, Atomic Bomb, Kix Cereal Premium, Instruction Sheet, Box ....*illus* 221
Sign, Merita Bread, Lone Ranger Safety Club, Cardboard, 1946, 16 x 26 In. 173
Toothbrush Holder, Lone Ranger On Silver, Rearing, c.1935........ 75
Toy, Lone Ranger Riding Silver, Lasso, Windup, Tin Lithograph, 1938, 7 In. 185

LONGWY WORKSHOP of Longwy, France, first made ceramic wares in 1798. The workshop is still in business. Most of the ceramic pieces found today are glazed with many colors to resemble cloisonne or other enameled metal. Many pieces were made with stylized figures and Art Deco designs. The factory used a variety of marks.

Creamer, Leaf Shape, Green Glaze, Veining, Loop Handle, c.1760, 2 x 4 In. 625
Lamp, Orientalist, Pottery, Bronze, Asian Style Base, Peonies, Electrified, 19 x 21 In., Pair........ 676
Pepper Pot, Faience, Flowers, Star, Pewter Top, c.1875, 4 In. 55
Plate, Red & Cream Flowers, Blue Ground, 9 In. 71
Vase, Cylindrical, Birds, Landscape, Elephant Head Stand, c.1890, 7 ½ x 10 ½ In. ....*illus* 492
Vase, The Curious, Nude Woman, Peering Over Edge, 18 ¼ x 7 ¾ In. 1210

LONHUDA POTTERY COMPANY of Steubenville, Ohio, was organized in 1892 by William Long, W. H. Hunter, and Alfred Day. Brown underglaze slip-decorated pottery was made. The firm closed in 1896. The company used many marks; the earliest included the letters LPCO.

LONHUDA

Vase, Brown, Cobalt Blue Violets, Red Clover, Pair, 5 ⅞ In. 181
Vase, Flowers, Violets, Clover, Brown Glaze, 5 ⅞ In., Pair........ 181

Lladro, Figurine, Queen Elizabeth II, Horse, No. 1275, 1974-86, 17 ½ In.
$488

DuMouchelles Art Gallery

Loetz, Basket, Gold Iridescent, White Opal, Upright Handle, Polished Pontil, c.1910, 16 In.
$370

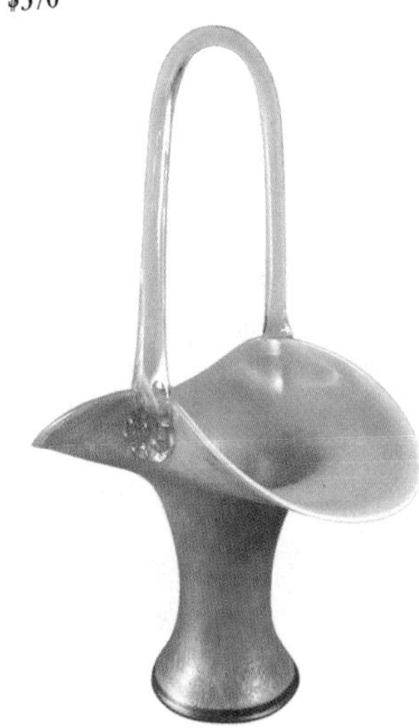

Ruby Lane

Loetz, Vase, Conch Shell, Stylized Seaweed Foot, Gold Iridescent, Oil Spot, Papillon, 12 In.
$1,185

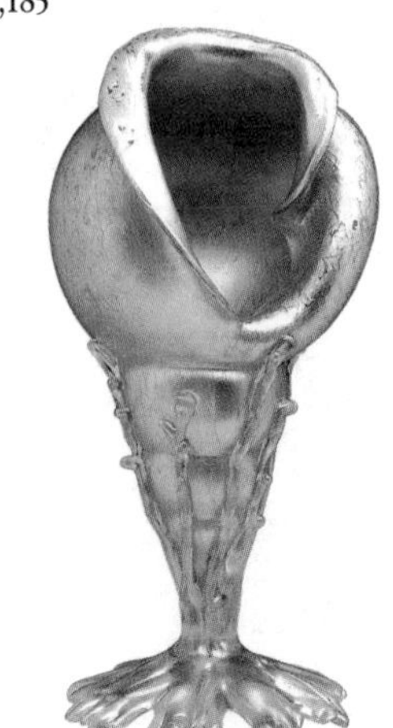

James D. Julia Auctioneers

Loetz, Vase, Green, Iridescent Oil Spots, Silver Overlay Flowers, Squat, c.1905, 3 In.
$550

Ruby Lane

Loetz, Vase, Iridescent, Silver Overlay, Flowers, Folded Rim, Austria, c.1900, 9 x 5 In.
$2,750

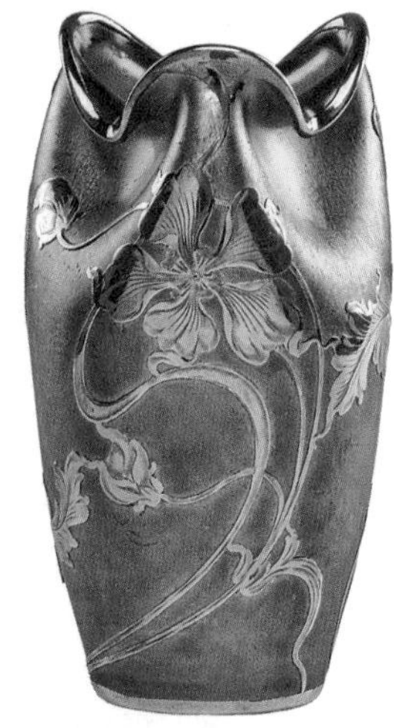

Rago Arts and Auction Center

Loetz, Vase, Peacock, Green Iridescent, Silver Threading, 4 Peacock Eyes, c.1899, 8 In.
$5,800

Ruby Lane

Vase, Harpist, Woman, White Dress, 1890s, 10 ¾ x 4 In. 320
Vase, Yellow, Brown, Denver, 2 Handles, 6 In. 1400

LOTUS WARE was made by the Knowles, Taylor & Knowles Company of East Liverpool, Ohio, from 1890 to 1900. Lotus Ware, a thin porcelain that resembles Belleek, was sometimes decorated outside the factory. Other types of ceramics that were made by the Knowles, Taylor & Knowles Company are listed under KTK.

Biscuit Jar, Blackberries, Vines, Flowers, 1890s 400
Bowl, Ruffled, Pink Flowers, Gold Trim, Gold Twig Base, 1891-96, 8 ½ In. 695
Ewer, White, Reticulated, 9 ½ In., Pair 236
Teapot, White, Gold Accents, 4 x 3 In. 399

LOW art tiles were made by the J. and J. G. Low Art Tile Works of Chelsea, Massachusetts, from 1877 to 1902. A variety of art and other tiles were made. Some of the tiles were made by a process called "natural," some were hand-modeled, and some were made mechanically.

J.&J.G.LOW

Tile, Backgammon, Table, Mother, Baby, Green, 1890, 4 ½ x 4 ½ In. 200
Tile, Flowers, Stippled, Blue, Green, 1890, 7 ¾ x 8 ½ In. 128
Tile, Portrait, Woman, Wheat Sheaves, Teal, 1890, 3 ⅛ In. 156
Tile, Putti, Musical Instruments, Dancing, Brown, Frame, 1910, 9 ¾ x 5 In. 350

LOY-NEL-ART, *see McCoy category.*

LUNCH BOXES and lunch pails have been used to carry lunches to school or work since the nineteenth century. Today, most collectors want either early tobacco advertising boxes or children's lunch boxes made since the 1930s. These boxes are made of metal or plastic. Boxes listed here include the original Thermos bottle inside the box unless otherwise indicated. Movie, television, and cartoon characters may be found in their own categories. Tobacco tin pails and lunch boxes are listed in the Advertising category.

Banana Splits, Vinyl, Fleegle & Drooper, Upright Handle, 1969 207
Buccaneer, Treasure Chest, Metal, Dome, Aladdin, 1957, 6 ½ In. .... *illus* 115
Carrier, Lacquered, Stacking, 4 Containers, Gilt Leaves, Japan, 15 x 13 ½ In. 106
Cowboy, Cowgirl, Cow, Basket Style, Tin Lithograph, 1940s, 7 x 5 In. 65
Dr. Seuss, Cat In The Hat, Fishbowl, Square, Embossed Metal, 1970 115
Home Town Airport, Dome, Metal, Handle, Aircraft, 1960, 7 In. 601
Incredible Hulk, Action Scenes, Embossed Metal, 1978, 7 In. 219
James Bond, Secret Agent, 007, Goldfinger, Metal, Disco Volante, 1966 1139
Jetsons, Dome, Metal, Hanna-Barbera, Aladdin, 1963 298
Junglebook, Mowgli, Baloo, Metal, Aladdin, 1966 126
Kiss, Band Photo Images, Metal, Plastic Thermos, Handle, 1977 253
Lost In Space, Metal, Dome, Handle, Latches, 1967 316
Major League Baseball MLB, Metal, Handle, Magnetic Game, 1968, 7 In. 316
Pac-Man, Metal, Ghosts, Yellow, Blue, Aladdin, 1980 115
Porky Pig, Porky's Lunch Wagon, Dome, Metal, Handle, 1959 196
Road Runner, Metal, Thermos, Wile E. Coyote, Rocks, Purple, 1970, 7 In. .... *illus* 190
Tin, Working Man's, Gold Paint, Bail Handle, Square, Cylindrical Neck, c.1900, 3 x 4 In. 115
Underdog, Kicking Villains, Sweet Polly Purebred, Metal, Universal, c.1974 .... *illus* 2296
Volkswagen Bus, Figural, Red & White, Metal, Handle, 1960s, 11 x 7 In. 115
Voyage To The Bottom Of The Sea, Seaview Submarine, Metal, Embossed, 1967 390

LUNEVILLE, a French faience factory, was established about 1730 by Jacques Chambrette. It is best known for its fine biscuit figures and groups and for large faience dogs and lions. The early pieces were unmarked. The firm was acquired by Keller and Guerin and is still working.

Asparagus Plate, Scalloped Rim, Basket Weave Border, Raised Asparagus, 9 In., 12 Piece 1250
Bowl, Old Strasbourg Pattern, Double Tulips, c.1880, 7 x 7 In. 50
Cachepot, Gilt Bronze Stand, Cobalt Blue, White Enamel Fleur-De-Lis, 13 x 8 In. 343
Compote, Violets, Leaf Border, c.1875, 9 x 4 ½ In. 150
Fish Platter, Tulip Border, Central Flowers, 24 x 10 In. 165
Jardiniere, Winged Griffin Handles, Flowers, Geometric Border, 16 x 9 In. 500
Plate, Eglantine Rose Pattern, Gilt Trim, 1800s, 8 In. 50
Plate, Old Strasbourg Pattern, Tulips, c.1880, 9 ½ In. 30
Tureen, Lid, Reticulated, Revebere Pattern, c.1875 625
Vase, Gourd, Loop Handle, Gray, Pink Glaze, Keller & Guerin, c.1900, 12 x 7 In. .... *illus* 26250

HOW TO DECLUTTER PROFITABLY!

Declutter, downsize, relocate, or settle an estate—these are words that bring problems and confusion to anyone. But for a collector or a collector's heirs, there are even more problems, more confusion, and often added guilt. Should I keep mother's collection of nutmeg graters? Will I ever use grandma's dishes or should I sell them? What do I do with my grown children's collections that are stored in my attic? How do I know what to price baseball cards, Barbie dolls, old electronic games, costume jewelry, a fifties prom dress, and the furniture I haven't used since 1950? The new job wants me to move to another state in two months—how fast can I declutter? Should I hire some help? Or should I sell it myself online or at a house sale?

There are many ways to solve these problems, but they all take time, work, and information. But remember the more work you do, the more money you will get. Also keep in mind that antiques dealers, shops, and galleries get retail prices, while most things sold privately online or in home sales get ½ to ⅓ of the retail price. Selling a collection takes time, information, and some unexpected emotional reactions. If it took 25 years to collect your treasures, you shouldn't be surprised when it takes a year to sell them, especially if you are a "quantity" collector with 400 toothpick holders, complete runs of mint comic books, or shelves filled with cameo glass vases. It's too late now to go back and keep accurate records, but provenance adds to value. So dig up what you remember, including sales slips, location, names, and history, and put it with the items. Be aware of the changes in the market. Some things like "brown furniture," including period Chippendale desks and Victorian oak furniture, have gone way down in price in the past 10 years. Only museum-quality pieces get the record prices reported in the papers. And limited editions, Royal Doulton figurines, Hummels, lady head planters, the average baseball card, coin silver, and Bakelite jewelry have gone out of style and are difficult to sell. But fifties modern furniture, studio glass, Picasso pottery, modernist jewelry, and technology like early TV sets, computers, or transistor radios have gone up.

Four Reasons to Declutter

1. The house is so full you can't find room to display your entire collection. The closets have clothes you haven't worn in years and the garage barely has room for the car. And you have stored unwanted or oversized parts of the collection in the attic and/or basement and can't remember everything that's there. You are decluttering to be able to enjoy the house and your collection, and to cut down on the extra work created by having a crowded house.
2. You need extra space in your home because relatives are moving in or because you are having physical problems and need to make the space open enough to accept a walker, a wheelchair, or even a cane or crutches.
3. You are moving to another house and need to "stage" the house for prospective buyers. You could just put all the excess collectibles, furniture, clothing, toys, etc. in a storage locker, but when you are packing you can also edit the collections.

4. You are sorting through household goods in a house that is part of an estate. There may be legal or family questions about the collections' value or ownership.

Each of these situations starts should start with an intelligent, unemotional way to sort everything in closets, cupboards, storage areas, and even the things hanging on walls or exhibited on shelves. Start with an idea of what rules you can follow to encourage yourself to get rid of some clutter. Will you keep any clothes you haven't worn for a year? Two years? Clothes that don't fit? Or are a color that you hate? Or are totally out of style or uncomfortable? How are you going to judge your collections? Have you lost interest in your tobacco signs, boxes, and tins in your large advertising collection? Or do you want to keep only the large, perfect pieces and try to sell the rest? If you need money, you might want to sell the largest, rarest items in the best condition because these are the most likely to get high prices. It helps to start with rules.

You will need to stock up on supplies like boxes, bags, stickers, pens, pencils, and maybe a tape measure and a magnifying glass. Use the latest *Kovels Antiques & Collectibles Price Guide* to find any information you have about the collections and other pieces. Gather bills, early photographs that show the furnishings (maybe with the kids and a Christmas tree, so you can guess when they were taken), and any dated insurance policies that lists decorative and fine art with a value. Old things can be researched in books and some are listed in this one. The quickest way to locate a book's name is to go online and search for the name or subject or partial name. It will show the author and the latest edition to ask for at your library.

Start with the easiest room first. Pick a room that hasn't much clutter, set up some card tables and three large boxes. Label one "Trash" and use it for the damaged, useless things you would put in a waste basket or garbage can. Include old check stubs, direction pamphlets for appliances you no longer own, all out-of-date medicine and cosmetics (but keep the fancy perfume bottles, powder boxes, and tins). Label another "Give Away or Sell." Use that to hold the things that are okay but no longer needed, like pans you don't use, old battered toys from the past 25 years, dishes that were part of an incomplete dinnerware set, and paperback books. (You should keep Barbie, her accessories, anything space related, robots, etc., to check on later.) You might want to give away some furniture or lamps. Label them with a sticker and put them near the Give Away or Sell box. The third box is "To Keep." The clothes that have followed your rules and have not been put in the Give Away or Sell box should be put on hangers or sorted into the now-empty drawers to keep. Small things go to the Keep box to be put away later. If you are displaying some of your antiques and collectibles like Staffordshire figures, Currier and Ives prints, or folk art, move them into a corner or under the card table and label the group "Collection." Then look around the room and be sure you have nothing stored under the bed, the chairs, on the walls, in cupboards, or on shelves that you should put in a box. Admire the spacious room. Congratulate yourself and take a break to call a friend, eat a snack, or plan the next attack on clutter.

This is the basic set of rules for each room and each of the four reasons to declutter. But what is the best way to handle collections, expensive antique furniture, and paintings? And the biggest problem—what to do with the Give-or- Sell box? Because you are a collector, it requires sorting for a second time.

Books have been written about how to remove clutter from a house, but the instructions often give no thought to the value of a collection like art pottery or Chase chrome. The authors often would not even know a collector could have a $5,000 Rookwood vase. If there is a change in your life that puts you in charge of immediately emptying a home and time is short, it may be best to just follow the basic suggestions. Instead of thinking of a Give-or-Sell box, just create a "Give Away" box and give as much as you can to friends and family. Then donate the rest to non-profit organizations and get an income tax deduction.

Suggestions on How to Declutter

1. Creating more space should be less difficult. If there is large antique or vintage furniture, closets filled with "I might wear these someday" clothes, and stored children's or parents' belongings, start with those. And include everyone. Grandma's collection of ironstone china has been saved for years and no one seems to want it, so plan to add it to the clutter-to-go list. Tell everyone the storage days are over, things must be moved in a month or they will be given away. If the owners complain, tell them they should rent a storage space. It might be a surprise to find the children's old text books, drawings from school days, old broken toys, etc., have no sentimental value and no resale value. The furniture, possibly some of the clothes, and toys that predate 1950 might require some research. (See page 6 TK to? for suggestions). The quickest and easiest way to sell these items is to have a house or garage sale, but that takes time, hard work, and enough know-how to run the sale, price the items, and know about security, permits, etc. You might want to hire an expert. If there is a large amount, there is another option. Hire a local company that will buy it all for a very, very low price and take it away. Anything done to declutter and make money involves time and money. The more time spent researching, the higher the selling price.
2. Selling the house also has special problems. To get the best price, realtors often suggest you paint some rooms, remove any personal items like family photos or portraits, and use a minimum of furniture in a contemporary style to make rooms look bigger. Small decorative pieces, equipment on kitchen shelves, garage stuff, etc., must go. Just keep a few large vases and some flowers. There are many TV shows and magazines that feature tricks used to encourage prospective buyers. While packing things to be taken out of the house, each item is handled so it is a good time to start editing collections. It will save work when unpacking in a new location and will save moving expenses. It might also be a time to think about anything related to the family or the neighborhood. Local historical societies might want pictures of past town events, yearbooks or uniforms from high schools, or letters about war experiences. Donations to museums and some other non-profits pay off in income tax deductions, pride, and a safe place for family history.
3. To move and stage the house, temporarily put things in a storage facility.
4. Sorting for an estate or a major "declutter" because you are moving are the most difficult ones to tackle. Everything must be given a value. Sales may involve legal issues. You and your adult family members should have a will. This is a true story: Jane was willed the antiques and her sister Mary was left the other furnishings. The deceased was a ninety-year-old collector and almost every item, including furniture, paintings, and almost everything but some kitchen pots and pans, was over 100 years old. Even the jewelry. The court ruled that almost everything was an antique and it went to Jane. She realized that was not the intent of the deceased, so she gave most of the furniture to her sister. Because of this, there were extra taxes to pay.

Don't let it get into a family argument or a legal tussle. Plan ahead with rules. Maybe each heir can put a color sticker on any special thing they want, and then the family can trade or bargain for the contested items. Perhaps you can have a bid-off with the money going equally to the others. Or have a family lottery. Try to even out the distribution of popular items by adding or subtracting cash, especially for art, furniture, and collections that have a high money value. Put everything out in plain sight on tables. It will help to have a computer nearby so you can find any names, hallmarks, or other identifying features that will help determine a price. If the family is contentious, it may help to have someone who understands antiques act as a referee. And it is more peaceful if there are no spouses or partners in on the final decisions. Sometimes emotional involvement can lead to problems.

The biggest headache is not what to throw out or give away, but how to sell the unwanted but valuable things. When downsizing, it's easy to get rid of the expensive things, but it's almost impossible to get the expected price if you want the original cost or more. No collectibles cost the same as they did 10 years ago, which is why everything must be studied. And if you use an appraiser (see list on the last page of this report) for the estate, ask for a wholesale, not a retail, replacement value. You could also find help from collectors' clubs that often have newsletters that take ads or announce that a collection is for sale. This is very helpful if the owner of the collectibles belonged to the club. It is a good idea to call the club if the Give-or-Sell box holds their collectible. Be aware that they will want things that are rare and in perfect condition.

HOW TO PRICE

There are several theories about pricing. Use high prices and offer a discount, often as high as 20%. Low prices should help sell things quickly, but if they are too low, they may make buyers wonder if your descriptions are accurate. If you are the seller, don't forget to add packing and shipping costs when figuring the price.

Be sure to keep complete records of your searches, where you got it, and any other information. The provenance (history) adds value. Also, record the searches that were failures. It is easy to forget what you did, and annoying when you realize you already looked at a website. Make sure notes include exact names of persons or businesses you contacted, phone numbers, dates called, email addresses, suggested prices, where the leads came from, timing for sale, and notes on any extras and problems.

There are different ways of selling a painting, a car, or a piece of jewelry. There are different sources of information, possible buyers, and even answers about whether it should be sold in an auction, shop or privately.

SUGGESTIONS, SOURCES, RESEARCH MATERIAL

PAINTINGS

Signed paintings can be looked up online or with the help of the signature on the picture and a library. Once you know who and when the painting was done, you can find recent prices online. If it's not mentioned online, it was probably not painted by a famous artist, so the painting has decorative value only (say, the cost of a similarly sized picture at a gift shop). Be sure it is a painting and not a lithograph or print. It may take an expert from an auction house, a dealer from an established shop, or an appraiser to tell you. Keep in mind that they all charge. Some will come to your home in hopes of buying, some charge by the hour for an opinion. A qualified appraiser should never offer to buy what is appraised. Ask for a wholesale appraisal, which is what a dealer might pay. It is less than the prices you see in reports of sales. A retail appraisal for donations to a non-profit organization will be higher.

The classic research book is *Benezit Dictionary of Artists* (Benezit is online at OxfordArtOnline.com). But there are many others that are limited to folk art, or outsider art, or specific countries or years. In many cities, the art museum librarians will help you learn the history and some recent auction prices. An online search also uncovers sources. You probably don't have a Rembrandt, but you might have a 30-year-old painting by a regional artist that could be worth thousands of dollars—or almost nothing.

FINE ART, SCULPTURE, DESIGN

The research for sculpture, glass, silver, furniture, even jewelry and wood carvings is the same as for paintings. Many artists made a variety of things. A famous name adds value. But some work by unknowns like samplers, quilts, glass bottles, posters, and advertising are pricey, and similar pieces can be found in books or online. Some things are so popular they have been reproduced. Your old blue glass flask that has Columbia with a Liberty cap molded on one side and an eagle molded on the other side may be the rare Kensington Glassworks bottle made in the 1830s. One sold this year for $133,000. Or it may be a copy made sometime within the last 50 years and worth $15. An online search for a similar piece sometimes gives information that leads to a price. LiveAuctioneers, Google images, Pinterest, and iCollect are a few sites that can help. It is said that there will soon be sites that use image recognition programs to recognize similar antiques.

FURNITURE

It is helpful to have bills, notes, or pictures that give clues to age. Look for names on the furniture and think about what is in style. All of the styles from William and Mary (1689-1702) to Victorian (1837-1901) are unpopular. Hottest is Mid century Modern (1930s-1980s), and later high style pieces especially those from famous Italian and Scandinavian designers. But copies are inexpensive. It probably takes an expert to tell originals from copies. Useable furniture can always be sold but some is very low priced. And some 18th-century pieces sold for thousands of dollars 10 years ago and now are worth just a few hundred. But Mid century Modern is in style and prices are high—much higher than they cost less than 50 years ago. Because of shipping costs, it is best to find a local place to sell furniture unless it is museum quality. Ask nearby antiques shops and dealers if they will buy it or take it on consignment. Send pictures to an auction gallery that runs ads that say they visit all parts of the country looking for antiques like yours. Original modern furniture made since the 1950s gets high prices, but there are reissues and revivals that sell for low prices. Arts and Crafts furniture from the famous Stickley companies and the Roycroft community, original Shaker community pieces, and Belter and other famous Victorian makers' pieces still sell well. Reproductions of Chippendale, Sheraton, and Hepplewhite are hard to sell unless they are quality reproductions made by Baker, Beacon Hill, or Kittinger since 1930.

Cupboard, double, Shaker, 77 in.

Lists

Kovels' Antiques & Collectibles Price Guide 2017

Kovels.com has a free price guide with over a million prices.

ADVERTISING

This is one of the most popular collectibles and one of the easiest to sell. Most collectors specialize in a limited interest like medicine, cars, petroliana (things related to cars), food, brand name products, tobacciana, beer, oatmeal boxes, signs that picture early factories, telephone-related material, sports, World Wars, ethnic ads, trade cards, and much more. There are specialty auctions that sell only advertising and, of course, they must get the items to sell, perhaps from your decluttering. Clubs, magazines, and newspapers about collecting, as well as the internet, are filled with information about buying, selling, and, of course, prices. Anything large with great graphics and in very good condition is wanted, and prices are high for unusual or very large examples. Talk to someone who is an advertising collector for clues to local buyers. The clubs often take paid For Sale ads for their publications. And their members may want to buy something you have but, like all buyers, they will need clear pictures of front, back, sides, marks, damage, and your selling price unless you go to an auctioneer or dealer.

Clubs & Publications

American Breweriana Association (ABA), americanbreweriana.org
Antique Advertising Association of America, pastimes.org
Brewery Collectibles Club of America, bcca.com
Coca-Cola, Coca-Cola Collectors Club, cocacolacollectors.club/wp
Eastern Coast Breweriana Association (ECBA), www.eastcoastbrew.com
McDonald's, McDonald's Collectors Club, mcdclub.com
National Association of Breweriana Advertising (NABA), naba.wildapricot.org

CLOTHING & TEXTILES

Clothing sells very differently than most things because pieces are usually bought to be worn, saved until vintage or older, then given to a costume collection or sold at a consignment shop. This is all less than 10 years old. Before 2010, no auction house wanted to sell old couture, and even today, most of the best men's clothing has few buyers. Consignment shops don't want a suit by Zegna or Brioni, but a dress or jacket by Pucci, Hermès, Tory Burch, or Burberry sells quickly. So do shoes by the most famous makers like Christian Louboutin and Manolo Blahnik. Hermès scarves are popular. A new favorite is workout clothes by Lululemon. It is hard to believe that someone who will pay $4,000 for a handbag will buy a bargain-priced used one at auction. Of course it must be in near-perfect condition. Plato's Closet, Material World, and Tradesy are national chains that buy and sell stylish clothes like Juicy Couture or Eileen Fisher. There are many local shops that sell high style, famous designer clothes, as well as workout and maternity clothes.

GLASS & BOTTLES

Bottle collectors are experts. They can tell great blue glass from ordinary blue glass because the color determines rarity and value. They know which flasks, bitters bottles, canning jars, and even milk bottles are special and, as the auction catalogs like to say, "highly collectible." There are bottle shows in all parts of the country and if you have a lot of "good" bottles, go and talk about what you have to the dealers and collectors who have rented tables to sell at the show. You can also learn a lot about what is valuable. Learn the descriptive words used by collectors like wax sealers, bitters, sodas, pontils, blob tops, mold marks, or bust and grind.

It is very, very difficult for a novice to identify most glass because there are so few pieces that are marked. Cameo glass, Dorflinger, Heisey, Hawkes, Lalique, Libbey, Orrefors, and other Scandinavian glass, Thomas Webb and Sons, and Tiffany, are some of the best known marks. Cut glass is sometimes marked on the flat glass surface inside a bowl. Full sets of formal glassware with cut or etched designs made in special shapes used for wine, water, and other drinks sell for much less than cost. They are not used for informal parties today.

Pressed and Depression glass can be identified by pattern, but a goblet or plate usually sells for less than $10.

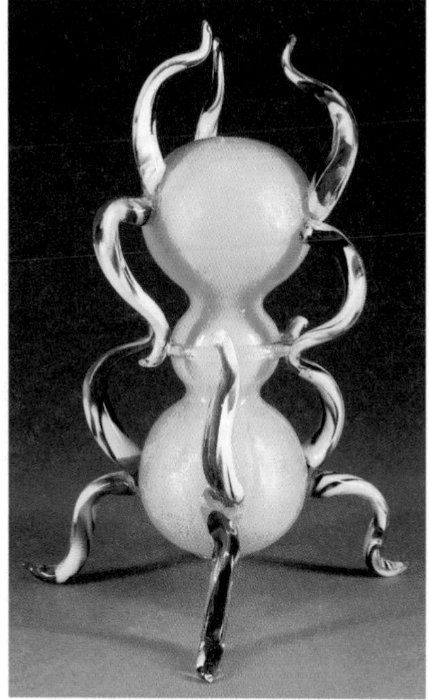

Sculpture, Yellow Two-Tiered Piccolo, D. Chihuly, 14 in.

Clubs & Publications

American Carnival Glass Association, myacga.com
American Cut Glass Association, cutglass.org
Antique Glass Salt & Sugar Shaker Club (AGSSSC), antiquesaltshakers.com
Early American Pattern Glass Society, eapgs.org
Federation of Historical Bottle Collectors, fohbc.org
Fenton Art Glass Collectors of America, fagainc.com
Fostoria Glass Society of America, fostoriaglass.org
Heisey Collectors of America, heiseymuseum.org
International Perfume Bottle Association, perfumebottles.org
Just Glass, justglass.com
Mt. Washington & Pairpoint Glass Society, mwpgs.net
National Cambridge Collector's Inc., cambridgeglass.org
National Depression Glass Association, ndga.net
National Imperial Glass Collectors Society, imperialglass.org
Paperweight Collectors Association, Inc., paperweight.org
Stretch Glass Society, stretchglasssociety.org
Tiffin Glass Museum, tiffinglass.org

Books

American Bottles & Flasks and Their Ancestry by Helen McKearin and Kenneth M. Wilson
Antique Trader Bottles Identification & Price Guide, 8th Edition by Michael Polak
The Collector's Guide to Old Fruit Jars: Red Book 9 by Douglas M. Leybourne Jr.

Marks Books

Glasmarken Lexikon 1600-1945 by Carolus Hartmann (written in German)
Glass Signatures, Trademarks and Trade Names by Anne Geffken Pullin

JEWELRY, WATCHES & CLOCKS

Sort the jewelry by the marks for gold, silver, platinum, plated, plastic, or other material. Gold and silver should be seen by a jeweler who will also recognize valuable stones, even the old mine diamonds that look like glass to most people. Elaborate vintage settings, stone cameos (not shell), unusual designs, and makers' names add value. Unusual American Indian, Mexican silver, and Mid-century Modern pieces can sell for thousands, but most pieces go for hundreds. It takes an expert to spot great stones and settings.

Clubs & Publications

National Association of Watch & Clock Collectors, www.nawcc.org

Website with marks

illusionjewels.com

POTTERY & PORCELAIN

This is probably the easiest thing to price and to sell. Most good pieces are marked. Large decorative vases and sculptures are popular. Marks, histories, pictures, and prices are online and in books. Sets of dishes are difficult to sell because styles have changed, and there is the added work of packing and shipping. They will sell at a house sale, but an average set of 12 six-piece place settings brings about $150 to $300 at a shop. There are many small clubs that can be found by searching online by company name.

Clubs & Publications

Flow Blue International Collectors' Club, flowblue.org

McCoy Pottery Collectors' Society, mccoypotterycollectorssociety.org

Red Wing Collectors Society, redwingcollectorssociety.org

Replacements, Ltd., Replacements.com (a matching service that buys and sells thousands of patterns of popular new and old dinnerware and many limited edition plates. Gives buying and selling prices and pictures the patterns.

Books of Pottery Marks

British Studio Potters' Marks by Eric Yates-Owen and Robert Fournier

Encyclopaedia of British Pottery and Porcelain Marks by Geoffrey A. Godden

Encyclopedia of Marks 1780-1980 by Arnold Kowalsky and Dorothy Kowalsky

Kovels' Dictionary of Marks—Pottery & Porcelain, 1650 to 1850 by Ralph and Terry Kovel

Kovels' New Dictionary of Marks—Pottery & Porcelain, 1850 to the Present by Ralph and Terry Kovel

Lehner's Encyclopedia of U.S. Marks on Pottery, Porcelain & Clay by Lois Lehner

Marks on German, Bohemian and Austrian Porcelain: 1710 to the present, Updated & Revised Edition by Robert E. Rontgen

Websites with marks

Kovels.com/Marks

porcelainmarksandmore.com

themarksproject.org (A Dictionary of American Studio Ceramics, 1946 to Present)

SILVER & OTHER METAL

Check marks and makers online or in books, and consider the meltdown price before you try to sell anything. Old sets of silver and tea services are very low priced today unless they are in the most modern design. Coin silver is out of style, has few collectors, and may be of unknown quality so it is not wanted for meltdown. English silver is well marked and makers are known, and there are still collectors of the 18th and 19th century pieces. Silver from other countries is usually less popular.

Books of marks

A Directory of American Silver, Pewter, and Silver Plate by Ralph and Terry Kovel

Encyclopedia of American Silver Manufacturers, Revised Fourth Edition by Dorothy T. Rainwater & Judy Redfield

Kovels' American Silver Marks, 1650 to the present by Ralph and Terry Kovel

IV
V
M Rd 2
7

English registry mark, 1842-1867

Website with marks

925-1000.com (Online Encyclopedia of Silver Marks, Hallmarks & Makers' Marks)

modernsilver.com (Includes mystery marks on silver pieces, including jewelry, tableware, and decorative pieces made in the United States, Mexico, and many European countries.)

SPORTS

There are shows, auctions, and very detailed price books for sports cards and memorabilia. Decoys and fishing paraphernalia have their own sites and shows. Hunting, fishing, skiing, marathons, swimming, surfing and almost any other sport has something wanted by collectors. There are community sales of used sports materials in many cities. Check your library or search online. There are shows in many states, and show dealers might want to buy your decluttered collection. Easy information to find.

Price Book

Beckett Baseball Card Price Guide #38 by Beckett Media

Beckettmedia.com has other publications covering baseball, basketball, football, hockey, and other sports

Website

antiquelures.com (Fishing)

TOYS & DOLLS & GAMES

Mechanical bank, Jonah & the Whale, 1890, 10 in.

Toys and dolls in good condition with most of the original look made before 1900 will be of interest to dealers and collectors and some sell for amazing prices. The experts know "anything that moves or makes noise" will interest collectors, and those who remember them from childhood have an emotional attachment to them. Best sellers that could bring thousands of dollars include iron mechanical banks, early tin toys, automatons, early robots and space-related toys, the original Barbie, and antique European dolls by famous makers—but they must be in excellent condition with original paint or clothing. Pristine examples of early toy cars and trucks, especially accurate models, are wanted. Trains do not follow the expected example. The early large gauge trains do not sell as well as the more recent O-gauge models.

Clubs & Publications

Dolls, United Federation of Doll Clubs, Inc. ufdc.org

Toys, Antique Toy Collectors of America, Inc., atca-club.org

Toys, Train Collectors Association (TCA), traincollectors.org

Books

The Collector's Encyclopedia of Dolls, Volume Two by Dorothy S., Elizabeth A., and Evelyn J. Coleman

Toys and Dolls Marks & Labels by Gwen White

MISCELLANEOUS

Don't discard anything unusual or over 50 years old until you check a possible market. Electric toasters, metal lunchboxes, outdoor metal furniture, gold-decorated cocktail glasses, transistor radios, radio tubes, telephone insulators, iron doorstops, decorative iron fences, even old working light bulbs, and much more may be wanted by a collector.

Clubs & Publications

American Bell Association, americanbell.org
Antique Doorknob Collectors of America, antiquedoorknobs.org
Antique Fan Collectors Association, fancollectors.org
The Early Typewriter Collectors' Association, www.etconline.org
Ephemera Society of America, ephemerasociety.org
Music Box Society International, mbsi.org
National Insulator Association, nia.org
National Toothpick Holder Collectors' Society, nthcs.org
Pressing Iron & Trivet Collectors of America, pressingironandtrivetcollectors.org
Wagner & Griswold Society, wag-society.org

Price Books

Goldmine Record Album Price Guide by Dave Thompson
Official Overstreet Comic Book Price Guide #38 by Robert M. Overstreet

DONATIONS

Charitable organizations have places where you can drop off household goods or clothing. Some will pick up items if you have enough. They will give you a form to be used with your income tax filing for a charitable donation deduction.

Dress for Success
Easter Seals
Goodwill Industries International
The Salvation Army
Volunteers of America
Other charities, like Hospice and Thriftique, have stores
Public Television auctions in many cities

APPRAISERS

There are many local appraisers, usually dealers or auction staff. Three national associations have members from all states who are vetted appraisers.

American Society of Appraisers
11107 Sunset Hills Rd.
Suite 310
Reston, VA 20190
800-ASA-VALU
(800-272-8258) or
703-478-2228
appraisers.org

Appraisers Association
of America, Inc.
212 West 35th Street
11th Floor South
New York, NY 10000
212-889-5404 Ext. 10
appraisersassociation.org

International Society of
Appraisers
225 West Wacker Drive
Suite 650
Chicago, Illinois 60606
312-981-6778
isa-appraisers.org

LUSTER glaze was meant to resemble copper, silver, or gold. The term *luster* includes any piece with some luster trim. It has been used since the sixteenth century. Some of the luster found today was made during the nineteenth century. The metallic glazes are applied on pottery. The finished color depends on the combination of the clay color and the glaze. Blue, orange, gold, and pearlized luster decorations were used by Japanese and German firms in the early 1900s. Fairyland Luster was made by Wedgwood in the 1900s. Tea Leaf pieces have their own category.

Fairyland luster is included in the Wedgwood category.
Silver, Mug, Transfer, Present For Writing Well, Child's, 2 ½ In. 325
Silver, Teapot, Sugar, Lid, Rosette Rim, Embossed Arch & Column, Oval, 6 ½ In. 83
Sunderland Luster Pieces are in the Sunderland category.

LUSTRES are mantel decorations or pedestal vases with many hanging glass prisms. The name really refers to the prisms, and it is proper to refer to a single glass prism as a lustre. Either spelling, luster or lustre, is correct.

Bohemian Glass, Green, Crystal, Prisms, c.1920, 14 ½ In., Pair.......... 162
Bohemian, White, Overlay, Cut To Blue, Painted Flower Sprays, 9 ⅝ In. 263
Cranberry Cut To Clear, Round Base, Bohemia, c.1900, 11 In. 184
Crystal Prisms, Brass Base, Flowers, Satin Glass, 15 x 5 ¾ In. 58
Cut Glass, Clear, Frost, 24 In., Pair 88
Cut Glass, Diamond Point Cutting, Panel Cut Standard, Prisms, Anglo-Irish, 9 x 5 In., Pair.......... 738
Cut Glass, Leaf, Grapevine, Cut Shades, Faceted Prisms, Electrified, 18 ¾ In. 375
Cut Glass, Topaz, Star Pattern Feet, Prisms, 27 ¼ In. 976
Girandole, Overlay, Green, Clear Pendants, Bohemian, 15 In., Pair 1125
Green, Frosted, Enamel, 12 x 6 In., Pair 125
Opaline Cut To Cranberry Glass, Enameled Decoration, Cut Prisms, 12 In., Pair.......... 96
Pink, Candlestick, Figural, Maiden With Urn Shape Holder, c.1810, 15 In., Pair..........*illus* 369
Pink, Strawberries, Gilt, Crystal Prisms, 15 ½ In., Pair.......... 148
Ruby Glass, Gilt Highlights, Cut Glass Prisms, 1900, 14 ⅛ In. 360
Ruby Glass, White Enamel Flowers, Green Leaves, White Dots, Crystal Prisms, 13 x 6 In. 354
White Cut To Cranberry, Spread Foot, Gilt, c.1890, 12 In., Pair 735

MACINTYRE, *see Moorcroft category.*

MAIZE glass was made by W.L. Libbey & Son Company of Toledo, Ohio, after 1889. The glass resembled an ear of corn. The leaves were usually green, but some pieces were made with blue or red leaves. The kernels of corn were light yellow, white, or light green.

Sugar Shaker, Custard Glass, Green, Brown, Leaves, 6 In. 118
Sugar Shaker, Oval, White Kernels, Green & Peach Leaves, Metal Lid, 6 In. ....*illus* 121
Vase, Custard Glass, Blue Leaves, Gilt, 1889, 7 ⅞ In. 168
Vase, Iridescent Gold, Light Blue Leaves, 1900, 6 ½ In. 149
Vase, Opaque White, Green Leaves, 1889, 6 ½ In. 36

MAJOLICA is a general term for any pottery glazed with an opaque tin enamel that conceals the color of the clay body. It has been made since the fourteenth century. Today's collector is most likely to find Victorian majolica. The heavy, colorful ware is rarely marked. Some famous makers include Minton; Griffen, Smith and Hill (marked *Etruscan*); and Chesapeake Pottery (marked *Avalon* or *Clifton*). Majolica made by Wedgwood is listed in the Wedgwood category.

Asparagus Tray, Green, Cream, 13 x 7 In. 48
Basin, Palissy Style, Blue, Lily Pads, Shells, Frog, 17 In. 3250
Bowl, Banana Bunch, White Monkeys, 14 x 16 ½ In. 354
Bowl, Blue, Yellow, Portrait, Profile, Flowers, 1800s, 14 In. 118
Bowl, Pond Decoration, Applied Frogs, Calla Lilies, Massier, 3 ½ In. 188
Bowl, Shell Shape, Pink, Green, 12 In. Diam. 90
Bowl, Sun Figure, Green, Yellow, Brown Glaze, c.1890, 9 In. Diam. 720
Butter, Yellow Flower, Leaves, Mauve Ground, 9 In. 97
Candlestick, Blackmore, Man, Jar On Head, Basket, 13 ½ x 4 In. 213
Centerpiece, Green, Italy, 5 x 13 ¾ In., 7 Piece 300
Centerpiece, Painted, Oval, Handles, Footed, Continental, c.1890, 5 ½ x 9 In. 48
Charger, 6 Gods & Goddesses, Blue Border, Marked Faenza 1885, 22 In. Diam. 1800
Charger, Applied Coiled Snake, Green, Palissy Ware, Portugal, 11 ½ In., Pair.......... 5250
Charger, Blue & Yellow, Villas, Garden, Rabbits, Birds, Insects, c.1740, 14 In. Diam. 1750
Charger, Renaissance Style, Tin Glazed Earthenware, Landscape, Putti, 1800s, 20 In. 708
Charger, Venetian, Blue, Yellow, Villa Scene, Rabbits, Birds, Insects, c.1750, 14 In. 2952
Cheese Bell, Stand, Domed Straw Beehive, Faux Wood Base, 14 In. 4375

Loetz, Vase, Rainbow, Square, Dimpled, Angular Ribbing, Blue, Yellow, Red, c.1890, 8 In.
$461

Skinner, Inc.

Lone Ranger, Ring, Atomic Bomb, Kix Cereal Premium, Instruction Sheet, Box
$221

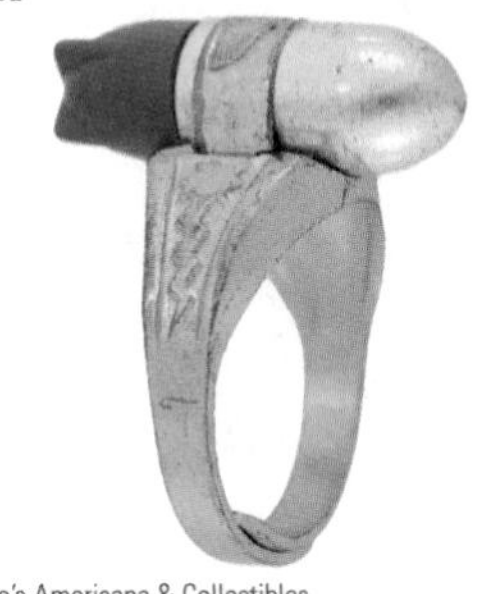

Hake's Americana & Collectibles

Longwy, Vase, Cylindrical, Birds, Landscape, Elephant Head Stand, c.1890, 7 ½ x 10 ½ In.
$492

Skinner, Inc.

Lunch Box, Buccaneer, Treasure Chest, Metal, Dome, Aladdin, 1957, 6 ½ In.
$115

Hake's Americana & Collectibles

Lunch Box, Road Runner, Metal, Thermos, Wile E. Coyote, Rocks, Purple, 1970, 7 In.
$190

Hake's Americana & Collectibles

Lunch Box, Underdog, Kicking Villains, Sweet Polly Purebred, Metal, Universal, c.1974
$2,296

Hake's Americana & Collectibles

Lunch Boxes

About 650 different children's metal lunch box designs have been made in the United States. The first, a Hopalong Cassidy lunch box, was made in 1951; and the last, a Rambo box, dates from 1985. Now children's lunch boxes are plastic.

Cheese Dish, Twig Molded Stand, Dome Lid, Cow Finial, George Jones, 13 x 12 In. *illus* 1250

Compote, Flowers, Wavy Rim, Multicolor, Flared Pedestal Foot, 5 x 9 In. 94

Decanter, Monkey Man, Wearing Suit, Hat, Square Base, 12 ¼ In. 200

Dish, Adam & Eve Laying In The Bottom, Italy, 3 x 8 In. 1599

Dish, Full Nest, Brown Feathered Bird, Perched, Grass, Rabbits, Ferns, 7 ½ x 13 In. 363

Dish, Leaf, Green, Yellow Center, 7 ¾ In., Pair 90

Ewer, Underplate, Palissy, Green Coleslaw, Insects, Lizards, c.1890, 11 In. 156

Figurine, Blackamoor, Multicolor, Serving, Terra-Cotta, 1900s, 37 ½ x 12 In., Pair 287

Figurine, Dog, Whippet, Sitting, 27 In. 1529

Figurine, Peacock, Green, Spain, 25 ½ x 14 ½ In. 210

Garniture, Cherub, Lion Heads, Blue, Green, 17 x 9 In. 105

Jardiniere, Applied Lemons, Green Ground, 16 ½ x 28 In. 750

Jardiniere, Blue Wash Interior, Ribbed White Exterior, Shells, 8 x 9 In. 438

Jardiniere, Figural Handles, Blue, Yellow, Tree, Leaves, Nuts, 10 x 9 ½ In., Pair 600

Jardiniere, Frie Onnaing, Handles, Gilt Detail, Blue, Red, c.1900, 8 x 13 ½ In. 180

Mug, Double Face, Husband & Wife, France, 6 ½ x 7 In. 60

Pedestal, Corinthian Capitals, Column, Cornucopia, Garlands, Masks, 47 In., Pair 2750

Pitcher, Battle Scene, Fortress, Mountains, Blue, Yellow, Italy, 11 In. 1945

Pitcher, Fish Shape, Gray, Curved Tail, 11 ½ In. 120

Pitcher, Fish Shape, Tail Curled Up Forming Handle, Open Mouth Spout, Glazed, 10 In. 130

Pitcher, Fish Shape, Tail Handle, Open Mouth, 9 In. 118

Pitcher, Flowers, Long Stem, Green, c.1900, 7 ½ In. 110

Pitcher, Leaping Fish, Blue, Foot, 11 In., Pair 110

Pitcher, Painted, Dog, Landscape, Dog Handle, Continental, c.1890, 6 x 7 In. 150

Planter, Figural, Grasshopper, J. Massier Fils, Vallauris, France, c.1910, 5 x 9 In. *illus* 1180

Plate, Blackberry, White Basket Weave, 10 In. 24

Plate, Landscape, Castelli, c.1760, 9 ¼ In., Pair 973

Plate, Leaf, Purple Rim, Handle, 9 In., 4 Piece 48

Plate, Multicolor, Cobalt Blue, Green, White, Rust, Leaves, Cantagalli, 11 In. 236

Punch Bowl, Enameled, Earthenware, Punch Figure, Bowl, Holly, George Jones, c.1870, 13 In. *illus* 3075

Punch Bowl, Turquoise Interior, Water Lilies, Marine Plants, 7 x 15 In. 90

Sculpture, Parrot, Red, Blue, Yellow, Wood Perch, 20 ½ x 8 In. 307

Server, Blue Bird, Perched, Leaf, 3 x 8 In. 120

Smoking Stand, Boy, Holding Hat, 2 Wells, 7 ½ x 7 ½ In. 182

Strainer, Underplate, Tripod, White, Italy, 9 ½ x 10 ½ In. 120

Tobacco Jar, Lid, Frog Smoking Pipe, Austria, 6 ¼ In. *illus* 132

Tray, Begonia Leaf, Yellow Rim, Stem Handle 36

Tray, Oak Leaf, Purple Rim, Stem Handle, 12 In. 49

Tureen, Lid, Crab Shape, Coral Branch Handle, Seaweed, 13 ½ In. 8125

Umbrella Stand, Graduated Bamboo Cylinders, Japan, c.1910, 17 x 25 In. 236

Umbrella Stand, Pierced, Square, Flowers, Leaves, Brown, 22 In. 519

Vase, Leaves, 2 Handles, Cream, Brown, F&A Gerbing, c.1900, 13 x 7 ½ In. 84

Wall Brackets, Bacchanalian Bust, Blond Hair, Fruit, 12 x 7 ½ In. 182

MALACHITE is a green stone with unusual layers or rings of darker green shades. It is often polished and used for decorative objects. Most malachite comes from Siberia or Australia.

Ashtray, Art Deco, 3 Horses, 5 ¼ In. 60

Box, Casket Shape, Hinged, Bronze Footed, 10 x 4 x 3 In. 2495

Decanter, Leaves, Henry Schlevogt, 1930s, 11 In. 595

Figurine, Lion, Art Deco, Carved, 1920s, Chinese, 3 ¼ In. 160

Figurine, Panda, Jewel Eyes, c.1900, 3 x 4 In. 975

Figurine, Whale, Tail Up, 2 ¾ x 1 ½ In. 95

Necklace, Beads, 14K Yellow Gold, 18 In. 150

Vase, Dancing Nudes, 1930s, 5 ¼ In. 149

Vase, Silver, Pieced Flowers, Leaves, Hexagonal, 13 x 8 In., Pair 15730

MAPS of all types have been collected for centuries. The earliest known printed maps were made in 1478. The first printed street map showed London in 1559. The first road maps for use by drivers of automobiles were made in 1901. Collectors buy maps that were pages of old books, as well as the multifolded road maps popular in this century.

America Sive India Nova, Hemispherical, Michael Mercator, Duisberg, c.1613, 15 x 19 In. 3068

America, Giovanni Botero, 1640, 9 ¾ x 6 ¾ In. 345

American Traveler, Guide To The U.S., H.S. Tanner, Phila., FDR's Copy, 1837, 6 x 4 In. 1121

Britain, Copper Plate, 7 Cartouches, Kings Of The Heptarchy, 23 ½ x 28 ½ In. 668

British & French Settlements, North America, 1755, 15 x 14 In. 720

California, Soil, Rainfall, Temperature, 1885, Frame, 23 x 30 In. 780
Colonial North, Cartouche, Beaver, Natives, Friars, Guillaume Delisle, 1703, 26 x 20 In. 1610
Colonial South, French & English Coat Of Arms, Hide, Arnoldus Montanus, 1671, 14 x 12 In. .. 805
England & Wales, Needlework On Silk, Beige, Brown, Square, Frame, 14 x 13 In. ....*illus* 316
English Empire, Ocean Of America Or West Indies, Revis'd J. Senex, c.1719, 20 x 24 In. 138
French Quarter, Le Vieux Carre De La Nouvelle Orleans, Litho, Barnes, 1942, 23 x 31 In. 275
General Atlas, Various Countries, City Plans, 50 Quarto Maps, Mitchell, 1862, 16 x 13 In. 885
Georgia, Part Of Carolina, Florida, Louisiana, Bowen, 1748, 15 x 19 In. 1888
Georgia, Pocket, Frame, J.H. Colton, New York, c.1861, 16 x 13 ½ In. 354
Globe, Celestial & Terrestrial, Turned Wood Base, Josiah Loring, c.1840, 17 In., Pair 7995
Globe, Celestial, Beige, Stand, France, 12 x 9 ¾ In. 600
Globe, Celestial, H. Hughes & Son, Mahogany Cased, Lift Lid, c.1920, 8 In. 2031
Globe, Library, Floor Model, Lacquer Finish, Replogle, c.1951, 51 ½ In. 2375
Globe, Silver & Gilt, Stand, Fish Shape Stem, Rope Trim, Waufgeschutzt, c.1980, 15 In. 4183
Globe, Terrestrial, Brass Stand, Paw Feet, 46 In. 299
Globe, Terrestrial, Bronze, 12 Engraved Gores, Multicolor, Stand, Newton, 1800s, 8 In. ....*illus* 1107
Globe, Terrestrial, Bronze, 8 In. 70
Globe, Terrestrial, Celestial, Mahogany Stand, Cary, England, c.1820, 36 x 18 In., 2 Piece.... 5100
Globe, Terrestrial, Cobalt Blue, Stand, 22 x 17 In. 129
Globe, Terrestrial, Compass, Stand, 42 x 34 In. 738
Globe, Terrestrial, Ebonized, Hanging, Brass Supports, 11 x 11 In. 540
Globe, Terrestrial, George III, Satinwood Tripod, Compass, J&W Cary, c.1815, 46 x 29 In. 21250
Globe, Terrestrial, Lacquer Brass, Desk, Half Meridian, Equator Ring, c.1900, 17 In. 2373
Globe, Terrestrial, Mahogany Stand, Compass, A.K. Johnston, c.1891, 41 x 23 In. 5000
Globe, Terrestrial, Paper Veneer, Wood Rings, Metal, Footed Base, c.1900, 23 In. 104
Globe, Terrestrial, Pocket, Hinged, Holbrook's Apparatus Mfg. Co., c.1850, 3 In.. 1625
Globe, Terrestrial, Resin, Multicolor, Copper Tone Stand, 38 x 16 In. 165
Globe, Terrestrial, Rotates, Semiprecious Stones, Brass Stand, 1900s, 21 x 12 ½ In. 195
Globe, Terrestrial, Stand, Tin, Zooming, Windup, Box, Gama, West Germany, 12 x 12 In. 350
Globe, Terrestrial, Tan, Mean Isothermal Lines, Stand, Rand, McNally, 38 x 24 In. 544
Italy, Hand Colored Engraving, Mounted On Board, 1708, 19 ¾ x 24 ¾ In. 183
Louisiana, Inset, Colored, D'Anville's Atlas, Harrison & Bowen, 1788, 13 x 21 In. 1185
Mississippi, Colored Lithograph, J. Bien, 1879, 26 ¼ x 22 ½ In. 375
New England, Johannes Baptista Homann, Engraving, 1716, 2 Page, 24 x 20 In. ....*illus* 1046
New York Wilderness, Blindstamped Cloth, Colton & Co., 1869, 4 x 6 In. 600
North America, Hand Colored Engraving, Alvin Jewett Johnson, 1867 24 x 18 In. 122
North America, Principal Divisions, William Duke Of Gloucester, 1573, 15 x 20 In. 1170
North Polar Region, 15 Panels, Linen, 31 ½ x 24 In. 276
Ohio, Inset Of Cleveland, Hand Colored, J.H. Colton, Mat, Frame, 1855, 17 x 20 In. 270
Ohio, Toledo War, Disputed Land, Ohio-Michigan Border, Leather Bound, c.1834, 13 x 10 In. 240
Panama & South America, Jan Janssonius, Copperplate Engraving, 17 ½ x 23 In.... 303
Paper, Globe Projection Map Of World, Watercolor, Ink, Schoolgirl, 1831, 22 x 33 In. 2706
Solar System, Sun, Cellarius, Schenk & Valck, 1708, 20 ½ x 17 In. 776
Southern Appalachian Region, Relief, Julius Bien, Frame, c.1902, 19 x 23 In. 1180
Texas, Indian Territory, Hand Colored, Tiantor Bros. & Merrill, 1800s, 21 ¼ x 30 In. 183
Turkish Empire, c.1875, 26 x 40 In. 861

MARBLE collectors pay highest prices for glass and sulphide marbles. The game of marbles has been popular since the days of the ancient Romans. American children were able to buy marbles by the mid-eighteenth century. Dutch glazed clay marbles were least expensive. Glazed pottery marbles, attributed to the Bennington potteries in Vermont, were of a better quality. Marbles made of pink marble were also available by the 1830s. Glass marbles seem to have been made later. By 1880, Samuel C. Dyke of South Akron, Ohio, was making clay marbles and The National Onyx Marble Company was making marbles of onyx. The Navarre Glass Marble Company of Navarre, Ohio, and M. B. Mishler of Ravenna, Ohio, made the glass marbles. Ohio remained the center of the marble industry, and the Akron-made Akro Agate brand became nationally known. Other pieces made by Akro Agate are listed in this book in the Akro Agate category. Sulphides are glass marbles with frosted white figures in the center.

End Of Day, Cane, Red, Blue, Green, Polished Pontil, 1890s, ¾ In. ....*illus* 85
Glass, Clear, Yellow, Red Spotting, End Of Day, Wisping Tail, Pontil, 1 In. 210
Glass, Orange, Blue, Yellow, Blue, Joseph's Coat, Pontil, 1 In. 150
Lutz, Amber Glass, Ribbon, $^{27}/_{32}$ In. 150
Lutz, Banded, Black Opaque, ⅞ In. 840
Lutz, Banded, Indian, Black Opaque Base, White, Blue, $^{11}/_{16}$ In. 390
Lutz, Ribbon, Brown, Clear Glass, $^{25}/_{32}$ In. 120

Luneville, Vase, Gourd, Loop Handle, Gray, Pink Glaze, Keller & Guerin, c.1900, 12 x 7 In.
$26,250

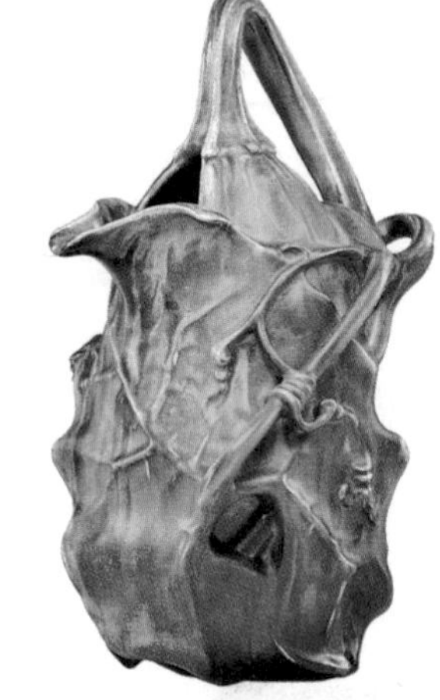

Rago Arts and Auction Center

Lustres, Pink, Candlestick, Figural, Maiden With Urn-Shape Holder, c.1810, 15 In., Pair
$369

Skinner, Inc.

Maize, Sugar Shaker, Oval, White Kernels, Green & Peach Leaves, Metal Lid, 6 In .
$121

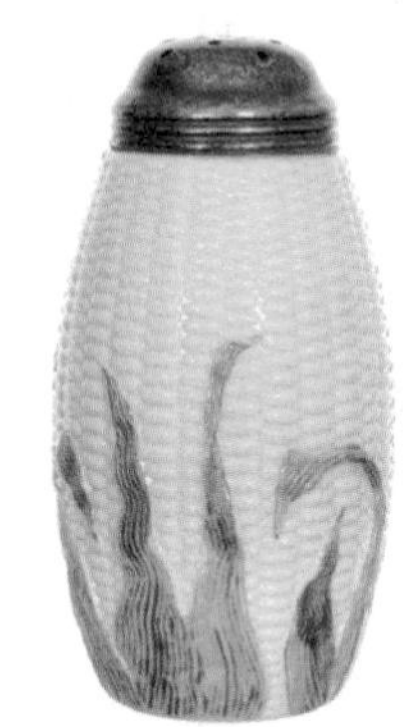

Woody Auction

M

Mica, Confetti, Spotting, Turquoise, Red, Pink, Yellow, Flakes, 25/64 In.	780
Millefiori, Paperweight, Red & White, Onionskin, 1 7/16 In.	330
Pinwheel, Arrows Pointing Center, 3 Black Bands, Green, Red, Chinese, 23/32 In.	210
Snowflake, Twist, Onionskin, Pink, White, Blue, Flakes Float, Pontil, 5/8 In.	60
Sulphide, Angel, Nude, Wings Spread, Flying Position, 1 13/16 In.	420
Sulphide, Vampire Bat, Spread Wing, Clear, Silver Effect, 1 13/16 In.	2400
Swirl, Ribbon Core, Shooter, Multicolor, c.1890, 1 3/4 In. *illus*	135

MARBLE CARVINGS, such as large or small figurines, groups of people or animals, and architectural decorations, have been a special art form since the time of the ancient Greeks. Reproductions, especially of large Victorian groups, are being made of a mixture using marble dust. These are very difficult to detect and collectors should be careful. Other carvings are listed under Alabaster.

Bacchante, Standing Nude, Holding Grapes, Goat, Vines, c.1900, 30 In.	2000
Buddha, Downcast Eyes, Serene Face, Long Earlobes, Wood Stand, 10 1/2 In. *illus*	3851
Bust, Bearded Man, 26 In.	263
Bust, Caesar, Gazing Forward, Turned Base, Italy, c.1860, 23 1/2 In.	1875
Bust, Child, Hands Together, Head Covering, 25 In.	146
Bust, Cicero, White Marble, Column, Italy, c.1890, 17-In. Bust, 40 In.	1200
Bust, Diana, Head Turned, Marble Base, Italy, 1900, 22 In.	406
Bust, Florentine Woman, Pietro Bazzanti, Italy, c.1850, 24 In. *illus*	2706
Bust, Goddess Diana, Tapered Pedestal, Guglielmo Pugi, 24 x 14 In.	2933
Bust, Head Of David, After Michelangelo, Italy, c.1900, 46 In. *illus*	9840
Bust, Joan Of Arc, Ferruzzi Virgilio, Florence, Italy, 1900s, 13 x 14 In.	660
Bust, Madame Du Barry, White, Breche Marble Base, c.1875, 28 In.	6250
Bust, Man, Curly Hair, White, Mounted, Square Base, Italy, 18 In.	2175
Bust, Marie Antoinette, Draped, Columnar Base, c.1890, 28 x 19 In.	2000
Bust, Neoclassical, Roman Style, Laurel Wreath, 20 x 12 In.	449
Bust, Niobe, Grieving For Her Children, Pedestal, c.1865, 65 x 12 In.	1750
Bust, Portrait Of Woman, Draped, Square Base, Signed, 1890, 28 x 18 In.	3250
Bust, Woman, Bonnet, Necklace, Gray Socle, P. Barzanti, Italy, c.1900, 28 In. *illus*	885
Bust, Woman, Classical, Rosette, 28 In.	70
Bust, Woman, Hat, Lace, Italy, 1900s, 10 x 9 1/4 In.	575
Bust, Woman, Off The Shoulder Dress, Coiffure, 26 In.	117
Bust, Woman, Reticulated Lace Trimmed Hat, Italy, 19 5/8 In.	668
Bust, Woman, Robes, Seminude, 30 In.	380
Bust, Woman, Victorian, Richard Westmacott The Younger, c.1859, 21 In.	3112
Bust, Young Woman, Head Wrap, Classical Clothing, 18 x 14 In.	1829
Figure, Maternal Love, Reclining Nude, Holding Child, 1930, 9 x 21 In.	1845
Figure, Seminude Woman, Faun, Decanter, Tambourine, 32 x 13 In.	1037
Obelisk, Beige, 18 1/2 In.	147
Obelisk, Dark Dusky Rose, 15 5/8 In., Pair	375
Obelisk, Pink, Black Veins, 12 1/2 In., Pair	250
Pedestal, Renaissance, 3 Columns, 35 x 13 In.	309
Pedestal, Roman Style Column, 4 Pillars, Squared Top, Gray, 44 x 9 1/2 In.	307
Pedestal, Swivel Top, Raised On Feet, 44 x 14 In.	1200
Pedestal, Variegated, Round Foot, 35 1/2 x 14 3/4 In., Pair	750
Plaque, Lamentation Of Christ, Gilt Trim, Frame, 1800s, 32 x 31 In.	1476
Reliquary, Grand Tour, Italy, 4 1/4 x 10 In.	3600
Statue, 3 Graces, Daughters Of Zeus, Nude, Embracing, c.1800, 23 x 14 In.	2250
Statue, Angel, Cloud, Caped Shoulders, Tiara, Ringlets, Spread Wings, 59 In.	13750
Statue, Angel, Trumpet, Full Round, Ringlets, c.1890, 59 1/2 In.	18750
Statue, Aphrodite, At Her Bath, Nude, Kneeling, Amphora, 24 1/2 x 13 In.	690
Statue, Bather, Woman, Nude, Drying Foot, Upswept Hair, 1700s, 62 In.	31980
Statue, Boy With Horn, Raised Arm, Italy, Signed, 32 In.	1000
Statue, Cherub, Holding Sheaf Of Wheat, 21 1/2 In.	1045
Statue, Children, Swing, Dog, 15 x 11 In.	176
Statue, Embrace, Mother, Father, Infant, Ralph Hurst, 18 In.	456
Statue, Fisher Girl, Standing, Earrings, Holding Basket, Fish, Italy, c.1880, 24 In.	791
Statue, Girl, Surprised By Lizard, Draped, Holding Flowers In Skirt, c.1860, 31 In.	10879
Statue, Hebe, Adamo Tadolini, Standing, Left Arm Raised, After A. Canova, 37 In.	23750
Statue, Horse, Prancing, Han Style, White, Chinese, 20th Century, 15 In.	590
Statue, Horses, Heads, 10 3/4 x 9 1/2 In.	1830
Statue, Lion, Male, Crouching, Marble Base, 52 3/4 x 55 In.	2587
Statue, Madonna, 36 In.	900

TIP

Old majolica pitchers have a glazed interior. Many reproduction majolica pitchers have bisque interiors.

Majolica, Cheese Dish, Twig Molded Stand, Dome Lid, Cow Finial, George Jones, 13 x 12 In.
$1,250

New Orleans (Cakebread)

Majolica, Planter, Figural, Grasshopper, J. Massier Fils, Vallauris, France, c.1910, 5 x 9 In.
$1,180

Brunk Auctions

Majolica, Punch Bowl, Enameled, Earthenware, Punch Figure, Bowl, Holly, George Jones, c.1870, 13 In.
$3,075

Skinner, Inc.

Majolica, Tobacco Jar, Lid, Frog Smoking Pipe, Austria, 6 ¼ In.
$132

Fox Auctions

Map, England & Wales, Needlework On Silk, Beige, Brown, Square, Frame, 14 x 13 In.
$316

Cottone Auctions

Map, Globe, Terrestrial, Bronze, 12 Engraved Gores, Multicolor, Stand, Newton, 1800s, 8 In.
$1,107

Skinner, Inc.

Map, New England, Johannes Baptista Homann, Engraving, 1716, 2 Page, 24 x 20 In.
$1,046

Skinner, Inc.

TIP

Do not mount old maps, prints, etc., on cardboard. The acid in the cardboard causes stains. Use an all rag board. An art store can help.

Marble, End Of Day, Cane, Red, Blue, Green, Polished Pontil, 1890s, ¾ In.
$85

Ruby Lane

Marble, Swirl, Ribbon Core, Shooter, Multicolor, c.1890, 1 ¾ In.
$135

Ruby Lane

Marble Carving, Buddha, Downcast Eyes, Serene Face, Long Earlobes, Wood Stand, 10 ½ In.
$3,851

James D. Julia Auctioneers

Marble Carving, Bust, Florentine Woman, Pietro Bazzanti, Italy, c.1850, 24 In.
$2,706

Cowan Auctions

Marble Carving, Bust, Head Of David, After Michelangelo, Italy, c.1900, 46 In.
$9,840

Skinner, Inc.

TIP
Marble will eventually react to rain and deteriorate. Keep marble ornaments out of the rain and frost.

Marble Carving, Bust, Woman, Bonnet, Necklace, Gray Socle, P. Barzanti, Italy, c.1900, 28 In.
$885

Brunk Auctions

Marble Carving, Statue, Venus Italica, Seminude, Drape, Side Glancing, Round Base, c.1860, 40 In.
$6,250

New Orleans (Cakebread)

Marblehead, Vase, Flying Geese, A. Aldrich, S. Tutt, Ship Mark, c.1910, 8 ½ x 7 In.
$6,250

Rago Arts and Auction Center

Marblehead, Vase, Green, Stylized Roses, Columns, Arthur Hennessey, Sarah Tutt, 1920s, 7 x 4 In.
$20,000

Rago Arts and Auction Center

Mardi Gras, Doubloon, Krewe Of Iris, New Orleans, Silver Tone, 1995, 1 ½ In.
$20

Rock Island Auction

Statue, Nude, Teasing Rearing Goat, Rectangular Base, c.1905, 12 x 27 In. 1250
Statue, Shrine, Buddha, Attendants, Dragon, 1900s, 37 ½ In. 354
Statue, Venus De Medici, Standing, Nude, Cherub At Feet, Round Base, c.1900, 24 In. 375
Statue, Venus Italica, Seminude, Drape, Side Glancing, Round Base, c.1860, 40 In. ....*illus* 6250
Statue, Wild Cat, Slope, 8 x 23 In. 292
Statue, Woman, Nude, Looking Over Shoulder, Seated, 28 In. 3750
Statue, Woman, Sitting, Deep Folds, 35 In. 2000
Vase, Bronze Mount, Gilt, Relief, Cylindrical, Lid, c.1875, 18 In., Pair 2140
Vase, Green, 12 ¼ In. 120

MARBLEHEAD POTTERY was founded in 1904 by Dr. J. Hall as a rehabilitative program for the patients of a Marblehead, Massachusetts, sanitarium. Two years later it was separated from the sanitarium and it continued operations until 1936. Many of the pieces were decorated with marine motifs.

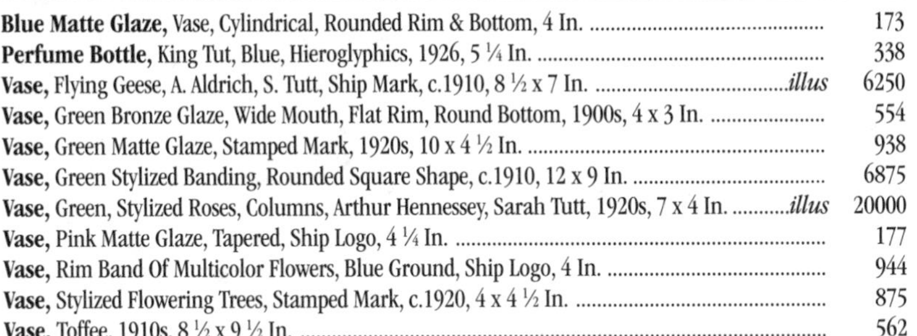

Blue Matte Glaze, Vase, Cylindrical, Rounded Rim & Bottom, 4 In. 173
Perfume Bottle, King Tut, Blue, Hieroglyphics, 1926, 5 ¼ In. 338
Vase, Flying Geese, A. Aldrich, S. Tutt, Ship Mark, c.1910, 8 ½ x 7 In. ....*illus* 6250
Vase, Green Bronze Glaze, Wide Mouth, Flat Rim, Round Bottom, 1900s, 4 x 3 In. 554
Vase, Green Matte Glaze, Stamped Mark, 1920s, 10 x 4 ½ In. 938
Vase, Green Stylized Banding, Rounded Square Shape, c.1910, 12 x 9 In. 6875
Vase, Green, Stylized Roses, Columns, Arthur Hennessey, Sarah Tutt, 1920s, 7 x 4 In. ....*illus* 20000
Vase, Pink Matte Glaze, Tapered, Ship Logo, 4 ¼ In. 177
Vase, Rim Band Of Multicolor Flowers, Blue Ground, Ship Logo, 4 In. 944
Vase, Stylized Flowering Trees, Stamped Mark, c.1920, 4 x 4 ½ In. 875
Vase, Toffee, 1910s, 8 ½ x 9 ½ In. 562

MARDI GRAS, French for "Fat Tuesday," was first celebrated in seventeenth-century Europe. The first celebration in America was held in Mobile, Alabama, in 1703. The first krewe, a parading or social club, was founded in 1856. Dozens have been formed since. The Mardi Gras Act, which made Fat Tuesday a legal holiday, was passed in Louisiana in 1875. Mardi Gras balls, carnivals, parties, and parades are held from January 6 until the Tuesday before the beginning of Lent. The most famous carnival and parades take place in New Orleans. Parades feature floats, elaborate costumes, masks, and "throws" of strings of beads, cups, doubloons, or small toys. Purple, green, and gold are traditional Mardi Gras colors. Mardi Gras memorabilia ranges from cheap plastic beads to expensive souvenirs from early celebrations.

Ball Invitation, Rex, 1986, Envelope, Heavenly Bodies, Blue, Gold, 1986 431
Dance Card, 1911, Twelfth Night Revelers, 4 ½ x 4 In. 184
Dance Card, Rex, 1912 246
Doubloon, Krewe Of Iris, New Orleans, Silver Tone, 1995, 1 ½ In. ....*illus* 20
Doubloon, Krewe Of Louisianians, Washington D.C., Gold Tone, 1985 ....*illus* 50
Parade Bulletin, 1892, Krewe Of Comus, Nippon Land Of Rising Sun, Litho 308
Parade Bulletin, 1892, Proteus, Dream Of Vegetable Kingdom, Litho, 28 x 42 In. 338
Parade Bulletin, 1892, Symbolism Of Colors, Lithograph 359
Parade Bulletin, 1904, Knights Of Momus, February 11, Walle & Co., 28 x 42 In. 384
Parade Bulletin, 1905, Lost Pleid, Krewe Of Comus, March 7, Walle & Co., 28 x 42 In. 610
Parade Bulletin, 1908, Krew Of Proteus, Light Of Asia, Lithograph, 28 x 42 In. 246
Parade Bulletin, 1923, Alice's Adventures In Wonderland, Searcy & Pfaff, 28 x 42 In. 246
Parade Bulletin, 1927, Wonderful Adventures Of Nils, 28 x 42 In. 184
Parade Bulletin, 1928, Famous Heroes & Heroines Of History, Searcy & Pfaff, 28 x 42 In. 369
Parade Bulletin, 1928, Transportation, Searcy & Pfaff, 28 x 42 ¼ In. 276
Parade Bulletin, 1929, The Adventures Of Hajji Baba, Searcy & Pfaff, 28 x 42 In. 184
Parade Bulletin, 1931, Broadcasting Old Favorites, Searcy & Pfaff, 28 x 42 In. 369
Pin, 1904, Mistick Krewe Of Comus, Izdubar, 3 In. 246
Pin, Krewe Favor, Snowflake Shape, White & Blue Enamel, Mithras Ball, 1985, 1 In. ....*illus* 55
Pin, Krewe Of Proteus Favor, Lamp Post, Street Sign, New Orleans, 1985, 1 ¾ In. ....*illus* 65

MARTIN BROTHERS of Middlesex, England, made Martinware, a salt-glazed stoneware, between 1873 and 1915. Many figural jugs and vases were made by the four brothers. Of special interest are the fanciful birds, usually made with removable heads. Most pieces have the incised name of the artists plus other information on the bottom.

Figurine, Green Lizard Creature, England, 1900, 2 ½ x 3 In. 5440
Jardiniere, Brown, Gray, 7 ⅛ In. 625
Jug, Face, Glazed Stoneware, Double-Sided, Robert W. Martin, 1908, 6 x 6 In. 2000
Tobacco Jar, Bird, Lid, Benjamin Disraeli, Incised, 1889, 14 In. ....*illus* 233000

TIP
Marble will scorch. A marble statue very close to the heat of a 100-watt lightbulb may be damaged.

Mardi Gras, Doubloon, Krewe Of Louisianians, Washington D.C., Gold Tone, 1985
$50

Ruby Lane

Mardi Gras, Pin, Krewe Favor, Snowflake Shape, White & Blue Enamel, Mithras Ball, 1985, 1 In.
$55

Ruby Lane

Mardi Gras, Pin, Krewe Of Proteus Favor, Lamp Post, Street Sign, New Orleans, 1985, 1 ¾ In.
$65

Ruby Lane

Martin Brothers, Tobacco Jar, Bird, Lid, Benjamin Disraeli, Incised, 1889, 14 In. $233,000

Phillips

Mary Gregory, Pitcher, Cherub, Flowers, Dark Green, c.1890, 6 x 3 ½ In. $90

Ruby Lane

Match Holder, Indian, Beaded, Lobed Top, Hanger, Dangling Beads, Green, Yellow, 1907, 7 x 5 In. $66

Old Barn Auctions

MARY GREGORY is the name used for a type of glass that is easily identified. White figures were painted on clear or colored glass as the decoration. The figures chosen were usually children at play. The first glass known as Mary Gregory was made in about 1870. Similar glass is made even today. The traditional story has been that the glass was made at the Boston & Sandwich Glass Company in Sandwich, Massachusetts, by a woman named Mary Gregory. Recent research has shown that none was made at Sandwich. In fact, all early Mary Gregory glass was made in Bohemia. Beginning in 1957, the Westmoreland Glass Co. made the first Mary Gregory–type decorations on American glassware. These pieces had simpler designs, less enamel paint, and more modern shapes. France, Italy, Germany, Switzerland, and England, as well as Bohemia, made this glassware. Children standing, not playing, were pictured after the 1950s.

Pitcher, Cherub, Flowers, Dark Green, c.1890, 6 x 3 ½ In. .... *illus* 90
Tray, Cranberry Glass, Round, 2 Human Figures, 12 In. 29

MASONIC, *see Fraternal category.*

MASON'S IRONSTONE was made by the English pottery of Charles J. Mason after 1813. Mason, of Lane Delph, was given a patent for this improved earthenware. He usually called it *Mason's Patent Ironstone China*. It resisted chipping and breaking, so it became popular for dinnerware and other table service dishes. Vases and other decorative pieces were also made. The ironstone was decorated with orange, blue, gold, and other colors, often in Japanese-inspired designs. The firm had financial difficulties but the molds and the name *Mason* were used by many owners through the years, including Francis Morley, Taylor Ashworth, George L. Ashworth, and John Shaw. Mason's joined the Wedgwood group in 1973 and the name was used for a few years and then dropped.

Bowl, Ironstone, Muted Ground, Black & Red, Coral-Like Pattern, 4 x 8 In. 118
Bowl, Ironstone, Yellow, Dragon, Scale Pattern, 3 ¾ x 8 In. 118
Cheese Dish Base, White, Underglaze Blue Transfer, Exotic Birds, c.1860, 20 In. 118
Cup & Saucer, Flowers, Regency, Blue, Demitasse.......... 43
Garniture Set, Ironstone, Red Flowers, Blue Fence, 3 Piece.......... 184
Plate, Niagara Falls, Maple Leaf, Brown, Transfer, 10 In. 76
Tureen, Lid, Platter, Multicolor Enamel, Imari Colors, c.1829, 6 x 11 ½ In. 378
Urn, Lid, Ironstone, Leaves, Birds, Green Handles, 13 x 5 ½ In. 207
Vase, Ironstone, Gold Fish Scale Pattern, Rectangular Orange Reserves, Man, 8 x 5 In. 236

MASSIER, a French art pottery, was made by brothers Jerome, Delphin, and Clement Massier in Vallauris and Golfe-Juan, France, in the late nineteenth and early twentieth centuries. It has an iridescent metallic luster glaze that resembles the Weller Sicardo pottery glaze. Most pieces are marked J. Massier. Massier may also be listed in the Majolica category.

Jardiniere, Pineapples, Branches, Purple, Green, Blue Luster, Round, 12 x 16 In. 1725
Umbrella Stand, Iris, 33 In. 125
Vase, Peacock Feathers, Red Metallic Glaze, Tapered, Swollen Shoulder, 8 ½ x 4 In. 750
Vase, Vallauris, Drawings, Crescent Moons, Circles, Diamonds, Animals, 14 ½ In. 1210

MATCH HOLDERS were made to hold the large wooden matches that were used in the nineteenth and twentieth centuries for a variety of purposes. The kitchen stove and the fireplace or furnace had to be lit regularly. One type of match holder was made to hang on the wall, another was designed to be kept on a tabletop. Of special interest today are match holders that have advertisements as part of the design.

Bulbous, Round Stepped Pedestal, Yellow, Green, Mottled, 1800s, 4 x 4 In. 1121
Ceresota Bread Flour, Boy Slicing Bread, Tin Litho, Die Cut, Embossed, 5 x 2 In. 235
Civil War Boot, Bootjack Striker, Base, Cast Iron, 5 x 5 In. 279
Dr. Shoop's Health Coffee, Tin, Yellow, 3 ⅜ x 4 ⅞ In. 228
Dubonnet, 1900 Grand Prix, Tapered Cup, Saucer Foot, Green, White, 3 x 3 In. 117
Elephant, Figural, Brass, Ivory Tusks, Standing, 2 ⅛ x 1 ½ In. 240
Football Player, Figural, Holding Ball, Metal, Marble Base.......... 171
Grape Design, Iron, Wall Bracket, c.1900, 9 x 5 In. 70
Hunting Bag, Antlers, Game, Cast Iron, 10 ½ In. 263
Indian, Beaded, Lobed Top, Hanger, Dangling Beads, Green, Yellow, 1907, 7 x 5 In. .... *illus* 66
Joyce & Company's Hosiery, No Flies On Green, Figural Fly, Cast Iron.......... 840
Man, Tasseled Hat, Pipe, Cooking Pot, Cast Metal, Marked, c.1890, 4 ½ In. .... *illus* 104
Marble, Cornish Red Serpentine, Lathe Turned, Rock Base, 3 ½ x 4 In. 150
Match Strike, Cut Glass, Ball Shape, Faceted, 3 x 4 In. 118
Napoleonic Soldier, Opening In Hat, Bronze, 6 ¾ x 8 In. 110

MATCH SAFES were designed to be carried in the pocket. Early matches were made with phosphorus and could ignite unexpectedly. The matches were safely stored in the tightly closed container. Match safes were made in sterling silver, plated silver, or other metals. The English call these "vesta boxes."

A Match For You At Any Time, Brass, Nickel Plate, Match, Initials, 1 ⅜ x 2 In. 240
Alligator, Sterling Silver, Mouth Hinged Lid, Gilt, Shiebler, c.1900, 2 In. 6573
Cherubs, Molded, Art Nouveau, Silver, Wm. B. Kerr & Co., c.1900, 2 ½ In. 450
Compliments Of Castleberg Jewelers, Washington, D.C., Silver, 3 In. 96
Copper Spider, Silver, Hammered Finish, Hinged Lid, c.1890, 2 ¼ In. 1135
Devil, Figural, Red Glass Eyes, Sterling Silver, 1 ¾ x 1 ¾ In. .... *illus* 210
Enamel Flowers, Silver, Hinged Lid, Scroll, Bottom Strike, 1898, 2 ⅜ In. 2390
Enamel, 18K Tiffany Gold, Cobalt Blue, Chased Leaves, Hinged Lid, c.1900, 2 In. 13145
Fish, Aquatic Scene, Oriental Style, Sterling Silver, Gorham, 2 ⅝ x 1 ½ In. 156
Flowers & Scroll, Silver, 15 Garnet Stars, Repousse, Gilt, Hinged Lid, c.1900, 2 In. 508
Girl With Flowing Hair, Sterling Silver, Embossed, Art Nouveau, 2 ½ In. 150
Gold Medal Flour, Washburn-Crosby Co., Flour Sack, Silver, 3 In. 156
Hardstone, 18K Gold, Enamel, Celtic Dragon Design, Stones, c.1900, 2 ⅜ In. 5938
Hidden Photo, Scrolling Leaves, Center Oval For Photo, Battin, 1896, 2 ¼ In. 50
Horse Head, Figural, Nickel Plate, 2 ¼ In. 60
Horse Head, Sterling Silver, Embossed, Flowers, Swirls, Round Top, 2 ½ In. 120
King Albert, High Grade Cigars, Silver, Whitehead & Hoag, 2 In. 120
Mother & Child, Swinging, Dolphins & Dragons, Sterling Silver, 1946, 2 ½ In. 100
Neptune, 2 Dolphins, Sterling Silver, Monogram, 2 ⅝ x 1 ⅝ In. 228
Nude Woman, Bat Wings, Silver Repousse, Inscribed, Hinged Lid, c.1905, 2 In. 1733
Outhouse, Nickel-Plated Brass, Seated Bare Man In Top Hat, c.1890, 2 In. .... *illus* 379
President Harrison, Figural, Profile, 2 ½ In. 210
Rampant Lion, Coat Of Arms, 18K Gold, Auspice Christo, T.B. Starr, 1 ¾ In. 510
Satyr & Bacchanal, 14K Gold, Repousse, Scroll Border, Kerr, c.1880, 2 ½ In. 1375
Silver, Art Nouveau, 2 ¾ In. 175
Silver, Gold Wash, Enamel Leaves, Multicolor, Peter Milyukov, c.1916, 2 x 1 In. 230
Standard Oil, Cylinder Oil, Barrels, Celluloid, Pocket, 3 x 1 ½ In. 242
Statue Of Liberty, Engraved, Diamond Torch, Quartz Paneled Base.......... 4250
Violin, Figural, 18K Gold, Engine Turned, Bail Loop Side, c.1900, 2 ½ In. 2750
Woman, At Seaside, Seminude, Lyre, Seagulls, Silver, Hinged Lid, c.1900, 2 ¼ In. 956
Woman, Profile, Bonnet, Repousse, Silver, Monogram, Hinged Lid, c.1890, 2 In. 1793
Woman, Smoking, Art Nouveau, Silver, Embossed, 2 ½ In. 210
Wreath, Shield, Spear, 14K Rose Gold, Repousse, Monogram, Carter, c.1893, 2 ½ In. 1494

MATT MORGAN, an English artist, was making pottery in Cincinnati, Ohio, by 1883. His pieces were decorated to resemble Moorish wares. Incised designs and colors were applied to raised panels on the pottery. Shiny or matte glazes were used. The company lasted less than two years.

MATT MORGAN —CIN. O— ART POTTERY Co

Ewer, Earthenware, Brown, Gilt, Corn Stalks, 6 ½ x 6 In. 1650
Perfume Jug, Small Bird, Wispy Grasses, Blue, 4 ¼ In. 484
Teapot, Butterfly, Cloud, Blue, Brown, Stick Handle, Gold Trim, 4 ½ In. 726
Vase, North American Loon, Rocky Shore, Limoges, 11 ¾ In. 1089

McCOY pottery was made in Roseville, Ohio. Nelson McCoy and J.W. McCoy established the Nelson McCoy Sanitary and Stoneware Company in Roseville, Ohio, in 1910. The firm made art pottery after 1926. In 1933 it became the Nelson McCoy Pottery Company. Pieces marked McCoy were made by the Nelson McCoy Pottery Company. Cookie jars were made from about 1940 until December 1990, when the McCoy factory closed. Since 1991 pottery with the McCoy mark has been made by firms unrelated to the original company. Because there was a company named Brush-McCoy, there is great confusion between Brush and Nelson McCoy pieces. See Brush category for more information.

McCoy

Basket, Leaves, Berries, Green Ground, 9 ½ In. 55
Bowl, Green, 9 In. 56
Cookie Jar, Globe, Airplane, 10 In. 123
Jardiniere, Green, Round, Marked, 9 In. 84
Jardiniere, Majolica, Yellow, Green, 8 ¼ x 10 In. 92
Planter, No Hunting Dog, Landscape, Fence, 12 ½ In. 52
Strawberry Jar, Bird Of Paradise, Green, 8 In. 40
Vase, Loy-Nel-Art, Brown, Flowers, 12 In. 92
Vase, Stoneware, Light Brown, Leaves, Handles, 7 In. 22

Match Holder, Man, Tasseled Hat, Pipe, Cooking Pot, Cast Metal, Marked, c.1890, 4 ½ In.
$104

Jeffrey S. Evans

Match Safe, Devil, Figural, Red Glass Eyes, Sterling Silver, 1 ¾ x 1 ¾ In.
$210

Showtime Auction Services

M

Match Safe, Outhouse, Nickel-Plated Brass, Seated Bare Man In Top Hat, c.1890, 2 In.
$379

Ruby Lane

McKee, Tumbler, Heart Band, Ruby, c.1897
$30

Ruby Lane

Medical, Cabinet, Apothecary, 30 Drawer, Doors, Bracket Base, New Eng., c.1810, 61 x 47 In.
$5,843

Skinner, Inc.

Medical, Cabinet, Apothecary, Elmwood, Stand, 80 Drawers, Labels, c.1625, 44 x 37 In.
$948

James D. Julia Auctioneers

TIP

An old cotton sock is a good polishing cloth. So is an old cloth diaper.

McKEE is a name associated with various glass enterprises in the United States since 1836, including J. & F. McKee (1850), Bryce, McKee & Co. (1850 to 1854), McKee and Brothers (1865), and National Glass Co. (1899). In 1903, the McKee Glass Company was formed in Jeannette, Pennsylvania. It became McKee Division of the Thatcher Glass Co. in 1951 and was bought out by the Jeannette Corporation in 1961. Pressed glass, kitchenwares, and tablewares were produced. Jeannette Corporation closed in the early 1980s. Additional pieces may be included in the Custard Glass and Depression Glass categories.

Bowl, Snappy, 3-Toed, 10 In. 46
Bowl, Toltec, Milk Glass, 3-Toed, 7 In. 27
Bowl, Toltec, Milk Glass, Round, 8 In. 31
Bread Tray, Deer & Pine Tree, Amber, 13 In. 92
Butter, Cover, Rock Crystal, Round 310
Candlestick, Plymouth Thumbprint, Square Base, 3 ½ In. 13
Candlestick, Ray, Milk Glass, 7 ¾ In. 30
Celery Dish, Martec, Milk Glass, Handle, 5 In. 39
Celery Dish, Quintec, 10 In. 17
Champagne, Rock Crystal, 6 Oz., 4 ¾ In. 9
Compote, Nortec, 7 ¾ In. 18
Compote, Orange, Black Rolled Rim, Art Deco, c.1925, 4 In. 28
Compote, Quintec, Crimped, 6 ½ In. 21
Compote, Yutec, 4 ½ In. 20
Cordial, Rock Crystal, Oz., 3 In. 10
Cordial, Rock Crystal, Red, Oz., 3 In. 65
Creamer, Laurel, French Ivory, Footed, 4 In. 16
Creamer, Plymouth Thumbprint, Milk Glass, 4 ½ In. 6
Creamer, Quintec, 4 In. 12
Creamer, Rock Crystal, Footed, Scalloped, 4 In. 20
Creamer, Toltec, Milk Glass, Sawtooth Rim, 3 ½ In. 6
Cup & Saucer, Laurel, Jade Green 28
Cup & Saucer, Rock Crystal, Footed 15
Dish, Crab, Red, 5 ¾ In. 11
Dish, Pickle, Rock Crystal, Scalloped, 7 In. 45
Goblet, Iced Tea, Opal, Milk Glass, 5 ½ In. 10
Goblet, Iced Tea, Rock Crystal, Concave, 12 Oz., 5 ¼ In. 43
Goblet, Water, Barberry, 6 In. 27
Goblet, Water, Bellflower, 6 In. 33
Goblet, Water, Feather, 5 ¾ In. 49
Goblet, Water, Queen, 6 In. 23
Goblet, Water, Rock Crystal, Red, 7 ½ Oz., 5 ¾ In. 32
Goblet, Water, Stippled Band, 6 In. 23
Jug, Tankard, Rock Crystal, 56 Oz., 11 In. 229
Nappy, Rock Crystal, 7 In. 19
Pin Tray, Open Hand, Milk Glass, 5 In. 20
Pitcher, Home, 48 Oz., 9 In. 56
Pitcher, Majestic, 64 Oz., 9 ½ In. 33
Pitcher, Rock Crystal, 54 Oz., 8 ½ In. 219
Plate, Bread & Butter, Rock Crystal, 6 ½ In. 17
Plate, Dinner, Rock Crystal, Scalloped, 11 ¼ In. 54
Punch Bowl, Hickman, 15 ¼ In. 145
Punch Bowl, Sextec, 13 ¾ In. 189
Punch Bowl, Stand, Aztec 189
Punch Bowl, The Concord, Crimped, 13 In. 39
Punch Bowl, Wiltec 153
Punch Cup, Martec, 2 ¼ In. 8
Punch Cup, Sextec, 1 ½ In. 12
Punch Cup, Teutonic, 2 ¼ In. 8
Punch Cup, Wiltec, 2 ¼ In. 11
Relish, Rock Crystal, 5 Sections, Round, 11 ¾ In. 34
Rose Bowl, Snappy, 3-Toed, 7 In. 49
Salt & Pepper, Puritan, Milk Glass, 4 ¼ In. 16
Salt & Pepper, Rock Crystal, Bulbous, 3 ⅝ In. 109
Sandwich Plate, Toltec, 10 In. 20
Sherbet, Laurel, French Ivory, 3 ½ In. 10
Sherbet, Lenox, Green, 4 ⅞ In. 18
Sherbet, Rock Crystal, Red, 3 ½ In. 66

Sugar, Lid, Rock Crystal, Footed, Handles, Scalloped, 6 ⅝ In. 56
Sugar, Toltec, Milk Glass, Footed, 3 ¼ In. 6
Torte Plate, Wiltec, 19 ¾ In. 82
Tray, Rock Crystal, Amber, Center Handle, Round, 10 In. 46
Tumbler, Feather, 4 In. 45
Tumbler, Heart Band, Ruby, c.1897 .... *illus* 30
Tumbler, Rock Crystal, Amber, Concave, 8 Oz., 4 ⅜ In. 26
Tumbler, Sextec, 8 Oz., 3 ⅞ In. 21
Tumbler, Virginia Cut 1, 8 Oz., 3 ¾ In. 18
Vase, Champion, Footed, Flared Rim, 12 In. 19
Vase, Cornucopia, Rock Crystal, 8 ½ x 3 ¾ In. 82
Vase, Fentec, Footed, Scalloped Rim, 8 ¼ In. 20
Vase, Rock Crystal, Footed, Cupped, Scalloped, 11 In. 92
Wine, Bellflower, 4 In. 39
Wine, Feather, 4 In. 21

MECHANICAL BANKS *are listed in the Bank category.*

MEDICAL office furniture, operating tools, microscopes, thermometers, and other paraphernalia used by doctors are included in this category. Veterinary collectibles are also included here. Medicine bottles are listed in the Bottle category. There are related collectibles listed under Dental.

Apothecary Tube Set, 11 Tubes, Glass Stoppers, Cork Stoppers, Leather Carrier, 7 x 3 In. 106
Cabinet, Apothecary, 12 Drawers, Bootjack Cutout Base, 1800s, 36 x 33 In. 994
Cabinet, Apothecary, 12 Drawers, Round Knobs, 12 x 19 In. 819
Cabinet, Apothecary, 18 Drawers, 1800s, 60 ½ x 18 ½ In. 2106
Cabinet, Apothecary, 28 Drawers, Yellow, 60 x 40 In. 1989
Cabinet, Apothecary, 30 Drawers, Doors, Bracket Base, New Eng., c.1810, 61 x 47 In. .... *illus* 5843
Cabinet, Apothecary, 32 Drawers, 1900s, 24 x 49 In. 555
Cabinet, Apothecary, Drawers, Oak, Glass, Harp Back, Swivel Showcase, 39 x 74 In. 456
Cabinet, Apothecary, Elmwood, Stand, 80 Drawers, Labels, c.1625, 44 x 37 In. .... *illus* 948
Cabinet, Apothecary, Pine, 30 Drawers, Old Red & White Paint, c.1875, 25 x 31 In. 2400
Cabinet, Apothecary, Red, Yellow, 33 ½ x 16 ½ In. 1404
Cabinet, Apothecary, Tiger Maple, 18 Drawers, Bracket Base, 1800s, 37 x 31 x 11 In. .... *illus* 3218
Chair, Convalescent, Leather, Hand Crank, 2-Wheel Axle, Brass, Pivot Wheel, c.1910 .... *illus* 1120
Chair, Examination, Converts, Table, Wood, Iron Base, R. Boericke, Pat. June 10, 1884 .... *illus* 224
Chair, Examination, Reclining, Leather, Arms, Foot Rest, Wood Base, 55 x 37 In. 114
Chair, Examination, Wood, Swivel Seat, Adjustable Back, Twisted Wire Base 168
Doctor's Bag, Leather, Push Button, Flip Over End, Hinged Sides, 1920s, 6 x 9 In. 220
Embalming Machine, 45 In. 153
Forceps, Obstetric, Stainless Steel, Sklar 30
Instrument Table, Iron Frame, Paint, Nickel Gallery, Glass Shelves, 1920s, 35 x 17 In. 196
Instruments, Surgeon's, Civil War Era, Case, 9 ½ In. 720
Instruments, Surgeon's, Scalpels, Bone Saw, Fitted Case, Civil War Era, 16 In. 3600
Invalid Chair, Carry Handles, Wood Frame, Caned Back, Seat, c.1910 78
Optician Test Set, American Optical Co., c.1900, 15 x 10 In. 118
Phrenology Head, Quack, L. N. Fowler, 17 x 8 In. 123
Phrenology Skull, Chalkware, S.R. Wells & Co., Paper Labels, c.1850, 10 In. .... *illus* 247
Quackery, Magneto-Electric Machine, Nervous Diseases, James W. Queen & Co., 4 x 8 In. 108
Scale, Floor Model, Porcelain, Balance Beam, Slide Measure, 5 Cent, 50 In. 270
Vampire Killing Kit, Case, Crucifix, Vials, Candles, Rosary, Stakes, 1892, 13 x 10 In. 1180
Waste Receptacle, Oak, Removable Liner, Foot Operated Lid, W.D. Allison, 22 x 11 In. 196

MEISSEN is a town in Germany where porcelain has been made since 1710. Any china made in the town can be called Meissen, although the famous Meissen factory made the finest porcelains of the area. The crossed swords mark of the great Meissen factory has been copied by many other firms in Germany and other parts of the world. Pieces of Meissen dinnerware in the Onion pattern are listed in their own category in this book.

Basket, 2 Handles, Multicolor Figural Head Terminals, Flowers, 1700s, 4 ¾ In. 277
Bowl, Gilt, Morning Glory, Matte Flowers, Leaves, Burnished, c.1960, 11 In., Pair 343
Box, Lid, Gilt, Multicolor, High Relief Allegorical Scenes, c.1860, 8 x 12 In. 7380
Cachepot, Lovers, Bacchus Head Handles, Pink, 4 ¾ x 5 In., Pair 1107
Cachepot, Yellow, Garden Scenes, Lovers, 7 x 8 ½ In. 1168
Chandelier, 15-Light, Porcelain, Flowering Scroll Branches, Putti, c.1900, 30 In. 25000

Medical, Cabinet, Apothecary, Tiger Maple, 18 Drawers, Bracket Base, 1800s, 37 x 31 x 11 In.
$3,218

Thomaston Place Auction

Medical, Chair, Convalescent, Leather, Hand Crank, 2-Wheel Axle, Brass, Pivot Wheel, c.1910
$1,120

Wickliffe Auctioneers

Medical, Chair, Examination, Converts, Table, Wood, Iron Base, R. Boericke, Pat. June 10, 1884
$224

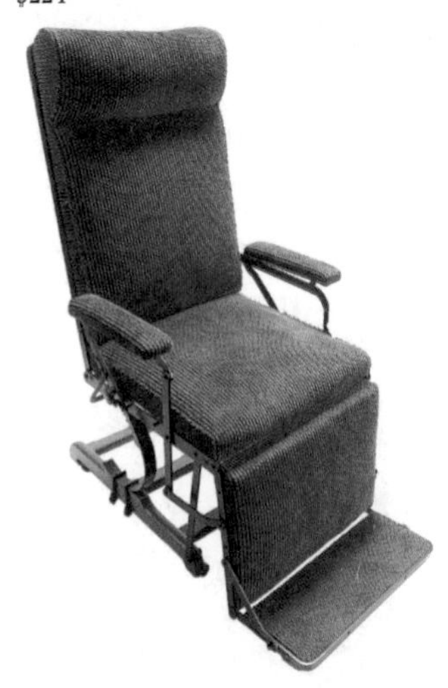

Wickliffe Auctioneers

Medical, Phrenology Skull, Chalkware, S.R. Wells & Co., Paper Labels, c.1850, 10 In.
$247

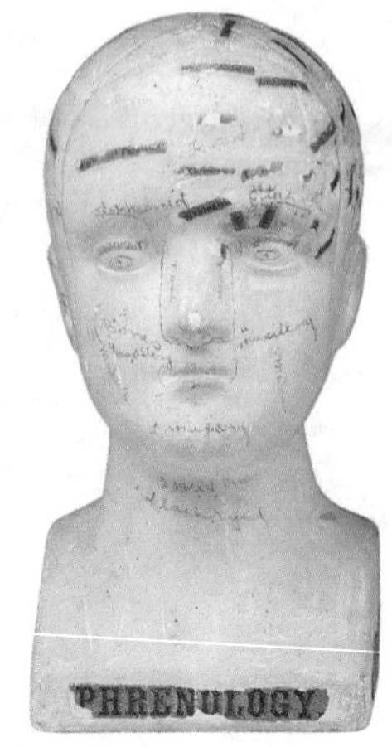

James D. Julia Auctioneers

Meissen, Figurine, Girl, Sheer Gown, Playing Bowls, Holding Ball, Gilt, Round Base, c.1900, 14 In.
$885

Brunk Auctions

Meissen, Figurine, Nodder, Asian Man, Tongue, Hands, Head Moves, Seated, c.1900, 5 ¾ In.
$3,075

Skinner, Inc.

Charger, Cranberry Colored Flowers, 1800s, 16 ½ In. 60
Charger, Group, Garden Landscape, Gilt Border, c.1870, 3 x 15 In. 400
Chocolate Pot, Flower Finial, Campsite, Barrels, 9 ¾ In. 584
Coffee Set, Coffeepot, Sugar & Creamer, Serpent Handle, 3 Piece 600
Compote, Canterbury Bells, Footed, Morning Glory, 11 In.. 149
Compote, Grape & Leaf, Gilt, 1880s, 5 x 8 In. 795
Cup & Saucer, Blue, White, Gilt, 3 In. 90
Cup & Saucer, Blue, White, Gilt, Flower Sprays, Ardalt Italian Display Holder, 3 In. 161
Cup & Saucer, Cobalt Blue, Repeating Gilt Stars, Gilt Interior, c.1890, 2 ¾ In. 83
Cup & Saucer, Gilt, Leaf, Stand, 5 In. 85
Cup & Saucer, Indian, Purple Flower Bouquets, Leaves, Gold Rim Trim, c.1850.... 47
Cup & Saucer, White Ground, Flower Shape, Handle, Gilt Trim, c.1910, 3 x 5 In. 83
Dish, Scalloped, Low Relief, Gilt Rim, Fruit & Leaf Reserves, 11 ¾ In. 104
Ewer, Air Element, Drapery Handle, Putti, Feathers, Juno, Relief, c.1880, 27 In. 8610
Ewer, Flower Encrusted, Leaf Form Handle, Birds, 25 In. 19375
Figurine, After The Bath, Seminude Woman, Towel, Adjusting Shoe, c.1900, 17 In. 3250
Figurine, Cupid, Anvil, 7 In. 195
Figurine, Girl, Dog, Mirror, Seated On Cushion, Painted, Gilt, c.1890, 5 ½ In. 759
Figurine, Girl, Sheer Gown, Playing Bowls, Holding Ball, Gilt, Round Base, c.1900, 14 In. ..*illus* 885
Figurine, Kingfisher, White Tree Stump, 12 In., Pair.... 1750
Figurine, Maiden, Lyre, Pink Drapery, Dolphin, Oval Base, 1800s, 7 ½ In. 923
Figurine, Maiden, Standing, Holding Book, Putto, Lyre, Music, c.1890, 12 In. 1625
Figurine, Man, Grafting Wood, Flower Print Coat, Gilt Base, Marked, c.1900, 7 In. 240
Figurine, Nodder, Asian Man, Laughing, Red Shoes, Crossed Swords Mark, 1900, 12 x 13 In. 10000
Figurine, Nodder, Asian Man, Tongue, Hands, Head Moves, Seated, c.1900, 5 ¾ In. ....*illus* 3075
Figurine, Parisian Wine Seller, Painted, 1900s, 5 ¼ x 2 ¼ In. 275
Figurine, Seated Child Drinking Tea, 4 In. 500
Figurine, White Marley Stallion, Blackamoor Groom, After J.J. Kaendler, 16 x 8 In. 840
Figurine, Woman, Flowers, Holding Flower, c.1911, 5 ¾ In. 1169
Figurine, Woman, Nude, Seated, Leg Up, Head Scarf, White Glaze, c.1939, 13 In. 717
Figurine, Woman, Selling Flowers, Marked, 7 In. 584
Figurine, Woman, With Cat, c.1900.... 1080
Group, 2 Putti, Playing Drum, Wearing Helmet, Shield, Suit Of Armor, c.1890, 6 In. 1000
Group, 4 Dancers, Flowers, Round Base, c.1934, 6 ¼ In. 1845
Group, Allegorical, Earth, Cybele, Seated On Lion, Cornucopia, Putti, c.1900, 9 In. 472
Group, Allegory Of Visual Arts, Cherubs At Easel, Busts, 6 In. ....*illus* 246
Group, Capturing The Tritons, 2 Women, Child, Fishing Net, Rocky Base, c.1860, 12 In. 5625
Group, Girl, Seated, Flower Dress, Boy With Flute, Round Base, c.1900, 6 x 5 In. 610
Group, Maiden, Seated, Boy, Sleeping, Cupid Gazing Over, c.1890, 14 In. 7500
Group, Man & Woman, Opera Singers, Gown, Soldier Uniform, c.1890, 9 In. 1187
Group, Man, Fur Hat, Ivy Garland, Woman, Scarf, Winter Scene, c.1890, 5 In. 984
Group, Men & Women, Dancing, Flowers, Instruments, c.1875, 9 x 7 ½ In. 1200
Group, Musicians, Woman, Mandolin, Cherub, Goat, Pyramid Shape, c.1930, 15 In. 1476
Group, Mythological, Woman, Hand On Globe, Telescope, Cherub, 1800s, 7 In. 1845
Group, Nymph, Seated On Bull, Garland, 2 Attendants, Flowers, c.1890, 9 In. 1250
Group, Porcelain, Apollo & Daphne, c.1900, 14 In. 1476
Group, Revelers, Dancing, Playing Music, Around Tree, Dog, c.1900, 19 In. 1500
Group, Silenus, On Donkey, Bacchantes, Oval Base, c.1875, 8 ½ x 8 In. 600
Group, Woman Musician, Man, Dog, 9 In. 1434
Plate, Birds, Pale Yellow Border, Gilt Rims, 8 ¾ In., 4 Piece.... 122
Plate, Relief Maple Leaf, Gilt & Green Enamel, c.1900, 8 ½ In. 95
Plate, Soup, Blue Flowers & Border, Crossed Swords Mark, 9 ¾ In., 6 Piece 92
Salt, Double, Girl, Sitting, Basket Cellars, 5 ¾ In. 299
Tea Set, Malerel Pattern, Teapot, Sugar & Creamer, Tray, 4 Piece.... 246
Teapot, Flowers, Multicolor, 9 ½ In. 549
Tray, Cobalt Blue, Flowers, 5 Shaped Medallions, Butterflies, 7 ½ x 11 In. 181
Tray, Dance Party, Landscape, c.1870, 17 ½ x 13 In. 800
Tray, Rococo Style, Flowers, Serpentine Rim, Scalloped Corners, Handles, 16 x 16 In. 127
Tray, White Ground, Multicolor Flowers, Gilded Rocaille Shells, 15 x 15 In. 738
Tureen, Lid, Oblong, Leaf Shape Handles, Flowers, Leaves, Marked, 10 x 15 In. 242
Tureen, Underplate, Cabbage Shape, Bouquets, Marked, c.1800, 7 ½ In. & 10 In. ....*illus* 738
Urn, Cobalt Blue, Parcel Gilt, Leaf Handles, Baluster, Saucer Foot, c.1890, 27 In., Pair 1187
Urn, White, Gilt Trim, Flared Rim, Scroll Handles, 12 In., Pair.... 177
Vase, Cornucopia, Fluted, Gilt, Putti, Standing On Rocky Base, c.1910, 11 In., Pair.... 554
Vase, Flared Rim, Entwined Snake Handles, Putto, c.1900, 11 In., Pair 1125

MERCURY GLASS, or silvered glass, was first made in the 1850s. It lost favor for a while but became popular again about 1910. It looks like a piece of silver.

Bowl, 5 x 12 ½ In. 172
Candleholder, Etched, Scrolling Leaves, Striping, 1880, 10 ½ x 5 In. 195
Dish, Leaf Shape, 10 x 8 In. 156
Orb, Engraved Design, 10 ½ In., Pair 61
Perfume Bottle, Dabber, Silver & Blue Spiral, Lay Down, 3 x 2 In. .... *illus* 50
Urn, Lid, 24 In., Pair 184
Urn, White, Enamel Leaves, Grapes, Lid, 1880, 12 x 4 ¾ In. 250
Vase, Bud, Flowers, Bird, Frosted, Painted, 1880, 8 ½ x 4 In. 250
Vase, Flowers, Bird, Frosted, Painted, 10 ½ x 4 In. 275
Vase, Flowers, Cylindrical, 20 ½ In. 78
Vase, Footed, 1880, 9 ½ x 3 ¼ In. 125
Vase, Leaves, Flared, Footed, France, c.1850, 13 ½ x 5 ½ In. .... *illus* 550
Vase, Trumpet Shape, Ball Support, Round Foot, 8 ¾ In., Pair 70

MERRIMAC POTTERY Company was founded by Thomas Nickerson in Newburyport, Massachusetts, in 1902. The company made art pottery, garden pottery, and reproductions of Roman pottery. The pottery burned to the ground in 1908.

Vase, Bronze, Green Glaze, Dripped, Cylindrical Neck, Rolled Rim, c.1905, 5 In. 492
Vase, Frothy Green, 11 ½ x 6 In. 625
Vase, Luster Crackle Glaze, Paper Label, c.1905, 2 ½ x 5 In. 375
Vase, Ribbed, Gunmetal Over Green Glaze, Swollen, Footed, c.1905, 15 x 12 In. .... *illus* 2250

METLOX POTTERIES was founded in 1927 in Manhattan Beach, California. Dinnerware was made beginning in 1931. Evan K. Shaw purchased the company in 1946 and expanded the number of patterns. Poppytrail (1946–89) and Vernonware (1958–80) were divisions of Metlox under E.K. Shaw's direction. The factory closed in 1989.

Antique Grape, Bowl, Cereal, 7 In. 21
California Contempora, Gravy Boat, Poppy Trail, 1950s 75
California Ivy, Bowl, Vegetable, Divided, 11 x 7 In. 35
California Ivy, Plate, Dinner, 10 In. 38
Cape Cod, Cup & Saucer 13
Homespun, Bowl, Pt. 42
Homespun, Chop Plate, 12 In. 29
Poppytrail, Dish, Relish, Ivy Decoration, Divided, Twig Handle, c.1950, 9 ¼ In. .... *illus* 20
Poppytrail, Platter, 13 x 10 In. 30
Red Rooster, Plate, Dinner, 10 In. 29
Salt & Pepper, Strawberry Shape, Red, 2 ½ In. 35
Tropicana, Cup & Saucer 14
Woodland Gold, Chop Plate, 13 In. 43
Woodland Gold, Teapot, Lid, 5 Cup, 5 In. 58

METTLACH, Germany, is a city where the Villeroy and Boch factories worked. Steins from the firm are marked with the word *Mettlach* or the castle mark. They date from about 1842. *PUG* means painted under glaze. The steins can be dated from the marks on the bottom, which include a date-number code. Other pieces may be listed in the Villeroy & Boch category.

Beaker, No. 2327-1141, Girl, Cavalier, Schlitt, ¼ Liter 74
Beer Tap, No. 2671, 3 Spigots, Ball Finial, 19 In. 420
Charger, Man Playing Flute, Flowers, Heinrich Schlitt, 17 In. .... *illus* 625
Charger, No. 2518, Town Of Meissen, Scenic, Etched, Gold Trim, 1911, 17 ½ In. .... *illus* 595
Charger, Stoneware, Greek Sailing Ship, Johannes Stahl, c.1899, 18 In. 270
Dispenser, Water, Mosaic, Lid, Curved Handles, Flowers, Leaves, Spout, 16 ½ In. .... *illus* 276
Ewer, Portrait, Cavalier, Lady On Reverse, Etched, Incised, C. Warth, 1897, 16 In. .... *illus* 499
Jardiniere, Art Nouveau, Flowers, Etched, Shaped Rim, Footed, No. 2415, 17 In. 240
Jardiniere, Squat, Footed, Wavy Rim, Tree, Flower Heads, 6 ½ In. 810
Pitcher, No. 2486, Otto Echmann, Art Nouveau, 5 Swans, 1897, 8 In. 360
Pitcher, Pouring, 2 Colors, Relief, 2-Piece Lid, Heraldic Vignettes, 13 ½ x 8 In. 238
Plaque, Cavalier, Standing Among Flowering Tree, Round, 17 In. 122
Plaque, No. 130/1044, Heidelberg Schloss, Castle Turret, Landscape, 12 In. 60
Plaque, No. 292/1044, Motivaus Basel, Architecture, Landscape, 12 ¼ In. Diam. 78
Plaque, No. 1044/1327, Paint Under Glass, Dwarf, Hands Nut To Squirrel, 8 In. 540
Plaque, No. 1044/5159, Harbor, Blue & White, Shore, Boats, Figures, 17 In. Diam. 144

Meissen, Group, Allegory Of Visual Arts, Cherubs At Easel, Busts, 6 In.
$246

Cowan Auctions

Meissen, Tureen, Underplate, Cabbage Shape, Bouquets, Marked, c.1800, 7 ½ In. & 10 In.
$738

New Orleans (Cakebread)

M

Mercury Glass, Perfume Bottle, Dabber, Silver & Blue Spiral, Lay Down, 3 x 2 In.
$50

Ruby Lane

Mercury Glass, Vase, Leaves, Flared, Footed, France, c.1850, 13 ½ x 5 ½ In.
$550

Ruby Lane

Merrimac, Vase, Ribbed, Gunmetal Over Green Glaze, Swollen, Footed, c.1905, 15 x 12 In.
$2,250

Rago Arts and Auction Center

Metlox, Poppytrail, Dish, Relish, Ivy Decoration, Divided, Twig Handle, c.1950, 9 ¼ In.
$20

Ruby Lane

Plaque, No. 2563, Bicycle Riders At Night, Etched, Round, 17 In. 1920
Plaque, No. 3166, Lohengrin's Departure With Swan Boat, Etched, Round, 17 In. 660
Plaque, No. 3225, Shield, Paint Under Glass, Austria, 13 x 11 In. 1440
Plaque, No. 6019, Cherub, Flowers, Leaves, 11 In. 25
Plaque, No. 7043, Cameo, Nudes Riding Dolphin, Blue & White, 21 In. Diam. 480
Punch Bowl, No. 2088, Etched, Drinking Scenes, Schlitt, Gnome On Underplate 570
Stein, Cameo Relief, Man With Harp, Grapevines, Inlaid Lid, 19th Century, 12 In. *illus* 995
Stein, First American Football Game, c.1905, 9 In. 240
Stein, Hops, Wheat, Flowers, Villeroy & Boch, 1909, ½ Liter, 8 ½ In. 338
Stein, No. 78, Ear Of Corn, 1 Liter 2873
Stein, No. 1526, Paint Over Glass, Bavaria Monument, Pewter Lid, 1 Liter 360
Stein, No. 1645, Tapestry, Etched, Pewter Lid, ½ Liter 84
Stein, No. 1675, Heidelberg Scene, Pewter Thumblift, Villeroy & Boch, c.1888, 8 In. 210
Stein, No. 1909/1176, Paint Under Glass, Man Shoots Dice With Devil, ½ Liter 192
Stein, No. 1915, Etched, Paint Under Glass, Cologne Cathedral, Inlaid Lid, ½ Liter 720
Stein, No. 2001C, Scholar Book, Relief, Inlaid Lid, ½ Liter 510
Stein, No. 2009, Etched, Embracing Couple, Inlaid Lid, ½ Liter 480
Stein, No. 2028, Pewter, Tavern Scene, Lid, 6 ¾ x 5 ¾ In. 215
Stein, No. 2052, Munich Child, Inlaid Lid, Cherub, Finial, 1895, ¼ Liter, 4 x 3 In. *illus* 325
Stein, No. 2074, Bird In Cage, Inlaid Lid, ½ Liter 1140
Stein, No. 2126, Occupational, Composers, Etched, 5 Liter 3840
Stein, No. 2183, Gnomes Drinking, PUG, Gnome Thumblift, 3 ¼ Liter, 14 ½ In. *illus* 445
Stein, No. 2277, Heidelberg, Etched, Inlaid Lid, ½ Liter 192
Stein, No. 2430, Cavalier, Drinking, Etched, Inlaid Lid, 3 Liter *illus* 570
Stein, No. 2685/179, Paint Under Glass, Radish Design, Art Nouveau, ½ Liter 720
Stein, No. 2715, Cameo, Zither Player, Couples Dancing, Inlaid Lid, ½ Liter 348
Stein, No. 2719, Occupational, Baker, Etched, Inlaid Lid, ½ Liter 1200
Stein, No. 2725, Occupational, Artist, Inlaid Lid, ½ Liter 3600
Stein, No. 2730, Occupational, Butcher, Etched, Inlaid Lid, ½ Liter 9000
Stein, No. 2887, Etched, Knights Drinking, Inlaid Lid, ½ Liter 300
Stein, No. 2934, Art Nouveau, Inlaid Lid, ½ Liter 456
Stein, No. 3170, People, Walking At Night, Holwein, Etched, Inlaid Lid, ½ Liter 420
Stein, No. 3202, Etched, Early Automobile, Inlaid Lid, ½ Liter 960
Stein, No. 3245, Art Nouveau Design, Etched, Inlaid Lid, ½ Liter 960
Stein, No. 3343, Skiers, 6-Sided, Pewter Mount, Square Handle, c.1905, 6 x 3 In. *illus* 1150
Tureen, Lid, Coral, Cameo Figures, Incised Mark, Ges Gesch, 1800s, 15 x 12 In. *illus* 595
Vase, No. 1870, Blue, Elephant Handles, 14 In., Pair 188
Vase, No. 2506, Mosaic, Flowers, Yellow, 16 In. 110
Vase, No. 2915, Etched, Art Nouveau, 13 ½ In. *illus* 395

MILK GLASS was named for its milky white color. It was first made in England during the 1700s. The height of its popularity in the United States was from 1870 to 1880. It is now correct to refer to some colored glass as blue milk glass, black milk glass, etc. Reproductions of milk glass are being made and sold in many stores. Related pieces may be listed in the Cosmos, Vallerysthal, and Westmoreland categories.

Ashtray, Openwork Rim, Ribbed Interior, 7 x 7 In. 13
Bowl, 4-Toed, Flowers, Scrolls, Jeannette Glass, 6 ¾ In. 15
Candy Dish, 3 Swan Handles & Finial, 5 ½ In. 45
Compote, Hobnail, Pie Crust Edge, Pedestal Base, 1900, 5 ½ x 8 In. *illus* 37
Compote, Openwork Rim, Anchor Hocking, 4 In. 13
Cookie Jar, Hobnail, Anchor Hocking, 6 In. 26
Dish, Hen On Nest Lid, Red Comb & Tail, 1930s, 4 ½ x 3 x 4 In. 30
Dish, Powder, Lid, Hobnail, White, 1950s, 4 ¾ In. *illus* 42
Lamp, White Leaves, Feather Shape, 16 In., Pair 50
Pitcher, Grapes, Leaves, Footed, Indiana Glass, 11 In. 28
Pitcher, Hobnail, Anchor Hocking, 7 ¼ In. 20
Planter, Rectangular, White, Scalloped Edge, Hazel Atlas, 8 x 4 ¼ x 2 ½ In. *illus* 10
Plate, Deviled Egg, 12 Wells, Gilt Edge, Shaped, 10 In. 30
Plate, Ruffled, 9 In., 6 Piece 6
Salt & Pepper, Ribbed, Hazel, 1930s, 4 ¾ In. 55
Slipper, Roses, 6 x 3 In. 40
Sugar, Octagonal, Angular Handles, Jeannette Glass, 4 ½ In. 11
Vase, Diamond Quilt Pattern, Bulbous, 6 In. 14
Vase, Embossed Grapes & Leaves, Scalloped Rim & Base, Footed, 6 In. 18
Vase, Flared, Footed, Scalloped Rim, Hobnail, Anchor Hocking, 9 ¾ In. 26

Mettlach, Charger, Man Playing Flute, Flowers, Heinrich Schlitt, 17 In.
$625

Ruby Lane

Mettlach, Charger, No. 2518, Town Of Meissen, Scenic, Etched, Gold Trim, 1911, 17 ½ In.
$595

Ruby Lane

Mettlach, Dispenser, Water, Mosaic, Lid, Curved Handles, Flowers, Leaves, Spout, 16 ½ In.
$276

The Stein Auction Company

Mettlach, Ewer, Portrait, Cavalier, Lady On Reverse, Etched, Incised, C. Warth, 1897, 16 In.
$499

Ruby Lane

Mettlach, Stein, Cameo Relief, Man With Harp, Grapevines, Inlaid Lid, 19th Century, 12 In.
$995

Ruby Lane

Mettlach, Stein, No. 2052, Munich Child, Inlaid Lid, Cherub, Finial, 1895, ¼ Liter, 4 x 3 In.
$325

Ruby Lane

Mettlach, Stein, No. 2183, Gnomes Drinking, PUG, Gnome Thumblift, 3 ¼ Liter, 14 ½ In.
$445

Ruby Lane

Mettlach, Stein, No. 2430, Cavalier, Drinking, Etched, Inlaid Lid, 3 Liter
$570

Fox Auctions

Mettlach, Stein, No. 3343, Skiers, 6-Sided, Pewter Mount, Square Handle, c.1905, 6 x 3 In.
$1,150

Ruby Lane

M

Mettlach, Tureen, Lid, Coral, Cameo Figures, Incised Mark, Ges Gesch, 1800s, 15 x 12 In.
$595

Ruby Lane

Mettlach, Vase, No. 2915, Etched, Art Nouveau, 13 ½ In.
$395

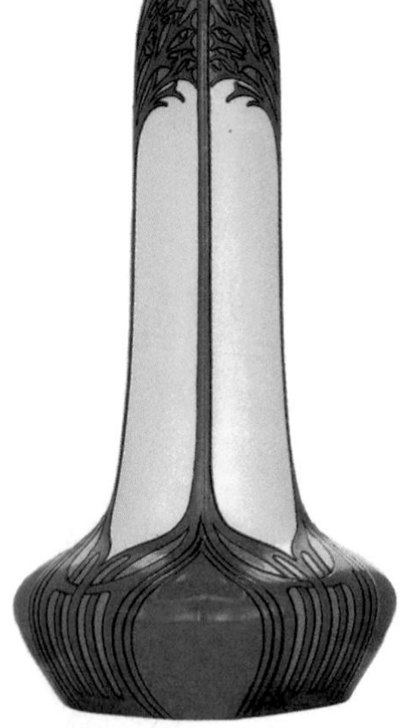

The Stein Auction Company

Milk Glass, Compote, Hobnail, Pie Crust Edge, Pedestal Base, 1900, 5 ½ x 8 In.
$37

Ruby Lane

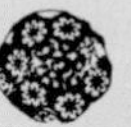

MILLEFIORI means, literally, a thousand flowers. Many small pieces of glass resembling flowers are grouped together to form a design. It is a type of glasswork popular in paperweights and some are listed in that category.

Beaker, Multicolor Flowers, Cylindrical, Blown Glass, 4 In. 96
Cruet, Murano, Twisted Clear Loop Handle, Pontil, 1960s, 5 ⅜ In. .... *illus* 65
Pitcher, Multicolor Flowers, Round Pedestal Foot, Loop Handle, 10 In. 144

MINTON china has been made in the Staffordshire region of England from 1793 to the present. The firm became part of the Royal Doulton Tableware Group in 1968, but the wares continued to be marked *Minton*. In 2009 the brand was bought by KPS Capital Partners of New York and became part of WWRD Holdings. The company no longer makes Minton china. Many marks have been used. The word *England* was added in 1891. Minton majolica is listed in this book in the Majolica category.

Charger, Children, Blowing A Feather, Kensington Gore, Signed I.I., c.1873, 20 In. .... *illus* 492
Cup & Saucer, Flower, Red, Gilt Leaves & Rim, Ring Handle, c.1810 64
Group, Ariadne & Panther, Parian, Marked, c.1850, 14 x 12 In. .... *illus* 1225
Oyster Server, 4 Tiers, Revolving, 1858, 12 In. 8125
Oyster Stand, Revolving, 4 Tiers, Earthenware, Enameled, Shells, Fish & Eel Handle, c.1863, 11 In. . *illus* 1599
Plate, Cup, Saucer, Soup, Salad, Bowl, Ardmore Pattern, c.1945, Service For 12 2900
Plate, Fish, Flags At Rim, Underwater Scenes, Albert H. Wright, 1900s, 8 ½ In. 123
Plate, Great Temple Near Zhehol Tartary, 9 ⅝ In. Diam. 554
Plate, Pate-Sur-Pate, Gilt Pattern No. 2575, 8 ⅞ In., 12 Piece 11250
Plate, Pate-Sur-Pate, Maiden, Draped Cloak, Crescent Moon, Dagger, c.1872, 9 In. 5855
Plate, Woman, Fuchsia Dress, Holding Tambourine, Gold Chain Link Border, 9 In. 125
Seafood Dish, Crab Shape, 12 Dark Blue Wells, Lid, 15 ¾ In. 5250
Tureen, Basket, Entwined Branches, Pigeons, Nesting Pigeon Finial, Lid, 11 ½ In. 1875
Urn, Serpents, Grotesques, Enamel, Christopher Dresser, Marked, 1874, 24 x 13 In. .... *illus* 8750
Vase, Gilt, Cherubs, Green Band, Swags, Handles, Pate-Sur-Pate, Lid, 13 In., Pair 10625
Vase, Gilt, White, Woman Picking Grapes, Stars, Pate-Sur-Pate, 19 In. 23750
Vase, Lily Of The Valley, Green, White, Leaves, Stems, Gilt, Round Foot, c.1850, 5 In. 179
Vase, Moon Flask, Orange-Red Ground, Cream Flowers, Leaves, 17 x 13 In. 330
Vase, Raised Flowers, Basket Weave, Attached Base, Blue, White, 6 ½ In. 156

MIRRORS *are listed in the Furniture category under Mirror.*

MOCHA pottery is an English-made product that was sold in America during the early 1800s. It is a heavy pottery with pale coffee-and-cream coloring. Designs of blue, brown, green, orange, black, or white were added to the pottery and given fanciful names, such as Tree, Snail Trail, or Moss. Mocha designs are sometimes found on pearlware. A few pieces of mocha ware were made in France, the United States, and other countries.

Bowl, Earthworm, Brown, Tan, Opaque White, Zigzag, Tan Band, 3 x 6 In. 106
Bowl, Earthworm, Rockingham Glaze, Yellowware, East Liverpool, Ohio, 5 x 11 In. 840
Bowl, Seaweed, Banding, Yellowware, c.1870, 7 x 14 ¾ In. 461
Bowl, Seaweed, Umber Band, Blue Band, 4 Black Bands, c.1850, 3 ½ x 5 In. 85
Bowl, Seaweed, White Band, Yellowware, 5 ⅜ x 11 ½ In. 95
Creamer, Earthworm, Looping, 5 In. 384
Creamer, Seaweed, Brown Plumes, Tan Band, Stripes, Loop Handle, 5 In. 531
Cup, Porridge, Seaweed Band, Loop Handle, Bulbous, Yellowware, 3 x 5 In. 189
Mug, Cat's-Eye, Reproduction, Don G. Carpentier, 6 ⅜ In. 443
Pepper Pot, Earthworm, Blue Band, Brown Stripes, Dome Lid, 4 ¼ In. .... *illus* 885
Pepper Pot, Geometric Designs, Diamonds & Bands, Dome Lid, Bulbous, 4 In. 354
Pitcher, Band, Bulbous, Ribbed Loop Handle, Yellowware, 7 ½ In. 1180
Pitcher, Bands, Blue Banded Lip, Brown Band, Trees, 7 ¾ In. 438
Pitcher, Bands, Twig, Brown Wavy Bands At Lip, Orange Band, c.1835, 7 In. 738
Pitcher, Cat's-Eye Decoration, 1800s, 4 ¾ In. .... *illus* 369
Pitcher, Cat's-Eye, Brown & White, Brown & Blue Bands, 6 In. .... *illus* 826
Pitcher, Cat's-Eye, Seaweed, Green Bands, 6 ¾ In. 2006
Pitcher, Earthworm, Blue, Brown, Gray, 1800s, 7 ½ In. 369
Salt, Bands, Sprig, Brown Band Border, Tan Ground, 1 ½ x 3 In. 148
Salt, Master, Cat's-Eye, Flared Pedestal Foot, 2 x 3 In. 189
Vase, Brown, Green Sponge Glaze, Yellow, Bands, Flared Neck, 1800s, 6 In. 270
Waste Bowl, Cat's-Eye, Green, Reticulated Star Border, 1800s, 7 In. Diam. 384

MONMOUTH POTTERY COMPANY started working in Monmouth, Illinois, in 1892. The pottery made a variety of utilitarian wares. It became part of Western Stoneware Company in 1906. The maple leaf mark was used until about 1930.

Bean Pot, Lid, Texas Longhorn, Brown, Tan, Loop Handles, Western Stoneware Mark .... *illus* 9
Carafe, Stoneware, Brown Sugar Glaze, Ribbed, Cylindrical Neck, Handle, c.1950, 10 ½ In. *illus* 24
Cookie Jar, Dark Brown Glaze, Impressed Lines, Marked, 11 x 7 In. 28
Crock, Salt Glaze, 6 x 6 In. 125
Mixing Bowl, Brown, Bands, ½ Gal., 8 ½ In. 40
Mug, Bill Of Fare, Gray, Blue, 4 ¾ x 2 ⅝ In. 10
Syrup, Lid, Salt Glaze, Ribbed, Bulbous, 11 In. 85
Vase, Blue, Leaf Design At Shoulder, 10 x 15 In. 120

MONT JOYE, *see Mt. Joye category.*

MOORCROFT pottery was first made in Burslem, England, in 1913. William Moorcroft had managed the art pottery department for James Macintyre & Company of England from 1898 to 1913. The Moorcroft pottery continues today, although William Moorcroft died in 1945. The earlier wares are similar to the modern ones, but color and marking will help indicate the age.

Bowl, Center, Pomegranate, Flat Rim, Red, Blue, Green, England, c.1920, 13 In. .... *illus* 1000
Bowl, Columbine, Dark Blue Ground, Footed, 1950s, 4 ½ In. 90
Bowl, Columbine, Dark Green Ground, Footed, 1950s, 4 ½ In. 100
Bowl, Coral Hibiscus, 1950, 10 In. 300
Bowl, Macintyre Florian, Freesia, Red Glaze, Cloud Patches, 3 ½ x 5 In. 708
Cup & Saucer, Pomegranate, Green Slip Mark, 2 x 5 ¼ In. 443
Ginger Jar, Lid, Hibiscus Flowers, 6 ½ In. 270
Lamp Base, Peacock, Round, Tapered, Green, Blue, c.1900, 11 x 10 In. 2000
Plaque, Impalas, Eight, On Savanna, Frame, 12 x 6 In. 354
Vase, Anemone, Blue, 1950s, 3 In. 125
Vase, Blue, Red, Yellow, Green, 4 ½ In. 175
Vase, Butterflies, Yellow Buttercups, Blue Ground, Leaves, CES Monogram, 10 In. 531
Vase, Cornflower Pattern, Beaker, Handles At Rim, Red, Yellow, c.1912, 12 In. 3107
Vase, Eventide, Tree, Hills, Green, Red, Orange, Blue, c.1960, 9 x 4 In. 4375
Vase, Eventide, Trees, Multicolor Gloss Glaze, Impressed Cobridge Mark, 8 In. 1652
Vase, Fish Design, Tapered Neck, c.1930, 8 In. 420
Vase, Flambe, Prunus Blossoms, Spider Web, JC Monogram, 9 ½ In. 192
Vase, Flowers, Blue, Bulbous, Trumpet Neck, Swirls, 5 ¼ In. 518
Vase, Hibiscus, 3 Blossoms, Incised Relief, Green Ground, 8 ½ In. 196
Vase, Hyacinth, Blue Ground, Cylindrical, 3 In. 125
Vase, Multicolor Leaves, Tapered, Flared Rim, Liberty & Co., 1900s, 15 In. 1888
Vase, Pansies, Pink & Purple, Blue Ground, Bulbous, Cylinder Neck, c.1950, 6 In. 185
Vase, Pansies, Violets, Yellow, Buds, Cream Ground, Genie Bottle, c.1916, 8 In. 1195
Vase, Pomegranate, Black Ground, Tapered, 7 ½ In., Pair 480
Vase, River Traffic, Squat, Ring Foot, Stick Neck, Flared Rim, Blue, Green, 12 In. 805

MORGANTOWN GLASS WORKS operated in Morgantown, West Virginia, from 1900 to 1974. Some of their wares are marked with an adhesive label that says *Old Morgantown Glass.*

Bell, American Beauty, Pink, 8 In. 53
Cocktail, Monroe Pattern, Ruby Color, Fluted, Knopped Stem, 6 x 4 In., 8 Piece 248
Tea, Monroe Pattern, Ruby Color, Flared Rim, Tapered, 7 x 4 In., 10 Piece 177
Vase, Snowball, c.1935, 7 In. 177
Wine, Cathay, 1920s, 6 In. 27

MORIAGE is a special type of raised decoration used on some Japanese pottery. Sometimes pieces of clay were shaped by hand and applied to the item; sometimes the clay was squeezed from a tube in the way we apply cake frosting. One type of moriage is called Dragonware by collectors.

Ewer, Irises, Leaf Designs, Green Ground, Black Handle, 10 In. 184
Ewer, Leaves, Stems, Scroll, Cylindrical, Bell Foot, Wavy Rim, Square Handle, 10 In. 183
Vase, Chrysanthemums, Daisies, Green Ground, Tapered, 8 ½ x 14 In. 615
Vase, Light Green, Birds, Red Faces, Handles, 11 In. 609
Vase, Lobed, High Square Handles, Roses, Gilt, Nippon Blue Mark, 12 x 6 In. .... *illus* 325
Vase, White Flowers, Green Ground, Nippon, 14 In. 123
Whiskey Jug, Elk, Forest, Wicker Basket Base, Stopper, 9 ¾ In. 406

Milk Glass, Dish, Powder, Lid, Hobnail, White, 1950s, 4 ¾ In.
$42

Ruby Lane

Milk Glass, Planter, Rectangular, White, Scalloped Edge, Hazel Atlas, 8 x 4 ¼ x 2 ½ In.
$10

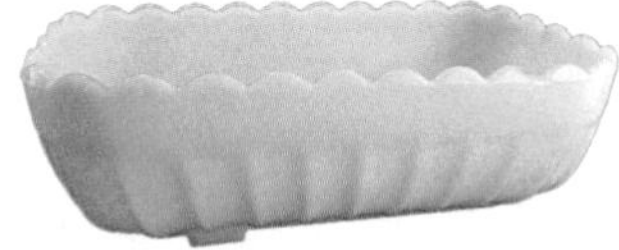

Ruby Lane

TIP
Milk glass will yellow with repeated washings in a dishwasher.

Millefiori, Cruet, Murano, Twisted Clear Loop Handle, Pontil, 1960s, 5 ⅜ In.
$65

Ruby Lane

Minton, Charger, Children, Blowing A Feather, Kensington Gore, Signed I.I., c.1873, 20 In.
$492

Cowan Auctions

Minton, Group, Ariadne & Panther, Parian, Marked, c.1850, 14 x 12 In.
$1,225

Neal Auctions

Minton, Oyster Stand, Revolving, 4 Tiers, Earthenware, Enameled, Shells, Fish & Eel Handle, c.1863, 11 In.
$1,599

Skinner, Inc.

Minton, Urn, Serpents, Grotesques, Enamel, Christopher Dresser, Marked, 1874, 24 x 13 In.
$8,750

Rago Arts and Auction Center

Mocha, Pepper Pot, Earthworm, Blue Band, Brown Stripes, Dome Lid, 4 ¼ In.
$885

Hess Auction Group

Mocha, Pitcher, Cat's-Eye Decoration, 1800s, 4 ¾ In.
$369

Cowan Auctions

Mocha, Pitcher, Cat's-Eye, Brown & White, Brown & Blue Bands, 6 In.
$826

Hess Auction Group

Monmouth, Bean Pot, Lid, Texas Longhorn, Brown, Tan, Loop Handles, Western Stoneware Mark
$9

Ruby Lane

Monmouth, Carafe, Stoneware, Brown Sugar Glaze, Ribbed, Cylindrical Neck, Handle, c.1950, 10 ½ In.
$24

Ruby Lane

MOSAIC TILE COMPANY of Zanesville, Ohio, was started by Karl Langerbeck and Herman Mueller in 1894. Many types of plain and ornamental tiles were made until 1959. The company closed in 1967. The company also made some ashtrays, bookends, and related giftwares. Most pieces are marked with the entwined MTC monogram.

Grizzly Bear, Blue Black Matt Glaze, Marked, 10 x 4 In. 169
Plaque, Lincoln, Hexagon, Blue, White, 2 ½ In. 36
Tile, The Lion In Love, 1900, 6 x 6 In. 150
Tray, Dog, Terrier, Black, White, 1935.......... 132

MOSER glass is made by a Bohemian (Czech) glasshouse founded by Ludwig Moser in 1857. Art Nouveau-type glassware and iridescent glassware were made. The most famous Moser glass is decorated with heavy enameling in gold and bright colors. The firm, Moser Glassworks, is still working in Karlovy Vary, Czech Republic. Few pieces of Moser glass are marked.

Bowl, Flowers, Enamel, Green To Yellow, 4 Blue Feet, 5 ½ x 12 In. 312
Bowl, Teal Blue Cut To Clear, Cased, Gilt Flowers, Scrolling Leaves, 6 x 9 In. 302
Box, Hinged Lid, Cranberry, Optic Ribbed, Translucent, Enamel, Fern Leaves, 3 x 4 In. 144
Box, Trinket, Oval, Gold Decoration, c.1875, 3 ¼ x 5 ½ In. ....*illus* 450
Casket, Cobalt Blue, Metal, Hinged, Beveled Dome Lid, Bail Handle, Ball Feet, 4 x 4 In. 351
Chalice, Emerald Glass, Crenulated Rim, Cartouches, Flowers, Woman, 14 x 7 In. 1815
Champagne Coupe, Cobalt Cut, Cartouches, Panels, Leaves, Turned Shaft, 5 In., 6 Piece.......... 544
Charger, Enameled, Karlsbad Landmarks, Shields, Hunters With Dogs, 12 ½ In. 2124
Chocolate Pot, Handled Cups, Enamel, Ruby Ovals, 8 ½ x 9 In., 5 Piece.......... 281
Compote, Enameled, Cranberry & Amber Glass, c.1890, 9 x 12 In. 420
Cruet, Cranberry, Peacock Eyes, Acanthus, 6 In. 412
Decanter Set, Clear Glass, Decanter, Glasses, Gilt, 10 ½ In., 7 Piece.......... 469
Decanter, Blue, Glowers, Gilt, Stopper, 12 ½ In. 156
Decanter, Cranberry Glass, Gilt, Tapered Octagonal Finial, Flowers, 13 ½ In. 242
Decanter, Enamel, Flower Heads, Vines, Faceted Stopper, Bulbous, c.1900, 9 In. 575
Decanter, Green Glass, Enameled Flowers, Gilt, Purple Stopper, 11 ¼ In. 59
Decanter, Red Glass, Gilt, Dish, 11 In., 2 Piece 338
Decanter, Red To Green, Enamel, Flowers, Acorns, Stopper, 13 ½ In. 218
Ewer, Gilt, Enameled Optic, Flattened Baluster, Applied Band, Spout, 9 In. 177
Goblet, Crystal, Spanish Royal Coat Of Arms, 6 In. ....*illus* 465
Goblet, Gilded Oak Leaves, Acorns, Shaped Stem, Green, 8 In. 192
Goblet, Rainbow Glass, Grape Bunches, Vines, Leaves, 7 In., Pair 2125
Goblet, Red Glass, Gilt, Bejeweled, Enameled, Footed, 4 x 2 ½ In., 9 Piece.......... 161
Goblet, Ruby, Cabochon, c.1885, 6 ¾ In. ....*illus* 145
Perfume Bottle, Amber, Red, Mottled, Enamel, Leaves, Gilt, Stopper, 12 In. 218
Pin Dish, Cased, Stippled Grapes & Leaves, Amber Handle, 2 x 6 In. 500
Pitcher, Amberina, Enamel, Grapevines, Bird, Insects, Amber Handle, 8 In. 1659
Pitcher, Cranberry, Vaseline, Bees, 10 ½ In. 363
Plate, Salad, Critallo, Enamel, Leaves, Deer, Yellow, Blue, Pink, Salviati, 8 In., 9 Piece.......... 295
Ruby Glass, Luster, Cut To Clear, Oval Medallions, 10 Cartouches, 12 ¾ x 6 In. 605
Sauce Bowl, Underplate, Gilt Rim, Roses, Optic Cut, Footed, 1900s, 6 ½ x 8 In. 183
Urn, Lid, Cranberry, Applied Medallion, Portrait, Brunette Woman, 15 x 6 In. 847
Vase, Amber, Blue, Applied Lizard, Round Foot, 8 ¼ x 3 ½ In. 242
Vase, Art Deco Style, Blue, Clear, Fluted, Petal Shape Rim, Faceted, Footed, 11 In., Pair.......... 154
Vase, Blue Cut To Clear, Gilt, Flowers, Footed, 12 x 6 ½ In., Pair.......... 605
Vase, Blue, Yellow Roses, Round Foot, 14 In. 60
Vase, Cobalt Blue, Faceted, 12-Sided Polygon, Flower Medallions, 4 ⅝ In. 242
Vase, Cranberry, Multicolor Oak Leaves, Insects, Applied Acorns, Gilt, 7 x 6 In. 2057
Vase, Dancing Nudes, Green Malachite, 1930s, 5 In. 289
Vase, Elephant Jungle Scene, Amethyst Glass, 1920s, 5 x 5 ½ In. 500
Vase, Enameled Cattails & Fish, Snake At Shoulder, Amber Glass Ground, 3 ¼ In. 533
Vase, Enameled, Ruby Glass, Cylindrical, Dragon & Flowers, Footed, c.1900, 13 In. 854
Vase, Faceted Sides, Clear To Amethyst, 2 High Relief Tigers, Parrot, 11 In. 4148
Vase, Gold Frieze Band, Faceted, 6 ¾ In. 238
Vase, Iris, Enamel, Green, White, Gold, Cylindrical, 11 In. 1107
Vase, Lavender Glass, Female Warrior, Gilt Ground, 8 x 5 ½ In. 124
Vase, Pansy, Enameled Glass, Shaded Clear To Violet, c.1900, 11 ¾ In. 270
Vase, Pillow, Clear, Oak Leaves, Acorns, Raised Parrot, Gold Scrolls, 4-Footed, 8 In. 1150
Vase, Pillow, Cranberry, Jeweled, Gilt, 4-Footed, 4 ¾ x 2 ¾ In. 726
Vase, Pillow, Parcel Gilt, Green, 2 Parrots, 4-Footed, Scroll, 4 ¾ x 4 ½ In. 605
Vase, Purple Cameo Grapevines, Grapes Cluster, Swirling White & Yellow Ground, 10 In. 356
Vase, Rococo Revival, Crystal, Gilt, Enamel, Faceted, Arched Top, Hexagonal, 11 In. 177

Moorcroft, Bowl, Center, Pomegranate, Flat Rim, Red, Blue, Green, England, c.1920, 13 In.
$1,000

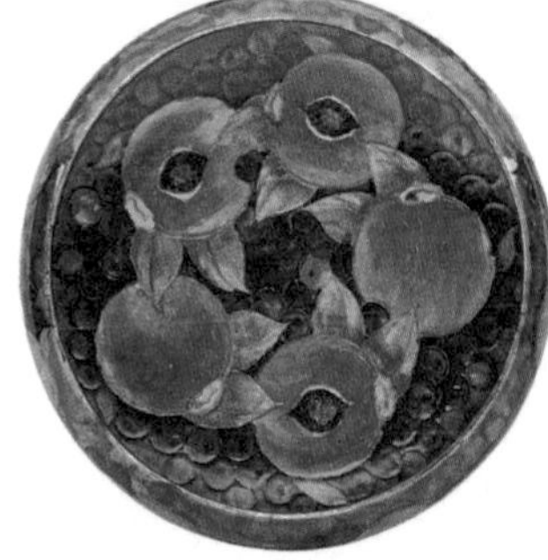

Rago Arts and Auction Center

Moriage, Vase, Lobed, High Square Handles, Roses, Gilt, Nippon Blue Mark, 12 x 6 In.
$325

Ruby Lane

Moser, Box, Trinket, Oval, Gold Decoration, c.1875, 3 ¼ x 5 ½ In.
$450

Ruby Lane

M

Moser, Goblet, Crystal, Spanish Royal Coat Of Arms, 6 In.
$465

Ruby Lane

Moser, Goblet, Ruby, Cabochon, c.1885, 6 ¾ In.
$145

Ruby Lane

Moser, Vase, Stag, Cranberry, Cut To Clear, c.1800, 9 ¾ x 4 In.
$140

Ruby Lane

Vase, Seahorses, Fish, Lavender, 7 ½ x 3 In. 1089
Vase, Stag, Cranberry, Cut To Clear, c.1800, 9 ¾ x 4 In. .... *illus* 140
Vase, Stick, Green, Gold & Silver Flowers, Scrollwork, Spread Foot, 16 In. 316
Vase, Tapered Square, Clear To Amethyst, Carved Blooming Tulips, c.1880, 16 In. 1016
Vase, Trumpet, Round Bottom, Fuchsia Blossoms, Ribbed, Purple To Clear, 6 In., Pair 259
Vase, Trumpet, Tapered, Lobed Stem, Footed, Flowers, 16 In. 432
Wine, Enameled Glass, Applied Flowers, 1800s, 6 In. 2040
Wine, Enameled Glass, Applied Petals, Footed, 6 ¾ In. 330

MOSS ROSE china was made by many firms from 1808 to 1900. It has a typical moss rose pictured as the design. The plant is not as popular now as it was in Victorian gardens, so the fuzz-covered bud is unfamiliar to most collectors. The dishes were usually decorated with pink and green flowers.

Ashtray, Square, Gilt, Homer Laughlin, 2 ¾ x 2 ¾ In., 4 Piece 12
Butter, Dome Lid, Pink, Green, White, Homer Laughlin, 4 x 7 ½ In. 20
Cup & Saucer, Gilt, Demitasse, Homer Laughlin, 2 Piece 24
Eggcup, Double, Pink, Homer Laughlin, 1940s, 3 ¾ In. 30
Sugar & Creamer, Homer Laughlin, 1949 34
Sugar, Lid, Homer Laughlin, 1949 24

MOTHER-OF-PEARL GLASS, or pearl satin glass, was first made in the 1850s in England and in Massachusetts. It was a special type of mold-blown satin glass with air bubbles in the glass, giving it a pearlized color. It has been reproduced. Mother-of-pearl shell objects are listed under Pearl.

Biscuit Jar, Lid, Diamond Quilted, Blue, 5 In. 259
Bottle, Satin, Pink Cased, Peacock-Eye, Engraved Silver Overlay, 5 In. 1534
Box, Basket Weave, Butterscotch Shaded To Yellow, Turret Top, 4 In. 288
Perfume Bottle, England, c.1890 .... *illus* 250

MOTORCYCLES and motorcycle accessories of all types are being collected today. Examples can be found that date back to the early twentieth century. Toy motorcycles are listed in the Toy category.

Carnival Ride, Indian, 2 Seater, Green, Wheels Roll, Belgium, 58 x 29 In. .... *illus* 915
Motorcycle, Harley-Davidson, Green, Red Stripes, Leather Seat, Patent 1916, 42 x 94 In. ....*illus* 22230
Sign, Harley-Davidson Oil, Is It Time For A Refill, Red, Black Border, 9 x 15 In. 600

MOUNT WASHINGTON, *see Mt. Washington category.*

MOVIE memorabilia of all types are collected. Animation Art, Games, Sheet Music, Toys, and some celebrity items are listed in their own section. A lobby card is usually 11 by 14 inches, but other sizes were also made. A set of lobby cards includes seven scene cards and one title card. An American one sheet, the standard movie poster, is 27 by 41 inches. A three sheet is 40 by 81 inches. A half sheet is 22 by 28 inches. A window card, made of cardboard, is 14 by 22 inches. An insert is 14 by 36 inches. A herald is a promotional item handed out to patrons. Press books, sent to exhibitors to promote a movie, contain ads and lists of what is available for advertising, i.e., posters, lobby cards. Press kits, sent to the media, contain photos and details about the movie, i.e., stars' biographies and interviews.

Art, Rebecca, A. Hitchcock, Oil On Canvas, L. Olivier & J. Fontaine, 1940, 20 x 18 In. 1064
Bust, Greta Garbo, White Plaster, Incised, Jane Jackson, 1930s, 6 ¼ In. 115
Button, Beat The Devil, Humphrey Bogart, Photo, Black & White, Glossy, 1953, 1 ½ In. 115
Herald, Memorium, Saratoga, Jean Harlow, 2-Sided, Photo, Last Movie, 1937, 5 x 7 In. 115
Lobby Card, No Census No Feeling, 3 Stooges, 1940, 14 x 11 In. 1080
Lobby Card, Phony Express, 3 Stooges, 1943, 14 x 11 In. 960
Membership Card, Button, Bela Lugosi Fan Club, Count Dracula, 1950s, 3 In. 1771
Photograph, Rain Man, Tom Cruise & Dustin Hoffman, Glossy, Signed, 1988, 8 x 10 In. 168
Photograph, Rocky III, Sylvester Stallone, Belt & Gloves, Signed, c.1982, 11 x 14 In. 144
Photograph, Still, Unforgiven, Clint Eastwood, Horseback, Signed, Glossy, 8 x 10 In. 173
Photograph, Still, West Side Story, Natalie Wood, Singing, Glossy, Signed, 1961, 8 x 10 In. 253
Poster, A Clockwork Orange, R-Rated, Science Fiction, 1971, 27 x 41 In. 131
Poster, Beat It, Harold Lloyd, 2 Cops, Man In Suit & Hat, Seated, Pathe, 30 x 44 In. 1100
Poster, Brides Of Dracula, Peter Cushing, Frida Jackson, Universal Int'l., 1960, 22 x 28 In. 100
Poster, Forbidden Planet, Robby Robot, Carrying Woman, Sci-Fi, 1958, 14 x 22 In. 316
Poster, Ghosts On The Loose, Bela Lugosi, East Side Kids, Ava Gardner, 1943, 22 x 28 In. 500
Poster, Goldfinger, James Bond 007, Sean Connery, 1964, 30 x 40 In. 10158
Poster, Hondo, John Wayne, Geraldine Page, Warner Bros., 1953, 14 x 36 In. 200

Poster, House Of Usher, Vincent Price, Mark Damon, 1960, 22 x 28 In. 100
Poster, I Was A Teenage Werewolf, Michael Landon, AIP, 1957, 11 x 14 In. 275
Poster, It's A Wonderful Life, James Stewart, Donna Reed, RKO, 1946, 11 x 14 In. 300
Poster, Jezebel, Bette Davis, Profile, Warner Brothers, 1938, 27 x 41 In. 7170
Poster, Lady For A Day, Warren William, Glenda Farrell, Columbia, 1933, 14 x 36 In. 325
Poster, Life Of Buffalo Bill, In 3 Reels, Vignettes, Imprinted, Frame, 49 x 25 In. .... *illus* 1185
Poster, Living On Velvet, K. Francis, W. William, G. Brent, First National, 1934, 14 x 3 In. 600
Poster, Moon Over Miami, Betty Grable, Swimsuit, Holding Ball, 1941, 27 x 41 In. 35850
Poster, Mrs. Doubtfire, Robin Williams & Sally Field, Signed, Frame, 42 x 24 In. 147
Poster, Ocean's 11, Frank Sinatra, Dean Martin, Warner Bros., 1960, 11 x 14 In. 300
Poster, One Flew Over The Cuckoo's Nest, Jack Nicholson, 1975, 27 x 41 In. 125
Poster, Press Sheet, Flying Ace, All Colored Cast, Silent, 1926, 44 x 28 In. 263
Poster, Revenge Of Frankenstein, Peter Cushing, Columbia, 1958, 22 x 28 In. 100
Poster, Song Of The Thin Man, William Powell, Myrna Loy, MGM, 1947, 22 x 28 In. 125
Poster, The Big Shot, Humphrey Bogart, I. Manning, Warner Bros., 1942, 14 x 36 In. 300
Poster, The Day The Earth Stood Still, Spaceman Carrying Woman, 1951, 27 x 41 In. 11353
Poster, The Fatal Warning, Helene Costello, Ralph Graves, Couple, Clock, 30 x 44 In. 225
Poster, The Littlest Rebel, Shirley Temple, Horses, Gold Frame, c.1935, 31 x 37 In. 732
Poster, The Lone Ranger, Clayton Moore, Warner Bros., Black, Red, White, 27 x 41 In. 176
Poster, The Maltese Falcon, Bogart, Lorre, Astor, Warner Bros., 1941, 45 x 61 In. 6700
Poster, The Monster Walks, Big Gorilla, Woman, Linen Mounted, 1938, 27 x 41 In. 419
Poster, The Plainsman, Gary Cooper, Jean Arthur, Paramount, 1936, 27 x 41 In. 1600
Poster, The Quick Gun, Audie Murphy, On Knees, Pistol, Columbia, 27 x 41 In. 120
Poster, The Secret Bride, Barbara Stanwyck, Warner Bros., 1934, 27 x 41 In. 3884
Poster, Wizard Of Oz, Yellow, 1955, 39 ½ x 29 ¾ In. 393
Prop, Gladiator Breast Plate, Stand, Steel, Leather, Articulate, 1920s, 58 x 24 In. 124
Theater Card, Frankenstein, Courage Club, RKO Orpheum, 1931, 2 x 3 ½ In. 310
Theater Seat, Folding Chair, Cast Iron, Paint, 2 Clown Men, Upholstery, 31 In. 671

MT. JOYE is an enameled cameo glass made in the late nineteenth and twentieth centuries by Saint-Hilaire Touvier de Varraux and Co. of Pantin, France. This same company made De Vez glass. Pieces were usually decorated with enameling. Most pieces are not marked.

Decanter, Bird & Poppy, Art Nouveau, Birds, Stopper, 10 ¾ In. 484
Vase, 2 Stylized Purple Flowers, Leaf, Textured Frosted Ground, Ruffled Rim, 3 In. 316
Vase, Art Nouveau, Mistletoe, Enamel, Gilt Relief, Opal Cabochon, Pyrite, 5 x 6 In. 483
Vase, Bulbous, Fan Shape Rim, Green Textured Ground, Gilt Flowers, c.1900, 9 In. 275
Vase, Cameo, Green Leaf Vines, Pea Pods, Ribbed, Textured, Gold Details, 6 ½ In. 325
Vase, Chipped Ice, Mint Green, Gilt Leaves, Cameo, 9 ¾ x 4 In. 484
Vase, Chipped Ice, Purple & Gold Flowers, Green Glass, 8 In. 156
Vase, Green Mottled Ground, Violets, Gold Textured Leaves, Bottle Shape, Stick Neck, 12 In. *illus* 805
Vase, Green, Enameled, Flowers, 12 In. 123
Vase, Green, Etched Purple Pansies, Enameled, Gilt, c.1910, 6 In. 388
Vase, Irises, Applied Handles, 8 x 5 In. 1089

MT. WASHINGTON Glass Works started in 1837 in South Boston, Massachusetts. In 1870 the company moved to New Bedford, Massachusetts. Many types of art glass were made there until 1894, when the company merged with Pairpoint Manufacturing Co. Amberina, Burmese, Crown Milano, Cut Glass, Peachblow, and Royal Flemish are each listed in their own category.

Biscuit Jar, Burmese Color, Silver Plate Lid, Yellow, Bamboo Stalks, 7 In. 302
Biscuit Jar, Glass, Painted, Pairpoint Fittings, c.1890, 5 x 6 ½ In. 150
Biscuit Jar, Pink & White Diagonal Stripe, Figural Lid, Turtle, 5 ½ In. 430
Bowl, Optic Rib, Fern Leaf, Applied Feet, Crimped Rim, 5 ½ x 10 ½ In. 4025
Bride's Basket, Griffin, Pink, Cameo, Square, Crimped, Pairpoint Stand, 10 In. 604
Bride's Basket, Griffin, Yellow, White, Cameo, Silver Plated Harp Stand, 12 In. 374
Candlestick, Blue Petal Socket, Clambroth Hexagonal Base, 8 In., Pair 185
Epergne, Central Trumpet, 3 Ruffled Horns, Pink, Clear, Yellow, 15 In. 2000
Pitcher, Clear, 3 Fish, Gold Enamel Seaweed, Gilt Fishnet Design, 8 In. .... *illus* 2075
Rose Bowl, Verona, Orange & Pink Wild Roses, Ribbed, Wavy Rim, 4 In. 173
Vase, Ball Shape, Footed, Loop Handles, Leaves, Applied Beads, 9 In. 2345
Vase, Bulbous, Ruffled Rim, Mythological Creature, Scroll, Rose, Gilt, 13 In. 4095
Vase, Chrysanthemums, Stylized Leaves, Yellow, Pink, Stick Neck, 11 In. 920
Vase, Colonial Ware, Camel, Gold Trim, Jar Shape, 3 Handles, 12 In. 13800
Vase, Cut Velvet, Pink, Diamond Design, Cane Sprigs, Gilded, 11 In. 1067
Vase, Enameled Panels, Geese, Gold Sun & Stars, Scrollwork, Tapered, 14 In. .... *illus* 8280
Vase, Jack-In-The-Pulpit, Blush Shaded To Green, Stippled Flowers, 10 In. 460

Mother-Of-Pearl, Perfume Bottle, England, c.1890, $250

Ruby Lane

Motorcycle, Carnival Ride, Indian, 2 Seater, Green, Wheels Roll, Belgium, 58 x 29 In. $915

Morphy Auctions

Motorcycle, Motorcycle, Harley-Davidson, Green, Red Stripes, Leather Seat, Patent 1916, 42 x 94 In. $22,230

James D. Julia Auctioneers

Movie, Poster, Life Of Buffalo Bill, In 3 Reels, Vignettes, Imprinted, Frame, 49 x 25 In.
$1,185

James D. Julia Auctioneers

Mt. Joye, Vase, Green Mottled Ground, Violets, Gold Textured Leaves, Bottle Shape, Stick Neck, 12 In.
$805

Early Auction Company

Mt. Washington, Pitcher, Clear, 3 Fish, Gold Enamel Seaweed, Gilt Fishnet Design, 8 In.
$2,075

James D. Julia Auctioneers

Vase, Lava Glass, Blue, Orange & Red Shards, Raspberry Ground, Gold Trim, 5 In. 1837
Vase, Lava Glass, Red, Purple, Blue & Green Shards, Inlay, Black Ground, 7 In. 2370

MULBERRY ware was made in the Staffordshire district of England from about 1850 to 1860. The dishes were decorated with a reddish brown transfer design, now called mulberry. Many of the patterns are similar to those used for flow blue and other Staffordshire transfer wares.

Urn, River, Mountains, Buildings, Paneled, Gothic Shape, c.1855, 7 ¾ In. 168

MULLER FRERES, French for Muller Brothers, made cameo and other glass from about 1895 to 1933. Their factory was first located in Luneville, then in nearby Croismare, France. Pieces were usually marked with the company name.

Ewer, Red Cameo Glass Owl, Tree, Yellow, Smokestack, Wavy Handle, 11 In. 14813
Lamp, 2-Light, Mushroom Shape, Signed Lorraine, Illuminates Base, Shade, 6 x 4 In. 334
Lamp, Luneville, Art Deco, Oscar Bach Style, Etched Shade, Orange Mottled, 13 x 7 In. 633
Vase, Art Deco, Geometric Shapes, Bulbous, 1920s, 10 In. 210
Vase, Bird, Prunus Branches, Green, Overlay, Cylindrical, Rolled Rim, c.1900, 4 In. 1434
Vase, Cameo Leaves, Stems, Berries, Brown, Orange, Mottled Blue, Bulbous, 5 In. 593
Vase, Cameo Roses, Pink, Yellow, Cream Ground, Bulbous, Flare Lip, 10 In. 2963
Vase, Cameo, Rhododendrons In Full Bloom, Red, Brown, Honey, Oval, 10 In. 863
Vase, Cameo, Scenic, Purple Trees, Pond, Frosted Ground, Pedestal Foot, 13 In. 356
Vase, Fish, Acid Etched, Cameo, Aquamarine, Signed, 1900s, 14 x 8 In. ....*illus* 12500
Vase, Flowers, Translucent Ground, 6 ¼ x 4 ½ In. 968
Vase, Luneville Cameo, Barren Trees, Lake, 12 In. 690
Vase, Luneville, Cameo Glass, Blue Flowers, Black Leaves, Mottled, c.1910, 12 x 7 In. 2337
Vase, Luneville, Cobalt Blue, Aqua Metallic, Bubble Design, Round, 12 In. 1380
Vase, Maroon, Red, Flowers, Clear Satin Ground, 8 ¼ x 5 In. 968
Vase, Orange Mottled, Burnt Umber, Black, Bulbous, Tapered, c.1930, 8 In. 154
Vase, Scenic, Lake, Trees, Shades Of Indigo, Tapered, Inverted Rim, 7 In. 230
Vase, Trumpet Flowers, Burgundy & Pink Over White, Cameo, 17 x 9 In. 2125

MUNCIE Clay Products Company was established by Charles Benham in Muncie, Indiana, in 1922. The company made pottery for the florist and giftshop trade. The company closed by 1939. Pieces are marked with the name *Muncie* or just with a system of numbers and letters, like *1A*.

Basket, Handle, Green Drip Over Rose Glaze, 11 ¾ x 7 ¾ In. 125
Candlestick, Glossy Brown Peachskin Glaze, Tapered, Base, 9 ½ In., Pair.......... 120
Lamp, Dancing Nudes, Paneled, Bronze Foot, c.1920, 28 In. 340
Pitcher, Green Over Mauve Matte Glaze, Triangle Spout, c.1920, 7 ½ In. 68
Pitcher, Ruba Rombic, Light Blue Gloss Glaze, Reuben Haley, 5 x 4 ½ In. 480
Vase, Black Glossy Glaze, Flared Rim, Footed, 1930s, 6 In. 50
Vase, Brown Peachskin Glaze, Handles, Shouldered, 6 x 7 ½ In. 100
Vase, Conical, Folded Design, Zigzag Rim, Spread Foot, Green, Orange Matte, 8 In. 575
Vase, Drip Over Purple Glaze, Pulled Ruffle Rim, 1930s, 6 In. ....*illus* 79
Vase, Eggshell Matte Glaze, Mauve To Moss, Stick Neck, 10 ½ In. 127
Vase, Fan Shape, Green, Pumpkin Glaze, Footed, Ruba Rombic, c.1928, 8 In. 995
Vase, Folded Design, Pointed Rim, Green Over Lavender, 4 In. 196
Vase, Green Glossy Glaze, Brown Speckles, Shouldered, 1930s, 6 In. 55
Vase, Green Matte Over Lilac Glaze, Oval, 3 ½ x 3 ¾ In. 60
Vase, Green Matte Over Lilac, Rolled Square Rim, 7 ¾ In. 120
Vase, Green Matte Over Rose, Squat, 3 ½ x 3 ¾ In. 65
Vase, Green, Orange Matte Glaze, Squat, High Handles, Tapered, Marked, c.1925, 6 x 8 In. .*illus* 149
Vase, Maroon, Handles, 1930s, 7 In. 90
Vase, Ruba Rombic, Lavender Matte Glaze, 4 x 5 In. 360
Vase, Ruba Rombic, Orange Matte Glaze, Green Drip, 6 x 4 In. 600
Vase, Ruba Rombic, Orange Peel Glaze, Reuben Haley, Muncie, c.1930, 4 x 4 In. 720
Vase, Ruba Rombic, Rose Glass Glaze, Reuben Haley, 4 x 4 ½ In. 600
Vase, Ruba Rombic, Rose Matte, Green Drip, 4 x 4 ¾ In. 204
Vase, White, Ribbed, Oval, 1930s, 7 ¼ x 3 ½ In. 55

MURANO, *see Glass-Venetian category.*

MUSIC boxes and musical instruments are listed here. Phonograph records, jukeboxes, phonographs, and sheet music are listed in other categories in this book.

Accordion, Plastic, Wood, Leather, Fabric, Silvio Sporani, Case, 1900s, 19 x 13 In. 172
Amplifier, Twin Reverb, Black, Fender, 1972, 26 x 23 In. 531

Banjo, 4-String, Tenor, Ludwig Kenmore, 1930s ... 287
Banjo, Kay, 5-String, 38 ½ In. ... 82
Box, 10 Tunes, Wood Case, Swiss, 5 ½ x 17 In. ... 369
Box, Boat On Calm Lake, 7-In. Metal Discs, Mira, 7 x 10 In. ... 371
Box, Carousel, 4 Horses, Dolls, Tent Top, Wood Base, Windup, 8 ½ In. ... 1896
Box, Cast Metal, Paint, Hinge Top, Seated Pirate, Faux Ivory Face, Swiss, 7 In. ... 93
Box, Comb, Inlay, Case, 6 x 22 ½ In. ... 330
Box, Cylinder, 1 Drum, 1 Comb, Hand Crank, 8 ¼ x 27 In. ... 1694
Box, Cylinder, 4 Tunes, Swiss, 11 ½ x 13 In. ... 168
Box, Cylinder, 6 Tunes, Inlay, Longue-Marche, J. Manger & Co., c.1870, 10 x 30 In. ... 6510
Box, Cylinder, 8 Tunes, Burled Walnut, Mother-Of-Pearl, Bells, Swiss, 15 ½ x 28 In. ... 2420
Box, Cylinder, 25 Discs, Stella By Mermod Freres, c.1900, 14 x 28 In. ... 2299
Box, Cylinder, Brass, 12 Tunes, Nicole Freres, 7 x 20 ¼ In. ... 800
Box, Cylinder, Inlay, Medallion, Flowers, 8 Tunes, 7 x 24 ½ In. ... 671
Box, Cylinder, Spring Motors, 6 Tunes, J. Manger & Co., c.1870, 10 x 30 x 15 In. ... 6510
Box, Cylinder, Swiss Chalet, Dancing Dolls, Mahogany, 37 x 37 In. ... 10540
Box, Cylinder, Walnut Inlaid Case, Lid, Brass Cartouche, Mother-Of-Pearl, 9 x 32 In. ... 1230
Box, Figural, Mother Playing Piano, 2 Dancing Children, Bisque, 9 In. ... 1200
Box, Inlay, Burl Veneer, Cowboy, Horse, Dog, Mariachi, 15 x 26 In. ... 180
Box, Interchangeable, Mahogany, Mermod Freres, Swiss, 26 ¼ x 13 In. ... 1500
Box, Jacot & Son, Sublime Harmonie, Cylinders, Mother-Of-Pearl Inlay, Lid, 33 x 17 In. ... 9300
Box, Mahogany, Carved, Regina, Disc, Baluster Gallery, Fluted Columns, c.1900, 86 In. ... 7500
Box, Mermod Freres, Stella Orchestral Grand, Mahogany, Carved, Disc, 27 x 44 In. ... 12520
Box, Oak Case, 9-In. Disc, Crank, Olympia, 33 Records, 9 x 12 In. ... 618
Box, Piccolo, Cylinder, Brass, Harpe Harmonique, 8 Tunes, Swiss, c.1900, 27 ½ In. ... 649
Box, Piccolo, Rosewood Inlay, Ebonized, Glass Top, Cylinder, 8 Tunes, 1800s, 26 x 12 In. ... 1062
Box, Polyphon, Walnut, 2 Sections, Glazed Door, Spandrels, 11 Discs, c.1890, 84 x 34 In. ... 5900
Box, Regina, Floor Model, Disc, Inlay, Painted, Hinged Top, c.1902, 40 x 23 In. ... 2040
Box, Regina, Mahogany Case, Table Top, Disc Player, Crank Handle, 13 x 29 In. ... 1770
Box, Regina, Table Top, Oak, Lid, Inside Artwork, Disc, c.1896, 21 x 19 In. ... 1952
Box, Reginaphone, Upright, Mahogany, Phonograph Attachments, 40 Discs, 40 x 22 In. ...*illus* 8680
Box, Reuge, Cigarette Holder, Gilt, Footed, Finial, 12 ¾ x 5 In. ... 120
Box, Reuge, Swill Cylinder, Musical Inlays Design, 3 Tunes, Key, 4 x 17 In. ... 988
Box, Rosewood, Cylinder, Stand, 25 x 10 In. ... 1195
Box, Rosewood, Inlay, Mahogany, Cast Bronze Handles, c.1890, 8 ⅝ x 25 ½ In. ... 1100
Box, Singing Bird, Cylinder, Chinese Folk Tunes, Mahogany, 17 x 25 x 34 In. ... 24800
Box, Singing Bird, Guilloche Enamel, Silver, Blue Enamel, Painted Courting Scene, 5 x 2 ½ In. 3540
Box, Singing Bird, In Cage, Tail Flap, Beaks Move, West Germany, 11 x 6 In. ... 602
Box, Singing Bird, Karl Griesbaum, Brown, Orange, Maroon, Bone Beak, Gilt Case, 4 x 2 ½ In. . 600
Box, Singing Bird, Karl Griesbaum, c.1880, 11 x 7 In. ... 302
Box, Singing Bird, Orchestral, 12 Chinese Tunes, Dolls, Bells, Drum, Mahogany, 17 x 25 In. ... 24800
Box, Singing Bird, Red, Blue, Windup, 11 x 6 In. ... 118
Box, Singing Bird, Wood, 2 ¼ x 4 ½ In. ... 531
Box, Stella Orchestral, Mahogany, Carved, Mermod Freres, 27 x 44 x 28 In. ... 12520
Box, Stella, Model 168, Mahogany, Table Top, Leaves, Drawer, c.1900, 22 x 29 In. ... 1952
Box, Sublime Harmonie, Cylinder, Mother-Of-Pearl, Jacot & Son, 33 x 14 x 10 In. ... 9300
Box, Swiss Chalet, Dancing Dolls, Automation, 37 x 37 ¼ x 20 In. ... 10540
Box, Symphonion Disc, Double Comb, Children, Instruments, Walnut, 9 x 18 x 14 In. ... 1240
Box, Symphonion Style, Rococo, Carved, Flowers, Cherubs, Dancers, Discs, 12 x 20 In. ... 3396
Box, Symphonion, Double Comb, Burl, Inlay, 12 Discs, Swiss, 19 ½ x 16 In. ... 1500
Box, Symphonion, Double Comb, Litho Under Glass, Children, Discs, 10 x 19 In. ... 1240
Bugle, Tin, Conical, Rectangular Handle, Bell Shape End, Mouth Piece, 27 In. ... 502
Chair, Black Forest, Inlay, Plays Music, Carved, Pierced, c.1910, 37 x 18 In. ...*illus* 1098
Drum Kit, White, Marine Pearl, George Way, Aristocrat, 1960, 5 Piece... 2185
Drum, Cow Hide, Round, Cone Shape, Tripod Legs, Africa, 19 ¾ x 28 In. ... 308
Dulcimer, Natural, Wood, Orb Shape, Stand, 1960s ... 53
Flute, Rosewood, Nickel Silver, Inscribed Case, Byron Holton, c.1850, 13 In. ... 1250
Flute, Silver, Gemeinhardt, Presentation Case, Carry-On Bag, Elkhart, 17 x 4 In. ... 702
Flute, Sterling Silver, Armstrong, Model 90, Case ... 153
Gong, Split, Silicon Bronze, Enameled Steel Base, Harry Bertoia, 1976, 60 In. ... 33750
Guitar, Acoustic, Fender, F-15, 6-String, 40 In... 71
Guitar, Angelica, D-412, Acoustic, Case, 40 In. ... 59
Guitar, Carlos, Model No. CN8, Acoustic, Case, 39 ½ In. ... 117
Guitar, Cromwell, Acoustic, Sunburst, Archtop, Mahogany V'd Neck, 1930s ... 359
Guitar, Electric, Fender, Mustang, Sonic Blue, Brazilian Rosewood Finger Board, 1965... 777
Guitar, Electric, Gibson, Red, Bass, U.S.A., 1960s ... 335

Mt. Washington, Vase, Enameled Panels, Geese, Gold Sun & Stars, Scrollwork, Tapered, 14 In.
$8,280

Early Auction Company

Muller Freres, Vase, Fish, Acid Etched, Cameo, Aquamarine, Signed, 1900s, 14 x 8 In.
$12,500

Rago Arts and Auction Center

Muncie, Vase, Drip Over Purple Glaze, Pulled Ruffle Rim, 1930s, 6 In.
$79

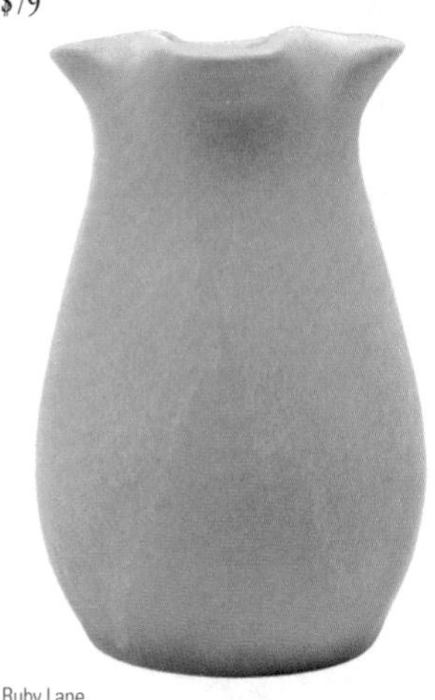

Ruby Lane

Muncie, Vase, Green, Orange Matte Glaze, Squat, High Handles, Tapered, Marked, c.1925, 6 x 8 In.
$149

Ruby Lane

Music, Box, Reginaphone, Upright, Mahogany, Phonograph Attachments, 40 Discs, 40 x 22 In.
$8,680

Forsythe's Auctions

Music, Chair, Black Forest, Inlay, Plays Music, Carved, Pierced, c.1910, 37 x 18 In.
$1,098

Morphy Auctions

Melodium, American Rosewood, c.1860, 32 x 51 In. 106
Organ, Jamboree, Electronic, Lowrey, c.1975, 37 x 46 In. 72
Piano, Grand, Wurlitzer, Model C153, Black Lacquered, Stool, 60 x 62 In. 6440
Pianoforte, Hepplewhite, Mahogany Inlay, Broderip & Wilkinson, London, 1807, 33 x 66 In. 590
Pianoforte, Inlay, Banding, Paneled Maple, Casters, John Geib & Son, 35 x 66 In. 2440
Snare Drum, Maple Shell, Loops, 15-In. Rosewood Sticks, 1860s, 11 x 14 In. 1125
Speaker, Cylinder, Pierced, 1800s, 11 x 8 In. 94
Stand, Ebonized, Mother-Of-Pearl, Urn Rest, Brass Standard, Scroll Feet, c.1850, 39 In. 1225
Synthesizer, Polymoog, Model 203A, Dampers, Case, Pedal, 31 x 49 In. 1660
Trumpet, Cornet, Brass King 602, Leather Carrying Case, 18 x 10 In. 60
Trumpet, Dragon Shape, Silver Plated Copper, Repousse Flowers, Tibet, 1900s, 20 In. 240
Trumpet, Indiana Brass, Silver Yamaha Mouthpiece, 1950s.......... 38
Viola, Lawrence Brown, Case, P.F. Reidl Bow, 16 In. 1298
Violin, G.A. Pfretzschner, Spruce Top, Curly Maple Back & Sides, Bow, 1920s.......... 287
Violin, John Carr Falkirk, Signed, 2 Bows, Wood Case, 1800s.......... 550
Violin, Josef Metzner, Sachsen, Tiger Maple, Spruce, Stradivarius Copy, Case, c.1900, 14 In. 556
Violin, Joseph Guamerius Cremonae Anno 1778 HIS, Copy, Germany, Case, Bow, 24 x 9 In. 265

MUSTACHE CUPS were popular from 1850 to 1900 when the large, flowing mustache was in style. A ledge of china or silver held the hair out of the liquid in the cup. This kept the mustache tidy and also kept the mustache wax from melting. Left-handed mustache cups are rare but are being reproduced.

Brown Flowers, Cream Ground, Raised Present, 3 ¼ In. 24
Flowers, 3 Loop Handle, Nippon 28
Flowers, Art Nouveau, Engraved, Attached Saucer, Barbour Bros., c.1890.......... 125
Grasses, Saucer, Belleek, 1st Black Mark, 2 Piece .... *illus* 454
Ivory Dots, Pink, Lusterware, 2 ¾ In. 48
Oriental Village Scene, Gilt Border, c.1891 325
Pastel Roses, Footed, Germany.......... 35
Peaches, Cherries, Walnut, Left Handed 510
Pink Rose Bouquet, 4 ½ In. 55
Purple Flowered Branch 20
Raised Flowers & Leaves, Pink, Blue, Gold Trim, Victorian, Germany, c.1900 45
Roses & Rope, Majolica, Saucer 485
Scuttle Style, Twig Handle, Flowers, Green Border, Germany.......... 52
Shells, Fishnet, Majolica, Turquoise, Red, Fielding Co., 2 ½ In. 175
Violets, Gold Trim, Saucer, Hammersley.......... 150

MZ AUSTRIA is the wording on a mark used by Moritz Zdekauer on porcelains made at his works in Altrolau, Austria, from 1884 to 1909. The mark was changed to MZ *Altrolau* in 1909, when the firm was purchased by C.M. Hutschenreuther. The firm operated under the name Altrolau Porcelain Factories from 1909 to 1945. It was nationalized after World War II. The pieces were decorated with lavish floral patterns and overglaze gold decoration. Full sets of dishes were made as well as vases, toilet sets, and other wares.

MZ Austria

Bonbon, Roses, Foldover Rim, Pearl Luster, 1900s, 2 x 7 ½ In. 60
Chocolate Pot, Roses, Gilt Bands, 9 ½ In. 17
Dish, Pink Roses, Gilt, Forget-Me-Nots, Daisies, White, c.1900, 7 x 5 ½ In. 19
Tray, Morning Glories, Signed A.E.U., 1914, 3¾ x 6½ In. .... *illus* 95

NAILSEA glass was made in the Bristol district in England from 1788 to 1873. The name also applies to glass made by many different factories, not just the Nailsea Glass House. Many pieces were made with loopings of either white or colored glass as decoration.

Bell, White Looping, Clear Handle, 9 In. 177
Bowl, White, Yellow, Ruffled Rim, 5 x 3 In. 198
Witch's Ball, 4-Color Glass, 4 In. .... *illus* 356

NAKARA is a trade name for a white glassware made about 1900 by the C. F. Monroe Company of Meriden, Connecticut. The glass was decorated in pastel colors. The glass was very similar to another glass, called Wave Crest, made by the company. The company closed in 1916. Boxes for use on a dressing table are the most commonly found Nakara pieces. The mark is not found on every piece.

NAKARA

Box, Collars & Cuffs, Flowers, Sage Green Ground, 8 x 6 In. 1200
Box, Hinged, Pink Flowers, White Slip Beading, 4-Footed, 4 x 3 In. 244
Dresser Box, Hinged, Mirror, Portrait, Woman, Rococo Scrolls, Round, 2 x 4 In. 425

Dresser Box, Woman's Portrait On Lid, Lavender, Pink, Enamel Beaded Garlands, 2 x 4 In. 201
Jewelry Box, Flowers, Green Ground, Reticulated, Hinged, 4-Footed, Round, 6 x 3 In. 725

NANKING is a type of blue-and-white porcelain made in China from the late 1700s to the early 1900s. It was shipped from the port of Nanking. It is similar to Canton wares listed in that category, but it is of better quality. The blue design was almost the same, a landscape, building, trees, and a bridge. But a person was sometimes on the bridge on a Nanking piece. The "spear and post" border was used, sometimes with gold added. Nanking sells for more than Canton.

Footbath, Blue & White, Figures, Mountains, Spearhead Border, Flat Rim, 1800s, 24 In. 1422
Milk Jug, Blue & White, Mountain Landscape, c.1750, 3 ¾ In. 418
Platter, Blue & White Border, Gold Rim, Floral Center, 12 ¼ In. 780
Tureen, Boar's Head Handles, Leaf Shape Finial, Landscapes, 1800s, 13 ½ x 9 ½ In. ....*illus* 593

NAPKIN RINGS were in fashion from 1869 to about 1900. They were made of silver, porcelain, wood, and other materials. They are still being made today. The most popular rings with collectors are the silver plated figural examples. Small, realistic figures were made to hold the ring. Good and poor reproductions of the more expensive rings are now being made and collectors must be very careful.

Bakelite, Bird, Butterscotch, 1940s ....*illus* 65
Brass, Trench Art, World War I, Gott Mit Uns Insignia, 1 ⅜ x 1 ⅞ In. 29
Clay, Blue Flowers, Brown Decoration, Cream Ground, Mexico, 3 ½ x 1 ½ In., 7 Piece........ 18
Cut Glass, Flat Star, Fan, 2 ¼ In. 118
Figural, Bakelite, Chicken, Yellow, Brown Beak, 2 ½ In. 35
Figural, Bakelite, Fish, 2 ¾ x 3 In. 20
Figural, Gold Plated, Enamel, Exotic Bird, 5 x 1 ½ In. 61
Figural, Silver Plate, 2 Cherubs, Forbes Silver Co., 3 ½ In. ....*illus* 395
Figural, Silver Plate, 2 Elves Holding Ring, Reed & Barton, c.1875, 4 In. ....*illus* 850
Figural, Silver Plate, 2 Rabbits, 3 ¼ In. 300
Figural, Silver Plate, Bird, Ring, Wheeled Cart, 3 ½ In. 610
Figural, Silver Plate, Buffalo, 2 ½ In. 360
Figural, Silver Plate, Child On Stomach, Ring On Back, 2 ¾ In. 450
Figural, Silver Plate, Child Playing, Holds Ring, Flared Rims, Meriden, 2 ½ In. 502
Figural, Silver Plate, Emu, Kangaroo, Map, Australia, Marked, EPNS, S&S, 1890-1910 ....*illus* 350
Figural, Silver Plate, Frog, Walking, Ring On Back, Reed & Barton 120
Figural, Silver Plate, Horse Pulling Cart, 2 ¾ x 3 ½ In., 4 Piece........ 1130
Figural, Silver Plate, Knight Standing Holding Torch, 4 In. 107
Figural, Silvertone, Reindeer, 3 ¼ x 3 In., 15 Piece 70
Figural, Sterling Silver, Reclining Child, Bird, Flowers, 3 In. 40
Metal, Hebrew Inscriptions, Bezalel, Jerusalem, 4 ½ In. 187
Silver Plate, Crossed Swords, Maple Leaf, Toronto Silver Plate Co., 1 ¾ In. ....*illus* 75
Silver Plate, Gold Washed, Applied Strapwork Medallion, Victorian, 12 Piece 1107
Silver, 3 Dancing Putti, Roses, Art Nouveau, Marked, 835, Germany, 1900s, 1 In. ....*illus* 135
Silver, Engraved, Roses & Swirls, Leaves, c.1900 98
Sterling, Geometric Designs, Flowers, Scalloped Rim, Russia, c.1908, 2 In. 180
Sterling Silver, Hexagonal, Engraved, England, 1944, 1 ⅜ x 1 ⅞ In. ....*illus* 110
Sterling, Leatherette Case, Walker & Hall, Sheffield, c.1915........ 59

NATZLER pottery was made by Gertrud Amon and Otto Natzler. They were born in Vienna, met in 1933, and established a studio in 1935. Gertrud threw thin-walled, simple, classical shapes on the wheel, while Otto developed glazes. A few months after Hitler's regime occupied Austria in 1938, they married and fled to the United States. The Natzlers set up a workshop in Los Angeles. After Gertrud's death in 1971, Otto continued creating pieces decorated with his distinctive glazes. Otto died in 2007.

Bowl, Brown & Caramel Mottled Glaze, Conical, Recessed Foot, c.1956, 4 x 6 ½ In. 1476
Bowl, Conical, Verdigris Crater Glaze, Wide Rim, Green, Silver, Purple, c.1974, 4 x 9 In. 4063
Bowl, Green, Brown, Crater Glaze, c.1955, 2 ¼ x 7 In. 4556
Bowl, Mystic Blue Glaze, Ring Foot, c.1955, 8 ½ In. 2309
Bowl, Porcelain, Blue, Dark Blue Rim, 3 ½ x 9 In. 1107
Bowl, Sloping Sides, Brown Matte, 6 ¾ In. 625
Bowl, Sloping Sides, Gray Matte, 8 ⅛ In. 813
Bowl, Sloping Sides, Yellow Matte, 13 In. 469
Bowl, Velvet Chartreuse Matte Glaze, Flared, Signed, 1940s, 4 x 6 In. ....*illus* 3125
Bowl, Wide Folded Rim, Tapered, Chartreuse Glaze, Signed, 4 x 7 x 5 In. 1500
Bowl, Yellow Interior, Black Mottled Exterior, 11 ¼ In. 2250

Mustache Cup, Grasses, Saucer, Belleek, 1st Black Mark, 2 Piece
$454

Jaremos Estate Liquidators

Mz Austria, Tray, Morning Glories, Signed A.E.U., 1914, 3 ¾ x 6 ½ In.
$95

Ruby Lane

Nailsea, Witch's Ball, 4-Color Glass, 4 In.
$356

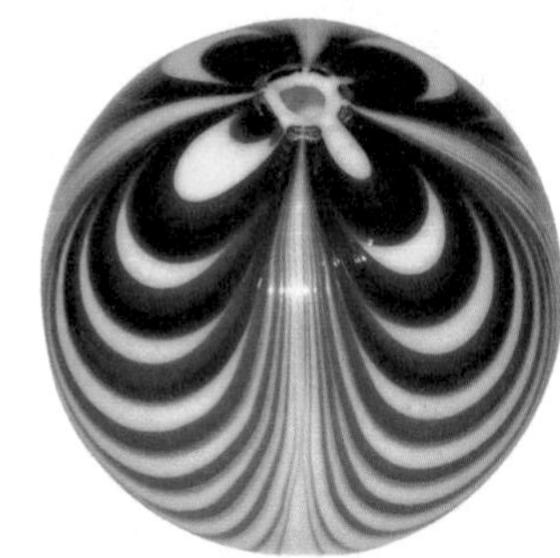

Ruby Lane

Collect by Color
An inexpensive and foolproof way to collect is by color. You can easily collect pottery that way. Buy light green, white, light blue, or any other color you like. Then display a large grouping on a table or shelf. Unmarked pieces are usually inexpensive. You can even use some large bowls and stands as bases for smaller pieces to build a jardiniere-like look.

Nanking, Tureen, Boar's Head Handles, Leaf Shape Finial, Landscapes, 1800s, 13 ½ x 9 ½ In.
$593

James D. Julia Auctioneers

Napkin Ring, Bakelite, Bird, Butterscotch, 1940s
$65

Ruby Lane

TIP
A household window cleaner with ammonia can be used to clean Bakelite.

N

Napkin Ring, Figural, Silver Plate, 2 Cherubs, Forbes Silver Co., 3 ½ In.
$395

Ruby Lane

TIP
To remove gum, put an ice cube in a zip-up plastic bag, then set it on the gum. When the gum hardens, hit it with a hammer and it will break off.

Vase, Blue, Tapered Neck, 15 ½ In. 2440
Vase, Yellow Glaze, Cylindrical, c.1960, 4 In. 547

NAUTICAL antiques are listed in this category. Any of the many objects that were made or used by the seafaring trade, including ship parts, models, and tools, are included. Other pieces may be found listed under Scrimshaw.

Anchor, H.B. Nevins, Brass, Marked, City Island, 32 In. 490
Anchor, Wrought Iron, Multiple Spikes, Loop Handle, 15 In. 270
Becket Handles, Ropework, Carved, Painted, Sawtooth Border, Swinging, 1800s, 12 x 6 In. 861
Bell Rope, Sailor's, Macrame, Painted, Iron & Brass Holder, c.1800, 10 x 2 In. 593
Binnacle, Compass, Constellation, Dome, Wilfred O. White & Sons ....*illus* 325
Binnacle, Compass, Ship's, Brass, Floating, 53 x 34 In. 1875
Binnacle, Compensating, Brass, Copper, US Navy, 1942, 53 x 28 In. 748
Binnacle, Whyte Thompson Co., Brass, Gimbal Compass, Domed Case, Glascow, 9 In. 240
Buoy, Spherical, Yellow, Cast Iron, Marked ORE, c.1900, 27 ½ In. 240
Canoe, Wood, Green Paint, Caned Seats, 4 Paddles, c.1930, 178 In. 1080
Chest, Painted, Dovetail, Signal Flags, Pennants, Harpoon, Hinged, c.1800, 11 x 28 x 13 In. 1722
Chronometer, Lange & Shone, Rosewood, Brass Cased, Steel Dial, Key, c.1900, 7 ¾ In. 1003
Chronometer, Marine, 8-Day, Brass Gimbals, Wood Case, c.1805, 8 x 8 In. 10000
Chronometer, Thomas Mercer Ltd., Mahogany, St. Albans, England, 6 ¾ x 7 In. 1046
Clock, Ship's, Chelsea, US Maritime Commission, Time Only, Key, Bronze Case, 7 x 2 ¾ In. 305
Clock, Ship's, Warren Eastbourne, Pewter Cased, 8 ½ x 7 In. 207
Compass, Gimbaled, Brass, Geo. B. Carpenter, Engraved D1207, Box, 7 ½ x 7 ½ In. ....*illus* 750
Compass, Pascali, Atkey & Sons, Gimbal, Brass, c.1800, 11 ¾ x 4 ½ In. 523
Compass, Ship's, Brass, Cylindrical Domed Case, Oil Compartment, 10 In. 424
Compass, Ship's, E.S. Ritchie & Sons, Boston, c.1929, 8 In. 120
Diorama, Yacht, Sachem II, Oil, Silk, Canvas, Frame, T. Willis, 1916, 13 x 17 In. ....*illus* 861
Figurehead, Chef De Marin, Tricorn Hat, Uniform, Holding Octant, c.1750, 52 In. 7110
Figurehead, Woman, Hand On Heart, Model, 48 x 13 In. 4680
Fishing Net Float, Glass, Blue Green, France, c.1915, 8 ½ x 9 ½ In. 210
Half-Model, Carved, Stained, Wood Backboard Mounted, 12 ½ x 46 In. 270
Lamp, Ship's, Dressel, 15 ½ In. 70
Lamp, Ship's, Mast Head, 17 ½ In. 81
Lantern, Lampads, 2-Light, Brass, Copper, Tag, R.C. Murrays, Glascow, 26 x 16 In. 391
Model, Battleship Missouri, Aircraft Carrier, Peace Table, Wood Crate, c.1945, 7 x 32 In. 671
Model, Boat, Sea Queen, Green & White Hull, Figural Sailor, Wood Stand, 20 x 65 In. 153
Model, Fishing Boat, Trawler, Wood & Glass Case, 44 x 28 In. 122
Model, Freighter, Great Lakes, Wood, Working, 2 Masts, 1923, 6 x 41 In. 720
Model, Freighter, Wood & Metal, Paint, Horace Boucher, c.1955, 51 In. 500
Model, Paddle Boat, Confederate, Stars & Bars, Flag, Glass Case, 43 x 19 In. 183
Model, Paddle Steamer, Mount Washington Boat, Side-Wheeler, Stand, 10 x 45 In. 244
Model, Pinewood, 2 Masts, 5 Sails, Corded Rope, Glass Case, Arnie Wegner, 24 x 31 In. 181
Model, River Barge, 2 Paddles, Cargo, White Hull, Red Deck, Pacific, c.1880, 16 x 33 In. 122
Model, River Boat, Wood & Paper, Sternwheeler, Bales Of Cotton, c.1900, 27 ½ In. 780
Model, Ship, Fran's Follies, Wood, Hand Crafted, 40 x 44 In. 300
Model, Ship, Queen Mary, Paper & Pasteboard, Green & Red Paint, c.1950, 72 In. 240
Model, Ship, USS Constellation, Carved, Sails, 33 x 42 In. 720
Model, Ship, Winatoo Hull, Black, Smokestack, 2 Mast, Sail, Case, 19 x 42 In. 915
Model, SS North Cornwall, Mirror Back, Mahogany Case, c.1924, 27 x 109 In. 1544
Model, Steam Tug, Pine, Alligatored Paint, Flag, Nameplate Scotten, 1930, 14 x 21 In. 875
Model, Steamboat, Stern Wheel, White, Red, Black, A.C. Payne, c.1890, 18 x 42 In. ....*illus* 3720
Model, Tall Ship, 2 Masts, 3 Sails, American Flag, Steven Lewis, 42 x 52 In. 153
Model, Tug Boat, Steam, Motorized, Glass Case, 45 x 25 In. 793
Model, Yankee Clipper Ship, 2 Masts, Wood, Stand, 25 In. 183
Motor, Outboard, Elgin, 7.5HP Model, West Bend, Wood Stand, 1957, 19 x 40 In. 671
Motor, Outboard, Mercury, 4 Cylinder, Open Fly Wheel, Tiller Handle, 1950s, 44 In. 2400
Octant, Elpalet Loring, Mahogany, Brass, Arched Crossbar, Inlaid, Numbers, c.1825, 17 In. 738
Propeller, Bronze, 1900s, 17 In. 145
Pulley Block, Marine, Wood, Metal, Cast Iron Hook, Tateno Seisakusho, Japan, 17 x 8 In. 71
Sea Chest Brackets, Rope, Braided, Blue Paint, c.1800, 7 ¾ In., Pair 330
Sea Chest Brackets, Rope, Braided, Leather Wrapped, Paint, 10 ½ In., Pair 300
Sea Chest, Green Paint, Nailed Construction, Iron Hinges, Rope Handles, Tools, 14 x 37 In. 356
Sea Chest, Pine, Dovetailed, Lidded Ditty Box, Intersecting Beckets, Rope, 16 x 41 In. 237
Sextant, Brass, Brown Wood Box, Carl Bamberg, 5 x 11 ¾ In. 431
Sextant, Mahogany Box, Gerrard, Liverpool, England, 1890s, 10 x 9 x 5 In. ....*illus* 1365

Napkin Ring, Figural, Silver Plate, 2 Elves Holding Ring, Reed & Barton, c.1875, 4 In.
$850

Ruby Lane

Napkin Ring, Figural, Silver Plate, Emu, Kangaroo, Map, Australia, Marked, EPNS, S&S, 1890-1910
$350

Ruby Lane

Napkin Ring, Silver Plate, Crossed Swords, Maple Leaf, Toronto Silver Plate Co., 1 ¾ In.
$75

Ruby Lane

Napkin Ring, Silver, 3 Dancing Putti, Roses, Art Nouveau, Marked, 835, Germany, 1900s, 1 In.
$135

Ruby Lane

Napkin Ring, Sterling Silver, Hexagonal, Engraved, England, 1944, 1 ⅜ x 1 ⅞ In.
$110

Ruby Lane

Natzler, Bowl, Velvet Chartreuse Matte Glaze, Flared, Signed, 1940s, 4 x 6 In.
$3,125

Los Angeles Modern Auctions

Nautical, Binnacle, Compass, Constellation, Dome, Wilfred O. White & Sons
$325

Ruby Lane

Nautical, Compass, Gimbaled, Brass, Geo. B. Carpenter, Engraved D1207, Box, 7 ½ x 7 ½ In.
$750

Ruby Lane

Nautical, Diorama, Yacht, Sachem II, Oil, Silk, Canvas, Frame, T. Willis, 1916, 13 x 17 In.
$861

Skinner, Inc.

Nautical, Model, Steamboat, Stern Wheel, White, Red, Black, A.C. Payne, c.1890, 18 x 42 In.
$3,720

Selkirk Auctioneers & Appraisers

Nautical, Sextant, Mahogany Box, Gerrard, Liverpool, England, 1890s, 10 x 9 x 5 In.
$1,365

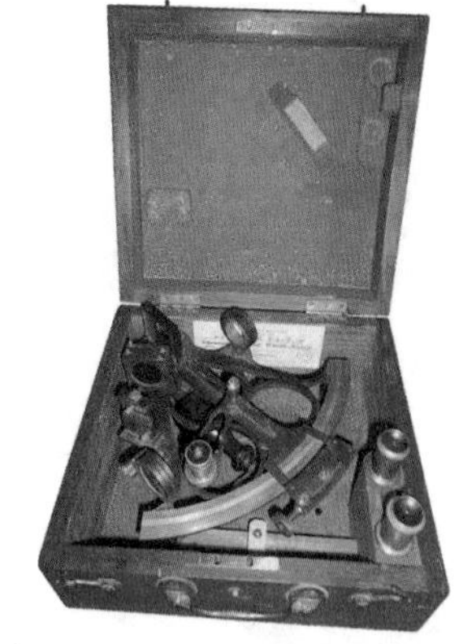

Ruby Lane

TIP

To remove a sticky price label from a piece of silver, heat it with a hair dryer to soften the adhesive. Then peel off the label. If there is sticky glue left, remove it with isopropyl alcohol.

Nautical, Ship's Wheel, Bronze, 6 Spokes, Teak Handles, 6 Lbs. 4 Oz., 18 In.
$400

Ruby Lane

Nautical, Stern Board, American Eagle, Carved, Painted, c.1925, 23 x 46 ½ In.
$3,555

James D. Julia Auctioneers

Nautical, Telegraph, Ship's, Brass, Pedestal, Wood, J.W. Ray & Co., Eng., c.1900, 47 In.
$840

Cowan Auctions

Sextant, Micrometer, Tamaya & Co., Japan, 11 x 11 In. 373
Sextant, Naval, Blackened Brass, Mahogany Case, c.1900, 10 x 10 In. 478
Ship Model, see Nautical, Model.
Ship's Wheel, Bronze, 6 Spokes, Teak Handles, 6 Lbs. 4 Oz., 18 In. .... *illus* 400
Ship's Wheel, Oak, 6 Turned Spindles, Iron Hub, Brass Trim Ring, Brass, 22 x 5 In. 138
Speaking Horn, Silver, Presentation, Engraved Steamship, Lighthouse, c.1855, 21 In. 18880
Stern Board, American Eagle, Carved, Painted, c.1925, 23 x 46 ½ In. .... *illus* 3555
Telegraph, Chas Cory & Son, Brass, Navigational Settings, 40 In. 550
Telegraph, J.W. Ray & Co., 2-Sided, Black Dial, Red, White, 52 x 19 In. 932
Telegraph, Ship's, Brass, Pedestal, Wood, J.W. Ray & Co., Eng., c.1900, 47 In. .... *illus* 840
Telescope, Single Draw, c.1870, 24 In. 208
Weather Station, Barometer, Hygrometer, Ship's Wheels, Airguide, 1950s, 9 x 5 In. .... *illus* 120

NETSUKES are small ivory, wood, metal, or porcelain pieces used as toggles on the end of the cord that held a Japanese money pouch or inro. The earliest date from the sixteenth century. Many are miniature carved works of art. This category also includes the ojime, the slide or string fastener that was used on the inro cord.

Bone, 3 Shells, Hermit Crab, Gilt Lacquered Case, Maple Leaves, 3 ¼ x 2 In. 732
Bone, Bean Pod, 3 In. 89
Bone, Figure In Low Relief, Applied Brown Pigment, 1 ½ x 1 ¾ In. 165
Boxwood, 3 Lions, Fighting, Intertwined In Circle, Signed Masamitsu, 1800, 1 ¼ x 1 ¼ In. 3198
Boxwood, Bean Pod Shape, 5 ¾ In. 242
Cherry, 2 Rodents, Amber, Marked, 1 ¾ In. 265
Chestnut, Wood, Carved, Small Insert Representing A Worm, 1 ½ x 2 In. 161
Ebony, Crying Boy, Seated, 1 ¼ In. 307
Ebony, Lion Seated On Right Hind Leg, Left Leg To Ear, 1800, 1 ¼ x 2 In. 800
Inro, Gold Lacquer, Interior Scene, Female Divinity, Clouds, Bow, Arrows, 3 ¾ x 2 ¼ In. 677
Inro, Gold, Black Lacquer, Bone Inlay, 2 Birds, Bonsai Tree, 3 ½ x 1 ¾ In. 861
Inro, Turtle Shell Shape, 3 Compartments, Wood Ojime, 3 Stacked Turtles, 3 x 4 ½ In. 817
Ivory, Basket With Vegetables, Gourds, Cucumbers, Woven, Corded Rim, 1 ½ x 1 In. 155
Karakuri, Dancing Performer, Coral Tongue, Mother-Of-Pearl, Fan, Bells, 1800s, 3 ¼ In. 738
Metal, Demon, Man On Reverse, 1 ¼ x 1 ½ In. 112
Porcelain, Emaciated Man, Carrying Sake Flask, 1800s, 3 In. 120
Porcelain, Monkey Head, Movable, Blue Robe, Carrying Fan, 3 ¾ In. .... *illus* 600
Wood, Bearded Sage, Staff, Double Gourd, Riding Fish, 3 ½ In. .... *illus* 350
Wood, Boy Resting On Buddha Hand, Holding Beads, Carved, 2 In. 207
Wood, Dragon, Manju, 2 In. 254
Wood, Ebonized, Skull & Snake, 1 ½ x 1 x 2 In. 183
Wood, Fungi, 2 Mushrooms, 2 x 1 ¾ In. 236
Wood, Lion, On Back, Peony, Branch, Leaves, Openwork Ball, Signed Minokoku, 1 x 2 In. 1968
Wood, Lion, Squatting, Open Mouth, Coiled Tail, 1800, 1 x 1 ⅜ In. 1169
Wood, Lychee, Carved Bone, Eagle Perching In Tree, Mount Fuji, Japan, 3 x 2 ½ In. 98
Wood, Rabbit, Seated, Carved, Lacquered, Signed, 1 ½ x 1 ¼ In. 124

NEW MARTINSVILLE Glass Manufacturing Company was established in 1901 in New Martinsville, West Virginia. It was bought and renamed the Viking Glass Company in 1944. In 1987 Kenneth Dalzell, former president of Fostoria Glass Company, purchased the factory and renamed it Dalzell-Viking. Production ceased in 1998.

Ancestral, Plate, Salad, 7 In. 8
Bookends, Horse, Rearing, 7 ½ In. 75
Bookends, Tiger, Seated, 8 In. 145
Canterbury, Bowl, Salad, Flared Rim, 3-Footed, 10 ½ In. 31
Canterbury, Candlestick, 5 In. 16
Canterbury, Plate, 7 ½ In. 15
Floral Oval, Bowl, Crimped, 8 ½ In. 20
Floral Oval, Compote, 8 In. 34
Floral Oval, Sherbet, 3 ½ In. 12
Floral Oval, Wine, 4 In. 11
Florentine, Sugar & Creamer, Tray 42
Florentine, Torte Plate, 13 ½ In. 24
Flower Basket, Bowl, Crimped, 12 In. 26
Flower Basket, Candlestick, 2-Light 20
Flower Basket, Compote, 4 In. 46
Flower Basket, Creamer, 3 ⅛ In. 16
Flower Basket, Relish, 3 Sections, Round, 7 ½ In. 32

Fortuna, Compote, 4 ¾ In. 17
Fortuna, Rose Bowl, 7 In. 16
Frontier, Cake Stand, Pedestal, 5 In. 35
Hostmaster, Cordial, 2 ⅞ In. 18
Hostmaster, Cup & Saucer, Amber 9
Hostmaster, Cup & Saucer, Ruby 26
Janice, Bonbon 30
Janice, Bowl, Footed, Blue, 12 In. 46
Janice, Cup & Saucer, Blue, Footed 21
Janice, Relish, 2 Sections, 8 In. 9
Janice, Sherbet, 2 ¼ In. 11
Janice, Sugar & Creamer 33
Moondrops, Ashtray, Round, Ruby, 4 In. 13
Moondrops, Butter, Round, Pink, ½ Lb. 46
Moondrops, Compote, 4 ⅛ In. 17
Moondrops, Cordial, Ruby, ¾ Oz., 2 ⅞ In. 28
Moondrops, Cup & Saucer, Amber 7
Moondrops, Relish, 3 Sections, Footed, Cobalt Blue, 8 In. 17
Moondrops, Sherbet, Ruby, 2 ⅝ In. 19
Moondrops, Tumbler, 3 ¼ In. 8
Moondrops, Whiskey, Floral, Ruby, Handle, 2 Oz., 2 ¾ In. 26
Moondrops, Wine, Ruby, 4 Oz., 4 In. 12
Pitcher, Horseshoe Daisy, Pressed Glass, Clear, 1912-22, 8 In. .... *illus* 75
Punch Bowl, Stand, Carnation, Scalloped Edge, 1904, 10 x 14 In. .... *illus* 285
Radiance, Butter, Cover, Round, ¼ Lb. 169
Radiance, Candy Dish, Footed, Handle, Ice Blue, 5 In. 24
Radiance, Punch Bowl, Flared, 11 In. 38
Radiance, Punch Cup, 2 ½ In. 5
Radiance, Punch Cup, Amber, 2 ⅜ In. 4
Radiance, Sugar & Creamer, Ruby 25
Rexford, Compote, 6 ¾ In. 18
Swan, Emerald Green, Clear Head & Neck, 1940-60, 7 In. .... *illus* 50
Teardrop, Candlestick, 2-Light 19
Wild Rose, Candlestick, 2-Light 15
Wild Rose, Relish, 3 Sections, 12 ¾ In. 22

NEWCOMB POTTERY was founded at Sophie Newcomb College, New Orleans, Louisiana, in 1895. The work continued through the 1940s. Pieces of this art pottery are marked with the printed letters *NC* and often have the incised initials of the artist and potter as well. A date letter code was printed on pieces made from 1901 to 1941. Most pieces have a matte glaze and incised decoration.

Bowl, Plums, Footed, Sadie Irvine, 4 x 7 In. 1887
Bowl, Spiderwort, Blue & Green Matte Glaze, Squat, Ring Foot, 1917, 2 x 4 In. 919
Bowl, Squat, Molded Rim, Blue Ground, Flowers, Leaves, c.1914, 4 x 6 In. 1353
Humidor, Witches, Black Cats, Lightning, Harriet Joor, 1902, 7 ½ x 6 In. .... *illus* 53125
Jar, Green & Brown High Glaze, Baluster Shape, Early 1900s, 5 ½ x 4 ½ In. 415
Plaque, Pine Trees, Frame, Henrietta Bailey, Label, 1915, 10 x 6 In. .... *illus* 4375
Plaque, Round, Peacock Feather Banding, Blue, Green, c.1915, 8 In. Diam. 3220
Plate, Blooming Daisies Border, Green, Blue, Yellow, 1913, 8 ¾ In. Diam. 1875
Vase, 4 Handles, Panels, Green, Pink, c.1932, 3 ⅞ In. 3178
Vase, Bloomed Daffodil, Grass Blades, Anna Francis Simpson, c.1924, 7 In. 1521
Vase, Blue Trees, Relief, Green Moss, Moon, Tapered, Swollen Shoulder, Signed, 9 In. 5036
Vase, Blue, Green, Pine Trees, Tapered, Shouldered, Rolled Rim, 1908, 7 x 4 In. 13750
Vase, Blue, Green, Pink, Cherries, Leaves, Shouldered, Tapered, 1924, 11 x 8 In. 3000
Vase, Cactus Flowers, Blue, Harriet Joor, 1902, 13 ½ x 5 ½ In. 9375
Vase, Clovers, Stylized Leaves, Blue, Green, Joseph Meyer, Marked, 1901, 15 In. .... *illus* 9800
Vase, Daffodils, Grass Blades, Blue Ground, c.1924, 7 In. 2694
Vase, Floral Matte Glaze, Irises, Pink, Blue, Green, Yellow, Sadie Irvine, 1918, 4 ⅜ In. 590
Vase, Flowers, Green, Blue, Oval, Shouldered, Rolled Rim, 1916, 6 x 4 In. 4375
Vase, Fuchsia, Leaves At Shoulder, White Ground, Henrietta Bailey, 1904, 8 ¼ x 7 In. 5938
Vase, Live Oaks, Spanish Moss, Fence, Anna F. Simpson, 1918, 10 x 8 In. .... *illus* 8750
Vase, Louisiana Irises, Blue & Green Underglaze, Henrietta Bailey, c.1908, 9 x 7 In. 14340
Vase, Matte Drip Glaze, 5 ¼ x 3 ¾ In. 580
Vase, Matte Glaze, Relief Flowers, Tapered, Sadie Irvine, 1924, 9 x 7 In. 1845
Vase, Moon & Moss, Blue, Green, Sadie Irvine, Jonathan Hunt, 1930, 5 ⅛ In. .... *illus* 2125

Nautical, Weather Station, Barometer, Hygrometer, Ship's Wheels, Airguide, 1950s, 9 x 5 In.
$120

Ruby Lane

China Mark

A mark with the words *Made in the People's Republic of China* was used starting in 1949. The mark appears on baskets, pottery, and other objects. *Made in China* was used from 1891 to 1949 and again starting in 1978.

Netsuke, Porcelain, Monkey Head, Movable, Blue Robe, Carrying Fan, 3 ¾ In.
$600

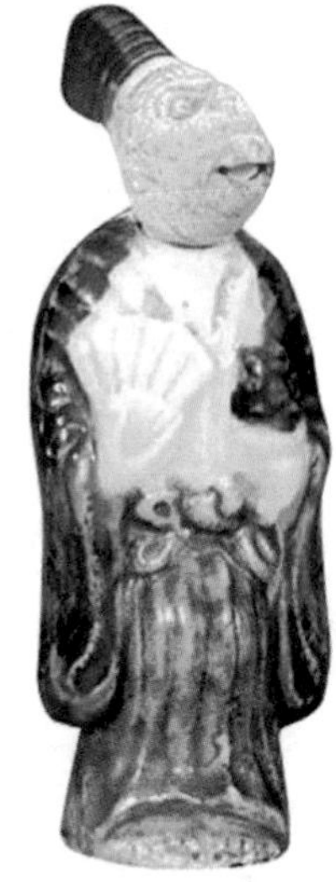

Ruby Lane

Netsuke, Wood, Bearded Sage, Staff, Double Gourd, Riding Fish, 3 ½ In.
$350

Ruby Lane

N

TIP
Dental wax (ask your orthodontist about it) is a good adhesive to keep figurines on shelves, or lids on teapots.

New Martinsville, Pitcher, Horseshoe Daisy, Pressed Glass, Clear, 1912-22, 8 In. $75

Ruby Lane

New Martinsville, Punch Bowl, Stand, Carnation, Scalloped Edge, 1904, 10 x 14 In. $285

Ruby Lane

New Martinsville, Swan, Emerald Green, Clear Head & Neck, 1940-60, 7 In. $50

Ruby Lane

Vase, Moon & Trees, Blue, Cylindrical, 7 In. 3689
Vase, Narcissus, Vellum Glaze, Cynthia Pugh Littlejohn, 1914, 3 x 5 ¾ In. 1476
Vase, Pine & Moon, Cabins, Matte Glaze, Blue, Green, Henrietta Bailey, 1925, 16 In. .... *illus* 22705
Vase, Pink Daffodils, Green Grass Blades, Bulbous, Anna Francis, c.1924, 7 In. 1521
Vase, Plantation Trees At Dawn, Spanish Moss, Anna Francis Simpson, 3 ½ x 4 ½ In. 2832
Vase, Scenic, Blues, Tapered, Sadie Irvine, Impressed Logo, 1928, 6 In. 2904
Vase, Spanish Moss, Trees, Bayou, Shouldered, c.1928, 5 ½ In. 2925
Vase, Stargazer Lilies, White Leaves, Blue Ground, Irene Keep, 1902, 13 ½ x 8 In. 6250
Vase, Stylized Pattern, Sadie Irvine, 1933, 3 ½ x 3 ½ In. 875
Vase, Trees, Spanish Moss, Full Moon, Blue, Green, Round, Flat Rim, 1933, 5 x 4 ½ In. 2250
Vase, Windmill Palms, Full Moon, Landscape, Anna Frances Simpson, 1921, 9 x 6 ¾ In. 10000

NILOAK POTTERY (*Kaolin* spelled backward) was made at the Hyten Brothers Pottery in Benton, Arkansas, between 1910 and 1947. Although the factory did make cast and molded wares, collectors are most interested in the marbleized art pottery line made of colored swirls of clay. It was called Mission Ware. By 1931 the company made castware, and many of these pieces were marked with the name *Hywood.*

NILOAK

Bowl, Lid, Marbleized, Brown, Cream, Red, 3 x 5 ½ In. 275
Bowl, Marbleized, Red, Blue Brown, Pat. No. 1657997, 2 ¾ x 6 ¼ In. 135
Candlestick, Marbleized, Brown, Cream, Paper Label, 8 ½ In., Pair 345
Cornucopia, Mauve Matte Finish, Ribbed, 9 x 5 ½ In. 55
Ewer, Flying Eagle, Stars, Blue Matte Glaze, 10 In. 45
Ewer, Green Matte, Flower, 11 In. 40
Flower Frog, Green Matte Glaze, Bulb Shape, Footed, Leaves, 5 x 4 In. 75
Jardiniere, Marbleized, Brown, Blue, Squat, Rolled Rim, 3 ¼ x 4 In. 90
Lamp Base, Electrolier, Mission Ware, Swirl, Red, Beige, Blue, Brown, 1910-24, 10 In. .... *illus* 195
Pitcher, Embossed Flowers, Pink, Square, 7 In. 30
Planter, Dutch Shoe Shape, Red, c.1930, 4 ¾ x 2 In. 40
Vase, Bud, Red Matte Glaze, Bulbous, Stick Neck, c.1936, 4 ½ In. 109
Vase, Marbleized, Ball Shape, Brown, Cream, Red, 4 ¼ x 5 In. 150
Vase, Marbleized, Blue, Brown, Cream, Bulbous, 8 ½ In. 160
Vase, Marbleized, Brown, Cream, Blue, Cylindrical, 5 ¾ x 3 ½ In. 110
Vase, Marbleized, Brown, Cream, Blue, Pinched Waist, Footed, 8 In. 225
Vase, Marbleized, Brown, Cream, Green, Tapered, 5 ¼ x 3 ¼ In. 135
Vase, Marbleized, Brown, Cream, Red, Corseted, 5 ½ x 3 ¼ In. 100
Vase, Marbleized, Dark Brown, Green, Rolled Rim, Footed, 8 ¼ In. 225
Vase, Marbleized, Flared Rim, Brown, Cream, 5 ¼ In. 110

NIPPON porcelain was made in Japan from 1891 to 1921. *Nippon* is the Japanese word for "Japan." A few firms continued to use the word *Nippon* on ceramics after 1921 as a part of the company name more than as an identification of the country of origin. More pieces marked *Nippon* will be found in the Dragonware, Moriage, and Noritake categories.

Hand Painted NIPPON

Bowl, Flowers, Pink & Blue, Gilt, Lid, Finial, 6 ¼ x 7 ½ In. 47
Charger, Bedouin, On Horseback, Molded Relief, Marked, c.1910, 15 In. 615
Chocolate Pot, Enamel, Landscape, Handle, Lid, Hand Painted, c.1900, 10 In. 61
Plate, Pink Roses, Beaded, Rounded Gilt Edge, c.1920, 5 x 5 In. 38
Salt & Pepper, Painted Faces, On Tray, 1930s, 1 ½ In., Tray 3 ½ x 1 ½ In. .... *illus* 25
Tea Set, Gilt, Landscapes, Teapot, 6 Cup & Saucers, Sugar & Creamer, 15 Piece 184
Vase, 2 Triangular, Handles, Green, Pink Flowers, Leaves, 4 ½ In. 30
Vase, Blown Out, Dimensional Sunflowers, Maple Leaf Stamp, 10 In. 443
Vase, Gilt, Green, Roses, Coralene, Handles, 3 ½ In. 531
Vase, Green, Pink Flower Banding, Gilt, Beading, Swollen, Loop Handles, c.1890, 6 In. 96
Vase, Roses, Leaves, Beaded, Square Handles, Narrow Mouth, c.1900, 8 x 6 In. 161

NODDERS, also called nodding figures or pagods, are figures with heads and hands that are attached to wires. Any slight movement causes the parts to move up and down. They were made in many countries during the eighteenth, nineteenth, and twentieth centuries. A few Art Deco designs are also known. Copies are being made. A more recent type of nodder is made of papier-mache or plastic. These often represent sports figures or comic characters. Sports nodders are listed in the Sports category.

Alligator, Ashtray, Open Mouth, Green, c.1950, 4 x 5 x 2 In. 32
Ashtray, Boy, Smoking Cigar, Hands In Pocket, Suspenders, Cast Iron, Japan, 4 x 4 In. 36
Bear Cubs, Holding Toes, Salt & Pepper, Porcelain, Japan, 2 x 3 x 2 In. 20
Beatnik Cat, Black, Playing Drum, Wood, 4 ½ In. 19

Newcomb, Humidor, Witches, Black Cats, Lightning, Harriet Joor, 1902, 7 ½ x 6 In.
$53,125

Rago Arts and Auction Center

Newcomb, Plaque, Pine Trees, Frame, Henrietta Bailey, Label, 1915, 10 x 6 In.
$4,375

Rago Arts and Auction Center

Newcomb, Vase, Clovers, Stylized Leaves, Blue, Green, Joseph Meyer, Marked, 1901, 15 In.
$9,800

Neal Auctions

Newcomb, Vase, Live Oaks, Spanish Moss, Fence, Anna F. Simpson, 1918, 10 x 8 In.
$8,750

Rago Arts and Auction Center

Newcomb, Vase, Moon & Moss, Blue, Green, Sadie Irvine, Jonathan Hunt, 1930, 5 ⅛ In.
$2,125

Neal Auctions

Newcomb, Vase, Pine & Moon, Cabins, Matte Glaze, Blue, Green, Henrietta Bailey, 1925, 16 In.
$22,705

Neal Auctions

Niloak, Lamp Base, Electrolier, Mission Ware, Swirl, Red, Beige, Blue, Brown, 1910-24, 10 In.
$195

Ruby Lane

Don't Throw It Away

Broken and damaged art pieces considered beyond repair sometimes were legally declared worthless and became the property of the insurance company that paid the owner for the loss. But the Salvage Art Institute borrowed the damaged art for an exhibition and let visitors touch a broken piece of a Jeff Koons artwork or handle a slashed painting. It inspired a conversation about why expensive artworks with repairable damage or minor imperfections are suddenly worthless and no longer called art. Some insurers do sell pieces that are legally worthless but are restored and then sold as repaired. They can recoup some of their loses and sometimes make a profit.

Nippon, Salt & Pepper, Painted Faces, On Tray, 1930s, 1 ½ In., Tray 3 ½ x 1 ½ In.
$25

Nodder, Foxy Grandpa & Old Woman, Painted, Papier-Mache, Germany, c.1890, 6 ½ In., Pair
$112

Theriault's

Nodder, Gentleman, Composition, Painted, Germany, 7 ½ In.
$118

Bertoia Auctions

Who's Huck?
"Huck" is the mark used by Flora Cable Huckfield on North Dakota School of Mines pottery. She worked there from 1924 to 1949.

Cat, Playing Instrument, Spelter, Germany, c.1900 ... 225
Clown, Green Coat, Big Black Shoes, Wood, Spain, c.1950, 3 ½ In. ... 18
Dog, Hound, Brown & White, Japan, 3 In. ... 22
Dog, Poodle, Spaghetti, Begging, White, Ceramic, 5 In. ... 50
Duck, Papier-Mache, Yellow, Blue, Red Tie, Germany, 5 In. ... 95
Dutch Girl, Dancing, Holding Basket, Bisque, c.1900, 6 In. ... 50
Dutch Girl, Hat, Green Shawl, Bisque, Germany, c.1900, 3 ½ In. ... 59
Elephant, Ashtray, Gray, On Back, Feet Up, Japan, c.1950, 3 x 4 x 3 In. ... 35
Foxy Grandpa & Old Woman, Painted, Papier-Mache, Germany, c.1890, 6 ½ In., Pair ... *illus* 112
Gentleman, Composition, Painted, Germany, 7 ½ In. ... *illus* 118
Goose, White, Celluloid, 1920s, 3 ½ In. ... 25
Hawaiian Girl, Green Skirt, Lei, Glancing Up, 6 ¼ In. ... 18
Hawaiian Hula Girl, Grass Skirt, c.1940, 5 ½ In. ... 78
Man, Porcelain, Hands In Pocket, Hat, Flowered Pants, Boots, Cane, Germany, 6 In. ... 42
Monk, Blond Hair, Holding Book & Mug, Porcelain, Japan, 6 ¼ In. ... 23
Policeman, Keystone Cop, Club, Bisque, Germany, 4 ½ In. ... 80
Salt & Pepper Shakers are listed in the Salt & Pepper category.
Woman, Gown, Nightcap, Holding Dog, Porcelain, 1900s, 7 In. ... 110
Woman, Red Polka Dot Dress, Seated, Hands On Lap, Bisque, 4 x 3 In. ... 100

NORITAKE porcelain was made in Japan after 1904 by Nippon Toki Kaisha. The best-known Noritake pieces are marked with the *M* in a wreath for the Morimura Brothers, a New York City distributing company. This mark was used until the early 1950s. There may be some helpful price information in the Nippon category, since prices are comparable. Noritake Azalea is listed in the Azalea category in this book.

Bowl, Pedestal, Cherry Blossoms, Lake, Silver Rim, c.1930, 7 ½ In. Diam. ... *illus* 59
Cake Plate, Christmas Ball, Handles, 10 ¾ In. ... 35
Candlestick, Egyptian Revival, Cone Shape, Painted, Desert Scene, c.1910, 8 In. ... 42
Creamer, Blue Moon ... 21
Cup & Saucer, Colburn ... 21
Cup & Saucer, Gilt, Cream Band, 23 Piece ... 56
Plate, Dinner, Cho San, c.1955, 10 ⅝ In. ... 8
Sugar & Creamer, Sunny Side ... 52
Sugar Shaker, Landscape, Painted, Gold Trim, Footed, 6 ½ In. ... *illus* 35
Teapot, Lorenzo, 5 In. ... 77
Tray, Trinket, Figural, Lady, Gold Iridescent, 5 ¼ x 4 ¾ In. ... 632
Willowbrook, Sugar & Creamer, Flowers, Scrollwork, 1979-87, 4 In. ... *illus* 65

NORSE POTTERY COMPANY started in Edgerton, Wisconsin, in 1903. In 1904 the company moved to Rockford, Illinois. The company made a black pottery, which resembled early bronze relics of the Scandinavian countries. The firm went out of business in 1913.

Bowl, 3 Crescent Man In The Moon Feet, Serpentine & Chain Design, 5 ¼ x 7 ½ In. ... 224
Jardiniere, 3 Paw Feet, Mythological Falcon Heads, 7 ½ x 11 ½ In. ... 767
Vase, Rolled Rim, 4 Attached Handles, Raised Fern Braches, 9 x 10 ½ In. ... 649

NORTH DAKOTA SCHOOL OF MINES was established in 1898 at the University of North Dakota. A ceramics course was established in 1910. Students made pieces from the clays found in the region. Although very early pieces were marked *U.N.D.*, most pieces were stamped with the full name of the university. After 1963 pieces were only marked with students' names.

Bowl, Turquoise, Brown, Stylized, Flora Huckfield, 8 In. ... 6250
Ewer, Pinched Sides, Melrose, 7 ¼ In. ... 110
Medallion, Blue Glaze, Central Flower, Parents Day, June 1936, 3 ¾ In. Diam. ... 160
Plaque, Horse Head, 5 ¼ In. Diam. ... 695
Vase, Barrel Shape, Blue & Green Bands, Signed JM, 5 ½ In. ... 900
Vase, Blue & Green Matte Glaze, Bell Shape, Incised, 1930s, 4 In. ... *illus* 460
Vase, Brown Matte Glaze, Rabbits, Blossoms, Panels, Elizabeth Bready, 3 ¾ In. ... 1895
Vase, Carved Flowers, Blue Stamp, Julia Mattson, 5 ½ x 4 ½ In. ... 995
Vase, Crystalline Glaze, Embossed Wheat, Green Glaze, c.1931, 3 ¼ x 7 In. ... 826
Vase, Feelie Shape, Green Drip Glaze, Dorothy Olson, 4 ¾ x 4 ¾ In. ... 275
Vase, Fish, Blue, Incised, Marie Thormodsgard, c.1913, 7 x 8 In. ... 2875
Vase, Glossy Blue Glaze, Julia Mattson, 6 ¼ In. ... 150
Vase, Glossy Blue Glaze, Shouldered, Carved Leaves, Hendrickson, 6 x 6 In. ... 365
Vase, Glossy Green Glaze, Ribbed, 2 ¾ x 2 ¼ In. ... 110
Vase, Green Drip Glaze, Oval, Julia Mattson, 6 ¼ In. ... 395

Vase, Green Glaze, Ribbed, Julia Mattson, 3 x 3 ½ In. 215
Vase, Green Matte Over Brown, Bulbous, 6 In. 215
Vase, Green Over Blue, Bulbous, Signed MC, 1928, 8 ½ In. 675
Vase, Native American, Reticulations, Marked, Ferock, 8 In. 1121
Vase, Orange Glaze, Flower & Leaf Band, Julia Mattson, 5 ½ In. 295
Vase, Shoulder, Painted Prairie Roses, Flora Huckfield, 1920s, 4 ¾ In. 895
Vase, Tan, Shouldered, Ribbed Neck, 1930s, 5 In. 450
Vase, Turkeys, Trees, Full Moon, Award Inscription, M. Cable, 1934, 8 In. ....*illus* 11875
Vase, Viking Ship, Julia Mattson, 3 x 3 ¾ In. 1095

NORTHWOOD glass was made by one of the glassmaking companies operated by Harry C. Northwood. His first company, Northwood Glass Co., was founded in Martins Ferry, Ohio, in 1887 and moved to Ellwood City, Pennsylvania, in 1892. The company closed in 1896. Later that same year, Harry Northwood opened the Northwood Co. in Indiana, Pennsylvania. Some pieces made at the Northwood Co. are marked "Northwood" in script. The Northwood Co. became part of a consortium called the National Glass Co. in 1899. Harry left National in 1901 to found the H. Northwood Co. in Wheeling, West Virginia. At the Wheeling factory, Harry Northwood and his brother Carl manufactured pressed and blown tableware and novelties in many colors that are collected today as custard, opalescent, goofus, carnival, and stretch glass. Pieces made between 1905 and about 1915 may have an underlined *N* trademark. Harry Northwood died in 1919, and the plant closed in 1925.

Acorn Burrs, Creamer, Amethyst 137
Acorn Burrs, Punch Cup, Amethyst 32
Alaska, Creamer & Spooner, Canary Yellow Opalescent, c.1897, 3 ¼ x 6 ¼ In. 12
Cherry & Cable, Butter, Cover, Round 99
Cherry & Cable, Pitcher, 56 Oz., 8 ½ In. 136
Cruet, Argonaut Shell, Custard Glass, Gilt, 6 ½ In. 450
Drapery, Butter, Cover, Blue Opalescent, Gold Trim, c.1904, 5 ½ x 8 In. 54
Drapery, Pitcher, White Opalescent, 64 Oz. 109
Everglades, Bowl, Fruit, Oval, Footed, White Opalescent, 5 ¼ In. 12
Everglades, Water Set, Pitcher, 2 Tumblers, Blue, Opalescent, 7 ½ x 7 In., 3 Piece 36
Grape & Cable, Bonbon, Amethyst, Notched Edge, Handles, Carnival Glass ....*illus* 62
Grape & Cable, Bowl, Crimped, Round, Green, 8 ¾ In. 36
Grape & Cable, Bowl, Fruit, Amethyst, 3 Curled Feet, c.1910, 10 ½ In. ....*illus* 450
Grape & Cable, Bowl, Fruit, Green, 4 ⅞ In. 21
Grape & Cable, Tumbler, Amethyst, 8 Oz., 3 ⅞ In. 31
Grape & Gothic Arches, Goblet, Water 25
Grape Frieze, Bonbon, Green, 6 ½ In. 29
Klondyke, Bowl, Triangular, 3-Footed, Blue Opalescent, 7 ¾ In. 16
Leaf & Beads, Bowl, 3-Footed, White Opalescent, 7 ⅝ In. 32
Leaf & Beads, Bowl, Crimped, Footed, White Opalescent, 8 ½ In. 37
Leaf & Beads, Bowl, Double Crimped, White Opalescent, 9 In. 48
Memphis, Bowl, Dessert, 4 ¾ In. 8
Memphis, Spooner, 3 ⅜ In. 23
Nearcut, Pitcher, 40 Oz., 8 ¼ In. 30
Peacock At The Fountain, Punch Cup, Cobalt, 2 ½ In. 34
Pearl Flowers, Bowl, Crimped, Round, 3-Footed, White Opalescent, 9 In. 40
Pitcher, Daisy & Fern, Opalescent, Ball Shape, Crimped Edge, 1894-1904, 8 ¾ In. ....*illus* 149
Roulette, Bowl, Crimped, Footed, Blue Opalescent, 8 ¼ In. 88
Scroll With Acanthus, Bowl, Flared, Footed, White, 9 In. 35
Scroll With Acanthus, Compote, Green, 5 In. 28
Singing Birds, Mug, Amethyst, 3 ½ In. 18
Spanish Lace, Sugar Shaker, Metal Lid, Clear Opalescent, c.1900, 3 In. 89
Swirl, Pitcher, Water, Blue Opalescent, Ball Shape Pitcher, c.1890, 9 ½ x 7 In. 48

NU-ART *see Imperial category.*

NUTCRACKERS of many types have been used through the centuries. At first the nutcracker was probably strong teeth or a hammer. But by the nineteenth century, many elaborate and ingenious types were made. Levers, screws, and hammer adaptations were the most popular. Because nutcrackers are still useful, they are still being made, some in the old styles.

Alligator, Metal, Bronze Tone, 7 ½ In. 84
Bearded Horned Goat Head, Wooden, Glass Eyes, Hand Carved, Hinged Handles, c.1880, 8 In. *illus* 195
Chipmunk, Black Forest, Black Glass Eyes, c.1890, 7 ¼ In. 155
Dog, Cast Iron, White Paint, c.1900, 12 x 5 In. 345
Dog, Cast Metal, Mechanical, Lift Tail Mouth Opens, 10 In. 12

Noritake, Bowl, Pedestal, Cherry Blossoms, Lake, Silver Rim, c.1930, 7 ½ In. Diam.
$59

Ruby Lane

Noritake, Sugar Shaker, Landscape, Painted, Gold Trim, Footed, 6 ½ In.
$35

Ruby Lane

N

TIP
Don't dry your china and crystal with a cloth that has been laundered with fabric softener. The softener may leave a film.

Noritake, Willowbrook, Sugar & Creamer, Flowers, Scrollwork, 1979-87, 4 In.
$65

Ruby Lane

North Dakota, Vase, Blue & Green Matte Glaze, Bell Shape, Incised, 1930s, 4 In.
$460

Humler & Nolan

North Dakota, Vase, Turkeys, Trees, Full Moon, Award Inscription, M. Cable, 1934, 8 In.
$11,875

Rago Arts and Auction Center

N

TIP

Do not display carnival glass made before 1910 in direct sunlight. The glass will turn purple or brown and the iridescent finish may fade.

Northwood, Grape & Cable, Bonbon, Amethyst, Notched Edge, Handles, Carnival Glass
$62

Ruby Lane

Dog, Iron, Standing, Open Mouth, Footed Shaped Base, Black, c.1880, 5 x 8 In. .... *illus* 259
Dwarf, Head, Carved Wood .... *illus* 120
Flowers, Vines, Iron, Chrome Finish 12
Jester's Head, Brass, c.1900, 7 ¼ In. 104
Monkey, Black Forest, Wood, 8 In. 495
Nude, Wood, Raised Arms, Folk Art, 1950s, 13 ½ In. 55
Parrot Head, Silver Plate, 6 In. 135
Parrot, Geometric Shape, Extended Tail, Green, Red, 8 x 5 ⅞ In. 295
Rabbit Head, Black Forest, Glass Eyes, c.1900, 8 In. 320
Ram, Black Forest, Glass Eyes, 7 ¼ In. 275
Soldier, Wood, Erzgebirge, 11 ½ In. 75
Squirrel, Iron, Silver Paint, Tail Moves Jaw To Crack, 6 x 8 ½ In. 106
Sterling Silver, Repousse Handles, Kirk & Sons, 7 In. 137
Walnut, Edwardian, Clothespin Shape, 8 ½ In. 180
Woman, Seminude, Figural, Wood, 13 ¼ In. 36
Wood, Bowl, Crank, 9 x 7 In. 12

NYMPHENBURG, *see Royal Nymphenburg.*

OCCUPIED JAPAN was printed on pottery, porcelain, toys, and other goods made during the American occupation of Japan after World War II, from 1947 to 1952. Collectors now search for these pieces. The items were made for export. Ceramic items are listed here. Toys are listed in the Toy category in this book.

OCCUPIED JAPAN

Bowl, Vegetable, Lid, Aladdin, Fantasia Pattern, 11 x 6 In. 59
Cigarette Box, Enamel Brass, Wood Lining, Footed, 4 x 3 In. 45
Cigarette Dispenser, Marquetry, Bird, Mechanical, 6 x 3 x 3 In. 76
Creamer, Blue & White, Pagoda, Bushes, 2 ½ In. 5
Creamer, Toby Style, Blue Jacket, Hat, 3 In. 10
Cup & Saucer, Spring Violets, Gilt Rim, Rossetti Co. 49
Cup, Demitasse, Leaves & Berries 15
Dish, Pastel Flowers, Open Handle, Spout, 6 x 5 x 1 In. 18
Figurine, Colonial Man, Striped Pants, Flowered Vest, 6 ½ In. 30
Figurine, Couple, Sitting, Playing Mandolin, 3 ¾ x 3 ¾ In. 18
Figurine, Girl, Wearing Kerchief, Flowers, Rabbit, 3 ⅞ In. 25
Figurine, Goose, Running, Red Feet & Beak, c.1947, 2 In. 16
Figurine, Woman, Blowing In The Wind, Art Deco, 4 ¾ In. 14
Figurine, Woman, Seated, Holding Rose, Beau, Holding Hat, Oval Base, 6 In. 125
Figurine, Woman, Southern Belle, Hat, Rosy Cheeks, 1940s, 6 In. 22
Lemon Server, Handle, Flowers, 5 ½ x 5 ½ In. 35
Salt & Pepper, Teapot Shape, Bouquet, 2 x 2 ½ In. 18
Trinket Box, Palm Trees, Pink Flamingos, 6-Footed, 4 x 2 x 2 In. 25
Vase, Baby On Tummy, Resting On Book, Mocco, 2 ½ x 3 ¼ In. 23

OFFICE TECHNOLOGY includes office equipment and related products, such as adding machines, calculators, and check-writing machines. Typewriters are in their own category in this book.

Check Writer, Model Y, Key, Safe Guard Check Writer Co., 9 ½ x 7 ¾ In. 148
Mail Sorting Wheel, Iron, Cast, Wood, Ferris Wheel Shape, 47 x 34 In. 875

OHR pottery was made in Biloxi, Mississippi, from 1883 to 1906 by George E. Ohr, a true eccentric. The pottery was made of very thin clay that was twisted, folded, and dented into odd, graceful shapes. Some pieces were lifelike models of hats, animal heads, or even a potato. Others were decorated with folded clay "snakes." Reproductions and reworked pieces are appearing on the market. These have been reglazed, or snakes and other embellishments have been added.

Bowl, Dimpled Sides, Ring Foot, Gunmetal Glaze, Stamped, c.1900, 2 ½ x 4 ½ In. 1000
Bowl, Dimpled, Squat, Folded Wavy Rim, Raspberry Speckled Glaze, c.1900, 3 x 5 In. 4688
Mug, Folded Rim, Loop Handle, Green, Raspberry, Blue, Gunmetal Glaze, c.1900, 5 In. 4375
Pitcher, Folded Rim, Cutout Handle, Ring Foot, Brown, Blue, Speckle Glaze, c.1900, 3 x 5 In. ... 2875
Puzzle Mug, Manganese, Lead, c.1900, 3 ½ x 3 ½ In. 780
Salt, Redware, Mottled Glaze, Round, Rolled Shoulder, Stamped Signature, 3 ⅛ In. 443
Teapot, In-Body Twist, Ear Handle, S-Spout, Green, Gunmetal Speckle Glaze, c.1900, 4 x 8 In. .. 18750
Vase, Crumpled, Ruffled Rim, Green Over Raspberry Drip Glaze, c.1900, 3 ½ x 5 In. 3750
Vase, Dimpled Body, Crimped Rim, Ribbon Handles, Mottled Glaze, c.1900, 4 In. .... *illus* 9560

Northwood, Grape & Cable, Bowl, Fruit, Amethyst, 3 Curled Feet, c.1910, 10 ½ In.
$450

Ruby Lane

TIP

Make up a new name for your mother's maiden name when asked for the answer to this security question. The real maiden name is too easy to find with searches of obituaries or early school records or geneology sites. A company will not know the real name. But be sure you remember the name.

Northwood, Pitcher, Daisy & Fern, Opalescent, Ball Shape, Crimped Edge, 1894-1904, 8 ¾ In.
$149

Ruby Lane

Nutcracker, Bearded Horned Goat Head, Wooden, Glass Eyes, Hand Carved, Hinged Handles, c.1880, 8 In.
$195

Ruby Lane

Nutcracker, Dog, Iron, Standing, Open Mouth, Footed Shaped Base, Black, c.1880, 5 x 8 In.
$259

Ruby Lane

Nutcracker, Dwarf, Head, Carved Wood
$120

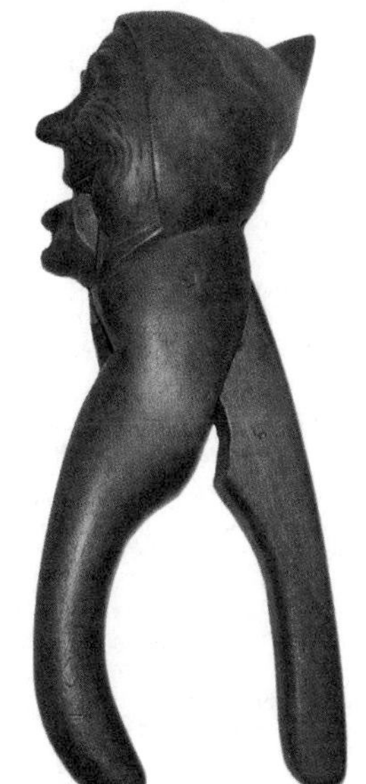

Fox Auctions

Ohr, Vase, Dimpled Body, Crimped Rim, Ribbon Handles, Mottled Glaze, c.1900, 4 In.
$9,560

Neal Auctions

Ohr, Vase, Green Gunmetal, Raspberry, Speckled Glaze, 2 Handles, Stamped, c.1900, 8 In.
$46,875

Rago Arts and Auction Center

Ohr, Vase, In-Body Twist, Gunmetal, Green, Brown Sponged Glaze, Stamped, c.1900, 6 ¾ In.
$6,875

Rago Arts and Auction Center

Ohr, Vase, In-Body Twist, Red, Green Glaze, Stamped, 1895-96, 5 x 3 ¼ In.
$20,000

Rago Arts and Auction Center

Ohr, Vase, Squat, Green & Blue Speckled Glaze, Yellow Splotches, c.1890, 4 x 4 In.
$1,500

Neal Auctions

Vase, Dimpled, Dark Blue, Torn & Folded Rim, 6 ½ x 5 ½ In. 5625
Vase, Dimples, Crinkled Neck, Ruffle Rim, Smokestack, Brown, Gunmetal Glaze, c.1900, 5 In. .. 7500
Vase, Flared Foot, Urn Body, Pinched Stick Neck, Ruffle Rim, Indigo, Pink Glaze, c.1900, 9 In. .. 6875
Vase, Gourd Shape, Gunmetal Black Glaze, Gray, Cylindrical Neck, 3 In. 2070
Vase, Green Gunmetal, Raspberry, Speckled Glaze, 2 Handles, Stamped, c.1900, 8 In. .... *illus* 46875
Vase, Gunmetal Over Mahogany, Aventurine Lip, 5 ¾ x 2 ¾ In. 3125
Vase, In-Body Twist, Gunmetal, Green, Brown Sponged Glaze, Stamped, c.1900, 6 ¾ In. ..... *illus* 6875
Vase, In-Body Twist, Red, Green Glaze, Stamped, 1895-96, 5 x 3 ¼ In. .... *illus* 20000
Vase, Mustard Ground, Crumpled, Dotted, Crimped Rim, Earthenware, 4 ¾ x 6 ½ In. 3600
Vase, Squat, Green & Blue Speckled Glaze, Yellow Splotches, c.1890, 4 x 4 In. .... *illus* 1500
Vase, Squat, Green, Blue, Speckled, 3 ½ x 3 ¾ In. 1500

OLD PARIS, *see Paris category.*

OLD SLEEPY EYE, *see Sleepy Eye category.*

ONION PATTERN, originally named bulb pattern, is a white ware decorated with cobalt blue or pink. Although it is commonly associated with Meissen, other companies made the pattern in the late nineteenth and the twentieth centuries. A rare type is called *red bud* because there are added red accents on the blue-and-white dishes.

Bowl, Blue, Pierced, Meissen, 1900s, 9 ½ In. 154
Cup & Saucer, Villeroy & Boch 46
Platter, Warming, Blue, Metal Frame, Handles, Cap Spout, Meissen, c.1910, 22 x 14 In. 173
Soup, Dish, Rim, Villeroy & Boch, 9 ⅛ In. 30
Tray, Blue, Ribbon, Bows, Meissen, 1900s, 15 ¾ In. 215
Tureen, Lid, Handles, Footed, Villeroy & Boch 350
Tureen, Soup, Handles, Lid, Underplate, Meissen, 13 x 9 In. 145

OPALESCENT GLASS is translucent glass that has the tones of the opal gemstone. It originated in England in the 1870s and is often found in pressed glassware made in Victorian times. Opalescent glass was first made in America in 1897 at the Northwood glassworks in Indiana, Pennsylvania. Some dealers use the terms *opaline* and *opalescent* for any of these translucent wares. More opalescent pieces may be listed in Hobnail, Pressed Glass, and other glass categories.

Basket, Canary Yellow, Footed, Jefferson Glass Co., c.1902, 7 x 8 In. 108
Bowl, Green, Wide Ruffled Rim, Swirls, 8 ½ In. .... *illus* 72
Epergne, Pink, Silver Plated Figural Centerpiece, c.1890, 13 ½ x 12 In. 360
Epergne, Ruffled Rim, Shaded Yellow To Cranberry, England, 1800s, 11 x 7 ½ In. 150
Epergne, Victorian, Cranberry, 5 Vases, Ruffled Rims, Scalloped Bowl, c.1890, 19 In. 330
Hobnail, Vase, Blue, Ruffled Edge, 5 ¼ In. .... *illus* 40
Jolly Bear, Bowl, Ruffled Rim, Jefferson Glass, c.1906, 9 In. 24
Raindrop, Bowl, Peach, Ruffled, Iridescent, Dugan Glass, c.1904, 9 In. 21
Sparrow & Grape, Charger, Gilt Metal Bezel Mount, 14 In. 295
Vase, Sea Creature Decoration, Seahorse Handles, 7 In. 238
Vase, White, Corn Shape, Dugan Glass, c.1905, 8 ½ x 3 ¼ In. 30
Wreath & Shell, Rose Bowl, Blue, Model Flint Glass, c.1900, 4 x 3 ¾ In. 12

OPALINE, or opal glass, was made in white, green, and other colors. The glass had a matte surface and a lack of transparency. It was often gilded or painted. It was a popular mid-nineteenth-century European glassware.

Bowl, Pink, Gilt, Gallery, France, 7 x 7 ½ In. 181
Box, Blue, Hinged Top, Chamfered Corners, Ormolu Mounts, 4 x 5 In. 484
Box, Metal Mount, Hinged Lid, 3 ½ In. 163
Girandole, Flared Scalloped Edged, Gilt, Blue, Suspended Prisms, 14 x 7 ½ In., Pair 610
Vase, Etruscan Painted, France, 41 In. 120
Vase, Stick, Lobed Bulbous Bottom, Pink, Gilded Scrolls, Flowers, 13 In. 354

OPERA GLASSES are needed because the stage is a long way from some of the seats at a play or an opera. Mother-of-pearl was a popular decoration on many French glasses.

Brass, C.W. Dixey, London, 5 x 4 ½ In. .... *illus* 289
Brass, Mother-Of-Pearl, 2 ¼ x 3 ⅞ In. 123
Enamel, Blue, Bouquets, Jeweled Dots, France, c.1880 895
Gold Plate, Green Braided Ribbons, Box, 4 ½ x 6 ⅜ In. 403
Mother-Of-Pearl, 3x18, Scope No. 2380, Goldtone Bag 88
Mother-Of-Pearl, Brass, Filigree, D.C. & H.S. Fink, 3 ¾ x 2 ¾ In. 70

Mother-Of-Pearl, Enamel, Braided Ribbon, Red, Flowers, Case, 3 ½ In. 676

Mother-Of-Pearl, Gold Plated Brass, Flowered Case, France, Birks, c.1800, 3 ½ x 1 ½ In. 729

Mother-Of-Pearl, Gold Plated, Telescoping, 2 Adjustments, Lemoire Paris, 4 x 10 In. 178

Mother-Of-Pearl, Lemoire Paris, France, 2 ¼ x 4 In., Pair 118

Mother-Of-Pearl, Red, Enamel Flowers, Lemoire, 3 ½ In. 676

Mother-Of-Pearl, Side Telescoping, Inscribed, Red Bag, Lemoire Paris, 4 x 10 In. 183

Mother-Of-Pearl, Telescoping, Inscribed, Chrome Plated, Lemoire Paris, 4 x 10 In. 121

Sevres Style, Portraits, Sky Blue, Gilt, 1 ⅝ x 3 ¾ In. 1045

Silvertone, Birds, Flowers, 1800s, 6 x 4 In. 299

ORPHAN ANNIE first appeared in the comics in 1924. The last strip ran in newspapers on June 13, 2010. The redheaded girl, her dog Sandy, and her friends were on the radio from 1930 to 1942. The first movie based on the strip was produced in 1932. A second movie was produced in 1938. A Broadway musical that opened in 1977, a movie based on the musical and produced in 1982, and a made-for-television movie based on the musical produced in 1999 made Annie popular again, and many toys, dishes, and other memorabilia have been made. A new adaptation of the movie based on the musical opened in 2014.

Button, Movie, Little Orphan Annie, Saturday April 14th, 1932, ⅞ In. 153

Comic Book, In The Thieves Den, Harold Gray, Whitman, 1944 115

Doll, Composition, Socket Head, Sculpted Hair, Blue Eyes, Jointed, Sandy, c.1925, 12 In. 399

Pastry Set, Rolling Pin, Muffin Cups, Pan, Recipe Book, Box, Transogram Co., 1930s 125

Ring, Magnifying, Secret Guard, Brass, Portrait, SG Initials, Quaker, 1941 460

Toy, Annie & Sandy, Skipping Rope, Walking Sandy, Marx, 5 ½ In. 125

Toy, Orphan Annie Skipping Rope, Sandy Carrying Suitcase, Tin, Windup, 5 ½ In. & 4 In. *illus* 108

ORREFORS Glassworks, located in the Swedish province of Smaaland, was established in 1898. The company is still making glass for use on the table or as decorations. There is renewed interest in the glass made in the modern styles of the 1940s and 1950s. In 1990, the company merged with Kosta Boda. Most vases and decorative pieces are signed with the etched name *Orrefors*.

Bowl, Black Ground, White Designs, Footed, Lars Hellsten, 5 x 11 In. 270

Bowl, Ravenna, Cobalt Blue, Controlled Bubble-Linked Circles, Red & Clear, Flared, 9 In. 1659

Bowl, Toprup Pattern, Signed, Sven Palmquist, 1960s, 7 x 2 ½ In. 150

Bowl, Wavy Rim, Fluted Sides, Jan Johansson, 7 x 12 In. 150

Candleholder, Ring Base, Corona, Textured, Marked, 5 ¾ x 1 ¾ In. 42

Candy Dish, Marin Cut, Tapered, Square, Clear, 3 x 7 In. 85

Cordial, Gustav Adolf, Etched, Woman Holding Flower, Square Stem, 3 ¼ x 3 In., 5 Piece 83

Decanter, Clear Crystal, Cut Stopper, Squared, Sloped Shoulder, 10 In. 46

Ice Bucket, Crystal, Clear, Round, Hinged Chrome Handle & Tongs, Signed, 9 In. 127

Vase, Apple Shape, Clear Glass, Stem Shape Lip, Marked, 1957, 15 x 12 In. *illus* 3750

Vase, Ariel, Cased, Signed, Ingeborg Lundin, Sweden, 1963, 5 ½ x 5 ½ In. *illus* 1375

Vase, Ariel, Girl, Dove, Black, Cobalt Blue, Wavy Rim, Ohrstrom, 1982, 8 x 5 In. *illus* 750

Vase, Ariel, Stylized Woman, Guitar Player In Boat, Geometrics, Cased, Amber, Blue, 7 In. 4148

Vase, Ariel, Woman's Profile, Dove, Flowers, Brown, Blue, Clear, Edvin Ohrstrom, 7 ½ In. 2360

Vase, Bird, Blue, Black, Edvin Ohrstrom, 5 ⅝ In. 1708

Vase, Bubble Design, Green & Blue, Round, Narrow, Tapered, 14 In. 184

Vase, Egg Shape, Clear & Green, Fish Design, Seaweed, Signed, 6 In. 350

Vase, Graal, Fish, Green Tint, Aquatic Plant Life, Etched, Edvard Hald, c.1950, 5 In. 380

Vase, Hexagonal Ball, Clear, Swimming Fish, Sea Plants, c.1930, 4 ½ In. 1188

Vase, Melon, Green, Etched, Ingeborg Lundin, Sweden, 1959, 12 ¼ x 13 In. 2125

Vase, Orange & Black, Horses, Round, Bulbous, Rolled Rim, c.1969, 5 ½ In. 374

Vase, Oval, Blue & Green Glass, Suspended In Clear, 1900s, 6 In. 308

Vase, Pear Shape, Deep Amethyst, Slip Graal, Signed, Edvard Hald, 7 In. *illus* 293

Vase, Sphere, Ingeborg Lundin, 1957, 14 ½ x 12 In. 3750

OTT & BREWER COMPANY operated the Etruria Pottery at Trenton, New Jersey, from 1871 to 1892. It started making belleek in 1882. The firm used a variety of marks that incorporated the initials *O & B*.

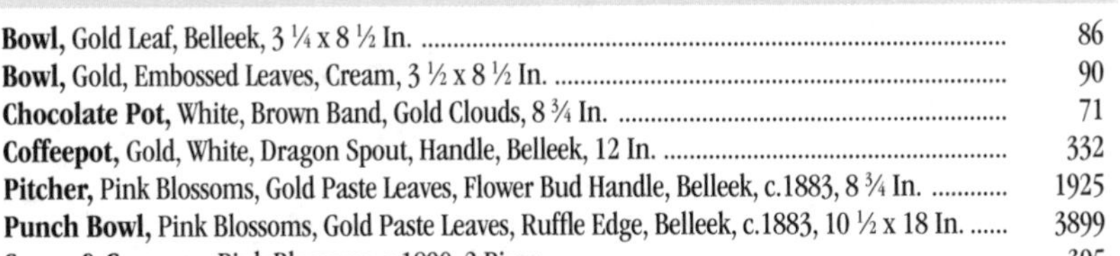

Bowl, Gold Leaf, Belleek, 3 ¼ x 8 ½ In. 86

Bowl, Gold, Embossed Leaves, Cream, 3 ½ x 8 ½ In. 90

Chocolate Pot, White, Brown Band, Gold Clouds, 8 ¾ In. 71

Coffeepot, Gold, White, Dragon Spout, Handle, Belleek, 12 In. 332

Pitcher, Pink Blossoms, Gold Paste Leaves, Flower Bud Handle, Belleek, c.1883, 8 ¾ In. 1925

Punch Bowl, Pink Blossoms, Gold Paste Leaves, Ruffle Edge, Belleek, c.1883, 10 ½ x 18 In. 3899

Sugar & Creamer, Pink Blossoms, c.1890, 2 Piece 395

Opalescent Glass, Bowl, Green, Wide Ruffled Rim, Swirls, 8 ½ In.
$72

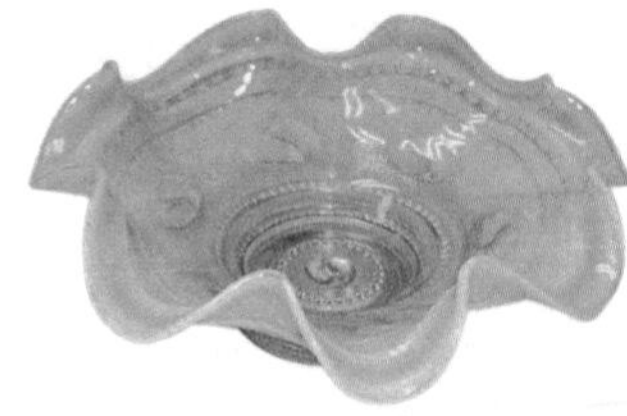

Ruby Lane

Opalescent, Hobnail, Vase, Blue, Ruffled Edge, 5 ¼ In.
$40

Ruby Lane

Opera Glasses, Brass, C.W. Dixey, London, 5 x 4 ½ In.
$289

Ruby Lane

Orphan Annie, Toy, Orphan Annie Skipping Rope, Sandy Carrying Suitcase, Tin, Windup, 5 ½ In. & 4 In.
$108

Rich Penn

Orrefors, Vase, Apple Shape, Clear Glass, Stem Shape Lip, Marked, 1957, 15 x 12 In.
$3,750

Rago Arts and Auction Center

Orrefors, Vase, Ariel, Cased, Signed, Ingeborg Lundin, Sweden, 1963, 5 ½ x 5 ½ In.
$1,375

Rago Arts and Auction Center

O

Orrefors, Vase, Ariel, Girl, Dove, Black, Cobalt Blue, Wavy Rim, Ohrstrom, 1982, 8 x 5 In.
$750

Rago Arts and Auction Center

OVERBECK POTTERY was made by four sisters named Overbeck at a pottery in Cambridge City, Indiana. They started in 1911. They made all types of vases, each one of a kind. Small, hand-modeled figurines are the most popular pieces with today's collectors. The factory continued until 1955, when the last of the four sisters died.

Figurine, Colonial Man, Striped Yellow Pants, Cane, Impressed Logo, 8 ¼ In. 767
Figurine, Robin Feeding Hungry Chicks, Impressed Logo, 3 ½ In. 649
Paperweight, Robin On Pink Flowers, Impressed Logo, 4 ¼ In. 142
Vase, Green Matte Glaze, Angled Handles, Impressed Mark, c.1910, 9 In. 908
Vase, Incised, Women Holding Umbrellas, Pink, Blue, Green, c.1920, 7 In. ....*illus* 5625
Vase, Vase, White Over Blue, Man Walking Animal, Flared Lip, 9 In. 3210

OWENS POTTERY was made in Zanesville, Ohio, from 1891 to 1928. The first art pottery was made after 1896. Utopian Ware, Cyrano, Navarre, Feroza, and Henri Deux were made. Pieces were usually marked with a form of the name *Owens*. About 1907, the firm began to make tile and discontinued the art pottery wares.

Bowl, Dogwood, Salt Glaze, Slip Blossoms, Wide Rim, Saucer Foot, 3 x 9 In. 345
Candlestick, White Glaze, Stick, Bell Shape Foot, Bowl Cup, 12 In., Pair.......... 949
Tankard, Utopian, Hunting Dogs, Cecil Exline, Signed, 17 In. 115
Vase, Elongated Oval, Cylinder Neck, Lotus, Grapes, Leaves, c.1900, 14 x 6 In. 313
Vase, Gourd Shape, Round Foot, Brown, Green, Blossoming Vines, c.1900, 9 In. 311
Vase, Henri Deux, Black, Brown, 1900, 6 ¾ x 9 In. 1188
Vase, Layered Glaze, White, Brown, Loop Handles, Flat Rim, Black Ankle, c.1962, 6 In. 150
Vase, Lily, Red Glaze, Oval, 4 Folded Handles, Signed, 12 In. 173
Vase, Lotus, Poppy, Creamy Ground, Swollen Shoulder, Walter Denny, 14 x 5 In. 313
Vase, Utopian, Indian Portrait, 1900, 21 ½ x 7 ½ In. 938
Vase, White Wave, Gray Matte Glaze Ground, Squeezebag Shape, Frank Ferrell, 8 ½ In. 649

OYSTER PLATES were popular from the 1880s. Each course at dinner was served in a special dish. The oyster plate had indentations shaped like oysters. Usually six oysters were held on a plate. There is no greater value to a plate with more oysters, although that myth continues to haunt antiques dealers. There are other plates for shellfish, including cockle plates and whelk plates. The appropriately shaped indentations are part of the design of these dishes.

5 Wells, Fish, Seaweed, Gilt Edge, Porcelain, 8 In. 175
6 Wells, Brown, Green, Pink Flowers, Haviland & Co., c.1880, 9 In. 250
6 Wells, Green, 10 In. 73
6 Wells, Pink & White, Feather & Shell Design, Wavy Rim, Porcelain, 9 In. Diam. 94
7 Wells, Blue, Central Well, Majolica, George Jones, England, 8 ¾ x 10 ½ In., Pair 984
7 Wells, Pink, Gold Trim, M Initial, Limoges, 9 ¼ In., 8 Piece 492

PADEN CITY GLASS MANUFACTURING COMPANY was established in 1916 at Paden City, West Virginia. The company made over twenty different colors of glass. The firm closed in 1951. Paden City Pottery may be listed in Dinnerware.

Biscayne, Berry Bowl, 5 In. 18
Buttercup, Cup & Saucer 32
Gazebo, Bowl, Flat Edge, 13 In. 35
Gazebo, Sugar & Creamer 30
Ivy, Platter, 13 In. 56
Tree, Toothpick Holder, c.1915 54

PAINTINGS listed in this book are not works by major artists but rather decorative paintings on ivory, board, or glass that would be of interest to the average collector. Watercolors on paper are listed under Picture. To learn the value of an oil painting by a listed artist, you must contact an expert in that area.

Acrylic On Canvas, Jasmine, 3 Female Figures, Nude, Flowers, Frame, 1941, 44 x 44 In. 345
Miniature, Oil On Ivory, Vicar, Sterling Locket Case, 19th Century, 2 x 1 ¾ In. 240
Miniature, Oil On Ivory, Woman, Red & Black Dress, Oval Gilt Frame, 2 ¾ x 2 In. 84
Miniature, Oil On Silk, Child At Altar, Bubble Glass, L.M. & C., France, 2 ⅝ x 2 In. 25
Oil On Board, Polo Match, White Birch Vs. Rolex, Frame, 1942, 17 x 18 In. 875
Oil On Board, Putti, Pasture Scene, Carved Ribbon, Oval, Frame, c.1900, 30 In., Pair 2706
Oil On Board, Sheep, Pasture, Dog On Rock, 13 ½ In. 345
Oil On Board, Spanish Dancer, Woman, Leaning Back, Holding Mask, c.1900, 28 x 25 In. 1434
Oil On Board, Steamship, Wilmington, American Flag, Passengers, A. Jacobsen, 18 x 36 In. 5166
Oil On Canvas, 2 Children With Dog, Wooded Landscape, Giltwood Frame, 1863, 50 x 40 In. 1968

Oil On Canvas, A Girl & Child With Red Flowers, Frame, c.1890, 25 x 20 In. 1845
Oil On Canvas, Arabian Water Carrier, Woman, Draped Top, Frame, c.1860, 32 x 22 In. 3936
Oil On Canvas, Arriving On Schell, Sailboats, Frame, c.1800, 16 x 24 In. 1599
Oil On Canvas, At The Bal Masque, Portrait, Woman, Giltwood Frame, 1876, 29 x 24 In. 3500
Oil On Canvas, Bassenthwait Lake, Trees, Mountains, Frame, 1850, 31 x 52 In. 3690
Oil On Canvas, Boy & Dog, Checked Dress & Pants, Seascape, Frame, 1800s, 27 x 22 In. 9225
Oil On Canvas, Cafe In Algeria, Robed Men, Inscribed, Frame, 1880, 20 x 40 In. 738
Oil On Canvas, Father Time, Overcome By Love, Hope, Beauty, Frame, c.1900, 44 x 57 In. 4750
Oil On Canvas, Game Players, Children Playing Dice, Oval, Frame, c.1810, 30 x 24 In. 4250
Oil On Canvas, Girl With Broken Pitcher, Oval, Giltwood Frame, 1800s, 39 x 32 In. 2250
Oil On Canvas, Girl, Checkered Dress, Book, Patterned Carpet, Frame, 1800s, 24 x 20 In. 3198
Oil On Canvas, Joining The Hunt, Woman On Horseback, Frame, 17 x 22 In. 937
Oil On Canvas, La Terreur, Portrait, Woman Looking To Side, Frightened, 1825, 22 x 18 In. 5000
Oil On Canvas, Landscape, Figures By A Forest, Frame, c.1910, 25 x 30 In. 1353
Oil On Canvas, Landscape, Figures, Meandering River, Giltwood Frame, c.1835, 20 x 30 In. 1353
Oil On Canvas, Lone Fisherman, Early Morning On River, Frame, c.1850, 30 x 50 In. 5250
Oil On Canvas, Master & His Hound, Seated Man, Red Coat, Dog, 1800s, 30 x 25 In. 3690
Oil On Canvas, Mother & Children, Seated, Gown, Frame, 1886, 12 x 10 In. 4000
Oil On Canvas, New Member Of The Family, Girls With Kitten, Frame, c.1890, 38 x 32 In. 1625
Oil On Canvas, Niagara Falls, Frame, 1800s, 23 ½ x 35 ½ In. ..... *illus* 2040
Oil On Canvas, Niagara Falls, Hudson River School, Gilt Frame, c.1850, 29 x 43 In. 3792
Oil On Canvas, Niagara Falls, Indians Looking At Falls, Stormy Sky, Henry Inman, 20 x 24 In. ..*illus* 17220
Oil On Canvas, Nude After Bath, Seated Woman, Frame, c.1900, 24 x 18 In. 1845
Oil On Canvas, Old Louisiana, Mansion, Columns, Willow Trees, Frame, c.1900, 16 x 20 In. 3444
Oil On Canvas, Peacock, Chickens, Marmaduke Cradock, c.1700, 22 x 56 In. 6000
Oil On Canvas, Penitent Magdalene, Seminude, Carved Giltwood Frame, 19 x 15 In. 1750
Oil On Canvas, Portrait Of Blue-Eyed Noblewoman, Giltwood Frame, c.1700, 15 x 12 In. 922
Oil On Canvas, Portrait, Captain George Leslie, Frame, 1800s, 11 ¾ x 10 In. 307
Oil On Canvas, Portrait, Lady In White, Under An Arbor, Frame, 1863, 44 x 34 In. 15625
Oil On Canvas, Portrait, Young Man, Yellow Jacket, Blue Cloak, Frame, c.1690, 14 x 12 In. 1875
Oil On Canvas, River Landscape, Figures, Trees, Frame, 25 x 30 In. 2250
Oil On Canvas, Rural Landscape, Farmhouse & Fence, Frame, 8 x 10 In. 2214
Oil On Canvas, Sacre Famiglia Con Santi, Italy, c.1700, Frame, 25 x 19 In. 3500
Oil On Canvas, Salmon, 2 Fish On Grassy Banks, Frame, c.1860, 20 x 37 In. 960
Oil On Canvas, Seated Boy, Blue Clothes, Leaning On Drum, c.1810, 42 x 35 In. 923
Oil On Canvas, Seated Woman, Nude, Long Hair, Tied Back, 1984, 31 x 24 In. 406
Oil On Canvas, Still Life, Fruit In Bowl, On Table, Frame, 1800s, 12 x 16 In. 400
Oil On Canvas, Subject Was Roses, Giltwood Frame, c.1900, 16 x 25 In. 13125
Oil On Canvas, Sunny Afternoon, Woman Looking Outside, Frame, c.1970, 16 x 20 In. 1168
Oil On Canvas, The Cardinals Aria, Signed, Frame, c.1910, 18 x 22 In. 1187
Oil On Canvas, The Plow, Farmer, Field, Dog Running Alongside, Frame, c.1900, 32 x 47 In. 3444
Oil On Canvas, Twin Girls, Both In Green Dresses, c.1850, 20 x 24 In. 480
Oil On Canvas, Une Discussion, Kittens, Food Bowl, c.1850, 26 x 32 In. 5750
Oil On Canvas, Venus Reclining, Satyr, Follower Of Titan, Italy, Frame, c.1570, 47 x 75 In. 4920
Oil On Canvas, Village Landscape, Bridge & Cottage, Frame, 1800s, 20 x 30 In. 1168
Oil On Canvas, Woman, Playing Lute, Children, Frame, Chinese Export, 1800s, 23 x 18 In. *illus* 4740
Oil On Canvas, Woman Seated At Desk, Long Dress, Carved Gilt Frame, c.1900, 24 x 20 In. 2214
Oil On Canvas, Yehudit On White Wicker Chair, Giltwood Frame, c.1950, 51 x 39 In. 3690
Oil On Ivory, Portrait Of Mary Queen Of Scotland, Oval, 2 ¾ x 2 In. 161
Oil On Masonite, Jolly Clown, Leo, Top Hat, Umbrella, c.1972, 24 x 39 In. 210
Oil On Masonite, Landscape, Clapboard House, Trees, Frame, 30 x 32 In. 660
Oil On Masonite, Nude Woman, Seated, Resting On Arm, Frame, 1960s, 19 x 23 In. 420
Oil On Masonite, Reclining Nude Woman, Brunette, Sheets, Frame, 1960s, 39 x 24 In. 660
Oil On Panel, At The Racetrack, Frame, c.1948, 43 x 43 In. 5166
Oil On Panel, The Memory, House On A Lane, Frame, 1893, 20 x 16 In. 1625
Oil Wash On Paper, Water Lilies & Trees Along Bayou, Glazed, Frame, c.1900, 18 x 29 In. 3000
Reverse On Glass, Mandarin, Garden, Consort, Children, Chinese, 1700s, 33 x 30 In. .....*illus* 4148
Reverse On Glass, Woman At Table, Flower, Chinese Export, 23 x 16 In. ..... *illus* 562

PAIRPOINT Manufacturing Company started in 1880 in New Bedford, Massachusetts. It soon joined with the glassworks nearby and made glass, silver-plated pieces, and lamps. Reverse-painted glass shades and molded shades known as "puffies" were part of the production until the 1930s. The company reorganized and changed its name several times but is still working today. Items listed here are glass or glass and metal. Silver-plated pieces are listed under Silver Plate.

Bell, Peachblow, Teardrop, Swirled Handle, 1970s, 11 In. 98
Bowl, Cut Glass, Daisy & Butterfly, 3 x 15 ¼ In. 172
Chandelier, Domed Shade, Flowers, Vine, Mottled Purple & Cream, 3 Chains, 16 In. 2666

Orrefors, Vase, Pear Shape, Deep Amethyst, Slip Graal, Signed, Edvard Hald, 7 In.
$293

Thomaston Place Auction

Overbeck, Vase, Incised, Women Holding Umbrellas, Pink, Blue, Green, c.1920, 7 In.
$5,625

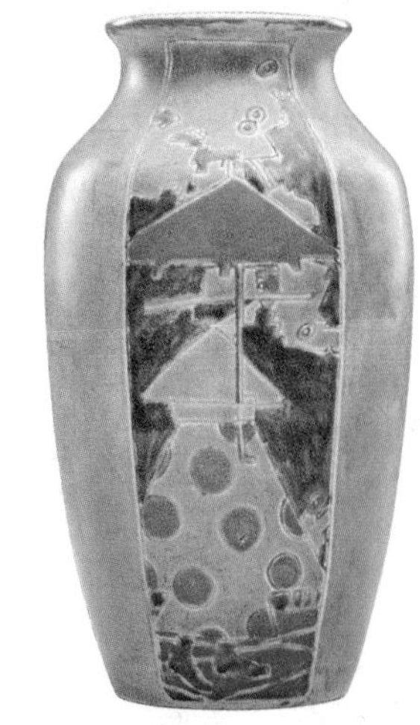

Rago Arts and Auction Center

TIP

The best burglary protection is a dog. Inmates from three Ohio prisons were surveyed and said timed lights, dead-bolt locks, and alarms are deterrents; but the thing most avoided by a professional thief is a noisy dog.

P

Painting, Oil On Canvas, Niagara Falls, Frame, 1800s, 23 ½ x 35 ½ In.
$2,040

Cowan Auctions

Painting, Oil On Canvas, Niagara Falls, Indians Looking At Falls, Stormy Sky, Henry Inman, 20 x 24 In.
$17,220

Skinner, Inc.

Painting, Oil On Canvas, Woman, Playing Lute, Children, Frame, Chinese Export, 1800s, 23 x 18 In.
$4,740

James D. Julia Auctioneers

Painting, Reverse On Glass, Mandarin, Garden, Consort, Children, Chinese, 1700s, 33 x 30 In.
$4,148

James D. Julia Auctioneers

Painting, Reverse On Glass, Woman At Table, Flower, Chinese Export, 23 x 16 In.
$562

New Orleans (Cakebread)

Pairpoint, Lamp, Chesterfield Shade, Venetian Harbor, Reverse Painted, 4-Arm Base, 22 In.
$11,500

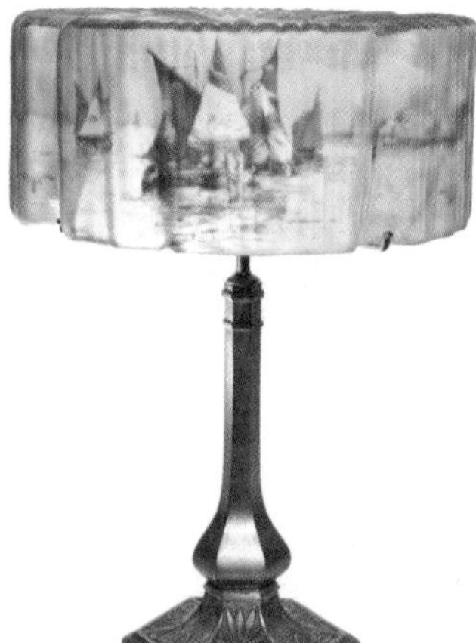

Early Auction Company

Cologne Bottle, Cut Glass, Savoy Pattern, Scalloped Base, Footed, c.1890, 9 ½ In. 177
Compote, Plums On Vine, Painted Bowl, Silver Footed Base, 2 Parts, c.1900, 6 x 8 In. 242
Lamp, Bird Of Paradise, 22 ½ x 18 In. 1150
Lamp, Chesterfield Shade, Venetian Harbor, Reverse Painted, 4-Arm Base, 22 In. ....*illus* 11500
Lamp, Directoire Style Shade, Reverse Painted, Marble Plinth Base, c.1910, 27 x 17 In. 984
Lamp, Glass Sphere, Controlled Bubbles, Polished Base, 7 ½ x 4 In. 236
Lamp, Puffy, Azalea, Pink, Red, White, Square Tapered Brass Base, Poppies, 22 In. 14813
Lamp, Puffy, Dogwood Shade, 4 Leafy Branch Supports, Flowerpot Base, 17 x 10 In. 9600
Lamp, Puffy, Papillon, Red, Pink, Cream, Copper Finish Base, Fleur-De-Lis Feet, 20 In. 3555
Lamp, Puffy, Reverse Painted, Hummingbird & Rose, 22 In. x 14 In. 5405
Lamp, Puffy, Roses, Square Flared Base, 20 ½ In. 5265
Lamp, Ravenna Shade, Garlands, Puffy, Frosted, Patinated Arched, Stepped Base, 24 In. 3125
Lamp, Reverse Painted Shade, Ships, Night Sky, Domed, Flared, Paneled Base, 17 In. 1778
Lamp, Shade, Poppies, 6-Sided, Silvered Metal, Glass & Marble Base, 27 In. 2250
Urn, Cobalt Blue, Silver Grapes, Leaves, Footed, 11 x 6 In. 236
Vase, Ambero, Yellow Green, Reverse Painted, Purple Grape Clusters, Footed, 8 In. 770

PALMER COX, *Brownies, see Brownies category.*

PAPER collectibles, including almanacs, catalogs, children's books, some greeting cards, stock certificates, and other paper ephemera, are listed here. Paper calendars are listed separately in the Calendar category. Paper items may be found in many other sections, such as Christmas and Movie.

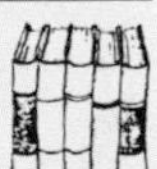

Autograph, Colonel Ellsworth, Letter To John Brown, Jr., 1873 1250
Bill, Sale Of Horse, Used In Revolutionary War, 1780, 8 x 7 ½ In. 219
Book, Big Little, Mother Goose, Hardcover, Nursery Rhymes, Illustrations, c.1934, 4 x 6 In. 345
Bookplate, Watercolor, Ink, Orange, Yellow, Green Bird, Abraham Person's Book, 1834, 6 x 3 In. 207
Certificate, Birth & Baptismal, Illuminated, Multicolor, Gabriel, Jesus, Children, 13 x 16 In. 649
Family Record, 2 Women, Urns, Watercolor, Rev. Henry Young, Penn., c.1842, 19 x 15 In. 2760
Family Record, Thomas & Betsey Alexander, 8 Children, Watercolor, Ink, Frame, c.1820, 18 In. . 625
Family Record, Watercolor, Ink, Patten Family, Marriage, 12 Children, c.1782, 14 In. 3075
Fraktur, Angel, Crossed Legs, Watercolor, Ink, John Kiehn, Pa., c.1808, 16 x 19 In. ....*illus* 4920
Fraktur, Beloved Friend, Fruit, Wreath, Pinprick, Watercolor, 1854, 9 x 10 ½ In. ....*illus* 413
Fraktur, Birth & Baptism, Tulips, Birds, Girl, Stags, Esther Rohrback, 1813, 9 x 13 In. 1534
Fraktur, Birth Record, Multicolor, Samuel Fisher, 1808, 7 x 5 ½ In. 2006
Fraktur, Birth, Watercolor, Ink, Cutout Border, Tulip, Hearts, Carolus Gabel, 1799, Penn., 15 In. 3120
Fraktur, Birth, Watercolor, Ink, Jacob Wiest, December 29, 1824, Samuel Bentz, Penn., 11 In. .. 1140
Fraktur, Bookplate, Bible Verse, Watercolor, Ink, Red, Yellow, Black, Frame, c.1815, 7 x 5 In. 1968
Fraktur, Bookplate, Flower, Heart, Verse, Watercolor, Christina Rithin, Pa., 1796, 5 x 2 ½ In. 561
Fraktur, Parrots, Verse, July 30, 1826, Geo. Walters, Watercolor, Ink, Pa., 14 x 10 In. ....*illus* 7995
Fraktur, Sampler, Hex Sign, Birds, Flowers, Soldier On Horse, Barbara Ebersol, 1864, 11 x 14 In. .. 5900
Fraktur, Symmetrical Birds & Branches, Heart, Inscription, Watercolor, Frame, 1838, 12 x 15 In. . 27060
Handbill, Concert, Rolling Stones, Ardwick Theatre, England, Sept. 28, 1966, 6 x 9 In. 288
House Blessing, Meditation On The 12 Hours, Flowers, Hearts, Henrich Otto, 1785, 16 x 13 In. 2832
Leaf, Illuminated, Book Of Hours, In Latin, Vellum, 2-Sided, Gold, Red, Blue, c.1500, 6 x 4 In. .. 210
Magazine, Playboy, Marilyn Monroe, 1st Issue, Golden Dreams Photo, 1953 2087
Manuscript, Naskhi Script, Arabic, Prisoners Execution, Persia, 1600s, 14 x 9 In. 533
Manuscript, New York Police Blotter, Ellsworth's Zouaves, Bound Folia, 1860 1125

PAPER DOLLS were probably inspired by the pantins, or jumping jacks, made in eighteenth-century Europe. By the 1880s, sheets of printed paper dolls and clothes were being made. The first paper doll books were made in the 1920s. Collectors prefer uncut sheets or books or boxed sets of paper dolls. Prices are about half as much if the pages have been cut.

Baby Sister, Queen Holden, Whitman, 1929, 9 In., Uncut 37
Dolly Dingle, Boyfriend, Nephew, 3 Pages, c.1920, 14 x 10 ¾ In., Uncut 30
Joan & Bobby, Costumes, Merrimack Publishing, 6 Pages, 1920s, 11 In., Uncut 12
Wee Patsy, 2 Dolls, 24 Costumes, Playhouse, Effanbee, 9 Pages, 7 x 10 ¾ In., Uncut 15

PAPERWEIGHTS must have first appeared along with paper in ancient Egypt. Today's collectors search for every type, from the very expensive French weights of the nineteenth century to the modern artist weights or advertising pieces. The glass tops of the paperweights sometimes have been nicked or scratched, and this type of damage can be removed by polishing. Some serious collectors think this type of repair is an alteration and will not buy a repolished weight; others think it is an acceptable technique of restoration that does not change the value. Baccarat paperweights are listed separately under Baccarat.

Angelfish, Blue & White, Pink & Green Fronds, Bubbles, 1996, 3 ¾ In. 400

Paper, Fraktur, Angel, Crossed Legs, Watercolor, Ink, John Kiehn, Pa., c.1808, 16 x 19 In.
$4,920

Skinner, Inc.

Paper, Fraktur, Beloved Friend, Fruit, Wreath, Pinprick, Watercolor, 1854, 9 x 10 ½ In.
$413

Hess Auction Group

Paper, Fraktur, Parrots, Verse, July 30, 1826, Geo. Walters, Watercolor, Ink, Pa., 14 x 10 In.
$7,995

Skinner, Inc.

This is an edited listing of current prices. Visit **Kovels.com** to check thousands of prices from previous years and sign up for free information on trends, tips, reproductions, marks, and more.

Paperweight, Brass, Nautical Sextant Shape, Brass, 3 In.
$69

Ruby Lane

Paperweight, Jade, Dragon In Relief, Oval, Green, Lavender, 3 x 2 In.
$799

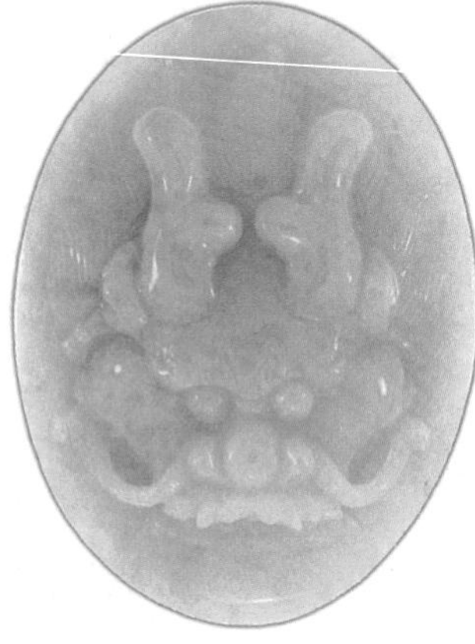

Ruby Lane

Paperweight, Stankard, Root People, Honeycomb, Bee, Ants, Flowers, Berries, 1998, 3 In.
$2,370

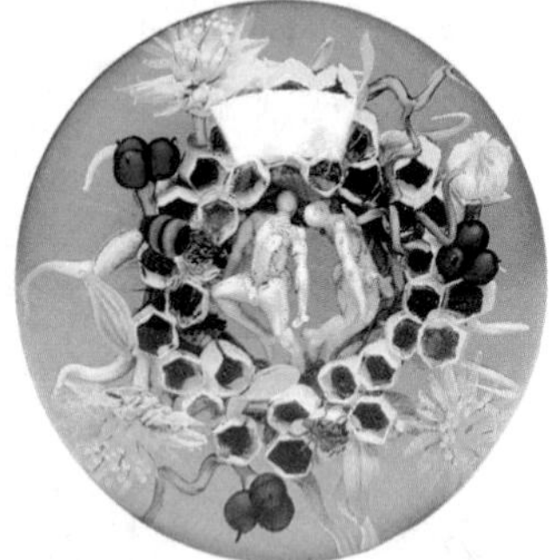

James D. Julia Auctioneers

TIP

Soak dirty pen points in all-purpose liquid household cleanser. After about 12 hours the metal should be clean.

Art Glass, 5-Petal Flower, Fireworks, Multicolor, Stone Ground, 3 ¼ In. 95
Art Glass, Blossoming Blue Flower, Central Bubble, 3 ½ In. 48
Art Glass, Pastel Ribbons & Swirls, 3 ¾ In. 125
Avon, Snowflake, Crystal, Domed, 3 ½ In. Diam. 12
Ayotte, Purple & Red Flowers, White Veining, Round, 3 ½ In. 741
Brass, Nautical Sextant Shape, Brass, 3 In. ....*illus* 69
Bull, Bronze, Cast, Brown Patina, Austria, 4 ½ x 2 ½ In. 81
Caithness, Aztec Rainflower, Abstract, Wedge Shape, Faceted, Fluted, 3 In. 250
Canary, Perched On Box Base, Cormandel Glaze, c.1935, 4 In. 359
Cat, Figural, Wine Madder Glaze, Seated, Looking Up, Base, c.1945, 7 In. 196
Clichy, Millefiori, Concentric Circles, Red, White, Pink, Blue, 2 ½ In. 2607
Crow, Perched, Looking Downward, Blue Over Tan Glaze, 1930, 3 In. 518
Dog, Cocker Spaniel, Glossy Black Glaze, Paw Up, Long Ears, 1953, 4 In. 196
Donkey, Standing, Ivory Matte Glaze, Plank Shape Base, 1937, 6 In. 195
Donofrio, Frog, Lily Pads, Lilies, Purple, Marked, 3 In. 423
Double Goose, Seated, Blue Over Gray Glaze, 1917, 4 In. 219
Elephant, Figural, Pale Blue High Glaze, Standing, c.1945, 4 In. 161
Elephant, Standing, 2 Clowns Caressing Trunk, Blue Over Tan Glaze, Base, 1923, 4 In. 259
Fish, Figural, Blue Over Tan Glaze, Open Mouth, Diamond Pattern Scales, 1928, 5 In. 805
Fox, Cast Iron, Red Paint, Sleeping, Curled Up, c.1950, 6 x 4 ½ In. 265
Fox, Reclining, Aventurine Glaze, Base, 1937, 2 x 6 In. 374
Frog, Silver, Bumps, 2 x 3 In. 228
Jablonski, Adam, Blown Glass, Modern Teardrop Shape, Amethyst, Clear, Poland, 7 In 210
Jade, Dragon In Relief, Oval, Green, Lavender, 3 x 2 In. ....*illus* 799
Kirk Stieff, Lion, Reclining, Pewter, Marked, 2 ¾ x 1 ½ In. 27
Lotton, Cased Pink Flowers, Tangled Black Vines, Metallic Core, 1988, 5 x 5 In. 259
Lotton, Mini Magnum, Tangled Cobalt Blue Vines, Leaves, Round, 4 x 6 In. 207
Lundberg, Stylized Angelfish, Blue Ground, Seaweed, Bubbles, 1874, 2 ¼ In. 115
Millefiori, Concentric Canes, Multicolor, Blue Overlay, 1970s, 3 In. Diam. 477
Monkey On Book, Figural, Seated, Gray Matte Glaze, Amber, 1928, 4 In. 138
Monkey, Seated, Knees To Chest, Nubian Black Glaze, 1938, 4 In. 207
Mouse, Sitting Up, Oval Base, Blue Over Brown Glaze, Glossy, 1937, 3 In. 3220
Murano, Bubbles, 2 Layers, 6 In. 71
Murano, Nautilus Shell Design, Gold Flecks, 1940s, 3 x 2 In. 125
New England, Canes, Concentric Circles, Orange, Green, Purple & Blue, 3 ¼ In. 618
New England, Pink Cog Canes, Blue Star, Running Rabbits, 2 ½ In. 237
Nude Woman, Figural, Seated, Head Tilted, Ivory Matte Glaze, Pottery, 1929, 4 ¼ In. 150
Potter At The Wheel, Round, Brown Glossy Glaze, Pottery, 1935, 4 In. Diam. 374
Redington, Jay, Scarab, Blue Aurene, Magenta & Gold Highlights, Engraved, 4 ¾ In. 118
Rooster, Standing, Multicolor, Flowing Tail, Square Base, Pottery, 1945, 5 In. 288
Rooster, Standing, Square Base, Pink, Black, Glossy Cream Glaze, Pottery, 1952, 5 In. 219
Sailing Ship, Waves, Base, Ivory Matte Glaze, Pottery, c.1924, 4 In. 138
Smith, G., White Flowers, Green Leaves, Red Raspberries, Rectangular, Faceted, 3 In. 1235
St. Louis, Grape Cluster, Mushroom Shape, Clear Cut, Faceted, 1900s, 2 ½ In. 708
Stankard, Blue Flowers, Green Leaves, Breaking Through Sandy Soil, 3 In. 1778
Stankard, Flowers, Bee, Root People, Word Canes, Lampworked Glass, 1997, 2 ½ x 3 In. 4063
Stankard, Root People, Berries, Ants, Bee, Honeycomb, Round, 3 In. 4148
Stankard, Root People, Honeycomb, Bee, Ants, Flowers, Berries, 1998, 3 In. ....*illus* 2370
Stankard, Root People, White Flowers, Buds, Soil, Round, 3 In. 2370
Stankard, Thin Leaf, Berries, Roots, Yellow, Signed, 1900s, 2 ¾ In. 605
Stankard, Thistle, Root, Rippled, 4 x 2 x 2 In. 6950
Stevens, Alfred, Lion, Seated, Bronze, Hammered, Brown Patina, Wellington, 1800s, 5 In. 196
Tiffany Style, Scarab, Iridescent Glass, 2 ½ x 4 ½ In. ....*illus* 250
Turtle, Head Up, Round Base, Brown Over Tan Matte Glaze, 1923, 2 ¼ In. 978
Turtle, Looking Up, Green Over Blue Matte Glaze, 1924, 2 ¼ In. 345
Winking Dog, Figural, Seated, Blue Over Tan Glaze, Matte, Floppy Ears, 1930, 4 In. 460
Ysart, Pink Flowers, White Ground, Domed, 3 In. 432

PAPIER-MACHE is made from paper mixed with glue, chalk, and other ingredients, then molded and baked. It becomes very hard and can be painted. Boxes, trays, and furniture were made of papier-mache. Some of the nineteenth-century pieces were decorated with mother-of-pearl. Papier-mache is still being used to make small toys, figures, candy containers, boxes, and other giftwares. Furniture made of papier-mache is listed in the Furniture category.

Automaton, Dog On Barrel, Popcorn Box On Nose, 32 In. 1220
Box, Gilt & Shell Inlaid, Flower Sprays, Leaves, Hinged Lid, c.1890 625
Box, Monument To Peter The Great, 2001, 3 ¼ x 1 ½ In. 24

Box, Mother-Of-Pearl Inlay, Grand Tour, 1800s, 11 ½ x 9 In. 234
Cigarette Case, Fiddler, Dancer, Woman, Trees, Hinged, Moscow, 1870s, 3 x 1 ¾ In. 395
Dish, William IV, Hunt Scene, Dog, Bird, Rushes, 10 ¾ In. 150
Face Screen, Round, Painted, Birds, Leaves, Gilt, Mahogany Handle, 16 x 9 In., Pair 176
Figure, Dog, Bull Terrier, Standing, Black & White, Erect Ears, Fur Collar, 17 In. 1400
Figure, Dog, Bulldog, Brown, Black Collar, 12 x 19 In. 960
Figure, Dog, Labrador Retriever, Black, 28 x 19 In. 420
Figure, Elephant, Parcel Gilt, Red, Gold, Painted Wheeled Platform, 56 x 69 In. 1750
Figure, Heron, Standing, Green, Blue, Yellow, Mexico, c.1942, 60 x 34 In. 460
Figure, Sheepdog, Shaggy, Signed W. Chazin, 21 x 10 In. 220
Figure, Sun In Hands, Orange, Purple, Sergio Bustamante, 27 ¾ x 19 ½ In. 847
Group, 2 Owls, On Stand, Red Orange, Sergio Bustamante, Signed, 30 In. 500
Hat Stand, Bust, Lady Duff, Painted, 1920s, 15 In. *illus* 384
Mask, Human Face, Paint, Patina, Mounted On Stand, France, c.1855, 14 x 8 In. 1187
Mask, Rooster, 14 x 17 In. 292
Shelf, Flowers, Hinged, Painted, Hanging Holes, 8 x 5 In. 110
Snuffbox, George Washington Portrait, Lacquered, Stobwasser, Germany, 1820s 4250
Tray, Central Reserve, Horse, Stall, Ebonized, Footed, Victorian, 19 ½ x 26 In. 210
Tray, Oval, Raised Edge, Gilt Border, Bamboo Stand, c.1825, 22 x 31 x 23 In. 553
Tray, Painted, Black Lacquer, Mixed Flower Center, Gilt Border, 19 x 24 ½ In. 92
Tray, Painted, Green, Scalloped, Birds, Bouquets, Garlands, Scrollwork, c.1900, 30 x 24 In. 461
Tray, Peacocks, Flowers, Fountain, Scrolled, Painted, 31 x 22 In. 665
Wine Coaster, Grapevines, Leaves, Gilt, Georgian Regency, c.1820, 4 ½ In. 165

PARASOL, *see Umbrella category.*

PARIAN is a fine-grained, hard-paste porcelain named for the marble it resembles. It was first made in England in 1846 and gained in favor in the United States about 1860. Figures, tea sets, vases, and other items were made of Parian at many English and American factories.

Box, Lid, Fox, Bird Under Paw, Basin Shape, Pedestal, Round Handles, 1800s, 5 x 6 In. 121
Bust, Man, Wavy Hair, Ruffled Shirt, 17 In. 200
Bust, Napoleon, 9 ⅜ In. 138
Figurine, Cupid's Kiss, Stepped Leaf Relief Base, Bird's Nest, c.1900, 24 x 10 ½ In. 178
Group, Ino & Infant Bacchus, Seated, Gown, Baby Laying In Lap, c.1850, 12 x 10 In. 189
Group, Nude, Woman, Grooming Lion, White, 11 ½ In. 313
Pitcher, Iris, Stems, Reeded Ground, Glazed, Frederick Dallas Pottery, c.1878, 5 ½ In. 354

PARIS, Vieux Paris, or Old Paris, is porcelain ware that is known to have been made in Paris in the eighteenth or early nineteenth century. These porcelains have no identifying mark but can be recognized by the whiteness of the porcelain and the lines and decorations. Gold decoration is often used.

Bowl, Flowers, Footed, 8 x 18 In. 450
Cachepot, Flowers, Parcel Gilt, Leaves, Legs, 1900s, 9 ½ x 8 In. 302
Epergne, Pink, Flower Transfer, Gilt Leaf Scalloped Edge, Fluted Vase, Metal Base, 25 x 16 In. 173
Figurine, Bohemian Man, Woman, Costumes, Gold Trim, c.1875, 14 In., Pair 1000
Figurine, Woman, Multicolor Dress, Gilt & Blue Base, Flowers, 1800s, 24 x 9 In. 431
Jardiniere, Reserves, Amorous Couple, Flowers, Waisted Oval Body, Leaf Handles, 11 x 19 In. 800
Pitcher, Woman, Formal Gown, Flowers, Baluster, Leaf Handle, 7 In. 210
Plate, Cornflowers In Center, Puce Flowers, Scalloped Gilt Rim, 1700s, 8 ½ In., 15 Piece 125
Plate, Gilt, Green, Center Bouquet, Flowers On Rim, Boyer St. De Feuillet, 9 In., 12 Piece 2432
Tazza, Gilt, Royal Blue, Tripartite Base, Paw Feet, Pinecones, Leaf Border, 5 ¾ x 9 ¼ In. 615
Tureen, Parcel Gilt, Fruit Finial, Dome Lid, 12 ½ x 13 ½ In. 425
Urn, Landscapes, Courting Couples, Gilt, Red, Orange, 1800s, 10 ¾ x 8 In. 610
Urn, White, Mask, Square Foot, 11 ¼ In. 120
Vase, Classical Scenes, Black Matte Ground, Gilt, Bulbous, Flared Neck, c.1880, 20 In., Pair 431
Vase, Flower Basket, Scroll Handles, Ram's Head Terminals, Bisque Swags, 12 In., Pair 2250
Vase, Flowers, Matte & Burnished Gilt, Swan Handles, 10 ¾ In., Pair *illus* 793
Vase, Fox & Boar Hunt, Gold Ground, Krater, 1820, 12 ¾ In. 6250
Vase, Gilt, Blue Ground, Landscapes, Interiors, 10 In., Pair 500
Vase, Gilt, Lilac, Lime Green Accents, 10 x 5 In., Pair 188
Vase, Mantel, Painted Reserves, Gold Accents, Floral Handles, 16 ½ In., Pair 300
Vase, Mother & Child, Landscape, Flowers, Pink, Gilt, 18 ½ x 13 In. 156
Vase, Multicolor Flowers, Gilt Handles, 14 ½ In. 188
Vase, Parcel Gilt, Oval, Flowers, Handles, Ribbon, 1900s, 16 x 10 ¾ In., Pair 484
Vase, Reserves, Birds, Roses, Blue, White, Flared, 11 ¼ x 8 ⅜ In. 307

Paperweight, Tiffany Style, Scarab, Iridescent Glass, 2 ½ x 4 ½ In.
$250

Papier-Mache, Hat Stand, Bust, Lady Duff, Painted, 1920s, 15 In.
$384

Hess Auction Group

Paris, Vase, Flowers, Matte & Burnished Gilt, Swan Handles, 10 ¾ In., Pair
$793

Neal Auctions

P

Pate-De-Verre, Bowl, Lilac & Jade Color, Openwork, Arrow Design, 1992, 8 x 10 In.
$3,375

Rago Arts and Auction Center

Pate-De-Verre, Figurine, Rooster, Green Glass, Yellow Feet, Rectangular Base, 5 ½ In.
$2,074

James D. Julia Auctioneers

Patent Model, Ironing Board, P. P. Harter, 1913, 7 ½ x 13 ¼ In.
$395

Ruby Lane

Names for Peachblow

Peachblow glass varies in color from one company to another. Even the names are confusing. Original trade ads used the term as one or two words. The companies themselves used different names in their ads: Coral, Peach Bloom, Peach Blow, Peach Skin, or Wild Rose.

PATE-DE-VERRE is an ancient technique in which glass is made by blending and refining powdered glass of different colors into molds. The process was revived by French glassmakers, especially Galle, around the end of the nineteenth century.

Bowl, Lilac & Jade Color, Openwork, Arrow Design, 1992, 8 x 10 In. ... *illus* 3375
Dish, Artist's Palette Shape, Amber, Leaves, Flowers, c.1920, 11 In. ... 2500
Figurine, Rooster, Green Glass, Yellow Feet, Rectangular Base, 5 ½ In. ... *illus* 2074
Lamp Shade, Umbrella Form Top, Folded, Turquoise Shaded To Blue, c.1920, 6 In. ... 1375
Plaque, Lizard Climbing Tree, Birds, Mottled, Raised Border, H. Crois, 10 x 7 In. ... 2963
Plaque, Rodent Eating Orange & Yellow Berries, Mottled Blue & White, 7 x 9 In. ... 3555
Tray, Nude Woman, Lying On Grassy Knoll, Swirling Green & Yellow, 7 x 3 In. ... 3259
Vase, Blue & Seafoam, Openwork, Zigzag Cutout Design, Round, 19 x 13 In. ... 6250
Vase, Lotus, Pink Blossom, Unfurling Aquamarine Leaves, 1900s, 18 x 11 In. ... 1968
Vase, Rose Passion, Flared, Molded Roses & Leaves, Amber, 1900s, 12 In. ... 1722

PATENT MODELS were required as part of a patent application for a United States patent until 1880. In 1926 the stored patent models were sold as a group by the U.S. Patent Office, and individual models are now appearing in the marketplace.

Canal Boat, Charles Hermance, Aluminum, Inscribed Label, 1872, 17 ½ In. ... 180
Ironing Board, P. P. Harter, 1913, 7 ½ x 13 ¼ In. ... *illus* 395
Window Guard, Gabriel Konigsberg, Wood, Cross Bars, Sliding Panes, 1874, 12 x 6 ½ In. ... 246

PATE-SUR-PATE means paste on paste. The design was made by painting layers of slip on the ceramic piece until a relief decoration was formed. The method was developed at the Sevres factory in France about 1850. It became even more famous at the English Minton factory about 1870. It has since been used by many potters to make both pottery and porcelain wares.

Plaque, Courting Couple, Green, Wooden Frame, Scrolls, Acanthus, 18 x 9 In. ... 250
Plaque, Lune De Meil, Taxile Doat, Signed, France, 1882, 8 ¾ x 6 ¼ In. ... *illus* 2250
Plaque, Nude Woman, Holding Cherub, Sheer Gown, String Of Cherubs, c.1907, 8 x 3 In. ... 3500
Plate, Meissen, Mythology, Cobalt Blue Over White, Gilt Bands, 8 ½ In. ... 1971
Urn, Cobalt Blue, Courting Couple, Germany, 15 x 7 In. ... 100
Vase, Bird, Leaves, Brown, Round, Flat, 6 x 7 In. ... 86
Vase, Dark, Putti, Butterfly, Gilt Decoration, 13 x 8 In., Pair ... 338
Vase, Ivory, Bird, Reeds, Umber, Gilt, Flattened Oval, Flared, Ring Handles, c.1890, 8 In. ... 598

PAUL REVERE POTTERY was made at several locations in and around Boston, Massachusetts, between 1906 and 1942. The pottery was operated as a settlement house program for teenage girls. Many pieces were signed *S.E.G.* for Saturday Evening Girls. The artists concentrated on children's dishes and tiles. Decorations were outlined in black and filled with color.

Bowl, House & Tree In Medallion, Shades Of Blue, S.E.G., 1920, 3 x 7 In. ... 369
Jar, Lid, Squirrel On Branch In Medallion, Blue, Tapered, S.E.G., c.1920, 5 In. ... 615
Mug Set, Tree In Medallion, Light & Dark Blue, A. Mangini, S.E.G., 3 ⅝ In., 6 Piece ... 1230
Pitcher, Blue, S.E.G., 6 x 5 In. ... 108
Pitcher, White Goose In Medallion, Light & Dark Blue, Handle, S.E.G., 4 ¼ In. ... 400
Plate, House Landscape In Medallion, Blue, Cutout Handles, S.E.G., 9 ½ In. ... 584
Sugar & Creamer, House Landscape In Medallion, Blue Ground, S.E.G., 1920, 4 In. ... 615
Teapot, House In Medallion, Light & Dark Blue, Mangini, Goodman, S.E.G., 5 In. ... 400
Vase, Band Of Hills & Trees, Cobalt Glaze, E. Geneco, S.E.G., 1908, 10 In. ... *illus* 1845
Vase, Daffodils, Cuerda Seca, Tapered, Rolled Rim, S. Galner, 1915, 11 In. ... *illus* 2625

PEACHBLOW glass was made by several factories beginning in the 1880s. New England peachblow is a one-layer glass shading from red to white. Mt. Washington peachblow shades from pink to bluish-white. Hobbs, Brockunier and Company of Wheeling, West Virginia, made Coral glass that it marketed as Peachblow. It shades from yellow to peach and is lined with white glass. Reproductions of all types of peachblow have been made. Related pieces may be listed under Gundersen and Webb Peachblow.

Cruet, Glossy, Opal Interior, Amber Handle, Faceted Stopper, Wheeling, 7 In. ... *illus* 230
Pitcher, Water, Bulbous, Applied Camphor Handle, 8 ¼ In. ... *illus* 288
Shaker, Powdered Sugar, Tapered, Shaded, Glossy, Pierced Screw Cap, 5 ¼ In. ... 690
Vase, Bottle Shape, Satin Glass, Peach To Fuchsia, Figural Dragon Pedestal, c.1900, 10 In. ... 750
Vase, Cased, Crimped Folded Mouth, Trumpet Neck, Stevens & Williams, c.1890, 14 In. ... 211
Vase, Clear Shaded To Cranberry, Enamel, Flower Handles, England, c.1890, 12 In. ... 390
Vase, Lily, Dark Pink Shaded To White, Inverted Saucer Foot, Ruffled Rim, 12 In. ... 356
Vase, Morgan, Cased, 5-Griffin Stand, Hobbs, Brockunier & Co., c.1890, 10 In. ... *illus* 413

Pate-Sur-Pate, Plaque, Lune De Meil, Taxile Doat, Signed, France, 1882, 8 ¾ x 6 ¼ In.
$2,250

Rago Arts and Auction Center

Paul Revere, Vase, Band Of Hills & Trees, Cobalt Glaze, E. Geneco, S.E.G., 1908, 10 In.
$1,845

Skinner, Inc.

Paul Revere, Vase, Daffodils, Cuerda Seca, Tapered, Rolled Rim, S. Galner, 1915, 11 In.
$2,625

Rago Arts and Auction Center

Peachblow, Cruet, Glossy, Opal Interior, Amber Handle, Faceted Stopper, Wheeling, 7 In.
$230

Early Auction Company

Peachblow, Pitcher, Water, Bulbous, Applied Camphor Handle, 8 ¼ In.
$288

Early Auction Company

TIP

The handle on a glass jug is a clue to the jug's age. About 1860 handles were applied at the bottom first, creating a thick blob, then drawn to the top and affixed to the edge. Before 1860 the handles were applied at the top first, then drawn toward the bottom, stuck to the body of the pitcher, and curled upward.

Peachblow, Vase, Morgan, Cased, 5-Griffin Stand, Hobbs, Brockunier & Co., c.1890, 10 In.
$413

Brunk Auctions

Peachblow, Vase, Stick, Glossy, Mahogany Shaded To Custard, Long Neck, Wheeling, 9 In.
$374

Early Auction Company

Peachblow, Vase, Stick, White & Yellow Daisies, Bulbous, Mt. Washington, 8 In.
$2,012

Early Auction Company

P

Peanuts, Button, Moon Landing, Snoopy, I'm On The Moon, Simon Simple, 1969, 1 ¾ In.
$240

Hake's Americana & Collectibles

Peanuts, Toy, Bus, Peanuts Special, Characters, Battery Operated, Tin Litho, Chein, 1966, 14 In.
$278

Hake's Americana & Collectibles

Tokens

If you find a box of old coins and coin-like items or "tokens," don't throw any away. Sometimes the things that are not real money have more value than coins. Streetcar tokens, political tokens, medallions commemorating special events, and even lodge tokens have value.

Pearlware, Jug, Marbled, Grooved Loop Handle, Applied Swags, Slip Ground Agate, c.1790, 5 In.
$1,046

Skinner, Inc.

Vase, Satin, Double Gourd Shape, Mt. Washington, 6 ¾ In. 575
Vase, Stick, Glossy, Mahogany Shaded To Custard, Long Neck, Wheeling, 9 In. .... *illus* 374
Vase, Stick, Glossy, Wheeling, 8 ½ In. 288
Vase, Stick, J.H. Hobbs, Brockunier & Co., c.1885, 9 ¼ In. 272
Vase, Stick, White & Yellow Daisies, Bulbous, Mt. Washington, 8 In. .... *illus* 2012
Vase, Wheeling, 6 ¾ x 6 ½ In. 298

PEANUTS is the title of a comic strip created by cartoonist Charles M. Schulz (1922–2000). The strip, drawn by Schulz from 1950 to 2000, features a group of children, including Charlie Brown and his sister Sally, Lucy Van Pelt and her brother Linus, Peppermint Patty, and Pig Pen, and an imaginative and independent beagle named Snoopy. The Peanuts gang has also been featured in books, television shows, and a Broadway musical.

Bobble Head, Lucy, Frowning, Red Dress, Black Square Base, 5 ½ In. 60
Button, Moon Landing, Snoopy, I'm On The Moon, Simon Simple, 1969, 1 ¾ In. .... *illus* 240
Comic Strip Art, Linus, Snoopy, Signed, Frame, 1970, 10 ¾ x 32 ¼ In. 13420
Figure, Schroeder, At Piano, Beethoven's Bust, Vinyl, c.1960, 7 ½ In. 480
Lunch Box, Snoopy, Woodstock, Metal, King-Seeley, c.1980 115
Nodder, Lucy, Porcelain, Blue Dress, 3 ¾ In. 24
Toy, Bus, Peanuts Special, Characters, Battery Operated, Tin Litho, Chein, 1966, 14 In. .... *illus* 278

PEARL items listed here are made of the natural mother-of-pearl from shells. Such natural pearl has been used to decorate furniture and small utilitarian objects for centuries. The glassware known as mother-of-pearl is listed by that name. Opera glasses made with natural pearl shell are listed under Opera Glasses.

Box, Inlay, Brown, Gilt Flowers, 2 Hinged Flaps, Japan, 9 ¼ x 21 ¾ In. 360
Card Case, Engraved, 4 x 3 In. 54
Card Case, Silver, Group In Garden, 4 ¼ x 3 ¾ In. 400
Desk Set, Dore Bronze, Shaped, Vine, Leaf, 2 Inkwells, 6 ½ x 8 In. 181
Dresser Box, Inlay, Bands, Keyhole, England, 1800s, 10 x 7 In. 97
Necessaire, Crystal Perfume Bottle, Silver Funnel, Pique Work, France, 1700s, 3 ¾ In. 1416
Sculpture, Mosaic, Inlaid, Abalone, Shell Shape, 40 ½ x 18 In. 95

PEARLWARE is an earthenware made by Josiah Wedgwood in 1779. It was copied by other potters in England. Pearlware is only slightly different in color from creamware and for many years collectors have confused the terms. Wedgwood pieces are listed in the Wedgwood category in this book. Most pearlware with mocha designs is listed under Mocha.

Pearl

Bowl, Double Stroke 3-Color Designs, 3 Blue Rings, 8 ¾ x 4 ⅜ In. 180
Figure, Lion, Standing, Stepped & Pierced Base, Portugal, c.1910, 4 ½ x 6 In. 86
Flask, Heart Shape, Multicolor, Sport Scenes, Staffordshire, c.1810, 6 In. 615
Group, Elephant, Curled Trunk, Tusks, Indian Driver, Staffordshire, 9 x 8 ¾ In. 7200
Group, Polito's Menagerie, Obadiah Sheratt, Staffordshire, 1820, 12 ¾ In. 11250
Jug, Marbled, Grooved Loop Handle, Applied Swags, Slip Ground Agate, c.1790, 5 In. .... *illus* 1046
Plaque, Lions, Pratt Type, High Relief, Oval, Leaf Border, c.1800, 17 In. 2706
Platter, Stand, Blue Transfer Print, River With Temple, Staffordshire, 1800s, 19 In. 923
Puzzle Jug, Plymouth, Pierced Neck, 3 Duck-Shaped Spouts, Flowers, c.1827, 5 In. 584
Teapot, Cabbage Rose, Black, Green, Red, Yellow, c.1840, 6 ¼ x 10 In. 210
Tureen, Lid, Blue Transfer, Lion's Head Finial & Handles, England, c.1810, 8 x 13 In. 180
Waste Bowl, Strawberry, Leafy Vine, Blue Border, Wide Rim, 1700s, 3 x 6 In. 177

PEKING GLASS is a Chinese cameo glass first made popular in the eighteenth century. The Chinese have continued to make this layered glass in the old manner, and many new pieces are now available that could confuse the average buyer.

Bowl, Emerald Green, 7 Lobes, Footed, c.1900, 8 ¾ In. 400
Bowl, Pink, Cats, Birds, Butterflies, Flowers, Ring Foot, 1700s, 6 In. 711
Censer, Lid, White, Molded, Reticulated, Flowers, Leaves, 6 x 7 ¾ In. 460
Cup, White, Basket Weave, Reticulated, Grotesque C-Scroll Handles, 9 ¼ In. 278
Disk, Ritual, Ruby Glass, Swirling Chih Lung, Clouds, 1700s, 8 In. Diam., Pair 8058
Jar, Cover, Peonies, Rockwork, Green Over White, Chinese, 1800s, 9 ¼ In. .... *illus* 610
Jar, Lid, Black Overlay Designs, c.1950, 10 x 6 In. 210
Jar, Pine, Prunus, Bamboo, Yellow & Turquoise, Rounded Square, c.1800, 4 In. 2370
Snuff Bottle, White, Flattened, Blue Cabochon Stopper, Spoon, 3 x 2 ½ In. 127
Vase, Birds, Branches, White, Blue Overlay, Chinese, 20th Century, 13 In., Pair .... *illus* 960
Vase, Bottle Shape, Dark Blue To Light, Peach Tree, Rocks, c.1800, 6 In. 533
Vase, Bottle Shape, Pale Blue, Chih Lung Hydras, c.1800, 6 In. 948

P

Vase, Bottle Shape, Red Cut To Snowflake, Flowers, c.1800, 11 In. 2074
Vase, Bottle Shape, Red To Yellow, Applied Jui Foot, 1700s, 10 In. ....*illus* 1067
Vase, Bottle Shape, Ring Foot, Pink, Green, Birds, Flowers, 1700s, 10 In. 7110
Vase, Bottle Shape, Transparent Red, Fluted Sides, Ring Foot, c.1800, 9 In. 7703
Vase, Bottle Shape, Turquoise, Globular, Long Neck, 1700s, 13 In., Pair 1422
Vase, Flowers, Leaves, Green, Pink, Yellow, Red, Oval, 1800s, 5 x 5 In. 1778
Vase, Lid, White Ground, Multicolor Plants, 1800s, 8 In. ....*illus* 3555
Vase, Orange, White, Wood Stand, Chinese, 9 In. 150
Vase, Pink & White, Court Lady In Reserve, Hexagonal, c.1800, 7 ¾ x 4 In. 676
Vase, White, Pink Overlay, Dragons, Swollen Shoulder, c.1800, 8 In. 4740
Vase, Yellow, Masks, Leaves, Globular, Trumpet Neck, Saucer Foot, 4 In. 2844

PENS replaced hand-cut quills as writing instruments in 1780, when the first steel pen point was made in England. But it was 100 years before the commercial pen was a common item. The fountain pen was invented in the 1830s but was not made in quantity until the 1880s. All types of old pens are collected. Float pens that feature small objects floating in a liquid as part of the handle are popular with collectors. Advertising pens are listed in the Advertising section of this book.

PEN

Calligraphy Set, Victorian, Rolled Gold, Sienna Amber, Banded Agate, Box, 1800s, 7 x 2 ½ In. . 380
Montblanc, Ballpoint, Black, Meisterstuck 146, Resin, 14K, 5 ½ x ¾ In. .... 126 to 230
Montblanc, Fountain, Peter I, The Great, Gold Plated, Green Resin, Box, 5 ⅝ In. 1250
Tiffany, Dip Pen, Pine Needle, Bronze, Waterman Nib, 6 ¾ In. 1003
Tiffany, Stylized Bamboo, 14K Gold, Marked, Tiffany & Co., 4 ⅛ In. ....*illus* 861
Wahl Eversharp, Fountain, 14K Gold Nib, Green Onyx, Desk Stand, 6 x 3 ½ In. 31

PEN & PENCIL

Combination Pen & Pencil, Mabie Todd, 14K Gold, Repousse Leaves, Scrolls, 4 ¼ In. 345

PENCILS were invented, so it is said, in 1565. The eraser was not added to the pencil until 1858. The automatic pencil was invented in 1863. Collectors today want advertising pencils or automatic pencils of unusual design. Boxes and sharpeners for pencils are also collected. Advertising pencils are listed in the Advertising category. Pencil boxes are listed in the Box category.

PENCIL

Architect, Sterling Silver, Edwardian, Built-In Ruler, c.1910, 12 In. 600
Conte, Case, Silver, Bows, Leaves, Monogram, Oak Garland, France, 1800s, 3 In. ....*illus* 175
Dixon, Lead, Red & Black, No. 998-H, U.S.A., 8 ½ In. 5
Mechanical, 9K Gold, Scrolls, Victorian, England, c.1900, 4 In. 465
Mechanical, 14K Gold, Embossed, Citrine, 4 ½ In. 447
Mechanical, Airship Shape, USS Los Angeles, Metal, Tail Slides Out, 1920s, 2 ½ In. 190
Mechanical, Black & White Enamel, Scrolls, In Memory Of, 19th Century, 3 ⅜ In. 495
Mechanical, Chatelaine, Victorian Rose, Gold Filled, Inlaid Abalone, c.1880, 3 ½ In. 250
Mechanical, Cross, Geometric, 14K Gold Filled, 2 ½ In. 185
Mechanical, Eversharp, 14K Gold Filled, Box 19
Mechanical, Goldtone, Art Deco, Curb Chain, c.1930, 3 ⅝ In. 65
Mechanical, Gun Shape, White Metal, Mahogany, 1800s, 4 In. 321
Mechanical, Mabie Todd, Gold Filled, Ornate, Box 199
Mechanical, Mabie, Hard Black Rubber, Gold Filled Rim, Pat. Oct. 3, 1854, 4 In. 120
Mechanical, Stanhope, Bellow, Wood, Metal, c.1880, 3 In. 957
Mechanical, Sterling Silver, Cartouche, Repousse, 3 ⅞ In. 135
Mechanical, Tiffany & Co., 14K Gold, Hexagonal, Monogram, 5 ½ In. 690
Mechanical, Wahl, Gold Filled, Chatelaine, Edwardian, Box, c.1920, 4 In. 65
S. Mordan Co., 9K Gold, Barley Corn Pattern, 4 In. 350
Sterling Silver, Enamel, Guilloche, Engraved, 1800s, 3 In. 75
Tiffany & Co., 14K Gold, Square Ribbed, Built-In Watch, Art Deco, c.1900 808
Victorian, Gold Filled, Repousse, End Ring, 5 ¼ In. 95

PENCIL SHARPENER

Alarm Clock, Nickel Plated, Glass Bezel, Germany, 1920s, 1 ¾ x 1 ¼ In. 169
Angell Co., Cast Iron, Tin Hopper, Wood Platform, Boston, 5 In. 619
Bakelite, Green, Key Chain, 1930s, 1 ¾ In. 25
Car, Sedan, Cast Metal, Red, Silver, Germany, 1 ¾ In. 75
Cash Register, Contado, Die Cast, 2 ½ x 2 In. 19
Clock Face, Metal, Fuchsia Paint, Japan, 1940s, 1 ½ x 1 In. 12
Dog, Bulldog's Head, Badger Collar, Black Metal, Occupied Japan, 1 ½ In. 90
Dog, Scottie, Bakelite, Red, 1 ¾ x 1 ¼ In. 52
Donald Duck, Waving, Decal, Round, c.1940, 1 ¹⁄₁₆ In. 36

Peking Glass, Jar, Cover, Peonies, Rockwork, Green Over White, Chinese, 1800s, 9 ¼ In.
$610

Neal Auctions

TIP
Never allow water to evaporate in a glass vase. It will leave a white residue that may be impossible to remove.

Peking Glass, Vase, Birds, Branches, White, Blue Overlay, Chinese, 20th Century, 13 In., Pair
$960

Cowan Auctions

Peking Glass, Vase, Bottle Shape, Red To Yellow, Applied Jui Foot, 1700s, 10 In.
$1,067

James D. Julia Auctioneers

Peking Glass, Vase, Lid, White Ground, Multicolor Plants, 1800s, 8 In.
$3,555

James D. Julia Auctioneers

Pen, Tiffany, Stylized Bamboo, 14K Gold, Marked, Tiffany & Co., 4 ⅛ In.
$861

Skinner, Inc.

Pencils, Conte, Case, Silver, Bows, Leaves, Monogram, Oak Garland, France, 1800s, 3 In.
$175

Ruby Lane

Pencil Sharpener, Machine, Cast Iron, Gears, Handle, E.S. Simpson, Patented, Sept. 2, 1884
$8,226

Auction Team Breker

Pepsi-Cola, Sign, Double Dash, Tin, Embossed, 17 x 6 ¼ In.
$240

Showtime Auction Services

Research Help
When doing research into the history of your antiques and collectibles, avoid depending on old books. Company materials, like original catalogs, are fine. New scientific methods, archaeological digs, and years of research have turned up many errors and myths found in early information. This year we made minor additions or corrections to over thirty paragraphs in this book.

Perfume Bottle, Atomizer, Glass, Swirled, Painted, Pansies, Pairpoint, 1894, 7 In.
$70

Ruby Lane

Perfume Bottle, Atomizer, Red, Iridescent Leaves, Charles Lotton, 1993, 8 ¾ In.
$531

Humler & Nolan

Perfume Bottle, Christian Dior, J'Appartiens, Dog Shape, Silk Box Doghouse, 1957, 7 In.
$67,650

Perfume Bottles Auction

Elephant, Trunk Up, Celluloid, 2 In. 60
Globe, Germany, 1920s, 3 ⅝ In. 155
Hand Crank, Maroon, Yellow, Painted, Ever Handy, Hunt Pen Co., 3 x 3 x 4 In. 18
Hand Pump, Die Cast, Spain, 3 ½ In. 29
Lamppost, 5 Lights, 5 In. 22
Machine, Cast Iron, Gears, Handle, E.S. Simpson, Patented, Sept. 2, 1884 .... *illus* 8226
Model KS, Boston Pencil Sharpener Co., c.1894 24
Phonograph, Play Me, 3 ¼ x 2 ½ In. 16
Pistol, Metal, Silver Paint, Germany, 3 In. 38
Sterling Silver, Cylindrical, 1 ½ x 1 ⅞ In. 195
Wall Mounted, Boston Model, KS, c.1894 24

PENNSBURY POTTERY worked in Morrisville, Pennsylvania, from 1950 to 1971. Full sets of dinnerware as well as many decorative items were made. Pieces are marked with the name of the factory.

Pennsbury Pottery

Amish, Cookie Jar, 7 ½ In. 85
Amish, Mug, 3 ⅛ In. 35
Red Rooster, Creamer, 2 ½ In. 12
Star, Plate, Locomotive, Central New Jersey R.R., 1870, c.1950, 7 x 5 In. 18

PEPSI-COLA, the drink and the name, was invented in 1898 but was not trademarked until 1903. The logo was changed from an elaborate script to the modern block letters in 1963. Several different logos have been used. Until 1951, the words *Pepsi* and *Cola* were separated by two dashes. These bottles are called "double dash." In 1951 the modern logo with a single hyphen was introduced. All types of advertising memorabilia are collected, and reproductions are being made.

PEPSI-COLA

Clock, Enjoy Pepsi Anytime!, Metal, Analog, Yellow Border, 32 x 45 ½ In. 180
Clock, Red, White & Blue, Round, Electric, 15 ½ In. Diam. 180
Clock, Think Young, Say Pepsi Please, Bottle Cap, Yellow, 1961, 16 x 16 In. 150
Cooler, Ice Chest, Drink Pepsi-Cola, Gray & Red, Handle, 1950s, 19 x 22 In. 336
Menu Board, Bottle Caps, Order Of The Day!, Metal Frame, 1950s, 21 x 13 ½ In. 390
Refrigerator, Hits The Spot, Bottle Cap Logo, Bottle, Blue, Frigidaire, 32 x 57 In. 1320
Sign, Ask For Pepsi-Cola, The Perfect Mixer, Celluloid, Blue, Red, White, Round, 9 In. 120
Sign, Bottle, 5 Cents, Tin, 46 x 16 In. 360
Sign, Buvez Pepsi, Yellow Border, Enameled Metal, Grommets, France, 13 x 29 In. 120
Sign, Chalkboard, Say Pepsi Please, Tin, Embossed, 27 x 19 In. 60
Sign, Double Dash, Tin, Embossed, 17 x 6 ¼ In. .... *illus* 240
Sign, Drink Pepsi-Cola Ice Cold, Bottle Cap, Plastic, Metal, Light-Up, 16 In. 360
Sign, Drink Pepsi-Cola, 5 Cents, Red, White, Blue, Tin, Embossed, 1940s, 30 x 10 In. 570
Sign, Pepsi-Cola, Bottle Cap Shape, Blue, Tin Embossed, Red, White, 1963, 28 In. Diam. 234
Thermometer, Bigger, Better, Bottle, Double Dash, Blue, Tin, 16 x 6 In. 125
Thermometer, Bottle Cap, Rounded Corners, Metal, Yellow, Red, Blue, 1950s, 27 In. 150
Thermometer, Have A Pepsi, Bottle Cap, Yellow, 1950s, 27 In. 225
Thermometer, Sign, Big Big Bottle, Hits The Spot, Tin Lithograph, 27 x 7 In. 480
Urn, Syrup, Lid, Blue, Green, Trees, Saucer Base, Porcelain, 18 In. 28800
Vending Machine, Roulette, Cooler, Bottle Cap, Blue, Round, Footed, 1940s, 28 x 48 In. 9760
Vending Machine, Royal Blue, Drink Pepsi-Cola, Bottle Cap, 27 x 78 In. 510

PERFUME BOTTLES are made of cut glass, pressed glass, art glass, silver, metal, enamel, and even plastic or porcelain. Although the small bottle to hold perfume was first made before the time of ancient Egypt, it is the nineteenth- and twentieth-century examples that interest today's collector. DeVilbiss Company has made atomizers of all types since 1888 but no longer makes the perfume bottle tops so popular with collectors. These were made from 1920 to 1968. The glass bottle may be by any of many manufacturers even if the atomizer is marked *DeVilbiss*. The word *factice*, which often appears in ads, refers to store display bottles. Glass or porcelain examples may be found under the appropriate name such as Lalique, Czechoslovakia, Glass-Bohemian, etc.

Asian Woman's Head, Figural, Crown Top, Germany, 1920s, 3 ½ In. 185
Atomizer, Airplane, Enameled Glass Bottle, Chromed Metalwork, 1930s, 7 In. 2460
Atomizer, Cranberry, Cut To Clear, Enamel, Gilt, c.1920, 7 ¾ In. 2460
Atomizer, Glass, Swirled, Painted, Pansies, Pairpoint, 1894, 7 In. .... *illus* 70
Atomizer, Purple, Blue, Iridescent, Gilt, Pallme-Koenig, 1880s, 4 ¾ In. 615
Atomizer, Red, Iridescent Leaves, Charles Lotton, 1993, 8 ¾ In. .... *illus* 531
Christian Dior, J'Appartiens, Dog Shape, Silk Box Doghouse, 1957, 7 In. .... *illus* 67650
Clear, Gilt Wheel Cut Drape, Tassel, Rose Bouquet Cover, 1960s, 8 In. 278
Cloisonne, Gilt Silver, Bottle Shape, Screw Cap, Stylized Flowers, Russia, 3 In. 590

Perfume Bottle, Cobalt Blue Over Clear, Blown, Faceted Body & Stopper, Tiers, 6 ½ In.
$144

Fox Auctions

Perfume Bottle, Man, Dandy, Painted, Leather Coat, Stopper, Parera Varon, 1951, 5 In.
$9,840

Perfume Bottles Auction

Perfume Bottle, Mickey Mouse, Porcelain, Luster Glaze, Marked, Made In Japan, 1930s, 5 In.
$369

Perfume Bottles Auction

Peters & Reed, Vase, Landsun, Scenic, Trees, Rolling Hills, 1910, 13 In.
$615

Ruby Lane

Peters & Reed, Vase, Moss Aztec, Daisies, Molded, Red Clay, Green Accents, c.1915, 6 In.
$60

Ruby Lane

Pewter, Bowl, Crimped, Marked, Standish Solid Pewter, Benedict, 2 ½ x 7 In.
$65

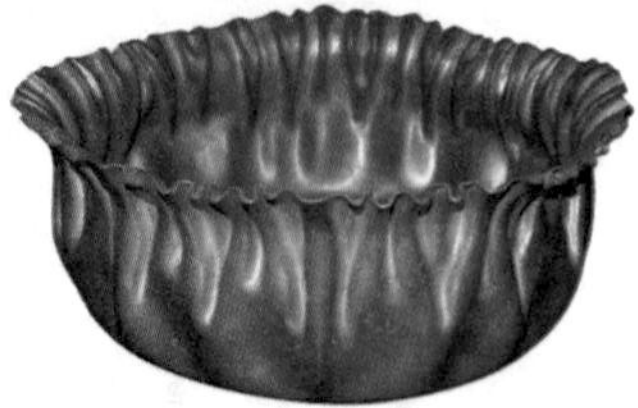

Ruby Lane

Cobalt Blue Over Clear, Blown, Faceted Body & Stopper, Tiers, 6 ½ In. .... *illus* 144
DeVilbiss, Atomizer, Black, Stylized Gold Leaves, Silver, Gilt Metal, 6 ¾ In. 1169
DeVilbiss, Atomizer, Blue, Iridescent, 1925, 10 In. 1107
DeVilbiss, Atomizer, Clear Shoulders, Frosted Blue Base, Gilt, 6 ¾ In. 738
DeVilbiss, Atomizer, Green, Red Poppies, Enamel, Gilt, 1926, 10 In. 800
DeVilbiss, Atomizer, Marigold, Signed .... 50 to 60
Enameled, Clear, Black, Red Beads, Molded Swirl Design, Stopper, c.1925, 3 In. 875
Flower Shape Stopper, Red To Clear, Oval Pattern, Bohemia, c.1900, 9 In. 500
Glass, Diamond Pattern, Clear, Round, Silver Hinge, H. Wilkenson, c.1901, 5 ⅜ In. 99
Gold Favrile, Applied Green Hearts & Vines, Stopper, Tiffany, 1913, 5 In. 1888
Green Opaline, Gilt Metal Carriage Mount, Palais Royal, 1880s, 14 In. 4305
Guerlain, Muguet, Clear, Onionskin Seal, Ribbon, 1920, 3 ¾ In. 738
Guerlain, Shalimar, Paneled, Shouldered, Footed, Gold Label, Blue Fan Stopper, 15 In. 741
Jasper Plaque, 3 Lions, Granite Shield, Silver Mount & Screw Cap, 2 ½ In. 826
Jovoy, Severem, Clear, Figural Frost Stopper, 1923, 4 In. 1230
Lancome, Magie, Silk Box, 1948, 4 ½ In. 277
Leaf Shape, Royal Blue Enamel, Flowers, Silver Repousse Cap, 3 ½ In. 413
Luzia, Scarabs, Molded Glass, Amber, Powder Decorated, Square, Lid, 1920s, 3 In. 633
Malachite, Carved Rose, 2 x 1 In. 50
Malachite, Cupids, Flower Garland, 6 In. 395
Man, Dandy, Painted, Leather Coat, Stopper, Parera Varon, 1951, 5 In. .... *illus* 9840
Mickey Mouse, Porcelain, Luster Glaze, Marked, Made In Japan, 1930s, 5 In. .... *illus* 369
Opaque White, Disk Shape, Gold Repousse Mount, Red, Green Enamel, c.1825, 3 In. 2242
Pierre Lionceau, Parfum Pour Blondes, Turquoise, Ocher Patina, 1926, 5 ⅞ In. 615
Pilgrim's Flask, Golden Trellis, Emerald Glass, Gilt Stopper, c.1765, 2 ¾ In. 1003
Rigaud, Pres De Vous, Multicolor Enamel, Gothic Script, Figures, Stopper, c.1930, 6 In. 1298
Sapphire Blue Glass, Filigree Layers, Gilt Hinged Cap, Applied Detail, c.1860, 2 ¾ In. 885
Schiaparelli, Shocking, Sleeping, Zut, Miniatures Set, Box, 2 ¼ In., 3 Piece 615
Schiaparelli, Snuff, Pipe Shape, Glass, 1939, 5 ⅜ In. 461
Schiaparelli, Succes Fou, Opaline Glass, Enameled, Heart Shape Box, 1953, 2 ½ In. 800
Swollen Oval, Rolled Rim, Gold Iridescent, Red, Orange, Swirls, Eickhold, 5 In. 29
Tank, Chrome Plated Metal, Atomizer, 1920s, 4 ¼ In. 3321
Vase Shape, Bamboo, Engraved, Bun Base, B. Sillars, Orient & Flume, 9 ¾ In. 384
Vase Shape, Blue Aurene, Raised Wreath, Textured Dogwood Blossoms, Leaves, 7 In. 295
Wine Barrel, Allegorical Tableaus, Enamel, Gilt Metal Dwarfs, Vienna, 1880s, 5 In. 14760
Woman, Black & Yellow Dress, Crown Top, Porcelain, Germany, 3 ⅜ In. 246

PETERS & REED POTTERY COMPANY of Zanesville, Ohio, was founded by John D. Peters and Adam Reed in 1897. Chromal, Landsun, Montene, Pereco, and Persian are some of the art lines that were made. The company, which became Zane Pottery in 1920 and Gonder Pottery in 1941, closed in 1957. Peters & Reed pottery was unmarked.

Bowl, Dragonfly, Footed, 2 ¼ x 5 ¼ In. 55
Column, Marbleized, Red, Black, Yellow, 6-Sided, 1920s, 9 x 4 In. 95
Cuspidor, Green Matte Glaze, 4 ½ x 7 ½ In. 165
Figurine, Dog, Bulldog, Seated, 13 In. 350
Figurine, Dog, Ivory, Brown Spots, Marked, 13 In. 172
Jardiniere, Pereco, Birds, 3 ½ x 6 ¾ In. 65
Mug, Brown Glaze, Grapes, Leaves, 5 ½ In. 35
Tankard, Brown Glaze, Grapes & Leaf Sprig, Scroll Handle, 5 ½ In. 75
Umbrella Stand, Moss Aztec, Woman In Flowing Dress, 20 ½ In. 266
Vase, Green Matte Glaze, Arts & Crafts, Ivy, 7 ½ In. 275
Vase, Green Matte Glaze, Pinched Waist, Grapes, c.1920, 11 ½ In. 75
Vase, Landsun, Scenic, Trees, Rolling Hills, 1910, 13 In. .... *illus* 615
Vase, Moss Aztec, Daisies, Molded, Red Clay, Green Accents, c.1915, 6 In. .... *illus* 60
Vase, Trumpet, Landsun, Blue, Beige, Brown, 5 In. 75
Vase, Vellum, Pink, Purple, Green, Blue, Stick Neck, Bud, c.1910, 10 In. 85

PETRUS REGOUT, *see Maastricht category.*

PEWABIC POTTERY was founded by Mary Chase Perry Stratton in 1903 in Detroit, Michigan. The company made many types of art pottery, including pieces with matte green glaze and an iridescent crystalline glaze. The company continued working until the death of Mary Stratton in 1961. It was reactivated by Michigan State University in 1968.

PEWABIC

Brooch, Seahorse, Oval, Blue & Yellow Pearlescent Glaze, 2 ⅝ In. 144
Dresser Box, Gunmetal, Shepherd, Animals, 2 x 3 ½ In. 204

Plaque, Fairytale, Scenic, Painted Green, 1998, 6 x 11 In. 108
Plate, Crackleware, Incised Swimming Ducks, Blue & White Glaze, 9 In. 590
Vase, Copper Glaze, Signed, Ira & Ella, c.1960, 6 x 5 ½ In. 675
Vase, Iridescent Glaze, Baluster, c.1910, 11 In. 960
Vase, Luster Glaze, Blue, Purple, Gray, Impressed Mark, 5 ¼ In. 472
Vase, Luster Glaze, Tan & Blue, Impressed Mark, Early 20th Century, 5 ¼ In. 484
Vase, Purple Lilies, Green Leaves, Blue Mottled Ground, 11 In. 200

PEWTER is a metal alloy of tin and lead. Some of the pewter made after 1840 has a slightly different composition and is called Britannia metal. This later type of pewter was worked by machine; the earlier pieces were made by hand. In the 1920s pewter came back into fashion and pieces were often marked *Genuine Pewter*. Eighteenth-, nineteenth-, and twentieth-century examples are listed here.

Basin, Flowers, Wrigglework, Engraved, Initials, Flat Rim, 1812, 2 ½ x 13 ½ In. 240
Basin, Round, Rolled Sides, Wide Molded Rim, 1800s, 3 ½ x 13 In. 165
Bowl, Crimped, Marked, Standish Solid Pewter, Benedict, 2 ½ x 7 In. ....*illus* 65
Bowl, Ettore Sottsass, Cast, Handles, Dust Bag, Box, c.1960, 2 ¼ x 17 ¾ In. 484
Bowl, Scalloped, 3-Footed, c.1930, 10 ½ x 3 ¾ In. 45
Bowl, Soup, Wide Flat Edge, Rolled Rim, Incised Line, Townsend & Compton, 13 In. 224
Box, Duck Shape, Lid, Jadeite Handle, Mother-Of-Pearl, Brass, Chinese, c.1890, 6 x 7 In. 123
Chalice, Engraved, Un. Assoc. Cong. Of Monteith, John McKerrow, Minister 1834, 1800s, 9 In. ... 212
Charger, Classical Images, Mars, God Of War, Continental, 18 ½ In. 63
Coffee & Tea Set, Teapot, Coffeepot, Hot Water Urn, Sugar & Creamer, Trays, 7 Piece 60
Coffeepot, Domed Top, Shaped Handle, Gooseneck Spout, Saucer Foot, c.1850, 11 In. 212
Dish, Sailboat Design, 3-Sided, 5 ¾ x 5 In. 45
Ewer, Gothic Style Decoration, Armorial Designs, Continental, 27 In. 219
Figure, Rabbit, Sitting, Tilted Head, Marked, c.1980, 1 In. 13
Figure, Rooster, Walking, 4 x 8 In., Pair 35
Flagon, French Normandy, Flared Foot Ring, c.1775, 12 In. 345
Flagon, Ring Finial, Double Bulbous Lid, Tapered, Boardman & Co., c.1835, 12 In. 502
Flask, Disc Shaped, Incised Circle Bands, Screw Spout, 5 In. 118
Lunch Box, 4 Lobes, Bail Handles, 2 Qilong, Footed, Fitted Interior, c.1900, 7 x 14 In. 504
Mirror, Flowers, Art Nouveau, 15 x 10 ½ In. 60
Monteith Bowl, Scalloped Shaped Rim, Ring Handles, Oval Base, 1700s, 7 ½ x 19 In. 1476
Plate, Engraved Rim, Crest, Arm Holding Scroll, Jonas Durand, c.1730, 9 ½ In. 738
Plate, Molded, Scenes Of 12 Apostles, Germany, 17th Century, 7 In. 246
Plate, Oval, Wide Flat Rim, Marked, B&O, Shield, England, 1800s, 14 x 18 In. 212
Porringer, Openwork Handle, Thomas Danforth Boardman, c.1845, 7 x 5 In. ....*illus* 450
Snuffbox, Stylized Flower Basket, 19th Century, 2 ¼ x 1 ½ In. 125
Sugar, Cover, Banded, Squat, Footed, Scroll Handles, 6 In. 360
Tankard, Incised Saints, Hexagonal, Twisted Handle, Lion's Feet, Lid, 1900s, 24 In. 688
Tankard, Touchmark, Stephen Maxwell, Scotland, c.1790, 9 ½ In. 344
Teapot, Black Paint Handle, Wafer Finial, Pedestal Foot, Sellew & Co., c.1850, 7 ½ In. 60
Teapot, Flowering Rose Stems, Incised, Knop, Jade Handle, 1800s, 5 In. 1558
Teapot, Squared Body, Saucer Foot, Loop Handle, Upturned Spout, Lid, 1800s, 8 ½ In. 49
Teaspoon, Molded, 19th Century, 5 ¾ In., 6 Piece 12
Tray, Art Nouveau, Flower Shape Handles, France, Marked, 14 ½ x 18 ½ In. 100
Vase, Art Nouveau, 3 Handles, Round Foot, 10 x 6 In. 54
Warming Dish, Hammered Bouge, Touchmarks, Thomas Griffin, London, c.1770, 13 In. 120
Warming Tray, Incised, Shaped Rim, Wood Handles, Reeded Base, Bun Feet, 4 x 22 In. 127

PHOENIX GLASS Company was founded in 1880 in Pennsylvania. The firm made commercial products, such as lampshades, bottles, and glassware. Collectors today are interested in the "Sculptured Artware" made by the company from the 1930s until the mid-1950s. Some pieces of Phoenix glass are very similar to those made by the Consolidated Lamp and Glass Company. Phoenix made Reuben Blue, lavender, and yellow pieces. These colors were not used by Consolidated. In 1970 Phoenix became a division of Anchor Hocking, which was sold to the Newell Group in 1987. The factory is still working.

Drink Set, Satin Glass, 8-Lobed Pitcher, 6 Tumblers, 8 ½ x 3 ¾ In., 7 Piece 363
Vase, Dancing Nudes, Coral Ribbons, Molded Glass, 11 In. 134
Vase, Dancing Nudes, White Ribbons, Blue, Molded Glass, 11 In. 120
Vase, Dogwood, Coral, White, Molded Glass, 10 ¾ In. 60
Vase, Foxgloves, Orange, Molded Glass, 10 ½ In. 32
Vase, Light Blue Flying Geese, White, Molded Glass, 9 ½ x 11 In. 58
Vase, White Flowers, Blue Ground, Molded Glass, 11 x 7 In. 60

Pewter, Porringer, Openwork Handle, Thomas Danforth Boardman, c.1845, 7 x 5 In.
$450

Cowan Auctions

An Old Wives' Tale

Recently some have thought that eating from pewter plates can give you lead poisoning. If that were true, most of our ancestors would have died before their time. It is safe to serve any type of food on either shiny or dull pewter. The same tin that is in pewter has been used for years in the cans that store our food.

Photography, Ambrotype, 2 Men In Fighting Stance, Shirtless, Red Sashes, Boots, ¼ Plate
$1,599

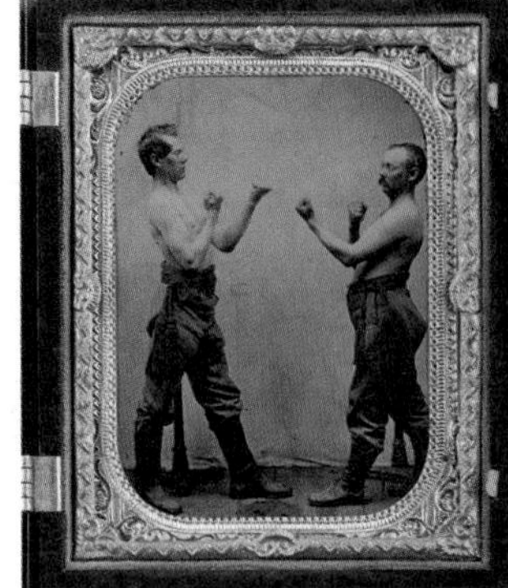

Cowan Auctions

TIP

Daguerreotype cases can be polished with liquid shoe wax (not polish).

Photography, Ambrotype, Tourists At Niagara Falls, N.Y., Babbitt, Pressed Paper Case, Full Plate
$1,080

Cowan Auctions

Photography, Cabinet Card, Miss Annie Oakley, Little Sure-Shot, Woodbury Type, 1890s
$2,760

Cowan Auctions

Photography, Carte De Visite, Confederate Captain John S. Lanier, Anderson, New Orleans
$2,040

Cowan Auctions

PHONOGRAPHS, invented by Thomas Edison in 1877, have been made by many firms. This category also includes other items associated with the phonograph. Jukeboxes and Records are listed in their own categories.

Admiral, Tabletop, Bakelite Cabinet, Scalloped Design Speaker, Radio, 1949, 16 x 10 In. 90
Cardinal, Portable, Plays 45s, Lid, Suitcase Style, 12 x 5 x 10 In. 12
Edison, Morning Glory Horn, Oak Case 357
Edison, S-160333, Brass Horn, Oak Casing, 12 In. 442
Edison, S-171575, Brass Horn, Oak Casing, Crank, 12 In. 472
Edison, Tabletop, Internal Horn, Oak Case, Hand Crank, 11 x 15 In. 336
Edison, Victor IV, Mahogany Horn, Columns, Plaque, 14 x 14 In. 1544
Lindstrom, Model 777, Child, Tin Lithograph, Yellow, Red, Electric, 13 x 7 In. 60
RCA Victor Talking Machine, Oak Laminate, Decal, Horn, Nickel Plate, c.1910, 26 x 22 In. 1020
Victor Victrola, Table Top, Hand Crank, Oak, Tiger Stripe Grain, Lid, 1915, 13 x 19 In. 244

PHOTOGRAPHY items are listed here. The first photograph was a view from a window in France taken in 1826. The commercially successful photograph started with the daguerreotype introduced in 1839. Today all sorts of photographs and photographic equipment are collected. Albums were popular in Victorian times. Cartes de visite, popular after 1854, were mounted on 2 ½-by-4-inch cardboard. Cabinet cards were introduced in 1866. These were mounted on 4 ¼-by-6 ½-inch cards. Stereo views are listed under Stereo Card. Stereoscopes are listed in their own section.

Albumen, Bellows Falls Stage House, Vermont, c.1845, 7 ¾ x 5 In. 240
Albumen, Niagara Falls, George Barker, c.1880, 19 x 33 In. 540
Ambrotype, 2 Men In Fighting Stance, Shirtless, Red Sashes, Boots, ¼ Plate.......... *illus* 1599
Ambrotype, Boy, Bowtie, Union Case, Octagonal, Scroll Design, S. Peck Co., ⅙ Plate.......... 165
Ambrotype, CSA Marine, Sword, Hat, Velvet Covered Octagonal Frame, c.1865, ⅙ Plate.......... 5750
Ambrotype, Drummer Boy, Hand Tinted, Embossed, Leather Case, c.1865, ⅙ Plate.......... 2250
Ambrotype, Soldiers With Muskets, Drummer, Union Case, ⅙ Plate.......... 1680
Ambrotype, Tourists At Niagara Falls, N.Y., Babbitt, Pressed Paper Case, Full Plate.......... *illus* 1080
Ambrotype, Warren Adams, Uniform, ¼ Plate.......... 16200
Ambrotype, Washington's Tomb, Mt. Vernon, Tinted, ½ Plate.......... 360
Cabinet Card, Buffalo Bill, Show Regalia, Woodbury Type, 1890s.......... 510
Cabinet Card, Miss Annie Oakley, Little Sure-Shot, Woodbury Type, 1890s.......... *illus* 2760
Cabinet Card, Sitting Bull, Seated, Holding Pipe, Bailey, Dix & Mead, 1882.......... 984
Camera, Ansco Ready Flash, Bottom Opening, 620 Film, 1953, 3 x 4 x 2 ½ In. 12
Camera, Bellows, Cherry, Carved, 5 x 7 Plate, A.J. Pipon, 1800s, 13 ½ x 31 ¼ In. 305
Camera, Brownie, Kodak, Leatherette Covered Card Box, 1900, 2 ¼ x 2 ¼ In. 619
Camera, Eastman Kodak, Daylight, String Set Sector Shutter, c.1890, 11 x 5 In. 531
Camera, Kodak, Brownie Target Six-20, Black, Handle, c.1950, 4 x 5 x 3 In. 28
Carte De Visite, Confederate Captain John S. Lanier, Anderson, New Orleans.......... *illus* 2040
Carte De Visite, Tintype, John Bugler, Train Robber, Portrait.......... 330
Daguerreotype, Boy Holding Gun, Dog, Full Case, ⅙ Plate.......... 523
Daguerreotype, Butcher, Knife & Sharpener, Full Case, ⅙ Plate.......... 720
Daguerreotype, Father & Son, Full Case, Mathew Brady, ¼ Plate.......... 400
Daguerreotype, Fireman, Bearded, Uniform, ⅙ Plate.......... 3480
Daguerreotype, Girl, Leaning On Table With Doll, Flower Case, ⅙ Plate.......... 308
Ferrotype, Badge, Jefferson Davis, Portrait, Octagonal, 1 In. 1200
Magic Lantern, Brass, Red Paint, Figural Lens Stand, Oil, Box, 13 ½ In. 270
Negative, Nitrate, Mary Pickford, Standing At Fireplace, 1930s, 8 x 10 In. 84
Photograph, Airship Akron, Gelatin Silver Print, M. Bourke-White, 1931, 20 x 26 In. .... *illus* 3125
Photograph, Chicago Cubs, Team Pose, Black & White, Mat, Frame, 1906, 22 x 26 In. 6871
Photograph, Council, Blackfeet, Silver Gelatin, Roland Reed, 1912, 11 x 14 In. 1140
Photograph, F.A. Rinehart, Indian, Spies On The Enemy, Crow, Platinum, 11 x 9 In. .... *illus* 720
Photograph, George A. Custer, Portrait, Profile, In Uniform, Black & White, 1876, 4 x 6 In. 1188
Photograph, Hopi Snake Priest, Platinum, Edward Curtis, 1907, 16 x 12 In. 738
Photograph, Jack Dempsey, Boxing Legend, Black & White, 12 x 14 In. 57
Photograph, Jeffrey Pine, Sentinel Dome, Yosemite, Ansel Adams, 1940, 7 ½ x 9 ½ In. 3690
Photograph, Marilyn Monroe, Color, White Fur Coat, Gloves, Frame, 26 x 39 In. 90
Photograph, Native American, Black Bear, Oglala Sioux, Platinum Print, 13 x 16 In. 1320
Photograph, Nevada Gambling Hall, Black & White, Frame, c.1910, 15 x 21 In. 60
Photograph, Thompkins Square, Black & White, Benches, Dog, 1974, 18 x 27 In. 460
Salt Print, Horse Drawn Wagons, General Store, c.1850, 7 x 5 In. 1107
Tintype, Armed Confederate Soldier, Hand Tinted, Scrolled Case, ⅙ Plate.......... *illus* 1800
Tintype, Armed Union Cavalryman, Scrolled Union Case, Civil War, ¼ Plate.......... *illus* 960
Tintype, Brevet Maj. Gen. George Armstrong Custer, Thermoplastic Case, c.1865, 4 ¼ x 3 In. 1599
Tintype, Confederate Soldier, Frock Coat, Holding Sword, Leather Case, c.1865, ¼ Plate.......... 5000

Photography, Photograph, Airship Akron, Gelatin Silver Print, M. Bourke-White, 1931, 20 x 26 In.
$3,125

Los Angeles Modern Auctions

Photography, Photograph, F.A. Rinehart, Indian, Spies On The Enemy, Crow, Platinum, 11 x 9 In.
$720

Cowan Auctions

TIP

Nineteenth-century photographs are more easily damaged than pictures from later years. They are more likely to fade or deteriorate. Color photos of any date often fade. Keep all photographs away from strong light.

TIP

You can clean oil, fingerprints, and dust from a photograph with a wad of white bread.

Photography, Tintype, Armed Confederate Soldier, Hand Tinted, Scrolled Case, ⅙ Plate
$1,800

Cowan Auctions

Photography, Tintype, Armed Union Cavalryman, Scrolled Union Case, Civil War, ¼ Plate
$960

Cowan Auctions

TIP
If you are in an area with earth tremors or windstorms, or even near a heavily traveled road or train track, you may have pictures that move on the wall. To keep them straight, use two picture hooks next to each other.

Piano Baby, Crawling, Girl, Bisque, Chipped Thumb & Toe, Germany, 5 ¾ In.
$65

Ruby Lane

Pickard, Pitcher, Water, Luster Grape Decoration, Limoges, Signed, Hessler, c.1930, 12 In.
$115

Early Auction Company

Tintype, Uniformed Firefighter, Trumpet, Bearded, Geometric Union Case, ¼ Plate 554
Tintype, Union Soldier, Armed With Musket, Embossed Leather Case, ⅙ Plate 350

PIANO BABY is a collector's term. About 1880, the well-decorated home had a shawl on the piano. Bisque figures of babies were designed to help hold the shawl in place. They usually range in size from 6 to 18 inches. Most of the figures were made in Germany. Reproductions are being made. Other piano babies may be listed under manufacturers' names.

Baby, Crawling, Gown, Collar, Rabbit, Kitten, Porcelain, Germany, 6 In. 135
Baby, Crawling, Holding Puppy, Bisque, Germany, 9 x 5 ¾ In. 70
Baby, Crawling, Sucking Thumb, Foot Raised, Nightgown, c.1890, 16 In. 129
Baby, Sitting, Blond, Gown Falling Off Shoulders, Gebruder Heubach, 3 In. 160
Boy, Sitting, Reading Book, Blue Romper, 4 ¼ In. 44
Crawling, Girl, Bisque, Chipped Thumb & Toe, Germany, 5 ¾ In. .... *illus* 65
Girl, Leaning Back, Leg Up, Yellow Dress, Porcelain, 5 ½ In. 20
Girl, Leaning On Arm, Curls, Holding Rabbit, Jumper, Germany, c.1900, 9 In. 99
Girl, Seated, Crossed Legs, Holding Bottle, Flowered Romper, 3 In. 132
Girl, Sitting, Dress, Lace Trim, Pink Bonnet, Porcelain, Germany, 2 In. 124
Girl, Sitting, Legs Crossed, Blond Curly Hair, Flowered Dress, Bow, 8 In. 195

PICKARD China Company was started in 1893 by Wilder Pickard. Hand-painted designs were used on china purchased from other sources. In the 1930s, the company began to make its own china wares in Chicago, Illinois. The company now makes many types of porcelains, including a successful line of limited edition collector plates.

Ashtray, Floral Chintz, Round, 3 In. .... 32 to 43
Jardiniere, Poinsettia, Gilt Trim, Marked, H. Tolley, 7 x 9 In. 559
Pitcher, Water Lilies, Buds, Leaves, Lake, Trees, Green, Gold, Round, Loop Handle, 6 In. 259
Pitcher, Water, Luster Grape Decoration, Limoges, Signed, Hessler, c.1930, 12 In. .... *illus* 115
Plate, Dinner, Greenbriar, 10 In. 38
Platter, Serving, Brocade, Oval, 12 In. 121
Sugar, Lid, Cameo 102

PICTURES, silhouettes, and other small decorative objects framed to hang on the wall are listed here. Some other types of pictures are listed in the Print and Painting categories.

Aquatint, Meet Of The Vine Hounds, Hunting, Frame, c.1810, 33 x 42 In. 180
Calligraphy, Spencerian, Soule College, New Orleans, Montgomery, 1870, 25 x 35 In. 922
Charcoal, Gouache, Oil, Girl With Cat, Jessie Wilcox Smith, c.1932, 17 x 9 In. 49450
Crayon, Study Of A Female Head, France, Frame, c.1790, 6 x 8 In. 1187
Crayon, Study Of Angels, Ascension Scene, Glazed, Italy, Frame, c.1800, 9 x 15 In. 1500
Cutwork, Pinprick, Flower Basket, Cream Paper, Black Cloth Ground, 1800s, 8 ½ x 10 In. 120
Cutwork, Solder's Farewell, Multicolor Papers, Frame, 7 ¼ x 7 In. 60
Gouache, Elephants In Combat, Gold, Soldiers, Mughal, 1700s, 7 x 11 In. 710
Gouache, Empress & Attendant Visiting Holy Man, Mughal, 1800s, 14 x 11 In. 644
Gouache, On Paper, Mughal Style, Indian Court, Nobleman, Frame, 30 ½ x 19 ½ In. 71
Gouache, Seated Holy Man, Flowers, Gold, Brown, Album, 1700s, 16 x 10 In. 1510
Gouache, Seated Imam, Flowers, Gold On Green, 1700s, 16 x 10 In. 888
Memorial, Etched Glass, Black Velvet Backing, Theodore Wm. Kelley, c.1889, 17 x 22 In. 62
Memorial, Nathan Brown, Urn, Inscription, Mourner, Willow Tree, Watercolor, c.1811, 12 In. ... 1335
Multicolor Panel, Jockeys, Fred Archer, Tommy Cannon, Riding Attire, 68 x 19 In., Pair 531
Needlework, Embroidery, Eglomise Frame, Silk, Painted, Mother, Children, c.1800, 10 x 12 In. 142
Needlework, Embroidery, Fighting Cockerels, Attacking, Sheltering, Bamboo, 37 x 30 In. 194
Needlework, Family Record, Fletcher, Wreaths, Sawtooth, Silk, Linen, Mass., 1822, 18 In. 984
Needlework, Medieval Saint, Lilies, Wool, Frame, c.1890, 41 x 37 In. 210
Needlework, Memorial, Watercolor, Silk, Lucy Mason, Aged 25, 1809, 22 x 24 In. .... *illus* 5100
Needlework, Mourning, Silk Thread, Ink, Flowers, Willow, Multicolor, Frame, 10 x 15 In. 2091
Needlework, Noah's Ark, Animals, Figures, Multicolor, Petit Point, 7 x 4 ½ In. 90
Needlework, Prince With Bird, Multicolor, Frame, 51 x 56 In. 84
Needlework, Silk, Mother, Daughter, Landscape, Elizabeth Lovering, 1809, 10 x 14 In. .... *illus* 4920
Needlework, Wool, Sailing Ship, 3-Masted, Lighthouse, England, c.1890, 15 x 21 In. .... *illus* 984
Paint, On Ivory, Woman's Portrait, Holding Rose, Painted Frame, 1800s, 5 ¾ x 5 In. .... *illus* 207
Paper, On Cloth, Cutwork, Urn, Flowers, Birds, Baltimore, Frame, 9 ½ x 7 ½ In. .... *illus* 180
Pastel, On Board, Portrait, Louis XVI, Oval, Glazed, Carved Gilt Frame, 1800s, 8 x 6 In. 875
Pastel, On Paper, Continental, Grapes, Apples, Orange, Gilt Frame, c.1900, 20 In. Diam. 676
Pastel, On Paper, Girl In Striped Sweater, Frame, c.1940, 24 x 18 In. 1168
Pastel, Portrait, Child Holding Doll, Cane, Gold Necklace, Frame, 1800s, 23 x 18 In. 240
Pen & Ink, Pinprick, Portrait, Woman, Primitive, 1800s, Frame, 6 ½ x 5 ½ In. 120

Pen & Ink, Portrait, Seated Man, J.M. Crawley, Frame, c.1836, 4 ¾ x 3 ¼ In. 480
Sandpaper, Classical Ruins, Soldier, Giltwood Frame, c.1850, 19 x 25 In. ....*illus* 1845
Set Design Sketch, Backdrop, Gouache, Ink, Raoul Pene De Bois, c.1950, 16 x 19 In. 138
Silhouette, Adelaide Dickenson, Age 13, Standing In Landscape, A. Edouart, 1843, 11 In. 308
Silhouette, Girl With Sticks, Marguerite Anne Molesworth, Gilt Frame, 1834, 10 x 8 In. 1080
Silhouette, Man & Woman, Hollow-Cut Portraits, Ink Details, Gilt Frame, N.H., 7 x 10 In. 677
Silkscreen, Town, Sun, Juan Romero, 1980, 31 x 31 In. 123
Theorem, Mourning, Woman At Monument, Trees, Painted Frame, c.1820, 16 x 19 In. ....*illus* 384
Theorem, Oil On Velvet, Basket Of Fruit, Wood Frame, c.1830, 22 x 27 In. 1500
Theorem, On Velvet, Basket Of Fruit, Frame, Signed, D. Ellinger, 17 ¾ x 22 In. ....*illus* 1003
Theorem, On Velvet, Urn, Fruit, Frame, 1800s, 14 x 20 In. 180
Theorem, Still Life, Fruit Basket, Velvet, Watercolor, Gilt Frame, 1800s, 15 x 18 In. ....*illus* 1599
Theorem, Watercolor, Basket Of Flowers, On Stone Slab, Frame, 17 x 22 In. 615
Theorem, Watercolor, Basket, Flowers, Multicolor, Giltwood Frame, 1800s, 19 x 20 In. 984
Theorem, Watercolor, Napoleon Viewing Tomb, Presentation, Frame, 12 x 10 In. ....*illus* 188
Theorem, Watercolor, On Velvet, Bowl, Flowers, Frame, Elizabeth Sherwood, 1829, 13 x 18 In. . 472
Theorem, Watercolor, On Velvet, Fruit, Marble Tabletop, 17 x 21 In. 2214
Theorem, Watercolor, On Velvet, Fruit, Tipped Bowl, Patterned Tablecloth, 15 x 21 In. 984
Theorem, Winter Scene, Richland, Pa., Signed, A. Wiest, 1970s, 10 ¼ x 12 In. 142
Watercolor & Ink, Red & Yellow Bird, In Flowers, Heart, Reeded Frame, c.1834, 7 x 5 In. 4551
Watercolor, Board, Figure Before An Adoring Crowd, Frame, 1800s, 5 x 7 In. 937
Watercolor, Church, Cottage, Feather Grain Painted Frame, Annie B. Musser, 11 x 13 In. 1534
Watercolor, Compass Star, Red, Mustard, Green, Painted Frame, c.1810, 7 x 7 In. ....*illus* 3321
Watercolor, Family At Table, Multicolor, Chinese, 15 x 10 In. 48
Watercolor, French Quarter Townhouse, Jim Blanchard, 1993, 22 x 30 In. 3444
Watercolor, Girl In Blue Dress, Holding Tabby Cat, Phebe Louisa Bonner, 1842, 7 x 8 In. 2006
Watercolor, Gold, On Wasli Paper, Court Scene, Women, Prince, India, c.1900, 13 x 9 In. ...*illus* 738
Watercolor, Little People, Walt Scott, 1950s, 7 ¼ x 10 ¼ In. 354
Watercolor, Memorial, Joseph Chandler, Jr. Family, Flag, Eagle, Frame, 1800s, 8 x 5 ½ In. 510
Watercolor, Mughal, Attendants, Holding Flower, Instrument, 1700s, 8 x 5 ½ In. ....*illus* 593
Watercolor, On Board, Ponte Vecchio, William Walcot, 1919, 23 ½ x 27 In. 1150
Watercolor, On Ivory, John Wright, Black Overcoat, Buff Waistcoat, Ebony Frame, 1833, 5 In. .. 523
Wax, Profile Of George Washington, Frame, 1800s, 4 ¼ x 3 ¼ In. ....*illus* 330
Woolwork, HMS Egret, 3-Masted Sailing Vessel, Banner, c.1800s, 10 ¾ x 11 ½ In. 590

PICTURE FRAMES *are listed in this book in the Furniture category under Frame.*

PIERCE, *see Howard Pierce category.*

PIGEON FORGE POTTERY was started in Pigeon Forge, Tennessee, in 1946. Red clay found near the pottery was used to make the pieces. Molded or thrown pottery with matte glaze and slip decoration was made. The pottery closed in 2000.

The Pigeon Forge Pottery Pigeon Forge Tenn

Bowl, Bird, Blue Slip, Off White Ground, Marked, c.1978, 11 ¾ In. 100
Bowl, Dogwood, Blossoms, Marked, 2 ¾ x 5 ¼ In. ....*illus* 49
Bowl, Yellow Matte Glaze, Ruffled Rim, T. Hoyle, 4 ⅜ In. 75
Figurine, Fox, Brown Glaze, Doug Ferguson, Marked, 5 x 11 In. 140
Figurine, Fox, Rust Over Brown High Glaze, Elongated Body, 5 x 11 In. 161
Figurine, Raccoon, Doug Ferguson, c.1965, 5 In. 15
Jug, Green Black Matrix Glaze, Handle, 7 In. 95
Pitcher, White Dogwood, Textured Tan Glaze, 4 ⅜ In. 30
Vase, Cylindrical, Brown & White Bubbled Glaze, 10 x 3 ¾ In. 110
Vase, Volcanic Glaze, U Shape, 2 Openings, 6 x 6 ¾ In. 70

PILLIN pottery was made by Polia (1909–1992) and William (1910–1985) Pillin, who set up a pottery in Los Angeles in 1948. William shaped, glazed, and fired the clay, and Polia painted the pieces, often with elongated figures of women, children, flowers, birds, fish, and other animals. Pieces are marked with a stylized Pillin signature.

W + P Pillin

Bowl, Dancers, Frothy White Over Brown, 10 ½ x 15 ¼ In. 1280
Bowl, Women Dancers, Tan Sponged Ground, Signed, 10 ½ x 15 In. 1250
Decanter Set, Decanter, 3 Cups, Multicolor Stripes, Horses, 15 x 3 ½ In., 5 Piece 640
Decanter Set, Horses, Blue, Green, Red, Tan Bands, Tapered, 15-In. Decanter, 5 Piece 625
Panel, Horses, Teal, Yellow, 2 Tiles, 16 ½ x 33 In. 3750
Plaque, Kidney Shape, Women, Brown, 12 x 6 In. 360
Plaque, Stylized Horses, 2 Tiles, Signed, Frame, Tiles 16 ½ x 33 In. 3750
Plate, Dancing Girl, Birds, Multicolor 250
Plate, Diamond Shape, Woman, Birds, Brown Rim, Signed, 7 ¼ x 6 ¼ In. ....*illus* 450

Picture, Needlework, Memorial, Watercolor, Silk, Lucy Mason, Aged 25, 1809, 22 x 24 In.
$5,100

Garth's Auctioneers & Appraisers

Picture, Needlework, Silk, Mother, Daughter, Landscape, Elizabeth Lovering, 1809, 10 x 14 In.
$4,920

Skinner, Inc.

Picture, Needlework, Wool, Sailing Ship, 3-Masted, Lighthouse, England, c.1890, 15 x 21 In.
$984

Skinner, Inc.

Picture, Paint, On Ivory, Woman's Portrait, Holding Rose, Painted Frame, 1800s, 5 ¾ x 5 In.
$207

Hess Auction Group

P

TIP

Never touch the surface of a watercolor or drawing. Lift unframed paper by the corners.

Picture, Paper On Cloth, Cutwork, Urn, Flowers, Birds, Baltimore, Frame, 9 ½ x 7 ½ In.
$180

Cowan Auctions

Picture, Sandpaper, Classical Ruins, Soldier, Giltwood Frame, c.1850, 19 x 25 In.
$1,845

Skinner, Inc.

Picture, Theorem, Mourning, Woman At Monument, Trees, Painted Frame, c.1820, 16 x 19 In.
$384

Hess Auction Group

Picture, Theorem, On Velvet, Basket Of Fruit, Frame, Signed, D. Ellinger, 17 ¾ x 22 In.
$1,003

Hess Auction Group

Picture, Theorem, Still Life, Fruit Basket, Velvet, Watercolor, Gilt Frame, 1800s, 15 x 18 In.
$1,599

Skinner, Inc.

Picture, Theorem, Watercolor, Napoleon Viewing Tomb, Presentation, Frame, 12 x 10 In.
$188

Garth's Auctioneers & Appraisers

Picture, Watercolor, Compass Star, Red, Mustard, Green, Painted Frame, c.1810, 7 x 7 In.
$3,321

Skinner, Inc.

Picture, Watercolor, Gold, On Wasli Paper, Court Scene, Women, Prince, India, c.1900, 13 x 9 In.
$738

Skinner, Inc.

Picture, Watercolor, Mughal, Attendants, Holding Flower, Instrument, 1700s, 8 x 5 ½ In.
$593

James D. Julia Auctioneers

P

Plate, Woman's Portrait, Multicolor 175
Vase, 3 Women, Lute, Purple, Blue, Green, Red, Cylindrical, Tapered, Signed, 15 In. 2070
Vase, Circus Performers With Horses, Shades Of Gray, Bulbous, 11 x 9 In. 1000
Vase, Cylinder, High Glaze, Women, 7 ⅜ In. 300
Vase, Seated Woman, Bird, High Glaze, Squat, Pinched Neck, Rolled Rim, 5 ½ In. 345
Vase, Stick, Gilt, Bird, Horse, 7 ½ In. 480
Vase, Woman & Bird, Girl & Horse, Blue, Green, Bottle Shape, Stick Neck, 7 ½ In. 460
Vase, Woman Holding Blue Bird, Rooster, Tree, High Glaze, Cylindrical, 7 In. 403
Vase, Woman On Horseback, Bird, Deer, Rounded Square Shape, Footed, 6 ¼ In. 431
Vase, Woman, Bird, Dancer, Tree, Spotted Deer, Signed, 5 ½ In. 472
Vase, Woman, Blue Scarf, Rooster, 6 ¼ x 3 ¾ In. 240
Vase, Woman, Striped Dress, Multicolor, Geometric Ground, 1940s, 12 x 4 In. 2300
Vase, Women Dancing & Playing Lute, Brown Horizontal Bands, Signed, 10 In. 375
Vase, Women Holding Birds & Flowers, Deep Tan Ground, Tapered, Flat Rim, 21 In. 1250
Vase, Women, Child, Cat, Rectangular, 11 x 4 x 3 ½ In. 1375
Vase, Women, Horse, Bird, Bulbous, Signed, 9 x 8 ½ In. ....*illus* 938
Vase, Women, Standing, Blue, Multicolor, Narrow Neck, 21 ½ x 7 In. 1500

PINCUSHION DOLLS are not really dolls and often were not even pincushions. Some collectors use the term "half-doll." The top half of each doll was made of porcelain. The edge of the half-doll was made with several small holes for thread, and the doll was stitched to a fabric body with a voluminous skirt. The finished figure was used to cover a hot pot of tea, powder box, pincushion, whiskbroom, or lamp. They were made in sizes from less than an inch to over 9 inches high. Most date from the early 1900s to the 1950s. Collectors often find just the porcelain doll without the fabric skirt.

Child, Blond, Bonnet, Molded Ribbons, 2 ¼ In. 125
Man, Clown, White, Black, Spiraled Collar, 2 ¼ In. 240
Pierrot, Bust, Black Skullcap, Ruffled Collar, Painted Face, Porcelain, 1920s, 2 x 2 In. ....*illus* 175
Woman, Arms Away, Rose In Hair, Blue Eyes, 6 ¾ In. 175
Woman, Curly Hair, Bonnet, Bow, Scarf, Holding Bouquet, Germany, 3 ¾ In. 45
Woman, Flapper, Mohair, Bracelets, 1920s, 4 In. 68
Woman, Gold Bodice, Extended Bisque Legs, 1900s, 5 In. 42
Woman, Masquerade, Black Mask, Green Bodice, Up-Do, 5 ¾ In. 437

PINK SLAG *pieces are listed in this book in the Slag Glass category.*

PIPES have been popular since tobacco was introduced to Europe by Sir Walter Raleigh. Carved wood, porcelain, ivory, and glass pipes and accessories may be listed here.

Figural, Boy On Rooster, Carved & Painted Wood, Tin-Lined Bowl, 1800s, 4 In. 561
Meerschaum, Carved, Amber Stem, Tribal Hunter, Lion, Gazelles, Case, c.1900, 5 ½ x 12 In. 799
Meerschaum, Carved, Nude, Fitted Case, Red Velvet Lining, 1800s, 10 x 5 ½ In. 330
Meerschaum, Man Mounting High Wheel Bicycle, Curved Upward, Signed, 6 In. 478
Meerschaum, Sultan's Head, Amber Stem, 6 ¼ In. ....*illus* 110
Patriotic, American Shield, Ceramic, Zouave Head, Fez, Painted, 7 ¾ In. 100
Pipe Box, Wood, Scrollwork Arched Top, 3 Drawers, 10 ½ x 21 In. 234
Pipe Rack, Native American Chief, Cast Iron, 1900s, 12 ½ x 6 ¼ In. 82
Tapper, Art Deco, 18K Yellow Gold, Flattened Rivet Nail, Ribbed Finger Grips, 2 ¾ In. 719
Wood, Black Forest, Antler, Stag & Leaf Design, Germany, c.1890, 21 In. 431

PIRKENHAMMER is a porcelain manufactory started in 1803 by Friedrich Holke and J. G. Lilst. It was located in Bohemia, now Brezova, Czech Republic. The company made tablewares usually decorated with views and flowers. Lithophanes were also made. The mark of the crossed hammers is easy to remember as the Pirkenhammer symbol.

Bowl, Bouquet, Multicolor, Basket Weave, Open Handles, Gilt Trim, 10 x 8 In. 35
Figurine, Dog, Springer Spaniel, Black, White, 8 x 3 In. 350
Figurine, Woman, Cat, Black & White, c.1920, 10 In. 420
Plate, Dessert, Aesthetic, Painted, Birds, Flowers, Figures, Cobalt, Gilt, 9 In., 12 Piece 374
Plate, Violet Paneled Border, Leaves, c.1914, 9 In. 135
Vase, Band Of Roses, Pink, Cream Ground, c.1910, 8 ¾ In. 185

PISGAH FOREST POTTERY was made in North Carolina beginning in 1926. The pottery was started by Walter B. Stephen, who had been making pottery in that location since 1914. The pottery continued in operation after his death in 1961. The most famous kinds of Pisgah Forest ware are the cameo type with designs made of raised glaze and the turquoise crackle glaze wares.

Candlestick, Seafoam Green, Arts & Crafts, 1931, 4 ½ In., Pair 68

Picture, Wax, Profile Of George Washington, Frame, 1800s, 4 ¼ x 3 ¼ In.
$330

Cowan Auctions

Pigeon Forge, Bowl, Dogwood, Blossoms, Marked, 2 ¾ x 5 ¼ In.
$49

Ruby Lane

Pillin, Plate, Diamond Shape, Woman, Birds, Brown Rim, Signed, 7 ¼ x 6 ¼ In.
$450

Ruby Lane

Pillin Pottery

Pillin vases by now are so expensive fakes are on the market. A real Pillin vase has a different scene on each side. The signature on a real piece is incised through a black glaze (early pieces) or signed with a blunt-pointed marker on red clay–colored glaze (later pieces).

TIP

All exterior doors in a house should be made of solid wood or metal. A determined burglar can break through a panel door.

Pillin, Vase, Women, Horse, Bird, Bulbous, Signed, 9 x 8 ½ In.
$938

Rago Arts and Auction Center

Pincushion Doll, Pierrot, Bust, Black Skullcap, Ruffled Collar, Painted Face, Porcelain, 1920s, 2 x 2 In.
$175

Ruby Lane

Pipe, Meerschaum, Sultan's Head, Amber Stem, 6 ¼ In.
$110

Ruby Lane

Jug, Turquoise, Brown Glaze, c.1935, 4 x 5 In. 68
Pitcher, Turquoise, Green Band, Raised Settlers, Horses, Wagons, Loop Handle, 7 In. 215
Vase, Baluster, Turquoise Crackle Glaze, c.1939, 6 ¼ In. 85
Vase, Crystalline, Cream & Brown, Drip Design, Rolled Rim, 1953, 6 In. .... *illus* 177

PLANTERS PEANUTS memorabilia are collected. Planters Nut and Chocolate Company was started in Wilkes-Barre, Pennsylvania, in 1906. The Mr. Peanut figure was adopted as a trademark in 1916. National advertising for Planters Peanuts started in 1918. The company was acquired by Standard Brands, Inc., in 1961. Standard Brands merged with Nabisco in 1981. Some of the Mr. Peanut jars and other memorabilia have been reproduced and, of course, new items are being made.

Box, My! These Planters Peanuts Are Delicious, Woman Aviator, 5 Cents, c.1940, 9 In. 300
Costume, Mr. Peanut, Fiberglass, Composition, 1940s, 50 x 18 In. .... *illus* 474
Crate, Planters Pennant, Salted Peanuts, Mr. Peanut, Wood, 18 ½ x 33 In. 300
Display Rack, Candy Bars, Z-Shape, Tin Lithograph, Peanut Specialties, 5 x 14 In. 719
Display, Shelf Sitter, Girl Holding Box Of Peanuts, Cardboard, 28 In. 510
Figure, Mr. Peanut, Jointed, Painted, Wood, c.1938, 9 In. 120
Figure, Mr. Peanut, Metal, Standing, Legs Crossed, Hand On Hip, Cane, 7 ½ In. 390
Jar, 6-Sided Glass, Enameled Label, Yellow Mr. Peanut, Lid, 1930s, 7 ½ x 8 In. 180
Jar, Lid, Clear Glass, Embossed, Squared, Ring Foot, 13 ½ In. 75
Jar, Planters Salted Peanuts, 5 Cents, Fishbowl, Glass, Embossed Lid, c.1930, 13 In. 270
Jar, Planters Salted Peanuts, Barrel Shape, Ribbed, Mr. Peanut Running, Lid, 13 x 8 In. 360
Pail, Peanut Butter, Mr. Peanut, Dog, Moon, Bail Handle, 1920s, 4 x 4 In. 127
Sign, Planters Lenten Specials, Mr. Peanut Pushing Cart, 1960s, 12 x 20 In. 115
Tin, Planters Salted Peanuts, Pennant, Pale Blue, Red, Lid 120
Wall Pocket, Mr. Peanut Head, Top Hat, Ceramic, 1960s, 7 x 12 In. 139

PLASTIC objects of all types are being collected. Some pieces are listed in other categories; gutta-percha cases are listed in the Photography category. Celluloid is in its own category.

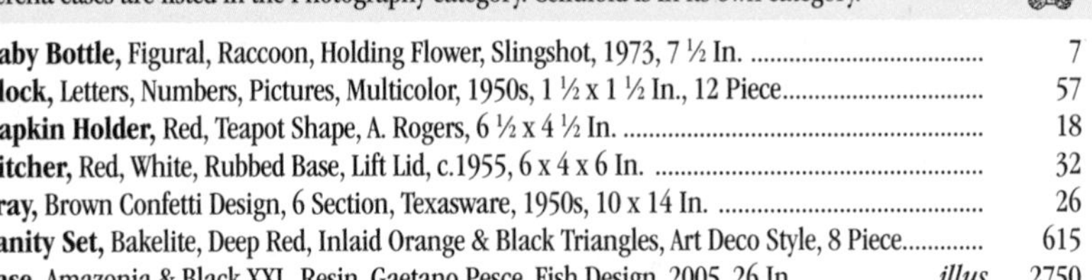

Baby Bottle, Figural, Raccoon, Holding Flower, Slingshot, 1973, 7 ½ In. 7
Block, Letters, Numbers, Pictures, Multicolor, 1950s, 1 ½ x 1 ½ In., 12 Piece 57
Napkin Holder, Red, Teapot Shape, A. Rogers, 6 ½ x 4 ½ In. 18
Pitcher, Red, White, Rubbed Base, Lift Lid, c.1955, 6 x 4 x 6 In. 32
Tray, Brown Confetti Design, 6 Section, Texasware, 1950s, 10 x 14 In. 26
Vanity Set, Bakelite, Deep Red, Inlaid Orange & Black Triangles, Art Deco Style, 8 Piece 615
Vase, Amazonia & Black XXL, Resin, Gaetano Pesce, Fish Design, 2005, 26 In. .... *illus* 2750
Vase, Spaghetti Special, Multicolor, Resin, G. Pesce, 2004, 25 In. .... *illus* 2500

PLATED AMBERINA was patented June 15, 1886, by Joseph Locke and made by the New England Glass Company. It is similar in color to amberina but is characterized by a cream colored or chartreuse lining (never white) and small ridges or ribs on the outside.

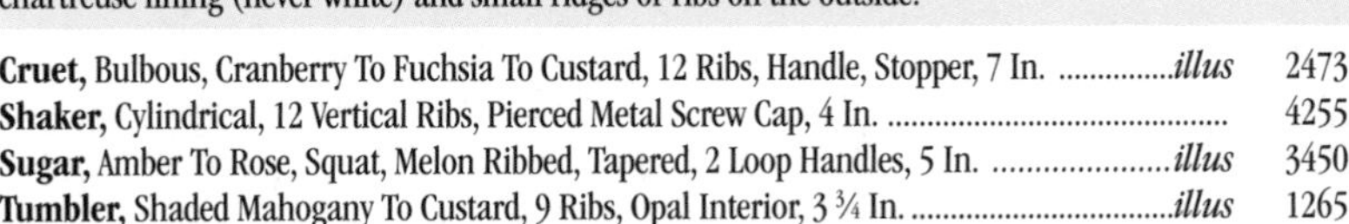

Cruet, Bulbous, Cranberry To Fuchsia To Custard, 12 Ribs, Handle, Stopper, 7 In. .... *illus* 2473
Shaker, Cylindrical, 12 Vertical Ribs, Pierced Metal Screw Cap, 4 In. 4255
Sugar, Amber To Rose, Squat, Melon Ribbed, Tapered, 2 Loop Handles, 5 In. .... *illus* 3450
Tumbler, Shaded Mahogany To Custard, 9 Ribs, Opal Interior, 3 ¾ In. .... *illus* 1265

PLIQUE-A-JOUR is an enameling process. The enamel is laid between thin raised metal lines and heated. The finished piece has transparent enamel held between the thin metal wires. It is different from cloisonne because it is translucent.

Bowl, Flowers, Leaves, Butterflies, Pink, Blue Scalloped Border, 5 ½ In. 389
Bowl, Peonies, Pierced Openwork, Panels, Multicolor, Footed, 7 x 4 In. 875
Bowl, Pink, Blue, Purple Flowers, Silver Rim, c.1900, 5 In. Diam. 676
Cup, Turquoise, Gold, Flowers, Wood Carved Vase, France, c.1900, 2 ½ In. 84
Thimble, Flower, Green, Blue, Gilt Trim, ¾ In. 35

POLITICAL memorabilia of all types, from buttons to banners, are collected. Items related to presidential candidates are the most popular, but collectors also search for material related to state and local offices. Memorabilia related to social causes, minor political parties, and protest movements are also included here. Many reproductions have been made. A jugate is a button with photographs of both the presidential and vice presidential candidates. In this list a button is round, usually with a straight pin or metal tab to secure it to a shirt. A pin is brass, often figural, sometimes attached to a ribbon.

Ashtray, General Chester Arthur, Portrait, Pottery, Rolled Rim, 4 In. 189

Badge, Brass Shell, McKinley, Portrait, Eagle Hanger, An Honest Dollar, c.1896, 5 x 7 In. 115
Badge, Harrison & Reid, Cardboard Photos, Brass Shell, Eagle Crest, 1892, 1 x 1 In. 552
Badge, Hayes, Glass, Oval, Union Veterans, Lithograph Portrait, Torchlight Parade, 1800s.......... 345
Bandanna, Garfield & Arthur, Jugate, Spread-Wing Eagles, Red, Border, 1880, 21 In. 177
Bandanna, Gen. Winfield Hancock, William English, Jugate, Eagles, Shields, 1880, 19 x 21 In. . 190
Bandanna, Harrison, Morton, Jugate, Campaign, Cotton, 1888, 23 x 22 In. ....*illus* 240
Bandanna, Harrison, Reid, Republican Protection, Jugate, 1892-1896, 21 x 22 In. ....*illus* 570
Bandanna, Roosevelt, Protection To America, Jugate, Eagle, Flag, Frame, 1904, 28 x 29 In. *illus* 1124
Bandanna, Taft, Sherman, Flag Ground, Portraits, Jugate, Capitol Building, 1908, 16 x 17 In. *illus* 485
Bandanna, We Want Teddy, Musical Score, Oval Portrait, Red, White, 1912, 18 x 18 In. ......*illus* 177
Bandanna, William H. Harrison, Portrait, Capitol Building, Lady Liberty, Silk, 1840, 29 x 27 In. 10755
Bandanna, William Henry Harrison, Medallions, Red, White, Cotton, 1840, 26 x 27 In. ......*illus* 1440
Bank, Donation, W. Wilson, Marshall, Celluloid, Chrome Plate, Jugate, c.1916, 3 x 2 In. 2988
Banner, For President, Wendell Willkie, Portrait, Flags, Eagle, 1940, 34 x 35 In. 380
Banner, John Breckinridge, Campaign, Portrait, 1860, 27 x 17 In. 95600
Banner, Smith, For President, 2 Stars, Portrait, Canvas, 1928, 60 x 39 In. 863
Booklet, Campaign Songster, Abraham Lincoln, Lyrics To Political Songs, 47 Pages, 1860, 4 x 6 In. 1793
Bookmark, Taft, Sherman, Figural, Teddy Bear, Heart, Aluminum, Die Cut, 2 ¾ In. ....*illus* 214
Bootjack, Franklin Roosevelt, Figural Donkey Head, Cast Iron, Paint, 1932, 5 x 11 In. .. 242 to 920
Bottle Stopper, John F. Kennedy, Cork, Painted, Stained, c.1960, 5 & 4 In., 3 Piece..................... 127
Box, McKinley, Portrait Bust, Porcelain, Paint, Gilt, Flowers, Shaped, Lid, 1896, 4 x 4 In. 388
Broom Torch, McKinley Portrait, Paper Label, c.1885, 64 In. 546
Button, Bryan & Stevenson, Capitol Dome, Rays, Jugate, Celluloid, 1 ½ In. 4428
Button, Bryan Leading Taft To The Voters Finish Line, Cartoon, 2 In. 805
Button, Bryan, Goldbugs Impaled On Pitchfork, Jugate, 1896, 1 In. 435
Button, Bryan, In Silver Horseshoe, Eagle, Stars, Stripes, Photo, Celluloid, c.1900, 1 ½ In. 2214
Button, BSU, In Black We Trust, Fist, Black & White, Civil Rights, c.1968, 3 ½ In. 238
Button, Citizens For McGovern, Volunteer Bucks County, 1972, 1 In. 234
Button, Core, Civil Rights, Apple Core, Artist's Palette, Lichtenstein, 1965, 1 ¾ In. ....*illus* 190
Button, DNC Obama Biden Heartland Team Rural Council, Jugate, 2008, 3 In. 115
Button, Franklin D. Roosevelt, For President, Portrait, V, Stars, Morse Code, 1944, 2 In. 195
Button, George Washington Inaugural, Copper, Gilt, Long Live President GW, 1 ½ In. 2825
Button, George Washington, Long Live The King, Inaugural, Copper, 1789, 1 ½ In. 4800
Button, Get Your . . . Off The Grass It's Dewey, Donkey Rebus, 1 ¾ In. ....*illus* 230
Button, I Dial For The Duke, Photo, Michael Dukakis On Phone, 2 ¼ In. 247
Button, I'm Still Madly For Adlai, Blue & White, Celluloid, 1956, 2 ¼ In. 254
Button, Inauguration Day, Eisenhower, Nixon, January 20th 1953, Jugate, 3 ½ In. 115
Button, Jugate, Hoover, Curtis, Tin Lithograph, Flag Design Ground, 2 ¼ In. ....*illus* 190
Button, Kennedy Is The Remedy, Photo, Red, White, Blue, 1960, 4 In. 2233
Button, March For Freedom Now, Footprint, Civil Rights, Blue & White, 1960, 2 ½ In. 716
Button, McKinley & Roosevelt, Commerce & Industry, Jugate, Scenes, Mertz, 1 ¼ In. 477
Button, Milk For Supervisor, Photo, Harvey Milk, Gay Rights Activist, c.1977, 1 ½ In. 348
Button, National Wheelmens McKinley & Hobart Club, Jugate, Celluloid, 1896, 1 ¼ In. 115
Button, Ohio Women For Landon, Yellow Flower, 1936 In Center, Lithograph, 13/16 In. 190
Button, Old Jim Crow Has Got To Go, Jobs, Negro Youth Fed., Civil Rights, 1930s, 1 In. 423
Button, Peace Sign, Doves, Red, White, Blue, Peter Max, 2 In. 98
Button, Reagan, Stylized Globe, Alternating Red & Blue Sections, White Letters, 2 ¼ In. 886
Button, School Integration Now!, Celluloid, Civil Rights, 1950s, 1 In. 278
Button, SDS, Dare To Struggle, Dare To Win, Civil Rights, Late 1960s, 1 ¼ In. 383
Button, Sit In Don't Give In, White Ground, Black Lettering, Civil Rights, c.1960, 1 In. 411
Button, Slogan, No Oil On Al, 2 Stars, Celluloid, Teapot Dome Reference, 1928, ¾ In. 115
Button, T. Roosevelt, La Fiesta De Las Flores, Los Angeles, Trumpeters, 1903, 1 ¼ In. 2321
Button, Taft, Swastika, Good Luck, W&H Back Paper, Jugate, 1908, 1 ½ In. 5514
Button, Truman, Barkley, Donkey, Red, White, 1948, 1 ¼ In. 460
Button, Truman, Portrait In Gold Wreath, Above Crossed Flags, Celluloid, 3 ½ In. 115
Button, Votes For Women, 12 Stars Around Border, Ehrman Back Paper, 1 In. 132
Button, Votes For Women, 1915, Golden Sunrise, Celluloid, ⅞ In. 115
Button, Wilson & General Pershing, Victory 1918, Crossed Flags, Jugate, 1 ½ In. 128
Button, Woodrow Wilson, The Man Of The Hour, Portrait Profile, Yellow, Blue, 1912, 2 In. 658
Button, Youth For Kennedy, Portrait, Photo, White & Red, Full Gloss, 1958, 2 ¼ In. 682
Button, Zachary Taylor, Rough & Ready, Brass, Portrait, Profile, 1848, 1 In. 263
Cane, Parade, Benjamin Harrison, Levi Morton, Metal Handle, Portraits, Jugate, 1888, 33 In. ... 690
Cane, Ulysses S. Grant Bust, Cast Iron, 1868, 34 In. 342
Charm, Grant & Colfax, Portraits, Top Loop, 2-Sided, Jugate, 1868, ½ In. 357
Charm, Harding, Brass, Nose Thumber, Mechanical, Top Hat, Tail, 2 In. 115
Cigar Band, Charles Evans Hughes, Portrait, Multicolor, 1916, 8 ½ In. 49

Pisgah Forest, Vase, Crystalline, Cream & Brown, Drip Design, Rolled Rim, 1953, 6 In.
$177

Brunk Auctions

Planters Peanuts, Costume, Mr. Peanut, Fiberglass, Composition, 1940s, 50 x 18 In.
$474

James D. Julia Auctioneers

Plastic, Vase, Amazonia & Black XXL, Resin, Gaetano Pesce, Fish Design, 2005, 26 In.
$2,750

Rago Arts and Auction Center

P

Plastic, Vase, Spaghetti Special, Multicolor, Resin, G. Pesce, 2004, 25 In.
$2,500

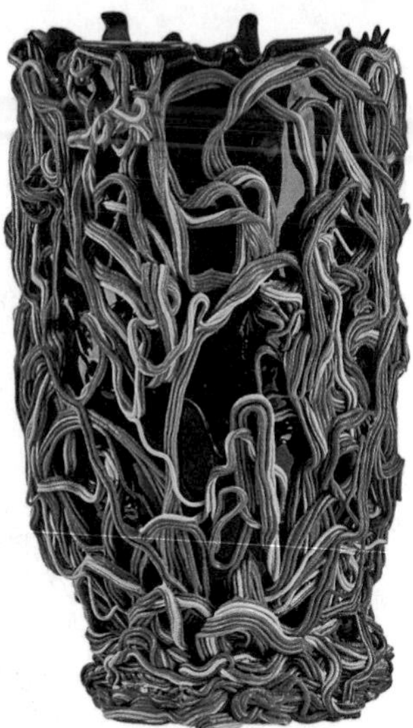

Rago Arts and Auction Center

Plated Amberina, Cruet, Bulbous, Cranberry To Fuchsia To Custard, 12 Ribs, Handle, Stopper, 7 In.
$2,473

Early Auction Company

Plated Amberina, Sugar, Amber To Rose, Squat, Melon Ribbed, Tapered, 2 Loop Handles, 5 In.
$3,450

Early Auction Company

Cigar Label, U.S. Grant, Robert E. Lee, Profiles, Fellow Citizens, Lithograph, 9 x 6 In. 388
Clock, Theodore Roosevelt, Rough Rider, On Horse, Cast Iron, c.1899, 9 x 11 In. 127
Coin Purse, Wm. Henry Harrison, Log Cabin, Bust, Silk, Pink, 2-Sided, 1840, 3 x 3 ½ In. 510
Cup Plate, Andrew Jackson, Portrait, Mulberry Transfer, 1828, 3 ¾ In. 316
Display, Adlai Stevenson, Figural Hat, Nodding Donkey, Red Plastic, Paper, 5 In. 72
Doorstop, Frog, I Croak For The Jackson Wagon, Cast Iron, c.1850, 5 In. 179
Drum, Parade, William Henry Harrison, Painted, Eagle, Shield, 1840, 20 In. 2271
Embroidery, Eagle, Spread Wings, Landing, American Flag Shield, c.1900, 20 x 16 In. 418
Flag, Campaign, Lincoln, Hamlin & S.R. Curtis, 33 Stars, Glazed Cotton, 17 x 22 In. 13800
Flag, Parade, Ulysses S. Grant, Glazed Cotton, Grant, Colfax, Bingham, 1868, 20 x 28 In. 4481
Gloves, I Like Ike, Frame, 11 x 9 In. 117
Hat, Harrison & Reid, G.O.P. Campaign, Felt, Jugate Inside, 1892, 12 x 10 In. ....*illus* 244
Hood Ornament, Charles Evans Hughes, Elephant, Wood, Paint, Flags, 13 x 8 In. 575
Kerchief, Wm. H. Harrison, Campaign, Ohio Farmer, Frame, 1840, 34 x 39 In. ....*illus* 6518
Label, Harry Truman, Beer Bottle & Neck, Ballantine's Burton Ale, c.1934, 3 x 4 In. 16
Lantern, Japanese, Hayes & Wheeler, Paper, Wire Handle, Candleholder, 1876, 7 ½ In. 153
Lantern, McKinley & Roosevelt, Full Dinner Pail, Punched Tin, Bail Handle, c.1900, 9 In. 2868
License Plate, Kennedy For President, John F., Green & White Metal, Full Size, 1960 299
Locket, Lincoln & Johnson, Brass, Book Shape, Photos Inside, c.1860, 1 x 1 In. 956
Map, World According To Ronald Reagan, c.1982, 24 x 36 In. 590
Mirror, Al Smith, Portrait, Round, Celluloid, Metal Collar, Pocket, 1928, 2 ¼ In. 307
Mirror, Warren G. Harding, Portrait, Elephants, Round, 2 In. 896
Mug, FDR, Figural, Face, Square Handle, White Glaze, c.1932, 7 In. 115
Mustard, McKinley, Full Dinner Pail, Metal Cup, Handle, 1900, 2 ¼ x 5 In. 232
Necktie, Jim Crow Must Go, Stick Figures, Maroon Ground, Civil Rights, 1940s, 48 In. 702
Paperweight, Zachary Taylor, Portrait, Bust, Sulphide Glass, Wine Color, White, 2 x 3 In. 1434
Pin Tray, Theodore Roosevelt, Teddy Bear, In Clown Suit, Giraffe, Tin Litho, 1906, 3 x 5 In. 239
Pin, Cleveland, Stevenson, Brass Shell Frame, Eagle Holding Banner, Jugate, 1892, 2 In. 886
Pin, McKinley & Hobart, Brass Bicycle, Paper, Jugate, 1896........ 508
Pin, Remember Pearl Harbor, Figural, Harbor, Plane, Palm Trees, Metal, c.1941, 2 x 3 In. 474
Pin, Theodore Roosevelt, Marvel Flour, Portrait, Round, Red, White, Blue, 1 ¼ In. 813
Pipe, Henry Clay, Portrait, Wood, Metal Bowl, c.1850, 10 In. 207
Pitcher, James Garfield, Brown Glaze, High Relief Portraits, 9 x 5 In. 153
Pitcher, Ulysses S. Grant, Portrait, Majolica, Ribbon, c.1872, 9 ¾ In. 345
Plaque, McKinley & Roosevelt, Bronze, Jugate, 10 ¼ x 13 ½ In. 847
Plate, Andrew Jackson, Portrait, Pink Luster, Shaped Rim, Leaf Border, c.1825, 9 In. 717
Plate, Lincoln White House Service, Royal Purple, Haviland, c.1861, 9 ½ In. ....*illus* 3900
Platter, Blaine, Logan, Milk Glass, Scalloped, Vine & Berry Border, Jugate, 1884, 9 x 13 In. 406
Poster, Black Panther Party, Crying Boy, Free Huey Button, Rifle On Back, 8 x 22 In. 294
Poster, Black Panther, Photographic, Newton & Seal, Standing With Guns, c.1971, 23 x 29 In. . 4428
Poster, Franklin Roosevelt, Roosevelt For President, Signed, c.1932, 59 x 29 In. ....*illus* 414
Poster, Teddy Roosevelt, Uncle Sam, He's Good Enough For Me!, 1904, 11 x 17 In. 167
Poster, Women Suffrage, Political Responsibility, Signed, c.1915, 12 x 36 In. 1315
Print, Abraham Lincoln, Portrait, Vignettes, Sangamo Ins. Co., Paper, 1865, 10 x 13 In. 179
Razor, Straight, Abraham Lincoln, Union & Freedom, Horn Handle, Case, 1864, 6 In. 1135
Razor, Straight, Wilson & Marshall, Wood Grain, Celluloid, Jugate, c.1912, 6 In. 115
Ribbon, Andrew Jackson, Bust, Funeral, Quote, Battle Scene, Silk, 1847, 3 x 8 In. 960
Ribbon, Campaign, Abraham Lincoln, American Flag, Union Motto, 1860, 8 x 3 In. ....*illus* 1777
Ribbon, Henry Clay, Portrait, Vignette, Farmer Of Ashland, Full Color, 1844, 6 ¼ In. 460
Ribbon, Martin Van Buren, Presidential Campaign, No Bank Monopoly, Silk, 1840, 2 x 7 In. 2040
Ribbon, Millard Fillmore, North Or South, Silk, Sullivan, Fischer, 2 ¼ x 7 In. 406
Ribbon, Press, McKinley, Portrait, Republican National League Convention, 1896, 9 In. 127
Ribbon, Woman's Suffrage Convention, Orange, Black, Fringe, N.Y., 1845, 6 In. 173
Ring, John Q. Adams, Gilt Brass, 4 Stars, Adams & Liberty Inscription, 1825, Woman's........ 4485
Scale, Cleveland & Harrison, Bisque Figures, Metal Hangers, Wood, c.1888, 6 In. ....*illus* 1019
Sewing Box, Andrew Jackson, Portrait Lid, Eagle, Under Glass, Removable Lid, 5 x 4 In. 2629
Stickpin, Andrew Johnson, Ivory, Profile, Half Round, 1800s, ¾ x 1 In. 1610
Stickpin, Blaine, Cardboard Photo, Eagle, Brass, Jugate, 2 In. 370
Stickpin, Chester A. Arthur, Cardboard Photo, Brass Shell, 1 In. 729
Stickpin, Roosevelt, Teddy Bear Holding Photo Of Taft, Brass, Celluloid, 2 ⅜ In. 127
Textile, Zachary Taylor, On Horseback, Roller Print Ground, 1848, 22 x 25 In. ....*illus* 861
Thermometer, Hoover's VP Charles Curtis, Celluloid, Round, Easel, 1932, 3 In. 604
Time Magazine Cover, Watergate Dynamite, How Much Damage, Signatures, 1973, 9 x 11 In. 487
Tin, Candy, Theodore Roosevelt, Portrait, Lithograph, Round, Lid, Scroll Design, 2 ½ In. 96
Torch, Benjamin Harrison, Figural Log Cabin, Tin, Torchlight Parades, 1888, 5 x 12 In. 3738
Toy, Teddy Roosevelt, Horseback, Mohair, Leather Saddle, Horsehair Mane, Steiff, 38 In. 7768

Plated Amberina, Tumbler, Shaded Mahogany To Custard, 9 Ribs, Opal Interior, 3 ¾ In.
$1,265

Early Auction Company

Political, Bandanna, Harrison, Morton, Jugate, Campaign, Cotton, 1888, 23 x 22 In.
$240

Cowan Auctions

Political, Bandanna, Harrison, Reid, Republican Protection, Jugate, 1892-1896, 21 x 22 In.
$570

Hake's Americana & Collectibles

TIP

You should not regild, resilver, or repaint political buttons or badges. It lowers the value.

Political, Bandanna, Roosevelt, Protection To America, Jugate, Eagle, Flag, Frame, 1904, 28 x 29 In.
$1,124

Hake's Americana & Collectibles

Political, Bandanna, Taft, Sherman, Flag Ground, Portraits, Jugate, Capitol Building, 1908, 16 x 17 In.
$485

Hake's Americana & Collectibles

Political, Bandanna, We Want Teddy, Musical Score, Oval Portrait, Red, White, 1912, 18 x 18 In.
$177

Hake's Americana & Collectibles

Political, Bandanna, William Henry Harrison, Medallions, Red, White, Cotton, 1840, 26 x 27 In.
$1,440

Cowan Auctions

Political, Bookmark, Taft, Sherman, Figural, Teddy Bear, Heart, Aluminum, Die Cut, 2 ¾ In.
$214

Hake's Americana & Collectibles

Political, Button, Core, Civil Rights, Apple Core, Artist's Palette, Lichtenstein, 1965, 1 ¾ In.
$190

Hake's Americana & Collectibles

Political, Button, Get Your . . . Off The Grass It's Dewey, Donkey Rebus, 1 ¾ In.
$230

Hake's Americana & Collectibles

Political, Button, Jugate, Hoover, Curtis, Tin Lithograph, Flag Design Ground, 2 ¼ In.
$190

Hake's Americana & Collectibles

Political, Hat, Harrison & Reid, G.O.P. Campaign, Felt, Jugate Inside, 1892, 12 x 10 In.
$244

Hake's Americana & Collectibles

"On the Curl"
For a political collector, "on the curl" has a special meaning. It indicates that the name of the maker is printed on the curled edge of a celluloid or tin campaign button.

Political, Kerchief, Wm. H. Harrison, Campaign, Ohio Farmer, Frame, 1840, 34 x 39 In.
$6,518

James D. Julia Auctioneers

Political, Plate, Lincoln White House Service, Royal Purple, Haviland, c.1861, 9 ½ In.
$3,900

Garth's Auctioneers & Appraisers

Political, Poster, Franklin Roosevelt, Roosevelt For President, Signed, c.1932, 59 x 29 In.
$414

James D. Julia Auctioneers

Political, Ribbon, Campaign, Abraham Lincoln, American Flag, Union Motto, 1860, 8 x 3 In.
$1,777

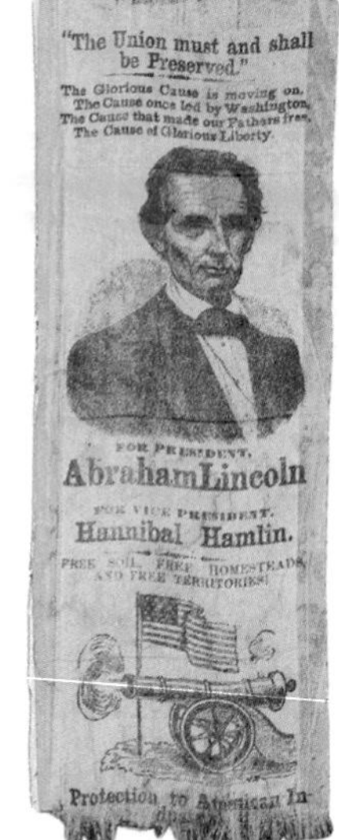

James D. Julia Auctioneers

Political, Scale, Cleveland & Harrison, Bisque Figures, Metal Hangers, Wood, c.1888, 6 In.
$1,019

Hake's Americana & Collectibles

Political, Textile, Zachary Taylor, On Horseback, Roller Print Ground, 1848, 22 x 25 In.
$861

Cowan Auctions

Tray, Alton Parker, Jefferson, Jackson, Shoes At H. Brueggen's, Metal, 1904, 17 In. ....*illus* 265
Watch Fob, Cox, Roosevelt, Portraits, Brass, Shield Shape, Jugate, 1920 170
Watch Fob, Teddy Roosevelt, Progressive Party, Sepia Photo, Portrait, 1912, 5 In. 238
Watch, Roosevelt & Fairbanks, Metal Case, Jugate, Pocket, 1900s 3364
Wrapper, Candy, Tilden & Hendricks, Portraits, Multicolor, 1876, 5 x 4 In. 448

POMONA glass is a clear glass with a soft amber border decorated with pale blue or rose-colored flowers and leaves. The colors are very, very pale. The background of the glass is covered with a network of fine lines. It was made from 1885 to 1888 by the New England Glass Company. First grind was made from April 1885 to June 1886. It was made by cutting a wax surface on the glass, then dipping it in acid. Second grind was a less expensive method of acid etching that was developed later.

Bowl, Fluted, Etched Design, 2 ½ x 5 ¼ In. 105
Pitcher, Flowers, Leaves, Multicolor, 7 x 7 In. 90
Tumbler, Pansy, Butterfly, New England Glass, 3 ¾ x 2 ¼ In. 150

PONTYPOOL, *see Tole category.*

POOLE POTTERY was founded by Jesse Carter in 1873 in Poole, England, and has operated under various names since then. The pottery operated as Carter & Co. for several years and established Carter, Stabler & Adams as a subsidiary in 1921. The company specialized in tiles, architectural ceramics, and garden ornaments. Tableware, bookends, candelabra, figures, vases, and other items have also been made. The name *Poole Pottery Ltd.* was taken in 1963. The company went bankrupt in 2003 but is in business today with new owners.

Casserole, Lid, Cornflower Blue, Retro Design, Round, 1950s, 8 In. 55
Casserole, Lid, Round, Stylized Blue Pea Pods, Cauliflower, Leaves, c.1955, 3 x 8 In. ....*illus* 55
Charger, Himalayan Poppy, Orange, Dark Blue, 15 In. 220
Cracker Jar, Blue Bird On Branch, Flowers, Knob Handles, 6 ½ x 5 ½ In. 40
Figurine, Dolphin In Waves, Blue, Black, c.1930, 6 ½ x 4 ¾ In. 40
Figurine, Seal, Holding Fish, Blue Green, 4 ¾ In. 260
Plate, Delphis, Yellow, Green, Orange, c.1974, 10 In. 130
Salt & Pepper, Stylized Flowers, Purple, Pink.. 40
Tray, Aegean, Green, Black, c.1973, 7 x 4 In. 30
Trinket Box, Odyssey Pattern, Lid, Red, Yellow, Round, 2 In. 93
Vase, Delphis, Slab Sides, Glossy Red, Green & Black Design, c.1970, 4 ¼ In. 65
Vase, Yellow Orange Poppies, Blue Ground, Footed, Oval, 10 In. 170
Wall Pocket, Yellow Orange Poppies, Blue Ground, 10 x 11 In. 230

POPEYE was introduced to the Thimble Theatre comic strip in 1929. The character became a favorite of readers. In 1932, an animated cartoon featuring Popeye was made by Paramount Studios. The cartoon series continued and became even more popular when it was shown on television starting in the 1950s. The full-length movie with Robin Williams as Popeye was made in 1980. KFS stands for King Features Syndicate, the distributor of the comic strip.

Alarm Clock, Popeye's Thimble Theatre, Metal Case, Round, Square Base, 4 ½ In. 450
Bank, Popeye Portrait, Corncob Pipe, Ceramic, U.S.A., 7 ½ In. 180
Display, Popeye Holding Sign, I Sez Wheatena Makes Muskle!, Cardboard, 46 In. 300
Doormat, Rug, Popeye, Olive Oyl, Brutus Playing Drum, Flute, Spinach, Frame, 37 x 23 In. 60
Doorstop, Full Figure, Removable Pipe, Cast Iron, Paint, King Features Syn., 1929, 9 In. ....*illus* 4425
Doorstop, Popeye Standing, Pipe, Cast Iron, Painted, Hubley, 1929, 9 In. .... 1020 to 3835
Fly Swatter, Popeye Cutouts, Metal, Painted Wood Handle, US Mfg. Corp., 1936 278
Game, Popeye Menu, Pinball, Tin Lithograph, 1935, Durable Toy & Novelty, 12 x 23 In. 270
Game, Target, Pin The Pipe On Popeye, Paper Poster, 1940, 27 x 15 In. 60
Jigger, Popeye & Olive Oyl, Dancing, Playing Accordion, Windup, Marx, 9 ½ In. 443
Lamp, Electric, Popeye Standing, Arm Around Stem, Cast Metal, Shade, 15 In. 275
Night-Light, Popeye Standing, Cast Metal, Tin, Paint, Base, Switch, 4 ½ In. 240
Pencil Sharpener, Popeye Holding Pencil, Bakelite, Yellow, King Features Syndicate, 2 In. 45
Puppet, Popeye, Talking, Vinyl Head, Cloth Felt Body, Box, 1967, 7 x 12 In. 175
Sign, Drink Popeye, I Yam What I Yam & I Yam Tops, Cardboard, c.1925, 23 x 15 In. 690
Sign, Popeye On Th' Radio, Fudgicle, Fudge Freeze, 5 Cents, Cardboard, 13 x 9 In. ....*illus* 184
Sign, Popeye Sailor Man, Book Promo, 50 Cents, Cardboard, Easel Back, 13 x 9 In. ....*illus* 184
Tapping Set, Popeye Images, Aluminum Sheets, Mallet, Punch, Cardboard Box, 1957, 11 x 15 In. 185
Toy, Car, Sports Roadster, Olive Oyl, Friction, 1950s, 8 ½ In. 190
Toy, Handcar, Popeye & Olive Oyl, Slinkys, Linemar, 6 ½ In. 480
Toy, Motorcycle, Spinach Patrol, Popeye Rider, 3 Wheels, Cast Iron, Paint, c.1930, 6 In. 390
Toy, Popeye & Rowboat, Moving Oars, Pressed Steel, Windup, c.1935, 15 In. 3600

Political, Tray, Alton Parker, Jefferson, Jackson, Shoes At H. Brueggen's, Metal, 1904, 17 In.
$265

Hake's Americana & Collectibles

Poole, Casserole, Lid, Round, Stylized Blue Pea Pods, Cauliflower, Leaves, c.1955, 3 x 8 In.
$55

Ruby Lane

Popeye, Doorstop, Full Figure, Removable Pipe, Cast Iron, Paint, King Features Syn., 1929, 9 In.
$4,425

Bertoia Auctions

This is an edited listing of current prices. Visit **Kovels.com** to check thousands of prices from previous years and sign up for free information on trends, tips, reproductions, marks, and more.

Popeye, Sign, Popeye On Th' Radio, Fudgicle, Fudge Freeze, 5 Cents, Cardboard, 13 x 9 In.
$184

Wm Morford

Popeye, Sign, Popeye Sailor Man, Book Promo, 50 Cents, Cardboard, Easel Back, 13 x 9 In.
$184

Wm Morford

Porcelain, Dresser Box, Lid, King On Throne, Figural, Victorian, 10 In.
$47

Hess Auction Group

Toy, Popeye Express, Pushing Wheelbarrow, Trunk With Parrot, Tin Litho, Clockwork, 8 ¼ In. .. 443
Toy, Popeye On Spinach Can, Smoking, Waving, Battery Operated, Linemar, Box, c.1958, 9 In. .. 1770
Toy, Popeye Punching Bag, Red Base, Tin Lithograph, Windup, 8 In. 1200
Toy, Popeye Skater, Tin Lithograph, Windup, Linemar, 6 ½ In. 450
Toy, Popeye The Champ, Popeye & Brutus Boxing, Tin, Celluloid, Windup, Marx, 7 In. 600
Toy, Popeye The Pilot, In Airplane, Propeller, Multicolor, Tin Lithograph, Marx, 8 ½ In. 250
Toy, Popeye Walking, Holding Parrot Cage, Tin, Windup, Marx, Box, 1920s, 8 ¼ In. 354
Toy, Popeye, Barrel Walking, Protruding Limbs, Tin Lithograph, Windup, Box, Chein, 7 In. 708
Toy, Popeye, Blowing Bubbles, Holding Can, Tin Litho, Battery Operated, Linemar, 12 In. 502
Toy, Popeye, Riding Tricycle, Cloth Pants, Tin Lithograph, King Features, 6 ¼ In. 531
Toy, Sand, Popeye & Olive Oyl, Holding Swee'Pea, Jeep, Tin Lithograph, 9 ½ In. 120
Whirligig, Folk Art, Wood, Carved, Painted, Black Base, c.1910, 17 ¼ x 23 In. 400

PORCELAIN factories that are well known are listed in this book under the factory name. This category lists pieces made by the less well-known factories. Additional pieces of porcelain are listed in this book in the categories Porcelain-Contemporary, Porcelain-Midcentury, and under the factory name.

Bowl, Applied Roses & Leaves, Reticulated, Cherub Finial, Lid, 7 In. 35
Bowl, Blue & White, Metal Mount, 16 x 15 In. 492
Bowl, Blue Plum, Round, Ruffled Rim, 3 Feet, Onondaga Pottery Co., 10 ½ In. 182
Bowl, Cherubs, Blue & White Striped Shells, Gilt, 2 Tiers, 27 ½ x 20 ½ In. 400
Bowl, Colonial Town, Dunham Style, Gilt Bronze Mount, 12 x 23 In. 531
Bowl, Flaring Cylindrical, Fruit Cluster, Flowers, Gilt Scrolls, 1810, 7 x 6 In. 438
Bowl, Flowers, Multicolor, 13 ½ In. 125
Bowl, Magic Flute Pattern, Bjorn Wiinblad, 3 ½ x 7 In. 98
Bowl, Vignettes, Flowers, Reticulated, Branch Handles, Royal Berlin, 4 x 12 In. 357
Box, Jewelry, Enamel, White Dots, 4-Footed, France, 2 ½ x 3 ¼ In. 54
Box, Sevres Style, Landscape, Lid, 6 ¼ In. 125
Bust, Marie Antoinette, Flowers In Hair, Robes, 22 x 14 In. 968
Bust, Woman, Gilt, Blonde, Elaborate Hat, Ruffles, Victorian, 7 x 4 In. 58
Cachepot, Pink, Flower Bouquet, Gilt Lip, Marked, 4 ¾ In. 156
Candleholder, Cat, Lying Down, Flowers, Pink, Yellow, Blue, White Ground, Persia, 6 x 7 In. 12
Centerpiece, 3 Graces, Holding Hands, Reticulated Basket Over Heads, Gilt, c.1920, 11 In. 1500
Centerpiece, Parcel Gilt, Women, Arms Crossed, Continental, 18 In. 275
Cheese Plate, Dome Lid, Red, White, Pinecone Finial, 8 x 10 ¼ In. 180
Chocolate Pot, Lid, Cobalt Blue, Etched Trellis Design, Silver Overlay, c.1900, 11 In. 750
Chocolate Set, Classical Scene, Green, Burgundy, Pot, Cups, Tray, Germany, 10 Piece 150
Chocolate Set, Ships On Water, Brown, Pot, 6 Cup & Saucers, Tray, 14 Piece 246
Coffeepot, Harbor View, Storage Tent, Pushing Barrels, Sailboats, Lid, 8 ⅝ In. 360
Compote, Boy, Girl, Baskets, Bunnies, Chicks, Sitzendorf, Germany, 12 ½ x 9 In. 60
Cup & Saucer, Flowers, Gilt Rim, 5 ¼ In. 63
Dish, 5 Reserves, Women In Courtyard, Gilt, Japan, 7 ¼ In. 47
Dish, Lid, Peasants Drinking, Landscape, Flowers, Butterflies, Painted, c.1810, 10 x 13 In. 236
Dish, Sweetmeat, Flowers, Painted, Gilt, Lobed, Bow Handles, 1800s, 7 ¾ x 7 In. 276
Dresser Box, Lid, King On Throne, Figural, Victorian, 10 In. *illus* 47
Figurine, 2 Children, Boat, Singing, Playing Flute, Italy, 6 ½ x 9 ¼ In. 106
Figurine, 2 Ladies, Lace Dresses, Grass, 7 ½ x 8 ¼ In. 94
Figurine, 4 Seasons, Painted, Multicolor, Red Anchor Mark, 9 ½ x 3 ¾ In., 4 Piece 922
Figurine, Bacchus, Holding Grapes, Foot On Ewer, Nude, 12 x 8 In. 461
Figurine, Bird, Leaves, Flowers, Tendrils, Ormolu, 7 x 7 ½ In. 424
Figurine, Dancer, Woman, Long Flowing Gown, Bent Arms, Stylized, White, c.1925, 15 In. 1750
Figurine, Dancing Couple, Pink Skirt, 12 x 11 In., Pair 125
Figurine, Dancing Woman, Green & Red Underglaze, 16 ¼ x 8 ¼ In. 720
Figurine, Dog, Doberman Pinscher, Snarling, 9 In. 63
Figurine, Empress, Seated, Multicolor, Glazed, c.1820, 13 ¾ x 8 ½ In. 77
Figurine, Girl, Country, Fruit Tree, Multicolor, 7 ¾ x 2 ½ In. 58
Figurine, Hunter, Rifle, Bronn, 20 x 10 In. 522
Figurine, Macaw, Perched On White Trunk, 16 In. 1375
Figurine, Parrots, Green Feathers, White Base, Vista Alegre, 15 ½ x 3 ¼ In. 360
Figurine, Parrots, Perching, Marked, Sitzendorf, 9 ¼ In., Pair 34
Figurine, Peasant Riding Devil, Red Pants, Russia, 6 ⅜ x 5 ¼ In. 153
Figurine, Seated Nude Woman, Blue Crowned V Mark, Continental, 12 ½ In. 375
Figurine, Walrus, Dark Gray, 14 x 23 In. 106
Figurine, Woodpecker, Orange, Black, Italy, 12 ½ x 9 In. 47
Flower Holder, Blooms & Buds, Blue, Green, Pink, Tan, Shaped Base, 1926, 5 In. 978

Flower, Pink Debutante, Purple Iris, Branch, Connoisseur Of Malvern, 10 ¾ In. 523
Group, Coach, Carried By 2 Men, Blue, White, France, 1878, 10 In. 369
Group, Couple Dancing, Pink Ruffled Skirt, Germany, 12 x 11 In. 120
Group, Courting Lovers, Seated Woman, Doting Man, Dog, 6 x 6 In. 123
Group, Horses, Coach, 14 x 5 ½ In. 30
Group, Men Talking, 1 Seated, 8 ½ In. 313
Group, Native American Elder & Youth, Bronn, 12 x 14 In. 738
Group, Woman & Child, Combing Hair, Green Cape, Dressing Table, 7 ½ x 7 ½ In. 400
Holy Water Font, Biscuit, White, Figure On Flower, Gothic Style Arch, c.1910, 15 x 8 In. 178
Jar, 2 Views Of Tower, Walled Town, Purple, White Ground, Lid, 6 ½ x 4 ¼ In., Pair 480
Jar, Battle Scenes, Flower Bouquets, Vertical Ribs, Raptor Finial, 12 ¾ In., Pair 302
Jar, Goldfish, Flowers, White Ground, Lid, 16 x 14 In. 215
Jar, Lid, Dragon, Blue & White, Melon Lobed, Pieced Wood Cover, c.1890, 10 In. 3835
Jardiniere, Coat Of Arms, White, 9 ¼ x 12 In., Pair 163
Jardiniere, Gilt, Flowers, Lion Head Handles, 1830, 6 ½ x 6 ½ In. 584
Jardiniere, Rainbow Colors, Birds, Flowers, 15 x 19 In. 118
Mirror, Cherubs, Flowers, White, Curvy, 35 x 19 In. 863
Mug, Bacchus & Cherubs, Multicolor, Relief Decoration, Ring Foot, Handle, ¾ Liter 96
Pipe, Regimental, Porcelain Bowl, Garde Ulan Regt., c.1910 312
Pitcher, Red Robin Shape, Beak Spout, Marked, Mr. Clemens To Mayme, 1907, 7 In. 115
Plant Stand, Tripod, Hanging Cauldron, Flowers, Brass Trim, Chain, England, 57 In. 480
Planter, Flower Garland, Roses, Pink, Gilt, Ruffle Rim, Curved Handles, c.1890, 12 In. 120
Plaque, Louis XV Style, Giltwood, Couples In Period Dress, Swag Base, 39 x 17 In., Pair 2337
Plaque, Marie Antoinette, Portrait, Painted, Giltwood Frame, c.1900, 15 x 13 In. 922
Plaque, Mother & Child, Painted, c.1890, 3 ½ x 2 ½ In. 123
Plaque, Ruth The Gleaner, Armful Of Wheat, Gilt Wood Openwork Frame, c.1900, 6 x 5 In. 840
Plaque, Woman, Gauzy Pink Dress, Garland, Pond, Trees, Bronze Frame, c.1900, 13 x 9 In. 1135
Plaque, Young Woman, Rose Color Classical Dress, Holding Vase, Gilt Frame, 18 x 10 In. 106
Plate, Bird, Landscape, Gilt, Blue, White, Neoclassical, 9 ½ In., Pair 38
Plate, Dessert, Flowers, Green Leaves, White Ground, Italy, 8 In., 8 Piece 215
Plate, Flowers, Pink, Green, Cauldon, England, 8 ¾ In., 11 Piece 147
Plate, Fruit, Painted, White Ground, Gilt Rim, C. Breton, 9 ⅜ In., 12 Piece 1800
Plate, Monkey Under Peach Tree, Deer, Birds, Insects, Wucai Enamel, Ming, 8 ¾ In. 2832
Plate, Sixteen Birds Of England, E. Donovan, 11 x 9 In., 16 Piece 207
Plate, White, Black Drawing, Pablo Picasso, Block Langenthal, 8 In., 12 Piece 270
Platter, Bird In Cartouche, Gilt Rosette, White Ground, Octagonal, c.1880, 15 x 11 In. 35
Punch Bowl, Grapevine, Germany, 6 ½ x 13 ⅝ In. 69
Punch Bowl, Green, Flowers, Figural Base, Dolphins, Sea Grass, c.1820, 9 ½ x 18 In. 344
Stand, Dessert, Flowers, Pink, Gilt Scrolling Leaves, 4 Tiers, Paw Feet, c.1830, 21 In. 1125
Sweetmeat Stand, Tiered, 10 Upturned Shell-Shape Dishes, Coral Base, c.1770, 10 In. 2500
Tazza, Applied Putto, Blue, Gilt Acanthus Feet, 30 ½ x 19 ½ In. 1342
Tea Set, Flowers, Blue Green, Fukugawa, 6 Cups & Saucers, 15 Piece 215
Tea Set, White, Blue Grapevine, Cherubs, Gilt Trim, Kornilov, c.1900, 4 Piece 1722
Teapot, Blue & White, Dragon, Rounded Body, Handle, Scrolling, 5 ½ x 7 In. 196
Teapot, Figures In Landscape, Enamel, Gilt, Globular, Twig Handle, Lid, c.1860, 11 In. 1793
Teapot, Lid, Globular, Loop Handle, Enamel Design, Bib Border, Flowers, Lowestoft, c.1787, 6 In. *illus* 2337
Tureen, Sauce, Stand, Branch Handles, Ogee Domed Lid, Flower Finial, 1800s, 6 x 9 In. 177
Tureen, White, Fluted, Lid, England, 11 x 13 In. 123
Urn, Arabesque Style, Figural Panels, Landscapes, Bronze Mount, Beast Handles, 14 In., Pair 6000
Urn, Lid, Finial, Green Ground, Gold Acanthus, Continental, 26 In. 188
Urn, Louis XVI, Bronze, Lid, Guilloche Base, Gilt Leaves, Allegorical, 14 x 5 In., Pair 984
Urn, Painted, Platinum Ground, Snake Shape Handles, Gilt, Masks, c.1890, 11 In., Pair 1000
Urn, Pink & White Glaze, Wide Rim, Upswept Handles, Pedestal Foot, 1935, 8 In. 115
Urn, Vienna Style, Genre Scenes, Blue, Marble Pedestal, Franz Dorfl, c.1900, 30 In 1250
Urn, Yellow Glaze, Seashell Handles, Pointed Lid, 1939, 13 In. 184
Urn, Yellow, Square Base, England, 13 In. 125
Vase, 3 White Geese, Mottled Blue Gray Ground, Baluster, 1934, 6 ¼ In. 1840
Vase, Applied White Flowers, Branch Shape Feet, 9 ¾ In. 250
Vase, Beaker, White Chrysanthemums, Pale Blue Ground, Ed Diers, 1904, 8 In. 316
Vase, Blue & White, Landscape, Estates, Cows, Booths Silicon China, 17 x 8 In., Pair 236
Vase, Blue & White, Mythical Beasts, Floral Panels, c.1500, 10 ½ In. 1353
Vase, Blue Birds, Flowers, Water, Mountains, Tapered, Squared Shoulder, 1920, 10 In. 2300
Vase, Blue, Roses, White Feathery Handles, 10 In. 24
Vase, Bottle Shape, Encrusted Flowers, Transfer Print, Meissen Style, c.1900, 6 In., Pair 500
Vase, Bottle Shape, Flower Encrusted, White Ground, c.1900, 9 ½ In., Pair 250
Vase, Bottle Shape, Green Matte Glaze, Oval, Long Neck, Footed, Marked, 7 ½ In. 253
Vase, Bud, Young Woman, Paris, Seine, Narrow Neck, Round Foot, France, 3 In. 363

Porcelain, Teapot, Lid, Globular, Loop Handle, Enamel Design, Bib Border, Flowers, Lowestoft, c.1787, 6 In.
$2,337

Skinner, Inc.

Porcelain-Asian, Figurine, Laughing Boy, Standing, Holding Jar, Lotus Blossom, 1600s, 11 In.
$492

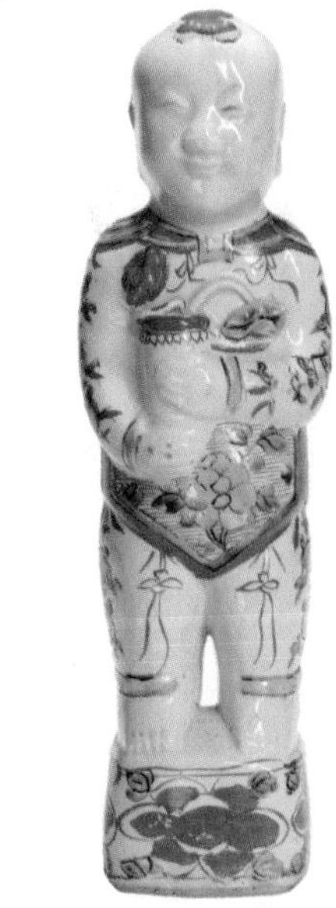

Skinner, Inc.

Porcelain-Asian, Ginger Jar, Lid, Blue & White, Children Playing, Garden, c.1900, 8 x 7 In.
$237

James D. Julia Auctioneers

Porcelain-Asian, Plate, Dragon, Phoenix In Flight, Iron Red & White, Gilt, c.1910, 10 In.
$356

James D. Julia Auctioneers

Porcelain-Asian, Vase, Blue, White, Reticulated, 6-Sided, Roosters, Flowers, c.1700, 5 In.
$2,952

Skinner, Inc.

Porcelain-Asian, Vase, Double Gourd, Dragon, Phoenix In Flight, Clouds, Waves, Red, White, 9 In.
$9,480

James D. Julia Auctioneers

Vase, Cartouche, Lobed, Rose Decoration, Gilt, Handles, Round Foot, Austria, 15 x 6 In. 122
Vase, Cobalt Blue, Asian Scenes, Dragon Mount, 1800s, France, 15 ¾ x 15 In. 1722
Vase, Cobalt Blue, Still-Life Flowers, 2 Handles, Faux Marble Base, 7 ½ In. 1125
Vase, Copper Red, Bottle Shape, Unglazed Foot, c.1900, 22 In. 1770
Vase, Cornucopia, Pink & Green Bouquets, Rococo, 9 ¼ In., Pair 375
Vase, Couple Talking, Green, Gilt, White, Swan Handles, 10 ¾ x 6 ¼ In. 126
Vase, Court Scenes, Panels, Chateau, Couples, Cobalt, Gilt, Leaf Swag Handles, 41 In. 5250
Vase, Double Gourd, Red & Purple Flambe Glaze, Triple Spout, 22 ¾ In. 3025
Vase, Double Gourd, White Matte, Footed, 7 ¼ In. 161
Vase, Flowers, Leaves, Scrolls, Elongated, Shaped Neck, Foo Dog Feet, 19 x 9 In., Pair 360
Vase, Gold Dangling Spiders, Web, Speckled Blue Gray, Drip, Wavy Rim, 6 In. 5175
Vase, Green, Landscape Reserves, Round Foot, 13 In. 163
Vase, Green, Woman In High Relief, Spring, Summer, Sitzendorf, Germany, 11 In., Pair 354
Vase, Parrot, Tulips, Brown, Yellow Tint, Tapered, Wide Rim, 1931, 8 In. 1035
Vase, Pear Shape, Bavarian Flowers, Flared Rim, Silver Overlay, c.1930, 8 In. 500
Vase, Pinecone & Needles, Brown, Yellow, Tapered Cylinder, 1902, 17 In. 575
Vase, Rouleau, Apple Green Over White Glaze, Galleried Rim, Gilt Edge, 1800s, 18 In. 531
Vase, Rouleau, Iron Red Flowers, Gilt Phoenix, Blue & White Bands, 22 In. 354
Vase, Sacrificial, Cobalt Blue Glaze, Bottle Shape, Marked, 11 ¾ In. 4720
Vase, Seaweed, Fish, Cream Wax Matte, Gray, Tan, Baluster, Hentschel, 1931, 7 In. 4255
Vase, Sevres Style, Gilt Bronze, Champleve, 28 In. 9375
Vase, Shell Shape, Blue, Applied Coral, Starfish, Shells, c.1879, 17 ½ In. 3750
Vase, Stick, White, Dogwood Blossoms, Iris Glaze, Squat, J. Wareham, 1898, 6 In. 230
Vase, Teadust Glaze, Footed, 1800s, 12 ½ In., Pair 1770
Vase, Trumpet, Pansies, Pink, White, Purple, Gilt, Squat, Russia, c.1860, 12 In. 6573
Vase, Yellow Glaze, Cylindrical, Rounded, Molded Rim, Ring Foot, 1915, 9 In. 115
Wall Pocket, Cupid, Bow, Quiver, Lovebird, Painted, Rococo Style, c.1890, 14 x 7 In. 875
Water Pot, Beehive, Clair-De-Lune Glaze, Domed, 3 ½ x 5 ¼ In. 861
Water Pot, Beehive, Peachbloom, Dragon Roundels, 6-Character Mark, 3 x 5 In. 492

PORCELAIN-ASIAN includes pieces made in China, Japan, Korea, and other Asian countries. Asian porcelain is also listed in Canton, Chinese Export, Imari, Japanese Coralene, Moriage, Nanking, Occupied Japan, Satsuma, Sumida, and other categories.

Bottle, Armorial, Lid, Flower Festoons, Eagle, Shield, Shaped, 4 ½ In. 406
Bowl, Blue & White, Landscapes, Calligraphy, 12 x 7 In. 197
Bowl, Blue & White, Leaves, Scalloped Edge, Recessed Foot, Japan, 2 ½ x 5 In. 41
Bowl, Dragons, Egg & Spinach Glaze, Bell Shaped, Ring Foot, c.1870, 4 In., Pair 216
Bowl, Figures, Pine Trees, Lanterns, Dragon, Wide Rim, Ring Foot, 1800s, 5 In. Diam. 306
Bowl, Flower Scrolls, Fret Border Inside, Metal Rim, 4 In. Diam. 5250
Bowl, Magenta Glaze, Gilt Edge, Bucket Shape, Flared Rim, 1800s, 6 x 3 In. 593
Bowl, Molded Petals, 2 Swimming Fish Inside, Tan, 5 In. Diam. 875
Bowl, Pale Blue, Crackled, Purple Splashes, Bubble Rings, Foot, 4 In. Diam. 618
Bowl, Tea, Lid, Blue & White, Landscape, Animals, Japan, 2 ¼ x 4 ¼ In. 24
Bowl, Yellow Glaze, Incised Vines & Lotus Blossoms, Ring Foot, 1900s, 3 x 7 In. 371
Box, Lid, Dragons, Blue & White, Rounded Square, Flower Form Corners, 9 x 6 In. 3555
Box, Sweetmeat, Woman, Trees, Round, 4 Sections, Ring Handles, 1800s, 7 In. 214
Brushpot, Blue & White, Landscape, Figures, 8 ¼ x 8 In. 275
Brushpot, Pine, Prunus, Bamboo, Cylindrical, Molded, Pierced, c.1800, 5 x 4 In. 371
Brushpot, Red & White, Flowers, Cylindrical, Waisted, Key Decoration, 1800s, 8 In. 3555
Censer, Teadust Glaze, Square, Faceted Sides, Squared Handles, Footed, 7 In. 124
Coffeepot, Lid, Lighthouse Shape, Enamel, Animals, Flowers, 1700s, 7 In. 400
Cup, Engraved Dragons, Clouds, Stem, Cylindrical Foot, Wide Rim, 6 In. Diam. 62
Cup, Pink, Dragon, Pearl, Clouds, Bell Shaped, 1800s, 3 x 3 In. 185
Dish, Insects Perched On Blossoming Stems, Vines, 1900s, 7 ½ In. Diam. 356
Dish, Millefleur, Vines & Leaves, Multicolor, Gilt Ground, c.1900, 9 In. Diam. 309
Double Gourd, White Matte Finish, 7 In. 336
Figurine, Blanc De Chine, Scholar, Heavy Robes, Signed, 8 ½ x 3 ½ In. 3552
Figurine, Buddhist Lion, Paw On Brocade Ball, Ribbon In Jaws, Plinth, 11 In. 429
Figurine, Foo Dog, Blue On White Glass, Cube Pedestal, Dragon, 22 x 11 In., Pair 610
Figurine, Laughing Boy, Standing, Holding Jar, Lotus Blossom, 1600s, 11 In. .... *illus* 492
Figurine, Rooster, Yellow, Cobalt, Brown, 11 In., Pair 461
Flask, Moon Shape, Blue & White, Cylindrical Neck, Scroll Handles, 1900s, 11 In. 1853
Flask, Pilgrim, Moon Shape, Stylized Lotus, Dragon Handles, 1800s, 19 In. 4940
Ginger Jar, Lid, Blue & White, Children Playing, Garden, c.1900, 8 x 7 In. .... *illus* 237
Hat Stand, Vase, Hexagonal, Cutout, Multicolored Flowers, 10 In. 183
Hibachi, Raised Flowers, Cobalt Leaves, Geometric Frieze, Japan, 13 x 19 In. 120

Incense Burner, Saddle, Stirrups, Hakata Style, Japan, 6 ¾ x 8 ½ In. 1830
Jar, Blue & White, Dragons, Chasing Flaming Pearl, Swollen Shoulder, 13 In. 247
Jar, Dome Lid, Mythical Beasts, Panels, Multicolor, Oval, 1600s, 14 In. 1593
Jar, Landscape, Evergreen & Prunus Trees, Blue, Red, 9 ¼ In. 93
Jar, Lid, Blue & White, Panels, Prunus, Cracked Ice, 10 In. 116
Jardiniere, Woman, Trees, Flowers, Round, Tapered, Flat Wide Rim, 16 x 18 In. 4270
Plate, Dragon, Phoenix In Flight, Iron Red & White, Gilt, c.1910, 10 In. ....*illus* 356
Platter, Blue & White, Birds & Flowers, Hexagonal, 1700s, 14 x 12 In. 770
Platter, Blue & White, Dragons, Flying, Clouds, Flames, Vine Border, c.1890, 17 In. 371
Tea Canister, Lid, Blue & White, Figures, Landscape, Square, 1900s, 7 In. 474
Tea Dispenser, Blue Asian Characters, Twisted Bands, Bung Hole, Handles, 1890s, 10 In. 54
Tea Set, Stripes, Gilt, Teapot, Sugar & Creamer, Kuznetsov, Russia, 3 Piece.......... 343
Teacup, White, Goldfish, Swimming, Gilt Rim, 1900s, 2 ½ In. Diam., Pair.......... 119
Umbrella Stand, Flowers, Leaves, Beige, Green, Red, Cylindrical, 20 In. 122
Urn, Lid, Flowers, Pierced, Handles, Gilt Bronze Mount, Foot, c.1890, 14 In. 3500
Vase, Beaker Shape, Blue & White, Dragons, Flowers, Flared Rim, 1800s, 14 In. 500
Vase, Beaker Shape, Scrolling Vine Band, Flowers, Flared Rim, 1900s, 18 In. 2779
Vase, Blue & White, 4 Beauties, Raised Dots, Waisted Neck, 17 In. 475
Vase, Blue & White, Bamboo, Prunus, Orchid, Inverted Pear Form, 8 In. 625
Vase, Blue & White, Dragon Chasing Flaming Pearl, Baluster, c.1900, 18 In. 2161
Vase, Blue & White, Dragon, Shou, Globular, Straight Neck, Lappet Band, 9 In. 5925
Vase, Blue & White, House, Landscape, Yellow Ground, Japan, 32 x 44 In. 1845
Vase, Blue & White, Leafy Vines, Flowers, Cylindrical, Flat Shoulder, 1900s, 10 In. 1544
Vase, Blue & White, Leaves, Squat, Recessed Foot, Metal Rim, 4 ¾ x 4 ¾ In. 130
Vase, Blue & White, Prunus Blossoms, Baluster, Waisted, Domed Lid, 1700s, 17 In. 1948
Vase, Blue & White, Rows Of Shou Symbols, Script, Baluster, 1900s, 18 In. 2666
Vase, Blue & White, Square, Inverted Neck, Mask & Ring Handles, 11 In. 948
Vase, Blue & White, Village, Pomegranate Handles, Flared Rim, c.1900, 23 In. 345
Vase, Blue, Geese, Oval, Bronze Reticulated Base, Leaf Rim, c.1890, 15 In., Pair.......... 1225
Vase, Blue, White, Reticulated, 6-Sided, Roosters, Flowers, c.1700, 5 In. ....*illus* 2952
Vase, Bottle Shape, Butterflies, Vines, Gilt, Flared Rim, Round Foot, 1900s, 16 In. 1304
Vase, Bottle Shape, Cream To Red Glaze, Lang Yao, c.1900, 15 x 9 In. 711
Vase, Bottle Shape, Flowers, Lizard Form Handles At Neck, 18 In. 153
Vase, Bottle Shape, Vines, Bats, Coral, Gilt, Garlic Top, 1900s, 7 In., Pair.......... 948
Vase, Bottle Shape, White, Gilt Roundels, Flared Rim, 1900s, 16 x 10 In. 1112
Vase, Crackle Glaze, Molded Ribs, Cylindrical, Inverted Neck, 1900s, 8 In. 432
Vase, Double Gourd, Blue & White, Bats, Stylized Flowers, Shells, 1900s, 9 In. 1235
Vase, Double Gourd, Blue & White, Running Horses, Flames, c.1600, 12 In. 711
Vase, Double Gourd, Dragon, Phoenix In Flight, Clouds, Waves, Red, White, 9 In. ....*illus* 9480
Vase, Dragon Cartouches, Flowers, Gourd Shape, Squared Base, 16 In. 139
Vase, Dragons, Flying, Flowers, Hexagonal, Tapered Shoulder, 1900s, 16 In. 119
Vase, Dragons, Vines, Tapering Cylinder, Squared Shoulder, 1900s, 15 In. 948
Vase, Dragons, Wucai Enamel Decoration, Octagonal, 9 ½ In. 93
Vase, Famille Verte, Figures, Flowers, Gilt Scrolls, 1800s, 21 In. 1225
Vase, Flambe Glaze, Red, Olive, Elephant Head Handles, Pear Shape, 1800s, 7 In. 652
Vase, Flowers, Scrolling Vines, Blue, Green, Flared Rim, 1900s, 16 In. 7410
Vase, Genie Bottle, Blue & White, Plantain Leaves, Pagoda, 1900s, 13 In. 207
Vase, Gray Crackled Glaze, Flattened Oval, Tube Handles At Neck, 7 In. 25478
Vase, Gray Crackled Glaze, Hexagonal, Tube Handles At Neck, 17 ½ In. 8645
Vase, Hu Shape, Figures In Landscape, Bat Handles, Gilt, c.1950, 15 x 11 In. ....*illus* 1778
Vase, Lid, White, Roosters, Flowers, Grass, Cylindrical, 12 In. 153
Vase, Painted, Gold Glaze, Tapered, Japan, 7 x 3 In., Pair.......... 480
Vase, Palace Garden, Trees, Rectangular, Foo Dog Lug Handles, 1800s, 12 In., Pair.......... 812
Vase, Panels, Figures, White Glaze, Downturned Rim, Scroll Handles, 24 In., Pair 875
Vase, Sang De Boeuf Glaze, High Shoulders, Tapering Neck, 19 ½ In. 377
Vase, Smokestack, Flying Dragons, Turquoise Glaze, Gilt, Ring Foot, 1900s, 12 In. 237
Vase, Teadust Glaze, Globular, Funnel Neck, Grotesque Handles, 8 In. 7410
Vase, Teadust Glaze, Raised Ribs, Flared Rim, Ring Handles, 1900s, 9 In. 865
Vase, Turquoise, Red Dragons, Phoenix, Baluster, Flared Rim, c.1780, 16 In. 290
Vase, White, Red Stylized Dragon, Mallet Shape, 1800s, 7 In. 830
Water Dropper, Tadpole, Figural, Short Tail, Red, Blue, White, Korea, 3 In. 1599

PORCELAIN-CHINESE is listed here. See also Canton, Chinese Export, Imari, Moriage, Nanking, and other categories.

Basket, Pierced, Oval, Applied Flowers, Gilt Spear Border, 3 ¾ x 9 In. 177
Bowl, 2 Five-Clawed Dragons, Waves, Pagoda, Calligraphy, 12 x 14 ½ In. 212

Porcelain-Asian, Vase, Hu Shape, Figures In Landscape, Bat Handles, Gilt, c.1950, 15 x 11 In.
$1,778

James D. Julia Auctioneers

TIP
When cleaning or repairing antiques, remember less is more.

Porcelain-Chinese, Deity, San Tsai, Figurine, On Throne, Court Costume, Wood Stand, 1700s, 11 In.
$3,851

James D. Julia Auctioneers

TIP
Use paper plates between your china plates to help prevent chipping.

PORCELAIN-CHINESE

Porcelain-Chinese, Ginger Jar, Lid, Black, Gilt Blossoms, Kangxi Mark, 19th Century, 11 In.
$975

Ruby Lane

Porcelain-Chinese, Plate, Thousand Flowers, Late 19th Century, 9 ¼ In. Diam.
$255

Ruby Lane

Porcelain-Chinese, Teapot, Blue, White, Landscape, Figures, Case, Silk Lined, c.1910, 6 x 7 In.
$356

James D. Julia Auctioneers

Porcelain-Chinese, Teapot, Cadogan Turquoise, Flowers, Leaves, Egg Shape, Handle, c.1900, 6 In.
$345

Cottone Auctions

Porcelain-Chinese, Vase, Blanc De Chine, Lion Mask Handles, Pinched Neck, c.1800, 14 In.
$2,460

Skinner, Inc.

Porcelain-Chinese, Vase, Blue & White, Flower Heads, Vines, Double Ring Mark, 1800s, 14 In.
$610

Neal Auctions

Porcelain-Chinese, Vase, Bottle Shape, Yellow Ground, Green Dragon, c.1800, 28 x 7 In.
$875

New Orleans (Cakebread)

Porcelain-Chinese, Vase, Landscape, Flowers, Tan Crackle Glaze, Famille Rose, 1800s, 18 In.
$474

James D. Julia Auctioneers

TIP

"Never invest your money in anything that eats or needs repainting." Wise words from Billy Rose, a successful showman and art collector.

Bowl, Bats, Green Dragons, Round, 3 ½ x 11 In. 181

Bowl, Birds, Cherry Blossoms, 3 ½ x 8 ¾ In. 720

Bowl, Blue & White, 16 ½ In. 250

Bowl, Blue & White, Red Cranes, Recessed Foot, 2 ¾ x 7 In. 41

Bowl, Blue & White, Water Dragon, Crossed Vajra Symbol, 4 x 8 ½ In. 2242

Bowl, Blue Glaze, White Carved Dragon, 3 ½ x 8 In. 799

Bowl, Bombe, Horses, 3-Footed, 3 ¼ x 3 ¾ In. 976

Bowl, Flowers, Ling Chih Mushrooms, Rock, Waves, Trees, Purple Ground, 5 In. 1659

Box, Famille Verte, Garden Pavilion, Women, 2-Part Interior, 7 ½ x 4 In. 360

Box, Lid, Dragons, Leaves, Wucai Enamel, Cushion Body, 6 x 6 In. 1195

Box, Paste, Peach Bloom Glaze, Round, Cover, 1 x 2 In. 3068

Brushpot, Blue & White, Scholar Figures, Landscape, 5 ¼ x 4 ¼ In. 184

Brushpot, Famille Verte, Square, Jadeite Finial, 5 In. 5015

Brushpot, Peach Bloom Glaze, Compressed Body, Raised Lip, 3 x 5 In. 492

Cachepot, Blue, White Rim, Bowstring Band, 5 x 6 ¼ In. 649

Cachepot, Flambe, Ormolu Mount, Lions, Mask Handles, Paw Feet, 11 ½ x 11 In. 3125

Censer, Flambe Glaze, Animal Head Handles, Rim Lip, Footed, 1800, 5 x 11 In. 413

Charger, Blue & White, Lattice, Flowers, Rockwork, C Scroll, 17 ⅜ In. 600

Charger, Cobalt Blue & White, Scholar's Rock, Panels, 1800s, 16 In. 196

Charger, Figures, Flowers, Scrolls, Bats, Iron Red, Gilt, 13 In. 368

Charger, Flowers, Bats, Sprigs, Diaper Pattern, Flared Scalloped Rim, 18 In. 600

Charger, Guangxu, Blue & White Dragon, Clouds, c.1890, 13 ¼ In. 90

Compote, Flowers, Yellow, Gilt, Enameled Metal, Pedestal Base, 4 x 7 In. 196

Deity, San Tsai, Figurine, On Throne, Court Costume, Wood Stand, 1700s, 11 In. *illus* 3851

Dish, Ru Type, Dragon, Light Green, 7 ½ In. 92

Figurine, Blanc De Chine, Kwan Yin, Crown, Beads, Lotus, 22 ½ In. 1140

Figurine, Blanc De Chine, Kwan Yin, Standing, 9 x 3 ¼ In. 360

Figurine, Foo Dog, Blue, Male, Female, 10 ¼ x 3 ¾ In., Pair 181

Figurine, Kwan Yin, Deer, Flower Basket, Blanc De Chine, 1900s, 15 x 6 In. 738

Figurine, Lychee Fruit, Leafy Stem, 2 ¼ In. 1250

Figurine, Phoenix, Standing On Rocks, Famille Rose, 1700s, 21 In. 2832

Figurine, Ram, Reclining, Kangxi Style, Turquoise Glaze, 1800s, 5 x 8 In., Pair 1534

Figurine, Resting Hotai On Brown Sack, Sancai Glaze, 4 ½ x 9 In. 142

Fishbowl, Blue & White, Landscape, Pagoda, Flowers At Rim, 17 x 20 In. 179

Ginger Jar, Lid, Black, Gilt Blossoms, Kangxi Mark, 19th Century, 11 In. *illus* 975

Group, Rearing Horse, 8 ¾ In. 188

Group, Rearing Horse, Jockey, 9 ¼ In. 188

Jar, Blue & White, 6-Character Mark, Lid, 12 ½ x 7 ¼ In., Pair 390

Jar, Blue & White, Baluster Shape, Dome Lid, Finial, 14 x 10 In. 127

Jar, Double Happiness, Blue & White, Blossoms, 1800s, 18 x 11 In. 442

Jar, Famille Verte, Bird, Red, Green, 15 In. 1845

Jar, Ginger, Lid, White Ground, Painted, 6 In., Pair 180

Jar, Kylin Figures, Garden, Foo Dog Knop, Clobbered, Oval, Domed Lid, c.1750, 16 In. 657

Jar, Lid, Dragons, Qianlong Mark, c.1890, 8 ¾ In. 2640

Jar, Peach, Lid, Multicolored Fruit, Famille Rose, Loop Handles, 6 x 7 In. 1127

Jar, Robin's-Egg Glaze, Applied Chilong & Bat, Black, Gilt, Oval, 1900s, 8 x 6 In. 830

Pillow Block, Painted, Berries, Flowers, Blue, Green, 5 ½ x 11 ½ In. 156

Planter, Figures, Enamel, c.1900, 3 ½ x 5 In., Pair 96

Planter, Underplate, Flowers, Vines, Flared Rim, 13 x 19 In., Pair 210

Plate, Thousand Flowers, Late 19th Century, 9 ¼ In. Diam. *illus* 255

Plaque, 2 Figures On Horseback, Tree, Pink Blossoms, 11 ¾ x 9 In. 6765

Plaque, Grasshopper, Grass Blade, Wood Frame, 1900s, 11 ¼ x 6 ¾ In. 484

Plaque, Painted, Legend, Famille Rose, Rosewood Frame, 23 x 15 ¾ In. 5490

Plaque, Painted, Monks, Famille Rose, Rosewood Frame, 23 x 15 ¾ In. 5795

Plate, Aster Flowers, Leaves, Blue & White, Scalloped Edge, 7 ¾ In., Pair 77

Plate, Blue & White, White Center, 8 ¼ In. 738

Plate, Curvy Octagonal Cartouche, Flowers, Fish Scales, Kites, 8 ½ In. 181

Plate, Famille Jaune, Symbols, Prosperous Longevity, Guangxu Marks, Footed, 10 In. 207

Punch Bowl, Blue, Central Medallion, Dragonfly, Flowers, Rocks, 13 In. 767

Screen, Table, Hardstone, Painted, Wood Frame, 7 ½ In., Pair 210

Teapot, 2 Women Studying, Gilt, Finial, 6 x 7 ½ In. 153

Teapot, Blue & Gold Decoration, Reed Handle, Berry Finial, c.1800, 6 x 10 In. 130

Teapot, Blue, White, Landscape, Figures, Case, Silk Lined, c.1910, 6 x 7 In. *illus* 356

Teapot, Butterfly, Birds, White, Famille Rose, Narrow Neck, 6 x 5 ½ In. 96

Teapot, Cadogan Turquoise, Flowers, Leaves, Egg Shape, Handle, c.1900, 6 In. *illus* 345

Teapot, Group, Lake, House, Straw Handle, c.1910, 6 x 3 In. 118

Porcelain-Contemporary, Bowl, Teal, Blue Textured Glaze, Stand, Cliff Lee, 1951, 6 x 9 In.
$2,370

James D. Julia Auctioneers

Porcelain-Contemporary, Sculpture, Balloon Dog, Metallic Glaze, Jeff Koons, 1995, 11 In.
$12,500

Rago Arts and Auction Center

Poster, Circus, Jeanette May, Acrobat, Hagenbeck-Wallace, Portrait, Women Acrobats, c.1937, 27 x 40 In.
$173

Hake's Americana & Collectibles

Poster, Concert, Grateful Dead, Be Mine, Carousel Ballroom, Feb. 14, 1968, 11 x 11 In.
$380

Hake's Americana & Collectibles

Poster, Concert, Jimi Hendrix Experience, Spectrum, Stiff Paper, 1 Show Only In Pa., 1969, 14 x 21 In.
$4,244

Hake's Americana & Collectibles

Potlid, Base, Jules Hauel Perfumer, Ben Franklin Bust, Red Transfer, 3 ½ In.
$288

Glass Works Auctions

Teapot, Monochrome Glaze, Yellow, Bamboo, 5 ½ In. 250
Umbrella Stand, Flowers, Hand Painted, 23 x 9 ¼ In. 660
Vase, Archers, Dragons Pursuing Flaming Pearl, Sancai Glaze, Marked, 9 In. 2390
Vase, Architectural Scene, Snow, Mountains, 1900s, 16 ¾ x 7 ½ In. 484
Vase, Begonia Shape, Blue Celadon, Bow String Borders, 11 In., Pair 4720
Vase, Blanc De Chine, Lion Mask Handles, Pinched Neck, c.1800, 14 In. *illus* 2460
Vase, Blue & White, 3 Abundances, Peach, Pomegranate, 6 ¼ In. 3835
Vase, Blue & White, Dragons, Flowers, Narrow Neck, 16 In. 369
Vase, Blue & White, Emperor Daoguang, Underglaze, Marked, 1800s, 14 In. 480
Vase, Blue & White, Flower Heads, Vines, Double Ring Mark, 1800s, 14 In. *illus* 610
Vase, Blue & White, Flying Dragon, Fire, Narrow Neck, 12 In. 246
Vase, Blue & White, Meiping Shape, Ming Style, Tapered, 14 x 9 In. 472
Vase, Blue & White, Tapered Neck, Footed, 17 x 9 In. 184
Vase, Blue & White, Wedding Joy, Long Neck, Flared, Leaves, 15 x 7 In. 136
Vase, Blue, Cartouche, Mountain Landscape, Openwork Panels, 9 In. 861
Vase, Blue, Purple, Conical Base, 15 ¼ In. 177
Vase, Bottle Shape, Famille Rose, Yellow, Stylized Bats, Flowers, 17 In. 4425
Vase, Bottle Shape, Teadust Glaze, Footed, 1800s, 13 ¼ In. 2596
Vase, Bottle Shape, Yellow Ground, Green Dragon, c.1800, 28 x 7 In. *illus* 875
Vase, Clair De Lune Glaze, Masks, Elephant Head Handles, 11 In. 2006
Vase, Court Scene, Landscape, 11 x 5 In., Pair 181
Vase, Flambe Glaze, Blue Drip, Peach Bloom Ground, 11 In. 180
Vase, Flambe Glaze, Red, Pale Green Mottling, 1800s, 36 x 7 In. 875
Vase, Flowers, Leaves, Cup-Shape Neck, Handles, 10 In. 307
Vase, Foo Dog, White, Iron Red, Cylindrical, 1800s, 11 In. 219
Vase, Ivory, Gadrooned Neck, Vine, Round Foot, 12 x 8 In. 1200
Vase, Kangxi, Peach Bloom Glaze, Amphora Shape, 5 ½ In. 1770
Vase, Landscape, Flowers, Tan Crackle Glaze, Famille Rose, 1800s, 18 In. *illus* 474
Vase, Moon, Ivory, Chrysanthemum, Scrolling Dragon Handles, 13 x 8 In. 1560
Vase, Oxblood, Bellows Shape, Black Sides, 12 x 7 In. 800
Vase, Pear Shape, Rust Glaze, Mottled Foot, 19th Century, 8 In. 826
Vase, People, Birds, Trees, Foo Dog, 22 ½ In. 236
Vase, Plum Flambe Glaze, Incised, Baluster, Ruffled Rim, 8 In. 450
Vase, Red, White Reserve, Children Playing, Landscape, 16 In. 177
Vase, Red, Yellow, Blue, Flattened, Narrow Neck, 11 In. 118
Vase, Reticulated, Medallions, 17 x 9 ½ In. 1180
Vase, Speckled Peach Bloom Glaze, Ringed Neck, 10 ⅛ In. 840
Vase, White, Double Handled, 9 ¼ In. 720
Vase, White, Lion Masks, 11 ½ In. 338
Water Pot, Beehive, Swirl Pattern, Stand, Kangxi Mark, 3 ½ In. 120
Water Pot, Beehive, White, Immortals, Famille Rose, Domed, 4 ½ x 5 In. 553

PORCELAIN-CONTEMPORARY lists pieces made by artists working after 1975.

Bowl, Brown Stripes, Mary Rogers, 1970s, 4 x 6 In. 188
Bowl, Light Gatherer, Signed, Rudolf Staffel, 5 x 6 ½ In. 813
Bowl, Teal, Blue Textured Glaze, Stand, Cliff Lee, 6 x 9 In. *illus* 2370
Figurine, Assumption, Crown, Green, Beige, Giuseppe Armani, 18 ½ In. 310
Figurine, Cream, Square, 3 Shaped Open Handles, R. Duckworth, 8 x 10 In. 3000
Group, La Pieta, Multicolor, Giuseppe Armani, 20 In. 253
Plate, Acrobats, Transfer Print, Jeff Koons, 10 ¼ In. 307
Sculpture, Balloon Dog, Metallic Glaze, Jeff Koons, 1995, 11 In. *illus* 12500
Sculpture, House Of Cards, Transfers, Decals, R. Shaw, c.2003, 13 x 9 In. 2812
Tea Set, Butterflies, White, Green Leaves, Gilt, A. Weatherly, 4 Piece 600
Teapot, Slits, Kappa Doll, White, Signed, Philip Cornelius, 1984, 8 x 8 In. 1188
Vase, 2 Men, 2 Dogs, 2 Birds, Mouse, Black, White, Etched, E. Eberle, 1985, 7 In. 2115
Vase, Yellow, Prickly Melon, Signed, Cliff Lee, 2007, 14 x 6 In. 3250

PORCELAIN-MIDCENTURY includes pieces made from the 1940s to about 1975.

Charger, Red Rim, Fitz & Floyd, 12 In., 12 Piece 215
Charger, Starburst, Cobalt Rim, Fitz & Floyd, 12 In., 8 Piece 185
Cookie Jar, Beehive, Water Works, Patti Warashina, c.1970, 10 x 10 x 5 In. 2640
Figurine, Angel, February, Wings, Halo, Red Heart, Napco, c.1950, 4 ½ In. 19
Figurine, Hobo With Guitar, Tiziano Galli, Italy, 9 x 11 In. 74
Fornasetti, Plate, Clown Face, Italy, 10 In. 213
Plate, Bar Mitzvah Boy, Transfer, Marked, Howard Kottler, 10 In. 584

Plate, Hunting, Sporting, Dog, White, Mustard Border, Hermes, 8 In., 4 Piece ... 1089
Teapot, Gray, Glazed, Cone Shape, Robert Hudson, 1972, 8 x 9 In. ... 3750
Tureen, Duck, Undertray, Handles, Multicolor, Fitz & Floyd, 8 x 18 In. ... 122
Vase, Bud, Red Glaze, Squat, Narrow Rim, Bulbous, G. Williams, c.1970, 4 x 5 In. ... 308
Vase, Hyacinth, White, Blue, Green Leaves, Swollen, 1945, 13 In. ... 805
Vase, Man In Profile, Transfer Print, Jean Cocteau, 1952, 9 ¾ x 5 In. ... 540

POSTCARDS were first legally permitted in Austria on October 1, 1869. The United States passed postal regulations allowing the card in 1872. Most of the picture postcards collected today date after 1910. The amount of postage can help to date a card. The rates are: 1872 (1 cent), 1917 (2 cents), 1919 (1 cent), 1925 (2 cents), 1928 (1 cent), 1952 (2 cents), 1958 (3 cents), 1963 (4 cents), 1968 (5 cents), 1971 (6 cents), 1973 (8 cents), 1975 (7 cents), 1976 (9 cents), 1978 (10 cents), March 1981 (12 cents), November 1981 (13 cents), 1985 (14 cents), 1988 (15 cents), 1991 (19 cents), 1995 (20 cents), 2001 (21 cents), 2002 (23 cents), 2006 (24 cents), 2007 (26 cents), 2008 (27 cents), 2009 (28 cents), 2011 (29 cents), 2012 (32 cents), 2013 (33 cents), 2014 (34 cents), 2016 (35 cents beginning January 17 and back to 34 cents beginning April 10). While most postcards sell for low prices, a small number bring high prices. Some of these are listed here.

Boonsborough, Kentucky, Daniel Boone Fort, 1915, 3 ½ x 5 In. ... 8
Seattle, Washington, Waterfront, c.1905 ... 7
SS Titanic, Thompson Dock, Ireland, Photograph ... 35
Wall Street Of New Orleans, Carondelet Street ... 6
Washington Taking Command Of Army, Farewell To Officers, 1903 ... 7
Woman, Long Dress, Foot Bridge, Gentleman, James Henderson & Sons, c.1900 ... 12

POSTERS have informed the public about news and entertainment events since ancient times. Nineteenth-century advertising and theatrical posters and twentieth-century movie and war posters are of special interest today. The price is determined by the artist, the condition, and the rarity. Other posters may be listed under Movie, Political, and World War I and II.

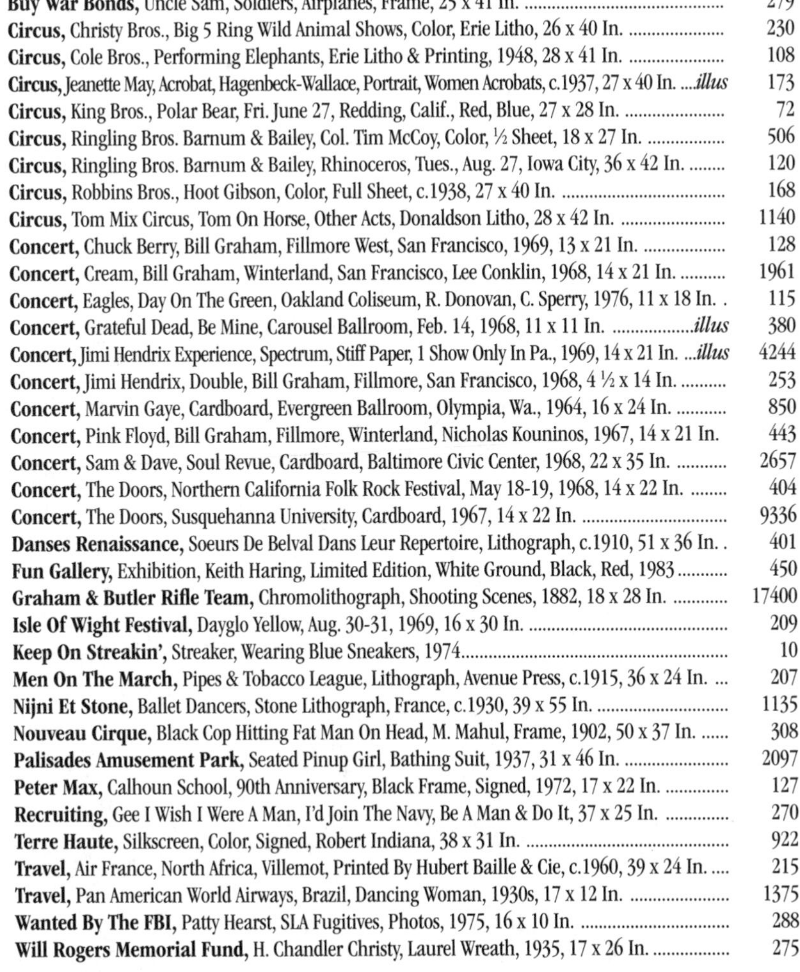
Buy War Bonds, Uncle Sam, Soldiers, Airplanes, Frame, 25 x 41 In. ... 279
Circus, Christy Bros., Big 5 Ring Wild Animal Shows, Color, Erie Litho, 26 x 40 In. ... 230
Circus, Cole Bros., Performing Elephants, Erie Litho & Printing, 1948, 28 x 41 In. ... 108
Circus, Jeanette May, Acrobat, Hagenbeck-Wallace, Portrait, Women Acrobats, c.1937, 27 x 40 In. ...*illus* 173
Circus, King Bros., Polar Bear, Fri. June 27, Redding, Calif., Red, Blue, 27 x 28 In. ... 72
Circus, Ringling Bros. Barnum & Bailey, Col. Tim McCoy, Color, ½ Sheet, 18 x 27 In. ... 506
Circus, Ringling Bros. Barnum & Bailey, Rhinoceros, Tues., Aug. 27, Iowa City, 36 x 42 In. ... 120
Circus, Robbins Bros., Hoot Gibson, Color, Full Sheet, c.1938, 27 x 40 In. ... 168
Circus, Tom Mix Circus, Tom On Horse, Other Acts, Donaldson Litho, 28 x 42 In. ... 1140
Concert, Chuck Berry, Bill Graham, Fillmore West, San Francisco, 1969, 13 x 21 In. ... 128
Concert, Cream, Bill Graham, Winterland, San Francisco, Lee Conklin, 1968, 14 x 21 In. ... 1961
Concert, Eagles, Day On The Green, Oakland Coliseum, R. Donovan, C. Sperry, 1976, 11 x 18 In. . 115
Concert, Grateful Dead, Be Mine, Carousel Ballroom, Feb. 14, 1968, 11 x 11 In. ...*illus* 380
Concert, Jimi Hendrix Experience, Spectrum, Stiff Paper, 1 Show Only In Pa., 1969, 14 x 21 In. ...*illus* 4244
Concert, Jimi Hendrix, Double, Bill Graham, Fillmore, San Francisco, 1968, 4 ½ x 14 In. ... 253
Concert, Marvin Gaye, Cardboard, Evergreen Ballroom, Olympia, Wa., 1964, 16 x 24 In. ... 850
Concert, Pink Floyd, Bill Graham, Fillmore, Winterland, Nicholas Kouninos, 1967, 14 x 21 In. 443
Concert, Sam & Dave, Soul Revue, Cardboard, Baltimore Civic Center, 1968, 22 x 35 In. ... 2657
Concert, The Doors, Northern California Folk Rock Festival, May 18-19, 1968, 14 x 22 In. ... 404
Concert, The Doors, Susquehanna University, Cardboard, 1967, 14 x 22 In. ... 9336
Danses Renaissance, Soeurs De Belval Dans Leur Repertoire, Lithograph, c.1910, 51 x 36 In. . 401
Fun Gallery, Exhibition, Keith Haring, Limited Edition, White Ground, Black, Red, 1983 ... 450
Graham & Butler Rifle Team, Chromolithograph, Shooting Scenes, 1882, 18 x 28 In. ... 17400
Isle Of Wight Festival, Dayglo Yellow, Aug. 30-31, 1969, 16 x 30 In. ... 209
Keep On Streakin', Streaker, Wearing Blue Sneakers, 1974 ... 10
Men On The March, Pipes & Tobacco League, Lithograph, Avenue Press, c.1915, 36 x 24 In. ... 207
Nijni Et Stone, Ballet Dancers, Stone Lithograph, France, c.1930, 39 x 55 In. ... 1135
Nouveau Cirque, Black Cop Hitting Fat Man On Head, M. Mahul, Frame, 1902, 50 x 37 In. ... 308
Palisades Amusement Park, Seated Pinup Girl, Bathing Suit, 1937, 31 x 46 In. ... 2097
Peter Max, Calhoun School, 90th Anniversary, Black Frame, Signed, 1972, 17 x 22 In. ... 127
Recruiting, Gee I Wish I Were A Man, I'd Join The Navy, Be A Man & Do It, 37 x 25 In. ... 270
Terre Haute, Silkscreen, Color, Signed, Robert Indiana, 38 x 31 In. ... 922
Travel, Air France, North Africa, Villemot, Printed By Hubert Baille & Cie, c.1960, 39 x 24 In. ... 215
Travel, Pan American World Airways, Brazil, Dancing Woman, 1930s, 17 x 12 In. ... 1375
Wanted By The FBI, Patty Hearst, SLA Fugitives, Photos, 1975, 16 x 10 In. ... 288
Will Rogers Memorial Fund, H. Chandler Christy, Laurel Wreath, 1935, 17 x 26 In. ... 275

Crossed Swords

Crossed swords are a mark used by the eighteenth-century Meissen pottery in Germany, but crossed swords have been used by dozens of other companies since then. Check in Kovels' books on pottery marks to learn more.

Pottery, Cadogan, Wine Ewer, Aubergine, Turquoise, Potted Peach Shape, 1800s, 7 ¼ In.
$945

Brunk Auctions

Pottery, Colander, Tin Glazed, Earthenware, Bowl, Affixed Pierced Cover, Flowers, c.1750, 9 In.
$861

Skinner, Inc.

Pottery, Figurine, Bactrian Camel, Standing, Saddlebags, Tang Style, Sancai Glazed, 21 x 17 In.
$413

Brunk Auctions

Pottery, Figurine, Warrior, On Rock, Raised Leg, Beard, Painted, Chinese, c.1900, 7 ½ In.
$246

Skinner, Inc.

Pottery, Flowerpot, Tin Glazed, Earthenware, Canted Sides, Pierced At Top, c.1760, 4 In.
$1,968

Skinner, Inc.

Pottery, Game Dish, Lid, Underplate, Basket Weave, Bird Finial, Drabware, England, 11 In.
$488

Neal Auctions

TIP

If your front entrance has glass windows or doors that give a view of your front hall, be sure the control pad for your alarm is out of sight. A burglar can look in to see if it is off.

POTLIDS are just that, lids for pots. Transfer-printed potlids had their heyday from the 1840s to the early 1900s. The English Staffordshire potteries made ceramic containers with decorative lids for bear's grease, shrimp or meat paste, cold cream, and toothpaste. Printed advertising and pictures of historical events, portraits of famous people, or scenic views were designed in black and white or color. Reproductions have been made.

Base, Jules Hauel Perfumer, Ben Franklin Bust, Red Transfer, 3 ½ In. .... *illus* 288
Fishmongers, Ironstone, Transferware, Felix Pratt, England, 1800s, 4 In. 145
Fishmongers, Pratt, 1800s, 4 ¼ In. 145
Gentleman, Child, Dog, Woman Selling Primroses, Pratt, Frame, 1840-1900, 5 ½ In. 100
Gentleman, Woman Selling Cherries, Dog, Pratt, Frame, 5 ½ In. 100
Lobster, Fish, Cat On Counter, Pratt, Frame, c.1840, 6 ½ In. 177
Men Playing Checkers, Woman, Child, Pratt, 4 ¼ x 2 In. 125
Room In Which Shakespeare Was Born, 1800s, 3 ½ In. 185
Shepherd Boy, Dog, Sheep, Pratt, c.1875, 4 x 2 In. 110
Strasbourg, Row Houses, Residents In Street, Pratt, c.1855, 5 x 2 In. 60
Strasbourg, Waterfront, Dock, Pratt, Mahogany Frame, 1840-1900, 6 In. 125
The Trooper, Man On Horse, Woman, Dog, Pratt, 1840-1900 50
Thistle, White, 5 ½ In. 12
Wolf & The Lamb, School Boys, Lamb, Pratt, 1840-1900, 4 ¼ In. 125
Woman, Selling Oranges To Gentleman, Pratt, Frame, 5 ½ In. 115

POTTERY and porcelain are different. Pottery is opaque; you can't see through it. Porcelain is translucent. If you hold a porcelain dish in front of a strong light, you will see the light through the dish. Porcelain is colder to the touch. Pottery is softer and easier to break and will stain more easily because it is porous. Porcelain is thinner, lighter, and more durable. Majolica, faience, and stoneware are all pottery. Additional pieces of pottery are listed in this book in the categories Pottery-Art, Pottery-Contemporary, Pottery-Midcentury, and under the factory name. For information about pottery makers and marks, see *Kovels' Dictionary of Marks—Pottery & Porcelain: 1650–1850* and *Kovels' New Dictionary of Marks—Pottery & Porcelain: 1850 to the Present.*

Biscuit Barrel, Agateware, Metal Rim, Handle, Cover, England, 6 ¾ In. 90
Bowl, Concentric Rings, Manganese Glaze, Wide Rim, 1800s, 11 In. Diam. 133
Bread Bin, Lid, Molded Vines, Labeled Bread, Mottled Green, Blue, Brown Glaze, 14 x 11 In. 240
Cadogan, Wine Ewer, Aubergine, Turquoise, Potted Peach Shape, 1800s, 7 ¼ In. .... *illus* 945
Censer, Lid, Turquoise Glaze, Octagonal, Foo Dog Handles, Curved Feet, 23 In. 1500
Charger, Center Flowers, Leaves, Moravian Style, Westmoore, Stamped, 14 ⅜ In. 92
Colander, Tin Glazed, Earthenware, Bowl, Affixed Pierced Cover, Flowers, c.1750, 9 In. .... *illus* 861
Figure, Christ, Sacred Heart, Matte Glaze, Burnished Gilt, Signed, Pattarino, 28 In. 93
Figurine, Bactrian Camel, Standing, Saddlebags, Tang Style, Sancai Glazed, 21 x 17 In. .... *illus* 413
Figurine, Stock Broker, Reading Ticket, Beige, Bencini, 1900s, 9 x 4 ¾ In. 58
Figurine, Ten Commandments, Edgardo Simone, 21 x 12 In. 510
Figurine, Warrior, On Rock, Raised Leg, Beard, Painted, Chinese, c.1900, 7 ½ In. .... *illus* 246
Flowerpot, Tin Glazed, Earthenware, Canted Sides, Pierced At Top, c.1760, 4 In. .... *illus* 1968
Game Dish, Lid, Underplate, Basket Weave, Bird Finial, Drabware, England, 11 In. .... *illus* 488
Group, Flowers, Pink, Green Leaves, 23 ½ In. 125
Jar, Alkaline Glaze, Drip, Pear Shape, Ear Handles, Lid, 15 In. 207
Jar, Cocoon, Painted Design, Pinched Neck, Flared Rim, Round Foot, 12 ½ In. 309
Jardiniere, Pedestal, Peacock In Tree, Phoenix Ware, Thomas Forester & Sons, 12 x 38 In. 531
Jug, Lines, Spots, Brown Glaze, 3 Applied Snakes, Narrow Neck, Snake Handle, 6 In. 1968
Jug, Salt Glaze, Cream & Orange, Swollen Oval, Tapered Bottom, Handle, 3 Gal., 16 In. 86
Plate, Tin Glazed, Earthenware, 8-Sided, Brown, Cartouches, Flowers, c.1750, 9 In. .... *illus* 492
Platter, Enamel, Earthenware, Turtle, Fish, Frogs, Lizards, Shells, Oval, Palissy Ware, c.1860, 16 In. .. *illus* 1968
Platter, Village, People At Well, Flowers On Rim, France, 19 In. 123
Posset Pot, Lid, Tin Glazed, Earthenware, 2 Scrolled Handles, Spout, c.1670, 6 In. .... *illus* 3075
Rattle, Bird, Figural, Seated, Mottled Glaze, Punched Rosettes, Oval Base, 1800s, 2 x 3 In. 885
Statue, Foo Dog, Sancai, Bells On Neck, Cub, Male, Female, 1900s, 41 In., Pair........ *illus* 1169
Tankard, Peacock, Roosting In Tree, Sun, Phoenix Ware, Thomas Forester & Sons, 13 ½ In. 472
Teapot, Lotus Flower, Lobed, Scroll Spout, Loop Handle, Lid, 7 In. 148
Teapot, Monster Spout & Finial, Bulbous, Loop Handle, Curved Feet, 7 ¼ In. 474
Vase, Blue To Brown Flambe Glaze, Tapered, Japan, c.1900, 4 ¾ x 5 In. 363
Vase, Double Gourd, Salt Glaze, Beige, Blue & Red Splatter, 7 In. 242
Vase, Granite Design, Medallions, Gilt, Marble, Bronze, Lid, Palmer, c.1776, 14 In. .... *illus* 1599
Vase, Green & Brown Glaze, Double Twist Handle, Ruffled Rim, Isaac Stahl, 1935, 6 In. 467
Vase, Green Crackle Glaze, Flared Mouth, Waisted Neck, 14 In. 687
Vase, Struggle For Life, Cream, Green, Louis Carrier-Belleuse, Choisy HB, c.1894, 15 ½ In. 1725
Wall Pocket, Man's Face, Mustache, Manganese Glaze, Leaf Crown, 1800s, 7 x 7 In. .... *illus* 224
Water Coupe, Peachbloom Glaze, Domed Shoulder, Roundels, Scrolls, c.1700, 3 x 5 In. .... *illus* 2583

Pottery, Plate, Tin Glazed, Earthenware, 8-Sided, Brown, Cartouches, Flowers, c.1750, 9 In.
$492

Skinner, Inc.

Pottery, Platter, Enamel, Earthenware, Turtle, Fish, Frogs, Lizards, Shells, Oval, Palissy Ware, c.1860, 16 In.
$1,968

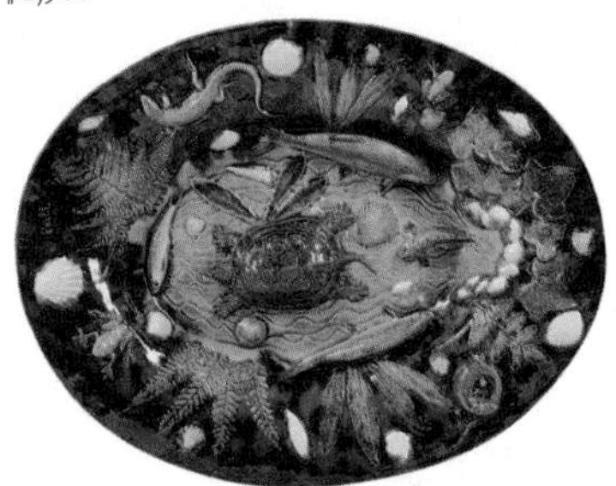

Skinner, Inc.

Pottery, Statue, Foo Dog, Sancai, Bells On Neck, Cub, Male, Female, 1900s, 41 In., Pair
$1,169

Skinner, Inc.

Art Pottery Fakes

In recent years art pottery fakes were being sold online by a United States company. They are copies, some bad, of Pillin, Natzler, and Ohr pottery. The Ohr pottery fakes have stilt marks on the bottom, something not seen on real Ohr. The Pillin mark is just wrong enough to be noticed. Watch out for them.

Pottery, Posset Pot, Lid, Tin Glazed, Earthenware, 2 Scrolled Handles, Spout, c.1670, 6 In.
$3,075

Skinner, Inc.

Pottery, Vase, Granite Design, Medallions, Gilt, Marble, Bronze, Lid, Palmer, c.1776, 14 In.
$1,599

Skinner, Inc.

Pottery, Wall Pocket, Man's Face, Mustache, Manganese Glaze, Leaf Crown, 1800s, 7 x 7 In.
$224

Hess Auction Group

Pottery, Water Coupe, Peachbloom Glaze, Domed Shoulder, Roundels, Scrolls, c.1700, 3 x 5 In.
$2,583

Skinner, Inc.

P

Schreckengost
Viktor Schreckengost, best known to collectors for his ceramic designs, including the famous Cowan Pottery Jazz Bowl, also did industrial designing. He designed pedal cars and bicycles for Murray Ohio Company of Cleveland.

Pottery-Art, Bowl, Brother Thomas Bezanson, Speckled, Purple Vellum Glaze, 2 x 5 In.
$351

Thomaston Place Auction

Pottery-Art, Jardiniere, Glazed Flowers, Butterflies, Metal Mounts, Openwork, 1880s, 13 x 15 In.
$1,875

Rago Arts and Auction Center

Pottery-Art, Plate, Toros, Glazed Earthenware, Stamped, Pablo Picasso, 1952, 8 In.
$1,750

Rago Arts and Auction Center

Pottery-Art, Vase, Flowers, Yellow Ground, John Bennett, 1877, 6 ¾ x 4 ¼ In.
$3,375

Rago Arts and Auction Center

Pottery-Art, Vase, Handle, Drip Glaze, Green & Brown Tones, W.J. Walley, c.1900, 10 ½ x 6 In.
$1,875

Rago Arts and Auction Center

Pottery-Art, Vase, Incised Leaves, Green Matte Glaze, Rolled Rim, Zark, c.1910, 5 x 5 In.
$1,000

Rago Arts and Auction Center

Pottery-Art, Sculpture, Female Electron, Lighting Bolt, Fountain, Blue, W. Gregory, c.1938, 47 In.
$50,000

Rago Arts and Auction Center

Pottery-Art, Vase, Leaves, Flame Painted, Incised Whalebone, T.A. Brouwer, 1900s, 5 x 6 In.
$6,250

Rago Arts and Auction Center

TIP
You can cover up a small chip in a piece of porcelain with a bit of colored nail polish. It comes in almost every color now.

P

POTTERY-ART. Art pottery was first made in America in Cincinnati, Ohio, during the 1870s. The pieces were hand thrown and hand decorated. The art pottery tradition continued until the 1930s when studio potters began making the more artistic wares. American, English, and Continental art pottery by less well-known makers is listed here. Most makers listed in *Kovels' American Art Pottery*, such as Arequipa, Ohr, Rookwood, Roseville, and Weller, are listed in their own categories in this book. More recent pottery is listed under the name of the maker or in another pottery category.

Ashtray, Pelican, Figural, Open Mouth, Ivory Glaze, 1939, 4 x 6 In. 138
Bowl, Applied Leaves, Glossy Bronze & Blue Matte Glazes, 5 ½ x 8 ¼ In. 1342
Bowl, Brother Thomas Bezanson, Speckled, Purple Vellum Glaze, 2 x 5 In. ....*illus* 351
Bowl, Carved Rosehips, Squat, Flat Rim, Green, Brown, Blue Matte, Feet, 1917, 3 x 6 In. 173
Bowl, Center Flower, Greek Key Border, Green Glaze, Red, Black, 1922, 6 In. Diam. 173
Bowl, Circles, Brown, Cream, Saucer Foot, Wide Rim, McIntosh, 5 x 15 In. 1125
Bowl, Eagle, Arrows, Tulips, Yellow, Isaac Stahl, 1940, 10 In. 550
Bowl, Pinecone, Squat, Blue Matte, Cutouts, 1909, 2 x 7 In. 374
Bust, Dante, Red Hat & Shirt, Marked, Wiener Werkstatte, Austria, 7 ½ In. 177
Charger, German Verse, Swan, Butterfly, Flowers, Yellow, Isaac Stahl, 1936, 9 In. 440
Compote, 3 Eagles Holding Bowl, Aventurine Glaze, Flat Wide Rim, 1923, 6 In. 173
Dish, 3 Elongated Figures, Green Glaze, Rounded, Man Ray, France, c.1950, 8 x 6 In. 1353
Ewer, Bird, Blossoms, Medallions, Enamel, Metallic Glaze, Aesthetic Period, Bretby, 17 In. 90
Figurine, Satyr, Maiden, Pierre Le Faguays, c.1925, 10 ¾ In. 1298
Jar, Stripes, Cream, Brown, Round, Rolled Rim, Curved Finial, Lid, McIntosh, 12 In. 2625
Jardiniere, Glazed Flowers, Butterflies, Metal Mounts, Openwork, 1880s, 13 x 15 In. ....*illus* 1875
Jardiniere, Glorious Fame Of Summer, Avon, 8 x 13 In. 3120
Jardiniere, Pedestal, Carved, Teal Blue High Glaze, Bretby, England, 34 x 12 In 120
Jardiniere, Purple & Pink Flowers, White Ground, Avon, 9 ½ In. 130
Mask, Metallic Brown Black Glaze, Marked, Arko, 9 In. 472
Pitcher, Woman, Birds, Flowers, Large Mouth, Thomas Stahl, 1936, 9 In. 990
Plate, Toros, Glazed Earthenware, Stamped, Pablo Picasso, 1952, 8 In. ....*illus* 1750
Plate, Turquoise, Black & White Crossed Stripes, Square, S. Hamada, 11 x 11 In. 610
Sculpture, Female Electron, Lighting Bolt, Fountain, Blue, W. Gregory, c.1938, 47 In. ....*illus* 50000
Sculpture, Reclining Woman, Art Nouveau, Bernard Bloch, 6 x 11 ½ In. 272
Teapot, Butterfly Design, Straight Spout, Lid, Stick Handle, 1882, 5 In. 690
Tray, Incised Spider & Web, Oval, Red Brown Glaze, 1902, 6 x 4 In. 1150
Umbrella Stand, White Flowers, Gold Rim, 23 ½ x 11 In. 96
Vase, Blue Flambe Glaze, Cylindrical, Flat Shoulder, Rolled Rim, 1910, 14 In. 3105
Vase, Blue, Textured, Applied Roses, Leaves & Vines, Fired On Gold, Oval, 18 In. 748
Vase, Brown, Green, Impressed Vance, Avon, 7 x 7 In. 360
Vase, Brown, Leaves, Square Body, Rectangular Neck, S. Hamada, 7 ¼ In. 976
Vase, Chinese Red Glaze, Paneled Body, Stick Neck, Raised Handles, 1910, 10 In. 805
Vase, Chrome Red, Bulbous, Ring-Turned Neck, Handles, Rainbow Pottery, c.1935, 11 In. 138
Vase, Chrome Red, Ring-Turned Neck, Bulbous, Handles, c.1936, 10 ½ In. 138
Vase, Cream, 2 Gray Glazed Sides, Square Base, Italy, 8 ½ x 5 In. 193
Vase, Dark Red Glaze, Iridescent Dark Silver Splash, Squat, 2 Handles, Dalpayrat, 4 In. 246
Vase, Distel, Handles, Floral Gloss Glaze, Marked, 6 ½ In. 266
Vase, Elephant Foot, Combed Veins, Raindrop Patterns, Mueller, 15 x 6 ½ In. 295
Vase, Flattened Circle, Cylindrical Mouth & Foot, Clay Slip, 1970s, 11 x 16 In. 5313
Vase, Flower Form, Art Nouveau, 11 In. 125
Vase, Flowerhead Shape, Lily, Flowers & Leaves, Blue Trim, 1946, 8 In. 460
Vase, Flowers, Green, Ruffled Rim, Double Handles, Isaac Stahl, c.1938, 9 In. 1045
Vase, Flowers, Yellow Ground, John Bennett, 1877, 6 ¾ x 4 ¼ In. ....*illus* 3375
Vase, Green Matte Glaze, Brown Leaves Around Shoulder, Squat, 1926, 5 In. 518
Vase, Green, Gourd Shape, Art Deco, L. Lourioux, 1929, 9 ½ x 4 ¼ In. 726
Vase, Handle, Drip Glaze, Green & Brown Tones, W.J. Walley, c.1900, 10 ½ x 6 In. ....*illus* 1875
Vase, Incised Leaves, Green Matte Glaze, Rolled Rim, Zark, c.1910, 5 x 5 In. ....*illus* 1000
Vase, Iridescent Green, 4 Applied Starfish, Paul Daschel, c.1900, 14 ⅝ In. 6132
Vase, Kezonta Ware, Ivory Faience, Scroll Work, Cincinnati Art Pottery, c.1900, 10 In. 153
Vase, Leaves, Flame Painted, Incised Whalebone, T.A. Brouwer, 1900s, 5 x 6 In. ....*illus* 6250
Vase, Mottled Green & Violet, Bulbous, Handles At Rim, c.1940, 7 In. 39
Vase, Mustard Base, Black Drip Glaze, Art Deco, Louis Dage, 10 ½ In. 420
Vase, Naked Men & Women Encircle, Figural, Ivory Glaze, Cylindrical, 1922, 5 In. 184
Vase, Pilgrim, Coal Tipple In Deep Wood, Full Moon, Clouds, Footed, 1880, 8 In. 1265
Vase, Raised Geometrics, Yellow, Orange, Teal, Tendril Handles, Wiener Werkstatte, 12 In. 1353
Vase, Serpents, Luster Glaze, Wing Shape Handles, Frederic Danton, 1900s, 13 ½ In. ....*illus* 1750
Vase, Shouldered, Tapered, Green Glaze, Dripped Over Brown, Rhead, c.1915, 7 In. ....*illus* 575
Vase, Slip Trailed Decoration, Green, Black, Orange, Double Gourd, Avon, Ohio, c.1902, 9 In. 900
Vase, Snowdrops, Yellow Ground, Mary Yancy, Iowa State, 5 x 4 ¼ In. ....*illus* 4063

Pottery-Art, Vase, Serpents, Luster Glaze, Wing Shape Handles, Frederic Danton, 1900s, 13 ½ In.
$1,750

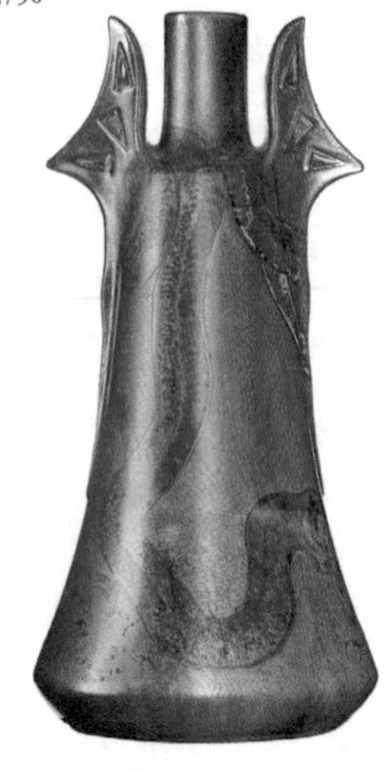

Rago Arts and Auction Center

Pottery-Art, Vase, Shouldered, Tapered, Green Glaze, Dripped Over Brown, Rhead, c.1915, 7 In.
$575

Humler & Nolan

Pottery-Art, Vase, Snowdrops, Yellow Ground, Mary Yancy, Iowa State, 5 x 4 ¼ In.
$4,063

Rago Arts and Auction Center

P

Pottery-Art, Vase, Squeezebag Design, Green & Yellow, Craven, c.1905, 11 In.
$5,635

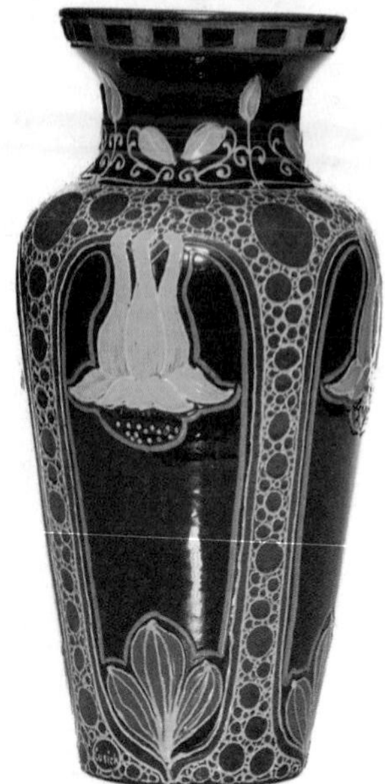

Humler & Nolan

Pottery-Contemporary, Bottle, Square, Rolled Lip, Blue, Brown, Circle Design, A. Green, c.1986, 11 In.
$510

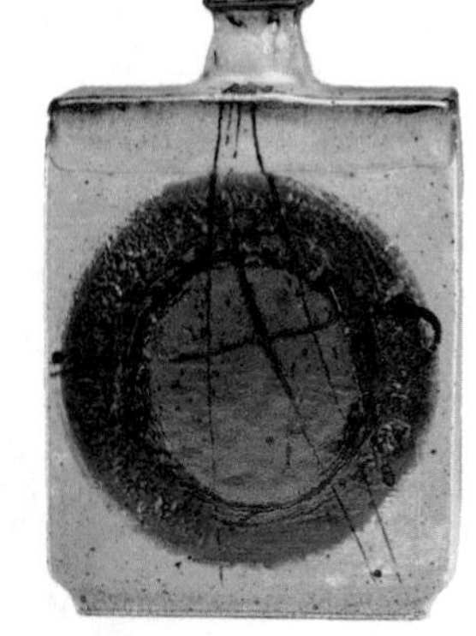

Sam Scott Pottery

Pottery-Contemporary, Bowl, Earthenware, Glaze, Glen Lukens, Signed, c.1960s, 2 x 10 In.
$1,000

Rago Arts and Auction Center

Vase, Square, Triangular Wings, Art Deco Geometrics, Frie Onnaing, France, 10 In., Pair........... 554
Vase, Squeezebag Design, Green & Yellow, Craven, c.1905, 11 In. ....*illus* 5635
Vase, Stacked Bulbs, Yellow, Blue Accent, Amaco, 8 ¾ x 5 In. 156
Vase, Stylized Flowers, Green Matte Glaze, Cylindrical, Shouldered, Flat Rim, 1910, 9 In. 2185
Vase, Tapered Cylinder, Mottled Green, Red Glaze, Gilt Bronze Cage, Trees, c.1910, 8 In. 359
Vase, Tapered, Shouldered, Cherry Blossom Band, Cream To Blue, Vellum, 1918, 8 In. 288
Vase, Tenmoku Glaze, Baluster, Charles F. Binns, 1930, 7 ¾ x 6 In. 11250
Vase, White Ground, Multicolor Leaves, Herman Kahler, 13 ½ x 7 In. 150

POTTERY-CONTEMPORARY lists pieces made by artists working about 1975 and later.

Basket, Stoneware, Twisted Handle, Chuck Hindes, c.1977, 13 ½ x 7 ½ In. 120
Bottle, Black, Red & White Stripes, Square, Albert Green, c.1980, 11 ½ x 7 ½ In. 780
Bottle, Square, Rolled Lip, Blue, Brown, Circle Design, A. Green, c.1986, 11 In. ....*illus* 510
Bowl, Abstract, Multicolor, White Ground, Robert Palusky, 13 In. 148
Bowl, Black, White, Etched Square, Circle, Rectangle, E. Eberle, 2 x 5 In. 446
Bowl, Blue & White, Clutch Purse Shape, Jon Middlemiss, 8 ¾ x 12 In. 240
Bowl, Blue, Green, Tan, Wavy Pattern, James Kaneko, 4 ½ x 12 In. 400
Bowl, Blue, White, Stoneware, Albert Green, c.1980, 3 ¾ x 6 In. 120
Bowl, Brown, Manganese, High Foot, Lucie Rie, 1974, 5 x 9 ¼ In. 6150
Bowl, Canyon, Raku, Signed, Wayne Higby, c.1986, 6 x 12 In. 3000
Bowl, Cobalt Blue, Cutout Rim, Elsa Rady, 1982, 4 ¾ x 12 ¼ In. 2040
Bowl, Earthenware, Glaze, Glen Lukens, Signed, c.1960s, 2 x 10 In. ....*illus* 1000
Bowl, Gold Luster Fish, Footed, Beatrice Wood, c.1980, 6 ½ x 8 In. ....*illus* 7500
Bowl, Gold, Fish, Blue Interior, Beatrice Wood, c.1980, 6 ½ x 7 ½ In. 7500
Bowl, Hollow Base, Richard Devore, 8 x 15 In. 3250
Bowl, Metallic, Drips, Round Foot, 8 x 18 In. 278
Bowl, Red Purple, Elsa Rady, 3 ½ In. 83
Bowl, Wood Fired, Green, Brown Drip, Chuck Hindes, c.1990, 3 x 6 ½ In. 240
Bust, Head On Head, Multicolor, Michael Lucero, 1985, 62 x 15 ½ In. 660
Chalice, Raku, Snout Animal, Annette McCormick, 1900, 7 x 5 ¼ In. 123
Charger, Blue & Yellow, White Ground, Wafta Midani, 1996, 23 In. 83
Charger, Raku, Mask, License Plates, Stamped, Erik Gronberg, 4 x 16 In. 875
Charger, Stylized Bird, Blue, Yellow Ground, Wafta Midani, 1999, 19 In. 83
Figure, Cube, Flower House, 5 Holes, F. Hundertwasser, Germany, 1983, 9 x 7 In. 2750
Figurine, Blue, Brown, Glass, Anish Kapoor, 1993, 11 x 10 In. 3125
Figurine, Couple Embracing, Akio Takamori, 9 ¼ x 8 In. 6710
Figurine, Masked Man, Multicolor, Viola Frey, 31 x 25 In. 10000
Figurine, Mouse, Twigs In Eyes, B. Cavener, 2009, 12 ¼ x 8 In. 9000
Group, Artist & Model, Multicolor, Lo Scricciolo, Italy, 9 ¾ In. 60
Jar, Black, Lid, Jerry Rothman, c.1983, 23 ½ x 15 In. 4500
Pitcher, Cream, Blue Plants, Marked, Maurice Grossman, 8 ¾ x 7 In. 86
Pitcher, Glossy Brown Stripes, Jacques Pouchein, c.1970, 7 ½ In. 120
Pitcher, Pillow, Blue & Green Squiggles, Betty Woodman, c.1981, 24 x 23 ½ In. 6600
Planter, Calabasas, Pink, Woman, Skirt, Marked, R.C. Gorman, 17 ¾ x 14 In. 544
Planter, Tire Shape, Beige, John Follis, 21 x 10 In. 325
Plaque, Human Finger Scribbles, R. Arneson, 14 In. Diam. 6000
Plaque, Nude, Modernist, Rough Finish, 11 ¼ x 7 In. 330
Plate, Adam & Eve, Wood Fired, Ken Ferguson, c.1984, 22 ½ In. 3000
Plate, Angle, Weathervane, White, Aaron Bohrod, 11 In. 70
Plate, Blue, Yellow, Red, Benday Dots, Roy Lichtenstein, 10 In. 180
Plate, Horse, Men, Hands, Signed, Viola Frey, c.1983, 25 In. 4500
Plate, Jazz Trumpeter, Brown, Cream Ground, Xavier De Callatay, 10 ¾ In. 246
Plate, Round, Smiley Face, Yellow, J.B. Blunk, 11 ¼ In. 458
Platter, Blue, Brown, Gray, Stripes, Asymmetrical, H. Takemoto, c.1959, 14 x 13 In. 2812
Platter, Bull's-Eye, Yellow, Branch Pattern, Albert Green, c.1970, 16 In. 300
Platter, Stoneware, White, Red Accents, Albert Green, c.1980, 15 ½ In. 480
Platter, Two Faces, Patterned, Andrea Gill, c.1980s, 7 ¾ x 12 In. 492
Platter, Zig-Zag, Birds, Checks, Ralph Bacerra, 1983, 24 x 19 In. 5535
Sculpture, 2 Parts, Pit Fired, Multicolor Paint, Gilt Inside, B. Bean, 9 x 10 In. 2125
Sculpture, Abstract, Muted Colors, Organic Form, Robert Lohman, 25 x 8 In. 120
Sculpture, Conditions Of Space No. 1, M. Smith, c.1998, 8 x 16 ½ In. 2952
Sculpture, Dango, Jun Kaneko, 1998, 36 x 42 In. 7200
Sculpture, Frog, Inside Oreo Cookie, Brown, Gilhooly, 1970s, 1 ¼ x 2 ½ In. ....*illus* 1188
Sculpture, Gold Teapot, Rocks, Gold Pond, K. Fukazawa, 3 ¾ x 11 ½ In. 900
Sculpture, Horse, Prancing, Raised Front Leg, Cloth-Covered Saddle, 21 x 25 In. ....*illus* 7187
Sculpture, Jun Kaneko, Stoneware, Painted, Glazed, 1989, 36 x 24 In. ....*illus* 23750

Sculpture, Kangaroo Head, Multicolor, Wool, Yarn, M. Lucero, 2003, 38 x 25 In. .... *illus* 10625
Sculpture, Linea II, White, Gordon Baldwin, 1998, 15 x 17 In. 3075
Sculpture, Lowenbrau Box, Signed, Victor Spinski, 8 x 16 x 11 In. 2000
Sculpture, Man, Hands In Pockets, Dog, Signed, Jack Earl, 1981, 26 In. 4688
Sculpture, Monolith, Painted Skull, Mark Chatterly, 1988, 36 x 5 In. 553
Sculpture, Ohio, Bill, Red Hat, Green Shirt, Pants, Jack Earl, c.1981, 26 ½ x 9 In. 4688
Sculpture, Purple, Yellow, Chuck Aydlett, 1987, 17 x 7 In. 360
Sculpture, Shift & Progression No. 5, Martin Smith, 12 x 9 ½ In. 5842
Sculpture, Valentina, White Blouse, Black Details, Nancy Castle, c.1983, 17 x 18 In. 1625
Sculpture, Vessel With 11 Elements, Tony Marsh, c.1990, 2 x 12 ½ In. 3240
Sculpture, Wake, Green, Beige, Adrian Arleo, c.1990, 40 x 10 In. 500
Shot Glass, Self Portrait, Robert Arneson, c.1979, 2 ⅜ In. 4059
Teapot, Hand Built, Glaze, Signed, John Gill, 1988, 7 ½ x 14 In. 1188
Teapot, Heart, Figural, Hiroshima III, Richard Notkin, 1989, 7 x 11 In. 14400
Teapot, Nude Woman, Figural, Akio Takamori, 9 ½ x 8 In. 2750
Teapot, Red, Green, Blue, Ralph Baccera, 12 x 17 ½ In. 10455
Teapot, Tire Shape, Tan, Richard Notkin, 1985, 2 ¾ x 8 In. 14760
Teapot, Visualizing A House, Multicolor, Eyeballs, Curly Handle, M. Lucero, 10 x 10 In. .... *illus* 5700
Teapot, Zanjo, Green, Dots, Small Cylindrical Spout, Lid, P. Cornelius, 1981, 8 x 6 In. .... *illus* 655
Vase, Ablil, Glazed, Claude Conover, 1970s, 22 x 12 In. 6250
Vase, Blue, Beige, Irregular Shape, Lid, Double Ring Handle, R. Turner, 12 x 12 In. 1536
Vase, Blue, Brown, Carved Abstract Design, Oval, Tobias Weissman, 1976, 16 In. 154
Vase, Brown Mottled Glaze, Handles, Stoneware, Mark Hewitt, Stamped 71, Lid, 17 In. .... *illus* 295
Vase, Brown, Pinched, Asymmetric, Richard Devore, c.1992, 16 x 12 In. 5843
Vase, Bulbous, Incised Design, Brown, White, Claude Conover, c.1950, 22 In. .... *illus* 7995
Vase, Bulbous, Red, Black Glaze, Small Opening, Alan Vigland, 10 ½ x 11 In. 330
Vase, Coastal Rock, Carved Sculpted, Iron Oxide, Anne Goldman, 1990s, 33 x 14 In. 1250
Vase, Cream & Red, Torn Paper Pattern, Rick Dillingham, c.1984, 6 x 5 In. 1200
Vase, Diagonal Rope-Like Waves, Richard Zane Smith, 1993, 11 x 13 In. 1500
Vase, Figure Study Complex Vessel, E. Eberle, 15 x 9 ½ In. 4522
Vase, Geometric Wave, Multifaceted, Graduated Tan, Ken Mihara, 1991, 9 ½ In. 1230
Vase, Gourd Shape, Many Stick Necks, 14 x 13 ½ In. 671
Vase, Gray Matte Glaze, Mottled Green Banding, Raku, Cut Rim, D. Roberts, 16 In. 123
Vase, Harry Stalhane, Yellow, Tan, Rust, 1953, 4 In. 395
Vase, Heron, Raku, Sgraffito, Frank Boyden, 5 ¾ x 7 In. 125
Vase, Large Zigzag, Signed, Wesley Anderegg, 1990s, 27 x 17 In. 750
Vase, Lucie Rie, Pink & Blue Swirl Volcanic Glaze, c.1979, 7 x 4 In. .... *illus* 5000
Vase, Madonna, Face, Handles, Red, Orange, Andrea Gill, c.1985, 19 x 9 ½ In. 738
Vase, Male & Female Figures, Speckled Mustard, Beatrice Wood, c.1960, 7 In. 1032
Vase, Melon Shape, Multicolor, Gold Interior, Bennett Bean, 8 x 7 ½ In. 1080
Vase, Mirror Glaze, Dark Gray, Hideaki Miyamura, 8 In. 1968
Vase, Moontang, Stoneware, Stripes, Glazed, Billy Bengston, 1957, 13 ¼ In. .... *illus* 4375
Vase, New York Skyline, Burnished, Lidya Buzio, 15 x 11 In. 7200
Vase, Panthers, Silver Leaf, 12 x 15 In. 215
Vase, Plaid, Multicolor, Rick Dillingham, c.1983, 10 x 9 ½ In. 4800
Vase, Prickly Melon, Imperial Yellow Glaze, Cliff Lee, 10 ¾ x 6 ½ In. 2625
Vase, Purple, Hideaki Miyamura, 6 In. 922
Vase, Purple, Red, Black, Richard Zane Smith, 1990, 10 ½ x 13 In. 400
Vase, Rain Storm, Tim Eberhardt, 2003, 8 ⅝ In. 200
Vase, Raku, Cream, Tan, Paul Soldner, 18 x 11 In. 1250
Vase, Salatan, Mahogany, Ron Artman, c.2005, 24 x 6 In. 500
Vase, Slit Foot, Lid, Marked, Karen Karnes, c.1988, 9 x 5 In. 2400
Vase, Stand, Blue & Brown Glaze, Handles, Signed, A. Hirondelle, c.1995, 7 x 22 In. 369
Vase, Stoneware, Combed Parallel Lines, Claude Conover, 20 In. .... *illus* 8610
Vase, Stoneware, Wood Fired, Chuck Hindes, c.1977, 20 x 6 ¼ In. 180
Vase, Tape Dispenser Shape, Rounded, Gordon Baldwin, 13 x 14 ¼ In. 1107
Vase, Triangular, Concave Base, Signed, Marek Cecula, 1985, 7 x 11 In., Pair 330
Vase, Venetian Blind Pattern, Black & White, Edward Eberle, 7 x 5 In. 450
Vase, White, Drawn On Japanese Figure, Michael Frimkiss, c.1973, 5 x 6 In. 1599
Water Barrel, Abstract Design, Lidya Buzio, 1982, 8 x 10 In. .... *illus* 2875

POTTERY-MIDCENTURY includes pieces made from the 1940s to about 1975.

Birdhouse, Brown, Thomas Stahl, c.1941, 7 In. 247
Bowl, Bird With Tuft, Slip Glaze, Picasso, Madoura, 1952, 6 In. 1888
Bowl, Fish, Blue & White, Wavy Dot Design Rim, J. Jensen, 1953, 7 In. Diam. 173
Bowl, Flower Head Shape, Gray, White Flowers & Butterflies, 1944, 8 In. 138

TIP
When you move, remember that there is no insurance coverage for breakage if the items are not packed by the shipper.

Pottery-Contemporary, Bowl, Gold Luster Fish, Footed, Beatrice Wood, c.1980, 6 ½ x 8 In.
$7,500

Los Angeles Modern Auctions

Pottery-Contemporary, Sculpture, Frog, Inside Oreo Cookie, Brown, Gilhooly, 1970s, 1 ¼ x 2 ½ In.
$1,188

Rago Arts and Auction Center

Pottery-Contemporary, Sculpture, Horse, Prancing, Raised Front Leg, Cloth-Covered Saddle, 21 x 25 In.
$7,187

New Orleans (Cakebread)

Pottery-Contemporary, Sculpture, Jun Kaneko, Stoneware, Painted, Glazed, 1989, 36 x 24 In.
$23,750

Los Angeles Modern Auctions

Pottery-Contemporary, Sculpture, Kangaroo Head, Multicolor, Wool, Yarn, M. Lucero, 2003, 38 x 25 In.
$10,625

Rago Arts and Auction Center

Pottery-Contemporary, Teapot, Visualizing A House, Multicolor, Eyeballs, Curly Handle, M. Lucero, 10 x 10 In.
$5,700

Sam Scott Pottery

Pottery-Contemporary, Teapot, Zanjo, Green, Dots, Small Cylindrical Spout, Lid, P. Cornelius, 1981, 8 x 6 In.
$655

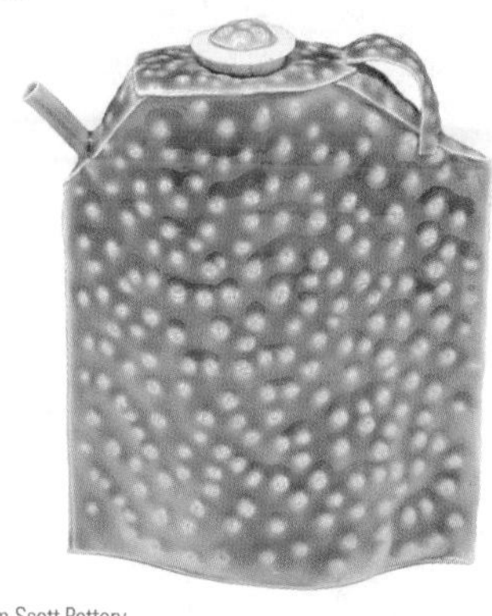

Sam Scott Pottery

Pottery-Contemporary, Vase, Brown Mottled Glaze, Handles, Stoneware, Mark Hewitt, Stamped 71, Lid, 17 In.
$295

Brunk Auctions

Pottery-Contemporary, Vase, Bulbous, Incised Design, Brown, White, Claude Conover, c.1950, 22 In.
$7,995

Skinner, Inc.

Pottery-Contemporary, Vase, Lucie Rie, Pink & Blue Swirl Volcanic Glaze, c.1979, 7 x 4 In.
$5,000

Rago Arts and Auction Center

Pottery-Contemporary, Vase, Moontang, Stoneware, Stripes, Glazed, Billy Bengston, 1957, 13 ¼ In.
$4,375

Los Angeles Modern Auctions

Pottery-Contemporary, Vase, Stoneware, Combed Parallel Lines, Claude Conover, 20 In.
$8,610

Skinner, Inc.

P

Bowl, Frog, Figural, Green Matt Glaze, Oval, Rolled Rim, 1903, 1 ¼ x 5 In. 1035
Bowl, Glazed, Blue, Tan, Peter Voulkos, 1951, 3 ½ x 8 ½ In. 2250
Bowl, Glazed, Red, Laura Andresen, 1953, 6 ¼ x 4 ¾ In. 1875
Bowl, Picador, Pablo Picasso, 1952, 5 ¾ x 5 ¾ In. 2250
Bowl, Pink Crackle Glaze, 4-Footed, Lukens, 15 ¼ In. 1952
Bowl, Sgraffito Lines, High Glaze Interior, Graphic Pattern, Bitossi, Raymor, 8 In. 275
Bowl, Turquoise Stippled Glaze, Purple Ground, Harding Black, c.1959, 2 x 6 In. 243
Charger, Brown, Yellow, Orange, Signed, Paul Soldner, 1975, 18 In. Diam. 1375
Cup & Saucer, R. Lichtenstein, Jackson China, 1966, Saucer 6 In., 24 Piece.......... *illus* 3250
Cup, Mummy Eagle, Adamson, 1975, 5 In. 63
Dish, Brown, Cream Overglaze, Signed, Paul Soldner, 1955, 9 ½ In. Diam. 1450
Dish, Impressed Rope, Brown Ground, Cartouches, Wide Rim, T. Shimaoka, 12 In. 3690
Dish, Impressed Rope, White Slip, Blue Green Center, Wide Rim, T. Shimaoka, 11 In. 738
Figurine, Mother & Child, Waylande Gregory, 1934, 8 ½ x 5 ¼ In. 861
Figurine, Tortoise & The Hare, Edris Eckhardt, c.1926, 5 ½ In. 472
Group, 3 Men On Their Knees, White, Steele Burden, 3 x 7 ¼ In. 615
Jar, Green Glaze, Teardrops, Lid, Harrison McIntosh, 1960, 10 x 6 ½ In. 1750
Jug, Red Drip Glaze, Handle, West Germany, 24 x 17 In. 193
Pitcher, Black, Vallauris, France, c.1950, 9 In. 300
Pitcher, Cream, Blue, Glazed, Engraved, Picasso, 8 ⅝ In. 9408
Pitcher, Incised Rubino, Vallauris, France, c.1960, 9 ⅛ In. 600
Pitcher, Owl, White & Blue, Loop Handle, Pablo Picasso, 1954, 10 In. 5000
Planter, Aqua Blue, Textured, Malcolm Leland, c.1963, 20 x 14 In. 1500
Plaque, Bull In Profile, Ivory, Brown, Green, Picasso, 1956, 10 In. 2829
Plaque, Face, Green, Brown, Bjorn Wiinblad, 1960, 29 ½ x 18 ½ In. 2560
Plaque, Man, Woman, Harris Strong, 1965, 23 x 5 In. 297
Plaque, Oval, Portrait, Yellow, Blue, Green, Bjorn Wiinblad, 1955, 22 x 14 In. 1440
Plate, Face In High Relief, Black Rim, Brown Ground, Picasso, 16 ¾ In. 8232
Plate, Fish, Earthenware, Mottled Brown, Cream, Green, Oval, P. Picasso, 16 In. 8610
Plate, People, Landscape, Stencil, Peter Voulkos, 1956, 2 ¾ x 15 ¼ In. 9375
Plate, Picasso, Little Horse No. 61, Blue, Black, Madoura, 1963, 10 In. 6250
Plate, Polo, Glazed, Stamped Cowan, Viktor Schreckengost, c.1929, 11 In. 812
Plate, Stylized Female Figures, Birds, Gray, 8-Sided, Thelma Winter, 13 In. 625
Platter, 5-Sided, Stripes, Brown, Blue, Henry Takemoto, Signed, 1959, 14 x 13 In. 2813
Platter, Stripes, Blue, Brown, Cream Ground, Signed, Henry Takemoto, 14 In. 2812
Sculpture, King Bird, Thelma Frazier Winter, Glaze, 1959, 26 x 12 In. .... *illus* 5625
Sculpture, Sinatra Swooners, Teenage Girls, Radio, J.H. Reich, 1940s, 6 x 6 In. .... *illus* 590
Vase, Blue Stripe, Madeline Speer, 12 x 5 In. 83
Vase, Blue Stripes, Brown Cross, Billy Al Bengston, c.1957, 13 x 6 ¼ In. 3500
Vase, Blue, Ken Price, 1958, 17 x 7 In. 8750
Vase, Brother Thomas Bezanson, Copper Red, Vermont, Signed, 1950s, 12 x 7 In. .... *illus* 4688
Vase, Brown Linear Decoration, Pear Shape, Hans Coper, c.1952, 8 ⅞ In. 7878
Vase, Brown, Blue, Partially Glazed, Squared, Ken Price, c.1958, 17 x 7 x 5 In. 8750
Vase, Circles Design, White, Brown, Flattened Oval, A. Prieto, 1950s, 12 In. 625
Vase, Cirrus Glaze, White Bonsai Tree, Pear Shape, Ring Foot, L. Holtkamp, 1953, 4 In. 173
Vase, Concentric Circles, Brown, Buff Ground, Bulbous, A. Prieto, 12 x 8 In. .... *illus* 1353
Vase, Couple, Picnic, Marked, Maija Grotell, 4 x 4 In. 2976
Vase, Earth Tone, Vivika & Otto Heino, 11 ½ In. 312
Vase, Earthenware, Glazed, Signed, Guido Gambone, Italy, 1960s, 19 x 7 ½ In. 2250
Vase, Farsta, Wilhelm Kage, Gustavsberg Studio, 1950, 6 x 6 In. .... *illus* 2500
Vase, Fish, White, Yellow & Black, Rounded Shoulders, 11 In. 120
Vase, Flaring, Blue, Tan, Brown, Swirls, Saucer Foot, M. Wildenhain, c.1950, 8 In. .... *illus* 1000
Vase, Geometric, 2 Sections, Blue, Brown, Ken Price, c.1958, 17 x 7 In. 8750
Vase, Lid, Purple, Red Copper Glaze, Ichthys Symbol, Br. T. Bezanson, 7 x 7 In. 2720
Vase, Lion Head, Mane, Figural, Lisa Larson, 1965, 5 ½ x 4 ½ In. 83
Vase, Multicolor, Round, Paul Soldner, 4 x 5 In. 180
Vase, Raku, Brown, Tapered, Small Hole, Paul Soldner, 1970, 17 x 7 ½ In. 1250
Vase, Red Chrome, Streaky Glaze, Flared, Handles At Neck, Bulbous, c.1945, 10 In. 196
Vase, Sunburst, Green, Blue, Signed, Michael Frinkess, 11 ¾ x 6 In. 2812

POWDER FLASKS AND POWDER HORNS were made to hold the gunpowder used in antique firearms. The early examples were made of horn or wood; later ones were of copper or brass.

POWDER FLASK

Brass, Eagle, Hands Shaking, Coat Of Arms, 1854, 9 ¾ x 4 In. 258
Copper, Brass, James Dixon & Sons, 1800, 7 ¾ x 3 ¼ In. 207
Tin, Civil War, Round, Leather Strap, 1860s, 4 ½ In. 138

Pottery-Contemporary, Water Barrel, Abstract Design, Lidya Buzio, 1982, 8 x 10 In.
$2,875

Los Angeles Modern Auctions

Pottery-Midcentury, Cup & Saucer, R. Lichtenstein, Jackson China, 1966, Saucer 6 In., 24 Piece
$3,250

Rago Arts and Auction Center

Pottery-Midcentury, Sculpture, King Bird, Thelma Frazier Winter, Glaze, 1959, 26 x 12 In.
$5,625

Rago Arts and Auction Center

P

Pottery-Midcentury, Sculpture, Sinatra Swooners, Teenage Girls, Radio, J.H. Reich, 1940s, 6 x 6 In.
$590

Humler & Nolan

Pottery-Midcentury, Vase, Brother Thomas Bezanson, Copper Red, Vermont, Signed, 1950s, 12 x 7 In.
$4,688

Rago Arts and Auction Center

Pottery-Midcentury, Vase, Concentric Circles, Brown, Buff Ground, Bulbous, A. Prieto, 12 x 8 In.
$1,353

Skinner, Inc.

POWDER HORN

Horn, Eagle, Spread Wing, Shield, Banner, Ship, Engraved, Ring-Turned Neck, c.1800, 16 In. ... 1353

Horn, Elijah Sexton, Son Of Liberty, Carved, Patina, Pewter Ferrule, c.1775, 15 In. ... 9480

Horn, Elk, Tree Of Life, Holy Eucharist, c.1850, 7 ½ x 3 In. ... 1121

Horn, George Washington Portrait, Artillery, Carved, England, c.1800, 18 In. ... 1080

Horn, Lion, Horse, Animals, Soldiers, Swords, Nathaniel Bartlett, 1755, 13 In. ... *illus* 8610

Horn, Pine Plug, Carved, Horse, Handler, Birds, John Rhodes, c.1777, 7 ⅜ In. ... 2460

Pine Plug, Iron Staple, Ticonderoga, Carved Designs, Timothy Woodins, c.1759, 14 In. ... 3690

PRATT ware means two different things. It was an early Staffordshire pottery, cream-colored with colored decorations, made by Felix Pratt during the late eighteenth century. There was also Pratt ware made with transfer designs during the mid-nineteenth century in Fenton, England. Reproductions of the transfer-printed Pratt are being made.

PRATT
FENTON

Bank, 2-Story Cottage, Children Looking Out Windows, 5 x 3 x 2 In. ... 425

Creamer, Cow Form, Sponged Decoration, Milkmaid ... 210

Figurine, Cobbler, Milkmaid, Painted, c.1800, 8 ½ In., Pair ... 177

Figurine, Lion, Reclining, c.1825, 4 In. ... 250

Figurine, Virgin Mary, Soft Paste, 9 ¾ In. ... 142

Meat Jar, Men, Hunting, Dogs, Quail, Rabbits, c.1856, 4 ½ In. ... 65

Mug, Fisherman, Horse & Cart, Castle, Angular Handle, Turquoise, 3 ¾ In. ... 105

Mug, Fisherman, Women With Baskets, Pink, Gilt Trim, 1840-1900 ... 90

Pitcher, Portraits, Admiral Nelson, Captain Berry, Ships, Embossed, c.1810, 5 In. ... *illus* 123

Plate, Cattle, Ruins, Herder, Turquoise Border, Gilt Trim, Transferware, 8 ½ In. ... 245

Plate, Pasture, Cows, Waterfall, Couple, Transferware, Turquoise Border, 7 ½ In. ... 245

PRESSED GLASS, or pattern glass, was first made in the United States in the 1820s after the invention of glass pressing machines. Hundreds of patterns of pressed glass were made in complete table settings. Although the Boston and Sandwich Works was the most famous of the pressed glass factories, there were about sixteen other factories making pressed glass from 1830 to 1850, and still more from 1850 to 1900, when pressed glass reached its greatest popularity. It is now being widely reproduced. The pattern names used in this listing are based on the information in the book *Pressed Glass in America* by John and Elizabeth Welker. There may be pieces of pressed glass listed in this book in other categories, such as Lamp, Ruby Glass, Sandwich Glass, and Souvenir.

Atlas, Pitcher, 12 In., 52 Oz. ... 102

Atterbury, Cake Stand, Milk Glass, 12 In. ... 72

Beautiful Lady, Compote, 6 In. ... 32

Candlestick, Frosted Dolphin, Scalloped Octagonal Cup, c.1890, 8 x 5 In., Pair ... 671

Cosmos pattern is listed in this book as its own category.

Cottage, Cake Stand, Pedestal, Adams & Bellaire, 1870s, 9 x 6 ½ In. ... 95

Dish, Sweetmeat, Lid, Cobalt Blue, Octagonal, Fluted Stem, Stepped Base, 7 ½ In. ... 3198

Ellipse & Circle, Vase, Blue, Gauffered Rim, Hexagonal Base, c.1850, 7 ¼ In. ... 246

Eye & Scale, Vase, Green, Scalloped Rim, New England Glass, 9 ½ In., Pair ... *illus* 2583

Fan & Star, Sugar & Creamer ... 25

Four Printie Block, Lamp, Hexagon Base, Cobalt Blue, c.1845, 11 ¼ In. ... 1722

Four Printie Block, Vase, Footed, c.1850, 9 ¾ In. ... 98

Frosted patterns may be listed under the name of the main pattern.

Hobnail pattern is in this book as its own category.

Lion, Sugar & Creamer, Gillinder ... 95

Loop, Lamp, White Opaque, Elongated, Hexagonal, Fluid Burner, c.1850, 4 ¾ In. ... 548

Loop, Vase, Amethyst, Gauffered Rim, 8-Sided Standard, Square Base, c.1840, 11 In. ... 1168

Loop, Vase, Blue, Gauffered Rim, 8-Sided Standard, Square Base, Boston & Sandwich, 9 In. ... 738

Moon & Star, Cologne Bottle, Stopper, Canary Yellow, Boston & Sandwich, c.1850, 7 In. ... 400

Quintec, Basket, Handle, Footed, Ruby, Smith Glass, 7 In. ... 26

Salt, Light Green, Scallop & Point Rim, 4-Footed, Jersey Glass Co., 2 x 3 In. ... *illus* 443

Sawtooth, Compote, Cover, Pedestal Base, c.1850, 12 x 8 In. ... 118

Spiral Ribs, Cruet, Sapphire Blue, Tapered, Tam-O'-Shanter Stopper, 6 ¾ In. ... 185

Three Printie Block, Lamp, Amethyst, Octagonal Standard, Square Base, 9 In. ... 1599

Tulip, Vase, Cobalt Blue, Flaring Hexagonal Foot, 9 ½ In. ... 5843

Twisted Loop, Vase, 8-Sided Standard, Square Base, Cobalt Blue, c.1840, 10 In. ... 1476

Twisted Loop, Vase, Amethyst, Hexagonal Stem, Round Foot, Scalloped Rim, 9 ½ In. ... 369

PRINT, in this listing, means any of many printed images produced on paper by one of the more common methods, such as lithography. The prints listed here are of interest primarily to the antiques collector, not the fine arts collector. Many of these prints were originally part of books. Other prints will be found in the Advertising, Currier & Ives, Movie, and Poster categories.

Appel, Karel, Looking Into The Infinite, Color Lithograph, Arches Paper, Signed, 28 x 41 In. ... 782

Audubon bird prints were originally issued as part of books printed from 1826 to 1854. They were issued in two sheet sizes, 26 ½ inches by 39 ½ inches and 11 inches by 7 inches. The height of a picture is listed before the width. The quadrupeds were issued in 28-by-22-inch prints. Later editions of the Audubon books were done in many sizes, and reprints of the books in the original sizes were also made. The words *After John James Audubon* appear on all of the prints, including the originals, because the pictures were made as copies of Audubon's original oil paintings. The bird pictures have been so popular they have been copied in myriad sizes using both old and new printing methods. This list includes originals and later copies because Audubon prints of all ages are sold in antiques shops.

J.W.Audubon

Audubon, American Flamingo, Octavo Edition, Gilt Frame, 8 ¼ x 6 In. 504
Audubon, Canada Goose, Volare Octavo Edition, Frame, 8 ½ x 6 In. 444
Audubon, Fish Hawk, Amsterdam Edition, Frame, 39 x 26 In. 738
Audubon, Florida Jay, Amsterdam Edition, Gilt Frame, 28 x 21 ½ In. 711
Audubon, Golden Eagle, Aquila Chrysaetos, Engraving, Havell, 38 x 25 In. 8260
Audubon, Ivory-Billed Woodpecker, 1 Male, 2 Females, Havell, Frame, 38 x 25 In. .... *illus* 16500
Audubon, Louisiana Heron, Octavo Edition, Frame, 6 ¼ x 8 In. 356
Audubon, Ruby-Throated Hummingbird, Bien Edition, Chromolithograph, 34 x 24 In. 1003
Audubon, Summer Or Wood Duck, Amsterdam Edition, Mahogany Frame, 37 x 26 In. 584
Audubon, White Pelican, Princeton Edition, Frame, 38 ½ x 25 ½ In. 732
Audubon, Wild Turkey, Female & Young, Color Lithograph, Mat, Frame, 26 x 39 In. 1037
Audubon, Wood Wren, Birds Of America, Frame, 1833, 37 ½ x 24 ¾ In. 590
Bacon, Francis, Human Body, Lithograph, Signed, Limited, 61 ¾ x 43 In. 12200
Catesby, Mark, Summer Redbird, Colored Engraving, Frame, 14 x 10 ¼ In. 944
Chagall, Marc, Vence, Cite Des Arts Et Des Fleurs, 1954, 27 x 18 ½ In. 300
Charcoal On Paper, Still Life, Champagne, Asparagus & Candles, Glazed, Frame, 27 x 22 In. .. 1125
Currier & Ives prints are listed in the Currier & Ives category.
Ede, Basil, White Pelican, Colored Lithograph, Signed, Frame, 1900s, 48 x 35 In. 1107
Erte, Alphabet, Color, Frame, 36 x 24 In. 48
Erte, Starstruck, Silkscreen, Frame, 33 x 24 In. 840
Hirschfeld, Albert, Tom Selleck, Etching, 1984, 12 ¼ x 9 ½ In. 177

Icart prints were made by Louis Icart, who worked in Paris from 1907 as an employee of a postcard company. He then started printing magazines and fashion brochures. About 1910 he created a series of etchings of fashionably dressed women, and he continued to make similar etchings until he died in 1950. He is well known as a printmaker, painter, and illustrator. Original etchings are much more expensive than the later photographic copies.

Icart, Le Jardin Japonaise, Mother, Daughter, Sitting At Table, 1932, 10 x 15 In. 795
Icart, Le Panier De Pommes, Girl, Apple Basket, Frame, 19 x 26 In. 400
Icart, Little Butterflies, Color Etching, Signed, Numbered, Gilt Wood Frame, 1926, 15 x 19 In. .. 759
Icart, The Letter, Woman, Looking Over Shoulder, Shawl, Frame, 18 x 26 In. 400

Jacoulet prints were designed by Paul Jacoulet (1902–1960), a Frenchman who spent most of his life in Japan. He was a master of Japanese woodblock print technique. Subjects included life in Japan, the South Seas, Korea, and China. His prints were sold by subscription and issued in series. Each series had a distinctive seal, such as a sparrow or butterfly. Most Jacoulet prints are approximately 15 x 10 inches.

Jacoulet, Downpour At Metalanim Ponape, Duck Seal, c.1935, 15 x 11 In. 600
Jacoulet, La Dansuse Coreene, Korean Dancer, 1960, 12 x 16 In. 675
Jacoulet, Le Bonze Errant, Wandering Priest, Woodblock, 12 x 16 In. 575

Japanese woodblock prints are listed as follows: Print, Japanese, name of artist, title or description, type, and size. Dealers use the following terms: Tate-e is a vertical composition. Yoko-e is a horizontal composition. The words Aiban (13 by 9 inches), Chuban (10 by 7 ½ inches), Hosoban (13 by 6 inches), Koban (7 by 4 inches), Nagaban (20 by 9 inches), Oban (15 by 10 inches), Shikishiban (8 by 9 inches), and Tanzaku (15 by 5 inches) denote approximate size. Modern versions of some of these prints have been made. Other woodblock prints that are not Japanese are listed under Print, Woodblock.

Japanese, Bijin, Landscape, Bonsai Tree, Children, Pagoda, Frame, 9 ¾ x 7 In. 12
Japanese, Kinoshita, Tomio, Ink, Stylized People, Eyes Closed, 1980, 34 x 23 In. .... *illus* 1230
Japanese, Kiyoshi Saito, Winter In Aizu, Houses, Trees, Man, Frame, 1970, 16 x 21 In. .... *illus* 2091
Japanese, Koitsu, Tsuchiya, Summer Moon At Miyajima, Mat, Frame, 10 ¼ x 15 ⅝ In. 828
Japanese, Sakamoto, Isamu, Temple Gate On Mountain, Red Chop Mark, c.1972, 24 x 18 In. ... 132
Japanese, Sung-Ch'uan, Chao, White Bird Peonies, c.1915, 70 x 23 In. 184
Japanese, Yoshida, Hiroshi, Yomei Gate At Nikko, Multicolor, Signed, c.1937, 15 x 9 ¾ In. 196
Lithograph, Miami Indian, Kneeling Hunter, Spear, Frame, 1924, 43 x 35 In. 570
Lithograph, Nocturne In Blue & Gold, Old Battersea Bridge, c.1915, 21 x 16 In. 2375

Pottery-Midcentury, Vase, Farsta, Wilhelm Kage, Gustavsberg Studio, 1950, 6 x 6 In.
$2,500

Los Angeles Modern Auctions

Pottery-Midcentury, Vase, Flaring, Blue, Tan, Brown, Swirls, Saucer Foot, M. Wildenhain, c.1950, 8 In.
$1,000

Rago Arts and Auction Center

Powder Horn, Horn, Lion, Horse, Animals, Soldiers, Swords, Nathaniel Bartlett, 1755, 13 In.
$8,610

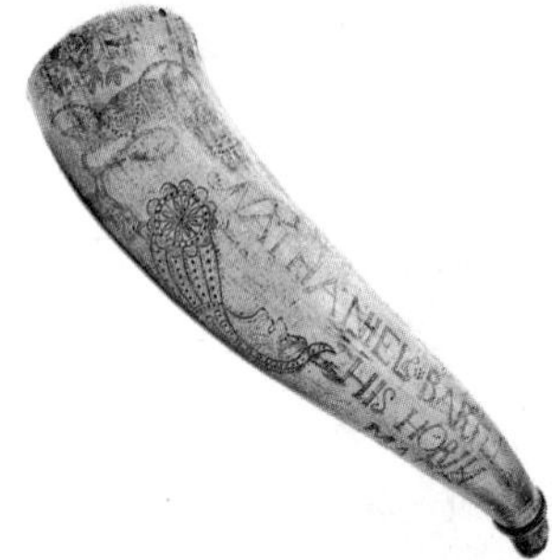

Skinner, Inc.

This is an edited listing of current prices. Visit **Kovels.com** to check thousands of prices from previous years and sign up for free information on trends, tips, reproductions, marks, and more.

Pratt, Pitcher, Portraits, Admiral Nelson, Captain Berry, Ships, Embossed, c.1810, 5 In.
$123

Cowan Auctions

Pressed Glass, Eye & Scale, Vase, Green, Scalloped Rim, New England Glass, 9 ½ In., Pair
$2,583

Skinner, Inc.

Pressed Glass, Salt, Light Green, Scallop & Point Rim, 4-Footed, Jersey Glass Co., 2 x 3 In.
$443

Hess Auction Group

Lithograph, Offset, Nebraska Evening, Thomas Hart Benton, 1941, 13 ½ x 10 ½ In. 834
Matisse, Henri, La Danseuse Creole, Lithograph, Mourlot Printer, Nice, France, 39 x 29 In. 793
McKenney & Hall, Chippewa Widow, Lithograph, Hand Colored, 1837-44, 20 x 14 In. 1107
McKenney & Hall, Lithograph, Ap-Pa-Noo-Se, Saukie Chief, 20 ½ x 15 ½ In. ....*illus* 420
Miro, Joan, Le Lezard Aux Plumes D'Or, Lithograph, Signed, Limited, 15 x 21 In. 1300
Mucha, Alphonse, Salome, L'Estampe Moderne, Color Lithograph, Signed, 1897, 21 x 16 In. 1298

Nutting prints are popular with collectors. Wallace Nutting is known for his pictures, furniture, and books. Collectors call his pictures Nutting prints although they are actually hand-colored photographs issued from 1900 to 1941. There are over 10,000 different titles. Wallace Nutting furniture is listed in the Furniture category.

Wallace Nutting

Nutting, A Touching Tale, Interior Scene, Girl Reading At Table, 16 x 12 In. 195
Nutting, All Smiles, Interior Scene, Girl, Mirror, Mat, Wood Frame, c.1920, 11 x 17 In. 165
Nutting, Blossom Cove, River Scene, Mat, Frame, c.1915, 14 x 11 In. 135
Nutting, Colonial Woman Sewing, Signed, Frame, 7 ¾ x 10 In. 49
Nutting, In The Brave Days Of Old, Mahogany Frame, 22 x 18 In. 350
Nutting, Lady Pembroke, Frame, 20 x 16 In. 325
Nutting, Patchwork Quilting, Mat, Frame, 12 x 10 In. 150

Parrish prints are wanted by collectors. Maxfield Frederick Parrish was an illustrator who lived from 1870 to 1966. He is best known as a designer of magazine covers, posters, calendars, and advertisements. His prints have been copied in recent years. Some Maxfield Parrish items may be listed in Advertising.

Maxfield Parrish

Parrish, Air Castle, Frame, 19 x 15 ¼ In. 324
Pond, Clayton, My Studio On Broome Street, Color Serigraph, Signed, 1971, 30 x 40 In. 190
Rockwell, Norman, Artist Critic, Lithograph, Frame, 28 ½ x 26 ½ In. 2400
Rockwell, Norman, Summer Stock, Lithograph, Frame, 22 x 18 In. 540
Ruscha, Ed, Raw, Lithograph, Signed, 10 ¾ x 21 ¼ In. 4250
Steffen, Bernard, Upland, Black & White Lithograph, Signed, Frame, 9 ½ x 13 In. 307
Stella, Frank, Engraving IX, Etching, Relief, Signed, Tyler Graphics, N.Y., 58 ½ x 49 In. 4000
Vasarely, Victor, Dom-Bor, Screenprint, Signed, Limited, 28 ¾ x 23 ¼ In. 425

Woodblock prints that are not in the Japanese tradition are listed here. Most were made in England and the United States during the Arts and Crafts period. Japanese woodblock prints are listed under Print, Japanese.

Woodblock, Bailey, Henrietta, Charcoal Schooners, Frame, 1932, 13 x 9 ¼ In. ....*illus* 1625
Woodblock, Baumann, Gustave, Mountain Gold, Signed, Mat, Frame, 1925, 10 x 11 In. .....*illus* 18750
Woodblock, Baumann, Gustave, Ranchos De Taos, Mat, Frame, Signed, 1930, 9 x 11 In. 12500
Woodblock, Baumann, Gustave, Taos Placita, Mat & Frame, Signed, 1947, 10 x 11 In. ....*illus* 1250
Woodblock, Patterson, Margaret, Trees, Road, House, Color, Signed, c.1900, 9 x 6 In. ....*illus* 2500

PURINTON POTTERY COMPANY was incorporated in Wellsville, Ohio, in 1936. The company moved to Shippenville, Pennsylvania, in 1941 and made a variety of hand-painted ceramic wares. By the 1950s Purinton was making dinnerware, souvenirs, cookie jars, and florist wares. The pottery closed in 1959.

Purinton Pottery

Apple, Bowl, Cereal, 5 ⅜ In. 10
Apple, Canister Set, Slipware, Flour, Sugar, Coffee, Tea, 1940s, 4 Piece ....*illus* 68
Apple, Chop Plate, Round, 11 In. 32
Apple, Cookie Jar, Lid, 7 ⅝ In. 124
Apple, Creamer, 10 Oz., 3 ¼ In. 15
Apple, Cup & Saucer 9
Apple, Dish, Pickle, 6 ⅛ In. 91
Apple, Jug, 80 Oz., 6 ½ In. 52
Apple, Plate, Dinner, 9 ¾ In. 17
Apple, Platter, Oval, 12 In. 43
Apple, Salt & Pepper, Jug Shape, Handle 12
Fruit, Creamer, 14 Oz., 4 ½ In. 15
Fruit, Creamer, 3 In. 18
Fruit, Jug, 12 Oz., 4 ½ In. 17
Fruit, Jug, Ice Lip, 5 ½ In. 26
Fruit, Tumbler, 4 ¾ In. 18
Heather Plaid, Cup & Saucer 12
Heather Plaid, Sugar, 3 ¼ In. 20

Intaglio, Bowl, Vegetable, Oval, Brown, 7 In.	16
Intaglio, Chop Plate, Round, Brown, 11 In.	39
Intaglio, Jug, Brown, 16 Oz., 4 ½ In.	26
Intaglio, Relish, 3 Sections, Center Handle, Brown, 9 In.	16
Normandy Plaid, Chop Plate, Round, 11 ¾ In.	43
Normandy Plaid, Cup & Saucer	6
Normandy Plaid, Plate, Salad, 6 ¾ In.	7
Normandy Plaid, Salt & Pepper	36
Normandy Plaid, Sugar, 3 In.	16
Normandy Plaid, Tumbler, 12 Oz., 4 ¾ In.	10
Petals, Syrup, Ball Shape, Handle, c.1950, 6 ½ In.	15
Pitcher, Ivy, Yellow Blossom, Slipware, Yellow, Green, Brown, c.1950, 7 ½ In. *illus*	35
Shooting Star, Vase, Ball Shape, 5 In.	35
Shooting Star, Vase, Flat Handles, 5 ⅝ In.	13

PURSES have been recognizable since the eighteenth century, when leather and needlework purses were preferred. Beaded purses became popular in the nineteenth century, went out of style, but are again in use. Mesh purses date from the 1880s and are still being made. How to carry a handkerchief and lipstick is a problem today for every woman, including the Queen of England.

Alligator, Brass Clasp, Compartments, Lucille De Paris, c.1960, 10 ½ x 7 ½ In. *illus*	550
Alligator, Tote, Black, Center Seam, Anne Klein	40
Basket, Nantucket Friendship, Bone Medallion, Whale Pulling Boat, 1991, 7 x 11 In. *illus*	123
Beaded, Art Deco, Enameled, Chain Link Handle, Morabito, 9 x 5 x 1 In.	278
Beaded, Drawstring, Courting Couple, Fringe, c.1920, 8 x 4 In.	125
Beaded, Minaudiere, Envelope, Clear, Gray, Black, Intaglio Closure, Judith Leiber, 3 x 6 In.	390
Beaded, Minaudiere, Satin, Beggar's Pouch, Multicolor, Shoulder Chain, J. Leiber, 1994, 5 In.	570
Caiman, Teal, Jeweled Medallion, ½ Gusseted Slip Pocket, Armenta, 6 ¼ x 12 In.	492
Calfskin, Black, Flap Top, CC Logo, 2 Pockets, Strap, Chanel, 8 ½ x 12 ¼ In.	484
Calfskin, Woven, Camel, Double Handles, Bottega Veneta, Italy, Dust Bag, 15 x 9 In. *illus*	725
Canvas, Hobo Style, Boulogne 35, Lined, Louis Vuitton, 12 x 14 In.	770
Canvas, Mini Looping, Monogram, Flap Closure, Leather Handle, Louis Vuitton, 7 x 11 In.	460
Canvas, Sac, Weekend PM, Top Zip, Rolled Handles, Louis Vuitton, 1987, 18 x 12 In.	472
Celluloid, Painted, Rhinestones, Snap Closure, Mirror, Art Deco, 1920s, 4 ¼ x 3 In. *illus*	115
Crocodile, Clutch, Red, Shiny, Oscar De La Renta, 6 ½ x 9 ½ In.	812
Crocodile, Green, Shiny, Top Handle, Ralph Lauren, 6 ½ x 7 ½ In.	625
Crocodile, Shoulder, Black, Matte, Marc Jacobs, 13 x 7 ½ In.	600
Crocodile, Tote, Cognac, Girelli, Tod's, 13 ½ In.	625
Crystal, Gold & Silver Trellis Design, Chain, Push Clasp, Judith Leiber, 1980s, 4 x 5 In.	1375
Crystals, Gold Frame, Leather, Tomato, Chain Strap, Judith Leiber, Box, 4 x 4 In. *illus*	1625
Fabric, Clutch, Green, Pleated, Tan Bakelite Crouching Wolf Handle, 7 x 9 ¾ In. *illus*	677
Fabric, Hunt Scene, Black, Gray, Green, Persian Style, Green Bakelite Clasp, France, 5 x 7 In.	338
Fabric, Leather, Borsa Magic Piccolo Zucca, Goldtone Hardware, Fendi, 8 ½ x 12 In.	368
Faux Leather, Clutch, Metallic Gold, 1950s, 5 x 7 In.	26
Goatskin, Blue, Le Talentueux, Goldtone Corners, Studs, Louis Vuitton, c.2003, 13 x 7 In.	1179
Karung, Gathered, Toggle Frame, Tiger's-Eye Cabochon, Judith Leiber, 1980s, 6 x 9 In.	2500
Leather, Alston, Wine, Silvertone Hardware, Monogram, Louis Vuitton, 7 ½ x 11 ½ In.	605
Leather, Black, Normandie, Ocean Liner Shape, Ship's Funnel Clasp, Anchor, France, 13 In.	1230
Leather, Bordeaux, Snap Closure, Cartier, 1900s, 15 x 19 In.	593
Leather, Bowler, Luxe Ligne, Metallic Gold, Braided Straps, Chain, Chanel, 17 x 7 In.	546
Leather, Brown Caviar, Silver Hardware, Pockets On Front, Zip Top, Chanel, 10 x 11 In.	825
Leather, Doctor Bag, Pull Button Closure, Lined, Monogram, 1800s, 4 x 8 In.	63
Leather, Mini Tote, Embroidered Ornaments, Handles, Intrecciato, Bottega Veneta, 7 x 12 In.	173
Leather, Parrot, Jackie At Psychologist's Form Board, Shoulder, 1950s, 11 x 7 In.	64
Leather, Quilted, Black, Shoulder Straps, Goldtone Hardware, Chanel, 14 x 11 In. *illus*	412
Leather, Shoulder, Black, Silver Hardware, Ferragamo, 11 ½ x 12 ½ In.	500
Leather, Shoulder, Red, Gathered, Salvatore Ferragamo, 12 ½ x 19 In.	210
Leather, Shoulder, Ricky, Dark Brown, Ralph Lauren, 9 x 15 ½ In.	525
Leather, Textured, Goldenrod, Hobo, Shoulder Strap, Buckle Ends, Zipper, Prada, 13 x 14 In.	2375
Leather, Tote, Purple, Classic D Bag, Tod's, 13 ½ In.	625
Lizard, Brown, Kelly, Goldtone Hardware, Hermes	2829
Lizard, Shoulder, Patchwork, Gold, Pink, Teal, Olive, Valentino, 4 x 10 In.	575
Lizard, Tote, Patchwork, Gold, Pink, Teal, Olive, Valentino, 11 x 12 In.	1375
Lucite, Clear Top, Diamonds, Marbleized Bottom, Charles S. Kahn, Miami, 1950s, 7 ¾ In. *illus*	119
Mesh, 14K Gold, Cabochon Sapphire Push Closure, 4 ½ In. *illus*	2706

Print, Audubon, Ivory-Billed Woodpecker, 1 Male, 2 Females, Havell, Frame, 38 x 25 In.
$16,500

Brunk Auctions

Print, Japanese, Kinoshita, Tomio, Ink, Stylized People, Eyes Closed, 1980, 34 x 23 In.
$1,230

Skinner, Inc.

Print, Japanese, Kiyoshi Saito, Winter In Aizu, Houses, Trees, Man, Frame, 1970, 16 x 21 In.
$2,091

Skinner, Inc.

Print, McKenney & Hall, Lithograph, Ap-Pa-Noo-Se, Saukie Chief, 20 ½ x 15 ½ In.
$420

Garth's Auctioneers & Appraisers

Print, Woodblock, Bailey, Henrietta, Charcoal Schooners, Frame, 1932, 13 x 9 ¼ In.
$1,625

Rago Arts and Auction Center

Print, Woodblock, Baumann, Gustave, Mountain Gold, Signed, Mat, Frame, 1925, 10 x 11 In.
$18,750

Rago Arts and Auction Center

Print, Woodblock, Baumann, Gustave, Taos Placita, Mat & Frame, Signed, 1947, 10 x 11 In.
$1,250

Rago Arts and Auction Center

Print, Woodblock, Patterson, Margaret, Trees, Road, House, Color, Signed, c.1900, 9 x 6 In.
$2,500

Rago Arts and Auction Center

Purinton, Apple, Canister Set, Slipware, Flour, Sugar, Coffee, Tea, 1940s, 4 Piece
$68

Ruby Lane

Mesh, El-Sah, Built-In Mirror, Multicolor, Silver, Whiting & Davis, 5 ¼ x 7 In. 450
Mesh, Princess Mary Style, Gold, Lace & Chain Fringe, Whiting & Davis, 5 x 7 In. 499
Mesh, Zebra Stripes, Brown, Gold, Silk Lining, 30-Inch Chain, Whiting & Davis, 4 ⅝ x 9 In. *illus* 85
Metal, Buddha, Rhinestones, Shoulder Chain, Judith Leiber, 1900s, 5 x 4 ½ In. ....*illus* 570
Metal, Clutch, Red & Gold, Oscar De La Renta, 4 x 7 In. 200
Metal, Leather, Foo Dog, Crystals, Chain Strap, Accessories, Judith Leiber, Box, 6 x 4 In. ......*illus* 2250
Minaudiere, Flowers, Stained Glass Style, Pink, Green, Teal, Judith Leiber, 1992, 4 x 7 In. 660
Minaudiere, New York City Skyline, Black & Silver, Judith Leiber, 3 x 4 ½ In. 660
Needlepoint, Clutch, Art Deco Circles, Rectangles, Squares, Blue, Tan, Purple, France, 5 x 8 In. 185
Needlepoint, Fox Hunt Scene, Leather, Suedette, Satin Lining, c.1953, 15 x 9 In. ....*illus* 325
Ostrich, Brown, Goldtone Hardware, Lucille De Paris, 7 ¾ x 10 ½ In. ....*illus* 215
Ostrich, Bucket Bag, Brown, White Stitching, Goldtone Hardware, Gucci, 7 ¼ x 7 In. 259
Ostrich, Kelly Bag, Goldtone Hardware, Clochette, Key, Sellier Style, Hermes, 13 In. ....*illus* 5185
Pigskin, Sac Mallette, Brown, Gilt Hardware, Velvet & Silk Lined, Hermes, 1950s, 10 In. 860
Pony Hair, Clutch, Black, Silver Hardware, Michael Kors, 5 x 11 In. 64
Pony Hair, Leopard Print, Miss Urbanette, Weekender, Dolce & Gabbana, 14 x 20 In. ....*illus* 5000
Python, Leather, Top Handle, Beige, Michael Kors, 8 x 13 In. 162
Rhinestones, Minaudiere, Gold Plate, Leather Interior, Chain Strap, Judith Leiber, 5 x 3 In. 325
Satin, Blue, Black, Teal, Intrecciaio, Adjustable Shoulder Strap, Bottega Veneta, 5 x 9 In. 184
Satin, Silver Crystal, Pouch, Flap, Designed For Nancy Reagan, Judith Leiber, Box, 1985.......... 2125
Satin, Tan, Faux Pearls, Minaudiere, Judith Leiber, 4 x 4 ½ In. 330
Suede, Clutch, Blondie, Brown, Gilt Metal Logo, Gucci, 1970s, 11 x 6 In. 695
Suede, Leather Handles, Compact, Mirror, Powder Puff, Elgin American, 1940s, 5 x 4 In. ....*illus* 110
Silk, Black, Evening, Gold Leaf Clasp, Lapis, Turquoise, Sapphires, Signed, Cartier, 10 In. 3567
Silver, Compact, Etched Flowers & Scrolls, Inset Buttonhole Watch, Chain, c.1900, 5 In. 185
Snakeskin, Clutch, Pleated, Goldtone Frame, White, Black Stones, Judith Leiber, 1894, 6 x 8 In. . 253
Snakeskin, Crystal, Black, Kiss Lock Closure, Black, Dust Bag, Judith Leiber, c.1950, 5 x 6 In. ... 150
Snakeskin, Miu, Shoulder, Purple, Pleats, 7 ½ x 10 In. 162
Suede, Ostrich, Hobo, Brown, Braided Sides, Ferragamo, 16 x 14 In. 150
Suede, Silk, Silk Interior, Mirror, Enamel Clasp, Cartier, 7 ⅞ In. ....*illus* 861
Velvet, Black, Evening, Metal Frame, Black & Green Bakelite & Diamond Trim, Art Deco, 7 In. .. 400
Velvet, Miu, Clutch, Brown, Chevron, 5 x 10 In. 118
Wallet, Men's, Black, Strap Across Middle, Metal Tag, Trifold, YSL, 4 x 3 In. 24
Wallet, Saffiano Leather, Emerald Green, Goldtone Hardware, Zipper Closure, 6 x 3 ½ In. 127
Wallet, Vernis Leather, Sarah, Brown, Burgundy, Flap, Snap Button, Louis Vuitton, 7 x 4 In. 276
Wood, Mother-Of-Pearl, Pushlock Closure, Optional Shoulder Strap, Judith Leiber, 5 x 2 In. 112
Wool, Plaid, Pleated, Tartan, Appliqued Felt Flowers, Soft Structure, Moschino, 9 x 13 In. 184
Yellow Gold, 14K, Braided Handle, William B. Kerr & Co., c.1910, 4 In. 2280

PYREX glass baking dishes were first made in 1915 by the Corning Glass Works. Pyrex dishes are made of a heat-resistant glass that can go from refrigerator or freezer to oven or microwave and are nice enough to put on the table. Clear glass dishes were made first. Pyrex Flameware, for use over a stovetop burner, was made from 1936 to 1979. A set of mixing bowls in four colors (blue, red, green, and yellow) was made beginning in 1947. After Corning sold its Pyrex brand to World Kitchen LLC in 1998, changes were made to the formula for the glass.

pyrex

Bowl, Lid, Yellow Square, c.1955, 9 x 9 x 3 In., 2 ½ Qt. 25
Bowl, Old Town, c.1965, 4 x 2 ½ In. 13
Butter, Cover, Crazy Daisy, Green, c.1950, ¼ Lb. 12
Carafe, Starburst, 32 Oz. 10
Casserole, Americana, Lid, Brown, Divided, c.1960, 12 x 8 In., 1 ½ Qt. 20
Casserole, Golden Acorn, Handles, 1960s, 1 ½ Qt. 17
Casserole, Lid, Blue Garland, Handles, 1 ½ Qt. 19
Casserole, Lid, Blue Snowflake, Garland, Tab Handles, Marked, 1950s, 1 ½ Qt. ....*illus* 28
Casserole, Lid, Brown Flowers, Handles, 8 ½ In. 17
Casserole, Lid, Divided, Sunflower, 1960s, 1 ½ Qt. 19
Casserole, Lid, Forest Fancies, Pt. 15
Casserole, Lid, Friendship Pattern, 2 ½ Qt. 42
Casserole, Lid, Frost Garland, c.1960, 1 ½ Qt. 65
Casserole, Lid, Gold Acorn, Divided, 1 ½ Qt. 9
Casserole, Lid, Gold Honeysuckle, 2 ½ Qt. 11
Casserole, Lid, Golden Acorn, Cream, Gold Design, 11 ¼ x 6 ¾ In. 32
Casserole, Lid, Old Orchard, Orange, Oval, Handles, 1 ½ Qt. 14
Casserole, Lid, Sandalwood, White On Tan, 6 ¼ In., Qt. 28
Casserole, Lid, Snowflake, Qt. 15

Purinton, Pitcher, Ivy, Yellow Blossom, Slipware, Yellow, Green, Brown, c.1950, 7 ½ In.
$35

Ruby Lane

Purse, Alligator, Brass Clasp, Compartments, Lucille De Paris, c.1960, 10 ½ x 7 ½ In.
$550

Ruby Lane

Purse, Basket, Nantucket Friendship, Bone Medallion, Whale Pulling Boat, 1991, 7 x 11 In.
$123

Skinner, Inc.

P

Purse, Calfskin, Woven, Camel, Double Handles, Bottega Veneta, Italy, Dust Bag, 15 x 9 In.
$725

Ruby Lane

Purse, Celluloid, Painted, Rhinestones, Snap Closure, Mirror, Art Deco, 1920s, 4 ¼ x 3 In.
$115

Ruby Lane

Purse, Crystals, Gold Frame, Leather, Tomato, Chain Strap, Judith Leiber, Box, 4 x 4 In.
$1,625

Heritage Auctions Galleries

Purse, Fabric, Clutch, Green, Pleated, Tan Bakelite Crouching Wolf Handle, 7 x 9 ¾ In.
$677

Skinner, Inc.

Purse, Leather, Quilted, Black, Shoulder Straps, Goldtone Hardware, Chanel, 14 x 11 In.
$412

Heritage Auctions Galleries

Purse, Lucite, Clear Top, Diamonds, Marbleized Bottom, Charles S. Kahn, Miami, 1950s, 7 ¾ In.
$119

Ruby Lane

Purse, Mesh, 14K Gold, Cabochon Sapphire Push Closure, 4 ½ In.
$2,706

Skinner, Inc.

Purse, Mesh, Zebra Stripes, Brown, Gold, Silk Lining, 30-inch Chain, Whiting & Davis, 4 ⅝ x 9 In.
$85

Ruby Lane

TIP

To date a mesh purse, look at the bottom edge. If it is zigzagged or fringed, it dates from the 1920–30 period.

Purse, Metal, Buddha, Rhinestones, Shoulder Chain, Judith Leiber, 1900s, 5 x 4 ½ In.
$570

Sloans & Kenyon

Purse, Metal, Leather, Foo Dog, Crystals, Chain Strap, Accessories, Judith Leiber, Box, 6 x 4 In.
$2,250

Heritage Auctions Galleries

Casserole, Lid, Spring Blossom, Pt. 18
Casserole, Lid, Trailing Flowers, Beige, Rust Design, c.1980, 2 ½ Qt. 10
Casserole, Lid, Verde 24, 1967-72 ....*illus* 12
Casserole, Lid, White Daisy, Flamingo Pink, 10 x 6 In., 1 ½ Qt. 26
Casserole, Lid, Woodland, White Flowers, Leaves, Tab Handles, 1978, 25 Oz. ....*illus* 11
Coffeepot, Clear, 4 Cup 38
Coffeepot, Clear, 9 Cup 80
Coffeepot, Flameware, Stainless Band, 6 Cup 34
Cup, Flamingo, Coral, Milk Glass 7
Dish, Lid, Amish Butterprint, Turquoise, 1950s, 6 ¾ x 4 ¼ x 3 ¼ In. 20
Dish, Lid, Sol Flower, 1960-70........*illus* 16
Dish, Lid, Sol Flower, Lid, 1960s, Qt. 16
Gravy Boat, Underplate, Old Towne Blue 10
Gravy Boat, Underplate, Spring Blossom, Green 22
Loaf Pan, Clear, Handles, Marked, 8 x 5 x 2 In. 34
Mixing Bowl Set, Nesting Amish Butterprint Turquoise, 4 Piece 119
Mixing Bowl Set, Nesting, New Dots, Orange, Yellow, Blue, Green, Corning, c.1968, 4 ....*illus* 245
Mixing Bowl, Amish Butterprint, Aqua On White, 2 ½ Qt., 10 In. .... 10 to 22
Mixing Bowl, Amish Butterprint, Orange On White, Cinderella, 4 Qt. 47
Mixing Bowl, Blue Horizon, 2 ½ Qt. 26
Mixing Bowl, Brittany Blue, 1 ½ Qt. 12
Mixing Bowl, Butterfly Gold, White Ground, 1970s, 1 ½ In. 10
Mixing Bowl, Cinderella Style, Dove Pattern, Red, 2 ½ In. 28
Mixing Bowl, Cinderella, Blue Snowflake Garland, 4 Qt. 34
Mixing Bowl, Cinderella, Gooseberry, Black & White, 1957, 1 ½ Pt. 12
Mixing Bowl, Colonial Mist, Cinderella, 4 Qt. 15
Mixing Bowl, Forest Fancies, 2 ½ Qt. 14
Mixing Bowl, Gooseberry, Yellow, Black, 1960s, 7 ½ In. 25
Mixing Bowl, Horizon Blue, 1970s, 2 ½ In. 34
Mixing Bowl, Spring Blossom, Crazy Daisy, Green, 1 ½ Qt. 10
Mixing Bowl, Spring, Blossom, Green, 8 ½ In. 23
Pan, Friendship, White, Red, 15 x 9 In. 30
Platter, Grecian Gray, Oval, 1960s, 9 ½ x 7 In. 5
Salt & Pepper, Spring Blossom, Milk Glass, Green, 3 ½ In. 14

Quezal

QUEZAL glass was made from 1901 to 1924 at the Queens, New York, company started by Martin Bach. Other glassware by other firms, such as Loetz, Steuben, and Tiffany, resembles this gold-colored iridescent glass. Martin Bach died in 1921. His son-in-law, Conrad Vahlsing Jr., went to work at the Lustre Art Company about 1920. Bach's son, Martin Bach Jr., worked at the Durand Art Glass division of the Vineland Flint Glass Works after 1924.

Bowl, Gold Iridescent, 15 ½ In. 438
Candlestick Holder, Gold Iridescent, Flat Disk, Candle Cup, Ring Handle, 2 ¼ x 4 ½ In. 173
Chandelier, Arts & Crafts, 6 Glass Shades, Cast Metal, Acanthus, Pulled Feather, 28 In. 1770
Cup & Saucer, Demitasse, Applied Handle, Red Tones, Signed, 2 ¾ In. 144
Lamp, Electric, Desk, Gooseneck, Glass Shade, Bronzed Metal, Feathered Glass, 17 ½ In. 885
Nut Dish, Iridescent, Red & Green Tones, Ribbed, Flared, Squat, Folded-In Rim, 1 x 2 ¾ In. 86
Shade, Green Snakeskin, Ribbed, Gold Iridescent Zipper Design, Signed, 5 ⅛ In. ....*illus* 1359
Shade, Opalescent Bell Shape, Opal Hooded Features, Gold Tipped, 2 ¼ x 5 ¼ In., 3 Piece 403
Shade, Opaque White, Green & Gold Pulled Feather, Gold Iridescent Interior, 16 In., Pair 210
Shade, Ribbed Tulip, Gold Iridescent, Signed, 5 ½ x 3 ½ In. 98
Vase, Gold & Green Swirls, 1900s, 10 x 4 In. 2000
Vase, Gold Iridescent Top Rim, White Calcite, Polished Base, 1900s, 8 In. 295
Vase, Gold Iridescent, Cream Hooked Feathers, Silver Overlay Daffodils, Bulbous, 7 In. 4323
Vase, Gold Iridescent, Pink & Blue Flashing, Silver Overlay, Urn Shape, Flare Rim, 7 In. 267
Vase, Green To Orange Iridescent, Disc Foot, 7 ½ x 4 ¾ In. 484
Vase, Green, Opal, Gold Swirls & Threading, 1900s, 11 x 8 In. ....*illus* 3000
Vase, Iridescent, Pulled Feather, Flower Shape, Flared Ruffle Rim, Green, c.1920, 7 In. 1315
Vase, Jack-In-The-Pulpit, Green & Gold Iridescent, Pulled Feathers, Bulbous Foot, 15 In. 6518
Vase, Jack-In-The-Pulpit, Green Pulled Feather, Gold Base, Signed, 8 ½ In. 3425
Vase, Orange Iridescent, Baluster Shape, Flared Rim, 8 x 4 In. 357
Vase, Pulled Feather, Applied Shell Shapes, Gold, Teal, 1900s, 15 ¼ x 5 In. 4063
Vase, Stemmed Buds, Gold Iridescent, Oil Spots, Pulled Green, Round Swirl Foot, 7 In. 1840
Vase, Sweet Pea, Opal, Iridescent, Pulled Wintergreen, Gold Tips, Onionskin Rim, 6 In. ....*illus* 1092
Vase, Triangular, Purple, Silver Scrolls, 9 ¾ In. 960

Purse, Needlepoint, Fox Hunt Scene, Leather, Suedette, Satin Lining, c.1953, 15 x 9 In.
$325

Ruby Lane

Purse, Ostrich, Brown, Goldtone Hardware, Lucille De Paris, 7 ¾ x 10 ½ In.
$215

Skinner, Inc.

Purse, Ostrich, Kelly Bag, Goldtone Hardware, Clochette, Key, Sellier Style, Hermes, 13 In.
$5,185

DuMouchelles Art Gallery

Q

Purse, Pony Hair, Leopard Print, Miss Urbanette, Weekender, Dolce & Gabbana, 14 x 20 In.
$5,000

New Orleans (Cakebread)

Purse, Suede, Leather Handles, Compact, Mirror, Powder Puff, Elgin American, 1940s, 5 x 4 In.
$110

Ruby Lane

Purse, Suede, Silk, Silk Interior, Mirror, Enamel Clasp, Cartier, 7 ⅞ In.
$861

Skinner, Inc.

Pyrex, Casserole, Lid, Blue Snowflake, Garland, Tab Handles, Marked, 1950s, 1 ½ Qt.
$28

Ruby Lane

QUILTS have been made since the seventeenth century. Early textiles were very precious and every scrap was saved to be reused. A quilt is a combination of fabrics joined to a filler and a backing by small stitched designs known as quilting. An appliqued quilt has pieces stitched to the top of a large piece of background fabric. A patchwork, or pieced, quilt is made of many small pieces stitched together. Embroidery can be added to either type.

Amish, Barn Raising, Multicolor Squares, Blue Border, Cotton, Ohio, 1945, 75 x 76 In. 2280
Amish, Patchwork, 9-Patch, Multicolor, Rayon, Mid 20th Century, 82 x 85 In. 590
Amish, Patchwork, Bowtie, Blue Border, Penn., 1930-40, 64 x 82 In. 660
Amish, Patchwork, Broken Dishes, Blue & Yellow Border, Cotton, Ohio, 1935, 74 x 84 In. 360
Amish, Patchwork, Star & Leaf, Yellow & Red, Green Ground, Square, Penn., c.1925, 84 In. 369
Amish, Sunshine & Shadow, Blue Border, Pink, Green, Cream, 86 x 84 In. 375
Amish, Sunshine & Shadow, Flower & Leaf Border, Rayon, Mid 20th Century, 82 x 84 In. 354
Appliqued, 6 Squares, Flower Basket, Red, Green, 1800s, 18 In. 212
Appliqued, Basket Of Flowers, White Ground, Red, Green, Orange, 1800s, 18 x 18 In. 236
Appliqued, Eagles, Stars, Maple Leaf, Moon Medallion, Vine Border, c.1904, 80 x 80 In. 2400
Appliqued, Oak Leaf, Names, Proverbs, Marianne Williams, 1800s, 63 x 74 In. 995
Appliqued, Patchwork, Carolina Lily, Red, Green, White, Cotton, H. Noble, 1846, 84 x 84 In. 1020
Appliqued, Pictorial, Cherry Tree, Potted Tulips, Birds, Animals, Red Border, 67 x 76 In. 130
Appliqued, Pumpkin Ground, Brown & Green Flowers, Sawtooth Border, 1800s, 80 x 87 In. 384
Appliqued, Redwork, White Ground, Wreaths, Women, Moon, Animals, 1901, 73 x 80 In. 540
Appliqued, Rose Of Sharon, Vine Border, Flower Baskets & Birds, Cotton, c.1860, 91 x 92 In. 1020
Appliqued, Rose Of Sharon, Vine Border, Red, Green, Yellow, 1875, 78 x 79 In. 540
Appliqued, Star & Sun, Eagle Corners, Red, Yellow, Green Bar Border, 83 x 85 In. 354
Appliqued, Sun Bonnet Sue, Embroidered, Feed Sack, Print, 1930s, 82 x 62 In. 245
Appliqued, Sunflower, Dresden Plate, Cotton, Calico, Aqua Border, c.1930, 84 x 70 In. ....*illus* 392
Appliqued, Tulip Vase, Diagonal Design, Red, Green, White, c.1860, 90 x 92 In. ....*illus* 785
Appliqued, Whig Rose, Feathered Plumes, Pink Print Binding, Cotton, 81 x 84 In. 540
Crazy, Silk, Velvet, Cotton, Taffeta, Greene Country, Va., 83 x 85 In. 354
Crazy, Wool, Silk, Velvet, 2-Sided, Square, Embroidered 1898, Signed, A.R. Long, 90, 74 In. .*illus* 395
Embroidered, 42 Panels, Vignettes, Red, White, Schlaggenwald, 65 x 76 In. 184
Mennonite, Patchwork, Flying Geese, Blue, Red, 60 x 60 In. 439
Mennonite, Patchwork, Sunshine & Shadow, Orange, Yellow, c.1900, 80 x 68 In. 492
Patchwork, 1-Patch Variation, Sawtooth Border, Red, Yellow, 76 x 71 In. 380
Patchwork, 4-Pointed Star, Green, Black, Red, 20th Century, 40 x 41 In. 189
Patchwork, 9-Patch, Geometric, Pennsylvania, 19th Century, 49 x 50 ½ In. 384
Patchwork, Basket Of Tulips, Penny White, 1850, 107 x 111 In. 177
Patchwork, Bethlehem Star, Jacob's Coat, Framed Border, 1800s, 89 x 89 In. ....*illus* 472
Patchwork, Blocks On Point, c.1900-30, 84 x 72 In. 350
Patchwork, Central Star, Red, Orange, Yellow, Pink Ground, c.1940, 78 x 78 In. 210
Patchwork, Chariot Wheels, Star & Garland Border, Red, Yellow, Gray, 83 x 87 In. 1250
Patchwork, Double Irish Chain, Marigold, Hunter Green, Cream Ground, 88 x 88 In. 123
Patchwork, Double Wedding Ring, Multicolor, Pastel, 1940s, 84 x 69 ½ In. 468
Patchwork, Floral, Geometric, Chintz Border, Copper Plate, Phila., c.1810, 106 x 116 In. 590
Patchwork, Flower Baskets, Scalloped Ribbon Edge, Multicolor, 1930s, 85 x 98 In. 210
Patchwork, Irish Chain Variation, Green, White, 1930s, 80 x 80 In. 263
Patchwork, Jacks On 6, 16 Blocks, Orange, Green, Black, c.1890, 89 x 90 In. ....*illus* 308
Patchwork, Joseph's Coat, Green & Red Banding, 84 x 76 In. 550
Patchwork, LeMoyne Star, Blue, Stitched Grid, White, Cut Out Corners, Cotton, 93 x 96 In. 150
Patchwork, Log Cabin, Multicolor, 1800s, 80 x 85 In. 322
Patchwork, Log Cabin, Pineapple, Red, Blue, 1800s, 80 x 80 In. 380
Patchwork, Lone Star, Satellite Stars, Multicolor, White Ground, 90 x 93 In. 351
Patchwork, Pine Burr, Red, Beige, White, c.1890, 75 x 75 In. ....*illus* 995
Patchwork, Pinwheel, Heart, Star, 4 Panels, Multicolor, Red Border, 80 x 82 In. 236
Patchwork, Rolling Stone Variation, Brown, Red, Green, 1800s, 82 x 64 In. 468
Patchwork, Sampler, Marriage Presentation, Signed, Lynn, Mass., 19th Century, 89 x 102 In. 295
Patchwork, Star & Wedding Band, Scalloped Edge, White Ground, Multicolor, 82 x 95 In. 295
Patchwork, Star Of Bethlehem, Prairie Point Border, Red, Yellow, Orange, 88 x 88 In. 497
Patchwork, Star, Yellow, White, Feathered Wreath Corners, Ohio, c.1920, 76 x 76 In. ....*illus* 625
Patchwork, Stars, Pink, Gray, Pennsylvania, Lebanon County, 80 x 80 In. 263
Patchwork, Stars, Red & Green, Cotton, Stitched Double Rows, 86 x 87 In. 570
Patchwork, Sunburst, Diamonds, Blue & White Dots Ground, c.1880, 82 x 82 In. 1046
Patchwork, Tumbling Blocks, Silk, Embroidered Center On Velvet, 1800s, 59 x 62 In. 205
Patchwork & Appliqued, 73 Album Squares, Names, Silk, Cotton, Nantucket, c.1860, 100 x 108 In. 1599
Patchwork & Appliqued, Flower, Diamond, Yellow, Red, 88 x 72 In. 230
Trapunto, White, Flower Baskets, Birds, Plumed Serpentine Border, c.1850, 74 x 81 In. 840

Pyrex, Casserole, Lid, Verde 24, 1967-72
$12

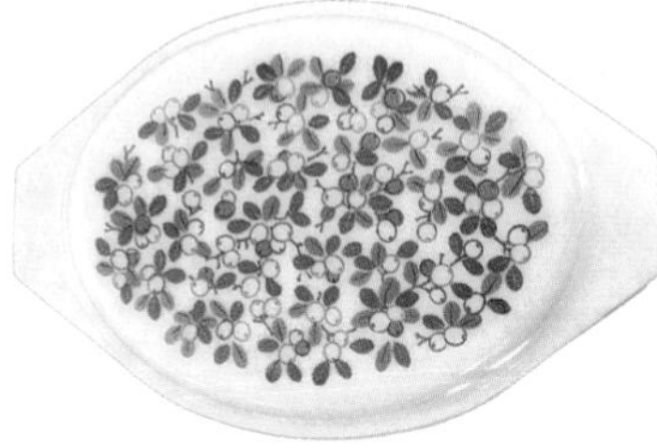

Pyrex, Casserole, Lid, Woodland, White Flowers, Leaves, Tab Handles, 1978, 25 Oz.
$11

Ruby Lane

Pyrex, Dish, Lid, Sol Flower Pattern, 1960-70
$16

Pyrex, Mixing Bowl Set, Nesting, New Dots, Orange, Yellow, Blue, Green, Corning, c.1968, 4
$245

Ruby Lane

Quezal, Shade, Green Snakeskin, Ribbed, Gold Iridescent Zipper Design, Signed, 5 ⅛ In.
$1,359

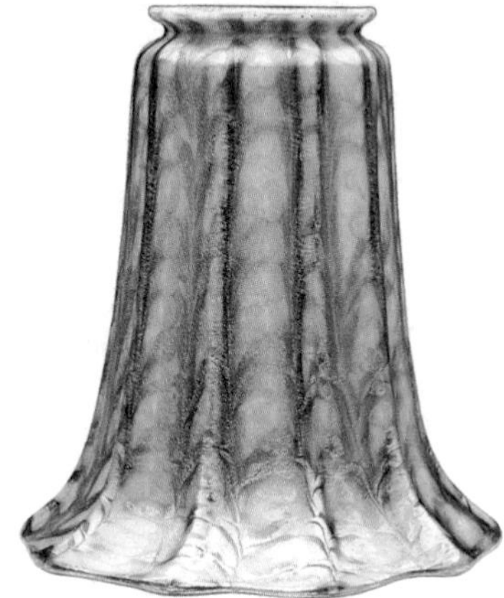

James D. Julia Auctioneers

Quezal, Vase, Green, Opal, Gold Swirls & Threading, 1900s, 11 x 8 In.
$3,000

Rago Arts and Auction Center

Quezal, Vase, Sweet Pea, Opal, Iridescent, Pulled Wintergreen, Gold Tips, Onionskin Rim, 6 In.
$1,092

Early Auction Company

Quilt, Appliqued, Sunflower, Dresden Plate, Cotton, Calico, Aqua Border, c.1930, 84 x 70 In.
$392

Ruby Lane

Quilt, Appliqued, Tulip Vase, Diagonal Design, Red, Green, White, c.1860, 90 x 92 In.
$785

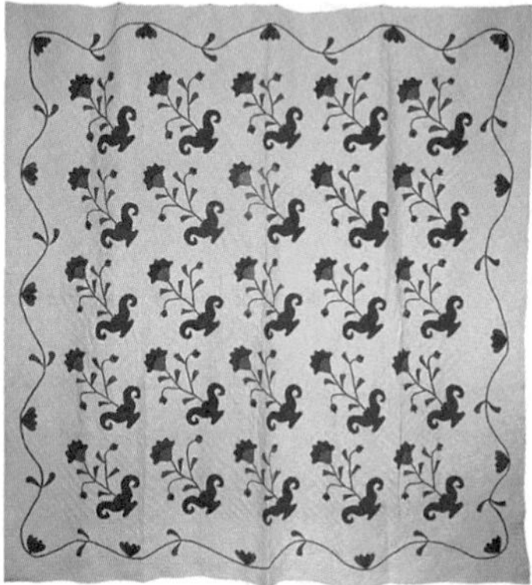

Ruby Lane

TIP
Quilts with a white background are more popular than those with a colored background—and the prices are higher.

Quilt, Crazy, Wool, Silk, Velvet, 2-Sided, Square, Embroidered 1898, Signed, A.R. Long, 90, 74 In.
$395

Ruby Lane

Q

TIP

If you can't hang your vintage quilt or coverlet you can display it on the guest room bed. The best storage for textiles avoids folding. Large textiles shoud be rolled.

Quilt, Patchwork, Bethlehem Star, Jacob's Coat, Framed Border, 1800s, 89 x 89 In.
$472

Hess Auction Group

Quilt, Patchwork, Jacks On 6, 16 Blocks, Orange, Green, Black, c.1890, 89 x 90 In.
$308

Cowan Auctions

Quilt, Patchwork, Pine Burr, Red, Beige, White, c.1890, 75 x 75 In.
$995

Ruby Lane

QUIMPER pottery has a long history. Tin-glazed, hand-painted pottery has been made in Quimper, France, since the late seventeenth century. The earliest firm was founded in 1708 by Pierre Bousquet. In 1782, Antoine de la Hubaudiere became the manager of the factory and the factory became known as the HB Factory (for Hubaudiere-Bousquet), de la Hubaudiere, or Grande Maison. Another firm, founded in 1772 by Francois Eloury, was known as Porquier. The third firm, founded by Guillaume Dumaine in 1778, was known as HR or Henriot Quimper. All three firms made similar pottery decorated with designs of Breton peasants and sea and flower motifs. The Eloury (Porquier) and Dumaine (Henriot) firms merged in 1913. Bousquet (HB) merged with the others in 1968. The group was sold to an American holding company in 1984. More changes followed, and in 2011 Jean-Pierre Le Goff became the owner and the name was changed to Henriot-Quimper.

Basket, Double Swan Neck Handle, Yellow, Blue, Heart, Flowers, 1900s, 11 x 13 In. 74
Candlestick, Peasant Woman, Bouquet, Yellow, Scalloped Base, 8 ½ In. 58
Candlestick, Pottery, Painted, Multicolor, Henriot, c.1940, 11 In., Pair 84
Dish, Flowers, Multicolor, Signed, 3 ½ x 1 In. 49
Eggcup, Peasant Man, Peasant Woman, Blue, Yellow, 4 In., Pair 59
Platter, Faience, Oval, Shaped Edge, Peasant, Trees, Flower Border, Henriot, 12 In. .... *illus* 122
Wall Pocket, Peasant Man, Wild Flowers, Triangular, 8 In. 65

RADIO broadcast receiving sets were first sold in New York City in 1910. They were used to pick up the experimental broadcasts of the day. The first commercial radios were made by Westinghouse Company for listeners of the experimental shows on KDKA Pittsburgh in 1920. Collectors today are interested in all early radios, especially those made of Bakelite plastic or decorated with blue mirrors. Figural advertising radios and transistor radios are also collected.

Admiral, Bakelite, Model 5Z, Chrome Columns, Grill Cloth, 1937, 11 x 8 x 7 In. 178
Coronado, Model C5D14AC, Bakelite, Sunburst Dial, 1942, 6 x 8 x 5 In. 115
Crosley Dashboard, Model D-25WE, Bakelite, Clock, Art Deco, 1953, 7 x 13 In. 84
Crosley, Art Deco, Dashboard, Tube, White, Gold Dial, 1950s, 6 ¾ x 12 In. 138
Crosley, Model D-25WE, AM, Clock, White Plastic, Gold Accents, Tabletop, 1951, 7 ½ In. 210
Crosley, Tube, Model 56TX, White, 1946, 12 x 7 x 7 In. 165
Fada, Brown, Yellow Trim, Bakelite, 6 ¼ x 10 In. 523
Howard, Model 518, AM, 6 Preset Stations, Floor Console, 1939, 42 In. 60
Multi Band, Wood Console, Dial On Front, Tube Panels, Floor Model, c.1939, 27 x 44 In. 793
Philco Jr., Model 80, AM, Wood, Cathedral, 1932, 12 x 13 In. 90
RCA Victor, Model R-7, Cathedral Cabinet, 8 Tube, Pilasters, Gothic Arches, 1931, 17 x 14 In. ... 105
RCA, Model 75X11, 5 Tube, 1947, 10 x 8 x 8 In. 139
RCA, Victor Model 115, Art Deco, Wood, Paneled Design, 14 x 7 ½ x 9 In. 240
Saba Freudenstandt, Tube, Wood Cabinet, 4 Speakers, Germany, 1950s, 15 x 24 In. 265
Stewart Warner, Varsity, Black & Red, 7 ½ In. 120
Westinghouse, Model WR-8-R, Columnaire, 2-Tone Wood, Round Dial, 1931, 60 In. 732
Zenith, Console, Model 15U269, 15 Tube, Walnut, Tear Shape Escutcheon, c.1938, 43 x 26 In. .. 577
Zenith, Model J616, AM, Deluxe, Bakelite, 13 In. 90

RAILROAD enthusiasts collect any train memorabilia. Everything is wanted, from oilcans to whole train cars. The Chessie System has a store that sells many reproductions of its old dinnerware and uniforms.

Clock, Pendleton Steam Service Control, Day & Night, Grand Central Terminal 220
Columns, Electric RR Equipment Co., Cast Iron, Fluted, Acanthus, 1800s, 42 In., Pair 510
Door, Caboose, Wood, Arched Top Window, Sliding Sash, 69 x 28 In. 106
Jacket, Waiter's, Rock Island & Pacific Railroad, Cotton, White, Size 48 23
Lamp, Norfolk & Western, Caboose Marker, Handlan St. Louis, Green, Red, Amber, 15 In. 146
Lantern, New York Central, Dietz No. 6, Red Globe, Embossed, 10 In. 82
Lock & Key, Lake Shore & Michigan Southern, NY Central, Brass, Cast Back, 1914-35 .... *illus* 225
Map, Michigan, c.1880, Frame, 13 ¼ x 10 ¼ In. 240
Plate, Baltimore & Ohio Railroad, Incline, Shell Border, Blue & White, 9 In. 240
Plate, Southern Pacific, 3 Sections, Griffon Pattern, Scammell, 10 ¾ In. 12
Reflector, Stimsonite No. 19, Round, 6 Lenses, Red, Black, 24 In. Diam. 120
Sign, Crossing, Colorless Reflectors, Black & White, 48 x 9 In. 120
Sign, Crossing, Stop, Look & Listen, Wood, Painted, Single Sided, 1800s, 15 x 52 In. 4130
Sign, Green, White, Delaware Ave., 5, Belt Line 3, 2-Sided, 13 x 22 In. 180
Sign, Slow, 2-Sided, c.1900, 24 In. Diam. 210
Sign, Subway, Exit, Cast Iron, Black, White, c.1915, 23 x 8 ½ In. 390
Sign, Trains Stopping To Do Work Must Leave Cars, Yellow, 20 x 22 In. 330
Sign, Warning, Structures On This Track Will Not Clear, Black, White, c.1900, 18 x 24 In. 270
Signal, Reflector Lights, Green, Yellow, 14 x 18 In. 90

Step Box, Pullman, Metal, Yellow Paint, 20 x 18 x 10 In. 94
Switch Key, Erie Railroad, Brass, F.S. Hardware.......... 29
Whistle, Conductor's, 3-Chamber, Brass, 5 ½ In. 65
Whistle, Steam, Brass, No. 125, Crane Mfg., 25 x 4 In. 690

RAZORS were used in ancient Egypt and subsequently wherever shaving was in fashion. The metal razor used in America until about 1870 was made in Sheffield, England. After 1870, machine-made hollow-ground razors were made in Germany or America. Plastic or bone handles were popular. The razor was often sold in a set of seven, one for each day of the week. The set was often kept by the barber who shaved the well-to-do man each day in the shop.

Celluloid Handle, Red, Inlaid Silver & Mother-Of-Pearl Flowers, Straight 29
Celluloid Handle, Silver Inlaid Alligator, Baurmann, Solingen, Germany.......... 285
Celluloid Handle, Silver Inlaid Butterfly & Flowers, Scalloped Edge Blade, Germany 114
Celluloid Handle, Straight, Molded, Cowboy, Jewels, Hibbard, Spencer & Bartlett.......... *illus* 485
Ivory Handle, Straight, Checkered, Carved, Inlay Pique, c.1825.......... 387
Mother-Of-Pearl Handle, Abalone Inlay, Straight Blade, Gold Mountain & Lake Scene.......... 456
Mother-Of-Pearl Handle, Carved Trim, Straight, Storr & Mortimer 570

REAMERS, or juice squeezers, have been known since 1767, although most of those collected today date from the twentieth century. Figural reamers are among the most prized.

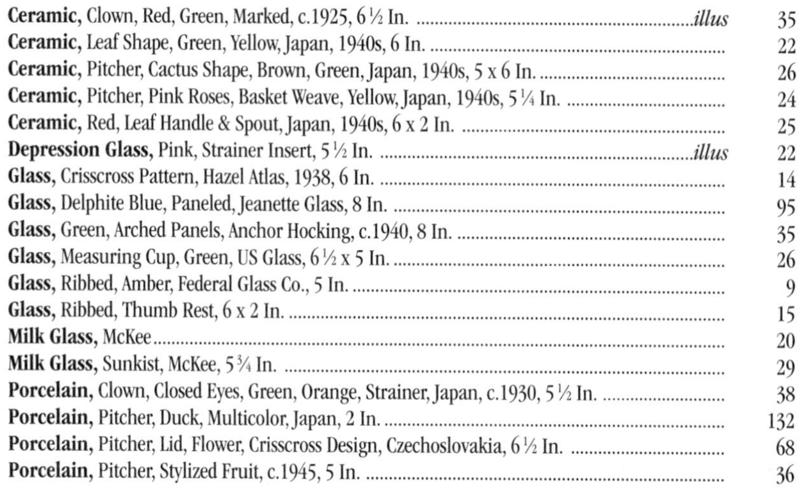

Ceramic, Clown, Red, Green, Marked, c.1925, 6 ½ In. .... *illus* 35
Ceramic, Leaf Shape, Green, Yellow, Japan, 1940s, 6 In. 22
Ceramic, Pitcher, Cactus Shape, Brown, Green, Japan, 1940s, 5 x 6 In. 26
Ceramic, Pitcher, Pink Roses, Basket Weave, Yellow, Japan, 1940s, 5 ¼ In. 24
Ceramic, Red, Leaf Handle & Spout, Japan, 1940s, 6 x 2 In. 25
Depression Glass, Pink, Strainer Insert, 5 ½ In. .... *illus* 22
Glass, Crisscross Pattern, Hazel Atlas, 1938, 6 In. 14
Glass, Delphite Blue, Paneled, Jeanette Glass, 8 In. 95
Glass, Green, Arched Panels, Anchor Hocking, c.1940, 8 In. 35
Glass, Measuring Cup, Green, US Glass, 6 ½ x 5 In. 26
Glass, Ribbed, Amber, Federal Glass Co., 5 In. 9
Glass, Ribbed, Thumb Rest, 6 x 2 In. 15
Milk Glass, McKee.......... 20
Milk Glass, Sunkist, McKee, 5 ¾ In. 29
Porcelain, Clown, Closed Eyes, Green, Orange, Strainer, Japan, c.1930, 5 ½ In. 38
Porcelain, Pitcher, Duck, Multicolor, Japan, 2 In. 132
Porcelain, Pitcher, Lid, Flower, Crisscross Design, Czechoslovakia, 6 ½ In. 68
Porcelain, Pitcher, Stylized Fruit, c.1945, 5 In. 36

RECORDS have changed size and shape through the years. The cylinder-shaped phonograph record for use with the early Edison models was made about 1889. Disc records were first made by 1894, the double-sided disc by 1904. High-fidelity records were first issued in 1944, the first vinyl disc in 1946, the first stereo record in 1958. The 78 RPM became the standard in 1926 but was discontinued in 1957. In 1932, the first 33⅓ RPM was made but was not sold commercially until 1948. In 1949, the 45 RPM was introduced. Compact discs became available in the U.S. in 1982 and many companies began phasing out the production of phonograph records. Vinyl records are popular again. People claim the sound is better on a vinyl recording and new recordings are being made. Some collectors want colored vinyl records. Vintage albums are collected for their cover art as well as for the fame of the artist and the music.

Beatles, Love Me Do, P.S. I Love You, Tollie Records, 45 RPM.......... 8
Beatles, Sgt. Pepper's Lonely Hearts Club Band, Capitol Records, 33 RPM, 1967 45
Dick Todd, Red Apple Cheeks, Daddy's Little Boy, Rainbow Records, 78 RPM, 9 ¾ In. 13
Doris Day, Day By Day, Columbia Records, 33 RPM, 1956.......... 15
Elvis Presley, All Shook Up, That's When Your Heartaches Begin, 45 RPM, 1957 5
Isley Brothers, This Old Heart Of Mine, LP, 1975.......... 23
Lady & The Tramp, Disney, 78 RPM, 1962.......... 12
Lawrence Welk, Christmas Music, 33 RPM, 1958.......... 8
Let's Have A Rhythm Band, Kids, Playing Instruments, Columbia, 1950s 10
Rick Nelson, Ricky, Imperial Records, 33 RPM, 1957 13
Rolling Stones, Flowers, Mono Records, LP, 1967.......... 28
Sergio Mendes & Brasil 66, Look Around, A & M Records, LP, 1966.......... 8
Sleeping Beauty, Peter Pan Records, 45 RPM, 1958.......... 25
Sly & The Family Stone, Greatest Hits, 33 RPM, 1970.......... 12
Sonny & Cher, Greatest Hits, LP, 1967 16

Quilt, Patchwork, Star, Yellow, White, Feathered Wreath Corners, Ohio, c.1920, 76 x 76 In.
$625

Ruby Lane

Quimper, Platter, Faience, Oval, Shaped Edge, Peasant, Trees, Flower Border, Henriot, 12 In.
$122

DuMouchelles Art Gallery

Railroad, Lock & Key, Lake Shore & Michigan Southern, NY Central, Brass, Cast Back, 1914-35
$225

Ruby Lane

78 Records

Old 78 records were made of shellac. Vinyl 78s were introduced around 1951. The records that followed were all vinyl.

Razor, Celluloid Handle, Straight, Molded, Cowboy, Jewels, Hibbard, Spencer & Bartlett
$485

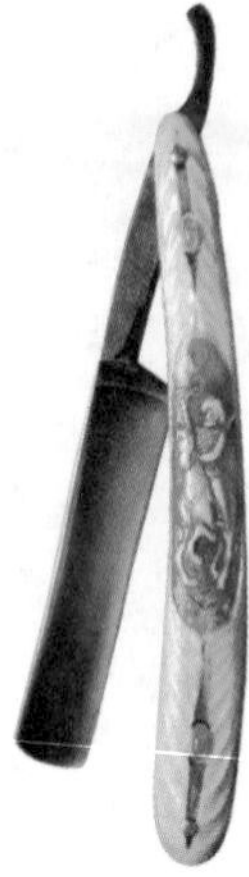

Showtime Auction Services

TIP
Store records on edge, straight up (not tipped) and in their sleeves.

Reamer, Ceramic, Clown, Red, Green, Marked, c.1925, 6 ½ In.
$35

Ruby Lane

Reamer, Depression Glass, Pink, Strainer Insert, 5 ½ In.
$22

Ruby Lane

The Jacksons, Hot Nights & City Lights, K-Tel Label, LP, 1979 15
Willie Nelson, Always On My Mind, 33 RPM, 1982 42

RED WING POTTERY of Red Wing, Minnesota, was a firm started in 1878. The company first made utilitarian pottery, including stoneware jugs and canning jars. In the 1920s art pottery was introduced. Many dinner sets and vases were made before the company closed in 1967. Rumrill pottery made by the Red Wing Pottery for George Rumrill is listed in its own category. For more prices, go to kovels.com.

Country Garden, Bowl, Vegetable, 9 ½ In. 54
Country Garden, Salt & Pepper 115
Crock, Wood & Wire Handles, 1913, 12 Gal., 18 In. 400
Flower Frog, Deer, Leaping, Cream & Tan, 1930s, 10 x 4 In. 95
Jardiniere, Cranes, Brushed Ware, c.1920, 5 x 8 In. .... *illus* 85
Jardiniere, U-Shape Handles, Blue Over Green, 1931, 5 x 7 In. 165
Lute Song, Plate, Dinner, 10 ¼ In. 20
Magnolia, Vase, Ribbed Base, 1940s, 9 In. .... *illus* 28
Pompeii, Gravy Boat, Lid, Underplate 48
Pompeii, Plate, Salad, 7 ½ In. 24
Pompeii, Salt & Pepper 32
Pompeii, Sugar & Creamer 54
Random Harvest, Platter, Oval, 15 x 10 In. 25
Spruce, Bowl, Green, 3-Footed, c.1930, 6 In. 61
Vase, 10-Sided, Foot Ring, 2-Tone Yellow Glaze, Arts & Crafts Design, 5 x 5 In. 110

REDWARE is a hard, red stoneware that originated in the late 1600s and continues to be made. The term is also used to describe any common clay pottery that is reddish in color.

Bank, Scroddled, Sphere, Round Pedestal Foot, Turned Finial, Signed, 1800s, 8 ½ In. 71
Bowl, Alternating Yellow & Green Stylized Leaves, Slip Glaze, 10 ½ In. 123
Bowl, Fruit, Red, Black Manganese Splotches, Wide Rolled Rim, 1800s, 5 x 10 In. 189
Bowl, Interior Glaze, Double Ear Handle, Signed John Headman, 1845, 6 x 15 In. 1320
Bowl, Lions, Lion Head Handles, Wide Rolled Rim, Tapered, 1978, 10 ¾ In. Diam. 83
Bowl, Potted Flower, Green, Yellow, Slip Decorated, 11 ½ In. 825
Bowl, Yellow Slip, Glazed, Molded Rim, Applied Loop Handles, Footed, 1800s, 5 x 6 ½ In. 1770
Butter, Incised Tulip & Star Design, Twist Border, Brown, Yellow, 1974, 3 x 4 In. 118
Canteen, Painted, Footed, Cork, Round, 6 ¼ x 5 In. 96
Chamberstick, Albany Slip Glaze, Deep Saucer Base, S. Routson, Ohio, 3 In. 240
Charger, 3 Sets Of Wavy Lines, Yellow Slip Decoration, 11 ½ In. 357
Charger, Bird & Flower, Sgraffito Decoration, Yellow Ground, Coggled Rim, 11 In. 2200
Charger, Colonial Fifer & Drummer, Yellow, Red, Green, 1980, 12 ¾ In. 94
Charger, Eagle, Shield, Olive Branches, Green & Yellow Glaze, Sgraffito, 1827, 12 In. 2714
Charger, Horse & Rider, Sword Drawn, Yellow Ground, Coggled, Lester Breininger, 12 In. 110
Charger, Potted Tulips, Yellow Ground, Coggled Rim, Lester Breininger, 12 In. 55
Charger, Tin Glaze, Ivory Ground, Blue Bands, Germany, 1800s, 14 In. 246
Charger, Tin Glaze, Ivory Ground, Green Bands, Orange Swag, Flowers, 14 ¾ In. 308
Charger, Yellow Slip, Coggle Wheel Edge, 1800s, 12 ¾ In. 106
Creamer, Raised Dots, Gold Decoration, Japan, 1940s-50s, 3 ½ x 5 In. .... *illus* 9
Crock, Apple Butter, Glazed, Applied Loop Handle, D. Swope & Son, 7 ¾ In. 472
Crock, Mottled Green Glaze, Cylindrical, Thick Rolled Rim, 7 ½ In. 240
Crock, Squared Rim, Marked, John Bell, Waynesboro, 7 ¾ x 6 ½ In. .... *illus* 135
Cup Plate, Slip Decorated, Pennsylvania, 1820-30, 4 In. .... *illus* 875
Cup Plate, Yellow Slip, Coggle Wheel Rim, 1800s, 4 In. 224
Cuspidor, Manganese Sponged Decoration, c.1875, 7 x 4 In. .... *illus* 175
Dish, Orange Brown, Wavy Lines, Straight Lines, Notched Rim, 12 ½ In. 132
Figurine, Bear, Walking, 9 ½ x 7 ½ In. 105
Figurine, Cat, Seated, Black Glaze, Red Paint, Square Base, c.1915, 11 In. 240
Flask, Log Cabin Shape, Molded, Open Chimney, 4 In. 180
Flowerpot, Attached Saucer Base, Green Glaze, Molded Rim, John Bell, 7 x 9 In. 384
Flowerpot, Manganese Glaze, Gadrooned Rim, Undertray, Handles, John Bell, c.1850, 7 In. 5100
Flowerpot, Mottled Glaze, Saucer Base, Molded Lip, Tapered, J. Bell, 6 x 7 In. 2242
Flowerpot, Splotched, Coggled Rim, Attached Saucer, Shenandoah Valley, Va., 8 In. 1560
Honey Pot, Lid, Lug Handles, Bulbous, Rolled Rim, Glazed, 7 In. 325
Jar, 8 Katsina Figures, Polished Slip, Squat, Rolled Rim, c.1975, 8 In. Diam. 4688
Jar, Apple Blossom, Carved, Teresita Naranjo, 7 ½ x 7 ½ In. .... *illus* 1800
Jar, Bird Finial, Lid, Handles, Embossed Flowers, Foltz, 9 ½ In. .... *illus* 177
Jar, Dark Green Mottled Glaze, U.S.A., c.1850, 8 In. 1125

Jar, Etched Banding, Inset Stones, Fish, Stippled, Bear Paw, Long Neck, c.1965, 6 In. 32500
Jar, Glazed Interior, Tooled Shoulder, Stamped John Bell, Waynesboro, 7 ½ x 6 ¾ In. 92
Jar, Lid, Dark Chocolate Glaze, Round, Shouldered, 1800s, 8 In. 118
Jar, Lid, Slip Decorated, Bulbous Shape, Applied Open Handles, Breininger, 1979, 9 ¾ In. 106
Jar, Mottled Glaze, Flared Rim, Coggle Wheel Rim, Ribbed Loop Handles, Bulbous, 11 In. 189
Jar, Storage, Mottled Glaze, Coggle Wheel Band, Flared Rim, Tapered Shoulder, 1800s, 4 In. 384
Jar, Storage, Mottled Glaze, Molded Rim, Oval, 1800s, 5 ¼ In. 142
Jar, Storage, Speckled Glaze, Lug Handles, 11 ¾ In. 240
Jug, Manganese Glaze, Handle, John Bell, Impressed Mark, c.1850, 7 In. 4800
Jug, Molded Spout, Ribbed Applied Loop Handle, Incised Rings, Glazed, Oval, 1800s, 13 In. 165
Keg, Brandy, Mottled Glaze, Incised Bands, Barrel Shape Body, Honeycomb Top, 5 In. 413
Loaf Pan, Oval, Red, Yellow Circles & Squiggle Design, 17 x 12 In. 71
Match Holder, Green & Yellow Mottled Glaze, Shenandoah Valley, c.1899, 3 ⅜ In. 531
Mold, Fish, Black Manganese, 1800s, 7 ½ x 8 ½ In. ....*illus* 106
Mold, Turk's Head, Glazed, 1800s, 3 ½ x 8 In. ....*illus* 30
Mold, Turk's Head, Mottled Glaze, Green Interior, 1800s, 12 ½ x 5 ½ In. 82
Mold, Turk's Head, Mustard Glaze, John Bell, Waynesboro, Pa., 6 ½ x 10 ½ In. 324
Mold, Turk's Head, Rockingham Glaze, 3 x 8 ½ In. 60
Pie Plate, Eagle & Tulip, Mottled Green, Brown, Jacob Medinger, 7 ¾ In. 770
Pie Plate, Green, Yellow, Brown, Slip Decoration, Coggled Rim, Dry Pottery, 8 In. 990
Pie Plate, Potted Tulip, Yellow Ground, Jacob Medinger, 7 ¾ In. 660
Pie Plate, Star & Circle, Coggled Rim, 9 In. 880
Pie Plate, Yellow Slip Star, Green Specks, 6 ¼ In. 300
Pitcher, Engine-Turned Base, Silvered Rim & Handle, Leafy Designs, c.1800, 7 In. 800
Pitcher, Manganese Speckles, Applied Ribbed Handle, 7 ½ In. 720
Pitcher, Mottled Glaze, Bulbous, Molded Rim, Applied Loop Handle, Ribbed, Squat, 7 ¾ In. 1003
Pitcher, Mottled Glaze, Flared Rim, Shaped Spout, Incised Bands, c.1899, 10 In. 649
Pitcher, Mottled Green, Brown, Orange, Coggled Band, Strap Handle, Jacob Medinger, 14 In. 1650
Pitcher, Ring Foot, Loop Handle, Flare Rim, Splotchy Color, 1800s, 6 In. 62
Pitcher, Slip Decorated, Cream & Green, France, c.1880, 8 ½ In. 165
Pitcher, Terra-Cotta, Orange, Slip Design, Cream, Green, Handle, c.1880, 9 In. ....*illus* 165
Pitcher, Yellow & Green Glaze, Shouldered, S. Bell & Sons, Virginia, c.1885, 10 In. 2750
Planter, Hanging, Glazed, Molded Rim, Incised Line, Tiered Drop Finial, 5 ½ In. 502
Planter, Mottled Glaze, Molded Lip, Tapered Body, Incised Ring, Saucer Base, 5 ¾ x 6 In. 413
Planter, Multicolor Mottled Glaze, Double Coggle Wheel Rim, Tapered Body, c.1899, 8 In. 502
Planter, Underplate, Eagle, Spread Wings, Flowers, Liberty For All, 10 x 12 In. 94
Plaque, Scalloped & Beaded Edge, Praying Angel, Acorns & Leaves, 1800s, 10 In. 266
Plate, Geometric Impressions, Rose Gonzales, 1928, 11 ½ In. 702
Plate, Green & Yellow Mottled, Glazed Sgraffito, Tulip Basket, Coggle Wheel Edge, 9 In. 413
Plate, Manganese & Yellow Slip, Scroll Design, W. Smith, 8 In. 2714
Plate, Merry Christmas, Incised Candle & Holly, Yellow, Green, Red, 1979, 10 In. 53
Plate, Mottled Glaze, 1800s, 8 ¼ In. 41
Plate, Red Rooster, Orange Ground, Sponge Design, Circles Border, 1977, 10 In. 35
Plate, Yellow Slip, Zigzag & Crisscross, Womelsdorf, Pa., Stamped, W. Smith, 7 In. ....*illus* 590
Platter, Houses On Hill, Trees, Animals, Rounded Corners, Yellow, Red, 1988, 19 x 13 In. 236
Platter, Oval, Yellow Slip Design, Coggle Wheel Rim, 1800s, 11 x 17 In. 561
Platter, Oval, Yellow Slip Design, Intertwining Bamboo, Sprigs, 16 In. 1062
Platter, Union Forever, 1776-1976, Eagle, Spread Wings, Yellow, Red, 1975, 12 x 16 In. 130
Platter, Yellow Slip Design, Love & Unity, Shooner, 12 x 15 In. 94
Platter, Yellow Slip, Coggle Wheel Rim, Pennsylvania, 1800s, 9 ½ x 12 ¾ In. ....*illus* 708
Puzzle Jug, 3 Spouts, Pierced Cut Collar, Bulbous Base, Scroddleware, 1885, 6 In. ....*illus* 118
Serving Dish, Lid, Lug Handles, Finial, Incised Roulettes, Sponge Design, 9 In. Diam. 118
Soap Dish, Glazed, Round, Molded Rim, Pierced Tray, 1800s, 3 x 5 In. 106
Sugar, Manganese Glaze, Applied, Molded Leaf, 1800s, 7 ½ In. 502
Teapot, Lid, Globular, Crabstock Handle & Spout, Boy In Tree Design, c.1750, 3 ½ In. 584
Tile, Bisque, Molded Seahorse, Leaves, A. Robertson, 1911, 2 ¾ In. 1500
Vase, Bust, Black Man, Glazed, Opening At Top Of Head, 1900s, 5 In. 178
Vase, Funnel Shape, Glazed, Hanging Hole, 12 x 4 In. 59
Vase, Landscape, Blue, Pink, Turquoise, White, Tapered, Chinese, 1900s, 20 In. 270
Vase, Strap Handles, Lead & Manganese Glaze, Coggled Band, Jacob Medinger, 11 ½ In. 550
Washboard, Wood Frame, Mottled Glaze, Marked Common Sense Wash Board, 13 ½ In. 472
Whistle, Bird Shape, Yellow & Orange Glaze, Hand Molded, 2 ¾ x 3 In. 590

REGOUT, *see Maastricht category.*

Red Wing, Jardiniere, Cranes, Brushed Ware, c.1920, 5 x 8 In.
$85

Ruby Lane

Red Wing, Magnolia, Vase, Ribbed Base, 1940s, 9 In.
$28

Ruby Lane

TIP

If you have an alarm system, program a strobe light attached to the outside of the house to go on if there is a break-in attempt. The light will frighten the burglar and will make it easy for the police to find the house.

R

Redware, Creamer, Raised Dots, Gold Decoration, Japan, 1940s-50s, 3 ½ x 5 In.
$9

Ruby Lane

Redware, Crock, Squared Rim, Marked, John Bell, Waynesboro, 7 ¾ x 6 ½ In.
$135

Ruby Lane

Redware, Cup Plate, Slip Decorated, Pennsylvania, 1820-30, 4 In.
$875

Ruby Lane

Redware, Cuspidor, Manganese Sponged Decoration, c.1875, 7 x 4 In.
$175

Ruby Lane

Redware, Jar, Apple Blossom, Carved, Teresita Naranjo, 7 ½ x 7 ½ In.
$1,800

Cowan Auctions

Redware, Jar, Bird Finial, Lid, Handles, Embossed Flowers, Foltz, 9 ½ In.
$177

Hess Auction Group

Redware, Mold, Fish, Black Manganese, 1800s, 7 ½ x 8 ½ In.
$106

Hess Auction Group

TIP

Do not light a cabinet filled with glass with light bulbs over 25 watts. Stronger bulbs generate too much heat. Some new types of bulbs are brighter and give off less heat.

Redware, Mold, Turk's Head, Glazed, 1800s, 3 ½ x 8 In.
$30

Hess Auction Group

Redware, Pitcher, Terra-Cotta, Orange, Slip Design, Cream, Green, Handle, c.1880, 9 In.
$165

Ruby Lane

Hang a Horseshoe for Good Luck

When you hang a horseshoe today for good luck, you hang it so the opening faces the ceiling. In earlier days, you wanted the horseshoe opening to face the floor. During the Depression of the 1930s, the superstition changed and the idea was to hold the luck in, not let it run to the floor.

RIDGWAY pottery has been made in the Staffordshire district in England since 1808 by a series of companies with the name Ridgway. Ridgway became part of Royal Doulton in the 1960s. The transfer-design dinner sets are the most widely known product. Other pieces of Ridgway may be listed under Flow Blue.

Bowl, Vegetable, Gainsborough, Flow Blue, Scrolls, Curlicues, Gilt, c. 1910, 9¼ In. ....*illus* 45
Bowl, Vegetable, Lid, Lugano Pattern, Blue & White, Footed, 11½ In. 150
Ewer, Black, Paneled Baluster, Scalloped, C-Scroll Handle, Scene, c.1845, 10 In. 325
Jug, Swan & Bulrush, Relief, Footed, Gray, Matte Salt Glaze, c.1852, 8 In. 395
Plate, Imari Colors, Anglesey, 9 In. ....*illus* 110
Plate, Insane Hospital Of Boston, Leaf & Scroll Border, Transfer, c.1825, 7 In. 140
Platter, Italian Rose, Flow Blue, c.1840, 19 x 15 In. 490
Platter, Londsale, Flow Blue, c.1912, 18 x 13 In. 120
Platter, Palestine, Octagonal, Blue & White, c.1841, 10¾ x 8¾ In. 210
Teapot, Oriental, Camel & Rider, Red Transfer, 6 x 10 In. 95

RIVIERA dinnerware was made by the Homer Laughlin Co. of Newell, West Virginia, from 1938 to 1950. The pattern was similar in coloring and in mood to Fiesta and Harlequin. The Riviera plates and cup handles were square. For more prices, go to kovels.com.

Cobalt Blue, Butter, Cover, ½ Lb. 130
Green, Bowl, Vegetable, Lid, Rectangular, 8¾ In. 86
Ivory, Platter, Oval, 11½ In. 24
Ivy Century, Platter, 13¼ x 10 In. ....*illus* 75
Medium Green, Sugar & Creamer 80
Turquoise, Butter, Cover, ½ Lb. 35

ROCKINGHAM, in the United States, is a pottery with a brown glaze that resembles tortoiseshell. It was made from 1840 to 1900 by many American potteries. Mottled brown Rockingham wares were first made in England at the Rockingham factory. Other types of ceramics were also made by the English firm. Related pieces may be listed in the Bennington category.

Candlestick, Glazed Yellow & Brown, Turned Stem, Flared Foot, 8½ In., Pair 649
Cuspidor, Grape Clusters, 8-Sided, Scalloped, Marked Speeler, Taylor & Bloor, 4 x 8 In. 95
Figurine, Dog, Spaniel, Seated, Embossed Platform, Yellowware, 10½ In. ....*illus* 142
Soap Dish, Yellowware, Glazed, Molded Rim, 2 x 6 In. 130
Urn, Coffee, Lid, Flint Enamel Yellow & Brown Glaze, Applied Handles, Pewter Spigot, 23 In. 330
Urn, Lid, Brameld, Painted, Vase Shape, Scrolling Leaf Footed, Multicolor, 11 In. 185

ROGERS, *see John Rogers category.*

ROOKWOOD pottery was made in Cincinnati, Ohio, beginning in 1880. All of this art pottery is marked, most with the famous flame mark. The *R* is reversed and placed back to back with the letter *P*. Flames surround the letters. After 1900, a Roman numeral was added to the mark to indicate the year. The company went bankrupt in 1941. It was bought and sold several times after that. For several years various owners tried to revive the pottery, but by 1967 it was out of business. The name and some of the molds were bought by a collector in 1982. In 2005, a group of Cincinnati investors bought the company and 3,700 original molds, the name, and trademark. Martin and Marilyn Wade bought the company in 2011. Today they make new items and remake some old items, architectural tile, art pottery, and special commissions. Pieces are marked with the RP mark and a Roman numeral for the four-digit date.

Ash Receiver, Matches, Cigars, Cigarettes, Marked, Jeanette Swing, 1903, 6 In. ....*illus* 590
Bookends, Polar Bear, Ivory Matte Glaze, Logo, 1965, 4 In. 413
Bookends, Rook, Tan Matte Glaze, 1916, 6½ x 6½ In. 246
Bookends, St. Francis Of Assisi, Brown Gray Glaze, Clothilda Zanetta, 1945, 7¾ In. ....*illus* 266
Bookends, Walking Polar Bear, Brown Mottled Matte Glaze, Shirayamadani, 4 x 7 In. 590
Candlestick, Arts & Crafts Design, Plum Matte Glaze, 1916, 9 In. 277
Candy Dish, One-Eyed Jack, Multicolor, Diamond Shape, Logo, Sallie Toohey, 1928, 9½ In. 472
Creamer, Pansies, Standard Glaze, Daniel Cook, Logo, Monogram, 1894, 2⅝ In. 266
Cruet, Brown, Yellow Flowers, 1902, 5 x 4 In. 325
Cup & Saucer, White, Flower, Leaf & Scroll Border, Black Slip, Sallie Toohey 120
Figurine, Colonial Woman, Standing, Long Dress, Yellow High Glaze, 1949, 8 In. 173
Humidor, Springer Spaniel Portrait, Logo, E.T. Hurley, 5 In. 413
Jar, Lid, Limoges Style, Birds, Oriental Grasses, Gold Highlights, 1885, 4⅞ In. ....*illus* 443
Jar, Potpourri, Lid, Flowering Branches, 1909, 5½ In. 288
Jug, Enameled Glaze, Bamboo Leaves, Waterfalls, Flying Birds, Gold Leaf, 5 x 3 In. 307
Jug, Perfume, Loop Handle, Swallow Flying, Grass, Green, Yellow, c.1884, 5 In. 288

Redware, Plate, Yellow Slip, Zigzag & Crisscross, Womelsdorf, Pa., Stamped, W. Smith, 7 In.
$590

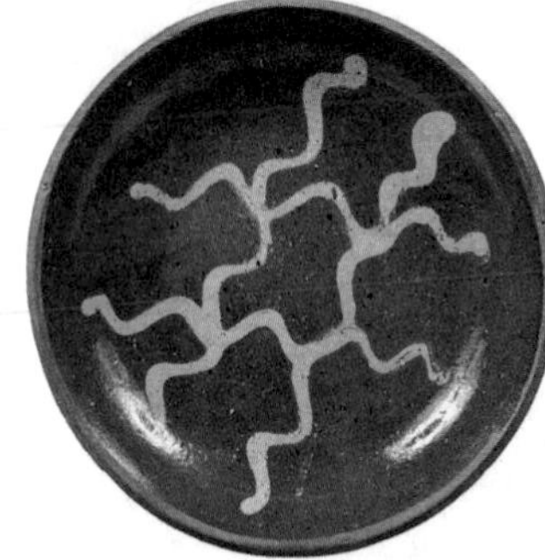

Hess Auction Group

Redware, Platter, Yellow Slip, Coggle Wheel Edge, Pennsylvania, 1800s, 9½ x 12¾ In.
$708

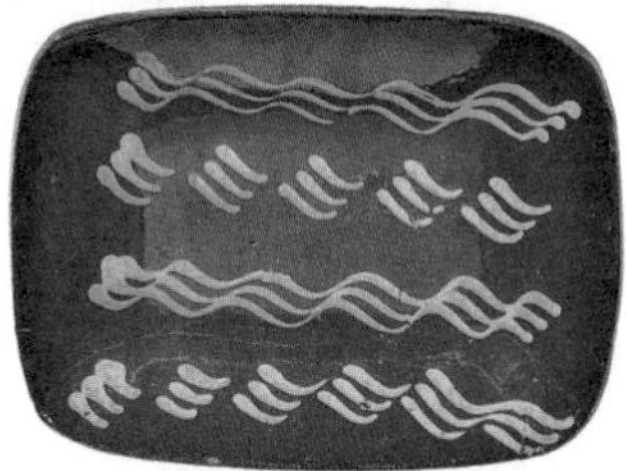

Hess Auction Group

Redware, Puzzle Jug, 3 Spouts, Pierced Cut Collar, Bulbous Base, Scroddleware, 1885, 6 In.
$118

Hess Auction Group

Rookwood Ink Stamp Mark

Henry Farny, who is now best known for his Western paintings, designed the ink stamp mark first used by Rookwood in 1881.

R

Ridgway, Bowl, Vegetable, Gainsborough, Flow Blue, Scrolls, Curlicues, Gilt, c. 1910, 9 ¼ In.
$45

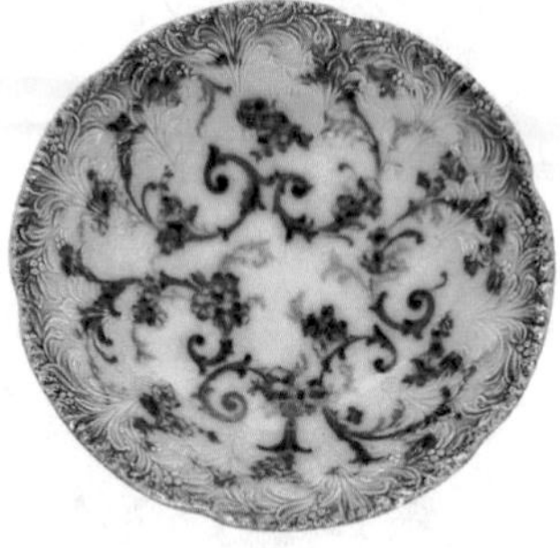

Ruby Lane

Ridgway, Plate, Imari Colors, Anglesey, 9 In.
$110

Ruby Lane

Riviera, Ivy Century, Platter, 13 ¼ x 10 In.
$75

Ruby Lane

Rockingham, Figurine, Dog, Spaniel, Seated, Embossed Platform, Yellowware, 10 ½ In.
$142

Hess Auction Group

Jug, Whiskey, Melon Shape, Stopper, Green Glaze, Lines, Handle, Marked, 1906, 8 In. .... *illus* 295
Lamp Vase, White Peony, Matte Glaze, Incised, Sallie Toohey, 1903, 11 ½ In. 354
Letter Holder, 1st U.S. Stamp, Divider, Light Blue High Glaze, 3 x 4 In. 81
Letter Holder, Fish, Jet Black Glaze, Green Interior, Shirayamadani, 1928, 7 x 13 In. 708
Match Holder, Leaf & Acorn, Blue Matte Glaze, Logo, 1922, 2 ½ x 2 In. 153
Mug, Tyg Type, Collie, Handles, E.T. Hurley, 1901, 6 In. 266
Paperweight, Blue Matte Glaze, Sallie Toohey, Logo, 1922, 3 x 4 In. 413
Paperweight, Cat, Gray, Logo, Arthur Conant, 1965, 4 ¼ In. 384
Paperweight, Cat, Napping On Plinth, Blue Black Glaze, William Hentschel, 1925, 5 ½ In. 531
Paperweight, Duck, Blue Mottled Gloss Glaze, Starkville, 1964, 2 ⅛ In. 83
Paperweight, Fish, Aventurine Glaze, Shirayamadani, 2 ½ x 5 In. .... *illus* 708
Paperweight, Fox, Ivory Matte Glaze, Square Base, Shirayamadani, 1934, 6 In. 403
Paperweight, Gazelle, Figural, Blue High Glaze, Standing, Square Base, 1951, 6 In. 138
Paperweight, Kitten, Lying Down, White Matte Glaze, David Seyler, Logo, 1945, 3 ½ In. 472
Paperweight, Monkey, Sitting On Book, Flipping Pages, Brown Glaze, 3 ½ x 4 In. 242
Paperweight, Squirrel, Brown, Green, Light Blue Matte Glaze, 1928, 4 ⅛ In. 413
Paperweight, Turtle, Gray Over Tan Matte Glaze, Box, 1922, 2 ¼ In. 708
Pencil Holder, Rook, Blue Crystalline Matte Glaze, Logo, 4 ¾ In. 266
Pitcher, Gold & Orange Ground, Yellow Roses, Bulbous, Wide Wavy Rim, 1887, 8 In. 575
Pitcher, Greek Key Band, Squared Handle, Blue Matte Glaze, 1911, 6 In. 115
Pitcher, Incised Flowers, Cream, Fired Gold, Cylindrical, Loop Handle, 1882, 11 In. 127
Pitcher, Squat, Scroll Handle, Ruffled Rim, Flowers, Pierced Silver Overlay, c.1892, 11 In. 3500
Plaque, Poppies, Wheat Stalks, Frame, Shirayamadani, 1931, 11 x 8 ¾ In. 5310
Plaque, Venice Canal, Gondolas, Vellum Glaze, Frame, Ed Diers, 1928, 8 x 9 ¾ In. .... *illus* 4720
Tile, Elephant, Blue Matte Glaze, Logo, 1921, 3 ⅝ In. 177
Tile, Rabbit, Vertical Ridges, Olive Green Glaze, Arts & Crafts Frame, 3 ½ x 3 ½ In. 767
Tile, Tea, Gaggle Of Geese, Meadow, Pond, Logo, 1943, 5 ½ x 5 ½ In. 212
Tile, Tea, Rabbits, Yellow Gloss Glaze, Green Tree Of Life, Flowers, 1940, 5 ½ In. 295
Tray, Clown, Smiling, Baggy Costume, Yellow, Black, Purple, Orange, Sallie Toohey, 4 x 6 In. 590
Tray, Figural Clown, Seated At Corner, Square, Orange, Black, 1929, 4 x 4 ½ In. 345
Tray, Image Of Pottery Building, Famous Gates, Aventurine Glaze, c.1958, 6 In. Diam.......... 115
Trivet, Black Crow, Blue & White Lattice Ground, Frame, 1945, 5 ½ In. 460
Trivet, Crane, Pastel, Logo, 1922, 5 ½ x 5 ½ In. 118
Trivet, Rook, Trellis Background, Oak Frame, Marked, 1922, 5 ⅝ In. .... *illus* 472
Vase, 2 Handles At Neck, Ivory Jewel Glaze, Flowers, Branches, 1923, 8 In. .... *illus* 531
Vase, 13 Swimming Fish, Iris Glaze, Logo, E.T. Hurley, 1905, 10 In. 3540
Vase, Angular Handles, Yellow, c.1928, 4 In. 95
Vase, Arches, Flowers, William Hentschel, Logo, Monogram, 4 ⅝ In. 266
Vase, Art Deco Design, Blue Cirrus Glaze, Loretta Holtkamp, 1953, 4 In. .... *illus* 590
Vase, Art Deco, Geometric Patterns, Tan, Cream, 1925, 7 x 5 ½ In. 325
Vase, Art Deco, Geometric Patterns, Vines, Green, Squeezebag, E. Barrett, 1928, 6 ¾ In. ...... *illus* 1534
Vase, Art Deco, Geometric, Brown, Green, Pink, Tan, Vellum, Lorinda Epply, 1931, 10 In. 8850
Vase, Banded, Birds, Blossoms, Vellum, Sara Sax, 1916, 9 x 4 ½ In. 2500
Vase, Birch Trees, Vellum Glaze, Oval, Flared Rim, E.T. Hurley, 1947, 7 ½ In. 690
Vase, Bird, Flowering Branch, Green Blue Ground, Jens Jensen, 1946, 11 ½ In. 390
Vase, Black Opal, 3 Flowers, Blue, Red, Yellow, Black, Green, Sara Sax, 1925, 18 In. 5546
Vase, Black Opal, Flowers, Blue Hazing, Harriet Wilcox, 1929, 5 In. 531
Vase, Blue Birds, Snow-Covered Tree, Albert Valentien, 1882, 13 ⅛ In. .... *illus* 12980
Vase, Blue Drip Over Mauve, Logo, 1930, 4 ⅛ In. 142
Vase, Blue Nacreous Glaze, Blue Pink Tints, Tapered, Saucer Foot, 1915, 9 In. 374
Vase, Blue, Yellow Wreath, Red Morning Glories, Matte Glaze, Coyne, 1924, 10 x 6 In. 767
Vase, Branches, Red Blossoms, Blue Birds, Katherine Van Horne, 1917, 7 In. .... *illus* 1534
Vase, Bud, Pinched Neck, Rolled Rim, Fruit Blossoms, Green, Yellow, c.1894, 5 In. 184
Vase, Butterflies, Blue, Cylindrical, c.1930, 6 ½ In. 288
Vase, Carp, Blue, Green, Tapered, Shouldered, Rolled Rim, 1905, 12 x 6 In. 6875
Vase, Carved Lotus Blossom Wrapping Around Rim, Round, Red Glaze, 1907, 4 In. 403
Vase, Chrysanthemums, Flame Mark, Elizabeth Neave Lincoln, 1919, 6 ¾ x 8 In. 938
Vase, Concentric Circles, Earl Menzel, Logo, 1953, 6 In. 266
Vase, Dark Blue High Gloss Glaze, Tapered, Molded Poppies, 1922, 11 In. 184
Vase, Diamond, Art Deco, Flared, Black, c.1930, 6 ½ In. 165
Vase, Flower Band, Leaves, Pink Glaze, 1926, 9 ½ In. 189
Vase, Flowers, Arts & Crafts, Green Matte, c.1912, 8 ½ In. 950
Vase, Flowers, Cream Ground, Tan Flowers, Jens Jensen, 1945, 6 In. 236
Vase, Flowers, Leaves, Earth Tone, Trumpet Shape, Flared Rim, 8 x 5 In. 395
Vase, Flowers, Squeezebag, Blue, Green, Black Glaze, E. Barrett, 1930, 5 ¼ In. 767
Vase, Green Leaves, Pink Flowers, Vellum, Lorinda Epply, 1907, 5 ½ In. 708

Vase, Green, Etched Tulip Design, Cylindrical, Shouldered, Rolled Rim, 1921, 9 In. 259
Vase, Hidatsu Chief, Lean Wolf, Pillow Shape, Grace Young, 1898, 9¾ In. ....*illus* 4130
Vase, Holly, Branches, Leaves, Green, Red, Brown Glaze, 1902, 7 In. 259
Vase, Hydrangea, Iris Glaze, Albert Valentien, 1902, 14 x 8 In. ....*illus* 3500
Vase, Incised Flowers, Ombroso Glaze, Red, Squat, Square Handles, 1914, 3 x 7 In. 173
Vase, Iris Glaze, Pink Thistles, Yellow Buds, Albert Valentien, 1905, 17½ In. 3540
Vase, Light Green, Flowers, Dark Green, Blue, Tapered, Shouldered, 1920, 7 In. 489
Vase, Lotus Blossoms, Elizabeth Lincoln, 1905, 5 In. 325
Vase, Lotus Flowers, Leaves, Pods, Black Glaze, Kataro Shirayamadani, 1927, 7½ In. 189
Vase, Molded Flower Design, Fan Shape, Round Foot, Blue Matte Glaze, 1937, 5 In. 219
Vase, Molded Flowers, Green Over Pink Matte Glazes, 1930, 6 In., Pair 177
Vase, Molded Flowers, Pink Matte Glaze, Tapered Cylinder, Round Foot, 1935, 6 In. 127
Vase, Molded Parrots, Light Blue Glaze, Cylindrical, Rounded Rim, 1929, 11 In. 138
Vase, Monet Pond Scene, Black Iris, Glazed, Marked, 1908, 5½ x 9½ In. 5490
Vase, Multicolor Flowers, Blue Ground, Vellum Glaze, Lenore Asbury, 1923, 8 In. 1121
Vase, Olive & Marigold Glaze, Lenore Asbury, Impressed Marks, 1903, 8½ In. 390
Vase, Orchid, Signed Lenore Ashbury, 1913, 7¼ x 4 In. 1100
Vase, Pink, Glowers, Signed Sallie E. Coyne, c.1926, 5½ x 2¾ In. 875
Vase, Prunus Branches, Double Vellum Glaze, K. Shirayamadani, 1923, 15½ In. ....*illus* 1625
Vase, Prunus, Yellow Blossoms, Peach Ground, Vellum Glaze, Lenore Asbury, 1931, 5 In. 177
Vase, Raised Flowers, Cream & Gray, Round, Bulbous, Flat Rim, 1945, 6 In. 150
Vase, Repeating Flower Panels, White Ground, Multicolor, Arthur Conant, 1920, 9 In. 472
Vase, Repeating Flowers, Orange, Purple, Green, Yellow Ground, Sara Sax, 1930, 4 In. 472
Vase, Rolled Rim, Girl & Deer, Molded, Green High Glaze, 1936, 7 In. 173
Vase, Rooks, Sitting On Window Sills, Blue Over Tan Glaze, 7¼ In. 443
Vase, Scenic, Trees, Flowers, Lake, Mountain, Arthur Conant, 1918, 8 In. 1416
Vase, Scenic, Trees, Sun, Sailboats, Iris Glaze, Fred Rothenbusch, 1905, 6½ In. 1298
Vase, Seashells At Neck & Around Shoulder, Crystalline Green Glaze, 1937, 8 In. 374
Vase, Spiral Ribbed, Rose Hips, Brown, Orange, Yellow, Ruffled Rim, Round, 1896, 5 In. 259
Vase, Swallow, Bamboo, Speckled Green Ground, Bulbous, A.M. Bookprinter, 1885, 3 In. 431
Vase, Tapered, Flowers, Blue, Green, Flat Lip, 1925, 6 In. 316
Vase, Tapered, Shouldered, Rolled Rim, Landscape, Trees, Blue, Green, 1920, 15 In. 2125
Vase, Thistle, Leaves, Flowers, Matte Glaze, Elizabeth Lincoln, 1928, 14⅝ In. ....*illus* 4720
Vase, Trumpet, Pinecones, Peach, Brown & Yellow, S. Sax, 1924, 11 In. 920
Vase, Trumpet, Rooster & Hen, Black Opal Glaze, A. Conant, 1922, 25 In. 3910
Vase, Uranium Glaze, Orange, Crackled & Puckered, Oval, Rolled Rim, 1961, 10 In. 431
Vase, Violets, Leaves, Tan, Blue, Chocolate Interior, Vellum, Fred Rothenbusch, 1930, 6 In. 826
Vase, Water Lily, Blue, 1945, 6 x 5 In. 345
Vase, White, Brown Magnolias, Blue Mottled Ground, Jens Jensen, Logo, 1943, 7 In. 354
Vase, Wide Rim, Yellow To Brown, Yellow Blossoms, Branches, c.1891, 5 In. 219
Vase, Yellow Flowers, Green Leaves, Pear Shape, Loop Handles, 1898, 5 In. 316
Vase, Yellow Glaze, Flowers, Gourd Shape, Melon Ribbed, 1929, 5 In. 460
Vase, Yellow Matte Ground, Louis Abel, c.1927, 17 In. 2124
Vase, Yellow Tulips, Iris Glaze, Rose Fechheimer, 1903, 10 In. 472
Wall Pocket, Molded Flowers, Light Blue Matte Glaze, Round Bottom, 1921, 6 In. 316

RORSTRAND was established near Stockholm, Sweden, in 1726. By the nineteenth century Rorstrand was making English-style earthenware, bone china, porcelain, ironstone china, and majolica. The company is still working and is now owned by Fiskars Sweden. The three-crown mark has been used since 1884.

Plate, Art Deco, Mint Green, Black, Ilse Claussen, c.1930, 7½ In., 4 Piece 363
Urn, Blue & White, Trees, Glade, Cattle, Cherub Handles, 24½ In. 80
Vase, Green, Chamotte & Gunnar Nylund, 1930s, 6 In. ....*illus* 270
Vase, Maple Leaves, Karl Lindstrom, 1900s, 16 x 6 In. 938
Vase, Pink Aquatic Skates, Green Waves, Integrated Handles, Logo, 8¾ In. 1003
Vase, Squat, Stoneware, Incised Swirls, Silver & Copper Color, c.1950, 13 x 10 In. 1000
Vase, Tapering, High Shoulder, Flamingos In Landscape, c.1940, 19 In. 1188

ROSALINE, *see Steuben category.*

ROSE BOWLS were popular during the 1880s. Rose petals were kept in the open bowl to add fragrance to a room, a popular idea in a time of limited personal hygiene. The glass bowls were made with crimped tops, which kept the petals inside. Many types of Victorian art glass were made into rose bowls.

Cameo Glass, Flowers, Leaves, Orange, White, Ruffled Rim, 4½ In. 299

Appraiser Problems

It's getting more difficult to obtain an appraisal for a work of art or an antique. Prices for many 18th-century antiques have gone down, while some pieces of modern art, old advertising and Chinese ceramics seem too high to be true. If you need an appraisal for tax or estate purposes and have an unusual or very valuable collection, you may not be able to find an expert whose appraisal will meet government guidelines. Even places like the Warhol Museum in Pittsburgh, Pennsylvania are not doing appraisals or authenticating pieces because the chances of facing a lawsuit are so high. Another reason? Forgeries abound.

Rookwood, Ash Receiver, Matches, Cigars, Cigarettes, Marked, Jeanette Swing, 1903, 6 In.
$590

Humler & Nolan

Rookwood, Bookends, St. Francis Of Assisi, Brown Gray Glaze, Clothilda Zanetta, 1945, 7¾ In.
$266

Humler & Nolan

R

Rookwood, Jar, Lid, Limoges Style, Birds, Oriental Grasses, Gold Highlights, 1885, 4 ⅞ In.
$443

Humler & Nolan

Rookwood, Jug, Whiskey, Melon Shape, Stopper, Green Glaze, Lines, Handle, Marked, 1906, 8 In.
$295

Humler & Nolan

Rookwood, Paperweight, Fish, Aventurine Glaze, Shirayamadani, 2 ½ x 5 In.
$708

Humler & Nolan

Rookwood, Plaque, Venice Canal, Gondolas, Vellum Glaze, Frame, Ed Diers, 1928, 8 x 9 ¾ In.
$4,720

Humler & Nolan

Rookwood, Trivet, Rook, Trellis Background, Oak Frame, Marked, 1922, 5 ⅝ In.
$472

Humler & Nolan

Rookwood, Vase, 2 Handles At Neck, Ivory Jewel Glaze, Flowers, Branches, 1923, 8 In.
$531

Rago Arts and Auction Center

Rookwood, Vase, Art Deco Design, Blue Cirrus Glaze, Loretta Holtkamp, 1953, 4 In.
$590

Humler & Nolan

Rookwood, Vase, Art Deco, Geometric Patterns, Vines, Green, Squeezebag, E. Barrett, 1928, 6 ¾ In.
$1,534

Humler & Nolan

Rookwood, Vase, Blue Birds, Snow-Covered Tree, Albert Valentien, 1882, 13 ⅛ In.
$12,980

Humler & Nolan

Rookwood, Vase, Branches, Red Blossoms, Blue Birds, Katherine Van Horne, 1917, 7 In.
$1,534

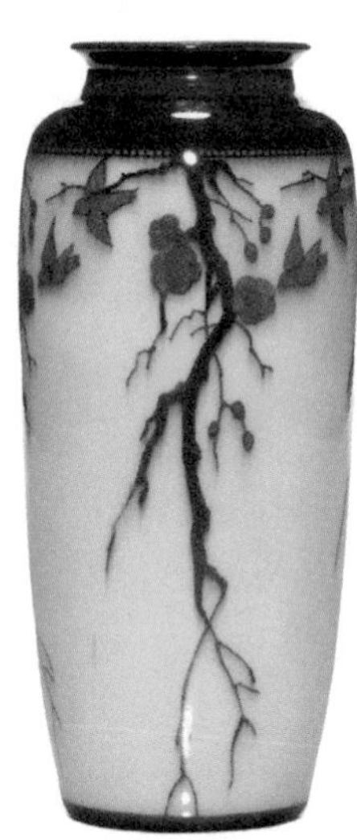

Humler & Nolan

Enamel, Fired Gold Glass, Continental, c.1900, 8 In. 84
Peachblow, Cased, Gold Flowers, 4¼ x 4 In. 65
Pink Roses, Cased, Dark Pink Interior, Satin Glass Exterior, 4½ x ¾ In. 28
Pink, Blue, Brown, Confetti, Hand Blown, Fluted, 3½ x 4½ In. 65

ROSE CANTON china is similar to Rose Mandarin and Rose Medallion, except that no people or birds are pictured in the decoration. It was made in China during the nineteenth and twentieth centuries in greens, pinks, and other colors.

Bowl, Stem, Lotus, Turquoise Interior, 5 In. 1875
Condiment Set, 11½ In., 9 Piece 123
Dish, Lotus, Turquoise Border, 10½ In. Diam. 2080
Plate, Pink, Green, Peonies, Butterflies, 10 In. 22
Platter, Oval, Butterflies, Peonies, 12¼ x 9½ In. 123
Saucer, Butterflies, Peonies, 5½ In., 12 Piece 110
Tureen, Butterflies, Peonies, 5 x 8½ In. 86
Vase, White, Narrow Mouth, Kingfisher, Lotus, Branch, Butterflies, 5½ In. 1968

ROSE MANDARIN china is similar to Rose Canton and Rose Medallion. If the panels in the design picture only people and not birds, it is Rose Mandarin.

Case, People, Interior Scenes, 25 x 12 In. 3146
Charger, 6 Triangular Cartouches, Butterflies, People, 14¾ In. 121
Hat Stand, People, Landscape, Calligraphy, Hexagon Shape, 10⅔ x 4⅚ In. 302
Platter, Oval, People, Flowers & Leaves, Gilt Trim, c.1900, 15 In. 84
Platter, Tree, People, Courtyard, 16 x 13 In. 1230
Punch Bowl, Courtly Figures, Flowers, Leaves, c.1950, 7 x 14 In. 244
Punch Bowl, Enamel, Gilt, Alternating Panels, Court Scenes, 8½ x 22 In. 5228
Punch Bowl, People, Interior Scenes, 12 In. 425
Punch Bowl, People, Landscapes, Lotus Blossoms, 1700s, 5 In. Diam. 1000
Teapot, People, Gold Accents In Women's Hair, Mid 19th Century, 7½ x 10 In. *illus* 375
Urn, Kod, Diapered Ground, 2 Pierced Handles, 1700s, 14¼ In. 649
Urn, Lid, Foo Dog Finial, Gilt Dragon Handles, Spread Foot, c.1790, 10 In. 944
Urn, People In Gardens, Chi Dragons In Relief, Foo Dog, 39 x 17 In. 307
Vase, Cylindrical, Trumpet Neck, Foo Dog Mask, Rings, 1800s, 25 In. 1230
Vase, People In Courtyard On Body & Neck, 17 x 7½ In. 246
Vase, Scenes Of Court Life, Flowers, Butterflies, Enamel, Gilt, 1800s, 17 In. *illus* 523
Vase, Women, Garden, Fences, Yellow Ground, 18½ x 10 In. 185

ROSE MEDALLION china was made in China during the nineteenth and twentieth centuries. It is a distinctive design with four or more panels of decoration around a central medallion that includes a bird or a peony. The panels show birds and people. The background is a design of tree peonies and leaves. Pieces are colored in greens, pinks, and other colors. It is similar to Rose Canton and Rose Mandarin.

Bowl, Lotus Flower Finial, Dome Lid, Alternating Panels, Pink Flowers, 5½ In. 181
Bowl, Underplate, Reticulated, Yellow, Multicolor, 1850, 9 x 7½ In. 495
Bowl, Vegetable, Gilt, 1850, 10½ x 8½ In. 510
Bowl, Vegetable, Multicolor Painted Butterflies, Flowers, Interior, Lid, 8 x 9½ In. 265
Candlestick, Tapered, Rolled Rim, Bell Foot, Figures, Leaves, c.1850, 9 In., Pair 122
Chamber Pot, Lid, Button Finial, Strap Handle, 1800s, 7 x 9 In. 92
Chop Plate, Gilt, 6 Triangular Panels, 1900s, 16 In. 800
Creamer, 1900, 4½ x 4½ In. 170
Dish, Leaf Shape, Pierced Handle, Green, Yellow, Orange, c.1880, 7 In. 108
Platter, 6 Reserves, Footed, Oval, c.1920, 15 In., Pair 180
Platter, Oval, Flowers, Birds, People, Scroll, 1800s, 13 x 10½ In. 138
Punch Bowl, Figures, Birds, Butterflies, Panels, 6 x 14 In. 492
Punch Bowl, Flowers & Leaves, People, Wide Rim, Round Foot, 23 In. Diam. 7500
Punch Bowl, Gilt, 1850, 6 x 14½ In. 1875
Punch Bowl, Group, Flowers, Peonies, 7 x 16 In. 461
Punch Bowl, Panels, Court Life, Birds, Flowers, 13½ In. Diam. 161
Punch Bowl, People, Birds, Butterflies, Flowers, 16 In. 1230
Soap Dish, Liner, Lid, 1850, 5 x 4 In. 700
Tea Set, Teapot, Sugar & Creamer, Tray, 4 Piece 151
Teapot, Gilt, Ball Finial, 1850, 8 x 11 In. 450
Teapot, Gilt, Bell Shape, 4 x 3½ In. 310
Teapot, Lid, Cylindrical, Flat Shoulder, Upright Handle, Curved Spout, c.1880, 6 In. 96

Rookwood, Vase, Hidatsu Chief, Lean Wolf, Pillow Shape, Grace Young, 1898, 9¾ In.
$4,130

Humler & Nolan

Rookwood, Vase, Hydrangea, Iris Glaze, Albert Valentien, 1902, 14 x 8 In.
$3,500

Rago Arts and Auction Center

Rookwood, Vase, Prunus Branches, Double Vellum Glaze, K. Shirayamadani, 1923, 15½ In.
$1,625

Rago Arts and Auction Center

Rookwood, Vase, Thistle, Leaves, Flowers, Matte Glaze, Elizabeth Lincoln, 1928, 14 5/8 In.
$4,720

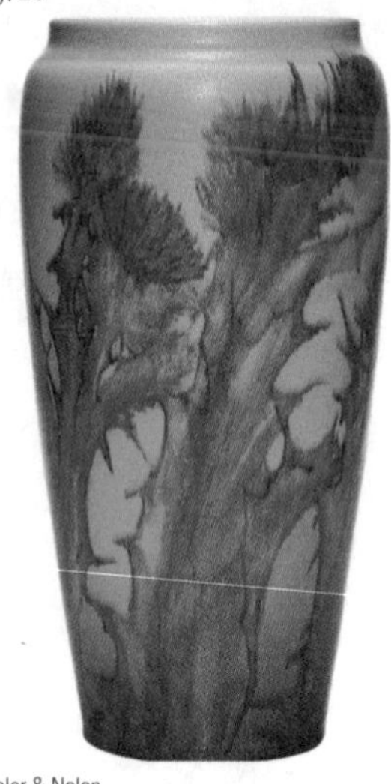

Humler & Nolan

Rorstrand, Vase, Green, Chamotte & Gunnar Nylund, 1930s, 6 In.
$270

Ruby Lane

Rose Mandarin, Teapot, People, Gold Accents In Women's Hair, Mid 19th Century, 7 ½ x 10 In.
$375

Ruby Lane

Tray, Oval, Flowers, People, Center Circle, c.1870, 17 In. 275
Urn, Dragons, Foo Dog Finial, 25 ½ x 10 ½ In. 922
Vase, Cased, Reticulated, Peonies, Birds, 20 5/8 x 12 3/8 In. 911
Vase, Courting Scenes, Bird & Flower Arrangements, 13 ¾ In., Pair 615
Vase, Dome Lid, Oval, Gilt Salamander Handles, 1800s, 20 In. 800
Vase, Figures, Flowers, Panels, Scenes, 1800s, 8 In. ....*illus* 122
Vase, Figures, Flowers, Panels, Scenes, Cylindrical, Flared Lip, 1800s, 15 ½ In. ....*illus* 153
Vase, Gilt, Enameled, Birds, Flowers, Insects, Foo Dogs, 1900s, 25 x 12 In., Pair 750
Vase, Globular, Elongated Neck, Gilt, Flowers, People, c.1890, 15 x 11 In. 508
Vase, Multicolor, Applied Handles, c.1900, 10 ¼ In. 540
Vase, People Seated At Table, Flowers, Elephant Head Ring Handles, 25 x 9 In., Pair 615
Vase, Seated People, Lotus Blossoms, 23 In. 615
Vase, Wood Base, Applied Foo Dogs, Dragons, Court Figures, 32 x 9 In. 861
Washbasin, Court Ladies, Garden, Carved Wood Stand, c.1900, 16 In. Diam. 615

ROSE O'NEILL, *see Kewpie category.*

ROSE TAPESTRY porcelain was made by the Royal Bayreuth factory of Tettau, Germany, during the late nineteenth century. The surface of the porcelain was pressed against a coarse fabric while it was still damp, and the impressions remained on the finished porcelain. It looks and feels like a textured cloth. Very skillful reproductions are being made that even include a variation of the Royal Bayreuth mark, so be careful when buying.

Basket, Bavaria Royal Bayreuth, Miniature, 4 In. 71
Creamer, Cylindrical, Pinched, Gold Handle, Royal Bayreuth c.1902, 3 In. 179
Pin Tray, Yellow Roses, Cloverleaf Shape, Ring Handle, c.1890, 4 x 5 In. 160
Plate, Gilt Trim, Royal Bayreuth, c.1910, 6 In. 36
Plate, Royal Bayreuth, c.1925, 6 In., Pair..........*illus* 78
Teapot, Lid, Roses, Daisies, Pink, Yellow, Gilt Handle, c.1910, 4 x 7 In. 125
Vase, Pink, Yellow, Cylindrical, 1900s, Royal Bayreuth, 5 ½ In. 65
Vase, Roses, Leaves, Pink, Red, Oval, Royal Bayreuth, c.1910, 5 x 4 In. 75
Vase, Shoe Shape, Roses, Daisies, Lace Holes, 5 In. 100

ROSENTHAL porcelain was made at the factory established in Selb, Bavaria, in 1891. The factory is still making fine-quality tablewares and figurines. A series of Christmas plates was made from 1910. Other limited edition plates have been made since 1971. In 1997 Rosenthal was acquired by the Waterford Wedgwood Group. Rosenthal was bought by Sambonet Paderno Industries, headquartered in Orfengo, Novara, Italy, in 2009. Rosenthal china is still being produced in Bavaria.

Bowl, Art Deco, Beige, Gilt Rim, Alternating Red & Orange Flowers, 2 ¼ x 9 In. 211
Bowl, Seated Monkey On Rim, c.1913, 8 In. 750
Candelabrum, Figural, Head, Black, Blue, Cone Shape Base, 14 ½ In. 625
Central Bouquet, Pink Roses, Ivory, 10 ½ In, 10 Piece 118
Charger, Classical Profile, Cobalt Blue Border, 14 In. 233
Coffeepot, Pansies, Pink, Purple, 22K Gold, 9 In. ....*illus* 50
Coffeepot, Warmer, Flash Design, Handle, Dorothy Hafner, 1900s, 11 x 9 In. ....*illus* 345
Ewer, White, Blue Putti, Silver Overlay, Etched Trellis & Scroll, c.1900, 14 In. 813
Figure, Clown, Seated, Playing Guitar, Poodle At His Feet, c.1920, 15 x 10 In. 688
Figurine, 2 Lovers, Nude Couple, Man Standing, Woman Seated, Kissing, c.1920, 15 In. 1063
Figurine, Arms Raised, Standing Figure, Robe, 17 In. 400
Figurine, Art Deco, Dancer, Blue Trim Skirt, Germany, 12 x 4 ½ In. 480
Figurine, Classic Rose, Arms Up, Priestly Robes, White, 17 In. 325
Figurine, Indian Dancer, Kneeling, c.1933, 6 x 3 In. 330
Figurine, Jay No. 1761, Multicolor, 1947, 11 In. 150
Figurine, Pair Of Lovers, Nude Man, Seated, Playing Flute, Woman At His Feet, c.1920, 15 In. ... 1063
Figurine, Sea Nymph, Kneeling, Holding Large Seashell, Drape, c.1920, 10 x 8 In. 750
Figurine, Stag, 14-Point Elk, Open Mouth, Porcelain, 1900s, 14 x 15 In. 1000
Figurine, Young Woman, Gazing Downward, One Leg Up, Drape, Octagonal Base, c.1936, 18 In. 3000
Mustache Cup, Woman, Rose Tree, Fern, Green 85
Tea Set, Flash, Pot, Tray, Plate, Sugar & Creamer, 5 Piece 100
Tea Set, Rainbow Pattern, Teapot, 6 Cups & Saucers, 6 Plates, Sugar & Creamer, Plate, 20 Piece 2583
Vase, Ball Shape, Trumpet Mouth, Cobalt Blue, Silver Overlay, Peacock, 1900s, 8 In. 213
Vase, Cylindrical, Ring Foot, Black, Silver Overlay, Flying Geese, c.1920, 8 In. 550
Vase, Daffodil, Multicolor, c.1930, 10 In. 90
Vase, Trumpet, Spread Foot, Blue, Silver Overlay, Flowering Branches, 1900s, 12 In. 188

ROSEVILLE POTTERY COMPANY was organized in Roseville, Ohio, in 1890. Another plant was opened in Zanesville, Ohio, in 1898. Many types of pottery were made until 1954. Early wares include Sgraffito, Olympic, and Rozane. Later lines were often made with molded decorations, especially flowers and fruit. Most pieces are marked *Roseville*. Many reproductions made in China have been offered for sale the past few years.

Roseville U.S.A.

Apple Blossom, Basket, 11 ½ In. 98
Apple Blossom, Ewer, Green, Brown Handle, 8 ¼ In. 57
Artcraft, Jardiniere, Stepped Handles, Mottled Orange, 10 x 15 In. 595
Bittersweet, Wall Pocket, Yellow, Triangular, 7 ½ x 4 ¾ In. 145
Blackberry, Candleholder, Brown, Green, 4 ¾ In. 365
Bleeding Heart, Vase, Handles, Green Glaze, Pointed Rim, Footed, 10 x 6 In. 295
Bushberry, Vase, Cornucopia Shape, Leave, Round Base, Marked, 6 In., Pair 180
Carnelian, Vase, Green, 6 ½ In. 134
Cherry Blossom, Vase, 5 In. 127
Clematis, Basket, Yellow, Brown, 7 ½ In. 86
Clematis, Vase, Blue, Square Handles, Ring Foot, Marked, 12 x 16 In. 90
Clematis, Vase, Oval, Swollen, Square Handles, Saucer Foot, Peach, Brown, 9 In., Pair 100
Cosmos, Vase, Green, Low Handles, Round Foot, 7 ¼ In. 58
Cremona, Vase, Fan Shape, Yellow Green, 5 In. 27
Dahlrose, Bowl, 6 ¾ In. 92
Dahlrose, Vase, 8 ¼ In. 46
Della Robbia, Vase, Daffodils, Rozane, F. Rhead, H. Smith, c.1910, 21 In. .... *illus* 15000
Della Robbia, Vase, Stylized Trees, Rozane, Incised Initials, c.1910, 10 In. .... *illus* 10000
Dogwood, Vase, Raised Flowers, Multicolor, 8 In. 301
Earlam, Strawberry Pot, Tan & Blue, Flared Rim, 8 x 7 ¼ In. 450
Falline, Vase, Brown, Green Pea Pods, Curved Handles, Foil Label, Marked, 6 In. 384
Ferella, Flower Frog, Brown, Rim, 9 ½ In. 356
Ferella, Vase, Pink Mottled Glaze, Green Accents, 1930s, 9 x 6 ¼ In. 775
Foxglove, Ewer, Leaves, Pointed Handle, Pedestal Foot, Purple To Mauve, 10 In. 210
Freesia, Vase, Green, 8 ⅜ In. 29
Fuchsia, Flower Frog, Blue, 3 ⅛ In. 22
Fuchsia, Vase, Blue, Green Leaves, Orange Flowers, Impressed Marks, 12 In. 189
Futura, Vase, Blue Sunray, Compressed Square, Base, 5 In. 173
Futura, Vase, Shooting Star, Blue, Green, Square Rim, Tapered, Panel, Dome Foot, 10 In. 196
Futura, Vase, The Bomb, Teal, Blue, 12 ¼ In. 649
Futura, Vase, Tombstone Shape, Flowering Branches, Amber, Blue Flowers, 6 In. 184
Gardenia, Basket, Mint, 12 In. 86
Imperial II, Wall Pocket, Red & Green Mottled, Cup Shape, Rolled Rim, 7 In. 196
Jardiniere, Multicolor Flowers, Stippled Ground, Yellow, 12 x 10 In. 90
Jonquil, Hanging Pot, Shouldered, Brown, Green, 5 x 7 In. 225
Luffa, Vase, Green, 8 ⅛ In. 104
Mock Orange, Ewer, Footed, 17 In. 250
Monticello, Vase, Handles, Blue, 5 ¼ In. 242
Monticello, Vase, Handles, Blue, Brown Bands, 5 In. 98
Morning Glory, Vase, Brown & Tan Glaze, White Flowers, Purple, Handles, 8 In. 561
Morning Glory, Vase, Pink, 9 ¼ In. 224
Moss, Vase, 12 ½ x 8 ½ In. 366
Moss, Wall Pocket, 10 ¾ In. 161
Orian, Vase, Blue, Round Base, 14 ¼ In. 86
Orian, Vase, Red, Green Interior, Handles, 8 ¼ In. 56
Orian, Vase, Tan, Green Interior, Handles, 8 ¼ In. 46
Pauleo, Vase, Crackle, 18 ⅝ In. 604
Pauleo, Vase, Cream, 16 In. 575
Pine Cone, Sconce, Triangular Backplate, Blue, Leaves, 8 In. 288
Pine Cone, Vase, 8 ¼ In. 184
Pine Cone, Vase, Flared, 7 In. 154
Pine Cone, Vase, Green Leaves, Blue Glaze, Flat Rim, Shaped Handles, Round Foot, 19 In. 374
Primrose, Basket, Tan, White Flowers, Footed, 4-Sided Handle, 10 x 6 In. 250
Primrose, Umbrella Stand, Blue, White Flowers, Footed, 21 x 9 In. 695
Raymor, Trivet, Orange, 7 In. 68
Rosecraft Panel, Urn, Matte Glaze, Brown, Flowers, Fruit, 8 ¼ In. 94
Rosecraft, Vase, Blue, Handles, 12 In. 63
Silhouette, Basket, Red, Handle, 10 ¼ In. 69
Sunflower, Vase, 5 In. 184
Sunflower, Vase, Green Leaves, Stems, Orange Flowers, Tapered, 10 ¼ In. 767

Rose Mandarin, Vase, Scenes Of Court Life, Flowers, Butterflies, Enamel, Gilt, 1800s, 17 In.
$523

Skinner, Inc.

Decorating Goes Big

Perhaps it started because the walls are full of paintings or the tables are covered with small collectibles, but the newest look, according to the fashionistas, is large sculptures inside the house. Folk art collectors have displayed carousel horses, cigar store Indians, and huge advertising signs for years.

Rose Medallion, Vase, Figures, Flowers, Panels, Scenes, 1800s, 8 In.
$122

DuMouchelles Art Gallery

Rose Medallion, Vase, Figures, Flowers, Panels, Scenes, Cylindrical, Flared Lip, 1800s, 15 ½ In.
$153

DuMouchelles Art Gallery

Rose Tapestry, Plate, Royal Bayreuth, c.1925, 6 In., Pair
$78

Ruby Lane

Rosenthal, Coffeepot, Pansies, Pink, Purple, 22K Gold, 9 In.
$50

Ruby Lane

Rosenthal, Coffeepot, Warmer, Flash Design, Handle, Dorothy Hafner, 1900s, 11 x 9 In.
$345

Cottone Auctions

Metric Dinnerware Sizes
The metric system was adopted in the United States by an Act of Congress in 1988, but sizes were not quickly changed. Dishes imported into the United States after that were often in metric sizes. A new metric dinner plate may be about ¼ inch too large to fit the shelf in a standard 1950s kitchen cabinet. Old patterns made from old molds are still made with sizes measured in inches.

Roseville, Della Robbia, Vase, Daffodils, Rozane, F. Rhead, H. Smith, c.1910, 21 In.
$15,000

Rago Arts and Auction Center

Roseville, Della Robbia, Vase, Stylized Trees, Rozane, Incised Initials, c.1910, 10 In.
$10,000

Rago Arts and Auction Center

Rowland & Marsellus, Plate, Don't Give Up On The Ship, Flow Blue, 1800s, 10 ¾ In.
$100

Ruby Lane

Roy Rogers, Button, King Of The Cowboys, Tin Litho, Photo Of Roy, 1 ⅜ In.
$173

Hake's Americana & Collectibles

R

Sunflower, Vase, Round, 4 In. 259
Sunflower, Vase, Tapered, Ear Handles, Blue, Green, Yellow, 10 In. 920
Velmoss, Vase, Green, Leaves, 9 In. 543
Velmoss, Vase, Handles, 7 In. 29
White Rose, Vase, Handles, Brown, Footed, 12 ¼ In. 345
Wincraft, Vase, Cornucopia, Yellow, Green, c.1945, 5 x 9 In. 60
Windsor, Vase, Blue, 2 Handles, 5 In. 278
Wisteria, Jardiniere, Pedestal, Brown, Green, Leaves, 28 In. 1078
Wisteria, Vase, 7 ¼ In. 109
Wisteria, Vase, Angled Handles, Blue Ground, 10 ½ In. 1154
Woodland, Vase, Hanging Flowers, Green, Gold, Tan Bisque Ground, Rozane, 6 In. 295
Zephyr Lily, Cookie Jar, Bulbous, Curved Handles, Lid, Green, Yellow, Pink, 11 In. 210

ROWLAND & MARSELLUS COMPANY is part of a mark that appears on historical Staffordshire dating from the late nineteenth and early twentieth centuries. *Rowland & Marsellus* is the mark used by an American importing company in New York City. The company worked from 1893 to about 1937. Some of the pieces may have been made by the British Anchor Pottery Co. of Longton, England, for export to a New York firm. Many American views were made. Of special interest to collectors are the plates with rolled edges, usually blue and white.

Plate, Albany, New York, Blue, Rolled Edge, 10 In. 98
Plate, Denver, Colorado, Blue, Rolled Edge, 10 In. 125
Plate, Don't Give Up On The Ship, Flow Blue, 1800s, 10 ¾ In. .... *illus* 100
Plate, Sherbrooke, Quebec, Blue, Rolled Edge, 10 In. 59
Plate, Trexlertown, Pennsylvania, Blue, Rolled Edge, 1924, 10 In. 95
Plate, William Shakespeare, Flow Blue, Rolled Edge, 10 In. 20

ROY ROGERS was born in 1911 in Cincinnati, Ohio. In the 1930s, he made a living as a singer; in 1935, his group started work at a Los Angeles radio station. He appeared in his first movie in 1937. From 1952 to 1957, he made 101 television shows. The other stars in the show were his wife, Dale Evans, his horse, Trigger, and his dog, Bullet. Roy Rogers memorabilia, including items from the Roy Rogers restaurants, are collected.

Button, King Of The Cowboys, Tin Litho, Photo Of Roy, 1 ⅜ In. .... *illus* 173
Cap Gun, Die Cast, White Metal, Signature, Flowers, Leaves, Rope, Geo. Schmidt Mfg., 8 In. 245
Doll, Dale Evans, Buttermilk, Full Size, Hartland Plastics, c.1950 125
Flashlight, Signal Siren, Pasture, Roy On Trigger, Lasso, White Fence, Plastic, 8 In. 58
Lantern, Electric, Red, Yellow, Blue, Bail Handle, Box, 8 x 4 x 4 In. 60
Pencil Case, Vinyl, Red, Roy Rogers On Trigger, Rearing, c.1962, 7 ½ x 2 ¾ In. 45
Pitcher, Head, King Of The Cowboys, Embossed, F & F Mold & Die, 4 ½ x 4 In. 65
Ring, Saddle, Sterling Silver, 1948, Size 4 ½ In. 115
Sign, Trick Lasso, Roy With Lasso, Multicolor, 3-D Easel, 1950s, 15 x 24 In. 244
Store Display, Roy Waving While Trigger Rears Up, Plastic, Wood Base, 39 In. 915
Toy, Horseshoe Set, No. 531, Tin Lithograph Base, Ohio Art Company, 1950s 48
Yo-Yo, Roy Rogers & Trigger, All Western Plastics, 1950s 15

ROYAL BAYREUTH is the name of a factory that was founded in Tettau, Bavaria, in 1794. It has continued to modern times. The marks have changed through the years. A stylized crest, the name Royal Bayreuth, and the word *Bavaria* appear in slightly different forms from 1870 to about 1919. Later dishes may include the words *U.S. Zone* (1945–1949), the year of the issue, or the word *Germany* instead of *Bavaria*. Related pieces may be found listed in the Rose Tapestry, Sand Babies, Snow Babies, and Sunbonnet Babies categories.

Berry Bowl, Lobed, Pink Roses, c.1910, 5 In. 45
Bowl, Elk, Bulbous, Head & Antlers, Brown, Footed, c.1902, 3 x 6 In. 287
Bowl, Figural Pumpkin, Stylized Leafy Ring Foot, Melon Ribbed, c.1900, 4 In. 131
Creamer, Clown, Bending Over, Ruffle Collar, Hat Forms Spout, c.1957, 4 In. 167
Creamer, Conch Shell, Green, Rust, Marked, 1910, 2 ½ x 5 In. .... *illus* 125
Cup & Saucer, Apple Shape On Leaf, Demitasse 76
Loving Cup, 3 Handles, Green, Cows In Pasture, 3 ⅜ In. 48
Loving Cup, 3 Handles, Tavern Scene, Musketeers, 1900s, 4 In. 65
Match Holder, Devil & Cards, Half Body, Hanging, Blue Mark, c.1930, 5 x 4 In. .... *illus* 150
Nappy, Oval, Figural Radish & Leaf, Root Forms Handle, Green, Red, c.1902, 8 In. 78
Pitcher, Chambermaid, Candle, Pink, Green, 6 ½ In. 135
Pitcher, King & Queen Face Cards, Figural Devil Handle, 5 In. 431
Pitcher, Tomato Shape, 3 ¾ In. 80
Plate, Shepherdess, Goats, Flowers In Apron, 9 In. 85

Royal Bayreuth, Creamer, Conch Shell, Green, Rust, Marked, 1910, 2 ½ x 5 In.
$125

Ruby Lane

Royal Bayreuth, Match Holder, Devil & Cards, Half Body, Hanging, Blue Mark, c.1930, 5 x 4 In.
$150

Potter & Potter

Royal Bonn, Urn, Lid, Flowers, Prunus, Sunrise, Gilt, Molded Base, Handles, c.1900, 15 x 14 In.
$984

New Orleans (Cakebread)

This is an edited listing of current prices. Visit **Kovels.com** to check thousands of prices from previous years and sign up for free information on trends, tips, reproductions, marks, and more.

Royal Bonn, Vase, Gold Luster, Marked, c.1900, 8 x 5 In.
$89

Ruby Lane

Royal Bonn, Vase, Old Dutch, Pink, Green, Marked, 1890-1923, 7 In.
$495

Ruby Lane

Royal Copenhagen, Bowl, Fluted, Blue, 6¾ In.
$85

Ruby Lane

Sugar & Creamer, Boy With Donkeys 90
Sugar, Lid, Tomato Shape, Red, 3¾ x 4¾ In. 36
Toothpick Holder, 3 Handles, Doing Laundry, 3 x 3¼ In. 74
Trinket Dish, Girl Walking Dog, Handle, 5 In. 75
Vase, Hunt Scene, Leaf Handles, Waisted, Green, c.1900, 5 x 6 In. 75
Vase, Sunset, Bulbous, Footed, c.1919, 4 In. 56

ROYAL BONN is the nineteenth- and twentieth-century trade name used by Franz Anton Mehlem, who had a pottery in Bonn, Germany, from 1836 to 1931. Porcelain and earthenware were made. The factory was purchased by Villeroy & Boch in 1921 and closed in 1931. Many marks were used, most including the name Bonn, the initials FM, and a crown.

Bowl, Flowers, Multicolor, c.1910, 10 In. 225
Clock, 8-Day, Strike Movement, Ansonia La Cerda, c.1904, 15 x 14 In. 2250
Jardiniere, Blue & White, Landscape, Shouldered, c.1900, 7 x 6 In. 560
Urn, Lid, Flowers Prunus, Sunrise, Gilt, Molded Base, Handles, c.1900, 15 x 14 In. ..... *illus* 984
Urn, Lid, Square Handles, Daisies, Gilt, Pedestal Foot, Finial, c.1880, 17 In. 167
Vase, Art Nouveau Shape, Mums, Forest Scene, M. Dirkmann, c.1900, 12 In. 499
Vase, Art Nouveau, Porcelain, Portrait, Scenic, Multicolor, Tapered, Gerhard, 11 In., Pair 480
Vase, Blooming Roses, Yellows, Oranges, White, Ball Shape, 7¼ In. 369
Vase, Bulbous, Stick Neck, Footed, Birds, c.1910, 10½ In. 344
Vase, Cabbage Roses, Multicolor, Gold Rim, Oval, c.1900, 8 x 5 In. 360
Vase, Flowers, Birds, Gilt, Pink, 25 In. 240
Vase, Flowers, Black Ground, 2 Handles, Flared Base, 11 In. 595
Vase, Flowers, Blue & Pink, Cream Ground, Footed, Handles, c.1880, 9 In. 200
Vase, Gold Luster, Marked, c.1900, 8 x 5 In. ..... *illus* 89
Vase, Hibiscus, Lavender Ground, Gilt, Shouldered, Handles, 14 x 8 In., Pair 545
Vase, Irises, Pink, Purple, Green Ground, Cylindrical, c.1890, 14 In. 250
Vase, Old Dutch, Pink, Green, Marked, 1890-1923, 7 In. ..... *illus* 495
Vase, Pink Ruffled Flowers, Blue, Green, 12 In. 47
Vase, Roses, Leaves, Gray & Pink, Bulbous, Swollen Neck, Rolled Rim, c.1890, 11 In. 120
Vase, Vase, Muscle, Brown, Cavalier, Blue Hat, 2 Handles, 8 In. 155

ROYAL COPENHAGEN porcelain and pottery have been made in Denmark since 1775. The Christmas plate series started in 1908. The figurines with pale blue and gray glazes have remained popular in this century and are still being made. Many other old and new style porcelains are made today.

Bowl, Bird, Purple, Yellow Breast, Flowers, White Ground, 10¾ In. 123
Bowl, Blue Fluted Lace, Square, 8 x 8 In. 110
Bowl, Fluted, Blue, 6¾ In. ..... *illus* 85
Bowl, Montieth, Flora Danica, Gilt, Flowers, 13 In. 4250
Cachepot, Flora Danica, Branch & Flower Handles, 1900s, 5 In. 819
Cachepot, Flora Danica, Twin Handles, Encrusted Flowers, 6½ In. 1200
Cake Plate, Flora Danica, Triangular, Yellow Flower, Leaves, 8 x 9 In. 1000
Candelabrum, 6-Light, Blue Fluted Full Lace, Grotesques, 1900s, 21½ In. 180
Charger, Fish, Swimming In Seaweed, Signed, 15¾ In. Diam 754
Compote, Flora Danica, Pedestal, 5½ x 8 In. 1680
Cup & Saucer, Blue & White, Ribbed, Demitasse 30
Cup & Saucer, Blue Fluted, Scalloped, 1969-74, 4 x 6 In., 12 Piece 1210
Cup & Saucer, Demitasse, Blue Flowers, 1940-80, 16 Piece 108
Dish, Flora Danica, Flower Sprigs, Leaves, Beaded Edge, c.1970, 13 In. 750
Dish, Pickle, Blue, Fluted, Half Lace, 9 x 7 In. 156
Dish, Trinket, Mermaid, White, 4 x 6 In. 50
Figurine, Boy, Raincoat, Holding Umbrella, 1970s, 7 In. 140
Figurine, Boy, Shirtless, White Hair, Flower Wreath, Round Base, c.1905, 6 In. 688
Figurine, Faun, Sitting, Frog, On Knee, 4¾ x 3½ In. ..... *illus* 295
Figurine, Girl With Dogs, Blue Dress, 6½ x 7 In. 108
Figurine, Hippocampus, Half Horse, Half Sea Creature, 3¾ x 7 In. 192
Figurine, Polar Bear, Seated, 9 x 17 In. 276
Figurine, Waves & Rock, Theodor Lundberg, 18¼ x 11¾ In. 484
Fruit Basket, Flora Danica, Reticulated, 9¼ In. 2500
Group, Amorous Couple, Wave & Rock, 18 In. ..... *illus* 366
Group, Goat & Kid, Blue, 4 x 6 In. 108
Group, Nude Couple, Kissing, Marked, 1970s, 18 In. 684
Jardiniere, Flowers, Reticulated Flare Neck, Gargoyle Handles, c.1924, 9 In. 1625
Plate, Dinner, Flora Danica, Cistus Helianthemum L, Gilt, 10 In. 472

R

Plate, Flora Danica, Reticulated, Purple Flower, 11 ¾ In. 938
Plate, Flora Danica, Reticulated, Small Yellow Flowers, 13 In. 1063
Plate, Frijsenborg, White, Gilt, Scalloped Rim, Flowers, 1900s, 8 In., 12 Piece 319
Plate, Luncheon, Flora Danica, Pierced, Fruits, 9 In., 6 Piece 4200
Plate, Pierced Edge, Flora Danica, Wintergreen, Gilt, 9 In. 484
Plate, Salad, Princess, 7 In. 30
Platter, Blue Fluted Lace, 10 x 13 In. 150
Platter, Flora Danica, 1967, 14 ¼ In. 610
Platter, Flora Danica, Oval, Pink Flowers, Broad Leaves, 17 In. 2250
Platter, Flora Danica, Oval, Yellow Flower, Lacy Leaves, 14 ½ In. 1875
Salt Dish, Flora Danica, Oval, Pink Flowers, Leaves, Petals, 1 ½ x 4 In. 484
Toothpick Holder, Blue & White, Fluted, Marked, 2 ¾ In. 92
Tureen, Flora Danica, Underplate, 15 ⅝ In. 5000
Vase, Cherry Blossom Branch, Dragonfly, c.1968, 5 ½ In. 50
Vase, Sailing Ship, Choppy Sea, Blue, White, Tapered, 17 ½ In. 163
Vase, Tapered, Bulbous Shoulder, Blossoming Blue Tulips, c.1900, 9 In. 1125
Vase, Trophy Shape, Ivy Gilt Handles, Danish Skyline, Greenhouse, 1868, 16 In. 2032

ROYAL CROWN DERBY COMPANY, LTD., is a name used on porcelain beginning in 1890. There is a complex family tree that includes the Derby, Crown Derby, and Royal Crown Derby porcelains. The Royal Crown Derby mark includes the name and a crown. The words *Made in England* were used after 1921. The company became part of Allied English Potteries Group in 1964. It was bought in 2000 and is now privately owned.

Bowl, Old Imari, Orange, White, Cobalt Blue, Octagonal, 5 x 11 ½ In. 615
Candlestick, Liners, Red Aves Pattern, 10 ½ x 5 ¼ In. 238
Demitasse Set, Imari Pattern, 8 Cups, 8 Saucers, 16 Piece 615
Figurine, Ptarmigan, White Grouse, Standing On Gray Mound, 1900s, 7 ½ In. 236
Plate, Dinner, Scalloped, Gadrooned Border, Gilt, Cobalt Blue, c.1890, 9 ½ In., 6 Piece 138
Platter, Gilt, Cobalt Blue, Flowers, 13 x 10 In. 123
Platter, Old Imari, Orange, White, Cobalt Blue, 14 In., Pair 492
Tea Set, Red Aves, Birds, Leaves, Teapot, Sugar, Creamer, 10 Cups, Saucer, 15 Piece 553
Urn, Cobalt Blue Ground, White, Gilt Detail, Multicolor Birds, 6 ¼ In., Pair 923
Urn, Gilt, Orange Poppies, Blue, Square Base, 1800s, 11 ¼ In. 360
Vase, Curved Handles, Ribbed Body, Green Crystalline Glaze, c.1940, 9 In. 207

ROYAL DOULTON is the name used on Doulton and Company pottery made from 1902 to the present. Doulton and Company of England was founded in 1853. Pieces made before 1902 are listed in this book under Doulton. Royal Doulton collectors search for the out-of-production figurines, character jugs, vases, and series wares. Some vases and animal figurines were made with a special red glaze called flambe. Sung and Chang glazed pieces are rare. The multicolored glaze is very thick and looks as if it were dropped on the clay. Bunnykins figurines were first made by Royal Doulton in 1939. In 2005 Royal Doulton was acquired by the Waterford Wedgwood Group, which was bought by KPS Capital Partners of New York in 2009 and became part of WWRD Holdings. Beatrix Potter bunny figurines were made by Beswick and are listed in that category.

Animal, Cat, Seated, Flambe, 11 ¾ x 7 ¼ In. .... 240 to 460
Animal, Dragon, Flambe, HN 3552, 7 ½ x 10 In. 240
Animal, Owl, Flambe, 12 In. 240
Animal, Owl, Flambe, Red, Black, Blue, Orange, 12 ¼ x 6 In. 230
Animal, Rhinoceros, Flambe, Red, Black, 10 x 15 ½ In. 373
Animal, Tiger, Flambe, HN 2646, 6 x 13 ½ In. 300

Royal Doulton character jugs depict the head and shoulders of the subject. They are made in four sizes: large, 5 ¼ to 7 inches; small, 3 ¼ to 4 inches; miniature, 2 ¼ to 2 ½ inches; and tiny, 1 ¼ inches. Toby jugs portray a seated, full figure.

Character Jug, Collector, Holds Jug, Left Handed, D 6796, 6 In. .... *illus* 186
Character Jug, Scaramouche, D 6558, Max Henk, 6 ¾ In. 325
Charger, Jackdaw Of Reims, Bishops & Abbot & Prior Were There, D 1648, 15 In. 58
Figurine, Accordion Man, Striped Shirt, Hat, HN 2172, 6 ½ In. 186
Figurine, Bridget, Curious Old Woman, HN 2070, 8 In. 95
Figurine, Enchantment, HN 2178, c.1956, 7 ½ In. 42
Figurine, Forty Winks, HN 1974 83
Figurine, Helmsman, Multicolor, Blue Cap, Green Overcoat, HN 2499, 9 In. 92
Figurine, In The Stocks, Red Coat, HN 2163, 6 ⅛ In. 248
Figurine, Jester, Seated, 1 Knee Bent, Pedestal, HN 2016, 10 In. .... *illus* 85
Figurine, Knight, Kneeling, Holding Sword, Multicolor Enamel, 1920, 9 ½ In. 2583

Royal Copenhagen, Figurine, Faun, Sitting, Frog, On Knee, 4 ¾ x 3 ½ In.
$295

Ruby Lane

Royal Copenhagen, Group, Amorous Couple, Wave & Rock, 18 In.
$366

DuMouchelles Art Gallery

Royal Doulton, Character Jug, Collector, Holds Jug, Left Handed, D 6796, 6 In.
$186

Ruby Lane

R

Royal Doulton, Figurine, Jester, Seated, 1 Knee Bent, Pedestal, HN 2016, 10 In.
$85

DuMouchelles Art Gallery

TIP
Sometimes glasses get a cloudy look from the lime deposits in hard water. Cover the cloudy part with wet potato peelings for 24 hours. Rinse and dry.

Royal Doulton, Figurine, One Of The Forty, Multicolor Enamel, c.1924, 6 ¾ In.
$2,460

Skinner, Inc.

Figurine, One Of The Forty, Multicolor Enamel, c.1924, 6 ¾ In. ... *illus* 2460
Figurine, Owd Willum, HN 2042, 1948, 6 ¾ In. ... 98 to 120
Figurine, Paisley Shawl, HN 1987, c.1960, 6 x 4 In. ... *illus* 190
Figurine, Piper, Michael Abberley, HN 2907 ... 52
Figurine, Potter, HN 1493, 7 In. ... 43
Figurine, Sairy Gamp, Green Dress, HN 2100, 7 ⅞ In. ... 25
Figurine, Simone, 1970, HN 2378, 7 ½ In. ... 84
Figurine, Strolling, Chic Woman With Greyhound, HN 3073, 14 In. ... 60
Figurine, The Cobbler, HN 1706, 8 In. ... 169
Jar, Lid, Chang Ware, Runny Glaze, Charles Noke, Harry Nixon, c.1925, 11 In. ... *illus* 9375
Mask, Marlene Dietrich, HN 1541 ... 148
Mask, Sweet Anne, HN 1590 ... 156
Mug, Santa Claus, 7 Piece ... 276
Pitcher, Washbasin, Watteau, Flow Blue, Wide Spout, Loop Handle, 13 In. ... 98
Plate, Scenic, Pembroke Castle, Ross Castle, C. Hart, 10 ¼ In., Pair ... 81
Sugar & Creamer, Old Trentham Sprays ... 24
Tankard, Nightwatchman, Kingsware, D 5478, 1900s, 5 ¾ In. ... 110
Tobacco Jar, Flambe Sung, Elephant Finial, Fred Moore, c.1930, 6 In. ... *illus* 795
Tobacco Jar, Lid, Scroll, Flowers, Minnie Waters, c.1925, 8 x 5 In. ... *illus* 200
Vase, Blue Flambe, Blue Tendrils, Signed, 9 In. ... 354
Vase, Chang, Yellow, Cream Glaze, Rust Highlights, C. Noke, Harry Nixon, 6 In. ... 885
Vase, Elongated, Flared, Knopped, Flowers, Green To Blue, 13 x 5 In., Pair ... 295
Vase, Flambe, Slender, Glazed, Red, Landscape, African Motif, 11 ½ x 4 ½ In. ... 153
Vase, Flambe, Veined, 13 ½ In. ... 180
Vase, Scenic, Iridescent Glaze, Painted Tree-Lined Lane, Mountains, 27 x 8 In. ... 150
Vase, Ships In Moonlight, Blue, 4 x 3 In. ... *illus* 375
Vase, Sung, 6-Lobe Gourd Shape, Veining, Charles Noke, Fred Moore, 7 In. ... *illus* 560
Vase, Tree-Lined Road, Cylindrical, R. Holdcroft, 8 ¼ In. ... 275

ROYAL DUX is the more common name for the Duxer Porzellanmanufaktur, which was founded by E. Eichler in Dux, Bohemia (now Duchcov, Czech Republic), in 1860. By the turn of the twentieth century, the firm specialized in porcelain statuary and busts of Art Nouveau–style maidens, large porcelain figures, and ornate vases with three-dimensional figures climbing on the sides. The firm is still in business. It is now part of Czesky Porcelan (Czech Porcelain).

Bowl, Figural, Art Nouveau, Sea Nymphs, Pedestal, c.1910, 16 x 18 In. ... 1107
Bowl, Seashell Shape, Molded Woman, Seated On Rocks, Doves, c.1890, 9 In. ... 388
Bust, Maiden, Hands On Face, c.1905, 18 In. ... 820
Centerpiece, Mermaid Stem, Shell On Shoulders, Porcelain Base, 12 In. ... 889
Figurine, Girl, Classical Attire, Flute, Sheep, Cobalt Blue Ground, c.1900, 20 x 10 In. ... 339
Figurine, Hunting Dog, Bird In Mouth, Cream, Gilt, Matte Glaze, c.1920, 7 x 14 In. ... 153
Figurine, Snake Charmer, 9 x 6 ½ In. ... 120
Figurine, Woman, Green Dress, Cloak, Carrying Vase, Rocks, Round Base, c.1900, 12 In. ... 359
Figurine, Woman, Masked Man, Cloaked, Lantern, Cobalt Blue, Round Base, 1900s, 20 In. ... 329
Figurine, Woman, With Basket, Painted, c.1920, 17 In. ... 120
Group, Courting Couple, Classical Attire, 18 In. ... 175
Group, Diana, Nude, Running With Hound, Art Deco, 14 ¼ In. ... 138
Vase, Art Nouveau, Figural, Woman, Bird, Grapes, 26 In. ... 242
Vase, Flower Shape, Applied Woman, Blue, Cream, Marked, c.1900, 14 In. ... *illus* 431
Vase, Nymph, 3 Shallow Basins, Overlapping Leaves, 7 ½ x 9 In. ... 181

ROYAL FLEMISH glass was made during the late 1880s in New Bedford, Massachusetts, by the Mt. Washington Glass Works. It is a colored satin glass decorated with dark colors and raised gold designs. The glass was patented in 1894. It was supposed to resemble stained glass windows.

Bowl, Round, Gilt Grids, Flowers, Gold Tracery, 4 x 11 In. ... 1840
Ewer, Chrysanthemums, Lavender Ground, Frosted, Gilt, Loop Handle, Wavy Rim, 14 In. ... 2666
Ewer, Coat Of Arms, Shield & Shamrock, Flowers, Dancing Dragons, Handle, 12 In. ... 5750
Mug, Frosted, Enameled Circles, Flowers, Twisted Handle, Mt. Washington, 7 In. ... *illus* 2818
Vase, Blackberry Design, Stippled, Berry Clusters, Red, Yellow, White, 8 ½ In. ... 4600
Vase, Bulbous, Stain Glass Panels, Raised Gilt Lines, Handles, Cup Mouth, 10 In. ... 3259
Vase, Cherub Slaying Dragon, Frosted, Raised Gilt Lines, Angular Handles, 16 In. ... 4148
Vase, Cylindrical, Enameled Panels, Winged Dragon, Ring Collar, 13 In. ... *illus* 8050
Vase, Gourd, Pansy Bouquets, Enamel, Frosted, Gold Tendrils, Sun Rays, 6 x 8 In. ... 1150
Vase, Raised Panels, Vines, Stippled Berries, Curled Reeded Handles, 8 In. ... *illus* 316
Vase, Tapered, Gilt Panels, Gold Enamel Dragon, Scrolling Flowers, Trifold Rim, 14 In. ... *illus* 5175

Royal Doulton, Figurine, Paisley Shawl, HN 1987, c.1960, 6 x 4 In.
$190

Ruby Lane

Royal Doulton, Jar, Lid, Chang Ware, Runny Glaze, Charles Noke, Harry Nixon, c.1925, 11 In.
$9,375

Rago Arts and Auction Center

TIP

Check the metal strips holding any heavy wall-hung shelves. After a few years, the shelf holder may develop "creep" and gradually bend away from the wall, spilling anything on it.

Transmutation Glazes

Potters at Royal Doulton created transmutation glazes during the early 1890s. Copper oxide and other chemicals were applied to the pottery, then the flow of oxygen to the kiln was reduced. This made an unpredictable glaze of reds, yellows, blues, and greens. Rouge flambé, first made in 1904, is still made.

Royal Doulton, Tobacco Jar, Flambe Sung, Elephant Finial, Fred Moore, c.1930, 6 In.
$795

Ruby Lane

Royal Doulton, Tobacco Jar, Lid, Scroll, Flowers, Minnie Waters, c.1925, 8 x 5 In.
$200

Ruby Lane

Royal Doulton, Vase, Ships In Moonlight, Blue, 4 x 3 In.
$375

Ruby Lane

Royal Doulton, Vase, Sung, 6-Lobe Gourd Shape, Veining, Charles Noke, Fred Moore, 7 In.
$560

Humler & Nolan

Royal Dux, Vase, Flower Shape, Applied Woman, Blue, Cream, Marked, c.1900, 14 In.
$431

Cowan Auctions

Royal Flemish, Mug, Frosted, Enameled Circles, Flowers, Twisted Handle, Mt. Washington, 7 In.
$2,818

Early Auction Company

Royal Flemish, Vase, Cylindrical, Enameled Panels, Winged Dragon, Ring Collar, 13 In.
$8,050

Early Auction Company

Royal Flemish, Vase, Raised Panels, Vines, Stippled Berries, Curled Reeded Handles, 8 In.
$316

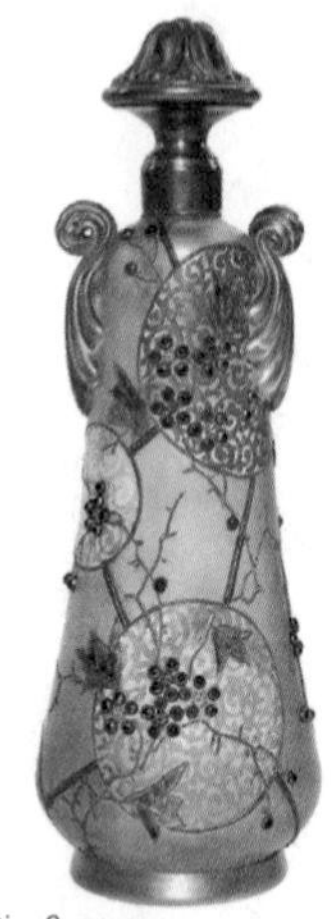

Early Auction Company

ROYAL HAEGER, *see Haeger category.*

ROYAL HICKMAN designed pottery, glass, silver, aluminum, furniture, lamps, and other items. From 1938 to 1944 and again from the 1950s to 1969, he worked for Haeger Potteries. Mr. Hickman operated his own pottery in Tampa, Florida, during the 1940s. He moved to California and worked for Vernon Potteries. During the last years of his life he lived in Guadalajara, Mexico, and continued designing for Royal Haeger. Pieces made in his pottery listed here are marked *Royal Hickman* or *Hickman*.

Figurine, Sailfish, Green Briar Drip Glaze, c.1942, 8 x 13 In. 45
Vase, Gladiola, Gray & White Drip Glaze, Sticker, c.1948, 10 x 11 In. 150
Vase, Swan Shape, Chartreuse Drip Glaze, 1940s, 13 ½ In. 300
Vase, Tropical Leaves, Relief, Peach Tan & Cream Glaze, Foil Label, 7 x 8 In. 60

ROYAL NYMPHENBURG is the modern name for the Nymphenburg porcelain factory, which was established at Neudeck-ob-der-Au, Germany, in 1753 and moved to Nymphenburg in 1761. The company is still in existence. Marks include a checkered shield topped by a crown, a crowned *CT* with the year, and a contemporary shield mark on reproductions of eighteenth-century porcelain.

Figurine, Lion Of Bavaria, Shield, Base, 5 x 4 ½ In. .... *illus* 275
Group, 4 Seasons, Blanc De Chine, Plinth Base, c.1910, 11 In. 240
Plate, Dessert, Wildflowers, After Rudolph Sieck, Germany, 8 In., 8 Piece 531

ROYAL RUDOLSTADT, *see Rudolstadt category.*

ROYAL VIENNA, *see Beehive category.*

ROYAL WORCESTER is a name used by collectors. Worcester porcelains were made in Worcester, England, from about 1751. The firm went through many different periods and name changes. It became the Worcester Royal Porcelain Company, Ltd., in 1862. Today collectors call the porcelains made after 1862 "Royal Worcester." In 1976, the firm merged with W.T. Copeland to become Royal Worcester Spode. The company was bought by the Portmeirion Group in 2009. Some early products of the factory are listed under Worcester. Related pieces may be listed under Copeland, Copeland Spode, and Spode.

Biscuit Jar, Plate, Melon Shape, Flowering Branches, Gilt, Ivory Ground, 1890s, 6 ¾ In. .....*illus* 325
Bottle Stopper, Porcelain, Dove, Blue & White, 3 ½ x 4 In. 20
Chop Plate, Lavinia Pattern, Marked, 12 ½ In. 49
Cup & Saucer, Black, Gilt, 2 Piece 71
Cup & Saucer, Lavinia Pattern, Gold Rim 29
Ewer, Hexagonal, Pierced, Pearls, Roses, Impressed, G. Owen, 6 ¾ In. 1815
Ewer, Pierced Handle, Faux Canary Jewels, Beading, Petals, c.1880, 17 In. 984
Figurine, Bisque, Chinese Men, Seated, 12 In., Pair 150
Figurine, Urn On Head, Urn On Hip, Robes, Pink, Barefoot, 31 In. 312
Jug, Cream Ground, Painted Flowers, Twig Handle, 9 x 6 In. 84
Jug, White Ground, Flowers, Purple, Gold Lip, England, 1875, 12 ¼ In. 92
Plate, Chantilly, Cream, Flower Center, Flowered Rim, 9 In., 8 Piece 184
Plate, Dessert, Fruit, Woodland Ground, Leafy Gilt Rims, 9 In., 12 Piece 8000
Plate, Service, Hyde Park Pattern, c.1966, 10 ½ In., 12 Piece 354
Plate, Service, Raised Gilt, Green, Faux Stone Border, 1940s, 10 In., 14 Piece 1799
Vase, Globular, Pierced Scrollwork, Swags, Bows, Sheep, 1910, 12 In. 8783
Vase, Reticulated, Grainger, 1889-1902, 13 In., Pair 308

ROYCROFT products were made by the Roycrofter community of East Aurora, New York, in the late nineteenth and early twentieth centuries. The community was founded by Elbert Hubbard, famous philosopher, writer, and artist. The workshops owned by the community made furniture, metalware, leatherwork, embroidery, and jewelry. A printshop produced many signs, books, and the magazines that promoted the sayings of Elbert Hubbard. Furniture by the Roycroft community is listed in the Furniture category.

Bookends, Copper, Hammered, Brown Patina, Sailboat, c.1910, 5 x 5 ½ In. 123
Bowl, Flying Saucer, Copper, Hammered, Marked, 2 ½ x 10 ½ In. 443
Candlestick, Copper, Hammered, Half Twist Stem, Spread Foot, 13 In., Pair 805
Case, Copper, Hammered, Ginko Leaves, Banding, 12 In. 403
Lamp, Brass-Washed Copper, Leaded Slag Glass Shade, Toothaker, 1920s, 20 In. .... *illus* 12500
Letter Holder, Copper, Hammered, Half Circle, 3 x 5 ½ In. 123

Sconce, Copper, Hammered, 8 ½ In. 153
Vase, Copper, Hammered, Bowl Shape Bottom, Trumpet Shape Neck, 12 In. 1180
Vase, Copper, Hammered, Scalloped Rim, Cupped Foot, 10 x 4 ½ In. 354

ROZANE, *see Roseville category.*

ROZENBURG worked at The Hague, Holland, from 1890 to 1914. The most important pieces were earthenware made in the early twentieth century with pale-colored Art Nouveau designs.

Jardiniere, Squat, Green, Brown, Yellow Shells, Open-Mouth Fish, 8 ½ x 15 In. 300
Vase, Bottle Shape, Flat, Eggshell, Gilt Crab, Green Sea Plants, c.1900, 11 In. 3585
Vase, Flask Shape, Eggshell, Flying Bird, Scrolling Branches, c.1904, 7 In. 4780
Vase, Red, Blue, Purple, Flowers, Double Handled, 14 x 6 In. 2640

RRP, or RRP Roseville, is the mark used by the firm of Robinson-Ransbottom. It is not a mark of the more famous Roseville Pottery. The Ransbottom brothers started a pottery in 1900 in Ironspot, Ohio. In 1920, they merged with the Robinson Clay Products Company of Akron, Ohio, to become Robinson-Ransbottom. The factory closed in 2005.

Jardiniere, Pedestal, Flowers, Green, Brown Glaze, c.1910, 22 In. .... *illus* 120
Vase, Centennial, Green, 9 ¼ In. 29
Vase, Cream, Red Flowers, Leaves, c.1928, 12 In. 23
Vase, Cream, Red, Flowers, Handles, 15 ½ In. 23

RS GERMANY is part of the wording in marks used by the Tillowitz, Germany, factory of Reinhold Schlegelmilch from 1914 until about 1945. The porcelain was sold decorated and undecorated. The Schlegelmilch families made porcelains marked in many ways. See also ES Germany, RS Poland, RS Prussia, RS Silesia, RS Suhl, and RS Tillowitz.

Bowl, Gold Leaves, 3 x 12 In. 30
Dish, Tulips, Pale Multicolor, Footed, 1920s, 9 x 7 In. 11
Jam Jar, Flower Bouquet, Pink, Green, Hand Painted, 3 x 3 In. 5
Sauceboat, Underplate, Roses, Yellow Ground, Gilt Design, 2 Piece 20
Sugar & Creamer, Lid, Flowers, 2 Piece 15

RS POLAND (German) is a mark used by the Reinhold Schlegelmilch factory at Tillowitz from about 1946 to 1956. After 1956, the factory made porcelain marked *PT Poland.* This is one of many of the RS marks used. See also ES Germany, RS Germany, RS Prussia, RS Silesia, RS Suhl, and RS Tillowitz.

Urn, Purple Flowers, Multicolor, 11 In. 113
Vase, Long Stemmed Roses, 9 ¾ In. 68

RS PRUSSIA appears in several marks used on porcelain before 1917. Reinhold Schlegelmilch started his porcelain works in Suhl, Germany, in 1869. See also ES Germany, RS Germany, RS Poland, RS Silesia, RS Suhl, and RS Tillowitz.

Biscuit Jar, Tray, Gilt, Flowers, Cream, Tillowitz, 5 x 7 ¾ In., 2 Piece 72
Bowl, Cobalt Blue, Flowers, Shaped Rim, 10 ½ In. 203
Bowl, Pink Roses, Scalloped Edge, Gold Rim, 8 In. 199
Chocolate Pot, Flowers, Leaves, Green, Pink, Octagonal, Lobed, 1920s, 7 x 10 In. 80
Chocolate Set, Pot, Cup & Saucer, Ribbed, Flowers, c.1900, 10 Piece 650
Dessert Set, Master Tray, Flowers, Signed, 6 ¼-In. Plate, 9 ½-In. Tray, 7 Piece 115
Plate, Pink, Flowers, Green Border, Gilt, 9 In. .... *illus* 116
Toothpick Holder, Poppy Flower, Leaves, Bud, Ribbed, 2 ¼ x 2 In. 50

RS SILESIA appears on porcelain made at the Reinhold Schlegelmilch factory in Tillowitz, Germany, from the 1920s to the 1940s. The Schlegelmilch families made porcelains marked in many ways. See also ES Germany, RS Germany, RS Poland, RS Prussia, RS Suhl, and RS Tillowitz.

Cake Plate, The King's Tent, Roses, Cream To Green, 1920s, 10 In. 45
Plate, Violets, Gold Rim, 7 ⅜ In. 37

RS SUHL is a mark used by the Reinhold Schlegelmilch factory in Suhl, Germany, between 1900 and 1917. The Schlegelmilch families made porcelains in many places. See also ES Germany, RS Germany, RS Poland, RS Prussia, RS Silesia, and RS Tillowitz.

Dresser Box, Egg Shape, Roses, Multicolor, 7 In. 250

Is It Pottery or Porcelain?

Porcelain is translucent. When a porcelain dish is held in front of a strong light, you see light through the dish. Pottery is opaque. You can't see through it.

If pottery is held in one hand and porcelain in the other, the porcelain will be colder to the touch.

If a dish is broken, a porcelain dish will chip with small shell-like breaks; pottery cracks on a line.

Pottery is softer and easier to break. Pottery will stain more easily. Porcelain is thinner, lighter, and more durable.

Royal Flemish, Vase, Tapered, Gilt Panels, Gold Enamel Dragon, Scrolling Flowers, Trifold Rim, 14 In.
$5,175

Early Auction Company

Royal Nymphenburg, Figurine, Lion Of Bavaria, Shield, Base, 5 x 4 ½ In.
$275

Ruby Lane

Royal Worchester, Biscuit Jar, Plate, Melon Shape, Flowering Branches, Gilt, Ivory Ground, 1890s, 6 ¾ In.
$325

Ruby Lane

TIP
Parchment lampshades can be cleaned with a cloth soaked in milk. Then wipe dry with a clean cloth.

Roycroft, Lamp, Brass-Washed Copper, Leaded Slag Glass Shade, Toothaker, 1920s, 20 In.
$12,500

Rago Arts and Auction Center

Down with the *Lusitania*
Roycroft founder Elbert Hubbard and his second wife, Alice, died on the British ocean liner *Lusitania* when it was sunk by a German submarine in 1915. The Roycroft shops were managed by Elbert Hubbard II until they closed in 1938.

Sugar & Creamer, Lid, Flowers, Beige To Green, Gold 150
Vase, Melon Eaters, 4 Women, Robes, Landscape, Red, Gold Border, c.1910, 7 x 3 In. 174

RS TILLOWITZ was marked on porcelain by the Reinhold Schlegelmilch factory at Tillowitz from the 1920s to the 1940s. Table services and ornamental pieces were made. See also ES Germany, RS Germany, RS Poland, RS Prussia, RS Silesia, and RS Suhl.

Bowl, Flowers, Multicolor, 5 In. 12
Bowl, Flowers, Pink, Yellow, Orange, Open Handles, 10 x 8 In. 185

RUBINA is a glassware that shades from red to clear. It was first made by George Duncan and Sons of Pittsburgh, Pennsylvania, in about 1885. This coloring was used on many types of glassware.

Celery Vase, Pinched Waist, 1800s, 6 In. 135
Cruet, Stopper, Ruffled Lip, 6 In. 50
Pitcher, Peace & Happiness, Etched Flowers, Buildings, Paneled, 9 In. 226
Spooner, Ruffled Square Top, c.1890, 3 ½ In. 150
Vase, Satin, Enameled, Red To White, Flowers, c.1905, 11 In. ....*illus* 500
Vase, Trumpet, Footed, Ruffled Edge, 8 x 5 In. 145

RUBINA VERDE is a Victorian glassware that was shaded from red to green. It was first made by Hobbs, Brockunier and Company of Wheeling, West Virginia, about 1890.

Compote, Figural, Silver Plate, Scalloped Bowl, Victorian, 1890, 11 x 8 In. 240
Umbrella Stand, Cameo, Fuchsia Flower Tendrils, Green, Gold, 24 x 8 In. 4025
Vase, Trumpet Shape, Blue, Green, Peacock Feathers, Scarlet Red, 12 In. 173

RUBY GLASS is the dark red color of a ruby, the precious gemstone. It was a popular Victorian color that never went completely out of style. The glass was shaped by many different processes to make many different types of ruby glass. There was a revival of interest in the 1940s when modern-shaped ruby table glassware became fashionable. Sometimes the red color is added to clear glass by a process called flashing or staining. Flashed glass is clear glass dipped in a colored glass, then pressed or cut. Stained glass has color painted on a clear glass. Then it is refired so the stain fuses with the glass. Pieces of glass colored in this way are indicated by the word *stained* in the description. Related items may be found in other categories, such as Cranberry Glass, Pressed Glass, and Souvenir.

Decanter, Flowers, Stopper, 14 ½ In., Pair 82
Goblet, Male Portrait, Gold Curlicues, Twisted Stem, 6 ¼ In., 6 Piece 118
Pitcher, Etched, Gilt, Leaves, Stopper, 11 ½ x 6 ½ In. 584
Punch Set, Roman Figures, 12 Goblets, 14 Piece 544
Vase, Art Nouveau, Dancing Nudes, Bacchantes, 7 In., Pair 184
Vase, Cornucopia Shape, Gilt Scrollwork, Hanging Prisms, c.1850, 10 x 11 In., Pair 812
Vase, Cut To Clear, Leaves, 8 ½ In. 37
Vase, Enamel, Applied Handles, Ruffled Top, 8 In. 51

RUDOLSTADT was a faience factory in the Thuringia region of Germany from 1720 to about 1791. In 1854, Ernst Bohne began working in the area. From about 1887 to 1918, the New York and Rudolstadt Pottery made decorated porcelain marked with the RW and crown familiar to collectors. This porcelain was imported by Lewis Straus and Sons of New York, which later became Nathan Straus and Sons. The word *Royal* was included in their import mark. Collectors often call it "Royal Rudolstadt." Most pieces found today were made in the late nineteenth or early twentieth century. Additional pieces may be listed in the Kewpie category.

Urn, Cover, Flower Design, Pomegranate Finial, Signed, 19 x 12 In. ....*illus* 950
Vase, Flowers, Blue Ground, Beaded, Oval, Triangular Base, c.1887, 14 In. 275
Vase, Pink, Gold Luster, Woman, Vase On Shoulder, Bottle Shape, Handles, 10 In. 431

RUGS have been used in the American home since the seventeenth century. The oriental rug of that time was often used on a table, not on the floor. Rag rugs, hooked rugs, and braided rugs were made by housewives from scraps of material. American Indian rugs are listed in the Indian category.

Abstract, Shag, Apple Slice Shape, Green, Blue, c.1950, 5 Ft. 5 In. x 3 Ft. 6 In. 238
Afshar, Navy Diamonds, Birds, Shrubs, Red, Ivory, Persia, 5 Ft. 4 In. x 3 Ft. 9 In. 369
After Paul Klee, Drummer Boy, Red, Black, Beige, Wool, 1871, 4 Ft. 4 In. x 2 Ft. 6 In. 544
Art Nouveau, William Morris, Stylized Flowers, Borders, 9 Ft. 6 In. x 7 Ft. 8 In. ....*illus* 800
Aubusson, Fragment, Center Flower, Leaves, Vine Border, 2 Ft. 2 In. x 2 Ft. 615

Aubusson, Medallion, Red Center, Tan, 4 Ft. 3 In. x 5 Ft. 9 In.	380
Aubusson, Rose, Flower Medallion, Scrolling, Tapestry Style, 1900s, 13 x 9 Ft.	236
Aubusson, Rosettes, Leaves, Vines, Peach, Green, Blue, Ivory, 10 Ft. 4 In. x 6 Ft. 9 In.	400
Bakhtiari, Garden Panel, Multicolor, Wool, Cotton, 1900s, 10 Ft. 4 In. x 6 Ft. 9 In.	414
Bakhtiari, Geometric & Abstract Flowers, Persia, 9 Ft. 9 In. x 7 Ft. 8 In.	1076
Bakhtiari, Gold Field, Paisley, Green, Red, Brown, Ivory, c.1890, 3 Ft. 8 In. x 4 Ft. 6 In.	413
Bidjar, Flowers & Medallions, Blue, Red, Tan, c.1900, Kurdish, 5 Ft. 2 In. x 4 Ft. *illus*	1610
Bokhara, Cranberry Color, Stepped Borders, Wool, Persian, 10 Ft. 4 In. x 8 Ft. 3 In.	587
Caucasian, Multicolor, Red Ground, Multiple Borders, c.1920, 2 Ft. 10 In. x 11 Ft. 10 In.	600
Caucasian, Runner, 4 Hooked Edge Medallions, Brown Ground, c.1930, 3 Ft. 9 In. x 8 Ft.	531
Chinese, Hand Knotted, Wool, Art Deco Style, Multicolor, Flowers, Leaves, 9 x 12 Ft. *illus*	2625
Chinese, Urns, Flowers, Cobalt Blue Ground, c.1950, 3 Ft. 11 In. x 6 Ft. 9 In.	177
Chinese, Wool, Green, Lavender, Brick Red, Nichols, Late 1930s, 4 Ft. x 2 Ft. 6 In. *illus*	775
Gabbeh, Blue, Diamonds, Cream, Rose, Tassels, Fringe, Wool, 5 Ft. 6 In. x 2 Ft. 9 In.	124
Gabbeh, Multicolor Geometric & Stylized Animals, Birds, Wool, 6 Ft. 7 In. x 4 Ft. 3 In.	426
Herati, Blue, Repeating Pattern, Cream Border, Linked Border, 10 Ft. 5 In. x 2 Ft. 8 In.	236
Heriz, Brick Red Ground, Blue Border, Iran, c.1910, 9 Ft. 7 In. x 11 Ft. 6 In.	4560
Heriz, Medallion, Red Field, Ivory Corners, Borders, Persia, 9 Ft. 6 In. x 17 Ft. 7 In. *illus*	1185
Heriz, Red Ground, Medallion, Blue, White, Green, Wool, Cotton, 16 Ft. 4 In. x 10 Ft. 7 In.	1003
Hooked, Alpha Epsilon, Multicolor, Wool, After Morris Louis, c.1970, 38 x 79 In.	1875
Hooked, Baby, Dog, Black Border, Flowers, 45 x 35 In.	994
Hooked, Clipper Ship, 3 Masts, Flags, Frame, Gilt Liner, c.1910, 15 x 19 In.	246
Hooked, Drum Shape, Shield, Wool, Cotton, c.1920, 31 x 20 In.	180
Hooked, Flowers, Dimensional Yarn Work, Leaf Border, c.1900, 30 x 60 In.	212
Hooked, Geometric Border, Striped Ground, 2 Spaniels, c.1900, 77 x 40 In.	799
Hooked, Geometric, Flowers, Green Border, 75 x 107 In.	702
Hooked, Green, Mottled & Red Border, Crashing Waves, c.1925, 35 x 47 In.	2091
Hooked, Horse, Brown, Tan, Striated, 40 x 40 In.	1053
Hooked, House, Trees, Fields, Blue, Green, Yellow, 44 x 31½ In.	175
Hooked, Log Cabin, Flower Border, Silk & Wool On Burlap, 1890s, 40 x 48 In.	540
Hooked, Main Street, Maine, Post Office, Grocer, Barber Shop, c.1920, 29 x 44 In. *illus*	351
Hooked, Mat, Polar Bear, Iceberg, Bleached, Rayon, Cotton, Silk Strips, Grenfell, 17 x 24 In.	400
Hooked, Mennonite, Brick Pattern, Wood Stretcher Frame, c.1910, 33½ x 61 In.	142
Hooked, Patriot Figure, Oval, Felt Border, Stars, Cotton Backing, 1900s, 31 x 25 In. *illus*	895
Hooked, Reclining Dog, Purple Striations, Faux Patchwork Rug, 27 x 18 In.	146
Hooked, Seated Dog, Grass, Black Border, 32 x 59 In.	409
Hooked, Spaniels, Fence, Garden, 43 x 23 In.	180
Hooked, Standing Horse, Scalloped & Fenced Border, Flowers, Natural, 44½ x 54 In.	240
Hooked, Trotting Horse, Sun, Tree, Brown, Tan, Orange, Stretcher, c.1900, 30 x 49 In.	3304
Hooked, Urn, Bouquet, Orange Ground, Brown Border, 31 x 17½ In.	204
Hooked, White Ground, Multicolor Flowers, Green Border, Wool, Oval, 1920, 67 x 41 In.	60
Hooked, White Horse Running, Flowers In Corners, c.1900, 25 x 39 In.	510
Hooked, Woman Holding Parasol, Scalloped Oval, Floral Corners, Black Ground, 37 x 25 In.	185
Hooked, Wool, Burlap Backing, House, Path, Flowers, Black Border, Fringe, c.1920, 36 x 60 In. *illus*	119
Hooked, Wreath, Violet Border, 71 x 104 In.	300
India, Hand Knotted, Wool, Vines, Flowers, Black, Beige, Wm. Morris, 10 Ft. x 13 Ft. 10 In. *illus*	1250
Isfahan, Medallion, Segmented, Compass Rose, Palmettes, Wool, Cotton, 11 Ft. x 8 Ft. 2 In.	316
Isfahan, Prayer, Vase, Mihrab, Birds, Arabesques, Silk, Wool, 3 Ft. 2 In. x 2 Ft. 4 In.	546
Karaba, Prayer, Stylized Medallions & Hands, c.1930, 3 Ft. 3 In. x 4 Ft. 3 In. *illus*	540
Kashan, Blue, Scrolling Vines, Flowers, Cream, Pink, Blue, Green, 1900s, 11 Ft. 2 In. x 8 Ft.	856
Kashan, Flowers, Ivory Field, Medallion, Blue, Cream, Green, 13 Ft. 7 In. x 9 Ft. 8 In.	1035
Kashan, Flowers, Leaves, Burgundy, Multiple Borders, Wool, 8 Ft. 3 In. x 5 Ft. 8 In.	240
Kashan, Medallion, Flowers, Red Field, c.1960, 9 Ft. 8 In. x 12 Ft. 9 In.	2360
Kashan, Medallion, Leaves, Cream, Stepped Borders, Wool, 15 Ft. 5 In. x 11 Ft. 8 In.	600
Kayseri, Prayer, Green Mihrab, Red, Green Panels, Silk, Anatolia, c.1900, 3 Ft. 8 In. x 5 Ft.	767
Kazak, Center Medallions, Diamond Shape, Flowers, Teal, Green, Brown, 11 Ft. x 4 Ft. 6 In.	726
Kazak, Cloud Band, Medallions, Red Ground, Quadrupeds, Birds, 1800s, 4 Ft. 4 In. x 7 Ft.	590
Kazak, White Square Medallion, Geometric Borders, 7 Ft. 6 In. x 6 Ft. 3 In.	6250
Kerman, Blue, Red, Gold Medallion, Flowers, Ivory Field, c.1940, 12 Ft. x 19 Ft. 2 In.	1298
Kerman, Ivory Ground, Medallion, Palmettes, Extensions, Borders, 17 Ft. 6 In. x 10 Ft. 8 In.	1553
Kerman, Medallion, Beige, Vines, Fuchsia Spandrels, Persia, 19 Ft. 7 In. x 12 Ft. 8 In.	1845
Kerman, Medallion, Flowers, Cream Ground, Multiple Borders, c.1900, 13 Ft. x 4 Ft. 4 In.	1200
Kilim, Multicolor Floral Bouquets, Garland Border, Fringe, 1900s, 10 Ft. 10 In. x 6 Ft.	177
Kilim, Orange Spirals, Yellow Ground, Wool, Chinese, French Accents, 8 x 10 Ft.	813
Kilim, Red, Blue, Yellow, Anatolian, c.1800, 12 Ft. 7 In. x 5 Ft.	11875

RRP, Jardiniere, Pedestal, Flowers, Green, Brown Glaze, c.1910, 22 In.
$120

Cowan Auctions

RS Prussia, Plate, Pink, Flowers, Green Border, Gilt, 9 In.
$116

Martin Auction Co.

Rubina, Vase, Satin, Enameled, Red To White, Flowers, c.1905, 11 In.
$500

Ruby Lane

R

Rudolstadt, Urn, Cover, Flower Design, Pomegranate Finial, Signed, 19 x 12 In. $950

Ruby Lane

Rug, Art Nouveau, William Morris, Stylized Flowers, Borders, 9 Ft. 6 In. x 7 Ft. 8 In. $800

Neal Auctions

Rug, Bidjar, Flowers & Medallions, Blue, Red, Tan, c.1900, Kurdish, 5 Ft. 2 In. x 4 Ft. $1,610

Cottone Auctions

Kilim, Yellow Clover, Blue Ground, Wool, French Accents, 9 Ft. 2 In. x 11 Ft. 10 In. 938
Kuba Kilim, Embroidered, Indigo, Green, Yellow, Red, White, c.1890, 12 x 6 Ft.......... *illus* 1481
Leopard Print, Einstein Moomjy, 10 Ft. 4 In. x 8 Ft. 8 In. 960
Lillihan, Red Ground, Flowers, Multicolor, Wool, Cotton, 1800s, 11 Ft. 8 In. x 16 Ft. 7 In. 1333
Luri, Paisley Design, Rosettes, Stepped Border, Multicolor, 6 Ft. 7 In. x 3 Ft. 10 In. 523
Luri, Red Ground, Flowering Tree, Blue Border, 1900s, Runner, 9 Ft. 9 In. x 2 Ft. 11 In. 874
Lut Zwieler, 3 Rows, Gold & Blue Octagons, Hooked Diamonds, Austria, 9 Ft. x 6 Ft. 7 In. 615
Mahal, Flower Lattice, Multicolor, Red Ground, Palmette, c.1930, 14 Ft. x 10 Ft. 6 In. 1722
Mahal, Red Ground, Geometric Border, Multicolor, Persia, 9 Ft. 4 In. x 11 Ft. 4 In. .... *illus* 4750
Mahal, Ziegler, Flowers, Blue Ground, Green, Red, Salmon, 1800s, 11 Ft. 8 In. x 17 Ft. 10 In. 3776
Midcentury, Abstract Pattern, Scrolls, Squiggles, Stripes, Multicolor, 4 Ft. 4 In. x 7 Ft. 2 In. 726
Modern, Alexander Calder, Red & Black Circles, Yellow Ground, 1975, 8 x 6 Ft.. 5227
Moroccan, Cross Medallion, Ram's Head, Wool, Cotton, 1900s, 9 Ft. 6 In. x 7 Ft. 7 In. 384
Needlepoint, Girl, Lamb, Flowers, Izella Tessier, Wall Hanging, Quebec, 1920, 59 x 32 In. ..*illus* 450
Oushak, Flowers, Salmon Ground, Green, Gold, Red, c.1900, 9 Ft. 3 In. x 11 Ft. 2 In. 1652
Oushak, Gold Center Medallion, Corners, Red Ground, Serrated Borders, c.1900, 12 x 15 Ft...... 7080
Persian, Black Diamond Center, Shrubs, Birds, Bracket Border, c.1875, 5 Ft. 4 In. x 4 Ft. 615
Persian, Flowers, Blue Ground, Roses, Urns, Leaves, Woven, Silk, 3 Ft. x 5 Ft.......... 847
Persian, Madonna & Child, Wool, Claret Red, 2 Ft. 6 In. x 2 Ft. ....*illus* 1450
Persian, Red Center Panel, Blue Medallion, Cobalt Blue, Tan, 1900s, 8 Ft. 9 In. x 12 Ft. 2 In. 472
Qashqai, Red Ground, Geometric Medallion, Flowers, Animals, Persia, 7 Ft. x 5 Ft. 3 In. 717
Rolakan, Wool, Blue & Cream, Medallions, Sweden, c.1965, 6 Ft. 6 In. x 4 Ft. 6 In. ....*illus* 1000
Rya, Shag Pile, Red Swirl Design, Wool, 5 Ft. 11 In. x 3 Ft. 11 In. 127
Sarouk, Blue Field, Floral Sprays, Palmette, Borders, Persia, c.1920, 19 Ft. 3 In. x 10 Ft.......... 2337
Sarouk, Flower Designs, Rust Ground, Blue Green Border, c.1900, 5 Ft. x 4 Ft. 11 In. 2360
Sarouk, Rose Field Center Panel, Flowers, Navy Ground, 4 Ft. x 6 Ft. 7 In. 413
Sarouk, Urn & Flowers, Burgundy Ground, c.1900, 3 Ft. 2 In. x 4 Ft. 9 In. 1062
Senneh, Diamond Medallion, Ivory Border, Navy Ground, Red, Gold, 4 Ft. 4 In. x 6 Ft. 2 In. 295
Shirvan, Soumak, 3 Blue Medallions, Red Ground, Ivory Borders, 1800s, 4 Ft. 4 In. x 5 Ft. 9 In. 472
Soumak, Runner, Semi-Antique, 5 Ft. x 18 Ft. 5 In. ....*illus* 562
Suzani, Embroidery, Red Flowers, Leaves, White Ground, c.1880, 7 Ft. 6 In. x 5 Ft. 13750
Suzani, Lakai, Embroidery, Red Circles, Leaves, c.1875, 6 Ft. 11 In. x 5 Ft.......... 5625
Turkmen Camel, Wool, Hand Knotted, 1885-1925, 5 Ft. 8½ In. x 2 Ft. 1 In. ....*illus* 1500
Verhen, Concentric Rectangles, Red, Blue, Stylized Flowers, Cotton, 5 Ft. 10 In. x 4 Ft. 7 In. 4000
Wool, Interlocking Diamonds, Edward Fields, 8 Ft. 7 In. x 5 Ft. 5 In. ....*illus* 250
Zanjan, Medallions, Herati Motifs, Multicolor, Leaves, Rosettes, c.1910, 6 Ft. 7 In. x 4 Ft. 3 In. ... 374

RUMRILL POTTERY was designed by George Rumrill of Little Rock, Arkansas. From 1933 to 1938, it was produced by the Red Wing Pottery of Red Wing, Minnesota. In January 1938, production was transferred to the Shawnee Pottery in Zanesville, Ohio. It was moved again in December of 1938 to Florence Pottery Company in Mt. Gilead, Ohio, where Rumrill ware continued to be manufactured until the pottery burned in 1941. It was then produced by Gonder Ceramic Arts in South Zanesville until early 1943.

RumRill

Bowl, Console, Looping Scroll Handles, Pink Matte Glaze, 6 x 11 In. 95
Bowl, Console, Pink Matte Glaze, Scroll Handles, 1935, 6 x 5 In. ....*illus* 79
Dish, Trumpet Flower, White Matte Glaze, 8 x 5¾ In. 76
Ewer, White Matte Glaze, Ribbed Handle & Spout, 9 In. 25
Jardiniere, Cranes, Cattails, Green, c.1920, 5½ x 8 In. 85
Urn, Deco Style, Yellow, Scroll Handles, 7 In. 80
Vase, Nude, Dancing, Art Deco, Rust Over Green, Handles, 7½ In. 422
Vase, Purple, Mottled, Ribbed, 2 Handles, 6¾ In. 50
Vase, Quatrefoil, Flaring Rim, Pink Matte Glaze, c.1937, 6½ In. 55
Vase, Scalloped, Flared, Leaf & Grape, 12 In. 65

RUSKIN is a British art pottery of the twentieth century. The Ruskin Pottery was started by William Howson Taylor, and his name was used as the mark until about 1899. The factory, at West Smethwick, Birmingham, England, stopped making new pieces in 1933 but continued to glaze and sell the remaining wares until 1935. The art pottery is noted for its exceptional glazes.

RUSKIN POTTERY WEST SMETHWICK

Bowl, Merging Blue & Yellow Crystalline Glaze, 1927, 8 In. 107
Plate, Green Souffle Glaze, 8¼ In. 66
Vase, Blue, Yellow, 5½ In. 79
Vase, Multicolor, Round Foot, 1913, 10¼ In. 857
Vase, Oxblood Glaze, Mottled, Stamped, 1926, 14 x 7 In. ....*illus* 3250
Vase, Yellow Pearlware Luster, 1920, 10 In. 225

R

Rug, Chinese, Hand Knotted, Wool, Art Deco Style, Multicolor, Flowers, Leaves, 9 x 12 Ft.
$2,625

Rago Arts and Auction Center

Rug, Chinese, Wool, Green, Lavender, Brick Red, Nichols, Late 1930s, 4 Ft. x 2 Ft. 6 In.
$775

Ruby Lane

Rug, Heriz, Medallion, Red Field, Ivory Corners, Borders, Persia, 9 Ft. 6 In. x 17 Ft. 7 In.
$1,185

James D. Julia Auctioneers

Rug, Hooked, Main Street, Maine, Post Office, Grocer, Barber Shop, c.1920, 29 x 44 In.
$351

Thomaston Place Auction

Rug, Hooked, Patriot Figure, Oval, Felt Border, Stars, Cotton Backing, 1900s, 31 x 25 In.
$895

Ruby Lane

Rug, Hooked, Wool, Burlap Backing, House, Path, Flowers, Black Border, Fringe, c.1920, 36 x 60 In.
$119

Ruby Lane

Orientals on the Wall
There is a modern safe way to hang an antique Oriental rug on the wall. Put a strip of 2-inch-wide Velcro on a strip of wood. Mount the wood on the wall. Hang the rug directly on the Velcro. The rug will stay in place and can be pulled loose to be cleaned.

Rug, India, Hand Knotted, Wool, Vines, Flowers, Black, Beige, Wm. Morris, 10 Ft. x 13 Ft. 10 In.
$1,250

Rago Arts and Auction Center

Rug, Karaba, Prayer, Stylized Medallions & Hands, c.1930, 3 Ft. 3 In. x 4 Ft. 3 In.
$540

Garth's Auctioneers & Appraisers

Rug, Kuba Kilim, Embroidered, Indigo, Green, Yellow, Red, White, c.1890, 12 x 6 Ft.
$1,481

James D. Julia Auctioneers

Rug, Mahal, Red Ground, Geometric Border, Multicolor, Persia, 9 Ft. 4 In. x 11 Ft. 4 In.
$4,750

New Orleans (Cakebread)

Rug, Needlepoint, Girl, Lamb, Flowers, Izella Tessier, Wall Hanging, Quebec, 1920, 59 x 32 In.
$450

Ruby Lane

Rug, Persian, Madonna & Child, Wool, Claret Red, 2 Ft. 6 In. x 2 Ft.
$1,450

Ruby Lane

Rug, Rolakan, Wool, Blue & Cream, Medallions, Sweden, c.1965, 6 Ft. 6 In. x 4 Ft. 6 In.
$1,000

Rago Arts and Auction Center

Rug, Soumak, Runner, Semi-Antique, 5 Ft. x 18 Ft. 5 In.
$562

New Orleans (Cakebread)

Rug, Turkmen Camel, Wool, Hand Knotted, 1885-1925, 5 Ft. 8 ½ In. x 2 Ft. 1 In.
$1,500

Ruby Lane

Rug, Wool, Interlocking Diamonds, Edward Fields, 8 Ft. 7 In. x 5 Ft. 5 In.
$250

Palm Beach Modern Auctions

TIP

Be sure your rug is clean before you store it. It is best to have light in the room to discourage moths. Be sure there is no excess humidity or extreme heat or cold. Don't use the garage or attic. Roll or fold it, and put the roll flat on the shelf, not standing up or leaning. Do not stack rugs on top of each other. Open the rug bundle once a year and put it flat in natural light for a few days.

R

RUSSEL WRIGHT designed dinnerware in modern shapes for many companies. Iroquois China Company, Harker China Company, Steubenville Pottery, and Justin Tharaud and Sons made dishes marked *Russel Wright.* The Steubenville wares, first made in 1938, are the most common today. Wright was a designer of domestic and industrial wares, including furniture, aluminum, radios, interiors, and glassware. A new company, Bauer Pottery Company of Los Angeles, is making Russel Wright's American Modern dishes using molds made from original pieces. The pottery is made in Highland, California. Pieces are marked *Russel Wright by Bauer Pottery California USA* . Russel Wright Dinnerware and other original pieces by Wright are listed here. For more prices, go to kovels.com.

Russel Wright MFG. BY STEUBENVILLE

American Modern, Bowl, Vegetable, Divided, Cedar, 14 x 10 In. 95
American Modern, Plate, Black Chutney, 10 x 12 In. 75
Apricot, Sauceboat, Lid, Handle, 6 In. 245
Avocado, Coffeepot, Lid, 5 In. 175
Avocado, Pitcher, Ball Shape, 1½ Qt. 115
Bean Brown, Casserole, Lid, 1 Qt. 138
Bookends, Moaninio, Nickel Plated, Metal, c.1930, 4¾ x 7 In. .... *illus* 7500
Iroquois Casual, Coffeepot, Parsley, 5 In. 150
Pink Sherbet, Butter, 8 x 4 In. 85

SABINO glass was made in the 1920s and 1930s in Paris, France. Founded by Marius-Ernest Sabino (1878–1961), the firm was noted for Art Deco lamps, vases, figurines, and animals in clear, colored, and opalescent glass. Production stopped during World War II but resumed in the 1960s with the manufacture of nude figurines and small opalescent glass animals. Pieces made in recent years are a slightly different color and can be recognized. Only vintage pieces are listed here.

Sabino France

Figurine, Poisson Saint George, Opalescent, Raised Mark, 4¼ x 4½ In. .... *illus* 150
Perfume Bottle, Opalescent Glass, Atomizer, 5½ In. 120
Vase, Opalescent, Square Base, Applied Shell Shapes, Tapered, 5 In. 180

SALOPIAN ware was made by the Caughley factory of England during the eighteenth century. The early pieces were blue and white with some colored decorations. Another ware referred to as Salopian is a late nineteenth-century tableware decorated with color transfers.

Salopian

Bowl, Cottage, Stag, Yellow, Green, Soft Paste, 3 x 6⅜ In. 272
Bowl, Stag & Cottage, Soft Paste, 3 x 6⅜ In. 266
Cup & Saucer, Cottage, Yellow, Green, Soft Paste, 5½ In. 60
Cup & Saucer, Milkmaid, Soft Paste, 5⅜ In. .... 153 to 157
Cup & Saucer, Multicolor, c.1810, 5½ In. .... *illus* 118

SALT AND PEPPER SHAKERS in matched sets were first used in the nineteenth century. Collectors are primarily interested in figural examples made after World War I. Huggers are pairs of shakers that appear to embrace each other. Many salt and pepper shakers are listed in other categories and can be located through the index at the back of this book.

Bear, Holding Shakers, Dee Beeb, Hong Kong, 6 x 4 In. .... *illus* 12
Bears, Huggers, Marked, Van Tellingen, Pat. Pending, 3 In. .... *illus* 30
Bell, Violets, Gold Handle, Norcrest 35
Birds, Yellow Wings, Clear Stem Bases, 4¾ In. 30
Dean Martin, Jerry Lewis, Heads, Napco Ceramics, 1950s, 3½ In. 115
Desk & Typewriter, 1980, Desk 4 x 2 In., Typewriter 2 x 2½ In. .... *illus* 16
Dog & Cat, Brown & Yellow Gingham, Brayton Laguna Pottery 25
Ears Of Corn, Japan, 8½ x 1½ In. .... *illus* 8
Elephant, Sitting, Trunk Up, Crystal, Gorham, 2 In. 15
Felix The Cat, Figural, Black & White, Ceramic, Germany, c.1920, 3 In. 115
Geisha, Red, Green, 3⅛ In. 28
Glass, Mother-Of-Pearl Lid, Engraved, c.1910, 3¼ In. 10
Goldtone & White, Square, 3 x 1 x 1 In. 45
Milk Glass, Black Aluminum Top & Letters, Hazel Glass, 4½ In. 49
Orange, Yellow Flowers, Ribbed, Gilt Top, Footed, Japan, 4 In. 28
Pagoda, Tiered, Hexagonal Base, Sterling Silver, c.1930, 2½ In. 118
Porcelain, Embossed, 6-Sided, Flared Base, Gold, c.1925, 4¾ In. 129
Shadowleaf, Green, Wallace China, 1950s, 3¾ In. 550
Silver Plate, Mountain Scene, Engraved, Japanese Comb Shape, c.1920, 2 x 1⅛ In. 295
Silver Plate, Owl, Figural, Gold Wash, Continental, 1900s, 2¾ x ¼ In. 847
Southwest Indians, Canoe, 7 x 3 In. 12

American Modern

American Modern dinnerware designed by Russel Wright (1905–76) was made by Steubenville Pottery Company, Steubenville, Ohio, from 1939 to 1959. In the 1950s, American Modern outsold all other dinnerware patterns in the United States. It was made in unfamiliar colors—muted tones called Seafoam Blue, Cedar Green, and Chutney. The dinner plate has no rim, the celery dish is a curved free-form, and the cups turn in at the rim.

Rumrill, Bowl, Console, Pink Matte Glaze, Scroll Handles, 1935, 6 x 5 In.
$79

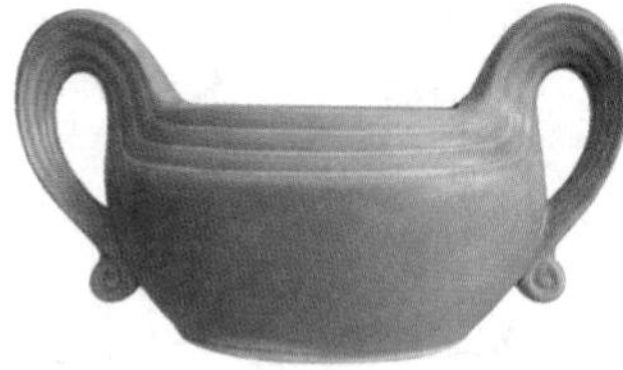

Ruby Lane

Ruskin, Vase, Oxblood Glaze, Mottled, Stamped, 1926, 14 x 7 In.
$3,250

Rago Arts and Auction Center

Russel Wright, Bookends, Moaninio, Nickel Plated, Metal, c.1930, 4¾ x 7 In.
$7,500

Rago Arts and Auction Center

Sabino, Figurine, Poisson Saint George, Opalescent, Raised Mark, 4 ¼ x 4 ½ In.
$150

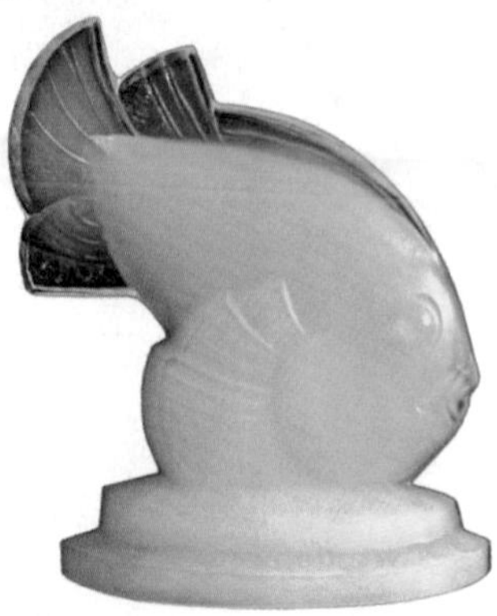

Ruby Lane

Salopian, Cup & Saucer, Multicolor, c.1810, 5 ½ In.
$118

Hess Auction Group

Salt & Pepper, Bear, Holding Shakers, Dee Beeb, Hong Kong, 6 x 4 In.
$12

TIP

Be sure to remove salt and pepper from shakers and dishes after use. Wash, then store.

Strawberry, Leaf Base, Red, Green, Ceramic, Cork Stopper, 1950s, 3 x 3 In. 12
Tiger Shark, Brown & Black, Ceramic, Japan, c.1970, 4¾ x 1 ½ In. 23
Tiger, Pink, Green, Patchwork, Cork Stopper, Napco, 2 ½ In. 15
Turkey, Multicolor, Japan, 1950s, 4 x 3 In. 8
Vegetables, Celery, Leek, Cabbage, Pepper, On Tomato Base, 5 Piece .... *illus* 20

SAMPLERS were made in America from the early 1700s. The best examples were made from 1790 to 1840. Long, narrow samplers are usually older than square ones. Early samplers just had stitching or alphabets. The later examples had numerals, borders, and pictorial decorations. Those with mottoes are mid-Victorian. A revival of interest in the 1930s produced simpler samplers, usually with mottoes.

ABCDE

Alphabet, Animals, Geometrics, Rebecca McConnell, Shippensburgh, 1807, 19 x 16 In. 250
Alphabet, Birds, Fruit Baskets, Sarah Stubbs Aldoth, Silk On Linen, 1811, 14 x 11 In. 300
Alphabet, Friendship, Joanna & Phillip Forever, Cross, Holland, 23 x 20 In. 120
Alphabet, Mary Jenkins, 1833, 12 ½ x 17 In. 72
Alphabet, Numbers, Bow, Flowers, Ruth Somerby, Silk On Linen, Newburyport, c.1803, 16 In. .. 738
Alphabet, Verse In Wreath, Urns, Cornucopia, Vine Border, Lydia Haines, 1826, Frame, 17 In. ... 1500
Alphabet, Verse, Border Design, Maple Frame, Rachel Furness, 1796, 16 ½ x 10 In. 420
Alphabet, Verse, Flowers, Ester Banks, 1828, 21 ½ x 16 ½ In. 409
Alphabet, Verse, Sarah Ann Stevenson, Kesgrave School, 1847, Silk, Wool, 14 In. .... *illus* 188
Alphabet, Verse, Urn, House With Fence, Eliza Shotwell, 1833, 16 x 14 In. 570
Family Crest, Red, Black, Cream, Marie Schulze, 1877, 16 x 14 ½ In. 132
Family Record, Flower Vine Border, Jacob & Gertrude Polhemus, Silk, 1802, 23 x 20 In. 780
Needlework, Female Arts In Usefulness, Needle Far Exceeds, Abigail Whitney, 1832, 17 x 12 In. 861
Pictorial, Alphabet, Flowers, Vines, Isabella Duncan, 1848, 15 ¼ x 12 ½ In. 780
Pictorial, Alphabet, Tree, Man, Woman, Line Border, Elisabeth Andrews, 1784, 16 x 11 In. 2880
Pictorial, House, Fence, Trees, Butterflies, Ann Jane Mazey, Aged 11, 1836, Wool, 18 x 14 In. 780
Pictorial, House, Peacocks, Miss Playfair Teacher Longforgan, Wool, Linen, 1840, 17 x 18 In. .. 531
Pictorial, Manse, Cricket Player, Caroline Martin, 1760, 17 x 12 ½ In. 1230
Pictorial, Map Of England, Schoolgirl, Vine Border, Ann Peach, Silk, c.1800, 18 x 17 In. .... *illus* 240
Verse, Adam & Eve, 2 Black Ships, Elizabeth Gill, Aged 12, 1821, Linen, 18 x 16 In. 500
Verse, Adam & Eve, Ann Robson, 1812, 25 x 19 ½ In. 409
Verse, Brick House, Pond, Swans, Dogs, Couple, Thank You To Uncle, Silk, 1816, 19 x 16 In. 600
Verse, Church, Tree, Adam & Eve, Serpents, Vine Border, Mary Hopley, 1840, 18 x 21 In. 492
Verse, Crown, Swans, Trees, N. Howell, 1858, Frame, 18 ¼ x 12 ½ In. 410
Verse, Crowns, Vine Border, Cherubs, Castle Tower, Urns, Mary Ann Clark, 1804, 16 x 12 In. 215
Verse, Flower Border, Angels, Birds, Sarah Potter, 1784, Silk On Wool, 20 x 15 In. 438
Verse, Flowers, Animals, Eliza Osborn, 1820, 15 x 12 In. 351
Verse, Hannah Catherine Crabb, 1823, Silk On Linen, 17 x 13 In. 330
Verse, Motto, Vines, Trellis, Trees, Birds, Flowers, Sarah Brown, 1824, 16 x 19 In. 472
Verse, Red Flowers, Boats, Trees, Mary Brearley, 1839, 16 x 17 In. 400
Verse, Religious, Roses, Animals, Children, Sarah Till, Aged 13, Frame, 1871, 27 x 28 In. .... *illus* 1424
Verse, Stars, Hearts, Diamonds, Candelabrum, New Jersey, 12 x 12 In. 518
Verse, Trees, Flowers, House, Sarah Roberts, 1819, 16 ½ x 13 In. 338

SAMSON and Company, a French firm specializing in the reproduction of collectible wares of many countries and periods, was founded in Paris in the early nineteenth century. Chelsea, Meissen, Famille Verte, and Chinese Export porcelain are some of the wares that have been reproduced by the company. The firm used a variety of marks on the reproductions. It closed in 1969.

Dish, Shell Shape, Faux Armorial, Scalloped, Ribbed Interior, Flowers, c.1900, 14 x 11 In. 136
Mug, Armorial, Multicolor Enamels, Flowers, Spear Shape Border, 1800s, 5 ½ In. 89
Plate, Armorial, Serpentine Rim, Puce Scale, Cartouche, Flowers, 9 In., Pair 178
Plate, Armorial, Serpentine Rim, Reticulated, Bellflower Garlands, Multicolor, 9 ½ In., Pair.......... 184
Tureen, Lid, Multicolor Flower Bouquets, Fluted, Embossed Lattice Border, 9 x 13 In. 71
Vase, Cupid & Maiden, Woodland, Sevres Style, 17 x 8 In. .... *illus* 2159

SANDWICH GLASS is any of the myriad types of glass made by the Boston & Sandwich Glass Company of Sandwich, Massachusetts, between 1825 and 1888. It is often very difficult to be sure whether a piece was really made at the Sandwich factory because so many types were made there and similar pieces were made at other glass factories. Additional pieces may be listed under Pressed Glass and in other related categories.

Candlestick, Columnar, Blue Socket, Clambroth Hexagonal Base, 7 ½ In., Pair.......... 185
Candlestick, Dolphin, Blue Ruffled Socket, Opaque White Square Base, 10 In., Pair 1968
Candlestick, No-Eyed Dolphin, Lemon Yellow, Square Stepped Base, 10 ¼ In., Pair.......... 492

Candlestick, Opalescent, Petal Socket, Hexagonal Base, 7 ⅜ In., Pair 400
Candlestick, Petal & Loop, Peacock Blue, 7 In., Pair 492
Candlestick, Yellow, Hexagonal, c.1850, 9 In., Pair .... *illus* 677
Cologne Bottle, Blown Molded, Diamond Point, Translucent Blue, c.1840, 6 ½ In. 354
Cologne Bottle, Star & Punty, Yellow Green, 6-Sided, Stopper, c.1850, 6 ⅝ In. 308
Lamp, Oil, Acanthus Leaf, Blue Font, Clambroth Stepped Base, 12 ⅜ In., Pair 523
Lamp, Oil, Octagonal Baluster Stem, Square Base, Amethyst, c.1850, 9 In. 480
Pitcher, Free-Blown, Black Globular Base, Lime Green Loop Design, 11 In. 3437
Vase, Tulip, Dark Blue, Octagonal Foot, 9 ⅞ In., Pair 3690
Vase, Tulip, Marbleized Blue, 8 Panels, Octagonal Foot, Scalloped Rim, 10 In., Pair 23370
Vase, Twisted Loop, Amethyst, Octagonal Stem, Ruffled Rim, Square Base, 10 ½ In. 492

SARREGUEMINES is the name of a French town that is used as part of a china mark. Utzschneider and Company, a porcelain factory, made ceramics in Sarreguemines, Lorraine, France, from about 1775. Transfer-printed wares and majolica were made in the nineteenth century. The nineteenth-century pieces, most often found today, usually have colorful transfer-printed decorations showing peasants in local costumes.

Bowl, Cobalt Blue, Gilt Bronze, Maidens, Claw Feet, Majolica, 1800s, 9 ½ x 26 In. .... *illus* 5843
Bowl, Grape Leaves, Vines, Clusters, Notched Rim, Green, Majolica, 12 In. 196
Fountain, Spout, Bowl, Multicolor, Shell Shape, 3 Piece 1180
Jardiniere, Double Ducks, Face To Face, Multicolor, 1880, 9 x 22 In. 522
Pitcher, Begging Dog, White, Gray, 9 x 6 ½ In. 42
Pitcher, Tan, Flat Ring, Round Foot, 8 ⅜ In. 250
Plaque, Partridges, Grasses, Cobalt Blue Ground, Oval, Leaf Handles, 24 x 16 In. 4428
Plate, Dessert, Grapevines, Notched Rim, Green, Majolica, 7 ¾ In., 4 Piece 120
Stein, No. 2784, Munich Child, Verse, Relief, Tree Trunk Handle, 1 Liter .... *illus* 660
Tobacco Jar, Rickshaw, Chinese Man, European Woman, Shaped Lid, 1875 1107

SASCHA BRASTOFF made decorative accessories, ceramics, enamels on copper, and plastics of his own design. He headed a factory, Sascha Brastoff of California, Inc., in West Los Angeles, from 1953 until about 1973. He died in 1993. Pieces signed with the signature *Sascha Brastoff* were his work and are the most expensive. Other pieces marked *Sascha B.* or with a stamped mark were made by others in his company. Pieces made by Matt Adams after he left the factory are listed here with his name.

Ashtray, Inuit Alaskan Home On Stilts, 3-Footed, 3 x 5 ¾ In. 39
Dish, Abstract, Gloss, Purple, Green, Gold, Rounded Triangle Shape, 9 ½ In. 12
Figurine, Polar Bears, Kissing, Green, Resin, 10 In., 2 Piece 36
Pipe, Rooftops, White, Blue, Green, Gold, 1953-62, 4 ¼ In. 35
Plate, 2 Igloos, Mountains, 8 In. 34
Tray, Enamel On Copper, Blue, Berries, 14 In. 30

SATIN GLASS is a late nineteenth-century art glass. It has a dull finish that is caused by hydrofluoric acid vapor treatment. Satin glass was made in many colors and sometimes has applied decorations. Satin glass is also listed by factory name, such as Webb, or in the Mother-of-Pearl category in this book.

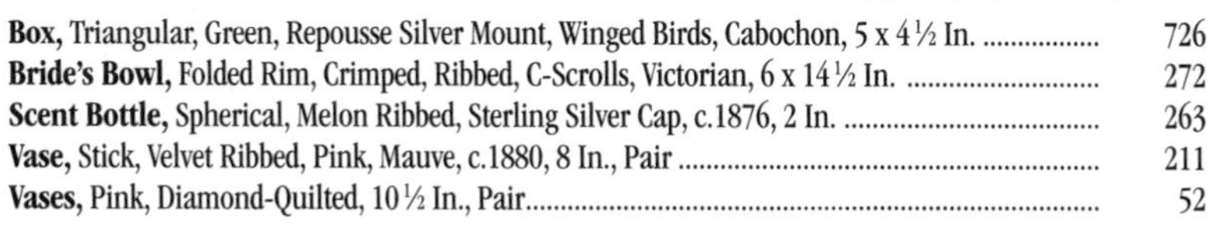

Box, Triangular, Green, Repousse Silver Mount, Winged Birds, Cabochon, 5 x 4 ½ In. 726
Bride's Bowl, Folded Rim, Crimped, Ribbed, C-Scrolls, Victorian, 6 x 14 ½ In. 272
Scent Bottle, Spherical, Melon Ribbed, Sterling Silver Cap, c.1876, 2 In. 263
Vase, Stick, Velvet Ribbed, Pink, Mauve, c.1880, 8 In., Pair 211
Vases, Pink, Diamond-Quilted, 10 ½ In., Pair 52

SATSUMA is a Japanese pottery with a distinctive creamy beige crackled glaze. Most of the pieces were decorated with blue, red, green, orange, or gold. Almost all Satsuma found today was made after 1860, especially during the Meiji Period, 1868–1912. During World War I, Americans could not buy undecorated European porcelains. Women who liked to make hand-painted porcelains at home began to decorate plain Satsuma. These pieces are known today as "American Satsuma."

Bowl, Figural Panels, Painted, Footed Wood Stand, c.1890, 10 x 5 ½ In. .... *illus* 2706
Bowl, Gilt, 4 People, Landscape, 2 x 11 In. 126
Bowl, Gilt, Buddhist Imagery, Signed Hododa, c.1900, 4 x 9 ½ In. 300
Bowl, Group, Landscape, Red, Purple, 4 ¾ x 11 In. 960
Bowl, Scalloped Edge, Crane Pattern, Gilded Clouds, 15 ½ x 6 ½ In. 909
Box, Samurai, Children, Landscape, Cartouches, Bands, Japan, 2 ½ x 2 ½ In. 308
Censer, Squat, Round, Enamels, Gilt, 2 Cartouches, Birds, Plum Blossom, 4 ¾ In. 492

Salt & Pepper, Bears, Huggers, Marked, Van Tellingen, Pat. Pending, 3 In.
$30

Salt & Pepper, Desk & Typewriter, 1980, Desk 4 x 2 In., Typewriter 2 x 2 ½ In.
$16

Salt & Pepper, Ears Of Corn, Japan, 8 ½ x 1 ½ In.
$8

Salt & Pepper, Vegetables, Celery, Leek, Cabbage, Pepper, On Tomato Base, 5 Piece
$20

S

Sampler, Alphabet, Verse, Sarah Ann Stevenson, Kesgrave School, 1847, Silk, Wool, 14 In.
$188

Garth's Auctioneers & Appraisers

Sampler, Pictorial, Map Of England, Schoolgirl, Vine Border, Ann Peach, Silk, c.1800, 18 x 17 In.
$240

Cowan Auctions

Sampler, Verse, Religious, Roses, Animals, Children, Sarah Till, Aged 13, Frame, 1871, 27 x 28 In.
$1,424

Ruby Lane

TIP

If you store fabrics in paper, be sure it is acid-free. An acidic paper can discolor a fabric in a year, damage it within three years.

Charger, Heavenly Figures, Raised Gold Accents, Fans, Flowers, 1800s, 12 In. ... 120
Charger, People, Landscape, Town, Gold, Tan, Multicolor, 12 In. ... 978
Charger, Round, Flowering Branches, Gold Border At Rim, 15 In. Diam. ... 500
Dish, Sage, Sitting, Animal Skin, Plants, Crane, Scholar's Rock, 11 In. ... 153
Flask, Moon, Figures, Landscape, Bamboo, Foo Dog Handles, c.1900, 11 x 8 In. ... *illus* 2645
Flask, Pilgrim, Geisha, Cherry Blossoms, Gold Border, Saucer Foot, c.1900, 12 In. ... *illus* 10980
Ginger Jar, Wire Lid, Gilt, Flowers, Leaves, Enamel, 6 x 5 In. ... 390
Jar, Woman, Lid, 6 ½ In. ... 86
Jardiniere, Gilt, Bronze Mounted, Dragon Handles, 4-Footed, 13 ½ x 15 In. ... 1107
Plate, Landscape, Figures, Bridge, Cream, Gilt, 1800s, 9 ½ In. Diam. ... 153
Plate, Leaves, Birds, Multicolor, 10 ⅛ In. ... 108
Vase, Birds, Branches, Blossoms, Gilt, Japan, 10 x 5 ½ In. ... 177
Vase, Bottle, Flowering Trees, Phoenixes, Wave, 5 ⅞ In. ... 185
Vase, Chatting Men, Hairy Chest, Teapot, Dragons, Calligraphy, 14 ½ In. ... 2250
Vase, Court & Religious Scenes, Marked, Royal Satsuma Cross, 5 In. ... *illus* 180
Vase, Cylindrical, Slight Spread, Millefiori, Figures, Lakeside Pavilion, 9 ½ In. ... 214
Vase, Double Gourd, Applied Rope, Bow, Gilt, Enamel, Scholars, Children, Japan, 15 ¼ In. ... 369
Vase, Figural Decorations, Phoenix, Marked, 1890, 3 ½ In. ... 90
Vase, Hexagonal, Tapered, Medallions, Figures, Landscapes, 12 In. ... 240
Vase, Landscape, Temple, Beige, Pink, Purple, Red, Pattern On Shoulders, 6 In., Pair ... 123
Vase, Multicolor, Gilt Outlines, Flowers, Recessed Foot, Red Ground, 7 ½ In. ... 319
Vase, Oval, Rolled Rim, Wood Base, Woman, Landscape, Black & Gold, 16 In. ... 244
Vase, Round, Tapered, Rolled Rim, Saucer Foot, Seated Man, Landscape, c.1900, 12 In. ... 122
Vase, Squat, Broad Shoulders, Pinched Neck, Flowers, Lappet Banding, 8 In. ... 194
Vase, Tapered, Shouldered, Trumpet Neck, Wavy Rim, Figures, 1800s, 19 In., Pair ... 244
Vase, Wisteria Blossoms, Leaves, White Ground, 7 ½ x 3 In. ... 240

SATURDAY EVENING GIRLS, *see Paul Revere Pottery category.*

SCALES have been made to weigh everything from babies to gold. Collectors search for all types. Most popular are small gold dust scales and special grocery scales.

Balance, Apothecary, Brass, Oak & Glass Case, Marble Base, 18 x 14 In. ... 120
Balance, Brass, Marble, 24 x 23 In. ... 240
Balance, Dodge Scale Co., Micrometer, Nickel, Marble Base, Plaque, 12 In. ... 976
Balance, J.A.L., Turned Support, Fleur-De-Lis Base, Portugal, 1800s, 23 In. ... 130
Balance, Kaufman Lattimer, Metal & Glass Case, Laboratory Equipment, 1950s, 20 x 20 In. ... 90
Balance, Marble Top, Level Gauge, Brass Weights, Oak Casing, 21 In. ... 188
Balance, Micrometer, Iron, Green Paint, Steel Screw Rod, Brass Tray & Plate, Yonkers, 16 In. ... 720
Balance, Pharmacy, Henry Troemner, Wood & Glass Case, Footed, Hinged Lid, 9 x 13 In. ... 180
Balance, Turnbull's Patent, Iron, Round Brass Dial, White Marble Tray, June 2, 1874, 24 In. ... 240
Balance, Village Dairy Co., Avery Of England, Cast Iron, Weights, Blue, 14 x 9 In. ... 210
Balance, Wood, Brass, Glass Tray, Computing Scale Co., Money Weight, 36 In. ... 600
Butcher's, Iron Cow, Scroll, Marble Platform, c.1900, 22 x 16 In. ... 360
Candy, Dayton No. 166, Beige, Decals, Scoop, 15 In. ... 730
Candy, Hobart, Fan, Scope, White Porcelain, 11 In. ... 90
Candy, Imperial Confectioners, 10 ½ In. ... 90
Candy, National, Porcelain, Fan Shape, Shield Logo, Enameled, 9 x 10 In. ... *illus* 976
Candy, Penny, Ives, Cast Iron, Girl, Basket In Lap, Seated Boy Center, Woven Basket, 9 In. ... 3088
Candy, Stimpson, Model 40, Green, Pinstriped, Brass, 16 x 16 In. ... 1220
Coin, Hanson, 1 Cent, 5 Cents, Carrying Case, Scoop, Sacks, 14 x 13 In. ... 90
Computing, Dayton, Cast Iron, Brass Trim, Glass Platform, 32 x 18 ¾ In. ... 544
Computing, Dayton, Fan Design, Full Weight & Correct Charge, Green Metal, 30 x 27 In. ... 741
Computing, Dayton, Iron Frame, Brass Beam, Pan & Plaque, c.1895, 15 x 26 In. ... 420
Egg, Farm Master, Screw, Leveling Device, Jiffy-Way Inc., Minn., 1940s, 5 ½ x 8 x 3 In. ... *illus* 55
Hanging, Brass, Copper, 3 Chains ... 49
Lollipop, Toledo Scale Co., White Cast Iron, Purse Stand, Brass Platform ... 2419
Pharmacy, Griffin & George Ltd., Brass, Shadowbox, Sliding Front Panel, 16 x 18 In. ... 342
Platform, Buffalo, Gilt Metal Beam, Iron, c.1890, 57 ½ x 19 In. ... 302
Store, National Store Specialty Co., Green, Scrolling Flowers, Footed, 10 x 12 In. ... 270
Store, Red Cast Iron, Gold Pinstripes, Howe, Brass Beams & Weights, 24 x 9 In. ... 90
Weighing, Chas. Forschner & Sons, Hanging, Iron, Brass, Wood Tray, Holds 30 Lb., 1912, 32 In. ... 120
Weighing, Floor, 1 Cent, Your Correct Weight For One Cent, Embossed, Keys, 72 In. ... 780
Weighing, Lollipop, Round Dial, Mirror Front, Chayney & Co., Green, Porcelain, 18 x 31 In. ... 120
Weighing, National Novelty Co., Floor, Cast Iron, Leaf Design, 5 Cents, Top Sign, Black, 68 In. .. 915
Weighing, National Scale & Hardware Co., Cast Iron, Lancaster, Pa., 28 x 28 In. ... 94

Samson, Vase, Cupid & Maiden, Woodland, Sevres Style, 17 x 8 In.
$2,159

Ruby Lane

Sandwich Glass, Candlestick, Yellow, Hexagonal, c.1850, 9 In., Pair
$677

Skinner, Inc.

Sarreguemines, Bowl, Cobalt Blue, Gilt Bronze, Maidens, Claw Feet, Majolica, 1800s, 9 ½ x 26 In.
$5,843

Skinner, Inc.

Sarreguemines, Stein, No. 2784, Munich Child, Verse, Relief, Tree Trunk Handle, 1 Liter
$660

Fox Auctions

Satsuma, Bowl, Figural Panels, Painted, Footed Wood Stand, c.1890, 10 x 5 ½ In.
$2,706

Neal Auctions

Satsuma, Flask, Moon, Figures, Landscape, Bamboo, Foo Dog Handles, c.1900, 11 x 8 In.
$2,645

Cottone Auctions

Broken Dishes

The French term for a mosaic made from broken dishes is *pique assiette.* The term is also used by English-speaking artists.

Satsuma, Flask, Pilgrim, Geisha, Cherry Blossoms, Gold Border, Saucer Foot, c.1900, 12 In.
$10,980

DuMouchelles Art Gallery

Satsuma, Vase, Court & Religious Scenes, Marked, Royal Satsuma Cross, 5 In.
$180

Cowan Auctions

Scale, Candy, National, Porcelain, Fan Shape, Shield Logo, Enameled, 9 x 10 In. $976

Morphy Auctions

Scale, Egg, Farm Master, Screw, Leveling Device, Jiffy-Way Inc., Minn., 1940s, 5 ½ x 8 x 3 In. $55

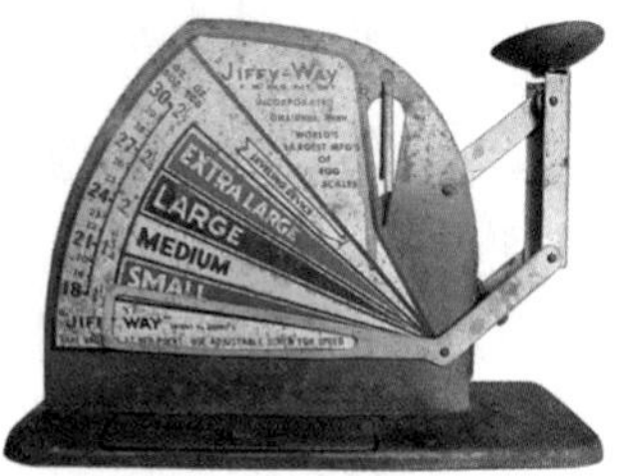

Ruby Lane

Scheier, Vase, Brown Glaze, Incised Pre-Columbian Style Figures, Fish, Marked, c.1955, 21 In. $3,075

Skinner, Inc.

TIP

Big dogs seem scary, but small dogs bark more. It's the bark that discourages a burglar.

Weighing, Nursery, Hanson Pediatric, Stork & Baby, Dial, White, 12 In. 30
Weighing, Peerless, Floor, Iron, Porcelain, Watch Your Weight & Keep Healthy, 16 x 69 In. 1440
Weighing, Watling, Porcelain, Lollipop, Floor, Brown & White, Porcelain, 71 In. 4270
Weight Set, Brass, Bell Shape, Open Handles, Graduated Size, ¼ Oz. To 7 Lb., 9 Piece 472

SCHAFER & VATER, makers of small ceramic items, are best known for their amusing figurals. The factory was located in Volkstedt-Rudolstadt, Germany, from 1890 to 1962. Some pieces are marked with the crown and *R* mark, but many are unmarked.

Bottle, Figural, A Wee Scotch, Baby Drinking Out Of Bottle, 4 ½ In. 98
Bottle, Figural, Bagpiper, A Little Scotch, 8 In. 155
Bottle, Figural, Flapper Girl, Holding Bottle & Glass, Porcelain, 6 ½ In. 225
Bottle, Figural, Nip, Baseball Player, Multicolor, c.1900, 4 ½ In. 135
Decanter Set, Decanter, 4 Cups, Tray, Dutch Man, Happy, Sad Faces, 6 Piece 233
Decanter Set, Decanter, 4 Cups, Tray, Skeleton, Poison, Brown, 6 Piece 242
Group, 2 Women, Bobble Heads, Teapot, Book Reading, 1920, 6 In. 726
Plate, Angel, Cupid, Fruit Border, Blue, White, Jasperware, 6 In. 95
Tea Set, Teapot, Sugar, Creamer, 2 Cup, Saucers, Pop-Eyed Faces, 7 Piece 726

SCHEIER POTTERY was made by Edwin Scheier (1910–2008) and his wife, Mary (1908–2007). They met while they both worked for the WPA, and married in 1937. In 1939, they established their studio, Hillcrock Pottery, in Glade Spring, Virginia. From 1940 to 1968, Edwin taught at the University of New Hampshire and Mary was artist-in-residence. They moved to Oaxaca, Mexico, in 1968 to study the arts and crafts of the Zapotec Indians. When the Scheiers moved to Green Valley, Arizona, in 1978, Ed returned to pottery, making some of his biggest and best-known pieces.

Scheier

Bowl, Female Half Face Joined To Fish, Gray Matte Glaze, 4 x 6 In. 923
Bowl, Overlapping Faces, Bird, Mottled Green Gray, M. & E. Scheier, 8 In. 246
Bowl, Tapered, Wide Rim, Tan Glaze, Figures, E. Scheier, 1960s, 7 x 13 In. 3375
Bowl, Tea, Faces & Fish, Blue & Blue Green Matte Glazes, 3 x 4 In. 215
Coupe, Footed, Figures, Glazed, Brown, Copper, White, E. Scheier, 1967, 13 In. 7500
Vase, Brown Glaze, Incised Pre-Columbian Style Figures, Fish, Marked, c.1955, 21 In. .... *illus* 3075
Vase, Copper Metallic Over Black Glazes, Hillcrock Pottery Logo, c.1939, 5 ⅜ In. .... *illus* 316
Vase, Cylindrical Neck, Stylized Figures, Blue, E. & M. Scheier, 1993, 13 In. .... *illus* 5625

SCHNEIDER GLASSWORKS was founded in 1917 at Epinay-sur-Seine, France, by Charles and Ernest Schneider. Art glass was made between 1918 and 1933. The company still produces clear crystal glass. See also the Le Verre Francais category.

Schneider

Compote, Mottled Pink, Purple Striped Stem & Foot, 3 Cream Bands, 12 x 14 In. 1791
Vase, 4 Black Flowers, Mottled Yellow, Brown, Purple & White, Bulbous, 7 In. 2311
Vase, Blue Foot, Mottled Orange & Blue, Split Lip Fold To Handles, Swollen, 13 In. 237
Vase, Brown Branches, Green Leaves, Padded Orange Berries, Shaped Stem & Foot, 18 In. 5187
Vase, Clear, Internal Red, Yellow & Orange, Iron Frame, Flower Handles, 6 x 13 In. 1606
Vase, Lilac, Internal Mottled Gold Bands, Navy Blue Foot, Signed, 15 In. 1791
Vase, Sparrows, Leaves, Triangular, Yellow Orange Mottled Base, c.1918, 6 ½ In. .... *illus* 800

SCIENTIFIC INSTRUMENTS of all kinds are included in this category. Other categories such as Barometer, Binoculars, Dental, Medical, Nautical, and Thermometer may also price scientific apparatus.

Chronometer, Parkinson & Frodsham, Brass, Mahogany Case, Key, c.1828, 7 In. .... *illus* 5045
Compass, Constellation, Iron, Glass Dome, 1950s, 8 x 17 x 11 In. 2390
Compass, Kelvin White & Wilfred White & Sons, 1900s, 9 ¾ x 8 In. 230
Compass, The Chicago Laboratory Supply & Scale Co., 10 ½ x 8 ¾ In. 153
Magnifying Glass, Cobalt Blue Crystal, Faceted Handle, 12 In. 750
Magnifying Glass, Yellow Gold, Rock Crystal, Jeweled Handle, 7 In. 858
Microscope, Brass, J. Zentmeyer, U.S. Navy Med. Dept., c.1855, 15 In. 2360
Microscope, Culpeper Type, Pillars, Eyepiece, Nuremberg, c.1850, 13 In. .... *illus* 1476
Microscope, Field, Lacquered Brass, Stepped Cylindrical, Case, 6 In. 183
Model, Engine, Live Steam, 2 Flywheels, Positive & Negative Connectors, 10 x 13 In. 303
Model, Engine, Stationary Steam, Hand Built, Wood Box, 9 ½ x 15 ½ In. 968
Model, Engine, Stuart, Horizontal, Iron, Cast, Brass, Steel, 5-In. Flywheel, Base, 7 ½ x 12 In. 968
Moisture Meter, Model MM-3, Irvington-Moore, Box, 4 x 6 ¾ x 8 In. .... *illus* 40
Octant, Spencer, Browning & Rust, Ebony, Brass, Mahogany Box, 12 In. 369
Periscope, Carl Zeiss, Polished Aluminum & Steel, c.1960, 45 In. 5125
Periscope, Trench, Military, Handle, Case, c.1944, 33 In. 253
Sextant, A. Prince, Wood Box, 1800s, 12 In. 688

Spyglass, U.S. Navy, WWII, 16 Power, Wood Case, 1942, 31 In. 311
Sundial, Diptych, Ivory, Engraved Pointer, Karner, 1600s, 2 ½ x 3 ½ In. .... *illus* 4305
Telescope, Brackenreg, Brass, Leather, 3 Draw, London, 36 ½ In. 1098
Telescope, Brass, Cased, 2 Sections, Adjustable Tripod Stand, c.1890, 48 x 33 In. 1180
Telescope, Dollond, Refracting, Case, 19th Century, Tripod, 46 ⅓ In. 726
Telescope, Doublet Of London, Brass, Folding Tripod, c.1890, 66 x 5 In. 2750
Telescope, Dumpy Level, Glass Bubble Level, 4 ½ x 11 In. 423
Telescope, Removable Lenses, Wood Case, 36 In. 717
Telescope, Ship's, Dollond, Brass, Tripod Base, 68 In. 2750
Temperature Gauge, Hermes, Compass, Barometer, Calendar, Cube, c.1950, 4 In. 4782
Transit, Surveyor's, Brass & Copper, Hinged Lid, 1920, 3 x 2 In. 119
Transit, Surveyor's, W. & L.E. Gurley, New York, Wood Box, c.1930, 2 Piece 330

SCRIMSHAW is bone or ivory or whale's teeth carved by sailors and others for entertainment during the sailing-ship days. Some scrimshaw was carved as early as 1800. There are modern scrimshanders making pieces today on bone, ivory, or plastic. Other pieces may be found in the Ivory and Nautical categories. Collectors should be aware of the recent laws limiting the buying and selling of scrimshaw and elephant ivory.

Busk, Lighthouse, Flags, Rocky Shore, 3-Masted Ship, 13 x 1 ½ In. 431
Busk, Whalebone, 4 Panels, Courtship Scene, Inked, Inscribed, 1800s, 12 In. 660
Busk, Whalebone, Heart, Flower, Pinwheel, Red & Green Accents, 13 In. 1230
Busk, Whalebone, Paneled, Heart, Potted Plants, Stars, Inked, 1800s, 13 ½ In. 1353
Ring, Ivory, Patriotic Interest, Red, Blue, Green, Eagle, Shield, 1800s, 1 In. 450
Tusk, Mammoth, Siberian, Stand, 13 x 29 In. 1495
Walrus Skull & Tusks, Depicting Walruses & Polar Bears, 27 In. 1593
Whale's Tooth, Clipper Ship, The French Frigate Incorruptible, c.1815, 2 ½ x 5 ½ In. 545
Whale's Tooth, Eagle, Stars, Arrows, Crossed Flags, Shield, Ship, Maiden, 1800s, 6 In. 1560
Whale's Tooth, Eels & Fish, Hand Carved, 18 In. 413
Whale's Tooth, Fashionably Dressed Woman, Late 19th Century, 7 ¼ In. 2706
Whale's Tooth, Lake, Mountains, Trees, 12 In. 236
Whale's Tooth, Vines, Flowers, Red & Green, 19th Century, 4 In. 1045
Whale's Tooth, Whaling Scene, Sperm Whale, Rigged Ship, American Ship, 6 In. 1121
Whale's Tooth, Woman, Holding Monkey, 1800s, 5 In. 584

SEG, *see Paul Revere Pottery category.*

SEVRES porcelain has been made in Sevres, France, since 1769. Many copies of the famous ware have been made. The name originally referred to the works of the Royal Porcelain factory. The name now includes any of the wares made in the town of Sevres, France. The entwined lines with a center letter used as the mark is one of the most forged marks in antiques. Be very careful to identify Sevres by quality, not just by mark.

Basket, Gilt, Pierced & Molded, Flared Rim, Leaf & Berry Wreath Band, c.1807, 11 In., Pair 3346
Bowl, Blue, Oval, Birds, Lovers, 11 x 8 In., Pair 400
Bowl, Centerpiece, Stand, Pate-Sur-Pate, Gilt Fret Border, Flower, France, 1891, 10 x 13 In. 2460
Bowl, Lid, Ormolu, 3-Footed, Cobalt Blue, Gilt, 2 Handles, Pineapple Finial, 7 ½ x 9 In. 408
Bowl, Maiden At Well, Farm Boy, Cherub, Blue Bands, Double Handles, 19 x 10 In. 1188
Box, Coffin Shape, Gilt Bronze, Red, 4-Footed, Paul Milet, 7 ¼ In. 238
Box, Hinged, Gilt Brass Mounts, Green, Turquoise Mottled, Brown Underglaze, 5 x 3 ½ In. 293
Cachepot, Battle Scenes, White Ground, 4 Acorn Finials, 4-Footed, 7 In., Pair 288
Cachepot, Blue Celeste, Flowers, Putti, 18th Century, 7 x 7 ¼ In. 2091
Centerpiece, Cherub, Clouds, Cornucopia, Blue, Gilt, Oval, 6 ½ x 10 In. 472
Compote, Blue, Cherubs In Reserves, Figural Cherub Supports, 20 ¼ In., Pair 5250
Compote, Cherubs, 4 Dolphin Supports, Dore Bronze Mounts, 7 ¾ x 10 In. 1045
Compote, Reticulated, White Ground, 6 In. 188
Cup & Saucer, Enameled Jewel Design, Gilt, Cobalt Blue Ground 3485
Cup & Saucer, Female Portrait, Profile, 1800s, Pair 9840
Dish, Blue Celeste, Gilt, People In Field, Houses, 6 ½ x 5 In., Pair 553
Dish, Green Glaze, White Center, Gilt, Flowers, Lozenge Shape, c.1809, 11 x 5 In., Pair 378
Dresser Box, Ormolu Mounts, Oval, Serpentine Border, Hinged Lid, Blue, Flowers, 7 x 4 ½ In. .. 81
Garniture Set, Courting Scenes, Blue, Urns, Centerpiece, 3 Piece 2214
Lamp Base, Peasant Girl, Dore Bronze, Rococo Gilt, Bands, Columnar, c.1910, 15 In. 59
Pedestal, Square Sides, Figures Climbing Ladders, Marble Base, Gilt Bronze, 42 In., Pair 1500
Pitcher, Looped Handle, Green, Brown Mottle, Gourd Shape, 1900, 8 x 6 x 5 In. 1125
Pitcher, Turquoise, Gilt, Cherubs, 1700s, 7 ½ In. 861
Plate, 6 Portraits, Celeste Blue, Jeweled Decoration, 11 ½ In. 1476

Scheier, Vase, Copper Metallic Over Black Glazes, Hillcrock Pottery Logo, c.1939, 5 ⅜ In.
$316

Humler & Nolan

Scheier, Vase, Cylindrical Neck, Stylized Figures, Blue, E. & M. Scheier, 1993, 13 In.
$5,625

Rago Arts and Auction Center

Schneider, Vase, Sparrows, Leaves, Triangular, Yellow Orange Mottled Base, c.1918, 6 ½ In.
$800

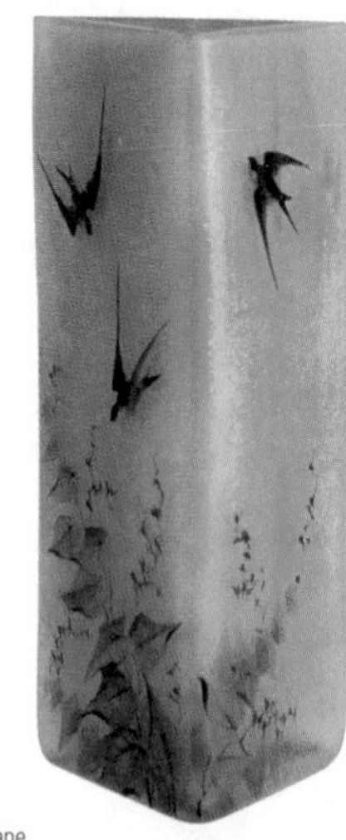

Ruby Lane

S

Scientific Instrument, Chronometer, Parkinson & Frodsham, Brass, Mahogany Case, Key, c.1828, 7 In.
$5,045

Ruby Lane

Scientific Instrument, Microscope, Culpeper Type, Pillars, Eyepiece, Nuremberg, c.1850, 13 In.
$1,476

Skinner, Inc.

Scientific Instrument, Moisture Meter, Model MM-3, Irvington-Moore, Box, 4 x 6¾ x 8 In.
$40

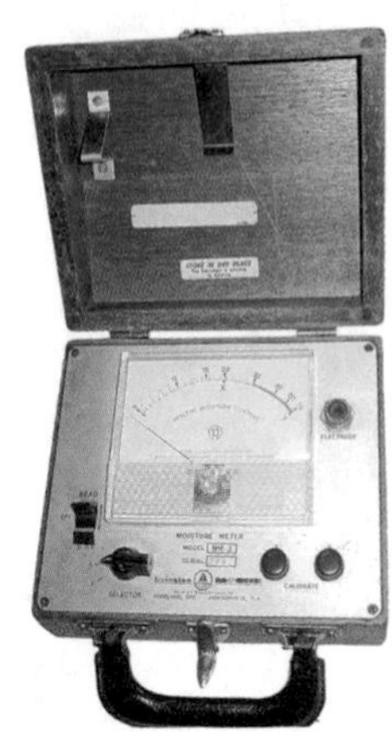

Ruby Lane

Plate, Blue, Soft Paste, Oval Cameos, Birds, Swags, 23⅓ In. 312
Plate, Footed, Crown, Flower Monogram, Shaped Rim, Flowers, Cherubs, c.1773, 8 In. 13750
Plate, Portrait, Cobalt Rim, 9¾ In., Pair 305
Potpourri, Gilt, Flower Swags, White Ground, 3 Supports, 7½ In., Pair 281
Sconce, 5-Light, Gilt Bronze, Baluster, Scroll Arms, Woman & Dove, c.1870, 20 In., Pair 3585
Stand, Dessert, Putti, Multicolor, 22 In. 768
Sugar, Children Playing, Lapis Blue, Gilt, Lid, Flower Finial, c.1757, 4¼ In. 2000
Tea Set, Pink Pompadour, Teapot, Cream, 2 Cup & Saucer, 6 Piece 1968
Urn, Blue, Courting Scene, Castle, Signed, 24 In. 338
Urn, Cherubs, Blue, Cherub Finial, Lid, 21 In. 1610
Urn, Cobalt Blue, Romantic Scenes, Gilt, 12¾ x 5 In., Pair 676
Urn, Courting Couples, Pink, Pinecone Finial, 18 In., Pair 1750
Urn, Gilt, Red Ground, Reserves, Lovers At Rest, Round Foot, 22½ x 8¾ In., Pair 1000
Urn, Lovers, Landscapes, Blue, Gilt, Egg & Dart Trim, Lid, c.1925, 26 x 11 In., Pair 4062
Urn, Pink Pompadour, Ormolu Mounts, 3 Portrait Panels, 11½ In., Pair 2337
Urn, Potpourri, Conical Lid, Flower Border, Winged Female Paw Feet, c.1900, 12 In. 549
Vase, Art Nouveau, Blue Flower Stems, Green Leaves, 11¾ In. 3900
Vase, Cobalt Blue, Figures In Robes, Round Foot, 21 x 8 In. 610
Vase, Cobalt Blue, Women At Lily Pond, Round Foot, 21 x 8 In. 549
Vase, Crystalline Glaze, Bubble Handles, Amber, Red, Porcelain, 1905, 9 x 3 In. .... *illus* 6250
Vase, Green, Gilt, Ormolu, Dome Lid, Urn Shaped Finial, Leaf Handles, 41 In. 2987
Vase, Group Landscapes, Fuchsia Ground, Feathers, Gilt Metal Mount, Lid, 18 In., Pair 1250
Vase, Ormolu Mount, Cherub, Musical Instruments, 7¾ In. 369
Vase, Pink, Gardens, Bronze Mount, Drop Ring Handles, 12 x 4 In. 605
Vase, Sea Green, Art Nouveau Portrait, Woman, Gold Highlights, Handles, 9½ In. .... *illus* 288
Vase, Shouldered, Cobalt Blue Glaze, Gilt Stars, Gilt Rim, 1930s, 43 x 17 In. 826

SEWER TILE figures were made by workers at the sewer tile and pipe factories in the Ohio area during the late nineteenth and early twentieth centuries. Figurines, small vases, and cemetery vases were favored. Often the finished vase was a piece of the original pipe with added decorations and markings. All types of sewer tile work are now considered folk art by collectors.

Ashtray, Chimney Shape, Tin Grate, Ohio, 6 In. 120
Bank, Pig, Seated, Upright Ears, Mottled Brown, c.1940, 10 In. 188
Bank, Pig, Standing, Incised Eyelashes, Ohio, c.1910, 13 In. .... *illus* 900
Bank, Piggy, Seated, Incised, Now You've Got Me On A Diet, Nov. 26, 1967, 10 In. 570
Birdhouse, Acorn Shape, 2 Parts, Mark, Walter Smith, Ohio, 1900s, 8 In. 840
Birdhouse, Conical Roof, Tooled Bark, Early 20th Century, 8½ In. 240
Birdhouse, Cylindrical, Ohio, 20th Century, 10 In. 660
Birdhouse, Cylindrical, Pointed Roof, Brown Glaze, Wood Base, Hangs, c.1915, 7 In. 570
Birdhouse, Ohio, 1800s, 11½ x 8½ x 9 In. .... *illus* 295
Birdhouse, Tooled Bark Surface, Wood Bottom, U.S.A., c.1950, 8 In. 300
Birdhouse, Tree Trunk Form, Conical Roof, Unglazed, Ohio, 8¼ In. 180
Bottle, Pig, Anatomically Correct Male, Tan Glaze, W.S. Dickey Co., Kansas, 5 In. 281
Chicken Waterer, c.1880, 12½ In. 300
Dice, Agateware Type, Unglazed, c.1900, 3¾ In., Pair 270
Downspout, Rectangular, Molded Lion's Head, Open Mouth Spout, Brown, 13 In. 180
Figure, Camel, Standing, Incised EJE, c.1950, 5½ In. 330
Figure, Dog, Collie, Standing, Yellow Glaze Details, 8 In. 300
Figure, Dog, Dachshund, Incised W, 1900s, 12¼ In. 469
Figure, Dog, Long Nose, Seated, Collar, Square Base, c.1900, 11½ In. 1140
Figure, Dog, Poodle, Sitting, Elongated Neck, Incised Hair, 1940s, 16 In. 150
Figure, Dog, Spaniel, Sitting, Speckled, 8 In. 66
Figure, Duck, Hand Molded, Incised Base EJE, 3 x 6 In. 413
Figure, Eagle, Standing, Spread Wings, Yellow & White Glaze, Rocky Base, c.1950, 11 In. 531
Figure, Frog, Mottled Brown, Orange, Head Up, c.1955, 9 In. 125
Figure, Lion, Reclining, 2-Tier Base, 5 x 7 In. 360
Figure, Lion, Reclining, Brown Glaze, Incised Features, Michigan, 1900s, 9½ In. 188
Figure, Owl, Sitting On Stump, Mottled Brown Glaze, 13 In. .... *illus* 246
Figure, Owl, Yellow Clay Eyes, Talons, c.1940, 12 In. 210
Figure, Pig, Standing, Incised Eyelashes, National Sewer Pipe, 8 x 13 In. 780
Figure, Skull, Human, Life Size, Signed Selzer, c.1939, 6 In. 780
Figure, Soldier, Standing, Uniform, Sword In Hand, c.1950, 13½ In. 540
Plaque, Relief, Last Supper, U.S.A., 1900s, 6 x 12 In. 120
Train, Steam Engine, Marked Mark RR, c.1920, 6½ x 13 In. 480
Umbrella Stand, Landscapes, Birds, Signed, Hill, 26 In. 63
Urn, Molded Design Around Shoulder, Tapered, c.1950, 19 In. 120

SEWING equipment of all types is collected, from sewing birds that held the cloth to tape measures, needle books, and old wooden spools. Sewing machines are included here. Needlework pictures are listed in the Picture category.

Basket, Woven, Straw, Birch, Lid, 6 x 10 In. ... 24
Basket, Woven, White, Blue Satin Lining, Swing Handle, Belding Corticelli, 12 x 9 x 5 In. ... 35
Box, Black Forest, Carved, Flowers, Grapevine Feet, Velvet Lined, c.1900, 9 x 9 In. ... 438
Box, Gilt Lacquer, Hinged Lid, Brass Handles, Dragon Feet, Drawer, Chinese Export, 15 x 11 In. 523
Box, Mosaic, Sandalwood, Ebony, Ivory Tools, Anglo-Indian, 5 ½ x 17 ½ In. ... 450
Box, Musical, Empire, Satinwood, Hinged Serpentine Dome Lid, Handle, 1800s, 3 x 8 In. ... 1020
Box, Pine, Gold & Black Paint, Vines, Swing Handle, Dome Lift Lid, c.1850, 7 x 8 In. ... 390
Box, Spool, Brainerd & Armstrong, Wood, 3 Drawers, Handles, 8 x 16 In. ... 127
Box, Wallpaper Cover, Removable Lid, Pincushion, Crisscross Design, 1800s, 5 x 4 In. ... 212
Box, Walnut, Bone Inlay, Stars, Scissors, Needle, Awl, Crochet Hook, 1864, 7 x 16 In. ... 960
Cabinet, Spool, Southern Gum, Eastlake Molding, 4 Drawers, Glass, Brass Pulls, 17 x 23 In. ... 330
Cabinet, Spool, Walnut, Mahogany, 8 Glass Front Drawers, 27 x 20 In. ... 438
Cabinet, Spool, see also the Advertising category under Cabinet, Spool.
Caddy, Turned Maple, Round, Pincushion Finial, 1800s, 4 x 6 In. ... 83
Dress Form, Blue, Cream, 40 In. ... 58
Dress Form, Stand, Blue, 4-Footed Base, Adjustable, 1940s, 58 In. ... 30
Loom, Maple, Mixed Woods, Dovetailed, Cased Tape, Wrought Iron Spool Handle, 15 In. ... 563
Loom, Wood, Twine, Miniature, 12 x 14 x 15 In. ... 60
Machine, Iron, Wood Case, Portable, Handle, Hand Crank, Singer, 15 In. ... 240
Machine, Victorian, Treadle, 36 x 18 In. ... 70
Needle Case, Mother-Of-Pearl, Beaded Edge, Carved Bird, c.1820, 3 ½ x 5 In. ... 872
Pattern, Dresses, Casual To Cocktail, Vogue, 1960s ... 8
Pattern, McCall, Dress, No. 9523, Size 12, 1953 ... 4
Pattern, Simplicity, Girl's Dress, No. 2190, Size 10, c.1935 ... 4
Pattern, Simplicity, Prairie Skirt & Top, No. 3978, 1952, Size 12 ... 20
Pattern, Woman's Dress Coat, Advance No. 8137, Bust 36, Waist 28, Hip 38, 1958 ... 11
Pincushion & Tape Measure, Stuffed Dog, Tongue Pulls Out, 5 x 3 In. ... 35
Pincushion Dolls are listed in their own category.
Pincushion, Bear, Carved, Black Forest, Glass Eyes, 3 ½ In. ... 235
Pincushion, Bulldog, Sitting, Chalkware, Japan, 2 ¾ In. ... 48
Pincushion, Mother-Of-Pearl, Children, Garden, Engraved, 2 In. Diam. ... 95
Pincushion, Upside Down Strawberry, 6 Dangling Strawberries, c.1940, 10 x 8 In. ... 45
Sock Darner, Wood, Egg Shape, 6 x 2 In. ... 16
Spool Cabinets are listed here or in the Advertising category under Cabinet, Spool.
Spool Shelf, Salmon Paint, 1800s, 23 x 8 In. ... 35
Study For Quilt, No. 34, Stitcher, Painted, Fabric, Pamela Studstill, Frame, 23 x 23 In. ... 1125
Tape Measure, Bakelite, Steel Tape, Red, Stanley, c.1935, 72 In. ... 12
Thimble, Rose Gold, Engraved Decoration, c.1900, ¾ x ⅝ In. ... 123
Thimble, Sterling Silver, Angels, Cherub, Stars, ⅝ In. ... 125
Thimble, Sterling Silver, Beaded Base, Germany, ¾ In. ... 35
Thread Dispenser, Wood, Berries, Leaves, Painted, c.1900, 2 x 3 In. ... 397
Yarn Holder, Wood, Clamp, Swift, 1800s, 21 In. ... 59
Yarn Winder, Chestnut, Fruitwood, Incised Measuring Circle, 1800s, 41 In. ... *illus* 41
Yarn Winder, Mixed Wood, Pennsylvania, 1800s, 39 ½ In. ... 12
Yarn Winder, Mixed Wood, Pennsylvania, 1800s, 42 In. ... 47
Yarn Winder, Mixed Wood, Turned Spindles, Legs, Carved, 1800s, 1825, 48 x 26 ½ In. ... 120
Yarn Winder, Wood, 1800, 35 In. ... 47

SHAKER items are characterized by simplicity, functionalism, and orderliness. There were many Shaker communities in America from the eighteenth century to the present day. The religious order made furniture, small wooden pieces, and packaged medicines, herbs, and jellies to sell to "outsiders." Other useful objects were made for use by members of the community. Shaker furniture is listed in this book in the Furniture category.

Applesauce Maker, Pine, Tin, Cast Iron, Apple Chute, Handle, c.1870, 14 x 24 In. ... *illus* 1440
Basket, Kindling, Splint, Black Ash, Hoop Handle, Mattress Ticking Lined, 16 x 20 In. ... 420
Basket, Sewing, Handle, Sabbathday Lake, 3 x 7 In. ... 369
Basket, Splint, Black Ash, Oval, Square Base, 3 Skids, Wrapped Rim, 2 Handles, 9 x 27 In. ... 780
Box, 2-Finger, Lid, Bentwood, Blue Painted, Copper Tacks, 1800s, 3 ½ x 10 In. ... 1888
Box, 2-Finger, Lid, Oval, Bentwood, Copper Tacks, 1800s, 3 ¾ x 2 ½ In. ... *illus* 384
Box, 2-Finger, Lid, Pine, Maple, Red Brown Paint, Round, c.1820, 3 x 4 In. ... 1920
Box, 2-Finger, Oval, Maple, Pine, Cherry, Yellow Paint, 1 ¾ x 4 ½ In. ... *illus* 4080
Box, 2-Finger, Red Paint, Metal Tacks, Oval, 1800, 3 ½ x 7 In. ... 150
Box, 4-Finger, Lid, Maple, Pine, Oval, White Paint, Iron Tacks, Maine, c.1830, 5 x 11 In. ... 780

Scientific Instrument, Sundial, Diptych, Ivory, Engraved Pointer, Karner, 1600s, 2 ½ x 3 ½ In.
$4,305

Skinner, Inc.

Sevres, Vase, Crystalline Glaze, Bubble Handles, Amber, Red, Porcelain, 1905, 9 x 3 In.
$6,250

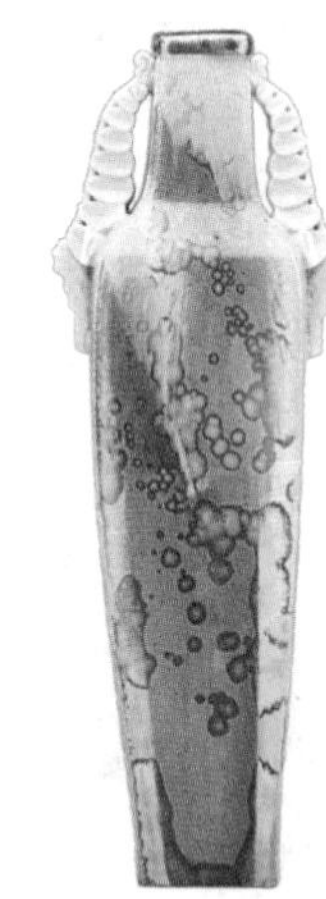

Rago Arts and Auction Center

Sevres, Vase, Sea Green, Art Nouveau Portrait, Woman, Gold Highlights, Handles, 9 ½ In.
$288

Early Auction Company

S

Sewer Tile, Bank, Pig, Standing, Incised Eyelashes, Ohio, c.1910, 13 In.
$900

Garth's Auctioneers & Appraisers

Sewer Tile, Birdhouse, Ohio, 1800s, 11 ½ x 8 ½ x 9 In.
$295

Hess Auction Group

Sewer Tile, Figure, Owl, Sitting On Stump, Mottled Brown Glaze, 13 In.
$246

Cowan Auctions

Box, 5-Finger, Lid, Maple, Pine, Oval, Cherry Red Paint, Copper Tacks, 5 ½ x 13 In. 960
Box, Candle, Hanging, Fruitwood, Figured, Beveled, Chamfered Sliding Lid, Peg Hole, 16 In. 1440
Box, Seed, Pine, Painted, Label, Shakers Genuine Garden Seeds, Mount Lebanon, N.Y., 23 In. 1920
Broom & Dustpan, Pine, Broom Corn, Tin Flared Dust Pan, Peg Ring, 15 In. 840
Bucket, Beveled Lid, Pine, Blue Paint, 2 Steel Straps, Porcelain Pull, 12 x 18 In. 1800
Bucket, Oak, Old Gray, Stencil, Corn, 2 Wrought Iron Bands, Riveted, Tall Ears, Rope, 10 In. 2760
Butter Bell, Maple, Dark Patina, 3 Holes, Turned Handle, Ball Top, 3 ¼ In. 600
Candle Dryer, Pine, Mortised & Pinned Frame, 7 Carved Holders, c.1830, 23 x 9 In. 600
Candlestick, Steel, Soldered Bobeche, Sliding Thumb Latch, Round Base, 12 x 5 In. 540
Carrier, Egg, Pine, Bent Maple Handles, Tin Latch & Hinges, Cardboard Separators, 12 In. 630
Carrier, Pine, Maple, Oval, 2-Finger, Hoop Handle, 5 Copper Tacks, c.1840, 6 x 11 x 8 In. 8400
Carrier, Poplar, Canted Sides, Dovetailed, Square Head Nails, Cutout Handles, 9 x 22 In. 720
Carrier, Utensil, Cherry, Pine, Red Stain, 5 Sections, Canted Rectangular Handle, 19 x 15 In. 3000
Carrier, Walnut, Rectangular, Dovetailed, Bottle, 28 Sections, Center Handle, 4 x 12 In. 1500
Carrier, Walnut, Varnish, Square, Canted Sides, Extended Base, Hoop Handle, 9 x 9 In. 5400
Churn, Mixed Wood, Vertical Staves, Elongated Handle, 1800s, 53 In. 325
Cloak, Sister's, Black Wool, Gathered Hood, Black Silk Ribbons, Wood Hangar, Me., 46 In. 660
Desk, Tabletop, Butternut, Pine, Red Stain, Slanted Lift Lid, Ink Drawer, Inscribed, 6 x 22 In. 2640
Dress, Cotton, Purple, Green Dots, Herringbone Pattern, Lace Trim, Pine Hangar.................... 360
Ladder, Folding, Walnut, 3 Steps, Mortised Construction, c.1840, 35 x 20 In. 3360
Mirror, Humility, Pine, Red Tinted Varnish, Silvered Glass, Enfield, Conn., 5 ¾ In. 1800
Mold, Bonnet, Standing, Maple, Cylindrical, Scribe Lines, X Base, New Lebanon, 35 In. 480
Mortar & Pestle, Burl Maple, Patina, Footed, 1830-40, 3 x 3 ½ In. ....*illus* 1680
Mortar & Pestle, Maple, Tiger Maple Handle, Curved Herb Masher, 3 x 5 In. 1140
Neckerchief, Silk, Raspberry Red Dyed, Small White Squares & Lines, 32 x 35 In. 270
Pantry Box, Bentwood, Wire Bail Handle, Lid, Peg & Nails, Red, 1800s, 7 x 10 In. 236
Pantry Box, Round, Lid, Dandelion Root, c.1880, 6 ¼ x 6 ¼ x 2 ½ In. 120
Peg Rail, Pine, Dark Stain, 13 Turned Pegs, c.1850, 50 In. 360
Rack, Drying, Pine, 2 Bars, 3 Vertical Posts, Lamb's Tongue Carving, Pegged, 39 x 76 In. 600
Rolling Pin, Maple, 2 Handles, Turned As 1 Piece, 3 ¾ x 32 In. 960
Sieve, Medicine, Maple, 2-Finger, Woven Silk Mesh, Copper Tacks, c.1820, 2 x 3 In. 1080
Sign, Shaker Store, Arrow, Pine, White Paint, Black Letters, Hanging Holes, 9 x 31 In. 2400
Sundial, Copper, Put Your Hands To Works, Give Your Hearts To God, 1938, 14 In. 1140
Taping Bench, Maple, Birch, 2 Threaded Screw Clamps, Splayed Legs, 28 In. 720

SHAVING MUGS were popular from 1860 to 1900. Many types were made, including occupational mugs featuring pictures of men's jobs. There were scuttle mugs, silver-plated mugs, glass-lined mugs, and others.

Cowboy, Lassoing Steer, Circle Handle, Gilt, 3 ¾ In. 450
Indian Chief With Headdress, Sterling Silver, Brush.................... 1140
Koken Barber Supply, Loop Handle, Saucer Base, Limoges, c.1915, 4 x 4 In. 30
Occupational, Baseball Theme, Crossed Bat & Ball, Ring Foot, White, Gilt, c.1900.................... 687
Occupational, Blacksmith, Shoeing Stallion, Loop Handle, Ring Foot, Gilt, 4 In. 191
Occupational, Bricklayer, Mason Laying Brick, Gilt, 4 In. 480
Occupational, Cattle Breeder, Butcher, Man Standing With Bull, Gilt.................... 120
Occupational, Church, Steeple, Rev. S. Lightfoot, Gilt Ring Foot, 4 In. 1560
Occupational, Druggist, Skull & Crossbones, White & Gilt, F.S. Lowery.................... 600
Occupational, Dry Goods, M.A. Morkman, S.D. Shaw Barber Shop Supply....................*illus* 120
Occupational, Harley-Davidson, Motorcycle, Gilt, Handle, Saucer Foot, 3 ½ In. 239
Occupational, Horse Trainer, Jos. Sroczck, Horse Head, Gilt 120
Occupational, Tailor, Man Sewing Pants, Gilt, 3 ¾ In. 180
Occupational, Tin Maker, Howard Burke, Man Working, Gilt.................... 840
Occupational, Tobacconist, Wm. Kinley, Crossed Cigars, White & Gilt.................... 60
Soap Dish, Spout, Loop Handle, Tin, c.1865, 3 In. 179

SHAWNEE POTTERY was started in Zanesville, Ohio, in 1937. The company made vases, novelty ware, flowerpots, planters, lamps, and cookie jars. Three dinnerware lines were made: Corn, Lobster Ware, and Valencia (a solid color line). White Corn pattern utility pieces were made in 1945. Corn King was made from 1946 to 1954; Corn Queen, with darker green leaves and lighter colored corn, from 1954 to 1961. Shawnee produced pottery for George Rumrill during the late 1930s. The company closed in 1961.

Shawnee USA

Cookie Jar, Owl, Winking, Green, Brown, Peach, c.1940, 11 ¾ In. ....*illus* 185
Cookie Jar, Smiley Pig, Blue Neckerchief, 11 In. 99
Cookie Jar, Winnie Pig, Hat, Clovers, Hands In Pocket, Green Collar, 11 In. 85
Creamer, Smiley Pig, Blue Neckerchief, 5 x 4 In. 140
Head Vase, Polynesian Woman, Black Hair, 5 ½ In. 49

S

Pitcher, Corn King, 8 In. 45
Planter, Bulb, Ivy Vine Pattern, Green Glaze, 7¾ x 3 In. 40
Planter, Bulb, Raised Tulips & Daisies, Swirling Leaves, Mauve, 1940s, 7 x 3 In. 36
Planter, Button Shoe, Sky Blue, 1940s, 4 x 2 In. 16
Salt & Pepper, Dutch Boy & Girl, c.1940, 5¼ In. 65
Salt & Pepper, Milk Can Shape, Blue & Red Dots, 1940s, 3½ In. 15
Salt & Pepper, Sailor Boy & Girlfriend, Creamy White, Red & Blue, 3½ In. 32
Salt & Pepper, Winking Owls, Cream, 3¼ x 2 In. 15
Teapot, Lid, Corn King, c.1950, 6½ In. 75
Toothbrush Holder, Woman, Blond, Hat, 5 In. 23
Vase, Burlap Textured, Yellow Interior, Square Base, 8 In. 38
Wall Pocket, Clock Face, Roman Numerals, Green, Yellow, 1950s, 6 x 5 In. 18

SHEARWATER POTTERY is a family business started in 1928 by Peter Anderson, with the help of his parents, Mr. and Mrs. G.W. Anderson Sr. The local Ocean Springs, Mississippi, clays were used to make the wares in the 1930s. The company was damaged by Hurricane Katrina in 2005 but was rebuilt and is still in business, now owned by Peter's four children.

Figurine, Cat, Heart Shape Face, Green Crystalline Glaze, Curled Tail, 10 In. 345
Figurine, Gulls, Gloss & Crystalline Glazes, Impressed Logo, 6 x 10 In. 295
Vase, Abstract Figural Decoration, 2002, 9 x 4¾ In. 240
Vase, Ducks, Waves, Blue, Green, Purple, Walter Anderson, c.1930, 6 In. 480
Vase, Light Blue Glaze, Impressed Circle Marks, 1930s, 4½ In., Pair.......... 368
Vase, Sea Gulls, Green, Black, Swirl Design, Round, Flat Rim, c.1990, 7 In. ....*illus* 690
Vase, Sea, Earth & Sky, Blue Glaze, Molded Pelicans, Fish, Horses, Birds, c.1940, 6 In. ....*illus* 5975
Vase, Street Scene, People, Multicolor Slip, Tapered, c.1988, 9 In. ....*illus* 4575
Vase, Stylized Pelicans, Waves, Small Birds, Deep Blue, White, 8⅞ x 4½ In. 9455

SHEET MUSIC from the past centuries is now collected. The favorites are examples with covers featuring artistic or historic pictures. Early sheet music covers were lithographed, but by the 1900s photographic reproductions were used. The early music was larger than more recent sheets, and you must watch out for examples that were trimmed to fit in a twentieth-century piano bench.

Broadway Blues, Sophie Tucker, W. Rossiter, Chicago, 1915, 10 x 14 In. 25
Dance Me Loose, Arthur Godfrey, Mel Howard, Lee Erwin, 1951 18
Donny Osmond, Twelfth Of Never, 1973.......... 9
Frosty The Snowman, Hill & Range Songs Inc., c.1950, 12 x 9 In. 9
Harp Of Old Erin & Banner Of Stars, De Marsan, 1861, 10 x 6½ In. 15
Hen & The Weather Vane, Cohan & Harris Publishing, 1908, 10½ x 14 In. 113
Lady In The Dark, Ginger Rogers, c.1943, 12 x 9 In. 7
On Wisconsin, March Song, Carl Beck, W.T. Purdy, 1910 149
Pride Of The Regiment, Mitchell W. Meyers, 1910, 4 Pages 75
She's Always A Woman, Billy Joel, 1977 14
Voluptuosa, Josephine Baker, Salabert, 10¼ x 13½ In. 131
Way Down In Dixie, E.L. Bolling, 1905, 10¾ x 13¾ In. 30
You Needed Me, Anne Murray, 1975.......... 12

SHEFFIELD *items are listed in the Silver Plate and Silver-English categories.*

SHELLEY first appeared on English ceramics about 1912. The Foley China Works started in England in 1860. Joseph Ball Shelley joined the company in 1862 and became a partner in 1872. Percy Shelley joined the firm in 1881. The company went through a series of name changes and in 1910 the then Foley China Company became Shelley China. In 1929 it became Shelley Potteries. The company was acquired in 1966 by Allied English Potteries, then merged with the Doulton group in 1971. The name Shelley was put into use again in 1980. A trio is the name for a cup, saucer, and cake plate set.

Bowl, Fruit, Blue, Dainty, 5 In. 53
Bowl, Vegetable, Bridesmaid, Oval, 10 In. 72
Cake Plate, Blue, Empress, Cutout Handles, 10 In. 96
Cup & Saucer, Bridesmaid, Footed.......... 15
Cup & Saucer, Daffodil Time, Demitasse 38
Cup & Saucer, Daffodil Time, Footed 46
Cup & Saucer, Heather, Gold Trim, Bone China, Made In England, 1940s ....*illus* 45
Cup & Saucer, Regent, 1938 29
Cup & Saucer, Sweet Vintage, Chester, Gold Trim, c.1932.......... 60
Cup & Saucer, Violets, Blue Trim, Miniature, Saucer 2½ In. ....*illus* 125

Sewing, Yarn Winder, Chestnut, Fruitwood, Incised Measuring Circle, 1800s, 41 In.
$41

Hess Auction Group

Shaker, Applesauce Maker, Pine, Tin, Cast Iron, Apple Chute, Handle, c.1870, 14 x 24 In.
$1,440

Willis Henry Auctions, Inc.

Shaker, Box, 2-Finger, Lid, Oval, Bentwood, Copper Tacks, 1800s, 3¾ x 2½ In.
$384

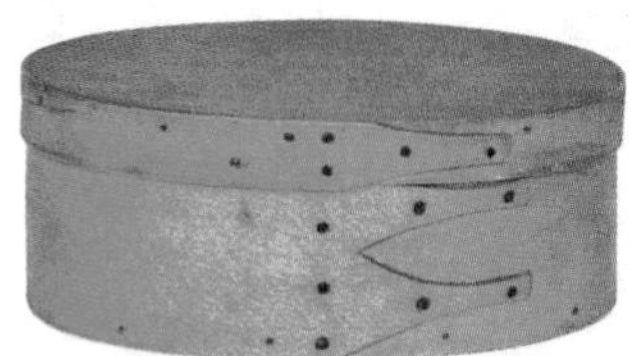

Hess Auction Group

TIP

A two-finger Shaker box really has three. Two are on the bottom, one is on the lid.

Shaker, Box, 2-Finger, Oval, Maple, Pine, Cherry, Yellow Paint, 1 ¾ x 4 ½ In.
$4,080

Willis Henry Auctions, Inc.

Shaker, Mortar & Pestle, Burl Maple, Patina, Footed, 1830-40, 3 x 3 ½ In.
$1,680

Willis Henry Auctions, Inc.

TIP
Avoid shopping at shows or shops with unpriced items. If you look eager or affluent, you may be charged more.

Shaving Mug, Occupational, Dry Goods, M.A. Morkman, S.D. Shaw Barber Shop Supply
$120

Showtime Auction Services

Shawnee, Cookie Jar, Owl, Winking, Green, Brown, Peach, c.1940, 11 ¾ In.
$185

Ruby Lane

Shearwater, Vase, Sea Gulls, Green, Black, Swirl Design, Round, Flat Rim, c.1990, 7 In.
$690

Humler & Nolan

Shearwater, Vase, Sea, Earth & Sky, Blue Glaze, Molded Pelicans, Fish, Horses, Birds, c.1940, 6 In.
$5,975

Neal Auctions

Shearwater, Vase, Street Scene, People, Multicolor Slip, Tapered, c.1988, 9 In.
$4,575

Neal Auctions

Shelley, Cup & Saucer, Heather, Gold Trim, Bone China, Made In England, 1940s
$45

Ruby Lane

Shelley, Cup & Saucer, Violets, Blue Trim, Miniature, Saucer 2 ½ In.
$125

Ruby Lane

S

Cup & Saucer, Woodland .... 36 to 45
Eggcup, Blue, Dainty, 3 In. 57
Gravy Boat, Bridal Rose, 8 In. 68
Jam Jar, Bridal Rose, Underplate 63
Mustache Cup, Green & Brown Ivy Pattern, Cream Ground 90
Nut Dish, Rosebud, Fluted, 4 In. 52
Plate, Bread & Butter, Blue, Empress, 6 In. 24
Plate, Dinner, Chippendale, Turquoise, 10 7/8 In. 36
Teapot, Melody, Chintz, Green, Lid, 5 1/2 x 8 1/2 In. 476

SHIRLEY TEMPLE, the famous movie star, was born in 1928. She made her first movie in 1932. She died in 2014. Thousands of items picturing Shirley have been and still are being made. Shirley Temple dolls were first made in 1934 by Ideal Toy Company. Millions of Shirley Temple cobalt blue glass dishes were made by Hazel Atlas Glass Company and U.S. Glass Company from 1934 to 1942. They were given away as premiums for Wheaties and Bisquick. A bowl, mug, and pitcher were made as a breakfast set. Some pieces were decorated with the picture of a very young Shirley, others used a picture of Shirley in her 1936 *Captain January* costume. Although collectors refer to a cobalt creamer, it is actually the 4 ½-inch-high milk pitcher from the breakfast set. Many of these items are being reproduced today. There was an auction of the costumes, dolls, and other memorablilia that belonged to Shirley Temple and had been saved by her mother. The auction brought $4.2 million in 2015.

Accordion, Pearlized Celluloid Finish, 12-Key, Rhinestone Fan Blades, 1935, 9 x 11 In. 4704
Bible, Red Leather, Gilt Edge, Sterling Silver Clasp, University Press, 1938, 8 x 5 In. 5040
Bowl, Honeycomb, Cobalt Blue, Scalloped Rim, 6 In. 8
Breakfast Set, Bowl, Mug, Pitcher, Portrait, Honeycomb, Hazel Glass, Blue 45
Brochure, Poor Little Rich Girl, 20th Century Fox, 14 Pages, 1936, 22 x 16 In. 560
Chum Club Badge, Octagonal, Red Gargoyle, Silver, Raised Letters, 1937, 1 In. 2016
Cradle, Doll's, Maple Finish, 1930s, 19 x 23 In. 3920
Doll Purse, Red Vinyl, White Script Signature, Cutout Handle, Ideal, 1950s .... *illus* 33
Doll, Captain January, Composition, Socket Head, Ringlets, Ideal, c.1936, 18 In. 456
Doll, Composition, Blond Curly Mohair Wig, Sleep Eyes, Ideal, 18 In. 12
Doll, Composition, Hazel Sleep & Flirting Eyes, Texas Outfit, Blond Mohair, 27 In. 9520
Doll, Composition, Sleep Eyes, Dress, Slip, Ideal, 20 In. 125
Doll, Composition, Sleep Eyes, Wig, Open Mouth, Dimples, Jointed, Ideal, 15 In. 125
Doll, Composition, Socket Head, Flirty Eyes, Curly Top Costume, Ideal, 1935, 25 In. 912
Doll, Composition, Socket Head, Sleep Eyes, Dimples, Mohair Ringlets, 1934, 18 In. 570
Doll, Vinyl, Wee Willie Winkie Scottish Outfit, Hat, Ideal, c.1955, 12 In. .... *illus* 85
Dress, Red Polka Dot, Puff Sleeve, Wavy Hem, Sash, Double Layer Skirt, 1934 84000
Magazine, Life, Portrait Photo, Teenager, Hat, Signed, 1942 115
Mug, Cobalt Blue, Portrait, Tapered Side, 3 5/8 In. 15
Outfit, Sailor Pants, Middy Blouse, Anchor, Eagle, Tie, White Poplin, Captain January, 1936 9520
Pitcher, Portrait, Cobalt Blue, Atlas Glass, 1930s, 4 3/4 In. 18
Pitcher, Portrait, Honeycomb Pattern, Cobalt Blue, c.1930, 4 1/2 In. 24
Ring, Sterling Silver, Blue Enamel, High Relief Portrait, Child's, Size 3 1/2 221
Saddle, Leather, Engraved, Shirley Smiling, Lasso Lettering, 23 x 25 In. 11200
Watercolor On Paper Board, Petal Flowers, Lavender Pot, Bird On Branch, c.1935, 17 x 13 In. 2912

SHRINER, *see Fraternal category.*

SILVER, *Sheffield, see Silver Plate; Silver-English categories.*

SILVER DEPOSIT glass was first made during the late nineteenth century. Solid sterling silver is applied to the glass by a chemical method so that a cutout design of silver metal appears against a clear or colored glass. It is sometimes called silver overlay.

Claret Jug, Trefoil Rim, Openwork Scrolls, Grape Leaves, Clusters, 15 1/2 In. 676
Decanter, Flowers, France, c.1900, 10 x 4 1/2 In. 259
Decanter, Whiskey, Conical, Paneled, Wheat Stalks, 8 1/2 In. 400
Pitcher, Chased Overlay, Leaves, Grapes, Wavy Rim, Handle, c.1900, 10 In. .... *illus* 450
Pitcher, Emerald, Blown Glass, Flowers, 8 3/4 In. 395
Vase, Iridescent Purple, Green, Dimpled, Flower Rim, c.1900, 11 In. 688

SILVER FLATWARE includes many of the current and out-of-production silver and silver-plated flatware patterns made in the past eighty years. Other silver is listed under Silver-American, Silver-English, etc. Most silver flatware sets that are missing a few pieces can be completed through the help of a silver matching service.

TIP
When the weather is bad, a farm auction will probably be good. Brave storms and cold and attend auctions in bad weather when the crowd is small and the prices low.

Shirley Temple, Doll Purse, Red Vinyl, White Script Signature, Cutout Handle, Ideal, 1950s
$33

Ruby Lane

Shirley Temple, Doll, Vinyl, Wee Willie Winkie Scottish Outfit, Hat, Ideal, c.1955, 12 In.
$85

Ruby Lane

S

Silver Deposit, Pitcher, Chased Overlay, Leaves, Grapes, Wavy Rim, Handle, c.1900, 10 In.
$450

Cowan Auctions

Silver Flatware Sterling, Bernadotte, Dinner Service For 12, Serving Fork & Spoon, Georg Jensen
$14,220

James D. Julia Auctioneers

Silver Flatware Sterling, Versailles, Punch Ladle, Woman, Harp, Gilt Washed Bowl, Gorham, 13 In.
$219

Sloans & Kenyon

SILVER FLATWARE PLATED

Algonquin, Spoon, Demitasse, Oneida, 1923, 4⅜ In. 15
Assyrian, Pickle Fork, Rogers Bros., 1947, 8 In. 20
Avalon, Coup Spoon, Wm. Rogers Mfg. Co., 1940, 7 In. 7
Camelot, Harvest, Grille Knife, American Silver Co., 1964, 9 In. 3
Coronation, Meat Fork, Oneida, 1936, 8⅜ In. 24
Fairoaks, Cream Ladle, Rockford S.P. Co., 1909, 5¾ In. 18
Lady Barbara, Meat Fork, Wm. Rogers & Son, 1959, 8½ In. 16
Lexington, Fork, Oneida, 1914, 7 In. 6
Malmaison, Dessert Fork, Christofle, Fitted Case, c.1967, 96 Piece 984
Mojeska, Butter Knife, Oneida, 1916, 7⅜ In. 6
Old Colony, Gravy Ladle, Rogers Bros., 1911, 7 In. 17
Old South, Teaspoon, Wm. Rogers, 1938, 6¼ In. 6
Vinea, Asparagus Server, Pierced, Christofle, 10 In. 108

SILVER FLATWARE STERLING

Acorn, Ladle, Double Scrolls, 4 Leaves, Georg Jensen, 7¾ In. 185
Acorn, Service For 12, Georg Jensen, 84 Piece 11070
Ailanthus, Ice Cream Spoon, Tiffany & Co., c.1900, 5½ In., 12 Piece 500
Baltimore Rose, Ladle, Repousse, Monogram, Flowers & Leaves, Schofield, 13 In. 150
Bernadotte, Dinner Service For 12, Serving Fork & Spoon, Georg Jensen ..... *illus* 14220
Bird's Nest, Cake Server, Gorham, 1865, 9⅛ In. 2300
Bird's Nest, Nut Scoop, Gilt, Gorham, c.1865, 9 In. 2125
Cactus, Demitasse Spoon, Georg Jensen, 4 In., 12 Piece 311
Calla Lily, Cake Server, Bright Cut, Whiting, c.1850, 11 In. 517
Chantilly, Dessert Fork, Gorham, c.1890, 5¾ In., 11 Piece 196
Greta, Knife, Stainless Steel Blade, O. Mogensen, 8 In., 10 Piece 161
King, Butter Spreader, Scalloped Shell, Dominick & Haff, 5½ In., 10 Piece 124
King, Dinner Fork, Monogram, Gelston Ladd & Co., 9 In., 12 Piece 366
King, Rice Spoon, Monogram, Hayden & Gregg, c.1850, 11½ In. 1062
Ladle, Scalloped, Fluted, Tapered Handle, Chased Leaves, Bird, Monogram, 12½ In. 155
Lily, Salad Servers, Whiting Division, 12½ In., Pair 176
Louis XIV, Ladle, Gorham, c.1870 538
Louis XIV, Salad Set, Bellflowers, Fluted Bowl, Tapered Handle, Towle, 9 x 3 In. 98
Mathilde, Spoon, Swollen, Scrolls, Scallop Shell, Jensen, 9 In. 154
Morning Glory, Ladle, Gorham, c.1865, 7 In. 313
Old Baronial, Vegetable Server, Serpentine Rim, Acanthus, c.1900, 9¾ x 3 In. 167
Raphael, Ladle, Gorham, c.1874, 13 In. 245
Tuscan Beaded, Salad Set, Gold Washing, Reticulated Bowl, 8 In. 138
Versailles, Punch Ladle, Woman, Harp, Gilt Washed Bowl, Gorham, 13 In. ..... *illus* 219

SILVER PLATE is not solid silver. It is a ware made of a metal, such as nickel or copper, that is covered with a thin coating of silver. The letters *EPNS* are often found on American and English silver-plated wares. *Sheffield* is a term with two meanings. Sometimes it refers to sterling silver made in the town of Sheffield, England. Sometimes it refers to an old form of plated silver.

Basket, Hexagonal, Reticulated Basket, Bail Handle, Meriden Britannia, 1900s, 10 In. 738
Basket, Pastry, Arched Handle, Repousse, Scrolling, Reticulated, Meriden Britannia, 8 x 10 In. . 354
Biscuit Barrel, 3-Arch Handle, Footed, 9 x 7½ In. 240
Biscuit Barrel, Round, Hinged Lid, Reticulated Foot, c.1900, 7¼ In. 240
Biscuit Box, Shell Form, Branchwork Supports, c.1900, 10 In. ..... *illus* 366
Biscuit Box, Shell Form, Folding, Gourd Shape, 9 x 6 In. 147
Bottle Cooler, Bleached Walnut, Stag Head Handles, Cylindrical, 14½ In., Pair 3250
Bottle Cooler, Fish, Resting On Back Fins, Figural, Hinged Neck, 15½ x 12 In. 847
Bowl, Handle, 4-Footed, Medallions, Roman Soldier, Dragon, Leaves, c.1870, 12½ In. 120
Box, 4 Seasons, Stylized Medallions, Handles, Germany, c.1900, 6 x 17 In. 1320
Bun Warmer, Oval, Dome Lid, Fluted, Claw Feet, Liners, Harrison Bros. & Howson, 9 x 14 In. ... 184
Butter Keeper, Cow Finial, Handles, Footed, Reed & Barton, c.1870, 6½ x 8 In. 210
Cake Plate, Handle, Footed Stand, Engraved Design, Repousse, c.1900, 12½ x 10 In. 108
Cardholder, Engraved, Acanthus Scrolls, Rondels, 4 x 2¾ In., Pair 300
Casket, Rococo Style, Gold Wash, 4 Ball Feet, Hinged Lid, Rogers, Smith & Co., 5 x 8 In. 124
Caviar Cooler, Square Base, Egg Shape Holder, Pedestal, St. James Of Brazil, 11 x 7 In. 540
Centerpiece, Entwined Grapevines, Basket, Frosted Glass Bowl, Tripod Feet, 19 x 10 In. 960
Centerpiece, Jugendstil, Standing Woman, Leaf Base, Glass Bowl, Germany, c.1900, 18 x 14 In. 1920
Centerpiece, Pierced Lid, Round Foot, Wide Rim, Etched, Low Relief, 5 x 11 In. 60
Centerpiece, Waisted Gadroon Standard, Cut Glass Bowl, Scrolls, c.1835, 13 In. ..... *illus* 812
Centerpiece, William IV, Baluster, Scroll Branches, Trumpet, Flowers, c.1835, 20 x 22 In. 2214

Chafing Dish, Victorian, Ram's Head, Ram's Foot, Flowers, 14 x 9 In. 84
Champagne Bucket, Yellow Ball, Handle, 22 ½ x 10 In. 123
Cigar Holder, Locomotive Shape, 8 Holders, Presented By Colonel Pratt, c.1880, 11 In. 1250
Claret Jug, Oval Glass Body, Swirls, Silver Gadroon Collar & Scroll Handle, 11 In. 593
Cocktail Shaker, Lighthouse Shape, Meriden, c.1930, 20 x 7 ¼ In. 5938
Cocktail Shaker, Penguin, Napier, 12 In. 1080
Cocktail Shaker, Penguins, Figural, Strap Handle, 12 ¾ In., Pair 3750
Coffee Urn, 2 Piece, Cylindrical Body, Tube Handles, France, 27 x 16 ½ In. 363
Compote, Baroque Style, Reticulated, Poland, 1800s, 6 ¾ x 8 In. 124
Compote, Basket, Grape Clusters, Leaves, Branch, Putti, Lioness, 12 In. 183
Compote, Tripod, Lotus Leaf, 3 Stems, Ivy Leaves, c.1860, 5 ¾ x 6 ½ In. 83
Container, Bear, Performing, Hinged Head, Forepaws Crossed, Glass Eyes, Italy, 20 In. 600
Cover, Meat, Armorial, Rocaille, Gadroon Banding, Handle, c.1810, 10 x 16 In., Pair 492
Cover, Meat, Dome Lid, Shields, Tray, Sheffield, c.1810, 10 x 25 In. 1416
Cup, Jester Handle, Monogram, Spiral Rim, Saucer Foot, 5 In. 35
Cup, Wood, Lid, 3 S-Shape Handles, Grapevine Banding, Clusters, ½ Liter 96
Dish Warmer, Napoleon III, Christofle, Oval, Rocaille Armorial Cartouches, Footed, 17 x 12 In. .. 468
Dish, Entree, Lid, Oval, Reeded Feet, Removable Interior Tray, Heraldic, 1900s, 12 x 15 In. 236
Dish, Pedestal, Handle, Etched, Meriden Britannia Company, 8 In. 24
Epergne, 4 Scrolled Arms, Openwork, Irises, Round Plateau, c.1900, 15 x 23 In. 799
Epergne, 5 Branch, Blossoms, Shells, Cut Glass Bowls, Square Base, 22 ½ In. 2250
Epergne, 5 Sections, Mirror Plates, Leaf & Scroll Berry Border, c.1865, 4 x 92 In. 10000
Figurine, Pheasant, Head Up, 1900s, 11 ½ In., Pair 125
Figurine, Pheasant, Weidlich Bros., 1900s, 16 In., Pair 1375
Figurine, Quail, Wood Plinth, 11 x 17 ½ In. 106
Fish Dish, Dome Lid, Warming Stand, Hot Water Compartment, Mazarin, c.1900, 13 x 28 In. ... 1968
Flask, R. Wallace & Sons, Clam Shell Shape, 6 In. 130
Flask, Sheffield, Monogram, Cartier, James Dixon & Son, England, 5 x 3 In. 112
Goblet, Flat Chased Decoration, England, 8 ¼ In., 6 Piece 275
Grape Stand, Fluted Bowl, Flower, Vine Hook, WH & SB, c.1900, 8 ¾ x 7 In. 225
Hot Water Urn, Bun Feet, Stylized Arms, Spigot, 16 x 14 In. 125
Hot Water Urn, Gadroon Banding, Stirrup Ringed Lion Masque Handles, 18 x 12 In. 437
Hot Water Urn, Georgian, Engraved Band, Lion Masque Handles, Old Sheffield, 17 x 12 In. 625
Hot Water Urn, Georgian, Gadroon Borders, Loop Handles, Lion Mask, c.1810, 18 In. 378
Hot Water Urn, Oval, Acanthus, Caryatid Handles, Dome Lid, Foot, c.1870, 21 x 18 In. 615
Hot Water Urn, Regency, Oval, Fluted Columns, Lion Masks, Sphinx Finial, 17 In. 250
Hot Water Urn, Regency, Upturned Handles, Pedestal, Ball Feet, Leafy Band, 19 In. .... *illus* 366
Jar, Honey Bee, Figural, Cranberry Glass Thorax, Mappin & Webb, 3 x 6 ½ In. 726
Jewelry Box, Gilt, Village Scenes, 4 Leafy Feet, Silk, 3 x 4 In. 108
Kettle, Hot Water, Stand, Melon Shape, Engraved, Scroll, Elkington & Co., 1853, 18 ⅜ In. 4425
Knife Rest, Crossed Torches, Ribbon Bow, Christofle & Apollo, 1 ½ x 3 ¾ In., 12 Piece 424
Letter Rack, Brass, Ball Feet, Christopher Dresser, Hukin & Heath, c.1880, 5 x 7 In. .... *illus* 938
Loving Cup, Woman, Hollowed Shirt, Raised Arms, Swinging Cup, 8 ½ In. 245
Meat Dish, Dome Lid, Leafy Handle, Oval, Scroll Feet, Well & Tree Dish, 13 x 26 In. 980
Mirror, Vanity, Art Nouveau, Standing Women Base, 19 x 8 ¾ In. 720
Model, Horse-Drawn Trolley Car, C.H. Zimmerman, Movable Parts, c.1900, 15 In. 1125
Paperclip, Dog, Hound, Glass Eyes, 6 In. 63
Paperclip, Fish, Glass Eyes, 6 In. 63
Pitcher, Art Nouveau, Vine Band, Scroll Handle, Meriden Brittania, c.1890, 8 x 8 In. 449
Pitcher, Water, Aesthetic, Insulated, Embossed, Meriden Britannia, 1885, 14 In. 922
Pitcher, Water, Stand, Swing Handle, 20 x 12 In. 52
Pitcher, Water, Victorian, Homan Silver Plate Company, 9 ¾ x 7 In. 80
Planter, Lion Mask Handles, 4-Footed, 7 x 8 ½ In. 153
Plaque, 4 Putti, Flowers, Elkington, 12 ½ In. 344
Plaque, Don Quixote, Battles Wineskins, Peasant Maids, Copper Electrotype, 15 x 21 In., Pair ... 984
Plateau, Applied Flower Band, Scroll Feet, Oak Backboard, England, 5 x 18 In. .... *illus* 1464
Plateau, Oblong, Reeded & Gadroon Frame, Hairy Paw Feet, 1800s, 26 x 16 In. 1673
Plateau, Round, Gadroon Border, Paw Scroll Feet, Beveled Mirror, 5 x 20 In. 531
Salt & Pepper, Turned Wood Shape, Borel, France, c.1970, 6 x 2 ⅛ In. 213
Salt Cellar, Spoon, Compote Shape, Dolphin Pedestal, 2 In., 12 Piece 274
Salver, Armorial, Round, Rose & Leaf Rim, Scroll Legs, Scrolling, Tray, c.1810, 20 In. 615
Server, Lazy Susan, Rotating Tray, Round Foot, 4 Handles, Cobalt Glass Liners, 13 x 28 In. 861
Server, Lid, Liner, Handles, Shaped Rim, Embossed, Sheffield, c.1920, 6 x 12 In. 49
Serving Dish, Lid, Handle, Art Nouveau, Reed & Barton, 6 x 11 In. 210
Serving Dish, Triple Bowl, Cast Scalloped Sea Shells, c.1900, 6 x 11 x 11 In. 109
Spoon, Souvenir, see Souvenir category.

Silver Plate, Biscuit Box, Shell Form, Branchwork Supports, c.1900, 10 In.
$366

Neal Auctions

Silver Plate, Centerpiece, Waisted Gadroon Standard, Cut Glass Bowl, Scrolls, c.1835, 13 In.
$812

New Orleans (Cakebread)

Silver Plate, Hot Water Urn, Regency, Upturned Handles, Pedestal, Ball Feet, Leafy Band, 19 In.
$366

Neal Auctions

Silver Plate, Letter Rack, Brass, Ball Feet, Christopher Dresser, Hukin & Heath, c.1880, 5 x 7 In.
$938

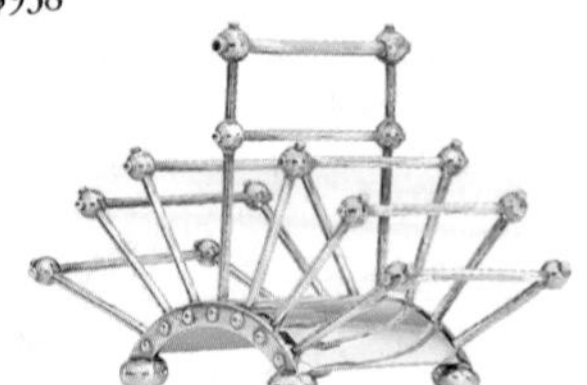

Rago Arts and Auction Center

Silver Plate, Plateau, Applied Flower Band, Scroll Feet, Oak Backboard, England, 5 x 18 In.
$1,464

Neal Auctions

Silver-American, Bowl, Fruit, Art Nouveau, Embossed Poppies, Monogram, Mauser Mfg., c.1900, 11 In.
$430

New Orleans (Cakebread)

TIP

When polishing silver, first remove all detachable parts like screw-on handles or finials. Rest the silver piece on a cloth in your lap, never on the table or other hard surface. Polish by rubbing in circles. If there are wooden handles or other parts, these should be waxed when the silver is cleaned.

Tea & Coffee Set, Plymouth, Gorham, c.1915, 5 Piece, 8 In. 677
Tea & Coffee Set, Rosewood, Coffeepot, Teapot, Sugar & Creamer, Tray, 5 Piece 72
Tea & Coffee Set, Teapot, Sugar & Creamer, Ebonized Wood, Modern, 3 Piece 272
Tea Set, Scrolling, 3 Pots, Wood Handles, Stand, Burner, Sugar, Creamer, Tray, Ellis-Barker 540
Tea Set, Teapot, Sugar & Creamer, Tray, Midcentury, 6 ½ x 16 In., 4 Piece 174
Tea Urn, Flowers, 4 Hairy Paw Feet, Base With Bun Feet, 18 x 9 In. 94
Tea Urn, Heart, Engraved Leaves, Ball & Claw Feet, 20 ½ In., Pair 1000
Tea Urn, Victorian, Double Handle, 4 Legs, Lamp, 13 ¾ In. 60
Teapot, Aesthetic, Rectangular, Pyramid Shape Lid, Scroll Handle, Footed, 10 x 9 In. 136
Teapot, Creamer, Tray, Vivianna Torun Bulow-Hube, Sweden, c.1965, 17 In. 330
Teapot, Flowers, Hinged Lid, 6 x 10 In. 204
Teapot, Mahogany Handle & Finial, Ilonka Karasz, 5 x 6 In. 120
Toast Rack, 4 Slots, England, 2 ¾ In. 75
Toast Warmer, 3 Divisions, Hinged Shell Lids, Pierced Inserts, Hood Feet, c.1880, 10 In. 266
Tray, Flowers, Leaf Scroll, Tubular Gallery, Handles, Ball Feet, c.1890, 21 x 15 In. 1062
Tray, Gallery, Openwork Sides, Handles, Bun Feet, Applied Heraldic Shield, c.1910, 27 In. 885
Tray, Handles, Shells, Scrolls, Clusters On Rim, Engraved, 18 x 28 In. 92
Tray, Oval, Faux Tortoiseshell, Penhaligon Silver Co., 4 x 16 In. 738
Tray, Relief Cast Border, Flowers, Scrolls, Stippled, Boulton & Watts, c.1755, 30 In. 120
Tray, Tea, Flowers, Scrolling, Handles, Ellis Barker, Birmingham, 1900s, 25 x 16 In. 366
Tray, Wild Boar Shape Handles, France, c.1910, 19 ¼ x 12 In. 277
Tureen, Lid, 4 Scrolled Feet, Relief Shells, Incised, Cartouches, Acanthus Handles, 11 x 15 In. 207
Tureen, Sauce, Dome Lid, Bulbous, Reeded Handles, Gadroon Rim, c.1835, 5 x 7 In., Pair 625
Tureen, Soup, George III, Old Sheffield, Navette Shape, Ring Handles, 6 x 6 ½ In., Pair 676
Tureen, Soup, Victorian, Oval, Rope Handles, Lion Masks, Flowers, 9 x 13 In. 240
Urn, Centerpiece, Jugendstil, Whiplash Handles, WMF Co., Germany, c.1900, 11 x 17 In. 840
Urn, Double Handle, Grape Branches, Leafy Scrolls, Webster-Wilcox, 11 x 10 In. 300
Urn, Neoclassical, Classical Figures, 27 ¾ In., Pair 1625
Vase, Rectangular, Flaring & Narrowing, Bottom To Top, Sabattini, c.1925, 10 In. 554
Warmer, Double Burner, George III Style, Aluminum Tray Insert, Asprey, 19 x 10 In. 178
Warming Dome, T. & J. Creswick, Sheffield, 12 x 19 In. 431
Wine Coaster, Molded Grape & Vine, Sheffield, 1800s, 7 ⅝ In., Pair 300
Wine Coaster, Relief Banded, Reclining Putti, Grapevines, 3 x 7 ½ In., Pair 210
Wine Cooler, Fluted, Ear Handles, 9 x 10 In. 153
Wine Cooler, Spiral, Fluted, Gadroon, Branch Handles, c.1835, 11 In., Pair 5000

SILVER-AMERICAN. American silver is listed here. Coin and sterling silver are included. Most of the sterling silver listed in this book is subdivided by country. There are also other pieces of silver and silver plate listed under special categories, such as Candelabrum, Napkin Ring, Silver Flatware, Silver Plate, Silver-Sterling, and Tiffany Silver. The meltdown price determines the value of solid silver items. These prices are based on silver values from June 2015 to April 2016.

Basket, Fixed Handle, Pierced Border, Trianon, 10 In. 750
Bowl, Bacchus, Pierce Undulating Rim, Gorham, 12 ¼ In. 276
Bowl, Beaded Rim, Square Foot, 8 x 11 In. 840
Bowl, Chased Rim, Leafy Scrolling, Shells, Gorham, c.1900 184
Bowl, Chippendale, Fluted Sides, Flat Bottom, Gorham, 1959, 9 ½ In. 180
Bowl, Chippendale, Paneled Sides, Monogram, Reed & Barton, 1931, 9 In. 180
Bowl, Dublin Pattern, Spaulding & Co., 9 ⅞ In. 240
Bowl, Flared Shell & Scrolls Rim, Cartouches, Round Foot, Gorham, 1927, 16 In. 1353
Bowl, Flowers, Scroll, Black, Starr & Frost, 13 ½ In. 610
Bowl, Fluted Basin, Pierced Rim, Scrolling Acanthus, 3 ¼ x 12 In. 518
Bowl, Footed, Gorham, 10 ¼ In. 549
Bowl, Francis I, Reed & Barton, 1907, 8 In. 1045
Bowl, Francis I, Reed & Barton, 1948, 11 ½ In. 461
Bowl, Francis I, Serpentine Rim, Lobed, Repousse, Reed & Barton, 12 x 3 In. 401
Bowl, Fruit, Art Nouveau, Embossed Poppies, Monogram, Mauser Mfg., c.1900, 11 In. .... *illus* 430
Bowl, Hammered, Straight-Sided, 5 Flutes, Rolled Rim, Arts & Crafts, A. Eicher, 7 In. 461
Bowl, Inverted Rim, Saucer Foot, Gorham, 1900s, 4 x 13 In. 944
Bowl, Latticed Lobes, Repousse Flowers, c.1925, 19 In. 4305
Bowl, Lily Pad, Oblong, Repousse, 12 ¾ x 8 In. 423
Bowl, Lucky, Horseshoe Shape, 4-Leaf Clovers, Reed & Barton, 3 x 2 ½ In. 189
Bowl, Marie Antoinette, Relief Designs, Monogram, Gorham, 11 In. 334
Bowl, Marked J.E. Caldwell & Co., 3 ½ x 13 In. 522
Bowl, Nancy Lee, Repousse Gadroon Rim, Bellflower Band, Reed & Barton, 1946, 9 x 2 In. 115
Bowl, Paul Revere Pattern, Flared Rim, Stepped Foot, Rogers Sterling, 4 x 9 In. 196

Bowl, Poppy Blossom, Wallace, 10 In. 302
Bowl, Poppy Design, Scalloped Rim, Wallace, 1900s, 10 In. 429
Bowl, Prelude, Round, Flared Repousse Rim, Leaves, International Silver Co., 10 In. 155
Bowl, Presentation, Engraved Inscription, Gorham, c.1950, 9 In. 338
Bowl, Ram's Head, Footed, Gorham, 3 ½ x 8 In. 369
Bowl, Repousse Border, Pedestal Foot, Loring Andrews Co., 6 x 12 In. 1403
Bowl, Round, Applied Die-Rolled Border, Footed, Ewan, Charleston, c.1850, 4 In. 4130
Bowl, Round, Urn, Swag, Flowers, Scrolling, Dominick & Haff, 10 In. 354
Bowl, Royal Danish, Molded Corners, International Silver, 12 In. 270
Bowl, Salem, Square, Lobed, Wavy Rim, Initial, Reed & Barton, 8 ½ In. 230
Bowl, Scalloped, Flared Rim, Oval, Reeded, Paw Feet, Reed & Barton, 4 x 13 In. 240
Bowl, Scalloped, Flowers, Footed, Towle, 4 ⅝ x 9 ¾ In. 341
Bowl, Shell Shape, Fluted, Repousse Scroll, R. Wallace & Sons, c.1890, 10 In. 466
Bowl, Squared, Shaped Rim, Randahl, 8 x 8 In. 319
Bowl, Stylized Engraved Leaves, Hallmark, Gorham, 8 x 2 In. 124
Bowl, Stylized Petal Shape, Lobed, Flat Rim, Watson, 2 x 10 In. 259
Bowl, Undulating Rim, Folded Edges, Chased Flowers, Martele, c.1906, 12 In. 9600
Bowl, Vegetable, Francis I, Round, Shaped Rim, 1907, 12 In. Diam., Pair 1500
Bowl, Vegetable, Lid, Removable Handle, Can Use As 2 Dishes, Trianon, 10 In. 1795
Bowl, Wide Rim, Round Pedestal Foot, Gyllenberg & Swanson, c.1930, 5 In. Diam. 98
Bowl, Windsor, Lobed, Flared Rim, Marked Reed & Barton, 12 x 9 In. 207
Bread Tray, Francis I, Reed & Barton, 12 x 7 In. 440
Butter, Conical Cover, Flower & Scroll Repousse, Banded Rim, Trifid Feet, c.1820, 7 In. 688
Candelabra are listed in the Candelabrum category.
Candlesticks are listed in their own category.
Cann, Cup, Scrolled Handle, Footed, John Ball, Mass., c.1752, 6 In. 4956
Charger, Repousse Floral Rim, Monogram, Kirk & Son, c.1930, 11 In., 6 Piece 3936
Charger, Scrolled Rim, Floral Scrollwork, Gorham, c.1915, 11 ½ In., 12 Piece 6765
Cigar Box, Hinged Lid, Andrew Taylor, 6 In. 210
Cigar Case, Figural 3 Cigars, Gilt Ribbon, Engraved, Gorham, c.1900, 5 In. 8125
Cigarette Box, Rectangular, Gorham, 5 In., Pair 210
Cigarette Case, 14K Yellow Gold, Stripe Design, Black, Starr & Gorham, 3 x 5 In. 173
Cocktail Fork, Etched Flowers, Diamond Cut, Bailey, Banks & Biddle, Box, 5 In., 12 Piece 109
Cocktail Shaker, Alphonse La Paglia, Round Base, Short Spout, 9 x 6 In. 4428
Cocktail Shaker, Georgian Revival, Beaded Trim, Handle, Chicago Silver, 11 In. 400
Cocktail Shaker, La Paglia, International, 9 ½ In. 1620
Cocktail Shaker, Reed & Barton, Tapered Cylinder, Dome Lid, 5 ½ x 4 In. 277
Coffee Set, Art Deco, Square, Stepped Decoration, Ebony Handles, 4 Piece 6765
Coffee Set, Diamond Pattern, Pointed Finial, Plastic Handle, Reed & Barton, 3 Piece 863
Coffee Set, Slender Lobed Body, Hammered, Whiting, c.1916, 4 Piece 861
Coffee Set, Trailing Leaves, Berry Clusters, Frank Smith, c.1900, 10 In., 3 Piece 584
Coffeepot, Christian Wiltberger, c.1793 3120
Coffeepot, Egg & Dart Decoration, Flower Finial, Bard & Lamont, c.1835, 10 In. 500
Coffeepot, Leafy Banding, Stodder & Frobisher, c.1815, 9 ¾ In. 438
Coffeepot, Lobed Body, Handles, Hyde & Goodrich, 12 ¾ In. 531
Coffeepot, Repousse, S. Kirk & Son, 10 In. 671
Coffeepot, Tapered, Dome Lid, Scroll Handle, Duck's Beak Spout, Baltimore, 1910, 10 x 6 In. 922
Cold Meat Fork, Les Six Fleurs, Pierced, 4 Tines, Reed & Barton, 8 In. 132
Compote, 3 Dolphin Supports, Robert Anstead, 5 x 9 ½ In. 221
Compote, Francis I, Fluted, Footed, Serpentine Rim, Scroll, Reed & Barton, 1950s, 8 x 5 In. 357
Compote, Francis I, Reed & Barton, 1949, 4 ¾ x 8 In. 522
Compote, Round Lobed Foot, 3 ¾ x 7 In., Pair 400
Compote, Scalloped, Flared Rim, Flowers, George A. Henckel & Co., c.1940, 8 x 4 In. 118
Compote, Square Foot, Trianon, 10 x 5 ¾ In. 75
Compote, Seville, Towle, 10 In. .... *illus* 425
Compote, Small Crest, Whiting, c.1905, 5 ½ In. .... *illus* 199
Cordial, Trumpet Shape, Green Wash, Marked, Gorham, 2 ¾ In. 61
Coupe, Footed, Falcons, Carnelian, Circle Base, Flared Rim, Gorham, 1930s, 3 x 5 In. 2125
Cream Jug, Egyptian Revival, Helmet Shape, Pharaonic Head, Ball, Black & Co., 7 In. 420
Cream Soup Spoon, Cast Handle, Blossoming Lilies, International Silver Co., 7 In., 6 Piece 196
Creamer, Lobed, Flared Lip, Scroll Handle, Shells, Flowers, c.1830, 7 In. 717
Creamer, Lobed, Faux Bois Handle, Hinged Lid, Charters, Cann & Dunn, c.1950, 7 In. 338
Creamer, Manning Family, Urn Shape, Flowers, Monogram, 4 In. 413
Creamer, Monogram, Repousse, Dominick & Haff, 5 ½ x 6 ¾ In. 183
Creamer, Stieff, Oval, Wide Spout, Loop Handle, Marked 139
Creamer, Urn Shape, Scroll Handle, Faceted Body, John Mood, 7 ¾ In. 1536

Invisible Mark

A new technique called acoustical imaging can be used to make rubbed-out hallmarks on silver visible again. A special type of image similar to an ultrasound can show the slight compression of the metal where the silver was stamped with the hallmark. Sounds like a good tool for museums and the very, very serious collector.

Silver-American, Compote, Seville, Towle, 10 In.
$425

Ruby Lane

Silver-American, Compote, Small Crest, Whiting, c.1905, 5 ½ In.
$199

Ruby Lane

TIP

It is best to hand wash silverware and not put it in a dishwasher. The force of the water may make the silver bump, the detergent may have some harmful ingredients, and the handles on vintage knives may come unglued.

S

Silver-American, Kettle, Stand, Lobed, Acorn Finial, Engraved, Charters, Cann & Dunn, c.1850, 16 In.
$2,829

Skinner, Inc.

Silver-American, Mug, Panels, Greek Key Band, Handle, John C. Moore & Son, N.Y., 3 ¾ In.
$461

New Orleans (Cakebread)

Silver-American, Mug, Presentation, Paneled, Engraved, Henry Fletcher, Coin, c.1850, 3 ⅝ In.
$826

Brunk Auctions

Croquette Server, Engraved Iris, Carter Brothers, 9 x 3 In. 293
Crumb Pan, Gallery, Leaves, Hyde & Goodrich, c.1800, 12 In. 240
Crumber, H.H. Curtis, c.1900, 13 In. 150
Dish, Chippendale, Serpentine Flared Rim, Ogee Border, International Silver, 12 x 9 In. 230
Dish, Coquille, Milled Laurel Edged Handle, C-Scroll Feet, Coin, c.1875, 5 x 4 In., Pair 615
Dish, Divided, Chippendale, Molded Rim, Frank Smith Silver Co., 11 In. 158
Dish, Dublin, Round, Scalloped, Fluted Edge, Tuttle Silversmiths, c.1955, 10 In. 196
Dish, Entree, Cartouche Paneled Shape, Handles, Reed & Barton, 11 In., Pair 826
Dish, Flower Shape, Leaf Spray, Blossoms, Reed & Barton, 1940, 14 In. 492
Dish, Fluted Edge, Square, Reed & Barton, c.1939, 8 ½ In. 180
Dish, Fluted, Footed, Ribbed Wide Border, Flared Rim, Reed & Barton, 1956, 11 x 8 In. 401
Dish, Footed, Lily, J.C. Boardman & Co., 2 ⅞ x 6 ⅞ In. 120
Dish, Lid, Oval, Guilloche Rim, Handles, Dome Lid, Lion Finial, Gorham, 10 In. 369
Dish, Oval, Flower Spray Rim, 2 Sections, Jacobi & Jenkins, c.1900, 13 In. 523
Dish, Reticulated Edge, Monogram, Chester, Billings & Son, c.1900, 7 In. 923
Dish, Scallop Shell Shape, Ribbed, Flared Rim, Ball Feet, Gorham, 1956, 6 x 6 In., 3 Piece 354
Dish, Scalloped, Fluted Seashell Design, Handle, Frank W. Smith, 11 x 9 In. 161
Dish, Shell Shape, Ball Footed, Gorham, 9 In. 120
Dish, Soup, Art Nouveau, Relief Violets Rim, Unger Bros., 1900s, 10 In. 360
Dish, Sweetmeat, Oval, Rococo Scroll Rim, Love Birds, Flowers, Gorham, c.1900, 7 x 6 In. 369
Dresser Box, Rococo Style, Domed, Girl With Flowing Hair, Mauser, c.1890, 5 x 3 In. 354
Dresser Set, Repousse Floral, Mirror, Tray, Gorham & Whiting, c.1886, 8 Piece 230
Egg Spoon, Gold Wash, Bird's Nest Pattern, Leaves, Twig Handle, Gorham, 4 In., 6 Piece 755
Epergne, 8-Light, Crystal Bowl, 18 ¾ In. 787
Ewer, Chased Flower Decoration, Relief, Reed & Barton, 9 In. 270
Ewer, Engraved, Hinged Lid, Gale & Hayden, 7 ½ In. 2838
Ewer, Urn Shape, Acanthus Handle, Rocaille Cartouche, S. Kirk, c.1846 In., 18 In. 2091
Eyeglass Case, Monogram Hinged Lid, Flowers, Scroll, c.1900, 5 ¼ In. 90
Fish Slice, Spoon, Repousse, 1800s, 11 In., Pair 72
Flask, Engine Turned, Cartouche, Napier, c.1930, 5 ¾ x 3 ⅞ In. 389
Flask, Japanesque, Partial Gilt, Dominick & Haff, c.1882, 6 In. 2125
Fork, Birds, On Branches, Child's, Whiting Mfg. Co., 1874 35
Fork, Gadroon, Gorham, 7 In. 51
Goblet, Bell Shape Bowls, Wallace, 1900s, 7 In., 10 Piece 780
Goblet, Cordial, Gorham, 2 In., 4 Piece 72
Goblet, Lord Saybrook, Tapered, International, 6 ½ To 6 ¾ In., 13 Piece 1534
Goblet, Out Swept Lip, Pedestal, Elgin Silversmiths, 1900s, 7 In., 6 Piece 413
Goblet, Puritan Pattern, Gorham, 6 ½ In., 6 Piece 671
Goblet, Repousse, Flower Garland, Beaded Border, c.1830, 5 In. 368
Goblet, Tapered Foot, International Silver, 6 x 3 In., 6 Piece 605
Gravy Boat, Underplate, Francis I, Reed & Barton, 1929 2200
Gravy Spoon, Buttercup, Button To Handle, Monogram, Gorham, 12 In. 173
Ice Cream Slice, Engraved Blade, Figural Stag Head Terminal, c.1855, 10 In. 531
Ice Cream Slice, Hollow Handle, Scrolls & Flower Heads, Redlich, c.1900, 15 In. 215
Ice Cream Spoon, Raphael, Arched, Textured, Gorham, c.1874, 4 ½ In., 11 Piece 112
Julep Cup, Tapered Cylinder, Stepped Rim, Kirk Stieff, 4 x 3 In. 293
Kettle, Stand, Lobed, Acorn Finial, Engraved, Charters, Cann & Dunn, c.1850, 16 In. ....*illus* 2829
Knife Set, Japonesque, Mixed Metals, Gorham, c.1890, 8 In., 6 Piece 732
Knife, Master Butter, Twist Handle, Coin, 1800s, 8 In. 95
Ladle, Fiddlehead, Melville & Co., c.1849, 13 ⅝ In. 687
Ladle, Gold Wash Bowl, Wavy Rim, Grapes, F.W. Smith, c.1890, 13 ¼ In. 363
Ladle, Gravy, Parcel Gilt, Round Bowl, Rosette, Portrait Medallion, c.1870, 7 In. 311
Ladle, Gravy, Shaped Bowl, Arched Handle, Rosette, Warrior, Gilt, c.1870, 8 In. 335
Ladle, Marked De Larue, 14 ½ In. 2126
Ladle, Medallion, 12 ½ In. 204
Ladle, Medallion, Flared Rim, Monogram, John Rudolph Wendt, 1862, 13 In. 738
Ladle, Oval Bowl, Shell Back Design, Monogram, Curved Handle, c.1820, 13 In. 508
Ladle, Rose Gold Bowl, Strawberry, Leaves, Medallion Handle, Box, c.1870, 8 In. 156
Ladle, Rounded Square Shape, Serpentine Rim, Twist Handle, Whiting Mfg., 12 x 4 In. 213
Ladle, Versailles, Gold Wash Round Bowl, Gorham, c.1888, 5 ¾ In. 300
Loving Cup, Grapes & Vine Band, Paneled, Swollen Shoulder, Whiting, 10 In. 1853
Magnifying Glass, Umbrella Handle, Stieff Rose, 14 In. 115
Money Clip, Horseshoe Shape, Ralph Lauren 122
Mug, Panels, Greek Key Band, Handle, John C. Moore & Son, N.Y., 3 ¾ In. ....*illus* 461
Mug, Presentation, Paneled, Engraved, Henry Fletcher, Coin, c.1850, 3 ⅝ In. ....*illus* 826
Mug, Trophy, Agriculture, Best Single Harness Horse, Georgia, Coin, 1851, 4 ½ In. ....*illus* 7670

S

Napkin Rings are listed in their own category.
Nut Scoop, Hooded, Gothic Dome, George Sharp, c.1866, 10 ½ In. 3250
Perfume Bottle, Enameled Violets & Leaves, Stopper, Gorham, 1897, 6 In. .... *illus* 2242
Pie Server, Engraved Blade, Applied Lily & Leaves Handle, c.1880, 9 In. 335
Pie Server, Wood & Hughes, c.1850, 10 In. 390
Pitcher, Arts & Crafts, Kalo Shops, Hammered, Monogram, Early 1900s, 7 In. 2460
Pitcher, Baluster, Fluted, Beaded Edges, Round Foot, c.1850, 7 In. 216
Pitcher, Baluster, Scroll Handle, Baltimore Silversmiths, 10 In. 300
Pitcher, Baluster, Wavy Wide Spout, Scroll Handle, Hearts, c.1850, 13 In. 1008
Pitcher, Bulbous, Ribbed Bottom, Ruffled Rim, Bigelow & Kennard, 8 In. 1235
Pitcher, Buttercup Pattern, Repousse Cartouche, Squat, Gorham, 7 ½ In. 948
Pitcher, Flowers, Trailing Scroll Rim, Monogram, George Shiebler, c.1900, 6 In. 861
Pitcher, Hammered, Applied Flowering Strawberry, 1900s, 9 ½ In. 1875
Pitcher, Lobed, Tapered, Scroll Handle, Applied Leaves, Adler, c.1950, 9 In. 330
Pitcher, Pear Shape, Scroll, Acanthus, Flowers, Medallions, T.B. Starr, c.1915, 7 In. 605
Pitcher, Repousse Bands, Hammered & Stippled Flowers, Gorham, 7 ½ In. 1304
Pitcher, Repousse Scrolls, Leaves & Vines, Bulbous Top, Footed, Durgin, 10 In. 2370
Pitcher, Shaped Spout, Greek Key Design, Classic Heads, Gorham, 1800s, 12 In. 2160
Pitcher, Squared Top Handle, International Silver Company, 8 ½ In. 484
Pitcher, Water, Art Nouveau, Urn Shape, Leaves, Iris, Reed & Barton, c.1900, 12 In. 9225
Pitcher, Water, Baltimore Rose, Repousse, Feather Crested Handle, Schofield, c.1925, 9 In. 1599
Pitcher, Water, Baluster, Elongated Spout, Allan Adler, 8 In. 584
Pitcher, Water, Baluster, Pronounced Spout, Angle Handle, Fisher, 9 x 9 ½ In. 425
Pitcher, Water, Grapes, Leaves, Branch Handles, Bird Finial, Lincoln & Foss, c.1850 885
Pitcher, Water, Hammered, Ivory Handle, Footed, Blossoms Band, DeMatteo, c.1940, 10 In. 900
Pitcher, Water, Helmet Shape, Scroll Handle, Monogram, Reed & Barton, 1941, 9 In. 590
Pitcher, Water, Lobed, Rolled Rims, C-Scroll Handle, Spread Foot, c.1815, 10 In. 1016
Pitcher, Water, Monogram, Mark, Gorham, 1921, 8 ¾ In. 276
Pitcher, Water, Octagonal, Pear Shape, Lobed, S-Scroll Handle, Reed & Barton, 10 In. 480
Pitcher, Water, Polar Bear On Ice Cap Figural Handle, Reeded Foot, 12 In. 299
Pitcher, Water, Shouldered, Squared Handle, Reeded Foot, Barbour, 8 In. 493
Plate, Francis I, Flower Shape, Panels, Festoons, Reed & Barton, 1907, 12 In., Pair 1250
Plate, Poppies, Repousse, Wallace Sterling, 10 ½ In. 302
Plate, Round, Monogram, Marked, Gorham, 10 In. 121
Plate, Serving, Raised Floral Rim, International Silver Co., 10 ½ In. 180
Plate, Serving, Raised Sides, Repousse, Gorham, 1958, 10 In. 180
Plate, Serving, Repousse Rim, Watson Co., 10 In. 210
Platter, Chippendale, Stepped Rim, Frank Smith Silver Co., 19 ½ In. 540
Platter, Lobed, Oval, Scrollwork Rim, Enameled Medallions, Gorham, 1899, 18 In. 861
Platter, Oblong, Art Deco Style, Incised Lines On Rim, Dominick & Haff, 18 x 12 In. 550
Platter, Oval, Shell & Scroll Rim, Durgin, c.1900, 19 In. 923
Platter, Oval, Undulating Border, Reticulated, Beaded Rim, Alvin, 1898, 12 x 10 In. 207
Platter, Round, Ruffled Rim, Towle, 15 In. 360
Platter, Trianon, 15 In. 1495
Platter, Trianon, 20 ¾ In. 2095
Platter, Well & Tree, Oval, Marked Codan, 19 ¾ In. 600
Porringer, Bulbous, Scrolled Berry Handle, A. La Paglia, c.1950, 4 ½ x 5 ½ In. .... *illus* 1045
Porringer, Cartouche, c.1750, 7 x 5 In. 2125
Porringer, Flared Rim, Bulbous, Scroll Handle, Paul Revere Jr., c.1770, 8 ½ x 5 ½ In. .... *illus* 39975
Punch Bowl, Arts & Crafts, Flared Rim, Short Foot, Marked Woolley, c.1910, 15 In. 1600
Punch Ladle, Gold Washed Basin, Wavy Rim, Grape Bunches, Frank W. Wilder, 13 ¼ In. 302
Punch Ladle, Oval Bowl, Double Spouts, Curved Handle, Durgin, 13 x 5 In. 374
Punch Set, Punch Bowl, 12 Cups, Ladle, Blue Enamel Liners, Towle, c.1950, 14 Piece 2220
Rattle, Mother Goose, Pearl Handle, Unger Brothers, c.1905, 3 ¾ In. 395
Salad Servers, Swedish Modern, Oval Bowl, Hammered Handle, Allan Adler, 10 In. 178
Salad Set, Baroque, Molded, Openwork, Scrolls, Shell Bowl, Monogram, Durgin, 9 In. 218
Salt & Pepper, Chased, Village, Dancers, Marshall Field & Co., 1903-40, 6 In. 189
Salt & Pepper, Repousse Flowers, 3 Legs, S. Kirk & Son, 4 ½ x 2 In. 153
Salt Cellar, Glass Liner, Baldwin & Miller, Spoon, Wallace, c.1910, 1 x 2 In., 4 Piece 167
Salt Cellar, Oval Barrel Shape, 2 Handles, Pedestal, Wallace, c.1800, 5 x 2 In., Pair 406
Salver, Piecrust Rim, Engraved, Bailey, Banks & Biddle, c.1910, 12 In. 677
Salver, Round, Shell & Scroll Rim, Scrolled Feet, J.E. Caldwell, c.1900, 12 In. 523
Sauceboat, Georgian, 5 ½ x 9 In., Pair 554
Sauceboat, Liner, Chatham Pattern, Hallmark, Durgin, 4 ½ x 8 & 8 x 5 ½ In. 184
Sauceboat, Oval Tray, Squared Handle, Shaped Rim, Frank W. Smith, 7 In. 127
Serving Spoon, Art Deco Style, Oval Bowl, Towle, c.1928, 8 ½ In., 6 Piece 165

Silver-American, Mug, Trophy, Agriculture, Best Single Harness Horse, Georgia, Coin, 1851, 4 ½ In.
$7,670

Brunk Auctions

Silver-American, Perfume Bottle, Enameled Violets & Leaves, Stopper, Gorham, 1897, 6 In.
$2,242

Brunk Auctions

Silver-American, Porringer, Bulbous, Scrolled Berry Handle, A. La Paglia, c.1950, 4 ½ x 5 ½ In.
$1,045

New Orleans (Cakebread)

S

Silver-American, Porringer, Flared Rim, Bulbous, Scroll Handle, Paul Revere Jr., c.1770, 8 ½ x 5 ½ In.
$39,975

Skinner, Inc.

Silver-American, Tea Set, Classical, Lobed, Banding, Coin, Marked, John Crawford, c.1830, 5 Piece
$1,536

Neal Auctions

Silver-American, Teapot, Bead Border, Lion Head Spout, c.1810, 8 ½ In.
$590

Brunk Auctions

TIP

To copy a silver hallmark, try this. Hold a candle under the mark so the candle soot covers the mark. After the silver cools, put a piece of transparent tape over the mark and push it down. Remove the tape and put it on a piece of paper. You should have a copy of the mark.

Serving Spoon, Berry, Shaped, Twist Stem, Grapes, Monogram, c.1870, 10 In. 538
Serving Spoon, Bird's Nest Pattern, Gorham, c.1890, 10 In. 1599
Serving Spoon, Engraved Strawberry Bowl, Twist Stem, c.1870, 9 In. 79
Serving Spoon, Reticulated Handles & Bowls, Victorian, Case, 1899, Pair 98
Serving Spoon, Twist Stem, Etched Medallion, Portrait, Coin, c.1870, 10 In. 239
Serving Stand, Round, Fluted Rim, Monogram, Wallace, 11 In. 270
Spoon, Marked GG, 9 In. 610
Sugar & Creamer, Art Nouveau, Round Foot, 6 ¼ In. 138
Sugar & Creamer, Dome Lid, Repousse, Scroll Handles, Lincoln & Foss, c.1850, 6 ½ & 7 In. 677
Sugar & Creamer, Gorham, 2 Piece 178
Sugar & Creamer, Molded Leaves, Spiders, Gilt, George Shiebler, c.1885, 3 x 4 In. 3690
Sugar & Creamer, Tray, Art Deco Style, Footed, Double Handles, Reed & Barton, 1952 413
Sugar, Basket Shape, Beaded Design, Hinged Handle, Chased Leaves, c.1850, 7 x 6 In. 630
Sugar, Out-Turned Bowl, Gallery Rim, Beaded, Square Base, Monogram, c.1795, 6 In. 777
Sugar, Repousse, Bulbous, Undulating Rim, Scroll Handles, Dominick & Haff, 3 x 5 In. 159
Sugar, Urn Shape Finial, Cast Leaftip Rim, Engraved, c.1815, 6 ¼ In. 338
Tankard, Coat Of Arms, Stepped Lid, Scroll Handle & Thumblift, N. Roosevelt, 8 In. 9840
Tasting Spoon, Twist Handle, Dominick & Haff, 15 In. 74
Tea & Coffee Set, Georgian Rose, Baroque Style, Reed & Barton, 5 Piece 944
Tea & Coffee Set, Kettle, Coffeepot, Teapot, Sugar & Creamer, Waste, Tray, Gorham, 7 Piece 4270
Tea & Coffee Set, Scroll Handles, Footed, Reed & Barton, 27 In., 5 Piece 1020
Tea & Coffee Set, Sugar & Creamer, Teapot, Coffeepot, 6 Piece 5980
Tea & Coffee Set, Teapot, Coffeepot, Sugar, Creamer, Waste, Repousse Flowers, 5 Piece 1845
Tea Caddy, Aesthetic, Hammered, Waves, Sea Creatures, Dominick & Haff, 1800s 2124
Tea Caddy, Repousse Flowers, Vines, Dominick & Haff, c.1890, 4 ½ In. 531
Tea Set, Classical, Lobed, Banding, Coin, Marked, John Crawford, c.1830, 5 Piece .... *illus* 1536
Tea Set, Engraved, Coffeepot, Teapot, Hot Water Pot, Sugar & Creamer, Waste, 7 Piece 2091
Tea Set, Exemplar, Teapot, Creamer, Sugar, Watson Co., 1820, 3 Piece 272
Tea Set, Squat, Bulbous, Repousse, Flowers, Whiting, c.1900, 5 In., 3 Piece 984
Tea Set, Water Kettle, Stand, Teapot, Sugar & Creamer, Waste, Tray, S. Kirk & Son, 6 Piece 13420
Tea Strainer, Art Nouveau, Repousse Flower Handle & Bowl, R. Wallace, 7 x 3 In. 109
Tea Strainer, Colonial Revival Style, Wood Handle, Marked Gorham, c.1966, 9 In. 124
Tea Strainer, Francis I, Reed & Barton, 1900s, 7 In., 12 Piece 1320
Tea Strainer, Repousse, Monogram, Jenkins & Jenkins, 3 ¾ In. 250
Tea Strainer, Teapot Shape, Gorham, 1 In. 65
Teakettle, Repousse, Stand, Flowers, Scroll, Burner, Bigelow Kennard & Co., 9 In. 923
Teapot, Bead Border, Lion Head Spout, c.1810, 8 ½ In. .... *illus* 590
Teapot, Lid, Ball Finial, Flared Neck, Scrolling, Shreve & Co., 5 x 7 In. 148
Teapot, Urn Shape, Engraved Acanthus Monogram, J.B. Hone & Co., 10 ¼ In. 984
Teaspoon, Chased Leaf Design, Oval Bowl, Elongated Handle, Towle, 6 In., 12 Piece 127
Tongs, Flat Handles, Marked, Woods, Freeman, North Carolina, Coin, c.1810, 5 ¾ In. .... *illus* 4425
Tongs, Medallion Pattern, Chicken Claw, Pierced Spatula, Gorham, c.1865, 13 In. 1718
Tongs, Openwork Spoon, Birds Foot Claw, Talon, Reed & Barton, 7 ¼ In. 283
Tray, Calling Card, Oval, Shaped Handles, Marked S. Kirk & Son, 10 x 5 In. 124
Tray, Center Monogram, Decorative Edge, Round, Reed & Barton, 15 In. 484
Tray, Chippendale Pattern, Shaped Rim, Gorham, Marked, 12 In. .... *illus* 995
Tray, Chippendale, Round, Fluted Edges, Shaped Rim, Gorham, 12 In. Diam. 345
Tray, Egg & Dart Molded Rim Edge, R. Wallace & Sons, 1900s, 12 In. 248
Tray, Floral Repousse Rim, Reticulated Flowers, Monogram, Durgin, 6 x 11 In. 150
Tray, Grapevine & Leaf Borders, S. Kirk & Son, Baltimore, 28 In. 4484
Tray, Pastry, Boat Shape, Reeded Rim, Hunt Silver Co., c.1940, 12 ½ x 7 In. 153
Tray, Pea Pod, La Paglia, 24 ½ x 14 In. 2475
Tray, Plymouth, Cartouche Shape, Handles, Reeded Border, Gorham, 1928, 25 In. 1534
Tray, Reticulated, 8 Petals, J.E. Caldwell, 14 ½ In. 976
Tray, Round, Scalloped Edge, International Silver Co., 14 In. 390
Tray, Round, Towle, 20 ½ In. 1440
Tray, Shaped Oval, Repousse Design, Sacrificial Scene, 2 Handles, c.1870, 36 x 23 In. 11950
Tray, Square, Stepped Geometric Banding, Reed & Barton, 1928, 12 x 13 In. 1750
Trophy Cup, Presentation, Deer Antler Handles, Gorham, c.1891, 5 x 10 In. 224
Trophy Cup, Tapered, Cylindrical, Angled Handles, Frank W. Smith, 9 ½ x 5 In. 219
Trophy, Goblet Shape, Scrolls, Inscribed, Best Stallion, Tom Thumb, c.1850, 7 In. .... *illus* 3068
Tureen, Lid, Monogram, Paneled, Finial, Handles, Shreve, Crump & Low, 12 In. 861
Vanity Set, Brush, Comb, Mirror, Blackinton & Co., c.1925, 3 Piece 275
Vase, Art Deco, Tapered, Scroll Handle, Footed, Monogram, Dominick & Haff, 15 In. 1560
Vase, Flutter Rim, Acanthus Capped, Scroll Handles, Dieges & Clust, c.1950, 22 In. 5228
Vase, Footed, Tapered, Wavy Rim, Engraved, George A. Henckel, c.1920, 17 In. 420

Vase, Footed, Weighted, International Silver Co., 8 In. 180
Vase, Plateau, Paneled, Rocaille Shells, Scrollwork, Garland, Durgin, c.1910, 14 In. 1476
Vase, Repousse Leaves & Scroll, Scroll Handles & Feet, c.1950, 22 In. 11875
Vase, Repousse, Acanthus Leaf, Flowers, Gorham, 1905, 15 In. 1875
Vase, Trumpet Shape, Medallions, Flowers, Scrolls, J.F. Fradley, 15 x 5 In. 605
Vase, Trumpet Shape, Octagonal Saucer Foot, William Durgin, 12 In. 151
Vase, Trumpet Shape, Round Foot, Wheel-Cut Crystal, Reed & Barton, 12 x 6 In. 180
Vase, Trumpet, Shaped Saucer Foot, Petal Rim, Webster Company, 14 In. 184
Wine Cooler, Louis XVI Reproduction, Ribbed, Baluster, Dominick & Haff, 8 x 7 In. 978
Wine, Lord Saybrook, International Silver Co., 4 ½ In., 8 Piece 240

SILVER-ASIAN
Tankard, Hinged Lid, Scrolled Handle, Bearded Man Spout, Bulbous, 1800s, 9 In. 984
Teakettle, Gilt, Round, Squat, Domed Lid, Birds, Flowers, Leaf Knop, 1800s, 10 In. 23423

SILVER-AUSTRALIAN
Centerpiece, Egg, Hinged Lid, Emu Finial, Ebonized Foot, c.1870, 7 x 5 In. 5075

SILVER-AUSTRIAN
Box, Engraving, Horse, The Shooting Pony, 9 x 7 ¼ In. 281
Cigarette Case, Art Deco, Shield Cartouche, Enameled Design, c.1920, 3 x 4 In. 127
Cigarette Case, Curved Square, Enamel, Couple Under Leaf, 1900s, 3 In. 1243
Ewer, Red, Curling Vine Handle, 5 ½ In. 750
Platter, Reeded Border, Marked J.C.K., c.1900, 28 In. 1000
Tray, Rectangular, Rounded Corners, Vincent Mayer's Sohne, 10 x 20 In. 375

SILVER-BURMESE
Bowl, Lotus Petals, Narrative Scene, 5 x 7 ¾ In. Diam. 1037
Bowl, Panels, Hammered, Animals, 7 x 12 ¾ In. Diam. 519
Bowl, Repousse, 3 Knob Feet, Figures Farming, c.1900, 10 In. .... *illus* 1422

SILVER-CANADIAN
Sauceboat, Stand, Footed, Leafy Open End Handle, Birks, 8 ½ In. 330

SILVER-CHINESE
Bowl, Chased Double Dragon Design, Footed, 4 ½ x 8 In. 1440
Bowl, Reticulated, Oval, Hinged Lid, Handle, 6 ½ x 4 In. 254
Box, Engraved, Shaped Sides, 2 ½ x 5 In. 184
Box, Repousse, Dragon, Monogram CRH, 9 ½ x 5 In. 1476
Butter, Cover, Knife, Round, Knop, c.1940, 5 In. 270
Cocktail Shaker, Dragon, Chinese Export, 9 ¾ x 4 In. 450
Cocktail Shaker, Incised Bamboo Branches, Signed Tuck Chang, 12 In. 922
Dragon Boat, Bolted, Carved Wood Base, Box, 4 x 7 In. 127
Figurine, Peacock, Enamel, Filigree, Enamel, Marked, c.1910, 5 In. 840
Figurine, Peacock, Filigree, Enamel, Lotus Flower, 6 x 6 ¾ In. 484
Hand Mirror & Brush, Birds, Plants, Relief, 10 ½ In. 369
Sugar Castor, Canton & Hong Kong, Wamg Hing, c.1890, 8 In. 1250
Tea Set, Bulbous Body Dragon, Hammered, Bamboo Handles, 6 In., 3 Piece 1722
Tea Set, Teapot, Sugar & Creamer, Leafy Branches, Bamboo Handles, 3 Piece 1320
Teapot, Lid, Hinged, 8 ½ x 6 In. 216
Tray, Round, 3 Scaly Dragons, Raised Border, Applied Dragon Mounts, Tripod, 13 ½ In. 1420
Wax Seal, Man, 19th Century, 1 ¼ In. .... *illus* 65

SILVER-CONTINENTAL
Basket, Center Bowl, Lobed, Scalloped, Reticulated, Round Foot, 8 ½ x 7 ¾ In. 338
Basket, Flowers, Reticulated Rim, Group Of Musicians, 3 x 9 ⅝ In. 308
Bowl, Vegetable, Rococo, Leaf Scroll Handles, 8 ⅞ x 13 In. 780
Box, Blue Agate, Applied Lapis Lazuli Ball Feet, 1800s, 1 x 4 In. 549
Charger, Shells, Flower Repousse Decoration, Hardstone Inset, 12 In. 406
Cigar Case, 3 Compartments, Chased Leaf Engraving, c.1910 345
Coffeepot, Flower Finial, Lobed Body, Wood Handle, 6 ½ In. 625
Ewer, Wine, Vase Shape Pitcher, Reticulated Handle, 12 In. 338
Figurine, Ship, Santa Maria, 9 In. 307
Fish Set, Knife, Fork, Shell Tip, Leafy Chased Handles, Continental, Board Box, 24 Piece 360
Incense Boat, Figural, Woman Finial, Italy, 1800s, 9 ½ x 7 ½ In. 330
Jardiniere, Flowers, Scrolls, Lobes, 4 Scroll Supports, Lions, 19 In. 3000
Ladle, Applied Edge, 14 In. 125
Pitcher, Beaded Waist, Engraved Medallions, Flowers, c.1850, 11 In. 1599
Pitcher, Flutter Rim, Flowering Vines, Cartouche, Monogram, c.1850, 13 In. 923
Plate, Marie Antoinette, 8 ½ In. 307

Silver-American, Tongs, Flat Handles, Marked, Woods, Freeman, North Carolina, Coin, c.1810, 5 ¾ In.
$4,425

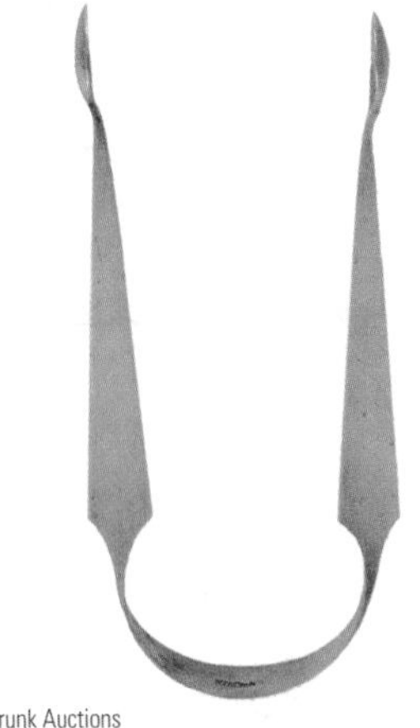

Brunk Auctions

Silver-American, Tray, Chippendale Pattern, Shaped Rim, Gorham, Marked, 12 In.
$995

Ruby Lane

Silver-American, Trophy, Goblet Shape, Scrolls, Inscribed, Best Stallion, Tom Thumb, c.1850, 7 In.
$3,068

Brunk Auctions

Silver-Burmese, Bowl, Repousse, 3 Knob Feet, Figures Farming, c.1900, 10 In.
$1,422

James D. Julia Auctioneers

Silver-Chinese, Wax Seal, Man, 19th Century, 1 ¼ In.
$65

Ruby Lane

Silver-Danish, Salad Servers, Pattern No. 57, Georg Jensen, c.1915, 8 ¾ In., Pair
$330

Cowan Auctions

Tray, Etched Melons, 17 ¼ In. 793
Vase, Bud, Lavender Purple, Guilloche Enamel, c.1910, 5 In. 1331
Wedding Cup, Woman, Bell-Shaped Skirt, Arms Holding Cup Up, 1870, 2 ½ In. 153

SILVER-DANISH

Bread Tray, Lobed, Scroll, Beaded Rim, Georg Jensen, 11 In. 1107
Coffee Set, Coffeepot, Sugar & Creamer, Ebony Handle, Urn Shape, 3 Piece 2551
Coffee Set, Cylindrical, Wide Vertical Ribs, S. Bernadotte, Jensen, c.1942, 3 Piece 4920
Cup, Flared, Lobed, Relief, Gold Wash, Svend Toxvaerd, c.1950, 2 ¾ In. 264
Dish, Oval, Blossom Handles, Georg Jensen, 1 ¾ x 12 ½ In. 1650
Lobster Pick, Georg Jensen, 7 ¼ In., 6 Piece 1200
Pitcher, Henning Koppel, 6 ¾ In. 1586
Pitcher, Rosewood Handle, Tapered Pear Shape, Karl Gustav Hansen, c.1958, 8 ½ In. 2187
Placecard Holder, Acorn Pattern, Rectangular Base, G. Jensen, 3 In., 8 Piece 2952
Salad Servers, Pattern No. 57, Georg Jensen, c.1915, 8 ¾ In., Pair .... *illus* 330
Salad Servers, Tulip Vase Tip, Reticulated, Beaded, G. Jensen, 9 In., 2 Piece 984
Salt & Pepper, Royal Blue Guilloche Enamel Cap, Mushroom Shape, 2 x 1 ½ In. 115
Sauce Pot, Wood Handle, 20 ½ x 7 In. 156
Sauceboat, Undertray, Hans Hansen, 1961, 3 ⅝ x 7 In. 790
Serving Fork, Spoon, Hammered, Marked O. Mogensen, 10 ¼ In. 265
Serving Set, Spoon, Fork, Openwork Berried Blossom Handle, 9 ½ In. 2188
Serving Spoon, Owl, Green Cabochon Eyes, G. Jensen, 10 In. 1046
Spoon, Demitasse, Blue Enamel Handle, Gold Wash, 3 ¾ In., 6 Piece 120
Spoon, Enamel Handle, Christmas, Michelsen, 1967, 6 ¼ In. 39
Spoon, No. 42, Georg Jensen, 10 ¼ In. 600
Sugar & Creamer, Urn Shape, Scrolled Handles, Georg Jensen, c.1944, 4 In. 984
Sugar, Handles, Georg Jensen, c.1927, 2 x 4 In. 975
Tazza, Stylized Leaves, Berries, Johan Rohde, Georg Jensen, c.1946, 13 x 14 In. .... *illus* 16250
Teapot, Ivory Handle, Franz Hingelberg, 8 x 7 ¼ In. 302
Tray, Round, Georg Jensen, c.1945, 14 In. Diam. 1944
Vase, Tapered, Block Foot, Round Tiered Pedestal Foot, G. Jensen, 1930s, 8 In. 3000
Wine Taster, Hammered, Inset 5 Kroner Coin, Loop Handle, 4 In. 150

SILVER-DUTCH

Ashtray, Repousse, 6 ¼ In. 276
Basket, Pierced, 4 Ball Feet, 2 ¼ x 3 ¾ In. 60
Bell, Windmill, Mouthpiece For Spinning Action, 7 ½ In. 185
Bottle, Harbor Scene, Beading, Windmill, Square Shape, 5 In. 374
Bowl, Brandy, Mascaron Handles, Oval, Repousse, Lattice & Scroll Ground, 1852, 10 In. 369
Box, Heart Shape, Cattle, Farming Scene, Hinged Lid, Scrolling, 2 ¾ x 2 In. 86
Box, Sugar, 1800s, 6 ¼ In. 360
Figure, Windmill, 13 In. 307
Hot Water Urn, Filigree Stand, Twisted Handles, c.1890, 10 In. 944
Hot Water Urn, Repousse, Scrolls, Putti, Reticulated Base, Partial Mark, c.1890, 10 In. .... *illus* 885
Spoon & Fork, Combination, Detachable Toothpick, Parcel Gilt, 6 In. 7780
Tray, 2 Handles, Oval, Beaded Border, Pierced Gallery, Scroll Leaves, 1910, 25 In. 1339

SILVER-EGYPTIAN

Dish, Chased, Molded, Geometric & Floral Designs, Scalloped Rim, 6 In. 132

SILVER-ENGLISH. English sterling silver is marked with a series of four or five small hallmarks. The standing lion mark is the most commonly seen sterling quality mark. The other marks indicate the city of origin, the maker, and the year of manufacture. These dates can be verified in many good books on silver. These prices are based on current silver values.

Basket, George III, Urn Shape, Reticulated, Glass Liner, C. Chesterman II, 7 In. 677
Berry Spoon, George William Adams, 1869 50
Biscuit Jar, Mappin & Webb, 5 ½ In. 151
Bonbon, Handle, Raised Base, Oval, Stewart Dawson Ltd., 1911, 4 ½ x 4 In. 200
Bowl, Armorial, Footed, Chased, Monogram, Paul Storr, c.1807, 5 x 9 ½ In. 2880
Bowl, George III, John Robbins, 1785, 5 x 8 In. 1792
Cafe Au Lait Pot, Turned Wood Handles, Birmingham, c.1946, 7 ⅜ In. 240
Cake Basket, Caryatids, Reticulated Body, Armorial Shield, Handle, 15 x 12 In. 8750
Cake Basket, George III, Oval, Openwork Flowers, Foot Ring, Engraved, Handle, 15 In. 2460
Cake Basket, Swing Handle, Pierced Rim, Flowers, Lobed, 1835, 14 In. 1530
Candelabra are listed in the Candelabrum category.
Candlesnuffer, Scissors Shape, Hallmarked, c.1840, 7 In. 91
Candlesticks are listed in their own category.

Candy Dish, Chrichton Brothers, 1914, 8 In. 183
Carving Set, Edwardian, Antler Handles, Pistol Grip, Sheffield, 12 x 15 In., 3 Piece 562
Castor, William & Mary, Lighthouse Shape, Dome Lid, Pierced, 1691, 7 In. .... *illus* 2832
Chalice, Repousse, Pedestal Stem, Round Foot, Mappin & Webb, 1904, 8 x 4 In. 293
Champagne Bucket, Stripes, Handles, Round Foot, 9 x 9 In. 338
Chocolate Pot, George V, Baluster, Hinged Dome Lid, Wood Handle, c.1919, 11 In. 438
Cigarette Case, Nude Woman, Black Hair, Gold Vermeil Compartments, 3 ½ x 3 In. 544
Cigarette Case, Nude Women, Etched Diamond Pattern Surface, 1927, 3 In. 726
Cigarette Case, Titanic, Enamel Medallion, J. Gloster Ltd., 1912, 3 ½ x 2 ½ In. 605
Coffeepot, Baluster, Dome Lid, Squirrel Finial, Wood Loop Handle, 1766, 11 In. 1530
Coffeepot, George I, Hinged Dome Lid, Cylindrical, Tapered, Wood Handle, c.1720, 9 In. 1320
Coffeepot, George II, Dome Lid, Wood Handle, Armorial, c.1757, 9 In. 800
Coffeepot, George II, Wood Scrolled Handle, Footed, Gurney & Cook, 1754, 9 In. 1320
Coffeepot, George III, Baluster, Urn Finial, Rocaille Cartouche, Flowers, 1783, 12 In. 1046
Coffeepot, High Shoulders, Leaf Handle, Hinged Lid, Gourd Finial, 11 In. 600
Coffeepot, Victorian, Medallions, Cartouche, Family Crest, Mappin & Webb, 11 In. 715
Compote, Flowers, Holland Aldwinckle & Slater, c.1901, 4 x 11 In. 236
Creamer, Figural Handle, 1911, 5 In. 338
Cruet Set, Victorian, Oval, Leaves, Flowers, 8 Bottles, George Angell, 1854-55, 13 ½ In. 1125
Cup & Lid, C-Scroll Handle, Mappin & Webb, 1963, 3 ⅝ x 7 In., 12 Piece 960
Cup, 2 Handles, William IV, Urn Shape, Repousse, Flowers, 1833, 10 x 8 In. 540
Dish Ring, Blue Glass Liner, Openwork, T. Weir & Son, Dublin, 1907, 3 ¾ x 8 In. 1121
Dish, George V, Arts & Crafts, Reticulated Grapevine Border, Handles, c.1914, 7 In 308
Dish, Lid, Dog Finial, Engraved, Gadroon Rim, Stand, S. Smith, 1872, 15 In., Pair .... *illus* 6765
Dish, Rope Edge, Paul Storr, 1806, 13 x 10 In. 10625
Dish, Spot Hammered, Center Fleur-De-Lis, Beaded, Omar Ramsden, 1927, 7 In. 573
Dish, Sweetmeat, Charles I, Scalloped, Lobed, Shell Handles, Flowers, 1634, 8 In. 3252
Egg Coddler, Edward VII, Burner, 4 Egg Holders, Roberts & Belk, 1905-06, 10 ½ In. 845
Finger Bowl, George I, Britannia, Round Foot, Thomas Mason, 1719, 2 x 4 In. 375
Fish Knife, Georgian Shape, Eley, Fearn & Chawner, c.1810, 12 In. 60
Fish Set, Mother-Of-Pearl, Oak Box, Jonathan Bell & Sons, c.1897, 6 ¾ In., 12 Piece 183
Flask, Hip, W.C. Griffiths, 1912, 4 x 2 ½ In. 550
Fruit Strainer, George III, Round, Gadroon, Shaped Handles, Hester Bateman, 12 In. 780
Goblet, Gilt, Stuart Devlin, 1976, 6 ¾ In. 183
Ice Bucket, RWB, Trefoil, Sheffield, 1965, 9 x 10 In. 1200
Ladle, Shell Shape, Hallmarks For Walter Tweedie, c.1777, 13 ½ In. 180
Ladle, William IV, Family Crest, John, Henry, Charles Lias, London, 1832-33, 14 In. 500
Marrow Scoop, Double End, 8 ¼ x 1 In. 244
Marrow Spoon, 2-Sided, c.1786, 8 ½ In. 110
Mug, George III, Banded Decoration, James Crawford, 1772, 6 In. 1875
Napkin Rings are listed in their own category.
Picture Frame, Art Nouveau, Frieze, Fruiting Vines, Flared Feet, 12 x 8 In. 840
Pitcher, George III, Baluster Shape, Acanthus Capped Handle, Engraved, 9 In. 2337
Porringer, Gadroon, Fluted Band, Central Cartouche, 1719, 2 In. 803
Punch Bowl, Louis XV Style, Lobed, C-Scrolls, Putti, Crystal Liner, 1700s, 7 x 13 In. 1422
Punch Bowl, Repousse, Nude Torsos, Winged Women, Charles Clement, 20 ½ x 13 In. 10625
Punch Ladle, Hallmarked London 1800-1801, 13 In. 153
Salt Cellar, Oval, Pedestal Base, Gilt Inside, Dorothy Langland, 1830s, 2 In., Pair 300
Salver, Engraved Boar's Head Crest, Footed, 10 In. 338
Salver, Engraved, Scalloped Rim, Shellwork, Scroll Feet, 11 In. 420
Salver, Family Crest, Oval, Footed, Hallmarked For William Bolton, 8 ½ x 6 ½ In. 276
Salver, George II, Shaped Rim, Scroll Border, Coat Of Arms, Paw Feet, 1747, 12 In. 1339
Salver, George III, Reeded Rim, Stippled Band, 3 Scroll Feet, 1790, 11 In. 900
Salver, George III, Shell & Scroll Rim, Engraved, Trailing Roses, 22 In. 3444
Salver, George V, Canted Square, Chippendale Rim, Scroll & Pad Feet, 16 x 16 In. 2125
Salver, Georgian, Piecrust Rim, Engraved Armorial, 3 Scroll Feet, 12 ½ In. 800
Salver, Round, Leafy Scroll Border, Coat Of Arms Center, 3-Footed, Eaton, 20 In. 3890
Salver, Undulating Rim, S-Scrolls, Lion Crest, Pad Feet, 7 ¾ In. 750
Sauceboat, George IV, Repousse, Footed, 1828, 4 ½ x 10 ¾ In. 600
Scissors, Flowers, Leaves, William Hutton & Sons, Box, 6 x 2 ¾ In. 60
Spoon Set, Demitasse, Enameled, Vermeil, Gold Wash, Turner & Simpson, 3 In., 6 Piece 293
Spoon, Elizabeth I, Parcel Gilt, Apostle, St. Jude, R. Hilliard, c.1590, 8 In. 2529
Spoon, James I, Parcel Gilt, Apostle, St. Andrew, 1619, 7 ¼ In. 2334
Spoon, Lace Back, Scrolling Leaves, Ribbed, Stephen Venables, c.1684, 7 ¼ In. 389
Strainer, George III, Dome Shape Bowl, Detachable Funnel, Marked, 1771, 5 x 3 In. 414
Sugar & Creamer, George III, Angular Handles, Edinburgh, 1802, 4 x 4 In. 180

Silver-Danish, Tazza, Stylized Leaves, Berries, Johan Rohde, Georg Jensen, c.1946, 13 x 14 In.
$16,250

Rago Arts and Auction Center

Silver-Dutch, Hot Water Urn, Repousse, Scrolls, Putti, Reticulated Base, Partial Mark, c.1890, 10 In.
$885

Brunk Auctions

Silver-English, Castor, William & Mary, Lighthouse Shape, Dome Lid, Pierced, 1691, 7 In.
$2,832

Brunk Auctions

S

Silver-English, Dish, Lid, Dog Finial, Engraved, Gadroon Rim, Stand, S. Smith, 1872, 15 In., Pair
$6,765

Skinner, Inc.

Silver-English, Teapot, George IV, Squat Round Body, Fluted, Phillip Rundell, 1823-24, 5 In.
$1,230

Skinner, Inc.

Silver-French, Claret Jug, Etched Glass, Openwork Mounts, Claude Doutre-Roussel, c.1885, 11 In.
$1,845

New Orleans (Cakebread)

TIP
An old hand-engraved monogram or decoration adds value to a piece of silver.

Sugar Basket, George III, Navette Shape, Glass Liner, Scrolling, Swing Handle, 7 x 6 In. 676
Sugar, Dome Lid, George I, Britannia Standard, Gilt, Thomas Gladwin, Pagoda Finial, 6 In. 1169
Tablespoon, Queen Anne, Dog Nose, William Scarlett, London, 1710, 7 ½ In. 389
Tankard, Charles II, Scroll Handle, Beading, Leaf Medallion, Dolphin, c.1675, 8 In. 7500
Tankard, George II, Baluster Shape, Dome Lid, Footed, Engraved Armorial, 8 In. 1353
Tankard, George II, Stepped Base, Engraved RS, Cartouche, R. A. Cox, 1758, 5 In. 1063
Tankard, William III, Tapered, Scroll Thumbpiece, 7 In. 2723
Tazza, Queen Anne, Round, Gadroon Border, Monogram, Trumpet Foot, 1705, 11 In. 5625
Tea & Coffee Set, Georgian, Edward Viners, Plated Water Kettle, Tray, 7 Piece 1080
Teapot, George III, Repousse, Bulbous, Footed, Bird's Head Handle, Elliott, c.1819, 3 x 7 In. 190
Teapot, George IV, Squat Round Body, Fluted, Phillip Rundell, 1823-24, 5 In. .... *illus* 1230
Teapot, Individual, Filigree Base, Burner, 5 x 4 In. 125
Teapot, Oval, Hinged Lid, 4 ¾ x 10 In. 420
Toast Rack, William IV, Footed, Leaves, Loop Top Handle, 1836, 5 x 7 In. 674
Tray Liner, Pierced, Engraved Coat Of Arms, Garrard & Co., 1839, 19 ½ x 14 In. 922
Tray, George III, Reticulated, Armorial, Monogram, 19 In. 923
Tray, Oval, Beaded Border, D-Shape Handles, Leaves, Paul Storr, c.1831, 32 In. 8365
Tray, Oval, Gadroon Edge, Engraved Armorial, c.1804, 23 In. 2706
Tray, Oval, Gallery, Crested, 22 ½ In. 180
Tray, Shaped Oval, Gadroon Border, Armorial Crest, P. Storr, c.1805, 23 x 17 In. 8750
Trophy Cup, Skegness Xmas Fat Stock Show, William Hutton & Sons, 8 x 4 In. 357
Tureen, Sauce, George III, Lid, Finial, Gadroon Rim, Acanthus Handle, Paw Feet, 6 In. 1722
Urn, Edward VII, Over, Reeded, Satyr, Edward Barnard & Sons, 11 In. 2990

SILVER-ETHIOPIAN

Coptic Cross, Openwork, Lucite Base, 26 ½ x 18 ¼ In. 230

SILVER-FRENCH

Bowl, Low, Applied Rosettes, Die-Rolled Border, c.1963, 1 x 6 In. 109
Bowl, Vegetable, Round, Serpentine, Lobed, Laurel & Ribbon Edge, Henri Freres, 9 ¼ In. 468
Chalice, Lid, Art Deco, Inscription, Finial, Saints, c.1940, 9 ¾ In. 738
Claret Jug, Etched Glass, Openwork Mounts, Claude Doutre-Roussel, c.1885, 11 In. .... *illus* 1845
Coffeepot, Pear Shape, Twig Handle, Spout, Flowers Branches, c.1890, 7 ¾ In. 767
Dish, Meat, Shells, Fluted Border, Leaves, 16 ¾ In. 600
Dish, Round, Scrolling Border, 11 ⅞ In., Pair 840
Fish Set, 3 Forks, 3 Spoons, Etched Blades, Relief Handles, 6 Piece 553
Jug, Spiral-Cut Glass, Silver Mounts, Flowers, 12 In. 1375
Melon Fork, First Standard, Shell & Thread, Gilt, Tetard Freres, 6 In., 12 Piece 812
Monstrance, Cross Finial, Sunburst, Center Window, Winged Angel Heads, c.1810, 25 x 12 In. .. 3690
Platter, Meat, Oval, Reeded Border, 19 In. 813
Salt, Master, Parcel Gilt, Acanthus, 2 Trays, Cardeilhac, 9 In., Pair 11685
Sauceboat, Shaped Rim, Undertray, 3 ¾ x 8 In. 400
Sauceboat, Shell Tipped, Raised Scroll Handles, Leafy Garlands, Stand, 6 x 12 ½ In. 840
Sauceboat, Stand, Louis XV, Spiral Fluted, Shell Tip, Double Branch Handles, 4 x 10 In. 420
Serving Set, Spoon, Fork, Profile Busts Of Louis XVI & Marie Antoinette, 2 Piece 276
Tea Strainer, Louis XVI, Marie Antoinette, 6 ⅜ In., Pair 430
Teakettle, Burner, Garland, Swag, Basket Weave, Flower Finial, Veyray, 19 x 13 In. 1920
Teaspoon, Gilt Washed, C-Scrolls, Shells, Maison Odiot, Box, 12 Piece 423
Tray, Chased, Chamfered Corners, Shell Engraving, 9 ½ In., Pair 840

SILVER-GERMAN

Basin, Gilt, Oval, Reeded, Leaf Scroll, Marked Adolf Sper, c.1844, 16 In. 5018
Basket, Fruit, Oval, Putti, Ducklings, Landscape, Wide Rim, c.1900, 15 x 11 In. 250
Basket, Reticulated, Footed, Handle, Storck & Sinsheimer, Hanau, c.1900, 15 x 12 In. 480
Beaker, Biedermeier, Tapered Oval, Gilt Interior, Monogram, c.1835, 4 In. .... *illus* 492
Beaker, Coins, Weapons, Claw On Ball Feet, c.1892, 7 In. 671
Beaker, Parcel Gilt, 2 Rows Of 6 Coins, Gilt Bands, 2 ¾ In. 2123
Bonbon, Swan Shape, Hinged Wings, Gilt Interiors, 9 ¾ In. 4668
Bowl, Art Deco, Handwrought, Ferdinand Richard Wilm, 10 In. 794
Bowl, Crystal Bowl, Four Swans, Wings Outstretched, Acanthus, 8 ¾ x 18 In. 2745
Bowl, Lobed, Hand Hammered, 3 Scrolled Feet, c.1900, 10 In. Diam. 338
Bowl, Octagonal, Pierced Panels, Roped Daisies & Clover, c.1900, 8 In. Diam. 669
Box, Cherub, Hexagon, Schleissner & Sohne, 1 x 3 In. 150
Box, Dancing Cherub, Oval, Hinged Lid, Storck & Sinsheimer, 5 ½ x 3 ½ In. 300
Box, Hanau, J. Kurz & Co., c.1890, 1 ⅜ In. 84
Box, Hinged Lid, Shaped, Chased Repousse, Portrait, Textured, Gilt, c.1900, 4 x 3 In. 448
Box, Oval, 2 Facing Portraits, Leaves, Wreaths, 6 x 4 In. 312

Brush, Clothing, Gold Wash, Oval, Domed Bristle Cushion, Repousse, 5 x 3 In. 89
Chalice, Lid, Wreath Finial, Robed Figures, Round Foot, Grapevines, c.1830, 13 In. 984
Compote, Reticulated Bowl, Portrait Medallions, Swags, Footed, c.1900, 7 ½ In. 431
Cup, Lid, Historismus, Neresheimer & Sohne, Knight Bust Top, 17 In. 1107
Decanter, Leafy Overlay, Glass Lining, Figural Finial, Wolf & Knell, c.1900, 11 In. 213
Decanter, Wine, Amber Crystal, Etched, Silver Mounted, Schleissner Sohne, 9 ½ x 4 In. 260
Dish, Art Deco, Fluted, Hammered, 4 Stepped Feet, Otto Walter, 8 x 2 In. 242
Dish, Shell, Openwork C-Scroll, Winged Figure, 3-Footed, 5 ¾ x 16 In. 1170
Dish, Sweetmeat, Gilt, Lobed Oval, Scroll Handles, Caryatid, c.1680, 7 ½ In. 7334
Figurine, Cockatoo, On Tree Trunk, Movable Wings & Head, 1900s, 10 ¾ In. 1168
Figurine, Cockerel, Raised Wings, Detachable, Neresheimer Of Hanau, c.1900, 9 In. 2334
Fork Set, 4 Tines, Long Handle, Ribbon, Bruckmann & Sohne, 8 In., 6 Piece 118
Kettle, Stand, Pear Shape, Spiral Fluting, Gooseneck Spout, Handle, c.1891, 16 In. .... *illus* 2750
Model, Galleon, 3 Masts, Billowing Sails, Ludwig Neresheimer, c.1925, 19 In. 5250
Nef, Gilt, 2-Masted, Sails, Pennants, Figures, c.1910, 19 x 16 In. 7200
Page Turner, Eagle Head, Ivorine Blade, Monogram, c.1900, 12 In. 590
Pastry Server, Rococo Style, Cast Flowers, Rocaille, Bruckman & Sohne, 9 x 2 In. 83
Plaque, Rabbit, Bird, Fruit, Vegetables, 16 x 22 In. 383
Plate, Dinner, Hallmarks, Reeded Rim, Engraved, 10 In., Pair 3998
Plate, Presentation, Trotting Club, Scrolling Leaves Rim, c.1930, 12 In. Diam. 242
Plate, Raised Decoration, Pierced, Simon Rosenau, 1910, 7 ¾ In. Diam. .... *illus* 680
Salt & Pepper, Baluster, Pierced Dome Lid, Pinecone Finial, Repousse, 4 x 1 ½ In. 144
Server, Repousse, Mary & Child, Openwork, 11 ¾ In. 144
Shaker, Flower Repousse, Acorn Shape Finials, 7 In., Pair 184
Tankard, Gilt Washed, Set With Hanover Thalers, 6 x 6 In. 3660
Tray, Oval, Handles, Flower Border, Flat Rim, Stamped, 1900s, 29 ½ x 16 In. 1000
Tray, Putti, 7 x 10 ¾ In. 553
Wedding Basket, Swing Handle, Openwork, Shaped Rim, Flowers, Medallions, 25 In. 2250
Wedding Cup, Woman, Swivel Cup, Embossed, Chased Rococo Panels, c.1915, 8 In. .... *illus* 522

SILVER-GREEK

Bowl, Lobed, Footed, Double Handles, Beaded, Round Foot, 11 x 10 In. 354
Goblet, Hand Hammered, Reeded Stem, Bell Foot, Ilias Lalaounis, 4 In., Pair 306
Vase, Hammered, Tapered Rim, Xeipoe, 7 x 4 ½ In. 177

SILVER-HUNGARIAN

Decanter, Vase Shape, Lid, Eagle Finial, Saucer Foot, c.1900, 11 In. 123
Tray, Art Nouveau, Oblong, Chased & Repousse, Serpentine Ribbons, 9 x 19 In. 363
Tray, Scrolls, Border, 13 In. .... *illus* 547

SILVER-INDIAN

Bowl, Chased Leafy Scrolls, Squat, Bulbous, Ring Foot, Flat Wide Rim, 3 x 6 In. 253

SILVER-IRISH

Bowl, Oval, Robert W. Smith, Dublin, Hallmark, c.1854, 12 x 8 In. 504
Bowl, Rosettes, Draping, Shell & Hoof Feet, Matthew West, 1788, 3 x 5 In. 165
Dish Ring, Edward VII, Pierced, Animals, Monogram, J. Smith, Dublin, 1906, 4 In. .... *illus* 738
Dish Ring, George III Style, Reticulated, Flared Foot, 1912, 8 In. Diam. 613
Jug, Gilt Interior, Royal Irish Silver Co., 1968, 8 ⅞ In. 875
Salt, Master, William IV, Parcel Gilt, Flower Repousse, 3 Paw Feet, Lion's Mask, 2 x 3 In. 500
Salver, Piecrust Border, Flowers, Shell, Central Cartouche, Coat Of Arms, 16 In. 5625
Salver, Shaped, Round, Shells, 4 Ball & Paw Feet, Coat Of Arms, c.1760, 16 ¾ In. 6000
Snuffer Stand, George II, Oval, Crest, Shaped Handle, Button Feet, 1700s, 8 In. 1125
Spoon, Engraved, Cartouche, 6-Point Star, 10 In. 104
Tray, George III, Oval, Reeded Handles, Coat Of Arms, Scroll Feet, 1800, 29 In. 6246
Tureen, Gadroon, Open Handles, Engraved Crest, Hallmarked For Dublin 1802, 12 x 19 In. 4920
Wine Cooler, 3 Swirling Handles, Twisted Stem, Spread Base, 1972, 20 In. 11478

SILVER-ITALIAN

Bowl, Oval, Flaring Rim, Turtle-Shape Feet, Mallards, Cattails, Frogs, 13 ½ In. Diam. 2750
Bowl, Scallop Shell, 2 Shell Feet, 2 Ball Feet, Hand Hammered, Buccellati, c.1950, 22 In. 10000
Bowl, Squat, Lobed, Ruffle Rim, Leaf Scroll Feet, c.1950, 24 x 18 In. 23900
Centerpiece, 3 Joined Shells, Conch Shell Feet, Buccellati, c.1968, 9 In. 5356
Compact, Mirror, Carved, Enamel, Country Maiden, Berry Picking Scene, c.1930, 2 x 1 x 5 In. . . 230
Cup, Gold Wash, Flared Rims, 4 In. 461
Figurine, Frog, Mario Buccellati, 2 ½ In. 594
Figurine, Ostrich, Standing, Gilt Legs, Feather Detail, Mubati, c.1968, 14 ⅜ In. 3634
Figurine, Standing, Head Down, Buccellati, c.1968, 15 In. 11095
Garniture, Fighting Cockerel, 9 ½ In., Pair 1353

Silver-German, Beaker, Biedermeier, Tapered Oval, Gilt Interior, Monogram, c.1835, 4 In.
$492

New Orleans (Cakebread)

Silver-German, Kettle, Stand, Pear Shape, Spiral Fluting, Gooseneck Spout, Handle, c.1891, 16 In.
$2,750

New Orleans (Cakebread)

Silver-German, Plate, Raised Decoration, Pierced, Simon Rosenau, 1910, 7 ¾ In. Diam.
$680

Ruby Lane

Silver-German, Wedding Cup, Woman, Swivel Cup, Embossed, Chased Rococo Panels, c.1915, 8 In.
$522

New Orleans (Cakebread)

Silver-Hungarian, Tray, Scrolls, Border, 13 In.
$547

Ruby Lane

Silver-Irish, Dish Ring, Edward VII, Pierced, Animals, Monogram, J. Smith, Dublin, 1906, 4 In.
$738

Skinner, Inc.

Silver-Mexican, Mustard Pot, Bird Handle, Glass Insert, Sanborns, 1950s, 3 In.
$85

Ruby Lane

Silver-Mexican, Pitcher, Water, Repousse, Flowers, Scrolls, Crest, c.1940, 12 x 11 In.
$875

New Orleans (Cakebread)

Silver-Mexican, Tureen, Lid, Pierced Support, Leaf Handles, Flower Finial, Sanborns, 11 In.
$1,140

Cowan Auctions

Silver-Persian, Figurine, Peacock, Hanging Bells, 3 In.
$125

Ruby Lane

Silver-Portuguese, Jug, Wine, Barrel Shape, Grapevine Rim, Handle, Reis Joalheiros, c.1950, 8 x 9 In.
$1,230

New Orleans (Cakebread)

Silver-Russian, Cigarette Case, Cossack Couple, Landscape, Buildings, c.1917, 4 ½ In.
$584

Skinner, Inc.

Hand Warmer, Oval, Perforated Dome Lid, Family Crest, Turned Wood Handle, 5 x 7 In. 6670
Mustard Pot, Spoon, Mushroom Shape, Buccellati, 4 x 3 ½ In. 1440
Plate, Serving, Radiant Lobes, Hammered, Scalloped Rim, Buccellati, 12 In. Diam. 1500
Salt & Pepper, Mushroom Shapes, Buccellati, 3 x 4 In. 1560
Vase, Flattened, Round, Hammered Sides, Ducks In Flight, Bulrushes, Italo Gori, 7 In. 1125

SILVER-JAPANESE

Bowl, Lobed Sides, 3 Scroll Legs, Flower Frog, 4 x 7 In. 123
Cigarette Case, Engraved Scrolling Leaves, Monogram, Cartouche, 6 x 3 In. 98
Ginger Jar, Repousse, Chrysanthemum, 1907, 14 In. 6875
Teapot, Bucket Shape, Hinged Spout Cap, Melon Finial, Taisho Period, 7 x 7 In. 861

SILVER-MEXICAN

Bowl, 2 Handles, 5 x 9 ½ In. 156
Bowl, Boat Shape, Wire Handles, Balls, Hand Hammered, c.1950, 8 ½ x 20 In. 1240
Bowl, Flat Rim, Round Stepped Foot, Pierced Base, c.1950, 6 x 6 In. 263
Bowl, Lid, Footed, c.1950, 2 ¼ x 5 ½ In. 123
Bowl, Lobed, Repousse Blooms & Leaves Band, C-Shape Handles, c.1950, 12 x 11 In. 1554
Bowl, Melon Ribbed, Wavy Rim, Spread Foot, c.1960, 3 x 5 In. 388
Bowl, Ribbed, Squat, 3 Loop Handles, Ball Design, c.1940, 7 In. Diam. 359
Bowl, Round, Shaped Banded Rim, Stepped Border, 3 Scroll Feet, c.1950, 12 In. 813
Bowl, Running Scrolls, Shaped Rim, Openwork Scroll Foot, 15 In. 500
Bowl, Scalloped Edge, Wide Rim, Saucer Foot, c.1940, 4 In. 568
Bowl, Semi-Round, Undulated Foot, Juventino Lopez Reyes, 1900s, 7 x 3 In. 173
Box, Figural Duck, Engraved Feather Design, Green Stone Eyes, c.1950, 7 In. 1016
Box, Inlay, Malachite, Lapis, Butterfly, Copper Feet, c.1950, 8 ¾ x 4 In. 216
Cigarette Box, Embossed, Flip Top, Filigreed, c.1920 61
Coffee Set, Coffeepot, Kettle, Stand, Sugar & Creamer, Tray, Chased Flowers, 6 Piece 2500
Coffeepot, Cylindrical, Straight Spout, Rosewood Handle, Jaguar Finial, c.1950, 9 In. 1375
Cup, Child's, Ducks, Cattle, Chicks, Birds, Sanborns, 3 x 1 ½ In. 121
Decanter, Genie Bottle Shape, Ruffled Mouth, Cork & Silver Stopper, 7 In. 2601
Dish, Sweetmeat, Underplate, Hammered, c.1950, 3 ¾ In., 4 Piece 123
Goblet, Inverted Bell Shape, Waisted Stem, Round Foot, c.1950, 6 x 3 In., 8 Piece 1045
Iced Tea Stirrer, Tea Leaf Shape Bowl, 5 Piece 50
Ladle, Salvador De La Serna, 12 ¾ x 3 ½ In. 123
Letter Opener, Letter Tray, Inset Amethyst, A.E.M., 12 x 8 In. 171
Mustard Pot, Bird Handle, Glass Insert, Sanborns, 1950s, 3 In. .... *illus* 85
Pitcher, Hammered, Bird Between Rim & Handle, Cockatoo, 9 In. 406
Pitcher, Salvador De La Serna, 5 ¾ x 7 ¾ In. 480
Pitcher, Stylized Dolphin Handle, Scroll Rim, c.1950, 11 In. 461
Pitcher, Toucan, Lapis Inlaid Handle & Eyes, Taxco, 13 ½ In. 767
Pitcher, Urn Shape Paneled Body, Alfredo Ortega & Sons, c.1950, 10 In. 423
Pitcher, Water, Repousse, Flowers, Scrolls, Crest, c.1940, 12 x 11 In. .... *illus* 875
Pitcher, Water, Taxco, Signed VM, c.1950, 8 ½ x 8 In. 400
Pitcher, Wide Mouth, Scrolling, C. Zurita, c.1960, 9 ½ In. 431
Relish, 3 Sections, Acanthus Leaf Trim, 15 x 11 In. 420
Sauce Ladle, Round Deep Bowl, Curved Handle, F. Ramierz, 6 ½ In. 53
Sauceboat, Figural Swan Shape, Gilt, Chassed Repousse Feathers, c.1980, 8 x 9 In. 1434
Sauceboat, Hammered Finish, Hook Handle, Footed, Wavy Rim, 3 In. 86
Spurs, Eagle Head On Shank, Engraved Design, Chain & Bucket Guard, c.1800, 6 In. 1534
Spurs, Presentation, Mexican War, Col. George T.M. Davis, Engraved, 1847 8125
Sugar & Creamer, Lobed, Round Foot, 1900s, 2 Piece 125
Syrup, Bulbous, Loop Handle, Hinged Lid, Beaded Round Foot, c.1950, 5 In. 500
Tea & Coffee Set, Coffeepot, Teapot, Spoon, Tray, 4 Piece 2040
Tea & Coffee Set, Kettle On Stand, Coffeepot, Teapot, Sugar & Creamer, Tray, 7 Piece 3997
Tea Set, 2 Teapots, Sugar & Creamer, Tray, Taxco, 5 Piece 2040
Tea Set, Pear Shape, Coffeepot, Teapot, Sugar & Creamer, Tray, 6 Piece 3690
Tray, 2 Handles, Scrollwork Rim, c.1955, 23 In. 615
Tray, Aztec Rose Border, Bud & Leaves, Sanborn, c.1950, 12 x 8 In. 275
Tray, Flared Lobed Rim, Scrolling, c.1950, 25 In. 738
Tray, Oval, Leafy Scroll Edge & Handles, Molded Ball Border, c.1950, 13 In. 469
Tray, Oval, Reeded Rim, Shaped Handles, c.1960, 16 x 25 ½ In. 1673
Tray, Oval, Scrolling Border, Handles, Sanborns, 1900s, 26 ¾ In. 2125
Tray, Rounded Edges, Scalloped Detail, 15 x 12 In. 334
Tray, Waiter, Oval, Flat Rim, 2 Rounded Handles, 24 x 16 In. 690
Tureen, Lid, Pierced Support, Leaf Handles, Flower Finial, Sanborns, 11 In. .... *illus* 1140
Tureen, Round, Lobed Body, Handles, Sanborns, Mexico City, 1900s, 7 x 11 In. 677

TIP
Do not put valuable silver in the dishwasher. The oxidation (the black color in the recessed parts of the raised pattern) will eventually be removed.

Silver-Sterling, Bowl, Gadroon Rim, Man, Bamboo Stalk, Paul Storr, 1812, 10 In. Diam.
$2,091

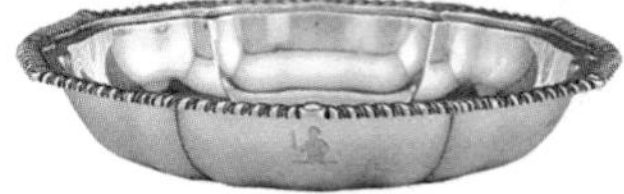

Cowan Auctions

Silver-Sterling, Card Case, Parcel Gilt, Woman, Parasol, Chain Handle, Gorham, c.1856, 4 In.
$800

Skinner, Inc.

Silver-Sterling, Cigar Lighter, Gimbaled, Wide Collar, Antelope Horn Twisted Handle, London, c.1898, 23 In.
$1,353

Skinner, Inc.

This is an edited listing of current prices. Visit **Kovels.com** to check thousands of prices from previous years and sign up for free information on trends, tips, reproductions, marks, and more.

Silver-Sterling, Cruet Set, Wood Base, Reticulated Frame, Engraved, Footed, c.1822, 10 In.
$984

Skinner, Inc.

Silver-Sterling, Cup, Embossed Hunt Scenes, Crowned Monogram, Continental, 1800s, 5 In.
$360

Cowan Auctions

Silver-Sterling, Hot Water Urn, George III, Reeded Handles, Gadroon, E.K., c.1810, 22 In.
$2,091

Skinner, Inc.

SILVER-NORWEGIAN

Nef, Plique-A-Jour, Enamel, Dragestil, Viking Ship, Dragon's Head Prow, c.1900, 6 In. 738
Salad Servers, Mountain Rose, David Andersen, 8 In., 2 Piece 123
Salt Spoon, Viking Ship, Glass Liner, 1 ½ x 3 In., 24 Piece 726
Sauce Ladle, Openwork Wide Handle, Leafy Scrolls, 6 In. 92

SILVER-PERSIAN

Box, Arabesque Design, Gold Wash Interior, Marked, 5 ¾ x 5 ¾ In. 322
Box, Hinged Lid, Repousse Birds, Flowers, Chased, Gilt, c.1900, 6 ½ x 6 ½ In. 1250
Charger, Music Players, Meditation, Hookahs, Scalloped, Signed, 14 In. 2583
Compote, Flowers, Leaves, Diamonds, Scallop, 7 ¾ In. 282
Decanter, Tree Of Life, Camels, Deer, Glass Liner, 11 ½ x 3 In. 2178
Plate, Footed, 12 ½ x 12 ½ In. 522
Vase, Engraved, Flowers, Birds, 1800s, 8 In. 369
Vase, Group, Landscape, 7 ½ In., Pair 375

SILVER-PERUVIAN

Basket, Flower, Filigree Bail Handle, Flared Rim, Flower Head Band, 6 ½ In. 677
Bowl, Spanish Colonial Style, Lobed Body, Roses, c.1950, 5 ½ x 12 ½ In. 615
Chalice, Round Foot, Urn Support, 10 ¾ In. 944
Cocktail Shaker, Figural Finial, Abstract Pattern, Welsch & Co., 10 In. 369
Dish, Jelly, Cantilevered Lid, Camusso, 1900s, 6 ¾ x 5 In. 123
Figurine, Peacock, Hanging Bells, 3 In. ......*illus* 125
Goblet, Repousse Inca Design, Figural Stem, Oval Domed Stepped Foot, 6 ½ x 3 In. 81
Tray, Scroll Border & Handles, Flowers, Leaves, 30 ½ x 17 ½ In. 1875

SILVER-POLISH

Cordial Set, 4 Cordials, 3 ½ In., Tray, 2 Handles, 1920-62, 12 In. 120
Cocktail Shaker, Baluster, Scroll Rim, Dome Lid, Gilt Interior, c.1938, 8 In. 478
Humidor, Faceted Hinged Lid, Wood Lined, Chased, 5 ½ x 3 ⅝ In. 242

SILVER-PORTUGUESE

Jug, Wine, Barrel Shape, Grapevine Rim, Handle, Reis Joalheiros, c.1950, 8 x 9 In. ......*illus* 1230
Serving Dish, 2 Handles, Chrysanthemum, Cast Rope, c.1938, 11 ¾ x 9 In. 850
Toothpick Holder, Footed Tray, Openwork Basket, Pierced Pear, Bird, c.1810, 6 ½ In. 590
Tray, Pierced, Round, Topazio, 11 In., Pair 480

SILVER-RUSSIAN. Russian silver is marked with the Cyrillic, or Russian, alphabet. The numbers 84, 88, or 91 indicate the silver content. Russian silver may be higher or lower than sterling standard. Other marks indicate maker, assayer, or city of manufacture. Many pieces of silver made in Russia are decorated with enamel. These prices are based on current silver values. Faberge pieces are listed in their own category. 88 91

Basket, Tray, Faux Basket Weave, Leafy Lid, 3 ½ x 6 In. 2415
Bonbon, Kresner, 10 ⅛ In. 200
Box, Scholar, Factory, Marked Orest Kurlykov, 4 x 3 In. 738
Centerpiece, Cut Glass Overlay, 7 ½ x 8 ½ In. 153
Chalice, Petal Design Base, Branchlike Stem, Inverted Bell Shape Cup, c.1860, 7 In. 334
Cigar Case, Double, Br. Hemple, 1925, 5 In. 270
Cigarette Case, Applied Insignia, Enameled Accents, 14K Gold, c.1889, 4 In. 677
Cigarette Case, Cossack Couple, Landscape, Buildings, c.1917, 4 ½ In. ......*illus* 584
Cigarette Case, Relief, Man Tilling Field, Magenta Oval Cabochon, c.1926, 4 x 4 In. 437
Cigarette Case, Rounded Corners, Enamel, Gem, Charms, Beetle, Horseshoe, 4 In. 2500
Creamer, Scroll Handle, Round Foot, 1844, 4 ½ x 6 ½ In. 180
Cup, Birds, Hooved Animals, Leaves, 3 In., Pair 1045
Cup, Vodka, Figural, Musician, Dancer, 3 In. 430
Egg, Faberge Style, Hunting, 3-Legged, 3 In. 522
Egg, Filigree, Lion Insert, Cabochons, 4 In. 338
Egg, Hunting Scenes, Moose Heads, Red Cabochons, 3-Footed, 3 In. 522
Egg, Tripod Base, Hoof Feet, 4 x 2 In. 1230
Ewer, Wine, Art Nouveau, Copper, Tapered, Lily Pad Bands, 13 In. 738
Figurine, Bear, Reclining, 6 In. 360
Figurine, Dog, Puppy, Crouching, 4 In. 390
Figurine, Rabbit, Seated, Red Cabochon Eyes, 4 In. 480
Frame, Blue Enamel, Partial Circle, Guilloche, Dot Dash, 3 ½ In. 625
Kovsh, Art Nouveau, Petr Baskakov, 1908-17, 14 In. 7500
Ladle, Assay Mark For Aleksandr Nilolayevich, c.1857, 14 In 108
Magnifier, Rose Cut Diamonds, Guilloche Enamel, 6 In. 800

S

Match Safe, Horseshoe Shape, Engraved Writings, c.1900, 2 ½ x 2 ½ In. 399
Salt, Spoon, Gilt, Enamel, Moscow, c.1930 750
Samovar, Double Headed Eagle, Hallmarked, 18 ½ In. 12300
Scoop, Elongated Handle, Enameled Flowers, Leaves, White Ground, c.1900, 4 In. 702
Serving Spoon, Gilt, Moscow Kremlin Building, Sokolov, 1896, 7 ⅝ In. 660
Sugar Basket, Gilt, Enamel, Footed, Curved Handle, Moscow, 5 ½ In. 2360
Sugar Tongs, Gold Wash, Fiddle Handle, Cloisonne, c.1890, 5 x 1 In. 207
Tea Strainer, Enamel, Blue Flowers, Leaves, Gold Wash, 4 ½ x 3 In., Pair 660
Tea Strainer, Gold Wash, Cloisonne Decoration On Handle, 6 x 2 In. 247
Teapot, Cylindrical Body, Pedestal Foot, Dome Lid, Flowers, Leaves, 1891, 6 ½ In. 531

SILVER-SPANISH

Benetier, Repousse, Oval, Coquille Shape, Leaves, Royal Arms Crest, c.1910, 7 x 11 In. 615
Brazier, Turned Wood Handles, Cabriole Legs, c.1800, 3 x 14 In. 325
Figurine, Pheasants, Erect Tail, Left Foot In Front, 3 x 9 In. 484
Incense Boat, Hinged Lid, Repousse Scroll & Leaves, Footed, c.1875, 4 In. 500
Kettle, Bulbous, Animal Head Spout, Hoofed Legs, Scroll Handle, c.1800, 10 In. 1200
Ladle, Engraved Flowering Vines, 1700s, 16 ½ x 4 In. 1560
Trophy, Urn, Backgammon, Handles, Acanthus, Berry Finial, 1955, 12 x 13 In. 605

SILVER-STERLING. Sterling silver is made with 925 parts silver out of 1,000 parts of metal. The word *sterling* is a quality guarantee used in the United States after about 1860. The word was used much earlier in England and Ireland. Pieces listed here are not identified by country. These prices are based on current silver values. Other pieces of sterling quality silver are listed under Silver-American, Silver-English, etc.

Ashtray, Egyptian Style, Anhk, Crook, 4 Troughs, 3 ¾ In. 60
Basket, Bail Handle, Round Stepped Pedestal, Scallop Rim, Lobed Swirl, 6 In. 610
Basket, Footed, Ribbed Edge, American, c.1925, 12 x 9 ½ In. 300
Basket, Reticulated, Openwork, Swing Handle, c.1908, 7 x 5 In. 86
Basket, Scallop Rim, Bail Handle, Scrolls, Portrait Medallion, 1862, 6 In. 738
Bowl, Aesthetic, Flared Rim, Round Foot, Pierced Vine Band, Flowers, c.1920, 4 x 9 In. 338
Bowl, Cut Glass, Repousse Flowers, Scrollwork, Prism Cut, 13 In. Diam. 1035
Bowl, Dome Lid, Repousse, Flowers & Scrolling, Fern Handles, 9 x 10 In. 351
Bowl, Flared Reticulated Border, Flared Repousse Rim, Footed, c.1890, 10 x 2 In. 190
Bowl, Flared Rim, Reticulated Roses, Leaves & Scroll, Footed, c.1900, 15 In. Diam. 2835
Bowl, Fluted Bowl, Stepped Border, Footed, Monogram, 9 ½ x 2 ½ In. 161
Bowl, Fruit, Oval, Upscrolled Handles, Chased Fruit, c.1935, 13 x 8 In. 1125
Bowl, Gadroon Rim, Man, Bamboo Stalk, Paul Storr, 1812, 10 In. Diam. *illus* 2091
Bowl, Molded Rim, Pedestal Foot, Incised Banding, Scroll, Star, 8 In. Diam. 840
Bowl, Northern Lights, Wide Flat Rim, Shaped Handles, c.1928, 12 In. 245
Bowl, Oval, Scroll, Scalloped Border, 1900s, 11 ¼ In., Pair 354
Bowl, Presentation, Virginia Carvel Pattern, Handles, Pedestal Foot, c.1924, 7 In. 109
Bowl, Repousse Grape Clusters, Shaped Rim, Monogram Center, 9 In. Diam. 230
Bowl, Repousse, Chinese Zodiac Animals, Flower Banding, c.1900, 7 In. 830
Bowl, Round, Footed, Tapered Body, Repousse Flared Border, 10 x 3 In. 236
Bowl, Shaped, Sea Scrolls, Repousse Fruit Bunches, Pedestal Foot, 6 x 12 In. 711
Bowl, Sherbet, Flared Rim, Weighted Base, 3 ½ In., 6 Piece 132
Bowl, Squat, Spherical, Repousse, Bands, Dancers, Deer, Leaves, 1900s, 8 x 13 In. 2214
Bowl, Stand, Wavy Rim, Incised Wreath, Ram's Heads, Swag, Garland, c.1900, 3 In. 420
Bowl, Undertray, Cast Frogs, Flowers, Engraved Monogram, c.1903, 7 In. 738
Bowl, Vegetable, Dome Lid, Serpentine Lobed, Shell Handles, c.1865, 7 x 9 In., Pair 3500
Bowl, Vegetable, Lid, Oval, Rococo Scroll Edge, Pinecone Rim, 1898, 5 x 14 In., Pair 4000
Bowl, Vegetable, Oval, Scroll Border, Acanthus, Monogram, Whiting Mfg., 10 x 8 In., Pair 541
Bowl, Vegetable, Repousse Flowers & Shells, Handles, Footed, c.1890, 12 In., Pair 2772
Box, Agate, Guilloche Enamel, Center Cartouche, Hinged Lid, c.1900, 5 x 4 In. 492
Box, Art Deco, Blue Enamel, Engraved, Cartier, Paris, London, New York, c.1930, 2 ½ x 9 In. 18880
Box, Frog, Figural, 2 Parts, Black Stone Eyes, 2 In. 92
Box, Gilt, Flower Basket, Cartouche, Plique-A-Jour, Guilloche Enamel, 3 x 2 In. 1353
Box, Polish Amber Lid, Etched, 3 x 3 ½ In. 240
Box, Venus Riding A Seahorse, Gilt Leafy Cartouche, 2 x 3 In. 322
Bread Plate, Leaf Rim, Round Foot, Flared Rim, Monogram, Gorham, 1930, 6 In., 12 Piece 604
Bread Tray, Oval, Engraving, Open Cartouche Ends, c.1900, 11 ½ x 6 In. 127
Butter, Dome Cover, Geometric Finial, Leaf Band Border, Flowers, c.1860, 6 x 7 In. 1000
Cake Plate, Repousse Grapes, Leaves, Vines, Shaped, Pedestal Foot, 15 In. Diam. 1348
Cake Stand, Ribbon & Fleur-De-Lis Border, Round, Bell Foot, 4 x 11 In. 173

Silver-Sterling, Kettle, Stand, George III, Bone Handle & Finial, Engraved, 11 ½ In.
$677

Cowan Auctions

Silver-Sterling, Loving Cup, Square, Dragonfly, Plants, Hammered, Handles, 1881, 6 In.
$4,305

Skinner, Inc.

Silver-Sterling, Sauceboat, Ribbed, Wide Spout, Handle, Pedestal Base, Coin, 6 x 8 In.
$889

James D. Julia Auctioneers

TIP

The acid or sulfur in eggs, onions, mayonnaise, tart salad dressing, and salt corrode silver or silver plate. Rinse dishes as soon as possible.

Silver-Sterling, Tablespoon, Paul Revere Touchmark, Monogram, Case, Coin, c.1790, 9 In., Pair
$10,665

James D. Julia Auctioneers

TIP

Clean silver with gilt, like berry spoons or salt dishes, with soap, warm water, and a sponge. Do not use abrasive polish.

Slag Glass, Purple, Bowl, Milk Glass Swirl, Hobnail, 3 ¾ x 4 ½ In.
$32

Ruby Lane

Sleepy Eye, Barrel Label, Sleepy Eye Cream, Indian's Head, 196 Lbs. Net When Packed, 17 In.
$164

North American Auction Co.

Candelabra are listed in the Candelabrum category.
Candlesticks are listed in their own category.
Card Case, Chased, Japanese Courtyard Scene, Landscape, 3 ½ x 2 In. 378
Card Case, Parcel Gilt, Woman, Parasol, Chain Handle, Gorham, c.1856, 4 In. .... *illus* 800
Castor Stand, Regency, Boat Shape, Column Supports, Molded Ram's Head, 1818, 10 In. 300
Centerpiece, Shaped Edge, Lobed, 4-Footed, 3 x 13 In. 246
Centerpiece, Sleigh, Bateau Shape, Scrolling, Harnessed Reindeer, c.1910, 24 In. 8750
Cigar Holder, Gold Wash, Oval, Tapered, Geometric Stripes, Monogram, 5 x 2 In. 92
Cigar Lighter, Gimbaled, Wide Collar, Antelope Horn Twisted Handle, London, c.1898, 23 In. . *illus* 1353
Cigarette Box, Japanese Castle, Mountains, Wood Liner, 6 x 3 In. 103
Cigarette Case, Pierced On Diagonal, 5 ½ x 3 In. 153
Coffee Set, Industrial Pattern, Riveted, Swan Spout, Angled Handle, c.1907, 3 Piece 978
Coffeepot, Baluster, Domed Lid, Eagle Head Spout, Wood Handle, 1755, 9 In. 13663
Compote, Round, Shaped Rim, Repousse Flowers, Trumpeting Foot, c.1935, 5 x 11 In. 984
Corn Holders, Figural, 3 In., 12 Piece 96
Creamer, Helmet Shape, Serpentine Rim, Angled Handle, Stepped Foot, 6 x 5 In. 121
Cruet Set, Wood Base, Reticulated Frame, Engraved, Footed, c.1822, 10 In. .... *illus* 984
Cruet, Frosted, Figural Stopper, 6 ½ In. 123
Cup, Embossed Hunt Scenes, Crowned Monogram, Continental, 1800s, 5 In. .... *illus* 360
Dish, Repousse Flowers, Scalloped Edge, Round, Middle Eastern, 6 In. 84
Dish, Repousse Rim, Pierced, Footed, Round, Middle Eastern, c.1920, 7 In. 192
Dish, Sweetmeat, George III, Pictorial, Enameled, Footed, c.1816, 4 x 3 In. 276
Epergne, Flared Trumpet, Pierced Leaves, Baluster Column, Tiers, 1919, 27 In. 11711
Ewer, Grapevine Relief, 4-Footed, S-Curve Handle, Grape Cluster, 13 ½ In. 1093
Ewer, Hinged Lid, Paneled Body, Grapes, Leaves, Flower Shape Foot, 1868, 14 In. 984
Figurine, Boy Riding Dolphin, Holding Dorsal Fin, Marble Base, 1979, 13 In. 11478
Figurine, Pheasants, Wings Outstretched, Glass Eyes, c.1950, 18 In., Pair 3998
Flask, Pocket, Curved, Twist Lid, Hinged Holder, Tooling, Monogram, 5 x 4 In. 83
Flask, Rounded, Basket Weave, Hinged Cap, Inscribed, c.1910, 7 x 4 In. 553
Frame, Fighting Lions, Cherubs, Rabbits, Victorian, c.1896, 7 x 5 In. 675
Grape Shears, Grape Leaf-Shape Handles, Vining, 7 ½ In. 236
Gravy Boat, Classical Shape, Curved Rim, Scroll Handle, 3-Footed, c.1950, 7 x 4 In. 63
Gravy Boat, Scalloped Rim, 3-Footed, 7 ½ In. 220
Hot Water Urn, Dome Lid, Oval, Calyx, Gadroons, Serpent Handles, c.1804, 18 In. 13125
Hot Water Urn, George III, Reeded Handles, Gadroon, E.K., c.1810, 22 In. .... *illus* 2091
Incense Burner, Double Gourd, Handles, Repousse, Tripod, Birds, c.1890, 13 x 9 In. 948
Jewelry Box, Lift Lid, Square, Monogram Lid, Initials 92
Kettle, Stand, Gadroon, Wood Handle, Finial, Victorian, c.1881, 12 x 9 In. 480
Kettle, Stand, George III, Bone Handle & Finial, Engraved, 11 ½ In. .... *illus* 677
Kettle, Stand, Oval, Gadroon, Rocaille, Turned In Rim, Stirrup Handle, c.1905, 14 In. 861
Loving Cup, Square, Dragonfly, Plants, Handles, Dominick & Haff, 1881, 6 In. .... *illus* 4305
Loving Cup, Urn Shape, Scroll Handles, Auto Trophy, Pedestal, 1909, 11 In. 2360
Money Clip, Alpaca, Basket Weave, 1 ⅞ x 1 In. 47
Money Clip, Cross Shape, Inset Amethyst, Aquamarine, Pearls, 1900s, 3 ½ In. 120
Napkin Rings are listed in their own category.
Nosegay Holder, Victorian, Trumpet Shape, Flower Shape, Pin & Ring, 6 x 2 In. 154
Page Turner, Victorian, Bone, Curved Handle, Flat Blade, Marked, 1896, 15 In. 308
Pitcher, Art Nouveau, Iris & Daffodil Design, Smokestack Shape, 1882, 9 In. 1260
Pitcher, Baluster, Fluted, Lobed, Flared Lip, Scroll Handle, Shell Feet, c.1840, 10 In. 1315
Pitcher, Baluster, Water Lily Spout, Cattail Handle, Leaf Molded Rim, Pedestal, c.1855, 15 In. ... 8750
Pitcher, Contemporary Style, Newport, Swollen Body, Handle, 7 ½ In. 660
Pitcher, Monogram, Round Foot, Leafy Handle, 9 ½ x 5 In. 442
Pitcher, Paneled Body, Wide Handle, Flowers, Monogram, c.1900, 9 In. 1722
Pitcher, Squat, Pear Shape, Hexagon, Serpentine Lobed, Scroll Handle, 11 x 10 In. 687
Pitcher, Stirrer, Tapering Oval, Molded Rim, Banding, Duck Beak Spout, 8 x 4 In. 2000
Plaque, Last Supper, 17 x 33 In. 615
Plateau, Centerpiece, Round, Turned Out Rim, 16 In. 590
Platter, George III, Shaped Oval, Gadroon, Leaf Border, Coat Of Arms, 1797, 24 In. 5855
Platter, Waiter, Round, Shaped Shell & Scroll Rim, Scroll Feet, c.1900, 13 In., Pair 1500
Platter, Washington Pattern, Oval, Squared Rim, 20 In. 582
Porringer, Pierced Scroll Handle, Flared Rim, Convex Base, c.1805, 8 In. 1107
Punch Ladle, Shell Design, Wavy Rim, 13 In. 115
Ritual Pot, Monster Head Handle & Spout, Doughnut Body, Emblems, 1800, 9 In. 1067
Salt & Pepper, Pagoda, Fence, Steep Roof, 2 x 2 In. 91
Salt Spoon, Repousse Flowers, 3 Lion Mask & Paw Feet, Ruffle Rim, 2 x 3 In. 115
Salver, Armorial, Scroll Feet, Engraved, Chippendale Rim, c.1901, 24 In. Diam. 2706

Salver, Round, Pierced Gallery Rim, Festoons, Beaded, Ribbon, Footed, c.1870, 16 In. 1107
Salver, Round, Rope Twist Border, Trumpet Foot, Coat Of Arms, 1700, 12 In. 10735
Sauceboat, Ribbed, Wide Spout, Handle, Pedestal Base, Coin, 6 x 8 In. .... *illus* 889
Sauceboat, Victorian, Figural Whippet Handle, Raised Paw, Splay Feet, c.1872, 6 In. 2583
Serving Spoon, Napoleon Figural Handle, Hand Tooled, 10 ½ In., Pair 307
Serving Spoon, Victorian, Fiddle Pattern, Squared Shoulder, c.1839, 12 In., Pair 1250
Silent Butler, Round, Hinged Lid, Turned Handle, Birds, Flowers, c.1950, 6 In. 185
Spoon, Souvenir, see Souvenir category.
Strawberry Fork, Fiddle Shape, Beaded Edge, 3 Tines, Monogram, 5 In., 6 Piece 98
Sugar Casket, Hinged Lid, Incised, Flattened Anthemion Foot, c.1900, 4 x 5 In. 120
Sugar, Lobed, Flower Band, Scroll Handles, Lid, Basket Finial, Stepped Foot, c.1850, 10 In. 1000
Sugar, Reticulated Bowl, Swing Handle, Cobalt Blue Glass Liner, 4 In. 75
Tablespoon, Paul Revere Touchmark, Monogram, Case, Coin, c.1790, 9 In., Pair .... *illus* 10665
Tankard, Dome Lid, Dog Shape Thumbpiece, Scrollwork, Cartouche, c.1868, 8 ½ In. 738
Tankard, Tapered, Molded Rim & Base, Flowers, Round Lid, Loop Handle, c.1700, 7 In. 2460
Tazza, Central Monogram, Reticulated Flutter Rim, Garlands, c.1950, 5 ½ In. 492
Tea & Coffee Set, Wood Scroll Handles, Footed, Lionel A. Crichton, c.1896, 6 Piece 2280
Tea Set, Teapot, Sugar & Creamer, Urn Shape, Ivory Handle, c.1930-60, 6 x 3 In. 625
Tea Strainer, Enamel, Light Blue Border, 4 ½ x 3 In. 165
Teakettle, Stand, Repousse Scroll, Flowers, Bird Mask Spout, 1855, 17 In. 2204
Teapot, Dome Lid, Squat, Bulbous, Gadroon, Flared Rim, Bone Finial, 5 x 11 In. 562
Teapot, Flowers, Leaves, Bird Finial, Hinged Lid, Scroll Feet, c.1832, 6 ½ In. 464
Teapot, Globular, Hinged Lid, Wheat Finial & Band, Stepped Foot, c.1830, 10 In. 896
Teapot, Hinged Dome Lid, Squat, Ivory S-Shape Handle, Ring Foot, c.1708, 6 In. 7170
Teapot, Square, Embossed Flowers, Shell Knees, Pad Feet, C. Thomas & G. Fox, 4 ½ x 8 In. 390
Tomato Server, Grotesque Mask, Ram's Head Terminus, Monogram, J. Stevenson, 8 In. 201
Tray, Edwardian, Scrolling Rim, Pierced Border, Vines, 1901, 26 In. Diam. 8783
Tray, Octagonal, 14 x 9 In. 300
Tray, Oval, Handles, Gadroon & Scalloped Border, Monogram, 1912, 28 x 17 In. 2489
Tray, Oval, Reeded Rim, 2 Handles, Leaves, Cartouche, Bracket Feet, c.1795, 26 In. 3690
Tray, Pierced Gallery, Ball Feet, 8 x 8 In. 216
Tray, Round, Jensen Style Blossom Handles, Monogram, c.1950, 15 ½ In. 492
Tray, Round, Openwork, Urns, Leaves, Lattice, 10 ½ In. 307
Tray, Round, Shaped Shell & Scroll Rim, Crest, Pad Feet, c.1755, 11 In. Diam. 1625
Tray, Scalloped, Shaped Edge, Leaves, Flowers, Handles, 1900s, 17 x 26 In. 1840
Tray, Serving, Molded Swirl Rim, Leafy Scrolled Swag Edge, 1900s, 16 In. Diam. 1188
Tray, Tea, Navette Shape, Upturned Ends, Integral Handles, c.1935, 22 x 14 In. 676
Tureen, Dome Lid Oval, Applied Grape Leaves, Tendrils, Arched Handles, 16 x 9 In. 984
Tureen, Lid, Oval, Shell & Scroll Rim & Handles, Bracket Feet, 1899, 15 In. 984
Urn, Lid, Baluster, Embossed Flowers, Openwork Ring Handles, 1900s, 13 x 10 In. 750
Vase, Enameled Tulips, Tapered, Serpentine Square, Round Dome Foot, 1897, 10 In. 1476
Vase, Trumpet, Openwork Edge, Laurel Swags, Shaped Rim, c.1909, 18 In. 2500
Whistle, Scrolling Leaves, c.1896, 1 In. 125
Wine Bottle Holder, Reticulated Grapevine, Grotesque Mask Handle, 1900s, 9 In. 2091
Wine Cooler, Cylindrical, Monteith Shape Rim, Scroll, Ring Handles, 10 x 9 In. 3000
Wine Cooler, Tapering Cylinder, Cabochon, Scroll, Lion Mask Handles, 10 x 9 In. 3000

SILVER-SWEDISH

Cigarette Case, Stockholm Stadshuset, Engraved, C.G. Halberg, 1950, 3 x 3 x In. 375
Demitasse Spoon, Open Flower & Lattice, Crown Top, 4 In. 28

SILVER-TURKISH

Cigarette Case, Niello, Etched, Floral Cartouche, Gold Wash Interior, 3 ¼ x 4 In. 248
Vase, Tapered Cylinder, Rococo Scrolls, Lattice, Villages, 1900s, 24 x 5 In. 406

SINCLAIRE cut glass was made by H.P. Sinclaire and Company of Corning, New York, between 1904 and 1929. He cut glass made at other factories until 1920. Pieces were made of crystal as well as amber, blue, green, or ruby glass. Only a small percentage of Sinclaire glass is marked with the *S* in a wreath.

Bowl, Central Star Of David, Hobstars, Scalloped & Serrated Rim, 8 x 2 In. 125
Centerpiece, Footed, Flat Rim, Amber, Signed, c.1910, 9 x 3 ½ In. 100
Sugar & Creamer, Engraved Flowers, Leaves, 1920s 60
Tray, Stemmed Flowers, Upward Curved Sides, Marked, c.1910, 11 x 7 In. 125
Vase, Bouquet, Footed, Rolled Rim, Shouldered, 13 In. 1400

SKIING, *see Sports category.*

Snow Babies, Figurine, Girl, Seated, Outreached Arms, Mittens, Bisque, c.1910, 1 ¾ In.
$75

Ruby Lane

Soapstone, Carving, Green, Roses & Birds, Clustered Leafy Branches, Footed, Chinese, 10 x 7 In.
$244

DuMouchelles Art Gallery

Soft Paste, Mug, Canary Yellow, Luster, Transfer, A Trifle For Eliza, Loop Handle, 2 ½ In.
$59

Hess Auction Group

Spangle Glass, Vase, Pink, Silver Mica Flakes, Lobed, Crimped Edge, Ruffled Rim, Pontil, England, c.1890, 10 In. $350

Ruby Lane

TIP

Always dust from the top down. The dust falls.

Spatter Glass, Vase, Mottled Cream, Red, Brown, Gold Spangles, Ruffled Rim, 9 In. $332

James D. Julia Auctioneers

Spatterware, Cup & Saucer, Cockscomb, Yellow, Red Flower, Green Leaves, Saucer 6 In. $944

Hess Auction Group

S

SLAG GLASS resembles a marble cake. It can be streaked with different colors. There were many types made from about 1880. Caramel slag is the incorrect name for chocolate glass. Pink slag was an American product made by Harry Bastow and Thomas E.A. Dugan at Indiana, Pennsylvania, about 1900. Purple and blue slag were made in American and English factories in the 1880s. Red slag is a very late Victorian and twentieth-century glass. Other colors are known but are of less importance to the collector. New versions of chocolate glass and colored slag glass have been made.

Bittersweet Orange, Dish, Yellow, Ruffled, Cream Rim, L.E. Smith, 5½ x 3 In. 38
Bittersweet Orange, Vase, Yellow, L. E. Smith, 15¾ In. 48
Caramel Slag is listed in the Imperial Glass category.
Green, Bowl, Starburst Pattern On Side & Bottom, White, 2 x 6½ In. 28
Green, Match Holder, Top Handle, Square Metal Mount, 3 x 3 In. 160
Green, Saltcellar, Swirled, Hexagon, Flower Stamp, 1½ x ⅞ In. 22
Green, Sugar & Spooner, Variegated, Atterbury Glass Company, 2 Piece 250
Pink, Cruet Set, Cruet, 2 Shakers, Tray, Forget-Me-Not, 4 Piece 64
Purple, Bowl, Milk Glass Swirl, Hobnail, 3¾ x 4½ In. .... *illus* 32
Red, Orange, Swan, White, Swirls, 3½ x 16 In. 45

SLEEPY EYE collectors look for anything bearing the image of the nineteenth-century Indian chief with the drooping eyelid. The Sleepy Eye Milling Co., Sleepy Eye, Minnesota, used his portrait in advertising from 1883 to 1921. It offered many premiums, including stoneware and pottery steins, crocks, bowls, mugs, and pitchers, all decorated with the famous profile of the Indian. The popular pottery was made by Weir Pottery Co. from c.1899 to 1905. Weir merged with six other potteries and became Western Stoneware in 1906. Western Stoneware Co. made blue and white Sleepy Eye from 1906 until 1937, long after the flour mill went out of business in 1921. Reproductions of the pitchers are being made today. The original pitchers came in only five sizes: 4 inches, 5 ¼ inches, 6 ½ inches, 8 inches, and 9 inches. The Sleepy Eye image was also used by companies unrelated to the flour mill.

Barrel Label, Sleepy Eye Cream, Indian's Head, 196 Lbs. Net When Packed, 17 In. .... *illus* 164
Crock, Cobalt Blue, Tan Ground, 5¾ x 6½ In., Pair 172
Fan, Sleepy Eye Flour & Cereal, Indian, Old Sleepy Eye, Ish-Tak-A-Bah, 13 x 6 In. 60
Label, Milling Barrel, Strong, Bakers, 21 x 21 213
Pitcher, Cobalt Blue, Beige, Indian Chief, Tepees, Trees, Signed, 8 x 6 In. 750
Pitcher, Cobalt Blue, White Ground, Indian Chief, 6¼ x 6½ In. 125
Poster, Indian Cloth, Central Portrait, Buffalo Hunt, Cloth, 21 x 22 In. 1220
Sign, The Meritorious Flour, Portrait, Tin Lithograph, Framed, 24 x 19½ In. 8540
Vase, Cylindrical, Blue, Gray, Beige Ground, 8½ In. 96

SLOT MACHINES *are included in the Coin-Operated Machine category.*

SNOW BABIES, made from bisque and spattered with glitter sand, were first manufactured in 1864 by Hertwig and Company of Thuringia. Other German and Japanese companies copied the Hertwig designs. Originally, Snow Babies were made of candy and used as Christmas decorations. There are also Snow Babies tablewares made by Royal Bayreuth. Copies of the small Snow Babies figurines are being made today and a line called "Snowbabies" was introduced by Department 56 in 1987. Don't confuse these with the original Snow Babies.

Figurine, Boy, Holding Tennis Racquet, 1920s, 1¾ In. 150
Figurine, Boy, Seated, Reaching Out, 2¼ In. 115
Figurine, Girl, Red Skirt, Pushing Snowball, c.1930, 2½ x 1¾ In. 165
Figurine, Girl, Red Skirt, Sitting On Large Snowball, 1¾ x 2 In. 150
Figurine, Girl, Riding Red Airplane, c.1930, 2½ x 2 In. 225
Figurine, Girl, Riding Snow Bear, Waving, 2 x 3 In. 325
Figurine, Girl, Seated, Outreached Arms, Mittens, Bisque, c.1910, 1¾ In. .... *illus* 75
Group, 2 Girls, Penguin, Snowball, c.1920, 1 x 2 In. 135
Group, 3 Elves, Red Outfits, c.1920, 2¾ x 1½ In. 165
Group, Boy & Girl In Igloo, c.1920, 4 x 3 In. 175
Group, Boys, Sledding On Snowbank, 1⅞ x 1½ In. 95
Group, Santa & Elf In Train, c.1910, 1½ x 3 In. 175

SNUFF BOTTLES *are listed in the Bottle category.*

SNUFFBOXES held snuff. Taking snuff was popular long before cigarettes became available. The gentleman or lady would take a small pinch of the ground tobacco or snuff in the fingers, then sniff it and sneeze. Snuffboxes were made of many materials, including gold, silver, enameled metal, and wood. Most snuffboxes date from the late eighteenth or early nineteenth centuries.

Celluloid, Mandarin Figure, Carved, Glass Eyes, Painted Hair, c.1800, 4¼ In. 1047

Cowrie Shell, Monogram, Silver Gilt, Ireland, 1818, 1 ¼ x 2 ¾ In. 540
Silver, Hinged Lid, Engraved Cyrillic Writing, Russia, 3 x 1 ¼ In. 121
Silver, Painted Courtly Cover, Guilloche Enameled Base, c.1900, 3 ¼ In. 738
Tortoiseshell, Silver Mounted, Oval Carnelian, Agate, c.1713, 4 In. 3890
Tortoiseshell, Silver, Mother-Of-Pearl, Birds, Acanthus, Curlicues, 3 ⅛ In. 1945
Wood, Leather, Book Shape, Drawer, c.1880, 2 x 4 x 5 In. 245

SOAPSTONE is a mineral that was used for foot warmers or griddles because of its heat-retaining properties. Soapstone was carved into figurines and bowls in many countries in the nineteenth and twentieth centuries. Most of the soapstone seen today is from China or Japan. It is still being carved in the old styles.

Bowl, Leaf Shape, Lizard Crawling Along Edge, 2 ¾ x 7 ½ In. 88
Carving, Green, Roses & Birds, Clustered Leafy Branches, Footed, Chinese, 10 x 7 In. .... *illus* 244
Figurine, Black Grouse, Head Turned Over Back, 7 x 6 In. 153
Figurine, Carved, Guanyin, Gown, Holding Scroll, Platform Base, c.1910, 7 In. 177
Group, Dragons, Flaming Pearl, Chinese, 10 x 13 In. 270
Sculpture, 2 Vases, Phoenix, Flowers, 16 x 9 In. 344
Seal, Carved Lion, Seated, Cub On Back, Wood Stand, Box, 2 In. 208
Seal, Columnar, Rounded Top, Red & Gray, Carved Bats & Clouds, Trees, c.1900, 5 In. 741
Seal, Orange Tone, Square Shaped, Bixie Finial, Mythical Figure, 3 ¼ In. 89
Seal, Oval, Carved Frog, Worm, Chinese Characters, Finley, 2 ½ In. 153
Seal, Rose Gray, Foo Dog Finial, Rectangular, c.1900, 2 In. 741
Seal, Stylized Sea Animal, Base, Carved, Chinese, 2 ½ x 3 In. 74

SOFT PASTE is a name for a type of pottery. Although it looks very much like porcelain, it is a chemically different material. Most of the soft-paste wares were made in the early nineteenth century. Other pieces may be listed under Gaudy Dutch or Leeds.

Bowl, Earthworm Design, Flared Rim, Ring Foot, Mocha, Blue, Green, Leaf Border, 3 x 5 In. 413
Dish, Cobalt Blue, White Flowers, 11 ¼ In. 180
Figurine, Asian Woman, Cup, Fire Glazed, Brown, Green, 13 In. 236
Group, Asian Woman, Girl, Fire Glazed, Brown, Green, 15 x 9 In. 236
Mug, Canary Yellow, Luster, Transfer, A Trifle For Eliza, Loop Handle, 2 ½ In. .... *illus* 59

SOUVENIRS of a trip—what could be more fun? Our ancestors enjoyed the same thing and souvenirs were made for almost every location. Most of the souvenir pottery and porcelain pieces of the nineteenth century were made in England or Germany, even if the picture showed a North American scene. In the twentieth century, the souvenir china business seems to have been dominated by the manufacturers in Japan, Taiwan, Hong Kong, England, and the United States. Another popular souvenir item is the souvenir spoon, made of sterling or silver plate. These are usually made in the country pictured on the spoon. Related pieces may be found in the Coronation and World's Fair categories.

Countertop Display, Postcards, Rotating, 4 Rows, 29 x 11 In. 458
Plaque, Pan-American Expo, Embossed Indian Chief, Round, Copper Flash, 1901, 5 In. 240
Plate, Mount Vernon, Delano Studios, Embossed Laurel Rim, 1950s, 10 In. 18
Spoon, Hawaii, Catamaran, King Kamehameha, Silver, Red Enamel, 5 ½ In. 125
Spoon, Louisville, Farm Scene, Silver, c.1900, 5 In. 48
Spoon, Twisted Handle, Heart Shape Bowl, Chicago, Sterling Silver, 4 In. 38
Spoon, Yale University, Silver, 1891, 4 In. 30

SPANGLE GLASS is multicolored glass made from odds and ends of colored glass rods. It includes metallic flakes of mica covered with gold, silver, nickel, or copper. Spangle glass is usually cased with a thin layer of clear glass over the multicolored layer. Similar glass is listed in the Vasa Murrhina category.

Banana Bowl, Cranberry, Silver Spangles, White, Flower Bouquet, 4 x 11 In. 277
Pitcher, Red, Amber, Applied Handle, 9 x 7 In. 96
Rose Bowl, Cranberry, Opal Glass, Clear Cased, Silver Spangle 75
Vase, Egg Shape, Gold Spangles, Yellow Opalescent To Clear, White, 4 x 3 ½ In. 79
Vase, Egg Shape, Silver Spangles, Blue Opalescent To Clear, White, 4 x 3 ½ In. 79
Vase, Pink, Mica Flakes, Gourd Shape, Ruffled Rim, Pink Interior, c.1890, 10 x 6 In. 350
Vase, Pink, Silver Mica Flakes, Lobed, Crimped Edge, Ruffled Rim, Pontil, England, c.1890, 10 In. *illus* 350

SPANISH LACE *is listed in the Opalescent category as Opaline Brocade.*

Spatterware, Cup & Saucer, Rainbow, Red & Blue, Central Bull's-Eye, Saucer 5 ⅞ In.
$106

Hess Auction Group

Spatterware, Mug, Peafowl On Branch, Blue, Green, Red, Child's, 2 ½ In.
$384

Hess Auction Group

Spatterware, Plate, Acorn, Purple Border, Teal, Green, 9 ¾ In.
$767

Hess Auction Group

TIP

Keep your keys next to your bed at night. If you hear someone in the house or breaking in, push the panic button and the alarm will go off. It should frighten a burglar or wake up the neighbors. (Test the car key to be sure the car is within range.)

Storage Lockers
Storage lockers available for rent were first built in the 1960s. The units store unneeded household furniture and belongings. Are we acquiring too many things? Moving more often? Or are houses smaller?

SPATTER GLASS is a multicolored glass made from many small pieces of different colored glass. It is sometimes called End-of-Day glass. It is still being made.

Bowl, Champagne, White Spatters, Blue Glass Festoon, Blown, 3 x 4 In. 65
Bowl, Internal Silver Speck, Ruffled Rim, 4 x 9 ½ In. 20
Bowl, Pink, Yellow, Star Shape, 1890-1900, 3 ¾ x 8 ½ In. 250
Pitcher, Red, Blue, Applied Blue Handle, 9 x 3 In. 225
Rose Bowl, Pink, Yellow, Chartreuse, 1800s, 3 x 3 ¾ In. 48
Vase, Green, Pink Spatter, White Ground, Satin Cut, Ruffle Rim, 9 In. 60
Vase, Green, White, 4 ½ x 10 In. 33
Vase, Mottled Cream, Red, Brown, Gold Spangles, Ruffled Rim, 9 In. .... *illus* 332
Vase, Orange, Red, Green, Blue, White, Ribbed, Ruffled Rim, 8 x 6 In. 65

SPATTERWARE and spongeware are terms that have changed in meaning in recent years, causing much confusion for collectors. Some say that *spatterware* is the term used by Americans, *sponged ware* or *spongeware* by the English. The earliest pieces were made in the late eighteenth century, but most of the spatterware found today was made from about 1800 to 1850. Early spatterware was made in the Staffordshire district of England for sale in America. Collectors also use the word *spatterware* to refer to kitchen crockery with added spatter made in America during the late nineteenth and early twentieth centuries. Spongeware is very similar to spatterware in appearance. Designs were applied to ceramics by daubing the color on with a sponge or cloth. Many collectors do not differentiate between spongeware and spatterware and use the names interchangeably. Modern pottery is being made to resemble old spatterware and spongeware, but careful examination will show it is new.

Creamer, Cockscomb, Yellow, Red Paneled, Molded Handle, c.1830s, 5 In. 1722
Cup & Saucer, Cockscomb, Yellow, Red Flower, Green Leaves, Saucer 6 In. .... *illus* 944
Cup & Saucer, Peafowl, Blue Ball Flower, Red, c.1830, 2 ¼ In. 369
Cup & Saucer, Rainbow, Red & Blue, Central Bull's-Eye, Saucer 5 ⅞ In. .... *illus* 106
Cup & Saucer, Tree, Blue, 6 In. 236
Dispenser, Barrel Shape, Spongeware, Blue Stripes, White, Metal Spigot, Lid, 16 x 11 In. 90
Mug, Peafowl On Branch, Blue, Green, Red, Child's, 2 ½ In. .... *illus* 384
Mustard Pot, Blue, White, Applied Handle, Lid, c.1860, 3 ¼ x 2 ¾ In. 185
Pitcher, Rainbow, 5 Colors, Molded Handle, Shell Spout, 1930s, 8 In. 1353
Pitcher, Tulip, Purple, Red & Blue, Paneled, Handle, c.1925, 6 In. 615
Plate, Acorn, Purple Border, Teal, Green, 9 ¾ In. .... *illus* 767
Plate, Acorn, Purple Spatter, Brown, Teal, Green, Adams, 9 ¼ In. 502
Plate, Blue, Tulip, Shaped Rim, Paneled, Green Leaves, Ironstone, 8 ½ In. 177
Plate, Columbine, Green, Daisy Border, Stick Spatter, Ironstone, 9 ¾ In. 142
Plate, Dahlia Pattern, Red & Blue Flowers, Purple Border, Ironstone, 8 ¼ In. 649
Plate, Delilah, Purple, Paneled, Red, Blue, 6-Panel Flower, 8 ⅜ In. 130
Plate, Festoon, Red & Blue, Paneled, Red & Green Sprig, 8 In. 2337
Plate, Peafowl, 3 Colors, Branch, Feather Edge, 8 ½ In. .... *illus* 236
Plate, Peafowl, Green Spatter, Red, Yellow, Blue, 9 In. 472
Plate, Rabbitware, Stick Spatter, Ironstone, 9 In. .... *illus* 106
Plate, Rabbitware, Virginia Stick Spatter, Green Frogs, Cabbages, Yellow Grassland, 9 In. 300
Plate, Rainbow, Purple & Blue, Ironstone, Bull's-Eye Border, 9 ½ In. .... *illus* 325
Plate, Schoolhouse, Blue Rim, Ironstone, Stamped, J. Goodwin, 8 ½ In. .... *illus* 443
Plate, Thistle, Purple, Bluebell Flower, Red Buds, Green Leaves, Ironstone, 8 In. 177
Plate, Tulip, Blue Spatter, Red, Green Leaves, 9 In. 502
Plate, Tulip, Purple, Paneled, Green Buds, c.1830, 10 ½ In. 430
Plate, Wigwam, Red Spatter, Paneled, Cream Ground, 1800s, 8 In. 212
Platter, Peafowl, Bird On Branch, Red Spatter, Blue, Yellow, Green, Ironstone, 8 ½ In. 118
Platter, Rainbow, Octagonal, c.1920, 12 ¼ x 9 ¼ In. 11685
Platter, Tulip, Blue, Red Bud, Octagonal, 13 ½ x 12 In. 1168
Platter, Tulip, Purple, Red & Blue, Octagonal, c.1825, 18 x 14 In. 5535
Salt, Purple & Blue, Footed, England, c.1930s, 2 ¼ In. 215
Sugar, Lid, Fort, Blue, Gray, Brown, Red, Green Trees, 4 ¾ In. 130
Sugar, Lid, Peafowl, Red, Yellow, Green, Ring Foot, Ironstone, 4 ½ In. 266
Sugar, Lid, Red Thistle, Yellow, Panel, c.1835, 8 In. 984
Sugar, Lid, Rooster, Red, Mustard, Blue, 4 ¾ In. 71
Sugar, Lid, Tulip, Memorial, 4 ¾ In. 53
Tea Set, Peafowl, Blue, Red, Yellow, Green, Child's, 9 Piece 443
Teapot, Lid, Peafowl, Blue, Paneled, Footed, c.1830, 9 ¼ In. 430
Teapot, Rainbow, Red & Green, Squat, Loop Handle, Gooseneck, 5 ½ In. .... *illus* 1062
Waste Bowl, Peafowl, Green, Blue, Yellow, Red, 3 x 5 ½ In. 354
Waste Bowl, Thistle, Red, Footed, c.1940, 9 In. 20191

Spatterware, Plate, Peafowl, 3 Colors, Branch, Feather Edge, 8 ½ In.
$236

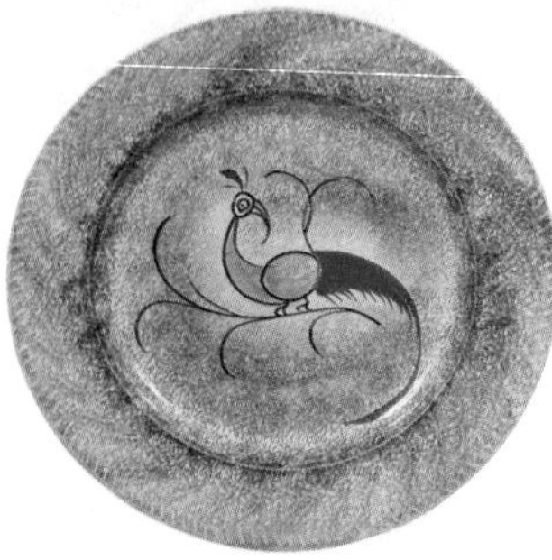

Hess Auction Group

Spatterware, Plate, Rabbitware, Stick Spatter, Ironstone, 9 In.
$106

Hess Auction Group

Spatterware, Plate, Rainbow, Purple & Blue, Ironstone, Bull's-Eye Border, 9 ½ In.
$325

Hess Auction Group

SPELTER is a synonym for a zinc alloy. Figurines, candlesticks, and other pieces were made of spelter and given a bronze or painted finish. The metal has been used since about the 1860s to make statues, tablewares, and lamps that resemble bronze. Spelter is soft and breaks easily. To test for spelter, scratch the base of the piece. Bronze is solid; spelter will show a silvery scratch.

Bust, Curly Beard, Anatole Guillot, 15 ½ x 8 ½ In. 338
Ewer, Bronzed, Victorian, Animals & Roses, 33 ¼ x 6 In. 302
Ewer, Tapered Bristol Glass, Pink Roses, Lion's Head Relief, 18 x 7 In. 584
Ewer, Winged Woman, Lion Mask On Torso, 24 ½ In. 281
Plaque, Relief, Classical Female Figures, Winged Putti, 9 ½ x 7 In., Pair 123
Sculpture, 2 Pheasants, Strutting, Marble Base, 13 x 24 In. 246
Sculpture, Cyclist, Cap, 100 Km. Marker, Paris, Marble Base, Signed Limousin, 11 ¾ In. 2918
Sculpture, Emile Louis Picault, Metal Worker, Tool, France, c.1850, 31 In. .... *illus* 720
Sculpture, Le Cid, Warrior, Cape, Helmet, Seated, Pensive, Engraved, 20 x 17 ½ In. 168
Sculpture, Nobleman, Coats, Long Hair, France, 16 In. 61
Sculpture, Satyr, Wine Skin, Patina, Marble Base, 20th Century, 22 In. 649
Sculpture, Warrior, Bronzed, Shield, Sword, 15 In. 153
Sculpture, Woman, Collecting Water, Vase, After August Moreau, 16 In. 71
Sculpture, Woman, Winged, Robed, After Julien Causse, France, 23 In. 210
Urn, Candleholders, Victorian, Late 19th Century, Lovebirds, 16 x 20 In., Pair 151
Vase, Figural, Man Standing Pensively By Tree, A De Rank, 22 ¾ x 9 ½ In. 126

SPINNING WHEELS in the corner have been symbols of earlier times for the past 100 years. Although spinning wheels date back to medieval days, the ones found today are rarely more than 200 years old. Because the style of the spinning wheel changed very little, it is often impossible to place an exact date on a wheel.

Castle Style, Mixed Wood, Pa., 1800s, 48 In. 118
Flax, Carved & Turned, Spindles, c.1810, 34 In. .... *illus* 115
Mixed Wood, 14-Spoke Wheel, Plank Deck, Turnings, 1800s, 57 x 64 In. .... *illus* 92

SPODE pottery, porcelain, and bone china were made by the Stoke-on-Trent factory of England founded by Josiah Spode about 1770. The firm became Copeland and Garrett from 1833 to 1847, then W.T. Copeland or W.T. Copeland and Sons until 1976. It then became Royal Worcester Spode Ltd. The company was bought by the Portmeirion Group in 2009. The word *Spode* appears on many pieces made by the factories. Most collectors include all the wares under the more familiar name of Spode. Porcelains are listed in this book by the name that appears on the piece. Related pieces may be listed under Copeland, Copeland Spode, and Royal Worcester.

Basket, Chestnut, On Stand, Creamware, Grapes, Leaves, Marked, c.1830, 3 x 10 In., Pair 615
Bowl, Blue, Japanese Flower Pattern, Gold Trim, 10 ½ In. 123
Cup & Saucer, Flared, Multicolor Flowers, Gilt Rim, c.1820, 3 ½ x 5 ½ In. 46
Dish, Sweetmeat, Scalloped Rim, Handles, Gilt, Grapes, Leaves, Reserves, 1800s, 10 x 9 In. 92
Lazy Susan, Tower Pattern, Central Tureen, 4 Covered Dishes, 10 x 22 In. 156
Pitcher, Celadon, Relief Birds & Dragonflies, 7 ½ x 5 ½ In., Pair 236
Plate, Greek, 4 Horses, Chariot, Greek Key Rim, 10 ½ In. 151
Plate, Luncheon, Gilt Trim, Blue Ground, Flower Border, Feathers, Birds, c.1810, 8 ¾ In. 554
Tea Service, Imari Style, Teapot, Sugar, Creamer, Cups, Saucers, Lazy Susan, 12 Piece 1440
Vase, Lid, Jasperware, Satyr Mask Handles, Dolphin Finial, Putti, Faun, Cupid, 14 In., Pair 2375

SPORTS equipment, sporting goods, brochures, and related items are listed here. Items are listed by sport. Other categories of interest are Bicycle, Card, Fishing, Sword, Toy, and Trap.

Baseball, Ball, Autographed, 16 Players, New York Yankees, Babe Ruth, Frame, c.1930 1560
Baseball, Ball, Autographed, Boston Red Sox, Team, Ted Williams, Rubber Center, 1959 230
Baseball, Ball, Autographed, Connie Mack, Reach Official League, c.1945 822
Baseball, Ball, Autographed, Mickey Mantle, Rawlings 270
Baseball, Ball, Autographed, Jackie Robinson, Best Wishes, 1960s 26290
Baseball, Bank, Save & Win With Jackie Robinson, Dime, Register, Tin Litho, 1950, 2 x 5 In. 404
Baseball, Banner, Champions, American League, Chicago, Silk, 1907, 18 x 28 In. 1080
Baseball, Bat, Commemorative, Hall Of Fame, June 12, 1939, H & B 6000
Baseball, Bat, Willie Mays, Game Used, Hillerich & Bradsby S2, Ball Marks, c.1956, 35 In. 5975
Baseball, Bat, Autographed, Michael Jordan, Wood, 1994, 33 ¾ x 2 ¼ In. 316
Baseball, Bottle, Whiskey, Red Sox, Whiskey One Ball, Player Up To Bat, Glass, Metal Cap, c.1910, 4 In. 696
Baseball, Button, Babe Ruth, Hello Babe, Portrait, Celluloid, 1930s, 1 In. 202
Baseball, Button, I'm Rooting For Jackie Robinson, Dodgers, Photo, c.1947, 1 ¼ In. 278
Baseball, Button, Leroy Satchel Paige, Cleveland Indians, CPB, 1949, 1 ¼ In. 259
Baseball, Button, Yankees, Joe DiMaggio, Portrait, Celluloid, 1 ¾ In. 153

Spatterware, Plate, Schoolhouse, Blue Rim, Ironstone, Stamped, J. Goodwin, 8 ½ In.
$443

Hess Auction Group

Spatterware, Teapot, Rainbow, Red & Green, Squat, Loop Handle, Gooseneck, 5 ½ In.
$1,062

Hess Auction Group

Spelter, Sculpture, Emile Louis Picault, Metal Worker, Tool, France, c.1850, 31 In.
$720

Cowan Auctions

Spinning Wheel, Flax, Carved & Turned, Spindles, c.1810, 34 In.
$115

Cottone Auctions

Spinning Wheel, Mixed Wood, 14-Spoke Wheel, Plank Deck, Turnings, 1800s, 57 x 64 In.
$92

Cowan Auctions

TIP
Fountain pens date from the 1880s, ballpoints from the mid-'40s, fiber-tip pens from the mid-'60s, and Sharpies from the mid-'70s. Don't be fooled by a forgery written with the wrong kind of pen.

Baseball, Button, Yankees, Lou Gehrig, Portrait, Domed, Celluloid, 1 3/4 In. ... 190
Baseball, Cap, Usher's, Brooklyn Dodgers, Red, Blue, Embroidered, 1950s, 7 1/4 In. ... 10200
Baseball, Catcher's Mitt, Yogi Berra, c.1960 ... 17925
Baseball, Child's Baseball Set, Mickey Mantle, Bat, Card, Ball, 22 In. ... 450
Baseball, Doll, Christy Mathewson, SABA, Speilwarenfabrik, 1920-35, 7 1/2 In. ... *illus* 288
Baseball, Pennant, Joe Jackson, Felt, Ferguson Bakery, 1916 ... *illus* 7200
Baseball, Pennant, On Bat, National Baseball Hall Of Fame, Blue & Yellow Felt, c.1965, 16 x 12 In. 20
Baseball, Photograph, J. DiMaggio, T. Williams, M. Mantle, Autographed, 24 x 28 In. ... 270
Baseball, Salt & Pepper, Ball & Glove, Pittsburgh Pirates, Cream & Red, 3 x 3 In. ... *illus* 15
Baseball, Souvenir, Straight Razor, World Series, Cubs & White Sox, Ivory, Germany, 1906, 6 In. 348
Baseball, Stickpin, Brass Shell, Hinged Baseball, BBC, Baseball Hat, Crossed Bats, 1890s, 3 In. .. 141
Baseball, Stickpin, Chicago Cubs, World's Record Breakers, Brass, Inset Ball, 1906, 2 5/8 In. ... 695
Baseball, Team Card, Kansas City Cowboys, Ball Park Dedication, Team Photo, 1886, 4 1/4 x 3 1/2 In. 2629
Baseball, Watch Fob, St. Louis Baseball Club, Leather, Brass, Embossed 98, 1936, 1 3/4 In. ... 153
Baseball, Wrapper, Babe Ruth, Ice Cream, Frame, 1922 ... *illus* 1440
Basketball, Poster, Harlem Globetrotters, Wilt Chamberlain, Suitcase, c.1958, 28 x 41 In. ... 305
Basketball, Scoreboard, School Gym, Red, Fair Play, 1950s, 59 x 7 x 42 In. ... 510
Bowling, Bag, Stan Musial, Leather, Bird Mowing Down Pins, Tooled Stan, Handles ... 1554
Bowling, Poster, Tournament, Madison Square Garden, Frame, 40 x 31 In. ... *illus* 671
Boxing, Belt, Diamond, Gold On Copper, Shield, Eagle, Slide, Leather Strap, 3 3/4 x 2 3/4 In. ... 414
Boxing, Photograph, Muhammad Ali, Boxing Trunks & Gloves, Glossy, Signed, 8 x 10 In. ... 190
Boxing, Pin, Cassius Clay, Portrait, Celluloid, 1 3/4 In. ... 182
Boxing, Program, Sugar Ray Leonard, Cardstock, 4 Pages, May 14, 1977, 5 x 8 In. ... 158
Boxing, Robe, Muhammad Ali, Fight Worn, Jimmy Young Fight, Satin, Red Trim, 1976 ... 31070
Cheerleading, Megaphone, Red, White, 39 In. ... 24
Equestrian, Tack, Brown, Sloped Lid, T, Templeton, 26 1/2 x 20 1/2 In., Pair ... 600
Equestrian, Tack, Brown, Yellow Trim, Templeton Stables, 24 x 36 In. ... 1320 to 1680
Equestrian, Tack, Mixed Wood, 2 Drawers, Cast Iron Horse Head, Paint, c.1985, 21 x 12 In. ... 570
Football, Ball, Cleveland Browns, NFL Championship Game Used, Wilson, Leather, 1954 ... 6573
Football, Helmet, Jim Thorpe,Game Worn, Aviator Style, Tan Leather, 1920s, Size 8 ... 17925
Football, Helmet, Leather, Hard Plastic, 6 x 5 1/2 In. ... 52
Football, Jersey, Joe Namath, White Durene, Green Twill 12, Namath, c.1972, Size 52 ... 12548
Golf, Bag, Jack Nicklaus, Tournament Used, Green & White Leather, MacGregor, 1970s ... 10158
Golf, Club Set, Walter Hagen, 4 Woods, 9 Irons, Putter, In Oak Display Case, Dated 1954 ... 156
Hockey, Equipment Bag, John Harrington, USA Olympics Used, Blue, Black, 1980, 36 In. ... 5079
Hockey, Gloves, Cowhide, Bob Cameron Brand, Magic Grip, Canada, c.1960, 13 1/2 In. ... 175
Hockey, Puck, Wayne Gretzky's, 1st NHL, Opening Game Used, Wood Plaque, 1979, 6 x 8 In. ... 2390
Hockey, Stick, Northland, 1979-80 N.Y. Rangers, 61 In. ... 59
Horse Racing, Helmet, Jockey Steve Cauthen, Triple Crown Race Worn, Goggles, 1978 ... 1434
Hunting, Duck Call, Magnum Style, Oak Barrel, Lanyard, Glynn Scobey, 1900s, 6 1/2 x 1 1/2 In. ... 32
Hunting, Turkey Call, Cedar, Box, True Tone, Roger Latham, 1950s, 2 1/2 x 11 In. ... 46
Pool, Table, Rosewood, Aluminum, Brunswick-Balke-Collender, c.1940, 112 x 63 In. ... 6050
Skateboard, Deck, Blue, Black, Dancing Person, After Keith Haring, 32 In. ... 184
Skateboard, Deck, Pink, Green, Dancing Line-Drawn People, After Keith Haring, 32 In. ... 123
Skateboard, Deck, Purple, Pink, Cow, After Andy Warhol, 32 In. ... 153
Skating, Ice Skates, Wood, Wrought Iron Blades, Primitive, 1800s, 13 In. ... 30
Soap Box Derby, Helmet, Red, White & Blue Logo, 1948 ... 42
Surfing, Board, Vintage Wave, Hollow, Yellow, Red, 77 x 20 In. ... 153
Tennis, Ball Dispensing Machine, Electric, Ball Boy, Automatic, 31 x 21 x 50 In. ... 90

STAFFORDSHIRE, England, has been a district making pottery and porcelain since the 1700s. Hundreds of kilns are still working in the area. Thousands of types of pottery and porcelain have been made in the many factories that worked and still work in the area. Some of the most famous factories have been listed separately, such as Adams, Davenport, Ridgway, Rowland & Marsellus, Royal Doulton, Royal Worcester, Spode, Wedgwood, and others. Some Staffordshire pieces are listed under categories like Fairing, Flow Blue, Mulberry, Shaving Mug, etc.

Bowl, Feeding Chickens, Blue, White, Riley, c.1825, 11 In. ... 725
Bowl, Footed, U.S. Capitol, Washington D.C., c.1830, 4 3/4 x 11 In. ... 3690
Bowl, Fruit, Blue Transfer, 5 1/2 x 11 In. ... 200
Bust, Black Basalt, Rev. George Whitefield, Sept 30, 1770, Enoch Wood, 12 In. ... 246
Bust, Czar Alexander, Military Dress, c.1815, 12 In. ... 500
Bust, Washington, Incised Medallion, Enoch Wood, 1818, 8 3/8 In. ... *illus* 3998
Cheese Wheel, Stand, Blue Willow, Boat Shape, Scrolled, Footed, 1800s, 8 x 17 In. ... 875
Coffeepot, Lid, Creamware, Chintz, Pear Shape, Double Strap, Striping, c.1770, 9 In. ... 7995
Coffeepot, Lid, Redware, Pear Shape, Basket Weave Handle, Fluted Spout, c.1770, 8 In. ... 461
Coffeepot, Lid, Redware, Pear Shape, Scrolled Handle, Fluted Spout, c.1770, 8 1/2 In. ... 369

Coffeepot, Lid, White Salt Glaze Stoneware, Landscape, Strap Handle, c.1760, 8 In. 861
Coffeepot, Seasons, Brown Transferware, Flower Finial, Scalloped, 8 x 12 In. ....*illus* 130
Compote, Shannon Pattern, Pedestal Foot, Blue Transfer, Ironstone, 6 x 11 In. ....*illus* 59
Creamer, Boating, Castles, Blue Transfer, Helmet Shape, Square Handle, 5 In. ....*illus* 59
Creamer, Lid, Agate, Pear Shape, Brown, Cream, Blue Underglaze, c.1760, 6 ½ In. 1600
Creamer, White, Flowers, Vase Shape, Salt Glaze, 3 ¼ In. 94
Cup, Combed Slipware, Loop Handle, Orange Buff Ground, Stripes, Scrolls, c.1695, 4 In. ....*illus* 18450
Cup, White Salt Glaze Stoneware, Handles, Leaf & Scrolled Handles, c.1765, 5 In. 2829
Ewer, Equestrian Scenes, Steeple Chase, 12 ½ In., Pair.................... 2750
Figure, Lion, Reclining, Glass Eyes, England, c.1850, 12 In., Pair 120
Figurine, Benjamin Franklin, Blue Coat, Titled Washington, 15 In. 156
Figurine, Benjamin Franklin, Holding Document & Tricorn Hat, 14 In. ....*illus* 240
Figurine, Brittania Enthroned, Woman Warrior, Flag, Lion, c.1820, 15 x 8 In. ....*illus* 585
Figurine, Cat, Multicolor, Integral Cobalt Base, Gilt, c.1910, 8 x 4 In., Pair.................... 183
Figurine, Cat, Seated, Solid Agate, Marbleized, Brown, White, Blue, c.1745, 5 In. ....*illus* 3444
Figurine, Deer, Seated, Grassy Base, Translucent Glaze, Earthenware, 4 ¾ In. 443
Figurine, Dog, King Charles Spaniel, Seated, White, Orange, c.1840, 10 In., Pair.................... 214
Figurine, Dog, Spaniel, Copper Luster Spots & Chains, 7 In., Pair....................................*illus* 270
Figurine, Dog, Spaniel, Red, White, 12 ½ x 9 ½ In., Pair.................... 30
Figurine, Dog, Whippet, Brown, White Base, Rabbits In Mouths, 8 x 7 In., Pair.................... 219
Figurine, Elephant, Standing, Jumbo, Naturalistic Base, 1800s, 10 ½ In. 2375
Figurine, Hunter, Horse, Dogs, Multicolor, John Peel, 1800s, 10 x 8 In. 316
Figurine, Man, Pony, Dog, Deer, Multicolor, 1800s, 11 ½ x 5 ¾ In. 287
Figurine, Royal Lion, Walton, Bocage, Multicolor, c.1810, 6 In. 369
Figurine, Violinist, Lead Glaze, Creamware, Translucent Green & Yellow, c.1760, 6 In. 431
Footbath, Blue Transfer Landscape, 1900s, 18 In. 94
Fruit Basket, Stand, Salt Glaze, Stoneware, Pierced Border, c.1760, 10 ½ In. 584
Group, Couple, Dog, Cobalt Blue Jacket, Swan, 1800s, 11 ½ x 7 In. 316
Group, Lion, Tiger, Multicolor, Tree, c.1850, 8 ¾ x 6 ½ In. 547
Jug, Cream, Handle, Oriental Decoration, Multicolor, 4 x 6 In. 52
Jug, Glazed Red Agate, Reeded Ear Shape Handle, Turned Banding, c.1780, 5 ½ In. 984
Loving Cup, Transferware, Blue, Rural Scenes, Footed, c.1829, 6 In. 165
Milk Pail, Blue & White, Bucket Shape, Flowers, Pure Milk, Copper Lid, 16 In. 1375
Mug, Toad, Relief Panels, 3 Drinking Men, Legend, 2 Handles, 5 x 5 ½ In. 50
Penholder, Whippet, Laying Down, Multicolor, Blue Base, 1800s, 3 ¾ x 4 ¾ In. 150
Pitcher, Commodore W. Bainbridge, War Of 1812, Naval Symbols, Transferware, 5 In. ....*illus* 780
Pitcher, Red Transfer, Fruit & Flower Border, Wavy Spout, Saucer Foot, 8 In. 71
Plate, 2 Ships, Cadmus, American Flag, Shell Border, Blue Transfer, 10 In. 390
Plate, America Independent, Eagle & Boat, Blue Transfer, Enoch Wood, 10 In. ....*illus* 154
Plate, Blue Transfer, States Pattern, Building, Observatory, Shaped Rim, 11 In.................... 153
Plate, Commemorative, Salt Glaze, Stoneware, Scalloped Rim, Lattice Border, 9 In. 2460
Plate, Dam & Waterworks, Philadelphia, Blue Transfer, 10 In. ....*illus* 443
Plate, Dinner, Cathedral, Fisherman & Couple At Pond, Blue Transfer, Clews, 10 In., 8 Piece...... 338
Plate, Doctor Syntax Returned From Tour, Flower Border, Transfer, Clews, 9 In. ....*illus* 59
Plate, Pittsfield, Massachusetts, Clews, 1800s, 10 ½ In. 117
Plate, Swags, Scrolls, For My Dear Girl, Transfer, Multicolor, c.1885, 6 In. 178
Plate, Upper Ferry Bridge Over The River Schuylkill, Blue Transfer, 8 ¾ In. ....*illus* 236
Plate, View Near Conway, Red Transfer, Adams, 9 ¼ In., Pair..*illus* 30
Platter, Arabian Nights Pattern, Blue Scene, Green Border, Wavy Rim, 11 x 13 In. ....*illus* 201
Platter, Bosphorus Pattern, Blue Transfer, Flower Border, Scallop Rim, 13 x 16 In. 95
Platter, Canova Pattern, Green Scene, Red Border, T. Mayer, 13 x 16 In. ....*illus* 177
Platter, Columbus, Ohio, Blue Transfer, Floral Border, c.1830, 14 x 11 ½ In. 900
Platter, Landing Gen. Lafayette, Castle Garden, Blue, Clews, 1824, 17 In. ....*illus* 420
Platter, Palestine Pattern, Red Transfer, Wavy Rim, 15 ¼ In. 106
Platter, Wild Rose, Blue Transfer, 16 ¾ In. 240
Soup, Dish, Octagon Boston Church, Blue Transfer, 10 In. ....*illus* 142
Stirrup Cup, Cow's Head, Translucent Underglaze, Creamware, 1700s, 5 In. ....*illus* 923
Tankard, Agate, Baluster, Ribbed Handle, Brown, Blue, Saucer Foot, c.1750, 7 In. 2460
Teapot, Camel Shape, Howdah, White Salt Glaze, Stoneware, c.1750, 7 ½ x 5 In. 400
Teapot, Lid, Agate, Squat, Faceted Spout, Ear Shape Handles, Mottled, c.1760, 6 In. 923
Teapot, Lid, Creamware, Globe Shape, Cabbage Leaf Spout, Leaf Handle, c.1790, 8 In. 308
Teapot, Lid, Creamware, Pierced Gallery, Double Strap Handles, 1700s, 8 ¾ In. 1046
Teapot, Lid, Cylindrical, Bamboo Shape Handle & Spout, Dragon, Brown, c.1750, 5 In. 523
Teapot, Lid, Globe Shape, Loop Handle, Leaf Spout, Multicolor, Huntsman, c.1770, 8 In. 615
Teapot, Lid, Globular, Crabstock Handle & Spout, Flowers, Flutist, c.1760, 4 In. 923
Teapot, Lid, Pectin Shell, Redware Ground, Speckles, Foo Dog Finial, c.1760, 6 In. 584

Sports, Baseball, Doll, Christy Mathewson, SABA, Speilwarenfabrik, 1920-35, 7 ½ In.
$288

Robert Edwards Auctions

Sports, Baseball, Pennant, Joe Jackson, Felt, Ferguson Bakery, 1916
$7,200

Robert Edwards Auctions

Sports, Baseball, Salt & Pepper, Ball & Glove, Pittsburgh Pirates, Cream & Red, 3 x 3 In.
$15

S

Sports, Baseball, Wrapper, Babe Ruth, Ice Cream, Frame, 1922
$1,440

Robert Edwards Auctions

Sports, Bowling, Poster, Tournament, Madison Square Garden, Frame, 40 x 31 In.
$671

Morphy Auctions

TIP

You can remove stickers from most things by spraying them with a lubricant.

Staffordshire, Bust, Washington, Incised Medallion, Enoch Wood, 1818, 8 ⅜ In.
$3,998

Skinner, Inc.

Teapot, Lid, Redware, Stand, Cylindrical, Leaf Framed Cartouche, Chinese Figures, c.1760 800
Teapot, Lid, Salt Glaze, Flowers, Crabstock Handle, Spout, Twig Finial, c.1760, 7 In. .... *illus* 400
Teapot, Lid, Salt Glaze, Stoneware, Globe Shape, Blue Enamel, Roses, c.1765, 4 ¾ In. 615
Teapot, Lid, Salt Glaze, Stoneware, Globe Shape, Crabstock Handle, c.1760, 5 ¾ In. 308
Teapot, Lid, Salt Glaze, Stoneware, Globe Shape, Crabstock Handle, Flowers, c.1755, 8 In. 400
Teapot, Lid, Salt Glaze, Stoneware, House Shape, Gooseneck, c.1760, 5 ½ In. 492
Teapot, Lid, Tortoiseshell Glazed Creamware, Crabstock Handle, Spout, c.1790, 7 In. 554
Tobacco Jar, Magenta Transfer, Sailing Ships, British Fleet, Conical Lid, c.1820, 9 In. 900
Toby Jugs are listed in their own category.
Tray, Landing Of Gen. LaFayette, Blue & White, Shaped Reticulated Edge, 12 x 10 In. 923
Tureen, Hen-On-Nest Cover, Brown Basket, 1850, 7 ¾ In. 200
Tureen, Sauce, Tray, Blue Transfer, Palace Of Linlithgow, c.1850, 9 In. 300
Tureen, Tan Hen-On-Nest Cover, Brown Basket, 1850, 11 ½ In. 200
Vase, Games Keeper, Purple Skirt, Green Cardigan, Dog, 1800s, 12 x 6 In. 58
Vase, Spill, 3 Children, Reading Book Together, 1850, 6 x 4 ½ In. 115
Vase, Spill, Dog & Child, 1850, 7 ¾ x 5 In. 125
Vase, Spill, Giraffe, Tree Stump, Yellow, Green, Black Spots, Mirrored Pair, 7 In. 960
Vase, Spill, Horse, China Leaves, 1850s, 6 ¼ x 5 In. 115
Vase, Spill, Horse, Stump, Applied Flowers & Leaves On Base, 9 x 13 In. 1320
Vase, Spill, Lamb, Standing By Tree Stump, Textured, Painted, 5 x 4 ½ In. 81
Vase, Spill, Robin Hood, Spaniel, Companion, Standing By Tree Trunk, Painted, 15 x 9 ½ In. 69

STAINLESS STEEL became available to artists and manufacturers about 1920. They used it to make flatware, tableware, and many decorative items.

Bookmark, Dangling Pearl, Mikimoto, 5 In. 55
Butter, Cover, Glass Insert, Reed & Barton, 1970s, 7 x 2 ½ In. 15
Carving Set, Lundofte, Knife, Fork, Honing Steel, Germany, 3 Piece 36
Cheese Slicer, Half-Circle Shape, Acme MGM Co., Pat. Pending, 5 ½ x 5 In. 18
Coaster, Cylinda-Line, Stelton, Denmark, c.1967, 3 ½ In., 6 Piece 60
Cocktail Shaker, Penguin, Web Feet, Wings, Restoration Hardware, 11 In. 95
Gravy Boat, Underplate, Reed & Barton, 9 x 5 x 3 In. 15
Ice Bucket, Bail Handle, Double Wall, Cylinda-Line, Stelton, Denmark, 1960s, 1 ¾ Pt. 225
Knife, Cake, Bakelite, 1940s, 9 In. 24
Ladle, Crystal Handle, Libretto Pattern, Oneida, 7 ¾ In. 12
Relish, 3 Sections, Cromargan, Sweden, 1950s, 9 ½ x 12 In. 35
Sculpture, Geometric, Abstract, Gary Slater, 49 In. 1295
Teapot, Ball Shape, Chantal, 8 x 9 In. 24

STANGL POTTERY traces its history back to the Fulper Pottery of New Jersey. In 1910, Johann Martin Stangl started working at Fulper. He left to work at Haeger Pottery from 1915 to 1920. Stangl returned to Fulper Pottery in 1920, became president in 1926, and changed the company name to Stangl Pottery in 1929. Stangl acquired the firm in 1930. The pottery is known for dinnerware and a line of bird figurines. Martin Stangl died in 1972 and the pottery was sold to Frank Wheaton Jr. of Wheaton Industries. Production continued until 1978, when Pfaltzgraff Pottery purchased the right to the Stangl trademark and the remaining inventory was liquidated. A single bird figurine is identified by a number. Figurines made up of two birds are identified by a number followed by the letter *D* indicating Double.

Amber Glo, Bowl, Vegetable, Round, 8 In. 30
Amber Glo, Chop Plate, 14 In. 53
Amber Glo, Plate, Dinner, 10 In. 20
Amber Glo, Soup, Dish, Lugged, 6 In. 13
Amber Glo, Sugar & Creamer 38
Apple Delight, Ashtray, 5 In. 6
Apple Delight, Bowl, Vegetable, Divided, Oval, 10 In. 12
Apple Delight, Butter, Cover 24
Apple Delight, Chop Plate, 12 In. 42
Apple Delight, Creamer, 6 Oz., 2 ¾ In. 16
Apple Delight, Gravy Boat 22
Apple Delight, Plate, Dinner, 10 In. 19
Aztec, Plate, Dinner, 10 In. 19
Bella Rosa, Chop Plate, 14 In. 40
Bella Rosa, Sugar & Creamer 47
Bird, Chestnut-Sided Warbler, Multicolor, 4 In. 100
Bird, Cliff Swallow, Blue, White Breasted, Black-Tipped Tail, 3 ⅝ x 4 ¾ In. 49
Bird, Crowing Rooster, Gloss Glaze, Multicolor, 5 ½ In. 201
Bird, Double White Crowned Pigeons, 12 ½ x 7 ½ In. 500

TIP
When removing a stain from fabrics or marble or any other surface, apply the stain cleaner from the edge to the center to avoid spreading the stain.

Staffordshire, Coffeepot, Seasons, Brown Transferware, Flower Finial, Scalloped, 8 x 12 In.
$130

Hess Auction Group

Staffordshire, Compote, Shannon Pattern, Pedestal Foot, Blue Transfer, Ironstone, 6 x 11 In.
$59

Hess Auction Group

Staffordshire, Creamer, Boating, Castles, Blue Transfer, Helmet Shape, Square Handle, 5 In.
$59

Hess Auction Group

Staffordshire, Cup, Combed Slipware, Loop Handle, Orange Buff Ground, Stripes, Scrolls, c.1695, 4 In.
$18,450

Skinner, Inc.

Staffordshire, Figurine, Benjamin Franklin, Holding Document & Tricorn Hat, 14 In.
$240

Cowan Auctions

New Use for Old Salts
Old salt and pepper shakers without tops can be used as small flower vases.

Staffordshire, Figurine, Brittania Enthroned, Woman Warrior, Flag, Lion, c.1820, 15 x 8 In.
$585

Thomaston Place Auction

Staffordshire, Figurine, Cat, Seated, Solid Agate, Marbleized, Brown, White, Blue, c.1745, 5 In.
$3,444

Skinner, Inc.

S

Staffordshire, Figurine, Dog, Spaniel, Copper Luster Spots & Chains, 7 In., Pair
$270

Cowan Auctions

Staffordshire, Pitcher, Commodore W. Bainbridge, War Of 1812, Naval Symbols, Transferware, 5 In.
$780

Cowan Auctions

Dinnerware in the Early 1900s
Dinnerware in the average American home in the early 1900s was usually English ironstone or American whiteware for everyday and porcelain from Limoges, France, especially Haviland, for "good" dishes.

Staffordshire, Plate, America Independent, Eagle & Boat, Blue Transfer, Enoch Wood, 10 In.
$154

Hess Auction Group

Staffordshire, Plate, Dam & Waterworks, Philadelphia, Blue Transfer, 10 In.
$443

Hess Auction Group

Staffordshire, Plate, Doctor Syntax Returned From Tour, Flower Border, Transfer, Clews, 9 In.
$59

Hess Auction Group

Staffordshire, Plate, Upper Ferry Bridge Over The River Schuylkill, Blue Transfer, 8 ¾ In.
$236

Hess Auction Group

Staffordshire, Plate, View Near Conway, Red Transfer, Adams, 9 ¼ In., Pair
$30

Hess Auction Group

Staffordshire, Platter, Arabian Nights Pattern, Blue Scene, Green Border, Wavy Rim, 11 x 13 In.
$201

Hess Auction Group

Bird, Hummingbird, Black Beak, Wing Tips, Red Back, Green Wings, 3 x 3¾ In. 60
Bird, Key West Quail Dove, 9¼ In. *illus* 53
Bird, Painted Bunting, No. 3452, Perched On Branch, Leaves, Marked, 6 x 5 In. *illus* 85
Bird, Titmouse, Blue Back, 2⅝ x 2 In. 45
Birds, Cockatoo, Double, No. 3405, 2 Pink Birds, Stamped, c.1941, 10 x 5 In. *illus* 165
Birds, Goldfinches, No. 3635, Mother, 3 Chicks, Perched, Branch, Marked, 13 In. *illus* 195
Carnival, Cup & Saucer 16
Carnival, Plate, Dinner, 10 In. 26
Chicory, Chop Plate, 12 In. 52
Chicory, Creamer, 8 Oz., 3½ In. 28
Chicory, Cup & Saucer 18
Chicory, Pitcher, 64 Oz., 6⅜ In. 72
Chicory, Plate, Dinner, 10 In. 24
Chicory, Teapot, Lid, 5 Cup, 4½ In. 97
Cosmos, Vase, Pillow, White Matte Glaze, 7 x 5 In. 36
Country Garden, Plate, Dinner, Flowers, Leaves, Turquoise Border, 10 In. Diam. *illus* 25
Country Life, Bowl, Vegetable, Round, Mallard, 8 In. 66
Country Life, Plate, Bread & Butter, Rooster, 6¼ In. 26
Country Life, Plate, Dinner, Rooster, 10 In. 58
Country Life, Plate, Salad, Cow, 8 In. 118
Country Life, Plate, Salad, Pig, 8 In. 107
Country Life, Salt & Pepper, Ducklings 102
Country Life, Soup, Dish, Duck, 7 In. 53
Country Life, Sugar, Lid, Rooster, 3 In. 56
Diana, Sugar, Lid 16
Diana, Teapot, Lid, 4 In. 29
El Rosa, Chop Plate, 12 In. 43
El Rosa, Creamer, 12 Oz., 3⅝ In. 21
El Rosa, Plate, Bread & Butter, 6 In. 5
Fairlawn, Creamer, 8 Oz., 3½ In. 26
Fairlawn, Plate, Dinner, 10 In. 54
Field Daisy, Plate, Bread & Butter, 6 In. 7
Field Daisy, Plate, Salad, 8 In. 11
First Love, Bowl, Vegetable, Round, 8 In. 15
First Love, Platter, Oval, 14 In. 25
Florentine, Bowl, Vegetable, Round, 8 In. 16
Florentine, Cup & Saucer 8
Florentine, Plate, Dinner, 11 In. 10
Florette, Creamer, 8 Oz., 3⅜ In. 15
Florette, Gravy Boat, Underplate 42
Golden Grape, Bowl, Vegetable, Divided, Oval, 10 In. 17
Golden Grape, Chop Plate, 14 In. 19
Golden Grape, Creamer, 8 Oz., 3 In. 9
Golden Grape, Eggcup, Double, 3 In. 11
Golden Grape, Salt & Pepper 18
Holly, Chop Plate, 12 In. 116
Holly, Cup & Saucer 13
Holly, Plate, Dinner, 10 In. 97
Lamp Base, Archers, Bow & Arrows, Yellow, Bulbous, 9½ In. *illus* 65
Lime, Chop Plate, Square, 12 In. 66
Magnolia, Ashtray, Center Cigarette Rests, Purple Flowers, Leaves, Marked, 8 x 3 In. *illus* 25
Mountain Laurel, Trinket Box, Lid, Terra Rose, Flowers, Scroll, Marked, 4 x 5 In. *illus* 65
Orchard Song, Relish, Bread Tray, Fruit, Green Leaves, Flared Rectangle, 11 x 7 In. *illus* 20
Paisley, Bowl, Vegetable, Round, 8 In. 14
Paisley, Cup & Saucer 5
Paisley, Plate, Bread & Butter, 6 In. 6
Pink Cosmos, Creamer 18
Pink Dogwood, Bowl, Vegetable, Round, Scalloped Rim, 8½ In. 26
Pink Dogwood, Creamer 14
Pitcher, Terra Rose, Yellow Tulip, Wide Spout, Loop Handle, 4⅝ In. *illus* 35
Prelude, Bowl, Vegetable, Round, 9 In. 20
Prelude, Chop Plate, 12 In. 19
Prelude, Cup & Saucer 9
Prelude, Eggcup, Double 11
Prelude, Sugar & Creamer, Pink Flower, Leaves, 3 In. & 3½ In. *illus* 15
Prelude, Sugar, Lid 28
Provincial, Bowl, Vegetable, Divided, Oval, 10 In. 15

Staffordshire, Platter, Canova Pattern, Green Scene, Red Border, T. Mayer, 13 x 16 In.
$177

Hess Auction Group

Staffordshire, Platter, Landing Gen. Lafayette, Castle Garden, Blue, Clews, 1824, 17 In.
$420

Cowan Auctions

Staffordshire, Soup, Dish, Octagon Boston Church, Blue Transfer, 10 In.
$142

Hess Auction Group

TIP

Keep a "mystery disaster" box. If you find a piece of veneer, an old screw, or even a porcelain rosebud, put it into the box until you are able to make the necessary repairs.

TIP
Rearrange your furniture so valuable silver or paintings can't be seen from the street.

Staffordshire, Stirrup Cup, Cow's Head, Translucent Underglaze, Creamware, 1700s, 5 In.
$923

Skinner, Inc.

Staffordshire, Teapot, Lid, Salt Glaze, Flowers, Crabstock Handle, Spout, Twig Finial, c.1760, 7 In.
$400

Skinner, Inc.

Stangl, Bird, Key West Quail Dove, 9 ¼ In.
$53

Hess Auction Group

Provincial, Cup & Saucer 13
Provincial, Gravy Boat 44
Provincial, Pitcher, 24 Oz., 4 ½ In. 36
Provincial, Platter, Oval, 13 In. 21
Sculptured Fruit, Creamer, Yellow & Green Paint, Loop Handle, 1950s, 5 ½ x 4 In. .... *illus* 30
Star Flower, Bowl, Fruit, 5 In. 17
Star Flower, Butter, Cover, ¼ Lb. 62
Star Flower, Chop Plate, 14 In. 53
Star Flower, Cup & Saucer 13
Star Flower, Plate, Bread & Butter, 6 In. 7
Star Flower, Serving Bowl, 9 ⅞ In. 48
Star Flower, Soup, Dish, Lugged, 6 In. 21
Star Flower, Teapot, Lid, 5 Cup, 4 ½ In. 134
Stardust, Cup & Saucer 8
Tulip, Teapot, Terra Rose, Yellow, Green Leaves, Lid, Leaf Finial, 6 x 10 In. .... *illus* 40
Wig Stand, Woman's Head, Round Pottery Base, Foil Label, 1960s, 15 In. .... *illus* 200
Wild Rose, Bowl, Vegetable, Divided, Oval, 10 In. 25
Wild Rose, Butter, Cover 53
Wild Rose, Chop Plate, 14 In. 36
Wild Rose, Coffeepot, Lid, 7 Cup, 7 ½ In. 109
Wild Rose, Cup & Saucer 9
Wild Rose, Gravy Boat, Underplate 21
Wild Rose, Pitcher, Water, 6 ⅜ In. 39
Wild Rose, Plate Dinner, 10 In. 27
Wild Rose, Soup, Dish, 7 ¾ In. 19
Wild Rose, Sugar & Creamer 38
Willow, Soup, Dish, Tab Handles, 5 In. 28

STAR TREK AND STAR WARS collectibles are included here. The original *Star Trek* television series ran from 1966 through 1969. The series spawned an animated TV series, three TV sequels, and a TV prequel. The first *Star Trek* movie was released in 1979 and eleven others followed, the most recent in 2013. The movie *Star Wars* opened in 1977. Sequels were released in 1980 and 1983; prequels in 1999, 2002, and 2005. *Star Wars: Episode VII* opened in 2015, which increased interest in *Star Wars* collectibles. The latest episode includes actors from the original cast. Other science fiction and fantasy collectibles can be found under Batman, Buck Rogers, Captain Marvel, Flash Gordon, Movie, Superman, and Toy.

STAR TREK
Coloring Set, Numbered Pencil, Pre-Sketched Pictures, 6 Colored Pencils, Box, 1967 348
Lunch Box, Dome, Ship, Characters, Handle, Metal, Latches, 1968 329
Toy, Gun, Astro-Buzz-Ray, Plastic, Buzzer Signal, Color Flashes, Box, 1967, 11 In. 422
Toy, Space Rifle, Tracer-Scope, Jet Disc, Hard Plastic, Blue, 1968, 18 In. 758
Toy, Transporter Room, Lithograph, Palitoy Bradgate, Box, 1974, 5 x 5 x 11 In. 230

STAR WARS
Action Figure, Boba Fett, Return Of The Jedi, Blaster Rifle, Tri-Logo Card, 1983, 6 x 9 In. 778
Action Figure, Darth Vader, Return Of The Jedi, Tri-Logo Card, 1983, 7 x 9 In. 222
Action Figure, Luke Skywalker, Imperial Storm Trooper, Helmet, Card, 1984, 4 In. .... *illus* 387
Action Figure, Luke Skywalker, Jedi Knight, Pistol, Light Saber, Robe, Card, 1983, 6 x 9 In. 115
Action Figure, Princess Leia Organa, Blaster Pistol, Vinyl Cape, Card, 1983, 7 x 9 In. 652
Action Figure, Return Of The Jedi, Lando Calrissian, Blister Card, 1983, 4 In. 127
Art Sheet, Concept, Characters With Different Look, Black & White, 1977, 11 x 14 In. 1793
Comic Book, No. 1, July, A New Hope, Marvel Comics, Roy Thomas Story, 1977 612
Ewok Staff, Prop, Caravan Of Courage, An Ewok Adventure, Curved Wood, 1984, 35 In. 604
Helmet, Storm Trooper, Plastic, White & Black, Promotional Marketing 1572
Still Photo, Return Of The Jedi, Cast, Signed, Glossy, c.1983, 8 x 10 In. 460
Toy, Millennium Falcon, The Empire Strikes Back, Box, 1979 176
Toy, TIE Fighter, Darth Vader, Kenner, Model No. 38040, 1978 66
Toy, X-Wing Fighter, Kenner, Model No. 38030, 1978 88

STEINS have been used by beer and ale drinkers for over 500 years. They have been made of ivory, porcelain, pottery, stoneware, faience, silver, pewter, wood, or glass in sizes up to nine gallons. Although some were made by Mettlach, Meissen, Capo-di-Monte, and other famous factories, most were made by less important German potteries. The words *Geschutz* or *Musterschutz* on a stein are the German words for "patented" or "registered design," not company names. Steins are still being made in the old styles. Lithophane steins may be found in the Lithophane category.

Character, Alligator, Porcelain, E. Bohne & Sohne, ½ Liter .... *illus* 336

Stangl, Bird, Painted Bunting, No. 3452, Perched On Branch, Leaves, Marked, 6 x 5 In. $85

Ruby Lane

Stangl, Birds, Cockatoo, Double, No. 3405, 2 Pink Birds, Stamped, c.1941, 10 x 5 In. $165

Ruby Lane

Stangl, Birds, Goldfinches, No. 3635, Mother, 3 Chicks, Perched, Branch, Marked, 13 In. $195

Ruby Lane

Stangl Birds

Stangl Pottery birds have been produced since 1939. During the 1940s, hundreds of thousands were made. The figurines were based on illustrations in James Audubon's *Birds of America* and Alexander Wilson's *American Ornithology.*

Stangl, Country Garden, Plate, Dinner, Flowers, Leaves, Turquoise Border, 10 In. Diam. $25

Ruby Lane

Stangl, Lamp Base, Archers, Bow & Arrows, Yellow, Bulbous, 9 ½ In. $65

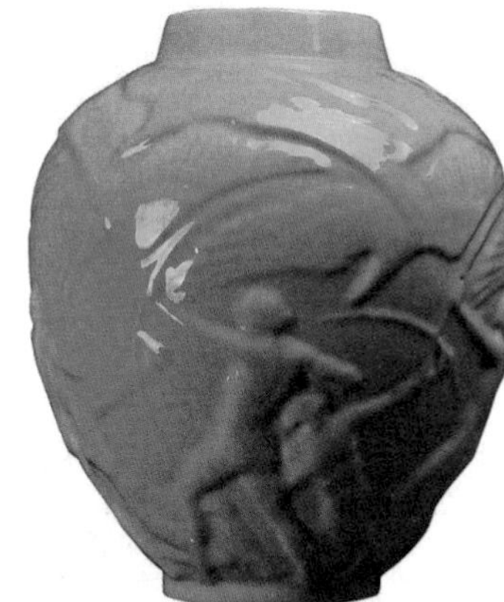

Ruby Lane

Stangl, Magnolia, Ashtray, Center Cigarette Rests, Purple Flowers, Leaves, Marked, 8 x 3 In. $25

Ruby Lane

Stangl, Mountain Laurel, Trinket Box, Lid, Terra Rose, Flowers, Scroll, Marked, 4 x 5 In. $65

Ruby Lane

Stangl, Orchard Song, Relish, Bread Tray, Fruit, Green Leaves, Flared Rectangle, 11 x 7 In. $20

Ruby Lane

Missing Lids

Many beer steins are missing their metal lids. In 1916, Germany needed metal for the war effort and citizens had to sell items made of gold, silver, brass, bronze, copper, and pewter to the government. The pewter steins and lids were melted for the war effort.

Stangl, Prelude, Sugar & Creamer, Pink Flower, Leaves, 3 In. & 3 ½ In.
$15

Ruby Lane

Stangl, Sculptured Fruit, Creamer, Yellow & Green Paint, Loop Handle, 1950s, 5 ½ x 4 In.
$30

Ruby Lane

Stangl, Tulip, Teapot, Terra Rose, Yellow, Green Leaves, Lid, Leaf Finial, 6 x 10 In.
$40

Ruby Lane

Character, Alligator, Porcelain, Marked Musterschutz, By Schierholz, ½ Liter 630
Character, Alligator, Seated, Curled Tail Handle, Shaped Base, Marzi & Remy, 6 In. .... *illus* 390
Character, Alligator, Seated, Open Mouth, Brown, Porcelain, Musterschutz, ½ Liter 510
Character, Asian Man's Face, Mustache, Pottery, Print Over Glaze, Hanke, ½ Liter .... *illus* 450
Character, Cat With Hangover, Paws Crossed, Bandage On Head, Porcelain, ½ Liter 480
Character, Clown, Smiling, Ruffled Collar, Party Hat, Porcelain, Schierholz, ½ Liter 2880
Character, Devil & Skull, Porcelain, E. Bohne & Sohne, ½ Liter 690
Character, Devil, Green Face, Black Horns, Smiling, Missing Teeth, Porcelain, Zinn, 7 In. 330
Character, Dice, Pottery, Marked 1781, ½ Liter 480
Character, Drunken Monkey, Porcelain, Musterschutz, By Schierholz, ½ Liter 348
Character, Fraternity Student, Eye Patch, Hat, Mustache, Hofbrauhaus, ½ Liter 750
Character, Gentleman Dog, Glasses, Hat, Pipe, Porcelain, Schierholz, ½ Liter 2160
Character, Gentleman Rabbit, Lid, Porcelain, Musterschutz, By Schierholz, ½ Liter 240
Character, Happy Radish, Porcelain, Schierholz, ½ Liter .... *illus* 288
Character, Heidelberg Teacher, Porcelain, Schierholz, ½ Liter 1020
Character, Hunter, Inlaid Lid, Pottery, Marked, J. Reinemann, ½ Liter 910
Character, King Ludwig, Made For Jos. M. Mayer, Porcelain, Schierholz, 1 ½ Liter 18000
Character, Man, Holding Cat, Top Hat, Pottery, Diesinger, ½ Liter 602
Character, Monkeys, Embossed, Lid, Figural Handle & Finial, Germany, c.1890, 9 In. .... *illus* 165
Character, Nurnberg Tower, Purple & Blue, Pewter Lid, Marked T.W., ¼ Liter 90
Character, Owl, Marked Musterschutz, By Schierholz, ½ Liter 960
Character, Pixie, Porcelain, Music Box Base, Schierholz, ½ Liter 960
Character, Rabbit Hunter, Porcelain, Inlaid Lid, R.P.M., ½ Liter 84
Character, Radish Woman, Porcelain, Schierholz, ½ Liter 3600
Character, Regimental, Skull, 2. Esk., Braunschweig, Porcelain, c.1909, ½ Liter 4560
Character, Satan, Figural Head, Porcelain, Pewter, Horns, E. Bohne & Sohne, c.1910, 5 In. *illus* 395
Character, Skull On Book, Bohne Porcelain, ½ Liter 348
Character, Skull, Porcelain, E. Bohne & Sohne, 1 Liter, 3 In. Diam. 420
Character, Student Fox, Porcelain, Amberg, ½ Liter 288
Character, Woman With Money Bag, Pottery, Marked 680, ½ Liter 240
Enameled Glass, Dueling Fraternal Student, Inscription, Pewter Band, Art Nouveau, 2 Liter 600
Enameled Glass, Man Looking Through Keyhole, Seminude Woman Inside, ½ Liter 192
Faience, Birds, Insects, Flowers, White Ground, Bulbous, Saucer Foot, Shaped Lid, 1 Liter 192
Faience, Leaping Deer, Pewter Lid, c.1775, 10 In. 300
Faience, Ostterreichischer Walzenkrug, Religious Scene, Pewter Lid & Footring, c.1800, 9 In. 1114
Faience, Pegasus & Mercury, Painted Under Glass, No. 5024/5394, 1 Liter 780
Faience, Potted Plant, Lid, North Germany, 1798, 1 Liter 480
Faience, Stylized Goat, Pewter Lid & Footring, Erfurter Walzenkrug, c.1750, 9 In. 600
Glass, Blown, Children, Picnic, Enameled, Amber, Pewter Lid, ¼ Liter 84
Glass, Blown, Cranberry, Pewter Overlay, Base & Lid, 1 Liter 168
Glass, Blown, Eagle, Enameled, Pewter Lid, Helmet Finial, 1899, ½ Liter 168
Glass, Blown, Stag, Wheel Engraved, Cut, Faceted, Pewter Lid & Strap, 1 Liter 288
Glass, Blown, White & Blue Swirl, Clear, c.1875, ½ Liter 1980
Glass, Cobalt Blue, Flowers, Horse Head Thumblift, 1 Liter 180
Glass, Cranberry Cut To Clear, Thistle & Fern Design, Sawtooth Base, Metal Lid, 10 In. .... *illus* 595
Glass, Flowers, Blue, White, Clear, Inlaid Porcelain Lid, Gambrinus, ½ Liter .... *illus* 900
Glass, Ruby Overlay, Flowers, Porcelain Inlay, Women, Silver Lid, Teeth Thumblift, ½ Liter 3600
Glass, Stag, Enameled, Blue, Flowers, Faceted Body, Silver Lid, c.1850, ½ Liter 840
Mettlach Steins are listed in the Mettlach category.
Military, Artillery Scene, Stoneware, Pewter Lid, 1893, 1 Liter 414
Military, Lithophane, 2 Seminude Women, Pewter Lid, Soldier, Germany, c.1896, 11 In. .... *illus* 395
Military, Third Reich, Erlangen, Stoneware, Pewter Lid, 1941, ½ Liter 133
Military, Third Reich, L. Komp. Pion. Batl., 45, Neu-Ulm, 1935, Swastika, Helmet, ½ Liter 324
Porcelain, 3 Men Drinking, Royal Vienna Type, Brass Lid, 7 In., 1 Liter 720
Porcelain, Bird, Flowers, Painted, Lithophane, Pewter Lid, ½ Liter 60
Porcelain, Enameled, Meinem Lieben Vater, Transfer, 13 Juli, 1914, Pewter Lid, ½ Liter 96
Porcelain, Heidelberg Scene, Painted Over Glass, Relief Perkeo Pewter Lid, ½ Liter 144
Porcelain, Satyr, Flowers, Painted, Royal Vienna Type, Beehive Mark, ⅓ Liter, 5 In. 1500
Porcelain, Student Shield, Skull & Crossbones, Painted Over Glass, ½ Liter 240
Porcelain, V & B Luxemburg, No. 24, Cavalier, Song Book Inlay Lid, ½ Liter 192
Pottery, 4 Seasons, Etched, Marked Gerz., 1346, Inlaid Lid, 2 Liter, 15 In. 330
Pottery, Golfer, O'Hara Dial Co., Inlaid Lid, 1903, ½ Liter 420
Pottery, Gymnastics, Pewter Lid, 1 Liter 60
Pottery, Incised Verse, Relief, Marked 11, Joliet Citizens Brewing Co., 1 Liter, 14 In. 12
Pottery, Jester, Cats, Transfer, Enameled, Hops Finial, ½ Liter 102

Pottery, Man On Bicycle, Transfer, Enameled, Majolica, Pewter Lid, R. Ditmar, ½ Liter 390
Pottery, Playing Cards, Etched, Square Body, Footed, Pewter Lid, ½ Liter........................... *illus* 120
Pottery, Weapons, Shield, Munich Child, Painted Over Glass, Relief Munich Lid, ½ Liter............ 168
Regimental, 6. Comp., Bayr. Inft. Regt. Nr. 3. Augsburg, Georg Helf, 1912-24, ½ Liter................. 348
Regimental, Flask, 1. Esk. Garde Kurassier Regt., Gefr. Wilhelm Schubert, 1910-13, ¼ Liter....... 840
Regimental, L. Batt., Feld Artl. Regt. Nr. 29 Ludwigsburg, Fahrer Wacher, c.1902, ½ Liter 204
Regimental, Roster, 5 Comp. Inft. Regt. Nr. 115 Darmstadt, Porcelain, c.1905, ½ Liter........ *illus* 240
Regimental, Roster, 6 Comp, Inft. Regt. Nr. 170, Offenburg, 2 Scenes, ½ Liter 252
Regimental, Roster, 9 Bat, 2 Scenes, Schiess-Schule, Eagle Thumblift, c.1905, ½ Liter............... 510
Regimental, Roster, Crew Finial, Eagle Thumblift, Pewter Strap, c.1907, 10½ In. 5640
Regimental, Sailor On Barrel, S.M.S. Wettin, Wilhelmshaven, Roster, Pottery, ½ Liter......... *illus* 7050
Regimental, Sanitats Comp. In Wurzburg, Medical Scene, Reinhard Schonherr, 1897, ½ Liter .. 360
Regimental, Stoneware, Kraftfahr Komp, Freuding Adolf, Car, Munich Lid, 1 Liter..................... 960
Salt Glaze, Courting Scene, Metal Lid, Tapered Cylinder, Renaissance Revival, 13 In. 77
Stoneware, Cupid, Wings, Top Hat, High Wheel Bicycle, Engraved Lid, 1898, 1 Liter 450
Stoneware, Hessen Coat Of Arms, Pewter Lid, Sarreguemines, Marked, 1 Liter............................ 1021
Stoneware, Munich Shooting Scene, Painted Over Glass, Relief Lid Man Shooting, ½ Liter 144
Stoneware, Rearing Horse, Blue Salt Glaze, Pewter Lid, Westerwalder Walzenkrug, c.1775, 8 In. 526
Stoneware, Tavern Scene, Etched, Pewter Lid & Handle, Simon P. Gerz, c.1890, 18 In. ....*illus* 325
Tankard, Wood, Pyrography, Portrait, Script, Hinged Lid, Acorn Finial, c.1910, 12 In. ....*illus* 129

STEREO CARDS that were made for stereoscope viewers became popular after 1840. Two almost identical pictures were mounted on a stiff cardboard backing so that, when viewed through a stereoscope, a three-dimensional picture could be seen. Value is determined by maker and by subject. These cards were made in quantity through the 1930s.

1020 Dearborn St., Chicago, Wagons, Horses, Whiting View Co.. 8
Devil's Hole Rock Formation, 1877 18
Hotel At Bouley Bay, Jersey Interest.. 25
Jerusalem, Fence, Figure, Sepia, Tissue Paper, 1850s... 55
Mamma Doll & Her Children, c.1890, 6⅞ x 3½ In. ....*illus* 35
St. Pierre, Rome, Tissue Paper, 1850s 65
Wreck Of The Louisa, T.B. Hutton... 100

STEREOSCOPES were used for viewing stereo cards. The hand viewer was invented by Oliver Wendell Holmes, although more complicated table models were used before his was produced in 1859. Do not confuse the stereoscope with the stereopticon, a magic lantern that used glass slides.

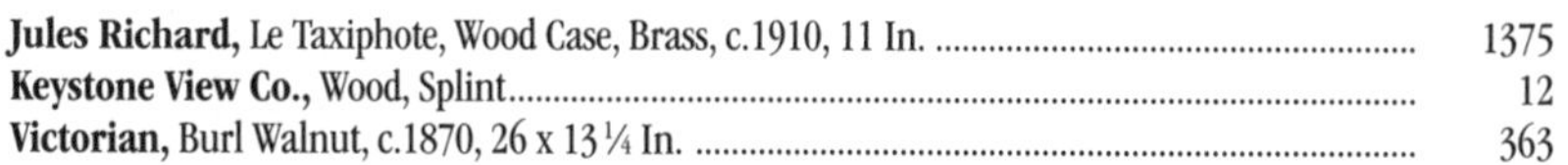

Jules Richard, Le Taxiphote, Wood Case, Brass, c.1910, 11 In. 1375
Keystone View Co., Wood, Splint... 12
Victorian, Burl Walnut, c.1870, 26 x 13¼ In. 363

STERLING SILVER, *see Silver-Sterling category.*

STEUBEN glass was made at the Steuben Glass Works of Corning, New York. The factory, founded by Frederick Carder and T.G. Hawkes Sr., was purchased by the Corning Glass Company. Corning continued to make glass called Steuben. Many types of art glass were made at Steuben. Aurene is an iridescent glass. Schottenstein Stores Inc. bought 80 percent of the business in 2008. The factory closed in 2011 and no more of this quality glass will be made. Additional pieces may be found in the Cluthra and Perfume Bottle categories.

Bottle, Dresser, Smoky Gray, Overall Threading, Rounded Square, Flower Stopper, 5 In. 259
Bowl, Calcite, Stretched Border, Gold Aurene Lip Wrap, Flared, 4¾ x 10 In. 259
Bowl, Centerpiece, Peony, c.1960, 6 x 14 In. 330
Bowl, Cranberry To Clear, Free-Form, Wavy Rim, Triangular Legs, c.1980, 6½ In. 369
Bowl, Gold Aurene Interior, Calcite Exterior, 8 x 3½ In. 161
Bowl, Green Jade, 6 x 12½ In. 177
Bowl, Intarsia, Raspberry Leaf & Vine, Flared, 6-Sided Foot, Signed, F. Carder, 8 x 6 In. 8295
Bowl, Plum Jade, Acid Cutback Medallions, Classical Busts, Drapery, Folded-In Rim, 6 In. 1235
Bowl, Scroll Feet, John Dreves, 1942, 7 x 3 In. 150
Bowl, Thick Wall, Inverted Piecrust Rim, Sphere Shapes In Rim, Signed, 6¼ x 8½ In. 259
Candlestick, Amethyst, Canterbury Pattern, 10 In. 978
Candlestick, Optic Swirled Body, Gold Ruby Rim, Flat Feet, 4¾ In., Pair 259
Candlestick, Orange Cintra Body, Blue Lip Wrap On Foot, Rim, 10 In., Pair 1035
Candlestick, Round Bowl, Star In Center, 1960s, 4⅛ x 6½ In. Diam., Pair 365
Cologne Bottle, Art Deco, Green Shading To Alabaster, Cased, 1920s, 7 In. 708
Cologne Bottle, Blue Aurene Cut To Pomona Green, Acid-Cut Back, Crystal Stopper, 6¾ In. 4140
Cologne Bottle, Blue Aurene, Melon Ribbed, 3 Curled Shell Feet, Stopper, 4¼ In. .... *illus* 920

Stangl, Wig Stand, Woman's Head, Round Pottery Base, Foil Label, 1960s, 15 In.
$200

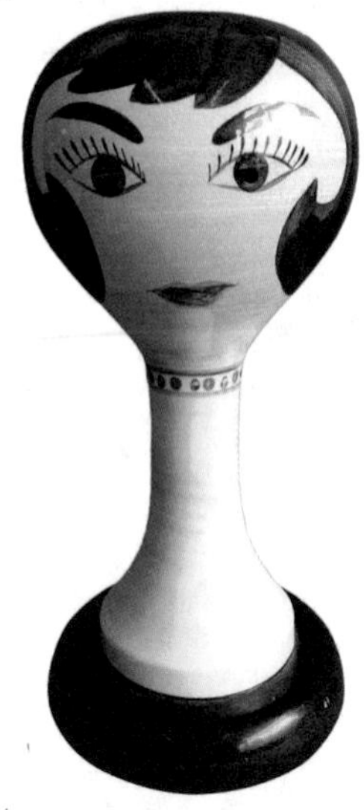

Ruby Lane

Star Wars, Action Figure, Luke Skywalker, Imperial Storm Trooper, Helmet, Card, 1984, 4 In.
$387

Hake's Americana & Collectibles

Pringles Can as Burial Wrap
The designer of the container for Pringle potato chips died in 2008, and as he requested, part of his ashes were bured in a Pringles can. The rest of his remains were put into urns given to family members.

Stein, Character, Alligator, Porcelain, E. Bohne & Sohne, ½ Liter
$336

The Stein Auction Company

Stein, Character, Alligator, Seated, Curled Tail Handle, Shaped Base, Marzi & Remy, 6 In.
$390

The Stein Auction Company

Stein, Character, Asian Man's Face, Mustache, Pottery, Print Over Glaze, Hanke, ½ Liter
$450

Fox Auctions

Stein, Character, Happy Radish, Porcelain, Schierholz, ½ Liter
$288

Fox Auctions

Stein, Character, Monkeys, Embossed, Lid, Figural Handle & Finial, Germany, c.1890, 9 In.
$165

Ruby Lane

Stein, Character, Satan, Figural Head, Porcelain, Pewter, Horns, E. Bohne & Sohne, c.1910, 5 In.
$395

Ruby Lane

Stein, Glass, Cranberry Cut To Clear, Thistle & Fern Design, Sawtooth Base, Metal Lid, 10 In.
$595

Ruby Lane

Stein, Glass, Flowers, Blue, White, Clear, Inlaid Porcelain Lid, Gambrinus, ½ Liter
$900

Fox Auctions

Stein, Military, Lithophane, 2 Seminude Women, Pewter Lid, Soldier, Germany, c.1896, 11 In.
$395

Ruby Lane

Don't Take Your Car to a Flea Market
Take your van, truck, or station wagon when you go to a farm auction, flea market, or out-of-town show. You never know when you'll find the dining room table of your dreams.

Cologne Bottle, Clear, Black & White Mottled Center, Controlled Bubbles, Stopper, 9 In. 10665
Cologne Bottle, Crystal, Mirror Black Threading, Stopper, 1920s, 4 ½ In. 531
Cologne Bottle, Ribbed Optic, Crystal, Silverine Rosa Stripes, Ball Stem, Stopper, 12 In. 1298
Compote, Calcite, Blue Aurene Inside, 6 In. 230
Compote, Lid, Gold Ruby, Flemish Blue Connectors & Rim, Cintra Pear Finial, 10 In. 1150
Console Set, Spiral Glass, 2 Candlesticks, Bowl, Signed F. Carder, 3 ⅝ x 14 In. & 4 In. 418
Console, Celeste Blue, Folded In Sides, 3 Applied Feet, 3 ¼ x 12 ¼ In. 144
Cordial, Thistle, Amethyst Cut To Clear, Flared, Clear Square Foot, 4 In., Pair 431
Cruet, Rosaline, Calcite, Blown Stopper, 6 ½ x 4 In., Pair 271
Figurine, Eagle, On Ball, Marked, 1900s, 5 x 13 x 4 In. 584
Figurine, Eagle, Signed, Presentation Case, 5 x 4 ¼ In. 523
Figurine, Koala, Box, Signed, 5 ½ In. 495
Figurine, Unicorn Head, Gilt Bronze Horn, Marked, c.1900, 3 ½ In. 1476
Goblet, Champagne, Pattern No. 6268, 3 ¾ In., 4 Piece 96
Lamp, Bronze, Shaped Harp, Steuben Intarsia Shade, Butterscotch, Platinum Waves, 57 In. 3396
Luminary, Art Deco, Intaglio Carved, Nude Man & Woman, Holding Inverted Vase, 9 x 11 In. ... 1121
Ornament, Mistletoe, Clear, Cultured Pearls, Silver, Gold, D. Pollard, c.1970, 6 In. 1599
Paperweight, Apple, 4 ½ x 3 ½ In. 118
Perfume Bottle, Blue Iridescent, Footed, Flame Stopper, Aurene, c.1915, 7 ½ In. .... *illus* 885
Perfume Bottle, Gold Aurene Crackle, Footed, DeVilbiss, c.1940, 7 In. 413
Perfume Bottle, Gold Aurene, Squat, Melon Ribbed, Ribbed Flame Stopper, 6 ½ In. 431
Perfume Bottle, Gold, Aurene, Engraved Flowers, Pearl Swags, Dabber, 5 ⅛ In. 738
Perfume Bottle, Green Jade, Tapered, Flattened Foot, Alabaster Teardrop Stopper, 10 In. 374
Perfume Bottle, Pomona Green, Melon Ribbed, Teardrop Stopper, 4 ¾ In. 230
Perfume Bottle, Selenium Red, Flint White Flame Stopper, Footed, Dabber, c.1910, 8 In. 767
Plate, Oriental Poppy, Smoky Purple, Opalescent Radiating Bands, 8 ½ In. 230
Plate, Rouge Flambe, Deep Red, Wide Flat Rim, 8 ¼ In. .... *illus* 4600
Punch Bowl, Cup Shape, Low Foot, G. Thompson, c.1950, 7 x 10 ¾ In. 492
Railroad Signal Lenses, Celeste Blue, Ribbed Disc, c.1935, 4 ½ x 4 ½ In., Pair 259
Scent Bottle, Blue Aurene, Bell Shape, Egg Shape Stopper, Signed, 6 In. .... *illus* 748
Scent Bottle, Yellow Jade, Bulbous, Cylindrical Neck, Flared Rim, Flattened Stopper, 5 In. 711
Sculpture, Alligator, Open Mouth, Air Bubbles, Scales, Houston, 3 x 11 In. 847
Sculpture, Cat, Seated, Green Tourmaline Eyes, P. Davidson, c.1973, 4 In. 308
Sculpture, Cathedral, Pointed Prism, Religious Statues, G. Thompson, c.1955, 15 In. 3198
Sculpture, Eagle, 7 x 7 In. 600
Sculpture, Nude, Reclining In Asymmetrical Block, Turntable Base, c.1970, 8 ½ In. 3198
Sculpture, Powerful Bull & Bear, Wall Street Symbols, c.1993, 5 & 4 In., Pair 861
Sculpture, Snail, Clear Shell, Vermeil Foot, Lapis Bead Eyes, P. Schelling, c.1970, 7 In. 1845
Shade, Orange Hooked Loop & Pulled Feather Design, Cream Ground, Ruffle Rim, 5 In. 830
Sherbet, Underplate, Gold Aurene, Calcite, Iridescence, 4 In. 776
Sugar & Creamer, Clear, Scroll Shape Handles, 3 In. 94
Table, Mosaic, Blue & Gold Aurene Tiles, Wrought Iron Frame, 1920s, 20 x 21 In. .... *illus* 3105
Tazza, Blue Aurene, Twist Stem, Flower Shape Bowl, Spread Foot, c.1920, 8 In. 625
Vase, 3 Stumps, Thorns, Blue Aurene, Platinum Iridescence, Signed, 6 ½ In. 575
Vase, 5 Prongs, Triangular, Jade Green, Alabaster Base, Scalloped Elevation, 12 x 11 In. 1955
Vase, Aquatic Scene, Acid-Cut Back, Black Over Jade, 1900s, 12 x 8 In. .... *illus* 4063
Vase, Aurene, Platinum, Green Hearts & Vines, Opal Millefiori Blossoms, 6 In. .... *illus* 2012
Vase, Blue Aurene, Engraved, Drilled Hole For Lamp, 12 In. 502
Vase, Blue Aurene, Green & Gold Iridescent, Urn Shape, Flared Rim, 7 In. 415
Vase, Blue Jade, Gold Iridescent Hooked Feathers On Shoulder, Bulbous, Squat, 2 In. 2074
Vase, Bud, Blue Aurene, Stick Shape, Saucer Foot, 8 In. 86
Vase, Bud, Gold Aurene, Tree Stump Shape, 3 Applied Stems, Signed, 6 In. 354
Vase, Calcite, Gold Aurene Inside, Flared, Undulating Rim, 5 In. 86
Vase, Calla Lily, Green Jade, Rectangular, 6 x 9 In. 460
Vase, Clear To Pink, Open Mouth, Flared Foot, c.1950, 6 x 5 ½ In. 308
Vase, Cluthra, Mottled Pink, Controlled Bubbles, Urn Shape, c.1925, 8 In. 625
Vase, Cluthra, Pink, Shouldered, Acid Etched Fleur-De-Lis, 8 In. .... *illus* 460
Vase, Cluthra, Pomona Green, Oval, Flared Rim, 8 In. 259
Vase, Cluthra, Urn Shape, Baccarat, Opaline Loop Handles, Clear Base, F. Carder, 10 In., Pair..... 738
Vase, Cup Shape, Clear, Round Base, 6 In. 154
Vase, Fan, Spanish Green, Applied Threading, Spread Foot, 8 ½ In. 144
Vase, Gold Aurene, Cream & Brown Vines, Cream & Green Hearts, Bulbous, 6 ½ In. 1422
Vase, Gold Aurene, Ring Foot, Lobed, Shouldered, Ruffled Rim, c.1900, 5 In. 488
Vase, Green Aurene, Iridescent Platinum Pulled Hearts & Vines, Shouldered, 7 ½ In. 4025
Vase, Green Jade, Matzu Pattern, Acid-Cut Back, Oval, Inward Folded Rim, 7 In. 489
Vase, Grotesque, Blue Jade, Handkerchief Form, Folded Rim, 6 ½ x 12 In. 1725
Vase, Moss Agate, Green, Shouldered, 11 ¾ In. 690

Stein, Pottery, Playing Cards, Etched, Square Body, Footed, Pewter Lid, ½ Liter
$120

Fox Auctions

Stein, Regimental, Roster, 5 Comp. Inft. Regt. Nr. 115 Darmstadt, Porcelain, c.1905, ½ Liter
$240

The Stein Auction Company

Stein, Regimental, Sailor On Barrel, S.M.S. Wettin, Wilhelmshaven, Roster, Pottery, ½ Liter
$7,050

The Stein Auction Company

S

Stein, Stoneware, Tavern Scene, Etched, Pewter Lid & Handle, Simon P. Gerz, c.1890, 18 In.
$325

Ruby Lane

Stein, Tankard, Wood, Pyrography, Portrait, Script, Hinged Lid, Acorn Finial, c.1910, 12 In.
$129

Ruby Lane

Stereo Card, Mamma Doll & Her Children, c.1890, 6 7⁄8 x 3 1⁄2 In.
$35

Ruby Lane

Steuben, Cologne Bottle, Blue Aurene, Melon Ribbed, 3 Curled Shell Feet, Stopper, 4 1⁄4 In.
$920

Early Auction Company

Steuben, Perfume Bottle, Blue Iridescent, Footed, Flame Stopper, Aurene, c.1915, 7 1⁄2 In.
$885

Brunk Auctions

Steuben, Plate, Rouge Flambe, Deep Red, Wide Flat Rim, 8 1⁄4 In.
$4,600

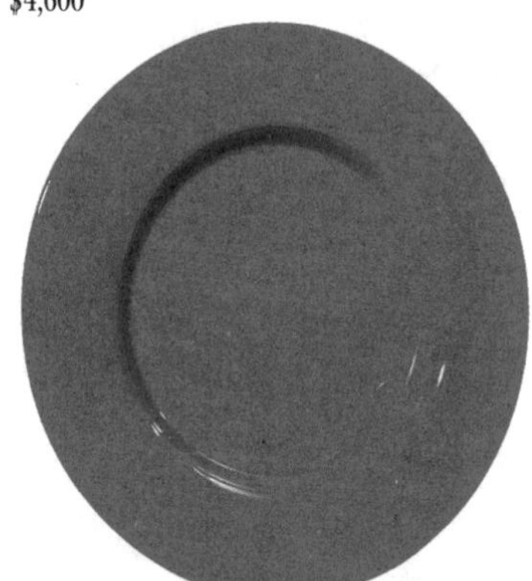

Early Auction Company

Steuben, Scent Bottle, Blue Aurene, Bell Shape, Egg Shape Stopper, Signed, 6 In.
$748

Early Auction Company

Steuben, Table, Mosaic, Blue & Gold Aurene Tiles, Wrought Iron Frame, 1920s, 20 x 21 In.
$3,105

Early Auction Company

Steuben, Vase, Aquatic Scene, Acid-Cut Back, Black Over Jade, 1900s, 12 x 8 In.
$4,063

Rago Arts and Auction Center

Vase, Organic, Flower Shape, Engraved, 7¾ In. 150
Vase, Oriental Poppy, Light Opalescent Stripes, Shouldered, Flared Rim, 5 In. 575
Vase, Red Aurene, Platinum Pulled Vine, Gold Inside, Shouldered, F. Carder, 9 In. 12074
Vase, Rosaline Stylized Flowers, Stems, Leaves, Textured Ground, 9½ In. .... *illus* 1185
Vase, Rosaline, Alabaster, Frederick Carder, Double Acid Etched, Branches, 7 x 8 In. 546
Vase, Rose Quartz, Crackled, Acid-Cut Back, Peacocks & Scrolls, Oval, 15¾ In. 1481
Vase, Stick, Blue Aurene, Iridescence, Footed, Signed, 8 In. 230
Vase, Stump, Gold Ruby, Clear Disc Foot, 3 Thorny Trunks, 6 In. .... *illus* 1006
Vase, Stump, Mirror Black, 3 Prongs, Thorns, Round Foot, 6 In. 805
Vase, Tyrian, Squat, Melon Ribbed, Elongated Neck, Platinum Hearts Vines, 4¼ In. 3450
Vase, White To Black At Rim, Cylindrical, Ring Foot, Flared Rim, Cluthra, 7 In. .... *illus* 403
Whimsy, Rouge Flambe, Sock Darner Shape, 6½ In. .... *illus* 1265
Whimsy, Sock Darner, Medium Blue Jade, Ball End, Elongated Handle, 6 In. 518

STEVENGRAPHS are woven pictures made like fancy ribbons. They were manufactured by Thomas Stevens of Coventry, England, and became popular in 1862. Most are marked *Woven in silk by Thomas Stevens* or were mounted on a cardboard that tells the story of the Stevengraph. Other similar ribbon pictures have been made in England and Germany.

Full Cry, Men & Woman, Fox Hunt, Frame, 7½ x 5¾ In. 475
Good Old Days, Horse Drawn Stagecoach, Men, Frame, 11½ x 8¾ In. 100
Struggle, Horse & Riders, Frame, 7½ x 10 In. 425

STEVENS & WILLIAMS of Stourbridge, England, made many types of glass, including layered, etched, cameo, and art glass, between the 1830s and 1930s. Some pieces are signed *S & W*. Many pieces are decorated with flowers, leaves, and other designs based on nature.

Cordial, Jade Cup, Alabaster Base, Carder Type, 6 In., 4 Piece 127
Perfume Bottle, Emerald Cut To Clear, Spirals, Silver Stopper, c.1900, 9 In. 2595
Perfume Bottle, Satin Glass, Green Shaded To Yellow, Raised Gilt, 1886, 4 In. 413
Perfume Bottle, Triple Cased Glass, Green, Pink, Cut To Clear, 9 In. 1107
Scent Bottle, Fish Shape, Silver Foil, Green Glass, Enamel, Gilt, Silver Tail, 5½ In. 4956
Toothpick Holder, Silveria, Foil Inclusions, Green Threading, Bulbous, Flared, 2 In. 3259
Vase, Blue, White Primrose, Butterfly, Rounded, Tapered, Cameo, 7 In. 1793
Vase, Brown Flowers & Persian Bands, Yellow Ground, Bottle Form, 12 In. 5333
Vase, Cranberry Flower, Crimped & Threaded Rim, Footed, 6¾ In. .... *illus* 256
Vase, Diamond Quilted, Mother-Of-Pearl, Rainbow, Fold-Down Top, 5½ In. 403
Vase, Exotic Birds, Flowering Branches, Burgundy Over Crystal, 6 x 7 In. 3565
Vase, Figural Blue Lizard, Amber Ribbed, Blue Lava Drips, Footed, 10 In. 259
Vase, Pull-Up, Pink, Orange, Yellow, Osiris, c.1887, 9 In. .... *illus* 1080
Vase, Red, Gold Scribble Design, Shouldered, Squat Neck, Flared, c.1920, 8 In. 250
Vase, Rose Du Barry, White Cut To Pink, Cameo, Oval, Tapered, 3¼ In. 518
Vase, Silveria, Blue, Purple, Red, Yellow, Green Threading, Pinched Sides, 13 In. 2903
Vase, Stick, Pompeiian Swirl, Shaded Blue, 8½ In. 690
Vase, Stick, Willow Green, Golden Ocher, Apple Blossom Branch, 7 In. 1534
Vase, Yellow, Pink Interior, Long Neck, c.1875, 8¼ x 2¾ In. 211

STIEGEL TYPE glass is listed here. It is almost impossible to be sure a piece was actually made by Stiegel, so the knowing collector refers to this glass as "Stiegel type." Henry William Stiegel, a colorful immigrant to the colonies, started his first factory in Pennsylvania in 1763. He remained in business until 1774. Glassware was made in a style popular in Europe at that time and was similar to the glass of many other makers. It was made of clear or colored glass and was decorated with enamel colors, mold blown designs, or etching.

Bottle, Cased, 2-Sided, Engraved Tulip, Leaves, 9¼ In. 71
Cup, Orange Petal Shape Decoration, Blue Daisies, Green Leaves, 3⅞ In. 119
Cup, Orange, Green, Yellow, Blue Flowers, Yellow Center, Applied Handle, 4 In. 60
Decanter, Goats, Leaves, Flowers, 9½ In. 150
Decanter, Roses, Stopper, 11 In. 220
Ogee Bowl, Dome Lid, Soda Lime, Copper Wheel Engraved, 10 In. 960

STONE includes those articles made of stones, coral, shells, and some other natural materials not listed elsewhere in this book. Micro mosaics (small decorative designs made by setting pieces of stone into a pattern), urns, vases, and other pieces made of natural stone are listed here. Stoneware is pottery and is listed in the Stoneware category. Alabaster, Jade, Malachite, Marble, and Soapstone are in their own categories.

Box, Cowrie Shell, Silver Plate Lid, Shell Shape, Engraved Village Scene, c.1900, 4 x 2½ In. *illus* 236

Steuben, Vase, Aurene, Platinum, Green Hearts & Vines, Opal Millefiori Blossoms, 6 In.
$2,012

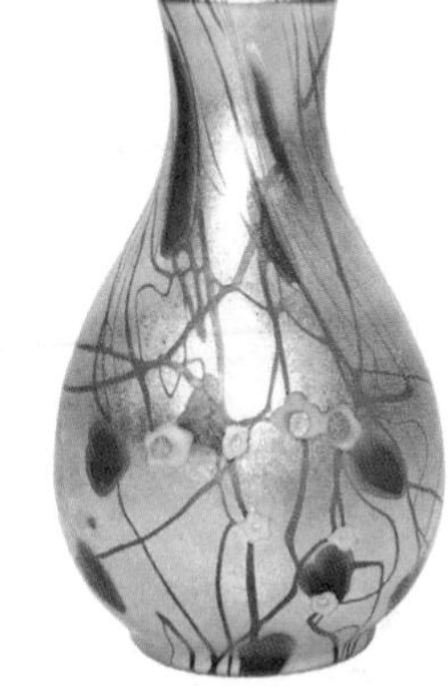

Early Auction Company

Steuben, Vase, Cluthra, Pink, Shouldered, Acid Etched Fleur-De-Lis, 8 In.
$460

Early Auction Company

Steuben, Vase, Rosaline Stylized Flowers, Stems, Leaves, Textured Ground, 9½ In.
$1,185

James D. Julia Auctioneers

Steuben, Vase, Stump, Gold Ruby, Clear Disc Foot, 3 Thorny Trunks, 6 In.
$1,006

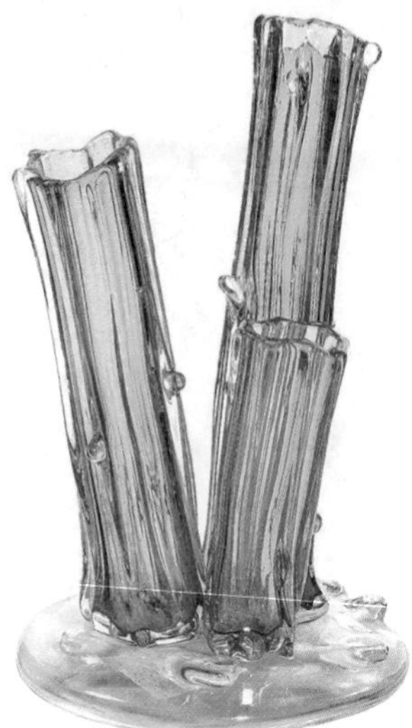

Early Auction Company

Steuben, Vase, White To Black At Rim, Cylindrical, Ring Foot, Flared Rim, Cluthra, 7 In.
$403

Early Auction Company

Steuben, Whimsy, Rouge Flambe, Sock Darner Shape, 6 ½ In.
$1,265

Early Auction Company

Censer, Lid, Jade, Green, Carved Design, Upright Pierced Handles, Drop Finial, 3 x 4 In. .....*illus* 299
Chalkboard, Slate, 2-Sided, Wood Frame, c.1900, 8 ¼ x 12 ¼ In. 42
Coral Branch, On Lucite Plinth, 7 ½ x 4 ½ In. 369
Coral, Pink, Branch, Oval Stained Wood, 3 ¼ x 7 ¼ In. 484
Ewer, Nautilus Shell, Gilt Metal Mount, Dolphins, 3 Handles, 13 x 8 In. 5700
Figure, 2 Women In Forest, Lapis Lazuli, Carved, Stand, 7 x 7 ½ In. 281
Figure, Buddha Head, Serene Expression, Tapered Square Socle, 1800s, 17 In. 1180
Figure, Buddha, Seated, Varada Mudra Gesture, Root, Carved, Snail Hair, 12 x 7 ½ In. 319
Figure, Bust, Man, Hair Combed Back, Limestone, Weathered Surface, 1900s, 23 In. 780
Figure, Bust, Woman, Flowing Hair, Modern, Cliff Fragua, 10 x 11 In. 154
Figure, Elder, Staff, Robes, Malachite, 6 ½ x 2 ½ In. 156
Figure, Fish Net, Fish, Carnelian, Agate, Free-Form, 7 x 5 In. 366
Figure, Foo Dog, Amethyst, Chinese, 5 x 2 In. 177
Figure, Frog, Hardstone, Mottled, Base, Chinese, 4 ¾ In. 210
Figure, Guanyin, Hair Up, Roses, Goose, Rose Quartz, 6 ½ x 3 In. 62
Figure, Head, Crystal, Carved, Chinese, 2 ½ x 2 In. 240
Figure, Heron, Rose Quartz, Chinese, 12 ½ x 8 ½ In. 413
Figure, Horse, Carved Hardstone, Reclining, Head Turned, c.1950, 9 x 12 In. 58
Figure, Parrot, Rose Quartz, Pink, Purple, 8 ½ In. 270
Figure, Phoenix, Figures, Coral, Red, 3 x 8 ½ In. 3327
Figure, Rabbit, Granite, 11 In. 1170
Figure, Rooster, Agate, Finial, Carnelian, 4 ⅞ In., Pair 74
Obelisk, Inlaid Flowering Vines, Malachite Leaves, Stepped Base, c.1890, 18 x 5 In., Pair 625
Pedestal, Molding, Carving, Lapis Lazuli Front, 43 In., Pair.....*illus* 214
Petrified Bamboo, 26 x 6 ¼ In. 369
Plaque, Centennial, Sandstone, Liberty Bell, Banner, Ernest Popeye Reed, 12 x 7 ½ In. 240
Plaque, Pietra Dura, Inlaid Musketeer Drinking, Barmaid With Tankard, 1900s, 12 x 7 In., Pair. 625
Scepter, Rose Quartz, Rock Crystal, France, 7 In. 420
Shell, Rock Crystal, Carved, Inlay, Coral, Turquoise, India, 9 ½ In. 984
Specimen, Coral, White, Lucite Base, 4 ½ x 13 ¼ In. 272
Tabletop, Slate, Faux Painted, Curling Leaves, Italy, 47 x 17 ½ In. 522
Urn, Lapis Lazuli, Lid, Tapered Body, Taotie Design, Wood Base, 7 x 2⁄4 In. 522
Vase, Lapis Lazuli, Bottle Shape, Flowering Vines, Phoenixes, 8 x 6 In. 1200
Vase, Malachite, Figural Handles, 5 x 3 ¼ In. 84
Vase, Rock Crystal, Cinnabar Sawtooth Shoulder, 4 ⅞ In. 360

STONEWARE is a coarse, glazed, and fired potter's ceramic that is used to make crocks, jugs, bowls, etc. It is often decorated with cobalt blue decorations. In the nineteenth and early twentieth centuries, potters often decorated crocks with blue numbers indicating the size of the container. A *2* meant 2 gallons. Stoneware is still being made. American stoneware is listed here.

Bank, Dome Top, Slot, Brown Glaze, Sprig & Leaf, Finial, Incised Alfred Nelson, 6 In. 325
Batter Bowl, Marked Chadler Maker, 1810-54, 7 ½ In. 531
Batter Jug, Albany Slip Glaze, Bail Handle, Tin Lid, 13 In. 180
Batter Jug, Cobalt Blue Leaf, Wire Bail Handle, Wood Grip, Tin Lid, 1 ½ Gal., 11 In. 649
Batter Jug, Cobalt Blue Leaves, Salt Glaze, Handle, Lid, Cowden, c.1885, 8 x 8 In. 1550
Bowl, Brown Glaze, Cream Ground, Japan, 2 ½ x 13 ½ In. 248
Chicken Feeder, Cobalt Blue Leaves, Ear Handles, Dome Top, Tiered Finial, 16 In. 2478
Chicken Waterer, Cobalt Blue Leaves, Highlights, Final, Applied Handles, 2 Gal., 15 In. 885
Churn, Blue Flower Spray, Albany, N.Y., Lug Handles, Wood Lid, 6 Gal., 18 In. 277
Churn, Blue Flowers, Molded Lip, Ear Handles, Bulbous, T. Harrington Lyons, 4 Gal., 16 In. 325
Churn, Blue Slip, Trailing Flowers & Leaves, 6 Gal., 1869, 22 In. 1003
Churn, Cobalt Blue Spitting Tulips, Salt Glaze, Lug Ear Handles, Impressed 2, c.1870, 2 Gal. 280
Churn, Double Handles, South Carolina, 3 Gal., 17 In. 115
Churn, Fowler, Beaver, Pa., Cobalt Blue Stencil, Spire & Duff, c.1870, 21 In. 570
Churn, White Glaze, Cobalt Blue Banding, Globe Pottery, Crooksville, 1902, 20 In. 960
Cistern, Glazed, Tan, Lipscobe & Co., 32 x 18 In. 250
Clock, Wine Pitcher Shape, Pedestal, Lion's Head, Ring, Germany, c.1910, 19 In. 84
Colander, Salt Glaze, Brown, Hanging Holes, 19th Century, 5 x 9 ½ In. 130
Cream Pot, Cobalt Blue Beehive Flower, Cowden & Wilcox, c.1870, 7 ¾ x 7 ⅝ In. 130
Creamer, Cobalt Blue Glaze Dipped, Tooled Rim, Shoulder, 4 ½ In. 600
Crock, 2 Hearts, Open Handles, Impressed Charlestown, Oval, c.1810, 10 ½ In. 660
Crock, 3 Flowers, Cobalt Blue, Oval, Squared Rim, Moore & Colvin, Middlebury, Ohio, 12 In. 390
Crock, 3, N. Clark & Co., 3 Gal. 403
Crock, Apple Butter, Cobalt Blue Closed Tulip, Cowden & Wilcox, c.1870, 7 x 7 ⅜ In. 100
Crock, Barrel Shape, Incised Blue Bands, Undulating Lines, 15 Gal., 24 In. 295
Crock, Bird, 1800s, 10 ½ x 11 In. 263

Stevens & Williams, Vase, Cranberry Flower, Crimped & Threaded Rim, Footed, 6 ¾ In.
$256

Ruby Lane

Stevens & Williams, Vase, Pull-Up, Pink, Orange, Yellow, Osiris, c.1887, 9 In.
$1,080

Ruby Lane

Stone, Box, Cowrie Shell, Silver Plate Lid, Shell Shape, Engraved Village Scene, c.1900, 4 x 2 ½ In.
$236

Brunk Auctions

Stone, Censer, Lid, Jade, Green, Carved Design, Upright Pierced Handles, Drop Finial, 3 x 4 In.
$299

Ruby Lane

Stone, Pedestal, Molding, Carving, Lapis Lazuli Front, 43 In., Pair
$214

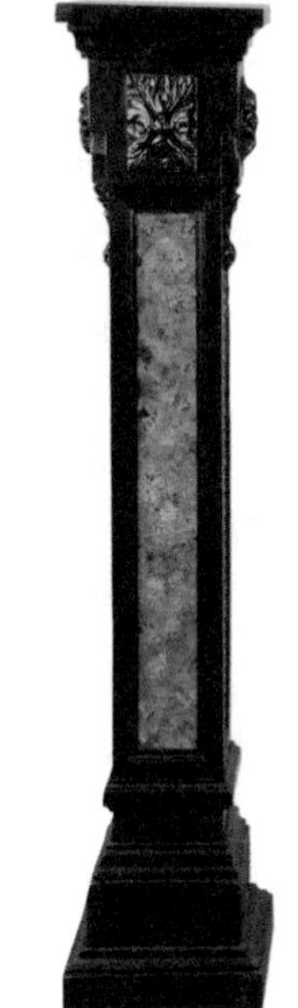

Morphy Auctions

Stoneware, Crock, Cobalt Blue Design, T.F. Reppert, Greensboro, Pa., Lug Handles, 1800s, 5 Gal.
$570

Cowan Auctions

Stoneware, Flowerpot, Glazed, Blue Flowers, Attached Saucer, 1800s, 6 ¾ x 8 In.
$325

Hess Auction Group

Stoneware, Flowerpot, Mottled Brown Glaze, Grape Cluster Handles, John Bell, Penn., 9 In.
$6,000

Cowan Auctions

Stoneware, Jar, Canning, Cobalt Blue Bird & Flowers, John Bell, Waynesboro, c.1890, 7 In.
$9,225

Skinner, Inc.

Stoneware, Jar, Cobalt Blue Stylized Flower, 2 Lug Handles, White's, Utica, 3 Gal., 11 In.
$60

Cowan Auctions

Stoneware, Jar, Olive Runny Glaze, Lug Handles, Nelson Bass, Stamped NB 7, c.1900, 17 In.
$708

Brunk Auctions

Stoneware, Jug, Alkaline Glaze, Brown, Strap Handle, Collar Rim, Shouldered, Edgefield, c.1850, 9 In.
$354

Brunk Auctions

Crock, Blue Flower, Burger Bro's, Rochester N.Y., Tan Salt Glaze, Closed Ears, 13 In. 242
Crock, Blue Slip Leaf, 4, Molded Rim, Incised Band, Tapered Body, 1800s, 13 In 295
Crock, Butter, Cobalt Blue Flowers, Double Ear Handles, Lid, 8 ½ x 5 In. 412
Crock, Cake, Blue Flowers, Leaves, Straight-Sided, Incised Bands, Lid, 6 x 9 In. 531
Crock, Cake, Cobalt Blue Flowers & Leaves, Ear Handles, Lid, 6 ½ x 9 ½ In. 649
Crock, Chicken, Pecking, Rady & Ryan, Ellenville, N.Y., 4 Gal., 12 x 11 In. 380
Crock, Cobalt Blue Bird, Riedinger & Caire, Poughkeepsie, N.Y., 11 x 12 In. 292
Crock, Cobalt Blue Bird, Riedinger & Caire, Poughkeepsie, 1800s, 10 ¼ x 11 In. 321
Crock, Cobalt Blue Chicken, Pecking Corn, Ear Handles, 2 Gal., Stamped, 9 ½ In. 224
Crock, Cobalt Blue Chicken, Pecking Corn, Molded Rim, Lug Handles, 9 ½ In. 443
Crock, Cobalt Blue Design, T.F. Reppert, Greensboro, Pa., Lug Handles, 1800s, 5 Gal. .... *illus* 570
Crock, Cobalt Blue Flower, 2, Impressed J, U.S.A., c.1850, 9 ½ In. 360
Crock, Cobalt Blue Flower, Impressed HB Pfaltzgraff, York, Pa., 11 ½ In. 390
Crock, Cobalt Blue Flowers, J.B. Caire & Co., Poughkeepsie, N.Y., 11 x 11 ½ In. 292
Crock, Cobalt Blue Freehand Flower, Salt Glaze, c.1890, 20 ½ x 15 ½ In. 300
Crock, Cobalt Blue Stencil, C.L. Williams & Company, 12, New Geneva, Pa., 22 In. 900
Crock, Cobalt Blue X Inside Reserve, Salt Glaze, 2 Applied Strap Handles, 1800s, 17 In. 1140
Crock, Cobalt Blue, 10-Part Leaf, 8 ¾ x 6 In. 108
Crock, Eagle, A. Conrad, Fayette Co., Pa., Gray, Blue Stencil, Ear Handles, 4 Gal., 14 In. 489
Crock, Flower, 3, Cobalt Blue, Gray Salt Glaze, John Burger, Rochester, Ear Handles, 3 Gal. 316
Crock, Flower, Cobalt Blue, N. Clark & Co., 5 Gal. 1150
Crock, Folk Art Lion, Cobalt Blue, Midwestern, c.1875, 12 In. 840
Crock, Glazed, Cobalt Blue Flowers, 5 Gal., 12 x 10 In. 108
Crock, Salt Glaze, Cylindrical, Lug Handles, Brown, Stamped EA Poe, 2 Gal., 11 In. 150
Crock, Snowflake, Blue Slip Design, Ear Handles, Molded Lip, 10 In. 189
Crock, Stencil, Lid, Demuth Snuff, Lancaster, Pa., 6 ½ In. 112
Crock, Stylized Cobalt Blue Flowers, William Rowley, Middlebury, O., 10 ½ In. 469
Cup, Textured Herringbone, Globular, Disc Shape Lip, Tapering Foot, c.1965, 4 In. 15838
Ewer, Flowers, Green, Shouldered, Trumpet Neck, Upright Spout, Lobed, Oval 8 In. 618
Ewer, Green Glaze, Hardwood Base, Squat, Loop Handle, Rolled Rim, c.1940, 6 ½ In. 1067
Figure, Spaniel, Seated, Cobalt Blue Glaze, Molded, 1800s, 6 ¾ In. 708
Flowerpot, Glazed, Blue Flowers, Attached Saucer, 1800s, 6 ¾ x 8 In. .... *illus* 325
Flowerpot, Mottled Brown Glaze, Grape Cluster Handles, John Bell, Penn., 9 In. .... *illus* 6000
Jar, Canning, 2 Cobalt Blue Stars, Stenciled, Pinched Neck, Rolled Rim, c.1870, 8 In. 420
Jar, Canning, Cobalt Blue Bird & Flowers, John Bell, Waynesboro, c.1890, 7 In. .... *illus* 9225
Jar, Canning, Salt Glaze, Coggle Wheel Design At Shoulder, Rolled Rim, 8 In. 173
Jar, Cobalt Blue Stripes, Oval, Flared Rim, Applied Handles, c.1800, 11 In. 1968
Jar, Cobalt Blue Stylized Flower, 2 Lug Handles, White's, Utica, 3 Gal., 11 In. .... *illus* 60
Jar, Cream Ground, 3 Dark Blue Characters, Japan, 4 ¼ In. 53
Jar, Gray, Blue Diagonal Stencil, James Hamilton, Greensboro, Pa., Qt., 8 In. 184
Jar, Immortals In Garden, Relief, Fahua, Blue & Purple Glaze, Stand, 1800s, 12 x 14 In. 5250
Jar, Incised Design, Pear Shape, Lid, Thrown, Signed, 13 ½ In. 201
Jar, Line Decoration, Inscribed 4, Lug Handles, T. Ritchie, Catawba Valley, 18 ½ In. 354
Jar, Olive Glaze, Incised 8, 4 Looped Handles, 17 ¾ In. 177
Jar, Olive Runny Glaze, Lug Handles, Nelson Bass, Stamped NB 7, c.1900, 17 In. .... *illus* 708
Jar, Tooled Shoulder, Lug Handles, James Hamilton, Greensboro, 12 Gal., 21 In. 1320
Jardiniere, Green, Oxblood Drip Glaze, Flowers, Dammouse, c.1900, 8 x 11 In. 3125
Jug, Alkaline Glaze, Brown, Strap Handle, Collar Rim, Shouldered, Edgefield, c.1850, 9 In. . *illus* 354
Jug, Bird, Fort Edward Pottery Co. 2, 16 In. 204
Jug, Bird, Splotches, Cobalt Blue, Handle, c.1775, 15 In. 400
Jug, Cobalt Blue Beehive Flower, Cowden & Wilcox, c.1870, 11 x 7 ⅞ In. 130
Jug, Cobalt Blue Bird, Impressed Mark, N.A. White & Son, Utica, 1800s, 2 Gal., 14 In. 480
Jug, Cobalt Blue Bird, Leaf, Slip Design, N.Y., 3 Gal., 15 ½ In. 325
Jug, Cobalt Blue Diamond Shape Stencil, Impressed 2, FH Cowden, c.1885, 14 x 9 In. 130
Jug, Cobalt Blue Flower, Incised, Glazed, D. Roberts, Utica, c.1830, 17 In. .... *illus* 2706
Jug, Cobalt Blue Flower, Swirl Stem, Leaf, Round, Pinched Mouth, 1800s, 18 In. 234
Jug, Cobalt Blue Scrolling Leaf Design, Salt Glaze, 1880s, 16 In. 276
Jug, Cobalt Blue Spitting Tulip, Impressed 3, Cowden & Wilcox, c.1870, 3 Gal. 160
Jug, Cobalt Blue Tulip, Oval, J.E. Sawyer, Ohio, c.1875, 15 ½ In. 360
Jug, Crescents & Tassels, Cobalt Blue, Incised, Commeraws, Hook, N.Y., 11 ½ In. 8610
Jug, Double Eagle Armorial, Pewter Lid, Reeded Neck, Octagonal Seal, Westerwald, 9 In. 1003
Jug, Face, Blue Glaze, Ears Stick Out, Teeth, B.B. Craig, 6 ½ In. 334
Jug, Running Bird, White's, Utica, 1800s, 3 Gal. 146
Jug, Sloop, General Pike, Huntington Oct 20th Y 1819, Blue, Gray Glaze, 13 In. 2340
Jug, Whiskey, Blue & White Banding, Funnel Top, Loop Handle, 1800s, 12 In. 37

Milk Pan, Salt Glaze, Slope Sided, Cobalt Blue 2, Pouring Spout, 5 ½ x 11 ⅞ In. 130
Pitcher, Albany Slip Glaze, Bulbous, 13 In. 118
Pitcher, Blue & White, Rooster Spout, Hunter Outside Castle, Utica, 8 ½ In. 28
Pitcher, Cobalt Blue Flower, Number 1, Bulbous, Molded Rim, 10 ½ In. 153
Pitcher, Cobalt Blue Flowers, Swollen, Loop Handle, Shaped Spout, 1800s, 10 In. 615
Pitcher, Cobalt Blue Tulip, Incised, Strap Handle, Cowden & Wilcox, Harrisburg, Pa., 10 In. 330
Pitcher, Cream, Cobalt Blue Design, Loop Handle, Uziah Kendall, c.1870, 10 In. 1320
Pitcher, Flower, Fence, 19th Century, 10 ½ In. 120
Pitcher, Flowers & Leaves, Cobalt Blue Slip Design, Shouldered, 9 In. 266
Pitcher, Milk, Salt Glaze, Cobalt Blue Flowers, Strap Handle, 7 ½ In. 330
Pitcher, Stoneware, Salt Glaze, Brown, Long Spout, c.1980, 9 ¾ x 9 ½ In. 240
Pitcher, Tanware, Brushwork, Blossoms, Flared Spout, c.1890, 6 In. 408
Stove Pipe, Blue Stencil, Jos. Eneix & Evans, New Geneva, Pa., 1800s, 23 ½ In. 944
Syrup, Paneled Scroll, 5 ¾ In. 70
Teapot, Lid, Pink Enamel, Flowers, Crabstock Handle, Spout, c.1760, 4 ½ In. *illus* 3321
Teapot, Lid, Red, Cylindrical, Loop Handle, Flowers, Leaves, Vines, c.1760, 3 ¼ In. *illus* 738
Teapot, Lid, Salt Glaze, Painted, Man Playing Horn, Crabstock Handle, c.1760, 4 x 6 In. *illus* 431
Teapot, Lid, Salt Glaze, White, Mansion Shape, Loop Handle, Nude Boy On Spout, c.1750, 5 In. *illus* 1599
Tree Stump, Tripod, 21 ½ x 17 In. 300
Urn, Lid, Wood Fired, Soda Ash Glaze, Brown, Tan, Mushroom Finial, D. Stuempfle, 9 In. 184
Vase, Mottled Volcanic Oxblood Drip Glaze, Hugh C. Robertson, 3 ¾ x 6 In. 1625
Vase, Nautical Scene, Trees, Blue, Cream, Salt Glaze, S. Frackelton, 1900s, 8 In. *illus* 11875
Vase, Oxblood Glaze, Hugh C. Robertson, 1896-1908, 8 x 3 In. 875
Wall Pocket, Face, Stoneware, Smiling, China Plate Teeth, Big Ears, Stamped, 7 In. 299
Water Cooler, Blue Leaves, Flowers, Molded Rim, Ear Handles, Incised, Spigot Hole, 15 In. 2242
Water Cooler, Cobalt Blue Flowers, 2 Handles, Saucer Foot, 1800s, 20 In. 649
Water Cooler, Cobalt Blue Stylized Bird & Leaf, Gray, Barrel, Charlestown, 13 In. 761
Water Cooler, Embossed Vines, Flowers, Label, Filtre Chamberland, 1800s, 20 ½ In. 277
Water Cooler, Flowers, Ice Water, Salt Glaze, Carved, Copper Spigot, Lid, 15 ½ In. 127
Water Cooler, Yellow Glaze, Green, Embossed Stag, Doe, Lid, Metal Spout, 5 Gal., 16 In. 443
Wine Bottle, Salt Glaze, Brown, Freckle Design, Pear Shape, Loop Handle, Stopper, c.1680, 9 In. *illus* 2214

STORE fixtures, cases, cutters, and other items that have no advertising as part of the decoration are listed here. Most items found in an old store are listed in the Advertising category in this book.

Bin, 3 Lift-Top Glass Doors, Bootjack Cutout Base, 26 x 64 In. 1521
Bin, Grain, 3 Iron Strap Hinges, 4 Interior Bins, Dovetail Construction, 28 ½ x 69 ½ In. 180
Bin, Spice, Pagoda Shape, Tin, 6-Sided, Revolving, American Can Co., 36 x 27 In. *illus* 3300
Cabinet, Display, Mahogany, Glass Front, Rear Door, Adjustable Shelves, Footed, 59 x 23 In. 418
Cabinet, Pie, Wood, Molded Nickel, Shelf, Glass Sides, 31 x 20 In. 106
Cabinet, Seed, Quartersawn Oak, 5 Slant Lid Hinge Top Bins, Glass Front Drawers, 1800s 1062
Case, Display, Art Deco, Nickel Over Steel, Trapezoid Shape, Hinged Doors, 70 x 28 In. 3009
Case, Display, Oak, Hinged Top, Glass, Holds 72 Canes, H. Pauk Sons, 54 x 24 In. *illus* 900
Chest, Seed, Pine, Painted, Various Size Drawers, Wood Knobs, 1800s, 41 x 40 In. 1845
Cigar Cutter, 14K Gold, Ruby, 6 Diamonds, Bulbous, Tapered, 1 ¼ In. 420
Cigar Cutter, Atlas, Curved End, Matte & Polished Stripes, Tiffany, 1 ⅜ x 2 In. 212
Cigar Cutter, Turtle, Figural, Cast Iron, Geschutzt 399
Coffee Grinders are listed in the Coffee Mill category.
Dispenser, Straw, Wood, Horizontal, Round Dials, 1950s, 8 x 8 x 5 In. 60
Display Case, Ribbons, Oak, Stepped Cornice, A.N. Russell & Sons, 28 x 6 In. 660
Display, Jewelry, Sunbursts, Corner Brackets, Reeded Legs, Drawer, Tabletop, 30 x 42 In. 1080
Egg Carrier, Ventilator, Dairy Supply Co., Hinged, Pat. 1898, 14 x 6 ¼ x 9 ¾ In. 180
Ledger, Receipt Log, Wallpaper Cover, Bookplate, Johannes S. Turner, c.1835, 13 x 8 In. 1121
Lighter, Cigar, Eldred Mfg., Jump Spark, Wood Case, Wireless, 15 x 9 ½ x 7 ½ In. 540
Lighter, Cigar, Electric, Cannon, Soldier, Nickel Plate, Wood Base, 7 ½ x 13 x 9 ½ In. 627
Lighter, Cigar, Figural Hand, Holding Nozzle, Threaded Pipe, Cast Iron, Round Base, 6 ½ In. 240
Mannequin, Wood, Papier-Mache, Cloth, Painted, Ball-Jointed, c.1865, 52 x 17 In. *illus* 1250
Milk Carrier, Miller Dairy, Blue Paint, Yellow Letters, Iron Bail Handle, 7 x 13 In. 266
Pail, Dairy Storage, Rustic, Wood Bands, Lid, Scandinavia, 1800s, 10 x 10 In. 100
Shoeshine, Twisted Wrought Iron, 50 x 24 In. 165
Showcase, Curved Glass, Arched Top, c.1900, 44 x 27 In. 787
Showcase, Oak, Curved Glass, H. Paulk & Sons, c.1900, 36 x 60 In. 726
Sign, Antique Shop, Black Letters, Cream Ground, 21 ¾ x 31 In. 468
Sign, Apothecary, Mortar & Pestle, Metal, Gold Painted, c.1900, 32 x 22 In. 800
Sign, Automobile Gasoline For Sale Here, Wood, 2-Sided, 22 x 62 In. 1062
Sign, Boots, Carved Pine, Figural Boot, Painted, Iron Rod, c.1850, 39 x 14 In. 948

Stoneware, Jug, Cobalt Blue Flower, Incised, Glazed, D. Roberts, Utica, c.1830, 17 In.
$2,706

Skinner, Inc.

Stoneware, Teapot, Lid, Pink Enamel, Flowers, Crabstock Handle, Spout, c.1760, 4 ½ In.
$3,321

Skinner, Inc.

Stoneware, Teapot, Lid, Red, Cylindrical, Loop Handle, Flowers, Leaves, Vines, c.1760, 3 ¼ In.
$738

Skinner, Inc.

TIP

The average burglar spends 60 seconds breaking into a house. If you can delay him with bars, locks, or other security measures, he may leave.

S

TIP
When ordering antiques by mail, do not send cash; send a check or charge them. Keep a copy of your order.

Stoneware, Teapot, Lid, Salt Glaze, Painted, Man Playing Horn, Crabstock Handle, c.1760, 4 x 6 In.
$431

Skinner, Inc.

Stoneware, Teapot, Lid, Salt Glaze, White, Mansion Shape, Loop Handle, Nude Boy On Spout, c.1750, 5 In.
$1,599

Skinner, Inc.

Stoneware, Vase, Nautical Scene, Trees, Blue, Cream, Salt Glaze, S. Frackelton, 1900s, 8 In.
$11,875

Rago Arts and Auction Center

Stoneware, Wine Bottle, Salt Glaze, Brown, Freckle Design, Pear Shape, Loop Handle, Stopper, c.1680, 9 In.
$2,214

Skinner, Inc.

Store, Bin, Spice, Pagoda Shape, Tin, 6-Sided, Revolving, American Can Co., 36 x 27 In.
$3,300

Showtime Auction Services

Store, Case, Display, Oak, Hinged Top, Glass, Holds 72 Canes, H. Pauk Sons, 54 x 24 In.
$900

Brunk Auctions

Store, Mannequin, Wood, Papier-Mache, Cloth, Painted, Ball-Jointed, c.1865, 52 x 17 In.
$1,250

New Orleans (Cakebread)

1876
The Colonial Revival started with the patriotism kindled by the 1876 Centennial Exhibition in Philadelphia. The old styles popular in the days of George Washington represented the security and standards of the founders of the country.

Sign, Centennial, Bangor, Maine, Molding, Arched Panel, Green Borders, 1876, 14 x 67 In. 450
Sign, Cobbler's, Shoe Shape, Curved Hanging Bracket, c.1890, 11 ½ In. ....*illus* 2091
Sign, Egg Crate, Wood, 24 x 46 In. 2340
Sign, Figural Cowboy Boot, Spur, Red Paint, Gilt, Sheet Iron, c.1880, 2-Sided, 29 x 19 In. 474
Sign, Fowl, Dead Or Alive, Eggs, Lodging & Extras, 19 ½ x 24 In. 234
Sign, Hat, Cast Iron, 10 ½ x 8 ½ In. 234
Sign, Ice Cream Cone Shape, Copper, Impressed 5 Cents, c.1920, 14 x 6 In. 160
Sign, Locksmith, Key Shape, Painted Red, Crackle Surface, Sheet Iron, 38 In. 826
Sign, Locksmith, Key Shape, Pierced Bow, Turned Shank, Gold Paint, 66 In. 584
Sign, Pocket Watch, Roman Numerals, Wind Lever, Iron Ring, 21 ½ x 16 In. 420
Sign, Pool & Billiards, Tables & Cues By The Hour, Shelf, Curved Top, 25 x 36 In. 120
Sign, Rooster, Sheet Metal, 22 x 24 In. 702
Sign, Shoe, Black, Shoes Repaired While You Wait, 22 ½ x 25 ½ In. 960
Sign, Teacher Of Piano, Metal, Black Ground, Yellow Letters, 10 x 9 In. 175
Sign, Today's Beef Prices, Black, Chalkboard, Book Shape, 29 x 30 In. 146
Sign, Top Hat, Bracket, Hanging Hand, 1800s, 43 x 38 ½ In. 4095
Sign, Welcome Inn, Wood, 46 x 23 In. 93
Sign, Your Photo, In A Minute, 15 Cents With A Frame, Aluminum, 22 x 17 In. 915
Workbench, Jewelry, Oak, Steel, France, c.1915, 35 x 30 In. 960

STOVES have been used in America for heating since the eighteenth century and for cooking since the nineteenth century. Most types of wood, coal, gas, kerosene, and even some electric stoves are collected.

Cook, Corner, Baked Enamel, Flowers, 3 Burners, Belgium, 38 ½ x 45 In. 250
Cook, Wood Burning, Belleville, Cast Iron, Chrome Trim, c.1910, 56 x 38 In. ....*illus* 244
Heating, Cast Iron, S.M. Howes Co., 25 x 21 In. 146
Heating, Ceramic, Baroque Style, Glazed, Marble Top, Glass, Cast Iron, Sweden, 40 In. 354
Heating, Ceramic, Baroque, 5 Sections, Brass Door, Drawer, Scandinavia, 1700s, 75 In. .....*illus* 1180
Heating, Coal, Tin Glaze, Art Nouveau, Majolica Tiles, 30 ½ x 48 In. 1331
Heating, Porcelain, Blue, Cast Iron, Pierced, Curved Doors, Deville & Cie, 22 x 21 In., Pair 430
Heating, Porcelain, Brown, Cast Iron, Door, De Dietrich & Cie, 17 x 21 In. 184
Heating, Terra-Cotta, White & Yellow Glaze, 2 Doors, Italy, 54 x 24 In. 338
Heating, Tilework, Continental, Blue, White, 1700s, 66 ½ x 32 ¼ In. 6875
Hibachi, Japanese Elm, Copper Basin, 5 Drawers, 14 x 28 In. 99
Shaker, Cast Iron, Rectangular Fire Box, Extended Coal Catcher, Scroll Legs, c.1850, 31 In. 420
Stove Plate, Cast Iron, Mary Ann Furnace, 1763, 22 x 16 ¾ In. 944
Stove Plate, Cast Iron, Tulips, Columns, Animals, Martic Furnace, Lancaster, 1761, 25 x 28 In. 826
Stove Plate, Sheet Iron, Running Horse Silhouette, Concave, c.1900, 24 x 27 In. 118

STRETCH GLASS is named for the strange stretch marks in the glass. It was made by many glass companies in the United States from about 1900 to the 1920s. It is iridescent. Most American stretch glass is molded; most European pieces are blown and may have a pontil mark.

Bowl, Orange To Purple Iridescent, Flared, 12 In. Diam. ....*illus* 30
Bowl, Red, 9 ¾ x 2 ½ In. 58
Bowl, Vaseline, Pheasant Etched, Gold Encrusted, 9 ¾ In. 25
Candlestick, Blue, Round Base, 8 In., Pair 22
Candlestick, Red, Iridescent, 8 ¼ In., Pair 161
Vase, Fan, Melon Ribs, Light Green, 7 ¾ In. 60
Vase, Green Swirl, Ruffled Rim, 7 ½ In. ....*illus* 45
Vase, Yellow, Clear, 15 In. 15

SUMIDA is a Japanese pottery that was made from about 1895 to 1941. Pieces are usually everyday objects—vases, jardinieres, bowls, teapots, and decorative tiles. Most pieces have a very heavy orange-red, blue, brown, black, green, purple, or off-white glaze, with raised three-dimensional figures as decorations. The unglazed part is painted red, green, black, or orange. Sumida is sometimes mistakenly called Sumida gawa, but true Sumida gawa is a softer pottery made in the early 1800s.

Figurine, Benkei, Red Dragon Wrapped Around Body, 6 x 3 ½ x 7 In. 225
Mug, Man, Climbing, High Relief, Signed, Japan, 5 In. 28
Teapot, Lid, Blue, Red, Signed, 5 ½ In. 115
Umbrella Stand, Men, Cliff, Bird, Branches, 24 x 8 In. 484
Vase, Applied Leaves & White Flowers, 18 x 10 In. 615
Vase, Men, Climbing Up Sides, Multicolor, 4 x 7 ½ In. 206

Store, Sign, Cobbler's, Shoe Shape, Curved Hanging Bracket, c.1890, 11 ½ In.
$2,091

Skinner, Inc.

Stove, Cook, Wood Burning, Belleville, Cast Iron, Chrome Trim, c.1910, 56 x 38 In.
$244

Morphy Auctions

Stove, Heating, Ceramic, Baroque, 5 Sections, Brass Door, Drawer, Scandinavia, 1700s, 75 In.
$1,180

Brunk Auctions

S

TIP
Do not put wire-stemmed artificial flowers in a valuable narrow neck glass vase. The stems will scratch and damage the vase.

Stretch Glass, Bowl, Orange To Purple Iridescent, Flared, 12 In. Diam.
$30

Ruby Lane

Stretch Glass, Vase, Green Swirl, Ruffled Rim, 7 ½ In.
$45

Ruby Lane

Sunbonnet Babies, Creamer, Gardening, Royal Bayreuth, Blue Mark, 3 ¾ In.
$205

Ruby Lane

SUNBONNET BABIES were introduced in 1900 in the book *The Sunbonnet Babies*. The stories were by Eulalie Osgood Grover, illustrated by Bertha Corbett. The children's faces were completely hidden by the sunbonnets. The children had been pictured in black and white before this time, but the color pictures in the book were immediately successful. The Royal Bayreuth China Company made a full line of children's dishes decorated with the Sunbonnet Babies. Some Sunbonnet Babies plates have been reproduced, but they are clearly marked.

Creamer, Gardening, Royal Bayreuth, Blue Mark, 3 ¾ In. .... *illus* 205
Pitcher, Ironing, Tuesday, Royal Bayreuth, 4 ½ In. 75
Pitcher, Mending, Thursday, Wavy Rim, c.1910, 3 ½ In. 95

SUNDERLAND luster is a name given to a special type of pink luster made by Leeds, Newcastle, and other English firms during the nineteenth century. The luster glaze is metallic and glossy and appears to have bubbles in it. Other pieces of luster are listed in the Luster category.

Cup & Saucer, Pink Luster, Leaves, Handleless, 3 ¼ x 5 ½ In., Pair 40
Mug, Cider, Clipper Ship, Forgive & Forget, 1850, 4 In. .... *illus* 195
Pitcher, Pink Luster, Soft Paste, Transferware, Iron Bridge, Compass, 9 ½ x 8 In. 590
Plaque, Prepare To Meet Thy God, 8 ¼ x 7 ½ In. 47
Punch Bowl, Pink Luster, Transferware, Forget-Me-Nots, Heraldry, Sailboat, 5 ½ x 11 In. 472
Punch Bowl, Pink Luster, Transferware, Maritime, Compass Rose, Poem, 5 ½ x 10 In. 354

SUPERMAN was created by two seventeen-year-olds in 1938. The first issue of *Action Comics* had the strip. Superman remains popular and became the hero of a radio show in 1940, cartoons in the 1940s, a television series, and several major movies.

Animation Art, Style Sheet, 24 Head Sketches, Pencil, Fleischer Studios, 1940s, 11 x 13 In. 3542
Belt & Buckle, Brass, Leather, Holding Chain, Fighting Scenes, 28 x 1 In. 230
Belt, Brown Leather, Brass Buckle, Pioneer, 1940s, 34 In. 335
Book, Cutouts, 4 Pages, Cardboard, Saalfield Pub. No. 1502, 1940, 10 ½ x 14 In. 791
Button, Superman In Flight, Sunday Mail Comics Club, 1940s, 1 In. 153
Button, Superman, Nancy & Sluggo, Sun Times Comic Capers Club, Tin Back, 1940s, 2 In. 575
Comic Book, Cover, No. 201, Dejected Clark Kent, Curt Swan, Pencil, 1994, 18 x 25 In. 1171
Comic Book, No. 9, March-April, Jerry Siegel, Fred Ray Cover, 1941 1227
Comic Book, No. 29, July-August, Prankster, Don Cameron, Joe Samachson, 1944 863
Cookie Jar, Man Of Steel, Chains Across Chest, Warner Bros. Exclusive, Box, 1992 72
Figure, Die Cut, Cardboard Figure, National Comic Publications, 1948 431
Figure, Lois Lane, S Symbol, Porcelain, Robert Tonner Doll Co., 1997, 16 & 19 In., Pair 190
Figure, Poseable, Mego, NPP Inc., 1972 285
Figure, Superman Standing, Hands On Hips, Brown & Red, 1940s, 6 In. 1684
Figure, Superman, Rubber Body, Plastic Head, Cloth Cape & Trunks, Box, 1979, 9 x 15 In. 529
Jigsaw Puzzle, Shows His Super Strength, 300 Piece, Box, 1940, 12 x 16 In. 825
Jumper, Outfit, Action Images, Cotton, Toddler, 1940s 2530
Lighter, DC Mascot Character, National Comics, Plated Metal, 2 ¼ x 2 ¼ In. 386
Milk Cap, Roberts Milk, Superman, Hands On Hips, 1 ⅝ In. 380
Picture, Punching Robot, Glow-In-The-Dark, Wood Frame, Mid 1940s, 8 x 10 In. 380
Playsuit, 3-Piece, Silk Screen, A.S. Fishbach, 1940 886
Pocket Watch, Flying Across Skyline, Metal, Box, Bradley, 1959, 2 In. Diam. 689
Portrait, Artboard, Colored Pencil, Profile, In Uniform, Joe Shuster, 7 x 10 In. 4302
Ring, Silvered Metal, Red Paint, Lightning Bolts, Planet, Superman, 1940 3479
Ring, Supermen Of America, Action Comics, Silver Luster, Red Paint, c.1939 10436
Toy, Motorcycle, Plastic, Vinyl Superman Rider, Box, 1980s, 11 x 10 In. 1151
Toy, Raygun, Krypto, Embossed, Daisy, Box, 10 ¼ x 8 ¼ In. 1020
Toy, Rollover Airplane, Rolls In Circles, Tin Litho, Clockwork, Marx, 1940, 6 In. .... *illus* 885
Toy, Tank, Superman Lifting Tank, Turret, Brown, Green, Battery Operated, Box, c.1958 2530
Wristwatch, Leather Band, Superman Standing, Hands On Hips, 1938 360

SUSIE COOPER began as a designer in 1925 working for the English firm A.E. Gray & Company. In 1932 she formed Susie Cooper Pottery, Ltd. In 1950 it became Susie Cooper China, Ltd., and the company made china and earthenware. In 1966 it was acquired by Josiah Wedgwood & Sons, Ltd. The name *Susie Cooper* appears with the company names on many pieces of ceramics.

Coffee Set, Coffeepot, Sugar, Creamer, 6 Cups, Saucers, 6 Spoons, Triangles, 1928, 15 Piece 1645
Coffee Set, Venetia, Coffeepot, Sugar & Creamer, 6 Cups & Saucers, 15 Piece 40
Jug, Earthenware, Turquoise Matte Glaze, Dimpled Body, 8 In. 56
Pitcher, Wedding Ring Pattern, Earthenware, c.1940, 3 In. .... *illus* 20

Pitcher, Yellow, Black, Color Blacks, Sgraffito, 6 ⅓ In. 253
Plate, Golfing Figure, Yellow Shirt, Cooper Crown Works Burslem, 1935, 7 In. 112

SWANKYSWIGS are small drinking glasses. In 1933, the Kraft Food Company began to market cheese spreads in these decorated, reusable glass tumblers. They were discontinued from 1941 to 1946, then made again from 1947 to 1958. Then plain glasses were used for most of the cheese, although a few special decorated Swankyswigs have been made since that time. For more prices, go to kovels.com.

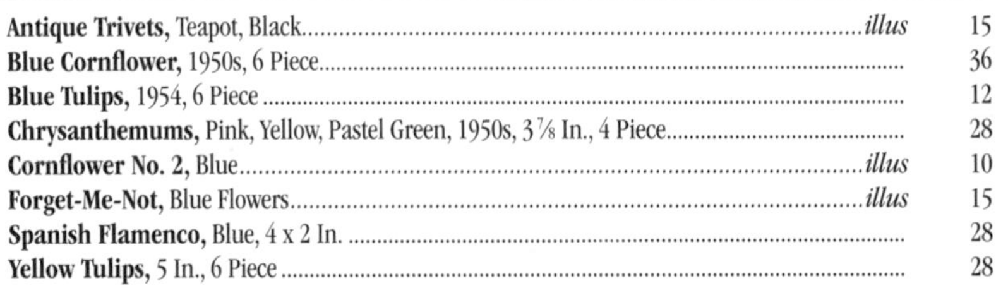

Antique Trivets, Teapot, Black.......... *illus* 15
Blue Cornflower, 1950s, 6 Piece.......... 36
Blue Tulips, 1954, 6 Piece 12
Chrysanthemums, Pink, Yellow, Pastel Green, 1950s, 3 ⅞ In., 4 Piece.......... 28
Cornflower No. 2, Blue.......... *illus* 10
Forget-Me-Not, Blue Flowers.......... *illus* 15
Spanish Flamenco, Blue, 4 x 2 In. 28
Yellow Tulips, 5 In., 6 Piece 28

SWASTIKA KERAMOS is a line of art pottery made from 1906 to 1908 by the Owen China Company of Minerva, Ohio. Many pieces were made with an iridescent glaze.

Vase, Bronze, Gold, Panels Of Swastikas, Black, 9 In. 400
Vase, Landscape, 1906-08, 8 x 3 ½ In. 640
Vase, Landscape, Trees, Handles, 8 In. 350
Vase, Red Iris, Green Leaves, 12 In. 140

SWORDS of all types that are of interest to collectors are listed here. The military dress sword with elaborate handle is probably the most wanted. A tsuba is a hand guard fitted to a Japanese sword between the handle and the blade. Be sure to display swords in a safe way, out of reach of children.

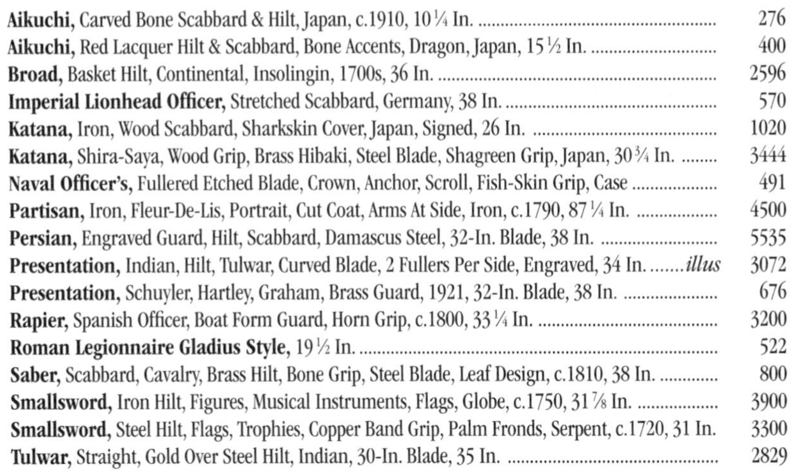

Aikuchi, Carved Bone Scabbard & Hilt, Japan, c.1910, 10 ¼ In. 276
Aikuchi, Red Lacquer Hilt & Scabbard, Bone Accents, Dragon, Japan, 15 ½ In. 400
Broad, Basket Hilt, Continental, Insolingin, 1700s, 36 In. 2596
Imperial Lionhead Officer, Stretched Scabbard, Germany, 38 In. 570
Katana, Iron, Wood Scabbard, Sharkskin Cover, Japan, Signed, 26 In. 1020
Katana, Shira-Saya, Wood Grip, Brass Hibaki, Steel Blade, Shagreen Grip, Japan, 30 ¾ In. 3444
Naval Officer's, Fullered Etched Blade, Crown, Anchor, Scroll, Fish-Skin Grip, Case 491
Partisan, Iron, Fleur-De-Lis, Portrait, Cut Coat, Arms At Side, Iron, c.1790, 87 ¼ In. 4500
Persian, Engraved Guard, Hilt, Scabbard, Damascus Steel, 32-In. Blade, 38 In. 5535
Presentation, Indian, Hilt, Tulwar, Curved Blade, 2 Fullers Per Side, Engraved, 34 In. .... *illus* 3072
Presentation, Schuyler, Hartley, Graham, Brass Guard, 1921, 32-In. Blade, 38 In. 676
Rapier, Spanish Officer, Boat Form Guard, Horn Grip, c.1800, 33 ¼ In. 3200
Roman Legionnaire Gladius Style, 19 ½ In. 522
Saber, Scabbard, Cavalry, Brass Hilt, Bone Grip, Steel Blade, Leaf Design, c.1810, 38 In. 800
Smallsword, Iron Hilt, Figures, Musical Instruments, Flags, Globe, c.1750, 31 ⅞ In. 3900
Smallsword, Steel Hilt, Flags, Trophies, Copper Band Grip, Palm Fronds, Serpent, c.1720, 31 In. 3300
Tulwar, Straight, Gold Over Steel Hilt, Indian, 30-In. Blade, 35 In. 2829

SYRACUSE is a trademark used by the Onondaga Pottery of Syracuse, New York. The company was established in 1871. The name became the Syracuse China Company in 1966. Syracuse China closed in 2009. It was known for fine dinnerware and restaurant china.

Bombay, Gravy Boat, Underplate, 9 In. 30
Clover, Gravy Boat, Underplate.......... 25
Coralbel, Bowl, Vegetable, 10 In. 21
Coralbel, Cup & Saucer, Platinum Trim, Footed, c.1955 .... *illus* 12
Dearborn, Sugar & Creamer.......... 68
Lady Louise, Bowl, Vegetable, Lid, 7 In. 110
Mayview, Gravy Boat, Federal Shape, Underplate, 7 ¾ In. 27
Romance, Bowl, Vegetable, Oval, 10 ½ In. 15
Romance, Gravy Boat, Underplate, 9 ½ In. 20
Wayside, Bowl, Round, 8 In. 59
Wayside, Platter, Round, 11 In. 25

TAPESTRY, *Porcelain, see Rose Tapestry category.*

Sunderland, Mug, Cider, Clipper Ship, Forgive & Forget, 1850, 4 In.
$195

Ruby Lane

Superman, Toy, Rollover Airplane, Rolls In Circles, Tin Litho, Clockwork, Marx, 1940, 6 In.
$885

Bertoia Auctions

Susie Cooper, Pitcher, Wedding Ring Pattern, Earthenware, c.1940, 3 In.
$20

Ruby Lane

TIP

If you are uncomfortable when trying to buy an antique, either because of the attitude of the dealer or some of the information you are given, walk away. There are other shops and other antiques.

S

Swankyswig, Antique Trivets, Teapot, Black
$15

Swankyswig, Cornflower No. 2, Blue
$10

TIP

If two tumblers get stuck when stacked, try putting cold water into the inside glass, then put both into hot water up to the lower rim.

Swankyswig, Forget-Me-Not, Blue Flowers
$15

TEA CADDY is the name for a small box made to hold tea leaves. In the eighteenth century, tea was very expensive and it was stored under lock and key. The first tea caddies were made with locks. By the nineteenth century, tea was more plentiful and the tea caddy was larger. Often there were two sections, one for green tea, one for black tea.

Black Lacquer Base, Pentagon Shape, 2 Canisters, Chinese Export, 11 x 6 In. 1320
Blue, Hexagonal, Scrolling Leaves, Brown Ground, 7 In., Pair.......... 826
Burl Veneer, Line Inlay, Coffin Shape, 2 Compartments, England, c.1800, 6 x 8 In. 660
Burl, Arched Top, Brass Washed Steel Accents, Mother-Of-Pearl, 9 x 6½ In. 260
Ceramic, Famille Rose, White, Flowers, Vine, Lid, Peach Finial, 5½ In. 185
Cherry, String Edge, Leather Lined, Double Hinged Lid, 1700s, 11½ x 5¾ In. 189
Cupid, Gilt, Cobalt Blue, Handles, Lid, 6 In. 344
Fruitwood, Apple Shape, Lock, 4 In. 1234
Fruitwood, Melon Shape, Stem, Silver Lined, Georgian, 5½ x 5 In. 1560
Fruitwood, Pear Shape, Foil Lined, c.1800, 6½ x 3½ In. ....*illus* 1168
Fruitwood, Pear Shape, George III, 1700s, 7½ x 5 In. ....*illus* 687
Gilt Bronze Boulle Style, Paw Feet, France, c.1880, 6 x 10¾ In. 1107
Gilt, Octagonal, Narrow Neck, Lid, 5½ x 3¾ In., Pair 183
Lacquer, Octagonal, Hinged Lid, Black, Gilt, Figures, Dragon Border, 8 x 15 In. 1560
Mahogany Veneer, Hinged Lid, Rectangular, Inlaid Shells, String Edges, 5 x 8 x 5 In. 308
Mahogany Veneer, Line Inlay, Oval Bowl Inside, 5 x 6 In. 510
Mahogany, Divided Interior, Bracket Feet, Handle, George II, c.1755, 7 x 10 In. 2500
Mahogany, George III, Crossbanded, Marquetry, 6 x 12 In. 375
Mahogany, Georgian, Crossbanded, 5½ x 7¼ In. 200
Mahogany, Inlaid Ovals, Flowers, Leaping Stag, c.1810, 5 x 7 In. 593
Mahogany, Inlay, Royal Navy Motifs, Acorns, Oak Leaves, 4 x 7 In. 363
Mahogany, Satinwood, 2 Compartments, 19th Century, 6 x 12 In. 302
Mahogany, Shell Inlay, Silver Paper Lining, 1800s, 4½ x 5 In. 123
Mahogany, Silver, Crossbanded, Inlay, Scrollwork, Coffin Lid, c.1790, 7 x 13 In. 1353
Mahogany, Square, Shaped Lid, Log Shape Handle, Footed, 1800s, 10 x 5 In. 153
Maple, Apple Shape, Applied Stem, Steel Lock, Hinged Lid, 1700s, 5½ x 4¼ In. ....*illus* 702
Maple, Coffin Shape, Pagoda Top, Hinged, Bone Pulls, Ball Feet, 6 x 7½ In. 484
Pewter, Gilt, Mountains, Houses, Trees, China, 6½ x 7 In., Pair.......... 184
Porcelain, Multicolor Flowers, Gilt, White Ground, 8-Sided, 4 x 3 x 2 In. 210
Porcelain, Red, Blue, White, Double Ring Mark, 7 In., Pair 184
Quillwork, Rolled Paper, 6-Sided, Faux Malachite Cameo, Hinged Lid, c.1800, 5 In. ....*illus* 2074
Quillwork, Wood, Flowers, Heart, 8-Sided, Ribbon, Metal Handle, 4 x 5 In. ....*illus* 400
Rosewood, Casket Shape, Mother-Of-Pearl Escutcheon, Ring Handles, c.1835, 8 x 13 In. 593
Rosewood, Coffin Shape, Dome Lid, 2 Compartments, England, 1800s, 5 x 10 In. 214
Rosewood, Mother-Of-Pearl, Inlaid, Coffin Shape, Sprigs, Bun Feet, 1800s, 7 x 12 In. 294
Rosewood, Pyramid Lid, 6 x 8 In. 344
Satinwood, Inlay, Flower Bouquet, Octagonal, 5 x 7½ In. 522
Satinwood, Marquetry, Inlay, Single Cube, Oval, Fan, Patera, George III, 5 x 4 In. 1089
Satinwood, Sycamore, String Inlay, Flower Heads, Ivory Escutcheon, 8 x 5 In. 2162
Silver, Armorial, Dome Lid, Finial, Engraved, Stevens & Huntley, 5 x 3½ In. 909
Silver, Bird In Oval, Falconer, Flutist, Woman, Lid, Gorham, 5 x 3 In. 600
Silver, Blossom, Georg Jensen, 5 x 3 In. 3965
Silver, Enamel Scenic Panels, Birds, Coral, Turquoise, Chinese, c.1910, 6½ In. 1560
Silver, Gold Wash, Birmingham, England, 1896, 19 x 15 In. 125
Silver, Lobed, Lid, Flame Finial, George Nathan & Ridley Hayes, Edwardian, 6 In. 427
Silver, Narrative Scenes, Lion Shape Feet, 5 x 7 In. 1599
Silver, Oval, Beaded Rims, Wood Finial, Nathan & R. Haynes, 1903, 6 x 5½ In. 390
Silver, Oval, Husk Banding, Ribbed, Hinged Dome Lid, George III, 1801, 6 In. 1721
Tin, Painted, Long-Tailed Bird, Leaves, 6-Sided, c.1810, 5 In. ....*illus* 1230
Tin, Painted, White, Green & Yellow Flower, Leaves, Japanned Ground, 1800s, 6 In. 1722
Tole, Black, Gold Bands, 18 In. 94
Tortoiseshell, Glass Knob Pulls, Regency, 5 x 8 In. 2420
Tortoiseshell, Hinged Lid, Inlay, Silver Plate Ring Pull, c.1800, 6 x 12 In. 2375
Tortoiseshell, Mother-Of-Pearl Inlay, Serpentine, Hinged Lid, c.1890, 7 x 5 In. 1875
Tortoiseshell, Octagonal, Oval Mother-Of-Pearl Escutcheon, 4¾ x 6½ In. 1089
Tortoiseshell, Silver Inlay, 2 Covered Compartments, Silver Lock Escutcheon, 7 x 4½ In. 1573
Tortoiseshell, Silver Inlay, Brass Pulls, 4 Ball Feet, Regency, 4½ x 6 In. 1452
Tropical Hardwood, Strapwork Lozenges, 2 Foil-Lined Compartments, c.1875, 6 x 13 In. 400
Walnut Veneered, Mahogany, Crossbanded, Hinged Lid, Georgian, c.1800, 4 x 4 In., Pair.......... 562
Walnut, Satinwood Marquetry, Dome Lid, Shield, Scroll, Hinge, Brass Knobs, 6 x 9 In. 544
White Brass, 6-Sided, Engraved, Flowers, Butterflies, Birds, 19th Century, 5 In. 110

TEA LEAF IRONSTONE dishes are named for their decorations. There was a superstition that it was lucky if a whole tea leaf unfolded at the bottom of your cup. This idea was translated into the pattern of dishes known as "tea leaf." By 1850 at least twelve English factories were making this pattern, and by the 1870s it was a popular pattern in many countries. The tea leaf was always a luster glaze on early wares, although now some pieces are made with a brown tea leaf. There are many variations of tea leaf designs, such as Teaberry, Pepper Leaf, and Gold Leaf. The designs were used on many different white ironstone shapes, such as Bamboo, Lily of the Valley, Empress, and Cumbow.

Ashtray, Red Cliff, 4 x 4 In. 17
Bone Dish, Red Cliff, 7 In. 16
Bowl, Dessert, Alfred Meakin, 4¾ In. 24
Bowl, Vegetable, A.J. Wilkinson, 7 x 7 In. 97
Bowl, Vegetable, Alfred Meakin, 7 x 7 In. 74
Bowl, Vegetable, Footed, Lid, Alfred Meakin, 9 x 9 In. 192
Bowl, Vegetable, Grindley, 9 In. 80
Bowl, Vegetable, Oval, A.J. Wilkinson, 8¾ In. 84
Bowl, Vegetable, Oval, Alfred Meakin, 9 In. 101
Bowl, Vegetable, Red Cliff, 6 x 6 In. 114
Bowl, Vegetable, Round, Adams, 9 In. 54
Bowl, Vegetable, Round, Wedgwood, 9 In. 127
Bowl, Vegetable, Wedgwood, 8 x 8 In. 109
Butter, Cover, Ribbed Corners, Alfred Meakin, ¼ Lb. 179
Cake Plate, Handles, Adams, 11¾ In. 104
Coffeepot, Lid, A.J. Wilkinson, 4 Cup, 6½ In. 233
Coffeepot, Lid, Alfred Meakin, 7 Cup, 7¼ In. 187
Coffeepot, Lid, Red Cliff, 5 Cup, 7 In. 155
Coffeepot, Lid, Wedgwood, 7 Cup, 7 In. 178
Creamer, Paneled, Adams, 8 Oz., 3 In. 27
Creamer, Red Cliff, 12 Oz., 5 In. 40
Cup & Saucer, Adams, Demitasse, 2 In. 49
Cup & Saucer, Red Cliff 24
Gravy Boat, Alfred Meakin 82
Gravy Boat, Furnivals 108
Gravy Boat, Grindley 108
Gravy Boat, Red Cliff 109
Gravy Boat, Underplate, Wedgwood 183
Nappy, Wedgwood, 4 In. 17
Pitcher, 64 Oz. 139
Pitcher, Adams, 32 Oz., 7 In. 103
Pitcher, Luster Glaze, Panels, Shaped Handle & Rim, Red Cliff, 1950s, 8 In. .... *illus* 119
Pitcher, Red Cliff, 40 Oz., 7¼ In. 62
Plate, Bread & Butter, Red Cliff, 6 In. 8
Plate, Dinner, Adams, 10 In. 26
Plate, Dinner, Grindley, 10 In. 35
Plate, Dinner, Mellor Taylor, 9¾ In. 10
Plate, Dinner, Red Cliff, 10 In. 13
Plate, Dinner, Wedgwood, 10 In. 21
Plate, Luncheon, A.J. Wilkinson, 9 In. 11
Plate, Luncheon, Alfred Meakin, 8¾ In. 14
Plate, Luncheon, Mellor Taylor, 9 In. 12
Plate, Salad, Anthony Shaw, 8 In. 14
Plate, Salad, Red Cliff, 8 In. 9
Platter, A.J. Wilkinson, 17 In. 249
Platter, Furnivals, 13 In. 62
Platter, Oval, Alfred Meakin, 16 In. 169
Platter, Oval, Anthony Shaw, 15 In. 73
Platter, Oval, Mellor Taylor, 11 In. 122
Platter, Ribbed Edge, Grindley, 15 In. 85
Relish, Handles, Alfred Meakin, 8½ In. 32
Salt & Pepper, Octagonal Foot, Adams 111
Soup, Dish, Adams, 8 In. 32
Soup, Dish, Mellor Taylor, 9 In. 34
Soup, Dish, Rim, Wedgwood, 9 In. 26
Sugar, Lid, Paneled, Adams, 4 In. 42
Sugar, Lid, Square, A.J. Wilkinson, 5 In. 112

Sword, Presentation, Indian, Hilt, Tulwar, Curved Blade, 2 Fullers Per Side, Engraved, 34 In.
$3,072

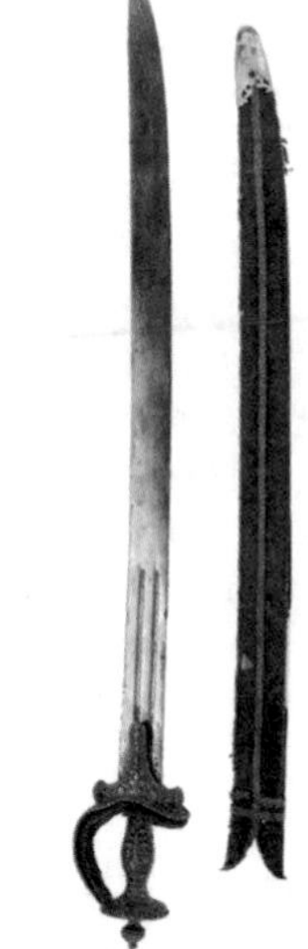

Freeman's Auctioneers & Appraisers

Syracuse, Coralbel, Cup & Saucer, Platinum Trim, Footed, c.1955
$12

Ruby Lane

Tea Caddy, Fruitwood, Pear Shape, Foil Lined, c.1800, 6½ x 3½ In.
$1,168

New Orleans (Cakebread)

Tea Caddy, Fruitwood, Pear Shape, George III, 1700s, 7 ½ x 5 In.
$687

New Orleans (Cakebread)

Tea Caddy, Maple, Apple Shape, Applied Stem, Steel Lock, Hinged Lid, 1700s, 5 ½ x 4 ¼ In.
$702

Thomaston Place Auction

Tea Caddy, Quillwork, Rolled Paper, 6-Sided, Faux Malachite Cameo, Hinged Lid, c.1800, 5 In.
$2,074

DuMouchelles Art Gallery

T

TIP

Don't hide all your valuables in one place. Burglars may miss some hiding places.

Tray, Rectangular, Anthony Shaw, 10 In. 56
Tureen, Lid, Red Cliff 278

TECO is the mark used on the art pottery line made by the American Terra Cotta and Ceramic Company of Terra Cotta and Chicago, Illinois. The company was an offshoot of the firm founded by William D. Gates in 1881. The Teco line was first made in 1885 but was not sold commercially until 1902. It continued in production until 1922. Over 500 designs were made in a variety of colors, shapes, and glazes. The company closed in 1930.

Figure, Elephant, Gray, Made For Westinghouse Building, Plinth Base, 17 x 20 In. .... *illus* 2530
Pitcher, Aventurine, Stamped, Terra-Cotta, Ill., c.1910, 4 x 5 In. 688
Vase, 3 Buttresses, Round Foot, Green, 11 ¾ x 5 ½ In. 1320
Vase, Beaker Shape, 4 Buttressed Handles, Brown Matte Glaze, Stamped, 1910, 7 x 4 In. 1500
Vase, Beaker Shape, Flared Foot, Flat Rim, 4 Loop Handles, Green, 1910, 15 x 10 In. 3750
Vase, Blue Glaze, Reticulated Design, Wavy Rim, Ring Foot, c.1910, 12 x 5 In. .... *illus* 1250
Vase, Buttressed, Terra-Cotta, Stamped, Ill., c.1910, 5 x 3 In. 750
Vase, Cylindrical, Flared Foot, 4 Buttressed Handles, Green, Stamped, 1910, 17 x 10 In. 9375
Vase, Cylindrical, Openwork Leaves Shoulder, Trumpet Neck, Green Matte, c.1902, 12 In. 6573
Vase, Elongated Lobed Oval, Flat Rim, Light Green, Stamped, 1910, 10 In. 2250
Vase, Green Glaze, Shouldered, Reticulated Elongated Leaves, Flared Rim, 11 x 4 In. 3000
Vase, Green, Cylindrical, 4 Squared Buttresses, 11 ¾ x 5 In. 1625
Vase, Green, Two Handles, 6 x 9 In. 1020
Vase, Narrow Neck, Green, 11 In. 369
Vase, Oblong Shape, Buttressed, Red Matte Glaze, Charcoaling, 6 In. 920
Vase, Rosehip Shape Rim, Green, 4-Footed, Stamped, 1910, 19 x 7 In. 1563
Vase, Squash Blossom, Green, Squat Bulbous Base, Flared Neck, Ruffled, 10 x 7 In. 1625
Vase, Squat, Twin Circle Cutout Handles, Green Matte Glaze, Charcoaling, 5 ½ In. 546

TEDDY BEARS were named for a president of the United States. The first teddy bear was a cuddly toy said to be inspired by a hunting trip made by Teddy Roosevelt in 1902. Morris and Rose Michtom started selling their stuffed bears as "teddy bears" and the name stayed. The Michtoms founded the Ideal Novelty and Toy Company. The German version of the teddy bear was made about the same time by the Steiff Company. There are many types of teddy bears and all are collected. The old ones are being reproduced. Other bears are listed in the Toy section.

Henry's, Mink, Tan, Brown Nose, Jointed, Glass Eyes, Tag, 1987, 12 In. 72
Hermann, Mohair, Tan, Jointed, 12 In. 42
Mohair, Tan, Humpback, Jointed, Glass Eyes, 20 In. 480
Mohair, White, Brown Nose, Center Seam Face, 5-Way Jointed, 20 In. 4537
Steiff, Beige, Swivel Head, Shoebutton Eyes, Stitched Details, Button In Ear, 12 In. .... *illus* 1416
Steiff, Bruin, Gold Fur, Shoebutton Eyes, Stitched Nose, Button In Ear, 18 In. 3835
Steiff, Mohair, Apricot, Shoebutton Eyes, c.1907, 12 In. 1560
Steiff, Mohair, Black, Jointed, Button In Ear, 4 In. 133
Steiff, Mohair, Brown Nose, Plastic Eyes, Camel Felt Pads, Silver Button, 11 In. 110
Steiff, Mohair, Golden, Humpback, Jointed, Button In Ear, 23 In. 240
Steiff, Mohair, White, Brown Nose, Jointed, Button In Ear, 3 ½ In. 133
Teddy B. Roosevelt, Laughing, Gold Mohair, Glass Eyes, Mouth Opens, 14 In. 1440

TELEPHONES are wanted by collectors if the phones are old enough or unusual enough. The first telephone may have been made in Havana, Cuba, in 1849, but it was not patented. The first publicly demonstrated phone was used in Frankfurt, Germany, in 1860. The phone made by Alexander Graham Bell was shown at the Centennial Exhibition in Philadelphia in 1876, but it was not until 1877 that the first private phones were installed. Collectors today want all types of old phones, phone parts, and advertising. Even recent figural phones are popular.

American Bell Telephone Co., Public, Wall Mount, Oak, Type 21, 8 x 32 x 13 In. .... *illus* 714
American Electric Telephone Co., Switchboard, Wood Case, Shelf, 11 x 26 In. 399
American Telegraph & Telephone Co., Candlestick Neck, Round Dial, Handle, 12 In. 300
Booth, Door, Wood, Paint, Glass Inserts, Seat & Shelf, 1940s, 30 ½ x 83 In. 150
Booth, Metal, Folding Door, Coin-Operated Rotary Phone, 1950s, 85 x 30 In. .... *illus* 266
Booth, Oak, Folding Door, Tin Liner, Seat, Rotary Phone, Western Electric, 89 x 31 In. .... *illus* 976
Case, Oak, c.1900, 20 In. 35
Ettore Sottsass, Gray, White, Boxy, Corded, Enorme, 5 x 12 In. 240
Illinois Telephone Co., Bell System, Oak, Wall Mount, Pay, c.1910, 17 x 21 In. 671
Jydsk Telefon, Desk, Denmark, c.1910, 12 x 6 In. 120
Kellogg, Crank, Added, Oak Wood Case, 1920 Style, 8 x 25 In. 210
Rotary, Lucite, Visible Wires, Black Handset, 18 x 8 In. 240
Western Electric, Rotary, Paint, Nickel Plate, Multi-Coin, c.1970, 6 x 19 In. 270

Tea Caddy, Quillwork, Wood, Flowers, Heart, 8-Sided, Ribbon, Metal Handle, 4 x 5 In.
$400

Cowan Auctions

Tea Caddy, Tin, Painted, Long-Tailed Bird, Leaves, 6-Sided, c.1810, 5 In.
$1,230

Skinner, Inc.

Tea Leaf Ironstone, Pitcher, Luster Glaze, Panels, Shaped Handle & Rim, Red Cliff, 1950s, 8 In.
$119

Ruby Lane

Teco, Figure, Elephant, Gray, Made For Westinghouse Building, Plinth Base, 17 x 20 In.
$2,530

Humler & Nolan

Teco, Vase, Blue Glaze, Reticulated Design, Wavy Rim, Ring Foot, c.1910, 12 x 5 In.
$1,250

Rago Arts and Auction Center

Teddy Bear, Steiff, Beige, Swivel Head, Shoebutton Eyes, Stitched Details, Button In Ear, 12 In.
$1,416

Bertoia Auctions

Telephone, American Bell Telephone Co., Public, Wall Mount, Oak, Type 21, 8 x 32 x 13 In.
$714

Showtime Auction Services

Telephone, Booth, Metal, Folding Door, Coin-Operated Rotary Phone, 1950s, 85 x 30 In.
$266

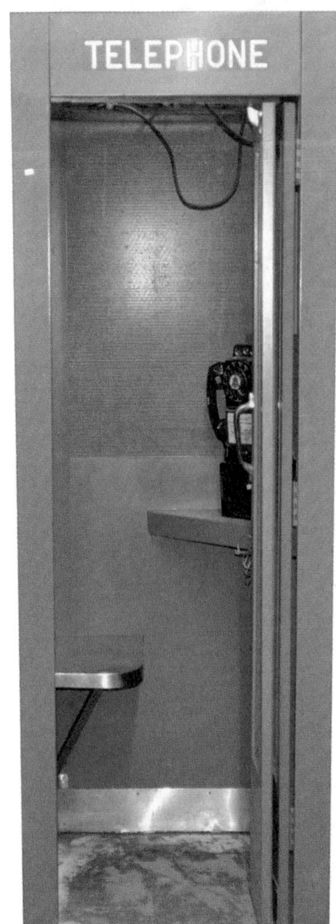

Hess Auction Group

T

Telephone, Booth, Oak, Folding Door, Tin Liner, Seat, Rotary Phone, Western Electric, 89 x 31 In.
$976

Morphy Auctions

Television, Philco, Predicta, Dark Model G-4242 M, Swivel Tube, Tubes, 1950s, 26 x 29 In.
$427

Morphy Auctions

Television, Philco, Predicta, Tube, Turquoise Console, Speaker Base, 1950s, 49 x 24 In.
$759

James D. Julia Auctioneers

TELEVISION sets are twentieth-century collectibles. Although the first television transmission took place in England in 1925, collectors find few sets that pre-date 1946. The first sets had only five channels, but by 1949 the additional UHF channels were included. The first color television set became available in 1951.

Philco, Predicta, 2-Tone Wood Stand, Front Speaker, 1950s, 46 In. 850

Philco, Predicta, Dark Model G-4242 M, Swivel Tube, Tubes, 1950s, 26 x 29 In. .... *illus* 427

Philco, Predicta, Tube, Turquoise Console, Speaker Base, 1950s, 49 x 24 In. .... *illus* 759

Philips, Keracolor, Spherical, White, 1970s, 36 In. 200

RCA Victor, Model 14-S-7073G, Black, White, Chevrons, Bronze Trim, 1957, 14 In. 37

TEPLITZ refers to art pottery manufactured by a number of companies in the Teplitz-Turn area of Bohemia during the late nineteenth and early twentieth centuries. Two of these companies were the Alexandra Works founded by Ernst Wahliss, and the Amphora Porcelain Works, run by Riessner, Stellmacher, and Kessel.

Bowl, Blue Bouquets, Urns, Yellow, Stippled Cream Glaze, Ernst Wahliss, 3 ½ x 7 In. 236

Card Tray, Figural Maiden, Flowers, Flowing Gown Forms Tray, 17 In. 2666

Compote, Pink Flowers, Jewels, Orange Peel Surface, Arched Leaf Handles, Footed, 6 x 11 In. ... 236

Ewer, Bearded Man Mask, Draped Woman Shape Handle, Wahliss, 13 ½ x 8 ½ In. 200

Ewer, Double Gourd, Enamel Accents, Loop Handle, Glazed, Amphora, 12 In. 58

Group, Porcelain, Robed Woman, Boy, Fountain, Garland, Austria, 24 ½ x 10 In. 2000

Pitcher, Elongated, Scrolled Flower Handle, Poppies, Ernst Wahliss, 1890s, 28 In. .... *illus* 3500

Pitcher, Figural, Black Man, Bag & Hat, Mouth Spout, Amphora, 12 In. 100

Vase, Art Nouveau, Beauty & Poppies, Woman's Portrait, Domed, Tapered, 12 x 7 In. 472

Vase, Bird, Vines, Green, Black, White & Red, 2 Loop Handles, Amphora, 16 In. 431

Vase, Eastern Dragon, Blue, Beige, Amphora, c.1900, 17 In. 7380

Vase, Green Metallic Glaze, Frog On Rim, Weed Stems, Leaves, c.1910, 9 ½ In. 308

Vase, Green, Mottled, Gilt, Bird, Insects, Flowers, Oval, Trumpet Neck, Handles, c.1900, 19 In. ... 113

Vase, Iris & Tulip Design, Crackle Ground, Swollen Shoulder, Saucer Foot, Amphora, 11 In. 356

Vase, Molded Dragon, Spiked Spine, Coiled, Cream Glaze, Gilt, Amphora, c.1900, 30 In. 6292

Vase, Molded Women, Flowing Green Hair, Gilt Flower, Spider Web, Wood Base, c.1910, 14 In. ... 3750

Vase, Octopus, Gold, Green, Modeled, Bulbous, 2 Tentacle Handles, Amphora, 9 In. .... *illus* 3851

Vase, Pear Shape, Wavy Rim, Up-Scrolled Handles, Poppies, Faux Jewels, 11 In. 431

Vase, Portrait, Maiden, Gilt Flowing Hair, Cream Flowers, Trees, Tapered, Amphora, 6 In. 2074

Vase, Seminude Woman, Reaching, Dangling Flower, 1900, 24 In. .... *illus* 10665

Vase, Stylized Fern, Gold Trim, Tapered, 4 Curling Leaf Handles, P. Daschel, 6 In. 1896

Vase, Tapered Cylinder, Marigolds, Jewels, Metallic Ground, Rim Band, 11 In. 690

Vase, Tapered, Paneled, Maiden Mask, Vine Handles, Green, Orange, 12 ½ In. 345

Vase, Urn Shape, Scroll Handles, Gilt, Green Ground, Courting Couple, Amphora, 11 In., Pair ... 756

Vase, Wasp, Flowers, Gilt Handles, Amphora, 7 In. 1107

Vase, Woman With Crown, Mottled Bands, Maroon, Cream, Flowers, Jewels, Amphora, 7 In. 3851

TERRA-COTTA is a special type of pottery. It ranges from pale orange to dark reddish-brown in color. The color comes from the clay, which is fired but not always glazed in the finished piece.

Bowl, Tin Glazed, Blue & White, Spain, 11 ½ In. 300

Bowl, Tin Glazed, Blue & White, Swags, White Center, 10 ½ In. 360

Bust, Albrecht Durer, Albert-Ernest Carrier-Belleuse, France, c.1875, 22 In. 3750

Bust, Apollo, Waisted Round Socle, Impressed Stamp, 13 In. 369

Bust, Classical, Boy, 1900s, 14 x 8 In. 1500

Bust, Madame Du Barry, Draped, Upswept Hair, Sideways Glancing, c.1900, 29 x 17 In. 1168

Bust, Napoleon, As Caesar, Laurel Wreath, c.1900, 23 x 12 In. 1250

Bust, Princessa D'Aragona, After Francesco Laurana, 18 x 16 ½ In. 1037

Bust, Rembrandt, Albert-Ernest Carrier-Belleuse, France, c.1875, 22 In. 1375

Bust, Ribbon Tied Hair, Double Strand Necklace, 16 ½ x 21 In. 9000

Bust, Richard III, Painted, Long Hair, Hat, Shaped Wood Base, Italy, 20 x 22 In. 1187

Bust, Roman, White Robes, 33 ½ In. 875

Bust, Woman, Rustic Walled City On Head, Hair In Chignon, 23 x 17 In. 3240

Figurine, Bulldog, Seated, Glass Eyes, Studded Collar, Austria, c.1900, 20 In. 3125

Figurine, Cupid & Psyche, Embracing, c.1900, 13 x 15 In. 1250

Figurine, Dog, Black Ears, Collar, 8 ½ In. 188

Figurine, Dog, In Boot, Glass Eyes, Lace-Up Shoe, 11 x 9 ½ In. 372

Figurine, Dwarf, Working With Metal Tools, Jon Maresch, 25 In. .... *illus* 780

Figurine, Goddess Diana, Holding Bird's Nest, Seated Dog, Pedestal, 69 x 19 In. 338

Figurine, Leopards, Reclining, Raised Paw, Crossed Paws, 1900s, 20 x 27 In., Pair 2500

Figurine, Monkey Family, Dressed In Sunday Best, On Brick Wall, Multicolor, 8 x 9 In. 351

Figurine, Woman, In Gown, Rosary, Holding Amphora, Carved Frieze, 70 In. 3998
Fish, Teal, Mouth Up, Tail Flipped Up, 36 x 14 In., Pair 863
Jar, Cat, Figural, Gray Tabby, Red Bow Around Neck, 10 ¼ In. 248
Pitcher, Picador, Bull, Picasso, Black Glaze, Narrow Mouth, Loop Handle, 1952, 6 In. 1968
Plaque, Relief, Woman Knits In Window, Painted, 13 x 16 In. 288
Potpourri Pot, Silver Mounts, Fluting, Rocaille, Scalloped, Roses, Russia, 1895, 6 In. 7665
Sculpture, Anthropomorphic, Multicolor, Bulbous Protrusions, 27 x 8 In. 605
Sculpture, Falcon, 25 x 21 In., Pair 2574
Sculpture, Foo Dog, White, Blue, Tan, Italy, 36 In. 207
Sculpture, Gatekeeper, Colonial Clothes, Keys, Horn, Holding Lantern, c.1900, 33 In. 83
Sculpture, Horse Head, Red & White Traces, Wood Stand, 13 x 11 In., Pair 3250
Sculpture, Horse, 1 Hoof Up, Standing, Wood Base, 24 In. 1625
Sculpture, Joseph, Mary Magdalene, Glass Eyes, Cork Base, Neapolitan, c.1900, 21 x 23 In. 3501
Sculpture, Putto & Cherub, Hunting, Oval Giltwood Base, c.1900, 20 ½ In. 980
Sculpture, Roman Female, Tarangra, 5 x 2 In. 338
Sculpture, Satyr, Shepherdess, 36 ½ x 13 ½ In. 720
Sculpture, Woman, Standing Barefoot, Harvesting Wheat, France, 25 In. 290
Statue, Maiden In Dress, Hat, Urn, Garden, c.1910, 27 In. *illus* 2000
Urn, 2 Handles, Square Base, 1900s, 25 ½ x 31 In. 375
Urn, Fluted, Square Base, 1900s, 33 x 26 In., Pair 500
Urn, Fronds, Boys, Pedestal, 2 Parts, 24 x 35 In. 175
Urn, High Relief, Handles, 20 ½ In., Pair 2750
Urn, High Shoulders, Square Base, White Paint, Lid, Finials, Italy, 33 x 13 In., Pair 2214
Vase, Egyptian Revival, Multicolor, Hieroglyph Design, 1800s, 33 In. 1230
Vase, Green, Thick Rim, 30 ½ x 17 ½ In. 2196
Vase, Red, Japanese Characters In Wide Band, c.1950, 10 ½ x 9 In. 297
Vinegar Pot, Yellow Glaze, Narrow Spout, c.1900, 9 x 8 x 6 In. 325

TEXTILES listed here include many types of printed fabrics and table and household linens. Some other textiles will be found under Clothing, Coverlet, Rug, Quilt, etc.

Banner, Carnival, Panamanian Family, Green, Monkeys, J.A. Record, c.1910, 69 x 88 In. *illus* 6765
Banner, Silk Embroidered, Eagle, Flag, Black Silk Mat Frame, c.1900, 18 x 18 In. *illus* 295
Beadwork, Legend Of Clovis, Silk Velvet, c.1859, 31 x 42 In. 615
Bell Pull, Glass Handle, Needlework, Linen Canvas, Crewelwork Patterns, c.1805, 90 In. *illus* 118
Blanket, Hudson's Bay, 4-Point, c.1935, 87 x 90 In., Pair *illus* 518
Book Cover, Burlap, Flame Stitch, Zigzag, Purple, Brown, White, c.1910, 3 ½ x 6 In. *illus* 201
Flag, American, 13 Stars, Applique, Silk, Francis Hopkinson Annin & Co., c.1890, 16 x 25 In. 1416
Flag, American, 13 Stars, Battle Of Cowpen's Pattern, Cotton, c.1876, 12 x 16 In. 960
Flag, American, 21 Stars, Red & White Stripes, Stars, Blue Cotton, c.1850, 49 x 77 In. 3444
Flag, American, 23 Stars, Wool, Applique, Jute Hoist, c.1870, 27 x 36 In. *illus* 3600
Flag, American, 26 Stars, Painted, Linen Hoist, Eyelets, 1837, 175 x 108 In. *illus* 1853
Flag, American, 34 Stars, Carried At Appomattox, Cavalry, Guidon, Silk, Frame, Civil War, 26 x 36 In. 26250
Flag, American, 35 Stars, Double Wreath, Civil War Era, Glazed Cotton, 19 x 29 In. 4613
Flag, American, 35 Stars, Medallion Pattern, Wool Bunting, Civil War, 1863, 93 x 70 In. 5250
Flag, American, 35 Stars, Wool Bunting, Whipped Eyelets, Civil War, 1861-64, 102 x 68 In. 1750
Flag, American, 36 Stars, Cotton, Frame, 1865-67, 17 x 11 In. 1200
Flag, American, 36 Stars, Frame, 8 x 11 ¾ In. 180
Flag, American, 36 Stars, Frame, 17 ½ x 21 ½ In. 480
Flag, American, 36 Stars, Wool, c.1865, 60 x 105 In. 1680
Flag, American, 38 Stars, Printed, Frame, 1876, 34 x 26 In. *illus* 330
Flag, American, 39 Stars, Frame, 15 ¼ x 19 In. 240
Flag, American, 40 Stars, Pressed Dyed On Muslin, Metal Bail, c.1889, 36 x 72 In. 368
Flag, American, 40 Stars, Wool, c.1889, 48 x 80 In. 660
Flag, American, 42 Stars, Uncut Piece, 106 x 24 In. 210
Flag, American, 50 Stars, Tassel, 48 x 68 ½ In. 58
Flag, American, 50 Stars, Tassel, 56 x 97 ½ In. 58
Flag, Colonies, Snake, Join Or Die, 22 x 32 In. 292
Flag, Parade, American, 26 Stars, Vertical Rows, 7-6-7-6, Cotton, 11 x 20 In. 780
Flag, Presidential, Gold Fringe, Coat Of Arms, 4 Silk Stars, Silk, c.1916-45, 72 x 116 In. 1440
Fragment, Apotheosis Of Washington, B. Franklin, Printed, c.1800, 21 x 31 In., 2 Piece *illus* 1353
Handkerchief, Boys Playing Cricket, Linen, Cream Color, Print Border, 14 x 14 In. 30
Needlepoint, Angel, Musical, Flowing Robe, Playing Harp, Multicolor, c.1920, 71 x 45 In. 69
Needlework, Embroidered, Silk Thread, Urn, Pumpkin, Serpent, Fruit, Frame, c.1899, 36 x 12 In. 106
Needlework, Embroidered, Silk, Classical Scene, Servant Pouring Water, c.1810, 21 x 17 In. 800
Needlework, Panel, 2 Mourning Woman At Tombstone, Cherub Overhead, Silk, 16 In. 125

Teplitz, Pitcher, Elongated, Scrolled Flower Handle, Poppies, Ernst Wahliss, 1890s, 28 In.
$3,500

Rago Arts and Auction Center

Teplitz, Vase, Octopus, Gold, Green, Modeled, Bulbous, 2 Tentacle Handles, Amphora, 9 In.
$3,851

James D. Julia Auctioneers

Teplitz, Vase, Seminude Woman, Reaching, Dangling Flower, 1900, 24 In.
$10,665

James D. Julia Auctioneers

T

Terra-Cotta, Figurine, Dwarf, Working With Metal Tools, Jon Maresch, 25 In.
$780

Fox Auctions

Terra-Cotta, Statue, Maiden In Dress, Hat, Urn, Garden, c.1910, 27 In.
$2,000

Ruby Lane

T

TIP

Never wash vintage silk, satin, banners, flags, or embroideries. Delicate fabrics may fade or the colors may run, and lightweight fabrics wear out very quickly.

Textile, Banner, Carnival, Panamanian Family, Green, Monkeys, J.A. Record, c.1910, 69 x 88 In.
$6,765

Skinner, Inc.

Textile, Banner, Silk Embroidered, Eagle, Flag, Black Silk Mat Frame, c.1900, 18 x 18 In.
$295

Brunk Auctions

Textile, Bell Pull, Glass Handle, Needlework, Linen Canvas, Crewelwork Patterns, c.1805, 90 In.
$118

Brunk Auctions

Textile, Blanket, Hudson's Bay, 4-Point, c.1935, 87 x 90 In., Pair
$518

Allard Auctions

Textile, Book Cover, Burlap, Flame Stitch, Zigzag, Purple, Brown, White, c.1910, 3 ½ x 6 In.
$201

Hess Auction Group

Panel, Baroque, Seasons, Gold, Garlands, Arches, Flemish, Pair, 71 x 27 In., Pair ... 2187
Panel, Deity On Throne, Holding Plaque, Ink On Silk, Frame, c.1600, 80 x 40 In. ... 18750
Panel, Dragons, Mushroom Shape Clouds, Brocade, Silk, Wool, Japan, c.1910, 64 x 42 In. ... 438
Panel, Embroidered, Antigone, Silk, Frame, 24 x 27 ½ In. ... 363
Panel, Embroidered, Border, Silk, Yellow, Blue, Block, Azerbaijan, 30 x 26 In. ... 10000
Panel, Embroidered, Central Geometric Design, Flowers, Morocco, c.1880, 17 x 84 In. ... 937
Panel, Embroidered, Elephant, Ceremonial Dress, Sequins, Gold Thread, India, 27 x 27 In. ... 47
Panel, Embroidered, Flowers, Multicolor, Cream Ground, 39 x 55 In. ... 100
Panel, Embroidered, Gold Dragons, Flaming Pearl, Clouds, Bats, Frame, c.1700, 28 x 62 In. ... 1250
Panel, Embroidered, Murder Of Feodor Godunov & Tsaritsa, Needlepoint, c.1880, 48 x 64 In. ... 2214
Panel, Embroidered, Navy Blue, Flowers, Waves, Silk, Chinese, 40 ¼ x 16 ½ In. ... 276
Panel, Embroidered, Peacock, Gold Beads, Sequins, Gilt, Frame, India, 27 x 27 In., Pair ... 65
Panel, Embroidered, Shoulao & Magu With Deer, Red Ground, 75 x 30 In. ... 413
Panel, Embroidered, Silk, Flowers, Butterflies, Chinese, Frame, Late 1800s, 27 x 15 In. ... 61
Panel, Embroidered, Silk, Green, Peony, Chrysanthemum, Garlands, 1800s, 80 x 54 In. ... 428
Panel, Embroidered, Silk, Watercolor, Boyarina & Prince, Russia, c.1900, 11 x 8 In. ... 63
Panel, Embroidered, Zodiac Medallions, Gilt Thread, Beads, Sequins, India, 45 x 55 In. ... 95
Panel, Flowers, Paisley, Linen, Ink Printed, Woodblock, Frame, 1800s, 52 x 35 In. ... 1375
Panel, Geometric, Dutch, 1920, 59 ½ x 38 In. ... 570
Panel, Needlework, Hansel & Gretel, Witch, Gingerbread House, Yarn, Black Felt, 27 x 33 In. ... 450
Panel, Needlework, Silk, Seated Scholar, Reading Scroll, Japan, 65 x 39 In. ... 120
Panel, Scroll Painting, Silk, Men On Hunt, Riding Horses, Mountains, Chinese, 61 x 32 In. ... 59
Panel, Silk, Hand Embroidered, Frame, 1958, 26 x 17 In., Pair ... 1560
Panel, Silk, Hand Embroidered, Frame, Chinese, c.1860, 12 In. ... 240
Panel, Silk, Yellow Ground, Stitched Peacock, Flowering Branches, 1800s, 47 x 48 In. ... 623
Panel, Velvet, Silk, Metal Thread, Red, Cream, Anatolia, c.1600, 50 x 22 In. ... 8125
Pillow, Needlepoint, Geometric Design, Multicolor Patchwork, Amish, 1930s, 18 In. ... *illus* 18
Table Cover, Silk Velvet, Peach, Red, Brown, Yellow Tassels, 36 In. ... 300
Table Runner, Marigold Ends, Gray, Green, Blue, Linen, Silk, G. Stickley, 1908, 47 x 17 In. ... 2000
Table Scarf, Needlework, Flower & Scroll Medallion, Urn, Tassels, Victorian, 60 x 60 In. ... 59
Tablecloth, Napkins, Linen, Cream, Ecru Lace Insertions, 116 x 63 In. & 20 x 20 In., 13 Piece ... 732
Tablecloth, Paisley, Center 8-Point Star, Red, Black, Gold, Rust, Fringe, 76 In. ... 885
Tapestry, 2 Peacocks, Flowering Branches, Embroidered, Frame, 1800s, 54 x 32 In. ... 1320
Tapestry, Abstract, Multicolor, Joan Miro, c.1970, 59 x 35 In. ... 570
Tapestry, Alexander The Great & Roxana, Multicolor, Flemish, 1600s, 112 x 163 In. ... 860
Tapestry, Armorial, Ferdinand II Of Aragon & Isabella I Of Castile Crest, 75 x 73 In. ... 938
Tapestry, Art Of Sword Fighting, Point De L'Halluin, France, 36 ½ x 57 In. ... 484
Tapestry, Birds Fighting, Rockwork, Fountain, Belgium, 1600s, 113 x 150 In. ... 12100
Tapestry, Bucolic Scene At Waterside, Women, Machine Made, 43 x 92 In. ... 150
Tapestry, Charles Lindbergh, Historic Flight, Airplane, Spirit Of St. Louis, 63 x 26 In. ... 183
Tapestry, Color Fields, Shag Pile, Geometric, Daga Ramsey, 72 x 32 In. ... 303
Tapestry, Courting Couple, Park, Chateau, Flowers Border, 1800s, 120 x 114 In. ... 3500
Tapestry, Courting Couple, Reclining Women, Frame, 55 x 66 In. ... 457
Tapestry, Courtly Couples, Wool, Cotton, Flower Border, France, 1800s, 47 x 59 In. ... *illus* 307
Tapestry, Family Of King Charles I, Eglomise Frame, England, 1800s, 21 x 15 In. ... *illus* 90
Tapestry, Figure Riding Unicorn, Griffin, Flowers, Vine, 41 x 57 ½ In. ... 176
Tapestry, Flemish Style, After Gobelin, Landscape, People, 78 x 53 In. ... 519
Tapestry, Forested Landscape, Flowery Border, 98 ½ x 58 ½ In. ... 1250
Tapestry, Garden Party, France, c.1900, 72 x 88 In. ... 3965
Tapestry, Girl, Lion, Unicorn, Man & Woman, Rosette, Cord, 32 x 64 In. ... 176
Tapestry, Landscape, Shepherd, Attendants, Sheep, Dogs, Trees, c.1705, 98 x 129 In. ... 2500
Tapestry, Lion, Animals, Rock, Frame, 29 ½ x 68 In. ... 396
Tapestry, Moravian Star, Cream, Blue, Red, 1800s, 88 x 46 In. ... 123
Tapestry, Needlepoint, Falcon, On Branch, Flowers, Gilt Cartouche Frame, 40 x 31 In. ... 434
Tapestry, Needlework, Frontiersman Hunter Figure, Long Rifle, Dog, c.1810, 20 x 16 In. ... 369
Tapestry, People In Courtly Dress, Landscape, Wool, Silk Accents, c.1590, 78 x 124 In. ... 5535
Tapestry, Putti, Flowers, Garlands, Cream, Dark Border, 43 x 82 In. ... 92
Tapestry, Putti, Woven Wool Panel, Green Velvet, Frame, c.1800, 20 x 8 ½ In., Pair ... 944
Tapestry, Quest, Holy Grail, Swords, Robes, Wool, Belgium, 54 x 77 In. ... 750
Tapestry, Silk Flower Blossoms, Jeweled, Multicolor, Gilt, 52 x 40 In. ... 207
Tapestry, Village, Animals, Man In Boat, Green, Brown, Silk Accents, 1700s, 88 x 94 In. ... 1230
Tapestry, Woman, Gathering Flowers, Serpent Biting Foot, c.1765, 117 x 192 In. ... 10000
Tapestry, Wool, Hunt Scene, Woods, Scrolling Leaf Borders, Belgium, 48 x 59 In. ... 578
Towel, Show, 3 Panels, Birds On Tree, Heart Design, Susana Long, 1823, 14 x 46 In. ... 153
Valance, Chinese Design, White Ground, Festival Tents, 60 x 60 In. ... 246
Wall Hanging, Balloons, Jute Fiber, Embroidered, After Calder, 1974, 70 x 48 In. ... *illus* 5313

TIP
Store textiles flat if possible. A hanger can cause fabrics to sag.

Textile, Flag, American, 23 Stars, Wool, Applique, Jute Hoist, c.1870, 27 x 36 In.
$3,600

Cowan Auctions

Textile, Flag, American, 26 Stars, Painted, Linen Hoist, Eyelets, 1837, 175 x 108 In.
$1,853

James D. Julia Auctioneers

Textile, Flag, American, 38 Stars, Printed, Frame, 1876, 34 x 26 In.
$330

Cowan Auctions

Textile, Fragment, Apotheosis Of Washington, B. Franklin, Printed, c.1800, 21 x 31 In., 2 Piece
$1,353

Skinner, Inc.

T

Textile, Pillow, Needlepoint, Geometric Design, Multicolor Patchwork, Amish, 1930s, 18 In.
$18

Hess Auction Group

Textile, Tapestry, Courtly Couples, Wool, Cotton, Flower Border, France, 1800s, 47 x 59 In.
$307

New Orleans (Cakebread)

Textile, Tapestry, Family Of King Charles I, Eglomise Frame, England, 1800s, 21 x 15 In.
$90

Cowan Auctions

TIP

Use your phone camera at a flea market. Record things you might want to buy later; record marks, etc. to look up.

Wall Hanging, Bright Squares, Screen Print, Tufted Nylon, Gerhard Richter, Germany, 29½ x 30½ In. 960
Wall Hanging, Moon, Bon Art, After Calder, Maguey Fiber, Guatemala, 1974, 5 x 7 In. 8125
Wall Hanging, Moon, Bon Art, After Calder, Maguey, Embroidered, 1974, 60 x 84 In. ....*illus* 9375
Wall Hanging, Stylized Red Orange Tulip Shape Stripes, Verner Panton, 30 x 26 In. 178

THERMOMETER is a name that comes from the Greek word for heat. The thermometer was invented in 1731 to measure the temperature of either water or air. All kinds of thermometers are collected, but those with advertising messages are the most popular.

Abbott's Bitters, Add Zest & Flavor To Beverages, Wood, 21 x 5¾ In. 184
Aluminum, Cast, Wall, Scientific Instrument Co., Detroit, c.1920, 12 x 2 In. 96
Ambulance, Wood, Paint, Ralph Robinson & Son Funeral Directors, c.1910, 15 x 4 In. 242
B-1 Lemon-Lime, More Zip In Every Sip, Tin, Striped, Embossed Bubble, 16 x 5 In. 244
Bronze, Classical Column, Black Slate Vase, Victorian, 11 x 4 In. 119
Calumet Baking Powder, Best By Test, Arched, Yellow, Red, Wood, 22 In. 330
Carter Inx, Arched Top, Porcelain, Red & White, 1915, 27 x 7 In. 210
Cherub, 4 Curved Feet, Bronze, Victorian, 11 In. ....*illus* 295
Coca-Cola, Drink Coca-Cola, Bottles, Leaf Design, Rounded, Tin, 1941, 16 x 7 In. 240
Cox's Shoes, Wood, Shoe Sole Shape, Patina, 21 x 5¾ In. 253
Dairy Queen, Country Fresh Flavor, Ice Cream Cone, Tin Litho, 1950s, 6 x 16 In. 336
Deer Pencils, Wood, Pencil Shape, Red & White Paint, 11 x 2 In. 575
Dwarf, Holding Thermometer, Wood, 10 In. ....*illus* 120
Fan Shape, Tassel, Metal, Bronze, 10 In. ....*illus* 295
Ford, Keep Me, I Bring You Good Luck, Horseshoe, Shamrocks, Mirrored, 10 In. 180
Hills Bros., Tea & Coffee, Man Drinking, Red, Yellow, Arch Top, 1915, 9 x 21 In. 1596
Hires Root Beer, Bottle Shape, Red, Orange, 1950s, 28½ In. 180
Hires, With Roots Barks Herbs, Since 1876, Bottle Shape, Orange, Brown 330
Iver Johnson Arms Co., Brass Frame, Standard Thermometer Co., c.1888, 9 In. 1450
Jacquin's Cordials, Liquor, Old Gaston, Rock & Rye Bottles, Round, 1950s, 12 In. 222
Kayo Chocolate, Bottle, Tin, 13 x 6 In. 225
Koca Nola, Great Tonic Drink, Wood, Arched Top, 24 In. 30
Louis XVI Style, Gilt Bronze, Glass, Pierced Crest, Wreaths, Torches, c.1900, 13 x 6 In. 430
M.F. Rentschler, Wines & Liquors, Wood, Whiskey Jug Shape, 12 In. ....*illus* 207
M.L. Goldman Optometrist, Wood, Blue, Arched Top, 8¼ In. 114
Mug Old Fashioned Root Beer, Belfast, Forecast Pleasure, Round, Tin, 1950, 9 In. 120
None Such Mince Meat, Like Mother Used To Make, Round, Yellow, Brown, 10 In. 257
Prestone Anti-Freeze, You're Safe & You Know It, Porcelain, Red, White, Blue, 37 In. 285
Prestone-Eveready, Anti-Freeze, Does Not Boil Away, Green, Red, Gold, Tin, 36 In. 375
Queen Bess Milk, Metal Frame, White, Red, Black, Blue, Round, 12 In. 120
Saint Paul Milk Co., Baby's Guardian, Pilgrims, Rounded, Celluloid, 6 x 2 In. 138
Sauer's Flavoring Extracts, 10 & 25 Cents, Wood, Arched Top, 7 x 24 In. 325
Shoes, Fitted By X-Ray, Wood, Shoe Sole Shape, 21 x 6 In. 518
Tums, Tin Litho, Glass Cylinder, Rotating, Wall, 3 Sides, Quality Drugs, 10 Cents, 17 In. 214
Vess Beverages, Chalkware, Sign, Grocer, Customer, Delivery Boy, 12 x 16 In. 122
Wards Vitovim Bread, Keeps Him Smiling, Baby Eating, Porcelain, 1915, 21 In. 854

TIFFANY is a name that appears on items made by Louis Comfort Tiffany, the American glass designer who worked from about 1879 to 1933. His work included iridescent glass, Art Nouveau styles of design, and original contemporary styles. He was also noted for stained glass windows, unusual lamps, bronze work, pottery, and silver. Tiffany & Company, often called "Tiffany," is also listed in this section. The company was started by Charles Lewis Tiffany and Teddy Young in 1837 in New York City. In 1853 the name was changed to Tiffany & Company. Louis Tiffany (1848–1933), Charles Tiffany's son, started his own business in 1879. It was named Louis Comfort Tiffany and Associated American Artists. In 1902 the name was changed to Tiffany Studios. Tiffany & Company is still working today and is best known for silver and fine jewelry. Louis worked for his father's company as a decorator in 1900 but at the same time was working for his Tiffany Studios. Other types of Tiffany are listed under Tiffany Glass, Tiffany Gold, Tiffany Pottery, or Tiffany Silver. The famous Tiffany lamps are listed in this section. Tiffany jewelry is listed in the Jewelry and Wristwatch categories. Some Tiffany Studio desk sets have matching clocks. They are listed here. Clocks made by Tiffany & Co. are listed in the Clock category. Reproductions of some types of Tiffany are being made.

Ashtray, Bronze, Ribbed Handles, Gold Dore, Marked, 4½ In. 177
Belt Buckle, 14K Yellow Gold, Slide, Pin Holder, Hoop Belt Holder, Monogram, 2 x 1 In. 299
Blotter Ends, Venetian, Cast Bronze, Dore Finish, Stamped, c.1910, 19 x 2½ In. 104
Blotter, Rocker, Grape Leaf, Caramel Slag Glass, Gold Dore, 2 x 6 In. 230
Blotter, Rocker, Nautical, Fish, Wave Edge, Bronze, Flower Form Handle, 5 In. 889
Bookends, Abalone, Grape Leaves & Clusters, Bronze Dore, 5 x 5 In. 2074

Bookends, Buddha, Seated On Dais, Arched, Bronze, Patinated, 6 In. 185
Bookends, Ninth Century, Blue & Green Glass Cabochons, Bronze Dore, 5 In. 2666
Bookmark, Owl, Red Stone Eyes, 14K Yellow Gold, Clip, Monogram, c.1930, 3 In. 659
Bowl, Bronze Dore, Marked, 9 In. 142
Bowl, Geometric, Bronze, Mother-Of-Pearl, Flared, Footed, 9 In. 384
Box, Bronze, Art Deco, Gold Patina, Blue & Green Enamel, 4 Ball Feet, 4 x 6 In. 1778
Box, Grape Leaf, Bronze, Green Slag Glass, Hinged Lid, Ball Feet, 4 x 3 In. 649
Box, Handkerchief, Pine Needle, Bronze, Beaded Edge, Green Slag Glass, 7 x 7 In. 1422
Calendar Holder, Grape Leaf, Easel Back, Gold Dore, 4 x 6 In. 316
Candelabrum, 4-Light, Bronze, Curved Arms, Inset Green Cabochons, Platform Foot, 13 In. 2252
Candlestick, 3-Light, Bronze, Blown Glass, Green, Spread Foot, 1900s, 15 x 6 In. *illus* 5000
Candlestick, Bronze, Blown Out Glass Cabochon, 4 Supports, Paw Feet, 11 In., Pair *illus* 1599
Candlestick, Dore Bronze, Buttress Top, Amphora Shape Candlecup, 18½ x 5¾ In., Pair 1476
Card Holder, Arts & Crafts, Bronze Dore, Marked Tiffany Studios, c.1910, 10 In. 125
Chalice, Thistle, Dore Bronze, Round Foot, Cone Shape Stem, Leaves, c.1907, 7½ In. 974
Chamberstick, Bronze Leaf Shape Platform, Reticulated Cups, Marked, 7 x 7 In. *illus* 7110
Chandelier, Copper, Tiered, Prisms, 4 Tulip Light Sockets, 8 Leaded Windows, 17½ x 5½ In. 4248
Clock, Bronze, Blue Mottled Enamel, 4 Ball Feet, Tiffany Furnaces, Art Deco, 6 In. 4740
Clock, Carriage, Grapevine, Bronze, Green Slag Glass, Porcelain Face, 5½ In. 3555
Clock, Carriage, Pine Needle, Slag Glass, Porcelain Dial, Gold Patina, 5¼ In. *illus* 2161
Compact, Wave, Mirror, Powder Compartment, 3 x 2½ In. 2760
Frame, Enamel, Calendar Sheets, Red, c.1920, 5¼ x 7¼ In. 6000
Heat Cap, Acid Etched Cutouts, Green, Brown Patina, 5 In. & 4 In., 2 Piece *illus* 1185
Inkstand, Round Base, Repousse, 2 Nude Men, Glass Melon Shape Well, 17 Oz. 1482
Inkwell, Applied Flowers & Garland, Claw Feet, c.1880, 5 In. 13000
Inkwell, Bookmark Pattern, Bronze Dore, 8 Panels, Glass Insert, 3 x 4 In. 474
Inkwell, Bronze, Zodiac, Hexagonal, Canted, Repousse Design, 3 x 6½ In. 235
Inkwell, Grape Leaf, Caramel Slag Glass, Gold Dore, Hinged Lid, 4 x 4 In. 259
Inkwell, Ninth Century, Green & Blue Jewels, Strapwork, Animals, Marked, 2 x 2½ In. 295
Inkwell, Wave, Gilt Bronze, c.1900 840
Inkwell, Zodiac, Bronze, Squat, Paneled, Round Lid, Glass Liner, c.1900, 4 In. 275
Lamp Base, Bronze, 3-Light, Swirls, Tendrils, Lily Pad Feet, Tiffany Studios, 18 In. *illus* 7406
Lamp Base, Harp, Gold Dore, Ruffled Platform Foot, Tiffany Studios, 55 In 830
Lamp Base, Lily, 3-Light, 3 Gooseneck Arms, Brown Patina, Tiffany Studios, 12¾ In. 1185
Lamp Base, Silvered Patina, Adjustable, 3-Light, Tiffany Studios, 19 To 23 In. 2110
Lamp Base, Stick, 4-Light, Ribbed Stem, 4-Footed, Round Base, Tiffany Studios, 25 In. *illus* 4444
Lamp Base, Student, Double, Artichoke, Beaded Trim, Adjustable Holders, 24 To 26 In. 2666
Lamp Screen, Moth, Yellow, Chain, c.1905, 2¼ x 3½ In. 4000
Lamp, 3-Light, Gold Dore Base, 3 Gold Iridescent Lily Shades, Marked, 13½ In. 3450
Lamp, 3-Light, Twisted Stem Base, Favrile Glass, Gilt Bronze, Engraved, c.1910, 16¼ In. 5000
Lamp, 12-Light, Iridescent Lily Shades, Gilt Bronze Lily Pad Base, 20½ In. *illus* 10925
Lamp, Amber Linenfold, Hammered Glass Panels, Bronze Stem, 1950, 26 In. *illus* 7110
Lamp, Apple Blossom Shade, Pink Mottled, Green, Square Base, Stepped, 20 In. 11070
Lamp, Apple Blossom Shade, Pink, Green Mottled, Cream & Brown, Bronze Urn Base, 22 In. 27255
Lamp, Begonia, Leaded Glass, Bronze Tree Base, Tiffany Studios, c.1905, 17 In. *illus* 137000
Lamp, Daffodil Shade, Bronze, Tiffany Studios, c.1905, 19 x 15 In. *illus* 75000
Lamp, Daffodil Shade, Yellow Mottled, Striated Brown & Amber, Bronze Urn Base, 19 In. 28736
Lamp, Desk, Bronze, Pine Needle, Blown Glass, Ribbed Base, c.1910, 12½ In. *illus* 3690
Lamp, Desk, Green Damascene Shade, Harp Base, Vertical Ribs, 18 In. 3851
Lamp, Desk, Green Iridescent Shade, Platinum Swirls, Bronze Base, Artichoke Foot, 17 In. 10498
Lamp, Dogwood Shade, 3-Light, Bronze, Spiral Coil, Copper Cap, 11 x 22 In. 8850
Lamp, Dogwood Shade, Green Mottled Geometric Ground, Bronze Base, Lily Pad Feet, 22 In. 32588
Lamp, Dragonfly Shade, Tree Base, Leaded Glass, Patinated Bronze, Impressed, 32 x 22 In. 112500
Lamp, Fleur-De-Lis Shade, Green, Amber & Cream, Geometric, Bronze Urn Base, 22 In. 8295
Lamp, Floor, Bronze, Handel Shade, Tripod Legs, Pad Feet, Shaped Frame Top, 55 In. 830
Lamp, Gilt Bronze, Favrile Glass, Gold Damascene Shade, Wave, Iridescent Bands, 15 x 8 In. 3795
Lamp, Glass Linenfold Shade, Paneled, Bronze Harp, Round Base, Cabriole Legs, 57 In. 6150
Lamp, Gold Iridescent, Swirled Spread Stem, Cone Shade, Hooked Feather, 15 In. 2015
Lamp, Green Damascene Shade, Bronze Base, Ribbed, Bulbous Platform, Lily Pad Feet, 23 In. 14820
Lamp, Hanger, Stalactite, Orange Iridescent, Drop Shape, Bronze Socket, Chain, 27 In. 1541
Lamp, Kerosene Font, Bronze, 3-Arm Spider, Tiffany Studios, 6¼ In 106
Lamp, Mosaic Glass, Chainmail, Bronze, Shade Engraved L.C.T., 1905, 26 x 16 In. *illus* 37000
Lamp, Mushroom Shade, Pulled Feather, Favrile, Vase Shape Base, c.1910, 17 In. 4500
Lamp, Oriental Poppy Shade, Bronze, Pigtail Finial, Tiffany Studios, c.1910, 78 In. *illus* 1066000
Lamp, Pony Begonia Shade, Tree Base, Leaded Glass, Bronze, Impressed, 17 x 13 In. 137000
Lamp, Spider Shade, Mushroom Base, Leaded Glass, Patinated Bronze, c.1905, 18 x 15 In. 110000

Textile, Wall Hanging, Balloons, Jute Fiber, Embroidered, After Calder, 1974, 70 x 48 In.
$5,313

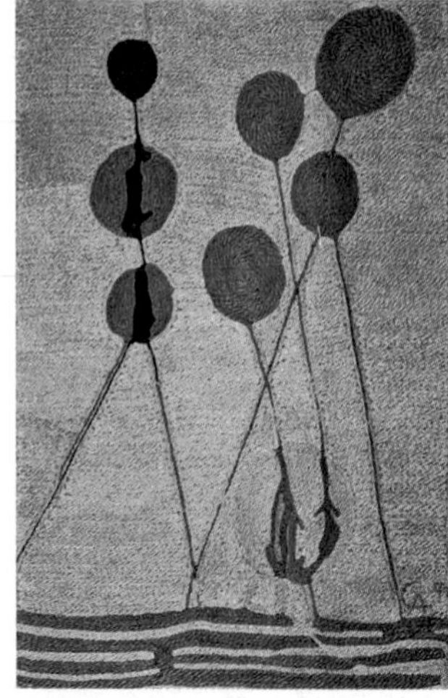

Rago Arts and Auction Center

Textile, Wall Hanging, Moon, Bon Art, After Calder, Maguey, Embroidered, 1974, 60 x 84 In.
$9,375

Rago Arts and Auction Center

Thermometer, Cherub, 4 Curved Feet, Bronze, Victorian, 11 In.
$295

Ruby Lane

This is an edited listing of current prices. Visit **Kovels.com** to check thousands of prices from previous years and sign up for free information on trends, tips, reproductions, marks, and more.

Thermometer, Dwarf, Holding Thermometer, Wood, 10 In.
$120

Fox Auctions

Thermometer, Fan Shape, Tassel, Metal, Bronze, 10 In.
$295

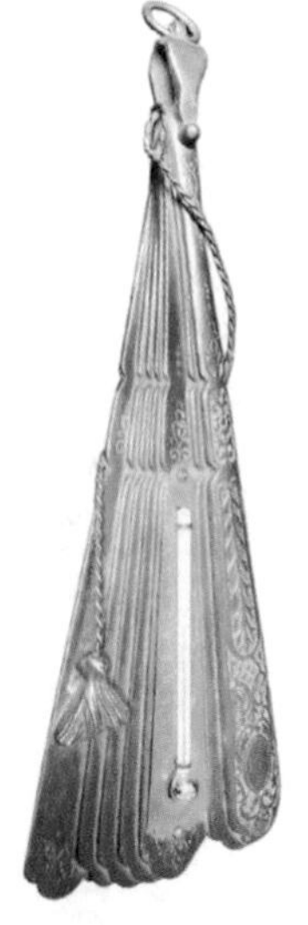

Ruby Lane

Thermometer, M.F. Rentschler, Wines & Liquors, Wood, Whiskey Jug Shape, 12 In.
$207

Glass Works Auctions

Lamp, Tulip Shade, Red & Pink, Mottled Leaves, Amber Ground, Bronze Ribbed Base, 23 In. 35198
Lamp, Turtleback, Favrile, Patinated Bronze, Impressed L.C.T., c.1905, 9 x 16 In. 32500
Lamp, Wisteria Shade, Bronze Tree Base, Patina, Leaded, Impressed Plate, c.1905, 27 x 18 In. ... 334000
Letter Holder, Bronze, Dore, White & Caramel Slag Glass, c.1920, 6 x 10 In. 480
Letter Holder, Grape Leaf Over Slag Glass, Gold Dore, 2 Sections, 5 x 6 In. 184
Letter Holder, Grape Leaf, Bronze, Green Slag Glass, Impressed, 6 x 10 In. 295
Letter Holder, Zodiac, Bronze, 2 Compartments, Marked, 6 x 9 ½ In. 253
Letter Opener, Bronze, Muscular Arm Holding Hammer Handle, c.1910, 8 In. 861
Paperweight, Bronze, Wave & Swirls, Iridescent Glass Center, Shaped, 4 x 3 In. 4444
Paperweight, Zodiac, Bronze, 2 x 3 ½ In. 900
Parasol Handle, Sterling, Abalone Inlay, Cast Shell, Scrolls, Marked, 1800s, 6 x 1 ½ In. 132
Sculpture, Kangaroo, Bronze, Stamped Tiffany & Co., c.1910, 9 ¾ x 7 In. ..... *illus* 938
Smoker Stand, Bronze, Adjustable, Patinated, Gold Dore Tray, Match Safe, c.1910, 28 x 10 In. . 1045
Thermometer, Desk, Pine Needle, Gilt Bronze, Beaded Border, c.1920, 9 In. 2750
Trinket Box, Pine Needle, Caramel Slag Glass, Hinged Lid, Ball Feet, 2 x 6 In. 288
Vase, Marigold Neck, Charcoal Black Leaves, Gold Edging, Gold Iridescent, 8 ½ In. 3776

TIFFANY GLASS

Bowl, Blue Favrile Glass, Ruffled Rim, L.C. Tiffany, 6 In. 960
Bowl, Blue Favrile, Ribbed, Scalloped Rim, Iridescent Gold Interior, c.1910, 3 x 6 In. 615
Bowl, Blue Iridescent, Favrile, Paper Label, 4 x 9 ¾ In. 1434
Bowl, Blue Iridescent, Flower Frog, Favrile, Signed, 4 x 10 ¼ In. ..... *illus* 956
Bowl, Centerpiece, Blue Iridescent, Vertical Ribs, Flared Rim, Favrile, 12 In. 2074
Bowl, Fruit, Gold Favrile, Pink, Purple, Squat, Ruffled Rim & Ribs, c.1900, 10 In. 2045
Bowl, Fruit, Wavy Lobes, Engraved Edge, 2 x 11 In. 632
Bowl, Gold Favrile, Footed, Iridescent, Pulled Handles, Signed, 3 ¾ In. 403
Bowl, Gold Iridescent, Ink Blue Tint, Squat, Ruffled Rim, c.1900, 4 In. 263
Bowl, Green, Bronze Overlay, 6 Ribs, Etched, L.C.T., c.1910, 5 x 6 ½ In. ..... *illus* 660
Bowl, King Tut Design, Ruffled Crinkled Rim, Favrile, 2 x 5 In. 374
Bowl, Lily Pad, Flower Frog, Signed, L.C. Tiffany, 12 ½ x 4 In. 1652
Bowl, Optic Ribbed Body, Onionskin Border, Favrile, Signed, 7 ¾ x 2 In. 144
Box, Desk, Bronze, Grapevine, Lift Lid, Green, Ball Feet, c.1915, 8 x 8 In. 3000
Candle Shade, Gold Iridescent, Pink & Platinum Highlights, Ruffled Rim, 3 ¼ In. 827
Candlestick, Favrile, Pink & White Feathered, Swollen Stem, Flower Cup, c.1900, 11 In. 625
Candlestick, Gold Favrile, Fluted Stems, Reeded Foot, Bulbous Cup, c.1910, 12 In., Pair 3750
Compote, Wisteria, Favrile, 3 ¼ x 3 In., Pair 738
Decanter, Gold Favrile, Bulbous, Stick Neck, Dimpled, Pinched Finial, c.1900, 11 In. 2032
Finger Bowl, Underplate, Gold Favrile, Blue Gold Iridescent, Purple Overtone, 6 x 4 ½ In. 288
Finger Bowl, Underplate, Gold Favrile, Ruffled Rim, Folded Design, c.1900, 6 In. 458
Glue Pot Holder, Green Glass, Bronze Grapevines, Cylindrical, Hinged Lid, c.1915, 4 In. 2125
Goblet, Water, Aquamarine, Favrile, Inscribed L.C.T., 8 ½ In. 345
Ice Bucket, Round, Upward Swirl Handles, Flared Rim, 6 In. 183
Paperweight, Turtleback, Gold Iridescent, Green Highlights, 5 x 4 In. 2713
Plate, Seafoam Green, Radiating Opalescent Bands, Signed, 8 ¾ In. 144
Salt, Favrile, Iridescent, 1 x 1 ¾ To 1 ¼ x 2 In., 4 Piece 142
Salt, Gold Iridescent, Pinched Rim, Marked, L.C.T., 2 ¾ In. 185
Salt Dip, Ruffled Rim, Iridescent, Favrile, Signed L.C.T., 2 ¾ In. Diam. ..... *illus* 395
Scarab, Molded, Transparent Green, 1 ¾ In. 400
Shade, Crocus, Yellow & Green Striated Buds, Green & Cream Ground, Domed, 16 In. 10073
Shade, Hooked Feather, Blue Iridescent, Green, Bullet Shape, 9 In. 3775
Shade, Inverted Dome, Gold Favrile, Iridescent Hooked Feather, L.C.T., 10 In. ..... *illus* 6518
Sherbet, Aquamarine Pastel, Signed, 2 ¼ x 4 ¾ In. 316
Tazza, Green Iridized Top, Laurel Leaf, Opalescent Stem, Base, Inscribed, 6 ¼ In. 575
Toothpick Holder, Vase Shape, Rolled Rim, Amber, Gold Favrile, c.1910, 1 ¾ In. 123
Tumbler, Gold Iridescent, Pinched Waist, 4 ¼ In. 173
Tumbler, Juice, Favrile, 8 Prunts, Gold Ground, Amber, Swollen, 4 In. 127
Vase, Amber, Green Pulled Feather, Bulbous, Swollen Neck, Favrile, c.1910, 2 In. 861
Vase, Blue & Purple, Gold Favrile, Urn Shape, Spread Foot, c.1900, 7 In. 1063
Vase, Blue Favrile, Tapered, Ribbed, Gold & Green Tones, Signed, 11 In. 1150
Vase, Blue Iridescent, Pinched Waist, Vertical X-Shape Ribs, Favrile, 5 In. 2963
Vase, Blue Iridescent, Flowers, Favrile, Bulbous, c.1917, 3 In. 1560
Vase, Blue, Undulating Gold Ensigns, Favrile, Signed, 10 In. 1035
Vase, Favrile, Flower Shape, Ribbed Body, Cupped Foot, Blue, Gold, Magenta, 13 In. 2124
Vase, Favrile, Trumpet Shape, Pulled Feather, Bronze Dore Base, Stamped, c.1900, 11 ½ In. 1000
Vase, Feathered, Blue, Favrile, Squat, Etched, 1901, 2 x 4 In. 2794
Vase, Flower Shape, Gold Iridescent, Favrile, c.1910, 10 ¾ In. 885
Vase, Flower Shape, Pink, Clear, Ruffled Rim, Narrow Stem, Round Foot, c.1915, 9 In. 48750

T

Tiffany, Candlestick, 3-Light, Bronze, Blown Glass, Green, Spread Foot, 1900s, 15 x 6 In.
$5,000

Rago Arts and Auction Center

Tiffany, Candlestick, Bronze, Blown Out Glass Cabochon, 4 Supports, Paw Feet, 11 In., Pair
$1,599

Cowan Auctions

Tiffany, Chamberstick, Bronze Leaf Shape Platform, Reticulated Cups, Marked, 7 x 7 In.
$7,110

James D. Julia Auctioneers

Tiffany, Clock, Carriage, Pine Needle, Slag Glass, Porcelain Dial, Gold Patina, 5 ¼ In.
$2,161

James D. Julia Auctioneers

Tiffany, Heat Cap, Acid Etched Cutouts, Green, Brown Patina, 5 In. & 4 In., 2 Piece
$1,185

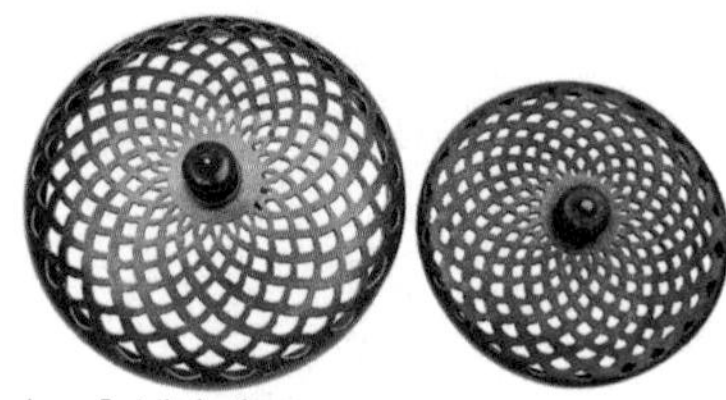

James D. Julia Auctioneers

Tiffany, Lamp Base, Bronze, 3-Light, Swirls, Tendrils, Lily Pad Feet, Tiffany Studios, 18 In.
$7,406

James D. Julia Auctioneers

TIP

Cheesecloth is a good polishing cloth.

Tiffany, Lamp Base, Stick, 4-Light, Ribbed Stem, 4-Footed, Round Base, Tiffany Studios, 25 In.
$4,444

James D. Julia Auctioneers

Tiffany, Lamp, 12-Light, Iridescent Lily Shades, Gilt Bronze Lily Pad Base, 20 ½ In.
$10,925

Cottone Auctions

T

Tiffany, Lamp, Amber Linenfold, Hammered Glass Panels, Bronze Stem, 1950, 26 In.
$7,110

James D. Julia Auctioneers

Tiffany, Lamp, Begonia, Leaded Glass, Bronze Tree Base, Tiffany Studios, c.1905, 17 In.
$137,000

Sotheby's

Tiffany, Lamp, Daffodil Shade, Bronze, Tiffany Studios, c.1905, 19 x 15 In.
$75,000

Sotheby's

TIP

Be careful removing a lightbulb from an old lamp with a glass shade. The Tiffany lily-shaped shades and others are made so that the shade is held in place by a screw-in bulb.

Tiffany, Lamp, Desk, Bronze, Pine Needle, Blown Glass, Ribbed Base, c.1910, 12 ½ In.
$3,690

Skinner, Inc.

Tiffany, Lamp, Mosaic Glass, Chainmail, Bronze, Shade Engraved L.C.T., 1905, 26 x 16 In.
$37,000

Sotheby's

Tiffany, Lamp, Oriental Poppy Shade, Bronze, Pigtail Finial, Tiffany Studios, c.1910, 78 In.
$1,066,000

Sotheby's

Tiffany, Sculpture, Kangaroo, Bronze, Stamped Tiffany & Co., c.1910, 9 ¾ x 7 In.
$938

Rago Arts and Auction Center

Vase, Flower Shape, Purple, Green, Gold Favrile, Ribbed Saucer Foot, Ruffle Rim, 18 In. 1126
Vase, Gold Cypriot Finish, Flowing Lava-Like Band, Gourd Shape, 4 In. 11258
Vase, Gold Favrile, Flower Shape, Etched, 1915, 8 x 3 ¾ In. 750
Vase, Gold Iridescent, Green Lily Pads & Vines, Bulbous, Favrile, 7 In. .... *illus* 1380
Vase, Gold Iridescent, Leaf & Vine, Blue, Purple, Pink, Bottle Shape, 14 In. 3555
Vase, Gold Iridescent, Opalescent, Green, Flower Shape, Saucer Foot, 13 In. 9480
Vase, Gold Iridescent, Pink & Purple, Pulled Feather, Bronze Cylindrical Neck, 6 In. 5925
Vase, Gold Iridescent, Pulled Feather, Green Favrile, Squat, Bulbous, Ring Foot, 6 In. 593
Vase, Gold Iridescent, Trumpet, Ball Standard Footed, Favrile, Signed, 16 ½ In. 1630
Vase, Golden Green Leaves, Trailing Vines, Gold Ground, Urn Shape, 11 In. 4025
Vase, Green Iridescent, Pulled Feather, Metallic, Favrile, Shouldered, c.1900, 6 In. 2390
Vase, Green Pulled Feather, Flower Shape, Ribbed Saucer Foot, Petal Rim, 9 In. 1185
Vase, Green, Gold Iridescent Swirls, Rim & Handles, Swollen Baluster, 7 ¾ In. 14220
Vase, Heart & Vine, Gold Favrile, Elongated Oval, 1912, 11 x 4 In. 1375
Vase, Iridescent, Green Leaf & Vine, Intaglio Carved, Gold Favrile, 12 In. 1067
Vase, Iridescent, Multicolor, Shouldered, Waisted Bottom, Flat Rim, Favrile, 1903, 4 In. 3125
Vase, King Tut, Blue Iridescent, Cream Zigzag, Signed, LCT, 11 ⅜ In. 14220
Vase, Lava, Favrile Glass, L.C. Tiffany, 6 In. 6000
Vase, Leaf & Vine Design, Green, Gold Iridescent Ground, Bulbous, Rolled Rim, 3 In. 1185
Vase, Long Stem, Round Foot, Flower Shape, Ruffles, Amber, Favrile, c.1900, 11 In. 2868
Vase, Metallic Hearts & Vines, Green Iridescent, Favrile, Bulbous, c.1900, 4 In. 2629
Vase, Millefiori, Gold & Green Iridescent, Leaf & Vine, Swollen, Favrile, 9 In. 5333
Vase, Narcissus, White Flowers, Beaker Shape, Paperweight, c.1916, 18 In. 41825
Vase, Orange To Red Favrile, Rolled Rim, c.1900, 7 ½ In. 1375
Vase, Pinched Waist, Lattice Belt Design, Amber, Gold Iridescent, Wide Rim, 4 In. 345
Vase, Pink, Undulating, Gold Favrile, Flower Shape, Wavy Rim, Round Foot, c.1900, 15 In. 1912
Vase, Platinum Iridescent, Blue & Gold, Hooked Feather, Purple Tendrils, 6 In. 13628
Vase, Pulled Feather, Flower Shape, Red, Green, Gilt Metal Base, Signed, 13 In. 1179
Vase, Pulled Feather, Gold, Green, Mauve, Ivory Opalescent Ground, Favrile, 5 x 6 ½ In. 861
Vase, Red Favrile, Pulled Feather, Etched L.C.T., 1906, 3 ¾ x 2 ¼ In. .... *illus* 3750
Vase, Silver Blue Iridescent, Green Heart & Vine, Bulbous, 9 In. 2500
Vase, Tel El Amarna, Gold Iridescent, Red & Platinum, Hooked Decoration, 7 ¾ In. .... *illus* 6037
Vase, Tel El Amarna, Green Iridescent, Cream & Gold Chain Neck, 9 In. 3555
Vase, Trailing Vine, Multicolor, Favrile, Double Gourd, c.1900, 9 In. 50788
Vase, Trumpet Shape, Ball Standard, Gold Iridescent, Favrile, Footed, Signed, 16 In. 1746
Vase, Trumpet, Round Gilt Bronze Foot, Gold Favrile, c.1920, 18 In. 2250
Vase, Twisting Clear & Yellow Glass, Favrile, Marked, 4 ¾ In. 554
Vase, Yellow, Platinum Pulled Feather & Band, Internal Vertical Stripes, 7 In. 1185
Water Sprinkler, Rose, Iridescent Gold, Pink, Favrile, Gooseneck, Squat, c.1900, 10 In. 5079
Window, Blue Mottled Geometric Panels, Green Leaves & Border, 46 x 15 In., Pair 14220

TIFFANY GOLD

Money Clip, 20th Century, 14K Yellow Gold, Marked Tiffany & Co., 2 x ¾ In. 480

TIFFANY POTTERY

Jar, Lid, Raised Milkweed Pods, Old Ivory Glaze, 1900s, 8 x 5 In. 12500
Vase, Artichoke, Ivory Bisque & Glaze, Pinched Waist, 11 In. 1725
Vase, Bisque, Embossed Beech Leaf Sprays, Incised LCT, 5 ½ In. 826
Vase, Embossed Leaves Around Collar, Crystalline Glaze, Tapered, 13 In. 20700

TIFFANY SILVER

Asparagus Fork, Chrysanthemum, c.1880, 10 In. 1312
Asparagus Tongs, Richelieu, Sterling, Monogram, c.1900, 7 ½ In. 523
Asparagus Tongs, Vine, Openwork Blade, Monogram, Mark, c.1900, 8 In. 649
Bowl, Clover, Openwork Repousse Edge, Engraved Monogram, 2 ½ x 9 In. 564
Bowl, Cut Rim, Reeded Ring Base, Tapered, c.1950, 4 x 9 In. 1046
Bowl, Flower Sprays, Gilt Brass Inset Frog, Overhang Rim, c.1930, 16 In. 1845
Bowl, Fruit, Clover, Octagonal, Lobed, Openwork Rim, Monogram, 1898, 10 In. 875
Bowl, Gilt, Scrolling Berries & Leaves, Lobed, Pierced Flared Rim, c.1904, 12 In. 984
Bowl, King Protea, Sterling, Ribbed, Scalloped Body, 3 Ball Feet, 5 x 3 In. 242
Bowl, Navette Shape, Leaf Capped Loop Handles, Flared Foot, 16 In. 1530
Bowl, Reticulated Border, Tapered Rim, Monogram, c.1914, 9 In. 265
Bowl, Reticulated Rim, Rocaille Shells, Scrolling, Flared, Oval, c.1907, 16 In. 1845
Bowl, Scalloped Rim, Footed, 3 x 9 In. 300
Bowl, Sterling, Round, Paneled Sides, c.1947, 9 In. 523
Bowl, Stylized Leaf Shape, Tripod Ball Feet, Marked, c.1960, 7 x 7 In. 153
Bowl, Vegetable, Lid, Chrysanthemum, Lobed, Stirrup Handles, c.1897, 8 x 11 In. 6562
Cake Basket, Twist Handle, Oval Rim, Spade Leaf Chasing, Footed, 11 x 11 In. 518
Cake Basket, Wavy Rim, Flower Clusters, Trellis Panels, 4 Paw Feet, 16 In. 1440

Tiffany Glass, Bowl, Blue Iridescent, Flower Frog, Favrile, Signed, 4 x 10 ¼ In.
$956

Neal Auctions

Tiffany Glass, Bowl, Green, Bronze Overlay, 6 Ribs, Etched, L.C.T., c.1910, 5 x 6 ½ In.
$660

Cowan Auctions

Tiffany Glass, Salt Dip, Ruffled Rim, Iridescent, Favrile, Signed L.C.T., 2 ¾ In. Diam.
$395

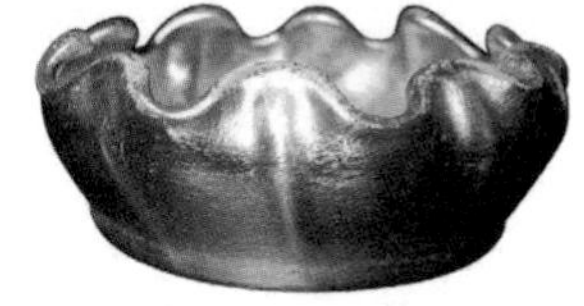

Ruby Lane

Tiffany Glass, Shade, Inverted Dome, Gold Favrile, Iridescent Hooked Feather, L.C.T., 10 In.
$6,518

James D. Julia Auctioneers

TIP

Black lights can detect repairs to antiques that are invisible to the eye, but be sure you use a longwave black light. A shortwave black light could injure your eyes or skin.

Tiffany Glass, Vase, Gold Iridescent, Green Lily Pads & Vines, Bulbous, Favrile, 7 In.
$1,380

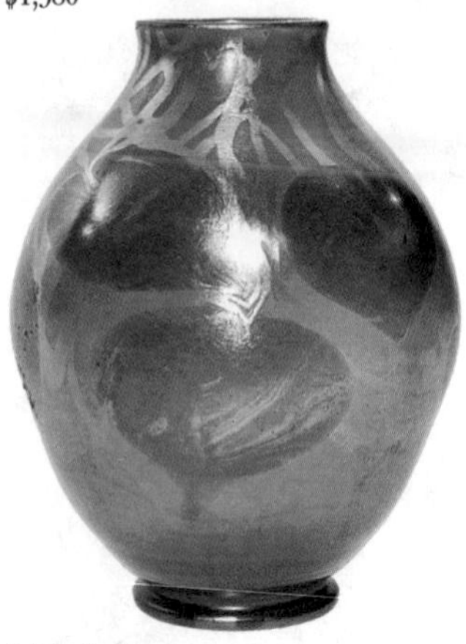

Early Auction Company

Tiffany Glass, Vase, Red Favrile, Pulled Feather, Etched L.C.T., 1906, 3 ¾ x 2 ¼ In.
$3,750

Rago Arts and Auction Center

Tiffany Glass, Vase, Tel El Amarna, Gold Iridescent, Red & Platinum, Hooked Decoration, 7 ¾ In.
$6,037

Early Auction Company

Candy Dish, Swan, Signed, c.1960, 3 ¼ x 8 In. 237
Castor, Mixed Metal, Copper, Beetle, Hammered, Bottle Shape, 5 In. 1230
Cigarette Case, 14K Gold, Rubies, Radiating Incision, c.1925, 3 x 3 ½ In. 308
Clock, Travel, Leaf, Oval, 2 ½ x 2 ½ In. 594
Cocktail Shaker, Cylindrical Lid, Diagonal Spout, Bracket Handle, 1900s, 10 x 5 In. 390
Coffeepot, Baluster, Urn Finial, Dome Lid, Hollow Handle, 1960s, 11 In. 732
Compote, Flared Rim, Knopped Stem, Round Base, 5 ½ x 6 In. 357
Creamer, Smokestack, Loop Handle, Flower Sprays, Gold Wash Interior, c.1865, 6 In. 1476
Creamer, Sterling, Mixed Metal, Gilt Interior, Fish, Butterfly, Flowers, c.1900, 3 In. 450
Cup, Hammered, Tapered, Cylindrical, Double Band Rim, Handle, Footed, 3 ¼ x 4 In. 265
Dish, Entree, Lid, Oval, Divided Liner, Stirrup Handle, c.1923, 5 x 11 In. 1476
Dish, Entree, Lid, Sterling, Faux Bois Loop Handle, Scalloped Rim, c.1891, 9 In. 3321
Dish, Family Crest, Dome Lid, Flower Below Finial, 4 ½ In. 688
Dish, Leaf Shape, Lobed, Round, Embossed Overlapping Stylized Leaves, c.1870, 9 ½ In. 738
Dish, Reticulated Leaf Border, Stepped Foot, Monogram, 9 ½ In. 357
Dish, Scallop Shell Shape, 2 ¾ In., 4 Piece 270
Fish Knife, Vine, Pomegranate, c.1891, 8 In. 1046
Fish Set, Vine, Sterling, 9 Daisy Forks, 12 Pomegranate Knives, 1872, 6 & 8 In. 4305
Fork, Colonial, Sterling, Elongated Ribbed Handle, 4 Tines, 7 In., 7 Piece 253
Fork, Luncheon, Chrysanthemum, Monogram, c.1891, 6 ¾ In., 24 Piece 1599
Jar, Lid, Acorn & Leaf Finial, Duck, Cattails, Scroll, Round, Footed, c.1970, 7 In. 1140
Jug, Hot Milk, Hinged Lid, Leaves, Stippled, Cartouche, Flowers, c.1865, 7 In. 1046
Jug, Hot Milk, Sterling, Monogram, Engraved, Flowers, Scrolls, 8 In. 615
Knife, Bolster Style, Tapered Square Handle, Monogram, 9 In., 12 Piece 242
Ladle, Round Bowl, Relief Flowers, Sterling, Curved Handle, Monogram, 13 In. 307
Ladle, Vine, Tomato, Leaves, Stippled Ground, Scalloped Bowl, 1872, 12 ½ In. 750
Ladle, Wave Edge, Sterling, Monogram, 10 ½ In. 369
Lettuce Fork, Old Ivy, Flared, Rounded Handle, 4 Tapered Tines, 7 x 2 In., Pair 184
Oyster Fork, King's Pattern, 3 Tines, c.1920, 6 In. 230
Pitcher, Aesthetic, Blossoms, Hammered, Beaded, Scrolls, c.1880, 8 ½ In. .... *illus* 10455
Pitcher, Baluster, Repousse Maple Leaves, Copper Veins, Beetle, Frog, c.1885, 10 In. 21250
Pitcher, Hammered, Dragonfly, Beetles & Insects, Tiffany & Co., 7 ½ In. .... *illus* 14663
Pitcher, Inverted Baluster Shape, Reeded Handle, Gadrooned, Footed, c.1907, 10 In. 1353
Pitcher, Round, Cylindrical Neck, 2 Raised Flower Bands, 7 In. 1482
Pitcher, Squat, Leaf Banding, Monogram, c.1900, 7 In. 1230
Pitcher, Sterling, Reeded Rim, Acanthus Handle, c.1947, 10 In. 1353
Pitcher, Tapered, Round Foot, Squared Handle, Wide Spout, Reeded Trim, 10 In. 948
Plate, Engraved Coat Of Arms, Scottish Clan MacLean, c.1930, 10 In. 246
Platter, Molded Rim, Banded Edge, Round, c.1951, 18 In. 1353
Sauce Ladle, Shell Shape, Fiddle Handle, Monogram, c.1905, 7 ½ x 3 In. 118
Sauceboat, Stiff Leaf Border, Oval Foot, 1873-91, 6 ½ x 9 ½ In. 813
Serving Spoon, Tiffany, Oval Bowl, Scroll, Monogram, c.1860, 8 ½ In., 4 Piece 283
Soup Ladle, Palm, c.1937, 12 In. 369
Spoon, Berry & Leaf Design, Ribbon Monogram, Lap Over Edge, 9 In. 529
Spoon, Chrysanthemum, Gold Wash, Reticulated, Scalloped Rim, 7 x 4 ½ In. 272
Sugar Castor, Colonial Revival, Sterling, Baluster Shape, Garland Leaves, 6 ¾ In., Pair 130
Tazza, Beaded, Cartouche, Flowers, Monogram, 1917, 3 ¼ In. 585
Tazza, Reticulated Cast Clover Rim, Footed, c.1907, 3 ½ In. 584
Tea Canister, Center Oak Leaf Wreath, Ribbon Tied, c.1896, 3 ½ In. 554
Tea Set, Repousse Vines, Bulbous, Vine Handles, Ellis & Young, 3 Piece 3555
Teapot, Greek Key, Burner, Stand, 11 ½ In. 829
Teaspoon, Jack & Jill, Gilded Bowl, Dated Monogram, c.1920, 6 In., 12 Piece 861
Tongs, Olympian, 7 In. 1001
Tray, Applied Border, Oval, 16 In. 1492
Tray, Grass & Stem, Gilt Fish & Crab, Shaped Square, Scroll Feet, c.1878, 9 In. 17925
Tray, Integrated Handles, Central Flowers, Octagonal, c.1907, 24 x 20 In. 3576
Tureen, Repousse, Flowers, Leaves, Stippled Ground, Footed, 1875, 8 In. .... *illus* 4270
Urn, Nautical, Lid, Cast Figure Finial, Anchors, Rope, c.1925, 16 In. 2040
Vase, Gilt, Chased Strapwork, Flared Neck, Pierced Rim, Supports, Oval, c.1895, 21 In. 10158
Vase, Inverted Baluster Shape, c.1938, 20 In. 7995
Vase, Putti, Flowers, c.1900, 12 In. 923
Vase, Scalloped Rim, Flowers, Vines, Long Neck, Bulb Body, 1902, 12 ½ In. 2000
Vase, Trophy, Medallion, Crossed Swords, Scale, Monogram, c.1920, 8 In. 253
Vase, Trumpet Shape, Paneled, Shaped Foot, c.1920, 12 In. 531
Vase, Trumpet Shape, Ribbed Morning Glories, Round Foot, 12 ½ x 4 In. 425
Vase, Trumpet, Round Foot, Monogram B, 1914, 20 In. 2500

TIFFIN Glass Company of Tiffin, Ohio, was a subsidiary of the United States Glass Co. of Pittsburgh, Pennsylvania, in 1892. The U.S. Glass Co. went bankrupt in 1963, and the Tiffin plant employees purchased the building and the inventory. They continued running it from 1963 to 1966, when it was sold to Continental Can Company. In 1969, it was sold to Interpace, and in 1980, it was closed. The black satin glass, made from 1923 to 1926, and the stemware of the last twenty years are the best-known products.

Admira, Sherbet, 4 ¾ In. 25
Admira, Tumbler, Iced Tea, 6 ½ In. 26
Alaris, Wine, 5 ¼ In. 41
Allegro, Cordial, 5 ¼ In. .... 29 to 41
Allegro, Goblet, Water, 7 In. 27
Allegro, Plate, Luncheon, 8 ¼ In. 31
Allegro, Tumbler, Juice, 5 In. 18
Florian, Tumbler, Iced Tea, 7 In. 28
Fordham, Goblet, Juice, 5 In. 28
Fordham, Goblet, Water, 7 In. 27
Fordham, Plate, Luncheon, 8 In. 16
Forever, Goblet, Water, 7 ¾ In. 10
Forever, Sherbet, 5 ½ In. 7
Forever, Tumbler, Iced Tea, 6 ¾ In. 8
Fremont, Goblet, Juice, 5 In. 14
Fremont, Tumbler, Iced Tea, 6 ½ In. 10
Garland, Cocktail, 5 ¼ In. 7
Garland, Wine, 6 In. 9
Georgian, Plate, Bread & Butter, Yellow, 6 In. 28
Golden Spring, Sherbet, 6 In. 8
Golden Spring, Wine, Claret, 7 In. 9
Golden Wheat, Goblet, Water, 6 ¼ In. 37
Goteberg, Cordial, 3 ½ In. 14
Goteberg, Goblet, Water, 6 ¼ In. 16
Grecian Star, Goblet, Juice, 3 ½ In. 9
Grecian Star, Punch Cup, 2 ¼ In. 7
Greenbriar, Goblet, Juice, 5 In. 19
Greenbriar, Goblet, Water, 6 ½ In. 15
Greenbriar, Plate, Luncheon, 8 In. 13
Hamilton, Goblet, Juice, 5 In. 24
Hamilton, Goblet, Water, 8 In. 36
Hamilton, Sherbet, 3 ½ In. 12
Hamilton, Wine, Claret, 6 In. 36
Iris, Cordial, 3 ¾ In. 18
Iris, Goblet, Water, 6 ¼ In. 21
Iris, Plate, Luncheon, 8 In. 17
Jap Lily, Punch Cup, 2 In. 9
Jubilee, Sherbet, 4 ½ In. 7
Julie, Goblet, Water, 8 ¼ In. 15
Julie, Tumbler, Iced Tea, 8 In. 7
Juliet, Goblet, Juice, 5 ¼ In. 13
Juliet, Goblet, Water, 5 ½ In. 12
Juliet, Sherbet, 4 ¼ In. 11
Jupiter, Cordial, 4 ¼ In. 18
Jupiter, Goblet, Water, 6 In. 13
Jupiter, Parfait, 6 ¼ In. 11
Jupiter, Sherbet, 4 ½ In. 21
Jupiter, Tumbler, Iced Tea, 6 In. 20
Keats, Sherbet, 4 ½ In. 10
Keats, Tumbler, Iced Tea, 6 ¾ In. 10
Keats, Wine, Claret, 5 ¼ In. 19
Keepsake, Sherbet, 5 ½ In. 7
Kimberley, Goblet, Water, 6 In. 28
King's Crown, Cocktail, 3 ¾ In. 6
King's Crown, Tumbler, Cranberry, 5 In. 21
Kingston, Sherbet, 5 ¼ In. 10
Kingston, Tumbler, Iced Tea, 6 In. 10
Kirsten, Goblet, Water, 6 In. 13
Kissing Birds, Lamp, Painted, Orange & Green, 10 ¾ In. .... *illus* 62

Tiffany Silver, Pitcher, Aesthetic, Blossoms, Hammered, Beaded, Scrolls, c.1880, 8 ½ In.
$10,455

Skinner, Inc.

TIP
Don't display silver on latex paint. It will tarnish quickly.

Tiffany Silver, Pitcher, Hammered, Dragonfly, Beetles & Insects, Tiffany & Co., 7 ½ In.
$14,663

Cottone Auctions

Tiffany Silver, Tureen, Repousse, Flowers, Leaves, Stippled Ground, Footed, 1875, 8 In.
$4,270

Neal Auctions

Tiffin, Kissing Birds, Lamp, Painted, Orange & Green, 10 ¾ In.
$62

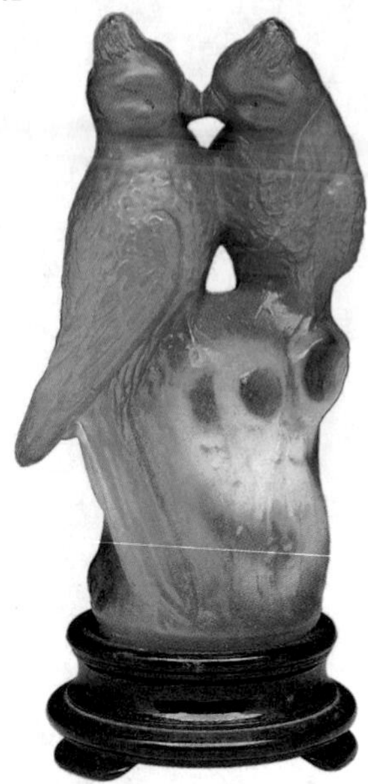

James D. Julia Auctioneers

Tile, Bacchus, Gio Ponti, Buildings, Trees, Ginori, Italy, c.1929, 16 ½ x 10 ½ In.
$5,312

Los Angeles Modern Auctions

TIP
August is the peak month for residential burglaries. April has the fewest home break-ins. Most home burglaries occur in the daytime and the average break-in lasts 17 minutes.

La Fleure, Bonbon, Yellow, 5 ¼ In. 33
La Fleure, Candlestick, Yellow, 3 ½ In. 35
La Fleure, Goblet, Water, Yellow, 8 ¼ In. 48
La Fleure, Plate, Bread & Butter, Yellow, 6 ¼ In. 23
La Salle, Sherbet, Yellow, 6 ¼ In. 11
Lady Carol, Cordial, 4 ¼ In. 23
Lady Carol, Goblet, Juice, 5 In. 21
Lady Carol, Goblet, Water, 6 ½ In. 13
Lady Carol, Plate, Luncheon, 8 In. 15
Lady Carol, Sherbet, 4 ½ In. 25
Lady Carol, Wine, Claret, 5 ¼ In. 9
Laurel Wreath, Sherbet, 5 ¼ In. 11
Laurel Wreath, Wine, 5 ¾ In. 35
Lexington, Goblet, Water, 6 ½ In. 8
Lexington, Sherbet, 5 In. 8
Lexington, Tumbler, Iced Tea, 7 In. 10
Linda, Goblet, Water, 6 ¼ In. 9
Linda, Plate, Luncheon, 8 In. 20
Linda, Tumbler, Iced Tea, 6 ½ In. 23
Linda, Wine, 5 ¼ In. 55
Lisette, Tumbler, Iced Tea, 6 ¾ In. 35
Manchester, Cordial, 4 In. 41
Manchester, Goblet, Water, 7 In. 40
Manchester, Plate, Luncheon, 8 In. 61
Manchester, Sherbet, 5 ¼ In. 12
Mansfield, Goblet, Water, 6 ½ In. 15
Mansfield, Sherbet, 5 In. 8
Mansfield, Wine, 6 In. 25
Marcia, Goblet, Juice, 5 ¼ In. 12
Marcia, Goblet, Water, 6 ½ In. 10
Marcia, Plate, Luncheon, 8 In. 8
Marcia, Tumbler, Iced Tea, 6 ¼ In. 8
Meadow Breeze, Tumbler, Iced Tea, 7 In. 10
Misty Leaf, Cordial, 4 In. 21
Misty Leaf, Goblet, Water, 6 ½ In. 15
Misty Leaf, Tumbler, Iced Tea, 7 In. 11
Moon & Star, Punch Cup, Ruby Flash, 2 ¼ In. 16
Moss Rose, Goblet, Water, 7 ¼ In. 46
Moss Rose, Plate, Luncheon, 8 In. 49
Mt. Vernon, Cordial, 4 ¼ In. 18
Mt. Vernon, Tumbler, Iced Tea, 6 In. 35
Nancy, Goblet, Water, 5 ½ In. 34
Nancy, Tumbler, Iced Tea, 6 In. 30
Octagon, Plate, Salad, Apple Green, 8 In. 18
Octagon, Plate, Salad, Pink, 7 In. 16
Paula, Cordial, 4 In. 23
Paula, Tumbler, Iced Tea, 7 In. 8
Peach Tree, Goblet, Water, 6 In. 13
Peach Tree, Sherbet, 4 ½ In. 8
Peach Tree, Tumbler, Iced Tea, 6 In. 8
Polka, Goblet, Water, 6 ½ In. 32
Prudence, Plate, Luncheon, 8 In. 13
Prudence, Tumbler, Iced Tea, 6 ¾ In. 9
Rambler Rose, Sherbet, Pink, 3 ¾ In. 21
Rambler Rose, Tumbler, Iced Tea, Pink, 5 ¼ In. 13
Valencia, Cordial, 6 In. 35

TILES have been used in most countries of the world as a sturdy building material for floors, roofs, fireplace surrounds, and surface toppings. The cuerda seca (dry cord) technique of decoration uses a greasy pigment to separate different glaze colors during firing. In cuenca (raised line) decorated tiles, the design is impressed, leaving ridges that separate the glaze colors. Many of the American tiles are listed in this book under the factory name.

Aries Astrological Sign, Don Schreckengost, 6 ¼ x 6 ¼ In. 141
Bacchus, Gio Ponti, Buildings, Trees, Ginori, Italy, c.1929, 16 ½ x 10 ½ In. *illus* 5312
Birds, Painted, Blue Ground, Flowers, 4 Squares, 12 x 12 In. 246

Ceramic, Middle Eastern Style, Scrolling Leaves, Turquoise, Green, Blue, White, 8 x 8 In. 207
Cityscape, Yellow, Purple, Midcentury, 12 x 12 In. 369
Delft, Still Life, Bird In Cage, Painted, 22 ½ x 17 In., 3 Piece 2000
Fruiting Branch, Glazed, M. Wildenhain, Pond Farm, c.1950, 7 x 9 In. 1000
Galleon Ship In Wind, Flag, Seahorse, Anchor & Ship's Wheel In Corners, Square, 18 In. 677
Qajar, Ceramic, 8-Point Star Shape, Underglaze Enameling, Animals, Persia, 8 x 8 In. 472
Volcanic Ash, Metal Oxide, Yellow Lichen, Signed Randy O'Brien, 13 x 13 In. 58
White Rabbit, Alice In Wonderland, Brown Slip, C. Pardee Works, 4 ¼ x 4 ¼ In. 1121
Zebra Scene, Pyramid, 15 Tiles On Plywood, Frame, Harris Strong, c.1933, 24 x 36 In. ......*illus* 345

TINWARE containers for household use have been made in America since the seventeenth century. The first tin utensils were brought from Europe, but by 1798, tin plate was imported and local tinsmiths made the wares. Painted tin is called tole and is listed separately. Some tin kitchen items may be found listed under Kitchen. The lithographed tin containers used to hold food and tobacco are listed in the Advertising category under Tin.

Fish Horn, Conical, Wire Ring Hanging Hook, 1800s, 15 ½ In. 47
Mold, Candle, 12 Tube, 10-In. Candle, Arch Foot Base, Tray Top, Handle, 8 x 5 In. 95
Mold, Candle, 12 Tube, Punch Upper Tray, 13 ½ x 6 In. 120
Mold, Candle, 72 Tube, Raised Rim, Wood Frame, Tapering Legs, 1800s, 33 ½ x 43 In. 1046
Nursing Bottle, Cone Shape, Hinged Dome Lid, Loop Handle, 1800s, 3 ¼ In. 83

TOBACCO CUTTERS *may be listed in either the Advertising or Store categories.*

TOBACCO JAR collectors search for those made in odd shapes and colors. Because tobacco needs special conditions of humidity and air, it has been stored in special containers since the eighteenth century.

Arts & Crafts, Sterling On Bronze, Humidor, 6 x 5 ½ In. 132
Blackamoor Schoolboy, Barrel, Humidor, Austria, 7 x 5 In. 216
Brass, Mooring Bollard, Tied With Rope, Nautical Trophies, Anchors, Chains, 10 ¾ In. 5749
Ceramic, Cream, Brown Bands, Inscribed Tabac, 8 ½ x 6 ¼ In., Pair 30
Coal Train Car Shape, Humidor, Inscribed C. & S.W.R., 6 x 13 In. 1125
Cylindrical, Humidor, 1919, 5 x 3 ½ In. 205
Dwarf Comes Out Of Bag, Terra-Cotta, Jon Maresch, 8 In. 120
Dwarf Comes Out Of Gourd, Terra-Cotta, Jon Maresch, 7 ½ In. 192
Falstaff, Figural, Seated, Throne, Cast Iron, Kratzenberg, Germany, c.1840 2375
Figural, Man, Drinking, Cigar Base, Humidor, Bohemia, 1900s, 9 In. 125
Figural, Woman, Bust, Ceramic, Art Nouveau, c.1900, 7 ½ In. ....*illus* 135
George V, Mahogany Inlay, Swags, Humidor, c.1900, 10 x 16 x 12 In. 338
Medieval Style, Metal Mount, Humidor, 11 x 13 ½ In. 720
Munich Child, Sitting On Box, Drinking, Terra-Cotta 503
Owl, Delft, Blue & White, Head Lid, Coat Of Arms, 10 ¼ In., Pair 1751
Silver Plate, Brass, Humidor, 17 ½ x 9 ½ In. 497
Skye Terrier, Egg Shape Box, Humidor, Wood, Anri, c.1926, 10 x 7 ½ In. 1450
Spanish Cedar, Maple Veneer, Inlay, Herring Bone, Humidor, 8 x 15 In. 84
Walnut, Cedar, Brass, Glass, Leather, Bookshelf Facade, Humidor, 8 x 13 In. 316

TOBY JUG is the name of a very special form of pitcher. It is shaped like the full figure of a man or woman. A pitcher that shows just the top half of a person is not correctly called a toby. More examples of toby jugs can be found under Royal Doulton and other factory names.

Brown Coat, Creamware, Multicolor Enamel, Staffordshire, 1700s, 9 ½ In. 738
Man, Seated, Holding Jug, Creamware, Staffordshire, c.1790, 9 ⅝ In. ....*illus* 584
Sponged Coat, Pearlware, Multicolor Enamel, Staffordshire, c.1790, 9 In. 369
Village Idiot, Multicolor Enamel, Blue Sponged Coat, Pratt, c.1790, 8 In. 1169

TOLE is painted tin. It is sometimes called japanned ware, pontypool, or toleware. Most nineteenth-century tole is painted with an orange-red or black background and multicolored decorations. Many recent versions of toleware are made and sold. Related items may be listed in the Tinware category.

Apple Tray, Flower, Japanned Ground, Crystallized Center, c.1830, 12 ½ In. 840
Box, Deed, Dome Lid, 1820, 5 ½ x 9 In. 351
Box, Document, Dome Lid, Blue Swag, Japanned Ground, Wire Handle, c.1860, 5 x 8 In. 510
Box, Document, Dome Lid, Pomegranates, Bail Handle, c.1810, 6 x 9 In. ....*illus* 1599
Box, Document, Dome Lid, Red Ground, 2 Birds, Brass Bail Handle, c.1830, 6 x 10 In. 6600
Box, Document, Shaped Lid, Green, Stenciled Building, Turrets, Handle, c.1850, 6 x 10 In. 60

Tile, Zebra Scene, Pyramid, 15 Tiles On Plywood, Frame, Harris Strong, c.1933, 24 x 36 In.
$345

Humler & Nolan

Tobacco Jar, Figural, Woman, Bust, Ceramic, Art Nouveau, c.1900, 7 ½ In.
$135

Ruby Lane

Toby Jug, Man, Seated, Holding Jug, Creamware, Staffordshire, c.1790, 9 ⅝ In.
$584

Skinner, Inc.

TIP
Drapes should be lined to protect the fabric from heat and sun, and to evenly distribute the weight of the fabric.

Tole, Box, Document, Dome Lid, Pomegranates, Bail Handle, c.1810, 6 x 9 In.
$1,599

Skinner, Inc.

Tole, Box, Painted, Red Flowers, Blossoms, Hasp, Dome Lid, Pa., c.1840, 5 ½ x 7 In.
$17,220

Skinner, Inc.

Tole, Coffeepot, Lighthouse Shape, Gooseneck Spout, Flowers, Black Ground, Penn., 10 In.
$2,950

Hess Auction Group

Box, Fire, Black Ground, Multicolor Design, Stand, Label, c.1870, 22 x 22 In. 183
Box, Oval, Hinged, Painted, Man Eating Pie, Judge Of Pie Iron Clad, 1800s, 3 x 10 In. 413
Box, Painted, Red Flowers, Blossoms, Hasp, Dome Lid, Pa., c.1840, 5 ½ x 7 In. .... *illus* 17220
Canister, Cylindrical, Smoke Design, Tapered Lid, Ribbing, 2 Handles, 1800s, 24 In. 236
Case, Display, Hanging, Figural Medallion, Green, Floral Sprays, 2 Shelves, 24 x 21 In. 793
Chest, Dower, Tulip Design, Bracket Feet, Lift Lid, 3 x 6 In. 83
Cistern, French Yellow, Pyramid Shape, Flowers, 21 x 7 ½ In. 390
Coffeepot, Dome Lid, Gooseneck Spout, Flared Foot, Flowers, Signed, c.1840, 11 In. 1652
Coffeepot, Lighthouse Shape, Dome Lid, Mushroom Finial, Red, Flowers, 1800s, 10 In. 944
Coffeepot, Lighthouse Shape, Gooseneck Spout, Flowers, Black Ground, Penn., 10 In. .... *illus* 2950
Coffeepot, Tulip Band, Yellow, Red, Tapered, c.1830-70, 9 ¼ x 6 ½ In. 400
Field Jug, Cylindrical, Lid, Tin, Hinged Spout, Wire Bail Handle, Smoke Design, 1800s, 17 In. ... 59
Footbath, Neoclassical Decoupage, 13 x 22 In. 343
Jardiniere, Crenellated, Yellow, Group, Nude, Trees, Fields, Estates, Handles, 12 In. 200
Jardiniere, Green, Cornucopia Shape, Hanging, 52 In. 478
Jardiniere, Landscape, Asian Figures, Umbrellas, 5 ½ x 8 ½ In., Pair 125
Lamp Base, Tea Urn, Nesting Birds, Leaves, Reticulated Base, Burner, 26 In. .... *illus* 239
Lilies, Black Pot, Long Stem, 33 In., Pair 1500
Mug, Tin, Roses, Tulips, Leaves, Red, Yellow, Green, 1800s, 6 In. 1476
Obelisk, Neoclassical Style, Faux Lapis Lazuli, Metal Base, c.1940, Italy, 22 x 6 In., Pair 922
Pail, Lid, Oval, Wire Bail Handle, Tomato & Leaf Design, 1800s, 2 In. 384
Palm Tree, Red Pot, 96 x 26 In. 400
Pineapple, Cast Iron, 38 ½ x 15 In. 600
Plaque, Virgin Mary, Oval, Sunburst Border, 35 x 26 ¾ In. 2760
Syrup, Red Flowers, Japanned Ground, Loop Handle, Lid, c.1860, 4 In. 660
Table, 2 Tiers, Black, Lacquer, Parcel Gilt, Removable Trays, 29 x 23 ¾ In. 423
Tea Caddy, Cylindrical, Lid, Red & Yellow Flowers, Green Leaves, 1800s, 5 In. 201
Teapot, Flowers, Bird's Neck Spout, Braced Handle, c.1830-70, 11 x 6 ½ In. 525
Tray, 3-Masted Ship, Half Sail, Flag, Gold Leaf & Acorn Border, Oval, 16 x 20 In. 1185
Tray, Center Flower Bouquet, Leafy Scroll Border, Shaped Rim, Black, Red, Orange, 25 In. 92
Tray, Chinoiserie Figures, Garden, Flower Border, Stenciled, Stand, 1800s, 19 x 30 In. 750
Tray, Classical Figures, Harp, Wreaths, Green, Red, Handles, 1900s, 22 x 29 ½ In. 121
Tray, Drying, Oval, Swirl Paint Design, Wire Handles, 1800s, 24 x 30 In. 472
Tray, Enamel Painting, Fruit Basket, Gold Details, Yellow Edge, 18 ½ x 13 ½ In. 77
Tray, Flower Bouquet, Yellow Ground, Gallery, France, 18 x 10 In. 73
Tray, George III, After Party Angling, By George Moreland, c.1800, 30 In. 1125
Tray, Grapes, Flowers, Yellow Decoration On Rim, 20 x 14 ¾ In. 90
Tray, Melons & Strawberries Still Life, Flat Rim, 1800s, 20 x 28 In. 115
Tray, Painted Center, Child, Dogs, Flat Edge, Oblong, 21 x 25 ½ In. 248
Tray, Patriotic, Liberty, Spread Wing Eagle, Flag, Shield, Open Handles, 18 x 24 In. 2370
Tray, Regency, Shepherd, Sheep, Estate, Trees, Pierced Gallery, 23 x 31 In. 236
Tray, Round, Scalloped Rim, Painted, Figures, Quayside Venice, Palace, Gilt Border, 23 In. 3125
Tray, Stenciled, Locomotive, 3 Cars, Bystanders, Flowers, Leaf Border, 1800s, 13 x 16 In. 885
Tray, Tin, Painted, Fruit Still Life, Mountain Scene, Leafy Border, c.1840, 22 x 30 In. 984
Tree, Bright Red Fruit, Green Leaves, Branches, Brown Pot, 26 In. 281
Umbrella Stand, Green, Compartments, Fist Form Handle, c.1880, 29 x 19 In. .... *illus* 531
Umbrella Stand, Repousse, Figures, Interior Scene, 21 x 18 In. 150
Urn, 10 Masks & Rings, Hexagonal Base, 44 In., Pair 3000
Urn, Lid, Japanned, Shield Shape, Ring Handles, Pagoda, Birds, 13 In., Pair .... *illus* 325
Wastepaper Can, Coat Of Arms, Lions, 12 x 10 ¼ In. 63

TOM MIX was born in 1880 and died in 1940. He was the hero of over 100 silent movies from 1910 to 1929, and 25 sound films from 1929 to 1935. There was a Ralston Tom Mix radio show from 1933 to 1950, but the original Tom Mix was not in the show. Tom Mix comics were published from 1942 to 1953.

Bracelet, Charm, Brass Link, 6 Gun, Steer Head, Tom On Tony, TM Logo, 1936, 7 In. 205
Button, Celluloid, Photo, Black & White, Round, 1935, ⅞ In. 230
Pin, Straight Shooter, Man On Horse, Red & Blue, Gold, Ralston, 2 In. 228
Poster, Circus, Big Top Scene, Canadian Mounties, c.1936, 27 x 41 In. 557
Poster, Circus, Jungle Oddities, Animals, c.1936, 27 x 41 In. 278
Poster, Circus, Portrait, Western Suit, Hat, Entertainment Insurance, c.1936, 19 x 27 In. 348
Poster, Circus, Tom Kneeling Next To Boy, One Of His Million Admirers, c.1937, 27 x 41 In. 483
Poster, Tom Mix Circus & Wild West, Horse Scenes, Lines Mounted, c.1936, 27 x 41 In. 253
Ring, 14K White Gold Finish, Shield, Star, Premium, Chicle Gum 1725
Ring, Deputy, Badge, Eagle & Shield, Star, White Gold Finish, Brass 506
Ring, Photo, Mystery Look-In, Tony & 6 Gun, Brass, Square, 1938 127

TOOLS of all sorts are listed here, but most are related to industry. Other tools may be found listed under Iron, Kitchen, Tinware, and Wooden.

Ax, Felling, Partial Haft, Broad Arrow, Marked Hawke, Wood Haft, Britain, c.1870, 11 ⅝ In. 615
Bench, Cobbler's, Grain Painted, Leather Covered Cutout Seat, 1800s, 19 x 46 In. 1121
Bench, Cobbler's, Painted, Bins, Slots, Tools, Dovetailed Drawers, c.1830, 44 x 37 In. ....*illus* 1778
Bench, Leather Worker's, Softwood, Painted Red, Drawer, Clamp, 30 In. ....*illus* 153
Brander, Iron, Loop Handle, Letter K, 45 ½ In. 39
Broadax, Wrought Iron, W. Beatty & Son, Lancaster, Pa., 12-In. Blade, 19-In. Shaft.........*illus* 118
Bucket, Sugar, Turned Rings, Flowers & Pussy Willow Vine, Iron Bands, c.1800, 9 x 7 In. 1003
Bullet Mold, Rifle, Sharps, .50 Caliber, ⅞ Bullet, Sprue Trimmer, 9 In. 1750
C Clamp, Jointed Corners, Wood, Octagonal Handle, 10 x 7 In. 55
Chest, Carpenter's, Paneled Lid, Reeded Block Panels, Spindle Handles, c.1800, 29 x 40 In. 531
Cobbler's Measuring Stick, Brass, Wood, France, c.1830, 13 ½ In. 149
Comb, Flax Carding, Forged Iron, France, 19th Century, 13 x 16 ½ In. 210
Corn Sheller, Wood & Brass, Crank Handle, Square Base, Salesman's Sample, 6 x 11 In. 513
Cultivator, 1 Row, Wood, Spoke Wagon Wheels, Brass Saddle Seat, 1866, 14 x 17 In. 2074
Drying Rack, Wood, Brown Paint, Mortised & Pegged, Shoe Feet, 1800s, 47 x 47 In. 12
Flashlight, Chrome, Red Plastic, Eveready, 1950s, 7 ½ In. 12
Graphotype, Dog Tag Machine, Typewriter Keyboard, Light, Clipboard, Tags, 46 In. 120
Key Cutting Machine, Corbin Cabinet Co., Countertop, Drawers, Wood Base, 14 x 14 In. 660
Ladder, Apple Picking, Wood, 5-Rung, 76 x 25 ½ In. 150
Lucet, Fruitwood, 2 Prongs, Hole, 1700s, 3 ¼ x 1 ¾ In. 45
Micrometer Level, Height, Toledo, Ohio, 24 In. 321
Perforating Machine, Cummins Co., Cast Iron, Black, Red, Pinstriping, c.1892, 17 x 17 In. 270
Plow, Walk Behind, Wood Body, Metal Hardware, Oliver Chilled, 8 ½ x 23 In. 8295
Saw, Bone Meat, Stainless Steel, Skyline, England, 10 ⅜ In. 12
Saw, Veneer, 2-Man, 50 x 27 In. 47
Seeder, Farm Implement, Wood, Cast Iron, Paint, 2 Spoke Wheels, Long Handle, 12 x 12 In. 114
Shovel, Wrought Iron, 25 ½ In. 23
Tobacco Shredder, Cast Iron, Wheel, Wood Handle, Shaped Apron, 14 In. 60
Trammel, Sawtooth, Wrought Iron, Adjustable, 1800s, 41 In. 224
Vacuum Cleaner, Everybody's Vacuum Cleaner, Pump, Cloth Bag, Box, 1913........ 75
Vacuum Cleaner, Hand, Success, Leather Bellows, Hutchison Mfg., Wilkinsburg, Pa., 51 In. 18
Wagon Jack, Wood, Metal, Crank, Conestoga, U.S.A., 1849, 20 In. 180
Wheelbarrow, Wood, Orange Paint, Spoked Wheel, Curved Handles, c.1900, 27 x 81 In. 236
Whiskey Still, White Metal, Pine Handle, Drum Shaped, 22 ¾ x 16 In. 211
Wine Corking Machine, Brass, Cast Iron, Pine Workbench, 39 x 13 In. 338
Wine Corking Machine, Cast Iron, France, 39 ¼ x 15 In. 276
Workbench, Oak, 2 Vises, Iron Dog Slots, Jameson Distillery, 1700s, 34 x 115 In. ....*illus* 2161
Workbox, Blacksmith's, Stand, French Provincial, Oak, Iron, Arched Handle, 24 x 18 In. 338

TOOTHBRUSH HOLDERS were part of every bowl and pitcher set in the late nineteenth century. Most were oblong covered dishes. About 1920, manufacturers started to make children's toothbrush holders shaped like animals or cartoon characters. A few modern toothbrush holders are still being made.

Cast Iron, Gold Glitter Lucite, Ball & Claw Feet, 3 x 4 In. 65
Castle, Beaded Edge, Lion Head Feet, Porcelain, Cylindrical, c.1870, 5 In. 50
Cowboy, Holster, Hat, Ceramic, Japan, 5 ½ In. ....*illus* 75
Ironstone, Cylindrical, Tea Leaf, Alfred Meakin, 4 ⅝ In. 45
Man, Boxing, Porcelain, 1920s, 5 x 3 x 2 In. 149
Nickel, Wall Mount, 5 Holes, c.1915, 2 ¾ In. 45
Panels, Glass, Repousse Sterling Silver Top, Hummingbird, Cylindrical, 7 In. 150
Three Little Pigs, Multicolor, Ceramic, Goldcastle, Japan, 4 x 4 x 2 In. 45

TOOTHPICK HOLDERS are sometimes called *toothpicks* by collectors. The variously shaped containers used to hold small wooden toothpicks are made of glass, china, or metal. Most of the toothpick holders are made of Victorian pressed glass. Additional items may be found in other categories, such as Bisque, Silver Plate, Slag Glass, etc.

Amberina, Diamond Quilted, Little Lord Fauntleroy Caddy, Tufts Silver, 3 In. ....*illus* 201
Basket Pattern, Blue, Boston & Sandwich, c.1850, 4 In. 338
Bisque, Teddy Roosevelt, Bear Cub, 3 ½ x 2 ¾ In. 90
Cranberry, Scalloped Rim, Cambridge Glass, c.1901, 2 In. 59
Daisy & Button, Pressed Glass, Hat, Vaseline, 2 ½ In. 25
King's Crown, Clear, Ruby Stain, 2 ½ In. 30

Tole, Lamp Base, Tea Urn, Nesting Birds, Leaves, Reticulated Base, Burner, 26 In.
$239

Neal Auctions

Tole, Umbrella Stand, Green, Compartments, Fist Form Handle, c.1880, 29 x 19 In.
$531

Neal Auctions

Tole, Urn, Lid, Japanned, Shield Shape, Ring Handles, Pagoda, Birds, 13 In., Pair
$325

Hess Auction Group

T

Tool, Bench, Cobbler's, Painted, Bins, Slots, Tools, Dovetailed Drawers, c.1830, 44 x 37 In.
$1,778

James D. Julia Auctioneers

Tool, Bench, Leather Worker's, Softwood, Painted Red, Drawer, Clamp, 30 In.
$153

Hess Auction Group

Tool, Broadax, Wrought Iron, W. Beatty & Son, Lancaster, Pa., 12-In. Blade, 19-In. Shaft
$118

Hess Auction Group

Tool, Workbench, Oak, 2 Vises, Iron Dog Slots, Jameson Distillery, 1700s, 34 x 115 In.
$2,161

James D. Julia Auctioneers

Paneled Sprig, Northwood, Clear Opalescent, 1½ In. 75
Sterling Silver, White Enamel, A. Michaelsen, Copenhagen, 2½ In. 172
Twisted Hobnail, Pressed Glass, Clear, 2¼ In. 20
Waffle & Star, Clear, c.1910, 2¼ In. 35

TORQUAY is the name given to ceramics by several potteries working near Torquay, England, from 1870 until 1962. Until about 1900, the potteries used local red clay to make classical-style art pottery vases and figurines. Then they turned to making souvenir wares. Items were dipped in colored slip and decorated with painted slip and sgraffito designs. They often had mottoes or proverbs, and scenes of cottages, ships, birds, or flowers. The Scandy design was a symmetrical arrangement of brushstrokes and spots done in colored slips. Potteries included Watcombe Pottery (1870–1962), Torquay Terra-Cotta Company (1875–1905), Aller Vale (1881–1924), Torquay Pottery (1908–1940), and Longpark (1883–1957).

TORQUAY

Cheese Keeper, Ship, Mousehole, Motto Ware, Royal Watcombe, 6 x 5 In. .... *illus* 135
Creamer, Motto Ware, Scandy, 3 x 3 In. 24
Cup, Cottage, It's An Ill Wind That Profits Nobody, Demitasse, 1950s, 2⅜ x 2½ In. 20
Hatpin Holder, Sailboat, A Place For Hatpins, c.1910, 5 In. 100
Jug, Scottish Toast, Green, Brown Tan, Pinched Spout, 6 x 6 In. 75
Tobacco Jar, Lid, Sailing Ship, Brown, Black, Tobacco Help Yerself, 5 x 3 In. 130

TORTOISESHELL is the shell of the tortoise. It has been used as inlay and to make small decorative objects since the seventeenth century. Some species of tortoise are now on the endangered species list, and old or new objects made from these shells cannot be sold legally.

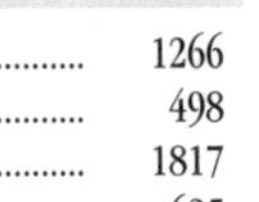

Box, Lid, Carved, Pierced, Figures, Leaves, Initial L, Round, 1800s, 4 In. 1266
Box, Paris Scenes, 6 x 4 In. 498
Clock, Silver Handle, Beaded Rim, Bun Feet, Ribbon Festoon, 1911, 4 In. 1817
Page Turner, Shaped Blade, Jeweled Scroll Bronze Handle, c.1890, 13½ In. 625
Trinket Box, Ivory Mounted, Engraved Leaves, Swing Handle, 1700s, 3½ x 12 In. 196

TORTOISESHELL GLASS was made during the 1800s and after by the Sandwich Glass Works of Massachusetts and some firms in Germany. Tortoiseshell glass is, of course, named for its resemblance to real shell from a tortoise. It has been reproduced.

Candleholder, Folded Rim, Footed, c.1950, 10 x 5 In., Pair 395
Vase, Boot Shape, Clear Rigaree Accents, c.1890, 3¾ In. 75
Vase, Trumpet, Footed, Flattened Rim, 1800s, 11 In. 50

TOY collectors have special clubs, magazines, and shows. Toys are designed to entice children, and today they have attracted new interest among adults who are still children at heart. All types of toys are collected. Tin toys, iron toys, battery-operated toys, and many others are collected by specialists. Dolls, Games, Teddy Bears, and Bicycles are listed in their own categories. Other toys may be found under company or celebrity names.

2 Boxers, Articulated, On Push Pull Slide, Tin Litho, Meier, Germany, Penny, 4 In. 1298
Action Figure, Bionic Woman, Blue Leisure Suit, Long Rooted Hair, Purse, Box, 1976, 12 In. 139
Action Figure, Captain Action, Uniform, Box, 1966, 9 x 12 In. 696
Action Figure, Dreadful Dracula, Suit, Cape, Glow-In-Dark Features, Plastic, Box, 1973 209
Action Figure, Frankenstein, Boots & Suit, Eyes & Hands Glow-In-Dark, Plastic, Box, 1973 261
Action Figure, Human Wolfman, Suit, Fur Cuffs, Glow-In-Dark Features, Plastic, Box, 1973 209
Action Figure, Indiana Jones, Raiders Of The Lost Ark, Leather Jacket, Hat, Gun, 1981, 12 In. 348
Action Figure, Man From U.N.C.L.E., Illya Kuryakin, Plastic, A.C. Gilbert, Box, 1965, 12 In. 285
Action Figure, Six Million Dollar Man, Maskatron, Weapon Arms, Box, 1976, 10 x 14 In. 262
Action Figure, Spider-Man, Window Box, Marvel Comics, 1979, 12½ In. 209
Action Figure, Wonder Woman, Posing Doll, Super Queens Series, Ideal, Box, 1967, 6 x 15 In. 5313
Adam The Porter, Walker, Pushes Luggage Cart, Tin Litho, Clockwork, Lehmann, 8 In. 1298
Airplane Spiral, Spring Support, 2 Airplanes, Tin Lithograph, Einfalt, Germany, Penny, 6½ In. 384
Airplane, Air Mail, Cast Iron, Embossed, Blue, Single Prop, Nickel Disc Wheels, Kenton, 8 In. 1062
Airplane, Bleriot, Tin Litho, Wings, Movable Celluloid Propellers, Germany 1920s, 9½ In. 5925
Airplane, Bremen, Iron, Ribbed, Embossed, 2 Passengers, Nickel Propeller, Hubley, 10 In. *illus* 2124
Airplane, DC-7 Airplane, Tin Lithograph, American Airlines, 4 Propellers, Light-Up, 25 x 8 In. 780
Airplane, Flight Jet, P-38, Red & White, Hubley, Mighty Metal, Box, 11 x 11 In. 125
Airplane, Lucky Boy, Cast Iron, Silver, Red Trim, Stars, Embossed Wings, Dent, 7 In. 472
Airplane, Ride 'Em, Keystone, Metal, Wood, Rubber Wheels, c.1910, 25 x 27½ In. 326
Airplane, Silver, Pan American Airways, 4 Engines, Marx, 1940, 27 In. 175
Airplane, Single Prop, Yellow, Red, Passengers, Windows, Kellerman, Germany, Penny, 5 In. 708

T

Airplane, Spirit Of St. Louis, Tin Lithograph, Felt-Dressed Pilot, Schuco, Friction, 4 ½ In. 561
Airport Set, Mighty Metal, Truck, Car, Fire Truck, Plane, Hubley, Box, 16 x 10 x 2 In. 200
Alligator, Tin Lithograph, Wheelless, Teeth Embossed Body, Penny, 3 In. 266
Alphabet Man, Schoolmaster, Cast Iron, Painted, Push Lever Hand Points, Letters, 11 In. ..*illus* 23600
Ambulance Van, Tin Litho, Red Cross Emblems, Driver, Crank, White, Lindstrom, 1920s, 8 In. . 354
Anti-Aircraft Gun, Rail Platform, Swivel Base, Tin, Lineol, Germany, 7 In. 649
Aquarium Figure, Creature From Black Lagoon, Plastic, Air Tube, Moves, Box, 1971, 6 In. 633
Arab Chief, Wood, Jointed, Dagger, Revolver, Cloth Clothes, Schoenhut, 8 ½ In. 1121
Avengers, Set, Metal, Plastic Figures, Lotus Elan, 1927 Bentley, Box, 1966, 3 & 4 In. 431
Avengers, Steel Sword Cane, Fluid Squirting Feature, Display Card, 1960s, 24 x ¾ In. 765
Ballerina, Tin Lithograph, Girl In Scottish Plaid Skirt, Winding Key, Germany, 5 In. 118
Balloon Vendor, Mechanical Arm, Tin Litho, Embossed, Kellermann, Germany, 6 In. ....*illus* 502
Barber Bear, Battery Operated, Box, Linemar, 9 ½ In. 450
Barber, Polishing Bald Man's Head, Tin Lithograph, Clockwork, F. Martin, 7 ¾ In. ....*illus* 2242
Barn & Silo, Sunnyfield Farms, Tin Lithograph, Red, Yellow, c.1955, 10 x 5 In. ....*illus* 50
Barney Google & Sparkplug, Statue, Plaster, Barney Riding Sparkplug, 1920s, 9 x 11 In. ...*illus* 385
Barney Google & Sparkplug, Wood, Jointed, Felt Clothes & Blanket, c.1922, 6 & 8 In. 472
Batmobile, Batman & Robin, Rocket Firing, Corgi 267, Box, 5 In. 735
Batmobile, Batman Driver, Tin Litho, Plastic Tailwings, Bat Symbols, Friction, 1966, 11 In. 1645
Battleship, Builder, Exploding, Wood, Puzzle, Spring-Loaded, Pop Cannon, 12 x 4 In. 237
Bears are also listed in the Teddy Bear category.
Bell Ringer, Young America, Red Platform, Embossed Letters, Large Spoke Wheels, 6 In. 3540
Bell, Baby Quieter, Gentleman Reading Evening News, Child On Leg, J. & E. Stevens, 7 In. 384
Bicycles that are large enough to ride are listed in the Bicycle category.
Bicycle Riders, 3 Racing, Striped Shirts, Round Track, Tin, Mechanical, France, c.1900, 9 ½ In. 1770
Big Bad Wolf, Bib Overalls, Ceramic, Painted, Glazed, 1930s, 7 In. 484
Blimp, Akron, Silver Paint, 3 Wheels, Steelcraft, Ohio, c.1933, 25 In. 325
Blocks, Alphabet, Paper Lithograph, Wood, Fisk & Little, Box, 1880s, 8 In. 195
Blocks, Building, U.S. Capitol, Cardboard, Litho, Makes 6 Buildings, Box, 8 x 21 In. 2360
Blondie's Jalopy, Blondie, Cookie, Dagwood, Alexander Heads, Tin Litho, Windup, 1935, 16 In. 886
Boat, Battleship, Gray, 2-Masted, Stack, Rails, Lifeboats, Guns, Cannons, Clockwork, Bing, 25 In. 3540
Boat, Destroyer, Gray, Red Hull, Guns On Deck, 2 Lifeboats, 4 Stacks, Bing, c.1912, 28 In. 5605
Boat, Ferry, Tin Lithograph, Windup, Walbert Manufacturing, Chicago, 13 ½ In. 300
Boat, Fire Fly Gunboat, Paper On Wood, Lithograph Details, American Eagle, Bliss, 17 In. 299
Boat, Ocean Liner, Gold, Black Bands, 3 White Decks, 3 Stacks, Bing, Series IV, c.1930, 16 In. 2950
Boat, Outboard, Tin Lithograph, Paint, Nickel Plate Motor, Windup, Japan, Box, 1940s, 6 In. 115
Boat, Racing Scull, 8-Man, Coxswain, Spoke Wheels, Cast Iron, U.S. Hardware, 1890s, 14 In. 2655
Boat, Riverboat, Paddlewheels On Sides, Center Flywheel, Tin Lithograph, Hess, Germany, 11 In. 295
Boat, Schooner, Paper Lithograph On Wood, Wheels, c.1890, 6 x 46 x 22 In. 610
Boat, Scull, 8-Man, Striped Shirts, Oars, Rowing Action, Tin, Clockwork, Gunthermann, 29 In. . 6490
Boat, Speedboat, Miss Southern, Wood, Copper Fittings & Nose, Rudder, Decals, Mengels, 15 In. 175
Boat, Speedboat, Remote Control, Tangerine Machine, Driver, Stand, 13 x 19 In. 427
Boat, Speedboat, Wood Body, Tin Lithograph Nose, Decal, Windup, Liberty, 15 ½ In. 100
Boat, Steamcraft Congo Launch, Steam Powered, Plastic, Atwood, Box, 1950s, 19 In. 115
Boat, Tanker Freighter, Red & Black Hull, Tin Litho, Catwalk, Lifeboats, Fleischmann, 20 In. 502
Boat, Tanker, Texaco, Plastic, AMF Wen-Mac, Stickers, Box, 1961, 27 In. 168
Boxers, 2 Black Men, Wearing Hats, Mechanical, Wood Platform, Ives, 11 ½ In. 7200
Boxers, 2 Men, Wheels, Tin Litho, Clockwork, Marked D.R.P., Germany, c.1920, 6 In. ....*illus* 212
Boy On Sled, Legs In Air, Yellow Trestle Sled, Wheels, Tin Litho, Meier, Germany, Penny, 3 In. ... 413
Boy On Sled, Pressed Steel, Friction, Dayton, 9 In. 325
Bumper Car, Pressed Steel, Red, Tin Lithograph Driver, Windup, Wyandotte, c.1950, 9 In. 144
Bus, Double-Decker, Red, Cast Iron, Decal, Nickel Spoke Wheels, Arcade, 8 In. ....*illus* 1062
Bus, Express, Tin Lithograph, Red, Green, Wolverine, Box, 14 In. 295
Bus, Greyhound, Cast Iron, Coast To Coast, Stencil, Blue, Rubber Tires, Arcade, 7 ½ In. 266
Bus, Honeymooners, Jackie Gleason, Tin Litho, Wolverine, Wood Wheels, 1955, 14 x 5 In. 350
Bus, Yellow Coach, Double-Decker, Cast Iron, Green, Rubber Tires, Arcade, 1920s, 13 In. ....*illus* 1652
Busy Lizzie, Woman Pushing Mop, Tin Lithograph, Clockwork, Germany, 7 In. ....*illus* 531
Butter & Egg Man, Duck, Tin, Walker, Louis Marx, Box, c.1935, 7 ½ In. ....*illus* 1560
Cackling Hen, Composition, Cardboard, Crank, Eggs, Windup, 1930, 5 x 2 In. ....*illus* 40
Camel, Riding, Standing, Mohair, Metal Carriage, Wheels, Pull Cord, Steiff, c.1935, 18 x 23 In. . 1422
Camper Trailer, Ham, Tee-Nee Custom, Aluminum, Doors, Cargo Hatch, 1950s, 48 x 23 In. *illus* 366
Cap Gun, Chinese Must Go, Trigger Leg Kicks, Cast Iron, Japanned Finish, Ives, 5 In. ....*illus* 472
Cap Gun, Sheriff, Repeating, Stevens, White Grip, Box... 114
Cap Gun, Texan 50 Shot Repeater, White Grip, Hubley, Box.. 120
Car & Trailer, Rambler Wagon, Shasta Trailer, Holiday Express, Bandai, c.1960, 22 In. .....*illus* 711
Car, 1910 Model, Garage, Tin, Windup, Orobr, Germany, 6 In., 8 ½ In. 575

Toothbrush Holder, Cowboy, Holster, Hat, Ceramic, Japan, 5 ½ In.
$75

Ruby Lane

Toothpick Holder, Amberina, Diamond Quilted, Little Lord Fauntleroy Caddy, Tufts Silver, 3 In.
$201

Early Auction Company

Torquay, Cheese Keeper, Ship, Mousehole, Motto Ware, Royal Watcombe, 6 x 5 In.
$135

Ruby Lane

TIP

Never leave the key under the doormat.

T

Toy, Airplane, Bremen, Iron, Ribbed, Embossed, 2 Passengers, Nickel Propeller, Hubley, 10 In.
$2,124

Bertoia Auctions

Toy, Alphabet Man, Schoolmaster, Cast Iron, Painted, Push Lever Hand Points, Letters, 11 In.
$23,600

Bertoia Auctions

Toy, Balloon Vendor, Mechanical Arm, Tin Litho, Embossed, Kellermann, Germany, 6 In.
$502

Bertoia Auctions

Car, Bump, 100 Heavy, Cast Iron, Outer Bumper Frame, Wheels, 17 ½ In. 900
Car, Chevrolet Corvette, Convertible, Plastic, Yellow, Red Seats, 1958, 6 ½ In. 115
Car, Chevrolet, Coupe, Cast Iron, Gray, Black, Silver Grille, Running Boards, Arcade, 8 In. 236
Car, Convertible, Plastic, Blue, Fix-It, Ideal, Box, 13 In. 95
Car, Corvette, Convertible, Die Cast Metal, Red Paint, Rubber Tires, Hubley, Box, 1954, 12 In. 239
Car, Coupe, Reo Royale, Yellow, Red Stripes, Nickel Grille, Side-Mounted Spare, Arcade, 9 In. 1652
Car, Dagwood The Driver, Comical Driver, Tin Lithograph, Clockwork, Marx, 8 In. ....*illus* 443
Car, Electric, Tin, Knapp, 12 ½ In. 3245
Car, Ferrari, 2 Door, Slide-Back Roof, Blue, Driver, Japan, 1960s, 11 ½ In. 472
Car, Ford, Model T, Flivver, Pressed Steel, Buddy L, 7 x 11 In. ....*illus* 413
Car, Funeral, Cast Iron, Black, Rear Doors Open, Plexiglas Windows, Motorcade Toys, 10 In. 443
Car, James Bond, Aston Martin DB5, Corgi, Open Roof, Ejector Seat, Slasher Blade, 1968, 4 In. .. 417
Car, Jeep, Willys, Lights, Trailer, Steel, Paint, Tin Litho Wheels, Horn, Marx, Box, 1950s, 11 In. ... 266
Car, LaSalle Sedan, 1934 Model, Die Cast, Light Blue, Tootsietoy, c.1936, 4 In. 235
Car, Matador Stocker, Steerable Gas Powered, Plastic, Cox, Box, 1974, 13 In. 253
Car, Mercedes, Hitler, SS Driver, Tin Lithograph, Tippco, Germany, 9 In. 3000
Car, Milton Berle, Crazy, Red Hat, Tin Lithograph, Windup, Marx, Box, 1950s, 6 x 6 In. 234
Car, Monkeemobile, The Monkees, Corgi, Die Cast Metal, Plastic, Engine, Box, 1967, 5 In. 209
Car, Munster Koach, Hard Plastic, Black & Red, Cardboard Box, 1964, 15 x 6 In. 506
Car, Police, 1953 Studebaker, Black & White, Tin, Marusan, c.1956, 6 In. 265
Car, Portly Driver, White Suit & Hat, Blows Horn, Tin, Clockwork, Lehmann, 7 In. 561
Car, Pressed Steel, Wyandotte, 1930s, 15 In. 245
Car, Race, Alfa Romeo, Light Blue, Clockwork, Box, France, c.1937, 20 In. 7080
Car, Race, Steel, Blue, 2 Figures, Crank Spring Drive, Dayton Friction Toy Co., c.1914, 12 In. 413
Car, Racing, Green, Tin Lithograph, Driver, Windup, Ferdinand Strauss Co., Box, c.1920, 8 In. .. 525
Car, Racing, Preston, Midgets Special, Gasoline, 1950s Style, Fiberglass, 33 x 73 In. ....*illus* 2318
Car, Red, 2 Door, Tin Lithograph, Nickel Plated Grille, Windup, Chad Valley, c.1947, 9 ¾ In. 177
Car, Roadster, Cast Iron, Red, Opening Rumble Seat, Spare On Back, Kilgore, 1920s, 8 In. 413
Car, Runabout, Open Top, Driver Holds Tiller, Red, Gold Trim, Tin Lithograph, Issmayer, 4 In. .. 767
Car, Sedan, 4 Doors, Tin Lithograph, Disc Wheels, Tippco, Germany, Late 1920s, 9 In. ....*illus* 738
Car, Soapbox Derby, Cracker 7, Super Turbo, Wood, Metal, 78 In. 310
Car, Sports, Convertible, Die Cast, Yellow Paint, Box, 7 In. 245
Car, Sports, Corvette, Custom, Die Cast Metal, Rubber Tires, Hubley, Box, 1954, 12 In. 239
Car, Touring, Cast Iron, Red, Yellow Spoke Wheels, Driver, Passenger Inside, Kenton, 7 ¾ In. 295
Car, Touring, Soft Top Style, Spoke Wheels, Driver, Light Green, Tin, Windup, Bing, 7 In. 944
Car, Turbo-Jet, Plastic Jet Car, Metal Lithograph Launch Station, Ideal Toy Corp., 1950s, 13 In. . 71
Car, Victoria, Touring Roundabout, Tin, Rubber Tires, Clockwork, Gunthermann, 6 In. .....*illus* 2655
Car, Volkswagen Beetle, Turquoise, Metal, Tonka, c.1955, 8 In. 40
Caribou, Stuffed Animal, Steiff, Detachable Antlers, Floor Display, 67 x 75 In. 732
Carousel, 3 Airplanes, Tower, Tin Lithograph, Germany USA Zone, 1950s, 9 In. 115
Carousel, 3 Riders On Horses, Scalloped Canopy, Flag, Tin, Clockwork, Germany, 9 In. 384
Carousel, Gondola Cars, Propeller, Wood Grain Metal Base, Canopy, Figures, c.1910, 13 In. 5249
Carousel, Musical, Papier-Mache Horses, Children Riders, Crank, 11 In. 3000
Cat Dozer, Yellow, Doepke D-6, 1954, 15 In. 260
Chickmobile, Peter Rabbit, Cast Iron, Lionel, 1930s, 9 In. 695
Climbing Monkey, Pull Cord, Penny, Distler, Germany, c.1910, 7 In. ....*illus* 275
Clown Drummer, Yellow Kid, Tin Horse, Platform, Converse, c.1920, 10 x 12 In. ....*illus* 118
Clown, On Roller Skates, Japan, T.P.S., Box, 6 In. 109
Clown, Playing Harp, Drum, Plink-Plunk Music, Gunthermann, 8 ½ In. 2598
Clown, Riding Pig, Painted, Tin, Gunthermann, Windup, 5 In. 505
Construction Set, Airplane, Mecavion, Red, Cream, Pontoons, Emblems, Box, Meccano, 12 In. 649
Dancers, Black, Wood Chest, Windup, Jointed Figures, Ives, c.1885, 3 ½ x 6 In. 345
Dancing Sailor, Tin, Blue Cloth Sailor Outfit, Clockwork, Lehmann, 7 ½ In. 354
Dancing, Les Valseurs, Waltzing Couple, Clothing, Windup, F. Martin, France, Box, 8 In. 4720
Dashboard, Green Hornet, Black Beauty, Plastic, Battery Operated, Keys, Box, 1966, 11 x 16 In. 14055
Delivery Van, EBO Express, Doors Open, Tin, Clockwork, Hans Eberl, Germany, 8 In. ....*illus* 413
Detective Set, Untouchables, Robert Stack, Eliot Ness, Box, Marx, 15 x 8 In. 450
Dirigible, Los Angeles, Cast Iron, Red, Nickel Disc Wheels, Kenton, 11 In. 1652
Disc Harrow, Tandem, Painted, Cast Iron, Arcade, Box, 5 ½ In. 1121
Display Card, Hot Wheels, Mongoose, Red, Tilt Up Car, Button, Sticker Sheets, 1970........*illus* 345
Dog In Kennel, Dog Goes In & Out, Yellow, Red, Green, Tin Litho, Crank, Penny, 3 In. 590
Dog, Black, White & Brown, Wire Tail, Little Snoopy, Pull Toy, Fisher-Price, 1965, 11 In. 20
Dog, Bulldog, Wood, Jointed, Ball-Jointed Neck, Schoenhut, 6 In. 354
Dog, Cuddly Dudley, Plush, Box Converts To Car, Mid 1960s, 28 In. 207
Dog, Dachshund, Shimmy Pup, Wood, Painted, Pull Toy, 24 ½ In. 130

Toy, Barber, Polishing Bald Man's Head, Tin Lithograph, Clockwork, F. Martin, 7 ¾ In.
$2,242

Bertoia Auctions

Toy, Barn & Silo, Sunnyfield Farms, Tin Lithograph, Red, Yellow, c.1955, 10 x 5 In.
$50

Ruby Lane

Toy, Barney Google & Sparkplug, Statue, Plaster, Barney Riding Sparkplug, 1920s, 9 x 11 In.
$385

Hake's Americana & Collectibles

Toy, Boxers, 2 Men, Wheels, Tin Litho, Clockwork, Marked D.R.P., Germany, c.1920, 6 In.
$212

Hess Auction Group

Toy, Bus, Double-Decker, Red, Cast Iron, Decal, Nickel Spoke Wheels, Arcade, 8 In.
$1,062

Bertoia Auctions

Toy, Bus, Yellow Coach, Double-Decker, Cast Iron, Green, Rubber Tires, Arcade, 1920s, 13 In.
$1,652

Bertoia Auctions

Toy, Busy Lizzie, Woman Pushing Mop, Tin Lithograph, Clockwork, Germany, 7 In.
$531

Bertoia Auctions

TIP

Don't buy a Fisher-Price toy with a broken part. It is very difficult to find a replacement. The parts that break, often the wheels, are the easiest to damage and so the least available to use for repairs. Newly made parts are too shiny and new-looking to be suitable.

T

Toy, Butter & Egg Man, Duck, Tin, Walker, Louis Marx, Box, c.1935, 7 ½ In.
$1,560

RSL Auction

Toy, Cackling Hen, Composition, Cardboard, Crank, Eggs, Windup, 1930, 5 x 2 In.
$40

Ruby Lane

Toy, Camper Trailer, Ham, Tee-Nee Custom, Aluminum, Doors, Cargo Hatch, 1950s, 48 x 23 In.
$366

Morphy Auctions

Toy, Cap Gun, Chinese Must Go, Trigger Leg Kicks, Cast Iron, Japanned Finish, Ives, 5 In.
$472

Bertoia Auctions

Toy, Car & Trailer, Rambler Wagon, Shasta Trailer, Holiday Express, Bandai, c.1960, 22 In.
$711

James D. Julia Auctioneers

Toy, Car, Dagwood The Driver, Comical Driver, Tin Lithograph, Clockwork, Marx, 8 In.
$443

Bertoia Auctions

Toy, Car, Ford, Model T, Flivver, Pressed Steel, Buddy L, 7 x 11 In.
$413

Hess Auction Group

Toy, Car, Racing, Preston, Midgets Special, Gasoline, 1950s Style, Fiberglass, 33 x 73 In.
$2,318

Morphy Auctions

TIP
Collectors pay higher prices for most plastic space-gun toys than for lithographed tin guns. The newer plastic toys have more futuristic designs.

Toy, Car, Sedan, 4 Doors, Tin Lithograph, Disc Wheels, Tippco, Germany, Late 1920s, 9 In.
$738

Bertoia Auctions

Toy, Car, Victoria, Touring Roundabout, Tin, Rubber Tires, Clockwork, Gunthermann, 6 In.
$2,655

Bertoia Auctions

Toy, Climbing Monkey, Pull Cord, Penny, Distler, Germany, c.1910, 7 In.
$275

Ruby Lane

Dog, St. Bernard, Mohair, Cast Iron Wheels, Jointed, Amber Glass Eyes, Steiff, 1900s, 11 In. 798

Dolls are listed in the Doll category.

Doll Carriage, Tin, Pink & Cream, Curlicue Handle, Marklin, 8 In. 2160

Doll Room Box, Parlor, Dolls, Walterhausen, Germany, c.1910, 12 x 12 In. *illus* 375

Dollhouse Furniture, Bedroom, Cottage Style, Wood, Light Green, Stencils, 1920s, 6 Piece 207

Dollhouse Furniture, Cradle, Yellow Slip Design, Alphabet, Redware, c.1860, 4 x 7 In. 210

Dollhouse, 2 Story, 4 Rooms, Balcony, Painted, Pediment, Christian Hacker, 24 x 24 In. 413

Dollhouse, 2 Story, Center Door, 5 Windows, Wood, Paper, Electrified, C. Hacker, 34 x 27 In. 2006

Dollhouse, 2 Story, Red & White, Glass Windows, Lift-Off, 1930s, 39 In. 300

Dollhouse, 2 Story, Wood, Paper, Front Porch, Blue Roof, Gottschalk, 22 x 8 x 13 In. 944

Dream Car, Futuristic Friction Toy, Convertible, Plastic, Chrome, Box, Mattel, 10 ½ In. 247

Drum, Eagle, Open Wings, American Flag, Punched Tin, Wood Bands, 1800s, 6 x 8 In. 701

Duck Pulling Ducklings In Cart, Pak, Tin Lithograph, Clockwork, Lehmann, 7 In. 236

Dumbo, Standing, Rubber Wheels, Riding, Steiff, Button In Ear, 21 x 31 In. 1003

Elephant, Circus Suit, Rings Bell, Banner, See Our Circus, Celluloid, Windup, Kuramochi, 9 In. 510

Elephant, Circus, Wood, Jointed, Stitched Cloth Blanket & Head Piece, Schoenhut 8 In. 384

Exploding Battleship Builder, Wood, Spring Loaded, Baker & Bennet Co., c.1905, 4 x 12 In. 237

Feeding Chickens, Hen House, Chickens Peck, Tin, Crank, Germany, Penny, 2 ½ In. 443

Felix The Cat, Figure, Wood, Jointed, Leather Ears, Schoenhut, 7 ½ In. 390

Felix The Cat, Sparkler, Tin Lithograph, Black & White, Chein, 5 In. 325

Ferdinand The Bull, Boy Pulling Tail, Tin, Windup, Japan, 9 ½ In. 71

Ferris Wheel, Clown Face On Support, 6 Gondolas, Tin Lithograph, Clockwork, Chein, 16 In. 207

Ferris Wheel, Tin Lithograph, Multicolor, Clown Face, Windup, Chein, 1930s, 17 x 13 In. 153

Fire Hose Carriage, Iron, Reel, Original Rope, 4 Red Spoke Wheels, 2 Horses, Dent, 23 In. 4720

Fire Truck, Aerial Ladder, Pressed Steel, Paint, Smith-Miller-MIC, Box, 1950s, 24 In. 443

Fire Truck, Cast Iron, Nickel Plated Stacks, Firemen, No. 2167, Painted, Hubley, 9 x 4 In. 127

Fire Truck, Hook & Ladder, Pressed Steel, Red, 4 Ladders, Boom, Reel, Buddy L, 1926, 25 In. 1652

Fire Truck, Pumper, Cast Iron, Nickel Plated Wheels, Paint, A.C. Williams Co., 1920s, 6 In. *illus* 225

Fire Truck, Pumper, Cast Iron, Red, Silver Boiler, Nickel Driver, Disc Wheels, Hubley, 11 In. 118

Fire Truck, Red, Cast Iron, Embossed, Silver Ladder & Driver, Hubley, 16 In. 384

Fire Truck, Red, Cast Iron, Nickel Hose, Reel & Bell, 6 Men, Arcade, c.1941, 13 In. 649

Fire Wagon, Driver, Horses, Boiler, Clockwork, Cast Iron, Ives, c.1890, 19 In. 1650

Fire Wagon, Ladder, Cast Iron, Gray, Yellow Spoke Wheels, Bell Ringer, 3 Horses, Dent, 30 In. 3540

Fire Wagon, Pumper, Cast Iron, Yellow, Nickel Boiler, Spokes, 2 Horses, Driver, Kenton, 21 In. 649

Fire Wagon, Pumper, Horse Drawn, Black, Gold Highlights, Red Wheels, Cast Iron, Ives, 19 In. 1062

Flintstones, Dino, Stroller, Pull Toy, Box, 1964, 19 ½ In. 210

Flintstones, Pals, Dino, Fred On Purple Dinosaur, Tin Lithograph, Rubber, Marx, Box, 8 In. 443

Flintstones, Tricycle, Celluloid Fred, Tin Cycle, Windup, Marx, Japan, Box, 4 In. 472

Floor Puncher, Clown, Clockwork, Celluloid Bag, Tin Lithograph, Chein, 8 In. 384

Flying Saucer, Sky Patrol, Red, Tin, Plastic Dome, Astronaut, Battery, Box, Japan, c.1960, 8 In. 171

Flying Saucer, Z-101, Tin Lithograph, Multicolor, Friction, Box, Japan, 7 In. 660

Foxy Grandpa In Rocker, Tin Head & Hands, Cloth Outfit, Curved Rockers, Windup, 8 In. 2950

Foxy Grandpa Skater, Arms & Legs Move, Tin, Germany, 8 In. 1416

Frankenstein, Vinyl, Tin Lithograph, Moves, Pants Drop, Red Face, Battery, Box, 1960s, 14 In. 253

Funicular Railway, 2 Coal Cars, Slanted Track, House At Top, M & K, Germany, 33 In. 944

Funny Face, Harold Lloyd, Tin, Walker, Louis Marx, Box, c.1930, 10 ½ In. *illus* 4890

Games are listed in the Game category.

Garage, Pressed Steel, 2 Bays, Toytown, 16 x 21 In. 649

Gas Pump, Cast Iron, Yellow, Red, Decal Dial, Arcade, 6 In. 472

Gazelle, Wood, Jointed, Painted Eyes, Leather Ears, Replaced Horns, Schoenhut, 6 In. *illus* 531

Gent Acrobat, Circus, Bisque Head, Wood, Jointed, Felt Costume, Bar Bell, Schoenhut, 8 In. 384

Giraffe, Circus, Wood, Jointed, Glass Eyes, Leather Ears, Schoenhut, 8 In. 177

Giraffe, Plush, Standing, Orange & Yellow, Furry Mane & Tail, Bead Eyes, Steiff 60

Gnomes, Sawing Wood, Meier, Germany, Penny, 4 In. 177

Going To The Fair, Woman, Blue Dress, Tin Litho, Windup, Lehmann, Germany, 6 In. *illus* 708

Gorilla, Circus, Wood, Jointed, Painted, Molded Ears, Schoenhut, 7 ¾ In. 1180

Grasshopper, Green, Cast Iron, Aluminum Legs, Articulated, Hubley, Pull Toy, 10 In. 384

Gun Truck, Anti-Aircraft, Tin, Cannon, Enclosed Cab, Figures, Clockwork, Gray, 10 ½ In. 236

Gun, Atomic Disintegrator, Metal, Red Handle, Hubley, 7 In. 250

Ham & Sam, Minstrel Team, Piano, Man Playing Banjo, Windup, Strauss, 1930s, 3 x 5 In. 292

Hand Puppet, Uncle Fester, Addams Family, Box, Filmways, 1964, 10 ½ In. 1265

Handcar, Moon Mullins & Kayo, Tin Lithograph, Paint, Marx, 6 ½ In. 150

Hansom Cab, Cast Iron, Open Front, Driver On Roof, House, Pratt & Letchworth, 11 In. 236

Hansom Cab, Dapper Driver, Top Hat, Passenger Seat, Horse, Red Wheels, c.1915, 12 In. 356

Hay Rake, Red, Yellow, Cast Iron, Arcade, Box, 7 In. 826

Battery-Operated Toys

Battery-operated toys were possible after C and D batteries became easily available after World War II. Many of the toys were made in Japan after the war, often using tin from discarded American drink cans left by soldiers.

Toy, Clown Drummer, Yellow Kid, Tin Horse, Platform, Converse, c.1920, 10 x 12 In.
$118

Bertoia Auctions

Toy, Delivery Van, EBO Express, Doors Open, Tin, Clockwork, Hans Eberl, Germany, 8 In.
$413

Bertoia Auctions

Toy, Display Card, Hot Wheels, Mongoose, Red, Tilt-Up Car, Button, Sticker Sheets, 1970
$345

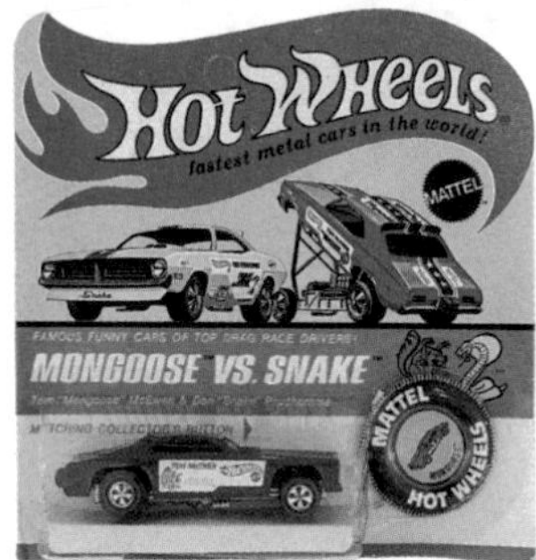

Hake's Americana & Collectibles

T

Toy, Doll Room Box, Parlor, Dolls, Walterhausen, Germany, c.1910, 12 x 12 In.
$375

Apple Tree Auction

TIP
Restoration of an old dollhouse should be restrained. Wash it, repair the structural problems, repaint as little as possible, and redecorate with appropriate old wallpaper fabrics and paint colors.

Toy, Fire Truck, Pumper, Cast Iron, Nickel Plated Wheels, Paint, A.C. Williams Co., 1920s, 6 In.
$225

Ruby Lane

Toy, Funny Face, Harold Lloyd, Tin, Walker, Louis Marx, Box, c.1930, 10 ½ In.
$4,890

RSL Auction

Hippo, Circus, Wood, Jointed, Glass Eyes, Carved Teeth, Schoenhut, 9 In. 325
Hobby Horse, Running, Old White Paint, Oil Cloth Saddle, 22 x 45 In. 300
Hoisting Tower, Pressed Steel, Buddy L, Illinois, c.1940, 38 ¼ In. 864
Horse Race, 3 Horses, Jockeys, Fence, Finish Line, Tin Litho, Germany, Penny, c.1920, 4 In. 649
Horse Race, Fence, Finish Sign, Tin Lithograph, Germany, Penny, c.1920, 4 In. 590
Horse, Black Stallion, Tin Base, Cast Wheels, Cutout Hearts, Bell, 9 ¼ In. 1422
Horse, Glider, Wood, Leather Ears & Saddle, Reins, 27 ½ x 33 ½ In. 377
Horse, On Platform, Bell, Tin Base, Cast Wheels, Early 1900s, 9 ¼ In. 1422
Horse, Pull, Standing, Painted Wood, Rollers, Yellow & Red, Signed, 1981, 10 In. 71
Horse, Push Pull, Wood, Carved, Painted Black Spots, Black Base, Red Edging & Wheels, 22 In. 523
Horse, Rocking, Poplar, Black & White Painted Horses, Red Rockers, Center Seat, c.1880, 45 In. 240
Horse, Rocking, Wood, Horsehair Mane & Tail, Black Burlap & Leather Bridle, 34 x 38 In. 360
Horse, Rocking, Wood, Paint, Yellow Ground, Blue, Green, Red, Seat, 1800s, 22 x 45 In. 2006
Horse, Rocking, Wood, Yellow Paint, Tack Leather Seat, Dovetailed, 1800s, 26 x 45 In. 2360
Horse, Wheels, Carved, Red, Saddle, Teeth, 44 x 40 In. 968
Humphrey Mobile, 3-Wheel Bike, House, Door, Tin Litho, Windup, 1950s, 9 In. 155
James Bond, Secret Agent 007, Assault Raider Kit, B.A.R.K. Attache Set, Box, 9 ¾ x 14 In. 1256
Jazzbo Jim, Banjo, Log Cabin Stage, Tin Lithograph, Windup, 10 ¼ In. 295
Jazzbo Jim, Dancer On Cabin Roof, Tin Lithograph, Clockwork, Unique Art, 10 In. 502
Joy Rider, Tin Litho, Multicolor, Windup, Driver's Head Spins, Wheels Turn, Marx, 8 x 6 In. 305
King Kong, Plush Body, Remote Control, The Mighty Kong, Box, 1960s, 11 In. 772
Knife, Khyber Bowie, Machete Style, Indiana Jones, Leather Scabbard, Branded, Box, 24 In. 115
Ladder Truck, Aerial, Studebaker Body, Pressed Steel, Clockwork, Kingsbury, c.1938, 23 In. 89
Le Petit Diabolo, Boy With Diabolo Stick, Clockwork, Fernand Martin, 8 In. 2360
Li'l Abner Dogpatch Band, Tin Lithograph, Clockwork, Unique Art, Box, 1945 325
Lion Tamer, Circus, Composition, Wood, Brown Hair, Blue Coat, Red Fez, Schoenhut, 8 In. 177
Lion, Mohair, Curly Mane, Amber Glass Eyes, Iron Wheel Base, Pull String, Steiff, 1915, 22 In. .. 741
Little Calculator, Schoolboy At Chalkboard, Math Problems, Tin, Clockwork, 7 In. 1298
Little Cook, Clockwork, Slices Carrots, Sticks Out Tongue, Clockwork, Martin, 8 In. .... *illus* 2124
Locomotive, Clockwork, Lion, Fire Hydrant, Tin, Cast Iron Wheels, Head Lamp, Bergman, 12 In. 3250
Magic Lantern, Projector, Wood Cabinet, Brass, Tin Chimney, England, 16 x 13 In. 432
Man & Woman, Walker, Arm In Arm, Dog At Side, Tin Litho, Flywheel, Lehmann, 6 In. 1298
Man Pulling Rickshaw, Woman Rider, Tin Lithograph, Clockwork, Lehmann, 7 In. 472
Man Wearing Kilt, Riding Scooter, Tin Litho, Disc Wheels, Windup, Germany, c.1922, 7 In. 1298
Merrymakers Band, Piano, 3 Mice, Tin, Painted, Windup, Marx, Box, 1930s, 9 x 9 In. 688
Merrymakers Band, Piano, 5 Mice Musicians, Marx, Tin Lithograph, Windup, 1930s, 5 x 5 x 5 In. 508
Minstrel Playing Banjo, Tin, Painted, Clockwork, Gunthermann, Germany, 8 In. 1534
Minstrel Show, Strums Banjo, Paper On Wood, Litho, Courier Lithograph Co., 1884, 10 In. 1062
Model Kit, Car, Woody, 1948 Model, Revell, Box, 1990s 20
Monkey, Climbing Palm Tree, Gravity, Tin Lithograph, Emporium Specialty Co., 1940s, 18 In. .. 89
Monkey, Climbing, Tin Lithograph, Pull String, Distler, Germany, Penny, 7 In. 295
Monkey, Cymbals, Fuzzy, Blue Hat, Windup, Germany, 8 In. 55
Monkey, Top Hat, Tin, Felt Suit, Cardboard Hat, Clockwork, Schuco, Germany, 6 In. .... *illus* 266
Monkey, Wood, Standing, Jointed, Felt Jumpsuit, Schoenhut, 8 In. 266
Mother Goose, Walker, Riding On Goose With Cat, Tin Litho, Windup, Marx, 1930s, 9 In. 336
Motorcycle & Rider, Headlight, Tin Lithograph, Meier, Germany, Penny, 4 In. .... *illus* 1534
Motorcycle, Evel Knievel, Stunt Cycle, Figure, Ideal, Box, 1975, 9 x 14 In. 634
Motorcycle, Harley-Davidson, Cast Iron, Rubber Tires, Spoke Wheels, Hubley, 9 In. .... *illus* 826
Motorcycle, Harley-Davidson, Hill Climber, Orange, Cast Iron, Nickel, Rubber, Hubley, 8 In. 6490
Motorcycle, Indian, Cast Iron, Green, 4 Cylinder, Rubber Tires, Police Driver, Hubley, 9 In. 1416
Motorcycle, Indian, Cast Iron, Red, Nickel Engine, Aluminum Handlebars, Hubley, 9 In. 1180
Motorcycle, Parcel Post, Driver, Harley-Davidson Decal, Cast Iron, Hubley, 10 In. 1560
Motorcycle, Police Dept. M.C., Driver, Tin, Crank, Japan 245
Motorcycle, Police Siren, Tin Lithograph, Windup, Box, Marx, c.1935, 3 x 8 x 5 In. 285
Motorcycle, Police, Hops On & Off, Circles, Mechanical, Modern Toys, Japan, 11 ½ In. 400
Motorcycle, Police, Red, Cast Iron, Electric Headlight, Rubber Tires, Hubley, 6 In. 266
Motorcycle, Policeman, Silver, Green Rider, Cast Iron, Nickel, Rubber, Kilgore, 6 ½ In. 1121
Motorcycle, Removable Policeman, Red, Cast Iron, Headlight, Hubley, c.1935, 8 In. 1180
Movie Viewer, Horrorscope, Werewolf, Frankenstein, Dracula, Box, 1964, 20 x 12 In. 2280
Mysterious Ball, Spiral Track, String, Windup, Tin Litho, F. Martin, 1906, 14 In. .... *illus* 711
Nanny Pushing Carriage, Baby Rocks, Tin, Windup, Germany, 8 In. 3835
Noah's Ark, Boat, Animal Figures, Carved, Painted, Hinged Roof, Germany, c.1900, 10 x 21 In. 1062
Noah's Ark, Pine, Painted, Hinged Lid, 111 Carved Animals, c.1900, 9 x 18 In. 840
Nodder, Figurine, Alice In Wonderland, Queen Of Hearts, Glazed Ceramic, 1950s, 6 In. .... *illus* 920
Pail, Kids On Beach, Tin Lithograph, Ohio Art Co., c.1930, 6 ½ In. 379
Pail, Lid, Felix The Cat, Riding Horse, Beach Scenes, Tin Litho, England, c.1925, 9 In. .... *illus* 1150

Pail, Stave Construction, Red Stars, Painted Blue, Wire Bail Handle, c.1875, 3 x 4 In. 2214
Parisian Woman, Walker, Green Felt Skirt & Hat, Fur Muff, Fernand Martin, 7 ½ In. 8260
Pedal Car, Airflow, Maroon, White Grille, Headlights, Bulb Horn, Steelcraft.1930s, 43 In. 1121
Pedal Car, Airplane, Army Pursuit, Eagle Decals, Stars, Wings, Propeller Turns, 47 In. 210
Pedal Car, Airplane, Pursuit, Steel, Blue, Yellow, Red Trim, Disc Wheels, Steelcraft, 1930s, 45 In. 590
Pedal Car, Airplane, Super Sonic Jet, Pressed Steel, Silver, Red Accents, Murray, 1950s, 45 In. 944
Pedal Car, American National, Toledo, Ohio, Painted Red, Black, 1930............................*illus* 3510
Pedal Car, Biplane, Yellow Paint, Curtis Moth, c.1930, 31-In. Wingspan....................................... 767
Pedal Car, BMC Special Racer, Red, Pressed Steel, Rubber Tires, 1950s, 41 In. 502
Pedal Car, Boat, Dolphin, White, Blue, Flag, Seat Cushion, Murray, 39 x 18 In. 444
Pedal Car, Boat, Murray, Li'l Beaver, Pressed Steel, Gray, Blue, Purple, 46 x 18 In. 1140
Pedal Car, Champion, Pink, Red Stripes, Chrome Hubs, Steering Wheel & Hood Ornament, 36 In. . 120
Pedal Car, Chevrolet, Pressed Steel, Yellow & Green, Maroon Leather, Steelcraft, c.1935, 38 In. . 1180
Pedal Car, Chrysler Airflow, American National, Plastic Windshield, 25 x 47 In. ....*illus* 2074
Pedal Car, Chrysler Town & Country, Pressed Steel, Wood, Disc Wheels, Stegar, 1940s, 42 In. 885
Pedal Car, Dodge, Steel, Painted, Rubber Tires, Gear Shift, American National, 36 In. 384
Pedal Car, Dude Wagon, Ford Model, Pressed Steel, Tailgate, Teal, Murray, c.1948, 40 In. 207
Pedal Car, Dump Truck, Chain Driven, Sand & Gravel Trailer, 1950s, 48 x 19 In. 300
Pedal Car, Fire Chief, Pressed Steel, Red, Black Fenders & Grille, Steelcraft, 49 In. 1534
Pedal Car, Fire Pumper, Pressed Steel, Red Paint, Decals, American National, 64 In. 2360
Pedal Car, Fire Truck, Murray, Dipside Fire Chief, Bell, Pressed Steel, Red, 1950s, 35 x 22 In. 120
Pedal Car, Fire Truck, Pontiac, Pressed Steel, Red, White, Wood Ladders, Murray, c.1949, 43 In. 118
Pedal Car, Fire Truck, Pressed Steel, Red Paint, Steelcraft, 31 In. 325
Pedal Car, Garton, Hot Rod, Pressed Steel, Pearlescent Paint, Blue, Decals, 1950s, 36 x 20 In. ... 390
Pedal Car, Jordan, Pressed Steel, Blue, Black, Nickel Trim, Spoke Wheels, Gendron, 55 In. 2242
Pedal Car, Jordan, Pressed Steel, Blue, Spoke Wheels, Gendron, 52 In. 4130
Pedal Car, Lincoln, Pressed Steel, Springs, Spoke Wheels, American National, 46 In. 1003
Pedal Car, Locomotive, Pressed Steel, Black, Red, Bell, No. 6400, Keystone, 26 In. 354
Pedal Car, Mercedes-Benz, Plastic, 300SL, Silver, Red, 1980s, 44 In. 236
Pedal Car, Open, Wood, Chain Drive, Upholstered, Spoke Wheels, 46 In. 266
Pedal Car, Packard, Shades Of Blue, Black, Steel, 1920s Style, American National, 47 In. 1062
Pedal Car, Plymouth, Steel, Maroon, Black Fenders, Steelcraft, 46 In. 1180
Pedal Car, Pontiac Station Wagon, Murray, Pressed Steel, Maroon, 1948, 46 In. 460
Pedal Car, Pontiac, Fire Truck, City Fire Department, Bell, Ladder Rail, Red, 1950s, 40 x 22 In. 180
Pedal Car, Pontiac, Pressed Steel, Maroon, Black Fenders, Luggage Bars, Steelcraft, 43 In. 1534
Pedal Car, Pressed Steel, Disc Wheels, Belgium Coupe Model, Torck, 43 In. 207
Pedal Car, Pressed Steel, Nickel Grille, American National Paige, c.1925, 59 In. 2950
Pedal Car, Ranch Wagon, Maroon, Steel, V8 On Grille, Rear Hand Rails, Murray, 1950s, 45 In. . 236
Pedal Car, Ranch Wagon, Pressed Steel, Disc Wheels, Rubber Tires, Murray, c.1940, 48 In. 472
Pedal Car, Roadster, Pressed Steel, Blue, Nickel Trim, Gendron, 1940s, 40 In. 561
Pedal Car, Rocket Ship, Pressed Steel, Red, Yellow, Air Force Decal, Robert, c.1950, 26 In. 1121
Pedal Car, Streak Sky, Pressed Steel, Rocket Body, Chain Drive, Red, White, 1950s, 46 In. 1298
Pedal Car, Stutz, Pressed Steel, Buick Style, Yellow, Black Grille, Steelcraft, 47 In. 1298
Pedal Car, Taxi, New York City Checker, Checker Pattern, Yellow, Decals, 34 In. 180
Phonograph, Gold Horn, Litho & Painted, Crank, Meier, Germany, Penny, 4 In. 207
Pig, Wood, Jointed, Painted, Humpty Dumpty Circus, Schoenhut, 7 ½ In. ....*illus* 295
Playset, Evel Knievel Stunt Stadium, Ramp, Hook, High Jump, Vinyl, Box, 1974, 46 In. 253
Playset, G.I. Joe Action Marine Demolition, Voltmeter, Detection Light, Box, 1966, 11 x 11 In. ... 424
Playset, Jurassic Park, Electronic Command Center, Box, Kenner, 1993, 16 ½ x 22 ½ In. 173
Playset, Marx Service Center, Gas Station, Repairs, Ramp, Sky View Parking Roof, Tin, 26 In. ... 177
Playset, Noah's Ark, Bird On Roof, Sliding Panel, Animals, Wood, 1894, 20 In., 100 Piece........... 1888
Playset, Planet Of The Apes, Treehouse, Rifles, Sticks, Net, Pole, c.1975, 18 x 22 In. 817
Playset, Tales Of Wells Fargo, Stagecoach, Horses, Cowboys, Box, c.1960, 16 x 27 In. 1497
Playset, Tootsietoy Funnies, With Action, 6 Comic Vehicles, Fitted Box, c.1930, 15 In. 3540
Playset, Tootsietoy Rol-Ezy, No. 5149, 10 3-In. Vehicles, Box 295
Playset, Walton's Farmhouse, 5 Rooms, Furniture, Cardboard Box, 1975, 26 x 38 In. 243
Polar Explorer, Sled, Muster Geschutzt, 2 Explorers, 2 Dogs, Tin, Germany, c.1915, 9 In. 1680
Pram, Felix The Cat, Tin Lithograph, Spain, 1920s, 5 ½ In. ....*illus* 236
Puppet, Charlie Chan, Vinyl Body, Ideal, Bagged, 1973, 12 In. 115
Puppet, Dr. Doolittle, Talking, Vinyl Head, Fabric Body, Hand, Box, 1967, 7 x 12 In. 115
Puppet, King Kong & Bobby Bond, Talking, Soft Vinyl Head, Felt Body, Box, 1966, 7 x 12 In. 385
Puppet, Little Ricky, I Love Lucy, Fabric Pajamas, Vinyl Head Hands & Feet, Box, 1953, 9 In. 253
Puppet, Man From U.N.C.L.E., Illya Kuryakin, Vinyl, Cloth, On Card, A.C. Gilbert, 1965, 13 In. .. 190
Puppet, Morticia, The Addams Family, Hand, Pink Body, Plastic Bag, Header Card, 1960s........... 416
Puppet, Pinocchio Type Figure, Elongated Nose, Wood Composition, 23 In. 556
Puppet, The Monkees, Talking, Soft Vinyl Heads, Fabric Body, Mattel, Box, 1966, 7 x 12 In. 508

Toy, Gazelle, Wood, Jointed, Painted Eyes, Leather Ears, Replaced Horns, Schoenhut, 6 In.
$531

Bertoia Auctions

Toy, Going To The Fair, Woman, Blue Dress, Tin Litho, Windup, Lehmann, Germany, 6 In.
$708

Bertoia Auctions

Toy, Little Cook, Clockwork, Slices Carrots, Sticks Out Tongue, Clockwork, Martin, 8 In.
$2,124

Bertoia Auctions

T

Toy, Monkey, Top Hat, Tin, Felt Suit, Cardboard Hat, Clockwork, Schuco, Germany, 6 In.
$266

Bertoia Auctions

Toy, Motorcycle & Rider, Headlight, Tin Lithograph, Meier, Germany, Penny, 4 In.
$1,534

Bertoia Auctions

Toy, Motorcycle, Harley-Davidson, Cast Iron, Rubber Tires, Spoke Wheels, Hubley, 9 In.
$826

Bertoia Auctions

Revolver, Leather Fringed Holster, Silver Rivets, 6 In. 12
Ringmaster, Circus, Composition, Wood, Jointed, Glass Eyes, Felt Suit, Staff Schoenhut, 7 In. ... 354
Robot, Answer Game Machine, Calculator, Flashes, Spins, Tin Litho, Box, Japan, 1960s, 14 In. .. 736
Robot, Blink-A-Gear, Tin Litho, Plastic, Gears In Chest, Batteries, Walks, Blinks, 1960s, 15 In. ... 337
Robot, Chime Trooper, Astronaut, Mechanical, Tin Lithograph, Japan, Box, 9 ½ In. 11400
Robot, Chrome, Hollow Eyes, Antenna Ears, Windup, Key, c.1950, 5 In. 30
Robot, Directional, Tin Lithograph, Japan, Box, 11 In. 2700
Robot, Lavender, Gang Of Five, Masudaya, Battery Operated, Japan, 14 ¾ In. .... *illus* 2006
Robot, Lost In Space, Plastic, Cardboard Inserts, 14 In. 600
Robot, Lost In Space, Plastic, Motorized, Red & Blue, Chest Light-Up, Box, 1966, 12 In. 386
Robot, Plastic Dome Head, Revolves, Flashes, Tin Litho, Box, Alps, Remote Control, 1950s, 9 In. 1139
Robot, TV Spaceman, Tin, Litho, Walks, Lights, Box, Alps, Japan, c.1959, 11 In. .... *illus* 614
Rocket Racer, Red, Green, Black, White Rubber Wheels, Wyandotte, 1935, 6 In. 95
Rocket, Sparkling, Tin Lithograph, V-1, USAF, Rubber Nose Cone, Japan, Box, 12 ½ In. 2280
Roller Coaster, 2 Cars, Tin Lithograph, Belt Driven, Windup, J. Chein, Box, c.1929, 18 In. 148
Rollo Chair, Black Man, Push Cart, Boardwalk, Tin, Windup, Strauss, Germany, 7 In. 720
Safariwagen, Land Rover, Painted, Resin Body, Removable Top, Steiff, Box, 1971-79, 10 In. 115
Sailor, Walking, Columbia, Tin, Painted, Windup, Lehmann, Germany, c.1900, 8 In. .... *illus* 280
Scale, Balance, Felix The Cat, Tin Litho, Removable Plates, Spain, 1920s, 5 ½ In. .... *illus* 148
Schoolhouse, Roof Opens, Classroom, Students, Wood, Papered, Furnishings, c.1900, 10 x 14 In. 1200
Scooter Wagon, Kroger, Country Club Super Speedster, Steel, Metalcraft, 33 In. .... *illus* 649
Seal, Red Collar, Tin Lithograph, Windup, Lehmann, 7 In. 295
Service Station, Tin Lithograph, Figures, Pumps, Folding Ramp, Marx, 10 x 13 In. 295
Sizzlers, High-Winder Set, Live Wire, Battery Powered Recharger, Mattel, 1971, 10 x 25 In. 173
Ski Boat, Bathing Beauty Figure, Tin Platform, Rubber, 10 In. 309
Sky Rangers, Airplane, Blimp Go-Round, Tin Litho, Multicolor, Unique Art, 1933, 24 x 9 In. 325
Sled, Dexter, Wood, Red Paint, Reindeer's Head, Gold Stripes & Curls, Iron Runners, 40 In. 502
Sled, Eagle, Red, Yellow Striping, Banner, E Pluribus Unum, 1800s, 43 x 18 ¼ In. .... *illus* 2875
Sled, Mixed Wood, Painted, Signed Gipsy, 19th Century, 32 In. .... *illus* 153
Sled, Painted, Stylized Landscape, Flowers, Red Frame & Runners, 19th Century, 32 x 14 In. 523
Sled, Pine, Iron, Painted Design, Winter Landscape, Pivoting Runners, c.1900, 68 In. 875
Sled, Wood, Paint, Finger Lakes Scene, Iron Runners, Geese Head Pulls, 1890s, 18 x 38 In. 2196
Soldier, Mounted, Green Platform, Tin Lithograph, Germany, Penny, 2 ¾ In. 384
Soldiers, Lead, All The Queen's Men, No. 1661, Britains, 11 Piece.......... 210
Soldiers, Lead, Britains, c.1920, 26 Piece 390
Soldiers, Lead, Britains, c.1925, 9 Piece 270
Space Gun, Tin, Multicolor, Characters, Clouds, Friction, Japan, 18 In. 150
Spaceship, Space Patrol, Mars-107, Tin Litho, Turret, Cannons, Blinking Lights, 1950s, 17 In. . 285
Spaceship, Tin Lithograph, Ship X-2, Red, Yellow, Gray, Friction, Box, 7 ½ In. 660
Sparkler, Felix The Cat, Tin, Spring Action Mechanism, Spins, Eyes Spark, c.1926, 2 ½ x 2 ½ In. .. *illus* 115
Sparky Robot, Tin Lithograph, Walks, Eyes Light Up, Illustrated Box, Yoshiya, 1950s, 7 ¾ In. ... 230
Store, Diorama, Wood, Paper, Bisque Storekeeper, Counter, Products, Germany, 12 x 21 In. 600
Store, Wood, Cutouts, Paint, 3-Sided, Shelves, Drawers, Doors, Counter, Scale, 22 x 28 In. 810
Strutting Sam, Dancing, Tin Lithograph, Multicolor, Box, 11 x 4 In. 242
Sulky, Jockey, Spoke Wheels, Cast Iron, Pratt & Letchworth, Buffalo Toy, Box, 8 In. 2006
Sunny Andy Cable Car, 2 Cars, Tin Lithograph, String Pull, Wolverine, Box, 10 x 23 In. 384
Sunny Suzy Washing Machine, Tin Litho, Wringer, Crank Handle, Tub, Wolverine, 8 ½ In. 108
Tank, Radar, Diver, WH-196, Pick Shovel, Tin Lithograph, Windup, Hausser, 10 In. 510
Tank, Space, Tin Lithograph, 3 Figures, Holding Guns, Remote Control, Explorer, Japan, 8 In. .. 204
Taxi, Amos 'N' Andy, Fresh Air, Tin Litho, Men & Dog, Marx, Box, 8 In. 826
Taxi, For Hire, White, Gold Trim, Die Cut Lamps, Uniformed Driver, Distler, Penny, 3 In. 413
Taxi, Pressed Steel, Orange & Black, Driver, Friction, Republic Tool Co., c.1926, 11 In. 207
Teddy Bears are also listed in the Teddy Bear category.
Teddy Roosevelt Safari, Wood, Jointed, Paint, Cloth, Leather, Rifle, Schoenhut, 8 In. 1534
Tiger Circus, Jointed Wood, Orange, Glass Eyes, Rope Tail, Leather Ears, Schoenhut, 7 In. 325
Tom Twist, Clown, Harlequin Pattern, Tin, Walker, Ferdinand Strauss, c.1925, 8 ¾ In. .... *illus* 390
Toonerville Trolley, Figure On Platform, Tin Litho, Clockwork, Fontaine Fox, c.1922, 7 In. 295
Tractor, Caterpillar, Driver, Climbing, Windup, Tin Lithograph, Marx, 1950s, 8 ¾ In. .... *illus* 47
Train Accessory, Bing, Station, Tin, Embossed Brick, Glass Window Inserts, 1 Gauge, 22 In. 6490
Train Accessory, Lionel, Icing Station, Red Roof, White Building.......... *illus* 46
Train Accessory, Marklin, Bridge, Suspension, 2 Towers, Flags, Enameled, 0 Gauge, 63 In. 21240
Train Accessory, Marklin, Buffet Bar & Fountain, Brick Pattern, Pumps Water, 6 In. 4720
Train Accessory, Marklin, Destination Board, Zugfahrt Nach, City Signs, c.1904, 8 In. 266
Train Accessory, Marklin, Direction Indicator, Arrow Boards, Innsbruck, Leipzig, 10 In. 2950
Train Accessory, Marklin, Freight Shed, Sliding Doors, Pivoting Derrick, 1 Gauge, 14 x 10 In. . 384
Train Accessory, Marklin, Gantry Crane, 2 Cranks, 16 In. 590

Toy, Mysterious Ball, Spiral Track, String, Windup, Tin Litho, F. Martin, 1906, 14 In.
$711

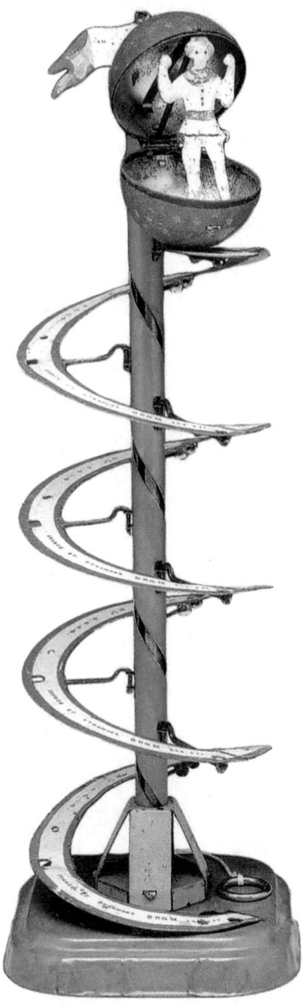

James D. Julia Auctioneers

Play in the Sand

Sand pails were first made in the late 1800s; any pail in good to excellent condition sells quickly. Best-known makers of pails were Chein, T. Cohn, Happynak, E. Rosen Co., and Ohio Art.

Toy, Pail, Lid, Felix The Cat, Riding Horse, Beach Scenes, Tin Litho, England, c.1925, 9 In.
$1,150

Hake's Americana & Collectibles

Toy, Pedal Car, American National, Toledo, Ohio, Painted Red, Black, 1930
$3,510

Showtime Auction Services

Toy, Pig, Wood, Jointed, Painted, Humpty Dumpty Circus, Schoenhut, 7 ½ In.
$295

Bertoia Auctions

Toy, Pram, Felix The Cat, Tin Lithograph, Spain, 1920s, 5 ½ In.
$236

Bertoia Auctions

Toy, Nodder, Figurine, Alice In Wonderland, Queen Of Hearts, Glazed Ceramic, 1950s, 6 In.
$920

Hake's Americana & Collectibles

Toy, Pedal Car, Chrysler Airflow, American National, Plastic Windshield, 25 x 47 In.
$2,074

Morphy Auctions

Toy, Robot, Lavender, Gang Of Five, Masudaya, Battery Operated, Japan, 14 ¾ In.
$2,006

Bertoia Auctions

Toy, Robot, TV Spaceman, Tin, Litho, Walks, Lights, Box, Alps, Japan, c.1959, 11 In.
$614

Hake's Americana & Collectibles

Toy, Sailor, Walking, Columbia, Tin, Painted, Windup, Lehmann, Germany, c.1900, 8 In.
$280

Theriault's

Toy, Scale, Balance, Felix The Cat, Tin Litho, Removable Plates, Spain, 1920s, 5 ½ In.
$148

Bertoia Auctions

Toy, Scooter Wagon, Kroger, Country Club Super Speedster, Steel, Metalcraft, 33 In.
$649

Bertoia Auctions

Toy, Sled, Eagle, Red, Yellow Striping, Banner, E Pluribus Unum, 1800s, 43 x 18 ¼ In.
$2,875

James D. Julia Auctioneers

Toy, Sled, Mixed Wood, Painted, Signed Gipsy, 19th Century, 32 In.
$153

Hess Auction Group

Toy, Sparkler, Felix The Cat, Tin, Spring Action Mechanism, Spins, Eyes Spark, c.1926, 2 ½ x 2 ½ In.
$115

Hake's Americana & Collectibles

Train Accessory, Marklin, Round House, 5 Tracks, Arched Doorways, 1 Gauge, 30 In. ... 325
Train Accessory, Marklin, Semaphore Signal, Red & White Pole, Compressed Air, 12 In. ... 443
Train Accessory, Marklin, Signal Bridge, Electric Lanterns, Trestle, Germany, 24 In. ... 266
Train Accessory, Marklin, Snow Plow, Orange, Gray, Black Plow Blade, 1 Gauge, 8 In. ... 1180
Train Accessory, Marklin, Station Yard, Freight Shed, Signal, Lamps, Crane, 29 In. ... 11210
Train Accessory, Marklin, Station, Show Tickets, Refreshments Room, Awnings, 12 x 14 In. ... 5400
Train Accessory, Marklin, Switch Stand & Signal, Enameled Brickwork, 1 Gauge, 11 In. ... 12980
Train Accessory, Marklin, Ticket Station, Enamel, Roof Opens, 1 Gauge, 14 x 10 In. ... *illus* 7670
Train Accessory, Marklin, Tunnel, Tin, Painted, 15 x 20 In. ... *illus* 2124
Train Car, Bachmann, Steam Locomotive, Tender, O Gauge 4-8-4, NY Central, 1900s, 17 In. ... 36
Train Car, Bassett-Lowke, Locomotive & Tender, Enterprise, Maroon, 4-4-0, O Gauge ... 295
Train Car, Bassett-Lowke, Locomotive, Duchess Of Montrose, Green, O Gauge, Insignia ... 1416
Train Car, Bassett-Lowke, Locomotive, George The Fifth, Black, O Gauge, Tender, 9 In. ... 295
Train Car, Bassett-Lowke, Locomotive, L&NWR, Black, Red Stripes, 4-4-2, O Gauge, 11 In. ... 325
Train Car, Big Boy, Akane, 4-8-8-4, Steam Locomotive, Tender, HO Gauge, Japan, 1900s... 390
Train Car, Bing Bassett-Lowke, Locomotive, Great Central Sir Sam Fay, Electric, 1 Gauge, 15 In. 1652
Train Car, Bing, Boxcar, Swift Refrigerator Line 7300, Swift's Premium Hams, Logo, 9 In. ... 118
Train Car, Bing, Locomotive, Flying Fox, Green, Black, 2-6-0, O Gauge, Clockwork, Tender ... 826
Train Car, Bing, Locomotive, Great Western, Green, O Gauge, Clockwork, 10 In. ... *illus* 295
Train Car, Buddy L, Boxcar, Pressed Steel, Red, Sliding Door, Decals, c.1930, 20 ½ In. ... 236
Train Car, Buddy L, Caboose, Pressed Steel, Red, Ladders, Decals, Outdoor, 18 In. ... 472
Train Car, Buddy L, Flat Car, Pressed Steel, Black Paint, 20 In. ... 177
Train Car, Buddy L, Locomotive Wrecking Crane, Outdoor Railroad Scale, c.1925, 36 x 13 In. .. 610
Train Car, Elettren, Pullman, Tin Lithograph, Blue, Cream, Lights, O Gauge, 16 ½ In. ... 236
Train Car, Fleischmann, Trolley Engine, 2-4-2, Green, O Gauge, Germany, 8 In. ... 148
Train Car, Handcar, Tin, Windup, Box, Japan, 1950s, 6 In. ... 95
Train Car, Knapp, Caboose, Tin, Painted, N.Y.C & H.R.R.R., 5860, 8 Wheels, 10 In. ... 767
Train Car, Lionel, Engine & Tender, Pink, c.1946 ... *illus* 316
Train Car, Lionel, Locomotive & Tender, Standard Gauge, 400E Metal, c.1997, 2 Piece ... 420
Train Car, Lionel, Locomotive, Standard Gauge, No. 8, c.1940, 11 In. ... 71
Train Car, Lionel, Master Engine, Jersey Central Train, O Gauge, c.1946 ... *illus* 402
Train Car, Lionel, Rapid Transit, Red & Yellow, O Gauge, c.1946 ... *illus* 52
Train Car, Marklin, Baggage Car, Gray, Stripes, O Gauge, Germany, 4 ¾ In. ... *illus* 1298
Train Car, Marklin, Box Cab, Brown, O Gauge, Center Pantograph, Electric, 0-4-0 ... *illus* 236
Train Car, Marklin, Boxcar, Heinz 57 Varieties, Pickle, Tomato Ketchup, Orange, Tin Litho, 7 In. 1180
Train Car, Marklin, Congressional Limited Combine, Sliding Doors, O Gauge, 6 ½ In. ... *illus* 944
Train Car, Marklin, Crane Car, Tin, Embossed, Rivet Accents, O Gauge, 6 x 8 In. ... *illus* 708
Train Car, Marklin, Locomotive & Tender, Midland, O Gauge, Electric, 4-4-0, 8 In. ... *illus* 413
Train Car, Marklin, Locomotive, Cast Iron, Clockwork, O Gauge, 12 In. ... 2655
Train Car, Marklin, Locomotive, Commodore Vanderbilt, Black, NYC Tender, O Gauge, 14 In. ... 5900
Train Car, Marklin, Passenger Car, Mustard, Green Roof, Celluloid Windows, 1 Gauge, 21 In. ... 1416
Train Car, Marklin, Passenger, Twentieth Century Limited, Red Stripes, Doors Open, 12 In. ... 1180
Train Car, Marklin, Pullman, Oneonta, Green, 12 Wheels, O Gauge, 20 ¾ In. ... 5900
Train Car, Marklin, Red Cross, Tin, Hinged Roof, Operating Table, 1 Gauge, 9 In. ... *illus* 531
Train Car, Marklin, Sleeping Car, Blue, Hinged Top, Lights, 8 Wheels, 1 Gauge, 13 In., Pair ... 413
Train Car, Marklin, Steeple Cab, Green, Pantograph On Roof, Headlight, 1 Gauge ... 443
Train Car, Marklin, Steeple Cab, Nickel Rails, Pantograph, Clockwork, O Gauge ... *illus* 590
Train Car, Marklin, Zeevish Freight Car, White, 8 Wheels, O Gauge, Germany, 6 In. ... *illus* 4425
Train Car, Marx, 2 Men, Tin, Pull Toy, 1920s, 9 ½ In. ... 175
Train Set, BJD, Buildings, Tunnel, Gatehouse, Tin Litho, Clockwork, Germany, 9 In. ... *illus* 325
Train Set, Flintstones, Village, Track, Tunnel, Bedrock Station, Box, 1979, 16 x 26 In. ... 115
Train Set, Ives, Blue Vagabond, Locomotive, Tender, 3 Passenger Cars, Blue, c.1930 ... 649
Train Set, Ives, No. 5, Locomotive, Tender, Club, Parlor, Cars, Box, 13-In. Engine ... 8260
Train Set, Lionel, Blue Comet, Locomotive, Tender, 3 Passenger Cars, Standard Gauge ... 3540
Train Set, Lionel, Flying Yankee, Silver, Red Top, No. 616, Diesel, 2 Cars, c.1935 ... 531
Train Set, Marklin, Locomotive, Passenger Car, 1 Gauge, 5 Piece ... 4720
Train Set, Tin Litho, Windup Train, Board, Town, Cardboard Box, 1950s, 13 x 22 In. ... 115
Train, Round Track, Tunnel, Square Base, Scenery, Tin Lithograph, Penny, 4 ½ In. ... 148
Train, Steam Locomotive & Tender, HO Gauge, Japan, 2-8-4, c.1950 ... 600
Tricycle, Clockwork, Gentleman Rider, Plaid Suit, Spoke Wheels, 10 In. ... 2192
Trolley, Horse, Consolidated Street RR, Painted, Cast Iron, c.1895, 13 In. ... 590
Trolley, Lower & Upper Decks, Canopy, Tin, Red & Yellow, Clockwork, Bing, 12 In. ... 325
Trolley, Pressed Steel, Open Bench, Yellow, Red, Black Wheels, Converse, 16 In. ... 295
Truck, Allied Van Lines, Pressed Steel, Orange, Doors Open, Buddy L, c.1940, 30 In. ... 531
Truck, Ambulance, Pressed Steel, White, Red Cross Emblems, Sturditoy, c.1929, 27 In. ... 2360
Truck, Arcade, Coal, Cast Iron, Green Paint, Rubber Tires, 10 In. ... 425

Toy, Tom Twist, Clown, Harlequin Pattern, Tin, Walker, Ferdinand Strauss, c.1925, 8 ¾ In.
$390

RSL Auction

Toy, Tractor, Caterpillar, Driver, Climbing, Windup, Tin Lithograph, Marx, 1950s, 8 ¾ In.
$47

Hess Auction Group

Toy, Train Accessory, Lionel, Icing Station, Red Roof, White Building
$46

Apple Tree Auction

TIP

"Lead rot" is a disease of lead soldiers and other lead toys. Gray dust forms on the soldier and eventually the toy will disintegrate. It is not contagious, but it often appears on a group of soldiers stored together because it is caused by oxidation brought on by the environment. It seems to appear if lead items are stored in new wooden cases (use metal cases). Old wooden cases that are sealed with latex paint seem safe.

Toy, Train Accessory, Marklin, Ticket Station, Enamel, Roof Opens, 1 Gauge, 14 x 10 In.
$7,670

Bertoia Auctions

Toy, Train Accessory, Marklin, Tunnel, Tin, Painted, 15 x 20 In.
$2,124

Bertoia Auctions

Toy, Train Car, Bing, Locomotive, Great Western, Green, O Gauge, Clockwork, 10 In.
$295

Bertoia Auctions

Toy, Train Car, Lionel, Master Engine, Jersey Central Train, O Gauge, c.1946
$402

Apple Tree Auction

Toy, Train Car, Lionel, Rapid Transit, Red & Yellow, O Gauge, c.1946
$52

Apple Tree Auction

Toy, Train Car, Marklin, Baggage Car, Gray, Stripes, O Gauge, Germany, 4 ¾ In.
$1,298

Bertoia Auctions

Toy, Train Car, Lionel, Engine & Tender, Pink, c.1946
$316

Apple Tree Auction

Toy, Train Car, Marklin, Box Cab, Brown, O Gauge, Center Pantograph, Electric, 0-4-0
$236

Bertoia Auctions

Toy, Train Car, Marklin, Congressional Limited Combine, Sliding Doors, O Gauge, 6 ½ In.
$944

Bertoia Auctions

Toy, Train Car, Marklin, Crane Car, Tin, Embossed, Rivet Accents, O Gauge, 6 x 8 In.
$708

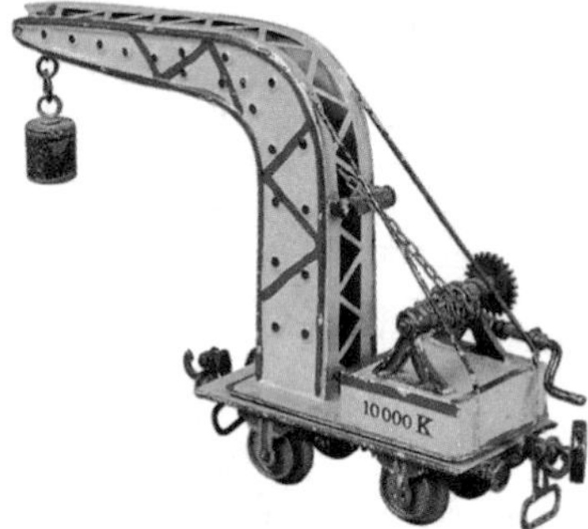

Bertoia Auctions

Toy, Train Car, Marklin, Locomotive & Tender, Midland, O Gauge, Electric, 4-4-0, 8 In.
$413

Bertoia Auctions

Truck, Army, Tin Litho, Green, Stars, Stencil, Marx, 1950s, 13 x 5 In. .... *illus* 110
Truck, Bulldozer, Cat Dozer, Aluminum, Paint, Rubber Treads, Hubley, Box, 1958, 10 In. 139
Truck, Cement Mixer, Jaeger, Cast Iron, Nickel Plated Drum & Scoop, Kenton, 6½ In. 354
Truck, Cement Mixer, Pressed Steel, Gray, Scoop, Revolving Drum, Buddy L, c.1925, 14 In. 561
Truck, Cement Mixer, Rotating Drum, Steel, Blue, White, Horn, Structo, 1960s, 16 In. 55
Truck, Cement, Blue Diamond, Die Cast, 3 Chutes, White, Blue, Smith-Miller, 18½ In. 708
Truck, Coal, Black Diamond Coal Co., Tin Litho, Dump Bed, Windup, Box, 1950s, 11 In. 228
Truck, Delivery Van, Cast Iron, Blue, Embossed, Flowers, Rubber Tires, Hubley, 1930s, 3½ In. ... 1416
Truck, Delivery Van, Peerless, Cast Iron, Embossed White On Grille, Arcade, 1929, 8 In. 21240
Truck, Delivery, Palmolive, Pressed Steel, Red Deco Body, Stake Side, Metalcraft, 1930s, 11 In. .. 2950
Truck, Delivery, Railroad Transfer, Steel, Yellow, Decals, Buddy L, Box, c.1949, 23 In. .... *illus* 2360
Truck, Digger, Mack Chassis, Cast Iron, Red, Green, Nickel Shovel, Rubber Tires, Hubley, 8 In. .. 561
Truck, Dump, Baby, Cast Iron, Red, Decals, Nickel Lift Bar, Arcade, 10 In. 207
Truck, Dump, Metallic Blue & Orange, Structo, 1957, 20 In. 110
Truck, Dump, Pressed Steel, Spring Loaded, Black, Red, Wyandotte, c.1930, 15 In. 95
Truck, Dump, Pressed Steel, Wood Handle Bar, Red, Green, Seat, Garland Red Flyer, 25 In. 472
Truck, Gas, Arcade Mack, Red, Gilt Accents, Rubber Tires, Spark Chain, Driver, 13 In. 2015
Truck, GMC, Texaco, Decals, Red & White Paint, Smith-Miller, 12¾ In. 125
Truck, Jaeger Mixer, Cast Iron, Nickel Cement Barrel, Kenton, 1940, 9½ In. .... *illus* 384
Truck, Meadow Gold Butter, Pressed Steel, Electric Light, Metalcraft, 1930s, 13 In. .... *illus* 443
Truck, North American Van Lines, Mack, Red, Yellow, Overhang, F. Thompson, 21 In. 1416
Truck, Pickup, A.C. Williams, Cast Iron, Patina, Wood Paneled, Spoke Wheels, 1920s, 7 In. 250
Truck, Pile Driver, Mighty Metal, Red, Hubley, 12 In. 75
Truck, Playset, Evel Knievel, Canyon Rig, Camping Accessories, Box, Ideal, 1975, 9 x 14 In. 354
Truck, Racing Transporter, M6, Matchbox, Box, c.1969, 5 In. 69
Truck, RCA-NBC Mobile TV, Rotating Cameraman, Tin Litho, Batteries, Box, Cragstan, 9 In. 780
Truck, Ride-On, Roberts Sealtest Milk, Gray & Red, Pressed Steel, Doors, Bell, 21 In. 420
Truck, Road Roller, Huber, Cast Iron, Green, Red Rollers, Nickel Grille & Tank, Hubley, 14 In. ... 767
Truck, Semi-Trailer, Mighty Metal, Red, Hubley, Box, 18 x 6 In. 225
Truck, Semi-Trailer, Power Shovel, Hubley, Box, 1960s, 21 x 9 In. 225
Truck, Steam Shovel, Cast Iron, Red, Embossed Panama On Sides, Hubley, c.1920, 9 In. 325
Truck, Steel Hauler, Ramps, Structo, 1951, 20 In. 95
Truck, Street Sweeper, The Elgin, Cast Iron, Nickel, Rubber Tires, Figure, Hubley, 8 In. 1416
Truck, Tanker, Streamline, Pressed Steel, Green, Rubber Tires, Wyandotte, 10 In. 285
Truck, Tow, Husky Wrecker, Pressed Steel, Paint, Dual Boom, Ny-Lint, Box, c.1970 115
Truck, Trailer, 3-Wheel, Red & White, Cushman Truckster, 7 x 10 In. 5795
Truck, U.S. Army, Troop Carrier, Clear Plastic, Pressed Steel, Green, 13 In. 120
Truck, Van, Military-TV, Army-TV Car, Green, Tin Lithograph, Friction, 6 In. 168
Turkey, On Wheels, Composition, Molded, Glass Eyes, Skittles Game Base, 16 In. .... *illus* 2124
Turtle, Spotted Shell, Composition, Feet On Wires, Spoke Wheels, Clockwork, 6 In. 354
Tyrolian Dancers, Tin Boy, Celluloid Girl, Clockwork, Schuco, c.1937, 5 In. 148
Van, U.S. Mail, Driver, Spoke Wheels, Yellow, Black, Tin Litho, A.C. Gilbert, 1930s, 8 In. 295
Violinist, Tin Head, Face, Hat & Violin, Cloth Pants & Jacket, Clockwork, F. Martin, 8 In. 826
Wagon, Circus, Driver On Roof, Overland, Cage, Red, White Bear, 2 Horses, Kenton, 14 In. 384
Wagon, Circus, Driver, 2 Lions, Scallop Top, Slats, Pressed Steel, 12 x 8 x 4 In. 60
Wagon, Circus, Driver, Big Show, Tin Litho, Cage, Animals, Die Cut Marquee, F. Strauss, 10 In. .. 561
Wagon, Circus, Driver, Overland, Band, Red, Gold Trim, 6 Musicians, 2 Horses, Kenton, 16 In. .. 561
Wagon, Circus, Driver, Royal, Band, Red, Gold, 6 Musicians, 4 Horses, Steel, Hubley, 21 In. 885
Wagon, Circus, Royal, Cage, Green & Gold, 2 Rhinos, 2 Horses, Cast Iron, Hubley, 15 In. 531
Wagon, Fire Boiler, Black, Boiler Moves Up & Down, Cast Iron, Clockwork, Ives, c.1890, 19 In. .. 1652
Wagon, Horse Drawn, U.S. Mail, Pull Toy, Tin Lithograph, Paint, 13 In. 130
Wagon, Milk, Tin, Milkman, Milk Jugs, Pure Milk, Paint, Spoke Wheels, 11 In. 556
Wagon, Milk, White, Red Wheels, Black Horse, Cast Iron, Kenton, Model 241, Box, 13 In. 216
Wagon, Phaeton, Black, Brown Seat, Woman Driver, Horse, Iron, Steel, Pratt & Letchworth, 16 In. . 885
Wagon, Pine, Stencils, Wagon Mfg. Co., Cedar Falls, Iowa, Cast Iron Wheels, 1907, 18 x 36 In. .. 450
Wagon, Wood, Painted, Green, Spoke Wheels, Acme Wagon Co., 1885, 27 x 42 In. 1003
Wagon, Wood, Red Wheels, Rubber Tires, Hand Brake, Peerless, Handle 156
Walking Ducks, 1 Large, 2 Small, Wings Flap, Tin, Windup, Gunthermann, 9 In. 443
Waltzing Couple, Harlequin Costumes, Tin Lithograph, Clockwork, Germany, 7 In. 590
Waltzing Woman Holding Muff, Tin, Painted, Blue, White, Gunthermann, 7½ In. 1888
Washer Woman, Basin On Stand, Tin, Cloth, Windup, Fernand Martin, 7 In. 2360
Washing Machine, 3 Little Pigs, Hand Crank, Footed, Yellow, Tin Lithograph, Chein, 8 In. 150
Washing Machine, Ringer, Maytag, Decal, Cast Iron, Paint, Hand Crank, Wheels, 7 In. 200
Windmill, Green, Brown, Tin, Germany, c.1915, Penny, 3 In. 120
Woman Chasing Rat With Broom, Tin, Windup, 7¼ In. 1652
Wyatt Earp, Gunfighter, Plastic, Hat & Guns, Box, Heartland, 9½ In. 450

Toy, Train Car, Marklin, Red Cross, Tin, Hinged Roof, Operating Table, 1 Gauge, 9 In.
$531

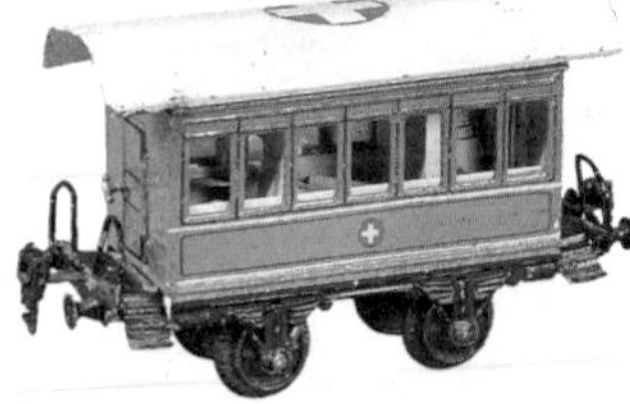

Bertoia Auctions

Toy, Train Car, Marklin, Steeple Cab, Nickel Rails, Pantograph, Clockwork, 0 Gauge
$590

Bertoia Auctions

Toy, Train Car, Marklin, Zeevish Freight Car, White, 8 Wheels, 0 Gauge, Germany, 6 In.
$4,425

Bertoia Auctions

Slinky Toy

Richard James invented the Slinky toy in 1945. It was the start of a successful toy company. But in about 1960, James left his wife, Betty, and six children to join a Bolivian religious cult. Betty discovered that her husband had given corporate money to the cult, leaving the firm in debt. She became CEO and made the company a success again by creating dozens of new Slinky toys. Richard James died in 1974. Betty died at age 90 in 2008.

Never Too Much Shopping
Have a bad day? Psychologists have proved that shopping is one way to combat depression. Cheer up. Rummage through some antiques for sale. You can even stay at home and look via your computer. Collecting can make you happy.

Toy, Train Set, BJD, Buildings, Tunnel, Gatehouse, Tin Litho, Clockwork, Germany, 9 In.
$325

Bertoia Auctions

Toy, Truck, Army, Tin Litho, Green, Stars, Stencil, Marx, 1950s, 13 x 5 In.
$110

Ruby Lane

Toy, Truck, Delivery, Railroad Transfer, Steel, Yellow, Decals, Buddy L, Box, c.1949, 23 In.
$2,360

Bertoia Auctions

Toy, Truck, Jaeger Mixer, Cast Iron, Nickel Cement Barrel, Kenton, 1940, 9 ½ In.
$384

Bertoia Auctions

Yeti, Abominable Snowman, Remote Control, Vinyl Face, Plush Body, Box, 1964, 11 In. 1581
Yogi Bear, Friction, Plastic Body, Jointed Running Legs, Box, 1960s, 7 In. 193
Zebra, Circus, Wood, Jointed, Cloth Mane, Leather Ears, Rope Tail, Schoenhut, 8 In. 236
Zebra, Wood, Jointed, Leather, Rope, Glass Eye, Painted, Schoenhut, 8 In. 443
Zeppelin, Graf Zeppelin, Propeller, Windup, Tin Lithograph, Marklin, 15 ½ In. 1140
Zeppelin, Little Giant, Painted, Pressed Steel, Wheels, Pull Toy, Katz, 1930s, 7 x 25 In. 520
Zeppelin, Rail, 0 Gauge, Clockwork, Marklin, c.1936, 12 In. 1062
Zeppelin, Tin Lithograph, Embossed, Windup, Tippco, 13 In. 325
Zig Zag, 2 Men, Rocking Car, Wheel On Sides, Tin Lithograph, Clockwork, Lehmann, 4 In. 767
Zilotone, Clown Plays Xylophone, Spinning Records, Tin, Pressed Steel, Wolverine, 8 In. 266

TRAMP ART is a form of folk art made since the Civil War. It is usually made from chip-carved cigar boxes. Examples range from small boxes and picture frames to full-sized pieces of furniture.

Box, Pedestal, Triangular Shapes, Velvet Interior, c.1890, 7 x 10 In. 680
Box, Pyramid Sections, Stepped Pedestal, Painted White, 11 ½ In. 94
Box, Wood, Green, Yellow, Lid, Handle, c.1900, 10 x 7 In. 3850
Bureau Box, Gilt Letters & Numbers, Lion Head Ring Handle, Paw Feet, 1892, 7 x 12 In. 236
Chair, Converts To Table, Chip Carved, 27 ¼ x 24 In. 1110
Chalet, Berg Weih Nacht, Christmas Tree, 12 x 7 In. 150
Crucifix, Carved, Block Base, Figure Of Christ, INRI Banner, Skull, Crossbones, c.1910, 20 In. ... 300
Frame, Chip Carved, Crosscut Corner, Stepped Layers, 1930s, 11 x 13 In. 285
House Model, Red Tin Roof, Green Frame, 13 x 15 In. 150
Jewelry Box, Brass, Mirror, 1900, 14 In. ....*illus* 595
Jar Holder, Bottle Caps, 2 Ring Handles, 1900s, 4 ⅜ x 10 ¼ x 5 In. 37
Lamp, Whimsical, Lighthouse Shape, 1930s, 19 x 10 In. 450
Mirror, Peaked Top, Heart, c.1890, 28 x 19 In. 1260
Plaque, Sampler Style, Birds, Sunflowers In Pots, Star, Heart, c.1885, 27 x 32 In. 665
Puzzle Chair, No Nails Or Glue, WP Initials On Backrest, 11 x 8 ¾ In. 154
Spice Chest, Walnut, Stepped Crest, Carved, Starburst, Hex Symbol, c.1900, 13 x 9 In. 1481
Trinket Box, Dome Lid, Trunk, Heart & Geometric Inlay, Block Feet, 1800s, 6 x 8 In. 83
Wall Cabinet, White Paint, 1 Shelf, 1 Door, 14 x 16 ½ In. 240

TRAPS for animals may be handmade. One of the most unusual is the mousetrap made so that when the mouse entered the trap, it was hit on the head with a mallet. Other traps were commercially manufactured and often are marked with the name of the manufacturer. Many traps were designed to be as humane as possible, and they would trap the live animal so it could be released in the woods.

Animal, Metal, Mesh, 1900s, 15 ½ x 8 In. 60
Animal, Steel, 2-In. Pressure Plate............ 10
Bear, No. 5 ATC, S. Newhouse, c.1927, 34 x 8 In. 833
Eel, Collapsible, Metal, France, 15 ½ x 8 In. 68
Minnow, Orvis, Glass, Wire ....*illus* 165
Mouse, No Kill, Wood, Copper, Metal, 5 ¼ x 4 In. 78
Squirrel Cage, Cottage Shape, Punched Star, Wheel, Tin & Wood, 1800s, 14 x 20 In. ....*illus* 266

TREEN, *see Wooden category.*

TRENCH ART is a form of folk art made by soldiers. Metal casings from bullets and mortar shells were cut and decorated to form useful objects, such as vases.

Artillery Shell, 2 Flags & U.S.A., c.1918, 13 ½ In. ....*illus* 90
Artillery Shell, Flowers, Butterfly, 12 ⅞ In. 90
Artillery Shell, Marked, 75 Dec. N. 872-175R, 100F No 527, 14 In. ....*illus* 60
Helmet, Doughboy, Landscape, American Flag, 6 x 13 In. 298
Letter Opener, Pierced 4-Leaf Clover, Crown Cartouche, 8 In. 90
Vase, Artillery Shell, Embossed Thistle Design, Stamped 75 DEC-H 892918-H, 12 In. ....*illus* 60

TRIVETS are now used to hold hot dishes. Most trivets of the late nineteenth and early twentieth centuries were made to hold hot irons. Iron or brass reproductions are being made of many of the old styles.

Brass, Wrought Iron, Round, Heart Shapes, England, 1800s, 5 ½ x 7 x 15 In. 35
Brass, Wrought Iron, Turned Wood Handle, Reticulated, Bird, Iron Stand, c.1800, 8 x 9 In. 106
Brass, Wrought Iron, Wood Handle, Reticulated, Animal Images, Iron Stand, 1700s, 12 x 10 In. 183
Cast Iron, Maple Leaf, 4 Legs, Marked, Ober, 5 ¼ In. ....*illus* 45
Iron, Pierced, Shaped Rear Leg, 17 ½ x 15 In. 200

Iron, Warming, Slotted Base, 6 Bars, c.1750-1820, 18¼ x 13 In. 120
Wrought Iron, 5 Hearts Design, Square Stem Legs, Black, Forged, 1700s, 2 x 8 In. 1778
Wrought Iron, Round, Shaped Flat Handle, Penny End, Hanging Eyelet, c.1800, 8 In. 325
Wrought Iron, Shield Shape, Ram's Horn Support, c.1800, 13 x 5 In. 154

TRUNKS of many types were made. The nineteenth-century sea chest was often handmade of unpainted wood. Brass-fitted camphorwood chests were brought back from the Orient. Leather-covered trunks were popular from the late eighteenth to mid-nineteenth centuries. By 1895, trunks were covered with canvas or decorated sheet metal. Embossed metal coverings were used from 1870 to 1910. By 1925, trunks were covered with vulcanized fiber or undecorated metal. Suitcases are listed here.

American Steamer, 24 x 32 In. 24
Blue Paint, Side Handles, Dovetailed Case, 1800s, 35 x 13 In. 47
Brass, Repousse, Continental, 19 x 29½ In. 660
Camelback, Oak Strapping, Embossed Tin, Lift-Out Tray, Lithographed Scenery, 29 x 36 In. 270
Canvas Exterior, Steamer, Chevron, Goyard, Brassbound, 3 Trays, c.1900, 27 x 48 In. 9840
Canvas, Steamer, Goyard, Monogram, Hinged Top, Brass, Removable Trays, c.1910, 26 x 44 In. 4613
George Domett, Pine, Hinged Dome Top, Wrought Iron Handles, 1800s, 10 x 24 In. 165
Gucci, Leather, Canvas, Hard Frame, Red & Green Stripes, 18 x 28 In. 472
Hardwood, Rosettes, Incised Hinges, Metal Bound, Side Handles, 1800s, 18 x 42 In. 960
Hartmann Co., Wardrobe, 6 Drawers, Key, 1920s, 41 x 25 x 22 In. 395
Hide Covered, Wood, Dome Top, Brass Tacks, Leather Bands, Fitted, c.1800, 27 In. 210
Lane, Wood Veneer, Pet Carrier, Bakelite Handle, Bars, Chain, Marked, c.1950, 17 x 24 In. 242
Leather Covered, Steamer Style, 21 x 22 x 20 In. 369
Leather, Brass Mounted, Chinese, 19 x 46 In. 300
Leather, Multicolor, Brass, Lift Top, Frame, Painted Scenes, Chinese, 1800s, 21 x 36 In. 531
Leather, Renaissance Style, Metal Bound, Footed, c.1900, 22 x 44½ In. 125
Leather, Studded, Brass, 10¼ x 25 In. 148
Louis Vuitton, Canvas, Monogram, Hinged Top, Leathers Handles, Tray, c.1910, 21 x 32 In. 8066
Louis Vuitton, Lift Top, Label, c.1890, 20½ x 23¾ In. 3540
Louis Vuitton, Logo, Tufted Interior, Saks & Co., 13 x 40 In. 4305
Louis Vuitton, Shoe & Hat, Hardwood, Canvas, Leather Handles, Brass, c.1930, 22 x 30 In. *illus* 10937
Louis Vuitton, Steamer, 2 Front Panels, 3 Clothbound Drawers, c.1880, 28 x 44 In. 4059
Louis Vuitton, Steamer, Canvas, Monogram, Webbed Interior, Tray, 1900s, 23 x 32 In. ......*illus* 6765
Louis Vuitton, Steamer, Monogram Canvas, Brass Hardware, Leather Trim, c.1910, 23 x 36 In. 5923
Louis Vuitton, Steamer, Wood, Canvas, Painted, Metal Edging, c.1860, 33 x 13 In. 1080
Louis Vuitton, Steamer, Wood, Canvas, Painted, Monogram, c.1920, 27 x 39 In. 2880
Louis Vuitton, Suit Carrier, Monogram Canvas, Leather Handle, 23 x 51 In. ....*illus* 312
Louis Vuitton, Suitcase, Brown Monogram Canvas, Leather Trim, 1970s, 16½ x 21½ In. 460
Louis Vuitton, Suitcase, Leather Handle, Brass Fittings, Canvas Straps, 31½ x 21 In. 2104
Louis Vuitton, Suitcase, Leather Trim, Open Interior, Leather Strap, Label, 17 x 13 In. ......*illus* 865
Louis Vuitton, Suitcase, Leather, Brass, Logos, 8 x 26 x 17 In. ....*illus* 1150
Louis Vuitton, Suitcase, Lift-Out Fabric Basket, Monogram, Label, 9 x 19½ x 19½ In. 1180
Louis Vuitton, Suitcase, Monogram 80, Hardside, Leather Accents, S Lock, 21 x 31 In. 550
Louis Vuitton, Suitcase, Monogram Canvas, c.1975, 22 x 26 In. 335
Louis Vuitton, Suitcase, Soft-Sided, Leather Corners, Brass, Stud Feet, 1970s, 31 x 26 In. 956
Louis Vuitton, Suitcase, Square Handle, Cloth Straps, c.1915, 8½ x 25½ In. 1187
Louis Vuitton, Train Case, Goldtone Hardware, Monogram, 8¾ x 12½ In. 330
Louis Vuitton, Train Case, Monogram Canvas, Stripe, Monogram, c.1900, 10 x 16 In. 4305
Louis Vuitton, Travel Bag, Keepall 60, Monogram Canvas, Leather Handles, 1985, 12 x 24 In. .. 506
Louis Vuitton, Trunk, Red & White Stripes, 23 x 44 In. 4888
Louis Vuitton, Wardrobe, Hardwood, Canvas, Leather Handles, Brass Trim, 26 x 56 In. 18750
Louis Vuitton, Wardrobe, Interior Tray, Drawers, Leather Handle, Monogram, c.1910, 45 x 27 In. .. 9840
Maison Goyard, Steamer, Canvas On Wood, Metal, Trays, Letter Rack, 20 x 40 In. 799
Mother-Of-Pearl, Lacquer, Flowers, Wood Stand, Chinese, 17¾ x 21¾ In. 854
Oak, Dome Top, Iron Strap, 28 x 45 In. 625
Painted, Dome Top, Vermont, 1800s, 37 x 19 In. 526
Pine, Dome Top, Dovetail, Unfinished, 18 x 40 In. 151
Pine, Immigrant's, Dome Top, Painted Design, Lock, Key, 1800s, 20 x 34 In. ....*illus* 210
Softwood, Immigrant's, Paint, Blue, Yellow Highlights, Faux Detail, 1863, 25 x 48 In. 266
Steamer, Canvas, Leather, Chevron, Brass Hardware, France, c.1935, 19 x 44 In. 4613
Tin, Carrying Case, Wood Slats, Punched Pennsylvania Dutch Symbols, 20 x 15 In. ....*illus* 474
Vinyl, Black & White Stripes, Chrome Handles, Velvet Lined, 20½ x 24 In., Pair.......... 138
Wilhelm Schmidt, Pine, Red Wash, Forged Handles, Baltimore, Germany, c.1850, 14 x 28 In. .. 96
Wood, Dome Top, Carved, Country Landscape, Flowers, Iron Strap, Norway, 21 x 23 In. 750
Wood, Dome Top, Carved, Dovetailed Case, Iron Lock Plate, Norway, 19½ x 11½ In. 594

TIP

Be sure you have photographs and descriptions of your collections in case of a robbery. Keep them in a safe place away from your house.

Toy, Truck, Meadow Gold Butter, Pressed Steel, Electric Light, Metalcraft, 1930s, 13 In.
$443

Bertoia Auctions

Toy, Turkey, On Wheels, Composition, Molded, Glass Eyes, Skittles Game Base, 16 In.
$2,124

Bertoia Auctions

Tramp Art, Jewelry Box, Brass, Mirror, 1900, 14 In.
$595

Ruby Lane

T

Trap, Minnow, Orvis, Glass, Wire
$165

Old Barn Auctions

Trap, Squirrel Cage, Cottage Shape, Punched Star, Wheel, Tin & Wood, 1800s, 14 x 20 In.
$266

Hess Auction Group

TIP

Musty odors in trunks are a constant problem. Try this system. Fill the trunk with wrinkled, crushed newspaper, close the lid for a week, remove and replace the papers. Repeat the process until the musty odor is gone. This system also helps with car interiors for tobacco odors, musty books if kept in a closed paper bag, and suitcases.

TUTHILL Cut Glass Company of Middletown, New York, worked from 1902 to 1923. Of special interest are the finely cut pieces of stemware and tableware.

Dish, Hobstars, Flowers, Pie Shape Wedges, Sawtooth Rim, 5 In. 45
Tray, Grape Bunches, Leaves, Hobstar Border, Tab Handles, 13 x 8 In. 1995
Vase, Cut Glass, Floral Cutting, Leaves, Honeycomb, Ruffled Sawtooth Rim, 12 In. 177

TYPEWRITER collectors divide typewriters into two main classifications: the index machine, which has a pointer and a dial for letter selection, and the keyboard machine, most commonly seen today. The first successful typewriter was made by Sholes and Glidden in 1874.

Electric, Smith-Corona 2200, Orson Welles Used, Slate Blue, c.1970, 14 x 13 In. 9063
Remington Portable, Case, Black Wood, 12 x 11 x 4 In. 145
Remington Portable, Model No. 1, Case, 1921, 11 x 10 In. ....*illus* 225
Tom Thumb Junior, Model 1602, Box, 10 x 7 x 4 In. 45
Underwood, Portable, Tennessee Williams Used, Cat On Hot Tin Roof, 1940s 4481

UHL POTTERY was made in Evansville, Indiana, in 1854. The pottery moved to Huntingburg, Indiana, in 1908. Stoneware and glazed pottery were made until the mid-1940s.

Churn, 3, Stomper, 3 Gal. 70
Jug, Ball Shape, Dark Rose Matte Glaze, Spout, Handle, 6 ½ x 7 ¼ In. 25
Jug, Lid, Brown, Cream Body, 5 Gal. 55
Pitcher, Grapes & Lattice, Blue Salt Glaze, Marked, 8 ¼ In. 24
Pitcher, Stoneware, Grape Clusters Hanging On Vines, Trellis, Blue, c.1915, 5 ¾ In. ....*illus* 275

UMBRELLA collectors like rain or shine. The first known umbrella was owned by King Louis XIII of France in 1637. The earliest umbrellas were sunshades, not designed to be used in the rain. The umbrella was embellished and redesigned many times. In 1852, the fluted steel rib style was developed and it has remained the most useful style.

Antelope Horn Handle, Black, c.1900, 35 ½ In. 149
Carved Dog's Head Handle, Glass Eyes, Moving Mouth, Leather Collar, Black, 25 In. 245
Cream Bakelite Handle, Brown, White Stripes, 1940s, 23 x 37 In. Diam. 65
From Jack To Nellie, Engraved, Gold Plating, Black, 1903, 36 ½ In. 425

UNION PORCELAIN WORKS was originally William Boch & Brothers, located in Greenpoint, New York. Thomas C. Smith bought the company in 1861 and renamed it Union Porcelain Works. The company went through a series of ownership changes and finally closed about 1922. The company made a fine quality white porcelain that was often decorated in clear, bright colors. Don't confuse this company with its competitor, Charles Cartlidge and Company, also in Greenpoint.

Liberty Cup, Bisque, Vignettes, Mercury, Justice, Liberty Handle, c.1877, 4 In. ....*illus* 840
Oyster Plate, 4 Wells, Pink Ground, Shell, c.1881, 8 ½ In., 8 Piece 2750
Oyster Plate, 4 Wells, Sauce, Shells, Sea Plants, Oval, Marked, UPW, c.1880, 8 ½ In. ....*illus* 310
Oyster Plate, 6 Wells, Seaweed, Sea Life, 9 ½ In., Pair 357
Vase, Birds, Flowers, Monkey Head Handles, Elizabeth Maurer, c.1900, 12 In. ....*illus* 2750

UNIVERSITY CITY POTTERY, of University, Missouri, worked from 1909 to 1915. Well-known artists, including Taxile Doat, Adelaide Alsop Robineau, and Frederick Hurten Rhead, worked there.

Figurine, Woman Kneeling, Stoneware, Porcelain-Like White Glaze, 1910s, 11 In. ....*illus* 1250
Panel, 4 Tiles, Peacock, Enamel, Square, Frederick Rhead, c.1910, 20 ½ In. ....*illus* 250000
Plaque, Nymph Of Spring, Light Blue, 4 ½ In. 632
Vase, Purple, Blue, Green, Porcelain, Taxile Doat, Signed, 3 ½ x 2 In. 1875
Vase, White, Crystalline, Porcelain, Emile Diffloth, Signed, 6 x 2 ½ In. 1250

UNIVERSITY OF NORTH DAKOTA, *see North Dakota School of Mines category.*

VAL ST. LAMBERT Cristalleries of Belgium was founded by Messieurs Kemlin and Lelievre in 1825. The company is still in operation. All types of table glassware and decorative glassware have been made. Pieces are often decorated with cut designs.

Bowl, Centerpiece, Flat Rim, Cut Diamond Pattern, Stylized Pineapples, 9 x 12 In. 378
Candlestick, Crystal, 13 In., Pair 270
Coaster, Zodiac Symbols, Etched Crystal, Floral Rim, 3 ½ In., 12 Piece 118
Vase, Cornucopia, Cranberry, Signed, 8 ½ x 5 ¾ x 4 In. 100
Vase, Flaring, Emerald Cut To Clear, Belgian, 1900s, 16 x 11 In. 1062

Trench Art, Artillery Shell, 2 Flags & U.S.A., c.1918, 13 ½ In.
$90

The Stein Auction Company

Trench Art, Artillery Shell, Marked, 75 Dec. N. 872-175R, 100F No 527, 14 In.
$60

The Stein Auction Company

Trench Art, Vase, Artillery Shell, Embossed Thistle Design, Stamped 75 DEC-H 892918-H, 12 In.
$60

Showtime Auction Services

Trivet, Cast Iron, Maple Leaf, 4 Legs, Marked, Ober, 5 ¼ In.
$45

Ruby Lane

Louis Vuitton

Watch for luggage by Louis Vuitton. The company has been in business since 1854, and its trunks sell for hundreds and even thousands of dollars.

Trunk, Louis Vuitton, Shoe & Hat, Hardwood, Canvas, Leather Handles, Brass, c.1930, 22 x 30 In.
$10,937

New Orleans (Cakebread)

Trunk, Louis Vuitton, Steamer, Canvas, Monogram, Webbed Interior, Tray, 1900s, 23 x 32 In.
$6,765

Skinner, Inc.

Trunk, Louis Vuitton, Suit Carrier, Monogram Canvas, Leather Handle, 23 x 51 In.
$312

New Orleans (Cakebread)

Trunk, Louis Vuitton, Suitcase, Leather Trim, Open Interior, Leather Strap, Label, 17 x 13 In.
$865

James D. Julia Auctioneers

Trunk, Louis Vuitton, Suitcase, Leather, Brass, Logos, 8 x 26 x 17 In.
$1,150

Cottone Auctions

Trunk, Pine, Immigrant's, Dome Top, Painted Design, Lock, Key, 1800s, 20 x 34 In.
$210

Garth's Auctioneers & Appraisers

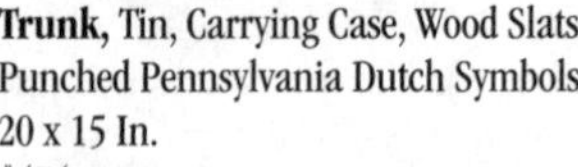

Trunk, Tin, Carrying Case, Wood Slats, Punched Pennsylvania Dutch Symbols, 20 x 15 In.
$474

James D. Julia Auctioneers

Typewriter, Remington Portable, Model No. 1, Case, 1921, 11 x 10 In.
$225

Ruby Lane

Uhl, Pitcher, Stoneware, Grape Clusters Hanging On Vines, Trellis, Blue, c.1915, 5 ¾ In.
$275

Ruby Lane

Vernon Kilns Plaid Patterns

Gingham (1949 to 1958), green and yellow plaid with a dark green border.

Homespun (1948 to 1958), cinnamon, green, and yellow.

Organdie (1940s and '50s), brown and yellow.

Tam O'Shanter (1949 to 1958), rust, chartreuse, and dark green.

Tweed (1950 to 1955), yellow and gray blue.

VALLERYSTHAL GLASSWORKS was founded in 1836 in Lorraine, France. In 1854, the firm became Klenglin et Cie. It made table and decorative glass, opaline, cameo, and art glass. A line of covered, pressed glass animal dishes was made in the nineteenth century. The firm is still working.

Candlestick, Glass Dolphin, Blue Opaline, 1900s, 8 x 5 In., Pair ... *illus* 199
Goblet, Blue, Opaline, 6 ½ x 3 ½ In., 10 Piece ... 420
Nesting Hen, Amber, 5 x 4 In. ... 64
Vase, Gourd Shape, Squash Blossoms, Butterflies, France, 1890s, 9 x 4 In. ... 1792

VAN BRIGGLE POTTERY was started by Artus Van Briggle in Colorado Springs, Colorado, after 1901. Van Briggle had been a decorator at Rookwood Pottery of Cincinnati, Ohio. He died in 1904 and his wife took over managing the pottery. One of the employees, Kenneth Stevenson, took over the company in 1969. He died in 1990 and his wife and son ran the pottery. She died in 2010 and the company closed in 2012. The wares usually had modeled relief decorations and a soft, dull glaze.

Dish, Indian Woman Kneeling, Washing, Turquoise, 6 ¼ In. ... 180
Ewer, Ribbed, Curved Handle, Upright Spout, High Gloss Amber Glaze, c.1960, 8 In. ... 108
Flower Frog, 3 Frogs, Brown, 5 In. ... 200
Flower Frog, Blue, Indigo, 5 In. ... 50
Tile, Stylized Flowers, Quartersawn Oak Frame, Butterfly Clips, 6 x 6 In., Pair ... 177
Vase, Flowers At Shoulder, Pink, 1902, 10 x 4 In. ... 2625
Vase, Gourd Shape, Blossoms, Celadon Glaze, AA Van Briggle, 1906, 6 x 3 In. ... *illus* 1063
Vase, Irises, Variegated Green Glaze, 1904, 13 ½ x 5 ½ In. ... 3500
Vase, Leaves, Curdled Green Glaze, Marked, c.1905, 9 ¾ x 5 In. ... *illus* 875
Vase, Lorelei, Nymph, Ming Turquoise, Baluster Shape, c.1900, 11 In. ... 437
Vase, Mulberry Glaze, Embossed Long Stem Flowers, Incised, 9 In. ... 224
Vase, Peach, Pink, Green, Glaze, Signed, 1903, 5 x 2 ½ In. ... 2250
Vase, Pinecones, Mountain Craig Brown, Incised, 1910s, 5 ½ x 11 In. ... 625
Vase, Stylized Flowers, Matte Violet Glaze, Cylindrical, Garlic Mouth, c.1910, 7 In. ... 231

VASELINE GLASS is a greenish-yellow glassware resembling petroleum jelly. Pressed glass of the 1870s was often made of vaseline-colored glass. Some vaseline glass is still being made in old and new styles. Additional pieces of vaseline glass may also be listed under Pressed Glass in this book.

Candlestick, Lobed Knop & Rim, Spread Base, 7 In., Pair ... *illus* 212
Candy Dish, Lid, Cut Glass ... 50
Compote, Gilt, Jeweled Rim, 5 ½ x 6 ½ In. ... 48
Compote, Optic Ribbed, John Walsh, 8 In. ... 48
Compote, Pedestal, Daisy & Button, Scalloped Edge, Lid, Belmont Glass, 12 ½ x 9 In. ... 390
Decanter, 3 Rings On Neck, Cut Glass, Stopper, Persia, 15 In ... 2214
Decanter, Blown, Cut, Gilt, Enamel, Bohemian, 1880s, 18 In. ... 1599
Decanter, Cone Shape, Finial, Persia, 15 In. ... 2214
Lamp, Art Deco Nude Woman, Outstretched Arms, Metal Base, 11 ½ x 11 In. ... 770
Rose Bowl, Melon Shape, Large Applied Pink Flowers, 5 x 6 In. ... 150
Sugar, Open, Wreathed Cherries, Scalloped Rim, L.G. Wright, 3 ¾ x 4 In. ... *illus* 45
Tumbler, Molded, 4 Circles, 4 Piece ... 84

VENETIAN GLASS, *see Glass-Venetian category.*

VENINI GLASS, *see Glass-Venetian category.*

VERLYS glass was made in Rouen, France, by the Societe Holophane Français, a company that started in 1920. It was made in Newark, Ohio, from 1935 to 1951. The art glass is either blown or molded. The American glass is signed with a diamond-point-scratched name, but the French pieces are marked with a molded signature. The designs resemble those used by Lalique.

Vase, Art Deco, Flower Heads, Leaves, 9 x 6 ½ In. ... 120
Vase, Art Deco, Thistle Branches, Opalescent, 9 ½ x 7 In. ... 150
Vase, Hydrangea Blossoms, Opalescent, Leafy Sprig Ground, Ring Foot, 6 x 7 In. ... 127
Vase, Thistle, Les Chardons, Opalescent, Cathedral Panels, Ring Foot, Tapered, 10 x 6 In. ... 259

VERNON KILNS was the name used by Vernon Potteries, Ltd. The company, which started in 1931 in Vernon, California, made dinnerware and figurines until it went out of business in 1958. The molds were bought by Metlox, which continued to make some patterns. Collectors search for the brightly colored dinnerware and the pieces designed by Rockwell Kent, Walt Disney, and Don Blanding. For more prices, go to kovels.com.

Anytime, Gravy Boat ... 18

Barkwood, Chop Plate, 13 In.	44
Barkwood, Cup & Saucer	8
Barkwood, Salt & Pepper	12
Barkwood, Sugar, Lid	10
Blossom Time, Creamer, Blue, 6 Oz.	39
Blossom Time, Plate, Bread & Butter, Blue, 6 ½ In.	14
Bouquet, Plate, Dinner, 10 ½ In.	16
Brown Eyed Susan, Chop Plate, 14 In.	42
Brown Eyed Susan, Cup & Saucer	8
Brown Eyed Susan, Plate, Bread & Butter, 6 In.	5
California Apple, Cup & Saucer	9
California Apple, Dish, Vegetable, Lid, Round	47
California Apple, Salt & Pepper, Handles, 3 In.	21
California Apple, Soup, Dish, Coupe, 7 In.	13
California Fruit, Cup & Saucer	11
California Fruit, Gravy Boat	36
California Fruit, Plate, Dinner, 10 In.	22
California Fruit, Salt & Pepper, 4 In.	34
Chintz, Cup & Saucer	15
Chintz, Plate, Dinner, 10 ½ In.	20
Country Cousins, Bowl, Vegetable, Round, 8 In.	17
Country Cousins, Cup & Saucer	6
Country Cousins, Pitcher, 32 Oz., 7 ¾ In.	21
Del Rey, Platter, Oval, 11 In.	19
Dolores, Bowl, Cereal, Lugged, 7 ½ In.	9
Dolores, Chop Plate, 14 In.	19
Dolores, Cup & Saucer	11
Dolores, Gravy Boat	20
Harvest, Chop Plate, 12 ½ In.	46
Hibiscus, Gravy Boat, Underplate	43
Hibiscus, Platter, Oval, 12 In.	18
Hibiscus, Relish, Handles, 10 In.	19
Hibiscus, Teapot, Lid, 4 Cup, 5 ½ In.	138
Linda, Cup & Saucer	18
Lotus, Cup & Saucer	13
Organdie, Cup & Saucer	8
Organdie, Salt & Pepper	12
Peach Blossom, Cup & Saucer	18
Peach Blossom, Plate, Dinner, 10 In.	14
Peach Blossom, Platter, Oval, 13 In.	30
Plate, Scenes Of Danville, Virginia, Transferware, Brown, c.1945, 10 ½ In. *illus*	26
Provincial Rose, Coffeepot, Lid, 6 Cup, 8 In.	54
Provincial Rose, Cup & Saucer	6
Rosalie, Coffeepot, Ultra Line, Flowers, Stems, Upside Down Handle, Lid, 1940s, 9 In. *illus*	62
Tam O'Shanter, Ashtray, Round, 4 In.	22
Tam O'Shanter, Chop Plate, 14 In.	56
Tam O'Shanter, Cup & Saucer	6
Tam O'Shanter, Gravy Boat, Plaid Design, c.1950, 4 x 7 In. *illus*	25
Tam O'Shanter, Jug, Bulbous, 32 Oz., 6 ⅝ In.	46
Tam O'Shanter, Plate, Bread & Butter, 6 ¼ In.	5
Tam O'Shanter, Plate, Dinner, 10 ½ In.	25
Tam O'Shanter, Platter, Oval, 14 In.	21
Tam O'Shanter, Salt & Pepper	12
Tickled Pink, Plate, Dinner, 10 In.	22
Tulips, Plate, Dinner, 10 In.	32
Tweed, Bowl, Vegetable, Round, Gray & Yellow, 9 In.	28
Tweed, Chop Plate, Gray & Yellow, 12 In.	34
Tweed, Cup & Saucer, Gray & Yellow	11
Tweed, Gravy Boat, Gray & Yellow	47
Tweed, Plate, Dinner, Gray & Yellow, 10 ½ In.	36
Tweed, Salt & Pepper, Gray & Yellow	29
Vernon's 1860, Cup & Saucer, Footed	9
Vernon's 1860, Platter, Oval, 16 In.	82
Vernon's 1860, Tureen, Underplate	276
Year Round, Plate, Salad, 7 ¾ In.	6
Young In Heart, Chop Plate, 12 In.	35

Union Porcelain Works, Liberty Cup, Bisque, Vignettes, Mercury, Justice, Liberty Handle, c.1877, 4 In.
$840

Cowan Auctions

Union Porcelain Works, Oyster Plate, 4 Wells, Sauce, Shells, Sea Plants, Oval, Marked, UPW, c.1880, 8 ½ In.
$310

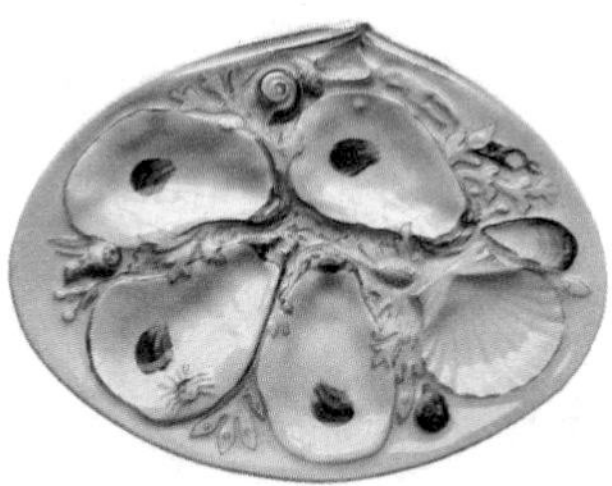

Ruby Lane

Union Porcelain Works, Vase, Birds, Flowers, Monkey Head Handles, Elizabeth Maurer, c.1900, 12 In.
$2,750

Rago Arts and Auction Center

University City, Figurine, Woman Kneeling, Stoneware, Porcelain-Like White Glaze, 1910s, 11 In.
$1,250

Rago Arts and Auction Center

University City, Panel, 4 Tiles, Peacock, Enamel, Square, Frederick Rhead, c.1910, 20 ½ In.
$250,000

Rago Arts and Auction Center

Vallerysthal, Candlestick, Glass Dolphin, Blue Opaline, 1900s, 8 x 5 In., Pair
$199

Ruby Lane

Van Briggle, Vase, Gourd Shape, Blossoms, Celadon Glaze, AA Van Briggle, 1906, 6 x 3 In.
$1,063

Rago Arts and Auction Center

Van Briggle, Vase, Leaves, Curdled Green Glaze, Marked, c.1905, 9 ¾ x 5 In.
$875

Rago Arts and Auction Center

Vaseline Glass, Candlestick, Lobed Knop & Rim, Spread Base, 7 In., Pair
$212

Hess Auction Group

Vaseline Glass, Sugar, Open, Wreathed Cherries, Scalloped Rim, L.G. Wright, 3 ¾ x 4 In.
$45

Ruby Lane

Vernon Kilns, Plate, Scenes Of Danville, Transferware, Brown, c.1945, 10 ½ In.
$26

Ruby Lane

Vernon Kilns, Rosalie, Coffeepot, Ultra Line, Flowers, Stems, Upside Down Handle, Lid, 1940s, 9 In.
$62

Ruby Lane

Vernon Kilns, Tam O'Shanter, Gravy Boat, Plaid Design, c.1950, 4 x 7 In.
$25

Ruby Lane

Young In Heart, Creamer, 8 Oz., 4 In. 15
Young In Heart, Plate, Dinner, 10 In. 17
Young In Heart, Relish, 8 In. 18

VERRE DE SOIE glass was first made by Frederick Carder at the Steuben Glass Works from about 1905 to 1930. It is an iridescent glass of soft white or very, very pale green. The name means "glass of silk," and it does resemble silk. Other factories have made verre de soie, and some of the English examples were made of different colors. Verre de soie is an art glass and is not related to the iridescent, pressed, white carnival glass mistakenly called by its name. Related pieces may be found in the Steuben category.

Bowl, 3 Applied Feet, 2 ¼ x 8 In. 66
Cologne Bottle, Footed, Melon Ribbed, Monogram, Flame Stopper, c.1910, 7 In. 413
Compote, Shaped Stem, Coral Lip Wrap, 6 ¼ In. 259
Perfume Bottle, Melon Ribbed, Light Blue Jade Teardrop Stopper, 4 ½ In. 86
Urn, Lid, Bulbous, Ball Stem, Saucer Foot, 3 Rigaree Handles, 13 In. 948
Tray, Serving, 3 Tiers, Silver Plate, 14 ¼ x 10 ¼ In. 77
Vase, Shouldered, Turquoise Rim, Etched Signature, F. Carder, 12 ½ In. 259

VIENNA, *see Beehive category.*

VIENNA ART plates are round metal serving trays produced at the turn of the century. The designs, copied from Royal Vienna porcelain plates, usually featured a portrait of a woman encircled by a wide, ornate border. Many were used as advertising or promotional items and were produced in Coshocton, Ohio, by J. F. Meeks Tuscarora Advertising Co. and H.D. Beach's Standard Advertising Co.

Plate, Woman, Bouffant Honey, Blond Hair, Red Rim, Gilt Leaves, 10 In. 25
Plate, Woman, Green Rim, White 5-Pointed Star, Thick Brunette Hair, 1905, 10 In. 91
Plate, Woman, Shoulders Out, Brunette, Tin, 10 In. 69
Plate, Woman In Garden, Fountain, Birds, Gold Rim, Tin, 10 In. .... *illus* 31

VILLEROY & BOCH POTTERY of Mettlach was founded in 1836. The firm made many types of wares, including the famous Mettlach steins. Collectors can be confused because although Villeroy & Boch made most of its pieces in the city of Mettlach, Germany, the company also had factories in other locations. The dating code impressed on the bottom of most pieces makes it possible to determine the age of the piece. Additional items, including steins and earthenware pieces marked with the famous castle mark or the word *Mettlach*, may be found in the Mettlach category.

Ashtray, Alt Amsterdam, Round, 5 ⅞ In. 14
Cake Plate, Le Cirque, Square, Handles, Circus, Elephant, Stars, 9 In. .... *illus* 55
Charger, Musician Holding Tin, 17 ⅜ In. 35
Chocolate Pot, Lid, Artemis, Gray Black, 4 Cup, 8 ¾ In. 135
Chop Plate, Forsa, 12 In. 75
Chop Plate, Normandie, 12 In. 91
Coffeepot, Lid, Alsace, 4 Cup, 5 ⅝ In. 71
Creamer, China Blue, Paneled, 8 Oz., 4 In. 32
Creamer, Fruit Garden, 9 Oz., 4 In. 30
Cup & Saucer, Ascoli, Demitasse 13
Cup & Saucer, Burgenland, Green 19
Eggcup, Burgenland, Maroon, 2 ⅛ In. 9
Eggcup, Forsa, 2 ¼ In. 26
Eggcup, Fruit Garden, 2 ⅛ In. 21
Gravy Boat, Anjou 142
Gravy Boat, Blue Castle 75
Lazy Susan, Blue Onion, Saxony, Black Ink Stamp, 1874-1909, 9 ½ x 14 In. 142
Pitcher, Forsa, 32 Oz., 5 In. 134
Plate, Dinner, Alt Amsterdam, 10 ½ In. 73
Plate, Dinner, Burgenland, Green, 9 ⅞ In. 38
Plate, Dinner, Palermo, 10 ½ In. 32
Plate, Dinner, Piccadilly, 10 ⅜ In. 40
Plate, Fairy Tale, Firebird, Couple On Wolf, 8 ¼ In. 40
Platter, Normandie, Oval, 15 In. 163
Platter, Rectangular, Rounded Corners, Flower, Vine Border, c.1900, 16 x 12 In. .... *illus* 95
Salt & Pepper, Alt Amsterdam 125
Salt & Pepper, Indian Summer 74
Soup, Dish, Alpina, Rim, Brown, 8 In. 8
Sugar, Lid, Alt Amsterdam, Handles, 2 ¾ In. 60

Vienna Art, Plate, Woman In Garden, Fountain, Birds, Gold Rim, Tin, 10 In.
$31

Morphy Auctions

Villeroy & Boch, Cake Plate, Le Cirque, Square, Handles, Circus, Elephant, Stars, 9 In.
$55

Ruby Lane

Villeroy & Boch, Platter, Rectangular, Rounded Corners, Flower, Vine Border, c.1900, 16 x 12 In.
$95

Ruby Lane

Villeroy & Boch

Villeroy & Boch began to make ceramics in contemporary shapes, designs, and colors in the 1960s. Important designers included Paloma Picasso and Keith Haring. In the 1980s, the company made tiles, sanitary wares, tableware, and crystal.

Villeroy & Boch, Tureen, Petite Fleur, Oval, Dome Lid, Flower Knob, Handles, c.1748, 9 x 12 In.
$65

Ruby Lane

Wade, Ashtray, Turtle, Brown, Porcelain, 1950s, 2 x 7 ¼ In.
$65

Ruby Lane

Wall Pocket, Bagpipe Shape, Pottery, Desvres, Flower Frog, France, 1800s, 6 ½ In.
$125

Ruby Lane

Warwick, Cheese Keeper, Lid, Pink Flowers, Handle, c.1900, 6 ¼ x 10 ¾ In.
$50

Ruby Lane

Sugar, Lid, Ascoli, 2 ½ In. 19
Teapot, Lid, Alt Amsterdam, 4 Cup, 5 In. 172
Tray, Petite Fleur Pattern, Handles, 8 ½ x 9 ½ In. 40
Tureen, Blue Castle, Handles, Dome Lid 375
Tureen, Petite Fleur, Oval, Dome Lid, Flower Knob, Handles, c.1748, 9 x 12 In. .... *illus* 65

VOLKMAR POTTERY was made by Charles Volkmar of New York from 1879 to about 1911. He was associated with several firms, including the Volkmar Ceramic Company, Volkmar and Cory, and Charles Volkmar and Son. He was hired by Durant Kilns of Bedford Village, New York, in 1910 to oversee production. Volkmar bought the business and after 1930 only the Volkmar name was used as a mark. Volkmar had been a painter, and his designs often look like oil paintings drawn on pottery.

VOLKMAR Corona N.Y

Mug, Flock Of Ducks, Blue Wash, Cylindrical, Tapering, Loop Handle, 6 In. 369
Vase, Bronze Green Matte Glaze, Marked, 15 ¾ In. 461

VOLKSTEDT was a soft-paste porcelain factory started in 1760 by Georg Heinrich Macheleid at Volkstedt, Thuringia. Volkstedt-Rudolstadt was a porcelain factory started at Volkstedt-Rudolstadt by Beyer and Bock in 1890. Most pieces seen in shops today are from the later factory.

B

Figurine, Woman, Dress, Flowers, Blue, Chair, Green, Tufted, Music Book, c.1945, 11 ⅞ In. 847
Figurine, Seated Nude, Art Deco, Blue Chair, Germany, c.1919, 6 ½ x 3 In. 156
Group, 18th Century Couple, Fortepiano, Germany, 10 ¾ x 12 In. 210
Group, Plateau, Dresden Lace, Musical Family, 2 Couples, 3 Children, Piano, Harp, 20 x 14 In. . 1438

WADE pottery is made by the Wade Group of Potteries started in 1810 near Burslem, England. Several potteries merged to become George Wade & Son, Ltd., early in the twentieth century, and other potteries have been added through the years. The best-known Wade pieces are the small figurines called Whimsies. They first were made in 1954. Special Whimsies were given away with Red Rose Tea beginning in 1967. The Disney figures are listed in this book in the Disneyana category.

WADE Figures c. 1936+

Ashtray, 2 Turtle Tagalongs, Brown, Green, 1950s, 7 ¼ In. 65
Ashtray, Turtle, Brown, Porcelain, 1950s, 2 x 7 ¼ In. .... *illus* 65
Bank, Truck, Thornton's Chocolates 1911, Brown Glaze, 1970s, 4 x 8 x 3 ¾ In. 28
Dish, Trinket, Irish Setter, Sleeping In Basket, 2 ½ x 3 In. 10
Figurine, Blynken, Seated, Blue Outfit, Flower Base, c.1950, 2 ⅜ In. 52
Figurine, Brown Bear, 1 ½ In. 6
Figurine, Budgerigar, Bird, On Flowering Branch, 1930s, 7 In. 396
Figurine, Cat & The Fiddle, c.1975, 2 ¾ In. 60
Figurine, Cockatoo, White, Head Twisted, c.1940, 7 In. 310
Figurine, Horse, Eating Grass, Palomino, 1950s, 2 In. 130
Figurine, Jill, Carrying Bucket, 3 In. 30
Figurine, Little Jack Horner, 1970s, 3 In. 35
Figurine, Little Tommy Tucker, c.1978, 2 ½ In. 45
Figurine, Old King Cole, Seated, 1 ⅜ In. 9
Figurine, Old Lady In A Shoe, 1970s, 3 In. 125
Figurine, Pindar The Panda, Black & White, c.1930, 4 In. 125
Jug, Stylized Plums, Purple, Burgundy, Copper Luster, c.1953, 6 ½ In. 48
Nut Dish, Figural, Pelican, White, Yellow Open Beak, c.1945, 6 x 7 ½ In. 243
Pitcher, Copper Luster, Running Stag, 4 In. 40
Sugar & Creamer, Berries, Twigs, 3 ½ In. 28
Trinket Box, Tortoise, Brown, 4 x 1 ½ In. 30
Vase, Flared Neck, Yellow Rose, Green Ground, c.1910, 7 ½ In. 39

WAHPETON POTTERY, *see Rosemeade category.*

WALL POCKETS were popular in the 1930s. They were made by many American and European factories. Glass, pottery, porcelain, majolica, chalkware, and metal wall pockets can be found in many fanciful shapes.

Bagpipe Shape, Pottery, Desvres, Flower Frog, France, 1800s, 6 ½ In. .... *illus* 125
Face, Mustache, Goatee, Leaf Crown, Manganese Glaze, Ceramic, 7 x 7 In. 230
Lattice, Wood, Undershelf, 33 x 19 ½ In., Pair 343
Majolica, Seahorses, Multicolor, Fantechi, 19 In. 778
Porcelain, Transfer Painted, Pink & Purple Flowers, Gien, c.1875, 13 ¼ x 6 ¾ In. 250
Wrought Metal, Green, Twist, Curls, Triangle, Basket, Italy, 1800s, 29 x 12 In., Pair 123

WALLACE NUTTING *photographs are listed under Print, Nutting. His reproduction furniture is listed under Furniture.*

WALRATH was a potter who worked in New York City; Rochester, New York; and at the Newcomb Pottery in New Orleans, Louisiana. Frederick Walrath died in 1920. Pieces listed here are from his Rochester period.

Paperweight, Green Matte Glaze, Reclining Nude, Incised, 4 ½ In. 531
Vase, Cylindrical, Flat Shoulder, Green, Beige, Blue, Trees, Landscape, c.1910, 7 In. 8125
Vase, Cylindrical, Waisted Rim, Stylized Roses, Green, Pink, Signed, 1911, 13 x 5 In. 13750
Vase, Pinched Waist, Stylized Pink Roses, Green Ground, 1912, 11 x 6 In. 9375

WALT DISNEY, *see Disneyana category.*

WALTER, *see A. Walter category.*

WARWICK china was made in Wheeling, West Virginia, in a pottery working from 1887 to 1951. Many pieces were made with hand painted or decal decorations. The most familiar Warwick has a shaded brown background. The name *Warwick* is part of the mark and sometimes the mysterious word *IOGA* is also included.

Cheese Keeper, Lid, Pink Flowers, Handle, c.1900, 6 ¼ x 10 ¾ In. .... *illus* 50
Chocolate Set, Pot, Cup & Saucer, Nasturtium, Cream To Brown, 13 In. 24
Pitcher, Brown, Poppies, Gold Trim, c.1900 100
Vase, Cloverleaf Shape, Brown, Nasturtiums, Yellow, Orange, 10 ½ x 5 ½ In. 300
Vase, Dogs, Fields, Fence, 11 ¾ In. 85
Vase, Portrait, Woman, 8 In. 40
Vase, Portrait, Woman, Pearls, Double Handle, 10 ½ In. 30
Vase, Woman With Pearls, Brown, Double Handle, Ioga, 10 ½ In. 29

WATCH pockets held the pocket watch that was important in Victorian times because it was not until World War I that the wristwatch was used. All types of watches are collected: silver, gold, or plated. Watches are listed here by company name or by style. Wristwatches are a separate category.

A. Saltzman, Hunting Case, 18K Gold, Black Enamel, Diamonds, Engraved Edge, Box, 1 ½ In. . 1230
Augustin Perrenoud, Hunting Case, 18K Gold, Carved, Sub Second, Key Wind 679
Bornand Geneve, Spiral Brequet, 15 Rubies, Silver, Carved Castle, Leaves 153
Cartier, Pendulette, Art Deco, Agate, Diamond, Goldtone Metal Dial, Blue Cabochons, 3 x 3 In. . 8487
Chain, 14K Yellow Gold, Interlocked Oval Bar Links, Beveled, 13 In. 242
Chain, Herringbone, 14K Yellow Gold, Spring Bar, 13 In. 863
Chain, Yellow Gold, Braided, 4-Sided Ornament, Red & White Agate, Victorian, 10 In. 277
Chance London, Open Face, 18K Gold, Goldtone Dial, Engraved Flowers, Key Wind, 1 ¾ In. 575
Charles E. Jacot, Hunting Case, Carved, 18K Yellow Gold, Flowers, c.1871, 1 ½ In. 863
Dudley, Mason's, Yellow Gold, Open Face, Engraved, Monogram, 1920s, Pocket 4063
Dudley, No. 2879, Skeleton, Open Face, 14K White Gold Filled, 19 Jewel, 1900s 4063
E. Howard Watch Co., 14K Gold Filled, Boston 300
Elgin, 14K Yellow Gold, Diamond, Fob With Charms, Woman's 1200
Elgin, 14K Yellow Gold, Swing Out, Steel Bezel, 15 Jewels 248
Elgin, Rounded Triangle, Indented Corners, Arabic, Gold Filled, Art Deco, Pocket 149
George Prior, Verge, Gilt Brass, Key Wind, Chain, c.1790, 2 ½ In. .... *illus* 615
Hamilton, 14K Yellow Gold, 17 Jewel, Woman's 124
Howard, 14K White Gold, 19 Jewel, Adjustment 5 Temperature, Embossed 401
Howard, 14K White Gold, Octagonal, 17 Jewel, Monogram, Box 319
Lapel, Art Nouveau, 18K Gold, Ruby, Diamond, Gold Dial, Engraving, 2 ¾ In. .... *illus* 984
Lohengrin, Exposition, Engraved Cover, 15 Rubies In Movement, Silver, 18K Gold, 1 ½ In. 403
Longines Wittnauer, Deco, 18K Gold, Open Face, Guilloche Gray Enamel, Woman's 834
Omega, 14K Yellow Gold, Swiss Unadjusted Movement, 17 Jewel 366
Omega, Platinum, Brushed, Silver Bar Markers, 17 Jewel, 1 ¾ In. 920
Patek Philippe, 18K Yellow Gold, Hunting Case, Marked, 2 In. Diam 2594
Pin, Edwardian, Diamonds, Blue Guilloche, Ivory Tone Dial, Platinum, Gold, 2 In. 1722
Reuge, Huntsman, Gold Plated, Musical Alarm, 17 Jewel, Figures, Castle, Box 909
Ring, Edwardian, 18K Gold, White Guilloche Bezel, Enamel, Diamonds, Size 7 1599
Robert Perry, Sterling Silver, Open Face, Engraved Masonic Symbols, c.1857, Pocket 240
S.E. Bailey & Graves, 18K Gold, Black Enamel Tracery, Seconds Dial, 1868, 1 ¾ In. 554
Schaffhausen, Stainless Steel, Open Face, Leather Pouch 425
W.C. Fields, 17 Jewels, Gold Metal Case, Any Man Who Hates Dogs, 1971 .... *illus* 463
Waltham, Hunting Case, Carved, Painted Sacred Heart, Rose & Fern Design 448
Waltham, Masonic, 14K Yellow Gold, Open Face, Repeater, c.1888, Pocket 1938

Watch, George Prior, Verge, Gilt Brass, Key Wind, Chain, c.1790, 2 ½ In.
$615

Skinner, Inc.

Watch, Lapel, Art Nouveau, 18K Gold, Ruby, Diamond, Gold Dial, Engraving, 2 ¾ In.
$984

Skinner, Inc.

Watch, W.C. Fields, 17 Jewels, Gold Metal Case, Any Man Who Hates Dogs, 1971
$463

Hake's Americana & Collectibles

WATCH FOBS were worn on watch chains. They were popular during Victorian times and after. Many styles, especially advertising designs, are still made today.

Allatt's Sports, Shield Shape, Sterling Silver, Chain, 1921, 1 ½ x 10 In. 50
Allis-Chalmers, Tractor, HD 21, Logo, Copper, 1 ¾ x 1 ½ In. 39
BC Equipment Co., International, Bulldozer, Brass, 1965, 1 ¾ x 1 ¾ In. 28
Illinois Sewing Machine Co., Nickel Plated, Letters, c.1890, 1 ½ x 1 ⅝ In. 125
Locket, Ruby, Diamonds, Chain, 14K Gold, Octagonal Lobed, c.1900, 4 In. ....*illus* 695
Patek Philippe, Repousse Figures, Leafy Scroll Border, c.1890, 1 ½ In. Diam. 1778
Rumely Thresher Co., Oil-Pull Logo, Tractor, Silver Bronze, c.1920, 1 x 1 ½ In. 245
Shield Shape, Rose Gold, Monogram, c.1920, 1 ¼ x ⅞ In. 119
Terex, GM, Embossed, Round, Brass, 1960s, 2 In. 65

WATERFORD type glass resembles the famous glass made from 1783 to 1851 in the Waterford Glass Works in Ireland. It is a clear glass that was often decorated by cutting. Modern glass is being made again in Waterford, Ireland, and is marketed under the name Waterford. Waterford merged with Wedgwood in 1986 to form the Waterford Wedgwood Group. Most Waterford Wedgwood assets were bought by KPS Capital Partners of New York in 2009 and became part of WWRD Holdings. WWRD was bought by Fiskars in 2015.

Bottle Stopper, Seahorse, 5 ½ In. 69
Bowl, Fruit, Lismore, Round Foot, 5 x 8 In. 122
Cake Plate, Comeragh, Pedestal Stand, Ireland, Marked, 5 x 10 In. 183
Centerpiece, Pedestal Foot, Flared Flat Rim, 8 x 10 In. 244
Champagne Flute, Lismore, 8 In., 6 Piece 240
Decanter Set, Colleen, Stopper, 6 Tumblers, Mahogany Tray, 6 ½ x 7 In. 637
Decanter, Glass, Cut Crystal, 9 x 4 In. & 3 ½ x 2 ¾ In. 83
Flower Arranger, Bulbous, Rolled Foot, Flat Rim, X-Design, 5 x 7 In. 122
Goblet, Wine Hock, Kylemore, Lismore, Crystal, 7 ½ In., 12 Piece 180
Lamp, Cut Glass, Cut, Bulbous Shade, Baluster, Ireland, 1900s, 19 In., Pair 1045
Ornament, 2 Turtle Doves, Box, 1983 38
Rose Bowl, Glandore, 1950s, 6 x 5 In. 60
Sherbet, Alana, 4 ⅛ In. 22
Vase, Cut Crystal, Tapered, Pedestal Base, 9 ¾ In. 120
Vase, Cylindrical, Clear Cut Crystal, Leaf Design, 10 In. 153
Wine, Lismore, 6 In., 6 Piece 360

WATT family members bought the Globe pottery of Crooksville, Ohio, in 1922. They made pottery mixing bowls and tableware of the type made by Globe. In 1935 they changed the production and made the pieces with the freehand decorations that are popular with collectors today. Apple, Starflower, Rooster, Tulip, and Autumn Foliage are the best-known patterns. Pansy, also called Rio Rose, was the earliest pattern. Apple, the most popular pattern, can be dated from the leaves. Originally, the apples had three leaves; after 1958 two leaves were used. The plant closed in 1965. For more prices, go to kovels.com.

Apple, Bowl, No. 6, 3-Leaf, 6 ¼ In. 41
Apple, Bowl, No. 7, 3-Leaf, Ribbed 56
Apple, Bowl, Lid, No. 67, 8 ½ In. 15
Apple, Bowl, Lid, No. 120, 5 In. 24
Apple, Bowl, No. 73, 3-Leaf, 9 ½ In. 85
Apple, Coffeepot, No. 115, 9 ¾ In. 1265
Apple, Pitcher, No. 16, 3-Leaf, Farmers Elevator Co., 6 ½ x 6 In. ....*illus* 49
Apple, Pitcher, No. 62, 3-Leaf, 4 ¼ In. 54
Apple, Salt & Pepper, Commemorative, Watt Collectors Assn., 1996, 4 In. 22
Apple, Sugar, No. 89, 3-Leaf, Mission, S.D., 4 ¼ In. 195
Autumn Foliage, Bowl, Spaghetti, No. 39, 13 In. 80
Autumn Foliage, Mixing Bowl, No. 65, c.1965, 12 Cup 195
Autumn Foliage, Salt & Pepper, 4 ¼ In. 34
Cherry, Salt & Pepper, 4 ½ In. 518
Double Apple, Pitcher, No. 15, 5 ½ In. 35
Open Apple, Bowl, Salad, No. 74, 5 ¼ In. 21
Pansy, Bowl, 8 In. 64
Pansy, Bowl, Cut Leaf, Bullseye, 10 ¾ In. 40
Rooster, Bowl, No. 8, Salesman's Sample, Oven Ware, 8 In. 115
Rooster, Bowl, No. 99, Oven Ware, 7 In. 7
Rooster, Bowl, Spaghetti, No. 24, Oven Ware, 8 In. 21
Rooster, Cheese Crock, No. 80, Oven Ware, 8 ½ In. 7

TIP

Do not pour detergent directly on stainless steel.

Watch Fob, Locket, Ruby, Diamonds, Chain, 14K Gold, Octagonal Lobed, c.1900, 4 In.
$695

Ruby Lane

Watt, Apple, Pitcher, No. 16, 3-Leaf, Farmers Elevator Co., 6 ½ x 6 In.
$49

Ruby Lane

Wave Crest, Plaque, Scrolls, Transfer, Figures In Garden, Gilt Metal Frame, 15 x 10 In.
$6,765

Nest Egg Auctions

Rooster, Mixing Bowl, No. 9, 9 In. 39
Rooster, Mixing Bowl, No. 65, 9 In. 59
Rooster, Pitcher, No. 69, Square, 8 In. 300
Starflower, Bowl, No. 74, 4-Petal, 5 ⅝ In. 45
Starflower, Creamer, No. 15, 5-Petal, 5 ½ In. 35
Starflower, Pitcher, 5-Petal, 5 ⅜ In. 45
Starflower, Pitcher, No. 15, 4-Petal, 2-Leaf, 5 ½ In. 75
Starflower, Pitcher, No. 16, 5-Petal, 6 ½ In. 32
Starflower, Pitcher, No. 17, 5-Petal, 8 In. 65
Starflower, Salt & Pepper, 4 ¼ In. 196
Tear Drop, Bowl, No. 5, Ribbed, 5 ¼ In. 29
Tear Drop, Pitcher, No. 15, 5 ⅜ In. 75
Tulip, Creamer, No. 15, 5 ⅜ In. 95

WATT, *Rio Rose, see Pansy*

WAVE CREST glass is an opaque white glassware manufactured by the Pairpoint Manufacturing Company of New Bedford, Massachusetts, and some French factories. It was decorated by the C.F. Monroe Company of Meriden, Connecticut. The glass was painted in pastel colors and decorated with flowers. The name Wave Crest was used starting in 1892.

WAVE CREST WARE

Box, Pink Rose, Iridescent Purple C-Scrolls, Shells, Lid, 5 x 4 ¾ In. 302
Brush Holder, Brass Ormolu, Floral Enamel, 9 x 4 ½ In. 345
Dresser Jar, Round, Squat, Pinched Waist, Metal Band, Flowers On Lid, 4 In. 69
Plaque, Scrolls, Transfer, Figures In Garden, Gilt Metal Frame, 15 x 10 In. .... *illus* 6765

WEAPONS listed here include instruments of combat other than guns, knives, rifles, or swords, and clothing worn in combat. Firearms made after 1900 are not listed in this book. Knives and Swords are listed in their own categories.

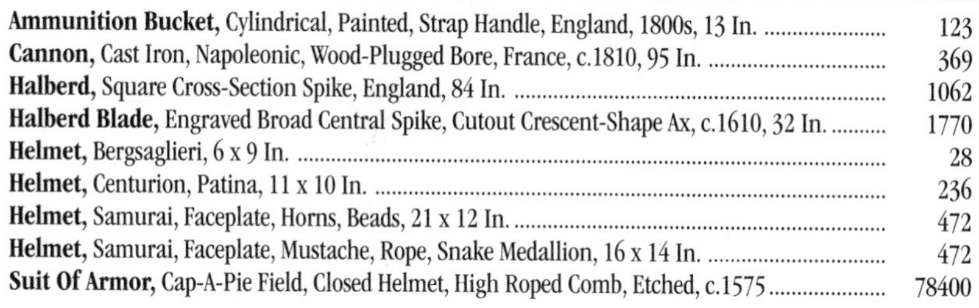

Ammunition Bucket, Cylindrical, Painted, Strap Handle, England, 1800s, 13 In. 123
Cannon, Cast Iron, Napoleonic, Wood-Plugged Bore, France, c.1810, 95 In. 369
Halberd, Square Cross-Section Spike, England, 84 In. 1062
Halberd Blade, Engraved Broad Central Spike, Cutout Crescent-Shape Ax, c.1610, 32 In. 1770
Helmet, Bergsaglieri, 6 x 9 In. 28
Helmet, Centurion, Patina, 11 x 10 In. 236
Helmet, Samurai, Faceplate, Horns, Beads, 21 x 12 In. 472
Helmet, Samurai, Faceplate, Mustache, Rope, Snake Medallion, 16 x 14 In. 472
Suit Of Armor, Cap-A-Pie Field, Closed Helmet, High Roped Comb, Etched, c.1575 78400

WEATHER VANES were used in seventeenth-century Boston. The direction of the wind was an indication of coming weather, important to the seafaring and farming communities. By the mid-nineteenth century, commercial weather vanes were made of metal. Many were shaped like animals. Ethan Allen, Dexter, and St. Julian are famous horses that were depicted. Today's collectors often consider weather vanes to be examples of folk art, even though they may not have been handmade.

Airplane, Sheet Metal, Front Mounted Propeller, Stand, c.1925, 21 x 24 In. 492
American Indian, Copper, Verdigris Patina, Full Body, 1900s, 27 In. 531
Angel Gabriel, Bronze, Floating, Trumpet, 34 In. 1220
Arm, Holding Book, Holding Forth, Arrow, Copper, Stand, c.1910, 19 x 42 In. 1440
Arrow, Leafy Tail, Copper, Cast Iron Spear Point, Gilt Trace, 1800s, 60 x 20 In. 885
Automobile, Copper & Metal, 20th Century, 16 x 24 x 10 In. .... *illus* 2760
Automobile, Model T, Copper, Embossed, Green, Brass Ornaments, 1900s, 13 x 17 In. .... *illus* 2963
Banner, Stylized Arrow, Pierced 1906, Zinc, Old White Paint, 20 x 28 In. 360
Baseball Pitcher, Copper, Windup Pose, Full Body, Stand, c.1980, 25 x 35 In. 711
Beaver, Copper, Full Body, Crosshatched Tail, Upright Ears, c.1910, 32 x 20 In. 1185
Billy Goat, Sheet Iron, 31 x 24 ½ In. 643
Boat, Metal, 2-Masted, Full Sail, Painted, 1900s, 13 x 16 In. 246
Bull, Cast Zinc Head, Copper Body, Full Body, Arrow, Gold Leaf, 1800s, 23 x 44 In. 18800
Bull, Copper, Molded, Gilt, 26 x 42 In. 2750
Bull, Copper, Molded, Zinc, A.B & W.T Westervelt, c.1900, 34 ½ x 46 In. 10000
Canada Goose, Layered Wood Panels, Painted, Iron & Wood Stand, 31 x 23 In. 277
Chicken, Arrow, 44 In. 168
Chief Massasiot, Full Body, Standing, Bow & Arrow, Patina, Base, c.1950, 45 In. 1200
Civil War Soldier, Full Body, 2-Sided, Cutout, Standing With Rifle, 35 In. 120
Codfish, Copper, Full Body, Repousse, Soldered Seams, Mounted, c.1950, 35 In. 2779
Colonel Sanders, Steel, Pointing Cane, Full Body, 2-Sided, Litho, Arrow, 1960s, 62 x 23 In. 1050

Weather Vane, Automobile, Copper & Metal, 20th Century, 16 x 24 x 10 In.
$2,760

Cottone Auctions

Weather Vane, Automobile, Model T, Copper, Embossed, Green, Brass Ornaments, 1900s, 13 x 17 In.
$2,963

James D. Julia Auctioneers

Weather Vane, Grasshopper, Copper, Hollow, Molded, Green Over Black, c.1910, 41 x 10 In.
$17,290

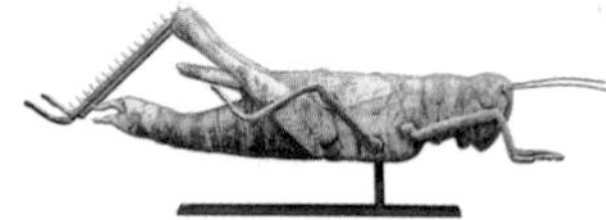

James D. Julia Auctioneers

Weather Vane, Pig, Copper, Molded, Curly Iron Tail, Green Verdigris, Gilt, c.1890, 20 x 35 In.
$14,813

James D. Julia Auctioneers

TIP

If you live in an old house and the locks are old, check the new types. There have been many improvements, and new locks provide much better security.

Weather Vane, Ram, Copper Sheets, Cast Lead Head, Soldered, 1800s, 27 x 36 In.
$14,220

James D. Julia Auctioneers

Weather Vane, Tobacco Bale, 2 Men, Sheet Metal, Riveted Frame, c.1900, 22 x 30 In.
$649

Brunk Auctions

Webb, Perfume Bottle, Green, Opal Flower, Butterfly, Cameo, Gorham Silver Flip Cap, 3 In.
$1,495

Early Auction Company

Webb, Perfume Bottle, Opal, Blue Tint Over Blue, Flowers, Cameo Stopper, c.1890, 5 In.
$826

Brunk Auctions

Confederate Soldier, Sheet Metal, Standing Guard, Upright Rifle, c.1900, 35 In. 708
Cow, Sheet Iron, Black Paint, 36 x 17 In. 205
Dove, Metal, Wings, Leafy Twig In Beak, 28 x 24 In. 1989
Eagle, Ball, Zinc Head, 23 x 13 In. 995
Eagle, Copper, Spread Wings, c.1900, 60 In. 1800
Eagle, Copper, Spread Wings, On Ball, Directional Arrow, Tree Limb Mount, 26 In. 549
Eagle, Copper, Spread Wings, On Ball, Zinc Head, A.L. Jewell, Waltham, Mass., 22 In. 3690
Eagle, Copper, Yellow Paint, Gilding, Full Body, Directional, Pole, c.1925, 50 In. 420
Feather, Milk Glass Insulator, 3 Legs, Cone Shape Finial, 22 In. 182
Fish, Copper, Full Body, c.1900, 10 x 25 In. 2214
Fish, Pine Plank, Carved, Mouth & Tailfin Detail, Sheet Iron Dorsal Fin, 35 In. 431
Fish, Wood & Copper, Full Body, Gilt, Triangular Fins, 25 ½ In. 531
Flamingo, Metal, Paint, Full Body, 1900s, 51 In. 184
Flight Of Geese, Copper, Directionals, 42 x 28 In. 146
Fox & Hound, Gilt, Full Body, Metal Stand, c.1880, 35 x 17 In. 1173
Gabriel, Wrought Iron, Angel Flying Blowing Trumpet, Steel, Rod Stand, 17 x 25 In. 948
Galleon Ship, 4 Masts, Patina, 22 x 23 ½ In. 1638
Gamecock, Pine, Silhouette, White Paint, Penn., 20 In. 720
Grasshopper, Copper, Full Body, Repousse, Gold Leaf, c.1900, 44 x 35 In. 13035
Grasshopper, Copper, Hollow, Molded, Green Over Black, c.1910, 41 x 10 In. ....*illus* 17290
Grasshopper, Wood, 6 x 21 In. 1053
Horse, Blackhawk Type, 26 x 20 In. 2574
Horse, Blackhawk, Running, Copper, Molded, Full Body, Flattened, Gilt, c.1890, 25 In. 4305
Horse, Leaping Through Hoop, Copper, Zinc, A. Jewell, Waltham, Mass., 17 x 36 In. 8750
Horse, Prancing, Sheet Copper, Applied Saddle & Blanket, Patina, c.1880, 13 x 17 In. 240
Horse, Racing, Copper, Verdigris, Zinc Ears, Bullet Hole, Boston, c.1890, 16 x 27 In. 2400
Horse, Running, Cast Iron, Copper, Full Body, Dexter, Stand, c.1890, 16 x 35 In. 2963
Horse, Running, Copper & Zinc, Full Body, Stand, 16 x 34 In. 1121
Horse, Running, Copper, 42 x 19 ½ In. 2223
Horse, Running, Copper, Molded Gilt, Cast Zinc Ears, Harris & Co., 18 x 27 In. 2829
Horse, Running, Copper, Zinc, 21 x 32 ½ In. 1500
Horse, Running, Sheet Copper, Silhouette, Verdigris Patina, Gilt, 10 In. 360
Horse, Sheet Copper, Cast Lead, Verdigris, Riveted Straps, Applied Ears, 42 x 36 In. 7688
Horse, Trotting, Copper, Zinc, 1800s, 32 x 17 In. 312
Horse, Trotting, Zinc, Full Body, Wood Base, 1800s, 19 x 28 In. 1003
Indian Silhouette, Bow, Sheet Iron, 1800s, 40 x 25 ½ In. 7080
Jockey, On Horse, Sheet Metal, Painted, 37 x 22 In. 468
Jockey, Rider, Carriage, Copper, 45 x 23 In. 492
Leaping Cat, Cast Zinc, Full Body, Copper Bar, c.1880, 12 x 24 In. 8295
Leaping Stag, Copper, 24 x 27 In. 6435
Native American, With Bow & Dog, 56 ½ x 31 In. 4387
Pig, Copper, Molded, Curly Iron Tail, Green Verdigris, Gilt, c.1890, 20 x 35 In. ....*illus* 14813
Pig, Lead & Copper, Full Body, Standing, Yellow, Weathered, c.1890, 20 x 36 In. 9263
Pig, Zinc, Full Body, Dimensional, Gilt Finish, Stand, 12 x 19 In. 1180
Quill, Copper, Spire, Base, c.1890, 28 x 48 In. 1481
Race Horse & Jockey, Copper, Verdigris, 18 x 30 In. 360
Ram, Copper Sheets, Cast Lead Head, Soldered, 1800s, 27 x 36 In. ....*illus* 14220
Rooster, Copper, Molded Gilt, Perched On Ball, Sheet Copper Tail, 34 x 30 In. 1107
Rooster, Lead, Gilded, Full Body, Iron Stand, 1800s, 16 x 18 In. 120
Sea Captain, Sheet Iron, Telescope, Sailor, Blowing Horn, Full Body, Paint, 34 x 30 In. 474
Spade, Gilt Tin, Flat Blade Shovel, Cutout Handle, Stand, 39 x 8 In. 494
Sperm Whale, Bronze, 1900s, 30 In. 1500
Squirrel, Heavy Gauge Sheet Metal, Glass Marble Eye, Scroll, Arrow, Base, 83 x 35 In. 5557
Statue Of Liberty, Gilt, Arrow, Feather, 23 x 26 In. 585
Swordfish, Cast White Metal, Weathered Gold Finish, c.1935, 34 ½ In. 277
Tobacco Bale, 2 Men, Sheet Metal, Riveted Frame, c.1900, 22 x 30 In. ....*illus* 649
Whale, Copper, Full Body, Open Mouth, Mounted On Stand, U.S.A., c.1980, 39 In. 2666
Witch, Metal, Flying On Broom, Cat, Full Body, Candleholder Base, c.1950, 43 In. 720
Witch, Sheet Metal, Silhouette, Crescent Moon, Base, c.1980, 18 x 36 In. 469

WEBB glass was made by Thomas Webb & Sons of Ambelcot, England. Many types of art and cameo glass were made by them during the Victorian era. Production ceased by 1991 and the factory was demolished in 1995. Webb Burmese and Webb Peachblow are special colored glasswares of the Victorian era. They are listed at the end of this section. Glassware that is not Burmese or Peachblow is included here.

Webb

Biscuit Jar, Cameo, Bulbous, Yellow Cut, Opal Flowers, Metal Collar, Handle, Lid, 5 x 6 In. 690

Bowl, Silver Mount, Cranberry Glass, Cameo, 9 ¼ In. 469
Finger Bowl, Green, Cameo Flowers, Flower & Geometric Border, Ruffled, 2 ½ In. 4025
Finger Bowl, Ruffled Rim, Green, Cameo Cut Flowers, Border, 2 ¼ x 5 ½ In. 1438
Perfume Bottle, Blue, White Leaves & Branches, Silver Hinged Lid, Oval, Laydown, 2 ¾ In. 1304
Perfume Bottle, Clematis, Cameo, Silver, Engraved Hinged Cap, c.1890, 4 ¾ In. 708
Perfume Bottle, Green, Opal Flower, Butterfly, Cameo, Gorham Silver Flip Cap, 3 In. .... *illus* 1495
Perfume Bottle, Opal, Blue Tint Over Blue, Flowers, Cameo Stopper, c.1890, 5 In. .... *illus* 826
Perfume Bottle, Queens Burmese, Maidenhair Fern, Enameled, Gilt, Silver, 4 ½ In. 708
Perfume Bottle, Red, White Apple Blossoms, Round, Silver Screw Cap, Flowers, 2 ½ In. 1304
Perfume Bottle, Yellow, White Leaves, 2 Wheat Stalks, Hammered Silver Lid, Laydown, 4 In. 1422
Pitcher, Satin Glass, Butterscotch Pearl, Raindrop, Reeded Handle, 7 In. 121
Plate, Cameo, Ivory, Stylized Leaves, Flowers, Tendrils, Bands, Brown, 9 In. 948
Plate, Flowers, Light Blue, Etched Overlapping Nested Arcs, Cameo, 7 ¼ In. 4148
Rose Bowl, Flowers, Opal Cut To Red, Citron Ground, Cameo Bands, 3 ¼ In. 575
Vase, Cameo, Aqua Blue Ground, Lilac Shading To White Flowers, Butterfly, 2 In. 661
Vase, Cameo, Peacock, Cherry Tree Branch, Flowers, Leaves, White, Red Iridescent, 11 In. 1067
Vase, Coralene, Diamond Quilted, Rose To Light Pink, Leaves, 10 ½ x 3 ¼ In. 363
Vase, Flowers, Butterfly, White Cut To Red, Citron Ground, Bulbous, Straight Neck, 5 ¼ In. 805
Vase, Foxglove, White Cut To Red, Citron Ground, Cameo, 10 ¾ In. .... *illus* 9200
Vase, Frosted Blue, Ivory Overlay, Flowering Jasmine Vines, Bulbous, Stick Neck, c.1900, 9 In. 4481
Vase, Globular, Cranberry Ground, Ivory Overlay, Flowers, Dragonfly, c.1900, 1 In. 478
Vase, Green Over Clear, Tulips, Acid Cut, Trumpet Neck, Flared Foot, 1920, 9 x 7 ½ In. 288
Vase, Quilted Satin, Cased Glass, Coral Shaded To Pink, Flared 4 ¼-In. Lip, 7 ½ x 5 In. 224
Vase, Red Flower, Padded, Clear Cameo Leaves & Vines, Bulbous, Stand-Up Rim, 4 x 3 In. 2370
Vase, Shouldered, Blue & Pink Enamel, Flowers & Vines, c.1880, 10 In. 287
Vase, White & Gray Flowers, Butterfly, Red Ground, Shouldered, 8 ½ In. 1778
Vase, White Cameo Vines, Leaves, Flowers, Frosted Yellow, Rope Band Foot, Bottle, 11 In. 1067
Vase, White Flowers & Fern, 2 Butterflies, Citron, Oval, Cylindrical Neck, Cameo, 9 In. 5036
Vase, White Flowers & Leaves, Cut To Cranberry, 5 In. 302
Vase, Wild Rose, Berries, Butterfly, Blue, White, Cameo Bands, Shouldered, 8 ½ In. 2588
Vase, Woodbine Vine, Orange Berries, Round, Tapered, Bulbous Shoulder, 6 x 6 In. 288

WEBB BURMESE is a shaded Victorian glass made by Thomas Webb & Sons of Stourbridge, England, from 1886. Pieces are shades of pink to yellow.

Cruet, Yellow, Pink, 7 ½ In. 20
Fairy Lamp, Domed Shade, Ruffled Base, Satin Finish, Glass Insert, 5 ¾ In. 259
Fairy Lamp, Shade, Enameled Berries, Leaves, Ruffled, Clarke Base, Cricklite, 6 In. .... *illus* 345

WEBB PEACHBLOW is a shaded Victorian glass made by Thomas Webb & Sons of Stourbridge, England, from 1885.

Bowl, Pinched, Ruffled Rim, 5 ¼ x 8 ¾ In. 240
Bride's Basket, Flowers, Silver Plate Frame, Cherub Medallions, 13 x 12 In. 1062
Cologne, Bulbous Body, Gold Enamel, Fishing Net, Embossed Silver Cap, 4 ½ In. 575
Pitcher, Flowers, Triform Mouth, Amber Glass Handle, 1890, 8 In. 372
Sweetmeat, Lid, Butterfly, Flowers, Branches, Silver Plate, Handle, 3 In. 189
Vase, Flowers, Berries, 1890, 5 ¼ In. 120
Vase, Flowers, Vine, 9 ½ x 5 ½ In. 98
Vase, Pink To Yellow, Bulbous, Wavy Folded Rim, Signed, 3 In. .... *illus* 150
Vase, Stick, Gold Leaves, Gourd Shape, 10 ¾ In. 132

WEDGWOOD, one of the world's most successful potteries, was founded by Josiah Wedgwood, who was considered a cripple by his brother and was forbidden to work at the family business. The pottery was established in England in 1759. The company used a variety of marks, including Wedgwood, Wedgwood & Bentley, Wedgwood & Sons, and Wedgwood's Stone China. A large variety of wares has been made, including the well-known jasperware, basalt, creamware, and even a limited amount of porcelain. There are two kinds of jasperware. One is made from two colors of clay; the other is made from one color of clay with a color dip to create the contrast in design. In 1986 Wedgwood and Waterford Crystal merged to form the Waterford Wedgwood Group. Most Waterford Wedgwood assets were bought by KPS Capital Partners of New York in 2009 and became part of WWRD Holdings. Some manufacturing will be transferred to Germany, Indonesia, and Slovakia. Other Wedgwood pieces may be listed under Flow Blue, Majolica, Tea Leaf Ironstone, or in other porcelain categories. WWRD was bought by Fiskars in 2015.

WEDGWOOD

Basket, Creamware, Armorial, Handles, c.1800, 3 x 12 In. 84
Bookends, Pan, Earthenware, Erling Olsen, c.1932, 6 ½ In. 1107

Webb, Vase, Foxglove, White Cut To Red, Citron Ground, Cameo, 10 ¾ In.
$9,200

Early Auction Company

Webb Burmese, Fairy Lamp, Shade, Enameled Berries, Leaves, Ruffled, Clarke Base, Cricklite, 6 In.
$345

Early Auction Company

Wedgewood with an E

The word *Wedgewood* is found on china that was not made by the famous factory of Josiah Wedgwood. William Smith and Company of Stockton on Tees, England, made a cream-colored ware marked "Wedgewood" from 1826 to 1848. The mark was a deliberate attempt to mislead the public and to misrepresent the china as that of the more famous factory.

Webb Peachblow, Vase, Pink To Yellow, Bulbous, Wavy Folded Rim, Signed, 3 In.
$150

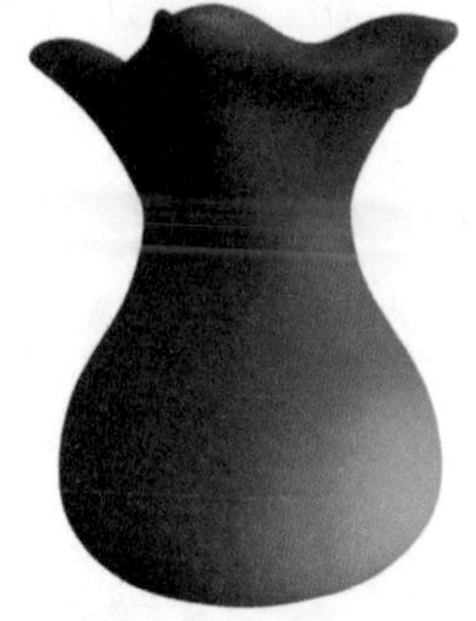

Ruby Lane

Wedgwood, Bough Pot, Lid, Jasperware, Blue, White Relief, Dancing Hours, Marked, 1800s, 6 In.
$1,353

Skinner, Inc.

Wedgwood, Bowl, Fairyland Luster, Castle On Road, 8-Sided, Marked, c.1920, 10 ¾ In.
$2,460

Skinner, Inc.

Wedgwood, Cann, Cup, Saucer, Jasper Dip, Tricolor, Diceware, Marked, 5 ⅜ In.
$923

Skinner, Inc.

Bookends, Stag & Tree, Earthenware, Erling Olsen, c.1932, 6 ½ In. 340
Bough Pot, Lid, Jasperware, Blue, White Relief, Dancing Hours, Marked, 1800s, 6 In. .... *illus* 1353
Bowl, Black Basalt, Acanthus, 1860s, 5 x 12 In. 345
Bowl, Dragon Luster, Mottled Blue, Mother-Of-Pearl Interior, Octagonal, c.1920, 9 In. 246
Bowl, Earthenware, Deer, Stylized Ground, Impressed Mark, Erling Olsen, 8 ½ In. 1353
Bowl, Fairyland Luster, Blue, Orange Mottled Interior, Flying Geese, Octagonal, 1920s, 4 x 9 In. 554
Bowl, Fairyland Luster, Castle On Road, 8-Sided, Marked, c.1920, 10 ¾ In. .... *illus* 2460
Bowl, Fairyland Luster, Elves, Bridge, Black Sky, Spider, Web, 8 ¾ In. 4062
Bowl, Fairyland Luster, Melba, Willow, Oriental Village, Boats, Lighthouse, Footed, 8 In. 1112
Bowl, Fairyland Luster, Paneled, Hummingbird Pattern, Octagonal, c.1917, 8 In. Diam. 813
Bowl, Fairyland Luster, Poplar Tree, Flame Ground, Woodland Bridge Inside, 11 In. 8651
Bowl, Fairyland Luster, Poplar Trees, Elves & Bell Branch, Ring Foot, c.1925, 4 x 9 In. 1875
Bowl, Fairyland Luster, Woodland Bridge, Midnight Sky, Octagonal, 9 In. Diam. 2074
Bowl, Fairyland Luster, Woodland Elves Patterns, Footed, Flared Rim, c.1920, 6 x 9 In. 3000
Bowl, Jasper Dip, Yellow, Applied Black Figures, Leaf Border, c.1930, 6 ¼ In. 800
Bowl, Lusterware, Gold Dragons, Blue Ground, Cranes, Daisy Jones, c.1915, 4 x 8 In. 495
Bowl, Museum Series, Diced Pattern, Blue, White, 1900s, 3 ½ x 7 ¾ In. 258
Box, Lid, Fairyland Luster, Nizami, Medallion, 4 Persian Gentlemen, Garden, 5 In. 23108
Bust, Mercury, Basalt, 18 In. 1250
Candlestick, Jasper Dip, Blue, Cylindrical, White Leaf Border, c.1800, 7 In., Pair 308
Candlestick, Yellow, Jasper Dip, White Banding, Black Figures, c.1930, 7 In., Pair 246
Cann, Cup, Saucer, Jasper Dip, Tricolor, Diceware, Marked, 5 ⅜ In. .... *illus* 923
Cassolette, Lid, Jasper Dip, Tricolor, Strapware, Candle Nozzle, 5 ¾ In. 523
Clock, Flower Bezel, Maiden Holding Bouquet, c.1880, 12 ¼ In. 523
Crocus Pot, Dome Lid, Holes, Basket Weave, Stoneware, Marked, c.1830, 7 In. .... *illus* 800
Cup & Saucer, Fairyland Luster, Nizami, Persian Man, Tree Stump, Gazelles 8295
Cup, Fairyland Luster, York, Leapfrogging Elves, Midnight Sky, 4 ⅝ In. 3259
Dish, Jasperware, Tricolor, Strapware, Blue, Yellow, White, Bamboo, Rope Border, 11 ¼ In. 1968
Dish, Leaf Shape, Majolica, Leaves Ring Blue Center, 11 In. 125
Figurine, Duiker, Tan, Gray, Raised Base, Skeaping Norman Wilson, 1959, 8 In. 1107
Figurine, Paintress, Seated Woman, Flower Dress, Shaped Base, 10 In. 305
Garden Seat, Rubens, Majolica, Rococo Design, Square Seat, Scrolled Legs, c.1900, 18 x 11 In. 1507
Group, Black Basalt, Faun & Bacchus, Standing, Tree Stump, c.1860, 18 ½ In. .... *illus* 1353
Ice Bucket, Lid, Jasperware, Blue, Silver Plate, Classical Women, 5 In. Diam. 50
Inkstand, Black Basalt, Double Inkpots, Fitted Rings, Multicolor Enamel, 7 ¾ In. 677
Jar, Canopic, Lid, Jasper Dip, Green, White Bands, Marked, 9 ½ In. .... *illus* 7995
Jardiniere, Jasper Dip, Blue, White Raised Garland, Classical Figures, 8 x 9 In. 120
Jug, Lid, Jasper Dip, Blue, Pear Shape, Leaf Handle & Spout, White Figures, c.1790, 9 In. 431
Malfrey Pot, Fairyland Luster, Woodland Elves, Bulbous, Squat, Gilt, c.1920, 4 In. 906
Mug, Jasper Dip, Blue, Classical Relief Figures, Twisted Handle, Silver Rim, c.1870, 5 In. 30
Pitcher, Black Basalt, Helmet Shape, Pedestal Foot, Bacchanalian Boys, c.1780, 11 In. 1476
Pitcher, Bowl, Queen's Ware, Cobble & Zoo, Daisy Makeig-Jones, 8 x 11 In. 492
Pitcher, Dragon Kenlock Ware, Basalt, 6 In. 100
Pitcher, Jasper Dip, Crimson, White Figures, Flowers, Bulbous, c.1920, 5 ¼ In. 308
Pitcher, Jasperware, Blue, Applied White Detail, 1800s, 6 ¾ In. 60
Pitcher, Queen's Ware, Multicolor, Dog, Landscape, Bulbous, c.1910, 8 ¼ In. 246
Pitcher, Queen's Ware, Painted, Stylized Trees, Impressed Mark, 1900s, 7 In. 185
Plaque, Fairyland Luster, Torches, Imps In River, Castle, Makeig-Jones, Frame, 13 x 10 In. 11850
Plate, Basket Weave, White, 11 ¼ In., 12 Piece 522
Plate, Belmar, Flower Baskets, 10 ⅜ In., 12 Piece 182
Plate, Dinner, Raised Gilt Scrolls, Latticework, Flowers, c.1940, 10 ½ In., 12 Piece 984
Plate, Fairyland Luster, Firbolgs, Purple, Turquoise, Red, Flower Rim, 10 ⅝ In. 3555
Plate, Green Leaf, Majolica, Etruria & Barlaston, c.1950, 8 In., 12 Piece 240
Plate, Luncheon, Grosvenor, White Ground, Flower Swags, Leaves, 1920s, 8 ¾ In., 12 Piece 242
Plate, Salad, Ventnor, Ivory Ground, Fruit Swags, Multicolor Urns, 1920s, 9 In., 12 Piece 183
Potpourri, Lid, Jasper Dip, Tricolor, Strapware, Lilac, Green, White, 8 ¼ In. 3075
Potpourri, Lid, Rosso Antico, Tropical Birds, Flowers, Loop Handles, c.1810, 12 In. .... *illus* 1599
Potpourri, Pierced Lid, Black Basalt, Globular, Loop Handles, Red Leaves, 1800s, 10 In. 800
Rum Kettle, Black, Lid, Basalt, Bail Handle, Marked, c.1800, 8 ½ In. 1230
Salad Set, Jasperware, Blue, Bowl, Salad Fork, Spoon, 1900s, 3 Piece 126
Sauceboat, Black Basalt, Loop Handles, Red & Cream Flower Band, c.1810, 8 In. 1169
Sugar, Lid, Jasper Dip, Tricolor, Diceware, White Leaves, Dome Lid, 1800s, 3 ½ In. 984
Tankard, Black Basalt, Oak Leaf Band, Textured Ground, Impressed, c.1790, 7 ⅜ In. .... *illus* 800
Tea Cup, Saucer, Jasper Dip, Blue, Applied White Classical Figures, c.1890, 4 ½ In. 738
Tea Cup, Saucer, Jasper Dip, Blue, Applied White Classical Figures, Striping, 5 In. 1600
Tea Set, Florentine, Turquoise, Teapot, Sugar, Lid, Creamer 167

Tea Set, Jasperware, Blue, Neoclassical Relief Figures, Teapot, Sugar, Lid, Creamer 104
Teapot, Jasperware, Crimson, White, 1920, 4 ¼ x 7 ¼ In. 575
Teapot, Lid, Black Basalt, Beehive, Molded Body, Impressed Mark, c.1810, 5 ¾ In. 5166
Teapot, Lid, Black, Basalt, Bronzed, Gilt Leaves In Relief, c.1890, 6 ½ In. ....*illus* 5228
Teapot, Lid, Jasper Dip, Blue, Leaf Handle & Spout, Leaves, Putti, c.1790, 8 In. 1230
Teapot, Lid, Jasper Dip, Tricolor, Diceware, Lilac, Green, White, c.1800, 3 ½ In. 1476
Teapot, Lid, Oval, Squat, White Prunus, Relief, Bamboo Handle & Spout, c.1810, 10 In. 2583
Telephone, Jasperware, Pink, Astral, 1900s, 7 x 9 ¾ In. 172
Tobacco Jar, Lid, Jasper Dip, Green, White Dancing Hours, Handles, 1906, 7 ¾ In. ....*illus* 369
Tray, Fairyland Luster, Lily, Garden Of Paradise, Daylight Ground, Gilt Geese, 13 In. 9263
Tray, Tea, Jasper Dip, Blue, White Classical Figures, Flowers, c.1890, 15 In. Diam. 984
Trinket Box, Pegasus, Blue, c.1850, 1 ¼ x 4 ¼ In. 161
Tureen, Soup, Underplate, Napoleon, Ivy Vine, White Ground, Handles, 12 & 9 x 11 In. 271
Umbrella Stand, Argenta Ware, Hexagonal, Bamboo Strapwork, 21 ¾ In. 1750
Umbrella Stand, Black & White, Landscape, 21 x 8 ¾ In. 250
Urn, Black Basalt, Flaring Shape, Relief, c.1850, 6 ¾ In. 210
Vase, Black Basalt, Shouldered, Rolled Rim, Bronze & Gilt Lilies, Leaves, 1880s, 9 In. 2337
Vase, Crimson Portland, White Classical Figures, Impressed, c.1910, 7 In. 1180
Vase, Fairyland Luster, Bifrost, Multicolor Rainbow, Castle, Fairies, 8 ½ In. 8295
Vase, Fairyland Luster, Brown Firbolgs, Red Ground, Gilt, Bottle Shape, Ring Foot, 8 In. 1007
Vase, Fairyland Luster, Butterflies, Pale Blue, Gilt, Spread Foot, c.1920, 8 In. 625
Vase, Fairyland Luster, Butterfly Women, Trees, Gilt, Purple, Trumpet Shape, 10 In. 3792
Vase, Fairyland Luster, Elves, Bridge, Footed, Flattened Rim, 8 ⅞ In. 4387
Vase, Fairyland Luster, Sycamore Tree, Feng Hwan & Bridge Panels, Flame Ground, 8 In. 9480
Vase, Fairyland Luster, Trumpet, Butterfly Women, Imps, Birds, Flame, 6 In., Pair 7703
Vase, Fairyland Luster, Trumpet, Hummingbird, Orange Mottled, Blue, Storks, 1900s, 12 In. 413
Vase, Fairyland Luster, Trumpet, Spread Foot, Butterfly Woman, Gilt, c.1920, 9 In. 1125
Vase, Hummingbird Luster, Blue Mottled Luster Ground, Gilt, c.1910, 9 In. 472
Vase, Jasper Dip, Light Blue, Pierced Disc Lid, Scalloped Rim, 1800s, 7 In. 800
Vase, Jasper Dip, Light Green, White Figures, Shouldered, Handles, 1800s, 8 In. 308
Vase, Lid, Black Basalt, Maiden Head Handles, Swirled Fluting, Swags, c.1775, 10 In. ....*illus* 1353
Vase, Lid, Black Basalt, Squat, Laurel & Berry Border, Swags, Cherubs, c.1780, 6 In. 800
Vase, Lid, Fairyland Luster, Candlemas Pattern, c.1920, 11 In. ....*illus* 4305
Vase, Lid, Fairyland Luster, Jewel Tree, Trees, Fairies, Mushrooms, Swollen, 11 ½ In. 3911
Vase, Lid, Jasper Dip, Black, White, Yellow, Diceware, c.1890, 9 In. ....*illus* 1353
Vase, Lid, Jasper Dip, Tricolor, Diceware, Leaf Handles, Applied Figures, 6 ¾ In. 400
Vase, Lid, Jasper Dip, Yellow, Bacchus Head Handles, Black Medallions, 12 In. ....*illus* 1230
Vase, Monkey, Green Glaze, Tropical Plants, Erling Olsen, c.1932, 9 In. ....*illus* 738

WELLER pottery was first made in 1872 in Fultonham, Ohio. The firm moved to Zanesville, Ohio, in 1882. Artwares were introduced in 1893. Hundreds of lines of pottery were produced, including Louwelsa, Eocean, Dickens Ware, and Sicardo, before the pottery closed in 1948.

LOUWELSA WELLER

Art Nouveau, Vase, Nautilus Shell, Woman's Portrait, Pastel, Impressed, 7 ¼ In. 201
Aurelian, Vase, Gladiolas, Virginia Adams, 1900, 17 ½ x 6 ½ In. 750
Aurelian, Vase, Pine Boughs, John Herold, 1900-10, 21 x 13 In. 938
Aurora, Vase, 2 Yellow Daisies, Pastel, 6 In. 266
Baldin, Jardiniere, Cream, Tan, Fruit, Pedestal, 31 ½ In. 238
Baldwin Apple, Jardiniere, Pedestal, 39 ½ In. 438
Cameo Jewel, Vase, Topless Woman, Robes, 1910-20, 13 ½ x 8 In. 1375
Coppertone, Bowl, Frog & Lily, Stamped, 3 ¼ x 15 ¾ In. 177
Coppertone, Figurine, Turtle, Shaped Shell, Head Out, Black Slip Bottom, 2 x 6 In. 345
Coppertone, Lawn Sprinkler, Frog, Green, Multicolor, 5 ¾ In. 590
Dedonatis, Vase, Ring Of Leaves, Berries, Multicolor, White Ground, Blue Bands, 3 ½ In. 354
Delta, Vase, Blue Nasturtium, Tapered, Flat Lip, Impressed Louwelsa, Madge Hurst, 8 In. 354
Dickens Ware, Jug, Bridge, Mt. Vernon Bridge Co., Ohio, Handles, 7 In. 354
Dickens Ware, Vase, Golfer, Stamped Mark, 1897-1905, 9 ¼ x 4 ½ In. ....*illus* 406
Eocean, Vase, Dragon, Bud, Eocean Green, Gray, White & Pink Glaze, 9 ½ In. 1180
Eocean, Vase, Raised Flowers, High Glaze, Cylindrical, Flared & Rolled Rim, 14 In. 390
Experimental, Vase, Lug Handles, Deep Red Glaze, Black Dragons, 6 In. 259
Figure, Kingfisher, On Twig, Flower Frog, Multicolor Glaze, 9 x 5 ¾ In. 184
Figure, Pelican, 1910s, 19 ½ x 20 In. 5000
Figure, Spaniel, Painted, Brown, Black, c.1930, 11 x 14 ¼ In. 604
Figure, Swan, Preening, 1910s, 15 x 22 In. 8750
Forest, Vase, Flared, Multicolor Matte Glaze, Oval, 4-Footed, 8 x 5 ¾ In. 171
Fru Russet, Vase, Green, Applied Woman, Flowy Dress, c.1905, 13 x 5 ½ In. 8125
Glendale, Vase, Parakeets, Multicolor, Paper Label, 9 In. 472

Wedgwood, Crocus Pot, Dome Lid, Holes, Basket Weave, Stoneware, Marked, c.1830, 7 In.
$800

Skinner, Inc.

Wedgwood, Group, Black Basalt, Faun & Bacchus, Standing, Tree Stump, c.1860, 18 ½ In.
$1,353

Skinner, Inc.

Wedgwood, Jar, Canopic, Lid, Jasper Dip, Green, White Bands, Marked, 9 ½ In.
$7,995

Skinner, Inc.

Wedgwood, Potpourri, Lid, Rosso Antico, Tropical Birds, Flowers, Loop Handles, c.1810, 12 In.
$1,599

Skinner, Inc.

Wedgwood, Tankard, Black Basalt, Oak Leaf Band, Textured Ground, Impressed, c.1790, 7 ⅜ In.
$800

Skinner, Inc.

Wedgwood, Teapot, Lid, Black, Basalt, Bronzed, Gilt Leaves In Relief, c.1890, 6 ½ In.
$5,228

Skinner, Inc.

Wedgwood, Tobacco Jar, Lid, Jasper Dip, Green, White Dancing Hours, Handles, 1906, 7 ¾ In.
$369

Skinner, Inc.

Wedgwood, Vase, Lid, Black Basalt, Maiden Head Handles, Swirled Fluting, Swags, c.1775, 10 In.
$1,353

Skinner, Inc.

Wedgwood, Vase, Lid, Fairyland Luster, Candlemas Pattern, c.1920, 11 In.
$4,305

Skinner, Inc.

Wedgwood, Vase, Lid, Jasper Dip, Black, White, Yellow, Diceware, c.1890, 9 In.
$1,353

Skinner, Inc.

Wedgwood, Vase, Lid, Jasper Dip, Yellow, Bacchus Head Handles, Black Medallions, 12 In.
$1,230

Skinner, Inc.

TIP

Iridescent pottery like Sicardo should be carefully cleaned. Wash in mild detergent and water. Rinse. Dry by buffing vigorously with dry, fluffy towels. Then polish with a silver cloth as if it were made of metal. Buff again with a clean towel.

Group, Coppertone, Frogs, Green, Embracing, 1920s, 16 ¾ x 11 ½ In. 5938
Hobart, Vase, Woman, Standing, Holding Skirt Out To Sides, Blue Matte Glaze, 10 ¾ In. 189
Hudson, Bowl, Blossoms, Brown, Green, Tan Ground, 1920s, 5 ½ x 2 In. 60
Hudson, Bowl, Flowers, Leaves, 5 x 2 In. 60
Hudson, Vase, Hollyhocks, Pastel Pink & White, Mae Timberlake, 12 In. 708
Hudson, Vase, Pink Dogwood Blossoms, Footed, Hester Pillsbury, 10 ¼ In. 354
Hudson, Vase, Snow Scene, Green Slip, Mae Timberlake, 7 In. 1180
Hudson, Vase, White Daisies, Lavender Ground, Handles, Sarah Timberlake, 5 ½ In. 177
Iris, Vase, Metallic Glaze, Signed, c.1915, 24 ½ x 13 In. ....*illus* 13750
Jap Birdimal, Vase, Geisha, Squeezebag, Frederick Rhead, c.1903, 10 In. ....*illus* 3375
Kingfisher, Pitcher, Perched On Branch, Cattails, Branch Handle, 8 ¼ In. 118
L'Art Nouveau, Cane Stand, Sunflowers, 1903-04, 34 x 6 ½ In. 2500
L'Art Nouveau, Vase, Egyptian Scene, Reclining Woman, 1903-04, 12 ½ x 8 In. 1750
Lasa, Vase, Cylindrical, Bell Foot, Rolled Rim, Blue & White Flowers, Gold, Amber, 6 In. 316
Lasa, Vase, Pine Trees, Landscape, 11 ½ x 5 ¼ In. 270
Louwelsa, Jardiniere, Peony Flowers, Brown, 7 ½ x 10 ½ In. 132
Louwelsa, Pitcher, Blackberries, Leaves, Red & Brown Glaze, 11 In. 225
Louwelsa, Vase, Tulips, Brown Shaded To Warm Gold Glaze, Urn Form, A. Haubrich, 16 In. 308
Malvern, Vase, Vines, Leaves, Pinched Waist, 5 ¾ In. 175
Matte Ware, Jardiniere, Sunflowers, Tan Ground, Etched, Frank Ferrell Monogram, 6 x 8 In. 118
Matte Ware, Vase, Arts & Crafts Style, Flowers In Slip, Incised, Frank Ferrell, 9 In. 502
Matte Ware, Vase, Squat, Twisted Handles, Green Mottle, Grapes, 5 x 9 ½ In. 374
Muskota, Flower Frog, Leda & The Swan, 6 ¾ In. 177
Pedestal, Green Glaze, Flared At Base & Top, Grotesque Masques, Mark, c.1925, 26 x 12 In. 311
Perfecto, Vase, Footed Pillow Shape, Rolled Rim, Portrait Of St. Bernard, Cream, 11 In. 1840
Rhead Faience, Tankard, Tall Trees, Green Leaves, Red Ground, Beaker Shape, Spout, 11 In. 1093
Sicardo, Bowl, Buttressed, Flowers, Swirls, Green, Purple Luster Interior, 2 ½ x 6 ½ In. 161
Sicardo, Vase, Daisies, Flower & Stem Band, Iridized, Signed, 9 ½ In. 502
Sicardo, Vase, Faceted, Iridescent Peacock Feather, Rounded, Tapered, 8 In. 896
Sicardo, Vase, Floral Pattern, Iridized Multicolor, Signed, 7 ¼ In. 1652
Sicardo, Vase, Lobed, Flowers, Multicolor, Signed Jacques Sicard, 1903-17, 11 x 7 In. 2625
Sicardo, Vase, Stylized Flowers, 4-Footed, 7 x 8 ¼ In. 384
Sicardo, Vase, Tapered, Rounded Bottom, Spiral Ribbed, Daisies, 11 ½ In. 633
Vase, Elongated Oval, Tapered, Bird, Branch, Coiled Snake, Green, Matte, 1905, 18 In. 8125
Warwick, Wall Pocket, Paper Label, 11 ½ x 4 In. 150
White & Decorated, Vase, Branches With Berries, Flowers, Gray Birds, 8 ¼ In. 826
Woodcraft, Ashtray, Oak Leaves, 6 x 2 In. 75
Woodcraft, Planter, Foxes, Multicolor, Impressed, 5 ¾ In. 189
Woodcraft, Vase, Apple Tree Stump, Black Faced Owl, Knothole, Flowers, 15 ½ In. 1298
Woodcraft, Vase, Tree Trunk, Owl, Impressed Mark, c.1910, 15 ½ In. ....*illus* 1331
Xenia, Vase, Flowers, Pastels, Impressed Name, 9 In. 708

WEMYSS ware was first made in 1882 by Robert Heron, the owner of Fife Pottery in Kirkaldy, Scotland. Large colorful flowers, hearts, and other symbols were hand painted on figurines, inkstands, jardinieres, candlesticks, buttons, pots, and other items. Fife Pottery closed in 1932. The molds and designs were used by a series of potteries until 1957. In 1985 the Wemyss name and designs were obtained by Griselda Hill. The Wemyss Ware trademark was registered in 1994. Modern Wemyss Ware in old styles is still being made.

Figurine, Pig, Cabbage Roses, Green Leaves, Hand Painted, Scotland, c.1900, 6 In. ....*illus* 825
Figurine, Pig, Sitting, Cabbage Rose, Red, c.1900, 6 x 4 ¾ In. 825
Washbowl & Jug, Cabbage Rose, Footed, c.1890, 10-In. Jug, 14-In. Washbowl 1919

WESTMORELAND GLASS was made by the Westmoreland Glass Company of Grapeville, Pennsylvania, from 1889 to 1984. The company made clear and colored glass of many varieties, such as milk glass, pressed glass, and slag glass.

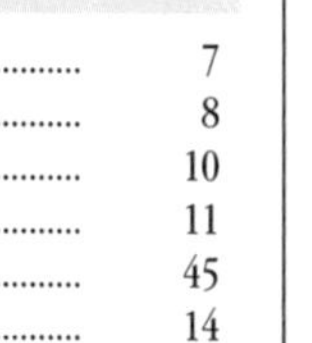

Ashburton, Sherbet, Amber, 3 ½ In. 7
Ashburton, Sherbet, Blue, 3 ⅝ In. 8
Ashburton, Tumbler, Old Fashioned, Yellow, 3 ⅞ In. 10
Ashburton, Wine, Claret, Yellow, 5 ¼ In. 11
Buzz Star, Compote, 8 In. 45
Buzz Star, Punch Cup, 2 ⅛ In. 14
Cherry & Grape, Creamer, Lid, Milk Glass, 3 ¾ In. 18
Cherry, Creamer, Milk Glass, 3 ¾ In. 16
Cherry, Honey Jar, Milk Glass, Lid, 5 ⅜ In. 21
China Rose, Basket, Milk Glass, Handle, 6 ¾ In. 20

TIP
The first place a burglar looks for valuables is in the bedroom. A better choice is in your garage or freezer.

Wedgwood, Vase, Monkey, Green Glaze, Tropical Plants, Erling Olsen, c.1932, 9 In.
$738

Skinner, Inc.

Weller, Dickens Ware, Vase, Golfer, Stamped Mark, 1897-1905, 9 ¼ x 4 ½ In.
$406

Rago Arts and Auction Center

W

This is an edited listing of current prices. Visit **Kovels.com** to check thousands of prices from previous years and sign up for free information on trends, tips, reproductions, marks, and more.

Weller, Iris, Vase, Metallic Glaze, Signed, c.1915, 24 ½ x 13 In.
$13,750

Rago Arts and Auction Center

TIP
Your collectibles will live best at the temperature and humidity that is comfortable for you. Not too hot, cold, wet, or dry.

Weller, Jap Birdimal, Vase, Geisha, Squeezebag, Frederick Rhead, c.1903, 10 In.
$3,375

Rago Arts and Auction Center

Weller, Woodcraft, Vase, Tree Trunk, Owl, Impressed Mark, c.1910, 15 ½ In.
$1,331

Humler & Nolan

Wemyss, Figurine, Pig, Cabbage Roses, Green Leaves, Hand Painted, Scotland, c.1900, 6 In.
$825

Ruby Lane

Westmoreland, Doric, Candlestick, Pink, Round Scrolled Foot, 1940s, 4 ½ x 4 In., Pair
$38

Ruby Lane

Westmoreland, Old Quilt, Creamer, Milk Glass, Shaped Rim, Ring Foot, c.1955, 4 x 4 In.
$15

Ruby Lane

Wheatley, Vase, Spread Foot, Green Matte Glaze, Incised Leaf Design, c.1910, 11 In.
$920

Humler & Nolan

Willets, Pitcher, Red & Purple Grapes, Hand Painted, Wavy Rim, Belleek, Signed, 1890s, 15 In.
$600

Ruby Lane

Della Robbia, Cocktail, 4 ⅜ In. ... 14
Della Robbia, Compote, Lid, Milk Glass, 7 In. ... 15
Della Robbia, Creamer ... 13
Della Robbia, Cup & Saucer ... 15
Della Robbia, Plate, Dinner, 10 ⅝ In. ... 64
Della Robbia, Punch Bowl, 12 In. ... 209
Della Robbia, Sherbet, 4 ¾ In. ... 11
Della Robbia, Sherbet, Milk Glass, 4 ⅞ In. ... 7
Della Robbia, Sugar ... 12
Della Robbia, Tumbler, 12 Oz. ... 13
Della Robbia, Tumbler, Iced Tea, Footed, Flared, 5 ¾ In. ... 13
Dolphin, Candlestick, Milk Glass, 4 ¼ In. ... 27
Doric, Banana Stand, Milk Glass, 11 In. ... 33
Doric, Candlestick, Milk Glass, 4 ½ In. ... 13
Doric, Candlestick, Pink, Round Scrolled Foot, 1940s, 4 ½ x 4 In., Pair ... *illus* 38
Doric, Compote, Milk Glass, 11 In. ... 29
Doric, Rose Bowl, Milk Glass, 3 ¾ In. ... 21
English Hobnail, Butter, Cover, Amber, ¼ Lb. ... 24
English Hobnail, Cocktail, Ruby Flash, 4 ½ In. ... 17
English Hobnail, Creamer, Footed, Amber, 4 ¼ In. ... 10
English Hobnail, Plate, Dinner, Amber, 9 ⅛ In. ... 58
Forget-Me-Knot, Sandwich, Plate, Milk Glass, 11 In. ... 18
Fruits, Punch Set, 8 Piece ... 189
Hearts, Dish, Heart Shape, Almond, 8 In. ... 15
Hobnail, Cup & Saucer ... 12
Hobnail, Vase, Ruby Flashed, Footed, Flared, 4 ¼ x 5 In. ... 14
Lattice Edge, Banana Stand, 8 In. ... 23
Leaf, Nut Dish, Footed, Milk Glass, 6 In. ... 19
Leaf, Plate, Luncheon, Milk Glass, 8 ½ In. ... 13
Old Quilt, Creamer, Milk Glass, Shaped Rim, Ring Foot, c.1955, 4 x 4 In. ... *illus* 15
Paneled Grape, Toothpick Holder, Purple ... 23
Peacock, Sugar, Lid, Milk Glass, Footed ... 21
Princess Feather, Plate, Luncheon, Amber, 8 In. ... 8
Quilt Pattern, Vase, Bell Rim, Milk Glass, 9 x 6 In. ... 24
Ring & Petal, Bowl, Flared, Footed, Milk Glass, 12 In. ... 21
Ring & Petal, Bowl, Footed, Milk Glass, 10 x 10 In. ... 35
Ring & Petal, Candlestick, Milk Glass, 3 ½ In. ... 12
Ring & Petal, Plate, Salad, Milk Glass, 8 ¼ In. ... 24
Rose & Lattice, Vase, Bulbous, Ruffled Rim, Milk Glass, Bud, 8 ¾ In. ... 19
Roses & Bows, Ashtray, 4 x 4 In. ... 19
Roses & Bows, Basket, Handle, 6 ¾ In. ... 21
Roses & Bows, Basket, Handle, Footed, 3 In. ... 15
Roses & Bows, Bell, Cameo, 6 In. ... 20
Roses & Bows, Candlestick, Square Base, 4 ⅝ In. ... 19
Roses & Bows, Compote, Lid ... 40
Roses & Bows, Compote, Lid, Milk Glass, 7 In. ... 32
Roses & Bows, Dish, Sweetmeat, Ruffled, Footed, 5 ⅛ In. ... 25
Roses & Bows, Napkin Ring, 6-Sided ... 43
Roses & Bows, Sugar, Lid, Footed ... 33
Roses & Bows, Trinket Box, Lid, Footed, 2 ¾ x 2 ¾ In. ... 38
Roses & Bows, Vase, Paneled, Footed, 6 In. ... 30
Roses & Bows, Vase, Scalloped, Footed, Bud, 10 ¾ In. ... 18
Shell & Jewel, Bowl, Round, 8 In. ... 40
Shell & Jewel, Tumbler, 8 Oz., 3 ¾ In. ... 27
Spoke & Rim, Bowl, Footed, Roses & Blue Dots, 10 ¼ In. ... 140
Square S, Plate, Dinner, White, 8 x 8 In. ... 16
Swan, Sugar, Milk Glass ... 19
Swan, Toothpick Holder, Black, 2 ⅜ In. ... 23
Swan, Vase, Milk Glass, 6 ½ In. ... 21
Swirl & Ball, Basket, Handle, Golden Sunset, 5 In. ... 20
Swirl & Ball, Candy Dish, Milk Glass, 4 ⅜ In. ... 9
Thousand Eye, Bowl, Oval, Flashed, 11 ½ In. ... 37
Thousand Eye, Candlestick, 5 In. ... 15
Thousand Eye, Cocktail, 4 ½ In. ... 8
Thousand Eye, Compote, Flashed, 4 ⅛ In. ... 21
Thousand Eye, Creamer, Flashed, 8 Oz., 3 ¾ In. ... 23
Thousand Eye, Cup & Saucer, Footed ... 12

Willow, Pepper Pot, Blue, Dome Lid, Bulbous, Flared Foot, Transfer, 1800s, 4 ¼ In.
$153

Hess Auction Group

Willow, Platter, Transfer, Spaniard Inn, Davenport, 1800s, 17 ½ x 22 In.
$165

Hess Auction Group

Window, Leaded, Frogs, Birds, Fish, Squirrel, Dragonfly, Spider, Square Panels, Glass, 18 x 24 In.
$570

Fox Auctions

TIP
Wipe glass dry with newspapers for a special shine.

Window, Stained Glass, Hanging Grapes, Vine, Frame, c.1900, 14 ¼ x 33 ¾ In.
$595

Ruby Lane

Window, Stained Glass, Mission Style Rose, Leaves, Arch, Frame, 83 x 22 In.
$900

Ruby Lane

Window, Stained Glass, Scenic, Sun, Rays, Lake, Mountains, Frame, c.1880, 30 x 29 In.
$1,500

Ruby Lane

TIP
Wooden items should be kept off a sunny windowsill. Direct sunlight will harm wood finishes.

Thousand Eye, Dish, Mayonnaise, 4 In. 26
Thousand Eye, Goblet, Water, Flashed, 6 ¾ In. 10
Thousand Eye, Plate, Salad, 7 In. 18
Thousand Eye, Relish, 3 Sections, 8 ¼ In. 27
Thousand Eye, Relish, 6 Sections, Round, 9 ¾ In. 20
Thousand Eye, Sherbet, 5 ⅛ In. 9
Thousand Eye, Sherbet, Flashed, 5 ¼ In. 9
Thousand Eye, Sugar, Footed, Handles, 5 ⅜ In. 21
Thousand Eye, Torte Plate, 14 In. 26
Thousand Eye, Torte Plate, 18 In. 79
Thousand Eye, Torte Plate, Ruby, 18 ¼ In. 184
Three Ball, Candlestick, 3 ½ In. 12
Three Ball, Torte Plate, 14 In. 27
Waterford, Candlestick, Ruby, 6 In. 27
Waterford, Candy Dish, Lid, Milk Glass, 6 ⅜ In. 18
Waterford, Compote, Crimped, Ruby, 5 ⅞ In. 23
Waterford, Compote, Ruffled, Ruby, 5 ½ In. 21
Waterford, Plate, 7 x 7 In. 6
Waterford, Sherbet, 3 ¾ In. 9
Waterford, Tumbler, Footed, 4 ¾ In. 8
Waterford, Vase, Double Crimped, Footed, Ruby, 6 In. 94
Waterford, Wine, Ruby, 2 Oz., 4 ⅜ In. 16
Wedding, Bowl, Lid, Ruby Flash, 9 ⅝ In. 47
Wedding, Candlestick, Milk Glass, 4 ½ In. 17

WHEATLEY POTTERY was founded by Thomas J. Wheatley in Cincinnati, Ohio. He had worked with the founders of the art pottery movement, including M. Louise McLaughlin of the Rookwood Pottery. He started T.J. Wheatley & Co. in 1880. That company was closed by 1884. Thomas Wheatley worked for Weller Pottery in Zanesville, Ohio, from 1897 to 1900. In 1903 he founded Wheatley Pottery Company in Cincinnati. Wheatley Pottery was purchased by the Cambridge Tile Manufacturing Company in 1927.

Vase, Ribbed Shoulder, Feathery Green Matte Glaze, 12 ½ In. 531
Vase, Spread Foot, Green Matte Glaze, Incised Leaf Design, c.1910, 11 In. .... *illus* 920
Plate, Mottled Brown, Green, Yellow, Squares, Embossed Rim, 9 ½ In. 181
Vase, 4 Panels, Gold, Blue, Leaves, 10 In. 31

WILLETS MANUFACTURING COMPANY of Trenton, New Jersey, began work in 1879. The company made belleek in the late 1880s and 1890s in shapes similar to those used by the Irish Belleek factory. It stopped working about 1912. A variety of marks were used, most including the name *Willets*.

Chalice, Round Foot, Bulbous Cup, Pink, Gooseberries, Gilt, c.1900, 11 In. 155
Cup, Saucer, Roses, Branches, Pink, Beaded Rim, Footed, Scalloped Handle, c.1910.......... 395
Dish, Heart Shape, Pink Roses, Leaves, Ruffled Gilt Edge, Marked, 6 In. 200
Pitcher, Red & Purple Grapes, Hand Painted, Wavy Rim, Belleek, Signed, 1890s, 15 In. .... *illus* 600
Plate, Purple Poppies, Buds, Pleated Edge, Gilt Trim, 8 ½ In. 225
Tankard, Cherries, Vines, Wide Spout, Dragon Handle, 9 In. 325
Tankard, Grape Bunches, Vines, Green, Purple, Gilt Handle, c.1900, 15 In. 1895
Vase, Trumpet, Roses, Stems, Marked, 15 ½ In. 432

WILLOW pattern has been made in England since 1780. The pattern has been copied by factories in many countries, including Germany, Japan, and the United States. It is still being made. Willow was named for a pattern that pictures a bridge, birds, willow trees, and a Chinese landscape. Most pieces are blue and white. Some made after 1900 are pink and white.

Casserole, Lid, Handles, 1960s, 10 x 7 In. 20
Pepper Pot, Blue, Dome Lid, Bulbous, Flared Foot, Transfer, 1800s, 4 ¼ In. .... *illus* 153
Platter, Doves, Bridge, Transfer, Staffordshire, c.1840, 18 x 14 In. 355
Platter, Transfer, Spaniard Inn, Davenport, 1800s, 17 ½ x 22 In. .... *illus* 165

WINDOW glass that was stained and beveled was popular for houses during the late nineteenth and early twentieth centuries. The old windows became popular with collectors in the 1970s; today, old and new examples are seen.

Leaded, 5 Green Tulips, Red & Brown Stems, 43 x 22 ½ In. 270
Leaded, Arch, Etched Flowers, Beveled, 2-Panel, 46 x 26 In. 330
Leaded, Arch, Scroll, Red, Green, Yellow, 30 x 25 In. 214

Leaded, Arches, Sunburst, 24¾ x 44 In., Pair 94
Leaded, Art Deco, Textured, Yellow, Green, Chevron, 46⅞ x 21½ In., Pair 246
Leaded, Art Nouveau, Center Tulip, 36½ x 27 In., Pair 307
Leaded, Arts & Crafts, Lilies, Pond, 33 x 11½ In. 122
Leaded, Bottle Glass, Green, Brown Border, Wood Frame, 77 x 28 In., Pair 600
Leaded, Church, Blue Flowers, Green Leaves, Arched Top Piece, 1873 144
Leaded, Clear Glass, Squares Pattern, Shapes, Side Panel, 67 x 17 In., Pair 115
Leaded, Crest, Red Lion, Green Banner, 10¾ x 8 In., 3 Piece 100
Leaded, Demilune, Blue, White, Flower, 38½ x 19 In. 175
Leaded, Demilune, Blue, White, Green, Flower, 41 x 20½ In. 175
Leaded, Diamond Pattern Mullions, Wood Frame, 30 x 20 In., Pair 108
Leaded, Feathered Arrow, Clear Glass, 38 x 13½ In., Pair 188
Leaded, Frogs, Birds, Fish, Squirrel, Dragonfly, Spider, Square Panels, Glass, 18 x 24 In. .....*illus* 570
Leaded, Geometric, Blue, Brown, Yellow, Purple, 56¾ x 25¾ In. 313
Leaded, Half Round, Stylized Peacock Feather Design, Circles, Rippled Glass, 75 x 49 In. 1126
Leaded, Landscape, Trees, Green, Tan, White, 34 x 35 In., Pair 343
Leaded, Leaves, Diamonds, Netting, Red, Blue, Wood Frame, 33 x 19 In. 100
Leaded, Leaves, Vines, Tan Sky, Green Border, Frame, 52 x 21 In. 240
Leaded, Monogram, Green, Black, White, 1800s, 36 x 36 In. 82
Leaded, Overlapping Circles, Frank Lloyd Wright, Parker House, 30⅜ x 21 In. 5750
Leaded, Reclining Lamb, Holding Banner, Cross, Round, 1800s, 14¼ In. 189
Leaded, Stained, Peacock, Flowers, Trees, Acrylic Glass, Frame, 1900s, 36 x 22 In. 104
Leaded, Town Crest, Canterbury, Multicolor, Shield, Lion, Banner, 48 x 27 In. 212
Leaded, Town Crest, Liverpool, Multicolor, Shield, Liver Bird, Branch, 50 x 25 In. 189
Leaded, Town Crest, Plymouth, Multicolor, Shield, Turrets, Banner, 49 x 23 In. 94
Leaded, Town Crest, Salisbury, Multicolor, Shield, Azure & Gold Stripes, 52 x 26 In. 59
Painted, Figures, Urns, Arch, Wood Frame, Iran, c.1967, 88½ x 37¼ In. 300
Slag Glass, Religious, Gothic Decoration, Roundels, Frame, c.1880, 51 x 29 In. 356
Stained, 12 Rectangles, 57 x 30 In., 5 Piece 125
Stained, Blue, Green, Purple Flower, Cast Iron, Half Circle, 38½ x 19 In. 117
Stained, Center Oval Reserve, Caramel Glass Surrounds, Leaves, 1900s, 55 x 26 In., Pair 1169
Stained, Dublin Inscription, Green, 2 Women Flanking Shield, Wood Frame, 30 x 25 In. 400
Stained, Landscape, Leafy Trees, Blue Border, Pine Frame, c.1880, 29 x 41 In. 397
Stained, Swirl Heart Design, Multicolor, Wood Frame, 1900s, 27 x 15 In. 115
Stained Glass, Hanging Grapes, Vine, Frame, c.1900, 14¼ x 33¾ In. ....*illus* 595
Stained Glass, Mission Style Rose, Leaves, Arch, Frame, 83 x 22 In. ....*illus* 900
Stained Glass, Scenic, Sun, Rays, Lake, Mountains, Frame, c.1880, 30 x 29 In. ....*illus* 1500
Swags, Facets, Ruby Jewels, c.1875, 39 x 39 In. 1476
Transom, Half Circle, 61 x 34 In. 322
Transom, Woman's Portrait, Scrolling, Flowers, c.1900, 15½ x 55½ In. 1320

WOOD CARVINGS and wooden pieces are listed separately in this book. There are also wooden pieces found in other categories, such as Folk Art, Kitchen, and Tool.

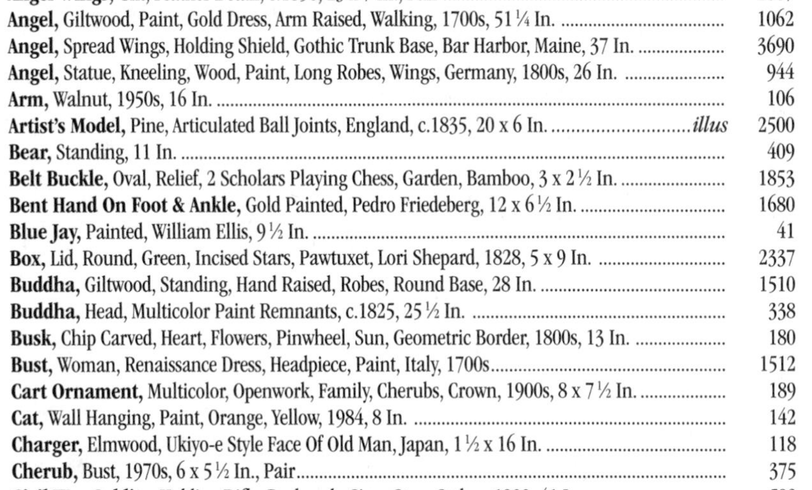

Angel Wings, Gilt, Feather Detail, c.1850, 23 x 7 In., Pair 1067
Angel, Giltwood, Paint, Gold Dress, Arm Raised, Walking, 1700s, 51¼ In. 1062
Angel, Spread Wings, Holding Shield, Gothic Trunk Base, Bar Harbor, Maine, 37 In. 3690
Angel, Statue, Kneeling, Wood, Paint, Long Robes, Wings, Germany, 1800s, 26 In. 944
Arm, Walnut, 1950s, 16 In. 106
Artist's Model, Pine, Articulated Ball Joints, England, c.1835, 20 x 6 In. ....*illus* 2500
Bear, Standing, 11 In. 409
Belt Buckle, Oval, Relief, 2 Scholars Playing Chess, Garden, Bamboo, 3 x 2½ In. 1853
Bent Hand On Foot & Ankle, Gold Painted, Pedro Friedeberg, 12 x 6½ In. 1680
Blue Jay, Painted, William Ellis, 9½ In. 41
Box, Lid, Round, Green, Incised Stars, Pawtuxet, Lori Shepard, 1828, 5 x 9 In. 2337
Buddha, Giltwood, Standing, Hand Raised, Robes, Round Base, 28 In. 1510
Buddha, Head, Multicolor Paint Remnants, c.1825, 25½ In. 338
Busk, Chip Carved, Heart, Flowers, Pinwheel, Sun, Geometric Border, 1800s, 13 In. 180
Bust, Woman, Renaissance Dress, Headpiece, Paint, Italy, 1700s 1512
Cart Ornament, Multicolor, Openwork, Family, Cherubs, Crown, 1900s, 8 x 7½ In. 189
Cat, Wall Hanging, Paint, Orange, Yellow, 1984, 8 In. 142
Charger, Elmwood, Ukiyo-e Style Face Of Old Man, Japan, 1½ x 16 In. 118
Cherub, Bust, 1970s, 6 x 5½ In., Pair 375
Civil War Soldier, Holding Rifle, Backpack, Cigar Store Style, c.1900, 41 In. 593
Civil War Soldier, Painted, Multicolor, 15½ In. 643
Crow, Platform Base, Marked Chas. Perdew, 12¼ In. 266

Wood Carving, Deer, Wharton Esherick, Marked WE, To JAP, 1940, 11 x 5 In.
$9,675

Rago Arts and Auction Center

Wood Carving, Artist's Model, Pine, Articulated Ball Joints, England, c.1835, 20 x 6 In.
$2,500

New Orleans (Cakebread)

Wood Carving, Fedora & Box, Koa, Perry Policicchio, Signed, 7 x 14 x 12½ In.
$1,180

Brunk Auctions

Wood Carving, Head, Milliner's, Marotte, Pine, Knotted Bun, Bonnet, c.1830, 12 ½ x 8 In.
$4,750

New Orleans (Cakebread)

Wood Carving, Mailbox Holder, Figural, Uncle Sam, Standing, Red, White & Blue Paint, 59 In.
$533

James D. Julia Auctioneers

TIP

If something looks strange or not quite right when you come home, don't be shy. Risk embarrassment and go to the neighbors for assistance.

Deer, Wharton Esherick, Marked WE, To JAP, 1940, 11 x 5 In. .... *illus* 9675
Dog, Painted, White & Black Spotted, Red Tongue, 1800s, 10 x 19 In. 7995
Dogs, Mother & 3 Pups, Glass Eyes, Black Forest, Switzerland, c.1900, 10 x 23 In. 19200
Don Quixote, Standing, Outstretched Arms, Book, Spain, 22 In. 246
Duck, Canvasback, Paint, White Feathers, Russet Head & Wing, Perched, c.1960, 3 In. 185
Eagle Head, Open Mouth, Tongue, Feathers, Blue & Red Paint, c.1980, 11 x 22 In. 237
Eagle, Federal, Gilt, Spread Wings, American Shield, c.1950, 25 x 72 In. 2400
Eagle, Perched On Globe, 1900s, 11 ½ In. 180
Elephant, Bone Inlay, 20 x 24 In. 1003
Elephant, Saddle, On Wagon, Flower Platform, Wheels, Nodding Head, c.1900, 33 x 36 In. 1168
Eureka, Miner Holding Gold Nugget, Pick Axe, Base, 81 x 28 In. 3965
Fedora & Box, Koa, Perry Policicchio, Signed, 7 x 14 x 12 ½ In. .... *illus* 1180
Fish, Pine, Incised Scales, Painted Glass Eyes, Stand, 1900s, 24 In. 469
Fish, Trout, Painted, Open Mouth, Oval Plaque, c.1900, 24 In. 720
Flask, Coconut, Face Shape, Round Opening As Mouth, Flags, Cannons, c.1880, 5 In. 245
Gavel, Preserved Fish Head, Glass Eyes, Wood Handle, 9 ½ x 7 In. 300
Gazelle, Karl Hagenauer, Walnut, Brass, Stylized, Austria, 13 In. 1035
Gnome, Black Forest, Seated, Holding Staff, 1950s, 7 ¾ In. 150
Goose, Spread Wings, Gilt Wood, Articulated Feathers, 1800s, 11 ½ In. 1888
Group, 4 Dogs, Black Forest, 13 In. 1750
Guanyin, Cherry & Amber, Robe, Peony Blossoms, Fan, Sword, 12 In. 115
Harlequins, Fruitwood, Mandolins, Italy, 36 x 32 In. 6613
Head, Milliner's, Marotte, Pine, Knotted Bun, Bonnet, c.1830, 12 ½ x 8 In. .... *illus* 4750
Heart In Hand, Square Base, Balsa Wood, Patina, 1900s, 12 In. 63
Helix, Mahogany, Pleated Swirl Design, Dal Fabbro, 1974, 21 x 25 In. 3750
Humidor, Tobacco, Skull, Entwined Snake, Frog Finial, Wood, 1800s, 6 ½ In. 266
Humpback Whale, Black White & Red Paint, c.1960, 18 x 5 In. 1968
Lustereibchen, Woman Holds Flower Behind Shield, 15 x 13 In. 1800
Mailbox Holder, Figural, Uncle Sam, Standing, Red, White & Blue Paint, 59 In. .... *illus* 533
Man, Holding Crop & Reins, Next To Horse, Base, Pine, c.1900, 14 In. 2706
Man, Smoking, Cap, Striped Shirt, Belt, Necktie, 9 x 6 In. 2808
Mannequin, Pine, Articulated, Patina, 1800s, 22 In. 875
Maquette Francaise, Equestrian, Walnut, Brass Joints, Iron Stand, c.1860, 30 x 33 In. .... *illus* 23750
Mask, Buffalo, Patterned Nose, Burkina Faso, 22 x 13 In. 1599
Model, Fish, Atlantic Salmon, Painted, Backboard Mounted, 1930s, 48 x 19 In. 1185
Model, Russian Orthodox Church, 32 x 15 In. 60
Mold, Cigar, 22 ¾ x 4 In. 99
Mold, Rococo, Leaves, Applied Designs, Wood Frame, 16 x 13 In. 242
Monk, Byzantine Style Features, Glass Eyes, Continental, 30 In. .... *illus* 390
Monkey, Articulated, Teak, Oak, Long Arms, K. Bojesen, Denmark, 1950s, 18 In. .... *illus* 4063
Mountain Climber, Hanging, Rope, Lantern, Black Forest, 1900s, 12 In. 343
Night Watchman, Lantern, Black Forest, 1900s, 20 ½ In. 192
Pan, Classical Figure, Draped, Holding Pipes, Painted, Parcel Gilt, 1800s, 63 In. 6150
Panel, Marquetry, Reindeer, Birds, Dog, Burled, Walnut, Oak, 20 x 10 ¼ In., 2 Piece 242
Panel, Martyrdom Of St. John Of Nepomuk, c.1725, 33 ¼ In. 1751
Panel, Oak, Caryatid, Birds, Angels, 1600s, 21 ½ In. 1167
Panel, Over The Door, Broken Arch Pediment, Doves, Fruit, c.1887, 23 x 73 In. 1500
Panel, Walnut, Choristers, Florence Cathedral, Della Robbia, 1888s, 39 x 38 In. 3884
Parrot, On Branch, Painted, Multicolor, Dan & Barbara Strawser, 1979, 24 In. 443
Pipe Rack, Figural Dwarf, Holding Branchwork, Round Base, 7 ½ In. .... *illus* 168
Plaque, Boxwood, High Relief, Mother Of God, Angels, Winged Seraph, Greek Inscription, 2 In. 1000
Plaque, Eagle With Banner, Spread Wings, c.1935, 7 x 35 In. 1778
Plaque, Eagle, Pine, Painted Shield, John Haley Bellamy, Maine, c.1900, 6 x 36 In. .... *illus* 8610
Plaque, Eagle, Spread Wings, Flag, Blue Ribbon, Painted, c.1900, 81 x 21 In. 3198
Plaque, Finback Whale, Painted, Signed, Clark Voorhees, c.1950, 18 x 4 In. 3690
Plaque, Marquetry, Asian Village, Palm Trees, 13 x 26 In. 120
Plaque, Marquetry, Courting Woman, Hunter, Carriage, 23 x 14 In. 72
Plaque, Marquetry, Fly Fisherman, Trout, Legend Label On Back, 17 x 26 In. 330
Plaque, Marquetry, Harbor Scene, Cat, Lobster, Fish Catch, Signed R. Barros, 36 x 44 In. 72
Plaque, Marquetry, Tiger, Landscape, Legend Label On Back, 16 x 25 In. 270
Plaque, Marquetry, Woman, Urn, 27 ¼ x 20 ¾ In. 72
Plaque, Monk, Holding Cup, Black Forest, Germany, c.1950, 14 x 8 In. 276
Plaque, Oak, 2 Angels, Holding Monstrance, Cascading Hair, Germany, 1700s, 24 x 11 In. 594
Plaque, Orca Whale, Teeth, Painted, C. Voorhees, Conn., 18 x 7 In. 1169
Plaque, Relief, Animals Pulling Cart, Figures, Landscape, Frame, c.1910, 27 x 18 In. 556
Plaque, Sperm Whale, Painted, Clark Voorhees, Marked, c.1950, 17 x 5 In. 3690

Wood Carving, Maquette Francaise, Equestrian, Walnut, Brass Joints, Iron Stand, c.1860, 30 x 33 In.
$23,750

New Orleans (Cakebread)

Wood Carving, Monk, Byzantine Style Features, Glass Eyes, Continental, 30 In.
$390

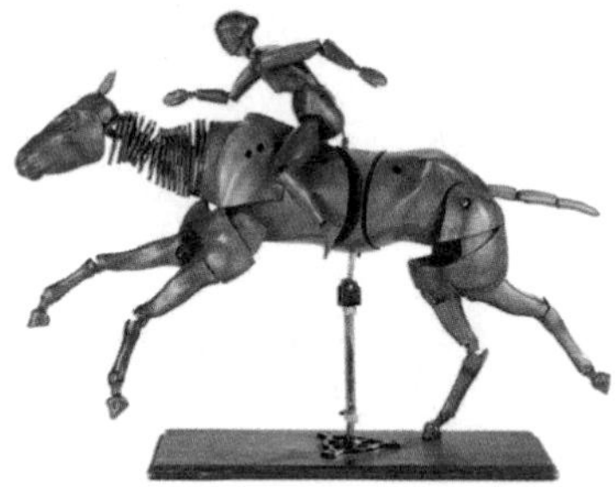

Cowan Auctions

Wood Carving, Monkey, Articulated, Teak, Oak, Long Arms, K. Bojesen, Denmark, 1950s, 18 In.
$4,063

Rago Arts and Auction Center

Wood Carving, Pipe Rack, Figural Dwarf, Holding Branchwork, Round Base, 7 ½ In.
$168

Fox Auctions

TIP

If you use an old wooden bowl for salad, treat it with mineral oil or walnut oil, not a regular wood polish.

Wood Carving, Santo, St. Anthony Of Padua, Painted, Gilded, Glass Eyes, Mexico, c.1850, 20 In.
$1,200

Cowan Auctions

Wood Carving, Plaque, Eagle, Pine, Painted Shield, John Haley Bellamy, Maine, c.1900, 6 x 36 In.
$8,610

Skinner, Inc.

Wood Carving, Putti, Carved, Painted, Gilt, Italy, c.1800, 31 x 20 In., Pair
$1,920

Neal Auctions

Wood Carving, Sculpture, Totems, Signed, Ida Rittenberg Kohlmeyer, 1985, 12 x 7 In.
$5,120

Neal Auctions

Wood Carving, Vase, Tulipwood, Turned, Etched Mark, Ed Moulthrop, Branded Cipher, 7 x 9 ¾ In.
$1,210

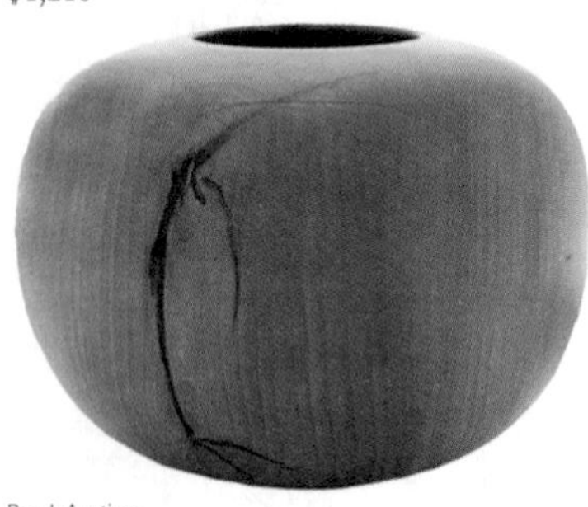

Brunk Auctions

Wood Carving, Water Buffalo, 2 Men On Back, Chinese
$200

Wood Carving, Whistler, Man Leaning On Lamppost, 19 In.
$360

Fox Auctions

Wooden, Bowl, Burl, Flared, Marked, TH, Dated, 1822, 20 ¾ In.
$600

Garth's Auctioneers & Appraisers

Wooden, Bowl, Burl, Rim, Footed Base, 1700s, 4 x 11 ½ In.
$885

Hess Auction Group

Wooden, Bowl, Burl, Scrubbed Surface, 1800s, 5 x 15 In.
$840

Garth's Auctioneers & Appraisers

Wooden, Bowl, Nut, Walnut, Grapes & Leaves, Biltmore, N.C., c.1910, 3 ⅝ x 9 In.
$826

Brunk Auctions

Wooden, Bowl, Pine, Beehive Turnings, Red Paint, c.1790, 3 x 9 In.
$474

James D. Julia Auctioneers

Wooden, Bowl, Spalted Hackberry, Bulbous, Squat, Wide Mouth, P. Moulthrop, 8 x 12 In.
$1,169

Skinner, Inc.

Wooden, Cup, Saffron, Lid, Poplar, Berries, Flowers, Lehnware, c.1892, 4 ½ In.
$413

Hess Auction Group

Policeman, Standing, Tall Hat, Walnut, Square Base, c.1898, 20 In. 711
Priest, Padre, Holding Devil Pincushion, Paint, John Cisney, c.1980, 20 x 38 In. 458
Putti, Carved, Painted, Gilt, Italy, c.1800, 31 x 20 In., Pair .... *illus* 1920
Rooster, Standing, Mouth Open, Painted, Carved, Square Base, 1900s, 36 In. 960
Santo, Jesus Christ, 24 ½ In. 605
Santo, Pine, Robes, Bent Arms, Thick Book, Pointy Nose, 20 ¾ x 6 ¾ In. 363
Santo, Pope St. Gregory VII, Fabric, Plaster, Miter, Gilt, c.1775, 31 In. 738
Santo, Red Top, Brocade Skirts, No Arms, 44 In. 1125
Santo, St. Anthony Of Padua, Painted, Gilded, Glass Eyes, Mexico, c.1850, 20 In. .... *illus* 1200
Santo, St. George, Spearing Dragon, Latin America, c.1910, 26 x 21 x 7 In. 922
Sculpture, Torso, Female, Teak, Rectangular Slab, Tiger's-Eye Nipples, c.2000, 25 ¾ x 13 In. 242
Sculpture, Totems, Signed, Ida Rittenberg Kohlmeyer, 1985, 12 x 7 In. .... *illus* 5120
Sheldrake, Mound Base, A. Elmer Crowell, Mass., c.1922, 3 In. 492
Shorebirds, Walter Cross, Nova Scotia, 28 x 7 In. 82
Snake, Root Wood, Painted Patina, Folk Art, 34 In. 531
Sphinx, Reclining, Stylized, Spheres In Hands, Red & Green Paint Trace, 1900s, 18 x 29 In. 406
Squirrel, Walnut, Eating Nut, Seated, Arched Base, Signed, 3 ¼ In. 83
St. Martin & The Beggar, Cedar, Tree Trunks, 27 In. 3501
Statue, Deity & Attendant, Longevity, Rosewood, Peach Staff, Lotus, c.1950, 15 In. 237
Statue, Mary Magdalene, Carved, Painted, c.1800, 35 In. 1080
Sword, Swordfish, Ship, Gloucester, Pine, Painted, Tapered, Scrolled Hilt, Inlaid W, 40 In. 1169
Train, On Bridge, 8 ½ x 48 In. 98
Turkey, Painted, Wood Base, Keith Collis, 27 In. 885
Turkish Journey, Multicolor, Wagon, Luggage, Betty Parsons, 1969, 19 x 10 In. 3480
Vase, Figured Tulipwood, Square Branded Cipher, Ed Moulthrop, 7 x 9 ¾ In. 4484
Vase, Georgia Purple Pine, Pinus Taeda, Ed Moulthrop, 10 x 14 In. 10890
Vase, Tulipwood, Turned, Etched Mark, Ed Moulthrop, Branded Cipher, 7 x 9 ¾ In. .... *illus* 1210
Vase, Wild Cherry, Square Branded Cipher, Philip Moulthrop, 9 ½ x 6 In. 726
Waddling Woman, Arm Raised, Albert Wein, 35 In. 2990
Wall Hanging, Sunburst, Distressed Gilt, 61 ½ x 42 ½ In. 1331
Wall Pocket, Openwork Crest, Man On Horse, Fiddle Player Panel, c.1910, 15 x 11 In. 188
Warbler, Perched On Rock, Paint, Yellow & Black, Red Stripe, c.1950, 2 ⅛ In. 246
Water Buffalo, 2 Men On Back, Chinese .... *illus* 200
Whistler, Leaning On Light Post, Arm Wrapped Around Pole, Windup, c.1900, 19 In. 580
Whistler, Man Leaning On Lamppost, 19 In. .... *illus* 360

WOODEN wares were used in all parts of the home. Wood was used for many containers and tools. Small wooden pieces are called *treenware* in England, but the term *woodenware* is more common in the United States. Additional pieces may be found in the Advertising, Kitchen, and Tool categories.

Book Holder, Sliding, Walnut, Goats, Leaves, Germany, c.1880, 22 x 11 In. 523
Bowl, Ash Burl, Oblong, Elongated Sides, Cutout Handles, 18 In. 3360
Bowl, Ash Leaf Maple, Square Branded Cipher, Ed Moulthrop, 3 ½ x 17 ¼ In. 6490
Bowl, Burl, Flared, Marked, TH, Dated, 1822, 20 ¾ In. .... *illus* 600
Bowl, Burl, Gouge Carved, Taper Shaved, 10 x 5 ½ In. 325
Bowl, Burl, Rim, Footed Base, 1700s, 4 x 11 ½ In. .... *illus* 885
Bowl, Burl, Round, Early 1800s, 2 x 6 In. 384
Bowl, Burl, Round, Footed, 1 ¾ x 4 ¼ In. 330
Bowl, Burl, Round, Turned, Raised Outer Collar, c.1840, 7 x 18 ½ In. 738
Bowl, Burl, Round, Turned, Squared Projecting Collar, New England, 6 x 18 In. 1845
Bowl, Burl, Scrubbed Surface, 1800s, 5 x 15 In. .... *illus* 840
Bowl, Burl, Turned, 5 ½ x 13 ¾ In. 780
Bowl, Burl, Turned, Cutout Banding, 1800s, 7 x 20 In. 236
Bowl, Burl, Woodlands, Oblong, Carved Handles, c.1810, 6 x 14 In. 3120
Bowl, Elm, Burl Integral Handle, Pot Shaped, c.1800, 5 x 8 In. 474
Bowl, Lid, Alaskan Diamond Willow, Applewood, Mahogany, Walnut, Robert Cutler, 5 x 17 In. 4114
Bowl, Lid, Louviere, Bird's-Eye Maple, Ebonized, Padauk, Plumwood, Inlay, Lambert, 5 x 7 In. 242
Bowl, Maple, Turned, Red, Matt Moulthrop, 6 ¾ x 11 In. 1815
Bowl, Nut, Walnut, Grapes & Leaves, Biltmore, N.C., c.1910, 3 ⅝ x 9 In. .... *illus* 826
Bowl, Pine, Beehive Turnings, Red Paint, c.1790, 3 x 9 In. .... *illus* 474
Bowl, Redwood Lace Bowl, David Ellsworth, 1986, 4 x 8 ½ In. 786
Bowl, Scoop, Burl, Oval, Extended & Pierced Trapezoid Handles, 9 x 19 x 17 In. 7380
Bowl, Shovel Shape Paddle, Hand Turned, Wide Rim, Round Base, c.1800, 10 In. Diam. 85
Bowl, Softwood, Ear Handles, c.1830-60, 8 x 20 In. 375
Bowl, Spalted Hackberry, Bulbous, Squat, Wide Mouth, P. Moulthrop, 8 x 12 In. .... *illus* 1169
Bowl, Teak, Finn Juhl, Kay Bojesen, 2 ¾ x 9 In. 1250

Wooden, Propeller, Laminated Maple, Copper Edge & Tips, Marked, c.1950, 94 ½ In.
$840

Garth's Auctioneers & Appraisers

Wooden, Salt, Master, Turned, Flowers, Footed, Joseph Lehnware, W. Heilig, 3 x 2 ½ In.
$189

Hess Auction Group

Wooden, Tray, Cutlery, Cherry, Splayed Sides, Cutout Handle, Dovetailed, Pa., 1800s, 15 x 8 In.
$649

Hess Auction Group

TIP

Wooden boxes, toys, or decoys should not be kept on the fireplace mantel or nearby floor areas when the fire is burning. The heat dries the wood and the paint. Unprotected wooden items on warm TV sets and stereos may also be damaged.

Worcester, Pitcher, Molded Cabbage, Mask Spout, Crescent Mark, Dr. Wall, c.1790, 11 ¾ In.
$708

Brunk Auctions

World War I, Hat, Kepi, Wool, Leather, Cotton Lining, Chin Strap, Brass, Infantry, France, 1914
$480

Cowan Auctions

World War I, Honor Cup, Luftwaffe, Silver, Eagles, Pedestal Foot, Marked, c.1980, 8 In.
$2,400

The Stein Auction Company

World War I, Military Cloth, Center Spread Wing Eagle, Iron Cross, Frame, 1914, 23 x 17 In.
$162

The Stein Auction Company

Propaganda Posters
During World War I, posters were used for propaganda purposes and to recruit soldiers. The most famous example is James Montgomery Flagg's 1917 "I Want You" poster that shows Uncle Sam pointing his finger at you.

World War I, Poster, Uncle Sam, I Want You For U.S. Army, J.M. Flagg, Copyright 1917, 40 x 30 In.
$4,688

Garth's Auctioneers & Appraisers

W

Bowl, Treen, Green Paint, Interior Patina, c.1860, 7 x 24 In. 660
Bowl, Walnut, Hammered Brass Rim, Square Foot, c.1850, 4 x 9 ½ In. 240
Brushpot, Bamboo, Cylindrical, 3 Scholars, Attendant, Pine Canopy, 6 In. 494
Brushpot, Bamboo, Cylindrical, Scholars In Landscape, 1800s, 5 x 7 In. 741
Brushpot, Bamboo, Immortals, 7 Figures, Pine Trees, 6 ¼ In. 813
Brushpot, Hardwood, Cylindrical, Beaded Edges, Honey Color, 8 x 9 In. 437
Brushpot, Zitan Wood, Flowers, Vines, 6 ½ In. 750
Brushpot, Zitan, Cylindrical, Reeded Top & Bottom, c.1800, 9 x 10 In. 3088
Bucket, Banded, Oak, Brass, Rope Handle, Coat Of Arms, Victorian, 17 x 12 x 19 In. 1100
Bucket, Currants, Stencil, Stave Construction, 3 Bentwood Hoops, Pegged Handle, 11 In. 523
Bucket, Lid, 2 Tapered Finger Staves, Gray Green Paint, Iron & Wood Handle, 6 ½ In. 861
Bucket, Lid, Oak, Poplar, Salmon Graining, Staves, Vines, Porcelain Knob, J. Lehn, c.1850, 9 In. .. 1625
Canister, Apple Shape, Lid, Turned Maple, Stem Finial, Treen, 3 x 3 In. 118
Canister, Lid, Peaseware, Tapered Cylinder, Carved Flower Design, Treen, c.1890, 5 In. 1140
Canister, Peaseware, Bulbous, Turned Maple, Ring Design, Urn Finial, Ring Foot, 1800s, 5 In. .. 502
Canister, Peaseware, Maple, Turned, Lift-Off Lid, 10 ½ In. 738
Canister, Turned Maple, Squat, Ring Turnings, Ring Foot, Lid, Treen, 1800s, 7 x 7 In. 236
Compote, Lid, Maple, Varnish, Acorn Finial, Peaseware, Ohio, Miniature, 3 In. 240
Container, Lid, Finial, Squat, Ring Foot, Banding, Treen, Peaseware, c.1890, 11 ½ In. 1800
Cup, Saffron, Lid, Poplar, Berries, Flowers, Lehnware, c.1892, 4 ½ In. .... *illus* 413
Devotional Panel, Gilt, Scenes Of Christ's Life, Enamel, Gilt Wood, Russia, 1700s, 10 In. 212
Dressing Set, Ebonized Rosewood Box, Brass Corners, Inlay, Handles, c.1870, 14 x 10 In. 360
Egg Crate, Slats Design, Top Handle, 12 ½ x 12 ½ In. 46
Eggcup, Maple, Sponge Decorated, Goblet Shape, Pedestal Base, Treen, 3 ¼ In. 266
Firkin, Blue, Swing Handle, 14 ½ x 13 ½ In. 234
Firkin, Blue, Swing Handle, 1800s, 9 x 8 ½ In. 234
Jar, Burl Wood, Dan Kvitka, Signed, 7 ¼ In. 250
Jar, Lid, Finial, Fan Design, Red & Yellow, Treen, c.1850, 3 ½ In. 1800
Jar, Round Pedestal Foot, Lid, Finial, Flat Rim, Maple, Peaseware, c.1890, 8 In. 120
Jar, Tobacco Leaf, Paint Decorated, Round, Swollen Shape, Flattened Knob, 8 In. 984
Jar, Treen, Maple, Original Vinegar Paint, Knob Finial, 7 ½ x 10 ½ In. 1320
Keg, Cherry Stave, Softwood Lid, Buzz Shaved Exterior, 12 ½ x 12 In. 210
Letter Box, Softwood, 3 Tiers, Hanging, Red Paint, 1800s, 17 x 11 In. 413
Libation Cup, Aloeswood, Scholars, Landscape, Wide Shaped Rim, c.1800, 6 In. 9480
Mixing Bowl, Chestnut, Beehive Turned, Green Paint, Shallow Foot, 1700s, 5 x 17 In. 1067
Plate, Green Ground, Pink & Red Flowers, 15 ½ In. 6
Pot, Lid, Wire Bail Handle, Bulbous, Ring Foot, Banding, Treen, Peaseware, c.1890, 7 In. 390
Propeller, Laminated Maple, Copper Edge & Tips, Marked, c.1950, 94 ½ In. .... *illus* 840
Propeller, Metal Clad, Partial Decal, Embossed Design Number, Hartzell, 72 In. 357
Salt, Master, Turned, Flowers, Footed, Joseph Lehnware, W. Heilig, 3 x 2 ½ In. .... *illus* 189
Shoe Holder, Carved Walnut, Swivel Top, Footed Base, 1800s, 16 ½ In. 59
Stocking Stretchers, Chamfered Edging, c.1840, 32 ½ x 9 In. 60
Sugar, Turned, Round, Dome Lid, Compressed, Yellow Paint, c.1800, 4 x 5 In. 618
Tray, Cutlery, Cherry, Splayed Sides, Cutout Handle, Dovetailed, Pa., 1800s, 15 x 8 In. .... *illus* 649
Tray, Mahogany, Rectangular, Waved Gallery, George III, 24 x 18 In. 2949
Tray, Pine, Blue Paint, Canted Sides, Shaped Handles, c.1810, 26 x 17 In. 1544
Urn, Maple, Varnish, Peaseware, Ohio, c.1870, 4 In. 240
Vase, Narrow Neck, 60 x 11 In. 196
Vase, Spalted Norway Maple Burl, David Ellsworth, 1984, 10 ½ x 5 ½ In. 708
Vase, Turned, Removable Copper Liner, 17 x 9 ¼ In. 270

WORCESTER porcelains were made in Worcester, England, from 1751. The firm went through many name changes and eventually, in 1862, became The Royal Worcester Porcelain Company Ltd. Collectors often refer to Dr. Wall, Barr, Flight, and other names that indicate time periods or artists at the factory. It became part of Royal Worcester Spode Ltd. in 1976. The company was bought by the Portmeirion Group in 2009. Related pieces may be found in the Royal Worcester category.

Basket, Butterflies, Hop Vine, Gilt Gadroon Rim, Handle, c.1813, 12 In. 1875
Basket, Chestnut, Lid, Stand, Quatrefoil Flowers, Applied Branch Handles, 10 In. 2375
Butter, Cover, Enameled Flowers, 18th Century, 3 ½ x 7 x 5 In. 738
Creamer, Flared Scalloped Shape, Cobalt Blue, White, Flowers, Scroll Handle, c.1770, 3 x 4 In. .. 269
Jug, Blue & White, Molded Leaves, Mask Spout, Scroll Handle, c.1755, 12 In. 296
Jug, Bulbous, Blue & White, Molded Cabbage Leaf, Scroll Handle, Flowers, c.1760, 10 In. 531
Jug, Cream, Chinoiserie, Beak Shape, Gilt, Multicolor Figures, c.1760, 3 ½ In. 246
Mug, Cylindrical, Loop Handle, Royal Lily Pattern, Blue, White, Gilt, c.1780, 4 In. 531
Pitcher, Molded Cabbage, Mask Spout, Crescent Mark, Dr. Wall, c.1790, 11 ¾ In. .... *illus* 708
Plate, Armorial, Salmon Ground, Stowe, Flight, Barr & Barr, 9 ½ In., Pair 12075

TIP

Never move an object that might explode. Call the local police bomb squad. Many accidents are caused by old souvenir hand grenades and firearms.

World War II, Helmet, German, Luftwaffe
$540

The Stein Auction Company

World War II, Statue, Carnival, Uncle Sam, V For Victory, Plaster, Red, White, Blue, Flat Back, 1940s
$285

Hake's Americana & Collectibles

World's Fair, Jewelry Box, 1904, St. Louis Exposition, Reverse Painted Lid, Cascade Garden, 3 In.
$118

Hess Auction Group

WPA, Vase, Bear Hunting Scene, Russell Crook, c.1910, 14 ¾ x 11 ½ In.
$5,625

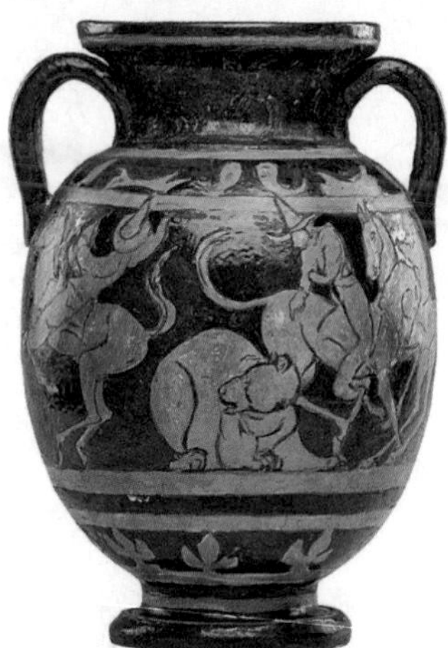

Rago Arts and Auction Center

Cocktail Watches Are Back in Style

Vintage watches, called cocktail watches, are back in style. The tiny watch face is hard to read and the watch must be wound each day, but it is worn with blue jeans or cocktail dresses as a vintage bracelet. Jeweled watches by name companies sell for thousands of dollars. Knock-off costume jewelry watches are inexpensive but have the same look.

Wristwatch, 14K Gold, Diamond, Ruby, Flip Top, Bracelet, Art Deco, Windup, 5 ¾ In.
$1,995

Ruby Lane

Platter, Faux Marble Ground, Seashells, Coral, Gilt Gadroon Rim, Barr & Barr, 22 ½ In. 8750
Teapot, Lid, Flower Knop, Globe Shape, Multicolor Enameled Birds, c.1770, 5 ½ In. 246
Tray, Rectangular, Canted Corners, Flower Sprays, Sprigs, Gilt Scroll, Cobalt Blue, c.1770, 17 In. 1076
Tureen, Lid, Cauliflower Shape, Enameled, Black Moth, c.1760, 4 In. 2460
Tureen, Lid, Underplate, Armorial, Apple Green, White, Gilt, Handles, Footed, c.1820, 10 In. 585
Vase, Drum Shape, Tripod Paws, Landscapes, 3 ⅝ In., 4 Piece 10000
Vase, Krater, Spire Finials, Portraits, Landscape, Loop Handles, Red, 32 ½ In., Pair 4375

WORLD WAR I and World War II souvenirs are collected today. Be careful not to store anything that includes live ammunition. Your local police will tell you how to dispose of the explosives. See also Sword and Trench Art.

WORLD WAR I

Hat, Kepi, Wool, Leather, Cotton Lining, Chin Strap, Brass, Infantry, France, 1914.......... *illus* 480
Helmet, Steel, Blue Letters, I.O.O.A. Band, Germany.......... 375
Honor Cup, Luftwaffe, Silver, Eagles, Pedestal Foot, Marked, c.1980, 8 In. .... *illus* 2400
Military Cloth, Center Spread Wing Eagle, Iron Cross, Frame, 1914, 23 x 17 In. .... *illus* 162
Poster, Are You 100 Percent American, Sackett & Wilhelm, 30 x 20 In. 59
Poster, Halt The Hun, Buy U.S. Government Bonds, Third Liberty Loan, 20 x 29 ½ In. 82
Poster, I Want You For U.S. Army, M. Flagg, 1917, 30 x 41 In. 5676
Poster, Join The Army Air Service, Eagles, Airplane, 20 ½ x 27 In. 995
Poster, Liberty War Bonds, Lend The Way They Fight, Soldiers, Frame, 44 x 32 In. 671
Poster, Over The Top For You, Soldier, Flag, 20 x 30 In. 117
Poster, Ring It Again, Liberty Bell, Sackett & Wilhelm Corp., 30 x 20 In. 117
Poster, Uncle Sam, I Want You For U.S. Army, J.M. Flagg, Copyright 1917, 40 x 30 In. .... *illus* 4688
Print, Recruitment, Colored Man Is No Slacker, Shaped Wood Frame, 26 x 22 In. 180
Ring, Motor Transport Corps, Spoked Wheel, Mercury's Winged Hat, Sterling, 1920.......... 115

WORLD WAR II

Badge, Army Air Force, Pilot Wings, Sterling, Clutch Back, Amico, c.1940, 3 In. 149
Compass, U.S. Navy, Metal Case, Brass Plate, 5 ⅜ In. 81
Creamer, Spring Lid, Pour Ring, Aluminum Goods Mfg. Co., 1941, 6 In. 16
Helmet, Brodie, KK II, Steel, 1942, 11 x 11 x 4 In. 126
Helmet, German, Luftwaffe.......... *illus* 540
Pin, Sweetheart Soldier, Articulated, World War II, 4 x 4 In. 35
Statue, Carnival, Uncle Sam, V For Victory, Plaster, Red, White, Blue, Flat Back, 1940s.......... *illus* 285
Statue, Saluting Bathing Beauty, Holding Flag, Military Cap, Composition, c.1940, 40 In. 750

WORLD'S FAIR souvenirs from all of the fairs are collected. The first fair was the Great Exhibition of 1851 in London. Some other important exhibitions and fairs include Philadelphia, 1876 (Centennial); Chicago, 1893 (World's Columbian); Buffalo, 1901 (Pan-American); St. Louis, 1904 (Louisiana Purchase); Portland, 1905 (Lewis & Clark Centennial Exposition); San Francisco, 1915 (Panama-Pacific); Philadelphia, 1926 (Sesquicentennial); Chicago, 1933 (Century of Progress); Cleveland, 1936 (Great Lakes); San Francisco, 1939 (Golden Gate International); New York, 1939 (World of Tomorrow); Seattle, 1962 (Century 21); New York, 1964; Montreal, 1967; Knoxville (Energy Turns the World) 1982; New Orleans, 1984; Tsukuba, Japan, 1985; Vancouver, Canada, 1986; Brisbane, Australia, 1988; Seville, Spain, 1992; Genoa, Italy, 1992; Seoul, South Korea, 1993; Lisbon, Portugal, 1998; Hanover, Germany, 2000; and Aichi, Japan, 2005. Memorabilia of fairs include directories, pictures, fabrics, ceramics, etc. Memorabilia from other similar celebrations may be listed in the Souvenir category.

Bank, 1893, Chicago, Administration Building, Cast Iron, Red & White Paint, Steeple, 6 x 6 In. 1020
Bracelet, 1933, A Century Of Progress, Logo, Bakelite, Brass Rings.......... 235
Fan, 1876, Philadelphia, Centennial Exposition, Painted, 11 ¼ x 20 ¾ In. 185
Ferris Wheel, 1900, Exposition Universelle De Paris, Wood, Paper, Wire, Box, 22 In. 1320
Jewelry Box, 1904, St. Louis Exposition, Reverse Painted Lid, Cascade Garden, 3 In. .... *illus* 118
Lamp, 1904, Louisiana Purchase Exposition, Man, Lifesaver, Lighthouse, Metal, 58 In. 2625
Medal, 1904, St. Louis, Commemorative, Shield Shape, Weinman, 2 ¾ x 2 ¾ In. 177
Medal, 1904, St. Louis, Louisiana Purchase Expo, Bronze, Weinman, 2 ½ In. 153
Pennant, 1939, New York, Frank Buck Jungleland, Leather, Signed, 4 ½ x 14 In. 316
Plate, 1939, 150th Anniversary Of George Washington, Homer Laughlin, 9 Piece.......... 210
Whiskbroom, 1933, Chicago, Parrot Head, Ceramic, Multicolor, 7 ½ In. 145

WPA is the abbreviation for Works Progress Administration, a program created by executive order in 1935 to provide jobs for millions of unemployed Americans. Artists were hired to create murals, paintings, drawings, and sculptures for public buildings. Pieces are marked *WPA* and may have the artist's name on them.

Vase, Bear Hunting Scene, Russell Crook, c.1910, 14 ¾ x 11 ½ In. .... *illus* 5625

WRISTWATCHES came into use during World War I. Wristwatches are listed here by manufacturer or as advertising or character watches. Wristwatches may also be listed in other categories. Pocket watches are listed in the Watch category.

14K Gold, Diamond, Ruby, Flip Top, Bracelet, Art Deco, Windup, 5 ¾ In. ... *illus* 1995
Abra, Art Deco, White Gold Case, Blue Ribbon Bracelet, Woman's ... 69
Art Deco, 14K Rose & Yellow Gold Case, Silver Tone Bracelet, 17 Jewel, Woman's ... 334
Baume & Mercier, 14K Gold, Dangle Rope Bracelet, Adjustable Band, 17 Jewel ... 708
Baume & Mercier, 18K Yellow Gold, Stirrup Shape Case, Sapphire Cabochons, Woman's ... 615
Benrus, 14K Gold, 17 Jewel, Textured Dial, Leather Band, 1 ¼ In. ... 230
Breitling, Chronographe, Stainless Steel, 17 Jewel, 1940s, 1 ½ In. ... 575
Breitling, Stainless Steel, Mechanical Wind Movement, 1950s ... 307
Bulgari, Enigma, Stainless Steel, Oval Dial, Arabic & Dots, Date, Rubber Strap, 6 ¾ In. ... 615
Bulova, 14K Yellow Gold, Diamond, Bezel Set, Woman's, 7 In. ... 378
Bulova, 18K Yellow Gold, Open Oval Link Bracelet, c.1972, Woman's, 7 ½ In. ... 780
Bulova, Accutron, 14K Yellow Gold, Textured Case, Orange, Turquoise, Woman's, ¾ In. ... 92
Bulova, Dive, Super Compressor, Stainless Steel, Waterproof ... 590
Bulova, Platinum, Round Face, Diamond Link Bracelet, 1900s, Woman's, 6 ½ In. ... 660
Bulova, Space View, Retro, Electronic Accutron Movement, 1965, 1 ¼ In. ... 374
Bulova, Tuxedo Tank Style, 10K Gold Filled, Horizontal Reeded Detail, ¾ In. ... 98
Cartier, Ballon Bleu, 18K White Gold, Engine Turned Dial, Roman Numerals, Date ... 13530
Cartier, Gold Plated, Sapphire Glass, 17 Jewel, Leather Band, 1960s, 7 ½ In. ... 602
Cartier, Panthere, 18K Gold, Diamond, Ivory Tone Dial, Diamond Bezel, Box ... *illus* 7995
Cartier, Santos, Stainless Steel, Screws, Ivory Dial, Quartz, Woman's, 6 In. ... 984
Cartier, Tank Basculante, Stainless Steel, Guilloche Dial, Manual Wind, Leather Band ... 2214
Cartier, Tank, Gold Over Silver, Leather Band, 1 In. ... 414
Cellini, 18K Yellow Gold, Oval Case, Weave Design Bracelet, Woman's, 6 In. ... 1947
Chopard, 18K Gold, Monte Carlo, Gold Dial, Block Link Bracelet, c.1980, Woman's ... 3120
Chopard, 18K White Gold, Mother-Of-Pearl Dial, Diamond Markers, Leather Band, c.1980 ... 3600
Dudley, 14K White Gold, Open Link Bracelet, Shaped Face, 1900s, Woman's, 7 In. ... 188
Ebel, 18K Yellow Gold, Diamond Time Marks, White Face, Link Bracelet, Woman's ... 1920
Eloga, Incabloc, 17 Jewel, Diamonds, 6 ¾ In. ... 360
Eterna, 18K Yellow Gold, White Dial, Diamond Markers, Link, c.1990, Woman's ... 2040
Fleuron, 17 Jewel, 18K Gold Bracelet, Hinged, Diamonds, Yin Yang Design, Woman's ... 600
Geneve, Golden Shadow, 18K Yellow Gold, Champagne Dial, Black Alligator Band, c.1970 ... 780
Girard Perregaux, Platinum, Diamond, Manual Wind, 6 ¼ In. ... 1845
Gotham, Art Deco, 14K Pink Gold, Diamond Marker, Gold Filled Band ... 184
Hamilton Electric, Trapezoidal Face, 2-Tone Dial, Leather Band, c.1950 ... 720
Hamilton, 14K White Gold, Oval Case, Elongated XO Link Bracelet, Woman's ... 242
Hamilton, Platinum, Diamond Case, Bracelet, Silvertone Dial, Woman's, 6 In. ... 920
Hardy Hayes, Platinum, Baguette & Round Diamonds, Bracelet, c.1905, Women's, 6 ½ In. ... 960
Harry Winston Avenue C, Tank, 18K White Gold, Diamonds, Leather Band, Woman's ... 7080
Hermes, H-Hour, White Dial, Goldtone Case, Leather Band, Woman's ... 1845
Hermes, Nantucket, 18K Gold, Swiss Quartz, Matte Finish Face, Box, Woman's, 1 ½ x 1 In. ... 1208
Jules Jergensen, 14K White Gold Tonneau Shape Case, Velvet Bracelet, Woman's ... 207
Longines, 14K Yellow Gold, Round Case, Integral Bracelet, Woman's ... 288
Longines, 14K Yellow Gold, Textured Mesh Dial, Bracelet, c.1980, 6 In. ... 826
Longines, Art Deco, 14K White Gold, Square, Top Hat Lugs, Diamond, Woman's ... 173
Longines, One Button Flyback, Chronograph, 5 Hands, 17 Jewel, Leather Band ... 1150
Longines, Tank, 14K Yellow Gold, Manual Wind, Lizard Band, 1900s ... 458
Lucien Piccard, 18K Yellow Gold, Textured Tonneau Case, Oval Bezel, Woman's ... 150
Mathey Tissot, 14K White Gold, Diamond, Marked, Woman's ... 900
Mathey Tissot, Art Deco, 14K White Gold, Diamonds, Flower Shape Lugs, Woman's ... 260
Omega Marine, Sliding Case, 14K Yellow Gold, White Dial, 1930s ... 2537
Omega, Constellation, Stainless Steel Case, Yellow Tone Accents, Woman's, 6 In. ... 299
Omega, Seamaster, Calendar, Automatic, Stainless Stain, 1 ¼ In. ... 587
Patek Philippe, Ellipse, Model 3546, 18K Yellow Gold, 1970s, 1 In. ... 4600
Patek Philippe, Rectangular, 18K Gold, Silver Dial, Gold Hands, 18 Jewel, 1935 ... 5100
Piaget, 18K Gold, Diamond Bezel, Green Jade Dial, Mesh Bracelet, 1970s, 6 ½ In. ... *illus* 3835
Piguet, 18K Yellow Gold, Stainless Steel & Gold Band, Tonneau Shape, 6 ½ In. ... 3500
Rolex, 14K Yellow Gold, Diamond, Air King, Black Dial, Leather Band, 9 ½ In. ... 4500
Rolex, 17K Gold, White Satin Dial, Engraved, 1964, 8 In. ... 2832
Rolex, 18K Yellow Gold, Diamond, Datejust, Oyster Perpetual, Woman's, 6 In. ... 5250
Rolex, 18K Yellow Gold, Stainless Steel & Diamond, Jubilee Band, Woman's, 6 ¾ In. ... 2500
Rolex, Oyster Perpetual, Chronometer, 14K Gold, Waffle Dial, 17 Jewel, c.1951 ... 1320
Rolex, Oyster, Chronometer, Perpetual, 14K Gold, 1 ¼ In. ... 2185
Rolex, Oyster, Perpetual, 18K Yellow Gold, Diamond, Day-Date, Blue Dial, 7 In. ... 8555
Rolex, Oyster, Perpetual, Stainless Steel Case, Coral Face, c.1960, 1 ¾ In. ... 2070

Wristwatch, Cartier, Panthere, 18K Gold, Diamond, Ivory Tone Dial, Diamond Bezel, Box
$7,995

Skinner, Inc.

Wristwatch, Piaget, 18K Gold, Diamond Bezel, Green Jade Dial, Mesh Bracelet, 1970s, 6 ½ In.
$3,835

Brunk Auctions

Wristwatch, Rose Gold, 17 Jewels, Stretch Band, Mechanical Wind, 6 ¾ In.
$279

Ruby Lane

Yellowware, Mixing Bowl, Brown Band, 7 x 15 ¾ In.
$153

Hess Auction Group

Zsolnay, Vase, Tulip, Multicolor Eosin Glaze, Leaves, Swirls, Footed, c.1900, 13 In.
$17,500

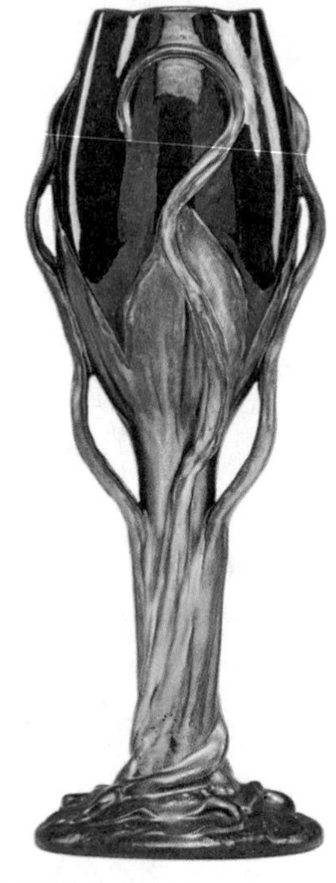

Rago Arts and Auction Center

Flea Market Tricks

Ever go to a flea market, buy something heavy, but not want to carry it around with you all day? Worried you will have trouble finding your way back to the booth? No problem. Ask the dealer to hold it and then pay for it. Take a picture with your phone of both the item and the number sign on the booth. You will have a way to find the booth again when it is time to pick up your purchase. Be sure the dealer's name is on your receipt as an added precaution.

Rolex, Presidential, Diamond Dial, Bezel, 18K Gold, 31 Jewel, Box, c.1989, Woman's 8280
Rolex, Stainless Steel, Diamond Dial & Bezel, 7 Million Series, c.1982, Woman's 1920
Rose Gold, 17 Jewels, Stretch Band, Mechanical Wind, 6 ¾ In. ..... *illus* 279
Seiko, Hi-Beat, Stainless Steel, Green Dial, Silver Stick Hands, Mesh Band, c.1971 123
Sellita, 14K Yellow Gold, Braided Bracelet, Tassels, Diamonds, 1900s, Woman's, 7 In. 960
Tag Heuer, Aquaracer, Diver's, Blue Guilloche Dial, Luminescent Hands, Quartz 780
Tiffany & Co., 18K Gold Case, Buckle, Quartz Movement, Leather Band, c.1940, 8 In. 3068
Vacheron Constantine & LeCoultre, Mystery, 14K White Gold, Leather Band, 1 ¼ In. 2013
Waltham, Art Deco, 14K White Gold, Enameled Bezel, Blue Lizard Band, Woman's 426
Zenith El Primo, Automatic Chronograph, Water Resistant, Leather Band 2006
Zenith, Automatic, 18K Yellow Gold, Goldtone Dial, Calendar Aperture, 1 ¼ In. 805
Zodiac, Chronograph, Fancy Bull Horn Lugs, Rose Gold-Filled Case, 1950s 708

YELLOWWARE is a heavy earthenware made of a yellowish clay. It varies in color from light yellow to orange-yellow. Many nineteenth- and twentieth-century kitchen bowls and jugs were made of yellowware. It was made in England and in the United States. Another form of pottery that is sometimes classed as yellowware is listed in this book in the Mocha category.

Bowl, 16 Blue & White Bands, Flat Rim, Ring Base, 15 ½ In. Diam. 90
Butter Tub, Blue Band, 4 ½ x 8 ½ In. 201
Colander, Flared Edge, Rolled Rim, Yellow, 3 ¼ x 10 ¼ In. 354
Colander, Panel & Scroll, Molded, 3 x 7 ¾ In. 94
Colander, White & Brown Band, 5 ¼ x 10 ¾ In. 118
Creamer, Blue Seaweed Banding, Bulbous, Flared Foot, Loop Handle, 5 In. 236
Crock, Mustard Glaze, Mottled White & Olive Band, Flattened Lid, 6 x 7 ⅜ In. 288
Jug, Man, Holding Hat In Air, Onlooker, Garlands Of Grapes, c.1850, 2 ¾ In. 145
Mixing Bowl, Blue & White Band, 6 x 13 ½ In. 71
Mixing Bowl, Brown Band, 7 x 15 ¾ In. ..... *illus* 153
Mixing Bowl, Wide Roll Rim, Ring Foot, Bands, 17 In. Diam. 325
Mold, Corn Pattern, Oval, Fluted Interior, 3 x 7 In. 47
Mold, Rabbit Shape, 3 ¾ x 8 ¼ In. 118
Pail, Oyster, Brown Band, Barrel Shape, 7 ¼ In. 130
Pepper, Dome Lid, Blue & White Bands, Smokestack, Pedestal Foot, 4 In. 472
Pitcher, Water, White & Brown Band, Signed Green & Co., 8 ½ In. 224
Rolling Pin, c.1900, 15 x 3 ¼ In. 399
Rolling Pin, Hollow Cast, Turned Software Handles, c.1890-1920, 14 x 3 In. 150
Salt, Blue Seaweed Design, Pedestal Foot, Yellow, 2 x 3 In. 472
Washboard, Brown Mottle Glaze, Pine Wood Frame, c.1840-60, 23 x 13 In. 200
Water Cooler, Barrel Shape, 1800s, 10 Gal., 21 ½ x 13 ½ In. 120

ZANESVILLE Art Pottery was founded in 1900 by David Schmidt in Zanesville, Ohio. The firm made faience umbrella stands, jardinieres, and pedestals. The company closed in 1920 and Weller bought the factory. Many pieces are marked with just the words *La Moro*.

LA MORO

Planter, Frogs, Green Glaze, c.1920, 8 x 3 In. 125
Urn, Grapevine, Grapes, Relief, Purple, Green, Beige Ground, 17 x 16 In. 72
Vase, Brown Drip Glaze, Shouldered, 4 x 5 In. 35
Vase, Flared Trumpet, Green Matte Glaze, 6 In. 115

ZSOLNAY pottery was made in Hungary after 1853 and was characterized by Persian, Art Nouveau, or Hungarian motifs. A series of new Zsolnay figurines with green-gold luster finish is available in many shops today. Early Zsolnay was not marked, but by 1878 the tower trademark was used.

Dish, Red, Brown, Oval, Fluted Edge, Impressed Leaves, c.1883, 8 ½ x 6 In. ..... 119 to 250
Figurine, Nude Maiden Lying On Ground, Head & Arms On Rock, Iridescent, 8 x 8 In. 5333
Group, Polar Bears, Green, 7 ½ In. 125
Pitcher, Female Figural Handle, Gold Iridescent, 4 ⅞ x 2 ½ In. 300
Pitcher, Oval, Stick Neck, Loop Handle, Sunrise, Flowers, Branches, Red, Blue, c.1899, 9 In. 7500
Stein, Majolica, Woman Warrior, Knight Thumblift, 2 Liter 2040
Vase, Applied Female Figure, Narrow Neck, Green, 9 x 5 In. 216
Vase, Bulbous, Pinched Neck, Pierced & Reticulated, Cup Mouth, 1900s, 8 In. 200
Vase, Geranium, Red, 9 x 5 ½ In. 7930
Vase, Gold & Green Iridescent Glaze, Amphora, Loop Handles, c.1890, 10 In. 338
Vase, Man Climbing Toward Seating Person, Green, 9 x 9 In. 1845
Vase, Melon Ribbed, Stick Neck, Flower Rim, Iridescent Green & Gold, 13 In. 345
Vase, Pilgrim Flask, Pecs, Loop Handles, Footed, Flowers, Vines, 6 ½ In. 118
Vase, Tapered, Shouldered, Bird & Flower Design, Eosin Glaze, c.1906, 21 x 10 In. 6250
Vase, Tulip, Multicolor Eosin Glaze, Leaves, Swirls, Footed, c.1900, 13 In. ..... *illus* 17500

INDEX

This index is computer-generated, making it as complete and accurate as possible. References in uppercase type are category listings. Those in lowercase letters refer to additional pages where pieces can be found. There is also an internal cross-referencing system used in the main part of the book, so if you look for a Kewpie doll in the Doll category, you will be told it is in its own category. There is additional information at the end of many paragraphs about where to find prices of pieces similar to yours.

A

B

C

D

E

F

G

Q

R

S

T

U

V

W

Y

Z

PHOTO CREDITS

We have included the name of the auction house or photographer with each pictured object. This is a list of the addresses of those who have contributed photographs and information for this book. Every dealer or auction has to buy antiques to have items to sell. Call or email a dealer or auction house if you want to discuss buying or selling. If you need an appraisal or advice, remember that appraising is part of their business and fees may be charged.

Accurate Auctions
2900 Jackson Highway
Sheffield, AL 34654
401-390-3139

Ahlers & Ogletree Auction Gallery
715 Miami Circle
Suite 210
Atlanta, GA 30324
aandoauctions.com
404-869-2478

Alex Cooper Auctioneers
908 York Rd.
Towson, MD 21204
Alexcooper.com
800-272-3145

Allard Auctions
P.O. Box 1030
St. Ignatius, MT 59865
allardauctions.com
406-745-0500

Bamfords Auctioneers and Valuers Ltd.
The Derby House
Chequers Road
Off Pentagon Island
Derby, United Kingdom DE21 6EN
www.bamfords-auctions.co.uk
+44 (0) 1332 210000

Bertoia Auctions
2141 DeMarco Dr.
Vineland, NJ 08360
bertoiaauctions.com
856-692-1881

Bill & Jill Insulators
103 Canterbury Court
Carlisle, MA 01741
Billandjillinsulators.com
978-369-0208

Brunk Auctions
P.O. Box 2135
Asheville, NC 28802
brunkauctions.com
828-254-6846

California Auctioneers & Appraisers
8597 Ventura Avenue
Ventura, CA 93001
californiaauctioneers.com
805-649-2686

Case Antiques Inc.
2240 Sutherland Ave.
Knoxville, TN 37919
Caseantiques.com
865-558-3033

Clars Auction Gallery
5644 Telegraph Ave.
Oakland, CA 94609
Clars.com
888-339-7600

Copake Auction Inc.
PO Box 47
Copake, NY 12516
copakeauction.com
518-329-1142

Cordier Auctions & Auctioneers
1500 Paxton St.
Harrisburg, PA 17104
Cordierauction.com
717-731-8662

Cottone Auctions
120 Court St.
Geneseo, NY 14454
cottoneauctions.com
585-243-1000

Cowan's Auctions
6270 Este Ave.
Cincinnati, OH 45232
cowanauctions.com
513-871-1670

Crocker Farm
15900 York Road
Sparks, MD 21152
crockerfarm.com
410-472-2016

Crown Auctions
101 Hicks Ave.
Medford, MA 02155
Crownauctions.com
781-324-4400

Dirk Soulis Auctions
529 W. lone Jack-Lee's Road
PO Box 17
Lone Jack, MO 64070
dirksoulisauctions.com
816-697-3830

DuMouchelles Art Gallery
409 East Jefferson Ave.
Detroit, MI 48226
dumouchelles.com
313-963-6255

Eagle Cap Collectibles Auction
Eaglecapcollectibles.com

Early American History Auctions
PO Box 3507
Rancho Santa Fe, CA 92067
earlyamerican.com
858-759-3290

Early Auction Co.
123 Main St.
Milford, OH 45150
earlyauctionco.com
513-831-4833

Enchantment Vintage Costume Jewelry
Vintagecostumejewels.com

Ewbank's
Burnt Common Auction Rooms
London Road
Woking, Surrey GU23 7LN
antiques@ewbankauction.co.uk
+44 (0) 1483 223101

Fairfield Auction
707 Main St.
Monroe, CT 06468
Fairfieldauction.com
203-880-5200

Fox Auctions
P.O. Box 4069
Vallejo, CA 94590
foxauctionsonline.com
631-553-3841

Fryer & Brown Auctioneers
The Old Mill
Cobham Park Road
Downside
Cobham, Surrey KT11 3PF
fryerandbrown.com
+44 (0) 1932 865026

Garth's Auctioneers & Appraisers
P.O. Box 369
Delaware, OH 43015
garths.com
740-362-4771

Glass Works Auctions
P.O. Box 38
Lambertville, NJ 08530
glswrk-auction.com
609-483-2683

Great Estates Auctioneers & Appraisers
40 Front Street
Port Jervis, NY 12771
greatestatesauctioneers.com
845-856-2001

Guyette & Deeter
PO Box 1170
St. Michaels, MD 21663
Guyetteanddeeter.com
410-745-0485

Hake's Americana & Collectibles
P.O. Box 12001
York, PA 17402
hakes.com
717-434-1600

Heritage Auctions
3500 Maple Ave., 17th Flr.
Dallas, TX 75219
Ha.com
214-528-3500

Hess Auction Group
768 Graystone Road
Manheim, PA 17545
hessauctiongroup.com
717-898-7284

Humler & Nolan
225 E. Sixth St., 4th Floor
Cincinnati, OH 45202
humlernolan.com
513-381-2041

James D. Julia Auctioneers
203 Skowhegan Rd.
Fairfield, Maine 04937
jamesdjulia.com
207-453-7125

Jaremos Estate Liquidators
2863 W. 95th St
Suite 143-223
Naperville, IL 60564
jaremos.com
630-248-7785

Jeffrey S. Evans & Associates
P.O. Box 2638
Harrisonburg, VA 22801
jefffreysevans.com
540-434-3939

Los Angeles Modern Auctions (LAMA)
16145 Hart St.
Van Nuys, CA 91406
lamodern.com
323-904-1950

Manifest Auctions
361 Woodruff Road
Greenville, SC 29607
manifestauctions.com
864-520-2208

Martin Auction Co.
100 Lick Creek Road
PO Box 2
Anna, IL 62906
martinauctionco.com
864-520-2208

McMasters Harris Auction Co.
1625 West Church St.
Newark, OH 43055
Mcmastersharris.com
800-842-3526

Milestone Auctions
3860 Ben Hur Avenue
Unit 8
Willoughby, OH 44094
milestoneauctions.com
440-527-8060

Morphy Auctions
2000 North Reading Road
Denver, PA 17517
morphyauctions.com
717-335-3435

Mossgreen Pty. Ltd.
926-930 High Streeet
Armadale Victoria, 3143
Australia

Neal Auction Co.
4038 Magazine St.
New Orleans, LA 70115
nealauction.com
800-467-5329

Nest Egg Auctions
758 Four Rod Road
Berlin, CT 06037
nesteggauctions.com
203-630-1400

New Orleans Auction Galleries
333 St. Joseph St.
New Orleans, LA 70130
neworleansauction.com
504-566-1849

NH Button Auctions
Manchester, NH 03103
NHbuttonauctions.com
603-627-2525

Norman C. Heckler & Co.
79 Bradford Corner Rd.
Woodstock Valley, CT 06282
hecklerauction.com
860-974-1634

North American Auction Co.
34156 East Frontage Road
Bozeman, MT 59715
northamericanauctioncompany.com
800-686-4216

Old Barn Auction
10040 State Route 224
Findlay, OH 45840
oldbarn.com
419-422-8531

Open Wire Insulator Services
28390 Saffron Ave.
Highland, CA 92346
Open-wire.com
909-862-9279

Palm Beach Modern Auctions
417 Bunker Rd.
West Palm Beach, FL 33405
modernauctions.com
561-586-5500

Perfume Bottles Auction
International Perfume Bottle Association
IPBA: perfumebottles.org
Perfumebottlesauction.com
800-942-0550

Phillips
450 Park Ave.
New York, NY 10022
Phillips.com
212-940-1300

Potter & Potter Auctions
3759 N. Ravenswood Ave., #121
Chicago, IL 60613
Potterauctions.com
773-472-1442

Rago Arts and Auction Center
333 North Main St.
Lambertville, NJ 08530
ragoarts.com
609-397-9374

Replacements Ltd.
P.O. Box 26029
Greensboro, NC 27420-6029
replacements.com
800-737-5223

Rich Penn Auctions
PO Box 1355
Waterloo, IA 50704
Richpennauctions.com
319-291-6688

Robert Edward Auctions
90 Gallowae
Watchung, NJ 07069
robertedwardauctions.com
908-226-9920

RSL Auction
P.O. Box 635
Oldwick, NJ 08858
rslauctionco.com
908-823-4049

Ruby Lane
381 Bush St., Suite 400
San Francisco, CA 94104
rubylane.com
415-362-7611

Sam Scott Pottery
samscottpottery.com

Selkirk Auctioneers & Appraisers
4739 McPherson Avenue
St. Louis, MO 63108
selkirkauctions.com
314-696-9041

Showtime Auction Services
22619 Monterey Dr.
Woodhaven, MI 48183
showtimeauctions.com
951-453-2415

Skinner Auctioneers & Appraisers
274 Cedar Hill St.
Marlborough, MA 01752
skinnerinc.com
508-970-3000

Stephenson's Auction
1005 Industrial Blvd
Southampton, PA
stephensonsauction.com
215-322-6182

Strawser Auction Group
200 North Main Street
P.O. Box 332
Wolcottville, IN 46795
strawserauctions.com
260-854-2859

The Cobb Auctioneers
Noone Falls Mill
50 Jaffrey Road
Peterborough, NH 03458
thecobbs.com
603-924-6361

The Stein Auction Co.
P.O. Box 136
Palatine, IL 60078
TSACO.com
847-991-5927

Theriault's
P.O. Box 151
Annapolis, MD 21404
theriaults.com
800-638-0422

Thomaston Place Auction Galleries
P.O. Box 300
Thomaston, ME 04861
thomastonauction.com
207-354-8141

Tradewinds Antiques & Auctions
PO Box 249
Manchester-by-the-Sea, MA 01929
Tradewindsantiques.com
978-526-4085

Treadway Toomey Auctions
C/O Treadway Gallery
2029 Madison Rd.
Cincinnati, OH 45208
treadwaygallery.com
513-321-6742

Wickliff Auctioneers
12232 Hancock St.
Carmel, IN 46032
Wickliffauctioneers.com
317-844-7253

Wm Morford Auctions
RD #2 Cobb Hill Rd.
Cazenovia, NY 13035
morfauction.com
315-662-7625

Woody Auction
P.O. Box 618
317 S. Forrest
Douglass, KS 67039
woodyauction.com
316-747-2694

Wright
1440 W. Hubbard St.
Chicago, IL 60642
wright20.com
312-563-0020